This Holy Bible

is presented to

Kelsea Pearson

by

Greg

on

_10/9/02_

Church Record

EVENT

MINISTER

CHURCH   DATE

EVENT

MINISTER

CHURCH   DATE

EVENT

MINISTER

CHURCH   DATE

EVENT

MINISTER

CHURCH   DATE

EVENT

MINISTER

CHURCH   DATE

EVENT

MINISTER

CHURCH   DATE

Marriages

HUSBAND

WIFE

PLACE   DATE

HUSBAND

WIFE

PLACE   DATE

HUSBAND

WIFE

PLACE   DATE

HUSBAND

WIFE

PLACE   DATE

HUSBAND

WIFE

PLACE   DATE

HUSBAND

WIFE

PLACE   DATE

Wife's Family Tree

NAME _____

BIRTHPLACE _____ DATE _____

BROTHERS AND SISTERS _____

_____

PARENTS

FATHER

NAME _____

BIRTHPLACE _____ DATE _____

MOTHER

NAME _____

BIRTHPLACE _____ DATE _____

GRANDPARENTS

PATERNAL

GRANDFATHER _____

BIRTHPLACE _____ DATE _____

GRANDMOTHER _____

BIRTHPLACE _____ DATE _____

MATERNAL

GRANDFATHER _____

BIRTHPLACE _____ DATE _____

GRANDMOTHER _____

BIRTHPLACE _____ DATE _____

GREAT-GRANDPARENTS

PATERNAL

GRANDFATHER'S FATHER _____

BIRTHPLACE _____ DATE _____

GRANDFATHER'S MOTHER _____

BIRTHPLACE _____ DATE _____

GRANDMOTHER'S FATHER _____

BIRTHPLACE _____ DATE _____

GRANDMOTHER'S MOTHER _____

BIRTHPLACE _____ DATE _____

MATERNAL

GRANDFATHER'S FATHER _____

BIRTHPLACE _____ DATE _____

GRANDFATHER'S MOTHER _____

BIRTHPLACE _____ DATE _____

GRANDMOTHER'S FATHER _____

BIRTHPLACE _____ DATE _____

GRANDMOTHER'S MOTHER _____

BIRTHPLACE _____ DATE _____

Husband's Family Tree

NAME _____

BIRTHPLACE _____ DATE _____

BROTHERS AND SISTERS _____

_____

PARENTS

FATHER   **MOTHER**

NAME _____   NAME _____

BIRTHPLACE _____ DATE ____   BIRTHPLACE _____ DATE ____

GRANDPARENTS

PATERNAL   **MATERNAL**

GRANDFATHER _____   GRANDFATHER _____

BIRTHPLACE _____ DATE ____   BIRTHPLACE _____ DATE ____

GRANDMOTHER _____   GRANDMOTHER _____

BIRTHPLACE _____ DATE ____   BIRTHPLACE _____ DATE ____

GREAT-GRANDPARENTS

PATERNAL   **MATERNAL**

GRANDFATHER'S FATHER _____   GRANDFATHER'S FATHER _____

BIRTHPLACE _____ DATE ____   BIRTHPLACE _____ DATE ____

GRANDFATHER'S MOTHER _____   GRANDFATHER'S MOTHER _____

BIRTHPLACE _____ DATE ____   BIRTHPLACE _____ DATE ____

GRANDMOTHER'S FATHER _____   GRANDMOTHER'S FATHER _____

BIRTHPLACE _____ DATE ____   BIRTHPLACE _____ DATE ____

GRANDMOTHER'S MOTHER _____   GRANDMOTHER'S MOTHER _____

BIRTHPLACE _____ DATE ____   BIRTHPLACE _____ DATE ____

Births

NAME _____ DATE _____

BORN TO _____

NAME _____ DATE _____

BORN TO _____

NAME _____ DATE _____

BORN TO _____

NAME _____ DATE _____

BORN TO _____

NAME _____ DATE _____

BORN TO _____

NAME _____ DATE _____

BORN TO _____

NAME _____ DATE _____

BORN TO _____

NAME _____ DATE _____

BORN TO _____

NAME _____ DATE _____

BORN TO _____

Deaths

NAME
_____

DATE
_____

NAME
_____

DATE
_____

NAME
_____

DATE
_____

NAME
_____

DATE
_____

NAME
_____

DATE
_____

NAME
_____

DATE
_____

NAME
_____

DATE
_____

NAME
_____

DATE
_____

NAME
_____

DATE
_____

Special Events

EVENT
_____

PLACE   DATE

EVENT
_____

PLACE   DATE

EVENT
_____

PLACE   DATE

EVENT
_____

PLACE   DATE

EVENT
_____

PLACE   DATE

EVENT
_____

PLACE   DATE

NEW INTERNATIONAL VERSION OF
The Holy Bible

The
HOLY
BIBLE

NEW INTERNATIONAL VERSION®

*Containing The Old Testament
and The New Testament*

ZONDERVAN™

GRAND RAPIDS, MICHIGAN 49530

Contents

Preface to The New International Version vii

THE BOOKS OF

The Old Testament

THE BOOKS OF

The New Testament

Alphabetical Order of

The Books of the Bible

Preface

THE NEW INTERNATIONAL VERSION is a completely new translation of the Holy Bible made by over a hundred scholars working directly from the best available Hebrew, Aramaic and Greek texts. It had its beginning in 1965 when, after several years of exploratory study by committees from the Christian Reformed Church and the National Association of Evangelicals, a group of scholars met at Palos Heights, Illinois, and concurred in the need for a new translation of the Bible in contemporary English. This group, though not made up of official church representatives, was transdenominational. Its conclusion was endorsed by a large number of leaders from many denominations who met in Chicago in 1966.

Responsibility for the new version was delegated by the Palos Heights group to a self-governing body of fifteen, the Committee on Bible Translation, composed for the most part of biblical scholars from colleges, universities and seminaries. In 1967 the New York Bible Society (now the International Bible Society) generously undertook the financial sponsorship of the project—a sponsorship that made it possible to enlist the help of many distinguished scholars. The fact that participants from the United States, Great Britain, Canada, Australia and New Zealand worked together gave the project its international scope. That they were from many denominations—including Anglican, Assemblies of God, Baptist, Brethren, Christian Reformed, Church of Christ, Evangelical Free, Lutheran, Mennonite, Methodist, Nazarene, Presbyterian, Wesleyan and other churches—helped to safeguard the translation from sectarian bias.

How it was made helps to give the New International Version its distinctiveness. The translation of each book was assigned to a team of scholars. Next, one of the Intermediate Editorial Committees revised the initial translation, with constant reference to the Hebrew, Aramaic or Greek. Their work then went to one of the General Editorial Committees, which checked it in detail and made another thorough revision. This revision in turn was carefully reviewed by the Committee on Bible Translation, which made further changes and then released the final version for publication. In this way the entire Bible underwent three revisions, during each of which the translation was examined for its faithfulness to the original languages and for its English style.

All this involved many thousands of hours of research and discussion regarding the meaning of the texts and the precise way of putting them into English. It may well be that no other translation has been made by a more thorough process of review and revision from committee to committee than this one.

From the beginning of the project, the Committee on Bible Translation held to certain goals for the New International Version: that it would be an accurate translation and one that would have clarity and literary quality and so prove suitable for public and private reading, teaching, preaching, memorizing and liturgical use. The Committee also sought to preserve some measure of continuity with the long tradition of translating the Scriptures into English.

In working toward these goals, the translators were united in their commitment to the authority and infallibility of the Bible as God's Word in written form. They believe that it contains the divine answer to the deepest needs of humanity, that it sheds unique light on our path in a dark world, and that it sets forth the way to our eternal well-being.

The first concern of the translators has been the accuracy of the translation and its fidelity to the thought of the biblical writers. They have weighed the significance of the lexical and grammatical details of the Hebrew, Aramaic and Greek texts. At the same time, they have striven for more than a word-for-word translation. Because thought patterns and syntax differ from language to language, faithful communication of the meaning of the writers of the Bible demands frequent modifications in sentence structure and constant regard for the contextual meanings of words.

A sensitive feeling for style does not always accompany scholarship. Accordingly the Committee on Bible Translation submitted the developing version to a number of stylistic consultants. Two of them read every book of both Old and New Testaments twice—once before and once after the last major revision—and made invaluable suggestions. Samples of the translation were tested for clarity and ease of reading by various kinds of people—young and old, highly educated and less well educated, ministers and laymen.

Concern for clear and natural English—that the New International Version should be idiomatic but not idiosyncratic, contemporary but not dated—motivated the translators and consultants. At the same time, they tried to reflect the differing styles of the biblical writers. In view of the international use of English, the translators sought to avoid obvious Americanisms on the one hand and obvious Anglicisms on the other. A British edition reflects the comparatively few differences of significant idiom and of spelling.

As for the traditional pronouns "thou," "thee" and "thine" in reference to the Deity, the translators judged that to use these archaisms (along with the old verb forms such as "doest," "wouldest" and "hadst") would violate accuracy in translation. Neither Hebrew, Aramaic nor Greek uses special pronouns for the persons of the Godhead. A present-day translation is not enhanced by forms that in the time of the King James Version were used in everyday speech, whether referring to God or man.

For the Old Testament the standard Hebrew text, the Masoretic Text as published in the latest editions of *Biblia Hebraica*, was used throughout. The Dead Sea Scrolls contain material bearing on an earlier stage of the Hebrew text. They were consulted, as were the Samaritan Pentateuch and the ancient scribal traditions relating to textual changes. Sometimes a variant Hebrew reading in the margin of the Masoretic Text was followed instead of the text itself. Such instances, being variants within the Masoretic tradition, are not specified by footnotes. In rare cases, words in the consonantal text were divided differently from the way they appear in the Masoretic Text. Footnotes indicate this. The translators also consulted the more important early versions—the Septuagint; Aquila, Symmachus and Theodotion; the Vulgate; the Syriac Peshitta; the Targums; and for the Psalms the *Juxta Hebraica* of Jerome. Readings from these versions were occasionally followed where the Masoretic Text seemed doubtful and where accepted principles of textual criticism showed that one or more of these textual witnesses appeared to provide the correct reading. Such instances are footnoted. Sometimes vowel letters and vowel signs did not, in the judgment of the translators, represent the correct vowels for the original consonantal text. Accordingly some words were read with a different set of vowels. These instances are usually not indicated by footnotes.

The Greek text used in translating the New Testament was an eclectic one. No other piece of ancient literature has such an abundance of manuscript witnesses as does the New Testament. Where existing manuscripts differ, the translators made their choice of readings according to accepted principles of New Testament textual criticism. Footnotes call attention to places where there was uncertainty about what the original text was. The best current printed texts of the Greek New Testament were used.

There is a sense in which the work of translation is never wholly finished. This

applies to all great literature and uniquely so to the Bible. In 1973 the New Testament in the New International Version was published. Since then, suggestions for corrections and revisions have been received from various sources. The Committee on Bible Translation carefully considered the suggestions and adopted a number of them. These were incorporated in the first printing of the entire Bible in 1978. Additional revisions were made by the Committee on Bible Translation in 1983 and appear in printings after that date.

As in other ancient documents, the precise meaning of the biblical texts is sometimes uncertain. This is more often the case with the Hebrew and Aramaic texts than with the Greek text. Although archaeological and linguistic discoveries in this century aid in understanding difficult passages, some uncertainties remain. The more significant of these have been called to the reader's attention in the footnotes.

In regard to the divine name *YHWH*, commonly referred to as the *Tetragrammaton*, the translators adopted the device used in most English versions of rendering that name as "Lord" in capital letters to distinguish it from *Adonai*, another Hebrew word rendered "Lord," for which small letters are used. Wherever the two names stand together in the Old Testament as a compound name of God, they are rendered "Sovereign Lord."

Because for most readers today the phrases "the Lord of hosts" and "God of hosts" have little meaning, this version renders them "the Lord Almighty" and "God Almighty." These renderings convey the sense of the Hebrew, namely, "he who is sovereign over all the 'hosts' (powers) in heaven and on earth, especially over the 'hosts' (armies) of Israel." For readers unacquainted with Hebrew this does not make clear the distinction between *Sabaoth* ("hosts" or "Almighty") and *Shaddai* (which can also be translated "Almighty"), but the latter occurs infrequently and is always footnoted. When *Adonai* and *YHWH Sabaoth* occur together, they are rendered "the Lord, the Lord Almighty."

As for other proper nouns, the familiar spellings of the King James Version are generally retained. Names traditionally spelled with "ch," except where it is final, are usually spelled in this translation with "k" or "c," since the biblical languages do not have the sound that "ch" frequently indicates in English—for example, in *chant*. For well-known names such as Zechariah, however, the traditional spelling has been retained. Variation in the spelling of names in the original languages has usually not been indicated. Where a person or place has two or more different names in the Hebrew, Aramaic or Greek texts, the more familiar one has generally been used, with footnotes where needed.

To achieve clarity the translators sometimes supplied words not in the original texts but required by the context. If there was uncertainty about such material, it is enclosed in brackets. Also for the sake of clarity or style, nouns, including some proper nouns, are sometimes substituted for pronouns, and vice versa. And though the Hebrew writers often shifted back and forth between first, second and third personal pronouns without change of antecedent, this translation often makes them uniform, in accordance with English style and without the use of footnotes.

Poetical passages are printed as poetry, that is, with indentation of lines and with separate stanzas. These are generally designed to reflect the structure of Hebrew poetry. This poetry is normally characterized by parallelism in balanced lines. Most of the poetry in the Bible is in the Old Testament, and scholars differ regarding the scansion of Hebrew lines. The translators determined the stanza divisions for the most part by analysis of the subject matter. The stanzas therefore serve as poetic paragraphs.

As an aid to the reader, italicized sectional headings are inserted in most of the books. They are not to be regarded as part of the NIV text, are not for oral reading, and are not intended to dictate the interpretation of the sections they head.

The footnotes in this version are of several kinds, most of which need no explanation. Those giving alternative translations begin with "Or" and generally

introduce the alternative with the last word preceding it in the text, except when it is a single-word alternative; in poetry quoted in a footnote a slant mark indicates a line division. Footnotes introduced by "Or" do not have uniform significance. In some cases two possible translations were considered to have about equal validity. In other cases, though the translators were convinced that the translation in the text was correct, they judged that another interpretation was possible and of sufficient importance to be represented in a footnote.

In the New Testament, footnotes that refer to uncertainty regarding the original text are introduced by "Some manuscripts" or similar expressions. In the Old Testament, evidence for the reading chosen is given first and evidence for the alternative is added after a semicolon (for example: Septuagint; Hebrew *father*). In such notes the term "Hebrew" refers to the Masoretic Text.

It should be noted that minerals, flora and fauna, architectural details, articles of clothing and jewelry, musical instruments and other articles cannot always be identified with precision. Also measures of capacity in the biblical period are particularly uncertain (see the table of weights and measures following the text).

Like all translations of the Bible, made as they are by imperfect man, this one undoubtedly falls short of its goals. Yet we are grateful to God for the extent to which he has enabled us to realize these goals and for the strength he has given us and our colleagues to complete our task. We offer this version of the Bible to him in whose name and for whose glory it has been made. We pray that it will lead many into a better understanding of the Holy Scriptures and a fuller knowledge of Jesus Christ the incarnate Word, of whom the Scriptures so faithfully testify.

The Committee on Bible Translation

June 1978
(Revised August 1983)

Names of the translators and editors may be secured from the International Bible Society, translation sponsors of the New International Version, 1820 Jet Stream Drive, Colorado Springs, Colorado, 80921-3696 U.S.A.

Introduction

The references in this Bible are conveniently located at the end of a verse, poetry line or paragraph. They appear in contrasting type to set them off from the text and are arranged in book order. Each reference can refer to the preceding sentence, the preceding paragraph or a concept within that paragraph.

The
Old Testament

Genesis

Introduction:

The word Genesis means "beginnings." The book of Genesis is about many beginnings—the beginning of the universe, the beginning of man and woman, the beginning of human sin, the beginning of God's promises and plans for salvation, and the beginning of a special relationship between Abraham and God. Genesis tells us about God's special people and his plan for their lives. Some of these people are: Adam and Eve, Noah, Abraham, Isaac, Jacob, and Joseph and his brothers.

Genesis is the first book in what is called the Pentateuch—a word that means five books, and includes the first five books of the Bible. These books are also known as the books of the law because they contain God's instructions and laws for the people of Israel. Genesis is included because it tells the history of how Israel became God's special people. These five books were most likely written by Moses, except for the last chapter of Deuteronomy which tells about Moses' death.

Outline of contents:

The Beginning

1 In the beginning God created the heavens and the earth. ²Now the earth was^a formless and empty, darkness was over the surface of the deep, and the Spirit of God was hovering over the waters. Ps 102:25; Jn 1:1-2

³And God said, "Let there be light," and there was light. ⁴God saw that the light was

---

^{a}2 Or possibly *became*

good, and he separated the light from the darkness. ⁵God called the light "day," and the darkness he called "night." And there was evening, and there was morning—the first day.

⁶And God said, "Let there be an expanse between the waters to separate water from water." ⁷So God made the expanse and separated the water under the expanse from the water above it. And it was so. ⁸God called the expanse "sky." And there was evening, and there was morning— the second day.   Ps 148:4

⁹And God said, "Let the water under the sky be gathered to one place, and let dry ground appear." And it was so. ¹⁰God called the dry ground "land," and the gathered waters he called "seas." And God saw that it was good.   Ps 33:7; 2Pe 3:5

¹¹Then God said, "Let the land produce vegetation: seed-bearing plants and trees on the land that bear fruit with seed in it, according to their various kinds." And it was so. ¹²The land produced vegetation: plants bearing seed according to their kinds and trees bearing fruit with seed in it according to their kinds. And God saw that it was good. ¹³And there was evening, and there was morning—the third day.   Ps 65:9-13

¹⁴And God said, "Let there be lights in the expanse of the sky to separate the day from the night, and let them serve as signs to mark seasons and days and years, ¹⁵and let them be lights in the expanse of the sky to give light on the earth." And it was so. ¹⁶God made two great lights—the greater light to govern the day and the lesser light to govern the night. He also made the stars. ¹⁷God set them in the expanse of the sky to give light on the earth, ¹⁸to govern the day and the night, and to separate light from darkness. And God saw that it was good. ¹⁹And there was evening, and there was morning—the fourth day.   Ps 74:16

²⁰And God said, "Let the water teem with living creatures, and let birds fly above the earth across the expanse of the sky." ²¹So God created the great creatures of the sea and every living and moving thing with which the water teems, according to their kinds, and every winged bird according to its kind. And God saw that it was good. ²²God blessed them and said, "Be fruitful and increase in number and fill the water in the seas, and let the birds increase on the earth." ²³And there was evening, and there was morning—the fifth day.

²⁴And God said, "Let the land produce living creatures according to their kinds: livestock, creatures that move along the ground, and wild animals, each according to its kind." And it was so. ²⁵God made the wild animals according to their kinds, the livestock according to their kinds, and all the creatures that move along the ground according to their kinds. And God saw that it was good. Ge 2:19

²⁶Then God said, "Let us make man in our image, in our likeness, and let them rule over the fish of the sea and the birds of the air, over the livestock, over all the earth,ᵃ and over all the creatures that move along the ground." Ps 100:3; Ac 17:28,29

²⁷So God created man in his own image,
in the image of God he created him;
male and female he created them. Ge 5:2; Mk 10:6; 1Co 11:7

²⁸God blessed them and said to them, "Be fruitful and increase in number; fill the earth and subdue it. Rule over the fish of the sea and the birds of the air and over every living creature that moves on the ground."

²⁹Then God said, "I give you every seed-bearing plant on the face of the whole earth and every tree that has fruit with seed in it. They will be yours for food. ³⁰And to all the beasts of the earth and all the birds of the air and all the creatures that move on the ground—everything that has the breath of life in it—I give every green plant for food." And it was so.

³¹God saw all that he had made, and it was very good. And there was evening, and there was morning—the sixth day. Ps 104:24

2 Thus the heavens and the earth were completed in all their vast array.

²By the seventh day God had finished the work he had been doing; so on the seventh day he restedᵇ from all his work. ³And God blessed the seventh day and made it holy, because on it he rested from all the work of creating that he had done.

Adam and Eve

⁴This is the account of the heavens and the earth when they were created.

When the Lᴏʀᴅ God made the earth and the heavens— ⁵and no shrub of the field had yet appeared on the earthᶜ and no plant of the field had yet sprung up, for the Lᴏʀᴅ God

ᵃ26 Hebrew; Syriac *all the wild animals* also in verse 6   ᵇ2 Or *ceased*; also in verse 3   ᶜ5 Or *land*;

had not sent rain on the earth[a] and there was no man to work the ground, [6]but streams[b] came up from the earth and watered the whole surface of the ground— [7]the LORD God formed the man[c] from the dust of the ground and breathed into his nostrils the breath of life, and the man became a living being. Ge 1:11-12

[8]Now the LORD God had planted a garden in the east, in Eden; and there he put the man he had formed. [9]And the LORD God made all kinds of trees grow out of the ground—trees that were pleasing to the eye and good for food. In the middle of the garden were the tree of life and the tree of the knowledge of good and evil. Is 51:3

[10]A river watering the garden flowed from Eden; from there it was separated into four headwaters. [11]The name of the first is the Pishon; it winds through the entire land of Havilah, where there is gold. [12](The gold of that land is good; aromatic resin[d] and onyx are also there.) [13]The name of the second river is the Gihon; it winds through the entire land of Cush.[e] [14]The name of the third river is the Tigris; it runs along the east side of Asshur. And the fourth river is the Euphrates. Nu 11:7; Da 10:4

[15]The LORD God took the man and put him in the Garden of Eden to work it and take care of it. [16]And the LORD God commanded the man, "You are free to eat from any tree in the garden; [17]but you must not eat from the tree of the knowledge of good and evil, for when you eat of it you will surely die." Dt 30:15

[18]The LORD God said, "It is not good for the man to be alone. I will make a helper suitable for him." 1Co 11:9; 1Ti 2:13

[19]Now the LORD God had formed out of the ground all the beasts of the field and all the birds of the air. He brought them to the man to see what he would name them; and whatever the man called each living creature, that was its name. [20]So the man gave names to all the livestock, the birds of the air and all the beasts of the field.

But for Adam[f] no suitable helper was found. [21]So the LORD God caused the man to fall into a deep sleep; and while he was sleeping, he took one of the man's ribs[g] and closed up the place with flesh. [22]Then the LORD God made a woman from the rib[h] he had taken out of the man, and he brought her to the man. Ge 3:20; Job 33:15

[23]The man said,

"This is now bone of my
      bones
   and flesh of my flesh;

---

[a]5 Or *land;* also in verse 6   [b]6 Or *mist*   [c]7 The Hebrew for *man (adam)* sounds like and may be related to the Hebrew for *ground (adamah);* it is also the name *Adam* (see Gen. 2:20).   [d]12 Or *good; pearls*   [e]13 Possibly southeast Mesopotamia   [f]20 Or *the man*   [g]21 Or *took part of the man's side*   [h]22 Or *part*

she shall be called 'woman,'[a]
for she was taken out of
man." Eph 5:28-30

24For this reason a man will leave his father and mother and be united to his wife, and they will become one flesh. Mt 19:5 25The man and his wife were both naked, and they felt no shame. Ge 3:7,10,11

The Fall of Man

3 Now the serpent was more crafty than any of the wild animals the LORD God had made. He said to the woman, "Did God really say, 'You must not eat from any tree in the garden'?" Rev 12:9 2The woman said to the serpent, "We may eat fruit from the trees in the garden, 3but God did say, 'You must not eat fruit from the tree that is in the middle of the garden, and you must not touch it, or you will die.'" Ge 2:16-17 4"You will not surely die," the serpent said to the woman. 5"For God knows that when you eat of it your eyes will be opened, and you will be like God, knowing good and evil." 6When the woman saw that the fruit of the tree was good for food and pleasing to the eye, and also desirable for gaining wisdom, she took some and ate it. She also gave some to her husband, who was with her, and he ate it. 7Then the eyes of both of them were opened, and

they realized they were naked; so they sewed fig leaves together and made coverings for themselves. 1Ti 2:14; Jas 1:14-15 8Then the man and his wife heard the sound of the LORD God as he was walking in the garden in the cool of the day, and they hid from the LORD God among the trees of the garden. 9But the LORD God called to the man, "Where are you?"

10He answered, "I heard you in the garden, and I was afraid because I was naked; so I hid."

11And he said, "Who told you that you were naked? Have you eaten from the tree that I commanded you not to eat from?"

12The man said, "The woman you put here with me—she gave me some fruit from the tree, and I ate it." Pr 28:13

13Then the LORD God said to the woman, "What is this you have done?"

The woman said, "The serpent deceived me, and I ate."

14So the LORD God said to the serpent, "Because you have done this,

"Cursed are you above all
　　the livestock
and all the wild animals!
You will crawl on your belly
　and you will eat dust
　all the days of your life.
15And I will put enmity
　between you and the
　　woman,
　and between your
　　offspring[b] and hers;

---

[a]23 The Hebrew for *woman* sounds like the Hebrew for *man*.　　[b]15 Or *seed*

he will crush*ᵃ* your head,
and you will strike his
heel."   Ro 16:20

¹⁶To the woman he said,

"I will greatly increase your
pains in childbearing;
with pain you will give
birth to children.   Ps 48:6
Your desire will be for your
husband,
and he will rule over you."

¹⁷To Adam he said, "Because
you listened to your wife and
ate from the tree about which I
commanded you, 'You must
not eat of it,'   Ge 2:17

"Cursed is the ground
because of you;   Ge 5:29
through painful toil you
will eat of it
all the days of your life.
¹⁸It will produce thorns and
thistles for you,   Job 31:40
and you will eat the plants
of the field.   Ps 104:14
¹⁹By the sweat of your brow
you will eat your food
until you return to the
ground,
since from it you were
taken;
for dust you are
and to dust you will
return."   Ge 2:7

²⁰Adam*ᵇ* named his wife
Eve,*ᶜ* because she would
become the mother of all the
living.   1Ti 2:13

²¹The LORD God made gar-
ments of skin for Adam and his
wife and clothed them. ²²And
the LORD God said, "The man
has now become like one of us,
knowing good and evil. He
must not be allowed to reach
out his hand and take also from
the tree of life and eat, and live
forever." ²³So the LORD God
banished him from the Garden
of Eden to work the ground
from which he had been taken.
²⁴After he drove the man out, he
placed on the east side*ᵈ* of the
Garden of Eden cherubim and a
flaming sword flashing back
and forth to guard the way to
the tree of life. Ge 2:9; Eze 10:1

Cain and Abel

4 Adam*ᵇ* lay with his wife
Eve, and she became preg-
nant and gave birth to Cain.*ᵉ*
She said, "With the help of the
LORD I have brought forth*ᶠ* a
man." ²Later she gave birth to
his brother Abel.

Now Abel kept flocks, and
Cain worked the soil. ³In the
course of time Cain brought
some of the fruits of the soil as
an offering to the LORD. ⁴But
Abel brought fat portions from
some of the firstborn of his
flock. The LORD looked with favor on Abel and his offering,
⁵but on Cain and his offering he
did not look with favor. So Cain
was very angry, and his face
was downcast.   Lev 3:16; Nu 18:17

---

*ᵃ15 Or strike   ᵇ20,1 Or The man   ᶜ20 Eve probably means living.   ᵈ24 Or placed
in front   ᵉ1 Cain sounds like the Hebrew for brought forth or acquired.   ᶠ1 Or have
acquired*

⁶Then the LORD said to Cain, "Why are you angry? Why is your face downcast? ⁷If you do what is right, will you not be accepted? But if you do not do what is right, sin is crouching at your door; it desires to have you, but you must master it."

⁸Now Cain said to his brother Abel, "Let's go out to the field."ᵃ And while they were in the field, Cain attacked his brother Abel and killed him.

⁹Then the LORD said to Cain, "Where is your brother Abel?"

"I don't know," he replied. "Am I my brother's keeper?"

¹⁰The LORD said, "What have you done? Listen! Your brother's blood cries out to me from the ground. ¹¹Now you are under a curse and driven from the ground, which opened its mouth to receive your brother's blood from your hand. ¹²When you work the ground, it will no longer yield its crops for you. You will be a restless wanderer on the earth."   Heb 12:24; Rev 6:10

¹³Cain said to the LORD, "My punishment is more than I can bear. ¹⁴Today you are driving me from the land, and I will be hidden from your presence; I will be a restless wanderer on the earth, and whoever finds me will kill me."   Nu 35:19

¹⁵But the LORD said to him, "Not soᵇ; if anyone kills Cain, he will suffer vengeance seven times over." Then the LORD put a mark on Cain so that no one who found him would kill him. ¹⁶So Cain went out from the LORD's presence and lived in the land of Nod,ᶜ east of Eden.

¹⁷Cain lay with his wife, and she became pregnant and gave birth to Enoch. Cain was then building a city, and he named it after his son Enoch. ¹⁸To Enoch was born Irad, and Irad was the father of Mehujael, and Mehujael was the father of Methushael, and Methushael was the father of Lamech.   Ps 49:11

¹⁹Lamech married two women, one named Adah and the other Zillah. ²⁰Adah gave birth to Jabal; he was the father of those who live in tents and raise livestock. ²¹His brother's name was Jubal; he was the father of all who play the harp and flute. ²²Zillah also had a son, Tubal-Cain, who forged all kinds of tools out ofᵈ bronze and iron. Tubal-Cain's sister was Naamah.   Ex 35:35

²³Lamech said to his wives,

"Adah and Zillah, listen to
     me;
wives of Lamech, hear my
     words.
I have killedᵉ a man for
     wounding me,
a young man for injuring
     me.

ᵃ8 Samaritan Pentateuch, Septuagint, Vulgate and Syriac; Masoretic Text does not have "Let's go out to the field."   ᵇ15 Septuagint, Vulgate and Syriac; Hebrew *Very well*
ᶜ16 *Nod* means *wandering* (see verses 12 and 14).   ᵈ22 Or *who instructed all who work in*   ᵉ23 Or *I will kill*

²⁴If Cain is avenged seven
   times,
   then Lamech seventy-seven
   times." Ge 9:5-6; Mt 18:22

²⁵Adam lay with his wife again, and she gave birth to a son and named him Seth,ᵃ saying, "God has granted me another child in place of Abel, since Cain killed him." ²⁶Seth also had a son, and he named him Enosh. Ge 4:8; 5:3

At that time men began to call onᵇ the name of the LORD.

From Adam to Noah

5 This is the written account of Adam's line.

When God created man, he made him in the likeness of God. ²He created them male and female and blessed them. And when they were created, he called them "man.ᶜ" Ge 1:27

³When Adam had lived 130 years, he had a son in his own likeness, in his own image; and he named him Seth. ⁴After Seth was born, Adam lived 800 years and had other sons and daughters. ⁵Altogether, Adam lived 930 years, and then he died.

⁶When Seth had lived 105 years, he became the fatherᵈ of Enosh. ⁷And after he became the father of Enosh, Seth lived 807 years and had other sons and daughters. ⁸Altogether, Seth lived 912 years, and then he died. Ge 4:26; Lk 3:38

⁹When Enosh had lived 90 years, he became the father of Kenan. ¹⁰And after he became the father of Kenan, Enosh lived 815 years and had other sons and daughters. ¹¹Altogether, Enosh lived 905 years, and then he died. 1Ch 1:2; Lk 3:37

¹²When Kenan had lived 70 years, he became the father of Mahalalel. ¹³And after he became the father of Mahalalel, Kenan lived 840 years and had other sons and daughters. ¹⁴Altogether, Kenan lived 910 years, and then he died. 1Ch 1:2

¹⁵When Mahalalel had lived 65 years, he became the father of Jared. ¹⁶And after he became the father of Jared, Mahalalel lived 830 years and had other sons and daughters. ¹⁷Altogether, Mahalalel lived 895 years, and then he died. Lk 3:37

¹⁸When Jared had lived 162 years, he became the father of Enoch. ¹⁹And after he became the father of Enoch, Jared lived 800 years and had other sons and daughters. ²⁰Altogether, Jared lived 962 years, and then he died. 1Ch 1:2

²¹When Enoch had lived 65 years, he became the father of Methuselah. ²²And after he became the father of Methuselah, Enoch walked with God 300 years and had other sons and daughters. ²³Altogether, Enoch lived 365 years. ²⁴Enoch walked with God; then

ᵃ25 Seth probably means granted. ᵇ26 Or to proclaim ᶜ2 Hebrew adam
ᵈ6 Father may mean ancestor; also in verses 7-26.

he was no more, because God took him away. ‎ Ge 6:9; 17:1; Jude 14

25When Methuselah had lived 187 years, he became the father of Lamech. 26And after he became the father of Lamech, Methuselah lived 782 years and had other sons and daughters. 27Altogether, Methuselah lived 969 years, and then he died.

28When Lamech had lived 182 years, he had a son. 29He named him Noah*a* and said, "He will comfort us in the labor and painful toil of our hands caused by the ground the LORD has cursed." 30After Noah was born, Lamech lived 595 years and had other sons and daughters. 31Altogether, Lamech lived 777 years, and then he died.

32After Noah was 500 years old, he became the father of Shem, Ham and Japheth.

The Flood

6 When men began to increase in number on the earth and daughters were born to them, 2the sons of God saw that the daughters of men were beautiful, and they married any of them they chose. 3Then the LORD said, "My Spirit will not contend with*b* man forever, for he is mortal*c*; his days will be a hundred and twenty years."

4The Nephilim were on the earth in those days—and also afterward—when the sons of God went to the daughters of men and had children by them. They were the heroes of old, men of renown. ‎ Nu 13:33

5The LORD saw how great man's wickedness on the earth had become, and that every inclination of the thoughts of his heart was only evil all the time. 6The LORD was grieved that he had made man on the earth, and his heart was filled with pain. 7So the LORD said, "I will wipe mankind, whom I have created, from the face of the earth—men and animals, and creatures that move along the ground, and birds of the air—for I am grieved that I have made them." 8But Noah found favor in the eyes of the LORD.

9This is the account of Noah.

Noah was a righteous man, blameless among the people of his time, and he walked with God. 10Noah had three sons: Shem, Ham and Japheth. ‎ Ge 17:1

11Now the earth was corrupt in God's sight and was full of violence. 12God saw how corrupt the earth had become, for all the people on earth had corrupted their ways. 13So God said to Noah, "I am going to put an end to all people, for the earth is filled with violence because of them. I am surely going to destroy both them and the earth. 14So make yourself an ark of cypress*d* wood; make rooms in it and coat it with pitch inside

---

a29 Noah sounds like the Hebrew for *comfort.*　　*b3* Or *My spirit will not remain in*
c3 Or *corrupt*　　*d14* The meaning of the Hebrew for this word is uncertain.

and out. [15]This is how you are to build it: The ark is to be 450 feet long, 75 feet wide and 45 feet high.[a] [16]Make a roof for it and finish[b] the ark to within 18 inches[c] of the top. Put a door in the side of the ark and make lower, middle and upper decks. [17]I am going to bring floodwaters on the earth to destroy all life under the heavens, every creature that has the breath of life in it. Everything on earth will perish. [18]But I will establish my covenant with you, and you will enter the ark—you and your sons and your wife and your sons' wives with you. [19]You are to bring into the ark two of all living creatures, male and female, to keep them alive with you. [20]Two of every kind of bird, of every kind of animal and of every kind of creature that moves along the ground will come to you to be kept alive. [21]You are to take every kind of food that is to be eaten and store it away as food for you and for them."   Ge 7:3; Ps 14:1-3

[22]Noah did everything just as God commanded him.   Ge 7:5

7 The LORD then said to Noah, "Go into the ark, you and your whole family, because I have found you righteous in this generation. [2]Take with you seven[d] of every kind of clean animal, a male and its mate, and two of every kind of unclean animal, a male and its mate,

[3]and also seven of every kind of bird, male and female, to keep their various kinds alive throughout the earth. [4]Seven days from now I will send rain on the earth for forty days and forty nights, and I will wipe from the face of the earth every living creature I have made."

[5]And Noah did all that the LORD commanded him.   Ge 6:22

[6]Noah was six hundred years old when the floodwaters came on the earth. [7]And Noah and his sons and his wife and his sons' wives entered the ark to escape the waters of the flood. [8]Pairs of clean and unclean animals, of birds and of all creatures that move along the ground, [9]male and female, came to Noah and entered the ark, as God had commanded Noah. [10]And after the seven days the floodwaters came on the earth.   Ge 5:32

[11]In the six hundredth year of Noah's life, on the seventeenth day of the second month—on that day all the springs of the great deep burst forth, and the floodgates of the heavens were opened. [12]And rain fell on the earth forty days and forty nights.   Ge 7:4,17; 8:2

[13]On that very day Noah and his sons, Shem, Ham and Japheth, together with his wife and the wives of his three sons, entered the ark. [14]They had with them every wild animal according to its kind, all livestock

---

[a]15 Hebrew *300 cubits long, 50 cubits wide and 30 cubits high* (about 140 meters long, 23 meters wide and 13.5 meters high)   [b]16 Or *Make an opening for light by finishing*   [c]16 Hebrew *a cubit* (about 0.5 meter)   [d]2 Or *seven pairs*; also in verse 3

accounting for the life of his fellow man.   Lev 17:10-16; Dt 12:16

6"Whoever sheds the blood of
    man,
  by man shall his blood be
    shed;   Ge 4:11
for in the image of God
  has God made man.   Ge 1:26

7As for you, be fruitful and increase in number; multiply on the earth and increase upon it."

8Then God said to Noah and to his sons with him: 9"I now establish my covenant with you and with your descendants after you 10and with every living creature that was with you—the birds, the livestock and all the wild animals, all those that came out of the ark with you—every living creature on earth. 11I establish my covenant with you: Never again will all life be cut off by the waters of a flood; never again will there be a flood to destroy the earth."

12And God said, "This is the sign of the covenant I am making between me and you and every living creature with you, a covenant for all generations to come: 13I have set my rainbow in the clouds, and it will be the sign of the covenant between me and the earth. 14Whenever I bring clouds over the earth and the rainbow appears in the clouds, 15I will remember my covenant between me and you and all living creatures of every kind. Never again will the waters become a flood to destroy all life. 16Whenever the rainbow appears in the clouds, I will see it and remember the everlasting covenant between God and all living creatures of every kind on the earth."   Ge 17:11; Eze 1:28

17So God said to Noah, "This is the sign of the covenant I have established between me and all life on the earth." Ge 9:12

The Sons of Noah

18The sons of Noah who came out of the ark were Shem, Ham and Japheth. (Ham was the father of Canaan.) 19These were the three sons of Noah, and from them came the people who were scattered over the earth.

20Noah, a man of the soil, proceeded*a* to plant a vineyard. 21When he drank some of its wine, he became drunk and lay uncovered inside his tent. 22Ham, the father of Canaan, saw his father's nakedness and told his two brothers outside. 23But Shem and Japheth took a garment and laid it across their shoulders; then they walked in backward and covered their father's nakedness. Their faces were turned the other way so that they would not see their father's nakedness.   Ge 19:35

24When Noah awoke from his wine and found out what his youngest son had done to him, 25he said,

"Cursed be Canaan!   Ge 27:12
  The lowest of slaves

a20 Or soil, was the first

will he be to his brothers."

26He also said,

"Blessed be the LORD, the
　God of Shem!
May Canaan be the slave of
　Shem. *a*　　　　　　1Ki 9:21
27May God extend the territory
　of Japheth*b*;　　　Ge 10:2-5
may Japheth live in the
　tents of Shem,　　Eph 2:13-14
and may Canaan be his*c*
　slave."

28After the flood Noah lived
350 years. 29Altogether, Noah
lived 950 years, and then he
died.　　　　　　　　Ge 2:17

The Table of Nations

10 This is the account of
Shem, Ham and Japheth,
Noah's sons, who themselves
had sons after the flood.

The Japhethites

2The sons*d* of Japheth:
Gomer, Magog, Madai,
Javan, Tubal, Meshech
and Tiras.
3The sons of Gomer:
Ashkenaz, Riphath and
Togarmah.　　　　　Jer 51:27
4The sons of Javan:
Elishah, Tarshish, the
Kittim and the Rodanim.*e*
5(From these the maritime
peoples spread out into

their territories by their
clans within their na-
tions, each with its own
language.)　　1Ch 1:5-7; Eze 27:12

The Hamites

6The sons of Ham:
Cush, Mizraim,*f* Put and
Canaan.　　　　　　2Ki 19:9
7The sons of Cush:
Seba, Havilah, Sabtah,
Raamah and Sabteca.
The sons of Raamah:
Sheba and Dedan.　1Ch 1:8-10

8Cush was the father*g* of
Nimrod, who grew to be a
mighty warrior on the earth.
9He was a mighty hunter before
the LORD; that is why it is said,
"Like Nimrod, a mighty hunter
before the LORD." 10The first
centers of his kingdom were
Babylon, Erech, Akkad and Calneh, in*h* Shinar.*i* 11From that
land he went to Assyria, where
he built Nineveh, Rehoboth Ir,*j*
Calah 12and Resen, which is between Nineveh and Calah; that
is the great city.　　Ge 11:9; Mic 5:6

13Mizraim was the father of
the Ludites, Anamites,
Lehabites, Naphtuhites,
14Pathrusites, Casluhites
(from whom the Philis-
tines came) and Caphto-
rites.　　　　　　　　Am 9:7
15Canaan was the father of

*a*26 Or *be his slave*　　*b*27 *Japheth* sounds like the Hebrew for *extend*.　　*c*27 Or *their*
*d*2 *Sons* may mean *descendants* or *successors* or *nations*; also in verses 3, 4, 6, 7, 20-23, 29
and 31.　　*e*4 Some manuscripts of the Masoretic Text and Samaritan Pentateuch (see
also Septuagint and 1 Chron. 1:7); most manuscripts of the Masoretic Text *Dodanim*
*f*6 That is, Egypt; also in verse 13　　*g*8 *Father* may mean *ancestor* or *predecessor* or
founder; also in verses 13, 15, 24 and 26.　　*h*10 Or *Erech and Akkad—all of them in*
*i*10 That is, Babylonia　　*j*11 Or *Nineveh with its city squares*

Sidon his firstborn,ᵃ and of the Hittites, ¹⁶Jebusites, Amorites, Girgashites, ¹⁷Hivites, Arkites, Sinites, ¹⁸Arvadites, Zemarites and Hamathites.   1Ch 1:11-13

Later the Canaanite clans scattered ¹⁹and the borders of Canaan reached from Sidon toward Gerar as far as Gaza, and then toward Sodom, Gomorrah, Admah and Zeboiim, as far as Lasha.   Ge 14:2

²⁰These are the sons of Ham by their clans and languages, in their territories and nations.

The Semites

²¹Sons were also born to Shem, whose older brother wasᵇ Japheth; Shem was the ancestor of all the sons of Eber.

²²The sons of Shem:
Elam, Asshur, Arphaxad, Lud and Aram.
²³The sons of Aram:
Uz, Hul, Gether and Meshech.ᶜ   Job 1:1; Jer 25:20
²⁴Arphaxad was the father ofᵈ Shelah,
and Shelah the father of Eber.   Lk 3:35
²⁵Two sons were born to Eber:
One was named Peleg,ᵉ because in his time the earth was divided; his brother was named Joktan.

²⁶Joktan was the father of Almodad, Sheleph, Hazarmaveth, Jerah, ²⁷Hadoram, Uzal, Diklah, ²⁸Obal, Abimael, Sheba, ²⁹Ophir, Havilah and Jobab. All these were sons of Joktan.   1Ch 1:17-23

³⁰The region where they lived stretched from Mesha toward Sephar, in the eastern hill country.

³¹These are the sons of Shem by their clans and languages, in their territories and nations.

³²These are the clans of Noah's sons, according to their lines of descent, within their nations. From these the nations spread out over the earth after the flood.   Ge 9:19; 10:1

The Tower of Babel

11 Now the whole world had one language and a common speech. ²As men moved eastward,ᶠ they found a plain in Shinarᵍ and settled there.   Ge 10:10; 14:1

³They said to each other, "Come, let's make bricks and bake them thoroughly." They used brick instead of stone, and tar for mortar. ⁴Then they said, "Come, let us build ourselves a city, with a tower that reaches to the heavens, so that we may make a name for ourselves and

---

ᵃ15 Or of the Sidonians, the foremost   ᵇ21 Or Shem, the older brother of   ᶜ23 See Septuagint and 1 Chron. 1:17; Hebrew Mash   ᵈ24 Hebrew; Septuagint father of Cainan, and Cainan was the father of   ᵉ25 Peleg means division.   ᶠ2 Or from the east; or in the east   ᵍ2 That is, Babylonia

not be scattered over the face of the whole earth." Ge 14:10

⁵But the LORD came down to see the city and the tower that the men were building. ⁶The LORD said, "If as one people speaking the same language they have begun to do this, then nothing they plan to do will be impossible for them. ⁷Come, let us go down and confuse their language so they will not understand each other." Ge 18:21

⁸So the LORD scattered them from there over all the earth, and they stopped building the city. ⁹That is why it was called Babel*a*—because there the LORD confused the language of the whole world. From there the LORD scattered them over the face of the whole earth. Ge 9:19

From Shem to Abram

¹⁰This is the account of Shem.

Two years after the flood, when Shem was 100 years old, he became the father*b* of Arphaxad. ¹¹And after he became the father of Arphaxad, Shem lived 500 years and had other sons and daughters. Ge 10:21-22

¹²When Arphaxad had lived 35 years, he became the father of Shelah. ¹³And after he became the father of Shelah, Arphaxad lived 403 years and had other sons and daughters.*c*

¹⁴When Shelah had lived 30 years, he became the father of Eber. ¹⁵And after he became the father of Eber, Shelah lived 403 years and had other sons and daughters. Lk 3:35

¹⁶When Eber had lived 34 years, he became the father of Peleg. ¹⁷And after he became the father of Peleg, Eber lived 430 years and had other sons and daughters. 1Ch 1:19; Lk 3:35

¹⁸When Peleg had lived 30 years, he became the father of Reu. ¹⁹And after he became the father of Reu, Peleg lived 209 years and had other sons and daughters. Lk 3:35

²⁰When Reu had lived 32 years, he became the father of Serug. ²¹And after he became the father of Serug, Reu lived 207 years and had other sons and daughters. Lk 3:35

²²When Serug had lived 30 years, he became the father of Nahor. ²³And after he became the father of Nahor, Serug lived 200 years and had other sons and daughters. Lk 3:34

²⁴When Nahor had lived 29 years, he became the father of Terah. ²⁵And after he became the father of Terah, Nahor lived 119 years and had other sons and daughters. Lk 3:34

²⁶After Terah had lived 70

---

*a*9 That is, Babylon; *Babel* sounds like the Hebrew for *confused.*   *b*10 *Father* may mean *ancestor;* also in verses 11-25.   *c*12,13 Hebrew; Septuagint (see also Luke 3:35, 36 and note at Gen. 10:24) *35 years, he became the father of Cainan. 13And after he became the father of Cainan, Arphaxad lived 430 years and had other sons and daughters, and then he died. When Cainan had lived 130 years, he became the father of Shelah. And after he became the father of Shelah, Cainan lived 330 years and had other sons and daughters*

years, he became the father of Abram, Nahor and Haran.

27This is the account of Terah.

Terah became the father of Abram, Nahor and Haran. And Haran became the father of Lot. 28While his father Terah was still alive, Haran died in Ur of the Chaldeans, in the land of his birth. 29Abram and Nahor both married. The name of Abram's wife was Sarai, and the name of Nahor's wife was Milcah; she was the daughter of Haran, the father of both Milcah and Iscah. 30Now Sarai was barren; she had no children. Ge 24:10

31Terah took his son Abram, his grandson Lot son of Haran, and his daughter-in-law Sarai, the wife of his son Abram, and together they set out from Ur of the Chaldeans to go to Canaan. But when they came to Haran, they settled there. Ge 15:7

32Terah lived 205 years, and he died in Haran. Jos 24:2

The Call of Abram

12 The LORD had said to Abram, "Leave your country, your people and your father's household and go to the land I will show you. Ac 7:2-3

2"I will make you into a great nation Ge 13:16
and I will bless you; Ge 24:1
I will make your name great,
and you will be a blessing.
3I will bless those who bless you,

and whoever curses you I will curse; Ge 27:29
and all peoples on earth will be blessed through you." Ge 15:5

4So Abram left, as the LORD had told him; and Lot went with him. Abram was seventy-five years old when he set out from Haran. 5He took his wife Sarai, his nephew Lot, all the possessions they had accumulated and the people they had acquired in Haran, and they set out for the land of Canaan, and they arrived there. Ge 11:27,31
6Abram traveled through the land as far as the site of the great tree of Moreh at Shechem. At that time the Canaanites were in the land. 7The LORD appeared to Abram and said, "To your offspring*a* I will give this land." So he built an altar there to the LORD, who had appeared to him. Ge 17:1; Dt 11:30
8From there he went on toward the hills east of Bethel and pitched his tent, with Bethel on the west and Ai on the east. There he built an altar to the LORD and called on the name of the LORD. 9Then Abram set out and continued toward the Negev. Ge 13:4; 20:1

Abram in Egypt

10Now there was a famine in the land, and Abram went down to Egypt to live there for a while because the famine was severe. 11As he was about to en-

a7 Or seed

sions, since he was living in Sodom. Ge 13:10; 19:17

13One who had escaped came and reported this to Abram the Hebrew. Now Abram was living near the great trees of Mamre the Amorite, a brother*a* of Eshcol and Aner, all of whom were allied with Abram. 14When Abram heard that his relative had been taken captive, he called out the 318 trained men born in his household and went in pursuit as far as Dan. 15During the night Abram divided his men to attack them and he routed them, pursuing them as far as Hobah, north of Damascus. 16He recovered all the goods and brought back his relative Lot and his possessions, together with the women and the other people. Ge 13:18; Jdg 7:16

17After Abram returned from defeating Kedorlaomer and the kings allied with him, the king of Sodom came out to meet him in the Valley of Shaveh (that is, the King's Valley). 1Sa 18:6

18Then Melchizedek king of Salem*b* brought out bread and wine. He was priest of God Most High, 19and he blessed Abram, saying,

"Blessed be Abram by God
    Most High,
  Creator*c* of heaven and
    earth.
20And blessed be*d* God Most
    High,

who delivered your
    enemies into your
    hand." Ge 24:27
Then Abram gave him a tenth of everything. Heb 7:4

21The king of Sodom said to Abram, "Give me the people and keep the goods for yourself." Ge 14:11,12

22But Abram said to the king of Sodom, "I have raised my hand to the LORD, God Most High, Creator of heaven and earth, and have taken an oath 23that I will accept nothing belonging to you, not even a thread or the thong of a sandal, so that you will never be able to say, 'I made Abram rich.' 24I will accept nothing but what my men have eaten and the share that belongs to the men who went with me—to Aner, Eshcol and Mamre. Let them have their share." Ge 14:19; 2Ki 5:16

God's Covenant With Abram

15 After this, the word of the LORD came to Abram in a vision: Ge 46:2

"Do not be afraid, Abram.
  I am your shield,*e* Ge 21:17
  your very great reward.*f*"

2But Abram said, "O Sovereign LORD, what can you give me since I remain childless and the one who will inherit*g* my estate is Eliezer of Damascus?" 3And Abram said, "You have given me no children; so a ser-

*a*13 Or *a relative;* or *an ally*   *b*18 That is, Jerusalem   *c*19 Or *Possessor;* also in
verse 22   *d*20 Or *And praise be to*   *e*1 Or *sovereign*   *f*1 Or *shield; / your reward
will be very great*   *g*2 The meaning of the Hebrew for this phrase is uncertain.

vant in my household will be my heir."　　　　　Ge 14:14; Ac 7:5

⁴Then the word of the LORD came to him: "This man will not be your heir, but a son coming from your own body will be your heir." ⁵He took him outside and said, "Look up at the heavens and count the stars—if indeed you can count them." Then he said to him, "So shall your offspring be."　　Gal 4:28

⁶Abram believed the LORD, and he credited it to him as righteousness.　　　　Gal 3:6

⁷He also said to him, "I am the LORD, who brought you out of Ur of the Chaldeans to give you this land to take possession of it."　　　　Ge 11:31; 13:17

⁸But Abram said, "O Sovereign LORD, how can I know that I will gain possession of it?"

⁹So the LORD said to him, "Bring me a heifer, a goat and a ram, each three years old, along with a dove and a young pigeon."　　　　Nu 19:2; Dt 21:3

¹⁰Abram brought all these to him, cut them in two and arranged the halves opposite each other; the birds, however, he did not cut in half. ¹¹Then birds of prey came down on the carcasses, but Abram drove them away.　　　　Lev 1:17; Jer 34:18

¹²As the sun was setting, Abram fell into a deep sleep, and a thick and dreadful darkness came over him. ¹³Then the LORD said to him, "Know for certain that your descendants

will be strangers in a country not their own, and they will be enslaved and mistreated four hundred years. ¹⁴But I will punish the nation they serve as slaves, and afterward they will come out with great possessions. ¹⁵You, however, will go to your fathers in peace and be buried at a good old age. ¹⁶In the fourth generation your descendants will come back here, for the sin of the Amorites has not yet reached its full measure."　　　Ge 2:21; Lev 18:28

¹⁷When the sun had set and darkness had fallen, a smoking firepot with a blazing torch appeared and passed between the pieces. ¹⁸On that day the LORD made a covenant with Abram and said, "To your descendants I give this land, from the river*a* of Egypt to the great river, the Euphrates— ¹⁹the land of the Kenites, Kenizzites, Kadmonites, ²⁰Hittites, Perizzites, Rephaites, ²¹Amorites, Canaanites, Girgashites and Jebusites."

Hagar and Ishmael

16 Now Sarai, Abram's wife, had borne him no children. But she had an Egyptian maidservant named Hagar; ²so she said to Abram, "The LORD has kept me from having children. Go, sleep with my maidservant; perhaps I can build a family through her."　　Ge 11:30

Abram agreed to what Sarai said. ³So after Abram had been

*a*18 Or *Wadi*

living in Canaan ten years, Sarai his wife took her Egyptian maidservant Hagar and gave her to her husband to be his wife. [4]He slept with Hagar, and she conceived. Ge 12:5; 16:1

When she knew she was pregnant, she began to despise her mistress. [5]Then Sarai said to Abram, "You are responsible for the wrong I am suffering. I put my servant in your arms, and now that she knows she is pregnant, she despises me. May the LORD judge between you and me." Ge 31:53

[6]"Your servant is in your hands," Abram said. "Do with her whatever you think best." Then Sarai mistreated Hagar; so she fled from her. Jos 9:25

[7]The angel of the LORD found Hagar near a spring in the desert; it was the spring that is beside the road to Shur. [8]And he said, "Hagar, servant of Sarai, where have you come from, and where are you going?" Ge 3:9; 21:17; 22:11

"I'm running away from my mistress Sarai," she answered.

[9]Then the angel of the LORD told her, "Go back to your mistress and submit to her." [10]The angel added, "I will so increase your descendants that they will be too numerous to count."

[11]The angel of the LORD also said to her:

"You are now with child
and you will have a son.
You shall name him
Ishmael,[a]   Ge 17:18
for the LORD has heard of
your misery.   Ge 39:20,21
[12]He will be a wild donkey of a
man;   Job 6:5
his hand will be against
everyone
and everyone's hand
against him,
and he will live in hostility
toward[b] all his brothers."

[13]She gave this name to the LORD who spoke to her: "You are the God who sees me," for she said, "I have now seen[c] the One who sees me." [14]That is why the well was called Beer Lahai Roi[d]; it is still there, between Kadesh and Bered. Ge 32:30

[15]So Hagar bore Abram a son, and Abram gave the name Ishmael to the son she had borne. [16]Abram was eighty-six years old when Hagar bore him Ishmael. Gal 4:22

The Covenant of Circumcision

17 When Abram was ninety-nine years old, the LORD appeared to him and said, "I am God Almighty[e]; walk before me and be blameless. [2]I will confirm my covenant between me and you and will greatly increase your numbers." Ge 15:18; 28:3

[3]Abram fell facedown, and God said to him, [4]"As for me, this is my covenant with you: You will be the father of many

---

[a]11 *Ishmael* means *God hears.*   [b]12 Or *live to the east / of*   [c]13 Or *seen the back of*
[d]14 *Beer Lahai Roi* means *well of the Living One who sees me.*   [e]1 Hebrew *El-Shaddai*

nations. ⁵No longer will you be called Abram*a*; your name will be Abraham,*b* for I have made you a father of many nations. ⁶I will make you very fruitful; I will make nations of you, and kings will come from you. ⁷I will establish my covenant as an everlasting covenant between me and you and your descendants after you for the generations to come, to be your God and the God of your descendants after you. ⁸The whole land of Canaan, where you are now an alien, I will give as an everlasting possession to you and your descendants after you; and I will be their God."   Ge 35:11

⁹Then God said to Abraham, "As for you, you must keep my covenant, you and your descendants after you for the generations to come. ¹⁰This is my covenant with you and your descendants after you, the covenant you are to keep: Every male among you shall be circumcised. ¹¹You are to undergo circumcision, and it will be the sign of the covenant between me and you. ¹²For the generations to come every male among you who is eight days old must be circumcised, including those born in your household or bought with money from a foreigner—those who are not your offspring. ¹³Whether born in your household or bought with your money, they must be cir-

cumcised. My covenant in your flesh is to be an everlasting covenant. ¹⁴Any uncircumcised male, who has not been circumcised in the flesh, will be cut off from his people; he has broken my covenant."   Ex 12:48; Ac 7:8

¹⁵God also said to Abraham, "As for Sarai your wife, you are no longer to call her Sarai; her name will be Sarah. ¹⁶I will bless her and will surely give you a son by her. I will bless her so that she will be the mother of nations; kings of peoples will come from her."   Ge 18:10

¹⁷Abraham fell facedown; he laughed and said to himself, "Will a son be born to a man a hundred years old? Will Sarah bear a child at the age of ninety?" ¹⁸And Abraham said to God, "If only Ishmael might live under your blessing!"   Ge 18:12

¹⁹Then God said, "Yes, but your wife Sarah will bear you a son, and you will call him Isaac.*c* I will establish my covenant with him as an everlasting covenant for his descendants after him. ²⁰And as for Ishmael, I have heard you: I will surely bless him; I will make him fruitful and will greatly increase his numbers. He will be the father of twelve rulers, and I will make him into a great nation. ²¹But my covenant I will establish with Isaac, whom Sarah will bear to you by this time next year." ²²When he had fin-

---

a5 Abram means *exalted father.*   *b5 Abraham* means *father of many.*   *c19 Isaac* means *he laughs.*

ished speaking with Abraham, God went up from him. Ge 21:2

23On that very day Abraham took his son Ishmael and all those born in his household or bought with his money, every male in his household, and circumcised them, as God told him. 24Abraham was ninety-nine years old when he was circumcised, 25and his son Ishmael was thirteen; 26Abraham and his son Ishmael were both circumcised on that same day. 27And every male in Abraham's household, including those born in his household or bought from a foreigner, was circumcised with him. Ge 14:14

The Three Visitors

18 The LORD appeared to Abraham near the great trees of Mamre while he was sitting at the entrance to his tent in the heat of the day. 2Abraham looked up and saw three men standing nearby. When he saw them, he hurried from the entrance of his tent to meet them and bowed low to the ground.

3He said, "If I have found favor in your eyes, my lord,a do not pass your servant by. 4Let a little water be brought, and then you may all wash your feet and rest under this tree. 5Let me get you something to eat, so you can be refreshed and then go on your way—now that you have come to your servant." Ge 43:24

"Very well," they answered, "do as you say."

6So Abraham hurried into the tent to Sarah. "Quick," he said, "get three seahsb of fine flour and knead it and bake some bread." Ge 19:3; 2Sa 13:8

7Then he ran to the herd and selected a choice, tender calf and gave it to a servant, who hurried to prepare it. 8He then brought some curds and milk and the calf that had been prepared, and set these before them. While they ate, he stood near them under a tree. Ge 19:3

9"Where is your wife Sarah?" they asked him. Ge 3:9

"There, in the tent," he said.

10Then the LORDc said, "I will surely return to you about this time next year, and Sarah your wife will have a son." Ro 9:9

Now Sarah was listening at the entrance to the tent, which was behind him. 11Abraham and Sarah were already old and well advanced in years, and Sarah was past the age of childbearing. 12So Sarah laughed to herself as she thought, "After I am worn out and my masterd is old, will I now have this pleasure?" Ge 17:17; Ro 4:19

13Then the LORD said to Abraham, "Why did Sarah laugh and say, 'Will I really have a child, now that I am old?' 14Is anything too hard for the LORD? I will return to you at the ap-

---

a3 Or O Lord   b6 That is, probably about 20 quarts (about 22 liters)   c10 Hebrew Then he   d12 Or husband

pointed time next year and Sarah will have a son."

¹⁵Sarah was afraid, so she lied and said, "I did not laugh."

But he said, "Yes, you did laugh."　　　　　　Ps 63:11; Mt 12:25

Abraham Pleads for Sodom

¹⁶When the men got up to leave, they looked down toward Sodom, and Abraham walked along with them to see them on their way. ¹⁷Then the LORD said, "Shall I hide from Abraham what I am about to do? ¹⁸Abraham will surely become a great and powerful nation, and all nations on earth will be blessed through him. ¹⁹For I have chosen him, so that he will direct his children and his household after him to keep the way of the LORD by doing what is right and just, so that the LORD will bring about for Abraham what he has promised him."　　　　Ge 19:24; Gal 3:8

²⁰Then the LORD said, "The outcry against Sodom and Gomorrah is so great and their sin so grievous ²¹that I will go down and see if what they have done is as bad as the outcry that has reached me. If not, I will know."　　　Ge 19:13; Eze 16:49-50

²²The men turned away and went toward Sodom, but Abraham remained standing before the LORD.ᵃ ²³Then Abraham approached him and said: "Will you sweep away the righteous with the wicked? ²⁴What if there are fifty righteous people in the city? Will you really sweep it away and not spareᵇ the place for the sake of the fifty righteous people in it? ²⁵Far be it from you to do such a thing—to kill the righteous with the wicked, treating the righteous and the wicked alike. Far be it from you! Will not the Judgeᶜ of all the earth do right?"　　Ge 19:1

²⁶The LORD said, "If I find fifty righteous people in the city of Sodom, I will spare the whole place for their sake."　　　Jer 5:1

²⁷Then Abraham spoke up again: "Now that I have been so bold as to speak to the Lord, though I am nothing but dust and ashes, ²⁸what if the number of the righteous is five less than fifty? Will you destroy the whole city because of five people?"　　Job 30:19; 42:6

"If I find forty-five there," he said, "I will not destroy it."

²⁹Once again he spoke to him, "What if only forty are found there?"

He said, "For the sake of forty, I will not do it."

³⁰Then he said, "May the Lord not be angry, but let me speak. What if only thirty can be found there?"　　Ge 44:18; Ex 32:22

He answered, "I will not do it if I find thirty there."

³¹Abraham said, "Now that I have been so bold as to speak to

ᵃ22 Masoretic Text; an ancient Hebrew scribal tradition *but the* LORD *remained standing before Abraham*　　ᵇ24 Or *forgive*; also in verse 26　　ᶜ25 Or *Ruler*

the Lord, what if only twenty can be found there?"

He said, "For the sake of twenty, I will not destroy it."

³²Then he said, "May the Lord not be angry, but let me speak just once more. What if only ten can be found there?"

He answered, "For the sake of ten, I will not destroy it."

³³When the LORD had finished speaking with Abraham, he left, and Abraham returned home. <small>Ge 17:22</small>

Sodom and Gomorrah Destroyed

19 The two angels arrived at Sodom in the evening, and Lot was sitting in the gateway of the city. When he saw them, he got up to meet them and bowed down with his face to the ground. ²"My lords," he said, "please turn aside to your servant's house. You can wash your feet and spend the night and then go on your way early in the morning." <small>Ge 18:22</small>

"No," they answered, "we will spend the night in the square." <small>Jdg 19:15,20</small>

³But he insisted so strongly that they did go with him and entered his house. He prepared a meal for them, baking bread without yeast, and they ate. ⁴Before they had gone to bed, all the men from every part of the city of Sodom—both young and old—surrounded the house. ⁵They called to Lot, "Where are the men who came to you to-night? Bring them out to us so that we can have sex with them." <small>Ge 18:6; Jdg 19:22</small>

⁶Lot went outside to meet them and shut the door behind him ⁷and said, "No, my friends. Don't do this wicked thing. ⁸Look, I have two daughters who have never slept with a man. Let me bring them out to you, and you can do what you like with them. But don't do anything to these men, for they have come under the protection of my roof." <small>Jdg 19:23; 2Pe 2:7</small>

⁹"Get out of our way," they replied. And they said, "This fellow came here as an alien, and now he wants to play the judge! We'll treat you worse than them." They kept bringing pressure on Lot and moved forward to break down the door.

¹⁰But the men inside reached out and pulled Lot back into the house and shut the door. ¹¹Then they struck the men who were at the door of the house, young and old, with blindness so that they could not find the door.

¹²The two men said to Lot, "Do you have anyone else here—sons-in-law, sons or daughters, or anyone else in the city who belongs to you? Get them out of here, ¹³because we are going to destroy this place. The outcry to the LORD against its people is so great that he has sent us to destroy it." <small>1Ch 21:15</small>

¹⁴So Lot went out and spoke to his sons-in-law, who were

pledged to marry[a] his daughters. He said, "Hurry and get out of this place, because the LORD is about to destroy the city!" But his sons-in-law thought he was joking.   Nu 16:21

15With the coming of dawn, the angels urged Lot, saying, "Hurry! Take your wife and your two daughters who are here, or you will be swept away when the city is punished."

16When he hesitated, the men grasped his hand and the hands of his wife and of his two daughters and led them safely out of the city, for the LORD was merciful to them. 17As soon as they had brought them out, one of them said, "Flee for your lives! Don't look back, and don't stop anywhere in the plain! Flee to the mountains or you will be swept away!"   Lk 18:13

18But Lot said to them, "No, my lords,[b] please! 19Your[c] servant has found favor in your[c] eyes, and you[c] have shown great kindness to me in sparing my life. But I can't flee to the mountains; this disaster will overtake me, and I'll die. 20Look, here is a town near enough to run to, and it is small. Let me flee to it—it is very small, isn't it? Then my life will be spared."   Ge 6:8; 24:12

21He said to him, "Very well, I will grant this request too; I will not overthrow the town you speak of. 22But flee there quickly, because I cannot do anything until you reach it." (That is why the town was called Zoar.[d])

23By the time Lot reached Zoar, the sun had risen over the land. 24Then the LORD rained down burning sulfur on Sodom and Gomorrah—from the LORD out of the heavens. 25Thus he overthrew those cities and the entire plain, including all those living in the cities—and also the vegetation in the land. 26But Lot's wife looked back, and she became a pillar of salt.   Lk 17:29

27Early the next morning Abraham got up and returned to the place where he had stood before the LORD. 28He looked down toward Sodom and Gomorrah, toward all the land of the plain, and he saw dense smoke rising from the land, like smoke from a furnace.   Ge 18:22

29So when God destroyed the cities of the plain, he remembered Abraham, and he brought Lot out of the catastrophe that overthrew the cities where Lot had lived.   2Pe 2:7

Lot and His Daughters

30Lot and his two daughters left Zoar and settled in the mountains, for he was afraid to stay in Zoar. He and his two daughters lived in a cave. 31One day the older daughter said to the younger, "Our father is old, and there is no man around

---

a14 Or were married to   b18 Or No, Lord; or No, my lord   c19 The Hebrew is singular.   d22 Zoar means small.

here to lie with us, as is the custom all over the earth. 32Let's get our father to drink wine and then lie with him and preserve our family line through our father." Ge 14:10; Dt 25:5

33That night they got their father to drink wine, and the older daughter went in and lay with him. He was not aware of it when she lay down or when she got up.

34The next day the older daughter said to the younger, "Last night I lay with my father. Let's get him to drink wine again tonight, and you go in and lie with him so we can preserve our family line through our father." 35So they got their father to drink wine that night also, and the younger daughter went and lay with him. Again he was not aware of it when she lay down or when she got up.

36So both of Lot's daughters became pregnant by their father. 37The older daughter had a son, and she named him Moab*a*; he is the father of the Moabites of today. 38The younger daughter also had a son, and she named him Ben-Ammi*b*; he is the father of the Ammonites of today. Dt 2:9,19

Abraham and Abimelech

20 Now Abraham moved on from there into the region of the Negev and lived between Kadesh and Shur. For a while he stayed in Gerar, 2and there Abraham said of his wife Sarah, "She is my sister." Then Abimelech king of Gerar sent for Sarah and took her. Ge 12:13; 26:7

3But God came to Abimelech in a dream one night and said to him, "You are as good as dead because of the woman you have taken; she is a married woman." Ge 26:10; Job 33:15

4Now Abimelech had not gone near her, so he said, "Lord, will you destroy an innocent nation? 5Did he not say to me, 'She is my sister,' and didn't she also say, 'He is my brother'? I have done this with a clear conscience and clean hands." Ge 18:25; 1Ki 9:4

6Then God said to him in the dream, "Yes, I know you did this with a clear conscience, and so I have kept you from sinning against me. That is why I did not let you touch her. 7Now return the man's wife, for he is a prophet, and he will pray for you and you will live. But if you do not return her, you may be sure that you and all yours will die." 1Sa 25:26; Job 42:8

8Early the next morning Abimelech summoned all his officials, and when he told them all that had happened, they were very much afraid. 9Then Abimelech called Abraham in and said, "What have you done to us? How have I wronged you that you have brought such

---

a37 Moab sounds like the Hebrew for *from father*. *b38 Ben-Ammi* means *son of my people*.

great guilt upon me and my kingdom? You have done things to me that should not be done." ¹⁰And Abimelech asked Abraham, "What was your reason for doing this?"   Ge 12:18

¹¹Abraham replied, "I said to myself, 'There is surely no fear of God in this place, and they will kill me because of my wife.' ¹²Besides, she really is my sister, the daughter of my father though not of my mother; and she became my wife. ¹³And when God had me wander from my father's household, I said to her, 'This is how you can show your love to me: Everywhere we go, say of me, "He is my brother."'"   Ge 12:12; 26:7

¹⁴Then Abimelech brought sheep and cattle and male and female slaves and gave them to Abraham, and he returned Sarah his wife to him. ¹⁵And Abimelech said, "My land is before you; live wherever you like."   Ge 12:16; 13:9; 34:10

¹⁶To Sarah he said, "I am giving your brother a thousand shekels[a] of silver. This is to cover the offense against you before all who are with you; you are completely vindicated."

¹⁷Then Abraham prayed to God, and God healed Abimelech, his wife and his slave girls so they could have children again, ¹⁸for the LORD had closed up every womb in Abimelech's household because of Abraham's wife Sarah.   Nu 12:13

The Birth of Isaac

21 Now the LORD was gracious to Sarah as he had said, and the LORD did for Sarah what he had promised. ²Sarah became pregnant and bore a son to Abraham in his old age, at the very time God had promised him. ³Abraham gave the name Isaac[b] to the son Sarah bore him. ⁴When his son Isaac was eight days old, Abraham circumcised him, as God commanded him. ⁵Abraham was a hundred years old when his son Isaac was born to him.   Ge 17:16

⁶Sarah said, "God has brought me laughter, and everyone who hears about this will laugh with me." ⁷And she added, "Who would have said to Abraham that Sarah would nurse children? Yet I have borne him a son in his old age."   Isa 54:1

Hagar and Ishmael Sent Away

⁸The child grew and was weaned, and on the day Isaac was weaned Abraham held a great feast. ⁹But Sarah saw that the son whom Hagar the Egyptian had borne to Abraham was mocking, ¹⁰and she said to Abraham, "Get rid of that slave woman and her son, for that slave woman's son will never share in the inheritance with my son Isaac."   Ge 16:15; 1Sa 1:23

¹¹The matter distressed Abraham greatly because it concerned his son. ¹²But God said

---

[a]16 That is, about 25 pounds (about 11.5 kilograms)   [b]3 *Isaac* means *he laughs*.

to him, "Do not be so distressed about the boy and your maidservant. Listen to whatever Sarah tells you, because it is through Isaac that your offspring*a* will be reckoned. ¹³I will make the son of the maidservant into a nation also, because he is your offspring."

¹⁴Early the next morning Abraham took some food and a skin of water and gave them to Hagar. He set them on her shoulders and then sent her off with the boy. She went on her way and wandered in the desert of Beersheba.   Ge 16:1; Jos 15:28

¹⁵When the water in the skin was gone, she put the boy under one of the bushes. ¹⁶Then she went off and sat down nearby, about a bowshot away, for she thought, "I cannot watch the boy die." And as she sat there nearby, she*b* began to sob.

¹⁷God heard the boy crying, and the angel of God called to Hagar from heaven and said to her, "What is the matter, Hagar? Do not be afraid; God has heard the boy crying as he lies there. ¹⁸Lift the boy up and take him by the hand, for I will make him into a great nation."   Ex 3:7

¹⁹Then God opened her eyes and she saw a well of water. So she went and filled the skin with water and gave the boy a drink.   Ge 16:7; Nu 22:31

²⁰God was with the boy as he grew up. He lived in the desert and became an archer. ²¹While he was living in the Desert of Paran, his mother got a wife for him from Egypt.   Ge 28:15

The Treaty at Beersheba

²²At that time Abimelech and Phicol the commander of his forces said to Abraham, "God is with you in everything you do. ²³Now swear to me here before God that you will not deal falsely with me or my children or my descendants. Show to me and the country where you are living as an alien the same kindness I have shown to you."

²⁴Abraham said, "I swear it."

²⁵Then Abraham complained to Abimelech about a well of water that Abimelech's servants had seized. ²⁶But Abimelech said, "I don't know who has done this. You did not tell me, and I heard about it only today."   Ge 26:15,20-22

²⁷So Abraham brought sheep and cattle and gave them to Abimelech, and the two men made a treaty. ²⁸Abraham set apart seven ewe lambs from the flock, ²⁹and Abimelech asked Abraham, "What is the meaning of these seven ewe lambs you have set apart by themselves?"   Ge 26:31; 31:44,53

³⁰He replied, "Accept these seven lambs from my hand as a witness that I dug this well."

³¹So that place was called

---

*a*12 Or *seed*   *b*16 Hebrew; Septuagint *the child*

Beersheba,[a] because the two men swore an oath there. Ge 26:33

³²After the treaty had been made at Beersheba, Abimelech and Phicol the commander of his forces returned to the land of the Philistines. ³³Abraham planted a tamarisk tree in Beersheba, and there he called upon the name of the Lord, the Eternal God. ³⁴And Abraham stayed in the land of the Philistines for a long time. Dt 33:27

Abraham Tested

22 Some time later God tested Abraham. He said to him, "Abraham!" Dt 8:2

"Here I am," he replied.

²Then God said, "Take your son, your only son, Isaac, whom you love, and go to the region of Moriah. Sacrifice him there as a burnt offering on one of the mountains I will tell you about." 2Ch 3:1; Heb 11:17

³Early the next morning Abraham got up and saddled his donkey. He took with him two of his servants and his son Isaac. When he had cut enough wood for the burnt offering, he set out for the place God had told him about. ⁴On the third day Abraham looked up and saw the place in the distance. ⁵He said to his servants, "Stay here with the donkey while I and the boy go over there. We will worship and then we will come back to you." Jos 8:10

⁶Abraham took the wood for the burnt offering and placed it on his son Isaac, and he himself carried the fire and the knife. As the two of them went on together, ⁷Isaac spoke up and said to his father Abraham, "Father?" Jdg 19:29; Jn 19:17

"Yes, my son?" Abraham replied.

"The fire and wood are here," Isaac said, "but where is the lamb for the burnt offering?" Lev 1:10; Rev 13:8

⁸Abraham answered, "God himself will provide the lamb for the burnt offering, my son." And the two of them went on together. Jn 1:29

⁹When they reached the place God had told him about, Abraham built an altar there and arranged the wood on it. He bound his son Isaac and laid him on the altar, on top of the wood. ¹⁰Then he reached out his hand and took the knife to slay his son. ¹¹But the angel of the Lord called out to him from heaven, "Abraham! Abraham!"

"Here I am," he replied.

¹²"Do not lay a hand on the boy," he said. "Do not do anything to him. Now I know that you fear God, because you have not withheld from me your son, your only son." 1Sa 15:22; 1Jn 4:9

¹³Abraham looked up and there in a thicket he saw a ram[b] caught by its horns. He went over and took the ram and sacri-

---

a31 Beersheba can mean *well of seven* or *well of the oath.*   *b13* Many manuscripts of the Masoretic Text, Samaritan Pentateuch, Septuagint and Syriac; most manuscripts of the Masoretic Text *a ram behind him.*

ficed it as a burnt offering instead of his son. ¹⁴So Abraham called that place The LORD Will Provide. And to this day it is said, "On the mountain of the LORD it will be provided." Ge 8:20

¹⁵The angel of the LORD called to Abraham from heaven a second time ¹⁶and said, "I swear by myself, declares the LORD, that because you have done this and have not withheld your son, your only son, ¹⁷I will surely bless you and make your descendants as numerous as the stars in the sky and as the sand on the seashore. Your descendants will take possession of the cities of their enemies, ¹⁸and through your offspring*a* all nations on earth will be blessed, because you have obeyed me."

¹⁹Then Abraham returned to his servants, and they set off together for Beersheba. And Abraham stayed in Beersheba.

Nahor's Sons

²⁰Some time later Abraham was told, "Milcah is also a mother; she has borne sons to your brother Nahor: ²¹Uz the firstborn, Buz his brother, Kemuel (the father of Aram), ²²Kesed, Hazo, Pildash, Jidlaph and Bethuel." ²³Bethuel became the father of Rebekah. Milcah bore these eight sons to Abraham's brother Nahor. ²⁴His concubine, whose name was Reumah, also had sons: Tebah, Gaham, Tahash and Maacah.

The Death of Sarah

23 Sarah lived to be a hundred and twenty-seven years old. ²She died at Kiriath Arba (that is, Hebron) in the land of Canaan, and Abraham went to mourn for Sarah and to weep over her. Ge 13:18; Jos 14:15

³Then Abraham rose from beside his dead wife and spoke to the Hittites.*b* He said, ⁴"I am an alien and a stranger among you. Sell me some property for a burial site here so I can bury my dead." Ge 10:15; 1 Ch 29:15

⁵The Hittites replied to Abraham, ⁶"Sir, listen to us. You are a mighty prince among us. Bury your dead in the choicest of our tombs. None of us will refuse you his tomb for burying your dead." Ge 20:7; 24:35

⁷Then Abraham rose and bowed down before the people of the land, the Hittites. ⁸He said to them, "If you are willing to let me bury my dead, then listen to me and intercede with Ephron son of Zohar on my behalf ⁹so he will sell me the cave of Machpelah, which belongs to him and is at the end of his field. Ask him to sell it to me for the full price as a burial site among you." Ge 25:9; 47:30

¹⁰Ephron the Hittite was sitting among his people and he replied to Abraham in the hearing of all the Hittites who had come to the gate of his city. ¹¹"No, my lord," he said. "Lis-

---

a18 Or *seed*   *b3* Or *the sons of Heth*; also in verses 5, 7, 10, 16, 18 and 20

ten to me; I give[a] you the field, and I give[a] you the cave that is in it. I give[a] it to you in the presence of my people. Bury your dead."

Ge 18:1; Ru 4:11

[12]Again Abraham bowed down before the people of the land [13]and he said to Ephron in their hearing, "Listen to me, if you will. I will pay the price of the field. Accept it from me so I can bury my dead there."

[14]Ephron answered Abraham, [15]"Listen to me, my lord; the land is worth four hundred shekels[b] of silver, but what is that between me and you? Bury your dead."

Ex 30:13; Eze 45:12

[16]Abraham agreed to Ephron's terms and weighed out for him the price he had named in the hearing of the Hittites: four hundred shekels of silver, according to the weight current among the merchants.

[17]So Ephron's field in Machpelah near Mamre—both the field and the cave in it, and all the trees within the borders of the field—was deeded [18]to Abraham as his property in the presence of all the Hittites who had come to the gate of the city. [19]Afterward Abraham buried his wife Sarah in the cave in the field of Machpelah near Mamre (which is at Hebron) in the land of Canaan. [20]So the field and the cave in it were deeded to Abraham by the Hittites as a burial site.

Ge 25:9; 50:13; Jos 14:13

Isaac and Rebekah

24 Abraham was now old and well advanced in years, and the LORD had blessed him in every way. [2]He said to the chief[c] servant in his household, the one in charge of all that he had, "Put your hand under my thigh. [3]I want you to swear by the LORD, the God of heaven and the God of earth, that you will not get a wife for my son from the daughters of the Canaanites, among whom I am living, [4]but will go to my country and my own relatives and get a wife for my son Isaac."

Ge 12:2; 10:18

[5]The servant asked him, "What if the woman is unwilling to come back with me to this land? Shall I then take your son back to the country you came from?"

Heb 11:15

[6]"Make sure that you do not take my son back there," Abraham said. [7]"The LORD, the God of heaven, who brought me out of my father's household and my native land and who spoke to me and promised me on oath, saying, 'To your offspring[d] I will give this land'—he will send his angel before you so that you can get a wife for my son from there. [8]If the woman is unwilling to come back with you, then you will be released from this oath of mine. Only do not take my son back there." [9]So the servant put his hand under

---

[a]11 Or *sell*   [b]15 That is, about 10 pounds (about 4.5 kilograms)   [c]2 Or *oldest*
[d]7 Or *seed*

the thigh of his master Abraham and swore an oath to him concerning this matter. Ge 12:7

¹⁰Then the servant took ten of his master's camels and left, taking with him all kinds of good things from his master. He set out for Aram Naharaim[a] and made his way to the town of Nahor. ¹¹He had the camels kneel down near the well outside the town; it was toward evening, the time the women go out to draw water. Ge 11:31

¹²Then he prayed, "O Lord, God of my master Abraham, give me success today, and show kindness to my master Abraham. ¹³See, I am standing beside this spring, and the daughters of the townspeople are coming out to draw water. ¹⁴May it be that when I say to a girl, 'Please let down your jar that I may have a drink,' and she says, 'Drink, and I'll water your camels too'—let her be the one you have chosen for your servant Isaac. By this I will know that you have shown kindness to my master." Ge 26:24

¹⁵Before he had finished praying, Rebekah came out with her jar on her shoulder. She was the daughter of Bethuel son of Milcah, who was the wife of Abraham's brother Nahor. ¹⁶The girl was very beautiful, a virgin; no man had ever lain with her. She went down to the spring, filled her jar and came up again.

¹⁷The servant hurried to meet her and said, "Please give me a little water from your jar."1Ki 17:10

¹⁸"Drink, my lord," she said, and quickly lowered the jar to her hands and gave him a drink. Ge 24:14,26

¹⁹After she had given him a drink, she said, "I'll draw water for your camels too, until they have finished drinking." ²⁰So she quickly emptied her jar into the trough, ran back to the well to draw more water, and drew enough for all his camels. ²¹Without saying a word, the man watched her closely to learn whether or not the Lord had made his journey successful. Ge 24:14,27

²²When the camels had finished drinking, the man took out a gold nose ring weighing a beka[b] and two gold bracelets weighing ten shekels.[c] ²³Then he asked, "Whose daughter are you? Please tell me, is there room in your father's house for us to spend the night?" Ge 24:47

²⁴She answered him, "I am the daughter of Bethuel, the son that Milcah bore to Nahor." ²⁵And she added, "We have plenty of straw and fodder, as well as room for you to spend the night." Ge 11:29; Jdg 19:19

²⁶Then the man bowed down and worshiped the Lord, ²⁷saying, "Praise be to the Lord, the God of my master Abraham, who has not abandoned his

---

[a]10 That is, Northwest Mesopotamia   [b]22 That is, about 1/5 ounce (about 5.5 grams)
[c]22 That is, about 4 ounces (about 110 grams)

kindness and faithfulness to my master. As for me, the LORD has led me on the journey to the house of my master's relatives."

²⁸The girl ran and told her mother's household about these things. ²⁹Now Rebekah had a brother named Laban, and he hurried out to the man at the spring. ³⁰As soon as he had seen the nose ring, and the bracelets on his sister's arms, and had heard Rebekah tell what the man said to her, he went out to the man and found him standing by the camels near the spring. ³¹"Come, you who are blessed by the LORD," he said. "Why are you standing out here? I have prepared the house and a place for the camels."   Ge 29:12

³²So the man went to the house, and the camels were unloaded. Straw and fodder were brought for the camels, and water for him and his men to wash their feet. ³³Then food was set before him, but he said, "I will not eat until I have told you what I have to say."   Ge 43:24

"Then tell us," Laban said.

³⁴So he said, "I am Abraham's servant. ³⁵The LORD has blessed my master abundantly, and he has become wealthy. He has given him sheep and cattle, silver and gold, menservants and maidservants, and camels and donkeys. ³⁶My master's wife Sarah has borne him a son in herᵃ old age, and he has given

him everything he owns. ³⁷And my master made me swear an oath, and said, 'You must not get a wife for my son from the daughters of the Canaanites, in whose land I live, ³⁸but go to my father's family and to my own clan, and get a wife for my son.'

³⁹"Then I asked my master, 'What if the woman will not come back with me?'   Ge 24:15

⁴⁰"He replied, 'The LORD, before whom I have walked, will send his angel with you and make your journey a success, so that you can get a wife for my son from my own clan and from my father's family. ⁴¹Then, when you go to my clan, you will be released from my oath even if they refuse to give her to you—you will be released from my oath.'   Ge 12:1; 24:7

⁴²"When I came to the spring today, I said, 'O LORD, God of my master Abraham, if you will, please grant success to the journey on which I have come. ⁴³See, I am standing beside this spring; if a maiden comes out to draw water and I say to her, "Please let me drink a little water from your jar," ⁴⁴and if she says to me, "Drink, and I'll draw water for your camels too," let her be the one the LORD has chosen for my master's son.'   Ge 24:11-14

⁴⁵"Before I finished praying in my heart, Rebekah came out, with her jar on her shoulder. She went down to the spring

ᵃ36 Or his

and drew water, and I said to her, 'Please give me a drink.' ⁴⁶"She quickly lowered her jar from her shoulder and said, 'Drink, and I'll water your camels too.' So I drank, and she watered the camels also. Ge 24:18

⁴⁷"I asked her, 'Whose daughter are you?'

"She said, 'The daughter of Bethuel son of Nahor, whom Milcah bore to him.' Ge 22:22

"Then I put the ring in her nose and the bracelets on her arms, ⁴⁸and I bowed down and worshiped the LORD. I praised the LORD, the God of my master Abraham, who had led me on the right road to get the granddaughter of my master's brother for his son. ⁴⁹Now if you will show kindness and faithfulness to my master, tell me; and if not, tell me, so I may know which way to turn." Ge 47:29

⁵⁰Laban and Bethuel answered, "This is from the LORD; we can say nothing to you one way or the other. ⁵¹Here is Rebekah; take her and go, and let her become the wife of your master's son, as the LORD has directed." Ge 31:24; Ps 118:23

⁵²When Abraham's servant heard what they said, he bowed down to the ground before the LORD. ⁵³Then the servant brought out gold and silver jewelry and articles of clothing and gave them to Rebekah; he also gave costly gifts to her brother and to her mother. ⁵⁴Then he

and the men who were with him ate and drank and spent the night there. Ge 45:22; Ex 3:22

When they got up the next morning, he said, "Send me on my way to my master." Ge 30:25 ⁵⁵But her brother and her mother replied, "Let the girl remain with us ten days or so; then you^a may go." Jdg 19:4

⁵⁶But he said to them, "Do not detain me, now that the LORD has granted success to my journey. Send me on my way so I may go to my master." Ge 24:12

⁵⁷Then they said, "Let's call the girl and ask her about it." ⁵⁸So they called Rebekah and asked her, "Will you go with this man?" Jdg 19:3

"I will go," she said. Ru 1:16

⁵⁹So they sent their sister Rebekah on her way, along with her nurse and Abraham's servant and his men. ⁶⁰And they blessed Rebekah and said to her,

"Our sister, may you
    increase
to thousands upon
    thousands; Ge 17:16
may your offspring possess
    the gates of their enemies."

⁶¹Then Rebekah and her maids got ready and mounted their camels and went back with the man. So the servant took Rebekah and left. Ge 16:1; 30:3

⁶²Now Isaac had come from Beer Lahai Roi, for he was living in the Negev. ⁶³He went out to

^a55 Or she

the field one evening to meditate,*a* and as he looked up, he saw camels approaching. ⁶⁴Rebekah also looked up and saw Isaac. She got down from her camel ⁶⁵and asked the servant, "Who is that man in the field coming to meet us?"   Ge 16:14

"He is my master," the servant answered. So she took her veil and covered herself.   Ge 38:14

⁶⁶Then the servant told Isaac all he had done. ⁶⁷Isaac brought her into the tent of his mother Sarah, and he married Rebekah. So she became his wife, and he loved her; and Isaac was comforted after his mother's death.

The Death of Abraham

25 Abraham took*b* another wife, whose name was Keturah. ²She bore him Zimran, Jokshan, Medan, Midian, Ishbak and Shuah. ³Jokshan was the father of Sheba and Dedan; the descendants of Dedan were the Asshurites, the Letushites and the Leummites. ⁴The sons of Midian were Ephah, Epher, Hanoch, Abida and Eldaah. All these were descendants of Keturah.   1Ch 1:32-33; Isa 60:6

⁵Abraham left everything he owned to Isaac. ⁶But while he was still living, he gave gifts to the sons of his concubines and sent them away from his son Isaac to the land of the east.

⁷Altogether, Abraham lived a hundred and seventy-five years. ⁸Then Abraham breathed his last and died at a good old age, an old man and full of years; and he was gathered to his people. ⁹His sons Isaac and Ishmael buried him in the cave of Machpelah near Mamre, in the field of Ephron son of Zohar the Hittite, ¹⁰the field Abraham had bought from the Hittites.*c* There Abraham was buried with his wife Sarah. ¹¹After Abraham's death, God blessed his son Isaac, who then lived near Beer Lahai Roi.

Ishmael's Sons

¹²This is the account of Abraham's son Ishmael, whom Sarah's maidservant, Hagar the Egyptian, bore to Abraham.

¹³These are the names of the sons of Ishmael, listed in the order of their birth: Nebaioth the firstborn of Ishmael, Kedar, Adbeel, Mibsam, ¹⁴Mishma, Dumah, Massa, ¹⁵Hadad, Tema, Jetur, Naphish and Kedemah. ¹⁶These were the sons of Ishmael, and these are the names of the twelve tribal rulers according to their settlements and camps. ¹⁷Altogether, Ishmael lived a hundred and thirty-seven years. He breathed his last and died, and he was gathered to his people. ¹⁸His descendants settled in the area from Havilah to Shur, near the border of Egypt, as you go toward Asshur. And they lived

---

a63 The meaning of the Hebrew for this word is uncertain.   *b1* Or *had taken*
c10 Or *the sons of Heth*

in hostility toward[a] all their brothers.   Ge 17:20; 1Ch 1:29-31

Jacob and Esau

[19]This is the account of Abraham's son Isaac.   Ge 2:4

Abraham became the father of Isaac, [20]and Isaac was forty years old when he married Rebekah daughter of Bethuel the Aramean from Paddan Aram[b] and sister of Laban the Aramean.   Ge 24:15,29; 31:20
[21]Isaac prayed to the LORD on behalf of his wife, because she was barren. The LORD answered his prayer, and his wife Rebekah became pregnant. [22]The babies jostled each other within her, and she said, "Why is this happening to me?" So she went to inquire of the LORD.
[23]The LORD said to her,

"Two nations are in your
    womb,   Ge 17:4
  and two peoples from
    within you will be
    separated;
one people will be stronger
    than the other,
and the older will serve the
    younger."   Ge 9:25

[24]When the time came for her to give birth, there were twin boys in her womb. [25]The first to come out was red, and his whole body was like a hairy garment; so they named him Esau.[c] [26]After this, his brother came out, with his hand grasping Esau's heel; so he was named Jacob.[d] Isaac was sixty years old when Rebekah gave birth to them.   Ge 27:11; 38:27
[27]The boys grew up, and Esau became a skillful hunter, a man of the open country, while Jacob was a quiet man, staying among the tents. [28]Isaac, who had a taste for wild game, loved Esau, but Rebekah loved Jacob. Ge 27:3
[29]Once when Jacob was cooking some stew, Esau came in from the open country, famished. [30]He said to Jacob, "Quick, let me have some of that red stew! I'm famished!" (That is why he was also called Edom.[e])   Ge 32:3; 2Ki 4:38
[31]Jacob replied, "First sell me your birthright."   Dt 21:16-17
[32]"Look, I am about to die," Esau said. "What good is the birthright to me?"
[33]But Jacob said, "Swear to me first." So he swore an oath to him, selling his birthright to Jacob.   Ge 21:23; Heb 12:16
[34]Then Jacob gave Esau some bread and some lentil stew. He ate and drank, and then got up and left.   Ge 25:30
So Esau despised his birthright.

Isaac and Abimelech

26 Now there was a famine in the land—besides the earlier famine of Abraham's time—and Isaac went to Abime-

---

[a]18 Or *lived to the east of*   [b]20 That is, Northwest Mesopotamia   [c]25 *Esau* may mean *hairy*; he was also called Edom, which means *red*.   [d]26 *Jacob* means *he grasps the heel* (figuratively, *he deceives*).   [e]30 *Edom* means *red*.

lech king of the Philistines in Gerar. ²The LORD appeared to Isaac and said, "Do not go down to Egypt; live in the land where I tell you to live. ³Stay in this land for a while, and I will be with you and will bless you. For to you and your descendants I will give all these lands and will confirm the oath I swore to your father Abraham. ⁴I will make your descendants as numerous as the stars in the sky and will give them all these lands, and through your offspring*a* all nations on earth will be blessed, ⁵because Abraham obeyed me and kept my requirements, my commands, my decrees and my laws." ⁶So Isaac stayed in Gerar.   Ge 12:10

⁷When the men of that place asked him about his wife, he said, "She is my sister," because he was afraid to say, "She is my wife." He thought, "The men of this place might kill me on account of Rebekah, because she is beautiful."   Ge 12:13

⁸When Isaac had been there a long time, Abimelech king of the Philistines looked down from a window and saw Isaac caressing his wife Rebekah. ⁹So Abimelech summoned Isaac and said, "She is really your wife! Why did you say, 'She is my sister'?"   Ge 10:14; 12:19

Isaac answered him, "Because I thought I might lose my life on account of her."

¹⁰Then Abimelech said,

"What is this you have done to us? One of the men might well have slept with your wife, and you would have brought guilt upon us."   Ge 20:9; Ex 32:21

¹¹So Abimelech gave orders to all the people: "Anyone who molests this man or his wife shall surely be put to death."

¹²Isaac planted crops in that land and the same year reaped a hundredfold, because the LORD blessed him. ¹³The man became rich, and his wealth continued to grow until he became very wealthy. ¹⁴He had so many flocks and herds and servants that the Philistines envied him. ¹⁵So all the wells that his father's servants had dug in the time of his father Abraham, the Philistines stopped up, filling them with earth.   Ge 24:35; Mt 13:8

¹⁶Then Abimelech said to Isaac, "Move away from us; you have become too powerful for us."   Ex 1:9; Jdg 11:7

¹⁷So Isaac moved away from there and encamped in the Valley of Gerar and settled there. ¹⁸Isaac reopened the wells that had been dug in the time of his father Abraham, which the Philistines had stopped up after Abraham died, and he gave them the same names his father had given them.   Ge 20:1

¹⁹Isaac's servants dug in the valley and discovered a well of fresh water there. ²⁰But the herdsmen of Gerar quarreled with Isaac's herdsmen and said,

*a*4 Or *seed*

"The water is ours!" So he named the well Esek, *a* because they disputed with him. ²¹Then they dug another well, but they quarreled over that one also; so he named it Sitnah. *b* ²²He moved on from there and dug another well, and no one quarreled over it. He named it Rehoboth, *c* saying, "Now the LORD has given us room and we will flourish in the land." Ge 13:7

²³From there he went up to Beersheba. ²⁴That night the LORD appeared to him and said, "I am the God of your father Abraham. Do not be afraid, for I am with you; I will bless you and will increase the number of your descendants for the sake of my servant Abraham." Ge 22:19

²⁵Isaac built an altar there and called on the name of the LORD. There he pitched his tent, and there his servants dug a well.

²⁶Meanwhile, Abimelech had come to him from Gerar, with Ahuzzath his personal adviser and Phicol the commander of his forces. ²⁷Isaac asked them, "Why have you come to me, since you were hostile to me and sent me away?" Ge 21:22

²⁸They answered, "We saw clearly that the LORD was with you; so we said, 'There ought to be a sworn agreement between us'—between us and you. Let us make a treaty with you ²⁹that you will do us no harm, just as we did not molest you but always treated you well and sent you away in peace. And now you are blessed by the LORD."

³⁰Isaac then made a feast for them, and they ate and drank. ³¹Early the next morning the men swore an oath to each other. Then Isaac sent them on their way, and they left him in peace. Ge 21:31; 31:54

³²That day Isaac's servants came and told him about the well they had dug. They said, "We've found water!" ³³He called it Shibah, *d* and to this day the name of the town has been Beersheba. *e* Ge 21:14,30

³⁴When Esau was forty years old, he married Judith daughter of Beeri the Hittite, and also Basemath daughter of Elon the Hittite. ³⁵They were a source of grief to Isaac and Rebekah.

Jacob Gets Isaac's Blessing

27 When Isaac was old and his eyes were so weak that he could no longer see, he called for Esau his older son and said to him, "My son." Ge 48:10

"Here I am," he answered.

²Isaac said, "I am now an old man and don't know the day of my death. ³Now then, get your weapons—your quiver and bow—and go out to the open country to hunt some wild game for me. ⁴Prepare me the kind of tasty food I like and bring it to me to eat, so that I

---

a20 Esek means *dispute.*   *b21 Sitnah* means *opposition.*   *c22 Rehoboth* means *room.*
d33 Shibah can mean *oath* or *seven.*   *e33 Beersheba* can mean *well of the oath* or *well of seven.*

may give you my blessing before I die." Ge 25:27; 47:29

⁵Now Rebekah was listening as Isaac spoke to his son Esau. When Esau left for the open country to hunt game and bring it back, ⁶Rebekah said to her son Jacob, "Look, I overheard your father say to your brother Esau, ⁷'Bring me some game and prepare me some tasty food to eat, so that I may give you my blessing in the presence of the LORD before I die.' ⁸Now, my son, listen carefully and do what I tell you: ⁹Go out to the flock and bring me two choice young goats, so I can prepare some tasty food for your father, just the way he likes it. ¹⁰Then take it to your father to eat, so that he may give you his blessing before he dies." Ge 25:27

¹¹Jacob said to Rebekah his mother, "But my brother Esau is a hairy man, and I'm a man with smooth skin. ¹²What if my father touches me? I would appear to be tricking him and would bring down a curse on myself rather than a blessing."

¹³His mother said to him, "My son, let the curse fall on me. Just do what I say; go and get them for me." Mt 27:25

¹⁴So he went and got them and brought them to his mother, and she prepared some tasty food, just the way his father liked it. ¹⁵Then Rebekah took the best clothes of Esau her older son, which she had in the house, and put them on her younger son Jacob. ¹⁶She also covered his hands and the smooth part of his neck with the goatskins. ¹⁷Then she handed to her son Jacob the tasty food and the bread she had made. Ge 25:28

¹⁸He went to his father and said, "My father."

"Yes, my son," he answered. "Who is it?"

¹⁹Jacob said to his father, "I am Esau your firstborn. I have done as you told me. Please sit up and eat some of my game so that you may give me your blessing." Ge 25:28; 27:4

²⁰Isaac asked his son, "How did you find it so quickly, my son?"

"The LORD your God gave me success," he replied. Ge 24:12

²¹Then Isaac said to Jacob, "Come near so I can touch you, my son, to know whether you really are my son Esau or not."

²²Jacob went close to his father Isaac, who touched him and said, "The voice is the voice of Jacob, but the hands are the hands of Esau." ²³He did not recognize him, for his hands were hairy like those of his brother Esau; so he blessed him. ²⁴"Are you really my son Esau?" he asked. Ge 27:16; 45:4

"I am," he replied.

²⁵Then he said, "My son, bring me some of your game to eat, so that I may give you my blessing." Ge 27:4

Jacob brought it to him and he ate; and he brought some wine and he drank. ²⁶Then his father Isaac said to him, "Come here, my son, and kiss me."

²⁷So he went to him and kissed him. When Isaac caught the smell of his clothes, he blessed him and said,

"Ah, the smell of my son
   is like the smell of a field
   that the LORD has blessed.
²⁸May God give you of
      heaven's dew   Dt 33:13
   and of earth's richness—
   an abundance of grain and
      new wine.   Nu 18:12
²⁹May nations serve you
   and peoples bow down to
      you.   2Sa 8:14
Be lord over your brothers,
   and may the sons of your
      mother bow down to
      you.   Ge 9:25
May those who curse you be
      cursed
   and those who bless you be
      blessed."   Ge 12:3

³⁰After Isaac finished blessing him and Jacob had scarcely left his father's presence, his brother Esau came in from hunting. ³¹He too prepared some tasty food and brought it to his father. Then he said to him, "My father, sit up and eat some of my game, so that you may give me your blessing."   Ge 27:4

³²His father Isaac asked him, "Who are you?"   Ge 27:18

"I am your son," he answered, "your firstborn, Esau."

³³Isaac trembled violently and said, "Who was it, then, that hunted game and brought it to me? I ate it just before you came and I blessed him—and indeed he will be blessed!"   Ge 28:3-4

³⁴When Esau heard his father's words, he burst out with a loud and bitter cry and said to his father, "Bless me—me too, my father!"   Ex 12:32; Heb 12:17

³⁵But he said, "Your brother came deceitfully and took your blessing."   Ge 27:19; Jer 9:4

³⁶Esau said, "Isn't he rightly named Jacob*a*? He has deceived me these two times: He took my birthright, and now he's taken my blessing!" Then he asked, "Haven't you reserved any blessing for me?"   Ge 25:26

³⁷Isaac answered Esau, "I have made him lord over you and have made all his relatives his servants, and I have sustained him with grain and new wine. So what can I possibly do for you, my son?"   Dt 16:13

³⁸Esau said to his father, "Do you have only one blessing, my father? Bless me too, my father!" Then Esau wept aloud.

³⁹His father Isaac answered him,

"Your dwelling will be
   away from the earth's
      richness,
   away from the dew of
      heaven above.   Ge 36:6
⁴⁰You will live by the sword
   and you will serve your
      brother.   Ge 9:25
But when you grow restless,
   you will throw his yoke
   from off your neck."   2Ki 8:20-22

---

*a*36 *Jacob* means *he grasps the heel* (figuratively, *he deceives*).

"Yes, we know him," they answered.

[6]Then Jacob asked them, "Is he well?" Ge 43:27

"Yes, he is," they said, "and here comes his daughter Rachel with the sheep." Ex 2:16

[7]"Look," he said, "the sun is still high; it is not time for the flocks to be gathered. Water the sheep and take them back to pasture."

[8]"We can't," they replied, "until all the flocks are gathered and the stone has been rolled away from the mouth of the well. Then we will water the sheep." Ge 24:13

[9]While he was still talking with them, Rachel came with her father's sheep, for she was a shepherdess. [10]When Jacob saw Rachel daughter of Laban, his mother's brother, and Laban's sheep, he went over and rolled the stone away from the mouth of the well and watered his uncle's sheep. [11]Then Jacob kissed Rachel and began to weep aloud. [12]He had told Rachel that he was a relative of her father and a son of Rebekah. So she ran and told her father. Ex 2:17

[13]As soon as Laban heard the news about Jacob, his sister's son, he hurried to meet him. He embraced him and kissed him and brought him to his home, and there Jacob told him all these things. [14]Then Laban said to him, "You are my own flesh and blood." Ge 24:29-31; Ex 4:27

Jacob Marries Leah and Rachel

After Jacob had stayed with him for a whole month, [15]Laban said to him, "Just because you are a relative of mine, should you work for me for nothing? Tell me what your wages should be." Ge 31:41

[16]Now Laban had two daughters; the name of the older was Leah, and the name of the younger was Rachel. [17]Leah had weak[a] eyes, but Rachel was lovely in form, and beautiful. [18]Jacob was in love with Rachel and said, "I'll work for you seven years in return for your younger daughter Rachel."

[19]Laban said, "It's better that I give her to you than to some other man. Stay here with me." [20]So Jacob served seven years to get Rachel, but they seemed like only a few days to him because of his love for her. Ge 31:15

[21]Then Jacob said to Laban, "Give me my wife. My time is completed, and I want to lie with her." Jdg 15:1

[22]So Laban brought together all the people of the place and gave a feast. [23]But when evening came, he took his daughter Leah and gave her to Jacob, and Jacob lay with her. [24]And Laban gave his servant girl Zilpah to his daughter as her maidservant. Jdg 14:2; Jn 10:1-2

[25]When morning came, there was Leah! So Jacob said to Laban, "What is this you have

*a*17 Or *delicate*

done to me? I served you for Rachel, didn't I? Why have you deceived me?" Ge 27:36

26Laban replied, "It is not our custom here to give the younger daughter in marriage before the older one. 27Finish this daughter's bridal week; then we will give you the younger one also, in return for another seven years of work." Jdg 14:12; 15:2

28And Jacob did so. He finished the week with Leah, and then Laban gave him his daughter Rachel to be his wife. 29Laban gave his servant girl Bilhah to his daughter Rachel as her maidservant. 30Jacob lay with Rachel also, and he loved Rachel more than Leah. And he worked for Laban another seven years. Ge 4:19; Dt 22:30

Jacob's Children

31When the LORD saw that Leah was not loved, he opened her womb, but Rachel was barren. 32Leah became pregnant and gave birth to a son. She named him Reuben,a for she said, "It is because the LORD has seen my misery. Surely my husband will love me now." Ps 127:3

33She conceived again, and when she gave birth to a son she said, "Because the LORD heard that I am not loved, he gave me this one too." So she named him Simeon.b Ex 6:15; Dt 21:15

34Again she conceived, and when she gave birth to a son she said, "Now at last my husband will become attached to me, because I have borne him three sons." So he was named Levi.c

35She conceived again, and when she gave birth to a son she said, "This time I will praise the LORD." So she named him Judah.d Then she stopped having children. Ge 49:8; Mt 1:2

30 When Rachel saw that she was not bearing Jacob any children, she became jealous of her sister. So she said to Jacob, "Give me children, or I'll die!" Ge 11:30; 1Sa 1:5

2Jacob became angry with her and said, "Am I in the place of God, who has kept you from having children?" Ge 20:18; 29:31

3Then she said, "Here is Bilhah, my maidservant. Sleep with her so that she can bear children for me and that through her I too can build a family." Ge 16:2; Job 3:12

4So she gave him her servant Bilhah as a wife. Jacob slept with her, 5and she became pregnant and bore him a son. 6Then Rachel said, "God has vindicated me; he has listened to my plea and given me a son." Because of this she named him Dan.e Ge 16:3-4; 30:9,18

7Rachel's servant Bilhah conceived again and bore Jacob a second son. 8Then Rachel said, "I have had a great struggle

---

a32 Reuben sounds like the Hebrew for *he has seen my misery*; the name means *see, a son.* b33 Simeon probably means *one who hears*. c34 Levi sounds like and may be derived from the Hebrew for *attached*. d35 Judah sounds like and may be derived from the Hebrew for *praise*. e6 Dan here means *he has vindicated*.

with my sister, and I have won." So she named him Naphtali.*ᵃ*

Ge 32:28; Mt 4:13

⁹When Leah saw that she had stopped having children, she took her maidservant Zilpah and gave her to Jacob as a wife. ¹⁰Leah's servant Zilpah bore Jacob a son. ¹¹Then Leah said, "What good fortune!"*ᵇ* So she named him Gad.*ᶜ*

Ge 29:16

¹²Leah's servant Zilpah bore Jacob a second son. ¹³Then Leah said, "How happy I am! The women will call me happy." So she named him Asher.*ᵈ*

Pr 31:28

¹⁴During wheat harvest, Reuben went out into the fields and found some mandrake plants, which he brought to his mother Leah. Rachel said to Leah, "Please give me some of your son's mandrakes."

Ge 25:30

¹⁵But she said to her, "Wasn't it enough that you took away my husband? Will you take my son's mandrakes too?"

Nu 16:9,13

"Very well," Rachel said, "he can sleep with you tonight in return for your son's mandrakes."

Eze 16:33

¹⁶So when Jacob came in from the fields that evening, Leah went out to meet him. "You must sleep with me," she said. "I have hired you with my son's mandrakes." So he slept with her that night.

Ge 30:14

¹⁷God listened to Leah, and she became pregnant and bore Jacob a fifth son. ¹⁸Then Leah said, "God has rewarded me for giving my maidservant to my husband." So she named him Issachar.*ᵉ*

Ge 46:13; Nu 1:8

¹⁹Leah conceived again and bore Jacob a sixth son. ²⁰Then Leah said, "God has presented me with a precious gift. This time my husband will treat me with honor, because I have borne him six sons." So she named him Zebulun.*ᶠ*

1Pe 3:7

²¹Some time later she gave birth to a daughter and named her Dinah.

Ge 34:1; 46:15

²²Then God remembered Rachel; he listened to her and opened her womb. ²³She became pregnant and gave birth to a son and said, "God has taken away my disgrace." ²⁴She named him Joseph,*ᵍ* and said, "May the LORD add to me another son."

1Sa 1:19-20; Lk 1:25

Jacob's Flocks Increase

²⁵After Rachel gave birth to Joseph, Jacob said to Laban, "Send me on my way so I can go back to my own homeland. ²⁶Give me my wives and children, for whom I have served you, and I will be on my way. You know how much work I've done for you."

Ge 24:54; 29:20

²⁷But Laban said to him, "If I have found favor in your eyes, please stay. I have learned by divination that*ʰ* the LORD has

---

ᵃ8 Naphtali means *my struggle.*   *ᵇ11 Or "A troop is coming!"*   *ᶜ11 Gad* can mean *good fortune* or *a troop.*   *ᵈ13 Asher* means *happy.*   *ᵉ18 Issachar* sounds like the Hebrew for *reward.*   *ᶠ20 Zebulun* probably means *honor.*   *ᵍ24 Joseph* means *may he add.*   *ʰ27 Or possibly have become rich and*

blessed me because of you." ²⁸He added, "Name your wages, and I will pay them."

²⁹Jacob said to him, "You know how I have worked for you and how your livestock has fared under my care. ³⁰The little you had before I came has increased greatly, and the LORD has blessed you wherever I have been. But now, when may I do something for my own household?" Ge 31:38-40

³¹"What shall I give you?" he asked.

"Don't give me anything," Jacob replied. "But if you will do this one thing for me, I will go on tending your flocks and watching over them: ³²Let me go through all your flocks today and remove from them every speckled or spotted sheep, every dark-colored lamb and every spotted or speckled goat. They will be my wages. ³³And my honesty will testify for me in the future, whenever you check on the wages you have paid me. Any goat in my possession that is not speckled or spotted, or any lamb that is not dark-colored, will be considered stolen." Ge 31:8; Ps 37:6

³⁴"Agreed," said Laban. "Let it be as you have said." ³⁵That same day he removed all the male goats that were streaked or spotted, and all the speckled or spotted female goats (all that had white on them) and all the dark-colored lambs, and he placed them in the care of his sons. ³⁶Then he put a three-day journey between himself and Jacob, while Jacob continued to tend the rest of Laban's flocks.

³⁷Jacob, however, took fresh-cut branches from poplar, almond and plane trees and made white stripes on them by peeling the bark and exposing the white inner wood of the branches. ³⁸Then he placed the peeled branches in all the watering troughs, so that they would be directly in front of the flocks when they came to drink. When the flocks were in heat and came to drink, ³⁹they mated in front of the branches. And they bore young that were streaked or speckled or spotted. ⁴⁰Jacob set apart the young of the flock by themselves, but made the rest face the streaked and dark-colored animals that belonged to Laban. Thus he made separate flocks for himself and did not put them with Laban's animals. ⁴¹Whenever the stronger females were in heat, Jacob would place the branches in the troughs in front of the animals so they would mate near the branches, ⁴²but if the animals were weak, he would not place them there. So the weak animals went to Laban and the strong ones to Jacob. ⁴³In this way the man grew exceedingly prosperous and came to own large flocks, and maidservants and menservants, and camels and donkeys. Ge 31:9-12; Jer 1:11

Jacob Flees From Laban

31 Jacob heard that Laban's sons were saying, "Jacob has taken everything our father owned and has gained all this wealth from what belonged to our father." ²And Jacob noticed that Laban's attitude toward him was not what it had been.

³Then the LORD said to Jacob, "Go back to the land of your fathers and to your relatives, and I will be with you."   Ge 28:15

⁴So Jacob sent word to Rachel and Leah to come out to the fields where his flocks were. ⁵He said to them, "I see that your father's attitude toward me is not what it was before, but the God of my father has been with me. ⁶You know that I've worked for your father with all my strength, ⁷yet your father has cheated me by changing my wages ten times. However, God has not allowed him to harm me. ⁸If he said, 'The speckled ones will be your wages,' then all the flocks gave birth to speckled young; and if he said, 'The streaked ones will be your wages,' then all the flocks bore streaked young. ⁹So God has taken away your father's livestock and has given them to me.

¹⁰"In breeding season I once had a dream in which I looked up and saw that the male goats mating with the flock were streaked, speckled or spotted. ¹¹The angel of God said to me in the dream, 'Jacob.' I answered, 'Here I am.' ¹²And he said, 'Look up and see that all the male goats mating with the flock are streaked, speckled or spotted, for I have seen all that Laban has been doing to you. ¹³I am the God of Bethel, where you anointed a pillar and where you made a vow to me. Now leave this land at once and go back to your native land.'" Ge 16:7

¹⁴Then Rachel and Leah replied, "Do we still have any share in the inheritance of our father's estate? ¹⁵Does he not regard us as foreigners? Not only has he sold us, but he has used up what was paid for us. ¹⁶Surely all the wealth that God took away from our father belongs to us and our children. So do whatever God has told you."

¹⁷Then Jacob put his children and his wives on camels, ¹⁸and he drove all his livestock ahead of him, along with all the goods he had accumulated in Paddan Aram,ᵃ to go to his father Isaac in the land of Canaan. Ge 27:41

¹⁹When Laban had gone to shear his sheep, Rachel stole her father's household gods. ²⁰Moreover, Jacob deceived Laban the Aramean by not telling him he was running away. ²¹So he fled with all he had, and crossing the River,ᵇ he headed for the hill country of Gilead.

Laban Pursues Jacob

²²On the third day Laban was told that Jacob had fled. ²³Tak-

---

ᵃ18 That is, Northwest Mesopotamia   ᵇ21 That is, the Euphrates

ing his relatives with him, he pursued Jacob for seven days and caught up with him in the hill country of Gilead. ²⁴Then God came to Laban the Aramean in a dream at night and said to him, "Be careful not to say anything to Jacob, either good or bad." Ge 13:8; 30:36

²⁵Jacob had pitched his tent in the hill country of Gilead when Laban overtook him, and Laban and his relatives camped there too. ²⁶Then Laban said to Jacob, "What have you done? You've deceived me, and you've carried off my daughters like captives in war. ²⁷Why did you run off secretly and deceive me? Why didn't you tell me, so I could send you away with joy and singing to the music of tambourines and harps? ²⁸You didn't even let me kiss my grandchildren and my daughters good-by. You have done a foolish thing. ²⁹I have the power to harm you; but last night the God of your father said to me, 'Be careful not to say anything to Jacob, either good or bad.' ³⁰Now you have gone off because you longed to return to your father's house. But why did you steal my gods?" Ge 12:18

³¹Jacob answered Laban, "I was afraid, because I thought you would take your daughters away from me by force. ³²But if you find anyone who has your gods, he shall not live. In the presence of our relatives, see for yourself whether there is anything of yours here with me; and if so, take it." Now Jacob did not know that Rachel had stolen the gods. Ge 20:11; 44:9

³³So Laban went into Jacob's tent and into Leah's tent and into the tent of the two maidservants, but he found nothing. After he came out of Leah's tent, he entered Rachel's tent. ³⁴Now Rachel had taken the household gods and put them inside her camel's saddle and was sitting on them. Laban searched through everything in the tent but found nothing.

³⁵Rachel said to her father, "Don't be angry, my lord, that I cannot stand up in your presence; I'm having my period." So he searched but could not find the household gods. Ex 20:12

³⁶Jacob was angry and took Laban to task. "What is my crime?" he asked Laban. "What sin have I committed that you hunt me down? ³⁷Now that you have searched through all my goods, what have you found that belongs to your household? Put it here in front of your relatives and mine, and let them judge between the two of us.

³⁸"I have been with you for twenty years now. Your sheep and goats have not miscarried, nor have I eaten rams from your flocks. ³⁹I did not bring you animals torn by wild beasts; I bore the loss myself. And you demanded payment from me for whatever was stolen by day or night. ⁴⁰This was my situation: The heat consumed me in the daytime and the cold at night,

me." 21So Jacob's gifts went on ahead of him, but he himself spent the night in the camp.

Jacob Wrestles With God

22That night Jacob got up and took his two wives, his two maidservants and his eleven sons and crossed the ford of the Jabbok. 23After he had sent them across the stream, he sent over all his possessions. 24So Jacob was left alone, and a man wrestled with him till daybreak. 25When the man saw that he could not overpower him, he touched the socket of Jacob's hip so that his hip was wrenched as he wrestled with the man. 26Then the man said, "Let me go, for it is daybreak."

But Jacob replied, "I will not let you go unless you bless me."

27The man asked him, "What is your name?"

"Jacob," he answered. Gen 33:27

28Then the man said, "Your name will no longer be Jacob, but Israel,a because you have struggled with God and with men and have overcome." Ge 35:10

29Jacob said, "Please tell me your name."   Ex 3:13; Jdg 13:17

But he replied, "Why do you ask my name?" Then he blessed him there.   Ge 25:11; Jdg 13:18

30So Jacob called the place Peniel,b saying, "It is because I saw God face to face, and yet my life was spared."   Ge 16:13

31The sun rose above him as he passed Peniel,c and he was limping because of his hip. 32Therefore to this day the Israelites do not eat the tendon attached to the socket of the hip, because the socket of Jacob's hip was touched near the tendon.

Jacob Meets Esau

33 Jacob looked up and there was Esau, coming with his four hundred men; so he divided the children among Leah, Rachel and the two maidservants. 2He put the maidservants and their children in front, Leah and her children next, and Rachel and Joseph in the rear. 3He himself went on ahead and bowed down to the ground seven times as he approached his brother. Ge 32:6

4But Esau ran to meet Jacob and embraced him; he threw his arms around his neck and kissed him. And they wept. 5Then Esau looked up and saw the women and children. "Who are these with you?" he asked.

Jacob answered, "They are the children God has graciously given your servant." Ps 127:3

6Then the maidservants and their children approached and bowed down. 7Next, Leah and her children came and bowed down. Last of all came Joseph and Rachel, and they too bowed down. Ge 30:24

8Esau asked, "What do you

---

a28 Israel means he struggles with God. Penuel, a variant of Peniel   b30 Peniel means face of God.   c31 Hebrew

mean by all these droves I met?"

"To find favor in your eyes, my lord," he said.   Ge 32:14-16

9But Esau said, "I already have plenty, my brother. Keep what you have for yourself."

10"No, please!" said Jacob. "If I have found favor in your eyes, accept this gift from me. For to see your face is like seeing the face of God, now that you have received me favorably. 11Please accept the present that was brought to you, for God has been gracious to me and I have all I need." And because Jacob insisted, Esau accepted it. Ge 43:3

12Then Esau said, "Let us be on our way; I'll accompany you."

13But Jacob said to him, "My lord knows that the children are tender and that I must care for the ewes and cows that are nursing their young. If they are driven hard just one day, all the animals will die. 14So let my lord go on ahead of his servant, while I move along slowly at the pace of the droves before me and that of the children, until I come to my lord in Seir." Isa 40:11

15Esau said, "Then let me leave some of my men with you."

"But why do that?" Jacob asked. "Just let me find favor in the eyes of my lord."   Ge 34:11

16So that day Esau started on his way back to Seir. 17Jacob, however, went to Succoth, where he built a place for himself and made shelters for his livestock. That is why the place is called Succoth. *a*   Ge 14:6

18After Jacob came from Paddan Aram, *b* he arrived safely at the *c* city of Shechem in Canaan and camped within sight of the city. 19For a hundred pieces of silver, *d* he bought from the sons of Hamor, the father of Shechem, the plot of ground where he pitched his tent. 20There he set up an altar and called it El Elohe Israel. *e*   Ge 4:26; Jos 24:1

Dinah and the Shechemites

34 Now Dinah, the daughter Leah had borne to Jacob, went out to visit the women of the land. 2When Shechem son of Hamor the Hivite, the ruler of that area, saw her, he took her and violated her. 3His heart was drawn to Dinah daughter of Jacob, and he loved the girl and spoke tenderly to her. 4And Shechem said to his father Hamor, "Get me this girl as my wife."   Ge 30:21; Dt 21:14

5When Jacob heard that his daughter Dinah had been defiled, his sons were in the fields with his livestock; so he kept quiet about it until they came home.   Ge 35:22

6Then Shechem's father Hamor went out to talk with Jacob.

a17 Succoth means *shelters.*   *b18* That is, Northwest Mesopotamia   *c18* Or *arrived at Shalem, a*   *d19* Hebrew *hundred kesitahs;* a kesitah was a unit of money of unknown weight and value.   *e20 El Elohe Israel* can mean *God, the God of Israel* or *mighty is the God of Israel.*

⁷Now Jacob's sons had come in from the fields as soon as they heard what had happened. They were filled with grief and fury, because Shechem had done a disgraceful thing in*a* Israel by lying with Jacob's daughter—a thing that should not be done.   Jdg 14:2-5

⁸But Hamor said to them, "My son Shechem has his heart set on your daughter. Please give her to him as his wife. ⁹Intermarry with us; give us your daughters and take our daughters for yourselves. ¹⁰You can settle among us; the land is open to you. Live in it, trade*b* in it, and acquire property in it."

¹¹Then Shechem said to Dinah's father and brothers, "Let me find favor in your eyes, and I will give you whatever you ask. ¹²Make the price for the bride and the gift I am to bring as great as you like, and I'll pay whatever you ask me. Only give me the girl as my wife."   Ge 32:5

¹³Because their sister Dinah had been defiled, Jacob's sons replied deceitfully as they spoke to Shechem and his father Hamor. ¹⁴They said to them, "We can't do such a thing; we can't give our sister to a man who is not circumcised. That would be a disgrace to us. ¹⁵We will give our consent to you on one condition only: that you become like us by circumcising all your males. ¹⁶Then we will give you our daughters and take your daughters for ourselves. We'll settle among you and become one people with you. ¹⁷But if you will not agree to be circumcised, we'll take our sister*c* and go."   Ge 17:14; Ex 12:48

¹⁸Their proposal seemed good to Hamor and his son Shechem. ¹⁹The young man, who was the most honored of all his father's household, lost no time in doing what they said, because he was delighted with Jacob's daughter. ²⁰So Hamor and his son Shechem went to the gate of their city to speak to their fellow townsmen. ²¹"These men are friendly toward us," they said. "Let them live in our land and trade in it; the land has plenty of room for them. We can marry their daughters and they can marry ours. ²²But the men will consent to live with us as one people only on the condition that our males be circumcised, as they themselves are. ²³Won't their livestock, their property and all their other animals become ours? So let us give our consent to them, and they will settle among us."   Ge 49:3; 1Ch 4:9

²⁴All the men who went out of the city gate agreed with Hamor and his son Shechem, and every male in the city was circumcised.   Ge 18:1; 23:10

²⁵Three days later, while all of them were still in pain, two of Jacob's sons, Simeon and Levi, Dinah's brothers, took their

*a*7 Or *against*   *b*10 Or *move about freely*; also in verse 21   *c*17 Hebrew *daughter*

swords and attacked the unsuspecting city, killing every male. [26]They put Hamor and his son Shechem to the sword and took Dinah from Shechem's house and left. [27]The sons of Jacob came upon the dead bodies and looted the city where[a] their sister had been defiled. [28]They seized their flocks and herds and donkeys and everything else of theirs in the city and out in the fields. [29]They carried off all their wealth and all their women and children, taking as plunder everything in the houses. Ge 48:22; 49:5-7

[30]Then Jacob said to Simeon and Levi, "You have brought trouble on me by making me a stench to the Canaanites and Perizzites, the people living in this land. We are few in number, and if they join forces against me and attack me, I and my household will be destroyed." Ex 5:21; 1Ch 16:19

[31]But they replied, "Should he have treated our sister like a prostitute?" Lev 19:29; Pr 6:34

Jacob Returns to Bethel

35 Then God said to Jacob, "Go up to Bethel and settle there, and build an altar there to God, who appeared to you when you were fleeing from your brother Esau." Ge 28:19

[2]So Jacob said to his household and to all who were with him, "Get rid of the foreign gods you have with you, and purify yourselves and change your clothes. [3]Then come, let us go up to Bethel, where I will build an altar to God, who answered me in the day of my distress and who has been with me wherever I have gone." [4]So they gave Jacob all the foreign gods they had and the rings in their ears, and Jacob buried them under the oak at Shechem. [5]Then they set out, and the terror of God fell upon the towns all around them so that no one pursued them. Ge 31:19; Jos 24:26

[6]Jacob and all the people with him came to Luz (that is, Bethel) in the land of Canaan. [7]There he built an altar, and he called the place El Bethel,[b] because it was there that God revealed himself to him when he was fleeing from his brother. Ge 28:19; 35:3

[8]Now Deborah, Rebekah's nurse, died and was buried under the oak below Bethel. So it was named Allon Bacuth. Ge 24:59

[9]After Jacob returned from Paddan Aram,[d] God appeared to him again and blessed him. [10]God said to him, "Your name is Jacob,[e] but you will no longer be called Jacob; your name will be Israel.[f]" So he named him Israel. Ge 32:28; Hos 12:4

[11]And God said to him, "I am God Almighty[g]; be fruitful and increase in number. A nation

---

[a]27 Or because [b]7 El Bethel means God of Bethel. [c]8 Allon Bacuth means oak of weeping. [d]9 That is, Northwest Mesopotamia; also in verse 26 [e]10 Jacob means he grasps the heel (figuratively, he deceives). [f]10 Israel means he struggles with God. [g]11 Hebrew El-Shaddai

and a community of nations will come from you, and kings will come from your body. ¹²The land I gave to Abraham and Isaac I also give to you, and I will give this land to your descendants after you." ¹³Then God went up from him at the place where he had talked with him.   Ge 17:1; 28:13

¹⁴Jacob set up a stone pillar at the place where God had talked with him, and he poured out a drink offering on it; he also poured oil on it. ¹⁵Jacob called the place where God had talked with him Bethel. *a*   Ge 28:18

The Deaths of Rachel and Isaac

¹⁶Then they moved on from Bethel. While they were still some distance from Ephrath, Rachel began to give birth and had great difficulty. ¹⁷And as she was having great difficulty in childbirth, the midwife said to her, "Don't be afraid, for you have another son." ¹⁸As she breathed her last—for she was dying—she named her son Ben-Oni. *b* But his father named him Benjamin. *c*   Ge 30:24; Ru 4:11

¹⁹So Rachel died and was buried on the way to Ephrath (that is, Bethlehem). ²⁰Over her tomb Jacob set up a pillar, and to this day that pillar marks Rachel's tomb.   Ge 48:7; 1Sa 10:2

²¹Israel moved on again and pitched his tent beyond Migdal Eder. ²²While Israel was living in that region, Reuben went in and slept with his father's concubine Bilhah, and Israel heard of it.   Ge 49:2; Jos 15:21

Jacob had twelve sons:
²³The sons of Leah: Ge 29:16
    Reuben the firstborn of Jacob,   Ge 43:33
    Simeon, Levi, Judah, Issachar and Zebulun.
²⁴The sons of Rachel:
    Joseph and Benjamin.
²⁵The sons of Rachel's maidservant Bilhah: Ge 37:2
    Dan and Naphtali.
²⁶The sons of Leah's maidservant Zilpah: Ge 37:2
    Gad and Asher.   Ge 30:13

These were the sons of Jacob, who were born to him in Paddan Aram.   Ge 25:20; 1Ch 2:1-2

²⁷Jacob came home to his father Isaac in Mamre, near Kiriath Arba (that is, Hebron), where Abraham and Isaac had stayed. ²⁸Isaac lived a hundred and eighty years. ²⁹Then he breathed his last and died and was gathered to his people, old and full of years. And his sons Esau and Jacob buried him.

Esau's Descendants

36 This is the account of Esau (that is, Edom).

²Esau took his wives from the women of Canaan: Adah daughter of Elon the Hittite, and Oholibamah

---

a15 Bethel means *house of God.*   *b18 Ben-Oni* means *son of my trouble.*   *c18 Benjamin* means *son of my right hand.*

daughter of Anah and granddaughter of Zibeon the Hivite— ³also Basemath daughter of Ishmael and sister of Nebaioth.   Ge 26:34

⁴Adah bore Eliphaz to Esau, Basemath bore Reuel, ⁵and Oholibamah bore Jeush, Jalam and Korah. These were the sons of Esau, who were born to him in Canaan.   Ge 36:18; 1Ch 1:35

⁶Esau took his wives and sons and daughters and all the members of his household, as well as his livestock and all his other animals and all the goods he had acquired in Canaan, and moved to a land some distance from his brother Jacob. ⁷Their possessions were too great for them to remain together; the land where they were staying could not support them both because of their livestock. ⁸So Esau (that is, Edom) settled in the hill country of Seir.   Ge 12:5; 13:6

⁹This is the account of Esau the father of the Edomites in the hill country of Seir.   Nu 20:18

¹⁰These are the names of Esau's sons:
Eliphaz, the son of Esau's wife Adah, and Reuel, the son of Esau's wife Basemath.   1Ch 1:35

¹¹The sons of Eliphaz:
Teman, Omar, Zepho, Gatam and Kenaz.   1Ch 1:45

¹²Esau's son Eliphaz also had a concubine named Timna, who bore him Amalek. These were grandsons of Esau's wife Adah.   Ex 17:8; Nu 24:20

¹³The sons of Reuel:
Nahath, Zerah, Shammah and Mizzah. These were grandsons of Esau's wife Basemath.   1Ch 1:37

¹⁴The sons of Esau's wife Oholibamah daughter of Anah and granddaughter of Zibeon, whom she bore to Esau:
Jeush, Jalam and Korah.

¹⁵These were the chiefs among Esau's descendants:
The sons of Eliphaz the firstborn of Esau:
Chiefs Teman, Omar, Zepho, Kenaz, ¹⁶Korah,ᵃ Gatam and Amalek. These were the chiefs descended from Eliphaz in Edom; they were grandsons of Adah.   1Ch 1:36

¹⁷The sons of Esau's son Reuel:
Chiefs Nahath, Zerah, Shammah and Mizzah. These were the chiefs descended from Reuel in Edom; they were grandsons of Esau's wife Basemath.   1Ch 1:35,37

¹⁸The sons of Esau's wife Oholibamah:

ᵃ16 Masoretic Text; Samaritan Pentateuch (see also Gen. 36:11 and 1 Chron. 1:36) does not have *Korah*.

Chiefs Jeush, Jalam and Korah. These were the chiefs descended from Esau's wife Oholibamah daughter of Anah.   1Ch 1:52

¹⁹These were the sons of Esau (that is, Edom), and these were their chiefs.   Ge 25:30; 1Ch 1:35

²⁰These were the sons of Seir the Horite, who were living in the region:

Lotan, Shobal, Zibeon, Anah, ²¹Dishon, Ezer and Dishan. These sons of Seir in Edom were Horite chiefs.   Ge 14:6; Dt 2:12

²²The sons of Lotan:

Hori and Homam.ᵃ Timna was Lotan's sister.

²³The sons of Shobal:

Alvan, Manahath, Ebal, Shepho and Onam.   1Ch 1:40

²⁴The sons of Zibeon:

Aiah and Anah. This is the Anah who discovered the hot springsᵇ in the desert while he was grazing the donkeys of his father Zibeon.   Jos 15:19

²⁵The children of Anah:

Dishon and Oholibamah daughter of Anah.   1Ch 1:52

²⁶The sons of Dishonᶜ:

Hemdan, Eshban, Ithran and Keran.

²⁷The sons of Ezer:

Bilhan, Zaavan and Akan.   1Ch 1:42

²⁸The sons of Dishan:

Uz and Aran.   Job 1:1

²⁹These were the Horite chiefs:

Lotan, Shobal, Zibeon, Anah, ³⁰Dishon, Ezer and Dishan. These were the Horite chiefs, according to their divisions, in the land of Seir.

The Rulers of Edom

³¹These were the kings who reigned in Edom before any Israelite king reignedᵈ:

³²Bela son of Beor became king of Edom. His city was named Dinhabah.

³³When Bela died, Jobab son of Zerah from Bozrah succeeded him as king.   Isa 34:6

³⁴When Jobab died, Husham from the land of the Temanites succeeded him as king.   Jer 49:7; Eze 25:13

³⁵When Husham died, Hadad son of Bedad, who defeated Midian in the country of Moab, succeeded him as king. His city was named Avith.

³⁶When Hadad died, Samlah from Masrekah succeeded him as king.

³⁷When Samlah died, Shaul from Rehoboth on the riverᵉ succeeded him as king.   Ge 26:22

³⁸When Shaul died, Baal-Hanan son of Acbor succeeded him as king.

ᵃ22 Hebrew *Hemam*, a variant of *Homam* (see 1 Chron. 1:39)   ᵇ24 Vulgate; Syriac *discovered water*; the meaning of the Hebrew for this word is uncertain.   ᶜ26 Hebrew *Dishan*, a variant of *Dishon*   ᵈ31 Or *before an Israelite king reigned over them*   ᵉ37 Possibly the Euphrates

³⁹When Baal-Hanan son of Acbor died, Hadad*ᵃ* succeeded him as king. His city was named Pau, and his wife's name was Mehetabel daughter of Matred, the daughter of Me-Zahab.   1Ch 1:50

⁴⁰These were the chiefs descended from Esau, by name, according to their clans and regions:

Timna, Alvah, Jetheth, ⁴¹Oholibamah, Elah, Pinon, ⁴²Kenaz, Teman, Mibzar, ⁴³Magdiel and Iram. These were the chiefs of Edom, according to their settlements in the land they occupied. 1Ch 1:51-54

This was Esau the father of the Edomites.

Joseph's Dreams

37 Jacob lived in the land where his father had stayed, the land of Canaan.

²This is the account of Jacob.

Joseph, a young man of seventeen, was tending the flocks with his brothers, the sons of Bilhah and the sons of Zilpah, his father's wives, and he brought their father a bad report about them.

³Now Israel loved Joseph more than any of his other sons, because he had been born to him in his old age; and he made a richly ornamented*ᵇ* robe for him. ⁴When his brothers saw that their father loved him more than any of them, they hated him and could not speak a kind word to him.   Ge 27:41; 44:20

⁵Joseph had a dream, and when he told it to his brothers, they hated him all the more. ⁶He said to them, "Listen to this dream I had: ⁷We were binding sheaves of grain out in the field when suddenly my sheaf rose and stood upright, while your sheaves gathered around mine and bowed down to it."   Ge 28:12

⁸His brothers said to him, "Do you intend to reign over us? Will you actually rule us?" And they hated him all the more because of his dream and what he had said.   Ge 49:26

⁹Then he had another dream, and he told it to his brothers. "Listen," he said, "I had another dream, and this time the sun and moon and eleven stars were bowing down to me."

¹⁰When he told his father as well as his brothers, his father rebuked him and said, "What is this dream you had? Will your mother and I and your brothers actually come and bow down to the ground before you?" ¹¹His brothers were jealous of him, but his father kept the matter in mind.   Ge 27:29; Ru 2:16

Joseph Sold by His Brothers

¹²Now his brothers had gone

ᵃ39 Many manuscripts of the Masoretic Text, Samaritan Pentateuch and Syriac (see also 1 Chron. 1:50); most manuscripts of the Masoretic Text *Hadar*   *ᵇ3* The meaning of the Hebrew for *richly ornamented* is uncertain; also in verses 23 and 32.

to graze their father's flocks near Shechem, ¹³and Israel said to Joseph, "As you know, your brothers are grazing the flocks near Shechem. Come, I am going to send you to them."

"Very well," he replied.

¹⁴So he said to him, "Go and see if all is well with your brothers and with the flocks, and bring word back to me." Then he sent him off from the Valley of Hebron.   Ge 13:18; 35:27

When Joseph arrived at Shechem, ¹⁵a man found him wandering around in the fields and asked him, "What are you looking for?"

¹⁶He replied, "I'm looking for my brothers. Can you tell me where they are grazing their flocks?"

¹⁷"They have moved on from here," the man answered. "I heard them say, 'Let's go to Dothan.'"   2Ki 6:13

So Joseph went after his brothers and found them near Dothan. ¹⁸But they saw him in the distance, and before he reached them, they plotted to kill him.   1Sa 19:1; Ac 23:12

¹⁹"Here comes that dreamer!" they said to each other. ²⁰"Come now, let's kill him and throw him into one of these cisterns and say that a ferocious animal devoured him. Then we'll see what comes of his dreams."   Ge 28:12; 37:32

²¹When Reuben heard this, he tried to rescue him from their hands. "Let's not take his life," he said. ²²"Don't shed any blood. Throw him into this cistern here in the desert, but don't lay a hand on him." Reuben said this to rescue him from them and take him back to his father.   Ge 29:32; 42:22

²³So when Joseph came to his brothers, they stripped him of his robe—the richly ornamented robe he was wearing— ²⁴and they took him and threw him into the cistern. Now the cistern was empty; there was no water in it.   Ge 49:23; Mt 27:28

²⁵As they sat down to eat their meal, they looked up and saw a caravan of Ishmaelites coming from Gilead. Their camels were loaded with spices, balm and myrrh, and they were on their way to take them down to Egypt.   Ps 45:8; Jer 8:22

²⁶Judah said to his brothers, "What will we gain if we kill our brother and cover up his blood? ²⁷Come, let's sell him to the Ishmaelites and not lay our hands on him; after all, he is our brother, our own flesh and blood." His brothers agreed.   Ge 4:10

²⁸So when the Midianite merchants came by, his brothers pulled Joseph up out of the cistern and sold him for twenty shekels*a* of silver to the Ishmaelites, who took him to Egypt.

²⁹When Reuben returned to the cistern and saw that Joseph was not there, he tore his clothes. ³⁰He went back to his

a28 That is, about 8 ounces (about 0.2 kilogram)

brothers and said, "The boy isn't there! Where can I turn now?" Ge 42:13,36; 44:13

³¹Then they got Joseph's robe, slaughtered a goat and dipped the robe in the blood. ³²They took the ornamented robe back to their father and said, "We found this. Examine it to see whether it is your son's robe." Ge 37:3; Rev 19:13

³³He recognized it and said, "It is my son's robe! Some ferocious animal has devoured him. Joseph has surely been torn to pieces." Ge 42:13; 44:28

³⁴Then Jacob tore his clothes, put on sackcloth and mourned for his son many days. ³⁵All his sons and daughters came to comfort him, but he refused to be comforted. "No," he said, "in mourning will I go down to the grave*ᵃ* to my son." So his father wept for him. 2Sa 3:31

³⁶Meanwhile, the Midianites*ᵇ* sold Joseph in Egypt to Potiphar, one of Pharaoh's officials, the captain of the guard. Ge 39:1

Judah and Tamar

38 At that time, Judah left his brothers and went down to stay with a man of Adullam named Hirah. ²There Judah met the daughter of a Canaanite man named Shua. He married her and lay with her; ³she became pregnant and gave birth to a son, who was named Er. ⁴She conceived again and gave birth to a son and named him Onan. ⁵She gave birth to still another son and named him Shelah. It was at Kezib that she gave birth to him. Jos 15:35

⁶Judah got a wife for Er, his firstborn, and her name was Tamar. ⁷But Er, Judah's firstborn, was wicked in the LORD's sight; so the LORD put him to death. ⁸Then Judah said to Onan, "Lie with your brother's wife and fulfill your duty to her as a brother-in-law to produce offspring for your brother." ⁹But Onan knew that the offspring would not be his; so whenever he lay with his brother's wife, he spilled his semen on the ground to keep from producing offspring for his brother. ¹⁰What he did was wicked in the LORD's sight; so he put him to death also. Dt 25:5; Ru 4:5

¹¹Judah then said to his daughter-in-law Tamar, "Live as a widow in your father's house until my son Shelah grows up." For he thought, "He may die too, just like his brothers." So Tamar went to live in her father's house. Ru 1:12-13

¹²After a long time Judah's wife, the daughter of Shua, died. When Judah had recovered from his grief, he went up to Timnah, to the men who were shearing his sheep, and his friend Hirah the Adullamite went with him. Jos 15:10; 19:43

¹³When Tamar was told,

---

*ᵃ*35 Hebrew *Sheol*   *ᵇ*36 Samaritan Pentateuch, Septuagint, Vulgate and Syriac (see also verse 28); Masoretic Text *Medanites*

"Your father-in-law is on his way to Timnah to shear his sheep," [14]she took off her widow's clothes, covered herself with a veil to disguise herself, and then sat down at the entrance to Enaim, which is on the road to Timnah. For she saw that, though Shelah had now grown up, she had not been given to him as his wife. Ge 31:19

[15]When Judah saw her, he thought she was a prostitute, for she had covered her face. [16]Not realizing that she was his daughter-in-law, he went over to her by the roadside and said, "Come now, let me sleep with you." Lev 18:15; Jdg 11:1; 16:1

"And what will you give me to sleep with you?" she asked.

[17]"I'll send you a young goat from my flock," he said.

"Will you give me something as a pledge until you send it?" she asked.

[18]He said, "What pledge should I give you?"

"Your seal and its cord, and the staff in your hand," she answered. So he gave them to her and slept with her, and she became pregnant by him. [19]After she left, she took off her veil and put on her widow's clothes again. Ge 41:42; 1Ki 21:8

[20]Meanwhile Judah sent the young goat by his friend the Adullamite in order to get his pledge back from the woman, but he did not find her. [21]He asked the men who lived there, "Where is the shrine prostitute who was beside the road at Enaim?" Ge 19:5; Lev 19:29

"There hasn't been any shrine prostitute here," they said.

[22]So he went back to Judah and said, "I didn't find her. Besides, the men who lived there said, 'There hasn't been any shrine prostitute here.'"

[23]Then Judah said, "Let her keep what she has, or we will become a laughingstock. After all, I did send her this young goat, but you didn't find her."

[24]About three months later Judah was told, "Your daughter-in-law Tamar is guilty of prostitution, and as a result she is now pregnant."

Judah said, "Bring her out and have her burned to death!"

[25]As she was being brought out, she sent a message to her father-in-law. "I am pregnant by the man who owns these," she said. And she added, "See if you recognize whose seal and cord and staff these are." Ge 37:32

[26]Judah recognized them and said, "She is more righteous than I, since I wouldn't give her to my son Shelah." And he did not sleep with her again.

[27]When the time came for her to give birth, there were twin boys in her womb. [28]As she was giving birth, one of them put out his hand; so the midwife took a scarlet thread and tied it on his wrist and said, "This one came out first." [29]But when he drew back his hand, his brother came out, and she said, "So this

is how you have broken out!"
And he was named Perez.[a]
30Then his brother, who had the
scarlet thread on his wrist, came
out and he was given the name
Zerah.[b]　　　　　Ge 25:24; 46:12

Joseph and Potiphar's Wife

39 Now Joseph had been
taken down to Egypt.
Potiphar, an Egyptian who was
one of Pharaoh's officials, the
captain of the guard, bought
him from the Ishmaelites who
had taken him there.　　Ge 37:28

2The LORD was with Joseph
and he prospered, and he lived
in the house of his Egyptian
master. 3When his master saw
that the LORD was with him and
that the LORD gave him success
in everything he did, 4Joseph
found favor in his eyes and
became his attendant. Potiphar
put him in charge of his household, and he entrusted to his
care everything he owned.
5From the time he put him in
charge of his household and of
all that he owned, the LORD
blessed the household of the
Egyptian because of Joseph.
The blessing of the LORD was on
everything Potiphar had, both
in the house and in the field. 6So
he left in Joseph's care everything he had; with Joseph in
charge, he did not concern himself with anything except the
food he ate.　　Ge 21:22; Jos 1:5

Now Joseph was well-built
and handsome, 7and after a
while his master's wife took notice of Joseph and said, "Come
to bed with me!"　　Ex 2:2; Pr 7:15

8But he refused. "With me in
charge," he told her, "my master does not concern himself
with anything in the house;
everything he owns he has entrusted to my care. 9No one is
greater in this house than I am.
My master has withheld nothing from me except you, because you are his wife. How
then could I do such a wicked
thing and sin against God?"
10And though she spoke to Joseph day after day, he refused
to go to bed with her or even be
with her.　　Ge 41:40; Pr 6:23

11One day he went into the
house to attend to his duties,
and none of the household servants was inside. 12She caught
him by his cloak and said,
"Come to bed with me!" But he
left his cloak in her hand and
ran out of the house.　　Ex 18:20

13When she saw that he had
left his cloak in her hand and
had run out of the house, 14she
called her household servants.
"Look," she said to them, "this
Hebrew has been brought to us
to make sport of us! He came in
here to sleep with me, but I
screamed. 15When he heard me
scream for help, he left his cloak
beside me and ran out of the
house."　　Ge 14:13; 21:9; Dt 22:24

16She kept his cloak beside
her until his master came home.
17Then she told him this story:

---

[a]29 Perez means breaking out.　　[b]30 Zerah can mean scarlet or brightness.

"That Hebrew slave you brought us came to me to make sport of me. ¹⁸But as soon as I screamed for help, he left his cloak beside me and ran out of the house." Ex 23:1; Dt 5:20

¹⁹When his master heard the story his wife told him, saying, "This is how your slave treated me," he burned with anger. ²⁰Joseph's master took him and put him in prison, the place where the king's prisoners were confined. Ps 105:18; Pr 6:34

But while Joseph was there in the prison, ²¹the LORD was with him; he showed him kindness and granted him favor in the eyes of the prison warden. ²²So the warden put Joseph in charge of all those held in the prison, and he was made responsible for all that was done there. ²³The warden paid no attention to anything under Joseph's care, because the LORD was with Joseph and gave him success in whatever he did. Ex 3:21

The Cupbearer and the Baker

40 Some time later, the cupbearer and the baker of the king of Egypt offended their master, the king of Egypt. ²Pharaoh was angry with his two officials, the chief cupbearer and the chief baker, ³and put them in custody in the house of the captain of the guard, in the same prison where Joseph was confined. ⁴The captain of the guard assigned them to Joseph, and he attended them. Est 2:21

After they had been in custody for some time, ⁵each of the two men—the cupbearer and the baker of the king of Egypt, who were being held in prison—had a dream the same night, and each dream had a meaning of its own. Ge 42:17

⁶When Joseph came to them the next morning, he saw that they were dejected. ⁷So he asked Pharaoh's officials who were in custody with him in his master's house, "Why are your faces so sad today?" Ne 2:2

⁸"We both had dreams," they answered, "but there is no one to interpret them." Ge 41:15-16

Then Joseph said to them, "Do not interpretations belong to God? Tell me your dreams."

⁹So the chief cupbearer told Joseph his dream. He said to him, "In my dream I saw a vine in front of me, ¹⁰and on the vine were three branches. As soon as it budded, it blossomed, and its clusters ripened into grapes. ¹¹Pharaoh's cup was in my hand, and I took the grapes, squeezed them into Pharaoh's cup and put the cup in his hand." Isa 27:6; 35:1-2

¹²"This is what it means," Joseph said to him. "The three branches are three days. ¹³Within three days Pharaoh will lift up your head and restore you to your position, and you will put Pharaoh's cup in his hand, just as you used to do when you were his cupbearer. ¹⁴But when all goes well with you, remember me and show me kindness; mention me to Pharaoh and get

me out of this prison. ¹⁵For I was forcibly carried off from the land of the Hebrews, and even here I have done nothing to deserve being put in a dungeon." Ge 41:12

¹⁶When the chief baker saw that Joseph had given a favorable interpretation, he said to Joseph, "I too had a dream: On my head were three baskets of bread. *a* ¹⁷In the top basket were all kinds of baked goods for Pharaoh, but the birds were eating them out of the basket on my head." Am 8:1-2

¹⁸"This is what it means," Joseph said. "The three baskets are three days. ¹⁹Within three days Pharaoh will lift off your head and hang you on a tree. *b* And the birds will eat away your flesh." Dt 21:22

²⁰Now the third day was Pharaoh's birthday, and he gave a feast for all his officials. He lifted up the heads of the chief cupbearer and the chief baker in the presence of his officials: ²¹He restored the chief cupbearer to his position, so that he once again put the cup into Pharaoh's hand, ²²but he hanged*c* the chief baker, just as Joseph had said to them in his interpretation. 2Ki 25:27

²³The chief cupbearer, however, did not remember Joseph; he forgot him. Ecc 1:11

Pharaoh's Dreams

41 When two full years had passed, Pharaoh had a dream: He was standing by the Nile, ²when out of the river there came up seven cows, sleek and fat, and they grazed among the reeds. ³After them, seven other cows, ugly and gaunt, came up out of the Nile and stood beside those on the riverbank. ⁴And the cows that were ugly and gaunt ate up the seven sleek, fat cows. Then Pharaoh woke up. Ex 1:22; Isa 19:6

⁵He fell asleep again and had a second dream: Seven heads of grain, healthy and good, were growing on a single stalk. ⁶After them, seven other heads of grain sprouted—thin and scorched by the east wind. ⁷The thin heads of grain swallowed up the seven healthy, full heads. Then Pharaoh woke up; it had been a dream.

⁸In the morning his mind was troubled, so he sent for all the magicians and wise men of Egypt. Pharaoh told them his dreams, but no one could interpret them for him. Da 2:1,3

⁹Then the chief cupbearer said to Pharaoh, "Today I am reminded of my shortcomings. ¹⁰Pharaoh was once angry with his servants, and he imprisoned me and the chief baker in the house of the captain of the guard. ¹¹Each of us had a dream the same night, and each dream had a meaning of its own. ¹²Now a young Hebrew was there with us, a servant of the captain of the guard. We told

---

*a*16 Or *three wicker baskets*   *b*19 Or *and impale you on a pole*   *c*22 Or *impaled*

him our dreams, and he interpreted them for us, giving each man the interpretation of his dream. 13And things turned out exactly as he interpreted them to us: I was restored to my position, and the other man was hanged.*a*"   Ge 37:36; 40:23

14So Pharaoh sent for Joseph, and he was quickly brought from the dungeon. When he had shaved and changed his clothes, he came before Pharaoh.   Ps 105:20; Da 2:25

15Pharaoh said to Joseph, "I had a dream, and no one can interpret it. But I have heard it said of you that when you hear a dream you can interpret it."

16"I cannot do it," Joseph replied to Pharaoh, "but God will give Pharaoh the answer he desires."   Da 2:30; 2Co 3:5

17Then Pharaoh said to Joseph, "In my dream I was standing on the bank of the Nile, 18when out of the river there came up seven cows, fat and sleek, and they grazed among the reeds. 19After them, seven other cows came up—scrawny and very ugly and lean. I had never seen such ugly cows in all the land of Egypt. 20The lean, ugly cows ate up the seven fat cows that came up first. 21But even after they ate them, no one could tell that they had done so; they looked just as ugly as before. Then I woke up.   Ge 41:1

22"In my dreams I also saw seven heads of grain, full and good, growing on a single stalk. 23After them, seven other heads sprouted—withered and thin and scorched by the east wind. 24The thin heads of grain swallowed up the seven good heads. I told this to the magicians, but none could explain it to me."

25Then Joseph said to Pharaoh, "The dreams of Pharaoh are one and the same. God has revealed to Pharaoh what he is about to do. 26The seven good cows are seven years, and the seven good heads of grain are seven years; it is one and the same dream. 27The seven lean, ugly cows that came up afterward are seven years, and so are the seven worthless heads of grain scorched by the east wind: They are seven years of famine.   Isa 46:11; Da 2:45

28"It is just as I said to Pharaoh: God has shown Pharaoh what he is about to do. 29Seven years of great abundance are coming throughout the land of Egypt, 30but seven years of famine will follow them. Then all the abundance in Egypt will be forgotten, and the famine will ravage the land. 31The abundance in the land will not be remembered, because the famine that follows it will be so severe. 32The reason the dream was given to Pharaoh in two forms is that the matter has been firmly decided by God, and God will do it soon.   Ge 47:13

---

*a*13 Or *impaled*

³³"And now let Pharaoh look for a discerning and wise man and put him in charge of the land of Egypt. ³⁴Let Pharaoh appoint commissioners over the land to take a fifth of the harvest of Egypt during the seven years of abundance. ³⁵They should collect all the food of these good years that are coming and store up the grain under the authority of Pharaoh, to be kept in the cities for food. ³⁶This food should be held in reserve for the country, to be used during the seven years of famine that will come upon Egypt, so that the country may not be ruined by the famine."   Ge 39:9; Est 2:3

³⁷The plan seemed good to Pharaoh and to all his officials. ³⁸So Pharaoh asked them, "Can we find anyone like this man, one in whom is the spirit of God*ᵃ*?"   Ge 45:16; Da 4:8-9

³⁹Then Pharaoh said to Joseph, "Since God has made all this known to you, there is no one so discerning and wise as you. ⁴⁰You shall be in charge of my palace, and all my people are to submit to your orders. Only with respect to the throne will I be greater than you."

Joseph in Charge of Egypt

⁴¹So Pharaoh said to Joseph, "I hereby put you in charge of the whole land of Egypt." ⁴²Then Pharaoh took his signet ring from his finger and put it on Joseph's finger. He dressed him in robes of fine linen and put a gold chain around his neck. ⁴³He had him ride in a chariot as his second-in-command,ᵇ and men shouted before him, "Make wayᶜ!" Thus he put him in charge of the whole land of Egypt.   Ge 42:6

⁴⁴Then Pharaoh said to Joseph, "I am Pharaoh, but without your word no one will lift hand or foot in all Egypt." ⁴⁵Pharaoh gave Joseph the name Zaphenath-Paneah and gave him Asenath daughter of Potiphera, priest of On,ᵈ to be his wife. And Joseph went throughout the land of Egypt.

⁴⁶Joseph was thirty years old when he entered the service of Pharaoh king of Egypt. And Joseph went out from Pharaoh's presence and traveled throughout Egypt. ⁴⁷During the seven years of abundance the land produced plentifully. ⁴⁸Joseph collected all the food produced in those seven years of abundance in Egypt and stored it in the cities. In each city he put the food grown in the fields surrounding it. ⁴⁹Joseph stored up huge quantities of grain, like the sand of the sea; it was so much that he stopped keeping records because it was beyond measure.

⁵⁰Before the years of famine came, two sons were born to Joseph by Asenath daughter of Potiphera, priest of On. ⁵¹Jo-

---

ᵃ38 Or of the gods   ᵇ43 Or in the chariot of his second-in-command; or in his second chariot   ᶜ43 Or Bow down   ᵈ45 That is, Heliopolis; also in verse 50

seph named his firstborn Manasseh[a] and said, "It is because God has made me forget all my trouble and all my father's household." [52]The second son he named Ephraim[b] and said, "It is because God has made me fruitful in the land of my suffering." *Ge 46:20; Nu 1:34*

[53]The seven years of abundance in Egypt came to an end, [54]and the seven years of famine began, just as Joseph had said. There was famine in all the other lands, but in the whole land of Egypt there was food. [55]When all Egypt began to feel the famine, the people cried to Pharaoh for food. Then Pharaoh told all the Egyptians, "Go to Joseph and do what he tells you." *Ps 105:16; Ac 7:11*

[56]When the famine had spread over the whole country, Joseph opened the storehouses and sold grain to the Egyptians, for the famine was severe throughout Egypt. [57]And all the countries came to Egypt to buy grain from Joseph, because the famine was severe in all the world. *Ge 42:5-6; 1Ch 27:25*

Joseph's Brothers Go to Egypt

42 When Jacob learned that there was grain in Egypt, he said to his sons, "Why do you just keep looking at each other?" [2]He continued, "I have heard that there is grain in Egypt. Go down there and buy some for us, so that we may live and not die." *Ge 43:8; Ac 7:12*

[3]Then ten of Joseph's brothers went down to buy grain from Egypt. [4]But Jacob did not send Benjamin, Joseph's brother, with the others, because he was afraid that harm might come to him. [5]So Israel's sons were among those who went to buy grain, for the famine was in the land of Canaan also.

[6]Now Joseph was the governor of the land, the one who sold grain to all its people. So when Joseph's brothers arrived, they bowed down to him with their faces to the ground. [7]As soon as Joseph saw his brothers, he recognized them, but he pretended to be a stranger and spoke harshly to them. "Where do you come from?" he asked.

"From the land of Canaan," they replied, "to buy food."

[8]Although Joseph recognized his brothers, they did not recognize him. [9]Then he remembered his dreams about them and said to them, "You are spies! You have come to see where our land is unprotected." *Ge 37:2*

[10]"No, my lord," they answered. "Your servants have come to buy food. [11]We are all the sons of one man. Your servants are honest men, not spies." *Ge 37:8; 44:7*

[12]"No!" he said to them.

---

[a]51 *Manasseh* sounds like and may be derived from the Hebrew for *forget*.
[b]52 *Ephraim* sounds like the Hebrew for *twice fruitful*.

"You have come to see where our land is unprotected."

¹³But they replied, "Your servants were twelve brothers, the sons of one man, who lives in the land of Canaan. The youngest is now with our father, and one is no more." Ge 43:7; 44:8

¹⁴Joseph said to them, "It is just as I told you: You are spies! ¹⁵And this is how you will be tested: As surely as Pharaoh lives, you will not leave this place unless your youngest brother comes here. ¹⁶Send one of your number to get your brother; the rest of you will be kept in prison, so that your words may be tested to see if you are telling the truth. If you are not, then as surely as Pharaoh lives, you are spies!" ¹⁷And he put them all in custody for three days. Ge 43:3

¹⁸On the third day, Joseph said to them, "Do this and you will live, for I fear God: ¹⁹If you are honest men, let one of your brothers stay here in prison, while the rest of you go and take grain back for your starving households. ²⁰But you must bring your youngest brother to me, so that your words may be verified and that you may not die." This they proceeded to do.

²¹They said to one another, "Surely we are being punished because of our brother. We saw how distressed he was when he pleaded with us for his life, but we would not listen; that's why this distress has come upon us." Ge 45:5; Hos 5:5

²²Reuben replied, "Didn't I tell you not to sin against the boy? But you wouldn't listen! Now we must give an accounting for his blood." ²³They did not realize that Joseph could understand them, since he was using an interpreter. Ge 37:22

²⁴He turned away from them and began to weep, but then turned back and spoke to them again. He had Simeon taken from them and bound before their eyes. Ge 43:30; 45:14-15

²⁵Joseph gave orders to fill their bags with grain, to put each man's silver back in his sack, and to give them provisions for their journey. After this was done for them, ²⁶they loaded their grain on their donkeys and left. Ge 44:1; Mt 5:44

²⁷At the place where they stopped for the night one of them opened his sack to get feed for his donkey, and he saw his silver in the mouth of his sack. ²⁸"My silver has been returned," he said to his brothers. "Here it is in my sack." Ge 43:21

Their hearts sank and they turned to each other trembling and said, "What is this that God has done to us?" Jos 2:11; Mk 5:33

²⁹When they came to their father Jacob in the land of Canaan, they told him all that had happened to them. They said, ³⁰"The man who is lord over the land spoke harshly to us and treated us as though we were spying on the land. ³¹But we said to him, 'We are honest men; we are not spies. ³²We

were twelve brothers, sons of one father. One is no more, and the youngest is now with our father in Canaan.'　　　Ge 44:24

33"Then the man who is lord over the land said to us, 'This is how I will know whether you are honest men: Leave one of your brothers here with me, and take food for your starving households and go. 34But bring your youngest brother to me so I will know that you are not spies but honest men. Then I will give your brother back to you, and you can trade*a* in the land.' "　　　Ge 34:10

35As they were emptying their sacks, there in each man's sack was his pouch of silver! When they and their father saw the money pouches, they were frightened. 36Their father Jacob said to them, "You have deprived me of my children. Joseph is no more and Simeon is no more, and now you want to take Benjamin. Everything is against me!"　　Ge 43:15,18; Job 3:25

37Then Reuben said to his father, "You may put both of my sons to death if I do not bring him back to you. Entrust him to my care, and I will bring him back."　　　Ge 39:4; 43:9

38But Jacob said, "My son will not go down there with you; his brother is dead and he is the only one left. If harm comes to him on the journey you are taking, you will bring my gray

head down to the grave*b* in sorrow."　　Ge 37:35; 44:29,34

The Second Journey to Egypt

43 Now the famine was still severe in the land. 2So when they had eaten all the grain they had brought from Egypt, their father said to them, "Go back and buy us a little more food."　　　Ge 12:10; 41:57

3But Judah said to him, "The man warned us solemnly, 'You will not see my face again unless your brother is with you.' 4If you will send our brother along with us, we will go down and buy food for you. 5But if you will not send him, we will not go down, because the man said to us, 'You will not see my face again unless your brother is with you.' "　　Ge 42:2; 44:23

6Israel asked, "Why did you bring this trouble on me by telling the man you had another brother?"　　Ge 17:5; 34:30

7They replied, "The man questioned us closely about ourselves and our family. 'Is your father still living?' he asked us. 'Do you have another brother?' We simply answered his questions. How were we to know he would say, 'Bring your brother down here'?"　　Ge 45:3

8Then Judah said to Israel his father, "Send the boy along with me and we will go at once, so that we and you and our children may live and not die. 9I myself will guarantee his safety;

---

a34 Or *move about freely*　　*b38* Hebrew *Sheol*

you can hold me personally responsible for him. If I do not bring him back to you and set him here before you, I will bear the blame before you all my life. [10]As it is, if we had not delayed, we could have gone and returned twice." Ge 42:2; 44:10

[11]Then their father Israel said to them, "If it must be, then do this: Put some of the best products of the land in your bags and take them down to the man as a gift—a little balm and a little honey, some spices and myrrh, some pistachio nuts and almonds. [12]Take double the amount of silver with you, for you must return the silver that was put back into the mouths of your sacks. Perhaps it was a mistake. [13]Take your brother also and go back to the man at once. [14]And may God Almighty[a] grant you mercy before the man so that he will let your other brother and Benjamin come back with you. As for me, if I am bereaved, I am bereaved." Ge 37:25; 42:25

[15]So the men took the gifts and double the amount of silver, and Benjamin also. They hurried down to Egypt and presented themselves to Joseph. [16]When Joseph saw Benjamin with them, he said to the steward of his house, "Take these men to my house, slaughter an animal and prepare dinner; they are to eat with me at noon." Ge 44:1; 45:9

[17]The man did as Joseph told him and took the men to Joseph's house. [18]Now the men were frightened when they were taken to his house. They thought, "We were brought here because of the silver that was put back into our sacks the first time. He wants to attack us and overpower us and seize us as slaves and take our donkeys." Ge 42:35; 44:14

[19]So they went up to Joseph's steward and spoke to him at the entrance to the house. [20]"Please, sir," they said, "we came down here the first time to buy food. [21]But at the place where we stopped for the night we opened our sacks and each of us found his silver—the exact weight—in the mouth of his sack. So we have brought it back with us. [22]We have also brought additional silver with us to buy food. We don't know who put our silver in our sacks." Ge 42:3; 43:12

[23]"It's all right," he said. "Don't be afraid. Your God, the God of your father, has given you treasure in your sacks; I received your silver." Then he brought Simeon out to them.

[24]The steward took the men into Joseph's house, gave them water to wash their feet and provided fodder for their donkeys. [25]They prepared their gifts for Joseph's arrival at noon, because they had heard that they were to eat there. Ge 18:4; 32:13

[a]14 Hebrew *El-Shaddai*

26When Joseph came home, they presented to him the gifts they had brought into the house, and they bowed down before him to the ground. 27He asked them how they were, and then he said, "How is your aged father you told me about? Is he still living?"   Ge 32:13; 37:7

28They replied, "Your servant our father is still alive and well." And they bowed low to pay him honor.   Ge 37:10; 44:24

29As he looked about and saw his brother Benjamin, his own mother's son, he asked, "Is this your youngest brother, the one you told me about?" And he said, "God be gracious to you, my son." 30Deeply moved at the sight of his brother, Joseph hurried out and looked for a place to weep. He went into his private room and wept there.

31After he had washed his face, he came out and, controlling himself, said, "Serve the food."   Ge 45:1; Isa 30:18

32They served him by himself, the brothers by themselves, and the Egyptians who ate with him by themselves, because Egyptians could not eat with Hebrews, for that is detestable to Egyptians. 33The men had been seated before him in the order of their ages, from the firstborn to the youngest; and they looked at each other in astonishment. 34When portions were served to them from Joseph's table, Benjamin's portion was five times as much as anyone else's. So they feasted and drank freely with him.

A Silver Cup in a Sack

44 Now Joseph gave these instructions to the steward of his house: "Fill the men's sacks with as much food as they can carry, and put each man's silver in the mouth of his sack. 2Then put my cup, the silver one, in the mouth of the youngest one's sack, along with the silver for his grain." And he did as Joseph said.   Ge 42:25; 43:16

3As morning dawned, the men were sent on their way with their donkeys. 4They had not gone far from the city when Joseph said to his steward, "Go after those men at once, and when you catch up with them, say to them, 'Why have you repaid good with evil? 5Isn't this the cup my master drinks from and also uses for divination? This is a wicked thing you have done.'"   Jdg 19:9; Ps 35:12

6When he caught up with them, he repeated these words to them. 7But they said to him, "Why does my lord say such things? Far be it from your servants to do anything like that! 8We even brought back to you from the land of Canaan the silver we found inside the mouths of our sacks. So why would we steal silver or gold from your master's house? 9If any of your servants is found to have it, he will die; and the rest of us will become my lord's slaves."

10"Very well, then," he said,

"let it be as you say. Whoever is found to have it will become my slave; the rest of you will be free from blame." Ge 43:9

11Each of them quickly lowered his sack to the ground and opened it. 12Then the steward proceeded to search, beginning with the oldest and ending with the youngest. And the cup was found in Benjamin's sack. 13At this, they tore their clothes. Then they all loaded their donkeys and returned to the city.

14Joseph was still in the house when Judah and his brothers came in, and they threw themselves to the ground before him. 15Joseph said to them, "What is this you have done? Don't you know that a man like me can find things out by divination?"

16"What can we say to my lord?" Judah replied. "What can we say? How can we prove our innocence? God has uncovered your servants' guilt. We are now my lord's slaves—we ourselves and the one who was found to have the cup."

17But Joseph said, "Far be it from me to do such a thing! Only the man who was found to have the cup will become my slave. The rest of you, go back to your father in peace."

18Then Judah went up to him and said: "Please, my lord, let your servant speak a word to my lord. Do not be angry with your servant, though you are equal to Pharaoh himself. 19My lord asked his servants, 'Do you have a father or a brother?' 20And we answered, 'We have an aged father, and there is a young son born to him in his old age. His brother is dead, and he is the only one of his mother's sons left, and his father loves him.' Ge 37:7; 41:40-44

21"Then you said to your servants, 'Bring him down to me so I can see him for myself.' 22And we said to my lord, 'The boy cannot leave his father; if he leaves him, his father will die.' 23But you told your servants, 'Unless your youngest brother comes down with you, you will not see my face again.' 24When we went back to your servant my father, we told him what my lord had said. Ge 42:11; 43:3

25"Then our father said, 'Go back and buy a little more food.' 26But we said, 'We cannot go down. Only if our youngest brother is with us will we go. We cannot see the man's face unless our youngest brother is with us.' Ge 42:2; 43:5

27"Your servant my father said to us, 'You know that my wife bore me two sons. 28One of them went away from me, and I said, "He has surely been torn to pieces." And I have not seen him since. 29If you take this one from me too and harm comes to him, you will bring my gray head down to the grave*a* in misery.' Ge 37:31-35; 46:19

30"So now, if the boy is not

*a*29 Hebrew *Sheol*; also in verse 31

with us when I go back to your servant my father and if my father, whose life is closely bound up with the boy's life, [31]sees that the boy isn't there, he will die. Your servants will bring the gray head of our father down to the grave in sorrow. [32]Your servant guaranteed the boy's safety to my father. I said, 'If I do not bring him back to you, I will bear the blame before you, my father, all my life!' 1Sa 18:1

[33]"Now then, please let your servant remain here as my lord's slave in place of the boy, and let the boy return with his brothers. [34]How can I go back to my father if the boy is not with me? No! Do not let me see the misery that would come upon my father." Jn 15:13

Joseph Makes Himself Known

45 Then Joseph could no longer control himself before all his attendants, and he cried out, "Have everyone leave my presence!" So there was no one with Joseph when he made himself known to his brothers. [2]And he wept so loudly that the Egyptians heard him, and Pharaoh's household heard about it.

[3]Joseph said to his brothers, "I am Joseph! Is my father still living?" But his brothers were not able to answer him, because they were terrified at his presence. Ge 43:27; Job 21:6

[4]Then Joseph said to his brothers, "Come close to me." When they had done so, he said, "I am your brother Joseph, the one you sold into Egypt! [5]And now, do not be distressed and do not be angry with yourselves for selling me here, because it was to save lives that God sent me ahead of you. [6]For two years now there has been famine in the land, and for the next five years there will not be plowing and reaping. [7]But God sent me ahead of you to preserve for you a remnant on earth and to save your lives by a great deliverance. [a] Ge 37:28

[8]"So then, it was not you who sent me here, but God. He made me father to Pharaoh, lord of his entire household and ruler of all Egypt. [9]Now hurry back to my father and say to him, 'This is what your son Joseph says: God has made me lord of all Egypt. Come down to me; don't delay. [10]You shall live in the region of Goshen and be near me—you, your children and grandchildren, your flocks and herds, and all you have. [11]I will provide for you there, because five years of famine are still to come. Otherwise you and your household and all who belong to you will become destitute.' Ge 41:43; Ac 7:14

[12]"You can see for yourselves, and so can my brother Benjamin, that it is really I who am speaking to you. [13]Tell my father about all the honor ac-

[a]7 Or save you as a great band of survivors

corded me in Egypt and about everything you have seen. And bring my father down here quickly." _{Ge 35:18; Mk 6:50}

¹⁴Then he threw his arms around his brother Benjamin and wept, and Benjamin embraced him, weeping. ¹⁵And he kissed all his brothers and wept over them. Afterward his brothers talked with him. _{Ge 29:11,13}

¹⁶When the news reached Pharaoh's palace that Joseph's brothers had come, Pharaoh and all his officials were pleased. ¹⁷Pharaoh said to Joseph, "Tell your brothers, 'Do this: Load your animals and return to the land of Canaan, ¹⁸and bring your father and your families back to me. I will give you the best of the land of Egypt and you can enjoy the fat of the land.' _{Ge 50:7; Ac 7:13}

¹⁹"You are also directed to tell them, 'Do this: Take some carts from Egypt for your children and your wives, and get your father and come. ²⁰Never mind about your belongings, because the best of all Egypt will be yours.' " _{Ge 45:21; 46:5}

²¹So the sons of Israel did this. Joseph gave them carts, as Pharaoh had commanded, and he also gave them provisions for their journey. ²²To each of them he gave new clothing, but to Benjamin he gave three hundred shekels[a] of silver and five sets of clothes. ²³And this is what he sent to his father: ten donkeys loaded with the best things of Egypt, and ten female donkeys loaded with grain and bread and other provisions for his journey. ²⁴Then he sent his brothers away, and as they were leaving he said to them, "Don't quarrel on the way!"

²⁵So they went up out of Egypt and came to their father Jacob in the land of Canaan. ²⁶They told him, "Joseph is still alive! In fact, he is ruler of all Egypt." Jacob was stunned; he did not believe them. ²⁷But when they told him everything Joseph had said to them, and when he saw the carts Joseph had sent to carry him back, the spirit of their father Jacob revived. ²⁸And Israel said, "I'm convinced! My son Joseph is still alive. I will go and see him before I die." _{Ge 37:31; 1Ki 10:7}

Jacob Goes to Egypt

46 So Israel set out with all that was his, and when he reached Beersheba, he offered sacrifices to the God of his father Isaac. _{Ge 28:13}

²And God spoke to Israel in a vision at night and said, "Jacob! Jacob!" _{Ge 15:1; Job 33:14}

"Here I am," he replied.

³"I am God, the God of your father," he said. "Do not be afraid to go down to Egypt, for I will make you into a great nation there. ⁴I will go down to Egypt with you, and I will surely bring you back again. And

---

_{a22 That is, about 7 1/2 pounds (about 3.5 kilograms)}

Joseph's own hand will close your eyes." Ge 28:13; 50:1

⁵Then Jacob left Beersheba, and Israel's sons took their father Jacob and their children and their wives in the carts that Pharaoh had sent to transport him. ⁶They also took with them their livestock and the possessions they had acquired in Canaan, and Jacob and all his offspring went to Egypt. ⁷He took with him to Egypt his sons and grandsons and his daughters and granddaughters—all his offspring. Ge 45:19; Dt 26:5

⁸These are the names of the sons of Israel (Jacob and his descendants) who went to Egypt:

Reuben the firstborn of Jacob. Ge 29:32
⁹The sons of Reuben: Ex 6:14
  Hanoch, Pallu, Hezron and Carmi. Nu 26:6
¹⁰The sons of Simeon: Ge 29:33
  Jemuel, Jamin, Ohad, Jakin, Zohar and Shaul the son of a Canaanite woman. Nu 26:13
¹¹The sons of Levi: Ge 29:34
  Gershon, Kohath and Merari. Ex 6:16
¹²The sons of Judah: Ge 29:35
  Er, Onan, Shelah, Perez and Zerah (but Er and Onan had died in the land of Canaan). Ge 38:7
  The sons of Perez: 1Ch 2:5

Hezron and Hamul. Nu 26:21
¹³The sons of Issachar: Ge 30:18
  Tola, Puah,ᵃ Jashubᵇ and Shimron. Nu 26:24
¹⁴The sons of Zebulun: Ge 30:20
  Sered, Elon and Jahleel.
¹⁵These were the sons Leah bore to Jacob in Paddan Aram,ᶜ besides his daughter Dinah. These sons and daughters of his were thirty-three in all. Ge 30:21

¹⁶The sons of Gad: Ge 30:11
  Zephon,ᵈ Haggi, Shuni, Ezbon, Eri, Arodi and Areli. Nu 26:15
¹⁷The sons of Asher: Ge 30:13
  Imnah, Ishvah, Ishvi and Beriah.
  Their sister was Serah.
  The sons of Beriah:
  Heber and Malkiel.
¹⁸These were the children born to Jacob by Zilpah, whom Laban had given to his daughter Leah—sixteen in all. Ge 16:1

¹⁹The sons of Jacob's wife Rachel: Ge 29:6
  Joseph and Benjamin. ²⁰In Egypt, Manasseh and Ephraim were born to Joseph by Asenath daughter of Potiphera, priest of On.ᵉ Ge 41:45
²¹The sons of Benjamin: Nu 26:38
  Bela, Beker, Ashbel, Gera, Naaman, Ehi, Rosh, Muppim, Huppim and Ard. Nu 26:40

ᵃ13 Samaritan Pentateuch and Syriac (see also 1 Chron. 7:1); Masoretic Text *Puvah*
ᵇ13 Samaritan Pentateuch and some Septuagint manuscripts (see also Num. 26:24 and 1 Chron. 7:1); Masoretic Text *Iob*   ᶜ15 That is, Northwest Mesopotamia
ᵈ16 Samaritan Pentateuch and Septuagint (see also Num. 26:15); Masoretic Text *Ziphion*
ᵉ20 That is, Heliopolis

²²These were the sons of Rachel who were born to Jacob—fourteen in all.   Ge 29:6

²³The son of Dan: Ge 30:6
     Hushim.   Nu 26:42
²⁴The sons of Naphtali: Ge 30:8
     Jahziel, Guni, Jezer and Shillem.
²⁵These were the sons born to Jacob by Bilhah, whom Laban had given to his daughter Rachel—seven in all.   Ge 24:61

²⁶All those who went to Egypt with Jacob—those who were his direct descendants, not counting his sons' wives—numbered sixty-six persons. ²⁷With the two sons[a] who had been born to Joseph in Egypt, the members of Jacob's family, which went to Egypt, were seventy[b] in all.

²⁸Now Jacob sent Judah ahead of him to Joseph to get directions to Goshen. When they arrived in the region of Goshen, ²⁹Joseph had his chariot made ready and went to Goshen to meet his father Israel. As soon as Joseph appeared before him, he threw his arms around his father[c] and wept for a long time.   Ge 29:11; 45:14-15
³⁰Israel said to Joseph, "Now I am ready to die, since I have seen for myself that you are still alive."   Ge 44:28; Lk 2:29-30
³¹Then Joseph said to his brothers and to his father's household, "I will go up and speak to Pharaoh and will say to him, 'My brothers and my father's household, who were living in the land of Canaan, have come to me. ³²The men are shepherds; they tend livestock, and they have brought along their flocks and herds and everything they own.' ³³When Pharaoh calls you in and asks, 'What is your occupation?' ³⁴you should answer, 'Your servants have tended livestock from our boyhood on, just as our fathers did.' Then you will be allowed to settle in the region of Goshen, for all shepherds are detestable to the Egyptians."

47 Joseph went and told Pharaoh, "My father and brothers, with their flocks and herds and everything they own, have come from the land of Canaan and are now in Goshen." ²He chose five of his brothers and presented them before Pharaoh.   Ge 45:10; 46:31

³Pharaoh asked the brothers, "What is your occupation?"

"Your servants are shepherds," they replied to Pharaoh, "just as our fathers were." ⁴They also said to him, "We have come to live here awhile, because the famine is severe in Canaan and your servants' flocks have no pasture. So now, please let your servants settle in Goshen."   Ge 46:34; Ru 1:1

⁵Pharaoh said to Joseph, "Your father and your brothers have come to you, ⁶and the land

---

[a]27 Hebrew; Septuagint *the nine children* footnote); Septuagint (see also Acts 7:14) *seventy-five*   [b]27 Hebrew (see also Exodus 1:5 and   [c]29 Hebrew *around him*

of Egypt is before you; settle your father and your brothers in the best part of the land. Let them live in Goshen. And if you know of any among them with special ability, put them in charge of my own livestock."

⁷Then Joseph brought his father Jacob in and presented him before Pharaoh. After Jacob blessed*ᵃ* Pharaoh, ⁸Pharaoh asked him, "How old are you?"

⁹And Jacob said to Pharaoh, "The years of my pilgrimage are a hundred and thirty. My years have been few and difficult, and they do not equal the years of the pilgrimage of my fathers." ¹⁰Then Jacob blessed*ᵇ* Pharaoh and went out from his presence.

¹¹So Joseph settled his father and his brothers in Egypt and gave them property in the best part of the land, the district of Rameses, as Pharaoh directed. ¹²Joseph also provided his father and his brothers and all his father's household with food, according to the number of their children.   Ex 1:11; Nu 33:3

Joseph and the Famine

¹³There was no food, however, in the whole region because the famine was severe; both Egypt and Canaan wasted away because of the famine. ¹⁴Joseph collected all the money that was to be found in Egypt and Canaan in payment for the grain they were buying, and he brought it to Pharaoh's palace.

¹⁵When the money of the people of Egypt and Canaan was gone, all Egypt came to Joseph and said, "Give us food. Why should we die before your eyes? Our money is used up." Ge 41:30

¹⁶"Then bring your livestock," said Joseph. "I will sell you food in exchange for your livestock, since your money is gone." ¹⁷So they brought their livestock to Joseph, and he gave them food in exchange for their horses, their sheep and goats, their cattle and donkeys. And he brought them through that year with food in exchange for all their livestock.   Ge 12:16; Ex 14:9

¹⁸When that year was over, they came to him the following year and said, "We cannot hide from our lord the fact that since our money is gone and our livestock belongs to you, there is nothing left for our lord except our bodies and our land. ¹⁹Why should we perish before your eyes—we and our land as well? Buy us and our land in exchange for food, and we with our land will be in bondage to Pharaoh. Give us seed so that we may live and not die, and that the land may not become desolate."   Ge 42:2; Ex 10:9

²⁰So Joseph bought all the land in Egypt for Pharaoh. The Egyptians, one and all, sold their fields, because the famine was too severe for them. The land became Pharaoh's, ²¹and Joseph reduced the people to

---

ᵃ7 Or *greeted*   *ᵇ10* Or *said farewell to*

servitude,*a* from one end of Egypt to the other. ²²However, he did not buy the land of the priests, because they received a regular allotment from Pharaoh and had food enough from the allotment Pharaoh gave them. That is why they did not sell their land. Ge 12:10; Ezr 7:24

²³Joseph said to the people, "Now that I have bought you and your land today for Pharaoh, here is seed for you so you can plant the ground. ²⁴But when the crop comes in, give a fifth of it to Pharaoh. The other four-fifths you may keep as seed for the fields and as food for yourselves and your households and your children."

²⁵"You have saved our lives," they said. "May we find favor in the eyes of our lord; we will be in bondage to Pharaoh." Ge 32:5

²⁶So Joseph established it as a law concerning land in Egypt— still in force today—that a fifth of the produce belongs to Pharaoh. It was only the land of the priests that did not become Pharaoh's. Ge 41:34

²⁷Now the Israelites settled in Egypt in the region of Goshen. They acquired property there and were fruitful and increased greatly in number. Ge 35:11

²⁸Jacob lived in Egypt seventeen years, and the years of his life were a hundred and forty-seven. ²⁹When the time drew near for Israel to die, he called for his son Joseph and said to him, "If I have found favor in your eyes, put your hand under my thigh and promise that you will show me kindness and faithfulness. Do not bury me in Egypt, ³⁰but when I rest with my fathers, carry me out of Egypt and bury me where they are buried." Ge 24:49; Dt 31:14

"I will do as you say," he said.

³¹"Swear to me," he said. Then Joseph swore to him, and Israel worshiped as he leaned on the top of his staff.*b* Ge 21:23

Manasseh and Ephraim

48 Some time later Joseph was told, "Your father is ill." So he took his two sons Manasseh and Ephraim along with him. ²When Jacob was told, "Your son Joseph has come to you," Israel rallied his strength and sat up on the bed. Ge 41:52

³Jacob said to Joseph, "God Almighty*c* appeared to me at Luz in the land of Canaan, and there he blessed me ⁴and said to me, 'I am going to make you fruitful and will increase your numbers. I will make you a community of peoples, and I will give this land as an everlasting possession to your descendants after you.' Ge 28:13,19

⁵"Now then, your two sons born to you in Egypt before I came to you here will be reckoned as mine; Ephraim and Ma-

---

*a*21 Samaritan Pentateuch and Septuagint (see also Vulgate); Masoretic Text *and he moved the people into the cities*   *b*31 Or *Israel bowed down at the head of his bed*
*c*3 Hebrew *El-Shaddai*

nasseh will be mine, just as Reuben and Simeon are mine. 6Any children born to you after them will be yours; in the territory they inherit they will be reckoned under the names of their brothers. 7As I was returning from Paddan, *a* to my sorrow Rachel died in the land of Canaan while we were still on the way, a little distance from Ephrath. So I buried her there beside the road to Ephrath" (that is, Bethlehem).   Ge 46:20

8When Israel saw the sons of Joseph, he asked, "Who are these?"   Ge 48:10

9"They are the sons God has given me here," Joseph said to his father.   Ge 33:5

Then Israel said, "Bring them to me so I may bless them."

10Now Israel's eyes were failing because of old age, and he could hardly see. So Joseph brought his sons close to him, and his father kissed them and embraced them.   Ge 27:1; 29:13

11Israel said to Joseph, "I never expected to see your face again, and now God has allowed me to see your children too."   Ge 45:26; Job 42:16

12Then Joseph removed them from Israel's knees and bowed down with his face to the ground. 13And Joseph took both of them, Ephraim on his right toward Israel's left hand and Manasseh on his left toward Israel's right hand, and brought them close to him. 14But Israel

reached out his right hand and put it on Ephraim's head, though he was the younger, and crossing his arms, he put his left hand on Manasseh's head, even though Manasseh was the firstborn.   Ge 42:6

15Then he blessed Joseph and said,   Ge 24:60

"May the God before whom
    my fathers
  Abraham and Isaac walked,
the God who has been my
    shepherd   Ge 49:24
  all my life to this day,
16the Angel who has delivered
    me from all harm   Ge 16:7
  —may he bless these boys.
May they be called by my
    name
  and the names of my
      fathers Abraham and
      Isaac,   Ge 28:13
and may they increase
      greatly
  upon the earth."   Ge 12:2

17When Joseph saw his father placing his right hand on Ephraim's head he was displeased; so he took hold of his father's hand to move it from Ephraim's head to Manasseh's head. 18Joseph said to him, "No, my father, this one is the firstborn; put your right hand on his head."   Ge 48:13-14

19But his father refused and said, "I know, my son, I know. He too will become a people, and he too will become great. Nevertheless, his younger

a7 That is, Northwest Mesopotamia

brother will be greater than he, and his descendants will become a group of nations." ²⁰He blessed them that day and said,

"In your*a* name will Israel
pronounce this blessing:
'May God make you like
Ephraim and
Manasseh.' "   Nu 1:33

So he put Ephraim ahead of Manasseh.

²¹Then Israel said to Joseph, "I am about to die, but God will be with you*b* and take you*b* back to the land of your*b* fathers. ²²And to you, as one who is over your brothers, I give the ridge of land*c* I took from the Amorites with my sword and my bow."

Jacob Blesses His Sons

49 Then Jacob called for his sons and said: "Gather around so I can tell you what will happen to you in days to come.   Nu 24:14; Isa 39:6

²"Assemble and listen, sons
of Jacob;   Jos 24:1
listen to your father Israel.

³"Reuben, you are my
firstborn,   Ge 29:32
my might, the first sign of
my strength,   Dt 21:17
excelling in honor, excelling
in power.   Ge 34:19; Dt 33:6
⁴Turbulent as the waters, you
will no longer excel,

for you went up onto your
father's bed,
onto my couch and
defiled it.   Ge 29:29

⁵"Simeon and Levi are
brothers—   Ge 29:33
their swords*d* are weapons
of violence.   Ge 34:25
⁶Let me not enter their
council,
let me not join their
assembly,   Ps 1:1
for they have killed men in
their anger
and hamstrung oxen as
they pleased.   Jos 11:6,9
⁷Cursed be their anger, so
fierce,
and their fury, so cruel!
I will scatter them in Jacob
and disperse them in Israel.

⁸"Judah,*e* your brothers will
praise you;   Ge 29:35
your hand will be on the
neck of your enemies;
your father's sons will bow
down to you.   Ge 9:25
⁹You are a lion's cub,
O Judah;   Ru 5:5
you return from the prey,
my son.   Nu 23:24
Like a lion he crouches and
lies down,
like a lioness—who dares to
rouse him?   Dt 33:7
¹⁰The scepter will not depart
from Judah,   Nu 24:17,19
nor the ruler's staff from
between his feet,

---

a20 The Hebrew is singular.   *b21* The Hebrew is plural.   *c22* Or *And to you I give one portion more than to your brothers—the portion*   *d5* The meaning of the Hebrew for this word is uncertain.   *e8* *Judah* sounds like and may be derived from the Hebrew for *praise.*

until he comes to whom it
belongs[a]
and the obedience of the
nations is his.   Ps 2:9
11He will tether his donkey to a
vine,   Jdg 5:10
his colt to the choicest
branch;   Dt 8:8
he will wash his garments in
wine,
his robes in the blood of
grapes.   Dt 32:14
12His eyes will be darker than
wine,
his teeth whiter than milk.[b]

13"Zebulun will live by the
seashore
and become a haven for
ships;
his border will extend
toward Sidon.   Ge 10:19

14"Issachar is a rawboned[c]
donkey
lying down between two
saddlebags.[d]   Jdg 5:16
15When he sees how good is
his resting place
and how pleasant is his
land,   Dt 33:18-19; Jos 19:17-23
he will bend his shoulder to
the burden
and submit to forced labor.

16"Dan[e] will provide justice for
his people
as one of the tribes of Israel.
17Dan will be a serpent by the
roadside,   Jdg 18:27

a viper along the path,   Dt 33:22
that bites the horse's heels
so that its rider tumbles
backward.

18"I look for your deliverance,
O Lord.   Ge 45:7

19"Gad[f] will be attacked by a
band of raiders,   Ge 30:11
but he will attack them at
their heels.   Dt 33:20

20"Asher's food will be rich;
he will provide delicacies fit
for a king.   Dt 33:24; Job 29:6

21"Naphtali is a doe set free
that bears beautiful fawns.[g]

22"Joseph is a fruitful vine,
a fruitful vine near a spring,
whose branches climb over
a wall.[h]   Ge 17:6
23With bitterness archers
attacked him;   1Ch 10:3
they shot at him with
hostility.   Ge 27:41
24But his bow remained
steady,   Job 29:20
his strong arms stayed[i]
limber,   Ps 18:34
because of the hand of the
Mighty One of Jacob,
because of the Shepherd,
the Rock of Israel,   Dt 32:4
25because of your father's God,
who helps you,   Ge 28:13
because of the Almighty,[j]
who blesses you

---

a10 Or until Shiloh comes; or until he comes to whom tribute belongs   b12 Or will be dull
from wine, / his teeth white from milk   c14 Or strong   d14 Or campfires   e16 Dan
here means he provides justice.   f19 Gad can mean attack and band of raiders.
g21 Or free; / he utters beautiful words   h22 Or Joseph is a wild colt, / a wild colt near a
spring, / a wild donkey on a terraced hill   i23,24 Or archers will attack . . . will shoot . . .
will remain . . . will stay   j25 Hebrew Shaddai

with blessings of the heavens
　　above,
blessings of the deep that
　　lies below,   Ge 27:28
blessings of the breast and
　　womb.   Dt 7:13
26Your father's blessings are
　　greater
than the blessings of the
　　ancient mountains,
thana the bounty of the
　　age-old hills.   Hab 3:6
Let all these rest on the head
　　of Joseph,   1Ch 5:1
on the brow of the prince
　　amongb his brothers.

27"Benjamin is a ravenous
　　wolf;   Ge 35:18
in the morning he devours
　　the prey,
in the evening he divides
　　the plunder."   Nu 31:11

28All these are the twelve
tribes of Israel, and this is what
their father said to them when
he blessed them, giving each
the blessing appropriate to him.

The Death of Jacob

29Then he gave them these instructions: "I am about to be
gathered to my people. Bury me
with my fathers in the cave in
the field of Ephron the Hittite,
30the cave in the field of Machpelah, near Mamre in Canaan,
which Abraham bought as a
burial place from Ephron the
Hittite, along with the field.
31There Abraham and his wife

Sarah were buried, there Isaac
and his wife Rebekah were buried, and there I buried Leah.
32The field and the cave in it
were bought from the Hit-
tites.c"   Ge 23:16; 25:8

33When Jacob had finished
giving instructions to his sons,
he drew his feet up into the bed,
breathed his last and was gathered to his people.   Ac 7:15

50 Joseph threw himself
upon his father and wept
over him and kissed him. 2Then
Joseph directed the physicians
in his service to embalm his father Israel. So the physicians
embalmed him, 3taking a full
forty days, for that was the time
required for embalming. And
the Egyptians mourned for him
seventy days.   Ge 37:34; 46:4

4When the days of mourning
had passed, Joseph said to
Pharaoh's court, "If I have
found favor in your eyes, speak
to Pharaoh for me. Tell him,
5'My father made me swear an
oath and said, "I am about to
die; bury me in the tomb I dug
for myself in the land of Canaan." Now let me go up and
bury my father; then I will re-
turn.'"   Ge 27:41; 2Sa 18:18

6Pharaoh said, "Go up and
bury your father, as he made
you swear to do."

7So Joseph went up to bury
his father. All Pharaoh's officials accompanied him—the
dignitaries of his court and all

a26 Or of my progenitors, / as great as   b26 Or the one separated from   c32 Or the sons
of Heth

the dignitaries of Egypt— [8]besides all the members of Joseph's household and his brothers and those belonging to his father's household. Only their children and their flocks and herds were left in Goshen. [9]Chariots and horsemen[a] also went up with him. It was a very large company.   Ge 45:16

[10]When they reached the threshing floor of Atad, near the Jordan, they lamented loudly and bitterly; and there Joseph observed a seven-day period of mourning for his father. [11]When the Canaanites who lived there saw the mourning at the threshing floor of Atad, they said, "The Egyptians are holding a solemn ceremony of mourning." That is why that place near the Jordan is called Abel Mizraim.[b]   1Sa 31:13; Job 2:13

[12]So Jacob's sons did as he had commanded them: [13]They carried him to the land of Canaan and buried him in the cave in the field of Machpelah, near Mamre, which Abraham had bought as a burial place from Ephron the Hittite, along with the field. [14]After burying his father, Joseph returned to Egypt, together with his brothers and all the others who had gone with him to bury his father.

Joseph Reassures His Brothers

[15]When Joseph's brothers saw that their father was dead, they said, "What if Joseph holds a grudge against us and pays us back for all the wrongs we did to him?" [16]So they sent word to Joseph, saying, "Your father left these instructions before he died: [17]'This is what you are to say to Joseph: I ask you to forgive your brothers the sins and the wrongs they committed in treating you so badly.' Now please forgive the sins of the servants of the God of your father." When their message came to him, Joseph wept.

[18]His brothers then came and threw themselves down before him. "We are your slaves," they said.   Ge 37:7; 43:18

[19]But Joseph said to them, "Don't be afraid. Am I in the place of God? [20]You intended to harm me, but God intended it for good to accomplish what is now being done, the saving of many lives. [21]So then, don't be afraid. I will provide for you and your children." And he reassured them and spoke kindly to them.   Ge 45:5; Ro 12:19

The Death of Joseph

[22]Joseph stayed in Egypt, along with all his father's family. He lived a hundred and ten years [23]and saw the third generation of Ephraim's children. Also the children of Makir son of Manasseh were placed at birth on Joseph's knees.[c]

---

[a]9 Or *charioteers* were counted as his   [b]11 *Abel Mizraim* means *mourning of the Egyptians*.   [c]23 That is,

²⁴Then Joseph said to his brothers, "I am about to die. But God will surely come to your aid and take you up out of this land to the land he promised on oath to Abraham, Isaac and Jacob." ²⁵And Joseph made the sons of Israel swear an oath and said, "God will surely come to your aid, and then you must carry my bones up from this place." Ge 48:21; Ex 3:16

²⁶So Joseph died at the age of a hundred and ten. And after they embalmed him, he was placed in a coffin in Egypt. Ex 1:6

Exodus

Introduction:

Exodus means "exit" or "departure." The title of this book comes from one of the greatest miracles of God's care for his people in the Old Testament—the Israelites being freed from slavery and leaving Egypt.

The book of Exodus continues the story of God's people, now called Israelites. The story of the Israelites began with Abraham in the book of Genesis.

From Moses' birth, God chose him for a special task—to lead the Israelites out of Egypt and to the land God had promised them, Canaan. Moses is the main character and author of this book. Although he was weak in his own strength, God made him strong with his power and encouragement (7:6–11). God showed his power to the Israelites and the Egyptians in the ten plagues (7:14–11:10); the last plague made it possible for the Israelites to leave Egypt. Before leaving Egypt they celebrated the Passover (12).

The Israelites began their journey protected and guided by God in a pillar of cloud by day and a pillar of fire by night. With Moses leading them they crossed the Red Sea (Sea of Reeds) and settled in the desert at the foot of Mount Sinai for about one year. Here God set up his covenant with the Israelites by giving them the laws for living and worshiping.

The covenant between God and Israel began a relationship in which Israel was identified as God's holy nation. God gave his people the Ten Commandments, priests, and a tabernacle to help them live lives that showed they were truly God's people.

Outline of contents:

Moses, God's leader (1:1–4:31)
The contest with Pharaoh (5:1–13:19)
From Egypt to Mount Sinai (13:20–19:2)
God's covenant and laws (19:3–24:8)
The tabernacle for worship (24:9–40:38)

The Israelites Oppressed

1 These are the names of the sons of Israel who went to Egypt with Jacob, each with his family: ²Reuben, Simeon, Levi and Judah; ³Issachar, Zebulun and Benjamin; ⁴Dan and Naphtali; Gad and Asher. ⁵The descendants of Jacob numbered seventy*a* in all; Joseph was already in Egypt.   Ge 46:8

⁶Now Joseph and all his brothers and all that generation died, ⁷but the Israelites were fruitful and multiplied greatly and became exceedingly numerous, so that the land was filled with them.   Ge 50:26

⁸Then a new king, who did not know about Joseph, came to power in Egypt. ⁹"Look," he said to his people, "the Israelites have become much too numerous for us. ¹⁰Come, we must deal shrewdly with them or they will become even more numerous and, if war breaks out, will join our enemies, fight against us and leave the country."   Jer 43:11; Ac 7:18-19

¹¹So they put slave masters over them to oppress them with forced labor, and they built Pithom and Rameses as store cities for Pharaoh. ¹²But the more they were oppressed, the more they multiplied and spread; so the Egyptians came to dread the Israelites ¹³and worked them ruthlessly. ¹⁴They made their lives bitter with hard labor in brick and mortar and with all kinds of work in the fields; in all their hard labor the Egyptians used them ruthlessly.   Ex 3:7; Dt 4:20

¹⁵The king of Egypt said to the Hebrew midwives, whose names were Shiphrah and Puah, ¹⁶"When you help the Hebrew women in childbirth and observe them on the delivery stool, if it is a boy, kill him; but if it is a girl, let her live." ¹⁷The midwives, however, feared God and did not do what the king of Egypt had told them to do; they let the boys live. ¹⁸Then the king of Egypt summoned the midwives and asked them, "Why have you done this? Why have you let the boys live?"   Ge 35:17; Ac 7:19

¹⁹The midwives answered Pharaoh, "Hebrew women are not like Egyptian women; they are vigorous and give birth before the midwives arrive."   Jos 2:4

²⁰So God was kind to the midwives and the people increased and became even more numerous. ²¹And because the midwives feared God, he gave them families of their own.   Isa 3:10

²²Then Pharaoh gave this order to all his people: "Every boy that is born*b* you must throw into the Nile, but let every girl live."   Ge 41:1; Ac 7:19

---

a5 Masoretic Text (see also Gen. 46:27); Dead Sea Scrolls and Septuagint (see also Acts 7:14 and note at Gen. 46:27) *seventy-five*   *b22* Masoretic Text; Samaritan Pentateuch, Septuagint and Targums *born to the Hebrews*

The Birth of Moses

2 Now a man of the house of Levi married a Levite woman, ²and she became pregnant and gave birth to a son. When she saw that he was a fine child, she hid him for three months. ³But when she could hide him no longer, she got a papyrus basket for him and coated it with tar and pitch. Then she placed the child in it and put it among the reeds along the bank of the Nile. ⁴His sister stood at a distance to see what would happen to him.

⁵Then Pharaoh's daughter went down to the Nile to bathe, and her attendants were walking along the river bank. She saw the basket among the reeds and sent her slave girl to get it. ⁶She opened it and saw the baby. He was crying, and she felt sorry for him. "This is one of the Hebrew babies," she said.

⁷Then his sister asked Pharaoh's daughter, "Shall I go and get one of the Hebrew women to nurse the baby for you?" Ru 4:16

⁸"Yes, go," she answered. And the girl went and got the baby's mother. ⁹Pharaoh's daughter said to her, "Take this baby and nurse him for me, and I will pay you." So the woman took the baby and nursed him. ¹⁰When the child grew older, she took him to Pharaoh's daughter and he became her son. She named him Moses,ᵃ saying, "I drew him out of the water." 1Sa 1:20; Ac 7:21

Moses Flees to Midian

¹¹One day, after Moses had grown up, he went out to where his own people were and watched them at their hard labor. He saw an Egyptian beating a Hebrew, one of his own people. ¹²Glancing this way and that and seeing no one, he killed the Egyptian and hid him in the sand. ¹³The next day he went out and saw two Hebrews fighting. He asked the one in the wrong, "Why are you hitting your fellow Hebrew?" Ac 7:23

¹⁴The man said, "Who made you ruler and judge over us? Are you thinking of killing me as you killed the Egyptian?" Then Moses was afraid and thought, "What I did must have become known." Ge 19:9; Ac 7:27

¹⁵When Pharaoh heard of this, he tried to kill Moses, but Moses fled from Pharaoh and went to live in Midian, where he sat down by a well. ¹⁶Now a priest of Midian had seven daughters, and they came to draw water and fill the troughs to water their father's flock. ¹⁷Some shepherds came along and drove them away, but Moses got up and came to their rescue and watered their flock.

¹⁸When the girls returned to Reuel their father, he asked them, "Why have you returned so early today?" Ex 3:1; Nu 10:29

ᵃ10 *Moses* sounds like the Hebrew for *draw out.*

¹⁹They answered, "An Egyptian rescued us from the shepherds. He even drew water for us and watered the flock."

²⁰"And where is he?" he asked his daughters. "Why did you leave him? Invite him to have something to eat." Ge 31:54

²¹Moses agreed to stay with the man, who gave his daughter Zipporah to Moses in marriage. ²²Zipporah gave birth to a son, and Moses named him Gershom,ᵃ saying, "I have become an alien in a foreign land." Ac 7:29

²³During that long period, the king of Egypt died. The Israelites groaned in their slavery and cried out, and their cry for help because of their slavery went up to God. ²⁴God heard their groaning and he remembered his covenant with Abraham, with Isaac and with Jacob. ²⁵So God looked on the Israelites and was concerned about them.

Moses and the Burning Bush

3 Now Moses was tending the flock of Jethro his father-in-law, the priest of Midian, and he led the flock to the far side of the desert and came to Horeb, the mountain of God. ²There the angel of the LORD appeared to him in flames of fire from within a bush. Moses saw that though the bush was on fire it did not burn up. ³So Moses thought, "I will go over and see this strange sight—why the bush does not burn up." Ex 2:18

⁴When the LORD saw that he had gone over to look, God called to him from within the bush, "Moses! Moses!" Ex 4:5

And Moses said, "Here I am." Ge 31:11

⁵"Do not come any closer," God said. "Take off your sandals, for the place where you are standing is holy ground." ⁶Then he said, "I am the God of your father, the God of Abraham, the God of Isaac and the God of Jacob." At this, Moses hid his face, because he was afraid to look at God. Jos 5:15

⁷The LORD said, "I have indeed seen the misery of my people in Egypt. I have heard them crying out because of their slave drivers, and I am concerned about their suffering. ⁸So I have come down to rescue them from the hand of the Egyptians and to bring them up out of that land into a good and spacious land, a land flowing with milk and honey—the home of the Canaanites, Hittites, Amorites, Perizzites, Hivites and Jebusites. ⁹And now the cry of the Israelites has reached me, and I have seen the way the Egyptians are oppressing them. ¹⁰So now, go. I am sending you to Pharaoh to bring my people the Israelites out of Egypt." Ex 2:25; Nu 10:9

¹¹But Moses said to God, "Who am I, that I should go to Pharaoh and bring the Israelites out of Egypt?" Ex 4:10; 6:12

ᵃ22 *Gershom* sounds like the Hebrew for *an alien there*.

¹²And God said, "I will be with you. And this will be the sign to you that it is I who have sent you: When you have brought the people out of Egypt, you*a* will worship God on this mountain."   Ge 31:3

¹³Moses said to God, "Suppose I go to the Israelites and say to them, 'The God of your fathers has sent me to you,' and they ask me, 'What is his name?' Then what shall I tell them?"

¹⁴God said to Moses, "I AM WHO I AM.*b* This is what you are to say to the Israelites: 'I AM has sent me to you.' "   Ex 6:3; Jn 8:58

¹⁵God also said to Moses, "Say to the Israelites, 'The LORD,*c* the God of your fathers—the God of Abraham, the God of Isaac and the God of Jacob—has sent me to you.' This is my name forever, the name by which I am to be remembered from generation to generation.   Ps 135:13; Hos 12:5

¹⁶"Go, assemble the elders of Israel and say to them, 'The LORD, the God of your fathers—the God of Abraham, Isaac and Jacob— appeared to me and said: I have watched over you and have seen what has been done to you in Egypt. ¹⁷And I have promised to bring you up out of your misery in Egypt into the land of the Canaanites, Hittites, Amorites, Perizzites, Hivites and Jebu-

sites—a land flowing with milk and honey.'   Ge 15:16; Ex 4:29

¹⁸"The elders of Israel will listen to you. Then you and the elders are to go to the king of Egypt and say to him, 'The LORD, the God of the Hebrews, has met with us. Let us take a three-day journey into the desert to offer sacrifices to the LORD our God.' ¹⁹But I know that the king of Egypt will not let you go unless a mighty hand compels him. ²⁰So I will stretch out my hand and strike the Egyptians with all the wonders that I will perform among them. After that, he will let you go.

²¹"And I will make the Egyptians favorably disposed toward this people, so that when you leave you will not go empty-handed. ²²Every woman is to ask her neighbor and any woman living in her house for articles of silver and gold and for clothing, which you will put on your sons and daughters. And so you will plunder the Egyptians."   Ex 11:3; Ps 105:37

Signs for Moses

4 Moses answered, "What if they do not believe me or listen to me and say, 'The LORD did not appear to you'?"   Ex 3:18

²Then the LORD said to him, "What is that in your hand?"

"A staff," he replied.   Ge 38:18

³The LORD said, "Throw it on the ground."

---

*a*12 The Hebrew is plural.   *b*14 Or *I WILL BE WHAT I WILL BE*   *c*15 The Hebrew for LORD sounds like and may be derived from the Hebrew for *I AM* in verse 14.

Moses threw it on the ground and it became a snake, and he ran from it. 4Then the LORD said to him, "Reach out your hand and take it by the tail." So Moses reached out and took hold of the snake and it turned back into a staff in his hand. 5"This," said the LORD, "is so that they may believe that the LORD, the God of their fathers—the God of Abraham, the God of Isaac and the God of Jacob—has appeared to you."

6Then the LORD said, "Put your hand inside your cloak." So Moses put his hand into his cloak, and when he took it out, it was leprous,*a* like snow.

7"Now put it back into your cloak," he said. So Moses put his hand back into his cloak, and when he took it out, it was restored, like the rest of his flesh. Nu 12:13; 2Ki 5:14

8Then the LORD said, "If they do not believe you or pay attention to the first miraculous sign, they may believe the second. 9But if they do not believe these two signs or listen to you, take some water from the Nile and pour it on the dry ground. The water you take from the river will become blood on the ground." Ex 7:19

10Moses said to the LORD, "O Lord, I have never been eloquent, neither in the past nor since you have spoken to your servant. I am slow of speech and tongue." Ex 6:12; Jer 1:6

11The LORD said to him, "Who gave man his mouth? Who makes him deaf or mute? Who gives him sight or makes him blind? Is it not I, the LORD? 12Now go; I will help you speak and will teach you what to say."

13But Moses said, "O Lord, please send someone else to do it." Jnh 1:1-3

14Then the LORD's anger burned against Moses and he said, "What about your brother, Aaron the Levite? I know he can speak well. He is already on his way to meet you, and his heart will be glad when he sees you. 15You shall speak to him and put words in his mouth; I will help both of you speak and will teach you what to do. 16He will speak to the people for you, and it will be as if he were your mouth and as if you were God to him. 17But take this staff in your hand so you can perform miraculous signs with it." Nu 23:5; Ps 77:20

Moses Returns to Egypt

18Then Moses went back to Jethro his father-in-law and said to him, "Let me go back to my own people in Egypt to see if any of them are still alive." Ex 2:21

Jethro said, "Go, and I wish you well."

19Now the LORD had said to Moses in Midian, "Go back to Egypt, for all the men who

---

*a*6 The Hebrew word was used for various diseases affecting the skin—not necessarily leprosy.

wanted to kill you are dead."
²⁰So Moses took his wife and sons, put them on a donkey and started back to Egypt. And he took the staff of God in his hand.   Ex 2:15; Ac 7:29

²¹The Lᴏʀᴅ said to Moses, "When you return to Egypt, see that you perform before Pharaoh all the wonders I have given you the power to do. But I will harden his heart so that he will not let the people go. ²²Then say to Pharaoh, 'This is what the Lᴏʀᴅ says: Israel is my firstborn son, ²³and I told you, "Let my son go, so he may worship me." But you refused to let him go; so I will kill your firstborn son.'"

²⁴At a lodging place on the way, the Lᴏʀᴅ met ⌊Moses⌋ᵃ and was about to kill him. ²⁵But Zipporah took a flint knife, cut off her son's foreskin and touched ⌊Moses'⌋ feet with it.ᵇ "Surely you are a bridegroom of blood to me," she said. ²⁶So the Lᴏʀᴅ let him alone. (At that time she said "bridegroom of blood," referring to circumcision.) Nu 22:22

²⁷The Lᴏʀᴅ said to Aaron, "Go into the desert to meet Moses." So he met Moses at the mountain of God and kissed him. ²⁸Then Moses told Aaron everything the Lᴏʀᴅ had sent him to say, and also about all the miraculous signs he had commanded him to perform.

²⁹Moses and Aaron brought together all the elders of the Israelites, ³⁰and Aaron told them

everything the Lᴏʀᴅ had said to Moses. He also performed the signs before the people, ³¹and they believed. And when they heard that the Lᴏʀᴅ was concerned about them and had seen their misery, they bowed down and worshiped.   Ex 3:16

Bricks Without Straw

5 Afterward Moses and Aaron went to Pharaoh and said, "This is what the Lᴏʀᴅ, the God of Israel, says: 'Let my people go, so that they may hold a festival to me in the desert.'"   Ex 3:18

²Pharaoh said, "Who is the Lᴏʀᴅ, that I should obey him and let Israel go? I do not know the Lᴏʀᴅ and I will not let Israel go."   Ex 3:19; Job 21:15

³Then they said, "The God of the Hebrews has met with us. Now let us take a three-day journey into the desert to offer sacrifices to the Lᴏʀᴅ our God, or he may strike us with plagues or with the sword."   Ex 3:18

⁴But the king of Egypt said, "Moses and Aaron, why are you taking the people away from their labor? Get back to your work!" ⁵Then Pharaoh said, "Look, the people of the land are now numerous, and you are stopping them from working."   Ge 12:2; Ex 1:11

⁶That same day Pharaoh gave this order to the slave drivers and foremen in charge of the people: ⁷"You are no longer to supply the people with straw

---

ᵃ24 Or ⌊Moses' son⌋; Hebrew *him*   ᵇ25 Or *and drew near* ⌊Moses'⌋ *feet*

for making bricks; let them go and gather their own straw. [8]But require them to make the same number of bricks as before; don't reduce the quota. They are lazy; that is why they are crying out, 'Let us go and sacrifice to our God.' [9]Make the work harder for the men so that they keep working and pay no attention to lies."   Ex 1:11

[10]Then the slave drivers and the foremen went out and said to the people, "This is what Pharaoh says: 'I will not give you any more straw. [11]Go and get your own straw wherever you can find it, but your work will not be reduced at all.' " [12]So the people scattered all over Egypt to gather stubble to use for straw. [13]The slave drivers kept pressing them, saying, "Complete the work required of you for each day, just as when you had straw." [14]The Israelite foremen appointed by Pharaoh's slave drivers were beaten and were asked, "Why didn't you meet your quota of bricks yesterday or today, as before?"

[15]Then the Israelite foremen went and appealed to Pharaoh: "Why have you treated your servants this way? [16]Your servants are given no straw, yet we are told, 'Make bricks!' Your servants are being beaten, but the fault is with your own people."

[17]Pharaoh said, "Lazy, that's what you are—lazy! That is why

you keep saying, 'Let us go and sacrifice to the LORD.' [18]Now get to work. You will not be given any straw, yet you must produce your full quota of bricks."

[19]The Israelite foremen realized they were in trouble when they were told, "You are not to reduce the number of bricks required of you for each day." [20]When they left Pharaoh, they found Moses and Aaron waiting to meet them, [21]and they said, "May the LORD look upon you and judge you! You have made us a stench to Pharaoh and his officials and have put a sword in their hand to kill us."

God Promises Deliverance

[22]Moses returned to the LORD and said, "O Lord, why have you brought trouble upon this people? Is this why you sent me? [23]Ever since I went to Pharaoh to speak in your name, he has brought trouble upon this people, and you have not rescued your people at all."   Nu 11:11

6 Then the LORD said to Moses, "Now you will see what I will do to Pharaoh: Because of my mighty hand he will let them go; because of my mighty hand he will drive them out of his country."   Ex 12:31

[2]God also said to Moses, "I am the LORD. [3]I appeared to Abraham, to Isaac and to Jacob as God Almighty,[a] but by my name the LORD[b] I did not make

---

a3 Hebrew *El-Shaddai*   *b3* See note at Exodus 3:15.

myself known to them.ᵃ ⁴I also established my covenant with them to give them the land of Canaan, where they lived as aliens. ⁵Moreover, I have heard the groaning of the Israelites, whom the Egyptians are enslaving, and I have remembered my covenant.   Ex 3:14; Ps 68:4

⁶"Therefore, say to the Israelites: 'I am the LORD, and I will bring you out from under the yoke of the Egyptians. I will free you from being slaves to them, and I will redeem you with an outstretched arm and with mighty acts of judgment. ⁷I will take you as my own people, and I will be your God. Then you will know that I am the LORD your God, who brought you out from under the yoke of the Egyptians. ⁸And I will bring you to the land I swore with uplifted hand to give to Abraham, to Isaac and to Jacob. I will give it to you as a possession. I am the LORD.' "   Nu 14:30; Dt 26:8

⁹Moses reported this to the Israelites, but they did not listen to him because of their discouragement and cruel bondage.

¹⁰Then the LORD said to Moses, ¹¹"Go, tell Pharaoh king of Egypt to let the Israelites go out of his country."   Ex 4:22

¹²But Moses said to the LORD, "If the Israelites will not listen to me, why would Pharaoh listen to me, since I speak with faltering lipsᵇ?"   Ex 4:10; Jer 1:6

Family Record of Moses and Aaron

¹³Now the LORD spoke to Moses and Aaron about the Israelites and Pharaoh king of Egypt, and he commanded them to bring the Israelites out of Egypt.   Ex 3:10

¹⁴These were the heads of their familiesᶜ: Nu 1:4

The sons of Reuben the firstborn son of Israel were Hanoch and Pallu, Hezron and Carmi. These were the clans of Reuben.   Ge 46:9

¹⁵The sons of Simeon were Jemuel, Jamin, Ohad, Jakin, Zohar and Shaul the son of a Canaanite woman. These were the clans of Simeon.   Ge 46:10

¹⁶These were the names of the sons of Levi according to their records: Gershon, Kohath and Merari. Levi lived 137 years.   Nu 3:17

¹⁷The sons of Gershon, by clans, were Libni and Shimei.   1Ch 6:17

¹⁸The sons of Kohath were Amram, Izhar, Hebron and Uzziel. Kohath lived 133 years.   1Ch 6:2,18

¹⁹The sons of Merari were Mahli and Mushi.   1Ch 6:19

These were the clans of Levi according to their records.

²⁰Amram married his fa-

ᵃ3 Or *Almighty, and by my name the* LORD *did I not let myself be known to them?*
ᵇ12 Hebrew *I am uncircumcised of lips;* also in verse 30   ᶜ14 The Hebrew for *families* here and in verse 25 refers to units larger than clans.

ther's sister Jochebed, who bore him Aaron and Moses. Amram lived 137 years.　Ex 2:1

²¹The sons of Izhar were Korah, Nepheg and Zicri.

²²The sons of Uzziel were Mishael, Elzaphan and Sithri.　Lev 10:4; Nu 3:30

²³Aaron married Elisheba, daughter of Amminadab and sister of Nahshon, and she bore him Nadab and Abihu, Eleazar and Ithamar.　Ru 4:19; 1Ch 2:10

²⁴The sons of Korah were Assir, Elkanah and Abiasaph. These were the Korahite clans.　Nu 26:11

²⁵Eleazar son of Aaron married one of the daughters of Putiel, and she bore him Phinehas.　Jos 24:33

These were the heads of the Levite families, clan by clan.

²⁶It was this same Aaron and Moses to whom the LORD said, "Bring the Israelites out of Egypt by their divisions." ²⁷They were the ones who spoke to Pharaoh king of Egypt about bringing the Israelites out of Egypt. It was the same Moses and Aaron.　Ex 7:14; Ps 77:20

Aaron to Speak for Moses

²⁸Now when the LORD spoke to Moses in Egypt, ²⁹he said to him, "I am the LORD. Tell Pharaoh king of Egypt everything I tell you."　Ex 7:2

³⁰But Moses said to the LORD, "Since I speak with faltering lips, why would Pharaoh listen to me?"　Ex 3:11; 4:10

7 Then the LORD said to Moses, "See, I have made you like God to Pharaoh, and your brother Aaron will be your prophet. ²You are to say everything I command you, and your brother Aaron is to tell Pharaoh to let the Israelites go out of his country. ³But I will harden Pharaoh's heart, and though I multiply my miraculous signs and wonders in Egypt, ⁴he will not listen to you. Then I will lay my hand on Egypt and with mighty acts of judgment I will bring out my divisions, my people the Israelites. ⁵And the Egyptians will know that I am the LORD when I stretch out my hand against Egypt and bring the Israelites out of it."　Ex 4:16

⁶Moses and Aaron did just as the LORD commanded them. ⁷Moses was eighty years old and Aaron eighty-three when they spoke to Pharaoh.　Ge 6:22

Aaron's Staff Becomes a Snake

⁸The LORD said to Moses and Aaron, ⁹"When Pharaoh says to you, 'Perform a miracle,' then say to Aaron, 'Take your staff and throw it down before Pharaoh,' and it will become a snake."　Isa 7:11; Jn 2:11

¹⁰So Moses and Aaron went to Pharaoh and did just as the LORD commanded. Aaron threw his staff down in front of Pharaoh and his officials, and it

became a snake. [11]Pharaoh then summoned wise men and sorcerers, and the Egyptian magicians also did the same things by their secret arts: [12]Each one threw down his staff and it became a snake. But Aaron's staff swallowed up their staffs. [13]Yet Pharaoh's heart became hard and he would not listen to them, just as the LORD had said.

The Plague of Blood

[14]Then the LORD said to Moses, "Pharaoh's heart is unyielding; he refuses to let the people go. [15]Go to Pharaoh in the morning as he goes out to the water. Wait on the bank of the Nile to meet him, and take in your hand the staff that was changed into a snake. [16]Then say to him, 'The LORD, the God of the Hebrews, has sent me to say to you: Let my people go, so that they may worship me in the desert. But until now you have not listened. [17]This is what the LORD says: By this you will know that I am the LORD: With the staff that is in my hand I will strike the water of the Nile, and it will be changed into blood. [18]The fish in the Nile will die, and the river will stink; the Egyptians will not be able to drink its water.'"   Ex 8:15

[19]The LORD said to Moses, "Tell Aaron, 'Take your staff and stretch out your hand over the waters of Egypt—over the streams and canals, over the ponds and all the reservoirs'—and they will turn to blood. Blood will be everywhere in Egypt, even in the wooden buckets and stone jars."   Ex 14:21; 2Ki 5:11

[20]Moses and Aaron did just as the LORD had commanded. He raised his staff in the presence of Pharaoh and his officials and struck the water of the Nile, and all the water was changed into blood. [21]The fish in the Nile died, and the river smelled so bad that the Egyptians could not drink its water. Blood was everywhere in Egypt.   Ps 105:29

[22]But the Egyptian magicians did the same things by their secret arts, and Pharaoh's heart became hard; he would not listen to Moses and Aaron, just as the LORD had said. [23]Instead, he turned and went into his palace, and did not take even this to heart. [24]And all the Egyptians dug along the Nile to get drinking water, because they could not drink the water of the river.

The Plague of Frogs

[25]Seven days passed after the LORD struck the Nile. [1]Then **8** the LORD said to Moses, "Go to Pharaoh and say to him, 'This is what the LORD says: Let my people go, so that they may worship me. [2]If you refuse to let them go, I will plague your whole country with frogs. [3]The Nile will teem with frogs. They will come up into your palace and your bedroom and onto your bed, into the houses of your officials and on your people, and into your ovens

and kneading troughs. ⁴The frogs will go up on you and your people and all your officials.' "   Ex 3:12,18; Ps 105:30

⁵Then the LORD said to Moses, "Tell Aaron, 'Stretch out your hand with your staff over the streams and canals and ponds, and make frogs come up on the land of Egypt.' "   Ex 7:19

⁶So Aaron stretched out his hand over the waters of Egypt, and the frogs came up and covered the land. ⁷But the magicians did the same things by their secret arts; they also made frogs come up on the land of Egypt.   Ps 78:45; 105:30

⁸Pharaoh summoned Moses and Aaron and said, "Pray to the LORD to take the frogs away from me and my people, and I will let your people go to offer sacrifices to the LORD."   Ex 9:27

⁹Moses said to Pharaoh, "I leave to you the honor of setting the time for me to pray for you and your officials and your people that you and your houses may be rid of the frogs, except for those that remain in the Nile."   Ex 9:5

¹⁰"Tomorrow," Pharaoh said.

Moses replied, "It will be as you say, so that you may know there is no one like the LORD our God. ¹¹The frogs will leave you and your houses, your officials and your people; they will remain only in the Nile."   Ex 9:14

¹²After Moses and Aaron left Pharaoh, Moses cried out to the LORD about the frogs he had brought on Pharaoh. ¹³And the LORD did what Moses asked. The frogs died in the houses, in the courtyards and in the fields. ¹⁴They were piled into heaps, and the land reeked of them. ¹⁵But when Pharaoh saw that there was relief, he hardened his heart and would not listen to Moses and Aaron, just as the LORD had said.   Ex 7:4; 9:33

The Plague of Gnats

¹⁶Then the LORD said to Moses, "Tell Aaron, 'Stretch out your staff and strike the dust of the ground,' and throughout the land of Egypt the dust will become gnats." ¹⁷They did this, and when Aaron stretched out his hand with the staff and struck the dust of the ground, gnats came upon men and animals. All the dust throughout the land of Egypt became gnats. ¹⁸But when the magicians tried to produce gnats by their secret arts, they could not. And the gnats were on men and animals.   Ex 4:2; Ps 105:31

¹⁹The magicians said to Pharaoh, "This is the finger of God." But Pharaoh's heart was hard and he would not listen, just as the LORD had said.   Ex 7:5; Ps 8:3

The Plague of Flies

²⁰Then the LORD said to Moses, "Get up early in the morning and confront Pharaoh as he goes to the water and say to him, 'This is what the LORD says: Let my people go, so that

they may worship me. ²¹If you do not let my people go, I will send swarms of flies on you and your officials, on your people and into your houses. The houses of the Egyptians will be full of flies, and even the ground where they are.   Ex 9:13

²²" 'But on that day I will deal differently with the land of Goshen, where my people live; no swarms of flies will be there, so that you will know that I, the LORD, am in this land. ²³I will make a distinction^a between my people and your people. This miraculous sign will occur tomorrow.' "   Ex 9:4; 10:23

²⁴And the LORD did this. Dense swarms of flies poured into Pharaoh's palace and into the houses of his officials, and throughout Egypt the land was ruined by the flies.   Ps 78:45

²⁵Then Pharaoh summoned Moses and Aaron and said, "Go, sacrifice to your God here in the land."   Ex 9:28; 10:16

²⁶But Moses said, "That would not be right. The sacrifices we offer the LORD our God would be detestable to the Egyptians. And if we offer sacrifices that are detestable in their eyes, will they not stone us? ²⁷We must take a three-day journey into the desert to offer sacrifices to the LORD our God, as he commands us."   Ge 43:32

²⁸Pharaoh said, "I will let you go to offer sacrifices to the LORD your God in the desert, but you must not go very far. Now pray for me."   Jer 37:3; Ac 8:24

²⁹Moses answered, "As soon as I leave you, I will pray to the LORD, and tomorrow the flies will leave Pharaoh and his officials and his people. Only be sure that Pharaoh does not act deceitfully again by not letting the people go to offer sacrifices to the LORD."   Ex 9:30; 10:11

³⁰Then Moses left Pharaoh and prayed to the LORD, ³¹and the LORD did what Moses asked: The flies left Pharaoh and his officials and his people; not a fly remained. ³²But this time also Pharaoh hardened his heart and would not let the people go.   Ex 7:14; 9:33

The Plague on Livestock

9 Then the LORD said to Moses, "Go to Pharaoh and say to him, 'This is what the LORD, the God of the Hebrews, says: "Let my people go, so that they may worship me." ²If you refuse to let them go and continue to hold them back, ³the hand of the LORD will bring a terrible plague on your livestock in the field—on your horses and donkeys and camels and on your cattle and sheep and goats. ⁴But the LORD will make a distinction between the livestock of Israel and that of Egypt, so that no animal belonging to the Israelites will die.' "   Lev 26:25

⁵The LORD set a time and said, "Tomorrow the LORD will

---

^a23 Septuagint and Vulgate; Hebrew *will put a deliverance*

do this in the land." 6And the next day the LORD did it: All the livestock of the Egyptians died, but not one animal belonging to the Israelites died. 7Pharaoh sent men to investigate and found that not even one of the animals of the Israelites had died. Yet his heart was unyielding and he would not let the people go.   Ex 7:14; 11:5

The Plague of Boils

8Then the LORD said to Moses and Aaron, "Take handfuls of soot from a furnace and have Moses toss it into the air in the presence of Pharaoh. 9It will become fine dust over the whole land of Egypt, and festering boils will break out on men and animals throughout the land."   Dt 28:27; 2Ki 20:7

10So they took soot from a furnace and stood before Pharaoh. Moses tossed it into the air, and festering boils broke out on men and animals. 11The magicians could not stand before Moses because of the boils that were on them and on all the Egyptians. 12But the LORD hardened Pharaoh's heart and he would not listen to Moses and Aaron, just as the LORD had said to Moses.   Ex 4:21; 8:18

The Plague of Hail

13Then the LORD said to Moses, "Get up early in the morning, confront Pharaoh and say to him, 'This is what the LORD, the God of the Hebrews, says: Let my people go, so that they may worship me, 14or this time I will send the full force of my plagues against you and against your officials and your people, so you may know that there is no one like me in all the earth. 15For by now I could have stretched out my hand and struck you and your people with a plague that would have wiped you off the earth. 16But I have raised you up*a* for this very purpose, that I might show you my power and that my name might be proclaimed in all the earth. 17You still set yourself against my people and will not let them go. 18Therefore, at this time tomorrow I will send the worst hailstorm that has ever fallen on Egypt, from the day it was founded till now. 19Give an order now to bring your livestock and everything you have in the field to a place of shelter, because the hail will fall on every man and animal that has not been brought in and is still out in the field, and they will die.' "   Ex 8:10; Pr 16:4

20Those officials of Pharaoh who feared the word of the LORD hurried to bring their slaves and their livestock inside. 21But those who ignored the word of the LORD left their slaves and livestock in the field.

22Then the LORD said to Moses, "Stretch out your hand toward the sky so that hail will

---

*a*16 Or *have spared you*

fall all over Egypt—on men and animals and on everything growing in the fields of Egypt." [23]When Moses stretched out his staff toward the sky, the LORD sent thunder and hail, and lightning flashed down to the ground. So the LORD rained hail on the land of Egypt; [24]hail fell and lightning flashed back and forth. It was the worst storm in all the land of Egypt since it had become a nation. [25]Throughout Egypt hail struck everything in the fields—both men and animals; it beat down everything growing in the fields and stripped every tree. [26]The only place it did not hail was the land of Goshen, where the Israelites were. Jos 10:11; Rev 16:21

[27]Then Pharaoh summoned Moses and Aaron. "This time I have sinned," he said to them. "The LORD is in the right, and I and my people are in the wrong. [28]Pray to the LORD, for we have had enough thunder and hail. I will let you go; you don't have to stay any longer."

[29]Moses replied, "When I have gone out of the city, I will spread out my hands in prayer to the LORD. The thunder will stop and there will be no more hail, so you may know that the earth is the LORD's. [30]But I know that you and your officials still do not fear the LORD God."

[31](The flax and barley were destroyed, since the barley had headed and the flax was in bloom. [32]The wheat and spelt, however, were not destroyed, because they ripen later.) Ru 1:22 [33]Then Moses left Pharaoh and went out of the city. He spread out his hands toward the LORD; the thunder and hail stopped, and the rain no longer poured down on the land. [34]When Pharaoh saw that the rain and hail and thunder had stopped, he sinned again: He and his officials hardened their hearts. [35]So Pharaoh's heart was hard and he would not let the Israelites go, just as the LORD had said through Moses. Ex 8:12

The Plague of Locusts

10 Then the LORD said to Moses, "Go to Pharaoh, for I have hardened his heart and the hearts of his officials so that I may perform these miraculous signs of mine among them [2]that you may tell your children and grandchildren how I dealt harshly with the Egyptians and how I performed my signs among them, and that you may know that I am the LORD." Ex 4:21; Dt 4:9

[3]So Moses and Aaron went to Pharaoh and said to him, "This is what the LORD, the God of the Hebrews, says: 'How long will you refuse to humble yourself before me? Let my people go, so that they may worship me. [4]If you refuse to let them go, I will bring locusts into your country tomorrow. [5]They will cover the face of the ground so that it cannot be seen. They will devour what little you have left after the

hail, including every tree that is growing in your fields. ⁶They will fill your houses and those of all your officials and all the Egyptians—something neither your fathers nor your forefathers have ever seen from the day they settled in this land till now.'" Then Moses turned and left Pharaoh.   1Ki 21:29; Rev 9:3

⁷Pharaoh's officials said to him, "How long will this man be a snare to us? Let the people go, so that they may worship the LORD their God. Do you not yet realize that Egypt is ruined?"   Ex 23:33; 1Sa 18:21

⁸Then Moses and Aaron were brought back to Pharaoh. "Go, worship the LORD your God," he said. "But just who will be going?"   Ex 8:8,25

⁹Moses answered, "We will go with our young and old, with our sons and daughters, and with our flocks and herds, because we are to celebrate a festival to the LORD."   Ex 12:37

¹⁰Pharaoh said, "The LORD be with you—if I let you go, along with your women and children! Clearly you are bent on evil. ᵃ ¹¹No! Have only the men go; and worship the LORD, since that's what you have been asking for." Then Moses and Aaron were driven out of Pharaoh's presence.   Ex 10:28

¹²And the LORD said to Moses, "Stretch out your hand over Egypt so that locusts will swarm over the land and devour everything growing in the fields, everything left by the hail."   Ex 7:19; 10:5,15

¹³So Moses stretched out his staff over Egypt, and the LORD made an east wind blow across the land all that day and all that night. By morning the wind had brought the locusts; ¹⁴they invaded all Egypt and settled down in every area of the country in great numbers. Never before had there been such a plague of locusts, nor will there ever be again. ¹⁵They covered all the ground until it was black. They devoured all that was left after the hail—everything growing in the fields and the fruit on the trees. Nothing green remained on tree or plant in all the land of Egypt.   Ps 78:46

¹⁶Pharaoh quickly summoned Moses and Aaron and said, "I have sinned against the LORD your God and against you. ¹⁷Now forgive my sin once more and pray to the LORD your God to take this deadly plague away from me."   Ex 8:8; 9:27

¹⁸Moses then left Pharaoh and prayed to the LORD. ¹⁹And the LORD changed the wind to a very strong west wind, which caught up the locusts and carried them into the Red Sea. ᵇ Not a locust was left anywhere in Egypt. ²⁰But the LORD hardened Pharaoh's heart, and he would not let the Israelites go.

ᵃ10 Or *Be careful, trouble is in store for you!* Reeds

ᵇ19 Hebrew *Yam Suph*; that is, Sea of

The Plague of Darkness

²¹Then the LORD said to Moses, "Stretch out your hand toward the sky so that darkness will spread over Egypt—darkness that can be felt." ²²So Moses stretched out his hand toward the sky, and total darkness covered all Egypt for three days. ²³No one could see anyone else or leave his place for three days. Yet all the Israelites had light in the places where they lived.   Dt 28:29

²⁴Then Pharaoh summoned Moses and said, "Go, worship the LORD. Even your women and children may go with you; only leave your flocks and herds behind."   Ge 45:10; Ex 10:8-10

²⁵But Moses said, "You must allow us to have sacrifices and burnt offerings to present to the LORD our God. ²⁶Our livestock too must go with us; not a hoof is to be left behind. We have to use some of them in worshiping the LORD our God, and until we get there we will not know what we are to use to worship the LORD."   Ge 8:20; Ex 18:12

²⁷But the LORD hardened Pharaoh's heart, and he was not willing to let them go. ²⁸Pharaoh said to Moses, "Get out of my sight! Make sure you do not appear before me again! The day you see my face you will die."

²⁹"Just as you say," Moses replied, "I will never appear before you again."   Heb 11:27

The Plague on the Firstborn

11 Now the LORD had said to Moses, "I will bring one more plague on Pharaoh and on Egypt. After that, he will let you go from here, and when he does, he will drive you out completely. ²Tell the people that men and women alike are to ask their neighbors for articles of silver and gold." ³(The LORD made the Egyptians favorably disposed toward the people, and Moses himself was highly regarded in Egypt by Pharaoh's officials and by the people.)

⁴So Moses said, "This is what the LORD says: 'About midnight I will go throughout Egypt. ⁵Every firstborn son in Egypt will die, from the firstborn son of Pharaoh, who sits on the throne, to the firstborn son of the slave girl, who is at her hand mill, and all the firstborn of the cattle as well. ⁶There will be loud wailing throughout Egypt—worse than there has ever been or ever will be again. ⁷But among the Israelites not a dog will bark at any man or animal.' Then you will know that the LORD makes a distinction between Egypt and Israel. ⁸All these officials of yours will come to me, bowing down before me and saying, 'Go, you and all the people who follow you!' After that I will leave." Then Moses, hot with anger, left Pharaoh.

⁹The LORD had said to Moses, "Pharaoh will refuse to listen to you—so that my wonders

may be multiplied in Egypt." ¹⁰Moses and Aaron performed all these wonders before Pharaoh, but the LORD hardened Pharaoh's heart, and he would not let the Israelites go out of his country.   Ex 4:21; 7:4

The Passover

12 The LORD said to Moses and Aaron in Egypt, ²"This month is to be for you the first month, the first month of your year. ³Tell the whole community of Israel that on the tenth day of this month each man is to take a lamb*a* for his family, one for each household. ⁴If any household is too small for a whole lamb, they must share one with their nearest neighbor, having taken into account the number of people there are. You are to determine the amount of lamb needed in accordance with what each person will eat. ⁵The animals you choose must be year-old males without defect, and you may take them from the sheep or the goats. ⁶Take care of them until the fourteenth day of the month, when all the people of the community of Israel must slaughter them at twilight. ⁷Then they are to take some of the blood and put it on the sides and tops of the doorframes of the houses where they eat the lambs. ⁸That same night they are to eat the meat roasted over the fire, along with bitter herbs, and bread made without yeast. ⁹Do not eat the meat raw or cooked in water, but roast it over the fire—head, legs and inner parts. ¹⁰Do not leave any of it till morning; if some is left till morning, you must burn it. ¹¹This is how you are to eat it: with your cloak tucked into your belt, your sandals on your feet and your staff in your hand. Eat it in haste; it is the LORD's Passover.   Lev 22:18-21; Dt 16:1

¹²"On that same night I will pass through Egypt and strike down every firstborn—both men and animals—and I will bring judgment on all the gods of Egypt. I am the LORD. ¹³The blood will be a sign for you on the houses where you are; and when I see the blood, I will pass over you. No destructive plague will touch you when I strike Egypt.   Nu 33:4

¹⁴"This is a day you are to commemorate; for the generations to come you shall celebrate it as a festival to the LORD—a lasting ordinance. ¹⁵For seven days you are to eat bread made without yeast. On the first day remove the yeast from your houses, for whoever eats anything with yeast in it from the first day through the seventh must be cut off from Israel. ¹⁶On the first day hold a sacred assembly, and another one on the seventh day. Do no work at all on these days, except to prepare

---

*a*3 The Hebrew word can mean *lamb* or *kid*; also in verse 4.

food for everyone to eat—that is all you may do. Nu 9:13

¹⁷"Celebrate the Feast of Unleavened Bread, because it was on this very day that I brought your divisions out of Egypt. Celebrate this day as a lasting ordinance for the generations to come. ¹⁸In the first month you are to eat bread made without yeast, from the evening of the fourteenth day until the evening of the twenty-first day. ¹⁹For seven days no yeast is to be found in your houses. And whoever eats anything with yeast in it must be cut off from the community of Israel, whether he is an alien or native-born. ²⁰Eat nothing made with yeast. Wherever you live, you must eat unleavened bread."

²¹Then Moses summoned all the elders of Israel and said to them, "Go at once and select the animals for your families and slaughter the Passover lamb. ²²Take a bunch of hyssop, dip it into the blood in the basin and put some of the blood on the top and on both sides of the doorframe. Not one of you shall go out the door of his house until morning. ²³When the Lord goes through the land to strike down the Egyptians, he will see the blood on the top and sides of the doorframe and will pass over that doorway, and he will not permit the destroyer to enter your houses and strike you down. Mk 14:12-16

²⁴"Obey these instructions as a lasting ordinance for you and your descendants. ²⁵When you enter the land that the Lord will give you as he promised, observe this ceremony. ²⁶And when your children ask you, 'What does this ceremony mean to you?' ²⁷then tell them, 'It is the Passover sacrifice to the Lord, who passed over the houses of the Israelites in Egypt and spared our homes when he struck down the Egyptians.'" Then the people bowed down and worshiped. ²⁸The Israelites did just what the Lord commanded Moses and Aaron.

²⁹At midnight the Lord struck down all the firstborn in Egypt, from the firstborn of Pharaoh, who sat on the throne, to the firstborn of the prisoner, who was in the dungeon, and the firstborn of all the livestock as well. ³⁰Pharaoh and all his officials and all the Egyptians got up during the night, and there was loud wailing in Egypt, for there was not a house without someone dead. Ex 11:4; Nu 35:27

The Exodus

³¹During the night Pharaoh summoned Moses and Aaron and said, "Up! Leave my people, you and the Israelites! Go, worship the Lord as you have requested. ³²Take your flocks and herds, as you have said, and go. And also bless me." Ex 8:8; 10:9,26

³³The Egyptians urged the people to hurry and leave the

country. "For otherwise," they said, "we will all die!" ³⁴So the people took their dough before the yeast was added, and carried it on their shoulders in kneading troughs wrapped in clothing. ³⁵The Israelites did as Moses instructed and asked the Egyptians for articles of silver and gold and for clothing. ³⁶The LORD had made the Egyptians favorably disposed toward the people, and they gave them what they asked for; so they plundered the Egyptians.   Ex 10:7

³⁷The Israelites journeyed from Rameses to Succoth. There were about six hundred thousand men on foot, besides women and children. ³⁸Many other people went up with them, as well as large droves of livestock, both flocks and herds. ³⁹With the dough they had brought from Egypt, they baked cakes of unleavened bread. The dough was without yeast because they had been driven out of Egypt and did not have time to prepare food for themselves.   Nu 11:4; 33:3

⁴⁰Now the length of time the Israelite people lived in Egyptᵃ was 430 years. ⁴¹At the end of the 430 years, to the very day, all the LORD's divisions left Egypt. ⁴²Because the LORD kept vigil that night to bring them out of Egypt, on this night all the Israelites are to keep vigil to honor the LORD for the generations to come.   Ac 7:6; Gal 3:17

Passover Restrictions

⁴³The LORD said to Moses and Aaron, "These are the regulations for the Passover: Nu 9:4

"No foreigner is to eat of it. ⁴⁴Any slave you have bought may eat of it after you have circumcised him, ⁴⁵but a temporary resident and a hired worker may not eat of it.   Ge 17:12-13

⁴⁶"It must be eaten inside one house; take none of the meat outside the house. Do not break any of the bones. ⁴⁷The whole community of Israel must celebrate it.   Nu 9:12; Jn 19:36

⁴⁸"An alien living among you who wants to celebrate the LORD's Passover must have all the males in his household circumcised; then he may take part like one born in the land. No uncircumcised male may eat of it. ⁴⁹The same law applies to the native-born and to the alien living among you."   Nu 9:14; Gal 3:28

⁵⁰All the Israelites did just what the LORD had commanded Moses and Aaron. ⁵¹And on that very day the LORD brought the Israelites out of Egypt by their divisions.   Ex 6:26; 12:28

Consecration of the Firstborn

13 The LORD said to Moses, ²"Consecrate to me every firstborn male. The first offspring of every womb among the Israelites belongs to me, whether man or animal."   Ex 22:29

³Then Moses said to the

ᵃ40 Masoretic Text; Samaritan Pentateuch and Septuagint *Egypt and Canaan*

people, "Commemorate this day, the day you came out of Egypt, out of the land of slavery, because the LORD brought you out of it with a mighty hand. Eat nothing containing yeast. ⁴Today, in the month of Abib, you are leaving. ⁵When the LORD brings you into the land of the Canaanites, Hittites, Amorites, Hivites and Jebusites—the land he swore to your forefathers to give you, a land flowing with milk and honey—you are to observe this ceremony in this month: ⁶For seven days eat bread made without yeast and on the seventh day hold a festival to the LORD. ⁷Eat unleavened bread during those seven days; nothing with yeast in it is to be seen among you, nor shall any yeast be seen anywhere within your borders. ⁸On that day tell your son, 'I do this because of what the LORD did for me when I came out of Egypt.' ⁹This observance will be for you like a sign on your hand and a reminder on your forehead that the law of the LORD is to be on your lips. For the LORD brought you out of Egypt with his mighty hand. ¹⁰You must keep this ordinance at the appointed time year after year.   Ex 12:15-20; Dt 16:3

¹¹"After the LORD brings you into the land of the Canaanites and gives it to you, as he promised on oath to you and your forefathers, ¹²you are to give over to the LORD the first offspring of every womb. All the firstborn males of your livestock belong to the LORD. ¹³Redeem with a lamb every firstborn donkey, but if you do not redeem it, break its neck. Redeem every firstborn among your sons.

¹⁴"In days to come, when your son asks you, 'What does this mean?' say to him, 'With a mighty hand the LORD brought us out of Egypt, out of the land of slavery. ¹⁵When Pharaoh stubbornly refused to let us go, the LORD killed every firstborn in Egypt, both man and animal. This is why I sacrifice to the LORD the first male offspring of every womb and redeem each of my firstborn sons.' ¹⁶And it will be like a sign on your hand and a symbol on your forehead that the LORD brought us out of Egypt with his mighty hand."

Crossing the Sea

¹⁷When Pharaoh let the people go, God did not lead them on the road through the Philistine country, though that was shorter. For God said, "If they face war, they might change their minds and return to Egypt." ¹⁸So God led the people around by the desert road toward the Red Sea. ᵃ The Israelites went up out of Egypt armed for battle.   Ex 14:11; Dt 17:16

¹⁹Moses took the bones of Joseph with him because Joseph had made the sons of Israel

ᵃ18 Hebrew *Yam Suph*; that is, Sea of Reeds

swear an oath. He had said, "God will surely come to your aid, and then you must carry my bones up with you from this place."[a]   Jos 24:32; Ac 7:16

20After leaving Succoth they camped at Etham on the edge of the desert. 21By day the LORD went ahead of them in a pillar of cloud to guide them on their way and by night in a pillar of fire to give them light, so that they could travel by day or night. 22Neither the pillar of cloud by day nor the pillar of fire by night left its place in front of the people.   Nu 33:6; Isa 4:5

14 Then the LORD said to Moses, 2"Tell the Israelites to turn back and encamp near Pi Hahiroth, between Migdol and the sea. They are to encamp by the sea, directly opposite Baal Zephon. 3Pharaoh will think, 'The Israelites are wandering around the land in confusion, hemmed in by the desert.' 4And I will harden Pharaoh's heart, and he will pursue them. But I will gain glory for myself through Pharaoh and all his army, and the Egyptians will know that I am the LORD." So the Israelites did this.   Nu 33:7; Ps 71:11

5When the king of Egypt was told that the people had fled, Pharaoh and his officials changed their minds about them and said, "What have we done? We have let the Israelites go and have lost their services!"

6So he had his chariot made ready and took his army with him. 7He took six hundred of the best chariots, along with all the other chariots of Egypt, with officers over all of them. 8The LORD hardened the heart of Pharaoh king of Egypt, so that he pursued the Israelites, who were marching out boldly. 9The Egyptians—all Pharaoh's horses and chariots, horsemen[b] and troops—pursued the Israelites and overtook them as they camped by the sea near Pi Hahiroth, opposite Baal Zephon.

10As Pharaoh approached, the Israelites looked up, and there were the Egyptians, marching after them. They were terrified and cried out to the LORD. 11They said to Moses, "Was it because there were no graves in Egypt that you brought us to the desert to die? What have you done to us by bringing us out of Egypt? 12Didn't we say to you in Egypt, 'Leave us alone; let us serve the Egyptians'? It would have been better for us to serve the Egyptians than to die in the desert!"

13Moses answered the people, "Do not be afraid. Stand firm and you will see the deliverance the LORD will bring you today. The Egyptians you see today you will never see again. 14The LORD will fight for you; you need only to be still."

15Then the LORD said to Moses, "Why are you crying

---

a19 See Gen. 50:25.   b9 Or charioteers; also in verses 17, 18, 23, 26 and 28

out to me? Tell the Israelites to move on. 16Raise your staff and stretch out your hand over the sea to divide the water so that the Israelites can go through the sea on dry ground. 17I will harden the hearts of the Egyptians so that they will go in after them. And I will gain glory through Pharaoh and all his army, through his chariots and his horsemen. 18The Egyptians will know that I am the LORD when I gain glory through Pharaoh, his chariots and his horsemen." Ex 4:21; Isa 10:26

19Then the angel of God, who had been traveling in front of Israel's army, withdrew and went behind them. The pillar of cloud also moved from in front and stood behind them, 20coming between the armies of Egypt and Israel. Throughout the night the cloud brought darkness to the one side and light to the other side; so neither went near the other all night long.

21Then Moses stretched out his hand over the sea, and all that night the LORD drove the sea back with a strong east wind and turned it into dry land. The waters were divided, 22and the Israelites went through the sea on dry ground, with a wall of water on their right and on their left. Ex 15:19; Isa 63:12

23The Egyptians pursued them, and all Pharaoh's horses and chariots and horsemen followed them into the sea. 24During the last watch of the night the LORD looked down from the pillar of fire and cloud at the Egyptian army and threw it into confusion. 25He made the wheels of their chariots come offa so that they had difficulty driving. And the Egyptians said, "Let's get away from the Israelites! The LORD is fighting for them against Egypt." Ex 13:21

26Then the LORD said to Moses, "Stretch out your hand over the sea so that the waters may flow back over the Egyptians and their chariots and horsemen." 27Moses stretched out his hand over the sea, and at daybreak the sea went back to its place. The Egyptians were fleeing towardb it, and the LORD swept them into the sea. 28The water flowed back and covered the chariots and horsemen—the entire army of Pharaoh that had followed the Israelites into the sea. Not one of them survived.

29But the Israelites went through the sea on dry ground, with a wall of water on their right and on their left. 30That day the LORD saved Israel from the hands of the Egyptians, and Israel saw the Egyptians lying dead on the shore. 31And when the Israelites saw the great power the LORD displayed against the Egyptians, the people feared the LORD and put

a25 Or He jammed the wheels of their chariots (see Samaritan Pentateuch, Septuagint and Syriac)   b27 Or from

their trust in him and in Moses
his servant.   Ps 106:8; Isa 43:3

The Song of Moses and Miriam

15 Then Moses and the Israelites sang this song to
the LORD: Nu 21:17

"I will sing to the LORD,
  for he is highly exalted.
The horse and its rider
  he has hurled into the sea.
[2]The LORD is my strength and
  my song;   Ps 18:1
he has become my
  salvation.   Ge 45:7
He is my God, and I will
  praise him,   Ge 28:21
my father's God, and I will
  exalt him.   Dt 10:21
[3]The LORD is a warrior;   Ex 14:14
  the LORD is his name.   Ex 3:15
[4]Pharaoh's chariots and his
  army
he has hurled into the sea.
The best of Pharaoh's officers
  are drowned in the Red
  Sea.[a]
[5]The deep waters have
  covered them;   Ex 14:28
they sank to the depths like
  a stone.   Ne 9:11

[6]"Your right hand, O LORD,
  was majestic in power. Ps 16:11
Your right hand, O LORD,
  shattered the enemy.   Ex 3:20
[7]In the greatness of your
  majesty
you threw down those who
  opposed you.   Dt 33:26

You unleashed your burning
  anger;   Ps 2:5
it consumed them like
  stubble.   Ex 24:17
[8]By the blast of your nostrils
  the waters piled up.   Jos 3:13
The surging waters stood
  firm like a wall;   Ex 14:22
the deep waters congealed
  in the heart of the sea.
[9]"The enemy boasted,
  'I will pursue, I will
  overtake them.   Ex 14:5-9
I will divide the spoils;   Jdg 5:30
  I will gorge myself on them.
I will draw my sword
  and my hand will destroy
  them.'
[10]But you blew with your
  breath,   Job 4:9
  and the sea covered them.
They sank like lead
  in the mighty waters.   Ne 9:11

[11]"Who among the gods is like
  you, O LORD?   Ex 8:10
Who is like you—
  majestic in holiness,   Lev 19:2
  awesome in glory,   Ex 14:4
  working wonders?   Ex 3:20
[12]You stretched out your right
  hand
and the earth swallowed
  them.   Ex 7:5; Nu 16:32

[13]"In your unfailing love you
  will lead
the people you have
  redeemed.   Ex 6:6; Ne 9:12
In your strength you will
  guide them
to your holy dwelling. Ps 68:16

---

[a]4 Hebrew *Yam Suph*; that is, Sea of Reeds; also in verse 22

¹⁴The nations will hear and
    tremble;   Ex 23:24
    anguish will grip the people
    of Philistia.   Ps 83:7
¹⁵The chiefs of Edom will be
    terrified,   Dt 2:4
    the leaders of Moab will be
    seized with trembling,
    the people*a* of Canaan will
    melt away;   Jos 2:9,24
¹⁶ terror and dread will fall
    upon them.   Ge 35:5
    By the power of your arm
    they will be as still as a
    stone—   1Sa 25:37
    until your people pass by,
    O LORD,
    until the people you
    bought*b* pass by.   Ps 74:2
¹⁷You will bring them in and
    plant them   Ex 23:20
    on the mountain of your
    inheritance—   Dt 33:19
    the place, O LORD, you made
    for your dwelling,
    the sanctuary, O Lord, your
    hands established.   Ps 78:69
¹⁸The LORD will reign
    for ever and ever."   Ge 21:33

¹⁹When Pharaoh's horses,
chariots and horsemen*c* went
into the sea, the LORD brought
the waters of the sea back over
them, but the Israelites walked
through the sea on dry ground.
²⁰Then Miriam the prophetess,
Aaron's sister, took a tambourine in her hand, and all the
women followed her, with tambourines and dancing. ²¹Miriam
sang to them:

"Sing to the LORD,
    for he is highly exalted.
The horse and its rider
    he has hurled into the sea."

The Waters of Marah and Elim

²²Then Moses led Israel from
the Red Sea and they went into
the Desert of Shur. For three
days they traveled in the desert
without finding water. ²³When
they came to Marah, they could
not drink its water because it
was bitter. (That is why the
place is called Marah.*d*) ²⁴So
the people grumbled against
Moses, saying, "What are we to
drink?"   Ge 25:18; Nu 33:8

²⁵Then Moses cried out to the
LORD, and the LORD showed
him a piece of wood. He threw
it into the water, and the water
became sweet.   Ex 14:10; 2Ki 2:21

There the LORD made a de-
cree and a law for them, and
there he tested them. ²⁶He said,
"If you listen carefully to the
voice of the LORD your God and
do what is right in his eyes, if
you pay attention to his commands and keep all his decrees,
I will not bring on you any of the
diseases I brought on the Egyptians, for I am the LORD, who
heals you."   Dt 7:12; Ps 66:10

²⁷Then they came to Elim,
where there were twelve
springs and seventy palm trees,
and they camped there near the
water.   Nu 33:9

---

*a*15 Or *rulers*   *b*16 Or *created*   *c*19 Or *charioteers*   *d*23 *Marah* means *bitter*.

Manna and Quail

16 The whole Israelite community set out from Elim and came to the Desert of Sin, which is between Elim and Sinai, on the fifteenth day of the second month after they had come out of Egypt. ²In the desert the whole community grumbled against Moses and Aaron. ³The Israelites said to them, "If only we had died by the LORD's hand in Egypt! There we sat around pots of meat and ate all the food we wanted, but you have brought us out into this desert to starve this entire assembly to death."   Nu 33:11-12

⁴Then the LORD said to Moses, "I will rain down bread from heaven for you. The people are to go out each day and gather enough for that day. In this way I will test them and see whether they will follow my instructions. ⁵On the sixth day they are to prepare what they bring in, and that is to be twice as much as they gather on the other days."   Dt 8:2; Jn 6:31

⁶So Moses and Aaron said to all the Israelites, "In the evening you will know that it was the LORD who brought you out of Egypt, ⁷and in the morning you will see the glory of the LORD, because he has heard your grumbling against him. Who are we, that you should grumble against us?" ⁸Moses also said, "You will know that it was the LORD when he gives you meat to eat in the evening and all the bread you want in the morning, because he has heard your grumbling against him. Who are we? You are not grumbling against us, but against the LORD."   Nu 16:28-30

⁹Then Moses told Aaron, "Say to the entire Israelite community, 'Come before the LORD, for he has heard your grumbling.'"   Nu 16:16

¹⁰While Aaron was speaking to the whole Israelite community, they looked toward the desert, and there was the glory of the LORD appearing in the cloud.   Nu 16:19; 1Ki 8:10

¹¹The LORD said to Moses, ¹²"I have heard the grumbling of the Israelites. Tell them, 'At twilight you will eat meat, and in the morning you will be filled with bread. Then you will know that I am the LORD your God.'"

¹³That evening quail came and covered the camp, and in the morning there was a layer of dew around the camp. ¹⁴When the dew was gone, thin flakes like frost on the ground appeared on the desert floor. ¹⁵When the Israelites saw it, they said to each other, "What is it?" For they did not know what it was.   Nu 11:31; Ps 78:27

Moses said to them, "It is the bread the LORD has given you to eat. ¹⁶This is what the LORD has commanded: 'Each one is to gather as much as he needs.

Take an omer*a* for each person you have in your tent.' " Jn 6:31

¹⁷The Israelites did as they were told; some gathered much, some little. ¹⁸And when they measured it by the omer, he who gathered much did not have too much, and he who gathered little did not have too little. Each one gathered as much as he needed. 2Co 8:15

¹⁹Then Moses said to them, "No one is to keep any of it until morning." Ex 12:10; 23:18

²⁰However, some of them paid no attention to Moses; they kept part of it until morning, but it was full of maggots and began to smell. So Moses was angry with them. Ex 32:19

²¹Each morning everyone gathered as much as he needed, and when the sun grew hot, it melted away. ²²On the sixth day, they gathered twice as much—two omers*b* for each person—and the leaders of the community came and reported this to Moses. ²³He said to them, "This is what the Lord commanded: 'Tomorrow is to be a day of rest, a holy Sabbath to the Lord. So bake what you want to bake and boil what you want to boil. Save whatever is left and keep it until morning.' " Ex 34:31; Lev 23:3

²⁴So they saved it until morning, as Moses commanded, and it did not stink or get maggots in it. ²⁵"Eat it today," Moses said,

"because today is a Sabbath to the Lord. You will not find any of it on the ground today. ²⁶Six days you are to gather it, but on the seventh day, the Sabbath, there will not be any." Ex 16:20

²⁷Nevertheless, some of the people went out on the seventh day to gather it, but they found none. ²⁸Then the Lord said to Moses, "How long will you*c* refuse to keep my commands and my instructions? ²⁹Bear in mind that the Lord has given you the Sabbath; that is why on the sixth day he gives you bread for two days. Everyone is to stay where he is on the seventh day; no one is to go out." ³⁰So the people rested on the seventh day. Ps 78:10; 107:11

³¹The people of Israel called the bread manna.*d* It was white like coriander seed and tasted like wafers made with honey. ³²Moses said, "This is what the Lord has commanded: 'Take an omer of manna and keep it for the generations to come, so they can see the bread I gave you to eat in the desert when I brought you out of Egypt.' " Nu 11:6-9

³³So Moses said to Aaron, "Take a jar and put an omer of manna in it. Then place it before the Lord to be kept for the generations to come." Heb 9:4

³⁴As the Lord commanded Moses, Aaron put the manna in front of the Testimony, that it might be kept. ³⁵The Israelites

*a*16 That is, probably about 2 quarts (about 2 liters); also in verses 18, 32, 33 and 36 *b*22 That is, probably about 4 quarts (about 4.5 liters) *c*28 The Hebrew is plural. *d*31 *Manna* means *What is it?* (see verse 15).

ate manna forty years, until they came to a land that was settled; they ate manna until they reached the border of Canaan.   Ex 25:16,21; Nu 17:10

36(An omer is one tenth of an ephah.)   Lev 5:11; Nu 5:15

Water From the Rock

17 The whole Israelite community set out from the Desert of Sin, traveling from place to place as the LORD commanded. They camped at Rephidim, but there was no water for the people to drink. 2So they quarreled with Moses and said, "Give us water to drink."   Ex 16:1

Moses replied, "Why do you quarrel with me? Why do you put the LORD to the test?"   Dt 6:16

3But the people were thirsty for water there, and they grumbled against Moses. They said, "Why did you bring us up out of Egypt to make us and our children and livestock die of thirst?"   Ex 16:2-3

4Then Moses cried out to the LORD, "What am I to do with these people? They are almost ready to stone me."   Nu 14:10

5The LORD answered Moses, "Walk on ahead of the people. Take with you some of the elders of Israel and take in your hand the staff with which you struck the Nile, and go. 6I will stand there before you by the rock at Horeb. Strike the rock, and water will come out of it for the people to drink." So Moses

did this in the sight of the elders of Israel. 7And he called the place Massah*a* and Meribah*b* because the Israelites quarreled and because they tested the LORD saying, "Is the LORD among us or not?"   Ex 7:20

The Amalekites Defeated

8The Amalekites came and attacked the Israelites at Rephidim. 9Moses said to Joshua, "Choose some of our men and go out to fight the Amalekites. Tomorrow I will stand on top of the hill with the staff of God in my hands."   Ge 36:12; Dt 25:17

10So Joshua fought the Amalekites as Moses had ordered, and Moses, Aaron and Hur went to the top of the hill. 11As long as Moses held up his hands, the Israelites were winning, but whenever he lowered his hands, the Amalekites were winning. 12When Moses' hands grew tired, they took a stone and put it under him and he sat on it. Aaron and Hur held his hands up—one on one side, one on the other—so that his hands remained steady till sunset. 13So Joshua overcame the Amalekite army with the sword.   Ex 24:14

14Then the LORD said to Moses, "Write this on a scroll as something to be remembered and make sure that Joshua hears it, because I will completely blot out the memory of Amalek from under heaven." 15Moses built an altar and

---

a7 Massah means *testing.*   *b7 Meribah* means *quarreling.*

called it The LORD is my Banner. [16]He said, "For hands were lifted up to the throne of the LORD. The[a] LORD will be at war against the Amalekites from generation to generation."   Ge 22:14; Nu 24:7

Jethro Visits Moses

18 Now Jethro, the priest of Midian and father-in-law of Moses, heard of everything God had done for Moses and for his people Israel, and how the LORD had brought Israel out of Egypt.   Ex 2:16; 6:6

[2]After Moses had sent away his wife Zipporah, his father-in-law Jethro received her [3]and her two sons. One son was named Gershom,[b] for Moses said, "I have become an alien in a foreign land"; [4]and the other was named Eliezer,[c] for he said, "My father's God was my helper; he saved me from the sword of Pharaoh."   Ex 4:25; Ac 7:29

[5]Jethro, Moses' father-in-law, together with Moses' sons and wife, came to him in the desert, where he was camped near the mountain of God. [6]Jethro had sent word to him, "I, your father-in-law Jethro, am coming to you with your wife and her two sons."   Ex 3:1, 12; 4:27

[7]So Moses went out to meet his father-in-law and bowed down and kissed him. They greeted each other and then went into the tent. [8]Moses told his father-in-law about everything the LORD had done to Pharaoh and the Egyptians for Israel's sake and about all the hardships they had met along the way and how the LORD had saved them.   Ge 29:13; Ex 4:27

[9]Jethro was delighted to hear about all the good things the LORD had done for Israel in rescuing them from the hand of the Egyptians. [10]He said, "Praise be to the LORD, who rescued you from the hand of the Egyptians and of Pharaoh, and who rescued the people from the hand of the Egyptians. [11]Now I know that the LORD is greater than all other gods, for he did this to those who had treated Israel arrogantly." [12]Then Jethro, Moses' father-in-law, brought a burnt offering and other sacrifices to God, and Aaron came with all the elders of Israel to eat bread with Moses' father-in-law in the presence of God.   Isa 63:7

[13]The next day Moses took his seat to serve as judge for the people, and they stood around him from morning till evening. [14]When his father-in-law saw all that Moses was doing for the people, he said, "What is this you are doing for the people? Why do you alone sit as judge, while all these people stand around you from morning till evening?"

[15]Moses answered him, "Because the people come to me to seek God's will. [16]Whenever

---

[a]16 Or "Because a hand was against the throne of the LORD, the   [b]3 Gershom sounds like the Hebrew for an alien there.   [c]4 Eliezer means my God is helper.

they have a dispute, it is brought to me, and I decide between the parties and inform them of God's decrees and laws." Ex 24:14; Dt 17:8

17Moses' father-in-law replied, "What you are doing is not good. 18You and these people who come to you will only wear yourselves out. The work is too heavy for you; you cannot handle it alone. 19Listen now to me and I will give you some advice, and may God be with you. You must be the people's representative before God and bring their disputes to him. 20Teach them the decrees and laws, and show them the way to live and the duties they are to perform. 21But select capable men from all the people—men who fear God, trustworthy men who hate dishonest gain—and appoint them as officials over thousands, hundreds, fifties and tens. 22Have them serve as judges for the people at all times, but have them bring every difficult case to you; the simple cases they can decide themselves. That will make your load lighter, because they will share it with you. 23If you do this and God so commands, you will be able to stand the strain, and all these people will go home satisfied."

24Moses listened to his father-in-law and did everything he said. 25He chose capable men from all Israel and made them leaders of the people, officials over thousands, hundreds, fifties and tens. 26They served as judges for the people at all times. The difficult cases they brought to Moses, but the simple ones they decided themselves. Dt 1:15; 2Ch 19:5

27Then Moses sent his father-in-law on his way, and Jethro returned to his own country.

At Mount Sinai

19 In the third month after the Israelites left Egypt—on the very day—they came to the Desert of Sinai. 2After they set out from Rephidim, they entered the Desert of Sinai, and Israel camped there in the desert in front of the mountain.

3Then Moses went up to God, and the LORD called to him from the mountain and said, "This is what you are to say to the house of Jacob and what you are to tell the people of Israel: 4'You yourselves have seen what I did to Egypt, and how I carried you on eagles' wings and brought you to myself. 5Now if you obey me fully and keep my covenant, then out of all nations you will be my treasured possession. Although the whole earth is mine, 6youª will be for me a kingdom of priests and a holy nation.' These are the words you are to speak to the Israelites." Ex 20:21

7So Moses went back and summoned the elders of the people and set before them all

ª5,6 Or possession, for the whole earth is mine. 6You

the words the LORD had commanded him to speak. 8The people all responded together, "We will do everything the LORD has said." So Moses brought their answer back to the LORD.   Ex 4:30; 24:3

9The LORD said to Moses, "I am going to come to you in a dense cloud, so that the people will hear me speaking with you and will always put their trust in you." Then Moses told the LORD what the people had said.

10And the LORD said to Moses, "Go to the people and consecrate them today and tomorrow. Have them wash their clothes 11and be ready by the third day, because on that day the LORD will come down on Mount Sinai in the sight of all the people. 12Put limits for the people around the mountain and tell them, 'Be careful that you do not go up the mountain or touch the foot of it. Whoever touches the mountain shall surely be put to death. 13He shall surely be stoned or shot with arrows; not a hand is to be laid on him. Whether man or animal, he shall not be permitted to live.' Only when the ram's horn sounds a long blast may they go up to the mountain."   1Sa 21:4; Heb 10:22

14After Moses had gone down the mountain to the people, he consecrated them, and they washed their clothes. 15Then he said to the people, "Prepare yourselves for the third day. Abstain from sexual relations."

16On the morning of the third day there was thunder and lightning, with a thick cloud over the mountain, and a very loud trumpet blast. Everyone in the camp trembled. 17Then Moses led the people out of the camp to meet with God, and they stood at the foot of the mountain. 18Mount Sinai was covered with smoke, because the LORD descended on it in fire. The smoke billowed up from it like smoke from a furnace, the whole mountaina trembled violently, 19and the sound of the trumpet grew louder and louder. Then Moses spoke and the voice of God answered him. b   Ps 81:7; Heb 12:18-19

20The LORD descended to the top of Mount Sinai and called Moses to the top of the mountain. So Moses went up 21and the LORD said to him, "Go down and warn the people so they do not force their way through to see the LORD and many of them perish. 22Even the priests, who approach the LORD, must consecrate themselves, or the LORD will break out against them."   Ex 3:5

23Moses said to the LORD, "The people cannot come up Mount Sinai, because you yourself warned us, 'Put limits

---

a18 Most Hebrew manuscripts; a few Hebrew manuscripts and Septuagint *all the people*
b19 Or *and God answered him with thunder*

around the mountain and set it apart as holy.'"

24The LORD replied, "Go down and bring Aaron up with you. But the priests and the people must not force their way through to come up to the LORD, or he will break out against them."

25So Moses went down to the people and told them.

The Ten Commandments

20 And God spoke all these words: Dt 5:22

2"I am the LORD your God, who brought you out of Egypt, out of the land of slavery.   Ge 17:7; Ex 13:3

3"You shall have no other gods before*a* me.   Ex 34:14

4"You shall not make for yourself an idol in the form of anything in heaven above or on the earth beneath or in the waters below. 5You shall not bow down to them or worship them; for I, the LORD your God, am a jealous God, punishing the children for the sin of the fathers to the third and fourth generation of those who hate me, 6but showing love to a thousand generations, of those who love me and keep my commandments.   Lev 26:1

7"You shall not misuse the name of the LORD your

God, for the LORD will not hold anyone guiltless who misuses his name.   Lev 19:12; Dt 6:13

8"Remember the Sabbath day by keeping it holy. 9Six days you shall labor and do all your work, 10but the seventh day is a Sabbath to the LORD your God. On it you shall not do any work, neither you, nor your son or daughter, nor your manservant or maidservant, nor your animals, nor the alien within your gates. 11For in six days the LORD made the heavens and the earth, the sea, and all that is in them, but he rested on the seventh day. Therefore the LORD blessed the Sabbath day and made it holy.   Ex 31:15

12"Honor your father and your mother, so that you may live long in the land the LORD your God is giving you.   Mt 15:4

13"You shall not murder.

14"You shall not commit adultery.   Lev 18:20; Mt 19:18

15"You shall not steal.   Lev 19:11

16"You shall not give false testimony against your neighbor.   Ex 23:1; Dt 5:20

17"You shall not covet your neighbor's house. You shall not covet your neighbor's wife, or his

a3 Or besides

manservant or maid-
servant, his ox or don-
key, or anything that be-
longs to your neigh-
bor." Lk 12:15; Ro 7:7

¹⁸When the people saw the
thunder and lightning and
heard the trumpet and saw the
mountain in smoke, they trembled with fear. They stayed at a
distance ¹⁹and said to Moses,
"Speak to us yourself and we
will listen. But do not have God
speak to us or we will die."

²⁰Moses said to the people,
"Do not be afraid. God has
come to test you, so that the fear
of God will be with you to keep
you from sinning." Dt 4:10

²¹The people remained at a
distance, while Moses ap-
proached the thick darkness
where God was. Ex 19:16; Dt 5:22

Idols and Altars

²²Then the LORD said to
Moses, "Tell the Israelites this:
'You have seen for yourselves
that I have spoken to you from
heaven: ²³Do not make any gods
to be alongside me; do not make
for yourselves gods of silver or
gods of gold. Ex 32:1; Ne 9:13

²⁴" 'Make an altar of earth for
me and sacrifice on it your burnt
offerings and fellowship offerings,^a your sheep and goats and
your cattle. Wherever I cause
my name to be honored, I will
come to you and bless you. ²⁵If
you make an altar of stones for

me, do not build it with dressed
stones, for you will defile it if
you use a tool on it. ²⁶And do
not go up to my altar on steps,
lest your nakedness be exposed
on it.' Lev 1:2; Dt 27:5

21
"These are the laws you
are to set before them:

Hebrew Servants

²"If you buy a Hebrew ser-
vant, he is to serve you for six
years. But in the seventh year,
he shall go free, without paying
anything. ³If he comes alone, he
is to go free alone; but if he has a
wife when he comes, she is to
go with him. ⁴If his master gives
him a wife and she bears him
sons or daughters, the woman
and her children shall belong to
her master, and only the man
shall go free. Lev 25:39-41; Jer 34:14

⁵"But if the servant declares,
'I love my master and my wife
and children and do not want to
go free,' ⁶then his master must
take him before the judges.^b He
shall take him to the door or the
doorpost and pierce his ear with
an awl. Then he will be his servant for life. Ex 22:8; Dt 15:16

⁷"If a man sells his daughter
as a servant, she is not to go free
as menservants do. ⁸If she does
not please the master who has
selected her for himself,^c he
must let her be redeemed. He
has no right to sell her to foreigners, because he has broken

^a24 Traditionally *peace offerings*   ^b6 Or *before God*   ^c8 Or *master so that he does not
choose her*

faith with her. ⁹If he selects her for his son, he must grant her the rights of a daughter. ¹⁰If he marries another woman, he must not deprive the first one of her food, clothing and marital rights. ¹¹If he does not provide her with these three things, she is to go free, without any payment of money.   Ne 5:5

Personal Injuries

¹²"Anyone who strikes a man and kills him shall surely be put to death. ¹³However, if he does not do it intentionally, but God lets it happen, he is to flee to a place I will designate. ¹⁴But if a man schemes and kills another man deliberately, take him away from my altar and put him to death.   Lev 24:16; Nu 35:22

¹⁵"Anyone who attacks*a* his father or his mother must be put to death.

¹⁶"Anyone who kidnaps another and either sells him or still has him when he is caught must be put to death.   Dt 24:7

¹⁷"Anyone who curses his father or mother must be put to death.   Mt 15:4; Mk 7:10

¹⁸"If men quarrel and one hits the other with a stone or with his fist*b* and he does not die but is confined to bed, ¹⁹the one who struck the blow will not be held responsible if the other gets up and walks around outside with his staff; however, he must pay the injured man for the loss of his time and see that he is completely healed.   2Sa 3:29

²⁰"If a man beats his male or female slave with a rod and the slave dies as a direct result, he must be punished, ²¹but he is not to be punished if the slave gets up after a day or two, since the slave is his property.

²²"If men who are fighting hit a pregnant woman and she gives birth prematurely*c* but there is no serious injury, the offender must be fined whatever the woman's husband demands and the court allows. ²³But if there is serious injury, you are to take life for life, ²⁴eye for eye, tooth for tooth, hand for hand, foot for foot, ²⁵burn for burn, wound for wound, bruise for bruise.   Dt 19:21

²⁶"If a man hits a manservant or maidservant in the eye and destroys it, he must let the servant go free to compensate for the eye. ²⁷And if he knocks out the tooth of a manservant or maidservant, he must let the servant go free to compensate for the tooth.

²⁸"If a bull gores a man or a woman to death, the bull must be stoned to death, and its meat must not be eaten. But the owner of the bull will not be held responsible. ²⁹If, however, the bull has had the habit of goring and the owner has been warned but has not kept it penned up and it kills a man or woman, the bull must be stoned

---

*a*15 Or *kills*   *b*18 Or *with a tool*   *c*22 Or *she has a miscarriage*

and the owner also must be put to death. ³⁰However, if payment is demanded of him, he may redeem his life by paying whatever is demanded. ³¹This law also applies if the bull gores a son or daughter. ³²If the bull gores a male or female slave, the owner must pay thirty shekels*a* of silver to the master of the slave, and the bull must be stoned. Ge 9:5; Nu 35:31

³³"If a man uncovers a pit or digs one and fails to cover it and an ox or a donkey falls into it, ³⁴the owner of the pit must pay for the loss; he must pay its owner, and the dead animal will be his. Lk 14:5

³⁵"If a man's bull injures the bull of another and it dies, they are to sell the live one and divide both the money and the dead animal equally. ³⁶However, if it was known that the bull had the habit of goring, yet the owner did not keep it penned up, the owner must pay, animal for animal, and the dead animal will be his. Ex 21:29

Protection of Property

22 "If a man steals an ox or a sheep and slaughters it or sells it, he must pay back five head of cattle for the ox and four sheep for the sheep. 2Sa 12:6

²"If a thief is caught breaking in and is struck so that he dies, the defender is not guilty of bloodshed; ³but if it happens*b*

after sunrise, he is guilty of bloodshed. Nu 35:27; Mt 24:43

"A thief must certainly make restitution, but if he has nothing, he must be sold to pay for his theft. Ex 21:2; Mt 18:25

⁴"If the stolen animal is found alive in his possession—whether ox or donkey or sheep—he must pay back double. Ge 43:12; 1Sa 12:5

⁵"If a man grazes his livestock in a field or vineyard and lets them stray and they graze in another man's field, he must make restitution from the best of his own field or vineyard. Ex 22:1

⁶"If a fire breaks out and spreads into thornbushes so that it burns shocks of grain or standing grain or the whole field, the one who started the fire must make restitution. Jdg 15:5

⁷"If a man gives his neighbor silver or goods for safekeeping and they are stolen from the neighbor's house, the thief, if he is caught, must pay back double. ⁸But if the thief is not found, the owner of the house must appear before the judges*c* to determine whether he has laid his hands on the other man's property. ⁹In all cases of illegal possession of an ox, a donkey, a sheep, a garment, or any other lost property about which somebody says, 'This is mine,' both parties are to bring their cases before the judges. The one whom the judges de-

---

*a*32 That is, about 12 ounces (about 0.3 kilogram)   *b*3 Or *if he strikes him*   *c*8 Or *before God*; also in verse 9

clare*a* guilty must pay back double to his neighbor.   Lev 6:2

10"If a man gives a donkey, an ox, a sheep or any other animal to his neighbor for safekeeping and it dies or is injured or is taken away while no one is looking, 11the issue between them will be settled by the taking of an oath before the LORD that the neighbor did not lay hands on the other person's property. The owner is to accept this, and no restitution is required. 12But if the animal was stolen from the neighbor, he must make restitution to the owner. 13If it was torn to pieces by a wild animal, he shall bring in the remains as evidence and he will not be required to pay for the torn animal.

14"If a man borrows an animal from his neighbor and it is injured or dies while the owner is not present, he must make restitution. 15But if the owner is with the animal, the borrower will not have to pay. If the animal was hired, the money paid for the hire covers the loss.   Lev 19:13

Social Responsibility

16"If a man seduces a virgin who is not pledged to be married and sleeps with her, he must pay the bride-price, and she shall be his wife. 17If her father absolutely refuses to give her to him, he must still pay the bride-price for virgins.   Dt 22:28

18"Do not allow a sorceress to live.   Lev 20:27; Dt 18:10

19"Anyone who has sexual relations with an animal must be put to death.   Lev 18:23; 20:15

20"Whoever sacrifices to any god other than the LORD must be destroyed.*b*   Lev 17:7; Dt 17:2-5

21"Do not mistreat an alien or oppress him, for you were aliens in Egypt.   Lev 19:33

22"Do not take advantage of a widow or an orphan. 23If you do and they cry out to me, I will certainly hear their cry. 24My anger will be aroused, and I will kill you with the sword; your wives will become widows and your children fatherless.   Dt 24:17

25"If you lend money to one of my people among you who is needy, do not be like a moneylender; charge him no interest.*c* 26If you take your neighbor's cloak as a pledge, return it to him by sunset, 27because his cloak is the only covering he has for his body. What else will he sleep in? When he cries out to me, I will hear, for I am compassionate.   Lev 25:35-37

28"Do not blaspheme God*d* or curse the ruler of your people.

29"Do not hold back offerings from your granaries or your vats.*e*   Ex 23:16; Lev 19:24

"You must give me the firstborn of your sons. 30Do the

---

*a*9 Or *whom God declares*   *b*20 The Hebrew term refers to the irrevocable giving over of things or persons to the LORD, often by totally destroying them.   *c*25 Or *excessive interest*   *d*28 Or *Do not revile the judges*   *e*29 The meaning of the Hebrew for this phrase is uncertain.

same with your cattle and your sheep. Let them stay with their mothers for seven days, but give them to me on the eighth day. Ex 13:2; Dt 15:19

³¹"You are to be my holy people. So do not eat the meat of an animal torn by wild beasts; throw it to the dogs. Lev 19:2

Laws of Justice and Mercy

23 "Do not spread false reports. Do not help a wicked man by being a malicious witness. Ex 20:16

²"Do not follow the crowd in doing wrong. When you give testimony in a lawsuit, do not pervert justice by siding with the crowd, ³and do not show favoritism to a poor man in his lawsuit. Dt 16:19

⁴"If you come across your enemy's ox or donkey wandering off, be sure to take it back to him. ⁵If you see the donkey of someone who hates you fallen down under its load, do not leave it there; be sure you help him with it. Dt 22:1-3; Ro 12:20

⁶"Do not deny justice to your poor people in their lawsuits. ⁷Have nothing to do with a false charge and do not put an innocent or honest person to death, for I will not acquit the guilty.

⁸"Do not accept a bribe, for a bribe blinds those who see and twists the words of the righteous. Dt 10:17; Job 15:34

⁹"Do not oppress an alien; you yourselves know how it feels to be aliens, because you were aliens in Egypt. Ex 22:21

Sabbath Laws

¹⁰"For six years you are to sow your fields and harvest the crops, ¹¹but during the seventh year let the land lie unplowed and unused. Then the poor among your people may get food from it, and the wild animals may eat what they leave. Do the same with your vineyard and your olive grove. Lev 25:3

¹²"Six days do your work, but on the seventh day do not work, so that your ox and your donkey may rest and the slave born in your household, and the alien as well, may be refreshed. Ex 20:8-11; Lk 13:14

¹³"Be careful to do everything I have said to you. Do not invoke the names of other gods; do not let them be heard on your lips. Dt 4:9; 1Ti 4:16

The Three Annual Festivals

¹⁴"Three times a year you are to celebrate a festival to me.

¹⁵"Celebrate the Feast of Unleavened Bread; for seven days eat bread made without yeast, as I commanded you. Do this at the appointed time in the month of Abib, for in that month you came out of Egypt.

"No one is to appear before me empty-handed. Ex 22:29

¹⁶"Celebrate the Feast of Harvest with the firstfruits of the crops you sow in your field.

"Celebrate the Feast of Ingathering at the end of the year, when you gather in your crops from the field. Ex 34:22; Dt 16:13

17"Three times a year all the men are to appear before the Sovereign LORD.   Dt 16:16

18"Do not offer the blood of a sacrifice to me along with anything containing yeast.   Ex 34:25

"The fat of my festival offerings must not be kept until morning.   Ex 12:8

19"Bring the best of the firstfruits of your soil to the house of the LORD your God.   Ex 22:29

"Do not cook a young goat in its mother's milk.   Dt 14:21

God's Angel to Prepare the Way

20"See, I am sending an angel ahead of you to guard you along the way and to bring you to the place I have prepared. 21Pay attention to him and listen to what he says. Do not rebel against him; he will not forgive your rebellion, since my Name is in him. 22If you listen carefully to what he says and do all that I say, I will be an enemy to your enemies and will oppose those who oppose you. 23My angel will go ahead of you and bring you into the land of the Amorites, Hittites, Perizzites, Canaanites, Hivites and Jebusites, and I will wipe them out. 24Do not bow down before their gods or worship them or follow their practices. You must demolish them and break their sacred stones to pieces. 25Worship the LORD your God, and his blessing will be on your food and water. I will take away sickness from among you, 26and none will miscarry or be barren in your land. I will give you a full life span.   Dt 18:19; Jer 30:20

27"I will send my terror ahead of you and throw into confusion every nation you encounter. I will make all your enemies turn their backs and run. 28I will send the hornet ahead of you to drive the Hivites, Canaanites and Hittites out of your way. 29But I will not drive them out in a single year, because the land would become desolate and the wild animals too numerous for you. 30Little by little I will drive them out before you, until you have increased enough to take possession of the land.   Dt 7:23

31"I will establish your borders from the Red Sea*a* to the Sea of the Philistines,*b* and from the desert to the River.*c* I will hand over to you the people who live in the land and you will drive them out before you. 32Do not make a covenant with them or with their gods. 33Do not let them live in your land, or they will cause you to sin against me, because the worship of their gods will certainly be a snare to you."   Jos 21:44

The Covenant Confirmed

24 Then he said to Moses, "Come up to the LORD, you and Aaron, Nadab and

a31 Hebrew *Yam Suph;* that is, Sea of Reeds   *b31* That is, the Mediterranean
c31 That is, the Euphrates

Abihu, and seventy of the elders of Israel. You are to worship at a distance, [2]but Moses alone is to approach the LORD; the others must not come near. And the people may not come up with him." Nu 11:16; 12:6-8

[3]When Moses went and told the people all the LORD's words and laws, they responded with one voice, "Everything the LORD has said we will do." [4]Moses then wrote down everything the LORD had said. Ex 19:8

He got up early the next morning and built an altar at the foot of the mountain and set up twelve stone pillars representing the twelve tribes of Israel. [5]Then he sent young Israelite men, and they offered burnt offerings and sacrificed young bulls as fellowship offerings[a] to the LORD. [6]Moses took half of the blood and put it in bowls, and the other half he sprinkled on the altar. [7]Then he took the Book of the Covenant and read it to the people. They responded, "We will do everything the LORD has said; we will obey."

[8]Moses then took the blood, sprinkled it on the people and said, "This is the blood of the covenant that the LORD has made with you in accordance with all these words." Heb 9:20

[9]Moses and Aaron, Nadab and Abihu, and the seventy elders of Israel went up [10]and saw the God of Israel. Under his feet was something like a pavement made of sapphire,[b] clear as the sky itself. [11]But God did not raise his hand against these leaders of the Israelites; they saw God, and they ate and drank. Eze 1:26; Rev 4:3

[12]The LORD said to Moses, "Come up to me on the mountain and stay here, and I will give you the tablets of stone, with the law and commands I have written for their instruction." Ex 32:15-16; Dt 4:13

[13]Then Moses set out with Joshua his aide, and Moses went up on the mountain of God. [14]He said to the elders, "Wait here for us until we come back to you. Aaron and Hur are with you, and anyone involved in a dispute can go to them."

[15]When Moses went up on the mountain, the cloud covered it, [16]and the glory of the LORD settled on Mount Sinai. For six days the cloud covered the mountain, and on the seventh day the LORD called to Moses from within the cloud. [17]To the Israelites the glory of the LORD looked like a consuming fire on top of the mountain. [18]Then Moses entered the cloud as he went on up the mountain. And he stayed on the mountain forty days and forty nights.

Offerings for the Tabernacle

25 The LORD said to Moses, [2]"Tell the Israelites to bring me an offering. You are to receive the offering for me from

─────────

[a]5 Traditionally *peace offerings* [b]10 Or *lapis lazuli*

each man whose heart prompts him to give. ³These are the offerings you are to receive from them: gold, silver and bronze; ⁴blue, purple and scarlet yarn and fine linen; goat hair; ⁵ram skins dyed red and hides of sea cows*a*; acacia wood; ⁶olive oil for the light; spices for the anointing oil and for the fragrant incense; ⁷and onyx stones and other gems to be mounted on the ephod and breastpiece.

⁸"Then have them make a sanctuary for me, and I will dwell among them. ⁹Make this tabernacle and all its furnishings exactly like the pattern I will show you.   Heb 9:1-2

The Ark

¹⁰"Have them make a chest of acacia wood—two and a half cubits long, a cubit and a half wide, and a cubit and a half high.*b* ¹¹Overlay it with pure gold, both inside and out, and make a gold molding around it. ¹²Cast four gold rings for it and fasten them to its four feet, with two rings on one side and two rings on the other. ¹³Then make poles of acacia wood and overlay them with gold. ¹⁴Insert the poles into the rings on the sides of the chest to carry it. ¹⁵The poles are to remain in the rings of this ark; they are not to be

removed. ¹⁶Then put in the ark the Testimony, which I will give you.   Dt 10:1-5; Heb 9:4

¹⁷"Make an atonement cover*c* of pure gold—two and a half cubits long and a cubit and a half wide.*d* ¹⁸And make two cherubim out of hammered gold at the ends of the cover. ¹⁹Make one cherub on one end and the second cherub on the other; make the cherubim of one piece with the cover, at the two ends. ²⁰The cherubim are to have their wings spread upward, overshadowing the cover with them. The cherubim are to face each other, looking toward the cover. ²¹Place the cover on top of the ark and put in the ark the Testimony, which I will give you. ²²There, above the cover between the two cherubim that are over the ark of the Testimony, I will meet with you and give you all my commands for the Israelites.   1Ki 8:7; Ro 3:25

The Table

²³"Make a table of acacia wood—two cubits long, a cubit wide and a cubit and a half high.*e* ²⁴Overlay it with pure gold and make a gold molding around it. ²⁵Also make around it a rim a handbreadth*f* wide and put a gold molding on the rim. ²⁶Make four gold rings for the table and fasten them to the

---

a5 That is, dugongs   *b10* That is, about 3 3/4 feet (about 1.1 meters) long and 2 1/4 feet (about 0.7 meter) wide and high   *c17* Traditionally *a mercy seat*   *d17* That is, about 3 3/4 feet (about 1.1 meters) long and 2 1/4 feet (about 0.7 meter) wide   *e23* That is, about 3 feet (about 0.9 meter) long and 1 1/2 feet (about 0.5 meter) wide and 2 1/4 feet (about 0.7 meter) high   *f25* That is, about 3 inches (about 8 centimeters)

four corners, where the four legs are. ²⁷The rings are to be close to the rim to hold the poles used in carrying the table. ²⁸Make the poles of acacia wood, overlay them with gold and carry the table with them. ²⁹And make its plates and dishes of pure gold, as well as its pitchers and bowls for the pouring out of offerings. ³⁰Put the bread of the Presence on this table to be before me at all times.   Nu 4:7; Heb 9:2

The Lampstand

³¹"Make a lampstand of pure gold and hammer it out, base and shaft; its flowerlike cups, buds and blossoms shall be of one piece with it. ³²Six branches are to extend from the sides of the lampstand—three on one side and three on the other. ³³Three cups shaped like almond flowers with buds and blossoms are to be on one branch, three on the next branch, and the same for all six branches extending from the lampstand. ³⁴And on the lampstand there are to be four cups shaped like almond flowers with buds and blossoms. ³⁵One bud shall be under the first pair of branches extending from the lampstand, a second bud under the second pair, and a third bud under the third pair—six branches in all. ³⁶The buds and branches shall all be of one piece with the lampstand, hammered out of pure gold.   Heb 9:2

³⁷"Then make its seven lamps and set them up on it so that they light the space in front of it. ³⁸Its wick trimmers and trays are to be of pure gold. ³⁹A talent*a* of pure gold is to be used for the lampstand and all these accessories. ⁴⁰See that you make them according to the pattern shown you on the mountain.

The Tabernacle

26 "Make the tabernacle with ten curtains of finely twisted linen and blue, purple and scarlet yarn, with cherubim worked into them by a skilled craftsman. ²All the curtains are to be the same size—twenty-eight cubits long and four cubits wide.*b* ³Join five of the curtains together, and do the same with the other five. ⁴Make loops of blue material along the edge of the end curtain in one set, and do the same with the end curtain in the other set. ⁵Make fifty loops on one curtain and fifty loops on the end curtain of the other set, with the loops opposite each other. ⁶Then make fifty gold clasps and use them to fasten the curtains together so that the tabernacle is a unit.   Ex 36:8-13

⁷"Make curtains of goat hair for the tent over the tabernacle—eleven altogether. ⁸All eleven curtains are to be the

---

a39 That is, about 75 pounds (about 34 kilograms)   *b2* That is, about 42 feet (about 12.5 meters) long and 6 feet (about 1.8 meters) wide

same size—thirty cubits long and four cubits wide. *a* ⁹Join five of the curtains together into one set and the other six into another set. Fold the sixth curtain double at the front of the tent. ¹⁰Make fifty loops along the edge of the end curtain in one set and also along the edge of the end curtain in the other set. ¹¹Then make fifty bronze clasps and put them in the loops to fasten the tent together as a unit. ¹²As for the additional length of the tent curtains, the half curtain that is left over is to hang down at the rear of the tabernacle. ¹³The tent curtains will be a cubit*b* longer on both sides; what is left will hang over the sides of the tabernacle so as to cover it. ¹⁴Make for the tent a covering of ram skins dyed red, and over that a covering of hides of sea cows.*c*   Ex 36:14-19

¹⁵"Make upright frames of acacia wood for the tabernacle. ¹⁶Each frame is to be ten cubits long and a cubit and a half wide,*d* ¹⁷with two projections set parallel to each other. Make all the frames of the tabernacle in this way. ¹⁸Make twenty frames for the south side of the tabernacle ¹⁹and make forty silver bases to go under them—two bases for each frame, one under each projection. ²⁰For the other side, the north side of the tabernacle, make twenty frames ²¹and forty

silver bases—two under each frame. ²²Make six frames for the far end, that is, the west end of the tabernacle, ²³and make two frames for the corners at the far end. ²⁴At these two corners they must be double from the bottom all the way to the top, and fitted into a single ring; both shall be like that. ²⁵So there will be eight frames and sixteen silver bases—two under each frame.

²⁶"Also make crossbars of acacia wood: five for the frames on one side of the tabernacle, ²⁷five for those on the other side, and five for the frames on the west, at the far end of the tabernacle. ²⁸The center crossbar is to extend from end to end at the middle of the frames. ²⁹Overlay the frames with gold and make gold rings to hold the crossbars. Also overlay the crossbars with gold.   Ex 36:31-34

³⁰"Set up the tabernacle according to the plan shown you on the mountain.   Ex 25:9

³¹"Make a curtain of blue, purple and scarlet yarn and finely twisted linen, with cherubim worked into it by a skilled craftsman. ³²Hang it with gold hooks on four posts of acacia wood overlaid with gold and standing on four silver bases. ³³Hang the curtain from the clasps and place the ark of the Testimony behind the curtain. The curtain will separate the Holy Place from the Most Holy

---

a8 That is, about 45 feet (about 13.5 meters) long and 6 feet (about 1.8 meters) wide
b13 That is, about 1 1/2 feet (about 0.5 meter)   *c14* That is, dugongs   *d16* That is, about 15 feet (about 4.5 meters) long and 2 1/4 feet (about 0.7 meter) wide

Place. ³⁴Put the atonement cover on the ark of the Testimony in the Most Holy Place. ³⁵Place the table outside the curtain on the north side of the tabernacle and put the lampstand opposite it on the south side.

³⁶"For the entrance to the tent make a curtain of blue, purple and scarlet yarn and finely twisted linen—the work of an embroiderer. ³⁷Make gold hooks for this curtain and five posts of acacia wood overlaid with gold. And cast five bronze bases for them.   Ex 36:37

The Altar of Burnt Offering

27 "Build an altar of acacia wood, three cubits*ᵃ* high; it is to be square, five cubits long and five cubits wide.*ᵇ* ²Make a horn at each of the four corners, so that the horns and the altar are of one piece, and overlay the altar with bronze. ³Make all its utensils of bronze—its pots to remove the ashes, and its shovels, sprinkling bowls, meat forks and firepans. ⁴Make a grating for it, a bronze network, and make a bronze ring at each of the four corners of the network. ⁵Put it under the ledge of the altar so that it is halfway up the altar. ⁶Make poles of acacia wood for the altar and overlay them with bronze. ⁷The poles are to be inserted into the rings so they will be on two sides of the altar when it is carried. ⁸Make the altar hollow, out of boards. It is to be made just as you were shown on the mountain.   Ex 25:40; Nu 4:14

The Courtyard

⁹"Make a courtyard for the tabernacle. The south side shall be a hundred cubits*ᶜ* long and is to have curtains of finely twisted linen, ¹⁰with twenty posts and twenty bronze bases and with silver hooks and bands on the posts. ¹¹The north side shall also be a hundred cubits long and is to have curtains, with twenty posts and twenty bronze bases and with silver hooks and bands on the posts.

¹²"The west end of the courtyard shall be fifty cubits*ᵈ* wide and have curtains, with ten posts and ten bases. ¹³On the east end, toward the sunrise, the courtyard shall also be fifty cubits wide. ¹⁴Curtains fifteen cubits*ᵉ* long are to be on one side of the entrance, with three posts and three bases, ¹⁵and curtains fifteen cubits long are to be on the other side, with three posts and three bases.

¹⁶"For the entrance to the courtyard, provide a curtain twenty cubits*ᶠ* long, of blue, purple and scarlet yarn and finely twisted linen—the work of an embroiderer—with four posts and four bases. ¹⁷All the

---

ᵃ1 That is, about 4 1/2 feet (about 1.3 meters) meters) long and wide   *ᶜ9* That is, about 150 feet (about 46 meters); also in verse 11 *ᵈ12* That is, about 75 feet (about 23 meters); also in verse 13   *ᵉ14* That is, about 22 1/2 feet (about 6.9 meters); also in verse 15   *ᶠ16* That is, about 30 feet (about 9 meters)   *ᵇ1* That is, about 7 1/2 feet (about 2.3 meters)

posts around the courtyard are to have silver bands and hooks, and bronze bases. ¹⁸The courtyard shall be a hundred cubits long and fifty cubits wide, *a* with curtains of finely twisted linen five cubits*b* high, and with bronze bases. ¹⁹All the other articles used in the service of the tabernacle, whatever their function, including all the tent pegs for it and those for the courtyard, are to be of bronze. Ex 36:37

Oil for the Lampstand

²⁰"Command the Israelites to bring you clear oil of pressed olives for the light so that the lamps may be kept burning. ²¹In the Tent of Meeting, outside the curtain that is in front of the Testimony, Aaron and his sons are to keep the lamps burning before the LORD from evening till morning. This is to be a lasting ordinance among the Israelites for the generations to come.

The Priestly Garments

28 "Have Aaron your brother brought to you from among the Israelites, along with his sons Nadab and Abihu, Eleazar and Ithamar, so they may serve me as priests. ²Make sacred garments for your brother Aaron, to give him dignity and honor. ³Tell all the skilled men to whom I have given wisdom in such matters that they are to make garments for Aaron, for his consecration, so he may serve me as priest. ⁴These are the garments they are to make: a breastpiece, an ephod, a robe, a woven tunic, a turban and a sash. They are to make these sacred garments for your brother Aaron and his sons, so they may serve me as priests. ⁵Have them use gold, and blue, purple and scarlet yarn, and fine linen. Nu 18:7

The Ephod

⁶"Make the ephod of gold, and of blue, purple and scarlet yarn, and of finely twisted linen—the work of a skilled craftsman. ⁷It is to have two shoulder pieces attached to two of its corners, so it can be fastened. ⁸Its skillfully woven waistband is to be like it—of one piece with the ephod and made with gold, and with blue, purple and scarlet yarn, and with finely twisted linen. Ex 25:7

⁹"Take two onyx stones and engrave on them the names of the sons of Israel ¹⁰in the order of their birth—six names on one stone and the remaining six on the other. ¹¹Engrave the names of the sons of Israel on the two stones the way a gem cutter engraves a seal. Then mount the stones in gold filigree settings ¹²and fasten them on the shoulder pieces of the ephod as memorial stones for the sons of Israel. Aaron is to bear the

---

a18 That is, about 150 feet (about 46 meters) long and 75 feet (about 23 meters) wide
b18 That is, about 7 1/2 feet (about 2.3 meters)

names on his shoulders as a memorial before the LORD. ¹³Make gold filigree settings ¹⁴and two braided chains of pure gold, like a rope, and attach the chains to the settings.

The Breastpiece

¹⁵"Fashion a breastpiece for making decisions—the work of a skilled craftsman. Make it like the ephod: of gold, and of blue, purple and scarlet yarn, and of finely twisted linen. ¹⁶It is to be square—a span[a] long and a span wide—and folded double. ¹⁷Then mount four rows of precious stones on it. In the first row there shall be a ruby, a topaz and a beryl; ¹⁸in the second row a turquoise, a sapphire[b] and an emerald; ¹⁹in the third row a jacinth, an agate and an amethyst; ²⁰in the fourth row a chrysolite, an onyx and a jasper.[c] Mount them in gold filigree settings. ²¹There are to be twelve stones, one for each of the names of the sons of Israel, each engraved like a seal with the name of one of the twelve tribes.   Ex 39:8-14; Lev 21:19-20

²²"For the breastpiece make braided chains of pure gold, like a rope. ²³Make two gold rings for it and fasten them to two corners of the breastpiece. ²⁴Fasten the two gold chains to the rings at the corners of the breastpiece, ²⁵and the other ends of the chains to the two

settings, attaching them to the shoulder pieces of the ephod at the front. ²⁶Make two gold rings and attach them to the other two corners of the breastpiece on the inside edge next to the ephod. ²⁷Make two more gold rings and attach them to the bottom of the shoulder pieces on the front of the ephod, close to the seam just above the waistband of the ephod. ²⁸The rings of the breastpiece are to be tied to the rings of the ephod with blue cord, connecting it to the waistband, so that the breastpiece will not swing out from the ephod.   Ex 39:17-21

²⁹"Whenever Aaron enters the Holy Place, he will bear the names of the sons of Israel over his heart on the breastpiece of decision as a continuing memorial before the LORD. ³⁰Also put the Urim and the Thummim in the breastpiece, so they may be over Aaron's heart whenever he enters the presence of the LORD. Thus Aaron will always bear the means of making decisions for the Israelites over his heart before the LORD.   Lev 8:8; Nu 27:21

Other Priestly Garments

³¹"Make the robe of the ephod entirely of blue cloth, ³²with an opening for the head in its center. There shall be a woven edge like a collar[d] around this opening, so that it

---

[a]16 That is, about 9 inches (about 22 centimeters)   [b]18 Or *lapis lazuli*   [c]20 The precise identification of some of these precious stones is uncertain.   [d]32 The meaning of the Hebrew for this word is uncertain.

will not tear. [33]Make pomegranates of blue, purple and scarlet yarn around the hem of the robe, with gold bells between them. [34]The gold bells and the pomegranates are to alternate around the hem of the robe. [35]Aaron must wear it when he ministers. The sound of the bells will be heard when he enters the Holy Place before the LORD and when he comes out, so that he will not die. Ex 39:22-26

[36]"Make a plate of pure gold and engrave on it as on a seal: HOLY TO THE LORD. [37]Fasten a blue cord to it to attach it to the turban; it is to be on the front of the turban. [38]It will be on Aaron's forehead, and he will bear the guilt involved in the sacred gifts the Israelites consecrate, whatever their gifts may be. It will be on Aaron's forehead continually so that they will be acceptable to the LORD.

[39]"Weave the tunic of fine linen and make the turban of fine linen. The sash is to be the work of an embroiderer. [40]Make tunics, sashes and headbands for Aaron's sons, to give them dignity and honor. [41]After you put these clothes on your brother Aaron and his sons, anoint and ordain them. Consecrate them so they may serve me as priests. Ex 39:41; Lev 16:4

[42]"Make linen undergarments as a covering for the body, reaching from the waist to the thigh. [43]Aaron and his sons must wear them whenever they enter the Tent of Meeting or approach the altar to minister in the Holy Place, so that they will not incur guilt and die.

"This is to be a lasting ordinance for Aaron and his descendants. Ex 27:21

Consecration of the Priests

29 "This is what you are to do to consecrate them, so they may serve me as priests: Take a young bull and two rams without defect. [2]And from fine wheat flour, without yeast, make bread, and cakes mixed with oil, and wafers spread with oil. [3]Put them in a basket and present them in it—along with the bull and the two rams. [4]Then bring Aaron and his sons to the entrance to the Tent of Meeting and wash them with water. [5]Take the garments and dress Aaron with the tunic, the robe of the ephod, the ephod itself and the breastpiece. Fasten the ephod on him by its skillfully woven waistband. [6]Put the turban on his head and attach the sacred diadem to the turban. [7]Take the anointing oil and anoint him by pouring it on his head. [8]Bring his sons and dress them in tunics [9]and put headbands on them. Then tie sashes on Aaron and his sons. [a] The priesthood is theirs by a lasting ordinance. In this way you shall ordain Aaron and his sons.

a9 Hebrew; Septuagint *on them*

¹⁰"Bring the bull to the front of the Tent of Meeting, and Aaron and his sons shall lay their hands on its head. ¹¹Slaughter it in the LORD's presence at the entrance to the Tent of Meeting. ¹²Take some of the bull's blood and put it on the horns of the altar with your finger, and pour out the rest of it at the base of the altar. ¹³Then take all the fat around the inner parts, the covering of the liver, and both kidneys with the fat on them, and burn them on the altar. ¹⁴But burn the bull's flesh and its hide and its offal outside the camp. It is a sin offering.   Ex 27:2; Lev 1:4

¹⁵"Take one of the rams, and Aaron and his sons shall lay their hands on its head. ¹⁶Slaughter it and take the blood and sprinkle it against the altar on all sides. ¹⁷Cut the ram into pieces and wash the inner parts and the legs, putting them with the head and the other pieces. ¹⁸Then burn the entire ram on the altar. It is a burnt offering to the LORD, a pleasing aroma, an offering made to the LORD by fire.   Ge 8:21; Lev 1:9; 8:18

¹⁹"Take the other ram, and Aaron and his sons shall lay their hands on its head. ²⁰Slaughter it, take some of its blood and put it on the lobes of the right ears of Aaron and his sons, on the thumbs of their right hands, and on the big toes of their right feet. Then sprinkle blood against the altar on all sides. ²¹And take some of the blood on the altar and some of the anointing oil and sprinkle it on Aaron and his garments and on his sons and their garments. Then he and his sons and their garments will be consecrated.

²²"Take from this ram the fat, the fat tail, the fat around the inner parts, the covering of the liver, both kidneys with the fat on them, and the right thigh. (This is the ram for the ordination.) ²³From the basket of bread made without yeast, which is before the LORD, take a loaf, and a cake made with oil, and a wafer. ²⁴Put all these in the hands of Aaron and his sons and wave them before the LORD as a wave offering. ²⁵Then take them from their hands and burn them on the altar along with the burnt offering for a pleasing aroma to the LORD an offering made to the LORD by fire. ²⁶After you take the breast of the ram for Aaron's ordination; wave it before the LORD as a wave offering, and it will be your share.

²⁷"Consecrate those parts of the ordination ram that belong to Aaron and his sons: the breast that was waved and the thigh that was presented. ²⁸This is always to be the regular share from the Israelites for Aaron and his sons. It is the contribution the Israelites are to make to the LORD from their fellowship offerings.ᵃ   Lev 7:31; Dt 18:3

ᵃ28 Traditionally *peace offerings*

29"Aaron's sacred garments will belong to his descendants so that they can be anointed and ordained in them. 30The son who succeeds him as priest and comes to the Tent of Meeting to minister in the Holy Place is to wear them seven days. Nu 20:28

31"Take the ram for the ordination and cook the meat in a sacred place. 32At the entrance to the Tent of Meeting, Aaron and his sons are to eat the meat of the ram and the bread that is in the basket. 33They are to eat these offerings by which atonement was made for their ordination and consecration. But no one else may eat them, because they are sacred. 34And if any of the meat of the ordination ram or any bread is left over till morning, burn it up. It must not be eaten, because it is sacred.

35"Do for Aaron and his sons everything I have commanded you, taking seven days to ordain them. 36Sacrifice a bull each day as a sin offering to make atonement. Purify the altar by making atonement for it, and anoint it to consecrate it. 37For seven days make atonement for the altar and consecrate it. Then the altar will be most holy, and whatever touches it will be holy. Lev 8:33; Heb 10:11

38"This is what you are to offer on the altar regularly each day: two lambs a year old. 39Offer one in the morning and the other at twilight. 40With the first lamb offer a tenth of an ephah*a* of fine flour mixed with a quarter of a hin*b* of oil from pressed olives, and a quarter of a hin of wine as a drink offering. 41Sacrifice the other lamb at twilight with the same grain offering and its drink offering as in the morning—a pleasing aroma, an offering made to the LORD by fire. Nu 28:3; Ezr 9:4-5

42"For the generations to come this burnt offering is to be made regularly at the entrance to the Tent of Meeting before the LORD. There I will meet you and speak to you; 43there also I will meet with the Israelites, and the place will be consecrated by my glory. Ex 30:8

44"So I will consecrate the Tent of Meeting and the altar and will consecrate Aaron and his sons to serve me as priests. 45Then I will dwell among the Israelites and be their God. 46They will know that I am the LORD their God, who brought them out of Egypt so that I might dwell among them. I am the LORD their God. Lev 21:15

The Altar of Incense

30 "Make an altar of acacia wood for burning incense. 2It is to be square, a cubit long and a cubit wide, and two cubits high*c*—its horns of one piece with it. 3Overlay the top and all the sides and the horns

---

a40 That is, probably about 2 quarts (about 2 liters)   *b40* That is, probably about 1 quart (about 1 liter)   *c2* That is, about 1 1/2 feet (about 0.5 meter) long and wide and about 3 feet (about 0.9 meter) high

with pure gold, and make a gold molding around it. 4Make two gold rings for the altar below the molding—two on opposite sides—to hold the poles used to carry it. 5Make the poles of acacia wood and overlay them with gold. 6Put the altar in front of the curtain that is before the ark of the Testimony—before the atonement cover that is over the Testimony—where I will meet with you.   Ex 25:11; 37:25

7"Aaron must burn fragrant incense on the altar every morning when he tends the lamps. 8He must burn incense again when he lights the lamps at twilight so incense will burn regularly before the LORD for the generations to come. 9Do not offer on this altar any other incense or any burnt offering or grain offering, and do not pour a drink offering on it. 10Once a year Aaron shall make atonement on its horns. This annual atonement must be made with the blood of the atoning sin offering for the generations to come. It is most holy to the LORD."   Lev 10:1; Nu 3:10

Atonement Money

11Then the LORD said to Moses, 12"When you take a census of the Israelites to count them, each one must pay the LORD a ransom for his life at the time he is counted. Then no plague will come on them when you number them. 13Each one who crosses over to those already counted is to give a half shekel,[a] according to the sanctuary shekel, which weighs twenty gerahs. This half shekel is an offering to the LORD. 14All who cross over, those twenty years old or more, are to give an offering to the LORD. 15The rich are not to give more than a half shekel and the poor are not to give less when you make the offering to the LORD to atone for your lives. 16Receive the atonement money from the Israelites and use it for the service of the Tent of Meeting. It will be a memorial for the Israelites before the LORD, making atonement for your lives."   Nu 26:2

Basin for Washing

17Then the LORD said to Moses, 18"Make a bronze basin, with its bronze stand, for washing. Place it between the Tent of Meeting and the altar, and put water in it. 19Aaron and his sons are to wash their hands and feet with water from it. 20Whenever they enter the Tent of Meeting, they shall wash with water so that they will not die. Also, when they approach the altar to minister by presenting an offering made to the LORD by fire, 21they shall wash their hands and feet so that they will not die. This is to be a lasting ordinance for Aaron and his de-

---

a13 That is, about 1/5 ounce (about 6 grams); also in verse 15

scendants for the generations to come."   <small>Ex 38:8; 40:31</small>

Anointing Oil

22Then the LORD said to Moses, 23"Take the following fine spices: 500 shekels[a] of liquid myrrh, half as much (that is, 250 shekels) of fragrant cinnamon, 250 shekels of fragrant cane, 24500 shekels of cassia—all according to the sanctuary shekel—and a hin[b] of olive oil. 25Make these into a sacred anointing oil, a fragrant blend, the work of a perfumer. It will be the sacred anointing oil. 26Then use it to anoint the Tent of Meeting, the ark of the Testimony, 27the table and all its articles, the lampstand and its accessories, the altar of incense, 28the altar of burnt offering and all its utensils, and the basin with its stand. 29You shall consecrate them so they will be most holy, and whatever touches them will be holy. <small>Ps 45:8</small>

30"Anoint Aaron and his sons and consecrate them so they may serve me as priests. 31Say to the Israelites, 'This is to be my sacred anointing oil for the generations to come. 32Do not pour it on men's bodies and do not make any oil with the same formula. It is sacred, and you are to consider it sacred. 33Whoever makes perfume like it and whoever puts it on anyone other

than a priest must be cut off from his people.'"   <small>Ex 30:25; Lev 8:12</small>

Incense

34Then the LORD said to Moses, "Take fragrant spices—gum resin, onycha and galbanum—and pure frankincense, all in equal amounts, 35and make a fragrant blend of incense, the work of a perfumer. It is to be salted and pure and sacred. 36Grind some of it to powder and place it in front of the Testimony in the Tent of Meeting, where I will meet with you. It shall be most holy to you. 37Do not make any incense with this formula for yourselves; consider it holy to the LORD. 38Whoever makes any like it to enjoy its fragrance must be cut off from his people."   <small>Ex 29:37; Lev 2:3</small>

Bezalel and Oholiab

31 Then the LORD said to Moses, 2"See, I have chosen Bezalel son of Uri, the son of Hur, of the tribe of Judah, 3and I have filled him with the Spirit of God, with skill, ability and knowledge in all kinds of crafts— 4to make artistic designs for work in gold, silver and bronze, 5to cut and set stones, to work in wood, and to engage in all kinds of craftsmanship. 6Moreover, I have appointed Oholiab son of Ahisamach, of the tribe of Dan, to

---

[a]23 That is, about 12 1/2 pounds (about 6 kilograms)   [b]24 That is, probably about 4 quarts (about 4 liters)

help him. Also I have given skill to all the craftsmen to make everything I have commanded you: [7]the Tent of Meeting, the ark of the Testimony with the atonement cover on it, and all the other furnishings of the tent— [8]the table and its articles, the pure gold lampstand and all its accessories, the altar of incense, [9]the altar of burnt offering and all its utensils, the basin with its stand— [10]and also the woven garments, both the sacred garments for Aaron the priest and the garments for his sons when they serve as priests, [11]and the anointing oil and fragrant incense for the Holy Place. They are to make them just as I commanded you."

The Sabbath

[12]Then the LORD said to Moses, [13]"Say to the Israelites, 'You must observe my Sabbaths. This will be a sign between me and you for the generations to come, so you may know that I am the LORD, who makes you holy.[a]   Eze 20:12

[14]" 'Observe the Sabbath, because it is holy to you. Anyone who desecrates it must be put to death; whoever does any work on that day must be cut off from his people. [15]For six days, work is to be done, but the seventh day is a Sabbath of rest, holy to the LORD. Whoever does any work on the Sabbath day must be put to death. [16]The Israelites are to observe the Sabbath, celebrating it for the generations to come as a lasting covenant. [17]It will be a sign between me and the Israelites forever, for in six days the LORD made the heavens and the earth, and on the seventh day he abstained from work and rested.' "   Ex 35:2

[18]When the LORD finished speaking to Moses on Mount Sinai, he gave him the two tablets of the Testimony, the tablets of stone inscribed by the finger of God.   Dt 4:13; 2Co 3:3

The Golden Calf

32 When the people saw that Moses was so long in coming down from the mountain, they gathered around Aaron and said, "Come, make us gods[b] who will go before us. As for this fellow Moses who brought us up out of Egypt, we don't know what has happened to him."   Dt 9:9; Ac 7:40

[2]Aaron answered them, "Take off the gold earrings that your wives, your sons and your daughters are wearing, and bring them to me." [3]So all the people took off their earrings and brought them to Aaron. [4]He took what they handed him and made it into an idol cast in the shape of a calf, fashioning it with a tool. Then they said, "These are your gods,[c] O Israel,

---

[a]13 Or who sanctifies you; or who sets you apart as holy   [b]1 Or a god; also in verses 23 and 31   [c]4 Or This is your god; also in verse 8

who brought you up out of Egypt." _{Ex 35:22}

⁵When Aaron saw this, he built an altar in front of the calf and announced, "Tomorrow there will be a festival to the LORD." ⁶So the next day the people rose early and sacrificed burnt offerings and presented fellowship offerings.ᵃ Afterward they sat down to eat and drink and got up to indulge in revelry. _{Lev 23:2; 2Ki 10:20}

⁷Then the LORD said to Moses, "Go down, because your people, whom you brought up out of Egypt, have become corrupt. ⁸They have been quick to turn away from what I commanded them and have made themselves an idol cast in the shape of a calf. They have bowed down to it and sacrificed to it and have said, 'These are your gods, O Israel, who brought you up out of Egypt.' _{Ge 6:11-12; 1Ki 12:28}

⁹"I have seen these people," the LORD said to Moses, "and they are a stiff-necked people. ¹⁰Now leave me alone so that my anger may burn against them and that I may destroy them. Then I will make you into a great nation." _{Ex 33:3,5}

¹¹But Moses sought the favor of the LORD his God. "O LORD," he said, "why should your anger burn against your people, whom you brought out of Egypt with great power and a mighty hand? ¹²Why should the Egyp-

tians say, 'It was with evil intent that he brought them out, to kill them in the mountains and to wipe them off the face of the earth'? Turn from your fierce anger; relent and do not bring disaster on your people. ¹³Remember your servants Abraham, Isaac and Israel, to whom you swore by your own self: 'I will make your descendants as numerous as the stars in the sky and I will give your descendants all this land I promised them, and it will be their inheritance forever.' " ¹⁴Then the LORD relented and did not bring on his people the disaster he had threatened. _{Dt 9:18,28}

¹⁵Moses turned and went down the mountain with the two tablets of the Testimony in his hands. They were inscribed on both sides, front and back. ¹⁶The tablets were the work of God; the writing was the writing of God, engraved on the tablets. _{Ex 31:18; Dt 9:15}

¹⁷When Joshua heard the noise of the people shouting, he said to Moses, "There is the sound of war in the camp." _{Ex 17:9}

¹⁸Moses replied:

"It is not the sound of
    victory,
 it is not the sound of defeat;
 it is the sound of singing
    that I hear."

¹⁹When Moses approached the camp and saw the calf and the dancing, his anger burned

ᵃ6 Traditionally *peace offerings*

and he threw the tablets out of his hands, breaking them to pieces at the foot of the mountain. ²⁰And he took the calf they had made and burned it in the fire; then he ground it to powder, scattered it on the water and made the Israelites drink it.

²¹He said to Aaron, "What did these people do to you, that you led them into such great sin?"   Ge 26:10

²²"Do not be angry, my lord," Aaron answered. "You know how prone these people are to evil. ²³They said to me, 'Make us gods who will go before us. As for this fellow Moses who brought us up out of Egypt, we don't know what has happened to him.' ²⁴So I told them, 'Whoever has any gold jewelry, take it off.' Then they gave me the gold, and I threw it into the fire, and out came this calf!"   Dt 9:24

²⁵Moses saw that the people were running wild and that Aaron had let them get out of control and so become a laughingstock to their enemies. ²⁶So he stood at the entrance to the camp and said, "Whoever is for the LORD, come to me." And all the Levites rallied to him. Ge 38:23

²⁷Then he said to them, "This is what the LORD, the God of Israel, says: 'Each man strap a sword to his side. Go back and forth through the camp from one end to the other, each killing his brother and friend and neighbor.' " ²⁸The Levites did as Moses commanded, and that day about three thousand of the people died. ²⁹Then Moses said, "You have been set apart to the LORD today, for you were against your own sons and brothers, and he has blessed you this day."   Dt 33:9

³⁰The next day Moses said to the people, "You have committed a great sin. But now I will go up to the LORD; perhaps I can make atonement for your sin."

³¹So Moses went back to the LORD and said, "Oh, what a great sin these people have committed! They have made themselves gods of gold. ³²But now, please forgive their sin—but if not, then blot me out of the book you have written."

³³The LORD replied to Moses, "Whoever has sinned against me I will blot out of my book. ³⁴Now go, lead the people to the place I spoke of, and my angel will go before you. However, when the time comes for me to punish, I will punish them for their sin."   Ex 3:17; Dt 29:20

³⁵And the LORD struck the people with a plague because of what they did with the calf Aaron had made.   Ex 32:4

33 Then the LORD said to Moses, "Leave this place, you and the people you brought up out of Egypt, and go up to the land I promised on oath to Abraham, Isaac and Jacob, saying, 'I will give it to your descendants.' ²I will send an angel before you and drive out the Canaanites, Amorites, Hittites, Perizzites, Hivites and Jebusites. ³Go up to the land flowing

with milk and honey. But I will not go with you, because you are a stiff-necked people and I might destroy you on the way."

⁴When the people heard these distressing words, they began to mourn and no one put on any ornaments. ⁵For the LORD had said to Moses, "Tell the Israelites, 'You are a stiff-necked people. If I were to go with you even for a moment, I might destroy you. Now take off your ornaments and I will decide what to do with you.'" ⁶So the Israelites stripped off their ornaments at Mount Horeb.   Ex 32:9; Nu 14:39

The Tent of Meeting

⁷Now Moses used to take a tent and pitch it outside the camp some distance away, calling it the "tent of meeting." Anyone inquiring of the LORD would go to the tent of meeting outside the camp. ⁸And whenever Moses went out to the tent, all the people rose and stood at the entrances to their tents, watching Moses until he entered the tent. ⁹As Moses went into the tent, the pillar of cloud would come down and stay at the entrance, while the LORD spoke with Moses. ¹⁰Whenever the people saw the pillar of cloud standing at the entrance to the tent, they all stood and worshiped, each at the entrance to his tent. ¹¹The LORD would speak to Moses face to face, as a man speaks with his friend. Then Moses would return to the camp, but his young aide Joshua son of Nun did not leave the tent.   Nu 16:27; Ps 99:7

Moses and the Glory of the LORD

¹²Moses said to the LORD, "You have been telling me, 'Lead these people,' but you have not let me know whom you will send with me. You have said, 'I know you by name and you have found favor with me.' ¹³If you are pleased with me, teach me your ways so I may know you and continue to find favor with you. Remember that this nation is your people."

¹⁴The LORD replied, "My Presence will go with you, and I will give you rest."   Isa 63:9

¹⁵Then Moses said to him, "If your Presence does not go with us, do not send us up from here. ¹⁶How will anyone know that you are pleased with me and with your people unless you go with us? What else will distinguish me and your people from all the other people on the face of the earth?"   Ex 34:9

¹⁷And the LORD said to Moses, "I will do the very thing you have asked, because I am pleased with you and I know you by name."   Jos 5:16(a)

¹⁸Then Moses said, "Now show me your glory."   Ex 16:7

¹⁹And the LORD said, "I will cause all my goodness to pass in front of you, and I will proclaim my name, the LORD, in your presence. I will have mercy on

whom I will have mercy, and I will have compassion on whom I will have compassion. ²⁰But," he said, "you cannot see my face, for no one may see me and live." _{Ge 32:20; Ro 9:15-16,18}

²¹Then the LORD said, "There is a place near me where you may stand on a rock. ²²When my glory passes by, I will put you in a cleft in the rock and cover you with my hand until I have passed by. ²³Then I will remove my hand and you will see my back; but my face must not be seen." _{Ps 27:5; 91:1}

The New Stone Tablets

34 The LORD said to Moses, "Chisel out two stone tablets like the first ones, and I will write on them the words that were on the first tablets, which you broke. ²Be ready in the morning, and then come up on Mount Sinai. Present yourself to me there on top of the mountain. ³No one is to come with you or be seen anywhere on the mountain; not even the flocks and herds may graze in front of the mountain." _{Ex 32:16}

⁴So Moses chiseled out two stone tablets like the first ones and went up Mount Sinai early in the morning, as the LORD had commanded him; and he carried the two stone tablets in his hands. ⁵Then the LORD came down in the cloud and stood there with him and proclaimed his name, the LORD. ⁶And he passed in front of Moses, proclaiming, "The LORD, the LORD, the compassionate and gracious God, slow to anger, abounding in love and faithfulness, ⁷maintaining love to thousands, and forgiving wickedness, rebellion and sin. Yet he does not leave the guilty unpunished; he punishes the children and their children for the sin of the fathers to the third and fourth generation." _{Ex 33:19; Dt 10:3}

⁸Moses bowed to the ground at once and worshiped. ⁹"O Lord, if I have found favor in your eyes," he said, "then let the Lord go with us. Although this is a stiff-necked people, forgive our wickedness and our sin, and take us as your inheritance." _{Ex 4:31; 33:15}

¹⁰Then the LORD said: "I am making a covenant with you. Before all your people I will do wonders never before done in any nation in all the world. The people you live among will see how awesome is the work that I, the LORD, will do for you. ¹¹Obey what I command you today. I will drive out before you the Amorites, Canaanites, Hittites, Perizzites, Hivites and Jebusites. ¹²Be careful not to make a treaty with those who live in the land where you are going, or they will be a snare among you. ¹³Break down their altars, smash their sacred stones and cut down their Asherah poles. *ᵃ* ¹⁴Do not wor-

---

ᵃ13 That is, symbols of the goddess Asherah

ship any other god, for the LORD, whose name is Jealous, is a jealous God. _{Ex 23:32; Dt 5:2}

15"Be careful not to make a treaty with those who live in the land; for when they prostitute themselves to their gods and sacrifice to them, they will invite you and you will eat their sacrifices. 16And when you choose some of their daughters as wives for your sons and those daughters prostitute themselves to their gods, they will lead your sons to do the same. _{Jdg 2:17; 1Co 8:4}

17"Do not make cast idols.

18"Celebrate the Feast of Unleavened Bread. For seven days eat bread made without yeast, as I commanded you. Do this at the appointed time in the month of Abib, for in that month you came out of Egypt.

19"The first offspring of every womb belongs to me, including all the firstborn males of your livestock, whether from herd or flock. 20Redeem the firstborn donkey with a lamb, but if you do not redeem it, break its neck. Redeem all your firstborn sons.

"No one is to appear before me empty-handed. _{Dt 16:16}

21"Six days you shall labor, but on the seventh day you shall rest; even during the plowing season and harvest you must rest. _{Ex 20:9-10; Lk 13:14}

22"Celebrate the Feast of Weeks with the firstfruits of the wheat harvest, and the Feast of Ingathering at the turn of the year.[a] 23Three times a year all your men are to appear before the Sovereign LORD, the God of Israel. 24I will drive out nations before you and enlarge your territory, and no one will covet your land when you go up three times each year to appear before the LORD your God. _{Ex 23:16}

25"Do not offer the blood of a sacrifice to me along with anything containing yeast, and do not let any of the sacrifice from the Passover Feast remain until morning. _{Ex 12:10; 23:18}

26"Bring the best of the firstfruits of your soil to the house of the LORD your God. _{Ex 22:29}

"Do not cook a young goat in its mother's milk." _{Ex 23:19}

27Then the LORD said to Moses, "Write down these words, for in accordance with these words I have made a covenant with you and with Israel." 28Moses was there with the LORD forty days and forty nights without eating bread or drinking water. And he wrote on the tablets the words of the covenant—the Ten Commandments. _{Ex 17:14; Dt 4:13}

The Radiant Face of Moses

29When Moses came down from Mount Sinai with the two tablets of the Testimony in his hands, he was not aware that his face was radiant because he had spoken with the LORD. 30When Aaron and all the Israel-

^a22 That is, in the fall

ites saw Moses, his face was radiant, and they were afraid to come near him. ³¹But Moses called to them; so Aaron and all the leaders of the community came back to him, and he spoke to them. ³²Afterward all the Israelites came near him, and he gave them all the commands the LORD had given him on Mount Sinai.   Ex 16:22; 32:15

³³When Moses finished speaking to them, he put a veil over his face. ³⁴But whenever he entered the LORD's presence to speak with him, he removed the veil until he came out. And when he came out and told the Israelites what he had been commanded, ³⁵they saw that his face was radiant. Then Moses would put the veil back over his face until he went in to speak with the LORD.   Ex 21:1; 2Co 3:13

Sabbath Regulations

35 Moses assembled the whole Israelite community and said to them, "These are the things the LORD has commanded you to do: ²For six days, work is to be done, but the seventh day shall be your holy day, a Sabbath of rest to the LORD. Whoever does any work on it must be put to death. ³Do not light a fire in any of your dwellings on the Sabbath day."

Materials for the Tabernacle

⁴Moses said to the whole Israelite community, "This is what

the LORD has commanded: ⁵From what you have, take an offering for the LORD. Everyone who is willing is to bring to the LORD an offering of gold, silver and bronze; ⁶blue, purple and scarlet yarn and fine linen; goat hair; ⁷ram skins dyed red and hides of sea cows*ᵃ*; acacia wood; ⁸olive oil for the light; spices for the anointing oil and for the fragrant incense; ⁹and onyx stones and other gems to be mounted on the ephod and breastpiece.

¹⁰"All who are skilled among you are to come and make everything the LORD has commanded: ¹¹the tabernacle with its tent and its covering, clasps, frames, crossbars, posts and bases; ¹²the ark with its poles and the atonement cover and the curtain that shields it; ¹³the table with its poles and all its articles and the bread of the Presence; ¹⁴the lampstand that is for light with its accessories, lamps and oil for the light; ¹⁵the altar of incense with its poles, the anointing oil and the fragrant incense; the curtain for the doorway at the entrance to the tabernacle; ¹⁶the altar of burnt offering with its bronze grating, its poles and all its utensils; the bronze basin with its stand; ¹⁷the curtains of the courtyard with its posts and bases, and the curtain for the entrance to the courtyard; ¹⁸the tent pegs for the tabernacle and for the courtyard, and their

---

*ᵃ*7 That is, dugongs; also in verse 23

ropes; [19]the woven garments worn for ministering in the sanctuary—both the sacred garments for Aaron the priest and the garments for his sons when they serve as priests." Ex 31:6

[20]Then the whole Israelite community withdrew from Moses' presence, [21]and everyone who was willing and whose heart moved him came and brought an offering to the LORD for the work on the Tent of Meeting, for all its service, and for the sacred garments. [22]All who were willing, men and women alike, came and brought gold jewelry of all kinds: brooches, earrings, rings and ornaments. They all presented their gold as a wave offering to the LORD. [23]Everyone who had blue, purple or scarlet yarn or fine linen, or goat hair, ram skins dyed red or hides of sea cows brought them. [24]Those presenting an offering of silver or bronze brought it as an offering to the LORD, and everyone who had acacia wood for any part of the work brought it. [25]Every skilled woman spun with her hands and brought what she had spun—blue, purple or scarlet yarn or fine linen. [26]And all the women who were willing and had the skill spun the goat hair. [27]The leaders brought onyx stones and other gems to be mounted on the ephod and breastpiece. [28]They also brought spices and olive oil for the light and for the anointing oil and for the fragrant incense. [29]All the Israelite men and women who were willing brought to the LORD freewill offerings for all the work the LORD through Moses had commanded them to do. Ex 25:2

Bezalel and Oholiab

[30]Then Moses said to the Israelites, "See, the LORD has chosen Bezalel son of Uri, the son of Hur, of the tribe of Judah, [31]and he has filled him with the Spirit of God, with skill, ability and knowledge in all kinds of crafts— [32]to make artistic designs for work in gold, silver and bronze, [33]to cut and set stones, to work in wood and to engage in all kinds of artistic craftsmanship. [34]And he has given both him and Oholiab son of Ahisamach, of the tribe of Dan, the ability to teach others. [35]He has filled them with skill to do all kinds of work as craftsmen, designers, embroiderers in blue, purple and scarlet yarn and fine linen, and weavers—all of them master craftsmen and designers. [1]So Bezalel, Oholiab and every skilled person to whom the LORD has given skill and ability to know how to carry out all the work of constructing the sanctuary are to do the work just as the Lord has commanded." Ex 31:1-6; 2Ch 2:14

36

[2]Then Moses summoned Bezalel and Oholiab and every skilled person to whom the LORD had given ability and who was willing to come and do the

work. ³They received from Moses all the offerings the Israelites had brought to carry out the work of constructing the sanctuary. And the people continued to bring freewill offerings morning after morning. ⁴So all the skilled craftsmen who were doing all the work on the sanctuary left their work ⁵and said to Moses, "The people are bringing more than enough for doing the work the LORD commanded to be done."   Ex 35:29

⁶Then Moses gave an order and they sent this word throughout the camp: "No man or woman is to make anything else as an offering for the sanctuary." And so the people were restrained from bringing more, ⁷because what they already had was more than enough to do all the work.   1Ki 7:47; 2Co 8:2,4

The Tabernacle

⁸All the skilled men among the workmen made the tabernacle with ten curtains of finely twisted linen and blue, purple and scarlet yarn, with cherubim worked into them by a skilled craftsman. ⁹All the curtains were the same size—twenty-eight cubits long and four cubits wide. *ᵃ* ¹⁰They joined five of the curtains together and did the same with the other five. ¹¹Then they made loops of blue material along the

edge of the end curtain in one set, and the same was done with the end curtain in the other set. ¹²They also made fifty loops on one curtain and fifty loops on the end curtain of the other set, with the loops opposite each other. ¹³Then they made fifty gold clasps and used them to fasten the two sets of curtains together so that the tabernacle was a unit.   Ex 26:1-14

¹⁴They made curtains of goat hair for the tent over the tabernacle—eleven altogether. ¹⁵All eleven curtains were the same size—thirty cubits long and four cubits wide. *ᵇ* ¹⁶They joined five of the curtains into one set and the other six into another set. ¹⁷Then they made fifty loops along the edge of the end curtain in one set and also along the edge of the end curtain in the other set. ¹⁸They made fifty bronze clasps to fasten the tent together as a unit. ¹⁹Then they made for the tent a covering of ram skins dyed red, and over that a covering of hides of sea cows. *ᶜ*   Ex 26:14; 40:19

²⁰They made upright frames of acacia wood for the tabernacle. ²¹Each frame was ten cubits long and a cubit and a half wide, *ᵈ* ²²with two projections set parallel to each other. They made all the frames of the tabernacle in this way. ²³They made twenty frames for the south side

---

ᵃ9 That is, about 42 feet (about 12.5 meters) long and 6 feet (about 1.8 meters) wide
ᵇ15 That is, about 45 feet (about 13.5 meters) long and 6 feet (about 1.8 meters) wide
ᶜ19 That is, dugongs   *ᵈ21* That is, about 15 feet (about 4.5 meters) long and 2 1/4 feet (about 0.7 meter) wide

of the tabernacle ²⁴and made forty silver bases to go under them—two bases for each frame, one under each projection. ²⁵For the other side, the north side of the tabernacle, they made twenty frames ²⁶and forty silver bases—two under each frame. ²⁷They made six frames for the far end, that is, the west end of the tabernacle, ²⁸and two frames were made for the corners of the tabernacle at the far end. ²⁹At these two corners the frames were double from the bottom all the way to the top and fitted into a single ring; both were made alike. ³⁰So there were eight frames and sixteen silver bases—two under each frame.   Ex 26:15-29

³¹They also made crossbars of acacia wood: five for the frames on one side of the tabernacle, ³²five for those on the other side, and five for the frames on the west, at the far end of the tabernacle. ³³They made the center crossbar so that it extended from end to end at the middle of the frames. ³⁴They overlaid the frames with gold and made gold rings to hold the crossbars. They also overlaid the crossbars with gold.   Ex 26:26

³⁵They made the curtain of blue, purple and scarlet yarn and finely twisted linen, with cherubim worked into it by a skilled craftsman. ³⁶They made four posts of acacia wood for it

and overlaid them with gold. They made gold hooks for them and cast their four silver bases. ³⁷For the entrance to the tent they made a curtain of blue, purple and scarlet yarn and finely twisted linen—the work of an embroiderer; ³⁸and they made five posts with hooks for them. They overlaid the tops of the posts and their bands with gold and made their five bases of bronze.   Ex 26:31-37; Mt 27:51

The Ark

37 Bezalel made the ark of acacia wood—two and a half cubits long, a cubit and a half wide, and a cubit and a half high.ᵃ ²He overlaid it with pure gold, both inside and out, and made a gold molding around it. ³He cast four gold rings for it and fastened them to its four feet, with two rings on one side and two rings on the other. ⁴Then he made poles of acacia wood and overlaid them with gold. ⁵And he inserted the poles into the rings on the sides of the ark to carry it.   Ex 25:12; 30:6

⁶He made the atonement cover of pure gold—two and a half cubits long and a cubit and a half wide.ᵇ ⁷Then he made two cherubim out of hammered gold at the ends of the cover. ⁸He made one cherub on one end and the second cherub on the other; at the two ends he made them of one piece with

---

ᵃ1 That is, about 3 3/4 feet (about 1.1 meters) long and 2 1/4 feet (about 0.7 meter) wide and high   ᵇ6 That is, about 3 3/4 feet (about 1.1 meters) long and 2 1/4 feet (about 0.7 meter) wide

the cover. ⁹The cherubim had their wings spread upward, overshadowing the cover with them. The cherubim faced each other, looking toward the cover.   Ex 25:17; Eze 41:18

The Table

¹⁰They*a* made the table of acacia wood—two cubits long, a cubit wide, and a cubit and a half high.*b* ¹¹Then they overlaid it with pure gold and made a gold molding around it. ¹²They also made around it a rim a handbreadth*c* wide and put a gold molding on the rim. ¹³They cast four gold rings for the table and fastened them to the four corners, where the four legs were. ¹⁴The rings were put close to the rim to hold the poles used in carrying the table. ¹⁵The poles for carrying the table were made of acacia wood and were overlaid with gold. ¹⁶And they made from pure gold the articles for the table—its plates and dishes and bowls and its pitchers for the pouring out of drink offerings.   Ex 25:23; Heb 9:2

The Lampstand

¹⁷They made the lampstand of pure gold and hammered it out, base and shaft; its flower-like cups, buds and blossoms were of one piece with it. ¹⁸Six branches extended from the sides of the lampstand—three on one side and three on the other. ¹⁹Three cups shaped like almond flowers with buds and blossoms were on one branch, three on the next branch and the same for all six branches extending from the lampstand. ²⁰And on the lampstand were four cups shaped like almond flowers with buds and blossoms. ²¹One bud was under the first pair of branches extending from the lampstand, a second bud under the second pair, and a third bud under the third pair—six branches in all. ²²The buds and the branches were all of one piece with the lampstand, hammered out of pure gold.   Ex 25:31-39; Heb 9:2

²³They made its seven lamps, as well as its wick trimmers and trays, of pure gold. ²⁴They made the lampstand and all its accessories from one talent*d* of pure gold.   Ex 40:4,25

The Altar of Incense

²⁵They made the altar of incense out of acacia wood. It was square, a cubit long and a cubit wide, and two cubits high*e*—its horns of one piece with it. ²⁶They overlaid the top and all the sides and the horns with pure gold, and made a gold molding around it. ²⁷They made two gold rings below the mold-

---

a10 Or *He*; also in verses 11-29   *b10* That is, about 3 feet (about 0.9 meter) long, 1 1/2 feet (about 0.5 meter) wide, and 2 1/4 feet (about 0.7 meter) high   *c12* That is, about 3 inches (about 8 centimeters)   *d24* That is, about 75 pounds (about 34 kilograms) *e25* That is, about 1 1/2 feet (about 0.5 meter) long and wide, and about 3 feet (about 0.9 meter) high

ing—two on opposite sides—to hold the poles used to carry it. ²⁸They made the poles of acacia wood and overlaid them with gold.   Ex 30:1-5; Heb 9:4

²⁹They also made the sacred anointing oil and the pure, fragrant incense—the work of a perfumer.   Ex 30:23; 39:38

The Altar of Burnt Offering

38 They^a built the altar of burnt offering of acacia wood, three cubits^b high; it was square, five cubits long and five cubits wide.^c ²They made a horn at each of the four corners, so that the horns and the altar were of one piece, and they overlaid the altar with bronze. ³They made all its utensils of bronze—its pots, shovels, sprinkling bowls, meat forks and firepans. ⁴They made a grating for the altar, a bronze network, to be under its ledge, halfway up the altar. ⁵They cast bronze rings to hold the poles for the four corners of the bronze grating. ⁶They made the poles of acacia wood and overlaid them with bronze. ⁷They inserted the poles into the rings so they would be on the sides of the altar for carrying it. They made it hollow, out of boards.

Basin for Washing

⁸They made the bronze basin and its bronze stand from the mirrors of the women who served at the entrance to the Tent of Meeting.   Ex 30:18; Dt 23:17

The Courtyard

⁹Next they made the courtyard. The south side was a hundred cubits^d long and had curtains of finely twisted linen, ¹⁰with twenty posts and twenty bronze bases, and with silver hooks and bands on the posts. ¹¹The north side was also a hundred cubits long and had twenty posts and twenty bronze bases, with silver hooks and bands on the posts. Ex 27:9-19

¹²The west end was fifty cubits^e wide and had curtains, with ten posts and ten bases, with silver hooks and bands on the posts. ¹³The east end, toward the sunrise, was also fifty cubits wide. ¹⁴Curtains fifteen cubits^f long were on one side of the entrance, with three posts and three bases, ¹⁵and curtains fifteen cubits long were on the other side of the entrance to the courtyard, with three posts and three bases. ¹⁶All the curtains around the courtyard were of finely twisted linen. ¹⁷The bases for the posts were bronze. The hooks and bands on the posts were silver, and their tops were overlaid with silver; so all the posts of the courtyard had silver bands.   Ex 27:14

¹⁸The curtain for the entrance

---

^a1 Or He; also in verses 2-9   ^b1 That is, about 4 1/2 feet (about 1.3 meters)
^c1 That is, about 7 1/2 feet (about 2.3 meters) long and wide   ^d9 That is, about 150 feet (about 46 meters)   ^e12 That is, about 75 feet (about 23 meters)   ^f14 That is, about 22 1/2 feet (about 6.9 meters)

to the courtyard was of blue, purple and scarlet yarn and finely twisted linen—the work of an embroiderer. It was twenty cubits*a* long and, like the curtains of the courtyard, five cubits*b* high, ¹⁹with four posts and four bronze bases. Their hooks and bands were silver, and their tops were overlaid with silver. ²⁰All the tent pegs of the tabernacle and of the surrounding courtyard were bronze.   Ex 27:16; 35:18

The Materials Used

²¹These are the amounts of the materials used for the tabernacle, the tabernacle of the Testimony, which were recorded at Moses' command by the Levites under the direction of Ithamar son of Aaron, the priest. ²²(Bezalel son of Uri, the son of Hur, of the tribe of Judah, made everything the LORD commanded Moses; ²³with him was Oholiab son of Ahisamach, of the tribe of Dan—a craftsman and designer, and an embroiderer in blue, purple and scarlet yarn and fine linen.) ²⁴The total amount of the gold from the wave offering used for all the work on the sanctuary was 29 talents and 730 shekels,*c* according to the sanctuary shekel. ²⁵The silver obtained from

those of the community who were counted in the census was 100 talents and 1,775 shekels,*d* according to the sanctuary shekel— ²⁶one beka per person, that is, half a shekel,*e* according to the sanctuary shekel, from everyone who had crossed over to those counted, twenty years old or more, a total of 603,550 men. ²⁷The 100 talents*f* of silver were used to cast the bases for the sanctuary and for the curtain—100 bases from the 100 talents, one talent for each base. ²⁸They used the 1,775 shekels*g* to make the hooks for the posts, to overlay the tops of the posts, and to make their bands.   Ex 30:12

²⁹The bronze from the wave offering was 70 talents and 2,400 shekels.*h* ³⁰They used it to make the bases for the entrance to the Tent of Meeting, the bronze altar with its bronze grating and all its utensils, ³¹the bases for the surrounding courtyard and those for its entrance and all the tent pegs for the tabernacle and those for the surrounding courtyard.

The Priestly Garments

39 From the blue, purple and scarlet yarn they made woven garments for ministering in the sanctuary. They also made sacred garments for

---

*a18 That is, about 30 feet (about 9 meters)   *b18 That is, about 7 1/2 feet (about 2.3 meters)   *c24 The weight of the gold was a little over one ton (about 1 metric ton).   *d25 The weight of the silver was a little over 3 3/4 tons (about 3.4 metric tons).   *e26 That is, about 1/5 ounce (about 5.5 grams)   *f27 That is, about 3 3/4 tons (about 3.4 metric tons)   *g28 That is, about 45 pounds (about 20 kilograms)   *h29 The weight of the bronze was about 2 1/2 tons (about 2.4 metric tons).

Aaron, as the LORD commanded Moses.   Ex 35:23

The Ephod

2They[a] made the ephod of gold, and of blue, purple and scarlet yarn, and of finely twisted linen. 3They hammered out thin sheets of gold and cut strands to be worked into the blue, purple and scarlet yarn and fine linen—the work of a skilled craftsman. 4They made shoulder pieces for the ephod, which were attached to two of its corners, so it could be fastened. 5Its skillfully woven waistband was like it—of one piece with the ephod and made with gold, and with blue, purple and scarlet yarn, and with finely twisted linen, as the LORD commanded Moses.   Ex 28:6-12

6They mounted the onyx stones in gold filigree settings and engraved them like a seal with the names of the sons of Israel. 7Then they fastened them on the shoulder pieces of the ephod as memorial stones for the sons of Israel, as the LORD commanded Moses.

The Breastpiece

8They fashioned the breastpiece—the work of a skilled craftsman. They made it like the ephod: of gold, and of blue, purple and scarlet yarn, and of finely twisted linen. 9It was square—a span[b] long and a span wide—and folded double. 10Then they mounted four rows of precious stones on it. In the first row there was a ruby, a topaz and a beryl; 11in the second row a turquoise, a sapphire[c] and an emerald; 12in the third row a jacinth, an agate and an amethyst; 13in the fourth row a chrysolite, an onyx and a jasper.[d] They were mounted in gold filigree settings. 14There were twelve stones, one for each of the names of the sons of Israel, each engraved like a seal with the name of one of the twelve tribes.   Ex 28:15-28

15For the breastpiece they made braided chains of pure gold, like a rope. 16They made two gold filigree settings and two gold rings, and fastened the rings to two of the corners of the breastpiece. 17They fastened the two gold chains to the rings at the corners of the breastpiece, 18and the other ends of the chains to the two settings, attaching them to the shoulder pieces of the ephod at the front. 19They made two gold rings and attached them to the other two corners of the breastpiece on the inside edge next to the ephod. 20Then they made two more gold rings and attached them to the bottom of the shoulder pieces on the front of the ephod, close to the seam just above the waistband of the ephod. 21They tied the rings of

a2 Or He; also in verses 7, 8 and 22   b9 That is, about 9 inches (about 22 centimeters)
c11 Or lapis lazuli   d13 The precise identification of some of these precious stones is uncertain.

the breastpiece to the rings of the ephod with blue cord, connecting it to the waistband so that the breastpiece would not swing out from the ephod—as the LORD commanded Moses.

Other Priestly Garments

²²They made the robe of the ephod entirely of blue cloth— the work of a weaver—²³with an opening in the center of the robe like the opening of a collar,ᵃ and a band around this opening, so that it would not tear. ²⁴They made pomegranates of blue, purple and scarlet yarn and finely twisted linen around the hem of the robe. ²⁵And they made bells of pure gold and attached them around the hem between the pomegranates. ²⁶The bells and pomegranates alternated around the hem of the robe to be worn for ministering, as the LORD commanded Moses.   Ex 28:24

²⁷For Aaron and his sons, they made tunics of fine linen—the work of a weaver— ²⁸and the turban of fine linen, the linen headbands and the undergarments of finely twisted linen. ²⁹The sash was of finely twisted linen and blue, purple and scarlet yarn—the work of an embroiderer—as the LORD commanded Moses.   Ex 28:31-34

³⁰They made the plate, the sacred diadem, out of pure gold and engraved on it, like an inscription on a seal: HOLY TO THE LORD. ³¹Then they fastened a blue cord to it to attach it to the turban, as the LORD commanded Moses.

Moses Inspects the Tabernacle

³²So all the work on the tabernacle, the Tent of Meeting, was completed. The Israelites did everything just as the LORD commanded Moses. ³³Then they brought the tabernacle to Moses: the tent and all its furnishings, its clasps, frames, crossbars, posts and bases; ³⁴the covering of ram skins dyed red, the covering of hides of sea cowsᵇ and the shielding curtain; ³⁵the ark of the Testimony with its poles and the atonement cover; ³⁶the table with all its articles and the bread of the Presence; ³⁷the pure gold lampstand with its row of lamps and all its accessories, and the oil for the light; ³⁸the gold altar, the anointing oil, the fragrant incense, and the curtain for the entrance to the tent; ³⁹the bronze altar with its bronze grating, its poles and all its utensils; the basin with its stand; ⁴⁰the curtains of the courtyard with its posts and bases, and the curtain for the entrance to the courtyard; the ropes and tent pegs for the courtyard; all the furnishings for the tabernacle, the Tent of Meeting; ⁴¹and the woven garments worn for ministering in

ᵃ23 The meaning of the Hebrew for this word is uncertain.   ᵇ34 That is, dugongs

the sanctuary, both the sacred garments for Aaron the priest and the garments for his sons when serving as priests.   Ex 25:9

⁴²The Israelites had done all the work just as the LORD had commanded Moses. ⁴³Moses inspected the work and saw that they had done it just as the LORD had commanded. So Moses blessed them.   Ex 35:10

Setting Up the Tabernacle

40 Then the LORD said to Moses: ²"Set up the tabernacle, the Tent of Meeting, on the first day of the first month. ³Place the ark of the Testimony in it and shield the ark with the curtain. ⁴Bring in the table and set out what belongs on it. Then bring in the lampstand and set up its lamps. ⁵Place the gold altar of incense in front of the ark of the Testimony and put the curtain at the entrance to the tabernacle.   Ex 12; Nu 9:1

⁶"Place the altar of burnt offering in front of the entrance to the tabernacle, the Tent of Meeting; ⁷place the basin between the Tent of Meeting and the altar and put water in it. ⁸Set up the courtyard around it and put the curtain at the entrance to the courtyard.   2Ki 16:14

⁹"Take the anointing oil and anoint the tabernacle and everything in it; consecrate it and all its furnishings, and it will be holy. ¹⁰Then anoint the altar of burnt offering and all its utensils; consecrate the altar, and it

will be most holy. ¹¹Anoint the basin and its stand and consecrate them.   Ex 29:36; 30:26

¹²"Bring Aaron and his sons to the entrance to the Tent of Meeting and wash them with water. ¹³Then dress Aaron in the sacred garments, anoint him and consecrate him so he may serve me as priest. ¹⁴Bring his sons and dress them in tunics. ¹⁵Anoint them just as you anointed their father, so they may serve me as priests. Their anointing will be to a priesthood that will continue for all generations to come." ¹⁶Moses did everything just as the LORD commanded him.   Ex 28:41; Nu 8:9

¹⁷So the tabernacle was set up on the first day of the first month in the second year. ¹⁸When Moses set up the tabernacle, he put the bases in place, erected the frames, inserted the crossbars and set up the posts. ¹⁹Then he spread the tent over the tabernacle and put the covering over the tent, as the LORD commanded him.   2Ch 1:3

²⁰He took the Testimony and placed it in the ark, attached the poles to the ark and put the atonement cover over it. ²¹Then he brought the ark into the tabernacle and hung the shielding curtain and shielded the ark of the Testimony, as the LORD commanded him.   Ex 25:16

²²Moses placed the table in the Tent of Meeting on the north side of the tabernacle outside the curtain ²³and set out the

bread on it before the LORD, as the LORD commanded him.

²⁴He placed the lampstand in the Tent of Meeting opposite the table on the south side of the tabernacle ²⁵and set up the lamps before the LORD, as the LORD commanded him.   Ex 25:31

²⁶Moses placed the gold altar in the Tent of Meeting in front of the curtain ²⁷and burned fragrant incense on it, as the LORD commanded him. ²⁸Then he put up the curtain at the entrance to the tabernacle.   Ge 6:22; Ex 30:1

²⁹He set the altar of burnt offering near the entrance to the tabernacle, the Tent of Meeting, and offered on it burnt offerings and grain offerings, as the LORD commanded him.   Ex 29:38

³⁰He placed the basin between the Tent of Meeting and the altar and put water in it for washing, ³¹and Moses and Aaron and his sons used it to wash their hands and feet. ³²They washed whenever they entered the Tent of Meeting or approached the altar, as the LORD commanded Moses.

³³Then Moses set up the courtyard around the tabernacle and altar and put up the curtain at the entrance to the courtyard. And so Moses finished the work.   Ex 27:9; 38:9-20

The Glory of the LORD

³⁴Then the cloud covered the Tent of Meeting, and the glory of the LORD filled the tabernacle. ³⁵Moses could not enter the Tent of Meeting because the cloud had settled upon it, and the glory of the LORD filled the tabernacle.   Lev 16:2; Nu 9:15-23

³⁶In all the travels of the Israelites, whenever the cloud lifted from above the tabernacle, they would set out; ³⁷but if the cloud did not lift, they did not set out—until the day it lifted. ³⁸So the cloud of the LORD was over the tabernacle by day, and fire was in the cloud by night, in the sight of all the house of Israel during all their travels.   Nu 9:17-23

Leviticus

Introduction:

Leviticus means "about the Levites." The Levites were God's priests, and the book of Leviticus contains many of the rules they needed to do their work—rules for worshiping God, making sacrifices, and handling everyday problems concerning cleanliness. Although many of the rules were given only for the Levites, the purpose of all the laws that were given was to help the Israelites worship and live as God's holy people. A key statement for the entire book is "Be holy, because I am holy." (11:44,45)

Outline of contents:

The Burnt Offering

1 The LORD called to Moses and spoke to him from the Tent of Meeting. He said, 2"Speak to the Israelites and say to them: 'When any of you brings an offering to the LORD, bring as your offering an animal from either the herd or the flock.   Ex 27:21; Nu 7:89

3" 'If the offering is a burnt offering from the herd, he is to offer a male without defect. He must present it at the entrance to the Tent of Meeting so that it[a] will be acceptable to the LORD. 4He is to lay his hand on the head of the burnt offering, and it will be accepted on his behalf to make atonement for him. 5He is to slaughter the young bull before the LORD, and then Aaron's sons the priests shall bring the blood and sprinkle it against the altar on all sides at the entrance to the Tent of Meeting. 6He is to skin the burnt

---

a3 Or he

offering and cut it into pieces. [7]The sons of Aaron the priest are to put fire on the altar and arrange wood on the fire. [8]Then Aaron's sons the priests shall arrange the pieces, including the head and the fat, on the burning wood that is on the altar. [9]He is to wash the inner parts and the legs with water, and the priest is to burn all of it on the altar. It is a burnt offering, an offering made by fire, an aroma pleasing to the LORD.

[10]" 'If the offering is a burnt offering from the flock, from either the sheep or the goats, he is to offer a male without defect. [11]He is to slaughter it at the north side of the altar before the LORD, and Aaron's sons the priests shall sprinkle its blood against the altar on all sides. [12]He is to cut it into pieces, and the priest shall arrange them, including the head and the fat, on the burning wood that is on the altar. [13]He is to wash the inner parts and the legs with water, and the priest is to bring all of it and burn it on the altar. It is a burnt offering, an offering made by fire, an aroma pleasing to the LORD.   Ex 29:11; Lev 3:12

[14]" 'If the offering to the LORD is a burnt offering of birds, he is to offer a dove or a young pigeon. [15]The priest shall bring it to the altar, wring off the head and burn it on the altar; its blood shall be drained out on the side of the altar. [16]He is to remove the crop with its contents[a] and throw it to the east side of the altar, where the ashes are. [17]He shall tear it open by the wings, not severing it completely, and then the priest shall burn it on the wood that is on the fire on the altar. It is a burnt offering, an offering made by fire, an aroma pleasing to the LORD.   Lev 5:7; Nu 4:13

The Grain Offering

2 " 'When someone brings a grain offering to the LORD, his offering is to be of fine flour. He is to pour oil on it, put incense on it [2]and take it to Aaron's sons the priests. The priest shall take a handful of the fine flour and oil, together with all the incense, and burn this as a memorial portion on the altar, an offering made by fire, an aroma pleasing to the LORD. [3]The rest of the grain offering belongs to Aaron and his sons; it is a most holy part of the offerings made to the LORD by fire.

[4]" 'If you bring a grain offering baked in an oven, it is to consist of fine flour: cakes made without yeast and mixed with oil, or[b] wafers made without yeast and spread with oil. [5]If your grain offering is prepared on a griddle, it is to be made of fine flour mixed with oil, and without yeast. [6]Crumble it and

---

[a]16 Or *crop and the feathers*; the meaning of the Hebrew for this word is uncertain.
[b]4 Or *and*

pour oil on it; it is a grain offering. ⁷If your grain offering is
cooked in a pan, it is to be made
of fine flour and oil. ⁸Bring the
grain offering made of these
things to the LORD; present it to
the priest, who shall take it to
the altar. ⁹He shall take out the
memorial portion from the
grain offering and burn it on the
altar as an offering made by fire,
an aroma pleasing to the LORD.
¹⁰The rest of the grain offering
belongs to Aaron and his sons;
it is a most holy part of the
offerings made to the LORD by
fire.

¹¹" 'Every grain offering you
bring to the LORD must be made
without yeast, for you are not to
burn any yeast or honey in an
offering made to the LORD by
fire. ¹²You may bring them to
the LORD as an offering of the
firstfruits, but they are not to be
offered on the altar as a pleasing
aroma. ¹³Season all your grain
offerings with salt. Do not leave
the salt of the covenant of your
God out of your grain offerings;
add salt to all your offerings.

¹⁴" 'If you bring a grain offering of firstfruits to the LORD, offer crushed heads of new grain
roasted in the fire. ¹⁵Put oil and
incense on it; it is a grain offering. ¹⁶The priest shall burn
the memorial portion of the
crushed grain and the oil, together with all the incense, as
an offering made to the LORD by
fire.   Nu 15:20; Dt 16:13

The Fellowship Offering

3 " 'If someone's offering is a
fellowship offering,ᵃ and he
offers an animal from the herd,
whether male or female, he is to
present before the LORD an animal without defect. ²He is to lay
his hand on the head of his offering and slaughter it at the entrance to the Tent of Meeting.
Then Aaron's sons the priests
shall sprinkle the blood against
the altar on all sides. ³From the
fellowship offering he is to
bring a sacrifice made to the
LORD by fire: all the fat that
covers the inner parts or is connected to them, ⁴both kidneys
with the fat on them near the
loins, and the covering of the
liver, which he will remove with
the kidneys. ⁵Then Aaron's
sons are to burn it on the altar
on top of the burnt offering that is on the burning
wood, as an offering made by
fire, an aroma pleasing to the
LORD.   Ex 29:13; Lev 7:11
⁶" 'If he offers an animal from
the flock as a fellowship offering
to the LORD, he is to offer a male
or female without defect. ⁷If he
offers a lamb, he is to present it
before the LORD. ⁸He is to lay his
hand on the head of his offering
and slaughter it in front of the
Tent of Meeting. Then Aaron's
sons shall sprinkle its blood
against the altar on all sides.
⁹From the fellowship offering
he is to bring a sacrifice made to
the LORD by fire: its fat, the en-

ᵃ1 Traditionally *peace offering*; also in verses 3, 6 and 9

tire fat tail cut off close to the backbone, all the fat that covers the inner parts or is connected to them, [10]both kidneys with the fat on them near the loins, and the covering of the liver, which he will remove with the kidneys. [11]The priest shall burn them on the altar as food, an offering made to the LORD by fire. Lev 22:21; Nu 15:5

[12]" 'If his offering is a goat, he is to present it before the LORD. [13]He is to lay his hand on its head and slaughter it in front of the Tent of Meeting. Then Aaron's sons shall sprinkle its blood against the altar on all sides. [14]From what he offers he is to make this offering to the LORD by fire: all the fat that covers the inner parts or is connected to them, [15]both kidneys with the fat on them near the loins, and the covering of the liver, which he will remove with the kidneys. [16]The priest shall burn them on the altar as food, an offering made by fire, a pleasing aroma. All the fat is the LORD's. Lev 1:10; 7:4

[17]" 'This is a lasting ordinance for the generations to come, wherever you live: You must not eat any fat or any blood.' "

The Sin Offering

4 The LORD said to Moses, [2]"Say to the Israelites: 'When anyone sins unintentionally and does what is for-bidden in any of the LORD's commands— Lev 5:15-18; Heb 9:7

[3]" 'If the anointed priest sins, bringing guilt on the people, he must bring to the LORD a young bull without defect as a sin of-fering for the sin he has commit-ted. [4]He is to present the bull at the entrance to the Tent of Meeting before the LORD. He is to lay his hand on its head and slaughter it before the LORD. [5]Then the anointed priest shall take some of the bull's blood and carry it into the Tent of Meeting. [6]He is to dip his finger into the blood and sprinkle some of it seven times before the LORD, in front of the curtain of the sanctuary. [7]The priest shall then put some of the blood on the horns of the altar of fra-grant incense that is before the LORD in the Tent of Meeting. The rest of the bull's blood he shall pour out at the base of the altar of burnt offering at the en-trance to the Tent of Meeting. [8]He shall remove all the fat from the bull of the sin offering—the fat that covers the inner parts or is connected to them, [9]both kid-neys with the fat on them near the loins, and the covering of the liver, which he will remove with the kidneys— [10]just as the fat is removed from the ox[a] sac-rificed as a fellowship offering.[b] Then the priest shall burn them on the altar of burnt offering. [11]But the hide of the bull and all

---

[a]10 The Hebrew word can include both male and female.   [b]10 Traditionally *peace offering*; also in verses 26, 31 and 35

its flesh, as well as the head and legs, the inner parts and offal— 12that is, all the rest of the bull—he must take outside the camp to a place ceremonially clean, where the ashes are thrown, and burn it in a wood fire on the ash heap.   Ex 28:41

13" 'If the whole Israelite community sins unintentionally and does what is forbidden in any of the LORD's commands, even though the community is unaware of the matter, they are guilty. 14When they become aware of the sin they committed, the assembly must bring a young bull as a sin offering and present it before the Tent of Meeting. 15The elders of the community are to lay their hands on the bull's head before the LORD, and the bull shall be slaughtered before the LORD. 16Then the anointed priest is to take some of the bull's blood into the Tent of Meeting. 17He shall dip his finger into the blood and sprinkle it before the LORD seven times in front of the curtain. 18He is to put some of the blood on the horns of the altar that is before the LORD in the Tent of Meeting. The rest of the blood he shall pour out at the base of the altar of burnt offering at the entrance to the Tent of Meeting. 19He shall remove all the fat from it and burn it on the altar, 20and do with this bull just as he did with the bull for the sin offering. In this way the priest will make atonement for them, and they will be forgiven. 21Then he shall take the bull outside the camp and burn it as he burned the first bull. This is the sin offering for the community.   Nu 15:24-26

22" 'When a leader sins unintentionally and does what is forbidden in any of the commands of the LORD his God, he is guilty. 23When he is made aware of the sin he committed, he must bring as his offering a male goat without defect. 24He is to lay his hand on the goat's head and slaughter it at the place where the burnt offering is slaughtered before the LORD. It is a sin offering. 25Then the priest shall take some of the blood of the sin offering with his finger and put it on the horns of the altar of burnt offering and pour out the rest of the blood at the base of the altar. 26He shall burn all the fat on the altar as he burned the fat of the fellowship offering. In this way the priest will make atonement for the man's sin, and he will be forgiven.   Lev 16:18

27" 'If a member of the community sins unintentionally and does what is forbidden in any of the LORD's commands, he is guilty. 28When he is made aware of the sin he committed, he must bring as his offering for the sin he committed a female goat without defect. 29He is to lay his hand on the head of the sin offering and slaughter it at the place of the burnt offering.

³⁰Then the priest is to take some of the blood with his finger and put it on the horns of the altar of burnt offering and pour out the rest of the blood at the base of the altar. ³¹He shall remove all the fat, just as the fat is removed from the fellowship offering, and the priest shall burn it on the altar as an aroma pleasing to the Lord. In this way the priest will make atonement for him, and he will be forgiven.   Lev 5:6

³²" 'If he brings a lamb as his sin offering, he is to bring a female without defect. ³³He is to lay his hand on its head and slaughter it for a sin offering at the place where the burnt offering is slaughtered. ³⁴Then the priest shall take some of the blood of the sin offering with his finger and put it on the horns of the altar of burnt offering and pour out the rest of the blood at the base of the altar. ³⁵He shall remove all the fat, just as the fat is removed from the lamb of the fellowship offering, and the priest shall burn it on the altar on top of the offerings made to the Lord by fire. In this way the priest will make atonement for him for the sin he has committed, and he will be forgiven.   Ex 29:38; Lev 1:4; 9:3

5 " 'If a person sins because he does not speak up when he hears a public charge to testify regarding something he has seen or learned about, he will be held responsible.   Pr 29:24

²" 'Or if a person touches anything ceremonially un- clean—whether the carcasses of unclean wild animals or of un- clean livestock or of unclean creatures that move along the ground—even though he is un- aware of it, he has become un- clean and is guilty.   Lev 11:11

³" 'Or if he touches human uncleanness—anything that would make him unclean— even though he is unaware of it, when he learns of it he will be guilty.

⁴" 'Or if a person thought- lessly takes an oath to do any- thing, whether good or evil—in any matter one might carelessly swear about—even though he is unaware of it, in any case when he learns of it he will be guilty.

⁵" 'When anyone is guilty in any of these ways, he must con- fess in what way he has sinned ⁶and, as a penalty for the sin he has committed, he must bring to the Lord a female lamb or goat from the flock as a sin offer- ing; and the priest shall make atonement for him for his sin.

⁷" 'If he cannot afford a lamb, he is to bring two doves or two young pigeons to the Lord as a penalty for his sin—one for a sin offering and the other for a burnt offering. ⁸He is to bring them to the priest, who shall first offer the one for the sin of- fering. He is to wring its head from its neck, not severing it completely, ⁹and is to sprinkle some of the blood of the sin of- fering against the side of the al- tar; the rest of the blood must be

drained out at the base of the altar. It is a sin offering. ¹⁰The priest shall then offer the other as a burnt offering in the prescribed way and make atonement for him for the sin he has committed, and he will be forgiven. _{Lev 1:14-17; 4:7; 12:8}

¹¹" 'If, however, he cannot afford two doves or two young pigeons, he is to bring as an offering for his sin a tenth of an ephah*ᵃ* of fine flour for a sin offering. He must not put oil or incense on it, because it is a sin offering. ¹²He is to bring it to the priest, who shall take a handful of it as a memorial portion and burn it on the altar on top of the offerings made to the LORD by fire. It is a sin offering. ¹³In this way the priest will make atonement for him for any of these sins he has committed, and he will be forgiven. The rest of the offering will belong to the priest, as in the case of the grain offering.' " _{Ex 16:36; Lev 2:1-2}

The Guilt Offering

¹⁴The LORD said to Moses: ¹⁵"When a person commits a violation and sins unintentionally in regard to any of the LORD's holy things, he is to bring to the LORD as a penalty a ram from the flock, one without defect and of the proper value in silver, according to the sanctuary shekel.ᵇ It is a guilt offering. ¹⁶He must make restitution for what he has failed to do in regard to the holy things, add a fifth of the value to that and give it all to the priest, who will make atonement for him with the ram as a guilt offering, and he will be forgiven. _{Ex 30:13}

¹⁷"If a person sins and does what is forbidden in any of the LORD's commands, even though he does not know it, he is guilty and will be held responsible. ¹⁸He is to bring to the priest as a guilt offering a ram from the flock, one without defect and of the proper value. In this way the priest will make atonement for him for the wrong he has committed unintentionally, and he will be forgiven. ¹⁹It is a guilt offering; he has been guilty ofᶜ wrongdoing against the LORD." _{Lev 6:6; 14:12}

6 The LORD said to Moses: ²"If anyone sins and is unfaithful to the LORD by deceiving his neighbor about something entrusted to him or left in his care or stolen, or if he cheats him, ³or if he finds lost property and lies about it, or if he swears falsely, or if he commits any such sin that people may do— ⁴when he thus sins and becomes guilty, he must return what he has stolen or taken by extortion, or what was entrusted to him, or the lost property he found, ⁵or whatever it was he swore falsely about. He must make restitution in full, add a fifth of the

value to it and give it all to the owner on the day he presents his guilt offering. ⁶And as a penalty he must bring to the priest, that is, to the LORD, his guilt offering, a ram from the flock, one without defect and of the proper value. ⁷In this way the priest will make atonement for him before the LORD, and he will be forgiven for any of these things he did that made him guilty." Lev 5:16; Nu 5:6

The Burnt Offering

⁸The LORD said to Moses: ⁹"Give Aaron and his sons this command: 'These are the regulations for the burnt offering: The burnt offering is to remain on the altar hearth throughout the night, till morning, and the fire must be kept burning on the altar. ¹⁰The priest shall then put on his linen clothes, with linen undergarments next to his body, and shall remove the ashes of the burnt offering that the fire has consumed on the altar and place them beside the altar. ¹¹Then he is to take off these clothes and put on others, and carry the ashes outside the camp to a place that is ceremonially clean. ¹²The fire on the altar must be kept burning; it must not go out. Every morning the priest is to add firewood and arrange the burnt offering on the fire and burn the fat of the

fellowship offerings*ᵃ* on it. ¹³The fire must be kept burning on the altar continuously; it must not go out. Ex 39:27; Lev 7:37

The Grain Offering

¹⁴" 'These are the regulations for the grain offering: Aaron's sons are to bring it before the LORD, in front of the altar. ¹⁵The priest is to take a handful of fine flour and oil, together with all the incense on the grain offering, and burn the memorial portion on the altar as an aroma pleasing to the LORD. ¹⁶Aaron and his sons shall eat the rest of it, but it is to be eaten without yeast in a holy place; they are to eat it in the courtyard of the Tent of Meeting. ¹⁷It must not be baked with yeast; I have given it as their share of the offerings made to me by fire. Like the sin offering and the guilt offering, it is most holy. ¹⁸Any male descendant of Aaron may eat it. It is his regular share of the offerings made to the LORD by fire for the generations to come. Whatever touches them will become holy.*ᵇ* " Lev 2:1; Eze 44:29

¹⁹The LORD also said to Moses, ²⁰"This is the offering Aaron and his sons are to bring to the LORD on the day he*ᶜ* is anointed: a tenth of an ephah*ᵈ* of fine flour as a regular grain offering, half of it in the morning and half in the evening.

---

*ᵃ*12 Traditionally *peace offerings*   *ᵇ*18 Or *Whoever touches them must be holy;* similarly in verse 27   *ᶜ*20 Or *each*   *ᵈ*20 That is, probably about 2 quarts (about 2 liters)

21Prepare it with oil on a griddle; bring it well-mixed and present the grain offering broken*a* in pieces as an aroma pleasing to the LORD. 22The son who is to succeed him as anointed priest shall prepare it. It is the LORD's regular share and is to be burned completely. 23Every grain offering of a priest shall be burned completely; it must not be eaten."

Ex 29:1; Lev 2:5

The Sin Offering

24The LORD said to Moses, 25"Say to Aaron and his sons: 'These are the regulations for the sin offering: The sin offering is to be slaughtered before the LORD in the place the burnt offering is slaughtered; it is most holy. 26The priest who offers it shall eat it; it is to be eaten in a holy place, in the courtyard of the Tent of Meeting. 27Whatever touches any of the flesh will become holy, and if any of the blood is spattered on a garment, you must wash it in a holy place. 28The clay pot the meat is cooked in must be broken; but if it is cooked in a bronze pot, the pot is to be scoured and rinsed with water. 29Any male in a priest's family may eat it; it is most holy. 30But any sin offering whose blood is brought into the Tent of Meeting to make atonement in the Holy Place must not be eaten; it must be burned.

The Guilt Offering

7 " 'These are the regulations for the guilt offering, which is most holy: 2The guilt offering is to be slaughtered in the place where the burnt offering is slaughtered, and its blood is to be sprinkled against the altar on all sides. 3All its fat shall be offered: the fat tail and the fat that covers the inner parts, 4both kidneys with the fat on them near the loins, and the covering of the liver, which is to be removed with the kidneys. 5The priest shall burn them on the altar as an offering made to the LORD by fire. It is a guilt offering. 6Any male in a priest's family may eat it, but it must be eaten in a holy place; it is most holy.

Ex 29:13; Lev 5:15

7" 'The same law applies to both the sin offering and the guilt offering: They belong to the priest who makes atonement with them. 8The priest who offers a burnt offering for anyone may keep its hide for himself. 9Every grain offering baked in an oven or cooked in a pan or on a griddle belongs to the priest who offers it, 10and every grain offering, whether mixed with oil or dry, belongs equally to all the sons of Aaron.

The Fellowship Offering

11" 'These are the regulations for the fellowship offering*b* a

---

a21 The meaning of the Hebrew for this word is uncertain.   *b11* Traditionally *peace offering*; also in verses 13-37

person may present to the LORD:

12" 'If he offers it as an expression of thankfulness, then along with this thank offering he is to offer cakes of bread made without yeast and mixed with oil, wafers made without yeast and spread with oil, and cakes of fine flour well-kneaded and mixed with oil. 13Along with his fellowship offering of thanksgiving he is to present an offering with cakes of bread made with yeast. 14He is to bring one of each kind as an offering, a contribution to the LORD; it belongs to the priest who sprinkles the blood of the fellowship offerings. 15The meat of his fellowship offering of thanksgiving must be eaten on the day it is offered; he must leave none of it till morning.   Lev 22:29

16" 'If, however, his offering is the result of a vow or is a freewill offering, the sacrifice shall be eaten on the day he offers it, but anything left over may be eaten on the next day. 17Any meat of the sacrifice left over till the third day must be burned up. 18If any meat of the fellowship offering is eaten on the third day, it will not be accepted. It will not be credited to the one who offered it, for it is impure; the person who eats any of it will be held responsible.   Lev 19:6-8; Nu 18:27

19" 'Meat that touches anything ceremonially unclean

must not be eaten; it must be burned up. As for other meat, anyone ceremonially clean may eat it. 20But if anyone who is unclean eats any meat of the fellowship offering belonging to the LORD, that person must be cut off from his people. 21If anyone touches something unclean—whether human uncleanness or an unclean animal or any unclean, detestable thing—and then eats any of the meat of the fellowship offering belonging to the LORD, that person must be cut off from his people.' "   Ge 17:14; Lev 22:3

Eating Fat and Blood Forbidden

22The LORD said to Moses, 23"Say to the Israelites: 'Do not eat any of the fat of cattle, sheep or goats. 24The fat of an animal found dead or torn by wild animals may be used for any other purpose, but you must not eat it. 25Anyone who eats the fat of an animal from which an offering by fire may be*a* made to the LORD must be cut off from his people. 26And wherever you live, you must not eat the blood of any bird or animal. 27If anyone eats blood, that person must be cut off from his people.' "   Ex 22:31; Lev 17:3

The Priests' Share

28The LORD said to Moses, 29"Say to the Israelites: 'Anyone who brings a fellowship offer-

a25 Or fire is

ing to the LORD is to bring part of it as his sacrifice to the LORD. ³⁰With his own hands he is to bring the offering made to the LORD by fire; he is to bring the fat, together with the breast, and wave the breast before the LORD as a wave offering. ³¹The priest shall burn the fat on the altar, but the breast belongs to Aaron and his sons. ³²You are to give the right thigh of your fellowship offerings to the priest as a contribution. ³³The son of Aaron who offers the blood and the fat of the fellowship offering shall have the right thigh as his share. ³⁴From the fellowship offerings of the Israelites, I have taken the breast that is waved and the thigh that is presented and have given them to Aaron the priest and his sons as their regular share from the Israelites.' "   Ex 29:24; Lev 3:1

³⁵This is the portion of the offerings made to the LORD by fire that were allotted to Aaron and his sons on the day they were presented to serve the LORD as priests. ³⁶On the day they were anointed, the LORD commanded that the Israelites give this to them as their regular share for the generations to come.   Lev 8:12,30

³⁷These, then, are the regulations for the burnt offering, the grain offering, the sin offering, the guilt offering, the ordination offering and the fellowship offering, ³⁸which the LORD gave Moses on Mount Sinai on the day he commanded the Israelites to bring their offerings to the LORD, in the Desert of Sinai.

The Ordination of Aaron and His Sons

8 The LORD said to Moses, ²"Bring Aaron and his sons, their garments, the anointing oil, the bull for the sin offering, the two rams and the basket containing bread made without yeast, ³and gather the entire assembly at the entrance to the Tent of Meeting." ⁴Moses did as the LORD commanded him, and the assembly gathered at the entrance to the Tent of Meeting.

⁵Moses said to the assembly, "This is what the LORD has commanded to be done." ⁶Then Moses brought Aaron and his sons forward and washed them with water. ⁷He put the tunic on Aaron, tied the sash around him, clothed him with the robe and put the ephod on him. He also tied the ephod to him by its skillfully woven waistband; so it was fastened on him. ⁸He placed the breastpiece on him and put the Urim and Thummim in the breastpiece. ⁹Then he placed the turban on Aaron's head and set the gold plate, the sacred diadem, on the front of it, as the LORD commanded Moses.   Ex 29:1; Ac 22:16

¹⁰Then Moses took the anointing oil and anointed the tabernacle and everything in it,

and so consecrated them. [11]He sprinkled some of the oil on the altar seven times, anointing the altar and all its utensils and the basin with its stand, to consecrate them. [12]He poured some of the anointing oil on Aaron's head and anointed him to consecrate him. [13]Then he brought Aaron's sons forward, put tunics on them, tied sashes around them and put headbands on them, as the LORD commanded Moses. Ex 30:26

[14]He then presented the bull for the sin offering, and Aaron and his sons laid their hands on its head. [15]Moses slaughtered the bull and took some of the blood, and with his finger he put it on all the horns of the altar to purify the altar. He poured out the rest of the blood at the base of the altar. So he consecrated it to make atonement for it. [16]Moses also took all the fat around the inner parts, the covering of the liver, and both kidneys and their fat, and burned it on the altar. [17]But the bull with its hide and its flesh and its offal he burned up outside the camp, as the LORD commanded Moses. Ex 29:10; Heb 9:22

[18]He then presented the ram for the burnt offering, and Aaron and his sons laid their hands on its head. [19]Then Moses slaughtered the ram and sprinkled the blood against the altar on all sides. [20]He cut the ram into pieces and burned the head, the pieces and the fat.

[21]He washed the inner parts and the legs with water and burned the whole ram on the altar as a burnt offering, a pleasing aroma, an offering made to the LORD by fire, as the LORD commanded Moses. Ex 29:15; Lev 1:8

[22]He then presented the other ram, the ram for the ordination, and Aaron and his sons laid their hands on its head. [23]Moses slaughtered the ram and took some of its blood and put it on the lobe of Aaron's right ear, on the thumb of his right hand and on the big toe of his right foot. [24]Moses also brought Aaron's sons forward and put some of the blood on the lobes of their right ears, on the thumbs of their right hands and on the big toes of their right feet. Then he sprinkled blood against the altar on all sides. [25]He took the fat, the fat tail, all the fat around the inner parts, the covering of the liver, both kidneys and their fat and the right thigh. [26]Then from the basket of bread made without yeast, which was before the LORD, he took a cake of bread, and one made with oil, and a wafer; he put these on the fat portions and on the right thigh. [27]He put all these in the hands of Aaron and his sons and waved them before the LORD as a wave offering. [28]Then Moses took them from their hands and burned them on the altar on top of the burnt offering as an ordination offering, a pleasing aroma, an offering made to the

LORD by fire. [29]He also took the breast—Moses' share of the ordination ram—and waved it before the LORD as a wave offering, as the LORD commanded Moses. Ex 29:19

[30]Then Moses took some of the anointing oil and some of the blood from the altar and sprinkled them on Aaron and his garments and on his sons and their garments. So he consecrated Aaron and his garments and his sons and their garments. Ex 30:30; Nu 3:3

[31]Moses then said to Aaron and his sons, "Cook the meat at the entrance to the Tent of Meeting and eat it there with the bread from the basket of ordination offerings, as I commanded, saying,[a] 'Aaron and his sons are to eat it.' [32]Then burn up the rest of the meat and the bread. [33]Do not leave the entrance to the Tent of Meeting for seven days, until the days of your ordination are completed, for your ordination will last seven days. [34]What has been done today was commanded by the LORD to make atonement for you. [35]You must stay at the entrance to the Tent of Meeting day and night for seven days and do what the LORD requires, so you will not die; for that is what I have been commanded." [36]So Aaron and his sons did everything the LORD commanded through Moses. Lev 6:16

The Priests Begin Their Ministry

9 On the eighth day Moses summoned Aaron and his sons and the elders of Israel. [2]He said to Aaron, "Take a bull calf for your sin offering and a ram for your burnt offering, both without defect, and present them before the LORD. [3]Then say to the Israelites: 'Take a male goat for a sin offering, a calf and a lamb—both a year old and without defect—for a burnt offering, [4]and an ox[b] and a ram for a fellowship offering[c] to sacrifice before the LORD, together with a grain offering mixed with oil. For today the LORD will appear to you.' " Lev 4:3; Eze 43:27

[5]They took the things Moses commanded to the front of the Tent of Meeting, and the entire assembly came near and stood before the LORD. [6]Then Moses said, "This is what the LORD has commanded you to do, so that the glory of the LORD may appear to you." Ex 16:7; 24:16

[7]Moses said to Aaron, "Come to the altar and sacrifice your sin offering and your burnt offering and make atonement for yourself and the people; sacrifice the offering that is for the people and make atonement for them, as the LORD has commanded."

[8]So Aaron came to the altar and slaughtered the calf as a sin offering for himself. [9]His sons brought the blood to him, and

---

[a]31 Or I was commanded: also in verses 18 and 19.   [b]4 The Hebrew word can include both male and female; [c]4 Traditionally peace offering; also in verses 18 and 22

he dipped his finger into the blood and put it on the horns of the altar; the rest of the blood he poured out at the base of the altar. 10On the altar he burned the fat, the kidneys and the covering of the liver from the sin offering, as the LORD commanded Moses; 11the flesh and the hide he burned up outside the camp. Lev 4:1-12; Eze 43:20

12Then he slaughtered the burnt offering. His sons handed him the blood, and he sprinkled it against the altar on all sides. 13They handed him the burnt offering piece by piece, including the head, and he burned them on the altar. 14He washed the inner parts and the legs and burned them on top of the burnt offering on the altar. Lev 10:19

15Aaron then brought the offering that was for the people. He took the goat for the people's sin offering and slaughtered it and offered it for a sin offering as he did with the first one. Lev 4:27-31

16He brought the burnt offering and offered it in the prescribed way. 17He also brought the grain offering, took a handful of it and burned it on the altar in addition to the morning's burnt offering. Lev 1:1-13

18He slaughtered the ox and the ram as the fellowship offering for the people. His sons handed him the blood, and he sprinkled it against the altar on all sides. 19But the fat portions of the ox and the ram—the fat tail, the layer of fat, the kidneys and

the covering of the liver— 20these they laid on the breasts, and then Aaron burned the fat on the altar. 21Aaron waved the breasts and the right thigh before the LORD as a wave offering, as Moses commanded.

22Then Aaron lifted his hands toward the people and blessed them. And having sacrificed the sin offering, the burnt offering and the fellowship offering, he stepped down. Ge 48:20; Lk 24:50

23Moses and Aaron then went into the Tent of Meeting. When they came out, they blessed the people; and the glory of the LORD appeared to all the people. 24Fire came out from the presence of the LORD and consumed the burnt offering and the fat portions on the altar. And when all the people saw it, they shouted for joy and fell facedown. Nu 14:10; 1Ki 18:39

The Death of Nadab and Abihu

10 Aaron's sons Nadab and Abihu took their censers, put fire in them and added incense; and they offered unauthorized fire before the LORD, contrary to his command. 2So fire came out from the presence of the LORD and consumed them, and they died before the LORD. 3Moses then said to Aaron, "This is what the LORD spoke of when he said:

" 'Among those who
     approach me
I will show myself holy;

in the sight of all the people I will be honored.'" Ex 14:4

Aaron remained silent.

[4]Moses summoned Mishael and Elzaphan, sons of Aaron's uncle Uzziel, and said to them, "Come here; carry your cousins outside the camp, away from the front of the sanctuary." [5]So they came and carried them, still in their tunics, outside the camp, as Moses ordered. Ex 6:22

[6]Then Moses said to Aaron and his sons Eleazar and Ithamar, "Do not let your hair become unkempt,[a] and do not tear your clothes, or you will die and the LORD will be angry with the whole community. But your relatives, all the house of Israel, may mourn for those the LORD has destroyed by fire. [7]Do not leave the entrance to the Tent of Meeting or you will die, because the LORD's anointing oil is on you." So they did as Moses said. Nu 16:22; Jos 7:1

[8]Then the LORD said to Aaron, [9]"You and your sons are not to drink wine or other fermented drink whenever you go into the Tent of Meeting, or you will die. This is a lasting ordinance for the generations to come. [10]You must distinguish between the holy and the common, between the unclean and the clean, [11]and you must teach the Israelites all the decrees the LORD has given them through Moses." Lev 20:25; Eze 44:21

[12]Moses said to Aaron and his remaining sons, Eleazar and Ithamar, "Take the grain offering left over from the offerings made to the LORD by fire and eat it prepared without yeast beside the altar, for it is most holy. [13]Eat it in a holy place, because it is your share and your sons' share of the offerings made to the LORD by fire; for so I have been commanded. [14]But you and your sons and your daughters may eat the breast that was waved and the thigh that was presented. Eat them in a ceremonially clean place; they have been given to you and your children as your share of the Israelites' fellowship offerings.[b] [15]The thigh that was presented and the breast that was waved must be brought with the fat portions of the offerings made by fire, to be waved before the LORD as a wave offering. This will be the regular share for you and your children, as the LORD has commanded." Ex 29:31; Lev 6:14

[16]When Moses inquired about the goat of the sin offering and found that it had been burned up, he was angry with Eleazar and Ithamar, Aaron's remaining sons, and asked, [17]"Why didn't you eat the sin offering in the sanctuary area? It is most holy; it was given to you to take away the guilt of the community by making atonement for them before the LORD. [18]Since its blood was not taken into the Holy Place, you should

---

[a]6 Or *Do not uncover your heads*   [b]14 Traditionally *peace offerings*

have eaten the goat in the sanctuary area, as I commanded."

[19]Aaron replied to Moses, "Today they sacrificed their sin offering and their burnt offering before the Lord, but such things as this have happened to me. Would the Lord have been pleased if I had eaten the sin offering today?" [20]When Moses heard this, he was satisfied.

Clean and Unclean Food

11 The Lord said to Moses and Aaron, [2]"Say to the Israelites: 'Of all the animals that live on land, these are the ones you may eat: [3]You may eat any animal that has a split hoof completely divided and that chews the cud.   Dt 14:3-21

[4]" 'There are some that only chew the cud or only have a split hoof, but you must not eat them. The camel, though it chews the cud, does not have a split hoof; it is ceremonially unclean for you. [5]The coney,[a] though it chews the cud, does not have a split hoof; it is unclean for you. [6]The rabbit, though it chews the cud, does not have a split hoof; it is unclean for you. [7]And the pig, though it has a split hoof completely divided, does not chew the cud; it is unclean for you. [8]You must not eat their meat or touch their carcasses; they are unclean for you.   Ac 10:14

[9]" 'Of all the creatures living in the water of the seas and the streams, you may eat any that have fins and scales. [10]But all creatures in the seas or streams that do not have fins and scales—whether among all the swarming things or among all the other living creatures in the water—you are to detest. [11]And since you are to detest them, you must not eat their meat and you must detest their carcasses. [12]Anything living in the water that does not have fins and scales is to be detestable to you.

[13]" 'These are the birds you are to detest and not eat because they are detestable: the eagle, the vulture, the black vulture, [14]the red kite, any kind of black kite, [15]any kind of raven, [16]the horned owl, the screech owl, the gull, any kind of hawk, [17]the little owl, the cormorant, the great owl, [18]the white owl, the desert owl, the osprey, [19]the stork, any kind of heron, the hoopoe and the bat.[b]   Dt 14:17

[20]" 'All flying insects that walk on all fours are to be detestable to you. [21]There are, however, some winged creatures that walk on all fours that you may eat: those that have jointed legs for hopping on the ground. [22]Of these you may eat any kind of locust, katydid, cricket or grasshopper. [23]But all other winged creatures that have four legs you are to detest.

[24]" 'You will make yourselves

---

[a]5 That is, the hyrax or rock badger   [b]19 The precise identification of some of the birds, insects and animals in this chapter is uncertain.

unclean by these; whoever touches their carcasses will be unclean till evening. 25Whoever picks up one of their carcasses must wash his clothes, and he will be unclean till evening.

26" 'Every animal that has a split hoof not completely divided or that does not chew the cud is unclean for you; whoever touches the carcass of any of them will be unclean. 27Of all the animals that walk on all fours, those that walk on their paws are unclean for you; whoever touches their carcasses will be unclean till evening. 28Anyone who picks up their carcasses must wash his clothes, and he will be unclean till evening. They are unclean for you.

29" 'Of the animals that move about on the ground, these are unclean for you: the weasel, the rat, any kind of great lizard, 30the gecko, the monitor lizard, the wall lizard, the skink and the chameleon. 31Of all those that move along the ground, these are unclean for you. Whoever touches them when they are dead will be unclean till evening. 32When one of them dies and falls on something, that article, whatever its use, will be unclean, whether it is made of wood, cloth, hide or sackcloth. Put it in water; it will be unclean till evening, and then it will be clean. 33If one of them falls into a clay pot, everything in it will be unclean, and you must break the pot. 34Any food that could be eaten but has water on it from such a pot is unclean, and any liquid that could be drunk from it is unclean. 35Anything that one of their carcasses falls on becomes unclean; an oven or cooking pot must be broken up. They are unclean, and you are to regard them as unclean. 36A spring, however, or a cistern for collecting water remains clean, but anyone who touches one of these carcasses is unclean. 37If a carcass falls on any seeds that are to be planted, they remain clean. 38But if water has been put on the seed and a carcass falls on it, it is unclean for you.

39" 'If an animal that you are allowed to eat dies, anyone who touches the carcass will be unclean till evening. 40Anyone who eats some of the carcass must wash his clothes, and he will be unclean till evening. Anyone who picks up the carcass must wash his clothes, and he will be unclean till evening.

41" 'Every creature that moves about on the ground is detestable; it is not to be eaten. 42You are not to eat any creature that moves about on the ground, whether it moves on its belly or walks on all fours or on many feet; it is detestable. 43Do not defile yourselves by any of these creatures. Do not make yourselves unclean by means of them or be made unclean by them. 44I am the LORD your God; consecrate yourselves and be holy, because I am holy. Do not make yourselves unclean by any creature that moves about

on the ground. 45I am the LORD who brought you up out of Egypt to be your God; therefore be holy, because I am holy.

46" 'These are the regulations concerning animals, birds, every living thing that moves in the water and every creature that moves about on the ground. 47You must distinguish between the unclean and the clean, between living creatures that may be eaten and those that may not be eaten.' " Lev 10:10

Purification After Childbirth

12 The LORD said to Moses, 2"Say to the Israelites: 'A woman who becomes pregnant and gives birth to a son will be ceremonially unclean for seven days, just as she is unclean during her monthly period. 3On the eighth day the boy is to be circumcised. 4Then the woman must wait thirty-three days to be purified from her bleeding. She must not touch anything sacred or go to the sanctuary until the days of her purification are over. 5If she gives birth to a daughter, for two weeks the woman will be unclean, as during her period. Then she must wait sixty-six days to be purified from her bleeding. Lev 15:19

6" 'When the days of her purification for a son or daughter are over, she is to bring to the priest at the entrance to the Tent of Meeting a year-old lamb

for a burnt offering and a young pigeon or a dove for a sin offering. 7He shall offer them before the LORD to make atonement for her, and then she will be ceremonially clean from her flow of blood. Lev 5:7; Lk 2:22

" 'These are the regulations for the woman who gives birth to a boy or a girl. 8If she cannot afford a lamb, she is to bring two doves or two young pigeons, one for a burnt offering and the other for a sin offering. In this way the priest will make atonement for her, and she will be clean.' " Lev 4:26; Lk 2:22-24

Regulations About Infectious Skin Diseases

13 The LORD said to Moses and Aaron, 2"When anyone has a swelling or a rash or a bright spot on his skin that may become an infectious skin disease,a he must be brought to Aaron the priest or to one of his sonsb who is a priest. 3The priest is to examine the sore on his skin, and if the hair in the sore has turned white and the sore appears to be more than skin deep,c it is an infectious skin disease. When the priest examines him, he shall pronounce him ceremonially unclean. 4If the spot on his skin is white but does not appear to be more than skin deep and the hair in it has not turned white,

---

a2 Traditionally *leprosy*; the Hebrew word was used for various diseases affecting the skin—not necessarily leprosy; also elsewhere in this chapter.   b2 Or *descendants*
c3 Or *be lower than the rest of the skin*; also elsewhere in this chapter

the priest is to put the infected person in isolation for seven days. ⁵On the seventh day the priest is to examine him, and if he sees that the sore is unchanged and has not spread in the skin, he is to keep him in isolation another seven days. ⁶On the seventh day the priest is to examine him again, and if the sore has faded and has not spread in the skin, the priest shall pronounce him clean; it is only a rash. The man must wash his clothes, and he will be clean. ⁷But if the rash does spread in his skin after he has shown himself to the priest to be pronounced clean, he must appear before the priest again. ⁸The priest is to examine him, and if the rash has spread in the skin, he shall pronounce him unclean; it is an infectious disease.   Lev 11:25; Dt 24:8

⁹"When anyone has an infectious skin disease, he must be brought to the priest. ¹⁰The priest is to examine him, and if there is a white swelling in the skin that has turned the hair white and if there is raw flesh in the swelling, ¹¹it is a chronic skin disease and the priest shall pronounce him unclean. He is not to put him in isolation, because he is already unclean.

¹²"If the disease breaks out all over his skin and, so far as the priest can see, it covers all the skin of the infected person from head to foot, ¹³the priest is to examine him, and if the disease has covered his whole body, he shall pronounce that person clean. Since it has all turned white, he is clean. ¹⁴But whenever raw flesh appears on him, he will be unclean. ¹⁵When the priest sees the raw flesh, he shall pronounce him unclean. The raw flesh is unclean; he has an infectious disease. ¹⁶Should the raw flesh change and turn white, he must go to the priest. ¹⁷The priest is to examine him, and if the sores have turned white, the priest shall pronounce the infected person clean; then he will be clean.

¹⁸"When someone has a boil on his skin and it heals, ¹⁹and in the place where the boil was, a white swelling or reddish-white spot appears, he must present himself to the priest. ²⁰The priest is to examine it, and if it appears to be more than skin deep and the hair in it has turned white, the priest shall pronounce him unclean. It is an infectious skin disease that has broken out where the boil was. ²¹But if, when the priest examines it, there is no white hair in it and it is not more than skin deep and has faded, then the priest is to put him in isolation for seven days. ²²If it is spreading in the skin, the priest shall pronounce him unclean; it is infectious. ²³But if the spot is unchanged and has not spread, it is only a scar from the boil, and the priest shall pronounce him clean.   Ex 9:9; Lev 14:37

²⁴"When someone has a burn on his skin and a reddish-white

or white spot appears in the raw flesh of the burn, ²⁵the priest is to examine the spot, and if the hair in it has turned white, and it appears to be more than skin deep, it is an infectious disease that has broken out in the burn. The priest shall pronounce him unclean; it is an infectious skin disease. ²⁶But if the priest examines it and there is no white hair in the spot and if it is not more than skin deep and has faded, then the priest is to put him in isolation for seven days. ²⁷On the seventh day the priest is to examine him, and if it is spreading in the skin, the priest shall pronounce him unclean; it is an infectious skin disease. ²⁸If, however, the spot is unchanged and has not spread in the skin but has faded, it is a swelling from the burn, and the priest shall pronounce him clean; it is only a scar from the burn.

²⁹"If a man or woman has a sore on the head or on the chin, ³⁰the priest is to examine the sore, and if it appears to be more than skin deep and the hair in it is yellow and thin, the priest shall pronounce that person unclean; it is an itch, an infectious disease of the head or chin. ³¹But if, when the priest examines this kind of sore, it does not seem to be more than skin deep and there is no black hair in it, then the priest is to put the infected person in isolation for seven days. ³²On the seventh day the priest is to examine the sore, and if the itch

has not spread and there is no yellow hair in it and it does not appear to be more than skin deep, ³³he must be shaved except for the diseased area, and the priest is to keep him in isolation another seven days. ³⁴On the seventh day the priest is to examine the itch, and if it has not spread in the skin and appears to be no more than skin deep, the priest shall pronounce him clean. He must wash his clothes, and he will be clean. ³⁵But if the itch does spread in the skin after he is pronounced clean, ³⁶the priest is to examine him, and if the itch has spread in the skin, the priest does not need to look for yellow hair; the person is unclean. ³⁷If, however, in his judgment it is unchanged and black hair has grown in it, the itch is healed. He is clean, and the priest shall pronounce him clean.   Lev 11:25; 14:8

³⁸"When a man or woman has white spots on the skin, ³⁹the priest is to examine them, and if the spots are dull white, it is a harmless rash that has broken out on the skin; that person is clean.

⁴⁰"When a man has lost his hair and is bald, he is clean. ⁴¹If he has lost his hair from the front of his scalp and has a bald forehead, he is clean. ⁴²But if he has a reddish-white sore on his bald head or forehead, it is an infectious disease breaking out on his head or forehead. ⁴³The priest is to examine him, and if

the swollen sore on his head or forehead is reddish-white like an infectious skin disease, [44]the man is diseased and is unclean. The priest shall pronounce him unclean because of the sore on his head.   2Ki 2:23; Eze 29:18

[45]"The person with such an infectious disease must wear torn clothes, let his hair be unkempt,[a] cover the lower part of his face and cry out, 'Unclean! Unclean!' [46]As long as he has the infection he remains unclean. He must live alone; he must live outside the camp.

Regulations About Mildew

[47]"If any clothing is contaminated with mildew—any woolen or linen clothing, [48]any woven or knitted material of linen or wool, any leather or anything made of leather— [49]and if the contamination in the clothing, or leather, or woven or knitted material, or any leather article, is greenish or reddish, it is a spreading mildew and must be shown to the priest. [50]The priest is to examine the mildew and isolate the affected article for seven days. [51]On the seventh day he is to examine it, and if the mildew has spread in the clothing, or the woven or knitted material, or the leather, whatever its use, it is a destructive mildew; the article is unclean. [52]He must burn up the clothing, or the woven or knitted material of wool or linen, or

any leather article that has the contamination in it, because the mildew is destructive; the article must be burned up.   Mk 1:44

[53]"But if, when the priest examines it, the mildew has not spread in the clothing, or the woven or knitted material, or the leather article, [54]he shall order that the contaminated article be washed. Then he is to isolate it for another seven days. [55]After the affected article has been washed, the priest is to examine it, and if the mildew has not changed its appearance, even though it has not spread, it is unclean. Burn it with fire, whether the mildew has affected one side or the other. [56]If, when the priest examines it, the mildew has faded after the article has been washed, he is to tear the contaminated part out of the clothing, or the leather, or the woven or knitted material. [57]But if it reappears in the clothing, or in the woven or knitted material, or in the leather article, it is spreading, and whatever has the mildew must be burned with fire. [58]The clothing, or the woven or knitted material, or any leather article that has been washed and is rid of the mildew, must be washed again, and it will be clean."   Lev 14:8

[59]These are the regulations concerning contamination by mildew in woolen or linen clothing, woven or knitted material, or any leather article, for

---

[a]45 Or *clothes, uncover his head*

pronouncing them clean or unclean.

Cleansing From Infectious Skin Diseases

14 The LORD said to Moses, 2"These are the regulations for the diseased person at the time of his ceremonial cleansing, when he is brought to the priest: 3The priest is to go outside the camp and examine him. If the person has been healed of his infectious skin disease,ª 4the priest shall order that two live clean birds and some cedar wood, scarlet yarn and hyssop be brought for the one to be cleansed. 5Then the priest shall order that one of the birds be killed over fresh water in a clay pot. 6He is then to take the live bird and dip it, together with the cedar wood, the scarlet yarn and the hyssop, into the blood of the bird that was killed over the fresh water. 7Seven times he shall sprinkle the one to be cleansed of the infectious disease and pronounce him clean. Then he is to release the live bird in the open fields.

8"The person to be cleansed must wash his clothes, shave off all his hair and bathe with water; then he will be ceremonially clean. After this he may come into the camp, but he must stay outside his tent for seven days. 9On the seventh day he must shave off all his hair; he must shave his head, his beard, his eyebrows and the rest of his hair. He must wash his clothes and bathe himself with water, and he will be clean.   Nu 8:7; 19:19; Dt 21:12

10"On the eighth day he must bring two male lambs and one ewe lamb a year old, each without defect, along with three-tenths of an ephahᵇ of fine flour mixed with oil for a grain offering, and one logᶜ of oil. 11The priest who pronounces him clean shall present both the one to be cleansed and his offerings before the LORD at the entrance to the Tent of Meeting.   Mt 8:4

12"Then the priest is to take one of the male lambs and offer it as a guilt offering, along with the log of oil; he shall wave them before the LORD as a wave offering. 13He is to slaughter the lamb in the holy place where the sin offering and the burnt offering are slaughtered. Like the sin offering, the guilt offering belongs to the priest; it is most holy. 14The priest is to take some of the blood of the guilt offering and put it on the lobe of the right ear of the one to be cleansed, on the thumb of his right hand and on the big toe of his right foot. 15The priest shall then take some of the log of oil, pour it in the palm of his own left hand, 16dip his right fore-

---

ª3 Traditionally *leprosy*; the Hebrew word was used for various diseases affecting the skin—not necessarily leprosy; also elsewhere in this chapter.   ᵇ10 That is, probably about 6 quarts (about 6.5 liters)   ᶜ10 That is, probably about 2/3 pint (about 0.3 liter); also in verses 12, 15, 21 and 24

finger into the oil in his palm, and with his finger sprinkle some of it before the LORD seven times. [17]The priest is to put some of the oil remaining in his palm on the lobe of the right ear of the one to be cleansed, on the thumb of his right hand and on the big toe of his right foot, on top of the blood of the guilt offering. [18]The rest of the oil in his palm the priest shall put on the head of the one to be cleansed and make atonement for him before the LORD. Lev 5:18

[19]"Then the priest is to sacrifice the sin offering and make atonement for the one to be cleansed from his uncleanness. After that, the priest shall slaughter the burnt offering [20]and offer it on the altar, together with the grain offering, and make atonement for him, and he will be clean. Lev 5:3

[21]"If, however, he is poor and cannot afford these, he must take one male lamb as a guilt offering to be waved to make atonement for him, together with a tenth of an ephah[a] of fine flour mixed with oil for a grain offering, a log of oil, [22]and two doves or two young pigeons, which he can afford, one for a sin offering and the other for a burnt offering. Lev 5:7; 15:30

[23]"On the eighth day he must bring them for his cleansing to the priest at the entrance to the Tent of Meeting, before the LORD. [24]The priest is to take the lamb for the guilt offering, together with the log of oil, and wave them before the LORD as a wave offering. [25]He shall slaughter the lamb for the guilt offering and take some of its blood and put it on the lobe of the right ear of the one to be cleansed, on the thumb of his right hand and on the big toe of his right foot. [26]The priest is to pour some of the oil into the palm of his own left hand, [27]and with his right forefinger sprinkle some of the oil from his palm seven times before the LORD. [28]Some of the oil in his palm he is to put on the same places he put the blood of the guilt offering—on the lobe of the right ear of the one to be cleansed, on the thumb of his right hand and on the big toe of his right foot. [29]The rest of the oil in his palm the priest shall put on the head of the one to be cleansed, to make atonement for him before the LORD. [30]Then he shall sacrifice the doves or the young pigeons, which the person can afford, [31]one[b] as a sin offering and the other as a burnt offering, together with the grain offering. In this way the priest will make atonement before the LORD on behalf of the one to be cleansed." Lev 5:7; 15:14

[32]These are the regulations for anyone who has an infectious skin disease and who can-

---

[a]21 That is, probably about 2 quarts (about 2 liters) Hebrew [31]such as the person can afford, one   [b]31 Septuagint and Syriac;

not afford the regular offerings for his cleansing. Lev 13:2

Cleansing From Mildew

33The LORD said to Moses and Aaron, 34"When you enter the land of Canaan, which I am giving you as your possession, and I put a spreading mildew in a house in that land, 35the owner of the house must go and tell the priest, 'I have seen something that looks like mildew in my house.' 36The priest is to order the house to be emptied before he goes in to examine the mildew, so that nothing in the house will be pronounced unclean. After this the priest is to go in and inspect the house. 37He is to examine the mildew on the walls, and if it has greenish or reddish depressions that appear to be deeper than the surface of the wall, 38the priest shall go out the doorway of the house and close it up for seven days. 39On the seventh day the priest shall return to inspect the house. If the mildew has spread on the walls, 40he is to order that the contaminated stones be torn out and thrown into an unclean place outside the town. 41He must have all the inside walls of the house scraped and the material that is scraped off dumped into an unclean place outside the town. 42Then they are to take other stones to replace these and take new clay and plaster the house. Ge 17:8

43"If the mildew reappears in the house after the stones have been torn out and the house scraped and plastered, 44the priest is to go and examine it and, if the mildew has spread in the house, it is a destructive mildew; the house is unclean. 45It must be torn down—its stones, timbers and all the plaster—and taken out of the town to an unclean place. Lev 13:51; Zec 5:4

46"Anyone who goes into the house while it is closed up will be unclean till evening. 47Anyone who sleeps or eats in the house must wash his clothes.

48"But if the priest comes to examine it and the mildew has not spread after the house has been plastered, he shall pronounce the house clean, because the mildew is gone. 49To purify the house he is to take two birds and some cedar wood, scarlet yarn and hyssop. 50He shall kill one of the birds over fresh water in a clay pot. 51Then he is to take the cedar wood, the hyssop, the scarlet yarn and the live bird, dip them into the blood of the dead bird and the fresh water, and sprinkle the house seven times. 52He shall purify the house with the bird's blood, the fresh water, the live bird, the cedar wood, the hyssop and the scarlet yarn. 53Then he is to release the live bird in the open fields outside the town. In this way he will make atonement for the house, and it will be clean." Lev 13:6

54These are the regulations for any infectious skin disease, for an itch, 55for mildew in cloth-

ing or in a house, ⁵⁶and for a swelling, a rash or a bright spot, ⁵⁷to determine when something is clean or unclean. Lev 10:10; 13:2

These are the regulations for infectious skin diseases and mildew.

Discharges Causing Uncleanness

15 The LORD said to Moses and Aaron, ²"Speak to the Israelites and say to them: 'When any man has a bodily discharge, the discharge is unclean. ³Whether it continues flowing from his body or is blocked, it will make him unclean. This is how his discharge will bring about uncleanness:

⁴" 'Any bed the man with a discharge lies on will be unclean, and anything he sits on will be unclean. ⁵Anyone who touches his bed must wash his clothes and bathe with water, and he will be unclean till evening. ⁶Whoever sits on anything that the man with a discharge sat on must wash his clothes and bathe with water, and he will be unclean till evening. Lev 11:25; 14:8

⁷" 'Whoever touches the man who has a discharge must wash his clothes and bathe with water, and he will be unclean till evening. Lev 22:5; Nu 19:19

⁸" 'If the man with the discharge spits on someone who is clean, that person must wash his clothes and bathe with

water, and he will be unclean till evening. Nu 12:14

⁹" 'Everything the man sits on when riding will be unclean, ¹⁰and whoever touches any of the things that were under him will be unclean till evening; whoever picks up those things must wash his clothes and bathe with water, and he will be unclean till evening. Nu 19:10

¹¹" 'Anyone the man with a discharge touches without rinsing his hands with water must wash his clothes and bathe with water, and he will be unclean till evening.

¹²" 'A clay pot that the man touches must be broken, and any wooden article is to be rinsed with water. Lev 6:28

¹³" 'When a man is cleansed from his discharge, he is to count off seven days for his ceremonial cleansing; he must wash his clothes and bathe himself with fresh water, and he will be clean. ¹⁴On the eighth day he must take two doves or two young pigeons and come before the LORD to the entrance to the Tent of Meeting and give them to the priest. ¹⁵The priest is to sacrifice them, the one for a sin offering and the other for a burnt offering. In this way he will make atonement before the LORD for the man because of his discharge. Lev 8:33; 14:22

¹⁶" 'When a man has an emission of semen, he must bathe his whole body with water, and he will be unclean till evening. ¹⁷Any clothing or leather that

has semen on it must be washed with water, and it will be unclean till evening. ¹⁸When a man lies with a woman and there is an emission of semen, both must bathe with water, and they will be unclean till evening. *Lev 22:4; Dt 23:10*

¹⁹ 'When a woman has her regular flow of blood, the impurity of her monthly period will last seven days, and anyone who touches her will be unclean till evening. *Lev 12:2*

²⁰ 'Anything she lies on during her period will be unclean, and anything she sits on will be unclean. ²¹Whoever touches her bed must wash his clothes and bathe with water, and he will be unclean till evening. ²²Whoever touches anything she sits on must wash his clothes and bathe with water, and he will be unclean till evening. ²³Whether it is the bed or anything she was sitting on, when anyone touches it, he will be unclean till evening. *Lev 15:27*

²⁴ 'If a man lies with her and her monthly flow touches him, he will be unclean for seven days; any bed he lies on will be unclean. *Lev 12:2; 18:19*

²⁵ 'When a woman has a discharge of blood for many days at a time other than her monthly period or has a discharge that continues beyond her period, she will be unclean as long as she has the discharge, just as in the days of her period. ²⁶Any bed she lies on while her discharge continues will be unclean, as is her bed during her monthly period, and anything she sits on will be unclean, as during her period. ²⁷Whoever touches them will be unclean; he must wash his clothes and bathe with water, and he will be unclean till evening. *Mt 9:20*

²⁸ 'When she is cleansed from her discharge, she must count off seven days, and after that she will be ceremonially clean. ²⁹On the eighth day she must take two doves or two young pigeons and bring them to the priest at the entrance to the Tent of Meeting. ³⁰The priest is to sacrifice one for a sin offering and the other for a burnt offering. In this way he will make atonement for her before the LORD for the uncleanness of her discharge. *Lev 14:22*

³¹ 'You must keep the Israelites separate from things that make them unclean, so they will not die in their uncleanness for defiling my dwelling place,ᵃ which is among them.' " *Nu 5:3*

³²These are the regulations for a man with a discharge, for anyone made unclean by an emission of semen, ³³for a woman in her monthly period, for a man or a woman with a discharge, and for a man who lies with a woman who is ceremonially unclean. *Lev 15:2*

ᵃ31 Or *my tabernacle*

The Day of Atonement

16 The LORD spoke to Moses after the death of the two sons of Aaron who died when they approached the LORD. ²The LORD said to Moses: "Tell your brother Aaron not to come whenever he chooses into the Most Holy Place behind the curtain in front of the atonement cover on the ark, or else he will die, because I appear in the cloud over the atonement cover. Ex 30:10; Lev 10:1

³"This is how Aaron is to enter the sanctuary area: with a young bull for a sin offering and a ram for a burnt offering. ⁴He is to put on the sacred linen tunic, with linen undergarments next to his body; he is to tie the linen sash around him and put on the linen turban. These are sacred garments; so he must bathe himself with water before he puts them on. ⁵From the Israelite community he is to take two male goats for a sin offering and a ram for a burnt offering. Lev 4:3

⁶"Aaron is to offer the bull for his own sin offering to make atonement for himself and his household. ⁷Then he is to take the two goats and present them before the LORD at the entrance to the Tent of Meeting. ⁸He is to cast lots for the two goats—one lot for the LORD and the other for the scapegoat.ᵃ ⁹Aaron shall bring the goat whose lot falls to the LORD and sacrifice it for a sin offering. ¹⁰But the goat chosen by lot as the scapegoat shall be presented alive before the LORD to be used for making atonement by sending it into the desert as a scapegoat. Lev 9:7

¹¹"Aaron shall bring the bull for his own sin offering to make atonement for himself and his household, and he is to slaughter the bull for his own sin offering. ¹²He is to take a censer full of burning coals from the altar before the LORD and two handfuls of finely ground fragrant incense and take them behind the curtain. ¹³He is to put the incense on the fire before the LORD, and the smoke of the incense will conceal the atonement cover above the Testimony, so that he will not die. ¹⁴He is to take some of the bull's blood and with his finger sprinkle it on the front of the atonement cover; then he shall sprinkle some of it with his finger seven times before the atonement cover. Ex 25:17; Lev 10:1

¹⁵"He shall then slaughter the goat for the sin offering for the people and take its blood behind the curtain and do with it as he did with the bull's blood: He shall sprinkle it on the atonement cover and in front of it. ¹⁶In this way he will make atonement for the Most Holy Place because of the uncleanness and rebellion of the Israelites, whatever their sins have been. He is to do the same for the Tent of Meeting, which is

ᵃ8 That is, the goat of removal; Hebrew *azazel*; also in verses 10 and 26

among them in the midst of their uncleanness. ¹⁷No one is to be in the Tent of Meeting from the time Aaron goes in to make atonement in the Most Holy Place until he comes out, having made atonement for himself, his household and the whole community of Israel. Heb 7:27

¹⁸"Then he shall come out to the altar that is before the LORD and make atonement for it. He shall take some of the bull's blood and some of the goat's blood and put it on all the horns of the altar. ¹⁹He shall sprinkle some of the blood on it with his finger seven times to cleanse it and to consecrate it from the uncleanness of the Israelites. Lev 4:25

²⁰"When Aaron has finished making atonement for the Most Holy Place, the Tent of Meeting and the altar, he shall bring forward the live goat. ²¹He is to lay both hands on the head of the live goat and confess over it all the wickedness and rebellion of the Israelites—all their sins— and put them on the goat's head. He shall send the goat away into the desert in the care of a man appointed for the task. ²²The goat will carry on itself all their sins to a solitary place; and the man shall release it in the desert. Ex 29:10; Lev 5:5

²³"Then Aaron is to go into the Tent of Meeting and take off the linen garments he put on before he entered the Most Holy Place, and he is to leave them

there. ²⁴He shall bathe himself with water in a holy place and put on his regular garments. Then he shall come out and sacrifice the burnt offering for himself and the burnt offering for the people, to make atonement for himself and for the people. ²⁵He shall also burn the fat of the sin offering on the altar. Eze 42:14

²⁶"The man who releases the goat as a scapegoat must wash his clothes and bathe himself with water; afterward he may come into the camp. ²⁷The bull and the goat for the sin offerings, whose blood was brought into the Most Holy Place to make atonement, must be taken outside the camp; their hides, flesh and offal are to be burned up. ²⁸The man who burns them must wash his clothes and bathe himself with water; afterward he may come into the camp. Ex 29:14; Lev 11:25

²⁹"This is to be a lasting ordinance for you: On the tenth day of the seventh month you must deny yourselves[a] and not do any work—whether native-born or an alien living among you— ³⁰because on this day atonement will be made for you, to cleanse you. Then, before the LORD, you will be clean from all your sins. ³¹It is a sabbath of rest, and you must deny yourselves; it is a lasting ordinance. ³²The priest who is anointed and ordained to succeed his father as high priest is

a29 Or must fast; also in verse 31

to make atonement. He is to put on the sacred linen garments [33]and make atonement for the Most Holy Place, for the Tent of Meeting and the altar, and for the priests and all the people of the community.   Nu 29:7

[34]"This is to be a lasting ordinance for you: Atonement is to be made once a year for all the sins of the Israelites."   Heb 9:7

And it was done, as the LORD commanded Moses.

Eating Blood Forbidden

17 The LORD said to Moses, [2]"Speak to Aaron and his sons and to all the Israelites and say to them: 'This is what the LORD has commanded: [3]Any Israelite who sacrifices an ox,[a] a lamb or a goat in the camp or outside of it [4]instead of bringing it to the entrance to the Tent of Meeting to present it as an offering to the LORD in front of the tabernacle of the LORD—that man shall be considered guilty of bloodshed; he has shed blood and must be cut off from his people. [5]This is so the Israelites will bring to the LORD the sacrifices they are now making in the open fields. They must bring them to the priest, that is, to the LORD, at the entrance to the Tent of Meeting and sacrifice them as fellowship offerings.[b] [6]The priest is to sprinkle the blood against the altar of the LORD at the entrance to the Tent

of Meeting and burn the fat as an aroma pleasing to the LORD. [7]They must no longer offer any of their sacrifices to the goat idols[c] to whom they prostitute themselves. This is to be a lasting ordinance for them and for the generations to come.'Dt 12:5-21

[8]"Say to them: 'Any Israelite or any alien living among them who offers a burnt offering or sacrifice [9]and does not bring it to the entrance to the Tent of Meeting to sacrifice it to the LORD—that man must be cut off from his people.   Lev 1:3; 3:7

[10]" 'Any Israelite or any alien living among them who eats any blood—I will set my face against that person who eats blood and will cut him off from his people. [11]For the life of a creature is in the blood, and I have given it to you to make atonement for yourselves on the altar; it is the blood that makes atonement for one's life. [12]Therefore I say to the Israelites, "None of you may eat blood, nor may an alien living among you eat blood."   Heb 9:22

[13]" 'Any Israelite or any alien living among you who hunts any animal or bird that may be eaten must drain out the blood and cover it with earth, [14]because the life of every creature is its blood. That is why I have said to the Israelites, "You must not eat the blood of any creature, because the life of every

---

[a]3 The Hebrew word can include both male and female.   [b]5 Traditionally *peace offerings*   [c]7 Or *demons*

creature is its blood; anyone who eats it must be cut off."

15" 'Anyone, whether native-born or alien, who eats anything found dead or torn by wild animals must wash his clothes and bathe with water, and he will be ceremonially unclean till evening; then he will be clean. 16But if he does not wash his clothes and bathe himself, he will be held responsible.' "   Ex 22:31; Dt 14:21

Unlawful Sexual Relations

18 The LORD said to Moses, 2"Speak to the Israelites and say to them: 'I am the LORD your God. 3You must not do as they do in Egypt, where you used to live, and you must not do as they do in the land of Canaan, where I am bringing you. Do not follow their practices. 4You must obey my laws and be careful to follow my decrees. I am the LORD your God. 5Keep my decrees and laws, for the man who obeys them will live by them. I am the LORD.   Ex 6:7

6" 'No one is to approach any close relative to have sexual relations. I am the LORD.

7" 'Do not dishonor your father by having sexual relations with your mother. She is your mother; do not have relations with her.   Lev 20:11; Dt 27:20

8" 'Do not have sexual relations with your father's wife; that would dishonor your father.   Ge 35:22; Dt 22:30

9" 'Do not have sexual relations with your sister, either your father's daughter or your mother's daughter, whether she was born in the same home or elsewhere.   Lev 20:17; Dt 27:22

10" 'Do not have sexual relations with your son's daughter or your daughter's daughter; that would dishonor you.

11" 'Do not have sexual relations with the daughter of your father's wife, born to your father; she is your sister.

12" 'Do not have sexual relations with your father's sister; she is your father's close relative.   Lev 20:19

13" 'Do not have sexual relations with your mother's sister, because she is your mother's close relative.   Lev 20:20

14" 'Do not dishonor your father's brother by approaching his wife to have sexual relations; she is your aunt.   Lev 20:20

15" 'Do not have sexual relations with your daughter-in-law. She is your son's wife; do not have relations with her.

16" 'Do not have sexual relations with your brother's wife; that would dishonor your brother.   Lev 20:21; Mt 14:4

17" 'Do not have sexual relations with both a woman and her daughter. Do not have sexual relations with either her son's daughter or her daughter's daughter; they are her close relatives. That is wickedness.

18" 'Do not take your wife's sister as a rival wife and have sexual relations with her while your wife is living.   Ge 30:1

19" 'Do not approach a

woman to have sexual relations during the uncleanness of her monthly period. Lev 15:24

20" 'Do not have sexual relations with your neighbor's wife and defile yourself with her.

21" 'Do not give any of your children to be sacrificed[a] to Molech, for you must not profane the name of your God. I am the LORD. Lev 20:2-5; Dt 12:31

22" 'Do not lie with a man as one lies with a woman; that is detestable. Lev 20:13; Ro 1:27

23" 'Do not have sexual relations with an animal and defile yourself with it. A woman must not present herself to an animal to have sexual relations with it; that is a perversion. Lev 20:15-16

24" 'Do not defile yourselves in any of these ways, because this is how the nations that I am going to drive out before you became defiled. 25Even the land was defiled; so I punished it for its sin, and the land vomited out its inhabitants. 26But you must keep my decrees and my laws. The native-born and the aliens living among you must not do any of these detestable things, 27for all these things were done by the people who lived in the land before you, and the land became defiled. 28And if you defile the land, it will vomit you out as it vomited out the nations that were before you. Lev 20:23

29" 'Everyone who does any of these detestable things— such persons must be cut off from their people. 30Keep my requirements and do not follow any of the detestable customs that were practiced before you came and do not defile yourselves with them. I am the LORD your God.' " Lev 22:9

Various Laws

19 The LORD said to Moses, 2"Speak to the entire assembly of Israel and say to them: 'Be holy because I, the LORD your God, am holy. 1Pe 1:16

3" 'Each of you must respect his mother and father, and you must observe my Sabbaths. I am the LORD your God.

4" 'Do not turn to idols or make gods of cast metal for yourselves. I am the LORD your God. Lev 11:44; Ps 96:5

5" 'When you sacrifice a fellowship offering[b] to the LORD, sacrifice it in such a way that it will be accepted on your behalf. 6It shall be eaten on the day you sacrifice it or on the next day; anything left over until the third day must be burned up. 7If any of it is eaten on the third day, it is impure and will not be accepted. 8Whoever eats it will be held responsible because he has desecrated what is holy to the LORD; that person must be cut off from his people. Lev 7:16-17

9" 'When you reap the harvest of your land, do not reap to the very edges of your field or gather the gleanings of your harvest. 10Do not go over your

---

a21 Or *to be passed through the fire*   b5 Traditionally *peace offering*

vineyard a second time or pick up the grapes that have fallen. Leave them for the poor and the alien. I am the LORD your God.

[11] "'Do not steal.   Ex 20:15

"'Do not lie.   Ex 20:16

"'Do not deceive one another.   Lev 6:2

[12] "'Do not swear falsely by my name and so profane the name of your God. I am the LORD.   Ex 20:7; Lev 18:21

[13] "'Do not defraud your neighbor or rob him.   Ex 20:15

"'Do not hold back the wages of a hired man overnight.

[14] "'Do not curse the deaf or put a stumbling block in front of the blind, but fear your God. I am the LORD.   Ex 4:11; Dt 27:18

[15] "'Do not pervert justice; do not show partiality to the poor or favoritism to the great, but judge your neighbor fairly.Ex 23:2

[16] "'Do not go about spreading slander among your people.

"'Do not do anything that endangers your neighbor's life. I am the LORD.   Ex 23:7; Dt 10:17

[17] "'Do not hate your brother in your heart. Rebuke your neighbor frankly so you will not share in his guilt.   1Jn 2:9

[18] "'Do not seek revenge or bear a grudge against one of your people, but love your neighbor as yourself. I am the LORD.   Ps 103:9; Ro 12:19

[19] "'Keep my decrees.   Ge 26:5

"'Do not mate different kinds of animals.

"'Do not plant your field with two kinds of seed.   Dt 22:9

"'Do not wear clothing woven of two kinds of material.

[20] "'If a man sleeps with a woman who is a slave girl promised to another man but who has not been ransomed or given her freedom, there must be due punishment. Yet they are not to be put to death, because she had not been freed. [21]The man, however, must bring a ram to the entrance to the Tent of Meeting for a guilt offering to the LORD. [22]With the ram of the guilt offering the priest is to make atonement for him before the LORD for the sin he has committed, and his sin will be forgiven.   Dt 22:23-27

[23] "'When you enter the land and plant any kind of fruit tree, regard its fruit as forbidden.[a] For three years you are to consider it forbidden[a]; it must not be eaten. [24]In the fourth year all its fruit will be holy, an offering of praise to the LORD. [25]But in the fifth year you may eat its fruit. In this way your harvest will be increased. I am the LORD your God.   Ex 22:29; Dt 12:17

[26] "'Do not eat any meat with the blood still in it.   Ge 9:4

"'Do not practice divination or sorcery.   Dt 18:10; 2Ki 17:17

[27] "'Do not cut the hair at the sides of your head or clip off the edges of your beard.   Lev 21:5

[28] "'Do not cut your bodies for the dead or put tattoo marks

[a]23 Hebrew *uncircumcised*

on yourselves. I am the LORD.

29"'Do not degrade your daughter by making her a prostitute, or the land will turn to prostitution and be filled with wickedness.   Dt 23:17

30"'Observe my Sabbaths and have reverence for my sanctuary. I am the LORD.   Lev 26:2

31"'Do not turn to mediums or seek out spiritists, for you will be defiled by them. I am the LORD your God.   Lev 20:6

32"'Rise in the presence of the aged, show respect for the elderly and revere your God. I am the LORD.   1Ki 12:8; Job 32:4

33"'When an alien lives with you in your land, do not mistreat him. 34The alien living with you must be treated as one of your native-born. Love him as yourself, for you were aliens in Egypt. I am the LORD your God.

35"'Do not use dishonest standards when measuring length, weight or quantity. 36Use honest scales and honest weights, an honest ephah*a* and an honest hin.*b* I am the LORD your God, who brought you out of Egypt.   Dt 25:13-16

37"'Keep all my decrees and all my laws and follow them. I am the LORD.' "   2Ki 17:37

Punishments for Sin

20 The LORD said to Moses, 2"Say to the Israelites: 'Any Israelite or any alien living in Israel who gives*c* any of his children to Molech must be put to death. The people of the community are to stone him. 3I will set my face against that man and I will cut him off from his people; for by giving his children to Molech, he has defiled my sanctuary and profaned my holy name. 4If the people of the community close their eyes when that man gives one of his children to Molech and they fail to put him to death, 5I will set my face against that man and his family and will cut off from their people both him and all who follow him in prostituting themselves to Molech.   Lev 18:21

6"'I will set my face against the person who turns to mediums and spiritists to prostitute himself by following them, and I will cut him off from his people.   Lev 19:31

7"'Consecrate yourselves and be holy, because I am the LORD your God. 8Keep my decrees and follow them. I am the LORD, who makes you holy.*d*

9"'If anyone curses his father or mother, he must be put to death. He has cursed his father or his mother, and his blood will be on his own head.   Dt 27:16

10"'If a man commits adultery with another man's wife— with the wife of his neighbor—both the adulterer and the adulteress must be put to death.   Ex 20:14; Dt 22:22

11"'If a man sleeps with his

---

a36 An ephah was a dry measure.   *b36* A hin was a liquid measure.   *c2* Or
sacrifices; also in verses 3 and 4   *d8* Or *who sanctifies you; or who sets you apart as holy*

father's wife, he has dishonored his father. Both the man and the woman must be put to death; their blood will be on their own heads. Lev 18:7-8

12" 'If a man sleeps with his daughter-in-law, both of them must be put to death. What they have done is a perversion; their blood will be on their own heads. Ge 11:31; Lev 18:15

13" 'If a man lies with a man as one lies with a woman, both of them have done what is detestable. They must be put to death; their blood will be on their own heads. Lev 18:22

14" 'If a man marries both a woman and her mother, it is wicked. Both he and they must be burned in the fire, so that no wickedness will be among you.

15" 'If a man has sexual relations with an animal, he must be put to death, and you must kill the animal. Lev 18:23

16" 'If a woman approaches an animal to have sexual relations with it, kill both the woman and the animal. They must be put to death; their blood will be on their own heads.

17" 'If a man marries his sister, the daughter of either his father or his mother, and they have sexual relations, it is a disgrace. They must be cut off before the eyes of their people. He has dishonored his sister and will be held responsible. Lev 18:9

18" 'If a man lies with a woman during her monthly period and has sexual relations with her, he has exposed the source of her flow, and she has also uncovered it. Both of them must be cut off from their people. Lev 15:24; 18:19

19" 'Do not have sexual relations with the sister of either your mother or your father, for that would dishonor a close relative; both of you would be held responsible. Lev 18:12

20" 'If a man sleeps with his aunt, he has dishonored his uncle. They will be held responsible; they will die childless.

21" 'If a man marries his brother's wife, it is an act of impurity; he has dishonored his brother. They will be childless.

22" 'Keep all my decrees and laws and follow them, so that the land where I am bringing you to live may not vomit you out. 23You must not live according to the customs of the nations I am going to drive out before you. Because they did all these things, I abhorred them. 24But I said to you, "You will possess their land; I will give it to you as an inheritance, a land flowing with milk and honey." I am the LORD your God, who has set you apart from the nations. Ex 3:8; Lev 18:25-28

25" 'You must therefore make a distinction between clean and unclean animals and between unclean and clean birds. Do not defile yourselves by any animal or bird or anything that moves along the ground—those which I have set apart as unclean for

you. ²⁶You are to be holy to me^a because I, the LORD, am holy, and I have set you apart from the nations to be my own. Ac 10:14

²⁷" 'A man or woman who is a medium or spiritist among you must be put to death. You are to stone them; their blood will be on their own heads.' "   Lev 19:31

Rules for Priests

21 The LORD said to Moses, "Speak to the priests, the sons of Aaron, and say to them: 'A priest must not make himself ceremonially unclean for any of his people who die, ²except for a close relative, such as his mother or father, his son or daughter, his brother, ³or an unmarried sister who is dependent on him since she has no husband—for her he may make himself unclean. ⁴He must not make himself unclean for people related to him by marriage,^b and so defile himself.

⁵" 'Priests must not shave their heads or shave off the edges of their beards or cut their bodies. ⁶They must be holy to their God and must not profane the name of their God. Because they present the offerings made to the LORD by fire, the food of their God, they are to be holy.

⁷" 'They must not marry women defiled by prostitution or divorced from their husbands, because priests are holy to their God. ⁸Regard them as holy, because they offer up the food of your God. Consider them holy, because I the LORD am holy—I who make you holy.^c   Ex 14:22; Lev 3:11

⁹" 'If a priest's daughter defiles herself by becoming a prostitute, she disgraces her father; she must be burned in the fire.   Ge 38:24; Lev 19:29

¹⁰" 'The high priest, the one among his brothers who has had the anointing oil poured on his head and who has been ordained to wear the priestly garments, must not let his hair become unkempt^d or tear his clothes. ¹¹He must not enter a place where there is a dead body. He must not make himself unclean, even for his father or mother, ¹²nor leave the sanctuary of his God or desecrate it, because he has been dedicated by the anointing oil of his God. I am the LORD.   Lev 10:6-7; 19:28

¹³" 'The woman he marries must be a virgin. ¹⁴He must not marry a widow, a divorced woman, or a woman defiled by prostitution, but only a virgin from his own people, ¹⁵so he will not defile his offspring among his people. I am the LORD, who makes him holy.^e' "

¹⁶The LORD said to Moses, ¹⁷"Say to Aaron: 'For the generations to come none of your descendants who has a defect may come near to offer the food of his God. ¹⁸No man who has any

---

^a26 Or *be my holy ones*   ^b4 Or *unclean as a leader among his people*   ^c8 Or *who sanctify you; or who set you apart as holy*   ^d10 Or *not uncover his head*   ^e15 Or *who sanctifies him; or who sets him apart as holy*

defect may come near: no man who is blind or lame, disfigured or deformed; ¹⁹no man with a crippled foot or hand, ²⁰or who is hunchbacked or dwarfed, or who has any eye defect, or who has festering or running sores or damaged testicles. ²¹No descendant of Aaron the priest who has any defect is to come near to present the offerings made to the LORD by fire. He has a defect; he must not come near to offer the food of his God. ²²He may eat the most holy food of his God, as well as the holy food; ²³yet because of his defect, he must not go near the curtain or approach the altar, and so desecrate my sanctuary. I am the LORD, who makes them holy.ᵃ' '' Lev 22:23; 2Sa 4:4

²⁴So Moses told this to Aaron and his sons and to all the Israelites.

22 The LORD said to Moses, ²''Tell Aaron and his sons to treat with respect the sacred offerings the Israelites consecrate to me, so they will not profane my holy name. I am the LORD. Ex 25:8; Lev 19:8

³''Say to them: 'For the generations to come, if any of your descendants is ceremonially unclean and yet comes near the sacred offerings that the Israelites consecrate to the LORD, that person must be cut off from my presence. I am the LORD. Lev 7:20

⁴'' 'If a descendant of Aaron has an infectious skin diseaseᵇ or a bodily discharge, he may not eat the sacred offerings until he is cleansed. He will also be unclean if he touches something defiled by a corpse or by anyone who has an emission of semen, ⁵or if he touches any crawling thing that makes him unclean, or any person who makes him unclean, whatever the uncleanness may be. ⁶The one who touches any such thing will be unclean till evening. He must not eat any of the sacred offerings unless he has bathed himself with water. ⁷When the sun goes down, he will be clean, and after that he may eat the sacred offerings, for they are his food. ⁸He must not eat anything found dead or torn by wild animals, and so become unclean through it. I am the LORD. Lev 11:24-28; Nu 18:11

⁹'' 'The priests are to keep my requirements so that they do not become guilty and die for treating them with contempt. I am the LORD, who makes them holy.ᶜ Ex 28:43; Lev 8:35

¹⁰'' 'No one outside a priest's family may eat the sacred offering, nor may the guest of a priest or his hired worker eat it. ¹¹But if a priest buys a slave with money, or if a slave is born in his household, that slave may eat his food. ¹²If a priest's daughter marries anyone other than a priest, she may not eat

---

ᵃ23 Or who sanctifies them; or who sets them apart as holy   ᵇ4 Traditionally leprosy; the Hebrew word was used for various diseases affecting the skin—not necessarily leprosy. ᶜ9 Or who sanctifies them; or who sets them apart as holy; also in verse 16

any of the sacred contributions. ¹³But if a priest's daughter becomes a widow or is divorced, yet has no children, and she returns to live in her father's house as in her youth, she may eat of her father's food. No unauthorized person, however, may eat any of it.   Ex 12:45

¹⁴" 'If anyone eats a sacred offering by mistake, he must make restitution to the priest for the offering and add a fifth of the value to it. ¹⁵The priests must not desecrate the sacred offerings the Israelites present to the LORD ¹⁶by allowing them to eat the sacred offerings and so bring upon them guilt requiring payment. I am the LORD, who makes them holy.' "   Lev 5:15

Unacceptable Sacrifices

¹⁷The LORD said to Moses, ¹⁸"Speak to Aaron and his sons and to all the Israelites and say to them: 'If any of you—either an Israelite or an alien living in Israel—presents a gift for a burnt offering to the LORD, either to fulfill a vow or as a freewill offering, ¹⁹you must present a male without defect from the cattle, sheep or goats in order that it may be accepted on your behalf. ²⁰Do not bring anything with a defect, because it will not be accepted on your behalf. ²¹When anyone brings from the herd or flock a fellowship offering^a to the LORD to ful-

fill a special vow or as a freewill offering, it must be without defect or blemish to be acceptable. ²²Do not offer to the LORD the blind, the injured or the maimed, or anything with warts or festering or running sores. Do not place any of these on the altar as an offering made to the LORD by fire. ²³You may, however, present as a freewill offering an ox^b or a sheep that is deformed or stunted, but it will not be accepted in fulfillment of a vow. ²⁴You must not offer to the LORD an animal whose testicles are bruised, crushed, torn or cut. You must not do this in your own land, ²⁵and you must not accept such animals from the hand of a foreigner and offer them as the food of your God. They will not be accepted on your behalf, because they are deformed and have defects.' "

²⁶The LORD said to Moses, ²⁷"When a calf, a lamb or a goat is born, it is to remain with its mother for seven days. From the eighth day on, it will be acceptable as an offering made to the LORD by fire. ²⁸Do not slaughter a cow or a sheep and its young on the same day.

²⁹"When you sacrifice a thank offering to the LORD, sacrifice it in such a way that it will be accepted on your behalf. ³⁰It must be eaten that same day; leave none of it till morning. I am the LORD.

---

^{a}21 Traditionally *peace offering* ^{b}23 The Hebrew word can include both male and female.

[31] "Keep my commands and follow them. I am the LORD. [32] Do not profane my holy name. I must be acknowledged as holy by the Israelites. I am the LORD, who makes[a] you holy[b] [33] and who brought you out of Egypt to be your God. I am the LORD."

23 The LORD said to Moses, [2] "Speak to the Israelites and say to them: 'These are my appointed feasts, the appointed feasts of the LORD, which you are to proclaim as sacred assemblies.
Nu 29:39; Eze 44:24

The Sabbath

[3] " 'There are six days when you may work, but the seventh day is a Sabbath of rest, a day of sacred assembly. You are not to do any work; wherever you live, it is a Sabbath to the LORD.

The Passover and Unleavened Bread

[4] " 'These are the LORD's appointed feasts, the sacred assemblies you are to proclaim at their appointed times: [5] The LORD's Passover begins at twilight on the fourteenth day of the first month. [6] On the fifteenth day of that month the LORD's Feast of Unleavened Bread begins; for seven days you must eat bread made without yeast. [7] On the first day hold a sacred assembly and do no

regular work. [8] For seven days present an offering made to the LORD by fire. And on the seventh day hold a sacred assembly and do no regular work.' " Ex 12:19

Firstfruits

[9] The LORD said to Moses, [10] "Speak to the Israelites and say to them: 'When you enter the land I am going to give you and you reap its harvest, bring to the priest a sheaf of the first grain you harvest. [11] He is to wave the sheaf before the LORD so it will be accepted on your behalf; the priest is to wave it on the day after the Sabbath. [12] On the day you wave the sheaf, you must sacrifice as a burnt offering to the LORD a lamb a year old without defect, [13] together with its grain offering of two-tenths of an ephah[c] of fine flour mixed with oil—an offering made to the LORD by fire, a pleasing aroma—and its drink offering of a quarter of a hin[d] of wine. [14] You must not eat any bread, or roasted or new grain, until the very day you bring this offering to your God. This is to be a lasting ordinance for the generations to come, wherever you live. Ex 23:19; Ro 11:16

Feast of Weeks

[15] " 'From the day after the Sabbath, the day you brought the sheaf of the wave offering, count off seven full weeks.

---

[a]32 Or made   [b]32 Or who sanctifies you; or who sets you apart as holy   [c]13 That is, probably about 4 quarts (about 4.5 liters); also in verse 17   [d]13 That is, probably about 1 quart (about 1 liter)

¹⁶Count off fifty days up to the day after the seventh Sabbath, and then present an offering of new grain to the LORD. ¹⁷From wherever you live, bring two loaves made of two-tenths of an ephah of fine flour, baked with yeast, as a wave offering of firstfruits to the LORD. ¹⁸Present with this bread seven male lambs, each a year old and without defect, one young bull and two rams. They will be a burnt offering to the LORD, together with their grain offerings and drink offerings—an offering made by fire, an aroma pleasing to the LORD. ¹⁹Then sacrifice one male goat for a sin offering and two lambs, each a year old, for a fellowship offering.ᵃ ²⁰The priest is to wave the two lambs before the LORD as a wave offering, together with the bread of the firstfruits. They are a sacred offering to the LORD for the priest. ²¹On that same day you are to proclaim a sacred assembly and do no regular work. This is to be a lasting ordinance for the generations to come, wherever you live. Ac 2:1

²²" 'When you reap the harvest of your land, do not reap to the very edges of your field or gather the gleanings of your harvest. Leave them for the poor and the alien. I am the LORD your God.' " Lev 19:9

Feast of Trumpets

²³The LORD said to Moses,

²⁴"Say to the Israelites: 'On the first day of the seventh month you are to have a day of rest, a sacred assembly commemorated with trumpet blasts. ²⁵Do no regular work, but present an offering made to the LORD by fire.' " Lev 25:9; Nu 29:1

Day of Atonement

²⁶The LORD said to Moses, ²⁷"The tenth day of this seventh month is the Day of Atonement. Hold a sacred assembly and deny yourselves,ᵇ and present an offering made to the LORD by fire. ²⁸Do no work on that day, because it is the Day of Atonement, when atonement is made for you before the LORD your God. ²⁹Anyone who does not deny himself on that day must be cut off from his people. ³⁰I will destroy from among his people anyone who does any work on that day. ³¹You shall do no work at all. This is to be a lasting ordinance for the generations to come, wherever you live. ³²It is a sabbath of rest for you, and you must deny yourselves. From the evening of the ninth day of the month until the following evening you are to observe your sabbath." Lev 16:29

Feast of Tabernacles

³³The LORD said to Moses, ³⁴"Say to the Israelites: 'On the fifteenth day of the seventh month the LORD's Feast of Tabernacles begins, and it lasts for

ᵃ19 Traditionally *peace offering*   ᵇ27 Or *and fast*; also in verses 29 and 32

seven days. ³⁵The first day is a sacred assembly; do no regular work. ³⁶For seven days present offerings made to the LORD by fire, and on the eighth day hold a sacred assembly and present an offering made to the LORD by fire. It is the closing assembly; do no regular work.   Ex 23:16

³⁷(" 'These are the LORD's appointed feasts, which you are to proclaim as sacred assemblies for bringing offerings made to the LORD by fire—the burnt offerings and grain offerings, sacrifices and drink offerings required for each day. ³⁸These offerings are in addition to those for the LORD's Sabbaths and*ᵃ* in addition to your gifts and whatever you have vowed and all the freewill offerings you give to the LORD.)   Lev 1:2; 2Ch 2:4

³⁹" 'So beginning with the fifteenth day of the seventh month, after you have gathered the crops of the land, celebrate the festival to the LORD for seven days; the first day is a day of rest, and the eighth day also is a day of rest. ⁴⁰On the first day you are to take choice fruit from the trees, and palm fronds, leafy branches and poplars, and rejoice before the LORD your God for seven days. ⁴¹Celebrate this as a festival to the LORD for seven days each year. This is to be a lasting ordinance for the generations to come; celebrate it in the seventh month. ⁴²Live in

booths for seven days: All native-born Israelites are to live in booths ⁴³so your descendants will know that I had the Israelites live in booths when I brought them out of Egypt. I am the LORD your God.' "   Ex 23:16

⁴⁴So Moses announced to the Israelites the appointed feasts of the LORD.   Lev 23:2

Oil and Bread Set Before the LORD

24 The LORD said to Moses, ²"Command the Israelites to bring you clear oil of pressed olives for the light so that the lamps may be kept burning continually. ³Outside the curtain of the Testimony in the Tent of Meeting, Aaron is to tend the lamps before the LORD from evening till morning, continually. This is to be a lasting ordinance for the generations to come. ⁴The lamps on the pure gold lampstand before the LORD must be tended continually.

⁵"Take fine flour and bake twelve loaves of bread, using two-tenths of an ephahᵇ for each loaf. ⁶Set them in two rows, six in each row, on the table of pure gold before the LORD. ⁷Along each row put some pure incense as a memorial portion to represent the bread and to be an offering made to the LORD by fire. ⁸This bread is to be set out before the LORD regularly, Sabbath after Sab-

---

ᵃ38 Or *These feasts are in addition to the LORD's Sabbaths, and these offerings are*   *ᵇ5* That is, probably about 4 quarts (about 4.5 liters)

bath, on behalf of the Israelites, as a lasting covenant. ⁹It belongs to Aaron and his sons, who are to eat it in a holy place, because it is a most holy part of their regular share of the offerings made to the LORD by fire."

A Blasphemer Stoned

¹⁰Now the son of an Israelite mother and an Egyptian father went out among the Israelites, and a fight broke out in the camp between him and an Israelite. ¹¹The son of the Israelite woman blasphemed the Name with a curse; so they brought him to Moses. (His mother's name was Shelomith, the daughter of Dibri the Danite.) ¹²They put him in custody until the will of the LORD should be made clear to them.   2Ki 6:33

¹³Then the LORD said to Moses: ¹⁴"Take the blasphemer outside the camp. All those who heard him are to lay their hands on his head, and the entire assembly is to stone him. ¹⁵Say to the Israelites: 'If anyone curses his God, he will be held responsible; ¹⁶anyone who blasphemes the name of the LORD must be put to death. The entire assembly must stone him. Whether an alien or native-born, when he blasphemes the Name, he must be put to death.   Lev 20:2; Dt 13:9

¹⁷" 'If anyone takes the life of a human being, he must be put to death. ¹⁸Anyone who takes the life of someone's animal must make restitution—life for life. ¹⁹If anyone injures his neighbor, whatever he has done must be done to him: ²⁰fracture for fracture, eye for eye, tooth for tooth. As he has injured the other, so he is to be injured. ²¹Whoever kills an animal must make restitution, but whoever kills a man must be put to death. ²²You are to have the same law for the alien and the native-born. I am the LORD your God.' "

²³Then Moses spoke to the Israelites, and they took the blasphemer outside the camp and stoned him. The Israelites did as the LORD commanded Moses.

The Sabbath Year

25 The LORD said to Moses on Mount Sinai, ²"Speak to the Israelites and say to them: 'When you enter the land I am going to give you, the land itself must observe a sabbath to the LORD. ³For six years sow your fields, and for six years prune your vineyards and gather their crops. ⁴But in the seventh year the land is to have a sabbath of rest, a sabbath to the LORD. Do not sow your fields or prune your vineyards. ⁵Do not reap what grows of itself or harvest the grapes of your untended vines. The land is to have a year of rest. ⁶Whatever the land yields during the sabbath year will be food for you—for yourself, your manservant and maidservant, and the hired worker and temporary resident who live among you, ⁷as well as for your livestock and the wild

animals in your land. Whatever the land produces may be eaten. _{Ex 23:10; Lev 26:35}

The Year of Jubilee

⁸" 'Count off seven sabbaths of years—seven times seven years—so that the seven sabbaths of years amount to a period of forty-nine years. ⁹Then have the trumpet sounded everywhere on the tenth day of the seventh month; on the Day of Atonement sound the trumpet throughout your land. ¹⁰Consecrate the fiftieth year and proclaim liberty throughout the land to all its inhabitants. It shall be a jubilee for you; each one of you is to return to his family property and each to his own clan. ¹¹The fiftieth year shall be a jubilee for you; do not sow and do not reap what grows of itself or harvest the untended vines. ¹²For it is a jubilee and is to be holy for you; eat only what is taken directly from the fields. _{Lev 23:24; Isa 61:1}

¹³" 'In this Year of Jubilee everyone is to return to his own property. _{Lev 25:10}

¹⁴" 'If you sell land to one of your countrymen or buy any from him, do not take advantage of each other. ¹⁵You are to buy from your countryman on the basis of the number of years since the Jubilee. And he is to sell to you on the basis of the number of years left for harvesting crops. ¹⁶When the years are many, you are to increase the price, and when the years are few, you are to decrease the price, because what he is really selling you is the number of crops. ¹⁷Do not take advantage of each other, but fear your God. I am the LORD your God.

¹⁸" 'Follow my decrees and be careful to obey my laws, and you will live safely in the land. ¹⁹Then the land will yield its fruit, and you will eat your fill and live there in safety. ²⁰You may ask, "What will we eat in the seventh year if we do not plant or harvest our crops?" ²¹I will send you such a blessing in the sixth year that the land will yield enough for three years. ²²While you plant during the eighth year, you will eat from the old crop and will continue to eat from it until the harvest of the ninth year comes in. _{Lev 26:10}

²³" 'The land must not be sold permanently, because the land is mine and you are but aliens and my tenants. ²⁴Throughout the country that you hold as a possession, you must provide for the redemption of the land.

²⁵" 'If one of your countrymen becomes poor and sells some of his property, his nearest relative is to come and redeem what his countryman has sold. ²⁶If, however, a man has no one to redeem it for him but he himself prospers and acquires sufficient means to redeem it, ²⁷he is to determine the value for the years since he sold it and refund the balance to the man to whom he sold it; he can then go back to his own prop-

erty. 28But if he does not acquire the means to repay him, what he sold will remain in the possession of the buyer until the Year of Jubilee. It will be returned in the Jubilee, and he can then go back to his property.   Lev 27:13; Ru 2:20

29" 'If a man sells a house in a walled city, he retains the right of redemption a full year after its sale. During that time he may redeem it. 30If it is not redeemed before a full year has passed, the house in the walled city shall belong permanently to the buyer and his descendants. It is not to be returned in the Jubilee. 31But houses in villages without walls around them are to be considered as open country. They can be redeemed, and they are to be returned in the Jubilee.

32" 'The Levites always have the right to redeem their houses in the Levitical towns, which they possess. 33So the property of the Levites is redeemable—that is, a house sold in any town they hold—and is to be returned in the Jubilee, because the houses in the towns of the Levites are their property among the Israelites. 34But the pastureland belonging to their towns must not be sold; it is their permanent possession.

35" 'If one of your countrymen becomes poor and is unable to support himself among you, help him as you would an alien or a temporary resident, so he can continue to live among you. 36Do not take interest of any kind*a* from him, but fear your God, so that your countryman may continue to live among you. 37You must not lend him money at interest or sell him food at a profit. 38I am the LORD your God, who brought you out of Egypt to give you the land of Canaan and to be your God.   Dt 15:8; Lk 6:35

39" 'If one of your countrymen becomes poor among you and sells himself to you, do not make him work as a slave. 40He is to be treated as a hired worker or a temporary resident among you; he is to work for you until the Year of Jubilee. 41Then he and his children are to be released, and he will go back to his own clan and to the property of his forefathers. 42Because the Israelites are my servants, whom I brought out of Egypt, they must not be sold as slaves. 43Do not rule over them ruthlessly, but fear your God. 1Ki 9:22

44" 'Your male and female slaves are to come from the nations around you; from them you may buy slaves. 45You may also buy some of the temporary residents living among you and members of their clans born in your country, and they will become your property. 46You can will them to your children

---

*a*36 Or *take excessive interest*; similarly in verse 37

as inherited property and can make them slaves for life, but you must not rule over your fellow Israelites ruthlessly.   Isa 56:3

47" 'If an alien or a temporary resident among you becomes rich and one of your countrymen becomes poor and sells himself to the alien living among you or to a member of the alien's clan, 48he retains the right of redemption after he has sold himself. One of his relatives may redeem him: 49An uncle or a cousin or any blood relative in his clan may redeem him. Or if he prospers, he may redeem himself. 50He and his buyer are to count the time from the year he sold himself up to the Year of Jubilee. The price for his release is to be based on the rate paid to a hired man for that number of years. 51If many years remain, he must pay for his redemption a larger share of the price paid for him. 52If only a few years remain until the Year of Jubilee, he is to compute that and pay for his redemption accordingly. 53He is to be treated as a man hired from year to year; you must see to it that his owner does not rule over him ruthlessly.   Job 7:1; Isa 16:14

54" 'Even if he is not redeemed in any of these ways, he and his children are to be released in the Year of Jubilee, 55for the Israelites belong to me as servants. They are my servants, whom I brought out of Egypt. I am the LORD your God.

Reward for Obedience

26 " 'Do not make idols or set up an image or a sacred stone for yourselves, and do not place a carved stone in your land to bow down before it. I am the LORD your God.

2" 'Observe my Sabbaths and have reverence for my sanctuary. I am the LORD.   Lev 19:30

3" 'If you follow my decrees and are careful to obey my commands, 4I will send you rain in its season, and the ground will yield its crops and the trees of the field their fruit. 5Your threshing will continue until grape harvest and the grape harvest will continue until planting, and you will eat all the food you want and live in safety in your land.   Lev 25:18; Dt 28:1

6" 'I will grant peace in the land, and you will lie down and no one will make you afraid. I will remove savage beasts from the land, and the sword will not pass through your country. 7You will pursue your enemies, and they will fall by the sword before you. 8Five of you will chase a hundred, and a hundred of you will chase ten thousand, and your enemies will fall by the sword before you.   Ps 29:11

9" 'I will look on you with favor and make you fruitful and increase your numbers, and I will keep my covenant with you. 10You will still be eating last year's harvest when you will have to move it out to make room for the new. 11I will put

my dwelling place[a] among you, and I will not abhor you. [12]I will walk among you and be your God, and you will be my people. [13]I am the LORD your God, who brought you out of Egypt so that you would no longer be slaves to the Egyptians; I broke the bars of your yoke and enabled you to walk with heads held high. Ge 17:6

Punishment for Disobedience

[14]" 'But if you will not listen to me and carry out all these commands, [15]and if you reject my decrees and abhor my laws and fail to carry out all my commands and so violate my covenant, [16]then I will do this to you: I will bring upon you sudden terror, wasting diseases and fever that will destroy your sight and drain away your life. You will plant seed in vain, because your enemies will eat it. [17]I will set my face against you so that you will be defeated by your enemies; those who hate you will rule over you, and you will flee even when no one is pursuing you. Dt 28:15; Mal 2:2

[18]" 'If after all this you will not listen to me, I will punish you for your sins seven times over. [19]I will break down your stubborn pride and make the sky above you like iron and the ground beneath you like bronze. [20]Your strength will be spent in vain, because your soil will not yield its crops, nor will the trees of the land yield their fruit. Dt 28:23; Isa 25:11

[21]" 'If you remain hostile toward me and refuse to listen to me, I will multiply your afflictions seven times over, as your sins deserve. [22]I will send wild animals against you, and they will rob you of your children, destroy your cattle and make you so few in number that your roads will be deserted. Ge 4:15

[23]" 'If in spite of these things you do not accept my correction but continue to be hostile toward me, [24]I myself will be hostile toward you and will afflict you for your sins seven times over. [25]And I will bring the sword upon you to avenge the breaking of the covenant. When you withdraw into your cities, I will send a plague among you, and you will be given into enemy hands. [26]When I cut off your supply of bread, ten women will be able to bake your bread in one oven, and they will dole out the bread by weight. You will eat, but you will not be satisfied. Ps 105:16; Jer 2:30

[27]" 'If in spite of this you still do not listen to me but continue to be hostile toward me, [28]then in my anger I will be hostile toward you, and I myself will punish you for your sins seven times over. [29]You will eat the flesh of your sons and the flesh of your daughters. [30]I will de-

---

[a]11 Or *my tabernacle*

stroy your high places, cut down your incense altars and pile your dead bodies on the lifeless forms of your idols, and I will abhor you. ³¹I will turn your cities into ruins and lay waste your sanctuaries, and I will take no delight in the pleasing aroma of your offerings. ³²I will lay waste the land, so that your enemies who live there will be appalled. ³³I will scatter you among the nations and will draw out my sword and pursue you. Your land will be laid waste, and your cities will lie in ruins. ³⁴Then the land will enjoy its sabbath years all the time that it lies desolate and you are in the country of your enemies; then the land will rest and enjoy its sabbaths. ³⁵All the time that it lies desolate, the land will have the rest it did not have during the sabbaths you lived in it.

³⁶" 'As for those of you who are left, I will make their hearts so fearful in the lands of their enemies that the sound of a windblown leaf will put them to flight. They will run as though fleeing from the sword, and they will fall, even though no one is pursuing them. ³⁷They will stumble over one another as though fleeing from the sword, even though no one is pursuing them. So you will not be able to stand before your enemies. ³⁸You will perish among the nations; the land of your enemies will devour you.

³⁹Those of you who are left will waste away in the lands of their enemies because of their sins; also because of their fathers' sins they will waste away.

⁴⁰" 'But if they will confess their sins and the sins of their fathers—their treachery against me and their hostility toward me, ⁴¹which made me hostile toward them so that I sent them into the land of their enemies—then when their uncircumcised hearts are humbled and they pay for their sin, ⁴²I will remember my covenant with Jacob and my covenant with Isaac and my covenant with Abraham, and I will remember the land. ⁴³For the land will be deserted by them and will enjoy its sabbaths while it lies desolate without them. They will pay for their sins because they rejected my laws and abhorred my decrees. ⁴⁴Yet in spite of this, when they are in the land of their enemies, I will not reject them or abhor them so as to destroy them completely, breaking my covenant with them. I am the LORD their God. ⁴⁵But for their sake I will remember the covenant with their ancestors whom I brought out of Egypt in the sight of the nations to be their God. I am the LORD.' " Eze 44:7; Lk 15:18

⁴⁶These are the decrees, the laws and the regulations that the LORD established on Mount Sinai between himself and the Israelites through Moses. Lev 7:38

Redeeming What Is the LORD's

27 The LORD said to Moses, ²"Speak to the Israelites and say to them: 'If anyone makes a special vow to dedicate persons to the LORD by giving equivalent values, ³set the value of a male between the ages of twenty and sixty at fifty shekels*ᵃ* of silver, according to the sanctuary shekel*ᵇ*; ⁴and if it is a female, set her value at thirty shekels.*ᶜ* ⁵If it is a person between the ages of five and twenty, set the value of a male at twenty shekels*ᵈ* and of a female at ten shekels.*ᵉ* ⁶If it is a person between one month and five years, set the value of a male at five shekels*ᶠ* of silver and that of a female at three shekels*ᵍ* of silver. ⁷If it is a person sixty years old or more, set the value of a male at fifteen shekels*ʰ* and of a female at ten shekels. ⁸If anyone making the vow is too poor to pay the specified amount, he is to present the person to the priest, who will set the value for him according to what the man making the vow can afford.   Ge 28:20

⁹" 'If what he vowed is an animal that is acceptable as an offering to the LORD, such an animal given to the LORD becomes holy. ¹⁰He must not exchange it or substitute a good one for a bad one, or a bad one for a good one; if he should substitute one animal for another, both it and the substitute become holy. ¹¹If what he vowed is a ceremonially unclean animal—one that is not acceptable as an offering to the LORD—the animal must be presented to the priest, ¹²who will judge its quality as good or bad. Whatever value the priest then sets, that is what it will be. ¹³If the owner wishes to redeem the animal, he must add a fifth to its value.   Lev 25:25; Dt 15:19

¹⁴" 'If a man dedicates his house as something holy to the LORD, the priest will judge its quality as good or bad. Whatever value the priest then sets, so it will remain. ¹⁵If the man who dedicates his house redeems it, he must add a fifth to its value, and the house will again become his.   Lev 27:13

¹⁶" 'If a man dedicates to the LORD part of his family land, its value is to be set according to the amount of seed required for it—fifty shekels of silver to a homer*ⁱ* of barley seed. ¹⁷If he dedicates his field during the Year of Jubilee, the value that has been set remains. ¹⁸But if he dedicates his field after the Jubilee, the priest will determine the value according to the number

---

ᵃ3 That is, about 1 1/4 pounds (about 0.6 kilogram); also in verse 16   *ᵇ3* That is, about 2/5 ounce (about 11.5 grams); also in verse 25   *ᶜ4* That is, about 12 ounces (about 0.3 kilogram)   *ᵈ5* That is, about 8 ounces (about 0.2 kilogram)   *ᵉ5* That is, about 4 ounces (about 110 grams); also in verse 7   *ᶠ6* That is, about 2 ounces (about 55 grams)   *ᵍ6* That is, about 1 1/4 ounces (about 35 grams)   *ʰ7* That is, about 6 ounces (about 170 grams)   *ⁱ16* That is, probably about 6 bushels (about 220 liters)

of years that remain until the next Year of Jubilee, and its set value will be reduced. [19]If the man who dedicates the field wishes to redeem it, he must add a fifth to its value, and the field will again become his. [20]If, however, he does not redeem the field, or if he has sold it to someone else, it can never be redeemed. [21]When the field is released in the Jubilee, it will become holy, like a field devoted to the Lord; it will become the property of the priests.[a]

[22]" 'If a man dedicates to the Lord a field he has bought, which is not part of his family land, [23]the priest will determine its value up to the Year of Jubilee, and the man must pay its value on that day as something holy to the Lord. [24]In the Year of Jubilee the field will revert to the person from whom he bought it, the one whose land it was. [25]Every value is to be set according to the sanctuary shekel, twenty gerahs to the shekel.   Ex 30:13; Lev 25:28

[26]" 'No one, however, may dedicate the firstborn of an animal, since the firstborn already belongs to the Lord; whether an ox[b] or a sheep, it is the Lord's. [27]If it is one of the un-clean animals, he may buy it back at its set value, adding a fifth of the value to it. If he does not redeem it, it is to be sold at its set value.   Ex 13:12; Lev 27:11

[28]" 'But nothing that a man owns and devotes[c] to the Lord—whether man or animal or family land—may be sold or redeemed; everything so devoted is most holy to the Lord.

[29]" 'No person devoted to de-struction[d] may be ransomed; he must be put to death.   Dt 7:26

[30]" 'A tithe of everything from the land, whether grain from the soil or fruit from the trees, belongs to the Lord; it is holy to the Lord. [31]If a man re-deems any of his tithe, he must add a fifth of the value to it. [32]The entire tithe of the herd and flock—every tenth animal that passes under the shep-herd's rod—will be holy to the Lord. [33]He must not pick out the good from the bad or make any substitution. If he does make a substitution, both the animal and its substitute become holy and cannot be re-deemed.' "   Dt 12:6; Mal 3:8

[34]These are the commands the Lord gave Moses on Mount Sinai for the Israelites.   Lev 26:46

---

[a]21 Or *priest*   [b]26 The Hebrew word can include both male and female.   [c]28 The Hebrew term refers to the irrevocable giving over of things or persons to the Lord. [d]29 The Hebrew term refers to the irrevocable giving over of things or persons to the Lord, often by totally destroying them.

Numbers

Introduction:

Numbers gets its name from the two accounts in chapters 1 and 26 of the numberings or countings of the people of Israel. Moses is the author of this book as well as the leader of the Israelites.

The first part of the book tells about Israel's year while camped at the foot of Mount Sinai. The second part of the book tells of the journey of Israel from Mount Sinai to the east side of the Dead Sea. The third part of the book tells of the preparations for entering and conquering Canaan.

Throughout the thirty-eight years of wandering in the desert, one thing became clear to Israel—God's constant care for them. He miraculously supplied the Israelites with manna, water and quails for their forty years in the desert. God loved and forgave his people continually even though they rebelled against him and their leaders.

Outline of contents:

Instructions for camping and marching (1:1–10:10)
From Sinai to the plains of Moab (10:11–21:35)
Balaam, Balak, and Israel (22:1–25:18)
Instructions for conquest and possession of the land of Canaan (26:1–36:13)

The Census

1 The LORD spoke to Moses in the Tent of Meeting in the Desert of Sinai on the first day of the second month of the second year after the Israelites came out of Egypt. He said: ²"Take a census of the whole Israelite community by their clans and families, listing every man by name, one by one. ³You and Aaron are to number by their divisions all the men in Israel twenty years old or more who are able to serve in the army. ⁴One man from each tribe, each the head of his family, is to help you. ⁵These are the names of the men who are to assist you: Ex 19:1

from Reuben, Elizur son of Shedeur;   Nu 17:2; 26:2
⁶from Simeon, Shelumiel son of Zurishaddai;   Nu 25:14
⁷from Judah, Nahshon son of Amminadab;   Ge 29:35

⁸from Issachar, Nethanel son of Zuar;   Ge 30:18

⁹from Zebulun, Eliab son of Helon;   Nu 10:16

¹⁰from the sons of Joseph:
from Ephraim, Elishama son of Ammihud;   Nu 2:18
from Manasseh, Gamaliel son of Pedahzur;   Nu 10:23

¹¹from Benjamin, Abidan son of Gideoni;   Nu 10:24

¹²from Dan, Ahiezer son of Ammishaddai;   Nu 2:25

¹³from Asher, Pagiel son of Ocran;   Nu 2:27; 10:26

¹⁴from Gad, Eliasaph son of Deuel;   Nu 2:24; 10:20

¹⁵from Naphtali, Ahira son of Enan."   Nu 2:29; 10:27

¹⁶These were the men appointed from the community, the leaders of their ancestral tribes. They were the heads of the clans of Israel.   Ex 18:25

¹⁷Moses and Aaron took these men whose names had been given, ¹⁸and they called the whole community together on the first day of the second month. The people indicated their ancestry by their clans and families, and the men twenty years old or more were listed by name, one by one, ¹⁹as the LORD commanded Moses. And so he counted them in the Desert of Sinai: Ezr 2:59; Heb 7:3

²⁰From the descendants of Reuben the firstborn son of Israel:

All the men twenty years old or more who were able to serve in the army were listed by name, one by one, according to the records of their clans and families. ²¹The number from the tribe of Reuben was 46,500.   Nu 26:7

²²From the descendants of Simeon:

All the men twenty years old or more who were able to serve in the army were counted and listed by name, one by one, according to the records of their clans and families. ²³The number from the tribe of Simeon was 59,300.   Ge 29:33; Nu 26:14

²⁴From the descendants of Gad:
All the men twenty years old or more who were able to serve in the army were listed by name, according to the records of their clans and families. ²⁵The number from the tribe of Gad was 45,650.

²⁶From the descendants of Judah:

All the men twenty years old or more who were able to serve in the army were listed by name, according to the records of their clans and families. ²⁷The number from the tribe of Judah was 74,600.

²⁸From the descendants of Issachar:

All the men twenty years old or more who were able to serve in the army were listed by name, ac-

cording to the records of their clans and families. ²⁹The number from the tribe of Issachar was 54,400.   Ge 30:18; Nu 26:25

³⁰From the descendants of Zebulun:

All the men twenty years old or more who were able to serve in the army were listed by name, according to the records of their clans and families. ³¹The number from the tribe of Zebulun was 57,400.   Ge 30:20; Nu 26:27

³²From the sons of Joseph:

From the descendants of Ephraim:

All the men twenty years old or more who were able to serve in the army were listed by name, according to the records of their clans and families. ³³The number from the tribe of Ephraim was 40,500.   Ge 49:26; Nu 26:37

³⁴From the descendants of Manasseh:

All the men twenty years old or more who were able to serve in the army were listed by name, according to the records of their clans and families. ³⁵The number from the tribe of Manasseh was 32,200.   Ge 41:51; Nu 26:28

³⁶From the descendants of Benjamin:

All the men twenty years old or more who were able to serve in the army were listed by name, according to the records of their clans and families. ³⁷The number from the tribe of Benjamin was 35,400.   Ge 35:18; Nu 26:41

³⁸From the descendants of Dan:

All the men twenty years old or more who were able to serve in the army were listed by name, according to the records of their clans and families. ³⁹The number from the tribe of Dan was 62,700.

⁴⁰From the descendants of Asher:

All the men twenty years old or more who were able to serve in the army were listed by name, according to the records of their clans and families. ⁴¹The number from the tribe of Asher was 41,500.

⁴²From the descendants of Naphtali:

All the men twenty years old or more who were able to serve in the army were listed by name, according to the records of their clans and families. ⁴³The number from the tribe of Naphtali was 53,400.   Ge 30:8; Nu 26:50

⁴⁴These were the men counted by Moses and Aaron and the

and that is the way they set out, each with his clan and family.

The Levites

3 This is the account of the family of Aaron and Moses at the time the LORD talked with Moses on Mount Sinai.   Ex 6:27

2The names of the sons of Aaron were Nadab the firstborn and Abihu, Eleazar and Ithamar. 3Those were the names of Aaron's sons, the anointed priests, who were ordained to serve as priests. 4Nadab and Abihu, however, fell dead before the LORD when they made an offering with unauthorized fire before him in the Desert of Sinai. They had no sons; so only Eleazar and Ithamar served as priests during the lifetime of their father Aaron.   Ex 6:23

5The LORD said to Moses, 6"Bring the tribe of Levi and present them to Aaron the priest to assist him. 7They are to perform duties for him and for the whole community at the Tent of Meeting by doing the work of the tabernacle. 8They are to take care of all the furnishings of the Tent of Meeting, fulfilling the obligations of the Israelites by doing the work of the tabernacle. 9Give the Levites to Aaron and his sons; they are the Israelites who are to be given wholly to him.ᵃ 10Appoint Aaron and his sons to serve as priests; anyone else who approaches the sanctuary must be put to death."   Nu 8:6-22; 18:6

11The LORD also said to Moses, 12"I have taken the Levites from among the Israelites in place of the first male offspring of every Israelite woman. The Levites are mine, 13for all the firstborn are mine. When I struck down all the firstborn in Egypt, I set apart for myself every firstborn in Israel, whether man or animal. They are to be mine. I am the LORD."

14The LORD said to Moses in the Desert of Sinai, 15"Count the Levites by their families and clans. Count every male a month old or more." 16So Moses counted them, as he was commanded by the word of the LORD.   Nu 1:19; 18:16

17These were the names of the sons of Levi: Ge 29:34
    Gershon, Kohath and Merari.   Ex 6:16; Jos 21:6
18These were the names of the Gershonite clans:
    Libni and Shimei.   Ex 6:17
19The Kohathite clans:
    Amram, Izhar, Hebron and Uzziel.   Ex 6:18
20The Merarite clans:
    Mahli and Mushi.   Ex 6:19
These were the Levite clans, according to their families.

21To Gershon belonged the clans of the Libnites and Shimeites; these were the Gershonite

---

ᵃ9 Most manuscripts of the Masoretic Text; some manuscripts of the Masoretic Text, Samaritan Pentateuch and Septuagint (see also Num. 8:16) *to me*

clans. 22The number of all the males a month old or more who were counted was 7,500. 23The Gershonite clans were to camp on the west, behind the tabernacle. 24The leader of the families of the Gershonites was Eliasaph son of Lael. 25At the Tent of Meeting the Gershonites were responsible for the care of the tabernacle and tent, its coverings, the curtain at the entrance to the Tent of Meeting, 26the curtains of the courtyard, the curtain at the entrance to the courtyard surrounding the tabernacle and altar, and the ropes—and everything related to their use. Ex 6:17; Nu 4:25

27To Kohath belonged the clans of the Amramites, Izharites, Hebronites and Uzzielites; these were the Kohathite clans. 28The number of all the males a month old or more was 8,600.ª The Kohathites were responsible for the care of the sanctuary. 29The Kohathite clans were to camp on the south side of the tabernacle. 30The leader of the families of the Kohathite clans was Elizaphan son of Uzziel. 31They were responsible for the care of the ark, the table, the lampstand, the altars, the articles of the sanctuary used in ministering, the curtain, and everything related to their use. 32The chief leader of the Levites was Eleazar son of Aaron, the priest. He was appointed over those who were responsible for the care of the sanctuary. 1Ch 26:23

33To Merari belonged the clans of the Mahlites and the Mushites; these were the Merarite clans. 34The number of all the males a month old or more who were counted was 6,200. 35The leader of the families of the Merarite clans was Zuriel son of Abihail; they were to camp on the north side of the tabernacle. 36The Merarites were appointed to take care of the frames of the tabernacle, its crossbars, posts, bases, all its equipment, and everything related to their use, 37as well as the posts of the surrounding courtyard with their bases, tent pegs and ropes. Ex 6:19; Nu 4:29-32

38Moses and Aaron and his sons were to camp to the east of the tabernacle, toward the sunrise, in front of the Tent of Meeting. They were responsible for the care of the sanctuary on behalf of the Israelites. Anyone else who approached the sanctuary was to be put to death.

39The total number of Levites counted at the LORD's command by Moses and Aaron according to their clans, including every male a month old or more, was 22,000.

40The LORD said to Moses,

ª28 Hebrew; some Septuagint manuscripts *8,300*

"Count all the firstborn Israelite males who are a month old or more and make a list of their names. ⁴¹Take the Levites for me in place of all the firstborn of the Israelites, and the livestock of the Levites in place of all the firstborn of the livestock of the Israelites. I am the LORD."   Nu 1:2

⁴²So Moses counted all the firstborn of the Israelites, as the LORD commanded him. ⁴³The total number of firstborn males a month old or more, listed by name, was 22,273.   Nu 3:39

⁴⁴The LORD also said to Moses, ⁴⁵"Take the Levites in place of all the firstborn of Israel, and the livestock of the Levites in place of their livestock. The Levites are to be mine. I am the LORD. ⁴⁶To redeem the 273 firstborn Israelites who exceed the number of the Levites, ⁴⁷collect five shekels[a] for each one, according to the sanctuary shekel, which weighs twenty gerahs. ⁴⁸Give the money for the redemption of the additional Israelites to Aaron and his sons."   Ex 13:13

⁴⁹So Moses collected the redemption money from those who exceeded the number redeemed by the Levites. ⁵⁰From the firstborn of the Israelites he collected silver weighing 1,365 shekels,[b] according to the sanctuary shekel. ⁵¹Moses gave the redemption money to Aaron and his sons, as he was com-

manded by the word of the LORD.   Nu 4:46-48

The Kohathites

4 The LORD said to Moses and Aaron: ²"Take a census of the Kohathite branch of the Levites by their clans and families. ³Count all the men from thirty to fifty years of age who come to serve in the work in the Tent of Meeting.   Nu 8:25; 1Ch 23:3

⁴"This is the work of the Kohathites in the Tent of Meeting: the care of the most holy things. ⁵When the camp is to move, Aaron and his sons are to go in and take down the shielding curtain and cover the ark of the Testimony with it. ⁶Then they are to cover this with hides of sea cows,[c] spread a cloth of solid blue over that and put the poles in place.   Nu 3:28; 1Ch 23:26

⁷"Over the table of the Presence they are to spread a blue cloth and put on it the plates, dishes and bowls, and the jars for drink offerings; the bread that is continually there is to remain on it. ⁸Over these they are to spread a scarlet cloth, cover that with hides of sea cows and put its poles in place.   Ex 25:30

⁹"They are to take a blue cloth and cover the lampstand that is for light, together with its lamps, its wick trimmers and trays, and all its jars for the oil used to supply it. ¹⁰Then they are to wrap it and all its accesso-

---

^a47 That is, about 2 ounces (about 55 grams) ^b50 That is, about 35 pounds (about 15.5 kilograms)   ^c6 That is, dugongs; also in verses 8, 10, 11, 12, 14 and 25

ries in a covering of hides of sea cows and put it on a carrying frame.   Ex 25:31; 25:38

[11]"Over the gold altar they are to spread a blue cloth and cover that with hides of sea cows and put its poles in place.

[12]"They are to take all the articles used for ministering in the sanctuary, wrap them in a blue cloth, cover that with hides of sea cows and put them on a carrying frame.   Nu 3:31

[13]"They are to remove the ashes from the bronze altar and spread a purple cloth over it. [14]Then they are to place on it all the utensils used for ministering at the altar, including the firepans, meat forks, shovels and sprinkling bowls. Over it they are to spread a covering of hides of sea cows and put its poles in place.   Lev 1:16; 1Ch 28:17

[15]"After Aaron and his sons have finished covering the holy furnishings and all the holy articles, and when the camp is ready to move, the Kohathites are to come to do the carrying. But they must not touch the holy things or they will die. The Kohathites are to carry those things that are in the Tent of Meeting.   Nu 7:9; 2Sa 6:6

[16]"Eleazar son of Aaron, the priest, is to have charge of the oil for the light, the fragrant incense, the regular grain offering and the anointing oil. He is to be in charge of the entire tabernacle and everything in it, including its holy furnishings and articles."   Ex 29:41; Nu 3:32

[17]The LORD said to Moses and Aaron, [18]"See that the Kohathite tribal clans are not cut off from the Levites. [19]So that they may live and not die when they come near the most holy things, do this for them: Aaron and his sons are to go into the sanctuary and assign to each man his work and what he is to carry. [20]But the Kohathites must not go in to look at the holy things, even for a moment, or they will die."   Ex 19:21; Nu 3:32

The Gershonites

[21]The LORD said to Moses, [22]"Take a census also of the Gershonites by their families and clans. [23]Count all the men from thirty to fifty years of age who come to serve in the work at the Tent of Meeting.   Nu 3:22

[24]"This is the service of the Gershonite clans as they work and carry burdens: [25]They are to carry the curtains of the tabernacle, the Tent of Meeting, its covering and the outer covering of hides of sea cows, the curtains for the entrance to the Tent of Meeting, [26]the curtains of the courtyard surrounding the tabernacle and altar, the curtain for the entrance, the ropes and all the equipment used in its service. The Gershonites are to do all that needs to be done with these things. [27]All their service, whether carrying or doing other work, is to be done under the direction of Aaron and his sons. You shall assign to them as their responsibility all

they are to carry. ²⁸This is the service of the Gershonite clans at the Tent of Meeting. Their duties are to be under the direction of Ithamar son of Aaron, the priest.   Ex 27:16; Nu 3:25

The Merarites

²⁹"Count the Merarites by their clans and families. ³⁰Count all the men from thirty to fifty years of age who come to serve in the work at the Tent of Meeting. ³¹This is their duty as they perform service at the Tent of Meeting: to carry the frames of the tabernacle, its crossbars, posts and bases, ³²as well as the posts of the surrounding courtyard with their bases, tent pegs, ropes, all their equipment and everything related to their use. Assign to each man the specific things he is to carry. ³³This is the service of the Merarite clans as they work at the Tent of Meeting under the direction of Ithamar son of Aaron, the priest."

The Numbering of the Levite Clans

³⁴Moses, Aaron and the leaders of the community counted the Kohathites by their clans and families. ³⁵All the men from thirty to fifty years of age who came to serve in the work in the Tent of Meeting, ³⁶counted by clans, were 2,750. ³⁷This was the total of all those in the Kohathite clans who served in the Tent of Meeting. Moses and Aaron

counted them according to the LORD's command through Moses.   Nu 4:3

³⁸The Gershonites were counted by their clans and families. ³⁹All the men from thirty to fifty years of age who came to serve in the work at the Tent of Meeting, ⁴⁰counted by their clans and families, were 2,630. ⁴¹This was the total of those in the Gershonite clans who served at the Tent of Meeting. Moses and Aaron counted them according to the LORD's command.   Ge 46:11; Nu 4:22

⁴²The Merarites were counted by their clans and families. ⁴³All the men from thirty to fifty years of age who came to serve in the work at the Tent of Meeting, ⁴⁴counted by their clans, were 3,200. ⁴⁵This was the total of those in the Merarite clans. Moses and Aaron counted them according to the LORD's command through Moses.   Nu 4:29

⁴⁶So Moses, Aaron and the leaders of Israel counted all the Levites by their clans and families. ⁴⁷All the men from thirty to fifty years of age who came to do the work of serving and carrying the Tent of Meeting ⁴⁸numbered 8,580. ⁴⁹At the LORD's command through Moses, each was assigned his work and told what to carry.

Thus they were counted, as the LORD commanded Moses.

The Purity of the Camp

5 The LORD said to Moses, ²"Command the Israelites to

send away from the camp anyone who has an infectious skin disease*a* or a discharge of any kind, or who is ceremonially unclean because of a dead body. ³Send away male and female alike; send them outside the camp so they will not defile their camp, where I dwell among them." ⁴The Israelites did this; they sent them outside the camp. They did just as the LORD had instructed Moses.

Restitution for Wrongs

⁵The LORD said to Moses, ⁶"Say to the Israelites: 'When a man or woman wrongs another in any way*b* and so is unfaithful to the LORD, that person is guilty ⁷and must confess the sin he has committed. He must make full restitution for his wrong, add one fifth to it and give it all to the person he has wronged. ⁸But if that person has no close relative to whom restitution can be made for the wrong, the restitution belongs to the LORD and must be given to the priest, along with the ram with which atonement is made for him. ⁹All the sacred contributions the Israelites bring to a priest will belong to him. ¹⁰Each man's sacred gifts are his own, but what he gives to the priest will belong to the priest.' "

Lev 6:2

The Test for an Unfaithful Wife

¹¹Then the LORD said to Moses, ¹²"Speak to the Israelites and say to them: 'If a man's wife goes astray and is unfaithful to him ¹³by sleeping with another man, and this is hidden from her husband and her impurity is undetected (since there is no witness against her and she has not been caught in the act), ¹⁴and if feelings of jealousy come over her husband and he suspects his wife and she is impure—or if he is jealous and suspects her even though she is not impure— ¹⁵then he is to take his wife to the priest. He must also take an offering of a tenth of an ephah*c* of barley flour on her behalf. He must not pour oil on it or put incense on it, because it is a grain offering for jealousy, a reminder offering to draw attention to guilt.   Ex 20:14

¹⁶" 'The priest shall bring her and have her stand before the LORD. ¹⁷Then he shall take some holy water in a clay jar and put some dust from the tabernacle floor into the water. ¹⁸After the priest has had the woman stand before the LORD, he shall loosen her hair and place in her hands the reminder offering, the grain offering for jealousy, while he himself holds the bitter water that brings a curse. ¹⁹Then the priest shall put the woman un-

---

a2 Traditionally *leprosy*; the Hebrew word was used for various diseases affecting the skin—not necessarily leprosy.   *b6* Or *woman commits any wrong common to mankind* *c15* That is, probably about 2 quarts (about 2 liters)

der oath and say to her, "If no other man has slept with you and you have not gone astray and become impure while married to your husband, may this bitter water that brings a curse not harm you. 20But if you have gone astray while married to your husband and you have defiled yourself by sleeping with a man other than your husband"— 21here the priest is to put the woman under this curse of the oath—"may the LORD cause your people to curse and denounce you when he causes your thigh to waste away and your abdomen to swell. a 22May this water that brings a curse enter your body so that your abdomen swells and your thigh wastes away. b"   Jos 6:26

" 'Then the woman is to say, "Amen. So be it."   Dt 27:15

23" 'The priest is to write these curses on a scroll and then wash them off into the bitter water. 24He shall have the woman drink the bitter water that brings a curse, and this water will enter her and cause bitter suffering. 25The priest is to take from her hands the grain offering for jealousy, wave it before the LORD and bring it to the altar. 26The priest is then to take a handful of the grain offering as a memorial offering and burn it on the altar; after that, he is to have the woman drink the water. 27If she has defiled her-

self and been unfaithful to her husband, then when she is made to drink the water that brings a curse, it will go into her and cause bitter suffering; her abdomen will swell and her thigh waste away, c and she will become accursed among her people. 28If, however, the woman has not defiled herself and is free from impurity, she will be cleared of guilt and will be able to have children.   Lev 8:27

29" 'This, then, is the law of jealousy when a woman goes astray and defiles herself while married to her husband, 30or when feelings of jealousy come over a man because he suspects his wife. The priest is to have her stand before the LORD and is to apply this entire law to her. 31The husband will be innocent of any wrongdoing, but the woman will bear the consequences of her sin.' "   Lev 5:1

The Nazirite

6 The LORD said to Moses, 2"Speak to the Israelites and say to them: 'If a man or woman wants to make a special vow, a vow of separation to the LORD as a Nazirite, 3he must abstain from wine and other fermented drink and must not drink vinegar made from wine or from other fermented drink. He must not drink grape juice or eat grapes or raisins. 4As long as he is a Nazirite, he must not eat

---

a21 Or causes you to have a miscarrying womb and barrenness   b22 Or body and cause you to be barren and have a miscarrying womb   c27 Or suffering; she will have barrenness and a miscarrying womb

anything that comes from the grapevine, not even the seeds or skins.   Jdg 13:5; 16:17

5" 'During the entire period of his vow of separation no razor may be used on his head. He must be holy until the period of his separation to the LORD is over; he must let the hair of his head grow long. 6Throughout the period of his separation to the LORD he must not go near a dead body. 7Even if his own father or mother or brother or sister dies, he must not make himself ceremonially unclean on account of them, because the symbol of his separation to God is on his head. 8Throughout the period of his separation he is consecrated to the LORD.   Nu 9:6; 1Sa 1:11

9" 'If someone dies suddenly in his presence, thus defiling the hair he has dedicated, he must shave his head on the day of his cleansing—the seventh day. 10Then on the eighth day he must bring two doves or two young pigeons to the priest at the entrance to the Tent of Meeting. 11The priest is to offer one as a sin offering and the other as a burnt offering to make atonement for him because he sinned by being in the presence of the dead body. That same day he is to consecrate his head. 12He must dedicate himself to the LORD for the period of his separation and must bring a year-old male lamb as a guilt of-

fering. The previous days do not count, because he became defiled during his separation.

13" 'Now this is the law for the Nazirite when the period of his separation is over. He is to be brought to the entrance to the Tent of Meeting. 14There he is to present his offerings to the LORD: a year-old male lamb without defect for a burnt offering, a year-old ewe lamb without defect for a sin offering, a ram without defect for a fellowship offering,[a] 15together with their grain offerings and drink offerings, and a basket of bread made without yeast—cakes made of fine flour mixed with oil, and wafers spread with oil.

16" 'The priest is to present them before the LORD and make the sin offering and the burnt offering. 17He is to present the basket of unleavened bread and is to sacrifice the ram as a fellowship offering to the LORD, together with its grain offering and drink offering.   Lev 1:3; 23:13

18" 'Then at the entrance to the Tent of Meeting, the Nazirite must shave off the hair that he dedicated. He is to take the hair and put it in the fire that is under the sacrifice of the fellowship offering.   Ac 21:24

19" 'After the Nazirite has shaved off the hair of his dedication, the priest is to place in his hands a boiled shoulder of the ram, and a cake and a wafer from the basket, both made

a14 Traditionally *peace offering*; also in verses 17 and 18

people of Reuben, brought his offering. _{Nu 1:5}

³¹His offering was one silver plate weighing a hundred and thirty shekels, and one silver sprinkling bowl weighing seventy shekels, both according to the sanctuary shekel, each filled with fine flour mixed with oil as a grain offering; ³²one gold dish weighing ten shekels, filled with incense; ³³one young bull, one ram and one male lamb a year old, for a burnt offering; ³⁴one male goat for a sin offering; ³⁵and two oxen, five rams, five male goats and five male lambs a year old, to be sacrificed as a fellowship offering. This was the offering of Elizur son of Shedeur.

³⁶On the fifth day Shelumiel son of Zurishaddai, the leader of the people of Simeon, brought his offering. _{Nu 1:6}

³⁷His offering was one silver plate weighing a hundred and thirty shekels, and one silver sprinkling bowl weighing seventy shekels, both according to the sanctuary shekel, each filled with fine flour mixed with oil as a grain offering; ³⁸one gold dish weighing ten shekels, filled with incense; ³⁹one young bull, one ram and one male lamb a year old, for a burnt offering; ⁴⁰one male goat for a sin of-

fering; ⁴¹and two oxen, five rams, five male goats and five male lambs a year old, to be sacrificed as a fellowship offering. This was the offering of Shelumiel son of Zurishaddai.

⁴²On the sixth day Eliasaph son of Deuel, the leader of the people of Gad, brought his offering. _{Nu 1:14}

⁴³His offering was one silver plate weighing a hundred and thirty shekels, and one silver sprinkling bowl weighing seventy shekels, both according to the sanctuary shekel, each filled with fine flour mixed with oil as a grain offering; ⁴⁴one gold dish weighing ten shekels, filled with incense; ⁴⁵one young bull, one ram and one male lamb a year old, for a burnt offering; ⁴⁶one male goat for a sin offering; ⁴⁷and two oxen, five rams, five male goats and five male lambs a year old, to be sacrificed as a fellowship offering. This was the offering of Eliasaph son of Deuel.

⁴⁸On the seventh day Elishama son of Ammihud, the leader of the people of Ephraim, brought his offering. _{Nu 1:10}

⁴⁹His offering was one silver plate weighing a hundred and thirty shekels, and one silver sprinkling bowl weighing seventy shekels, both according to the sanc-

tuary shekel, each filled with fine flour mixed with oil as a grain offering; ⁵⁰one gold dish weighing ten shekels, filled with incense; ⁵¹one young bull, one ram and one male lamb a year old, for a burnt offering; ⁵²one male goat for a sin offering; ⁵³and two oxen, five rams, five male goats and five male lambs a year old, to be sacrificed as a fellowship offering. This was the offering of Elishama son of Ammihud.   Heb 10:4

⁵⁴On the eighth day Gamaliel son of Pedahzur, the leader of the people of Manasseh, brought his offering.   Nu 1:10
⁵⁵His offering was one silver plate weighing a hundred and thirty shekels, and one silver sprinkling bowl weighing seventy shekels, both according to the sanctuary shekel, each filled with fine flour mixed with oil as a grain offering; ⁵⁶one gold dish weighing ten shekels, filled with incense; ⁵⁷one young bull, one ram and one male lamb a year old, for a burnt offering; ⁵⁸one male goat for a sin offering; ⁵⁹and two oxen, five rams, five male goats and five male lambs a year old, to be sacrificed as a fellowship offering. This was the offering of Gamaliel son of Pedahzur.

⁶⁰On the ninth day Abidan son of Gideoni, the leader of the people of Benjamin, brought his offering.   Nu 1:11
⁶¹His offering was one silver plate weighing a hundred and thirty shekels, and one silver sprinkling bowl weighing seventy shekels, both according to the sanctuary shekel, each filled with fine flour mixed with oil as a grain offering; ⁶²one gold dish weighing ten shekels, filled with incense; ⁶³one young bull, one ram and one male lamb a year old, for a burnt offering; ⁶⁴one male goat for a sin offering; ⁶⁵and two oxen, five rams, five male goats and five male lambs a year old, to be sacrificed as a fellowship offering. This was the offering of Abidan son of Gideoni.

⁶⁶On the tenth day Ahiezer son of Ammishaddai, the leader of the people of Dan, brought his offering.   Nu 1:12
⁶⁷His offering was one silver plate weighing a hundred and thirty shekels, and one silver sprinkling bowl weighing seventy shekels, both according to the sanctuary shekel, each filled with fine flour mixed with oil as a grain offering; ⁶⁸one gold dish weighing ten shekels, filled with incense; ⁶⁹one young bull, one ram and one male lamb a year old, for a burnt offering;

70one male goat for a sin offering; 71and two oxen, five rams, five male goats and five male lambs a year old, to be sacrificed as a fellowship offering. This was the offering of Ahiezer son of Ammishaddai.   Heb 10:4

72On the eleventh day Pagiel son of Ocran, the leader of the people of Asher, brought his offering.   Nu 1:13

73His offering was one silver plate weighing a hundred and thirty shekels, and one silver sprinkling bowl weighing seventy shekels, both according to the sanctuary shekel, each filled with fine flour mixed with oil as a grain offering; 74one gold dish weighing ten shekels, filled with incense; 75one young bull, one ram and one male lamb a year old, for a burnt offering; 76one male goat for a sin offering; 77and two oxen, five rams, five male goats and five male lambs a year old, to be sacrificed as a fellowship offering. This was the offering of Pagiel son of Ocran.

78On the twelfth day Ahira son of Enan, the leader of the people of Naphtali, brought his offering.   Nu 1:15

79His offering was one silver plate weighing a hundred and thirty shekels, and one silver sprinkling bowl weighing seventy shekels, both according to the sanctuary shekel, each filled with fine flour mixed with oil as a grain offering; 80one gold dish weighing ten shekels, filled with incense; 81one young bull, one ram and one male lamb a year old, for a burnt offering; 82one male goat for a sin offering; 83and two oxen, five rams, five male goats and five male lambs a year old, to be sacrificed as a fellowship offering. This was the offering of Ahira son of Enan.

84These were the offerings of the Israelite leaders for the dedication of the altar when it was anointed: twelve silver plates, twelve silver sprinkling bowls and twelve gold dishes. 85Each silver plate weighed a hundred and thirty shekels, and each sprinkling bowl seventy shekels. Altogether, the silver dishes weighed two thousand four hundred shekels,a according to the sanctuary shekel. 86The twelve gold dishes filled with incense weighed ten shekels each, according to the sanctuary shekel. Altogether, the gold dishes weighed a hundred and twenty shekels. b 87The total number of animals for the burnt offering came to twelve

---

a85 That is, about 60 pounds (about 28 kilograms)   b86 That is, about 3 pounds (about 1.4 kilograms)

young bulls, twelve rams and twelve male lambs a year old, together with their grain offering. Twelve male goats were used for the sin offering. 88The total number of animals for the sacrifice of the fellowship offering came to twenty-four oxen, sixty rams, sixty male goats and sixty male lambs a year old. These were the offerings for the dedication of the altar after it was anointed. Nu 4:14

89When Moses entered the Tent of Meeting to speak with the LORD, he heard the voice speaking to him from between the two cherubim above the atonement cover on the ark of the Testimony. And he spoke with him. Ex 33:9; Ps 80:1

Setting Up the Lamps

8 The LORD said to Moses, 2"Speak to Aaron and say to him, 'When you set up the seven lamps, they are to light the area in front of the lampstand.'" Ex 25:37; Lev 24:3

3Aaron did so; he set up the lamps so that they faced forward on the lampstand, just as the LORD commanded Moses. 4This is how the lampstand was made: It was made of hammered gold—from its base to its blossoms. The lampstand was made exactly like the pattern the LORD had shown Moses.

The Setting Apart of the Levites

5The LORD said to Moses:

6"Take the Levites from among the other Israelites and make them ceremonially clean. 7To purify them, do this: Sprinkle the water of cleansing on them; then have them shave their whole bodies and wash their clothes, and so purify themselves. 8Have them take a young bull with its grain offering of fine flour mixed with oil; then you are to take a second young bull for a sin offering. 9Bring the Levites to the front of the Tent of Meeting and assemble the whole Israelite community. 10You are to bring the Levites before the LORD, and the Israelites are to lay their hands on them. 11Aaron is to present the Levites before the LORD as a wave offering from the Israelites, so that they may be ready to do the work of the LORD.

12"After the Levites lay their hands on the heads of the bulls, use the one for a sin offering to the LORD and the other for a burnt offering, to make atonement for the Levites. 13Have the Levites stand in front of Aaron and his sons and then present them as a wave offering to the LORD. 14In this way you are to set the Levites apart from the other Israelites, and the Levites will be mine. Ex 29:10; Nu 3:12

15"After you have purified the Levites and presented them as a wave offering, they are to come to do their work at the Tent of Meeting. 16They are the Israelites who are to be given wholly to me. I have taken them

as my own in place of the first-born, the first male offspring from every Israelite woman. [17]Every firstborn male in Israel, whether man or animal, is mine. When I struck down all the firstborn in Egypt, I set them apart for myself. [18]And I have taken the Levites in place of all the firstborn sons in Israel. [19]Of all the Israelites, I have given the Levites as gifts to Aaron and his sons to do the work at the Tent of Meeting on behalf of the Israelites and to make atonement for them so that no plague will strike the Israelites when they go near the sanctuary."

[20]Moses, Aaron and the whole Israelite community did with the Levites just as the LORD commanded Moses. [21]The Levites purified themselves and washed their clothes. Then Aaron presented them as a wave offering before the LORD and made atonement for them to purify them. [22]After that, the Levites came to do their work at the Tent of Meeting under the supervision of Aaron and his sons. They did with the Levites just as the LORD commanded Moses.   Ge 35:2; Nu 16:47

[23]The LORD said to Moses, [24]"This applies to the Levites: Men twenty-five years old or more shall come to take part in the work at the Tent of Meeting, [25]but at the age of fifty, they must retire from their regular service and work no longer. [26]They may assist their brothers in performing their duties at the Tent of Meeting, but they themselves must not do the work. This, then, is how you are to assign the responsibilities of the Levites."   Nu 4:3; 1Ch 23:3

The Passover

9 The LORD spoke to Moses in the Desert of Sinai in the first month of the second year after they came out of Egypt. He said, [2]"Have the Israelites celebrate the Passover at the appointed time. [3]Celebrate it at the appointed time, at twilight on the fourteenth day of this month, in accordance with all its rules and regulations."   Nu 1:1

[4]So Moses told the Israelites to celebrate the Passover, [5]and they did so in the Desert of Sinai at twilight on the fourteenth day of the first month. The Israelites did everything just as the LORD commanded Moses. Ex 12:11

[6]But some of them could not celebrate the Passover on that day because they were ceremonially unclean on account of a dead body. So they came to Moses and Aaron that same day [7]and said to Moses, "We have become unclean because of a dead body, but why should we be kept from presenting the LORD's offering with the other Israelites at the appointed time?"   Ex 18:15; Nu 27:2

[8]Moses answered them, "Wait until I find out what the LORD commands concerning you."   Nu 27:5; Ps 85:8

[9]Then the LORD said to Moses, [10]"Tell the Israelites:

'When any of you or your descendants are unclean because of a dead body or are away on a journey, they may still celebrate the LORD's Passover. ¹¹They are to celebrate it on the fourteenth day of the second month at twilight. They are to eat the lamb, together with unleavened bread and bitter herbs. ¹²They must not leave any of it till morning or break any of its bones. When they celebrate the Passover, they must follow all the regulations. ¹³But if a man who is ceremonially clean and not on a journey fails to celebrate the Passover, that person must be cut off from his people because he did not present the LORD's offering at the appointed time. That man will bear the consequences of his sin.   Ex 12:8

¹⁴" 'An alien living among you who wants to celebrate the LORD's Passover must do so in accordance with its rules and regulations. You must have the same regulations for the alien and the native-born.' "   Ex 12:19

The Cloud Above the Tabernacle

¹⁵On the day the tabernacle, the Tent of the Testimony, was set up, the cloud covered it. From evening till morning the cloud above the tabernacle looked like fire. ¹⁶That is how it continued to be; the cloud covered it, and at night it looked like fire. ¹⁷Whenever the cloud lifted from above the Tent, the Israelites set out; wherever the cloud settled, the Israelites encamped. ¹⁸At the LORD's command the Israelites set out, and at his command they encamped. As long as the cloud stayed over the tabernacle, they remained in camp. ¹⁹When the cloud remained over the tabernacle a long time, the Israelites obeyed the LORD's order and did not set out. ²⁰Sometimes the cloud was over the tabernacle only a few days; at the LORD's command they would encamp, and then at his command they would set out. ²¹Sometimes the cloud stayed only from evening till morning, and when it lifted in the morning, they set out. Whether by day or by night, whenever the cloud lifted, they set out. ²²Whether the cloud stayed over the tabernacle for two days or a month or a year, the Israelites would remain in camp and not set out; but when it lifted, they would set out. ²³At the LORD's command they encamped, and at the LORD's command they set out. They obeyed the LORD's order, in accordance with his command through Moses.   Ex 13:21; Lev 8:35

The Silver Trumpets

10 The LORD said to Moses: ²"Make two trumpets of hammered silver, and use them for calling the community together and for having the camps set out. ³When both are sounded, the whole community is to assemble before you at the en-

trance to the Tent of Meeting. ⁴If only one is sounded, the leaders—the heads of the clans of Israel—are to assemble before you. ⁵When a trumpet blast is sounded, the tribes camping on the east are to set out. ⁶At the sounding of a second blast, the camps on the south are to set out. The blast will be the signal for setting out. ⁷To gather the assembly, blow the trumpets, but not with the same signal.

⁸"The sons of Aaron, the priests, are to blow the trumpets. This is to be a lasting ordinance for you and the generations to come. ⁹When you go into battle in your own land against an enemy who is oppressing you, sound a blast on the trumpets. Then you will be remembered by the LORD your God and rescued from your enemies. ¹⁰Also at your times of rejoicing—your appointed feasts and New Moon festivals—you are to sound the trumpets over your burnt offerings and fellowship offerings,ᵃ and they will be a memorial for you before your God. I am the LORD your God."   Jdg 2:18; Ps 106:4

The Israelites Leave Sinai

¹¹On the twentieth day of the second month of the second year, the cloud lifted from above the tabernacle of the Testimony. ¹²Then the Israelites set out from the Desert of Sinai and traveled from place to place un-

til the cloud came to rest in the Desert of Paran. ¹³They set out, this first time, at the LORD's command through Moses. Nu 9:17

¹⁴The divisions of the camp of Judah went first, under their standard. Nahshon son of Amminadab was in command. ¹⁵Nethanel son of Zuar was over the division of the tribe of Issachar, ¹⁶and Eliab son of Helon was over the division of the tribe of Zebulun. ¹⁷Then the tabernacle was taken down, and the Gershonites and Merarites, who carried it, set out.   Nu 2:3-9

¹⁸The divisions of the camp of Reuben went next, under their standard. Elizur son of Shedeur was in command. ¹⁹Shelumiel son of Zurishaddai was over the division of the tribe of Simeon, ²⁰and Eliasaph son of Deuel was over the division of the tribe of Gad. ²¹Then the Kohathites set out, carrying the holy things. The tabernacle was to be set up before they arrived.   Nu 2:10-16

²²The divisions of the camp of Ephraim went next, under their standard. Elishama son of Ammihud was in command. ²³Gamaliel son of Pedahzur was over the division of the tribe of Manasseh, ²⁴and Abidan son of Gideoni was over the division of the tribe of Benjamin.   Nu 2:24

²⁵Finally, as the rear guard for all the units, the divisions of the camp of Dan set out, under their standard. Ahiezer son of Ammishaddai was in com-

ᵃ10 Traditionally *peace offerings*

mand. ²⁶Pagiel son of Ocran was over the division of the tribe of Asher, ²⁷and Ahira son of Enan was over the division of the tribe of Naphtali. ²⁸This was the order of march for the Israelite divisions as they set out.

²⁹Now Moses said to Hobab son of Reuel the Midianite, Moses' father-in-law, "We are setting out for the place about which the LORD said, 'I will give it to you.' Come with us and we will treat you well, for the LORD has promised good things to Israel."   Ex 2:18; Jdg 4:11

³⁰He answered, "No, I will not go; I am going back to my own land and my own people."

³¹But Moses said, "Please do not leave us. You know where we should camp in the desert, and you can be our eyes. ³²If you come with us, we will share with you whatever good things the LORD gives us."   Job 29:15

³³So they set out from the mountain of the LORD and traveled for three days. The ark of the covenant of the LORD went before them during those three days to find them a place to rest. ³⁴The cloud of the LORD was over them by day when they set out from the camp.   Dt 1:33

³⁵Whenever the ark set out, Moses said,

"Rise up, O LORD!
  May your enemies be
    scattered;
  may your foes flee before
    you."   Dt 7:10; Ps 68:1

³⁶Whenever it came to rest, he said,

"Return, O LORD,
  to the countless thousands
    of Israel."   Ge 15:5; Isa 52:8

Fire From the LORD

11 Now the people complained about their hardships in the hearing of the LORD, and when he heard them his anger was aroused. Then fire from the LORD burned among them and consumed some of the outskirts of the camp. ²When the people cried out to Moses, he prayed to the LORD and the fire died down. ³So that place was called Taberah,ᵃ because fire from the LORD had burned among them. Lev 10:2

Quail From the LORD

⁴The rabble with them began to crave other food, and again the Israelites started wailing and said, "If only we had meat to eat! ⁵We remember the fish we ate in Egypt at no cost—also the cucumbers, melons, leeks, onions and garlic. ⁶But now we have lost our appetite; we never see anything but this manna!"

⁷The manna was like coriander seed and looked like resin. ⁸The people went around gathering it, and then ground it in a handmill or crushed it in a mortar. They cooked it in a pot or made it into cakes. And it tasted like something made with olive oil. ⁹When the dew settled on

---

ᵃ3 *Taberah* means *burning*.

the camp at night, the manna also came down. Ex 16:31

¹⁰Moses heard the people of every family wailing, each at the entrance to his tent. The LORD became exceedingly angry, and Moses was troubled. ¹¹He asked the LORD, "Why have you brought this trouble on your servant? What have I done to displease you that you put the burden of all these people on me? ¹²Did I conceive all these people? Did I give them birth? Why do you tell me to carry them in my arms, as a nurse carries an infant, to the land you promised on oath to their forefathers? ¹³Where can I get meat for all these people? They keep wailing to me, 'Give us meat to eat!' ¹⁴I cannot carry all these people by myself; the burden is too heavy for me. ¹⁵If this is how you are going to treat me, put me to death right now—if I have found favor in your eyes—and do not let me face my own ruin." Ps 78:21; Isa 40:11

¹⁶The LORD said to Moses: "Bring me seventy of Israel's elders who are known to you as leaders and officials among the people. Have them come to the Tent of Meeting, that they may stand there with you. ¹⁷I will come down and speak with you there, and I will take of the Spirit that is on you and put the Spirit on them. They will help you carry the burden of the people so that you will not have to carry it alone. Ex 3:16; 1Sa 10:6

¹⁸"Tell the people: 'Consecrate yourselves in preparation for tomorrow, when you will eat meat. The LORD heard you when you wailed, "If only we had meat to eat! We were better off in Egypt!" Now the LORD will give you meat, and you will eat it. ¹⁹You will not eat it for just one day, or two days, or five, ten or twenty days, ²⁰but for a whole month—until it comes out of your nostrils and you loathe it—because you have rejected the LORD, who is among you, and have wailed before him, saying, "Why did we ever leave Egypt?" ' " Ex 19:10

²¹But Moses said, "Here I am among six hundred thousand men on foot, and you say, 'I will give them meat to eat for a whole month!' ²²Would they have enough if flocks and herds were slaughtered for them? Would they have enough if all the fish in the sea were caught for them?" Ex 12:37; Mt 15:33

²³The LORD answered Moses, "Is the LORD's arm too short? You will now see whether or not what I say will come true for you." Nu 23:19; Isa 50:2

²⁴So Moses went out and told the people what the LORD had said. He brought together seventy of their elders and had them stand around the Tent. ²⁵Then the LORD came down in the cloud and spoke with him, and he took of the Spirit that was on him and put the Spirit on the seventy elders. When the Spirit rested on them, they

prophesied, but they did not do so again. *a*   Nu 12:5; 1Sa 10:6

26However, two men, whose names were Eldad and Medad, had remained in the camp. They were listed among the elders, but did not go out to the Tent. Yet the Spirit also rested on them, and they prophesied in the camp. 27A young man ran and told Moses, "Eldad and Medad are prophesying in the camp."   1Ch 12:18; Rev 1:10

28Joshua son of Nun, who had been Moses' aide since youth, spoke up and said, "Moses, my lord, stop them!"

29But Moses replied, "Are you jealous for my sake? I wish that all the LORD's people were prophets and that the LORD would put his Spirit on them!" 30Then Moses and the elders of Israel returned to the camp.

31Now a wind went out from the LORD and drove quail in from the sea. It brought them*b* down all around the camp to about three feet*c* above the ground, as far as a day's walk in any direction. 32All that day and night and all the next day the people went out and gathered quail. No one gathered less than ten homers. *d* Then they spread them out all around the camp. 33But while the meat was still between their teeth and before it could be consumed, the anger of the LORD burned against the people, and he struck them

with a severe plague. 34Therefore the place was named Kibroth Hattaavah,*e* because there they buried the people who had craved other food.   Ex 16:13; Ps 78:30

35From Kibroth Hattaavah the people traveled to Hazeroth and stayed there.   Nu 12:16; 33:17

Miriam and Aaron Oppose Moses

12 Miriam and Aaron began to talk against Moses because of his Cushite wife, for he had married a Cushite. 2"Has the LORD spoken only through Moses?" they asked. "Hasn't he also spoken through us?" And the LORD heard this.   Ex 2:21

3(Now Moses was a very humble man, more humble than anyone else on the face of the earth.)   Nu 20:10; Mt 11:29

4At once the LORD said to Moses, Aaron and Miriam, "Come out to the Tent of Meeting, all three of you." So the three of them came out. 5Then the LORD came down in a pillar of cloud; he stood at the entrance to the Tent and summoned Aaron and Miriam. When both of them stepped forward, 6he said, "Listen to my words: Nu 11:25; 16:19

"When a prophet of the
     LORD is among you,
I reveal myself to him in
     visions,   Ge 15:1
I speak to him in dreams.

---

*a*25 Or *prophesied and continued to do so*   *b*31 Or *They flew*   *c*31 Hebrew *two cubits* (about 1 meter)   *d*32 That is, probably about 60 bushels (about 2.2 kiloliters)   *e*34 *Kibroth Hattaavah* means *graves of craving*.

7But this is not true of my
    servant Moses;
  he is faithful in all my
    house.   Dt 34:5; Ps 105:26
8With him I speak face to face,
    clearly and not in riddles;
  he sees the form of the
    LORD.   Ex 20:4; Job 19:26
  Why then were you not
    afraid
    to speak against my servant
    Moses?"   Ex 24:23

9The anger of the LORD
burned against them, and he
left them.   Ge 17:22; Ex 4:14

10When the cloud lifted from
above the Tent, there stood
Miriam—leprous,ᵃ like snow.
Aaron turned toward her and
saw that she had leprosy; 11and
he said to Moses, "Please, my
lord, do not hold against us the
sin we have so foolishly committed. 12Do not let her be like a
stillborn infant coming from its
mother's womb with its flesh
half eaten away."   Dt 24:9

13So Moses cried out to the
LORD, "O God, please heal
her!"

14The LORD replied to Moses,
"If her father had spit in her
face, would she not have been
in disgrace for seven days? Confine her outside the camp for
seven days; after that she can be
brought back." 15So Miriam was
confined outside the camp for
seven days, and the people did
not move on till she was
brought back.   Lev 13:46; Dt 25:9

16After that, the people left
Hazeroth and encamped in the
Desert of Paran.   Ge 21:21; Nu 11:35

Exploring Canaan

13 The LORD said to Moses,
2"Send some men to ex-
plore the land of Canaan, which
I am giving to the Israelites.
From each ancestral tribe send
one of its leaders."   Dt 1:22

3So at the LORD's command
Moses sent them out from the
Desert of Paran. All of them
were leaders of the Israelites.
4These are their names: Nu 1:16

from the tribe of Reuben,
    Shammua son of Zaccur;
5from the tribe of Simeon,
    Shaphat son of Hori;
6from the tribe of Judah,
    Caleb son of Jephunneh;
7from the tribe of Issachar,
    Igal son of Joseph;
8from the tribe of Ephraim,
    Hoshea son of Nun;   Nu 11:28
9from the tribe of Benjamin,
    Palti son of Raphu;
10from the tribe of Zebulun,
    Gaddiel son of Sodi;
11from the tribe of Manasseh
    (a tribe of Joseph), Gaddi
    son of Susi;
12from the tribe of Dan, Am-
    miel son of Gemalli;
13from the tribe of Asher, Se-
    thur son of Michael;
14from the tribe of Naphtali,
    Nahbi son of Vophsi;
15from the tribe of Gad, Geuel
    son of Maki.

ᵃ10 The Hebrew word was used for various diseases affecting the skin—not necessarily
leprosy.

16These are the names of the men Moses sent to explore the land. (Moses gave Hoshea son of Nun the name Joshua.) Dt 32:44

17When Moses sent them to explore Canaan, he said, "Go up through the Negev and on into the hill country. 18See what the land is like and whether the people who live there are strong or weak, few or many. 19What kind of land do they live in? Is it good or bad? What kind of towns do they live in? Are they unwalled or fortified? 20How is the soil? Is it fertile or poor? Are there trees on it or not? Do your best to bring back some of the fruit of the land." (It was the season for the first ripe grapes.)

21So they went up and explored the land from the Desert of Zin as far as Rehob, toward Lebo*a* Hamath. 22They went up through the Negev and came to Hebron, where Ahiman, Sheshai and Talmai, the descendants of Anak, lived. (Hebron had been built seven years before Zoan in Egypt.) 23When they reached the Valley of Eshcol,*b* they cut off a branch bearing a single cluster of grapes. Two of them carried it on a pole between them, along with some pomegranates and figs. 24That place was called the Valley of Eshcol because of the cluster of grapes the Israelites cut off there. 25At the end of forty days they returned from exploring the land.   Jos 15:13; 19:28

Report on the Exploration

26They came back to Moses and Aaron and the whole Israelite community at Kadesh in the Desert of Paran. There they reported to them and to the whole assembly and showed them the fruit of the land. 27They gave Moses this account: "We went into the land to which you sent us, and it does flow with milk and honey! Here is its fruit. 28But the people who live there are powerful, and the cities are fortified and very large. We even saw descendants of Anak there. 29The Amalekites live in the Negev; the Hittites, Jebusites and Amorites live in the hill country; and the Canaanites live near the sea and along the Jordan."   Ex 3:8; Nu 32:8

30Then Caleb silenced the people before Moses and said, "We should go up and take possession of the land, for we can certainly do it."   Nu 14:6

31But the men who had gone up with him said, "We can't attack those people; they are stronger than we are." 32And they spread among the Israelites a bad report about the land they had explored. They said, "The land we explored devours those living in it. All the people we saw there are of great size. 33We saw the Nephilim there (the descendants of Anak come from the Nephilim). We seemed like grasshoppers in our own

---

*a*21 Or *toward the entrance to*   *b*23 *Eshcol* means *cluster;* also in verse 24.

eyes, and we looked the same to them." Nu 14:36; Am 2:9

The People Rebel

14 That night all the people of the community raised their voices and wept aloud. ²All the Israelites grumbled against Moses and Aaron, and the whole assembly said to them, "If only we had died in Egypt! Or in this desert! ³Why is the LORD bringing us to this land only to let us fall by the sword? Our wives and children will be taken as plunder. Wouldn't it be better for us to go back to Egypt?" ⁴And they said to each other, "We should choose a leader and go back to Egypt." Nu 11:1; Dt 1:39

⁵Then Moses and Aaron fell facedown in front of the whole Israelite assembly gathered there. ⁶Joshua son of Nun and Caleb son of Jephunneh, who were among those who had explored the land, tore their clothes ⁷and said to the entire Israelite assembly, "The land we passed through and explored is exceedingly good. ⁸If the LORD is pleased with us, he will lead us into that land, a land flowing with milk and honey, and will give it to us. ⁹Only do not rebel against the LORD. And do not be afraid of the people of the land, because we will swallow them up. Their protection is gone, but the LORD is with us. Do not be afraid of them." Nu 16:4; Jdg 11:35

¹⁰But the whole assembly talked about stoning them. Then the glory of the LORD appeared at the Tent of Meeting to all the Israelites. ¹¹The LORD said to Moses, "How long will these people treat me with contempt? How long will they refuse to believe in me, in spite of all the miraculous signs I have performed among them? ¹²I will strike them down with a plague and destroy them, but I will make you into a nation greater and stronger than they." Ex 17:4; Ps 78:22

¹³Moses said to the LORD, "Then the Egyptians will hear about it! By your power you brought these people up from among them. ¹⁴And they will tell the inhabitants of this land about it. They have already heard that you, O LORD, are with these people and that you, O LORD, have been seen face to face, that your cloud stays over them, and that you go before them in a pillar of cloud by day and a pillar of fire by night. ¹⁵If you put these people to death all at one time, the nations who have heard this report about you will say, ¹⁶'The LORD was not able to bring these people into the land he promised them on oath; so he slaughtered them in the desert.' Jos 2:9; Ps 106:23

¹⁷"Now may the Lord's strength be displayed, just as you have declared: ¹⁸'The LORD is slow to anger, abounding in love and forgiving sin and rebellion. Yet he does not leave the guilty unpunished; he punishes

the children for the sin of the fathers to the third and fourth generation.' ¹⁹In accordance with your great love, forgive the sin of these people, just as you have pardoned them from the time they left Egypt until now."

²⁰The Lord replied, "I have forgiven them, as you asked. ²¹Nevertheless, as surely as I live and as surely as the glory of the Lord fills the whole earth, ²²not one of the men who saw my glory and the miraculous signs I performed in Egypt and in the desert but who disobeyed me and tested me ten times— ²³not one of them will ever see the land I promised on oath to their forefathers. No one who has treated me with contempt will ever see it. ²⁴But because my servant Caleb has a different spirit and follows me wholeheartedly, I will bring him into the land he went to, and his descendants will inherit it. ²⁵Since the Amalekites and Canaanites are living in the valleys, turn back tomorrow and set out toward the desert along the route to the Red Sea.ᵃ" Ps 106:23

²⁶The Lord said to Moses and Aaron: ²⁷"How long will this wicked community grumble against me? I have heard the complaints of these grumbling Israelites. ²⁸So tell them, 'As surely as I live, declares the Lord, I will do to you the very things I heard you say: ²⁹In this desert your bodies will

fall—every one of you twenty years old or more who was counted in the census and who has grumbled against me. ³⁰Not one of you will enter the land I swore with uplifted hand to make your home, except Caleb son of Jephunneh and Joshua son of Nun. ³¹As for your children that you said would be taken as plunder, I will bring them in to enjoy the land you have rejected. ³²But you—your bodies will fall in this desert. ³³Your children will be shepherds here for forty years, suffering for your unfaithfulness, until the last of your bodies lies in the desert. ³⁴For forty years—one year for each of the forty days you explored the land—you will suffer for your sins and know what it is like to have me against you.' ³⁵I, the Lord, have spoken, and I will surely do these things to this whole wicked community, which has banded together against me. They will meet their end in this desert; here they will die."Ex 16:12

³⁶So the men Moses had sent to explore the land, who returned and made the whole community grumble against him by spreading a bad report about it— ³⁷these men responsible for spreading the bad report about the land were struck down and died of a plague before the Lord. ³⁸Of the men who went to explore the land, only Joshua son of Nun and

---

ᵃ25 Hebrew *Yam Suph*; that is, Sea of Reeds

Caleb son of Jephunneh survived. Nu 13:4-16; Jos 14:6

39When Moses reported this to all the Israelites, they mourned bitterly. 40Early the next morning they went up toward the high hill country. "We have sinned," they said. "We will go up to the place the LORD promised." Ex 33:4

41But Moses said, "Why are you disobeying the LORD's command? This will not succeed! 42Do not go up, because the LORD is not with you. You will be defeated by your enemies, 43for the Amalekites and Canaanites will face you there. Because you have turned away from the LORD, he will not be with you and you will fall by the sword." Nu 13:29; Dt 1:42

44Nevertheless, in their presumption they went up toward the high hill country, though neither Moses nor the ark of the LORD's covenant moved from the camp. 45Then the Amalekites and Canaanites who lived in that hill country came down and attacked them and beat them down all the way to Hormah. Nu 21:3; Dt 1:43

Supplementary Offerings

15 The LORD said to Moses, 2"Speak to the Israelites and say to them: 'After you enter the land I am giving you as a home 3and you present to the LORD offerings made by fire, from the herd or the flock, as an aroma pleasing to the LORD—whether burnt offerings or sacrifices, for special vows or freewill offerings or festival offerings— 4then the one who brings his offering shall present to the LORD a grain offering of a tenth of an ephah*a* of fine flour mixed with a quarter of a hin*b* of oil. 5With each lamb for the burnt offering or the sacrifice, prepare a quarter of a hin of wine as a drink offering. Lev 23:10

6" 'With a ram prepare a grain offering of two-tenths of an ephah*c* of fine flour mixed with a third of a hin*d* of oil, 7and a third of a hin of wine as a drink offering. Offer it as an aroma pleasing to the LORD. Nu 28:12

8" 'When you prepare a young bull as a burnt offering or sacrifice, for a special vow or a fellowship offering*e* to the LORD, 9bring with the bull a grain offering of three-tenths of an ephah*f* of fine flour mixed with half a hin*g* of oil. 10Also bring half a hin of wine as a drink offering. It will be an offering made by fire, an aroma pleasing to the LORD. 11Each bull or ram, each lamb or young goat, is to be prepared in this manner. 12Do this for each one, for as many as you prepare.

---

*a*4 That is, probably about 2 quarts (about 2 liters)   *b*4 That is, probably about 1 quart (about 1 liter); also in verse 5   *c*6 That is, probably about 4 quarts (about 4.5 liters)   *d*6 That is, probably about 1 1/4 quarts (about 1.2 liters); also in verse 7   *e*8 Traditionally *peace offering*   *f*9 That is, probably about 6 quarts (about 6.5 liters)   *g*9 That is, probably about 2 quarts (about 2 liters); also in verse 10

¹³" 'Everyone who is native-born must do these things in this way when he brings an offering made by fire as an aroma pleasing to the LORD. ¹⁴For the generations to come, whenever an alien or anyone else living among you presents an offering made by fire as an aroma pleasing to the LORD, he must do exactly as you do. ¹⁵The community is to have the same rules for you and for the alien living among you; this is a lasting ordinance for the generations to come. You and the alien shall be the same before the LORD: ¹⁶The same laws and regulations will apply both to you and to the alien living among you.' " Lev 16:29

¹⁷The LORD said to Moses, ¹⁸"Speak to the Israelites and say to them: 'When you enter the land to which I am taking you ¹⁹and you eat the food of the land, present a portion as an offering to the LORD. ²⁰Present a cake from the first of your ground meal and present it as an offering from the threshing floor. ²¹Throughout the generations to come you are to give this offering to the LORD from the first of your ground meal.

Offerings for Unintentional Sins

²²" 'Now if you unintentionally fail to keep any of these commands the LORD gave Moses— ²³any of the LORD's commands to you through him, from the day the LORD gave them and continuing through the generations to come— ²⁴and if this is done unintentionally without the community being aware of it, then the whole community is to offer a young bull for a burnt offering as an aroma pleasing to the LORD, along with its prescribed grain offering and drink offering, and a male goat for a sin offering. ²⁵The priest is to make atonement for the whole Israelite community, and they will be forgiven, for it was not intentional and they have brought to the LORD for their wrong an offering made by fire and a sin offering. ²⁶The whole Israelite community and the aliens living among them will be forgiven, because all the people were involved in the unintentional wrong. Lev 4:2; Nu 6:15

²⁷" 'But if just one person sins unintentionally, he must bring a year-old female goat for a sin offering. ²⁸The priest is to make atonement before the LORD for the one who erred by sinning unintentionally, and when atonement has been made for him, he will be forgiven. ²⁹One and the same law applies to everyone who sins unintentionally, whether he is a native-born Israelite or an alien. Lev 4:27; Nu 8:12

³⁰" 'But anyone who sins defiantly, whether native-born or alien, blasphemes the LORD, and that person must be cut off from his people. ³¹Because he has despised the LORD's word and broken his commands, that

person must surely be cut off; his guilt remains on him.' "

The Sabbath-Breaker Put to Death

³²While the Israelites were in the desert, a man was found gathering wood on the Sabbath day. ³³Those who found him gathering wood brought him to Moses and Aaron and the whole assembly, ³⁴and they kept him in custody, because it was not clear what should be done to him. ³⁵Then the LORD said to Moses, "The man must die. The whole assembly must stone him outside the camp." ³⁶So the assembly took him outside the camp and stoned him to death, as the LORD commanded Moses.   Ex 31:14; Ac 7:58

Tassels on Garments

³⁷The LORD said to Moses, ³⁸"Speak to the Israelites and say to them: 'Throughout the generations to come you are to make tassels on the corners of your garments, with a blue cord on each tassel. ³⁹You will have these tassels to look at and so you will remember all the commands of the LORD, that you may obey them and not prostitute yourselves by going after the lusts of your own hearts and eyes. ⁴⁰Then you will remember to obey all my commands and will be consecrated to your God. ⁴¹I am the LORD your God, who brought you out of Egypt to be

your God. I am the LORD your God.' "   Dt 22:12; Ps 73:27

Korah, Dathan and Abiram

16 Korah son of Izhar, the son of Kohath, the son of Levi, and certain Reubenites—Dathan and Abiram, sons of Eliab, and On son of Peleth—became insolent*ᵃ* ²and rose up against Moses. With them were 250 Israelite men, well-known community leaders who had been appointed members of the council. ³They came as a group to oppose Moses and Aaron and said to them, "You have gone too far! The whole community is holy, every one of them, and the LORD is with them. Why then do you set yourselves above the LORD's assembly?"   Nu 26:9; Jude 11

⁴When Moses heard this, he fell facedown. ⁵Then he said to Korah and all his followers: "In the morning the LORD will show who belongs to him and who is holy, and he will have that person come near him. The man he chooses he will cause to come near him. ⁶You, Korah, and all your followers are to do this: Take censers ⁷and tomorrow put fire and incense in them before the LORD. The man the LORD chooses will be the one who is holy. You Levites have gone too far!"   Lev 10:3; Nu 14:5

⁸Moses also said to Korah, "Now listen, you Levites! ⁹Isn't it enough for you that the God

*ᵃ*1 Or *Peleth—took men*

of Israel has separated you from the rest of the Israelite community and brought you near himself to do the work at the LORD's tabernacle and to stand before the community and minister to them? ¹⁰He has brought you and all your fellow Levites near himself, but now you are trying to get the priesthood too. ¹¹It is against the LORD that you and all your followers have banded together. Who is Aaron that you should grumble against him?"

¹²Then Moses summoned Dathan and Abiram, the sons of Eliab. But they said, "We will not come! ¹³Isn't it enough that you have brought us up out of a land flowing with milk and honey to kill us in the desert? And now you also want to lord it over us? ¹⁴Moreover, you haven't brought us into a land flowing with milk and honey or given us an inheritance of fields and vineyards. Will you gouge out the eyes of*ᵃ* these men? No, we will not come!"   Ac 7:27

¹⁵Then Moses became very angry and said to the LORD, "Do not accept their offering. I have not taken so much as a donkey from them, nor have I wronged any of them."   Ex 4:14; 1Sa 12:3

¹⁶Moses said to Korah, "You and all your followers are to appear before the LORD tomorrow—you and they and Aaron. ¹⁷Each man is to take his censer and put incense in it—250 censers in all—and present it before

the LORD. You and Aaron are to present your censers also." ¹⁸So each man took his censer, put fire and incense in it, and stood with Moses and Aaron at the entrance to the Tent of Meeting. ¹⁹When Korah had gathered all his followers in opposition to them at the entrance to the Tent of Meeting, the glory of the LORD appeared to the entire assembly. ²⁰The LORD said to Moses and Aaron, ²¹"Separate yourselves from this assembly so I can put an end to them at once."   Nu 14:10; Eze 8:11

²²But Moses and Aaron fell facedown and cried out, "O God, God of the spirits of all mankind, will you be angry with the entire assembly when only one man sins?"   Nu 14:5

²³Then the LORD said to Moses, ²⁴"Say to the assembly, 'Move away from the tents of Korah, Dathan and Abiram.'"

²⁵Moses got up and went to Dathan and Abiram, and the elders of Israel followed him. ²⁶He warned the assembly, "Move back from the tents of these wicked men! Do not touch anything belonging to them, or you will be swept away because of all their sins." ²⁷So they moved away from the tents of Korah, Dathan and Abiram. Dathan and Abiram had come out and were standing with their wives, children and little ones at the entrances to their tents.   Ex 19:7

²⁸Then Moses said, "This is

ᵃ14 Or you make slaves of; or you deceive

how you will know that the LORD has sent me to do all these things and that it was not my idea: ²⁹If these men die a natural death and experience only what usually happens to men, then the LORD has not sent me. ³⁰But if the LORD brings about something totally new, and the earth opens its mouth and swallows them, with everything that belongs to them, and they go down alive into the grave,^a then you will know that these men have treated the LORD with contempt." Ex 3:12; Job 31:2

³¹As soon as he finished saying all this, the ground under them split apart ³²and the earth opened its mouth and swallowed them, with their households and all Korah's men and all their possessions. ³³They went down alive into the grave, with everything they owned; the earth closed over them, and they perished and were gone from the community. ³⁴At their cries, all the Israelites around them fled, shouting, "The earth is going to swallow us too!"

³⁵And fire came out from the LORD and consumed the 250 men who were offering the incense. Nu 11:1-3; Rev 11:5

³⁶The LORD said to Moses, ³⁷"Tell Eleazar son of Aaron, the priest, to take the censers out of the smoldering remains and scatter the coals some distance away, for the censers are holy— ³⁸the censers of the men who

sinned at the cost of their lives. Hammer the censers into sheets to overlay the altar, for they were presented before the LORD and have become holy. Let them be a sign to the Israelites."

³⁹So Eleazar the priest collected the bronze censers brought by those who had been burned up, and he had them hammered out to overlay the altar, ⁴⁰as the LORD directed him through Moses. This was to remind the Israelites that no one except a descendant of Aaron should come to burn incense before the LORD, or he would become like Korah and his followers. 2Ch 26:18

⁴¹The next day the whole Israelite community grumbled against Moses and Aaron. "You have killed the LORD's people," they said. Ps 106:25

⁴²But when the assembly gathered in opposition to Moses and Aaron and turned toward the Tent of Meeting, suddenly the cloud covered it and the glory of the LORD appeared. ⁴³Then Moses and Aaron went to the front of the Tent of Meeting, ⁴⁴and the LORD said to Moses, ⁴⁵"Get away from this assembly so I can put an end to them at once." And they fell facedown. Ex 16:7; Nu 14:10

⁴⁶Then Moses said to Aaron, "Take your censer and put incense in it, along with fire from the altar, and hurry to the assembly to make atonement for them. Wrath has come out from

^a30 Hebrew *Sheol*; also in verse 33

the LORD; the plague has started." ⁴⁷So Aaron did as Moses said, and ran into the midst of the assembly. The plague had already started among the people, but Aaron offered the incense and made atonement for them. ⁴⁸He stood between the living and the dead, and the plague stopped. ⁴⁹But 14,700 people died from the plague, in addition to those who had died because of Korah. ⁵⁰Then Aaron returned to Moses at the entrance to the Tent of Meeting, for the plague had stopped.   Nu 8:19; Ps 106:29

The Budding of Aaron's Staff

17 The LORD said to Moses, ²"Speak to the Israelites and get twelve staffs from them, one from the leader of each of their ancestral tribes. Write the name of each man on his staff. ³On the staff of Levi write Aaron's name, for there must be one staff for the head of each ancestral tribe. ⁴Place them in the Tent of Meeting in front of the Testimony, where I meet with you. ⁵The staff belonging to the man I choose will sprout, and I will rid myself of this constant grumbling against you by the Israelites."   Ge 32:10

⁶So Moses spoke to the Israelites, and their leaders gave him twelve staffs, one for the leader of each of their ancestral tribes, and Aaron's staff was among them. ⁷Moses placed the staffs before the LORD in the Tent of the Testimony.   Ex 38:21; Nu 18:2

⁸The next day Moses entered the Tent of the Testimony and saw that Aaron's staff, which represented the house of Levi, had not only sprouted but had budded, blossomed and produced almonds. ⁹Then Moses brought out all the staffs from the LORD's presence to all the Israelites. They looked at them, and each man took his own staff.   Nu 1:50; Heb 9:4

¹⁰The LORD said to Moses, "Put back Aaron's staff in front of the Testimony, to be kept as a sign to the rebellious. This will put an end to their grumbling against me, so that they will not die." ¹¹Moses did just as the LORD commanded him.   Ps 66:7

¹²The Israelites said to Moses, "We will die! We are lost, we are all lost! ¹³Anyone who even comes near the tabernacle of the LORD will die. Are we all going to die?"   Nu 1:51; Jdg 13:22

Duties of Priests and Levites

18 The LORD said to Aaron, "You, your sons and your father's family are to bear the responsibility for offenses against the sanctuary, and you and your sons alone are to bear the responsibility for offenses against the priesthood. ²Bring your fellow Levites from your ancestral tribe to join you and assist you when you and your sons minister before the Tent of the Testimony. ³They are to be responsible to you and are to perform all the duties of the Tent, but they must not go near

the furnishings of the sanctuary or the altar, or both they and you will die. ⁴They are to join you and be responsible for the care of the Tent of Meeting—all the work at the Tent—and no one else may come near where you are.   Ex 28:38; Nu 3:10

⁵"You are to be responsible for the care of the sanctuary and the altar, so that wrath will not fall on the Israelites again. ⁶I myself have selected your fellow Levites from among the Israelites as a gift to you, dedicated to the LORD to do the work at the Tent of Meeting. ⁷But only you and your sons may serve as priests in connection with everything at the altar and inside the curtain. I am giving you the service of the priesthood as a gift. Anyone else who comes near the sanctuary must be put to death."   Lev 6:12; Nu 16:46

Offerings for Priests and Levites

⁸Then the LORD said to Aaron, "I myself have put you in charge of the offerings presented to me; all the holy offerings the Israelites give me I give to you and your sons as your portion and regular share. ⁹You are to have the part of the most holy offerings that is kept from the fire. From all the gifts they bring me as most holy offerings, whether grain or sin or

guilt offerings, that part belongs to you and your sons. ¹⁰Eat it as something most holy; every male shall eat it. You must regard it as holy.   Lev 2:1; 6:16

¹¹"This also is yours: whatever is set aside from the gifts of all the wave offerings of the Israelites. I give this to you and your sons and daughters as your regular share. Everyone in your household who is ceremonially clean may eat it.   Ex 29:26

¹²"I give you all the finest olive oil and all the finest new wine and grain they give the LORD as the firstfruits of their harvest. ¹³All the land's firstfruits that they bring to the LORD will be yours. Everyone in your household who is ceremonially clean may eat it.   Ex 23:19

¹⁴"Everything in Israel that is devotedᵃ to the LORD is yours. ¹⁵The first offspring of every womb, both man and animal, that is offered to the LORD is yours. But you must redeem every firstborn son and every firstborn male of unclean animals. ¹⁶When they are a month old, you must redeem them at the redemption price set at five shekelsᵇ of silver, according to the sanctuary shekel, which weighs twenty gerahs.   Lev 27:21

¹⁷"But you must not redeem the firstborn of an ox, a sheep or a goat; they are holy. Sprinkle their blood on the altar and burn their fat as an offering

---

ᵃ14 The Hebrew term refers to the irrevocable giving over of things or persons to the LORD.   ᵇ16 That is, about 2 ounces (about 55 grams)

made by fire, an aroma pleasing to the LORD. [18]Their meat is to be yours, just as the breast of the wave offering and the right thigh are yours. [19]Whatever is set aside from the holy offerings the Israelites present to the LORD I give to you and your sons and daughters as your regular share. It is an everlasting covenant of salt before the LORD for both you and your offspring." Ex 29:13; Lev 3:2

[20]The LORD said to Aaron, "You will have no inheritance in their land, nor will you have any share among them; I am your share and your inheritance among the Israelites. Dt 10:9

[21]"I give to the Levites all the tithes in Israel as their inheritance in return for the work they do while serving at the Tent of Meeting. [22]From now on the Israelites must not go near the Tent of Meeting, or they will bear the consequences of their sin and will die. [23]It is the Levites who are to do the work at the Tent of Meeting and bear the responsibility for offenses against it. This is a lasting ordinance for the generations to come. They will receive no inheritance among the Israelites. [24]Instead, I give to the Levites as their inheritance the tithes that the Israelites present as an offering to the LORD. That is why I said concerning them: 'They will have no inheritance among the Israelites.' " Lev 27:30-33

[25]The LORD said to Moses, [26]"Speak to the Levites and say to them: 'When you receive from the Israelites the tithe I give you as your inheritance, you must present a tenth of that tithe as the LORD's offering. [27]Your offering will be reckoned to you as grain from the threshing floor or juice from the winepress. [28]In this way you also will present an offering to the LORD from all the tithes you receive from the Israelites. From these tithes you must give the LORD's portion to Aaron the priest. [29]You must present as the LORD's portion the best and holiest part of everything given to you.' Lev 7:18; Ne 10:38

[30]"Say to the Levites: 'When you present the best part, it will be reckoned to you as the product of the threshing floor or the winepress. [31]You and your households may eat the rest of it anywhere, for it is your wages for your work at the Tent of Meeting. [32]By presenting the best part of it you will not be guilty in this matter; then you will not defile the holy offerings of the Israelites, and you will not die.' " Lev 19:8; 22:15

The Water of Cleansing

19 The LORD said to Moses and Aaron: [2]"This is a requirement of the law that the LORD has commanded: Tell the Israelites to bring you a red heifer without defect or blemish and that has never been under a yoke. [3]Give it to Eleazar the priest; it is to be taken outside the camp and slaughtered in his

presence. ⁴Then Eleazar the priest is to take some of its blood on his finger and sprinkle it seven times toward the front of the Tent of Meeting. ⁵While he watches, the heifer is to be burned—its hide, flesh, blood and offal. ⁶The priest is to take some cedar wood, hyssop and scarlet wool and throw them onto the burning heifer. ⁷After that, the priest must wash his clothes and bathe himself with water. He may then come into the camp, but he will be ceremonially unclean till evening. ⁸The man who burns it must also wash his clothes and bathe with water, and he too will be unclean till evening.   Dt 21:3

⁹"A man who is clean shall gather up the ashes of the heifer and put them in a ceremonially clean place outside the camp. They shall be kept by the Israelite community for use in the water of cleansing; it is for purification from sin. ¹⁰The man who gathers up the ashes of the heifer must also wash his clothes, and he too will be unclean till evening. This will be a lasting ordinance both for the Israelites and for the aliens living among them.   Ex 29:31

¹¹"Whoever touches the dead body of anyone will be unclean for seven days. ¹²He must purify himself with the water on the third day and on the seventh day; then he will be clean. But if he does not purify himself on the third and seventh days, he will not be clean. ¹³Whoever touches the dead body of anyone and fails to purify himself defiles the LORD's tabernacle. That person must be cut off from Israel. Because the water of cleansing has not been sprinkled on him, he is unclean; his uncleanness remains on him.

¹⁴"This is the law that applies when a person dies in a tent: Anyone who enters the tent and anyone who is in it will be unclean for seven days, ¹⁵and every open container without a lid fastened on it will be unclean.   Lev 6:28; Nu 31:20

¹⁶"Anyone out in the open who touches someone who has been killed with a sword or someone who has died a natural death, or anyone who touches a human bone or a grave, will be unclean for seven days.   1Ki 13:2

¹⁷"For the unclean person, put some ashes from the burned purification offering into a jar and pour fresh water over them. ¹⁸Then a man who is ceremonially clean is to take some hyssop, dip it in the water and sprinkle the tent and all the furnishings and the people who were there. He must also sprinkle anyone who has touched a human bone or a grave or someone who has been killed or someone who has died a natural death. ¹⁹The man who is clean is to sprinkle the unclean person on the third and seventh days, and on the seventh day he is to purify him. The person being cleansed must wash his clothes and bathe with water, and that

evening he will be clean. ²⁰But if a person who is unclean does not purify himself, he must be cut off from the community, because he has defiled the sanctuary of the LORD. The water of cleansing has not been sprinkled on him, and he is unclean. ²¹This is a lasting ordinance for them.   Eze 36:25; Heb 10:22

"The man who sprinkles the water of cleansing must also wash his clothes, and anyone who touches the water of cleansing will be unclean till evening. ²²Anything that an unclean person touches becomes unclean, and anyone who touches it becomes unclean till evening."   Ex 27:21; Lev 5:2

Water From the Rock

20 In the first month the whole Israelite community arrived at the Desert of Zin, and they stayed at Kadesh. There Miriam died and was buried.   Nu 33:36; Dt 1:46

²Now there was no water for the community, and the people gathered in opposition to Moses and Aaron. ³They quarreled with Moses and said, "If only we had died when our brothers fell dead before the LORD! ⁴Why did you bring the LORD's community into this desert, that we and our livestock should die here? ⁵Why did you bring us up out of Egypt to this terrible place? It has no grain or figs, grapevines or pomegranates. And there is no water to drink!"

⁶Moses and Aaron went from the assembly to the entrance to the Tent of Meeting and fell facedown, and the glory of the LORD appeared to them. ⁷The LORD said to Moses, ⁸"Take the staff, and you and your brother Aaron gather the assembly together. Speak to that rock before their eyes and it will pour out its water. You will bring water out of the rock for the community so they and their livestock can drink."   Ex 17:6

⁹So Moses took the staff from the LORD's presence, just as he commanded him. ¹⁰He and Aaron gathered the assembly together in front of the rock and Moses said to them, "Listen, you rebels, must we bring you water out of this rock?" ¹¹Then Moses raised his arm and struck the rock twice with his staff. Water gushed out, and the community and their livestock drank.   Ps 106:32; Isa 33:21

¹²But the LORD said to Moses and Aaron, "Because you did not trust in me enough to honor me as holy in the sight of the Israelites, you will not bring this community into the land I give them."   Nu 27:14; Dt 32:51

¹³These were the waters of Meribah,ᵃ where the Israelites quarreled with the LORD and where he showed himself holy among them.   Ex 17:7; Dt 33:8

ᵃ13 *Meribah* means *quarreling.*

Edom Denies Israel Passage

[14]Moses sent messengers from Kadesh to the king of Edom, saying:

"This is what your brother Israel says: You know about all the hardships that have come upon us. [15]Our forefathers went down into Egypt, and we lived there many years. The Egyptians mistreated us and our fathers, [16]but when we cried out to the LORD, he heard our cry and sent an angel and brought us out of Egypt.

"Now we are here at Kadesh, a town on the edge of your territory. [17]Please let us pass through your country. We will not go through any field or vineyard, or drink water from any well. We will travel along the king's highway and not turn to the right or to the left until we have passed through your territory." Ge 25:30

[18]But Edom answered:

"You may not pass through here; if you try, we will march out and attack you with the sword." Nu 21:23

[19]The Israelites replied:

"We will go along the main road, and if we or our livestock drink any of your water, we will pay for it. We only want to pass through on foot—nothing else." Dt 2:6

[20]Again they answered:

"You may not pass through."

Then Edom came out against them with a large and powerful army. [21]Since Edom refused to let them go through their territory, Israel turned away from them. Nu 21:23; Dt 2:8

The Death of Aaron

[22]The whole Israelite community set out from Kadesh and came to Mount Hor. [23]At Mount Hor, near the border of Edom, the LORD said to Moses and Aaron, [24]"Aaron will be gathered to his people. He will not enter the land I give the Israelites, because both of you rebelled against my command at the waters of Meribah. [25]Get Aaron and his son Eleazar and take them up Mount Hor. [26]Remove Aaron's garments and put them on his son Eleazar, for Aaron will be gathered to his people; he will die there." Nu 33:37

[27]Moses did as the LORD commanded: They went up Mount Hor in the sight of the whole community. [28]Moses removed Aaron's garments and put them on his son Eleazar. And Aaron died there on top of the mountain. Then Moses and Eleazar came down from the mountain, [29]and when the whole community learned that Aaron had died, the entire house of Israel mourned for him thirty days.

Arad Destroyed

21 When the Canaanite king of Arad, who lived in the Negev, heard that Israel was coming along the road to Atharim, he attacked the Israelites and captured some of them. ²Then Israel made this vow to the LORD: "If you will deliver these people into our hands, we will totally destroy*a* their cities." ³The LORD listened to Israel's plea and gave the Canaanites over to them. They completely destroyed them and their towns; so the place was named Hormah.*b*   Nu 33:40

The Bronze Snake

⁴They traveled from Mount Hor along the route to the Red Sea,*c* to go around Edom. But the people grew impatient on the way; ⁵they spoke against God and against Moses, and said, "Why have you brought us up out of Egypt to die in the desert? There is no bread! There is no water! And we detest this miserable food!"   Nu 20:22

⁶Then the LORD sent venomous snakes among them; they bit the people and many Israelites died. ⁷The people came to Moses and said, "We sinned when we spoke against the LORD and against you. Pray that the LORD will take the snakes

away from us." So Moses prayed for the people.   Dt 8:15

⁸The LORD said to Moses, "Make a snake and put it up on a pole; anyone who is bitten can look at it and live." ⁹So Moses made a bronze snake and put it up on a pole. Then when anyone was bitten by a snake and looked at the bronze snake, he lived.   2 Ki 18:4; Jn 3:14

The Journey to Moab

¹⁰The Israelites moved on and camped at Oboth. ¹¹Then they set out from Oboth and camped in Iye Abarim, in the desert that faces Moab toward the sunrise. ¹²From there they moved on and camped in the Zered Valley. ¹³They set out from there and camped alongside the Arnon, which is in the desert extending into Amorite territory. The Arnon is the border of Moab, between Moab and the Amorites. ¹⁴That is why the Book of the Wars of the LORD says: Ge 36:35; Nu 33:43

". . . Waheb in Suphah*d* and the ravines,
  the Arnon ¹⁵and*e* the slopes of the ravines
that lead to the site of Ar
and lie along the border of Moab."   1 Sa 17:47

¹⁶From there they continued on to Beer, the well where the

*a*2 The Hebrew term refers to the irrevocable giving over of things or persons to the LORD, often by totally destroying them; also in verse 3.   *b*3 *Hormah* means *destruction.*   *c*4 Hebrew *Yam Suph;* that is, Sea of Reeds   *d*14 The meaning of the Hebrew for this phrase is uncertain.   *e*14,15 Or *"I have been given from Suphah and the ravines / of the Arnon* ¹⁵*to*

LORD said to Moses, "Gather the people together and I will give them water."   Nu 25:1

¹⁷Then Israel sang this song:

"Spring up, O well!
  Sing about it,
¹⁸about the well that the
      princes dug,
  that the nobles of the
      people sank—
  the nobles with scepters
      and staffs."   Ex 15:1; Ps 105:2

Then they went from the desert to Mattanah, ¹⁹from Mattanah to Nahaliel, from Nahaliel to Bamoth, ²⁰and from Bamoth to the valley in Moab where the top of Pisgah overlooks the wasteland.   Nu 23:14; Dt 3:17

Defeat of Sihon and Og

²¹Israel sent messengers to say to Sihon king of the Amorites:

²²"Let us pass through your country. We will not turn aside into any field or vineyard, or drink water from any well. We will travel along the king's highway until we have passed through your territory."   Ge 3:3

²³But Sihon would not let Israel pass through his territory. He mustered his entire army and marched out into the desert against Israel. When he reached Jahaz, he fought with Israel. ²⁴Israel, however, put him to the sword and took over his land from the Arnon to the Jabbok, but only as far as the Am-

monites, because their border was fortified. ²⁵Israel captured all the cities of the Amorites and occupied them, including Heshbon and all its surrounding settlements. ²⁶Heshbon was the city of Sihon king of the Amorites, who had fought against the former king of Moab and had taken from him all his land as far as the Arnon.   Nu 20:21

²⁷That is why the poets say:

"Come to Heshbon and let it
      be rebuilt;
  let Sihon's city be restored.

²⁸"Fire went out from
      Heshbon,
  a blaze from the city of
      Sihon.
  It consumed Ar of Moab,
  the citizens of Arnon's
      heights.   Isa 15:2; Jer 48:45
²⁹Woe to you, O Moab!
  You are destroyed,
      O people of Chemosh!
  He has given up his sons as
      fugitives
  and his daughters as
      captives
  to Sihon king of the
      Amorites.   Ru 1:15; 2Ki 23:13
³⁰"But we have overthrown
      them;
  Heshbon is destroyed all
      the way to Dibon.   Nu 32:3
  We have demolished them as
      far as Nophah,
  which extends to Medeba."

³¹So Israel settled in the land of the Amorites.   Nu 13:29
³²After Moses had sent spies to Jazer, the Israelites captured

its surrounding settlements and drove out the Amorites who were there. ³³Then they turned and went up along the road toward Bashan, and Og king of Bashan and his whole army marched out to meet them in battle at Edrei.   Nu 32:1; Jer 48:32

³⁴The LORD said to Moses, "Do not be afraid of him, for I have handed him over to you, with his whole army and his land. Do to him what you did to Sihon king of the Amorites, who reigned in Heshbon." Dt 3:2

³⁵So they struck him down, together with his sons and his whole army, leaving them no survivors. And they took possession of his land.   Jos 9:10

Balak Summons Balaam

22 Then the Israelites traveled to the plains of Moab and camped along the Jordan across from Jericho.ᵃ   Nu 21:11

²Now Balak son of Zippor saw all that Israel had done to the Amorites, ³and Moab was terrified because there were so many people. Indeed, Moab was filled with dread because of the Israelites.   Nu 23:1-3

⁴The Moabites said to the elders of Midian, "This horde is going to lick up everything around us, as an ox licks up the grass of the field."   Ge 19:37

So Balak son of Zippor, who was king of Moab at that time, ⁵sent messengers to summon Balaam son of Beor, who was at Pethor, near the River,ᵇ in his native land. Balak said: Dt 23:4

"A people has come out of Egypt; they cover the face of the land and have settled next to me. ⁶Now come and put a curse on these people, because they are too powerful for me. Perhaps then I will be able to defeat them and drive them out of the country. For I know that those you bless are blessed, and those you curse are cursed."   Nu 23:7; 24:9

⁷The elders of Moab and Midian left, taking with them the fee for divination. When they came to Balaam, they told him what Balak had said.   Ge 30:27

⁸"Spend the night here," Balaam said to them, "and I will bring you back the answer the LORD gives me." So the Moabite princes stayed with him.   Nu 22:19

⁹God came to Balaam and asked, "Who are these men with you?"   Ge 20:3

¹⁰Balaam said to God, "Balak son of Zippor, king of Moab, sent me this message: ¹¹'A people that has come out of Egypt covers the face of the land. Now come and put a curse on them for me. Perhaps then I will be able to fight them and drive them away.'"

¹²But God said to Balaam, "Do not go with them. You

ᵃ1 Hebrew *Jordan of Jericho*; possibly an ancient name for the Jordan River   ᵇ5 That is, the Euphrates

must not put a curse on those people, because they are blessed." Ge 12:2; Nu 23:20

[13]The next morning Balaam got up and said to Balak's princes, "Go back to your own country, for the LORD has refused to let me go with you."

[14]So the Moabite princes returned to Balak and said, "Balaam refused to come with us."

[15]Then Balak sent other princes, more numerous and more distinguished than the first. [16]They came to Balaam and said:

"This is what Balak son of Zippor says: Do not let anything keep you from coming to me, [17]because I will reward you handsomely and do whatever you say. Come and put a curse on these people for me."   Nu 24:11

[18]But Balaam answered them, "Even if Balak gave me his palace filled with silver and gold, I could not do anything great or small to go beyond the command of the LORD my God. [19]Now stay here tonight as the others did, and I will find out what else the LORD will tell me."   Nu 24:13; 1Ki 22:14

[20]That night God came to Balaam and said, "Since these men have come to summon you, go with them, but do only what I tell you."   Nu 23:5

Balaam's Donkey

[21]Balaam got up in the morning, saddled his donkey and went with the princes of Moab. [22]But God was very angry when he went, and the angel of the LORD stood in the road to oppose him. Balaam was riding on his donkey, and his two servants were with him. [23]When the donkey saw the angel of the LORD standing in the road with a drawn sword in his hand, she turned off the road into a field. Balaam beat her to get her back on the road.   Ex 4:14; 2Pe 2:15

[24]Then the angel of the LORD stood in a narrow path between two vineyards, with walls on both sides. [25]When the donkey saw the angel of the LORD, she pressed close to the wall, crushing Balaam's foot against it. So he beat her again.   Jdg 6:12

[26]Then the angel of the LORD moved on ahead and stood in a narrow place where there was no room to turn, either to the right or to the left. [27]When the donkey saw the angel of the LORD, she lay down under Balaam, and he was angry and beat her with his staff. [28]Then the LORD opened the donkey's mouth, and she said to Balaam, "What have I done to you to make you beat me these three times?"   Nu 11:1; 2Pe 2:16

[29]Balaam answered the donkey, "You have made a fool of me! If I had a sword in my hand, I would kill you right now."

[30]The donkey said to Balaam, "Am I not your own donkey, which you have always ridden, to this day? Have I been in the habit of doing this to you?"

"No," he said.

31Then the LORD opened Balaam's eyes, and he saw the angel of the LORD standing in the road with his sword drawn. So he bowed low and fell face-down. Ge 21:19; Jos 5:13-15

32The angel of the LORD asked him, "Why have you beaten your donkey these three times? I have come here to oppose you because your path is a reckless one before me.*a* 33The donkey saw me and turned away from me these three times. If she had not turned away, I would certainly have killed you by now, but I would have spared her."

34Balaam said to the angel of the LORD, "I have sinned. I did not realize you were standing in the road to oppose me. Now if you are displeased, I will go back." Ge 39:9; Nu 14:40

35The angel of the LORD said to Balaam, "Go with the men, but speak only what I tell you." So Balaam went with the princes of Balak.

36When Balak heard that Balaam was coming, he went out to meet him at the Moabite town on the Arnon border, at the edge of his territory. 37Balak said to Balaam, "Did I not send you an urgent summons? Why didn't you come to me? Am I really not able to reward you?"

38"Well, I have come to you now," Balaam replied. "But can I say just anything? I must speak only what God puts in my mouth." Nu 23:5,26

39Then Balaam went with Balak to Kiriath Huzoth. 40Balak sacrificed cattle and sheep, and gave some to Balaam and the princes who were with him. 41The next morning Balak took Balaam up to Bamoth Baal, and from there he saw part of the people. Nu 23:1; Eze 45:23

Balaam's First Oracle

23 Balaam said, "Build me seven altars here, and prepare seven bulls and seven rams for me." 2Balak did as Balaam said, and the two of them offered a bull and a ram on each altar. Nu 22:40; 23:14

3Then Balaam said to Balak, "Stay here beside your offering while I go aside. Perhaps the LORD will come to meet with me. Whatever he reveals to me I will tell you." Then he went off to a barren height. Nu 23:15

4God met with him, and Balaam said, "I have prepared seven altars, and on each altar I have offered a bull and a ram."

5The LORD put a message in Balaam's mouth and said, "Go back to Balak and give him this message." Ex 4:12; Isa 59:21

6So he went back to him and found him standing beside his offering, with all the princes of Moab. 7Then Balaam uttered his oracle: Nu 22:5; Jos 24:9

"Balak brought me from
    Aram,

---

a32 The meaning of the Hebrew for this clause is uncertain.

the king of Moab from the
    eastern mountains.   2Ki 5:1
'Come,' he said, 'curse Jacob
    for me;
    come, denounce Israel.'
[8]How can I curse
    those whom God has not
      cursed?   Nu 22:12
  How can I denounce
    those whom the LORD has
      not denounced?   Isa 43:13
[9]From the rocky peaks I see
    them,
  from the heights I view
    them.   Nu 22:41
I see a people who live apart
and do not consider
    themselves one
  of the nations.Ex 33:16; Dt 32:8
[10]Who can count the dust of
    Jacob
  or number the fourth part
    of Israel?   Ge 13:16
Let me die the death of the
    righteous,
  and may my end be like
    theirs!"   Ps 37:37; 116:15

[11]Balak said to Balaam, "What
have you done to me? I brought
you to curse my enemies, but
you have done nothing but
bless them!"   Nu 24:10; Jos 24:10
[12]He answered, "Must I not
speak what the LORD puts in my
mouth?"   Nu 22:20,38

Balaam's Second Oracle

[13]Then Balak said to him,
"Come with me to another
place where you can see them;
you will see only a part but not
all of them. And from there,
curse them for me." [14]So he took
him to the field of Zophim on
the top of Pisgah, and there he
built seven altars and offered a
bull and a ram on each altar.

[15]Balaam said to Balak, "Stay
here beside your offering while
I meet with him over there."

[16]The LORD met with Balaam
and put a message in his mouth
and said, "Go back to Balak and
give him this message." Nu 22:38

[17]So he went to him and
found him standing beside his
offering, with the princes of
Moab. Balak asked him, "What
did the LORD say?"

[18]Then he uttered his oracle:

"Arise, Balak, and listen;
  hear me, son of Zippor.
[19]God is not a man, that he
    should lie,
  nor a son of man, that he
    should change his mind.
Does he speak and then not
    act?
Does he promise and not
    fulfill?   2Sa 7:25; Ps 119:38
[20]I have received a command
    to bless;
  he has blessed, and I
    cannot change it.   Nu 24:1
[21]"No misfortune is seen in
    Jacob,
  no misery observed in
    Israel.[a]
The LORD their God is with
    them;
  the shout of the King is
    among them.   Ps 32:2

[a]21 Or He has not looked on Jacob's offenses / or on the wrongs found in Israel.

²²God brought them out of
   Egypt;
   they have the strength of a
      wild ox.   Nu 24:8; Dt 33:17
²³There is no sorcery against
   Jacob,
   no divination against Israel.
It will now be said of Jacob
   and of Israel, 'See what
      God has done!'   Ge 30:27
²⁴The people rise like a lioness;
   they rouse themselves like a
      lion
   that does not rest till he
      devours his prey
   and drinks the blood of his
      victims."   Ge 49:9

²⁵Then Balak said to Balaam,
"Neither curse them at all nor
bless them at all!"
   ²⁶Balaam answered, "Did I
not tell you I must do whatever
the LORD says?"   Nu 22:18,20

Balaam's Third Oracle

²⁷Then Balak said to Balaam,
"Come, let me take you to another place. Perhaps it will
please God to let you curse
them for me from there." ²⁸And
Balak took Balaam to the top of
Peor, overlooking the wasteland.   Nu 24:10; Dt 3:29
   ²⁹Balaam said, "Build me
seven altars here, and prepare
seven bulls and seven rams for
me." ³⁰Balak did as Balaam had
said, and offered a bull and a
ram on each altar.

24 Now when Balaam saw
that it pleased the LORD
to bless Israel, he did not resort

to sorcery as at other times, but
turned his face toward the
desert. ²When Balaam looked
out and saw Israel encamped
tribe by tribe, the Spirit of God
came upon him ³and he uttered
his oracle: Nu 11:25; 23:23

"The oracle of Balaam son of
      Beor,
   the oracle of one whose eye
      sees clearly,
⁴the oracle of one who hears
      the words of God,
   who sees a vision from the
      Almighty,ᵃ
   who falls prostrate, and
      whose eyes are opened:

⁵"How beautiful are your
      tents, O Jacob,
   your dwelling places,
      O Israel!   Jer 4:20; Mal 2:12
⁶"Like valleys they spread
      out,
   like gardens beside a river,
   like aloes planted by the
      LORD,
   like cedars beside the
      waters.   Ps 1:3; 104:6
⁷Water will flow from their
      buckets;
   their seed will have
      abundant water.

"Their king will be greater
      than Agag;
   their kingdom will be
      exalted.   2Sa 5:12

⁸"God brought them out of
      Egypt;
   they have the strength of a
      wild ox.

ᵃ4 Hebrew *Shaddai*; also in verse 16

They devour hostile nations
and break their bones in
pieces;
with their arrows they
pierce them.   Jer 50:17
⁹Like a lion they crouch and
lie down,
like a lioness—who dares to
rouse them?   Nu 23:34

"May those who bless you be
blessed
and those who curse you be
cursed!"   Ge 12:3; 27:29

¹⁰Then Balak's anger burned
against Balaam. He struck his
hands together and said to him,
"I summoned you to curse my
enemies, but you have blessed
them these three times. ¹¹Now
leave at once and go home! I
said I would reward you handsomely, but the LORD has kept
you from being rewarded."

¹²Balaam answered Balak,
"Did I not tell the messengers
you sent me, ¹³'Even if Balak
gave me his palace filled with
silver and gold, I could not do
anything of my own accord,
good or bad, to go beyond the
command of the LORD—and I
must say only what the LORD
says'? ¹⁴Now I am going back to
my people, but come, let me
warn you of what this people
will do to your people in days to
come."   Nu 22:18; Mic 6:5

Balaam's Fourth Oracle

¹⁵Then he uttered his oracle:

"The oracle of Balaam son of
Beor,
the oracle of one whose eye
sees clearly,
¹⁶the oracle of one who hears
the words of God,
who has knowledge from
the Most High,
who sees a vision from the
Almighty,
who falls prostrate, and
whose eyes are opened:

¹⁷"I see him, but not now;
I behold him, but not near.
A star will come out of Jacob;
a scepter will rise out of
Israel.
He will crush the foreheads
of Moab,
the skulls*a* of*b* all the sons
of Sheth.*c*   Mt 2:2; Rev 1:7
¹⁸Edom will be conquered;
Seir, his enemy, will be
conquered,
but Israel will grow strong.
¹⁹A ruler will come out of Jacob
and destroy the survivors of
the city."   2Sa 8:14; Mic 5:2

Balaam's Final Oracles

²⁰Then Balaam saw Amalek
and uttered his oracle:

"Amalek was first among the
nations,
but he will come to ruin at
last."   Ex 17:14; Dt 25:19

²¹Then he saw the Kenites
and uttered his oracle:

---

a17 Samaritan Pentateuch (see also Jer. 48:45); the meaning of the word in the Masoretic
Text is uncertain.   *b17* Or possibly *Moab, / batter*   *c17* Or *all the noisy boasters*

"Your dwelling place is
    secure,
  your nest is set in a rock;
22yet you Kenites will be
      destroyed
    when Asshur takes you
      captive." Ge 10:22; 15:19

23Then he uttered his oracle:

"Ah, who can live when God
    does this?ᵃ
24 Ships will come from the
      shores of Kittim;
  they will subdue Asshur and
      Eber,
    but they too will come to
      ruin." Ge 10:4,21

25Then Balaam got up and returned home and Balak went
his own way. Nu 22:5; 31:8

Moab Seduces Israel

25 While Israel was staying
     in Shittim, the men began
to indulge in sexual immorality
with Moabite women, 2who invited them to the sacrifices to
their gods. The people ate and
bowed down before these gods.
3So Israel joined in worshiping
the Baal of Peor. And the
LORD's anger burned against
them. Mic 6:5; 1Co 10:20
  4The LORD said to Moses,
"Take all the leaders of these
people, kill them and expose
them in broad daylight before
the LORD, so that the LORD's
fierce anger may turn away
from Israel." Dt 4:3; 13:17
  5So Moses said to Israel's
judges, "Each of you must put
to death those of your men who
have joined in worshiping the
Baal of Peor." Ex 32:27
  6Then an Israelite man
brought to his family a Midianite woman right before the eyes
of Moses and the whole assembly of Israel while they were
weeping at the entrance to the
Tent of Meeting. 7When Phinehas son of Eleazar, the son of
Aaron, the priest, saw this, he
left the assembly, took a spear
in his hand 8and followed the
Israelite into the tent. He drove
the spear through both of
them—through the Israelite
and into the woman's body.
Then the plague against the Israelites was stopped; 9but those
who died in the plague numbered 24,000. Nu 14:1; Jos 22:13

  10The LORD said to Moses,
11"Phinehas son of Eleazar, the
son of Aaron, the priest, has
turned my anger away from the
Israelites; for he was as zealous
as I am for my honor among
them, so that in my zeal I did
not put an end to them. 12There-
fore tell him I am making my
covenant of peace with him.
13He and his descendants will
have a covenant of a lasting
priesthood, because he was
zealous for the honor of his God
and made atonement for the Israelites." Ex 20:5; Mal 2:14
  14The name of the Israelite
who was killed with the Midian-

ᵃ23 Masoretic Text; with a different word division of the Hebrew *A people will gather from
the north*.

ite woman was Zimri son of Salu, the leader of a Simeonite family. ¹⁵And the name of the Midianite woman who was put to death was Cozbi daughter of Zur, a tribal chief of a Midianite family.   Nu 1:6; 31:8

¹⁶The Lord said to Moses, ¹⁷"Treat the Midianites as enemies and kill them, ¹⁸because they treated you as enemies when they deceived you in the affair of Peor and their sister Cozbi, the daughter of a Midianite leader, the woman who was killed when the plague came as a result of Peor."   Nu 31:7

The Second Census

26 After the plague the Lord said to Moses and Eleazar son of Aaron, the priest, ²"Take a census of the whole Israelite community by families—all those twenty years old or more who are able to serve in the army of Israel." ³So on the plains of Moab by the Jordan across from Jericho, ᵃ Moses and Eleazar the priest spoke with them and said, ⁴"Take a census of the men twenty years old or more, as the Lord commanded Moses."   Ex 30:12; Nu 33:48

These were the Israelites who came out of Egypt:

⁵The descendants of Reuben, the firstborn son of Israel, were:
   through Hanoch, the Hanochite clan;

   through Pallu, the Palluite clan;
   ⁶through Hezron, the Hezronite clan;
   through Carmi, the Carmite clan.   Nu 1:20; 1Ch 5:3

⁷These were the clans of Reuben; those numbered were 43,730.

⁸The son of Pallu was Eliab, ⁹and the sons of Eliab were Nemuel, Dathan and Abiram. The same Dathan and Abiram were the community officials who rebelled against Moses and Aaron and were among Korah's followers when they rebelled against the Lord. ¹⁰The earth opened its mouth and swallowed them along with Korah, whose followers died when the fire devoured the 250 men. And they served as a warning sign. ¹¹The line of Korah, however, did not die out.   Dt 32:16; Ps 106:30

¹²The descendants of Simeon by their clans were:
   through Nemuel, the Nemuelite clan;
   through Jamin, the Jaminite clan;
   through Jakin, the Jakinite clan;
   ¹³through Zerah, the Zerahite clan;
   through Shaul, the Shaulite clan.   1Ki 19:10; 1Ch 4:24
¹⁴These were the clans of Simeon; there were 22,200 men.

ᵃ3 Hebrew *Jordan of Jericho;* possibly an ancient name for the Jordan River; also in verse 63

15The descendants of Gad by their clans were:

through Zephon, the Zephonite clan;

through Haggi, the Haggite clan;

through Shuni, the Shunite clan;

16through Ozni, the Oznite clan;

through Eri, the Erite clan;

17through Arodi,[a] the Arodite clan;

through Areli, the Arelite clan.   Ge 46:16

18These were the clans of Gad; those numbered were 40,500.

19Er and Onan were sons of Judah, but they died in Canaan. 20The descendants of Judah by their clans were:

through Shelah, the Shelanite clan;

through Perez, the Perezite clan;   Ge 38:5; Jos 7:17

through Zerah, the Zerahite clan.

21The descendants of Perez were:

through Hezron, the Hezronite clan;

through Hamul, the Hamulite clan.   Ge 38:29

22These were the clans of Judah; those numbered were 76,500.

23The descendants of Issachar by their clans were:

through Tola, the Tolaite clan;

through Puah, the Puite[b] clan;

24through Jashub, the Jashubite clan;

through Shimron, the Shimronite clan.   Ge 46:13

25These were the clans of Issachar; those numbered were 64,300.   Ge 30:18; Nu 1:29

26The descendants of Zebulun by their clans were:

through Sered, the Seredite clan;

through Elon, the Elonite clan;

through Jahleel, the Jahleelite clan.   Nu 1:30

27These were the clans of Zebulun; those numbered were 60,500.   Ge 30:20

28The descendants of Joseph by their clans through Manasseh and Ephraim were: Nu 1:32

29The descendants of Manasseh:

through Makir, the Makirite clan (Makir was the father of Gilead);

through Gilead, the Gileadite clan.   Nu 1:34; Jdg 11:1

30These were the descendants of Gilead:

through Iezer, the Iezerite clan;

through Helek, the Helekite clan;

31through Asriel, the Asrielite clan;

through Shechem, the Shechemite clan;

---

a17 Samaritan Pentateuch and Syriac (see also Gen. 46:16); Masoretic Text *Arod*
b23 Samaritan Pentateuch, Septuagint, Vulgate and Syriac (see also 1 Chron. 7:1); Masoretic Text *through Puvah, the Punite*

³²through Shemida, the Shemidaite clan;
through Hepher, the Hepherite clan.   Nu 27:1; Jos 17:2
³³(Zelophehad son of Hepher had no sons; he had only daughters, whose names were Mahlah, Noah, Hoglah, Milcah and Tirzah.)   Nu 27:3; 1Ch 7:15

³⁴These were the clans of Manasseh; those numbered were 52,700.   Nu 1:35

³⁵These were the descendants of Ephraim by their clans:
through Shuthelah, the Shuthelahite clan;
through Beker, the Bekerite clan;
through Tahan, the Tahanite clan.   Nu 1:32
³⁶These were the descendants of Shuthelah:
through Eran, the Eranite clan.

³⁷These were the clans of Ephraim; those numbered were 32,500.   Nu 1:33

These were the descendants of Joseph by their clans.

³⁸The descendants of Benjamin by their clans were:
through Bela, the Belaite clan;
through Ashbel, the Ashbelite clan;
through Ahiram, the Ahiramite clan;

³⁹through Shupham,ᵃ the Shuphamite clan;
through Hupham, the Huphamite clan.   Ge 46:21
⁴⁰The descendants of Bela through Ard and Naaman were:
through Ard,ᵇ the Ardite clan;
through Naaman, the Naamite clan.   1Ch 8:3
⁴¹These were the clans of Benjamin; those numbered were 45,600.   Nu 1:37

⁴²These were the descendants of Dan by their clans:
through Shuham, the Shuhamite clan.   Ge 46:23; Nu 1:38
These were the clans of Dan:
⁴³All of them were Shuhamite clans; and those numbered were 64,400.   Nu 1:39

⁴⁴The descendants of Asher by their clans were:
through Imnah, the Imnite clan;
through Ishvi, the Ishvite clan;
through Beriah, the Beriite clan;
⁴⁵and through the descendants of Beriah:
through Heber, the Heberite clan;
through Malkiel, the Malkielite clan.   Nu 1:40
⁴⁶(Asher had a daughter named Serah.)   1Ch 7:30

ᵃ39 A few manuscripts of the Masoretic Text, Samaritan Pentateuch, Vulgate and Syriac (see also Septuagint); most manuscripts of the Masoretic Text *Shephupham*
ᵇ40 Samaritan Pentateuch and Vulgate (see also Septuagint); Masoretic Text does not have *through Ard*.

47These were the clans of Asher; those numbered were 53,400.

48The descendants of Naphtali by their clans were:

through Jahzeel, the Jahzeelite clan;

through Guni, the Gunite clan;

49through Jezer, the Jezerite clan;

through Shillem, the Shillemite clan.   Ge 30:8

50These were the clans of Naphtali; those numbered were 45,400.   Nu 1:43

51The total number of the men of Israel was 601,730.   Ex 12:37

52The LORD said to Moses, 53"The land is to be allotted to them as an inheritance based on the number of names. 54To a larger group give a larger inheritance, and to a smaller group a smaller one; each is to receive its inheritance according to the number of those listed. 55Be sure that the land is distributed by lot. What each group inherits will be according to the names for its ancestral tribe. 56Each inheritance is to be distributed by lot among the larger and smaller groups."   Nu 33:54; Jos 11:23

57These were the Levites who were counted by their clans:

through Gershon, the Gershonite clan;

through Kohath, the Kohathite clan;

through Merari, the Merarite clan.   Ge 46:11

58These also were Levite clans:

the Libnite clan,

the Hebronite clan,

the Mahlite clan,

the Mushite clan,

the Korahite clan.   Ex 6:20

(Kohath was the forefather of Amram; 59the name of Amram's wife was Jochebed, a descendant of Levi, who was born to the Levites^a in Egypt. To Amram she bore Aaron, Moses and their sister Miriam. 60Aaron was the father of Nadab and Abihu, Eleazar and Ithamar. 61But Nadab and Abihu died when they made an offering before the LORD with unauthorized fire.)   Lev 10:1; Nu 3:2

62All the male Levites a month old or more numbered 23,000. They were not counted along with the other Israelites because they received no inheritance among them.   Nu 1:47; 3:39

63These are the ones counted by Moses and Eleazar the priest when they counted the Israelites on the plains of Moab by the Jordan across from Jericho. 64Not one of them was among those counted by Moses and Aaron the priest when they counted the Israelites in the Desert of Sinai. 65For the LORD had told those Israelites they

a59 Or Jochebed, a daughter of Levi, who was born to Levi

would surely die in the desert, and not one of them was left except Caleb son of Jephunneh and Joshua son of Nun.   Nu 22:1

Zelophehad's Daughters

27 The daughters of Zelophehad son of Hepher, the son of Gilead, the son of Makir, the son of Manasseh, belonged to the clans of Manasseh son of Joseph. The names of the daughters were Mahlah, Noah, Hoglah, Milcah and Tirzah. They approached ²the entrance to the Tent of Meeting and stood before Moses, Eleazar the priest, the leaders and the whole assembly, and said, ³"Our father died in the desert. He was not among Korah's followers, who banded together against the LORD, but he died for his own sin and left no sons. ⁴Why should our father's name disappear from his clan because he had no son? Give us property among our father's relatives."   Nu 9:8; 26:33

⁵So Moses brought their case before the LORD ⁶and the LORD said to him, ⁷"What Zelophehad's daughters are saying is right. You must certainly give them property as an inheritance among their father's relatives and turn their father's inheritance over to them.   Nu 36:2

⁸"Say to the Israelites, 'If a man dies and leaves no son, turn his inheritance over to his daughter. ⁹If he has no daughter, give his inheritance to his brothers. ¹⁰If he has no brothers, give his inheritance to his father's brothers. ¹¹If his father had no brothers, give his inheritance to the nearest relative in his clan, that he may possess it. This is to be a legal requirement for the Israelites, as the LORD commanded Moses.'"   Nu 35:29

Joshua to Succeed Moses

¹²Then the LORD said to Moses, "Go up this mountain in the Abarim range and see the land I have given the Israelites. ¹³After you have seen it, you too will be gathered to your people, as your brother Aaron was, ¹⁴for when the community rebelled at the waters in the Desert of Zin, both of you disobeyed my command to honor me as holy before their eyes." (These were the waters of Meribah Kadesh, in the Desert of Zin.)   Nu 33:47

¹⁵Moses said to the LORD, ¹⁶"May the LORD, the God of the spirits of all mankind, appoint a man over this community ¹⁷to go out and come in before them, one who will lead them out and bring them in, so the LORD's people will not be like sheep without a shepherd."   Nu 16:22

¹⁸So the LORD said to Moses, "Take Joshua son of Nun, a man in whom is the spirit,ᵃ and lay your hand on him. ¹⁹Have him stand before Eleazar the priest and the entire assembly and commission him in their

ᵃ18 Or Spirit

presence. ²⁰Give him some of your authority so the whole Israelite community will obey him. ²¹He is to stand before Eleazar the priest, who will obtain decisions for him by inquiring of the Urim before the LORD. At his command he and the entire community of the Israelites will go out, and at his command they will come in."   Dt 34:9

²²Moses did as the LORD commanded him. He took Joshua and had him stand before Eleazar the priest and the whole assembly. ²³Then he laid his hands on him and commissioned him, as the LORD instructed through Moses.   Dt 3:28

Daily Offerings

28 The LORD said to Moses, ²"Give this command to the Israelites and say to them: 'See that you present to me at the appointed time the food for my offerings made by fire, as an aroma pleasing to me.' ³Say to them: 'This is the offering made by fire that you are to present to the LORD: two lambs a year old without defect, as a regular burnt offering each day. ⁴Prepare one lamb in the morning and the other at twilight, ⁵together with a grain offering of a tenth of an ephah*ᵃ* of fine flour mixed with a quarter of a hin*ᵇ* of oil from pressed olives. ⁶This is the regular burnt offering instituted at Mount Sinai as a pleasing aroma, an offering made to the LORD by fire. ⁷The accompanying drink offering is to be a quarter of a hin of fermented drink with each lamb. Pour out the drink offering to the LORD at the sanctuary. ⁸Prepare the second lamb at twilight, along with the same kind of grain offering and drink offering that you prepare in the morning. This is an offering made by fire, an aroma pleasing to the LORD.   Lev 3:11; Nu 29:6

Sabbath Offerings

⁹" 'On the Sabbath day, make an offering of two lambs a year old without defect, together with its drink offering and a grain offering of two-tenths of an ephah*ᶜ* of fine flour mixed with oil. ¹⁰This is the burnt offering for every Sabbath, in addition to the regular burnt offering and its drink offering.   Mt 12:5

Monthly Offerings

¹¹" 'On the first of every month, present to the LORD a burnt offering of two young bulls, one ram and seven male lambs a year old, all without defect. ¹²With each bull there is to be a grain offering of three-tenths of an ephah*ᵈ* of fine flour mixed with oil; with the ram, a grain offering of two-tenths of an ephah of fine flour mixed

---

ᵃ5 That is, probably about 2 quarts (about 2 liters); also in verses 13, 21 and 29
ᵇ5 That is, probably about 1 quart (about 1 liter); also in verses 7 and 14   *ᶜ9* That is, probably about 4 quarts (about 4.5 liters); also in verses 12, 20 and 28   *ᵈ12* That is, probably about 6 quarts (about 6.5 liters); also in verses 20 and 28

with oil; [13]and with each lamb, a grain offering of a tenth of an ephah of fine flour mixed with oil. This is for a burnt offering, a pleasing aroma, an offering made to the LORD by fire. [14]With each bull there is to be a drink offering of half a hin[a] of wine; with the ram, a third of a hin[b]; and with each lamb, a quarter of a hin. This is the monthly burnt offering to be made at each new moon during the year. [15]Besides the regular burnt offering with its drink offering, one male goat is to be presented to the LORD as a sin offering.   Lev 5:15; Nu 10:10

The Passover

[16]" 'On the fourteenth day of the first month the LORD's Passover is to be held. [17]On the fifteenth day of this month there is to be a festival; for seven days eat bread made without yeast. [18]On the first day hold a sacred assembly and do no regular work. [19]Present to the LORD an offering made by fire, a burnt offering of two young bulls, one ram and seven male lambs a year old, all without defect. [20]With each bull prepare a grain offering of three-tenths of an ephah of fine flour mixed with oil; with the ram, two-tenths; [21]and with each of the seven lambs, one-tenth. [22]Include one male goat as a sin offering to make atonement for you. [23]Prepare these in addition to the regular morning burnt offering. [24]In this way prepare the food for the offering made by fire every day for seven days as an aroma pleasing to the LORD; it is to be prepared in addition to the regular burnt offering and its drink offering. [25]On the seventh day hold a sacred assembly and do no regular work.   Ex 12:16

Feast of Weeks

[26]" 'On the day of firstfruits, when you present to the LORD an offering of new grain during the Feast of Weeks, hold a sacred assembly and do no regular work. [27]Present a burnt offering of two young bulls, one ram and seven male lambs a year old as an aroma pleasing to the LORD. [28]With each bull there is to be a grain offering of three-tenths of an ephah of fine flour mixed with oil; with the ram, two-tenths; [29]and with each of the seven lambs, one-tenth. [30]Include one male goat to make atonement for you. [31]Prepare these together with their drink offerings, in addition to the regular burnt offering and its grain offering. Be sure the animals are without defect.   Ex 23:16; Dt 16:10

Feast of Trumpets

29 " 'On the first day of the seventh month hold a sacred assembly and do no regular work. It is a day for you to sound the trumpets. [2]As an

---

[a]14 That is, probably about 2 quarts (about 2 liters)   [b]14 That is, probably about 1 1/4 quarts (about 1.2 liters)

aroma pleasing to the LORD, prepare a burnt offering of one young bull, one ram and seven male lambs a year old, all without defect. ³With the bull prepare a grain offering of three-tenths of an ephah*a* of fine flour mixed with oil; with the ram, two-tenths*b*; ⁴and with each of the seven lambs, one-tenth. *c* ⁵Include one male goat as a sin offering to make atonement for you. ⁶These are in addition to the monthly and daily burnt offerings with their grain offerings and drink offerings as specified. They are offerings made to the LORD by fire—a pleasing aroma.   Lev 1:9; Nu 28:3

Day of Atonement

⁷" 'On the tenth day of this seventh month hold a sacred assembly. You must deny yourselves*d* and do no work. ⁸Present as an aroma pleasing to the LORD a burnt offering of one young bull, one ram and seven male lambs a year old, all without defect. ⁹With the bull prepare a grain offering of three-tenths of an ephah of fine flour mixed with oil; with the ram, two-tenths; ¹⁰and with each of the seven lambs, one-tenth. ¹¹Include one male goat as a sin offering, in addition to the sin offering for atonement and the regular burnt offering with its grain offering, and their drink offerings.   Lev 16:3; Ac 27:9

Feast of Tabernacles

¹²" 'On the fifteenth day of the seventh month, hold a sacred assembly and do no regular work. Celebrate a festival to the LORD for seven days. ¹³Present an offering made by fire as an aroma pleasing to the LORD, a burnt offering of thirteen young bulls, two rams and fourteen male lambs a year old, all without defect. ¹⁴With each of the thirteen bulls prepare a grain offering of three-tenths of an ephah of fine flour mixed with oil; with each of the two rams, two-tenths; ¹⁵and with each of the fourteen lambs, one-tenth. ¹⁶Include one male goat as a sin offering, in addition to the regular burnt offering with its grain offering and drink offering.   Lev 23:24; Nu 28:2

¹⁷" 'On the second day prepare twelve young bulls, two rams and fourteen male lambs a year old, all without defect. ¹⁸With the bulls, rams and lambs, prepare their grain offerings and drink offerings according to the number specified. ¹⁹Include one male goat as a sin offering, in addition to the regular burnt offering with its grain offering, and their drink offerings.   Lev 23:36; Nu 15:12

²⁰" 'On the third day prepare eleven bulls, two rams and fourteen male lambs a year old, all without defect. ²¹With the bulls,

---

a3 That is, probably about 6 quarts (about 6.5 liters); also in verses 9 and 14   *b3* That is, probably about 4 quarts (about 4.5 liters); also in verses 9 and 14   *c4* That is, probably about 2 quarts (about 2 liters); also in verses 10 and 15   *d7* Or *must fast*

rams and lambs, prepare their grain offerings and drink offerings according to the number specified. ²²Include one male goat as a sin offering, in addition to the regular burnt offering with its grain offering and drink offering. Nu 28:15

²³" 'On the fourth day prepare ten bulls, two rams and fourteen male lambs a year old, all without defect. ²⁴With the bulls, rams and lambs, prepare their grain offerings and drink offerings according to the number specified. ²⁵Include one male goat as a sin offering, in addition to the regular burnt offering with its grain offering and drink offering.

²⁶" 'On the fifth day prepare nine bulls, two rams and fourteen male lambs a year old, all without defect. ²⁷With the bulls, rams and lambs, prepare their grain offerings and drink offerings according to the number specified. ²⁸Include one male goat as a sin offering, in addition to the regular burnt offering with its grain offering and drink offering. Nu 15:24

²⁹" 'On the sixth day prepare eight bulls, two rams and fourteen male lambs a year old, all without defect. ³⁰With the bulls, rams and lambs, prepare their grain offerings and drink offerings according to the number specified. ³¹Include one male goat as a sin offering, in addi-

tion to the regular burnt offering with its grain offering and drink offering.

³²" 'On the seventh day prepare seven bulls, two rams and fourteen male lambs a year old, all without defect. ³³With the bulls, rams and lambs, prepare their grain offerings and drink offerings according to the number specified. ³⁴Include one male goat as a sin offering, in addition to the regular burnt offering with its grain offering and drink offering.

³⁵" 'On the eighth day hold an assembly and do no regular work. ³⁶Present an offering made by fire as an aroma pleasing to the LORD, a burnt offering of one bull, one ram and seven male lambs a year old, all without defect. ³⁷With the bull, the ram and the lambs, prepare their grain offerings and drink offerings according to the number specified. ³⁸Include one male goat as a sin offering, in addition to the regular burnt offering with its grain offering and drink offering. Lev 1:9; 23:36

³⁹" 'In addition to what you vow and your freewill offerings, prepare these for the LORD at your appointed feasts: your burnt offerings, grain offerings, drink offerings and fellowship offerings.ᵃ' " Lev 23:2; 1Ch 23:31

⁴⁰Moses told the Israelites all that the LORD commanded him.

ᵃ39 Traditionally *peace offerings*

Vows

30 Moses said to the heads of the tribes of Israel: "This is what the LORD commands: 2When a man makes a vow to the LORD or takes an oath to obligate himself by a pledge, he must not break his word but must do everything he said.   Dt 23:21; Job 22:27

3"When a young woman still living in her father's house makes a vow to the LORD or obligates herself by a pledge 4and her father hears about her vow or pledge but says nothing to her, then all her vows and every pledge by which she obligated herself will stand. 5But if her father forbids her when he hears about it, none of her vows or the pledges by which she obligated herself will stand; the LORD will release her because her father has forbidden her.

6"If she marries after she makes a vow or after her lips utter a rash promise by which she obligates herself 7and her husband hears about it but says nothing to her, then her vows or the pledges by which she obligated herself will stand. 8But if her husband forbids her when he hears about it, he nullifies the vow that obligates her or the rash promise by which she obligates herself, and the LORD will release her.   Lev 5:4

9"Any vow or obligation taken by a widow or divorced woman will be binding on her. 10"If a woman living with her husband makes a vow or obligates herself by a pledge under oath 11and her husband hears about it but says nothing to her and does not forbid her, then all her vows or the pledges by which she obligated herself will stand. 12But if her husband nullifies them when he hears about them, then none of the vows or pledges that came from her lips will stand. Her husband has nullified them, and the LORD will release her. 13Her husband may confirm or nullify any vow she makes or any sworn pledge to deny herself. 14But if her husband says nothing to her about it from day to day, then he confirms all her vows or the pledges binding on her. He confirms them by saying nothing to her when he hears about them. 15If, however, he nullifies them some time after he hears about them, then he is responsible for her guilt."   Eph 5:22; Col 3:18

16These are the regulations the LORD gave Moses concerning relationships between a man and his wife, and between a father and his young daughter still living in his house.   Ex 15:26

Vengeance on the Midianites

31 The LORD said to Moses, 2"Take vengeance on the Midianites for the Israelites. After that, you will be gathered to your people."   Nu 20:26

3So Moses said to the people, "Arm some of your men to go to war against the Midianites and to carry out the LORD's ven-

geance on them. ⁴Send into battle a thousand men from each of the tribes of Israel." ⁵So twelve thousand men armed for battle, a thousand from each tribe, were supplied from the clans of Israel. ⁶Moses sent them into battle, a thousand from each tribe, along with Phinehas son of Eleazar, the priest, who took with him articles from the sanctuary and the trumpets for signaling. Nu 10:2; Jdg 11:36

⁷They fought against Midian, as the LORD commanded Moses, and killed every man. ⁸Among their victims were Evi, Rekem, Zur, Hur and Reba—the five kings of Midian. They also killed Balaam son of Beor with the sword. ⁹The Israelites captured the Midianite women and children and took all the Midianite herds, flocks and goods as plunder. ¹⁰They burned all the towns where the Midianites had settled, as well as all their camps. ¹¹They took all the plunder and spoils, including the people and animals, ¹²and brought the captives, spoils and plunder to Moses and Eleazar the priest and the Israelite assembly at their camp on the plains of Moab, by the Jordan across from Jericho.ᵃ

¹³Moses, Eleazar the priest and all the leaders of the community went to meet them outside the camp. ¹⁴Moses was angry with the officers of the army—the commanders of thousands and commanders of hundreds—who returned from the battle. Ex 18:21; Dt 1:15

¹⁵"Have you allowed all the women to live?" he asked them. ¹⁶"They were the ones who followed Balaam's advice and were the means of turning the Israelites away from the LORD in what happened at Peor, so that a plague struck the LORD's people. ¹⁷Now kill all the boys. And kill every woman who has slept with a man, ¹⁸but save for yourselves every girl who has never slept with a man. 2Pe 2:15

¹⁹"All of you who have killed anyone or touched anyone who was killed must stay outside the camp seven days. On the third and seventh days you must purify yourselves and your captives. ²⁰Purify every garment as well as everything made of leather, goat hair or wood."

²¹Then Eleazar the priest said to the soldiers who had gone into battle, "This is the requirement of the law that the LORD gave Moses: ²²Gold, silver, bronze, iron, tin, lead ²³and anything else that can withstand fire must be put through the fire, and then it will be clean. But it must also be purified with the water of cleansing. And whatever cannot withstand fire must be put through that water. ²⁴On the seventh day wash your clothes and you will be clean. Then you may come into the camp." Nu 8:7

ᵃ12 Hebrew *Jordan of Jericho*; possibly an ancient name for the Jordan River

Dividing the Spoils

25The LORD said to Moses, 26"You and Eleazar the priest and the family heads of the community are to count all the people and animals that were captured. 27Divide the spoils between the soldiers who took part in the battle and the rest of the community. 28From the soldiers who fought in the battle, set apart as tribute for the LORD one out of every five hundred, whether persons, cattle, donkeys, sheep or goats. 29Take this tribute from their half share and give it to Eleazar the priest as the LORD's part. 30From the Israelites' half, select one out of every fifty, whether persons, cattle, donkeys, sheep, goats or other animals. Give them to the Levites, who are responsible for the care of the LORD's tabernacle." 31So Moses and Eleazar the priest did as the LORD commanded Moses.   Nu 1:4; Jos 22:8

32The plunder remaining from the spoils that the soldiers took was 675,000 sheep, 3372,000 cattle, 3461,000 donkeys 35and 32,000 women who had never slept with a man.   Ge 49:27

36The half share of those who fought in the battle was:

337,500 sheep, 37of which the tribute for the LORD was 675;

3836,000 cattle, of which the tribute for the LORD was 72;

3930,500 donkeys, of which

the tribute for the LORD was 61;

4016,000 people, of which the tribute for the LORD was 32.   Lev 15:23; Job 41:11

41Moses gave the tribute to Eleazar the priest as the LORD's part, as the LORD commanded Moses.   Nu 5:9; 18:8

42The half belonging to the Israelites, which Moses set apart from that of the fighting men— 43the community's half—was 337,500 sheep, 4436,000 cattle, 4530,500 donkeys 46and 16,000 people. 47From the Israelites' half, Moses selected one out of every fifty persons and animals, as the LORD commanded him, and gave them to the Levites, who were responsible for the care of the LORD's tabernacle.

48Then the officers who were over the units of the army—the commanders of thousands and commanders of hundreds— went to Moses 49and said to him, "Your servants have counted the soldiers under our command, and not one is missing. 50So we have brought as an offering to the LORD the gold articles each of us acquired—armlets, bracelets, signet rings, earrings and necklaces—to make atonement for ourselves before the LORD."

51Moses and Eleazar the priest accepted from them the gold—all the crafted articles. 52All the gold from the commanders of thousands and commanders of hundreds that

Moses and Eleazar presented as a gift to the LORD weighed 16,-750 shekels. *a* 53Each soldier had taken plunder for himself. 54Moses and Eleazar the priest accepted the gold from the commanders of thousands and commanders of hundreds and brought it into the Tent of Meeting as a memorial for the Israelites before the LORD.   Dt 20:14

The Transjordan Tribes

32 The Reubenites and Gadites, who had very large herds and flocks, saw that the lands of Jazer and Gilead were suitable for livestock. 2So they came to Moses and Eleazar the priest and to the leaders of the community, and said, 3"Ataroth, Dibon, Jazer, Nimrah, Heshbon, Elealeh, Sebam, Nebo and Beon— 4the land the LORD subdued before the people of Israel—are suitable for livestock, and your servants have livestock. 5If we have found favor in your eyes," they said, "let this land be given to your servants as our possession. Do not make us cross the Jordan."   Ex 12:38; Nu 21:32

6Moses said to the Gadites and Reubenites, "Shall your countrymen go to war while you sit here? 7Why do you discourage the Israelites from going over into the land the LORD has given them? 8This is what your fathers did when I sent them from Kadesh Barnea to look over the land. 9After they went up to the Valley of Eshcol and viewed the land, they discouraged the Israelites from entering the land the LORD had given them. 10The LORD's anger was aroused that day and he swore this oath: 11'Because they have not followed me wholeheartedly, not one of the men twenty years old or more who came up out of Egypt will see the land I promised on oath to Abraham, Isaac and Jacob— 12not one except Caleb son of Jephunneh the Kenizzite and Joshua son of Nun, for they followed the LORD wholeheartedly.' 13The LORD's anger burned against Israel and he made them wander in the desert forty years, until the whole generation of those who had done evil in his sight was gone.   Nu 13:27

14"And here you are, a brood of sinners, standing in the place of your fathers and making the LORD even more angry with Israel. 15If you turn away from following him, he will again leave all this people in the desert, and you will be the cause of their destruction."   2Ch 7:20; Ps 78:59

16Then they came up to him and said, "We would like to build pens here for our livestock and cities for our women and children. 17But we are ready to arm ourselves and go ahead of the Israelites until we have brought them to their place. Meanwhile our women and

a52 That is, about 420 pounds (about 190 kilograms)

children will live in fortified cities, for protection from the inhabitants of the land. ¹⁸We will not return to our homes until every Israelite has received his inheritance. ¹⁹We will not receive any inheritance with them on the other side of the Jordan, because our inheritance has come to us on the east side of the Jordan."   Jos 4:12; 22:1-4

²⁰Then Moses said to them, "If you will do this—if you will arm yourselves before the LORD for battle, ²¹and if all of you will go armed over the Jordan before the LORD until he has driven his enemies out before him— ²²then when the land is subdued before the LORD, you may return and be free from your obligation to the LORD and to Israel. And this land will be your possession before the LORD.

²³"But if you fail to do this, you will be sinning against the LORD; and you may be sure that your sin will find you out. ²⁴Build cities for your women and children, and pens for your flocks, but do what you have promised."   Ge 4:7; Nu 30:2

²⁵The Gadites and Reubenites said to Moses, "We your servants will do as our lord commands. ²⁶Our children and wives, our flocks and herds will remain here in the cities of Gilead. ²⁷But your servants, every man armed for battle, will cross over to fight before the LORD, just as our lord says."   Jos 1:14

²⁸Then Moses gave orders about them to Eleazar the priest and Joshua son of Nun and to the family heads of the Israelite tribes. ²⁹He said to them, "If the Gadites and Reubenites, every man armed for battle, cross over the Jordan with you before the LORD, then when the land is subdued before you, give them the land of Gilead as their possession. ³⁰But if they do not cross over with you armed, they must accept their possession with you in Canaan."   Jos 1:13

³¹The Gadites and Reubenites answered, "Your servants will do what the LORD has said. ³²We will cross over before the LORD into Canaan armed, but the property we inherit will be on this side of the Jordan."

³³Then Moses gave to the Gadites, the Reubenites and the half-tribe of Manasseh son of Joseph the kingdom of Sihon king of the Amorites and the kingdom of Og king of Bashan—the whole land with its cities and the territory around them. Nu 21:24

³⁴The Gadites built up Dibon, Ataroth, Aroer, ³⁵Atroth Shophan, Jazer, Jogbehah, ³⁶Beth Nimrah and Beth Haran as fortified cities, and built pens for their flocks. ³⁷And the Reubenites rebuilt Heshbon, Elealeh and Kiriathaim, ³⁸as well as Nebo and Baal Meon (these names were changed) and Sibmah. They gave names to the cities they rebuilt.   Dt 2:36

³⁹The descendants of Makir son of Manasseh went to Gilead, captured it and drove out the Amorites who were there.

⁴⁰So Moses gave Gilead to the Makirites, the descendants of Manasseh, and they settled there. ⁴¹Jair, a descendant of Manasseh, captured their settlements and called them Havvoth Jair.ᵃ ⁴²And Nobah captured Kenath and its surrounding settlements and called it Nobah after himself.   Jdg 10:4

Stages in Israel's Journey

33 Here are the stages in the journey of the Israelites when they came out of Egypt by divisions under the leadership of Moses and Aaron. ²At the Lord's command Moses recorded the stages in their journey. This is their journey by stages: Ex 17:1; Ps 77:20

³The Israelites set out from Rameses on the fifteenth day of the first month, the day after the Passover. They marched out boldly in full view of all the Egyptians, ⁴who were burying all their firstborn, whom the Lord had struck down among them; for the Lord had brought judgment on their gods.   Nu 10:2

⁵The Israelites left Rameses and camped at Succoth. ⁶They left Succoth and camped at Etham, on the edge of the desert.   Ex 13:20

⁷They left Etham, turned back to Pi Hahiroth, to the east of Baal Zephon, and camped near Migdol.   Ex 14:9

⁸They left Pi Hahirothᵇ and passed through the sea into the desert, and when they had traveled for three days in the Desert of Etham, they camped at Marah.   Ex 14:22; 15:23

⁹They left Marah and went to Elim, where there were twelve springs and seventy palm trees, and they camped there.   Ex 15:27

¹⁰They left Elim and camped by the Red Sea.ᶜ

¹¹They left the Red Sea and camped in the Desert of Sin.   Ex 16:1

¹²They left the Desert of Sin and camped at Dophkah.

¹³They left Dophkah and camped at Alush.

¹⁴They left Alush and camped at Rephidim, where there was no water for the people to drink.   Ex 15:22

¹⁵They left Rephidim and camped in the Desert of Sinai.   Ex 19:1

¹⁶They left the Desert of Sinai and camped at Kibroth Hattaavah.   Nu 11:34

¹⁷They left Kibroth Hattaavah and camped at Hazeroth.   Nu 11:35

¹⁸They left Hazeroth and camped at Rithmah.

¹⁹They left Rithmah and camped at Rimmon Perez.

ᵃ41 Or *them the settlements of Jair*   ᵇ8 Many manuscripts of the Masoretic Text, Samaritan Pentateuch and Vulgate; most manuscripts of the Masoretic Text *left from before Hahiroth*   ᶜ10 Hebrew *Yam Suph*; that is, Sea of Reeds; also in verse 11

²⁰They left Rimmon Perez and camped at Libnah. Jos 10:29

²¹They left Libnah and camped at Rissah.

²²They left Rissah and camped at Kehelathah.

²³They left Kehelathah and camped at Mount Shepher.

²⁴They left Mount Shepher and camped at Haradah.

²⁵They left Haradah and camped at Makheloth.

²⁶They left Makheloth and camped at Tahath.

²⁷They left Tahath and camped at Terah.

²⁸They left Terah and camped at Mithcah.

²⁹They left Mithcah and camped at Hashmonah.

³⁰They left Hashmonah and camped at Moseroth.

³¹They left Moseroth and camped at Bene Jaakan. Dt 10:6

³²They left Bene Jaakan and camped at Hor Haggidgad.

³³They left Hor Haggidgad and camped at Jotbathah. Dt 10:7

³⁴They left Jotbathah and camped at Abronah.

³⁵They left Abronah and camped at Ezion Geber. Dt 2:8

³⁶They left Ezion Geber and camped at Kadesh, in the Desert of Zin. Nu 13:21

³⁷They left Kadesh and camped at Mount Hor, on the border of Edom. ³⁸At the LORD's command Aaron the priest went up Mount Hor, where he died on the first day of the fifth month of the fortieth year after the Israelites came out of Egypt. ³⁹Aaron was a hundred and twenty-three years old when he died on Mount Hor. Nu 20:22; 27:13

⁴⁰The Canaanite king of Arad, who lived in the Negev of Canaan, heard that the Israelites were coming. Ge 10:18; Nu 21:1

⁴¹They left Mount Hor and camped at Zalmonah.

⁴²They left Zalmonah and camped at Punon.

⁴³They left Punon and camped at Oboth. Nu 21:10

⁴⁴They left Oboth and camped at Iye Abarim, on the border of Moab. Nu 21:11

⁴⁵They left Iyim*ᵃ* and camped at Dibon Gad.

⁴⁶They left Dibon Gad and camped at Almon Diblathaim.

⁴⁷They left Almon Diblathaim and camped in the mountains of Abarim, near Nebo. Nu 27:12

⁴⁸They left the mountains of Abarim and camped on the plains of Moab by the Jordan across from Jericho.*ᵇ*

⁴⁹There on the plains of Moab they camped along

ᵃ45 That is, Iye Abarim   *ᵇ48* Hebrew *Jordan of Jericho*; possibly an ancient name for the Jordan River; also in verse 50

the Jordan from Beth Jeshimoth to Abel Shittim.   Nu 22:1

⁵⁰On the plains of Moab by
the Jordan across from Jericho
the LORD said to Moses,
⁵¹"Speak to the Israelites and
say to them: 'When you cross
the Jordan into Canaan, ⁵²drive
out all the inhabitants of the
land before you. Destroy all
their carved images and their
cast idols, and demolish all their
high places. ⁵³Take possession
of the land and settle in it, for I
have given you the land to possess. ⁵⁴Distribute the land by
lot, according to your clans. To
a larger group give a larger inheritance, and to a smaller
group a smaller one. Whatever
falls to them by lot will be theirs.
Distribute it according to your
ancestral tribes.   Lev 16:8; Nu 34:2

⁵⁵" 'But if you do not drive
out the inhabitants of the land,
those you allow to remain will
become barbs in your eyes and
thorns in your sides. They will
give you trouble in the land
where you will live. ⁵⁶And then
I will do to you what I plan to do
to them.' "   Nu 14:28; Jos 23:13

Boundaries of Canaan

34 The LORD said to Moses,
²"Command the Israel-
ites and say to them: 'When you
enter Canaan, the land that will
be allotted to you as an inheritance will have these boundaries: Ge 17:8; Eze 47:15

³" 'Your southern side will include some of the Desert of Zin
along the border of Edom. On
the east, your southern boundary will start from the end of the
Salt Sea,ᵃ ⁴cross south of Scor-
pionᵇ Pass, continue on to Zin
and go south of Kadesh Barnea.
Then it will go to Hazar Addar
and over to Azmon, ⁵where it
will turn, join the Wadi of Egypt
and end at the Sea.ᶜ   Jos 15:1-3

⁶" 'Your western boundary
will be the coast of the Great
Sea. This will be your boundary
on the west.   Jos 1:4; Eze 47:10

⁷" 'For your northern boundary, run a line from the Great
Sea to Mount Hor ⁸and from
Mount Hor to Leboᵈ Hamath.
Then the boundary will go to
Zedad, ⁹continue to Ziphron
and end at Hazar Enan. This
will be your boundary on the
north.   Nu 13:21; Eze 47:15-17

¹⁰" 'For your eastern boundary, run a line from Hazar Enan
to Shepham. ¹¹The boundary
will go down from Shepham to
Riblah on the east side of Ain
and continue along the slopes
east of the Sea of Kinnereth.ᵉ
¹²Then the boundary will go
down along the Jordan and end
at the Salt Sea.   Jos 15:5; 2Ki 23:33

" 'This will be your land, with
its boundaries on every side.' "

¹³Moses commanded the Israelites: "Assign this land by lot
as an inheritance. The LORD has
ordered that it be given to the

ᵃ3 That is, the Dead Sea; also in verse 12   ᵇ4 Hebrew *Akrabbim*   ᶜ5 That is, the
Mediterranean; also in verses 6 and 7   ᵈ8 Or *to the entrance to*   ᵉ11 That is, Galilee

nine and a half tribes, [14]because the families of the tribe of Reuben, the tribe of Gad and the half-tribe of Manasseh have received their inheritance. [15]These two and a half tribes have received their inheritance on the east side of the Jordan of Jericho,[a] toward the sunrise." Jos 14:1

[16]The LORD said to Moses, [17]"These are the names of the men who are to assign the land for you as an inheritance: Eleazar the priest and Joshua son of Nun. [18]And appoint one leader from each tribe to help assign the land. [19]These are their names: Nu 11:28; Jos 14:1

Caleb son of Jephunneh,
    from the tribe of Judah;
[20]Shemuel son of Ammihud,
    from the tribe of Simeon;
[21]Elidad son of Kislon,
    from the tribe of Benjamin;
[22]Bukki son of Jogli,
    the leader from the tribe of Dan;
[23]Hanniel son of Ephod,
    the leader from the tribe of Manasseh son of Joseph;
[24]Kemuel son of Shiphtan,
    the leader from the tribe of Ephraim son of Joseph;
[25]Elizaphan son of Parnach,
    the leader from the tribe of Zebulun;
[26]Paltiel son of Azzan,
    the leader from the tribe of Issachar;
[27]Ahihud son of Shelomi,
    the leader from the tribe of Asher;
[28]Pedahel son of Ammihud,
    the leader from the tribe of Naphtali."   Ge 29:33; Nu 1:32

[29]These are the men the LORD commanded to assign the inheritance to the Israelites in the land of Canaan.   Nu 34:19

Towns for the Levites

35 On the plains of Moab by the Jordan across from Jericho,[b] the LORD said to Moses, [2]"Command the Israelites to give the Levites towns to live in from the inheritance the Israelites will possess. And give them pasturelands around the towns. [3]Then they will have towns to live in and pasturelands for their cattle, flocks and all their other livestock.   Nu 22:1

[4]"The pasturelands around the towns that you give the Levites will extend out fifteen hundred feet[c] from the town wall. [5]Outside the town, measure three thousand feet[d] on the east side, three thousand on the south side, three thousand on the west and three thousand on the north, with the town in the center. They will have this area as pastureland for the towns.

Cities of Refuge

[6]"Six of the towns you give

---

[a]15 Jordan of Jericho was possibly an ancient name for the Jordan River.   [b]1 Hebrew Jordan of Jericho; possibly an ancient name for the Jordan River   [c]4 Hebrew a thousand cubits (about 450 meters)   [d]5 Hebrew two thousand cubits (about 900 meters)

the Levites will be cities of refuge, to which a person who has killed someone may flee. In addition, give them forty-two other towns. ⁷In all you must give the Levites forty-eight towns, together with their pasturelands. ⁸The towns you give the Levites from the land the Israelites possess are to be given in proportion to the inheritance of each tribe: Take many towns from a tribe that has many, but few from one that has few."

⁹Then the LORD said to Moses: ¹⁰"Speak to the Israelites and say to them: 'When you cross the Jordan into Canaan, ¹¹select some towns to be your cities of refuge, to which a person who has killed someone accidentally may flee. ¹²They will be places of refuge from the avenger, so that a person accused of murder may not die before he stands trial before the assembly. ¹³These six towns you give will be your cities of refuge. ¹⁴Give three on this side of the Jordan and three in Canaan as cities of refuge. ¹⁵These six towns will be a place of refuge for Israelites, aliens and any other people living among them, so that anyone who has killed another accidentally can flee there.   Ex 21:13; Nu 33:51

¹⁶" 'If a man strikes someone with an iron object so that he dies, he is a murderer; the murderer shall be put to death. ¹⁷Or if anyone has a stone in his hand that could kill, and he strikes someone so that he dies, he is a murderer; the murderer shall be put to death. ¹⁸Or if anyone has a wooden object in his hand that could kill, and he hits someone so that he dies, he is a murderer; the murderer shall be put to death. ¹⁹The avenger of blood shall put the murderer to death; when he meets him, he shall put him to death. ²⁰If anyone with malice aforethought shoves another or throws something at him intentionally so that he dies ²¹or if in hostility he hits him with his fist so that he dies, that person shall be put to death; he is a murderer. The avenger of blood shall put the murderer to death when he meets him.   Ex 21:12; Lev 24:17

²²" 'But if without hostility someone suddenly shoves another or throws something at him unintentionally ²³or, without seeing him, drops a stone on him that could kill him, and he dies, then since he was not his enemy and he did not intend to harm him, ²⁴the assembly must judge between him and the avenger of blood according to these regulations. ²⁵The assembly must protect the one accused of murder from the avenger of blood and send him back to the city of refuge to which he fled. He must stay there until the death of the high priest, who was anointed with the holy oil.   Ex 21:13; 28:41

²⁶" 'But if the accused ever goes outside the limits of the

city of refuge to which he has fled ²⁷and the avenger of blood finds him outside the city, the avenger of blood may kill the accused without being guilty of murder. ²⁸The accused must stay in his city of refuge until the death of the high priest; only after the death of the high priest may he return to his own property.

²⁹" 'These are to be legal requirements for you throughout the generations to come, wherever you live. Nu 27:11

³⁰" 'Anyone who kills a person is to be put to death as a murderer only on the testimony of witnesses. But no one is to be put to death on the testimony of only one witness. Dt 17:6

³¹" 'Do not accept a ransom for the life of a murderer, who deserves to die. He must surely be put to death. Ex 21:30; Job 6:22

³²" 'Do not accept a ransom for anyone who has fled to a city of refuge and so allow him to go back and live on his own land before the death of the high priest.

³³" 'Do not pollute the land where you are. Bloodshed pollutes the land, and atonement cannot be made for the land on which blood has been shed, except by the blood of the one who shed it. ³⁴Do not defile the land where you live and where I dwell, for I, the LORD, dwell among the Israelites.' " Ge 4:10

Inheritance of Zelophehad's Daughters

36 The family heads of the clan of Gilead son of Makir, the son of Manasseh, who were from the clans of the descendants of Joseph, came and spoke before Moses and the leaders, the heads of the Israelite families. ²They said, "When the LORD commanded my lord to give the land as an inheritance to the Israelites by lot, he ordered you to give the inheritance of our brother Zelophehad to his daughters. ³Now suppose they marry men from other Israelite tribes; then their inheritance will be taken from our ancestral inheritance and added to that of the tribe they marry into. And so part of the inheritance allotted to us will be taken away. ⁴When the Year of Jubilee for the Israelites comes, their inheritance will be added to that of the tribe into which they marry, and their property will be taken from the tribal inheritance of our forefathers."

⁵Then at the LORD's command Moses gave this order to the Israelites: "What the tribe of the descendants of Joseph is saying is right. ⁶This is what the LORD commands for Zelophehad's daughters: They may marry anyone they please as long as they marry within the tribal clan of their father. ⁷No inheritance in Israel is to pass

from tribe to tribe, for every Israelite shall keep the tribal land inherited from his forefathers. [8]Every daughter who inherits land in any Israelite tribe must marry someone in her father's tribal clan, so that every Israelite will possess the inheritance of his fathers. [9]No inheritance may pass from tribe to tribe, for each Israelite tribe is to keep the land it inherits." Lev 25:23; 1Ch 23:22

[10]So Zelophehad's daughters did as the LORD commanded Moses. [11]Zelophehad's daughters—Mahlah, Tirzah, Hoglah, Milcah and Noah—married their cousins on their father's side. [12]They married within the clans of the descendants of Manasseh son of Joseph, and their inheritance remained in their father's clan and tribe. Nu 27:1

[13]These are the commands and regulations the LORD gave through Moses to the Israelites on the plains of Moab by the Jordan across from Jericho.[a]

Deuteronomy

Introduction:

Deuteronomy means "second law." After forty years the Israelites were about to enter the Promised Land of Canaan. But before they did, Moses wanted to remind them of their history, all that God and had done for them, and the laws they had to continue to obey as God's chosen people.

His first speech reminded the people of God's goodness to them through their journey and his giving them the land of Canaan. Moses' second speech was a summary of God's laws including the Ten Commandments. Moses told the people to "love the LORD your God with all your heart and with all your soul and with all your strength" in order to continue to enjoy God's blessing. Moses also emphasized the fact that to keep their relationship right with God, the people had to teach their children to love the Lord and obey his commandments.

Deuteronomy ends with the people of Israel being reminded of the covenant God had made with them (29), Joshua's appointment to be the new leader (31), and Moses' death (34). It is generally accepted that Moses wrote Deuteronomy except for the chapter about his death.

Outline of contents:

The Command to Leave Horeb

1 These are the words Moses spoke to all Israel in the desert east of the Jordan—that is, in the Arabah—opposite Suph, between Paran and Tophel, Laban, Hazeroth and Dizahab. ²(It takes eleven days to go from Horeb to Kadesh Barnea by the Mount Seir road.)

³In the fortieth year, on the first day of the eleventh month, Moses proclaimed to the Israel-

ites all that the LORD had commanded him concerning them. ⁴This was after he had defeated Sihon king of the Amorites, who reigned in Heshbon, and at Edrei had defeated Og king of Bashan, who reigned in Ashtaroth. Nu 21:23; Dt 8:2

⁵East of the Jordan in the territory of Moab, Moses began to expound this law, saying:

⁶The LORD our God said to us at Horeb, "You have stayed long enough at this mountain. ⁷Break camp and advance into the hill country of the Amorites; go to all the neighboring peoples in the Arabah, in the mountains, in the western foothills, in the Negev and along the coast, to the land of the Canaanites and to Lebanon, as far as the great river, the Euphrates. ⁸See, I have given you this land. Go in and take possession of the land that the LORD swore he would give to your fathers—to Abraham, Isaac and Jacob—and to their descendants after them." Nu 10:13; Jos 10:5

The Appointment of Leaders

⁹At that time I said to you, "You are too heavy a burden for me to carry alone. ¹⁰The LORD your God has increased your numbers so that today you are as many as the stars in the sky. ¹¹May the LORD, the God of your fathers, increase you a thousand times and bless you as he has promised! ¹²But how can I bear your problems and your burdens and your disputes all by myself? ¹³Choose some wise, understanding and respected men from each of your tribes, and I will set them over you."

¹⁴You answered me, "What you propose to do is good."

¹⁵So I took the leading men of your tribes, wise and respected men, and appointed them to have authority over you—as commanders of thousands, of hundreds, of fifties and of tens and as tribal officials. ¹⁶And I charged your judges at that time: Hear the disputes between your brothers and judge fairly, whether the case is between brother Israelites or between one of them and an alien. ¹⁷Do not show partiality in judging; hear both small and great alike. Do not be afraid of any man, for judgment belongs to God. Bring me any case too hard for you, and I will hear it. ¹⁸And at that time I told you everything you were to do.

Spies Sent Out

¹⁹Then, as the LORD our God commanded us, we set out from Horeb and went toward the hill country of the Amorites through all that vast and dreadful desert that you have seen, and so we reached Kadesh Barnea. ²⁰Then I said to you, "You have reached the hill country of the Amorites, which the LORD our God is giving us. ²¹See, the LORD your God has given you the land. Go up and take possession of it as the LORD, the

God of your fathers, told you. Do not be afraid; do not be discouraged." Dt 8:15; Jos 1:9

22Then all of you came to me and said, "Let us send men ahead to spy out the land for us and bring back a report about the route we are to take and the towns we will come to." Nu 13:1-3 23The idea seemed good to me; so I selected twelve of you, one man from each tribe. 24They left and went up into the hill country, and came to the Valley of Eshcol and explored it. 25Taking with them some of the fruit of the land, they brought it down to us and reported, "It is a good land that the LORD our God is giving us." Nu 13:27; Jos 1:2

Rebellion Against the LORD

26But you were unwilling to go up; you rebelled against the command of the LORD your God. 27You grumbled in your tents and said, "The LORD hates us; so he brought us out of Egypt to deliver us into the hands of the Amorites to destroy us. 28Where can we go? Our brothers have made us lose heart. They say, 'The people are stronger and taller than we are; the cities are large, with walls up to the sky. We even saw the Anakites there.'" Nu 14:1-4 29Then I said to you, "Do not be terrified; do not be afraid of them. 30The LORD your God, who is going before you, will fight for you, as he did for you in Egypt, before your very eyes, 31and in the desert. There you saw how the LORD your God carried you, as a father carries his son, all the way you went until you reached this place."

32In spite of this, you did not trust in the LORD your God, 33who went ahead of you on your journey, in fire by night and in a cloud by day, to search out places for you to camp and to show you the way you should go. Nu 10:33; Ps 106:24

34When the LORD heard what you said, he was angry and solemnly swore: 35"Not a man of this evil generation shall see the good land I swore to give your forefathers, 36except Caleb son of Jephunneh. He will see it, and I will give him and his descendants the land he set his feet on, because he followed the LORD wholeheartedly." Nu 14:23 37Because of you the LORD became angry with me also and said, "You shall not enter it, either. 38But your assistant, Joshua son of Nun, will enter it. Encourage him, because he will lead Israel to inherit it. 39And the little ones that you said would be taken captive, your children who do not yet know good from bad—they will enter the land. I will give it to them and they will take possession of it. 40But as for you, turn around and set out toward the desert along the route to the Red Sea.a" Dt 3:28; Ps 106:32

a40 Hebrew Yam Suph; that is, Sea of Reeds

⁴¹Then you replied, "We have sinned against the LORD. We will go up and fight, as the LORD our God commanded us." So every one of you put on his weapons, thinking it easy to go up into the hill country.   Nu 14:40

⁴²But the LORD said to me, "Tell them, 'Do not go up and fight, because I will not be with you. You will be defeated by your enemies.'"   Nu 14:41-43

⁴³So I told you, but you would not listen. You rebelled against the LORD's command and in your arrogance you marched up into the hill country. ⁴⁴The Amorites who lived in those hills came out against you; they chased you like a swarm of bees and beat you down from Seir all the way to Hormah. ⁴⁵You came back and wept before the LORD, but he paid no attention to your weeping and turned a deaf ear to you. ⁴⁶And so you stayed in Kadesh many days—all the time you spent there.   Ps 118:12

Wanderings in the Desert

2 Then we turned back and set out toward the desert along the route to the Red Sea,*a* as the LORD had directed me. For a long time we made our way around the hill country of Seir.

²Then the LORD said to me, ³"You have made your way around this hill country long enough; now turn north. ⁴Give the people these orders: 'You are about to pass through the territory of your brothers the descendants of Esau, who live in Seir. They will be afraid of you, but be very careful. ⁵Do not provoke them to war, for I will not give you any of their land, not even enough to put your foot on. I have given Esau the hill country of Seir as his own. ⁶You are to pay them in silver for the food you eat and the water you drink.' "   Nu 20:14

⁷The LORD your God has blessed you in all the work of your hands. He has watched over your journey through this vast desert. These forty years the LORD your God has been with you, and you have not lacked anything.   Dt 8:2-4

⁸So we went on past our brothers the descendants of Esau, who live in Seir. We turned from the Arabah road, which comes up from Elath and Ezion Geber, and traveled along the desert road of Moab.   Nu 20:21

⁹Then the LORD said to me, "Do not harass the Moabites or provoke them to war, for I will not give you any part of their land. I have given Ar to the descendants of Lot as a possession."   Nu 21:15

¹⁰(The Emites used to live there—a people strong and numerous, and as tall as the Anakites. ¹¹Like the Anakites, they too were considered Rephaites, but the Moabites called them Emites. ¹²Horites used to live in Seir, but the descendants of

a1 Hebrew Yam Suph; that is, Sea of Reeds

Esau drove them out. They destroyed the Horites from before them and settled in their place, just as Israel did in the land the LORD gave them as their possession.)   Ge 14:5; Nu 13:22,33

13And the LORD said, "Now get up and cross the Zered Valley." So we crossed the valley.

14Thirty-eight years passed from the time we left Kadesh Barnea until we crossed the Zered Valley. By then, that entire generation of fighting men had perished from the camp, as the LORD had sworn to them. 15The LORD's hand was against them until he had completely eliminated them from the camp.

16Now when the last of these fighting men among the people had died, 17the LORD said to me, 18"Today you are to pass by the region of Moab at Ar. 19When you come to the Ammonites, do not harass them or provoke them to war, for I will not give you possession of any land belonging to the Ammonites. I have given it as a possession to the descendants of Lot." Nu 21:15

20(That too was considered a land of the Rephaites, who used to live there; but the Ammonites called them Zamzummites. 21They were a people strong and numerous, and as tall as the Anakites. The LORD destroyed them from before the Ammonites, who drove them out and settled in their place. 22The LORD had done the same for the descendants of Esau, who lived in Seir, when he destroyed the Horites from before them. They drove them out and have lived in their place to this day. 23And as for the Avvites who lived in villages as far as Gaza, the Caphtorites coming out from Caphtor[a] destroyed them and settled in their place.)   Jos 13:3

Defeat of Sihon King of Heshbon

24"Set out now and cross the Arnon Gorge. See, I have given into your hand Sihon the Amorite, king of Heshbon, and his country. Begin to take possession of it and engage him in battle. 25This very day I will begin to put the terror and fear of you on all the nations under heaven. They will hear reports of you and will tremble and be in anguish because of you."   Jdg 11:18

26From the desert of Kedemoth I sent messengers to Sihon king of Heshbon offering peace and saying, 27"Let us pass through your country. We will stay on the main road; we will not turn aside to the right or to the left. 28Sell us food to eat and water to drink for their price in silver. Only let us pass through on foot— 29as the descendants of Esau, who live in Seir, and the Moabites, who live in Ar, did for us—until we cross the Jordan into the land the LORD our God is giving us." 30But Sihon king of Heshbon refused to

a23 That is, Crete

let us pass through. For the LORD your God had made his spirit stubborn and his heart obstinate in order to give him into your hands, as he has now done.   Nu 21:21; Dt 20:10

31The LORD said to me, "See, I have begun to deliver Sihon and his country over to you. Now begin to conquer and possess his land."   Ge 12:7; Dt 1:8

32When Sihon and all his army came out to meet us in battle at Jahaz, 33the LORD our God delivered him over to us and we struck him down, together with his sons and his whole army. 34At that time we took all his towns and completely destroyed[a] them—men, women and children. We left no survivors. 35But the livestock and the plunder from the towns we had captured we carried off for ourselves. 36From Aroer on the rim of the Arnon Gorge, and from the town in the gorge, even as far as Gilead, not one town was too strong for us. The LORD our God gave us all of them. 37But in accordance with the command of the LORD our God, you did not encroach on any of the land of the Ammonites, neither the land along the course of the Jabbok nor that around the towns in the hills.   Nu 21:23; Dt 3:6

Defeat of Og King of Bashan

3 Next we turned and went up along the road toward Bashan, and Og king of Bashan with his whole army marched out to meet us in battle at Edrei. 2The LORD said to me, "Do not be afraid of him, for I have handed him over to you with his whole army and his land. Do to him what you did to Sihon king of the Amorites, who reigned in Heshbon."   Nu 21:33

3So the LORD our God also gave into our hands Og king of Bashan and all his army. We struck them down, leaving no survivors. 4At that time we took all his cities. There was not one of the sixty cities that we did not take from them—the whole region of Argob, Og's kingdom in Bashan. 5All these cities were fortified with high walls and with gates and bars, and there were also a great many unwalled villages. 6We completely destroyed[a] them, as we had done with Sihon king of Heshbon, destroying[a] every city—men, women and children. 7But all the livestock and the plunder from their cities we carried off for ourselves.   Dt 2:24

8So at that time we took from these two kings of the Amorites the territory east of the Jordan, from the Arnon Gorge as far as Mount Hermon. 9(Hermon is called Sirion by the Sidonians; the Amorites call it Senir.) 10We took all the towns on the plateau, and all Gilead, and all Bashan as far as Salecah and Edrei,

---

[a]34,6 The Hebrew term refers to the irrevocable giving over of things or persons to the LORD, often by totally destroying them.

towns of Og's kingdom in Bashan. ¹¹(Only Og king of Bashan was left of the remnant of the Rephaites. His bed*ᵃ* was made of iron and was more than thirteen feet long and six feet wide.*ᵇ* It is still in Rabbah of the Ammonites.) Nu 32:33; Ps 29:6

Division of the Land

¹²Of the land that we took over at that time, I gave the Reubenites and the Gadites the territory north of Aroer by the Arnon Gorge, including half the hill country of Gilead, together with its towns. ¹³The rest of Gilead and also all of Bashan, the kingdom of Og, I gave to the half tribe of Manasseh. (The whole region of Argob in Bashan used to be known as a land of the Rephaites. ¹⁴Jair, a descendant of Manasseh, took the whole region of Argob as far as the border of the Geshurites and the Maacathites; it was named after him, so that to this day Bashan is called Havvoth Jair.*ᶜ*) ¹⁵And I gave Gilead to Makir. ¹⁶But to the Reubenites and the Gadites I gave the territory extending from Gilead down to the Arnon Gorge (the middle of the gorge being the border) and out to the Jabbok River, which is the border of the Ammonites. ¹⁷Its western border was the Jordan in the Arabah, from Kinnereth to the Sea of the Arabah (the Salt Sea*ᵈ*), below the slopes of Pisgah.

¹⁸I commanded you at that time: "The LORD your God has given you this land to take possession of it. But all your able-bodied men, armed for battle, must cross over ahead of your brother Israelites. ¹⁹However, your wives, your children and your livestock (I know you have much livestock) may stay in the towns I have given you, ²⁰until the LORD gives rest to your brothers as he has to you, and they too have taken over the land that the LORD your God is giving them, across the Jordan. After that, each of you may go back to the possession I have given you." Nu 32:17; Jos 1:14

Moses Forbidden to Cross the Jordan

²¹At that time I commanded Joshua: "You have seen with your own eyes all that the LORD your God has done to these two kings. The LORD will do the same to all the kingdoms over there where you are going. ²²Do not be afraid of them; the LORD your God himself will fight for you." Dt 1:29; 2Ch 32:8

²³At that time I pleaded with the LORD: ²⁴"O Sovereign LORD, you have begun to show to your servant your greatness and your strong hand. For what god is there in heaven or on earth

---

*ᵃ*11 Or *sarcophagus*   *ᵇ*11 Hebrew *nine cubits long and four cubits wide* (about 4 meters long and 1.8 meters wide)   *ᶜ*14 Or *called the settlements of Jair*   *ᵈ*17 That is, the Dead Sea

who can do the deeds and mighty works you do? 25Let me go over and see the good land beyond the Jordan—that fine hill country and Lebanon."

26But because of you the LORD was angry with me and would not listen to me. "That is enough," the LORD said. "Do not speak to me anymore about this matter. 27Go up to the top of Pisgah and look west and north and south and east. Look at the land with your own eyes, since you are not going to cross this Jordan. 28But commission Joshua, and encourage and strengthen him, for he will lead this people across and will cause them to inherit the land that you will see." 29So we stayed in the valley near Beth Peor. Nu 27:12; Dt 1:37

Obedience Commanded

4 Hear now, O Israel, the decrees and laws I am about to teach you. Follow them so that you may live and may go in and take possession of the land that the LORD, the God of your fathers, is giving you. 2Do not add to what I command you and do not subtract from it, but keep the commands of the LORD your God that I give you. Lev 18:4

3You saw with your own eyes what the LORD did at Baal Peor. The LORD your God destroyed from among you everyone who followed the Baal of Peor, 4but all of you who held fast to the LORD your God are still alive today. Nu 25:4; Ps 106:28

5See, I have taught you decrees and laws as the LORD my God commanded me, so that you may follow them in the land you are entering to take possession of it. 6Observe them carefully, for this will show your wisdom and understanding to the nations, who will hear about all these decrees and say, "Surely this great nation is a wise and understanding people." 7What other nation is so great as to have their gods near them the way the LORD our God is near us whenever we pray to him? 8And what other nation is so great as to have such righteous decrees and laws as this body of laws I am setting before you today? Dt 30:19

9Only be careful, and watch yourselves closely so that you do not forget the things your eyes have seen or let them slip from your heart as long as you live. Teach them to your children and to their children after them. 10Remember the day you stood before the LORD your God at Horeb, when he said to me, "Assemble the people before me to hear my words so that they may learn to revere me as long as they live in the land and may teach them to their children." 11You came near and stood at the foot of the mountain while it blazed with fire to the very heavens, with black clouds and deep darkness. 12Then the LORD spoke to you out of the fire. You heard the sound of words but saw no

form; there was only a voice.
13He declared to you his covenant, the Ten Command-
ments, which he commanded
you to follow and then wrote
them on two stone tablets.
14And the LORD directed me at
that time to teach you the decrees and laws you are to follow
in the land that you are crossing
the Jordan to possess.   Ge 18:19

Idolatry Forbidden

15You saw no form of any
kind the day the LORD spoke to
you at Horeb out of the fire.
Therefore watch yourselves
very carefully, 16so that you do
not become corrupt and make
for yourselves an idol, an image
of any shape, whether formed
like a man or a woman, 17or like
any animal on earth or any bird
that flies in the air, 18or like any
creature that moves along the
ground or any fish in the waters
below. 19And when you look up
to the sky and see the sun, the
moon and the stars—all the
heavenly array—do not be enticed into bowing down to them
and worshiping things the
LORD your God has appor-
tioned to all the nations under
heaven. 20But as for you, the
LORD took you and brought you
out of the iron-smelting furnace, out of Egypt, to be the
people of his inheritance, as you
now are.   Dt 17:3; Jdg 2:19
21The LORD was angry with
me because of you, and he solemnly swore that I would not
cross the Jordan and enter the
good land the LORD your God is
giving you as your inheritance.
22I will die in this land; I will not
cross the Jordan; but you are
about to cross over and take
possession of that good land.
23Be careful not to forget the
covenant of the LORD your God
that he made with you; do not
make for yourselves an idol in
the form of anything the LORD
your God has forbidden. 24For
the LORD your God is a consuming fire, a jealous God.   Dt 1:37
25After you have had children
and grandchildren and have
lived in the land a long time—if
you then become corrupt and
make any kind of idol, doing
evil in the eyes of the LORD your
God and provoking him to anger, 26I call heaven and earth as
witnesses against you this day
that you will quickly perish
from the land that you are crossing the Jordan to possess. You
will not live there long but will
certainly be destroyed. 27The
LORD will scatter you among the
peoples, and only a few of you
will survive among the nations
to which the LORD will drive
you. 28There you will worship
man-made gods of wood and
stone, which cannot see or hear
or eat or smell. 29But if from
there you seek the LORD your
God, you will find him if you
look for him with all your heart
and with all your soul. 30When
you are in distress and all these
things have happened to you,
then in later days you will return to the LORD your God and

obey him. [31]For the LORD your God is a merciful God; he will not abandon or destroy you or forget the covenant with your forefathers, which he confirmed to them by oath.   2Ki 17:17

The LORD Is God

[32]Ask now about the former days, long before your time, from the day God created man on the earth; ask from one end of the heavens to the other. Has anything so great as this ever happened, or has anything like it ever been heard of? [33]Has any other people heard the voice of God[a] speaking out of fire, as you have, and lived? [34]Has any god ever tried to take for himself one nation out of another nation, by testings, by miraculous signs and wonders, by war, by a mighty hand and an outstretched arm, or by great and awesome deeds, like all the things the LORD your God did for you in Egypt before your very eyes?   Ex 20:22; Dt 32:7

[35]You were shown these things so that you might know that the LORD is God; besides him there is no other. [36]From heaven he made you hear his voice to discipline you. On earth he showed you his great fire, and you heard his words from out of the fire. [37]Because he loved your forefathers and chose their descendants after them, he brought you out of Egypt by his Presence and his great strength, [38]to drive out before you nations greater and stronger than you and to bring you into their land to give it to you for your inheritance, as it is today.   Ex 19:19; 1Sa 2:2

[39]Acknowledge and take to heart this day that the LORD is God in heaven above and on the earth below. There is no other. [40]Keep his decrees and commands, which I am giving you today, so that it may go well with you and your children after you and that you may live long in the land the LORD your God gives you for all time.

Cities of Refuge

[41]Then Moses set aside three cities east of the Jordan, [42]to which anyone who had killed a person could flee if he had unintentionally killed his neighbor without malice aforethought. He could flee into one of these cities and save his life. [43]The cities were these: Bezer in the desert plateau, for the Reubenites; Ramoth in Gilead, for the Gadites; and Golan in Bashan, for the Manassites.   Ex 21:13

Introduction to the Law

[44]This is the law Moses set before the Israelites. [45]These are the stipulations, decrees and laws Moses gave them when they came out of Egypt [46]and were in the valley near Beth Peor east of the Jordan, in the land of Sihon king of the Amo-

[a]33 Or of a god

rites, who reigned in Heshbon and was defeated by Moses and the Israelites as they came out of Egypt. ⁴⁷They took possession of his land and the land of Og king of Bashan, the two Amorite kings east of the Jordan. ⁴⁸This land extended from Aroer on the rim of the Arnon Gorge to Mount Siyon*a* (that is, Hermon), ⁴⁹and included all the Arabah east of the Jordan, as far as the Sea of the Arabah,*b* below the slopes of Pisgah.   Nu 21:26

The Ten Commandments

5 Moses summoned all Israel and said:

Hear, O Israel, the decrees and laws I declare in your hearing today. Learn them and be sure to follow them. ²The LORD our God made a covenant with us at Horeb. ³It was not with our fathers that the LORD made this covenant, but with us, with all of us who are alive here today. ⁴The LORD spoke to you face to face out of the fire on the mountain. ⁵(At that time I stood between the LORD and you to declare to you the word of the LORD, because you were afraid of the fire and did not go up the mountain.) And he said:

⁶"I am the LORD your God, who brought you out of Egypt, out of the land of slavery.   Ex 13:3; Lev 26:1
⁷"You shall have no other gods before*c* me.

⁸"You shall not make for yourself an idol in the form of anything in heaven above or on the earth beneath or in the waters below. ⁹You shall not bow down to them or worship them; for I, the LORD your God, am a jealous God, punishing the children for the sin of the fathers to the third and fourth generation of those who hate me, ¹⁰but showing love to a thousand generations of those who love me and keep my commandments.   Ex 34:7; Jer 32:18

¹¹"You shall not misuse the name of the LORD your God, for the LORD will not hold anyone guiltless who misuses his name.   Lev 19:12; Ps 139:20

¹²"Observe the Sabbath day by keeping it holy, as the LORD your God has commanded you. ¹³Six days you shall labor and do all your work, ¹⁴but the seventh day is a Sabbath to the LORD your God. On it you shall not do any work, neither you, nor your son or daughter, nor your manservant or maidservant, nor your ox, your donkey or any of your animals, nor the

---

a48 Hebrew; Syriac (see also Deut. 3:9) *Sirion besides*   *b49* That is, the Dead Sea   *c7* Or

alien within your gates, so that your manservant and maidservant may rest, as you do. ¹⁵Remember that you were slaves in Egypt and that the LORD your God brought you out of there with a mighty hand and an outstretched arm. Therefore the LORD your God has commanded you to observe the Sabbath day.   Ge 2:2; Dt 4:34

¹⁶"Honor your father and your mother, as the LORD your God has commanded you, so that you may live long and that it may go well with you in the land the LORD your God is giving you.   Lev 19:3; Mal 1:6

¹⁷"You shall not murder.

¹⁸"You shall not commit adultery.   Lev 20:10; Mt 19:18

¹⁹"You shall not steal.   Lev 19:11

²⁰"You shall not give false testimony against your neighbor.   Ex 23:1

²¹"You shall not covet your neighbor's wife. You shall not set your desire on your neighbor's house or land, his manservant or maidservant, his ox or donkey, or anything that belongs to your neighbor."   Ro 7:7

²²These are the commandments the LORD proclaimed in a loud voice to your whole assembly there on the mountain from out of the fire, the cloud and the deep darkness; and he added nothing more. Then he wrote them on two stone tablets and gave them to me.   Ex 20:21

²³When you heard the voice out of the darkness, while the mountain was ablaze with fire, all the leading men of your tribes and your elders came to me. ²⁴And you said, "The LORD our God has shown us his glory and his majesty, and we have heard his voice from the fire. Today we have seen that a man can live even if God speaks with him. ²⁵But now, why should we die? This great fire will consume us, and we will die if we hear the voice of the LORD our God any longer. ²⁶For what mortal man has ever heard the voice of the living God speaking out of fire, as we have, and survived? ²⁷Go near and listen to all that the LORD our God says. Then tell us whatever the LORD our God tells you. We will listen and obey."   Ex 19:19; Dt 18:16

²⁸The LORD heard you when you spoke to me and the LORD said to me, "I have heard what this people said to you. Everything they said was good. ²⁹Oh, that their hearts would be inclined to fear me and keep all my commands always, so that it might go well with them and their children forever!   Dt 18:17

³⁰"Go, tell them to return to their tents. ³¹But you stay here with me so that I may give you all the commands, decrees and

laws you are to teach them to follow in the land I am giving them to possess." Ex 24:12

³²So be careful to do what the LORD your God has commanded you; do not turn aside to the right or to the left. ³³Walk in all the way that the LORD your God has commanded you, so that you may live and prosper and prolong your days in the land that you will possess.

Love the LORD Your God

6 These are the commands, decrees and laws the LORD your God directed me to teach you to observe in the land that you are crossing the Jordan to possess, ²so that you, your children and their children after them may fear the LORD your God as long as you live by keeping all his decrees and commands that I give you, and so that you may enjoy long life. ³Hear, O Israel, and be careful to obey so that it may go well with you and that you may increase greatly in a land flowing with milk and honey, just as the LORD, the God of your fathers, promised you. Ex 20:20

⁴Hear, O Israel: The LORD our God, the LORD is one.^a ⁵Love the LORD your God with all your heart and with all your soul and with all your strength. ⁶These commandments that I give you today are to be upon your hearts. ⁷Impress them on your children. Talk about them when you sit at home and when you walk along the road, when you lie down and when you get up. ⁸Tie them as symbols on your hands and bind them on your foreheads. ⁹Write them on the doorframes of your houses and on your gates. Dt 10:12; Mk 12:29

¹⁰When the LORD your God brings you into the land he swore to your fathers, to Abraham, Isaac and Jacob, to give you—a land with large, flourishing cities you did not build, ¹¹houses filled with all kinds of good things you did not provide, wells you did not dig, and vineyards and olive groves you did not plant—then when you eat and are satisfied, ¹²be careful that you do not forget the LORD, who brought you out of Egypt, out of the land of slavery. Dt 8:10

¹³Fear the LORD your God, serve him only and take your oaths in his name. ¹⁴Do not follow other gods, the gods of the peoples around you; ¹⁵for the LORD your God, who is among you, is a jealous God and his anger will burn against you, and he will destroy you from the face of the land. ¹⁶Do not test the LORD your God as you did at Massah. ¹⁷Be sure to keep the commands of the LORD your God and the stipulations and decrees he has given you. ¹⁸Do what is right and good in the LORD's sight, so that it may go

---

^a4 Or *The LORD our God is one LORD*; or *The LORD is our God, the LORD is one*; or *The LORD is our God, the LORD alone*

well with you and you may go in and take over the good land that the LORD promised on oath to your forefathers, ¹⁹thrusting out all your enemies before you, as the LORD said.   Dt 4:24

²⁰In the future, when your son asks you, "What is the meaning of the stipulations, decrees and laws the LORD our God has commanded you?" ²¹tell him: "We were slaves of Pharaoh in Egypt, but the LORD brought us out of Egypt with a mighty hand. ²²Before our eyes the LORD sent miraculous signs and wonders—great and terrible—upon Egypt and Pharaoh and his whole household. ²³But he brought us out from there to bring us in and give us the land that he promised on oath to our forefathers. ²⁴The LORD commanded us to obey all these decrees and to fear the LORD our God, so that we might always prosper and be kept alive, as is the case today. ²⁵And if we are careful to obey all this law before the LORD our God, as he has commanded us, that will be our righteousness."   Dt 10:12

Driving Out the Nations

7 When the LORD your God brings you into the land you are entering to possess and drives out before you many nations—the Hittites, Girgashites, Amorites, Canaanites, Perizzites, Hivites and Jebusites, seven nations larger and stronger than you— ²and when the LORD your God has delivered them over to you and you have defeated them, then you must destroy them totally.ᵃ Make no treaty with them, and show them no mercy. ³Do not intermarry with them. Do not give your daughters to their sons or take their daughters for your sons, ⁴for they will turn your sons away from following me to serve other gods, and the LORD's anger will burn against you and will quickly destroy you. ⁵This is what you are to do to them: Break down their altars, smash their sacred stones, cut down their Asherah polesᵇ and burn their idols in the fire. ⁶For you are a people holy to the LORD your God. The LORD your God has chosen you out of all the peoples on the face of the earth to be his people, his treasured possession.   Dt 31:3

⁷The LORD did not set his affection on you and choose you because you were more numerous than other peoples, for you were the fewest of all peoples. ⁸But it was because the LORD loved you and kept the oath he swore to your forefathers that he brought you out with a mighty hand and redeemed you from the land of slavery, from the power of Pharaoh king of Egypt. ⁹Know therefore that the LORD your God is God; he is the

---

ᵃ2 The Hebrew term refers to the irrevocable giving over of things or persons to the LORD, often by totally destroying them; also in verse 26.   ᵇ5 That is, symbols of the goddess Asherah; here and elsewhere in Deuteronomy

faithful God, keeping his covenant of love to a thousand generations of those who love him and keep his commands. 10But

those who hate him he will
repay to their face by
destruction;
he will not be slow to repay
to their face those who
hate him.   Dt 10:22; Ne 1:5

11Therefore, take care to follow the commands, decrees and laws I give you today.

12If you pay attention to these laws and are careful to follow them, then the LORD your God will keep his covenant of love with you, as he swore to your forefathers. 13He will love you and bless you and increase your numbers. He will bless the fruit of your womb, the crops of your land—your grain, new wine and oil—the calves of your herds and the lambs of your flocks in the land that he swore to your forefathers to give you. 14You will be blessed more than any other people; none of your men or women will be childless, nor any of your livestock without young. 15The LORD will keep you free from every disease. He will not inflict on you the horrible diseases you knew in Egypt, but he will inflict them on all who hate you. 16You must destroy all the peoples the LORD your God gives over to you. Do not look on them with pity and do not serve their gods, for that will be a snare to you.   Dt 28:1

17You may say to yourselves, "These nations are stronger than we are. How can we drive them out?" 18But do not be afraid of them; remember well what the LORD your God did to Pharaoh and to all Egypt. 19You saw with your own eyes the great trials, the miraculous signs and wonders, the mighty hand and outstretched arm, with which the LORD your God brought you out. The LORD your God will do the same to all the peoples you now fear. 20Moreover, the LORD your God will send the hornet among them until even the survivors who hide from you have perished. 21Do not be terrified by them, for the LORD your God, who is among you, is a great and awesome God. 22The LORD your God will drive out those nations before you, little by little. You will not be allowed to eliminate them all at once, or the wild animals will multiply around you. 23But the LORD your God will deliver them over to you, throwing them into great confusion until they are destroyed. 24He will give their kings into your hand, and you will wipe out their names from under heaven. No one will be able to stand up against you; you will destroy them. 25The images of their gods you are to burn in the fire. Do not covet the silver and gold on them, and do not take it for yourselves, or you will be ensnared by it, for it is detestable to the LORD your God. 26Do not bring a

detestable thing into your house or you, like it, will be set apart for destruction. Utterly abhor and detest it, for it is set apart for destruction. Dt 10:17

Do Not Forget the LORD

8 Be careful to follow every command I am giving you today, so that you may live and increase and may enter and possess the land that the LORD promised on oath to your forefathers. ²Remember how the LORD your God led you all the way in the desert these forty years, to humble you and to test you in order to know what was in your heart, whether or not you would keep his commands. ³He humbled you, causing you to hunger and then feeding you with manna, which neither you nor your fathers had known, to teach you that man does not live on bread alone but on every word that comes from the mouth of the LORD. ⁴Your clothes did not wear out and your feet did not swell during these forty years. ⁵Know then in your heart that as a man disciplines his son, so the LORD your God disciplines you. Dt 4:1

⁶Observe the commands of the LORD your God, walking in his ways and revering him. ⁷For the LORD your God is bringing you into a good land—a land with streams and pools of water, with springs flowing in the valleys and hills; ⁸a land with wheat and barley, vines and fig trees, pomegranates, olive oil and honey; ⁹a land where bread will not be scarce and you will lack nothing; a land where the rocks are iron and you can dig copper out of the hills. Dt 5:33; Ps 106:24

¹⁰When you have eaten and are satisfied, praise the LORD your God for the good land he has given you. ¹¹Be careful that you do not forget the LORD your God, failing to observe his commands, his laws and his decrees that I am giving you this day. ¹²Otherwise, when you eat and are satisfied, when you build fine houses and settle down, ¹³and when your herds and flocks grow large and your silver and gold increase and all you have is multiplied, ¹⁴then your heart will become proud and you will forget the LORD your God, who brought you out of Egypt, out of the land of slavery. ¹⁵He led you through the vast and dreadful desert, that thirsty and waterless land, with its venomous snakes and scorpions. He brought you water out of hard rock. ¹⁶He gave you manna to eat in the desert, something your fathers had never known, to humble and to test you so that in the end it might go well with you. ¹⁷You may say to yourself, "My power and the strength of my hands have produced this wealth for me." ¹⁸But remember the LORD your God, for it is he who gives you the ability to produce wealth, and so confirms his cov-

enant, which he swore to your forefathers, as it is today. Nu 21:6

19If you ever forget the LORD your God and follow other gods and worship and bow down to them, I testify against you today that you will surely be destroyed. 20Like the nations the LORD destroyed before you, so you will be destroyed for not obeying the LORD your God.

Not Because of Israel's Righteousness

9 Hear, O Israel. You are now about to cross the Jordan to go in and dispossess nations greater and stronger than you, with large cities that have walls up to the sky. 2The people are strong and tall—Anakites! You know about them and have heard it said: "Who can stand up against the Anakites?" 3But be assured today that the LORD your God is the one who goes across ahead of you like a devouring fire. He will destroy them; he will subdue them before you. And you will drive them out and annihilate them quickly, as the LORD has promised you. Nu 13:22; Dt 31:3

4After the LORD your God has driven them out before you, do not say to yourself, "The LORD has brought me here to take possession of this land because of my righteousness." No, it is on account of the wickedness of these nations that the LORD is going to drive them out before you. 5It is not because of your righteousness or your integrity that you are going in to take possession of their land; but on account of the wickedness of these nations, the LORD your God will drive them out before you, to accomplish what he swore to your fathers, to Abraham, Isaac and Jacob. 6Understand, then, that it is not because of your righteousness that the LORD your God is giving you this good land to possess, for you are a stiff-necked people. Ge 12:7; Dt 8:17

The Golden Calf

7Remember this and never forget how you provoked the LORD your God to anger in the desert. From the day you left Egypt until you arrived here, you have been rebellious against the LORD. 8At Horeb you aroused the LORD's wrath so that he was angry enough to destroy you. 9When I went up on the mountain to receive the tablets of stone, the tablets of the covenant that the LORD had made with you, I stayed on the mountain forty days and forty nights; I ate no bread and drank no water. 10The LORD gave me two stone tablets inscribed by the finger of God. On them were all the commandments the LORD proclaimed to you on the mountain out of the fire, on the day of the assembly. Ex 32:7-10

11At the end of the forty days and forty nights, the LORD gave me the two stone tablets, the tablets of the covenant. 12Then

the LORD told me, "Go down from here at once, because your people whom you brought out of Egypt have become corrupt. They have turned away quickly from what I commanded them and have made a cast idol for themselves." Ge 7:4; Dt 4:16

13And the LORD said to me, "I have seen this people, and they are a stiff-necked people indeed! 14Let me alone, so that I may destroy them and blot out their name from under heaven. And I will make you into a nation stronger and more numerous than they." Nu 14:12; Dt 10:16

15So I turned and went down from the mountain while it was ablaze with fire. And the two tablets of the covenant were in my hands. a 16When I looked, I saw that you had sinned against the LORD your God; you had made for yourselves an idol cast in the shape of a calf. You had turned aside quickly from the way that the LORD had commanded you. 17So I took the two tablets and threw them out of my hands, breaking them to pieces before your eyes. Ex 32:15

18Then once again I fell prostrate before the LORD for forty days and forty nights; I ate no bread and drank no water, because of all the sin you had committed, doing what was evil in the LORD's sight and so provoking him to anger. 19I feared the anger and wrath of the LORD, for he was angry enough with

you to destroy you. But again the LORD listened to me. 20And the LORD was angry enough with Aaron to destroy him, but at that time I prayed for Aaron too. 21Also I took that sinful thing of yours, the calf you had made, and burned it in the fire. Then I crushed it and ground it to powder as fine as dust and threw the dust into a stream that flowed down the mountain. Ex 34:28; Heb 12:21

22You also made the LORD angry at Taberah, at Massah and at Kibroth Hattaavah. Nu 11:3

23And when the LORD sent you out from Kadesh Barnea, he said, "Go up and take possession of the land I have given you." But you rebelled against the command of the LORD your God. You did not trust him or obey him. 24You have been rebellious against the LORD ever since I have known you. Nu 14:9

25I lay prostrate before the LORD those forty days and forty nights because the LORD had said he would destroy you. 26I prayed to the LORD and said, "O Sovereign LORD, do not destroy your people, your own inheritance that you redeemed by your great power and brought out of Egypt with a mighty hand. 27Remember your servants Abraham, Isaac and Jacob. Overlook the stubbornness of this people, their wickedness and their sin. 28Otherwise, the country from which

---

a15 Or And I had the two tablets of the covenant with me, one in each hand

you brought us will say, 'Because the LORD was not able to take them into the land he had promised them, and because he hated them, he brought them out to put them to death in the desert.' ²⁹But they are your people, your inheritance that you brought out by your great power and your outstretched arm." Ge 7:4; Ex 33:13

Tablets Like the First Ones

10 At that time the LORD said to me, "Chisel out two stone tablets like the first ones and come up to me on the mountain. Also make a wooden chest.ᵃ ²I will write on the tablets the words that were on the first tablets, which you broke. Then you are to put them in the chest." Ex 34:1-2; 2Ch 5:10

³So I made the ark out of acacia wood and chiseled out two stone tablets like the first ones, and I went up on the mountain with the two tablets in my hands. ⁴The LORD wrote on these tablets what he had written before, the Ten Commandments he had proclaimed to you on the mountain, out of the fire, on the day of the assembly. And the LORD gave them to me. ⁵Then I came back down the mountain and put the tablets in the ark I had made, as the LORD commanded me, and they are there now. Ex 37:1

⁶(The Israelites traveled from the wells of the Jaakanites to Moserah. There Aaron died and was buried, and Eleazar his son succeeded him as priest. ⁷From there they traveled to Gudgodah and on to Jotbathah, a land with streams of water. ⁸At that time the LORD set apart the tribe of Levi to carry the ark of the covenant of the LORD, to stand before the LORD to minister and to pronounce blessings in his name, as they still do today. ⁹That is why the Levites have no share or inheritance among their brothers; the LORD is their inheritance, as the LORD your God told them.) Nu 33:30

¹⁰Now I had stayed on the mountain forty days and nights, as I did the first time, and the LORD listened to me at this time also. It was not his will to destroy you. ¹¹"Go," the LORD said to me, "and lead the people on their way, so that they may enter and possess the land that I swore to their fathers to give them." Ex 33:17; Dt 9:18

Fear the LORD

¹²And now, O Israel, what does the LORD your God ask of you but to fear the LORD your God, to walk in all his ways, to love him, to serve the LORD your God with all your heart and with all your soul, ¹³and to observe the LORD's commands and decrees that I am giving you today for your own good? ¹⁴To the LORD your God belong the heavens, even the

ᵃ1 That is, an ark

highest heavens, the earth and everything in it. [15]Yet the LORD set his affection on your forefathers and loved them, and he chose you, their descendants, above all the nations, as it is today. [16]Circumcise your hearts, therefore, and do not be stiffnecked any longer. [17]For the LORD your God is God of gods and Lord of lords, the great God, mighty and awesome, who shows no partiality and accepts no bribes. [18]He defends the cause of the fatherless and the widow, and loves the alien, giving him food and clothing. [19]And you are to love those who are aliens, for you yourselves were aliens in Egypt. [20]Fear the LORD your God and serve him. Hold fast to him and take your oaths in his name. [21]He is your praise; he is your God, who performed for you those great and awesome wonders you saw with your own eyes. [22]Your forefathers who went down into Egypt were seventy in all, and now the LORD your God has made you as numerous as the stars in the sky.   1Ki 8:27

Love and Obey the LORD

11 Love the LORD your God and keep his requirements, his decrees, his laws and his commands always. [2]Remember today that your children were not the ones who saw and experienced the discipline of the LORD your God: his majesty, his mighty hand, his outstretched arm; [3]the signs he performed and the things he did in the heart of Egypt, both to Pharaoh king of Egypt and to his whole country; [4]what he did to the Egyptian army, to its horses and chariots, how he overwhelmed them with the waters of the Red Sea[a] as they were pursuing you, and how the LORD brought lasting ruin on them. [5]It was not your children who saw what he did for you in the desert until you arrived at this place, [6]and what he did to Dathan and Abiram, sons of Eliab the Reubenite, when the earth opened its mouth right in the middle of all Israel and swallowed them up with their households, their tents and every living thing that belonged to them. [7]But it was your own eyes that saw all these great things the LORD has done.

[8]Observe therefore all the commands I am giving you today, so that you may have the strength to go in and take over the land that you are crossing the Jordan to possess, [9]and so that you may live long in the land that the LORD swore to your forefathers to give to them and their descendants, a land flowing with milk and honey. [10]The land you are entering to take over is not like the land of Egypt, from which you have come, where you planted your seed and irrigated it by foot as in

---

[a]4 Hebrew *Yam Suph*; that is, Sea of Reeds

a vegetable garden. ¹¹But the land you are crossing the Jordan to take possession of is a land of mountains and valleys that drinks rain from heaven. ¹²It is a land the LORD your God cares for; the eyes of the LORD your God are continually on it from the beginning of the year to its end.   Dt 8:7; Jos 1:7; 1Ki 8:29

¹³So if you faithfully obey the commands I am giving you today—to love the LORD your God and to serve him with all your heart and with all your soul— ¹⁴then I will send rain on your land in its season, both autumn and spring rains, so that you may gather in your grain, new wine and oil. ¹⁵I will provide grass in the fields for your cattle, and you will eat and be satisfied.   Dt 6:17; Joel 2:23

¹⁶Be careful, or you will be enticed to turn away and worship other gods and bow down to them. ¹⁷Then the LORD's anger will burn against you, and he will shut the heavens so that it will not rain and the ground will yield no produce, and you will soon perish from the good land the LORD is giving you. ¹⁸Fix these words of mine in your hearts and minds; tie them as symbols on your hands and bind them on your foreheads. ¹⁹Teach them to your children, talking about them when you sit at home and when you walk along the road, when you lie down and when you get up.

²⁰Write them on the doorframes of your houses and on your gates, ²¹so that your days and the days of your children may be many in the land that the LORD swore to give your forefathers, as many as the days that the heavens are above the earth.   Dt 29:18; 1Ki 17:1; Ps 145:4

²²If you carefully observe all these commands I am giving you to follow—to love the LORD your God, to walk in all his ways and to hold fast to him— ²³then the LORD will drive out all these nations before you, and you will dispossess nations larger and stronger than you. ²⁴Every place where you set your foot will be yours: Your territory will extend from the desert to Lebanon, and from the Euphrates River to the western sea.ᵃ ²⁵No man will be able to stand against you. The LORD your God, as he promised you, will put the terror and fear of you on the whole land, wherever you go.   Dt 6:17; Jos 1:30

²⁶See, I am setting before you today a blessing and a curse— ²⁷the blessing if you obey the commands of the LORD your God that I am giving you today; ²⁸the curse if you disobey the commands of the LORD your God and turn from the way that I command you today by following other gods, which you have not known. ²⁹When the LORD your God has brought you into the land you are entering to

ᵃ24 That is, the Mediterranean

possess, you are to proclaim on Mount Gerizim the blessings, and on Mount Ebal the curses. [30]As you know, these mountains are across the Jordan, west of the road,[a] toward the setting sun, near the great trees of Moreh, in the territory of those Canaanites living in the Arabah in the vicinity of Gilgal. [31]You are about to cross the Jordan to enter and take possession of the land the LORD your God is giving you. When you have taken it over and are living there, [32]be sure that you obey all the decrees and laws I am setting before you today.   Dt 30:1; Jos 8:30

The One Place of Worship

12 These are the decrees and laws you must be careful to follow in the land that the LORD, the God of your fathers, has given you to possess—as long as you live in the land. [2]Destroy completely all the places on the high mountains and on the hills and under every spreading tree where the nations you are dispossessing worship their gods. [3]Break down their altars, smash their sacred stones and burn their Asherah poles in the fire; cut down the idols of their gods and wipe out their names from those places.   Dt 4:9

[4]You must not worship the LORD your God in their way. [5]But you are to seek the place the LORD your God will choose from among all your tribes to put his Name there for his dwelling. To that place you must go; [6]there bring your burnt offerings and sacrifices, your tithes and special gifts, what you have vowed to give and your freewill offerings, and the firstborn of your herds and flocks. [7]There, in the presence of the LORD your God, you and your families shall eat and shall rejoice in everything you have put your hand to, because the LORD your God has blessed you.   1Ki 5:5; Jer 10:2

[8]You are not to do as we do here today, everyone as he sees fit, [9]since you have not yet reached the resting place and the inheritance the LORD your God is giving you. [10]But you will cross the Jordan and settle in the land the LORD your God is giving you as an inheritance, and he will give you rest from all your enemies around you so that you will live in safety. [11]Then to the place the LORD your God will choose as a dwelling for his Name—there you are to bring everything I command you: your burnt offerings and sacrifices, your tithes and special gifts, and all the choice possessions you have vowed to the LORD. [12]And there rejoice before the LORD your God, you, your sons and daughters, your menservants and maidservants, and the Levites from your towns, who have no allotment

[a]30 Or Jordan, westward

or inheritance of their own. [13]Be careful not to sacrifice your burnt offerings anywhere you please. [14]Offer them only at the place the LORD will choose in one of your tribes, and there observe everything I command you. <small>Dt 11:31; Jos 22:23</small>

[15]Nevertheless, you may slaughter your animals in any of your towns and eat as much of the meat as you want, as if it were gazelle or deer, according to the blessing the LORD your God gives you. Both the ceremonially unclean and the clean may eat it. [16]But you must not eat the blood; pour it out on the ground like water. [17]You must not eat in your own towns the tithe of your grain and new wine and oil, or the firstborn of your herds and flocks, or whatever you have vowed to give, or your freewill offerings or special gifts. [18]Instead, you are to eat them in the presence of the LORD your God at the place the LORD your God will choose—you, your sons and daughters, your menservants and maidservants, and the Levites from your towns—and you are to rejoice before the LORD your God in everything you put your hand to. [19]Be careful not to neglect the Levites as long as you live in your land.

[20]When the LORD your God has enlarged your territory as he promised you, and you crave meat and say, "I would like some meat," then you may eat as much of it as you want. [21]If the place where the LORD your God chooses to put his Name is too far away from you, you may slaughter animals from the herds and flocks the LORD has given you, as I have commanded you, and in your own towns you may eat as much of them as you want. [22]Eat them as you would gazelle or deer. Both the ceremonially unclean and the clean may eat. [23]But be sure you do not eat the blood, because the blood is the life, and you must not eat the life with the meat. [24]You must not eat the blood; pour it out on the ground like water. [25]Do not eat it, so that it may go well with you and your children after you, because you will be doing what is right in the eyes of the LORD.

[26]But take your consecrated things and whatever you have vowed to give, and go to the place the LORD will choose. [27]Present your burnt offerings on the altar of the LORD your God, both the meat and the blood. The blood of your sacrifices must be poured beside the altar of the LORD your God, but you may eat the meat. [28]Be careful to obey all these regulations I am giving you, so that it may always go well with you and your children after you, because you will be doing what is good and right in the eyes of the LORD your God. <small>Nu 5:9-10; Dt 4:40</small>

[29]The LORD your God will cut off before you the nations you are about to invade and dispossess. But when you have driven

them out and settled in their land, ³⁰and after they have been destroyed before you, be careful not to be ensnared by inquiring about their gods, saying, "How do these nations serve their gods? We will do the same." ³¹You must not worship the LORD your God in their way, because in worshiping their gods, they do all kinds of detestable things the LORD hates. They even burn their sons and daughters in the fire as sacrifices to their gods.   Jos 23:4

³²See that you do all I command you; do not add to it or take away from it.   Dt 4:2

Worshiping Other Gods

13 If a prophet, or one who foretells by dreams, appears among you and announces to you a miraculous sign or wonder, ²and if the sign or wonder of which he has spoken takes place, and he says, "Let us follow other gods" (gods you have not known) "and let us worship them," ³you must not listen to the words of that prophet or dreamer. The LORD your God is testing you to find out whether you love him with all your heart and with all your soul. ⁴It is the LORD your God you must follow, and him you must revere. Keep his commands and obey him; serve him and hold fast to him. ⁵That prophet or dreamer must be put to death, because he preached rebellion against the LORD your God, who

brought you out of Egypt and redeemed you from the land of slavery; he has tried to turn you from the way the LORD your God commanded you to follow. You must purge the evil from among you.   2Ki 23:3; Mt 24:24

⁶If your very own brother, or your son or daughter, or the wife you love, or your closest friend secretly entices you, saying, "Let us go and worship other gods" (gods that neither you nor your fathers have known, ⁷gods of the peoples around you, whether near or far, from one end of the land to the other), ⁸do not yield to him or listen to him. Show him no pity. Do not spare him or shield him. ⁹You must certainly put him to death. Your hand must be the first in putting him to death, and then the hands of all the people. ¹⁰Stone him to death, because he tried to turn you away from the LORD your God, who brought you out of Egypt, out of the land of slavery. ¹¹Then all Israel will hear and be afraid, and no one among you will do such an evil thing again.   Dt 17:2-7; Pr 1:10

¹²If you hear it said about one of the towns the LORD your God is giving you to live in ¹³that wicked men have arisen among you and have led the people of their town astray, saying, "Let us go and worship other gods" (gods you have not known), ¹⁴then you must inquire, probe and investigate it thoroughly. And if it is true and it has been

proved that this detestable thing has been done among you, ¹⁵you must certainly put to the sword all who live in that town. Destroy it completely,ᵃ both its people and its livestock. ¹⁶Gather all the plunder of the town into the middle of the public square and completely burn the town and all its plunder as a whole burnt offering to the LORD your God. It is to remain a ruin forever, never to be rebuilt. ¹⁷None of those condemned thingsᵃ shall be found in your hands, so that the LORD will turn from his fierce anger; he will show you mercy, have compassion on you, and increase your numbers, as he promised on oath to your forefathers, ¹⁸because you obey the LORD your God, keeping all his commands that I am giving you today and doing what is right in his eyes. Ex 22:20; Jos 6:24

Clean and Unclean Food

14 You are the children of the LORD your God. Do not cut yourselves or shave the front of your heads for the dead, ²for you are a people holy to the LORD your God. Out of all the peoples on the face of the earth, the LORD has chosen you to be his treasured possession. ³Do not eat any detestable thing. ⁴These are the animals you may eat: the ox, the sheep, the goat, ⁵the deer, the gazelle, the roe deer, the wild goat, the ibex, the antelope and the mountain sheep.ᵇ ⁶You may eat any animal that has a split hoof divided in two and that chews the cud. ⁷However, of those that chew the cud or that have a split hoof completely divided you may not eat the camel, the rabbit or the coney.ᶜ Although they chew the cud, they do not have a split hoof; they are ceremonially unclean for you. ⁸The pig is also unclean; although it has a split hoof, it does not chew the cud. You are not to eat their meat or touch their carcasses. Job 39:1; Ac 10:14

⁹Of all the creatures living in the water, you may eat any that has fins and scales. ¹⁰But anything that does not have fins and scales you may not eat; for you it is unclean.

¹¹You may eat any clean bird. ¹²But these you may not eat: the eagle, the vulture, the black vulture, ¹³the red kite, the black kite, any kind of falcon, ¹⁴any kind of raven, ¹⁵the horned owl, the screech owl, the gull, any kind of hawk, ¹⁶the little owl, the great owl, the white owl, ¹⁷the desert owl, the osprey, the cormorant, ¹⁸the stork, any kind of heron, the hoopoe and the bat. Isa 13:21; Zep 2:14

¹⁹All flying insects that swarm are unclean to you; do not eat them. ²⁰But any winged

---

ᵃ15,17 The Hebrew term refers to the irrevocable giving over of things or persons to the LORD, often by totally destroying them.   ᵇ5 The precise identification of some of the birds and animals in this chapter is uncertain.   ᶜ7 That is, the hyrax or rock badger

creature that is clean you may eat. Lev 11:20; 20:25

21Do not eat anything you find already dead. You may give it to an alien living in any of your towns, and he may eat it, or you may sell it to a foreigner. But you are a people holy to the LORD your God. Lev 11:39

Do not cook a young goat in its mother's milk. Ex 23:19

Tithes

22Be sure to set aside a tenth of all that your fields produce each year. 23Eat the tithe of your grain, new wine and oil, and the firstborn of your herds and flocks in the presence of the LORD your God at the place he will choose as a dwelling for his Name, so that you may learn to revere the LORD your God always. 24But if that place is too distant and you have been blessed by the LORD your God and cannot carry your tithe (because the place where the LORD will choose to put his Name is so far away), 25then exchange your tithe for silver, and take the silver with you and go to the place the LORD your God will choose. 26Use the silver to buy whatever you like: cattle, sheep, wine or other fermented drink, or anything you wish. Then you and your household shall eat there in the presence of the LORD your God and rejoice. 27And do not neglect the Levites living in your towns, for they have no allotment or inheritance of their own. Lev 27:30

28At the end of every three years, bring all the tithes of that year's produce and store it in your towns, 29so that the Levites (who have no allotment or inheritance of their own) and the aliens, the fatherless and the widows who live in your towns may come and eat and be satisfied, and so that the LORD your God may bless you in all the work of your hands. Dt 26:12

The Year for Canceling Debts

15 At the end of every seven years you must cancel debts. 2This is how it is to be done: Every creditor shall cancel the loan he has made to his fellow Israelite. He shall not require payment from his fellow Israelite or brother, because the LORD's time for canceling debts has been proclaimed. 3You may require payment from a foreigner, but you must cancel any debt your brother owes you. 4However, there should be no poor among you, for in the land the LORD your God is giving you to possess as your inheritance, he will richly bless you, 5if only you fully obey the LORD your God and are careful to follow all these commands I am giving you today. 6For the LORD your God will bless you as he has promised, and you will lend to many nations but will borrow from none. You will rule over many nations but none will rule over you. Dt 31:10

7If there is a poor man among your brothers in any of the

towns of the land that the LORD your God is giving you, do not be hardhearted or tightfisted toward your poor brother. [8]Rather be openhanded and freely lend him whatever he needs. [9]Be careful not to harbor this wicked thought: "The seventh year, the year for canceling debts, is near," so that you do not show ill will toward your needy brother and give him nothing. He may then appeal to the LORD against you, and you will be found guilty of sin. [10]Give generously to him and do so without a grudging heart; then because of this the LORD your God will bless you in all your work and in everything you put your hand to. [11]There will always be poor people in the land. Therefore I command you to be openhanded toward your brothers and toward the poor and needy in your land.

Freeing Servants

[12]If a fellow Hebrew, a man or a woman, sells himself to you and serves you six years, in the seventh year you must let him go free. [13]And when you release him, do not send him away empty-handed. [14]Supply him liberally from your flock, your threshing floor and your winepress. Give to him as the LORD your God has blessed you. [15]Remember that you were slaves in Egypt and the LORD your God redeemed you. That is why I give you this command today. _{Dt 16:12; Jer 34:14}

[16]But if your servant says to you, "I do not want to leave you," because he loves you and your family and is well off with you, [17]then take an awl and push it through his ear lobe into the door, and he will become your servant for life. Do the same for your maidservant.

[18]Do not consider it a hardship to set your servant free, because his service to you these six years has been worth twice as much as that of a hired hand. And the LORD your God will bless you in everything you do.

The Firstborn Animals

[19]Set apart for the LORD your God every firstborn male of your herds and flocks. Do not put the firstborn of your oxen to work, and do not shear the firstborn of your sheep. [20]Each year you and your family are to eat them in the presence of the LORD your God at the place he will choose. [21]If an animal has a defect, is lame or blind, or has any serious flaw, you must not sacrifice it to the LORD your God. [22]You are to eat it in your own towns. Both the ceremonially unclean and the clean may eat it, as if it were gazelle or deer. [23]But you must not eat the blood; pour it out on the ground like water. _{Ex 13:2; Dt 12:5-7}

Passover

16 Observe the month of Abib and celebrate the Passover of the LORD your God, because in the month of Abib he

brought you out of Egypt by night. ²Sacrifice as the Passover to the LORD your God an animal from your flock or herd at the place the LORD will choose as a dwelling for his Name. ³Do not eat it with bread made with yeast, but for seven days eat unleavened bread, the bread of affliction, because you left Egypt in haste—so that all the days of your life you may remember the time of your departure from Egypt. ⁴Let no yeast be found in your possession in all your land for seven days. Do not let any of the meat you sacrifice on the evening of the first day remain until morning.   Ex 12:2; 1Co 5:8

⁵You must not sacrifice the Passover in any town the LORD your God gives you ⁶except in the place he will choose as a dwelling for his Name. There you must sacrifice the Passover in the evening, when the sun goes down, on the anniversary*a* of your departure from Egypt. ⁷Roast it and eat it at the place the LORD your God will choose. Then in the morning return to your tents. ⁸For six days eat unleavened bread and on the seventh day hold an assembly to the LORD your God and do no work.   Ex 12:42; Mt 26:17

Feast of Weeks

⁹Count off seven weeks from the time you begin to put the sickle to the standing grain. ¹⁰Then celebrate the Feast of Weeks to the LORD your God by giving a freewill offering in proportion to the blessings the LORD your God has given you. ¹¹And rejoice before the LORD your God at the place he will choose as a dwelling for his Name—you, your sons and daughters, your menservants and maidservants, the Levites in your towns, and the aliens, the fatherless and the widows living among you. ¹²Remember that you were slaves in Egypt, and follow carefully these decrees.   Ex 23:16; Dt 15:15

Feast of Tabernacles

¹³Celebrate the Feast of Tabernacles for seven days after you have gathered the produce of your threshing floor and your winepress. ¹⁴Be joyful at your Feast—you, your sons and daughters, your menservants and maidservants, and the Levites, the aliens, the fatherless and the widows who live in your towns. ¹⁵For seven days celebrate the Feast to the LORD your God at the place the LORD will choose. For the LORD your God will bless you in all your harvest and in all the work of your hands, and your joy will be complete.   Ex 23:16; Lev 23:39

¹⁶Three times a year all your men must appear before the LORD your God at the place he will choose: at the Feast of Unleavened Bread, the Feast of Weeks and the Feast of Taber-

a6 Or down, at the time of day

nacles. No man should appear before the LORD empty-handed: [17]Each of you must bring a gift in proportion to the way the LORD your God has blessed you.

Judges

[18]Appoint judges and officials for each of your tribes in every town the LORD your God is giving you, and they shall judge the people fairly. [19]Do not pervert justice or show partiality. Do not accept a bribe, for a bribe blinds the eyes of the wise and twists the words of the righteous. [20]Follow justice and justice alone, so that you may live and possess the land the LORD your God is giving you.

Worshiping Other Gods

[21]Do not set up any wooden Asherah pole[a] beside the altar you build to the LORD your God, [22]and do not erect a sacred stone, for these the LORD your God hates.   Ex 34:13; Dt 7:5

17 Do not sacrifice to the LORD your God an ox or a sheep that has any defect or flaw in it, for that would be detestable to him.   Dt 15:21

[2]If a man or woman living among you in one of the towns the LORD gives you is found doing evil in the eyes of the LORD your God in violation of his covenant, [3]and contrary to my command has worshiped other gods, bowing down to them or to the sun or the moon or the stars of the sky, [4]and this has been brought to your attention, then you must investigate it thoroughly. If it is true and it has been proved that this detestable thing has been done in Israel, [5]take the man or woman who has done this evil deed to your city gate and stone that person to death. [6]On the testimony of two or three witnesses a man shall be put to death, but no one shall be put to death on the testimony of only one witness. [7]The hands of the witnesses must be the first in putting him to death, and then the hands of all the people. You must purge the evil from among you.   Nu 35:30

Law Courts

[8]If cases come before your courts that are too difficult for you to judge—whether bloodshed, lawsuits or assaults—take them to the place the LORD your God will choose. [9]Go to the priests, who are Levites, and to the judge who is in office at that time. Inquire of them and they will give you the verdict. [10]You must act according to the decisions they give you at the place the LORD will choose. Be careful to do everything they direct you to do. [11]Act according to the law they teach you and the decisions they give you. Do not turn aside from what they tell you, to the right or to the left. [12]The man who shows contempt for

---

[a]21 Or *Do not plant any tree dedicated to Asherah*

the judge or for the priest who stands ministering there to the LORD your God must be put to death. You must purge the evil from Israel. ¹³All the people will hear and be afraid, and will not be contemptuous again.   Dt 12:5

The King

¹⁴When you enter the land the LORD your God is giving you and have taken possession of it and settled in it, and you say, "Let us set a king over us like all the nations around us," ¹⁵be sure to appoint over you the king the LORD your God chooses. He must be from among your own brothers. Do not place a foreigner over you, one who is not a brother Israelite. ¹⁶The king, moreover, must not acquire great numbers of horses for himself or make the people return to Egypt to get more of them, for the LORD has told you, "You are not to go back that way again." ¹⁷He must not take many wives, or his heart will be led astray. He must not accumulate large amounts of silver and gold.   1Sa 8:5

¹⁸When he takes the throne of his kingdom, he is to write for himself on a scroll a copy of this law, taken from that of the priests, who are Levites. ¹⁹It is to be with him, and he is to read it all the days of his life so that he may learn to revere the LORD his God and follow carefully all the words of this law and these decrees ²⁰and not consider himself better than his brothers and

turn from the law to the right or to the left. Then he and his descendants will reign a long time over his kingdom in Israel. Dt 31:24

Offerings for Priests and Levites

18 The priests, who are Levites—indeed the whole tribe of Levi—are to have no allotment or inheritance with Israel. They shall live on the offerings made to the LORD by fire, for that is their inheritance. ²They shall have no inheritance among their brothers; the LORD is their inheritance, as he promised them.   Nu 18:20; 1Co 9:13

³This is the share due the priests from the people who sacrifice a bull or a sheep: the shoulder, the jowls and the inner parts. ⁴You are to give them the firstfruits of your grain, new wine and oil, and the first wool from the shearing of your sheep, ⁵for the LORD your God has chosen them and their descendants out of all your tribes to stand and minister in the LORD's name always.

⁶If a Levite moves from one of your towns anywhere in Israel where he is living, and comes in all earnestness to the place the LORD will choose, ⁷he may minister in the name of the LORD his God like all his fellow Levites who serve there in the presence of the LORD. ⁸He is to share equally in their benefits, even though he has received money

from the sale of family posses-
sions.   1Ki 18:32; Ne 12:44

Detestable Practices

⁹When you enter the land the
LORD your God is giving you,
do not learn to imitate the detestable ways of the nations
there. ¹⁰Let no one be found
among you who sacrifices his
son or daughter in*a* the fire,
who practices divination or sorcery, interprets omens, engages
in witchcraft, ¹¹or casts spells, or
who is a medium or spiritist or
who consults the dead. ¹²Any-
one who does these things is
detestable to the LORD, and because of these detestable practices the LORD your God will
drive out those nations before
you. ¹³You must be blameless
before the LORD your God. Mt 5:48

The Prophet

¹⁴The nations you will dispossess listen to those who practice
sorcery or divination. But as for
you, the LORD your God has not
permitted you to do so. ¹⁵The
LORD your God will raise up for
you a prophet like me from
among your own brothers. You
must listen to him. ¹⁶For this is
what you asked of the LORD
your God at Horeb on the day of
the assembly when you said,
"Let us not hear the voice of the
LORD our God nor see this great
fire anymore, or we will die."
¹⁷The LORD said to me: "What
they say is good. ¹⁸I will raise up

for them a prophet like you
from among their brothers; I
will put my words in his mouth,
and he will tell them everything
I command him. ¹⁹If anyone
does not listen to my words that
the prophet speaks in my name,
I myself will call him to account.
²⁰But a prophet who presumes
to speak in my name anything I
have not commanded him to
say, or a prophet who speaks in
the name of other gods, must be
put to death."   Dt 13:1; Jn 4:25-26

²¹You may say to yourselves,
"How can we know when a
message has not been spoken
by the LORD?" ²²If what a
prophet proclaims in the name
of the LORD does not take place
or come true, that is a message
the LORD has not spoken. That
prophet has spoken presump-
tuously. Do not be afraid of
him.   Dt 13:2; Jer 28:9

Cities of Refuge

19 When the LORD your God
has destroyed the nations
whose land he is giving you,
and when you have driven
them out and settled in their
towns and houses, ²then set
aside for yourselves three cities
centrally located in the land the
LORD your God is giving you to
possess. ³Build roads to them
and divide into three parts the
land the LORD your God is giving you as an inheritance, so
that anyone who kills a man
may flee there.   Dt 6:10-11

---

a10 Or *who makes his son or daughter pass through*

⁴This is the rule concerning the man who kills another and flees there to save his life—one who kills his neighbor unintentionally, without malice aforethought. ⁵For instance, a man may go into the forest with his neighbor to cut wood, and as he swings his ax to fell a tree, the head may fly off and hit his neighbor and kill him. That man may flee to one of these cities and save his life. ⁶Otherwise, the avenger of blood might pursue him in a rage, overtake him if the distance is too great, and kill him even though he is not deserving of death, since he did it to his neighbor without malice aforethought. ⁷This is why I command you to set aside for yourselves three cities.   Nu 35:12

⁸If the LORD your God enlarges your territory, as he promised on oath to your forefathers, and gives you the whole land he promised them, ⁹because you carefully follow all these laws I command you today—to love the LORD your God and to walk always in his ways—then you are to set aside three more cities. ¹⁰Do this so that innocent blood will not be shed in your land, which the LORD your God is giving you as your inheritance, and so that you will not be guilty of bloodshed.   Ex 34:24; Pr 6:17

¹¹But if a man hates his neighbor and lies in wait for him, assaults and kills him, and then flees to one of these cities, ¹²the elders of his town shall send for him, bring him back from the city, and hand him over to the avenger of blood to die. ¹³Show him no pity. You must purge from Israel the guilt of shedding innocent blood, so that it may go well with you.   1Jn 3:15

¹⁴Do not move your neighbor's boundary stone set up by your predecessors in the inheritance you receive in the land the LORD your God is giving you to possess.   Dt 27:17; Job 24:2

Witnesses

¹⁵One witness is not enough to convict a man accused of any crime or offense he may have committed. A matter must be established by the testimony of two or three witnesses.   Dt 17:6

¹⁶If a malicious witness takes the stand to accuse a man of a crime, ¹⁷the two men involved in the dispute must stand in the presence of the LORD before the priests and the judges who are in office at the time. ¹⁸The judges must make a thorough investigation, and if the witness proves to be a liar, giving false testimony against his brother, ¹⁹then do to him as he intended to do to his brother. You must purge the evil from among you. ²⁰The rest of the people will hear of this and be afraid, and never again will such an evil thing be done among you. ²¹Show no pity: life for life, eye for eye, tooth for tooth, hand for hand, foot for foot.   Ex 23:1; Pr 19:5

Going to War

20 When you go to war against your enemies and see horses and chariots and an army greater than yours, do not be afraid of them, because the LORD your God, who brought you up out of Egypt, will be with you. ²When you are about to go into battle, the priest shall come forward and address the army. ³He shall say: "Hear, O Israel, today you are going into battle against your enemies. Do not be fainthearted or afraid; do not be terrified or give way to panic before them. ⁴For the LORD your God is the one who goes with you to fight for you against your enemies to give you victory." *1Sa 17:32; Ps 20:7*

⁵The officers shall say to the army: "Has anyone built a new house and not dedicated it? Let him go home, or he may die in battle and someone else may dedicate it. ⁶Has anyone planted a vineyard and not begun to enjoy it? Let him go home, or he may die in battle and someone else enjoy it. ⁷Has anyone become pledged to a woman and not married her? Let him go home, or he may die in battle and someone else marry her." ⁸Then the officers shall add, "Is any man afraid or fainthearted? Let him go home so that his brothers will not become disheartened too." ⁹When the officers have fin-

ished speaking to the army, they shall appoint commanders over it. *Dt 24:5; 1Co 9:7*

¹⁰When you march up to attack a city, make its people an offer of peace. ¹¹If they accept and open their gates, all the people in it shall be subject to forced labor and shall work for you. ¹²If they refuse to make peace and they engage you in battle, lay siege to that city. ¹³When the LORD your God delivers it into your hand, put to the sword all the men in it. ¹⁴As for the women, the children, the livestock and everything else in the city, you may take these as plunder for yourselves. And you may use the plunder the LORD your God gives you from your enemies. ¹⁵This is how you are to treat all the cities that are at a distance from you and do not belong to the nations nearby. *Dt 2:26; 1Ch 22:2*

¹⁶However, in the cities of the nations the LORD your God is giving you as an inheritance, do not leave alive anything that breathes. ¹⁷Completely destroy[a] them—the Hittites, Amorites, Canaanites, Perizzites, Hivites and Jebusites—as the LORD your God has commanded you. ¹⁸Otherwise, they will teach you to follow all the detestable things they do in worshiping their gods, and you will sin against the LORD your God.

[a]17 The Hebrew term refers to the irrevocable giving over of things or persons to the LORD, often by totally destroying them.

¹⁹When you lay siege to a city for a long time, fighting against it to capture it, do not destroy its trees by putting an ax to them, because you can eat their fruit. Do not cut them down. Are the trees of the field people, that you should besiege them?*ᵃ* ²⁰However, you may cut down trees that you know are not fruit trees and use them to build siege works until the city at war with you falls.　　　Jer 6:6

Atonement for an Unsolved Murder

21 If a man is found slain, lying in a field in the land the LORD your God is giving you to possess, and it is not known who killed him, ²your elders and judges shall go out and measure the distance from the body to the neighboring towns. ³Then the elders of the town nearest the body shall take a heifer that has never been worked and has never worn a yoke ⁴and lead her down to a valley that has not been plowed or planted and where there is a flowing stream. There in the valley they are to break the heifer's neck. ⁵The priests, the sons of Levi, shall step forward, for the LORD your God has chosen them to minister and to pronounce blessings in the name of the LORD and to decide all cases of dispute and assault. ⁶Then all the elders of the town nearest the body shall wash their hands over the heifer whose neck was broken in the valley, ⁷and they shall declare: "Our hands did not shed this blood, nor did our eyes see it done. ⁸Accept this atonement for your people Israel, whom you have redeemed, O LORD, and do not hold your people guilty of the blood of an innocent man." And the bloodshed will be atoned for. ⁹So you will purge from yourselves the guilt of shedding innocent blood, since you have done what is right in the eyes of the LORD.　　　Dt 17:8-11

Marrying a Captive Woman

¹⁰When you go to war against your enemies and the LORD your God delivers them into your hands and you take captives, ¹¹if you notice among the captives a beautiful woman and are attracted to her, you may take her as your wife. ¹²Bring her into your home and have her shave her head, trim her nails ¹³and put aside the clothes she was wearing when captured. After she has lived in your house and mourned her father and mother for a full month, then you may go to her and be her husband and she shall be your wife. ¹⁴If you are not pleased with her, let her go wherever she wishes. You must not sell her or treat her as a slave, since you have dishonored her.　　　Lev 14:9; Jos 21:44

---

*ᵃ*19 Or *down to use in the siege, for the fruit trees are for the benefit of man.*

The Right of the Firstborn

15If a man has two wives, and he loves one but not the other, and both bear him sons but the firstborn is the son of the wife he does not love, 16when he wills his property to his sons, he must not give the rights of the firstborn to the son of the wife he loves in preference to his actual firstborn, the son of the wife he does not love. 17He must acknowledge the son of his unloved wife as the firstborn by giving him a double share of all he has. That son is the first sign of his father's strength. The right of the firstborn belongs to him. Ge 49:3; 1Ch 26:10

A Rebellious Son

18If a man has a stubborn and rebellious son who does not obey his father and mother and will not listen to them when they discipline him, 19his father and mother shall take hold of him and bring him to the elders at the gate of his town. 20They shall say to the elders, "This son of ours is stubborn and rebellious. He will not obey us. He is a profligate and a drunkard." 21Then all the men of his town shall stone him to death. You must purge the evil from among you. All Israel will hear of it and be afraid. Ps 78:8; Isa 30:1

Various Laws

22If a man guilty of a capital offense is put to death and his body is hung on a tree, 23you must not leave his body on the tree overnight. Be sure to bury him that same day, because anyone who is hung on a tree is under God's curse. You must not desecrate the land the LORD your God is giving you as an inheritance. Jos 8:29; Mt 26:66

22 If you see your brother's ox or sheep straying, do not ignore it but be sure to take it back to him. 2If the brother does not live near you or if you do not know who he is, take it home with you and keep it until he comes looking for it. Then give it back to him. 3Do the same if you find your brother's donkey or his cloak or anything he loses. Do not ignore it. Ex 23:4

4If you see your brother's donkey or his ox fallen on the road, do not ignore it. Help him get it to its feet. Ex 23:5; 1Co 9:9

5A woman must not wear men's clothing, nor a man wear women's clothing, for the LORD your God detests anyone who does this.

6If you come across a bird's nest beside the road, either in a tree or on the ground, and the mother is sitting on the young or on the eggs, do not take the mother with the young. 7You may take the young, but be sure to let the mother go, so that it may go well with you and you may have a long life. Lev 22:28

8When you build a new house, make a parapet around your roof so that you may not bring the guilt of bloodshed on

your house if someone falls from the roof. _{Jos 2:8; 1Sa 9:25}

⁹Do not plant two kinds of seed in your vineyard; if you do, not only the crops you plant but also the fruit of the vineyard will be defiled.ᵃ _{Lev 19:19}

¹⁰Do not plow with an ox and a donkey yoked together. _{2Co 6:14}

¹¹Do not wear clothes of wool and linen woven together.

¹²Make tassels on the four corners of the cloak you wear.

Marriage Violations

¹³If a man takes a wife and, after lying with her, dislikes her ¹⁴and slanders her and gives her a bad name, saying, "I married this woman, but when I approached her, I did not find proof of her virginity," ¹⁵then the girl's father and mother shall bring proof that she was a virgin to the town elders at the gate. ¹⁶The girl's father will say to the elders, "I gave my daughter in marriage to this man, but he dislikes her. ¹⁷Now he has slandered her and said, 'I did not find your daughter to be a virgin.' But here is the proof of my daughter's virginity." Then her parents shall display the cloth before the elders of the town, ¹⁸and the elders shall take the man and punish him. ¹⁹They shall fine him a hundred shekels of silverᵇ and give them to the girl's father, because this man has given an Israelite virgin a bad name. She shall con-

tinue to be his wife; he must not divorce her as long as he lives.

²⁰If, however, the charge is true and no proof of the girl's virginity can be found, ²¹she shall be brought to the door of her father's house and there the men of her town shall stone her to death. She has done a disgraceful thing in Israel by being promiscuous while still in her father's house. You must purge the evil from among you. _{Dt 17:4}

²²If a man is found sleeping with another man's wife, both the man who slept with her and the woman must die. You must purge the evil from Israel. _{Jn 8:5}

²³If a man happens to meet in a town a virgin pledged to be married and he sleeps with her, ²⁴you shall take both of them to the gate of that town and stone them to death—the girl because she was in a town and did not scream for help, and the man because he violated another man's wife. You must purge the evil from among you.

²⁵But if out in the country a man happens to meet a girl pledged to be married and rapes her, only the man who has done this shall die. ²⁶Do nothing to the girl; she has committed no sin deserving death. This case is like that of someone who attacks and murders his neighbor, ²⁷for the man found the girl out in the country, and though the betrothed girl screamed,

---

ᵃ9 Or *be forfeited to the sanctuary*   ᵇ19 That is, about 2 1/2 pounds (about 1 kilogram)

there was no one to rescue her.

²⁸If a man happens to meet a virgin who is not pledged to be married and rapes her and they are discovered, ²⁹he shall pay the girl's father fifty shekels of silver.ᵃ He must marry the girl, for he has violated her. He can never divorce her as long as he lives.   Ex 22:16

³⁰A man is not to marry his father's wife; he must not dishonor his father's bed.   Dt 27:20

Exclusion From the Assembly

23 No one who has been emasculated by crushing or cutting may enter the assembly of the LORD.   Ne 13:1

²No one born of a forbidden marriageᵇ nor any of his descendants may enter the assembly of the LORD, even down to the tenth generation.

³No Ammonite or Moabite or any of his descendants may enter the assembly of the LORD, even down to the tenth generation. ⁴For they did not come to meet you with bread and water on your way when you came out of Egypt, and they hired Balaam son of Beor from Pethor in Aram Naharaimᶜ to pronounce a curse on you. ⁵However, the LORD your God would not listen to Balaam but turned the curse into a blessing for you, because the LORD your God loves you. ⁶Do not seek a treaty of friend-

ship with them as long as you live.   Dt 2:28; Mt 5:43

⁷Do not abhor an Edomite, for he is your brother. Do not abhor an Egyptian, because you lived as an alien in his country. ⁸The third generation of children born to them may enter the assembly of the LORD.Ge 25:26

Uncleanness in the Camp

⁹When you are encamped against your enemies, keep away from everything impure. ¹⁰If one of your men is unclean because of a nocturnal emission, he is to go outside the camp and stay there. ¹¹But as evening approaches he is to wash himself, and at sunset he may return to the camp. Lev 15:16

¹²Designate a place outside the camp where you can go to relieve yourself. ¹³As part of your equipment have something to dig with, and when you relieve yourself, dig a hole and cover up your excrement. ¹⁴For the LORD your God moves about in your camp to protect you and to deliver your enemies to you. Your camp must be holy, so that he will not see among you anything indecent and turn away from you.

Miscellaneous Laws

¹⁵If a slave has taken refuge with you, do not hand him over to his master. ¹⁶Let him live

---

ᵃ29 That is, about 1 1/4 pounds (about 0.6 kilogram)   ᵇ2 Or one of illegitimate birth
ᶜ4 That is, Northwest Mesopotamia

among you wherever he likes and in whatever town he chooses. Do not oppress him.

¹⁷No Israelite man or woman is to become a shrine prostitute. ¹⁸You must not bring the earnings of a female prostitute or of a male prostitute*a* into the house of the LORD your God to pay any vow, because the LORD your God detests them both.

¹⁹Do not charge your brother interest, whether on money or food or anything else that may earn interest. ²⁰You may charge a foreigner interest, but not a brother Israelite, so that the LORD your God may bless you in everything you put your hand to in the land you are entering to possess. Lev 25:36

²¹If you make a vow to the LORD your God, do not be slow to pay it, for the LORD your God will certainly demand it of you and you will be guilty of sin. ²²But if you refrain from making a vow, you will not be guilty. ²³Whatever your lips utter you must be sure to do, because you made your vow freely to the LORD your God with your own mouth. Nu 30:2; Ac 5:4

²⁴If you enter your neighbor's vineyard, you may eat all the grapes you want, but do not put any in your basket. ²⁵If you enter your neighbor's grainfield, you may pick kernels with your hands, but you must not put a sickle to his standing grain.

24 If a man marries a woman who becomes displeasing to him because he finds something indecent about her, and he writes her a certificate of divorce, gives it to her and sends her from his house, ²and if after she leaves his house she becomes the wife of another man, ³and her second husband dislikes her and writes her a certificate of divorce, gives it to her and sends her from his house, or if he dies, ⁴then her first husband, who divorced her, is not allowed to marry her again after she has been defiled. That would be detestable in the eyes of the LORD. Do not bring sin upon the land the LORD your God is giving you as an inheritance. Dt 22:13; Jer 3:1

⁵If a man has recently married, he must not be sent to war or have any other duty laid on him. For one year he is to be free to stay at home and bring happiness to the wife he has married. Dt 20:7

⁶Do not take a pair of millstones—not even the upper one—as security for a debt, because that would be taking a man's livelihood as security.

⁷If a man is caught kidnapping one of his brother Israelites and treats him as a slave or sells him, the kidnapper must die. You must purge the evil from among you. Ex 21:16; 1Co 5:13

⁸In cases of leprous*b* diseases

---

a18 Hebrew *of a dog*   *b8* The Hebrew word was used for various diseases affecting the skin—not necessarily leprosy.

be very careful to do exactly as the priests, who are Levites, instruct you. You must follow carefully what I have commanded them. ⁹Remember what the LORD your God did to Miriam along the way after you came out of Egypt.   Lev 13:2

¹⁰When you make a loan of any kind to your neighbor, do not go into his house to get what he is offering as a pledge. ¹¹Stay outside and let the man to whom you are making the loan bring the pledge out to you. ¹²If the man is poor, do not go to sleep with his pledge in your possession. ¹³Return his cloak to him by sunset so that he may sleep in it. Then he will thank you, and it will be regarded as a righteous act in the sight of the LORD your God.   Ex 22:26

¹⁴Do not take advantage of a hired man who is poor and needy, whether he is a brother Israelite or an alien living in one of your towns. ¹⁵Pay him his wages each day before sunset, because he is poor and is counting on it. Otherwise he may cry to the LORD against you, and you will be guilty of sin.

¹⁶Fathers shall not be put to death for their children, nor children put to death for their fathers; each is to die for his own sin.   2Ki 14:6; Jer 31:29

¹⁷Do not deprive the alien or the fatherless of justice, or take the cloak of the widow as a pledge. ¹⁸Remember that you were slaves in Egypt and the LORD your God redeemed you from there. That is why I command you to do this.   Dt 10:18

¹⁹When you are harvesting in your field and you overlook a sheaf, do not go back to get it. Leave it for the alien, the fatherless and the widow, so that the LORD your God may bless you in all the work of your hands. ²⁰When you beat the olives from your trees, do not go over the branches a second time. Leave what remains for the alien, the fatherless and the widow. ²¹When you harvest the grapes in your vineyard, do not go over the vines again. Leave what remains for the alien, the fatherless and the widow. ²²Remember that you were slaves in Egypt. That is why I command you to do this.   Lev 19:9; Dt 10:19

25 When men have a dispute, they are to take it to court and the judges will decide the case, acquitting the innocent and condemning the guilty. ²If the guilty man deserves to be beaten, the judge shall make him lie down and have him flogged in his presence with the number of lashes his crime deserves, ³but he must not give him more than forty lashes. If he is flogged more than that, your brother will be degraded in your eyes.   Dt 19:17

⁴Do not muzzle an ox while it is treading out the grain.   1Co 9:9

⁵If brothers are living together and one of them dies without a son, his widow must not marry outside the family. Her husband's brother shall

take her and marry her and fulfill the duty of a brother-in-law to her. 6The first son she bears shall carry on the name of the dead brother so that his name will not be blotted out from Israel. Ge 38:9; Ru 4:10

7However, if a man does not want to marry his brother's wife, she shall go to the elders at the town gate and say, "My husband's brother refuses to carry on his brother's name in Israel. He will not fulfill the duty of a brother-in-law to me." 8Then the elders of his town shall summon him and talk to him. If he persists in saying, "I do not want to marry her," 9his brother's widow shall go up to him in the presence of the elders, take off one of his sandals, spit in his face and say, "This is what is done to the man who will not build up his brother's family line." 10That man's line shall be known in Israel as The Family of the Unsandaled. Ru 4:1-2

11If two men are fighting and the wife of one of them comes to rescue her husband from his assailant, and she reaches out and seizes him by his private parts, 12you shall cut off her hand. Show her no pity. Dt 7:2

13Do not have two differing weights in your bag—one heavy, one light. 14Do not have two differing measures in your house—one large, one small. 15You must have accurate and honest weights and measures, so that you may live long in the land the LORD your God is giv-

ing you. 16For the LORD your God detests anyone who does these things, anyone who deals dishonestly. Pr 11:1; Mic 6:11

17Remember what the Amalekites did to you along the way when you came out of Egypt. 18When you were weary and worn out, they met you on your journey and cut off all who were lagging behind; they had no fear of God. 19When the LORD your God gives you rest from all the enemies around you in the land he is giving you to possess as an inheritance, you shall blot out the memory of Amalek from under heaven. Do not forget!

Firstfruits and Tithes

26 When you have entered the land the LORD your God is giving you as an inheritance and have taken possession of it and settled in it, 2take some of the firstfruits of all that you produce from the soil of the land the LORD your God is giving you and put them in a basket. Then go to the place the LORD your God will choose as a dwelling for his Name 3and say to the priest in office at the time, "I declare today to the LORD your God that I have come to the land the LORD swore to our forefathers to give us." 4The priest shall take the basket from your hands and set it down in front of the altar of the LORD your God. 5Then you shall declare before the LORD your God: "My father was a wandering

Aramean, and he went down into Egypt with a few people and lived there and became a great nation, powerful and numerous. ⁶But the Egyptians mistreated us and made us suffer, putting us to hard labor. ⁷Then we cried out to the LORD, the God of our fathers, and the LORD heard our voice and saw our misery, toil and oppression. ⁸So the LORD brought us out of Egypt with a mighty hand and an outstretched arm, with great terror and with miraculous signs and wonders. ⁹He brought us to this place and gave us this land, a land flowing with milk and honey; ¹⁰and now I bring the firstfruits of the soil that you, O LORD, have given me." Place the basket before the LORD your God and bow down before him. ¹¹And you and the Levites and the aliens among you shall rejoice in all the good things the LORD your God has given to you and your household.

¹²When you have finished setting aside a tenth of all your produce in the third year, the year of the tithe, you shall give it to the Levite, the alien, the fatherless and the widow, so that they may eat in your towns and be satisfied. ¹³Then say to the LORD your God: "I have removed from my house the sacred portion and have given it to the Levite, the alien, the fatherless and the widow, according to all you commanded. I

have not turned aside from your commands nor have I forgotten any of them. ¹⁴I have not eaten any of the sacred portion while I was in mourning, nor have I removed any of it while I was unclean, nor have I offered any of it to the dead. I have obeyed the LORD my God; I have done everything you commanded me. ¹⁵Look down from heaven, your holy dwelling place, and bless your people Israel and the land you have given us as you promised on oath to our forefathers, a land flowing with milk and honey.'' Ex 22:29; Hos 9:4

Follow the LORD's Commands

¹⁶The LORD your God commands you this day to follow these decrees and laws; carefully observe them with all your heart and with all your soul. ¹⁷You have declared this day that the LORD is your God and that you will walk in his ways, that you will keep his decrees, commands and laws, and that you will obey him. ¹⁸And the LORD has declared this day that you are his people, his treasured possession as he promised, and that you are to keep all his commands. ¹⁹He has declared that he will set you in praise, fame and honor high above all the nations he has made and that you will be a people holy to the LORD your God, as he promised.

The Altar on Mount Ebal

27 Moses and the elders of Israel commanded the people: "Keep all these commands that I give you today. ²When you have crossed the Jordan into the land the Lord your God is giving you, set up some large stones and coat them with plaster. ³Write on them all the words of this law when you have crossed over to enter the land the Lord your God is giving you, a land flowing with milk and honey, just as the Lord, the God of your fathers, promised you. ⁴And when you have crossed the Jordan, set up these stones on Mount Ebal, as I command you today, and coat them with plaster. ⁵Build there an altar to the Lord your God, an altar of stones. Do not use any iron tool upon them. ⁶Build the altar of the Lord your God with fieldstones and offer burnt offerings on it to the Lord your God. ⁷Sacrifice fellowship offerings*ᵃ* there, eating them and rejoicing in the presence of the Lord your God. ⁸And you shall write very clearly all the words of this law on these stones you have set up." Ps 78:7; Isa 8:1

Curses From Mount Ebal

⁹Then Moses and the priests, who are Levites, said to all Israel, "Be silent, O Israel, and listen! You have now become the people of the Lord your God. ¹⁰Obey the Lord your God and follow his commands and decrees that I give you today."

¹¹On the same day Moses commanded the people:

¹²When you have crossed the Jordan, these tribes shall stand on Mount Gerizim to bless the people: Simeon, Levi, Judah, Issachar, Joseph and Benjamin. ¹³And these tribes shall stand on Mount Ebal to pronounce curses: Reuben, Gad, Asher, Zebulun, Dan and Naphtali.

¹⁴The Levites shall recite to all the people of Israel in a loud voice:

¹⁵"Cursed is the man who carves an image or casts an idol—a thing detestable to the Lord, the work of the craftsman's hands—and sets it up in secret." Ex 20:4; 1Ki 11:5

Then all the people shall say, "Amen!"

¹⁶"Cursed is the man who dishonors his father or his mother." Ge 31:35; Lev 20:9

Then all the people shall say, "Amen!"

¹⁷"Cursed is the man who moves his neighbor's boundary stone." Dt 19:14

Then all the people shall say, "Amen!"

¹⁸"Cursed is the man who leads the blind astray on the road." Lev 19:14

Then all the people shall say, "Amen!"

¹⁹"Cursed is the man

ᵃ7 Traditionally *peace offerings*

who withholds justice from the alien, the fatherless or the widow." Ex 22:21; Dt 24:19

Then all the people shall say, "Amen!"

²⁰"Cursed is the man who sleeps with his father's wife, for he dishonors his father's bed." Lev 18:7

Then all the people shall say, "Amen!"

²¹"Cursed is the man who has sexual relations with any animal." Ex 22:19

Then all the people shall say, "Amen!"

²²"Cursed is the man who sleeps with his sister, the daughter of his father or the daughter of his mother." Lev 18:9; 20:17

Then all the people shall say, "Amen!"

²³"Cursed is the man who sleeps with his mother-in-law." Lev 20:14

Then all the people shall say, "Amen!"

²⁴"Cursed is the man who kills his neighbor secretly." Ge 4:23; Ex 21:12

Then all the people shall say, "Amen!"

²⁵"Cursed is the man who accepts a bribe to kill an innocent person." Ex 23:7-8

Then all the people shall say, "Amen!"

²⁶"Cursed is the man who does not uphold the words of this law by carrying them out." Dt 28:15

Then all the people shall say, "Amen!"

Blessings for Obedience

28 If you fully obey the LORD your God and carefully follow all his commands I give you today, the LORD your God will set you high above all the nations on earth. ²All these blessings will come upon you and accompany you if you obey the LORD your God: Nu 24:7

³You will be blessed in the city and blessed in the country. Ge 39:5; Ps 144:15

⁴The fruit of your womb will be blessed, and the crops of your land and the young of your livestock—the calves of your herds and the lambs of your flocks. Ge 49:25; Ps 107:38

⁵Your basket and your kneading trough will be blessed.

⁶You will be blessed when you come in and blessed when you go out.

⁷The LORD will grant that the enemies who rise up against you will be defeated before you. They will come at you from one direction but flee from you in seven. Lev 26:8,17; 2Ch 6:34

⁸The LORD will send a blessing on your barns and on everything you put your hand to. The LORD your God will bless you in the land he is giving you. Lev 25:21; Dt 15:4

⁹The LORD will establish you as his holy people, as he promised you on oath, if you keep the commands of the LORD your

God and walk in his ways.
¹⁰Then all the peoples on earth
will see that you are called by
the name of the LORD, and they
will fear you. ¹¹The LORD will
grant you abundant prosperity—in the fruit of your womb,
the young of your livestock and
the crops of your ground—in
the land he swore to your forefathers to give you.   1Ki 8:43
¹²The LORD will open the
heavens, the storehouse of his
bounty, to send rain on your
land in season and to bless all
the work of your hands. You
will lend to many nations but
will borrow from none. ¹³The
LORD will make you the head,
not the tail. If you pay attention
to the commands of the LORD
your God that I give you this
day and carefully follow them,
you will always be at the top,
never at the bottom. ¹⁴Do not
turn aside from any of the commands I give you today, to the
right or to the left, following
other gods and serving them.

Curses for Disobedience

¹⁵However, if you do not
obey the LORD your God and do
not carefully follow all his commands and decrees I am giving
you today, all these curses will
come upon you and overtake
you: Jos 23:15; Mal 2:2

¹⁶You will be cursed in
the city and cursed in the
country.
¹⁷Your basket and your

kneading trough will be
cursed.
¹⁸The fruit of your womb
will be cursed, and the
crops of your land, and the
calves of your herds and the
lambs of your flocks.
¹⁹You will be cursed
when you come in and
cursed when you go out.

²⁰The LORD will send on you
curses, confusion and rebuke in
everything you put your hand
to, until you are destroyed and
come to sudden ruin because of
the evil you have done in forsaking him. ᵃ ²¹The LORD will
plague you with diseases until
he has destroyed you from the
land you are entering to possess. ²²The LORD will strike you
with wasting disease, with fever and inflammation, with
scorching heat and drought,
with blight and mildew, which
will plague you until you perish. ²³The sky over your head
will be bronze, the ground
beneath you iron. ²⁴The LORD
will turn the rain of your country into dust and powder; it will
come down from the skies until
you are destroyed.   Dt 4:26
²⁵The LORD will cause you to
be defeated before your enemies. You will come at them
from one direction but flee from
them in seven, and you will
become a thing of horror to all
the kingdoms on earth. ²⁶Your
carcasses will be food for all the
birds of the air and the beasts of

ᵃ20 Hebrew me

the earth, and there will be no one to frighten them away. ²⁷The LORD will afflict you with the boils of Egypt and with tumors, festering sores and the itch, from which you cannot be cured. ²⁸The LORD will afflict you with madness, blindness and confusion of mind. ²⁹At midday you will grope about like a blind man in the dark. You will be unsuccessful in everything you do; day after day you will be oppressed and robbed, with no one to rescue you.   Isa 1:6

³⁰You will be pledged to be married to a woman, but another will take her and ravish her. You will build a house, but you will not live in it. You will plant a vineyard, but you will not even begin to enjoy its fruit. ³¹Your ox will be slaughtered before your eyes, but you will eat none of it. Your donkey will be forcibly taken from you and will not be returned. Your sheep will be given to your enemies, and no one will rescue them. ³²Your sons and daughters will be given to another nation, and you will wear out your eyes watching for them day after day, powerless to lift a hand. ³³A people that you do not know will eat what your land and labor produce, and you will have nothing but cruel oppression all your days. ³⁴The sights you see will drive you mad. ³⁵The LORD will afflict your knees and legs with painful boils that cannot be cured,

spreading from the soles of your feet to the top of your head.

³⁶The LORD will drive you and the king you set over you to a nation unknown to you or your fathers. There you will worship other gods, gods of wood and stone. ³⁷You will become a thing of horror and an object of scorn and ridicule to all the nations where the LORD will drive you.

³⁸You will sow much seed in the field but you will harvest little, because locusts will devour it. ³⁹You will plant vineyards and cultivate them but you will not drink the wine or gather the grapes, because worms will eat them. ⁴⁰You will have olive trees throughout your country but you will not use the oil, because the olives will drop off. ⁴¹You will have sons and daughters but you will not keep them, because they will go into captivity. ⁴²Swarms of locusts will take over all your trees and the crops of your land.   Jdg 6:5; Mic 6:15

⁴³The alien who lives among you will rise above you higher and higher, but you will sink lower and lower. ⁴⁴He will lend to you, but you will not lend to him. He will be the head, but you will be the tail.   Dt 26:19

⁴⁵All these curses will come upon you. They will pursue you and overtake you until you are destroyed, because you did not obey the LORD your God and observe the commands and decrees he gave you. ⁴⁶They will be a sign and a wonder to you and your descendants forever.

⁴⁷Because you did not serve the LORD your God joyfully and gladly in the time of prosperity, ⁴⁸therefore in hunger and thirst, in nakedness and dire poverty, you will serve the enemies the LORD sends against you. He will put an iron yoke on your neck until he has destroyed you.

⁴⁹The LORD will bring a nation against you from far away, from the ends of the earth, like an eagle swooping down, a nation whose language you will not understand, ⁵⁰a fierce-looking nation without respect for the old or pity for the young. ⁵¹They will devour the young of your livestock and the crops of your land until you are destroyed. They will leave you no grain, new wine or oil, nor any calves of your herds or lambs of your flocks until you are ruined. ⁵²They will lay siege to all the cities throughout your land until the high fortified walls in which you trust fall down. They will besiege all the cities throughout the land the LORD your God is giving you. Jer 5:15

⁵³Because of the suffering that your enemy will inflict on you during the siege, you will eat the fruit of the womb, the flesh of the sons and daughters the LORD your God has given you. ⁵⁴Even the most gentle and sensitive man among you will have no compassion on his own brother or the wife he loves or his surviving children, ⁵⁵and he will not give to one of them any of the flesh of his children that he is eating. It will be all he has left because of the suffering your enemy will inflict on you during the siege of all your cities. ⁵⁶The most gentle and sensitive woman among you—so sensitive and gentle that she would not venture to touch the ground with the sole of her foot—will begrudge the husband she loves and her own son or daughter ⁵⁷the afterbirth from her womb and the children she bears. For she intends to eat them secretly during the siege and in the distress that your enemy will inflict on you in your cities. Lev 26:29; Isa 47:1

⁵⁸If you do not carefully follow all the words of this law, which are written in this book, and do not revere this glorious and awesome name—the LORD your God— ⁵⁹the LORD will send fearful plagues on you and your descendants, harsh and prolonged disasters, and severe and lingering illnesses. ⁶⁰He will bring upon you all the diseases of Egypt that you dreaded, and they will cling to you. ⁶¹The LORD will also bring on you every kind of sickness and disaster not recorded in this Book of the Law, until you are destroyed. ⁶²You who were as numerous as the stars in the sky will be left but few in number, because you did not obey the LORD your God. ⁶³Just as it pleased the LORD to make you prosper and increase in number, so it will please him to ruin and destroy you. You will be

uprooted from the land you are entering to possess.   Dt 31:24

⁶⁴Then the LORD will scatter you among all nations, from one end of the earth to the other. There you will worship other gods—gods of wood and stone, which neither you nor your fathers have known. ⁶⁵Among those nations you will find no repose, no resting place for the sole of your foot. There the LORD will give you an anxious mind, eyes weary with longing, and a despairing heart. ⁶⁶You will live in constant suspense, filled with dread both night and day, never sure of your life. ⁶⁷In the morning you will say, "If only it were evening!" and in the evening, "If only it were morning!"—because of the terror that will fill your hearts and the sights that your eyes will see. ⁶⁸The LORD will send you back in ships to Egypt on a journey I said you should never make again. There you will offer yourselves for sale to your enemies as male and female slaves, but no one will buy you.   Dt 4:27

Renewal of the Covenant

29 These are the terms of the covenant the LORD commanded Moses to make with the Israelites in Moab, in addition to the covenant he had made with them at Horeb. Lev 7:38

²Moses summoned all the Israelites and said to them:

Your eyes have seen all that the LORD did in Egypt to Pharaoh, to all his officials and to all his land. ³With your own eyes you saw those great trials, those miraculous signs and great wonders. ⁴But to this day the LORD has not given you a mind that understands or eyes that see or ears that hear. ⁵During the forty years that I led you through the desert, your clothes did not wear out, nor did the sandals on your feet. ⁶You ate no bread and drank no wine or other fermented drink. I did this so that you might know that I am the LORD your God.   Ex 19:4

⁷When you reached this place, Sihon king of Heshbon and Og king of Bashan came out to fight against us, but we defeated them. ⁸We took their land and gave it as an inheritance to the Reubenites, the Gadites and the half-tribe of Manasseh.   Nu 21:21-24; Dt 3:12

⁹Carefully follow the terms of this covenant, so that you may prosper in everything you do. ¹⁰All of you are standing today in the presence of the LORD your God—your leaders and chief men, your elders and officials, and all the other men of Israel, ¹¹together with your children and your wives, and the aliens living in your camps who chop your wood and carry your water. ¹²You are standing here in order to enter into a covenant with the LORD your God, a covenant the LORD is making with you this day and sealing with an oath, ¹³to confirm you this day

as his people, that he may be your God as he promised you and as he swore to your fathers, Abraham, Isaac and Jacob. [14]I am making this covenant, with its oath, not only with you [15]who are standing here with us today in the presence of the LORD our God but also with those who are not here today.

[16]You yourselves know how we lived in Egypt and how we passed through the countries on the way here. [17]You saw among them their detestable images and idols of wood and stone, of silver and gold. [18]Make sure there is no man or woman, clan or tribe among you today whose heart turns away from the LORD our God to go and worship the gods of those nations; make sure there is no root among you that produces such bitter poison. _{Dt 11:16; Heb 12:15}

[19]When such a person hears the words of this oath, he invokes a blessing on himself and therefore thinks, "I will be safe, even though I persist in going my own way." This will bring disaster on the watered land as well as the dry. *a* [20]The LORD will never be willing to forgive him; his wrath and zeal will burn against that man. All the curses written in this book will fall upon him, and the LORD will blot out his name from under heaven. [21]The LORD will single him out from all the tribes of Israel for disaster, according to

all the curses of the covenant written in this Book of the Law.

[22]Your children who follow you in later generations and foreigners who come from distant lands will see the calamities that have fallen on the land and the diseases with which the LORD has afflicted it. [23]The whole land will be a burning waste of salt and sulfur—nothing planted, nothing sprouting, no vegetation growing on it. It will be like the destruction of Sodom and Gomorrah, Admah and Zeboiim, which the LORD overthrew in fierce anger. [24]All the nations will ask: "Why has the LORD done this to this land? Why this fierce, burning anger?" _{1Ki 9:8; Jer 19:8}

[25]And the answer will be: "It is because this people abandoned the covenant of the LORD, the God of their fathers, the covenant he made with them when he brought them out of Egypt. [26]They went off and worshiped other gods and bowed down to them, gods they did not know, gods he had not given them. [27]Therefore the LORD's anger burned against this land, so that he brought on it all the curses written in this book. [28]In furious anger and in great wrath the LORD uprooted them from their land and thrust them into another land, as it is now." _{2Ch 7:20}

[29]The secret things belong to the LORD our God, but the

---

a19 Or way, in order to add drunkenness to thirst."

things revealed belong to us and to our children forever, that we may follow all the words of this law. Jn 5:39; Ac 1:7

Prosperity After Turning to the LORD

30 When all these blessings and curses I have set before you come upon you and you take them to heart wherever the LORD your God disperses you among the nations, ²and when you and your children return to the LORD your God and obey him with all your heart and with all your soul according to everything I command you today, ³then the LORD your God will restore your fortunes*a* and have compassion on you and gather you again from all the nations where he scattered you. ⁴Even if you have been banished to the most distant land under the heavens, from there the LORD your God will gather you and bring you back. ⁵He will bring you to the land that belonged to your fathers, and you will take possession of it. He will make you more prosperous and numerous than your fathers. ⁶The LORD your God will circumcise your hearts and the hearts of your descendants, so that you may love him with all your heart and with all your soul, and live. ⁷The LORD your God will put all these curses on your enemies who hate and perse-

cute you. ⁸You will again obey the LORD and follow all his commands I am giving you today. ⁹Then the LORD your God will make you most prosperous in all the work of your hands and in the fruit of your womb, the young of your livestock and the crops of your land. The LORD will again delight in you and make you prosperous, just as he delighted in your fathers, ¹⁰if you obey the LORD your God and keep his commands and decrees that are written in this Book of the Law and turn to the LORD your God with all your heart and with all your soul.

The Offer of Life or Death

¹¹Now what I am commanding you today is not too difficult for you or beyond your reach. ¹²It is not up in heaven, so that you have to ask, "Who will ascend into heaven to get it and proclaim it to us so we may obey it?" ¹³Nor is it beyond the sea, so that you have to ask, "Who will cross the sea to get it and proclaim it to us so we may obey it?" ¹⁴No, the word is very near you; it is in your mouth and in your heart so you may obey it.

¹⁵See, I set before you today life and prosperity, death and destruction. ¹⁶For I command you today to love the LORD your God, to walk in his ways, and to keep his commands, decrees and laws; then you will live and increase, and the LORD your

*a*3 Or *will bring you back from captivity*

God will bless you in the land you are entering to possess.

¹⁷But if your heart turns away and you are not obedient, and if you are drawn away to bow down to other gods and worship them, ¹⁸I declare to you this day that you will certainly be destroyed. You will not live long in the land you are crossing the Jordan to enter and possess. Dt 4:26; 8:19

¹⁹This day I call heaven and earth as witnesses against you that I have set before you life and death, blessings and curses. Now choose life, so that you and your children may live ²⁰and that you may love the LORD your God, listen to his voice, and hold fast to him. For the LORD is your life, and he will give you many years in the land he swore to give to your fathers, Abraham, Isaac and Jacob. Ge 12:7

Joshua to Succeed Moses

31 Then Moses went out and spoke these words to all Israel: ²"I am now a hundred and twenty years old and I am no longer able to lead you. The LORD has said to me, 'You shall not cross the Jordan.' ³The LORD your God himself will cross over ahead of you. He will destroy these nations before you, and you will take possession of their land. Joshua also will cross over ahead of you, as the LORD said. ⁴And the LORD will do to them what he did to Sihon and Og, the kings of the Amorites, whom he destroyed along with

their land. ⁵The LORD will deliver them to you, and you must do to them all that I have commanded you. ⁶Be strong and courageous. Do not be afraid or terrified because of them, for the LORD your God goes with you; he will never leave you nor forsake you." Dt 3:27; Heb 13:5

⁷Then Moses summoned Joshua and said to him in the presence of all Israel, "Be strong and courageous, for you must go with this people into the land that the LORD swore to their forefathers to give them, and you must divide it among them as their inheritance. ⁸The LORD himself goes before you and will be with you; he will never leave you nor forsake you. Do not be afraid; do not be discouraged."

The Reading of the Law

⁹So Moses wrote down this law and gave it to the priests, the sons of Levi, who carried the ark of the covenant of the LORD, and to all the elders of Israel. ¹⁰Then Moses commanded them: "At the end of every seven years, in the year for canceling debts, during the Feast of Tabernacles, ¹¹when all Israel comes to appear before the LORD your God at the place he will choose, you shall read this law before them in their hearing. ¹²Assemble the people—men, women and children, and the aliens living in your towns—so they can listen and learn to fear the LORD your God and follow carefully all the

words of this law. ¹³Their children, who do not know this law, must hear it and learn to fear the LORD your God as long as you live in the land you are crossing the Jordan to possess."

Israel's Rebellion Predicted

¹⁴The LORD said to Moses, "Now the day of your death is near. Call Joshua and present yourselves at the Tent of Meeting, where I will commission him." So Moses and Joshua came and presented themselves at the Tent of Meeting.   Dt 32:49

¹⁵Then the LORD appeared at the Tent in a pillar of cloud, and the cloud stood over the entrance to the Tent. ¹⁶And the LORD said to Moses: "You are going to rest with your fathers, and these people will soon prostitute themselves to the foreign gods of the land they are entering. They will forsake me and break the covenant I made with them. ¹⁷On that day I will become angry with them and forsake them; I will hide my face from them, and they will be destroyed. Many disasters and difficulties will come upon them, and on that day they will ask, 'Have not these disasters come upon us because our God is not with us?' ¹⁸And I will certainly hide my face on that day because of all their wickedness in turning to other gods.   Ex 33:9

¹⁹"Now write down for yourselves this song and teach it to the Israelites and have them sing it, so that it may be a witness for me against them. ²⁰When I have brought them into the land flowing with milk and honey, the land I promised on oath to their forefathers, and when they eat their fill and thrive, they will turn to other gods and worship them, rejecting me and breaking my covenant. ²¹And when many disasters and difficulties come upon them, this song will testify against them, because it will not be forgotten by their descendants. I know what they are disposed to do, even before I bring them into the land I promised them on oath." ²²So Moses wrote down this song that day and taught it to the Israelites.

²³The LORD gave this command to Joshua son of Nun: "Be strong and courageous, for you will bring the Israelites into the land I promised them on oath, and I myself will be with you."

²⁴After Moses finished writing in a book the words of this law from beginning to end, ²⁵he gave this command to the Levites who carried the ark of the covenant of the LORD: ²⁶"Take this Book of the Law and place it beside the ark of the covenant of the LORD your God. There it will remain as a witness against you. ²⁷For I know how rebellious and stiff-necked you are. If you have been rebellious against the LORD while I am still alive and with you, how much more will you rebel after I die! ²⁸Assemble before me all the elders of your tribes and all your officials, so

that I can speak these words in their hearing and call heaven and earth to testify against them. ²⁹For I know that after my death you are sure to become utterly corrupt and to turn from the way I have commanded you. In days to come, disaster will fall upon you because you will do evil in the sight of the LORD and provoke him to anger by what your hands have made." Ex 23:21; Dt 9:27

The Song of Moses

³⁰And Moses recited the words of this song from beginning to end in the hearing of the whole assembly of Israel:

32 Listen, O heavens, and I will speak;
hear, O earth, the words of my mouth. Ps 49:1
²Let my teaching fall like rain and my words descend like dew,
like showers on new grass, like abundant rain on tender plants. Isa 55:11

³I will proclaim the name of the LORD. Ex 33:19
Oh, praise the greatness of our God! Dt 3:24
⁴He is the Rock, his works are perfect,
and all his ways are just.
A faithful God who does no wrong,
upright and just is he. Ps 92:15

⁵They have acted corruptly toward him;
to their shame they are no longer his children,
but a warped and crooked generation. ᵃ Mt 17:17; Lk 9:41
⁶Is this the way you repay the LORD,
O foolish and unwise people?
Is he not your Father, your Creator, ᵇ
who made you and formed you? Ps 116:12

⁷Remember the days of old; consider the generations long past. Job 8:8; Ps 44:1
Ask your father and he will tell you,
your elders, and they will explain to you. Job 15:18
⁸When the Most High gave the nations their inheritance,
when he divided all mankind,
he set up boundaries for the peoples
according to the number of the sons of Israel. ᶜ Ge 11:8
⁹For the LORD's portion is his people,
Jacob his allotted inheritance. Ps 73:26; Jer 10:16

¹⁰In a desert land he found him,
in a barren and howling waste. Dt 8:15; Job 12:24
He shielded him and cared for him;

ᵃ5 Or Corrupt are they and not his children, / a generation warped and twisted to their shame   ᵇ6 Or Father, who bought you   ᶜ8 Masoretic Text; Dead Sea Scrolls (see also Septuagint) sons of God

he guarded him as the
apple of his eye,
[11]like an eagle that stirs up its
nest
and hovers over its young,
that spreads its wings to
catch them
and carries them on its
pinions.
[12]The LORD alone led him;
no foreign god was with
him.   Jdg 2:12; Ps 106:9

[13]He made him ride on the
heights of the land
and fed him with the fruit
of the fields.   Dt 33:29
He nourished him with
honey from the rock,
and with oil from the flinty
crag,   Job 29:6
[14]with curds and milk from
herd and flock
and with fattened lambs
and goats,
with choice rams of Bashan
and the finest kernels of
wheat.   Ps 65:9
You drank the foaming blood
of the grape.   Ge 49:11

[15]Jeshurun[a] grew fat and
kicked;
filled with food, he became
heavy and sleek.   Dt 33:5
He abandoned the God who
made him
and rejected the Rock his
Savior.   Isa 58:2
[16]They made him jealous with
their foreign gods
and angered him with their
detestable idols.   1Co 10:22

[17]They sacrificed to demons,
which are not God—
gods they had not known,
gods that recently
appeared,
gods your fathers did not
fear.   Ex 22:20; Jdg 5:8
[18]You deserted the Rock, who
fathered you;
you forgot the God who
gave you birth.   Ps 106:21

[19]The LORD saw this and
rejected them
because he was angered by
his sons and daughters.
[20]"I will hide my face from
them," he said,
"and see what their end
will be;
for they are a perverse
generation,
children who are unfaithful.
[21]They made me jealous by
what is no god
and angered me with their
worthless idols.   Nu 25:11
I will make them envious by
those who are not a
people;
I will make them angry by a
nation that has no
understanding.   Ro 10:19
[22]For a fire has been kindled by
my wrath,
one that burns to the realm
of death[b] below.   Jer 15:14
It will devour the earth and
its harvests
and set afire the
foundations of the
mountains.

---

[a]15 *Jeshurun* means *the upright one*, that is, Israel.   [b]22 Hebrew *to Sheol*

²³"I will heap calamities upon
    them
  and spend my arrows
    against them.   Dt 29:21
²⁴I will send wasting famine
    against them,
  consuming pestilence and
    deadly plague;
I will send against them the
    fangs of wild beasts,
  the venom of vipers that
    glide in the dust.   Dt 28:22
²⁵In the street the sword will
    make them childless;
  in their homes terror will
    reign.
  Young men and young
    women will perish,
  infants and gray-haired
    men.   2Ch 36:17
²⁶I said I would scatter them
  and blot out their memory
    from mankind,
²⁷but I dreaded the taunt of the
    enemy,
  lest the adversary
    misunderstand
and say, 'Our hand has
    triumphed;
  the Lord has not done all
    this.' "   Isa 10:13

²⁸They are a nation without
    sense,
  there is no discernment in
    them.   Isa 1:3; 27:11
²⁹If only they were wise and
    would understand this
  and discern what their end
    will be!   Ps 81:13
³⁰How could one man chase a
    thousand,
  or two put ten thousand to
    flight,

unless their Rock had sold
    them,
  unless the Lord had given
    them up?   Lev 26:8
³¹For their rock is not like our
    Rock,
  as even our enemies
    concede.   Ge 49:24; 1Sa 2:2
³²Their vine comes from the
    vine of Sodom
  and from the fields of
    Gomorrah.   Jer 23:14
Their grapes are filled with
    poison,
  and their clusters with
    bitterness.   Job 6:4
³³Their wine is the venom of
    serpents,
  the deadly poison of cobras.

³⁴"Have I not kept this in
    reserve
  and sealed it in my vaults?
³⁵It is mine to avenge; I will
    repay.
  In due time their foot will
    slip;
their day of disaster is near
  and their doom rushes
    upon them."   Ro 12:19

³⁶The Lord will judge his
    people
  and have compassion on
    his servants
when he sees their strength
    is gone
  and no one is left, slave or
    free.   Ps 135:14
³⁷He will say: "Now where are
    their gods,
  the rock they took refuge
    in,
³⁸the gods who ate the fat of
    their sacrifices

and drank the wine of their
  drink offerings?   Jer 2:28
Let them rise up to help you!
Let them give you shelter!

39"See now that I myself am
    He!
  There is no god besides me.
  I put to death and I bring to
    life,
  I have wounded and I will
    heal,
  and no one can deliver out
    of my hand.   Ps 50:22
40I lift my hand to heaven and
    declare:
  As surely as I live forever,
41when I sharpen my flashing
    sword
  and my hand grasps it in
    judgment,
  I will take vengeance on my
    adversaries
  and repay those who hate
    me.   Ge 14:22
42I will make my arrows drunk
    with blood,
  while my sword devours
    flesh:
  the blood of the slain and the
    captives,
  the heads of the enemy
    leaders."   2Sa 2:26

43Rejoice, O nations, with his
    people,a,b
  for he will avenge the blood
    of his servants;
  he will take vengeance on his
    enemies
  and make atonement for his
    land and people.   Ro 15:10

44Moses came with Joshuac
son of Nun and spoke all the
words of this song in the hearing of the people. 45When
Moses finished reciting all these
words to all Israel, 46he said to
them, "Take to heart all the
words I have solemnly declared
to you this day, so that you may
command your children to obey
carefully all the words of this
law. 47They are not just idle
words for you—they are your
life. By them you will live long
in the land you are crossing the
Jordan to possess."   Nu 13:8

Moses to Die on Mount Nebo

48On that same day the LORD
told Moses, 49"Go up into the
Abarim Range to Mount Nebo
in Moab, across from Jericho,
and view Canaan, the land I am
giving the Israelites as their own
possession. 50There on the
mountain that you have
climbed you will die and be
gathered to your people, just as
your brother Aaron died on
Mount Hor and was gathered to
his people. 51This is because
both of you broke faith with me
in the presence of the Israelites
at the waters of Meribah Kadesh
in the Desert of Zin and because
you did not uphold my holiness
among the Israelites. 52There-
fore, you will see the land only
from a distance; you will not enter the land I am giving to the
people of Israel."   Nu 27:12

---

a43 Or Make his people rejoice, O nations   b43 Masoretic Text; Dead Sea Scrolls (see
also Septuagint) people, / and let all the angels worship him /   c44 Hebrew Hoshea, a
variant of Joshua

Moses Blesses the Tribes

33 This is the blessing that Moses the man of God pronounced on the Israelites before his death. ²He said: Jos 14:6

"The LORD came from Sinai
    and dawned over them
        from Seir;
    he shone forth from Mount
        Paran. Jos 11:17; Ps 50:2
He came with*a* myriads of
        holy ones
    from the south, from his
        mountain slopes.*b* Ps 89:7
³Surely it is you who love the
        people;
    all the holy ones are in your
        hand. Dt 4:37; 7:6
At your feet they all bow
        down,
    and from you receive
        instruction,
⁴the law that Moses gave us,
    the possession of the
        assembly of Jacob.
⁵He was king over Jeshurun*c*
    when the leaders of the
        people assembled,
    along with the tribes of
        Israel. Nu 23:21; 1Sa 10:19

⁶"Let Reuben live and not die,
    nor*d* his men be few."

⁷And this he said about
Judah:

"Hear, O LORD, the cry of
        Judah;
    bring him to his people.
With his own hands he
        defends his cause.

Oh, be his help against his
        foes!"

⁸About Levi he said:

"Your Thummim and Urim
        belong
    to the man you favored.
You tested him at Massah;
    you contended with him at
        the waters of Meribah.
⁹He said of his father and
        mother,
    'I have no regard for them.'
He did not recognize his
        brothers
    or acknowledge his own
        children,
but he watched over your
        word
    and guarded your
        covenant. Ps 61:5; Mal 2:5
¹⁰He teaches your precepts to
        Jacob
    and your law to Israel. Ne 8:18
He offers incense before you
    and whole burnt offerings
        on your altar. Ps 51:19
¹¹Bless all his skills, O LORD,
    and be pleased with the
        work of his hands.
Smite the loins of those who
        rise up against him;
    strike his foes till they rise
        no more."

¹²About Benjamin he said:

"Let the beloved of the LORD
        rest secure in him,
    for he shields him all day
        long,

---

*a*2 Or *from*   *b*2 The meaning of the Hebrew for this phrase is uncertain.
*c*5 *Jeshurun* means *the upright one,* that is, Israel; also in verse 26.   *d*6 Or *but let*

and the one the LORD loves
  rests between his
  shoulders."

13About Joseph he said:

"May the LORD bless his land
  with the precious dew from
    heaven above
  and with the deep waters
    that lie below;
14with the best the sun brings
    forth
  and the finest the moon can
    yield;
15with the choicest gifts of the
    ancient mountains
  and the fruitfulness of the
    everlasting hills;
16with the best gifts of the
    earth and its
    fullness
  and the favor of him who
    dwelt in the burning
    bush.
  Let all these rest on the head
    of Joseph,
  on the brow of the prince
    among*a* his brothers.
17In majesty he is like a
    firstborn bull;
  his horns are the horns of a
    wild ox.   Nu 23:22; 1Sa 2:10
  With them he will gore the
    nations,
  even those at the ends of
    the earth.   1Ki 22:11
  Such are the ten thousands
    of Ephraim;
  such are the thousands of
    Manasseh."   Ge 41:52

18About Zebulun he said:

"Rejoice, Zebulun, in your
  going out,
  and you, Issachar, in your
    tents.   Ge 30:20
19They will summon peoples to
    the mountain
  and there offer sacrifices of
    righteousness;
  they will feast on the
    abundance of the
    seas,
  on the treasures hidden in
    the sand."   Ps 4:5; Isa 2:3

20About Gad he said:

"Blessed is he who enlarges
  Gad's domain!
  Gad lives there like a lion,
  tearing at arm or head.   Ge 30:11
21He chose the best land for
    himself;
  the leader's portion was
    kept for him.   Nu 32:1-5
  When the heads of the
    people assembled,
  he carried out the LORD's
    righteous will,
  and his judgments
    concerning Israel."Jos 22:1-3

22About Dan he said:

"Dan is a lion's cub,
  springing out of Bashan."

23About Naphtali he said:

"Naphtali is abounding with
  the favor of the LORD
  and is full of his blessing;
  he will inherit southward to
    the lake."   Ge 30:8; 49:21

24About Asher he said:

a16 Or of the one separated from

"Most blessed of sons is
    Asher;
let him be favored by his
    brothers,
and let him bathe his feet in
    oil.   Ge 30:13; 49:20
25The bolts of your gates will
    be iron and bronze,
and your strength will
    equal your days.   Ne 3:3

26"There is no one like the God
    of Jeshurun,
who rides on the heavens
    to help you
and on the clouds in his
    majesty.   2Sa 22:10; Ps 68:4
27The eternal God is your
    refuge,
and underneath are the
    everlasting arms.   Ps 90:1
He will drive out your enemy
    before you,
saying, 'Destroy him!'   Dt 7:2
28So Israel will live in safety
    alone;
Jacob's spring is secure
in a land of grain and new
    wine,
where the heavens drop
    dew.   Ge 27:28; Ps 16:9
29Blessed are you, O Israel!
Who is like you,
a people saved by the
    LORD?   Ps 144:15
He is your shield and helper
and your glorious sword.
Your enemies will cower
    before you,
and you will trample down
    their high places. a" Ex 18:4

The Death of Moses

34 Then Moses climbed
Mount Nebo from the
plains of Moab to the top of Pisgah, across from Jericho. There
the LORD showed him the
whole land—from Gilead to
Dan, 2all of Naphtali, the territory of Ephraim and Manasseh,
all the land of Judah as far as the
western sea, b 3the Negev and
the whole region from the Valley of Jericho, the City of Palms,
as far as Zoar. 4Then the LORD
said to him, "This is the land I
promised on oath to Abraham,
Isaac and Jacob when I said, 'I
will give it to your descendants.' I have let you see it with
your eyes, but you will not cross
over into it."   Ge 12:7; Dt 32:49

5And Moses the servant of
the LORD died there in Moab, as
the LORD had said. 6He buried
him c in Moab, in the valley opposite Beth Peor, but to this day
no one knows where his grave
is. 7Moses was a hundred and
twenty years old when he died,
yet his eyes were not weak nor
his strength gone. 8The Israelites grieved for Moses in the
plains of Moab thirty days, until
the time of weeping and mourning was over.   Nu 12:7; 2Sa 11:27

9Now Joshua son of Nun was
filled with the spirit d of wisdom
because Moses had laid his
hands on him. So the Israelites
listened to him and did what

---

a29 Or *will tread upon their bodies*
    buried   d9 Or *Spirit*   b2 That is, the Mediterranean   c6 Or *He was*

the LORD had commanded Moses. Isa 11:2; Ac 6:6

10Since then, no prophet has risen in Israel like Moses, whom the LORD knew face to face, 11who did all those miraculous signs and wonders the LORD sent him to do in Egypt—to Pharaoh and to all his officials and to his whole land. 12For no one has ever shown the mighty power or performed the awesome deeds that Moses did in the sight of all Israel. Dt 18:15

Joshua

Introduction:

This book has the name of its leading character as its title. Joshua had been chosen and appointed by God just before Moses' death.

The book of Joshua is the story of both Joshua and Israel as they, with God's help, conquered the Promised Land—Canaan. The people miraculously crossed the Jordan River and conquered the town of Jericho. Then, with God's help again, they quickly took possession of all the main areas of Canaan.

Before Joshua died, he reminded the people of God's covenant promises to them. He instructed the people to keep on loving and obeying God. Publicly, he spoke of his own willingness to serve God when he said ". . . choose for yourselves this day whom you will serve, . . . But as for me and my household, we will serve the LORD" (24:15).

Outline of contents:

The LORD Commands Joshua

1 After the death of Moses the servant of the LORD, the LORD said to Joshua son of Nun, Moses' aide: 2"Moses my servant is dead. Now then, you and all these people, get ready to cross the Jordan River into the land I am about to give to them—to the Israelites. 3I will give you every place where you set your foot, as I promised Moses. 4Your territory will extend from the desert to Lebanon, and from the great river, the Euphrates—all the Hittite country—to the Great Sea[a] on the west. 5No one will be able to stand up against you all the days of your life. As I was with Moses, so I will be with you; I will never leave you nor forsake you.   Dt 7:24; 34:5; Ezr 4:20

6"Be strong and courageous, because you will lead these

---

[a]4 That is, the Mediterranean

people to inherit the land I swore to their forefathers to give them. ⁷Be strong and very courageous. Be careful to obey all the law my servant Moses gave you; do not turn from it to the right or to the left, that you may be successful wherever you go. ⁸Do not let this Book of the Law depart from your mouth; meditate on it day and night, so that you may be careful to do everything written in it. Then you will be prosperous and successful. ⁹Have I not commanded you? Be strong and courageous. Do not be terrified; do not be discouraged, for the LORD your God will be with you wherever you go." 2Sa 2:7

¹⁰So Joshua ordered the officers of the people: ¹¹"Go through the camp and tell the people, 'Get your supplies ready. Three days from now you will cross the Jordan here to go in and take possession of the land the LORD your God is giving you for your own.'" Jos 3:2

¹²But to the Reubenites, the Gadites and the half-tribe of Manasseh, Joshua said, ¹³"Remember the command that Moses the servant of the LORD gave you: 'The LORD your God is giving you rest and has granted you this land.' ¹⁴Your wives, your children and your livestock may stay in the land that Moses gave you east of the Jordan, but all your fighting men, fully armed, must cross over ahead of your brothers. You are to help your brothers ¹⁵until the LORD gives them rest, as he has done for you, and until they too have taken possession of the land that the LORD your God is giving them. After that, you may go back and occupy your own land, which Moses the servant of the LORD gave you east of the Jordan toward the sunrise." Nu 32:33; Jos 22:1-4

¹⁶Then they answered Joshua, "Whatever you have commanded us we will do, and wherever you send us we will go. ¹⁷Just as we fully obeyed Moses, so we will obey you. Only may the LORD your God be with you as he was with Moses. ¹⁸Whoever rebels against your word and does not obey your words, whatever you may command them, will be put to death. Only be strong and courageous!" Nu 27:20

Rahab and the Spies

2 Then Joshua son of Nun secretly sent two spies from Shittim. "Go, look over the land," he said, "especially Jericho." So they went and entered the house of a prostitute*a* named Rahab and stayed there. ²The king of Jericho was told, "Look! Some of the Israelites have come here tonight to spy out the land." ³So the king of Jericho sent this message to Rahab: "Bring out the men who came to you and entered your

---

*a*1 Or possibly *an innkeeper*

house, because they have come to spy out the whole land."

⁴But the woman had taken the two men and hidden them. She said, "Yes, the men came to me, but I did not know where they had come from. ⁵At dusk, when it was time to close the city gate, the men left. I don't know which way they went. Go after them quickly. You may catch up with them." ⁶(But she had taken them up to the roof and hidden them under the stalks of flax she had laid out on the roof.) ⁷So the men set out in pursuit of the spies on the road that leads to the fords of the Jordan, and as soon as the pursuers had gone out, the gate was shut.   Nu 22:1; Jos 6:22

⁸Before the spies lay down for the night, she went up on the roof ⁹and said to them, "I know that the LORD has given this land to you and that a great fear of you has fallen on us, so that all who live in this country are melting in fear because of you. ¹⁰We have heard how the LORD dried up the water of the Red Sea*a* for you when you came out of Egypt, and what you did to Sihon and Og, the two kings of the Amorites east of the Jordan, whom you completely destroyed.*b* ¹¹When we heard of it, our hearts melted and everyone's courage failed because of you, for the LORD your God is God in heaven above and on the earth below. ¹²Now then, please swear to me by the LORD that you will show kindness to my family, because I have shown kindness to you. Give me a sure sign ¹³that you will spare the lives of my father and mother, my brothers and sisters, and all who belong to them, and that you will save us from death."

¹⁴"Our lives for your lives!" the men assured her. "If you don't tell what we are doing, we will treat you kindly and faithfully when the LORD gives us the land."   Jdg 1:24; 1Ki 20:39

¹⁵So she let them down by a rope through the window, for the house she lived in was part of the city wall. ¹⁶Now she had said to them, "Go to the hills so the pursuers will not find you. Hide yourselves there three days until they return, and then go on your way."   Jer 38:6

¹⁷The men said to her, "This oath you made us swear will not be binding on us ¹⁸unless, when we enter the land, you have tied this scarlet cord in the window through which you let us down, and unless you have brought your father and mother, your brothers and all your family into your house. ¹⁹If anyone goes outside your house into the street, his blood will be on his own head; we will not be responsible. As for anyone who is in the house with you, his blood will be on our head if a hand is

---

a10 Hebrew *Yam Suph*; that is, Sea of Reeds   *b10* The Hebrew term refers to the irrevocable giving over of things or persons to the LORD, often by totally destroying them.

laid on him. ²⁰But if you tell what we are doing, we will be released from the oath you made us swear." Ge 24:8; Mt 27:25

²¹"Agreed," she replied. "Let it be as you say." So she sent them away and they departed. And she tied the scarlet cord in the window.

²²When they left, they went into the hills and stayed there three days, until the pursuers had searched all along the road and returned without finding them. ²³Then the two men started back. They went down out of the hills, forded the river and came to Joshua son of Nun and told him everything that had happened to them. ²⁴They said to Joshua, "The LORD has surely given the whole land into our hands; all the people are melting in fear because of us."

Crossing the Jordan

3 Early in the morning Joshua and all the Israelites set out from Shittim and went to the Jordan, where they camped before crossing over. ²After three days the officers went throughout the camp, ³giving orders to the people: "When you see the ark of the covenant of the LORD your God, and the priests, who are Levites, carrying it, you are to move out from your positions and follow it. ⁴Then you will know which way to go, since you have never been this way

before. But keep a distance of about a thousand yards[a] between you and the ark; do not go near it." Nu 35:5; Jos 2:1

⁵Joshua told the people, "Consecrate yourselves, for tomorrow the LORD will do amazing things among you." Ex 29:1

⁶Joshua said to the priests, "Take up the ark of the covenant and pass on ahead of the people." So they took it up and went ahead of them.

⁷And the LORD said to Joshua, "Today I will begin to exalt you in the eyes of all Israel, so they may know that I am with you as I was with Moses. ⁸Tell the priests who carry the ark of the covenant: 'When you reach the edge of the Jordan's waters, go and stand in the river.' " Jos 1:5; 4:14; 1Ch 29:25

⁹Joshua said to the Israelites, "Come here and listen to the words of the LORD your God. ¹⁰This is how you will know that the living God is among you and that he will certainly drive out before you the Canaanites, Hittites, Hivites, Perizzites, Girgashites, Amorites and Jebusites. ¹¹See, the ark of the covenant of the Lord of all the earth will go into the Jordan ahead of you. ¹²Now then, choose twelve men from the tribes of Israel, one from each tribe. ¹³And as soon as the priests who carry the ark of the LORD—the Lord of all the earth—set foot in the Jordan, its waters flowing down-

---

ᵃ4 Hebrew *about two thousand cubits* (about 900 meters)

stream will be cut off and stand up in a heap." Jos 4:7

¹⁴So when the people broke camp to cross the Jordan, the priests carrying the ark of the covenant went ahead of them. ¹⁵Now the Jordan is at flood stage all during harvest. Yet as soon as the priests who carried the ark reached the Jordan and their feet touched the water's edge, ¹⁶the water from upstream stopped flowing. It piled up in a heap a great distance away, at a town called Adam in the vicinity of Zarethan, while the water flowing down to the Sea of the Arabah (the Salt Sea*a*) was completely cut off. So the people crossed over opposite Jericho. ¹⁷The priests who carried the ark of the covenant of the LORD stood firm on dry ground in the middle of the Jordan, while all Israel passed by until the whole nation had completed the crossing on dry ground. Ex 14:22; Ps 132:8

4 When the whole nation had finished crossing the Jordan, the LORD said to Joshua, ²"Choose twelve men from among the people, one from each tribe, ³and tell them to take up twelve stones from the middle of the Jordan from right where the priests stood and to carry them over with you and put them down at the place where you stay tonight." Dt 27:2

⁴So Joshua called together the twelve men he had appointed from the Israelites, one from each tribe, ⁵and said to them, "Go over before the ark of the LORD your God into the middle of the Jordan. Each of you is to take up a stone on his shoulder, according to the number of the tribes of the Israelites, ⁶to serve as a sign among you. In the future, when your children ask you, 'What do these stones mean?' ⁷tell them that the flow of the Jordan was cut off before the ark of the covenant of the LORD. When it crossed the Jordan, the waters of the Jordan were cut off. These stones are to be a memorial to the people of Israel forever." Ex 12:26; Jos 2:12

⁸So the Israelites did as Joshua commanded them. They took twelve stones from the middle of the Jordan, according to the number of the tribes of the Israelites, as the LORD had told Joshua; and they carried them over with them to their camp, where they put them down. ⁹Joshua set up the twelve stones that had been*b* in the middle of the Jordan at the spot where the priests who carried the ark of the covenant had stood. And they are there to this day. Ex 28:21; 1Sa 7:12

¹⁰Now the priests who carried the ark remained standing in the middle of the Jordan until everything the LORD had commanded Joshua was done by the people, just as Moses had directed Joshua. The people

---

*a*16 That is, the Dead Sea   *b*9 Or *Joshua also set up twelve stones*

hurried over, [11]and as soon as all of them had crossed, the ark of the LORD and the priests came to the other side while the people watched. [12]The men of Reuben, Gad and the half-tribe of Manasseh crossed over, armed, in front of the Israelites, as Moses had directed them. [13]About forty thousand armed for battle crossed over before the LORD to the plains of Jericho for war.   Ex 13:18; Nu 32:27

[14]That day the LORD exalted Joshua in the sight of all Israel; and they revered him all the days of his life, just as they had revered Moses.   Jos 3:7

[15]Then the LORD said to Joshua, [16]"Command the priests carrying the ark of the Testimony to come up out of the Jordan."   Ex 25:22

[17]So Joshua commanded the priests, "Come up out of the Jordan."

[18]And the priests came up out of the river carrying the ark of the covenant of the LORD. No sooner had they set their feet on the dry ground than the waters of the Jordan returned to their place and ran at flood stage as before.   Ex 14:27; Jos 3:15

[19]On the tenth day of the first month the people went up from the Jordan and camped at Gilgal on the eastern border of Jericho. [20]And Joshua set up at Gilgal the twelve stones they had taken out of the Jordan. [21]He said to the Israelites, "In the future when your descendants ask their fathers, 'What do these stones mean?' [22]tell them, 'Israel crossed the Jordan on dry ground.' [23]For the LORD your God dried up the Jordan before you until you had crossed over. The LORD your God did to the Jordan just what he had done to the Red Sea[a] when he dried it up before us until we had crossed over. [24]He did this so that all the peoples of the earth might know that the hand of the LORD is powerful and so that you might always fear the LORD your God."   Dt 11:30; Ps 89:13

Circumcision at Gilgal

5 Now when all the Amorite kings west of the Jordan and all the Canaanite kings along the coast heard how the LORD had dried up the Jordan before the Israelites until we had crossed over, their hearts melted and they no longer had the courage to face the Israelites.

[2]At that time the LORD said to Joshua, "Make flint knives and circumcise the Israelites again." [3]So Joshua made flint knives and circumcised the Israelites at Gibeath Haaraloth.[b]   Ex 4:25

[4]Now this is why he did so: All those who came out of Egypt—all the men of military age—died in the desert on the way after leaving Egypt. [5]All the

---

[a]23 Hebrew Yam Suph; that is, Sea of Reeds foreskins.   [b]3 Gibeath Haaraloth means hill of

people that came out had been circumcised, but all the people born in the desert during the journey from Egypt had not. 6The Israelites had moved about in the desert forty years until all the men who were of military age when they left Egypt had died, since they had not obeyed the LORD. For the LORD had sworn to them that they would not see the land that he had solemnly promised their fathers to give us, a land flowing with milk and honey. 7So he raised up their sons in their place, and these were the ones Joshua circumcised. They were still uncircumcised because they had not been circumcised on the way. 8And after the whole nation had been circumcised, they remained where they were in camp until they were healed.

9Then the LORD said to Joshua, "Today I have rolled away the reproach of Egypt from you." So the place has been called Gilgal*a* to this day.

10On the evening of the fourteenth day of the month, while camped at Gilgal on the plains of Jericho, the Israelites celebrated the Passover. 11The day after the Passover, that very day, they ate some of the produce of the land: unleavened bread and roasted grain. 12The manna stopped the day after*b* they ate this food from the land; there was no longer any manna for the Israelites, but that year they ate of the produce of Canaan.   Ex 12:6; 16:35; Lev 23:14

The Fall of Jericho

13Now when Joshua was near Jericho, he looked up and saw a man standing in front of him with a drawn sword in his hand. Joshua went up to him and asked, "Are you for us or for our enemies?"   Ge 18:2

14"Neither," he replied, "but as commander of the army of the LORD I have now come." Then Joshua fell facedown to the ground in reverence, and asked him, "What message does my Lord*c* have for his servant?"   Ge 17:3; 19:1

15The commander of the LORD's army replied, "Take off your sandals, for the place where you are standing is holy." And Joshua did so.

6 Now Jericho was tightly shut up because of the Israelites. No one went out and no one came in.

2Then the LORD said to Joshua, "See, I have delivered Jericho into your hands, along with its king and its fighting men. 3March around the city once with all the armed men. Do this for six days. 4Have seven priests carry trumpets of rams' horns in front of the ark. On the seventh day, march around the city seven times, with the priests blowing the trumpets. 5When you hear them sound a long blast on the

---

a9 Gilgal sounds like the Hebrew for *roll.*   *b12* Or *the day*   *c14* Or *lord*

trumpets, have all the people give a loud shout; then the wall of the city will collapse and the people will go up, every man straight in." Lev 25:9; Jos 24:11

6So Joshua son of Nun called the priests and said to them, "Take up the ark of the covenant of the LORD and have seven priests carry trumpets in front of it." 7And he ordered the people, "Advance! March around the city, with the armed guard going ahead of the ark of the LORD." Ex 14:15; 1Sa 4:3

8When Joshua had spoken to the people, the seven priests carrying the seven trumpets before the LORD went forward, blowing their trumpets, and the ark of the LORD's covenant followed them. 9The armed guard marched ahead of the priests who blew the trumpets, and the rear guard followed the ark. All this time the trumpets were sounding. 10But Joshua had commanded the people, "Do not give a war cry, do not raise your voices, do not say a word until the day I tell you to shout. Then shout!" 11So he had the ark of the LORD carried around the city, circling it once. Then the people returned to camp and spent the night there.

12Joshua got up early the next morning and the priests took up the ark of the LORD. 13The seven priests carrying the seven trumpets went forward, marching before the ark of the LORD and blowing the trumpets. The armed men went ahead of them and the rear guard followed the ark of the LORD, while the trumpets kept sounding. 14So on the second day they marched around the city once and returned to the camp. They did this for six days. Jos 6:4

15On the seventh day, they got up at daybreak and marched around the city seven times in the same manner, except that on that day they circled the city seven times. 16The seventh time around, when the priests sounded the trumpet blast, Joshua commanded the people, "Shout! For the LORD has given you the city! 17The city and all that is in it are to be devoteda to the LORD. Only Rahab the prostituteb and all who are with her in her house shall be spared, because she hid the spies we sent. 18But keep away from the devoted things, so that you will not bring about your own destruction by taking any of them. Otherwise you will make the camp of Israel liable to destruction and bring trouble on it. 19All the silver and gold and the articles of bronze and iron are sacred to the LORD and must go into his treasury." Nu 31:22; 1Ki 18:44

20When the trumpets sounded, the people shouted, and at the sound of the trumpet, when the people gave a loud shout,

---

a17 The Hebrew term refers to the irrevocable giving over of things or persons to the LORD, often by totally destroying them; also in verses 18 and 21.   b17 Or possibly innkeeper; also in verses 22 and 25

the wall collapsed; so every man charged straight in, and they took the city. 21They devoted the city to the LORD and destroyed with the sword every living thing in it—men and women, young and old, cattle, sheep and donkeys. Heb 11:30

22Joshua said to the two men who had spied out the land, "Go into the prostitute's house and bring her out and all who belong to her, in accordance with your oath to her." 23So the young men who had done the spying went in and brought out Rahab, her father and mother and brothers and all who belonged to her. They brought out her entire family and put them in a place outside the camp of Israel. Jos 2:14; Heb 11:31

24Then they burned the whole city and everything in it, but they put the silver and gold and the articles of bronze and iron into the treasury of the LORD's house. 25But Joshua spared Rahab the prostitute, with her family and all who belonged to her, because she hid the men Joshua had sent as spies to Jericho—and she lives among the Israelites to this day.

26At that time Joshua pronounced this solemn oath: "Cursed before the LORD is the man who undertakes to rebuild this city, Jericho: 1Sa 14:24

"At the cost of his firstborn
 son
will he lay its foundations;
at the cost of his youngest
 will he set up its gates."

27So the LORD was with Joshua, and his fame spread throughout the land. Jos 9:1

Achan's Sin

7 But the Israelites acted unfaithfully in regard to the devoted things *a*; Achan son of Carmi, the son of Zimri, *b* the son of Zerah, of the tribe of Judah, took some of them. So the LORD's anger burned against Israel. Nu 1:4; Jos 6:18

2Now Joshua sent men from Jericho to Ai, which is near Beth Aven to the east of Bethel, and told them, "Go up and spy out the region." So the men went up and spied out Ai. Jos 18:12

3When they returned to Joshua, they said, "Not all the people will have to go up against Ai. Send two or three thousand men to take it and do not weary all the people, for only a few men are there." 4So about three thousand men went up; but they were routed by the men of Ai, 5who killed about thirty-six of them. They chased the Israelites from the city gate as far as the stone quarries *c* and struck them down on the slopes. At this the hearts of the

a1 The Hebrew term refers to the irrevocable giving over of things or persons to the LORD, often by totally destroying them; also in verses 11, 12, 13 and 15. *b1* See Septuagint and 1 Chron. 2:6; Hebrew *Zabdi*; also in verses 17 and 18. *c5* Or *as far as Shebarim*

people melted and became like water. _{Lev 26:17; Nu 2:10}

6Then Joshua tore his clothes and fell facedown to the ground before the ark of the LORD, remaining there till evening. The elders of Israel did the same, and sprinkled dust on their heads. 7And Joshua said, "Ah, Sovereign LORD, why did you ever bring this people across the Jordan to deliver us into the hands of the Amorites to destroy us? If only we had been content to stay on the other side of the Jordan! 8O Lord, what can I say, now that Israel has been routed by its enemies? 9The Canaanites and the other people of the country will hear about this and they will surround us and wipe out our name from the earth. What then will you do for your own great name?" _{Rev 18:19}

10The LORD said to Joshua, "Stand up! What are you doing down on your face? 11Israel has sinned; they have violated my covenant, which I commanded them to keep. They have taken some of the devoted things; they have stolen, they have lied, they have put them with their own possessions. 12That is why the Israelites cannot stand against their enemies; they turn their backs and run because they have been made liable to destruction. I will not be with you anymore unless you destroy whatever among you is devoted to destruction. _{Dt 29:27}

13"Go, consecrate the people. Tell them, 'Consecrate yourselves in preparation for tomorrow; for this is what the LORD, the God of Israel, says: That which is devoted is among you, O Israel. You cannot stand against your enemies until you remove it. _{Lev 11:44}

14" 'In the morning, present yourselves tribe by tribe. The tribe that the LORD takes shall come forward clan by clan; the clan that the LORD takes shall come forward family by family; and the family that the LORD takes shall come forward man by man. 15He who is caught with the devoted things shall be destroyed by fire, along with all that belongs to him. He has violated the covenant of the LORD and has done a disgraceful thing in Israel!' " _{1Sa 10:19}

16Early the next morning Joshua had Israel come forward by tribes, and Judah was taken. 17The clans of Judah came forward, and he took the Zerahites. He had the clan of the Zerahites come forward by families, and Zimri was taken. 18Joshua had his family come forward man by man, and Achan son of Carmi, the son of Zimri, the son of Zerah, of the tribe of Judah, was taken. _{Nu 26:20}

19Then Joshua said to Achan, "My son, give glory to the LORD,*a* the God of Israel, and give him the praise.*b* Tell me

_{a19} A solemn charge to tell the truth   _{b19} Or *and confess to him*

what you have done; do not hide it from me."   Jer 13:16

20Achan replied, "It is true! I have sinned against the LORD, the God of Israel. This is what I have done: 21When I saw in the plunder a beautiful robe from Babylonia,*a* two hundred shekels*b* of silver and a wedge of gold weighing fifty shekels,*c* I coveted them and took them. They are hidden in the ground inside my tent, with the silver underneath."   Ge 34:29; Eph 5:5

22So Joshua sent messengers, and they ran to the tent, and there it was, hidden in his tent, with the silver underneath. 23They took the things from the tent, brought them to Joshua and all the Israelites and spread them out before the LORD.

24Then Joshua, together with all Israel, took Achan son of Zerah, the silver, the robe, the gold wedge, his sons and daughters, his cattle, donkeys and sheep, his tent and all that he had, to the Valley of Achor. 25Joshua said, "Why have you brought this trouble on us? The LORD will bring trouble on you today."   Jos 15:7; Hos 2:15

Then all Israel stoned him, and after they had stoned the rest, they burned them. 26Over Achan they heaped up a large pile of rocks, which remains to this day. Then the LORD turned from his fierce anger. Therefore that place has been called the Valley of Achor*d* ever since.

Ai Destroyed

8 Then the LORD said to Joshua, "Do not be afraid; do not be discouraged. Take the whole army with you, and go up and attack Ai. For I have delivered into your hands the king of Ai, his people, his city and his land. 2You shall do to Ai and its king as you did to Jericho and its king, except that you may carry off their plunder and livestock for yourselves. Set an ambush behind the city."   Dt 1:21

3So Joshua and the whole army moved out to attack Ai. He chose thirty thousand of his best fighting men and sent them out at night 4with these orders: "Listen carefully. You are to set an ambush behind the city. Don't go very far from it. All of you be on the alert. 5I and all those with me will advance on the city, and when the men come out against us, as they did before, we will flee from them. 6They will pursue us until we have lured them away from the city, for they will say, 'They are running away from us as they did before.' So when we flee from them, 7you are to rise up from ambush and take the city. The LORD your God will give it into your hand. 8When you have taken the city, set it on fire. Do what the LORD has com-

---

*a*21 Hebrew *Shinar*   *b*21 That is, about 5 pounds (about 2.3 kilograms)   *c*21 That is, about 1 1/4 pounds (about 0.6 kilogram)   *d*26 *Achor* means *trouble*.

manded. See to it; you have my orders." Jdg 7:7; 20:29-38

⁹Then Joshua sent them off, and they went to the place of ambush and lay in wait between Bethel and Ai, to the west of Ai—but Joshua spent that night with the people. 2Ch 13:13

¹⁰Early the next morning Joshua mustered his men, and he and the leaders of Israel marched before them to Ai. ¹¹The entire force that was with him marched up and approached the city and arrived in front of it. They set up camp north of Ai, with the valley between them and the city. ¹²Joshua had taken about five thousand men and set them in ambush between Bethel and Ai, to the west of the city. ¹³They had the soldiers take up their positions—all those in the camp to the north of the city and the ambush to the west of it. That night Joshua went into the valley. Ge 22:3; Jos 7:6

¹⁴When the king of Ai saw this, he and all the men of the city hurried out early in the morning to meet Israel in battle at a certain place overlooking the Arabah. But he did not know that an ambush had been set against him behind the city. ¹⁵Joshua and all Israel let themselves be driven back before them, and they fled toward the desert. ¹⁶All the men of Ai were called to pursue them, and they pursued Joshua and were lured away from the city. ¹⁷Not a man remained in Ai or Bethel who

did not go after Israel. They left the city open and went in pursuit of Israel. Jos 15:61; Jdg 20:34

¹⁸Then the LORD said to Joshua, "Hold out toward Ai the javelin that is in your hand, for into your hand I will deliver the city." So Joshua held out his javelin toward Ai. ¹⁹As soon as he did this, the men in the ambush rose quickly from their position and rushed forward. They entered the city and captured it and quickly set it on fire.

²⁰The men of Ai looked back and saw the smoke of the city rising against the sky, but they had no chance to escape in any direction, for the Israelites who had been fleeing toward the desert had turned back against their pursuers. ²¹For when Joshua and all Israel saw that the ambush had taken the city and that smoke was going up from the city, they turned around and attacked the men of Ai. ²²The men of the ambush also came out of the city against them, so that they were caught in the middle, with Israelites on both sides. Israel cut them down, leaving them neither survivors nor fugitives. ²³But they took the king of Ai alive and brought him to Joshua.

²⁴When Israel had finished killing all the men of Ai in the fields and in the desert where they had chased them, and when every one of them had been put to the sword, all the Israelites returned to Ai and killed those who were in it.

25Twelve thousand men and women fell that day—all the people of Ai. 26For Joshua did not draw back the hand that held out his javelin until he had destroyed[a] all who lived in Ai. 27But Israel did carry off for themselves the livestock and plunder of this city, as the LORD had instructed Joshua. Dt 20:16-18

28So Joshua burned Ai and made it a permanent heap of ruins, a desolate place to this day. 29He hung the king of Ai on a tree and left him there until evening. At sunset, Joshua ordered them to take his body from the tree and throw it down at the entrance of the city gate. And they raised a large pile of rocks over it, which remains to this day. Dt 13:16; Jn 19:31

The Covenant Renewed at Mount Ebal

30Then Joshua built on Mount Ebal an altar to the LORD, the God of Israel, 31as Moses the servant of the LORD had commanded the Israelites. He built it according to what is written in the Book of the Law of Moses— an altar of uncut stones, on which no iron tool had been used. On it they offered to the LORD burnt offerings and sacrificed fellowship offerings.[b] 32There, in the presence of the Israelites, Joshua copied on stones the law of Moses, which he had written. 33All Israel, aliens and citizens alike, with their elders, officials and judges, were standing on both sides of the ark of the covenant of the LORD, facing those who carried it—the priests, who were Levites. Half of the people stood in front of Mount Gerizim and half of them in front of Mount Ebal, as Moses the servant of the LORD had formerly commanded when he gave instructions to bless the people of Israel. Dt 11:29

34Afterward, Joshua read all the words of the law—the blessings and the curses—just as it is written in the Book of the Law. 35There was not a word of all that Moses had commanded that Joshua did not read to the whole assembly of Israel, including the women and children, and the aliens who lived among them. Ex 12:38; Dt 31:11

The Gibeonite Deception

9 Now when all the kings west of the Jordan heard about these things—those in the hill country, in the western foothills, and along the entire coast of the Great Sea[c] as far as Lebanon (the kings of the Hittites, Amorites, Canaanites, Perizzites, Hivites and Jebusites)— 2they came together to make war against Joshua and Israel.

3However, when the people of Gibeon heard what Joshua

---

[a]26 The Hebrew term refers to the irrevocable giving over of things or persons to the LORD, often by totally destroying them.   [b]31 Traditionally peace offerings   [c]1 That is, the Mediterranean

had done to Jericho and Ai, [4]they resorted to a ruse: They went as a delegation whose donkeys were loaded[a] with worn-out sacks and old wineskins, cracked and mended. [5]The men put worn and patched sandals on their feet and wore old clothes. All the bread of their food supply was dry and moldy. [6]Then they went to Joshua in the camp at Gilgal and said to him and the men of Israel, "We have come from a distant country; make a treaty with us." Ge 26:28; Jos 10:10

[7]The men of Israel said to the Hivites, "But perhaps you live near us. How then can we make a treaty with you?"

[8]"We are your servants," they said to Joshua. 2Ki 10:5

But Joshua asked, "Who are you and where do you come from?"

[9]They answered: "Your servants have come from a very distant country because of the fame of the LORD your God. For we have heard reports of him: all that he did in Egypt, [10]and all that he did to the two kings of the Amorites east of the Jordan—Sihon king of Heshbon, and Og king of Bashan, who reigned in Ashtaroth. [11]And our elders and all those living in our country said to us, 'Take provisions for your journey; go and meet them and say to them, "We are your servants; make a

treaty with us." ' [12]This bread of ours was warm when we packed it at home on the day we left to come to you. But now see how dry and moldy it is. [13]And these wineskins that we filled were new, but see how cracked they are. And our clothes and sandals are worn out by the very long journey." Dt 20:15

[14]The men of Israel sampled their provisions but did not inquire of the LORD. [15]Then Joshua made a treaty of peace with them to let them live, and the leaders of the assembly ratified it by oath. Nu 27:21; Ps 106:34

[16]Three days after they made the treaty with the Gibeonites, the Israelites heard that they were neighbors, living near them. [17]So the Israelites set out and on the third day came to their cities: Gibeon, Kephirah, Beeroth and Kiriath Jearim. [18]But the Israelites did not attack them, because the leaders of the assembly had sworn an oath to them by the LORD, the God of Israel. Jos 18:25; Ps 15:4

The whole assembly grumbled against the leaders, [19]but all the leaders answered, "We have given them our oath by the LORD, the God of Israel, and we cannot touch them now. [20]This is what we will do to them: We will let them live, so that wrath will not fall on us for breaking the oath we swore to them." [21]They continued, "Let them

---

[a]4 Most Hebrew manuscripts; some Hebrew manuscripts, Vulgate and Syriac (see also Septuagint) *They prepared provisions and loaded their donkeys*

live, but let them be woodcutters and water carriers for the entire community." So the leaders' promise to them was kept.

²²Then Joshua summoned the Gibeonites and said, "Why did you deceive us by saying, 'We live a long way from you,' while actually you live near us? ²³You are now under a curse: You will never cease to serve as woodcutters and water carriers for the house of my God."   Ge 9:25

²⁴They answered Joshua, "Your servants were clearly told how the LORD your God had commanded his servant Moses to give you the whole land and to wipe out all its inhabitants from before you. So we feared for our lives because of you, and that is why we did this. ²⁵We are now in your hands. Do to us whatever seems good and right to you."   Dt 7:1; Jer 26:14

²⁶So Joshua saved them from the Israelites, and they did not kill them. ²⁷That day he made the Gibeonites woodcutters and water carriers for the community and for the altar of the LORD at the place the LORD would choose. And that is what they are to this day.   Ex 1:11; Dt 29:11

The Sun Stands Still

10 Now Adoni-Zedek king of Jerusalem heard that Joshua had taken Ai and totally destroyed[a] it, doing to Ai and its king as he had done to Jeri-

cho and its king, and that the people of Gibeon had made a treaty of peace with Israel and were living near them. ²He and his people were very much alarmed at this, because Gibeon was an important city, like one of the royal cities; it was larger than Ai, and all its men were good fighters. ³So Adoni-Zedek king of Jerusalem appealed to Hoham king of Hebron, Piram king of Jarmuth, Japhia king of Lachish and Debir king of Eglon. ⁴"Come up and help me attack Gibeon," he said, "because it has made peace with Joshua and the Israelites."   Jdg 1:7

⁵Then the five kings of the Amorites—the kings of Jerusalem, Hebron, Jarmuth, Lachish and Eglon—joined forces. They moved up with all their troops and took up positions against Gibeon and attacked it.   Nu 13:29

⁶The Gibeonites then sent word to Joshua in the camp at Gilgal: "Do not abandon your servants. Come up to us quickly and save us! Help us, because all the Amorite kings from the hill country have joined forces against us."   Dt 11:30; Jos 5:10

⁷So Joshua marched up from Gilgal with his entire army, including all the best fighting men. ⁸The LORD said to Joshua, "Do not be afraid of them; I have given them into your hand. Not one of them will be able to withstand you."   Jos 8:1

---

a1 The Hebrew term refers to the irrevocable giving over of things or persons to the LORD, often by totally destroying them; also in verses 28, 35, 37, 39 and 40.

⁹After an all-night march from Gilgal, Joshua took them by surprise. ¹⁰The Lord threw them into confusion before Israel, who defeated them in a great victory at Gibeon. Israel pursued them along the road going up to Beth Horon and cut them down all the way to Azekah and Makkedah. ¹¹As they fled before Israel on the road down from Beth Horon to Azekah, the Lord hurled large hailstones down on them from the sky, and more of them died from the hailstones than were killed by the swords of the Israelites.   Jdg 5:20; 1Sa 13:18

¹²On the day the Lord gave the Amorites over to Israel, Joshua said to the Lord in the presence of Israel: Am 2:9

"O sun, stand still over
    Gibeon,
O moon, over the Valley of
    Aijalon."   Jdg 1:35; 1Sa 14:31
¹³So the sun stood still,
    and the moon stopped,
till the nation avenged itself
    on*a* its enemies,

as it is written in the Book of Jashar.   2Sa 1:18
The sun stopped in the middle of the sky and delayed going down about a full day. ¹⁴There has never been a day like it before or since, a day when the Lord listened to a man. Surely the Lord was fighting for Israel!

¹⁵Then Joshua returned with all Israel to the camp at Gilgal.

Five Amorite Kings Killed

¹⁶Now the five kings had fled and hidden in the cave at Makkedah. ¹⁷When Joshua was told that the five kings had been found hiding in the cave at Makkedah, ¹⁸he said, "Roll large rocks up to the mouth of the cave, and post some men there to guard it. ¹⁹But don't stop! Pursue your enemies, attack them from the rear and don't let them reach their cities, for the Lord your God has given them into your hand."Ps 68:12

²⁰So Joshua and the Israelites destroyed them completely—almost to a man—but the few who were left reached their fortified cities. ²¹The whole army then returned safely to Joshua in the camp at Makkedah, and no one uttered a word against the Israelites.

²²Joshua said, "Open the mouth of the cave and bring those five kings out to me." ²³So they brought the five kings out of the cave—the kings of Jerusalem, Hebron, Jarmuth, Lachish and Eglon. ²⁴When they had brought these kings to Joshua, he summoned all the men of Israel and said to the army commanders who had come with him, "Come here and put your feet on the necks of these kings." So they came forward and placed their feet on their necks.   Dt 7:24; Isa 51:23

²⁵Joshua said to them, "Do not be afraid; do not be dis-

---

*a*13 Or *nation triumphed over*

couraged. Be strong and courageous. This is what the LORD will do to all the enemies you are going to fight." ²⁶Then Joshua struck and killed the kings and hung them on five trees, and they were left hanging on the trees until evening. ²⁷At sunset Joshua gave the order and they took them down from the trees and threw them into the cave where they had been hiding. At the mouth of the cave they placed large rocks, which are there to this day.

²⁸That day Joshua took Makkedah. He put the city and its king to the sword and totally destroyed everyone in it. He left no survivors. And he did to the king of Makkedah as he had done to the king of Jericho.

Southern Cities Conquered

²⁹Then Joshua and all Israel with him moved on from Makkedah to Libnah and attacked it. ³⁰The LORD also gave that city and its king into Israel's hand. The city and everyone in it Joshua put to the sword. He left no survivors there. And he did to its king as he had done to the king of Jericho. Nu 33:20

³¹Then Joshua and all Israel with him moved on from Libnah to Lachish; he took up positions against it and attacked it. ³²The LORD handed Lachish over to Israel, and Joshua took it on the second day. The city and everyone in it he put to the sword, just as he had done to Libnah. ³³Meanwhile, Horam king of Gezer had come up to help Lachish, but Joshua defeated him and his army—until no survivors were left. 2Ki 14:19

³⁴Then Joshua and all Israel with him moved on from Lachish to Eglon; they took up positions against it and attacked it. ³⁵They captured it that same day and put it to the sword and totally destroyed everyone in it, just as they had done to Lachish.

³⁶Then Joshua and all Israel with him went up from Eglon to Hebron and attacked it. ³⁷They took the city and put it to the sword, together with its king, its villages and everyone in it. They left no survivors. Just as at Eglon, they totally destroyed it and everyone in it. Jdg 1:10

³⁸Then Joshua and all Israel with him turned around and attacked Debir. ³⁹They took the city, its king and its villages, and put them to the sword. Everyone in it they totally destroyed. They left no survivors. They did to Debir and its king as they had done to Libnah and its king and to Hebron. Jdg 1:11

⁴⁰So Joshua subdued the whole region, including the hill country, the Negev, the western foothills and the mountain slopes, together with all their kings. He left no survivors. He totally destroyed all who breathed, just as the LORD, the God of Israel, had commanded. ⁴¹Joshua subdued them from Kadesh Barnea to Gaza and from the whole region of Go-

shen to Gibeon. ⁴²All these kings and their lands Joshua conquered in one campaign, because the LORD, the God of Israel, fought for Israel.   Dt 20:16-17

⁴³Then Joshua returned with all Israel to the camp at Gilgal.

Northern Kings Defeated

11 When Jabin king of Hazor heard of this, he sent word to Jobab king of Madon, to the kings of Shimron and Acshaph, ²and to the northern kings who were in the mountains, in the Arabah south of Kinnereth, in the western foothills and in Naphoth Dorᵃ on the west; ³to the Canaanites in the east and west; to the Amorites, Hittites, Perizzites and Jebusites in the hill country; and to the Hivites below Hermon in the region of Mizpah. ⁴They came out with all their troops and a large number of horses and chariots—a huge army, as numerous as the sand on the seashore. ⁵All these kings joined forces and made camp together at the Waters of Merom, to fight against Israel.

⁶The LORD said to Joshua, "Do not be afraid of them, because by this time tomorrow I will hand all of them over to Israel, slain. You are to hamstring their horses and burn their chariots."   Ge 49:6; 2Sa 8:4

⁷So Joshua and his whole army came against them suddenly at the Waters of Merom and attacked them, ⁸and the LORD gave them into the hand of Israel. They defeated them and pursued them all the way to Greater Sidon, to Misrephoth Maim, and to the Valley of Mizpah on the east, until no survivors were left. ⁹Joshua did to them as the LORD had directed: He hamstrung their horses and burned their chariots.   Jos 13:6

¹⁰At that time Joshua turned back and captured Hazor and put its king to the sword. (Hazor had been the head of all these kingdoms.) ¹¹Everyone in it they put to the sword. They totally destroyedᵇ them, not sparing anything that breathed, and he burned up Hazor itself.

¹²Joshua took all these royal cities and their kings and put them to the sword. He totally destroyed them, as Moses the servant of the LORD had commanded. ¹³Yet Israel did not burn any of the cities built on their mounds—except Hazor, which Joshua burned. ¹⁴The Israelites carried off for themselves all the plunder and livestock of these cities, but all the people they put to the sword until they completely destroyed them, not sparing anyone that breathed. ¹⁵As the LORD commanded his servant Moses, so Moses commanded Joshua, and

---

ᵃ2 Or *in the heights of Dor*   ᵇ11 The Hebrew term refers to the irrevocable giving over of things or persons to the LORD, often by totally destroying them; also in verses 12, 20 and 21.

Joshua did it; he left nothing undone of all that the LORD commanded Moses. Nu 33:50-52

16So Joshua took this entire land: the hill country, all the Negev, the whole region of Goshen, the western foothills, the Arabah and the mountains of Israel with their foothills, 17from Mount Halak, which rises toward Seir, to Baal Gad in the Valley of Lebanon below Mount Hermon. He captured all their kings and struck them down, putting them to death. 18Joshua waged war against all these kings for a long time. 19Except for the Hivites living in Gibeon, not one city made a treaty of peace with the Israelites, who took them all in battle. 20For it was the LORD himself who hardened their hearts to wage war against Israel, so that he might destroy them totally, exterminating them without mercy, as the LORD had commanded Moses. Dt 7:16; Jos 10:41

21At that time Joshua went and destroyed the Anakites from the hill country: from Hebron, Debir and Anab, from all the hill country of Judah, and from all the hill country of Israel. Joshua totally destroyed them and their towns. 22No Anakites were left in Israelite territory; only in Gaza, Gath and Ashdod did any survive. 23So Joshua took the entire land, just as the LORD had directed Moses, and he gave it as an inheritance to Israel according to their tribal divisions. Nu 13:33

Then the land had rest from war. Ex 33:14; Jos 14:15

List of Defeated Kings

12 These are the kings of the land whom the Israelites had defeated and whose territory they took over east of the Jordan, from the Arnon Gorge to Mount Hermon, including all the eastern side of the Arabah:

2Sihon king of the Amorites,
　who reigned in Heshbon.
He ruled from Aroer on the rim of the Arnon Gorge—from the middle of the gorge—to the Jabbok River, which is the border of the Ammonites. This included half of Gilead. 3He also ruled over the eastern Arabah from the Sea of Kinneretha to the Sea of the Arabah (the Salt Seab), to Beth Jeshimoth, and then southward below the slopes of Pisgah. Nu 21:20; Jdg 11:19

4And the territory of Og king of Bashan,
　one of the last of the Rephaites, who reigned in Ashtaroth and Edrei. 5He ruled over Mount Hermon, Salecah, all of Bashan to the border of the people of Geshur and Maacah, and half of Gilead to the border of Sihon king of Heshbon. Nu 21:21

6Moses, the servant of the

---

a3 That is, Galilee　　b3 That is, the Dead Sea

LORD, and the Israelites conquered them. And Moses the servant of the LORD gave their land to the Reubenites, the Gadites and the half-tribe of Manasseh to be their possession.

7These are the kings of the land that Joshua and the Israelites conquered on the west side of the Jordan, from Baal Gad in the Valley of Lebanon to Mount Halak, which rises toward Seir (their lands Joshua gave as an inheritance to the tribes of Israel according to their tribal divisions— 8the hill country, the western foothills, the Arabah, the mountain slopes, the desert and the Negev—the lands of the Hittites, Amorites, Canaanites, Perizzites, Hivites and Jebusites):   Jos 11:17; Ezr 9:1

9the king of Jericho   one
    the king of Ai (near
        Bethel)   one
10the king of Jerusalem   one
    the king of Hebron   one
11the king of Jarmuth   one
    the king of Lachish   one
12the king of Eglon   one
    the king of Gezer   one
13the king of Debir   one
    the king of Geder   one
14the king of Hormah   one
    the king of Arad   one
15the king of Libnah   one
    the king of Adullam   one
16the king of Makkedah   one
    the king of Bethel   one
17the king of Tappuah   one
    the king of Hepher   one
18the king of Aphek   one

the king of Lasharon   one
19the king of Madon   one
    the king of Hazor   one
20the king of Shimron
        Meron   one
    the king of Acshaph   one
21the king of Taanach   one
    the king of Megiddo   one
22the king of Kedesh   one
    the king of Jokneam in
        Carmel   one
23the king of Dor (in
        Naphoth Dora)   one
    the king of Goyim in
        Gilgal   one
24the king of Tirzah   one
thirty-one kings in all.   Ps 135:11

Land Still to Be Taken

13 When Joshua was old and well advanced in years, the LORD said to him, "You are very old, and there are still very large areas of land to be taken over.   Ge 24:1; Jos 14:10

2"This is the land that remains: all the regions of the Philistines and Geshurites: 3from the Shihor River on the east of Egypt to the territory of Ekron on the north, all of it counted as Canaanite (the territory of the five Philistine rulers in Gaza, Ashdod, Ashkelon, Gath and Ekron—that of the Avvites); 4from the south, all the land of the Canaanites, from Arah of the Sidonians as far as Aphek, the region of the Amorites, 5the area of the Gebalitesb; and all Leba-

---

a23 Or in the heights of Dor   b5 That is, the area of Byblos

non to the east, from Baal Gad below Mount Hermon to Lebo*a* Hamath. Jdg 3:3

6"As for all the inhabitants of the mountain regions from Lebanon to Misrephoth Maim, that is, all the Sidonians, I myself will drive them out before the Israelites. Be sure to allocate this land to Israel for an inheritance, as I have instructed you, 7and divide it as an inheritance among the nine tribes and half of the tribe of Manasseh." Jos 11:8

Division of the Land East of the Jordan

8The other half of Manasseh,*b* the Reubenites and the Gadites had received the inheritance that Moses had given them east of the Jordan, as he, the servant of the LORD, had assigned it to them. Jos 12:6; 18:7

9It extended from Aroer on the rim of the Arnon Gorge, and from the town in the middle of the gorge, and included the whole plateau of Medeba as far as Dibon, 10and all the towns of Sihon king of the Amorites, who ruled in Heshbon, out to the border of the Ammonites. 11It also included Gilead, the territory of the people of Geshur and Maacah, all of Mount Hermon and all Bashan as far as Salecah— 12that is, the whole kingdom of Og in Bashan,

who had reigned in Ashtaroth and Edrei and had survived as one of the last of the Rephaites. Moses had defeated them and taken over their land. 13But the Israelites did not drive out the people of Geshur and Maacah, so they continue to live among the Israelites to this day. Ge 14:5; Dt 2:36

14But to the tribe of Levi he gave no inheritance, since the offerings made by fire to the LORD, the God of Israel, are their inheritance, as he promised them. Dt 18:1-2; Jos 14:3

15This is what Moses had given to the tribe of Reuben, clan by clan:

16The territory from Aroer on the rim of the Arnon Gorge, and from the town in the middle of the gorge, and the whole plateau past Medeba 17to Heshbon and all its towns on the plateau, including Dibon, Bamoth Baal, Beth Baal Meon, 18Jahaz, Kedemoth, Mephaath, 19Kiriathaim, Sibmah, Zereth Shahar on the hill in the valley, 20Beth Peor, the slopes of Pisgah, and Beth Jeshimoth 21—all the towns on the plateau and the entire realm of Sihon king of the Amorites, who ruled at Heshbon. Moses had defeated him and the Midianite chiefs, Evi, Rekem, Zur,

---

*a*5 Or *to the entrance to*   *b*8 Hebrew *With it* (that is, with the other half of Manasseh)

Hur and Reba—princes allied with Sihon—who lived in that country. [22]In addition to those slain in battle, the Israelites had put to the sword Balaam son of Beor, who practiced divination. [23]The boundary of the Reubenites was the bank of the Jordan. These towns and their villages were the inheritance of the Reubenites, clan by clan. 1Sa 30:28

[24]This is what Moses had given to the tribe of Gad, clan by clan:

[25]The territory of Jazer, all the towns of Gilead and half the Ammonite country as far as Aroer, near Rabbah; [26]and from Heshbon to Ramath Mizpah and Betonim, and from Mahanaim to the territory of Debir; [27]and in the valley, Beth Haram, Beth Nimrah, Succoth and Zaphon with the rest of the realm of Sihon king of Heshbon (the east side of the Jordan, the territory up to the end of the Sea of Kinnereth[a]). [28]These towns and their villages were the inheritance of the Gadites, clan by clan. Nu 21:32

[29]This is what Moses had given to the half-tribe of Manasseh, that is, to half the family of the descendants of Manasseh, clan by clan:

[30]The territory extending from Mahanaim and including all of Bashan, the entire realm of Og king of Bashan—all the settlements of Jair in Bashan, sixty towns, [31]half of Gilead, and Ashtaroth and Edrei (the royal cities of Og in Bashan). This was for the descendants of Makir son of Manasseh— for half of the sons of Makir, clan by clan. Nu 32:41

[32]This is the inheritance Moses had given when he was in the plains of Moab across the Jordan east of Jericho. [33]But to the tribe of Levi, Moses had given no inheritance; the LORD, the God of Israel, is their inheritance, as he promised them.

Division of the Land West of the Jordan

14 Now these are the areas the Israelites received as an inheritance in the land of Canaan, which Eleazar the priest, Joshua son of Nun and the heads of the tribal clans of Israel allotted to them. [2]Their inheritances were assigned by lot to the nine-and-a-half tribes, as the LORD had commanded through Moses. [3]Moses had granted the two-and-a-half tribes their inheritance east of the Jordan but had not granted the Levites an inheritance among the rest, [4]for the sons of Joseph had become two tribes—Manasseh and

Ephraim. The Levites received no share of the land but only towns to live in, with pasturelands for their flocks and herds. [5]So the Israelites divided the land, just as the LORD had commanded Moses. Nu 34:13; Ps 16:6

Hebron Given to Caleb

[6]Now the men of Judah approached Joshua at Gilgal, and Caleb son of Jephunneh the Kenizzite said to him, "You know what the LORD said to Moses the man of God at Kadesh Barnea about you and me. [7]I was forty years old when Moses the servant of the LORD sent me from Kadesh Barnea to explore the land. And I brought him back a report according to my convictions, [8]but my brothers who went up with me made the hearts of the people melt with fear. I, however, followed the LORD my God wholeheartedly. [9]So on that day Moses swore to me, 'The land on which your feet have walked will be your inheritance and that of your children forever, because you have followed the LORD my God wholeheartedly.'[a] Nu 14:24; Dt 11:30

[10]"Now then, just as the LORD promised, he has kept me alive for forty-five years since the time he said this to Moses, while Israel moved about in the desert. So here I am today, eighty-five years old! [11]I am still as strong today as the day

Moses sent me out; I'm just as vigorous to go out to battle now as I was then. [12]Now give me this hill country that the LORD promised me that day. You yourself heard then that the Anakites were there and their cities were large and fortified, but, the LORD helping me, I will drive them out just as he said."

[13]Then Joshua blessed Caleb son of Jephunneh and gave him Hebron as his inheritance. [14]So Hebron has belonged to Caleb son of Jephunneh the Kenizzite ever since, because he followed the LORD, the God of Israel, wholeheartedly. [15](Hebron used to be called Kiriath Arba after Arba, who was the greatest man among the Anakites.)

Then the land had rest from war. Jdg 3:11; 1Ki 4:24

Allotment for Judah

15 The allotment for the tribe of Judah, clan by clan, extended down to the territory of Edom, to the Desert of Zin in the extreme south. Nu 34:3

[2]Their southern boundary started from the bay at the southern end of the Salt Sea,[b] [3]crossed south of Scorpion[c] Pass, continued on to Zin and went over to the south of Kadesh Barnea. Then it ran past Hezron up to Addar and curved around to Karka. [4]It then passed along to Azmon and joined the Wadi of Egypt,

---

[a]9 Deut. 1:36   [b]2 That is, the Dead Sea; also in verse 5   [c]3 Hebrew Akrabbim

ending at the sea. This is their[a] southern boundary.

5The eastern boundary is the Salt Sea as far as the mouth of the Jordan.

The northern boundary started from the bay of the sea at the mouth of the Jordan, 6went up to Beth Hoglah and continued north of Beth Arabah to the Stone of Bohan son of Reuben. 7The boundary then went up to Debir from the Valley of Achor and turned north to Gilgal, which faces the Pass of Adummim south of the gorge. It continued along to the waters of En Shemesh and came out at En Rogel. 8Then it ran up the Valley of Ben Hinnom along the southern slope of the Jebusite city (that is, Jerusalem). From there it climbed to the top of the hill west of the Hinnom Valley at the northern end of the Valley of Rephaim. 9From the hilltop the boundary headed toward the spring of the waters of Nephtoah, came out at the towns of Mount Ephron and went down toward Baalah (that is, Kiriath Jearim). 10Then it curved westward from Baalah to Mount Seir, ran along the northern slope of Mount Jearim (that is, Kesalon), continued down to

Beth Shemesh and crossed to Timnah. 11It went to the northern slope of Ekron, turned toward Shikkeron, passed along to Mount Baalah and reached Jabneel. The boundary ended at the sea. Dt 11:30; 2Ki 14:11

12The western boundary is the coastline of the Great Sea.[b]

These are the boundaries around the people of Judah by their clans. Nu 34:6

13In accordance with the LORD's command to him, Joshua gave to Caleb son of Jephunneh a portion in Judah—Kiriath Arba, that is, Hebron. (Arba was the forefather of Anak.) 14From Hebron Caleb drove out the three Anakites—Sheshai, Ahiman and Talmai—descendants of Anak. 15From there he marched against the people living in Debir (formerly called Kiriath Sepher). 16And Caleb said, "I will give my daughter Acsah in marriage to the man who attacks and captures Kiriath Sepher." 17Othniel son of Kenaz, Caleb's brother, took it; so Caleb gave his daughter Acsah to him in marriage. 1Sa 25:3

18One day when she came to Othniel, she urged him[c] to ask her father for a field. When she got off her donkey, Caleb asked her, "What can I do for you?"

---

a4 Hebrew your   b12 That is, the Mediterranean; also in verse 47   c18 Hebrew and some Septuagint manuscripts; other Septuagint manuscripts (see also note at Judges 1:14) Othniel, he urged her

¹⁹She replied, "Do me a special favor. Since you have given me land in the Negev, give me also springs of water." So Caleb gave her the upper and lower springs.   Jos 10:40

²⁰This is the inheritance of the tribe of Judah, clan by clan:

²¹The southernmost towns of the tribe of Judah in the Negev toward the boundary of Edom were:

Kabzeel, Eder, Jagur, ²²Kinah, Dimonah, Adadah, ²³Kedesh, Hazor, Ithnan, ²⁴Ziph, Telem, Bealoth, ²⁵Hazor Hadattah, Kerioth Hezron (that is, Hazor), ²⁶Amam, Shema, Moladah, ²⁷Hazar Gaddah, Heshmon, Beth Pelet, ²⁸Hazar Shual, Beersheba, Biziothiah, ²⁹Baalah, Iim, Ezem, ³⁰Eltolad, Kesil, Hormah, ³¹Ziklag, Madmannah, Sansannah, ³²Lebaoth, Shilhim, Ain and Rimmon—a total of twenty-nine towns and their villages.   2Sa 23:20; Zec 14:10

³³In the western foothills:

Eshtaol, Zorah, Ashnah, ³⁴Zanoah, En Gannim, Tappuah, Enam, ³⁵Jarmuth, Adullam, Socoh, Azekah, ³⁶Shaaraim, Adithaim and Gederah (or Gederothaim)ᵃ—fourteen towns and their villages.   Jdg 13:25

³⁷Zenan, Hadashah, Migdal Gad, ³⁸Dilean, Mizpah, Joktheel, ³⁹Lachish, Boz-

kath, Eglon, ⁴⁰Cabbon, Lahmas, Kitlish, ⁴¹Gederoth, Beth Dagon, Naamah and Makkedah—sixteen towns and their villages.   2Ki 14:7

⁴²Libnah, Ether, Ashan, ⁴³Iphtah, Ashnah, Nezib, ⁴⁴Keilah, Aczib and Mareshah—nine towns and their villages.   Nu 33:20; 1Ch 6:59

⁴⁵Ekron, with its surrounding settlements and villages; ⁴⁶west of Ekron, all that were in the vicinity of Ashdod, together with their villages; ⁴⁷Ashdod, its surrounding settlements and villages; and Gaza, its settlements and villages, as far as the Wadi of Egypt and the coastline of the Great Sea.   Nu 34:6; Jos 11:22

⁴⁸In the hill country:

Shamir, Jattir, Socoh, ⁴⁹Dannah, Kiriath Sannah (that is, Debir), ⁵⁰Anab, Eshtemoh, Anim, ⁵¹Goshen, Holon and Giloh—eleven towns and their villages.   Jdg 10:1

⁵²Arab, Dumah, Eshan, ⁵³Janim, Beth Tappuah, Aphekah, ⁵⁴Humtah, Kiriath Arba (that is, Hebron) and Zior—nine towns and their villages.   Ge 25:14

⁵⁵Maon, Carmel, Ziph, Juttah, ⁵⁶Jezreel, Jokdeam, Zanoah, ⁵⁷Kain, Gibeah and Timnah—ten towns and their villages.   Jdg 10:12; 1Ch 11:31

⁵⁸Halhul, Beth Zur, Ge-

ᵃ36 Or Gederah and Gederothaim

dor, ⁵⁹Maarath, Beth Anoth
and Eltekon—six towns and
their villages.   1Ch 2:45

⁶⁰Kiriath Baal (that is,
Kiriath Jearim) and Rab-
bah—two towns and their
villages.   Dt 3:11; Jos 9:17

⁶¹In the desert:

Beth Arabah, Middin,
Secacah, ⁶²Nibshan, the
City of Salt and En Ge-
di—six towns and their villages.   Jos 8:15; Eze 47:10

⁶³Judah could not dislodge
the Jebusites, who were living
in Jerusalem; to this day the Jebusites live there with the people
of Judah.   Jdg 1:21; Eze 48:7

Allotment for Ephraim and Manasseh

16 The allotment for Joseph began at the Jor-
dan of Jericho,ᵃ east of the
waters of Jericho, and went
up from there through the
desert into the hill country
of Bethel. ²It went on from
Bethel (that is, Luz),ᵇ
crossed over to the territory
of the Arkites in Ataroth,
³descended westward to
the territory of the Japhle-
tites as far as the region of
Lower Beth Horon and on
to Gezer, ending at the sea.
⁴So Manasseh and Ephraim, the
descendants of Joseph, received
their inheritance.   Jos 18:5

⁵This was the territory of
Ephraim, clan by clan:

The boundary of their in-
heritance went from Ata-
roth Addar in the east to
Upper Beth Horon ⁶and
continued to the sea. From
Micmethath on the north it
curved eastward to Taanath
Shiloh, passing by it to Janoah on the east. ⁷Then it
went down from Janoah
to Ataroth and Naarah,
touched Jericho and came
out at the Jordan. ⁸From
Tappuah the border went
west to the Kanah Ravine
and ended at the sea. This
was the inheritance of the
tribe of the Ephraimites,
clan by clan. ⁹It also included all the towns and
their villages that were set
aside for the Ephraimites
within the inheritance of
the Manassites.   2Ki 15:29

¹⁰They did not dislodge the Canaanites living in Gezer; to this
day the Canaanites live among
the people of Ephraim but are
required to do forced labor.

17 This was the allotment
for the tribe of Manasseh
as Joseph's firstborn, that is, for
Makir, Manasseh's firstborn.
Makir was the ancestor of the
Gileadites, who had received
Gilead and Bashan because the
Makirites were great soldiers.
²So this allotment was for the
rest of the people of Ma-

ᵃ1 *Jordan of Jericho* was possibly an ancient name for the Jordan River.
ᵇ2 Septuagint; Hebrew *Bethel to Luz*

nasseh—the clans of Abiezer, Helek, Asriel, Shechem, Hepher and Shemida. These are the other male descendants of Manasseh son of Joseph by their clans.   Nu 1:34; 1Ch 7:19

³Now Zelophehad son of Hepher, the son of Gilead, the son of Makir, the son of Manasseh, had no sons but only daughters, whose names were Mahlah, Noah, Hoglah, Milcah and Tirzah. ⁴They went to Eleazar the priest, Joshua son of Nun, and the leaders and said, "The LORD commanded Moses to give us an inheritance among our brothers." So Joshua gave them an inheritance along with the brothers of their father, according to the LORD's command. ⁵Manasseh's share consisted of ten tracts of land besides Gilead and Bashan east of the Jordan, ⁶because the daughters of the tribe of Manasseh received an inheritance among the sons. The land of Gilead belonged to the rest of the descendants of Manasseh.   Nu 27:1; Jos 13:30-31

⁷The territory of Manasseh extended from Asher to Micmethath east of Shechem. The boundary ran southward from there to include the people living at En Tappuah. ⁸(Manasseh had the land of Tappuah, but Tappuah itself, on the boundary of Manasseh, belonged to the Ephraimites.) ⁹Then the boundary continued south to the Kanah Ravine. There were towns belonging to Ephraim lying among the towns of Manasseh, but the boundary of Manasseh was the northern side of the ravine and ended at the sea. ¹⁰On the south the land belonged to Ephraim, on the north to Manasseh. The territory of Manasseh reached the sea and bordered Asher on the north and Issachar on the east.   Jdg 1:31; Eze 48:5

¹¹Within Issachar and Asher, Manasseh also had Beth Shan, Ibleam and the people of Dor, Endor, Taanach and Megiddo, together with their surrounding settlements (the third in the list is Naphoth*ᵃ*).   1Sa 31:10

¹²Yet the Manassites were not able to occupy these towns, for the Canaanites were determined to live in that region. ¹³However, when the Israelites grew stronger, they subjected the Canaanites to forced labor but did not drive them out completely.   Jos 15:63; Jdg 1:27-28

¹⁴The people of Joseph said to Joshua, "Why have you given us only one allotment and one portion for an inheritance? We are a numerous people and the LORD has blessed us abundantly."   Nu 26:28-37

¹⁵"If you are so numerous," Joshua answered, "and if the hill country of Ephraim is too

ᵃ11 That is, Naphoth Dor

small for you, go up into the forest and clear land for yourselves there in the land of the Perizzites and Rephaites." 2Sa 18:6

16The people of Joseph replied, "The hill country is not enough for us, and all the Canaanites who live in the plain have iron chariots, both those in Beth Shan and its settlements and those in the Valley of Jezreel." Jdg 1:19; 1Sa 29:1

17But Joshua said to the house of Joseph—to Ephraim and Manasseh—"You are numerous and very powerful. You will have not only one allotment 18but the forested hill country as well. Clear it, and its farthest limits will be yours; though the Canaanites have iron chariots and though they are strong, you can drive them out." Eze 48:5

Division of the Rest of the Land

18 The whole assembly of the Israelites gathered at Shiloh and set up the Tent of Meeting there. The country was brought under their control, 2but there were still seven Israelite tribes who had not yet received their inheritance. Jdg 18:31

3So Joshua said to the Israelites: "How long will you wait before you begin to take possession of the land that the LORD, the God of your fathers, has given you? 4Appoint three men from each tribe. I will send them out to make a survey of the land and to write a description of it,

according to the inheritance of each. Then they will return to me. 5You are to divide the land into seven parts. Judah is to remain in its territory on the south and the house of Joseph in its territory on the north. 6After you have written descriptions of the seven parts of the land, bring them here to me and I will cast lots for you in the presence of the LORD our God. 7The Levites, however, do not get a portion among you, because the priestly service of the LORD is their inheritance. And Gad, Reuben and the half-tribe of Manasseh have already received their inheritance on the east side of the Jordan. Moses the servant of the LORD gave it to them." Lev 16:8; Mic 2:5

8As the men started on their way to map out the land, Joshua instructed them, "Go and make a survey of the land and write a description of it. Then return to me, and I will cast lots for you here at Shiloh in the presence of the LORD." 9So the men left and went through the land. They wrote its description on a scroll, town by town, in seven parts, and returned to Joshua in the camp at Shiloh. 10Joshua then cast lots for them in Shiloh in the presence of the LORD, and there he distributed the land to the Israelites according to their tribal divisions. Nu 34:13; Jer 7:12

Allotment for Benjamin

11The lot came up for the tribe of Benjamin, clan by clan. Their al-

lotted territory lay between the tribes of Judah and Joseph:

¹²On the north side their boundary began at the Jordan, passed the northern slope of Jericho and headed west into the hill country, coming out at the desert of Beth Aven. ¹³From there it crossed to the south slope of Luz (that is, Bethel) and went down to Ataroth Addar on the hill south of Lower Beth Horon.   Ge 28:19

¹⁴From the hill facing Beth Horon on the south the boundary turned south along the western side and came out at Kiriath Baal (that is, Kiriath Jearim), a town of the people of Judah. This was the western side.

¹⁵The southern side began at the outskirts of Kiriath Jearim on the west, and the boundary came out at the spring of the waters of Nephtoah. ¹⁶The boundary went down to the foot of the hill facing the Valley of Ben Hinnom, north of the Valley of Rephaim. It continued down the Hinnom Valley along the southern slope of the Jebusite city and so to En Rogel. ¹⁷It then curved north, went to En Shemesh, continued to Geliloth, which faces the Pass of Adummim, and ran down to the Stone of Bohan

son of Reuben. ¹⁸It continued to the northern slope of Beth Arabahᵃ and on down into the Arabah. ¹⁹It then went to the northern slope of Beth Hoglah and came out at the northern bay of the Salt Sea,ᵇ at the mouth of the Jordan in the south. This was the southern boundary.   Ge 14:3

²⁰The Jordan formed the boundary on the eastern side.

These were the boundaries that marked out the inheritance of the clans of Benjamin on all sides.   1Sa 9:1

²¹The tribe of Benjamin, clan by clan, had the following cities:
Jericho, Beth Hoglah, Emek Keziz, ²²Beth Arabah, Zemaraim, Bethel, ²³Avvim, Parah, Ophrah, ²⁴Kephar Ammoni, Ophni and Geba—twelve towns and their villages.   2Ch 13:4; Isa 10:29
²⁵Gibeon, Ramah, Beeroth, ²⁶Mizpah, Kephirah, Mozah, ²⁷Rekem, Irpeel, Taralah, ²⁸Zelah, Haeleph, the Jebusite city (that is, Jerusalem), Gibeah and Kiriath—fourteen towns and their villages.   Jdg 4:5
This was the inheritance of Benjamin for its clans.   Eze 48:23

Allotment for Simeon

19 The second lot came out for the tribe of Simeon, clan by clan. Their inheritance

lay within the territory of Judah.
²It included: Ge 49:7; Jdg 1:3

Beersheba (or Sheba),ᵃ
Moladah, ³Hazar Shual,
Balah, Ezem, ⁴Eltolad,
Bethul, Hormah, ⁵Ziklag,
Beth Marcaboth, Hazar
Susah, ⁶Beth Lebaoth and
Sharuhen—thirteen towns
and their villages; Ge 21:14
⁷Ain, Rimmon, Ether and
Ashan—four towns and
their villages— ⁸and all the
villages around these towns
as far as Baalath Beer
(Ramah in the Negev). Jos 15:32
This was the inheritance of the
tribe of the Simeonites, clan by
clan. ⁹The inheritance of the
Simeonites was taken from the
share of Judah, because Judah's
portion was more than they
needed. So the Simeonites received their inheritance within
the territory of Judah. Ge 49:7

Allotment for Zebulun

¹⁰The third lot came up for
Zebulun, clan by clan: Jos 21:7

The boundary of their in-
heritance went as far as Sarid. ¹¹Going west it ran to
Maralah, touched Dab-
besheth, and extended to
the ravine near Jokneam.
¹²It turned east from Sarid
toward the sunrise to the
territory of Kisloth Tabor
and went on to Daberath
and up to Japhia. ¹³Then it
continued eastward to Gath
Hepher and Eth Kazin; it

came out at Rimmon and
turned toward Neah.
¹⁴There the boundary went
around on the north to
Hannathon and ended at
the Valley of Iphtah El. ¹⁵In-
cluded were Kattath, Na-
halal, Shimron, Idalah and
Bethlehem. There were
twelve towns and their villages. Ge 35:19; 1Ch 6:72
¹⁶These towns and their villages
were the inheritance of Zebulun, clan by clan. Eze 48:26

Allotment for Issachar

¹⁷The fourth lot came out for Issachar, clan by clan. ¹⁸Their territory included: Ge 30:18

Jezreel, Kesulloth, Shu-
nem, ¹⁹Hapharaim, Shion,
Anaharath, ²⁰Rabbith, Kishion, Ebez, ²¹Remeth, En
Gannim, En Haddah and
Beth Pazzez. ²²The bound-
ary touched Tabor, Sha-
hazumah and Beth She-
mesh, and ended at the Jordan. There were sixteen
towns and their villages.
²³These towns and their villages
were the inheritance of the tribe
of Issachar, clan by clan. Ge 49:15

Allotment for Asher

²⁴The fifth lot came out for the
tribe of Asher, clan by clan.
²⁵Their territory included: Jos 17:7

Helkath, Hali, Beten,
Acshaph, ²⁶Allammelech,
Amad and Mishal. On the
west the boundary touched

ᵃ2 Or Beersheba, Sheba; 1 Chron. 4:28 does not have Sheba.

Carmel and Shihor Libnath. ²⁷It then turned east toward Beth Dagon, touched Zebulun and the Valley of Iphtah El, and went north to Beth Emek and Neiel, passing Cabul on the left. ²⁸It went to Abdon,ᵃ Rehob, Hammon and Kanah, as far as Greater Sidon. ²⁹The boundary then turned back toward Ramah and went to the fortified city of Tyre, turned toward Hosah and came out at the sea in the region of Aczib, ³⁰Ummah, Aphek and Rehob. There were twenty-two towns and their villages.   1Ki 18:19

³¹These towns and their villages were the inheritance of the tribe of Asher, clan by clan.   Ge 30:13

Allotment for Naphtali

³²The sixth lot came out for Naphtali, clan by clan:

³³Their boundary went from Heleph and the large tree in Zaanannim, passing Adami Nekeb and Jabneel to Lakkum and ending at the Jordan. ³⁴The boundary ran west through Aznoth Tabor and came out at Hukkok. It touched Zebulun on the south, Asher on the west and the Jordanᵇ on the east. ³⁵The fortified cities were Ziddim, Zer, Hammath, Rakkath, Kinnereth, ³⁶Adamah, Ramah, Hazor, ³⁷Kedesh, Edrei, En Hazor, ³⁸Iron, Migdal El, Horem, Beth Anath and Beth Shemesh. There were nineteen towns and their villages.Jdg 4:11

³⁹These towns and their villages were the inheritance of the tribe of Naphtali, clan by clan. Eze 48:3

Allotment for Dan

⁴⁰The seventh lot came out for the tribe of Dan, clan by clan. ⁴¹The territory of their inheritance included:

Zorah, Eshtaol, Ir Shemesh, ⁴²Shaalabbin, Aijalon, Ithlah, ⁴³Elon, Timnah, Ekron, ⁴⁴Eltekeh, Gibbethon, Baalath, ⁴⁵Jehud, Bene Berak, Gath Rimmon, ⁴⁶Me Jarkon and Rakkon, with the area facing Joppa.

⁴⁷(But the Danites had difficulty taking possession of their territory, so they went up and attacked Leshem, took it, put it to the sword and occupied it. They settled in Leshem and named it Dan after their forefather.)   Dt 3:14; Jdg 18:1

⁴⁸These towns and their villages were the inheritance of the tribe of Dan, clan by clan.   Ge 30:6

Allotment for Joshua

⁴⁹When they had finished dividing the land into its allotted portions, the Israelites gave Joshua son of Nun an inheritance among them, ⁵⁰as the LORD had commanded. They

---

ᵃ28 Some Hebrew manuscripts (see also Joshua 21:30); most Hebrew manuscripts Ebron
ᵇ34 Septuagint; Hebrew west, and Judah, the Jordan,

gave him the town he asked for—Timnath Serah[a] in the hill country of Ephraim. And he built up the town and settled there.   Jos 24:30; Jdg 2:9

51These are the territories that Eleazar the priest, Joshua son of Nun and the heads of the tribal clans of Israel assigned by lot at Shiloh in the presence of the Lord at the entrance to the Tent of Meeting. And so they finished dividing the land.   Jos 23:4

Cities of Refuge

20 Then the Lord said to Joshua: 2"Tell the Israelites to designate the cities of refuge, as I instructed you through Moses, 3so that anyone who kills a person accidentally and unintentionally may flee there and find protection from the avenger of blood.   Nu 35:12

4"When he flees to one of these cities, he is to stand in the entrance of the city gate and state his case before the elders of that city. Then they are to admit him into their city and give him a place to live with them. 5If the avenger of blood pursues him, they must not surrender the one accused, because he killed his neighbor unintentionally and without malice aforethought. 6He is to stay in that city until he has stood trial before the assembly and until the death of the high priest who is serving at that time. Then he

may go back to his own home in the town from which he fled."

7So they set apart Kedesh in Galilee in the hill country of Naphtali, Shechem in the hill country of Ephraim, and Kiriath Arba (that is, Hebron) in the hill country of Judah. 8On the east side of the Jordan of Jericho[b] they designated Bezer in the desert on the plateau in the tribe of Reuben, Ramoth in Gilead in the tribe of Gad, and Golan in Bashan in the tribe of Manasseh. 9Any of the Israelites or any alien living among them who killed someone accidentally could flee to these designated cities and not be killed by the avenger of blood prior to standing trial before the assembly.

Towns for the Levites

21 Now the family heads of the Levites approached Eleazar the priest, Joshua son of Nun, and the heads of the other tribal families of Israel 2at Shiloh in Canaan and said to them, "The Lord commanded through Moses that you give us towns to live in, with pasturelands for our livestock." 3So, as the Lord had commanded, the Israelites gave the Levites the following towns and pasturelands out of their own inheritance: Lev 25:32; Nu 35:2-3

4The first lot came out for the Kohathites, clan by clan. The Levites who were descendants

---

a50 Also known as *Timnath Heres* (see Judges 2:9)   b8 *Jordan of Jericho* was possibly an ancient name for the Jordan River.

of Aaron the priest were allotted thirteen towns from the tribes of Judah, Simeon and Benjamin. [5]The rest of Kohath's descendants were allotted ten towns from the clans of the tribes of Ephraim, Dan and half of Manasseh.   Nu 3:17; Jos 21:26

[6]The descendants of Gershon were allotted thirteen towns from the clans of the tribes of Issachar, Asher, Naphtali and the half-tribe of Manasseh in Bashan.   Ge 30:18; Nu 3:17

[7]The descendants of Merari, clan by clan, received twelve towns from the tribes of Reuben, Gad and Zebulun.   Ex 6:16

[8]So the Israelites allotted to the Levites these towns and their pasturelands, as the LORD had commanded through Moses.   Nu 35:2

[9]From the tribes of Judah and Simeon they allotted the following towns by name [10](these towns were assigned to the descendants of Aaron who were from the Kohathite clans of the Levites, because the first lot fell to them):

[11]They gave them Kiriath Arba (that is, Hebron), with its surrounding pastureland, in the hill country of Judah. (Arba was the forefather of Anak.) [12]But the fields and villages around the city they had given to Caleb son of Jephunneh as his possession.   Ge 23:2

[13]So to the descendants of Aaron the priest they gave Hebron (a city of refuge for one accused of murder), Libnah, [14]Jattir, Eshtemoa, [15]Holon, Debir, [16]Ain, Juttah and Beth Shemesh, together with their pasturelands—nine towns from these two tribes.   Nu 33:20

[17]And from the tribe of Benjamin they gave them Gibeon, Geba, [18]Anathoth and Almon, together with their pasturelands—four towns.   Ne 11:31; Jer 32:7

[19]All the towns for the priests, the descendants of Aaron, were thirteen, together with their pasturelands.   2Ch 31:15

[20]The rest of the Kohathite clans of the Levites were allotted towns from the tribe of Ephraim:

[21]In the hill country of Ephraim they were given Shechem (a city of refuge for one accused of murder) and Gezer, [22]Kibzaim and Beth Horon, together with their pasturelands—four towns.   Jos 10:33; 1Sa 1:1

[23]Also from the tribe of Dan they received Eltekeh, Gibbethon, [24]Aijalon and Gath Rimmon, together with their pasturelands—four towns.   Jos 19:44

[25]From half the tribe of Manasseh they received Taanach and Gath Rimmon, together with their pasturelands—two towns.

[26]All these ten towns and their

pasturelands were given to the rest of the Kohathite clans.

27The Levite clans of the Gershonites were given:

from the half-tribe of Manasseh,

Golan in Bashan (a city of refuge for one accused of murder) and Be Eshtarah, together with their pasturelands—two towns;
28from the tribe of Issachar, Kishion, Daberath, 29Jarmuth and En Gannim, together with their pasturelands—four towns;   Ge 30:18
30from the tribe of Asher, Mishal, Abdon, 31Helkath and Rehob, together with their pasturelands—four towns;   Jos 17:7; 19:28
32from the tribe of Naphtali, Kedesh in Galilee (a city of refuge for one accused of murder), Hammoth Dor and Kartan, together with their pasturelands—three towns.   Nu 35:6
33All the towns of the Gershonite clans were thirteen, together with their pasturelands.

34The Merarite clans (the rest of the Levites) were given:

from the tribe of Zebulun, Jokneam, Kartah, 35Dimnah and Nahalal, together with their pasturelands—four towns;   Jos 12:22; 19:15
36from the tribe of Reuben, Bezer, Jahaz, 37Kedemoth and Mephaath, together with their pasturelands— four towns;   Nu 21:23

38from the tribe of Gad, Ramoth in Gilead (a city of refuge for one accused of murder), Mahanaim, 39Heshbon and Jazer, together with their pasturelands—four towns in all.
40All the towns allotted to the Merarite clans, who were the rest of the Levites, were twelve.

41The towns of the Levites in the territory held by the Israelites were forty-eight in all, together with their pasturelands. 42Each of these towns had pasturelands surrounding it; this was true for all these towns.

43So the LORD gave Israel all the land he had sworn to give their forefathers, and they took possession of it and settled there. 44The LORD gave them rest on every side, just as he had sworn to their forefathers. Not one of their enemies withstood them; the LORD handed all their enemies over to them. 45Not one of all the LORD's good promises to the house of Israel failed; every one was fulfilled.   Dt 34:4

Eastern Tribes Return Home

22 Then Joshua summoned the Reubenites, the Gadites and the half-tribe of Manasseh 2and said to them, "You have done all that Moses the servant of the LORD commanded, and you have obeyed me in everything I commanded. 3For a long time now—to this very day—you have not deserted your brothers but have car-

ried out the mission the LORD your God gave you. ⁴Now that the LORD your God has given your brothers rest as he promised, return to your homes in the land that Moses the servant of the LORD gave you on the other side of the Jordan. ⁵But be very careful to keep the commandment and the law that Moses the servant of the LORD gave you: to love the LORD your God, to walk in all his ways, to obey his commands, to hold fast to him and to serve him with all your heart and all your soul."

⁶Then Joshua blessed them and sent them away, and they went to their homes. ⁷(To the half-tribe of Manasseh Moses had given land in Bashan, and to the other half of the tribe Joshua gave land on the west side of the Jordan with their brothers.) When Joshua sent them home, he blessed them, ⁸saying, "Return to your homes with your great wealth—with large herds of livestock, with silver, gold, bronze and iron, and a great quantity of clothing—and divide with your brothers the plunder from your enemies."   Ex 39:43; Isa 9:3

⁹So the Reubenites, the Gadites and the half-tribe of Manasseh left the Israelites at Shiloh in Canaan to return to Gilead, their own land, which they had acquired in accordance with the command of the LORD through Moses.   Nu 32:26

¹⁰When they came to Geliloth near the Jordan in the land of Canaan, the Reubenites, the Gadites and the half-tribe of Manasseh built an imposing altar there by the Jordan. ¹¹And when the Israelites heard that they had built the altar on the border of Canaan at Geliloth near the Jordan on the Israelite side, ¹²the whole assembly of Israel gathered at Shiloh to go to war against them.   Isa 19:19

¹³So the Israelites sent Phinehas son of Eleazar, the priest, to the land of Gilead—to Reuben, Gad and the half-tribe of Manasseh. ¹⁴With him they sent ten of the chief men, one for each of the tribes of Israel, each the head of a family division among the Israelite clans. Nu 25:7

¹⁵When they went to Gilead—to Reuben, Gad and the half-tribe of Manasseh—they said to them: ¹⁶"The whole assembly of the LORD says: 'How could you break faith with the God of Israel like this? How could you turn away from the LORD and build yourselves an altar in rebellion against him now? ¹⁷Was not the sin of Peor enough for us? Up to this very day we have not cleansed ourselves from that sin, even though a plague fell on the community of the LORD! ¹⁸And are you now turning away from the LORD?   1Sa 13:13

" 'If you rebel against the LORD today, tomorrow he will be angry with the whole community of Israel. ¹⁹If the land you possess is defiled, come over to the LORD's land, where

the LORD's tabernacle stands, and share the land with us. But do not rebel against the LORD or against us by building an altar for yourselves, other than the altar of the LORD our God. ²⁰When Achan son of Zerah acted unfaithfully regarding the devoted things,ᵃ did not wrath come upon the whole community of Israel? He was not the only one who died for his sin.' "

²¹Then Reuben, Gad and the half-tribe of Manasseh replied to the heads of the clans of Israel: ²²"The Mighty One, God, the LORD! The Mighty One, God, the LORD! He knows! And let Israel know! If this has been in rebellion or disobedience to the LORD, do not spare us this day. ²³If we have built our own altar to turn away from the LORD and to offer burnt offerings and grain offerings, or to sacrifice fellowship offeringsᵇ on it, may the LORD himself call us to account.   1Sa 20:16; Ps 50:1

²⁴"No! We did it for fear that some day your descendants might say to ours, 'What do you have to do with the LORD, the God of Israel? ²⁵The LORD has made the Jordan a boundary between us and you—you Reubenites and Gadites! You have no share in the LORD.' So your descendants might cause ours to stop fearing the LORD.

²⁶"That is why we said, 'Let us get ready and build an al-

tar—but not for burnt offerings or sacrifices.' ²⁷On the contrary, it is to be a witness between us and you and the generations that follow, that we will worship the LORD at his sanctuary with our burnt offerings, sacrifices and fellowship offerings. Then in the future your descendants will not be able to say to ours, 'You have no share in the LORD.'   Dt 12:6; Isa 19:20

²⁸"And we said, 'If they ever say this to us, or to our descendants, we will answer: Look at the replica of the LORD's altar, which our fathers built, not for burnt offerings and sacrifices, but as a witness between us and you.'   Ge 21:30

²⁹"Far be it from us to rebel against the LORD and turn away from him today by building an altar for burnt offerings, grain offerings and sacrifices, other than the altar of the LORD our God that stands before his tabernacle."   Ex 26:1; Jos 24:16

³⁰When Phinehas the priest and the leaders of the community—the heads of the clans of the Israelites—heard what Reuben, Gad and Manasseh had to say, they were pleased. ³¹And Phinehas son of Eleazar, the priest, said to Reuben, Gad and Manasseh, "Today we know that the LORD is with us, because you have not acted unfaithfully toward the LORD in this matter. Now you have res-

---

ᵃ20 The Hebrew term refers to the irrevocable giving over of things or persons to the LORD, often by totally destroying them.   ᵇ23 Traditionally *peace offerings*; also in verse 27

citizens of Jericho fought against you, as did also the Amorites, Perizzites, Canaanites, Hittites, Girgashites, Hivites and Jebusites, but I gave them into your hands. 12I sent the hornet ahead of you, which drove them out before you— also the two Amorite kings. You did not do it with your own sword and bow. 13So I gave you a land on which you did not toil and cities you did not build; and you live in them and eat from vineyards and olive groves that you did not plant.'   Ex 14:29; Dt 6:10-11

14"Now fear the LORD and serve him with all faithfulness. Throw away the gods your forefathers worshiped beyond the River and in Egypt, and serve the LORD. 15But if serving the LORD seems undesirable to you, then choose for yourselves this day whom you will serve, whether the gods your forefathers served beyond the River, or the gods of the Amorites, in whose land you are living. But as for me and my household, we will serve the LORD."

16Then the people answered, "Far be it from us to forsake the LORD to serve other gods! 17It was the LORD our God himself who brought us and our fathers up out of Egypt, from that land of slavery, and performed those great signs before our eyes. He protected us on our entire journey and among all the nations through which we traveled. 18And the LORD drove out be-

fore us all the nations, including the Amorites, who lived in the land. We too will serve the LORD, because he is our God."

19Joshua said to the people, "You are not able to serve the LORD. He is a holy God; he is a jealous God. He will not forgive your rebellion and your sins. 20If you forsake the LORD and serve foreign gods, he will turn and bring disaster on you and make an end of you, after he has been good to you."   Lev 11:44; Hos 13:11

21But the people said to Joshua, "No! We will serve the LORD."

22Then Joshua said, "You are witnesses against yourselves that you have chosen to serve the LORD."   Ru 4:10; Ps 119:30

"Yes, we are witnesses," they replied.   Dt 25:9

23"Now then," said Joshua, "throw away the foreign gods that are among you and yield your hearts to the LORD, the God of Israel."   1Ki 8:58

24And the people said to Joshua, "We will serve the LORD our God and obey him."   Ex 19:8

25On that day Joshua made a covenant for the people, and there at Shechem he drew up for them decrees and laws. 26And Joshua recorded these things in the Book of the Law of God. Then he took a large stone and set it up there under the oak near the holy place of the LORD.

27"See!" he said to all the people. "This stone will be a witness against us. It has heard all the words the LORD has said

to us. It will be a witness against you if you are untrue to your God." Pr 30:9; Hab 2:11

Buried in the Promised Land

28Then Joshua sent the people away, each to his own inheritance. Jdg 2:6; 21:23-24

29After these things, Joshua son of Nun, the servant of the LORD, died at the age of a hundred and ten. 30And they buried him in the land of his inheritance, at Timnath Seraha in the hill country of Ephraim, north of Mount Gaash. Jdg 1:1; 2Sa 23:30

31Israel served the LORD throughout the lifetime of Joshua and of the elders who outlived him and who had experienced everything the LORD had done for Israel. Jdg 2:7

32And Joseph's bones, which the Israelites had brought up from Egypt, were buried at Shechem in the tract of land that Jacob bought for a hundred pieces of silverb from the sons of Hamor, the father of Shechem. This became the inheritance of Joseph's descendants. Ge 33:19

33And Eleazar son of Aaron died and was buried at Gibeah, which had been allotted to his son Phinehas in the hill country of Ephraim. Jos 22:13; 1Sa 9:4

---

a30 Also known as *Timnath Heres* (see Judges 2:9)   b32 Hebrew *hundred kesitahs*; a kesitah was a unit of money of unknown weight and value.

Judges

Introduction:

This book tells of Israel's history for the period between the death of Joshua and the ministry of Samuel. This time period was known for its heroes—called judges—who ruled the tribes of Israel.

The events in Judges followed a certain pattern:
1. The Israelites lived in peace while serving and loving God.
2. The Israelites forgot God and worshiped idols.
3. God punished his people by sending a neighboring nation to fight and rule over them.
4. The Israelites turned to God and asked for forgiveness.
5. God forgave his people and saved them by sending a judge to help conquer their enemy.

This pattern of events repeated itself many times during this time period in Israel's history.

A total of fifteen judges are listed for their leadership. The best-known judges are Deborah, Gideon and Samson.

Outline of contents:

Israel Fights the Remaining Canaanites

1 After the death of Joshua, the Israelites asked the LORD, "Who will be the first to go up and fight for us against the Canaanites?" Jos 24:29; Jdg 20:18

²The LORD answered, "Judah is to go; I have given the land into their hands." Ge 49:10

³Then the men of Judah said to the Simeonites their brothers, "Come up with us into the territory allotted to us, to fight against the Canaanites. We in turn will go with you into yours." So the Simeonites went with them. Jdg 1:17

⁴When Judah attacked, the LORD gave the Canaanites and Perizzites into their hands and they struck down ten thousand men at Bezek. ⁵It was there that they found Adoni-Bezek and fought against him, putting to rout the Canaanites and Periz-

zites. ⁶Adoni-Bezek fled, but they chased him and caught him, and cut off his thumbs and big toes.   Ge 13:7; Jos 3:10

⁷Then Adoni-Bezek said, "Seventy kings with their thumbs and big toes cut off have picked up scraps under my table. Now God has paid me back for what I did to them." They brought him to Jerusalem, and he died there.   Lev 24:19

⁸The men of Judah attacked Jerusalem also and took it. They put the city to the sword and set it on fire.   Jos 15:63; 2Sa 5:6

⁹After that, the men of Judah went down to fight against the Canaanites living in the hill country, the Negev and the western foothills. ¹⁰They advanced against the Canaanites living in Hebron (formerly called Kiriath Arba) and defeated Sheshai, Ahiman and Talmai.   Nu 13:17; Jos 15:14

¹¹From there they advanced against the people living in Debir (formerly called Kiriath Sepher). ¹²And Caleb said, "I will give my daughter Acsah in marriage to the man who attacks and captures Kiriath Sepher." ¹³Othniel son of Kenaz, Caleb's younger brother, took it; so Caleb gave his daughter Acsah to him in marriage.

¹⁴One day when she came to Othniel, she urged him*a* to ask her father for a field. When she got off her donkey, Caleb asked her, "What can I do for you?"

¹⁵She replied, "Do me a special favor. Since you have given me land in the Negev, give me also springs of water." Then Caleb gave her the upper and lower springs.   Nu 13:6

¹⁶The descendants of Moses' father-in-law, the Kenite, went up from the City of Palms*b* with the men of Judah to live among the people of the Desert of Judah in the Negev near Arad.

¹⁷Then the men of Judah went with the Simeonites their brothers and attacked the Canaanites living in Zephath, and they totally destroyed*c* the city. Therefore it was called Hormah.*d* ¹⁸The men of Judah also took*e* Gaza, Ashkelon and Ekron—each city with its territory.

¹⁹The LORD was with the men of Judah. They took possession of the hill country, but they were unable to drive the people from the plains, because they had iron chariots. ²⁰As Moses had promised, Hebron was given to Caleb, who drove from it the three sons of Anak. ²¹The Benjamites, however, failed to dislodge the Jebusites, who were living in Jerusalem; to this day the Jebusites live there with the Benjamites.   Jos 10:36; 17:16

²²Now the house of Joseph attacked Bethel, and the LORD was with them. ²³When they

---

*a*14 Hebrew; Septuagint and Vulgate *Othniel, he urged her*   *b*16 That is, Jericho
*c*17 The Hebrew term refers to the irrevocable giving over of things or persons to the LORD, often by totally destroying them.   *d*17 *Hormah* means *destruction.*
*e*18 Hebrew; Septuagint *Judah did not take*

sent men to spy out Bethel (formerly called Luz), 24the spies saw a man coming out of the city and they said to him, "Show us how to get into the city and we will see that you are treated well." 25So he showed them, and they put the city to the sword but spared the man and his whole family. 26He then went to the land of the Hittites, where he built a city and called it Luz, which is its name to this day.

Jdg 10:9; Eze 16:3

27But Manasseh did not drive out the people of Beth Shan or Taanach or Dor or Ibleam or Megiddo and their surrounding settlements, for the Canaanites were determined to live in that land. 28When Israel became strong, they pressed the Canaanites into forced labor but never drove them out completely. 29Nor did Ephraim drive out the Canaanites living in Gezer, but the Canaanites continued to live there among them. 30Neither did Zebulun drive out the Canaanites living in Kitron or Nahalol, who remained among them; but they did subject them to forced labor. 31Nor did Asher drive out those living in Acco or Sidon or Ahlab or Aczib or Helbah or Aphek or Rehob, 32and because of this the people of Asher lived among the Canaanite inhabitants of the land. 33Neither did Naphtali drive out those living in Beth Shemesh or Beth Anath; but the Naphtalites too lived among the Canaanite inhabitants of the land, and those living in Beth Shemesh and Beth Anath became forced laborers for them. 34The Amorites confined the Danites to the hill country, not allowing them to come down into the plain. 35And the Amorites were determined also to hold out in Mount Heres, Aijalon and Shaalbim, but when the power of the house of Joseph increased, they too were pressed into forced labor. 36The boundary of the Amorites was from Scorpion*a* Pass to Sela and beyond.

1Ki 9:21; Ps 106:34

The Angel of the LORD at Bokim

2 The angel of the LORD went up from Gilgal to Bokim and said, "I brought you up out of Egypt and led you into the land that I swore to give to your forefathers. I said, 'I will never break my covenant with you, 2and you shall not make a covenant with the people of this land, but you shall break down their altars.' Yet you have disobeyed me. Why have you done this? 3Now therefore I tell you that I will not drive them out before you; they will be thorns in your sides and their gods will be a snare to you."

Dt 7:9

4When the angel of the LORD had spoken these things to all the Israelites, the people wept aloud, 5and they called that

a36 Hebrew *Akrabbim*

place Bokim.ᵃ There they offered sacrifices to the LORD.

Disobedience and Defeat

⁶After Joshua had dismissed the Israelites, they went to take possession of the land, each to his own inheritance. ⁷The people served the LORD throughout the lifetime of Joshua and of the elders who outlived him and who had seen all the great things the LORD had done for Israel.   Jos 24:28

⁸Joshua son of Nun, the servant of the LORD, died at the age of a hundred and ten. ⁹And they buried him in the land of his inheritance, at Timnath Heresᵇ in the hill country of Ephraim, north of Mount Gaash.   Jos 1:1

¹⁰After that whole generation had been gathered to their fathers, another generation grew up, who knew neither the LORD nor what he had done for Israel. ¹¹Then the Israelites did evil in the eyes of the LORD and served the Baals. ¹²They forsook the LORD, the God of their fathers, who had brought them out of Egypt. They followed and worshiped various gods of the peoples around them. They provoked the LORD to anger ¹³because they forsook him and served Baal and the Ashtoreths. ¹⁴In his anger against Israel the LORD handed them over to raiders who plundered them. He sold them to their enemies all around, whom they were no longer able to resist. ¹⁵Whenever Israel went out to fight, the hand of the LORD was against them to defeat them, just as he had sworn to them. They were in great distress.   Gal 4:8

¹⁶Then the LORD raised up judges,ᶜ who saved them out of the hands of these raiders. ¹⁷Yet they would not listen to their judges but prostituted themselves to other gods and worshiped them. Unlike their fathers, they quickly turned from the way in which their fathers had walked, the way of obedience to the LORD's commands. ¹⁸Whenever the LORD raised up a judge for them, he was with the judge and saved them out of the hands of their enemies as long as the judge lived; for the LORD had compassion on them as they groaned under those who oppressed and afflicted them. ¹⁹But when the judge died, the people returned to ways even more corrupt than those of their fathers, following other gods and serving and worshiping them. They refused to give up their evil practices and stubborn ways.   Ac 13:20

²⁰Therefore the LORD was very angry with Israel and said, "Because this nation has violated the covenant that I laid down for their forefathers and has not listened to me, ²¹I will no longer drive out before them any of the

---

ᵃ5 *Bokim* means *weepers.*   ᵇ9 Also known as *Timnath Serah* (see Joshua 19:50 and 24:30)   ᶜ16 Or *leaders;* similarly in verses 17-19

nations Joshua left when he died. [22]I will use them to test Israel and see whether they will keep the way of the LORD and walk in it as their forefathers did." [23]The LORD had allowed those nations to remain; he did not drive them out at once by giving them into the hands of Joshua.   Ge 22:1; Jos 23:16

3 These are the nations the LORD left to test all those Israelites who had not experienced any of the wars in Canaan [2](he did this only to teach warfare to the descendants of the Israelites who had not had previous battle experience): [3]the five rulers of the Philistines, all the Canaanites, the Sidonians, and the Hivites living in the Lebanon mountains from Mount Baal Hermon to Lebo[a] Hamath. [4]They were left to test the Israelites to see whether they would obey the LORD's commands, which he had given their forefathers through Moses.   Ex 15:25; Jos 13:3

[5]The Israelites lived among the Canaanites, Hittites, Amorites, Perizzites, Hivites and Jebusites. [6]They took their daughters in marriage and gave their own daughters to their sons, and served their gods.

Othniel

[7]The Israelites did evil in the eyes of the LORD; they forgot the LORD their God and served the Baals and the Asherahs. [8]The anger of the LORD burned against Israel so that he sold them into the hands of Cushan-Rishathaim king of Aram Naharaim,[b] to whom the Israelites were subject for eight years. [9]But when they cried out to the LORD, he raised up for them a deliverer, Othniel son of Kenaz, Caleb's younger brother, who saved them. [10]The Spirit of the LORD came upon him, so that he became Israel's judge[c] and went to war. The LORD gave Cushan-Rishathaim king of Aram into the hands of Othniel, who overpowered him. [11]So the land had peace for forty years, until Othniel son of Kenaz died. Dt 4:9

Ehud

[12]Once again the Israelites did evil in the eyes of the LORD, and because they did this evil the LORD gave Eglon king of Moab power over Israel. [13]Getting the Ammonites and Amalekites to join him, Eglon came and attacked Israel, and they took possession of the City of Palms.[d] [14]The Israelites were subject to Eglon king of Moab for eighteen years.   Jdg 2:11

[15]Again the Israelites cried out to the LORD, and he gave them a deliverer—Ehud, a left-handed man, the son of Gera the Benjamite. The Israelites sent him with tribute to Eglon king of Moab. [16]Now Ehud had

[a]3 Or to the entrance to   [b]8 That is, Northwest Mesopotamia   [c]10 Or leader
[d]13 That is, Jericho

made a double-edged sword about a foot and a half[a] long, which he strapped to his right thigh under his clothing. [17]He presented the tribute to Eglon king of Moab, who was a very fat man. [18]After Ehud had presented the tribute, he sent on their way the men who had carried it. [19]At the idols[b] near Gilgal he himself turned back and said, "I have a secret message for you, O king."   1Ch 12:2

The king said, "Quiet!" And all his attendants left him.

[20]Ehud then approached him while he was sitting alone in the upper room of his summer palace[c] and said, "I have a message from God for you." As the king rose from his seat, [21]Ehud reached with his left hand, drew the sword from his right thigh and plunged it into the king's belly. [22]Even the handle sank in after the blade, which came out his back. Ehud did not pull the sword out, and the fat closed in over it. [23]Then Ehud went out to the porch[d]; he shut the doors of the upper room behind him and locked them.

[24]After he had gone, the servants came and found the doors of the upper room locked. They said, "He must be relieving himself in the inner room of the house." [25]They waited to the point of embarrassment, but when he did not open the doors of the room, they took a key and unlocked them. There they saw their lord fallen to the floor, dead.   1Sa 24:3; 2Ki 2:17

[26]While they waited, Ehud got away. He passed by the idols and escaped to Seirah. [27]When he arrived there, he blew a trumpet in the hill country of Ephraim, and the Israelites went down with him from the hills, with him leading them.   Jdg 6:34; 2Sa 2:28

[28]"Follow me," he ordered, "for the LORD has given Moab, your enemy, into your hands." So they followed him down and, taking possession of the fords of the Jordan that led to Moab, they allowed no one to cross over. [29]At that time they struck down about ten thousand Moabites, all vigorous and strong; not a man escaped. [30]That day Moab was made subject to Israel, and the land had peace for eighty years.   Jos 2:7

Shamgar

[31]After Ehud came Shamgar son of Anath, who struck down six hundred Philistines with an oxgoad. He too saved Israel.

Deborah

4 After Ehud died, the Israelites once again did evil in the eyes of the LORD. [2]So the LORD sold them into the hands of Jabin, a king of Canaan, who reigned in Hazor. The commander of his army was Sisera,

---

[a]16 Hebrew a cubit (about 0.5 meter)   [b]19 Or the stone quarries; also in verse 26
[c]20 The meaning of the Hebrew for this phrase is uncertain.   [d]23 The meaning of the Hebrew for this word is uncertain.

who lived in Harosheth Haggoyim. ³Because he had nine hundred iron chariots and had cruelly oppressed the Israelites for twenty years, they cried to the LORD for help. Jdg 2:19

⁴Deborah, a prophetess, the wife of Lappidoth, was leading*a* Israel at that time. ⁵She held court under the Palm of Deborah between Ramah and Bethel in the hill country of Ephraim, and the Israelites came to her to have their disputes decided. ⁶She sent for Barak son of Abinoam from Kedesh in Naphtali and said to him, "The LORD, the God of Israel, commands you: 'Go, take with you ten thousand men of Naphtali and Zebulun and lead the way to Mount Tabor. ⁷I will lure Sisera, the commander of Jabin's army, with his chariots and his troops to the Kishon River and give him into your hands.'" Ps 83:9

⁸Barak said to her, "If you go with me, I will go; but if you don't go with me, I won't go."

⁹"Very well," Deborah said, "I will go with you. But because of the way you are going about this,*b* the honor will not be yours, for the LORD will hand Sisera over to a woman." So Deborah went with Barak to Kedesh, ¹⁰where he summoned Zebulun and Naphtali. Ten thousand men followed him, and Deborah also went with him. Jos 12:22

¹¹Now Heber the Kenite had left the other Kenites, the descendants of Hobab, Moses' brother-in-law,*c* and pitched his tent by the great tree in Zaanannim near Kedesh. Nu 10:29

¹²When they told Sisera that Barak son of Abinoam had gone up to Mount Tabor, ¹³Sisera gathered together his nine hundred iron chariots and all the men with him, from Harosheth Haggoyim to the Kishon River.

¹⁴Then Deborah said to Barak, "Go! This is the day the LORD has given Sisera into your hands. Has not the LORD gone ahead of you?" So Barak went down Mount Tabor, followed by ten thousand men. ¹⁵At Barak's advance, the LORD routed Sisera and all his chariots and army by the sword, and Sisera abandoned his chariot and fled on foot. ¹⁶But Barak pursued the chariots and army as far as Harosheth Haggoyim. All the troops of Sisera fell by the sword; not a man was left. Dt 9:3

¹⁷Sisera, however, fled on foot to the tent of Jael, the wife of Heber the Kenite, because there were friendly relations between Jabin king of Hazor and the clan of Heber the Kenite.

¹⁸Jael went out to meet Sisera and said to him, "Come, my lord, come right in. Don't be afraid." So he entered her tent, and she put a covering over him. Jdg 4:17

a4 Traditionally *judging*   *b9* Or *But on the expedition you are undertaking*   *c11* Or
father-in-law

¹⁹"I'm thirsty," he said. "Please give me some water." She opened a skin of milk, gave him a drink, and covered him up.   Ge 18:8; Jdg 5:25

²⁰"Stand in the doorway of the tent," he told her. "If someone comes by and asks you, 'Is anyone here?' say 'No.'"

²¹But Jael, Heber's wife, picked up a tent peg and a hammer and went quietly to him while he lay fast asleep, exhausted. She drove the peg through his temple into the ground, and he died.   Ge 2:21

²²Barak came by in pursuit of Sisera, and Jael went out to meet him. "Come," she said, "I will show you the man you're looking for." So he went in with her, and there lay Sisera with the tent peg through his temple—dead.   Jdg 5:27

²³On that day God subdued Jabin, the Canaanite king, before the Israelites. ²⁴And the hand of the Israelites grew stronger and stronger against Jabin, the Canaanite king, until they destroyed him.   Ne 9:24

The Song of Deborah

5 On that day Deborah and Barak son of Abinoam sang this song: Ex 15:1; Ps 32:7

²"When the princes in Israel
   take the lead,
  when the people willingly
    offer themselves—
  praise the LORD!   2Ch 17:16

³"Hear this, you kings! Listen,
   you rulers!
I will sing to^a the LORD, I
  will sing;
I will make music to^b the
  LORD, the God of Israel.

⁴"O LORD, when you went
  out from Seir,
when you marched from
  the land of Edom,
the earth shook, the heavens
  poured,
the clouds poured down
  water.   Dt 33:2; Ps 68:8
⁵The mountains quaked
  before the LORD, the
  One of Sinai,
before the LORD, the God of
  Israel.   Ex 19:18; Isa 64:3

⁶"In the days of Shamgar son
  of Anath,
in the days of Jael, the
  roads were abandoned;
travelers took to winding
  paths.   Lev 26:22
⁷Village life^c in Israel ceased,
  ceased until I,^{d} Deborah,
  arose,
arose a mother in Israel.
⁸When they chose new gods,
  war came to the city gates,
and not a shield or spear was
  seen
among forty thousand in
  Israel.   Nu 25:7; Dt 32:17
⁹My heart is with Israel's
  princes,
with the willing volunteers
  among the people.
Praise the LORD!

---

^{a}3 Or of ^{b}3 Or / with song I will praise ^{c}7 Or Warriors ^{d}7 Or you

¹⁰"You who ride on white
        donkeys,
    sitting on your saddle
        blankets,
    and you who walk along
        the road,
    consider ¹¹the voice of the
        singers*a* at the watering
        places.
    They recite the righteous
        acts of the LORD,
    the righteous acts of his
        warriors*b* in Israel. Ge 49:11

    "Then the people of the
        LORD
    went down to the city
        gates.
¹²'Wake up, wake up,
        Deborah!
    Wake up, wake up, break
        out in song! Ps 57:8
    Arise, O Barak!
    Take captive your captives,
        O son of Abinoam.' Ps 68:18

¹³"Then the men who were left
        came down to the nobles;
    the people of the LORD
        came to me with the
        mighty.
¹⁴Some came from Ephraim,
        whose roots were in
        Amalek;
    Benjamin was with the
        people who followed
        you. Ge 41:52
    From Makir captains came
        down,
    from Zebulun those who
        bear a commander's
        staff. Nu 34:21

¹⁵The princes of Issachar were
        with Deborah;
    yes, Issachar was with
        Barak,
    rushing after him into the
        valley.
    In the districts of Reuben
        there was much searching
        of heart. Ge 30:18; Jdg 4:4
¹⁶Why did you stay among the
        campfires*c*
    to hear the whistling for the
        flocks?
    In the districts of Reuben
        there was much searching
        of heart.
¹⁷Gilead stayed beyond the
        Jordan.
    And Dan, why did he
        linger by the ships?
    Asher remained on the coast
        and stayed in his coves.
¹⁸The people of Zebulun risked
        their very lives;
    so did Naphtali on the
        heights of the field. Ge 30:20

¹⁹"Kings came, they fought;
    the kings of Canaan fought
    at Taanach by the waters of
        Megiddo,
    but they carried off no
        silver, no plunder. Jos 11:5
²⁰From the heavens the stars
        fought,
    from their courses they
        fought against
        Sisera. Jos 10:11
²¹The river Kishon swept them
        away,
    the age-old river, the river
        Kishon. Jos 1:6; Jdg 4:7

*a*11 Or *archers*; the meaning of the Hebrew for this word is uncertain.   *b*11 Or
villagers   *c*16 Or *saddlebags*

March on, my soul; be
    strong!
22Then thundered the horses'
    hoofs—
galloping, galloping go his
    mighty steeds.   Jer 8:16
23'Curse Meroz,' said the angel
    of the LORD.
'Curse its people bitterly,
because they did not come to
    help the LORD,
to help the LORD against the
    mighty.'   1Sa 18:17

24"Most blessed of women be
    Jael,
the wife of Heber the
    Kenite,
most blessed of
    tent-dwelling women.
25He asked for water, and she
    gave him milk;
in a bowl fit for nobles she
    brought him curdled
    milk.   Ge 18:8; Jdg 4:19
26Her hand reached for the
    tent peg,
her right hand for the
    workman's hammer.
She struck Sisera, she
    crushed his head,
she shattered and pierced
    his temple.   Jdg 4:21
27At her feet he sank,
    he fell; there he lay.
At her feet he sank, he fell;
where he sank, there he
    fell—dead.   Jdg 4:22

28"Through the window
    peered Sisera's mother;
behind the lattice she cried
    out,

'Why is his chariot so long in
    coming?
Why is the clatter of his
    chariots delayed?'   Pr 7:6
29The wisest of her ladies
    answer her;
indeed, she keeps saying to
    herself,
30'Are they not finding and
    dividing the spoils:
a girl or two for each man,
colorful garments as
    plunder for Sisera,
colorful garments
    embroidered,
highly embroidered
    garments for my neck—
all this as plunder?'   Ex 15:9

31"So may all your enemies
    perish, O LORD!
But may they who love you
    be like the sun
when it rises in its
    strength."   2Sa 23:4; Ps 19:4

Then the land had peace forty
years.   Jdg 3:11

Gideon

6 Again the Israelites did evil
    in the eyes of the LORD, and
for seven years he gave them
into the hands of the Midianites. 2Because the power of
Midian was so oppressive, the
Israelites prepared shelters for
themselves in mountain clefts,
caves and strongholds. 3When-
ever the Israelites planted their
crops, the Midianites, Amalekites and other eastern peoples
invaded the country. 4They
camped on the land and ruined

the crops all the way to Gaza and did not spare a living thing for Israel, neither sheep nor cattle nor donkeys. ⁵They came up with their livestock and their tents like swarms of locusts. It was impossible to count the men and their camels; they invaded the land to ravage it. ⁶Midian so impoverished the Israelites that they cried out to the LORD for help.   Jdg 2:11; Jer 49:32

⁷When the Israelites cried to the LORD because of Midian, ⁸he sent them a prophet, who said, "This is what the LORD, the God of Israel, says: I brought you up out of Egypt, out of the land of slavery. ⁹I snatched you from the power of Egypt and from the hand of all your oppressors. I drove them from before you and gave you their land. ¹⁰I said to you, 'I am the LORD your God; do not worship the gods of the Amorites, in whose land you live.' But you have not listened to me."   Jos 24:15; Jdg 3:9

¹¹The angel of the LORD came and sat down under the oak in Ophrah that belonged to Joash the Abiezrite, where his son Gideon was threshing wheat in a winepress to keep it from the Midianites. ¹²When the angel of the LORD appeared to Gideon, he said, "The LORD is with you, mighty warrior."   Rev 2:17

¹³"But sir," Gideon replied, "if the LORD is with us, why has all this happened to us? Where are all his wonders that our fathers told us about when they said, 'Did not the LORD bring us up out of Egypt?' But now the LORD has abandoned us and put us into the hand of Midian."

¹⁴The LORD turned to him and said, "Go in the strength you have and save Israel out of Midian's hand. Am I not sending you?"   2Ki 14:27; Heb 11:34

¹⁵"But Lord,ᵃ" Gideon asked, "how can I save Israel? My clan is the weakest in Manasseh, and I am the least in my family."

¹⁶The LORD answered, "I will be with you, and you will strike down all the Midianites together."   Ex 3:12; Jos 1:5

¹⁷Gideon replied, "If now I have found favor in your eyes, give me a sign that it is really you talking to me. ¹⁸Please do not go away until I come back and bring my offering and set it before you."

And the LORD said, "I will wait until you return."   Ge 24:14

¹⁹Gideon went in, prepared a young goat, and from an ephahᵇ of flour he made bread without yeast. Putting the meat in a basket and its broth in a pot, he brought them out and offered them to him under the oak.   Ge 18:7-8; Jdg 13:15

²⁰The angel of God said to him, "Take the meat and the unleavened bread, place them on this rock, and pour out the broth." And Gideon did so. ²¹With the tip of the staff that

ᵃ15 Or sir   ᵇ19 That is, probably about 3/5 bushel (about 22 liters)

was in his hand, the angel of the LORD touched the meat and the unleavened bread. Fire flared from the rock, consuming the meat and the bread. And the angel of the LORD disappeared. ²²When Gideon realized that it was the angel of the LORD, he exclaimed, "Ah, Sovereign LORD! I have seen the angel of the LORD face to face!" Jdg 13:19

²³But the LORD said to him, "Peace! Do not be afraid. You are not going to die." Da 10:19

²⁴So Gideon built an altar to the LORD there and called it The LORD is Peace. To this day it stands in Ophrah of the Abiezrites. Ge 22:14; Jos 18:23

²⁵That same night the LORD said to him, "Take the second bull from your father's herd, the one seven years old.^a Tear down your father's altar to Baal and cut down the Asherah pole^b beside it. ²⁶Then build a proper kind of^c altar to the LORD your God on the top of this height. Using the wood of the Asherah pole that you cut down, offer the second^d bull as a burnt offering." Ex 34:13

²⁷So Gideon took ten of his servants and did as the LORD told him. But because he was afraid of his family and the men of the town, he did it at night rather than in the daytime.

²⁸In the morning when the men of the town got up, there was Baal's altar, demolished, with the Asherah pole beside it cut down and the second bull sacrificed on the newly built altar! 1Ki 16:32; 2Ki 21:3

²⁹They asked each other, "Who did this?"

When they carefully investigated, they were told, "Gideon son of Joash did it."

³⁰The men of the town demanded of Joash, "Bring out your son. He must die, because he has broken down Baal's altar and cut down the Asherah pole beside it."

³¹But Joash replied to the hostile crowd around him, "Are you going to plead Baal's cause? Are you trying to save him? Whoever fights for him shall be put to death by morning! If Baal really is a god, he can defend himself when someone breaks down his altar." ³²So that day they called Gideon "Jerub-Baal,^e" saying, "Let Baal contend with him," because he broke down Baal's altar. 1Sa 24:15

³³Now all the Midianites, Amalekites and other eastern peoples joined forces and crossed over the Jordan and camped in the Valley of Jezreel. ³⁴Then the Spirit of the LORD came upon Gideon, and he blew a trumpet, summoning the Abiezrites to follow him. ³⁵He sent messengers throughout Manasseh, calling them to arms, and also into Asher, Zebulun and Naphtali, so that

---

^a25 Or *Take a full-grown, mature bull from your father's herd*   ^b25 That is, a symbol of the goddess Asherah; here and elsewhere in Judges   ^c26 Or *build with layers of stone an*   ^d26 Or *full-grown*; also in verse 28   ^e32 *Jerub-Baal* means *let Baal contend*.

they too went up to meet them.

³⁶Gideon said to God, "If you will save Israel by my hand as you have promised— ³⁷look, I will place a wool fleece on the threshing floor. If there is dew only on the fleece and all the ground is dry, then I will know that you will save Israel by my hand, as you said." ³⁸And that is what happened. Gideon rose early the next day; he squeezed the fleece and wrung out the dew—a bowlful of water. Job 31:20

³⁹Then Gideon said to God, "Do not be angry with me. Let me make just one more request. Allow me one more test with the fleece. This time make the fleece dry and the ground covered with dew." ⁴⁰That night God did so. Only the fleece was dry; all the ground was covered with dew. Ge 18:32; Isa 38:7

Gideon Defeats the Midianites

7 Early in the morning, Jerub-Baal (that is, Gideon) and all his men camped at the spring of Harod. The camp of Midian was north of them in the valley near the hill of Moreh. ²The LORD said to Gideon, "You have too many men for me to deliver Midian into their hands. In order that Israel may not boast against me that her own strength has saved her, ³announce now to the people, 'Anyone who trembles with fear may turn back and leave Mount Gilead.'" So twenty-

two thousand men left, while ten thousand remained. Jdg 6:32

⁴But the LORD said to Gideon, "There are still too many men. Take them down to the water, and I will sift them for you there. If I say, 'This one shall go with you,' he shall go; but if I say, 'This one shall not go with you,' he shall not go." 1Sa 14:6

⁵So Gideon took the men down to the water. There the LORD told him, "Separate those who lap the water with their tongues like a dog from those who kneel down to drink." ⁶Three hundred men lapped with their hands to their mouths. All the rest got down on their knees to drink. Ge 14:14

⁷The LORD said to Gideon, "With the three hundred men that lapped I will save you and give the Midianites into your hands. Let all the other men go, each to his own place." ⁸So Gideon sent the rest of the Israelites to their tents but kept the three hundred, who took over the provisions and trumpets of the others. Jos 8:7; 1Sa 14:6

Now the camp of Midian lay below him in the valley. ⁹During that night the LORD said to Gideon, "Get up, go down against the camp, because I am going to give it into your hands. ¹⁰If you are afraid to attack, go down to the camp with your servant Purah ¹¹and listen to what they are saying. Afterward, you will be encouraged to attack the camp." So he and Purah his servant went down to

the outposts of the camp. ¹²The Midianites, the Amalekites and all the other eastern peoples had settled in the valley, thick as locusts. Their camels could no more be counted than the sand on the seashore.   Jos 2:24

¹³Gideon arrived just as a man was telling a friend his dream. "I had a dream," he was saying. "A round loaf of barley bread came tumbling into the Midianite camp. It struck the tent with such force that the tent overturned and collapsed."

¹⁴His friend responded, "This can be nothing other than the sword of Gideon son of Joash, the Israelite. God has given the Midianites and the whole camp into his hands."   Jdg 6:11

¹⁵When Gideon heard the dream and its interpretation, he worshiped God. He returned to the camp of Israel and called out, "Get up! The LORD has given the Midianite camp into your hands." ¹⁶Dividing the three hundred men into three companies, he placed trumpets and empty jars in the hands of all of them, with torches inside.

¹⁷"Watch me," he told them. "Follow my lead. When I get to the edge of the camp, do exactly as I do. ¹⁸When I and all who are with me blow our trumpets, then from all around the camp blow yours and shout, 'For the LORD and for Gideon.'"   Jdg 3:27

¹⁹Gideon and the hundred men with him reached the edge of the camp at the beginning of the middle watch, just after they had changed the guard. They blew their trumpets and broke the jars that were in their hands. ²⁰The three companies blew the trumpets and smashed the jars. Grasping the torches in their left hands and holding in their right hands the trumpets they were to blow, they shouted, "A sword for the LORD and for Gideon!" ²¹While each man held his position around the camp, all the Midianites ran, crying out as they fled.   1Ch 21:12

²²When the three hundred trumpets sounded, the LORD caused the men throughout the camp to turn on each other with their swords. The army fled to Beth Shittah toward Zererah as far as the border of Abel Meholah near Tabbath. ²³Israelites from Naphtali, Asher and all Manasseh were called out, and they pursued the Midianites. ²⁴Gideon sent messengers throughout the hill country of Ephraim, saying, "Come down against the Midianites and seize the waters of the Jordan ahead of them as far as Beth Barah."

So all the men of Ephraim were called out and they took the waters of the Jordan as far as Beth Barah. ²⁵They also captured two of the Midianite leaders, Oreb and Zeeb. They killed Oreb at the rock of Oreb, and Zeeb at the winepress of Zeeb. They pursued the Midianites and brought the heads of Oreb and Zeeb to Gideon, who was by the Jordan.   Ps 83:11

Zebah and Zalmunna

8 Now the Ephraimites asked Gideon, "Why have you treated us like this? Why didn't you call us when you went to fight Midian?" And they criticized him sharply.　　　Jdg 12:1

2But he answered them, "What have I accomplished compared to you? Aren't the gleanings of Ephraim's grapes better than the full grape harvest of Abiezer? 3God gave Oreb and Zeeb, the Midianite leaders, into your hands. What was I able to do compared to you?" At this, their resentment against him subsided.　　　Nu 26:30

4Gideon and his three hundred men, exhausted yet keeping up the pursuit, came to the Jordan and crossed it. 5He said to the men of Succoth, "Give my troops some bread; they are worn out, and I am still pursuing Zebah and Zalmunna, the kings of Midian."　　　Ge 33:17

6But the officials of Succoth said, "Do you already have the hands of Zebah and Zalmunna in your possession? Why should we give bread to your troops?"　　　Jdg 7:15; 1Sa 25:11

7Then Gideon replied, "Just for that, when the Lord has given Zebah and Zalmunna into my hand, I will tear your flesh with desert thorns and briers."

8From there he went up to Peniel*a* and made the same request of them, but they answered as the men of Succoth had. 9So he said to the men of Peniel, "When I return in triumph, I will tear down this tower."　　　Ge 32:30; 1Ki 12:25

10Now Zebah and Zalmunna were in Karkor with a force of about fifteen thousand men, all that were left of the armies of the eastern peoples; a hundred and twenty thousand swordsmen had fallen. 11Gideon went up by the route of the nomads east of Nobah and Jogbehah and fell upon the unsuspecting army. 12Zebah and Zalmunna, the two kings of Midian, fled, but he pursued them and captured them, routing their entire army.　　　Nu 32:42; Isa 9:4

13Gideon son of Joash then returned from the battle by the Pass of Heres. 14He caught a young man of Succoth and questioned him, and the young man wrote down for him the names of the seventy-seven officials of Succoth, the elders of the town. 15Then Gideon came and said to the men of Succoth, "Here are Zebah and Zalmunna, about whom you taunted me by saying, 'Do you already have the hands of Zebah and Zalmunna in your possession? Why should we give bread to your exhausted men?'" 16He took the elders of the town and taught the men of Succoth a lesson by punishing them with desert thorns and briers. 17He also pulled down the tower of

---

a8 Hebrew *Penuel,* a variant of *Peniel*; also in verses 9 and 17

Peniel and killed the men of the town. _{Jdg 6:11; 1Sa 14:12}

¹⁸Then he asked Zebah and Zalmunna, "What kind of men did you kill at Tabor?"

"Men like you," they answered, "each one with the bearing of a prince." _{Jos 19:22}

¹⁹Gideon replied, "Those were my brothers, the sons of my own mother. As surely as the LORD lives, if you had spared their lives, I would not kill you." ²⁰Turning to Jether, his oldest son, he said, "Kill them!" But Jether did not draw his sword, because he was only a boy and was afraid. _{Nu 14:21}

²¹Zebah and Zalmunna said, "Come, do it yourself. 'As is the man, so is his strength.'" So Gideon stepped forward and killed them, and took the ornaments off their camels' necks.

Gideon's Ephod

²²The Israelites said to Gideon, "Rule over us—you, your son and your grandson—because you have saved us out of the hand of Midian."

²³But Gideon told them, "I will not rule over you, nor will my son rule over you. The LORD will rule over you." ²⁴And he said, "I do have one request, that each of you give me an earring from your share of the plunder." (It was the custom of the Ishmaelites to wear gold earrings.) _{Ge 35:4; 1Sa 12:12}

²⁵They answered, "We'll be glad to give them." So they spread out a garment, and each man threw a ring from his plunder onto it. ²⁶The weight of the gold rings he asked for came to seventeen hundred shekels,^a not counting the ornaments, the pendants and the purple garments worn by the kings of Midian or the chains that were on their camels' necks. ²⁷Gideon made the gold into an ephod, which he placed in Ophrah, his town. All Israel prostituted themselves by worshiping it there, and it became a snare to Gideon and his family. _{Ne 11:2}

Gideon's Death

²⁸Thus Midian was subdued before the Israelites and did not raise its head again. During Gideon's lifetime, the land enjoyed peace forty years. _{Ps 83:2}

²⁹Jerub-Baal son of Joash went back home to live. ³⁰He had seventy sons of his own, for he had many wives. ³¹His concubine, who lived in Shechem, also bore him a son, whom he named Abimelech. ³²Gideon son of Joash died at a good old age and was buried in the tomb of his father Joash in Ophrah of the Abiezrites. _{2Sa 11:21; 2Ki 10:1}

³³No sooner had Gideon died than the Israelites again prostituted themselves to the Baals. They set up Baal-Berith as their god and ³⁴did not remember the LORD their God, who had rescued them from the hands of all

---

^a26 That is, about 43 pounds (about 19.5 kilograms)

their enemies on every side. ³⁵They also failed to show kindness to the family of Jerub-Baal (that is, Gideon) for all the good things he had done for them.

Abimelech

9 Abimelech son of Jerub-Baal went to his mother's brothers in Shechem and said to them and to all his mother's clan, ²"Ask all the citizens of Shechem, 'Which is better for you: to have all seventy of Jerub-Baal's sons rule over you, or just one man?' Remember, I am your flesh and blood."

³When the brothers repeated all this to the citizens of Shechem, they were inclined to follow Abimelech, for they said, "He is our brother." ⁴They gave him seventy shekels*ᵃ* of silver from the temple of Baal-Berith, and Abimelech used it to hire reckless adventurers, who became his followers. ⁵He went to his father's home in Ophrah and on one stone murdered his seventy brothers, the sons of Jerub-Baal. But Jotham, the youngest son of Jerub-Baal, escaped by hiding. ⁶Then all the citizens of Shechem and Beth Millo gathered beside the great tree at the pillar in Shechem to crown Abimelech king.   Ge 29:15

⁷When Jotham was told about this, he climbed up on the top of Mount Gerizim and shouted to them, "Listen to me, citizens of Shechem, so that God may lis-

ten to you. ⁸One day the trees went out to anoint a king for themselves. They said to the olive tree, 'Be our king.'   Dt 11:29

⁹"But the olive tree answered, 'Should I give up my oil, by which both gods and men are honored, to hold sway over the trees?'   Ps 52:8

¹⁰"Next, the trees said to the fig tree, 'Come and be our king.'

¹¹"But the fig tree replied, 'Should I give up my fruit, so good and sweet, to hold sway over the trees?'

¹²"Then the trees said to the vine, 'Come and be our king.'

¹³"But the vine answered, 'Should I give up my wine, which cheers both gods and men, to hold sway over the trees?'   Ge 14:18; Ecc 2:3

¹⁴"Finally all the trees said to the thornbush, 'Come and be our king.'

¹⁵"The thornbush said to the trees, 'If you really want to anoint me king over you, come and take refuge in my shade; but if not, then let fire come out of the thornbush and consume the cedars of Lebanon!'   Isa 30:2

¹⁶"Now if you have acted honorably and in good faith when you made Abimelech king, and if you have been fair to Jerub-Baal and his family, and if you have treated him as he deserves— ¹⁷and to think that my father fought for you, risked his life to rescue you from the hand of Midian ¹⁸(but

---

*ᵃ*4 That is, about 1 3/4 pounds (about 0.8 kilogram)

today you have revolted against my father's family, murdered his seventy sons on a single stone, and made Abimelech, the son of his slave girl, king over the citizens of Shechem because he is your brother)— ¹⁹if then you have acted honorably and in good faith toward Jerub-Baal and his family today, may Abimelech be your joy, and may you be his, too! ²⁰But if you have not, let fire come out from Abimelech and consume you, citizens of Shechem and Beth Millo, and let fire come out from you, citizens of Shechem and Beth Millo, and consume Abimelech!"   1Sa 19:5; Ps 119:109

²¹Then Jotham fled, escaping to Beer, and he lived there because he was afraid of his brother Abimelech.   Nu 21:16; 2Sa 20:14

²²After Abimelech had governed Israel three years, ²³God sent an evil spirit between Abimelech and the citizens of Shechem, who acted treacherously against Abimelech. ²⁴God did this in order that the crime against Jerub-Baal's seventy sons, the shedding of their blood, might be avenged on their brother Abimelech and on the citizens of Shechem, who had helped him murder his brothers. ²⁵In opposition to him these citizens of Shechem set men on the hilltops to ambush and rob everyone who passed by, and this was reported to Abimelech.   Nu 35:33; 1Sa 16:14

²⁶Now Gaal son of Ebed moved with his brothers into Shechem, and its citizens put their confidence in him. ²⁷After they had gone out into the fields and gathered the grapes and trodden them, they held a festival in the temple of their god. While they were eating and drinking, they cursed Abimelech. ²⁸Then Gaal son of Ebed said, "Who is Abimelech, and who is Shechem, that we should be subject to him? Isn't he Jerub-Baal's son, and isn't Zebul his deputy? Serve the men of Hamor, Shechem's father! Why should we serve Abimelech? ²⁹If only this people were under my command! Then I would get rid of him. I would say to Abimelech, 'Call out your whole army!' "ᵃ   2Sa 15:4; Isa 16:10

³⁰When Zebul the governor of the city heard what Gaal son of Ebed said, he was very angry. ³¹Under cover he sent messengers to Abimelech, saying, "Gaal son of Ebed and his brothers have come to Shechem and are stirring up the city against you. ³²Now then, during the night you and your men should come and lie in wait in the fields. ³³In the morning at sunrise, advance against the city. When Gaal and his men come out against you, do whatever your hand finds to do."

³⁴So Abimelech and all his troops set out by night and took up concealed positions near

ᵃ29 Septuagint; Hebrew *him." Then he said to Abimelech, "Call out your whole army!"*

Shechem in four companies. ³⁵Now Gaal son of Ebed had gone out and was standing at the entrance to the city gate just as Abimelech and his soldiers came out from their hiding place. Ps 32:7; Jer 49:10

³⁶When Gaal saw them, he said to Zebul, "Look, people are coming down from the tops of the mountains!"

Zebul replied, "You mistake the shadows of the mountains for men."

³⁷But Gaal spoke up again: "Look, people are coming down from the center of the land, and a company is coming from the direction of the soothsayers' tree." Eze 38:12

³⁸Then Zebul said to him, "Where is your big talk now, you who said, 'Who is Abimelech that we should be subject to him?' Aren't these the men you ridiculed? Go out and fight them!" Jdg 9:28-29

³⁹So Gaal led out ᵃ the citizens of Shechem and fought Abimelech. ⁴⁰Abimelech chased him, and many fell wounded in the flight—all the way to the entrance to the gate. ⁴¹Abimelech stayed in Arumah, and Zebul drove Gaal and his brothers out of Shechem. Ge 35:4

⁴²The next day the people of Shechem went out to the fields, and this was reported to Abimelech. ⁴³So he took his men, divided them into three companies and set an ambush in the fields. When he saw the people coming out of the city, he rose to attack them. ⁴⁴Abimelech and the companies with him rushed forward to a position at the entrance to the city gate. Then two companies rushed upon those in the fields and struck them down. ⁴⁵All that day Abimelech pressed his attack against the city until he had captured it and killed its people. Then he destroyed the city and scattered salt over it. Jos 8:2; Jdg 7:16

⁴⁶On hearing this, the citizens in the tower of Shechem went into the stronghold of the temple of El-Berith. ⁴⁷When Abimelech heard that they had assembled there, ⁴⁸he and all his men went up Mount Zalmon. He took an ax and cut off some branches, which he lifted to his shoulders. He ordered the men with him, "Quick! Do what you have seen me do!" ⁴⁹So all the men cut branches and followed Abimelech. They piled them against the stronghold and set it on fire over the people inside. So all the people in the tower of Shechem, about a thousand men and women, also died.

⁵⁰Next Abimelech went to Thebez and besieged it and captured it. ⁵¹Inside the city, however, was a strong tower, to which all the men and women—all the people of the city—fled. They locked themselves in and climbed up on the tower roof. ⁵²Abimelech went to

ᵃ39 Or Gaal went out in the sight of

the tower and stormed it. But as he approached the entrance to the tower to set it on fire, ⁵³a woman dropped an upper millstone on his head and cracked his skull.   2Sa 11:21; Jer 25:10

⁵⁴Hurriedly he called to his armor-bearer, "Draw your sword and kill me, so that they can't say, 'A woman killed him.'" So his servant ran him through, and he died. ⁵⁵When the Israelites saw that Abimelech was dead, they went home.   1Sa 31:4

⁵⁶Thus God repaid the wickedness that Abimelech had done to his father by murdering his seventy brothers. ⁵⁷God also made the men of Shechem pay for all their wickedness. The curse of Jotham son of Jerub-Baal came on them.   Ps 94:23

Tola

10 After the time of Abimelech a man of Issachar, Tola son of Puah, the son of Dodo, rose to save Israel. He lived in Shamir, in the hill country of Ephraim. ²He led^a Israel twenty-three years; then he died, and was buried in Shamir.

Jair

³He was followed by Jair of Gilead, who led Israel twenty-two years. ⁴He had thirty sons, who rode thirty donkeys. They controlled thirty towns in Gilead, which to this day are called Havvoth Jair. ^b ⁵When Jair died, he was buried in Kamon. Nu 32:41

Jephthah

⁶Again the Israelites did evil in the eyes of the Lord. They served the Baals and the Ashtoreths, and the gods of Aram, the gods of Sidon, the gods of Moab, the gods of the Ammonites and the gods of the Philistines. And because the Israelites forsook the Lord and no longer served him, ⁷he became angry with them. He sold them into the hands of the Philistines and the Ammonites, ⁸who that year shattered and crushed them. For eighteen years they oppressed all the Israelites on the east side of the Jordan in Gilead, the land of the Amorites. ⁹The Ammonites also crossed the Jordan to fight against Judah, Benjamin and the house of Ephraim; and Israel was in great distress. ¹⁰Then the Israelites cried out to the Lord, "We have sinned against you, forsaking our God and serving the Baals."

¹¹The Lord replied, "When the Egyptians, the Amorites, the Ammonites, the Philistines, ¹²the Sidonians, the Amalekites and the Maonites^c oppressed you and you cried to me for help, did I not save you from their hands? ¹³But you have forsaken me and served other gods, so I will no longer save you. ¹⁴Go and cry out to the

---

^a2 Traditionally *judged*; also in verse 3   ^b4 Or *called the settlements of Jair*
^c12 Hebrew; some Septuagint manuscripts *Midianites*

gods you have chosen. Let them save you when you are in trouble!" Ex 14:30; Dt 32:37

15But the Israelites said to the LORD, "We have sinned. Do with us whatever you think best, but please rescue us now." 16Then they got rid of the foreign gods among them and served the LORD. And he could bear Israel's misery no longer.

17When the Ammonites were called to arms and camped in Gilead, the Israelites assembled and camped at Mizpah. 18The leaders of the people of Gilead said to each other, "Whoever will launch the attack against the Ammonites will be the head of all those living in Gilead."

11 Jephthah the Gileadite was a mighty warrior. His father was Gilead; his mother was a prostitute. 2Gilead's wife also bore him sons, and when they were grown up, they drove Jephthah away. "You are not going to get any inheritance in our family," they said, "because you are the son of another woman." 3So Jephthah fled from his brothers and settled in the land of Tob, where a group of adventurers gathered around him and followed him. 2Sa 10:6; Heb 11:32

4Some time later, when the Ammonites made war on Israel, 5the elders of Gilead went to get Jephthah from the land of Tob. 6"Come," they said, "be our commander, so we can fight the Ammonites." Jdg 10:9

7Jephthah said to them,

"Didn't you hate me and drive me from my father's house? Why do you come to me now, when you're in trouble?" Ge 26:16

8The elders of Gilead said to him, "Nevertheless, we are turning to you now; come with us to fight the Ammonites, and you will be our head over all who live in Gilead." Jdg 10:18

9Jephthah answered, "Suppose you take me back to fight the Ammonites and the LORD gives them to me—will I really be your head?"

10The elders of Gilead replied, "The LORD is our witness; we will certainly do as you say." 11So Jephthah went with the elders of Gilead, and the people made him head and commander over them. And he repeated all his words before the LORD in Mizpah. Ge 31:50

12Then Jephthah sent messengers to the Ammonite king with the question: "What do you have against us that you have attacked our country?"

13The king of the Ammonites answered Jephthah's messengers, "When Israel came up out of Egypt, they took away my land from the Arnon to the Jabbok, all the way to the Jordan. Now give it back peaceably."

14Jephthah sent back messengers to the Ammonite king, 15saying:

"This is what Jephthah says: Israel did not take the land of Moab or the land of the Ammonites. 16But when

they came up out of Egypt, Israel went through the desert to the Red Sea[a] and on to Kadesh. [17]Then Israel sent messengers to the king of Edom, saying, 'Give us permission to go through your country,' but the king of Edom would not listen. They sent also to the king of Moab, and he refused. So Israel stayed at Kadesh.　Dt 2:19

[18]"Next they traveled through the desert, skirted the lands of Edom and Moab, passed along the eastern side of the country of Moab, and camped on the other side of the Arnon. They did not enter the territory of Moab, for the Arnon was its border.　Nu 20:21

[19]"Then Israel sent messengers to Sihon king of the Amorites, who ruled in Heshbon, and said to him, 'Let us pass through your country to our own place.' [20]Sihon, however, did not trust Israel[b] to pass through his territory. He mustered all his men and encamped at Jahaz and fought with Israel.　Nu 21:23; Jos 12:2

[21]"Then the LORD, the God of Israel, gave Sihon and all his men into Israel's hands, and they defeated them. Israel took over all the land of the Amorites who lived in that country,

[22]capturing all of it from the Arnon to the Jabbok and from the desert to the Jordan.　Nu 21:24; Dt 2:26

[23]"Now since the LORD, the God of Israel, has driven the Amorites out before his people Israel, what right have you to take it over? [24]Will you not take what your god Chemosh gives you? Likewise, whatever the LORD our God has given us, we will possess. [25]Are you better than Balak son of Zippor, king of Moab? Did he ever quarrel with Israel or fight with them? [26]For three hundred years Israel occupied Heshbon, Aroer, the surrounding settlements and all the towns along the Arnon. Why didn't you retake them during that time? [27]I have not wronged you, but you are doing me wrong by waging war against me. Let the LORD, the Judge,[c] decide the dispute this day between the Israelites and the Ammonites."　Nu 21:29; 2Ch 20:12

[28]The king of Ammon, however, paid no attention to the message Jephthah sent him.

[29]Then the Spirit of the LORD came upon Jephthah. He crossed Gilead and Manasseh, passed through Mizpah of Gilead, and from there he advanced against the Ammonites.

---

[a]16 Hebrew *Yam Suph*; that is, Sea of Reeds agreement for Israel　[c]27 Or *Ruler*　　[b]20 Or *however, would not make an*

³⁰And Jephthah made a vow to the LORD: "If you give the Ammonites into my hands, ³¹whatever comes out of the door of my house to meet me when I return in triumph from the Ammonites will be the LORD's, and I will sacrifice it as a burnt offering." Lev 1:3; Jdg 3:10

³²Then Jephthah went over to fight the Ammonites, and the LORD gave them into his hands. ³³He devastated twenty towns from Aroer to the vicinity of Minnith, as far as Abel Keramim. Thus Israel subdued Ammon. Eze 27:17

³⁴When Jephthah returned to his home in Mizpah, who should come out to meet him but his daughter, dancing to the sound of tambourines! She was an only child. Except for her he had neither son nor daughter. ³⁵When he saw her, he tore his clothes and cried, "Oh! My daughter! You have made me miserable and wretched, because I have made a vow to the LORD that I cannot break."

³⁶"My father," she replied, "you have given your word to the LORD. Do to me just as you promised, now that the LORD has avenged you of your enemies, the Ammonites. ³⁷But grant me this one request," she said. "Give me two months to roam the hills and weep with my friends, because I will never marry." 2Sa 18:19; Lk 1:38

³⁸"You may go," he said. And he let her go for two months. She and the girls went into the hills and wept because she would never marry. ³⁹After the two months, she returned to her father and he did to her as he had vowed. And she was a virgin.

From this comes the Israelite custom ⁴⁰that each year the young women of Israel go out for four days to commemorate the daughter of Jephthah the Gileadite.

Jephthah and Ephraim

12 The men of Ephraim called out their forces, crossed over to Zaphon and said to Jephthah, "Why did you go to fight the Ammonites without calling us to go with you? We're going to burn down your house over your head." Jdg 8:1

²Jephthah answered, "I and my people were engaged in a great struggle with the Ammonites, and although I called, you didn't save me out of their hands. ³When I saw that you wouldn't help, I took my life in my hands and crossed over to fight the Ammonites, and the LORD gave me the victory over them. Now why have you come up today to fight me?" Dt 20:4

⁴Jephthah then called together the men of Gilead and fought against Ephraim. The Gileadites struck them down because the Ephraimites had said, "You Gileadites are renegades from Ephraim and Manasseh." ⁵The Gileadites captured the fords of the Jordan leading to Ephraim, and when-

ever a survivor of Ephraim said, "Let me cross over," the men of Gilead asked him, "Are you an Ephraimite?" If he replied, "No," ⁶they said, "All right, say 'Shibboleth.'" If he said, "Sibboleth," because he could not pronounce the word correctly, they seized him and killed him at the fords of the Jordan. Forty-two thousand Ephraimites were killed at that time.   1Ki 17:1

⁷Jephthah led*ᵃ* Israel six years. Then Jephthah the Gileadite died, and was buried in a town in Gilead.   Heb 11:32

Ibzan, Elon and Abdon

⁸After him, Ibzan of Bethlehem led Israel. ⁹He had thirty sons and thirty daughters. He gave his daughters away in marriage to those outside his clan, and for his sons he brought in thirty young women as wives from outside his clan. Ibzan led Israel seven years. ¹⁰Then Ibzan died, and was buried in Bethlehem.   Ge 35:19

¹¹After him, Elon the Zebulunite led Israel ten years. ¹²Then Elon died, and was buried in Aijalon in the land of Zebulun.   Jos 10:12

¹³After him, Abdon son of Hillel, from Pirathon, led Israel. ¹⁴He had forty sons and thirty grandsons, who rode on seventy donkeys. He led Israel eight years. ¹⁵Then Abdon son of Hillel died, and was buried at Pira-

thon in Ephraim, in the hill country of the Amalekites.

The Birth of Samson

13 Again the Israelites did evil in the eyes of the LORD, so the LORD delivered them into the hands of the Philistines for forty years.   Jdg 14:4

²A certain man of Zorah, named Manoah, from the clan of the Danites, had a wife who was sterile and remained childless. ³The angel of the LORD appeared to her and said, "You are sterile and childless, but you are going to conceive and have a son. ⁴Now see to it that you drink no wine or other fermented drink and that you do not eat anything unclean, ⁵because you will conceive and give birth to a son. No razor may be used on his head, because the boy is to be a Nazirite, set apart to God from birth, and he will begin the deliverance of Israel from the hands of the Philistines." Jos 19:41

⁶Then the woman went to her husband and told him, "A man of God came to me. He looked like an angel of God, very awesome. I didn't ask him where he came from, and he didn't tell me his name. ⁷But he said to me, 'You will conceive and give birth to a son. Now then, drink no wine or other fermented drink and do not eat anything unclean, because the boy will be a Nazirite of God from birth until the day of his death.'" 1Sa 2:27

ᵃ7 Traditionally *judged*; also in verses 8-14

8Then Manoah prayed to the LORD: "O Lord, I beg you, let the man of God you sent to us come again to teach us how to bring up the boy who is to be born."   Jdg 16:28; Hab 3:1

9God heard Manoah, and the angel of God came again to the woman while she was out in the field; but her husband Manoah was not with her. 10The woman hurried to tell her husband, "He's here! The man who appeared to me the other day!"

11Manoah got up and followed his wife. When he came to the man, he said, "Are you the one who talked to my wife?"   Jdg 13:8

"I am," he said.

12So Manoah asked him, "When your words are fulfilled, what is to be the rule for the boy's life and work?"

13The angel of the LORD answered, "Your wife must do all that I have told her. 14She must not eat anything that comes from the grapevine, nor drink any wine or other fermented drink nor eat anything unclean. She must do everything I have commanded her."   Lev 10:9

15Manoah said to the angel of the LORD, "We would like you to stay until we prepare a young goat for you."   Ge 18:5; Jdg 6:19

16The angel of the LORD replied, "Even though you detain me, I will not eat any of your food. But if you prepare a burnt offering, offer it to the LORD."

(Manoah did not realize that it was the angel of the LORD.)

17Then Manoah inquired of the angel of the LORD, "What is your name, so that we may honor you when your word comes true?"   Ge 32:29

18He replied, "Why do you ask my name? It is beyond understanding. a" 19Then Manoah took a young goat, together with the grain offering, and sacrificed it on a rock to the LORD. And the LORD did an amazing thing while Manoah and his wife watched: 20As the flame blazed up from the altar toward heaven, the angel of the LORD ascended in the flame. Seeing this, Manoah and his wife fell with their faces to the ground. 21When the angel of the LORD did not show himself again to Manoah and his wife, Manoah realized that it was the angel of the LORD.   Isa 9:6

22"We are doomed to die!" he said to his wife. "We have seen God!"   Dt 5:26; Jdg 6:22

23But his wife answered, "If the LORD had meant to kill us, he would not have accepted a burnt offering and grain offering from our hands, nor shown us all these things or now told us this."   Ps 25:14

24The woman gave birth to a boy and named him Samson. He grew and the LORD blessed him, 25and the Spirit of the LORD began to stir him while he was

a18 Or is wonderful

in Mahaneh Dan, between Zorah and Eshtaol.   Heb 11:32

Samson's Marriage

14 Samson went down to Timnah and saw there a young Philistine woman. ²When he returned, he said to his father and mother, "I have seen a Philistine woman in Timnah; now get her for me as my wife."   Ge 21:21; Jdg 13:24

³His father and mother replied, "Isn't there an acceptable woman among your relatives or among all our people? Must you go to the uncircumcised Philistines to get a wife?"   Ge 24:4

But Samson said to his father, "Get her for me. She's the right one for me." ⁴(His parents did not know that this was from the LORD, who was seeking an occasion to confront the Philistines; for at that time they were ruling over Israel.) ⁵Samson went down to Timnah together with his father and mother. As they approached the vineyards of Timnah, suddenly a young lion came roaring toward him. ⁶The Spirit of the LORD came upon him in power so that he tore the lion apart with his bare hands as he might have torn a young goat. But he told neither his father nor his mother what he had done. ⁷Then he went down and talked with the woman, and he liked her.   Jos 11:20; 1Sa 17:35

⁸Some time later, when he went back to marry her, he turned aside to look at the lion's carcass. In it was a swarm of bees and some honey, ⁹which he scooped out with his hands and ate as he went along. When he rejoined his parents, he gave them some, and they too ate it. But he did not tell them that he had taken the honey from the lion's carcass.

¹⁰Now his father went down to see the woman. And Samson made a feast there, as was customary for bridegrooms. ¹¹When he appeared, he was given thirty companions.   Ge 29:22

¹²"Let me tell you a riddle," Samson said to them. "If you can give me the answer within the seven days of the feast, I will give you thirty linen garments and thirty sets of clothes. ¹³If you can't tell me the answer, you must give me thirty linen garments and thirty sets of clothes."   Ge 29:27; Eze 17:2

"Tell us your riddle," they said. "Let's hear it."

¹⁴He replied,

"Out of the eater, something to eat;
out of the strong,
something sweet."   Jdg 14:18

For three days they could not give the answer.

¹⁵On the fourth*ᵃ* day, they said to Samson's wife, "Coax your husband into explaining the riddle for us, or we will burn you and your father's house-

---

ᵃ15 Some Septuagint manuscripts and Syriac; Hebrew *seventh*

hold to death. Did you invite us here to rob us?" Ecc 7:26

[16]Then Samson's wife threw herself on him, sobbing, "You hate me! You don't really love me. You've given my people a riddle, but you haven't told me the answer." Jdg 16:15

"I haven't even explained it to my father or mother," he replied, "so why should I explain it to you?" [17]She cried the whole seven days of the feast. So on the seventh day he finally told her, because she continued to press him. She in turn explained the riddle to her people.

[18]Before sunset on the seventh day the men of the town said to him,

"What is sweeter than honey?
What is stronger than a lion?" Jdg 15:14

Samson said to them,

"If you had not plowed with my heifer,
you would not have solved my riddle."

[19]Then the Spirit of the LORD came upon him in power. He went down to Ashkelon, struck down thirty of their men, stripped them of their belongings and gave their clothes to those who had explained the riddle. Burning with anger, he went up to his father's house. [20]And Samson's wife was given to the friend who had attended him at his wedding. 1Sa 11:6

Samson's Vengeance on the Philistines

15 Later on, at the time of wheat harvest, Samson took a young goat and went to visit his wife. He said, "I'm going to my wife's room." But her father would not let him go in.

[2]"I was so sure you thoroughly hated her," he said, "that I gave her to your friend. Isn't her younger sister more attractive? Take her instead." Jdg 14:20

[3]Samson said to them, "This time I have a right to get even with the Philistines; I will really harm them." [4]So he went out and caught three hundred foxes and tied them tail to tail in pairs. He then fastened a torch to every pair of tails, [5]lit the torches and let the foxes loose in the standing grain of the Philistines. He burned up the shocks and standing grain, together with the vineyards and olive groves. Ex 22:6; 2Sa 14:30-31

[6]When the Philistines asked, "Who did this?" they were told, "Samson, the Timnite's son-in-law, because his wife was given to his friend." Jdg 14:20

So the Philistines went up and burned her and her father to death. [7]Samson said to them, "Since you've acted like this, I won't stop until I get my revenge on you." [8]He attacked them viciously and slaughtered many of them. Then he went down and stayed in a cave in the rock of Etam. Ge 38:24

[9]The Philistines went up and

camped in Judah, spreading out near Lehi. ¹⁰The men of Judah asked, "Why have you come to fight us?"   Jdg 15:14,17,19

"We have come to take Samson prisoner," they answered, "to do to him as he did to us."

¹¹Then three thousand men from Judah went down to the cave in the rock of Etam and said to Samson, "Don't you realize that the Philistines are rulers over us? What have you done to us?"   Ps 106:40-42

He answered, "I merely did to them what they did to me."

¹²They said to him, "We've come to tie you up and hand you over to the Philistines."

Samson said, "Swear to me that you won't kill me yourselves."   Ge 47:31

¹³"Agreed," they answered. "We will only tie you up and hand you over to them. We will not kill you." So they bound him with two new ropes and led him up from the rock. ¹⁴As he approached Lehi, the Philistines came toward him shouting. The Spirit of the LORD came upon him in power. The ropes on his arms became like charred flax, and the bindings dropped from his hands. ¹⁵Finding a fresh jawbone of a donkey, he grabbed it and struck down a thousand men.   Jos 2:6; Jdg 16:11

¹⁶Then Samson said,

"With a donkey's jawbone

I have made donkeys of
    them. ᵃ
With a donkey's jawbone
I have killed a thousand
    men."   Jer 22:19

¹⁷When he finished speaking, he threw away the jawbone; and the place was called Ramath Lehi. ᵇ   Jdg 15:9

¹⁸Because he was very thirsty, he cried out to the LORD, "You have given your servant this great victory. Must I now die of thirst and fall into the hands of the uncircumcised?" ¹⁹Then God opened up the hollow place in Lehi, and water came out of it. When Samson drank, his strength returned and he revived. So the spring was called En Hakkore, ᶜ and it is still there in Lehi.   Jdg 16:28

²⁰Samson led ᵈ Israel for twenty years in the days of the Philistines.   Jdg 16:31; Heb 11:32

Samson and Delilah

16 One day Samson went to Gaza, where he saw a prostitute. He went in to spend the night with her. ²The people of Gaza were told, "Samson is here!" So they surrounded the place and lay in wait for him all night at the city gate. They made no move during the night, saying, "At dawn we'll kill him."   1Sa 19:11; Ps 118:10

³But Samson lay there only until the middle of the night.

ᵃ16 Or *made a heap or two*; the Hebrew for *donkey* sounds like the Hebrew for *heap.*
ᵇ17 *Ramath Lehi* means *jawbone hill.*   ᶜ19 *En Hakkore* means *caller's spring.*
ᵈ20 Traditionally *judged*

Then he got up and took hold of the doors of the city gate, together with the two posts, and tore them loose, bar and all. He lifted them to his shoulders and carried them to the top of the hill that faces Hebron.   Jos 10:36

⁴Some time later, he fell in love with a woman in the Valley of Sorek whose name was Delilah. ⁵The rulers of the Philistines went to her and said, "See if you can lure him into showing you the secret of his great strength and how we can overpower him so we may tie him up and subdue him. Each one of us will give you eleven hundred shekels*a* of silver."   Ge 24:67

⁶So Delilah said to Samson, "Tell me the secret of your great strength and how you can be tied up and subdued."   1Ki 21:7

⁷Samson answered her, "If anyone ties me with seven fresh thongs*b* that have not been dried, I'll become as weak as any other man."

⁸Then the rulers of the Philistines brought her seven fresh thongs that had not been dried, and she tied him with them. ⁹With men hidden in the room, she called to him, "Samson, the Philistines are upon you!" But he snapped the thongs as easily as a piece of string snaps when it comes close to a flame. So the secret of his strength was not discovered.   Jdg 16:12

¹⁰Then Delilah said to Samson, "You have made a fool of me; you lied to me. Come now, tell me how you can be tied."

¹¹He said, "If anyone ties me securely with new ropes that have never been used, I'll become as weak as any other man."   Jdg 15:13

¹²So Delilah took new ropes and tied him with them. Then, with men hidden in the room, she called to him, "Samson, the Philistines are upon you!" But he snapped the ropes off his arms as if they were threads.

¹³Delilah then said to Samson, "Until now, you have been making a fool of me and lying to me. Tell me how you can be tied."   Jdg 16:10,15

He replied, "If you weave the seven braids of my head into the fabric on the loom and tighten it with the pin, I'll become as weak as any other man." So while he was sleeping, Delilah took the seven braids of his head, wove them into the fabric ¹⁴and*c* tightened it with the pin.

Again she called to him, "Samson, the Philistines are upon you!" He awoke from his sleep and pulled up the pin and the loom, with the fabric.   Jdg 16:9

¹⁵Then she said to him, "How can you say, 'I love you,' when you won't confide in me? This is the third time you have made a fool of me and haven't told

a5 That is, about 28 pounds (about 13 kilograms)   *b7* Or *bowstrings*; also in verses 8 and 9   *c13,14* Some Septuagint manuscripts; Hebrew *"I can, if you weave the seven braids of my head into the fabric on the loom." ¹⁴So she*

me the secret of your great strength." [16]With such nagging she prodded him day after day until he was tired to death.

[17]So he told her everything. "No razor has ever been used on my head," he said, "because I have been a Nazirite set apart to God since birth. If my head were shaved, my strength would leave me, and I would become as weak as any other man." Nu 6:2; Mic 7:5

[18]When Delilah saw that he had told her everything, she sent word to the rulers of the Philistines, "Come back once more; he has told me everything." So the rulers of the Philistines returned with the silver in their hands. [19]Having put him to sleep on her lap, she called a man to shave off the seven braids of his hair, and so began to subdue him. [a] And his strength left him. 1Sa 5:8

[20]Then she called, "Samson, the Philistines are upon you!"

He awoke from his sleep and thought, "I'll go out as before and shake myself free." But he did not know that the LORD had left him. Jos 7:12; 1Sa 16:14

[21]Then the Philistines seized him, gouged out his eyes and took him down to Gaza. Binding him with bronze shackles, they set him to grinding in the prison. [22]But the hair on his head began to grow again after it had been shaved. Jer 47:1

The Death of Samson

[23]Now the rulers of the Philistines assembled to offer a great sacrifice to Dagon their god and to celebrate, saying, "Our god has delivered Samson, our enemy, into our hands." 1Sa 5:2

[24]When the people saw him, they praised their god, saying,

"Our god has delivered our enemy
into our hands,
the one who laid waste our land
and multiplied our slain."

[25]While they were in high spirits, they shouted, "Bring out Samson to entertain us." So they called Samson out of the prison, and he performed for them. Jdg 9:27; Ru 3:7

When they stood him among the pillars, [26]Samson said to the servant who held his hand, "Put me where I can feel the pillars that support the temple, so that I may lean against them." [27]Now the temple was crowded with men and women; all the rulers of the Philistines were there, and on the roof were about three thousand men and women watching Samson perform. [28]Then Samson prayed to the LORD, "O Sovereign LORD, remember me. O God, please strengthen me just once more, and let me with one blow get revenge on the Philistines for my two eyes." [29]Then Samson reached toward the two

---

[a]19 Hebrew; some Septuagint manuscripts *and he began to weaken*

central pillars on which the temple stood. Bracing himself against them, his right hand on the one and his left hand on the other, ³⁰Samson said, "Let me die with the Philistines!" Then he pushed with all his might, and down came the temple on the rulers and all the people in it. Thus he killed many more when he died than while he lived. _{Jos 2:8; Jer 15:15}

³¹Then his brothers and his father's whole family went down to get him. They brought him back and buried him between Zorah and Eshtaol in the tomb of Manoah his father. He had led*ᵃ* Israel twenty years.

Micah's Idols

17 Now a man named Micah from the hill country of Ephraim ²said to his mother, "The eleven hundred shekels*ᵇ* of silver that were taken from you and about which I heard you utter a curse—I have that silver with me; I took it." _{Jdg 18:2}

Then his mother said, "The Lᴏʀᴅ bless you, my son!" _{Ru 2:20}

³When he returned the eleven hundred shekels of silver to his mother, she said, "I solemnly consecrate my silver to the Lᴏʀᴅ for my son to make a carved image and a cast idol. I will give it back to you." _{Ex 20:4}

⁴So he returned the silver to his mother, and she took two hundred shekels*ᶜ* of silver and gave them to a silversmith, who made them into the image and the idol. And they were put in Micah's house. _{Ex 32:4; Isa 17:8}

⁵Now this man Micah had a shrine, and he made an ephod and some idols and installed one of his sons as his priest. ⁶In those days Israel had no king; everyone did as he saw fit.

⁷A young Levite from Bethlehem in Judah, who had been living within the clan of Judah, ⁸left that town in search of some other place to stay. On his way*ᵈ* he came to Micah's house in the hill country of Ephraim. _{Mt 2:1}

⁹Micah asked him, "Where are you from?"

"I'm a Levite from Bethlehem in Judah," he said, "and I'm looking for a place to stay."_{Ru 1:1}

¹⁰Then Micah said to him, "Live with me and be my father and priest, and I'll give you ten shekels*ᵉ* of silver a year, your clothes and your food." ¹¹So the Levite agreed to live with him, and the young man was to him like one of his sons. ¹²Then Micah installed the Levite, and the young man became his priest and lived in his house. ¹³And Micah said, "Now I know that the Lᴏʀᴅ will be good to me, since this Levite has become my priest." _{Nu 18:7}

Danites Settle in Laish

18 In those days Israel had no king. _{Jdg 17:6}

---

*ᵃ*31 Traditionally *judged*   *ᵇ*2 That is, about 28 pounds (about 13 kilograms)
*ᶜ*4 That is, about 5 pounds (about 2.3 kilograms)   *ᵈ*8 Or *To carry on his profession*
*ᵉ*10 That is, about 4 ounces (about 110 grams)

And in those days the tribe of the Danites was seeking a place of their own where they might settle, because they had not yet come into an inheritance among the tribes of Israel. ²So the Danites sent five warriors from Zorah and Eshtaol to spy out the land and explore it. These men represented all their clans. They told them, "Go, explore the land."   Nu 21:32; Jos 19:47

The men entered the hill country of Ephraim and came to the house of Micah, where they spent the night. ³When they were near Micah's house, they recognized the voice of the young Levite; so they turned in there and asked him, "Who brought you here? What are you doing in this place? Why are you here?"   Jdg 17:1,7

⁴He told them what Micah had done for him, and said, "He has hired me and I am his priest."   Jdg 17:12

⁵Then they said to him, "Please inquire of God to learn whether our journey will be successful."   1Sa 14:18; 2Sa 5:19

⁶The priest answered them, "Go in peace. Your journey has the LORD's approval."   1Ki 22:6

⁷So the five men left and came to Laish, where they saw that the people were living in safety, like the Sidonians, unsuspecting and secure. And since their land lacked nothing, they were prosperous.ᵃ Also, they lived a long way from the Sidonians and had no relationship with anyone else.ᵇ   Ge 34:25; Jos 19:47

⁸When they returned to Zorah and Eshtaol, their brothers asked them, "How did you find things?"

⁹They answered, "Come on, let's attack them! We have seen that the land is very good. Aren't you going to do something? Don't hesitate to go there and take it over. ¹⁰When you get there, you will find an unsuspecting people and a spacious land that God has put into your hands, a land that lacks nothing whatever."   Nu 13:30; Dt 8:9

¹¹Then six hundred men from the clan of the Danites, armed for battle, set out from Zorah and Eshtaol. ¹²On their way they set up camp near Kiriath Jearim in Judah. This is why the place west of Kiriath Jearim is called Mahaneh Danᶜ to this day. ¹³From there they went on to the hill country of Ephraim and came to Micah's house.

¹⁴Then the five men who had spied out the land of Laish said to their brothers, "Do you know that one of these houses has an ephod, other household gods, a carved image and a cast idol? Now you know what to do." ¹⁵So they turned in there and went to the house of the young Levite at Micah's place and greeted him. ¹⁶The six hundred Danites, armed for battle, stood

---

ᵃ7 The meaning of the Hebrew for this clause is uncertain.   ᵇ7 Hebrew; some Septuagint manuscripts *with the Arameans*   ᶜ12 *Mahaneh Dan* means *Dan's camp.*

at the entrance to the gate. ¹⁷The five men who had spied out the land went inside and took the carved image, the ephod, the other household gods and the cast idol while the priest and the six hundred armed men stood at the entrance to the gate.   Ge 31:19

¹⁸When these men went into Micah's house and took the carved image, the ephod, the other household gods and the cast idol, the priest said to them, "What are you doing?"

¹⁹They answered him, "Be quiet! Don't say a word. Come with us, and be our father and priest. Isn't it better that you serve a tribe and clan in Israel as priest rather than just one man's household?" ²⁰Then the priest was glad. He took the ephod, the other household gods and the carved image and went along with the people. ²¹Putting their little children, their livestock and their possessions in front of them, they turned away and left.   Job 21:5

²²When they had gone some distance from Micah's house, the men who lived near Micah were called together and overtook the Danites. ²³As they shouted after them, the Danites turned and said to Micah, "What's the matter with you that you called out your men to fight?"   2Ki 6:28

²⁴He replied, "You took the gods I made, and my priest, and went away. What else do I have? How can you ask, 'What's the matter with you?' "

²⁵The Danites answered, "Don't argue with us, or some hot-tempered men will attack you, and you and your family will lose your lives." ²⁶So the Danites went their way, and Micah, seeing that they were too strong for him, turned around and went back home.

²⁷Then they took what Micah had made, and his priest, and went on to Laish, against a peaceful and unsuspecting people. They attacked them with the sword and burned down their city. ²⁸There was no one to rescue them because they lived a long way from Sidon and had no relationship with anyone else. The city was in a valley near Beth Rehob.   Jos 19:47

The Danites rebuilt the city and settled there. ²⁹They named it Dan after their forefather Dan, who was born to Israel—though the city used to be called Laish. ³⁰There the Danites set up for themselves the idols, and Jonathan son of Gershom, the son of Moses,^a and his sons were priests for the tribe of Dan until the time of the captivity of the land. ³¹They continued to use the idols Micah had made, all the time the house of God was in Shiloh.   Ex 2:22; 1Ki 15:20

---

^a30 An ancient Hebrew scribal tradition, some Septuagint manuscripts and Vulgate; Masoretic Text *Manasseh*

A Levite and His Concubine

19 In those days Israel had no king.

Now a Levite who lived in a remote area in the hill country of Ephraim took a concubine from Bethlehem in Judah. ²But she was unfaithful to him. She left him and went back to her father's house in Bethlehem, Judah. After she had been there four months, ³her husband went to her to persuade her to return. He had with him his servant and two donkeys. She took him into her father's house, and when her father saw him, he gladly welcomed him. ⁴His father-in-law, the girl's father, prevailed upon him to stay; so he remained with him three days, eating and drinking, and sleeping there. Ex 32:6; Ru 1:1

⁵On the fourth day they got up early and he prepared to leave, but the girl's father said to his son-in-law, "Refresh yourself with something to eat; then you can go." ⁶So the two of them sat down to eat and drink together. Afterward the girl's father said, "Please stay tonight and enjoy yourself." ⁷And when the man got up to go, his father-in-law persuaded him, so he stayed there that night. ⁸On the morning of the fifth day, when he rose to go, the girl's father said, "Refresh yourself. Wait till afternoon!" So the two of them ate together. Ge 18:5

⁹Then when the man, with his concubine and his servant, got up to leave, his father-in-law, the girl's father, said, "Now look, it's almost evening. Spend the night here; the day is nearly over. Stay and enjoy yourself. Early tomorrow morning you can get up and be on your way home." ¹⁰But, unwilling to stay another night, the man left and went toward Jebus (that is, Jerusalem), with his two saddled donkeys and his concubine. Ge 10:16; Jos 15:8

¹¹When they were near Jebus and the day was almost gone, the servant said to his master, "Come, let's stop at this city of the Jebusites and spend the night." Jos 3:10; Jdg 1:21

¹²His master replied, "No. We won't go into an alien city, whose people are not Israelites. We will go on to Gibeah." ¹³He added, "Come, let's try to reach Gibeah or Ramah and spend the night in one of those places." ¹⁴So they went on, and the sun set as they neared Gibeah in Benjamin. ¹⁵There they stopped to spend the night. They went and sat in the city square, but no one took them into his home for the night. 1Sa 10:26; Heb 11:13

¹⁶That evening an old man from the hill country of Ephraim, who was living in Gibeah (the men of the place were Benjamites), came in from his work in the fields. ¹⁷When he looked and saw the traveler in the city square, the old man asked, "Where are you going? Where did you come from?"

¹⁸He answered, "We are on

our way from Bethlehem in Judah to a remote area in the hill country of Ephraim where I live. I have been to Bethlehem in Judah and now I am going to the house of the LORD. No one has taken me into his house. ¹⁹We have both straw and fodder for our donkeys and bread and wine for ourselves your servants—me, your maidservant, and the young man with us. We don't need anything."   Jdg 18:31

²⁰"You are welcome at my house," the old man said. "Let me supply whatever you need. Only don't spend the night in the square." ²¹So he took him into his house and fed his donkeys. After they had washed their feet, they had something to eat and drink.   Ge 24:32

²²While they were enjoying themselves, some of the wicked men of the city surrounded the house. Pounding on the door, they shouted to the old man who owned the house, "Bring out the man who came to your house so we can have sex with him."   Ge 19:4; Dt 13:13

²³The owner of the house went outside and said to them, "No, my friends, don't be so vile. Since this man is my guest, don't do this disgraceful thing. ²⁴Look, here is my virgin daughter, and his concubine. I will bring them out to you now, and you can use them and do to them whatever you wish. But to this man, don't do such a disgraceful thing."   Ge 19:8; 34:7

²⁵But the men would not listen to him. So the man took his concubine and sent her outside to them, and they raped her and abused her throughout the night, and at dawn they let her go. ²⁶At daybreak the woman went back to the house where her master was staying, fell down at the door and lay there until daylight.   Jdg 20:5; 1Sa 31:4

²⁷When her master got up in the morning and opened the door of the house and stepped out to continue on his way, there lay his concubine, fallen in the doorway of the house, with her hands on the threshold. ²⁸He said to her, "Get up; let's go." But there was no answer. Then the man put her on his donkey and set out for home.

²⁹When he reached home, he took a knife and cut up his concubine, limb by limb, into twelve parts and sent them into all the areas of Israel. ³⁰Everyone who saw it said, "Such a thing has never been seen or done, not since the day the Israelites came up out of Egypt. Think about it! Consider it! Tell us what to do!"   Jdg 20:7; 1Sa 11:7

Israelites Fight the Benjamites

20 Then all the Israelites from Dan to Beersheba and from the land of Gilead came out as one man and assembled before the LORD in Mizpah. ²The leaders of all the people of the tribes of Israel took their places in the assem-

bly of the people of God, four hundred thousand soldiers armed with swords. ³(The Benjamites heard that the Israelites had gone up to Mizpah.) Then the Israelites said, "Tell us how this awful thing happened."

⁴So the Levite, the husband of the murdered woman, said, "I and my concubine came to Gibeah in Benjamin to spend the night. ⁵During the night the men of Gibeah came after me and surrounded the house, intending to kill me. They raped my concubine, and she died. ⁶I took my concubine, cut her into pieces and sent one piece to each region of Israel's inheritance, because they committed this lewd and disgraceful act in Israel. ⁷Now, all you Israelites, speak up and give your verdict."　　Jos 7:15; Jdg 15:57

⁸All the people rose as one man, saying, "None of us will go home. No, not one of us will return to his house. ⁹But now this is what we'll do to Gibeah: We'll go up against it as the lot directs. ¹⁰We'll take ten men out of every hundred from all the tribes of Israel, and a hundred from a thousand, and a thousand from ten thousand, to get provisions for the army. Then, when the army arrives at Gibeah ᵃ in Benjamin, it can give them what they deserve for all this vileness done in Israel." ¹¹So all the men of Israel got to-gether and united as one man against the city.　　Lev 16:8

¹²The tribes of Israel sent men throughout the tribe of Benjamin, saying, "What about this awful crime that was committed among you? ¹³Now surrender those wicked men of Gibeah so that we may put them to death and purge the evil from Israel."

But the Benjamites would not listen to their fellow Israelites. ¹⁴From their towns they came together at Gibeah to fight against the Israelites. ¹⁵At once the Benjamites mobilized twenty-six thousand swordsmen from their towns, in addition to seven hundred chosen men from those living in Gibeah. ¹⁶Among all these soldiers there were seven hundred chosen men who were left-handed, each of whom could sling a stone at a hair and not miss.

¹⁷Israel, apart from Benjamin, mustered four hundred thousand swordsmen, all of them fighting men.

¹⁸The Israelites went up to Bethel ᵇ and inquired of God. They said, "Who of us shall go first to fight against the Benjamites?"　　Jos 12:9; Jdg 18:5

The Lord replied, "Judah shall go first."　　Ge 49:10

¹⁹The next morning the Israelites got up and pitched camp near Gibeah. ²⁰The men of Israel went out to fight the Benjamites and took up battle positions

---

ᵃ10 One Hebrew manuscript; most Hebrew manuscripts Geba, a variant of Gibeah
ᵇ18 Or to the house of God; also in verse 26

against them at Gibeah. ²¹The Benjamites came out of Gibeah and cut down twenty-two thousand Israelites on the battlefield that day. ²²But the men of Israel encouraged one another and again took up their positions where they had stationed themselves the first day. ²³The Israelites went up and wept before the LORD until evening, and they inquired of the LORD. They said, "Shall we go up again to battle against the Benjamites, our brothers?"   Nu 14:1

The LORD answered, "Go up against them."

²⁴Then the Israelites drew near to Benjamin the second day. ²⁵This time, when the Benjamites came out from Gibeah to oppose them, they cut down another eighteen thousand Israelites, all of them armed with swords.   Jdg 20:21

²⁶Then the Israelites, all the people, went up to Bethel, and there they sat weeping before the LORD. They fasted that day until evening and presented burnt offerings and fellowship offerings^a to the LORD. ²⁷And the Israelites inquired of the LORD. (In those days the ark of the covenant of God was there, ²⁸with Phinehas son of Eleazar, the son of Aaron, ministering before it.) They asked, "Shall we go up again to battle with Benjamin our brother, or not?"

The LORD responded, "Go,

for tomorrow I will give them into your hands."   Jos 2:24

²⁹Then Israel set an ambush around Gibeah. ³⁰They went up against the Benjamites on the third day and took up positions against Gibeah as they had done before. ³¹The Benjamites came out to meet them and were drawn away from the city. They began to inflict casualties on the Israelites as before, so that about thirty men fell in the open field and on the roads— the one leading to Bethel and the other to Gibeah.   Jos 8:2

³²While the Benjamites were saying, "We are defeating them as before," the Israelites were saying, "Let's retreat and draw them away from the city to the roads."   Jdg 20:39

³³All the men of Israel moved from their places and took up positions at Baal Tamar, and the Israelite ambush charged out of its place on the west^b of Gibeah. ^c ³⁴Then ten thousand of Israel's finest men made a frontal attack on Gibeah. The fighting was so heavy that the Benjamites did not realize how near disaster was. ³⁵The LORD defeated Benjamin before Israel, and on that day the Israelites struck down 25,100 Benjamites, all armed with swords. ³⁶Then the Benjamites saw that they were beaten.   Jos 8:19; 1Sa 9:21

Now the men of Israel had given way before Benjamin, be-

---

^a26 Traditionally *peace offerings*   ^b33 Some Septuagint manuscripts and Vulgate; the meaning of the Hebrew for this word is uncertain.   ^c33 Hebrew *Geba*, a variant of *Gibeah*

cause they relied on the ambush they had set near Gibeah. ³⁷The men who had been in ambush made a sudden dash into Gibeah, spread out and put the whole city to the sword. ³⁸The men of Israel had arranged with the ambush that they should send up a great cloud of smoke from the city, ³⁹and then the men of Israel would turn in the battle.   Jos 8:15,20

The Benjamites had begun to inflict casualties on the men of Israel (about thirty), and they said, "We are defeating them as in the first battle." ⁴⁰But when the column of smoke began to rise from the city, the Benjamites turned and saw the smoke of the whole city going up into the sky. ⁴¹Then the men of Israel turned on them, and the men of Benjamin were terrified, because they realized that disaster had come upon them. ⁴²So they fled before the Israelites in the direction of the desert, but they could not escape the battle. And the men of Israel who came out of the towns cut them down there. ⁴³They surrounded the Benjamites, chased them and easily[a] overran them in the vicinity of Gibeah on the east. ⁴⁴Eighteen thousand Benjamites fell, all of them valiant fighters. ⁴⁵As they turned and fled toward the desert to the rock of Rimmon, the Israelites cut down five thousand men along the roads. They kept pressing after the Benjamites as far as Gidom and struck down two thousand more.   1Sa 10:26; Ps 78:9

⁴⁶On that day twenty-five thousand Benjamite swordsmen fell, all of them valiant fighters. ⁴⁷But six hundred men turned and fled into the desert to the rock of Rimmon, where they stayed four months. ⁴⁸The men of Israel went back to Benjamin and put all the towns to the sword, including the animals and everything else they found. All the towns they came across they set on fire.   1Sa 9:21

Wives for the Benjamites

21 The men of Israel had taken an oath at Mizpah: "Not one of us will give his daughter in marriage to a Benjamite."   Jos 9:18; Jdg 20:1

²The people went to Bethel,[b] where they sat before God until evening, raising their voices and weeping bitterly. ³"O LORD, the God of Israel," they cried, "why has this happened to Israel? Why should one tribe be missing from Israel today?"

⁴Early the next day the people built an altar and presented burnt offerings and fellowship offerings.[c]   Jdg 20:26; 2Sa 24:25

⁵Then the Israelites asked, "Who from all the tribes of Israel has failed to assemble before the LORD?" For they had

---

[a]43 The meaning of the Hebrew for this word is uncertain.   [b]2 Or to the house of God
[c]4 Traditionally peace offerings

taken a solemn oath that anyone who failed to assemble before the LORD at Mizpah should certainly be put to death. Jdg 20:1

6Now the Israelites grieved for their brothers, the Benjamites. "Today one tribe is cut off from Israel," they said. 7"How can we provide wives for those who are left, since we have taken an oath by the LORD not to give them any of our daughters in marriage?" 8Then they asked, "Which one of the tribes of Israel failed to assemble before the LORD at Mizpah?" They discovered that no one from Jabesh Gilead had come to the camp for the assembly. 9For when they counted the people, they found that none of the people of Jabesh Gilead were there. Jos 9:18; 1Sa 11:1

10So the assembly sent twelve thousand fighting men with instructions to go to Jabesh Gilead and put to the sword those living there, including the women and children. 11"This is what you are to do," they said. "Kill every male and every woman who is not a virgin." 12They found among the people living in Jabesh Gilead four hundred young women who had never slept with a man, and they took them to the camp at Shiloh in Canaan. Nu 31:17; Jos 18:1

13Then the whole assembly sent an offer of peace to the Benjamites at the rock of Rimmon. 14So the Benjamites returned at that time and were given the women of Jabesh Gilead who had been spared. But there were not enough for all of them.

15The people grieved for Benjamin, because the LORD had made a gap in the tribes of Israel. 16And the elders of the assembly said, "With the women of Benjamin destroyed, how shall we provide wives for the men who are left? 17The Benjamite survivors must have heirs," they said, "so that a tribe of Israel will not be wiped out. 18We can't give them our daughters as wives, since we Israelites have taken this oath: 'Cursed be anyone who gives a wife to a Benjamite.' 19But look, there is the annual festival of the LORD in Shiloh, to the north of Bethel, and east of the road that goes from Bethel to Shechem, and to the south of Lebonah." Jos 16:1; 1Sa 1:3

20So they instructed the Benjamites, saying, "Go and hide in the vineyards 21and watch. When the girls of Shiloh come out to join in the dancing, then rush from the vineyards and each of you seize a wife from the girls of Shiloh and go to the land of Benjamin. 22When their fathers or brothers complain to us, we will say to them, 'Do us a kindness by helping them, because we did not get wives for them during the war, and you are innocent, since you did not give your daughters to them.'"

23So that is what the Benjamites did. While the girls were dancing, each man caught one

and carried her off to be his wife. Then they returned to their inheritance and rebuilt the towns and settled in them.

24At that time the Israelites left that place and went home to their tribes and clans, each to his own inheritance.

25In those days Israel had no king; everyone did as he saw fit.

Ruth

Introduction:

This book is named after the leading character whose story is told here. It may have been written during the reign of David, whose ancestry is traced in the final verses to his great-grandfather Boaz, whose wife was Ruth.

Ruth tells the story of an Israelite couple who moved to Moab during a famine in Canaan. The husband and his two sons died, leaving the mother (Naomi) alone with her two daughters-in-law (Orpah and Ruth). Naomi decided to move back to Israel and Ruth insisted on going back with her. Back in Israel, they looked to their relative Boaz for help and Ruth finally married Boaz. From their family came the royal family of David and the Messiah, Jesus Christ.

This book teaches us much about love and devotion. It also teaches us of God's concern for our everyday needs and that he is working out his plan for salvation.

Outline of contents:

Naomi's departure from Israel and her return (1:1–22)
Ruth's welcome (2:1–3:18)
Boaz and Ruth (4:1–22)

Naomi and Ruth

1 In the days when the judges ruled, *a* there was a famine in the land, and a man from Bethlehem in Judah, together with his wife and two sons, went to live for a while in the country of Moab. ²The man's name was Elimelech, his wife's name Naomi, and the names of his two sons were Mahlon and Kilion. They were Ephrathites from Bethlehem, Judah. And they went to Moab and lived there. Jdg 2:16-18; 1Sa 16:18

³Now Elimelech, Naomi's husband, died, and she was left with her two sons. ⁴They married Moabite women, one named Orpah and the other Ruth. After they had lived there about ten years, ⁵both Mahlon and Kilion also died, and Naomi was left without her two sons and her husband. Ge 35:19

⁶When she heard in Moab

a1 Traditionally *judged*

that the LORD had come to the aid of his people by providing food for them, Naomi and her daughters-in-law prepared to return home from there. [7]With her two daughters-in-law she left the place where she had been living and set out on the road that would take them back to the land of Judah.   Ex 4:31

[8]Then Naomi said to her two daughters-in-law, "Go back, each of you, to your mother's home. May the LORD show kindness to you, as you have shown to your dead and to me. [9]May the LORD grant that each of you will find rest in the home of another husband."   Ge 38:11

Then she kissed them and they wept aloud [10]and said to her, "We will go back with you to your people."   Ge 27:27; Nu 25:6

[11]But Naomi said, "Return home, my daughters. Why would you come with me? Am I going to have any more sons, who could become your husbands? [12]Return home, my daughters; I am too old to have another husband. Even if I thought there was still hope for me—even if I had a husband tonight and then gave birth to sons— [13]would you wait until they grew up? Would you remain unmarried for them? No, my daughters. It is more bitter for me than for you, because the LORD's hand has gone out against me!"   Dt 25:5; 1Sa 30:6

[14]At this they wept again. Then Orpah kissed her mother-in-law good-by, but Ruth clung to her.   Dt 10:20; Mic 7:6

[15]"Look," said Naomi, "your sister-in-law is going back to her people and her gods. Go back with her."   Dt 25:7; Jos 24:14

[16]But Ruth replied, "Don't urge me to leave you or to turn back from you. Where you go I will go, and where you stay I will stay. Your people will be my people and your God my God. [17]Where you die I will die, and there I will be buried. May the LORD deal with me, be it ever so severely, if anything but death separates you and me." [18]When Naomi realized that Ruth was determined to go with her, she stopped urging her.

[19]So the two women went on until they came to Bethlehem. When they arrived in Bethlehem, the whole town was stirred because of them, and the women exclaimed, "Can this be Naomi?"   Jdg 17:7; Mt 21:10

[20]"Don't call me Naomi,[a]" she told them. "Call me Mara,[b] because the Almighty[c] has made my life very bitter. [21]I went away full, but the LORD has brought me back empty. Why call me Naomi? The LORD has afflicted[d] me; the Almighty has brought misfortune upon me."   Job 1:21; Ps 91:1

[22]So Naomi returned from

---

[a]20 Naomi means pleasant; also in verse 21.   [b]20 Mara means bitter.   [c]20 Hebrew Shaddai; also in verse 21   [d]21 Or has testified against

Moab accompanied by Ruth the Moabitess, her daughter-in-law, arriving in Bethlehem as the barley harvest was beginning. Ex 9:31; 2Sa 21:9

Ruth Meets Boaz

2 Now Naomi had a relative on her husband's side, from the clan of Elimelech, a man of standing, whose name was Boaz. 1Sa 9:1; Pr 7:4

²And Ruth the Moabitess said to Naomi, "Let me go to the fields and pick up the leftover grain behind anyone in whose eyes I find favor." Lev 19:9

Naomi said to her, "Go ahead, my daughter." ³So she went out and began to glean in the fields behind the harvesters. As it turned out, she found herself working in a field belonging to Boaz, who was from the clan of Elimelech. 2Ki 4:18; Jer 9:22

⁴Just then Boaz arrived from Bethlehem and greeted the harvesters, "The LORD be with you!" Jdg 6:12; Lk 1:28

"The LORD bless you!" they called back. Ge 28:3; Nu 6:24

⁵Boaz asked the foreman of his harvesters, "Whose young woman is that?"

⁶The foreman replied, "She is the Moabitess who came back from Moab with Naomi. ⁷She said, 'Please let me glean and gather among the sheaves behind the harvesters.' She went into the field and has worked steadily from morning till now,

except for a short rest in the shelter." Ru 1:22; 2Sa 4:5

⁸So Boaz said to Ruth, "My daughter, listen to me. Don't go and glean in another field and don't go away from here. Stay here with my servant girls. ⁹Watch the field where the men are harvesting, and follow along after the girls. I have told the men not to touch you. And whenever you are thirsty, go and get a drink from the water jars the men have filled."

¹⁰At this, she bowed down with her face to the ground. She exclaimed, "Why have I found such favor in your eyes that you notice me—a foreigner?" Ps 41:1

¹¹Boaz replied, "I've been told all about what you have done for your mother-in-law since the death of your husband—how you left your father and mother and your homeland and came to live with a people you did not know before. ¹²May the LORD repay you for what you have done. May you be richly rewarded by the LORD, the God of Israel, under whose wings you have come to take refuge." Ps 18:20; Isa 55:5

¹³"May I continue to find favor in your eyes, my lord," she said. "You have given me comfort and have spoken kindly to your servant—though I do not have the standing of one of your servant girls." Ge 18:3

¹⁴At mealtime Boaz said to her, "Come over here. Have some bread and dip it in the wine vinegar." Ge 3:19; Ru 2:18

When she sat down with the harvesters, he offered her some roasted grain. She ate all she wanted and had some left over. 15As she got up to glean, Boaz gave orders to his men, "Even if she gathers among the sheaves, don't embarrass her. 16Rather, pull out some stalks for her from the bundles and leave them for her to pick up, and don't rebuke her."   Ge 37:10

17So Ruth gleaned in the field until evening. Then she threshed the barley she had gathered, and it amounted to about an ephah.ᵃ 18She carried it back to town, and her mother-in-law saw how much she had gathered. Ruth also brought out and gave her what she had left over after she had eaten enough.   Lev 19:36; Jdg 6:11

19Her mother-in-law asked her, "Where did you glean today? Where did you work? Blessed be the man who took notice of you!"   Ru 2:10; Ps 41:1

Then Ruth told her mother-in-law about the one at whose place she had been working. "The name of the man I worked with today is Boaz," she said.

20"The LORD bless him!" Naomi said to her daughter-in-law. "He has not stopped showing his kindness to the living and the dead." She added, "That man is our close relative; he is one of our kinsman-redeemers."   Jdg 17:2; Ru 3:9

21Then Ruth the Moabitess said, "He even said to me, 'Stay with my workers until they finish harvesting all my grain.'"

22Naomi said to Ruth her daughter-in-law, "It will be good for you, my daughter, to go with his girls, because in someone else's field you might be harmed."

23So Ruth stayed close to the servant girls of Boaz to glean until the barley and wheat harvests were finished. And she lived with her mother-in-law.

Ruth and Boaz at the Threshing Floor

3 One day Naomi her mother-in-law said to her, "My daughter, should I not try to find a homeᵇ for you, where you will be well provided for? 2Is not Boaz, with whose servant girls you have been, a kinsman of ours? Tonight he will be winnowing barley on the threshing floor. 3Wash and perfume yourself, and put on your best clothes. Then go down to the threshing floor, but don't let him know you are there until he has finished eating and drinking. 4When he lies down, note the place where he is lying. Then go and uncover his feet and lie down. He will tell you what to do."   Lev 2:14; 2Sa 14:2

5"I will do whatever you say," Ruth answered. 6So she went down to the threshing

ᵃ17 That is, probably about 3/5 bushel (about 22 liters)   ᵇ1 Hebrew find rest (see Ruth 1:9)

floor and did everything her mother-in-law told her to do.

⁷When Boaz had finished eating and drinking and was in good spirits, he went over to lie down at the far end of the grain pile. Ruth approached quietly, uncovered his feet and lay down. ⁸In the middle of the night something startled the man, and he turned and discovered a woman lying at his feet.

⁹"Who are you?" he asked.

"I am your servant Ruth," she said. "Spread the corner of your garment over me, since you are a kinsman-redeemer."

¹⁰"The LORD bless you, my daughter," he replied. "This kindness is greater than that which you showed earlier: You have not run after the younger men, whether rich or poor. ¹¹And now, my daughter, don't be afraid. I will do for you all you ask. All my fellow townsmen know that you are a woman of noble character. ¹²Although it is true that I am near of kin, there is a kinsman-redeemer nearer than I. ¹³Stay here for the night, and in the morning if he wants to redeem, good; let him redeem. But if he is not willing, as surely as the LORD lives I will do it. Lie here until morning."   Jdg 17:2; Mt 22:24

¹⁴So she lay at his feet until morning, but got up before anyone could be recognized; and he said, "Don't let it be known that a woman came to the threshing floor."   Nu 18:27; 2Co 8:21

¹⁵He also said, "Bring me the shawl you are wearing and hold it out." When she did so, he poured into it six measures of barley and put it on her. Then he*a* went back to town.   Isa 3:22

¹⁶When Ruth came to her mother-in-law, Naomi asked, "How did it go, my daughter?"

Then she told her everything Boaz had done for her ¹⁷and added, "He gave me these six measures of barley, saying, 'Don't go back to your mother-in-law empty-handed.' "

¹⁸Then Naomi said, "Wait, my daughter, until you find out what happens. For the man will not rest until the matter is settled today."   Ps 37:3-5

Boaz Marries Ruth

4 Meanwhile Boaz went up to the town gate and sat there. When the kinsman-redeemer he had mentioned came along, Boaz said, "Come over here, my friend, and sit down." So he went over and sat down.   Ge 18:1

²Boaz took ten of the elders of the town and said, "Sit here," and they did so. ³Then he said to the kinsman-redeemer, "Naomi, who has come back from Moab, is selling the piece of land that belonged to our brother Elimelech. ⁴I thought I should bring the matter to your attention and suggest that you buy it in the presence of these

---

*a15 Most Hebrew manuscripts; many Hebrew manuscripts, Vulgate and Syriac *she*

seated here and in the presence of the elders of my people. If you will redeem it, do so. But if you[a] will not, tell me, so I will know. For no one has the right to do it except you, and I am next in line." Ex 3:16; Jer 32:7-8

"I will redeem it," he said.

5Then Boaz said, "On the day you buy the land from Naomi and from Ruth the Moabitess, you acquire[b] the dead man's widow, in order to maintain the name of the dead with his property." Ge 38:8; Ru 3:13

6At this, the kinsman-redeemer said, "Then I cannot redeem it because I might endanger my own estate. You redeem it yourself. I cannot do it." Lev 25:25; Dt 25:7

7(Now in earlier times in Israel, for the redemption and transfer of property to become final, one party took off his sandal and gave it to the other. This was the method of legalizing transactions in Israel.) Dt 25:7-9

8So the kinsman-redeemer said to Boaz, "Buy it yourself." And he removed his sandal.

9Then Boaz announced to the elders and all the people, "Today you are witnesses that I have bought from Naomi all the property of Elimelech, Kilion and Mahlon. 10I have also acquired Ruth the Moabitess, Mahlon's widow, as my wife, in order to maintain the name of the dead with his property, so

that his name will not disappear from among his family or from the town records. Today you are witnesses!" Dt 25:6; Isa 8:2

11Then the elders and all those at the gate said, "We are witnesses. May the LORD make the woman who is coming into your home like Rachel and Leah, who together built up the house of Israel. May you have standing in Ephrathah and be famous in Bethlehem. 12Through the offspring the LORD gives you by this young woman, may your family be like that of Perez, whom Tamar bore to Judah." Ge 35:16; Dt 25:9

The Genealogy of David

13So Boaz took Ruth and she became his wife. Then he went to her, and the LORD enabled her to conceive, and she gave birth to a son. 14The women said to Naomi: "Praise be to the LORD, who this day has not left you without a kinsman-redeemer. May he become famous throughout Israel! 15He will renew your life and sustain you in your old age. For your daughter-in-law, who loves you and who is better to you than seven sons, has given him birth." Ge 29:32; 1Sa 1:8

16Then Naomi took the child, laid him in her lap and cared for him. 17The women living there said, "Naomi has a son." And they named him Obed. He was

a4 Many Hebrew manuscripts, Septuagint, Vulgate and Syriac; most Hebrew manuscripts he   b5 Hebrew; Vulgate and Syriac Naomi, you acquire Ruth the Moabitess,

the father of Jesse, the father of David.　　　1Sa 16:1; Ps 72:20

[18]This, then, is the family line of Perez:　　　Ge 38:29; Mt 1:3-6

Perez was the father of Hezron,
[19]Hezron the father of Ram,
Ram the father of Amminadab,

[20]Amminadab the father of Nahshon,
Nahshon the father of Salmon,[a]
[21]Salmon the father of Boaz,
Boaz the father of Obed,
[22]Obed the father of Jesse,
and Jesse the father of David.　　　Ex 6:23; Nu 7:12

---

[a]20 A few Hebrew manuscripts, some Septuagint manuscripts and Vulgate (see also verse 21 and Septuagint of 1 Chron. 2:11); most Hebrew manuscripts *Salma*

1 Samuel

Introduction:

The book of 1 Samuel records the lives of Samuel and Saul, and much of the life of David. First Samuel begins with the birth of Samuel and his training in the temple. It describes how he led Israel as prophet, priest and judge.

When the people of Israel demanded a king, Samuel, by God's leading, anointed Saul to be the first king of Israel. But Saul was disobedient to God and God rejected him as king. Then Samuel secretly anointed David to take Saul's place. The struggles between Saul and David make up the rest of this book. Although we learn much of these people's disobedience there is a stronger emphasis on their goodness and obedience to God.

It was during this part of Israel's history that the nation changed from judges as leaders to having a king as their neighboring nations had. Samuel, as prophet, priest and judge, had a great deal of influence throughout this time period.

Outline of contents:

The Birth of Samuel

1 There was a certain man from Ramathaim, a Zuphite[a] from the hill country of Ephraim, whose name was Elkanah son of Jeroham, the son of Elihu, the son of Tohu, the son of Zuph, an Ephraimite. ²He had two wives; one was called Hannah and the other Peninnah. Peninnah had children, but Hannah had none.

³Year after year this man went up from his town to worship and sacrifice to the LORD Almighty at Shiloh, where Hophni and Phinehas, the two sons of Eli, were priests of the LORD. ⁴Whenever the day came for Elkanah to sacrifice, he

---

a1 Or from Ramathaim Zuphim

would give portions of the meat to his wife Peninnah and to all her sons and daughters. ⁵But to Hannah he gave a double portion because he loved her, and the LORD had closed her womb. ⁶And because the LORD had closed her womb, her rival kept provoking her in order to irritate her. ⁷This went on year after year. Whenever Hannah went up to the house of the LORD, her rival provoked her till she wept and would not eat. ⁸Elkanah her husband would say to her, "Hannah, why are you weeping? Why don't you eat? Why are you downhearted? Don't I mean more to you than ten sons?"   Ps 102:4

⁹Once when they had finished eating and drinking in Shiloh, Hannah stood up. Now Eli the priest was sitting on a chair by the doorpost of the LORD's temple.ᵃ ¹⁰In bitterness of soul Hannah wept much and prayed to the LORD. ¹¹And she made a vow, saying, "O LORD Almighty, if you will only look upon your servant's misery and remember me, and not forget your servant but give her a son, then I will give him to the LORD for all the days of his life, and no razor will ever be used on his head."   Jdg 13:7; 1Sa 3:3

¹²As she kept on praying to the LORD, Eli observed her mouth. ¹³Hannah was praying in her heart, and her lips were moving but her voice was not heard. Eli thought she was drunk ¹⁴and said to her, "How long will you keep on getting drunk? Get rid of your wine."

¹⁵"Not so, my lord," Hannah replied, "I am a woman who is deeply troubled. I have not been drinking wine or beer; I was pouring out my soul to the LORD. ¹⁶Do not take your servant for a wicked woman; I have been praying here out of my great anguish and grief."

¹⁷Eli answered, "Go in peace, and may the God of Israel grant you what you have asked of him."   2Ki 5:19

¹⁸She said, "May your servant find favor in your eyes." Then she went her way and ate something, and her face was no longer downcast.   Ge 18:3; Ru 2:13

¹⁹Early the next morning they arose and worshiped before the LORD and then went back to their home at Ramah. Elkanah lay with Hannah his wife, and the LORD remembered her. ²⁰So in the course of time Hannah conceived and gave birth to a son. She named him Samuel,ᵇ saying, "Because I asked the LORD for him."   Ex 2:10; Jos 18:25

Hannah Dedicates Samuel

²¹When the man Elkanah went up with all his family to offer the annual sacrifice to the LORD and to fulfill his vow, ²²Hannah did not go. She said to her husband, "After the boy is weaned, I will take him and

---

ᵃ9 That is, tabernacle   ᵇ20 *Samuel* sounds like the Hebrew for *heard of God.*

present him before the LORD, and he will live there always."

23"Do what seems best to you," Elkanah her husband told her. "Stay here until you have weaned him; only may the LORD make good his*a* word." So the woman stayed at home and nursed her son until she had weaned him. Ge 25:21; Nu 30:7

24After he was weaned, she took the boy with her, young as he was, along with a three-year-old bull,*b* an ephah*c* of flour and a skin of wine, and brought him to the house of the LORD at Shiloh. 25When they had slaughtered the bull, they brought the boy to Eli, 26and she said to him, "As surely as you live, my lord, I am the woman who stood here beside you praying to the LORD. 27I prayed for this child, and the LORD has granted me what I asked of him. 28So now I give him to the LORD. For his whole life he will be given over to the LORD." And he worshiped the LORD there. Jos 18:1; Jdg 13:7

Hannah's Prayer

2 Then Hannah prayed and said:

"My heart rejoices in the
  LORD;
  in the LORD my horn*d* is
  lifted high.
My mouth boasts over my
  enemies,

for I delight in your
  deliverance. Ps 89:17

2"There is no one holy*e* like
  the LORD;
there is no one besides you;
there is no Rock like our
  God. 2Sa 22:32; Isa 40:25

3"Do not keep talking so
  proudly
or let your mouth speak
  such arrogance,
for the LORD is a God who
  knows,
and by him deeds are
  weighed. 1Ki 8:39; Pr 16:2

4"The bows of the warriors
  are broken,
but those who stumbled are
  armed with strength.
5Those who were full hire
  themselves out for food,
but those who were hungry
  hunger no more. Lk 1:53
She who was barren has
  borne seven children,
but she who has had many
  sons pines away. Ps 113:9

6"The LORD brings death and
  makes alive;
he brings down to the
  grave*f* and raises up.
7The LORD sends poverty and
  wealth;
he humbles and he exalts.
8He raises the poor from the
  dust
and lifts the needy from the
  ash heap;

---

*a*23 Masoretic Text; Dead Sea Scrolls, Septuagint and Syriac *your*   *b*24 Dead Sea Scrolls, Septuagint and Syriac; Masoretic Text *with three bulls*   *c*24 That is, probably about 3/5 bushel (about 22 liters)   *d*1 *Horn* here symbolizes strength; also in verse 10.   *e*2 Or *no Holy One*   *f*6 Hebrew *Sheol*

he seats them with princes
and has them inherit a
    throne of honor. Ps 113:7-8

"For the foundations of the
    earth are the LORD's;
upon them he has set the
    world. Job 15:7; Ps 104:5
⁹He will guard the feet of his
    saints,
but the wicked will be
    silenced in darkness.

"It is not by strength that one
    prevails;
¹⁰ those who oppose the
    LORD will be shattered.
He will thunder against them
    from heaven;
  the LORD will judge the
    ends of the earth. Ps 18:13

"He will give strength to his
    king
and exalt the horn of his
    anointed." Ps 59:16; Lk 1:69

¹¹Then Elkanah went home to
Ramah, but the boy ministered
before the LORD under Eli the
priest. Jos 18:25; 1Sa 3:1

Eli's Wicked Sons

¹²Eli's sons were wicked men;
they had no regard for the
LORD. ¹³Now it was the practice
of the priests with the people
that whenever anyone offered a
sacrifice and while the meat was
being boiled, the servant of the
priest would come with a three-
pronged fork in his hand. ¹⁴He
would plunge it into the pan or
kettle or caldron or pot, and the
priest would take for himself
whatever the fork brought up.
This is how they treated all the
Israelites who came to Shiloh.
¹⁵But even before the fat was
burned, the servant of the priest
would come and say to the man
who was sacrificing, "Give the
priest some meat to roast; he
won't accept boiled meat from
you, but only raw." Jer 2:8
¹⁶If the man said to him, "Let
the fat be burned up first, and
then take whatever you want,"
the servant would then answer,
"No, hand it over now; if you
don't, I'll take it by force." Lev 3:3
¹⁷This sin of the young men
was very great in the LORD's
sight, for theyᵃ were treating
the LORD's offering with contempt. Nu 14:11; Mal 2:7-9
¹⁸But Samuel was ministering
before the LORD—a boy wearing
a linen ephod. ¹⁹Each year his
mother made him a little robe
and took it to him when she
went up with her husband to
offer the annual sacrifice. ²⁰Eli
would bless Elkanah and his
wife, saying, "May the LORD
give you children by this
woman to take the place of the
one she prayed for and gave to
the LORD." Then they would go
home. ²¹And the LORD was gracious to Hannah; she conceived
and gave birth to three sons and
two daughters. Meanwhile, the
boy Samuel grew up in the presence of the LORD. 2Sa 6:14
²²Now Eli, who was very old,

ᵃ17 Or *men*

heard about everything his sons were doing to all Israel and how they slept with the women who served at the entrance to the Tent of Meeting. ²³So he said to them, "Why do you do such things? I hear from all the people about these wicked deeds of yours. ²⁴No, my sons; it is not a good report that I hear spreading among the LORD's people. ²⁵If a man sins against another man, God*a* may mediate for him; but if a man sins against the LORD, who will intercede for him?" His sons, however, did not listen to their father's rebuke, for it was the LORD's will to put them to death. Ex 38:8; Jos 11:20

²⁶And the boy Samuel continued to grow in stature and in favor with the LORD and with men. Pr 3:4; Lk 2:52

Prophecy Against the House of Eli

²⁷Now a man of God came to Eli and said to him, "This is what the LORD says: 'Did I not clearly reveal myself to your father's house when they were in Egypt under Pharaoh? ²⁸I chose your father out of all the tribes of Israel to be my priest, to go up to my altar, to burn incense, and to wear an ephod in my presence. I also gave your father's house all the offerings made with fire by the Israelites. ²⁹Why do you*b* scorn my sacrifice and offering that I pre-

scribed for my dwelling? Why do you honor your sons more than me by fattening yourselves on the choice parts of every offering made by my people Israel?' Ex 28:1; Dt 12:5

³⁰"Therefore the LORD, the God of Israel, declares: 'I promised that your house and your father's house would minister before me forever.' But now the LORD declares: 'Far be it from me! Those who honor me I will honor, but those who despise me will be disdained. ³¹The time is coming when I will cut short your strength and the strength of your father's house, so that there will not be an old man in your family line ³²and you will see distress in my dwelling. Although good will be done to Israel, in your family line there will never be an old man. ³³Every one of you that I do not cut off from my altar will be spared only to blind your eyes with tears and to grieve your heart, and all your descendants will die in the prime of life. Ex 29:9

³⁴" 'And what happens to your two sons, Hophni and Phinehas, will be a sign to you—they will both die on the same day. ³⁵I will raise up for myself a faithful priest, who will do according to what is in my heart and mind. I will firmly establish his house, and he will minister before my anointed one always. ³⁶Then everyone left in your family line will come

---

*a*25 Or *the judges*   *b*29 The Hebrew is plural.

and bow down before him for a piece of silver and a crust of bread and plead, "Appoint me to some priestly office so I can have food to eat.' '"   1Ki 13:3

The LORD Calls Samuel

3 The boy Samuel ministered before the LORD under Eli. In those days the word of the LORD was rare; there were not many visions.   Ps 74:9; Am 8:11

²One night Eli, whose eyes were becoming so weak that he could barely see, was lying down in his usual place. ³The lamp of God had not yet gone out, and Samuel was lying down in the temple*a* of the LORD, where the ark of God was. ⁴Then the LORD called Samuel.   Lev 24:2-4; 1Sa 4:15

Samuel answered, "Here I am." ⁵And he ran to Eli and said, "Here I am; you called me."

But Eli said, "I did not call; go back and lie down." So he went and lay down.

⁶Again the LORD called, "Samuel!" And Samuel got up and went to Eli and said, "Here I am; you called me."

"My son," Eli said, "I did not call; go back and lie down."

⁷Now Samuel did not yet know the LORD: The word of the LORD had not yet been revealed to him.   Jer 1:2; Am 3:7

⁸The LORD called Samuel a third time, and Samuel got up

and went to Eli and said, "Here I am; you called me."

Then Eli realized that the LORD was calling the boy. ⁹So Eli told Samuel, "Go and lie down, and if he calls you, say, 'Speak, LORD, for your servant is listening.' " So Samuel went and lay down in his place.   Ps 85:8

¹⁰The LORD came and stood there, calling as at the other times, "Samuel! Samuel!"

Then Samuel said, "Speak, for your servant is listening."

¹¹And the LORD said to Samuel: "See, I am about to do something in Israel that will make the ears of everyone who hears of it tingle. ¹²At that time I will carry out against Eli everything I spoke against his family—from beginning to end. ¹³For I told him that I would judge his family forever because of the sin he knew about; his sons made themselves contemptible,*b* and he failed to restrain them. ¹⁴Therefore, I swore to the house of Eli, 'The guilt of Eli's house will never be atoned for by sacrifice or offering.' "   2Ki 21:12; Jer 19:3

¹⁵Samuel lay down until morning and then opened the doors of the house of the LORD. He was afraid to tell Eli the vision, ¹⁶but Eli called him and said, "Samuel, my son."

Samuel answered, "Here I am."

¹⁷"What was it he said to

*a*3 That is, tabernacle   *b*13 Masoretic Text; an ancient Hebrew scribal tradition and Septuagint *sons blasphemed God*

you?" Eli asked. "Do not hide it from me. May God deal with you, be it ever so severely, if you hide from me anything he told you." [18]So Samuel told him everything, hiding nothing from him. Then Eli said, "He is the LORD; let him do what is good in his eyes." Ru 1:17; Jer 23:28

[19]The LORD was with Samuel as he grew up, and he let none of his words fall to the ground. [20]And all Israel from Dan to Beersheba recognized that Samuel was attested as a prophet of the LORD. [21]The LORD continued to appear at Shiloh, and there he revealed himself to Samuel through his word. Ge 21:22

4 And Samuel's word came to all Israel. Jdg 20:1

The Philistines Capture the Ark

Now the Israelites went out to fight against the Philistines. The Israelites camped at Ebenezer, and the Philistines at Aphek. [2]The Philistines deployed their forces to meet Israel, and as the battle spread, Israel was defeated by the Philistines, who killed about four thousand of them on the battlefield. [3]When the soldiers returned to camp, the elders of Israel asked, "Why did the LORD bring defeat upon us today before the Philistines? Let us bring the ark of the LORD's covenant from Shiloh, so that

it[a] may go with us and save us from the hand of our enemies."

[4]So the people sent men to Shiloh, and they brought back the ark of the covenant of the LORD Almighty, who is enthroned between the cherubim. And Eli's two sons, Hophni and Phinehas, were there with the ark of the covenant of God.

[5]When the ark of the LORD's covenant came into the camp, all Israel raised such a great shout that the ground shook. [6]Hearing the uproar, the Philistines asked, "What's all this shouting in the Hebrew camp?"

When they learned that the ark of the LORD had come into the camp, [7]the Philistines were afraid. "A god has come into the camp," they said. "We're in trouble! Nothing like this has happened before. [8]Woe to us! Who will deliver us from the hand of these mighty gods? They are the gods who struck the Egyptians with all kinds of plagues in the desert. [9]Be strong, Philistines! Be men, or you will be subject to the Hebrews, as they have been to you. Be men, and fight!" Ex 12:30

[10]So the Philistines fought, and the Israelites were defeated and every man fled to his tent. The slaughter was very great; Israel lost thirty thousand foot soldiers. [11]The ark of God was captured, and Eli's two sons, Hophni and Phinehas, died.

[a]3 Or *he*

Death of Eli

¹²That same day a Benjamite ran from the battle line and went to Shiloh, his clothes torn and dust on his head. ¹³When he arrived, there was Eli sitting on his chair by the side of the road, watching, because his heart feared for the ark of God. When the man entered the town and told what had happened, the whole town sent up a cry.   Jos 7:6; Eze 24:26

¹⁴Eli heard the outcry and asked, "What is the meaning of this uproar?"

The man hurried over to Eli, ¹⁵who was ninety-eight years old and whose eyes were set so that he could not see. ¹⁶He told Eli, "I have just come from the battle line; I fled from it this very day."   1Sa 3:2; 2Sa 1:4

Eli asked, "What happened, my son?"

¹⁷The man who brought the news replied, "Israel fled before the Philistines, and the army has suffered heavy losses. Also your two sons, Hophni and Phinehas, are dead, and the ark of God has been captured."

¹⁸When he mentioned the ark of God, Eli fell backward off his chair by the side of the gate. His neck was broken and he died, for he was an old man and heavy. He had led[a] Israel forty years.   Jdg 2:16; 1Sa 2:31

¹⁹His daughter-in-law, the wife of Phinehas, was pregnant and near the time of delivery. When she heard the news that the ark of God had been captured and that her father-in-law and her husband were dead, she went into labor and gave birth, but was overcome by her labor pains. ²⁰As she was dying, the women attending her said, "Don't despair; you have given birth to a son." But she did not respond or pay any attention.

²¹She named the boy Ichabod,[b] saying, "The glory has departed from Israel"—because of the capture of the ark of God and the deaths of her father-in-law and her husband. ²²She said, "The glory has departed from Israel, for the ark of God has been captured."   Ps 106:20

The Ark in Ashdod and Ekron

5 After the Philistines had captured the ark of God, they took it from Ebenezer to Ashdod. ²Then they carried the ark into Dagon's temple and set it beside Dagon. ³When the people of Ashdod rose early the next day, there was Dagon, fallen on his face on the ground before the ark of the LORD! They took Dagon and put him back in his place. ⁴But the following morning when they rose, there was Dagon, fallen on his face on the ground before the ark of the LORD! His head and hands had been broken off and were lying on the threshold; only his body remained. ⁵That is why to this

---

a18 Traditionally *judged*   *b21* Ichabod means *no glory*.

day neither the priests of Dagon nor any others who enter Dagon's temple at Ashdod step on the threshold. _{Jdg 16:23}

⁶The LORD's hand was heavy upon the people of Ashdod and its vicinity; he brought devastation upon them and afflicted them with tumors.^a ⁷When the men of Ashdod saw what was happening, they said, "The ark of the god of Israel must not stay here with us, because his hand is heavy upon us and upon Dagon our god." ⁸So they called together all the rulers of the Philistines and asked them, "What shall we do with the ark of the god of Israel?" _{Ex 9:3}

They answered, "Have the ark of the god of Israel moved to Gath." So they moved the ark of the God of Israel. _{Jos 11:22}

⁹But after they had moved it, the LORD's hand was against that city, throwing it into a great panic. He afflicted the people of the city, both young and old, with an outbreak of tumors.^b ¹⁰So they sent the ark of God to Ekron. _{Jos 13:3; 1Sa 7:13}

As the ark of God was entering Ekron, the people of Ekron cried out, "They have brought the ark of the god of Israel around to us to kill us and our people." ¹¹So they called together all the rulers of the Philistines and said, "Send the ark of the god of Israel away; let it go back to its own place, or it^c

will kill us and our people." For death had filled the city with panic; God's hand was very heavy upon it. ¹²Those who did not die were afflicted with tumors, and the outcry of the city went up to heaven. _{1Sa 4:8}

The Ark Returned to Israel

6 When the ark of the LORD had been in Philistine territory seven months, ²the Philistines called for the priests and the diviners and said, "What shall we do with the ark of the LORD? Tell us how we should send it back to its place." _{Ex 7:11}

³They answered, "If you return the ark of the god of Israel, do not send it away empty, but by all means send a guilt offering to him. Then you will be healed, and you will know why his hand has not been lifted from you." _{Ex 22:29; Lev 5:15}

⁴The Philistines asked, "What guilt offering should we send to him?"

They replied, "Five gold tumors and five gold rats, according to the number of the Philistine rulers, because the same plague has struck both you and your rulers. ⁵Make models of the tumors and of the rats that are destroying the country, and pay honor to Israel's god. Perhaps he will lift his hand from you and your gods and your land. ⁶Why do you harden your hearts as the Egyptians and

---

^a6 Hebrew; Septuagint and Vulgate *tumors. And rats appeared in their land, and death and destruction were throughout the city*   ^b9 Or *with tumors in the groin* (see Septuagint)   ^c11 Or *he*

Pharaoh did? When he[a] treated them harshly, did they not send the Israelites out so they could go on their way?   Jos 7:19

7"Now then, get a new cart ready, with two cows that have calved and have never been yoked. Hitch the cows to the cart, but take their calves away and pen them up. 8Take the ark of the LORD and put it on the cart, and in a chest beside it put the gold objects you are sending back to him as a guilt offering. Send it on its way, 9but keep watching it. If it goes up to its own territory, toward Beth Shemesh, then the LORD has brought this great disaster on us. But if it does not, then we will know that it was not his hand that struck us and that it happened to us by chance."

10So they did this. They took two such cows and hitched them to the cart and penned up their calves. 11They placed the ark of the LORD on the cart and along with it the chest containing the gold rats and the models of the tumors. 12Then the cows went straight up toward Beth Shemesh, keeping on the road and lowing all the way; they did not turn to the right or to the left. The rulers of the Philistines followed them as far as the border of Beth Shemesh.   Nu 20:19

13Now the people of Beth Shemesh were harvesting their wheat in the valley, and when they looked up and saw the ark, they rejoiced at the sight. 14The cart came to the field of Joshua of Beth Shemesh, and there it stopped beside a large rock. The people chopped up the wood of the cart and sacrificed the cows as a burnt offering to the LORD. 15The Levites took down the ark of the LORD, together with the chest containing the gold objects, and placed them on the large rock. On that day the people of Beth Shemesh offered burnt offerings and made sacrifices to the LORD. 16The five rulers of the Philistines saw all this and then returned that same day to Ekron.   2Sa 24:22

17These are the gold tumors the Philistines sent as a guilt offering to the LORD—one each for Ashdod, Gaza, Ashkelon, Gath and Ekron. 18And the number of the gold rats was according to the number of Philistine towns belonging to the five rulers—the fortified towns with their country villages. The large rock, on which[b] they set the ark of the LORD, is a witness to this day in the field of Joshua of Beth Shemesh.   Jos 13:3; 1Sa 5:8

19But God struck down some of the men of Beth Shemesh, putting seventy[c] of them to death because they had looked into the ark of the LORD. The people mourned because of the heavy blow the LORD had dealt them, 20and the men of Beth

---

[a]6 That is, God   [b]18 A few Hebrew manuscripts (see also Septuagint); most Hebrew manuscripts *villages as far as Greater Abel, where*   [c]19 A few Hebrew manuscripts; most Hebrew manuscripts and Septuagint 50,070

Shemesh asked, "Who can stand in the presence of the LORD, this holy God? To whom will the ark go up from here?" ²¹Then they sent messengers to the people of Kiriath Jearim, saying, "The Philistines have returned the ark of the LORD. Come down and take it up to your place." ¹So the men of Kiriath Jearim came and took up the ark of the LORD. They took it to Abinadab's house on the hill and consecrated Eleazar his son to guard the ark of the LORD.   Jos 9:17

Samuel Subdues the Philistines at Mizpah

²It was a long time, twenty years in all, that the ark remained at Kiriath Jearim, and all the people of Israel mourned and sought after the LORD. ³And Samuel said to the whole house of Israel, "If you are returning to the LORD with all your hearts, then rid yourselves of the foreign gods and the Ashtoreths and commit yourselves to the LORD and serve him only, and he will deliver you out of the hand of the Philistines." ⁴So the Israelites put away their Baals and Ashtoreths, and served the LORD only.   1Ch 13:5

⁵Then Samuel said, "Assemble all Israel at Mizpah and I will intercede with the LORD for you." ⁶When they had assembled at Mizpah, they drew water and poured it out before the LORD. On that day they fasted and there they confessed, "We have sinned against the LORD." And Samuel was leaderª of Israel at Mizpah.   Ps 99:6

⁷When the Philistines heard that Israel had assembled at Mizpah, the rulers of the Philistines came up to attack them. And when the Israelites heard of it, they were afraid because of the Philistines. ⁸They said to Samuel, "Do not stop crying out to the LORD our God for us, that he may rescue us from the hand of the Philistines." ⁹Then Samuel took a suckling lamb and offered it up as a whole burnt offering to the LORD. He cried out to the LORD on Israel's behalf, and the LORD answered him.

¹⁰While Samuel was sacrificing the burnt offering, the Philistines drew near to engage Israel in battle. But that day the LORD thundered with loud thunder against the Philistines and threw them into such a panic that they were routed before the Israelites. ¹¹The men of Israel rushed out of Mizpah and pursued the Philistines, slaughtering them along the way to a point below Beth Car.   1Sa 2:10

¹²Then Samuel took a stone and set it up between Mizpah and Shen. He named it Ebenezer,ᵇ saying, "Thus far has the LORD helped us." ¹³So the Philistines were subdued and did not invade Israelite territory again.   Jos 4:9; Jdg 13:5

ª6 Traditionally *judge*   ᵇ12 *Ebenezer* means *stone of help.*

Throughout Samuel's lifetime, the hand of the LORD was against the Philistines. ¹⁴The towns from Ekron to Gath that the Philistines had captured from Israel were restored to her, and Israel delivered the neighboring territory from the power of the Philistines. And there was peace between Israel and the Amorites. ^{Jos 13:3; Jdg 1:34}

¹⁵Samuel continued as judge over Israel all the days of his life. ¹⁶From year to year he went on a circuit from Bethel to Gilgal to Mizpah, judging Israel in all those places. ¹⁷But he always went back to Ramah, where his home was, and there he also judged Israel. And he built an altar there to the LORD. ^{1Sa 12:11}

Israel Asks for a King

8 When Samuel grew old, he appointed his sons as judges for Israel. ²The name of his firstborn was Joel and the name of his second was Abijah, and they served at Beersheba. ³But his sons did not walk in his ways. They turned aside after dishonest gain and accepted bribes and perverted justice. ^{Dt 16:18}

⁴So all the elders of Israel gathered together and came to Samuel at Ramah. ⁵They said to him, "You are old, and your sons do not walk in your ways; now appoint a king to lead*ᵃ* us, such as all the other nations have." ^{Dt 17:14; 1Sa 7:17}

⁶But when they said, "Give us a king to lead us," this displeased Samuel; so he prayed to the LORD. ⁷And the LORD told him: "Listen to all that the people are saying to you; it is not you they have rejected, but they have rejected me as their king. ⁸As they have done from the day I brought them up out of Egypt until this day, forsaking me and serving other gods, so they are doing to you. ⁹Now listen to them; but warn them solemnly and let them know what the king who will reign over them will do." ^{Ex 16:8}

¹⁰Samuel told all the words of the LORD to the people who were asking him for a king. ¹¹He said, "This is what the king who will reign over you will do: He will take your sons and make them serve with his chariots and horses, and they will run in front of his chariots. ¹²Some he will assign to be commanders of thousands and commanders of fifties, and others to plow his ground and reap his harvest, and still others to make weapons of war and equipment for his chariots. ¹³He will take your daughters to be perfumers and cooks and bakers. ¹⁴He will take the best of your fields and vineyards and olive groves and give them to his attendants. ¹⁵He will take a tenth of your grain and of your vintage and give it to his officials and attendants. ¹⁶Your menservants and maidservants and the best of your cattle*ᵇ* and

---

ᵃ5 Traditionally *judge*; also in verses 6 and 20　　*ᵇ16* Septuagint; Hebrew *young men*

donkeys he will take for his own use. ¹⁷He will take a tenth of your flocks, and you yourselves will become his slaves. ¹⁸When that day comes, you will cry out for relief from the king you have chosen, and the LORD will not answer you in that day." 2Sa 15:1

¹⁹But the people refused to listen to Samuel. "No!" they said. "We want a king over us. ²⁰Then we will be like all the other nations, with a king to lead us and to go out before us and fight our battles." Isa 50:2

²¹When Samuel heard all that the people said, he repeated it before the LORD. ²²The LORD answered, "Listen to them and give them a king." Jdg 11:11

Then Samuel said to the men of Israel, "Everyone go back to his town."

Samuel Anoints Saul

9 There was a Benjamite, a man of standing, whose name was Kish son of Abiel, the son of Zeror, the son of Becorath, the son of Aphiah of Benjamin. ²He had a son named Saul, an impressive young man without equal among the Israelites—a head taller than any of the others. 1Sa 10:24; 1Ch 9:39

³Now the donkeys belonging to Saul's father Kish were lost, and Kish said to his son Saul, "Take one of the servants with you and go and look for the donkeys." ⁴So he passed

through the hill country of Ephraim and through the area around Shalisha, but they did not find them. They went on into the district of Shaalim, but the donkeys were not there. Then he passed through the territory of Benjamin, but they did not find them. Jos 24:33

⁵When they reached the district of Zuph, Saul said to the servant who was with him, "Come, let's go back, or my father will stop thinking about the donkeys and start worrying about us." 1Sa 1:1; 10:2

⁶But the servant replied, "Look, in this town there is a man of God; he is highly respected, and everything he says comes true. Let's go there now. Perhaps he will tell us what way to take." Dt 33:1; Jdg 13:6

⁷Saul said to his servant, "If we go, what can we give the man? The food in our sacks is gone. We have no gift to take to the man of God. What do we have?" 1Ki 14:3; 2Ki 8:8

⁸The servant answered him again. "Look," he said, "I have a quarter of a shekel*ᵃ* of silver. I will give it to the man of God so that he will tell us what way to take." ⁹(Formerly in Israel, if a man went to inquire of God, he would say, "Come, let us go to the seer," because the prophet of today used to be called a seer.) 2Sa 24:11; 1Ch 9:22

¹⁰"Good," Saul said to his servant. "Come, let's go." So they

---

ᵃ8 That is, about 1/10 ounce (about 3 grams)

set out for the town where the man of God was.

[11]As they were going up the hill to the town, they met some girls coming out to draw water, and they asked them, "Is the seer here?"   Ge 24:13; Ex 2:16

[12]"He is," they answered. "He's ahead of you. Hurry now; he has just come to our town today, for the people have a sacrifice at the high place. [13]As soon as you enter the town, you will find him before he goes up to the high place to eat. The people will not begin eating until he comes, because he must bless the sacrifice; afterward, those who are invited will eat. Go up now; you should find him about this time."   Nu 28:11-15

[14]They went up to the town, and as they were entering it, there was Samuel, coming toward them on his way up to the high place.   1Sa 13:11

[15]Now the day before Saul came, the LORD had revealed this to Samuel: [16]"About this time tomorrow I will send you a man from the land of Benjamin. Anoint him leader over my people Israel; he will deliver my people from the hand of the Philistines. I have looked upon my people, for their cry has reached me."   2Ki 11:12

[17]When Samuel caught sight of Saul, the LORD said to him, "This is the man I spoke to you about; he will govern my people."   1Sa 16:12

[18]Saul approached Samuel in the gateway and asked, "Would you please tell me where the seer's house is?"   2Sa 15:27

[19]"I am the seer," Samuel replied. "Go up ahead of me to the high place, for today you are to eat with me, and in the morning I will let you go and will tell you all that is in your heart. [20]As for the donkeys you lost three days ago, do not worry about them; they have been found. And to whom is all the desire of Israel turned, if not to you and all your father's family?"   Ezr 6:8

[21]Saul answered, "But am I not a Benjamite, from the smallest tribe of Israel, and is not my clan the least of all the clans of the tribe of Benjamin? Why do you say such a thing to me?"

[22]Then Samuel brought Saul and his servant into the hall and seated them at the head of those who were invited—about thirty in number. [23]Samuel said to the cook, "Bring the piece of meat I gave you, the one I told you to lay aside."

[24]So the cook took up the leg with what was on it and set it in front of Saul. Samuel said, "Here is what has been kept for you. Eat, because it was set aside for you for this occasion, from the time I said, 'I have invited guests.'" And Saul dined with Samuel that day.   Lev 7:34

[25]After they came down from the high place to the town, Samuel talked with Saul on the roof of his house. [26]They rose about daybreak and Samuel called to Saul on the roof, "Get ready, and I will send you on your

way." When Saul got ready, he and Samuel went outside together. 27As they were going down to the edge of the town, Samuel said to Saul, "Tell the servant to go on ahead of us"—and the servant did so—"but you stay here awhile, so that I may give you a message from God." Dt 22:8

10 Then Samuel took a flask of oil and poured it on Saul's head and kissed him, saying, "Has not the LORD anointed you leader over his inheritance?*a* 2When you leave me today, you will meet two men near Rachel's tomb, at Zelzah on the border of Benjamin. They will say to you, 'The donkeys you set out to look for have been found. And now your father has stopped thinking about them and is worried about you. He is asking, "What shall I do about my son?"' 2Ki 9:1

3"Then you will go on from there until you reach the great tree of Tabor. Three men going up to God at Bethel will meet you there. One will be carrying three young goats, another three loaves of bread, and another a skin of wine. 4They will greet you and offer you two loaves of bread, which you will accept from them. Ge 35:8

5"After that you will go to Gibeah of God, where there is a Philistine outpost. As you approach the town, you will meet a procession of prophets coming down from the high place with lyres, tambourines, flutes and harps being played before them, and they will be prophesying. 6The Spirit of the LORD will come upon you in power, and you will prophesy with them; and you will be changed into a different person. 7Once these signs are fulfilled, do whatever your hand finds to do, for God is with you. 2Ki 3:15

8"Go down ahead of me to Gilgal. I will surely come down to you to sacrifice burnt offerings and fellowship offerings,*b* but you must wait seven days until I come to you and tell you what you are to do." 1Sa 13:8

Saul Made King

9As Saul turned to leave Samuel, God changed Saul's heart, and all these signs were fulfilled that day. 10When they arrived at Gibeah, a procession of prophets met him; the Spirit of God came upon him in power, and he joined in their prophesying. 11When all those who had formerly known him saw him prophesying with the prophets, they asked each other, "What is this that has happened to the son of Kish? Is Saul also among the prophets?" Dt 13:2; 1Sa 10:6

12A man who lived there answered, "And who is their father?" So it became a saying: "Is Saul also among the prophets?"

---

a1 Hebrew; Septuagint and Vulgate *over his people Israel? You will reign over the* LORD'S *people and save them from the power of their enemies round about. And this will be a sign to you that the* LORD *has anointed you leader over his inheritance:*   *b8* Traditionally *peace offerings*

13After Saul stopped prophesying, he went to the high place.

14Now Saul's uncle asked him and his servant, "Where have you been?" 1Sa 14:50

"Looking for the donkeys," he said. "But when we saw they were not to be found, we went to Samuel." 1Sa 9:3

15Saul's uncle said, "Tell me what Samuel said to you."

16Saul replied, "He assured us that the donkeys had been found." But he did not tell his uncle what Samuel had said about the kingship. 1Sa 9:20

17Samuel summoned the people of Israel to the LORD at Mizpah 18and said to them, "This is what the LORD, the God of Israel, says: 'I brought Israel up out of Egypt, and I delivered you from the power of Egypt and all the kingdoms that oppressed you.' 19But you have now rejected your God, who saves you out of all your calamities and distresses. And you have said, 'No, set a king over us.' So now present yourselves before the LORD by your tribes and clans." 1Sa 7:5; Ps 68:20

20When Samuel brought all the tribes of Israel near, the tribe of Benjamin was chosen. 21Then he brought forward the tribe of Benjamin, clan by clan, and Matri's clan was chosen. Finally Saul son of Kish was chosen. But when they looked for him, he was not to be found. 22So they inquired further of the LORD, "Has the man come here yet?" Jdg 18:5; Est 3:7

And the LORD said, "Yes, he has hidden himself among the baggage."

23They ran and brought him out, and as he stood among the people he was a head taller than any of the others. 24Samuel said to all the people, "Do you see the man the LORD has chosen? There is no one like him among all the people." 1Sa 9:2; 2Sa 21:6

Then the people shouted, "Long live the king!"

25Samuel explained to the people the regulations of the kingship. He wrote them down on a scroll and deposited it before the LORD. Then Samuel dismissed the people, each to his own home. Dt 17:14-20; 2Ki 11:12

26Saul also went to his home in Gibeah, accompanied by valiant men whose hearts God had touched. 27But some troublemakers said, "How can this fellow save us?" They despised him and brought him no gifts. But Saul kept silent. Jdg 19:14

Saul Rescues the City of Jabesh

11 Nahash the Ammonite went up and besieged Jabesh Gilead. And all the men of Jabesh said to him, "Make a treaty with us, and we will be subject to you." Jdg 21:8

2But Nahash the Ammonite replied, "I will make a treaty with you only on the condition that I gouge out the right eye of every one of you and so bring disgrace on all Israel." Nu 16:14

³The elders of Jabesh said to him, "Give us seven days so we can send messengers throughout Israel; if no one comes to rescue us, we will surrender to you."   Jdg 2:16; 1Sa 8:4

⁴When the messengers came to Gibeah of Saul and reported these terms to the people, they all wept aloud. ⁵Just then Saul was returning from the fields, behind his oxen, and he asked, "What is wrong with the people? Why are they weeping?" Then they repeated to him what the men of Jabesh had said. Jdg 2:4; 2Sa 21:6

⁶When Saul heard their words, the Spirit of God came upon him in power, and he burned with anger. ⁷He took a pair of oxen, cut them into pieces, and sent the pieces by messengers throughout Israel, proclaiming, "This is what will be done to the oxen of anyone who does not follow Saul and Samuel." Then the terror of the LORD fell on the people, and they turned out as one man. ⁸When Saul mustered them at Bezek, the men of Israel numbered three hundred thousand and the men of Judah thirty thousand. Jdg 3:10; 20:2

⁹They told the messengers who had come, "Say to the men of Jabesh Gilead, 'By the time the sun is hot tomorrow, you will be delivered.'" When the messengers went and reported this to the men of Jabesh, they were elated. ¹⁰They said to the Ammonites, "Tomorrow we will surrender to you, and you can do to us whatever seems good to you." 1Sa 11:3

¹¹The next day Saul separated his men into three divisions; during the last watch of the night they broke into the camp of the Ammonites and slaughtered them until the heat of the day. Those who survived were scattered, so that no two of them were left together. Jdg 7:16

Saul Confirmed as King

¹²The people then said to Samuel, "Who was it that asked, 'Shall Saul reign over us?' Bring these men to us and we will put them to death."

¹³But Saul said, "No one shall be put to death today, for this day the LORD has rescued Israel." 2Sa 19:22; 1Ch 11:14

¹⁴Then Samuel said to the people, "Come, let us go to Gilgal and there reaffirm the kingship." ¹⁵So all the people went to Gilgal and confirmed Saul as king in the presence of the LORD. There they sacrificed fellowship offeringsᵃ before the LORD, and Saul and all the Israelites held a great celebration.

Samuel's Farewell Speech

12 Samuel said to all Israel, "I have listened to everything you said to me and have set a king over you. ²Now you have a king as your leader. As

---

ᵃ15 Traditionally *peace offerings*

for me, I am old and gray, and my sons are here with you. I have been your leader from my youth until this day. ³Here I stand. Testify against me in the presence of the LORD and his anointed. Whose ox have I taken? Whose donkey have I taken? Whom have I cheated? Whom have I oppressed? From whose hand have I accepted a bribe to make me shut my eyes? If I have done any of these, I will make it right." Nu 16:15; 1Sa 8:7

⁴"You have not cheated or oppressed us," they replied. "You have not taken anything from anyone's hand." Ac 23:9

⁵Samuel said to them, "The LORD is witness against you, and also his anointed is witness this day, that you have not found anything in my hand."

"He is witness," they said.

⁶Then Samuel said to the people, "It is the LORD who appointed Moses and Aaron and brought your forefathers up out of Egypt. ⁷Now then, stand here, because I am going to confront you with evidence before the LORD as to all the righteous acts performed by the LORD for you and your fathers.

⁸"After Jacob entered Egypt, they cried to the LORD for help, and the LORD sent Moses and Aaron, who brought your forefathers out of Egypt and settled them in this place. Ex 2:23

⁹"But they forgot the LORD their God; so he sold them into the hand of Sisera, the commander of the army of Hazor, and into the hands of the Philistines and the king of Moab, who fought against them. ¹⁰They cried out to the LORD and said, 'We have sinned; we have forsaken the LORD and served the Baals and the Ashtoreths. But now deliver us from the hands of our enemies, and we will serve you.' ¹¹Then the LORD sent Jerub-Baal, ᵃ Barak, ᵇ Jephthah and Samuel, ᶜ and he delivered you from the hands of your enemies on every side, so that you lived securely. Jdg 3:7

¹²"But when you saw that Nahash king of the Ammonites was moving against you, you said to me, 'No, we want a king to rule over us'—even though the LORD your God was your king. ¹³Now here is the king you have chosen, the one you asked for; see, the LORD has set a king over you. ¹⁴If you fear the LORD and serve and obey him and do not rebel against his commands, and if both you and the king who reigns over you follow the LORD your God—good! ¹⁵But if you do not obey the LORD, and if you rebel against his commands, his hand will be against you, as it was against your fathers. Jos 24:20; 2Sa 5:2

¹⁶"Now then, stand still and see this great thing the LORD is

---

ᵃ11 Also called *Gideon*   ᵇ11 Some Septuagint manuscripts and Syriac; Hebrew *Bedan*
ᶜ11 Hebrew; some Septuagint manuscripts and Syriac *Samson*

about to do before your eyes! [17]Is it not wheat harvest now? I will call upon the LORD to send thunder and rain. And you will realize what an evil thing you did in the eyes of the LORD when you asked for a king."

[18]Then Samuel called upon the LORD, and that same day the LORD sent thunder and rain. So all the people stood in awe of the LORD and of Samuel. Ex 14:31

[19]The people all said to Samuel, "Pray to the LORD your God for your servants so that we will not die, for we have added to all our other sins the evil of asking for a king." Ex 8:8; Jos 5:18

[20]"Do not be afraid," Samuel replied. "You have done all this evil; yet do not turn away from the LORD, but serve the LORD with all your heart. [21]Do not turn away after useless idols. They can do you no good, nor can they rescue you, because they are useless. [22]For the sake of his great name the LORD will not reject his people, because the LORD was pleased to make you his own. [23]As for me, far be it from me that I should sin against the LORD by failing to pray for you. And I will teach you the way that is good and right. [24]But be sure to fear the LORD and serve him faithfully with all your heart; consider what great things he has done for you. [25]Yet if you persist in doing evil, both you and your king will be swept away." Dt 11:16

Samuel Rebukes Saul

13 Saul was ⌊thirty⌋[a] years old when he became king, and he reigned over Israel ⌊forty-⌋[b] two years.

[2]Saul[c] chose three thousand men from Israel; two thousand were with him at Micmash and in the hill country of Bethel, and a thousand were with Jonathan at Gibeah in Benjamin. The rest of the men he sent back to their homes. 1Sa 10:26; Isa 10:28

[3]Jonathan attacked the Philistine outpost at Geba, and the Philistines heard about it. Then Saul had the trumpet blown throughout the land and said, "Let the Hebrews hear!" [4]So all Israel heard the news: "Saul has attacked the Philistine outpost, and now Israel has become a stench to the Philistines." And the people were summoned to join Saul at Gilgal. 1Sa 10:5

[5]The Philistines assembled to fight Israel, with three thousand[d] chariots, six thousand charioteers, and soldiers as numerous as the sand on the seashore. They went up and camped at Micmash, east of Beth Aven. [6]When the men of Israel saw that their situation was critical and that their army was hard pressed, they hid in caves and thickets, among the

---

[a]1 A few late manuscripts of the Septuagint; Hebrew does not have *thirty*. [b]1 See the round number in Acts 13:21; Hebrew does not have *forty-*. [c]1,2 Or *and when he had reigned over Israel two years,* [2]*he* [d]5 Some Septuagint manuscripts and Syriac; Hebrew *thirty thousand*

rocks, and in pits and cisterns. [7]Some Hebrews even crossed the Jordan to the land of Gad and Gilead.   Nu 32:33; Jos 7:2

Saul remained at Gilgal, and all the troops with him were quaking with fear. [8]He waited seven days, the time set by Samuel; but Samuel did not come to Gilgal, and Saul's men began to scatter. [9]So he said, "Bring me the burnt offering and the fellowship offerings.[a]" And Saul offered up the burnt offering. [10]Just as he finished making the offering, Samuel arrived, and Saul went out to greet him.   2Sa 24:25

[11]"What have you done?" asked Samuel.

Saul replied, "When I saw that the men were scattering, and that you did not come at the set time, and that the Philistines were assembling at Micmash, [12]I thought, 'Now the Philistines will come down against me at Gilgal, and I have not sought the LORD's favor.' So I felt compelled to offer the burnt offering."   Jos 10:43; Ps 119:58

[13]"You acted foolishly," Samuel said. "You have not kept the command the LORD your God gave you; if you had, he would have established your kingdom over Israel for all time. [14]But now your kingdom will not endure; the LORD has sought out a man after his own heart and appointed him leader of his people, because you have not kept the LORD's command."

[15]Then Samuel left Gilgal[b] and went up to Gibeah in Benjamin, and Saul counted the men who were with him. They numbered about six hundred.   1Sa 14:2

Israel Without Weapons

[16]Saul and his son Jonathan and the men with them were staying in Gibeah[c] in Benjamin, while the Philistines camped at Micmash. [17]Raiding parties went out from the Philistine camp in three detachments. One turned toward Ophrah in the vicinity of Shual, [18]another toward Beth Horon, and the third toward the borderland overlooking the Valley of Zeboim facing the desert.   1Sa 14:15

[19]Not a blacksmith could be found in the whole land of Israel, because the Philistines had said, "Otherwise the Hebrews will make swords or spears!" [20]So all Israel went down to the Philistines to have their plowshares, mattocks, axes and sickles[d] sharpened. [21]The price was two thirds of a shekel[e] for sharpening plowshares and mattocks, and a third of a shekel[f] for sharpening forks and axes and for repointing goads.   Nu 25:7; 2Ki 24:14

---

[a]9 Traditionally *peace offerings*   [b]15 Hebrew; Septuagint *Gilgal and went his way; the rest of the people went after Saul to meet the army, and they went out of Gilgal*   [c]16 Two Hebrew manuscripts; most Hebrew manuscripts *Geba*, a variant of *Gibeah*   [d]20 Septuagint; Hebrew *plowshares*   [e]21 Hebrew *pim*; that is, about 1/4 ounce (about 8 grams)   [f]21 That is, about 1/8 ounce (about 4 grams)

²²So on the day of the battle not a soldier with Saul and Jonathan had a sword or spear in his hand; only Saul and his son Jonathan had them.   1Ch 9:39

Jonathan Attacks the Philistines

²³Now a detachment of Philistines had gone out to the pass at

14 Micmash. ¹One day Jonathan son of Saul said to the young man bearing his armor, "Come, let's go over to the Philistine outpost on the other side." But he did not tell his father.   1Sa 14:4

²Saul was staying on the outskirts of Gibeah under a pomegranate tree in Migron. With him were about six hundred men, ³among whom was Ahijah, who was wearing an ephod. He was a son of Ichabod's brother Ahitub son of Phinehas, the son of Eli, the LORD's priest in Shiloh. No one was aware that Jonathan had left.   1Sa 13:15; Ps 78:60

⁴On each side of the pass that Jonathan intended to cross to reach the Philistine outpost was a cliff; one was called Bozez, and the other Seneh. ⁵One cliff stood to the north toward Micmash, the other to the south toward Geba.   1Sa 13:23

⁶Jonathan said to his young armor-bearer, "Come, let's go over to the outpost of those uncircumcised fellows. Perhaps the LORD will act in our behalf.

Nothing can hinder the LORD from saving, whether by many or by few."   Jdg 7:4

⁷"Do all that you have in mind," his armor-bearer said. "Go ahead; I am with you heart and soul."

⁸Jonathan said, "Come, then; we will cross over toward the men and let them see us. ⁹If they say to us, 'Wait there until we come to you,' we will stay where we are and not go up to them. ¹⁰But if they say, 'Come up to us,' we will climb up, because that will be our sign that the LORD has given them into our hands."   Jdg 7:9-14

¹¹So both of them showed themselves to the Philistine outpost. "Look!" said the Philistines. "The Hebrews are crawling out of the holes they were hiding in." ¹²The men of the outpost shouted to Jonathan and his armor-bearer, "Come up to us and we'll teach you a lesson."   Jdg 8:16; 1Sa 13:6

So Jonathan said to his armor-bearer, "Climb up after me; the LORD has given them into the hand of Israel."   2Sa 5:24

¹³Jonathan climbed up, using his hands and feet, with his armor-bearer right behind him. The Philistines fell before Jonathan, and his armor-bearer followed and killed behind him. ¹⁴In that first attack Jonathan and his armor-bearer killed some twenty men in an area of about half an acre. ª

ª14 Hebrew *half a yoke*; a "yoke" was the land plowed by a yoke of oxen in one day.

Israel Routs the Philistines

[15]Then panic struck the whole army—those in the camp and field, and those in the outposts and raiding parties—and the ground shook. It was a panic sent by God. [a]   1Sa 13:17; 2Ki 7:6

[16]Saul's lookouts at Gibeah in Benjamin saw the army melting away in all directions. [17]Then Saul said to the men who were with him, "Muster the forces and see who has left us." When they did, it was Jonathan and his armor-bearer who were not there.   2Sa 18:24; Isa 52:8

[18]Saul said to Ahijah, "Bring the ark of God." (At that time it was with the Israelites.)[b] [19]While Saul was talking to the priest, the tumult in the Philistine camp increased more and more. So Saul said to the priest, "Withdraw your hand."

[20]Then Saul and all his men assembled and went to the battle. They found the Philistines in total confusion, striking each other with their swords. [21]Those Hebrews who had previously been with the Philistines and had gone up with them to their camp went over to the Israelites who were with Saul and Jonathan. [22]When all the Israelites who had hidden in the hill country of Ephraim heard that the Philistines were on the run, they joined the battle in hot pursuit. [23]So the Lord rescued Israel that day, and the battle moved on beyond Beth Aven.

Jonathan Eats Honey

[24]Now the men of Israel were in distress that day, because Saul had bound the people under an oath, saying, "Cursed be any man who eats food before evening comes, before I have avenged myself on my enemies!" So none of the troops tasted food.   Jos 6:26

[25]The entire army[c] entered the woods, and there was honey on the ground. [26]When they went into the woods, they saw the honey oozing out, yet no one put his hand to his mouth, because they feared the oath. [27]But Jonathan had not heard that his father had bound the people with the oath, so he reached out the end of the staff that was in his hand and dipped it into the honeycomb. He raised his hand to his mouth, and his eyes brightened.[d] [28]Then one of the soldiers told him, "Your father bound the army under a strict oath, saying, 'Cursed be any man who eats food today!' That is why the men are faint."   Ps 19:10

[29]Jonathan said, "My father has made trouble for the country. See how my eyes brightened[e] when I tasted a little of this honey. [30]How much better it would have been if the men had eaten today some of the

---

[a]15 Or a terrible panic   [b]18 Hebrew; Septuagint "Bring the ephod." (At that time he wore the ephod before the Israelites.)   [c]25 Or Now all the people of the land   [d]27 Or his strength was renewed   [e]29 Or my strength was renewed

plunder they took from their enemies. Would not the slaughter of the Philistines have been even greater?" 1Ki 18:18

31That day, after the Israelites had struck down the Philistines from Micmash to Aijalon, they were exhausted. 32They pounced on the plunder and, taking sheep, cattle and calves, they butchered them on the ground and ate them, together with the blood. 33Then someone said to Saul, "Look, the men are sinning against the LORD by eating meat that has blood in it."

"You have broken faith," he said. "Roll a large stone over here at once." 34Then he said, "Go out among the men and tell them, 'Each of you bring me your cattle and sheep, and slaughter them here and eat them. Do not sin against the LORD by eating meat with blood still in it.'" Lev 19:26

So everyone brought his ox that night and slaughtered it there. 35Then Saul built an altar to the LORD; it was the first time he had done this. 1Sa 7:17

36Saul said, "Let us go down after the Philistines by night and plunder them till dawn, and let us not leave one of them alive."

"Do whatever seems best to you," they replied.

But the priest said, "Let us inquire of God here." Ge 25:22

37So Saul asked God, "Shall I go down after the Philistines? Will you give them into Israel's hand?" But God did not answer him that day. 2Sa 22:42

38Saul therefore said, "Come here, all you who are leaders of the army, and let us find out what sin has been committed today. 39As surely as the LORD who rescues Israel lives, even if it lies with my son Jonathan, he must die." But not one of the men said a word. Jos 7:11

40Saul then said to all the Israelites, "You stand over there; I and Jonathan my son will stand over here."

"Do what seems best to you," the men replied.

41Then Saul prayed to the LORD, the God of Israel, "Give me the right answer."[a] And Jonathan and Saul were taken by lot, and the men were cleared. 42Saul said, "Cast the lot between me and Jonathan my son." And Jonathan was taken. Pr 16:33; Jnh 1:7

43Then Saul said to Jonathan, "Tell me what you have done."

So Jonathan told him, "I merely tasted a little honey with the end of my staff. And now must I die?" 1Sa 14:27

44Saul said, "May God deal with me, be it ever so severely, if you do not die, Jonathan."

45But the men said to Saul, "Should Jonathan die—he who has brought about this great deliverance in Israel? Never! As

---

a41 Hebrew; Septuagint "Why have you not answered your servant today? If the fault is in me or my son Jonathan, respond with Urim, but if the men of Israel are at fault, respond with Thummim."

surely as the LORD lives, not a hair of his head will fall to the ground, for he did this today with God's help." So the men rescued Jonathan, and he was not put to death. 2Sa 14:11

⁴⁶Then Saul stopped pursuing the Philistines, and they withdrew to their own land.

⁴⁷After Saul had assumed rule over Israel, he fought against their enemies on every side: Moab, the Ammonites, Edom, the kings*a* of Zobah, and the Philistines. Wherever he turned, he inflicted punishment on them.*b* ⁴⁸He fought valiantly and defeated the Amalekites, delivering Israel from the hands of those who had plundered them. 2Sa 10:6; 1Ch 4:43

Saul's Family

⁴⁹Saul's sons were Jonathan, Ishvi and Malki-Shua. The name of his older daughter was Merab, and that of the younger was Michal. ⁵⁰His wife's name was Ahinoam daughter of Ahimaaz. The name of the commander of Saul's army was Abner son of Ner, and Ner was Saul's uncle. ⁵¹Saul's father Kish and Abner's father Ner were sons of Abiel. 1Ch 8:33

⁵²All the days of Saul there was bitter war with the Philistines, and whenever Saul saw a mighty or brave man, he took him into his service. 1Sa 8:11

The LORD Rejects Saul as King

15 Samuel said to Saul, "I am the one the LORD sent to anoint you king over his people Israel; so listen now to the message from the LORD. ²This is what the LORD Almighty says: 'I will punish the Amalekites for what they did to Israel when they waylaid them as they came up from Egypt. ³Now go, attack the Amalekites and totally destroy*c* everything that belongs to them. Do not spare them; put to death men and women, children and infants, cattle and sheep, camels and donkeys.'" 1Sa 9:16; 2Sa 1:8

⁴So Saul summoned the men and mustered them at Telaim—two hundred thousand foot soldiers and ten thousand men from Judah. ⁵Saul went to the city of Amalek and set an ambush in the ravine. ⁶Then he said to the Kenites, "Go away, leave the Amalekites so that I do not destroy you along with them; for you showed kindness to all the Israelites when they came up out of Egypt." So the Kenites moved away from the Amalekites. Nu 24:22

⁷Then Saul attacked the Amalekites all the way from Havilah to Shur, to the east of Egypt. ⁸He took Agag king of the Amalekites alive, and all his

a47 Masoretic Text; Dead Sea Scrolls and Septuagint *king*   *b47* Hebrew; Septuagint *he was victorious*   *c3* The Hebrew term refers to the irrevocable giving over of things or persons to the LORD, often by totally destroying them; also in verses 8, 9, 15, 18, 20 and 21.

people he totally destroyed with the sword. ⁹But Saul and the army spared Agag and the best of the sheep and cattle, the fat calves[a] and lambs—everything that was good. These they were unwilling to destroy completely, but everything that was despised and weak they totally destroyed. Ex 17:8; 1Sa 14:48

¹⁰Then the word of the LORD came to Samuel: ¹¹"I am grieved that I have made Saul king, because he has turned away from me and has not carried out my instructions." Samuel was troubled, and he cried out to the LORD all that night. Job 21:14

¹²Early in the morning Samuel got up and went to meet Saul, but he was told, "Saul has gone to Carmel. There he has set up a monument in his own honor and has turned and gone on down to Gilgal." Jos 15:55

¹³When Samuel reached him, Saul said, "The LORD bless you! I have carried out the LORD's instructions." Ru 3:10

¹⁴But Samuel said, "What then is this bleating of sheep in my ears? What is this lowing of cattle that I hear?"

¹⁵Saul answered, "The soldiers brought them from the Amalekites; they spared the best of the sheep and cattle to sacrifice to the LORD your God, but we totally destroyed the rest." Ge 3:12; Pr 28:13

¹⁶"Stop!" Samuel said to Saul.

"Let me tell you what the LORD said to me last night."

"Tell me," Saul replied.

¹⁷Samuel said, "Although you were once small in your own eyes, did you not become the head of the tribes of Israel? The LORD anointed you king over Israel. ¹⁸And he sent you on a mission, saying, 'Go and completely destroy those wicked people, the Amalekites; make war on them until you have wiped them out.' ¹⁹Why did you not obey the LORD? Why did you pounce on the plunder and do evil in the eyes of the LORD?" Ex 3:11; 1Sa 14:32

²⁰"But I did obey the LORD," Saul said. "I went on the mission the LORD assigned me. I completely destroyed the Amalekites and brought back Agag their king. ²¹The soldiers took sheep and cattle from the plunder, the best of what was devoted to God, in order to sacrifice them to the LORD your God at Gilgal." 1Sa 28:18

²²But Samuel replied:

"Does the LORD delight in
    burnt offerings and
    sacrifices
  as much as in obeying the
    voice of the LORD?
To obey is better than
    sacrifice,
  and to heed is better than
    the fat of rams. Ps 40:6-8
²³For rebellion is like the sin of
    divination,

---

a9 Or *the grown bulls*; the meaning of the Hebrew for this phrase is uncertain.

and arrogance like the evil
   of idolatry.
Because you have rejected
   the word of the LORD,
he has rejected you as
   king."   Dt 18:10; 1Sa 13:13

²⁴Then Saul said to Samuel, "I have sinned. I violated the LORD's command and your instructions. I was afraid of the people and so I gave in to them. ²⁵Now I beg you, forgive my sin and come back with me, so that I may worship the LORD." Pr 29:25

²⁶But Samuel said to him, "I will not go back with you. You have rejected the word of the LORD, and the LORD has rejected you as king over Israel!"

²⁷As Samuel turned to leave, Saul caught hold of the hem of his robe, and it tore. ²⁸Samuel said to him, "The LORD has torn the kingdom of Israel from you today and has given it to one of your neighbors—to one better than you. ²⁹He who is the Glory of Israel does not lie or change his mind; for he is not a man, that he should change his mind."   1Ki 11:31; Heb 7:21

³⁰Saul replied, "I have sinned. But please honor me before the elders of my people and before Israel; come back with me, so that I may worship the LORD your God." ³¹So Samuel went back with Saul, and Saul worshiped the LORD.   Jn 12:43

³²Then Samuel said, "Bring me Agag king of the Amalekites."

Agag came to him confidently,[a] thinking, "Surely the bitterness of death is past."

³³But Samuel said,

"As your sword has made
   women childless,
so will your mother be
   childless among
   women."   Jer 18:21

And Samuel put Agag to death before the LORD at Gilgal.

³⁴Then Samuel left for Ramah, but Saul went up to his home in Gibeah of Saul. ³⁵Until the day Samuel died, he did not go to see Saul again, though Samuel mourned for him. And the LORD was grieved that he had made Saul king over Israel.

Samuel Anoints David

16 The LORD said to Samuel, "How long will you mourn for Saul, since I have rejected him as king over Israel? Fill your horn with oil and be on your way; I am sending you to Jesse of Bethlehem. I have chosen one of his sons to be king."

²But Samuel said, "How can I go? Saul will hear about it and kill me."

The LORD said, "Take a heifer with you and say, 'I have come to sacrifice to the LORD.' ³Invite Jesse to the sacrifice, and I will show you what to do. You are to anoint for me the one I indicate."   Dt 17:15; 1Sa 20:29

⁴Samuel did what the LORD

ᵃ32 Or *him trembling, yet*

said. When he arrived at Bethlehem, the elders of the town trembled when they met him. They asked, "Do you come in peace?" 2Ki 9:17; Lk 2:4

5Samuel replied, "Yes, in peace; I have come to sacrifice to the LORD. Consecrate yourselves and come to the sacrifice with me." Then he consecrated Jesse and his sons and invited them to the sacrifice. Ex 19:10

6When they arrived, Samuel saw Eliab and thought, "Surely the LORD's anointed stands here before the LORD." 1Sa 17:13

7But the LORD said to Samuel, "Do not consider his appearance or his height, for I have rejected him. The LORD does not look at the things man looks at. Man looks at the outward appearance, but the LORD looks at the heart." Ps 147:10

8Then Jesse called Abinadab and had him pass in front of Samuel. But Samuel said, "The LORD has not chosen this one either." 9Jesse then had Shammah pass by, but Samuel said, "Nor has the LORD chosen this one." 10Jesse had seven of his sons pass before Samuel, but Samuel said to him, "The LORD has not chosen these." 11So he asked Jesse, "Are these all the sons you have?" 1Sa 17:13

"There is still the youngest," Jesse answered, "but he is tending the sheep." Ge 37:2; 2Sa 7:8

Samuel said, "Send for him;

we will not sit down*a* until he arrives."

12So he sent and had him brought in. He was ruddy, with a fine appearance and handsome features. 1Sa 9:17; Ac 7:20

Then the LORD said, "Rise and anoint him; he is the one."

13So Samuel took the horn of oil and anointed him in the presence of his brothers, and from that day on the Spirit of the LORD came upon David in power. Samuel then went to Ramah. Jdg 11:29; 2Sa 22:51

David in Saul's Service

14Now the Spirit of the LORD had departed from Saul, and an evil*b* spirit from the LORD tormented him. Jdg 16:20

15Saul's attendants said to him, "See, an evil spirit from God is tormenting you. 16Let our lord command his servants here to search for someone who can play the harp. He will play when the evil spirit from God comes upon you, and you will feel better." 2Ch 29:26-27; Ps 49:4

17So Saul said to his attendants, "Find someone who plays well and bring him to me."

18One of the servants answered, "I have seen a son of Jesse of Bethlehem who knows how to play the harp. He is a brave man and a warrior. He speaks well and is a fine-looking

---

*a*11 Some Septuagint manuscripts; Hebrew *not gather around*   *b*14 Or *injurious*; also in verses 15, 16 and 23

man. And the LORD is with him."   2Sa 17:8; 1Ch 22:11

¹⁹Then Saul sent messengers to Jesse and said, "Send me your son David, who is with the sheep." ²⁰So Jesse took a donkey loaded with bread, a skin of wine and a young goat and sent them with his son David to Saul.   1Sa 17:15; Pr 18:16

²¹David came to Saul and entered his service. Saul liked him very much, and David became one of his armor-bearers. ²²Then Saul sent word to Jesse, saying, "Allow David to remain in my service, for I am pleased with him."   Ge 41:46; Pr 22:29

²³Whenever the spirit from God came upon Saul, David would take his harp and play. Then relief would come to Saul; he would feel better, and the evil spirit would leave him.

David and Goliath

17 Now the Philistines gathered their forces for war and assembled at Socoh in Judah. They pitched camp at Ephes Dammim, between Socoh and Azekah. ²Saul and the Israelites assembled and camped in the Valley of Elah and drew up their battle line to meet the Philistines. ³The Philistines occupied one hill and the Israelites another, with the valley between them.   2Ch 28:18

⁴A champion named Goliath, who was from Gath, came out of the Philistine camp. He was over nine feet[a] tall. ⁵He had a bronze helmet on his head and wore a coat of scale armor of bronze weighing five thousand shekels[b]; ⁶on his legs he wore bronze greaves, and a bronze javelin was slung on his back. ⁷His spear shaft was like a weaver's rod, and its iron point weighed six hundred shekels.[c] His shield bearer went ahead of him.   2Sa 21:19; 1Ch 11:23

⁸Goliath stood and shouted to the ranks of Israel, "Why do you come out and line up for battle? Am I not a Philistine, and are you not the servants of Saul? Choose a man and have him come down to me. ⁹If he is able to fight and kill me, we will become your subjects; but if I overcome him and kill him, you will become our subjects and serve us." ¹⁰Then the Philistine said, "This day I defy the ranks of Israel! Give me a man and let us fight each other." ¹¹On hearing the Philistine's words, Saul and all the Israelites were dismayed and terrified.   2Sa 21:21

¹²Now David was the son of an Ephrathite named Jesse, who was from Bethlehem in Judah. Jesse had eight sons, and in Saul's time he was old and well advanced in years. ¹³Jesse's three oldest sons had followed Saul to the war: The firstborn was Eliab; the second, Abinadab; and the third, Shammah.

---

[a]4 Hebrew *was six cubits and a span* (about 3 meters)   [b]5 That is, about 125 pounds (about 57 kilograms)   [c]7 That is, about 15 pounds (about 7 kilograms)

¹⁴David was the youngest. The three oldest followed Saul, ¹⁵but David went back and forth from Saul to tend his father's sheep at Bethlehem. Ge 35:19; Ps 132:6

¹⁶For forty days the Philistine came forward every morning and evening and took his stand.

¹⁷Now Jesse said to his son David, "Take this ephah^a of roasted grain and these ten loaves of bread for your brothers and hurry to their camp. ¹⁸Take along these ten cheeses to the commander of their unit.^b See how your brothers are and bring back some assurance^c from them. ¹⁹They are with Saul and all the men of Israel in the Valley of Elah, fighting against the Philistines." Ge 37:14

²⁰Early in the morning David left the flock with a shepherd, loaded up and set out, as Jesse had directed. He reached the camp as the army was going out to its battle positions, shouting the war cry. ²¹Israel and the Philistines were drawing up their lines facing each other. ²²David left his things with the keeper of supplies, ran to the battle lines and greeted his brothers. ²³As he was talking with them, Goliath, the Philistine champion from Gath, stepped out from his lines and shouted his usual defiance, and David heard it. ²⁴When the Israelites saw the man, they all ran from him in great fear. Jos 1:11

²⁵Now the Israelites had been saying, "Do you see how this man keeps coming out? He comes out to defy Israel. The king will give great wealth to the man who kills him. He will also give him his daughter in marriage and will exempt his father's family from taxes in Israel." Jos 15:16; 1Sa 18:17

²⁶David asked the men standing near him, "What will be done for the man who kills this Philistine and removes this disgrace from Israel? Who is this uncircumcised Philistine that he should defy the armies of the living God?" 1Sa 11:2

²⁷They repeated to him what they had been saying and told him, "This is what will be done for the man who kills him."

²⁸When Eliab, David's oldest brother, heard him speaking with the men, he burned with anger at him and asked, "Why have you come down here? And with whom did you leave those few sheep in the desert? I know how conceited you are and how wicked your heart is; you came down only to watch the battle."

²⁹"Now what have I done?" said David. "Can't I even speak?" ³⁰He then turned away to someone else and brought up the same matter, and the men answered him as before. ³¹What David said was overheard and reported to Saul, and Saul sent for him.

---

^a17 That is, probably about 3/5 bushel (about 22 liters)   ^b18 Hebrew *thousand*
^c18 Or *some token;* or *some pledge of spoils*

³²David said to Saul, "Let no one lose heart on account of this Philistine; your servant will go and fight him."   Dt 20:3; Ps 18:45

³³Saul replied, "You are not able to go out against this Philistine and fight him; you are only a boy, and he has been a fighting man from his youth." Nu 13:31

³⁴But David said to Saul, "Your servant has been keeping his father's sheep. When a lion or a bear came and carried off a sheep from the flock, ³⁵I went after it, struck it and rescued the sheep from its mouth. When it turned on me, I seized it by its hair, struck it and killed it. ³⁶Your servant has killed both the lion and the bear; this uncircumcised Philistine will be like one of them, because he has defied the armies of the living God. ³⁷The LORD who delivered me from the paw of the lion and the paw of the bear will deliver me from the hand of this Philistine."   1Ch 11:22; Job 10:16

Saul said to David, "Go, and the LORD be with you."

³⁸Then Saul dressed David in his own tunic. He put a coat of armor on him and a bronze helmet on his head. ³⁹David fastened on his sword over the tunic and tried walking around, because he was not used to them.   Ge 41:42

"I cannot go in these," he said to Saul, "because I am not used to them." So he took them off. ⁴⁰Then he took his staff in his hand, chose five smooth stones from the stream, put them in the pouch of his shepherd's bag and, with his sling in his hand, approached the Philistine.   Jdg 20:16

⁴¹Meanwhile, the Philistine, with his shield bearer in front of him, kept coming closer to David. ⁴²He looked David over and saw that he was only a boy, ruddy and handsome, and he despised him. ⁴³He said to David, "Am I a dog, that you come at me with sticks?" And the Philistine cursed David by his gods. ⁴⁴"Come here," he said, "and I'll give your flesh to the birds of the air and the beasts of the field!"   Ps 123:3; Pr 16:18

⁴⁵David said to the Philistine, "You come against me with sword and spear and javelin, but I come against you in the name of the LORD Almighty, the God of the armies of Israel, whom you have defied. ⁴⁶This day the LORD will hand you over to me, and I'll strike you down and cut off your head. Today I will give the carcasses of the Philistine army to the birds of the air and the beasts of the earth, and the whole world will know that there is a God in Israel. ⁴⁷All those gathered here will know that it is not by sword or spear that the LORD saves; for the battle is the LORD's, and he will give all of you into our hands."   2Ch 32:8; Ps 44:6

⁴⁸As the Philistine moved closer to attack him, David ran quickly toward the battle line to meet him. ⁴⁹Reaching into his bag and taking out a stone, he

slung it and struck the Philistine on the forehead. The stone sank into his forehead, and he fell facedown on the ground.

⁵⁰So David triumphed over the Philistine with a sling and a stone; without a sword in his hand he struck down the Philistine and killed him. _{1Sa 25:29}

⁵¹David ran and stood over him. He took hold of the Philistine's sword and drew it from the scabbard. After he killed him, he cut off his head with the sword. _{1Sa 21:9; Heb 11:34}

When the Philistines saw that their hero was dead, they turned and ran. ⁵²Then the men of Israel and Judah surged forward with a shout and pursued the Philistines to the entrance of Gath*ᵃ* and to the gates of Ekron. Their dead were strewn along the Shaaraim road to Gath and Ekron. ⁵³When the Israelites returned from chasing the Philistines, they plundered their camp. ⁵⁴David took the Philistine's head and brought it to Jerusalem, and he put the Philistine's weapons in his own tent. _{Jos 15:11,36}

⁵⁵As Saul watched David going out to meet the Philistine, he said to Abner, commander of the army, "Abner, whose son is that young man?" _{1Sa 16:21}

Abner replied, "As surely as you live, O king, I don't know."

⁵⁶The king said, "Find out whose son this young man is."

⁵⁷As soon as David returned from killing the Philistine, Abner took him and brought him before Saul, with David still holding the Philistine's head. ⁵⁸"Whose son are you, young man?" Saul asked him.

David said, "I am the son of your servant Jesse of Bethlehem." _{Ru 4:17; 1Sa 17:12}

Saul's Jealousy of David

18 After David had finished talking with Saul, Jonathan became one in spirit with David, and he loved him as himself. ²From that day Saul kept David with him and did not let him return to his father's house. ³And Jonathan made a covenant with David because he loved him as himself. ⁴Jonathan took off the robe he was wearing and gave it to David, along with his tunic, and even his sword, his bow and his belt.

⁵Whatever Saul sent him to do, David did it so successfully*ᵇ* that Saul gave him a high rank in the army. This pleased all the people, and Saul's officers as well. _{2Sa 5:2}

⁶When the men were returning home after David had killed the Philistine, the women came out from all the towns of Israel to meet King Saul with singing and dancing, with joyful songs and with tambourines and lutes. ⁷As they danced, they sang:

"Saul has slain his
thousands,

---

*ᵃ*52 Some Septuagint manuscripts; Hebrew *a valley*   *ᵇ*5 Or *wisely*

and David his tens of thousands." Ex 15:20

⁸Saul was very angry; this refrain galled him. "They have credited David with tens of thousands," he thought, "but me with only thousands. What more can he get but the kingdom?" ⁹And from that time on Saul kept a jealous eye on David. 1Sa 13:14; 15:23

¹⁰The next day an evil*a* spirit from God came forcefully upon Saul. He was prophesying in his house, while David was playing the harp, as he usually did. Saul had a spear in his hand ¹¹and he hurled it, saying to himself, "I'll pin David to the wall." But David eluded him twice. 1Sa 16:14

¹²Saul was afraid of David, because the LORD was with David but had left Saul. ¹³So he sent David away from him and gave him command over a thousand men, and David led the troops in their campaigns. ¹⁴In everything he did he had great success,*b* because the LORD was with him. ¹⁵When Saul saw how successful*c* he was, he was afraid of him. ¹⁶But all Israel and Judah loved David, because he led them in their campaigns.

¹⁷Saul said to David, "Here is my older daughter Merab. I will give her to you in marriage; only serve me bravely and fight the battles of the LORD." For Saul said to himself, "I will not raise a hand against him. Let the Philistines do that!" 1Sa 17:25

¹⁸But David said to Saul, "Who am I, and what is my family or my father's clan in Israel, that I should become the king's son-in-law?" ¹⁹So*d* when the time came for Merab, Saul's daughter, to be given to David, she was given in marriage to Adriel of Meholah. 2Sa 7:18

²⁰Now Saul's daughter Michal was in love with David, and when they told Saul about it, he was pleased. ²¹"I will give her to him," he thought, "so that she may be a snare to him and so that the hand of the Philistines may be against him." So Saul said to David, "Now you have a second opportunity to become my son-in-law." Ge 29:26

²²Then Saul ordered his attendants: "Speak to David privately and say, 'Look, the king is pleased with you, and his attendants all like you; now become his son-in-law.'"

²³They repeated these words to David. But David said, "Do you think it is a small matter to become the king's son-in-law? I'm only a poor man and little known." Ge 34:11; 1Sa 17:18

²⁴When Saul's servants told him what David had said, ²⁵Saul replied, "Say to David, 'The king wants no other price for the bride than a hundred Philistine foreskins, to take revenge on his enemies.'" Saul's plan was to have David fall by the hands of the Philistines.

²⁶When the attendants told

---

*a*10 Or *injurious*   *b*14 Or *he was very wise*   *c*15 Or *wise*   *d*19 Or *However,*

David these things, he was pleased to become the king's son-in-law. So before the allotted time elapsed, 27David and his men went out and killed two hundred Philistines. He brought their foreskins and presented the full number to the king so that he might become the king's son-in-law. Then Saul gave him his daughter Michal in marriage. 2Sa 3:14

28When Saul realized that the LORD was with David and that his daughter Michal loved David, 29Saul became still more afraid of him, and he remained his enemy the rest of his days.

30The Philistine commanders continued to go out to battle, and as often as they did, David met with more success*a* than the rest of Saul's officers, and his name became well known.

Saul Tries to Kill David

19 Saul told his son Jonathan and all the attendants to kill David. But Jonathan was very fond of David 2and warned him, "My father Saul is looking for a chance to kill you. Be on your guard tomorrow morning; go into hiding and stay there. 3I will go out and stand with my father in the field where you are. I'll speak to him about you and will tell you what I find out." 1Sa 18:1; 20:12

4Jonathan spoke well of David to Saul his father and said to him, "Let not the king do wrong to his servant David; he has not wronged you, and what he has done has benefited you greatly. 5He took his life in his hands when he killed the Philistine. The LORD won a great victory for all Israel, and you saw it and were glad. Why then would you do wrong to an innocent man like David by killing him for no reason?" 1Sa 20:32

6Saul listened to Jonathan and took this oath: "As surely as the LORD lives, David will not be put to death."

7So Jonathan called David and told him the whole conversation. He brought him to Saul, and David was with Saul as before. 1Sa 16:21; 18:10

8Once more war broke out, and David went out and fought the Philistines. He struck them with such force that they fled before him. 1Sa 23:5

9But an evil*b* spirit from the LORD came upon Saul as he was sitting in his house with his spear in his hand. While David was playing the harp, 10Saul tried to pin him to the wall with his spear, but David eluded him as Saul drove the spear into the wall. That night David made good his escape. Jdg 9:23

11Saul sent men to David's house to watch it and to kill him in the morning. But Michal, David's wife, warned him, "If you don't run for your life tonight, tomorrow you'll be killed." 12So Michal let David down through

a30 Or *David acted more wisely*   *b9* Or *injurious*

a window, and he fled and escaped. [13]Then Michal took an idol[a] and laid it on the bed, covering it with a garment and putting some goats' hair at the head. Jdg 16:2; Ac 9:25

[14]When Saul sent the men to capture David, Michal said, "He is ill." Jos 2:5

[15]Then Saul sent the men back to see David and told them, "Bring him up to me in his bed so that I may kill him." [16]But when the men entered, there was the idol in the bed, and at the head was some goats' hair.

[17]Saul said to Michal, "Why did you deceive me like this and send my enemy away so that he escaped?" 2Sa 2:22

Michal told him, "He said to me, 'Let me get away. Why should I kill you?' "

[18]When David had fled and made his escape, he went to Samuel at Ramah and told him all that Saul had done to him. Then he and Samuel went to Naioth and stayed there. [19]Word came to Saul: "David is in Naioth at Ramah"; [20]so he sent men to capture him. But when they saw a group of prophets prophesying, with Samuel standing there as their leader, the Spirit of God came upon Saul's men and they also prophesied. [21]Saul was told about it, and he sent more men, and they prophesied too. Saul sent men a third time, and they

also prophesied. [22]Finally, he himself left for Ramah and went to the great cistern at Secu. And he asked, "Where are Samuel and David?" Nu 11:25; 1Sa 7:17

"Over in Naioth at Ramah," they said.

[23]So Saul went to Naioth at Ramah. But the Spirit of God came even upon him, and he walked along prophesying until he came to Naioth. [24]He stripped off his robes and also prophesied in Samuel's presence. He lay that way all that day and night. This is why people say, "Is Saul also among the prophets?" 1Sa 10:13; Isa 20:2

David and Jonathan

20 Then David fled from Naioth at Ramah and went to Jonathan and asked, "What have I done? What is my crime? How have I wronged your father, that he is trying to take my life?" 1Sa 24:9; Ps 90:14

[2]"Never!" Jonathan replied. "You are not going to die! Look, my father doesn't do anything, great or small, without confiding in me. Why would he hide this from me? It's not so!" 1Sa 19:1

[3]But David took an oath and said, "Your father knows very well that I have found favor in your eyes, and he has said to himself, 'Jonathan must not know this or he will be grieved.' Yet as surely as the LORD lives and as you live, there is only a step between me and death."

---

[a]13 Hebrew teraphim; also in verse 16

⁴Jonathan said to David, "Whatever you want me to do, I'll do for you." 1Sa 31:2

⁵So David said, "Look, tomorrow is the New Moon festival, and I am supposed to dine with the king; but let me go and hide in the field until the evening of the day after tomorrow. ⁶If your father misses me at all, tell him, 'David earnestly asked my permission to hurry to Bethlehem, his hometown, because an annual sacrifice is being made there for his whole clan.' ⁷If he says, 'Very well,' then your servant is safe. But if he loses his temper, you can be sure that he is determined to harm me. ⁸As for you, show kindness to your servant, for you have brought him into a covenant with you before the LORD. If I am guilty, then kill me yourself! Why hand me over to your father?" Nu 10:10; 2Sa 14:32

⁹"Never!" Jonathan said. "If I had the least inkling that my father was determined to harm you, wouldn't I tell you?"

¹⁰David asked, "Who will tell me if your father answers you harshly?"

¹¹"Come," Jonathan said, "let's go out into the field." So they went there together.

¹²Then Jonathan said to David: "By the LORD, the God of Israel, I will surely sound out my father by this time the day after tomorrow! If he is favorably disposed toward you, will I not send you word and let you know? ¹³But if my father is inclined to harm you, may the LORD deal with me, be it ever so severely, if I do not let you know and send you away safely. May the LORD be with you as he has been with my father. ¹⁴But show me unfailing kindness like that of the LORD as long as I live, so that I may not be killed, ¹⁵and do not ever cut off your kindness from my family—not even when the LORD has cut off every one of David's enemies from the face of the earth." Ru 1:17; 2Sa 9:7

¹⁶So Jonathan made a covenant with the house of David, saying, "May the LORD call David's enemies to account." ¹⁷And Jonathan had David reaffirm his oath out of love for him, because he loved him as he loved himself. Jos 9:18; 1Sa 18:1

¹⁸Then Jonathan said to David: "Tomorrow is the New Moon festival. You will be missed, because your seat will be empty. ¹⁹The day after tomorrow, toward evening, go to the place where you hid when this trouble began, and wait by the stone Ezel. ²⁰I will shoot three arrows to the side of it, as though I were shooting at a target. ²¹Then I will send a boy and say, 'Go, find the arrows.' If I say to him, 'Look, the arrows are on this side of you; bring them here,' then come, because, as surely as the LORD lives, you are safe; there is no danger. ²²But if I say to the boy, 'Look, the arrows are beyond you,' then you must go, be-

cause the LORD has sent you away. ²³And about the matter you and I discussed— remember, the LORD is witness between you and me forever." 1Sa 19:2; 2Ki 13:15

²⁴So David hid in the field, and when the New Moon festival came, the king sat down to eat. ²⁵He sat in his customary place by the wall, opposite Jonathan,ᵃ and Abner sat next to Saul, but David's place was empty. ²⁶Saul said nothing that day, for he thought, "Something must have happened to David to make him ceremonially unclean—surely he is unclean." ²⁷But the next day, the second day of the month, David's place was empty again. Then Saul said to his son Jonathan, "Why hasn't the son of Jesse come to the meal, either yesterday or today?" Ps 81:3

²⁸Jonathan answered, "David earnestly asked me for permission to go to Bethlehem. ²⁹He said, 'Let me go, because our family is observing a sacrifice in the town and my brother has ordered me to be there. If I have found favor in your eyes, let me get away to see my brothers.' That is why he has not come to the king's table." Ge 8:20

³⁰Saul's anger flared up at Jonathan and he said to him, "You son of a perverse and rebellious woman! Don't I know that you have sided with the son of Jesse to your own shame

and to the shame of the mother who bore you? ³¹As long as the son of Jesse lives on this earth, neither you nor your kingdom will be established. Now send and bring him to me, for he must die!" Dt 21:20; 1Sa 23:17

³²"Why should he be put to death? What has he done?" Jonathan asked his father. ³³But Saul hurled his spear at him to kill him. Then Jonathan knew that his father intended to kill David. 1Sa 18:11; Mt 27:23

³⁴Jonathan got up from the table in fierce anger; on that second day of the month he did not eat, because he was grieved at his father's shameful treatment of David. 1Sa 28:20

³⁵In the morning Jonathan went out to the field for his meeting with David. He had a small boy with him, ³⁶and he said to the boy, "Run and find the arrows I shoot." As the boy ran, he shot an arrow beyond him. ³⁷When the boy came to the place where Jonathan's arrow had fallen, Jonathan called out after him, "Isn't the arrow beyond you?" ³⁸Then he shouted, "Hurry! Go quickly! Don't stop!" The boy picked up the arrow and returned to his master. ³⁹(The boy knew nothing of all this; only Jonathan and David knew.) ⁴⁰Then Jonathan gave his weapons to the boy and said, "Go, carry them back to town." Ru 2:10; 1Sa 24:8

⁴¹After the boy had gone, Da-

ᵃ25 Septuagint; Hebrew *wall. Jonathan arose*

vid got up from the south side of the stone, and bowed down before Jonathan three times, with his face to the ground. Then they kissed each other and wept together—but David wept the most. _{Ru 2:10; 2Sa 1:2}

⁴²Jonathan said to David, "Go in peace, for we have sworn friendship with each other in the name of the LORD, saying, 'The LORD is witness between you and me, and between your descendants and my descendants forever.'" Then David left, and Jonathan went back to the town. _{1Sa 1:17; 2Sa 1:26}

David at Nob

21 David went to Nob, to Ahimelech the priest. Ahimelech trembled when he met him, and asked, "Why are you alone? Why is no one with you?" _{1Sa 22:19; Ne 11:32}

²David answered Ahimelech the priest, "The king charged me with a certain matter and said to me, 'No one is to know anything about your mission and your instructions.' As for my men, I have told them to meet me at a certain place. ³Now then, what do you have on hand? Give me five loaves of bread, or whatever you can find."

⁴But the priest answered David, "I don't have any ordinary bread on hand; however, there is some consecrated bread here—provided the men have

kept themselves from women."

⁵David replied, "Indeed women have been kept from us, as usual whenever*a* I set out. The men's things*b* are holy even on missions that are not holy. How much more so today!" ⁶So the priest gave him the consecrated bread, since there was no bread there except the bread of the Presence that had been removed from before the LORD and replaced by hot bread on the day it was taken away.

⁷Now one of Saul's servants was there that day, detained before the LORD; he was Doeg the Edomite, Saul's head shepherd.

⁸David asked Ahimelech, "Don't you have a spear or a sword here? I haven't brought my sword or any other weapon, because the king's business was urgent."

⁹The priest replied, "The sword of Goliath the Philistine, whom you killed in the Valley of Elah, is here; it is wrapped in a cloth behind the ephod. If you want it, take it; there is no sword here but that one."_{1Sa 17:51}

David said, "There is none like it; give it to me."

David at Gath

¹⁰That day David fled from Saul and went to Achish king of Gath. ¹¹But the servants of Achish said to him, "Isn't this David, the king of the land? Isn't he the one they sing about in their dances:

---

*a*5 Or *from us in the past few days since*   *b*5 Or *bodies*

" 'Saul has slain his
thousands,
and David his tens of
thousands'?" 1Sa 25:13

¹²David took these words to heart and was very much afraid of Achish king of Gath. ¹³So he pretended to be insane in their presence; and while he was in their hands he acted like a madman, making marks on the doors of the gate and letting saliva run down his beard.

¹⁴Achish said to his servants, "Look at the man! He is insane! Why bring him to me? ¹⁵Am I so short of madmen that you have to bring this fellow here to carry on like this in front of me? Must this man come into my house?"

David at Adullam and Mizpah

22 David left Gath and escaped to the cave of Adullam. When his brothers and his father's household heard about it, they went down to him there. ²All those who were in distress or in debt or discontented gathered around him, and he became their leader. About four hundred men were with him.

³From there David went to Mizpah in Moab and said to the king of Moab, "Would you let my father and mother come and stay with you until I learn what God will do for me?" ⁴So he left them with the king of Moab, and they stayed with him as long as David was in the stronghold.

⁵But the prophet Gad said to David, "Do not stay in the stronghold. Go into the land of Judah." So David left and went to the forest of Hereth. 2Sa 24:11

Saul Kills the Priests of Nob

⁶Now Saul heard that David and his men had been discovered. And Saul, spear in hand, was seated under the tamarisk tree on the hill at Gibeah, with all his officials standing around him. ⁷Saul said to them, "Listen, men of Benjamin! Will the son of Jesse give all of you fields and vineyards? Will he make all of you commanders of thousands and commanders of hundreds? ⁸Is that why you have all conspired against me? No one tells me when my son makes a covenant with the son of Jesse. None of you is concerned about me or tells me that my son has incited my servant to lie in wait for me, as he does today." Jdg 4:5

⁹But Doeg the Edomite, who was standing with Saul's officials, said, "I saw the son of Jesse come to Ahimelech son of Ahitub at Nob. ¹⁰Ahimelech inquired of the LORD for him; he also gave him provisions and the sword of Goliath the Philistine." Ge 25:22; 1Sa 14:3

¹¹Then the king sent for the priest Ahimelech son of Ahitub and his father's whole family, who were the priests at Nob, and they all came to the king. ¹²Saul said, "Listen now, son of Ahitub."

"Yes, my lord," he answered.

13Saul said to him, "Why have you conspired against me, you and the son of Jesse, giving him bread and a sword and inquiring of God for him, so that he has rebelled against me and lies in wait for me, as he does today?"   1Sa 22:8

14Ahimelech answered the king, "Who of all your servants is as loyal as David, the king's son-in-law, captain of your bodyguard and highly respected in your household? 15Was that day the first time I inquired of God for him? Of course not! Let not the king accuse your servant or any of his father's family, for your servant knows nothing at all about this whole affair."   1Sa 19:4-5

16But the king said, "You will surely die, Ahimelech, you and your father's whole family."

17Then the king ordered the guards at his side: "Turn and kill the priests of the LORD, because they too have sided with David. They knew he was fleeing, yet they did not tell me."

But the king's officials were not willing to raise a hand to strike the priests of the LORD.

18The king then ordered Doeg, "You turn and strike down the priests." So Doeg the Edomite turned and struck them down. That day he killed eighty-five men who wore the linen ephod. 19He also put to the sword Nob, the town of the priests, with its men and women, its children and infants, and its cattle, donkeys and sheep.   1Sa 2:18; 15:3

20But Abiathar, a son of Ahimelech son of Ahitub, escaped and fled to join David. 21He told David that Saul had killed the priests of the LORD. 22Then David said to Abiathar: "That day, when Doeg the Edomite was there, I knew he would be sure to tell Saul. I am responsible for the death of your father's whole family. 23Stay with me; don't be afraid; the man who is seeking your life is seeking mine also. You will be safe with me."   1Sa 23:6; 1Ki 2:26

David Saves Keilah

23 When David was told, "Look, the Philistines are fighting against Keilah and are looting the threshing floors," 2he inquired of the LORD, saying, "Shall I go and attack these Philistines?"   Jos 15:44; 2Sa 5:19

The LORD answered him, "Go, attack the Philistines and save Keilah."

3But David's men said to him, "Here in Judah we are afraid. How much more, then, if we go to Keilah against the Philistine forces!"

4Once again David inquired of the LORD, and the LORD answered him, "Go down to Keilah, for I am going to give the Philistines into your hand." 5So David and his men went to Keilah, fought the Philistines and

carried off their livestock. He inflicted heavy losses on the Philistines and saved the people of Keilah. 6(Now Abiathar son of Ahimelech had brought the ephod down with him when he fled to David at Keilah.)   Jos 8:7

Saul Pursues David

7Saul was told that David had gone to Keilah, and he said, "God has handed him over to me, for David has imprisoned himself by entering a town with gates and bars." 8And Saul called up all his forces for battle, to go down to Keilah to besiege David and his men.   Ps 31:21

9When David learned that Saul was plotting against him, he said to Abiathar the priest, "Bring the ephod." 10David said, "O LORD, God of Israel, your servant has heard definitely that Saul plans to come to Keilah and destroy the town on account of me. 11Will the citizens of Keilah surrender me to him? Will Saul come down, as your servant has heard? O LORD, God of Israel, tell your servant."   1Sa 22:20; 30:7

And the LORD said, "He will."

12Again David asked, "Will the citizens of Keilah surrender me and my men to Saul?" 1Sa 23:20

And the LORD said, "They will."

13So David and his men, about six hundred in number, left Keilah and kept moving from place to place. When Saul was told that David had es-caped from Keilah, he did not go there.   1Sa 22:2; 25:13

14David stayed in the desert strongholds and in the hills of the Desert of Ziph. Day after day Saul searched for him, but God did not give David into his hands.   Jos 15:24; Ps 54:3-4

15While David was at Horesh in the Desert of Ziph, he learned that Saul had come out to take his life. 16And Saul's son Jonathan went to David at Horesh and helped him find strength in God. 17"Don't be afraid," he said. "My father Saul will not lay a hand on you. You will be king over Israel, and I will be second to you. Even my father Saul knows this." 18The two of them made a covenant before the LORD. Then Jonathan went home, but David remained at Horesh.   1Sa 30:6

19The Ziphites went up to Saul at Gibeah and said, "Is not David hiding among us in the strongholds at Horesh, on the hill of Hakilah, south of Jeshimon? 20Now, O king, come down whenever it pleases you to do so, and we will be responsible for handing him over to the king."   1Sa 26:1; Ps 54:3

21Saul replied, "The LORD bless you for your concern for me. 22Go and make further preparation. Find out where David usually goes and who has seen him there. They tell me he is very crafty. 23Find out about all the hiding places he uses and come back to me with definite

information. *a* Then I will go with you; if he is in the area, I will track him down among all the clans of Judah." *1Sa 22:8*

²⁴So they set out and went to Ziph ahead of Saul. Now David and his men were in the Desert of Maon, in the Arabah south of Jeshimon. ²⁵Saul and his men began the search, and when David was told about it, he went down to the rock and stayed in the Desert of Maon. When Saul heard this, he went into the Desert of Maon in pursuit of David. *Jos 15:55; 1Sa 26:1*

²⁶Saul was going along one side of the mountain, and David and his men were on the other side, hurrying to get away from Saul. As Saul and his forces were closing in on David and his men to capture them, ²⁷a messenger came to Saul, saying, "Come quickly! The Philistines are raiding the land." ²⁸Then Saul broke off his pursuit of David and went to meet the Philistines. That is why they call this place Sela Hammahlekoth. *b* ²⁹And David went up from there and lived in the strongholds of En Gedi. *Ps 17:9*

David Spares Saul's Life

24 After Saul returned from pursuing the Philistines, he was told, "David is in the Desert of En Gedi." ²So Saul took three thousand chosen men from all Israel and set out to look for David and his men near the Crags of the Wild Goats. *Jos 15:62; 1Sa 26:2*

³He came to the sheep pens along the way; a cave was there, and Saul went in to relieve himself. David and his men were far back in the cave. ⁴The men said, "This is the day the LORD spoke of when he said*c* to you, 'I will give your enemy into your hands for you to deal with as you wish.'" Then David crept up unnoticed and cut off a corner of Saul's robe. *Jdg 3:24*

⁵Afterward, David was conscience-stricken for having cut off a corner of his robe. ⁶He said to his men, "The LORD forbid that I should do such a thing to my master, the LORD's anointed, or lift my hand against him; for he is the anointed of the LORD." ⁷With these words David rebuked his men and did not allow them to attack Saul. And Saul left the cave and went his way. *1Sa 26:11; 2Sa 24:10*

⁸Then David went out of the cave and called out to Saul, "My lord the king!" When Saul looked behind him, David bowed down and prostrated himself with his face to the ground. ⁹He said to Saul, "Why do you listen when men say, 'David is bent on harming you'? ¹⁰This day you have seen with your own eyes how the LORD delivered you into my hands in the cave. Some urged me to kill

---

*a*23 Or *me at Nacon*   *b*28 *Sela Hammahlekoth* means *rock of parting.*   *c*4 Or *"Today the* LORD *is saying*

you, but I spared you; I said, 'I will not lift my hand against my master, because he is the LORD's anointed.' [11]See, my father, look at this piece of your robe in my hand! I cut off the corner of your robe but did not kill you. Now understand and recognize that I am not guilty of wrongdoing or rebellion. I have not wronged you, but you are hunting me down to take my life. [12]May the LORD judge between you and me. And may the LORD avenge the wrongs you have done to me, but my hand will not touch you. [13]As the old saying goes, 'From evildoers come evil deeds,' so my hand will not touch you.　　1Sa 26:20; Ps 7:3

[14]"Against whom has the king of Israel come out? Whom are you pursuing? A dead dog? A flea? [15]May the LORD be our judge and decide between us. May he consider my cause and uphold it; may he vindicate me by delivering me from your hand."　　1Sa 17:43; Ps 35:1

[16]When David finished saying this, Saul asked, "Is that your voice, David my son?" And he wept aloud. [17]"You are more righteous than I," he said. "You have treated me well, but I have treated you badly. [18]You have just now told me of the good you did to me; the LORD delivered me into your hands, but you did not kill me. [19]When a man finds his enemy, does he let him get away unharmed?

May the LORD reward you well for the way you treated me today. [20]I know that you will surely be king and that the kingdom of Israel will be established in your hands. [21]Now swear to me by the LORD that you will not cut off my descendants or wipe out my name from my father's family."　　1Sa 26:17; 2Sa 21:6-8

[22]So David gave his oath to Saul. Then Saul returned home, but David and his men went up to the stronghold.　　1Sa 23:29

David, Nabal and Abigail

25 Now Samuel died, and all Israel assembled and mourned for him; and they buried him at his home in Ramah.

Then David moved down into the Desert of Maon.[a] [2]A certain man in Maon, who had property there at Carmel, was very wealthy. He had a thousand goats and three thousand sheep, which he was shearing in Carmel. [3]His name was Nabal and his wife's name was Abigail. She was an intelligent and beautiful woman, but her husband, a Calebite, was surly and mean in his dealings.　　Jos 15:55

[4]While David was in the desert, he heard that Nabal was shearing sheep. [5]So he sent ten young men and said to them, "Go up to Nabal at Carmel and greet him in my name. [6]Say to him: 'Long life to you! Good health to you and your house-

---

[a]1 Some Septuagint manuscripts; Hebrew *Paran*

hold! And good health to all that is yours! 2Sa 24:10; 1Ch 12:18

7" 'Now I hear that it is sheep-shearing time. When your shepherds were with us, we did not mistreat them, and the whole time they were at Carmel nothing of theirs was missing. 8Ask your own servants and they will tell you. Therefore be favorable toward my young men, since we come at a festive time. Please give your servants and your son David whatever you can find for them.' " 2Sa 13:23

9When David's men arrived, they gave Nabal this message in David's name. Then they waited.

10Nabal answered David's servants, "Who is this David? Who is this son of Jesse? Many servants are breaking away from their masters these days. 11Why should I take my bread and water, and the meat I have slaughtered for my shearers, and give it to men coming from who knows where?" Jdg 9:28

12David's men turned around and went back. When they arrived, they reported every word. 13David said to his men, "Put on your swords!" So they put on their swords, and David put on his. About four hundred men went up with David, while two hundred stayed with the supplies. Nu 31:27; 1Sa 21:10

14One of the servants told Nabal's wife Abigail: "David sent messengers from the desert to give our master his greetings, but he hurled insults at them. 15Yet these men were very good to us. They did not mistreat us, and the whole time we were out in the fields near them nothing was missing. 16Night and day they were a wall around us all the time we were herding our sheep near them. 17Now think it over and see what you can do, because disaster is hanging over our master and his whole household. He is such a wicked man that no one can talk to him." Ex 14:22; 1Sa 13:10

18Abigail lost no time. She took two hundred loaves of bread, two skins of wine, five dressed sheep, five seahs^a of roasted grain, a hundred cakes of raisins and two hundred cakes of pressed figs, and loaded them on donkeys. 19Then she told her servants, "Go on ahead; I'll follow you." But she did not tell her husband Nabal.

20As she came riding her donkey into a mountain ravine, there were David and his men descending toward her, and she met them. 21David had just said, "It's been useless—all my watching over this fellow's property in the desert so that nothing of his was missing. He has paid me back evil for good. 22May God deal with David,^{b} be it ever so severely, if by morn-

---

^{a}18 That is, probably about a bushel (about 37 liters) ^{b}22 Some Septuagint
manuscripts; Hebrew *with David's enemies*

ing I leave alive one male of all who belong to him!" Ps 109:5

²³When Abigail saw David, she quickly got off her donkey and bowed down before David with her face to the ground. ²⁴She fell at his feet and said: "My lord, let the blame be on me alone. Please let your servant speak to you; hear what your servant has to say. ²⁵May my lord pay no attention to that wicked man Nabal. He is just like his name—his name is Fool, and folly goes with him. But as for me, your servant, I did not see the men my master sent.

²⁶"Now since the LORD has kept you, my master, from bloodshed and from avenging yourself with your own hands, as surely as the LORD lives and as you live, may your enemies and all who intend to harm my master be like Nabal. ²⁷And let this gift, which your servant has brought to my master, be given to the men who follow you. ²⁸Please forgive your servant's offense, for the LORD will certainly make a lasting dynasty for my master, because he fights the LORD's battles. Let no wrongdoing be found in you as long as you live. ²⁹Even though someone is pursuing you to take your life, the life of my master will be bound securely in the bundle of the living by the LORD your God. But the lives of your enemies he will hurl away as from the pocket of a sling. ³⁰When the LORD has done for my master every good thing he

promised concerning him and has appointed him leader over Israel, ³¹my master will not have on his conscience the staggering burden of needless bloodshed or of having avenged himself. And when the LORD has brought my master success, remember your servant." Heb 10:30

³²David said to Abigail, "Praise be to the LORD, the God of Israel, who has sent you today to meet me. ³³May you be blessed for your good judgment and for keeping me from bloodshed this day and from avenging myself with my own hands. ³⁴Otherwise, as surely as the LORD, the God of Israel, lives, who has kept me from harming you, if you had not come quickly to meet me, not one male belonging to Nabal would have been left alive by daybreak." Ge 24:27; Ex 18:10

³⁵Then David accepted from her hand what she had brought him and said, "Go home in peace. I have heard your words and granted your request."

³⁶When Abigail went to Nabal, he was in the house holding a banquet like that of a king. He was in high spirits and very drunk. So she told him nothing until daybreak. ³⁷Then in the morning, when Nabal was sober, his wife told him all these things, and his heart failed him and he became like a stone. ³⁸About ten days later, the LORD struck Nabal and he died. Pr 20:1

³⁹When David heard that Nabal was dead, he said, "Praise

be to the LORD, who has upheld my cause against Nabal for treating me with contempt. He has kept his servant from doing wrong and has brought Nabal's wrongdoing down on his own head." 1Sa 24:15; 1Ki 2:44

Then David sent word to Abigail, asking her to become his wife. 40His servants went to Carmel and said to Abigail, "David has sent us to you to take you to become his wife."

41She bowed down with her face to the ground and said, "Here is your maidservant, ready to serve you and wash the feet of my master's servants." 42Abigail quickly got on a donkey and, attended by her five maids, went with David's messengers and became his wife. 43David had also married Ahinoam of Jezreel, and they both were his wives. 44But Saul had given his daughter Michal, David's wife, to Paltiel[a] son of Laish, who was from Gallim. 1Sa 27:3

David Again Spares Saul's Life

26 The Ziphites went to Saul at Gibeah and said, "Is not David hiding on the hill of Hakilah, which faces Jeshimon?" 1Sa 23:19,24

2So Saul went down to the Desert of Ziph, with his three thousand chosen men of Israel, to search there for David. 3Saul made his camp beside the road on the hill of Hakilah facing Je-

shimon, but David stayed in the desert. When he saw that Saul had followed him there, 4he sent out scouts and learned that Saul had definitely arrived.[b]

5Then David set out and went to the place where Saul had camped. He saw where Saul and Abner son of Ner, the commander of the army, had lain down. Saul was lying inside the camp, with the army encamped around him. 1Sa 14:50; 17:55

6David then asked Ahimelech the Hittite and Abishai son of Zeruiah, Joab's brother, "Who will go down into the camp with me to Saul?" Jdg 7:10; 1Ch 2:16

"I'll go with you," said Abishai.

7So David and Abishai went to the army by night, and there was Saul, lying asleep inside the camp with his spear stuck in the ground near his head. Abner and the soldiers were lying around him.

8Abishai said to David, "Today God has delivered your enemy into your hands. Now let me pin him to the ground with one thrust of my spear; I won't strike him twice." 1Sa 24:4

9But David said to Abishai, "Don't destroy him! Who can lay a hand on the LORD's anointed and be guiltless? 10As surely as the LORD lives," he said, "the LORD himself will strike him; either his time will come and he will die, or he will go into battle

a44 Hebrew *Palti*, a variant of *Paltiel*   b4 Or *had come to Nacon*

and perish. ¹¹But the LORD forbid that I should lay a hand on the LORD's anointed. Now get the spear and water jug that are near his head, and let's go."

¹²So David took the spear and water jug near Saul's head, and they left. No one saw or knew about it, nor did anyone wake up. They were all sleeping, because the LORD had put them into a deep sleep.   Ge 2:21; Jdg 4:21

¹³Then David crossed over to the other side and stood on top of the hill some distance away; there was a wide space between them. ¹⁴He called out to the army and to Abner son of Ner, "Aren't you going to answer me, Abner?"   1Sa 14:50-51

Abner replied, "Who are you who calls to the king?"

¹⁵David said, "You're a man, aren't you? And who is like you in Israel? Why didn't you guard your lord the king? Someone came to destroy your lord the king. ¹⁶What you have done is not good. As surely as the LORD lives, you and your men deserve to die, because you did not guard your master, the LORD's anointed. Look around you. Where are the king's spear and water jug that were near his head?"

¹⁷Saul recognized David's voice and said, "Is that your voice, David my son?"   1Sa 24:16

David replied, "Yes it is, my lord the king." ¹⁸And he added, "Why is my lord pursuing his servant? What have I done, and what wrong am I guilty of? ¹⁹Now let my lord the king listen to his servant's words. If the LORD has incited you against me, then may he accept an offering. If, however, men have done it, may they be cursed before the LORD! They have now driven me from my share in the LORD's inheritance and have said, 'Go, serve other gods.' ²⁰Now do not let my blood fall to the ground far from the presence of the LORD. The king of Israel has come out to look for a flea—as one hunts a partridge in the mountains."   1Sa 24:14

²¹Then Saul said, "I have sinned. Come back, David my son. Because you considered my life precious today, I will not try to harm you again. Surely I have acted like a fool and have erred greatly."   1Sa 15:24; Ps 72:14

²²"Here is the king's spear," David answered. "Let one of your young men come over and get it. ²³The LORD rewards every man for his righteousness and faithfulness. The LORD delivered you into my hands today, but I would not lay a hand on the LORD's anointed. ²⁴As surely as I valued your life today, so may the LORD value my life and deliver me from all trouble."   1Sa 24:12; Ps 54:7

²⁵Then Saul said to David, "May you be blessed, my son David; you will do great things and surely triumph."   Ru 2:12

So David went on his way, and Saul returned home.

David Among the Philistines

27 But David thought to himself, "One of these days I will be destroyed by the hand of Saul. The best thing I can do is to escape to the land of the Philistines. Then Saul will give up searching for me anywhere in Israel, and I will slip out of his hand." ^{1Ch 29:28}

²So David and the six hundred men with him left and went over to Achish son of Maoch king of Gath. ³David and his men settled in Gath with Achish. Each man had his family with him, and David had his two wives: Ahinoam of Jezreel and Abigail of Carmel, the widow of Nabal. ⁴When Saul was told that David had fled to Gath, he no longer searched for him. ^{1Sa 25:13; 1Ki 2:39}

⁵Then David said to Achish, "If I have found favor in your eyes, let a place be assigned to me in one of the country towns, that I may live there. Why should your servant live in the royal city with you?"

⁶So on that day Achish gave him Ziklag, and it has belonged to the kings of Judah ever since. ⁷David lived in Philistine territory a year and four months.

⁸Now David and his men went up and raided the Geshurites, the Girzites and the Amalekites. (From ancient times these peoples had lived in the land extending to Shur and Egypt.) ⁹Whenever David attacked an area, he did not leave a man or woman alive, but took sheep and cattle, donkeys and camels, and clothes. Then he returned to Achish. ^{Ex 15:22}

¹⁰When Achish asked, "Where did you go raiding today?" David would say, "Against the Negev of Judah" or "Against the Negev of Jerahmeel" or "Against the Negev of the Kenites." ¹¹He did not leave a man or woman alive to be brought to Gath, for he thought, "They might inform on us and say, 'This is what David did.'" And such was his practice as long as he lived in Philistine territory. ¹²Achish trusted David and said to himself, "He has become so odious to his people, the Israelites, that he will be my servant forever."

Saul and the Witch of Endor

28 In those days the Philistines gathered their forces to fight against Israel. Achish said to David, "You must understand that you and your men will accompany me in the army." ^{1Sa 29:1}

²David said, "Then you will see for yourself what your servant can do."

Achish replied, "Very well, I will make you my bodyguard for life." ^{1Sa 29:2}

³Now Samuel was dead, and all Israel had mourned for him and buried him in his own town of Ramah. Saul had expelled the mediums and spiritists from the land. ^{Lev 19:31; 1Sa 25:1}

⁴The Philistines assembled

and came and set up camp at Shunem, while Saul gathered all the Israelites and set up camp at Gilboa. ⁵When Saul saw the Philistine army, he was afraid; terror filled his heart. ⁶He inquired of the LORD, but the LORD did not answer him by dreams or Urim or prophets. ⁷Saul then said to his attendants, "Find me a woman who is a medium, so I may go and inquire of her."   2Sa 1:6; 1Ch 10:13

"There is one in Endor," they said.   Jos 17:11; Ps 83:10

⁸So Saul disguised himself, putting on other clothes, and at night he and two men went to the woman. "Consult a spirit for me," he said, "and bring up for me the one I name."   Isa 8:19

⁹But the woman said to him, "Surely you know what Saul has done. He has cut off the mediums and spiritists from the land. Why have you set a trap for my life to bring about my death?"   Job 18:10; Pr 31:4

¹⁰Saul swore to her by the LORD, "As surely as the LORD lives, you will not be punished for this."

¹¹Then the woman asked, "Whom shall I bring up for you?"

"Bring up Samuel," he said.

¹²When the woman saw Samuel, she cried out at the top of her voice and said to Saul, "Why have you deceived me? You are Saul!"   Ge 27:36

¹³The king said to her, "Don't be afraid. What do you see?"

The woman said, "I see a spiritᵃ coming up out of the ground."   Lev 19:31; 2Ch 33:6

¹⁴"What does he look like?" he asked.

"An old man wearing a robe is coming up," she said.   1Sa 15:27

Then Saul knew it was Samuel, and he bowed down and prostrated himself with his face to the ground.

¹⁵Samuel said to Saul, "Why have you disturbed me by bringing me up?"

"I am in great distress," Saul said. "The Philistines are fighting against me, and God has turned away from me. He no longer answers me, either by prophets or by dreams. So I have called on you to tell me what to do."   Jdg 16:20; 1Sa 14:37

¹⁶Samuel said, "Why do you consult me, now that the LORD has turned away from you and become your enemy? ¹⁷The LORD has done what he predicted through me. The LORD has torn the kingdom out of your hands and given it to one of your neighbors—to David. ¹⁸Because you did not obey the LORD or carry out his fierce wrath against the Amalekites, the LORD has done this to you today. ¹⁹The LORD will hand over both Israel and you to the Philistines, and tomorrow you and your sons will be with me. The LORD will also hand over

ᵃ13 Or see spirits; or see gods

the army of Israel to the Philistines." _{1Sa 15:28; 1Ch 8:33}

²⁰Immediately Saul fell full length on the ground, filled with fear because of Samuel's words. His strength was gone, for he had eaten nothing all that day and night.

²¹When the woman came to Saul and saw that he was greatly shaken, she said, "Look, your maidservant has obeyed you. I took my life in my hands and did what you told me to do. ²²Now please listen to your servant and let me give you some food so you may eat and have the strength to go on your way." _{Jdg 12:3; 1Sa 19:5}

²³He refused and said, "I will not eat." _{1Ki 21:4}

But his men joined the woman in urging him, and he listened to them. He got up from the ground and sat on the couch. _{2Ki 5:13}

²⁴The woman had a fattened calf at the house, which she butchered at once. She took some flour, kneaded it and baked bread without yeast. ²⁵Then she set it before Saul and his men, and they ate. That same night they got up and left.

Achish Sends David Back to Ziklag

29 The Philistines gathered all their forces at Aphek, and Israel camped by the spring in Jezreel. ²As the Philistine rulers marched with their units of hundreds and thousands, David and his men were marching at the rear with Achish. ³The commanders of the Philistines asked, "What about these Hebrews?" _{Jos 17:16; 1Sa 28:1}

Achish replied, "Is this not David, who was an officer of Saul king of Israel? He has already been with me for over a year, and from the day he left Saul until now, I have found no fault in him." _{1Sa 27:7; 1Ch 2:19}

⁴But the Philistine commanders were angry with him and said, "Send the man back, that he may return to the place you assigned him. He must not go with us into battle, or he will turn against us during the fighting. How better could he regain his master's favor than by taking the heads of our own men? ⁵Isn't this the David they sang about in their dances:

" 'Saul has slain his
        thousands,
    and David his tens of
        thousands'?" _{1Ch 12:19}

⁶So Achish called David and said to him, "As surely as the LORD lives, you have been reliable, and I would be pleased to have you serve with me in the army. From the day you came to me until now, I have found no fault in you, but the rulers don't approve of you. ⁷Turn back and go in peace; do nothing to displease the Philistine rulers."

⁸"But what have I done?" asked David. "What have you found against your servant from the day I came to you until

now? Why can't I go and fight against the enemies of my lord the king?"

⁹Achish answered, "I know that you have been as pleasing in my eyes as an angel of God; nevertheless, the Philistine commanders have said, 'He must not go up with us into battle.' ¹⁰Now get up early, along with your master's servants who have come with you, and leave in the morning as soon as it is light." 2Sa 14:17; 1Ch 12:19

¹¹So David and his men got up early in the morning to go back to the land of the Philistines, and the Philistines went up to Jezreel. 2Sa 4:4

David Destroys the Amalekites

30 David and his men reached Ziklag on the third day. Now the Amalekites had raided the Negev and Ziklag. They had attacked Ziklag and burned it, ²and had taken captive the women and all who were in it, both young and old. They killed none of them, but carried them off as they went on their way. 1Sa 15:7; 27:8

³When David and his men came to Ziklag, they found it destroyed by fire and their wives and sons and daughters taken captive. ⁴So David and his men wept aloud until they had no strength left to weep. ⁵David's two wives had been captured—Ahinoam of Jezreel and Abigail, the widow of Nabal of Carmel. ⁶David was greatly distressed because the men were talking of stoning him; each one was bitter in spirit because of his sons and daughters. But David found strength in the LORD his God. Ge 31:26; Ex 17:4

⁷Then David said to Abiathar the priest, the son of Ahimelech, "Bring me the ephod." Abiathar brought it to him, ⁸and David inquired of the LORD, "Shall I pursue this raiding party? Will I overtake them?"

"Pursue them," he answered. "You will certainly overtake them and succeed in the rescue." Ge 14:16

⁹David and the six hundred men with him came to the Besor Ravine, where some stayed behind, ¹⁰for two hundred men were too exhausted to cross the ravine. But David and four hundred men continued the pursuit. 1Sa 27:2; 30:9

¹¹They found an Egyptian in a field and brought him to David. They gave him water to drink and food to eat— ¹²part of a cake of pressed figs and two cakes of raisins. He ate and was revived, for he had not eaten any food or drunk any water for three days and three nights. Jdg 15:19

¹³David asked him, "To whom do you belong, and where do you come from?"

He said, "I am an Egyptian, the slave of an Amalekite. My master abandoned me when I became ill three days ago. ¹⁴We raided the Negev of the Kerethites and the territory belong-

ing to Judah and the Negev of Caleb. And we burned Ziklag."

¹⁵David asked him, "Can you lead me down to this raiding party?"

He answered, "Swear to me before God that you will not kill me or hand me over to my master, and I will take you down to them." Dt 23:15

¹⁶He led David down, and there they were, scattered over the countryside, eating, drinking and reveling because of the great amount of plunder they had taken from the land of the Philistines and from Judah. ¹⁷David fought them from dusk until the evening of the next day, and none of them got away, except four hundred young men who rode off on camels and fled. ¹⁸David recovered everything the Amalekites had taken, including his two wives. ¹⁹Nothing was missing: young or old, boy or girl, plunder or anything else they had taken. David brought everything back. ²⁰He took all the flocks and herds, and his men drove them ahead of the other livestock, saying, "This is David's plunder." 2Sa 1:8; Lk 12:19

²¹Then David came to the two hundred men who had been too exhausted to follow him and who were left behind at the Besor Ravine. They came out to meet David and the people with him. As David and his men approached, he greeted them. ²²But all the evil men and troublemakers among David's followers said, "Because they did not go out with us, we will not share with them the plunder we recovered. However, each man may take his wife and children and go." Dt 13:13; 1Sa 30:10

²³David replied, "No, my brothers, you must not do that with what the LORD has given us. He has protected us and handed over to us the forces that came against us. ²⁴Who will listen to what you say? The share of the man who stayed with the supplies is to be the same as that of him who went down to the battle. All will share alike." ²⁵David made this a statute and ordinance for Israel from that day to this. Nu 31:27

²⁶When David arrived in Ziklag, he sent some of the plunder to the elders of Judah, who were his friends, saying, "Here is a present for you from the plunder of the LORD's enemies." Ge 33:11; 1Sa 25:27

²⁷He sent it to those who were in Bethel, Ramoth Negev and Jattir; ²⁸to those in Aroer, Siphmoth, Eshtemoa ²⁹and Racal; to those in the towns of the Jerahmeelites and the Kenites; ³⁰to those in Hormah, Bor Ashan, Athach ³¹and Hebron; and to those in all the other places where David and his men had roamed. Nu 13:22; Jos 15:48

Saul Takes His Life

31 Now the Philistines fought against Israel; the Israelites fled before them, and many fell slain on Mount Gil-

boa. ²The Philistines pressed hard after Saul and his sons, and they killed his sons Jonathan, Abinadab and Malki-Shua. ³The fighting grew fierce around Saul, and when the archers overtook him, they wounded him critically.　1Sa 28:4

⁴Saul said to his armor-bearer, "Draw your sword and run me through, or these uncircumcised fellows will come and run me through and abuse me."

But his armor-bearer was terrified and would not do it; so Saul took his own sword and fell on it. ⁵When the armor-bearer saw that Saul was dead, he too fell on his sword and died with him. ⁶So Saul and his three sons and his armor-bearer and all his men died together that same day.　1Sa 26:10; 2Sa 1:6-10

⁷When the Israelites along the valley and those across the Jordan saw that the Israelite army had fled and that Saul and his sons had died, they abandoned their towns and fled. And the Philistines came and occupied them.

⁸The next day, when the Philistines came to strip the dead, they found Saul and his three sons fallen on Mount Gilboa. ⁹They cut off his head and stripped off his armor, and they sent messengers throughout the land of the Philistines to proclaim the news in the temple of their idols and among their people. ¹⁰They put his armor in the temple of the Ashtoreths and fastened his body to the wall of Beth Shan.　Jdg 2:13; 2Sa 1:20

¹¹When the people of Jabesh Gilead heard of what the Philistines had done to Saul, ¹²all their valiant men journeyed through the night to Beth Shan. They took down the bodies of Saul and his sons from the wall of Beth Shan and went to Jabesh, where they burned them. ¹³Then they took their bones and buried them under a tamarisk tree at Jabesh, and they fasted seven days.　1Sa 11:3

2 Samuel

Introduction:

Second Samuel continues the story of the beginning of Israel's kingdom. It starts with Saul's death. Then it describes David's forty-year reign. Some of the best-known stories are the capture of Jerusalem, David's sin with Bathsheba, and Absalom's rebellion.

Outline of contents:

David Hears of Saul's Death

1 After the death of Saul, David returned from defeating the Amalekites and stayed in Ziklag two days. ²On the third day a man arrived from Saul's camp, with his clothes torn and with dust on his head. When he came to David, he fell to the ground to pay him honor. 1Sa 31:6

³"Where have you come from?" David asked him.

He answered, "I have escaped from the Israelite camp."

⁴"What happened?" David asked. "Tell me."

He said, "The men fled from the battle. Many of them fell and died. And Saul and his son Jonathan are dead." 1Sa 4:16

⁵Then David said to the young man who brought him the report, "How do you know that Saul and his son Jonathan are dead?"

⁶"I happened to be on Mount Gilboa," the young man said, "and there was Saul, leaning on his spear, with the chariots and riders almost upon him. ⁷When he turned around and saw me, he called out to me, and I said, 'What can I do?' 1Sa 28:4; 31:2-4

⁸"He asked me, 'Who are you?'

"'An Amalekite,' I answered. 1Sa 15:2; 30:13

⁹"Then he said to me, 'Stand over me and kill me! I am in the throes of death, but I'm still alive.' Jdg 9:54

¹⁰"So I stood over him and killed him, because I knew that after he had fallen he could not survive. And I took the crown that was on his head and the band on his arm and have brought them here to my lord."

¹¹Then David and all the men with him took hold of their

clothes and tore them. ¹²They mourned and wept and fasted till evening for Saul and his son Jonathan, and for the army of the LORD and the house of Israel, because they had fallen by the sword.   Ge 37:29; 2Sa 3:31

¹³David said to the young man who brought him the report, "Where are you from?"

"I am the son of an alien, an Amalekite," he answered.

¹⁴David asked him, "Why were you not afraid to lift your hand to destroy the LORD's anointed?"   1Sa 12:3; 26:9

¹⁵Then David called one of his men and said, "Go, strike him down!" So he struck him down, and he died. ¹⁶For David had said to him, "Your blood be on your own head. Your own mouth testified against you when you said, 'I killed the LORD's anointed.' "   2Sa 4:12

David's Lament for Saul and Jonathan

¹⁷David took up this lament concerning Saul and his son Jonathan, ¹⁸and ordered that the men of Judah be taught this lament of the bow (it is written in the Book of Jashar):   2Ch 35:25

¹⁹"Your glory, O Israel, lies
    slain on your heights.
  How the mighty have
    fallen!   2Sa 23:8; Ps 29:1

²⁰"Tell it not in Gath,
    proclaim it not in the streets
    of Ashkelon,

lest the daughters of the
    Philistines be glad,
  lest the daughters of the
    uncircumcised rejoice.

²¹"O mountains of Gilboa,
    may you have neither dew
    nor rain,
  nor fields that yield
    offerings ˻of grain˼.
For there the shield of the
    mighty was defiled,
  the shield of Saul—no
    longer rubbed with oil.

²²From the blood of the slain,
  from the flesh of the
    mighty,
the bow of Jonathan did not
    turn back,
  the sword of Saul did not
    return unsatisfied.   Isa 34:6

²³"Saul and Jonathan—
  in life they were loved and
    gracious,
  and in death they were not
    parted.
They were swifter than
    eagles,
  they were stronger than
    lions.   Dt 28:49; Jdg 14:18

²⁴"O daughters of Israel,
    weep for Saul,
  who clothed you in scarlet
    and finery,
  who adorned your
    garments with
    ornaments of gold.   Jdg 5:30

²⁵"How the mighty have fallen
    in battle!
  Jonathan lies slain on your
    heights.   2Sa 1:19,27
²⁶I grieve for you, Jonathan my
    brother;

you were very dear to me.
Your love for me was
    wonderful,
more wonderful than that
    of women.   1Sa 18:1

27"How the mighty have
    fallen!
The weapons of war have
    perished!"   1Sa 2:4

David Anointed King Over Judah

2 In the course of time, David inquired of the LORD. "Shall I go up to one of the towns of Judah?" he asked.   1Sa 13:2

The LORD said, "Go up."

David asked, "Where shall I go?"

"To Hebron," the LORD answered.   Ge 13:18; 2Sa 23:19

²So David went up there with his two wives, Ahinoam of Jezreel and Abigail, the widow of Nabal of Carmel. ³David also took the men who were with him, each with his family, and they settled in Hebron and its towns. ⁴Then the men of Judah came to Hebron and there they anointed David king over the house of Judah.   1Sa 25:43

When David was told that it was the men of Jabesh Gilead who had buried Saul, ⁵he sent messengers to the men of Jabesh Gilead to say to them, "The LORD bless you for showing this kindness to Saul your master by burying him. ⁶May the LORD now show you kind-

ness and faithfulness, and I too will show you the same favor because you have done this. ⁷Now then, be strong and brave, for Saul your master is dead, and the house of Judah has anointed me king over them."   Jdg 5:21; 1Sa 23:21

War Between the Houses of David and Saul

⁸Meanwhile, Abner son of Ner, the commander of Saul's army, had taken Ish-Bosheth son of Saul and brought him over to Mahanaim. ⁹He made him king over Gilead, Ashuri*a* and Jezreel, and also over Ephraim, Benjamin and all Israel.   2Sa 14:50; 1Ch 12:29

¹⁰Ish-Bosheth son of Saul was forty years old when he became king over Israel, and he reigned two years. The house of Judah, however, followed David. ¹¹The length of time David was king in Hebron over the house of Judah was seven years and six months.   2Sa 5:5

¹²Abner son of Ner, together with the men of Ish-Bosheth son of Saul, left Mahanaim and went to Gibeon. ¹³Joab son of Zeruiah and David's men went out and met them at the pool of Gibeon. One group sat down on one side of the pool and one group on the other side.   Jos 9:3

¹⁴Then Abner said to Joab, "Let's have some of the young men get up and fight hand to hand in front of us."

a9 Or *Asher*

"All right, let them do it," Joab said.

¹⁵So they stood up and were counted off—twelve men for Benjamin and Ish-Bosheth son of Saul, and twelve for David. ¹⁶Then each man grabbed his opponent by the head and thrust his dagger into his opponent's side, and they fell down together. So that place in Gibeon was called Helkath Hazzurim. *ᵃ*   Jdg 3:21

¹⁷The battle that day was very fierce, and Abner and the men of Israel were defeated by David's men.   1Sa 17:8; 2Sa 31:1

¹⁸The three sons of Zeruiah were there: Joab, Abishai and Asahel. Now Asahel was as fleet-footed as a wild gazelle. ¹⁹He chased Abner, turning neither to the right nor to the left as he pursued him. ²⁰Abner looked behind him and asked, "Is that you, Asahel?"   2Sa 3:39

"It is," he answered.

²¹Then Abner said to him, "Turn aside to the right or to the left; take on one of the young men and strip him of his weapons." But Asahel would not stop chasing him.

²²Again Abner warned Asahel, "Stop chasing me! Why should I strike you down? How could I look your brother Joab in the face?"   2Sa 3:27

²³But Asahel refused to give up the pursuit; so Abner thrust the butt of his spear into Asahel's stomach, and the spear came out through his back. He fell there and died on the spot. And every man stopped when he came to the place where Asahel had fallen and died.   2Sa 4:6

²⁴But Joab and Abishai pursued Abner, and as the sun was setting, they came to the hill of Ammah, near Giah on the way to the wasteland of Gibeon. ²⁵Then the men of Benjamin rallied behind Abner. They formed themselves into a group and took their stand on top of a hill.

²⁶Abner called out to Joab, "Must the sword devour forever? Don't you realize that this will end in bitterness? How long before you order your men to stop pursuing their brothers?"

²⁷Joab answered, "As surely as God lives, if you had not spoken, the men would have continued the pursuit of their brothers until morning. *ᵇ*"

²⁸So Joab blew the trumpet, and all the men came to a halt; they no longer pursued Israel, nor did they fight anymore.

²⁹All that night Abner and his men marched through the Arabah. They crossed the Jordan, continued through the whole Bithron *ᶜ* and came to Mahanaim.   Ge 32:2; Dt 3:17

³⁰Then Joab returned from pursuing Abner and assembled

ᵃ16 Helkath Hazzurim means *field of daggers* or *field of hostilities.* *ᵇ27* Or *spoken this morning, the men would not have taken up the pursuit of their brothers;* or *spoken, the men would have given up the pursuit of their brothers by morning* *ᶜ29* Or *morning;* or *ravine;* the meaning of the Hebrew for this word is uncertain.

all his men. Besides Asahel, nineteen of David's men were found missing. [31]But David's men had killed three hundred and sixty Benjamites who were with Abner. [32]They took Asahel and buried him in his father's tomb at Bethlehem. Then Joab and his men marched all night and arrived at Hebron by daybreak.   Ge 49:29; 1Sa 20:6

3 The war between the house of Saul and the house of David lasted a long time. David grew stronger and stronger, while the house of Saul grew weaker and weaker.   1Ki 14:30

[2]Sons were born to David in Hebron:

His firstborn was Amnon the son of Ahinoam of Jezreel;

[3]his second, Kileab the son of Abigail the widow of Nabal of Carmel;

the third, Absalom the son of Maacah daughter of Talmai king of Geshur;

[4]the fourth, Adonijah the son of Haggith;

the fifth, Shephatiah the son of Abital;

[5]and the sixth, Ithream the son of David's wife Eglah.

These were born to David in Hebron.   2Sa 13:1

Abner Goes Over to David

[6]During the war between the house of Saul and the house of David, Abner had been strengthening his own position in the house of Saul. [7]Now Saul had had a concubine named Rizpah daughter of Aiah. And Ish-Bosheth said to Abner, "Why did you sleep with my father's concubine?"   1Sa 14:50

[8]Abner was very angry because of what Ish-Bosheth said and he answered, "Am I a dog's head—on Judah's side? This very day I am loyal to the house of your father Saul and to his family and friends. I haven't handed you over to David. Yet now you accuse me of an offense involving this woman! [9]May God deal with Abner, be it ever so severely, if I do not do for David what the LORD promised him on oath [10]and transfer the kingdom from the house of Saul and establish David's throne over Israel and Judah from Dan to Beersheba." [11]Ish-Bosheth did not dare to say another word to Abner, because he was afraid of him.   2Sa 9:8

[12]Then Abner sent messengers on his behalf to say to David, "Whose land is it? Make an agreement with me, and I will help you bring all Israel over to you."

[13]"Good," said David. "I will make an agreement with you. But I demand one thing of you: Do not come into my presence unless you bring Michal daughter of Saul when you come to see me." [14]Then David sent messengers to Ish-Bosheth son of Saul, demanding, "Give me my wife Michal, whom I betrothed to myself for the price of a hundred Philistine foreskins."

[15]So Ish-Bosheth gave orders

and had her taken away from her husband Paltiel son of La-ish. [16]Her husband, however, went with her, weeping behind her all the way to Bahurim. Then Abner said to him, "Go back home!" So he went back.

[17]Abner conferred with the elders of Israel and said, "For some time you have wanted to make David your king. [18]Now do it! For the LORD promised David, 'By my servant David I will rescue my people Israel from the hand of the Philistines and from the hand of all their enemies.'" Jdg 11:11; 1Sa 9:16

[19]Abner also spoke to the Benjamites in person. Then he went to Hebron to tell David everything that Israel and the whole house of Benjamin wanted to do. [20]When Abner, who had twenty men with him, came to David at Hebron, David prepared a feast for him and his men. [21]Then Abner said to David, "Let me go at once and assemble all Israel for my lord the king, so that they may make a compact with you, and that you may rule over all that your heart desires." So David sent Abner away, and he went in peace.

Joab Murders Abner

[22]Just then David's men and Joab returned from a raid and brought with them a great deal of plunder. But Abner was no longer with David in Hebron, because David had sent him away, and he had gone in peace. [23]When Joab and all the soldiers with him arrived, he was told that Abner son of Ner had come to the king and that the king had sent him away and that he had gone in peace. 1Sa 27:8

[24]So Joab went to the king and said, "What have you done? Look, Abner came to you. Why did you let him go? Now he is gone! [25]You know Abner son of Ner; he came to deceive you and observe your movements and find out everything you are doing." 1Sa 29:6; Isa 37:28

[26]Joab then left David and sent messengers after Abner, and they brought him back from the well of Sirah. But David did not know it. [27]Now when Abner returned to Hebron, Joab took him aside into the gateway, as though to speak with him privately. And there, to avenge the blood of his brother Asahel, Joab stabbed him in the stomach, and he died. 2Sa 2:23

[28]Later, when David heard about this, he said, "I and my kingdom are forever innocent before the LORD concerning the blood of Abner son of Ner. [29]May his blood fall upon the head of Joab and upon all his father's house! May Joab's house never be without someone who has a running sore or leprosy[a] or who leans on a

---

[a]29 The Hebrew word was used for various diseases affecting the skin—not necessarily leprosy.

crutch or who falls by the sword or who lacks food.'' Dt 21:9

³⁰(Joab and his brother Abishai murdered Abner because he had killed their brother Asahel in the battle at Gibeon.) 2Sa 2:23

³¹Then David said to Joab and all the people with him, ''Tear your clothes and put on sackcloth and walk in mourning in front of Abner.'' King David himself walked behind the bier. ³²They buried Abner in Hebron, and the king wept aloud at Abner's tomb. All the people wept also. Ps 30:11; Pr 24:17

³³The king sang this lament for Abner:

''Should Abner have died as
    the lawless die? Ge 50:10
³⁴ Your hands were not
    bound,
    your feet were not fettered.
You fell as one falls before
    wicked men.'' Job 36:8

And all the people wept over him again.

³⁵Then they all came and urged David to eat something while it was still day; but David took an oath, saying, ''May God deal with me, be it ever so severely, if I taste bread or anything else before the sun sets!''

³⁶All the people took note and were pleased; indeed, everything the king did pleased them. ³⁷So on that day all the people and all Israel knew that the king had no part in the murder of Abner son of Ner. 2Sa 3:28

³⁸Then the king said to his men, ''Do you not realize that a prince and a great man has fallen in Israel this day? ³⁹And today, though I am the anointed king, I am weak, and these sons of Zeruiah are too strong for me. May the LORD repay the evildoer according to his evil deeds!'' 2Sa 1:19; 1Ki 2:32

Ish-Bosheth Murdered

4 When Ish-Bosheth son of Saul heard that Abner had died in Hebron, he lost courage, and all Israel became alarmed. ²Now Saul's son had two men who were leaders of raiding bands. One was named Baanah and the other Recab; they were sons of Rimmon the Beerothite from the tribe of Benjamin—Beeroth is considered part of Benjamin, ³because the people of Beeroth fled to Gittaim and have lived there as aliens to this day. 2Sa 3:27; Ne 11:33

⁴(Jonathan son of Saul had a son who was lame in both feet. He was five years old when the news about Saul and Jonathan came from Jezreel. His nurse picked him up and fled, but as she hurried to leave, he fell and became crippled. His name was Mephibosheth.) 2Sa 9:6

⁵Now Recab and Baanah, the sons of Rimmon the Beerothite, set out for the house of Ish-Bosheth, and they arrived there in the heat of the day while he was taking his noonday rest. ⁶They went into the inner part of the house as if to get some wheat, and they stabbed him in the stomach. Then Recab and

his brother Baanah slipped away. 2Sa 2:8; Rev 2:7

7They had gone into the house while he was lying on the bed in his bedroom. After they stabbed and killed him, they cut off his head. Taking it with them, they traveled all night by way of the Arabah. 8They brought the head of Ish-Bosheth to David at Hebron and said to the king, "Here is the head of Ish-Bosheth son of Saul, your enemy, who tried to take your life. This day the LORD has avenged my lord the king against Saul and his offspring."

9David answered Recab and his brother Baanah, the sons of Rimmon the Beerothite, "As surely as the LORD lives, who has delivered me out of all trouble, 10when a man told me, 'Saul is dead,' and thought he was bringing good news, I seized him and put him to death in Ziklag. That was the reward I gave him for his news! 11How much more—when wicked men have killed an innocent man in his own house and on his own bed—should I not now demand his blood from your hand and rid the earth of you!" 1Ki 1:29

12So David gave an order to his men, and they killed them. They cut off their hands and feet and hung the bodies by the pool in Hebron. But they took the head of Ish-Bosheth and buried it in Abner's tomb at Hebron. 2Sa 1:15; 3:32

David Becomes King Over Israel

5 All the tribes of Israel came to David at Hebron and said, "We are your own flesh and blood. 2In the past, while Saul was king over us, you were the one who led Israel on their military campaigns. And the LORD said to you, 'You will shepherd my people Israel, and you will become their ruler.'" 1Sa 18:13

3When all the elders of Israel had come to King David at Hebron, the king made a compact with them at Hebron before the LORD, and they anointed David king over Israel. 2Sa 3:21

4David was thirty years old when he became king, and he reigned forty years. 5In Hebron he reigned over Judah seven years and six months, and in Jerusalem he reigned over all Israel and Judah thirty-three years. 2Sa 2:11; Lk 3:23

David Conquers Jerusalem

6The king and his men marched to Jerusalem to attack the Jebusites, who lived there. The Jebusites said to David, "You will not get in here; even the blind and the lame can ward you off." They thought, "David cannot get in here." 7Nevertheless, David captured the fortress of Zion, the City of David.

8On that day, David said, "Anyone who conquers the Jebusites will have to use the water

shaft*a* to reach those 'lame and blind' who are David's enemies.*b*'' That is why they say, ''The 'blind and lame' will not enter the palace.''   2Ki 20:20

9David then took up residence in the fortress and called it the City of David. He built up the area around it, from the supporting terraces*c* inward. 10And he became more and more powerful, because the LORD God Almighty was with him.   2Sa 3:1; 1Ki 9:15

11Now Hiram king of Tyre sent messengers to David, along with cedar logs and carpenters and stonemasons, and they built a palace for David. 12And David knew that the LORD had established him as king over Israel and had exalted his kingdom for the sake of his people Israel.   Nu 24:7; 2Ch 2:3

13After he left Hebron, David took more concubines and wives in Jerusalem, and more sons and daughters were born to him. 14These are the names of the children born to him there: Shammua, Shobab, Nathan, Solomon, 15Ibhar, Elishua, Nepheg, Japhia, 16Elishama, Eliada and Eliphelet.   Dt 17:17; 1Ch 3:5

David Defeats the Philistines

17When the Philistines heard that David had been anointed king over Israel, they went up in full force to search for him, but David heard about it and went down to the stronghold. 18Now the Philistines had come and spread out in the Valley of Rephaim; 19so David inquired of the LORD, ''Shall I go and attack the Philistines? Will you hand them over to me?''   2Sa 23:14

The LORD answered him, ''Go, for I will surely hand the Philistines over to you.''

20So David went to Baal Perazim, and there he defeated them. He said, ''As waters break out, the LORD has broken out against my enemies before me.'' So that place was called Baal Perazim. *d* 21The Philistines abandoned their idols there, and David and his men carried them off.   Isa 28:21; 46:2

22Once more the Philistines came up and spread out in the Valley of Rephaim; 23so David inquired of the LORD, and he answered, ''Do not go straight up, but circle around behind them and attack them in front of the balsam trees. 24As soon as you hear the sound of marching in the tops of the balsam trees, move quickly, because that will mean the LORD has gone out in front of you to strike the Philistine army.'' 25So David did as the LORD commanded him, and he struck down the Philistines all the way from Gibeon*e* to Gezer.   Jdg 4:14; 2Sa 8:12; Isa 28:21

*a*8 Or *use scaling hooks*   *b*8 Or *are hated by David*   *c*9 Or *the Millo*   *d*20 Baal Perazim *means* the lord who breaks out.   *e*25 Septuagint (see also 1 Chron. 14:16); Hebrew *Geba*

The Ark Brought to Jerusalem

6 David again brought together out of Israel chosen men, thirty thousand in all. ²He and all his men set out from Baalah of Judah*ᵃ* to bring up from there the ark of God, which is called by the Name,*ᵇ* the name of the LORD Almighty, who is enthroned between the cherubim that are on the ark. ³They set the ark of God on a new cart and brought it from the house of Abinadab, which was on the hill. Uzzah and Ahio, sons of Abinadab, were guiding the new cart ⁴with the ark of God on it,*ᶜ* and Ahio was walking in front of it. ⁵David and the whole house of Israel were celebrating with all their might before the LORD, with songs*ᵈ* and with harps, lyres, tambourines, sistrums and cymbals. Lev 24:16; 1Sa 6:7

⁶When they came to the threshing floor of Nacon, Uzzah reached out and took hold of the ark of God, because the oxen stumbled. ⁷The LORD's anger burned against Uzzah because of his irreverent act; therefore God struck him down and he died there beside the ark of God. Nu 4:15; 1Sa 6:19

⁸Then David was angry because the LORD's wrath had broken out against Uzzah, and to this day that place is called Perez Uzzah.*ᵉ* Ge 38:29; Ps 7:11

⁹David was afraid of the LORD that day and said, "How can the ark of the LORD ever come to me?" ¹⁰He was not willing to take the ark of the LORD to be with him in the City of David. Instead, he took it aside to the house of Obed-Edom the Gittite. ¹¹The ark of the LORD remained in the house of Obed-Edom the Gittite for three months, and the LORD blessed him and his entire household.

¹²Now King David was told, "The LORD has blessed the household of Obed-Edom and everything he has, because of the ark of God." So David went down and brought up the ark of God from the house of Obed-Edom to the City of David with rejoicing. ¹³When those who were carrying the ark of the LORD had taken six steps, he sacrificed a bull and a fattened calf. ¹⁴David, wearing a linen ephod, danced before the LORD with all his might, ¹⁵while he and the entire house of Israel brought up the ark of the LORD with shouts and the sound of trumpets. 1Ki 8:1; Ps 47:5

¹⁶As the ark of the LORD was entering the City of David, Michal daughter of Saul watched

---

*ᵃ*2 That is, Kiriath Jearim; Hebrew *Baale Judah*, a variant of *Baalah of Judah*   *ᵇ*2 Hebrew; Septuagint and Vulgate do not have *the Name*.   *ᶜ*3,4 Dead Sea Scrolls and some Septuagint manuscripts; Masoretic Text *cart* ⁴*and they brought it with the ark of God from the house of Abinadab, which was on the hill*   *ᵈ*5 See Dead Sea Scrolls, Septuagint and 1 Chronicles 13:8; Masoretic Text *celebrating before the LORD with all kinds of instruments made of pine.*   *ᵉ*8 *Perez Uzzah* means *outbreak against Uzzah.*

from a window. And when she saw King David leaping and dancing before the LORD, she despised him in her heart.

¹⁷They brought the ark of the LORD and set it in its place inside the tent that David had pitched for it, and David sacrificed burnt offerings and fellowship offerings^a before the LORD. ¹⁸After he had finished sacrificing the burnt offerings and fellowship offerings, he blessed the people in the name of the LORD Almighty. ¹⁹Then he gave a loaf of bread, a cake of dates and a cake of raisins to each person in the whole crowd of Israelites, both men and women. And all the people went to their homes.   1Ch 15:1; Hos 3:1

²⁰When David returned home to bless his household, Michal daughter of Saul came out to meet him and said, "How the king of Israel has distinguished himself today, disrobing in the sight of the slave girls of his servants as any vulgar fellow would!"   Jdg 9:4; 1Sa 19:14

²¹David said to Michal, "It was before the LORD, who chose me rather than your father or anyone from his house when he appointed me ruler over the LORD's people Israel—I will celebrate before the LORD. ²²I will become even more undignified than this, and I will be humiliated in my own eyes. But by these slave girls you spoke of, I will be held in honor."   1Sa 13:14

²³And Michal daughter of Saul had no children to the day of her death.   Isa 22:14

God's Promise to David

7 After the king was settled in his palace and the LORD had given him rest from all his enemies around him, ²he said to Nathan the prophet, "Here I am, living in a palace of cedar, while the ark of God remains in a tent."   Ex 26:1; Ac 7:46

³Nathan replied to the king, "Whatever you have in mind, go ahead and do it, for the LORD is with you."   1Ki 8:17; Ps 132:1-5

⁴That night the word of the LORD came to Nathan, saying:

⁵"Go and tell my servant David, 'This is what the LORD says: Are you the one to build me a house to dwell in? ⁶I have not dwelt in a house from the day I brought the Israelites up out of Egypt to this day. I have been moving from place to place with a tent as my dwelling. ⁷Wherever I have moved with all the Israelites, did I ever say to any of their rulers whom I commanded to shepherd my people Israel, "Why have you not built me a house of cedar?"'   1Ki 5:3-5

⁸"Now then, tell my servant David, 'This is what the LORD Almighty says: I took you from the pasture and from following the

^a17 Traditionally *peace offerings*; also in verse 18

flock to be ruler over my people Israel. 9I have been with you wherever you have gone, and I have cut off all your enemies from before you. Now I will make your name great, like the names of the greatest men of the earth. 10And I will provide a place for my people Israel and will plant them so that they can have a home of their own and no longer be disturbed. Wicked people will not oppress them anymore, as they did at the beginning 11and have done ever since the time I appointed leaders*a* over my people Israel. I will also give you rest from all your enemies.   Ps 78:70

" 'The Lord declares to you that the Lord himself will establish a house for you: 12When your days are over and you rest with your fathers, I will raise up your offspring to succeed you, who will come from your own body, and I will establish his kingdom. 13He is the one who will build a house for my Name, and I will establish the throne of his kingdom forever. 14I will be his father, and he will be my son. When he does wrong, I will punish him with the rod of men, with floggings inflicted by men. 15But my

love will never be taken away from him, as I took it away from Saul, whom I removed from before you. 16Your house and your kingdom will endure forever before me*b*; your throne will be established forever.' "   1Ki 2:1; Ps 89:36

17Nathan reported to David all the words of this entire revelation.

David's Prayer

18Then King David went in and sat before the Lord, and he said:

"Who am I, O Sovereign Lord, and what is my family, that you have brought me this far? 19And as if this were not enough in your sight, O Sovereign Lord, you have also spoken about the future of the house of your servant. Is this your usual way of dealing with man, O Sovereign Lord?   Ex 3:11; Isa 55:8

20"What more can David say to you? For you know your servant, O Sovereign Lord. 21For the sake of your word and according to your will, you have done this great thing and made it known to your servant.

22"How great you are, O Sovereign Lord! There is no one like you, and there is no

---

*a*11 Traditionally *judges*   *b*16 Some Hebrew manuscripts and Septuagint; most Hebrew manuscripts *you*

God but you, as we have heard with our own ears. 23And who is like your people Israel—the one nation on earth that God went out to redeem as a people for himself, and to make a name for himself, and to perform great and awesome wonders by driving out nations and their gods from before your people, whom you redeemed from Egypt?ᵃ 24You have established your people Israel as your very own forever, and you, O LORD, have become their God.   Dt 26:18; Ps 48:1

25"And now, LORD God, keep forever the promise you have made concerning your servant and his house. Do as you promised, 26so that your name will be great forever. Then men will say, 'The LORD Almighty is God over Israel!' And the house of your servant David will be established before you.

27"O LORD Almighty, God of Israel, you have revealed this to your servant, saying, 'I will build a house for you.' So your servant has found courage to offer you this prayer. 28O Sovereign LORD, you are God! Your words are trustworthy, and you have promised these good things

to your servant. 29Now be pleased to bless the house of your servant, that it may continue forever in your sight; for you, O Sovereign LORD, have spoken, and with your blessing the house of your servant will be blessed forever."   Jn 17:17

David's Victories

8 In the course of time, David defeated the Philistines and subdued them, and he took Metheg Ammah from the control of the Philistines.   Ps 60:8

2David also defeated the Moabites. He made them lie down on the ground and measured them off with a length of cord. Every two lengths of them were put to death, and the third length was allowed to live. So the Moabites became subject to David and brought tribute.

3Moreover, David fought Hadadezer son of Rehob, king of Zobah, when he went to restore his control along the Euphrates River. 4David captured a thousand of his chariots, seven thousand charioteersᵇ and twenty thousand foot soldiers. He hamstrung all but a hundred of the chariot horses.

5When the Arameans of Damascus came to help Hadadezer king of Zobah, David struck down twenty-two thousand of them. 6He put garrisons

ᵃ23 See Septuagint and 1 Chron. 17:21; Hebrew *wonders for your land and before your people, whom you redeemed from Egypt, from the nations and their gods.*   ᵇ4 Septuagint (see also Dead Sea Scrolls and 1 Chron. 18:4); Masoretic Text *captured seventeen hundred of his charioteers*

in the Aramean kingdom of Damascus, and the Arameans became subject to him and brought tribute. The LORD gave David victory wherever he went. 2Sa 10:19; 1Ki 11:24

7David took the gold shields that belonged to the officers of Hadadezer and brought them to Jerusalem. 8From Tebah*a* and Berothai, towns that belonged to Hadadezer, King David took a great quantity of bronze.

9When Tou*b* king of Hamath heard that David had defeated the entire army of Hadadezer, 10he sent his son Joram*c* to King David to greet him and congratulate him on his victory in battle over Hadadezer, who had been at war with Tou. Joram brought with him articles of silver and gold and bronze. 1Ki 8:65

11King David dedicated these articles to the LORD, as he had done with the silver and gold from all the nations he had subdued: 12Edom*d* and Moab, the Ammonites and the Philistines, and Amalek. He also dedicated the plunder taken from Hadadezer son of Rehob, king of Zobah. Nu 24:20; 1Ki 7:51

13And David became famous after he returned from striking down eighteen thousand Edomites*e* in the Valley of Salt.

14He put garrisons through-

out Edom, and all the Edomites became subject to David. The LORD gave David victory wherever he went. Nu 24:17

David's Officials

15David reigned over all Israel, doing what was just and right for all his people. 16Joab son of Zeruiah was over the army; Jehoshaphat son of Ahilud was recorder; 17Zadok son of Ahitub and Ahimelech son of Abiathar were priests; Seraiah was secretary; 18Benaiah son of Jehoiada was over the Kerethites and Pelethites; and David's sons were royal advisers.*f*

David and Mephibosheth

9 David asked, "Is there anyone still left of the house of Saul to whom I can show kindness for Jonathan's sake?"

2Now there was a servant of Saul's household named Ziba. They called him to appear before David, and the king said to him, "Are you Ziba?" 2Sa 16:1-4

"Your servant," he replied.

3The king asked, "Is there no one still left of the house of Saul to whom I can show God's kindness?"

Ziba answered the king, "There is still a son of Jonathan; he is crippled in both feet."

a8 See some Septuagint manuscripts (see also 1 Chron. 18:8); Hebrew *Betah*.
b9 Hebrew *Toi*, a variant of *Tou*; also in verse 10   *c10* A variant of *Hadoram*
d12 Some Hebrew manuscripts, Septuagint and Syriac (see also 1 Chron. 18:11); most Hebrew manuscripts *Aram*   *e13* A few Hebrew manuscripts, Septuagint and Syriac (see also 1 Chron. 18:12); most Hebrew manuscripts *Aram* (that is, Arameans)
f18 Or *were priests*

4"Where is he?" the king asked.

Ziba answered, "He is at the house of Makir son of Ammiel in Lo Debar." 2Sa 17:27-29

5So King David had him brought from Lo Debar, from the house of Makir son of Ammiel.

6When Mephibosheth son of Jonathan, the son of Saul, came to David, he bowed down to pay him honor. Ge 37:7; 2Sa 16:4

David said, "Mephibosheth!"

"Your servant," he replied.

7"Don't be afraid," David said to him, "for I will surely show you kindness for the sake of your father Jonathan. I will restore to you all the land that belonged to your grandfather Saul, and you will always eat at my table." 2Sa 19:28; Jer 52:33

8Mephibosheth bowed down and said, "What is your servant, that you should notice a dead dog like me?" 2Sa 16:9

9Then the king summoned Ziba, Saul's servant, and said to him, "I have given your master's grandson everything that belonged to Saul and his family. 10You and your sons and your servants are to farm the land for him and bring in the crops, so that your master's grandson may be provided for. And Mephibosheth, grandson of your master, will always eat at my table." (Now Ziba had fifteen sons and twenty servants.)

11Then Ziba said to the king, "Your servant will do whatever my lord the king commands his servant to do." So Mephibosheth ate at David's[a] table like one of the king's sons. Job 36:7

12Mephibosheth had a young son named Mica, and all the members of Ziba's household were servants of Mephibosheth. 13And Mephibosheth lived in Jerusalem, because he always ate at the king's table, and he was crippled in both feet. 2Sa 4:4; 1Ch 8:34

David Defeats the Ammonites

10 In the course of time, the king of the Ammonites died, and his son Hanun succeeded him as king. 2David thought, "I will show kindness to Hanun son of Nahash, just as his father showed kindness to me." So David sent a delegation to express his sympathy to Hanun concerning his father.

When David's men came to the land of the Ammonites, 3the Ammonite nobles said to Hanun their lord, "Do you think David is honoring your father by sending men to you to express sympathy? Hasn't David sent them to you to explore the city and spy it out and overthrow it?" 4So Hanun seized David's men, shaved off half of each man's beard, cut off their garments in the middle at the buttocks, and sent them away.

a11 Septuagint; Hebrew *my*

⁵When David was told about this, he sent messengers to meet the men, for they were greatly humiliated. The king said, "Stay at Jericho till your beards have grown, and then come back."

⁶When the Ammonites realized that they had become a stench in David's nostrils, they hired twenty thousand Aramean foot soldiers from Beth Rehob and Zobah, as well as the king of Maacah with a thousand men, and also twelve thousand men from Tob. Ge 24:30

⁷On hearing this, David sent Joab out with the entire army of fighting men. ⁸The Ammonites came out and drew up in battle formation at the entrance to their city gate, while the Arameans of Zobah and Rehob and the men of Tob and Maacah were by themselves in the open country. 2Sa 2:18; 1Ki 10:16

⁹Joab saw that there were battle lines in front of him and behind him; so he selected some of the best troops in Israel and deployed them against the Arameans. ¹⁰He put the rest of the men under the command of Abishai his brother and deployed them against the Ammonites. ¹¹Joab said, "If the Arameans are too strong for me, then you are to come to my rescue; but if the Ammonites are too strong for you, then I will come to rescue you. ¹²Be strong and let us fight bravely for our people and the cities of our God. The LORD will do what is good in his sight." 1Sa 26:6

¹³Then Joab and the troops with him advanced to fight the Arameans, and they fled before him. ¹⁴When the Ammonites saw that the Arameans were fleeing, they fled before Abishai and went inside the city. So Joab returned from fighting the Ammonites and came to Jerusalem. 2Sa 8:12; 1Ki 20:13-21

¹⁵After the Arameans saw that they had been routed by Israel, they regrouped. ¹⁶Hadadezer had Arameans brought from beyond the River*a*; they went to Helam, with Shobach the commander of Hadadezer's army leading them. 2Sa 8:3

¹⁷When David was told of this, he gathered all Israel, crossed the Jordan and went to Helam. The Arameans formed their battle lines to meet David and fought against him. ¹⁸But they fled before Israel, and David killed seven hundred of their charioteers and forty thousand of their foot soldiers. *b* He also struck down Shobach the commander of their army, and he died there. ¹⁹When all the kings who were vassals of Hadadezer saw that they had been defeated by Israel, they made peace with the Israelites and became subject to them. 1Ch 19:18

So the Arameans were afraid

---

*a*16 That is, the Euphrates   *b*18 Some Septuagint manuscripts (see also 1 Chron. 19:18); Hebrew *horsemen*

to help the Ammonites any-more. 1Ki 11:25; 2Ki 5:1

David and Bathsheba

11 In the spring, at the time when kings go off to war, David sent Joab out with the king's men and the whole Israelite army. They destroyed the Ammonites and besieged Rabbah. But David remained in Jerusalem. 1Ki 20:22; 1Ch 20:1

²One evening David got up from his bed and walked around on the roof of the palace. From the roof he saw a woman bathing. The woman was very beautiful, ³and David sent someone to find out about her. The man said, "Isn't this Bathsheba, the daughter of Eliam and the wife of Uriah the Hittite?" ⁴Then David sent messengers to get her. She came to him, and he slept with her. (She had purified herself from her uncleanness.) Then[a] she went back home. ⁵The woman conceived and sent word to David, saying, "I am pregnant." Dt 22:8

⁶So David sent this word to Joab: "Send me Uriah the Hittite." And Joab sent him to David. ⁷When Uriah came to him, David asked him how Joab was, how the soldiers were and how the war was going. ⁸Then David said to Uriah, "Go down to your house and wash your feet." So Uriah left the palace, and a gift from the king was sent after him. ⁹But Uriah slept at the entrance to the palace with all his master's servants and did not go down to his house. 1Ch 11:41

¹⁰When David was told, "Uriah did not go home," he asked him, "Haven't you just come from a distance? Why didn't you go home?" 2Sa 7:2

¹¹Uriah said to David, "The ark and Israel and Judah are staying in tents, and my master Joab and my lord's men are camped in the open fields. How could I go to my house to eat and drink and lie with my wife? As surely as you live, I will not do such a thing!" 1Sa 21:5

¹²Then David said to him, "Stay here one more day, and tomorrow I will send you back." So Uriah remained in Jerusalem that day and the next. ¹³At David's invitation, he ate and drank with him, and David made him drunk. But in the evening Uriah went out to sleep on his mat among his master's servants; he did not go home.

¹⁴In the morning David wrote a letter to Joab and sent it with Uriah. ¹⁵In it he wrote, "Put Uriah in the front line where the fighting is fiercest. Then withdraw from him so he will be struck down and die." 1Ki 21:8

¹⁶So while Joab had the city under siege, he put Uriah at a place where he knew the strongest defenders were. ¹⁷When the men of the city came out and fought against Joab, some of the men in David's

---

a4 Or *with her. When she purified herself from her uncleanness,*

army fell; moreover, Uriah the Hittite died. 2Sa 11:21

[18]Joab sent David a full account of the battle. [19]He instructed the messenger: "When you have finished giving the king this account of the battle, [20]the king's anger may flare up, and he may ask you, 'Why did you get so close to the city to fight? Didn't you know they would shoot arrows from the wall? [21]Who killed Abimelech son of Jerub-Besheth[a]? Didn't a woman throw an upper millstone on him from the wall, so that he died in Thebez? Why did you get so close to the wall?' If he asks you this, then say to him, 'Also, your servant Uriah the Hittite is dead.' " Jdg 9:50-54

[22]The messenger set out, and when he arrived he told David everything Joab had sent him to say. [23]The messenger said to David, "The men overpowered us and came out against us in the open, but we drove them back to the entrance to the city gate. [24]Then the archers shot arrows at your servants from the wall, and some of the king's men died. Moreover, your servant Uriah the Hittite is dead."

[25]David told the messenger, "Say this to Joab: 'Don't let this upset you; the sword devours one as well as another. Press the attack against the city and destroy it.' Say this to encourage Joab."

[26]When Uriah's wife heard that her husband was dead, she mourned for him. [27]After the time of mourning was over, David had her brought to his house, and she became his wife and bore him a son. But the thing David had done displeased the LORD. Dt 34:8

Nathan Rebukes David

12 The LORD sent Nathan to David. When he came to him, he said, "There were two men in a certain town, one rich and the other poor. [2]The rich man had a very large number of sheep and cattle, [3]but the poor man had nothing except one little ewe lamb he had bought. He raised it, and it grew up with him and his children. It shared his food, drank from his cup and even slept in his arms. It was like a daughter to him.

[4]"Now a traveler came to the rich man, but the rich man refrained from taking one of his own sheep or cattle to prepare a meal for the traveler who had come to him. Instead, he took the ewe lamb that belonged to the poor man and prepared it for the one who had come to him." Jer 14:8

[5]David burned with anger against the man and said to Nathan, "As surely as the LORD lives, the man who did this deserves to die! [6]He must pay for that lamb four times over, because he did such a thing and had no pity." 1Ki 20:40

[a]21 Also known as Jerub-Baal (that is, Gideon)

⁷Then Nathan said to David, "You are the man! This is what the Lord, the God of Israel, says: 'I anointed you king over Israel, and I delivered you from the hand of Saul. ⁸I gave your master's house to you, and your master's wives into your arms. I gave you the house of Israel and Judah. And if all this had been too little, I would have given you even more. ⁹Why did you despise the word of the Lord by doing what is evil in his eyes? You struck down Uriah the Hittite with the sword and took his wife to be your own. You killed him with the sword of the Ammonites. ¹⁰Now, therefore, the sword will never depart from your house, because you despised me and took the wife of Uriah the Hittite to be your own.' 2Sa 13:28; 1Ki 20:42

¹¹"This is what the Lord says: 'Out of your own household I am going to bring calamity upon you. Before your very eyes I will take your wives and give them to one who is close to you, and he will lie with your wives in broad daylight. ¹²You did it in secret, but I will do this thing in broad daylight before all Israel.' " 2Sa 11:4-15

¹³Then David said to Nathan, "I have sinned against the Lord." Ge 13:13; Nu 22:34

Nathan replied, "The Lord has taken away your sin. You are not going to die. ¹⁴But because by doing this you have made the enemies of the Lord show utter contempt,ᵃ the son born to you will die." Pr 28:13

¹⁵After Nathan had gone home, the Lord struck the child that Uriah's wife had borne to David, and he became ill. ¹⁶David pleaded with God for the child. He fasted and went into his house and spent the nights lying on the ground. ¹⁷The elders of his household stood beside him to get him up from the ground, but he refused, and he would not eat any food with them. 1Sa 25:38; Da 6:18

¹⁸On the seventh day the child died. David's servants were afraid to tell him that the child was dead, for they thought, "While the child was still living, we spoke to David but he would not listen to us. How can we tell him the child is dead? He may do something desperate."

¹⁹David noticed that his servants were whispering among themselves and he realized the child was dead. "Is the child dead?" he asked.

"Yes," they replied, "he is dead."

²⁰Then David got up from the ground. After he had washed, put on lotions and changed his clothes, he went into the house of the Lord and worshiped. Then he went to his own house,

---

ᵃ14 Masoretic Text; an ancient Hebrew scribal tradition *this you have shown utter contempt for the Lord*

and at his request they served him food, and he ate. Mt 6:17

21His servants asked him, "Why are you acting this way? While the child was alive, you fasted and wept, but now that the child is dead, you get up and eat!" Jdg 20:26

22He answered, "While the child was still alive, I fasted and wept. I thought, 'Who knows? The LORD may be gracious to me and let the child live.' 23But now that he is dead, why should I fast? Can I bring him back again? I will go to him, but he will not return to me." Jnh 3:9

24Then David comforted his wife Bathsheba, and he went to her and lay with her. She gave birth to a son, and they named him Solomon. The LORD loved him; 25and because the LORD loved him, he sent word through Nathan the prophet to name him Jedidiah.a 1Ch 22:9

26Meanwhile Joab fought against Rabbah of the Ammonites and captured the royal citadel. 27Joab then sent messengers to David, saying, "I have fought against Rabbah and taken its water supply. 28Now muster the rest of the troops and besiege the city and capture it. Otherwise I will take the city, and it will be named after me." Dt 3:11

29So David mustered the entire army and went to Rabbah, and attacked and captured it. 30He took the crown from the head of their kingb—its weight was a talentc of gold, and it was set with precious stones—and it was placed on David's head. He took a great quantity of plunder from the city 31and brought out the people who were there, consigning them to labor with saws and with iron picks and axes, and he made them work at brickmaking.d He did this to all the Ammonite towns. Then David and his entire army returned to Jerusalem. Est 8:15

Amnon and Tamar

13 In the course of time, Amnon son of David fell in love with Tamar, the beautiful sister of Absalom son of David. 2Sa 3:2; 1Ch 3:9

2Amnon became frustrated to the point of illness on account of his sister Tamar, for she was a virgin, and it seemed impossible for him to do anything to her.

3Now Amnon had a friend named Jonadab son of Shimeah, David's brother. Jonadab was a very shrewd man. 4He asked Amnon, "Why do you, the king's son, look so haggard morning after morning? Won't you tell me?" 1Sa 16:9

Amnon said to him, "I'm in love with Tamar, my brother Absalom's sister."

5"Go to bed and pretend to be ill," Jonadab said. "When your father comes to see you, say to

---

a25 Jedidiah means loved by the LORD. b30 Or of Milcom (that is, Molech) c30 That is, about 75 pounds (about 34 kilograms) d31 The meaning of the Hebrew for this clause is uncertain.

him, 'I would like my sister Tamar to come and give me something to eat. Let her prepare the food in my sight so I may watch her and then eat it from her hand.' "

6So Amnon lay down and pretended to be ill. When the king came to see him, Amnon said to him, "I would like my sister Tamar to come and make some special bread in my sight, so I may eat from her hand."

7David sent word to Tamar at the palace: "Go to the house of your brother Amnon and prepare some food for him." 8So Tamar went to the house of her brother Amnon, who was lying down. She took some dough, kneaded it, made the bread in his sight and baked it. 9Then she took the pan and served him the bread, but he refused to eat.

"Send everyone out of here," Amnon said. So everyone left him. 10Then Amnon said to Tamar, "Bring the food here into my bedroom so I may eat from your hand." And Tamar took the bread she had prepared and brought it to her brother Amnon in his bedroom. 11But when she took it to him to eat, he grabbed her and said, "Come to bed with me, my sister." Ge 39:12

12"Don't, my brother!" she said to him. "Don't force me. Such a thing should not be done in Israel! Don't do this wicked thing. 13What about me? Where could I get rid of my disgrace? And what about you? You would be like one of the wicked fools in Israel. Please speak to the king; he will not keep me from being married to you." 14But he refused to listen to her, and since he was stronger than she, he raped her. Lev 20:17

15Then Amnon hated her with intense hatred. In fact, he hated her more than he had loved her. Amnon said to her, "Get up and get out!"

16"No!" she said to him. "Sending me away would be a greater wrong than what you have already done to me."

But he refused to listen to her. 17He called his personal servant and said, "Get this woman out of here and bolt the door after her." 18So his servant put her out and bolted the door after her. She was wearing a richly ornamenteda robe, for this was the kind of garment the virgin daughters of the king wore. 19Tamar put ashes on her head and tore the ornamentedb robe she was wearing. She put her hand on her head and went away, weeping aloud as she went. Ge 37:3; Da 9:3

20Her brother Absalom said to her, "Has that Amnon, your brother, been with you? Be quiet now, my sister; he is your brother. Don't take this thing to heart." And Tamar lived in her

---

a18 The meaning of the Hebrew for this phrase is uncertain.   b19 The meaning of the Hebrew for this word is uncertain.

brother Absalom's house, a desolate woman.   2Sa 14:24

²¹When King David heard all this, he was furious. ²²Absalom never said a word to Amnon, either good or bad; he hated Amnon because he had disgraced his sister Tamar.   Ge 31:24

Absalom Kills Amnon

²³Two years later, when Absalom's sheepshearers were at Baal Hazor near the border of Ephraim, he invited all the king's sons to come there. ²⁴Absalom went to the king and said, "Your servant has had shearers come. Will the king and his officials please join me?"   1Sa 25:7

²⁵"No, my son," the king replied. "All of us should not go; we would only be a burden to you." Although Absalom urged him, he still refused to go, but gave him his blessing.

²⁶Then Absalom said, "If not, please let my brother Amnon come with us."

The king asked him, "Why should he go with you?" ²⁷But Absalom urged him, so he sent with him Amnon and the rest of the king's sons.

²⁸Absalom ordered his men, "Listen! When Amnon is in high spirits from drinking wine and I say to you, 'Strike Amnon down,' then kill him. Don't be afraid. Have not I given you this order? Be strong and brave." ²⁹So Absalom's men did to Am-

non what Absalom had ordered. Then all the king's sons got up, mounted their mules and fled.   Ru 3:7; 2Sa 3:3

³⁰While they were on their way, the report came to David: "Absalom has struck down all the king's sons; not one of them is left." ³¹The king stood up, tore his clothes and lay down on the ground; and all his servants stood by with their clothes torn.

³²But Jonadab son of Shimeah, David's brother, said, "My lord should not think that they killed all the princes; only Amnon is dead. This has been Absalom's expressed intention ever since the day Amnon raped his sister Tamar. ³³My lord the king should not be concerned about the report that all the king's sons are dead. Only Amnon is dead."   2Sa 19:19

³⁴Meanwhile, Absalom had fled.

Now the man standing watch looked up and saw many people on the road west of him, coming down the side of the hill. The watchman went and told the king, "I see men in the direction of Horonaim, on the side of the hill."ᵃ   2Sa 18:24

³⁵Jonadab said to the king, "See, the king's sons are here; it has happened just as your servant said."

³⁶As he finished speaking, the king's sons came in, wailing loudly. The king, too, and all his servants wept very bitterly.

ᵃ34 Septuagint; Hebrew does not have this sentence.

³⁷Absalom fled and went to Talmai son of Ammihud, the king of Geshur. But King David mourned for his son every day.

³⁸After Absalom fled and went to Geshur, he stayed there three years. ³⁹And the spirit of the king*ᵃ* longed to go to Absalom, for he was consoled concerning Amnon's death.   Ge 38:12

Absalom Returns to Jerusalem

14 Joab son of Zeruiah knew that the king's heart longed for Absalom. ²So Joab sent someone to Tekoa and had a wise woman brought from there. He said to her, "Pretend you are in mourning. Dress in mourning clothes, and don't use any cosmetic lotions. Act like a woman who has spent many days grieving for the dead. ³Then go to the king and speak these words to him." And Joab put the words in her mouth.   Ru 3:3; 2Sa 13:39

⁴When the woman from Tekoa went*ᵇ* to the king, she fell with her face to the ground to pay him honor, and she said, "Help me, O king!"   2Ki 6:26-28

⁵The king asked her, "What is troubling you?"

She said, "I am indeed a widow; my husband is dead. ⁶I your servant had two sons. They got into a fight with each other in the field, and no one was there to separate them. One struck the other and killed him. ⁷Now the whole clan has risen up against your servant; they say, 'Hand over the one who struck his brother down, so that we may put him to death for the life of his brother whom he killed; then we will get rid of the heir as well.' They would put out the only burning coal I have left, leaving my husband neither name nor descendant on the face of the earth."   Nu 35:19

⁸The king said to the woman, "Go home, and I will issue an order in your behalf."   1Sa 25:35

⁹But the woman from Tekoa said to him, "My lord the king, let the blame rest on me and on my father's family, and let the king and his throne be without guilt."   1Sa 25:24; Mt 27:25

¹⁰The king replied, "If anyone says anything to you, bring him to me, and he will not bother you again."

¹¹She said, "Then let the king invoke the LORD his God to prevent the avenger of blood from adding to the destruction, so that my son will not be destroyed."   Nu 35:12,21

"As surely as the LORD lives," he said, "not one hair of your son's head will fall to the ground."   1Sa 14:45; Mt 10:30

¹²Then the woman said, "Let your servant speak a word to my lord the king."

*ᵃ*39 Dead Sea Scrolls and some Septuagint manuscripts; Masoretic Text *But the spirit of David the king*   *ᵇ*4 Many Hebrew manuscripts, Septuagint, Vulgate and Syriac; most Hebrew manuscripts *spoke*

"Speak," he replied.

13The woman said, "Why then have you devised a thing like this against the people of God? When the king says this, does he not convict himself, for the king has not brought back his banished son? 14Like water spilled on the ground, which cannot be recovered, so we must die. But God does not take away life; instead, he devises ways so that a banished person may not remain estranged from him.   2Sa 12:7; Heb 9:27

15"And now I have come to say this to my lord the king because the people have made me afraid. Your servant thought, 'I will speak to the king; perhaps he will do what his servant asks. 16Perhaps the king will agree to deliver his servant from the hand of the man who is trying to cut off both me and my son from the inheritance God gave us.'   Ex 34:9; Dt 32:9

17"And now your servant says, 'May the word of my lord the king bring me rest, for my lord the king is like an angel of God in discerning good and evil. May the LORD your God be with you.'"   1Ki 3:9; Da 2:21

18Then the king said to the woman, "Do not keep from me the answer to what I am going to ask you."

"Let my lord the king speak," the woman said.

19The king asked, "Isn't the hand of Joab with you in all this?"

The woman answered, "As surely as you live, my lord the king, no one can turn to the right or to the left from anything my lord the king says. Yes, it was your servant Joab who instructed me to do this and who put all these words into the mouth of your servant. 20Your servant Joab did this to change the present situation. My lord has wisdom like that of an angel of God—he knows everything that happens in the land."

21The king said to Joab, "Very well, I will do it. Go, bring back the young man Absalom."

22Joab fell with his face to the ground to pay him honor, and he blessed the king. Joab said, "Today your servant knows that he has found favor in your eyes, my lord the king, because the king has granted his servant's request."   Ge 47:7

23Then Joab went to Geshur and brought Absalom back to Jerusalem. 24But the king said, "He must go to his own house; he must not see my face." So Absalom went to his own house and did not see the face of the king.   2Ki 3:13; 13:37

25In all Israel there was not a man so highly praised for his handsome appearance as Absalom. From the top of his head to the sole of his foot there was no blemish in him. 26Whenever he cut the hair of his head—he used to cut his hair from time to time when it became too heavy for him—he would weigh it, and its weight was two hun-

dred shekels[a] by the royal standard.

27Three sons and a daughter were born to Absalom. The daughter's name was Tamar, and she became a beautiful woman.   2Sa 8:18; 13:1

28Absalom lived two years in Jerusalem without seeing the king's face. 29Then Absalom sent for Joab in order to send him to the king, but Joab refused to come to him. So he sent a second time, but he refused to come. 30Then he said to his servants, "Look, Joab's field is next to mine, and he has barley there. Go and set it on fire." So Absalom's servants set the field on fire.   Ex 9:31

31Then Joab did go to Absalom's house and he said to him, "Why have your servants set my field on fire?"   Jdg 15:5

32Absalom said to Joab, "Look, I sent word to you and said, 'Come here so I can send you to the king to ask, "Why have I come from Geshur? It would be better for me if I were still there!" ' Now then, I want to see the king's face, and if I am guilty of anything, let him put me to death."   1Sa 20:8; 2Sa 3:3

33So Joab went to the king and told him this. Then the king summoned Absalom, and he came in and bowed down with his face to the ground before the king. And the king kissed Absalom.   Ge 33:4; Lk 15:20

Absalom's Conspiracy

15 In the course of time, Absalom provided himself with a chariot and horses and with fifty men to run ahead of him. 2He would get up early and stand by the side of the road leading to the city gate. Whenever anyone came with a complaint to be placed before the king for a decision, Absalom would call out to him, "What town are you from?" He would answer, "Your servant is from one of the tribes of Israel." 3Then Absalom would say to him, "Look, your claims are valid and proper, but there is no representative of the king to hear you." 4And Absalom would add, "If only I were appointed judge in the land! Then everyone who has a complaint or case could come to me and I would see that he gets justice."

5Also, whenever anyone approached him to bow down before him, Absalom would reach out his hand, take hold of him and kiss him. 6Absalom behaved in this way toward all the Israelites who came to the king asking for justice, and so he stole the hearts of the men of Israel.   Isa 49:23; Ro 16:18

7At the end of four[b] years, Absalom said to the king, "Let me go to Hebron and fulfill a vow I made to the LORD. 8While your servant was living at Geshur in Aram, I made this vow:

---

[a]26 That is, about 5 pounds (about 2.3 kilograms)
Syriac and Josephus; Hebrew *forty*   [b]7 Some Septuagint manuscripts,

'If the Lord takes me back to Jerusalem, I will worship the Lord in Hebron.ᵃ'"   Ge 28:20

⁹The king said to him, "Go in peace." So he went to Hebron.

¹⁰Then Absalom sent secret messengers throughout the tribes of Israel to say, "As soon as you hear the sound of the trumpets, then say, 'Absalom is king in Hebron.'" ¹¹Two hundred men from Jerusalem had accompanied Absalom. They had been invited as guests and went quite innocently, knowing nothing about the matter. ¹²While Absalom was offering sacrifices, he also sent for Ahithophel the Gilonite, David's counselor, to come from Giloh, his hometown. And so the conspiracy gained strength, and Absalom's following kept on increasing.   1Ki 1:34; Ps 3:1

David Flees

¹³A messenger came and told David, "The hearts of the men of Israel are with Absalom."

¹⁴Then David said to all his officials who were with him in Jerusalem, "Come! We must flee, or none of us will escape from Absalom. We must leave immediately, or he will move quickly to overtake us and bring ruin upon us and put the city to the sword."   2Sa 19:9; Ps 132:1

¹⁵The king's officials answered him, "Your servants are ready to do whatever our lord the king chooses."

¹⁶The king set out, with his entire household following him; but he left ten concubines to take care of the palace. ¹⁷So the king set out, with all the people following him, and they halted at a place some distance away. ¹⁸All his men marched past him, along with all the Kerethites and Pelethites; and all the six hundred Gittites who had accompanied him from Gath marched before the king.

¹⁹The king said to Ittai the Gittite, "Why should you come along with us? Go back and stay with King Absalom. You are a foreigner, an exile from your homeland. ²⁰You came only yesterday. And today shall I make you wander about with us, when I do not know where I am going? Go back, and take your countrymen. May kindness and faithfulness be with you."2Sa 18:2

²¹But Ittai replied to the king, "As surely as the Lord lives, and as my lord the king lives, wherever my lord the king may be, whether it means life or death, there will your servant be."   Ru 1:16-17; Pr 17:17

²²David said to Ittai, "Go ahead, march on." So Ittai the Gittite marched on with all his men and the families that were with him.

²³The whole countryside wept aloud as all the people passed by. The king also crossed the Kidron Valley, and

---

ᵃ8 Some Septuagint manuscripts; Hebrew does not have *in Hebron.*

all the people moved on toward the desert. 1Sa 11:4; Jn 18:1

24Zadok was there, too, and all the Levites who were with him were carrying the ark of the covenant of God. They set down the ark of God, and Abiathar offered sacrifices*a* until all the people had finished leaving the city. Nu 4:15; 2Sa 8:17

25Then the king said to Zadok, "Take the ark of God back into the city. If I find favor in the LORD's eyes, he will bring me back and let me see it and his dwelling place again. 26But if he says, 'I am not pleased with you,' then I am ready; let him do to me whatever seems good to him." 2Sa 22:20; Ps 43:3

27The king also said to Zadok the priest, "Aren't you a seer? Go back to the city in peace, with your son Ahimaaz and Jonathan son of Abiathar. You and Abiathar take your two sons with you. 28I will wait at the fords in the desert until word comes from you to inform me." 29So Zadok and Abiathar took the ark of God back to Jerusalem and stayed there.

30But David continued up the Mount of Olives, weeping as he went; his head was covered and he was barefoot. All the people with him covered their heads too and were weeping as they went up. 31Now David had been told, "Ahithophel is among the conspirators with Absalom." So David prayed, "O LORD, turn Ahithophel's counsel into foolishness." Est 6:12; Ps 30:5

32When David arrived at the summit, where people used to worship God, Hushai the Arkite was there to meet him, his robe torn and dust on his head. 33David said to him, "If you go with me, you will be a burden to me. 34But if you return to the city and say to Absalom, 'I will be your servant, O king; I was your father's servant in the past, but now I will be your servant,' then you can help me by frustrating Ahithophel's advice. 35Won't the priests Zadok and Abiathar be there with you? Tell them anything you hear in the king's palace. 36Their two sons, Ahimaaz son of Zadok and Jonathan son of Abiathar, are there with them. Send them to me with anything you hear."

37So David's friend Hushai arrived at Jerusalem as Absalom was entering the city. 1Ch 27:33

David and Ziba

16 When David had gone a short distance beyond the summit, there was Ziba, the steward of Mephibosheth, waiting to meet him. He had a string of donkeys saddled and loaded with two hundred loaves of bread, a hundred cakes of raisins, a hundred cakes of figs and a skin of wine. 2Sa 9:1-13

2The king asked Ziba, "Why have you brought these?"

Ziba answered, "The don-

a24 Or Abiathar went up

keys are for the king's household to ride on, the bread and fruit are for the men to eat, and the wine is to refresh those who become exhausted in the desert." 2Sa 17:27-29

³The king then asked, "Where is your master's grandson?" 2Sa 9:9-10

Ziba said to him, "He is staying in Jerusalem, because he thinks, 'Today the house of Israel will give me back my grandfather's kingdom.'" 2Sa 9:2

⁴Then the king said to Ziba, "All that belonged to Mephibosheth is now yours." 2Sa 4:4

"I humbly bow," Ziba said. "May I find favor in your eyes, my lord the king."

Shimei Curses David

⁵As King David approached Bahurim, a man from the same clan as Saul's family came out from there. His name was Shimei son of Gera, and he cursed as he came out. ⁶He pelted David and all the king's officials with stones, though all the troops and the special guard were on David's right and left. ⁷As he cursed, Shimei said, "Get out, get out, you man of blood, you scoundrel! ⁸The LORD has repaid you for all the blood you shed in the household of Saul, in whose place you have reigned. The LORD has handed the kingdom over to your son Absalom. You have come to ruin because you are a man of blood!" 1Ki 2:8-9; Ps 55:3

⁹Then Abishai son of Zeruiah said to the king, "Why should this dead dog curse my lord the king? Let me go over and cut off his head." 1Sa 26:6; Lk 9:54

¹⁰But the king said, "What do you and I have in common, you sons of Zeruiah? If he is cursing because the LORD said to him, 'Curse David,' who can ask, 'Why do you do this?'" 2Sa 19:22

¹¹David then said to Abishai and all his officials, "My son, who is of my own flesh, is trying to take my life. How much more, then, this Benjamite! Leave him alone; let him curse, for the LORD has told him to. ¹²It may be that the LORD will see my distress and repay me with good for the cursing I am receiving today." Ge 45:5; Ro 8:28

¹³So David and his men continued along the road while Shimei was going along the hillside opposite him, cursing as he went and throwing stones at him and showering him with dirt. ¹⁴The king and all the people with him arrived at their destination exhausted. And there he refreshed himself.

The Advice of Hushai and Ahithophel

¹⁵Meanwhile, Absalom and all the men of Israel came to Jerusalem, and Ahithophel was with him. ¹⁶Then Hushai the Arkite, David's friend, went to Absalom and said to him, "Long live the king! Long live the king!" 2Sa 15:32,37

¹⁷Absalom asked Hushai, "Is

this the love you show your friend? Why didn't you go with your friend?" 2Sa 19:25; Pr 17:17

18Hushai said to Absalom, "No, the one chosen by the LORD, by these people, and by all the men of Israel—his I will be, and I will remain with him. 19Furthermore, whom should I serve? Should I not serve the son? Just as I served your father, so I will serve you." 2Sa 15:34

20Absalom said to Ahithophel, "Give us your advice. What should we do?"

21Ahithophel answered, "Lie with your father's concubines whom he left to take care of the palace. Then all Israel will hear that you have made yourself a stench in your father's nostrils, and the hands of everyone with you will be strengthened." 22So they pitched a tent for Absalom on the roof, and he lay with his father's concubines in the sight of all Israel. 1Sa 13:4; Zec 8:13

23Now in those days the advice Ahithophel gave was like that of one who inquires of God. That was how both David and Absalom regarded all of Ahithophel's advice.

17 Ahithophel said to Absalom, "I woulda choose twelve thousand men and set out tonight in pursuit of David. 2I wouldb attack him while he is weary and weak. I wouldb strike him with terror, and then all the people with him will flee. I wouldb strike down only the

king 3and bring all the people back to you. The death of the man you seek will mean the return of all; all the people will be unharmed." 4This plan seemed good to Absalom and to all the elders of Israel. 2Sa 15:12

5But Absalom said, "Summon also Hushai the Arkite, so we can hear what he has to say." 6When Hushai came to him, Absalom said, "Ahithophel has given this advice. Should we do what he says? If not, give us your opinion."

7Hushai replied to Absalom, "The advice Ahithophel has given is not good this time. 8You know your father and his men; they are fighters, and as fierce as a wild bear robbed of her cubs. Besides, your father is an experienced fighter; he will not spend the night with the troops. 9Even now, he is hidden in a cave or some other place. If he should attack your troops first,c whoever hears about it will say, 'There has been a slaughter among the troops who follow Absalom.' 10Then even the bravest soldier, whose heart is like the heart of a lion, will melt with fear, for all Israel knows that your father is a fighter and that those with him are brave. Hos 13:8

11"So I advise you: Let all Israel, from Dan to Beersheba—as numerous as the sand on the seashore—be gathered to you, with you yourself leading them into battle. 12Then we will attack

a1 Or Let me   b2 Or will   c9 Or When some of the men fall at the first attack

him wherever he may be found, and we will fall on him as dew settles on the ground. Neither he nor any of his men will be left alive. [13]If he withdraws into a city, then all Israel will bring ropes to that city, and we will drag it down to the valley until not even a piece of it can be found."   Jdg 20:1; Mic 1:6

[14]Absalom and all the men of Israel said, "The advice of Hushai the Arkite is better than that of Ahithophel." For the LORD had determined to frustrate the good advice of Ahithophel in order to bring disaster on Absalom.   2Sa 15:34; Ne 4:15

[15]Hushai told Zadok and Abiathar, the priests, "Ahithophel has advised Absalom and the elders of Israel to do such and such, but I have advised them to do so and so. [16]Now send a message immediately and tell David, 'Do not spend the night at the fords in the desert; cross over without fail, or the king and all the people with him will be swallowed up.'"   2Sa 15:28,35

[17]Jonathan and Ahimaaz were staying at En Rogel. A servant girl was to go and inform them, and they were to go and tell King David, for they could not risk being seen entering the city. [18]But a young man saw them and told Absalom. So the two of them left quickly and went to the house of a man in Bahurim. He had a well in his courtyard, and they climbed down into it. [19]His wife took a covering and spread it out over the opening of the well and scattered grain over it. No one knew anything about it.   Jos 15:7

[20]When Absalom's men came to the woman at the house, they asked, "Where are Ahimaaz and Jonathan?"   Ex 1:19; 1Sa 19:12

The woman answered them, "They crossed over the brook."[a] The men searched but found no one, so they returned to Jerusalem.

[21]After the men had gone, the two climbed out of the well and went to inform King David. They said to him, "Set out and cross the river at once; Ahithophel has advised such and such against you." [22]So David and all the people with him set out and crossed the Jordan. By daybreak, no one was left who had not crossed the Jordan. 2Sa 17:15-16

[23]When Ahithophel saw that his advice had not been followed, he saddled his donkey and set out for his house in his hometown. He put his house in order and then hanged himself. So he died and was buried in his father's tomb.   2Ki 20:1; Mt 27:5

[24]David went to Mahanaim, and Absalom crossed the Jordan with all the men of Israel. [25]Absalom had appointed Amasa over the army in place of Joab. Amasa was the son of a

---

[a]20 Or "They passed by the sheep pen toward the water."

man named Jether,[a] an Israelite[b] who had married Abigail,[c] the daughter of Nahash and sister of Zeruiah the mother of Joab. [26]The Israelites and Absalom camped in the land of Gilead. Ge 32:2; 2Sa 20:9-12

[27]When David came to Mahanaim, Shobi son of Nahash from Rabbah of the Ammonites, and Makir son of Ammiel from Lo Debar, and Barzillai the Gileadite from Rogelim [28]brought bedding and bowls and articles of pottery. They also brought wheat and barley, flour and roasted grain, beans and lentils,[d] [29]honey and curds, sheep, and cheese from cows' milk for David and his people to eat. For they said, "The people have become hungry and tired and thirsty in the desert." 1Ki 2:7

Absalom's Death

18 David mustered the men who were with him and appointed over them commanders of thousands and commanders of hundreds. [2]David sent the troops out—a third under the command of Joab, a third under Joab's brother Abishai son of Zeruiah, and a third under Ittai the Gittite. The king told the troops, "I myself will surely march out with you." Ex 18:25; 1Sa 11:11

[3]But the men said, "You must not go out; if we are forced to flee, they won't care about us. Even if half of us die, they won't care; but you are worth ten thousand of us.[e] It would be better now for you to give us support from the city." 2Sa 21:17

[4]The king answered, "I will do whatever seems best to you."

So the king stood beside the gate while all the men marched out in units of hundreds and of thousands. [5]The king commanded Joab, Abishai and Ittai, "Be gentle with the young man Absalom for my sake." And all the troops heard the king giving orders concerning Absalom to each of the commanders. 2Sa 18:12

[6]The army marched into the field to fight Israel, and the battle took place in the forest of Ephraim. [7]There the army of Israel was defeated by David's men, and the casualties that day were great—twenty thousand men. [8]The battle spread out over the whole countryside, and the forest claimed more lives that day than the sword.

[9]Now Absalom happened to meet David's men. He was riding his mule, and as the mule went under the thick branches of a large oak, Absalom's head got caught in the tree. He was

---

[a]25 Hebrew *Ithra*, a variant of *Jether*   [b]25 Hebrew and some Septuagint manuscripts; other Septuagint manuscripts (see also 1 Chron. 2:17) *Ishmaelite* or *Jezreelite*
[c]25 Hebrew *Abigal*, a variant of *Abigail*   [d]28 Most Septuagint manuscripts and Syriac; Hebrew *lentils, and roasted grain*   [e]3 Two Hebrew manuscripts, some Septuagint manuscripts and Vulgate; most Hebrew manuscripts *care; for now there are ten thousand like us*

left hanging in midair, while the mule he was riding kept on going. 2Sa 14:26

[10]When one of the men saw this, he told Joab, "I just saw Absalom hanging in an oak tree."

[11]Joab said to the man who had told him this, "What! You saw him? Why didn't you strike him to the ground right there? Then I would have had to give you ten shekels[a] of silver and a warrior's belt." 1Sa 18:4; 2Sa 3:39

[12]But the man replied, "Even if a thousand shekels[b] were weighed out into my hands, I would not lift my hand against the king's son. In our hearing the king commanded you and Abishai and Ittai, 'Protect the young man Absalom for my sake.'[c] [13]And if I had put my life in jeopardy[d]—and nothing is hidden from the king—you would have kept your distance from me." 2Sa 14:19-20

[14]Joab said, "I'm not going to wait like this for you." So he took three javelins in his hand and plunged them into Absalom's heart while Absalom was still alive in the oak tree. [15]And ten of Joab's armor-bearers surrounded Absalom, struck him and killed him. 2Sa 2:18

[16]Then Joab sounded the trumpet, and the troops stopped pursuing Israel, for Joab halted them. [17]They took Absalom, threw him into a big pit in the forest and piled up a large heap of rocks over him. Meanwhile, all the Israelites fled to their homes. 2Sa 2:28

[18]During his lifetime Absalom had taken a pillar and erected it in the King's Valley as a monument to himself, for he thought, "I have no son to carry on the memory of my name." He named the pillar after himself, and it is called Absalom's Monument to this day. Ge 14:17

David Mourns

[19]Now Ahimaaz son of Zadok said, "Let me run and take the news to the king that the LORD has delivered him from the hand of his enemies." 2Sa 15:36

[20]"You are not the one to take the news today," Joab told him. "You may take the news another time, but you must not do so today, because the king's son is dead."

[21]Then Joab said to a Cushite, "Go, tell the king what you have seen." The Cushite bowed down before Joab and ran off.

[22]Ahimaaz son of Zadok again said to Joab, "Come what may, please let me run behind the Cushite."

But Joab replied, "My son, why do you want to go? You don't have any news that will bring you a reward."

---

[a]11 That is, about 4 ounces (about 115 grams)   [b]12 That is, about 25 pounds (about 11 kilograms)   [c]12 A few Hebrew manuscripts, Septuagint, Vulgate and Syriac; most Hebrew manuscripts may be translated *Absalom, whoever you may be.*   [d]13 Or *Otherwise, if I had acted treacherously toward him*

²³He said, "Come what may, I want to run."

So Joab said, "Run!" Then Ahimaaz ran by way of the plain[a] and outran the Cushite.

²⁴While David was sitting between the inner and outer gates, the watchman went up to the roof of the gateway by the wall. As he looked out, he saw a man running alone. ²⁵The watchman called out to the king and reported it.   2Ki 9:17

The king said, "If he is alone, he must have good news." And the man came closer and closer.

²⁶Then the watchman saw another man running, and he called down to the gatekeeper, "Look, another man running alone!"

The king said, "He must be bringing good news, too."1Ki 4:42

²⁷The watchman said, "It seems to me that the first one runs like Ahimaaz son of Zadok."   2Ki 9:20

"He's a good man," the king said. "He comes with good news."   1Ki 1:42

²⁸Then Ahimaaz called out to the king, "All is well!" He bowed down before the king with his face to the ground and said, "Praise be to the LORD your God! He has delivered up the men who lifted their hands against my lord the king."2Sa 14:4

²⁹The king asked, "Is the young man Absalom safe?"

Ahimaaz answered, "I saw great confusion just as Joab was about to send the king's servant and me, your servant, but I don't know what it was."

³⁰The king said, "Stand aside and wait here." So he stepped aside and stood there.

³¹Then the Cushite arrived and said, "My lord the king, hear the good news! The LORD has delivered you today from all who rose up against you."Jdg 5:31

³²The king asked the Cushite, "Is the young man Absalom safe?"

The Cushite replied, "May the enemies of my lord the king and all who rise up to harm you be like that young man."1Sa 25:26

³³The king was shaken. He went up to the room over the gateway and wept. As he went, he said: "O my son Absalom! My son, my son Absalom! If only I had died instead of you—O Absalom, my son, my son!"   Ex 32:32; 2Sa 19:4

19 Joab was told, "The king is weeping and mourning for Absalom." ²And for the whole army the victory that day was turned into mourning, because on that day the troops heard it said, "The king is grieving for his son." ³The men stole into the city that day as men steal in who are ashamed when they flee from battle. ⁴The king covered his face and cried aloud, "O my son Absalom! O Absalom, my son, my son!"

⁵Then Joab went into the house to the king and said, "To-

_____
[a]23 That is, the plain of the Jordan

day you have humiliated all your men, who have just saved your life and the lives of your sons and daughters and the lives of your wives and concubines. ⁶You love those who hate you and hate those who love you. You have made it clear today that the commanders and their men mean nothing to you. I see that you would be pleased if Absalom were alive today and all of us were dead. ⁷Now go out and encourage your men. I swear by the LORD that if you don't go out, not a man will be left with you by nightfall. This will be worse for you than all the calamities that have come upon you from your youth till now." <small>Pr 14:28; Mt 5:46</small>

⁸So the king got up and took his seat in the gateway. When the men were told, "The king is sitting in the gateway," they all came before him. <small>2Sa 15:2</small>

David Returns to Jerusalem

Meanwhile, the Israelites had fled to their homes. ⁹Throughout the tribes of Israel, the people were all arguing with each other, saying, "The king delivered us from the hand of our enemies; he is the one who rescued us from the hand of the Philistines. But now he has fled the country because of Absalom; ¹⁰and Absalom, whom we anointed to rule over us, has died in battle. So why do you say nothing about bringing the king back?" <small>2Sa 8:1-14</small>

¹¹King David sent this message to Zadok and Abiathar, the priests: "Ask the elders of Judah, 'Why should you be the last to bring the king back to his palace, since what is being said throughout Israel has reached the king at his quarters? ¹²You are my brothers, my own flesh and blood. So why should you be the last to bring back the king?' ¹³And say to Amasa, 'Are you not my own flesh and blood? May God deal with me, be it ever so severely, if from now on you are not the commander of my army in place of Joab.'" <small>2Sa 15:24; 17:25</small>

¹⁴He won over the hearts of all the men of Judah as though they were one man. They sent word to the king, "Return, you and all your men." ¹⁵Then the king returned and went as far as the Jordan. <small>Jos 5:9; Jdg 20:1</small>

Now the men of Judah had come to Gilgal to go out and meet the king and bring him across the Jordan. ¹⁶Shimei son of Gera, the Benjamite from Bahurim, hurried down with the men of Judah to meet King David. ¹⁷With him were a thousand Benjamites, along with Ziba, the steward of Saul's household, and his fifteen sons and twenty servants. They rushed to the Jordan, where the king was. ¹⁸They crossed at the ford to take the king's household over and to do whatever he wished. <small>Ge 43:16; 2Sa 16:5</small>

When Shimei son of Gera crossed the Jordan, he fell prostrate before the king ¹⁹and said

to him, "May my lord not hold me guilty. Do not remember how your servant did wrong on the day my lord the king left Jerusalem. May the king put it out of his mind. 20For I your servant know that I have sinned, but today I have come here as the first of the whole house of Joseph to come down and meet my lord the king."

21Then Abishai son of Zeruiah said, "Shouldn't Shimei be put to death for this? He cursed the LORD's anointed."

22David replied, "What do you and I have in common, you sons of Zeruiah? This day you have become my adversaries! Should anyone be put to death in Israel today? Do I not know that today I am king over Israel?" 23So the king said to Shimei, "You shall not die." And the king promised him on oath.

24Mephibosheth, Saul's grandson, also went down to meet the king. He had not taken care of his feet or trimmed his mustache or washed his clothes from the day the king left until the day he returned safely. 25When he came from Jerusalem to meet the king, the king asked him, "Why didn't you go with me, Mephibosheth?"

26He said, "My lord the king, since I your servant am lame, I said, 'I will have my donkey saddled and will ride on it, so I can go with the king.' But Ziba my servant betrayed me. 27And he has slandered your servant to my lord the king. My lord the king is like an angel of God; so do whatever pleases you. 28All my grandfather's descendants deserved nothing but death from my lord the king, but you gave your servant a place among those who eat at your table. So what right do I have to make any more appeals to the king?"

29The king said to him, "Why say more? I order you and Ziba to divide the fields."

30Mephibosheth said to the king, "Let him take everything, now that my lord the king has arrived home safely."

31Barzillai the Gileadite also came down from Rogelim to cross the Jordan with the king and to send him on his way from there. 32Now Barzillai was a very old man, eighty years of age. He had provided for the king during his stay in Mahanaim, for he was a very wealthy man. 33The king said to Barzillai, "Cross over with me and stay with me in Jerusalem, and I will provide for you."

34But Barzillai answered the king, "How many more years will I live, that I should go up to Jerusalem with the king? 35I am now eighty years old. Can I tell the difference between what is good and what is not? Can your servant taste what he eats and drinks? Can I still hear the voices of men and women singers? Why should your servant be an added burden to my lord the king? 36Your servant will

cross over the Jordan with the king for a short distance, but why should the king reward me in this way? ³⁷Let your servant return, that I may die in my own town near the tomb of my father and mother. But here is your servant Kimham. Let him cross over with my lord the king. Do for him whatever pleases you."

³⁸The king said, "Kimham shall cross over with me, and I will do for him whatever pleases you. And anything you desire from me I will do for you."

³⁹So all the people crossed the Jordan, and then the king crossed over. The king kissed Barzillai and gave him his blessing, and Barzillai returned to his home.   Ge 31:55; 47:7

⁴⁰When the king crossed over to Gilgal, Kimham crossed with him. All the troops of Judah and half the troops of Israel had taken the king over.

⁴¹Soon all the men of Israel were coming to the king and saying to him, "Why did our brothers, the men of Judah, steal the king away and bring him and his household across the Jordan, together with all his men?"   Jdg 8:1; 12:1

⁴²All the men of Judah answered the men of Israel, "We did this because the king is closely related to us. Why are you angry about it? Have we eaten any of the king's provisions? Have we taken anything for ourselves?"

⁴³Then the men of Israel an-swered the men of Judah, "We have ten shares in the king; and besides, we have a greater claim on David than you have. So why do you treat us with con-tempt? Were we not the first to speak of bringing back our king?"   2Sa 5:1; 1Ki 11:30-31

But the men of Judah re-sponded even more harshly than the men of Israel.

Sheba Rebels Against David

20 Now a troublemaker named Sheba son of Bicri, a Benjamite, happened to be there. He sounded the trumpet and shouted,

"We have no share in David,
  no part in Jesse's son!
Every man to his tent,
  O Israel!"   1Ki 12:16; 2Ch 10:16

²So all the men of Israel de-serted David to follow Sheba son of Bicri. But the men of Judah stayed by their king all the way from the Jordan to Jerusalem.

³When David returned to his palace in Jerusalem, he took the ten concubines he had left to take care of the palace and put them in a house under guard. He provided for them, but did not lie with them. They were kept in confinement till the day of their death, living as widows.

⁴Then the king said to Amasa, "Summon the men of Judah to come to me within three days, and be here your-self." ⁵But when Amasa went to summon Judah, he took longer

than the time the king had set for him.   2Sa 17:25; 19:13

6David said to Abishai, "Now Sheba son of Bicri will do us more harm than Absalom did. Take your master's men and pursue him, or he will find fortified cities and escape from us." 7So Joab's men and the Kerethites and Pelethites and all the mighty warriors went out under the command of Abishai. They marched out from Jerusalem to pursue Sheba son of Bicri.

8While they were at the great rock in Gibeon, Amasa came to meet them. Joab was wearing his military tunic, and strapped over it at his waist was a belt with a dagger in its sheath. As he stepped forward, it dropped out of its sheath.   Jos 9:3; 2Sa 2:18

9Joab said to Amasa, "How are you, my brother?" Then Joab took Amasa by the beard with his right hand to kiss him. 10Amasa was not on his guard against the dagger in Joab's hand, and Joab plunged it into his belly, and his intestines spilled out on the ground. Without being stabbed again, Amasa died. Then Joab and his brother Abishai pursued Sheba son of Bicri.   Mt 26:49; 1Ki 2:5

11One of Joab's men stood beside Amasa and said, "Whoever favors Joab, and whoever is for David, let him follow Joab!" 12Amasa lay wallowing in his blood in the middle of the road, and the man saw that all the

troops came to a halt there. When he realized that everyone who came up to Amasa stopped, he dragged him from the road into a field and threw a garment over him. 13After Amasa had been removed from the road, all the men went on with Joab to pursue Sheba son of Bicri.   2Sa 2:23

14Sheba passed through all the tribes of Israel to Abel Beth Maacah*a* and through the entire region of the Berites, who gathered together and followed him. 15All the troops with Joab came and besieged Sheba in Abel Beth Maacah. They built a siege ramp up to the city, and it stood against the outer fortifications. While they were battering the wall to bring it down, 16a wise woman called from the city, "Listen! Listen! Tell Joab to come here so I can speak to him." 17He went toward her, and she asked, "Are you Joab?"

"I am," he answered.

She said, "Listen to what your servant has to say."

"I'm listening," he said.

18She continued, "Long ago they used to say, 'Get your answer at Abel,' and that settled it. 19We are the peaceful and faithful in Israel. You are trying to destroy a city that is a mother in Israel. Why do you want to swallow up the LORD's inheritance?"   Dt 2:26; 1Sa 26:19

20"Far be it from me!" Joab replied, "Far be it from me to

----

a 14 Or *Abel, even Beth Maacah*; also in verse 15

swallow up or destroy! [21]That is not the case. A man named Sheba son of Bicri, from the hill country of Ephraim, has lifted up his hand against the king, against David. Hand over this one man, and I'll withdraw from the city."

The woman said to Joab, "His head will be thrown to you from the wall."   2Sa 4:8

[22]Then the woman went to all the people with her wise advice, and they cut off the head of Sheba son of Bicri and threw it to Joab. So he sounded the trumpet, and his men dispersed from the city, each returning to his home. And Joab went back to the king in Jerusalem.

[23]Joab was over Israel's entire army; Benaiah son of Jehoiada was over the Kerethites and Pelethites; [24]Adoniram[a] was in charge of forced labor; Jehoshaphat son of Ahilud was recorder; [25]Sheva was secretary; Zadok and Abiathar were priests; [26]and Ira the Jairite was David's priest.   2Sa 8:16-18

The Gibeonites Avenged

21 During the reign of David, there was a famine for three successive years; so David sought the face of the LORD. The LORD said, "It is on account of Saul and his bloodstained house; it is because he put the Gibeonites to death."

[2]The king summoned the Gibeonites and spoke to them. (Now the Gibeonites were not a part of Israel but were survivors of the Amorites; the Israelites had sworn to spare them, but Saul in his zeal for Israel and Judah had tried to annihilate them.) [3]David asked the Gibeonites, "What shall I do for you? How shall I make amends so that you will bless the LORD's inheritance?"   Jos 9:3,15

[4]The Gibeonites answered him, "We have no right to demand silver or gold from Saul or his family, nor do we have the right to put anyone in Israel to death."   Nu 35:33-34

"What do you want me to do for you?" David asked.

[5]They answered the king, "As for the man who destroyed us and plotted against us so that we have been decimated and have no place anywhere in Israel, [6]let seven of his male descendants be given to us to be killed and exposed before the LORD at Gibeah of Saul—the LORD's chosen one."   1Sa 10:24

So the king said, "I will give them to you."

[7]The king spared Mephibosheth son of Jonathan, the son of Saul, because of the oath before the LORD between David and Jonathan son of Saul. [8]But the king took Armoni and Mephibosheth, the two sons of Aiah's daughter Rizpah, whom she had borne to Saul, together with the five sons of Saul's

---

[a]24 Some Septuagint manuscripts (see also 1 Kings 4:6 and 5:14); Hebrew *Adoram*

daughter Merab,[a] whom she had borne to Adriel son of Barzillai the Meholathite. [9]He handed them over to the Gibeonites, who killed and exposed them on a hill before the LORD. All seven of them fell together; they were put to death during the first days of the harvest, just as the barley harvest was beginning.   Ru 1:22; 2Sa 4:4

[10]Rizpah daughter of Aiah took sackcloth and spread it out for herself on a rock. From the beginning of the harvest till the rain poured down from the heavens on the bodies, she did not let the birds of the air touch them by day or the wild animals by night. [11]When David was told what Aiah's daughter Rizpah, Saul's concubine, had done, [12]he went and took the bones of Saul and his son Jonathan from the citizens of Jabesh Gilead. (They had taken them secretly from the public square at Beth Shan, where the Philistines had hung them after they struck Saul down on Gilboa.) [13]David brought the bones of Saul and his son Jonathan from there, and the bones of those who had been killed and exposed were gathered up. 1Sa 17:44

[14]They buried the bones of Saul and his son Jonathan in the tomb of Saul's father Kish, at Zela in Benjamin, and did everything the king com-manded. After that, God answered prayer in behalf of the land.   Jos 18:28; 1Ch 8:34

Wars Against the Philistines

[15]Once again there was a battle between the Philistines and Israel. David went down with his men to fight against the Philistines, and he became exhausted. [16]And Ishbi-Benob, one of the descendants of Rapha, whose bronze spearhead weighed three hundred shekels[b] and who was armed with a new sword, said he would kill David. [17]But Abishai son of Zeruiah came to David's rescue; he struck the Philistine down and killed him. Then David's men swore to him, saying, "Never again will you go out with us to battle, so that the lamp of Israel will not be extinguished."   2Sa 18:3; Ps 132:17

[18]In the course of time, there was another battle with the Philistines, at Gob. At that time Sibbecai the Hushathite killed Saph, one of the descendants of Rapha.   1Ch 11:29; 27:11

[19]In another battle with the Philistines at Gob, Elhanan son of Jaare-Oregim[c] the Bethlehemite killed Goliath[d] the Gittite, who had a spear with a shaft like a weaver's rod. 1Sa 17:4

[20]In still another battle, which took place at Gath, there was a huge man with six fingers on

---

[a]8 Two Hebrew manuscripts, some Septuagint manuscripts and Syriac (see also 1 Samuel 18:19); most Hebrew and Septuagint manuscripts *Michal*   [b]16 That is, about 7 1/2 pounds (about 3.5 kilograms)   [c]19 Or *son of Jair the weaver*   [d]19 Hebrew and Septuagint; 1 Chron. 20:5 *son of Jair killed Lahmi the brother of Goliath*

each hand and six toes on each foot—twenty-four in all. He also was descended from Rapha. ²¹When he taunted Israel, Jonathan son of Shimeah, David's brother, killed him.

²²These four were descendants of Rapha in Gath, and they fell at the hands of David and his men.   2Ki 12:17; 1Ch 20:8

David's Song of Praise

22 David sang to the LORD the words of this song when the LORD delivered him from the hand of all his enemies and from the hand of Saul. ²He said: Ex 15:1

"The LORD is my rock, my
    fortress and my
    deliverer;
³ my God is my rock, in
    whom I take refuge,
  my shield and the horn^a of
    my salvation. Ge 15:1; Ps 31:3
He is my stronghold, my
    refuge and my savior—
  from violent men you save
    me.   Ps 9:9; 52:7
⁴I call to the LORD, who is
    worthy of praise,
  and I am saved from my
    enemies.   Ps 48:1; 145:3

⁵"The waves of death swirled
    about me;
  the torrents of destruction
    overwhelmed me.   Jnh 2:3
⁶The cords of the grave^b
    coiled around me;

the snares of death
    confronted me.   Ps 116:3
⁷In my distress I called to the
    LORD;
  I called out to my God. Ge 35:3
From his temple he heard my
    voice;
  my cry came to his ears.

⁸"The earth trembled and
    quaked,
  the foundations of the
    heavens^c shook;
  they trembled because he
    was angry.   Jdg 5:4; Ps 77:18
⁹Smoke rose from his nostrils;
  consuming fire came from
    his mouth,
  burning coals blazed out
    of it.   Ps 97:3; Heb 12:29
¹⁰He parted the heavens and
    came down;
  dark clouds were under his
    feet.   1Ki 8:12; Ps 104:3
¹¹He mounted the cherubim
    and flew;
  he soared^d on the wings of
    the wind.   Ge 3:24; Ps 104:3
¹²He made darkness his
    canopy around him—
  the dark^e rain clouds of the
    sky.   Ex 19:9; Ps 97:2
¹³Out of the brightness of his
    presence
  bolts of lightning blazed
    forth.   Job 37:3; Ps 77:18
¹⁴The LORD thundered from
    heaven;
  the voice of the Most High
    resounded.   1Sa 2:10

---

^a3 *Horn* here symbolizes strength.   ^b6 Hebrew *Sheol*   ^c8 Hebrew; Vulgate and Syriac (see also Psalm 18:7) *mountains*   ^d11 Many Hebrew manuscripts (see also Psalm 18:10); most Hebrew manuscripts *appeared*   ^e12 Septuagint and Vulgate (see also Psalm 18:11); Hebrew *massed*

15He shot arrows and scattered
   the enemies,
 bolts of lightning and
   routed them.   Dt 32:33
16The valleys of the sea were
   exposed
 and the foundations of the
   earth laid bare
 at the rebuke of the LORD,
 at the blast of breath from
   his nostrils.   Ps 6:1; Na 1:4

17"He reached down from on
   high and took hold of
   me;
 he drew me out of deep
   waters.   Ex 2:10; Ps 144:7
18He rescued me from my
   powerful enemy,
 from my foes, who were
   too strong for me.   Lk 1:71
19They confronted me in the
   day of my disaster,
 but the LORD was my
   support.   Ps 23:4
20He brought me out into a
   spacious place;
 he rescued me because he
   delighted in me.   Ps 31:8

21"The LORD has dealt with me
   according to my
   righteousness;
 according to the cleanness
   of my hands he has
   rewarded me.   Ps 24:4
22For I have kept the ways of
   the LORD;
 I have not done evil by
   turning from my God.
23All his laws are before me;

I have not turned away
   from his decrees.   Dt 6:4-9
24I have been blameless before
   him
 and have kept myself from
   sin.   Ge 7:1; Eph 1:4
25The LORD has rewarded me
   according to my
   righteousness,
 according to my cleanness[a]
   in his sight.   1Sa 16:23

26"To the faithful you show
   yourself faithful,
 to the blameless you show
   yourself blameless,
27to the pure you show
   yourself pure,
 but to the crooked you
   show yourself shrewd.
28You save the humble,
 but your eyes are on the
   haughty to bring them
   low.   Ps 72:12; Isa 2:12
29You are my lamp, O LORD;
 the LORD turns my
   darkness into light.   Ps 27:1
30With your help I can advance
   against a troop[b];
 with my God I can scale a
   wall.

31"As for God, his way is
   perfect;
 the word of the LORD is
   flawless.   Dt 32:4; Mt 5:48
 He is a shield
 for all who take refuge in
   him.   Ge 15:1
32For who is God besides the
   LORD?

---

[a]25 Hebrew; Septuagint and Vulgate (see also Psalm 18:24) *to the cleanness of my hands*
[b]30 Or *can run through a barricade*

And who is the Rock except
our God? 1Sa 2:2; 2Sa 7:22
[33]It is God who arms me with
strength[a]
and makes my way perfect.
[34]He makes my feet like the
feet of a deer;
he enables me to stand on
the heights. Hab 3:19
[35]He trains my hands for
battle;
my arms can bend a bow of
bronze. Ps 144:1; Zec 9:13
[36]You give me your shield of
victory;
you stoop down to make
me great. Eph 6:16
[37]You broaden the path
beneath me,
so that my ankles do not
turn. Pr 4:11-12

[38]"I pursued my enemies and
crushed them;
I did not turn back till they
were destroyed. Ex 15:9
[39]I crushed them completely,
and they could not rise;
they fell beneath my feet.
[40]You armed me with strength
for battle;
you made my adversaries
bow at my feet. Jos 10:24
[41]You made my enemies turn
their backs in flight,
and I destroyed my foes.
[42]They cried for help, but there
was no one to save
them—
to the LORD, but he did not
answer. 1Sa 28:6; Ps 50:22

[43]I beat them as fine as the
dust of the earth;
I pounded and trampled
them like mud in the
streets. 2Ki 13:7; Isa 10:6

[44]"You have delivered me from
the attacks of my people;
you have preserved me as
the head of nations. 2Sa 3:1
People I did not know are
subject to me,
[45] and foreigners come
cringing to me;
as soon as they hear me,
they obey me. Isa 55:3-5
[46]They all lose heart;
they come trembling[b] from
their strongholds. Mic 7:17

[47]"The LORD lives! Praise be to
my Rock!
Exalted be God, the Rock,
my Savior! Dt 32:15; Ps 89:26
[48]He is the God who avenges
me,
who puts the nations under
me,
[49] who sets me free from my
enemies. Ps 140:1; 144:2
You exalted me above my
foes;
from violent men you
rescued me. Ps 27:6
[50]Therefore I will praise you,
O LORD, among the
nations;
I will sing praises to your
name. Pr 9:11; Ro 15:9
[51]He gives his king great
victories;

[a]33 Dead Sea Scrolls, some Septuagint manuscripts, Vulgate and Syriac (see also
Psalm 18:32); Masoretic Text *who is my strong refuge* [b]46 Some Septuagint manuscripts and Vulgate (see also Psalm 18:45); Masoretic Text *they arm themselves.*

he shows unfailing
    kindness to his
    anointed,
to David and his
    descendants forever."

The Last Words of David

23 These are the last words
of David:

"The oracle of David son of
    Jesse,
  the oracle of the man
    exalted by the Most
    High,
the man anointed by the God
    of Jacob,
Israel's singer of songs[a]:

2"The Spirit of the LORD
    spoke through me;
  his word was on my
    tongue.   Mt 22:43; 2Pe 1:21
3The God of Israel spoke,
  the Rock of Israel said to
    me:
'When one rules over men in
    righteousness,
  when he rules in the fear of
    God,
4he is like the light of morning
    at sunrise
on a cloudless morning,
like the brightness after rain
  that brings the grass from
    the earth.'   Dt 32:4

5"Is not my house right with
    God?
Has he not made with me
  an everlasting covenant,

arranged and secured in
    every part?
Will he not bring to fruition
    my salvation
and grant me my every
    desire?   Ps 89:29; Isa 55:3
6But evil men are all to be cast
    aside like thorns,
which are not gathered
    with the hand.   Mt 13:40-41
7Whoever touches thorns
  uses a tool of iron or the
    shaft of a spear;
  they are burned up where
    they lie."   Mt 3:10; Heb 6:8

David's Mighty Men

8These are the names of David's mighty men:

Josheb-Basshebeth,[b] a Tah-
kemonite,[c] was chief of the
Three; he raised his spear
against eight hundred men,
whom he killed[d] in one encounter.   2Sa 17:10; 1Ch 27:2
9Next to him was Eleazar son
of Dodai the Ahohite. As one of
the three mighty men, he was
with David when they taunted
the Philistines gathered at Pas
Dammim,[e] for battle. Then the
men of Israel retreated, 10but he
stood his ground and struck
down the Philistines till his
hand grew tired and froze to the
sword. The LORD brought about
a great victory that day. The
troops returned to Eleazar, but
only to strip the dead.   1Ch 27:4

---

[a]1 Or Israel's beloved singer   [b]8 Hebrew; some Septuagint manuscripts suggest
Ish-Bosheth, that is, Esh-Baal (see also 1 Chron. 11:11 Jashobeam).   [c]8 Probably a
variant of Hacmonite (see 1 Chron. 11:11)   [d]8 Some Septuagint manuscripts (see also
1 Chron. 11:11); Hebrew and other Septuagint manuscripts Three; it was Adino the Eznite
who killed eight hundred men   [e]9 See 1 Chron. 11:13; Hebrew gathered there.

¹¹Next to him was Shammah son of Agee the Hararite. When the Philistines banded together at a place where there was a field full of lentils, Israel's troops fled from them. ¹²But Shammah took his stand in the middle of the field. He defended it and struck the Philistines down, and the LORD brought about a great victory.   1Ch 11:27

¹³During harvest time, three of the thirty chief men came down to David at the cave of Adullam, while a band of Philistines was encamped in the Valley of Rephaim. ¹⁴At that time David was in the stronghold, and the Philistine garrison was at Bethlehem. ¹⁵David longed for water and said, "Oh, that someone would get me a drink of water from the well near the gate of Bethlehem!" ¹⁶So the three mighty men broke through the Philistine lines, drew water from the well near the gate of Bethlehem and carried it back to David. But he refused to drink it; instead, he poured it out before the LORD. ¹⁷"Far be it from me, O LORD, to do this!" he said. "Is it not the blood of men who went at the risk of their lives?" And David would not drink it.   Ge 38:1

Such were the exploits of the three mighty men.

¹⁸Abishai the brother of Joab son of Zeruiah was chief of the Three.*a* He raised his spear against three hundred men, whom he killed, and so he became as famous as the Three. ¹⁹Was he not held in greater honor than the Three? He became their commander, even though he was not included among them.   1Sa 26:6; 1Ch 11:20

²⁰Benaiah son of Jehoiada was a valiant fighter from Kabzeel, who performed great exploits. He struck down two of Moab's best men. He also went down into a pit on a snowy day and killed a lion. ²¹And he struck down a huge Egyptian. Although the Egyptian had a spear in his hand, Benaiah went against him with a club. He snatched the spear from the Egyptian's hand and killed him with his own spear. ²²Such were the exploits of Benaiah son of Jehoiada; he too was as famous as the three mighty men. ²³He was held in greater honor than any of the Thirty, but he was not included among the Three. And David put him in charge of his bodyguard.   Jos 15:21; 2Sa 8:18

²⁴Among the Thirty were:
    Asahel the brother of Joab,
    Elhanan son of Dodo from Bethlehem,   2Sa 2:18
²⁵Shammah the Harodite,
    Elika the Harodite,   Jdg 7:1
²⁶Helez the Paltite,
    Ira son of Ikkesh from Tekoa,   1Ch 27:10

---

a18 Most Hebrew manuscripts (see also 1 Chron. 11:20); two Hebrew manuscripts and Syriac *Thirty*

²⁷Abiezer from Anathoth,
Mebunnai^a the Hushath-
ite,   1Ch 27:12
²⁸Zalmon the Ahohite,
Maharai the Netopha-
thite,   2Ki 25:23
²⁹Heled^b son of Baanah the
Netophathite,
Ithai son of Ribai from
Gibeah in Benjamin,
³⁰Benaiah the Pirathonite,
Hiddai^c from the ravines
of Gaash,   Jdg 12:13
³¹Abi-Albon the Arbathite,
Azmaveth the Barhumite,
³²Eliahba the Shaalbonite,
the sons of Jashen,
Jonathan ³³son of^d Sham-
mah the Hararite,
Ahiam son of Sharar^e the
Hararite,   Jos 19:42
³⁴Eliphelet son of Ahasbai
the Maacathite,
Eliam son of Ahithophel
the Gilonite,   Dt 3:14
³⁵Hezro the Carmelite,
Paarai the Arbite,   Jos 12:22
³⁶Igal son of Nathan from
Zobah,
the son of Hagri,^f   1Sa 14:47
³⁷Zelek the Ammonite,
Naharai the Beerothite,
the armor-bearer of Joab
son of Zeruiah,   Jos 9:17
³⁸Ira the Ithrite,
Gareb the Ithrite

³⁹and Uriah the Hittite.
There were thirty-seven in
all.

David Counts the Fighting Men

24 Again the anger of the
LORD burned against Is-
rael, and he incited David
against them, saying, "Go and
take a census of Israel and
Judah."   1Ch 27:23; Job 1:6

²So the king said to Joab and
the army commanders^g with
him, "Go throughout the tribes
of Israel from Dan to Beersheba
and enroll the fighting men, so
that I may know how many
there are."   Jdg 20:1; 2Sa 3:10

³But Joab replied to the king,
"May the LORD your God multi-
ply the troops a hundred times
over, and may the eyes of my
lord the king see it. But why
does my lord the king want to
do such a thing?"   Dt 1:11; 2Sa 2:18

⁴The king's word, however,
overruled Joab and the army
commanders; so they left the
presence of the king to enroll
the fighting men of Israel.

⁵After crossing the Jordan,
they camped near Aroer, south
of the town in the gorge, and
then went through Gad and on
to Jazer. ⁶They went to Gilead
and the region of Tahtim Hod-

---

^a27 Hebrew; some Septuagint manuscripts (see also 1 Chron. 11:29) *Sibbecai*
^b29 Some Hebrew manuscripts and Vulgate (see also 1 Chron. 11:30); most Hebrew
manuscripts *Heleb*   ^c30 Hebrew; some Septuagint manuscripts (see also
1 Chron. 11:32) *Hurai*   ^d33 Some Septuagint manuscripts (see also 1 Chron. 11:34);
Hebrew does not have *son of.*   ^e33 Hebrew; some Septuagint manuscripts (see also
1 Chron. 11:35) *Sacar*   ^f36 Some Septuagint manuscripts (see also 1 Chron. 11:38);
Hebrew *Haggadi*   ^g2 Septuagint (see also verse 4 and 1 Chron. 21:2); Hebrew *Joab
the army commander*

shi, and on to Dan Jaan and around toward Sidon. 7Then they went toward the fortress of Tyre and all the towns of the Hivites and Canaanites. Finally, they went on to Beersheba in the Negev of Judah.   Jos 13:9

8After they had gone through the entire land, they came back to Jerusalem at the end of nine months and twenty days.

9Joab reported the number of the fighting men to the king: In Israel there were eight hundred thousand able-bodied men who could handle a sword, and in Judah five hundred thousand.

10David was conscience-stricken after he had counted the fighting men, and he said to the LORD, "I have sinned greatly in what I have done. Now, O LORD, I beg you, take away the guilt of your servant. I have done a very foolish thing."

11Before David got up the next morning, the word of the LORD had come to Gad the prophet, David's seer: 12"Go and tell David, 'This is what the LORD says: I am giving you three options. Choose one of them for me to carry out against you.' "   1Sa 22:5; 1Ch 21:12

13So Gad went to David and said to him, "Shall there come upon you three*a* years of famine in your land? Or three months of fleeing from your enemies while they pursue you? Or three days of plague in your land? Now then, think it over

and decide how I should answer the one who sent me."

14David said to Gad, "I am in deep distress. Let us fall into the hands of the LORD, for his mercy is great; but do not let me fall into the hands of men."

15So the LORD sent a plague on Israel from that morning until the end of the time designated, and seventy thousand of the people from Dan to Beersheba died. 16When the angel stretched out his hand to destroy Jerusalem, the LORD was grieved because of the calamity and said to the angel who was afflicting the people, "Enough! Withdraw your hand." The angel of the LORD was then at the threshing floor of Araunah the Jebusite.   Ge 6:6; 1Ch 27:24

17When David saw the angel who was striking down the people, he said to the LORD, "I am the one who has sinned and done wrong. These are but sheep. What have they done? Let your hand fall upon me and my family."   Ps 74:1; Jer 49:20

David Builds an Altar

18On that day Gad went to David and said to him, "Go up and build an altar to the LORD on the threshing floor of Araunah the Jebusite." 19So David went up, as the LORD had commanded through Gad. 20When Araunah looked and saw the king and his men coming

---

a13 Septuagint (see also 1 Chron. 21:12); Hebrew *seven*

toward him, he went out and bowed down before the king with his face to the ground.

21Araunah said, "Why has my lord the king come to his servant?"

"To buy your threshing floor," David answered, "so I can build an altar to the LORD, that the plague on the people may be stopped." Nu 16:44-50

22Araunah said to David, "Let my lord the king take whatever pleases him and offer it up. Here are oxen for the burnt offering, and here are threshing sledges and ox yokes for the wood. 23O king, Araunah gives

all this to the king." Araunah also said to him, "May the LORD your God accept you." 1Sa 6:14

24But the king replied to Araunah, "No, I insist on paying you for it. I will not sacrifice to the LORD my God burnt offerings that cost me nothing."

So David bought the threshing floor and the oxen and paid fifty shekels*a* of silver for them. 25David built an altar to the LORD there and sacrificed burnt offerings and fellowship offerings. *b* Then the LORD answered prayer in behalf of the land, and the plague on Israel was stopped. 1Sa 7:17; 2Sa 21:14

---

a24 That is, about 1 1/4 pounds (about 0.6 kilogram)   *b25* Traditionally *peace offerings*

1 Kings

Introduction:

Beginning with Solomon's reign (about 971 B.C.) 1 Kings records the history of Israel through the divided kingdom to the death of Ahaziah, the son of Ahab. Chapters 3 through 11 describe Solomon's reign, including the building of the temple and the palace in Jerusalem.

Rehoboam, Solomon's son, took the throne after Solomon's death but lost the northern part of the kingdom to Jeroboam. After this the northern kingdom was known as Israel, and the southern kingdom was called Judah. The last chapters of 1 Kings tell about the evil King Ahab and God's prophet Elijah, who condemned Ahab's wickedness and Israel's disobedience.

Because the author of 1 and 2 Kings was interested in Israel's faithfulness to God and his covenant he wrote about each king showing how he/she was faithful or unfaithful to God. The author often used the phrase, "did what was right in the eyes of the LORD," or "did evil in the eyes of the LORD," to describe the goodness or wickedness of the king.

Like Judges the author records that when Israel was obedient God brought peace to the land, but when the people were disobedient and worshiped idols the land of Israel suffered wars and other disasters.

Outline of contents:

Adonijah Sets Himself Up as King

1 When King David was old and well advanced in years, he could not keep warm even when they put covers over him.

²So his servants said to him, "Let us look for a young virgin to attend the king and take care of him. She can lie beside him so that our lord the king may keep warm."

³Then they searched throughout Israel for a beautiful girl and found Abishag, a Shunammite, and brought her to the king. ⁴The girl was very beautiful; she took care of the king and waited on him, but the king had no intimate relations with her. _{Jos 19:18; 1Ki 2:17}

⁵Now Adonijah, whose mother was Haggith, put himself forward and said, "I will be king." So he got chariots and horses^a ready, with fifty men to run ahead of him. ⁶(His father had never interfered with him by asking, "Why do you behave as you do?" He was also very handsome and was born next after Absalom.) _{1Sa 8:11; 2Sa 3:4}

⁷Adonijah conferred with Joab son of Zeruiah and with Abiathar the priest, and they gave him their support. ⁸But Zadok the priest, Benaiah son of Jehoiada, Nathan the prophet, Shimei and Rei^b and David's special guard did not join Adonijah. _{1Ki 22:20; 2Sa 8:18}

⁹Adonijah then sacrificed sheep, cattle and fattened calves at the Stone of Zoheleth near En Rogel. He invited all his brothers, the king's sons, and all the men of Judah who were royal officials, ¹⁰but he did not invite Nathan the prophet or Benaiah or the special guard or his brother Solomon. _{2Sa 17:17}

¹¹Then Nathan asked Bathsheba, Solomon's mother, "Have you not heard that Adonijah, the son of Haggith, has become king without our lord David's knowing it? ¹²Now then, let me advise you how you can save your own life and the life of your son Solomon. ¹³Go in to King David and say to him, 'My lord the king, did you not swear to me your servant: "Surely Solomon your son shall be king after me, and he will sit on my throne"? Why then has Adonijah become king?' ¹⁴While you are still there talking to the king, I will come in and confirm what you have said." _{2Sa 3:4}

¹⁵So Bathsheba went to see the aged king in his room, where Abishag the Shunammite was attending him. ¹⁶Bathsheba bowed low and knelt before the king.

"What is it you want?" the king asked.

¹⁷She said to him, "My lord, you yourself swore to me your servant by the LORD your God: 'Solomon your son shall be king after me, and he will sit on my throne.' ¹⁸But now Adonijah has become king, and you, my lord the king, do not know about it. ¹⁹He has sacrificed great numbers of cattle, fattened calves, and sheep, and has invited all the king's sons, Abiathar the priest and Joab the commander of the army, but he has not invited Solomon your servant. ²⁰My lord the king, the eyes of all Israel are on you, to learn from you who will sit on

the throne of my lord the king after him. 21Otherwise, as soon as my lord the king is laid to rest with his fathers, I and my son Solomon will be treated as criminals." Dt 31:16; 1Ki 2:10

22While she was still speaking with the king, Nathan the prophet arrived. 23And they told the king, "Nathan the prophet is here." So he went before the king and bowed with his face to the ground.

24Nathan said, "Have you, my lord the king, declared that Adonijah shall be king after you, and that he will sit on your throne? 25Today he has gone down and sacrificed great numbers of cattle, fattened calves, and sheep. He has invited all the king's sons, the commanders of the army and Abiathar the priest. Right now they are eating and drinking with him and saying, 'Long live King Adonijah!' 26But me your servant, and Zadok the priest, and Benaiah son of Jehoiada, and your servant Solomon he did not invite. 27Is this something my lord the king has done without letting his servants know who should sit on the throne of my lord the king after him?" 1Sa 10:24

David Makes Solomon King

28Then King David said, "Call in Bathsheba." So she came into the king's presence and stood before him.

29The king then took an oath: "As surely as the LORD lives, who has delivered me out of every trouble, 30I will surely carry out today what I swore to you by the LORD, the God of Israel: Solomon your son shall be king after me, and he will sit on my throne in my place." 2Sa 4:9

31Then Bathsheba bowed low with her face to the ground and, kneeling before the king, said, "May my lord King David live forever!" Ne 2:3; Da 2:4

32King David said, "Call in Zadok the priest, Nathan the prophet and Benaiah son of Jehoiada." When they came before the king, 33he said to them: "Take your lord's servants with you and set Solomon my son on my own mule and take him down to Gihon. 34There have Zadok the priest and Nathan the prophet anoint him king over Israel. Blow the trumpet and shout, 'Long live King Solomon!' 35Then you are to go up with him, and he is to come and sit on my throne and reign in my place. I have appointed him ruler over Israel and Judah."

36Benaiah son of Jehoiada answered the king, "Amen! May the LORD, the God of my lord the king, so declare it. 37As the LORD was with my lord the king, so may he be with Solomon to make his throne even greater than the throne of my lord King David!" Jos 1:5

38So Zadok the priest, Nathan the prophet, Benaiah son of Jehoiada, the Kerethites and the Pelethites went down and put Solomon on King David's mule and escorted him to Gihon.

³⁹Zadok the priest took the horn of oil from the sacred tent and anointed Solomon. Then they sounded the trumpet and all the people shouted, "Long live King Solomon!" ⁴⁰And all the people went up after him, playing flutes and rejoicing greatly, so that the ground shook with the sound.   2Ki 11:12; Ps 89:20

⁴¹Adonijah and all the guests who were with him heard it as they were finishing their feast. On hearing the sound of the trumpet, Joab asked, "What's the meaning of all the noise in the city?"   2Ch 23:12-13

⁴²Even as he was speaking, Jonathan son of Abiathar the priest arrived. Adonijah said, "Come in. A worthy man like you must be bringing good news."   2Sa 15:27; 18:26

⁴³"Not at all!" Jonathan answered. "Our lord King David has made Solomon king. ⁴⁴The king has sent with him Zadok the priest, Nathan the prophet, Benaiah son of Jehoiada, the Kerethites and the Pelethites, and they have put him on the king's mule, ⁴⁵and Zadok the priest and Nathan the prophet have anointed him king at Gihon. From there they have gone up cheering, and the city resounds with it. That's the noise you hear. ⁴⁶Moreover, Solomon has taken his seat on the royal throne. ⁴⁷Also, the royal officials have come to congratulate our lord King David, saying, 'May your God make Solomon's name more famous than yours

and his throne greater than yours!' And the king bowed in worship on his bed ⁴⁸and said, 'Praise be to the LORD, the God of Israel, who has allowed my eyes to see a successor on my throne today.'"   Dt 17:18; 1Ki 3:6

⁴⁹At this, all Adonijah's guests rose in alarm and dispersed. ⁵⁰But Adonijah, in fear of Solomon, went and took hold of the horns of the altar. ⁵¹Then Solomon was told, "Adonijah is afraid of King Solomon and is clinging to the horns of the altar. He says, 'Let King Solomon swear to me today that he will not put his servant to death with the sword.'"   Ex 27:2

⁵²Solomon replied, "If he shows himself to be a worthy man, not a hair of his head will fall to the ground; but if evil is found in him, he will die." ⁵³Then King Solomon sent men, and they brought him down from the altar. And Adonijah came and bowed down to King Solomon, and Solomon said, "Go to your home."   1Sa 14:45

David's Charge to Solomon

2 When the time drew near for David to die, he gave a charge to Solomon his son.

²"I am about to go the way of all the earth," he said. "So be strong, show yourself a man, ³and observe what the LORD your God requires: Walk in his ways, and keep his decrees and commands, his laws and requirements, as written in the Law of Moses, so that you may

prosper in all you do and wherever you go, [4]and that the LORD may keep his promise to me: 'If your descendants watch how they live, and if they walk faithfully before me with all their heart and soul, you will never fail to have a man on the throne of Israel.'   Jos 23:14

[5]"Now you yourself know what Joab son of Zeruiah did to me—what he did to the two commanders of Israel's armies, Abner son of Ner and Amasa son of Jether. He killed them, shedding their blood in peacetime as if in battle, and with that blood stained the belt around his waist and the sandals on his feet. [6]Deal with him according to your wisdom, but do not let his gray head go down to the grave[a] in peace.   2Sa 3:27; Pr 20:26

[7]"But show kindness to the sons of Barzillai of Gilead and let them be among those who eat at your table. They stood by me when I fled from your brother Absalom.   Ge 40:14; 2Sa 19:31

[8]"And remember, you have with you Shimei son of Gera, the Benjamite from Bahurim, who called down bitter curses on me the day I went to Mahanaim. When he came down to meet me at the Jordan, I swore to him by the LORD: 'I will not put you to death by the sword.' [9]But now, do not consider him innocent. You are a man of wisdom; you will know what to do to him. Bring his gray head

down to the grave in blood."

[10]Then David rested with his fathers and was buried in the City of David. [11]He had reigned forty years over Israel—seven years in Hebron and thirty-three in Jerusalem. [12]So Solomon sat on the throne of his father David, and his rule was firmly established.   2Ch 1:1; Ac 2:39

Solomon's Throne Established

[13]Now Adonijah, the son of Haggith, went to Bathsheba, Solomon's mother. Bathsheba asked him, "Do you come peacefully?"   1Sa 16:4; 2Sa 3:4

He answered, "Yes, peacefully." [14]Then he added, "I have something to say to you."

"You may say it," she replied.

[15]"As you know," he said, "the kingdom was mine. All Israel looked to me as their king. But things changed, and the kingdom has gone to my brother; for it has come to him from the LORD. [16]Now I have one request to make of you. Do not refuse me."   1Ki 1:5; 1Ch 22:9

"You may make it," she said.

[17]So he continued, "Please ask King Solomon—he will not refuse you—to give me Abishag the Shunammite as my wife."

[18]"Very well," Bathsheba replied, "I will speak to the king for you."

[19]When Bathsheba went to King Solomon to speak to him

[a]6 Hebrew *Sheol*; also in verse 9

for Adonijah, the king stood up to meet her, bowed down to her and sat down on his throne. He had a throne brought for the king's mother, and she sat down at his right hand.   Ps 45:9

²⁰"I have one small request to make of you," she said. "Do not refuse me."

The king replied, "Make it, my mother; I will not refuse you."

²¹So she said, "Let Abishag the Shunammite be given in marriage to your brother Adonijah."   1Ki 1:3

²²King Solomon answered his mother, "Why do you request Abishag the Shunammite for Adonijah? You might as well request the kingdom for him—after all, he is my older brother—yes, for him and for Abiathar the priest and Joab son of Zeruiah!"   2Sa 12:8; 1Ch 3:2

²³Then King Solomon swore by the LORD: "May God deal with me, be it ever so severely, if Adonijah does not pay with his life for this request! ²⁴And now, as surely as the LORD lives—he who has established me securely on the throne of my father David and has founded a dynasty for me as he promised—Adonijah shall be put to death today!" ²⁵So King Solomon gave orders to Benaiah son of Jehoiada, and he struck down Adonijah and he died.   Ru 1:17

²⁶To Abiathar the priest the king said, "Go back to your fields in Anathoth. You deserve to die, but I will not put you to death now, because you carried the ark of the Sovereign LORD before my father David and shared all my father's hardships." ²⁷So Solomon removed Abiathar from the priesthood of the LORD, fulfilling the word the LORD had spoken at Shiloh about the house of Eli.   Jos 21:18

²⁸When the news reached Joab, who had conspired with Adonijah though not with Absalom, he fled to the tent of the LORD and took hold of the horns of the altar. ²⁹King Solomon was told that Joab had fled to the tent of the LORD and was beside the altar. Then Solomon ordered Benaiah son of Jehoiada, "Go, strike him down!"   Ex 27:2

³⁰So Benaiah entered the tent of the LORD and said to Joab, "The king says, 'Come out!' "

But he answered, "No, I will die here."

Benaiah reported to the king, "This is how Joab answered me."

³¹Then the king commanded Benaiah, "Do as he says. Strike him down and bury him, and so clear me and my father's house of the guilt of the innocent blood that Joab shed. ³²The LORD will repay him for the blood he shed, because without the knowledge of my father David he attacked two men and killed them with the sword. Both of them—Abner son of Ner, commander of Israel's army, and Amasa son of Jether, commander of Judah's army—were better men and

more upright than he. ³³May the guilt of their blood rest on the head of Joab and his descendants forever. But on David and his descendants, his house and his throne, may there be the LORD's peace forever." Dt 19:13

³⁴So Benaiah son of Jehoiada went up and struck down Joab and killed him, and he was buried on his own land*a* in the desert. ³⁵The king put Benaiah son of Jehoiada over the army in Joab's position and replaced Abiathar with Zadok the priest.

³⁶Then the king sent for Shimei and said to him, "Build yourself a house in Jerusalem and live there, but do not go anywhere else. ³⁷The day you leave and cross the Kidron Valley, you can be sure you will die; your blood will be on your own head." Lev 20:9; 2Sa 16:5

³⁸Shimei answered the king, "What you say is good. Your servant will do as my lord the king has said." And Shimei stayed in Jerusalem for a long time.

³⁹But three years later, two of Shimei's slaves ran off to Achish son of Maacah, king of Gath, and Shimei was told, "Your slaves are in Gath." ⁴⁰At this, he saddled his donkey and went to Achish at Gath in search of his slaves. So Shimei went away and brought the slaves back from Gath. 1Sa 27:2; 2Sa 19:16-23

⁴¹When Solomon was told that Shimei had gone from

Jerusalem to Gath and had returned, ⁴²the king summoned Shimei and said to him, "Did I not make you swear by the LORD and warn you, 'On the day you leave to go anywhere else, you can be sure you will die'? At that time you said to me, 'What you say is good. I will obey.' ⁴³Why then did you not keep your oath to the LORD and obey the command I gave you?" 2Sa 19:23; Eze 17:19

⁴⁴The king also said to Shimei, "You know in your heart all the wrong you did to my father David. Now the LORD will repay you for your wrongdoing. ⁴⁵But King Solomon will be blessed, and David's throne will remain secure before the LORD forever." 1Sa 25:39; 2Sa 16:5-13

⁴⁶Then the king gave the order to Benaiah son of Jehoiada, and he went out and struck Shimei down and killed him.

The kingdom was now firmly established in Solomon's hands. 2Ch 1:1

Solomon Asks for Wisdom

3 Solomon made an alliance with Pharaoh king of Egypt and married his daughter. He brought her to the City of David until he finished building his palace and the temple of the LORD, and the wall around Jerusalem. ²The people, however, were still sacrificing at the high places, because a temple had not yet been built for the

---

a34 Or buried in his tomb

Name of the LORD. ³Solomon showed his love for the LORD by walking according to the statutes of his father David, except that he offered sacrifices and burned incense on the high places.   Dt 6:5; 1Ki 7:8

⁴The king went to Gibeon to offer sacrifices, for that was the most important high place, and Solomon offered a thousand burnt offerings on that altar. ⁵At Gibeon the LORD appeared to Solomon during the night in a dream, and God said, "Ask for whatever you want me to give you."   1Ki 9:2; 2Ch 1:3

⁶Solomon answered, "You have shown great kindness to your servant, my father David, because he was faithful to you and righteous and upright in heart. You have continued this great kindness to him and have given him a son to sit on his throne this very day.   1Ki 1:48

⁷"Now, O LORD my God, you have made your servant king in place of my father David. But I am only a little child and do not know how to carry out my duties. ⁸Your servant is here among the people you have chosen, a great people, too numerous to count or number. ⁹So give your servant a discerning heart to govern your people and to distinguish between right and wrong. For who is able to govern this great people of yours?"   Nu 27:17; Jas 1:5

¹⁰The Lord was pleased that Solomon had asked for this. ¹¹So God said to him, "Since you have asked for this and not for long life or wealth for yourself, nor have asked for the death of your enemies but for discernment in administering justice, ¹²I will do what you have asked. I will give you a wise and discerning heart, so that there will never have been anyone like you, nor will there ever be. ¹³Moreover, I will give you what you have not asked for—both riches and honor—so that in your lifetime you will have no equal among kings. ¹⁴And if you walk in my ways and obey my statutes and commands as David your father did, I will give you a long life." ¹⁵Then Solomon awoke—and he realized it had been a dream.

He returned to Jerusalem, stood before the ark of the Lord's covenant and sacrificed burnt offerings and fellowship offerings. *a* Then he gave a feast for all his court.   Est 1:3; Da 5:1

A Wise Ruling

¹⁶Now two prostitutes came to the king and stood before him. ¹⁷One of them said, "My lord, this woman and I live in the same house. I had a baby while she was there with me. ¹⁸The third day after my child was born, this woman also had a baby. We were alone; there was no one in the house but the two of us.   Nu 27:2

a15 Traditionally *peace offerings*

¹⁹"During the night this woman's son died because she lay on him. ²⁰So she got up in the middle of the night and took my son from my side while I your servant was asleep. She put him by her breast and put her dead son by my breast. ²¹The next morning, I got up to nurse my son—and he was dead! But when I looked at him closely in the morning light, I saw that it wasn't the son I had borne." Ru 4:16

²²The other woman said, "No! The living one is my son; the dead one is yours."

But the first one insisted, "No! The dead one is yours; the living one is mine." And so they argued before the king.

²³The king said, "This one says, 'My son is alive and your son is dead,' while that one says, 'No! Your son is dead and mine is alive.' "

²⁴Then the king said, "Bring me a sword." So they brought a sword for the king. ²⁵He then gave an order: "Cut the living child in two and give half to one and half to the other."

²⁶The woman whose son was alive was filled with compassion for her son and said to the king, "Please, my lord, give her the living baby! Don't kill him!"

But the other said, "Neither I nor you shall have him. Cut him in two!"

²⁷Then the king gave his ruling: "Give the living baby to the first woman. Do not kill him; she is his mother."

²⁸When all Israel heard the verdict the king had given, they held the king in awe, because they saw that he had wisdom from God to administer justice.

Solomon's Officials and Governors

4 So King Solomon ruled over all Israel. ²And these were his chief officials:

Azariah son of Zadok—the priest; 1Ch 6:10; 2Ch 26:17
³Elihoreph and Ahijah, sons of Shisha—secretaries;
Jehoshaphat son of Ahilud—recorder; 2Sa 8:16-17
⁴Benaiah son of Jehoiada—commander in chief;
Zadok and Abiathar—priests; 2Sa 8:18
⁵Azariah son of Nathan—in charge of the district officers;
Zabud son of Nathan—a priest and personal adviser to the king; 1Ch 27:33
⁶Ahishar—in charge of the palace;
Adoniram son of Abda—in charge of forced labor.

⁷Solomon also had twelve district governors over all Israel, who supplied provisions for the king and the royal household. Each one had to provide supplies for one month in the year. ⁸These are their names:

Ben-Hur—in the hill country of Ephraim; Jos 24:33
⁹Ben-Deker—in Makaz, Sha-

albim, Beth Shemesh and Elon Bethhanan; _{Jdg 1:35}

10Ben-Hesed—in Arubboth (Socoh and all the land of Hepher were his); _{Jos 15:35}

11Ben-Abinadab—in Naphoth Dor*ᵃ* (he was married to Taphath daughter of Solomon); _{Jos 11:2}

12Baana son of Ahilud—in Taanach and Megiddo, and in all of Beth Shan next to Zarethan below Jezreel, from Beth Shan to Abel Meholah across to Jokmeam; _{Jos 17:11}

13Ben-Geber—in Ramoth Gilead (the settlements of Jair son of Manasseh in Gilead were his, as well as the district of Argob in Bashan and its sixty large walled cities with bronze gate bars); _{Nu 32:41}

14Ahinadab son of Iddo—in Mahanaim; _{Jos 13:26}

15Ahimaaz—in Naphtali (he had married Basemath daughter of Solomon);

16Baana son of Hushai—in Asher and in Aloth;

17Jehoshaphat son of Paruah—in Issachar;

18Shimei son of Ela—in Benjamin; _{1Ki 1:8}

19Geber son of Uri—in Gilead (the country of Sihon king of the Amorites and the country of Og king of Bashan). He was the only governor over the district. _{Dt 3:8-10; Jos 12:2}

Solomon's Daily Provisions

20The people of Judah and Israel were as numerous as the sand on the seashore; they ate, they drank and they were happy. 21And Solomon ruled over all the kingdoms from the River*ᵇ* to the land of the Philistines, as far as the border of Egypt. These countries brought tribute and were Solomon's subjects all his life. _{Ge 32:12; 2Ch 9:26}

22Solomon's daily provisions were thirty cors*ᶜ* of fine flour and sixty cors*ᵈ* of meal, 23ten head of stall-fed cattle, twenty of pasture-fed cattle and a hundred sheep and goats, as well as deer, gazelles, roebucks and choice fowl. 24For he ruled over all the kingdoms west of the River, from Tiphsah to Gaza, and had peace on all sides. 25During Solomon's lifetime Judah and Israel, from Dan to Beersheba, lived in safety, each man under his own vine and fig tree. _{1Ki 10:5; Jer 23:6}

26Solomon had four*ᵉ* thousand stalls for chariot horses, and twelve thousand horses.*ᶠ*

27The district officers, each in his month, supplied provisions for King Solomon and all who came to the king's table. They saw to it that nothing was lacking. 28They also brought to the

---

ᵃ11 Or *in the heights of Dor*   *ᵇ21* That is, the Euphrates; also in verse 24   *ᶜ22* That is, probably about 185 bushels (about 6.6 kiloliters)   *ᵈ22* That is, probably about 375 bushels (about 13.2 kiloliters)   *ᵉ26* Some Septuagint manuscripts (see also 2 Chron. 9:25); Hebrew *forty*   *ᶠ26* Or *charioteers*

proper place their quotas of barley and straw for the chariot horses and the other horses.

Solomon's Wisdom

29God gave Solomon wisdom and very great insight, and a breadth of understanding as measureless as the sand on the seashore. 30Solomon's wisdom was greater than the wisdom of all the men of the East, and greater than all the wisdom of Egypt. 31He was wiser than any other man, including Ethan the Ezrahite—wiser than Heman, Calcol and Darda, the sons of Mahol. And his fame spread to all the surrounding nations. 32He spoke three thousand proverbs and his songs numbered a thousand and five. 33He described plant life, from the cedar of Lebanon to the hyssop that grows out of walls. He also taught about animals and birds, reptiles and fish. 34Men of all nations came to listen to Solomon's wisdom, sent by all the kings of the world, who had heard of his wisdom.　　1Ki 3:12

Preparations for Building the Temple

5 When Hiram king of Tyre heard that Solomon had been anointed king to succeed his father David, he sent his envoys to Solomon, because he had always been on friendly terms with David. 2Solomon sent back this message to Hiram:　　2Sa 5:11; 1Ch 14:1

3"You know that because of the wars waged against my father David from all sides, he could not build a temple for the Name of the LORD his God until the LORD put his enemies under his feet. 4But now the LORD my God has given me rest on every side, and there is no adversary or disaster. 5I intend, therefore, to build a temple for the Name of the LORD my God, as the LORD told my father David, when he said, 'Your son whom I will put on the throne in your place will build the temple for my Name.'　　2Sa 7:13; 1Ch 22:8

6"So give orders that cedars of Lebanon be cut for me. My men will work with yours, and I will pay you for your men whatever wages you set. You know that we have no one so skilled in felling timber as the Sidonians."　　1Ch 14:1; 22:4

7When Hiram heard Solomon's message, he was greatly pleased and said, "Praise be to the LORD today, for he has given David a wise son to rule over this great nation."　　1Ki 10:9

8So Hiram sent word to Solomon:

"I have received the message you sent me and will do all you want in providing the cedar and pine logs. 9My men will haul them down from Lebanon

to the sea, and I will float them in rafts by sea to the place you specify. There I will separate them and you can take them away. And you are to grant my wish by providing food for my royal household." Ezr 3:7; Ac 12:20

[10]In this way Hiram kept Solomon supplied with all the cedar and pine logs he wanted, [11]and Solomon gave Hiram twenty thousand cors[a] of wheat as food for his household, in addition to twenty thousand baths[b,c] of pressed olive oil. Solomon continued to do this for Hiram year after year. [12]The LORD gave Solomon wisdom, just as he had promised him. There were peaceful relations between Hiram and Solomon, and the two of them made a treaty. 1Ki 3:12; 2Ch 2:10

[13]King Solomon conscripted laborers from all Israel—thirty thousand men. [14]He sent them off to Lebanon in shifts of ten thousand a month, so that they spent one month in Lebanon and two months at home. Adoniram was in charge of the forced labor. [15]Solomon had seventy thousand carriers and eighty thousand stonecutters in the hills, [16]as well as thirty-three hundred[d] foremen who super-

vised the project and directed the workmen. [17]At the king's command they removed from the quarry large blocks of quality stone to provide a foundation of dressed stone for the temple. [18]The craftsmen of Solomon and Hiram and the men of Gebal[e] cut and prepared the timber and stone for the building of the temple. 1Ki 9:15

Solomon Builds the Temple

6 In the four hundred and eightieth[f] year after the Israelites had come out of Egypt, in the fourth year of Solomon's reign over Israel, in the month of Ziv, the second month, he began to build the temple of the LORD. 2Ch 3:1-2; Ac 7:47

[2]The temple that King Solomon built for the LORD was sixty cubits long, twenty wide and thirty high.[g] [3]The portico at the front of the main hall of the temple extended the width of the temple, that is twenty cubits,[h] and projected ten cubits[i] from the front of the temple. [4]He made narrow clerestory windows in the temple. [5]Against the walls of the main hall and inner sanctuary he built a structure around the building, in which there were side rooms. [6]The lowest floor was five cu-

---

*a11 That is, probably about 125,000 bushels (about 4,400 kiloliters) (see also 2 Chron. 2:10); Hebrew *twenty cors*   *b11 Septuagint   *c11 That is, about 115,000 gallons (about 440 kiloliters)   *d16 Hebrew; some Septuagint manuscripts (see also 2 Chron. 2:2, 18) *thirty-six hundred*   *e18 That is, Byblos   *f1 Hebrew; Septuagint *four hundred and fortieth*   *g2 That is, about 90 feet (about 27 meters) long and 30 feet (about 9 meters) wide and 45 feet (about 13.5 meters) high   *h3 That is, about 30 feet (about 9 meters)   *i3 That is, about 15 feet (about 4.5 meters)

bits*a* wide, the middle floor six cubits*b* and the third floor seven.*c* He made offset ledges around the outside of the temple so that nothing would be inserted into the temple walls.

⁷In building the temple, only blocks dressed at the quarry were used, and no hammer, chisel or any other iron tool was heard at the temple site while it was being built.   Dt 27:5

⁸The entrance to the lowest*d* floor was on the south side of the temple; a stairway led up to the middle level and from there to the third. ⁹So he built the temple and completed it, roofing it with beams and cedar planks. ¹⁰And he built the side rooms all along the temple. The height of each was five cubits, and they were attached to the temple by beams of cedar. ss 1:17

¹¹The word of the LORD came to Solomon: ¹²"As for this temple you are building, if you follow my decrees, carry out my regulations and keep all my commands and obey them, I will fulfill through you the promise I gave to David your father. ¹³And I will live among the Israelites and will not abandon my people Israel."   1Ki 12:22

¹⁴So Solomon built the temple and completed it. ¹⁵He lined its interior walls with cedar boards, paneling them from the floor of the temple to the ceiling, and covered the floor of the temple with planks of pine. ¹⁶He partitioned off twenty cubits*e* at the rear of the temple with cedar boards from floor to ceiling to form within the temple an inner sanctuary, the Most Holy Place. ¹⁷The main hall in front of this room was forty cubits*f* long. ¹⁸The inside of the temple was cedar, carved with gourds and open flowers. Everything was cedar; no stone was to be seen.   Ps 74:6; Ac 7:47

¹⁹He prepared the inner sanctuary within the temple to set the ark of the covenant of the LORD there. ²⁰The inner sanctuary was twenty cubits long, twenty wide and twenty high.*g* He overlaid the inside with pure gold, and he also overlaid the altar of cedar. ²¹Solomon covered the inside of the temple with pure gold, and he extended gold chains across the front of the inner sanctuary, which was overlaid with gold. ²²So he overlaid the whole interior with gold. He also overlaid with gold the altar that belonged to the inner sanctuary.

²³In the inner sanctuary he made a pair of cherubim of olive wood, each ten cubits*h* high. ²⁴One wing of the first cherub was five cubits long, and the other wing five cubits—ten cu-

---

a6 That is, about 7 1/2 feet (about 2.3 meters); also in verses 10 and 24   *b6* That is, about 9 feet (about 2.7 meters)   *c6* That is, about 10 1/2 feet (about 3.1 meters)   *d8* Septuagint; Hebrew *middle*   *e16* That is, about 30 feet (about 9 meters)   *f17* That is, about 60 feet (about 18 meters) long, wide and high   *g20* That is, about 30 feet (about 9 meters) long, wide and high   *h23* That is, about 15 feet (about 4.5 meters)

bits from wing tip to wing tip. 25The second cherub also measured ten cubits, for the two cherubim were identical in size and shape. 26The height of each cherub was ten cubits. 27He placed the cherubim inside the innermost room of the temple, with their wings spread out. The wing of one cherub touched one wall, while the wing of the other touched the other wall, and their wings touched each other in the middle of the room. 28He overlaid the cherubim with gold.   2Ch 3:10-12; Eze 9:3

29On the walls all around the temple, in both the inner and outer rooms, he carved cherubim, palm trees and open flowers. 30He also covered the floors of both the inner and outer rooms of the temple with gold.   Ex 36:8; Eze 41:18

31For the entrance of the inner sanctuary he made doors of olive wood with five-sided jambs. 32And on the two olive wood doors he carved cherubim, palm trees and open flowers, and overlaid the cherubim and palm trees with beaten gold. 33In the same way he made four-sided jambs of olive wood for the entrance to the main hall. 34He also made two pine doors, each having two leaves that turned in sockets. 35He carved cherubim, palm trees and open flowers on them

and overlaid them with gold hammered evenly over the carvings.   Eze 41:23-25

36And he built the inner courtyard of three courses of dressed stone and one course of trimmed cedar beams.   1Ki 7:12

37The foundation of the temple of the LORD was laid in the fourth year, in the month of Ziv. 38In the eleventh year in the month of Bul, the eighth month, the temple was finished in all its details according to its specifications. He had spent seven years building it.   1Ch 28:19

Solomon Builds His Palace

7 It took Solomon thirteen years, however, to complete the construction of his palace. 2He built the Palace of the Forest of Lebanon a hundred cubits long, fifty wide and thirty high,*a* with four rows of cedar columns supporting trimmed cedar beams. 3It was roofed with cedar above the beams that rested on the columns—forty-five beams, fifteen to a row. 4Its windows were placed high in sets of three, facing each other. 5All the doorways had rectangular frames; they were in the front part in sets of three, facing each other.*b* 6He made a colonnade fifty cubits long and thirty wide.*c* In front of it was a portico, and in

a2 That is, about 150 feet (about 46 meters) long, 75 feet (about 23 meters) wide and 45 feet (about 13.5 meters) high   *b5* The meaning of the Hebrew for this verse is uncertain.   *c6* That is, about 75 feet (about 23 meters) long and 45 feet (about 13.5 meters) wide

front of that were pillars and an overhanging roof.

⁷He built the throne hall, the Hall of Justice, where he was to judge, and he covered it with cedar from floor to ceiling. *a* ⁸And the palace in which he was to live, set farther back, was similar in design. Solomon also made a palace like this hall for Pharaoh's daughter, whom he had married.   1Ki 6:15; 2Ch 8:11

⁹All these structures, from the outside to the great courtyard and from foundation to eaves, were made of blocks of high-grade stone cut to size and trimmed with a saw on their inner and outer faces. ¹⁰The foundations were laid with large stones of good quality, some measuring ten cubits *b* and some eight. *c* ¹¹Above were high-grade stones, cut to size, and cedar beams. ¹²The great courtyard was surrounded by a wall of three courses of dressed stone and one course of trimmed cedar beams, as was the inner courtyard of the temple of the LORD with its portico.

The Temple's Furnishings

¹³King Solomon sent to Tyre and brought Huram, *d* ¹⁴whose mother was a widow from the tribe of Naphtali and whose father was a man of Tyre and a craftsman in bronze. Huram was highly skilled and experienced in all kinds of bronze work. He came to King Solomon and did all the work assigned to him.   2Ch 2:13; 4:11

¹⁵He cast two bronze pillars, each eighteen cubits high and twelve cubits around, *e* by line. ¹⁶He also made two capitals of cast bronze to set on the tops of the pillars; each capital was five cubits *f* high. ¹⁷A network of interwoven chains festooned the capitals on top of the pillars, seven for each capital. ¹⁸He made pomegranates in two rows *g* encircling each network to decorate the capitals on top of the pillars. *h* He did the same for each capital. ¹⁹The capitals on top of the pillars in the portico were in the shape of lilies, four cubits *i* high. ²⁰On the capitals of both pillars, above the bowl-shaped part next to the network, were the two hundred pomegranates in rows all around. ²¹He erected the pillars at the portico of the temple. The pillar to the south he named Jakin *j* and the one to the north Boaz. *k* ²²The capitals on top were in the shape of lilies. And

---

a7 Vulgate and Syriac; Hebrew *floor*   *b10* That is, about 15 feet (about 4.5 meters)
c10 That is, about 12 feet (about 3.6 meters)   *d13* Hebrew *Hiram,* a variant of *Huram;*
also in verses 40 and 45   *e15* That is, about 27 feet (about 8.1 meters) high and 18 feet
(about 5.4 meters) around   *f16* That is, about 7 1/2 feet (about 2.3 meters); also in
verse 23   *g18* Two Hebrew manuscripts and Septuagint; most Hebrew manuscripts
made the pillars, and there were two rows   *h18* Many Hebrew manuscripts and Syriac;
most Hebrew manuscripts *pomegranates*   *i19* That is, about 6 feet (about 1.8 meters);
also in verse 38   *j21* *Jakin* probably means *he establishes.*   *k21* *Boaz* probably means
in him is strength.

so the work on the pillars was completed.   2Ki 25:17; 2Ch 3:15

23He made the Sea of cast metal, circular in shape, measuring ten cubits[a] from rim to rim and five cubits high. It took a line of thirty cubits[b] to measure around it. 24Below the rim, gourds encircled it—ten to a cubit. The gourds were cast in two rows in one piece with the Sea.

25The Sea stood on twelve bulls, three facing north, three facing west, three facing south and three facing east. The Sea rested on top of them, and their hindquarters were toward the center. 26It was a handbreadth[c] in thickness, and its rim was like the rim of a cup, like a lily blossom. It held two thousand baths.[d]   2Ch 4:4; Jer 52:20

27He also made ten movable stands of bronze; each was four cubits long, four wide and three high.[e] 28This is how the stands were made: They had side panels attached to uprights. 29On the panels between the uprights were lions, bulls and cherubim—and on the uprights as well. Above and below the lions and bulls were wreaths of hammered work. 30Each stand had four bronze wheels with bronze axles, and each had a basin resting on four supports, cast with wreaths on each side. 31On the

inside of the stand there was an opening that had a circular frame one cubit[f] deep. This opening was round, and with its basework it measured a cubit and a half.[g] Around its opening there was engraving. The panels of the stands were square, not round. 32The four wheels were under the panels, and the axles of the wheels were attached to the stand. The diameter of each wheel was a cubit and a half. 33The wheels were made like chariot wheels; the axles, rims, spokes and hubs were all of cast metal.   2Ki 16:17

34Each stand had four handles, one on each corner, projecting from the stand. 35At the top of the stand there was a circular band half a cubit[h] deep. The supports and panels were attached to the top of the stand. 36He engraved cherubim, lions and palm trees on the surfaces of the supports and on the panels, in every available space, with wreaths all around. 37This is the way he made the ten stands. They were all cast in the same molds and were identical in size and shape.   2Ch 4:14

38He then made ten bronze basins, each holding forty baths[i] and measuring four cubits across, one basin to go on each of the ten stands. 39He

---

a23 That is, about 15 feet (about 4.5 meters)   b23 That is, about 45 feet (about 13.5 meters)   c26 That is, about 3 inches (about 8 centimeters)   d26 That is, probably about 11,500 gallons (about 44 kiloliters); the Septuagint does not have this sentence. e27 That is, about 6 feet (about 1.8 meters) long and wide and about 4 1/2 feet (about 1.3 meters) high   f31 That is, about 1 1/2 feet (about 0.5 meter)   g31 That is, about 2 1/4 feet (about 0.7 meter); also in verse 32   h35 That is, about 3/4 foot (about 0.2 meter)   i38 That is, about 230 gallons (about 880 liters)

placed five of the stands on the south side of the temple and five on the north. He placed the Sea on the south side, at the southeast corner of the temple. 40He also made the basins and shovels and sprinkling bowls.

So Huram finished all the work he had undertaken for King Solomon in the temple of the LORD:

41the two pillars;

the two bowl-shaped capitals on top of the pillars;

the two sets of network decorating the two bowl-shaped capitals on top of the pillars;

42the four hundred pomegranates for the two sets of network (two rows of pomegranates for each network, decorating the bowl-shaped capitals on top of the pillars);

43the ten stands with their ten basins;

44the Sea and the twelve bulls under it;

45the pots, shovels and sprinkling bowls.   2Ch 4:16

All these objects that Huram made for King Solomon for the temple of the LORD were of burnished bronze. 46The king had them cast in clay molds in the plain of the Jordan between Succoth and Zarethan. 47Solomon left all these things unweighed, because there were so many; the weight of the bronze was not determined.   Jos 13:27

48Solomon also made all the furnishings that were in the LORD's temple:

the golden altar;

the golden table on which was the bread of the Presence;

49the lampstands of pure gold (five on the right and five on the left, in front of the inner sanctuary);

the gold floral work and lamps and tongs;

50the pure gold basins, wick trimmers, sprinkling bowls, dishes and censers;

and the gold sockets for the doors of the innermost room, the Most Holy Place, and also for the doors of the main hall of the temple.   Ex 39:32-33

51When all the work King Solomon had done for the temple of the LORD was finished, he brought in the things his father David had dedicated—the silver and gold and the furnishings—and he placed them in the treasuries of the LORD's temple.   2Sa 8:11; Jer 27:19

The Ark Brought to the Temple

8 Then King Solomon summoned into his presence at Jerusalem the elders of Israel, all the heads of the tribes and the chiefs of the Israelite families, to bring up the ark of the LORD's covenant from Zion, the City of David. 2All the men of Israel

came together to King Solomon at the time of the festival in the month of Ethanim, the seventh month. Lev 23:34; 2Ch 7:8

3When all the elders of Israel had arrived, the priests took up the ark, 4and they brought up the ark of the LORD and the Tent of Meeting and all the sacred furnishings in it. The priests and Levites carried them up, 5and King Solomon and the entire assembly of Israel that had gathered about him were before the ark, sacrificing so many sheep and cattle that they could not be recorded or counted.

6The priests then brought the ark of the LORD's covenant to its place in the inner sanctuary of the temple, the Most Holy Place, and put it beneath the wings of the cherubim. 7The cherubim spread their wings over the place of the ark and overshadowed the ark and its carrying poles. 8These poles were so long that their ends could be seen from the Holy Place in front of the inner sanctuary, but not from outside the Holy Place; and they are still there today. 9There was nothing in the ark except the two stone tablets that Moses had placed in it at Horeb, where the LORD made a covenant with the Israelites after they came out of Egypt. 2Sa 6:17; Heb 9:4

10When the priests withdrew from the Holy Place, the cloud filled the temple of the LORD. 11And the priests could not perform their service because of the cloud, for the glory of the LORD filled his temple. 2Ch 7:2

12Then Solomon said, "The LORD has said that he would dwell in a dark cloud; 13I have indeed built a magnificent temple for you, a place for you to dwell forever." 2Sa 22:10; Ps 132:14

14While the whole assembly of Israel was standing there, the king turned around and blessed them. 15Then he said: 2Sa 6:18

"Praise be to the LORD, the God of Israel, who with his own hand has fulfilled what he promised with his own mouth to my father David. For he said, 16'Since the day I brought my people Israel out of Egypt, I have not chosen a city in any tribe of Israel to have a temple built for my Name to be there, but I have chosen David to rule my people Israel.' Dt 12:5; Lk 1:68

17"My father David had it in his heart to build a temple for the Name of the LORD, the God of Israel. 18But the LORD said to my father David, 'Because it was in your heart to build a temple for my Name, you did well to have this in your heart. 19Nevertheless, you are not the one to build the temple, but your son, who is your own flesh and blood—he is the one who will build the temple for my Name.' 2Sa 7:5; 1Ch 22:7

20"The LORD has kept the

promise he made: I have succeeded David my father and now I sit on the throne of Israel, just as the LORD promised, and I have built the temple for the Name of the LORD, the God of Israel. 21I have provided a place there for the ark, in which is the covenant of the LORD that he made with our fathers when he brought them out of Egypt." 1Ch 28:6

Solomon's Prayer of Dedication

22Then Solomon stood before the altar of the LORD in front of the whole assembly of Israel, spread out his hands toward heaven 23and said:

"O LORD, God of Israel, there is no God like you in heaven above or on earth below—you who keep your covenant of love with your servants who continue wholeheartedly in your way. 24You have kept your promise to your servant David my father; with your mouth you have promised and with your hand you have fulfilled it—as it is today. Dt 7:9; Ne 1:5

25"Now LORD, God of Israel, keep for your servant David my father the promises you made to him when you said, 'You shall never fail to have a man to sit before me on the throne of Israel, if only your sons are careful in all they do to walk before me as you have done.' 26And now, O God of Israel, let your word that you promised your servant David my father come true.

27"But will God really dwell on earth? The heavens, even the highest heaven, cannot contain you. How much less this temple I have built! 28Yet give attention to your servant's prayer and his plea for mercy, O LORD my God. Hear the cry and the prayer that your servant is praying in your presence this day. 29May your eyes be open toward this temple night and day, this place of which you said, 'My Name shall be there,' so that you will hear the prayer your servant prays toward this place. 30Hear the supplication of your servant and of your people Israel when they pray toward this place. Hear from heaven, your dwelling place, and when you hear, forgive. 2Ch 2:6

31"When a man wrongs his neighbor and is required to take an oath and he comes and swears the oath before your altar in this temple, 32then hear from heaven and act. Judge between your servants, condemning the guilty and bringing down on his own head what he has done. Declare the innocent not

guilty, and so establish his innocence. Ex 22:11; Dt 25:1

33"When your people Israel have been defeated by an enemy because they have sinned against you, and when they turn back to you and confess your name, praying and making supplication to you in this temple, 34then hear from heaven and forgive the sin of your people Israel and bring them back to the land you gave to their fathers.

35"When the heavens are shut up and there is no rain because your people have sinned against you, and when they pray toward this place and confess your name and turn from their sin because you have afflicted them, 36then hear from heaven and forgive the sin of your servants, your people Israel. Teach them the right way to live, and send rain on the land you gave your people for an inheritance. Dt 28:24

37"When famine or plague comes to the land, or blight or mildew, locusts or grasshoppers, or when an enemy besieges them in any of their cities, whatever disaster or disease may come, 38and when a prayer or plea is made by any of your people Israel—each one aware of the afflictions of his own heart, and spreading out his hands

toward this temple— 39then hear from heaven, your dwelling place. Forgive and act; deal with each man according to all he does, since you know his heart (for you alone know the hearts of all men), 40so that they will fear you all the time they live in the land you gave our fathers. Lev 26:26; Ps 130:4

41"As for the foreigner who does not belong to your people Israel but has come from a distant land because of your name— 42for men will hear of your great name and your mighty hand and your outstretched arm—when he comes and prays toward this temple, 43then hear from heaven, your dwelling place, and do whatever the foreigner asks of you, so that all the peoples of the earth may know your name and fear you, as do your own people Israel, and may know that this house I have built bears your Name. Dt 3:24

44"When your people go to war against their enemies, wherever you send them, and when they pray to the LORD toward the city you have chosen and the temple I have built for your Name, 45then hear from heaven their prayer and their plea, and uphold their cause. 1Ch 5:20; Ps 9:4

46"When they sin against you—for there is no one

who does not sin—and you become angry with them and give them over to the enemy, who takes them captive to his own land, far away or near; ⁴⁷and if they have a change of heart in the land where they are held captive, and repent and plead with you in the land of their conquerors and say, 'We have sinned, we have done wrong, we have acted wickedly'; ⁴⁸and if they turn back to you with all their heart and soul in the land of their enemies who took them captive, and pray to you toward the land you gave their fathers, toward the city you have chosen and the temple I have built for your Name; ⁴⁹then from heaven, your dwelling place, hear their prayer and their plea, and uphold their cause. ⁵⁰And forgive your people, who have sinned against you; forgive all the offenses they have committed against you, and cause their conquerors to show them mercy; ⁵¹for they are your people and your inheritance, whom you brought out of Egypt, out of that iron-smelting furnace.   Pr 20:9

⁵²"May your eyes be open to your servant's plea and to the plea of your people Israel, and may you listen to them whenever they cry out to you. ⁵³For

you singled them out from all the nations of the world to be your own inheritance, just as you declared through your servant Moses when you, O Sovereign LORD, brought our fathers out of Egypt."   Ex 19:5

⁵⁴When Solomon had finished all these prayers and supplications to the LORD, he rose from before the altar of the LORD, where he had been kneeling with his hands spread out toward heaven. ⁵⁵He stood and blessed the whole assembly of Israel in a loud voice, saying:

⁵⁶"Praise be to the LORD, who has given rest to his people Israel just as he promised. Not one word has failed of all the good promises he gave through his servant Moses. ⁵⁷May the LORD our God be with us as he was with our fathers; may he never leave us nor forsake us. ⁵⁸May he turn our hearts to him, to walk in all his ways and to keep the commands, decrees and regulations he gave our fathers. ⁵⁹And may these words of mine, which I have prayed before the LORD, be near to the LORD our God day and night, that he may uphold the cause of his servant and the cause of his people Israel according to each day's need, ⁶⁰so that all the peoples of the earth may know that the LORD is

God and that there is no other. [61]But your hearts must be fully committed to the LORD our God, to live by his decrees and obey his commands, as at this time."

The Dedication of the Temple

[62]Then the king and all Israel with him offered sacrifices before the LORD. [63]Solomon offered a sacrifice of fellowship offerings[a] to the LORD: twenty-two thousand cattle and a hundred and twenty thousand sheep and goats. So the king and all the Israelites dedicated the temple of the LORD.   Ezr 6:16

[64]On that same day the king consecrated the middle part of the courtyard in front of the temple of the LORD, and there he offered burnt offerings, grain offerings and the fat of the fellowship offerings, because the bronze altar before the LORD was too small to hold the burnt offerings, the grain offerings and the fat of the fellowship offerings.   2Ch 4:1; Eze 43:13-17

[65]So Solomon observed the festival at that time, and all Israel with him—a vast assembly, people from Lebo[b] Hamath to the Wadi of Egypt. They celebrated it before the LORD our God for seven days and seven days more, fourteen days in all. [66]On the following day he sent the people away. They blessed the king and then went home, joyful and glad in heart for all the good things the LORD had done for his servant David and his people Israel.   Ex 18:9; 2Ch 7:8

The LORD Appears to Solomon

9 When Solomon had finished building the temple of the LORD and the royal palace, and had achieved all he had desired to do, [2]the LORD appeared to him a second time, as he had appeared to him at Gibeon. [3]The LORD said to him: 1Ki 3:5

"I have heard the prayer and plea you have made before me; I have consecrated this temple, which you have built, by putting my Name there forever. My eyes and my heart will always be there.   2Ki 20:5

[4]"As for you, if you walk before me in integrity of heart and uprightness, as David your father did, and do all I command and observe my decrees and laws, [5]I will establish your royal throne over Israel forever, as I promised David your father when I said, 'You shall never fail to have a man on the throne of Israel.'   Ge 17:1; 1Ch 22:10

[6]"But if you[c] or your sons turn away from me and do not observe the commands and decrees I have given you[c] and go off to serve

---

[a]63 Traditionally *peace offerings*; also in verse 64   [b]65 Or *from the entrance to*
[c]6 The Hebrew is plural.

other gods and worship them, [7]then I will cut off Israel from the land I have given them and will reject this temple I have consecrated for my Name. Israel will then become a byword and an object of ridicule among all peoples. [8]And though this temple is now imposing, all who pass by will be appalled and will scoff and say, 'Why has the LORD done such a thing to this land and to this temple?' [9]People will answer, 'Because they have forsaken the LORD their God, who brought their fathers out of Egypt, and have embraced other gods, worshiping and serving them—that is why the LORD brought all this disaster on them.'" 2Sa 7:14

Solomon's Other Activities

[10]At the end of twenty years, during which Solomon built these two buildings—the temple of the LORD and the royal palace— [11]King Solomon gave twenty towns in Galilee to Hiram king of Tyre, because Hiram had supplied him with all the cedar and pine and gold he wanted. [12]But when Hiram went from Tyre to see the towns that Solomon had given him, he was not pleased with them.

[13]"What kind of towns are these you have given me, my brother?" he asked. And he called them the Land of Cabul,[a] a name they have to this day. [14]Now Hiram had sent to the king 120 talents[b] of gold. Jos 19:27

[15]Here is the account of the forced labor King Solomon conscripted to build the LORD's temple, his own palace, the supporting terraces,[c] the wall of Jerusalem, and Hazor, Megiddo and Gezer. [16](Pharaoh king of Egypt had attacked and captured Gezer. He had set it on fire. He killed its Canaanite inhabitants and then gave it as a wedding gift to his daughter, Solomon's wife. [17]And Solomon rebuilt Gezer.) He built up Lower Beth Horon, [18]Baalath, and Tadmor[d] in the desert, within his land, [19]as well as all his store cities and the towns for his chariots and for his horses[e]— whatever he desired to build in Jerusalem, in Lebanon and throughout all the territory he ruled. 1Ki 5:13; Ps 45:12

[20]All the people left from the Amorites, Hittites, Perizzites, Hivites and Jebusites (these peoples were not Israelites), [21]that is, their descendants remaining in the land, whom the Israelites could not exterminate[f]—these Solomon conscripted for his slave labor force,

---

[a]13 *Cabul* sounds like the Hebrew for *good-for-nothing*.   [b]14 That is, about 4 1/2 tons (about 4 metric tons)   [c]15 Or *the Millo*; also in verse 24   [d]18 The Hebrew may also be read *Tamar*.   [e]19 Or *charioteers*   [f]21 The Hebrew term refers to the irrevocable giving over of things or persons to the LORD, often by totally destroying them.

as it is to this day. 22But Solomon did not make slaves of any of the Israelites; they were his fighting men, his government officials, his officers, his captains, and the commanders of his chariots and charioteers. 23They were also the chief officials in charge of Solomon's projects—550 officials supervising the men who did the work.   1Ki 5:16; 2Ch 8:7

24After Pharaoh's daughter had come up from the City of David to the palace Solomon had built for her, he constructed the supporting terraces.   1Ki 3:1

25Three times a year Solomon sacrificed burnt offerings and fellowship offerings[a] on the altar he had built for the LORD, burning incense before the LORD along with them, and so fulfilled the temple obligations.

26King Solomon also built ships at Ezion Geber, which is near Elath in Edom, on the shore of the Red Sea.[b] 27And Hiram sent his men—sailors who knew the sea—to serve in the fleet with Solomon's men. 28They sailed to Ophir and brought back 420 talents[c] of gold, which they delivered to King Solomon.   Nu 33:35

The Queen of Sheba Visits Solomon

10 When the queen of Sheba heard about the fame of Solomon and his relation to the name of the LORD, she came to test him with hard questions. 2Arriving at Jerusalem with a very great caravan—with camels carrying spices, large quantities of gold, and precious stones—she came to Solomon and talked with him about all that she had on her mind. 3Solomon answered all her questions; nothing was too hard for the king to explain to her. 4When the queen of Sheba saw all the wisdom of Solomon and the palace he had built, 5the food on his table, the seating of his officials, the attending servants in their robes, his cupbearers, and the burnt offerings he made at[d] the temple of the LORD, she was overwhelmed.

6She said to the king, "The report I heard in my own country about your achievements and your wisdom is true. 7But I did not believe these things until I came and saw with my own eyes. Indeed, not even half was told me; in wisdom and wealth you have far exceeded the report I heard. 8How happy your men must be! How happy your officials, who continually stand before you and hear your wisdom! 9Praise be to the LORD your God, who has delighted in you and placed you on the throne of Israel. Because of the LORD's eternal love for Israel, he

---

a25 Traditionally *peace offerings*   b26 Hebrew *Yam Suph*; that is, Sea of Reeds
c28 That is, about 16 tons (about 14.5 metric tons)   d5 Or *the ascent by which he went up to*

has made you king, to maintain justice and righteousness."

¹⁰And she gave the king 120 talents*a* of gold, large quantities of spices, and precious stones. Never again were so many spices brought in as those the queen of Sheba gave to King Solomon. 1Ki 9:28; Isa 60:6

¹¹(Hiram's ships brought gold from Ophir; and from there they brought great cargoes of almugwood*b* and precious stones. ¹²The king used the almugwood to make supports for the temple of the LORD and for the royal palace, and to make harps and lyres for the musicians. So much almugwood has never been imported or seen since that day.) 2Ch 9:10-11

¹³King Solomon gave the queen of Sheba all she desired and asked for, besides what he had given her out of his royal bounty. Then she left and returned with her retinue to her own country.

Solomon's Splendor

¹⁴The weight of the gold that Solomon received yearly was 666 talents,*c* ¹⁵not including the revenues from merchants and traders and from all the Arabian kings and the governors of the land. 1Ki 9:28; 2Ch 9:13-28

¹⁶King Solomon made two hundred large shields of hammered gold; six hundred bekas*d*

of gold went into each shield. ¹⁷He also made three hundred small shields of hammered gold, with three minas*e* of gold in each shield. The king put them in the Palace of the Forest of Lebanon. 2Sa 8:7; 1Ki 17:2

¹⁸Then the king made a great throne inlaid with ivory and overlaid with fine gold. ¹⁹The throne had six steps, and its back had a rounded top. On both sides of the seat were armrests, with a lion standing beside each of them. ²⁰Twelve lions stood on the six steps, one at either end of each step. Nothing like it had ever been made for any other kingdom. ²¹All King Solomon's goblets were gold, and all the household articles in the Palace of the Forest of Lebanon were pure gold. Nothing was made of silver, because silver was considered of little value in Solomon's days. ²²The king had a fleet of trading ships*f* at sea along with the ships of Hiram. Once every three years it returned, carrying gold, silver and ivory, and apes and baboons. 2Ch 9:17

²³King Solomon was greater in riches and wisdom than all the other kings of the earth. ²⁴The whole world sought audience with Solomon to hear the wisdom God had put in his heart. ²⁵Year after year, everyone who came brought a

---

*a*10 That is, about 4 1/2 tons (about 4 metric tons) *b*11 Probably a variant of *algumwood*; also in verse 12 *c*14 That is, about 25 tons (about 23 metric tons) *d*16 That is, about 7 1/2 pounds (about 3.5 kilograms) *e*17 That is, about 3 3/4 pounds (about 1.7 kilograms) *f*22 Hebrew *of ships of Tarshish*

gift—articles of silver and gold, robes, weapons and spices, and horses and mules. 1Ki 3:13

26Solomon accumulated chariots and horses; he had fourteen hundred chariots and twelve thousand horses,*a* which he kept in the chariot cities and also with him in Jerusalem. 27The king made silver as common in Jerusalem as stones, and cedar as plentiful as sycamore-fig trees in the foothills. 28Solomon's horses were imported from Egypt*b* and from Kue*c*—the royal merchants purchased them from Kue. 29They imported a chariot from Egypt for six hundred shekels*d* of silver, and a horse for a hundred and fifty.*e* They also exported them to all the kings of the Hittites and of the Arameans.Dt 17:16

Solomon's Wives

11 King Solomon, however, loved many foreign women besides Pharaoh's daughter—Moabites, Ammonites, Edomites, Sidonians and Hittites. 2They were from nations about which the LORD had told the Israelites, "You must not intermarry with them, because they will surely turn your hearts after their gods." Nevertheless, Solomon held fast to them in love. 3He had seven hundred wives of royal birth and three hundred concubines, and his wives led him astray.

4As Solomon grew old, his wives turned his heart after other gods, and his heart was not fully devoted to the LORD his God, as the heart of David his father had been. 5He followed Ashtoreth the goddess of the Sidonians, and Molech*f* the detestable god of the Ammonites. 6So Solomon did evil in the eyes of the LORD; he did not follow the LORD completely, as David his father had done. Dt 17:17

7On a hill east of Jerusalem, Solomon built a high place for Chemosh the detestable god of Moab, and for Molech the detestable god of the Ammonites. 8He did the same for all his foreign wives, who burned incense and offered sacrifices to their gods. Nu 21:29; 2Ki 23:13

9The LORD became angry with Solomon because his heart had turned away from the LORD, the God of Israel, who had appeared to him twice. 10Although he had forbidden Solomon to follow other gods, Solomon did not keep the LORD's command. 11So the LORD said to Solomon, "Since this is your attitude and you have not kept my covenant and my decrees, which I commanded you, I will most certainly tear the kingdom away from you and give it to one of your subordinates. 12Nevertheless, for the sake of David your father, I will not do it during your lifetime. I

---

a26 Or *charioteers*   *b28* Or possibly *Muzur*, a region in Cilicia; also in verse 29   *c28* Probably *Cilicia*   *d29* That is, about 15 pounds (about 7 kilograms)   *e29* That is, about 3 3/4 pounds (about 1.7 kilograms)   *f5* Hebrew *Milcom*; also in verse 33

will tear it out of the hand of your son. [13]Yet I will not tear the whole kingdom from him, but will give him one tribe for the sake of David my servant and for the sake of Jerusalem, which I have chosen." 2Sa 7:15; 1Ki 3:5

Solomon's Adversaries

[14]Then the LORD raised up against Solomon an adversary, Hadad the Edomite, from the royal line of Edom. [15]Earlier when David was fighting with Edom, Joab the commander of the army, who had gone up to bury the dead, had struck down all the men in Edom. [16]Joab and all the Israelites stayed there for six months, until they had destroyed all the men in Edom. [17]But Hadad, still only a boy, fled to Egypt with some Edomite officials who had served his father. [18]They set out from Midian and went to Paran. Then taking men from Paran with them, they went to Egypt, to Pharaoh king of Egypt, who gave Hadad a house and land and provided him with food.   1Ch 18:12

[19]Pharaoh was so pleased with Hadad that he gave him a sister of his own wife, Queen Tahpenes, in marriage. [20]The sister of Tahpenes bore him a son named Genubath, whom Tahpenes brought up in the royal palace. There Genubath lived with Pharaoh's own children.

[21]While he was in Egypt, Hadad heard that David rested with his fathers and that Joab the commander of the army was also dead. Then Hadad said to Pharaoh, "Let me go, that I may return to my own country."

[22]"What have you lacked here that you want to go back to your own country?" Pharaoh asked.

"Nothing," Hadad replied, "but do let me go!"

[23]And God raised up against Solomon another adversary, Rezon son of Eliada, who had fled from his master, Hadadezer king of Zobah. [24]He gathered men around him and became the leader of a band of rebels when David destroyed the forces[a] of Zobah; the rebels went to Damascus, where they settled and took control. [25]Rezon was Israel's adversary as long as Solomon lived, adding to the trouble caused by Hadad. So Rezon ruled in Aram and was hostile toward Israel. 2Sa 8:3

Jeroboam Rebels Against Solomon

[26]Also, Jeroboam son of Nebat rebelled against the king. He was one of Solomon's officials, an Ephraimite from Zeredah, and his mother was a widow named Zeruah. 2Ch 13:6

[27]Here is the account of how he rebelled against the king: Solomon had built the supporting terraces[b] and had filled in the gap in the wall of the city of David his father. [28]Now Jero-

---

[a]24 Hebrew *destroyed them*   [b]27 Or *the Millo*

boam was a man of standing, and when Solomon saw how well the young man did his work, he put him in charge of the whole labor force of the house of Joseph. 1Ki 9:24

29About that time Jeroboam was going out of Jerusalem, and Ahijah the prophet of Shiloh met him on the way, wearing a new cloak. The two of them were alone out in the country, 30and Ahijah took hold of the new cloak he was wearing and tore it into twelve pieces. 31Then he said to Jeroboam, "Take ten pieces for yourself, for this is what the LORD, the God of Israel, says: 'See, I am going to tear the kingdom out of Solomon's hand and give you ten tribes. 32But for the sake of my servant David and the city of Jerusalem, which I have chosen out of all the tribes of Israel, he will have one tribe. 33I will do this because they have*a* forsaken me and worshiped Ashtoreth the goddess of the Sidonians, Chemosh the god of the Moabites, and Molech the god of the Ammonites, and have not walked in my ways, nor done what is right in my eyes, nor kept my statutes and laws as David, Solomon's father, did. Jdg 2:13; 1Ki 14:2

34" 'But I will not take the whole kingdom out of Solomon's hand; I have made him ruler all the days of his life for the sake of David my servant, whom I chose and who observed my commands and statutes. 35I will take the kingdom from his son's hands and give you ten tribes. 36I will give one tribe to his son so that David my servant may always have a lamp before me in Jerusalem, the city where I chose to put my Name. 37However, as for you, I will take you, and you will rule over all that your heart desires; you will be king over Israel. 38If you do whatever I command you and walk in my ways and do what is right in my eyes by keeping my statutes and commands, as David my servant did, I will be with you. I will build you a dynasty as enduring as the one I built for David and will give Israel to you. 39I will humble David's descendants because of this, but not forever.' " Dt 17:19; 1Ki 12:17

40Solomon tried to kill Jeroboam, but Jeroboam fled to Egypt, to Shishak the king, and stayed there until Solomon's death. 1Ki 12:12; 2Ch 12:2

Solomon's Death

41As for the other events of Solomon's reign—all he did and the wisdom he displayed—are they not written in the book of the annals of Solomon? 42Solomon reigned in Jerusalem over all Israel forty years. 43Then he rested with his fathers and was buried in the city of David his

---

a33 Hebrew; Septuagint, Vulgate and Syriac *because he has*

father. And Rehoboam his son succeeded him as king.   2Ch 9:29

Israel Rebels Against Rehoboam

12 Rehoboam went to Shechem, for all the Israelites had gone there to make him king. ²When Jeroboam son of Nebat heard this (he was still in Egypt, where he had fled from King Solomon), he returned from[a] Egypt. ³So they sent for Jeroboam, and he and the whole assembly of Israel went to Rehoboam and said to him: ⁴"Your father put a heavy yoke on us, but now lighten the harsh labor and the heavy yoke he put on us, and we will serve you."   1Sa 8:11; 2Ch 10:1

⁵Rehoboam answered, "Go away for three days and then come back to me." So the people went away.   1Ki 12:12

⁶Then King Rehoboam consulted the elders who had served his father Solomon during his lifetime. "How would you advise me to answer these people?" he asked.   1Ki 4:2

⁷They replied, "If today you will be a servant to these people and serve them and give them a favorable answer, they will always be your servants."   Pr 15:1

⁸But Rehoboam rejected the advice the elders gave him and consulted the young men who had grown up with him and were serving him. ⁹He asked them, "What is your advice?

How should we answer these people who say to me, 'Lighten the yoke your father put on us'?"   Lev 19:32

¹⁰The young men who had grown up with him replied, "Tell these people who have said to you, 'Your father put a heavy yoke on us, but make our yoke lighter'—tell them, 'My little finger is thicker than my father's waist. ¹¹My father laid on you a heavy yoke; I will make it even heavier. My father scourged you with whips; I will scourge you with scorpions.'"

¹²Three days later Jeroboam and all the people returned to Rehoboam, as the king had said, "Come back to me in three days." ¹³The king answered the people harshly. Rejecting the advice given him by the elders, ¹⁴he followed the advice of the young men and said, "My father made your yoke heavy; I will make it even heavier. My father scourged you with whips; I will scourge you with scorpions." ¹⁵So the king did not listen to the people, for this turn of events was from the LORD, to fulfill the word the LORD had spoken to Jeroboam son of Nebat through Ahijah the Shilonite.   Ex 1:14; 1Ki 11:29

¹⁶When all Israel saw that the king refused to listen to them, they answered the king:

"What share do we have in
     David,
   what part in Jesse's son?

_a2 Or_ he remained in

To your tents, O Israel!
  Look after your own house,
    O David!''   2Sa 20:1; Isa 7:17

So the Israelites went home.
[17]But as for the Israelites who were living in the towns of Judah, Rehoboam still ruled over them.   1Ki 11:36

[18]King Rehoboam sent out Adoniram,[a] who was in charge of forced labor, but all Israel stoned him to death. King Rehoboam, however, managed to get into his chariot and escape to Jerusalem. [19]So Israel has been in rebellion against the house of David to this day.

[20]When all the Israelites heard that Jeroboam had returned, they sent and called him to the assembly and made him king over all Israel. Only the tribe of Judah remained loyal to the house of David.   1Ki 1:13

[21]When Rehoboam arrived in Jerusalem, he mustered the whole house of Judah and the tribe of Benjamin—a hundred and eighty thousand fighting men—to make war against the house of Israel and to regain the kingdom for Rehoboam son of Solomon.   1Ki 14:30; 2Ch 11:1

[22]But this word of God came to Shemaiah the man of God: [23]"Say to Rehoboam son of Solomon king of Judah, to the whole house of Judah and Benjamin, and to the rest of the people, [24]'This is what the LORD says: Do not go up to fight against

your brothers, the Israelites. Go home, every one of you, for this is my doing.' " So they obeyed the word of the LORD and went home again, as the LORD had ordered.   Dt 33:1; 2Ch 12:5-7

Golden Calves at Bethel and Dan

[25]Then Jeroboam fortified Shechem in the hill country of Ephraim and lived there. From there he went out and built up Peniel.[b]   Jdg 8:8; 9:45

[26]Jeroboam thought to himself, "The kingdom will now likely revert to the house of David. [27]If these people go up to offer sacrifices at the temple of the LORD in Jerusalem, they will again give their allegiance to their lord, Rehoboam king of Judah. They will kill me and return to King Rehoboam."   Dt 12:5-6

[28]After seeking advice, the king made two golden calves. He said to the people, "It is too much for you to go up to Jerusalem. Here are your gods, O Israel, who brought you up out of Egypt." [29]One he set up in Bethel, and the other in Dan. [30]And this thing became a sin; the people went even as far as Dan to worship the one there.   Ex 32:8

[31]Jeroboam built shrines on high places and appointed priests from all sorts of people, even though they were not Levites. [32]He instituted a festival on the fifteenth day of the

---

[a]18 Some Septuagint manuscripts and Syriac (see also 1 Kings 4:6 and 5:14); Hebrew *Adoram*   [b]25 Hebrew *Penuel*, a variant of *Peniel*

eighth month, like the festival held in Judah, and offered sacrifices on the altar. This he did in Bethel, sacrificing to the calves he had made. And at Bethel he also installed priests at the high places he had made. 33On the fifteenth day of the eighth month, a month of his own choosing, he offered sacrifices on the altar he had built at Bethel. So he instituted the festival for the Israelites and went up to the altar to make offerings.

The Man of God From Judah

13 By the word of the LORD a man of God came from Judah to Bethel, as Jeroboam was standing by the altar to make an offering. 2He cried out against the altar by the word of the LORD: "O altar, altar! This is what the LORD says: 'A son named Josiah will be born to the house of David. On you he will sacrifice the priests of the high places who now make offerings here, and human bones will be burned on you.'" 3That same day the man of God gave a sign: "This is the sign the LORD has declared: The altar will be split apart and the ashes on it will be poured out." 2Ki 23:15; Isa 7:14

4When King Jeroboam heard what the man of God cried out against the altar at Bethel, he stretched out his hand from the altar and said, "Seize him!" But the hand he stretched out toward the man shriveled up, so that he could not pull it back. 5Also, the altar was split apart and its ashes poured out according to the sign given by the man of God by the word of the LORD.

6Then the king said to the man of God, "Intercede with the LORD your God and pray for me that my hand may be restored." So the man of God interceded with the LORD, and the king's hand was restored and became as it was before.   Ac 8:24

7The king said to the man of God, "Come home with me and have something to eat, and I will give you a gift."   1Sa 9:7

8But the man of God answered the king, "Even if you were to give me half your possessions, I would not go with you, nor would I eat bread or drink water here. 9For I was commanded by the word of the LORD: 'You must not eat bread or drink water or return by the way you came.'" 10So he took another road and did not return by the way he had come to Bethel.   Nu 22:18; 1Co 5:11

11Now there was a certain old prophet living in Bethel, whose sons came and told him all that the man of God had done there that day. They also told their father what he had said to the king. 12Their father asked them, "Which way did he go?" And his sons showed him which road the man of God from Judah had taken. 13So he said to his sons, "Saddle the donkey for me." And when they had saddled the donkey for him, he mounted it 14and rode after the man of God. He found him sit-

ting under an oak tree and asked, "Are you the man of God who came from Judah?"

"I am," he replied.

¹⁵So the prophet said to him, "Come home with me and eat."

¹⁶The man of God said, "I cannot turn back and go with you, nor can I eat bread or drink water with you in this place. ¹⁷I have been told by the word of the LORD: 'You must not eat bread or drink water there or return by the way you came.'"

¹⁸The old prophet answered, "I too am a prophet, as you are. And an angel said to me by the word of the LORD: 'Bring him back with you to your house so that he may eat bread and drink water.'" (But he was lying to him.) ¹⁹So the man of God returned with him and ate and drank in his house.   1Ki 22:6

²⁰While they were sitting at the table, the word of the LORD came to the old prophet who had brought him back. ²¹He cried out to the man of God who had come from Judah, "This is what the LORD says: 'You have defied the word of the LORD and have not kept the command the LORD your God gave you. ²²You came back and ate bread and drank water in the place where he told you not to eat or drink. Therefore your body will not be buried in the tomb of your fathers.'"   1Ki 15:26; 20:35

²³When the man of God had finished eating and drinking, the prophet who had brought him back saddled his donkey

for him. ²⁴As he went on his way, a lion met him on the road and killed him, and his body was thrown down on the road, with both the donkey and the lion standing beside it. ²⁵Some people who passed by saw the body thrown down there, with the lion standing beside the body, and they went and reported it in the city where the old prophet lived.   1Ki 20:36

²⁶When the prophet who had brought him back from his journey heard of it, he said, "It is the man of God who defied the word of the LORD. The LORD has given him over to the lion, which has mauled him and killed him, as the word of the LORD had warned him."

²⁷The prophet said to his sons, "Saddle the donkey for me," and they did so. ²⁸Then he went out and found the body thrown down on the road, with the donkey and the lion standing beside it. The lion had neither eaten the body nor mauled the donkey. ²⁹So the prophet picked up the body of the man of God, laid it on the donkey, and brought it back to his own city to mourn for him and bury him. ³⁰Then he laid the body in his own tomb, and they mourned over him and said, "Oh, my brother!"   Jer 22:18

³¹After burying him, he said to his sons, "When I die, bury me in the grave where the man of God is buried; lay my bones beside his bones. ³²For the message he declared by the word of

the LORD against the altar in Bethel and against all the shrines on the high places in the towns of Samaria will certainly come true." 1Ki 16:24; 2Ki 23:18

³³Even after this, Jeroboam did not change his evil ways, but once more appointed priests for the high places from all sorts of people. Anyone who wanted to become a priest he consecrated for the high places. ³⁴This was the sin of the house of Jeroboam that led to its downfall and to its destruction from the face of the earth.

Ahijah's Prophecy Against Jeroboam

14 At that time Abijah son of Jeroboam became ill, ²and Jeroboam said to his wife, "Go, disguise yourself, so you won't be recognized as the wife of Jeroboam. Then go to Shiloh. Ahijah the prophet is there— the one who told me I would be king over this people. ³Take ten loaves of bread with you, some cakes and a jar of honey, and go to him. He will tell you what will happen to the boy." ⁴So Jeroboam's wife did what he said and went to Ahijah's house in Shiloh. 1Sa 9:7

Now Ahijah could not see; his sight was gone because of his age. ⁵But the LORD had told Ahijah, "Jeroboam's wife is coming to ask you about her son, for he is ill, and you are to give her such and such an answer. When she arrives, she will pretend to be someone else." 2Sa 14:2

⁶So when Ahijah heard the sound of her footsteps at the door, he said, "Come in, wife of Jeroboam. Why this pretense? I have been sent to you with bad news. ⁷Go, tell Jeroboam that this is what the LORD, the God of Israel, says: 'I raised you up from among the people and made you a leader over my people Israel. ⁸I tore the kingdom away from the house of David and gave it to you, but you have not been like my servant David, who kept my commands and followed me with all his heart, doing only what was right in my eyes. ⁹You have done more evil than all who lived before you. You have made for yourself other gods, idols made of metal; you have provoked me to anger and thrust me behind your back.

¹⁰" 'Because of this, I am going to bring disaster on the house of Jeroboam. I will cut off from Jeroboam every last male in Israel—slave or free. I will burn up the house of Jeroboam as one burns dung, until it is all gone. ¹¹Dogs will eat those belonging to Jeroboam who die in the city, and the birds of the air will feed on those who die in the country. The LORD has spoken!'

¹²"As for you, go back home. When you set foot in your city, the boy will die. ¹³All Israel will mourn for him and bury him. He is the only one belonging to Jeroboam who will be buried,

because he is the only one in the house of Jeroboam in whom the LORD, the God of Israel, has found anything good.   2Ch 12:12

¹⁴"The LORD will raise up for himself a king over Israel who will cut off the family of Jeroboam. This is the day! What? Yes, even now.ᵃ ¹⁵And the LORD will strike Israel, so that it will be like a reed swaying in the water. He will uproot Israel from this good land that he gave to their forefathers and scatter them beyond the River,ᵇ because they provoked the LORD to anger by making Asherah poles.ᶜ ¹⁶And he will give Israel up because of the sins Jeroboam has committed and has caused Israel to commit."   Dt 12:3

¹⁷Then Jeroboam's wife got up and left and went to Tirzah. As soon as she stepped over the threshold of the house, the boy died. ¹⁸They buried him, and all Israel mourned for him, as the LORD had said through his servant the prophet Ahijah.   1Ki 15:33

¹⁹The other events of Jeroboam's reign, his wars and how he ruled, are written in the book of the annals of the kings of Israel. ²⁰He reigned for twenty-two years and then rested with his fathers. And Nadab his son succeeded him as king.   2Ch 13:2

Rehoboam King of Judah

²¹Rehoboam son of Solomon was king in Judah. He was forty-one years old when he became king, and he reigned seventeen years in Jerusalem, the city the LORD had chosen out of all the tribes of Israel in which to put his Name. His mother's name was Naamah; she was an Ammonite.   1Ki 11:1

²²Judah did evil in the eyes of the LORD. By the sins they committed they stirred up his jealous anger more than their fathers had done. ²³They also set up for themselves high places, sacred stones and Asherah poles on every high hill and under every spreading tree. ²⁴There were even male shrine prostitutes in the land; the people engaged in all the detestable practices of the nations the LORD had driven out before the Israelites.   Dt 23:17; 2Ch 12:1

²⁵In the fifth year of King Rehoboam, Shishak king of Egypt attacked Jerusalem. ²⁶He carried off the treasures of the temple of the LORD and the treasures of the royal palace. He took everything, including all the gold shields Solomon had made. ²⁷So King Rehoboam made bronze shields to replace them and assigned these to the commanders of the guard on duty at the entrance to the royal palace. ²⁸Whenever the king went to the LORD's temple, the guards bore the shields, and afterward they returned them to the guardroom.   2Ch 12:2

ᵃ14 The meaning of the Hebrew for this sentence is uncertain.   ᵇ15 That is, the Euphrates   ᶜ15 That is, symbols of the goddess Asherah; here and elsewhere in 1 Kings

²⁹As for the other events of Rehoboam's reign, and all he did, are they not written in the book of the annals of the kings of Judah? ³⁰There was continual warfare between Rehoboam and Jeroboam. ³¹And Rehoboam rested with his fathers and was buried with them in the City of David. His mother's name was Naamah; she was an Ammonite. And Abijah*ᵃ* his son succeeded him as king.

Abijah King of Judah

15 In the eighteenth year of the reign of Jeroboam son of Nebat, Abijah*ᵇ* became king of Judah, ²and he reigned in Jerusalem three years. His mother's name was Maacah daughter of Abishalom.*ᶜ*　2Ch 13:2

³He committed all the sins his father had done before him; his heart was not fully devoted to the LORD his God, as the heart of David his forefather had been. ⁴Nevertheless, for David's sake the LORD his God gave him a lamp in Jerusalem by raising up a son to succeed him and by making Jerusalem strong. ⁵For David had done what was right in the eyes of the LORD and had not failed to keep any of the LORD's commands all the days of his life—except in the case of Uriah the Hittite.

⁶There was war between Rehoboam*ᵈ* and Jeroboam throughout ₗAbijah'sⱼ lifetime. ⁷As for the other events of Abijah's reign, and all he did, are they not written in the book of the annals of the kings of Judah? There was war between Abijah and Jeroboam. ⁸And Abijah rested with his fathers and was buried in the City of David. And Asa his son succeeded him as king.　2Ch 13:2

Asa King of Judah

⁹In the twentieth year of Jeroboam king of Israel, Asa became king of Judah, ¹⁰and he reigned in Jerusalem forty-one years. His grandmother's name was Maacah daughter of Abishalom.

¹¹Asa did what was right in the eyes of the LORD, as his father David had done. ¹²He expelled the male shrine prostitutes from the land and got rid of all the idols his fathers had made. ¹³He even deposed his grandmother Maacah from her position as queen mother, because she had made a repulsive Asherah pole. Asa cut the pole down and burned it in the Kidron Valley. ¹⁴Although he did not remove the high places, Asa's heart was fully committed to the LORD all his life. ¹⁵He brought into the temple of the LORD the silver and gold and

ᵃ31 Some Hebrew manuscripts and Septuagint (see also 2 Chron. 12:16); most Hebrew manuscripts *Abijam*　*ᵇ1* Some Hebrew manuscripts and Septuagint (see also 2 Chron. 12:16); most Hebrew manuscripts *Abijam;* also in verses 7 and 8　*ᶜ2* A variant of *Absalom;* also in verse 10　*ᵈ6* Most Hebrew manuscripts; some Hebrew manuscripts and Syriac *Abijam* (that is, Abijah)

the articles that he and his father had dedicated. 1Ki 14:24

16There was war between Asa and Baasha king of Israel throughout their reigns. 17Baasha king of Israel went up against Judah and fortified Ramah to prevent anyone from leaving or entering the territory of Asa king of Judah. Jos 18:25

18Asa then took all the silver and gold that was left in the treasuries of the LORD's temple and of his own palace. He entrusted it to his officials and sent them to Ben-Hadad son of Tabrimmon, the son of Hezion, the king of Aram, who was ruling in Damascus. 19"Let there be a treaty between me and you," he said, "as there was between my father and your father. See, I am sending you a gift of silver and gold. Now break your treaty with Baasha king of Israel so he will withdraw from me." 2Ki 12:18

20Ben-Hadad agreed with King Asa and sent the commanders of his forces against the towns of Israel. He conquered Ijon, Dan, Abel Beth Maacah and all Kinnereth in addition to Naphtali. 21When Baasha heard this, he stopped building Ramah and withdrew to Tirzah. 22Then King Asa issued an order to all Judah—no one was exempt—and they carried away from Ramah the stones and timber Baasha had been using there. With them King Asa built up Geba in Benjamin, and also Mizpah. 2Sa 20:14

23As for all the other events of Asa's reign, all his achievements, all he did and the cities he built, are they not written in the book of the annals of the kings of Judah? In his old age, however, his feet became diseased. 24Then Asa rested with his fathers and was buried with them in the city of his father David. And Jehoshaphat his son succeeded him as king.

Nadab King of Israel

25Nadab son of Jeroboam became king of Israel in the second year of Asa king of Judah, and he reigned over Israel two years. 26He did evil in the eyes of the LORD, walking in the ways of his father and in his sin, which he had caused Israel to commit. 1Ki 12:30; 14:20

27Baasha son of Ahijah of the house of Issachar plotted against him, and he struck him down at Gibbethon, a Philistine town, while Nadab and all Israel were besieging it. 28Baasha killed Nadab in the third year of Asa king of Judah and succeeded him as king. 1Ki 14:14

29As soon as he began to reign, he killed Jeroboam's whole family. He did not leave Jeroboam anyone that breathed, but destroyed them all, according to the word of the LORD given through his servant Ahijah the Shilonite— 30because of the sins Jeroboam had committed and had caused Israel to commit, and because he provoked the LORD, the God of Israel, to anger. 1Ki 13:34

³¹As for the other events of Nadab's reign, and all he did, are they not written in the book of the annals of the kings of Israel? ³²There was war between Asa and Baasha king of Israel throughout their reigns.   1Ki 11:41

Baasha King of Israel

³³In the third year of Asa king of Judah, Baasha son of Ahijah became king of all Israel in Tirzah, and he reigned twenty-four years. ³⁴He did evil in the eyes of the LORD, walking in the ways of Jeroboam and in his sin, which he had caused Israel to commit.   1Ki 14:17; 2Ki 15:14

16 Then the word of the LORD came to Jehu son of Hanani against Baasha: ²"I lifted you up from the dust and made you leader of my people Israel, but you walked in the ways of Jeroboam and caused my people Israel to sin and to provoke me to anger by their sins. ³So I am about to consume Baasha and his house, and I will make your house like that of Jeroboam son of Nebat. ⁴Dogs will eat those belonging to Baasha who die in the city, and the birds of the air will feed on those who die in the country."

⁵As for the other events of Baasha's reign, what he did and his achievements, are they not written in the book of the annals of the kings of Israel? ⁶Baasha rested with his fathers and was buried in Tirzah. And Elah his son succeeded him as king.

⁷Moreover, the word of the LORD came through the prophet Jehu son of Hanani to Baasha and his house, because of all the evil he had done in the eyes of the LORD, provoking him to anger by the things he did, and becoming like the house of Jeroboam—and also because he destroyed it.   1Ki 6:11; 15:27,29

Elah King of Israel

⁸In the twenty-sixth year of Asa king of Judah, Elah son of Baasha became king of Israel, and he reigned in Tirzah two years.   2Ki 9:31

⁹Zimri, one of his officials, who had command of half his chariots, plotted against him. Elah was in Tirzah at the time, getting drunk in the home of Arza, the man in charge of the palace at Tirzah. ¹⁰Zimri came in, struck him down and killed him in the twenty-seventh year of Asa king of Judah. Then he succeeded him as king.   Ge 24:2

¹¹As soon as he began to reign and was seated on the throne, he killed off Baasha's whole family. He did not spare a single male, whether relative or friend. ¹²So Zimri destroyed the whole family of Baasha, in accordance with the word of the LORD spoken against Baasha through the prophet Jehu— ¹³because of all the sins Baasha and his son Elah had committed and had caused Israel to commit, so that they provoked the LORD, the God of Israel, to anger by their worthless idols.

¹⁴As for the other events of

Elah's reign, and all he did, are they not written in the book of the annals of the kings of Israel?

Zimri King of Israel

15In the twenty-seventh year of Asa king of Judah, Zimri reigned in Tirzah seven days. The army was encamped near Gibbethon, a Philistine town. 16When the Israelites in the camp heard that Zimri had plotted against the king and murdered him, they proclaimed Omri, the commander of the army, king over Israel that very day there in the camp. 17Then Omri and all the Israelites with him withdrew from Gibbethon and laid siege to Tirzah. 18When Zimri saw that the city was taken, he went into the citadel of the royal palace and set the palace on fire around him. So he died, 19because of the sins he had committed, doing evil in the eyes of the LORD and walking in the ways of Jeroboam and in the sin he had committed and had caused Israel to commit.

20As for the other events of Zimri's reign, and the rebellion he carried out, are they not written in the book of the annals of the kings of Israel? 2Ki 11:14

Omri King of Israel

21Then the people of Israel were split into two factions; half supported Tibni son of Ginath for king, and the other half supported Omri. 22But Omri's followers proved stronger than those of Tibni son of Ginath. So Tibni died and Omri became king.

23In the thirty-first year of Asa king of Judah, Omri became king of Israel, and he reigned twelve years, six of them in Tirzah. 24He bought the hill of Samaria from Shemer for two talents*a* of silver and built a city on the hill, calling it Samaria, after Shemer, the name of the former owner of the hill. 1Ki 15:33

25But Omri did evil in the eyes of the LORD and sinned more than all those before him. 26He walked in all the ways of Jeroboam son of Nebat and in his sin, which he had caused Israel to commit, so that they provoked the LORD, the God of Israel, to anger by their worthless idols. Dt 4:25; Mic 6:16

27As for the other events of Omri's reign, what he did and the things he achieved, are they not written in the book of the annals of the kings of Israel? 28Omri rested with his fathers and was buried in Samaria. And Ahab his son succeeded him as king. 1Ki 13:32

Ahab Becomes King of Israel

29In the thirty-eighth year of Asa king of Judah, Ahab son of Omri became king of Israel, and he reigned in Samaria over Israel twenty-two years. 30Ahab son of Omri did more evil in the eyes of the LORD than any of

*a24 That is, about 150 pounds (about 70 kilograms)

those before him. ³¹He not only considered it trivial to commit the sins of Jeroboam son of Nebat, but he also married Jezebel daughter of Ethbaal king of the Sidonians, and began to serve Baal and worship him. ³²He set up an altar for Baal in the temple of Baal that he built in Samaria. ³³Ahab also made an Asherah pole and did more to provoke the LORD, the God of Israel, to anger than did all the kings of Israel before him.

³⁴In Ahab's time, Hiel of Bethel rebuilt Jericho. He laid its foundations at the cost of his firstborn son Abiram, and he set up its gates at the cost of his youngest son Segub, in accordance with the word of the LORD spoken by Joshua son of Nun. Jos 6:26

Elijah Fed by Ravens

17 Now Elijah the Tishbite, from Tishbe*a* in Gilead, said to Ahab, "As the LORD, the God of Israel, lives, whom I serve, there will be neither dew nor rain in the next few years except at my word." Jdg 12:4

²Then the word of the LORD came to Elijah: ³"Leave here, turn eastward and hide in the Kerith Ravine, east of the Jordan. ⁴You will drink from the brook, and I have ordered the ravens to feed you there." Job 38:41

⁵So he did what the LORD had told him. He went to the Kerith Ravine, east of the Jordan, and stayed there. ⁶The ravens brought him bread and meat in the morning and bread and meat in the evening, and he drank from the brook. Ex 16:8

The Widow at Zarephath

⁷Some time later the brook dried up because there had been no rain in the land. ⁸Then the word of the LORD came to him: ⁹"Go at once to Zarephath of Sidon and stay there. I have commanded a widow in that place to supply you with food." ¹⁰So he went to Zarephath. When he came to the town gate, a widow was there gathering sticks. He called to her and asked, "Would you bring me a little water in a jar so I may have a drink?" ¹¹As she was going to get it, he called, "And bring me, please, a piece of bread." Ob 20

¹²"As surely as the LORD your God lives," she replied, "I don't have any bread—only a handful of flour in a jar and a little oil in a jug. I am gathering a few sticks to take home and make a meal for myself and my son, that we may eat it—and die."

¹³Elijah said to her, "Don't be afraid. Go home and do as you have said. But first make a small cake of bread for me from what you have and bring it to me, and then make something for yourself and your son. ¹⁴For this is what the LORD, the God of Israel, says: 'The jar of flour will not be used up and the jug of oil

---

a1 Or Tishbite, of the settlers

will not run dry until the day the LORD gives rain on the land.'"   Lk 4:25-26

15She went away and did as Elijah had told her. So there was food every day for Elijah and for the woman and her family. 16For the jar of flour was not used up and the jug of oil did not run dry, in keeping with the word of the LORD spoken by Elijah.   Ge 5:24

17Some time later the son of the woman who owned the house became ill. He grew worse and worse, and finally stopped breathing. 18She said to Elijah, "What do you have against me, man of God? Did you come to remind me of my sin and kill my son?"   Lk 5:8

19"Give me your son," Elijah replied. He took him from her arms, carried him to the upper room where he was staying, and laid him on his bed. 20Then he cried out to the LORD, "O LORD my God, have you brought tragedy also upon this widow I am staying with, by causing her son to die?" 21Then he stretched himself out on the boy three times and cried to the LORD, "O LORD my God, let this boy's life return to him!"   2Ki 4:33

22The LORD heard Elijah's cry, and the boy's life returned to him, and he lived. 23Elijah picked up the child and carried him down from the room into the house. He gave him to his mother and said, "Look, your son is alive!"   1Ki 18:21; Heb 11:35

24Then the woman said to Eli-

jah, "Now I know that you are a man of God and that the word of the LORD from your mouth is the truth."   Ps 119:43; Jn 16:30

Elijah and Obadiah

18 After a long time, in the third year, the word of the LORD came to Elijah: "Go and present yourself to Ahab, and I will send rain on the land." 2So Elijah went to present himself to Ahab.   1Ki 17:1

Now the famine was severe in Samaria, 3and Ahab had summoned Obadiah, who was in charge of his palace. (Obadiah was a devout believer in the LORD. 4While Jezebel was killing off the LORD's prophets, Obadiah had taken a hundred prophets and hidden them in two caves, fifty in each, and had supplied them with food and water.) 5Ahab had said to Obadiah, "Go through the land to all the springs and valleys. Maybe we can find some grass to keep the horses and mules alive so we will not have to kill any of our animals." 6So they divided the land they were to cover, Ahab going in one direction and Obadiah in another.

7As Obadiah was walking along, Elijah met him. Obadiah recognized him, bowed down to the ground, and said, "Is it really you, my lord Elijah?"

8"Yes," he replied. "Go tell your master, 'Elijah is here.' "

9"What have I done wrong," asked Obadiah, "that you are handing your servant over to

Ahab to be put to death? ¹⁰As surely as the LORD your God lives, there is not a nation or kingdom where my master has not sent someone to look for you. And whenever a nation or kingdom claimed you were not there, he made them swear they could not find you. ¹¹But now you tell me to go to my master and say, 'Elijah is here.' ¹²I don't know where the Spirit of the LORD may carry you when I leave you. If I go and tell Ahab and he doesn't find you, he will kill me. Yet I your servant have worshiped the LORD since my youth. ¹³Haven't you heard, my lord, what I did while Jezebel was killing the prophets of the LORD? I hid a hundred of the LORD's prophets in two caves, fifty in each, and supplied them with food and water. ¹⁴And now you tell me to go to my master and say, 'Elijah is here.' He will kill me!"   1Ki 17:3

¹⁵Elijah said, "As the LORD Almighty lives, whom I serve, I will surely present myself to Ahab today."   1Ki 17:1

Elijah on Mount Carmel

¹⁶So Obadiah went to meet Ahab and told him, and Ahab went to meet Elijah. ¹⁷When he saw Elijah, he said to him, "Is that you, you troubler of Israel?"   Jos 7:25; 1Ki 21:20

¹⁸"I have not made trouble for Israel," Elijah replied. "But you and your father's family have. You have abandoned the LORD's commands and have fol-

lowed the Baals. ¹⁹Now summon the people from all over Israel to meet me on Mount Carmel. And bring the four hundred and fifty prophets of Baal and the four hundred prophets of Asherah, who eat at Jezebel's table."   Jos 19:26; 1Ki 16:33

²⁰So Ahab sent word throughout all Israel and assembled the prophets on Mount Carmel. ²¹Elijah went before the people and said, "How long will you waver between two opinions? If the LORD is God, follow him; but if Baal is God, follow him."   Jos 24:15; Mt 6:24

But the people said nothing.

²²Then Elijah said to them, "I am the only one of the LORD's prophets left, but Baal has four hundred and fifty prophets. ²³Get two bulls for us. Let them choose one for themselves, and let them cut it into pieces and put it on the wood but not set fire to it. I will prepare the other bull and put it on the wood but not set fire to it. ²⁴Then you call on the name of your god, and I will call on the name of the LORD. The god who answers by fire—he is God."   1Ki 19:10

Then all the people said, "What you say is good."

²⁵Elijah said to the prophets of Baal, "Choose one of the bulls and prepare it first, since there are so many of you. Call on the name of your god, but do not light the fire." ²⁶So they took the bull given them and prepared it.

Then they called on the name

of Baal from morning till noon. "O Baal, answer us!" they shouted. But there was no response; no one answered. And they danced around the altar they had made. Isa 44:17

27At noon Elijah began to taunt them. "Shout louder!" he said. "Surely he is a god! Perhaps he is deep in thought, or busy, or traveling. Maybe he is sleeping and must be awakened." 28So they shouted louder and slashed themselves with swords and spears, as was their custom, until their blood flowed. 29Midday passed, and they continued their frantic prophesying until the time for the evening sacrifice. But there was no response, no one answered, no one paid attention.

30Then Elijah said to all the people, "Come here to me." They came to him, and he repaired the altar of the LORD, which was in ruins. 31Elijah took twelve stones, one for each of the tribes descended from Jacob, to whom the word of the LORD had come, saying, "Your name shall be Israel." 32With the stones he built an altar in the name of the LORD, and he dug a trench around it large enough to hold two seahs*a* of seed. 33He arranged the wood, cut the bull into pieces and laid it on the wood. Then he said to them, "Fill four large jars with water and pour it on the offering and on the wood." 1Ki 19:10

34"Do it again," he said, and they did it again.

"Do it a third time," he ordered, and they did it the third time. 35The water ran down around the altar and even filled the trench.

36At the time of sacrifice, the prophet Elijah stepped forward and prayed: "O LORD, God of Abraham, Isaac and Israel, let it be known today that you are God in Israel and that I am your servant and have done all these things at your command. 37Answer me, O LORD, answer me, so these people will know that you, O LORD, are God, and that you are turning their hearts back again." Nu 16:28; Jos 4:24

38Then the fire of the LORD fell and burned up the sacrifice, the wood, the stones and the soil, and also licked up the water in the trench. Lev 9:24; 1Ch 21:26

39When all the people saw this, they fell prostrate and cried, "The LORD—he is God! The LORD—he is God!" Ps 46:10

40Then Elijah commanded them, "Seize the prophets of Baal. Don't let anyone get away!" They seized them, and Elijah had them brought down to the Kishon Valley and slaughtered there. Dt 13:5

41And Elijah said to Ahab, "Go, eat and drink, for there is the sound of a heavy rain." 42So Ahab went off to eat and drink, but Elijah climbed to the top of Carmel, bent down to the

a32 That is, probably about 13 quarts (about 15 liters)

ground and put his face between his knees. Jas 5:18

43"Go and look toward the sea," he told his servant. And he went up and looked.

"There is nothing there," he said.

Seven times Elijah said, "Go back." 2Ki 5:10

44The seventh time the servant reported, "A cloud as small as a man's hand is rising from the sea." Jos 6:15

So Elijah said, "Go and tell Ahab, 'Hitch up your chariot and go down before the rain stops you.'"

45Meanwhile, the sky grew black with clouds, the wind rose, a heavy rain came on and Ahab rode off to Jezreel. 46The power of the LORD came upon Elijah and, tucking his cloak into his belt, he ran ahead of Ahab all the way to Jezreel.

Elijah Flees to Horeb

19 Now Ahab told Jezebel everything Elijah had done and how he had killed all the prophets with the sword. 2So Jezebel sent a messenger to Elijah to say, "May the gods deal with me, be it ever so severely, if by this time tomorrow I do not make your life like that of one of them." 1Ki 16:31

3Elijah was afraid[a] and ran for his life. When he came to Beersheba in Judah, he left his servant there, 4while he himself went a day's journey into the desert. He came to a broom tree, sat down under it and prayed that he might die. "I have had enough, LORD," he said. "Take my life; I am no better than my ancestors." 5Then he lay down under the tree and fell asleep. Ge 31:21; Nu 11:15

All at once an angel touched him and said, "Get up and eat." 6He looked around, and there by his head was a cake of bread baked over hot coals, and a jar of water. He ate and drank and then lay down again.

7The angel of the LORD came back a second time and touched him and said, "Get up and eat, for the journey is too much for you." 8So he got up and ate and drank. Strengthened by that food, he traveled forty days and forty nights until he reached Horeb, the mountain of God. 9There he went into a cave and spent the night. Dt 9:9; Mt 4:2

The LORD Appears to Elijah

And the word of the LORD came to him: "What are you doing here, Elijah?" Ge 3:9

10He replied, "I have been very zealous for the LORD God Almighty. The Israelites have rejected your covenant, broken down your altars, and put your prophets to death with the sword. I am the only one left, and now they are trying to kill me too." 1Ki 18:22; Ro 11:3

11The LORD said, "Go out and stand on the mountain in the

a3 Or Elijah saw

presence of the Lord, for the Lord is about to pass by."

Then a great and powerful wind tore the mountains apart and shattered the rocks before the Lord, but the Lord was not in the wind. After the wind there was an earthquake, but the Lord was not in the earthquake. ¹²After the earthquake came a fire, but the Lord was not in the fire. And after the fire came a gentle whisper. ¹³When Elijah heard it, he pulled his cloak over his face and went out and stood at the mouth of the cave. _{Ex 3:6; Job 4:16}

Then a voice said to him, "What are you doing here, Elijah?"

¹⁴He replied, "I have been very zealous for the Lord God Almighty. The Israelites have rejected your covenant, broken down your altars, and put your prophets to death with the sword. I am the only one left, and now they are trying to kill me too." _{1Ki 18:22; Ro 11:3}

¹⁵The Lord said to him, "Go back the way you came, and go to the Desert of Damascus. When you get there, anoint Hazael king over Aram. ¹⁶Also, anoint Jehu son of Nimshi king over Israel, and anoint Elisha son of Shaphat from Abel Meholah to succeed you as prophet. ¹⁷Jehu will put to death any who escape the sword of Hazael, and Elisha will put to death any who escape the sword of Jehu. ¹⁸Yet I reserve seven thousand in Israel—all whose knees have not bowed down to Baal and all whose mouths have not kissed him."

The Call of Elisha

¹⁹So Elijah went from there and found Elisha son of Shaphat. He was plowing with twelve yoke of oxen, and he himself was driving the twelfth pair. Elijah went up to him and threw his cloak around him. ²⁰Elisha then left his oxen and ran after Elijah. "Let me kiss my father and mother good-by," he said, "and then I will come with you." _{2Ki 2:8, 14; Lk 9:61}

"Go back," Elijah replied. "What have I done to you?"

²¹So Elisha left him and went back. He took his yoke of oxen and slaughtered them. He burned the plowing equipment to cook the meat and gave it to the people, and they ate. Then he set out to follow Elijah and became his attendant. _{1Sa 6:14}

Ben-Hadad Attacks Samaria

20 Now Ben-Hadad king of Aram mustered his entire army. Accompanied by thirty-two kings with their horses and chariots, he went up and besieged Samaria and attacked it. ²He sent messengers into the city to Ahab king of Israel, saying, "This is what Ben-Hadad says: ³'Your silver and gold are mine, and the best of your wives and children are mine.' "

⁴The king of Israel answered, "Just as you say, my lord the king. I and all I have are yours."

⁵The messengers came again and said, "This is what Ben-Hadad says: 'I sent to demand your silver and gold, your wives and your children. ⁶But about this time tomorrow I am going to send my officials to search your palace and the houses of your officials. They will seize everything you value and carry it away.'"

⁷The king of Israel summoned all the elders of the land and said to them, "See how this man is looking for trouble! When he sent for my wives and my children, my silver and my gold, I did not refuse him."

⁸The elders and the people all answered, "Don't listen to him or agree to his demands."

⁹So he replied to Ben-Hadad's messengers, "Tell my lord the king, 'Your servant will do all you demanded the first time, but this demand I cannot meet.'" They left and took the answer back to Ben-Hadad.

¹⁰Then Ben-Hadad sent another message to Ahab: "May the gods deal with me, be it ever so severely, if enough dust remains in Samaria to give each of my men a handful."   1Ki 19:2

¹¹The king of Israel answered, "Tell him: 'One who puts on his armor should not boast like one who takes it off.'"   Pr 27:1

¹²Ben-Hadad heard this message while he and the kings were drinking in their tents,ᵃ and he ordered his men: "Pre-pare to attack." So they pre-pared to attack the city.   1Ki 16:9

Ahab Defeats Ben-Hadad

¹³Meanwhile a prophet came to Ahab king of Israel and an-nounced, "This is what the LORD says: 'Do you see this vast army? I will give it into your hand today, and then you will know that I am the LORD.'"ᴶᵈᵍ ⁶:⁸

¹⁴"But who will do this?" asked Ahab.

The prophet replied, "This is what the LORD says: 'The young officers of the provincial com-manders will do it.'"

"And who will start the bat-tle?" he asked.   Jdg 1:1

The prophet answered, "You will."

¹⁵So Ahab summoned the young officers of the provincial commanders, 232 men. Then he assembled the rest of the Israel-ites, 7,000 in all. ¹⁶They set out at noon while Ben-Hadad and the 32 kings allied with him were in their tents getting drunk. ¹⁷The young officers of the provincial commanders went out first.   1Ki 16:9

Now Ben-Hadad had dis-patched scouts, who reported, "Men are advancing from Sa-maria."

¹⁸He said, "If they have come out for peace, take them alive; if they have come out for war, take them alive."   2Ki 14:8-12

¹⁹The young officers of the provincial commanders

ᵃ12 Or in Succoth; also in verse 16

marched out of the city with the army behind them ²⁰and each one struck down his opponent. At that, the Arameans fled, with the Israelites in pursuit. But Ben-Hadad king of Aram escaped on horseback with some of his horsemen. ²¹The king of Israel advanced and overpowered the horses and chariots and inflicted heavy losses on the Arameans.

²²Afterward, the prophet came to the king of Israel and said, "Strengthen your position and see what must be done, because next spring the king of Aram will attack you again."

²³Meanwhile, the officials of the king of Aram advised him, "Their gods are gods of the hills. That is why they were too strong for us. But if we fight them on the plains, surely we will be stronger than they. ²⁴Do this: Remove all the kings from their commands and replace them with other officers. ²⁵You must also raise an army like the one you lost—horse for horse and chariot for chariot—so we can fight Israel on the plains. Then surely we will be stronger than they." He agreed with them and acted accordingly.

²⁶The next spring Ben-Hadad mustered the Arameans and went up to Aphek to fight against Israel. ²⁷When the Israelites were also mustered and given provisions, they marched out to meet them. The Israelites camped opposite them like two small flocks of goats, while the Arameans covered the countryside. *Jdg 6:6; 2Ki 13:17*

²⁸The man of God came up and told the king of Israel, "This is what the LORD says: 'Because the Arameans think the LORD is a god of the hills and not a god of the valleys, I will deliver this vast army into your hands, and you will know that I am the LORD.'" *Ex 6:7; Jer 16:19-21*

²⁹For seven days they camped opposite each other, and on the seventh day the battle was joined. The Israelites inflicted a hundred thousand casualties on the Aramean foot soldiers in one day. ³⁰The rest of them escaped to the city of Aphek, where the wall collapsed on twenty-seven thousand of them. And Ben-Hadad fled to the city and hid in an inner room. *1Ki 22:25; Ps 62:4*

³¹His officials said to him, "Look, we have heard that the kings of the house of Israel are merciful. Let us go to the king of Israel with sackcloth around our waists and ropes around our heads. Perhaps he will spare your life." *Ge 37:34; Job 41:3*

³²Wearing sackcloth around their waists and ropes around their heads, they went to the king of Israel and said, "Your servant Ben-Hadad says: 'Please let me live.'"

The king answered, "Is he still alive? He is my brother."

³³The men took this as a good sign and were quick to pick up his word. "Yes, your brother Ben-Hadad!" they said.

"Go and get him," the king said. When Ben-Hadad came out, Ahab had him come up into his chariot.

34"I will return the cities my father took from your father," Ben-Hadad offered. "You may set up your own market areas in Damascus, as my father did in Samaria." 1Ki 15:20; 2Sa 8:6

Ahab said, "On the basis of a treaty I will set you free." So he made a treaty with him, and let him go. Ex 23:32

A Prophet Condemns Ahab

35By the word of the LORD one of the sons of the prophets said to his companion, "Strike me with your weapon," but the man refused. 2Ki 2:3; Am 7:14

36So the prophet said, "Because you have not obeyed the LORD, as soon as you leave me a lion will kill you." And after the man went away, a lion found him and killed him. 1Ki 13:24

37The prophet found another man and said, "Strike me, please." So the man struck him and wounded him. 38Then the prophet went and stood by the road waiting for the king. He disguised himself with his headband down over his eyes. 39As the king passed by, the prophet called out to him, "Your servant went into the thick of the battle, and someone came to me with a captive and said, 'Guard this man. If he is missing, it will be your life for his life, or you must pay a talent[a] of silver.' 40While your servant was busy here and there, the man disappeared." 2Ki 10:24

"That is your sentence," the king of Israel said. "You have pronounced it yourself." 2Sa 12:5

41Then the prophet quickly removed the headband from his eyes, and the king of Israel recognized him as one of the prophets. 42He said to the king, "This is what the LORD says: 'You have set free a man I had determined should die.[b] Therefore it is your life for his life, your people for his people.'" 43Sullen and angry, the king of Israel went to his palace in Samaria. 1Ki 21:4; Jer 48:10

Naboth's Vineyard

21 Some time later there was an incident involving a vineyard belonging to Naboth the Jezreelite. The vineyard was in Jezreel, close to the palace of Ahab king of Samaria. 2Ahab said to Naboth, "Let me have your vineyard to use for a vegetable garden, since it is close to my palace. In exchange I will give you a better vineyard or, if you prefer, I will pay you whatever it is worth." 2Ki 9:21

3But Naboth replied, "The LORD forbid that I should give you the inheritance of my fathers." Lev 25:23; Nu 36:7

---

a39 That is, about 75 pounds (about 34 kilograms) b42 The Hebrew term refers to the irrevocable giving over of things or persons to the LORD, often by totally destroying them.

⁴So Ahab went home, sullen and angry because Naboth the Jezreelite had said, "I will not give you the inheritance of my fathers." He lay on his bed sulking and refused to eat.   1Ki 20:43

⁵His wife Jezebel came in and asked him, "Why are you so sullen? Why won't you eat?"

⁶He answered her, "Because I said to Naboth the Jezreelite, 'Sell me your vineyard; or if you prefer, I will give you another vineyard in its place.' But he said, 'I will not give you my vineyard.' "

⁷Jezebel his wife said, "Is this how you act as king over Israel? Get up and eat! Cheer up. I'll get you the vineyard of Naboth the Jezreelite."   1Sa 8:14

⁸So she wrote letters in Ahab's name, placed his seal on them, and sent them to the elders and nobles who lived in Naboth's city with him. ⁹In those letters she wrote:

> "Proclaim a day of fasting and seat Naboth in a prominent place among the people. ¹⁰But seat two scoundrels opposite him and have them testify that he has cursed both God and the king. Then take him out and stone him to death."

¹¹So the elders and nobles who lived in Naboth's city did as Jezebel directed in the letters she had written to them. ¹²They proclaimed a fast and seated Naboth in a prominent place among the people. ¹³Then two scoundrels came and sat opposite him and brought charges against Naboth before the people, saying, "Naboth has cursed both God and the king." So they took him outside the city and stoned him to death. ¹⁴Then they sent word to Jezebel: "Naboth has been stoned and is dead."   2Ki 9:26; Isa 58:4

¹⁵As soon as Jezebel heard that Naboth had been stoned to death, she said to Ahab, "Get up and take possession of the vineyard of Naboth the Jezreelite that he refused to sell you. He is no longer alive, but dead." ¹⁶When Ahab heard that Naboth was dead, he got up and went down to take possession of Naboth's vineyard.

¹⁷Then the word of the LORD came to Elijah the Tishbite: ¹⁸"Go down to meet Ahab king of Israel, who rules in Samaria. He is now in Naboth's vineyard, where he has gone to take possession of it. ¹⁹Say to him, 'This is what the LORD says: Have you not murdered a man and seized his property?' Then say to him, 'This is what the LORD says: In the place where dogs licked up Naboth's blood, dogs will lick up your blood—yes, yours!' "   Ps 9:12

²⁰Ahab said to Elijah, "So you have found me, my enemy!"

"I have found you," he answered, "because you have sold yourself to do evil in the eyes of the LORD. ²¹I am going to bring

disaster on you. I will consume your descendants and cut off from Ahab every last male in Israel—slave or free. ²²I will make your house like that of Jeroboam son of Nebat and that of Baasha son of Ahijah, because you have provoked me to anger and have caused Israel to sin.'

²³"And also concerning Jezebel the LORD says: 'Dogs will devour Jezebel by the wall of*a* Jezreel.'

1Ki 15:29; 2Ki 9:10

²⁴"Dogs will eat those belonging to Ahab who die in the city, and the birds of the air will feed on those who die in the country."

Dt 28:26; 1Ki 14:11

²⁵(There was never a man like Ahab, who sold himself to do evil in the eyes of the LORD, urged on by Jezebel his wife. ²⁶He behaved in the vilest manner by going after idols, like the Amorites the LORD drove out before Israel.)

Ge 15:16; 1Ki 14:9

²⁷When Ahab heard these words, he tore his clothes, put on sackcloth and fasted. He lay in sackcloth and went around meekly.

2Sa 3:31; Isa 38:15

²⁸Then the word of the LORD came to Elijah the Tishbite: ²⁹"Have you noticed how Ahab has humbled himself before me? Because he has humbled himself, I will not bring this disaster in his day, but I will bring it on his house in the days of his son."

Ex 32:14; 2Ki 9:25

Micaiah Prophesies Against Ahab

22 For three years there was no war between Aram and Israel. ²But in the third year Jehoshaphat king of Judah went down to see the king of Israel. ³The king of Israel had said to his officials, "Don't you know that Ramoth Gilead belongs to us and yet we are doing nothing to retake it from the king of Aram?"

Dt 4:43; 2Ch 18:2

⁴So he asked Jehoshaphat, "Will you go with me to fight against Ramoth Gilead?"

2Ki 3:7

Jehoshaphat replied to the king of Israel, "I am as you are, my people as your people, my horses as your horses." ⁵But Jehoshaphat also said to the king of Israel, "First seek the counsel of the LORD."

Ex 33:7; 2Ki 3:11

⁶So the king of Israel brought together the prophets—about four hundred men—and asked them, "Shall I go to war against Ramoth Gilead, or shall I refrain?"

1Ki 18:19

"Go," they answered, "for the Lord will give it into the king's hand."

Jdg 18:6; 1Ki 13:18

⁷But Jehoshaphat asked, "Is there not a prophet of the LORD here whom we can inquire of?"

⁸The king of Israel answered Jehoshaphat, "There is still one man through whom we can inquire of the LORD, but I hate him because he never prophesies anything good about me, but al-

---

a23 Most Hebrew manuscripts; a few Hebrew manuscripts, Vulgate and Syriac (see also 2 Kings 9:26) *the plot of ground at*

ways bad. He is Micaiah son of Imlah." _{Isa 5:20; Am 5:10}

"The king should not say that," Jehoshaphat replied.

⁹So the king of Israel called one of his officials and said, "Bring Micaiah son of Imlah at once."

¹⁰Dressed in their royal robes, the king of Israel and Jehoshaphat king of Judah were sitting on their thrones at the threshing floor by the entrance of the gate of Samaria, with all the prophets prophesying before them. ¹¹Now Zedekiah son of Kenaanah had made iron horns and he declared, "This is what the Lord says: 'With these you will gore the Arameans until they are destroyed.' " _{Jdg 6:37}

¹²All the other prophets were prophesying the same thing. "Attack Ramoth Gilead and be victorious," they said, "for the Lord will give it into the king's hand."

¹³The messenger who had gone to summon Micaiah said to him, "Look, as one man the other prophets are predicting success for the king. Let your word agree with theirs, and speak favorably."

¹⁴But Micaiah said, "As surely as the Lord lives, I can tell him only what the Lord tells me." _{Nu 22:18; 1Sa 3:17}

¹⁵When he arrived, the king asked him, "Micaiah, shall we go to war against Ramoth Gilead, or shall I refrain?"

"Attack and be victorious,"

he answered, "for the Lord will give it into the king's hand."

¹⁶The king said to him, "How many times must I make you swear to tell me nothing but the truth in the name of the Lord?"

¹⁷Then Micaiah answered, "I saw all Israel scattered on the hills like sheep without a shepherd, and the Lord said, 'These people have no master. Let each one go home in peace.' " _{Nu 27:17}

¹⁸The king of Israel said to Jehoshaphat, "Didn't I tell you that he never prophesies anything good about me, but only bad?"

¹⁹Micaiah continued, "Therefore hear the word of the Lord: I saw the Lord sitting on his throne with all the host of heaven standing around him on his right and on his left. ²⁰And the Lord said, 'Who will entice Ahab into attacking Ramoth Gilead and going to his death there?' _{Isa 6:1; Da 7:9}

"One suggested this, and another that. ²¹Finally, a spirit came forward, stood before the Lord and said, 'I will entice him.'

²²" 'By what means?' the Lord asked. _{Jdg 9:23; 2Th 2:11}

" 'I will go out and be a lying spirit in the mouths of all his prophets,' he said.

" 'You will succeed in enticing him,' said the Lord. 'Go and do it.'

²³"So now the Lord has put a lying spirit in the mouths of all these prophets of yours. The

LORD has decreed disaster for you." Dt 13:3; Eze 14:9

²⁴Then Zedekiah son of Kenaanah went up and slapped Micaiah in the face. "Which way did the spirit fromᵃ the LORD go when he went from me to speak to you?" he asked.

²⁵Micaiah replied, "You will find out on the day you go to hide in an inner room." 1Ki 20:30

²⁶The king of Israel then ordered, "Take Micaiah and send him back to Amon the ruler of the city and to Joash the king's son ²⁷and say, 'This is what the king says: Put this fellow in prison and give him nothing but bread and water until I return safely.'" 2Ch 16:10; Jer 20:2

²⁸Micaiah declared, "If you ever return safely, the LORD has not spoken through me." Then he added, "Mark my words, all you people!" Nu 16:29; Dt 18:22

Ahab Killed at Ramoth Gilead

²⁹So the king of Israel and Jehoshaphat king of Judah went up to Ramoth Gilead. ³⁰The king of Israel said to Jehoshaphat, "I will enter the battle in disguise, but you wear your royal robes." So the king of Israel disguised himself and went into battle.

³¹Now the king of Aram had ordered his thirty-two chariot commanders, "Do not fight with anyone, small or great, except the king of Israel." ³²When the chariot commanders saw Jehoshaphat, they thought, "Surely this is the king of Israel." So they turned to attack him, but when Jehoshaphat cried out, ³³the chariot commanders saw that he was not the king of Israel and stopped pursuing him. 2Ch 18:30

³⁴But someone drew his bow at random and hit the king of Israel between the sections of his armor. The king told his chariot driver, "Wheel around and get me out of the fighting. I've been wounded." ³⁵All day long the battle raged, and the king was propped up in his chariot facing the Arameans. The blood from his wound ran onto the floor of the chariot, and that evening he died. ³⁶As the sun was setting, a cry spread through the army: "Every man to his town; everyone to his land!" 2Ki 14:12; 2Ch 35:23

³⁷So the king died and was brought to Samaria, and they buried him there. ³⁸They washed the chariot at a pool in Samaria (where the prostitutes bathed),ᵇ and the dogs licked up his blood, as the word of the LORD had declared. 1Ki 21:19

³⁹As for the other events of Ahab's reign, including all he did, the palace he built and inlaid with ivory, and the cities he fortified, are they not written in the book of the annals of the kings of Israel? ⁴⁰Ahab rested with his fathers. And Ahaziah his son succeeded him as king.

ᵃ24 Or Spirit of   ᵇ38 Or Samaria and cleaned the weapons

Jehoshaphat King of Judah

41Jehoshaphat son of Asa became king of Judah in the fourth year of Ahab king of Israel. 42Jehoshaphat was thirty-five years old when he became king, and he reigned in Jerusalem twenty-five years. His mother's name was Azubah daughter of Shilhi. 43In everything he walked in the ways of his father Asa and did not stray from them; he did what was right in the eyes of the LORD. The high places, however, were not removed, and the people continued to offer sacrifices and burn incense there. 44Jehoshaphat was also at peace with the king of Israel.   2Ch 30:41

45As for the other events of Jehoshaphat's reign, the things he achieved and his military exploits, are they not written in the book of the annals of the kings of Judah? 46He rid the land of the rest of the male shrine prostitutes who remained there even after the reign of his father Asa. 47There was then no king in Edom; a deputy ruled.

48Now Jehoshaphat built a fleet of trading ships*a* to go to Ophir for gold, but they never set sail—they were wrecked at Ezion Geber. 49At that time Ahaziah son of Ahab said to Jehoshaphat, "Let my men sail with your men," but Jehoshaphat refused.   Nu 33:35; 1Ki 9:26

50Then Jehoshaphat rested with his fathers and was buried with them in the city of David his father. And Jehoram his son succeeded him.   2Ch 21:1

Ahaziah King of Israel

51Ahaziah son of Ahab became king of Israel in Samaria in the seventeenth year of Jehoshaphat king of Judah, and he reigned over Israel two years. 52He did evil in the eyes of the LORD, because he walked in the ways of his father and mother and in the ways of Jeroboam son of Nebat, who caused Israel to sin. 53He served and worshiped Baal and provoked the LORD, the God of Israel, to anger, just as his father had done.   Jdg 2:11; 1Ki 15:26

2 Kings

Introduction:

Second Kings continues the stories of the great prophets Elijah and Elisha. It also tells the history of the northern kingdom of Israel and the southern kingdom of Judah until they were both finally conquered. Israel was conquered by Assyria in 722 B.C. and Judah was conquered by the Babylonians in 586 B.C. In both kingdoms God's prophets continually warned the people that God would punish them if they did not repent from their sins.

Outline of contents:

The LORD's Judgment on Ahaziah

1 After Ahab's death, Moab rebelled against Israel. ²Now Ahaziah had fallen through the lattice of his upper room in Samaria and injured himself. So he sent messengers, saying to them, "Go and consult Baal-Zebub, the god of Ekron, to see if I will recover from this injury."   Jdg 18:5; 2Sa 8:2

³But the angel of the LORD said to Elijah the Tishbite, "Go up and meet the messengers of the king of Samaria and ask them, 'Is it because there is no God in Israel that you are going off to consult Baal-Zebub, the god of Ekron?' ⁴Therefore this is what the LORD says: 'You will not leave the bed you are lying on. You will certainly die!' " So Elijah went.   1Ki 17:1; Ps 41:8

⁵When the messengers returned to the king, he asked them, "Why have you come back?"

⁶"A man came to meet us," they replied. "And he said to us, 'Go back to the king who sent you and tell him, "This is what the LORD says: Is it because there is no God in Israel that you are sending men to consult Baal-Zebub, the god of Ekron? Therefore you will not leave the bed you are lying on. You will certainly die!" ' "

⁷The king asked them, "What

kind of man was it who came to meet you and told you this?"

⁸They replied, "He was a man with a garment of hair and with a leather belt around his waist." Mt 3:4; Mk 1:6

The king said, "That was Elijah the Tishbite."

⁹Then he sent to Elijah a captain with his company of fifty men. The captain went up to Elijah, who was sitting on the top of a hill, and said to him, "Man of God, the king says, 'Come down!'" 2Ki 6:14; Isa 3:3

¹⁰Elijah answered the captain, "If I am a man of God, may fire come down from heaven and consume you and your fifty men!" Then fire fell from heaven and consumed the captain and his men. Lk 9:54

¹¹At this the king sent to Elijah another captain with his fifty men. The captain said to him, "Man of God, this is what the king says, 'Come down at once!'"

¹²"If I am a man of God," Elijah replied, "may fire come down from heaven and consume you and your fifty men!" Then the fire of God fell from heaven and consumed him and his fifty men.

¹³So the king sent a third captain with his fifty men. This third captain went up and fell on his knees before Elijah. "Man of God," he begged, "please have respect for my life and the lives of these fifty men,

your servants! ¹⁴See, fire has fallen from heaven and consumed the first two captains and all their men. But now have respect for my life!"

¹⁵The angel of the LORD said to Elijah, "Go down with him; do not be afraid of him." So Elijah got up and went down with him to the king. Isa 51:12

¹⁶He told the king, "This is what the LORD says: Is it because there is no God in Israel for you to consult that you have sent messengers to consult Baal-Zebub, the god of Ekron? Because you have done this, you will never leave the bed you are lying on. You will certainly die!" ¹⁷So he died, according to the word of the LORD that Elijah had spoken. 2Ki 8:15

Because Ahaziah had no son, Joram*ᵃ* succeeded him as king in the second year of Jehoram son of Jehoshaphat king of Judah. ¹⁸As for all the other events of Ahaziah's reign, and what he did, are they not written in the book of the annals of the kings of Israel? 2Ki 3:1

Elijah Taken Up to Heaven

2 When the LORD was about to take Elijah up to heaven in a whirlwind, Elijah and Elisha were on their way from Gilgal. ²Elijah said to Elisha, "Stay here; the LORD has sent me to Bethel." Ge 5:24; 1Ki 19:11

But Elisha said, "As surely as the LORD lives and as you live, I

ᵃ17 Hebrew Jehoram, a variant of Joram

will not leave you." So they went down to Bethel. Ru 1:16

³The company of the prophets at Bethel came out to Elisha and asked, "Do you know that the LORD is going to take your master from you today?" 1Sa 10:15

"Yes, I know," Elisha replied, "but do not speak of it."

⁴Then Elijah said to him, "Stay here, Elisha; the LORD has sent me to Jericho."

And he replied, "As surely as the LORD lives and as you live, I will not leave you." So they went to Jericho. Jos 3:16

⁵The company of the prophets at Jericho went up to Elisha and asked him, "Do you know that the LORD is going to take your master from you today?"

"Yes, I know," he replied, "but do not speak of it."

⁶Then Elijah said to him, "Stay here; the LORD has sent me to the Jordan." Jos 3:8,15

And he replied, "As surely as the LORD lives and as you live, I will not leave you." So the two of them walked on. Ru 1:16

⁷Fifty men of the company of the prophets went and stood at a distance, facing the place where Elijah and Elisha had stopped at the Jordan. ⁸Elijah took his cloak, rolled it up and struck the water with it. The water divided to the right and to the left, and the two of them crossed over on dry ground.

⁹When they had crossed, Elijah said to Elisha, "Tell me, what can I do for you before I am taken from you?"

"Let me inherit a double portion of your spirit," Elisha replied. Nu 11:17; Dt 21:17

¹⁰"You have asked a difficult thing," Elijah said, "yet if you see me when I am taken from you, it will be yours—otherwise not."

¹¹As they were walking along and talking together, suddenly a chariot of fire and horses of fire appeared and separated the two of them, and Elijah went up to heaven in a whirlwind. ¹²Elisha saw this and cried out, "My father! My father! The chariots and horsemen of Israel!" And Elisha saw him no more. Then he took hold of his own clothes and tore them apart. 2Ki 6:17

¹³He picked up the cloak that had fallen from Elijah and went back and stood on the bank of the Jordan. ¹⁴Then he took the cloak that had fallen from him and struck the water with it. "Where now is the LORD, the God of Elijah?" he asked. When he struck the water, it divided to the right and to the left, and he crossed over. 1Ki 19:19

¹⁵The company of the prophets from Jericho, who were watching, said, "The spirit of Elijah is resting on Elisha." And they went to meet him and bowed to the ground before him. ¹⁶"Look," they said, "we your servants have fifty able men. Let them go and look for your master. Perhaps the Spirit of the LORD has picked him up and set him down on some mountain or in some valley."

"No," Elisha replied, "do not send them."

¹⁷But they persisted until he was too ashamed to refuse. So he said, "Send them." And they sent fifty men, who searched for three days but did not find him. ¹⁸When they returned to Elisha, who was staying in Jericho, he said to them, "Didn't I tell you not to go?"   Jdg 3:25; 2Ki 8:11

Healing of the Water

¹⁹The men of the city said to Elisha, "Look, our lord, this town is well situated, as you can see, but the water is bad and the land is unproductive."

²⁰"Bring me a new bowl," he said, "and put salt in it." So they brought it to him.   1Sa 26:11

²¹Then he went out to the spring and threw the salt into it, saying, "This is what the LORD says: 'I have healed this water. Never again will it cause death or make the land unproductive.'" ²²And the water has remained wholesome to this day, according to the word Elisha had spoken.   Ex 15:25; 2Ki 4:41

Elisha Is Jeered

²³From there Elisha went up to Bethel. As he was walking along the road, some youths came out of the town and jeered at him. "Go on up, you baldhead!" they said. "Go on up, you baldhead!" ²⁴He turned around, looked at them and called down a curse on them in the name of the LORD. Then two bears came out of the woods and mauled forty-two of the youths. ²⁵And he went on to Mount Carmel and from there returned to Samaria.   2Ch 30:10

Moab Revolts

3 Joram*a* son of Ahab became king of Israel in Samaria in the eighteenth year of Jehoshaphat king of Judah, and he reigned twelve years. ²He did evil in the eyes of the LORD, but not as his father and mother had done. He got rid of the sacred stone of Baal that his father had made. ³Nevertheless he clung to the sins of Jeroboam son of Nebat, which he had caused Israel to commit; he did not turn away from them.   2Ki 1:17

⁴Now Mesha king of Moab raised sheep, and he had to supply the king of Israel with a hundred thousand lambs and with the wool of a hundred thousand rams. ⁵But after Ahab died, the king of Moab rebelled against the king of Israel. ⁶So at that time King Joram set out from Samaria and mobilized all Israel. ⁷He also sent this message to Jehoshaphat king of Judah: "The king of Moab has rebelled against me. Will you go with me to fight against Moab?"

"I will go with you," he replied. "I am as you are, my people as your people, my horses as your horses."

---

a1 Hebrew *Jehoram*, a variant of *Joram*; also in verse 6

⁸"By what route shall we attack?" he asked.

"Through the Desert of Edom," he answered.

⁹So the king of Israel set out with the king of Judah and the king of Edom. After a roundabout march of seven days, the army had no more water for themselves or for the animals with them.   1Ki 22:47

¹⁰"What!" exclaimed the king of Israel. "Has the LORD called us three kings together only to hand us over to Moab?"   Pr 19:3

¹¹But Jehoshaphat asked, "Is there no prophet of the LORD here, that we may inquire of the LORD through him?"   Ge 25:22

An officer of the king of Israel answered, "Elisha son of Shaphat is here. He used to pour water on the hands of Elijah.ᵃ"

¹²Jehoshaphat said, "The word of the LORD is with him." So the king of Israel and Jehoshaphat and the king of Edom went down to him.   Nu 11:7

¹³Elisha said to the king of Israel, "What do we have to do with each other? Go to the prophets of your father and the prophets of your mother."

"No," the king of Israel answered, "because it was the LORD who called us three kings together to hand us over to Moab."   Ru 1:15

¹⁴Elisha said, "As surely as the LORD Almighty lives, whom I serve, if I did not have respect for the presence of Jehoshaphat king of Judah, I would not look at you or even notice you. ¹⁵But now bring me a harpist."   1Sa 10:5

While the harpist was playing, the hand of the LORD came upon Elisha ¹⁶and he said, "This is what the LORD says: Make this valley full of ditches. ¹⁷For this is what the LORD says: You will see neither wind nor rain, yet this valley will be filled with water, and you, your cattle and your other animals will drink. ¹⁸This is an easy thing in the eyes of the LORD; he will also hand Moab over to you. ¹⁹You will overthrow every fortified city and every major town. You will cut down every good tree, stop up all the springs, and ruin every good field with stones."

²⁰The next morning, about the time for offering the sacrifice, there it was—water flowing from the direction of Edom! And the land was filled with water.   Ex 17:6; 29:41

²¹Now all the Moabites had heard that the kings had come to fight against them; so every man, young and old, who could bear arms was called up and stationed on the border. ²²When they got up early in the morning, the sun was shining on the water. To the Moabites across the way, the water looked red—like blood. ²³"That's blood!" they said. "Those kings must have fought and slaughtered each other. Now to the plunder, Moab!"   Ge 19:37

ᵃ11 That is, he was Elijah's personal servant.

24But when the Moabites came to the camp of Israel, the Israelites rose up and fought them until they fled. And the Israelites invaded the land and slaughtered the Moabites. 25They destroyed the towns, and each man threw a stone on every good field until it was covered. They stopped up all the springs and cut down every good tree. Only Kir Hareseth was left with its stones in place, but men armed with slings surrounded it and attacked it as well. Isa 16:7; Jer 48:31

26When the king of Moab saw that the battle had gone against him, he took with him seven hundred swordsmen to break through to the king of Edom, but they failed. 27Then he took his firstborn son, who was to succeed him as king, and offered him as a sacrifice on the city wall. The fury against Israel was great; they withdrew and returned to their own land.

The Widow's Oil

4 The wife of a man from the company of the prophets cried out to Elisha, "Your servant my husband is dead, and you know that he revered the LORD. But now his creditor is coming to take my two boys as his slaves." Lev 25:39

2Elisha replied to her, "How can I help you? Tell me, what do you have in your house?"

"Your servant has nothing there at all," she said, "except a little oil." 1Ki 17:12

3Elisha said, "Go around and ask all your neighbors for empty jars. Don't ask for just a few. 4Then go inside and shut the door behind you and your sons. Pour oil into all the jars, and as each is filled, put it to one side."

5She left him and afterward shut the door behind her and her sons. They brought the jars to her and she kept pouring. 6When all the jars were full, she said to her son, "Bring me another one."

But he replied, "There is not a jar left." Then the oil stopped flowing.

7She went and told the man of God, and he said, "Go, sell the oil and pay your debts. You and your sons can live on what is left." 1Ki 12:22

The Shunammite's Son Restored to Life

8One day Elisha went to Shunem. And a well-to-do woman was there, who urged him to stay for a meal. So whenever he came by, he stopped there to eat. 9She said to her husband, "I know that this man who often comes our way is a holy man of God. 10Let's make a small room on the roof and put in it a bed and a table, a chair and a lamp for him. Then he can stay there whenever he comes to us."

11One day when Elisha came, he went up to his room and lay down there. 12He said to his servant Gehazi, "Call the Shunammite." So he called her, and she

stood before him. 13Elisha said to him, "Tell her, 'You have gone to all this trouble for us. Now what can be done for you? Can we speak on your behalf to the king or the commander of the army?'" 2Ki 8:1

She replied, "I have a home among my own people."

14"What can be done for her?" Elisha asked.

Gehazi said, "Well, she has no son and her husband is old."

15Then Elisha said, "Call her." So he called her, and she stood in the doorway. 16"About this time next year," Elisha said, "you will hold a son in your arms." Ge 18:10

"No, my lord," she objected. "Don't mislead your servant, O man of God!"

17But the woman became pregnant, and the next year about that same time she gave birth to a son, just as Elisha had told her.

18The child grew, and one day he went out to his father, who was with the reapers. 19"My head! My head!" he said to his father. Ge 8:22; Ru 2:3

His father told a servant, "Carry him to his mother." 20After the servant had lifted him up and carried him to his mother, the boy sat on her lap until noon, and then he died. 21She went up and laid him on the bed of the man of God, then shut the door and went out.

22She called her husband and said, "Please send me one of the servants and a donkey so I can go to the man of God quickly and return."

23"Why go to him today?" he asked. "It's not the New Moon or the Sabbath." Nu 10:10; 1Ch 23:31

"It's all right," she said.

24She saddled the donkey and said to her servant, "Lead on; don't slow down for me unless I tell you." 25So she set out and came to the man of God at Mount Carmel. 1Ki 18:20

When he saw her in the distance, the man of God said to his servant Gehazi, "Look! There's the Shunammite! 26Run to meet her and ask her, 'Are you all right? Is your husband all right? Is your child all right?'"

"Everything is all right," she said.

27When she reached the man of God at the mountain, she took hold of his feet. Gehazi came over to push her away, but the man of God said, "Leave her alone! She is in bitter distress, but the LORD has hidden it from me and has not told me why." 1Sa 1:15

28"Did I ask you for a son, my lord?" she said. "Didn't I tell you, 'Don't raise my hopes'?"

29Elisha said to Gehazi, "Tuck your cloak into your belt, take my staff in your hand and run. If you meet anyone, do not greet him, and if anyone greets you, do not answer. Lay my staff on the boy's face." 1Ki 18:46

30But the child's mother said, "As surely as the LORD lives and as you live, I will not leave

you." So he got up and followed her.   2Ki 2:2

³¹Gehazi went on ahead and laid the staff on the boy's face, but there was no sound or response. So Gehazi went back to meet Elisha and told him, "The boy has not awakened."

³²When Elisha reached the house, there was the boy lying dead on his couch. ³³He went in, shut the door on the two of them and prayed to the LORD. ³⁴Then he got on the bed and lay upon the boy, mouth to mouth, eyes to eyes, hands to hands. As he stretched himself out upon him, the boy's body grew warm. ³⁵Elisha turned away and walked back and forth in the room and then got on the bed and stretched out upon him once more. The boy sneezed seven times and opened his eyes.   1Ki 17:20; 2Ki 8:5

³⁶Elisha summoned Gehazi and said, "Call the Shunammite." And he did. When she came, he said, "Take your son." ³⁷She came in, fell at his feet and bowed to the ground. Then she took her son and went out.

Death in the Pot

³⁸Elisha returned to Gilgal and there was a famine in that region. While the company of the prophets was meeting with him, he said to his servant, "Put on the large pot and cook some stew for these men."   2Ki 2:1

³⁹One of them went out into the fields to gather herbs and found a wild vine. He gathered some of its gourds and filled the fold of his cloak. When he returned, he cut them up into the pot of stew, though no one knew what they were. ⁴⁰The stew was poured out for the men, but as they began to eat it, they cried out, "O man of God, there is death in the pot!" And they could not eat it.   Jnh 4:6

⁴¹Elisha said, "Get some flour." He put it into the pot and said, "Serve it to the people to eat." And there was nothing harmful in the pot.   Ex 15:25

Feeding of a Hundred

⁴²A man came from Baal Shalishah, bringing the man of God twenty loaves of barley bread baked from the first ripe grain, along with some heads of new grain. "Give it to the people to eat," Elisha said. 1Sa 9:4

⁴³"How can I set this before a hundred men?" his servant asked.

But Elisha answered, "Give it to the people to eat. For this is what the LORD says: 'They will eat and have some left over.'" ⁴⁴Then he set it before them, and they ate and had some left over, according to the word of the LORD.   Mt 14:20; Lk 9:13

Naaman Healed of Leprosy

5 Now Naaman was commander of the army of the king of Aram. He was a great man in the sight of his master and highly regarded, because through him the LORD had given victory to Aram. He was a

valiant soldier, but he had leprosy.[a]

Ge 10:22; Lk 4:27

²Now bands from Aram had gone out and had taken captive a young girl from Israel, and she served Naaman's wife. ³She said to her mistress, "If only my master would see the prophet who is in Samaria! He would cure him of his leprosy." 2Ki 6:23

⁴Naaman went to his master and told him what the girl from Israel had said. ⁵"By all means, go," the king of Aram replied. "I will send a letter to the king of Israel." So Naaman left, taking with him ten talents[b] of silver, six thousand shekels[c] of gold and ten sets of clothing. ⁶The letter that he took to the king of Israel read: "With this letter I am sending my servant Naaman to you so that you may cure him of his leprosy." 1Sa 9:7

⁷As soon as the king of Israel read the letter, he tore his robes and said, "Am I God? Can I kill and bring back to life? Why does this fellow send someone to me to be cured of his leprosy? See how he is trying to pick a quarrel with me!" Ge 30:2

⁸When Elisha the man of God heard that the king of Israel had torn his robes, he sent him this message: "Why have you torn your robes? Have the man come to me and he will know that there is a prophet in Israel." ⁹So Naaman went with his horses and chariots and stopped at the door of Elisha's house. ¹⁰Elisha sent a messenger to say to him, "Go, wash yourself seven times in the Jordan, and your flesh will be restored and you will be cleansed." 1Ki 22:7; Jn 9:7

¹¹But Naaman went away angry and said, "I thought that he would surely come out to me and stand and call on the name of the LORD his God, wave his hand over the spot and cure me of my leprosy. ¹²Are not Abana and Pharpar, the rivers of Damascus, better than any of the waters of Israel? Couldn't I wash in them and be cleansed?" So he turned and went off in a rage. Ex 7:19; Isa 8:6

¹³Naaman's servants went to him and said, "My father, if the prophet had told you to do some great thing, would you not have done it? How much more, then, when he tells you, 'Wash and be cleansed'!" ¹⁴So he went down and dipped himself in the Jordan seven times, as the man of God had told him, and his flesh was restored and became clean like that of a young boy. 2Ki 6:21; Job 33:25

¹⁵Then Naaman and all his attendants went back to the man of God. He stood before him and said, "Now I know that there is no God in all the world except in Israel. Please accept now a gift from your servant."

¹⁶The prophet answered, "As surely as the LORD lives, whom

a1 The Hebrew word was used for various diseases affecting the skin—not necessarily leprosy; also in verses 3, 6, 7, 11 and 27.   *b5* That is, about 750 pounds (about 340 kilograms)   *c5* That is, about 150 pounds (about 70 kilograms)

I serve, I will not accept a thing." And even though Naaman urged him, he refused.

17"If you will not," said Naaman, "please let me, your servant, be given as much earth as a pair of mules can carry, for your servant will never again make burnt offerings and sacrifices to any other god but the LORD. 18But may the LORD forgive your servant for this one thing: When my master enters the temple of Rimmon to bow down and he is leaning on my arm and I bow there also— when I bow down in the temple of Rimmon, may the LORD forgive your servant for this."   Ex 20:24; 2Ki 7:2

19"Go in peace," Elisha said.

After Naaman had traveled some distance, 20Gehazi, the servant of Elisha the man of God, said to himself, "My master was too easy on Naaman, this Aramean, by not accepting from him what he brought. As surely as the LORD lives, I will run after him and get something from him."   Ex 20:7; 1Sa 1:17

21So Gehazi hurried after Naaman. When Naaman saw him running toward him, he got down from the chariot to meet him. "Is everything all right?" he asked.

22"Everything is all right," Gehazi answered. "My master sent me to say, 'Two young men from the company of the prophets have just come to me from the hill country of Ephraim. Please give them a talent[a] of silver and two sets of clothing.' "   Ge 45:22; 2Ki 4:26

23"By all means, take two talents," said Naaman. He urged Gehazi to accept them, and then tied up the two talents of silver in two bags, with two sets of clothing. He gave them to two of his servants, and they carried them ahead of Gehazi. 24When Gehazi came to the hill, he took the things from the servants and put them away in the house. He sent the men away and they left. 25Then he went in and stood before his master Elisha.   Jos 7:1; 2Ki 15:19

"Where have you been, Gehazi?" Elisha asked.

"Your servant didn't go anywhere," Gehazi answered.

26But Elisha said to him, "Was not my spirit with you when the man got down from his chariot to meet you? Is this the time to take money, or to accept clothes, olive groves, vineyards, flocks, herds, or menservants and maidservants? 27Naaman's leprosy will cling to you and to your descendants forever." Then Gehazi went from Elisha's presence and he was leprous, as white as snow.

An Axhead Floats

6 The company of the prophets said to Elisha, "Look, the place where we meet with you is too small for us. 2Let us go to

---

[a]22 That is, about 75 pounds (about 34 kilograms)

the Jordan, where each of us can get a pole; and let us build a place there for us to live."1Sa 10:5

And he said, "Go."

3Then one of them said, "Won't you please come with your servants?"　　　2Ki 5:23

"I will," Elisha replied. 4And he went with them.

They went to the Jordan and began to cut down trees. 5As one of them was cutting down a tree, the iron axhead fell into the water. "Oh, my lord," he cried out, "it was borrowed!"

6The man of God asked, "Where did it fall?" When he showed him the place, Elisha cut a stick and threw it there, and made the iron float. 7"Lift it out," he said. Then the man reached out his hand and took it.　　　Ex 15:25; 2Ki 2:21

Elisha Traps Blinded Arameans

8Now the king of Aram was at war with Israel. After conferring with his officers, he said, "I will set up my camp in such and such a place."　　　2Ki 8:28-29

9The man of God sent word to the king of Israel: "Beware of passing that place, because the Arameans are going down there." 10So the king of Israel checked on the place indicated by the man of God. Time and again Elisha warned the king, so that he was on his guard in such places.　　Ps 5:11; Jer 11:18

11This enraged the king of Aram. He summoned his offi-

cers and demanded of them, "Will you not tell me which of us is on the side of the king of Israel?"

12"None of us, my lord the king," said one of his officers, "but Elisha, the prophet who is in Israel, tells the king of Israel the very words you speak in your bedroom."

13"Go, find out where he is," the king ordered, "so I can send men and capture him." The report came back: "He is in Dothan." 14Then he sent horses and chariots and a strong force there. They went by night and surrounded the city.　　Ge 37:17

15When the servant of the man of God got up and went out early the next morning, an army with horses and chariots had surrounded the city. "Oh, my lord, what shall we do?" the servant asked.

16"Don't be afraid," the prophet answered. "Those who are with us are more than those who are with them."　　2Ch 32:7

17And Elisha prayed, "O LORD, open his eyes so he may see." Then the LORD opened the servant's eyes, and he looked and saw the hills full of horses and chariots of fire all around Elisha.　　2Ki 2:11

18As the enemy came down toward him, Elisha prayed to the LORD, "Strike these people with blindness." So he struck them with blindness, as Elisha had asked.　　Ge 19:11; Ac 13:11

19Elisha told them, "This is not the road and this is not the

city. Follow me, and I will lead you to the man you are looking for." And he led them to Samaria.

20After they entered the city, Elisha said, "LORD, open the eyes of these men so they can see." Then the LORD opened their eyes and they looked, and there they were, inside Samaria.

21When the king of Israel saw them, he asked Elisha, "Shall I kill them, my father? Shall I kill them?"   2Ki 5:13; 8:9

22"Do not kill them," he answered. "Would you kill men you have captured with your own sword or bow? Set food and water before them so that they may eat and drink and then go back to their master." 23So he prepared a great feast for them, and after they had finished eating and drinking, he sent them away, and they returned to their master. So the bands from Aram stopped raiding Israel's territory.   Dt 20:11

Famine in Besieged Samaria

24Some time later, Ben-Hadad king of Aram mobilized his entire army and marched up and laid siege to Samaria. 25There was a great famine in the city; the siege lasted so long that a donkey's head sold for eighty shekels*a* of silver, and a quarter of a cab*b* of seed pods*c* for five shekels. *d*   Dt 28:52; Isa 36:12

26As the king of Israel was passing by on the wall, a woman cried to him, "Help me, my lord the king!"

27The king replied, "If the LORD does not help you, where can I get help for you? From the threshing floor? From the winepress?" 28Then he asked her, "What's the matter?"   Jer 19:9

She answered, "This woman said to me, 'Give up your son so we may eat him today, and tomorrow we'll eat my son.' 29So we cooked my son and ate him. The next day I said to her, 'Give up your son so we may eat him,' but she had hidden him."Lev 26:29

30When the king heard the woman's words, he tore his robes. As he went along the wall, the people looked, and there, underneath, he had sackcloth on his body. 31He said, "May God deal with me, be it ever so severely, if the head of Elisha son of Shaphat remains on his shoulders today!" 1Ki 21:27

32Now Elisha was sitting in his house, and the elders were sitting with him. The king sent a messenger ahead, but before he arrived, Elisha said to the elders, "Don't you see how this murderer is sending someone to cut off my head? Look, when the messenger comes, shut the door and hold it shut against him. Is not the sound of his master's footsteps behind him?"   1Ki 18:4; Eze 8:1

---

*a*25 That is, about 2 pounds (about 1 kilogram)   *b*25 That is, probably about 1/2 pint (about 0.3 liter)   *c*25 Or *of dove's dung*   *d*25 That is, about 2 ounces (about 55 grams)

33While he was still talking to them, the messenger came down to him. And the king said, "This disaster is from the LORD. Why should I wait for the LORD any longer?"   Job 2:9

7 Elisha said, "Hear the word of the LORD. This is what the LORD says: About this time tomorrow, a seah*a* of flour will sell for a shekel*b* and two seahs*c* of barley for a shekel at the gate of Samaria."   2Ki 7:16

2The officer on whose arm the king was leaning said to the man of God, "Look, even if the LORD should open the floodgates of the heavens, could this happen?"   2Ki 5:18; Mal 3:10

"You will see it with your own eyes," answered Elisha, "but you will not eat any of it!"

The Siege Lifted

3Now there were four men with leprosy*d* at the entrance of the city gate. They said to each other, "Why stay here until we die? 4If we say, 'We'll go into the city'—the famine is there, and we will die. And if we stay here, we will die. So let's go over to the camp of the Arameans and surrender. If they spare us, we live; if they kill us, then we die."

5At dusk they got up and went to the camp of the Arameans. When they reached the edge of the camp, not a man was there, 6for the Lord had caused the Arameans to hear the sound of chariots and horses and a great army, so that they said to one another, "Look, the king of Israel has hired the Hittite and Egyptian kings to attack us!" 7So they got up and fled in the dusk and abandoned their tents and their horses and donkeys. They left the camp as it was and ran for their lives.   Ps 48:4-6; Eze 1:24

8The men who had leprosy reached the edge of the camp and entered one of the tents. They ate and drank, and carried away silver, gold and clothes, and went off and hid them. They returned and entered another tent and took some things from it and hid them also.

9Then they said to each other, "We're not doing right. This is a day of good news and we are keeping it to ourselves. If we wait until daylight, punishment will overtake us. Let's go at once and report this to the royal palace."   2Sa 18:27

10So they went and called out to the city gatekeepers and told them, "We went into the Aramean camp and not a man was there—not a sound of anyone—only tethered horses and donkeys, and the tents left just as they were." 11The gatekeepers shouted the news, and

a1 That is, probably about 7 quarts (about 7.3 liters); also in verses 16 and 18
b1 That is, about 2/5 ounce (about 11 grams); also in verses 16 and 18   *c1* That is, probably about 13 quarts (about 15 liters); also in verses 16 and 18   *d3* The Hebrew word is used for various diseases affecting the skin—not necessarily leprosy; also in verse 8.

it was reported within the palace.

12The king got up in the night and said to his officers, "I will tell you what the Arameans have done to us. They know we are starving; so they have left the camp to hide in the countryside, thinking, 'They will surely come out, and then we will take them alive and get into the city.'" Jos 8:4; 2Ki 6:25-29

13One of his officers answered, "Have some men take five of the horses that are left in the city. Their plight will be like that of all the Israelites left here—yes, they will only be like all these Israelites who are doomed. So let us send them to find out what happened."

14So they selected two chariots with their horses, and the king sent them after the Aramean army. He commanded the drivers, "Go and find out what has happened." 15They followed them as far as the Jordan, and they found the whole road strewn with the clothing and equipment the Arameans had thrown away in their headlong flight. So the messengers returned and reported to the king. 16Then the people went out and plundered the camp of the Arameans. So a seah of flour sold for a shekel, and two seahs of barley sold for a shekel, as the LORD had said. Job 27:22

17Now the king had put the officer on whose arm he leaned in charge of the gate, and the people trampled him in the gateway, and he died, just as the man of God had foretold when the king came down to his house. 18It happened as the man of God had said to the king: "About this time tomorrow, a seah of flour will sell for a shekel and two seahs of barley for a shekel at the gate of Samaria." 2Ki 6:32

19The officer had said to the man of God, "Look, even if the LORD should open the floodgates of the heavens, could this happen?" The man of God had replied, "You will see it with your own eyes, but you will not eat any of it!" 20And that is exactly what happened to him, for the people trampled him in the gateway, and he died. Job 20:23

The Shunammite's Land Restored

8 Now Elisha had said to the woman whose son he had restored to life, "Go away with your family and stay for a while wherever you can, because the LORD has decreed a famine in the land that will last seven years." 2The woman proceeded to do as the man of God said. She and her family went away and stayed in the land of the Philistines seven years. 2Ki 4:35

3At the end of the seven years she came back from the land of the Philistines and went to the king to beg for her house and land. 4The king was talking to Gehazi, the servant of the man of God, and had said, "Tell me

about all the great things Elisha has done." ⁵Just as Gehazi was telling the king how Elisha had restored the dead to life, the woman whose son Elisha had brought back to life came to beg the king for her house and land.

Gehazi said, "This is the woman, my lord the king, and this is her son whom Elisha restored to life." ⁶The king asked the woman about it, and she told him.

Then he assigned an official to her case and said to him, "Give back everything that belonged to her, including all the income from her land from the day she left the country until now."   Ne 5:12

Hazael Murders Ben-Hadad

⁷Elisha went to Damascus, and Ben-Hadad king of Aram was ill. When the king was told, "The man of God has come all the way up here," ⁸he said to Hazael, "Take a gift with you and go to meet the man of God. Consult the Lord through him; ask him, 'Will I recover from this illness?'"   1Ki 19:15

⁹Hazael went to meet Elisha, taking with him as a gift forty camel-loads of all the finest wares of Damascus. He went in and stood before him, and said, "Your son Ben-Hadad king of Aram has sent me to ask, 'Will I recover from this illness?'"

¹⁰Elisha answered, "Go and say to him, 'You will certainly

recover'; butᵃ the Lord has revealed to me that he will in fact die." ¹¹He stared at him with a fixed gaze until Hazael felt ashamed. Then the man of God began to weep.   Isa 38:1

¹²"Why is my lord weeping?" asked Hazael.

"Because I know the harm you will do to the Israelites," he answered. "You will set fire to their fortified places, kill their young men with the sword, dash their little children to the ground, and rip open their pregnant women."   Hos 13:16

¹³Hazael said, "How could your servant, a mere dog, accomplish such a feat?"   1Sa 17:43

"The Lord has shown me that you will become king of Aram," answered Elisha. 1Ki 19:15

¹⁴Then Hazael left Elisha and returned to his master. When Ben-Hadad asked, "What did Elisha say to you?" Hazael replied, "He told me that you would certainly recover." ¹⁵But the next day he took a thick cloth, soaked it in water and spread it over the king's face, so that he died. Then Hazael succeeded him as king.   2Ki 1:17

Jehoram King of Judah

¹⁶In the fifth year of Joram son of Ahab king of Israel, when Jehoshaphat was king of Judah, Jehoram son of Jehoshaphat began his reign as king of Judah. ¹⁷He was thirty-two years old when he became king, and he

ᵃ10 The Hebrew may also be read *Go and say*, '*You will certainly not recover*,' *for*.

reigned in Jerusalem eight years. ¹⁸He walked in the ways of the kings of Israel, as the house of Ahab had done, for he married a daughter of Ahab. He did evil in the eyes of the LORD. ¹⁹Nevertheless, for the sake of his servant David, the LORD was not willing to destroy Judah. He had promised to maintain a lamp for David and his descendants forever.   2Ch 21:1-4

²⁰In the time of Jehoram, Edom rebelled against Judah and set up its own king. ²¹So Jehoram*a* went to Zair with all his chariots. The Edomites surrounded him and his chariot commanders, but he rose up and broke through by night; his army, however, fled back home. ²²To this day Edom has been in rebellion against Judah. Libnah revolted at the same time.   1Ki 22:47; 2Ch 21:10

²³As for the other events of Jehoram's reign, and all he did, are they not written in the book of the annals of the kings of Judah? ²⁴Jehoram rested with his fathers and was buried with them in the City of David. And Ahaziah his son succeeded him as king.   2Ch 21:20; 22:1

Ahaziah King of Judah

²⁵In the twelfth year of Joram son of Ahab king of Israel, Ahaziah son of Jehoram king of Judah began to reign. ²⁶Ahaziah was twenty-two years old when he became king, and he reigned in Jerusalem one year. His mother's name was Athaliah, a granddaughter of Omri king of Israel. ²⁷He walked in the ways of the house of Ahab and did evil in the eyes of the LORD, as the house of Ahab had done, for he was related by marriage to Ahab's family.   2Ki 9:29

²⁸Ahaziah went with Joram son of Ahab to war against Hazael king of Aram at Ramoth Gilead. The Arameans wounded Joram; ²⁹so King Joram returned to Jezreel to recover from the wounds the Arameans had inflicted on him at Ramoth*b* in his battle with Hazael king of Aram.   Dt 4:43; 2Ki 9:21

Then Ahaziah son of Jehoram king of Judah went down to Jezreel to see Joram son of Ahab, because he had been wounded.

Jehu Anointed King of Israel

9 The prophet Elisha summoned a man from the company of the prophets and said to him, "Tuck your cloak into your belt, take this flask of oil with you and go to Ramoth Gilead. ²When you get there, look for Jehu son of Jehoshaphat, the son of Nimshi. Go to him, get him away from his companions and take him into an inner room. ³Then take the flask and pour the oil on his head and declare, 'This is what the LORD says: I anoint you king over Is-

---

*a*21 Hebrew *Joram*, a variant of *Jehoram*; also in verses 23 and 24   *b*29 Hebrew *Ramah*, a variant of *Ramoth*

rael.' Then open the door and run; don't delay!''   2Ki 8:28

⁴So the young man, the prophet, went to Ramoth Gilead. ⁵When he arrived, he found the army officers sitting together. "I have a message for you, commander," he said.

"For which of us?" asked Jehu.

"For you, commander," he replied.

⁶Jehu got up and went into the house. Then the prophet poured the oil on Jehu's head and declared, "This is what the LORD, the God of Israel, says: 'I anoint you king over the LORD's people Israel. ⁷You are to destroy the house of Ahab your master, and I will avenge the blood of my servants the prophets and the blood of all the LORD's servants shed by Jezebel. ⁸The whole house of Ahab will perish. I will cut off from Ahab every last male in Israel—slave or free. ⁹I will make the house of Ahab like the house of Jeroboam son of Nebat and like the house of Baasha son of Ahijah. ¹⁰As for Jezebel, dogs will devour her on the plot of ground at Jezreel, and no one will bury her.' " Then he opened the door and ran.

¹¹When Jehu went out to his fellow officers, one of them asked him, "Is everything all right? Why did this madman come to you?"   Jer 29:26; Jn 10:20

"You know the man and the sort of things he says," Jehu replied.

¹²"That's not true!" they said. "Tell us."

Jehu said, "Here is what he told me: 'This is what the LORD says: I anoint you king over Israel.' "

¹³They hurried and took their cloaks and spread them under him on the bare steps. Then they blew the trumpet and shouted, "Jehu is king!"   Mt 21:8

Jehu Kills Joram and Ahaziah

¹⁴So Jehu son of Jehoshaphat, the son of Nimshi, conspired against Joram. (Now Joram and all Israel had been defending Ramoth Gilead against Hazael king of Aram, ¹⁵but King Joram*a* had returned to Jezreel to recover from the wounds the Arameans had inflicted on him in the battle with Hazael king of Aram.) Jehu said, "If this is the way you feel, don't let anyone slip out of the city to go and tell the news in Jezreel." ¹⁶Then he got into his chariot and rode to Jezreel, because Joram was resting there and Ahaziah king of Judah had gone down to see him.   2Ki 8:28; 2Ch 22:17

¹⁷When the lookout standing on the tower in Jezreel saw Jehu's troops approaching, he called out, "I see some troops coming."   1Sa 14:16; Isa 21:6

"Get a horseman," Joram ordered. "Send him to meet them

---

*a15 Hebrew *Jehoram*, a variant of *Joram*; also in verses 17 and 21-24

and ask, 'Do you come in peace?' " 1Sa 16:4

¹⁸The horseman rode off to meet Jehu and said, "This is what the king says: 'Do you come in peace?' "

"What do you have to do with peace?" Jehu replied. "Fall in behind me."

The lookout reported, "The messenger has reached them, but he isn't coming back."

¹⁹So the king sent out a second horseman. When he came to them he said, "This is what the king says: 'Do you come in peace?' " 1Ki 11:36; 15:4

Jehu replied, "What do you have to do with peace? Fall in behind me." 2Ch 21:7

²⁰The lookout reported, "He has reached them, but he isn't coming back either. The driving is like that of Jehu son of Nimshi—he drives like a madman."

²¹"Hitch up my chariot," Joram ordered. And when it was hitched up, Joram king of Israel and Ahaziah king of Judah rode out, each in his own chariot, to meet Jehu. They met him at the plot of ground that had belonged to Naboth the Jezreelite. ²²When Joram saw Jehu he asked, "Have you come in peace, Jehu?" 1Ki 21:1; 2Ch 22:7

"How can there be peace," Jehu replied, "as long as all the idolatry and witchcraft of your mother Jezebel abound?" 1Ki 18:19

²³Joram turned about and fled, calling out to Ahaziah, "Treachery, Ahaziah!" 2Ki 11:14

²⁴Then Jehu drew his bow and shot Joram between the shoulders. The arrow pierced his heart and he slumped down in his chariot. ²⁵Jehu said to Bidkar, his chariot officer, "Pick him up and throw him on the field that belonged to Naboth the Jezreelite. Remember how you and I were riding together in chariots behind Ahab his father when the LORD made this prophecy about him: ²⁶'Yesterday I saw the blood of Naboth and the blood of his sons, declares the LORD, and I will surely make you pay for it on this plot of ground, declares the LORD.'ᵃ Now then, pick him up and throw him on that plot, in accordance with the word of the LORD." 1Ki 21:19; 22:34

²⁷When Ahaziah king of Judah saw what had happened, he fled up the road to Beth Haggan.ᵇ Jehu chased him, shouting, "Kill him too!" They wounded him in his chariot on the way up to Gur near Ibleam, but he escaped to Megiddo and died there. ²⁸His servants took him by chariot to Jerusalem and buried him with his fathers in his tomb in the City of David. ²⁹(In the eleventh year of Joram son of Ahab, Ahaziah had become king of Judah.) 2Ki 23:29

Jezebel Killed

³⁰Then Jehu went to Jezreel.

ᵃ26 See 1 Kings 21:19.   ᵇ27 Or fled by way of the garden house

see that no servants of the LORD are here with you—only ministers of Baal." 24So they went in to make sacrifices and burnt offerings. Now Jehu had posted eighty men outside with this warning: "If one of you lets any of the men I am placing in your hands escape, it will be your life for his life." Jos 2:14; 1Ki 20:39

25As soon as Jehu had finished making the burnt offering, he ordered the guards and officers: "Go in and kill them; let no one escape." So they cut them down with the sword. The guards and officers threw the bodies out and then entered the inner shrine of the temple of Baal. 26They brought the sacred stone out of the temple of Baal and burned it. 27They demolished the sacred stone of Baal and tore down the temple of Baal, and people have used it for a latrine to this day. 1Ki 18:40

28So Jehu destroyed Baal worship in Israel. 29However, he did not turn away from the sins of Jeroboam son of Nebat, which he had caused Israel to commit—the worship of the golden calves at Bethel and Dan. Ex 32:4; 1Ki 19:17

30The LORD said to Jehu, "Because you have done well in accomplishing what is right in my eyes and have done to the house of Ahab all I had in mind to do, your descendants will sit on the throne of Israel to the fourth generation." 31Yet Jehu

was not careful to keep the law of the LORD, the God of Israel, with all his heart. He did not turn away from the sins of Jeroboam, which he had caused Israel to commit. 2Ki 15:12

32In those days the LORD began to reduce the size of Israel. Hazael overpowered the Israelites throughout their territory 33east of the Jordan in all the land of Gilead (the region of Gad, Reuben and Manasseh), from Aroer by the Arnon Gorge through Gilead to Bashan.

34As for the other events of Jehu's reign, all he did, and all his achievements, are they not written in the book of the annals of the kings of Israel? 1Ki 15:31

35Jehu rested with his fathers and was buried in Samaria. And Jehoahaz his son succeeded him as king. 36The time that Jehu reigned over Israel in Samaria was twenty-eight years. 2Ki 13:1

Athaliah and Joash

11 When Athaliah the mother of Ahaziah saw that her son was dead, she proceeded to destroy the whole royal family. 2But Jehosheba, the daughter of King Jehoram[a] and sister of Ahaziah, took Joash son of Ahaziah and stole him away from among the royal princes, who were about to be murdered. She put him and his nurse in a bedroom to hide him from Athaliah; so he was not killed. 3He remained hidden

a2 Hebrew *Joram*, a variant of *Jehoram*

with his nurse at the temple of the Lord for six years while Athaliah ruled the land. 2Ki 8:18

⁴In the seventh year Jehoiada sent for the commanders of units of a hundred, the Carites and the guards and had them brought to him at the temple of the Lord. He made a covenant with them and put them under oath at the temple of the Lord. Then he showed them the king's son. ⁵He commanded them, saying, "This is what you are to do: You who are in the three companies that are going on duty on the Sabbath—a third of you guarding the royal palace, ⁶a third at the Sur Gate, and a third at the gate behind the guard, who take turns guarding the temple— ⁷and you who are in the other two companies that normally go off Sabbath duty are all to guard the temple for the king. ⁸Station yourselves around the king, each man with his weapon in his hand. Anyone who approaches your ranksᵃ must be put to death. Stay close to the king wherever he goes." 1Ki 14:27; 1Ch 9:25

⁹The commanders of units of a hundred did just as Jehoiada the priest ordered. Each one took his men—those who were going on duty on the Sabbath and those who were going off duty—and came to Jehoiada the priest. ¹⁰Then he gave the commanders the spears and shields that had belonged to King Da-vid and that were in the temple of the Lord. ¹¹The guards, each with his weapon in his hand, stationed themselves around the king—near the altar and the temple, from the south side to the north side of the temple.

¹²Jehoiada brought out the king's son and put the crown on him; he presented him with a copy of the covenant and proclaimed him king. They anointed him, and the people clapped their hands and shouted, "Long live the king!" 2Ki 23:3

¹³When Athaliah heard the noise made by the guards and the people, she went to the people at the temple of the Lord. ¹⁴She looked and there was the king, standing by the pillar, as the custom was. The officers and the trumpeters were beside the king, and all the people of the land were rejoicing and blowing trumpets. Then Athaliah tore her robes and called out, "Treason! Treason!" 1Ki 1:39; 2Ki 9:23

¹⁵Jehoiada the priest ordered the commanders of units of a hundred, who were in charge of the troops: "Bring her out between the ranksᵇ and put to the sword anyone who follows her." For the priest had said, "She must not be put to death in the temple of the Lord." ¹⁶So they seized her as she reached the place where the horses enter the palace grounds, and there she was put to death. 1Ki 2:30

ᵃ8 Or approaches the precincts   ᵇ15 Or out from the precincts

¹⁷Jehoiada then made a covenant between the LORD and the king and people that they would be the LORD's people. He also made a covenant between the king and the people. ¹⁸All the people of the land went to the temple of Baal and tore it down. They smashed the altars and idols to pieces and killed Mattan the priest of Baal in front of the altars.　Dt 12:3; 2Sa 5:3

Then Jehoiada the priest posted guards at the temple of the LORD. ¹⁹He took with him the commanders of hundreds, the Carites, the guards and all the people of the land, and together they brought the king down from the temple of the LORD and went into the palace, entering by way of the gate of the guards. The king then took his place on the royal throne, ²⁰and all the people of the land rejoiced. And the city was quiet, because Athaliah had been slain with the sword at the palace.

²¹Joash*a* was seven years old when he began to reign.　2Ch 24:1

Joash Repairs the Temple

12 In the seventh year of Jehu, Joash*b* became king, and he reigned in Jerusalem forty years. His mother's name was Zibiah; she was from Beersheba. ²Joash did what was right in the eyes of the LORD all the years Jehoiada the priest instructed him. ³The high places,

however, were not removed; the people continued to offer sacrifices and burn incense there.　Dt 12:25; 2Ki 18:4

⁴Joash said to the priests, "Collect all the money that is brought as sacred offerings to the temple of the LORD—the money collected in the census, the money received from personal vows and the money brought voluntarily to the temple. ⁵Let every priest receive the money from one of the treasurers, and let it be used to repair whatever damage is found in the temple."　2Ki 22:4

⁶But by the twenty-third year of King Joash the priests still had not repaired the temple. ⁷Therefore King Joash summoned Jehoiada the priest and the other priests and asked them, "Why aren't you repairing the damage done to the temple? Take no more money from your treasurers, but hand it over for repairing the temple." ⁸The priests agreed that they would not collect any more money from the people and that they would not repair the temple themselves.　2Ch 24:5-6

⁹Jehoiada the priest took a chest and bored a hole in its lid. He placed it beside the altar, on the right side as one enters the temple of the LORD. The priests who guarded the entrance put into the chest all the money that was brought to the temple of

---

*a*21 Hebrew *Jehoash*, a variant of *Joash* verses 2, 4, 6, 7 and 18　　*b*1 Hebrew *Jehoash*, a variant of *Joash*; also in

the LORD. ¹⁰Whenever they saw that there was a large amount of money in the chest, the royal secretary and the high priest came, counted the money that had been brought into the temple of the LORD and put it into bags. ¹¹When the amount had been determined, they gave the money to the men appointed to supervise the work on the temple. With it they paid those who worked on the temple of the LORD—the carpenters and builders, ¹²the masons and stonecutters. They purchased timber and dressed stone for the repair of the temple of the LORD, and met all the other expenses of restoring the temple.

¹³The money brought into the temple was not spent for making silver basins, wick trimmers, sprinkling bowls, trumpets or any other articles of gold or silver for the temple of the LORD; ¹⁴it was paid to the workmen, who used it to repair the temple. ¹⁵They did not require an accounting from those to whom they gave the money to pay the workers, because they acted with complete honesty. ¹⁶The money from the guilt offerings and sin offerings was not brought into the temple of the LORD; it belonged to the priests.   Lev 5:14-19; 1Ki 7:51

¹⁷About this time Hazael king of Aram went up and attacked Gath and captured it. Then he turned to attack Jerusalem. ¹⁸But Joash king of Judah took all the sacred objects dedicated by his fathers—Jehoshaphat, Jehoram and Ahaziah, the kings of Judah—and the gifts he himself had dedicated and all the gold found in the treasuries of the temple of the LORD and of the royal palace, and he sent them to Hazael king of Aram, who then withdrew from Jerusalem.   1Ki 15:21; 2Ki 8:12

¹⁹As for the other events of the reign of Joash, and all he did, are they not written in the book of the annals of the kings of Judah? ²⁰His officials conspired against him and assassinated him at Beth Millo, on the road down to Silla. ²¹The officials who murdered him were Jozabad son of Shimeath and Jehozabad son of Shomer. He died and was buried with his fathers in the City of David. And Amaziah his son succeeded him as king.   2Ki 14:5

Jehoahaz King of Israel

13 In the twenty-third year of Joash son of Ahaziah king of Judah, Jehoahaz son of Jehu became king of Israel in Samaria, and he reigned seventeen years. ²He did evil in the eyes of the LORD by following the sins of Jeroboam son of Nebat, which he had caused Israel to commit, and he did not turn away from them. ³So the LORD's anger burned against Israel, and for a long time he kept them under the power of Hazael king of Aram and Ben-Hadad his son.   Dt 31:17; 1Ki 12:26

⁴Then Jehoahaz sought the LORD's favor, and the LORD listened to him, for he saw how severely the king of Aram was oppressing Israel. ⁵The LORD provided a deliverer for Israel, and they escaped from the power of Aram. So the Israelites lived in their own homes as they had before. ⁶But they did not turn away from the sins of the house of Jeroboam, which he had caused Israel to commit; they continued in them. Also, the Asherah pole*ᵃ* remained standing in Samaria.   1Ki 16:33

⁷Nothing had been left of the army of Jehoahaz except fifty horsemen, ten chariots and ten thousand foot soldiers, for the king of Aram had destroyed the rest and made them like the dust at threshing time.   Am 1:3

⁸As for the other events of the reign of Jehoahaz, all he did and his achievements, are they not written in the book of the annals of the kings of Israel? ⁹Jehoahaz rested with his fathers and was buried in Samaria. And Jehoash*ᵇ* his son succeeded him as king.   2Ki 10:35

Jehoash King of Israel

¹⁰In the thirty-seventh year of Joash king of Judah, Jehoash son of Jehoahaz became king of Israel in Samaria, and he reigned sixteen years. ¹¹He did evil in the eyes of the LORD and did not turn away from any of the sins of Jeroboam son of Nebat, which he had caused Israel to commit; he continued in them.

¹²As for the other events of the reign of Jehoash, all he did and his achievements, including his war against Amaziah king of Judah, are they not written in the book of the annals of the kings of Israel? ¹³Jehoash rested with his fathers, and Jeroboam succeeded him on the throne. Jehoash was buried in Samaria with the kings of Israel.

¹⁴Now Elisha was suffering from the illness from which he died. Jehoash king of Israel went down to see him and wept over him. "My father! My father!" he cried. "The chariots and horsemen of Israel!"   Hos 1:1

¹⁵Elisha said, "Get a bow and some arrows," and he did so. ¹⁶"Take the bow in your hands," he said to the king of Israel. When he had taken it, Elisha put his hands on the king's hands.   1Sa 20:20; 1Ch 5:18

¹⁷"Open the east window," he said, and he opened it. "Shoot!" Elisha said, and he shot. "The LORD's arrow of victory, the arrow of victory over Aram!" Elisha declared. "You will completely destroy the Arameans at Aphek."   1Ki 20:26

¹⁸Then he said, "Take the arrows," and the king took them. Elisha told him, "Strike the

ᵃ6 That is, a symbol of the goddess Asherah; here and elsewhere in 2 Kings
ᵇ9 Hebrew *Joash*, a variant of *Jehoash*; also in verses 12-14 and 25

ground." He struck it three times and stopped. ¹⁹The man of God was angry with him and said, "You should have struck the ground five or six times; then you would have defeated Aram and completely destroyed it. But now you will defeat it only three times." 2Ki 13:25

²⁰Elisha died and was buried.

Now Moabite raiders used to enter the country every spring. ²¹Once while some Israelites were burying a man, suddenly they saw a band of raiders; so they threw the man's body into Elisha's tomb. When the body touched Elisha's bones, the man came to life and stood up on his feet. 2Ki 5:2

²²Hazael king of Aram oppressed Israel throughout the reign of Jehoahaz. ²³But the LORD was gracious to them and had compassion and showed concern for them because of his covenant with Abraham, Isaac and Jacob. To this day he has been unwilling to destroy them or banish them from his presence. Ex 2:24; 1Ki 19:17

²⁴Hazael king of Aram died, and Ben-Hadad his son succeeded him as king. ²⁵Then Jehoash son of Jehoahaz recaptured from Ben-Hadad son of Hazael the towns he had taken in battle from his father Jehoahaz. Three times Jehoash defeated him, and so he recovered the Israelite towns. 2Ki 10:32

Amaziah King of Judah

14 In the second year of Jehoash[a] son of Jehoahaz king of Israel, Amaziah son of Joash king of Judah began to reign. ²He was twenty-five years old when he became king, and he reigned in Jerusalem twenty-nine years. His mother's name was Jehoaddin; she was from Jerusalem. ³He did what was right in the eyes of the LORD, but not as his father David had done. In everything he followed the example of his father Joash. ⁴The high places, however, were not removed; the people continued to offer sacrifices and burn incense there. 2Ki 12:3; 13:10

⁵After the kingdom was firmly in his grasp, he executed the officials who had murdered his father the king. ⁶Yet he did not put the sons of the assassins to death, in accordance with what is written in the Book of the Law of Moses where the LORD commanded: "Fathers shall not be put to death for their children, nor children put to death for their fathers; each is to die for his own sins."[b] 2Ki 12:20

⁷He was the one who defeated ten thousand Edomites in the Valley of Salt and captured Sela in battle, calling it Joktheel, the name it has to this day. Jdg 1:36; 2Sa 8:13

⁸Then Amaziah sent messengers to Jehoash son of Jehoahaz, the son of Jehu, king of Israel,

---

*a*1 Hebrew *Joash,* a variant of *Jehoash;* also in verses 13, 23 and 27   *b*6 Deut. 24:16

with the challenge: "Come, meet me face to face." 2Ch 25:17

⁹But Jehoash king of Israel replied to Amaziah king of Judah: "A thistle in Lebanon sent a message to a cedar in Lebanon, 'Give your daughter to my son in marriage.' Then a wild beast in Lebanon came along and trampled the thistle underfoot. ¹⁰You have indeed defeated Edom and now you are arrogant. Glory in your victory, but stay at home! Why ask for trouble and cause your own downfall and that of Judah also?"

¹¹Amaziah, however, would not listen, so Jehoash king of Israel attacked. He and Amaziah king of Judah faced each other at Beth Shemesh in Judah. ¹²Judah was routed by Israel, and every man fled to his home. ¹³Jehoash king of Israel captured Amaziah king of Judah, the son of Joash, the son of Ahaziah, at Beth Shemesh. Then Jehoash went to Jerusalem and broke down the wall of Jerusalem from the Ephraim Gate to the Corner Gate—a section about six hundred feet long.ᵃ ¹⁴He took all the gold and silver and all the articles found in the temple of the LORD and in the treasuries of the royal palace. He also took hostages and returned to Samaria. 1Ki 22:36; Ne 8:16

¹⁵As for the other events of the reign of Jehoash, what he did and his achievements, including his war against Ama-

ziah king of Judah, are they not written in the book of the annals of the kings of Israel? ¹⁶Jehoash rested with his fathers and was buried in Samaria with the kings of Israel. And Jeroboam his son succeeded him as king.

¹⁷Amaziah son of Joash king of Judah lived for fifteen years after the death of Jehoash son of Jehoahaz king of Israel. ¹⁸As for the other events of Amaziah's reign, are they not written in the book of the annals of the kings of Judah? 2Ch 25:25-28

¹⁹They conspired against him in Jerusalem, and he fled to Lachish, but they sent men after him to Lachish and killed him there. ²⁰He was brought back by horse and was buried in Jerusalem with his fathers, in the City of David. Jos 10:31; 2Ki 9:28

²¹Then all the people of Judah took Azariah,ᵇ who was sixteen years old, and made him king in place of his father Amaziah. ²²He was the one who rebuilt Elath and restored it to Judah after Amaziah rested with his fathers. 2Ch 26:23; Isa 1:1

Jeroboam II King of Israel

²³In the fifteenth year of Amaziah son of Joash king of Judah, Jeroboam son of Jehoash king of Israel became king in Samaria, and he reigned forty-one years. ²⁴He did evil in the eyes of the LORD and did not turn away from any of the sins of Jeroboam son of Nebat, which he had

---

ᵃ13 Hebrew *four hundred cubits* (about 180 meters)   ᵇ21 Also called *Uzziah*

caused Israel to commit. 25He was the one who restored the boundaries of Israel from Lebo[a] Hamath to the Sea of the Arabah,[b] in accordance with the word of the LORD, the God of Israel, spoken through his servant Jonah son of Amittai, the prophet from Gath Hepher.

26The LORD had seen how bitterly everyone in Israel, whether slave or free, was suffering; there was no one to help them. 27And since the LORD had not said he would blot out the name of Israel from under heaven, he saved them by the hand of Jeroboam son of Jehoash.   Dt 32:36; 2Ki 13:4

28As for the other events of Jeroboam's reign, all he did, and his military achievements, including how he recovered for Israel both Damascus and Hamath, which had belonged to Yaudi,[c] are they not written in the book of the annals of the kings of Israel? 29Jeroboam rested with his fathers, the kings of Israel. And Zechariah his son succeeded him as king.   2Sa 8:5

Azariah King of Judah

15 In the twenty-seventh year of Jeroboam king of Israel, Azariah son of Amaziah king of Judah began to reign. 2He was sixteen years old when he became king, and he reigned in Jerusalem fifty-two years. His mother's name was Jecoliah; she was from Jerusalem. 3He did what was right in the eyes of the LORD, just as his father Amaziah had done. 4The high places, however, were not removed; the people continued to offer sacrifices and burn incense there.   1Ki 14:8; 2Ki 14:21

5The LORD afflicted the king with leprosy[d] until the day he died, and he lived in a separate house.[e] Jotham the king's son had charge of the palace and governed the people of the land.   Lev 13:46; Mic 1:1

6As for the other events of Azariah's reign, and all he did, are they not written in the book of the annals of the kings of Judah? 7Azariah rested with his fathers and was buried near them in the City of David. And Jotham his son succeeded him as king.   2Ch 26:23; Isa 6:1

Zechariah King of Israel

8In the thirty-eighth year of Azariah king of Judah, Zechariah son of Jeroboam became king of Israel in Samaria, and he reigned six months. 9He did evil in the eyes of the LORD, as his fathers had done. He did not turn away from the sins of Jeroboam son of Nebat, which he had caused Israel to commit.

10Shallum son of Jabesh conspired against Zechariah. He attacked him in front of the

---

a25 Or *from the entrance to*   b25 That is, the Dead Sea   c28 Or *Judah*   d5 The Hebrew word was used for various diseases affecting the skin—not necessarily leprosy.   e5 Or *in a house where he was relieved of responsibility*

people,[a] assassinated him and succeeded him as king. [11]The other events of Zechariah's reign are written in the book of the annals of the kings of Israel. [12]So the word of the LORD spoken to Jehu was fulfilled: "Your descendants will sit on the throne of Israel to the fourth generation."[b]   2Ki 12:20

Shallum King of Israel

[13]Shallum son of Jabesh became king in the thirty-ninth year of Uzziah king of Judah, and he reigned in Samaria one month. [14]Then Menahem son of Gadi went from Tirzah up to Samaria. He attacked Shallum son of Jabesh in Samaria, assassinated him and succeeded him as king.   1Sa 13:32; 1Ki 15:33

[15]The other events of Shallum's reign, and the conspiracy he led, are written in the book of the annals of the kings of Israel. [16]At that time Menahem, starting out from Tirzah, attacked Tiphsah and everyone in the city and its vicinity, because they refused to open their gates. He sacked Tiphsah and ripped open all the pregnant women.

Menahem King of Israel

[17]In the thirty-ninth year of Azariah king of Judah, Menahem son of Gadi became king of Israel, and he reigned in Samaria ten years. [18]He did evil in the eyes of the LORD. During his entire reign he did not turn away from the sins of Jeroboam son of Nebat, which he had caused Israel to commit.   1Ki 15:26

[19]Then Pul[c] king of Assyria invaded the land, and Menahem gave him a thousand talents[d] of silver to gain his support and strengthen his own hold on the kingdom. [20]Menahem exacted this money from Israel. Every wealthy man had to contribute fifty shekels[e] of silver to be given to the king of Assyria. So the king of Assyria withdrew and stayed in the land no longer.   2Ki 12:18; 1Ch 5:6

[21]As for the other events of Menahem's reign, and all he did, are they not written in the book of the annals of the kings of Israel? [22]Menahem rested with his fathers. And Pekahiah his son succeeded him as king.

Pekahiah King of Israel

[23]In the fiftieth year of Azariah king of Judah, Pekahiah son of Menahem became king of Israel in Samaria, and he reigned two years. [24]Pekahiah did evil in the eyes of the LORD. He did not turn away from the sins of Jeroboam son of Nebat, which he had caused Israel to commit. [25]One of his chief officers, Pekah son of Remaliah, conspired against him. Taking fifty men of Gilead with him, he assassinated Pekahiah, along with Argob and Arieh, in the

[a]10 Hebrew; some Septuagint manuscripts in Ibleam   [b]12 2 Kings 10:30   [c]19 Also called Tiglath-Pileser   [d]19 That is, about 37 tons (about 34 metric tons)   [e]20 That is, about 1 1/4 pounds (about 0.6 kilogram)

citadel of the royal palace at Samaria. So Pekah killed Pekahiah and succeeded him as king.

26The other events of Pekahiah's reign, and all he did, are written in the book of the annals of the kings of Israel.

Pekah King of Israel

27In the fifty-second year of Azariah king of Judah, Pekah son of Remaliah became king of Israel in Samaria, and he reigned twenty years. 28He did evil in the eyes of the LORD. He did not turn away from the sins of Jeroboam son of Nebat, which he had caused Israel to commit.   Isa 7:4

29In the time of Pekah king of Israel, Tiglath-Pileser king of Assyria came and took Ijon, Abel Beth Maacah, Janoah, Kedesh and Hazor. He took Gilead and Galilee, including all the land of Naphtali, and deported the people to Assyria. 30Then Hoshea son of Elah conspired against Pekah son of Remaliah. He attacked and assassinated him, and then succeeded him as king in the twentieth year of Jotham son of Uzziah.   2Ki 17:6

31As for the other events of Pekah's reign, and all he did, are they not written in the book of the annals of the kings of Israel?   1Ki 15:31

Jotham King of Judah

32In the second year of Pekah son of Remaliah king of Israel, Jotham son of Uzziah king of Judah began to reign. 33He was twenty-five years old when he became king, and he reigned in Jerusalem sixteen years. His mother's name was Jerusha daughter of Zadok. 34He did what was right in the eyes of the LORD, just as his father Uzziah had done. 35The high places, however, were not removed; the people continued to offer sacrifices and burn incense there. Jotham rebuilt the Upper Gate of the temple of the LORD.

36As for the other events of Jotham's reign, and what he did, are they not written in the book of the annals of the kings of Judah? 37(In those days the LORD began to send Rezin king of Aram and Pekah son of Remaliah against Judah.) 38Jotham rested with his fathers and was buried with them in the City of David, the city of his father. And Ahaz his son succeeded him as king.   2Ch 16:5

Ahaz King of Judah

16 In the seventeenth year of Pekah son of Remaliah, Ahaz son of Jotham king of Judah began to reign. 2Ahaz was twenty years old when he became king, and he reigned in Jerusalem sixteen years. Unlike David his father, he did not do what was right in the eyes of the LORD his God. 3He walked in the ways of the kings of Israel and even sacrificed his son in*a*

*a*3 Or *even made his son pass through*

the fire, following the detestable ways of the nations the LORD had driven out before the Israelites. ⁴He offered sacrifices and burned incense at the high places, on the hilltops and under every spreading tree.   Isa 1:1

⁵Then Rezin king of Aram and Pekah son of Remaliah king of Israel marched up to fight against Jerusalem and besieged Ahaz, but they could not overpower him. ⁶At that time, Rezin king of Aram recovered Elath for Aram by driving out the men of Judah. Edomites then moved into Elath and have lived there to this day.   2Ki 15:37

⁷Ahaz sent messengers to say to Tiglath-Pileser king of Assyria, "I am your servant and vassal. Come up and save me out of the hand of the king of Aram and of the king of Israel, who are attacking me." ⁸And Ahaz took the silver and gold found in the temple of the LORD and in the treasuries of the royal palace and sent it as a gift to the king of Assyria. ⁹The king of Assyria complied by attacking Damascus and capturing it. He deported its inhabitants to Kir and put Rezin to death.   2Ki 15:29

¹⁰Then King Ahaz went to Damascus to meet Tiglath-Pileser king of Assyria. He saw an altar in Damascus and sent to Uriah the priest a sketch of the altar, with detailed plans for its construction. ¹¹So Uriah the priest built an altar in accordance with all the plans that King Ahaz had sent from Damascus and finished it before King Ahaz returned. ¹²When the king came back from Damascus and saw the altar, he approached it and presented offeringsᵃ on it. ¹³He offered up his burnt offering and grain offering, poured out his drink offering, and sprinkled the blood of his fellowship offeringsᵇ on the altar. ¹⁴The bronze altar that stood before the LORD he brought from the front of the temple—from between the new altar and the temple of the LORD—and put it on the north side of the new altar.   Isa 8:2

¹⁵King Ahaz then gave these orders to Uriah the priest: "On the large new altar, offer the morning burnt offering and the evening grain offering, the king's burnt offering and his grain offering, and the burnt offering of all the people of the land, and their grain offering and their drink offering. Sprinkle on the altar all the blood of the burnt offerings and sacrifices. But I will use the bronze altar for seeking guidance." ¹⁶And Uriah the priest did just as King Ahaz had ordered.

¹⁷King Ahaz took away the side panels and removed the basins from the movable stands. He removed the Sea from the bronze bulls that supported it and set it on a stone base. ¹⁸He

ᵃ12 Or and went up   ᵇ13 Traditionally peace offerings

took away the Sabbath canopy[a] that had been built at the temple and removed the royal entryway outside the temple of the LORD, in deference to the king of Assyria.   1Ki 7:27

19As for the other events of the reign of Ahaz, and what he did, are they not written in the book of the annals of the kings of Judah? 20Ahaz rested with his fathers and was buried with them in the City of David. And Hezekiah his son succeeded him as king.   Isa 14:28

Hoshea Last King of Israel

17 In the twelfth year of Ahaz king of Judah, Hoshea son of Elah became king of Israel in Samaria, and he reigned nine years. 2He did evil in the eyes of the LORD, but not like the kings of Israel who preceded him.   2Ki 15:30

3Shalmaneser king of Assyria came up to attack Hoshea, who had been Shalmaneser's vassal and had paid him tribute. 4But the king of Assyria discovered that Hoshea was a traitor, for he had sent envoys to So[b] king of Egypt, and he no longer paid tribute to the king of Assyria, as he had done year by year. Therefore Shalmaneser seized him and put him in prison. 5The king of Assyria invaded the entire land, marched against Samaria and laid siege to it for three years. 6In the ninth year of

Hoshea, the king of Assyria captured Samaria and deported the Israelites to Assyria. He settled them in Halah, in Gozan on the Habor River and in the towns of the Medes.   Hos 10:14

Israel Exiled Because of Sin

7All this took place because the Israelites had sinned against the LORD their God, who had brought them up out of Egypt from under the power of Pharaoh king of Egypt. They worshiped other gods 8and followed the practices of the nations the LORD had driven out before them, as well as the practices that the kings of Israel had introduced. 9The Israelites secretly did things against the LORD their God that were not right. From watchtower to fortified city they built themselves high places in all their towns. 10They set up sacred stones and Asherah poles on every high hill and under every spreading tree. 11At every high place they burned incense, as the nations whom the LORD had driven out before them had done. They did wicked things that provoked the LORD to anger. 12They worshiped idols, though the LORD had said, "You shall not do this."[c] 13The LORD warned Israel and Judah through all his prophets and seers: "Turn from your evil ways. Observe my commands and decrees, in

---

a18 Or *the dais of his throne* (see Septuagint)   b4 Or *to Sais, to the; So* is possibly an
abbreviation for *Osorkon*.   c12 Exodus 20:4, 5

accordance with the entire Law that I commanded your fathers to obey and that I delivered to you through my servants the prophets." Ex 14:15; Jer 18:11

¹⁴But they would not listen and were as stiff-necked as their fathers, who did not trust in the LORD their God. ¹⁵They rejected his decrees and the covenant he had made with their fathers and the warnings he had given them. They followed worthless idols and themselves became worthless. They imitated the nations around them although the LORD had ordered them, "Do not do as they do," and they did the things the LORD had forbidden them to do. Ex 32:9

¹⁶They forsook all the commands of the LORD their God and made for themselves two idols cast in the shape of calves, and an Asherah pole. They bowed down to all the starry hosts, and they worshiped Baal. ¹⁷They sacrificed their sons and daughters inᵃ the fire. They practiced divination and sorcery and sold themselves to do evil in the eyes of the LORD, provoking him to anger.   Lev 19:26

¹⁸So the LORD was very angry with Israel and removed them from his presence. Only the tribe of Judah was left, ¹⁹and even Judah did not keep the commands of the LORD their God. They followed the practices Israel had introduced. ²⁰Therefore the LORD rejected all

the people of Israel; he afflicted them and gave them into the hands of plunderers, until he thrust them from his presence.

²¹When he tore Israel away from the house of David, they made Jeroboam son of Nebat their king. Jeroboam enticed Israel away from following the LORD and caused them to commit a great sin. ²²The Israelites persisted in all the sins of Jeroboam and did not turn away from them ²³until the LORD removed them from his presence, as he had warned through all his servants the prophets. So the people of Israel were taken from their homeland into exile in Assyria, and they are still there.   Jdg 6:8; 1Ki 11:11

Samaria Resettled

²⁴The king of Assyria brought people from Babylon, Cuthah, Avva, Hamath and Sepharvaim and settled them in the towns of Samaria to replace the Israelites. They took over Samaria and lived in its towns. ²⁵When they first lived there, they did not worship the LORD; so he sent lions among them and they killed some of the people. ²⁶It was reported to the king of Assyria: "The people you deported and resettled in the towns of Samaria do not know what the god of that country requires. He has sent lions among them, which are killing them off, be-

ᵃ17 Or *They made their sons and daughters pass through*

cause the people do not know what he requires." Ezr 4:2

²⁷Then the king of Assyria gave this order: "Have one of the priests you took captive from Samaria go back to live there and teach the people what the god of the land requires." ²⁸So one of the priests who had been exiled from Samaria came to live in Bethel and taught them how to worship the LORD.

²⁹Nevertheless, each national group made its own gods in the several towns where they settled, and set them up in the shrines the people of Samaria had made at the high places. ³⁰The men from Babylon made Succoth Benoth, the men from Cuthah made Nergal, and the men from Hamath made Ashima; ³¹the Avvites made Nibhaz and Tartak, and the Sepharvites burned their children in the fire as sacrifices to Adrammelech and Anammelech, the gods of Sepharvaim. ³²They worshiped the LORD, but they also appointed all sorts of their own people to officiate for them as priests in the shrines at the high places. ³³They worshiped the LORD, but they also served their own gods in accordance with the customs of the nations from which they had been brought. 1Ki 12:31

³⁴To this day they persist in their former practices. They neither worship the LORD nor adhere to the decrees and ordinances, the laws and commands that the LORD gave the descendants of Jacob, whom he named Israel. ³⁵When the LORD made a covenant with the Israelites, he commanded them: "Do not worship any other gods or bow down to them, serve them or sacrifice to them. ³⁶But the LORD, who brought you up out of Egypt with mighty power and outstretched arm, is the one you must worship. To him you shall bow down and to him offer sacrifices. ³⁷You must always be careful to keep the decrees and ordinances, the laws and commands he wrote for you. Do not worship other gods. ³⁸Do not forget the covenant I have made with you, and do not worship other gods. ³⁹Rather, worship the LORD your God; it is he who will deliver you from the hand of all your enemies." Ex 20:5

⁴⁰They would not listen, however, but persisted in their former practices. ⁴¹Even while these people were worshiping the LORD, they were serving their idols. To this day their children and grandchildren continue to do as their fathers did. 1Ki 18:21; Ezr 4:2

Hezekiah King of Judah

18 In the third year of Hoshea son of Elah king of Israel, Hezekiah son of Ahaz king of Judah began to reign. ²He was twenty-five years old when he became king, and he reigned in Jerusalem twenty-nine years. His mother's name

was Abijah*ᵃ* daughter of Zechariah. ³He did what was right in the eyes of the LORD, just as his father David had done. ⁴He removed the high places, smashed the sacred stones and cut down the Asherah poles. He broke into pieces the bronze snake Moses had made, for up to that time the Israelites had been burning incense to it. (It was called*ᵇ* Nehushtan.*ᶜ*) Hos 1:1

⁵Hezekiah trusted in the LORD, the God of Israel. There was no one like him among all the kings of Judah, either before him or after him. ⁶He held fast to the LORD and did not cease to follow him; he kept the commands the LORD had given Moses. ⁷And the LORD was with him; he was successful in whatever he undertook. He rebelled against the king of Assyria and did not serve him. ⁸From watchtower to fortified city, he defeated the Philistines, as far as Gaza and its territory. 2Ki 19:10

⁹In King Hezekiah's fourth year, which was the seventh year of Hoshea son of Elah king of Israel, Shalmaneser king of Assyria marched against Samaria and laid siege to it. ¹⁰At the end of three years the Assyrians took it. So Samaria was captured in Hezekiah's sixth year, which was the ninth year of Hoshea king of Israel. ¹¹The king of Assyria deported Israel to Assyria and settled them in Halah, in Gozan on the Habor River and in towns of the Medes. ¹²This happened because they had not obeyed the LORD their God, but had violated his covenant—all that Moses the servant of the LORD commanded. They neither listened to the commands nor carried them out. 1Sa 36:1; Da 9:6

¹³In the fourteenth year of King Hezekiah's reign, Sennacherib king of Assyria attacked all the fortified cities of Judah and captured them. ¹⁴So Hezekiah king of Judah sent this message to the king of Assyria at Lachish: "I have done wrong. Withdraw from me, and I will pay whatever you demand of me." The king of Assyria exacted from Hezekiah king of Judah three hundred talents*ᵈ* of silver and thirty talents*ᵉ* of gold. ¹⁵So Hezekiah gave him all the silver that was found in the temple of the LORD and in the treasuries of the royal palace. Isa 1:7

¹⁶At this time Hezekiah king of Judah stripped off the gold with which he had covered the doors and doorposts of the temple of the LORD, and gave it to the king of Assyria. 2Ch 29:3

Sennacherib Threatens Jerusalem

¹⁷The king of Assyria sent his supreme commander, his chief officer and his field commander

---

ᵃ2 Hebrew *Abi,* a variant of *Abijah*   *ᵇ4* Or *He called it*   *ᶜ4 Nehushtan* sounds like the Hebrew for *bronze* and *snake* and *unclean thing.*   *ᵈ14* That is, about 11 tons (about 10 metric tons)   *ᵉ14* That is, about 1 ton (about 1 metric ton)

with a large army, from Lachish to King Hezekiah at Jerusalem. They came up to Jerusalem and stopped at the aqueduct of the Upper Pool, on the road to the Washerman's Field. ¹⁸They called for the king; and Eliakim son of Hilkiah the palace administrator, Shebna the secretary, and Joah son of Asaph the recorder went out to them.Ne 2:14

¹⁹The field commander said to them, "Tell Hezekiah:

" 'This is what the great king, the king of Assyria, says: On what are you basing this confidence of yours? ²⁰You say you have strategy and military strength—but you speak only empty words. On whom are you depending, that you rebel against me? ²¹Look now, you are depending on Egypt, that splintered reed of a staff, which pierces a man's hand and wounds him if he leans on it! Such is Pharaoh king of Egypt to all who depend on him. ²²And if you say to me, "We are depending on the LORD our God"—isn't he the one whose high places and altars Hezekiah removed, saying to Judah and Jerusalem, "You must worship before this altar in Jerusalem"? Job 4:6; Eze 29:6

²³" 'Come now, make a bargain with my master, the king of Assyria: I will give you two thousand horses—if you can put riders on them! ²⁴How can you repulse one officer of the least of my master's officials, even though you are depending on Egypt for chariots and horsemen[a]? ²⁵Furthermore, have I come to attack and destroy this place without word from the LORD? The LORD himself told me to march against this country and destroy it.' " 2Ki 19:6; Isa 10:8

²⁶Then Eliakim son of Hilkiah, and Shebna and Joah said to the field commander, "Please speak to your servants in Aramaic, since we understand it. Don't speak to us in Hebrew in the hearing of the people on the wall." Ezr 4:7

²⁷But the commander replied, "Was it only to your master and you that my master sent me to say these things, and not to the men sitting on the wall—who, like you, will have to eat their own filth and drink their own urine?"

²⁸Then the commander stood and called out in Hebrew: "Hear the word of the great king, the king of Assyria! ²⁹This is what the king says: Do not let Hezekiah deceive you. He cannot deliver you from my hand. ³⁰Do not let Hezekiah persuade you to trust in the LORD when he says, 'The LORD will surely deliver us; this city will not be

---

[a]24 Or charioteers

given into the hand of the king of Assyria.'   2Ki 19:10; 2Ch 32:15

31"Do not listen to Hezekiah. This is what the king of Assyria says: Make peace with me and come out to me. Then every one of you will eat from his own vine and fig tree and drink water from his own cistern, 32until I come and take you to a land like your own, a land of grain and new wine, a land of bread and vineyards, a land of olive trees and honey. Choose life and not death!   1Ki 4:25

"Do not listen to Hezekiah, for he is misleading you when he says, 'The LORD will deliver us.' 33Has the god of any nation ever delivered his land from the hand of the king of Assyria? 34Where are the gods of Hamath and Arpad? Where are the gods of Sepharvaim, Hena and Ivvah? Have they rescued Samaria from my hand? 35Who of all the gods of these countries has been able to save his land from me? How then can the LORD deliver Jerusalem from my hand?"   2Ki 19:12

36But the people remained silent and said nothing in reply, because the king had commanded, "Do not answer him."

37Then Eliakim son of Hilkiah the palace administrator, Shebna the secretary and Joah son of Asaph the recorder went to Hezekiah, with their clothes torn, and told him what the field commander had said.

Jerusalem's Deliverance Foretold

19 When King Hezekiah heard this, he tore his clothes and put on sackcloth and went into the temple of the LORD. 2He sent Eliakim the palace administrator, Shebna the secretary and the leading priests, all wearing sackcloth, to the prophet Isaiah son of Amoz. 3They told him, "This is what Hezekiah says: This day is a day of distress and rebuke and disgrace, as when children come to the point of birth and there is no strength to deliver them. 4It may be that the LORD your God will hear all the words of the field commander, whom his master, the king of Assyria, has sent to ridicule the living God, and that he will rebuke him for the words the LORD your God has heard. Therefore pray for the remnant that still survives."

5When King Hezekiah's officials came to Isaiah, 6Isaiah said to them, "Tell your master, 'This is what the LORD says: Do not be afraid of what you have heard—those words with which the underlings of the king of Assyria have blasphemed me. 7Listen! I am going to put such a spirit in him that when he hears a certain report, he will return to his own country, and there I will have him cut down with the sword.'"

8When the field commander heard that the king of Assyria

had left Lachish, he withdrew and found the king fighting against Libnah. 2Ki 18:14

⁹Now Sennacherib received a report that Tirhakah, the Cushite[a] king of Egypt, was marching out to fight against him. So he again sent messengers to Hezekiah with this word: ¹⁰"Say to Hezekiah king of Judah: Do not let the god you depend on deceive you when he says, 'Jerusalem will not be handed over to the king of Assyria.' ¹¹Surely you have heard what the kings of Assyria have done to all the countries, destroying them completely. And will you be delivered? ¹²Did the gods of the nations that were destroyed by my forefathers deliver them: the gods of Gozan, Haran, Rezeph and the people of Eden who were in Tel Assar? ¹³Where is the king of Hamath, the king of Arpad, the king of the city of Sepharvaim, or of Hena or Ivvah?" 2Ki 18:5; Jer 49:23

Hezekiah's Prayer

¹⁴Hezekiah received the letter from the messengers and read it. Then he went up to the temple of the LORD and spread it out before the LORD. ¹⁵And Hezekiah prayed to the LORD: "O LORD, God of Israel, enthroned between the cherubim, you alone are God over all the kingdoms of the earth. You have made heaven and earth. ¹⁶Give ear, O LORD, and hear; open your eyes, O LORD, and see; listen to the words Sennacherib has sent to insult the living God. 2Ki 5:7; Ps 31:2

¹⁷"It is true, O LORD, that the Assyrian kings have laid waste these nations and their lands. ¹⁸They have thrown their gods into the fire and destroyed them, for they were not gods but only wood and stone, fashioned by men's hands. ¹⁹Now, O LORD our God, deliver us from his hand, so that all kingdoms on earth may know that you alone, O LORD, are God."

Isaiah Prophesies Sennacherib's Fall

²⁰Then Isaiah son of Amoz sent a message to Hezekiah: "This is what the LORD, the God of Israel, says: I have heard your prayer concerning Sennacherib king of Assyria. ²¹This is the word that the LORD has spoken against him: 1Ki 9:3; Isa 37:21

" 'The Virgin Daughter of
　Zion
despises you and mocks
　you.
The Daughter of Jerusalem
　tosses her head as you flee.
²²Who is it you have insulted
　and blasphemed?
Against whom have you
　raised your voice
and lifted your eyes in pride?
Against the Holy One of
　Israel! 2Ki 18:25; Ps 71:22
²³By your messengers

you have heaped insults on
the Lord.
And you have said,
"With my many chariots
I have ascended the heights
of the mountains,
the utmost heights of
Lebanon.   Ps 20:7
I have cut down its tallest
cedars,
the choicest of its pines.
I have reached its remotest
parts,
the finest of its forests.
24I have dug wells in foreign
lands
and drunk the water there.
With the soles of my feet
I have dried up all the
streams of Egypt."   Isa 19:6

25" 'Have you not heard?
Long ago I ordained it.
In days of old I planned it;
now I have brought it to
pass,
that you have turned fortified
cities
into piles of stone.   Isa 40:21
26Their people, drained of
power,
are dismayed and put to
shame.   Isa 13:7; Eze 7:17
They are like plants in the
field,
like tender green shoots,
like grass sprouting on the
roof,
scorched before it grows
up.   Job 8:12; Ps 129:6

27" 'But I know where you stay
and when you come and go
and how you rage against
me.   Ps 139:1-4

28Because you rage against me
and your insolence has
reached my ears,
I will put my hook in your
nose
and my bit in your mouth,
and I will make you return
by the way you came.'

29"This will be the sign for
you, O Hezekiah:

"This year you will eat what
grows by itself,
and the second year what
springs from that.
But in the third year sow and
reap,
plant vineyards and eat
their fruit.   Ps 107:37; Lk 2:12
30Once more a remnant of the
house of Judah
will take root below and
bear fruit above.   Isa 5:24
31For out of Jerusalem will
come a remnant,
and out of Mount Zion a
band of survivors.   Isa 66:19

The zeal of the LORD Almighty
will accomplish this.   Isa 9:7

32"Therefore this is what the
LORD says concerning the king
of Assyria:

"He will not enter this city
or shoot an arrow here.
He will not come before it
with shield
or build a siege ramp
against it.   Isa 37:33
33By the way that he came he
will return;
he will not enter this city,
declares the LORD.

34I will defend this city and
save it,
for my sake and for the
sake of David my
servant." 2Ki 20:6

35That night the angel of the LORD went out and put to death a hundred and eighty-five thousand men in the Assyrian camp. When the people got up the next morning—there were all the dead bodies! 36So Sennacherib king of Assyria broke camp and withdrew. He returned to Nineveh and stayed there.

37One day, while he was worshiping in the temple of his god Nisroch, his sons Adrammelech and Sharezer cut him down with the sword, and they escaped to the land of Ararat. And Esarhaddon his son succeeded him as king. 2Ki 17:31

Hezekiah's Illness

20 In those days Hezekiah became ill and was at the point of death. The prophet Isaiah son of Amoz went to him and said, "This is what the LORD says: Put your house in order, because you are going to die; you will not recover."

2Hezekiah turned his face to the wall and prayed to the LORD, 3"Remember, O LORD, how I have walked before you faithfully and with wholehearted devotion and have done what is good in your eyes." And Hezekiah wept bitterly.

4Before Isaiah had left the middle court, the word of the LORD came to him: 5"Go back and tell Hezekiah, the leader of my people, 'This is what the LORD, the God of your father David, says: I have heard your prayer and seen your tears; I will heal you. On the third day from now you will go up to the temple of the LORD. 6I will add fifteen years to your life. And I will deliver you and this city from the hand of the king of Assyria. I will defend this city for my sake and for the sake of my servant David.'" Ps 39:12

7Then Isaiah said, "Prepare a poultice of figs." They did so and applied it to the boil, and he recovered. Ex 9:9; Isa 38:21

8Hezekiah had asked Isaiah, "What will be the sign that the LORD will heal me and that I will go up to the temple of the LORD on the third day from now?"

9Isaiah answered, "This is the LORD's sign to you that the LORD will do what he has promised: Shall the shadow go forward ten steps, or shall it go back ten steps?" Jer 44:29

10"It is a simple matter for the shadow to go forward ten steps," said Hezekiah. "Rather, have it go back ten steps."

11Then the prophet Isaiah called upon the LORD, and the LORD made the shadow go back the ten steps it had gone down on the stairway of Ahaz. Jos 10:13

Envoys From Babylon

12At that time Merodach-Baladan son of Baladan king of Babylon sent Hezekiah letters

and a gift, because he had heard of Hezekiah's illness. [13]Hezekiah received the messengers and showed them all that was in his storehouses—the silver, the gold, the spices and the fine oil—his armory and everything found among his treasures. There was nothing in his palace or in all his kingdom that Hezekiah did not show them.

[14]Then Isaiah the prophet went to King Hezekiah and asked, "What did those men say, and where did they come from?"

"From a distant land," Hezekiah replied. "They came from Babylon."

[15]The prophet asked, "What did they see in your palace?"

"They saw everything in my palace," Hezekiah said. "There is nothing among my treasures that I did not show them."

[16]Then Isaiah said to Hezekiah, "Hear the word of the LORD: [17]The time will surely come when everything in your palace, and all that your fathers have stored up until this day, will be carried off to Babylon. Nothing will be left, says the LORD. [18]And some of your descendants, your own flesh and blood, that will be born to you, will be taken away, and they will become eunuchs in the palace of the king of Babylon."

[19]"The word of the LORD you have spoken is good," Hezekiah replied. For he thought, "Will there not be peace and security in my lifetime?" 1Sa 3:18

[20]As for the other events of Hezekiah's reign, all his achievements and how he made the pool and the tunnel by which he brought water into the city, are they not written in the book of the annals of the kings of Judah? [21]Hezekiah rested with his fathers. And Manasseh his son succeeded him as king.

Manasseh King of Judah

21 Manasseh was twelve years old when he became king, and he reigned in Jerusalem fifty-five years. His mother's name was Hephzibah. [2]He did evil in the eyes of the LORD, following the detestable practices of the nations the LORD had driven out before the Israelites. [3]He rebuilt the high places his father Hezekiah had destroyed; he also erected altars to Baal and made an Asherah pole, as Ahab king of Israel had done. He bowed down to all the starry hosts and worshiped them. [4]He built altars in the temple of the LORD, of which the LORD had said, "In Jerusalem I will put my Name." [5]In both courts of the temple of the LORD, he built altars to all the starry hosts. [6]He sacrificed his own son in[a] the fire, practiced sorcery and divination, and consulted mediums and spiritists. He did much evil in the

[a]6 Or *He made his own son pass through*

eyes of the LORD, provoking him to anger. Lev 18:21; 2Ki 16:3

7He took the carved Asherah pole he had made and put it in the temple, of which the LORD had said to David and to his son Solomon, "In this temple and in Jerusalem, which I have chosen out of all the tribes of Israel, I will put my Name forever. 8I will not again make the feet of the Israelites wander from the land I gave their forefathers, if only they will be careful to do everything I commanded them and will keep the whole Law that my servant Moses gave them." 9But the people did not listen. Manasseh led them astray, so that they did more evil than the nations the LORD had destroyed before the Israelites. Dt 16:21; Ps 29:12

10The LORD said through his servants the prophets: 11"Manasseh king of Judah has committed these detestable sins. He has done more evil than the Amorites who preceded him and has led Judah into sin with his idols. 12Therefore this is what the LORD, the God of Israel, says: I am going to bring such disaster on Jerusalem and Judah that the ears of everyone who hears of it will tingle. 13I will stretch out over Jerusalem the measuring line used against Samaria and the plumb line used against the house of Ahab. I will wipe out Jerusalem as one wipes a dish, wiping it and turning it upside down. 14I will forsake the remnant of my in-heritance and hand them over to their enemies. They will be looted and plundered by all their foes, 15because they have done evil in my eyes and have provoked me to anger from the day their forefathers came out of Egypt until this day." 2Ki 24:3

16Moreover, Manasseh also shed so much innocent blood that he filled Jerusalem from end to end—besides the sin that he had caused Judah to commit, so that they did evil in the eyes of the LORD. 2Ki 24:4; Ps 10:11

17As for the other events of Manasseh's reign, and all he did, including the sin he committed, are they not written in the book of the annals of the kings of Judah? 18Manasseh rested with his fathers and was buried in his palace garden, the garden of Uzza. And Amon his son succeeded him as king.

Amon King of Judah

19Amon was twenty-two years old when he became king, and he reigned in Jerusalem two years. His mother's name was Meshullemeth daughter of Haruz; she was from Jotbah. 20He did evil in the eyes of the LORD, as his father Manasseh had done. 21He walked in all the ways of his father; he worshiped the idols his father had worshiped, and bowed down to them. 22He forsook the LORD, the God of his fathers, and did not walk in the way of the LORD.

23Amon's officials conspired against him and assassinated

the king in his palace. ²⁴Then the people of the land killed all who had plotted against King Amon, and they made Josiah his son king in his place.   Zep 1:1

²⁵As for the other events of Amon's reign, and what he did, are they not written in the book of the annals of the kings of Judah? ²⁶He was buried in his grave in the garden of Uzza. And Josiah his son succeeded him as king.   2Ki 21:18; Mt 1:10

The Book of the Law Found

22 Josiah was eight years old when he became king, and he reigned in Jerusalem thirty-one years. His mother's name was Jedidah daughter of Adaiah; she was from Bozkath. ²He did what was right in the eyes of the LORD and walked in all the ways of his father David, not turning aside to the right or to the left.   Dt 5:32; Jos 15:39

³In the eighteenth year of his reign, King Josiah sent the secretary, Shaphan son of Azaliah, the son of Meshullam, to the temple of the LORD. He said: ⁴"Go up to Hilkiah the high priest and have him get ready the money that has been brought into the temple of the LORD, which the doorkeepers have collected from the people. ⁵Have them entrust it to the men appointed to supervise the work on the temple. And have these men pay the workers who repair the temple of the LORD— ⁶the carpenters, the builders and the masons. Also have

them purchase timber and dressed stone to repair the temple. ⁷But they need not account for the money entrusted to them, because they are acting faithfully."   2Ch 34:20; Ezr 7:1

⁸Hilkiah the high priest said to Shaphan the secretary, "I have found the Book of the Law in the temple of the LORD." He gave it to Shaphan, who read it. ⁹Then Shaphan the secretary went to the king and reported to him: "Your officials have paid out the money that was in the temple of the LORD and have entrusted it to the workers and supervisors at the temple." ¹⁰Then Shaphan the secretary informed the king, "Hilkiah the priest has given me a book." And Shaphan read from it in the presence of the king.   Dt 31:24

¹¹When the king heard the words of the Book of the Law, he tore his robes. ¹²He gave these orders to Hilkiah the priest, Ahikam son of Shaphan, Acbor son of Micaiah, Shaphan the secretary and Asaiah the king's attendant: ¹³"Go and inquire of the LORD for me and for the people and for all Judah about what is written in this book that has been found. Great is the LORD's anger that burns against us because our fathers have not obeyed the words of this book; they have not acted in accordance with all that is written there concerning us."   Am 2:4

¹⁴Hilkiah the priest, Ahikam, Acbor, Shaphan and Asaiah went to speak to the prophetess

Huldah, who was the wife of Shallum son of Tikvah, the son of Harhas, keeper of the wardrobe. She lived in Jerusalem, in the Second District.   Ex 15:20

15She said to them, "This is what the LORD, the God of Israel, says: Tell the man who sent you to me, 16'This is what the LORD says: I am going to bring disaster on this place and its people, according to everything written in the book the king of Judah has read. 17Because they have forsaken me and burned incense to other gods and provoked me to anger by all the idols their hands have made,*a* my anger will burn against this place and will not be quenched.' 18Tell the king of Judah, who sent you to inquire of the LORD, 'This is what the LORD, the God of Israel, says concerning the words you heard: 19Because your heart was responsive and you humbled yourself before the LORD when you heard what I have spoken against this place and its people, that they would become accursed and laid waste, and because you tore your robes and wept in my presence, I have heard you, declares the LORD. 20Therefore I will gather you to your fathers, and you will be buried in peace. Your eyes will not see all the disaster I am going to bring on this place.' "

So they took her answer back to the king.

Josiah Renews the Covenant

23 Then the king called together all the elders of Judah and Jerusalem. 2He went up to the temple of the LORD with the men of Judah, the people of Jerusalem, the priests and the prophets—all the people from the least to the greatest. He read in their hearing all the words of the Book of the Covenant, which had been found in the temple of the LORD. 3The king stood by the pillar and renewed the covenant in the presence of the LORD—to follow the LORD and keep his commands, regulations and decrees with all his heart and all his soul, thus confirming the words of the covenant written in this book. Then all the people pledged themselves to the covenant.   Dt 31:11

4The king ordered Hilkiah the high priest, the priests next in rank and the doorkeepers to remove from the temple of the LORD all the articles made for Baal and Asherah and all the starry hosts. He burned them outside Jerusalem in the fields of the Kidron Valley and took the ashes to Bethel. 5He did away with the pagan priests appointed by the kings of Judah to burn incense on the high places of the towns of Judah and on those around Jerusalem—those who burned incense to Baal, to the sun and moon, to the constellations and to all the starry

---

a17 Or *by everything they have done*

hosts. [6]He took the Asherah pole from the temple of the LORD to the Kidron Valley outside Jerusalem and burned it there. He ground it to powder and scattered the dust over the graves of the common people. [7]He also tore down the quarters of the male shrine prostitutes, which were in the temple of the LORD and where women did weaving for Asherah. 2Ki 25:18

[8]Josiah brought all the priests from the towns of Judah and desecrated the high places, from Geba to Beersheba, where the priests had burned incense. He broke down the shrines[a] at the gates—at the entrance to the Gate of Joshua, the city governor, which is on the left of the city gate. [9]Although the priests of the high places did not serve at the altar of the LORD in Jerusalem, they ate unleavened bread with their fellow priests.

[10]He desecrated Topheth, which was in the Valley of Ben Hinnom, so no one could use it to sacrifice his son or daughter in[b] the fire to Molech. [11]He removed from the entrance to the temple of the LORD the horses that the kings of Judah had dedicated to the sun. They were in the court near the room of an official named Nathan-Melech. Josiah then burned the chariots dedicated to the sun. Isa 30:33

[12]He pulled down the altars the kings of Judah had erected on the roof near the upper room of Ahaz, and the altars Manasseh had built in the two courts of the temple of the LORD. He removed them from there, smashed them to pieces and threw the rubble into the Kidron Valley. [13]The king also desecrated the high places that were east of Jerusalem on the south of the Hill of Corruption—the ones Solomon king of Israel had built for Ashtoreth the vile goddess of the Sidonians, for Chemosh the vile god of Moab, and for Molech[c] the detestable god of the people of Ammon. [14]Josiah smashed the sacred stones and cut down the Asherah poles and covered the sites with human bones. Jer 19:13

[15]Even the altar at Bethel, the high place made by Jeroboam son of Nebat, who had caused Israel to sin—even that altar and high place he demolished. He burned the high place and ground it to powder, and burned the Asherah pole also. [16]Then Josiah looked around, and when he saw the tombs that were there on the hillside, he had the bones removed from them and burned on the altar to defile it, in accordance with the word of the LORD proclaimed by the man of God who foretold these things. Jos 7:2; 1Ki 12:33

[17]The king asked, "What is that tombstone I see?"

---

[a]8 Or *high places*　　[b]10 Or *to make his son or daughter pass through*　　[c]13 Hebrew *Milcom*

The men of the city said, "It marks the tomb of the man of God who came from Judah and pronounced against the altar of Bethel the very things you have done to it."   1Ki 13:1,30

18"Leave it alone," he said. "Don't let anyone disturb his bones." So they spared his bones and those of the prophet who had come from Samaria.

19Just as he had done at Bethel, Josiah removed and defiled all the shrines at the high places that the kings of Israel had built in the towns of Samaria that had provoked the LORD to anger. 20Josiah slaughtered all the priests of those high places on the altars and burned human bones on them. Then he went back to Jerusalem.   2Ch 34:6

21The king gave this order to all the people: "Celebrate the Passover to the LORD your God, as it is written in this Book of the Covenant." 22Not since the days of the judges who led Israel, nor throughout the days of the kings of Israel and the kings of Judah, had any such Passover been observed. 23But in the eighteenth year of King Josiah, this Passover was celebrated to the LORD in Jerusalem.   Dt 16:2

24Furthermore, Josiah got rid of the mediums and spiritists, the household gods, the idols and all the other detestable things seen in Judah and Jerusalem. This he did to fulfill the requirements of the law written in the book that Hilkiah the priest had discovered in the temple of the LORD. 25Neither before nor after Josiah was there a king like him who turned to the LORD as he did—with all his heart and with all his soul and with all his strength, in accordance with all the Law of Moses.   Dt 18:11; Jer 22:15

26Nevertheless, the LORD did not turn away from the heat of his fierce anger, which burned against Judah because of all that Manasseh had done to provoke him to anger. 27So the LORD said, "I will remove Judah also from my presence as I removed Israel, and I will reject Jerusalem, the city I chose, and this temple, about which I said, 'There shall my Name be.' a"

28As for the other events of Josiah's reign, and all he did, are they not written in the book of the annals of the kings of Judah?

29While Josiah was king, Pharaoh Neco king of Egypt went up to the Euphrates River to help the king of Assyria. King Josiah marched out to meet him in battle, but Neco faced him and killed him at Megiddo. 30Josiah's servants brought his body in a chariot from Megiddo to Jerusalem and buried him in his own tomb. And the people of the land took Jehoahaz son of Josiah and anointed him and made him king in place of his father.   2Ki 9:28; Jer 46:2

a27 1 Kings 8:29

Jehoahaz King of Judah

31Jehoahaz was twenty-three years old when he became king, and he reigned in Jerusalem three months. His mother's name was Hamutal daughter of Jeremiah; she was from Libnah. 32He did evil in the eyes of the LORD, just as his fathers had done. 33Pharaoh Neco put him in chains at Riblah in the land of Hamath*a* so that he might not reign in Jerusalem, and he imposed on Judah a levy of a hundred talents*b* of silver and a talent*c* of gold. 34Pharaoh Neco made Eliakim son of Josiah king in place of his father Josiah and changed Eliakim's name to Jehoiakim. But he took Jehoahaz and carried him off to Egypt, and there he died. 35Jehoiakim paid Pharaoh Neco the silver and gold he demanded. In order to do so, he taxed the land and exacted the silver and gold from the people of the land according to their assessments.   1Ch 3:15; 2Ch 36:4

Jehoiakim King of Judah

36Jehoiakim was twenty-five years old when he became king, and he reigned in Jerusalem eleven years. His mother's name was Zebidah daughter of Pedaiah; she was from Rumah. 37And he did evil in the eyes of the LORD, just as his fathers had done.   1Ki 15:26; Jer 26:1

24 During Jehoiakim's reign, Nebuchadnezzar king of Babylon invaded the land, and Jehoiakim became his vassal for three years. But then he changed his mind and rebelled against Nebuchadnezzar. 2The LORD sent Babylonian,*d* Aramean, Moabite and Ammonite raiders against him. He sent them to destroy Judah, in accordance with the word of the LORD proclaimed by his servants the prophets. 3Surely these things happened to Judah according to the LORD's command, in order to remove them from his presence because of the sins of Manasseh and all he had done, 4including the shedding of innocent blood. For he had filled Jerusalem with innocent blood, and the LORD was not willing to forgive.   2Ki 18:25

5As for the other events of Jehoiakim's reign, and all he did, are they not written in the book of the annals of the kings of Judah? 6Jehoiakim rested with his fathers. And Jehoiachin his son succeeded him as king.   Jer 22:18-19; Eze 19:1

7The king of Egypt did not march out from his own country again, because the king of Babylon had taken all his territory, from the Wadi of Egypt to the Euphrates River.   Jer 46:2

Jehoiachin King of Judah

8Jehoiachin was eighteen

---

*a*33 Hebrew; Septuagint (see also 2 Chron. 36:3) *Neco at Riblah in Hamath removed him*
*b*33 That is, about 3 3/4 tons (about 3.4 metric tons)   *c*33 That is, about 75 pounds
(about 34 kilograms)   *d*2 Or *Chaldean*

years old when he became king, and he reigned in Jerusalem three months. His mother's name was Nehushta daughter of Elnathan; she was from Jerusalem. [9]He did evil in the eyes of the LORD, just as his father had done.   1Ch 3:16

[10]At that time the officers of Nebuchadnezzar king of Babylon advanced on Jerusalem and laid siege to it, [11]and Nebuchadnezzar himself came up to the city while his officers were besieging it. [12]Jehoiachin king of Judah, his mother, his attendants, his nobles and his officials all surrendered to him.

In the eighth year of the reign of the king of Babylon, he took Jehoiachin prisoner. [13]As the LORD had declared, Nebuchadnezzar removed all the treasures from the temple of the LORD and from the royal palace, and took away all the gold articles that Solomon king of Israel had made for the temple of the LORD. [14]He carried into exile all Jerusalem: all the officers and fighting men, and all the craftsmen and artisans—a total of ten thousand. Only the poorest people of the land were left.

[15]Nebuchadnezzar took Jehoiachin captive to Babylon. He also took from Jerusalem to Babylon the king's mother, his wives, his officials and the leading men of the land. [16]The king of Babylon also deported to Babylon the entire force of seven thousand fighting men, strong and fit for war, and a thousand craftsmen and artisans. [17]He made Mattaniah, Jehoiachin's uncle, king in his place and changed his name to Zedekiah.

Zedekiah King of Judah

[18]Zedekiah was twenty-one years old when he became king, and he reigned in Jerusalem eleven years. His mother's name was Hamutal daughter of Jeremiah; she was from Libnah. [19]He did evil in the eyes of the LORD, just as Jehoiakim had done. [20]It was because of the LORD's anger that all this happened to Jerusalem and Judah, and in the end he thrust them from his presence.   2Ki 23:31

The Fall of Jerusalem

Now Zedekiah rebelled against the king of Babylon.

25 So in the ninth year of Zedekiah's reign, on the tenth day of the tenth month, Nebuchadnezzar king of Babylon marched against Jerusalem with his whole army. He encamped outside the city and built siege works all around it. [2]The city was kept under siege until the eleventh year of King Zedekiah. [3]By the ninth day of the ₍fourth₎[a] month the famine in the city had become so severe that there was no food for the people to eat. [4]Then the city wall was broken through, and the whole army fled at night

[a]3 See Jer. 52:6.

through the gate between the two walls near the king's garden, though the Babylonians[a] were surrounding the city. They fled toward the Arabah,[b] [5]but the Babylonian[c] army pursued the king and overtook him in the plains of Jericho. All his soldiers were separated from him and scattered, [6]and he was captured. He was taken to the king of Babylon at Riblah, where sentence was pronounced on him. [7]They killed the sons of Zedekiah before his eyes. Then they put out his eyes, bound him with bronze shackles and took him to Babylon.   Dt 28:36; Eze 24:2

[8]On the seventh day of the fifth month, in the nineteenth year of Nebuchadnezzar king of Babylon, Nebuzaradan commander of the imperial guard, an official of the king of Babylon, came to Jerusalem. [9]He set fire to the temple of the LORD, the royal palace and all the houses of Jerusalem. Every important building he burned down. [10]The whole Babylonian army, under the commander of the imperial guard, broke down the walls around Jerusalem. [11]Nebuzaradan the commander of the guard carried into exile the people who remained in the city, along with the rest of the populace and those who had gone over to the king of Babylon. [12]But the commander left behind some of the poorest people of the land to work the vineyards and fields.   Isa 60:7

[13]The Babylonians broke up the bronze pillars, the movable stands and the bronze Sea that were at the temple of the LORD and they carried the bronze to Babylon. [14]They also took away the pots, shovels, wick trimmers, dishes and all the bronze articles used in the temple service. [15]The commander of the imperial guard took away the censers and sprinkling bowls—all that were made of pure gold or silver.   1Ki 7:50

[16]The bronze from the two pillars, the Sea and the movable stands, which Solomon had made for the temple of the LORD, was more than could be weighed. [17]Each pillar was twenty-seven feet[d] high. The bronze capital on top of one pillar was four and a half feet[e] high and was decorated with a network and pomegranates of bronze all around. The other pillar, with its network, was similar.   1Ki 7:47,15-22

[18]The commander of the guard took as prisoners Seraiah the chief priest, Zephaniah the priest next in rank and the three doorkeepers. [19]Of those still in the city, he took the officer in charge of the fighting men and five royal advisers. He also took the secretary who was chief officer in charge of conscripting the

---

[a]4 Or Chaldeans; also in verses 13, 25 and 26   [b]4 Or the Jordan Valley   [c]5 Or Chaldean; also in verses 10 and 24   [d]17 Hebrew eighteen cubits (about 8.1 meters)   [e]17 Hebrew three cubits (about 1.3 meters)

people of the land and sixty of his men who were found in the city. ²⁰Nebuzaradan the commander took them all and brought them to the king of Babylon at Riblah. ²¹There at Riblah, in the land of Hamath, the king had them executed.

So Judah went into captivity, away from her land.

²²Nebuchadnezzar king of Babylon appointed Gedaliah son of Ahikam, the son of Shaphan, to be over the people he had left behind in Judah. ²³When all the army officers and their men heard that the king of Babylon had appointed Gedaliah as governor, they came to Gedaliah at Mizpah—Ishmael son of Nethaniah, Johanan son of Kareah, Seraiah son of Tanhumeth the Netophathite, Jaazaniah the son of the Maacathite, and their men. ²⁴Gedaliah took an oath to reassure them and their men. "Do not be afraid of the Babylonian officials," he said. "Settle down in the land and serve the king of Babylon, and it will go well with you." 2Ki 22:12; Jer 40:5

²⁵In the seventh month, however, Ishmael son of Nethaniah, the son of Elishama, who was of royal blood, came with ten men and assassinated Gedaliah and also the men of Judah and the Babylonians who were with him at Mizpah. ²⁶At this, all the people from the least to the greatest, together with the army officers, fled to Egypt for fear of the Babylonians. Jer 43:7

Jehoiachin Released

²⁷In the thirty-seventh year of the exile of Jehoiachin king of Judah, in the year Evil-Merodach*a* became king of Babylon, he released Jehoiachin from prison on the twenty-seventh day of the twelfth month. ²⁸He spoke kindly to him and gave him a seat of honor higher than those of the other kings who were with him in Babylon. ²⁹So Jehoiachin put aside his prison clothes and for the rest of his life ate regularly at the king's table. ³⁰Day by day the king gave Jehoiachin a regular allowance as long as he lived. 1Ki 8:50

---

1 Chronicles

Introduction:

Although the books of Chronicles seem like a repeat of Samuel and Kings they aren't. The Chronicles were written for the exiles who had returned to Israel after the Babylonian captivity to remind them they were from the royal line of David and were God's chosen people. The main theme is that God is always faithful to his covenant.

For these reasons 1 Chronicles begins with an outline of history from Adam through the death of King Saul. The rest of the book is about the reign of King David. These books serve as both a warning and encouragement to the Jews to be faithful to the covenant.

Outline of contents:
      List of generations (1:1–9:44)
      The reign of David (10:1–29:30)

Historical Records From Adam to Abraham

To Noah's Sons

1 Adam, Seth, Enosh, ²Kenan, Mahalalel, Jared, ³Enoch, Methuselah, Lamech, Noah.

⁴The sons of Noah:*a*
    Shem, Ham and Japheth.

The Japhethites

⁵The sons*b* of Japheth:
    Gomer, Magog, Madai, Javan, Tubal, Meshech and Tiras.   Ge 10:2-4

⁶The sons of Gomer:
    Ashkenaz, Riphath*c* and Togarmah.
⁷The sons of Javan:
    Elishah, Tarshish, the Kittim and the Rodanim.

The Hamites

⁸The sons of Ham:
    Cush, Mizraim,*d* Put and Canaan.   Ge 10:6
⁹The sons of Cush:
    Seba, Havilah, Sabta, Raamah and Sabteca.
The sons of Raamah:

---

*a*4 Septuagint; Hebrew does not have *The sons of Noah:*   *b*5 *Sons* may mean *descendants* or *successors* or *nations*; also in verses 6-10, 17 and 20.   *c*6 Many Hebrew manuscripts and Vulgate (see also Septuagint and Gen. 10:3); most Hebrew manuscripts *Diphath*   *d*8 That is, Egypt; also in verse 11

Sheba and Dedan.

¹⁰Cush was the father*ᵃ* of Nimrod, who grew to be a mighty warrior on earth.

¹¹Mizraim was the father of the Ludites, Anamites, Lehabites, Naphtuhites, ¹²Pathrusites, Casluhites (from whom the Philistines came) and Caphtorites. Dt 2:23

¹³Canaan was the father of Sidon his firstborn,ᵇ and of the Hittites, ¹⁴Jebusites, Amorites, Girgashites, ¹⁵Hivites, Arkites, Sinites, ¹⁶Arvadites, Zemarites and Hamathites. Ge 10:15

The Semites

¹⁷The sons of Shem:

Elam, Asshur, Arphaxad, Lud and Aram. Ge 10:22

The sons of Aramᶜ:

Uz, Hul, Gether and Meshech.

¹⁸Arphaxad was the father of Shelah,

and Shelah the father of Eber.

¹⁹Two sons were born to Eber:

One was named Peleg,ᵈ because in his time the earth was divided; his brother was named Joktan.

²⁰Joktan was the father of

Almodad, Sheleph, Hazarmaveth, Jerah, ²¹Hadoram, Uzal, Diklah, ²²Obal,ᵉ Abimael, Sheba, ²³Ophir, Havilah and Jobab. All these were sons of Joktan. Ge 10:26

²⁴Shem, Arphaxad,ᶠ Shelah,

²⁵Eber, Peleg, Reu,

²⁶Serug, Nahor, Terah

²⁷and Abram (that is, Abraham). Lk 3:34-36

The Family of Abraham

²⁸The sons of Abraham:

Isaac and Ishmael. Ge 21:2

Descendants of Hagar

²⁹These were their descendants:

Nebaioth the firstborn of Ishmael, Kedar, Adbeel, Mibsam, ³⁰Mishma, Dumah, Massa, Hadad, Tema, ³¹Jetur, Naphish and Kedemah. These were the sons of Ishmael.

Descendants of Keturah

³²The sons born to Keturah, Abraham's concubine:

Zimran, Jokshan, Medan, Midian, Ishbak and Shuah.

The sons of Jokshan:

Sheba and Dedan. Ge 22:24

³³The sons of Midian:

ᵃ10 Father *may mean* ancestor *or* predecessor *or* founder; *also in verses 11, 13, 18 and 20.*
ᵇ13 Or of the Sidonians, the foremost   *ᶜ17 One Hebrew manuscript and some Septuagint manuscripts (see also Gen. 10:23); most Hebrew manuscripts do not have this line.*   *ᵈ19* Peleg *means* division.   *ᵉ22 Some Hebrew manuscripts and Syriac (see also Gen. 10:28); most Hebrew manuscripts* Ebal   *ᶠ24 Hebrew; some Septuagint manuscripts* Arphaxad, Cainan *(see also note at Gen. 11:10)*

Ephah, Epher, Hanoch, Abida and Eldaah. All these were descendants of Keturah.

Descendants of Sarah

34Abraham was the father of Isaac.

The sons of Isaac:
Esau and Israel.　Lk 3:34

Esau's Sons

35The sons of Esau:
Eliphaz, Reuel, Jeush, Jalam and Korah.　Ge 36:19
36The sons of Eliphaz:
Teman, Omar, Zepho,a Gatam and Kenaz;
by Timna: Amalek.b
37The sons of Reuel:
Nahath, Zerah, Shammah and Mizzah.　Ge 36:17

The People of Seir in Edom

38The sons of Seir:
Lotan, Shobal, Zibeon, Anah, Dishon, Ezer and Dishan.　Ge 36:20-28
39The sons of Lotan:
Hori and Homam. Timna was Lotan's sister.
40The sons of Shobal:
Alvan,c Manahath, Ebal, Shepho and Onam.

The sons of Zibeon:
Aiah and Anah.　Ge 36:2

41The son of Anah:
Dishon.

The sons of Dishon:
Hemdan,d Eshban, Ithran and Keran.
42The sons of Ezer:
Bilhan, Zaavan and Akan.e

The sons of Dishanf:
Uz and Aran.

The Rulers of Edom

43These were the kings who reigned in Edom before any Israelite king reignedg:

Bela son of Beor, whose city was named Dinhabah.　Ge 36:41-43
44When Bela died, Jobab son of Zerah from Bozrah succeeded him as king.　Isa 34:6
45When Jobab died, Husham from the land of the Temanites succeeded him as king.　Ge 36:4
46When Husham died, Hadad son of Bedad, who defeated Midian in the country of Moab, succeeded him as king. His city was named Avith.
47When Hadad died, Samlah from Masrekah succeeded him as king.　Ge 36:37
48When Samlah died, Shaul from Rehoboth on the riv-

---

a36 Many Hebrew manuscripts, some Septuagint manuscripts and Syriac (see also Gen. 36:11); most Hebrew manuscripts *Zephi*　b36 Some Septuagint manuscripts (see also Gen. 36:12); Hebrew *Gatam, Kenaz, Timna and Amalek*　c40 Many Hebrew manuscripts and some Septuagint manuscripts (see also Gen. 36:23); most Hebrew manuscripts *Alian*　d41 Many Hebrew manuscripts and some Septuagint manuscripts (see also Gen. 36:26); most Hebrew manuscripts *Hamran*　e42 Many Hebrew and Septuagint manuscripts (see also Gen. 36:27); most Hebrew manuscripts *Zaavan, Jaakan*　f42 Hebrew *Dishon*, a variant of *Dishan*　g43 Or *before an Israelite king reigned over them*

er^a succeeded him as king.

⁴⁹When Shaul died, Baal-Hanan son of Acbor succeeded him as king.

⁵⁰When Baal-Hanan died, Hadad succeeded him as king. His city was named Pau,^b and his wife's name was Mehetabel daughter of Matred, the daughter of Me-Zahab. ⁵¹Hadad also died.   Ge 36:40

The chiefs of Edom were:
Timna, Alvah, Jetheth, ⁵²Oholibamah, Elah, Pinon, ⁵³Kenaz, Teman, Mibzar, ⁵⁴Magdiel and Iram. These were the chiefs of Edom.

Israel's Sons

2 These were the sons of Israel:
Reuben, Simeon, Levi, Judah, Issachar, Zebulun, ²Dan, Joseph, Benjamin, Naphtali, Gad and Asher.

Judah

To Hezron's Sons

³The sons of Judah:
Er, Onan and Shelah. These three were born to him by a Canaanite woman, the daughter of Shua. Er, Judah's firstborn, was wicked in the LORD's sight; so the LORD put him to death. ⁴Tamar, Judah's daughter-in-law, bore him Perez and Zerah. Judah had five sons in all.   Ge 38:29; Mt 1:3

⁵The sons of Perez:
Hezron and Hamul.   Ge 46:12

⁶The sons of Zerah:
Zimri, Ethan, Heman, Calcol and Darda^c—five in all.   Jos 7:1

⁷The son of Carmi: 1Ki 4:31
Achar,^d who brought trouble on Israel by violating the ban on taking devoted things.^e   Jos 6:18; 7:1

⁸The son of Ethan:
Azariah.

⁹The sons born to Hezron were:
Jerahmeel, Ram and Caleb.^f   Nu 26:21

From Ram Son of Hezron

¹⁰Ram was the father of Amminadab, and Amminadab the father of Nahshon, the leader of the people of Judah. ¹¹Nahshon was the father of Salmon,^g Salmon the father of Boaz, ¹²Boaz the father of Obed and Obed the father of Jesse.   Nu 1:7

---

^a48 Possibly the Euphrates   ^b50 Many Hebrew manuscripts, some Septuagint manuscripts, Vulgate and Syriac (see also Gen. 36:39); most Hebrew manuscripts *Pai* ^c6 Many Hebrew manuscripts, some Septuagint manuscripts and Syriac (see also 1 Kings 4:31); most Hebrew manuscripts *Dara*   ^d7 *Achar* means *trouble*; *Achar* is called *Achan* in Joshua.   ^e7 The Hebrew term refers to the irrevocable giving over of things or persons to the LORD, often by totally destroying them.   ^f9 Hebrew *Kelubai*, a variant of *Caleb*   ^g11 Septuagint (see also Ruth 4:21); Hebrew *Salma*

¹³Jesse was the father of Eliab his firstborn; the second son was Abinadab, the third Shimea, ¹⁴the fourth Nethanel, the fifth Raddai, ¹⁵the sixth Ozem and the seventh David. ¹⁶Their sisters were Zeruiah and Abigail. Zeruiah's three sons were Abishai, Joab and Asahel. ¹⁷Abigail was the mother of Amasa, whose father was Jether the Ishmaelite.

1Sa 16:6; 2Sa 2:18

Caleb Son of Hezron

¹⁸Caleb son of Hezron had children by his wife Azubah (and by Jerioth). These were her sons: Jesher, Shobab and Ardon. ¹⁹When Azubah died, Caleb married Ephrath, who bore him Hur. ²⁰Hur was the father of Uri, and Uri the father of Bezalel.

²¹Later, Hezron lay with the daughter of Makir the father of Gilead (he had married her when he was sixty years old), and she bore him Segub. ²²Segub was the father of Jair, who controlled twenty-three towns in Gilead. ²³(But Geshur and Aram captured Havvoth Jair,ᵃ as well as Kenath with its surrounding settlements—sixty towns.) All

these were descendants of Makir the father of Gilead.

Nu 27:1; Dt 3:14

²⁴After Hezron died in Caleb Ephrathah, Abijah the wife of Hezron bore him Ashhur the fatherᵇ of Tekoa.

1Ch 4:5

Jerahmeel Son of Hezron

²⁵The sons of Jerahmeel the firstborn of Hezron:
Ram his firstborn, Bunah, Oren, Ozem andᶜ Ahijah. ²⁶Jerahmeel had another wife, whose name was Atarah; she was the mother of Onam.

²⁷The sons of Ram the firstborn of Jerahmeel:
Maaz, Jamin and Eker.

²⁸The sons of Onam:
Shammai and Jada.
The sons of Shammai:
Nadab and Abishur.

²⁹Abishur's wife was named Abihail, who bore him Ahban and Molid.

³⁰The sons of Nadab:
Seled and Appaim. Seled died without children.

³¹The son of Appaim:
Ishi, who was the father of Sheshan.
Sheshan was the father of Ahlai.

1Ch 1:34-35

³²The sons of Jada, Shammai's brother:
Jether and Jonathan. Jether died without children.

ᵃ23 Or captured the settlements of Jair   ᵇ24 Father may mean civic leader or military leader; also in verses 42, 45, 49-52 and possibly elsewhere.   ᶜ25 Or Oren and Ozem, by

[33]The sons of Jonathan:
Peleth and Zaza.

These were the descendants of Jerahmeel.

[34]Sheshan had no sons—only daughters.

He had an Egyptian servant named Jarha. [35]Sheshan gave his daughter in marriage to his servant Jarha, and she bore him Attai.

[36]Attai was the father of Nathan,
Nathan the father of Zabad,
[37]Zabad the father of Ephlal,
Ephlal the father of Obed,
[38]Obed the father of Jehu,
Jehu the father of Azariah,
[39]Azariah the father of Helez,
Helez the father of Eleasah,
[40]Eleasah the father of Sismai,
Sismai the father of Shallum,
[41]Shallum the father of Jekamiah,
and Jekamiah the father of Elishama.   1Ch 11:41

The Clans of Caleb

[42]The sons of Caleb the brother of Jerahmeel:
Mesha his firstborn, who was the father of Ziph,
and his son Mareshah,[a]

who was the father of Hebron.   1Ch 2:18-19
[43]The sons of Hebron:
Korah, Tappuah, Rekem and Shema. [44]Shema was the father of Raham, and Raham the father of Jorkeam. Rekem was the father of Shammai. [45]The son of Shammai was Maon, and Maon was the father of Beth Zur.   Jos 15:55
[46]Caleb's concubine Ephah was the mother of Haran, Moza and Gazez. Haran was the father of Gazez.
[47]The sons of Jahdai:
Regem, Jotham, Geshan, Pelet, Ephah and Shaaph.
[48]Caleb's concubine Maacah was the mother of Sheber and Tirhanah. [49]She also gave birth to Shaaph the father of Madmannah and to Sheva the father of Macbenah and Gibea. Caleb's daughter was Acsah. [50]These were the descendants of Caleb.   Jos 15:31

The sons of Hur the firstborn of Ephrathah:
Shobal the father of Kiriath Jearim, [51]Salma the father of Bethlehem, and Hareph the father of Beth Gader.   1Ch 4:4
[52]The descendants of Shobal the father of Kiriath Jearim were:
Haroeh, half the Manahathites, [53]and the clans of Kiriath Jearim: the Ith-

---

[a]42 The meaning of the Hebrew for this phrase is uncertain.

rites, Puthites, Shumath-ites and Mishraites. From these descended the Zo-rathites and Eshtaolites.

⁵⁴The descendants of Salma:
Bethlehem, the Netopha-thites, Atroth Beth Joab, half the Manahathites, the Zorites, ⁵⁵and the clans of scribes^a who lived at Jabez: the Tira-thites, Shimeathites and Sucathites. These are the Kenites who came from Hammath, the father of the house of Recab.^b   Ezr 2:22

The Sons of David

3 These were the sons of Da-vid born to him in Hebron:
The firstborn was Amnon the son of Ahinoam of Jezreel;
the second, Daniel the son of Abigail of Carmel;
²the third, Absalom the son of Maacah daughter of Talmai king of Geshur;
the fourth, Adonijah the son of Haggith;
³the fifth, Shephatiah the son of Abital;
and the sixth, Ithream, by his wife Eglah.   2Sa 3:3
⁴These six were born to David in Hebron, where he reigned seven years and six months.   2Sa 5:5
David reigned in Jerusalem

thirty-three years, ⁵and these were the children born to him there:
Shammua,^c Shobab, Na-than and Solomon. These four were by Bathsheba^d daughter of Ammiel. ⁶There were also Ibhar, Elishua,^e Eliphelet, ⁷No-gah, Nepheg, Japhia, ⁸Elishama, Eliada and Eliphelet—nine in all. ⁹All these were the sons of Da-vid, besides his sons by his concubines. And Ta-mar was their sister.   2Sa 11:3

The Kings of Judah

¹⁰Solomon's son was Reho-boam,
Abijah his son,
Asa his son,
Jehoshaphat his son,
¹¹Jehoram^f his son,
Ahaziah his son,
Joash his son,
¹²Amaziah his son,
Azariah his son,
Jotham his son,
¹³Ahaz his son,
Hezekiah his son,
Manasseh his son,
¹⁴Amon his son,
Josiah his son.   1Ki 15:1
¹⁵The sons of Josiah:
Johanan the firstborn,
Jehoiakim the second son,
Zedekiah the third,

---

^a55 Or of the Sopherites   ^b55 Or father of Beth Recab   ^c5 Hebrew Shimea, a variant of Shammua   ^d5 One Hebrew manuscript and Vulgate (see also Septuagint and 2 Samuel 11:3); most Hebrew manuscripts Bathshua   ^e6 Two Hebrew manuscripts (see also 2 Samuel 5:15 and 1 Chron. 14:5); most Hebrew manuscripts Elishama ^f11 Hebrew Joram, a variant of Jehoram

Shallum the fourth.   Jer 37:1

16The successors of Jehoiakim:
Jehoiachin[a] his son,
and Zedekiah.   2Ki 24:18

The Royal Line After the Exile

17The descendants of Jehoia-
chin the captive:
Shealtiel his son, 18Malki-
ram, Pedaiah, Shenazzar,
Jekamiah, Hoshama and
Nedabiah.   Ezr 3:2

19The sons of Pedaiah:
Zerubbabel and Shimei.
The sons of Zerubbabel:
Meshullam and Hana-
niah.
Shelomith was their sis-
ter.   Ezr 2:2; Ne 7:7

20There were also five others:
Hashubah, Ohel, Bere-
kiah, Hasadiah and Ju-
shab-Hesed.

21The descendants of Han-
aniah:
Pelatiah and Jeshaiah,
and the sons of Rephaiah,
of Arnan, of Obadiah and
of Shecaniah.

22The descendants of Sheca-
niah:
Shemaiah and his sons:
Hattush, Igal, Bariah,
Neariah and Shaphat—
six in all.   Ezr 8:2-3

23The sons of Neariah:
Elioenai, Hizkiah and Az-
rikam—three in all.

24The sons of Elioenai:

Hodaviah, Eliashib, Pelaiah, Akkub, Johanan, De-
laiah and Anani—seven
in all.

Other Clans of Judah

4 The descendants of Judah:
Perez, Hezron, Carmi,
Hur and Shobal.   Nu 26:21

2Reaiah son of Shobal was
the father of Jahath, and
Jahath the father of Ahu-
mai and Lahad. These
were the clans of the Zo-
rathites.   1Ch 2:52

3These were the sons[b] of
Etam:
Jezreel, Ishma and Id-
bash. Their sister was
named Hazzelelponi. 4Pe-
nuel was the father of Gedor, and Ezer the father of
Hushah.
These were the descend-
ants of Hur, the firstborn
of Ephrathah and father[c]
of Bethlehem.   1Ch 2:50

5Ashhur the father of Tekoa
had two wives, Helah
and Naarah.   1Ch 2:24

6Naarah bore him Ahuzzam,
Hepher, Temeni and
Haahashtari. These were
the descendants of Naa-
rah.

7The sons of Helah:
Zereth, Zohar, Ethnan,
8and Koz, who was the fa-
ther of Anub and Haz-
zobebah and of the clans
of Aharhel son of Harum.

---

a16 Hebrew *Jeconiah*, a variant of *Jehoiachin*; also in verse 17   b3 Some Septuagint
manuscripts (see also Vulgate); Hebrew *father*   c4 *Father* may mean *civic leader* or
military leader; also in verses 12, 14, 17, 18 and possibly elsewhere.

⁹Jabez was more honorable than his brothers. His mother had named him Jabez,ᵃ saying, "I gave birth to him in pain." ¹⁰Jabez cried out to the God of Israel, "Oh, that you would bless me and enlarge my territory! Let your hand be with me, and keep me from harm so that I will be free from pain." And God granted his request.

¹¹Kelub, Shuhah's brother, was the father of Mehir, who was the father of Eshton. ¹²Eshton was the father of Beth Rapha, Paseah and Tehinnah the father of Ir Nahash.ᵇ These were the men of Recah.

¹³The sons of Kenaz:
Othniel and Seraiah. Jos 15:17
The sons of Othniel:
Hathath and Meonothai.ᶜ
¹⁴Meonothai was the father of Ophrah.
Seraiah was the father of Joab,
the father of Ge Harashim.ᵈ It was called this because its people were craftsmen. Ne 11:35
¹⁵The sons of Caleb son of Jephunneh:
Iru, Elah and Naam.
The son of Elah:
Kenaz.
¹⁶The sons of Jehallelel:
Ziph, Ziphah, Tiria and Asarel.
¹⁷The sons of Ezrah:

Jether, Mered, Epher and Jalon. One of Mered's wives gave birth to Miriam, Shammai and Ishbah the father of Eshtemoa. ¹⁸(His Judean wife gave birth to Jered the father of Gedor, Heber the father of Soco, and Jekuthiel the father of Zanoah.) These were the children of Pharaoh's daughter Bithiah, whom Mered had married. Ex 15:20; Jos 15:34

¹⁹The sons of Hodiah's wife, the sister of Naham:
the father of Keilah the Garmite, and Eshtemoa the Maacathite.
²⁰The sons of Shimon:
Amnon, Rinnah, Ben-Hanan and Tilon.
The descendants of Ishi:
Zoheth and Ben-Zoheth.
²¹The sons of Shelah son of Judah:
Er the father of Lecah, Laadah the father of Mareshah and the clans of the linen workers at Beth Ashbea, ²²Jokim, the men of Cozeba, and Joash and Saraph, who ruled in Moab and Jashubi Lehem. (These records are from ancient times.) ²³They were the potters who lived at Netaim and Gederah; they stayed there and worked for the king. Ge 38:5

ᵃ9 *Jabez* sounds like the Hebrew for *pain*.   ᵇ12 Or *of the city of Nahash*   ᶜ13 Some Septuagint manuscripts and Vulgate; Hebrew does not have *and Meonothai*.   ᵈ14 *Ge Harashim* means *valley of craftsmen*.

Simeon

24The descendants of Simeon:
Nemuel, Jamin, Jarib, Zerah and Shaul;
25Shallum was Shaul's son, Mibsam his son and Mishma his son.   Ge 29:33
26The descendants of Mishma:
Hammuel his son, Zaccur his son and Shimei his son.

27Shimei had sixteen sons and six daughters, but his brothers did not have many children; so their entire clan did not become as numerous as the people of Judah. 28They lived in Beersheba, Moladah, Hazar Shual, 29Bilhah, Ezem, Tolad, 30Bethuel, Hormah, Ziklag, 31Beth Marcaboth, Hazar Susim, Beth Biri and Shaaraim. These were their towns until the reign of David. 32Their surrounding villages were Etam, Ain, Rimmon, Token and Ashan—five towns— 33and all the villages around these towns as far as Baalath.a These were their settlements. And they kept a genealogical record.   Jos 19:2

34Meshobab, Jamlech, Joshah son of Amaziah, 35Joel, Jehu son of Joshibiah, the son of Seraiah, the son of Asiel, 36also Elioenai, Jaakobah, Jeshohaiah, Asaiah, Adiel, Jesimiel, Benaiah, 37and Ziza son of Shiphi, the son of Allon, the son of Jedaiah, the son of Shimri, the son of Shemaiah.

38The men listed above by name were leaders of their clans. Their families increased greatly, 39and they went to the outskirts of Gedor to the east of the valley in search of pasture for their flocks. 40They found rich, good pasture, and the land was spacious, peaceful and quiet. Some Hamites had lived there formerly.   Jos 15:58

41The men whose names were listed came in the days of Hezekiah king of Judah. They attacked the Hamites in their dwellings and also the Meunites who were there and completely destroyedb them, as is evident to this day. Then they settled in their place, because there was pasture for their flocks. 42And five hundred of these Simeonites, led by Pelatiah, Neariah, Rephaiah and Uzziel, the sons of Ishi, invaded the hill country of Seir. 43They killed the remaining Amalekites who had escaped, and they have lived there to this day.

Reuben

5 The sons of Reuben the firstborn of Israel (he was the firstborn, but when he defiled his father's marriage bed, his rights as firstborn were given to the sons of Joseph son of Israel;

---

a33 Some Septuagint manuscripts (see also Joshua 19:8); Hebrew *Baal*   b41 The Hebrew term refers to the irrevocable giving over of things or persons to the LORD, often by totally destroying them.

so he could not be listed in the genealogical record in accordance with his birthright, ²and though Judah was the strongest of his brothers and a ruler came from him, the rights of the firstborn belonged to Joseph)— ³the sons of Reuben the firstborn of Israel:

Hanoch, Pallu, Hezron and Carmi.   Ge 29:32

⁴The descendants of Joel:

Shemaiah his son, Gog his son,

Shimei his son, ⁵Micah his son,

Reaiah his son, Baal his son,

⁶and Beerah his son, whom Tiglath-Pileser[a] king of Assyria took into exile. Beerah was a leader of the Reubenites.   2Ch 28:20

⁷Their relatives by clans, listed according to their genealogical records:

Jeiel the chief, Zechariah, ⁸and Bela son of Azaz, the son of Shema, the son of Joel. They settled in the area from Aroer to Nebo and Baal Meon. ⁹To the east they occupied the land up to the edge of the desert that extends to the Euphrates River, because their livestock had increased in Gilead.   Jos 13:15

¹⁰During Saul's reign they waged war against the Hagrites, who were defeated at their hands; they occupied the dwellings of the Hagrites throughout the entire region east of Gilead.1Ch 27:31

Gad

¹¹The Gadites lived next to them in Bashan, as far as Salecah:

¹²Joel was the chief, Shapham the second, then Janai and Shaphat, in Bashan.   Jos 13:24

¹³Their relatives, by families, were:

Michael, Meshullam, Sheba, Jorai, Jacan, Zia and Eber—seven in all.

¹⁴These were the sons of Abihail son of Huri, the son of Jaroah, the son of Gilead, the son of Michael, the son of Jeshishai, the son of Jahdo, the son of Buz.

¹⁵Ahi son of Abdiel, the son of Guni, was head of their family.

¹⁶The Gadites lived in Gilead, in Bashan and its outlying villages, and on all the pasturelands of Sharon as far as they extended.1Ch 27:29

¹⁷All these were entered in the genealogical records during the reigns of Jotham king of Judah and Jeroboam king of Israel.   2Ki 14:23; 15:32

¹⁸The Reubenites, the Gadites and the half-tribe of Manasseh had 44,760 men ready for military service—able-bodied men who could handle shield and

---

a6 Hebrew Tilgath-Pilneser, a variant of Tiglath-Pileser; also in verse 26

sword, who could use a bow, and who were trained for battle. [19]They waged war against the Hagrites, Jetur, Naphish and Nodab. [20]They were helped in fighting them, and God handed the Hagrites and all their allies over to them, because they cried out to him during the battle. He answered their prayers, because they trusted in him. [21]They seized the livestock of the Hagrites—fifty thousand camels, two hundred fifty thousand sheep and two thousand donkeys. They also took one hundred thousand people captive, [22]and many others fell slain, because the battle was God's. And they occupied the land until the exile.   Nu 1:3

The Half-Tribe of Manasseh

[23]The people of the half-tribe of Manasseh were numerous; they settled in the land from Bashan to Baal Hermon, that is, to Senir (Mount Hermon).   1Ch 7:14

[24]These were the heads of their families: Epher, Ishi, Eliel, Azriel, Jeremiah, Hodaviah and Jahdiel. They were brave warriors, famous men, and heads of their families. [25]But they were unfaithful to the God of their fathers and prostituted themselves to the gods of the peoples of the land, whom God had destroyed before them. [26]So the God of Israel stirred up the spirit of Pul king of Assyria (that is, Tiglath-Pileser king of Assyria), who took the Reubenites, the Gadites and the half-tribe of Manasseh into exile. He took them to Halah, Habor, Hara and the river of Gozan, where they are to this day. 1Ch 9:1

Levi

6 The sons of Levi:
Gershon, Kohath and Merari.   Ex 6:16; Nu 3:17

[2]The sons of Kohath:
Amram, Izhar, Hebron and Uzziel.   Ex 6:18

[3]The children of Amram:
Aaron, Moses and Miriam.

The sons of Aaron:
Nadab, Abihu, Eleazar and Ithamar.   Lev 10:1

[4]Eleazar was the father of Phinehas,
Phinehas the father of Abishua,
[5]Abishua the father of Bukki,
Bukki the father of Uzzi,
[6]Uzzi the father of Zerahiah,
Zerahiah the father of Meraioth,
[7]Meraioth the father of Amariah,
Amariah the father of Ahitub,
[8]Ahitub the father of Zadok,
Zadok the father of Ahimaaz,
[9]Ahimaaz the father of Azariah,
Azariah the father of Johanan,
[10]Johanan the father of Azariah (it was he who served as priest in the

temple Solomon built in Jerusalem),

[11]Azariah the father of Amariah,

Amariah the father of Ahitub,

[12]Ahitub the father of Zadok,

Zadok the father of Shallum,

[13]Shallum the father of Hilkiah,

Hilkiah the father of Azariah,

[14]Azariah the father of Seraiah,

and Seraiah the father of Jehozadak.   2Sa 8:17

[15]Jehozadak was deported when the LORD sent Judah and Jerusalem into exile by the hand of Nebuchadnezzar.   2Ki 25:18; Ne 12:1

[16]The sons of Levi: Gershon,[a] Kohath and Merari.   Ex 6:16

[17]These are the names of the sons of Gershon: Libni and Shimei.   Ex 6:17

[18]The sons of Kohath: Amram, Izhar, Hebron and Uzziel.   Ge 46:11

[19]The sons of Merari: Mahli and Mushi.   Nu 3:36

These are the clans of the Levites listed according to their fathers:

[20]Of Gershon:

Libni his son, Jehath his son,

Zimmah his son, [21]Joah his son,

Iddo his son, Zerah his son

and Jeatherai his son.

[22]The descendants of Kohath: Amminadab his son, Korah his son,

Assir his son, [23]Elkanah his son,

Ebiasaph his son, Assir his son,

[24]Tahath his son, Uriel his son,

Uzziah his son and Shaul his son.   Ex 6:24; 1Ch 15:5

[25]The descendants of Elkanah: Amasai, Ahimoth,

[26]Elkanah his son,[b] Zophai his son,

Nahath his son, [27]Eliab his son,

Jeroham his son, Elkanah his son

and Samuel his son.[c]   1Sa 1:1

[28]The sons of Samuel: Joel[d] the firstborn and Abijah the second son.   1Sa 8:2

[29]The descendants of Merari: Mahli, Libni his son, Shimei his son, Uzzah his son,

[30]Shimea his son, Haggiah his son

---

[a]16 Hebrew *Gershom*, a variant of *Gershon*; also in verses 17, 20, 43, 62 and 71
[b]26 Some Hebrew manuscripts, Septuagint and Syriac; most Hebrew manuscripts *Ahimoth* [26]*and Elkanah. The sons of Elkanah:*   [c]27 Some Septuagint manuscripts (see also 1 Samuel 1:19,20 and 1 Chron. 6:33,34); Hebrew does not have *and Samuel his son.*
[d]28 Some Septuagint manuscripts and Syriac (see also 1 Samuel 8:2 and 1 Chron. 6:33); Hebrew does not have *Joel.*

and Asaiah his son.

The Temple Musicians

³¹These are the men David put in charge of the music in the house of the LORD after the ark came to rest there. ³²They ministered with music before the tabernacle, the Tent of Meeting, until Solomon built the temple of the LORD in Jerusalem. They performed their duties according to the regulations laid down for them.   1Ch 25:1; Ne 12:45

³³Here are the men who served, together with their sons:

From the Kohathites:
Heman, the musician,
the son of Joel, the son of Samuel,
³⁴the son of Elkanah, the son of Jeroham,
the son of Eliel, the son of Toah,
³⁵the son of Zuph, the son of Elkanah,
the son of Mahath, the son of Amasai,
³⁶the son of Elkanah, the son of Joel,
the son of Azariah, the son of Zephaniah,
³⁷the son of Tahath, the son of Assir,
the son of Ebiasaph, the son of Korah,
³⁸the son of Izhar, the son of Kohath,
the son of Levi, the son of Israel;   Ex 6:21; 1Ki 4:31

³⁹and Heman's associate Asaph, who served at his right hand:
Asaph son of Berekiah, the son of Shimea,
⁴⁰the son of Michael, the son of Baaseiah,^a
the son of Malkijah, ⁴¹the son of Ethni,
the son of Zerah, the son of Adaiah,
⁴²the son of Ethan, the son of Zimmah,
the son of Shimei, ⁴³the son of Jahath,
the son of Gershon, the son of Levi;   1Ch 15:17

⁴⁴and from their associates, the Merarites, at his left hand:
Ethan son of Kishi, the son of Abdi,
the son of Malluch, ⁴⁵the son of Hashabiah,
the son of Amaziah, the son of Hilkiah,
⁴⁶the son of Amzi, the son of Bani,
the son of Shemer, ⁴⁷the son of Mahli,
the son of Mushi, the son of Merari,
the son of Levi.   1Ch 15:17

⁴⁸Their fellow Levites were assigned to all the other duties of the tabernacle, the house of God. ⁴⁹But Aaron and his descendants were the ones who presented offerings on the altar of burnt offering and on the altar of incense in connection

---

^a40 Most Hebrew manuscripts; some Hebrew manuscripts, one Septuagint manuscript and Syriac *Maaseiah*

with all that was done in the Most Holy Place, making atonement for Israel, in accordance with all that Moses the servant of God had commanded. Ex 30:7

⁵⁰These were the descendants of Aaron:
Eleazar his son, Phinehas his son,
Abishua his son, ⁵¹Bukki his son,
Uzzi his son, Zerahiah his son,
⁵²Meraioth his son, Amariah his son,
Ahitub his son, ⁵³Zadok his son
and Ahimaaz his son.

⁵⁴These were the locations of their settlements allotted as their territory (they were assigned to the descendants of Aaron who were from the Kohathite clan, because the first lot was for them): Nu 31:10
⁵⁵They were given Hebron in Judah with its surrounding pasturelands. ⁵⁶But the fields and villages around the city were given to Caleb son of Jephunneh. ⁵⁷So the descendants of Aaron were given Hebron (a city of refuge), and Libnah,ᵃ Jattir, Eshtemoa, ⁵⁸Hilen, Debir, ⁵⁹Ashan, Juttahᵇ and Beth Shemesh, together with their pasturelands. ⁶⁰And from the tribe of Benjamin they were given Gibeon,ᶜ Geba, Alemeth and Anathoth, together with their pasturelands.
These towns, which were distributed among the Kohathite clans, were thirteen in all.
⁶¹The rest of Kohath's descendants were allotted ten towns from the clans of half the tribe of Manasseh. Jos 21:5
⁶²The descendants of Gershon, clan by clan, were allotted thirteen towns from the tribes of Issachar, Asher and Naphtali, and from the part of the tribe of Manasseh that is in Bashan.
⁶³The descendants of Merari, clan by clan, were allotted twelve towns from the tribes of Reuben, Gad and Zebulun.
⁶⁴So the Israelites gave the Levites these towns and their pasturelands. ⁶⁵From the tribes of Judah, Simeon and Benjamin they allotted the previously named towns. Nu 35:1-8
⁶⁶Some of the Kohathite clans were given as their territory towns from the tribe of Ephraim.
⁶⁷In the hill country of Ephraim they were given Shechem (a city of refuge), and Gezer,ᵈ ⁶⁸Jokmeam, Beth Horon, ⁶⁹Aijalon and Gath Rimmon, together with their pasturelands.
⁷⁰And from half the tribe

ᵃ57 See Joshua 21:13; Hebrew given the cities of refuge: Hebron, Libnah.   ᵇ59 Syriac (see also Septuagint and Joshua 21:16); Hebrew does not have Juttah.   ᶜ60 See Joshua 21:17; Hebrew does not have Gibeon.   ᵈ67 See Joshua 21:21; Hebrew given the cities of refuge: Shechem, Gezer.

of Manasseh the Israelites gave Aner and Bileam, together with their pasturelands, to the rest of the Kohathite clans.

71The Gershonites received the following: 1Ch 23:7

From the clan of the half-tribe of Manasseh
they received Golan in Bashan and also Ashtaroth, together with their pasturelands;   Jos 20:8

72from the tribe of Issachar
they received Kedesh, Daberath, 73Ramoth and Anem, together with their pasturelands;   Jos 19:12

74from the tribe of Asher
they received Mashal, Abdon, 75Hukok and Rehob, together with their pasturelands;   Jos 19:28

76and from the tribe of Naphtali
they received Kedesh in Galilee, Hammon and Kiriathaim, together with their pasturelands.   Nu 32:37

77The Merarites (the rest of the Levites) received the following:

From the tribe of Zebulun
they received Jokneam, Kartah,ª Rimmono and Tabor, together with their pasturelands;   Nu 3:36

78from the tribe of Reuben across the Jordan east of Jericho
they received Bezer in the desert, Jahzah, 79Kedemoth and Mephaath, together with their pasturelands;   Dt 2:26; Jos 20:8

80and from the tribe of Gad they received Ramoth in Gilead, Mahanaim, 81Heshbon and Jazer, together with their pasturelands.   Ge 32:2; Nu 21:26

Issachar

7 The sons of Issachar:
Tola, Puah, Jashub and Shimron—four in all. Ge 46:13

2The sons of Tola:
Uzzi, Rephaiah, Jeriel, Jahmai, Ibsam and Samuel—heads of their families. During the reign of David, the descendants of Tola listed as fighting men in their genealogy numbered 22,600.   2Sa 24:1-2

3The son of Uzzi:
Izrahiah.

The sons of Izrahiah:
Michael, Obadiah, Joel and Isshiah. All five of them were chiefs. 4According to their family genealogy, they had 36,000 men ready for battle, for they had many wives and children.

5The relatives who were fighting men belonging to all the clans of Issachar, as listed in their genealogy, were 87,000 in all.   1Ch 6:62

ª77 See Septuagint and Joshua 21:34; Hebrew does not have *Jokneam, Kartah.*

Benjamin

⁶Three sons of Benjamin:
Bela, Beker and Jediael.
⁷The sons of Bela:
Ezbon, Uzzi, Uzziel, Jerimoth and Iri, heads of
families—five in all. Their
genealogical record listed
22,034 fighting men.
⁸The sons of Beker:
Zemirah, Joash, Eliezer,
Elioenai, Omri, Jeremoth,
Abijah, Anathoth and
Alemeth. All these were
the sons of Beker. ⁹Their
genealogical record listed
the heads of families and
20,200 fighting men.
¹⁰The son of Jediael:
Bilhan.

The sons of Bilhan:
Jeush, Benjamin, Ehud,
Kenaanah, Zethan, Tar-
shish and Ahishahar.
¹¹All these sons of Jediael
were heads of families.
There were 17,200 fight-
ing men ready to go out to
war.
¹²The Shuppites and Hup-
pites were the descend-
ants of Ir, and the Hush-
ites the descendants of
Aher.   Nu 26:39

Naphtali

¹³The sons of Naphtali:
Jahziel, Guni, Jezer and
Shillemᵃ—the descend-
ants of Bilhah.   Ge 46:24

Manasseh

¹⁴The descendants of Ma-
nasseh:
Asriel was his descendant
through his Aramean con-
cubine. She gave birth to
Makir the father of Gilead.
¹⁵Makir took a wife from
among the Huppites and
Shuppites. His sister's
name was Maacah.   1Ch 5:23
Another descendant was
named Zelophehad, who
had only daughters.
¹⁶Makir's wife Maacah
gave birth to a son and
named him Peresh. His
brother was named She-
resh, and his sons were
Ulam and Rakem.
¹⁷The son of Ulam:
Bedan.
These were the sons of Gilead son of Makir, the son
of Manasseh. ¹⁸His sister
Hammoleketh gave birth
to Ishhod, Abiezer and
Mahlah.   Nu 26:30; 1Sa 12:11
¹⁹The sons of Shemida were:
Ahian, Shechem, Likhi
and Aniam.   Jos 17:2

Ephraim

²⁰The descendants of
Ephraim:
Shuthelah, Bered his son,
Tahath his son, Eleadah
his son,
Tahath his son, ²¹Zabad
his son
and Shuthelah his son.

ᵃ13 Some Hebrew and Septuagint manuscripts (see also Gen. 46:24 and Num. 26:49);
most Hebrew manuscripts *Shallum*

Ezer and Elead were killed by the native-born men of Gath, when they went down to seize their livestock. ²²Their father Ephraim mourned for them many days, and his relatives came to comfort him. ²³Then he lay with his wife again, and she became pregnant and gave birth to a son. He named him Beriah,^a because there had been misfortune in his family. ²⁴His daughter was Sheerah, who built Lower and Upper Beth Horon as well as Uzzen Sheerah.

²⁵Rephah was his son, Resheph his son,^b
Telah his son, Tahan his son,
²⁶Ladan his son, Ammihud his son,
Elishama his son, ²⁷Nun his son
and Joshua his son.   Ex 24:13

²⁸Their lands and settlements included Bethel and its surrounding villages, Naaran to the east, Gezer and its villages to the west, and Shechem and its villages all the way to Ayyah and its villages. ²⁹Along the borders of Manasseh were Beth Shan, Taanach, Megiddo and Dor, together with their villages. The descendants of Joseph son of Israel lived in these towns.   Jos 10:33; 16:7

Asher

³⁰The sons of Asher:
Imnah, Ishvah, Ishvi and Beriah. Their sister was Serah.   Nu 1:40
³¹The sons of Beriah:
Heber and Malkiel, who was the father of Birzaith.
³²Heber was the father of Japhlet, Shomer and Hotham and of their sister Shua.
³³The sons of Japhlet:
Pasach, Bimhal and Ashvath.
These were Japhlet's sons.
³⁴The sons of Shomer:
Ahi, Rohgah,^c Hubbah and Aram.
³⁵The sons of his brother Helem:
Zophah, Imna, Shelesh and Amal.
³⁶The sons of Zophah:
Suah, Harnepher, Shual, Beri, Imrah, ³⁷Bezer, Hod, Shamma, Shilshah, Ithran^d and Beera.
³⁸The sons of Jether:
Jephunneh, Pispah and Ara.
³⁹The sons of Ulla:
Arah, Hanniel and Rizia.
⁴⁰All these were descendants of Asher—heads of families, choice men, brave warriors and outstanding leaders. The number of men ready for battle, as

---

^a23 Beriah sounds like the Hebrew for misfortune. Hebrew does not have his son.   ^b25 Some Septuagint manuscripts; ^c34 Or of his brother Shomer: Rohgah   ^d37 Possibly a variant of Jether

listed in their genealogy, was 26,000.

1Ch 7:30

The Genealogy of Saul the Benjamite

8 Benjamin was the father of Bela his firstborn,
Ashbel the second son, Aharah the third,
²Nohah the fourth and Rapha the fifth.

Ge 46:21

³The sons of Bela were:
Addar, Gera, Abihud,ᵃ ⁴Abishua, Naaman, Ahoah, ⁵Gera, Shephuphan and Huram.

2Sa 23:9

⁶These were the descendants of Ehud, who were heads of families of those living in Geba and were deported to Manahath:

⁷Naaman, Ahijah, and Gera, who deported them and who was the father of Uzza and Ahihud.

⁸Sons were born to Shaharaim in Moab after he had divorced his wives Hushim and Baara. ⁹By his wife Hodesh he had Jobab, Zibia, Mesha, Malcam, ¹⁰Jeuz, Sakia and Mirmah. These were his sons, heads of families. ¹¹By Hushim he had Abitub and Elpaal.

¹²The sons of Elpaal:
Eber, Misham, Shemed (who built Ono and Lod with its surrounding villages), ¹³and Beriah and Shema, who were heads of families of those living in Aijalon and who drove out the inhabitants of Gath.

Ezr 2:33; Ne 6:2

¹⁴Ahio, Shashak, Jeremoth, ¹⁵Zebadiah, Arad, Eder, ¹⁶Michael, Ishpah and Joha were the sons of Beriah.

¹⁷Zebadiah, Meshullam, Hizki, Heber, ¹⁸Ishmerai, Izliah and Jobab were the sons of Elpaal.

¹⁹Jakim, Zicri, Zabdi, ²⁰Elienai, Zillethai, Eliel, ²¹Adaiah, Beraiah and Shimrath were the sons of Shimei.

²²Ishpan, Eber, Eliel, ²³Abdon, Zicri, Hanan, ²⁴Hananiah, Elam, Anthothijah, ²⁵Iphdeiah and Penuel were the sons of Shashak.

²⁶Shamsherai, Shehariah, Athaliah, ²⁷Jaareshiah, Elijah and Zicri were the sons of Jeroham.

²⁸All these were heads of families, chiefs as listed in their genealogy, and they lived in Jerusalem.

²⁹Jeielᵇ the fatherᶜ of Gibeon lived in Gibeon.

Jos 9:3

His wife's name was Maacah, ³⁰and his firstborn son was Abdon, followed by Zur, Kish, Baal, Ner,ᵈ

ᵃ3 Or *Gera the father of Ehud*   ᵇ29 Some Septuagint manuscripts (see also 1 Chron. 9:35); Hebrew does not have *Jeiel*.   ᶜ29 *Father* may mean *civic leader* or *military leader*.   ᵈ30 Some Septuagint manuscripts (see also 1 Chron. 9:36); Hebrew does not have *Ner*.

Nadab, [31]Gedor, Ahio, Zeker [32]and Mikloth, who was the father of Shimeah. They too lived near their relatives in Jerusalem. *1Ch 9:35-38*

[33]Ner was the father of Kish, Kish the father of Saul, and Saul the father of Jonathan, Malki-Shua, Abinadab and Esh-Baal.[a]

[34]The son of Jonathan:

Merib-Baal,[b] who was the father of Micah. *2Sa 9:12*

[35]The sons of Micah:

Pithon, Melech, Tarea and Ahaz. *1Ch 9:41*

[36]Ahaz was the father of Jehoaddah, Jehoaddah was the father of Alemeth, Azmaveth and Zimri, and Zimri was the father of Moza. [37]Moza was the father of Binea; Raphah was his son, Eleasah his son and Azel his son. *1Ch 9:43*

[38]Azel had six sons, and these were their names:

Azrikam, Bokeru, Ishmael, Sheariah, Obadiah and Hanan. All these were the sons of Azel.

[39]The sons of his brother Eshek:

Ulam his firstborn, Jeush the second son and Eliphelet the third. [40]The sons of Ulam were brave warriors who could handle the bow. They had many sons and grandsons—150 in all.

All these were the descendants of Benjamin. *Nu 26:38*

9 All Israel was listed in the genealogies recorded in the book of the kings of Israel.

The People in Jerusalem

The people of Judah were taken captive to Babylon because of their unfaithfulness. [2]Now the first to resettle on their own property in their own towns were some Israelites, priests, Levites and temple servants. *Jos 9:27; Ezr 2:43*

[3]Those from Judah, from Benjamin, and from Ephraim and Manasseh who lived in Jerusalem were:

[4]Uthai son of Ammihud, the son of Omri, the son of Imri, the son of Bani, a descendant of Perez son of Judah. *Ge 28:39; 46:12*

[5]Of the Shilonites:

Asaiah the firstborn and his sons.

[6]Of the Zerahites:

Jeuel.

The people from Judah numbered 690.

[7]Of the Benjamites:

Sallu son of Meshullam, the son of Hodaviah, the son of Hassenuah; *Ge 35:18*

[8]Ibneiah son of Jeroham; Elah son of Uzzi, the son of Micri; and Meshullam son of Shephatiah, the son of Reuel, the son of Ibnijah.

[9]The people from Benja-

---

a33 Also known as *Ish-Bosheth*   *b34* Also known as *Mephibosheth*

min, as listed in their genealogy, numbered 956. All these men were heads of their families.

¹⁰Of the priests:

Jedaiah; Jehoiarib; Jakin;

¹¹Azariah son of Hilkiah, the son of Meshullam, the son of Zadok, the son of Meraioth, the son of Ahitub, the official in charge of the house of God;

¹²Adaiah son of Jeroham, the son of Pashhur, the son of Malkijah; and Maasai son of Adiel, the son of Jahzerah, the son of Meshullam, the son of Meshillemith, the son of Immer.   Ezr 2:38; Jer 21:1

¹³The priests, who were heads of families, numbered 1,760. They were able men, responsible for ministering in the house of God.

¹⁴Of the Levites:

Shemaiah son of Hasshub, the son of Azrikam, the son of Hashabiah, a Merarite; ¹⁵Bakbakkar, Heresh, Galal and Mattaniah son of Mica, the son of Zicri, the son of Asaph; ¹⁶Obadiah son of Shemaiah, the son of Galal, the son of Jeduthun; and Berekiah son of Asa, the son of Elkanah, who lived in the villages of the Netophathites.   Ne 11:15-19

¹⁷The gatekeepers:

Shallum, Akkub, Talmon, Ahiman and their brothers, Shallum their chief ¹⁸being stationed at the King's Gate on the east, up to the present time. These were the gatekeepers belonging to the camp of the Levites. ¹⁹Shallum son of Kore, the son of Ebiasaph, the son of Korah, and his fellow gatekeepers from his family (the Korahites) were responsible for guarding the thresholds of the Tent*a* just as their fathers had been responsible for guarding the entrance to the dwelling of the LORD. ²⁰In earlier times Phinehas son of Eleazar was in charge of the gatekeepers, and the LORD was with him. ²¹Zechariah son of Meshelemiah was the gatekeeper at the entrance to the Tent of Meeting.   1Ch 26:1

²²Altogether, those chosen to be gatekeepers at the thresholds numbered 212. They were registered by genealogy in their villages. The gatekeepers had been assigned to their positions of trust by David and Samuel the seer. ²³They and their descendants were in charge of guarding the gates of the house of the LORD—the house called the Tent. ²⁴The gatekeepers were on the four sides: east,

a 19 That is, the temple; also in verses 21 and 23

west, north and south. ²⁵Their brothers in their villages had to come from time to time and share their duties for seven-day periods. ²⁶But the four principal gatekeepers, who were Levites, were entrusted with the responsibility for the rooms and treasuries in the house of God. ²⁷They would spend the night stationed around the house of God, because they had to guard it; and they had charge of the key for opening it each morning.   2Ki 11:5; Isa 22:22

²⁸Some of them were in charge of the articles used in the temple service; they counted them when they were brought in and when they were taken out. ²⁹Others were assigned to take care of the furnishings and all the other articles of the sanctuary, as well as the flour and wine, and the oil, incense and spices. ³⁰But some of the priests took care of mixing the spices. ³¹A Levite named Mattithiah, the firstborn son of Shallum the Korahite, was entrusted with the responsibility for baking the offering bread. ³²Some of their Kohathite brothers were in charge of preparing for every Sabbath the bread set out on the table.   Lev 24:8; 1Ch 23:29

³³Those who were musicians, heads of Levite families, stayed in the rooms of the temple and were exempt from other duties because they were responsible for the work day and night.

³⁴All these were heads of Levite families, chiefs as listed in their genealogy, and they lived in Jerusalem.   Jos 10:1

The Genealogy of Saul

³⁵Jeiel the father*ᵃ* of Gibeon lived in Gibeon.   1Ch 8:29
His wife's name was Maacah, ³⁶and his firstborn son was Abdon, followed by Zur, Kish, Baal, Ner, Nadab, ³⁷Gedor, Ahio, Zechariah and Mikloth. ³⁸Mikloth was the father of Shimeam. They too lived near their relatives in Jerusalem.

³⁹Ner was the father of Kish, Kish the father of Saul, and Saul the father of Jonathan, Malki-Shua, Abinadab and Esh-Baal.*ᵇ*

⁴⁰The son of Jonathan:
Merib-Baal,*ᶜ* who was the father of Micah.   2Sa 4:4

⁴¹The sons of Micah:
Pithon, Melech, Tahrea and Ahaz.*ᵈ*   1Ch 8:35

⁴²Ahaz was the father of Jadah, Jadah*ᵉ* was the father of Alemeth, Azmaveth and Zimri, and Zimri was the father of Moza. ⁴³Moza was the father of Binea; Rephaiah was his son, Eleasah his son and Azel his son. 1Ch 8:36

ᵃ35 *Father* may mean *civic leader* or *military leader.*   *ᵇ39* Also known as *Ish-Bosheth*   *ᶜ40* Also known as *Mephibosheth*   *ᵈ41* Vulgate and Syriac (see also Septuagint and 1 Chron. 8:35); Hebrew does not have *and Ahaz.*   *ᵉ42* Some Hebrew manuscripts and Septuagint (see also 1 Chron. 8:36); most Hebrew manuscripts *Jarah, Jarah*

44Azel had six sons, and these were their names:

Azrikam, Bokeru, Ishmael, Sheariah, Obadiah and Hanan. These were the sons of Azel.

Saul Takes His Life

10 Now the Philistines fought against Israel; the Israelites fled before them, and many fell slain on Mount Gilboa. 2The Philistines pressed hard after Saul and his sons, and they killed his sons Jonathan, Abinadab and Malki-Shua. 3The fighting grew fierce around Saul, and when the archers overtook him, they wounded him.   1Sa 31:1-2

4Saul said to his armor-bearer, "Draw your sword and run me through, or these uncircumcised fellows will come and abuse me."

But his armor-bearer was terrified and would not do it; so Saul took his own sword and fell on it. 5When the armor-bearer saw that Saul was dead, he too fell on his sword and died. 6So Saul and his three sons died, and all his house died together.

7When all the Israelites in the valley saw that the army had fled and that Saul and his sons had died, they abandoned their towns and fled. And the Philistines came and occupied them.

8The next day, when the Philistines came to strip the dead, they found Saul and his sons fallen on Mount Gilboa. 9They stripped him and took his head and his armor, and sent messengers throughout the land of the Philistines to proclaim the news among their idols and their people. 10They put his armor in the temple of their gods and hung up his head in the temple of Dagon.   1Sa 5:2; 31:10

11When all the inhabitants of Jabesh Gilead heard of everything the Philistines had done to Saul, 12all their valiant men went and took the bodies of Saul and his sons and brought them to Jabesh. Then they buried their bones under the great tree in Jabesh, and they fasted seven days.   Jdg 21:8; 1Sa 14:52

13Saul died because he was unfaithful to the LORD; he did not keep the word of the LORD and even consulted a medium for guidance, 14and did not inquire of the LORD. So the LORD put him to death and turned the kingdom over to David son of Jesse.   1Sa 13:13; 1Ch 12:23

David Becomes King Over Israel

11 All Israel came together to David at Hebron and said, "We are your own flesh and blood. 2In the past, even while Saul was king, you were the one who led Israel on their military campaigns. And the LORD your God said to you, 'You will shepherd my people Israel, and you will become their ruler.' "   2Sa 5:1; Ps 78:71

3When all the elders of Israel had come to King David at He-

bron, he made a compact with them at Hebron before the LORD, and they anointed David king over Israel, as the LORD had promised through Samuel.

David Conquers Jerusalem

⁴David and all the Israelites marched to Jerusalem (that is, Jebus). The Jebusites who lived there ⁵said to David, "You will not get in here." Nevertheless, David captured the fortress of Zion, the City of David. Jos 3:10

⁶David had said, "Whoever leads the attack on the Jebusites will become commander-in-chief." Joab son of Zeruiah went up first, and so he received the command. 2Sa 2:13; 8:16

⁷David then took up residence in the fortress, and so it was called the City of David. ⁸He built up the city around it, from the supporting terraces*a* to the surrounding wall, while Joab restored the rest of the city. ⁹And David became more and more powerful, because the LORD Almighty was with him.

David's Mighty Men

¹⁰These were the chiefs of David's mighty men—they, together with all Israel, gave his kingship strong support to extend it over the whole land, as the LORD had promised— ¹¹this is the list of David's mighty men: 2Sa 17:10; 1Ch 12:23

Jashobeam,*b* a Hacmonite,

was chief of the officers*c*; he raised his spear against three hundred men, whom he killed in one encounter. 2Sa 23:8

¹²Next to him was Eleazar son of Dodai the Ahohite, one of the three mighty men. ¹³He was with David at Pas Dammim when the Philistines gathered there for battle. At a place where there was a field full of barley, the troops fled from the Philistines. ¹⁴But they took their stand in the middle of the field. They defended it and struck the Philistines down, and the LORD brought about a great victory.

¹⁵Three of the thirty chiefs came down to David to the rock at the cave of Adullam, while a band of Philistines was encamped in the Valley of Rephaim. ¹⁶At that time David was in the stronghold, and the Philistine garrison was at Bethlehem. ¹⁷David longed for water and said, "Oh, that someone would get me a drink of water from the well near the gate of Bethlehem!" ¹⁸So the Three broke through the Philistine lines, drew water from the well near the gate of Bethlehem and carried it back to David. But he refused to drink it; instead, he poured it out before the LORD. ¹⁹"God forbid that I should do this!" he said. "Should I drink the blood of these men who went at the risk of their lives?" Because they risked their lives

---

*a*8 Or *the Millo*   *b*11 Possibly a variant of *Jashob-Baal*   *c*11 Or *Thirty*; some Septuagint manuscripts *Three* (see also 2 Samuel 23:8)

to bring it back, David would not drink it. _{1Ch 14:9; Isa 17:5}

Such were the exploits of the three mighty men.

²⁰Abishai the brother of Joab was chief of the Three. He raised his spear against three hundred men, whom he killed, and so he became as famous as the Three. ²¹He was doubly honored above the Three and became their commander, even though he was not included among them. _{1Sa 26:6; 2Sa 23:18}

²²Benaiah son of Jehoiada was a valiant fighter from Kabzeel, who performed great exploits. He struck down two of Moab's best men. He also went down into a pit on a snowy day and killed a lion. ²³And he struck down an Egyptian who was seven and a half feet^a tall. Although the Egyptian had a spear like a weaver's rod in his hand, Benaiah went against him with a club. He snatched the spear from the Egyptian's hand and killed him with his own spear. ²⁴Such were the exploits of Benaiah son of Jehoiada; he too was as famous as the three mighty men. ²⁵He was held in greater honor than any of the Thirty, but he was not included among the Three. And David put him in charge of his bodyguard. _{Jos 15:21; 1Sa 17:36}

²⁶The mighty men were:

Asahel the brother of Joab,

Elhanan son of Dodo from Bethlehem, _{2Sa 2:18}

²⁷Shammoth the Harorite,

Helez the Pelonite, _{1Ch 27:8}

²⁸Ira son of Ikkesh from Tekoa,

Abiezer from Anathoth,

²⁹Sibbecai the Hushathite,

Ilai the Ahohite, _{2Sa 21:18}

³⁰Maharai the Netophathite,

Heled son of Baanah the Netophathite, _{2Sa 23:29}

³¹Ithai son of Ribai from Gibeah in Benjamin,

Benaiah the Pirathonite,

³²Hurai from the ravines of Gaash,

Abiel the Arbathite,

³³Azmaveth the Baharumite,

Eliahba the Shaalbonite,

³⁴the sons of Hashem the Gizonite,

Jonathan son of Shagee the Hararite,

³⁵Ahiam son of Sacar the Hararite,

Eliphal son of Ur,

³⁶Hepher the Mekerathite,

Ahijah the Pelonite,

³⁷Hezro the Carmelite,

Naarai son of Ezbai, _{2Sa 23:35}

³⁸Joel the brother of Nathan,

Mibhar son of Hagri,

³⁹Zelek the Ammonite,

Naharai the Berothite, the armor-bearer of Joab son of Zeruiah, _{1Ch 18:15}

⁴⁰Ira the Ithrite,

Gareb the Ithrite,

^a23 Hebrew *five cubits* (about 2.3 meters)

⁴¹Uriah the Hittite,
Zabad son of Ahlai, 2Sa 11:6
⁴²Adina son of Shiza the
Reubenite, who was chief
of the Reubenites, and
the thirty with him,
⁴³Hanan son of Maacah,
Joshaphat the Mithnite,
⁴⁴Uzzia the Ashterathite,
Shama and Jeiel the sons
of Hotham the Aroerite,
⁴⁵Jediael son of Shimri,
his brother Joha the Ti-
zite,
⁴⁶Eliel the Mahavite,
Jeribai and Joshaviah the
sons of Elnaam,
Ithmah the Moabite,
⁴⁷Eliel, Obed and Jaasiel the
Mezobaite.

Warriors Join David

12 These were the men who
came to David at Ziklag,
while he was banished from the
presence of Saul son of Kish
(they were among the warriors
who helped him in battle; ²they
were armed with bows and
were able to shoot arrows or to
sling stones right-handed or
left-handed; they were kinsmen
of Saul from the tribe of Benjamin): Jdg 3:15; 1Sa 27:2

³Ahiezer their chief and
Joash the sons of Shemaah
the Gibeathite; Jeziel and
Pelet the sons of Azmaveth;
Beracah, Jehu the Ana-
thothite, ⁴and Ishmaiah the
Gibeonite, a mighty man
among the Thirty, who was

a leader of the Thirty; Jeremiah, Jahaziel, Johanan,
Jozabad the Gederathite,
⁵Eluzai, Jerimoth, Bealiah,
Shemariah and Shephatiah
the Haruphite; ⁶Elkanah, Isshiah, Azarel, Joezer and
Jashobeam the Korahites;
⁷and Joelah and Zebadiah
the sons of Jeroham from
Gedor. Jos 15:36,58

⁸Some Gadites defected to
David at his stronghold in the
desert. They were brave warriors, ready for battle and able to
handle the shield and spear.
Their faces were the faces of
lions, and they were as swift as
gazelles in the mountains. 2Sa 2:18
⁹Ezer was the chief,
Obadiah the second in command, Eliab the third,
¹⁰Mishmannah the fourth,
Jeremiah the fifth,
¹¹Attai the sixth, Eliel the seventh,
¹²Johanan the eighth, El-
zabad the ninth,
¹³Jeremiah the tenth and
Macbannai the eleventh.
¹⁴These Gadites were army
commanders; the least was a
match for a hundred, and the
greatest for a thousand. ¹⁵It was
they who crossed the Jordan in
the first month when it was
overflowing all its banks, and
they put to flight everyone living in the valleys, to the east
and to the west. Lev 26:8; Jos 3:15
¹⁶Other Benjamites and some
men from Judah also came to

David in his stronghold. [17]David went out to meet them and said to them, "If you have come to me in peace, to help me, I am ready to have you unite with me. But if you have come to betray me to my enemies when my hands are free from violence, may the God of our fathers see it and judge you."

[18]Then the Spirit came upon Amasai, chief of the Thirty, and he said:

"We are yours, O David!
  We are with you, O son of
    Jesse!
Success, success to you,
  and success to those who
    help you,
  for your God will help
    you."   2Sa 17:25; 1Ch 28:12

So David received them and made them leaders of his raiding bands.

[19]Some of the men of Manasseh defected to David when he went with the Philistines to fight against Saul. (He and his men did not help the Philistines because, after consultation, their rulers sent him away. They said, "It will cost us our heads if he deserts to his master Saul.") [20]When David went to Ziklag, these were the men of Manasseh who defected to him: Adnah, Jozabad, Jediael, Michael, Jozabad, Elihu and Zillethai, leaders of units of a thousand in Manasseh. [21]They helped David against raiding bands, for all of them were brave warriors, and they were commanders in his army. [22]Day after day men came to help David, until he had a great army, like the army of God.[a]   1Sa 29:2

Others Join David at Hebron

[23]These are the numbers of the men armed for battle who came to David at Hebron to turn Saul's kingdom over to him, as the LORD had said: 2Sa 2:3-4

[24]men of Judah, carrying shield and spear—6,800 armed for battle;

[25]men of Simeon, warriors ready for battle—7,100;

[26]men of Levi—4,600, [27]including Jehoiada, leader of the family of Aaron, with 3,700 men, [28]and Zadok, a brave young warrior, with 22 officers from his family;   1Ch 6:8

[29]men of Benjamin, Saul's kinsmen—3,000, most of whom had remained loyal to Saul's house until then;   2Sa 2:8-9

[30]men of Ephraim, brave warriors, famous in their own clans—20,800;

[31]men of half the tribe of Manasseh, designated by name to come and make David king—18,000;

[32]men of Issachar, who understood the times and knew what Israel should do—200 chiefs, with all

a22 Or *a great and mighty army*

their relatives under their command; Est 1:13

³³men of Zebulun, experienced soldiers prepared for battle with every type of weapon, to help David with undivided loyalty—50,000; Ps 12:2

³⁴men of Naphtali—1,000 officers, together with 37,000 men carrying shields and spears;

³⁵men of Dan, ready for battle—28,600;

³⁶men of Asher, experienced soldiers prepared for battle—40,000;

³⁷and from east of the Jordan, men of Reuben, Gad and the half-tribe of Manasseh, armed with every type of weapon—120,000.

³⁸All these were fighting men who volunteered to serve in the ranks. They came to Hebron fully determined to make David king over all Israel. All the rest of the Israelites were also of one mind to make David king. ³⁹The men spent three days there with David, eating and drinking, for their families had supplied provisions for them. ⁴⁰Also, their neighbors from as far away as Issachar, Zebulun and Naphtali came bringing food on donkeys, camels, mules and oxen. There were plentiful supplies of flour, fig cakes, raisin cakes, wine, oil, cattle and sheep, for there was joy in Israel. 1Ch 9:1

Bringing Back the Ark

13 David conferred with each of his officers, the commanders of thousands and commanders of hundreds. ²He then said to the whole assembly of Israel, "If it seems good to you and if it is the will of the LORD our God, let us send word far and wide to the rest of our brothers throughout the territories of Israel, and also to the priests and Levites who are with them in their towns and pasturelands, to come and join us. ³Let us bring the ark of our God back to us, for we did not inquire of^a it^b during the reign of Saul." ⁴The whole assembly agreed to do this, because it seemed right to all the people.

⁵So David assembled all the Israelites, from the Shihor River in Egypt to Lebo^c Hamath, to bring the ark of God from Kiriath Jearim. ⁶David and all the Israelites with him went to Baalah of Judah (Kiriath Jearim) to bring up from there the ark of God the LORD, who is enthroned between the cherubim—the ark that is called by the Name. Jos 15:9; 1Ch 15:3

⁷They moved the ark of God from Abinadab's house on a new cart, with Uzzah and Ahio guiding it. ⁸David and all the Israelites were celebrating with all their might before God, with songs and with harps, lyres, tambourines, cymbals and trumpets. 1Sa 7:1; 2Sa 6:5

^a3 Or *we neglected*   ^b3 Or *him*   ^c5 Or *to the entrance to*

9When they came to the threshing floor of Kidon, Uzzah reached out his hand to steady the ark, because the oxen stumbled. 10The LORD's anger burned against Uzzah, and he struck him down because he had put his hand on the ark. So he died there before God. 2Sa 6:6

11Then David was angry because the LORD's wrath had broken out against Uzzah, and to this day that place is called Perez Uzzah. *a* 1Ch 15:13

12David was afraid of God that day and asked, "How can I ever bring the ark of God to me?" 13He did not take the ark to be with him in the City of David. Instead, he took it aside to the house of Obed-Edom the Gittite. 14The ark of God remained with the family of Obed-Edom in his house for three months, and the LORD blessed his household and everything he had. 1Ch 26:4-5

David's House and Family

14 Now Hiram king of Tyre sent messengers to David, along with cedar logs, stonemasons and carpenters to build a palace for him. 2And David knew that the LORD had established him as king over Israel and that his kingdom had been highly exalted for the sake of his people Israel. 2Sa 5:11

3In Jerusalem David took more wives and became the fa-ther of more sons and daughters. 4These are the names of the children born to him there: Shammua, Shobab, Nathan, Solomon, 5Ibhar, Elishua, Elpelet, 6Nogah, Nepheg, Japhia, 7Elishama, Beeliada *b* and Eliphelet. 2Sa 5:16; 1Ch 3:1

David Defeats the Philistines

8When the Philistines heard that David had been anointed king over all Israel, they went up in full force to search for him, but David heard about it and went out to meet them. 9Now the Philistines had come and raided the Valley of Rephaim; 10so David inquired of God: "Shall I go and attack the Philistines? Will you hand them over to me?" Jos 15:8; 1Ch 11:1

The LORD answered him, "Go, I will hand them over to you."

11So David and his men went up to Baal Perazim, and there he defeated them. He said, "As waters break out, God has broken out against my enemies by my hand." So that place was called Baal Perazim. *c* 12The Philistines had abandoned their gods there, and David gave orders to burn them in the fire.

13Once more the Philistines raided the valley; 14so David inquired of God again, and God answered him, "Do not go straight up, but circle around them and attack them in front of

---

a11 Perez Uzzah means outbreak against Uzzah. Perazim means the lord who breaks out. 　　*b7 A variant of Eliada* 　　*c11 Baal*

the balsam trees. ¹⁵As soon as you hear the sound of marching in the tops of the balsam trees, move out to battle, because that will mean God has gone out in front of you to strike the Philistine army." ¹⁶So David did as God commanded him, and they struck down the Philistine army, all the way from Gibeon to Gezer.   Jos 9:3; 2Sa 5:22

¹⁷So David's fame spread throughout every land, and the LORD made all the nations fear him.   Jos 6:27; 2Ch 26:8

The Ark Brought to Jerusalem

15 After David had constructed buildings for himself in the City of David, he prepared a place for the ark of God and pitched a tent for it. ²Then David said, "No one but the Levites may carry the ark of God, because the LORD chose them to carry the ark of the LORD and to minister before him forever."   Nu 4:15; 1Ch 16:1

³David assembled all Israel in Jerusalem to bring up the ark of the LORD to the place he had prepared for it. ⁴He called together the descendants of Aaron and the Levites: 1Ch 13:5

⁵From the descendants of Kohath,
Uriel the leader and 120 relatives;   1Ch 6:24

⁶from the descendants of Merari,

Asaiah the leader and 220 relatives;

⁷from the descendants of Gershon,ᵃ
Joel the leader and 130 relatives;

⁸from the descendants of Elizaphan,
Shemaiah the leader and 200 relatives;   Ex 8:22

⁹from the descendants of Hebron,
Eliel the leader and 80 relatives;   Ex 6:18

¹⁰from the descendants of Uzziel,
Amminadab the leader and 112 relatives.

¹¹Then David summoned Zadok and Abiathar the priests, and Uriel, Asaiah, Joel, Shemaiah, Eliel and Amminadab the Levites. ¹²He said to them, "You are the heads of the Levitical families; you and your fellow Levites are to consecrate yourselves and bring up the ark of the LORD, the God of Israel, to the place I have prepared for it. ¹³It was because you, the Levites, did not bring it up the first time that the LORD our God broke out in anger against us. We did not inquire of him about how to do it in the prescribed way." ¹⁴So the priests and Levites consecrated themselves in order to bring up the ark of the LORD, the God of Israel. ¹⁵And the Levites carried the ark of God with the poles on their shoulders, as Moses had com-

ᵃ7 Hebrew *Gershom*, a variant of *Gershon*

manded in accordance with the word of the LORD.   1Ch 12:28

16David told the leaders of the Levites to appoint their brothers as singers to sing joyful songs, accompanied by musical instruments: lyres, harps and cymbals.   1Ch 6:31; Ps 68:25

17So the Levites appointed Heman son of Joel; from his brothers, Asaph son of Berekiah; and from their brothers the Merarites, Ethan son of Kushaiah; 18and with them their brothers next in rank: Zechariah,*a* Jaaziel, Shemiramoth, Jehiel, Unni, Eliab, Benaiah, Maaseiah, Mattithiah, Eliphelehu, Mikneiah, Obed-Edom and Jeiel,*b* the gatekeepers.

19The musicians Heman, Asaph and Ethan were to sound the bronze cymbals; 20Zechariah, Aziel, Shemiramoth, Jehiel, Unni, Eliab, Maaseiah and Benaiah were to play the lyres according to *alamoth,c* 21and Mattithiah, Eliphelehu, Mikneiah, Obed-Edom, Jeiel and Azaziah were to play the harps, directing according to *sheminith.c* 22Kenaniah the head Levite was in charge of the singing; that was his responsibility because he was skillful at it.

23Berekiah and Elkanah were to be doorkeepers for the ark. 24Shebaniah, Joshaphat, Nethanel, Amasai, Zechariah, Benaiah and Eliezer the priests were to blow trumpets before the ark of God. Obed-Edom and Jehiah were also to be doorkeepers for the ark.   2Ki 25:18

25So David and the elders of Israel and the commanders of units of a thousand went to bring up the ark of the covenant of the LORD from the house of Obed-Edom, with rejoicing. 26Because God had helped the Levites who were carrying the ark of the covenant of the LORD, seven bulls and seven rams were sacrificed. 27Now David was clothed in a robe of fine linen, as were all the Levites who were carrying the ark, and as were the singers, and Kenaniah, who was in charge of the singing of the choirs. David also wore a linen ephod. 28So all Israel brought up the ark of the covenant of the LORD with shouts, with the sounding of rams' horns and trumpets, and of cymbals, and the playing of lyres and harps.   2Ch 1:4

29As the ark of the covenant of the LORD was entering the City of David, Michal daughter of Saul watched from a window. And when she saw King David dancing and celebrating, she despised him in her heart.

16 They brought the ark of God and set it inside the tent that David had pitched for

---

a18 Three Hebrew manuscripts and most Septuagint manuscripts (see also verse 20 and 1 Chron. 16:5); most Hebrew manuscripts *Zechariah son and* or *Zechariah, Ben and*   *b18* Hebrew; Septuagint (see also verse 21) *Jeiel and Azaziah*   *c20,21* Probably a musical term

it, and they presented burnt offerings and fellowship offerings[a] before God. [2]After David had finished sacrificing the burnt offerings and fellowship offerings, he blessed the people in the name of the LORD. [3]Then he gave a loaf of bread, a cake of dates and a cake of raisins to each Israelite man and woman.

[4]He appointed some of the Levites to minister before the ark of the LORD, to make petition, to give thanks, and to praise the LORD, the God of Israel: [5]Asaph was the chief, Zechariah second, then Jeiel, Shemiramoth, Jehiel, Mattithiah, Eliab, Benaiah, Obed-Edom and Jeiel. They were to play the lyres and harps, Asaph was to sound the cymbals, [6]and Benaiah and Jahaziel the priests were to blow the trumpets regularly before the ark of the covenant of God.   Ex 25:10; 1Ch 15:2

David's Psalm of Thanks

[7]That day David first committed to Asaph and his associates this psalm of thanks to the LORD: 2Sa 23:1; Ps 47:7

[8]Give thanks to the LORD, call
   on his name;
  make known among the
    nations what he has
    done.   2Ki 19:19; Ps 107:1
[9]Sing to him, sing praise to
   him;

  tell of all his wonderful
    acts.   Ex 15:1; Ps 7:17
[10]Glory in his holy name;
  let the hearts of those who
    seek the LORD rejoice.
[11]Look to the LORD and his
   strength;
  seek his face always.   Ps 24:6
[12]Remember the wonders he
   has done,
  his miracles, and the
    judgments he
    pronounced,
[13]O descendants of Israel his
   servant,
  O sons of Jacob, his chosen
    ones.   Dt 4:34; Ps 77:11
[14]He is the LORD our God;
  his judgments are in all the
    earth.   Ps 48:10; Isa 26:9
[15]He remembers[b] his covenant
   forever,
  the word he commanded,
    for a thousand
    generations,
[16]the covenant he made with
   Abraham,
  the oath he swore to Isaac.
[17]He confirmed it to Jacob as a
   decree,
  to Israel as an everlasting
    covenant:
[18]"To you I will give the land
   of Canaan
  as the portion you will
    inherit."   Ge 35:9-12
[19]When they were but few in
   number,
  few indeed, and strangers
    in it,   Ge 34:30; Dt 7:7

---

[a]1 Traditionally *peace offerings*; also in verse 2 also Psalm 105:8); Hebrew *Remember*

[b]15 Some Septuagint manuscripts (see

²⁰they^a wandered from nation
 to nation,
 from one kingdom to
  another.   Ge 20:13
²¹He allowed no man to
 oppress them;
 for their sake he rebuked
  kings: Ge 12:17
²²"Do not touch my anointed
 ones;
 do my prophets no harm."

²³Sing to the LORD, all the
 earth;
 proclaim his salvation day
  after day.   Ps 96:1-13
²⁴Declare his glory among the
 nations,
 his marvelous deeds among
  all peoples.   Isa 42:12
²⁵For great is the LORD and
 most worthy of praise;
 he is to be feared above all
  gods.   Ps 48:1; 89:7
²⁶For all the gods of the
 nations are idols,
 but the LORD made the
  heavens.   Ps 8:3; 102:25
²⁷Splendor and majesty are
 before him;
 strength and joy in his
  dwelling place.
²⁸Ascribe to the LORD,
 O families of nations,
 ascribe to the LORD glory
  and strength,
²⁹ ascribe to the LORD the
  glory due his name.
Bring an offering and come
 before him;
 worship the LORD in the
splendor of his^b
 holiness.   Dt 15:14; 2Ch 20:21
³⁰Tremble before him, all the
 earth!
The world is firmly
 established; it cannot
  be moved.   Ps 2:11; 99:1
³¹Let the heavens rejoice, let
 the earth be glad;
 let them say among the
  nations, "The LORD
  reigns!"   Ps 93:1; Isa 49:13
³²Let the sea resound, and all
 that is in it;
 let the fields be jubilant,
  and everything in them!
³³Then the trees of the forest
 will sing,
 they will sing for joy before
  the LORD,
 for he comes to judge the
  earth.   1Sa 2:10; Isa 55:12

³⁴Give thanks to the LORD, for
 he is good;
 his love endures forever.
³⁵Cry out, "Save us, O God
 our Savior;
 gather us and deliver us
  from the nations,
 that we may give thanks to
  your holy name,
 that we may glory in your
  praise."   Ps 106:47
³⁶Praise be to the LORD, the
 God of Israel,
 from everlasting to
  everlasting.   1Ki 8:15

Then all the people said
"Amen" and "Praise the
LORD."

---

^a18-20 One Hebrew manuscript, Septuagint and Vulgate (see also Psalm 105:12); most
Hebrew manuscripts *inherit,* / ¹⁹*though you are but few in number,* / *few indeed, and strangers
in it."* / ²⁰*They* ^b29 Or LORD *with the splendor of*

37David left Asaph and his associates before the ark of the covenant of the LORD to minister there regularly, according to each day's requirements. 38He also left Obed-Edom and his sixty-eight associates to minister with them. Obed-Edom son of Jeduthun, and also Hosah, were gatekeepers.

39David left Zadok the priest and his fellow priests before the tabernacle of the LORD at the high place in Gibeon 40to present burnt offerings to the LORD on the altar of burnt offering regularly, morning and evening, in accordance with everything written in the Law of the LORD, which he had given Israel. 41With them were Heman and Jeduthun and the rest of those chosen and designated by name to give thanks to the LORD, "for his love endures forever." 42Heman and Jeduthun were responsible for the sounding of the trumpets and cymbals and for the playing of the other instruments for sacred song. The sons of Jeduthun were stationed at the gate.   Ex 29:38

43Then all the people left, each for his own home, and David returned home to bless his family.   2Sa 6:19-20

God's Promise to David

17 After David was settled in his palace, he said to Nathan the prophet, "Here I am, living in a palace of cedar, while the ark of the covenant of the LORD is under a tent."1Ch 15:1

2Nathan replied to David, "Whatever you have in mind, do it, for God is with you."

3That night the word of God came to Nathan, saying:

4"Go and tell my servant David, 'This is what the LORD says: You are not the one to build me a house to dwell in. 5I have not dwelt in a house from the day I brought Israel up out of Egypt to this day. I have moved from one tent site to another, from one dwelling place to another. 6Wherever I have moved with all the Israelites, did I ever say to any of their leaders*a* whom I commanded to shepherd my people, "Why have you not built me a house of cedar?" '   1Ch 14:1; 28:3

7"Now then, tell my servant David, 'This is what the LORD Almighty says: I took you from the pasture and from following the flock, to be ruler over my people Israel. 8I have been with you wherever you have gone, and I have cut off all your enemies from before you. Now I will make your name like the names of the greatest men of the earth. 9And I will provide a place for my people Israel and will plant them so that they can have a home

a6 Traditionally *judges*; also in verse 10

of their own and no longer be disturbed. Wicked people will not oppress them anymore, as they did at the beginning ¹⁰and have done ever since the time I appointed leaders over my people Israel. I will also subdue all your enemies.

" 'I declare to you that the LORD will build a house for you: ¹¹When your days are over and you go to be with your fathers, I will raise up your offspring to succeed you, one of your own sons, and I will establish his kingdom. ¹²He is the one who will build a house for me, and I will establish his throne forever. ¹³I will be his father, and he will be my son. I will never take my love away from him, as I took it away from your predecessor. ¹⁴I will set him over my house and my kingdom forever; his throne will be established forever.' "   1Ch 22:10; Jer 33:17

¹⁵Nathan reported to David all the words of this entire revelation.

David's Prayer

¹⁶Then King David went in and sat before the LORD, and he said:

"Who am I, O LORD God, and what is my family, that you have brought me this far? ¹⁷And as if this were not enough in your sight, O God, you have spoken about the future of the house of your servant. You have looked on me as though I were the most exalted of men, O LORD God.

¹⁸"What more can David say to you for honoring your servant? For you know your servant, ¹⁹O LORD. For the sake of your servant and according to your will, you have done this great thing and made known all these great promises.   Isa 37:35

²⁰"There is no one like you, O LORD, and there is no God but you, as we have heard with our own ears. ²¹And who is like your people Israel—the one nation on earth whose God went out to redeem a people for himself, and to make a name for yourself, and to perform great and awesome wonders by driving out nations from before your people, whom you redeemed from Egypt? ²²You made your people Israel your very own forever, and you, O LORD, have become their God.   Isa 44:6; 46:9

²³"And now, LORD, let the promise you have made concerning your servant and his house be established forever. Do as you promised, ²⁴so that it will be established and that your name will be great forever. Then men will say, 'The LORD Almighty, the God

over Israel, is Israel's God!' And the house of your servant David will be established before you.   1Ki 8:25

25"You, my God, have revealed to your servant that you will build a house for him. So your servant has found courage to pray to you. 26O LORD, you are God! You have promised these good things to your servant. 27Now you have been pleased to bless the house of your servant, that it may continue forever in your sight; for you, O LORD, have blessed it, and it will be blessed forever."   Ps 16:11

David's Victories

18 In the course of time, David defeated the Philistines and subdued them, and he took Gath and its surrounding villages from the control of the Philistines.   2Sa 8:1-18

2David also defeated the Moabites, and they became subject to him and brought tribute.

3Moreover, David fought Hadadezer king of Zobah, as far as Hamath, when he went to establish his control along the Euphrates River. 4David captured a thousand of his chariots, seven thousand charioteers and twenty thousand foot soldiers. He hamstrung all but a hundred of the chariot horses.   1Ch 19:6

5When the Arameans of Damascus came to help Hadad-

ezer king of Zobah, David struck down twenty-two thousand of them. 6He put garrisons in the Aramean kingdom of Damascus, and the Arameans became subject to him and brought tribute. The LORD gave David victory everywhere he went.   2Ki 16:9; 1Ch 19:6

7David took the gold shields carried by the officers of Hadadezer and brought them to Jerusalem. 8From Tebah[a] and Cun, towns that belonged to Hadadezer, David took a great quantity of bronze, which Solomon used to make the bronze Sea, the pillars and various bronze articles.   1Ki 7:23

9When Tou king of Hamath heard that David had defeated the entire army of Hadadezer king of Zobah, 10he sent his son Hadoram to King David to greet him and congratulate him on his victory in battle over Hadadezer, who had been at war with Tou. Hadoram brought all kinds of articles of gold and silver and bronze.   2Sa 8:9; 10:16

11King David dedicated these articles to the LORD, as he had done with the silver and gold he had taken from all these nations: Edom and Moab, the Ammonites and the Philistines, and Amalek.   Nu 24:18; 2Sa 1:1

12Abishai son of Zeruiah struck down eighteen thousand Edomites in the Valley of Salt. 13He put garrisons in Edom, and all the Edomites became subject

---

a8 Hebrew *Tibhath,* a variant of *Tebah*

to David. The LORD gave David victory everywhere he went.

David's Officials

[14]David reigned over all Israel, doing what was just and right for all his people. [15]Joab son of Zeruiah was over the army; Jehoshaphat son of Ahilud was recorder; [16]Zadok son of Ahitub and Ahimelech[a] son of Abiathar were priests; Shavsha was secretary; [17]Benaiah son of Jehoiada was over the Kerethites and Pelethites; and David's sons were chief officials at the king's side.

1Ch 29:26

The Battle Against the Ammonites

19 In the course of time, Nahash king of the Ammonites died, and his son succeeded him as king. [2]David thought, "I will show kindness to Hanun son of Nahash, because his father showed kindness to me." So David sent a delegation to express his sympathy to Hanun concerning his father.

2Sa 10:1

When David's men came to Hanun in the land of the Ammonites to express sympathy to him, [3]the Ammonite nobles said to Hanun, "Do you think David is honoring your father by sending men to you to express sympathy? Haven't his men come to you to explore and spy out the country and overthrow it?" [4]So Hanun seized David's men, shaved them, cut off their garments in the middle at the buttocks, and sent them away.

[5]When someone came and told David about the men, he sent messengers to meet them, for they were greatly humiliated. The king said, "Stay at Jericho till your beards have grown, and then come back."

[6]When the Ammonites realized that they had become a stench in David's nostrils, Hanun and the Ammonites sent a thousand talents[b] of silver to hire chariots and charioteers from Aram Naharaim,[c] Aram Maacah and Zobah. [7]They hired thirty-two thousand chariots and charioteers, as well as the king of Maacah with his troops, who came and camped near Medeba, while the Ammonites were mustered from their towns and moved out for battle.

[8]On hearing this, David sent Joab out with the entire army of fighting men. [9]The Ammonites came out and drew up in battle formation at the entrance to their city, while the kings who had come were by themselves in the open country.

2Sa 10:7

[10]Joab saw that there were battle lines in front of him and behind him; so he selected some of the best troops in Israel and deployed them against the Arameans. [11]He put the rest of the

[a]16 Some Hebrew manuscripts, Vulgate and Syriac (see also 2 Samuel 8:17); most Hebrew manuscripts *Abimelech*   [b]6 That is, about 37 tons (about 34 metric tons)   [c]6 That is, Northwest Mesopotamia

men under the command of Abishai his brother, and they were deployed against the Ammonites. [12]Joab said, "If the Arameans are too strong for me, then you are to rescue me; but if the Ammonites are too strong for you, then I will rescue you. [13]Be strong and let us fight bravely for our people and the cities of our God. The LORD will do what is good in his sight."

[14]Then Joab and the troops with him advanced to fight the Arameans, and they fled before him. [15]When the Ammonites saw that the Arameans were fleeing, they too fled before his brother Abishai and went inside the city. So Joab went back to Jerusalem. 2Sa 10:13

[16]After the Arameans saw that they had been routed by Israel, they sent messengers and had Arameans brought from beyond the River,[a] with Shophach the commander of Hadadezer's army leading them. 2Sa 10:15

[17]When David was told of this, he gathered all Israel and crossed the Jordan; he advanced against them and formed his battle lines opposite them. David formed his lines to meet the Arameans in battle, and they fought against him. [18]But they fled before Israel, and David killed seven thousand of their charioteers and forty thousand of their foot soldiers. He

also killed Shophach the commander of their army. 1Ch 9:1

[19]When the vassals of Hadadezer saw that they had been defeated by Israel, they made peace with David and became subject to him.

So the Arameans were not willing to help the Ammonites anymore. 2Sa 10:19

The Capture of Rabbah

20 In the spring, at the time when kings go off to war, Joab led out the armed forces. He laid waste the land of the Ammonites and went to Rabbah and besieged it, but David remained in Jerusalem. Joab attacked Rabbah and left it in ruins. [2]David took the crown from the head of their king[b]— its weight was found to be a talent[c] of gold, and it was set with precious stones—and it was placed on David's head. He took a great quantity of plunder from the city [3]and brought out the people who were there, consigning them to labor with saws and with iron picks and axes. David did this to all the Ammonite towns. Then David and his entire army returned to Jerusalem. Dt 29:11; Am 1:13-15

War With the Philistines

[4]In the course of time, war broke out with the Philistines, at Gezer. At that time Sibbecai the Hushathite killed Sippai,

---

*a*16 That is, the Euphrates pounds (about 34 kilograms)   *b*2 Or *of Milcom,* that is, Molech   *c*2 That is, about 75

one of the descendants of the Rephaites, and the Philistines were subjugated. _{Jos 10:33}

5In another battle with the Philistines, Elhanan son of Jair killed Lahmi the brother of Goliath the Gittite, who had a spear with a shaft like a weaver's rod. _{1Sa 17:7; 2Sa 21:19}

6In still another battle, which took place at Gath, there was a huge man with six fingers on each hand and six toes on each foot—twenty-four in all. He also was descended from Rapha. 7When he taunted Israel, Jonathan son of Shimea, David's brother, killed him.

8These were descendants of Rapha in Gath, and they fell at the hands of David and his men.

David Numbers the Fighting Men

21 Satan rose up against Israel and incited David to take a census of Israel. 2So David said to Joab and the commanders of the troops, "Go and count the Israelites from Beersheba to Dan. Then report back to me so that I may know how many there are." _{2Ch 18:21}

3But Joab replied, "May the LORD multiply his troops a hundred times over. My lord the king, are they not all my lord's subjects? Why does my lord want to do this? Why should he bring guilt on Israel?" _{Dt 1:11}

4The king's word, however,

overruled Joab; so Joab left and went throughout Israel and then came back to Jerusalem. 5Joab reported the number of the fighting men to David: In all Israel there were one million one hundred thousand men who could handle a sword, including four hundred and seventy thousand in Judah. _{1Ch 9:1}

6But Joab did not include Levi and Benjamin in the numbering, because the king's command was repulsive to him. 7This command was also evil in the sight of God; so he punished Israel. _{1Ch 27:24}

8Then David said to God, "I have sinned greatly by doing this. Now, I beg you, take away the guilt of your servant. I have done a very foolish thing."

9The LORD said to Gad, David's seer, 10"Go and tell David, 'This is what the LORD says: I am giving you three options. Choose one of them for me to carry out against you.'" _{1Sa 22:5}

11So Gad went to David and said to him, "This is what the LORD says: 'Take your choice: 12three years of famine, three months of being swept away*a* before your enemies, with their swords overtaking you, or three days of the sword of the LORD—days of plague in the land, with the angel of the LORD ravaging every part of Israel.' Now then, decide how I should answer the one who sent me."

13David said to Gad, "I am in

---

a12 Hebrew; Septuagint and Vulgate (see also 2 Samuel 24:13) *of fleeing*

deep distress. Let me fall into the hands of the LORD, for his mercy is very great; but do not let me fall into the hands of men." Ps 6:4; 130:4

[14]So the LORD sent a plague on Israel, and seventy thousand men of Israel fell dead. [15]And God sent an angel to destroy Jerusalem. But as the angel was doing so, the LORD saw it and was grieved because of the calamity and said to the angel who was destroying the people, "Enough! Withdraw your hand." The angel of the LORD was then standing at the threshing floor of Araunah[a] the Jebusite. 1Ch 27:24; Ps 125:2

[16]David looked up and saw the angel of the LORD standing between heaven and earth, with a drawn sword in his hand extended over Jerusalem. Then David and the elders, clothed in sackcloth, fell facedown. Nu 14:5

[17]David said to God, "Was it not I who ordered the fighting men to be counted? I am the one who has sinned and done wrong. These are but sheep. What have they done? O LORD my God, let your hand fall upon me and my family, but do not let this plague remain on your people." 2Sa 7:8; Ps 74:1

[18]Then the angel of the LORD ordered Gad to tell David to go up and build an altar to the LORD on the threshing floor of Araunah the Jebusite. [19]So Da-

vid went up in obedience to the word that Gad had spoken in the name of the LORD. 2Ch 3:1

[20]While Araunah was threshing wheat, he turned and saw the angel; his four sons who were with him hid themselves. [21]Then David approached, and when Araunah looked and saw him, he left the threshing floor and bowed down before David with his face to the ground.

[22]David said to him, "Let me have the site of your threshing floor so I can build an altar to the LORD, that the plague on the people may be stopped. Sell it to me at the full price."

[23]Araunah said to David, "Take it! Let my lord the king do whatever pleases him. Look, I will give the oxen for the burnt offerings, the threshing sledges for the wood, and the wheat for the grain offering. I will give all this."

[24]But King David replied to Araunah, "No, I insist on paying the full price. I will not take for the LORD what is yours, or sacrifice a burnt offering that costs me nothing."

[25]So David paid Araunah six hundred shekels[b] of gold for the site. [26]David built an altar to the LORD there and sacrificed burnt offerings and fellowship offerings.[c] He called on the LORD, and the LORD answered him with fire from heaven on the altar of burnt offering. 2Sa 24:24

---

[a]15 Hebrew *Ornan*, a variant of *Araunah*; also in verses 18-28   [b]25 That is, about 15 pounds (about 7 kilograms)   [c]26 Traditionally *peace offerings*

27Then the LORD spoke to the angel, and he put his sword back into its sheath. 28At that time, when David saw that the LORD had answered him on the threshing floor of Araunah the Jebusite, he offered sacrifices there. 29The tabernacle of the LORD, which Moses had made in the desert, and the altar of burnt offering were at that time on the high place at Gibeon. 30But David could not go before it to inquire of God, because he was afraid of the sword of the angel of the LORD.　　　　Jos 9:3

22 Then David said, "The house of the LORD God is to be here, and also the altar of burnt offering for Israel." Ge 28:17

Preparations for the Temple

2So David gave orders to assemble the aliens living in Israel, and from among them he appointed stonecutters to prepare dressed stone for building the house of God. 3He provided a large amount of iron to make nails for the doors of the gateways and for the fittings, and more bronze than could be weighed. 4He also provided more cedar logs than could be counted, for the Sidonians and Tyrians had brought large numbers of them to David.　　1Ki 5:17
5David said, "My son Solomon is young and inexperienced, and the house to be built for the LORD should be of great magnificence and fame and splendor in the sight of all the nations. Therefore I will make preparations for it." So David made extensive preparations before his death.　　1Ch 29:1

6Then he called for his son Solomon and charged him to build a house for the LORD, the God of Israel. 7David said to Solomon: "My son, I had it in my heart to build a house for the Name of the LORD my God. 8But this word of the LORD came to me: 'You have shed much blood and have fought many wars. You are not to build a house for my Name, because you have shed much blood on the earth in my sight. 9But you will have a son who will be a man of peace and rest, and I will give him rest from all his enemies on every side. His name will be Solomon,a and I will grant Israel peace and quiet during his reign. 10He is the one who will build a house for my Name. He will be my son, and I will be his father. And I will establish the throne of his kingdom over Israel forever.'　　2Sa 7:13; Ac 7:47

11"Now, my son, the LORD be with you, and may you have success and build the house of the LORD your God, as he said you would. 12May the LORD give you discretion and understanding when he puts you in command over Israel, so that you may keep the law of the LORD

---

a9 *Solomon* sounds like and may be derived from the Hebrew for *peace.*

your God. 13Then you will have success if you are careful to observe the decrees and laws that the LORD gave Moses for Israel. Be strong and courageous. Do not be afraid or discouraged.

14"I have taken great pains to provide for the temple of the LORD a hundred thousand talents*a* of gold, a million talents*b* of silver, quantities of bronze and iron too great to be weighed, and wood and stone. And you may add to them. 15You have many workmen: stonecutters, masons and carpenters, as well as men skilled in every kind of work 16in gold and silver, bronze and iron—craftsmen beyond number. Now begin the work, and the LORD be with you."   1Ch 29:2-5

17Then David ordered all the leaders of Israel to help his son Solomon. 18He said to them, "Is not the LORD your God with you? And has he not granted you rest on every side? For he has handed the inhabitants of the land over to me, and the land is subject to the LORD and to his people. 19Now devote your heart and soul to seeking the LORD your God. Begin to build the sanctuary of the LORD God, so that you may bring the ark of the covenant of the LORD and the sacred articles belonging to God into the temple that will be built for the Name of the LORD."   1Ch 28:1; 2Ch 7:14

The Levites

23 When David was old and full of years, he made his son Solomon king over Israel.

2He also gathered together all the leaders of Israel, as well as the priests and Levites. 3The Levites thirty years old or more were counted, and the total number of men was thirty-eight thousand. 4David said, "Of these, twenty-four thousand are to supervise the work of the temple of the LORD and six thousand are to be officials and judges. 5Four thousand are to be gatekeepers and four thousand are to praise the LORD with the musical instruments I have provided for that purpose."

6David divided the Levites into groups corresponding to the sons of Levi: Gershon, Kohath and Merari.   2Ch 8:14

Gershonites

7Belonging to the Gershonites: Ladan and Shimei.   1Ch 6:71

8The sons of Ladan:
Jehiel the first, Zetham and Joel—three in all.

9The sons of Shimei:
Shelomoth, Haziel and Haran—three in all.
These were the heads of the families of Ladan.

10And the sons of Shimei:
Jahath, Ziza,*c* Jeush and Beriah.

---

a14 That is, about 3,750 tons (about 3,450 metric tons)   *b14* That is, about 37,500 tons (about 34,500 metric tons)   *c10* One Hebrew manuscript, Septuagint and Vulgate (see also verse 11); most Hebrew manuscripts *Zina*

These were the sons of Shimei—four in all. ¹¹Jahath was the first and Ziza the second, but Jeush and Beriah did not have many sons; so they were counted as one family with one assignment.

Kohathites

¹²The sons of Kohath:
Amram, Izhar, Hebron and Uzziel—four in all.
¹³The sons of Amram:
Aaron and Moses.
Aaron was set apart, he and his descendants forever, to consecrate the most holy things, to offer sacrifices before the LORD, to minister before him and to pronounce blessings in his name forever. ¹⁴The sons of Moses the man of God were counted as part of the tribe of Levi.   Ex 6:20
¹⁵The sons of Moses:
Gershom and Eliezer.
¹⁶The descendants of Gershom:
Shubael was the first.
¹⁷The descendants of Eliezer:
Rehabiah was the first.
Eliezer had no other sons, but the sons of Rehabiah were very numerous.
¹⁸The sons of Izhar:
Shelomith was the first.
¹⁹The sons of Hebron:
Jeriah the first, Amariah the second, Jahaziel the

third and Jekameam the fourth.   1Ch 24:23; 26:31
²⁰The sons of Uzziel:
Micah the first and Isshiah the second.

Merarites

²¹The sons of Merari:
Mahli and Mushi.
The sons of Mahli:
Eleazar and Kish.   1Ch 6:19
²²Eleazar died without having sons: he had only daughters. Their cousins, the sons of Kish, married them.   Nu 36:8
²³The sons of Mushi: 1Ch 24:28
Mahli, Eder and Jerimoth—three in all.   1Ch 24:30

²⁴These were the descendants of Levi by their families—the heads of families as they were registered under their names and counted individually, that is, the workers twenty years old or more who served in the temple of the LORD. ²⁵For David had said, "Since the LORD, the God of Israel, has granted rest to his people and has come to dwell in Jerusalem forever, ²⁶the Levites no longer need to carry the tabernacle or any of the articles used in its service." ²⁷According to the last instructions of David, the Levites were counted from those twenty years old or more.

²⁸The duty of the Levites was to help Aaron's descendants in the service of the temple of the LORD: to be in charge of the courtyards, the side rooms, the purification of all sacred things

and the performance of other duties at the house of God. 29They were in charge of the bread set out on the table, the flour for the grain offerings, the unleavened wafers, the baking and the mixing, and all measurements of quantity and size. 30They were also to stand every morning to thank and praise the LORD. They were to do the same in the evening 31and whenever burnt offerings were presented to the LORD on Sabbaths and at New Moon festivals and at appointed feasts. They were to serve before the LORD regularly in the proper number and in the way prescribed for them.

32And so the Levites carried out their responsibilities for the Tent of Meeting, for the Holy Place and, under their brothers the descendants of Aaron, for the service of the temple of the LORD. Nu 3:6; 1Ch 6:48

The Divisions of Priests

24 These were the divisions of the sons of Aaron:

The sons of Aaron were Nadab, Abihu, Eleazar and Ithamar. 2But Nadab and Abihu died before their father did, and they had no sons; so Eleazar and Ithamar served as the priests. 3With the help of Zadok a descendant of Eleazar and Ahimelech a descendant of Ithamar, David separated them into divisions for their appointed order of ministering. 4A larger number of leaders were found among Eleazar's de-

scendants than among Ithamar's, and they were divided accordingly: sixteen heads of families from Eleazar's descendants and eight heads of families from Ithamar's descendants. 5They divided them impartially by drawing lots, for there were officials of the sanctuary and officials of God among the descendants of both Eleazar and Ithamar. Lev 10:2

6The scribe Shemaiah son of Nethanel, a Levite, recorded their names in the presence of the king and of the officials: Zadok the priest, Ahimelech son of Abiathar and the heads of families of the priests and of the Levites—one family being taken from Eleazar and then one from Ithamar. 1Ch 8:16

7The first lot fell to Jehoiarib,
the second to Jedaiah, Ezr 2:36
8the third to Harim,
the fourth to Seorim, Ezr 2:39
9the fifth to Malkijah,
the sixth to Mijamin,
10the seventh to Hakkoz,
the eighth to Abijah, Ne 12:4
11the ninth to Jeshua,
the tenth to Shecaniah,
12the eleventh to Eliashib,
the twelfth to Jakim,
13the thirteenth to Huppah,
the fourteenth to Jesheb-eab,
14the fifteenth to Bilgah,
the sixteenth to Immer, Ezr 2:37
15the seventeenth to Hezir,
the eighteenth to Happizzez, Ne 10:20

¹⁶the nineteenth to Pethahiah,
the twentieth to Jehezkel,
¹⁷the twenty-first to Jakin,
the twenty-second to Ga-
mul,
¹⁸the twenty-third to Delaiah
and the twenty-fourth to
Maaziah.

¹⁹This was their appointed order of ministering when they
entered the temple of the LORD,
according to the regulations
prescribed for them by their
forefather Aaron, as the LORD,
the God of Israel, had commanded him.   1Ch 9:25

The Rest of the Levites

²⁰As for the rest of the descendants of Levi:
from the sons of Amram:
Shubael;
from the sons of Shubael:
Jehdeiah.   1Ch 23:6
²¹As for Rehabiah, from his
sons:
Isshiah was the first. 1Ch 23:7
²²From the Izharites: Shelomoth;
from the sons of Shelo-
moth: Jahath.   1Ch 23:18
²³The sons of Hebron: Jeriah
the first,ᵃ Amariah the
second, Jahaziel the third
and Jekameam the
fourth.   1Ch 23:19
²⁴The son of Uzziel: Micah;
from the sons of Micah:
Shamir.

²⁵The brother of Micah: Isshiah;
from the sons of Isshiah:
Zechariah.
²⁶The sons of Merari: Mahli
and Mushi.
The son of Jaaziah: Beno.
²⁷The sons of Merari:
from Jaaziah: Beno, Sho-
ham, Zaccur and Ibri.
²⁸From Mahli: Eleazar, who
had no sons.
²⁹From Kish: the son of Kish:
Jerahmeel.
³⁰And the sons of Mushi:
Mahli, Eder and Jeri-
moth.

These were the Levites, according to their families. ³¹They
also cast lots, just as their brothers the descendants of Aaron
did, in the presence of King David and of Zadok, Ahimelech,
and the heads of families of the
priests and of the Levites. The
families of the oldest brother
were treated the same as those
of the youngest.   1Ch 24:5

The Singers

25 David, together with the
commanders of the army,
set apart some of the sons of
Asaph, Heman and Jeduthun
for the ministry of prophesying,
accompanied by harps, lyres
and cymbals. Here is the list of
the men who performed this
service: 1Ch 6:33; 15:16

²From the sons of Asaph:

ᵃ23 Two Hebrew manuscripts and some Septuagint manuscripts (see also
1 Chron. 23:19); most Hebrew manuscripts *The sons of Jeriah:*

Zaccur, Joseph, Nethaniah and Asarelah. The sons of Asaph were under the supervision of Asaph, who prophesied under the king's supervision.

³As for Jeduthun, from his sons: Gedaliah, Zeri, Jeshaiah, Shimei,ᵃ Hashabiah and Mattithiah, six in all, under the supervision of their father Jeduthun, who prophesied, using the harp in thanking and praising the LORD.   1Ch 16:41-42

⁴As for Heman, from his sons: Bukkiah, Mattaniah, Uzziel, Shubael and Jerimoth; Hananiah, Hanani, Eliathah, Giddalti and Romamti-Ezer; Joshbekashah, Mallothi, Hothir and Mahazioth. ⁵All these were sons of Heman the king's seer. They were given him through the promises of God to exalt him.ᵇ God gave Heman fourteen sons and three daughters.   1Ch 6:33

⁶All these men were under the supervision of their fathers for the music of the temple of the LORD, with cymbals, lyres and harps, for the ministry at the house of God. Asaph, Jeduthun and Heman were under the supervision of the king. ⁷Along with their relatives—all of them trained and skilled in music for the LORD—they numbered 288. ⁸Young and old alike, teacher as well as student, cast lots for their duties.   1Ch 15:16-17

⁹The first lot, which was for Asaph, fell to Joseph,
    his sons and
    relatives,ᶜ   12ᵈ
the second to Gedaliah,
    he and his relatives
    and sons,   12
¹⁰the third to Zaccur,
    his sons and relatives, 12
¹¹the fourth to Izri,ᵉ
    his sons and relatives, 12
¹²the fifth to Nethaniah,
    his sons and relatives, 12
¹³the sixth to Bukkiah,
    his sons and relatives, 12
¹⁴the seventh to Jesarelah,ᶠ
    his sons and relatives, 12
¹⁵the eighth to Jeshaiah,
    his sons and relatives, 12
¹⁶the ninth to Mattaniah,
    his sons and relatives, 12
¹⁷the tenth to Shimei,
    his sons and relatives, 12
¹⁸the eleventh to Azarel,ᵍ
    his sons and relatives, 12
¹⁹the twelfth to Hashabiah,
    his sons and relatives, 12
²⁰the thirteenth to Shubael,
    his sons and relatives, 12
²¹the fourteenth to
    Mattithiah,
    his sons and relatives, 12
²²the fifteenth to Jerimoth,
    his sons and relatives, 12
²³the sixteenth to Hananiah,

ᵃ3 One Hebrew manuscript and some Septuagint manuscripts (see also verse 17); most Hebrew manuscripts do not have *Shimei*.   ᵇ5 Hebrew *exalt the horn*   ᶜ9 See Septuagint; Hebrew does not have *his sons and relatives*.   ᵈ9 See the total in verse 7; Hebrew does not have *twelve*.   ᵉ11 A variant of *Zeri*   ᶠ14 A variant of *Asarelah*   ᵍ18 A variant of *Uzziel*

his sons and relatives, 12
²⁴the seventeenth to
Joshbekashah,
his sons and relatives, 12
²⁵the eighteenth to Hanani,
his sons and relatives, 12
²⁶the nineteenth to Mallothi,
his sons and relatives, 12
²⁷the twentieth to Eliathah,
his sons and relatives, 12
²⁸the twenty-first to Hothir,
his sons and relatives, 12
²⁹the twenty-second to
Giddalti,
his sons and relatives, 12
³⁰the twenty-third to
Mahazioth,
his sons and relatives, 12
³¹the twenty-fourth to
Romamti-Ezer,
his sons and relatives, 12

The Gatekeepers

26 The divisions of the gatekeepers: 1Ch 9:17

From the Korahites: Me-
shelemiah son of Kore,
one of the sons of Asaph.
²Meshelemiah had sons:
Zechariah the firstborn,
Jediael the second,
Zebadiah the third,
Jathniel the fourth,
³Elam the fifth,
Jehohanan the sixth
and Eliehoenai the sev-
enth.   1Ch 9:21
⁴Obed-Edom also had sons:
Shemaiah the firstborn,
Jehozabad the second,
Joah the third,
Sacar the fourth,
Nethanel the fifth,

⁵Ammiel the sixth,
Issachar the seventh
and Peullethai the eighth.
(For God had blessed
Obed-Edom.)   1Ch 15:18

⁶His son Shemaiah also had
sons, who were leaders in
their father's family be-
cause they were very ca-
pable men. ⁷The sons of
Shemaiah: Othni, Repha-
el, Obed and Elzabad; his
relatives Elihu and Sema-
kiah were also able men.
⁸All these were descend-
ants of Obed-Edom; they
and their sons and their
relatives were capable
men with the strength to
do the
work—descendants of
Obed-Edom, 62 in all.
⁹Meshelemiah had sons and
relatives, who were able
men—18 in all.

¹⁰Hosah the Merarite had
sons: Shimri the first (although he was not the
firstborn, his father had
appointed him the first),
¹¹Hilkiah the second,
Tabaliah the third and
Zechariah the fourth. The
sons and relatives of
Hosah were 13 in all. Dt 21:16
¹²These divisions of the gate-
keepers, through their chief
men, had duties for ministering
in the temple of the LORD, just
as their relatives had. ¹³Lots
were cast for each gate, according to their families, young and
old alike.   1Ch 9:22; 24:5

¹⁴The lot for the East Gate fell to Shelemiah.ᵃ Then lots were cast for his son Zechariah, a wise counselor, and the lot for the North Gate fell to him. ¹⁵The lot for the South Gate fell to Obed-Edom, and the lot for the storehouse fell to his sons. ¹⁶The lots for the West Gate and the Shalleketh Gate on the upper road fell to Shuppim and Hosah.   1Ch 9:18; 2Ch 25:24

Guard was alongside of guard: ¹⁷There were six Levites a day on the east, four a day on the north, four a day on the south and two at a time at the storehouse. ¹⁸As for the court to the west, there were four at the road and two at the court itself.

¹⁹These were the divisions of the gatekeepers who were descendants of Korah and Merari.

The Treasurers and Other Officials

²⁰Their fellow Levites wereᵇ in charge of the treasuries of the house of God and the treasuries for the dedicated things.   2Sa 24:5

²¹The descendants of Ladan, who were Gershonites through Ladan and who were heads of families belonging to Ladan the Gershonite, were Jehieli, ²²the sons of Jehieli, Zetham and his brother Joel. They were in charge of the treasuries of the temple of the LORD.   1Ch 23:7

²³From the Amramites, the Izharites, the Hebronites and the Uzzielites: Nu 3:27

²⁴Shubael, a descendant of Gershom son of Moses, was the officer in charge of the treasuries. ²⁵His relatives through Eliezer: Rehabiah his son, Jeshaiah his son, Joram his son, Zicri his son and Shelomith his son. ²⁶Shelomith and his relatives were in charge of all the treasuries for the things dedicated by King David, by the heads of families who were the commanders of thousands and commanders of hundreds, and by the other army commanders. ²⁷Some of the plunder taken in battle they dedicated for the repair of the temple of the LORD. ²⁸And everything dedicated by Samuel the seer and by Saul son of Kish, Abner son of Ner and Joab son of Zeruiah, and all the other dedicated things were in the care of Shelomith and his relatives.   1Ch 23:16

²⁹From the Izharites: Kenaniah and his sons were assigned duties away from the temple, as officials and judges over Israel.

³⁰From the Hebronites: Hashabiah and his relatives—seventeen hundred able men—were responsible in Israel west of the Jordan for all the work

of the LORD and for the king's service. [31]As for the Hebronites, Jeriah was their chief according to the genealogical records of their families. In the fortieth year of David's reign a search was made in the records, and capable men among the Hebronites were found at Jazer in Gilead. [32]Jeriah had twenty-seven hundred relatives, who were able men and heads of families, and King David put them in charge of the Reubenites, the Gadites and the half-tribe of Manasseh for every matter pertaining to God and for the affairs of the king.

Army Divisions

27 This is the list of the Israelites—heads of families, commanders of thousands and commanders of hundreds, and their officers, who served the king in all that concerned the army divisions that were on duty month by month throughout the year. Each division consisted of 24,000 men.

[2]In charge of the first division, for the first month, was Jashobeam son of Zabdiel. There were 24,000 men in his division. [3]He was a descendant of Perez and chief of all the army officers for the first month.   2Sa 23:8

[4]In charge of the division for the second month was Dodai the Ahohite; Mikloth was the leader of his division. There were 24,000 men in his division.   2Sa 23:9

[5]The third army commander, for the third month, was Benaiah son of Jehoiada the priest. He was chief and there were 24,000 men in his division. [6]This was the Benaiah who was a mighty man among the Thirty and was over the Thirty. His son Ammizabad was in charge of his division.   2Sa 23:20

[7]The fourth, for the fourth month, was Asahel the brother of Joab; his son Zebadiah was his successor. There were 24,000 men in his division.   2Sa 2:18

[8]The fifth, for the fifth month, was the commander Shamhuth the Izrahite. There were 24,000 men in his division.   1Ch 11:27

[9]The sixth, for the sixth month, was Ira the son of Ikkesh the Tekoite. There were 24,000 men in his division.

[10]The seventh, for the seventh month, was Helez the Pelonite, an Ephraimite. There were 24,000 men in his division.   2Sa 23:26

[11]The eighth, for the eighth month, was Sibbecai the Hushathite, a Zerahite. There were 24,000 men in his division.   2Sa 21:18

[12]The ninth, for the ninth month, was Abiezer the Anathothite, a Benjamite.

There were 24,000 men in his division.   2Sa 23:27

¹³The tenth, for the tenth month, was Maharai the Netophathite, a Zerahite. There were 24,000 men in his division.   2Sa 23:28

¹⁴The eleventh, for the eleventh month, was Benaiah the Pirathonite, an Ephraimite. There were 24,000 men in his division.   1Ch 11:31

¹⁵The twelfth, for the twelfth month, was Heldai the Netophathite, from the family of Othniel. There were 24,-000 men in his division.

Officers of the Tribes

¹⁶The officers over the tribes of Israel:

over the Reubenites: Eliezer son of Zicri;

over the Simeonites: Shephatiah son of Maacah;

¹⁷over Levi: Hashabiah son of Kemuel;

over Aaron: Zadok;   1Ch 26:30

¹⁸over Judah: Elihu, a brother of David;

over Issachar: Omri son of Michael;   Dt 33:7

¹⁹over Zebulun: Ishmaiah son of Obadiah;

over Naphtali: Jerimoth son of Azriel;   Jdg 1:30

²⁰over the Ephraimites: Hoshea son of Azaziah;

over half the tribe of Manasseh: Joel son of Pedaiah;

²¹over the half-tribe of Ma-

nasseh in Gilead: Iddo son of Zechariah;

over Benjamin: Jaasiel son of Abner;

²²over Dan: Azarel son of Jeroham.

These were the officers over the tribes of Israel.   Nu 1:39

²³David did not take the number of the men twenty years old or less, because the LORD had promised to make Israel as numerous as the stars in the sky. ²⁴Joab son of Zeruiah began to count the men but did not finish. Wrath came on Israel on account of this numbering, and the number was not entered in the book*a* of the annals of King David.   2Sa 24:1; 1Ch 21:14

The King's Overseers

²⁵Azmaveth son of Adiel was in charge of the royal storehouses.

Jonathan son of Uzziah was in charge of the storehouses in the outlying districts, in the towns, the villages and the watchtowers.   2Ch 32:28

²⁶Ezri son of Kelub was in charge of the field workers who farmed the land.   Ge 2:15

²⁷Shimei the Ramathite was in charge of the vineyards.

Zabdi the Shiphmite was in charge of the produce of the vineyards for the wine vats.

²⁸Baal-Hanan the Gederite was in charge of the olive and sycamore-fig trees in the western foothills.

*a*24 Septuagint; Hebrew *number*

Joash was in charge of the supplies of olive oil. 1Ki 10:27

29Shitrai the Sharonite was in charge of the herds grazing in Sharon.

Shaphat son of Adlai was in charge of the herds in the valleys. SS 2:1; Isa 33:9

30Obil the Ishmaelite was in charge of the camels.

Jehdeiah the Meronothite was in charge of the donkeys.

31Jaziz the Hagrite was in charge of the flocks.

All these were the officials in charge of King David's property. 1Ch 5:10

32Jonathan, David's uncle, was a counselor, a man of insight and a scribe. Jehiel son of Hacmoni took care of the king's sons.

33Ahithophel was the king's counselor. 2Sa 15:12,37

Hushai the Arkite was the king's friend. 34Ahithophel was succeeded by Jehoiada son of Benaiah and by Abiathar.

Joab was the commander of the royal army. 1Sa 22:20

David's Plans for the Temple

28 David summoned all the officials of Israel to assemble at Jerusalem: the officers over the tribes, the commanders of the divisions in the service of the king, the commanders of thousands and commanders of hundreds, and the officials in charge of all the property and livestock belonging to the king and his sons, together with the palace officials, the mighty men and all the brave warriors. 1Ch 22:17

2King David rose to his feet and said: "Listen to me, my brothers and my people. I had it in my heart to build a house as a place of rest for the ark of the covenant of the LORD, for the footstool of our God, and I made plans to build it. 3But God said to me, 'You are not to build a house for my Name, because you are a warrior and have shed blood.' 1Sa 10:7; 2Sa 7:5

4"Yet the LORD, the God of Israel, chose me from my whole family to be king over Israel forever. He chose Judah as leader, and from the house of Judah he chose my family, and from my father's sons he was pleased to make me king over all Israel. 5Of all my sons—and the LORD has given me many—he has chosen my son Solomon to sit on the throne of the kingdom of the LORD over Israel. 6He said to me: 'Solomon your son is the one who will build my house and my courts, for I have chosen him to be my son, and I will be his father. 7I will establish his kingdom forever if he is unswerving in carrying out my commands and laws, as is being done at this time.' 2Ch 6:6

8"So now I charge you in the sight of all Israel and of the assembly of the LORD, and in the hearing of our God: Be careful to follow all the commands of the LORD your God, that you

may possess this good land and pass it on as an inheritance to your descendants forever. Dt 6:1

9"And you, my son Solomon, acknowledge the God of your father, and serve him with wholehearted devotion and with a willing mind, for the LORD searches every heart and understands every motive behind the thoughts. If you seek him, he will be found by you; but if you forsake him, he will reject you forever. 10Consider now, for the LORD has chosen you to build a temple as a sanctuary. Be strong and do the work." 1Ch 22:13; 29:19

11Then David gave his son Solomon the plans for the portico of the temple, its buildings, its storerooms, its upper parts, its inner rooms and the place of atonement. 12He gave him the plans of all that the Spirit had put in his mind for the courts of the temple of the LORD and all the surrounding rooms, for the treasuries of the temple of God and for the treasuries for the dedicated things. 13He gave him instructions for the divisions of the priests and Levites, and for all the work of serving in the temple of the LORD, as well as for all the articles to be used in its service. 14He designated the weight of gold for all the gold articles to be used in various kinds of service, and the weight of silver for all the silver articles to be used in various kinds of service: 15the weight of gold for

the gold lampstands and their lamps, with the weight for each lampstand and its lamps; and the weight of silver for each silver lampstand and its lamps, according to the use of each lampstand; 16the weight of gold for each table for consecrated bread; the weight of silver for the silver tables; 17the weight of pure gold for the forks, sprinkling bowls and pitchers; the weight of gold for each gold dish; the weight of silver for each silver dish; 18and the weight of the refined gold for the altar of incense. He also gave him the plan for the chariot, that is, the cherubim of gold that spread their wings and shelter the ark of the covenant of the LORD. Ex 25:40; 30:1-10

19"All this," David said, "I have in writing from the hand of the LORD upon me, and he gave me understanding in all the details of the plan." 1Ki 6:38

20David also said to Solomon his son, "Be strong and courageous, and do the work. Do not be afraid or discouraged, for the LORD God, my God, is with you. He will not fail you or forsake you until all the work for the service of the temple of the LORD is finished. 21The divisions of the priests and Levites are ready for all the work on the temple of God, and every willing man skilled in any craft will help you in all the work. The officials and all the people will obey your every command."

Gifts for Building the Temple

29 Then King David said to the whole assembly: "My son Solomon, the one whom God has chosen, is young and inexperienced. The task is great, because this palatial structure is not for man but for the LORD God. ²With all my resources I have provided for the temple of my God—gold for the gold work, silver for the silver, bronze for the bronze, iron for the iron and wood for the wood, as well as onyx for the settings, turquoise,ᵃ stones of various colors, and all kinds of fine stone and marble—all of these in large quantities. ³Besides, in my devotion to the temple of my God I now give my personal treasures of gold and silver for the temple of my God, over and above everything I have provided for this holy temple: ⁴three thousand talentsᵇ of gold (gold of Ophir) and seven thousand talentsᶜ of refined silver, for the overlaying of the walls of the buildings, ⁵for the gold work and the silver work, and for all the work to be done by the craftsmen. Now, who is willing to consecrate himself today to the LORD?"

⁶Then the leaders of families, the officers of the tribes of Israel, the commanders of thousands and commanders of hundreds, and the officials in charge of the king's work gave willingly. ⁷They gave toward the work on the temple of God five thousand talentsᵈ and ten thousand daricsᵉ of gold, ten thousand talentsᶠ of silver, eighteen thousand talentsᵍ of bronze and a hundred thousand talentsʰ of iron. ⁸Any who had precious stones gave them to the treasury of the temple of the LORD in the custody of Jehiel the Gershonite. ⁹The people rejoiced at the willing response of their leaders, for they had given freely and wholeheartedly to the LORD. David the king also rejoiced greatly.   1Ch 27:1

David's Prayer

¹⁰David praised the LORD in the presence of the whole assembly, saying,

"Praise be to you, O LORD,
   God of our father Israel,
   from everlasting to
   everlasting.   Ps 72:18
¹¹Yours, O LORD, is the
      greatness and the power
   and the glory and the
      majesty and the
      splendor,
   for everything in heaven
      and earth is yours. Mt 6:13
   Yours, O LORD, is the
      kingdom;

ᵃ2 The meaning of the Hebrew for this word is uncertain.   ᵇ4 That is, about 110 tons (about 100 metric tons)   ᶜ4 That is, about 260 tons (about 240 metric tons)   ᵈ7 That is, about 190 tons (about 170 metric tons)   ᵉ7 That is, about 185 pounds (about 84 kilograms)   ᶠ7 That is, about 375 tons (about 345 metric tons)   ᵍ7 That is, about 675 tons (about 610 metric tons)   ʰ7 That is, about 3,750 tons (about 3,450 metric tons)

you are exalted as head
over all.   Rev 5:13
12Wealth and honor come from
you;
you are the ruler of all
things.
In your hands are strength
and power
to exalt and give strength to
all.   2Ch 1:12; Ro 11:36
13Now, our God, we give you
thanks,
and praise your glorious
name.

14"But who am I, and who are
my people, that we should be
able to give as generously as
this? Everything comes from
you, and we have given you
only what comes from your
hand. 15We are aliens and
strangers in your sight, as were
all our forefathers. Our days on
earth are like a shadow, without
hope. 16O Lord our God, as for
all this abundance that we have
provided for building you a
temple for your Holy Name, it
comes from your hand, and all
of it belongs to you. 17I know,
my God, that you test the heart
and are pleased with integrity.
All these things have I given
willingly and with honest intent. And now I have seen with
joy how willingly your people
who are here have given to you.
18O Lord, God of our fathers
Abraham, Isaac and Israel, keep
this desire in the hearts of your
people forever, and keep their
hearts loyal to you. 19And give

my son Solomon the whole-
hearted devotion to keep your
commands, requirements and
decrees and to do everything to
build the palatial structure for
which I have provided."

20Then David said to the
whole assembly, "Praise the
Lord your God." So they all
praised the Lord, the God of
their fathers; they bowed low
and fell prostrate before the
Lord and the king.

Solomon Acknowledged as King

21The next day they made
sacrifices to the Lord and
presented burnt offerings to
him: a thousand bulls, a thousand rams and a thousand male
lambs, together with their drink
offerings, and other sacrifices in
abundance for all Israel. 22They
ate and drank with great joy in
the presence of the Lord that
day.   1Ki 8:62; 1Ch 12:40
Then they acknowledged
Solomon son of David as king a
second time, anointing him before the Lord to be ruler and
Zadok to be priest. 23So Solomon sat on the throne of the
Lord as king in place of his father David. He prospered and
all Israel obeyed him. 24All the
officers and mighty men, as
well as all of King David's sons,
pledged their submission to
King Solomon.   1Sa 2:35
25The Lord highly exalted

Solomon in the sight of all Israel and bestowed on him royal splendor such as no king over Israel ever had before.   2Ch 1:1

The Death of David

26David son of Jesse was king over all Israel. 27He ruled over Israel forty years—seven in Hebron and thirty-three in Jerusalem. 28He died at a good old age, having enjoyed long life, wealth and honor. His son Solomon succeeded him as king.   1Ch 18:14

29As for the events of King David's reign, from beginning to end, they are written in the records of Samuel the seer, the records of Nathan the prophet and the records of Gad the seer, 30together with the details of his reign and power, and the circumstances that surrounded him and Israel and the kingdoms of all the other lands.

2 Chronicles

Introduction:

Second Chronicles continues the history of David's royal line. Chapters 1–9 describe the building of the temple during Solomon's reign. Chapters 10–36 follow the history of the southern kingdom of Judah to the final destruction of Jerusalem and the people being taken captive to Babylon.

This book, like 1 Chronicles, shows that the people's relationship to God was most important. When the author wrote about the kings he measured them on the basis of their faithfulness to God. The reigns of evil kings are reported by the author quickly, while the reigns of good kings are described in more detail.

Outline of contents:

The reign of Solomon (1:1–9:31)
The kings of Judah (10:1–36:14)
The destruction of Jerusalem (36:15–23)

Solomon Asks for Wisdom

1 Solomon son of David established himself firmly over his kingdom, for the LORD his God was with him and made him exceedingly great.   1Ki 2:12

²Then Solomon spoke to all Israel—to the commanders of thousands and commanders of hundreds, to the judges and to all the leaders in Israel, the heads of families— ³and Solomon and the whole assembly went to the high place at Gibeon, for God's Tent of Meeting was there, which Moses the LORD's servant had made in the desert. ⁴Now David had brought up the ark of God from Kiriath Jearim to the place he had prepared for it, because he had pitched a tent for it in Jerusalem. ⁵But the bronze altar that Bezalel son of Uri, the son of Hur, had made was in Gibeon in front of the tabernacle of the LORD; so Solomon and the assembly inquired of him there. ⁶Solomon went up to the bronze altar before the LORD in the Tent of Meeting and offered a thousand burnt offerings on it.

⁷That night God appeared to Solomon and said to him, "Ask for whatever you want me to give you."   1Ki 3:5-6; 2Ch 7:12

⁸Solomon answered God, "You have shown great kindness to David my father and have made me king in his place. ⁹Now, LORD God, let your promise to my father David be confirmed, for you have made me king over a people who are as numerous as the dust of the earth. ¹⁰Give me wisdom and knowledge, that I may lead this people, for who is able to govern this great people of yours?"

¹¹God said to Solomon, "Since this is your heart's desire and you have not asked for wealth, riches or honor, nor for the death of your enemies, and since you have not asked for a long life but for wisdom and knowledge to govern my people over whom I have made you king, ¹²therefore wisdom and knowledge will be given you. And I will also give you wealth, riches and honor, such as no king who was before you ever had and none after you will have." Dt 17:17; 1Ki 3:11-13

¹³Then Solomon went to Jerusalem from the high place at Gibeon, from before the Tent of Meeting. And he reigned over Israel.

¹⁴Solomon accumulated chariots and horses; he had fourteen hundred chariots and twelve thousand horses,ᵃ which he kept in the chariot cities and also with him in Jerusa-

lem. ¹⁵The king made silver and gold as common in Jerusalem as stones, and cedar as plentiful as sycamore-fig trees in the foothills. ¹⁶Solomon's horses were imported from Egyptᵇ and from Kueᶜ—the royal merchants purchased them from Kue. ¹⁷They imported a chariot from Egypt for six hundred shekelsᵈ of silver, and a horse for a hundred and fifty.ᵉ They also exported them to all the kings of the Hittites and of the Arameans. SS 1:9

Preparations for Building the Temple

2 Solomon gave orders to build a temple for the Name of the LORD and a royal palace for himself. ²He conscripted seventy thousand men as carriers and eighty thousand as stonecutters in the hills and thirty-six hundred as foremen over them. 1Ki 5:5; 2Ch 10:14

³Solomon sent this message to Hiramᶠ king of Tyre: 2Sa 5:11

"Send me cedar logs as you did for my father David when you sent him cedar to build a palace to live in. ⁴Now I am about to build a temple for the Name of the LORD my God and to dedicate it to him for burning fragrant incense before him, for setting out the consecrated bread regularly,

---

ᵃ14 Or charioteers   ᵇ16 Or possibly Muzur, a region in Cilicia; also in verse 17   ᶜ16 Probably Cilicia   ᵈ17 That is, about 15 pounds (about 7 kilograms)   ᵉ17 That is, about 3 3/4 pounds (about 1.7 kilograms) also in verses 11 and 12   ᶠ3 Hebrew Huram, a variant of Hiram;

and for making burnt offerings every morning and evening and on Sabbaths and New Moons and at the appointed feasts of the LORD our God. This is a lasting ordinance for Israel. Dt 12:5

5"The temple I am going to build will be great, because our God is greater than all other gods. 6But who is able to build a temple for him, since the heavens, even the highest heavens, cannot contain him? Who then am I to build a temple for him, except as a place to burn sacrifices before him? 1Ki 8:27; 1Ch 16:25

7"Send me, therefore, a man skilled to work in gold and silver, bronze and iron, and in purple, crimson and blue yarn, and experienced in the art of engraving, to work in Judah and Jerusalem with my skilled craftsmen, whom my father David provided. 1Ch 22:16

8"Send me also cedar, pine and algum*a* logs from Lebanon, for I know that your men are skilled in cutting timber there. My men will work with yours 9to provide me with plenty of lumber, because the temple I build must be large and magnificent. 10I will give your servants, the woodsmen who cut the timber,

twenty thousand cors*b* of ground wheat, twenty thousand cors of barley, twenty thousand baths*c* of wine and twenty thousand baths of olive oil." 2Ch 9:10-11

11Hiram king of Tyre replied by letter to Solomon:

"Because the LORD loves his people, he has made you their king." 1Ki 10:9

12And Hiram added:

"Praise be to the LORD, the God of Israel, who made heaven and earth! He has given King David a wise son, endowed with intelligence and discernment, who will build a temple for the LORD and a palace for himself. Ps 33:6; 102:25

13"I am sending you Huram-Abi, a man of great skill, 14whose mother was from Dan and whose father was from Tyre. He is trained to work in gold and silver, bronze and iron, stone and wood, and with purple and blue and crimson yarn and fine linen. He is experienced in all kinds of engraving and can execute any design given to him. He will work with your craftsmen and with those of my lord, David your father.

15"Now let my lord send his servants the wheat and

---

a8 Probably a variant of *almug;* possibly juniper bushels (about 4,400 kiloliters)   *c10* That is, probably about 115,000 gallons (about 440 kiloliters)   *b10* That is, probably about 125,000

barley and the olive oil and wine he promised, [16]and we will cut all the logs from Lebanon that you need and will float them in rafts by sea down to Joppa. You can then take them up to Jerusalem."   Jos 19:46; Ezr 3:7

[17]Solomon took a census of all the aliens who were in Israel, after the census his father David had taken; and they were found to be 153,600. [18]He assigned 70,000 of them to be carriers and 80,000 to be stonecutters in the hills, with 3,600 foremen over them to keep the people working.   1Ch 22:2; 2Ch 8:8

Solomon Builds the Temple

3 Then Solomon began to build the temple of the LORD in Jerusalem on Mount Moriah, where the LORD had appeared to his father David. It was on the threshing floor of Araunah[a] the Jebusite, the place provided by David. [2]He began building on the second day of the second month in the fourth year of his reign.   Ezr 5:11; Ac 7:47

[3]The foundation Solomon laid for building the temple of God was sixty cubits long and twenty cubits wide[b] (using the cubit of the old standard). [4]The portico at the front of the temple was twenty cubits[c] long across

the width of the building and twenty cubits[d] high.   Eze 41:2

He overlaid the inside with pure gold. [5]He paneled the main hall with pine and covered it with fine gold and decorated it with palm tree and chain designs. [6]He adorned the temple with precious stones. And the gold he used was gold of Parvaim. [7]He overlaid the ceiling beams, doorframes, walls and doors of the temple with gold, and he carved cherubim on the walls.   Ge 3:24; Ezr 40:16

[8]He built the Most Holy Place, its length corresponding to the width of the temple—twenty cubits long and twenty cubits wide. He overlaid the inside with six hundred talents[e] of fine gold. [9]The gold nails weighed fifty shekels.[f] He also overlaid the upper parts with gold.   Ex 26:33; 1Ki 6:16

[10]In the Most Holy Place he made a pair of sculptured cherubim and overlaid them with gold. [11]The total wingspan of the cherubim was twenty cubits. One wing of the first cherub was five cubits[g] long and touched the temple wall, while its other wing, also five cubits long, touched the wing of the other cherub. [12]Similarly one wing of the second cherub was five cubits long and touched the

---

[a]1 Hebrew Ornan, a variant of Araunah; also in verses 8, 11 and 13   [b]3 That is, about 90 feet (about 27 meters)   [c]4 That is, about 30 feet (about 9 meters); also in verse 15   [d]4 Some Septuagint and Syriac manuscripts; Hebrew and a hundred and twenty   [e]8 That is, about 23 tons (about 21 metric tons)   [f]9 That is, about 1 1/4 pounds (about 0.6 kilogram)   [g]11 That is, about 7 1/2 feet (about 2.3 meters)

other temple wall, and its other wing, also five cubits long, touched the wing of the first cherub. 13The wings of these cherubim extended twenty cubits. They stood on their feet, facing the main hall. *a*   Ex 25:18

14He made the curtain of blue, purple and crimson yarn and fine linen, with cherubim worked into it.   Ex 26:31; Heb 9:3

15In the front of the temple he made two pillars, which together, were thirty-five cubits*b* long, each with a capital on top measuring five cubits. 16He made interwoven chains*c* and put them on top of the pillars. He also made a hundred pomegranates and attached them to the chains. 17He erected the pillars in the front of the temple, one to the south and one to the north. The one to the south he named Jakin*d* and the one to the north Boaz. *e*   1Ki 7:15,17

The Temple's Furnishings

4 He made a bronze altar twenty cubits long, twenty cubits wide and ten cubits high.*f* 2He made the Sea of cast metal, circular in shape, measuring ten cubits from rim to rim and five cubits*g* high. It took a line of thirty cubits*h* to measure around it. 3Below the rim, figures of bulls encircled it—ten to a cubit. *i* The bulls were cast in two rows in one piece with the Sea.   1Ki 8:64; Rev 4:6

4The Sea stood on twelve bulls, three facing north, three facing west, three facing south and three facing east. The Sea rested on top of them, and their hindquarters were toward the center. 5It was a handbreadth*j* in thickness, and its rim was like the rim of a cup, like a lily blossom. It held three thousand baths. *k*   Eze 48:30-34; Rev 21:13

6He then made ten basins for washing and placed five on the south side and five on the north. In them the things to be used for the burnt offerings were rinsed, but the Sea was to be used by the priests for washing.   Ex 30:18; 1Ki 7:38

7He made ten gold lampstands according to the specifications for them and placed them in the temple, five on the south side and five on the north.   Ex 25:40; 1Ki 7:49

8He made ten tables and placed them in the temple, five on the south side and five on the north. He also made a hundred gold sprinkling bowls.

9He made the courtyard of the priests, and the large court and the doors for the court, and

---

*a*13 Or *facing inward*   *b*15 That is, about 52 feet (about 16 meters)   *c*16 Or possibly *made chains in the inner sanctuary*; the meaning of the Hebrew for this phrase is uncertain. *d*17 *Jakin* probably means *he establishes.*   *e*17 *Boaz* probably means *in him is strength.* *f*1 That is, about 30 feet (about 9 meters) long and wide, and about 15 feet (about 4.5 meters) high   *g*2 That is, about 7 1/2 feet (about 2.3 meters)   *h*2 That is, about 45 feet (about 13.5 meters)   *i*3 That is, about 1 1/2 feet (about 0.5 meter)   *j*5 That is, about 3 inches (about 8 centimeters)   *k*5 That is, about 17,500 gallons (about 66 kiloliters)

overlaid the doors with bronze. [10]He placed the Sea on the south side, at the southeast corner.

[11]He also made the pots and shovels and sprinkling bowls.

So Huram finished the work he had undertaken for King Solomon in the temple of God:

[12]the two pillars;

the two bowl-shaped capitals on top of the pillars;

the two sets of network decorating the two bowl-shaped capitals on top of the pillars;

[13]the four hundred pomegranates for the two sets of network (two rows of pomegranates for each network, decorating the bowl-shaped capitals on top of the pillars);

[14]the stands with their basins;

[15]the Sea and the twelve bulls under it;

[16]the pots, shovels, meat forks and all related articles.   1Ki 7:27-30

All the objects that Huram-Abi made for King Solomon for the temple of the LORD were of polished bronze. [17]The king had them cast in clay molds in the plain of the Jordan between Succoth and Zarethan.[a] [18]All these things that Solomon made amounted to so much that the weight of the bronze was not determined.   Ge 33:17; 1Ki 7:23

[19]Solomon also made all the furnishings that were in God's temple:

the golden altar;

the tables on which was the bread of the Presence;

[20]the lampstands of pure gold with their lamps, to burn in front of the inner sanctuary as prescribed; Ex 25:31

[21]the gold floral work and lamps and tongs (they were solid gold);

[22]the pure gold wick trimmers, sprinkling bowls, dishes and censers; and the gold doors of the temple: the inner doors to the Most Holy Place and the doors of the main hall.

5 When all the work Solomon had done for the temple of the LORD was finished, he brought in the things his father David had dedicated—the silver and gold and all the furnishings—and he placed them in the treasuries of God's temple.   2Sa 8:11; 1Ki 7:51

The Ark Brought to the Temple

[2]Then Solomon summoned to Jerusalem the elders of Israel, all the heads of the tribes and the chiefs of the Israelite families, to bring up the ark of the LORD's covenant from Zion, the City of David. [3]And all the men of Israel came together to the king at the time of the festival in the seventh month.   Nu 3:31

[a]17 Hebrew *Zeredatha*, a variant of *Zarethan*

4When all the elders of Israel had arrived, the Levites took up the ark, 5and they brought up the ark and the Tent of Meeting and all the sacred furnishings in it. The priests, who were Levites, carried them up; 6and King Solomon and the entire assembly of Israel that had gathered about him were before the ark, sacrificing so many sheep and cattle that they could not be recorded or counted. 1Ch 15:2

7The priests then brought the ark of the LORD's covenant to its place in the inner sanctuary of the temple, the Most Holy Place, and put it beneath the wings of the cherubim. 8The cherubim spread their wings over the place of the ark and covered the ark and its carrying poles. 9These poles were so long that their ends, extending from the ark, could be seen from in front of the inner sanctuary, but not from outside the Holy Place; and they are still there today. 10There was nothing in the ark except the two tablets that Moses had placed in it at Horeb, where the LORD made a covenant with the Israelites after they came out of Egypt. Rev 11:19

11The priests then withdrew from the Holy Place. All the priests who were there had consecrated themselves, regardless of their divisions. 12All the Levites who were musicians—Asaph, Heman, Jeduthun and their sons and relatives—stood on the east side of the altar, dressed in fine linen and playing cymbals, harps and lyres. They were accompanied by 120 priests sounding trumpets. 13The trumpeters and singers joined in unison, as with one voice, to give praise and thanks to the LORD. Accompanied by trumpets, cymbals and other instruments, they raised their voices in praise to the LORD and sang:

"He is good;
    his love endures forever."

Then the temple of the LORD was filled with a cloud, 14and the priests could not perform their service because of the cloud, for the glory of the LORD filled the temple of God. Ex 40:34

6 Then Solomon said, "The LORD has said that he would dwell in a dark cloud; 2I have built a magnificent temple for you, a place for you to dwell forever." Ex 19:9; Ps 135:21

3While the whole assembly of Israel was standing there, the king turned around and blessed them. 4Then he said:

"Praise be to the LORD, the God of Israel, who with his hands has fulfilled what he promised with his mouth to my father David. For he said, 5'Since the day I brought my people out of Egypt, I have not chosen a city in any tribe of Israel to have a temple built for my Name to be there, nor have I chosen anyone to be the leader over my people Is-

rael. ⁶But now I have chosen Jerusalem for my Name to be there, and I have chosen David to rule my people Israel.' Dt 12:5; 1Ch 28:4

⁷"My father David had it in his heart to build a temple for the Name of the LORD, the God of Israel. ⁸But the LORD said to my father David, 'Because it was in your heart to build a temple for my Name, you did well to have this in your heart. ⁹Nevertheless, you are not the one to build the temple, but your son, who is your own flesh and blood—he is the one who will build the temple for my Name.' 1Ch 17:2; Ac 7:46

¹⁰"The LORD has kept the promise he made. I have succeeded David my father and now I sit on the throne of Israel, just as the LORD promised, and I have built the temple for the Name of the LORD, the God of Israel. ¹¹There I have placed the ark, in which is the covenant of the LORD that he made with the people of Israel." Dt 10:2; Ps 25:10

Solomon's Prayer of Dedication

¹²Then Solomon stood before the altar of the LORD in front of the whole assembly of Israel and spread out his hands.

¹³Now he had made a bronze platform, five cubitsᵃ long, five cubits wide and three cubitsᵇ high, and had placed it in the center of the outer court. He stood on the platform and then knelt down before the whole assembly of Israel and spread out his hands toward heaven. ¹⁴He said: Ne 8:4; Ps 95:6

"O LORD, God of Israel, there is no God like you in heaven or on earth—you who keep your covenant of love with your servants who continue wholeheartedly in your way. ¹⁵You have kept your promise to your servant David my father; with your mouth you have promised and with your hand you have fulfilled it—as it is today. Dt 7:9

¹⁶"Now LORD, God of Israel, keep for your servant David my father the promises you made to him when you said, 'You shall never fail to have a man to sit before me on the throne of Israel, if only your sons are careful in all they do to walk before me according to my law, as you have done.' ¹⁷And now, O LORD, God of Israel, let your word that you promised your servant David come true. 2Sa 7:13

¹⁸"But will God really dwell on earth with men? The heavens, even the

---

ᵃ13 That is, about 7 1/2 feet (about 2.3 meters) 1.3 meters)

ᵇ13 That is, about 4 1/2 feet (about

highest heavens, cannot contain you. How much less this temple I have built! ¹⁹Yet give attention to your servant's prayer and his plea for mercy, O LORD my God. Hear the cry and the prayer that your servant is praying in your presence. ²⁰May your eyes be open toward this temple day and night, this place of which you said you would put your Name there. May you hear the prayer your servant prays toward this place. ²¹Hear the supplications of your servant and of your people Israel when they pray toward this place. Hear from heaven, your dwelling place; and when you hear, forgive.   Isa 40:22

²²"When a man wrongs his neighbor and is required to take an oath and he comes and swears the oath before your altar in this temple, ²³then hear from heaven and act. Judge between your servants, repaying the guilty by bringing down on his own head what he has done. Declare the innocent not guilty and so establish his innocence.

²⁴"When your people Israel have been defeated by an enemy because they have sinned against you and when they turn back and confess your name, praying and making supplication before you in this temple, ²⁵then hear from heaven and forgive the sin of your people Israel and bring them back to the land you gave to them and their fathers.   Lev 26:17; 2Ch 7:14

²⁶"When the heavens are shut up and there is no rain because your people have sinned against you, and when they pray toward this place and confess your name and turn from their sin because you have afflicted them, ²⁷then hear from heaven and forgive the sin of your servants, your people Israel. Teach them the right way to live, and send rain on the land you gave your people for an inheritance.   Lev 26:19; Dt 11:17

²⁸"When famine or plague comes to the land, or blight or mildew, locusts or grasshoppers, or when enemies besiege them in any of their cities, whatever disaster or disease may come, ²⁹and when a prayer or plea is made by any of your people Israel—each one aware of his afflictions and pains, and spreading out his hands toward this temple— ³⁰then hear from heaven, your dwelling place. Forgive, and deal with each man according to all he does, since you know his heart (for you alone know the hearts of men), ³¹so that they will fear you and walk in your ways all

the time they live in the land you gave our fathers.

32"As for the foreigner who does not belong to your people Israel but has come from a distant land because of your great name and your mighty hand and your outstretched arm—when he comes and prays toward this temple, 33then hear from heaven, your dwelling place, and do whatever the foreigner asks of you, so that all the peoples of the earth may know your name and fear you, as do your own people Israel, and may know that this house I have built bears your Name. 2Ch 9:6; Ac 8:27

34"When your people go to war against their enemies, wherever you send them, and when they pray to you toward this city you have chosen and the temple I have built for your Name, 35then hear from heaven their prayer and their plea, and uphold their cause. Dt 28:7

36"When they sin against you—for there is no one who does not sin—and you become angry with them and give them over to the enemy, who takes them captive to a land far away or near; 37and if they have a change of heart in the land where they are held captive, and repent and plead

with you in the land of their captivity and say, 'We have sinned, we have done wrong and acted wickedly'; 38and if they turn back to you with all their heart and soul in the land of their captivity where they were taken, and pray toward the land you gave their fathers, toward the city you have chosen and toward the temple I have built for your Name; 39then from heaven, your dwelling place, hear their prayer and their pleas, and uphold their cause. And forgive your people, who have sinned against you. 2Ch 30:9; Job 15:14

40"Now, my God, may your eyes be open and your ears attentive to the prayers offered in this place. 2Ch 7:15

41"Now arise, O LORD God, and come to
   your resting place,
you and the ark of your
   might. 1Ch 28:2; Ps 3:7
May your priests,
   O LORD God, be
   clothed with
   salvation,
may your saints rejoice
   in your goodness.
42O LORD God, do not
   reject your anointed
   one.
Remember the great
   love promised to
   David your
   servant." Ps 2:2; 89:24

The Dedication of the Temple

7 When Solomon finished praying, fire came down from heaven and consumed the burnt offering and the sacrifices, and the glory of the LORD filled the temple. ²The priests could not enter the temple of the LORD because the glory of the LORD filled it. ³When all the Israelites saw the fire coming down and the glory of the LORD above the temple, they knelt on the pavement with their faces to the ground, and they worshiped and gave thanks to the LORD, saying,

"He is good;
his love endures forever."

⁴Then the king and all the people offered sacrifices before the LORD. ⁵And King Solomon offered a sacrifice of twenty-two thousand head of cattle and a hundred and twenty thousand sheep and goats. So the king and all the people dedicated the temple of God. ⁶The priests took their positions, as did the Levites with the LORD's musical instruments, which King David had made for praising the LORD and which were used when he gave thanks, saying, "His love endures forever." Opposite the Levites, the priests blew their trumpets, and all the Israelites were standing.   1Ki 8:62

⁷Solomon consecrated the middle part of the courtyard in front of the temple of the LORD, and there he offered burnt offerings and the fat of the fellowship offerings,ᵃ because the bronze altar he had made could not hold the burnt offerings, the grain offerings and the fat portions.   Ex 29:13; 1Ki 8:64-66

⁸So Solomon observed the festival at that time for seven days, and all Israel with him—a vast assembly, people from Leboᵇ Hamath to the Wadi of Egypt. ⁹On the eighth day they held an assembly, for they had celebrated the dedication of the altar for seven days and the festival for seven days more. ¹⁰On the twenty-third day of the seventh month he sent the people to their homes, joyful and glad in heart for the good things the LORD had done for David and Solomon and for his people Israel.   Lev 23:36; 2Ch 30:26

The LORD Appears to Solomon

¹¹When Solomon had finished the temple of the LORD and the royal palace, and had succeeded in carrying out all he had in mind to do in the temple of the LORD and in his own palace, ¹²the LORD appeared to him at night and said: 1Ch 28:20

"I have heard your prayer and have chosen this place for myself as a temple for sacrifices.   Dt 12:5,11

¹³"When I shut up the heavens so that there is no

rain, or command locusts to devour the land or send a plague among my people, [14]if my people, who are called by my name, will humble themselves and pray and seek my face and turn from their wicked ways, then will I hear from heaven and will forgive their sin and will heal their land. [15]Now my eyes will be open and my ears attentive to the prayers offered in this place. [16]I have chosen and consecrated this temple so that my Name may be there forever. My eyes and my heart will always be there.

[17]"As for you, if you walk before me as David your father did, and do all I command, and observe my decrees and laws, [18]I will establish your royal throne, as I covenanted with David your father when I said, 'You shall never fail to have a man to rule over Israel.'

[19]"But if you[a] turn away and forsake the decrees and commands I have given you[a] and go off to serve other gods and worship them, [20]then I will uproot Israel from my land, which I have given them, and will reject this temple I have consecrated for my Name. I will make it a byword and an object of ridicule among all peoples. [21]And though this temple is now so imposing, all who pass by will be appalled and say, 'Why has the LORD done such a thing to this land and to this temple?' [22]People will answer, 'Because they have forsaken the LORD, the God of their fathers, who brought them out of Egypt, and have embraced other gods, worshiping and serving them—that is why he brought all this disaster on them.' "

Dt 28:15; Jer 19:8

Solomon's Other Activities

8 At the end of twenty years, during which Solomon built the temple of the LORD and his own palace, [2]Solomon rebuilt the villages that Hiram[b] had given him, and settled Israelites in them. [3]Solomon then went to Hamath Zobah and captured it. [4]He also built up Tadmor in the desert and all the store cities he had built in Hamath. [5]He rebuilt Upper Beth Horon and Lower Beth Horon as fortified cities, with walls and with gates and bars, [6]as well as Baalath and all his store cities, and all the cities for his chariots and for his horses[c]—whatever he desired to build in Jerusalem, in Lebanon and throughout all the territory he ruled.

Jos 19:44; 2Sa 7:2

[7]All the people left from the Hittites, Amorites, Perizzites,

---

[a]19 The Hebrew is plural.   [b]2 Hebrew *Huram*, a variant of *Hiram*; also in verse 18
[c]6 Or *charioteers*

Hivites and Jebusites (these peoples were not Israelites), [8]that is, their descendants remaining in the land, whom the Israelites had not destroyed—these Solomon conscripted for his slave labor force, as it is to this day. [9]But Solomon did not make slaves of the Israelites for his work; they were his fighting men, commanders of his captains, and commanders of his chariots and charioteers. [10]They were also King Solomon's chief officials—two hundred and fifty officials supervising the men.   Ezr 9:1

[11]Solomon brought Pharaoh's daughter up from the City of David to the palace he had built for her, for he said, "My wife must not live in the palace of David king of Israel, because the places the ark of the LORD has entered are holy."   1Ki 3:1

[12]On the altar of the LORD that he had built in front of the portico, Solomon sacrificed burnt offerings to the LORD, [13]according to the daily requirement for offerings commanded by Moses for Sabbaths, New Moons and the three annual feasts—the Feast of Unleavened Bread, the Feast of Weeks and the Feast of Tabernacles. [14]In keeping with the ordinance of his father David, he appointed the divisions of the priests for their duties, and the Levites to lead the praise and to assist the priests according to each day's requirement. He also appointed the gatekeepers by divisions for the various gates, because this was what David the man of God had ordered. [15]They did not deviate from the king's commands to the priests or to the Levites in any matter, including that of the treasuries.   Ex 29:38; 1Ch 24:1

[16]All Solomon's work was carried out, from the day the foundation of the temple of the LORD was laid until its completion. So the temple of the LORD was finished.

[17]Then Solomon went to Ezion Geber and Elath on the coast of Edom. [18]And Hiram sent him ships commanded by his own officers, men who knew the sea. These, with Solomon's men, sailed to Ophir and brought back four hundred and fifty talents[a] of gold, which they delivered to King Solomon.

The Queen of Sheba Visits Solomon

9 When the queen of Sheba heard of Solomon's fame, she came to Jerusalem to test him with hard questions. Arriving with a very great caravan—with camels carrying spices, large quantities of gold, and precious stones—she came to Solomon and talked with him about all she had on her mind. [2]Solomon answered all her questions; nothing was too hard for him to explain to her. [3]When the queen of Sheba saw the wis-

---

[a]18 That is, about 17 tons (about 16 metric tons)

dom of Solomon, as well as the palace he had built, 4the food on his table, the seating of his officials, the attending servants in their robes, the cupbearers in their robes and the burnt offerings he made at*a* the temple of the LORD, she was overwhelmed. 1Ki 5:12; Mt 12:42

5She said to the king, "The report I heard in my own country about your achievements and your wisdom is true. 6But I did not believe what they said until I came and saw with my own eyes. Indeed, not even half the greatness of your wisdom was told me; you have far exceeded the report I heard. 7How happy your men must be! How happy your officials, who continually stand before you and hear your wisdom! 8Praise be to the LORD your God, who has delighted in you and placed you on his throne as king to rule for the LORD your God. Because of the love of your God for Israel and his desire to uphold them forever, he has made you king over them, to maintain justice and righteousness." 2Ch 6:32

9Then she gave the king 120 talents*b* of gold, large quantities of spices, and precious stones. There had never been such spices as those the queen of Sheba gave to King Solomon.

10(The men of Hiram and the men of Solomon brought gold from Ophir; they also brought algumwood*c* and precious stones. 11The king used the algumwood to make steps for the temple of the LORD and for the royal palace, and to make harps and lyres for the musicians. Nothing like them had ever been seen in Judah.) 1Ki 10:11

12King Solomon gave the queen of Sheba all she desired and asked for; he gave her more than she had brought to him. Then she left and returned with her retinue to her own country.

Solomon's Splendor

13The weight of the gold that Solomon received yearly was 666 talents,*d* 14not including the revenues brought in by merchants and traders. Also all the kings of Arabia and the governors of the land brought gold and silver to Solomon. 1Ki 10:14

15King Solomon made two hundred large shields of hammered gold; six hundred bekas*e* of hammered gold went into each shield. 16He also made three hundred small shields of hammered gold, with three hundred bekas*f* of gold in each shield. The king put them in the Palace of the Forest of Lebanon.

17Then the king made a great throne inlaid with ivory and overlaid with pure gold. 18The throne had six steps, and a footstool of gold was attached to it.

a4 Or *the ascent by which he went up to*   *b9* That is, about 4 1/2 tons (about 4 metric tons)   *c10* Probably a variant of *almugwood*   *d13* That is, about 25 tons (about 23 metric tons)   *e15* That is, about 7 1/2 pounds (about 3.5 kilograms)   *f16* That is, about 3 3/4 pounds (about 1.7 kilograms)

On both sides of the seat were armrests, with a lion standing beside each of them. [19]Twelve lions stood on the six steps, one at either end of each step. Nothing like it had ever been made for any other kingdom. [20]All King Solomon's goblets were gold, and all the household articles in the Palace of the Forest of Lebanon were pure gold. Nothing was made of silver, because silver was considered of little value in Solomon's day. [21]The king had a fleet of trading ships[a] manned by Hiram's[b] men. Once every three years it returned, carrying gold, silver and ivory, and apes and baboons. 1Ki 22:39; 2Ch 20:36-37

[22]King Solomon was greater in riches and wisdom than all the other kings of the earth. [23]All the kings of the earth sought audience with Solomon to hear the wisdom God had put in his heart. [24]Year after year, everyone who came brought a gift—articles of silver and gold, and robes, weapons and spices, and horses and mules. 1Ki 4:34; 2Ch 1:12

[25]Solomon had four thousand stalls for horses and chariots, and twelve thousand horses,[c] which he kept in the chariot cities and also with him in Jerusalem. [26]He ruled over all the kings from the River[d] to the land of the Philistines, as far as the border of Egypt. [27]The king made silver as common in Jerusalem as stones, and cedar as plentiful as sycamore-fig trees in the foothills. [28]Solomon's horses were imported from Egypt[e] and from all other countries. 1Sa 8:11; Ps 92:8

Solomon's Death

[29]As for the other events of Solomon's reign, from beginning to end, are they not written in the records of Nathan the prophet, in the prophecy of Ahijah the Shilonite and in the visions of Iddo the seer concerning Jeroboam son of Nebat? [30]Solomon reigned in Jerusalem over all Israel forty years. [31]Then he rested with his fathers and was buried in the city of David his father. And Rehoboam his son succeeded him as king. 1Ki 11:29; 2Ch 10:2

Israel Rebels Against Rehoboam

10 Rehoboam went to Shechem, for all the Israelites had gone there to make him king. [2]When Jeroboam son of Nebat heard this (he was in Egypt, where he had fled from King Solomon), he returned from Egypt. [3]So they sent for Jeroboam, and he and all Israel went to Rehoboam and said to him: [4]"Your father put a heavy yoke on us, but now lighten the harsh labor and the heavy yoke

---

[a]21 Hebrew *of ships that could go to Tarshish*   [b]21 Hebrew *Huram*, a variant of *Hiram*
[c]25 Or *charioteers*   [d]26 That is, the Euphrates   [e]28 Or possibly *Muzur*, a region in Cilicia

he put on us, and we will serve you." 1Ki 11:40; 2Ch 2:2

[5]Rehoboam answered, "Come back to me in three days." So the people went away.

[6]Then King Rehoboam consulted the elders who had served his father Solomon during his lifetime. "How would you advise me to answer these people?" he asked. Job 8:8-9

[7]They replied, "If you will be kind to these people and please them and give them a favorable answer, they will always be your servants." Pr 15:1

[8]But Rehoboam rejected the advice the elders gave him and consulted the young men who had grown up with him and were serving him. [9]He asked them, "What is your advice? How should we answer these people who say to me, 'Lighten the yoke your father put on us'?" 2Sa 17:14; Pr 13:20

[10]The young men who had grown up with him replied, "Tell the people who have said to you, 'Your father put a heavy yoke on us, but make our yoke lighter'—tell them, 'My little finger is thicker than my father's waist. [11]My father laid on you a heavy yoke; I will make it even heavier. My father scourged you with whips; I will scourge you with scorpions.'"

[12]Three days later Jeroboam and all the people returned to Rehoboam, as the king had said, "Come back to me in three days." [13]The king answered them harshly. Rejecting the advice of the elders, [14]he followed the advice of the young men and said, "My father made your yoke heavy; I will make it even heavier. My father scourged you with whips; I will scourge you with scorpions." [15]So the king did not listen to the people, for this turn of events was from God, to fulfill the word the LORD had spoken to Jeroboam son of Nebat through Ahijah the Shilonite. 1Ki 12:12

[16]When all Israel saw that the king refused to listen to them, they answered the king: 1Ch 9:1

"What share do we have in David,
    what part in Jesse's son?
To your tents, O Israel!
    Look after your own house,
        O David!" 2Sa 20:1

So all the Israelites went home. [17]But as for the Israelites who were living in the towns of Judah, Rehoboam still ruled over them.

[18]King Rehoboam sent out Adoniram,[a] who was in charge of forced labor, but the Israelites stoned him to death. King Rehoboam, however, managed to get into his chariot and escape to Jerusalem. [19]So Israel has been in rebellion against the house of David to this day.

11 When Rehoboam arrived in Jerusalem, he mus-

---

[a]18 Hebrew Hadoram, a variant of Adoniram

tered the house of Judah and Benjamin—a hundred and eighty thousand fighting men—to make war against Israel and to regain the kingdom for Rehoboam. 1Ki 12:21-24

2But this word of the LORD came to Shemaiah the man of God: 3"Say to Rehoboam son of Solomon king of Judah and to all the Israelites in Judah and Benjamin, 4'This is what the LORD says: Do not go up to fight against your brothers. Go home, every one of you, for this is my doing.'" So they obeyed the words of the LORD and turned back from marching against Jeroboam. 2Ch 2:15

Rehoboam Fortifies Judah

5Rehoboam lived in Jerusalem and built up towns for defense in Judah: 6Bethlehem, Etam, Tekoa, 7Beth Zur, Soco, Adullam, 8Gath, Mareshah, Ziph, 9Adoraim, Lachish, Azekah, 10Zorah, Aijalon and Hebron. These were fortified cities in Judah and Benjamin. 11He strengthened their defenses and put commanders in them, with supplies of food, olive oil and wine. 12He put shields and spears in all the cities, and made them very strong. So Judah and Benjamin were his. Jos 10:20

13The priests and Levites from all their districts throughout Israel sided with him. 14The Levites even abandoned their pasturelands and property, and came to Judah and Jerusalem because Jeroboam and his sons

had rejected them as priests of the LORD. 15And he appointed his own priests for the high places and for the goat and calf idols he had made. 16Those from every tribe of Israel who set their hearts on seeking the LORD, the God of Israel, followed the Levites to Jerusalem to offer sacrifices to the LORD, the God of their fathers. 17They strengthened the kingdom of Judah and supported Rehoboam son of Solomon three years, walking in the ways of David and Solomon during this time. Nu 35:2-5; 2Ch 12:1

Rehoboam's Family

18Rehoboam married Mahalath, who was the daughter of David's son Jerimoth and of Abihail, the daughter of Jesse's son Eliab. 19She bore him sons: Jeush, Shemariah and Zaham. 20Then he married Maacah daughter of Absalom, who bore him Abijah, Attai, Ziza and Shelomith. 21Rehoboam loved Maacah daughter of Absalom more than any of his other wives and concubines. In all, he had eighteen wives and sixty concubines, twenty-eight sons and sixty daughters. 1Sa 16:6

22Rehoboam appointed Abijah son of Maacah to be the chief prince among his brothers, in order to make him king. 23He acted wisely, dispersing some of his sons throughout the districts of Judah and Benjamin, and to all the fortified cities. He gave them abundant provisions

LORD, the God of your fathers, for you will not succeed." 2Ch 2:4

13Now Jeroboam had sent troops around to the rear, so that while he was in front of Judah the ambush was behind them. 14Judah turned and saw that they were being attacked at both front and rear. Then they cried out to the LORD. The priests blew their trumpets 15and the men of Judah raised the battle cry. At the sound of their battle cry, God routed Jeroboam and all Israel before Abijah and Judah. 16The Israelites fled before Judah, and God delivered them into their hands. 17Abijah and his men inflicted heavy losses on them, so that there were five hundred thousand casualties among Israel's able men. 18The men of Israel were subdued on that occasion, and the men of Judah were victorious because they relied on the LORD, the God of their fathers. Jos 8:9; Ps 22:5

19Abijah pursued Jeroboam and took from him the towns of Bethel, Jeshanah and Ephron, with their surrounding villages. 20Jeroboam did not regain power during the time of Abijah. And the LORD struck him down and he died. 1Sa 25:38

21But Abijah grew in strength. He married fourteen wives and had twenty-two sons and sixteen daughters.

22The other events of Abijah's reign, what he did and what he said, are written in the annotations of the prophet Iddo.

14 And Abijah rested with his fathers and was buried in the City of David. And Asa his son succeeded him as king, and in his days the country was at peace for ten years.

Asa King of Judah

2Asa did what was good and right in the eyes of the LORD his God. 3He removed the foreign altars and the high places, smashed the sacred stones and cut down the Asherah poles.a 4He commanded Judah to seek the LORD, the God of their fathers, and to obey his laws and commands. 5He removed the high places and incense altars in every town in Judah, and the kingdom was at peace under him. 6He built up the fortified cities of Judah, since the land was at peace. No one was at war with him during those years, for the LORD gave him rest. Ex 34:13

7"Let us build up these towns," he said to Judah, "and put walls around them, with towers, gates and bars. The land is still ours, because we have sought the LORD our God; we sought him and he has given us rest on every side." So they built and prospered. 1Ch 22:9

8Asa had an army of three hundred thousand men from Judah, equipped with large shields and with spears, and two hundred and eighty thou-

a3 That is, symbols of the goddess Asherah; here and elsewhere in 2 Chronicles

2 CHRON...

Benjamin, armed
sand [...] shields and with
with [...] these were brave
bow...men. 1Ch 21:1

[...] the Cushite marched
...ainst them with a vast
... and three hundred chari-
...and came as far as Mare-
...1. ¹⁰Asa went out to meet
..., and they took up battle po-
...ons in the Valley of Zepha-
...ah near Mareshah. 2Ch 11:8

¹¹Then Asa called to the LORD his God and said, "LORD, there is no one like you to help the powerless against the mighty. Help us, O LORD our God, for we rely on you, and in your name we have come against this vast army. O LORD, you are our God; do not let man prevail against you." 2Ch 13:14; Ps 79:9

¹²The LORD struck down the Cushites before Asa and Judah. The Cushites fled, ¹³and Asa and his army pursued them as far as Gerar. Such a great number of Cushites fell that they could not recover; they were crushed before the LORD and his forces. The men of Judah carried off a large amount of plunder. ¹⁴They destroyed all the villages around Gerar, for the terror of the LORD had fallen upon them. They plundered all these villages, since there was much booty there. ¹⁵They also attacked the camps of the herdsmen and carried off droves of sheep and goats and camels.

Then they returned to Jerusalem. Ge 35:5; 1Ki 8:45

Asa's Reform

15 The Spirit of God came upon Azariah son of Oded. ²He went out to meet Asa and said to him, "Listen to me, Asa and all Judah and Benjamin. The LORD is with you when you are with him. If you seek him, he will be found by you, but if you forsake him, he will forsake you. ³For a long time Israel was without the true God, without a priest to teach and without the law. ⁴But in their distress they turned to the LORD, the God of Israel, and sought him, and he was found by them. ⁵In those days it was not safe to travel about, for all the inhabitants of the lands were in great turmoil. ⁶One nation was being crushed by another and one city by another, because God was troubling them with every kind of distress. ⁷But as for you, be strong and do not give up, for your work will be rewarded." 2Ch 7:14

⁸When Asa heard these words and the prophecy of Azariah son of[b] Oded the prophet, he took courage. He removed the detestable idols from the whole land of Judah and Benjamin and from the towns he had captured in the hills of Ephraim. He repaired the altar of the

---

a9 Hebrew *with an army of a thousand thousands* or *with an army of thousands upon thousands*   *b8* Vulgate and Syriac (see also Septuagint and verse 1); Hebrew does not have *Azariah son of.*

moth, Jehonathan, Adonijah, Tobijah and Tob-Adonijah—and the priests Elishama and Jehoram. ⁹They taught throughout Judah, taking with them the Book of the Law of the LORD; they went around to all the towns of Judah and taught the people.

¹⁰The fear of the LORD fell on all the kingdoms of the lands surrounding Judah, so that they did not make war with Jehoshaphat. ¹¹Some Philistines brought Jehoshaphat gifts and silver as tribute, and the Arabs brought him flocks: seven thousand seven hundred rams and seven thousand seven hundred goats.

¹²Jehoshaphat became more and more powerful; he built forts and store cities in Judah ¹³and had large supplies in the towns of Judah. He also kept experienced fighting men in Jerusalem. ¹⁴Their enrollment by families was as follows:

From Judah, commanders of units of 1,000:
    Adnah the commander, with 300,000 fighting men;
    ¹⁵next, Jehohanan the commander, with 280,000;
    ¹⁶next, Amasiah son of Zicri, who volunteered himself for the service of the LORD, with 200,000.
¹⁷From Benjamin:
    Eliada, a valiant soldier, with 200,000 men armed with bows and shields;

¹⁸next, Jehozabad, with 180,000 men armed for battle.

¹⁹These were the men who served the king, besides those he stationed in the fortified cities throughout Judah.

Micaiah Prophesies Against Ahab

18 Now Jehoshaphat had great wealth and honor, and he allied himself with Ahab by marriage. ²Some years later he went down to visit Ahab in Samaria. Ahab slaughtered many sheep and cattle for him and the people with him and urged him to attack Ramoth Gilead. ³Ahab king of Israel asked Jehoshaphat king of Judah, "Will you go with me against Ramoth Gilead?"

Jehoshaphat replied, "I am as you are, and my people as your people; we will join you in the war." ⁴But Jehoshaphat also said to the king of Israel, "First seek the counsel of the LORD."

⁵So the king of Israel brought together the prophets—four hundred men—and asked them, "Shall we go to war against Ramoth Gilead, or shall I refrain?"

"Go," they answered, "for God will give it into the king's hand."

⁶But Jehoshaphat asked, "Is there not a prophet of the LORD here whom we can inquire of?"

⁷The king of Israel answered Jehoshaphat, "There is still one

man through whom we can inquire of the LORD, but I hate him because he never prophesies anything good about me, but always bad. He is Micaiah son of Imlah." 1Ki 22:8

"The king should not say that," Jehoshaphat replied.

8So the king of Israel called one of his officials and said, "Bring Micaiah son of Imlah at once."

9Dressed in their royal robes, the king of Israel and Jehoshaphat king of Judah were sitting on their thrones at the threshing floor by the entrance to the gate of Samaria, with all the prophets prophesying before them. 10Now Zedekiah son of Kenaanah had made iron horns, and he declared, "This is what the LORD says: 'With these you will gore the Arameans until they are destroyed.'" Ru 4:1

11All the other prophets were prophesying the same thing. "Attack Ramoth Gilead and be victorious," they said, "for the LORD will give it into the king's hand." 2Ch 22:5

12The messenger who had gone to summon Micaiah said to him, "Look, as one man the other prophets are predicting success for the king. Let your word agree with theirs, and speak favorably."

13But Micaiah said, "As surely as the LORD lives, I can tell him only what my God says."

14When he arrived, the king asked him, "Micaiah, shall we go to war against Ramoth

Gilead, or shall I refrain?"

"Attack and be victorious," he answered, "for they will be given into your hand."

15The king said to him, "How many times must I make you swear to tell me nothing but the truth in the name of the LORD?"

16Then Micaiah answered, "I saw all Israel scattered on the hills like sheep without a shepherd, and the LORD said, 'These people have no master. Let each one go home in peace.'" 1Ch 9:1

17The king of Israel said to Jehoshaphat, "Didn't I tell you that he never prophesies anything good about me, but only bad?"

18Micaiah continued, "Therefore hear the word of the LORD: I saw the LORD sitting on his throne with all the host of heaven standing on his right and on his left. 19And the LORD said, 'Who will entice Ahab king of Israel into attacking Ramoth Gilead and going to his death there?' Da 7:9

"One suggested this, and another that. 20Finally, a spirit came forward, stood before the LORD and said, 'I will entice him.'

"'By what means?' the LORD asked. Job 1:6

21"'I will go and be a lying spirit in the mouths of all his prophets,' he said. 1Ch 21:1

"'You will succeed in enticing him,' said the LORD. 'Go and do it.'

22"So now the LORD has put a lying spirit in the mouths of

these prophets of yours. The LORD has decreed disaster for you."

²³Then Zedekiah son of Kenaanah went up and slapped Micaiah in the face. "Which way did the spirit from*a* the LORD go when he went from me to speak to you?" he asked.

²⁴Micaiah replied, "You will find out on the day you go to hide in an inner room."

²⁵The king of Israel then ordered, "Take Micaiah and send him back to Amon the ruler of the city and to Joash the king's son, ²⁶and say, 'This is what the king says: Put this fellow in prison and give him nothing but bread and water until I return safely.'"

²⁷Micaiah declared, "If you ever return safely, the LORD has not spoken through me." Then he added, "Mark my words, all you people!"

Ahab Killed at Ramoth Gilead

²⁸So the king of Israel and Jehoshaphat king of Judah went up to Ramoth Gilead. ²⁹The king of Israel said to Jehoshaphat, "I will enter the battle in disguise, but you wear your royal robes." So the king of Israel disguised himself and went into battle.

³⁰Now the king of Aram had ordered his chariot commanders, "Do not fight with anyone, small or great, except the king of Israel." ³¹When the chariot commanders saw Jehoshaphat, they thought, "This is the king of Israel." So they turned to attack him, but Jehoshaphat cried out, and the LORD helped him. God drew them away from him, ³²for when the chariot commanders saw that he was not the king of Israel, they stopped pursuing him.

³³But someone drew his bow at random and hit the king of Israel between the sections of his armor. The king told the chariot driver, "Wheel around and get me out of the fighting. I've been wounded." ³⁴All day long the battle raged, and the king of Israel propped himself up in his chariot facing the Arameans until evening. Then at sunset he died.

19 When Jehoshaphat king of Judah returned safely to his palace in Jerusalem, ²Jehu the seer, the son of Hanani, went out to meet him and said to the king, "Should you help the wicked and love*b* those who hate the LORD? Because of this, the wrath of the LORD is upon you. ³There is, however, some good in you, for you have rid the land of the Asherah poles and have set your heart on seeking God."

Jehoshaphat Appoints Judges

⁴Jehoshaphat lived in Jerusalem, and he went out again among the people from Beersheba to the hill country of

---

a23 Or *Spirit of*   *b2* Or *and make alliances with*

Ephraim and turned them back to the Lord, the God of their fathers. ⁵He appointed judges in the land, in each of the fortified cities of Judah. ⁶He told them, "Consider carefully what you do, because you are not judging for man but for the Lord, who is with you whenever you give a verdict. ⁷Now let the fear of the Lord be upon you. Judge carefully, for with the Lord our God there is no injustice or partiality or bribery." Ge 18:25; Dt 10:17

⁸In Jerusalem also, Jehoshaphat appointed some of the Levites, priests and heads of Israelite families to administer the law of the Lord and to settle disputes. And they lived in Jerusalem. ⁹He gave them these orders: "You must serve faithfully and wholeheartedly in the fear of the Lord. ¹⁰In every case that comes before you from your fellow countrymen who live in the cities—whether bloodshed or other concerns of the law, commands, decrees or ordinances—you are to warn them not to sin against the Lord; otherwise his wrath will come on you and your brothers. Do this, and you will not sin.

¹¹"Amariah the chief priest will be over you in any matter concerning the Lord, and Zebadiah son of Ishmael, the leader of the tribe of Judah, will be over you in any matter concern-

ing the king, and the Levites will serve as officials before you. Act with courage, and may the Lord be with those who do well." 1Ch 28:20

Jehoshaphat Defeats Moab and Ammon

20 After this, the Moabites and Ammonites with some of the Meunites*ᵃ* came to make war on Jehoshaphat. Ps 83:6

²Some men came and told Jehoshaphat, "A vast army is coming against you from Edom,ᵇ from the other side of the Sea.ᶜ It is already in Hazazon Tamar" (that is, En Gedi). ³Alarmed, Jehoshaphat resolved to inquire of the Lord, and he proclaimed a fast for all Judah. ⁴The people of Judah came together to seek help from the Lord; indeed, they came from every town in Judah to seek him. Ge 14:7; Ezr 8:23

⁵Then Jehoshaphat stood up in the assembly of Judah and Jerusalem at the temple of the Lord in the front of the new courtyard ⁶and said:

"O Lord, God of our fathers, are you not the God who is in heaven? You rule over all the kingdoms of the nations. Power and might are in your hand, and no one can withstand you. ⁷O our God, did you not drive out the inhabitants of this

---

ᵃ1 Some Septuagint manuscripts; Hebrew *Ammonites* most Hebrew manuscripts, Septuagint and Vulgate *Aram*   *ᵇ2* One Hebrew manuscript; *ᶜ2* That is, the Dead Sea

land before your people Israel and give it forever to the descendants of Abraham your friend? ⁸They have lived in it and have built in it a sanctuary for your Name, saying, ⁹'If calamity comes upon us, whether the sword of judgment, or plague or famine, we will stand in your presence before this temple that bears your Name and will cry out to you in our distress, and you will hear us and save us.'   Dt 4:39; Isa 41:8

¹⁰"But now here are men from Ammon, Moab and Mount Seir, whose territory you would not allow Israel to invade when they came from Egypt; so they turned away from them and did not destroy them. ¹¹See how they are repaying us by coming to drive us out of the possession you gave us as an inheritance. ¹²O our God, will you not judge them? For we have no power to face this vast army that is attacking us. We do not know what to do, but our eyes are upon you."

¹³All the men of Judah, with their wives and children and little ones, stood there before the LORD.   Ezr 8:21

¹⁴Then the Spirit of the LORD came upon Jahaziel son of Zechariah, the son of Benaiah, the son of Jeiel, the son of Mattaniah, a Levite and descendant of Asaph, as he stood in the assembly.   1Ch 12:18; 2Ch 15:1

¹⁵He said: "Listen, King Jehoshaphat and all who live in Judah and Jerusalem! This is what the LORD says to you: 'Do not be afraid or discouraged because of this vast army. For the battle is not yours, but God's. ¹⁶Tomorrow march down against them. They will be climbing up by the Pass of Ziz, and you will find them at the end of the gorge in the Desert of Jeruel. ¹⁷You will not have to fight this battle. Take up your positions; stand firm and see the deliverance the LORD will give you, O Judah and Jerusalem. Do not be afraid; do not be discouraged. Go out to face them tomorrow, and the LORD will be with you.' "   2Ch 32:7

¹⁸Jehoshaphat bowed with his face to the ground, and all the people of Judah and Jerusalem fell down in worship before the LORD. ¹⁹Then some Levites from the Kohathites and Korahites stood up and praised the LORD, the God of Israel, with very loud voice.   Ex 4:31

²⁰Early in the morning they left for the Desert of Tekoa. As they set out, Jehoshaphat stood and said, "Listen to me, Judah and people of Jerusalem! Have faith in the LORD your God and you will be upheld; have faith in his prophets and you will be successful." ²¹After consulting the people, Jehoshaphat appointed men to sing to the LORD and to praise him for the splen-

dor of his[a] holiness as they went out at the head of the army, saying: 1Ch 16:29; Isa 7:9

"Give thanks to the LORD,
    for his love endures
    forever." 2Ch 5:13

22As they began to sing and praise, the LORD set ambushes against the men of Ammon and Moab and Mount Seir who were invading Judah, and they were defeated. 23The men of Ammon and Moab rose up against the men from Mount Seir to destroy and annihilate them. After they finished slaughtering the men from Seir, they helped to destroy one another. 2Ch 13:13

24When the men of Judah came to the place that overlooks the desert and looked toward the vast army, they saw only dead bodies lying on the ground; no one had escaped. 25So Jehoshaphat and his men went to carry off their plunder, and they found among them a great amount of equipment and clothing[b] and also articles of value—more than they could take away. There was so much plunder that it took three days to collect it. 26On the fourth day they assembled in the Valley of Beracah, where they praised the LORD. This is why it is called the Valley of Beracah[c] to this day.

27Then, led by Jehoshaphat, all the men of Judah and Jerusalem returned joyfully to Jerusa-

lem, for the LORD had given them cause to rejoice over their enemies. 28They entered Jerusalem and went to the temple of the LORD with harps and lutes and trumpets. Ne 12:43

29The fear of God came upon all the kingdoms of the countries when they heard how the LORD had fought against the enemies of Israel. 30And the kingdom of Jehoshaphat was at peace, for his God had given him rest on every side. Dt 2:25

The End of Jehoshaphat's Reign

31So Jehoshaphat reigned over Judah. He was thirty-five years old when he became king of Judah, and he reigned in Jerusalem twenty-five years. His mother's name was Azubah daughter of Shilhi. 32He walked in the ways of his father Asa and did not stray from them; he did what was right in the eyes of the LORD. 33The high places, however, were not removed, and the people still had not set their hearts on the God of their fathers. 1Ki 22:41-43

34The other events of Jehoshaphat's reign, from beginning to end, are written in the annals of Jehu son of Hanani, which are recorded in the book of the kings of Israel. 1Ki 16:1,7

35Later, Jehoshaphat king of Judah made an alliance with Ahaziah king of Israel, who was

---

[a]21 Or *him with the splendor of Hebrew manuscripts corpses*   [b]25 Some Hebrew manuscripts and Vulgate; most   [c]26 *Beracah* means *praise.*

guilty of wickedness. ³⁶He agreed with him to construct a fleet of trading ships.*a* After these were built at Ezion Geber, ³⁷Eliezer son of Dodavahu of Mareshah prophesied against Jehoshaphat, saying, "Because you have made an alliance with Ahaziah, the LORD will destroy what you have made." The ships were wrecked and were not able to set sail to trade.*b*

21 Then Jehoshaphat rested with his fathers and was buried with them in the City of David. And Jehoram his son succeeded him as king. ²Jehoram's brothers, the sons of Jehoshaphat, were Azariah, Jehiel, Zechariah, Azariahu, Michael and Shephatiah. All these were sons of Jehoshaphat king of Israel.*c* ³Their father had given them many gifts of silver and gold and articles of value, as well as fortified cities in Judah, but he had given the kingdom to Jehoram because he was his firstborn son.   1Ch 3:11; 2Ch 11:23

Jehoram King of Judah

⁴When Jehoram established himself firmly over his father's kingdom, he put all his brothers to the sword along with some of the princes of Israel. ⁵Jehoram was thirty-two years old when he became king, and he reigned in Jerusalem eight years. ⁶He walked in the ways of the kings of Israel, as the house of Ahab had done, for he married a daughter of Ahab. He did evil in the eyes of the LORD. ⁷Nevertheless, because of the covenant the LORD had made with David, the LORD was not willing to destroy the house of David. He had promised to maintain a lamp for him and his descendants forever.   Jdg 9:5; 2Sa 7:15

⁸In the time of Jehoram, Edom rebelled against Judah and set up its own king. ⁹So Jehoram went there with his officers and all his chariots. The Edomites surrounded him and his chariot commanders, but he rose up and broke through by night. ¹⁰To this day Edom has been in rebellion against Judah.

Libnah revolted at the same time, because Jehoram had forsaken the LORD, the God of his fathers. ¹¹He had also built high places on the hills of Judah and had caused the people of Jerusalem to prostitute themselves and had led Judah astray.   Lev 20:5

¹²Jehoram received a letter from Elijah the prophet, which said: 2Ki 1:16-17

"This is what the LORD, the God of your father David, says: 'You have not walked in the ways of your father Jehoshaphat or of Asa king of Judah. ¹³But you have walked in the ways of the kings of Israel, and you have led Judah and the people of Jerusalem to pros-

---

a36 Hebrew *of ships that could go to Tarshish*   *b37* Hebrew *sail for Tarshish*   *c2* That is, Judah, as frequently in 2 Chronicles

titute themselves, just as the house of Ahab did. You have also murdered your own brothers, members of your father's house, men who were better than you. ¹⁴So now the LORD is about to strike your people, your sons, your wives and everything that is yours, with a heavy blow. ¹⁵You yourself will be very ill with a lingering disease of the bowels, until the disease causes your bowels to come out.' "

¹⁶The LORD aroused against Jehoram the hostility of the Philistines and of the Arabs who lived near the Cushites. ¹⁷They attacked Judah, invaded it and carried off all the goods found in the king's palace, together with his sons and wives. Not a son was left to him except Ahaziah,[a] the youngest.　　2Ch 17:10

¹⁸After all this, the LORD afflicted Jehoram with an incurable disease of the bowels. ¹⁹In the course of time, at the end of the second year, his bowels came out because of the disease, and he died in great pain. His people made no fire in his honor, as they had for his fathers.

²⁰Jehoram was thirty-two years old when he became king, and he reigned in Jerusalem eight years. He passed away, to no one's regret, and was buried in the City of David, but not in the tombs of the kings.　2Ch 24:25

Ahaziah King of Judah

22 The people of Jerusalem made Ahaziah, Jehoram's youngest son, king in his place, since the raiders, who came with the Arabs into the camp, had killed all the older sons. So Ahaziah son of Jehoram king of Judah began to reign.　2Ch 21:17; 33:25

²Ahaziah was twenty-two[b] years old when he became king, and he reigned in Jerusalem one year. His mother's name was Athaliah, a granddaughter of Omri.　2Ch 21:6

³He too walked in the ways of the house of Ahab, for his mother encouraged him in doing wrong. ⁴He did evil in the eyes of the LORD, as the house of Ahab had done, for after his father's death they became his advisers, to his undoing. ⁵He also followed their counsel when he went with Joram[c] son of Ahab king of Israel to war against Hazael king of Aram at Ramoth Gilead. The Arameans wounded Joram; ⁶so he returned to Jezreel to recover from the wounds they had inflicted on him at Ramoth[d] in his battle with Hazael king of Aram.

Then Ahaziah[e] son of Jehoram king of Judah went

---

*a*17 Hebrew *Jehoahaz,* a variant of *Ahaziah*
Syriac (see also 2 Kings 8:26); Hebrew *forty-two*
Joram; also in verses 6 and 7　　*d*6 Hebrew *Ramah,* a variant of *Ramoth*
Hebrew manuscripts, Septuagint, Vulgate and Syriac (see also 2 Kings 8:29); most
Hebrew manuscripts *Azariah*

*b*2 Some Septuagint manuscripts and
*c*5 Hebrew *Jehoram,* a variant of
*e*6 Some

down to Jezreel to see Joram son of Ahab because he had been wounded. 1Ki 19:15; 2Ch 18:1

7Through Ahaziah's visit to Joram, God brought about Ahaziah's downfall. When Ahaziah arrived, he went out with Joram to meet Jehu son of Nimshi, whom the LORD had anointed to destroy the house of Ahab. 8While Jehu was executing judgment on the house of Ahab, he found the princes of Judah and the sons of Ahaziah's relatives, who had been attending Ahaziah, and he killed them. 9He then went in search of Ahaziah, and his men captured him while he was hiding in Samaria. He was brought to Jehu and put to death. They buried him, for they said, "He was a son of Jehoshaphat, who sought the LORD with all his heart." So there was no one in the house of Ahaziah powerful enough to retain the kingdom.

Athaliah and Joash

10When Athaliah the mother of Ahaziah saw that her son was dead, she proceeded to destroy the whole royal family of the house of Judah. 11But Jehosheba,a the daughter of King Jehoram, took Joash son of Ahaziah and stole him away from among the royal princes who were about to be murdered and put him and his nurse in a bedroom. Because Jehosheba,a the daughter of King Jehoram and

wife of the priest Jehoiada, was Ahaziah's sister, she hid the child from Athaliah so she could not kill him. 12He remained hidden with them at the temple of God for six years while Athaliah ruled the land. 2Ki 11:1-3

23 In the seventh year Jehoiada showed his strength. He made a covenant with the commanders of units of a hundred: Azariah son of Jeroham, Ishmael son of Jehohanan, Azariah son of Obed, Maaseiah son of Adaiah, and Elishaphat son of Zicri. 2They went throughout Judah and gathered the Levites and the heads of Israelite families from all the towns. When they came to Jerusalem, 3the whole assembly made a covenant with the king at the temple of God. 2Sa 7:12; 2Ki 11:4

Jehoiada said to them, "The king's son shall reign, as the LORD promised concerning the descendants of David. 4Now this is what you are to do: A third of you priests and Levites who are going on duty on the Sabbath are to keep watch at the doors, 5a third of you at the royal palace and a third at the Foundation Gate, and all the other men are to be in the courtyards of the temple of the LORD. 6No one is to enter the temple of the LORD except the priests and Levites on duty; they may enter because they are consecrated, but all the other men are to guard what the LORD has as-

a11 Hebrew Jehoshabeath, a variant of Jehosheba

signed to them.*ᵃ* ⁷The Levites are to station themselves around the king, each man with his weapons in his hand. Anyone who enters the temple must be put to death. Stay close to the king wherever he goes."   Zec 3:7

⁸The Levites and all the men of Judah did just as Jehoiada the priest ordered. Each one took his men—those who were going on duty on the Sabbath and those who were going off duty—for Jehoiada the priest had not released any of the divisions. ⁹Then he gave the commanders of units of a hundred the spears and the large and small shields that had belonged to King David and that were in the temple of God. ¹⁰He stationed all the men, each with his weapon in his hand, around the king—near the altar and the temple, from the south side to the north side of the temple.

¹¹Jehoiada and his sons brought out the king's son and put the crown on him; they presented him with a copy of the covenant and proclaimed him king. They anointed him and shouted, "Long live the king!"   Ex 25:16; Dt 17:18

¹²When Athaliah heard the noise of the people running and cheering the king, she went to them at the temple of the LORD. ¹³She looked, and there was the king, standing by his pillar at the entrance. The officers and the trumpeters were beside the king, and all the people of the land were rejoicing and blowing trumpets, and singers with musical instruments were leading the praises. Then Athaliah tore her robes and shouted, "Treason! Treason!"   2Ch 34:11

¹⁴Jehoiada the priest sent out the commanders of units of a hundred, who were in charge of the troops, and said to them: "Bring her out between the ranksᵇ and put to the sword anyone who follows her." For the priest had said, "Do not put her to death at the temple of the LORD." ¹⁵So they seized her as she reached the entrance of the Horse Gate on the palace grounds, and there they put her to death.   Ne 3:28; Jer 31:40

¹⁶Jehoiada then made a covenant that he and the people and the kingᶜ would be the LORD's people. ¹⁷All the people went to the temple of Baal and tore it down. They smashed the altars and idols and killed Mattan the priest of Baal in front of the altars.   Dt 13:9; 2Ch 29:10

¹⁸Then Jehoiada placed the oversight of the temple of the LORD in the hands of the priests, who were Levites, to whom David had made assignments in the temple, to present the burnt offerings of the LORD as written in the Law of Moses, with rejoicing and singing, as David had ordered. ¹⁹He also

---

ᵃ6 Or *to observe the LORD's command ˌnot to enterˌ*   *ᵇ14* Or *out from the precincts*
ᶜ16 Or *covenant between ˌthe LORDˌ and the people and the king that they* (see 2 Kings 11:17)

stationed doorkeepers at the gates of the Lord's temple so that no one who was in any way unclean might enter.   1Ch 23:6

²⁰He took with him the commanders of hundreds, the nobles, the rulers of the people and all the people of the land and brought the king down from the temple of the Lord. They went into the palace through the Upper Gate and seated the king on the royal throne, ²¹and all the people of the land rejoiced. And the city was quiet, because Athaliah had been slain with the sword.

Joash Repairs the Temple

24 Joash was seven years old when he became king, and he reigned in Jerusalem forty years. His mother's name was Zibiah; she was from Beersheba. ²Joash did what was right in the eyes of the Lord all the years of Jehoiada the priest. ³Jehoiada chose two wives for him, and he had sons and daughters.   2Ki 11:21; 2Ch 26:5

⁴Some time later Joash decided to restore the temple of the Lord. ⁵He called together the priests and Levites and said to them, "Go to the towns of Judah and collect the money due annually from all Israel, to repair the temple of your God. Do it now." But the Levites did not act at once.   Mt 17:24

⁶Therefore the king summoned Jehoiada the chief priest and said to him, "Why haven't you required the Levites to bring in from Judah and Jerusalem the tax imposed by Moses the servant of the Lord and by the assembly of Israel for the Tent of the Testimony?"   Ex 30:12

⁷Now the sons of that wicked woman Athaliah had broken into the temple of God and had used even its sacred objects for the Baals.   2Ch 21:17

⁸At the king's command, a chest was made and placed outside, at the gate of the temple of the Lord. ⁹A proclamation was then issued in Judah and Jerusalem that they should bring to the Lord the tax that Moses the servant of God had required of Israel in the desert. ¹⁰All the officials and all the people brought their contributions gladly, dropping them into the chest until it was full. ¹¹Whenever the chest was brought in by the Levites to the king's officials and they saw that there was a large amount of money, the royal secretary and the officer of the chief priest would come and empty the chest and carry it back to its place. They did this regularly and collected a great amount of money. ¹²The king and Jehoiada gave it to the men who carried out the work required for the temple of the Lord. They hired masons and carpenters to restore the Lord's temple, and also workers in iron and bronze to repair the temple.

¹³The men in charge of the work were diligent, and the repairs progressed under them. They rebuilt the temple of God

according to its original design and reinforced it. ¹⁴When they had finished, they brought the rest of the money to the king and Jehoiada, and with it were made articles for the LORD's temple: articles for the service and for the burnt offerings, and also dishes and other objects of gold and silver. As long as Jehoiada lived, burnt offerings were presented continually in the temple of the LORD. Ne 10:39

¹⁵Now Jehoiada was old and full of years, and he died at the age of a hundred and thirty. ¹⁶He was buried with the kings in the City of David, because of the good he had done in Israel for God and his temple. 2Ch 21:2

The Wickedness of Joash

¹⁷After the death of Jehoiada, the officials of Judah came and paid homage to the king, and he listened to them. ¹⁸They abandoned the temple of the LORD, the God of their fathers, and worshiped Asherah poles and idols. Because of their guilt, God's anger came upon Judah and Jerusalem. ¹⁹Although the LORD sent prophets to the people to bring them back to him, and though they testified against them, they would not listen. 2Ch 19:2; Jer 7:25

²⁰Then the Spirit of God came upon Zechariah son of Jehoiada the priest. He stood before the people and said, "This is what God says: 'Why do you disobey the LORD's commands? You will not prosper. Because you have forsaken the LORD, he has forsaken you.'" Nu 14:41; 2Ch 15:2

²¹But they plotted against him, and by order of the king they stoned him to death in the courtyard of the LORD's temple. ²²King Joash did not remember the kindness Zechariah's father Jehoiada had shown him but killed his son, who said as he lay dying, "May the LORD see this and call you to account."

²³At the turn of the year,ᵃ the army of Aram marched against Joash; it invaded Judah and Jerusalem and killed all the leaders of the people. They sent all the plunder to their king in Damascus. ²⁴Although the Aramean army had come with only a few men, the LORD delivered into their hands a much larger army. Because Judah had forsaken the LORD, the God of their fathers, judgment was executed on Joash. ²⁵When the Arameans withdrew, they left Joash severely wounded. His officials conspired against him for murdering the son of Jehoiada the priest, and they killed him in his bed. So he died and was buried in the City of David, but not in the tombs of the kings. Lev 26:25; 2Ki 12:17

²⁶Those who conspired against him were Zabad,ᵇ son of Shimeath an Ammonite woman, and Jehozabad, son of Shimrithᶜ a Moabite woman.

ᵃ23 Probably in the spring   ᵇ26 A variant of *Jozabad*   ᶜ26 A variant of *Shomer*

[27]The account of his sons, the many prophecies about him, and the record of the restoration of the temple of God are written in the annotations on the book of the kings. And Amaziah his son succeeded him as king.

Amaziah King of Judah

25 Amaziah was twenty-five years old when he became king, and he reigned in Jerusalem twenty-nine years. His mother's name was Jehoaddin[a]; she was from Jerusalem. [2]He did what was right in the eyes of the LORD, but not wholeheartedly. [3]After the kingdom was firmly in his control, he executed the officials who had murdered his father the king. [4]Yet he did not put their sons to death, but acted in accordance with what is written in the Law, in the Book of Moses, where the LORD commanded: "Fathers shall not be put to death for their children, nor children put to death for their fathers; each is to die for his own sins."[b]   2Ki 14:1-6

[5]Amaziah called the people of Judah together and assigned them according to their families to commanders of thousands and commanders of hundreds for all Judah and Benjamin. He then mustered those twenty years old or more and found that there were three hundred thousand men ready for military service, able to handle the spear and shield. [6]He also hired a hundred thousand fighting men from Israel for a hundred talents[c] of silver.   Nu 1:3

[7]But a man of God came to him and said, "O king, these troops from Israel must not march with you, for the LORD is not with Israel—not with any of the people of Ephraim. [8]Even if you go and fight courageously in battle, God will overthrow you before the enemy, for God has the power to help or to overthrow."   2Ch 14:11; 16:2-9

[9]Amaziah asked the man of God, "But what about the hundred talents I paid for these Israelite troops?"

The man of God replied, "The LORD can give you much more than that."   Pr 10:22

[10]So Amaziah dismissed the troops who had come to him from Ephraim and sent them home. They were furious with Judah and left for home in a great rage.

[11]Amaziah then marshaled his strength and led his army to the Valley of Salt, where he killed ten thousand men of Seir. [12]The army of Judah also captured ten thousand men alive, took them to the top of a cliff and threw them down so that all were dashed to pieces. 2Ki 14:7

[13]Meanwhile the troops that Amaziah had sent back and had not allowed to take part in the

---

[a]1 Hebrew *Jehoaddan*, a variant of *Jehoaddin*   [b]4 Deut. 24:16   [c]6 That is, about 3 3/4 tons (about 3.4 metric tons); also in verse 9

war raided Judean towns from Samaria to Beth Horon. They killed three thousand people and carried off great quantities of plunder.

14When Amaziah returned from slaughtering the Edomites, he brought back the gods of the people of Seir. He set them up as his own gods, bowed down to them and burned sacrifices to them. 15The anger of the Lord burned against Amaziah, and he sent a prophet to him, who said, "Why do you consult this people's gods, which could not save their own people from your hand?"   2Ch 28:23

16While he was still speaking, the king said to him, "Have we appointed you an adviser to the king? Stop! Why be struck down?"

So the prophet stopped but said, "I know that God has determined to destroy you, because you have done this and have not listened to my counsel."

17After Amaziah king of Judah consulted his advisers, he sent this challenge to Jehoash*a* son of Jehoahaz, the son of Jehu, king of Israel: "Come, meet me face to face."

18But Jehoash king of Israel replied to Amaziah king of Judah: "A thistle in Lebanon sent a message to a cedar in Lebanon, 'Give your daughter to my son in marriage.' Then a wild beast in Lebanon came along and trampled the thistle underfoot. 19You say to yourself that you have defeated Edom, and now you are arrogant and proud. But stay at home! Why ask for trouble and cause your own downfall and that of Judah also?"   Jdg 9:8-15; 2Ch 26:16

20Amaziah, however, would not listen, for God so worked that he might hand them over to Jehoash*u*, because they sought the gods of Edom. 21So Jehoash king of Israel attacked. He and Amaziah king of Judah faced each other at Beth Shemesh in Judah. 22Judah was routed by Israel, and every man fled to his home. 23Jehoash king of Israel captured Amaziah king of Judah, the son of Joash, the son of Ahaziah,*b* at Beth Shemesh. Then Jehoash brought him to Jerusalem and broke down the wall of Jerusalem from the Ephraim Gate to the Corner Gate—a section about six hundred feet*c* long. 24He took all the gold and silver and all the articles found in the temple of God that had been in the care of Obed-Edom, together with the palace treasures and the hostages, and returned to Samaria.

25Amaziah son of Joash king of Judah lived for fifteen years after the death of Jehoash son of Jehoahaz king of Israel. 26As for the other events of Amaziah's

---

*a*17 Hebrew *Joash*, a variant of *Jehoash*; also in verses 18, 21, 23 and 25   *b*23 Hebrew *Jehoahaz*, a variant of *Ahaziah*   *c*23 Hebrew *four hundred cubits* (about 180 meters)

reign, from beginning to end, are they not written in the book of the kings of Judah and Israel? ²⁷From the time that Amaziah turned away from following the LORD, they conspired against him in Jerusalem and he fled to Lachish, but they sent men after him to Lachish and killed him there. ²⁸He was brought back by horse and was buried with his fathers in the City of Judah.

Uzziah King of Judah

26 Then all the people of Judah took Uzziah,[a] who was sixteen years old, and made him king in place of his father Amaziah. ²He was the one who rebuilt Elath and restored it to Judah after Amaziah rested with his fathers.   2Ch 22:1

³Uzziah was sixteen years old when he became king, and he reigned in Jerusalem fifty-two years. His mother's name was Jecoliah; she was from Jerusalem. ⁴He did what was right in the eyes of the LORD, just as his father Amaziah had done. ⁵He sought God during the days of Zechariah, who instructed him in the fear[b] of God. As long as he sought the LORD, God gave him success.   2Ch 24:2

⁶He went to war against the Philistines and broke down the walls of Gath, Jabneh and Ashdod. He then rebuilt towns near Ashdod and elsewhere among the Philistines. ⁷God helped him against the Philistines and against the Arabs who lived in Gur Baal and against the Meunites. ⁸The Ammonites brought tribute to Uzziah, and his fame spread as far as the border of Egypt, because he had become very powerful.   2Ch 21:16; Isa 14:29

⁹Uzziah built towers in Jerusalem at the Corner Gate, at the Valley Gate and at the angle of the wall, and he fortified them. ¹⁰He also built towers in the desert and dug many cisterns, because he had much livestock in the foothills and in the plain. He had people working his fields and vineyards in the hills and in the fertile lands, for he loved the soil.   2Ch 25:23

¹¹Uzziah had a well-trained army, ready to go out by divisions according to their numbers as mustered by Jeiel the secretary and Maaseiah the officer under the direction of Hananiah, one of the royal officials. ¹²The total number of family leaders over the fighting men was 2,600. ¹³Under their command was an army of 307,500 men trained for war, a powerful force to support the king against his enemies. ¹⁴Uzziah provided shields, spears, helmets, coats of armor, bows and slingstones for the entire army. ¹⁵In Jerusalem he made machines designed by skillful men for use on the towers and on the corner defenses to shoot arrows and

---

a1 Also called *Azariah*   *b5* Many Hebrew manuscripts, Septuagint and Syriac; other Hebrew manuscripts *vision*

hurl large stones. His fame spread far and wide, for he was greatly helped until he became powerful. 2Ch 25:5; Jer 46:4

16But after Uzziah became powerful, his pride led to his downfall. He was unfaithful to the LORD his God, and entered the temple of the LORD to burn incense on the altar of incense. 17Azariah the priest with eighty other courageous priests of the LORD followed him in. 18They confronted him and said, "It is not right for you, Uzziah, to burn incense to the LORD. That is for the priests, the descendants of Aaron, who have been consecrated to burn incense. Leave the sanctuary, for you have been unfaithful; and you will not be honored by the LORD God." Nu 16:39; 18:1-7

19Uzziah, who had a censer in his hand ready to burn incense, became angry. While he was raging at the priests in their presence before the incense altar in the LORD's temple, leprosya broke out on his forehead. 20When Azariah the chief priest and all the other priests looked at him, they saw that he had leprosy on his forehead, so they hurried him out. Indeed, he himself was eager to leave, because the LORD had afflicted him. Nu 12:10

21King Uzziah had leprosy until the day he died. He lived in a separate houseb —leprous,

and excluded from the temple of the LORD. Jotham his son had charge of the palace and governed the people of the land. 22The other events of Uzziah's reign, from beginning to end, are recorded by the prophet Isaiah son of Amoz. 23Uzziah rested with his fathers and was buried near them in a field for burial that belonged to the kings, for people said, "He had leprosy." And Jotham his son succeeded him as king.

Jotham King of Judah

27 Jotham was twenty-five years old when he became king, and he reigned in Jerusalem sixteen years. His mother's name was Jerusha daughter of Zadok. 2He did what was right in the eyes of the LORD, just as his father Uzziah had done, but unlike him he did not enter the temple of the LORD. The people, however, continued their corrupt practices. 3Jotham rebuilt the Upper Gate of the temple of the LORD and did extensive work on the wall at the hill of Ophel. 4He built towns in the Judean hills and forts and towers in the wooded areas. 2Ki 15:5; Ne 3:26

5Jotham made war on the king of the Ammonites and conquered them. That year the Ammonites paid him a hundred talentsc of silver, ten thousand

---

a19 The Hebrew word was used for various diseases affecting the skin—not necessarily leprosy; also in verses 20, 21 and 23. b21 Or *in a house where he was relieved of responsibilities* c5 That is, about 3 3/4 tons (about 3.4 metric tons)

cors*a* of wheat and ten thousand cors of barley. The Ammonites brought him the same amount also in the second and third years.   Ge 19:38

6Jotham grew powerful because he walked steadfastly before the LORD his God.   2Ch 26:5

7The other events in Jotham's reign, including all his wars and the other things he did, are written in the book of the kings of Israel and Judah. 8He was twenty-five years old when he became king, and he reigned in Jerusalem sixteen years. 9Jotham rested with his fathers and was buried in the City of David. And Ahaz his son succeeded him as king.   2Ki 15:36

Ahaz King of Judah

28 Ahaz was twenty years old when he became king, and he reigned in Jerusalem sixteen years. Unlike David his father, he did not do what was right in the eyes of the LORD. 2He walked in the ways of the kings of Israel and also made cast idols for worshiping the Baals. 3He burned sacrifices in the Valley of Ben Hinnom and sacrificed his sons in the fire, following the detestable ways of the nations the LORD had driven out before the Israelites. 4He offered sacrifices and burned incense at the high places, on the hilltops and under every spreading tree.   1Ch 3:13

5Therefore the LORD his God handed him over to the king of Aram. The Arameans defeated him and took many of his people as prisoners and brought them to Damascus.

He was also given into the hands of the king of Israel, who inflicted heavy casualties on him. 6In one day Pekah son of Remaliah killed a hundred and twenty thousand soldiers in Judah—because Judah had forsaken the LORD, the God of their fathers. 7Zicri, an Ephraimite warrior, killed Maaseiah the king's son, Azrikam the officer in charge of the palace, and Elkanah, second to the king. 8The Israelites took captive from their kinsmen two hundred thousand wives, sons and daughters. They also took a great deal of plunder, which they carried back to Samaria.

9But a prophet of the LORD named Oded was there, and he went out to meet the army when it returned to Samaria. He said to them, "Because the LORD, the God of your fathers, was angry with Judah, he gave them into your hand. But you have slaughtered them in a rage that reaches to heaven. 10And now you intend to make the men and women of Judah and Jerusalem your slaves. But aren't you also guilty of sins against the LORD your God? 11Now listen to me! Send back your fellow countrymen you have taken as prisoners, for the

LORD's fierce anger rests on you." 2Ch 11:4; Ezr 9:6

12Then some of the leaders in Ephraim—Azariah son of Jehohanan, Berekiah son of Meshillemoth, Jehizkiah son of Shallum, and Amasa son of Hadlai—confronted those who were arriving from the war. 13"You must not bring those prisoners here," they said, "or we will be guilty before the LORD. Do you intend to add to our sin and guilt? For our guilt is already great, and his fierce anger rests on Israel." Ps 78:49

14So the soldiers gave up the prisoners and plunder in the presence of the officials and all the assembly. 15The men designated by name took the prisoners, and from the plunder they clothed all who were naked. They provided them with clothes and sandals, food and drink, and healing balm. All those who were weak they put on donkeys. So they took them back to their fellow countrymen at Jericho, the City of Palms, and returned to Samaria. 2Ki 6:22

16At that time King Ahaz sent to the kinga of Assyria for help. 17The Edomites had again come and attacked Judah and carried away prisoners, 18while the Philistines had raided towns in the foothills and in the Negev of Judah. They captured and occupied Beth Shemesh, Aijalon and Gederoth, as well as Soco, Timnah and Gimzo, with their surrounding villages. 19The LORD had humbled Judah because of Ahaz king of Israel,b for he had promoted wickedness in Judah and had been most unfaithful to the LORD. 20Tiglath-Pileserc king of Assyria came to him, but he gave him trouble instead of help. 21Ahaz took some of the things from the temple of the LORD and from the royal palace and from the princes and presented them to the king of Assyria, but that did not help him. 2Ki 16:7

22In his time of trouble King Ahaz became even more unfaithful to the LORD. 23He offered sacrifices to the gods of Damascus, who had defeated him; for he thought, "Since the gods of the kings of Aram have helped them, I will sacrifice to them so they will help me." But they were his downfall and the downfall of all Israel. Jer 5:3

24Ahaz gathered together the furnishings from the temple of God and took them away.d He shut the doors of the LORD's temple and set up altars at every street corner in Jerusalem. 25In every town in Judah he built high places to burn sacrifices to other gods and provoked the LORD, the God of his fathers, to anger. 2Ch 29:19; Mal 1:10

26The other events of his reign and all his ways, from beginning to end, are written in the

---

a16 One Hebrew manuscript, Septuagint and Vulgate (see also 2 Kings 16:7); most Hebrew manuscripts kings   b19 That is, Judah, as frequently in 2 Chronicles   c20 Hebrew Tilgath-Pilneser, a variant of Tiglath-Pileser   d24 Or and cut them up

book of the kings of Judah and Israel. ²⁷Ahaz rested with his fathers and was buried in the city of Jerusalem, but he was not placed in the tombs of the kings of Israel. And Hezekiah his son succeeded him as king.   2Ch 21:20

Hezekiah Purifies the Temple

29 Hezekiah was twenty-five years old when he became king, and he reigned in Jerusalem twenty-nine years. His mother's name was Abijah daughter of Zechariah. ²He did what was right in the eyes of the LORD, just as his father David had done.   1Ch 3:13; 2Ch 34:2

³In the first month of the first year of his reign, he opened the doors of the temple of the LORD and repaired them. ⁴He brought in the priests and the Levites, assembled them in the square on the east side ⁵and said: "Listen to me, Levites! Consecrate yourselves now and consecrate the temple of the LORD, the God of your fathers. Remove all defilement from the sanctuary. ⁶Our fathers were unfaithful; they did evil in the eyes of the LORD our God and forsook him. They turned their faces away from the LORD's dwelling place and turned their backs on him. ⁷They also shut the doors of the portico and put out the lamps. They did not burn incense or present any burnt offerings at the sanctuary to the God of Israel. ⁸Therefore, the anger of the LORD has fallen on Judah and Jerusalem; he has made

them an object of dread and horror and scorn, as you can see with your own eyes. ⁹This is why our fathers have fallen by the sword and why our sons and daughters and our wives are in captivity. ¹⁰Now I intend to make a covenant with the LORD, the God of Israel, so that his fierce anger will turn away from us. ¹¹My sons, do not be negligent now, for the LORD has chosen you to stand before him and serve him, to minister before him and to burn incense."

¹²Then these Levites set to work: Nu 3:17-20

from the Kohathites,
    Mahath son of Amasai
    and Joel son of Azariah;
from the Merarites,
    Kish son of Abdi and Azariah son of Jehallelel;
from the Gershonites,
    Joah son of Zimmah and
    Eden son of Joah;
¹³from the descendants of Elizaphan,   Ex 6:22
    Shimri and Jeiel;
from the descendants of
    Asaph,   1Ch 6:39
    Zechariah and Mattaniah;
¹⁴from the descendants of
    Heman,
    Jehiel and Shimei;
from the descendants of
    Jeduthun,
    Shemaiah and Uzziel.

¹⁵When they had assembled their brothers and consecrated themselves, they went in to purify the temple of the LORD, as the king had ordered, following the word of the LORD. ¹⁶The

priests went into the sanctuary of the LORD to purify it. They brought out to the courtyard of the LORD's temple everything unclean that they found in the temple of the LORD. The Levites took it and carried it out to the Kidron Valley. ¹⁷They began the consecration on the first day of the first month, and by the eighth day of the month they reached the portico of the LORD. For eight more days they consecrated the temple of the LORD itself, finishing on the sixteenth day of the first month.   2Sa 15:23

¹⁸Then they went in to King Hezekiah and reported: "We have purified the entire temple of the LORD, the altar of burnt offering with all its utensils, and the table for setting out the consecrated bread, with all its articles. ¹⁹We have prepared and consecrated all the articles that King Ahaz removed in his unfaithfulness while he was king. They are now in front of the LORD's altar."   2Ch 28:24

²⁰Early the next morning King Hezekiah gathered the city officials together and went up to the temple of the LORD. ²¹They brought seven bulls, seven rams, seven male lambs and seven male goats as a sin offering for the kingdom, for the sanctuary and for Judah. The king commanded the priests, the descendants of Aaron, to offer these on the altar of the LORD. ²²So they slaughtered the bulls, and the priests took the blood and sprinkled it on the altar; next they slaughtered the rams and sprinkled their blood on the altar; then they slaughtered the lambs and sprinkled their blood on the altar. ²³The goats for the sin offering were brought before the king and the assembly, and they laid their hands on them. ²⁴The priests then slaughtered the goats and presented their blood on the altar for a sin offering to atone for all Israel, because the king had ordered the burnt offering and the sin offering for all Israel.

²⁵He stationed the Levites in the temple of the LORD with cymbals, harps and lyres in the way prescribed by David and Gad the king's seer and Nathan the prophet; this was commanded by the LORD through his prophets. ²⁶So the Levites stood ready with David's instruments, and the priests with their trumpets.   1Ch 25:6

²⁷Hezekiah gave the order to sacrifice the burnt offering on the altar. As the offering began, singing to the LORD began also, accompanied by trumpets and the instruments of David king of Israel. ²⁸The whole assembly bowed in worship, while the singers sang and the trumpeters played. All this continued until the sacrifice of the burnt offering was completed.   1Sa 16:16

²⁹When the offerings were finished, the king and everyone present with him knelt down and worshiped. ³⁰King Hezekiah and his officials ordered the Levites to praise the LORD

with the words of David and of Asaph the seer. So they sang praises with gladness and bowed their heads and worshiped.   2Ch 20:18

[31]Then Hezekiah said, "You have now dedicated yourselves to the LORD. Come and bring sacrifices and thank offerings to the temple of the LORD." So the assembly brought sacrifices and thank offerings, and all whose hearts were willing brought burnt offerings.   Heb 13:15-16

[32]The number of burnt offerings the assembly brought was seventy bulls, a hundred rams and two hundred male lambs—all of them for burnt offerings to the LORD. [33]The animals consecrated as sacrifices amounted to six hundred bulls and three thousand sheep and goats. [34]The priests, however, were too few to skin all the burnt offerings; so their kinsmen the Levites helped them until the task was finished and until other priests had been consecrated, for the Levites had been more conscientious in consecrating themselves than the priests had been. [35]There were burnt offerings in abundance, together with the fat of the fellowship offerings[a] and the drink offerings that accompanied the burnt offerings.

So the service of the temple of the LORD was reestablished. [36]Hezekiah and all the people rejoiced at what God had brought about for his people, because it was done so quickly.

Hezekiah Celebrates the Passover

30 Hezekiah sent word to all Israel and Judah and also wrote letters to Ephraim and Manasseh, inviting them to come to the temple of the LORD in Jerusalem and celebrate the Passover to the LORD, the God of Israel. [2]The king and his officials and the whole assembly in Jerusalem decided to celebrate the Passover in the second month. [3]They had not been able to celebrate it at the regular time because not enough priests had consecrated themselves and the people had not assembled in Jerusalem. [4]The plan seemed right both to the king and to the whole assembly. [5]They decided to send a proclamation throughout Israel, from Beersheba to Dan, calling the people to come to Jerusalem and celebrate the Passover to the LORD, the God of Israel. It had not been celebrated in large numbers according to what was written.   1Ch 9:1

[6]At the king's command, couriers went throughout Israel and Judah with letters from the king and from his officials, which read:

"People of Israel, return to the LORD, the God of Abraham, Isaac and Israel,

a35 Traditionally *peace offerings*

that he may return to you who are left, who have escaped from the hand of the kings of Assyria. ⁷Do not be like your fathers and brothers, who were unfaithful to the LORD, the God of their fathers, so that he made them an object of horror, as you see. ⁸Do not be stiffnecked, as your fathers were; submit to the LORD. Come to the sanctuary, which he has consecrated forever. Serve the LORD your God, so that his fierce anger will turn away from you. ⁹If you return to the LORD, then your brothers and your children will be shown compassion by their captors and will come back to this land, for the LORD your God is gracious and compassionate. He will not turn his face from you if you return to him."   Ps 78:8,57

¹⁰The couriers went from town to town in Ephraim and Manasseh, as far as Zebulun, but the people scorned and ridiculed them. ¹¹Nevertheless, some men of Asher, Manasseh and Zebulun humbled themselves and went to Jerusalem. ¹²Also in Judah the hand of God was on the people to give them unity of mind to carry out what the king and his officials had ordered, following the word of the LORD.   2Ch 36:16

¹³A very large crowd of people assembled in Jerusalem to celebrate the Feast of Unleavened Bread in the second month. ¹⁴They removed the altars in Jerusalem and cleared away the incense altars and threw them into the Kidron Valley.   Nu 28:16; 2Ch 28:24

¹⁵They slaughtered the Passover lamb on the fourteenth day of the second month. The priests and the Levites were ashamed and consecrated themselves and brought burnt offerings to the temple of the LORD. ¹⁶Then they took up their regular positions as prescribed in the Law of Moses the man of God. The priests sprinkled the blood handed to them by the Levites. ¹⁷Since many in the crowd had not consecrated themselves, the Levites had to kill the Passover lambs for all those who were not ceremonially clean and could not consecrate their lambs to the LORD. ¹⁸Although most of the many people who came from Ephraim, Manasseh, Issachar and Zebulun had not purified themselves, yet they ate the Passover, contrary to what was written. But Hezekiah prayed for them, saying, "May the LORD, who is good, pardon everyone ¹⁹who sets his heart on seeking God—the LORD, the God of his fathers—even if he is not clean according to the rules of the sanctuary." ²⁰And the LORD heard Hezekiah and healed the people.   2Ch 29:34

²¹The Israelites who were present in Jerusalem celebrated

the Feast of Unleavened Bread for seven days with great rejoicing, while the Levites and priests sang to the LORD every day, accompanied by the LORD's instruments of praise.[a]

22Hezekiah spoke encouragingly to all the Levites, who showed good understanding of the service of the LORD. For the seven days they ate their assigned portion and offered fellowship offerings[b] and praised the LORD, the God of their fathers.

23The whole assembly then agreed to celebrate the festival seven more days; so for another seven days they celebrated joyfully. 24Hezekiah king of Judah provided a thousand bulls and seven thousand sheep and goats for the assembly, and the officials provided them with a thousand bulls and ten thousand sheep and goats. A great number of priests consecrated themselves. 25The entire assembly of Judah rejoiced, along with the priests and Levites and all who had assembled from Israel, including the aliens who had come from Israel and those who lived in Judah. 26There was great joy in Jerusalem, for since the days of Solomon son of David king of Israel there had been nothing like this in Jerusalem. 27The priests and the Levites stood to bless the people, and God heard them, for their

prayer reached heaven, his holy dwelling place.   Ex 39:43; 2Ch 7:9

31 When all this had ended, the Israelites who were there went out to the towns of Judah, smashed the sacred stones and cut down the Asherah poles. They destroyed the high places and the altars throughout Judah and Benjamin and in Ephraim and Manasseh. After they had destroyed all of them, the Israelites returned to their own towns and to their own property.

Contributions for Worship

2Hezekiah assigned the priests and Levites to divisions—each of them according to their duties as priests or Levites—to offer burnt offerings and fellowship offerings,[b] to minister, to give thanks and to sing praises at the gates of the LORD's dwelling. 3The king contributed from his own possessions for the morning and evening burnt offerings and for the burnt offerings on the Sabbaths, New Moons and appointed feasts as written in the Law of the LORD. 4He ordered the people living in Jerusalem to give the portion due the priests and Levites so they could devote themselves to the Law of the LORD. 5As soon as the order went out, the Israelites generously gave the firstfruits of their grain, new wine, oil and honey

---

a21 Or *priests praised the* LORD *every day with resounding instruments belonging to the* LORD
b22,2 Traditionally *peace offerings*

and all that the fields produced. They brought a great amount, a tithe of everything. 6The men of Israel and Judah who lived in the towns of Judah also brought a tithe of their herds and flocks and a tithe of the holy things dedicated to the LORD their God, and they piled them in heaps. 7They began doing this in the third month and finished in the seventh month. 8When Hezekiah and his officials came and saw the heaps, they praised the LORD and blessed his people Israel.   2Ch 29:9; Ps 144:13-15

9Hezekiah asked the priests and Levites about the heaps; 10and Azariah the chief priest, from the family of Zadok, answered, "Since the people began to bring their contributions to the temple of the LORD, we have had enough to eat and plenty to spare, because the LORD has blessed his people, and this great amount is left over."   2Sa 8:17; Eze 44:30

11Hezekiah gave orders to prepare storerooms in the temple of the LORD, and this was done. 12Then they faithfully brought in the contributions, tithes and dedicated gifts. Conaniah, a Levite, was in charge of these things, and his brother Shimei was next in rank. 13Jehiel, Azaziah, Nahath, Asahel, Jerimoth, Jozabad, Eliel, Ismakiah, Mahath and Benaiah were supervisors under Conaniah and Shimei his brother, by appointment of King Hezekiah and Azariah the official in charge of the temple of God.   2Ch 35:9

14Kore son of Imnah the Levite, keeper of the East Gate, was in charge of the freewill offerings given to God, distributing the contributions made to the LORD and also the consecrated gifts. 15Eden, Miniamin, Jeshua, Shemaiah, Amariah and Shecaniah assisted him faithfully in the towns of the priests, distributing to their fellow priests according to their divisions, old and young alike.

16In addition, they distributed to the males three years old or more whose names were in the genealogical records—all who would enter the temple of the LORD to perform the daily duties of their various tasks, according to their responsibilities and their divisions. 17And they distributed to the priests enrolled by their families in the genealogical records and likewise to the Levites twenty years old or more, according to their responsibilities and their divisions. 18They included all the little ones, the wives, and the sons and daughters of the whole community listed in these genealogical records. For they were faithful in consecrating themselves.   2Ch 29:12

19As for the priests, the descendants of Aaron, who lived on the farm lands around their towns or in any other towns, men were designated by name to distribute portions to every

male among them and to all who were recorded in the genealogies of the Levites.

²⁰This is what Hezekiah did throughout Judah, doing what was good and right and faithful before the LORD his God. ²¹In everything that he undertook in the service of God's temple and in obedience to the law and the commands, he sought his God and worked wholeheartedly. And so he prospered.   2Ki 20:3

Sennacherib Threatens Jerusalem

32 After all that Hezekiah had so faithfully done, Sennacherib king of Assyria came and invaded Judah. He laid siege to the fortified cities, thinking to conquer them for himself. ²When Hezekiah saw that Sennacherib had come and that he intended to make war on Jerusalem, ³he consulted with his officials and military staff about blocking off the water from the springs outside the city, and they helped him. ⁴A large force of men assembled, and they blocked all the springs and the stream that flowed through the land. "Why should the kings*a* of Assyria come and find plenty of water?" they said. ⁵Then he worked hard repairing all the broken sections of the wall and building towers on it. He built another wall outside that one and reinforced the supporting terraces*b*

of the City of David. He also made large numbers of weapons and shields.   Isa 36:1

⁶He appointed military officers over the people and assembled them before him in the square at the city gate and encouraged them with these words: ⁷"Be strong and courageous. Do not be afraid or discouraged because of the king of Assyria and the vast army with him, for there is a greater power with us than with him. ⁸With him is only the arm of flesh, but with us is the LORD our God to help us and to fight our battles." And the people gained confidence from what Hezekiah the king of Judah said.   Dt 31:6

⁹Later, when Sennacherib king of Assyria and all his forces were laying siege to Lachish, he sent his officers to Jerusalem with this message for Hezekiah king of Judah and for all the people of Judah who were there: Jos 10:3,31

¹⁰"This is what Sennacherib king of Assyria says: On what are you basing your confidence, that you remain in Jerusalem under siege? ¹¹When Hezekiah says, 'The LORD our God will save us from the hand of the king of Assyria,' he is misleading you, to let you die of hunger and thirst. ¹²Did not Hezekiah himself remove this god's high places and altars, saying to

---

a4 Hebrew; Septuagint and Syriac *king*   *b5* Or *the Millo*

Judah and Jerusalem, 'You must worship before one altar and burn sacrifices on it'? _{Isa 37:10; Eze 29:16}

¹³"Do you not know what I and my fathers have done to all the peoples of the other lands? Were the gods of those nations ever able to deliver their land from my hand? ¹⁴Who of all the gods of these nations that my fathers destroyed has been able to save his people from me? How then can your god deliver you from my hand? ¹⁵Now do not let Hezekiah deceive you and mislead you like this. Do not believe him, for no god of any nation or kingdom has been able to deliver his people from my hand or the hand of my fathers. How much less will your god deliver you from my hand!" _{1Sa 37:10}

¹⁶Sennacherib's officers spoke further against the LORD God and against his servant Hezekiah. ¹⁷The king also wrote letters insulting the LORD, the God of Israel, and saying this against him: "Just as the gods of the peoples of the other lands did not rescue their people from my hand, so the god of Hezekiah will not rescue his people from my hand." ¹⁸Then they called out in Hebrew to the people of Jerusalem who were on the wall, to terrify them and make them afraid in order to capture the city. ¹⁹They spoke about the God of Jerusalem as they did about the gods of the other peoples of the world—the work of men's hands. _{Isa 37:14}

²⁰King Hezekiah and the prophet Isaiah son of Amoz cried out in prayer to heaven about this. ²¹And the LORD sent an angel, who annihilated all the fighting men and the leaders and officers in the camp of the Assyrian king. So he withdrew to his own land in disgrace. And when he went into the temple of his god, some of his sons cut him down with the sword. _{Ge 19:13; Isa 1:15}

²²So the LORD saved Hezekiah and the people of Jerusalem from the hand of Sennacherib king of Assyria and from the hand of all others. He took care of them[a] on every side. ²³Many brought offerings to Jerusalem for the LORD and valuable gifts for Hezekiah king of Judah. From then on he was highly regarded by all the nations. _{1Sa 10:27; 2Ch 9:24}

Hezekiah's Pride, Success and Death

²⁴In those days Hezekiah became ill and was at the point of death. He prayed to the LORD, who answered him and gave him a miraculous sign. ²⁵But Hezekiah's heart was proud and he did not respond to the kindness shown him; therefore the LORD's wrath was

---

_a22 Hebrew; Septuagint and Vulgate *He gave them rest*

on him and on Judah and Jerusalem. 26Then Hezekiah repented of the pride of his heart, as did the people of Jerusalem; therefore the LORD's wrath did not come upon them during the days of Hezekiah.   2Ki 14:10

27Hezekiah had very great riches and honor, and he made treasuries for his silver and gold and for his precious stones, spices, shields and all kinds of valuables. 28He also made buildings to store the harvest of grain, new wine and oil; and he made stalls for various kinds of cattle, and pens for the flocks. 29He built villages and acquired great numbers of flocks and herds, for God had given him very great riches.   1Ch 29:12

30It was Hezekiah who blocked the upper outlet of the Gihon spring and channeled the water down to the west side of the City of David. He succeeded in everything he undertook. 31But when envoys were sent by the rulers of Babylon to ask him about the miraculous sign that had occurred in the land, God left him to test him and to know everything that was in his heart.   2Ki 18:17

32The other events of Hezekiah's reign and his acts of devotion are written in the vision of the prophet Isaiah son of Amoz in the book of the kings of Judah and Israel. 33Hezekiah rested with his fathers and was buried on the hill where the tombs of David's descendants are. All Judah and the people of Jerusalem honored him when he died. And Manasseh his son succeeded him as king.   2Ki 18:19

Manasseh King of Judah

33 Manasseh was twelve years old when he became king, and he reigned in Jerusalem fifty-five years. 2He did evil in the eyes of the LORD, following the detestable practices of the nations the LORD had driven out before the Israelites. 3He rebuilt the high places his father Hezekiah had demolished; he also erected altars to the Baals and made Asherah poles. He bowed down to all the starry hosts and worshiped them. 4He built altars in the temple of the LORD, of which the LORD had said, "My Name will remain in Jerusalem forever." 5In both courts of the temple of the LORD, he built altars to all the starry hosts. 6He sacrificed his sons in a the fire in the Valley of Ben Hinnom, practiced sorcery, divination and witchcraft, and consulted mediums and spiritists. He did much evil in the eyes of the LORD, provoking him to anger.   1Ch 3:13

7He took the carved image he had made and put it in God's temple, of which God had said to David and to his son Solomon, "In this temple and in Jerusalem, which I have chosen out of all the tribes of Israel, I

a6 Or *He made his sons pass through*

will put my Name forever. ⁸I will not again make the feet of the Israelites leave the land I assigned to your forefathers, if only they will be careful to do everything I commanded them concerning all the laws, decrees and ordinances given through Moses." ⁹But Manasseh led Judah and the people of Jerusalem astray, so that they did more evil than the nations the LORD had destroyed before the Israelites.   2Sa 7:10; 2Ch 7:16

¹⁰The LORD spoke to Manasseh and his people, but they paid no attention. ¹¹So the LORD brought against them the army commanders of the king of Assyria, who took Manasseh prisoner, put a hook in his nose, bound him with bronze shackles and took him to Babylon. ¹²In his distress he sought the favor of the LORD his God and humbled himself greatly before the God of his fathers. ¹³And when he prayed to him, the LORD was moved by his entreaty and listened to his plea; so he brought him back to Jerusalem and to his kingdom. Then Manasseh knew that the LORD is God.   Dt 28:36; 2Ch 6:37

¹⁴Afterward he rebuilt the outer wall of the City of David, west of the Gihon spring in the valley, as far as the entrance of the Fish Gate and encircling the hill of Ophel; he also made it much higher. He stationed military commanders in all the fortified cities in Judah.   1Ki 1:33

¹⁵He got rid of the foreign gods and removed the image from the temple of the LORD, as well as all the altars he had built on the temple hill and in Jerusalem; and he threw them out of the city. ¹⁶Then he restored the altar of the LORD and sacrificed fellowship offerings[a] and thank offerings on it, and told Judah to serve the LORD, the God of Israel. ¹⁷The people, however, continued to sacrifice at the high places, but only to the LORD their God.   2Ki 23:12

¹⁸The other events of Manasseh's reign, including his prayer to his God and the words the seers spoke to him in the name of the LORD, the God of Israel, are written in the annals of the kings of Israel.[b] ¹⁹His prayer and how God was moved by his entreaty, as well as all his sins and unfaithfulness, and the sites where he built high places and set up Asherah poles and idols before he humbled himself—all are written in the records of the seers.[c] ²⁰Manasseh rested with his fathers and was buried in his palace. And Amon his son succeeded him as king.   2Ch 6:37

Amon King of Judah

²¹Amon was twenty-two years old when he became king, and he reigned in Jerusalem two

---

[a]16 Traditionally *peace offerings*   [b]18 That is, Judah, as frequently in 2 Chron.
[c]19 One Hebrew manuscript and Septuagint; most Hebrew manuscripts *of Hozai*

years. ²²He did evil in the eyes of the LORD, as his father Manasseh had done. Amon worshiped and offered sacrifices to all the idols Manasseh had made. ²³But unlike his father Manasseh, he did not humble himself before the LORD; Amon increased his guilt.   1Ch 3:14

²⁴Amon's officials conspired against him and assassinated him in his palace. ²⁵Then the people of the land killed all who had plotted against King Amon, and they made Josiah his son king in his place.   2Ch 22:1

Josiah's Reforms

34 Josiah was eight years old when he became king, and he reigned in Jerusalem thirty-one years. ²He did what was right in the eyes of the LORD and walked in the ways of his father David, not turning aside to the right or to the left. ³In the eighth year of his reign, while he was still young, he began to seek the God of his father David. In his twelfth year he began to purge Judah and Jerusalem of high places, Asherah poles, carved idols and cast images. ⁴Under his direction the altars of the Baals were torn down; he cut to pieces the incense altars that were above them, and smashed the Asherah poles, the idols and the images. These he broke to pieces and scattered over the graves of those who had sacrificed to them. ⁵He burned the bones of the priests on their altars, and so he purged Judah and Jerusalem. ⁶In the towns of Manasseh, Ephraim and Simeon, as far as Naphtali, and in the ruins around them, ⁷he tore down the altars and the Asherah poles and crushed the idols to powder and cut to pieces all the incense altars throughout Israel. Then he went back to Jerusalem.   1Ch 16:11

⁸In the eighteenth year of Josiah's reign, to purify the land and the temple, he sent Shaphan son of Azaliah and Maaseiah the ruler of the city, with Joah son of Joahaz, the recorder, to repair the temple of the LORD his God.   2Ki 22:3-20

⁹They went to Hilkiah the high priest and gave him the money that had been brought into the temple of God, which the Levites who were the doorkeepers had collected from the people of Manasseh, Ephraim and the entire remnant of Israel and from all the people of Judah and Benjamin and the inhabitants of Jerusalem. ¹⁰Then they entrusted it to the men appointed to supervise the work on the LORD's temple. These men paid the workers who repaired and restored the temple. ¹¹They also gave money to the carpenters and builders to purchase dressed stone, and timber for joists and beams for the buildings that the kings of Judah had allowed to fall into ruin.   1Ch 6:13; 2Ch 24:12

¹²The men did the work faithfully. Over them to direct them

were Jahath and Obadiah, Levites descended from Merari, and Zechariah and Meshullam, descended from Kohath. The Levites—all who were skilled in playing musical instruments— [13]had charge of the laborers and supervised all the workers from job to job. Some of the Levites were secretaries, scribes and doorkeepers. 2Ki 12:15

The Book of the Law Found

[14]While they were bringing out the money that had been taken into the temple of the LORD, Hilkiah the priest found the Book of the Law of the LORD that had been given through Moses. [15]Hilkiah said to Shaphan the secretary, "I have found the Book of the Law in the temple of the LORD." He gave it to Shaphan. 2Ki 22:8

[16]Then Shaphan took the book to the king and reported to him: "Your officials are doing everything that has been committed to them. [17]They have paid out the money that was in the temple of the LORD and have entrusted it to the supervisors and workers." [18]Then Shaphan the secretary informed the king, "Hilkiah the priest has given me a book." And Shaphan read from it in the presence of the king.

[19]When the king heard the words of the Law, he tore his robes. [20]He gave these orders to Hilkiah, Ahikam son of Shaphan, Abdon son of Micah,[a] Shaphan the secretary and Asaiah the king's attendant: [21]"Go and inquire of the LORD for me and for the remnant in Israel and Judah about what is written in this book that has been found. Great is the LORD's anger that is poured out on us because our fathers have not kept the word of the LORD; they have not acted in accordance with all that is written in this book." Dt 28:3-68; La 2:4

[22]Hilkiah and those the king had sent with him[b] went to speak to the prophetess Huldah, who was the wife of Shallum son of Tokhath,[c] the son of Hasrah,[d] keeper of the wardrobe. She lived in Jerusalem, in the Second District. Ex 15:20

[23]She said to them, "This is what the LORD, the God of Israel, says: Tell the man who sent you to me, [24]'This is what the LORD says: I am going to bring disaster on this place and its people—all the curses written in the book that has been read in the presence of the king of Judah. [25]Because they have forsaken me and burned incense to other gods and provoked me to anger by all that their hands have made,[e] my anger will be poured out on this place and will not be quenched.' [26]Tell the king of Judah, who sent you to inquire of the LORD,

---

[a]20 Also called *Acbor son of Micaiah*   [b]22 One Hebrew manuscript, Vulgate and Syriac; most Hebrew manuscripts do not have *had sent with him*.   [c]22 Also called *Tikvah*   [d]22 Also called *Harhas*   [e]25 Or *by everything they have done*

'This is what the LORD, the God of Israel, says concerning the words you heard: ²⁷Because your heart was responsive and you humbled yourself before God when you heard what he spoke against this place and its people, and because you humbled yourself before me and tore your robes and wept in my presence, I have heard you, declares the LORD. ²⁸Now I will gather you to your fathers, and you will be buried in peace. Your eyes will not see all the disaster I am going to bring on this place and on those who live here.' "   2Ch 32:26; Pr 16:4

So they took her answer back to the king.

²⁹Then the king called together all the elders of Judah and Jerusalem. ³⁰He went up to the temple of the LORD with the men of Judah, the people of Jerusalem, the priests and the Levites—all the people from the least to the greatest. He read in their hearing all the words of the Book of the Covenant, which had been found in the temple of the LORD. ³¹The king stood by his pillar and renewed the covenant in the presence of the LORD—to follow the LORD and keep his commands, regulations and decrees with all his heart and all his soul, and to obey the words of the covenant written in this book.   2Ki 23:2

³²Then he had everyone in Jerusalem and Benjamin pledge themselves to it; the people of Jerusalem did this in accordance with the covenant of God, the God of their fathers.

³³Josiah removed all the detestable idols from all the territory belonging to the Israelites, and he had all who were present in Israel serve the LORD their God. As long as he lived, they did not fail to follow the LORD, the God of their fathers.

Josiah Celebrates the Passover

35 Josiah celebrated the Passover to the LORD in Jerusalem, and the Passover lamb was slaughtered on the fourteenth day of the first month. ²He appointed the priests to their duties and encouraged them in the service of the LORD's temple. ³He said to the Levites, who instructed all Israel and who had been consecrated to the LORD: "Put the sacred ark in the temple that Solomon son of David king of Israel built. It is not to be carried about on your shoulders. Now serve the LORD your God and his people Israel. ⁴Prepare yourselves by families in your divisions, according to the directions written by David king of Israel and by his son Solomon.

⁵"Stand in the holy place with a group of Levites for each subdivision of the families of your fellow countrymen, the lay people. ⁶Slaughter the Passover lambs, consecrate yourselves and prepare the lambs for your fellow countrymen, doing what

the LORD commanded through Moses." Lev 11:44

7Josiah provided for all the lay people who were there a total of thirty thousand sheep and goats for the Passover offerings, and also three thousand cattle—all from the king's own possessions. 2Ch 30:24

8His officials also contributed voluntarily to the people and the priests and Levites. Hilkiah, Zechariah and Jehiel, the administrators of God's temple, gave the priests twenty-six hundred Passover offerings and three hundred cattle. 9Also Conaniah along with Shemaiah and Nethanel, his brothers, and Hashabiah, Jeiel and Jozabad, the leaders of the Levites, provided five thousand Passover offerings and five hundred head of cattle for the Levites.

10The service was arranged and the priests stood in their places with the Levites in their divisions as the king had ordered. 11The Passover lambs were slaughtered, and the priests sprinkled the blood handed to them, while the Levites skinned the animals. 12They set aside the burnt offerings to give them to the subdivisions of the families of the people to offer to the LORD, as is written in the Book of Moses. They did the same with the cattle. 13They roasted the Passover animals over the fire as prescribed, and boiled the holy offerings in pots, caldrons and pans and served them quickly to all the people. 14After this, they made preparations for themselves and for the priests, because the priests, the descendants of Aaron, were sacrificing the burnt offerings and the fat portions until nightfall. So the Levites made preparations for themselves and for the Aaronic priests. 2Ch 30:16

15The musicians, the descendants of Asaph, were in the places prescribed by David, Asaph, Heman and Jeduthun the king's seer. The gatekeepers at each gate did not need to leave their posts, because their fellow Levites made the preparations for them. 1Ch 25:1

16So at that time the entire service of the LORD was carried out for the celebration of the Passover and the offering of burnt offerings on the altar of the LORD, as King Josiah had ordered. 17The Israelites who were present celebrated the Passover at that time and observed the Feast of Unleavened Bread for seven days. 18The Passover had not been observed like this in Israel since the days of the prophet Samuel; and none of the kings of Israel had ever celebrated such a Passover as did Josiah, with the priests, the Levites and all Judah and Israel who were there with the people of Jerusalem. 19This Passover was celebrated in the eighteenth year of Josiah's reign.

The Death of Josiah

20After all this, when Josiah

had set the temple in order, Neco king of Egypt went up to fight at Carchemish on the Euphrates, and Josiah marched out to meet him in battle. 21But Neco sent messengers to him, saying, "What quarrel is there between you and me, O king of Judah? It is not you I am attacking at this time, but the house with which I am at war. God has told me to hurry; so stop opposing God, who is with me, or he will destroy you."   Isa 10:9

22Josiah, however, would not turn away from him, but disguised himself to engage him in battle. He would not listen to what Neco had said at God's command but went to fight him on the plain of Megiddo. 1Sa 28:8

23Archers shot King Josiah, and he told his officers, "Take me away; I am badly wounded." 24So they took him out of his chariot, put him in the other chariot he had and brought him to Jerusalem, where he died. He was buried in the tombs of his fathers, and all Judah and Jerusalem mourned for him.

25Jeremiah composed laments for Josiah, and to this day all the men and women singers commemorate Josiah in the laments. These became a tradition in Israel and are written in the Laments.   Ge 50:10; 2Ch 34:28

26The other events of Josiah's reign and his acts of devotion, according to what is written in the Law of the LORD— 27all the events, from beginning to end, are written in the book of the kings of Israel and Judah. 1And the people of the land took Jehoahaz son of Josiah and made him king in Jerusalem in place of his father.

36

Jehoahaz King of Judah

2Jehoahaz[a] was twenty-three years old when he became king, and he reigned in Jerusalem three months. 3The king of Egypt dethroned him in Jerusalem and imposed on Judah a levy of a hundred talents[b] of silver and a talent[c] of gold. 4The king of Egypt made Eliakim, a brother of Jehoahaz, king over Judah and Jerusalem and changed Eliakim's name to Jehoiakim. But Neco took Eliakim's brother Jehoahaz and carried him off to Egypt.   Jer 22:10-12

Jehoiakim King of Judah

5Jehoiakim was twenty-five years old when he became king, and he reigned in Jerusalem eleven years. He did evil in the eyes of the LORD his God. 6Nebuchadnezzar king of Babylon attacked him and bound him with bronze shackles to take him to Babylon. 7Nebuchadnezzar also took to Babylon articles from the temple of the LORD and put them in his temple[d] there.   Ezr 1:7; Jer 22:18

---

a2 Hebrew *Joahaz*, a variant of *Jehoahaz*; also in verse 4   b3 That is, about 3 3/4 tons (about 3.4 metric tons)   c3 That is, about 75 pounds (about 34 kilograms)   d7 Or *palace*

⁸The other events of Jehoiakim's reign, the detestable things he did and all that was found against him, are written in the book of the kings of Israel and Judah. And Jehoiachin his son succeeded him as king.

Jehoiachin King of Judah

⁹Jehoiachin was eighteen*a* years old when he became king, and he reigned in Jerusalem three months and ten days. He did evil in the eyes of the LORD. ¹⁰In the spring, King Nebuchadnezzar sent for him and brought him to Babylon, together with articles of value from the temple of the LORD, and he made Jehoiachin's uncle,*b* Zedekiah, king over Judah and Jerusalem.   Jer 22:24-28

Zedekiah King of Judah

¹¹Zedekiah was twenty-one years old when he became king, and he reigned in Jerusalem eleven years. ¹²He did evil in the eyes of the LORD his God and did not humble himself before Jeremiah the prophet, who spoke the word of the LORD. ¹³He also rebelled against King Nebuchadnezzar, who had made him take an oath in God's name. He became stiff-necked and hardened his heart and would not turn to the LORD, the God of Israel. ¹⁴Furthermore, all the leaders of the priests and the people became more and more unfaithful, following all the detestable practices of the nations and defiling the temple of the LORD, which he had consecrated in Jerusalem.   2Ki 24:17

The Fall of Jerusalem

¹⁵The LORD, the God of their fathers, sent word to them through his messengers again and again, because he had pity on his people and on his dwelling place. ¹⁶But they mocked God's messengers, despised his words and scoffed at his prophets until the wrath of the LORD was aroused against his people and there was no remedy. ¹⁷He brought up against them the king of the Babylonians,*c* who killed their young men with the sword in the sanctuary, and spared neither young man nor young woman, old man or aged. God handed all of them over to Nebuchadnezzar. ¹⁸He carried to Babylon all the articles from the temple of God, both large and small, and the treasures of the LORD's temple and the treasures of the king and his officials. ¹⁹They set fire to God's temple and broke down the wall of Jerusalem; they burned all the palaces and destroyed everything of value there.   Isa 5:4

²⁰He carried into exile to Babylon the remnant, who escaped from the sword, and they

---

a9 One Hebrew manuscript, some Septuagint manuscripts and Syriac (see also 2 Kings 24:8); most Hebrew manuscripts *eight*   *b10* Hebrew *brother*, that is, relative (see 2 Kings 24:17)   *c17* Or *Chaldeans*

became servants to him and his sons until the kingdom of Persia came to power. ²¹The land enjoyed its sabbath rests; all the time of its desolation it rested, until the seventy years were completed in fulfillment of the word of the LORD spoken by Jeremiah.   Lev 26:44

²²In the first year of Cyrus king of Persia, in order to fulfill the word of the LORD spoken by Jeremiah, the LORD moved the heart of Cyrus king of Persia to make a proclamation throughout his realm and to put it in writing: Isa 44:28; 45:1

²³"This is what Cyrus king of Persia says:

" 'The LORD, the God of heaven, has given me all the kingdoms of the earth and he has appointed me to build a temple for him at Jerusalem in Judah. Anyone of his people among you—may the LORD his God be with him, and let him go up.' "   Jdg 4:10

Ezra

Introduction:

The book of Ezra tells about the return of the Jews from exile in Babylon. It begins in 539 B.C. with the decree of Cyrus, king of Persia, which allowed the people to go back to Jerusalem under the leadership of Zerubbabel. The people enthusiastically began rebuilding the temple and resumed sacrifices. But for eighteen years they were delayed by their enemies from the north. Finally, in 521 B.C. a decree from Darius, king of Persia, let them finish. The people completed and dedicated the temple in 515 B.C.

In 458 B.C. Ezra, the priest, returned to Jerusalem with another group of Babylonian exiles. He taught the people the law and reformed their religious life so the other nations around them could see they were God's chosen nation.

Ezra is the author of the books of Ezra and Nehemiah.

Outline of contents:

The first exiles return to the land of Judah (1:1–2:70)
The temple is rebuilt (3:1–6:22)
Ezra's return and ministry (7:1–10:44)

Cyrus Helps the Exiles to Return

1 In the first year of Cyrus king of Persia, in order to fulfill the word of the LORD spoken by Jeremiah, the LORD moved the heart of Cyrus king of Persia to make a proclamation throughout his realm and to put it in writing: Jer 25:12

2"This is what Cyrus king of Persia says:

" 'The LORD, the God of heaven, has given me all the kingdoms of the earth and he has appointed me to build a temple for him at Jerusalem in Judah. 3Anyone of his people among you—may his God be with him, and let him go up to Jerusalem in Judah and build the temple of the LORD, the God of Israel, the God who is in Jerusalem. 4And the people of any place where survivors may now be living are to provide

him with silver and gold, with goods and livestock, and with freewill offerings for the temple of God in Jerusalem.'" Nu 15:3; Isa 44:28

5Then the family heads of Judah and Benjamin, and the priests and Levites—everyone whose heart God had moved—prepared to go up and build the house of the LORD in Jerusalem. 6All their neighbors assisted them with articles of silver and gold, with goods and livestock, and with valuable gifts, in addition to all the freewill offerings. 7Moreover, King Cyrus brought out the articles belonging to the temple of the LORD, which Nebuchadnezzar had carried away from Jerusalem and had placed in the temple of his god.a 8Cyrus king of Persia had them brought by Mithredath the treasurer, who counted them out to Sheshbazzar the prince of Judah. Php 2:13

9This was the inventory:

gold dishes	30
silver dishes	1,000
silver pansb	29
10gold bowls	30
matching silver bowls	410
other articles	1,000

11In all, there were 5,400 articles of gold and of silver. Sheshbazzar brought all these along when the exiles came up from Babylon to Jerusalem. 1Ki 7:50

The List of the Exiles Who Returned

2 Now these are the people of the province who came up from the captivity of the exiles, whom Nebuchadnezzar king of Babylon had taken captive to Babylon (they returned to Jerusalem and Judah, each to his own town, 2in company with Zerubbabel, Jeshua, Nehemiah, Seraiah, Reelaiah, Mordecai, Bilshan, Mispar, Bigvai, Rehum and Baanah): 2Ch 36:20

The list of the men of the people of Israel:

3the descendants of Parosh	2,172
4of Shephatiah	372
5of Arah	775
6of Pahath-Moab (through the line of Jeshua and Joab)	2,812
7of Elam	1,254
8of Zattu	945
9of Zaccai	760
10of Bani	642
11of Bebai	623
12of Azgad	1,222
13of Adonikam	666
14of Bigvai	2,056
15of Adin	454
16of Ater (through Hezekiah)	98
17of Bezai	323
18of Jorah	112
19of Hashum	223
20of Gibbar	95
21the men of Bethlehem	123
22of Netophah	56

a7 Or gods   b9 The meaning of the Hebrew for this word is uncertain.

²³of Anathoth   128
²⁴of Azmaveth   42
²⁵of Kiriath Jearim,ᵃ
  Kephirah and
  Beeroth   743
²⁶of Ramah and Geba   621
²⁷of Micmash   122
²⁸of Bethel and Ai   223
²⁹of Nebo   52
³⁰of Magbish   156
³¹of the other Elam   1,254
³²of Harim   320
³³of Lod, Hadid and
  Ono   725
³⁴of Jericho   345
³⁵of Senaah   3,630

³⁶The priests: 1Ch 24:7

the descendants of
  Jedaiah (through the
  family of Jeshua)   973
³⁷of Immer   1,052
³⁸of Pashhur   1,247
³⁹of Harim   1,017

⁴⁰The Levites: Ge 39:34; Nu 3:9

the descendants of Jeshua
  and Kadmiel (through
  the line of Hodaviah) 74

⁴¹The singers: 1Ch 15:16

the descendants of
  Asaph   128

⁴²The gatekeepers of the
temple: 1Sa 3:15; 1Ch 9:17

the descendants of
  Shallum, Ater, Talmon,
  Akkub, Hatita and
  Shobai   139

⁴³The temple servants: 1Ch 9:2

the descendants of
  Ziha, Hasupha,
  Tabbaoth,
⁴⁴Keros, Siaha, Padon,
⁴⁵Lebanah, Hagabah,
  Akkub,
⁴⁶Hagab, Shalmai, Hanan,
⁴⁷Giddel, Gahar, Reaiah,
⁴⁸Rezin, Nekoda, Gazzam,
⁴⁹Uzza, Paseah, Besai,
⁵⁰Asnah, Meunim,
  Nephussim,
⁵¹Bakbuk, Hakupha,
  Harhur,
⁵²Bazluth, Mehida,
  Harsha,
⁵³Barkos, Sisera, Temah,
⁵⁴Neziah and Hatipha

⁵⁵The descendants of the
servants of Solomon: Ne 7:57

the descendants of
  Sotai, Hassophereth,
  Peruda,
⁵⁶Jaala, Darkon, Giddel,
⁵⁷Shephatiah, Hattil,
  Pokereth-Hazzebaim and
  Ami

⁵⁸The temple servants and
  the descendants of the
  servants of Solomon 392

⁵⁹The following came up
from the towns of Tel
Melah, Tel Harsha, Kerub,
Addon and Immer, but
they could not show that
their families were descended from Israel: Nu 1:18

⁶⁰The descendants of
  Delaiah, Tobiah and
  Nekoda   652

ᵃ25 See Septuagint (see also Neh. 7:29); Hebrew *Kiriath Arim.*

⁶¹And from among the priests: 2Sa 17:27

The descendants of
Hobaiah, Hakkoz and
Barzillai (a man who had
married a daughter of
Barzillai the Gileadite
and was called by that
name).
⁶²These searched for their
family records, but they
could not find them and so
were excluded from the
priesthood as unclean.
⁶³The governor ordered
them not to eat any of the
most sacred food until there
was a priest ministering
with the Urim and Thummim. Lev 2:3,10; Nu 3:10

⁶⁴The whole company
numbered 42,360, ⁶⁵besides
their 7,337 menservants
and maidservants; and they
also had 200 men and
women singers. ⁶⁶They had
736 horses, 245 mules, ⁶⁷435
camels and 6,720 donkeys.

⁶⁸When they arrived at the
house of the LORD in Jerusalem,
some of the heads of the families
gave freewill offerings
toward the rebuilding of the
house of God on its site. ⁶⁹According
to their ability they gave
to the treasury for this work 61,-
000 drachmas*a* of gold, 5,000
minas*b* of silver and 100 priestly
garments. Ex 25:2; Ezr 8:25-34
⁷⁰The priests, the Levites, the

singers, the gatekeepers and
the temple servants settled in
their own towns, along with
some of the other people, and
the rest of the Israelites settled
in their towns. 1Ch 9:2; Ne 11:3-4

Rebuilding the Altar

3 When the seventh month
came and the Israelites had
settled in their towns, the
people assembled as one man in
Jerusalem. ²Then Jeshua son of
Jozadak and his fellow priests
and Zerubbabel son of Shealtiel
and his associates began to
build the altar of the God of Israel
to sacrifice burnt offerings
on it, in accordance with what is
written in the Law of Moses the
man of God. ³Despite their fear
of the peoples around them,
they built the altar on its foundation
and sacrificed burnt offerings
on it to the LORD, both
the morning and evening sacrifices.
⁴Then in accordance with
what is written, they celebrated
the Feast of Tabernacles with
the required number of burnt
offerings prescribed for each
day. ⁵After that, they presented
the regular burnt offerings, the
New Moon sacrifices and the
sacrifices for all the appointed
sacred feasts of the LORD, as
well as those brought as freewill
offerings to the LORD. ⁶On the
first day of the seventh month
they began to offer burnt offerings
to the LORD, though the

a69 That is, about 1,100 pounds (about 500 kilograms)
(about 2.9 metric tons) *b69* That is, about 3 tons

foundation of the LORD's temple had not yet been laid. Ne 7:73

Rebuilding the Temple

7Then they gave money to the masons and carpenters, and gave food and drink and oil to the people of Sidon and Tyre, so that they would bring cedar logs by sea from Lebanon to Joppa, as authorized by Cyrus king of Persia. 1Ch 22:15; Isa 35:2; 60:13

8In the second month of the second year after their arrival at the house of God in Jerusalem, Zerubbabel son of Shealtiel, Jeshua son of Jozadak and the rest of their brothers (the priests and the Levites and all who had returned from the captivity to Jerusalem) began the work, appointing Levites twenty years of age and older to supervise the building of the house of the LORD. 9Jeshua and his sons and brothers and Kadmiel and his sons (descendants of Hodaviah[a]) and the sons of Henadad and their sons and brothers—all Levites—joined together in supervising those working on the house of God. Ezr 2:40; Zec 4:9

10When the builders laid the foundation of the temple of the LORD, the priests in their vestments and with trumpets, and the Levites (the sons of Asaph) with cymbals, took their places to praise the LORD, as prescribed by David king of Israel. 11With praise and thanksgiving they sang to the LORD: 1Ch 16:6

"He is good;
    his love to Israel endures
        forever." 1Ch 16:34

And all the people gave a great shout of praise to the LORD, because the foundation of the house of the LORD was laid. 12But many of the older priests and Levites and family heads, who had seen the former temple, wept aloud when they saw the foundation of this temple being laid, while many others shouted for joy. 13No one could distinguish the sound of the shouts of joy from the sound of weeping, because the people made so much noise. And the sound was heard far away.

Opposition to the Rebuilding

4 When the enemies of Judah and Benjamin heard that the exiles were building a temple for the LORD, the God of Israel, 2they came to Zerubbabel and to the heads of the families and said, "Let us help you build because, like you, we seek your God and have been sacrificing to him since the time of Esarhaddon king of Assyria, who brought us here." 2Ki 17:24

3But Zerubbabel, Jeshua and the rest of the heads of the families of Israel answered, "You have no part with us in building a temple to our God. We alone will build it for the LORD, the God of Israel, as King Cyrus, the king of Persia, commanded us." Ezr 1:1-4; Ne 2:20

a9 Hebrew Yehudah, probably a variant of Hodaviah

⁴Then the peoples around them set out to discourage the people of Judah and make them afraid to go on building. *a* ⁵They hired counselors to work against them and frustrate their plans during the entire reign of Cyrus king of Persia and down to the reign of Darius king of Persia.   Ezr 3:3; 5:5

Later Opposition Under Xerxes and Artaxerxes

⁶At the beginning of the reign of Xerxes, *b* they lodged an accusation against the people of Judah and Jerusalem.   Da 9:1

⁷And in the days of Artaxerxes king of Persia, Bishlam, Mithredath, Tabeel and the rest of his associates wrote a letter to Artaxerxes. The letter was written in Aramaic script and in the Aramaic language. *c,d*   2Ki 18:26

⁸Rehum the commanding officer and Shimshai the secretary wrote a letter against Jerusalem to Artaxerxes the king as follows:

⁹Rehum the commanding officer and Shimshai the secretary, together with the rest of their associates—the judges and officials over the men from Tripolis, Persia, *e* Erech and Babylon, the Elamites of Susa, ¹⁰and the other people whom the great and honorable Ashur-

banipal *f* deported and settled in the city of Samaria and elsewhere in Trans-Euphrates.   Ne 1:1; Da 8:2

¹¹(This is a copy of the letter they sent him.)

To King Artaxerxes,

From your servants, the men of Trans-Euphrates:

¹²The king should know that the Jews who came up to us from you have gone to Jerusalem and are rebuilding that rebellious and wicked city. They are restoring the walls and repairing the foundations.   Ezr 5:3,9

¹³Furthermore, the king should know that if this city is built and its walls are restored, no more taxes, tribute or duty will be paid, and the royal revenues will suffer. ¹⁴Now since we are under obligation to the palace and it is not proper for us to see the king dishonored, we are sending this message to inform the king, ¹⁵so that a search may be made in the archives of your predecessors. In these records you will find that this city is a rebellious city, troublesome to kings and provinces, a place of rebellion from ancient times. That is why this city was de-

---

*a*4 Or *and troubled them as they built*   *b*6 Hebrew *Ahasuerus,* a variant of Xerxes' Persian name   *c*7 Or *written in Aramaic and translated*   *d*7 The text of Ezra 4:8— 6:18 is in Aramaic   *e*9 Or *officials, magistrates and governors over the men from* *f*10 Aramaic *Osnappar,* a variant of Ashurbanipal

stroyed. 16We inform the king that if this city is built and its walls are restored, you will be left with nothing in Trans-Euphrates.   Ezr 7:24

17The king sent this reply:

To Rehum the commanding officer, Shimshai the secretary and the rest of their associates living in Samaria and elsewhere in Trans-Euphrates: Ezr 4:10

Greetings.

18The letter you sent us has been read and translated in my presence. 19I issued an order and a search was made, and it was found that this city has a long history of revolt against kings and has been a place of rebellion and sedition. 20Jerusalem has had powerful kings ruling over the whole of Trans-Euphrates, and taxes, tribute and duty were paid to them. 21Now issue an order to these men to stop work, so that this city will not be rebuilt until I so order. 22Be careful not to neglect this matter. Why let this threat grow, to the detriment of the royal interests?   1Ki 4:21; Ps 72:8; Da 6:2

23As soon as the copy of the letter of King Artaxerxes was read to Rehum and Shimshai the secretary and their asso-

ciates, they went immediately to the Jews in Jerusalem and compelled them by force to stop.   Ezr 4:9; Pr 4:16

24Thus the work on the house of God in Jerusalem came to a standstill until the second year of the reign of Darius king of Persia.   Da 9:25; Hag 1:15; Zec 1:1

Tattenai's Letter to Darius

5 Now Haggai the prophet and Zechariah the prophet, a descendant of Iddo, prophesied to the Jews in Judah and Jerusalem in the name of the God of Israel, who was over them. 2Then Zerubbabel son of Shealtiel and Jeshua son of Jozadak set to work to rebuild the house of God in Jerusalem. And the prophets of God were with them, helping them.   Hag 1:1

3At that time Tattenai, governor of Trans-Euphrates, and Shethar-Bozenai and their associates went to them and asked, "Who authorized you to rebuild this temple and restore this structure?" 4They also asked, "What are the names of the men constructing this building?" a 5But the eye of their God was watching over the elders of the Jews, and they were not stopped until a report could go to Darius and his written reply be received.   Ezr 6:6; Ps 33:18

6This is a copy of the letter that Tattenai, governor of Trans-Euphrates, and Shethar-

a4 See Septuagint; Aramaic 4We told them the names of the men constructing this building.

Bozenai and their associates, the officials of Trans-Euphrates, sent to King Darius. 7The report they sent him read as follows:

To King Darius:

Cordial greetings.

8The king should know that we went to the district of Judah, to the temple of the great God. The people are building it with large stones and placing the timbers in the walls. The work is being carried on with diligence and is making rapid progress under their direction.   Ezr 5:2

9We questioned the elders and asked them, "Who authorized you to rebuild this temple and restore this structure?" 10We also asked them their names, so that we could write down the names of their leaders for your information.   Ezr 4:12

11This is the answer they gave us:

"We are the servants of the God of heaven and earth, and we are rebuilding the temple that was built many years ago, one that a great king of Israel built and finished. 12But because our fathers angered the God of heaven, he handed them over to Nebuchadnezzar the Chaldean,

king of Babylon, who destroyed this temple and deported the people to Babylon.   1Ki 6:1; 2Ch 36:16

13"However, in the first year of Cyrus king of Babylon, King Cyrus issued a decree to rebuild this house of God. 14He even removed from the templeᵃ of Babylon the gold and silver articles of the house of God, which Nebuchadnezzar had taken from the temple in Jerusalem and brought to the templeᵃ in Babylon.

"Then King Cyrus gave them to a man named Sheshbazzar, whom he had appointed governor, 15and he told him, 'Take these articles and go and deposit them in the temple in Jerusalem. And rebuild the house of God on its site.' 16So this Sheshbazzar came and laid the foundations of the house of God in Jerusalem. From that day to the present it has been under construction but is not yet finished."   Ezr 1:7; 3:10

17Now if it pleases the king, let a search be made in the royal archives of Babylon to see if King Cyrus did in fact issue a decree to rebuild this house of God in Jerusalem. Then let the king send us his decision in this matter.   Ezr 4:15; 6:1-2

ᵃ14 Or palace

The Decree of Darius

6 King Darius then issued an order, and they searched in the archives stored in the treasury at Babylon. [2]A scroll was found in the citadel of Ecbatana in the province of Media, and this was written on it: Ezr 4:15

Memorandum:

[3]In the first year of King Cyrus, the king issued a decree concerning the temple of God in Jerusalem:

Let the temple be rebuilt as a place to present sacrifices, and let its foundations be laid. It is to be ninety feet[a] high and ninety feet wide, [4]with three courses of large stones and one of timbers. The costs are to be paid by the royal treasury. [5]Also, the gold and silver articles of the house of God, which Nebuchadnezzar took from the temple in Jerusalem and brought to Babylon, are to be returned to their places in the temple in Jerusalem; they are to be deposited in the house of God. 1Ch 29:2; Ezr 1:7; Hag 2:3

[6]Now then, Tattenai, governor of Trans-Euphrates, and Shethar-Bozenai and you, their fellow officials of that province, stay away from there. [7]Do not interfere with the work on this temple of God. Let the governor of the Jews and the Jewish elders rebuild this house of God on its site.

[8]Moreover, I hereby decree what you are to do for these elders of the Jews in the construction of this house of God:

The expenses of these men are to be fully paid out of the royal treasury, from the revenues of Trans-Euphrates, so that the work will not stop, [9]Whatever is needed—young bulls, rams, male lambs for burnt offerings to the God of heaven, and wheat, salt, wine and oil, as requested by the priests in Jerusalem—must be given them daily without fail, [10]so that they may offer sacrifices pleasing to the God of heaven and pray for the well-being of the king and his sons. 1Sa 9:20; Ezr 7:23

[11]Furthermore, I decree that if anyone changes this edict, a beam is to be pulled from his house and he is to be lifted up and impaled on it. And for this crime his house is to be made a pile of rubble. [12]May God, who has caused his Name to dwell there, overthrow any king or people who lifts a hand to change this decree or to destroy this temple in Jerusalem. Dt 12:5; Da 2:5

[a]3 Aramaic *sixty cubits* (about 27 meters)

I Darius have decreed it. Let it be carried out with diligence.

Completion and Dedication of the Temple

¹³Then, because of the decree King Darius had sent, Tattenai, governor of Trans-Euphrates, and Shethar-Bozenai and their associates carried it out with diligence. ¹⁴So the elders of the Jews continued to build and prosper under the preaching of Haggai the prophet and Zechariah, a descendant of Iddo. They finished building the temple according to the command of the God of Israel and the decrees of Cyrus, Darius and Artaxerxes, kings of Persia. ¹⁵The temple was completed on the third day of the month Adar, in the sixth year of the reign of King Darius. Ezr 5:1; Zec 4:9

¹⁶Then the people of Israel—the priests, the Levites and the rest of the exiles—celebrated the dedication of the house of God with joy. ¹⁷For the dedication of this house of God they offered a hundred bulls, two hundred rams, four hundred male lambs and, as a sin offering for all Israel, twelve male goats, one for each of the tribes of Israel. ¹⁸And they installed the priests in their divisions and the Levites in their groups for the service of God at Jerusalem, according to what is written in the Book of Moses. Nu 3:6; 1Ki 8:63

The Passover

¹⁹On the fourteenth day of the first month, the exiles celebrated the Passover. ²⁰The priests and Levites had purified themselves and were all ceremonially clean. The Levites slaughtered the Passover lamb for all the exiles, for their brothers the priests and for themselves. ²¹So the Israelites who had returned from the exile ate it, together with all who had separated themselves from the unclean practices of their Gentile neighbors in order to seek the Lord, the God of Israel. ²²For seven days they celebrated with joy the Feast of Unleavened Bread, because the Lord had filled them with joy by changing the attitude of the king of Assyria, so that he assisted them in the work on the house of God, the God of Israel.

Ezra Comes to Jerusalem

7 After these things, during the reign of Artaxerxes king of Persia, Ezra son of Seraiah, the son of Azariah, the son of Hilkiah, ²the son of Shallum, the son of Zadok, the son of Ahitub, ³the son of Amariah, the son of Azariah, the son of Meraioth, ⁴the son of Zerahiah, the son of Uzzi, the son of Bukki, ⁵the son of Abishua, the son of Phinehas, the son of Eleazar, the son of Aaron the chief priest— ⁶this Ezra came up from Babylon. He was a teacher well versed in the Law of Moses,

which the LORD, the God of Israel, had given. The king had granted him everything he asked, for the hand of the LORD his God was on him. ⁷Some of the Israelites, including priests, Levites, singers, gatekeepers and temple servants, also came up to Jerusalem in the seventh year of King Artaxerxes.   Ezr 8:1

⁸Ezra arrived in Jerusalem in the fifth month of the seventh year of the king. ⁹He had begun his journey from Babylon on the first day of the first month, and he arrived in Jerusalem on the first day of the fifth month, for the gracious hand of his God was on him. ¹⁰For Ezra had devoted himself to the study and observance of the Law of the LORD, and to teaching its decrees and laws in Israel.   Dt 33:10

King Artaxerxes' Letter to Ezra

¹¹This is a copy of the letter King Artaxerxes had given to Ezra the priest and teacher, a man learned in matters concerning the commands and decrees of the LORD for Israel:

¹²ªArtaxerxes, king of kings,   Eze 26:7; Da 2:37

To Ezra the priest, a teacher of the Law of the God of heaven:

Greetings.

¹³Now I decree that any of the Israelites in my kingdom, including priests and Levites, who wish to go to Jerusalem with you, may go. ¹⁴You are sent by the king and his seven advisers to inquire about Judah and Jerusalem with regard to the Law of your God, which is in your hand. ¹⁵Moreover, you are to take with you the silver and gold that the king and his advisers have freely given to the God of Israel, whose dwelling is in Jerusalem, ¹⁶together with all the silver and gold you may obtain from the province of Babylon, as well as the freewill offerings of the people and priests for the temple of their God in Jerusalem. ¹⁷With this money be sure to buy bulls, rams and male lambs, together with their grain offerings and drink offerings, and sacrifice them on the altar of the temple of your God in Jerusalem.   Est 1:14

¹⁸You and your brother Jews may then do whatever seems best with the rest of the silver and gold, in accordance with the will of your God. ¹⁹Deliver to the God of Jerusalem all the articles entrusted to you for worship in the temple of your God. ²⁰And anything else needed for the temple of your God that you may have occasion

---

ª12 The text of Ezra 7:12-26 is in Aramaic.

to supply, you may provide from the royal treasury. Ezr 6:4

21Now I, King Artaxerxes, order all the treasurers of Trans-Euphrates to provide with diligence whatever Ezra the priest, a teacher of the Law of the God of heaven, may ask of you— 22up to a hundred talents[a] of silver, a hundred cors[b] of wheat, a hundred baths[c] of wine, a hundred baths[c] of olive oil, and salt without limit. 23Whatever the God of heaven has prescribed, let it be done with diligence for the temple of the God of heaven. Why should there be wrath against the realm of the king and of his sons? 24You are also to know that you have no authority to impose taxes, tribute or duty on any of the priests, Levites, singers, gatekeepers, temple servants or other workers at this house of God. Ezr 6:10

25And you, Ezra, in accordance with the wisdom of your God, which you possess, appoint magistrates and judges to administer justice to all the people of Trans-Euphrates—all who know the laws of your God. And you are to teach any who do not know them. 26Whoever does not obey the law of your God and the law of the king must surely be punished by death, banishment, confiscation of property, or imprisonment.

27Praise be to the LORD, the God of our fathers, who has put it into the king's heart to bring honor to the house of the LORD in Jerusalem in this way 28and who has extended his good favor to me before the king and his advisers and all the king's powerful officials. Because the hand of the LORD my God was on me, I took courage and gathered leading men from Israel to go up with me. 1Ch 29:12; Ezr 5:5

List of the Family Heads Returning With Ezra

8 These are the family heads and those registered with them who came up with me from Babylon during the reign of King Artaxerxes: Ezr 7:7

2of the descendants of Phinehas, Gershom;

of the descendants of Ithamar, Daniel;

of the descendants of David, Hattush 3of the descendants of Shecaniah;

of the descendants of Parosh, Zechariah, and with him were registered 150 men; Ezr 2:3

4of the descendants of Pahath-Moab, Eliehoenai

---

[a]22 That is, about 3 3/4 tons (about 3.4 metric tons)   [b]22 That is, probably about 600 bushels (about 22 kiloliters)   [c]22 That is, probably about 600 gallons (about 2.2 kiloliters)

son of Zerahiah, and with him 200 men; Ezr 2:6

5of the descendants of Zattu,[a] Shecaniah son of Jahaziel, and with him 300 men;

6of the descendants of Adin, Ebed son of Jonathan, and with him 50 men;

7of the descendants of Elam, Jeshaiah son of Athaliah, and with him 70 men;

8of the descendants of Shephatiah, Zebadiah son of Michael, and with him 80 men;

9of the descendants of Joab, Obadiah son of Jehiel, and with him 218 men;

10of the descendants of Bani,[b] Shelomith son of Josiphiah, and with him 160 men;

11of the descendants of Bebai, Zechariah son of Bebai, and with him 28 men;

12of the descendants of Azgad, Johanan son of Hakkatan, and with him 110 men;

13of the descendants of Adonikam, the last ones, whose names were Eliphelet, Jeuel and Shemaiah, and with them 60 men; Ezr 2:13

14of the descendants of Bigvai, Uthai and Zaccur, and with them 70 men.

The Return to Jerusalem

15I assembled them at the canal that flows toward Ahava, and we camped there three days. When I checked among the people and the priests, I found no Levites there. 16So I summoned Eliezer, Ariel, Shemaiah, Elnathan, Jarib, Elnathan, Nathan, Zechariah and Meshullam, who were leaders, and Joiarib and Elnathan, who were men of learning, 17and I sent them to Iddo, the leader in Casiphia. I told them what to say to Iddo and his kinsmen, the temple servants in Casiphia, so that they might bring attendants to us for the house of our God. 18Because the gracious hand of our God was on us, they brought us Sherebiah, a capable man, from the descendants of Mahli son of Levi, the son of Israel, and Sherebiah's sons and brothers, 18 men; 19and Hashabiah, together with Jeshaiah from the descendants of Merari, and his brothers and nephews, 20 men. 20They also brought 220 of the temple servants—a body that David and the officials had established to assist the Levites. All were registered by name. 1 Ch 9:2; Ezr 2:43

21There, by the Ahava Canal, I proclaimed a fast, so that we might humble ourselves before our God and ask him for a safe journey for us and our children,

---

a5 Some Septuagint manuscripts (also 1 Esdras 8:32); Hebrew does not have *Zattu*.
b10 Some Septuagint manuscripts (also 1 Esdras 8:36); Hebrew does not have *Bani*.

with all our possessions. ²²I was ashamed to ask the king for soldiers and horsemen to protect us from enemies on the road, because we had told the king, "The gracious hand of our God is on everyone who looks to him, but his great anger is against all who forsake him." ²³So we fasted and petitioned our God about this, and he answered our prayer.   Dt 31:17; Ne 2:9

²⁴Then I set apart twelve of the leading priests, together with Sherebiah, Hashabiah and ten of their brothers, ²⁵and I weighed out to them the offering of silver and gold and the articles that the king, his advisers, his officials and all Israel present there had donated for the house of our God. ²⁶I weighed out to them 650 talents*a* of silver, silver articles weighing 100 talents,*b* 100 talents*b* of gold, ²⁷20 bowls of gold valued at 1,000 darics,*c* and two fine articles of polished bronze, as precious as gold.   Ezr 7:15

²⁸I said to them, "You as well as these articles are consecrated to the LORD. The silver and gold are a freewill offering to the LORD, the God of your fathers. ²⁹Guard them carefully until you weigh them out in the chambers of the house of the LORD in Jerusalem before the leading priests and the Levites and the family heads of Israel." ³⁰Then the priests and Levites received the silver and gold and sacred articles that had been weighed out to be taken to the house of our God in Jerusalem.

³¹On the twelfth day of the first month we set out from the Ahava Canal to go to Jerusalem. The hand of our God was on us, and he protected us from enemies and bandits along the way. ³²So we arrived in Jerusalem, where we rested three days.

³³On the fourth day, in the house of our God, we weighed out the silver and gold and the sacred articles into the hands of Meremoth son of Uriah, the priest. Eleazar son of Phinehas was with him, and so were the Levites Jozabad son of Jeshua and Noadiah son of Binnui. ³⁴Everything was accounted for by number and weight, and the entire weight was recorded at that time.   Ne 3:4; 11:16

³⁵Then the exiles who had returned from captivity sacrificed burnt offerings to the God of Israel: twelve bulls for all Israel, ninety-six rams, seventy-seven male lambs and, as a sin offering, twelve male goats. All this was a burnt offering to the LORD. ³⁶They also delivered the king's orders to the royal satraps and to the governors of Trans-Euphrates, who then gave assistance to the people and to the house of God.   Ezr 7:21

---

a26 That is, about 25 tons (about 22 metric tons)   *b26* That is, about 3 3/4 tons (about 3.4 metric tons)   *c27* That is, about 19 pounds (about 8.5 kilograms)

Ezra's Prayer About Intermarriage

9 After these things had been done, the leaders came to me and said, "The people of Israel, including the priests and the Levites, have not kept themselves separate from the neighboring peoples with their detestable practices, like those of the Canaanites, Hittites, Perizzites, Jebusites, Ammonites, Moabites, Egyptians and Amorites. 2They have taken some of their daughters as wives for themselves and their sons, and have mingled the holy race with the peoples around them. And the leaders and officials have led the way in this unfaithfulness." Ex 22:31; 1Ki 9:20; Ezr 6:21

3When I heard this, I tore my tunic and cloak, pulled hair from my head and beard and sat down appalled. 4Then everyone who trembled at the words of the God of Israel gathered around me because of this unfaithfulness of the exiles. And I sat there appalled until the evening sacrifice. Nu 14:6; Ezr 10:3

5Then, at the evening sacrifice, I rose from my self-abasement, with my tunic and cloak torn, and fell on my knees with my hands spread out to the Lord my God 6and prayed:

"O my God, I am too ashamed and disgraced to lift up my face to you, my God, because our sins are higher than our heads and our guilt has reached to the heavens. 7From the days of our forefathers until now, our guilt has been great. Because of our sins, we and our kings and our priests have been subjected to the sword and captivity, to pillage and humiliation at the hand of foreign kings, as it is today. Dt 28:64; 2Ch 28:9

8"But now, for a brief moment, the Lord our God has been gracious in leaving us a remnant and giving us a firm place in his sanctuary, and so our God gives light to our eyes and a little relief in our bondage. 9Though we are slaves, our God has not deserted us in our bondage. He has shown us kindness in the sight of the kings of Persia: He has granted us new life to rebuild the house of our God and repair its ruins, and he has given us a wall of protection in Judah and Jerusalem. Ne 9:36; Ps 13:3

10"But now, O our God, what can we say after this? For we have disregarded the commands 11you gave through your servants the prophets when you said: 'The land you are entering to possess is a land polluted by the corruption of its peoples. By their detestable practices they have filled it with their impurity from one end to the other. 12Therefore, do not give your daughters in marriage

to their sons or take their daughters for your sons. Do not seek a treaty of friendship with them at any time, that you may be strong and eat the good things of the land and leave it to your children as an everlasting inheritance.'   Dt 11:8; Ps 103:17

13"What has happened to us is a result of our evil deeds and our great guilt, and yet, our God, you have punished us less than our sins have deserved and have given us a remnant like this. 14Shall we again break your commands and intermarry with the peoples who commit such detestable practices? Would you not be angry enough with us to destroy us, leaving us no remnant or survivor? 15O LORD, God of Israel, you are righteous! We are left this day as a remnant. Here we are before you in our guilt, though because of it not one of us can stand in your presence."   Ne 13:27; Ps 130:3

The People's Confession of Sin

10 While Ezra was praying and confessing, weeping and throwing himself down before the house of God, a large crowd of Israelites—men, women and children—gathered around him. They too wept bitterly. 2Then Shecaniah son of Jehiel, one of the descendants of Elam, said to Ezra, "We have been unfaithful to our God by marrying foreign women from the peoples around us. But in spite of this, there is still hope for Israel. 3Now let us make a covenant before our God to send away all these women and their children, in accordance with the counsel of my lord and of those who fear the commands of our God. Let it be done according to the Law. 4Rise up; this matter is in your hands. We will support you, so take courage and do it."   2Ch 20:9

5So Ezra rose up and put the leading priests and Levites and all Israel under oath to do what had been suggested. And they took the oath. 6Then Ezra withdrew from before the house of God and went to the room of Jehohanan son of Eliashib. While he was there, he ate no food and drank no water, because he continued to mourn over the unfaithfulness of the exiles.   Dt 9:18; Ne 5:12; Ps 102:4

7A proclamation was then issued throughout Judah and Jerusalem for all the exiles to assemble in Jerusalem. 8Anyone who failed to appear within three days would forfeit all his property, in accordance with the decision of the officials and elders, and would himself be expelled from the assembly of the exiles.

9Within the three days, all the men of Judah and Benjamin had gathered in Jerusalem. And on

the twentieth day of the ninth month, all the people were sitting in the square before the house of God, greatly distressed by the occasion and because of the rain. ¹⁰Then Ezra the priest stood up and said to them, "You have been unfaithful; you have married foreign women, adding to Israel's guilt. ¹¹Now make confession to the LORD, the God of your fathers, and do his will. Separate yourselves from the peoples around you and from your foreign wives." Ezr 1:5; 7:21; Ne 9:2

¹²The whole assembly responded with a loud voice: "You are right! We must do as you say. ¹³But there are many people here and it is the rainy season; so we cannot stand outside. Besides, this matter cannot be taken care of in a day or two, because we have sinned greatly in this thing. ¹⁴Let our officials act for the whole assembly. Then let everyone in our towns who has married a foreign woman come at a set time, along with the elders and judges of each town, until the fierce anger of our God in this matter is turned away from us." ¹⁵Only Jonathan son of Asahel and Jahzeiah son of Tikvah, supported by Meshullam and Shabbethai the Levite, opposed this. Jos 6:5; 2Ch 29:10; Ne 11:16

¹⁶So the exiles did as was proposed. Ezra the priest selected men who were family heads, one from each family division, and all of them designated by name. On the first day of the tenth month they sat down to investigate the cases, ¹⁷and by the first day of the first month they finished dealing with all the men who had married foreign women. Ezr 4:1

Those Guilty of Intermarriage

¹⁸Among the descendants of the priests, the following had married foreign women: Jdg 3:6

From the descendants of Jeshua son of Jozadak, and his brothers: Maaseiah, Eliezer, Jarib and Gedaliah. ¹⁹(They all gave their hands in pledge to put away their wives, and for their guilt they each presented a ram from the flock as a guilt offering.) ²⁰From the descendants of Immer: 1Ch 24:14
Hanani and Zebadiah.
²¹From the descendants of Harim: 1Ch 24:8
Maaseiah, Elijah, Shemaiah, Jehiel and Uzziah.
²²From the descendants of Pashhur: 1Ch 9:12
Elioenai, Maaseiah, Ishmael, Nethanel, Jozabad and Elasah.

²³Among the Levites: Ne 8:7

Jozabad, Shimei, Kelaiah (that is Kelita), Pethahiah, Judah and Eliezer.
²⁴From the singers:
Eliashib. Ne 3:1; 12:10

From the gatekeepers:
Shallum, Telem and Uri.

25And among the other Israelites:

From the descendants of
Parosh: Ezr 2:3
Ramiah, Izziah, Malkijah,
Mijamin, Eleazar, Mal-
kijah and Benaiah.
26From the descendants of
Elam:
Mattaniah, Zechariah,
Jehiel, Abdi, Jeremoth
and Elijah.
27From the descendants of
Zattu:
Elioenai, Eliashib, Mat-
taniah, Jeremoth, Zabad
and Aziza.
28From the descendants of
Bebai:
Jehohanan, Hananiah,
Zabbai and Athlai.
29From the descendants of
Bani:
Meshullam, Malluch,
Adaiah, Jashub, Sheal
and Jeremoth.
30From the descendants of
Pahath-Moab:
Adna, Kelal, Benaiah,
Maaseiah, Mattaniah,
Bezalel, Binnui and Ma-
nasseh.

31From the descendants of
Harim:
Eliezer, Ishijah, Malkijah,
Shemaiah, Shimeon,
32Benjamin, Malluch and
Shemariah.
33From the descendants of
Hashum:
Mattenai, Mattattah,
Zabad, Eliphelet, Jere-
mai, Manasseh and
Shimei.
34From the descendants of
Bani:
Maadai, Amram, Uel,
35Benaiah, Bedeiah, Kelu-
hi, 36Vaniah, Meremoth,
Eliashib, 37Mattaniah,
Mattenai and Jaasu.
38From the descendants of
Binnui:a
Shimei, 39Shelemiah, Na-
than, Adaiah, 40Mac-
nadebai, Shashai, Sharai,
41Azarel, Shelemiah,
Shemariah, 42Shallum,
Amariah and Joseph.
43From the descendants of
Nebo:
Jeiel, Mattithiah, Zabad,
Zebina, Jaddai, Joel and
Benaiah.

44All these had married foreign women, and some of them
had children by these wives.b

---

a37,38 See Septuagint (also 1 Esdras 9:34); Hebrew Jaasu 38and Bani and Binnui,
b44 Or and they sent them away with their children

Nehemiah

Introduction:

Nehemiah continues the history of the Jews who returned from exile in Babylon. Nehemiah gave up his job as cupbearer to Artaxerxes, the Persian king, to become governor of Jerusalem. Nehemiah went to Jerusalem in 444 B.C., almost 100 years after the return of the first exiles. Nehemiah led the people in repairing the walls of Jerusalem and with Ezra provided leadership for the people. An important part of this book is the description of the importance of prayer to Nehemiah.

Outline of contents:

Nehemiah's Prayer

1 The words of Nehemiah son of Hacaliah:

In the month of Kislev in the twentieth year, while I was in the citadel of Susa, ²Hanani, one of my brothers, came from Judah with some other men, and I questioned them about the Jewish remnant that survived the exile, and also about Jerusalem. Jer 52:28; Zec 7:1

³They said to me, "Those who survived the exile and are back in the province are in great trouble and disgrace. The wall of Jerusalem is broken down, and its gates have been burned with fire." Ne 2:17; Isa 22:9

⁴When I heard these things, I sat down and wept. For some days I mourned and fasted and prayed before the God of heaven. ⁵Then I said: Ezr 9:4

"O LORD, God of heaven, the great and awesome God, who keeps his covenant of love with those who love him and obey his commands, ⁶let your ear be attentive and your eyes open to hear the prayer your servant is praying before you day and night for your servants, the people of Israel. I confess the sins we Israelites, including myself and my father's house, have committed against you. ⁷We have acted very wickedly toward you. We

have not obeyed the commands, decrees and laws you gave your servant Moses. Ne 4:14; Ps 106:6

8"Remember the instruction you gave your servant Moses, saying, 'If you are unfaithful, I will scatter you among the nations, 9but if you return to me and obey my commands, then even if your exiled people are at the farthest horizon, I will gather them from there and bring them to the place I have chosen as a dwelling for my Name.' Lev 26:33; Dt 30:4

10"They are your servants and your people, whom you redeemed by your great strength and your mighty hand. 11O Lord, let your ear be attentive to the prayer of this your servant and to the prayer of your servants who delight in revering your name. Give your servant success today by granting him favor in the presence of this man." Isa 51:9

I was cupbearer to the king.

Artaxerxes Sends Nehemiah to Jerusalem

2 In the month of Nisan in the twentieth year of King Artaxerxes, when wine was brought for him, I took the wine and gave it to the king. I had not been sad in his presence before; 2so the king asked me, "Why does your face look so sad when

you are not ill? This can be nothing but sadness of heart." Ezr 4:7

I was very much afraid, 3but I said to the king, "May the king live forever! Why should my face not look sad when the city where my fathers are buried lies in ruins, and its gates have been destroyed by fire?" Ne 1:3; Da 2:4

4The king said to me, "What is it you want?"

Then I prayed to the God of heaven, 5and I answered the king, "If it pleases the king and if your servant has found favor in his sight, let him send me to the city in Judah where my fathers are buried so that I can rebuild it."

6Then the king, with the queen sitting beside him, asked me, "How long will your journey take, and when will you get back?" It pleased the king to send me; so I set a time. Ne 5:14

7I also said to him, "If it pleases the king, may I have letters to the governors of Trans-Euphrates, so that they will provide me safe-conduct until I arrive in Judah? 8And may I have a letter to Asaph, keeper of the king's forest, so he will give me timber to make beams for the gates of the citadel by the temple and for the city wall and for the residence I will occupy?" And because the gracious hand of my God was upon me, the king granted my requests. 9So I went to the governors of Trans-Euphrates and gave them the king's letters. The king had also

sent army officers and cavalry with me. _{Ezr 8:22,36}

[10]When Sanballat the Horonite and Tobiah the Ammonite official heard about this, they were very much disturbed that someone had come to promote the welfare of the Israelites.

Nehemiah Inspects Jerusalem's Walls

[11]I went to Jerusalem, and after staying there three days [12]I set out during the night with a few men. I had not told anyone what my God had put in my heart to do for Jerusalem. There were no mounts with me except the one I was riding on. _{Ge 40:13}

[13]By night I went out through the Valley Gate toward the Jackal[a] Well and the Dung Gate, examining the walls of Jerusalem, which had been broken down, and its gates, which had been destroyed by fire. [14]Then I moved on toward the Fountain Gate and the King's Pool, but there was not enough room for my mount to get through; [15]so I went up the valley by night, examining the wall. Finally, I turned back and reentered through the Valley Gate. [16]The officials did not know where I had gone or what I was doing, because as yet I had said nothing to the Jews or the priests or nobles or officials or any others who would be doing the work.

[17]Then I said to them, "You see the trouble we are in: Jerusa-lem lies in ruins, and its gates have been burned with fire. Come, let us rebuild the wall of Jerusalem, and we will no longer be in disgrace." [18]I also told them about the gracious hand of my God upon me and what the king had said to me.

They replied, "Let us start rebuilding." So they began this good work. _{Ezr 5:5; Ne 1:3}

[19]But when Sanballat the Horonite, Tobiah the Ammonite official and Geshem the Arab heard about it, they mocked and ridiculed us. "What is this you are doing?" they asked. "Are you rebelling against the king?" _{Ne 2:10; 6:6; Ps 44:13}

[20]I answered them by saying, "The God of heaven will give us success. We his servants will start rebuilding, but as for you, you have no share in Jerusalem or any claim or historic right to it." _{Ezr 4:1,3; Ac 8:21}

Builders of the Wall

3 Eliashib the high priest and his fellow priests went to work and rebuilt the Sheep Gate. They dedicated it and set its doors in place, building as far as the Tower of the Hundred, which they dedicated, and as far as the Tower of Hananel. [2]The men of Jericho built the adjoining section, and Zaccur son of Imri built next to them. _{Jer 31:38}

[3]The Fish Gate was rebuilt by the sons of Hassenaah. They laid its beams and put its doors

_{a13 Or Serpent or Fig}

and bolts and bars in place. [4]Meremoth son of Uriah, the son of Hakkoz, repaired the next section. Next to him Meshullam son of Berekiah, the son of Meshezabel, made repairs, and next to him Zadok son of Baana also made repairs. [5]The next section was repaired by the men of Tekoa, but their nobles would not put their shoulders to the work under their supervisors. [a]

2Ch 33:14

[6]The Jeshanah[b] Gate was repaired by Joiada son of Paseah and Meshullam son of Besodeiah. They laid its beams and put its doors and bolts and bars in place. [7]Next to them, repairs were made by men from Gibeon and Mizpah—Melatiah of Gibeon and Jadon of Meronoth—places under the authority of the governor of Trans-Euphrates. [8]Uzziel son of Harhaiah, one of the goldsmiths, repaired the next section; and Hananiah, one of the perfumemakers, made repairs next to that. They restored[c] Jerusalem as far as the Broad Wall. [9]Rephaiah son of Hur, ruler of a half-district of Jerusalem, repaired the next section. [10]Adjoining this, Jedaiah son of Harumaph made repairs opposite his house, and Hattush son of Hashabneiah made repairs next to him. [11]Malkijah son of

Harim and Hasshub son of Pahath-Moab repaired another section and the Tower of the Ovens. [12]Shallum son of Hallohesh, ruler of a half-district of Jerusalem, repaired the next section with the help of his daughters.

Jos 9:3; Ne 12:39

[13]The Valley Gate was repaired by Hanun and the residents of Zanoah. They rebuilt it and put its doors and bolts and bars in place. They also repaired five hundred yards[d] of the wall as far as the Dung Gate.

Ne 2:13

[14]The Dung Gate was repaired by Malkijah son of Recab, ruler of the district of Beth Hakkerem. He rebuilt it and put its doors and bolts and bars in place.

Jer 6:1

[15]The Fountain Gate was repaired by Shallun son of Col-Hozeh, ruler of the district of Mizpah. He rebuilt it, roofing it over and putting its doors and bolts and bars in place. He also repaired the wall of the Pool of Siloam,[e] by the King's Garden, as far as the steps going down from the City of David. [16]Beyond him, Nehemiah son of Azbuk, ruler of a half-district of Beth Zur, made repairs up to a point opposite the tombs[f] of David, as far as the artificial pool and the House of the Heroes.

2Ki 20:20; Jn 9:7

---

[a]5 Or their Lord or the governor   [b]6 Or Old   [c]8 Or They left out part of   [d]13 Hebrew a thousand cubits (about 450 meters)   [e]15 Hebrew Shelah, a variant of Shiloah, that is, Siloam   [f]16 Hebrew; Septuagint, some Vulgate manuscripts and Syriac tomb

17Next to him, the repairs were made by the Levites under Rehum son of Bani. Beside him, Hashabiah, ruler of half the district of Keilah, carried out repairs for his district. 18Next to him, the repairs were made by their countrymen under Binnui*a* son of Henadad, ruler of the other half-district of Keilah. 19Next to him, Ezer son of Jeshua, ruler of Mizpah, repaired another section, from a point facing the ascent to the armory as far as the angle. 20Next to him, Baruch son of Zabbai zealously repaired another section, from the angle to the entrance of the house of Eliashib the high priest. 21Next to him, Meremoth son of Uriah, the son of Hakkoz, repaired another section, from the entrance of Eliashib's house to the end of it.

22The repairs next to him were made by the priests from the surrounding region. 23Beyond them, Benjamin and Hasshub made repairs in front of their house; and next to them, Azariah son of Maaseiah, the son of Ananiah, made repairs beside his house. 24Next to him, Binnui son of Henadad repaired another section, from Azariah's house to the angle and the corner, 25and Palal son of Uzai worked opposite the angle and the tower projecting from the upper palace near the court of the guard. Next to him, Pedaiah son of Parosh 26and the temple servants living on the hill of Ophel made repairs up to a point opposite the Water Gate toward the east and the projecting tower. 27Next to them, the men of Tekoa repaired another section, from the great projecting tower to the wall of Ophel.

28Above the Horse Gate, the priests made repairs, each in front of his own house. 29Next to them, Zadok son of Immer made repairs opposite his house. Next to him, Shemaiah son of Shecaniah, the guard at the East Gate, made repairs. 30Next to him, Hananiah son of Shelemiah, and Hanun, the sixth son of Zalaph, repaired another section. Next to them, Meshullam son of Berekiah made repairs opposite his living quarters. 31Next to him, Malkijah, one of the goldsmiths, made repairs as far as the house of the temple servants and the merchants, opposite the Inspection Gate, and as far as the room above the corner; 32and between the room above the corner and the Sheep Gate the goldsmiths and merchants made repairs.

Opposition to the Rebuilding

4 When Sanballat heard that we were rebuilding the wall, he became angry and was greatly incensed. He ridiculed the Jews, 2and in the presence of his associates and the army of

---

a18 Two Hebrew manuscripts and Syriac (see also Septuagint and verse 24); most Hebrew manuscripts *Bavvai*

Samaria, he said, "What are those feeble Jews doing? Will they restore their wall? Will they offer sacrifices? Will they finish in a day? Can they bring the stones back to life from those heaps of rubble—burned as they are?" Ne 2:10; Ps 79:1

3Tobiah the Ammonite, who was at his side, said, "What they are building—if even a fox climbed up on it, he would break down their wall of stones!" Ne 2:19; Job 13:12

4Hear us, O our God, for we are despised. Turn their insults back on their own heads. Give them over as plunder in a land of captivity. 5Do not cover up their guilt or blot out their sins from your sight, for they have thrown insults in the face of*a* the builders. Ps 69:27; Jer 18:23

6So we rebuilt the wall till all of it reached half its height, for the people worked with all their heart.

7But when Sanballat, Tobiah, the Arabs, the Ammonites and the men of Ashdod heard that the repairs to Jerusalem's walls had gone ahead and that the gaps were being closed, they were very angry. 8They all plotted together to come and fight against Jerusalem and stir up trouble against it. 9But we prayed to our God and posted a guard day and night to meet this threat. Ne 2:10; Ps 50:15

10Meanwhile, the people in Judah said, "The strength of the laborers is giving out, and there is so much rubble that we cannot rebuild the wall." 1Ch 23:4

11Also our enemies said, "Before they know it or see us, we will be right there among them and will kill them and put an end to the work."

12Then the Jews who lived near them came and told us ten times over, "Wherever you turn, they will attack us."

13Therefore I stationed some of the people behind the lowest points of the wall at the exposed places, posting them by families, with their swords, spears and bows. 14After I looked things over, I stood up and said to the nobles, the officials and the rest of the people, "Don't be afraid of them. Remember the Lord, who is great and awesome, and fight for your brothers, your sons and your daughters, your wives and your homes." Dt 1:29; 2Sa 10:12

15When our enemies heard that we were aware of their plot and that God had frustrated it, we all returned to the wall, each to his own work. 2Sa 17:14; Job 5:12

16From that day on, half of my men did the work, while the other half were equipped with spears, shields, bows and armor. The officers posted themselves behind all the people of Judah 17who were building the wall. Those who carried materials did their work with one

a5 Or have provoked you to anger before

hand and held a weapon in the other, [18]and each of the builders wore his sword at his side as he worked. But the man who sounded the trumpet stayed with me. Nu 10:2; Ps 149:6

[19]Then I said to the nobles, the officials and the rest of the people, "The work is extensive and spread out, and we are widely separated from each other along the wall. [20]Wherever you hear the sound of the trumpet, join us there. Our God will fight for us!" Ex 14:14

[21]So we continued the work with half the men holding spears, from the first light of dawn till the stars came out. [22]At that time I also said to the people, "Have every man and his helper stay inside Jerusalem at night, so they can serve us as guards by night and workmen by day." [23]Neither I nor my brothers nor my men nor the guards with me took off our clothes; each had his weapon, even when he went for water.[a]

Nehemiah Helps the Poor

5 Now the men and their wives raised a great outcry against their Jewish brothers. [2]Some were saying, "We and our sons and daughters are numerous; in order for us to eat and stay alive, we must get grain." Lev 25:35; Dt 15:7

[3]Others were saying, "We are mortgaging our fields, our vine-

yards and our homes to get grain during the famine." Ge 47:23

[4]Still others were saying, "We have had to borrow money to pay the king's tax on our fields and vineyards. [5]Although we are of the same flesh and blood as our countrymen and though our sons are as good as theirs, yet we have to subject our sons and daughters to slavery. Some of our daughters have already been enslaved, but we are powerless, because our fields and our vineyards belong to others." Lev 25:39-43; Ezr 4:13

[6]When I heard their outcry and these charges, I was very angry. [7]I pondered them in my mind and then accused the nobles and officials. I told them, "You are exacting usury from your own countrymen!" So I called together a large meeting to deal with them [8]and said: "As far as possible, we have bought back our Jewish brothers who were sold to the Gentiles. Now you are selling your brothers, only for them to be sold back to us!" They kept quiet, because they could find nothing to say.

[9]So I continued, "What you are doing is not right. Shouldn't you walk in the fear of our God to avoid the reproach of our Gentile enemies? [10]I and my brothers and my men are also lending the people money and grain. But let the exacting of usury stop! [11]Give back to them immediately their fields, vine-

---

[a]23 The meaning of the Hebrew for this clause is uncertain.

yards, olive groves and houses, and also the usury you are charging them—the hundredth part of the money, grain, new wine and oil." Ex 22:25; Isa 52:5

[12]"We will give it back," they said. "And we will not demand anything more from them. We will do as you say." Ezr 10:5

Then I summoned the priests and made the nobles and officials take an oath to do what they had promised. [13]I also shook out the folds of my robe and said, "In this way may God shake out of his house and possessions every man who does not keep this promise. So may such a man be shaken out and emptied!" Ne 8:6; Mt 10:14

At this the whole assembly said, "Amen," and praised the LORD. And the people did as they had promised. Dt 27:15-26

[14]Moreover, from the twentieth year of King Artaxerxes, when I was appointed to be their governor in the land of Judah, until his thirty-second year—twelve years—neither I nor my brothers ate the food allotted to the governor. [15]But the earlier governors—those preceding me—placed a heavy burden on the people and took forty shekels[a] of silver from them in addition to food and wine. Their assistants also lorded it over the people. But out of reverence for God I did not act like that. [16]Instead, I devoted myself to the work on this wall. All my men were assembled there for the work; we[b] did not acquire any land. Ne 2:6; Hag 1:1

[17]Furthermore, a hundred and fifty Jews and officials ate at my table, as well as those who came to us from the surrounding nations. [18]Each day one ox, six choice sheep and some poultry were prepared for me, and every ten days an abundant supply of wine of all kinds. In spite of all this, I never demanded the food allotted to the governor, because the demands were heavy on these people.

[19]Remember me with favor, O my God, for all I have done for these people. 2Ki 20:3; Ne 1:8

Further Opposition to the Rebuilding

6 When word came to Sanballat, Tobiah, Geshem the Arab and the rest of our enemies that I had rebuilt the wall and not a gap was left in it—though up to that time I had not set the doors in the gates— [2]Sanballat and Geshem sent me this message: "Come, let us meet together in one of the villages[c] on the plain of Ono."

But they were scheming to harm me; [3]so I sent messengers to them with this reply: "I am carrying on a great project and cannot go down. Why should the work stop while I leave it and go down to you?" [4]Four

---

[a]15 That is, about 1 pound (about 0.5 kilogram)   [b]16 Most Hebrew manuscripts; some Hebrew manuscripts, Septuagint, Vulgate and Syriac I   [c]2 Or in Kephirim

times they sent me the same message, and each time I gave them the same answer.

5Then, the fifth time, Sanballat sent his aide to me with the same message, and in his hand was an unsealed letter 6in which was written: Ne 2:10

"It is reported among the nations—and Geshem*a* says it is true—that you and the Jews are plotting to revolt, and therefore you are building the wall. Moreover, according to these reports you are about to become their king 7and have even appointed prophets to make this proclamation about you in Jerusalem: 'There is a king in Judah!' Now this report will get back to the king; so come, let us confer together." Ne 2:19

8I sent him this reply: "Nothing like what you are saying is happening; you are just making it up out of your head."

9They were all trying to frighten us, thinking, "Their hands will get too weak for the work, and it will not be completed."

But I prayed, "Now strengthen my hands."

10One day I went to the house of Shemaiah son of Delaiah, the son of Mehetabel, who was shut in at his home. He said, "Let us meet in the house of God, inside the temple, and let us close the temple doors, because men are coming to kill you—by night they are coming to kill you."

11But I said, "Should a man like me run away? Or should one like me go into the temple to save his life? I will not go!" 12I realized that God had not sent him, but that he had prophesied against me because Tobiah and Sanballat had hired him. 13He had been hired to intimidate me so that I would commit a sin by doing this, and then they would give me a bad name to discredit me. Jer 20:10; Eze 13:22

14Remember Tobiah and Sanballat, O my God, because of what they have done; remember also the prophetess Noadiah and the rest of the prophets who have been trying to intimidate me. Ne 13:29; Eze 13:17

The Completion of the Wall

15So the wall was completed on the twenty-fifth of Elul, in fifty-two days. 16When all our enemies heard about this, all the surrounding nations were afraid and lost their self-confidence, because they realized that this work had been done with the help of our God. Ne 2:10

17Also, in those days the nobles of Judah were sending many letters to Tobiah, and replies from Tobiah kept coming to them. 18For many in Judah were under oath to him, since he was son-in-law to Shecaniah

*a*6 Hebrew *Gashmu*, a variant of *Geshem*

son of Arah, and his son Jehohanan had married the daughter of Meshullam son of Berekiah. ¹⁹Moreover, they kept reporting to me his good deeds and then telling him what I said. And Tobiah sent letters to intimidate me.

7 After the wall had been rebuilt and I had set the doors in place, the gatekeepers and the singers and the Levites were appointed. ²I put in charge of Jerusalem my brother Hanani, along with*a* Hananiah the commander of the citadel, because he was a man of integrity and feared God more than most men do. ³I said to them, "The gates of Jerusalem are not to be opened until the sun is hot. While the gatekeepers are still on duty, have them shut the doors and bar them. Also appoint residents of Jerusalem as guards, some at their posts and some near their own houses."

The List of the Exiles Who Returned

⁴Now the city was large and spacious, but there were few people in it, and the houses had not yet been rebuilt. ⁵So my God put it into my heart to assemble the nobles, the officials and the common people for registration by families. I found the genealogical record of those who had been the first to return. This is what I found written there:

⁶These are the people of the province who came up from the captivity of the exiles whom Nebuchadnezzar king of Babylon had taken captive (they returned to Jerusalem and Judah, each to his own town, ⁷in company with Zerubbabel, Jeshua, Nehemiah, Azariah, Raamiah, Nahamani, Mordecai, Bilshan, Mispereth, Bigvai, Nehum and Baanah):

2Ch 36:20; Ezr 2:2

The list of the men of Israel:

⁸the descendants of
Parosh 2,172
⁹of Shephatiah 372
¹⁰of Arah 652
¹¹of Pahath-Moab
(through the line of
Jeshua and Joab) 2,818
¹²of Elam 1,254
¹³of Zattu 845
¹⁴of Zaccai 760
¹⁵of Binnui 648
¹⁶of Bebai 628
¹⁷of Azgad 2,322
¹⁸of Adonikam 667
¹⁹of Bigvai 2,067
²⁰of Adin 655
²¹of Ater (through
Hezekiah) 98
²²of Hashum 328
²³of Bezai 324
²⁴of Hariph 112
²⁵of Gibeon 95

²⁶the men of Bethlehem
and Netophah 188
²⁷of Anathoth 128
²⁸of Beth Azmaveth 42

a2 Or Hanani, that is,

29of Kiriath Jearim,
Kephirah and
Beeroth   743
30of Ramah and Geba   621
31of Micmash   122
32of Bethel and Ai   123
33of the other Nebo   52
34of the other Elam   1,254
35of Harim   320
36of Jericho   345
37of Lod, Hadid
and Ono   721
38of Senaah   3,930

39The priests: Ezr 2:36

the descendants of
Jedaiah (through the
family of Jeshua)   973
40of Immer   1,052
41of Pashhur   1,247
42of Harim   1,017

43The Levites: Ezr 2:40

the descendants of Jeshua
(through Kadmiel
through the line of
Hodaviah)   74

44The singers: Ne 11:23

the descendants of
Asaph   148

45The gatekeepers: 1Ch 9:17

the descendants of
Shallum, Ater, Talmon,
Akkub, Hatita and
Shobai   138

46The temple servants: Ne 3:26

the descendants of
Ziha, Hasupha,
Tabbaoth,
47Keros, Sia, Padon,

48Lebana, Hagaba,
Shalmai,
49Hanan, Giddel, Gahar,
50Reaiah, Rezin, Nekoda,
51Gazzam, Uzza, Paseah,
52Besai, Meunim,
Nephussim,
53Bakbuk, Hakupha,
Harhur,
54Bazluth, Mehida,
Harsha,
55Barkos, Sisera, Temah,
56Neziah and Hatipha

57The descendants of the servants of Solomon: Ezr 2:55

the descendants of
Sotai, Sophereth, Perida,
58Jaala, Darkon, Giddel,
59Shephatiah, Hattil,
Pokereth-Hazzebaim and
Amon

60The temple servants and
the descendants of the
servants of Solomon   392

61The following came up
from the towns of Tel
Melah, Tel Harsha, Kerub,
Addon and Immer, but
they could not show that
their families were descended from Israel:

62the descendants of
Delaiah, Tobiah and
Nekoda   642

63And from among the
priests: Ezr 2:61

the descendants of

Hobaiah, Hakkoz and Barzillai (a man who had married a daughter of Barzillai the Gileadite and was called by that name).

⁶⁴These searched for their family records, but they could not find them and so were excluded from the priesthood as unclean. ⁶⁵The governor, therefore, ordered them not to eat any of the most sacred food until there should be a priest ministering with the Urim and Thummim. Ex 28:30

⁶⁶The whole company numbered 42,360, ⁶⁷besides their 7,337 menservants and maidservants; and they also had 245 men and women singers. ⁶⁸There were 736 horses, 245 mules,ᵃ ⁶⁹435 camels and 6,720 donkeys.

⁷⁰Some of the heads of the families contributed to the work. The governor gave to the treasury 1,000 drachmasᵇ of gold, 50 bowls and 530 garments for priests. ⁷¹Some of the heads of the families gave to the treasury for the work 20,000 drachmasᶜ of gold and 2,200 minasᵈ of silver. ⁷²The total given by the rest of the people was 20,000 drach-mas of gold, 2,000 minasᵉ of silver and 67 garments for priests. Ex 25:2; Ne 8:9

⁷³The priests, the Levites, the gatekeepers, the singers and the temple servants, along with certain of the people and the rest of the Israelites, settled in their own towns. Ezr 3:1; Ne 1:10

Ezra Reads the Law

When the seventh month came and the Israelites had settled in their towns, **8** ¹all the people assembled as one man in the square before the Water Gate. They told Ezra the scribe to bring out the Book of the Law of Moses, which the LORD had commanded for Israel. Dt 28:61; Ezr 7:26; Ne 3:26

²So on the first day of the seventh month Ezra the priest brought the Law before the assembly, which was made up of men and women and all who were able to understand. ³He read it aloud from daybreak till noon as he faced the square before the Water Gate in the presence of the men, women and others who could understand. And all the people listened attentively to the Book of the Law. Lev 23:34; Dt 31:11; Ne 3:26

⁴Ezra the scribe stood on a high wooden platform built for the occasion. Beside him on his right stood Mattithiah, Shema,

---

ᵃ68 Some Hebrew manuscripts (see also Ezra 2:66); most Hebrew manuscripts do not have this verse.   ᵇ70 That is, about 19 pounds (about 8.5 kilograms)   ᶜ71 That is, about 375 pounds (about 170 kilograms); also in verse 72   ᵈ71 That is, about 1 1/3 tons (about 1.2 metric tons)   ᵉ72 That is, about 1 1/4 tons (about 1.1 metric tons)

Anaiah, Uriah, Hilkiah and Maaseiah; and on his left were Pedaiah, Mishael, Malkijah, Hashum, Hashbaddanah, Zechariah and Meshullam.

5Ezra opened the book. All the people could see him because he was standing above them; and as he opened it, the people all stood up. 6Ezra praised the LORD, the great God; and all the people lifted their hands and responded, "Amen! Amen!" Then they bowed down and worshiped the LORD with their faces to the ground.   Jdg 3:20; Ezr 9:5

7The Levites—Jeshua, Bani, Sherebiah, Jamin, Akkub, Shabbethai, Hodiah, Maaseiah, Kelita, Azariah, Jozabad, Hanan and Pelaiah—instructed the people in the Law while the people were standing there. 8They read from the Book of the Law of God, making it clear*a* and giving the meaning so that the people could understand what was being read.   2Ch 17:7

9Then Nehemiah the governor, Ezra the priest and scribe, and the Levites who were instructing the people said to them all, "This day is sacred to the LORD your God. Do not mourn or weep." For all the people had been weeping as they listened to the words of the Law.   Dt 12:7; 16:14-15; Ne 7:1

10Nehemiah said, "Go and enjoy choice food and sweet drinks, and send some to those who have nothing prepared. This day is sacred to our Lord. Do not grieve, for the joy of the LORD is your strength."   Est 9:22

11The Levites calmed all the people, saying, "Be still, for this is a sacred day. Do not grieve."

12Then all the people went away to eat and drink, to send portions of food and to celebrate with great joy, because they now understood the words that had been made known to them.

13On the second day of the month, the heads of all the families, along with the priests and the Levites, gathered around Ezra the scribe to give attention to the words of the Law. 14They found written in the Law, which the LORD had commanded through Moses, that the Israelites were to live in booths during the feast of the seventh month 15and that they should proclaim this word and spread it throughout their towns and in Jerusalem: "Go out into the hill country and bring back branches from olive and wild olive trees, and from myrtles, palms and shade trees, to make booths"—as it is written.*b*   Ex 23:16; Lev 23:40; Dt 16:16

16So the people went out and brought back branches and built themselves booths on their own roofs, in their courtyards, in the courts of the house of God and in the square by the Water Gate and the one by the Gate of Ephraim. 17The whole company

---

a8 Or *God, translating it*   *b15* See Lev. 23:37-40.

that had returned from exile built booths and lived in them. From the days of Joshua son of Nun until that day, the Israelites had not celebrated it like this. And their joy was very great.   1Ki 8:2; Ne 3:26; Hos 12:9

[18]Day after day, from the first day to the last, Ezra read from the Book of the Law of God. They celebrated the feast for seven days, and on the eighth day, in accordance with the regulation, there was an assembly.   Lev 23:36; Dt 31:11; Ezr 3:4

The Israelites Confess Their Sins

9 On the twenty-fourth day of the same month, the Israelites gathered together, fasting and wearing sackcloth and having dust on their heads. [2]Those of Israelite descent had separated themselves from all foreigners. They stood in their places and confessed their sins and the wickedness of their fathers. [3]They stood where they were and read from the Book of the Law of the LORD their God for a quarter of the day, and spent another quarter in confession and in worshiping the LORD their God. [4]Standing on the stairs were the Levites—Jeshua, Bani, Kadmiel, Shebaniah, Bunni, Sherebiah, Bani and Kenani—who called with loud voices to the LORD their God. [5]And the Levites—Jeshua, Kadmiel, Bani,

Hashabneiah, Sherebiah, Hodiah, Shebaniah and Pethahiah—said: "Stand up and praise the LORD your God, who is from everlasting to everlasting. [a]"

"Blessed be your glorious name, and may it be exalted above all blessing and praise. [6]You alone are the LORD. You made the heavens, even the highest heavens, and all their starry host, the earth and all that is on it, the seas and all that is in them. You give life to everything, and the multitudes of heaven worship you.

[7]"You are the LORD God, who chose Abram and brought him out of Ur of the Chaldeans and named him Abraham. [8]You found his heart faithful to you, and you made a covenant with him to give to his descendants the land of the Canaanites, Hittites, Amorites, Perizzites, Jebusites and Girgashites. You have kept your promise because you are righteous.   Ge 1:1; Ps 95:5

[9]"You saw the suffering of our forefathers in Egypt; you heard their cry at the Red Sea.[b] [10]You sent miraculous signs and wonders against Pharaoh, against all his officials and all the people of his land, for you knew how arrogantly the Egyptians treated them.

[a]5 Or God for ever and ever   [b]9 Hebrew Yam Suph; that is, Sea of Reeds

You made a name for yourself, which remains to this day. ¹¹You divided the sea before them, so that they passed through it on dry ground, but you hurled their pursuers into the depths, like a stone into mighty waters. ¹²By day you led them with a pillar of cloud, and by night with a pillar of fire to give them light on the way they were to take.   Ex 14:10; Ps 78:13

¹³"You came down on Mount Sinai; you spoke to them from heaven. You gave them regulations and laws that are just and right, and decrees and commands that are good. ¹⁴You made known to them your holy Sabbath and gave them commands, decrees and laws through your servant Moses. ¹⁵In their hunger you gave them bread from heaven and in their thirst you brought them water from the rock; you told them to go in and take possession of the land you had sworn with uplifted hand to give them.   Ex 19:19

¹⁶"But they, our forefathers, became arrogant and stiff-necked, and did not obey your commands. ¹⁷They refused to listen and failed to remember the miracles you performed among them. They became stiff-necked and in their rebellion appointed a leader in order to return to their slavery. But you are a forgiving God, gracious and compassionate, slow to anger and abounding in love. Therefore you did not desert them, ¹⁸even when they cast for themselves an image of a calf and said, 'This is your god, who brought you up out of Egypt,' or when they committed awful blasphemies.

¹⁹"Because of your great compassion you did not abandon them in the desert. By day the pillar of cloud did not cease to guide them on their path, nor the pillar of fire by night to shine on the way they were to take. ²⁰You gave your good Spirit to instruct them. You did not withhold your manna from their mouths, and you gave them water for their thirst. ²¹For forty years you sustained them in the desert; they lacked nothing, their clothes did not wear out nor did their feet become swollen.   Ex 16:15; Dt 8:4; Ps 23:3

²²"You gave them kingdoms and nations, allotting to them even the remotest frontiers. They took over the country of Sihon*a* king

---

a22 One Hebrew manuscript and Septuagint; most Hebrew manuscripts *Sihon, that is, the country of the*

of Heshbon and the country of Og king of Bashan. [23]You made their sons as numerous as the stars in the sky, and you brought them into the land that you told their fathers to enter and possess. [24]Their sons went in and took possession of the land. You subdued before them the Canaanites, who lived in the land; you handed the Canaanites over to them, along with their kings and the peoples of the land, to deal with them as they pleased. [25]They captured fortified cities and fertile land; they took possession of houses filled with all kinds of good things, wells already dug, vineyards, olive groves and fruit trees in abundance. They ate to the full and were well-nourished; they reveled in your great goodness.   Nu 21:21; Ps 23:6

[26]"But they were disobedient and rebelled against you; they put your law behind their backs. They killed your prophets, who had admonished them in order to turn them back to you; they committed awful blasphemies. [27]So you handed them over to their enemies, who oppressed them. But when they were oppressed they cried out to you. From heaven you heard them, and in your great compassion you gave them deliverers, who rescued them from the hand of their enemies.   Nu 25:17; Jdg 2:12

[28]"But as soon as they were at rest, they again did what was evil in your sight. Then you abandoned them to the hand of their enemies so that they ruled over them. And when they cried out to you again, you heard from heaven, and in your compassion you delivered them time after time.   Jdg 3:11

[29]"You warned them to return to your law, but they became arrogant and disobeyed your commands. They sinned against your ordinances, by which a man will live if he obeys them. Stubbornly they turned their backs on you, became stiff-necked and refused to listen. [30]For many years you were patient with them. By your Spirit you admonished them through your prophets. Yet they paid no attention, so you handed them over to the neighboring peoples. [31]But in your great mercy you did not put an end to them or abandon them, for you are a gracious and merciful God.   Zec 7:11

[32]"Now therefore, O our God, the great, mighty and awesome God, who keeps his covenant of love, do not let all this hardship seem trifling in your eyes—the hardship that has come

upon us, upon our kings and leaders, upon our priests and prophets, upon our fathers and all your people, from the days of the kings of Assyria until today. 33In all that has happened to us, you have been just; you have acted faithfully, while we did wrong. 34Our kings, our leaders, our priests and our fathers did not follow your law; they did not pay attention to your commands or the warnings you gave them. 35Even while they were in their kingdom, enjoying your great goodness to them in the spacious and fertile land you gave them, they did not serve you or turn from their evil ways.

36"But see, we are slaves today, slaves in the land you gave our forefathers so they could eat its fruit and the other good things it produces. 37Because of our sins, its abundant harvest goes to the kings you have placed over us. They rule over our bodies and our cattle as they please. We are in great distress. Dt 28:33; Ezr 9:9

The Agreement of the People

38"In view of all this, we are making a binding agreement, putting it in writing, and our leaders, our Levites and our priests are affixing their seals to it." 2Ch 23:16; Ne 10:29; Isa 44:5

10 Those who sealed it were:

Nehemiah the governor, the son of Hacaliah.

Zedekiah, 2Seraiah, Azariah, Jeremiah, Ezr 2:2
3Pashhur, Amariah, Malkijah, 1Ch 9:12
4Hattush, Shebaniah, Malluch,
5Harim, Meremoth, Obadiah, 1Ch 24:8
6Daniel, Ginnethon, Baruch,
7Meshullam, Abijah, Mijamin,
8Maaziah, Bilgai and Shemaiah.

These were the priests. Ne 12:1

9The Levites:

Jeshua son of Azaniah, Binnui of the sons of Henadad, Kadmiel,
10and their associates: Shebaniah,
Hodiah, Kelita, Pelaiah, Hanan,
11Mica, Rehob, Hashabiah,
12Zaccur, Sherebiah, Shebaniah,
13Hodiah, Bani and Beninu.

14The leaders of the people:

Parosh, Pahath-Moab, Elam, Zattu, Bani,
15Bunni, Azgad, Bebai,
16Adonijah, Bigvai, Adin,
17Ater, Hezekiah, Azzur,
18Hodiah, Hashum, Bezai,
19Hariph, Anathoth, Nebai,
20Magpiash, Meshullam, Hezir, 1Ch 24:15
21Meshezabel, Zadok, Jaddua,

²²Pelatiah, Hanan, Anaiah, ²³Hoshea, Hananiah, Hasshub,　　　　　　　　Ne 7:2

²⁴Hallohesh, Pilha, Shobek, ²⁵Rehum, Hashabnah, Maaseiah, ²⁶Ahiah, Hanan, Anan, ²⁷Malluch, Harim and Baanah.

²⁸"The rest of the people—priests, Levites, gatekeepers, singers, temple servants and all who separated themselves from the neighboring peoples for the sake of the Law of God, together with their wives and all their sons and daughters who are able to understand— ²⁹all these now join their brothers the nobles, and bind themselves with a curse and an oath to follow the Law of God given through Moses the servant of God and to obey carefully all the commands, regulations and decrees of the LORD our Lord.

³⁰"We promise not to give our daughters in marriage to the peoples around us or take their daughters for our sons.　　Ex 34:16; Ne 13:23

³¹"When the neighboring peoples bring merchandise or grain to sell on the Sabbath, we will not buy from them on the Sabbath or on any holy day. Every seventh year we will forgo working the land and will cancel all debts.　　Dt 15:1

³²"We assume the responsibility for carrying out the commands to give a third of a shekelᵃ each year for the service of the house of our God: ³³for the bread set out on the table; for the regular grain offerings and burnt offerings; for the offerings on the Sabbaths, New Moon festivals and appointed feasts; for the holy offerings; for sin offerings to make atonement for Israel; and for all the duties of the house of our God.　　Ps 81:3

³⁴"We—the priests, the Levites and the people—have cast lots to determine when each of our families is to bring to the house of our God at set times each year a contribution of wood to burn on the altar of the LORD our God, as it is written in the Law.

³⁵"We also assume responsibility for bringing to the house of the LORD each year the firstfruits of our crops and of every fruit tree.　　Nu 18:12; Dt 26:2

³⁶"As it is also written in the Law, we will bring the firstborn of our sons and of our cattle, of our herds and of our flocks to the house of our God, to the priests ministering there.　　Nu 18:15

ᵃ32 That is, about 1/8 ounce (about 4 grams)

³⁷"Moreover, we will bring to the storerooms of the house of our God, to the priests, the first of our ground meal, of our ˌgrainˌ offerings, of the fruit of all our trees and of our new wine and oil. And we will bring a tithe of our crops to the Levites, for it is the Levites who collect the tithes in all the towns where we work. ³⁸A priest descended from Aaron is to accompany the Levites when they receive the tithes, and the Levites are to bring a tenth of the tithes up to the house of our God, to the storerooms of the treasury. ³⁹The people of Israel, including the Levites, are to bring their contributions of grain, new wine and oil to the storerooms where the articles for the sanctuary are kept and where the ministering priests, the gatekeepers and the singers stay.   Lev 27:30; Eze 44:30

"We will not neglect the house of our God."   Ne 13:11

The New Residents of Jerusalem

11 Now the leaders of the people settled in Jerusalem, and the rest of the people cast lots to bring one out of every ten to live in Jerusalem, the holy city, while the remaining nine were to stay in their own towns. ²The people commended all the men who volunteered to live in Jerusalem. Ne 7:4

³These are the provincial leaders who settled in Jerusalem (now some Israelites, priests, Levites, temple servants and descendants of Solomon's servants lived in the towns of Judah, each on his own property in the various towns, ⁴while other people from both Judah and Benjamin lived in Jerusalem):   Ezr 1:5; 2:1

From the descendants of Judah:

Athaiah son of Uzziah, the son of Zechariah, the son of Amariah, the son of Shephatiah, the son of Mahalalel, a descendant of Perez; ⁵and Maaseiah son of Baruch, the son of Col-Hozeh, the son of Hazaiah, the son of Adaiah, the son of Joiarib, the son of Zechariah, a descendant of Shelah. ⁶The descendants of Perez who lived in Jerusalem totaled 468 able men.

⁷From the descendants of Benjamin:

Sallu son of Meshullam, the son of Joed, the son of Pedaiah, the son of Kolaiah, the son of Maaseiah, the son of Ithiel, the son of Jeshaiah, ⁸and his followers, Gabbai and Sallai—928 men. ⁹Joel son of Zicri was their chief officer, and Judah son of Hassenuah was over the Second District of the city.

¹⁰From the priests:

Jedaiah; the son of Joiarib; Jakin; ¹¹Seraiah son of Hilkiah, the son of Meshullam, the son of Zadok, the son of Meraioth, the son of Ahitub, supervisor in the house of God, ¹²and their associates, who carried on work for the temple—822 men; Adaiah son of Jeroham, the son of Pelaliah, the son of Amzi, the son of Zechariah, the son of Pashhur, the son of Malkijah, ¹³and his associates, who were heads of families—242 men; Amashsai son of Azarel, the son of Ahzai, the son of Meshillemoth, the son of Immer, ¹⁴and his*a* associates, who were able men—128. Their chief officer was Zabdiel son of Haggedolim.   1Ch 9:10

¹⁵From the Levites:

Shemaiah son of Hasshub, the son of Azrikam, the son of Hashabiah, the son of Bunni; ¹⁶Shabbethai and Jozabad, two of the heads of the Levites, who had charge of the outside work of the house of God; ¹⁷Mattaniah son of Mica, the son of Zabdi, the son of Asaph, the director who led in thanksgiving and prayer; Bakbukiah, second among his associates; and Abda son of Shammua, the son of Galal, the son of Jeduthun.

¹⁸The Levites in the holy city totaled 284.   Ezr 10:15; Ne 12:8

¹⁹The gatekeepers:

Akkub, Talmon and their associates, who kept watch at the gates—172 men.

²⁰The rest of the Israelites, with the priests and Levites, were in all the towns of Judah, each on his ancestral property.

²¹The temple servants lived on the hill of Ophel, and Ziha and Gishpa were in charge of them.   Ezr 2:43; Ne 3:26

²²The chief officer of the Levites in Jerusalem was Uzzi son of Bani, the son of Hashabiah, the son of Mattaniah, the son of Mica. Uzzi was one of Asaph's descendants, who were the singers responsible for the service of the house of God. ²³The singers were under the king's orders, which regulated their daily activity.   1Ch 9:15; Ne 7:44

²⁴Pethahiah son of Meshezabel, one of the descendants of Zerah son of Judah, was the king's agent in all affairs relating to the people.   Ge 38:30

²⁵As for the villages with their fields, some of the people of Judah lived in Kiriath Arba and its surrounding settlements, in Dibon and its settlements, in Jekabzeel and its villages, ²⁶in Jeshua, in Moladah, in Beth Pelet, ²⁷in Hazar Shual, in Beersheba and its settlements, ²⁸in Ziklag, in Meconah and its settlements, ²⁹in En Rimmon, in

Zorah, in Jarmuth, ³⁰Zanoah, Adullam and their villages, in Lachish and its fields, and in Azekah and its settlements. So they were living all the way from Beersheba to the Valley of Hinnom.   Jos 15:26; 1Sa 27:6

³¹The descendants of the Benjamites from Geba lived in Micmash, Aija, Bethel and its settlements, ³²in Anathoth, Nob and Ananiah, ³³in Hazor, Ramah and Gittaim, ³⁴in Hadid, Zeboim and Neballat, ³⁵in Lod and Ono, and in the Valley of the Craftsmen.   1Sa 13:18; Isa 10:29

³⁶Some of the divisions of the Levites of Judah settled in Benjamin.

Priests and Levites

12 These were the priests and Levites who returned with Zerubbabel son of Shealtiel and with Jeshua: Ezr 2:2; Zec 4:6
Seraiah, Jeremiah, Ezra,
²Amariah, Malluch, Hattush,
³Shecaniah, Rehum, Meremoth,
⁴Iddo, Ginnethon,ᵃ Abijah,
⁵Mijamin,ᵇ Moadiah, Bilgah,
⁶Shemaiah, Joiarib, Jedaiah,
⁷Sallu, Amok, Hilkiah and Jedaiah.
These were the leaders of the priests and their associates in the days of Jeshua.

⁸The Levites were Jeshua, Binnui, Kadmiel, Sherebiah, Judah, and also Mattaniah, who, together with his associates, was in charge of the songs of thanksgiving. ⁹Bakbukiah and Unni, their associates, stood opposite them in the services.   Ezr 2:2; Ne 11:17

¹⁰Jeshua was the father of Joiakim, Joiakim the father of Eliashib, Eliashib the father of Joiada, ¹¹Joiada the father of Jonathan, and Jonathan the father of Jaddua.   Ezr 10:24; Ne 3:20

¹²In the days of Joiakim, these were the heads of the priestly families:
of Seraiah's family, Meraiah;
of Jeremiah's, Hananiah;
¹³of Ezra's, Meshullam;
of Amariah's, Jehohanan;
¹⁴of Malluch's, Jonathan;
of Shecaniah's,ᶜ Joseph;
¹⁵of Harim's, Adna;
of Meremoth's,ᵈ Helkai;
¹⁶of Iddo's, Zechariah;
of Ginnethon's, Meshullam;
¹⁷of Abijah's, Zicri;   1Ch 24:10
of Miniamin's and of Moadiah's, Piltai;
¹⁸of Bilgah's, Shammua;
of Shemaiah's, Jehonathan;
¹⁹of Joiarib's, Mattenai;
of Jedaiah's, Uzzi;
²⁰of Sallu's, Kallai;
of Amok's, Eber;
²¹of Hilkiah's, Hashabiah;

ᵃ4 Many Hebrew manuscripts and Vulgate (see also Neh. 12:16); most Hebrew manuscripts *Ginnethoi*.   ᵇ5 A variant of *Miniamin*   ᶜ14 Very many Hebrew manuscripts, some Septuagint manuscripts and Syriac (see also Neh. 12:3); most Hebrew manuscripts *Shebaniah's*   ᵈ15 Some Septuagint manuscripts (see also Neh. 12:3); Hebrew *Meraioth's*

of Jedaiah's, Nethanel.

22The family heads of the Levites in the days of Eliashib, Joiada, Johanan and Jaddua, as well as those of the priests, were recorded in the reign of Darius the Persian. 23The family heads among the descendants of Levi up to the time of Johanan son of Eliashib were recorded in the book of the annals. 24And the leaders of the Levites were Hashabiah, Sherebiah, Jeshua son of Kadmiel, and their associates, who stood opposite them to give praise and thanksgiving, one section responding to the other, as prescribed by David the man of God.   2Ch 8:14; Ezr 2:40; Ne 11:17

25Mattaniah, Bakbukiah, Obadiah, Meshullam, Talmon and Akkub were gatekeepers who guarded the storerooms at the gates. 26They served in the days of Joiakim son of Jeshua, the son of Jozadak, and in the days of Nehemiah the governor and of Ezra the priest and scribe.   Ezr 7:6,11

Dedication of the Wall of Jerusalem

27At the dedication of the wall of Jerusalem, the Levites were sought out from where they lived and were brought to Jerusalem to celebrate joyfully the dedication with songs of thanksgiving and with the music of cymbals, harps and lyres. 28The singers also were brought together from the region around Jerusalem—from the villages of the Netophathites, 29from Beth Gilgal, and from the area of Geba and Azmaveth, for the singers had built villages for themselves around Jerusalem. 30When the priests and Levites had purified themselves ceremonially, they purified the people, the gates and the wall.

31I had the leaders of Judah go up on top*a* of the wall. I also assigned two large choirs to give thanks. One was to proceed on top*b* of the wall to the right, toward the Dung Gate. 32Hoshaiah and half the leaders of Judah followed them, 33along with Azariah, Ezra, Meshullam, 34Judah, Benjamin, Shemaiah, Jeremiah, 35as well as some priests with trumpets, and also Zechariah son of Jonathan, the son of Shemaiah, the son of Mattaniah, the son of Micaiah, the son of Zaccur, the son of Asaph, 36and his associates—Shemaiah, Azarel, Milalai, Gilalai, Maai, Nethanel, Judah and Hanani—with musical instruments prescribed by David the man of God. Ezra the scribe led the procession. 37At the Fountain Gate they continued directly up the steps of the City of David on the ascent to the wall and passed above the house of David to the Water Gate on the east.   1Ch 15:16; Ne 2:13

38The second choir proceeded in the opposite direction. I fol-

*a*31 Or go alongside   *b*31 Or proceed alongside

lowed them on top[a] of the wall, together with half the people—past the Tower of the Ovens to the Broad Wall, [39]over the Gate of Ephraim, the Jeshanah[b] Gate, the Fish Gate, the Tower of Hananel and the Tower of the Hundred, as far as the Sheep Gate. At the Gate of the Guard they stopped. Ne 3:11

[40]The two choirs that gave thanks then took their places in the house of God; so did I, together with half the officials, [41]as well as the priests—Eliakim, Maaseiah, Miniamin, Micaiah, Elioenai, Zechariah and Hananiah with their trumpets— [42]and also Maaseiah, Shemaiah, Eleazar, Uzzi, Jehohanan, Malkijah, Elam and Ezer. The choirs sang under the direction of Jezrahiah. [43]And on that day they offered great sacrifices, rejoicing because God had given them great joy. The women and children also rejoiced. The sound of rejoicing in Jerusalem could be heard far away.

[44]At that time men were appointed to be in charge of the storerooms for the contributions, firstfruits and tithes. From the fields around the towns they were to bring into the storerooms the portions required by the Law for the priests and the Levites, for Judah was pleased with the ministering priests and Levites. [45]They performed the service of their God and the service of purification, as did also the singers and gatekeepers, according to the commands of David and his son Solomon. [46]For long ago, in the days of David and Asaph, there had been directors for the singers and for the songs of praise and thanksgiving to God. [47]So in the days of Zerubbabel and of Nehemiah, all Israel contributed the daily portions for the singers and gatekeepers. They also set aside the portion for the other Levites, and the Levites set aside the portion for the descendants of Aaron. Ps 137:4

Nehemiah's Final Reforms

13 On that day the Book of Moses was read aloud in the hearing of the people and there it was found written that no Ammonite or Moabite should ever be admitted into the assembly of God, [2]because they had not met the Israelites with food and water but had hired Balaam to call a curse down on them. (Our God, however, turned the curse into a blessing.) [3]When the people heard this law, they excluded from Israel all who were of foreign descent. Dt 23:3; Ne 9:2

[4]Before this, Eliashib the priest had been put in charge of the storerooms of the house of our God. He was closely associated with Tobiah, [5]and he had provided him with a large room

formerly used to store the grain offerings and incense and temple articles, and also the tithes of grain, new wine and oil prescribed for the Levites, singers and gatekeepers, as well as the contributions for the priests.

⁶But while all this was going on, I was not in Jerusalem, for in the thirty-second year of Artaxerxes king of Babylon I had returned to the king. Some time later I asked his permission ⁷and came back to Jerusalem. Here I learned about the evil thing Eliashib had done in providing Tobiah a room in the courts of the house of God. ⁸I was greatly displeased and threw all Tobiah's household goods out of the room. ⁹I gave orders to purify the rooms, and then I put back into them the equipment of the house of God, with the grain offerings and the incense.   2Ch 29:5

¹⁰I also learned that the portions assigned to the Levites had not been given to them, and that all the Levites and singers responsible for the service had gone back to their own fields. ¹¹So I rebuked the officials and asked them, "Why is the house of God neglected?" Then I called them together and stationed them at their posts.

¹²All Judah brought the tithes of grain, new wine and oil into the storerooms. ¹³I put Shelemiah the priest, Zadok the scribe, and a Levite named Pedaiah in charge of the storerooms and made Hanan son of Zaccur, the son of Mattaniah,

their assistant, because these men were considered trustworthy. They were made responsible for distributing the supplies to their brothers. Ne 10:39

¹⁴Remember me for this, O my God, and do not blot out what I have so faithfully done for the house of my God and its services.   2Ki 20:3; Ne 5:19

¹⁵In those days I saw men in Judah treading winepresses on the Sabbath and bringing in grain and loading it on donkeys, together with wine, grapes, figs and all other kinds of loads. And they were bringing all this into Jerusalem on the Sabbath. Therefore I warned them against selling food on that day. ¹⁶Men from Tyre who lived in Jerusalem were bringing in fish and all kinds of merchandise and selling them in Jerusalem on the Sabbath to the people of Judah. ¹⁷I rebuked the nobles of Judah and said to them, "What is this wicked thing you are doing— desecrating the Sabbath day? ¹⁸Didn't your forefathers do the same things, so that our God brought all this calamity upon us and upon this city? Now you are stirring up more wrath against Israel by desecrating the Sabbath."   Ex 20:8; Jer 44:23

¹⁹When evening shadows fell on the gates of Jerusalem before the Sabbath, I ordered the doors to be shut and not opened until the Sabbath was over. I stationed some of my own men at

the gates so that no load could be brought in on the Sabbath day. ²⁰Once or twice the merchants and sellers of all kinds of goods spent the night outside Jerusalem. ²¹But I warned them and said, "Why do you spend the night by the wall? If you do this again, I will lay hands on you." From that time on they no longer came on the Sabbath. ²²Then I commanded the Levites to purify themselves and go and guard the gates in order to keep the Sabbath day holy.

Remember me for this also, O my God, and show mercy to me according to your great love.

²³Moreover, in those days I saw men of Judah who had married women from Ashdod, Ammon and Moab. ²⁴Half of their children spoke the language of Ashdod or the language of one of the other peoples, and did not know how to speak the language of Judah. ²⁵I rebuked them and called curses down on them. I beat some of the men and pulled out their hair. I made them take an oath in God's name and said: "You are not to give your daughters in marriage to their sons, nor

are you to take their daughters in marriage for your sons or for yourselves. ²⁶Was it not because of marriages like these that Solomon king of Israel sinned? Among the many nations there was no king like him. He was loved by his God, and God made him king over all Israel, but even he was led into sin by foreign women. ²⁷Must we hear now that you too are doing all this terrible wickedness and are being unfaithful to our God by marrying foreign women?" Ezr 9:2

²⁸One of the sons of Joiada son of Eliashib the high priest was son-in-law to Sanballat the Horonite. And I drove him away from me. Ezr 10:24; Ne 2:10

²⁹Remember them, O my God, because they defiled the priestly office and the covenant of the priesthood and of the Levites. Nu 25:13; Ne 1:8; Mal 2:4

³⁰So I purified the priests and the Levites of everything foreign, and assigned them duties, each to his own task. ³¹I also made provision for contributions of wood at designated times, and for the firstfruits.

Remember me with favor, O my God. Ge 8:1; Ne 1:8

Esther

Introduction:

The setting for the book of Esther is Susa, the Persian capital, during the time of Xerxes, who ruled Persia from 486–465 B.C. The book tells the story of a beautiful Jewish girl whom King Xerxes chose to be his queen. When Haman plotted to murder all the Jews, Queen Esther's cousin Mordecai persuaded Esther to try to save her people. Risking her own life, she appealed to the king and rescued the Jews.

Although the name of God does not appear in this book, his care for his chosen people is clearly shown. This exciting story of the rescue of the Jews is celebrated annually during the Feast of Purim, at which time the book of Esther is read out loud.

Outline of contents:

Esther made queen (1:1–2:23)
Haman's plot to destroy the Jews (3:1–5:14)
The Jews win (6:1–10:3)

Queen Vashti Deposed

1 This is what happened during the time of Xerxes,[a] the Xerxes who ruled over 127 provinces stretching from India to Cush[b]: ²At that time King Xerxes reigned from his royal throne in the citadel of Susa, ³and in the third year of his reign he gave a banquet for all his nobles and officials. The military leaders of Persia and Media, the princes, and the nobles of the provinces were present. _{1Ki 3:15; Ezr 4:6; Est 2:8}

⁴For a full 180 days he displayed the vast wealth of his kingdom and the splendor and glory of his majesty. ⁵When these days were over, the king gave a banquet, lasting seven days, in the enclosed garden of the king's palace, for all the people from the least to the greatest, who were in the citadel of Susa. ⁶The garden had hangings of white and blue linen, fastened with cords of white linen and purple material to silver rings on marble pillars.

---

[a]1 Hebrew *Ahasuerus*, a variant of Xerxes' Persian name; here and throughout Esther
[b]1 That is, the upper Nile region

There were couches of gold and silver on a mosaic pavement of porphyry, marble, mother-of-pearl and other costly stones. 7Wine was served in goblets of gold, each one different from the other, and the royal wine was abundant, in keeping with the king's liberality. 8By the king's command each guest was allowed to drink in his own way, for the king instructed all the wine stewards to serve each man what he wished.   Eze 23:41

9Queen Vashti also gave a banquet for the women in the royal palace of King Xerxes.

10On the seventh day, when King Xerxes was in high spirits from wine, he commanded the seven eunuchs who served him—Mehuman, Biztha, Harbona, Bigtha, Abagtha, Zethar and Carcas— 11to bring before him Queen Vashti, wearing her royal crown, in order to display her beauty to the people and nobles, for she was lovely to look at. 12But when the attendants delivered the king's command, Queen Vashti refused to come. Then the king became furious and burned with anger.

13Since it was customary for the king to consult experts in matters of law and justice, he spoke with the wise men who understood the times 14and were closest to the king— Carshena, Shethar, Admatha, Tarshish, Meres, Marsena and Memucan, the seven nobles of Persia and Media who had special access to the king and were highest in the kingdom.   2Ki 25:19; 1Ch 12:32; Ezr 7:14

15"According to law, what must be done to Queen Vashti?" he asked. "She has not obeyed the command of King Xerxes that the eunuchs have taken to her."

16Then Memucan replied in the presence of the king and the nobles, "Queen Vashti has done wrong, not only against the king but also against all the nobles and the peoples of all the provinces of King Xerxes. 17For the queen's conduct will become known to all the women, and so they will despise their husbands and say, 'King Xerxes commanded Queen Vashti to be brought before him, but she would not come.' 18This very day the Persian and Median women of the nobility who have heard about the queen's conduct will respond to all the king's nobles in the same way. There will be no end of disrespect and discord.

19"Therefore, if it pleases the king, let him issue a royal decree and let it be written in the laws of Persia and Media, which cannot be repealed, that Vashti is never again to enter the presence of King Xerxes. Also let the king give her royal position to someone else who is better than she. 20Then when the king's edict is proclaimed throughout all his vast realm, all the women will respect their husbands, from the least to the greatest."

21The king and his nobles

were pleased with this advice, so the king did as Memucan proposed. [22]He sent dispatches to all parts of the kingdom, to each province in its own script and to each people in its own language, proclaiming in each people's tongue that every man should be ruler over his own household.   Ne 13:24; 1Ti 2:12

Esther Made Queen

2 Later when the anger of King Xerxes had subsided, he remembered Vashti and what she had done and what he had decreed about her. [2]Then the king's personal attendants proposed, "Let a search be made for beautiful young virgins for the king. [3]Let the king appoint commissioners in every province of his realm to bring all these beautiful girls into the harem at the citadel of Susa. Let them be placed under the care of Hegai, the king's eunuch, who is in charge of the women; and let beauty treatments be given to them. [4]Then let the girl who pleases the king be queen instead of Vashti." This advice appealed to the king, and he followed it.   1Ki 1:2; Est 7:10

[5]Now there was in the citadel of Susa a Jew of the tribe of Benjamin, named Mordecai son of Jair, the son of Shimei, the son of Kish, [6]who had been carried into exile from Jerusalem by Nebuchadnezzar king of Babylon, among those taken captive with Jehoiachin[a] king of Judah. [7]Mordecai had a cousin named Hadassah, whom he had brought up because she had neither father nor mother. This girl, who was also known as Esther, was lovely in form and features, and Mordecai had taken her as his own daughter when her father and mother died.   1Sa 9:1; 2Ki 24:15; Da 5:13

[8]When the king's order and edict had been proclaimed, many girls were brought to the citadel of Susa and put under the care of Hegai. Esther also was taken to the king's palace and entrusted to Hegai, who had charge of the harem. [9]The girl pleased him and won his favor. Immediately he provided her with her beauty treatments and special food. He assigned to her seven maids selected from the king's palace and moved her and her maids into the best place in the harem.   Ne 1:1; Da 1:5

[10]Esther had not revealed her nationality and family background, because Mordecai had forbidden her to do so. [11]Every day he walked back and forth near the courtyard of the harem to find out how Esther was and what was happening to her.

[12]Before a girl's turn came to go in to King Xerxes, she had to complete twelve months of beauty treatments prescribed for the women, six months with oil of myrrh and six with perfumes and cosmetics. [13]And this

---

[a]6 Hebrew *Jeconiah*, a variant of *Jehoiachin*

is how she would go to the king: Anything she wanted was given her to take with her from the harem to the king's palace. [14]In the evening she would go there and in the morning return to another part of the harem to the care of Shaashgaz, the king's eunuch who was in charge of the concubines. She would not return to the king unless he was pleased with her and summoned her by name. Pr 27:9

[15]When the turn came for Esther (the girl Mordecai had adopted, the daughter of his uncle Abihail) to go to the king, she asked for nothing other than what Hegai, the king's eunuch who was in charge of the harem, suggested. And Esther won the favor of everyone who saw her. [16]She was taken to King Xerxes in the royal residence in the tenth month, the month of Tebeth, in the seventh year of his reign. Est 9:29; Ps 45:14

[17]Now the king was attracted to Esther more than to any of the other women, and she won his favor and approval more than any of the other virgins. So he set a royal crown on her head and made her queen instead of Vashti. [18]And the king gave a great banquet, Esther's banquet, for all his nobles and officials. He proclaimed a holiday throughout the provinces and distributed gifts with royal liberality. 1Ki 3:15; Est 1:7,11

Mordecai Uncovers a Conspiracy

[19]When the virgins were assembled a second time, Mordecai was sitting at the king's gate. [20]But Esther had kept secret her family background and nationality just as Mordecai had told her to do, for she continued to follow Mordecai's instructions as she had done when he was bringing her up. Est 4:2; 5:13

[21]During the time Mordecai was sitting at the king's gate, Bigthana[a] and Teresh, two of the king's officers who guarded the doorway, became angry and conspired to assassinate King Xerxes. [22]But Mordecai found out about the plot and told Queen Esther, who in turn reported it to the king, giving credit to Mordecai. [23]And when the report was investigated and found to be true, the two officials were hanged on a gallows.[b] All this was recorded in the book of the annals in the presence of the king. Est 6:2

Haman's Plot to Destroy the Jews

3 After these events, King Xerxes honored Haman son of Hammedatha, the Agagite, elevating him and giving him a seat of honor higher than that of all the other nobles. [2]All the royal officials at the king's gate knelt down and paid honor to Haman, for the king had com-

---

[a]21 Hebrew *Bigthan*, a variant of *Bigthana* similarly elsewhere in Esther

[b]23 Or *were hung* (or *impaled*) *on poles;*

manded this concerning him. But Mordecai would not kneel down or pay him honor.

³Then the royal officials at the king's gate asked Mordecai, "Why do you disobey the king's command?" ⁴Day after day they spoke to him but he refused to comply. Therefore they told Haman about it to see whether Mordecai's behavior would be tolerated, for he had told them he was a Jew.   Ge 39:10; Da 3:12

⁵When Haman saw that Mordecai would not kneel down or pay him honor, he was enraged. ⁶Yet having learned who Mordecai's people were, he scorned the idea of killing only Mordecai. Instead Haman looked for a way to destroy all Mordecai's people, the Jews, throughout the whole kingdom of Xerxes.   Ps 83:4; Pr 16:25

⁷In the twelfth year of King Xerxes, in the first month, the month of Nisan, they cast the *pur* (that is, the lot) in the presence of Haman to select a day and month. And the lot fell onᵃ the twelfth month, the month of Adar.   Lev 16:8; Ezr 6:15; Est 9:24

⁸Then Haman said to King Xerxes, "There is a certain people dispersed and scattered among the peoples in all the provinces of your kingdom whose customs are different from those of all other people and who do not obey the king's laws; it is not in the king's best interest to tolerate them. ⁹If it pleases the king, let a decree be issued to destroy them, and I will put ten thousand talentsᵇ of silver into the royal treasury for the men who carry out this business."   Est 7:4; Da 6:13; Ac 16:20

¹⁰So the king took his signet ring from his finger and gave it to Haman son of Hammedatha, the Agagite, the enemy of the Jews. ¹¹"Keep the money," the king said to Haman, "and do with the people as you please."

¹²Then on the thirteenth day of the first month the royal secretaries were summoned. They wrote out in the script of each province and in the language of each people all Haman's orders to the king's satraps, the governors of the various provinces and the nobles of the various peoples. These were written in the name of King Xerxes himself and sealed with his own ring. ¹³Dispatches were sent by couriers to all the king's provinces with the order to destroy, kill and annihilate all the Jews—young and old, women and little children—on a single day, the thirteenth day of the twelfth month, the month of Adar, and to plunder their goods. ¹⁴A copy of the text of the edict was to be issued as law in every province and made known to the people of every nationality so they would be ready for that day.   1Ki 21:8

ᵃ7 Septuagint; Hebrew does not have *And the lot fell on.*   ᵇ9 That is, about 375 tons (about 345 metric tons)

¹⁵Spurred on by the king's command, the couriers went out, and the edict was issued in the citadel of Susa. The king and Haman sat down to drink, but the city of Susa was bewildered.   Est 1:10; 8:15

Mordecai Persuades Esther to Help

4 When Mordecai learned of all that had been done, he tore his clothes, put on sackcloth and ashes, and went out into the city, wailing loudly and bitterly. ²But he went only as far as the king's gate, because no one clothed in sackcloth was allowed to enter it. ³In every province to which the edict and order of the king came, there was great mourning among the Jews, with fasting, weeping and wailing. Many lay in sackcloth and ashes.   Ps 30:11; Eze 27:30

⁴When Esther's maids and eunuchs came and told her about Mordecai, she was in great distress. She sent clothes for him to put on instead of his sackcloth, but he would not accept them. ⁵Then Esther summoned Hathach, one of the king's eunuchs assigned to attend her, and ordered him to find out what was troubling Mordecai and why.

⁶So Hathach went out to Mordecai in the open square of the city in front of the king's gate. ⁷Mordecai told him everything that had happened to him, including the exact amount of money Haman had promised to pay into the royal treasury for the destruction of the Jews. ⁸He also gave him a copy of the text of the edict for their annihilation, which had been published in Susa, to show to Esther and explain it to her, and he told him to urge her to go into the king's presence to beg for mercy and plead with him for her people.   Est 3:9; 7:4

⁹Hathach went back and reported to Esther what Mordecai had said. ¹⁰Then she instructed him to say to Mordecai, ¹¹"All the king's officials and the people of the royal provinces know that for any man or woman who approaches the king in the inner court without being summoned the king has but one law: that he be put to death. The only exception to this is for the king to extend the gold scepter to him and spare his life. But thirty days have passed since I was called to go to the king."   Ps 125:3; Da 2:9

¹²When Esther's words were reported to Mordecai, ¹³he sent back this answer: "Do not think that because you are in the king's house you alone of all the Jews will escape. ¹⁴For if you remain silent at this time, relief and deliverance for the Jews will arise from another place, but you and your father's family will perish. And who knows but that you have come to royal position for such a time as this?"

¹⁵Then Esther sent this reply to Mordecai: ¹⁶"Go, gather to-

gether all the Jews who are in Susa, and fast for me. Do not eat or drink for three days, night or day. I and my maids will fast as you do. When this is done, I will go to the king, even though it is against the law. And if I perish, I perish." 2Ch 20:3; Est 5:1

¹⁷So Mordecai went away and carried out all of Esther's instructions.

Esther's Request to the King

5 On the third day Esther put on her royal robes and stood in the inner court of the palace, in front of the king's hall. The king was sitting on his royal throne in the hall, facing the entrance. ²When he saw Queen Esther standing in the court, he was pleased with her and held out to her the gold scepter that was in his hand. So Esther approached and touched the tip of the scepter. Est 4:11; Eze 16:13

³Then the king asked, "What is it, Queen Esther? What is your request? Even up to half the kingdom, it will be given you." Est 7:2; Da 5:16; Mk 6:23

⁴"If it pleases the king," replied Esther, "let the king, together with Haman, come today to a banquet I have prepared for him."

⁵"Bring Haman at once," the king said, "so that we may do what Esther asks." Est 6:14

So the king and Haman went to the banquet Esther had prepared. ⁶As they were drinking wine, the king again asked Esther, "Now what is your peti-

tion? It will be given you. And what is your request? Even up to half the kingdom, it will be granted." Est 1:10; 7:2

⁷Esther replied, "My petition and my request is this: ⁸If the king regards me with favor and if it pleases the king to grant my petition and fulfill my request, let the king and Haman come tomorrow to the banquet I will prepare for them. Then I will answer the king's question."

Haman's Rage Against Mordecai

⁹Haman went out that day happy and in high spirits. But when he saw Mordecai at the king's gate and observed that he neither rose nor showed fear in his presence, he was filled with rage against Mordecai. ¹⁰Nevertheless, Haman restrained himself and went home. Pr 14:17

Calling together his friends and Zeresh, his wife, ¹¹Haman boasted to them about his vast wealth, his many sons, and all the ways the king had honored him and how he had elevated him above the other nobles and officials. ¹²"And that's not all," Haman added. "I'm the only person Queen Esther invited to accompany the king to the banquet she gave. And she has invited me along with the king tomorrow. ¹³But all this gives me no satisfaction as long as I see that Jew Mordecai sitting at the king's gate." Job 22:29; Pr 16:18

¹⁴His wife Zeresh and all his

friends said to him, "Have a gallows built, seventy-five feet[a] high, and ask the king in the morning to have Mordecai hanged on it. Then go with the king to the dinner and be happy." This suggestion delighted Haman, and he had the gallows built.   Est 6:4; 7:9

Mordecai Honored

6 That night the king could not sleep; so he ordered the book of the chronicles, the record of his reign, to be brought in and read to him. [2]It was found recorded there that Mordecai had exposed Bigthana and Teresh, two of the king's officers who guarded the doorway, who had conspired to assassinate King Xerxes.   Da 6:18

[3]"What honor and recognition has Mordecai received for this?" the king asked.

"Nothing has been done for him," his attendants answered.

[4]The king said, "Who is in the court?" Now Haman had just entered the outer court of the palace to speak to the king about hanging Mordecai on the gallows he had erected for him.

[5]His attendants answered, "Haman is standing in the court."

"Bring him in," the king ordered.

[6]When Haman entered, the king asked him, "What should be done for the man the king delights to honor?"

Now Haman thought to himself, "Who is there that the king would rather honor than me?" [7]So he answered the king, "For the man the king delights to honor, [8]have them bring a royal robe the king has worn and a horse the king has ridden, one with a royal crest placed on its head. [9]Then let the robe and horse be entrusted to one of the king's most noble princes. Let them robe the man the king delights to honor, and lead him on the horse through the city streets, proclaiming before him, 'This is what is done for the man the king delights to honor!'"

[10]"Go at once," the king commanded Haman. "Get the robe and the horse and do just as you have suggested for Mordecai the Jew, who sits at the king's gate. Do not neglect anything you have recommended."

[11]So Haman got the robe and the horse. He robed Mordecai, and led him on horseback through the city streets, proclaiming before him, "This is what is done for the man the king delights to honor!"   Ge 41:42

[12]Afterward Mordecai returned to the king's gate. But Haman rushed home, with his head covered in grief, [13]and told Zeresh his wife and all his friends everything that had happened to him.   2Sa 15:30

His advisers and his wife Zeresh said to him, "Since Mordecai, before whom your down-

[a]14 Hebrew *fifty cubits* (about 23 meters)

fall has started, is of Jewish origin, you cannot stand against him—you will surely come to ruin!" [14]While they were still talking with him, the king's eunuchs arrived and hurried Haman away to the banquet Esther had prepared.   1Ki 3:15; Est 5:10

Haman Hanged

7 So the king and Haman went to dine with Queen Esther, [2]and as they were drinking wine on that second day, the king again asked, "Queen Esther, what is your petition? It will be given you. What is your request? Even up to half the kingdom, it will be granted."

[3]Then Queen Esther answered, "If I have found favor with you, O king, and if it pleases your majesty, grant me my life—this is my petition. And spare my people—this is my request. [4]For I and my people have been sold for destruction and slaughter and annihilation. If we had merely been sold as male and female slaves, I would have kept quiet, because no such distress would justify disturbing the king.[a]"

[5]King Xerxes asked Queen Esther, "Who is he? Where is the man who has dared to do such a thing?"

[6]Esther said, "The adversary and enemy is this vile Haman."

Then Haman was terrified before the king and queen. [7]The king got up in a rage, left his wine and went out into the palace garden. But Haman, realizing that the king had already decided his fate, stayed behind to beg Queen Esther for his life.

[8]Just as the king returned from the palace garden to the banquet hall, Haman was falling on the couch where Esther was reclining.   Est 1:6; Jn 13:23

The king exclaimed, "Will he even molest the queen while she is with me in the house?"

As soon as the word left the king's mouth, they covered Haman's face. [9]Then Harbona, one of the eunuchs attending the king, said, "A gallows seventy-five feet[b] high stands by Haman's house. He had it made for Mordecai, who spoke up to help the king."   Est 1:10; 5:14

The king said, "Hang him on it!" [10]So they hanged Haman on the gallows he had prepared for Mordecai. Then the king's fury subsided.   Ge 40:22; Ps 7:16

The King's Edict in Behalf of the Jews

8 That same day King Xerxes gave Queen Esther the estate of Haman, the enemy of the Jews. And Mordecai came into the presence of the king, for Esther had told how he was related to her. [2]The king took off his signet ring, which he had reclaimed from Haman, and presented it to Mordecai. And

[a]4 Or *quiet, but the compensation our adversary offers cannot be compared with the loss the king would suffer*   [b]9 Hebrew *fifty cubits* (about 23 meters)

Esther appointed him over Haman's estate.   Pr 22:22; Da 2:48

³Esther again pleaded with the king, falling at his feet and weeping. She begged him to put an end to the evil plan of Haman the Agagite, which he had devised against the Jews. ⁴Then the king extended the gold scepter to Esther and she arose and stood before him.

⁵"If it pleases the king," she said, "and if he regards me with favor and thinks it the right thing to do, and if he is pleased with me, let an order be written overruling the dispatches that Haman son of Hammedatha, the Agagite, devised and wrote to destroy the Jews in all the king's provinces. ⁶For how can I bear to see disaster fall on my people? How can I bear to see the destruction of my family?"

⁷King Xerxes replied to Queen Esther and to Mordecai the Jew, "Because Haman attacked the Jews, I have given his estate to Esther, and they have hanged him on the gallows. ⁸Now write another decree in the king's name in behalf of the Jews as seems best to you, and seal it with the king's signet ring—for no document written in the king's name and sealed with his ring can be revoked."

⁹At once the royal secretaries were summoned—on the twenty-third day of the third month, the month of Sivan. They wrote out all Mordecai's orders to the Jews, and to the satraps, governors and nobles of the 127 provinces stretching from India to Cush.ᵃ These orders were written in the script of each province and the language of each people and also to the Jews in their own script and language. ¹⁰Mordecai wrote in the name of King Xerxes, sealed the dispatches with the king's signet ring, and sent them by mounted couriers, who rode fast horses especially bred for the king.   Ne 13:24; Est 1:1; 3:12

¹¹The king's edict granted the Jews in every city the right to assemble and protect themselves; to destroy, kill and annihilate any armed force of any nationality or province that might attack them and their women and children; and to plunder the property of their enemies. ¹²The day appointed for the Jews to do this in all the provinces of King Xerxes was the thirteenth day of the twelfth month, the month of Adar. ¹³A copy of the text of the edict was to be issued as law in every province and made known to the people of every nationality so that the Jews would be ready on that day to avenge themselves on their enemies.   Est 3:13

¹⁴The couriers, riding the royal horses, raced out, spurred on by the king's command. And the edict was also issued in the citadel of Susa.   Est 3:15

ᵃ9 That is, the upper Nile region

¹⁵Mordecai left the king's presence wearing royal garments of blue and white, a large crown of gold and a purple robe of fine linen. And the city of Susa held a joyous celebration. ¹⁶For the Jews it was a time of happiness and joy, gladness and honor. ¹⁷In every province and in every city, wherever the edict of the king went, there was joy and gladness among the Jews, with feasting and celebrating. And many people of other nationalities became Jews because fear of the Jews had seized them.   Est 3:15; Ps 35:27

Triumph of the Jews

9 On the thirteenth day of the twelfth month, the month of Adar, the edict commanded by the king was to be carried out. On this day the enemies of the Jews had hoped to overpower them, but now the tables were turned and the Jews got the upper hand over those who hated them. ²The Jews assembled in their cities in all the provinces of King Xerxes to attack those seeking their destruction. No one could stand against them, because the people of all the other nationalities were afraid of them. ³And all the nobles of the provinces, the satraps, the governors and the king's administrators helped the Jews, because fear of Mordecai had seized them. ⁴Mordecai was prominent in the palace; his reputation spread throughout the provinces, and he became more and more powerful.   Est 8:12

⁵The Jews struck down all their enemies with the sword, killing and destroying them, and they did what they pleased to those who hated them. ⁶In the citadel of Susa, the Jews killed and destroyed five hundred men. ⁷They also killed Parshandatha, Dalphon, Aspatha, ⁸Poratha, Adalia, Aridatha, ⁹Parmashta, Arisai, Aridai and Vaizatha, ¹⁰the ten sons of Haman son of Hammedatha, the enemy of the Jews. But they did not lay their hands on the plunder.   Ezr 4:6; Est 5:11; Ps 127:3

¹¹The number of those slain in the citadel of Susa was reported to the king that same day. ¹²The king said to Queen Esther, "The Jews have killed and destroyed five hundred men and the ten sons of Haman in the citadel of Susa. What have they done in the rest of the king's provinces? Now what is your petition? It will be given you. What is your request? It will also be granted."

¹³"If it pleases the king," Esther answered, "give the Jews in Susa permission to carry out this day's edict tomorrow also, and let Haman's ten sons be hanged on gallows."   Dt 21:22-23

¹⁴So the king commanded that this be done. An edict was issued in Susa, and they hanged the ten sons of Haman. ¹⁵The Jews in Susa came together on the fourteenth day of the month of Adar, and they put to death

in Susa three hundred men, but they did not lay their hands on the plunder.   Ezr 6:11; Est 8:11

¹⁶Meanwhile, the remainder of the Jews who were in the king's provinces also assembled to protect themselves and get relief from their enemies. They killed seventy-five thousand of them but did not lay their hands on the plunder. ¹⁷This happened on the thirteenth day of the month of Adar, and on the fourteenth they rested and made it a day of feasting and joy.   Dt 25:19; 1Ki 3:15; Est 4:14

Purim Celebrated

¹⁸The Jews in Susa, however, had assembled on the thirteenth and fourteenth, and then on the fifteenth they rested and made it a day of feasting and joy.

¹⁹That is why rural Jews—those living in villages—observe the fourteenth of the month of Adar as a day of joy and feasting, a day for giving presents to each other.

²⁰Mordecai recorded these events, and he sent letters to all the Jews throughout the provinces of King Xerxes, near and far, ²¹to have them celebrate annually the fourteenth and fifteenth days of the month of Adar ²²as the time when the Jews got relief from their enemies, and as the month when their sorrow was turned into joy

and their mourning into a day of celebration. He wrote them to observe the days as days of feasting and joy and giving presents of food to one another and gifts to the poor.   Ps 30:11-12

²³So the Jews agreed to continue the celebration they had begun, doing what Mordecai had written to them. ²⁴For Haman son of Hammedatha, the Agagite, the enemy of all the Jews, had plotted against the Jews to destroy them and had cast the *pur* (that is, the lot) for their ruin and destruction. ²⁵But when the plot came to the king's attention,ᵃ he issued written orders that the evil scheme Haman had devised against the Jews should come back onto his own head, and that he and his sons should be hanged on the gallows. ²⁶(Therefore these days were called Purim, from the word *pur*.) Because of everything written in this letter and because of what they had seen and what had happened to them, ²⁷the Jews took it upon themselves to establish the custom that they and their descendants and all who join them should without fail observe these two days every year, in the way prescribed and at the time appointed. ²⁸These days should be remembered and observed in every generation by every family, and in every province and in every city. And

ᵃ25 Or *when Esther came before the king*

these days of Purim should never cease to be celebrated by the Jews, nor should the memory of them die out among their descendants.   Est 3:7; Ps 7:16

²⁹So Queen Esther, daughter of Abihail, along with Mordecai the Jew, wrote with full authority to confirm this second letter concerning Purim. ³⁰And Mordecai sent letters to all the Jews in the 127 provinces of the kingdom of Xerxes—words of goodwill and assurance— ³¹to establish these days of Purim at their designated times, as Mordecai the Jew and Queen Esther had decreed for them, and as they had established for themselves and their descendants in regard to their times of fasting and lamentation. ³²Esther's decree confirmed these regulations about Purim, and it was written down in the records.   Est 2:15

The Greatness of Mordecai

10 King Xerxes imposed tribute throughout the empire, to its distant shores. ²And all his acts of power and might, together with a full account of the greatness of Mordecai to which the king had raised him, are they not written in the book of the annals of the kings of Media and Persia? ³Mordecai the Jew was second in rank to King Xerxes, preeminent among the Jews, and held in high esteem by his many fellow Jews, because he worked for the good of his people and spoke up for the welfare of all the Jews.   Ge 41:40; Est 8:15

Job

Introduction:

The book of Job is named for its main character, a righteous man who was very rich. Even after losing everything he owned and suffering from a terrible sickness, Job still confessed his love for God.

The book questions the reasons for suffering, especially the suffering of people who love God and are good. Job's friends insisted he was suffering as punishment for his sin. Job defended himself by insisting that he had done nothing seriously wrong and then expressed his trust in God.

Then God spoke and showed his mighty power. Job finally admitted that God is too great and wonderful for us to understand.

Outline of contents:

Prologue

1 In the land of Uz there lived a man whose name was Job. This man was blameless and upright; he feared God and shunned evil. ²He had seven sons and three daughters, ³and he owned seven thousand sheep, three thousand camels, five hundred yoke of oxen and five hundred donkeys, and had a large number of servants. He was the greatest man among all the people of the East.   Eze 14:14

⁴His sons used to take turns holding feasts in their homes, and they would invite their three sisters to eat and drink with them. ⁵When a period of feasting had run its course, Job would send and have them purified. Early in the morning he would sacrifice a burnt offering for each of them, thinking,

"Perhaps my children have sinned and cursed God in their hearts." This was Job's regular custom.   Ge 8:20; 1Ki 21:10

Job's First Test

⁶One day the angels[a] came to present themselves before the LORD, and Satan[b] also came with them. ⁷The LORD said to Satan, "Where have you come from?"   Job 2:1; Ps 109:6; Lk 22:31

Satan answered the LORD, "From roaming through the earth and going back and forth in it."   Ge 3:1; 1Pe 5:8

⁸Then the LORD said to Satan, "Have you considered my servant Job? There is no one on earth like him; he is blameless and upright, a man who fears God and shuns evil."   Ps 25:12

⁹"Does Job fear God for nothing?" Satan replied. ¹⁰"Have you not put a hedge around him and his household and everything he has? You have blessed the work of his hands, so that his flocks and herds are spread throughout the land. ¹¹But stretch out your hand and strike everything he has, and he will surely curse you to your face."

¹²The LORD said to Satan, "Very well, then, everything he has is in your hands, but on the man himself do not lay a finger."   Job 2:6; Lk 4:6; 1Co 10:13

Then Satan went out from the presence of the LORD.

¹³One day when Job's sons and daughters were feasting and drinking wine at the oldest brother's house, ¹⁴a messenger came to Job and said, "The oxen were plowing and the donkeys were grazing nearby, ¹⁵and the Sabeans attacked and carried them off. They put the servants to the sword, and I am the only one who has escaped to tell you!"   Ge 36:24; Job 9:24

¹⁶While he was still speaking, another messenger came and said, "The fire of God fell from the sky and burned up the sheep and the servants, and I am the only one who has escaped to tell you!"   Lev 10:2; Nu 11:1

¹⁷While he was still speaking, another messenger came and said, "The Chaldeans formed three raiding parties and swept down on your camels and carried them off. They put the servants to the sword, and I am the only one who has escaped to tell you!"   Ge 11:28; Job 9:24

¹⁸While he was still speaking, yet another messenger came and said, "Your sons and daughters were feasting and drinking wine at the oldest brother's house, ¹⁹when suddenly a mighty wind swept in from the desert and struck the four corners of the house. It collapsed on them and they are dead, and I am the only one who has escaped to tell you!"

²⁰At this, Job got up and tore his robe and shaved his head. Then he fell to the ground in worship ²¹and said: Ge 37:29

---

a6 Hebrew *the sons of God*   *b6* *Satan* means *accuser.*

"Naked I came from my
mother's womb,
and naked I will depart.*a*
The LORD gave and the LORD
has taken away;   Ru 1:21
may the name of the LORD
be praised."   1Th 5:18

22In all this, Job did not sin by
charging God with wrong-
doing.   Job 2:10; Ps 39:1

Job's Second Test

2 On another day the angels*b*
came to present themselves
before the LORD, and Satan also
came with them to present himself before him. 2And the LORD
said to Satan, "Where have you
come from?"   Ge 6:2; Job 1:6

Satan answered the LORD,
"From roaming through the
earth and going back and forth
in it."   Ge 3:1

3Then the LORD said to Satan,
"Have you considered my servant Job? There is no one on
earth like him; he is blameless
and upright, a man who fears
God and shuns evil. And he still
maintains his integrity, though
you incited me against him to
ruin him without any reason."

4"Skin for skin!" Satan replied. "A man will give all he
has for his own life. 5But stretch
out your hand and strike his
flesh and bones, and he will
surely curse you to your face."

6The LORD said to Satan,
"Very well, then, he is in your

hands; but you must spare his
life."   Job 1:12; 2Co 12:7

7So Satan went out from the
presence of the LORD and afflicted Job with painful sores from
the soles of his feet to the top of
his head. 8Then Job took a piece
of broken pottery and scraped
himself with it as he sat among
the ashes.   Job 42:6; Mt 11:21

9His wife said to him, "Are
you still holding on to your integrity? Curse God and die!"

10He replied, "You are talking
like a foolish*c* woman. Shall we
accept good from God, and not
trouble?"   Job 1:21; La 3:38

In all this, Job did not sin in
what he said.   Job 6:24; Jas 1:12

Job's Three Friends

11When Job's three friends,
Eliphaz the Temanite, Bildad
the Shuhite and Zophar the Naamathite, heard about all the
troubles that had come upon
him, they set out from their
homes and met together by
agreement to go and sympathize with him and comfort
him. 12When they saw him from
a distance, they could hardly
recognize him; they began to
weep aloud, and they tore their
robes and sprinkled dust on
their heads. 13Then they sat on
the ground with him for seven
days and seven nights. No one
said a word to him, because
they saw how great his suffer-
ing was.   Ge 25:2; 50:10; Jos 7:6

*a*21 Or *will return there*   *b*1 Hebrew *the sons of God*   *c*10 The Hebrew word
rendered *foolish* denotes moral deficiency.

Job Speaks

3 After this, Job opened his mouth and cursed the day of his birth. ²He said: Jer 15:10

³"May the day of my birth
    perish,
  and the night it was said,
    'A boy is born!'   Job 10:18
⁴That day—may it turn to
    darkness;
  may God above not care
    about it;
  may no light shine upon it.
⁵May darkness and deep
    shadow*ᵃ* claim it once
    more;   Job 10:21
  may a cloud settle over it;
  may blackness overwhelm
    its light.
⁶That night—may thick
    darkness seize it;   Job 23:17
  may it not be included
    among the days of the
    year
  nor be entered in any of the
    months.
⁷May that night be barren;
  may no shout of joy be
    heard in it.   Ps 20:5; 33:3
⁸May those who curse days*ᵇ*
    curse that day,
  those who are ready to
    rouse Leviathan.   Job 41:10
⁹May its morning stars
    become dark;
  may it wait for daylight in
    vain
  and not see the first rays of
    dawn,   Job 41:18
¹⁰for it did not shut the doors
    of the womb on me

to hide trouble from my
    eyes.

¹¹"Why did I not perish at
    birth,
  and die as I came from the
    womb?   Job 10:18
¹²Why were there knees to
    receive me   Isa 66:12
  and breasts that I might be
    nursed?
¹³For now I would be lying
    down in peace;   Job 17:13
  I would be asleep and at
    rest   Job 10:22
¹⁴with kings and counselors of
    the earth,   Job 12:17
  who built for themselves
    places now lying in
    ruins,   Job 15:28
¹⁵with rulers who had gold,
  who filled their houses with
    silver.   Job 12:21; 15:29
¹⁶Or why was I not hidden in
    the ground like a
    stillborn child,   Ps 58:8; Ecc 6:3
  like an infant who never
    saw the light of day? Ps 71:6
¹⁷There the wicked cease from
    turmoil,   Job 30:26; Ecc 4:2
  and there the weary are at
    rest.
¹⁸Captives also enjoy their
    ease;   Isa 51:14
  they no longer hear the
    slave driver's shout. Job 39:7
¹⁹The small and the great are
    there,   Job 9:22; Ecc 12:5
  and the slave is freed from
    his master.

²⁰"Why is light given to those
    in misery,

ᵃ5 Or *and the shadow of death*   *ᵇ8* Or *the sea*

and life to the bitter of soul,
²¹to those who long for death
    that does not come, Rev 9:6
who search for it more than
    for hidden treasure, Pr 2:4
²²who are filled with gladness
    and rejoice when they reach
    the grave? Job 7:16; Ecc 4:3
²³Why is life given to a man
    whose way is hidden, Pr 4:19
    whom God has hedged in?
²⁴For sighing comes to me
    instead of food; Ps 5:1
    my groans pour out like
    water. Ps 42:3-4
²⁵What I feared has come upon
    me;
    what I dreaded has
    happened to me. Job 7:9
²⁶I have no peace, no
    quietness; Isa 48:22
    I have no rest, but only
    turmoil." Job 7:4; 10:18

Eliphaz

4 Then Eliphaz the Temanite
   replied: Ge 36:11; Job 15:1

²"If someone ventures a word
    with you, will you be
    impatient?
    But who can keep from
    speaking? Job 32:20
³Think how you have
    instructed many, Job 29:23
    how you have strengthened
    feeble hands. Job 26:2
⁴Your words have supported
    those who stumbled;
    you have strengthened
    faltering knees. Job 29:11
⁵But now trouble comes to
    you, and you are
    discouraged; Jos 1:9

it strikes you, and you are
    dismayed. Job 6:14
⁶Should not your piety be
    your confidence Ps 27:3
    and your blameless ways
    your hope? Ge 6:9

⁷"Consider now: Who, being
    innocent, has ever
    perished? Job 5:11; Ps 37:25
    Where were the upright
    ever destroyed? Job 8:20
⁸As I have observed, those
    who plow evil Job 5:3
    and those who sow trouble
    reap it. Ps 7:15; Pr 22:8
⁹At the breath of God they are
    destroyed; Ex 15:10; Job 41:21
    at the blast of his anger
    they perish. Job 40:13; Isa 25:7
¹⁰The lions may roar and
    growl, Ps 22:13
    yet the teeth of the great
    lions are broken. Ps 58:6
¹¹The lion perishes for lack of
    prey, Job 27:11
    and the cubs of the lioness
    are scattered. Job 5:4

¹²"A word was secretly
    brought to me, Job 32:13
    my ears caught a whisper
    of it. Job 26:14; 33:14
¹³Amid disquieting dreams in
    the night,
    when deep sleep falls on
    men, Job 33:15
¹⁴fear and trembling seized me
    and made all my bones
    shake. Job 21:6; Jer 23:9
¹⁵A spirit glided past my face,
    and the hair on my body
    stood on end. Da 5:6; Mt 14:26
¹⁶It stopped,

but I could not tell what it
was.
A form stood before my eyes,
and I heard a hushed voice:
¹⁷'Can a mortal be more
righteous than God? Job 9:2
Can a man be more pure
than his Maker? Job 10:3
¹⁸If God places no trust in his
servants, Job 15:15; Heb 1:14
if he charges his angels
with error, Job 25:5
¹⁹how much more those who
live in houses of clay,
whose foundations are in
the dust,
who are crushed more Job 5:4
readily than a moth!
²⁰Between dawn and dusk
they are broken to
pieces;
unnoticed, they perish
forever. Job 20:7; Ps 89:47
²¹Are not the cords of their
tent pulled up, Job 8:22
so that they die without
wisdom?'ᵃ Job 36:12; Pr 5:23

5 "Call if you will, but who
will answer you? Hab 1:2
To which of the holy ones
will you turn? Job 15:15
²Resentment kills a fool, Job 21:15
and envy slays the simple.
³I myself have seen a fool
taking root, Ps 37:35
but suddenly his house was
cursed. Job 24:18; Pr 6:15
⁴His children are far from
safety,
crushed in court without a
defender. Job 4:11; 20:10
 Ps 109:12; Am 5:12

⁵The hungry consume his
harvest, Lev 26:16; Job 20:18
taking it even from among
thorns,
and the thirsty pant after
his wealth.
⁶For hardship does not spring
from the soil,
nor does trouble sprout
from the ground. Job 4:8
⁷Yet man is born to trouble
as surely as sparks fly
upward. Job 10:17; 15:35

⁸"But if it were I, I would
appeal to God;
I would lay my cause before
him. Job 8:5; Ps 35:23
⁹He performs wonders that
cannot be fathomed, Ps 78:4
miracles that cannot be
counted. Ps 71:15
¹⁰He bestows rain on the earth;
he sends water upon the
countryside. Job 36:28; 37:6
¹¹The lowly he sets on high,
and those who mourn are
lifted to safety. Mt 5:4; Jas 4:10
¹²He thwarts the plans of the
crafty, Ne 4:15; Ps 33:10
so that their hands achieve
no success. Job 12:23
¹³He catches the wise in their
craftiness, Job 37:24; Isa 29:14
and the schemes of the wily
are swept away. Job 9:4
¹⁴Darkness comes upon them
in the daytime; Job 15:22
at noon they grope as in the
night. Job 18:5; Am 8:9
¹⁵He saves the needy from the
sword in their mouth;

ᵃ21 Some interpreters end the quotation after verse 17.

he saves them from the
clutches of the
powerful.
16So the poor have hope,
and injustice shuts its
mouth. Job 20:19; Ps 107:42

17"Blessed is the man whom
God corrects; Ps 94:12
so do not despise the
discipline of the
Almighty. *a* Pr 3:11; Jer 31:18
18For he wounds, but he also
binds up; Ps 147:3
he injures, but his hands
also heal. Dt 32:39
19From six calamities he will
rescue you; Da 3:17
in seven no harm will befall
you. Ps 34:19; 91:10
20In famine he will ransom you
from death, Ps 33:19
and in battle from the
stroke of the sword.Ps 22:20
21You will be protected from
the lash of the tongue,
and need not fear when
destruction comes. Ps 31:20
22You will laugh at destruction
and famine, Job 8:21
and need not fear the beasts
of the earth. Ps 91:13
23For you will have a covenant
with the stones of the
field, Ps 91:12; Isa 28:15
and the wild animals will be
at peace with you. Job 40:20
24You will know that your tent
is secure; Job 12:6
you will take stock of your
property and find
nothing missing. Job 8:6

25You will know that your
children will be many,
and your descendants like
the grass of the earth.
26You will come to the grave in
full vigor, Ge 15:15; Dt 11:21
like sheaves gathered in
season. Pr 3:21-26
27"We have examined this, and
it is true.
So hear it and apply it to
yourself." Job 8:5; 32:10,17

Job

6 Then Job replied:
2"If only my anguish could
be weighed
and all my misery be placed
on the scales! Job 31:6; Pr 11:1
3It would surely outweigh the
sand of the seas— Pr 27:3
no wonder my words have
been impetuous. Job 7:11
4The arrows of the Almighty
are in me, Job 7:20; Ps 38:2
my spirit drinks in their
poison; Job 21:20; 34:6
God's terrors are marshaled
against me. Job 9:34; 30:15
5Does a wild donkey bray
when it has grass, Job 30:7
or an ox bellow when it has
fodder? Job 24:6; Isa 30:24
6Is tasteless food eaten
without salt,
or is there flavor in the
white of an egg*b*? Job 33:20
7I refuse to touch it;
such food makes me ill.

---

*a*17 Hebrew *Shaddai*; here and throughout Job
this phrase is uncertain.

*b*6 The meaning of the Hebrew for

⁸"Oh, that I might have my
    request,
  that God would grant what
    I hope for,   Job 14:13
⁹that God would be willing to
    crush me,   Job 19:2
  to let loose his hand and cut
    me off!   Nu 11:15; Ps 31:22
¹⁰Then I would still have this
    consolation—   Job 2:11
  my joy in unrelenting
    pain—   Ps 38:17; Jer 4:19
  that I had not denied the
    words of the Holy One.

¹¹"What strength do I have,
    that I should still hope?
  What prospects, that I
    should be patient?
¹²Do I have the strength of
    stone?
  Is my flesh bronze?   Job 26:2
¹³Do I have any power to help
    myself,
  now that success has been
    driven from me?

¹⁴"A despairing man should
    have the devotion of his
    friends,   Job 4:5; Ps 38:11
  even though he forsakes
    the fear of the Almighty.
¹⁵But my brothers are as
    undependable as
    intermittent streams,
  as the streams that overflow
¹⁶when darkened by thawing
    ice
  and swollen with melting
    snow,   Ps 147:18
¹⁷but that cease to flow in the
    dry season,
  and in the heat vanish from
    their channels.   Job 24:19

¹⁸Caravans turn aside from
    their routes;
  they go up into the
    wasteland and perish.
¹⁹The caravans of Tema look
    for water,   Ge 25:15
  the traveling merchants of
    Sheba look in hope.   Ge 10:7
²⁰They are distressed, because
    they had been confident;
  they arrive there, only to be
    disappointed.   Jer 14:3
²¹Now you too have proved to
    be of no help;
  you see something dreadful
    and are afraid.   Ps 38:11
²²Have I ever said, 'Give
    something on my behalf,
  pay a ransom for me from
    your wealth,   Job 33:24
²³deliver me from the hand of
    the enemy,
  ransom me from the
    clutches of the ruthless'?

²⁴"Teach me, and I will be
    quiet;   Job 2:10; Ps 39:1
  show me where I have been
    wrong.   Job 19:4
²⁵How painful are honest
    words!   Ecc 12:11
  But what do your
    arguments prove?
²⁶Do you mean to correct what
    I say,
  and treat the words of a
    despairing man as wind?
²⁷You would even cast lots for
    the fatherless   Eze 24:6
  and barter away your
    friend.

²⁸"But now be so kind as to
    look at me.   Job 9:15

Would I lie to your face?
²⁹Relent, do not be unjust; Job 19:6
  reconsider, for my integrity
    is at stake. ᵃ   Job 9:21
³⁰Is there any wickedness on
    my lips?   Job 27:4
  Can my mouth not discern
    malice?   Job 12:11

7 "Does not man have hard
  service on earth? Job 14:14
  Are not his days like those
    of a hired man?   Lev 25:50
²Like a slave longing for the
    evening shadows,   Job 14:1
  or a hired man waiting
    eagerly for his wages,
³so I have been allotted
    months of futility,
  and nights of misery have
    been assigned to me.
⁴When I lie down I think,
    'How long before I get
    up?'   Dt 28:67
  The night drags on, and I
    toss till dawn.
⁵My body is clothed with
    worms and scabs,   Job 17:14
  my skin is broken and
    festering.   Dt 28:35

⁶"My days are swifter than a
    weaver's shuttle,   Job 9:25
  and they come to an end
    without hope.   Job 13:15
⁷Remember, O God, that my
    life is but a breath; Ps 78:39
  my eyes will never see
    happiness again.   Job 10:20
⁸The eye that now sees me
    will see me no longer;
  you will look for me, but I
    will be no more.   Job 20:9

⁹As a cloud vanishes and is
    gone,   Job 3:25
  so he who goes down to the
    graveᵇ does not return.
¹⁰He will never come to his
    house again;
  his place will know him no
    more.   Job 18:21; Ps 37:10

¹¹"Therefore I will not keep
    silent;   Job 9:35; 13:13
  I will speak out in the
    anguish of my spirit,
  I will complain in the
    bitterness of my soul.
¹²Am I the sea, or the monster
    of the deep,   Job 38:8-11
  that you put me under
    guard?   Isa 1:14
¹³When I think my bed will
    comfort me
  and my couch will ease my
    complaint,   Job 19:27
¹⁴even then you frighten me
    with dreams
  and terrify me with visions,
¹⁵so that I prefer strangling
    and death,   1Ki 19:4
  rather than this body of
    mine.   Job 6:9; Rev 9:6
¹⁶I despise my life; I would not
    live forever.   Job 9:21
  Let me alone; my days have
    no meaning.   Ps 39:13

¹⁷"What is man that you make
    so much of him,
  that you give him so much
    attention,   Job 4:19; Ps 8:4
¹⁸that you examine him every
    morning   Ps 73:14
  and test him every
    moment?   Job 23:10; Ps 17:3

ᵃ29 Or *my righteousness still stands*   ᵇ9 Hebrew *Sheol*

¹⁹Will you never look away
    from me,
  or let me alone even for an
    instant? Job 9:18
²⁰If I have sinned, what have I
    done to you, Job 35:6
  O watcher of men?
  Why have you made me your
    target? Job 6:4
  Have I become a burden to
    you?ᵃ
²¹Why do you not pardon my
    offenses
  and forgive my sins? Job 9:28
  For I will soon lie down in
    the dust; Job 10:9; Ps 7:5
  you will search for me, but I
    will be no more." Job 3:13

Bildad

8 Then Bildad the Shuhite re-
    plied: Job 18:1; 25:1

²"How long will you say such
    things? Job 11:2; 18:2
  Your words are a blustering
    wind. 2Ch 36:16
³Does God pervert justice?
  Does the Almighty pervert
    what is right? Ge 18:25
⁴When your children sinned
    against him,
  he gave them over to the
    penalty of their sin. Job 1:19
⁵But if you will look to God
  and plead with the
    Almighty, Job 5:8; 9:15
⁶if you are pure and upright,
  even now he will rouse
    himself on your behalf

and restore you to your
    rightful place. Job 5:24
⁷Your beginnings will seem
    humble,
  so prosperous will your
    future be. Job 21:13; Jer 29:11

⁸"Ask the former generations
  and find out what their
    fathers learned,
⁹for we were born only
    yesterday and know
    nothing, Ge 47:9
  and our days on earth are
    but a shadow. 2Ch 10:6
¹⁰Will they not instruct you
    and tell you? Pr 1:8
  Will they not bring forth
    words from their
    understanding? Pr 2:1-2
¹¹Can papyrus grow tall where
    there is no marsh? Job 40:21
  Can reeds thrive without
    water? Isa 19:6; 35:7
¹²While still growing and
    uncut,
  they wither more quickly
    than grass. 2Ki 19:26
¹³Such is the destiny of all who
    forget God; Ps 9:17; 37:38
  so perishes the hope of the
    godless. Job 6:9; Pr 10:28
¹⁴What he trusts in is fragileᵇ;
  what he relies on is a
    spider's web. Job 27:18; Isa 59:5
¹⁵He leans on his web, but it
    gives way;
  he clings to it, but it does
    not hold. Mt 7:26
¹⁶He is like a well-watered
    plant in the sunshine,

ᵃ20 A few manuscripts of the Masoretic Text, an ancient Hebrew scribal tradition and
Septuagint; most manuscripts of the Masoretic Text *I have become a burden to myself.*
ᵇ14 The meaning of the Hebrew for this word is uncertain.

spreading its shoots over
the garden; Ps 80:11; Jer 11:16
¹⁷it entwines its roots around a
pile of rocks
and looks for a place among
the stones.
¹⁸But when it is torn from its
spot,
that place disowns it and
says, 'I never saw you.'
¹⁹Surely its life withers away,
andᵃ from the soil other
plants grow. Ps 119:90

²⁰"Surely God does not reject a
blameless man Job 1:1
or strengthen the hands of
evildoers. Ge 18:25
²¹He will yet fill your mouth
with laughter Job 5:22
and your lips with shouts of
joy. Job 35:10; Ps 47:5
²²Your enemies will be clothed
in shame, Job 27:7
and the tents of the wicked
will be no more." Job 18:6

Job

9 Then Job replied:
²"Indeed, I know that this
is true.
But how can a mortal be
righteous before God?
³Though one wished to
dispute with him, Job 40:5
he could not answer him
one time out of a
thousand. Job 10:2; 37:19
⁴His wisdom is profound, his
power is vast. Job 11:6
Who has resisted him and
come out unscathed?

⁵He moves mountains
without their
knowing it
and overturns them in his
anger. Ps 18:7; Mt 17:20
⁶He shakes the earth from its
place
and makes its pillars
tremble. Job 26:14; Isa 2:21
⁷He speaks to the sun and it
does not shine; Isa 34:4
he seals off the light of the
stars. Isa 13:10; Jer 4:23
⁸He alone stretches out the
heavens Ge 1:1,8
and treads on the waves of
the sea. Job 38:16; Ps 77:19
⁹He is the Maker of the Bear
and Orion, Job 32:22
the Pleiades and the
constellations of the
south. Ge 1:16
¹⁰He performs wonders that
cannot be fathomed,
miracles that cannot be
counted. Dt 6:22; Job 5:9
¹¹When he passes me, I cannot
see him;
when he goes by, I cannot
perceive him. Job 23:8-9
¹²If he snatches away, who can
stop him? Nu 23:20; Job 11:10
Who can say to him, 'What
are you doing?' Dt 32:39
¹³God does not restrain his
anger; Nu 14:18; Job 10:15
even the cohorts of Rahab
cowered at his feet. Job 26:12
¹⁴"How then can I dispute
with him?
How can I find words to
argue with him?

ᵃ19 Or Surely all the joy it has / is that

¹⁵Though I were innocent, I
    could not answer him;
I could only plead with my
    Judge for mercy.   Job 8:5
¹⁶Even if I summoned him and
    he responded,
I do not believe he would
    give me a hearing. Job 13:22
¹⁷He would crush me with a
    storm   Job 16:12; Ps 83:15
and multiply my wounds
    for no reason.   Job 16:14
¹⁸He would not let me regain
    my breath
but would overwhelm me
    with misery.   Job 7:19
¹⁹If it is a matter of strength,
    he is mighty!   Ne 9:32
And if it is a matter of
    justice, who will
    summon him*a*?   Jer 49:19
²⁰Even if I were innocent, my
    mouth would condemn
    me;
if I were blameless, it would
    pronounce me guilty.

²¹"Although I am blameless,
I have no concern for
    myself;   Nu 11:15; Job 10:1; 34:6
I despise my own life.
²²It is all the same; that is why
    I say,
'He destroys both the
    blameless and the
    wicked.'   Job 3:19; Eze 21:3
²³When a scourge brings
    sudden death,
he mocks the despair of the
    innocent.   Job 24:1; Ps 64:4
²⁴When a land falls into the
    hands of the wicked,
he blindfolds its judges.

If it is not he, then who is
    it?   Job 12:9; Isa 41:20
²⁵"My days are swifter than a
    runner;   Job 7:6
they fly away without a
    glimpse of joy.   Job 10:10
²⁶They skim past like boats of
    papyrus,   Job 24:18; Ps 46:3
like eagles swooping down
    on their prey.   Job 39:29
²⁷If I say, 'I will forget my
    complaint,   Job 7:11
I will change my
    expression, and smile,'
²⁸I still dread all my sufferings,
for I know you will not hold
    me innocent.   Ex 34:7
²⁹Since I am already found
    guilty,
why should I struggle in
    vain?   Ps 37:33
³⁰Even if I washed myself with
    soap*b*   Mal 3:2
and my hands with
    washing soda,   Job 17:9
³¹you would plunge me into a
    slime pit   Ps 35:7; Na 3:6
so that even my clothes
    would detest me.   Job 7:20

³²"He is not a man like me that
    I might answer him, Nu 23:19
that we might confront each
    other in court.
³³If only there were someone
    to arbitrate between us,
to lay his hand upon us
    both,   1Sa 2:25
³⁴someone to remove God's
    rod from me,   Job 21:9
so that his terror would
    frighten me no more.

---

*a*19 See Septuagint; Hebrew *me*.   *b*30 Or *snow*

35Then I would speak up
  without fear of him,
  but as it now stands with
  me, I cannot. Job 7:15

10 "I loathe my very life;
  therefore I will give free
  rein to my complaint
and speak out in the
  bitterness of my soul.
2I will say to God: Do not
  condemn me, Job 13:3
  but tell me what charges
  you have against me.
3Does it please you to oppress
  me, Job 9:22
  to spurn the work of your
  hands, Ge 1:26
  while you smile on the
  schemes of the wicked?
4Do you have eyes of flesh?
  Do you see as a mortal
  sees? 1Sa 16:7
5Are your days like those of a
  mortal
  or your years like those of a
  man, Job 36:26; Ps 39:5
6that you must search out my
  faults
  and probe after my sin—
7though you know that I am
  not guilty Job 6:29
  and that no one can rescue
  me from your hand?

8"Your hands shaped me and
  made me. Ge 2:7
  Will you now turn and
  destroy me? 2Sa 14:14
9Remember that you molded
  me like clay. Job 4:9
  Will you now turn me to
  dust again? Job 7:21

10Did you not pour me out like
  milk
  and curdle me like cheese,
11clothe me with skin and flesh
  and knit me together with
  bones and sinews? Ps 139:13
12You gave me life and showed
  me kindness, Ge 2:7
  and in your providence
  watched over my spirit.

13"But this is what you
  concealed in your heart,
  and I know that this was in
  your mind: Job 23:13
14If I sinned, you would be
  watching me Job 13:27
  and would not let my
  offense go unpunished.
15If I am guilty—woe to me!
  Even if I am innocent, I
  cannot lift my head, Job 9:13
  for I am full of shame
  and drowned in[a] my
  affliction. Ps 25:16
16If I hold my head high, you
  stalk me like a lion Ps 7:2
  and again display your
  awesome power against
  me. Job 5:9
17You bring new witnesses
  against me 1Ki 21:10
  and increase your anger
  toward me; Ru 1:21
  your forces come against
  me wave upon wave. Job 5:7

18"Why then did you bring me
  out of the womb? Job 3:8
  I wish I had died before any
  eye saw me. Job 3:26
19If only I had never come into
  being,

a15 Or *and aware of*

or had been carried straight
from the womb to the
grave!   Job 3:3; Jer 15:10
²⁰Are not my few days almost
over?   Job 7:7
Turn away from me so I can
have a moment's joy
²¹before I go to the place of no
return,   2Sa 12:23
to the land of gloom and
deep shadow,ᵃ   Job 3:5
²²to the land of deepest night,
of deep shadow and
disorder,
where even the light is like
darkness."   1Sa 2:9

Zophar

11 Then Zophar the Naamathite replied: Job 2:11

²"Are all these words to go
unanswered?   Job 8:2
Is this talker to be
vindicated?   Ge 41:6
³Will your idle talk reduce
men to silence?   Eph 4:29
Will no one rebuke you
when you mock?   Job 12:4
⁴You say to God, 'My beliefs
are flawless   Job 9:21
and I am pure in your
sight.'   Job 10:7
⁵Oh, how I wish that God
would speak,   Ex 20:19
that he would open his lips
against you
⁶and disclose to you the
secrets of wisdom,   Job 9:4
for true wisdom has two
sides.

Know this: God has even
forgotten some of your
sin.   Ezr 9:13
⁷"Can you fathom the
mysteries of God?   Job 5:9
Can you probe the limits of
the Almighty?   Ecc 3:11
⁸They are higher than the
heavens—what can you
do?   Ge 15:5; Eph 3:18
They are deeper than the
depths of the graveᵇ—
what can you know?
⁹Their measure is longer than
the earth   Eph 3:19-20
and wider than the sea.
¹⁰"If he comes along and
confines you in prison
and convenes a court, who
can oppose him?   Job 9:12
¹¹Surely he recognizes
deceitful men;
and when he sees evil, does
he not take note?   Job 10:4
¹²But a witless man can no
more become wise
than a wild donkey's colt
can be born a man.ᶜ
¹³"Yet if you devote your heart
to him   1Sa 7:3; Ps 78:8
and stretch out your hands
to him,   Ex 9:29; Job 5:8
¹⁴if you put away the sin that
is in your hand   Jos 24:14
and allow no evil to dwell
in your tent,   Ps 101:4
¹⁵then you will lift up your face
without shame;   Job 22:26
you will stand firm and
without fear.

ᵃ21 Or *and the shadow of death; also in verse 22*   ᵇ8 Hebrew *than Sheol*   ᶜ12 Or *wild*
donkey can be born tame

¹⁶You will surely forget your
     trouble,
  recalling it only as waters
     gone by.   Jos 7:5
¹⁷Life will be brighter than
     noonday,   Job 22:28
  and darkness will become
     like morning.   Job 17:12
¹⁸You will be secure, because
     there is hope;
  you will look about you and
     take your rest in safety.
¹⁹You will lie down, with no
     one to make you afraid,
  and many will court your
     favor.   Isa 45:14
²⁰But the eyes of the wicked
     will fail,   Dt 28:65
  and escape will elude them;
     their hope will become a
     dying gasp."   Job 8:13

Job

12 Then Job replied:

  ²"Doubtless you are the
     people,
  and wisdom will die with
     you!   Job 15:8; 17:10
³But I have a mind as well as
     you;
  I am not inferior to you.
  Who does not know all
     these things?   Job 13:2

⁴"I have become a
     laughingstock to my
     friends,   Ge 38:23
  though I called upon God
     and he answered—Ps 91:15
  a mere laughingstock,
     though righteous and
     blameless!   Job 6:29

⁵Men at ease have contempt
     for misfortune   Ps 123:4
  as the fate of those whose
     feet are slipping.   Ps 17:5
⁶The tents of marauders are
     undisturbed,   Job 5:24
  and those who provoke
     God are secure—   Job 9:24
  those who carry their god
     in their hands. ᵃ

⁷"But ask the animals, and
     they will teach you, Job 35:11
  or the birds of the air, and
     they will tell you;   Mt 6:26
⁸or speak to the earth, and it
     will teach you,
  or let the fish of the sea
     inform you.
⁹Which of all these does not
     know   Isa 1:3
  that the hand of the LORD
     has done this?   Job 9:24
¹⁰In his hand is the life of
     every creature   Da 5:23
  and the breath of all
     mankind.   Ge 2:7
¹¹Does not the ear test words
  as the tongue tastes food?
¹²Is not wisdom found among
     the aged?   1Ki 4:2
  Does not long life bring
     understanding?   Job 17:4

¹³"To God belong wisdom and
     power;   Job 9:4; Pr 21:30
  counsel and understanding
     are his.   Nu 23:19
¹⁴What he tears down cannot
     be rebuilt;   Job 16:9
  the man he imprisons
     cannot be released.   Job 9:3

ᵃ6 Or *secure / in what God's hand brings them*

15If he holds back the waters,
  there is drought; Dt 28:22
if he lets them loose, they
  devastate the land. Ge 7:24
16To him belong strength and
  victory; Job 9:4
  both deceived and deceiver
  are his. 2Ch 18:22
17He leads counselors away
  stripped Job 19:9
and makes fools of judges.
18He takes off the shackles put
  on by kings Ps 107:14
and ties a loincloth*a* around
  their waist. Job 34:18
19He leads priests away
  stripped
  and overthrows men long
  established. Dt 24:15
20He silences the lips of trusted
  advisers
  and takes away the
  discernment of elders.
21He pours contempt on nobles
  and disarms the mighty.
22He reveals the deep things of
  darkness 1Co 4:5
  and brings deep shadows
  into the light. Job 3:5
23He makes nations great, and
  destroys them; Ps 2:1
  he enlarges nations, and
  disperses them. Ex 34:24
24He deprives the leaders of
  the earth of their reason;
  he sends them wandering
  through a trackless
  waste. Ps 107:40
25They grope in darkness with
  no light; Dt 28:29
  he makes them stagger like
  drunkards. Ps 107:27

13 "My eyes have seen all
  this, Job 9:24
my ears have heard and
  understood it.
2What you know, I also know;
  I am not inferior to you.
3But I desire to speak to the
  Almighty Job 5:17; 40:2
and to argue my case with
  God. Job 5:8; 9:14-20
4You, however, smear me
  with lies; Ps 119:69
you are worthless
  physicians, all of
  you! Job 6:15
5If only you would be
  altogether silent! Jdg 18:19
For you, that would be
  wisdom. Pr 17:28
6Hear now my argument;
  listen to the plea of my lips.
7Will you speak wickedly on
  God's behalf?
  Will you speak deceitfully
  for him? Job 12:16
8Will you show him partiality?
  Will you argue the case for
  God?
9Would it turn out well if he
  examined you? Job 9:3
  Could you deceive him as
  you might deceive
  men?
10He would surely rebuke you
  if you secretly showed
  partiality. Lev 19:15
11Would not his splendor
  terrify you? Job 31:23
  Would not the dread of him
  fall on you? Ex 3:6
12Your maxims are proverbs of
  ashes;

a18 Or shackles of kings / and ties a belt

your defenses are defenses
of clay.   Ne 4:2-3

13"Keep silent and let me
speak;   Job 7:11
then let come to me what
may.   Job 9:21
14Why do I put myself in
jeopardy
and take my life in my
hands?   Jdg 9:17
15Though he slay me, yet will I
hope in him;   Ps 23:4
I will surely*a* defend my
ways to his face.   Job 5:8
16Indeed, this will turn out for
my deliverance,   Ps 30:5
for no godless man would
dare come before him!
17Listen carefully to my words;
let your ears take in what I
say.
18Now that I have prepared my
case,   Job 23:4; 37:19
I know I will be vindicated.
19Can anyone bring charges
against me?   Job 40:4
If so, I will be silent and
die.   Job 3:13; 9:15

20"Only grant me these two
things, O God,
and then I will not hide
from you:
21Withdraw your hand far
from me,   Ex 9:3
and stop frightening me
with your terrors.   Job 6:4
22Then summon me and I will
answer,   Job 9:35
or let me speak, and you
reply.   Job 9:16

23How many wrongs and sins
have I committed?   1Sa 26:18
Show me my offense and
my sin.   Job 7:21; 9:21
24Why do you hide your face
and consider me your
enemy?   Dt 32:20; Job 16:9
25Will you torment a
windblown leaf?   Lev 26:36
Will you chase after dry
chaff?   Job 21:18
26For you write down bitter
things against me
and make me inherit the
sins of my youth.   Job 18:7
27You fasten my feet in
shackles;   Ge 40:15
you keep close watch on all
my paths   Job 10:14
by putting marks on the
soles of my feet.

28"So man wastes away like
something rotten,
like a garment eaten by
moths.   Ps 39:11; 102:26

14 "Man born of woman
is of few days and full of
trouble.   Ge 3:17; Job 10:20
2He springs up like a flower
and withers away;   Ps 103:15
like a fleeting shadow, he
does not endure.   Job 4:20
3Do you fix your eye on such
a one?   Ps 8:4; 144:3
Will you bring him*b* before
you for judgment?   Job 7:18
4Who can bring what is pure
from the impure?   Job 4:17
No one!   Job 9:30
5Man's days are determined;

---

*a*15 Or *He will surely slay me; I have no hope — / yet I will*   *b*3 Septuagint, Vulgate and
Syriac; Hebrew *me*

you have decreed the
number of his
months
and have set limits he
cannot exceed. Ac 17:26
⁶So look away from him and
let him alone, Job 7:19
till he has put in his time
like a hired man. Ps 39:13

⁷"At least there is hope for a
tree: Job 19:10; Ps 52:5
If it is cut down, it will
sprout again,
and its new shoots will not
fail. Isa 6:13
⁸Its roots may grow old in the
ground
and its stump die in the
soil, Isa 11:1; 53:2
⁹yet at the scent of water it
will bud Job 29:19
and put forth shoots like a
plant. Lev 26:4; Eze 34:27
¹⁰But man dies and is laid low;
he breathes his last and is
no more. Job 10:21; 13:19
¹¹As water disappears from the
sea
or a riverbed becomes
parched and dry, 2Sa 14:14
¹²so man lies down and does
not rise;
till the heavens are no
more, men will not
awake
or be roused from their
sleep. Ps 102:26; Ac 3:21

¹³"If only you would hide me
in the grave[a] Job 7:9
and conceal me till your
anger has passed! Ps 30:5

If only you would set me a
time
and then remember me! Job 6:8
¹⁴If a man dies, will he live
again?
All the days of my hard
service Job 7:1
I will wait for my renewal[b]
to come. 2Ki 6:33
¹⁵You will call and I will
answer you; Job 13:22
you will long for the
creature your hands
have made. Job 10:3
¹⁶Surely then you will count
my steps Job 10:4
but not keep track of my
sin. 1Co 13:5
¹⁷My offenses will be sealed up
in a bag; Dt 32:34; Jer 32:10
you will cover over my sin.
¹⁸"But as a mountain erodes
and crumbles Eze 38:20
and as a rock is moved from
its place, Job 18:4
¹⁹as water wears away stones
and torrents wash away the
soil, Ge 7:23; Eze 13:13
so you destroy man's hope.
²⁰You overpower him once for
all, and he is gone; Job 4:20
you change his
countenance and send
him away. Job 7:10
²¹If his sons are honored, he
does not know it;
if they are brought low, he
does not see it. Job 21:21
²²He feels but the pain of his
own body Ps 38:7
and mourns only for
himself." Job 21:21

Eliphaz

15 Then Eliphaz the Temanite replied:
                                     Job 4:1

2"Would a wise man answer
    with empty notions
  or fill his belly with the hot
    east wind?   Ge 41:6
3Would he argue with useless
    words,
  with speeches that have no
    value?   Ne 4:2-3
4But you even undermine
    piety
  and hinder devotion to
    God.   Job 25:6
5Your sin prompts your
    mouth;   Job 11:6
  you adopt the tongue of the
    crafty.   Job 5:13
6Your own mouth condemns
    you, not mine;
  your own lips testify
    against you.   Job 9:15

7"Are you the first man ever
    born?   Job 38:21
  Were you brought forth
    before the hills?   1Sa 2:8
8Do you listen in on God's
    council?   Job 29:4; Isa 9:6
  Do you limit wisdom to
    yourself?   Job 12:2
9What do you know that we
    do not know?
  What insights do you have
    that we do not have?
10The gray-haired and the aged
    are on our side,   Job 12:12
  men even older than your
    father.   2Ch 10:6
11Are God's consolations not
    enough for you,   Ge 37:35
  words spoken gently to
    you?   Dt 8:3
12Why has your heart carried
    you away,   Job 11:13
  and why do your eyes
    flash,
13so that you vent your rage
    against God   Pr 29:11
  and pour out such words
    from your mouth?   Ps 94:4

14"What is man, that he could
    be pure,
  or one born of woman, that
    he could be righteous?
15If God places no trust in his
    holy ones,   Job 5:1
  if even the heavens are not
    pure in his eyes,   Job 4:18
16how much less man, who is
    vile and corrupt,   Lev 5:2
  who drinks up evil like
    water!   Job 20:12

17"Listen to me and I will
    explain to you;
  let me tell you what I have
    seen,   Job 4:8
18what wise men have
    declared,
  hiding nothing received
    from their fathers   Dt 32:7
19(to whom alone the land was
    given   Ge 12:1
  when no alien passed
    among them):
20All his days the wicked man
    suffers torment,   Isa 8:22
  the ruthless through all the
    years stored up for him.
21Terrifying sounds fill his
    ears;   1Sa 3:11
  when all seems well,
    marauders attack him.

22He despairs of escaping the
   darkness;   Job 5:14
   he is marked for the sword.
23He wanders about—food for
   vultures*a*;   Ps 109:10
   he knows the day of
   darkness is at hand.
24Distress and anguish fill him
   with terror;   Isa 8:22
   they overwhelm him, like a
   king poised to attack,
25because he shakes his fist at
   God   Ps 44:16
   and vaunts himself against
   the Almighty,   Job 11:8
26defiantly charging against
   him
   with a thick, strong shield.

27"Though his face is covered
   with fat
   and his waist bulges with
   flesh,   Jdg 3:17
28he will inhabit ruined towns
   and houses where no one
   lives,   Isa 5:9
   houses crumbling to rubble.
29He will no longer be rich and
   his wealth will not
   endure,   Job 3:15
   nor will his possessions
   spread over the land.
30He will not escape the
   darkness;   Job 5:14
   a flame will wither his
   shoots,   Job 8:19; 16:7
   and the breath of God's
   mouth will carry him
   away.   Ex 15:10; Isa 40:23
31Let him not deceive himself
   by trusting what is
   worthless,   Job 31:5; Isa 30:12

for he will get nothing in
   return.   Job 20:7
32Before his time he will be
   paid in full,   Ecc 7:17
   and his branches will not
   flourish.
33He will be like a vine
   stripped of its unripe
   grapes,   Hab 3:17
   like an olive tree shedding
   its blossoms.   Job 4:20
34For the company of the
   godless will be barren,
   and fire will consume the
   tents of those who love
   bribes.   Ex 23:8; Heb 10:27
35They conceive trouble and
   give birth to evil;   Job 5:7
   their womb fashions
   deceit."

Job

16

Then Job replied:
2"I have heard many
   things like these;
   miserable comforters are
   you all!   Job 6:15; Ps 69:20
3Will your long-winded
   speeches never end?
   What ails you that you keep
   on arguing?   Job 6:26
4I also could speak like you,
   if you were in my place;
   I could make fine speeches
   against you
   and shake my head at you.
5But my mouth would
   encourage you;
   comfort from my lips would
   bring you relief.   Job 29:25

*a*23 Or *about, looking for food*

⁶"Yet if I speak, my pain is
    not relieved;
and if I refrain, it does not
    go away.   Job 6:3
⁷Surely, O God, you have
    worn me out;   Jdg 8:5
you have devastated my
    entire household.   Job 1:19
⁸You have bound me—and it
    has become a witness;
my gauntness rises up and
    testifies against me.
⁹God assails me and tears me
    in his anger   Job 12:14
and gnashes his teeth at
    me;   Job 30:21; Ps 35:16
my opponent fastens on me
    his piercing eyes. Job 13:24
¹⁰Men open their mouths to
    jeer at me;   Ps 22:13
they strike my cheek in
    scorn   Isa 50:6
and unite together against
    me.   Job 11:3; Ps 27:3
¹¹God has turned me over to
    evil men
and thrown me into the
    clutches of the wicked.
¹²All was well with me, but he
    shattered me;
he seized me by the neck
    and crushed me.   Job 9:17
He has made me his target;
¹³   his archers surround me.
Without pity, he pierces my
    kidneys   Job 20:24
and spills my gall on the
    ground.
¹⁴Again and again he bursts
    upon me;   Job 9:17
he rushes at me like a
    warrior.   Joel 2:7

¹⁵"I have sewed sackcloth over
    my skin   Ge 37:34
and buried my brow in the
    dust.   Job 2:8
¹⁶My face is red with weeping,
    deep shadows ring my
    eyes;   Job 2:7; 17:7
¹⁷yet my hands have been free
    of violence   Isa 55:7
and my prayer is pure. Job 6:28
¹⁸"O earth, do not cover my
    blood;   Ge 4:10
may my cry never be laid to
    rest!   Job 19:24; Ps 5:2
¹⁹Even now my witness is in
    heaven;   Ge 31:50; Job 22:12
my advocate is on high.
²⁰My intercessor is my friend[a]
as my eyes pour out tears to
    God;   La 2:19
²¹on behalf of a man he pleads
    with God   1Ki 8:45
as a man pleads for his
    friend.
²²"Only a few years will pass
before I go on the journey
    of no return.   Job 10:21
17 ¹My spirit is broken,
    my days are cut short,
the grave awaits me.   Ps 88:3-4
²Surely mockers surround me;
my eyes must dwell on
    their hostility. Job 6:14; 11:3
³"Give me, O God, the pledge
    you demand.   Ps 35:2
Who else will put up
    security for me?   Pr 6:1
⁴You have closed their minds
    to understanding;   Job 12:12
therefore you will not let
    them triumph.

---

a20 Or *My friends treat me with scorn*

⁵If a man denounces his
    friends for reward, Ex 22:15
  the eyes of his children will
    fail. Job 11:20

⁶"God has made me a byword
    to everyone, 1Ki 9:7
  a man in whose face people
    spit. Nu 12:14
⁷My eyes have grown dim
    with grief; Job 16:8
  my whole frame is but a
    shadow. Job 2:12
⁸Upright men are appalled at
    this;
  the innocent are aroused
    against the ungodly.
⁹Nevertheless, the righteous
    will hold to their ways,
  and those with clean hands
    will grow stronger. Ps 84:7

¹⁰"But come on, all of you, try
    again!
  I will not find a wise man
    among you. Job 12:2
¹¹My days have passed, my
    plans are shattered,
  and so are the desires of my
    heart. Job 7:6
¹²These men turn night into
    day; Isa 50:11
  in the face of darkness they
    say, 'Light is near.' Job 5:17
¹³If the only home I hope for is
    the grave,ᵃ 2Sa 14:14
  if I spread out my bed in
    darkness, Ps 139:8
¹⁴if I say to corruption, 'You
    are my father,' Job 13:28
  and to the worm, 'My
    mother' or 'My sister,'
¹⁵where then is my hope? Job 4:19

Who can see any hope for
    me? Ps 31:22
¹⁶Will it go down to the gates
    of deathᵃ? Job 7:9
  Will we descend together
    into the dust?" Ge 2:7

Bildad

18 Then Bildad the Shuhite
  replied: Job 8:1

²"When will you end these
    speeches? Job 8:2
  Be sensible, and then we
    can talk.
³Why are we regarded as
    cattle Job 12:7
  and considered stupid in
    your sight? Ps 73:22
⁴You who tear yourself to
    pieces in your anger,
  is the earth to be
    abandoned for your
    sake?
  Or must the rocks be
    moved from their place?

⁵"The lamp of the wicked is
    snuffed out; Job 21:17
  the flame of his fire stops
    burning. Job 12:25
⁶The light in his tent becomes
    dark; Job 5:14
  the lamp beside him goes
    out. Job 11:17
⁷The vigor of his step is
    weakened; Ps 18:36
  his own schemes throw him
    down. Job 15:6
⁸His feet thrust him into a net
  and he wanders into its
    mesh.
⁹A trap seizes him by the heel;

ᵃ13,16 Hebrew *Sheol*

a snare holds him fast. Pr 5:22

[10]A noose is hidden for him on
the ground; Pr 7:22
a trap lies in his path. Ps 140:5

[11]Terrors startle him on every
side Job 15:21
and dog his every step.

[12]Calamity is hungry for him;
disaster is ready for him
when he falls. Job 15:23

[13]It eats away parts of his skin;
death's firstborn devours
his limbs. Zec 14:12

[14]He is torn from the security
of his tent Job 8:22
and marched off to the king
of terrors. Job 15:24

[15]Fire resides[a] in his tent; Job 20:26
burning sulfur is scattered
over his dwelling. Ge 19:24

[16]His roots dry up below
and his branches wither
above. Isa 5:24

[17]The memory of him perishes
from the earth; Dt 32:26
he has no name in the
land.

[18]He is driven from light into
darkness Job 5:14
and is banished from the
world. Job 11:20

[19]He has no offspring or
descendants among his
people, Ps 21:10; 37:28
no survivor where once he
lived. 2Ki 10:11

[20]Men of the west are appalled
at his fate; Ps 37:13
men of the east are seized
with horror.

[21]Surely such is the dwelling of
an evil man; Isa 57:20

such is the place of one
who knows not God.''

Job

19 Then Job replied:

[2]''How long will you
torment me Job 13:25
and crush me with words?

[3]Ten times now you have
reproached me; Job 20:3
shamelessly you attack me.

[4]If it is true that I have gone
astray,
my error remains my
concern alone. Job 6:24

[5]If indeed you would exalt
yourselves above me
and use my humiliation
against me,

[6]then know that God has
wronged me Job 6:29
and drawn his net around
me. Job 10:3; 18:8

[7]''Though I cry, 'I've been
wronged!' I get no
response; Job 30:20
though I call for help, there
is no justice. Job 30:24

[8]He has blocked my way so I
cannot pass; La 3:7
he has shrouded my paths
in darkness. Job 3:26

[9]He has stripped me of my
honor Ge 43:28; Job 12:17
and removed the crown
from my head. Job 2:8

[10]He tears me down on every
side till I am gone; Job 12:14
he uproots my hope like a
tree. Job 7:6; 14:7

---

[a]15 Or *Nothing he had remains*

[11]His anger burns against me;
he counts me among his
enemies. Job 13:24
[12]His troops advance in force;
they build a siege ramp
against me Job 16:10
and encamp around my
tent. Job 3:23

[13]"He has alienated my
brothers from me; Ps 69:8
my acquaintances are
completely estranged
from me. Job 16:7; 42:11
[14]My kinsmen have gone
away;
my friends have forgotten
me. 2Sa 15:12; Job 12:4
[15]My guests and my
maidservants count
me a stranger; Ge 14:14
they look upon me as an
alien.
[16]I summon my servant, but he
does not answer,
though I beg him with my
own mouth.
[17]My breath is offensive to my
wife;
I am loathsome to my own
brothers. Ps 38:5
[18]Even the little boys scorn me;
when I appear, they
ridicule me. Job 16:10
[19]All my intimate friends
detest me; Job 6:14; 30:10
those I love have turned
against me. Jn 13:18
[20]I am nothing but skin and
bones; Job 2:5

I have escaped with only
the skin of my teeth.[a]

[21]"Have pity on me, my
friends, have pity, Job 6:14
for the hand of God has
struck me. Jdg 2:15
[22]Why do you pursue me as
God does? Job 13:25
Will you never get enough
of my flesh? Ps 14:4

[23]"Oh, that my words were
recorded,
that they were written on a
scroll, Ex 17:14; Ps 40:7
[24]that they were inscribed with
an iron tool on[b] lead, Jer 17:1
or engraved in rock forever!
[25]I know that my Redeemer[c]
lives, Ex 6:6; 1Sa 14:39
and that in the end he will
stand upon the earth.[d]
[26]And after my skin has been
destroyed,
yet[e] in[f] my flesh I will see
God; Nu 12:8; Mt 5:8
[27]I myself will see him
with my own eyes—I, and
not another. Lk 2:30
How my heart yearns
within me! Ps 42:1

[28]"If you say, 'How we will
hound him, Job 13:25
since the root of the trouble
lies in him,[g]'
[29]you should fear the sword
yourselves;

<hr>

[a]20 Or only my gums   [b]24 Or and   [c]25 Or defender   [d]25 Or upon my grave
[e]26 Or And after I awake, / though this body has been destroyed, / then   [f]26 Or / apart
from   [g]28 Many Hebrew manuscripts, Septuagint and Vulgate; most Hebrew
manuscripts me

for wrath will bring
  punishment by the
  sword,   Job 15:22
and then you will know
  that there is
  judgment. *a* ''   Job 27:13-23

Zophar

20 Then Zophar the Naama-
thite replied: Job 2:11

2''My troubled thoughts
  prompt me to answer
because I am greatly
  disturbed.   Ps 42:5
3I hear a rebuke that
  dishonors me,   Job 19:3
and my understanding
  inspires me to reply.

4''Surely you know how it has
  been from of old,   Dt 4:32
ever since man *b* was placed
  on the earth,
5that the mirth of the wicked
  is brief,   Ps 94:3; La 1:20
the joy of the godless lasts
  but a moment.   Job 8:12
6Though his pride reaches to
  the heavens   Job 33:17
and his head touches the
  clouds,   Isa 14:13-14
7he will perish forever, like
  his own dung;   Job 4:20
those who have seen him
  will say, 'Where is he?'
8Like a dream he flies away,
  no more to be found,
banished like a vision of the
  night.   Job 27:20
9The eye that saw him will not
  see him again;

his place will look on him
  no more.   Job 7:8
10His children must make
  amends to the poor;
his own hands must give
  back his wealth.   Job 3:15
11The youthful vigor that fills
  his bones   Job 13:26
will lie with him in the
  dust.   Job 17:16

12''Though evil is sweet in his
  mouth   Job 15:16
and he hides it under his
  tongue,   Ps 10:7; 140:3
13though he cannot bear to let
  it go
and keeps it in his mouth,
14yet his food will turn sour in
  his stomach;   Pr 20:17
it will become the venom of
  serpents within him.
15He will spit out the riches he
  swallowed;   Lev 18:25
God will make his stomach
  vomit them up.
16He will suck the poison of
  serpents;   Dt 32:32
the fangs of an adder will
  kill him.   Dt 32:24
17He will not enjoy the
  streams,
the rivers flowing with
  honey and cream.   Ps 36:8
18What he toiled for he must
  give back uneaten;   Job 5:5
he will not enjoy the profit
  from his trading.   Ps 109:11
19For he has oppressed the
  poor and left them
  destitute;   Job 5:16
he has seized houses he did
  not build.   Isa 5:8

---

*a*29 Or / that you may come to know the Almighty   *b*4 Or Adam

²⁰"Surely he will have no
　　respite from his craving;
　he cannot save himself by
　　his treasure.　　　Pr 11:4
²¹Nothing is left for him to
　　devour;
　his prosperity will not
　　endure.　　　Job 7:8
²²In the midst of his plenty,
　　distress will overtake
　　him;　　　Jdg 2:15; Job 21:17
　the full force of misery will
　　come upon him.
²³When he has filled his belly,
　God will vent his burning
　　anger against him　La 4:11
　and rain down his blows
　　upon him.　　　Ps 78:30-31
²⁴Though he flees from an iron
　　weapon,　　　Isa 24:18
　a bronze-tipped arrow
　　pierces him.　　　Job 15:22
²⁵He pulls it out of his back,
　the gleaming point out of
　　his liver.
　Terrors will come over him;
²⁶　total darkness lies in wait
　　for his treasures.　Job 5:14
　A fire unfanned will
　　consume him　　Job 15:34
　and devour what is left in
　　his tent.　　　Job 18:15
²⁷The heavens will expose his
　　guilt;
　the earth will rise up
　　against him.　　　Dt 31:28
²⁸A flood will carry off his
　　house,ᵃ　　　Dt 28:31
　rushing watersᵃ on the day
　　of God's wrath.　Job 21:17
²⁹Such is the fate God allots
　　the wicked,

the heritage appointed for
　them by God."　　Job 15:20

Job

21 Then Job replied:
²"Listen carefully to my
　　words;　　　Job 13:17
　let this be the consolation
　　you give me.
³Bear with me while I speak,
　and after I have spoken,
　　mock on.　　　Job 6:14; 11:3

⁴"Is my complaint directed to
　　man?　　　Job 7:11
　Why should I not be
　　impatient?　　　Job 6:3
⁵Look at me and be
　　astonished;
　clap your hand over your
　　mouth.　　　Jdg 18:19
⁶When I think about this, I am
　　terrified;　　　Ge 45:3
　trembling seizes my body.
⁷Why do the wicked live on,
　growing old and increasing
　　in power?　　　Job 9:24
⁸They see their children
　　established around
　　them,
　their offspring before their
　　eyes.　　　Ps 17:14; Mal 3:15
⁹Their homes are safe and free
　　from fear;　　　Job 5:24
　the rod of God is not upon
　　them.　　　Job 9:34
¹⁰Their bulls never fail to
　　breed;
　their cows calve and do not
　　miscarry.　　　Ex 23:26
¹¹They send forth their
　　children as a flock;　Ps 78:52

ᵃ28 Or *The possessions in his house will be carried off, / washed away*

their little ones dance
about.

[12]They sing to the music of
tambourine and harp;
they make merry to the
sound of the flute.   Ge 4:21

[13]They spend their years in
prosperity   Job 8:7
and go down to the grave[a]
in peace.[b]   Job 24:19

[14]Yet they say to God, 'Leave
us alone!   Job 4:17
We have no desire to know
your ways.   Dt 32:15

[15]Who is the Almighty, that we
should serve him?
What would we gain by
praying to him?'   Job 5:2

[16]But their prosperity is not in
their own hands,
so I stand aloof from the
counsel of the wicked.

[17]"Yet how often is the lamp of
the wicked snuffed out?
How often does calamity
come upon them,   Job 18:12
the fate God allots in his
anger?   Job 20:22,28

[18]How often are they like straw
before the wind,
like chaff swept away by a
gale?   Job 13:25; Pr 10:25

[19]It is said, 'God stores up a
man's punishment for
his sons.'   Ex 20:5
Let him repay the man
himself, so that he will
know it!   Jer 25:14

[20]Let his own eyes see his
destruction;   Ex 32:33

let him drink of the wrath
of the Almighty.[c]   Job 20:28

[21]For what does he care about
the family he leaves
behind   Job 14:22
when his allotted months
come to an end?   Job 14:5

[22]"Can anyone teach
knowledge to God,   Job 35:11
since he judges even the
highest?   Job 4:18; Ps 82:1

[23]One man dies in full vigor,
completely secure and at
ease,   Job 3:13

[24]his body[d] well nourished,
his bones rich with marrow.

[25]Another man dies in
bitterness of soul,   Job 10:1
never having enjoyed
anything good.

[26]Side by side they lie in the
dust,   Job 17:16
and worms cover them
both.   Job 7:5; 24:20

[27]"I know full well what you
are thinking,
the schemes by which you
would wrong me.

[28]You say, 'Where now is the
great man's house,   Job 1:3
the tents where wicked
men lived?'   Job 8:22

[29]Have you never questioned
those who travel?
Have you paid no regard to
their accounts—

[30]that the evil man is spared
from the day of
calamity,   Job 31:3

---

[a]13 Hebrew *Sheol*   [b]13 Or *in an instant*
exclamations and 19 and 20 as declarations.
word is uncertain.

[c]17-20 Verses 17 and 18 may be taken as
[d]24 The meaning of the Hebrew for this

that he is delivered from[a]
the day of wrath? Job 20:22
31Who denounces his conduct
to his face?
Who repays him for what
he has done? Job 34:11
32He is carried to the grave,
and watch is kept over his
tomb. Isa 14:18
33The soil in the valley is sweet
to him; Job 3:22
all men follow after him,
and a countless throng
goes[b] before him. Job 3:19

34"So how can you console me
with your nonsense?
Nothing is left of your
answers but falsehood!"

Eliphaz

22 Then Eliphaz the Temanite replied: Job 4:1

2"Can a man be of benefit to
God? Lk 17:10
Can even a wise man
benefit him? Job 7:17
3What pleasure would it give
the Almighty if you
were righteous? Ps 143:2
What would he gain if your
ways were blameless?

4"Is it for your piety that he
rebukes you
and brings charges against
you? Job 9:3; 19:29
5Is not your wickedness great?
Are not your sins endless?
6You demanded security from
your brothers for no
reason; 2Ki 4:1

you stripped men of their
clothing, leaving them
naked. Ex 22:27
7You gave no water to the
weary Mt 10:42
and you withheld food
from the hungry, Job 29:12
8though you were a powerful
man, owning land—
an honored man, living
on it. Job 12:19; Isa 3:3
9And you sent widows away
empty-handed Job 24:3
and broke the strength of
the fatherless. Job 6:27
10That is why snares are all
around you, Job 18:9
why sudden peril terrifies
you, Job 15:21
11why it is so dark you cannot
see, Job 5:14
and why a flood of water
covers you. Ge 7:23

12"Is not God in the heights of
heaven? Job 11:8
And see how lofty are the
highest stars!
13Yet you say, 'What does God
know? Ps 10:11; 59:7
Does he judge through
such darkness? Ps 139:11
14Thick clouds veil him, so he
does not see us Job 26:9
as he goes about in the
vaulted heavens.' Job 37:18
15Will you keep to the old path
that evil men have trod?
16They were carried off before
their time, Job 15:32
their foundations washed
away by a flood. Ge 7:23

---

[a]30 Or *man is reserved for the day of calamity, / that he is brought forth to
countless throng went*   [b]33 Or / *as a*

17They said to God, 'Leave us
alone!
What can the Almighty do
to us?'   Job 21:15
18Yet it was he who filled their
houses with good
things,   Job 12:6
so I stand aloof from the
counsel of the wicked.

19"The righteous see their ruin
and rejoice;   Ps 5:11
the innocent mock them,
saying,   Job 21:3
20'Surely our foes are
destroyed,   Ps 18:39
and fire devours their
wealth.'   Job 15:30

21"Submit to God and be at
peace with him;   Isa 26:3
in this way prosperity will
come to you.   Job 8:7
22Accept instruction from his
mouth   Dt 8:3
and lay up his words in
your heart.   Job 6:10
23If you return to the
Almighty, you will be
restored: Isa 31:6
If you remove wickedness
far from your tent   Job 11:14
24and assign your nuggets to
the dust,   Job 28:6
your gold of Ophir to the
rocks in the ravines,
25then the Almighty will be
your gold,   Job 31:24
the choicest silver for you.
26Surely then you will find
delight in the Almighty
and will lift up your face to
God.   Job 11:15; 33:26

27You will pray to him, and he
will hear you,   Job 5:27
and you will fulfill your
vows.   Nu 30:2
28What you decide on will be
done,   Ps 103:11
and light will shine on your
ways.   Job 33:28
29When men are brought low
and you say, 'Lift them
up!'   Est 5:12
then he will save the
downcast.   Ps 18:27
30He will deliver even one who
is not innocent,   Isa 1:18
who will be delivered
through the cleanness of
your hands."   2Sa 22:21

Job

23

Then Job replied:

2"Even today my
complaint is bitter;   Job 7:11
his hand*a* is heavy in spite
of*b* my groaning.   Ps 6:6
3If only I knew where to find
him;
if only I could go to his
dwelling!   Dt 4:29
4I would state my case before
him   Job 13:18
and fill my mouth with
arguments.   Job 9:15
5I would find out what he
would answer me,   Job 11:5
and consider what he
would say.
6Would he oppose me with
great power?   Job 9:4
No, he would not press
charges against me.   Job 6:4

---

*a*2 Septuagint and Syriac; Hebrew / *the hand on me*   *b*2 Or *heavy on me in*

⁷There an upright man could
    present his case before
    him,   Ge 3:8; Job 1:1
and I would be delivered
    forever from my judge.

⁸"But if I go to the east, he is
    not there;
if I go to the west, I do not
    find him.
⁹When he is at work in the
    north, I do not see him;
when he turns to the south,
    I catch no glimpse of
    him.   Job 9:11
¹⁰But he knows the way that I
    take;   Job 27:6; Ps 7:9
when he has tested me, I
    will come forth as gold.
¹¹My feet have closely followed
    his steps;   Ps 17:5
I have kept to his way
    without turning aside.
¹²I have not departed from the
    commands of his lips;
I have treasured the words
    of his mouth more than
    my daily bread.   Mt 4:4

¹³"But he stands alone, and
    who can oppose him?
He does whatever he
    pleases.   Job 10:13; Isa 55:11
¹⁴He carries out his decree
    against me,
and many such plans he
    still has in store.   1Th 3:3
¹⁵That is why I am terrified
    before him;   Ge 45:3
when I think of all this, I
    fear him.   Jos 24:14
¹⁶God has made my heart
    faint;   Dt 20:3
the Almighty has terrified
    me.   Ex 3:6

¹⁷Yet I am not silenced by the
    darkness,   Job 3:6
by the thick darkness that
    covers my face.

24 "Why does the Almighty
    not set times for
    judgment?   Job 9:23; 14:5
Why must those who know
    him look in vain for such
    days?   Job 15:20; Ac 1:7
²Men move boundary stones;
they pasture flocks they
    have stolen.   Ex 20:15
³They drive away the
    orphan's donkey
and take the widow's ox in
    pledge.   Job 6:27
⁴They thrust the needy from
    the path   Job 29:16
and force all the poor of the
    land into hiding.   Job 30:25
⁵Like wild donkeys in the
    desert,   Ge 16:12
the poor go about their
    labor of foraging food;
the wasteland provides
    food for their
    children.
⁶They gather fodder in the
    fields   Job 6:5
and glean in the vineyards
    of the wicked.   Ru 2:22
⁷Lacking clothes, they spend
    the night naked;
they have nothing to cover
    themselves in the cold.
⁸They are drenched by
    mountain rains   Da 4:25
and hug the rocks for lack
    of shelter.   Jdg 6:2; La 4:5
⁹The fatherless child is
    snatched from the
    breast;   Dt 24:17; Job 29:17

the infant of the poor is
    seized for a debt.   Ps 14:4
10Lacking clothes, they go
    about naked;   Dt 24:12-13
they carry the sheaves, but
    still go hungry.   Lev 19:9
11They crush olives among the
    terraces^a;
they tread the winepresses,
    yet suffer thirst.   Isa 5:2
12The groans of the dying rise
    from the city,
and the souls of the
    wounded cry out for
    help.   Job 12:19
But God charges no one
    with wrongdoing.   Job 9:23

13"There are those who rebel
    against the light,   Job 38:15
who do not know its ways
    or stay in its paths.   Job 17:12
14When daylight is gone, the
    murderer rises up
and kills the poor and
    needy;   Isa 3:15
in the night he steals forth
    like a thief.   Ps 10:9
15The eye of the adulterer
    watches for dusk;   Pr 7:8-9
he thinks, 'No eye will see
    me,'   Ps 10:11
and he keeps his face
    concealed.
16In the dark, men break into
    houses,   Ex 22:2
but by day they shut
    themselves in;
they want nothing to do
    with the light.

17For all of them, deep
    darkness is their
    morning^b;
they make friends with the
    terrors of darkness. ^c

18"Yet they are foam on the
    surface of the water;
their portion of the land is
    cursed,   Job 5:3
so that no one goes to the
    vineyards.
19As heat and drought snatch
    away the melted snow,
so the grave^d snatches away
    those who have sinned.
20The womb forgets them,
    the worm feasts on them;
evil men are no longer
    remembered   Job 18:17
but are broken like a tree.
21They prey on the barren and
    childless woman,
and to the widow show no
    kindness.   Job 22:9
22But God drags away the
    mighty by his power;
though they become
    established, they have
    no assurance of life.
23He may let them rest in a
    feeling of security,
but his eyes are on their
    ways.   2Ch 16:9; Job 10:4
24For a little while they are
    exalted, and then they
    are gone;   2Ki 19:35
they are brought low and
    gathered up like all
    others;   Job 3:19

---

^a11 Or olives between the millstones; the meaning of the Hebrew for this word is
uncertain.   ^b17 Or them, their morning is like the shadow of death   ^c17 Or of the
shadow of death   ^d19 Hebrew Sheol

they are cut off like heads
  of grain.   Isa 17:5

25"If this is not so, who can
    prove me false
  and reduce my words to
    nothing?"   Job 6:28

Bildad

25 Then Bildad the Shuhite
        replied: Job 8:1

2"Dominion and awe belong
    to God;   Job 9:4; Ps 47:9
  he establishes order in the
    heights of heaven.   2Ch 20:6
3Can his forces be numbered?
  Upon whom does his light
    not rise?   Mt 5:45
4How then can a man be
    righteous before God?
  How can one born of
    woman be pure?   Job 4:17
5If even the moon is not
    bright   Job 31:26
  and the stars are not pure
    in his eyes,   Job 4:18
6how much less man, who is
    but a maggot—
  a son of man, who is only a
    worm!"   Job 4:19; Ps 80:17

Job

26 Then Job replied:
    2"How you have helped
      the powerless!   Job 6:12
  How you have saved the
    arm that is feeble!   Job 4:3
3What advice you have
    offered to one without
    wisdom!
  And what great insight you
    have displayed!   Job 34:35

4Who has helped you utter
    these words?
  And whose spirit spoke
    from your mouth?   1Ki 22:24

5"The dead are in deep
    anguish,   Ps 88:10
  those beneath the waters
    and all that live in them.
6Death*a* is naked before God;
  Destruction*b* lies
    uncovered.   Job 10:22
7He spreads out the northern
    ⌊skies⌋ over empty space;
  he suspends the earth over
    nothing.   Job 38:6
8He wraps up the waters in
    his clouds,   Job 36:27
  yet the clouds do not burst
    under their weight.
9He covers the face of the full
    moon,
  spreading his clouds
    over it.   2Sa 22:10
10He marks out the horizon on
    the face of the waters
  for a boundary between
    light and darkness.
11The pillars of the heavens
    quake,   2Sa 22:8
  aghast at his rebuke.
12By his power he churned up
    the sea;   Ex 14:21
  by his wisdom he cut Rahab
    to pieces.   Job 9:13; 12:13
13By his breath the skies
    became fair;   Job 9:8
  his hand pierced the gliding
    serpent.   Isa 27:1
14And these are but the outer
    fringe of his works;
  how faint the whisper we
    hear of him!   Job 4:12

a6 Hebrew *Sheol*   *b6* Hebrew *Abaddon*

Who then can understand
the thunder of his
power?" Job 9:6

27 And Job continued his
discourse: Job 29:1

2"As surely as God lives, who
has denied me justice,
the Almighty, who has
made me taste bitterness
of soul, 1Sa 1:10; Job 23:16

3as long as I have life within
me,
the breath of God in my
nostrils, Ge 2:7

4my lips will not speak
wickedness,
and my tongue will utter no
deceit. Job 6:28; 12:16

5I will never admit you are in
the right;
till I die, I will not deny my
integrity. Job 2:9; 10:7

6I will maintain my
righteousness and never
let go of it; Job 29:14
my conscience will not
reproach me as long as I
live. Ac 23:1; Ro 2:15

7"May my enemies be like the
wicked, Job 8:22
my adversaries like the
unjust! Job 31:35

8For what hope has the
godless when he is cut
off, Job 8:13
when God takes away his
life? Nu 16:22

9Does God listen to his cry
when distress comes upon
him? Dt 1:45; 1Sa 8:18

10Will he find delight in the
Almighty? Job 22:26

Will he call upon God at all
times?

11"I will teach you about the
power of God;
the ways of the Almighty I
will not conceal. Job 36:23

12You have all seen this
yourselves.
Why then this meaningless
talk?

13"Here is the fate God allots
to the wicked,
the heritage a ruthless man
receives from the
Almighty: Job 16:19

14However many his children,
their fate is the sword;
his offspring will never
have enough to eat. Job 4:11

15The plague will bury those
who survive him,
and their widows will not
weep for them. Ps 78:64

16Though he heaps up silver
like dust 1Ki 10:27
and clothes like piles of
clay, Zec 9:3

17what he lays up the
righteous will wear, Ps 39:6
and the innocent will divide
his silver. Ex 3:22

18The house he builds is like a
moth's cocoon, Job 8:22
like a hut made by a
watchman. Isa 1:8

19He lies down wealthy, but
will do so no more; Job 3:13
when he opens his eyes, all
is gone. Job 14:20

20Terrors overtake him like a
flood; Job 15:21
a tempest snatches him
away in the night. Job 20:8

²¹The east wind carries him
   off, and he is gone;
  it sweeps him out of his
   place.   Job 7:10
²²It hurls itself against him
   without mercy   Jer 13:14
  as he flees headlong from
   its power.   2Ki 7:15
²³It claps its hands in derision
  and hisses him out of his
   place.   Nu 24:10

28 "There is a mine for
   silver
  and a place where gold is
   refined.   Ps 12:6
²Iron is taken from the earth,
  and copper is smelted from
   ore.   Dt 8:9
³Man puts an end to the
   darkness;   Ecc 1:13
  he searches the farthest
   recesses
  for ore in the blackest
   darkness.   Job 26:10
⁴Far from where people dwell
   he cuts a shaft,
        2Sa 5:8
  in places forgotten by the
   foot of man;
  far from men he dangles
   and sways.
⁵The earth, from which food
   comes,   Ge 1:29
  is transformed below as by
   fire;
⁶sapphires*a* come from its
   rocks,   Isa 54:11
  and its dust contains
   nuggets of gold. Job 22:24
⁷No bird of prey knows that
   hidden path,

  no falcon's eye has seen it.
⁸Proud beasts do not set foot
   on it,   Job 41:34
  and no lion prowls there.
⁹Man's hand assaults the
   flinty rock   Dt 8:15
  and lays bare the roots of
   the mountains.   Jnh 2:6
¹⁰He tunnels through the rock;
  his eyes see all its treasures.
¹¹He searches*b* the sources of
   the rivers   Ge 7:11
  and brings hidden things to
   light.   Isa 48:6
¹²"But where can wisdom be
   found?   Pr 1:20; 8:1
  Where does understanding
   dwell?
¹³Man does not comprehend
   its worth;   Pr 3:13
  it cannot be found in the
   land of the living. Dt 29:29
¹⁴The deep says, 'It is not in
   me';   Ps 42:7
  the sea says, 'It is not with
   me.'   Dt 30:13
¹⁵It cannot be bought with the
   finest gold,
  nor can its price be weighed
   in silver.   Pr 3:13-14
¹⁶It cannot be bought with the
   gold of Ophir,   Ge 10:29
  with precious onyx or
   sapphires.   Ex 24:10
¹⁷Neither gold nor crystal can
   compare with it, Ps 119:72
  nor can it be had for jewels
   of gold.
¹⁸Coral and jasper are not
   worthy of mention; Pr 3:15

a6 Or *lapis lazuli;* also in verse 16   *b11* Septuagint, Aquila and Vulgate; Hebrew *He*
dams up

the price of wisdom is
  beyond rubies.   Pr 8:11
¹⁹The topaz of Cush cannot
  compare with it;   Ex 28:17
it cannot be bought with
  pure gold.   Pr 3:14-15

²⁰"Where then does wisdom
  come from?
Where does understanding
  dwell?   Job 9:4
²¹It is hidden from the eyes of
  every living thing,
concealed even from the
  birds of the air.
²²Destruction[a] and Death say,
  'Only a rumor of it has
  reached our ears.'   Job 20:26
²³God understands the way
  to it
and he alone knows where
  it dwells,   Job 9:4; Ecc 3:11
²⁴for he views the ends of the
  earth   Job 36:32; 37:3
and sees everything under
  the heavens.   Jos 3:11
²⁵When he established the
  force of the wind
and measured out the
  waters,   Job 12:15
²⁶when he made a decree for
  the rain   Job 36:28
and a path for the
  thunderstorm,   Job 36:33
²⁷then he looked at wisdom
  and appraised it;
he confirmed it and
  tested it.   Pr 3:19; 8:22-31
²⁸And he said to man,
  'The fear of the Lord—that
  is wisdom,
and to shun evil is
  understanding.' "   Ps 11:5

29 Job continued his discourse: Job 27:1

²"How I long for the months
  gone by,   Ge 31:30
for the days when God
  watched over me,   Jer 1:12
³when his lamp shone upon
  my head
and by his light I walked
  through darkness!   Job 11:17
⁴Oh, for the days when I was
  in my prime,
when God's intimate
  friendship blessed my
  house,   Job 15:8; Ps 25:14
⁵when the Almighty was still
  with me
and my children were
  around me,   Ps 127:3-5
⁶when my path was drenched
  with cream   Job 20:17
and the rock poured out for
  me streams of olive oil.

⁷"When I went to the gate of
  the city   Job 5:4
and took my seat in the
  public square,
⁸the young men saw me and
  stepped aside   1Ti 5:1
and the old men rose to
  their feet;   Lev 19:32
⁹the chief men refrained from
  speaking   Job 31:21
and covered their mouths
  with their hands;   Jdg 18:19
¹⁰the voices of the nobles were
  hushed,
and their tongues stuck to
  the roof of their mouths.
¹¹Whoever heard me spoke
  well of me,

a22 Hebrew *Abaddon*

and those who saw me
commended me, Job 4:4
[12]because I rescued the poor
who cried for help, Job 24:4
and the fatherless who had
none to assist him. Dt 24:17
[13]The man who was dying
blessed me; Job 31:20
I made the widow's heart
sing. Dt 10:18
[14]I put on righteousness as my
clothing; 2Sa 8:15
justice was my robe and my
turban. Job 19:9
[15]I was eyes to the blind Nu 10:31
and feet to the lame. Job 4:4
[16]I was a father to the needy;
I took up the case of the
stranger. Ex 18:26; Job 4:4
[17]I broke the fangs of the
wicked
and snatched the victims
from their teeth. Job 24:9

[18]"I thought, 'I will die in my
own house,
my days as numerous as
the grains of sand. Ps 1:1-3
[19]My roots will reach to the
water, Nu 24:6
and the dew will lie all
night on my
branches.
[20]My glory will remain fresh
in me, Ps 92:14
the bow ever new in my
hand.' Ge 49:24; Job 30:11

[21]"Men listened to me
expectantly,
waiting in silence for my
counsel.

[22]After I had spoken, they
spoke no more;
my words fell gently on
their ears. Dt 32:2
[23]They waited for me as for
showers
and drank in my words as
the spring rain. Job 4:3
[24]When I smiled at them, they
scarcely believed it;
the light of my face was
precious to them. [a] Nu 6:25
[25]I chose the way for them and
sat as their chief; Job 21:28
I dwelt as a king among his
troops; Job 1:3
I was like one who comforts
mourners. Job 4:4

30

"But now they mock me,
men younger than I,
whose fathers I would have
disdained
to put with my sheep dogs.
[2]Of what use was the strength
of their hands to me,
since their vigor had gone
from them?
[3]Haggard from want and
hunger,
they roamed[b] the parched
land
in desolate wastelands at
night. Job 24:5
[4]In the brush they gathered
salt herbs, Job 39:6
and their food[c] was the root
of the broom tree. 1Ki 19:4
[5]They were banished from
their fellow men,
shouted at as if they were
thieves.

[a]24 The meaning of the Hebrew for this clause is uncertain.   [b]3 Or gnawed   [c]4 Or
fuel

⁶They were forced to live in
   the dry stream beds,
among the rocks and in
   holes in the ground.
⁷They brayed among the
   bushes   Job 39:5-6
and huddled in the
   undergrowth.
⁸A base and nameless brood,
   they were driven out of the
   land.   Job 18:18

⁹"And now their sons mock
   me in song;   Job 16:10
I have become a byword
   among them.   Job 17:6
¹⁰They detest me and keep
   their distance;   Job 19:19
they do not hesitate to spit
   in my face.   Dt 25:9
¹¹Now that God has unstrung
   my bow and afflicted
   me,   Ge 12:17
they throw off restraint in
   my presence.   Job 41:13
¹²On my right the tribe*ᵃ*
   attacks;   Ps 109:6
they lay snares for my feet,
they build their siege ramps
   against me.   Job 16:10
¹³They break up my road;
they succeed in destroying
   me—   Isa 3:12
without anyone's helping
   them. *ᵇ*   Job 10:3
¹⁴They advance as through a
   gaping breach;   2Ki 25:4
amid the ruins they come
   rolling in.
¹⁵Terrors overwhelm me;   Ex 3:6
my dignity is driven away
   as by the wind,

my safety vanishes like a
   cloud.   Job 3:25

¹⁶"And now my life ebbs
   away;   Job 3:24
days of suffering grip me.
¹⁷Night pierces my bones;
my gnawing pains never
   rest.   Dt 28:35
¹⁸In his great power ⌞God⌟
   becomes like clothing to
   me*ᶜ*;   Job 9:4
he binds me like the neck of
   my garment.
¹⁹He throws me into the mud,
and I am reduced to dust
   and ashes.   Ge 3:19

²⁰"I cry out to you, O God, but
   you do not answer;   Job 19:7
I stand up, but you merely
   look at me.
²¹You turn on me ruthlessly;
with the might of your
   hand you attack me.
²²You snatch me up and drive
   me before the wind;
you toss me about in the
   storm.   Job 9:17
²³I know you will bring me
   down to death,   2Sa 14:14
to the place appointed for
   all the living.   Job 3:19

²⁴"Surely no one lays a hand
   on a broken man   Ps 145:14
when he cries for help in
   his distress.   Job 19:7
²⁵Have I not wept for those in
   trouble?   Lk 19:41
Has not my soul grieved for
   the poor?   Job 24:4

ᵃ12 The meaning of the Hebrew for this word is uncertain.   *ᵇ13* Or *me. / 'No one can
help him,' ⌞they say⌟.*   *ᶜ18* Hebrew; Septuagint ⌞God⌟ *grasps my clothing*

²⁶Yet when I hoped for good,
     evil came;
 when I looked for light,
     then came darkness. Job 3:6
²⁷The churning inside me
     never stops;   Ps 38:8
 days of suffering confront
     me.
²⁸I go about blackened, but not
     by the sun;   Job 17:14
 I stand up in the assembly
     and cry for help.   Job 19:7
²⁹I have become a brother of
     jackals,   Ps 44:19
 a companion of owls.   Ps 102:6
³⁰My skin grows black and
     peels;   La 3:4
 my body burns with fever.
³¹My harp is tuned to
     mourning,   Ge 8:8
 and my flute to the sound
     of wailing.   Ge 4:21

31 "I made a covenant with
       my eyes   Pr 4:25
 not to look lustfully at a
     girl.   Ex 20:14
²For what is man's lot from
     God above,   Nu 26:55
 his heritage from the
     Almighty on high? Job 16:19
³Is it not ruin for the wicked,
 disaster for those who do
     wrong?   Job 34:22
⁴Does he not see my ways
 and count my every step?

⁵"If I have walked in
     falsehood
 or my foot has hurried after
     deceit—   Job 15:31
⁶let God weigh me in honest
     scales   Lev 19:36; Ps 139:23

and he will know that I am
     blameless—   Ge 6:9
⁷if my steps have turned from
     the path,   Job 23:11
 if my heart has been led by
     my eyes,
 or if my hands have been
     defiled,   Job 9:30; Ps 7:3
⁸then may others eat what I
     have sown,   Job 5:5
 and may my crops be
     uprooted.   Mic 6:15

⁹"If my heart has been enticed
     by a woman,   Dt 11:16
 or if I have lurked at my
     neighbor's door,
¹⁰then may my wife grind
     another man's grain,
 and may other men sleep
     with her.   Dt 28:30
¹¹For that would have been
     shameful,   Pr 6:32-33
 a sin to be judged.   Ge 38:24
¹²It is a fire that burns to
     Destructionᵃ;   Job 15:30
 it would have uprooted my
     harvest.

¹³"If I have denied justice to
     my menservants and
     maidservants   Dt 5:14
 when they had a grievance
     against me,   Ex 21:2-11
¹⁴what will I do when God
     confronts me?   Job 33:5
 What will I answer when
     called to account?   Ps 10:13
¹⁵Did not he who made me in
     the womb make them?
 Did not the same one form
     us both within our
     mothers?   Job 10:3

ᵃ12 Hebrew *Abaddon*

¹⁶"If I have denied the desires
    of the poor   Lev 25:17
  or let the eyes of the widow
    grow weary,   Job 22:9
¹⁷if I have kept my bread to
    myself,
  not sharing it with the
    fatherless—   Job 6:27
¹⁸but from my youth I reared
    him as would a father,
  and from my birth I guided
    the widow—   Isa 51:18
¹⁹if I have seen anyone
    perishing for lack of
    clothing,   Job 22:6
  or a needy man without a
    garment,   Job 24:4
²⁰and his heart did not bless
    me   Job 29:13
  for warming him with the
    fleece from my sheep,
²¹if I have raised my hand
    against the fatherless,
  knowing that I had
    influence in court,   Job 29:7
²²then let my arm fall from the
    shoulder,
  let it be broken off at the
    joint.   Nu 15:30; Job 5:15
²³For I dreaded destruction
    from God,   Job 10:3
  and for fear of his splendor
    I could not do such
    things.   Job 13:11

²⁴"If I have put my trust in
    gold   Job 22:25
  or said to pure gold, 'You
    are my security,'   Mt 6:24
²⁵if I have rejoiced over my
    great wealth,   Ge 12:16
  the fortune my hands had
    gained,   Job 22:24

²⁶if I have regarded the sun in
    its radiance   Ge 1:16
  or the moon moving in
    splendor,   Job 25:5
²⁷so that my heart was secretly
    enticed   Dt 11:16
  and my hand offered them
    a kiss of homage,   Jer 8:2
²⁸then these also would be sins
    to be judged,   Ge 38:24
  for I would have been
    unfaithful to God on
    high.   Nu 11:20; Eze 3:16

²⁹"If I have rejoiced at my
    enemy's misfortune   Nu 14:1
  or gloated over the trouble
    that came to him—   Pr 17:5
³⁰I have not allowed my mouth
    to sin
  by invoking a curse against
    his life—   Job 5:3; Ro 12:14
³¹if the men of my household
    have never said,
  'Who has not had his fill of
    Job's meat?'—   Job 22:7
³²but no stranger had to spend
    the night in the street,
  for my door was always
    open to the traveler—
³³if I have concealed my sin as
    men do,^a   Ps 32:5
  by hiding my guilt in my
    heart   Ge 3:8
³⁴because I so feared the crowd
  and so dreaded the
    contempt of the clans
  that I kept silent and would
    not go outside   Ps 32:3

³⁵("Oh, that I had someone to
    hear me!   Job 9:24
  I sign now my defense—let

---

^a33 Or *as Adam did*

the Almighty answer
me;
let my accuser put his
indictment in writing.
[36]Surely I would wear it on my
shoulder,   Ex 28:12
I would put it on like a
crown.   Job 29:14
[37]I would give him an account
of my every step;   Job 11:11
like a prince I would
approach him.)—   Job 21:28

[38]"if my land cries out against
me   Ge 4:10
and all its furrows are wet
with tears,   Ps 65:10
[39]if I have devoured its yield
without payment   1Ki 21:19
or broken the spirit of its
tenants,   Lev 19:13
[40]then let briers come up
instead of wheat   Mt 13:7
and weeds instead of
barley."   Zep 2:9

The words of Job are ended.

Elihu

32 So these three men
stopped answering Job,
because he was righteous in his
own eyes. [2]But Elihu son of
Barakel the Buzite, of the family
of Ram, became very angry with
Job for justifying himself rather
than God. [3]He was also angry
with the three friends, because
they had found no way to refute
Job, and yet had condemned
him.[a] [4]Now Elihu had waited
before speaking to Job because

they were older than he. [5]But
when he saw that the three men
had nothing more to say, his anger was aroused.   Job 32:10; 42:7
[6]So Elihu son of Barakel the
Buzite said:

"I am young in years,
and you are old;   Job 15:10
that is why I was fearful,
not daring to tell you what I
know.
[7]I thought, 'Age should
speak;
advanced years should
teach wisdom.'   1Ch 29:15
[8]But it is the spirit[b] in a man,
the breath of the Almighty,
that gives him
understanding.   Job 12:13
[9]It is not only the old[c] who
are wise,   1Co 1:26
not only the aged who
understand what is
right.   Ps 119:100

[10]"Therefore I say: Listen to
me;   Job 33:1
I too will tell you what I
know.   Job 5:27
[11]I waited while you spoke,
I listened to your reasoning;
while you were searching for
words,
[12] I gave you my full
attention.
But not one of you has
proved Job wrong;
none of you has answered
his arguments.
[13]Do not say, 'We have found
wisdom;   Job 4:12

---

[a]3 Masoretic Text; an ancient Hebrew scribal tradition *Job, and so had condemned God*
[b]8 Or *Spirit*; also in verse 18   [c]9 Or *many*; or *great*

let God refute him, not
man.' Job 11:5
¹⁴But Job has not marshaled
his words against me,
and I will not answer him
with your arguments.

¹⁵"They are dismayed and
have no more to say;
words have failed them.
¹⁶Must I wait, now that they
are silent,
now that they stand there
with no reply?
¹⁷I too will have my say;
I too will tell what I know.
¹⁸For I am full of words,
and the spirit within me
compels me; Ac 4:20
¹⁹inside I am like bottled-up
wine,
like new wineskins ready to
burst. Jer 20:9; Am 3:8
²⁰I must speak and find relief;
I must open my lips and
reply. Job 4:2
²¹I will show partiality to no
one, Lev 19:15; Mt 22:16
nor will I flatter any man;
²²for if I were skilled in
flattery,
my Maker would soon take
me away. Job 4:17

33 "But now, Job, listen to
my words; Job 32:10
pay attention to everything
I say. Job 6:28
²I am about to open my
mouth;
my words are on the tip of
my tongue.

³My words come from an
upright heart; 1Ki 3:6
my lips sincerely speak
what I know. Job 6:28
⁴The Spirit of God has made
me; Ge 1:2; Job 10:3
the breath of the Almighty
gives me life. Job 27:3
⁵Answer me then, if you can;
prepare yourself and
confront me. Job 13:18
⁶I am just like you before God;
I too have been taken from
clay. Job 4:19
⁷No fear of me should alarm
you,
nor should my hand be
heavy upon you. Job 9:34

⁸"But you have said in my
hearing—
I heard the very words—
⁹'I am pure and without sin;
I am clean and free from
guilt. Job 2:9
¹⁰Yet God has found fault with
me;
he considers me his enemy.
¹¹He fastens my feet in
shackles; Job 13:27
he keeps close watch on all
my paths.'" Job 14:16

¹²"But I tell you, in this you
are not right,
for God is greater than
man. Job 5:9; Ps 8:4
¹³Why do you complain to him
that he answers none of
man's words[a]? Job 11:8
¹⁴For God does speak—now
one way, now another—

---

[a]13 Or that he does not answer for any of his actions

though man may not
    perceive it.   Job 4:12
15In a dream, in a vision of the
    night,   Da 2:19; Ac 16:9
when deep sleep falls on
    men   Ge 2:21
as they slumber in their
    beds,
16he may speak in their ears
and terrify them with
    warnings,   Job 6:4; Ps 88:15
17to turn man from
    wrongdoing
and keep him from pride,
18to preserve his soul from the
    pit,a   Ps 28:1; 30:9
his life from perishing by
    the sword.b   Job 15:20
19Or a man may be chastened
    on a bed of pain   Ge 17:1
with constant distress in his
    bones,   Job 16:16
20so that his very being finds
    food repulsive   Ps 102:4
and his soul loathes the
    choicest meal.   Job 3:24
21His flesh wastes away to
    nothing,
and his bones, once
    hidden, now stick out.
22His soul draws near to the
    pit,c
and his life to the
    messengers of death. d

23"Yet if there is an angel on
    his side
as a mediator, one out of a
    thousand,   Gal 3:19
to tell a man what is right
    for him,   Job 36:9-10

24to be gracious to him and
    say,
'Spare him from going
    down to the pite;
I have found a ransom for
    him'—   Job 6:22
25then his flesh is renewed like
    a child's;   Ps 103:5
it is restored as in the days
    of his youth.   2Ki 5:14
26He prays to God and finds
    favor with him,   Job 5:15
he sees God's face and
    shouts for joy;   Ezr 3:13
he is restored by God to his
    righteous state.   Ps 13:5
27Then he comes to men and
    says,
'I sinned, and perverted
    what was right,   Lk 15:21
but I did not get what I
    deserved.   Ezr 9:13
28He redeemed my soul from
    going down to the pit,f
and I will live to enjoy the
    light.'   Job 22:28

29"God does all these things to
    a man—   Ps 139:16
twice, even three times—
30to turn back his soul from the
    pit,g   Jas 5:19
that the light of life may
    shine on him.   Ps 49:19

31"Pay attention, Job, and
    listen to me;   Jer 23:8
be silent, and I will speak.
32If you have anything to say,
    answer me;
speak up, for I want you to
    be cleared.   Job 6:29

---

a18 Or preserve him from the grave   b18 Or from crossing the River   c22 Or He draws
near to the grave   d22 Or to the dead   e24 Or grave   f28 Or redeemed me from
going down to the grave   g30 Or turn him back from the grave

33But if not, then listen to me;
 be silent, and I will teach
  you wisdom." Job 6:24

34 Then Elihu said:

2"Hear my words, you
  wise men;
 listen to me, you men of
  learning. Job 32:10
3For the ear tests words
 as the tongue tastes food.
4Let us discern for ourselves
  what is right; Job 12:12
 let us learn together what is
  good. 1Th 5:21

5"Job says, 'I am innocent,
 but God denies me justice.
6Although I am right,
 I am considered a liar; Job 6:28
 although I am guiltless, Job 9:21
  his arrow inflicts an
  incurable wound.' Job 6:4
7What man is like Job,
 who drinks scorn like
  water? Job 9:21
8He keeps company with
  evildoers;
 he associates with wicked
  men. Job 22:15
9For he says, 'It profits a man
  nothing
 when he tries to please
  God.' Job 9:29-31

10"So listen to me, you men of
  understanding. Job 32:10
 Far be it from God to do
  evil, Ge 18:25
 from the Almighty to do
  wrong. Dt 32:4
11He repays a man for what he
  has done; Job 21:31

he brings upon him what
  his conduct deserves.
12It is unthinkable that God
  would do wrong, Tit 1:2
 that the Almighty would
  pervert justice. Job 8:3
13Who appointed him over the
  earth? Heb 1:2
 Who put him in charge of
  the whole world? Job 36:23
14If it were his intention
 and he withdrew his spirit[a]
  and breath, Ge 6:3
15all mankind would perish
  together Ge 6:13
 and man would return to
  the dust. Ge 2:7

16"If you have understanding,
  hear this;
 listen to what I say. Job 32:10
17Can he who hates justice
  govern? 2Sa 23:3-4
 Will you condemn the just
  and mighty One? Job 10:7
18Is he not the One who says
  to kings, 'You are
  worthless,'
 and to nobles, 'You are
  wicked,' Job 12:18
19who shows no partiality to
  princes
 and does not favor the rich
  over the poor, Lev 19:15
 for they are all the work of
  his hands? Job 10:3
20They die in an instant, in the
  middle of the night;
 the people are shaken and
  they pass away;
 the mighty are removed
  without human hand.

a14 Or *Spirit*

²¹"His eyes are on the ways of
    men;   Jer 32:19
  he sees their every step.
²²There is no dark place, no
    deep shadow,   Ps 74:20
  where evildoers can hide.
²³God has no need to examine
    men further,   Ps 11:4
  that they should come
    before him for
    judgment.   Job 11:11
²⁴Without inquiry he shatters
    the mighty   Isa 8:9
  and sets up others in their
    place.   Da 2:21
²⁵Because he takes note of their
    deeds,   Job 11:11
  he overthrows them in the
    night and they are
    crushed.   Pr 5:21-28
²⁶He punishes them for their
    wickedness   Ge 6:5
  where everyone can see
    them,
²⁷because they turned from
    following him   Ps 14:3
  and had no regard for any
    of his ways.   1Sa 15:11
²⁸They caused the cry of the
    poor to come before
    him,
  so that he heard the cry of
    the needy.   Ex 22:23
²⁹But if he remains silent, who
    can condemn him?   Ro 8:34
  If he hides his face, who
    can see him?   Ps 13:1
  Yet he is over man and
    nation alike,   Ps 83:18
³⁰ to keep a godless man from
    ruling,   Job 8:13

  from laying snares for the
    people.   Ps 25:15
³¹"Suppose a man says to God,
  'I am guilty but will offend
    no more.   Ps 51:5
³²Teach me what I cannot see;
  if I have done wrong, I will
    not do so again.'   Job 33:27
³³Should God then reward you
    on your terms,
  when you refuse to repent?
  You must decide, not I;
  so tell me what you know.
³⁴"Men of understanding
    declare,
  wise men who hear me say
    to me,
³⁵'Job speaks without
    knowledge;   Job 35:16
  his words lack insight.' Job 26:3
³⁶Oh, that Job might be tested
    to the utmost
  for answering like a wicked
    man!   Job 6:29; 22:15
³⁷To his sin he adds rebellion;
  scornfully he claps his
    hands among us   Job 27:23
  and multiplies his words
    against God."   Job 35:16

35 Then Elihu said:
²"Do you think this is
    just?
  You say, 'I will be cleared
    by God.ᵃ'   Job 2:9
³Yet you ask him, 'What profit
    is it to me,ᵇ
  and what do I gain by not
    sinning?'   Job 9:29-31
⁴"I would like to reply to you

---

and to your friends with
you.

[5]Look up at the heavens and
see; Ge 15:5
gaze at the clouds so high
above you. Job 11:7-9
[6]If you sin, how does that
affect him?
If your sins are many, what
does that do to him?
[7]If you are righteous, what do
you give to him, Ro 11:35
or what does he receive
from your hand? 1Co 4:7
[8]Your wickedness affects only
a man like yourself,
and your righteousness
only the sons of men.

[9]"Men cry out under a load of
oppression; Ex 2:23
they plead for relief from
the arm of the powerful.
[10]But no one says, 'Where is
God my Maker, Job 4:17
who gives songs in the
night, Job 8:21; Ps 42:8
[11]who teaches more to us than
to[a] the beasts of the
earth Job 12:7; 21:22
and makes us wiser than[b]
the birds of the air?'
[12]He does not answer when
men cry out 1Sa 8:18
because of the arrogance of
the wicked. Job 15:25
[13]Indeed, God does not listen
to their empty plea;
the Almighty pays no
attention to it. Dt 1:45
[14]How much less, then, will he
listen

when you say that you do
not see him, Job 9:11
that your case is before him
and you must wait for him,
[15]and further, that his anger
never punishes Job 9:24
and he does not take the
least notice of
wickedness.[c] Job 18:5
[16]So Job opens his mouth with
empty talk; Tit 1:10
without knowledge he
multiplies words." Job 34:25

36

Elihu continued:
[2]"Bear with me a little
longer and I will show
you
that there is more to be said
in God's behalf.
[3]I get my knowledge from
afar; Job 6:28
I will ascribe justice to my
Maker. Job 4:17
[4]Be assured that my words are
not false; Job 13:6
one perfect in knowledge is
with you. Job 37:5

[5]"God is mighty, but does not
despise men; Job 9:4
he is mighty, and firm in
his purpose. Nu 23:19
[6]He does not keep the wicked
alive Job 34:26
but gives the afflicted their
rights. Job 4:10
[7]He does not take his eyes off
the righteous; Job 11:11
he enthrones them with
kings Ps 113:8

---

[a]11 Or *teaches us by*   [b]11 Or *us wise by*   [c]15 Symmachus, Theodotion and Vulgate;
the meaning of the Hebrew for this word is uncertain.

and exalts them forever.
⁸But if men are bound in
chains, 2Sa 3:34
held fast by cords of
affliction, Ps 119:67
⁹he tells them what they have
done—
that they have sinned
arrogantly. Job 15:25
¹⁰He makes them listen to
correction Job 33:16
and commands them to
repent of their evil. Jdg 6:8
¹¹If they obey and serve him,
they will spend the rest of
their days in prosperity
and their years in
contentment. Ex 8:22
¹²But if they do not listen,
they will perish by the
sword ᵃ Lev 26:38
and die without
knowledge. Job 4:21

¹³"The godless in heart harbor
resentment; Job 15:12
even when he fetters them,
they do not cry for help.
¹⁴They die in their youth, Job 15:32
among male prostitutes of
the shrines. Dt 23:17
¹⁵But those who suffer he
delivers in their
suffering; 2Co 12:10
he speaks to them in their
affliction. Job 33:16

¹⁶"He is wooing you from the
jaws of distress Hos 2:14
to a spacious place free
from restriction, Ps 118:5

to the comfort of your table
laden with choice food.
¹⁷But now you are laden with
the judgment due the
wicked; Job 20:29
judgment and justice have
taken hold of you. Job 22:11
¹⁸Be careful that no one entices
you by riches;
do not let a large bribe turn
you aside. Ex 23:8
¹⁹Would your wealth
or even all your mighty
efforts
sustain you so you would
not be in distress? Ps 49:6
²⁰Do not long for the night,
to drag people away from
their homes. ᵇ Job 34:20
²¹Beware of turning to evil,
which you seem to prefer to
affliction. Heb 11:25

²²"God is exalted in his power.
Who is a teacher like him?
²³Who has prescribed his ways
for him, Job 34:13
or said to him, 'You have
done wrong'? Ge 18:25
²⁴Remember to extol his work,
which men have praised in
song. Ex 15:1
²⁵All mankind has seen it;
men gaze on it from afar.
²⁶How great is God—beyond
our understanding!
The number of his years is
past finding out. Ge 21:33

²⁷"He draws up the drops of
water, Job 26:8

ᵃ12 Or will cross the River   ᵇ20 The meaning of the Hebrew for verses 18-20 is uncertain.

which distill as rain to the
   streams[a];   2Sa 1:21
28the clouds pour down their
   moisture
and abundant showers fall
   on mankind.   Job 5:10
29Who can understand how he
   spreads out the clouds,
how he thunders from his
   pavilion?   Ps 29:3
30See how he scatters his
   lightning about him,
bathing the depths of the
   sea.   Ps 68:22
31This is the way he governs[b]
   the nations   Dt 28:23-24
and provides food in
   abundance.   Ps 104:14-15
32He fills his hands with
   lightning
and commands it to strike
   its mark.   Job 28:24
33His thunder announces the
   coming storm;   Job 37:5
even the cattle make known
   its approach.[c]   Job 28:26

37 "At this my heart
      pounds   Ps 38:10
and leaps from its place.
2Listen! Listen to the roar of
   his voice,   Job 32:10
to the rumbling that comes
   from his mouth.   Ps 18:13
3He unleashes his lightning
   beneath the whole
   heaven
   and sends it to the ends of   2Sa 22:13
   the earth.   Job 36:32
4After that comes the sound
   of his roar;

he thunders with his
   majestic voice.   Ex 20:19
When his voice resounds,
   he holds nothing back.
5God's voice thunders in
   marvelous ways;   1Sa 2:10
he does great things
   beyond our
   understanding.   Job 5:9
6He says to the snow, 'Fall on
   the earth,'   Dt 28:12
and to the rain shower, 'Be
   a mighty downpour.'
7So that all men he has made
   may know his work,
he stops every man from
   his labor.[d]   Ps 104:19-23
8The animals take cover;   Job 28:26
they remain in their dens.
9The tempest comes out from
   its chamber,   Ps 50:3
the cold from the driving
   winds.   Ps 147:17
10The breath of God produces
   ice,
and the broad waters
   become frozen.   Job 39:29-30
11He loads the clouds with
   moisture;   Job 26:8
he scatters his lightning
   through them.   Job 28:26
12At his direction they swirl
   around
over the face of the whole
   earth
to do whatever he
   commands them.   Ps 147:16
13He brings the clouds to
   punish men,   Ge 7:4
or to water his earth[e] and
   show his love.   1Ki 18:45

a27 Or distill from the mist as rain   b31 Or nourishes   c33 Or announces his coming—
/ the One zealous against evil   d7 Or / he fills all men with fear by his power   e13 Or to
favor them

14"Listen to this, Job; Job 32:10
stop and consider God's
wonders. Job 5:9
15Do you know how God
controls the clouds
and makes his lightning
flash? Job 36:30,32
16Do you know how the clouds
hang poised, Job 36:29
those wonders of him who
is perfect in knowledge?
17You who swelter in your
clothes
when the land lies hushed
under the south wind,
18can you join him in
spreading out the
skies,
hard as a mirror of cast
bronze? Dt 28:23

19"Tell us what we should say
to him; Ro 8:26
we cannot draw up our case
because of our darkness.
20Should he be told that I want
to speak?
Would any man ask to be
swallowed up?
21Now no one can look at the
sun, Jdg 5:31
bright as it is in the skies
after the wind has swept
them clean.
22Out of the north he comes in
golden splendor; Ps 19:5
God comes in awesome
majesty. Ex 24:17
23The Almighty is beyond our
reach and exalted in
power; Job 5:9
in his justice and great

righteousness, he does
not oppress. Job 4:17
24Therefore, men revere him,
for does he not have regard
for all the wise in
heart?a" Job 5:13; Eph 5:15

The LORD Speaks

38 Then the LORD answered
Job out of the storm. He
said: Ex 14:21; Job 11:5

2"Who is this that darkens my
counsel 1Ki 22:5
with words without
knowledge? Job 34:35
3Brace yourself like a man;
I will question you,
and you shall answer me.

4"Where were you when I laid
the earth's foundation?
Tell me, if you understand.
5Who marked off its
dimensions? Surely you
know! Ps 102:25
Who stretched a measuring
line across it? Jer 31:39
6On what were its footings
set, Pr 8:25
or who laid its
cornerstone— Job 26:7
7while the morning stars sang
together Ge 1:16
and all the angelsb shouted
for joy? 1Ki 22:19

8"Who shut up the sea behind
doors Ps 33:7
when it burst forth from the
womb, Ge 1:9-10
9when I made the clouds its
garment

a24 Or for he does not have regard for any who think they are wise.   b7 Hebrew the sons of God

and wrapped it in thick
darkness,   Ge 1:2
¹⁰when I fixed limits for it
and set its doors and bars in
place,   Ne 3:3; Job 7:12
¹¹when I said, 'This far you
may come and no
farther;
here is where your proud
waves halt'?   Ps 65:7

¹²"Have you ever given orders
to the morning,   Ps 57:5
or shown the dawn its
place,   Ps 74:16
¹³that it might take the earth
by the edges
and shake the wicked out
of it?   Job 8:22; Ps 104:35
¹⁴The earth takes shape like
clay under a seal;   Ex 28:11
its features stand out like
those of a garment.
¹⁵The wicked are denied their
light,   Dt 28:29
and their upraised arm is
broken.   Ge 17:14

¹⁶"Have you journeyed to the
springs of the sea
or walked in the recesses of
the deep?   Ge 1:7
¹⁷Have the gates of death been
shown to you?   Job 33:22
Have you seen the gates of
the shadow of death*a*?
¹⁸Have you comprehended the
vast expanses of the
earth?   Job 28:24
Tell me, if you know all
this.

¹⁹"What is the way to the
abode of light?

And where does darkness
reside?   Ge 1:4
²⁰Can you take them to their
places?
Do you know the paths to
their dwellings?   Job 24:13
²¹Surely you know, for you
were already born!
You have lived so many
years!   Job 15:7

²²"Have you entered the
storehouses of the
snow
or seen the storehouses of
the hail,   Ps 105:32
²³which I reserve for times of
trouble,   Ps 27:5
for days of war and battle?
²⁴What is the way to the place
where the lightning is
dispersed,   Job 28:24
or the place where the east
winds are scattered over
the earth?   Job 27:21
²⁵Who cuts a channel for the
torrents of rain,
and a path for the
thunderstorm,   Job 28:26
²⁶to water a land where no
man lives,   Job 36:27
a desert with no one in it,
²⁷to satisfy a desolate
wasteland
and make it sprout with
grass?   Job 28:26
²⁸Does the rain have a father?
Who fathers the drops of
dew?   2Sa 1:21
²⁹From whose womb comes
the ice?
Who gives birth to the frost
from the heavens

a17 Or gates of deep shadows

³⁰when the waters become
hard as stone,
when the surface of the
deep is frozen? Job 37:10

³¹"Can you bind the beautiful*ª*
Pleiades?
Can you loose the cords of
Orion? Job 9:9
³²Can you bring forth the
constellations in their
seasons*ᵇ* 2Ki 23:5
or lead out the Bear*ᶜ* with
its cubs? Ge 1:16
³³Do you know the laws of the
heavens? Ps 148:6
Can you set up ⌊God's*ᵈ*⌋
dominion over the
earth?

³⁴"Can you raise your voice to
the clouds
and cover yourself with a
flood of water? Job 5:10
³⁵Do you send the lightning
bolts on their way? Job 36:32
Do they report to you,
'Here we are'?
³⁶Who endowed the heart*ᵉ*
with wisdom Job 9:4
or gave understanding to
the mind*ᵉ*?
³⁷Who has the wisdom to
count the clouds?
Who can tip over the water
jars of the heavens Jos 3:16
³⁸when the dust becomes hard
and the clods of earth stick
together? 1Ki 18:45
³⁹"Do you hunt the prey for
the lioness

and satisfy the hunger of
the lions Ge 49:9
⁴⁰when they crouch in their
dens Job 37:8
or lie in wait in a thicket?
⁴¹Who provides food for the
raven Ge 1:30; 8:7
when its young cry out to
God
and wander about for lack
of food? Ps 147:9

39 "Do you know when the
mountain goats give
birth? Dt 14:5
Do you watch when the
doe bears her fawn?
²Do you count the months till
they bear?
Do you know the time they
give birth? Ge 31:7-9
³They crouch down and bring
forth their young;
their labor pains are ended.
⁴Their young thrive and grow
strong in the wilds;
they leave and do not
return.

⁵"Who let the wild donkey go
free? Ge 16:12
Who untied his ropes?
⁶I gave him the wasteland as
his home, Job 24:5
the salt flats as his habitat.
⁷He laughs at the commotion
in the town; Job 5:22
he does not hear a driver's
shout. Job 3:18
⁸He ranges the hills for his
pasture Isa 32:20

ª31 Or *the twinkling;* or *the chains of the* *ᵇ32* Or *the morning star in its season*
ᶜ32 Or *out Leo*   *ᵈ33* Or *his;* or *their* *ᵉ36* The meaning of the Hebrew for this word
is uncertain.

and searches for any green
  thing.

9"Will the wild ox consent to
    serve you?   Nu 23:22
  Will he stay by your
    manger at night?   Ge 42:27
10Can you hold him to the
    furrow with a harness?
  Will he till the valleys
    behind you?
11Will you rely on him for his
    great strength?   Job 40:16
  Will you leave your heavy
    work to him?
12Can you trust him to bring in
    your grain
  and gather it to your
    threshing floor?

13"The wings of the ostrich
    flap joyfully,
  but they cannot compare
    with the pinions and
    feathers of the stork. Zec 5:9
14She lays her eggs on the
    ground
  and lets them warm in the
    sand,
15unmindful that a foot may
    crush them,
  that some wild animal may
    trample them.   2Ki 14:9
16She treats her young harshly,
    as if they were not hers;
  she cares not that her labor
    was in vain,   La 4:3
17for God did not endow her
    with wisdom
  or give her a share of good
    sense.   Job 21:22
18Yet when she spreads her
    feathers to run,
  she laughs at horse and
    rider.   Job 5:22

19"Do you give the horse his
    strength
  or clothe his neck with a
    flowing mane?
20Do you make him leap like a
    locust,   Joel 2:4-5
  striking terror with his
    proud snorting?   Job 41:25
21He paws fiercely, rejoicing in
    his strength,
  and charges into the fray.
22He laughs at fear, afraid of
    nothing;   Job 5:22
  he does not shy away from
    the sword.
23The quiver rattles against his
    side,   Isa 5:28
  along with the flashing
    spear and lance.   Na 3:3
24In frenzied excitement he
    eats up the ground;
  he cannot stand still when
    the trumpet sounds.
25At the blast of the trumpet he
    snorts, 'Aha!'   Jos 6:5
  He catches the scent of
    battle from afar,
  the shout of commanders
    and the battle cry.   Jer 8:6

26"Does the hawk take flight
    by your wisdom
  and spread his wings
    toward the south?   Jer 8:7
27Does the eagle soar at your
    command
  and build his nest on high?
28He dwells on a cliff and stays
    there at night;
  a rocky crag is his
    stronghold.   Jer 49:16
29From there he seeks out his
    food;   Job 9:26
  his eyes detect it from afar.

³⁰His young ones feast on
   blood,
  and where the slain are,
     there is he." Mt 24:28

40 The LORD said to Job:
  ²"Will the one who
   contends with the
   Almighty correct him?
  Let him who accuses God
   answer him!" Job 9:15

³Then Job answered the
LORD:

⁴"I am unworthy—how can I
   reply to you? Job 42:6
  I put my hand over my
   mouth. Jdg 18:19
⁵I spoke once, but I have no
   answer— Job 9:3
  twice, but I will say no
   more." Job 9:15

⁶Then the LORD spoke to Job
out of the storm: Ex 14:21

⁷"Brace yourself like a man;
  I will question you,
  and you shall answer me.

⁸"Would you discredit my
   justice? Job 15:25
  Would you condemn me to
   justify yourself? Job 2:3
⁹Do you have an arm like
   God's, 2Ch 32:8
  and can your voice thunder
   like his? Isa 6:8
¹⁰Then adorn yourself with
   glory and splendor,
  and clothe yourself in
   honor and majesty. Ps 45:3

¹¹Unleash the fury of your
   wrath, Job 20:28
  look at every proud man
   and bring him low, Ps 18:27
¹²look at every proud man and
   humble him, Ps 10:4
  crush the wicked where
   they stand. Ps 60:12
¹³Bury them all in the dust
   together; Nu 16:31-34
  shroud their faces in the
   grave. Job 4:9
¹⁴Then I myself will admit to
   you
  that your own right hand
   can save you. Ex 15:6

¹⁵"Look at the behemoth,ᵃ
  which I made along with
   you Job 9:9
  and which feeds on grass
   like an ox. Isa 11:7
¹⁶What strength he has in his
   loins, Job 39:11
  what power in the muscles
   of his belly! Job 41:9
¹⁷His tailᵇ sways like a cedar;
  the sinews of his thighs are
   close-knit.
¹⁸His bones are tubes of
   bronze,
  his limbs like rods of iron.
¹⁹He ranks first among the
   works of God, Job 41:33
  yet his Maker can approach
   him with his sword.Ge 3:24
²⁰The hills bring him their
   produce, Ps 104:14
  and all the wild animals
   play nearby. Ps 104:26
²¹Under the lotus plants he
   lies,

ᵃ15 Possibly the hippopotamus or the elephant   ᵇ17 Possibly trunk

hidden among the reeds in
the marsh.   Ge 41:2

22The lotuses conceal him in
their shadow;
the poplars by the stream
surround him.   Ps 1:3

23When the river rages, he is
not alarmed;   Isa 8:7
he is secure, though the
Jordan should surge
against his mouth.   Jos 3:1

24Can anyone capture him by
the eyes,ᵃ
or trap him and pierce his
nose?   2Ki 19:28

41 "Can you pull in the
leviathanᵇ with a
fishhook   Am 4:2
or tie down his tongue with
a rope?

2Can you put a cord through
his nose   Job 40:24
or pierce his jaw with a
hook?   Eze 19:4

3Will he keep begging you for
mercy?   1Ki 20:31
Will he speak to you with
gentle words?

4Will he make an agreement
with you
for you to take him as your
slave for life?   Ex 21:6

5Can you make a pet of him
like a bird
or put him on a leash for
your girls?

6Will traders barter for him?
Will they divide him up
among the merchants?

7Can you fill his hide with
harpoons

or his head with fishing
spears?   Job 40:24

8If you lay a hand on him,
you will remember the
struggle and never do it
again!   Job 3:8

9Any hope of subduing him is
false;
the mere sight of him is
overpowering.   Job 40:16

10No one is fierce enough to
rouse him.   Job 3:8
Who then is able to stand
against me?   2Ch 20:6

11Who has a claim against me
that I must pay?   Job 34:33
Everything under heaven
belongs to me.   Jos 3:11

12"I will not fail to speak of his
limbs,   Job 40:18
his strength and his
graceful form.   Job 39:11

13Who can strip off his outer
coat?
Who would approach him
with a bridle?   Job 30:11

14Who dares open the doors of
his mouth,   Ps 22:13
ringed about with his
fearsome teeth?

15His back hasᶜ rows of shields
tightly sealed together;Job 40:17

16each is so close to the next
that no air can pass
between.

17They are joined fast to one
another;
they cling together and
cannot be parted.

18His snorting throws out
flashes of light;

ᵃ24 Or by a water hole   ᵇ1 Possibly the crocodile   ᶜ15 Or His pride is his

his eyes are like the rays of
dawn. *Job 3:9*

19Firebrands stream from his
mouth; *Da 10:6*
sparks of fire shoot out.

20Smoke pours from his
nostrils *Ps 18:8*
as from a boiling pot over a
fire of reeds.

21His breath sets coals ablaze,
and flames dart from his
mouth. *Isa 10:17*

22Strength resides in his neck;
dismay goes before him.

23The folds of his flesh are
tightly joined;
they are firm and
immovable.

24His chest is hard as rock,
hard as a lower millstone.

25When he rises up, the
mighty are terrified;
they retreat before his
thrashing. *Job 3:8*

26The sword that reaches him
has no effect,
nor does the spear or the
dart or the javelin. *Jos 8:18*

27Iron he treats like straw
and bronze like rotten
wood.

28Arrows do not make him
flee; *Ps 91:5*
slingstones are like chaff to
him.

29A club seems to him but a
piece of straw;
he laughs at the rattling of
the lance. *Job 5:22*

30His undersides are jagged
potsherds,
leaving a trail in the mud
like a threshing sledge.

31He makes the depths churn
like a boiling caldron
and stirs up the sea like a
pot of ointment. *Eze 32:2*

32Behind him he leaves a
glistening wake;
one would think the deep
had white hair.

33Nothing on earth is his
equal— *Job 40:19*
a creature without fear.

34He looks down on all that are
haughty; *Ps 18:29*
he is king over all that are
proud." *Job 28:8*

Job

42 Then Job replied to the
LORD:

2"I know that you can do all
things; *Ge 18:14*
no plan of yours can be
thwarted. *2Ch 20:6*

3You asked, ⌞'Who is this that
obscures my counsel
without knowledge?'⌟
Surely I spoke of things I
did not understand,
things too wonderful for me
to know. *Job 5:9*

4"You said, ⌞'Listen now, and
I will speak;⌟
I will question you,
and you shall answer me.'

5My ears had heard of you
but now my eyes have seen
you. *Jdg 13:22*

6Therefore I despise myself
and repent in dust and
ashes." *Ex 10:3; Job 34:33*

Epilogue

7After the LORD had said these things to Job, he said to Eliphaz the Temanite, "I am angry with you and your two friends, because you have not spoken of me what is right, as my servant Job has. 8So now take seven bulls and seven rams and go to my servant Job and sacrifice a burnt offering for yourselves. My servant Job will pray for you, and I will accept his prayer and not deal with you according to your folly. You have not spoken of me what is right, as my servant Job has." 9So Eliphaz the Temanite, Bildad the Shuhite and Zophar the Naamathite did what the LORD told them; and the LORD accepted Job's prayer.   Job 2:11

10After Job had prayed for his friends, the LORD made him prosperous again and gave him twice as much as he had before. 11All his brothers and sisters and everyone who had known him before came and ate with him in his house. They comforted and consoled him over all the trouble the LORD had brought upon him, and each one gave him a piece of silver*a* and a gold ring.   Dt 30:3; Job 19:13; Ps 14:7

12The LORD blessed the latter part of Job's life more than the first. He had fourteen thousand sheep, six thousand camels, a thousand yoke of oxen and a thousand donkeys. 13And he also had seven sons and three daughters. 14The first daughter he named Jemimah, the second Keziah and the third Keren-Happuch. 15Nowhere in all the land were there found women as beautiful as Job's daughters, and their father granted them an inheritance along with their brothers.   Job 1:10

16After this, Job lived a hundred and forty years; he saw his children and their children to the fourth generation. 17And so he died, old and full of years.

---

*a*11 Hebrew *him a kesitah*; a kesitah was a unit of money of unknown weight and value.

Psalms

Introduction:

The Psalms are poems or songs of praise, worship, thankfulness, and repentance, and each one of them is complete by itself. They also show a variety of feelings, emotions, attitudes and interests.

Of the 150 Psalms, one hundred of them are thought to be written by the following authors: David—73; Asaph—12; Sons of Korah—10; Moses—1; Heman the Ezrahite—1; Ethan the Ezrahite—1; and one or two by Solomon. The rest of the Psalms have no recorded author.

Because the Psalms are written by so many people, from different time periods, and they show such a variety of emotions they have had a world-wide appeal and are familiar and loved by many people.

Hebrew poetry often uses pairs of lines. The second line either repeats the thought of the first or gives an opposite. Look for these pairs of lines as you read the Psalms.

Outline of contents:

BOOK I

Psalms 1–41

Psalm 1

¹Blessed is the man   Dt 33:29
who does not walk in the
counsel of the wicked
or stand in the way of
sinners   Ge 49:6; Ps 26:9
or sit in the seat of mockers.
²But his delight is in the law
of the LORD,   Ps 112:1
and on his law he meditates
day and night.   Ge 24:63
³He is like a tree planted by
streams of water,   Nu 24:6
which yields its fruit in
season   Ps 92:14
and whose leaf does not
wither.   Isa 1:30

Whatever he does prospers.

4Not so the wicked!
    They are like chaff   Job 13:25
    that the wind blows away.
5Therefore the wicked will not
    stand in the judgment,
    nor sinners in the assembly
    of the righteous.   Ps 35:18

6For the LORD watches over
    the way of the
    righteous,   Ps 37:18
    but the way of the wicked
    will perish.   Lev 26:38

Psalm 2

1Why do the nations
    conspire*a*
    and the peoples plot in
    vain?   Ps 21:11
2The kings of the earth take
    their stand   Ps 48:4
    and the rulers gather
    together
  against the LORD
    and against his Anointed
    One.*b*   Ac 4:25-26
3"Let us break their chains,"
    they say,   Job 36:8
    "and throw off their
    fetters."   2Sa 3:34

4The One enthroned in
    heaven laughs;   Isa 37:16
    the Lord scoffs at them.
5Then he rebukes them in his
    anger   Ps 6:1
    and terrifies them in his
    wrath, saying,   Ps 21:9
6"I have installed my King*c*
    on Zion, my holy hill." Ex 15:17

7I will proclaim the decree of
the LORD:

He said to me, "You are my
    Son*d*;   Mt 3:17
    today I have become your
    Father. *e*   2Sa 7:14
8Ask of me,
    and I will make the nations
    your inheritance,   Job 22:26
    the ends of the earth your
    possession.   Ps 22:27
9You will rule them with an
    iron scepter*f*;   Ge 49:10
    you will dash them to
    pieces like pottery."

10Therefore, you kings, be
    wise;   Pr 27:11
    be warned, you rulers of
    the earth.   Ps 141:6
11Serve the LORD with fear
    and rejoice with trembling.
12Kiss the Son, lest he be angry
    and you be destroyed in
    your way,
    for his wrath can flare up in a
    moment.   Dt 9:8
    Blessed are all who take
    refuge in him.   Ps 5:11

Psalm 3

A psalm of David. When he fled
from his son Absalom.

1O LORD, how many are my
    foes!
    How many rise up against
    me!
2Many are saying of me,

---

*a*1 Hebrew; Septuagint *rage*   *b*2 Or *anointed one*   *c*6 Or *king*   *d*7 Or *son*; also in
verse 12   *e*7 Or *have begotten you*   *f*9 Or *will break them with a rod of iron*

"God will not deliver him."
Selah[a]

[3]But you are a shield around
me, O LORD;   Ge 15:1
you bestow glory on me
and lift[b] up my head.
[4]To the LORD I cry aloud,
and he answers me from
his holy hill.   *Selah*

[5]I lie down and sleep;   Lev 26:6
I wake again, because the
LORD sustains me.   Ps 17:15
[6]I will not fear the tens of
thousands   Job 11:15
drawn up against me on
every side.   Ps 118:11

[7]Arise, O LORD!   2Ch 6:41
Deliver me, O my God!
Strike all my enemies on the
jaw;   Job 16:10
break the teeth of the
wicked.   Job 29:17

[8]From the LORD comes
deliverance.   Ps 27:1
May your blessing be on
your people.   *Selah*

Psalm 4

For the director of music. With
stringed instruments.
A psalm of David.

[1]Answer me when I call to
you,   Ps 13:3
O my righteous God.
Give me relief from my
distress;   Ge 32:7

be merciful to me and hear
my prayer.   Ps 17:6

[2]How long, O men, will you
turn my glory into
shame[c]?   Ex 16:7; 2Ki 19:26
How long will you love
delusions and seek false
gods[d]?   *Selah*
[3]Know that the LORD has set
apart the godly for
himself;   Ps 12:1
the LORD will hear when I
call to him.   Ps 6:8

[4]In your anger do not sin;
when you are on your beds,
search your hearts and be
silent.   *Selah*
[5]Offer right sacrifices
and trust in the LORD.   Ps 31:6

[6]Many are asking, "Who can
show us any good?"
Let the light of your face
shine upon us, O LORD.
[7]You have filled my heart
with greater joy   Ac 14:17
than when their grain and
new wine abound.   Ge 27:28
[8]I will lie down and sleep in
peace,   Lev 26:6
for you alone, O LORD,
make me dwell in safety.

Psalm 5

For the director of music. For
flutes. A psalm of David.

[1]Give ear to my words,
O LORD,   1Ki 8:29
consider my sighing.   Ps 38:9

---

[a]2 A word of uncertain meaning, occurring frequently in the Psalms; possibly a musical
term   [b]3 Or LORD, / my Glorious One, who lifts   [c]2 Or *you dishonor my Glorious One*
[d]2 Or *seek lies*

²Listen to my cry for help,
my King and my God,
for to you I pray.   Ps 44:4
³In the morning, O Lord, you
hear my voice;   Isa 28:19
in the morning I lay my
requests before you
and wait in expectation.

⁴You are not a God who takes
pleasure in evil;
with you the wicked cannot
dwell.   Ps 1:5
⁵The arrogant cannot stand in
your presence;   Ps 73:3
you hate all who do wrong.
⁶You destroy those who tell
lies;   Pr 19:22
bloodthirsty and deceitful
men
the Lord abhors.

⁷But I, by your great mercy,
will come into your house;
in reverence will I bow down
toward your holy temple.
⁸Lead me, O Lord, in your
righteousness   Ps 23:3
because of my enemies—
make straight your way
before me.   1Ki 8:36

⁹Not a word from their mouth
can be trusted;
their heart is filled with
destruction.
Their throat is an open grave;
with their tongue they
speak deceit.   Ps 12:2
¹⁰Declare them guilty, O God!
Let their intrigues be their
downfall.
Banish them for their many
sins,   La 1:5

for they have rebelled
against you.   Ps 78:40

¹¹But let all who take refuge in
you be glad;
let them ever sing for joy.
Spread your protection over
them,
that those who love your
name may rejoice in
you.   Job 22:19
¹²For surely, O Lord, you
bless the righteous;
you surround them with
your favor as with a
shield.   Ge 15:1

Psalm 6

For the director of music. With
stringed instruments. According
to sheminith.ᵃ A psalm of David.

¹O Lord, do not rebuke me in
your anger   Ps 2:5
or discipline me in your
wrath.
²Be merciful to me, Lord, for I
am faint;   Ps 61:2
O Lord, heal me, for my
bones are in agony. Ps 22:14
³My soul is in anguish.   Job 7:11
How long, O Lord, how
long?   1Sa 1:14

⁴Turn, O Lord, and deliver
me;   Ps 25:16
save me because of your
unfailing love.   Ps 13:5
⁵No one remembers you
when he is dead.
Who praises you from the
graveᵇ?   Ps 30:9

ᵃTitle: Probably a musical term   ᵇ5 Hebrew Sheol

⁶I am worn out from
   groaning; Jdg 8:5; Job 3:24
all night long I flood my
   bed with weeping Job 16:16
and drench my couch with
   tears. Job 7:3
⁷My eyes grow weak with
   sorrow; Job 16:8
they fail because of all my
   foes.

⁸Away from me, all you who
   do evil,
for the LORD has heard my Ps 119:115
   weeping.
⁹The LORD has heard my cry
   for mercy; Ps 28:6
the LORD accepts my
   prayer.
¹⁰All my enemies will be
   ashamed and dismayed;
they will turn back in
   sudden disgrace. Ps 40:14

Psalm 7

A *shiggaion*ᵃ of David, which he
sang to the LORD concerning
Cush, a Benjamite.

¹O LORD my God, I take
   refuge in you; Ps 2:12
save and deliver me from
   all who pursue me,
²or they will tear me like a
   lion Ge 49:9
and rip me to pieces with
   no one to rescue me.

³O LORD my God, if I have
   done this

and there is guilt on my
   hands— Isa 59:3
⁴if I have done evil to him
   who is at peace with me
or without cause have
   robbed my foe— Ps 35:7
⁵then let my enemy pursue
   and overtake me; Ex 15:9
let him trample my life to
   the ground 2Sa 22:43
and make me sleep in the
   dust. *Selah*

⁶Arise, O LORD, in your
   anger; 2Ch 6:41
rise up against the rage of
   my enemies. Ps 138:7
Awake, my God; decree
   justice. Ps 35:23
⁷Let the assembled peoples
   gather around you.
Rule over them from on
   high; Ps 68:18
⁸ let the LORD judge the
   peoples. 1Ch 16:33
Judge me, O LORD, according
   to my righteousness,
according to my integrity,
   O Most High. Ge 3:5
⁹O righteous God, Jer 11:20
who searches minds and
   hearts, 1Ch 28:9
bring to an end the violence
   of the wicked
and make the righteous
   secure. Ps 37:23

¹⁰My shieldᵇ is God Most
   High, Ps 3:3
who saves the upright in
   heart. Job 33:3

ᵃTitle: Probably a literary or musical term   ᵇ10 Or *sovereign*

¹¹God is a righteous judge,
a God who expresses his
wrath every day.   Dt 9:8
¹²If he does not relent,   Eze 3:19
heᵃ will sharpen his sword;
he will bend and string his
bow.   2Sa 22:35
¹³He has prepared his deadly
weapons;
he makes ready his flaming
arrows.   Ps 11:2

¹⁴He who is pregnant with evil
and conceives trouble gives
birth to disillusionment.
¹⁵He who digs a hole and
scoops it out
falls into the pit he has
made.   Job 4:8; Ps 35:7
¹⁶The trouble he causes recoils
on himself;
his violence comes down on
his own head.

¹⁷I will give thanks to the LORD
because of his
righteousness   Ps 5:8
and will sing praise to the
name of the LORD Most
High.   Ge 14:18

Psalm 8

For the director of music.
According to *gittith.*ᵇ
A psalm of David.

¹O LORD, our Lord,
how majestic is your name
in all the earth!   1Ch 16:10

You have set your glory
above the heavens.   Ps 57:5
²From the lips of children and
infants
you have ordained praiseᶜ
because of your enemies,
to silence the foe and the
avenger.   Ps 143:12

³When I consider your
heavens,   Ge 15:5
the work of your fingers,
the moon and the stars,
which you have set in
place,   Ge 1:16
⁴what is man that you are
mindful of him,
the son of man that you
care for him?   1Ch 29:14
⁵You made him a little lower
than the heavenly
beingsᵈ   Ge 1:26
and crowned him with
glory and honor.   Ps 21:5

⁶You made him ruler over the
works of your hands;
you put everything under
his feet: Heb 2:6-8
⁷all flocks and herds,   Ge 13:5
and the beasts of the field,
⁸the birds of the air,
and the fish of the sea,
all that swim the paths of
the seas.   Ge 1:26

⁹O LORD, our Lord,
how majestic is your name
in all the earth!

ᵃ12 Or *If a man does not repent, / God*   ᵇTitle: Probably a musical term   ᶜ2 Or
strength   ᵈ5 Or *than God*

Psalm 9[a]

For the director of music. To ˌthe
tune of ˌ"The Death of the Son."
A psalm of David.

[1]I will praise you, O LORD,
   with all my heart;   Ps 86:12
I will tell of all your
   wonders.   Dt 4:34
[2]I will be glad and rejoice in
   you;   Job 22:19
I will sing praise to your
   name, O Most High.

[3]My enemies turn back;
   they stumble and perish
   before you.
[4]For you have upheld my
   right and my cause;
you have sat on your
   throne, judging
   righteously.   Ps 11:4
[5]You have rebuked the
   nations and destroyed
   the wicked;   Ge 20:7
you have blotted out their
   name for ever and ever.
[6]Endless ruin has overtaken
   the enemy,
you have uprooted their
   cities;   Dt 29:28
even the memory of them
   has perished.   Ps 34:16

[7]The LORD reigns forever;
   he has established his
   throne for judgment.
[8]He will judge the world in
   righteousness;   Ps 7:11
he will govern the peoples
   with justice.   Ps 11:7

[9]The LORD is a refuge for the
   oppressed,   Dt 33:27
a stronghold in times of
   trouble.   Ps 32:7
[10]Those who know your name
   will trust in you,   Ps 91:14
for you, LORD, have never
   forsaken those who seek
   you.   Ps 70:4

[11]Sing praises to the LORD,
   enthroned in Zion;   Ps 2:6
proclaim among the nations
   what he has done.   Ps 18:49
[12]For he who avenges blood
   remembers;   2Sa 4:11
he does not ignore the cry
   of the afflicted.   Ps 10:17

[13]O LORD, see how my
   enemies persecute me!
Have mercy and lift me up
   from the gates of death,
[14]that I may declare your
   praises   Ps 51:15
in the gates of the Daughter
   of Zion   2Ki 19:21
and there rejoice in your
   salvation.   Ps 13:5
[15]The nations have fallen into
   the pit they have dug;
their feet are caught in the
   net they have hidden.
[16]The LORD is known by his
   justice;
the wicked are ensnared by
   the work of their hands.
        Higgaion.[b] *Selah*
[17]The wicked return to the
   grave,[c]   Nu 16:30

[a]Psalms 9 and 10 may have been originally a single acrostic poem, the stanzas of which
begin with the successive letters of the Hebrew alphabet. In the Septuagint they
constitute one psalm.   [b]16 Or *Meditation*; possibly a musical notation
[c]17 Hebrew *Sheol*

all the nations that forget
    God.   Job 8:13
[18]But the needy will not always
    be forgotten,
  nor the hope of the afflicted
    ever perish.   Ps 25:3

[19]Arise, O Lord, let not man
    triumph;   Ps 3:7
  let the nations be judged in
    your presence.   Ps 110:6
[20]Strike them with terror,
    O Lord;   Ge 35:5
  let the nations know they
    are but men.   *Selah*

Psalm 10 [a]

[1]Why, O Lord, do you stand
    far off?   Ps 22:1
  Why do you hide yourself
    in times of trouble?   Ps 13:1

[2]In his arrogance the wicked
    man hunts down the
    weak,   Job 20:19
  who are caught in the
    schemes he devises.
[3]He boasts of the cravings of
    his heart;   Ps 49:6
  he blesses the greedy and
    reviles the Lord.   Job 1:5
[4]In his pride the wicked does
    not seek him;
  in all his thoughts there is
    no room for God.   Ps 36:1
[5]His ways are always
    prosperous;
  he is haughty and your
    laws are far from him;

  he sneers at all his enemies.
[6]He says to himself, "Nothing
    will shake me;
  I'll always be happy and
    never have trouble."
[7]His mouth is full of curses
    and lies and threats;
  trouble and evil are under
    his tongue.   Job 20:12
[8]He lies in wait near the
    villages;   Ps 37:32
  from ambush he murders
    the innocent,   Hos 6:9
  watching in secret for his
    victims.
[9]He lies in wait like a lion in
    cover;
  he lies in wait to catch the
    helpless;
  he catches the helpless and
    drags them off in his
    net.   Job 18:8
[10]His victims are crushed, they
    collapse;   Job 9:17
  they fall under his strength.
[11]He says to himself, "God has
    forgotten;   Job 22:13
  he covers his face and never
    sees."   Job 22:14

[12]Arise, Lord! Lift up your
    hand, O God.   Ps 17:7
  Do not forget the helpless.
[13]Why does the wicked man
    revile God?
  Why does he say to
    himself,
  "He won't call me to
    account"?   Job 31:14
[14]But you, O God, do see
    trouble and grief;   Ps 22:11

---

[a]Psalms 9 and 10 may have been originally a single acrostic poem, the stanzas of which
begin with the successive letters of the Hebrew alphabet. In the Septuagint they
constitute one psalm.

you consider it to take it in
 hand.
The victim commits himself
 to you; Ps 37:5
you are the helper of the
 fatherless. Dt 33:29
¹⁵Break the arm of the wicked
 and evil man; Job 31:22
call him to account for his
 wickedness
that would not be found
 out.

¹⁶The LORD is King for ever
 and ever; Ex 15:18
the nations will perish from
 his land. Dt 8:20
¹⁷You hear, O LORD, the desire
 of the afflicted; Ps 9:12
you encourage them, and
 you listen to their cry,
¹⁸defending the fatherless and
 the oppressed, Ps 9:9
in order that man, who is of
 the earth, may terrify no
 more.

Psalm 11

For the director of music. Of
David.

¹In the LORD I take refuge.
 How then can you say to
 me:
"Flee like a bird to your
 mountain. Ps 50:11
²For look, the wicked bend
 their bows; 2Sa 22:35
they set their arrows
 against the strings Ps 7:13
to shoot from the shadows
 at the upright in heart. Job 33:3

³When the foundations are
 being destroyed, Ps 18:15
what can the righteous
 do*a*?"

⁴The LORD is in his holy
 temple; 1Ki 8:48
the LORD is on his heavenly
 throne. 2Ch 6:18
He observes the sons of men;
 his eyes examine them.
⁵The LORD examines the
 righteous, Dt 7:13
but the wicked*b* and those
 who love violence
his soul hates. Job 28:28
⁶On the wicked he will rain
fiery coals and burning
 sulfur; Ge 19:24
a scorching wind will be
 their lot. Ge 41:6

⁷For the LORD is righteous,
 he loves justice; Ps 9:8
upright men will see his
 face. Ps 17:15

Psalm 12

For the director of music.
According to *sheminith.* *c*
A psalm of David.

¹Help, LORD, for the godly are
 no more; Isa 57:1
the faithful have vanished
 from among men.
²Everyone lies to his neighbor;
 their flattering lips speak
 with deception. Ps 5:9

³May the LORD cut off all
 flattering lips Pr 26:28
and every boastful tongue

---

*a*3 Or *what is the Righteous One doing*   *b*5 Or *The* LORD, *the Righteous One, examines the*
wicked, /   *c*Title: Probably a musical term

4that says, "We will triumph
with our tongues; Pr 18:21
we own our lips^a—who is
our master?"

5"Because of the oppression
of the weak Ps 44:24
and the groaning of the
needy, Ps 6:6
I will now arise," says the
LORD. Ps 3:7
"I will protect them from
those who malign
them." Ps 34:6
6And the words of the LORD
are flawless, 2Sa 22:31
like silver refined in a
furnace of clay, Job 23:10
purified seven times.

7O LORD, you will keep us
safe Ps 16:1
and protect us from such
people forever. Ps 37:28
8The wicked freely strut about
when what is vile is
honored among men.

Psalm 13

For the director of music.
A psalm of David.

1How long, O LORD? Will you
forget me forever? Ps 42:9
How long will you hide
your face from me?
2How long must I wrestle
with my thoughts Ps 42:4
and every day have sorrow
in my heart?
How long will my enemy
triumph over me? Ps 94:3

3Look on me and answer,
O LORD my God. Ps 9:12
Give light to my eyes, or I
will sleep in death;
4my enemy will say, "I have
overcome him," Ps 25:2
and my foes will rejoice
when I fall. Ps 38:16

5But I trust in your unfailing
love; Ps 6:4
my heart rejoices in your
salvation. Job 33:26
6I will sing to the LORD,
for he has been good to me.

Psalm 14

For the director of music. Of
David.

1The fool^b says in his heart,
"There is no God." Ps 10:4
They are corrupt, their deeds
are vile;
there is no one who does
good.

2The LORD looks down from
heaven Job 41:34
on the sons of men
to see if there are any who
understand, Ps 92:6
any who seek God. Ezr 6:21
3All have turned aside, 1Sa 8:3
they have together become
corrupt; 2Pe 2:7
there is no one who does
good, 1Ki 8:46
not even one. Ro 3:10-12

4Will evildoers never learn—
those who devour my
people as men eat bread

---

^a4 Or / our lips are our plowshares   ^b1 The Hebrew words rendered *fool* in Psalms
denote one who is morally deficient.

and who do not call on the
LORD? Ps 79:6
⁵There they are, overwhelmed
with dread,
for God is present in the
company of the
righteous.
⁶You evildoers frustrate the
plans of the poor,
but the LORD is their refuge.

⁷Oh, that salvation for Israel
would come out of Zion!
When the LORD restores the
fortunes of his people,
let Jacob rejoice and Israel
be glad! Dt 30:3

Psalm 15

A psalm of David.

¹LORD, who may dwell in
your sanctuary? Ex 25:8
Who may live on your holy
hill? Ex 15:17

²He whose walk is blameless
and who does what is
righteous, Ge 6:9
who speaks the truth from
his heart Pr 16:13
³ and has no slander on his
tongue, Lev 19:16
who does his neighbor no
wrong
and casts no slur on his
fellowman,
⁴who despises a vile man
but honors those who fear
the LORD, Job 19:9
who keeps his oath Dt 23:21
even when it hurts,

⁵who lends his money
without usury Ex 22:25
and does not accept a bribe
against the innocent.

He who does these things
will never be shaken. Job 29:18

Psalm 16

A *miktam*ᵃ of David.

¹Keep me safe, O God, Ps 12:7
for in you I take refuge. Pr 2:12

²I said to the LORD, "You are
my Lord; Ps 31:14
apart from you I have no
good thing." Ps 73:25
³As for the saints who are in
the land, Ps 101:6
they are the glorious ones
in whom is all my
delight.ᵇ
⁴The sorrows of those will
increase Ps 32:10
who run after other gods.
I will not pour out their
libations of blood
or take up their names on
my lips. Ex 23:13

⁵LORD, you have assigned me
my portion and my cup;
you have made my lot
secure. Job 31:2
⁶The boundary lines have
fallen for me in pleasant
places; Dt 19:14
surely I have a delightful
inheritance. Job 22:26

⁷I will praise the LORD, who
counsels me; Ps 73:24

ᵃTitle: Probably a literary or musical term
land / and the nobles in whom all delight, I said:
ᵇ3 Or *As for the pagan priests who are in the*

even at night my heart
   instructs me.   Job 35:10
⁸I have set the LORD always
   before me.
Because he is at my right
   hand,   1Ki 2:19
I will not be shaken.   Ps 15:5

⁹Therefore my heart is glad
   and my tongue rejoices;
my body also will rest
   secure,   Dt 33:28
¹⁰because you will not
   abandon me to the
   grave,ᵃ   Nu 16:30
nor will you let your Holy
   Oneᵇ see decay.   2Ki 19:22
¹¹You have madeᶜ known to
   me the path of life;
you will fill me with joy in
   your presence,   Ac 2:25-28
with eternal pleasures at
   your right hand.   Ps 21:6

Psalm 17

A prayer of David.

¹Hear, O LORD, my righteous
   plea;   Ps 30:10
listen to my cry.   Ps 5:2
Give ear to my prayer—
   it does not rise from
   deceitful lips.   Isa 29:13
²May my vindication come
   from you;   Ps 24:5
may your eyes see what is
   right.   Ps 99:4

³Though you probe my heart
   and examine me at
   night,   Ps 139:1
though you test me, you
   will find nothing;   Job 7:18

I have resolved that my
   mouth will not sin.
⁴As for the deeds of men—
   by the word of your lips
I have kept myself
   from the ways of the
   violent.
⁵My steps have held to your
   paths;   Job 23:11
my feet have not slipped.

⁶I call on you, O God, for you
   will answer me;   Ps 86:7
give ear to me and hear my
   prayer.   Ps 116:2
⁷Show the wonder of your
   great love,   Ps 31:21
you who save by your right
   hand   Ps 10:12
those who take refuge in
   you from their foes.
⁸Keep me as the apple of your
   eye;   Dt 32:10
hide me in the shadow of
   your wings   Ru 2:12
⁹from the wicked who assail
   me,
from my mortal enemies
   who surround me.

¹⁰They close up their callous
   hearts,   Ps 73:7
and their mouths speak
   with arrogance.   1Sa 2:3
¹¹They have tracked me down,
   they now surround me,
with eyes alert, to throw me
   to the ground.   Ps 88:17
¹²They are like a lion hungry
   for prey,   Ps 7:2
like a great lion crouching
   in cover.

ᵃ10 Hebrew *Sheol*   ᵇ10 Or *your faithful one*   ᶜ11 Or *You will make*

¹³Rise up, O Lᴏʀᴅ, confront
 them, bring them down;
rescue me from the wicked
 by your sword.   Ps 35:8
¹⁴O Lᴏʀᴅ, by your hand save
 me from such men,
from men of this world
 whose reward is in this
 life.   Ps 49:17

You still the hunger of those
 you cherish;
their sons have plenty,
and they store up wealth
 for their children.   Isa 2:7
¹⁵And I—in righteousness I
 will see your face;
when I awake, I will be
 satisfied with seeing
 your likeness.   Nu 12:8

Psalm 18

For the director of music. Of
David the servant of the Lᴏʀᴅ. He
sang to the Lᴏʀᴅ the words of this
song when the Lᴏʀᴅ delivered
him from the hand of all his
enemies and from the hand of
Saul. He said:

¹I love you, O Lᴏʀᴅ, my
 strength.   Ex 15:2

²The Lᴏʀᴅ is my rock, my
 fortress and my
 deliverer;   Ps 40:17
my God is my rock, in
 whom I take refuge.
He is my shield and the
 hornᵃ of my salvation,
 my stronghold.   1Sa 2:1
³I call to the Lᴏʀᴅ, who is
 worthy of praise,   1Ch 16:25

and I am saved from my
 enemies.   Ps 9:13
⁴The cords of death entangled
 me;   Ps 116:3
the torrents of destruction
 overwhelmed me.   Ps 93:4
⁵The cords of the graveᵇ
 coiled around me;
the snares of death
 confronted me.   Pr 13:14
⁶In my distress I called to the
 Lᴏʀᴅ;   Ps 30:2
I cried to my God for help.
From his temple he heard my
 voice;   Ps 66:19
my cry came before him,
 into his ears.   Job 16:18

⁷The earth trembled and
 quaked,   Ps 97:4
and the foundations of the
 mountains shook;   Jdg 5:5
they trembled because he
 was angry.   Job 9:5
⁸Smoke rose from his nostrils;
consuming fire came from
 his mouth,   Ex 15:7
burning coals blazed out
 of it.   Pr 25:22
⁹He parted the heavens and
 came down;   Ge 11:5
dark clouds were under his
 feet.   Ex 20:21
¹⁰He mounted the cherubim
 and flew;   Ge 3:24
he soared on the wings of
 the wind.   Ps 104:3
¹¹He made darkness his
 covering, his canopy
 around him—   Job 22:14
the dark rain clouds of the
 sky.

─────────
ᵃ2 *Horn* here symbolizes strength.   ᵇ5 Hebrew *Sheol*

¹²Out of the brightness of his
    presence clouds
    advanced,   Ps 104:2
  with hailstones and bolts of
    lightning.   Job 10:11
¹³The LORD thundered from
    heaven;   Ex 9:23
  the voice of the Most High
    resounded. ^a
¹⁴He shot his arrows and
    scattered ⸤the enemies⸥,
  great bolts of lightning and
    routed them.   Jdg 4:15
¹⁵The valleys of the sea were
    exposed
  and the foundations of the
    earth laid bare   Ps 11:3
  at your rebuke, O LORD,
  at the blast of breath from
    your nostrils.   Ex 15:8

¹⁶He reached down from on
    high and took hold of
    me;
  he drew me out of deep
    waters.   Ps 69:2
¹⁷He rescued me from my
    powerful enemy,   Ps 38:19
  from my foes, who were
    too strong for me. Jdg 18:26
¹⁸They confronted me in the
    day of my disaster,   Pr 1:27
  but the LORD was my
    support.   Ps 20:2
¹⁹He brought me out into a
    spacious place;   Ps 31:8
  he rescued me because he
    delighted in me.   Nu 14:8

²⁰The LORD has dealt with me
    according to my
    righteousness;   1Sa 26:23

    according to the cleanness
      of my hands he has
      rewarded me.   Ru 2:12
²¹For I have kept the ways of
    the LORD;   2Ch 34:33
  I have not done evil by
    turning from my God.
²²All his laws are before me;
  I have not turned away
    from his decrees.
²³I have been blameless before
    him   Ge 6:9
  and have kept myself from
    sin.
²⁴The LORD has rewarded me
    according to my
    righteousness,   1Sa 26:23
  according to the cleanness
    of my hands in his sight.

²⁵To the faithful you show
    yourself faithful,   Ps 25:10
  to the blameless you show
    yourself blameless,
²⁶to the pure you show
    yourself pure,   Pr 15:26
  but to the crooked you
    show yourself shrewd.
²⁷You save the humble
  but bring low those whose
    eyes are haughty.   Job 41:34
²⁸You, O LORD, keep my lamp
    burning;   1Ki 11:36
  my God turns my darkness
    into light.   Job 29:3
²⁹With your help I can advance
    against a troop^b;
  with my God I can scale a
    wall.

³⁰As for God, his way is
    perfect;   Dt 32:4

---

^a13 Some Hebrew manuscripts and Septuagint (see also 2 Samuel 22:14); most Hebrew
manuscripts *resounded, / amid hailstones and bolts of lightning*   ^b29 Or *can run through a
barricade*

the word of the LORD is
flawless.   Ps 12:6
He is a shield
for all who take refuge in
him.   Ps 3:3; 2:12
³¹For who is God besides the
LORD?   Dt 4:35
And who is the Rock except
our God?   Ge 49:24
³²It is God who arms me with
strength   1Pe 5:10
and makes my way perfect.
³³He makes my feet like the
feet of a deer;   Ps 42:1
he enables me to stand on
the heights.   Dt 32:13
³⁴He trains my hands for
battle;   Ps 144:1
my arms can bend a bow of
bronze.
³⁵You give me your shield of
victory,
and your right hand
sustains me;   Ps 3:5
you stoop down to make
me great.
³⁶You broaden the path
beneath me,   Ps 31:8
so that my ankles do not
turn.   Job 18:7

³⁷I pursued my enemies and
overtook them;   Lev 26:7
I did not turn back till they
were destroyed.
³⁸I crushed them so that they
could not rise;   Ps 36:12
they fell beneath my feet.
³⁹You armed me with strength
for battle;   Isa 45:5
you made my adversaries
bow at my feet.   Ps 47:3
⁴⁰You made my enemies turn
their backs in flight,   Jos 7:12

and I destroyed my foes.
⁴¹They cried for help, but there
was no one to save
them—   2Ki 14:26
to the LORD, but he did not
answer.   1Sa 8:18
⁴²I beat them as fine as dust
borne on the wind;
I poured them out like mud
in the streets.   Dt 9:21

⁴³You have delivered me from
the attacks of the people;
you have made me the
head of nations;   2Sa 8:1-14
people I did not know are
subject to me.   Isa 55:5
⁴⁴As soon as they hear me,
they obey me;
foreigners cringe before me.
⁴⁵They all lose heart;
they come trembling from
their strongholds.   Ps 9:9

⁴⁶The LORD lives! Praise be to
my Rock!   Ex 33:22
Exalted be God my Savior!
⁴⁷He is the God who avenges
me,   Ge 4:24
who subdues nations under
me,   Jdg 4:23
⁴⁸ who saves me from my
enemies.   Ps 7:10
You exalted me above my
foes;
from violent men you
rescued me.   Ps 140:1
⁴⁹Therefore I will praise you
among the nations,
O LORD;   Ps 9:11
I will sing praises to your
name.   Ps 7:17
⁵⁰He gives his king great
victories;

he shows unfailing
kindness to his
anointed,   2Sa 23:1
to David and his
descendants forever.

Psalm 19

For the director of music.
A psalm of David.

¹The heavens declare the
glory of God;   Ps 89:5
the skies proclaim the work
of his hands.   Ps 8:6
²Day after day they pour forth
speech;
night after night they
display knowledge.Ps 74:16
³There is no speech or
language
where their voice is not
heard.ᵃ
⁴Their voiceᵇ goes out into all
the earth,
their words to the ends of
the world.   Ro 10:18

In the heavens he has
pitched a tent for the
sun,   Job 36:29
5 which is like a bridegroom
coming forth from his
pavilion,   Joel 2:16
like a champion rejoicing to
run his course.   1Sa 17:4
⁶It rises at one end of the
heavens   Dt 30:4
and makes its circuit to the
other;   Ps 113:3
nothing is hidden from its
heat.

⁷The law of the LORD is
perfect,   Ps 119:142
reviving the soul.   Ps 23:3
The statutes of the LORD are
trustworthy,   Ps 93:5
making wise the simple.
⁸The precepts of the LORD are
right,   Ps 33:4
giving joy to the heart.
The commands of the LORD
are radiant,
giving light to the eyes. Ezr 9:8
⁹The fear of the LORD is pure,
enduring forever.   Ps 34:11
The ordinances of the LORD
are sure
and altogether righteous.
¹⁰They are more precious than
gold,   Job 22:24
than much pure gold;
they are sweeter than honey,
than honey from the comb.
¹¹By them is your servant
warned;
in keeping them there is
great reward.

¹²Who can discern his errors?
Forgive my hidden faults.
¹³Keep your servant also from
willful sins;   Nu 15:30
may they not rule over me.
Then will I be blameless,
innocent of great
transgression.   Ge 6:9

¹⁴May the words of my mouth
and the meditation of
my heart
be pleasing in your sight,
O LORD, my Rock and my
Redeemer.   Ex 6:6

ᵃ3 Or *They have no speech, there are no words; / no sound is heard from them*
ᵇ4 Septuagint, Jerome and Syriac; Hebrew *line*

Psalm 20

For the director of music.
A psalm of David.

¹May the Lord answer you
when you are in
distress;   Ps 4:1
may the name of the God of
Jacob protect you.   Pr 59:1
²May he send you help from
the sanctuary   Nu 3:28
and grant you support from
Zion.   Ps 2:6
³May he remember all your
sacrifices   Ac 10:4
and accept your burnt
offerings.   *Selah*
⁴May he give you the desire of
your heart   Ps 21:2
and make all your plans
succeed.   Ps 140:8
⁵We will shout for joy when
you are victorious   Job 3:7
and will lift up our banners
in the name of our God.
May the Lord grant all your
requests.   1Sa 1:17

⁶Now I know that the Lord
saves his anointed;   Pr 28:8
he answers him from his
holy heaven
with the saving power of
his right hand.   Job 40:14
⁷Some trust in chariots and
some in horses,   Dt 17:16
but we trust in the name of
the Lord our God.
⁸They are brought to their
knees and fall,   Ps 27:2
but we rise up and stand
firm.   Job 11:15

⁹O Lord, save the king!
Answer*ᵃ* us when we call!

Psalm 21

For the director of music.
A psalm of David.

¹O Lord, the king rejoices in
your strength.   1Sa 2:10
How great is his joy in the
victories you give!
²You have granted him the
desire of his heart
and have not withheld the
request of his lips.   *Selah*
³You welcomed him with rich
blessings
and placed a crown of pure
gold on his head.   Zec 6:11
⁴He asked you for life, and
you gave it to him—
length of days, for ever and
ever.   Ps 10:16
⁵Through the victories you
gave, his glory is great;
you have bestowed on him
splendor and majesty.
⁶Surely you have granted him
eternal blessings
and made him glad with
the joy of your presence.
⁷For the king trusts in the
Lord;   2Ki 18:5
through the unfailing love
of the Most High
he will not be shaken.

⁸Your hand will lay hold on
all your enemies;
your right hand will seize
your foes.   Isa 10:10

ᵃ9 Or save! / O King, answer

⁹At the time of your
  appearing
  you will make them like a
  fiery furnace.
In his wrath the LORD will
  swallow them up,
  and his fire will consume
  them.   Dt 32:22
¹⁰You will destroy their
  descendants from the
  earth,
  their posterity from
  mankind.   Dt 28:18
¹¹Though they plot evil against
  you   Ps 2:1
  and devise wicked
  schemes, they cannot
  succeed;   Job 10:3
¹²for you will make them turn
  their backs   Ex 23:27
  when you aim at them with
  drawn bow.

¹³Be exalted, O LORD, in your
  strength;   Ps 18:1
  we will sing and praise
  your might.

Psalm 22

For the director of music. To the
tune of "The Doe of the
Morning." A psalm of David.

¹My God, my God, why have
  you forsaken me?   Job 6:15
Why are you so far from
  saving me,
so far from the words of my
  groaning?   Job 3:24; Ps 10:1
²O my God, I cry out by day,
  but you do not answer,
  by night, and am not silent.

³Yet you are enthroned as the
  Holy One;   2Ki 19:22
  you are the praise of Israel. ᵃ
⁴In you our fathers put their
  trust;
  they trusted and you
  delivered them.   Ps 78:53
⁵They cried to you and were
  saved;   1Ch 5:20
  in you they trusted and
  were not disappointed.

⁶But I am a worm and not a
  man,   Job 4:19
  scorned by men and
  despised by the people.
⁷All who see me mock me;
  they hurl insults, shaking
  their heads: Mk 15:29
⁸"He trusts in the LORD;
  let the LORD rescue him.
Let him deliver him,
  since he delights in him."

⁹Yet you brought me out of
  the womb;   Job 10:18
  you made me trust in you
  even at my mother's breast.
¹⁰From birth I was cast upon
  you;   Ps 71:6; Isa 46:3
  from my mother's womb
  you have been my God.
¹¹Do not be far from me,
  for trouble is near   Ps 10:14
  and there is no one to help.

¹²Many bulls surround me;
  strong bulls of Bashan
  encircle me.   Dt 32:14
¹³Roaring lions tearing their
  prey   Eze 22:25
  open their mouths wide
  against me.   La 3:46
¹⁴I am poured out like water,

ᵃ3 Or *Yet you are holy,* / *enthroned on the praises of Israel*

and all my bones are out of
   joint.   Ps 6:2
My heart has turned to wax;
   it has melted away within
   me.   Jos 7:5
¹⁵My strength is dried up like a
   potsherd,   Isa 45:9
   and my tongue sticks to the
   roof of my mouth;   Ps 137:6
you lay me*a* in the dust of
   death.   Job 7:21
¹⁶Dogs have surrounded me;
   a band of evil men has
   encircled me,   Php 3:2
   they have pierced*b* my
   hands and my feet.   Isa 51:9
¹⁷I can count all my bones;
   people stare and gloat over
   me.   Ps 25:2; Lk 23:35
¹⁸They divide my garments
   among them
   and cast lots for my
   clothing.   Mt 27:35; Mk 9:12

¹⁹But you, O LORD, be not far
   off;
O my Strength, come
   quickly to help me.   Ps 18:1
²⁰Deliver my life from the
   sword,   Job 5:20
my precious life from the
   power of the dogs.   Ps 35:17
²¹Rescue me from the mouth of
   the lions;   Job 4:10
save*c* me from the horns of
   the wild oxen.   Nu 23:22

²²I will declare your name to
   my brothers;
in the congregation I will
   praise you.   Ps 26:12

²³You who fear the LORD,
   praise him!   Ps 33:2
All you descendants of
   Jacob, honor him!   Ps 50:15
Revere him, all you
   descendants of Israel!
²⁴For he has not despised or
   disdained   Ps 102:17
   the suffering of the afflicted
   one;   Ps 9:12
he has not hidden his face
   from him   Ps 13:1
but has listened to his cry
   for help.   Job 24:12

²⁵From you comes the theme
   of my praise in the great
   assembly;   Ps 26:12
before those who fear you*d*
   will I fulfill my vows.
²⁶The poor will eat and be
   satisfied;   Ps 107:9
they who seek the LORD
   will praise him—   Ps 40:16
may your hearts live
   forever!
²⁷All the ends of the earth
   will remember and turn to
   the LORD,   Ps 2:8
and all the families of the
   nations
   will bow down before him,
²⁸for dominion belongs to the
   LORD   Ps 47:7
and he rules over the
   nations.

²⁹All the rich of the earth will
   feast and worship;   Ps 45:12
all who go down to the dust
   will kneel before him—

---

*a*15 Or / I am laid   *b*16 Some Hebrew manuscripts, Septuagint and Syriac; most
Hebrew manuscripts / like the lion,   *c*21 Or / you have heard   *d*25 Hebrew him

those who cannot keep
themselves alive.   Ps 89:48
³⁰Posterity will serve him;
future generations will be
told about the Lord.
³¹They will proclaim his
righteousness   Ps 5:8
to a people yet unborn—
for he has done it.   Lk 18:31

Psalm 23

A psalm of David.

¹The Lord is my shepherd, I
shall not be in want. Ps 34:9
² He makes me lie down in
green pastures,
he leads me beside quiet
waters,   Ps 36:8
³ he restores my soul.   Ps 19:7
He guides me in paths of
righteousness   Ps 5:8
for his name's sake.   Ps 25:11
⁴Even though I walk
through the valley of the
shadow of death,ᵃ   Job 3:5
I will fear no evil,   Ps 3:6
for you are with me;   Ps 16:8
your rod and your staff,
they comfort me.

⁵You prepare a table before
me   Job 36:16
in the presence of my
enemies.
You anoint my head with oil;
my cup overflows.   Ps 16:5
⁶Surely goodness and love
will follow me   Ne 9:25
all the days of my life,

and I will dwell in the house
of the Lord
forever.

Psalm 24

Of David. A psalm.

¹The earth is the Lord's, and
everything in it,   Ex 9:29
the world, and all who live
in it;   1Co 10:26
²for he founded it upon the
seas
and established it upon the
waters.   Ps 104:3

³Who may ascend the hill of
the Lord?   Ps 2:6
Who may stand in his holy
place?   Ps 15:1
⁴He who has clean hands and
a pure heart,   2Sa 22:21
who does not lift up his
soul to an idol   Eze 18:15
or swear by what is false.ᵇ
⁵He will receive blessing from
the Lord   Dt 11:26
and vindication from God
his Savior.   Ps 17:2
⁶Such is the generation of
those who seek him,
who seek your face, O God
of Jacob.ᶜ   Selah

⁷Lift up your heads, O you
gates;   Ps 118:19
be lifted up, you ancient
doors,
that the King of glory may
come in.   Pr 44:4; Zec 9:9

ᵃ4 Or through the darkest valley   ᵇ4 Or swear falsely   ᶜ6 Two Hebrew manuscripts
and Syriac (see also Septuagint); most Hebrew manuscripts face, Jacob

⁸Who is this King of glory?
The LORD strong and
mighty,   1Ch 29:11
the LORD mighty in battle.
⁹Lift up your heads, O you
gates;
lift them up, you ancient
doors,
that the King of glory may
come in.
¹⁰Who is he, this King of
glory?
The LORD Almighty—   1Sa 1:11
he is the King of glory.
Selah

Psalm 25 ᵃ

Of David.

¹To you, O LORD, I lift up my
soul;   Ps 143:8
² in you I trust, O my God.
Do not let me be put to
shame,
nor let my enemies triumph
over me.
³No one whose hope is in you
will ever be put to shame,
but they will be put to shame
who are treacherous
without excuse.   Ps 22:5

⁴Show me your ways,
O LORD,
teach me your paths;   Job 34:32
⁵guide me in your truth and
teach me,   Ps 31:3
for you are God my Savior,
and my hope is in you all
day long.   Ps 33:20

⁶Remember, O LORD, your
great mercy and love,
for they are from of old.
⁷Remember not the sins of my
youth   Job 13:26
and my rebellious ways;
according to your love
remember me,   Ps 6:4
for you are good, O LORD.

⁸Good and upright is the
LORD;   Ps 92:15
therefore he instructs
sinners in his ways.
⁹He guides the humble in
what is right   Ps 23:3
and teaches them his way.
¹⁰All the ways of the LORD are
loving and faithful Ps 18:25
for those who keep the
demands of his
covenant.   Ps 103:18
¹¹For the sake of your name,
O LORD,   Ex 9:16
forgive my iniquity, though
it is great.   Ex 34:9
¹²Who, then, is the man that
fears the LORD?   Job 1:8
He will instruct him in the
way chosen for him.
¹³He will spend his days in
prosperity,   Dt 30:15
and his descendants will
inherit the land.   Nu 14:24
¹⁴The LORD confides in those
who fear him;   Pr 3:32
he makes his covenant
known to them.   Ge 17:2
¹⁵My eyes are ever on the
LORD,   2Ch 20:12
for only he will release my
feet from the snare.

ᵃThis psalm is an acrostic poem, the verses of which begin with the successive letters of
the Hebrew alphabet.

¹⁶Turn to me and be gracious
to me, Nu 6:25; Ps 6:4
for I am lonely and
afflicted. Ps 68:6
¹⁷The troubles of my heart
have multiplied; 1Ki 1:29
free me from my anguish.
¹⁸Look upon my affliction and
my distress 2Sa 16:12
and take away all my sins.
¹⁹See how my enemies have
increased Ps 3:1
and how fiercely they hate
me! Ps 35:19
²⁰Guard my life and rescue me;
let me not be put to shame,
for I take refuge in you.
²¹May integrity and
uprightness protect me,
because my hope is in you.

²²Redeem Israel, O God,
from all their troubles! Ps 130:8

Psalm 26

Of David.

¹Vindicate me, O LORD,
for I have led a blameless
life; 1Sa 24:15; Ps 15:2
I have trusted in the LORD
without wavering. Ps 22:4
²Test me, O LORD, and try
me, Ps 66:10
examine my heart and my
mind; Dt 6:6
³for your love is ever before
me, Ps 6:4
and I walk continually in
your truth. Ps 40:11
⁴I do not sit with deceitful
men, Ps 1:1
nor do I consort with
hypocrites; Ps 28:3

⁵I abhor the assembly of
evildoers Ps 139:21
and refuse to sit with the
wicked.
⁶I wash my hands in
innocence, Ps 73:13
and go about your altar,
O LORD,
⁷proclaiming aloud your
praise Isa 42:12
and telling of all your
wonderful deeds. Jos 3:5
⁸I love the house where you
live, O LORD, Ps 122:6
the place where your glory
dwells. Ex 29:43

⁹Do not take away my soul
along with sinners,
my life with bloodthirsty
men, Ps 5:6
¹⁰in whose hands are wicked
schemes, Ps 21:11
whose right hands are full
of bribes. Job 36:18
¹¹But I lead a blameless life;
redeem me and be merciful
to me. Ps 31:5

¹²My feet stand on level
ground; Ps 27:11
in the great assembly I will
praise the LORD. Ps 22:25

Psalm 27

Of David.

¹The LORD is my light and my
salvation— 2Sa 22:29
whom shall I fear?
The LORD is the stronghold
of my life— Ps 9:9

of whom shall I be afraid?
²When evil men advance
    against me
to devour my flesh,*a*
when my enemies and my
    foes attack me,
they will stumble and fall.
³Though an army besiege me,
    my heart will not fear; Ge 4:7
though war break out against
    me,
even then will I be
    confident.   Job 4:6

⁴One thing I ask of the LORD,
    this is what I seek: Lk 10:42
that I may dwell in the house
    of the LORD
all the days of my life, Ps 23:6
to gaze upon the beauty of
    the LORD
and to seek him in his
    temple.
⁵For in the day of trouble
he will keep me safe in his
    dwelling;   Ps 12:7
he will hide me in the shelter
    of his tabernacle   Ps 17:8
and set me high upon a
    rock.   Ps 40:2
⁶Then my head will be exalted
above the enemies who
    surround me;   Ps 22:12
at his tabernacle will I
    sacrifice with shouts of
    joy;   Ezr 3:13
I will sing and make music
    to the LORD.   Ps 33:2

⁷Hear my voice when I call,
    O LORD;   Ps 5:3; 18:6
be merciful to me and
    answer me.   Ps 4:1

⁸My heart says of you, "Seek
    his*b* face!"   1Ch 16:11
Your face, LORD, I will seek.
⁹Do not hide your face from
    me,   Dt 31:17
do not turn your servant
    away in anger;   Ps 2:5
you have been my helper.
Do not reject me or forsake
    me,   Dt 4:31; Ps 37:28
O God my Savior.   Ps 18:46
¹⁰Though my father and
    mother forsake me,
the LORD will receive me.
¹¹Teach me your way, O LORD;
lead me in a straight path
because of my oppressors.
¹²Do not turn me over to the
    desire of my foes,
for false witnesses rise up
    against me,   Dt 19:16
breathing out violence.

¹³I am still confident of this:
    I will see the goodness of
    the LORD   Ex 33:19
in the land of the living.
¹⁴Wait for the LORD;   Ps 33:20
    be strong and take heart
    and wait for the LORD.

Psalm 28

Of David.

¹To you I call, O LORD my
    Rock;
do not turn a deaf ear to
    me.   Dt 1:45
For if you remain silent, Est 4:14
    I will be like those who
    have gone down to the
    pit.   Job 33:18

---

*a*2 Or *to slander me*   *b*8 Or *To you, O my heart, he has said, "Seek my*

²Hear my cry for mercy   Ps 17:1
　as I call to you for help,
　as I lift up my hands   Ps 63:4
　　toward your Most Holy
　　　Place.   Ps 5:7

³Do not drag me away with
　　the wicked,
　with those who do evil,
　who speak cordially with
　　their neighbors
　but harbor malice in their
　　hearts.   Ps 12:2
⁴Repay them for their deeds
　and for their evil work;
　repay them for what their
　　hands have done   Ps 62:12
　and bring back upon them
　　what they deserve.   La 3:64
⁵Since they show no regard
　　for the works of the
　　LORD
　and what his hands have
　　done,   Isa 5:12
　he will tear them down
　　and never build them up
　　again.

⁶Praise be to the LORD,   Ge 24:27
　for he has heard my cry for
　　mercy.
⁷The LORD is my strength and
　　my shield;   Ps 18:1
　my heart trusts in him, and
　　I am helped.   Ps 13:5
　My heart leaps for joy   Dt 16:15
　and I will give thanks to
　　him in song.   Ps 33:3

⁸The LORD is the strength of
　　his people,   Ps 18:1
　a fortress of salvation for
　　his anointed one.   Ex 15:2

⁹Save your people and bless
　　your inheritance;   1Ch 16:35
　be their shepherd and carry
　　them forever.   Dt 1:31

Psalm 29

A psalm of David.

¹Ascribe to the LORD,
　　O mighty ones,   2Sa 1:19
　ascribe to the LORD glory
　　and strength.   Ps 8:1
²Ascribe to the LORD the glory
　　due his name;
　worship the LORD in the
　　splendor of his*a*
　　holiness.   1Ch 16:29

³The voice of the LORD is over
　　the waters;   Job 37:5
　the God of glory thunders,
　the LORD thunders over the
　　mighty waters.   Ex 15:10
⁴The voice of the LORD is
　　powerful;   Ps 68:33
　the voice of the LORD is
　　majestic.
⁵The voice of the LORD breaks
　　the cedars;
　the LORD breaks in pieces
　　the cedars of Lebanon.
⁶He makes Lebanon skip like
　　a calf,   Ps 114:4
　Sirion*b* like a young wild
　　ox.   Dt 3:9; Job 39:9
⁷The voice of the LORD strikes
　　with flashes of lightning.
⁸The voice of the LORD shakes
　　the desert;
　the LORD shakes the Desert
　　of Kadesh.   Nu 13:26

---

*a*2 Or LORD *with the splendor of*   *b*6 That is, Mount Hermon

⁹The voice of the Lord twists
the oaks*a*   Nu 13:32
and strips the forests bare.
And in his temple all cry,
"Glory!"   Ps 26:8

¹⁰The Lord sits*b* enthroned
over the flood;   Ge 6:17
the Lord is enthroned as
King forever.   Ex 15:18
¹¹The Lord gives strength to
his people;   Ps 18:1
the Lord blesses his people
with peace.   Lev 26:6

Psalm 30

A psalm. A song. For the
dedication of the temple.*c* Of
David.

¹I will exalt you, O Lord,
for you lifted me out of the
depths   Job 11:8
and did not let my enemies
gloat over me.   Ps 22:17
²O Lord my God, I called to
you for help   Ps 5:2
and you healed me.   Nu 12:13
³O Lord, you brought me up
from the grave*d*;   Ps 16:10
you spared me from going
down into the pit.   Ps 28:1

⁴Sing to the Lord, you saints
of his;   Ps 16:3
praise his holy name.   Ex 3:15
⁵For his anger lasts only a
moment,   Job 14:13
but his favor lasts a lifetime;
weeping may remain for a
night,   2Sa 15:30

but rejoicing comes in the
morning.   2Co 4:17

⁶When I felt secure, I said,
"I will never be shaken."
⁷O Lord, when you favored
me,
you made my mountain*e*
stand firm;
but when you hid your face,
I was dismayed.   Dt 31:17

⁸To you, O Lord, I called;
to the Lord I cried for
mercy:
⁹"What gain is there in my
destruction,*f*
in my going down into the
pit?   Job 33:18
Will the dust praise you?
Will it proclaim your
faithfulness?   Ps 6:5
¹⁰Hear, O Lord, and be
merciful to me;   Ps 4:1
O Lord, be my help."

¹¹You turned my wailing into
dancing;   Ex 15:20; Est 4:1
you removed my sackcloth
and clothed me with joy,
¹²that my heart may sing to
you and not be silent.
O Lord my God, I will give
you thanks forever.   Ps 44:8

Psalm 31

For the director of music.
A psalm of David.

¹In you, O Lord, I have taken
refuge;   Ps 7:1
let me never be put to
shame;

---

*a*9 Or Lord *makes the deer give birth*   *b*10 Or *sat*   *c*Title: Or *palace*   *d*3 Hebrew
Sheol   *e*7 Or *hill country*   *f*9 Or *there if I am silenced*

deliver me in your
   righteousness.   Ps 5:8
2Turn your ear to me,   Ps 6:4
   come quickly to my rescue;
be my rock of refuge,   2Sa 22:3
   a strong fortress to save me.
3Since you are my rock and
   my fortress,   Ps 18:2
for the sake of your name
   lead and guide me.   Ps 23:2
4Free me from the trap that is
   set for me,   1Sa 28:9
for you are my refuge.   Ps 9:9
5Into your hands I commit my
   spirit;   Lk 23:46
redeem me, O LORD, the
   God of truth.   Isa 45:19

6I hate those who cling to
   worthless idols;   Dt 32:21
I trust in the LORD.   Ps 4:5
7I will be glad and rejoice in
   your love,
for you saw my affliction
   and knew the anguish of
   my soul.   Ps 13:3
8You have not handed me
   over to the enemy   Dt 32:30
but have set my feet in a
   spacious place.   2Sa 22:20

9Be merciful to me, O LORD,
   for I am in distress;   Ps 4:1
my eyes grow weak with
   sorrow,   Ps 6:7
my soul and my body with
   grief.   Ps 63:1
10My life is consumed by
   anguish
and my years by groaning;
   my strength fails because of
   my affliction,a   Ps 25:18
and my bones grow weak.

11Because of all my enemies,
   I am the utter contempt of
   my neighbors;   Ps 38:11
I am a dread to my friends—
   those who see me on the
   street flee from me.
12I am forgotten by them as
   though I were dead;
I have become like broken
   pottery.
13For I hear the slander of
   many;   Lev 19:16
   there is terror on every side;
they conspire against me
   and plot to take my life.

14But I trust in you, O LORD;
   I say, "You are my God."
15My times are in your hands;
   deliver me from my
   enemies
and from those who pursue
   me.
16Let your face shine on your
   servant;   Nu 6:25
   save me in your unfailing
   love.   Ps 6:4
17Let me not be put to shame,
   O LORD,   Ps 22:5
for I have cried out to you;
but let the wicked be put to
   shame
   and lie silent in the grave.b
18Let their lying lips be
   silenced,   Ps 120:2
for with pride and
   contempt
they speak arrogantly
   against the righteous.

19How great is your goodness,
   which you have stored up
   for those who fear you,

a10 Or guilt   b17 Hebrew Sheol

which you bestow in the
　　sight of men　　　*Ps 23:5*
on those who take refuge in
　　you.　　　*Ps 2:12*
20In the shelter of your
　　presence you hide them
from the intrigues of men;
in your dwelling you keep
　　them safe
from accusing tongues.

21Praise be to the LORD,　　*Ps 28:6*
　　for he showed his
　　wonderful love to me
when I was in a besieged
　　city.　　　*1Sa 23:7*
22In my alarm I said,　　*Ps 116:11*
　　"I am cut off from your
　　sight!"
Yet you heard my cry for
　　mercy　　　*Ps 6:9*
when I called to you for
　　help.

23Love the LORD, all his saints!
The LORD preserves the
　　faithful,　　　*Ps 18:25*
but the proud he pays back
　　in full.　　　*Dt 32:41*
24Be strong and take heart,
　　all you who hope in the
　　LORD.　　　*Ps 27:14*

Psalm 32

Of David. A *maskil.* *a*

1Blessed is he
　　whose transgressions are
　　forgiven,
　　whose sins are covered.
2Blessed is the man
　　whose sin the LORD does
　　not count against him

and in whose spirit is no
　　deceit.　　　*Jn 1:47*
3When I kept silent,　　*Job 31:34*
　　my bones wasted away
through my groaning all
　　day long.　　　*Job 3:24*
4For day and night
　　your hand was heavy upon
　　me;　　　*1Sa 5:6*
my strength was sapped
　　as in the heat of summer.
　　　　　　　　　　Selah
5Then I acknowledged my sin
　　to you
and did not cover up my
　　iniquity.　　　*Job 31:33*
I said, "I will confess　　*Pr 28:13*
　　my transgressions to the
　　LORD"—
and you forgave
　　the guilt of my sin.　　*Selah*
6Therefore let everyone who
　　is godly pray to you
while you may be found;
surely when the mighty
　　waters rise,　　*Ps 69:1*
they will not reach him.
7You are my hiding place;
　　you will protect me from
　　trouble　　　*Ps 9:9*
and surround me with
　　songs of deliverance.
　　　　　　　　　　Selah
8I will instruct you and teach
　　you in the way you
　　should go;　　*Ps 34:11*
I will counsel you and
　　watch over you.　　*Ps 33:18*
9Do not be like the horse or
　　the mule,

*a*Title: Probably a literary or musical term

which have no
understanding
but must be controlled by bit
and bridle Job 30:11
or they will not come to
you.
¹⁰Many are the woes of the
wicked, Ro 2:9
but the LORD's unfailing
love
surrounds the man who
trusts in him. Ps 4:5

¹¹Rejoice in the LORD and be
glad, you righteous;
sing, all you who are
upright in heart!

Psalm 33

¹Sing joyfully to the LORD,
you righteous; Ps 5:11
it is fitting for the upright to
praise him. Ps 11:7
²Praise the LORD with the
harp; Ge 4:21
make music to him on the
ten-stringed lyre. Ps 92:3
³Sing to him a new song; Ps 40:3
play skillfully, and shout
for joy. Job 3:7

⁴For the word of the LORD is
right and true; Ps 19:8
he is faithful in all he does.
⁵The LORD loves
righteousness and
justice; Ps 11:7
the earth is full of his
unfailing love. Ps 6:4

⁶By the word of the LORD
were the heavens made,

their starry host by the
breath of his mouth.
⁷He gathers the waters of the
sea into jars*a*; Jos 3:16
he puts the deep into
storehouses.
⁸Let all the earth fear the
LORD; Dt 6:13
let all the people of the
world revere him. Dt 14:23
⁹For he spoke, and it came to
be;
he commanded, and it
stood firm. Ps 148:5
¹⁰The LORD foils the plans of
the nations; Isa 44:25
he thwarts the purposes of
the peoples.
¹¹But the plans of the LORD
stand firm forever, Nu 23:19
the purposes of his heart
through all generations.

¹²Blessed is the nation whose
God is the LORD, Ps 144:15
the people he chose for his
inheritance. Ex 34:9; Dt 7:6
¹³From heaven the LORD looks
down Ps 53:2
and sees all mankind; Job 28:24
¹⁴from his dwelling place he
watches 1Ki 8:39
all who live on earth—
¹⁵he who forms the hearts of
all, Job 10:8
who considers everything
they do. Jer 32:19
¹⁶No king is saved by the size
of his army; 1Sa 14:6
no warrior escapes by his
great strength.
¹⁷A horse is a vain hope for
deliverance; Ps 20:7

a7 Or sea as into a heap

despite all its great strength
it cannot save.
¹⁸But the eyes of the LORD are
on those who fear him,
on those whose hope is in
his unfailing love,   Ps 6:4
¹⁹to deliver them from death
and keep them alive in
famine.   Job 5:20

²⁰We wait in hope for the
LORD;   Ps 27:14
he is our help and our
shield.
²¹In him our hearts rejoice,
for we trust in his holy
name.   Ps 30:4
²²May your unfailing love rest
upon us, O LORD,   Ps 6:4
even as we put our hope in
you.

Psalm 34 ᵃ

Of David. When he pretended to
be insane before Abimelech, who
drove him away, and he left.

¹I will extol the LORD at all
times;   Ps 71:6
his praise will always be on
my lips.
²My soul will boast in the
LORD;   Ps 44:8
let the afflicted hear and
rejoice.   Ps 69:32
³Glorify the LORD with me;
let us exalt his name
together.   Ex 15:2

⁴I sought the LORD, and he
answered me;   Ps 77:2

he delivered me from all my
fears.   Ps 18:43
⁵Those who look to him are
radiant;   Ex 34:29
their faces are never
covered with shame.
⁶This poor man called, and
the LORD heard him;
he saved him out of all his
troubles.   Ps 25:17
⁷The angel of the LORD
encamps around those
who fear him,
and he delivers them.   Ge 32:1

⁸Taste and see that the LORD
is good;   Heb 6:5
blessed is the man who
takes refuge in him.
⁹Fear the LORD, you his
saints,   Dt 6:13
for those who fear him lack
nothing.   Ps 23:1
¹⁰The lions may grow weak
and hungry,
but those who seek the
LORD lack no good
thing.   Ps 23:1

¹¹Come, my children, listen to
me;   Ps 66:16
I will teach you the fear of
the LORD.   Ps 32:8
¹²Whoever of you loves life
and desires to see many
good days,   Ecc 3:13
¹³keep your tongue from evil
and your lips from speaking
lies.   1Pe 2:23
¹⁴Turn from evil and do good;
seek peace and pursue it.

ᵃThis psalm is an acrostic poem, the verses of which begin with the successive letters of
the Hebrew alphabet.

15The eyes of the LORD are on
the righteous   Job 23:10
and his ears are attentive to
their cry;   Mal 3:16
16the face of the LORD is
against those who do
evil,   Lev 17:10
to cut off the memory of
them from the earth.

17The righteous cry out, and
the LORD hears them;
he delivers them from all
their troubles.   Ps 145:19
18The LORD is close to the
brokenhearted   Ps 51:1
and saves those who are
crushed in spirit.

19A righteous man may have
many troubles,   Ps 25:17
but the LORD delivers him
from them all;   Job 5:19
20he protects all his bones,
not one of them will be
broken.   Jn 19:36

21Evil will slay the wicked;
the foes of the righteous
will be condemned. Ps 7:9
22The LORD redeems his
servants;   Ex 6:6
no one will be condemned
who takes refuge in him.

Psalm 35

Of David.

1Contend, O LORD, with those
who contend with me;
fight against those who
fight against me.   Ex 14:14

2Take up shield and buckler;
arise and come to my aid.
3Brandish spear and javelin*a*
against those who pursue
me.   Nu 25:7; Jos 8:18
Say to my soul,
"I am your salvation." Ps 27:1

4May those who seek my life
be disgraced and put to
shame;   Ps 25:3
may those who plot my ruin
be turned back in dismay.
5May they be like chaff before
the wind,   Job 13:25
with the angel of the LORD
driving them away;
6may their path be dark and
slippery,
with the angel of the LORD
pursuing them.
7Since they hid their net for
me without cause   Ps 7:4
and without cause dug a pit
for me,   Job 9:31
8may ruin overtake them by
surprise—   Isa 47:11
may the net they hid
entangle them,
may they fall into the pit, to
their ruin.   Ps 7:15
9Then my soul will rejoice in
the LORD   Ps 2:11
and delight in his salvation.
10My whole being will exclaim,
"Who is like you, O LORD?
You rescue the poor from
those too strong for
them,   Ps 18:17
the poor and needy from
those who rob them."

*a*3 Or *and block the way*

[11]Ruthless witnesses come
    forward;   Ex 23:1
they question me on things
    I know nothing about.
[12]They repay me evil for good
    and leave my soul forlorn.
[13]Yet when they were ill, I put
    on sackcloth   2Sa 3:31
and humbled myself with
    fasting.   Job 30:25
When my prayers returned
    to me unanswered,
[14] I went about mourning
    as though for my friend or
    brother.   Ps 38:6
I bowed my head in grief
    as though weeping for my
    mother.
[15]But when I stumbled, they
    gathered in glee;   Job 31:29
attackers gathered against
    me when I was
    unaware.
They slandered me without
    ceasing.   Job 16:10
[16]Like the ungodly they
    maliciously mocked[a];
they gnashed their teeth at
    me.   Job 16:9
[17]O Lord, how long will you
    look on?   Ps 6:3
Rescue my life from their
    ravages,
my precious life from these
    lions.   Ps 22:21
[18]I will give you thanks in the
    great assembly;   Ps 22:25
among throngs of people I
    will praise you.   Ps 42:4

[19]Let not those gloat over me
who are my enemies
    without cause;   Ps 9:13

let not those who hate me
    without reason   Ps 38:19
maliciously wink the eye.
[20]They do not speak peaceably,
but devise false accusations
against those who live
    quietly in the land.   Ps 38:12
[21]They gape at me and say,
    "Aha! Aha!   Ps 40:15
With our own eyes we have
    seen it."

[22]O Lord, you have seen this;
    be not silent.   Ex 3:7
Do not be far from me,
    O Lord.   Ps 10:1
[23]Awake, and rise to my
    defense!   Ps 17:13
Contend for me, my God
    and Lord.   1Sa 24:15
[24]Vindicate me in your
    righteousness, O Lord
    my God;
do not let them gloat over
    me.   Ps 22:17
[25]Do not let them think, "Aha,
    just what we wanted!"
or say, "We have
    swallowed him up."

[26]May all who gloat over my
    distress   Ps 4:1
be put to shame and
    confusion;   Job 8:22
may all who exalt themselves
    over me   Job 19:5
be clothed with shame and
    disgrace.
[27]May those who delight in my
    vindication   Ps 9:4
shout for joy and gladness;
may they always say, "The
    Lord be exalted,

[a]16 Septuagint; Hebrew may mean *ungodly circle of mockers*.

who delights in the
 well-being of his
 servant." Ps 147:11
28My tongue will speak of your
 righteousness Ps 5:8
and of your praises all day
 long. Ps 71:15

Psalm 36

For the director of music. Of
David the servant of the LORD.

1An oracle is within my heart
 concerning the sinfulness of
 the wicked:a Job 21:16
There is no fear of God
 before his eyes. Job 23:15
2For in his own eyes he
 flatters himself
too much to detect or hate
 his sin. Dt 29:19
3The words of his mouth are
 wicked and deceitful;
he has ceased to be wise
 and to do good. Ps 94:8
4Even on his bed he plots evil;
 he commits himself to a
 sinful course Isa 65:2
and does not reject what is
 wrong. Ps 52:3

5Your love, O LORD, reaches
 to the heavens,
your faithfulness to the
 skies. Ps 57:10
6Your righteousness is like the
 mighty mountains, Ps 68:15
your justice like the great
 deep. Ge 1:2
O LORD, you preserve both
 man and beast. Ne 9:6

7 How priceless is your
 unfailing love! Ps 6:4
Both high and low among
 men
find b refuge in the shadow
 of your wings. Ru 2:12
8They feast on the abundance
 of your house; Ps 65:4
you give them drink from
 your river of delights.
9For with you is the fountain
 of life; Ps 87:7
in your light we see light.

10Continue your love to those
 who know you, Jer 31:3
your righteousness to the
 upright in heart. Ps 7:10
11May the foot of the proud
 not come against me,
nor the hand of the wicked
 drive me away. Ps 71:4
12See how the evildoers lie
 fallen—
thrown down, not able to
 rise! Ps 18:38

Psalm 37 c

Of David.

1Do not fret because of evil
 men
or be envious of those who
 do wrong; Pr 3:31
2for like the grass they will
 soon wither, 2Ki 19:26
like green plants they will
 soon die away. Ps 90:6

3Trust in the LORD and do
 good;

a1 Or heart: / Sin proceeds from the wicked.
heavenly beings and men / find   cThis psalm is an acrostic poem, the stanzas of which
begin with the successive letters of the Hebrew alphabet.   b7 Or love, O God! / Men find; or love! / Both

dwell in the land and enjoy
  safe pasture.   Eze 34:14
⁴Delight yourself in the LORD
  and he will give you the
  desires of your heart.

⁵Commit your way to the
  LORD;
  trust in him and he will do
  this: Ps 4:5
⁶He will make your
  righteousness shine like
  the dawn,   Job 11:17
  the justice of your cause
  like the noonday sun.

⁷Be still before the LORD and
  wait patiently for him;
  do not fret when men
  succeed in their ways,
  when they carry out their
  wicked schemes.   Ps 21:11

⁸Refrain from anger and turn
  from wrath;   Eph 4:31
  do not fret—it leads only to
  evil.
⁹For evil men will be cut off,
  but those who hope in the
  LORD will inherit the
  land.   Ps 25:13

¹⁰A little while, and the wicked
  will be no more;   Job 7:10
  though you look for them,
  they will not be found.
¹¹But the meek will inherit the
  land   Nu 14:24
  and enjoy great peace. Lev 26:6

¹²The wicked plot against the
  righteous   Ps 2:1
  and gnash their teeth at
  them;   Job 16:9
¹³but the Lord laughs at the
  wicked,

for he knows their day is
  coming.   1Sa 26:10

¹⁴The wicked draw the sword
  and bend the bow   Ps 22:20
to bring down the poor and
  needy,   Ps 35:10
to slay those whose ways
  are upright.
¹⁵But their swords will pierce
  their own hearts,   Ps 9:16
  and their bows will be
  broken.   1Sa 2:4

¹⁶Better the little that the
  righteous have
  than the wealth of many
  wicked;   Pr 15:16
¹⁷for the power of the wicked
  will be broken,   Job 38:15
  but the LORD upholds the
  righteous.   Ps 41:12

¹⁸The days of the blameless are
  known to the LORD,
  and their inheritance will
  endure forever.   Ps 44:21
¹⁹In times of disaster they will
  not wither;
  in days of famine they will
  enjoy plenty.

²⁰But the wicked will perish:
  The LORD's enemies will be
  like the beauty of the
  fields,
  they will vanish—vanish
  like smoke.   Ps 68:2

²¹The wicked borrow and do
  not repay,
  but the righteous give
  generously;   Lev 25:35
²²those the LORD blesses will
  inherit the land,

but those he curses will be
cut off. Job 5:3

23If the LORD delights in a
man's way, Nu 14:8
he makes his steps firm;
24though he stumble, he will
not fall, Ps 7:9
for the LORD upholds him
with his hand. 2Ch 9:8

25I was young and now I am
old,
yet I have never seen the
righteous forsaken
or their children begging
bread. Ps 111:5; Heb 13:5
26They are always generous
and lend freely; Lev 25:35
their children will be
blessed. Dt 28:4

27Turn from evil and do good;
then you will dwell in the
land forever. Nu 24:21
28For the LORD loves the just
and will not forsake his
faithful ones. Dt 7:6

They will be protected
forever,
but the offspring of the
wicked will be cut off;
29the righteous will inherit the
land Pr 2:21
and dwell in it forever.

30The mouth of the righteous
man utters wisdom,
and his tongue speaks what
is just. Ps 49:3
31The law of his God is in his
heart; Dt 6:6
his feet do not slip. Dt 32:35

32The wicked lie in wait for the
righteous, Ps 11:5
seeking their very lives;
33but the LORD will not leave
them in their power
or let them be condemned
when brought to trial.

34Wait for the LORD
and keep his way. Ps 27:14
He will exalt you to inherit
the land;
when the wicked are cut
off, you will see it.

35I have seen a wicked and
ruthless man
flourishing like a green tree
in its native soil, Job 5:3
36but he soon passed away and
was no more;
though I looked for him, he
could not be found. Ps 12:7

37Consider the blameless,
observe the upright;Ps 11:7
there is a futurea for the
man of peace. Isa 57:1-2
38But all sinners will be
destroyed; Ps 73:19
the futureb of the wicked
will be cut off.

39The salvation of the
righteous comes from
the LORD; Ps 3:8
he is their stronghold in
time of trouble. Ps 9:9
40The LORD helps them and
delivers them; 1Ch 5:20
he delivers them from the
wicked and saves them,
because they take refuge in
him. Ps 2:12

---

a37 Or there will be posterity   b38 Or posterity

Psalm 38

A psalm of David. A petition.

¹O LORD, do not rebuke me in
  your anger
  or discipline me in your
    wrath.   Ps 6:1
²For your arrows have pierced
  me,   Job 6:4
  and your hand has come
    down upon me.
³Because of your wrath there
    is no health in my body;
  my bones have no
    soundness because of
    my sin.   Job 33:19
⁴My guilt has overwhelmed
  me   Ps 40:12
  like a burden too heavy to
    bear.   Nu 11:14

⁵My wounds fester and are
    loathsome   Ps 147:3
  because of my sinful folly.
⁶I am bowed down and
    brought very low;   Ps 57:6
  all day long I go about
    mourning.   Ps 35:14
⁷My back is filled with searing
    pain;   Job 14:22
  there is no health in my
    body.
⁸I am feeble and utterly
    crushed;   Ps 34:18
  I groan in anguish of heart.

⁹All my longings lie open
    before you, O Lord;
  my sighing is not hidden
    from you.   Job 3:24
¹⁰My heart pounds, my
    strength fails me;   Ps 31:10
  even the light has gone
    from my eyes.   Ps 6:7

¹¹My friends and companions
  avoid me because of my
    wounds;
  my neighbors stay far
    away.
¹²Those who seek my life set
    their traps,   Ps 31:4
  those who would harm me
    talk of my ruin;   Ps 35:4
  all day long they plot
    deception.
¹³I am like a deaf man, who
    cannot hear,   Ps 115:6
  like a mute, who cannot
    open his mouth;
¹⁴I have become like a man
    who does not hear,
  whose mouth can offer no
    reply.
¹⁵I wait for you, O LORD;
  you will answer, O Lord
    my God.   Ps 17:6
¹⁶For I said, "Do not let them
    gloat   Ps 22:17
  or exalt themselves over me
    when my foot slips."

¹⁷For I am about to fall,
  and my pain is ever with
    me.   Ps 37:24
¹⁸I confess my iniquity;   Lev 26:40
  I am troubled by my sin.
¹⁹Many are those who are my
    vigorous enemies;
  those who hate me without
    reason are numerous.
²⁰Those who repay my good
    with evil   Ge 44:4
  slander me when I pursue
    what is good.   Ps 54:5

²¹O LORD, do not forsake me;
  be not far from me, O my
    God.   Ps 27:9

22Come quickly to help me,
 O Lord my Savior. 1Ch 16:35

Psalm 39

For the director of music. For
Jeduthun. A psalm of David.

1I said, "I will watch my ways
 and keep my tongue from
 sin; Job 1:22; Ps 34:13
I will put a muzzle on my
 mouth Job 6:24
 as long as the wicked are in
 my presence."
2But when I was silent and
 still, Ps 77:4
 not even saying anything
 good,
 my anguish increased. Ps 6:3
3My heart grew hot within
 me, Lk 24:32
 and as I meditated, the fire
 burned; Ps 1:2
 then I spoke with my
 tongue:

4"Show me, O Lord, my life's
 end
 and the number of my
 days; Job 14:5
 let me know how fleeting is
 my life. Ge 47:9
5You have made my days a
 mere handbreadth; Job 10:20
 the span of my years is as
 nothing before you.
 Each man's life is but a
 breath. Selah
6Man is a mere phantom as he
 goes to and fro: Job 8:9
 He bustles about, but only
 in vain; Ps 127:2
 he heaps up wealth, not
 knowing who will get it.

7"But now, Lord, what do I
 look for?
 My hope is in you. Ps 9:18
8Save me from all my
 transgressions; Ps 6:4
 do not make me the scorn
 of fools. Dt 28:37
9I was silent; I would not
 open my mouth, Ps 38:13
 for you are the one who has
 done this. Isa 38:15
10Remove your scourge from
 me;
 I am overcome by the blow
 of your hand. 2Ch 21:14
11You rebuke and discipline
 men for their sin; Dt 28:20
 you consume their wealth
 like a moth— Ps 90:7
 each man is but a breath.
 Selah

12"Hear my prayer, O Lord,
 listen to my cry for help;
 be not deaf to my weeping.
For I dwell with you as an
 alien, Lev 25:23
 a stranger, as all my fathers
 were. Ge 47:9
13Look away from me, that I
 may rejoice again
 before I depart and am no
 more." Job 10:21

Psalm 40

For the director of music. Of
David. A psalm.

1I waited patiently for the
 Lord; Ps 37:7
 he turned to me and heard
 my cry. Ps 6:9
2He lifted me out of the slimy
 pit, Job 9:31

out of the mud and mire;
he set my feet on a rock
  and gave me a firm place to
    stand.   Ps 27:5; 31:8
[3]He put a new song in my
    mouth,   Ps 28:7
  a hymn of praise to our
    God.   Ps 52:6
Many will see and fear
  and put their trust in the
    LORD.   Ex 14:31

[4]Blessed is the man
  who makes the LORD his
    trust,   Ps 34:8; 84:12
  who does not look to the
    proud,   Ps 101:5
  to those who turn aside to
    false gods.[a]   Dt 31:20
[5]Many, O LORD my God,
  are the wonders you have
    done.   Dt 4:34
The things you planned for
    us
  no one can recount to you;
  were I to speak and tell of
    them,
  they would be too many to
    declare.   Ps 71:15

[6]Sacrifice and offering you did
    not desire,   1Sa 15:22
  but my ears you have
    pierced[b,c];   Ex 21:6
  burnt offerings and sin
    offerings
  you did not require.
[7]Then I said, "Here I am, I
    have come—
  it is written about me in the
    scroll.[d]   Job 19:23

[8]I desire to do your will, O my
    God;   Mt 26:39; Heb 10:5-7
  your law is within my
    heart."   Dt 6:6

[9]I proclaim righteousness in
    the great assembly;
  I do not seal my lips,
  as you know, O LORD.
[10]I do not hide your
    righteousness in my
    heart;
  I speak of your faithfulness
    and salvation.   Ps 89:1
  I do not conceal your love
    and your truth
  from the great assembly.

[11]Do not withhold your mercy
    from me, O LORD;   Zec 1:12
  may your love and your
    truth always protect me.
[12]For troubles without number
    surround me;   Ps 25:17
  my sins have overtaken me,
    and I cannot see.   Ps 38:4
They are more than the hairs
    of my head,   Ps 69:4
  and my heart fails within
    me.   Ps 73:26

[13]Be pleased, O LORD, to save
    me;
  O LORD, come quickly to
    help me.   Ps 22:19
[14]May all who seek to take my
    life   1Sa 20:1
  be put to shame and
    confusion;   Est 9:2
  may all who desire my ruin
  be turned back in disgrace.

---

[a]4 Or to falsehood   [b]6 Hebrew; Septuagint but a body you have prepared for me (see also
Symmachus and Theodotion)   [c]6 Or opened   [d]7 Or come / with the scroll written for
me

15May those who say to me,
"Aha! Aha!"   Ps 35:21
be appalled at their own
shame.
16But may all who seek you
rejoice and be glad in
you;
may those who love your
salvation always say,
"The LORD be exalted!"

17Yet I am poor and needy;
may the Lord think of me.
You are my help and my
deliverer;   Ps 18:2
O my God, do not delay.

Psalm 41

For the director of music.
A psalm of David.

1Blessed is he who has regard
for the weak;   Job 24:4
the LORD delivers him in
times of trouble.   Ps 25:17
2The LORD will protect him
and preserve his life;
he will bless him in the land
and not surrender him to
the desire of his foes.
3The LORD will sustain him on
his sickbed   Ps 6:6
and restore him from his
bed of illness.   2Sa 13:5

4I said, "O LORD, have mercy
on me;   Ps 6:2
heal me, for I have sinned
against you."   Dt 32:39
5My enemies say of me in
malice,

"When will he die and his
name perish?"   Ps 38:12
6Whenever one comes to see
me,
he speaks falsely, while his
heart gathers slander;
then he goes out and
spreads it abroad.   Lev 19:16

7All my enemies whisper
together against me;
they imagine the worst for
me, saying,
8"A vile disease has beset
him;
he will never get up from
the place where he lies."
9Even my close friend, whom
I trusted,   2Sa 15:12
he who shared my bread,
has lifted up his heel
against me.   Nu 30:2

10But you, O LORD, have
mercy on me;
raise me up, that I may
repay them.   Ps 3:3
11I know that you are pleased
with me,   Nu 14:8
for my enemy does not
triumph over me.   Ps 25:2
12In my integrity you uphold
me   Ps 18:35; 25:21
and set me in your presence
forever.

13Praise be to the LORD, the
God of Israel,   Ps 72:18
from everlasting to
everlasting.
Amen and Amen.   Ps 72:19

BOOK II

Psalms 42–72

Psalm 42[a]

For the director of music. A *maskil*[b] of the Sons of Korah.

[1]As the deer pants for streams
    of water,   Ps 18:33
so my soul pants for you,
    O God.   Job 19:27
[2]My soul thirsts for God, for
    the living God.   Jos 3:10
When can I go and meet
    with God?   Ps 43:4
[3]My tears have been my food
    day and night,   Job 3:24
while men say to me all day
    long,
    "Where is your God?" Ps 79:10
[4]These things I remember
    as I pour out my soul: 1Sa 1:15
how I used to go with the
    multitude,
leading the procession to
    the house of God,   Ps 55:14
with shouts of joy and
    thanksgiving   Ezr 3:13
    among the festive
    throng.

[5]Why are you downcast,
    O my soul?
    Why so disturbed within
    me?   Ps 38:6
                                        Job 20:2
Put your hope in God,   Ps 25:5
    for I will yet praise him,
    my Savior and [6]my God.

My[c] soul is downcast within
    me;
therefore I will remember
    you   Ps 63:6
from the land of the Jordan,
    the heights of Hermon—
    from Mount Mizar.   Dt 3:8
[7]Deep calls to deep   Ge 1:2
    in the roar of your
    waterfalls;
all your waves and breakers
    have swept over me.   Ps 69:2

[8]By day the LORD directs his
    love,   Ps 57:3
    at night his song is with
    me—   Ps 16:7; 77:6
    a prayer to the God of my
    life.   Ps 133:3

[9]I say to God my Rock,   Ps 18:31
    "Why have you forgotten
    me?   Ps 10:11
Why must I go about
    mourning,   Ps 35:14
    oppressed by the enemy?"
[10]My bones suffer mortal
    agony   Ps 6:2
    as my foes taunt me,   Dt 32:27
saying to me all day long,
    "Where is your God?"

[11]Why are you downcast,
    O my soul?
    Why so disturbed within
    me?
Put your hope in God,
    for I will yet praise him,
    my Savior and my God. Ps 43:5

---

[a]In many Hebrew manuscripts Psalms 42 and 43 constitute one psalm.   [b]Title:
Probably a literary or musical term   [c]5,6 A few Hebrew manuscripts, Septuagint and
Syriac; most Hebrew manuscripts *praise him for his saving help.* / [6]*O my God, my*

Psalm 43[a]

[1]Vindicate me, O God,
    and plead my cause against
        an ungodly nation;   Jdg 6:31
    rescue me from deceitful
        and wicked men.   Ps 36:3
[2]You are God my stronghold.
    Why have you rejected me?
    Why must I go about
        mourning,   Ps 35:14
    oppressed by the enemy?
[3]Send forth your light and
        your truth,   Ps 27:1
    let them guide me;   Ps 25:5
    let them bring me to your
        holy mountain,   Ps 2:6
    to the place where you
        dwell.   2Sa 15:25
[4]Then will I go to the altar of
        God,   Ps 42:2
    to God, my joy and my
        delight.   Ps 26:6
    I will praise you with the
        harp,   Ge 4:21
    O God, my God.

[5]Why are you downcast,
        O my soul?
    Why so disturbed within
        me?
    Put your hope in God,
    for I will yet praise him,
    my Savior and my God.   Ps 42:6

Psalm 44

For the director of music. Of the
Sons of Korah. A *maskil.*[b]

[1]We have heard with our ears,
        O God;   2Sa 7:22
    our fathers have told us
    what you did in their days,
        in days long ago.   Dt 32:7
[2]With your hand you drove
        out the nations   Jos 3:10
    and planted our fathers;
    you crushed the peoples
        and made our fathers
            flourish.   Jdg 4:23; Ps 80:9
[3]It was not by their sword that
        they won the land, Jos 24:12
    nor did their arm bring
        them victory;
    it was your right hand, your
        arm,   Ex 15:16; Ps 78:54
    and the light of your face,
        for you loved them. Ps 89:15

[4]You are my King and my
        God,   Ps 5:2; 24:7
    who decrees[c] victories for
        Jacob.   Ps 21:5
[5]Through you we push back
        our enemies;   Jos 23:5
    through your name we
        trample our foes.   Ps 60:12
[6]I do not trust in my bow,
    my sword does not bring
        me victory;   Ge 48:22
[7]but you give us victory over
        our enemies,   Dt 20:4
    you put our adversaries to
        shame.   Job 8:22
[8]In God we make our boast all
        day long,   Ps 34:2
    and we will praise your
        name forever.   *Selah*

[9]But now you have rejected
        and humbled us;   Ps 43:2
    you no longer go out with
        our armies.   Jos 7:12

---

[a]In many Hebrew manuscripts Psalms 42 and 43 constitute one psalm.   [b]Title:
Probably a literary or musical term   [c]4 Septuagint, Aquila and Syriac; Hebrew *King,
O God; / command*

10You made us retreat before
   the enemy,   Lev 26:17
and our adversaries have
   plundered us.   Jdg 2:14
11You gave us up to be
   devoured like sheep
and have scattered us
   among the nations.Lev 26:33
12You sold your people for a
   pittance,   Dt 32:30
gaining nothing from their
   sale.

13You have made us a reproach
   to our neighbors,   2Ch 29:8
the scorn and derision of
   those around us.   Eze 23:32
14You have made us a byword
   among the nations;   1Ki 9:7
the peoples shake their
   heads at us.   2Ki 19:21
15My disgrace is before me all
   day long,   Ge 20:33
and my face is covered with
   shame   Ps 34:5
16at the taunts of those who
   reproach and revile me,
because of the enemy, who
   is bent on revenge.

17All this happened to us,
   though we had not
   forgotten you   Dt 6:12
or been false to your
   covenant.
18Our hearts had not turned
   back;   Ps 119:51
our feet had not strayed
   from your path.
19But you crushed us and
   made us a haunt for
   jackals   Job 30:29

and covered us over with
   deep darkness.   Job 3:5

20If we had forgotten the name
   of our God   Dt 32:18
or spread out our hands to
   a foreign god,   Ex 20:3
21would not God have
   discovered it,
since he knows the secrets
   of the heart?   1Sa 16:7
22Yet for your sake we face
   death all day long;
we are considered as sheep
   to be slaughtered.   Isa 53:7

23Awake, O Lord! Why do you
   sleep?   Ps 78:65
Rouse yourself! Do not
   reject us forever.   Ps 74:1
24Why do you hide your face
   and forget our misery and
   oppression?   Ps 13:1

25We are brought down to the
   dust;   Ps 119:25
our bodies cling to the
   ground.
26Rise up and help us;   Nu 10:35
   redeem us because of your
   unfailing love.   Ps 6:4

Psalm 45

For the director of music. To the
tune of "Lilies." Of the Sons of
Korah. A *maskil.* [a] A wedding
song.

1My heart is stirred by a noble
   theme
as I recite my verses for the
   king;

---

[a]Title: Probably a literary or musical term

my tongue is the pen of a
skillful writer.

2You are the most excellent of
men
and your lips have been
anointed with grace,
since God has blessed you
forever.   Ps 21:6
3Gird your sword upon your
side, O mighty one;
clothe yourself with
splendor and majesty.
4In your majesty ride forth
victoriously   Rev 6:2
in behalf of truth, humility
and righteousness;
let your right hand display
awesome deeds.   Ps 21:8
5Let your sharp arrows pierce
the hearts of the king's
enemies;   Ps 9:13
let the nations fall beneath
your feet.
6Your throne, O God, will last
for ever and ever;   Ge 21:33
a scepter of justice will be
the scepter of your
kingdom.
7You love righteousness and
hate wickedness;   Ps 11:5
therefore God, your God,
has set you above your
companions
by anointing you with the
oil of joy.   Ps 2:2
8All your robes are fragrant
with myrrh and aloes
and cassia;   Ge 37:25
from palaces adorned with
ivory   1Ki 22:39
the music of the strings
makes you glad.   Ps 144:9

9Daughters of kings are
among your honored
women;   SS 6:8
at your right hand is the
royal bride in gold of
Ophir.   Isa 62:5
10Listen, O daughter, consider
and give ear: Ru 1:11
Forget your people and
your father's house.
11The king is enthralled by
your beauty;   Est 1:11
honor him, for he is your
lord.   Eph 5:33
12The Daughter of Tyre will
come with a gift, *a*
men of wealth will seek
your favor.   Jos 19:29
13All glorious is the princess
within ˌher chamberˌ;
her gown is interwoven
with gold.   Ex 39:3
14In embroidered garments she
is led to the king;   Jdg 5:30
her virgin companions
follow her   SS 1:3
and are brought to you.
15They are led in with joy and
gladness;   Est 8:17
they enter the palace of the
king.
16Your sons will take the place
of your fathers;
you will make them princes
throughout the land.
17I will perpetuate your
memory through all
generations;   Ex 3:15
therefore the nations will
praise you for ever and
ever.   Ps 21:4

a12 Or A Tyrian robe is among the gifts

Psalm 46

For the director of music. Of the Sons of Korah. According to *alamoth.* [a] A song.

[1] God is our refuge and
    strength,   Ps 9:9
an ever-present help in
    trouble.   Ps 34:18
[2] Therefore we will not fear,
    though the earth give
    way   Ps 82:5
and the mountains fall into
    the heart of the sea,
[3] though its waters roar and
    foam   Ps 93:3
and the mountains quake
    with their surging. *Selah*

[4] There is a river whose
    streams make glad the
    city of God,   Ps 48:1
the holy place where the
    Most High dwells.
[5] God is within her, she will
    not fall;   Ps 125:1
God will help her at break
    of day.   1Ch 5:20
[6] Nations are in uproar,   Ps 74:23
    kingdoms fall;   Ps 68:32
he lifts his voice, the earth
    melts.   Ps 29:3

[7] The LORD Almighty is with
    us;   Ge 21:22
the God of Jacob is our
    fortress.   *Selah*

[8] Come and see the works of
    the LORD,   Ps 66:5
the desolations he has
    brought on the earth.

[9] He makes wars cease to the
    ends of the earth;
he breaks the bow and
    shatters the spear,
he burns the shields [b] with
    fire.   Isa 9:5
[10] "Be still, and know that I am
    God;   Dt 4:35
I will be exalted among the
    nations,   Ps 18:46
I will be exalted in the
    earth."
[11] The LORD Almighty is with
    us;   Ps 20:1
the God of Jacob is our
    fortress.   *Selah*

Psalm 47

For the director of music. Of the Sons of Korah. A psalm.

[1] Clap your hands, all you
    nations;   2Ki 11:12
shout to God with cries of
    joy.   Ps 33:3
[2] How awesome is the LORD
    Most High,   Ge 14:18
the great King over all the
    earth!   Ps 2:6
[3] He subdued nations under
    us,   Ps 18:39
peoples under our feet.
[4] He chose our inheritance for
    us,   Ps 2:8
the pride of Jacob, whom
    he loved.   *Selah*

[5] God has ascended amid
    shouts of joy,   Ps 68:18
the LORD amid the
    sounding of trumpets.

[a] Title: Probably a musical term   [b] 9 Or *chariots*

⁶Sing praises to God, sing
   praises;   *2Sa 22:50*
sing praises to our King,
   sing praises.

⁷For God is the King of all the
   earth;   *Zec 14:9*
sing to him a psalm*ᵃ* of
   praise.   *1Ch 16:7*
⁸God reigns over the nations;
   God is seated on his holy
   throne.   *1Ki 22:19*
⁹The nobles of the nations
   assemble
as the people of the God of
   Abraham,
for the kings*ᵇ* of the earth
   belong to God;   *Job 25:2*
he is greatly exalted.   *Ps 46:10*

Psalm 48

A song. A psalm of the Sons of
   Korah.

¹Great is the LORD, and most
   worthy of praise,   *Ps 86:10*
in the city of our God, his
   holy mountain.   *Dt 33:19*
²It is beautiful in its loftiness,
   the joy of the whole earth.
Like the utmost heights of
   Zaphon*ᶜ* is Mount Zion,
the*ᵈ* city of the Great King.
³God is in her citadels;   *Ps 122:7*
he has shown himself to be
   her fortress.   *Ps 18:2*

⁴When the kings joined
   forces,
when they advanced
   together,   *2Sa 10:1-19*

⁵they saw ⌊her⌋ and were
   astounded;
they fled in terror.   *Ex 15:16*
⁶Trembling seized them there,
   pain like that of a woman in
   labor.   *Ge 3:16*
⁷You destroyed them like
   ships of Tarshish   *Ge 10:4*
shattered by an east wind.

⁸As we have heard,
   so have we seen
in the city of the LORD
   Almighty,
in the city of our God:
   God makes her secure
   forever.   *Selah*

⁹Within your temple, O God,
   we meditate on your
   unfailing love.   *Ps 39:3*
¹⁰Like your name, O God,
   your praise reaches to the
   ends of the earth;
your right hand is filled
   with righteousness.
¹¹Mount Zion rejoices,
   the villages of Judah are
   glad
because of your judgments.

¹²Walk about Zion, go around
   her,
   count her towers,   *Ne 3:1*
¹³consider well her ramparts,
   view her citadels,   *Hab 2:1*
that you may tell of them to
   the next generation.
¹⁴For this God is our God for
   ever and ever;
he will be our guide even to
   the end.   *Ps 25:5*

ᵃ7 Or *a maskil (probably a literary or musical term)*
refer to a sacred mountain or the direction north.
northern side / of the
   ᵇ9 Or *shields*   *ᶜ2 Zaphon can*
ᵈ2 Or *earth, / Mount Zion, on the*

Psalm 49

For the director of music. Of the Sons of Korah. A psalm.

¹Hear this, all you peoples;
   listen, all who live in this
      world,   Ps 33:8
²both low and high,
   rich and poor alike: Ps 62:9
³My mouth will speak words
   of wisdom;   Ps 37:30
   the utterance from my heart
      will give understanding.
⁴I will turn my ear to a
   proverb;   Ps 78:2
   with the harp I will
      expound my riddle: Nu 12:8

⁵Why should I fear when evil
   days come,   Ps 23:4
   when wicked deceivers
      surround me—
⁶those who trust in their
   wealth   Job 22:25
   and boast of their great
      riches?   Job 36:19
⁷No man can redeem the life
   of another
   or give to God a ransom for
      him—
⁸the ransom for a life is costly,
   no payment is ever
      enough—   Mt 16:26
⁹that he should live on forever
   and not see decay.   Ps 16:10

¹⁰For all can see that wise men
   die;   Ecc 2:16
   the foolish and the
      senseless alike perish

and leave their wealth to
   others.   Lk 12:20
¹¹Their tombs will remain their
   houses[a] forever,   Mk 5:3
   their dwellings for endless
      generations,   Ps 106:31
   though they had[b] named
      lands after themselves.

¹²But man, despite his riches,
   does not endure;   Job 14:2
   he is[c] like the beasts that
      perish.   2Pe 2:12

¹³This is the fate of those who
   trust in themselves,
   and of their followers, who
      approve their sayings.
                               Selah
¹⁴Like sheep they are destined
   for the grave,[d]   Jer 43:11
   and death will feed on
      them.
   The upright will rule over
      them in the morning;
   their forms will decay in the
      grave,[d]
   far from their princely
      mansions.
¹⁵But God will redeem my life[e]
   from the grave;   Ps 56:13
   he will surely take me to
      himself.   *Selah*

¹⁶Do not be overawed when a
   man grows rich,
   when the splendor of his
      house increases;
¹⁷for he will take nothing with
   him when he dies,   1Ti 6:7

---

[a]11 Septuagint and Syriac; Hebrew *In their thoughts their houses will remain*   [b]11 Or / *for they have*   [c]12 Hebrew; Septuagint and Syriac read verse 12 the same as verse 20.   [d]14 Hebrew *Sheol;* also in verse 15   [e]15 Or *soul*

his splendor will not
    descend with him.   Ps 17:14
[18]Though while he lived he
    counted himself
    blessed—   Ps 10:6
and men praise you when
    you prosper—
[19]he will join the generation of
    his fathers,   Ge 15:15
who will never see the light
    of life.   Job 33:30

[20]A man who has riches
    without understanding
is like the beasts that
    perish.   Pr 16:16

Psalm 50

A psalm of Asaph.

[1]The Mighty One, God, the
    LORD,   Jos 22:22
speaks and summons the
    earth
from the rising of the sun
    to the place where it
    sets.
[2]From Zion, perfect in beauty,
    God shines forth.   Dt 33:2
[3]Our God comes and will not
    be silent;   Isa 42:14
a fire devours before him,
and around him a tempest
    rages.   Job 37:9
[4]He summons the heavens
    above,
and the earth, that he may
    judge his people: Heb 10:30
[5]"Gather to me my
    consecrated ones,   Dt 7:6

who made a covenant with
    me by sacrifice."   Ex 24:7
[6]And the heavens proclaim
    his righteousness,   Ps 19:1
for God himself is judge.
                        Selah

[7]"Hear, O my people, and I
    will speak,
O Israel, and I will testify
    against you: Heb 2:4
I am God, your God.   Ex 20:2
[8]I do not rebuke you for your
    sacrifices   2Sa 22:16
or your burnt offerings,
    which are ever before
    me.   Ps 40:6
[9]I have no need of a bull from
    your stall   Lev 1:5
or of goats from your
    pens,
[10]for every animal of the forest
    is mine,   Ps 104:20
and the cattle on a
    thousand hills.   Ps 104:24
[11]I know every bird in the
    mountains,   Mt 6:26
and the creatures of the
    field are mine.   Ps 8:7
[12]If I were hungry I would not
    tell you,
for the world is mine, and
    all that is in it.   Dt 10:14
[13]Do I eat the flesh of bulls
    or drink the blood of
    goats?
[14]Sacrifice thank offerings to
    God,   Ezr 1:4
fulfill your vows to the
    Most High,   Nu 30:2
[15]and call upon me in the day
    of trouble;   Ps 4:1

I will deliver you, and you
  will honor me.''   Ps 22:23

¹⁶But to the wicked, God says:

''What right have you to
    recite my laws
  or take my covenant on
    your lips?   Ps 25:10
¹⁷You hate my instruction
  and cast my words behind
    you.   1Ki 14:9
¹⁸When you see a thief, you
    join with him;   Ro 1:32
  you throw in your lot with
    adulterers.   Job 22:15
¹⁹You use your mouth for evil
  and harness your tongue to
    deceit.   Ps 10:7
²⁰You speak continually
    against your brother
  and slander your own
    mother's son.   Mt 10:21
²¹These things you have done
    and I kept silent;   Isa 42:14
  you thought I was
    altogether^a like you.
  But I will rebuke you
  and accuse you to your
    face.   Ps 6:1; 85:5

²²''Consider this, you who
    forget God,   Job 8:13
  or I will tear you to pieces,
    with none to rescue:
²³He who sacrifices thank
    offerings honors me,
  and he prepares the way
  so that I may show him^b
    the salvation of God.''

Psalm 51

For the director of music.
A psalm of David. When the
prophet Nathan came to him
after David had committed
adultery with Bathsheba.

¹Have mercy on me, O God,
  according to your unfailing
    love;   Ps 25:7
  according to your great
    compassion   Ne 9:27
  blot out my transgressions.
²Wash away all my iniquity
  and cleanse me from my
    sin.   Ru 3:3; Pr 20:30

³For I know my
    transgressions,
  and my sin is always before
    me.   Isa 59:12
⁴Against you, you only, have
    I sinned   1Sa 15:24
  and done what is evil in
    your sight,   Ge 20:6
  so that you are proved right
    when you speak
  and justified when you
    judge.   Ro 3:4
⁵Surely I was sinful at birth,
  sinful from the time my
    mother conceived me.
⁶Surely you desire truth in the
    inner parts^c;
  you teach^d me wisdom in
    the inmost place.   Job 9:4

⁷Cleanse me with hyssop, and
    I will be clean;   Isa 4:4
  wash me, and I will be
    whiter than snow.   Isa 1:18

---

^a21 Or *thought the 'I AM' was*   ^b23 Or *and to him who considers his way / I will show*
^c6 The meaning of the Hebrew for this phrase is uncertain.   ^d6 Or *you desired . . . ; /
you taught*

⁸Let me hear joy and
    gladness;   Isa 35:10
  let the bones you have
    crushed rejoice.   Ex 12:46
⁹Hide your face from my sins
  and blot out all my iniquity.

¹⁰Create in me a pure heart,
    O God,   Ps 24:4
  and renew a steadfast spirit
    within me.   Eze 18:31
¹¹Do not cast me from your
    presence   Ge 4:14
  or take your Holy Spirit
    from me.   Ps 106:33
¹²Restore to me the joy of your
    salvation   Job 33:26
  and grant me a willing
    spirit, to sustain me.

¹³Then I will teach
    transgressors your
    ways,
  and sinners will turn back
    to you.   Ps 1:1
¹⁴Save me from bloodguilt,
    O God,   Ps 39:8
  the God who saves me,
  and my tongue will sing of
    your righteousness.   Ps 5:8
¹⁵O Lord, open my lips,   Ex 4:15
  and my mouth will declare
    your praise.
¹⁶You do not delight in
    sacrifice, or I would
    bring it;   1Sa 15:22
  you do not take pleasure in
    burnt offerings.
¹⁷The sacrifices of God are[a] a
    broken spirit;   Pr 15:8
  a broken and contrite heart,
  O God, you will not
    despise.   Mt 11:29

¹⁸In your good pleasure make
    Zion prosper;   Ps 102:16
  build up the walls of
    Jerusalem.   Ps 69:35
¹⁹Then there will be righteous
    sacrifices,   Dt 33:19
  whole burnt offerings to
    delight you;   Ps 66:13
  then bulls will be offered on
    your altar.   Ps 66:15

Psalm 52

For the director of music. A
maskil[b] of David. When Doeg the
Edomite had gone to Saul and
told him: "David has gone to the
house of Ahimelech."

¹Why do you boast of evil,
    you mighty man?
  Why do you boast all day
    long,   Ps 10:3
  you who are a disgrace in
    the eyes of God?
²Your tongue plots
    destruction;   Ps 5:9
  it is like a sharpened razor,
  you who practice deceit.
³You love evil rather than
    good,   Ex 10:10
  falsehood rather than
    speaking the truth. *Selah*
⁴You love every harmful
    word,
  O you deceitful tongue!

⁵Surely God will bring you
    down to everlasting
    ruin:
  He will snatch you up and
    tear you from your tent;
  he will uproot you from the
    land of the living.   *Selah*

---

*a*17 Or *My sacrifice, O God, is*   *b*Title: Probably a literary or musical term

⁶The righteous will see and
    fear;
  they will laugh at him,
    saying,   Job 22:19
⁷"Here now is the man
  who did not make God his
    stronghold   2Sa 22:3
  but trusted in his great
    wealth   Ps 49:6
  and grew strong by
    destroying others!"

⁸But I am like an olive tree
  flourishing in the house of
    God;   Ps 1:3
  I trust in God's unfailing love
    for ever and ever.   Ps 6:4
⁹I will praise you forever for
    what you have done;
  in your name I will hope,
    for your name is good.
  I will praise you in the
    presence of your saints.

Psalm 53

For the director of music.
According to *mahalath.* ª A *maskil* ᵇ
of David.

¹The fool says in his heart,
  "There is no God."   Ps 10:4
  They are corrupt, and their
    ways are vile;
  there is no one who does
    good.

²God looks down from
    heaven   Ps 33:13
  on the sons of men
  to see if there are any who
    understand,   Ps 82:5
  any who seek God.   2Ch 15:2
³Everyone has turned away,

they have together become
    corrupt;
  there is no one who does
    good,
  not even one.   Ro 3:10-12

⁴Will the evildoers never
    learn—
  those who devour my
    people as men eat bread
  and who do not call on
    God?
⁵There they were,
    overwhelmed with
    dread,   Lev 26:17
  where there was nothing to
    dread.
  God scattered the bones of
    those who attacked you;
  you put them to shame, for
    God despised them.

⁶Oh, that salvation for Israel
    would come out of Zion!
  When God restores the
    fortunes of his people,
  let Jacob rejoice and Israel
    be glad!

Psalm 54

For the director of music. With
stringed instruments. A *maskil* ᵇ of
David. When the Ziphites had
gone to Saul and said, "Is not
David hiding among us?"

¹Save me, O God, by your
    name;
  vindicate me by your   Ps 20:1
    might.   2Ch 20:6
²Hear my prayer, O God;
  listen to the words of my
    mouth.   Ps 4:1

ªTitle: Probably a musical term   ᵇTitle: Probably a literary or musical term

³Strangers are attacking me;
  ruthless men seek my life—
  men without regard for
    God.   *Selah*

⁴Surely God is my help;   1Ch 5:20
  the Lord is the one who
    sustains me.   Ps 18:35

⁵Let evil recoil on those who
    slander me;   Dt 32:35
  in your faithfulness destroy
    them.   Ps 89:49

⁶I will sacrifice a freewill
    offering to you;   Lev 7:12
  I will praise your name,
    O LORD,   Ps 44:8
  for it is good.   Ps 52:9
⁷For he has delivered me from
    all my troubles,   Ps 34:6
  and my eyes have looked in
    triumph on my foes.

Psalm 55

For the director of music. With
stringed instruments. A *maskil*ᵃ of
David.

¹Listen to my prayer, O God,
  do not ignore my plea; Ps 27:9
² hear me and answer me.
  My thoughts trouble me and
    I am distraught 1Sa 1:15-16
³ at the voice of the enemy,
  at the stares of the wicked;
  for they bring down suffering
    upon me   2Sa 16:6-8
  and revile me in their
    anger.   Ps 44:16

⁴My heart is in anguish within
    me;   Ps 6:3

the terrors of death assail
    me.   Job 18:11
⁵Fear and trembling have
    beset me;   Job 4:14
  horror has overwhelmed
    me.   Dt 28:67
⁶I said, "Oh, that I had the
    wings of a dove!
  I would fly away and be at
    rest—
⁷I would flee far away
  and stay in the desert; *Selah*
⁸I would hurry to my place of
    shelter,   Ps 31:20
  far from the tempest and
    storm."   Ps 77:18

⁹Confuse the wicked, O Lord,
  confound their speech,
  for I see violence and strife
    in the city.   Ps 11:5
¹⁰Day and night they prowl
    about on its walls;   1Pe 5:8
  malice and abuse are
    within it.
¹¹Destructive forces are at
    work in the city;   Ps 5:9
  threats and lies never leave
    its streets.   Ps 10:7

¹²If an enemy were insulting
    me,
  I could endure it;
  if a foe were raising himself
    against me,
  I could hide from him.
¹³But it is you, a man like
    myself,
  my companion, my close
    friend,   2Sa 15:12
¹⁴with whom I once enjoyed
    sweet fellowship   Ac 1:16

ᵃTitle: Probably a literary or musical term

as we walked with the
   throng at the house of
   God.   Ps 42:4

15Let death take my enemies
   by surprise;   Ps 64:7
let them go down alive to
   the grave,ᵃ   Ps 49:14
for evil finds lodging
   among them.

16But I call to God,
   and the LORD saves me.
17Evening, morning and noon
   I cry out in distress,   Ps 141:2
   and he hears my voice.
18He ransoms me unharmed
   from the battle waged
      against me,
   even though many oppose
      me.
19God, who is enthroned
   forever,   Ex 15:18
   will hear them and afflict
      them—   Selah
men who never change their
      ways
   and have no fear of God.

20My companion attacks his
   friends;   Ps 7:4
   he violates his covenant.
21His speech is smooth as
   butter,   Ps 12:2
   yet war is in his heart;
his words are more soothing
   than oil,   Pr 5:3
   yet they are drawn swords.

22Cast your cares on the LORD
   and he will sustain you;
   he will never let the
      righteous fall.   Ps 15:5

23But you, O God, will bring
   down the wicked
   into the pit of corruption;
bloodthirsty and deceitful
   men   Ps 5:6
will not live out half their
   days.   Job 15:32

But as for me, I trust in you.

Psalm 56

For the director of music. To the
tune of "A Dove on Distant
Oaks." Of David. A miktam.ᵇ
When the Philistines had seized
him in Gath.

1Be merciful to me, O God,
   for men hotly pursue
      me;   Ps 57:1-3
   all day long they press their
      attack.   Ps 17:9
2My slanderers pursue me all
   day long;   Ps 35:25
   many are attacking me in
      their pride.   Ps 35:1

3When I am afraid,   Ps 55:4-5
   I will trust in you.   Ps 55:23
4In God, whose word I praise,
   in God I trust; I will not be
      afraid.   Ps 27:1
   What can mortal man do to
      me?   Ps 118:6

5All day long they twist my
   words;   Ps 41:7
   they are always plotting to
      harm me.
6They conspire, they lurk,
   they watch my steps,
   eager to take my life.   Ps 71:10

ᵃ15 Hebrew Sheol   ᵇTitle: Probably a literary or musical term

⁷On no account let them
  escape;   Pr 19:5
in your anger, O God, bring
  down the nations.   Ps 36:12
⁸Record my lament;
  list my tears on your
  scroll*ᵃ*—   2Ki 20:5
  are they not in your record?

⁹Then my enemies will turn
  back   Ps 9:3
when I call for help.   Ps 102:2
By this I will know that God
  is for me.   Nu 14:8
¹⁰In God, whose word I praise,
  in the LORD, whose word I
  praise—
¹¹in God I trust; I will not be
  afraid.
What can man do to me?

¹²I am under vows to you,
  O God;   Ps 50:14
I will present my thank
  offerings to you.
¹³For you have delivered me*ᵇ*
  from death   Ps 30:3
and my feet from
  stumbling,
that I may walk before God
  in the light of life.*ᶜ*   Job 33:30

Psalm 57

For the director of music. ⌐To the
tune of⌐ "Do Not Destroy." Of
David. A *miktam.*ᵈ When he had
fled from Saul into the cave.

¹Have mercy on me, O God,
  have mercy on me,
for in you my soul takes
  refuge.   Ps 2:12

I will take refuge in the
  shadow of your wings
until the disaster has
  passed.   Isa 26:20

²I cry out to God Most High,
  to God, who fulfills ⌐his
  purpose⌐ for me.   Ps 138:8
³He sends from heaven and
  saves me,   Ps 18:9
rebuking those who hotly
  pursue me;   *Selah*
God sends his love and his
  faithfulness.   Ps 25:10

⁴I am in the midst of lions;
I lie among ravenous
  beasts—
men whose teeth are spears
  and arrows,
whose tongues are sharp
  swords.   Ps 55:21

⁵Be exalted, O God, above the
  heavens;
let your glory be over all the
  earth.   Ps 108:5

⁶They spread a net for my
  feet—   Ps 10:9
I was bowed down in
  distress.   Ps 38:6
They dug a pit in my path—
but they have fallen into it
  themselves.   *Selah*

⁷My heart is steadfast, O God,
  my heart is steadfast; Ps 112:7
I will sing and make music.
⁸Awake, my soul!
Awake, harp and lyre!
I will awaken the dawn.

ᵃ8 Or / *put my tears in your wineskin*   *ᵇ13* Or *my soul*   *ᶜ13* Or *the land of the living*
*ᵈ*Title: Probably a literary or musical term

⁹I will praise you, O Lord,
    among the nations;
  I will sing of you among the
    peoples.
¹⁰For great is your love,
    reaching to the heavens;
  your faithfulness reaches to
    the skies.   Ps 36:5

¹¹Be exalted, O God, above the
    heavens;   Ps 8:1
  let your glory be over all the
    earth.

Psalm 58

For the director of music. ˌTo the
tune ofˌ "Do Not Destroy." Of
David. A *miktam.* ᵃ

¹Do you rulers indeed speak
    justly?   Ps 82:2
  Do you judge uprightly
    among men?
²No, in your heart you devise
    injustice,   Mt 15:19
  and your hands mete out
    violence on the earth.
³Even from birth the wicked
    go astray;
  from the womb they are
    wayward and speak lies.
⁴Their venom is like the
    venom of a snake,   Nu 21:6
  like that of a cobra that has
    stopped its ears,
⁵that will not heed the tune of
    the charmer,   Ps 81:11
  however skillful the
    enchanter may be.

⁶Break the teeth in their
    mouths, O God;   Ps 3:7

tear out, O Lᴏʀᴅ, the fangs
    of the lions!   Job 4:10
⁷Let them vanish like water
    that flows away;   Lev 26:36
  when they draw the bow,
    let their arrows be
    blunted.   Ps 11:2
⁸Like a slug melting away as it
    moves along,   Isa 13:7
  like a stillborn child, may
    they not see the sun.

⁹Before your pots can feel ˌthe
    heat ofˌ the thorns—
  whether they be green or
    dry—the wicked will be
    swept away.ᵇ   Job 7:10
¹⁰The righteous will be glad
    when they are
    avenged,
  when they bathe their feet
    in the blood of the
    wicked.   Ps 68:23
¹¹Then men will say,
  "Surely the righteous still
    are rewarded;   Ge 15:1
  surely there is a God who
    judges the earth."   Ge 18:25

Psalm 59

For the director of music. ˌTo the
tune ofˌ "Do Not Destroy." Of
David. A *miktam.* ᵃ When Saul had
sent men to watch David's house
in order to kill him.

¹Deliver me from my enemies,
    O God;   Ps 143:9
  protect me from those who
    rise up against me.   Ps 20:1

ᵃTitle: Probably a literary or musical term
verse is uncertain.

ᵇ9 The meaning of the Hebrew for this

²Deliver me from evildoers
and save me from
bloodthirsty men. Ps 26:9

³See how they lie in wait for
me!
Fierce men conspire against
me Ps 56:6
for no offense or sin of
mine, O LORD.
⁴I have done no wrong, yet
they are ready to attack
me. Mt 5:11
Arise to help me; look on
my plight! Ps 13:3
⁵O LORD God Almighty, the
God of Israel, Ps 69:6
rouse yourself to punish all
the nations; Ps 44:23
show no mercy to wicked
traitors. *Selah*

⁶They return at evening,
snarling like dogs, Ps 22:16
and prowl about the city.
⁷See what they spew from
their mouths— Ps 94:4
they spew out swords from
their lips, Ps 55:21
and they say, "Who can
hear us?" Job 22:13
⁸But you, O LORD, laugh at
them; Ps 37:13
you scoff at all those
nations. Ps 2:4

⁹O my Strength, I watch for
you; Ps 18:1
you, O God, are my
fortress, ¹⁰my loving
God. Ps 9:9

God will go before me
and will let me gloat over
those who slander me.
¹¹But do not kill them, O Lord
our shield,ᵃ Ps 3:3
or my people will forget.
In your might make them
wander about,
and bring them down.
¹²For the sins of their mouths,
for the words of their lips,
let them be caught in their
pride. Isa 2:12
For the curses and lies they
utter,
13 consume them in wrath,
consume them till they are
no more. Ps 104:35
Then it will be known to the
ends of the earth
that God rules over Jacob.
Selah

¹⁴They return at evening,
snarling like dogs,
and prowl about the city.
¹⁵They wander about for food
and howl if not satisfied.
¹⁶But I will sing of your
strength, Ps 108:1
in the morning I will sing of
your love; Ps 5:3
for you are my fortress,
my refuge in times of
trouble. Dt 4:30

¹⁷O my Strength, I sing praise
to you;
you, O God, are my
fortress, my loving
God.

ᵃ11 Or *sovereign*

Psalm 60

For the director of music. To the tune of, "The Lily of the Covenant." A miktam[a] of David. For teaching. When he fought Aram Naharaim[b] and Aram Zobah,[c] and when Joab returned and struck down twelve thousand Edomites in the Valley of Salt.

[1]You have rejected us, O God, and burst forth upon us; you have been angry—now restore us! Ps 79:5
[2]You have shaken the land and torn it open; Ps 18:7 mend its fractures, for it is quaking. 2Ch 7:14
[3]You have shown your people desperate times; Ps 71:20 you have given us wine that makes us stagger.

[4]But for those who fear you, you have raised a banner Isa 5:26 to be unfurled against the bow. *Selah*

[5]Save us and help us with your right hand, Job 40:14 that those you love may be delivered. Dt 33:12
[6]God has spoken from his sanctuary: "In triumph I will parcel out Shechem Ge 12:6 and measure off the Valley of Succoth. Ge 33:17
[7]Gilead is mine, and Manasseh is mine; Jos 13:31 Ephraim is my helmet, Judah my scepter. Nu 34:19

[8]Moab is my washbasin, upon Edom I toss my sandal; over Philistia I shout in triumph." 2Sa 8:1
[9]Who will bring me to the fortified city? Who will lead me to Edom?
[10]Is it not you, O God, you who have rejected us and no longer go out with our armies? Jos 7:12
[11]Give us aid against the enemy, for the help of man is worthless. Ps 146:3
[12]With God we will gain the victory, and he will trample down our enemies. Job 40:12

Psalm 61

For the director of music. With stringed instruments. Of David.

[1]Hear my cry, O God; Ps 64:1 listen to my prayer. Ps 4:1

[2]From the ends of the earth I call to you, I call as my heart grows faint; Ps 6:2 lead me to the rock that is higher than I. Ps 18:2
[3]For you have been my refuge, Ps 9:9 a strong tower against the foe. Ps 59:9

[4]I long to dwell in your tent forever Ps 15:1

[a]Title: Probably a literary or musical term   [b]Title: That is, Arameans of Northwest Mesopotamia   [c]Title: That is, Arameans of central Syria

and take refuge in the
shelter of your wings.
Selah

[5]For you have heard my
vows, O God;   Nu 30:2
you have given me the
heritage of those who
fear your name.   Ex 6:3

[6]Increase the days of the
king's life,   1Ki 3:14
his years for many
generations.   Ps 21:4
[7]May he be enthroned in
God's presence forever;
appoint your love and
faithfulness to protect
him.   Ps 40:11

[8]Then will I ever sing praise to
your name   Ps 7:17
and fulfill my vows day
after day.   Nu 30:2

Psalm 62

For the director of music. For
Jeduthun. A psalm of David.

[1]My soul finds rest in God
alone;   Ps 5:3
my salvation comes from
him.
[2]He alone is my rock and my
salvation;   Ps 18:31
he is my fortress, I will
never be shaken.   Ps 59:9

[3]How long will you assault a
man?
Would all of you throw him
down—
this leaning wall, this
tottering fence?   Isa 30:13

[4]They fully intend to topple
him
from his lofty place;
they take delight in lies.
With their mouths they bless,
but in their hearts they
curse.   *Selah*

[5]Find rest, O my soul, in God
alone;
my hope comes from him.
[6]He alone is my rock and my
salvation;
he is my fortress, I will not
be shaken.
[7]My salvation and my honor
depend on God[a];
he is my mighty rock, my
refuge.   Ps 61:3
[8]Trust in him at all times,
O people;   Ps 37:5
pour out your hearts to
him,   1Sa 1:15
for God is our refuge.   *Selah*

[9]Lowborn men are but a
breath,   Ps 49:2
the highborn are but a lie;
if weighed on a balance, they
are nothing;   Isa 40:15
together they are only a
breath.
[10]Do not trust in extortion
or take pride in stolen
goods;   Isa 61:8
though your riches increase,
do not set your heart on
them.   Job 31:25

[11]One thing God has spoken,
two things have I heard:
that you, O God, are strong,
[12]   and that you, O Lord, are
loving.   Ps 86:5

---

[a]7 Or / God Most High is my salvation and my honor

Surely you will reward each
person
according to what he has
done.   Job 21:31

Psalm 63

A psalm of David. When he was
in the Desert of Judah.

1O God, you are my God,
  earnestly I seek you;   Ps 42:2
my soul thirsts for you,
  my body longs for you,
in a dry and weary land
  where there is no water.

2I have seen you in the
  sanctuary   Ps 15:1
and beheld your power and
  your glory.   Ex 16:7
3Because your love is better
  than life,   Ps 36:7
my lips will glorify you.
4I will praise you as long as I
  live,   Ps 104:33
and in your name I will lift
  up my hands.   Ps 28:2
5My soul will be satisfied as
  with the richest of
  foods;
with singing lips my mouth
  will praise you.   Ps 36:8

6On my bed I remember you;
  I think of you through the
  watches of the night.
7Because you are my help,
  I sing in the shadow of your
  wings.   Ru 2:12
8My soul clings to you;   Nu 32:12
  your right hand upholds
  me.   Ps 41:12

9They who seek my life will
  be destroyed;   Ps 40:14
they will go down to the
  depths of the earth.
10They will be given over to
  the sword   Jer 18:21
and become food for
  jackals.   La 5:18
11But the king will rejoice in
  God;
all who swear by God's
  name will praise him,
while the mouths of liars
  will be silenced.   Job 5:16

Psalm 64

For the director of music.
A psalm of David.

1Hear me, O God, as I voice
  my complaint;   Ps 142:2
protect my life from the
  threat of the enemy.
2Hide me from the conspiracy
  of the wicked,   Ps 56:6
from that noisy crowd of
  evildoers.

3They sharpen their tongues
  like swords   Ps 55:21
and aim their words like
  deadly arrows.   Ps 7:13
4They shoot from ambush at
  the innocent man;   Job 9:23
they shoot at him suddenly,
  without fear.   Ps 55:19

5They encourage each other in
  evil plans,
they talk about hiding their
  snares;   Ps 91:3

they say, "Who will see
them[a]?"   Job 22:13
6They plot injustice and say,
"We have devised a perfect
plan!"
Surely the mind and heart
of man are cunning.

7But God will shoot them with
arrows;
suddenly they will be
struck down.
8He will turn their own
tongues against them
and bring them to ruin;
all who see them will shake
their heads in scorn.

9All mankind will fear;
they will proclaim the
works of God
and ponder what he has
done.   Jer 51:10
10Let the righteous rejoice in
the LORD   Job 22:19
and take refuge in him;
let all the upright in heart
praise him!   Ps 32:11

Psalm 65

For the director of music.
A psalm of David. A song.

1Praise awaits[b] you, O God,
in Zion;   Ps 2:6
to you our vows will be
fulfilled.   Dt 23:21
2O you who hear prayer,
to you all men will come.
3When we were overwhelmed
by sins,   Ps 40:12

you forgave[c] our
transgressions.   Ps 79:9
4Blessed are those you choose
and bring near to live in
your courts!   Nu 16:5
We are filled with the good
things of your house,
of your holy temple.   Ps 36:8

5You answer us with
awesome deeds of
righteousness,   Dt 4:34
O God our Savior,   Ps 18:46
the hope of all the ends of
the earth   Ps 48:10
and of the farthest seas,
6who formed the mountains
by your power,   Am 4:13
having armed yourself with
strength,   Ps 18:1
7who stilled the roaring of the
seas,   Ps 89:9
the roaring of their waves,
and the turmoil of the
nations.   Dt 32:41
8Those living far away fear
your wonders;
where morning dawns and
evening fades
you call forth songs of joy.

9You care for the land and
water it;   Lev 26:4
you enrich it abundantly.
The streams of God are filled
with water
to provide the people with
grain,   Ge 27:28
for so you have ordained
it.[d]
10You drench its furrows
and level its ridges;

a5 Or us   b1 Or befits; the meaning of the Hebrew for this word is uncertain.
c3 Or made atonement for   d9 Or for that is how you prepare the land

you soften it with showers
and bless its crops.   Dt 32:2
[11]You crown the year with
    your bounty,   Dt 28:12
and your carts overflow
    with abundance.   Job 36:28
[12]The grasslands of the desert
    overflow;   Job 28:26
the hills are clothed with
    gladness.   Ps 98:8
[13]The meadows are covered
    with flocks   Ps 144:13
and the valleys are mantled
    with grain;   Ps 72:16
they shout for joy and sing.

Psalm 66

For the director of music. A song.
A psalm.

[1]Shout with joy to God, all the
    earth!   Ps 81:1
[2] Sing the glory of his name;
make his praise glorious!
[3]Say to God, "How awesome
    are your deeds!   Dt 7:21
So great is your power
that your enemies cringe
    before you.   2Sa 22:45
[4]All the earth bows down to
    you;   Ps 22:27
they sing praise to you,
they sing praise to your
    name."   Selah

[5]Come and see what God has
    done,
how awesome his works in
    man's behalf!   Ps 106:22
[6]He turned the sea into dry
    land,   Ge 8:1
they passed through the
    waters on foot—   1Co 10:1
come, let us rejoice in him.

[7]He rules forever by his
    power,   Ex 15:18
his eyes watch the
    nations—   Ex 3:8
let not the rebellious rise up
    against him.   Selah

[8]Praise our God, O peoples,
let the sound of his praise
    be heard;
[9]he has preserved our lives
and kept our feet from
    slipping.   Dt 32:35
[10]For you, O God, tested us;
    you refined us like silver.
[11]You brought us into prison
and laid burdens on our
    backs.   Ge 3:17
[12]You let men ride over our
    heads;   Isa 51:23
we went through fire and
    water,
but you brought us to a
    place of abundance.

[13]I will come to your temple
    with burnt offerings
and fulfill my vows to
    you—   Ps 22:25
[14]vows my lips promised and
    my mouth spoke
when I was in trouble.
[15]I will sacrifice fat animals to
    you
and an offering of rams;
I will offer bulls and goats.
    Selah

[16]Come and listen, all you who
    fear God;   Ps 34:11
let me tell you what he has
    done for me.   Ps 71:15
[17]I cried out to him with my
    mouth;

his praise was on my
tongue.
¹⁸If I had cherished sin in my
heart,
the Lord would not have
listened;   Dt 1:45
¹⁹but God has surely listened
and heard my voice in
prayer.   Ps 18:6
²⁰Praise be to God,
who has not rejected my
prayer   Ps 22:24
or withheld his love from
me!

Psalm 67

For the director of music. With
stringed instruments. A psalm.
A song.

¹May God be gracious to us
and bless us
and make his face shine
upon us,   *Selah*
²that your ways may be
known on earth,
your salvation among all
nations.   Isa 40:5

³May the peoples praise you,
O God;
may all the peoples praise
you.
⁴May the nations be glad and
sing for joy,   Ps 100:1-2
for you rule the peoples
justly   Ps 9:4
and guide the nations of the
earth.   *Selah*
⁵May the peoples praise you,
O God;

may all the peoples praise
you.

⁶Then the land will yield its
harvest,   Ge 8:22
and God, our God, will
bless us.   Ge 12:2
⁷God will bless us,
and all the ends of the earth
will fear him.   Ps 33:8

Psalm 68

For the director of music. Of
David. A psalm. A song.

¹May God arise, may his
enemies be scattered;
may his foes flee before
him.   Nu 10:35
²As smoke is blown away by
the wind,   Ps 37:20
may you blow them away;
as wax melts before the fire,
may the wicked perish
before God.   Nu 10:35
³But may the righteous be
glad
and rejoice before God;
may they be happy and
joyful.   Ps 64:10

⁴Sing to God, sing praise to
his name,   2Sa 22:50
extol him who rides on the
clouds^a—   Ex 20:21
his name is the LORD—
and rejoice before him.   Ex 6:3
⁵A father to the fatherless, a
defender of widows,
is God in his holy dwelling.
⁶God sets the lonely in
families,^b   Ps 113:9

^a4 Or / *prepare the way for him who rides through the deserts*   ^b6 Or *the desolate in a homeland*

he leads forth the prisoners
    with singing;   Ps 79:11
but the rebellious live in a
    sun-scorched land.   Isa 35:7

⁷When you went out before
    your people, O God,
    when you marched through
        the wasteland,   *Selah*
⁸the earth shook,   2Sa 22:8
    the heavens poured down
        rain,   Jdg 5:4
    before God, the One of Sinai,
    before God, the God of
        Israel.   Jdg 5:5
⁹You gave abundant showers,
    O God;   Dt 32:2
    you refreshed your weary
        inheritance.
¹⁰Your people settled in it,
    and from your bounty,
        O God, you provided
        for the poor.   Ps 65:9

¹¹The Lord announced the
        word,
    and great was the company
        of those who proclaimed
        it: Lk 2:13
¹²"Kings and armies flee in
        haste;   Jos 10:16
    in the camps men divide
        the plunder.   Jdg 5:30
¹³Even while you sleep among
        the campfires,ᵃ   Ge 49:14
    the wings of ˻my˼ dove are
        sheathed with silver,
    its feathers with shining
        gold."
¹⁴When the Almightyᵇ
    scattered the kings in
        the land,   2Sa 22:15

it was like snow fallen on
    Zalmon.   Jdg 9:48

¹⁵The mountains of Bashan are
    majestic mountains;
    rugged are the mountains
        of Bashan.
¹⁶Why gaze in envy, O rugged
        mountains,
    at the mountain where God
        chooses to reign,   Dt 12:5
    where the LORD himself will
        dwell forever?   Ps 132:14
¹⁷The chariots of God are tens
        of thousands   2Ki 2:11
    and thousands of
        thousands;   Da 7:10
    the Lord ˻has come˼ from
        Sinai into his sanctuary.
¹⁸When you ascended on high,
    you led captives in your
        train;   Jdg 5:12
    you received gifts from
        men,   Eph 4:8
    even fromᶜ the rebellious—
    that you,ᵈ O LORD God,
        might dwell there.

¹⁹Praise be to the Lord, to God
        our Savior,   Ps 65:5
    who daily bears our
        burdens.   *Selah*
²⁰Our God is a God who saves;
    from the Sovereign LORD
        comes escape from
        death.   Ps 56:13

²¹Surely God will crush the
        heads of his enemies,
    the hairy crowns of those
        who go on in their sins.
²²The Lord says, "I will bring
        them from Bashan;

ᵃ13 Or *saddlebags*   ᵇ14 Hebrew *Shaddai*   ᶜ18 Or *gifts for men, / even*   ᵈ18 Or *they*

I will bring them from the
  depths of the sea,   Job 36:30
23that you may plunge your
  feet in the blood of your
  foes,   Ps 58:10
while the tongues of your
  dogs have their share."

24Your procession has come
  into view, O God,
the procession of my God
  and King into the
  sanctuary.   Ps 63:2
25In front are the singers, after
  them the musicians;
with them are the maidens
  playing tambourines.
26Praise God in the great
  congregation;   Ps 22:22
praise the LORD in the
  assembly of Israel. Lev 19:2
27There is the little tribe of
  Benjamin, leading
  them,
there the great throng of
  Judah's princes,
and there the princes of
  Zebulun and of
  Naphtali.   Jdg 5:18

28Summon your power,
  O God*a*;   Ex 9:16
show us your strength,
  O God, as you have
  done before.   Isa 26:12
29Because of your temple at
  Jerusalem
kings will bring you gifts.
30Rebuke the beast among the
  reeds,   Isa 27:1
the herd of bulls among the
  calves of the nations.

Humbled, may it bring bars
  of silver.
Scatter the nations who
  delight in war.   Ps 120:7
31Envoys will come from
  Egypt;   Isa 19:19
Cush*b* will submit herself to
  God.   Isa 11:11

32Sing to God, O kingdoms of
  the earth,   Ps 46:6
sing praise to the Lord,
                          Selah
33to him who rides the ancient
  skies above,   Dt 33:26
who thunders with mighty
  voice.   Ps 29:4
34Proclaim the power of God,
  whose majesty is over
  Israel,   Ps 45:3
whose power is in the
  skies.
35You are awesome, O God, in
  your sanctuary;   Ge 28:17
the God of Israel gives
  power and strength to
  his people.   Ps 29:11

Praise be to God!   Ps 28:6

Psalm 69

For the director of music. To the
tune of "Lilies." Of David.

1Save me, O God,
for the waters have come
  up to my neck.   Ps 32:6
2I sink in the miry depths,
  where there is no foothold.
I have come into the deep
  waters;
the floods engulf me.

---

a28 Many Hebrew manuscripts, Septuagint and Syriac; most Hebrew manuscripts *Your
God has summoned power for you*   *b31* That is, the upper Nile region

³I am worn out calling for
help;   Ps 6:6
my throat is parched.
My eyes fail,   Ps 119:82
looking for my God.
⁴Those who hate me without
reason   Jn 15:25
outnumber the hairs of my
head;
many are my enemies
without cause,   Ps 35:19
those who seek to destroy
me.   Ps 40:14
I am forced to restore
what I did not steal.

⁵You know my folly, O God;
my guilt is not hidden from
you.   Ps 44:21

⁶May those who hope in you
not be disgraced because of
me,
O Lord, the LORD
Almighty;
may those who seek you
not be put to shame
because of me,
O God of Israel.
⁷For I endure scorn for your
sake,   Ps 39:8
and shame covers my face.
⁸I am a stranger to my
brothers,
an alien to my own
mother's sons;   Ps 31:11
⁹for zeal for your house
consumes me,   Jn 2:17
and the insults of those
who insult you fall on
me.   Ps 89:50-51
¹⁰When I weep and fast,   Ps 35:13
I must endure scorn;
¹¹when I put on sackcloth,
people make sport of me.

¹²Those who sit at the gate
mock me,   Ge 18:1
and I am the song of the
drunkards.   Job 30:9

¹³But I pray to you, O LORD,
in the time of your favor;
in your great love, O God,
answer me with your sure
salvation.
¹⁴Rescue me from the mire,
do not let me sink;
deliver me from those who
hate me,
from the deep waters.   Ps 144:7
¹⁵Do not let the floodwaters
engulf me   Ps 124:4-5
or the depths swallow me
up   Nu 16:33
or the pit close its mouth
over me.   Ps 28:1
¹⁶Answer me, O LORD, out of
the goodness of your
love;   Ps 63:3
in your great mercy turn to
me.
¹⁷Do not hide your face from
your servant;   Ps 22:24
answer me quickly, for I am
in trouble.   Ps 50:15
¹⁸Come near and rescue me;
redeem me because of my
foes.   Ps 49:15

¹⁹You know how I am scorned,
disgraced and shamed;
all my enemies are before
you.   Ps 22:6
²⁰Scorn has broken my heart
and has left me helpless;
I looked for sympathy, but
there was none,
for comforters, but I found
none.   Job 16:2
²¹They put gall in my food

and gave me vinegar for my
  thirst.   Mt 27:34

22May the table set before them
  become a snare;
may it become retribution
  and*a* a trap.   1Sa 28:9
23May their eyes be darkened
  so they cannot see,
and their backs be bent
  forever.   Ro 11:9-10
24Pour out your wrath on
  them;   Ps 79:6
let your fierce anger
  overtake them.
25May their place be deserted;
let there be no one to dwell
  in their tents.   Ac 1:20
26For they persecute those you
  wound
and talk about the pain of
  those you hurt.   Job 19:22
27Charge them with crime
  upon crime;   Ne 4:5
do not let them share in
  your salvation.   Ps 109:14
28May they be blotted out of
  the book of life   Ex 32:32
and not be listed with the
  righteous.   Eze 13:9

29I am in pain and distress;
may your salvation, O God,
  protect me.   Ps 20:1

30I will praise God's name in
  song   Ps 28:7
and glorify him with
  thanksgiving.   Ps 34:3
31This will please the LORD
  more than an ox,
more than a bull with its
  horns and hoofs.   Ps 51:16

32The poor will see and be
  glad—   Ps 34:2
you who seek God, may
  your hearts live!   Ps 22:26
33The LORD hears the needy
  and does not despise his
  captive people.   Ps 12:5

34Let heaven and earth praise
  him,
the seas and all that move
  in them,   Ps 96:11
35for God will save Zion   Ob 17
and rebuild the cities of
  Judah.   Ezr 9:9
Then people will settle there
  and possess it;
36 the children of his servants
  will inherit it,   Ps 25:13
and those who love his
  name will dwell there.

Psalm 70

*For the director of music. Of
David. A petition.*

1Hasten, O God, to save me;
O LORD, come quickly to
  help me.   Ps 22:19
2May those who seek my life
be put to shame and
  confusion;   Ps 35:4
may all who desire my ruin
be turned back in disgrace.
3May those who say to me,
  "Aha! Aha!"   Ps 35:21
turn back because of their
  shame.
4But may all who seek you
rejoice and be glad in you;
may those who love your
  salvation always say,

---

*a*22 Or *snare / and their fellowship become*

"Let God be exalted!" Ps 35:27

⁵Yet I am poor and needy;
  come quickly to me, O God.
You are my help and my
    deliverer; Ps 18:2
  O Lord, do not delay.

Psalm 71

¹In you, O Lord, I have taken
    refuge; Dt 23:15
  let me never be put to
    shame. Ps 22:5
²Rescue me and deliver me in
    your righteousness;
  turn your ear to me and
    save me. 2Ki 19:16
³Be my rock of refuge,
  to which I can always go;
  give the command to save
    me,
  for you are my rock and my
    fortress. Ps 18:2
⁴Deliver me, O my God, from
    the hand of the wicked,
  from the grasp of evil and
    cruel men. Ge 48:16

⁵For you have been my hope,
    O Sovereign Lord,
  my confidence since my
    youth. Job 4:6
⁶From birth I have relied on
    you; Ps 22:10
  you brought me forth from
    my mother's womb.
  I will ever praise you. Ps 9:1
⁷I have become like a portent
    to many, Dt 28:46
  but you are my strong
    refuge. 2Sa 22:3
⁸My mouth is filled with your
    praise, Ps 51:15

declaring your splendor all
    day long. Ps 96:6
⁹Do not cast me away when I
    am old; Ps 92:14
  do not forsake me when my
    strength is gone. Dt 4:31
¹⁰For my enemies speak
    against me; Ps 3:7
  those who wait to kill me
    conspire together. Ex 1:10
¹¹They say, "God has forsaken
    him; Ps 9:10
  pursue him and seize him,
  for no one will rescue him."
¹²Be not far from me, O God;
  come quickly, O my God,
    to help me. Ps 22:19
¹³May my accusers perish in
    shame; Jer 18:19
  may those who want to
    harm me
  be covered with scorn and
    disgrace. Ps 70:2

¹⁴But as for me, I will always
    have hope; Ps 25:3
  I will praise you more and
    more.
¹⁵My mouth will tell of your
    righteousness, Ps 51:14
  of your salvation all day
    long,
  though I know not its
    measure.
¹⁶I will come and proclaim
    your mighty acts,
    O Sovereign Lord; Ps 9:1
  I will proclaim your
    righteousness, yours
    alone.
¹⁷Since my youth, O God, you
    have taught me, Dt 4:5
  and to this day I declare
    your marvelous deeds.

18Even when I am old and
    gray,   Isa 46:4
  do not forsake me,
    O God,
  till I declare your power to
    the next generation,
  your might to all who are to
    come.   Job 8:8

19Your righteousness reaches
    to the skies, O God,
  you who have done great
    things.   Ps 126:2
  Who, O God, is like you?
20Though you have made me
    see troubles, many and
    bitter,   Ps 25:17
  you will restore my life
    again;   Ps 80:3
  from the depths of the earth
    you will again bring me up.
21You will increase my honor
    and comfort me once again.

22I will praise you with the
    harp   Ps 33:2
  for your faithfulness, O my
    God;
  I will sing praise to you with
    the lyre,   Job 21:12
  O Holy One of Israel.
23My lips will shout for joy
    when I sing praise to you—
  I, whom you have
    redeemed.   Ex 15:13
24My tongue will tell of your
    righteous acts
  all day long,   Ps 35:28
  for those who wanted to
    harm me   Est 9:2
  have been put to shame
    and confusion.

Psalm 72

Of Solomon.

1Endow the king with your
    justice, O God,   Dt 1:16
  the royal son with your
    righteousness.
2He willª judge your people in
    righteousness,   Isa 9:7
  your afflicted ones with
    justice.
3The mountains will bring
    prosperity to the people,
  the hills the fruit of
    righteousness.
4He will defend the afflicted
    among the people   Ps 9:12
  and save the children of the
    needy;   Isa 11:4
  he will crush the oppressor.

5He will endureᵇ as long as
    the sun,   1Sa 13:13
  as long as the moon,
    through all generations.
6He will be like rain falling on
    a mown field,   Dt 32:2
  like showers watering the
    earth.
7In his days the righteous will
    flourish;   Ps 92:12
  prosperity will abound till
    the moon is no more.

8He will rule from sea to sea
  and from the Riverᶜ to the
    ends of the earth.ᵈ
9The desert tribes will bow
    before him
  and his enemies will lick
    the dust.

ª2 Or *May he;* similarly in verses 3-11 and 17
feared   ᶜ8 That is, the Euphrates   ᵇ5 Septuagint; Hebrew *You will be*   ᵈ8 Or *the end of the land*

¹⁰The kings of Tarshish and of
      distant shores   Est 10:1
  will bring tribute to him;
  the kings of Sheba and Seba
  will present him gifts.
¹¹All kings will bow down to
      him
                        Ge 27:29
  and all nations will serve
      him.
                        Ezr 1:2

¹²For he will deliver the needy
      who cry out,
  the afflicted who have no
      one to help.
¹³He will take pity on the weak
      and the needy   Isa 60:10
  and save the needy from
      death.
¹⁴He will rescue them from
      oppression and violence,
  for precious is their blood in
      his sight.   1Sa 26:21

¹⁵Long may he live!
  May gold from Sheba be
      given him.   Ge 10:7
  May people ever pray for
      him
  and bless him all day long.
¹⁶Let grain abound throughout
      the land;   Ge 27:28
  on the tops of the hills may
      it sway.
  Let its fruit flourish like
      Lebanon;   Ps 92:12
  let it thrive like the grass of
      the field.   Nu 22:4
¹⁷May his name endure
      forever;   Ex 3:15
  may it continue as long as
      the sun.   Ps 89:36

All nations will be blessed
      through him,
  and they will call him
      blessed.   Ge 12:3

¹⁸Praise be to the LORD God,
      the God of Israel,
  who alone does marvelous
      deeds.   Job 5:9
¹⁹Praise be to his glorious
      name forever;   2Sa 7:26
  may the whole earth be
      filled with his glory.
      Amen and Amen.   Ps 41:13

²⁰This concludes the prayers of
      David son of Jesse. Ru 4:17

BOOK III

Psalms 73–89

Psalm 73

A psalm of Asaph.

¹Surely God is good to Israel,
  to those who are pure in
      heart.   Ps 24:4

²But as for me, my feet had
      almost slipped;   Dt 32:35
  I had nearly lost my
      foothold.   Ps 69:2
³For I envied the arrogant
  when I saw the prosperity
      of the wicked.   Job 9:24

⁴They have no struggles;
  their bodies are healthy and
      strong.ᵃ

ᵃ4 With a different word division of the Hebrew; Masoretic Text struggles at their death; /
their bodies are healthy

5They are free from the
burdens common to
man;   Eze 23:42
they are not plagued by
human ills.
6Therefore pride is their
necklace;   Lev 26:19
they clothe themselves with
violence.   Ge 6:11
7From their callous hearts
comes iniquity*a*;   Ps 17:10
the evil conceits of their
minds know no limits.
8They scoff, and speak with
malice;   Ps 41:5
in their arrogance they
threaten oppression.
9Their mouths lay claim to
heaven,
and their tongues take
possession of the earth.
10Therefore their people turn
to them
and drink up waters in
abundance.*b*
11They say, "How can God
know?
Does the Most High have
knowledge?"
12This is what the wicked are
like—
always carefree, they
increase in wealth.   Ps 49:6
13Surely in vain have I kept my
heart pure;   Job 9:29-31
in vain have I washed my
hands in innocence.
14All day long I have been
plagued;
I have been punished every
morning.

15If I had said, "I will speak
thus,"
I would have betrayed your
children.
16When I tried to understand
all this,   Ecc 8:17
it was oppressive to me
17till I entered the sanctuary of
God;   Ex 15:17
then I understood their
final destiny.   Job 8:13

18Surely you place them on
slippery ground;   Dt 32:35
you cast them down to
ruin.   Ps 17:13
19How suddenly are they
destroyed,   Dt 28:20
completely swept away by
terrors!   Ge 19:15
20As a dream when one
awakes,   Job 20:8
so when you arise, O Lord,
you will despise them as
fantasies.   Pr 12:11

21When my heart was grieved
and my spirit embittered,
22I was senseless and ignorant;
I was a brute beast before
you.   Ps 49:10,12

23Yet I am always with you;
you hold me by my right
hand.   Ge 48:13
24You guide me with your
counsel,   Ps 48:14
and afterward you will take
me into glory.
25Whom have I in heaven but
you?   Ps 16:2
And earth has nothing I
desire besides you.   Php 3:8

---

a7 Syriac (see also Septuagint); Hebrew *Their eyes bulge with fat*   *b10* The meaning of
the Hebrew for this verse is uncertain.

²⁶My flesh and my heart may
        fail,   Ps 31:10
    but God is the strength of
        my heart   Ps 18:1
    and my portion forever.

²⁷Those who are far from you
        will perish;   Ps 34:21
    you destroy all who are
        unfaithful to you.   Lev 6:2
²⁸But as for me, it is good to be
        near God.   Zep 3:2
    I have made the Sovereign
        LORD my refuge;   Ps 9:9
    I will tell of all your deeds.

Psalm 74

A *maskil*[a] of Asaph.

¹Why have you rejected us
        forever, O God?   Ps 43:2
    Why does your anger
        smolder against the
        sheep of your pasture?
²Remember the people you
        purchased of old,   Dt 32:7
    the tribe of your
        inheritance, whom you
        redeemed—   Ex 15:13
    Mount Zion, where you
        dwelt.   Ps 2:6
³Turn your steps toward these
        everlasting ruins,   Isa 44:26
    all this destruction the
        enemy has brought on
        the sanctuary.

⁴Your foes roared in the place
        where you met with us;
    they set up their standards
        as signs.   Nu 2:2
⁵They behaved like men
        wielding axes

[a]Title: Probably a literary or musical term

to cut through a thicket of
        trees.   Jer 46:22
⁶They smashed all the carved
        paneling   1Ki 6:18
    with their axes and
        hatchets.
⁷They burned your sanctuary
        to the ground;
    they defiled the dwelling
        place of your Name.
⁸They said in their hearts,
    "We will crush them
        completely!"   Ps 94:5
    They burned every place
        where God was
        worshiped in the land.
⁹We are given no miraculous
        signs;   Ex 4:17
    no prophets are left,   1Sa 3:1
    and none of us knows how
        long this will be.

¹⁰How long will the enemy
        mock you, O God?   Ps 6:3
    Will the foe revile your
        name forever?   Ps 44:16
¹¹Why do you hold back your
        hand, your right hand?
    Take it from the folds of
        your garment and
        destroy them!   Ne 5:13

¹²But you, O God, are my king
        from of old;   Ps 2:6
    you bring salvation upon
        the earth.   Ps 27:1
¹³It was you who split open
        the sea by your power;
    you broke the heads of the
        monster in the waters.
¹⁴It was you who crushed the
        heads of Leviathan   Job 3:8

and gave him as food to the
creatures of the desert.
[15]It was you who opened up
springs and streams;
you dried up the ever
flowing rivers.   Ex 14:29
[16]The day is yours, and yours
also the night;
you established the sun and
moon.   Ps 136:7-9
[17]It was you who set all the
boundaries of the earth;
you made both summer
and winter.   Ge 8:22

[18]Remember how the enemy
has mocked you,
O LORD,
how foolish people have
reviled your name.   Dt 32:6
[19]Do not hand over the life of
your dove to wild
beasts;   Ge 8:8
do not forget the lives of
your afflicted people
forever.   Ps 9:18
[20]Have regard for your
covenant,   Ge 6:18
because haunts of violence
fill the dark places of the
land.   Job 34:22
[21]Do not let the oppressed
retreat in disgrace;   Ps 9:9
may the poor and needy
praise your name.   Ps 35:10

[22]Rise up, O God, and defend
your cause;   Ps 17:13
remember how fools mock
you all day long.   Ps 53:1
[23]Do not ignore the clamor of
your adversaries,   Isa 31:4
the uproar of your enemies,
which rises continually.

Psalm 75

For the director of music. To the
tune of "Do Not Destroy." A
psalm of Asaph. A song.

[1]We give thanks to you,
O God,
we give thanks, for your
Name is near;   Ps 145:18
men tell of your wonderful
deeds.   Jos 3:5

[2]You say, "I choose the
appointed time;   Ex 13:10
it is I who judge uprightly.
[3]When the earth and all its
people quake,   Isa 24:19
it is I who hold its pillars
firm.   *Selah*
[4]To the arrogant I say, 'Boast
no more,'   1Sa 2:3
and to the wicked, 'Do not
lift up your horns.   Zec 1:21
[5]Do not lift your horns against
heaven;
do not speak with
outstretched neck.' "

[6]No one from the east or the
west
or from the desert can exalt
a man.
[7]But it is God who judges:
He brings one down, he
exalts another.   1Sa 2:7
[8]In the hand of the LORD is a
cup
full of foaming wine mixed
with spices;   Pr 23:30
he pours it out, and all the
wicked of the earth
drink it down to its very
dregs.   Isa 51:17

⁹As for me, I will declare this
forever;   Ps 40:10
I will sing praise to the God
of Jacob.   Ps 108:1
¹⁰I will cut off the horns of all
the wicked,
but the horns of the
righteous will be lifted
up.   Ps 89:17; 92:10

Psalm 76

For the director of music. With
stringed instruments. A psalm of
Asaph. A song.

¹In Judah God is known;
his name is great in Israel.
²His tent is in Salem,   Ge 14:18
his dwelling place in Zion.
³There he broke the flashing
arrows,   Eze 39:9
the shields and the swords,
the weapons of war.
                        Selah

⁴You are resplendent with
light,   Ps 36:9
more majestic than
mountains rich with
game.
⁵Valiant men lie plundered,
they sleep their last sleep;
not one of the warriors
can lift his hands.
⁶At your rebuke, O God of
Jacob,   Ps 50:21
both horse and chariot lie
still.   Ex 15:1
⁷You alone are to be feared.
Who can stand before you
when you are angry?

⁸From heaven you
pronounced judgment,
and the land feared and
was quiet—   1Ch 16:30
⁹when you, O God, rose up to
judge,   Ps 9:8
to save all the afflicted of
the land.   *Selah*
¹⁰Surely your wrath against
men brings you praise,
and the survivors of your
wrath are restrained. *ᵃ*
¹¹Make vows to the LORD your
God and fulfill them;
let all the neighboring lands
bring gifts to the One to be
feared.   2Ch 32:23
¹²He breaks the spirit of rulers;
he is feared by the kings of
the earth.

Psalm 77

For the director of music. For
Jeduthun. Of Asaph. A psalm.

¹I cried out to God for help;
I cried out to God to hear
me.
²When I was in distress, I
sought the Lord;   Ge 32:7
at night I stretched out
untiring hands   Ex 9:29
and my soul refused to be
comforted.   Ge 37:35

³I remembered you, O God,
and I groaned;   Ex 2:23
I mused, and my spirit
grew faint.   *Selah*
⁴You kept my eyes from
closing;

---

*ᵃ10 Or Surely the wrath of men brings you praise, / and with the remainder of wrath you arm
yourself*

I was too troubled to speak.
⁵I thought about the former
       days,   Dt 32:7
   the years of long ago;
⁶I remembered my songs in
       the night.
   My heart mused and my
       spirit inquired:

⁷"Will the Lord reject forever?
   Will he never show his
       favor again?   Ps 85:1
⁸Has his unfailing love
       vanished forever?   Ps 6:4
   Has his promise failed for
       all time?   2Pe 3:9
⁹Has God forgotten to be
       merciful?   Ps 25:6
   Has he in anger withheld
       his compassion?"   Selah

¹⁰Then I thought, "To this I
       will appeal:
   the years of the right hand
       of the Most High."   Ex 15:6
¹¹I will remember the deeds of
       the LORD;
   yes, I will remember your
       miracles of long ago.
¹²I will meditate on all your
       works   Ge 24:63
   and consider all your
       mighty deeds.   Ps 143:5

¹³Your ways, O God, are holy.
   What god is so great as our
       God?   Ex 15:11
¹⁴You are the God who
       performs miracles;   Ex 3:20
   you display your power
       among the peoples.
¹⁵With your mighty arm you
       redeemed your people,

   the descendants of Jacob
       and Joseph.   Selah

¹⁶The waters saw you, O God,
   the waters saw you and
       writhed;   Ps 114:4
   the very depths were
       convulsed.
¹⁷The clouds poured down
       water,   Jdg 5:4
   the skies resounded with
       thunder;   Ex 9:23
   your arrows flashed back
       and forth.   Dt 32:23
¹⁸Your thunder was heard in
       the whirlwind,   Ps 55:8
   your lightning lit up the
       world;   2Sa 22:13
   the earth trembled and
       quaked.   Jdg 5:4
¹⁹Your path led through the
       sea,   Job 9:8
   your way through the
       mighty waters,
   though your footprints
       were not seen.

²⁰You led your people like a
       flock   Ps 78:52
   by the hand of Moses and
       Aaron.   Ex 4:16

Psalm 78

A *maskil*[a] of Asaph.

¹O my people, hear my
       teaching;   Isa 51:4
   listen to the words of my
       mouth.
²I will open my mouth in
       parables,   Ps 49:4
   I will utter hidden things,
       things from of old—

─────────────────
[a]Title: Probably a literary or musical term

³what we have heard and
    known,
  what our fathers have told
    us.   Jdg 6:13
⁴We will not hide them from
    their children;   Dt 11:19
  we will tell the next
    generation   Dt 32:7
  the praiseworthy deeds of
    the LORD,   Ps 26:7
  his power, and the wonders
    he has done.   Job 5:9
⁵He decreed statutes for Jacob
  and established the law in
    Israel,
  which he commanded our
    forefathers
  to teach their children,
⁶so the next generation would
    know them,
  even the children yet to be
    born,   Ps 22:31
  and they in turn would tell
    their children.
⁷Then they would put their
    trust in God
  and would not forget his
    deeds   Dt 6:12
  but would keep his
    commands.   Dt 5:29
⁸They would not be like their
    forefathers—   2Ch 30:7
  a stubborn and rebellious
    generation,   Ex 23:21
  whose hearts were not loyal
    to God,
  whose spirits were not
    faithful to him.

⁹The men of Ephraim, though
    armed with bows,   1Ch 12:2
  turned back on the day of
    battle;   Jdg 20:39

¹⁰they did not keep God's
    covenant   Jos 7:11
  and refused to live by his
    law.   Ex 16:28
¹¹They forgot what he had
    done,   Ps 106:13
  the wonders he had shown
    them.
¹²He did miracles in the sight
    of their fathers   Ne 9:17
  in the land of Egypt, in the
    region of Zoan.   Nu 13:22
¹³He divided the sea and led
    them through;   Ex 14:21
  he made the water stand
    firm like a wall.   Ex 14:22
¹⁴He guided them with the
    cloud by day
  and with light from the fire
    all night.   Ex 13:21
¹⁵He split the rocks in the
    desert   Nu 20:11
  and gave them water as
    abundant as the seas;
¹⁶he brought streams out of a
    rocky crag
  and made water flow down
    like rivers.

¹⁷But they continued to sin
    against him,   Dt 9:22
  rebelling in the desert
    against the Most High.
¹⁸They willfully put God to the
    test   Ex 17:2
  by demanding the food
    they craved.   Ex 15:24
¹⁹They spoke against God,
    saying,   Nu 21:5
  "Can God spread a table in
    the desert?
²⁰When he struck the rock,
    water gushed out,   Nu 20:11

and streams flowed
    abundantly.
But can he also give us food?
Can he supply meat for his
    people?" Nu 11:18
21When the LORD heard them,
    he was very angry;
his fire broke out against
    Jacob, Nu 11:1
and his wrath rose against
    Israel,
22for they did not believe in
    God
or trust in his deliverance.
23Yet he gave a command to
    the skies above
and opened the doors of
    the heavens; Ge 7:11
24he rained down manna for
    the people to eat, Ex 16:4
he gave them the grain of
    heaven.
25Men ate the bread of angels;
he sent them all the food
    they could eat.
26He let loose the east wind
    from the heavens Nu 11:31
and led forth the south
    wind by his power.
27He rained meat down on
    them like dust,
flying birds like sand on the
    seashore. Ex 16:13
28He made them come down
    inside their camp,
all around their tents.
29They ate till they had more
    than enough, Nu 11:20
for he had given them what
    they craved.
30But before they turned from
    the food they craved,
even while it was still in
    their mouths, Nu 11:33

31God's anger rose against
    them;
he put to death the
    sturdiest among them,
cutting down the young
    men of Israel. Isa 10:16

32In spite of all this, they kept
    on sinning;
in spite of his wonders,
    they did not believe.
33So he ended their days in
    futility Nu 14:29,35
and their years in terror.
34Whenever God slew them,
    they would seek him;
they eagerly turned to him
    again.
35They remembered that God
    was their Rock, Ge 49:24
that God Most High was
    their Redeemer. Dt 9:26
36But then they would flatter
    him with their mouths,
lying to him with their
    tongues; Eze 33:31
37their hearts were not loyal to
    him, Ac 8:21
they were not faithful to his
    covenant.
38Yet he was merciful; Ex 34:6
he forgave their iniquities
and did not destroy them.
Time after time he restrained
    his anger Job 9:13
and did not stir up his full
    wrath.
39He remembered that they
    were but flesh, Ge 6:3
a passing breeze that does
    not return. Job 7:7

40How often they rebelled
    against him in the desert

and grieved him in the
  wasteland!   Eph 4:30
⁴¹Again and again they put
  God to the test;   Ex 17:2
  they vexed the Holy One of
  Israel.   2Ki 19:22
⁴²They did not remember his
  power—   Jdg 3:7
  the day he redeemed them
  from the oppressor,
⁴³the day he displayed his
  miraculous signs in
  Egypt,   Ex 10:1
  his wonders in the region of
  Zoan.   Ex 3:20
⁴⁴He turned their rivers to
  blood;   Ex 7:20
  they could not drink from
  their streams.
⁴⁵He sent swarms of flies that
  devoured them,   Ex 8:24
  and frogs that devastated
  them.   Ex 8:2,6
⁴⁶He gave their crops to the
  grasshopper,   Na 3:15
  their produce to the locust.
⁴⁷He destroyed their vines
  with hail   Ex 9:23
  and their sycamore-figs
  with sleet.
⁴⁸He gave over their cattle to
  the hail,
  their livestock to bolts of
  lightning.   Ex 9:25
⁴⁹He unleashed against them
  his hot anger,   Ex 15:7
  his wrath, indignation and
  hostility—
  a band of destroying
  angels.   Ge 19:13
⁵⁰He prepared a path for his
  anger;
  he did not spare them from
  death

but gave them over to the
  plague.
⁵¹He struck down all the
  firstborn of Egypt,   Ex 12:12
  the firstfruits of manhood
  in the tents of Ham.
⁵²But he brought his people
  out like a flock;   Job 21:11
  he led them like sheep
  through the desert.
⁵³He guided them safely, so
  they were unafraid;
  but the sea engulfed their
  enemies.   Ex 15:7
⁵⁴Thus he brought them to the
  border of his holy land,
  to the hill country his right
  hand had taken.   Ps 44:3
⁵⁵He drove out nations before
  them   Ps 44:2
  and allotted their lands to
  them as an inheritance;
  he settled the tribes of Israel
  in their homes.
⁵⁶But they put God to the test
  and rebelled against the
  Most High;
  they did not keep his
  statutes.
⁵⁷Like their fathers they were
  disloyal and faithless,
  as unreliable as a faulty
  bow.   Ex 20:27
⁵⁸They angered him with their
  high places;   Lev 26:30
  they aroused his jealousy
  with their idols.   Ex 20:4
⁵⁹When God heard them, he
  was very angry;   Lev 26:28
  he rejected Israel
  completely.   Dt 32:19
⁶⁰He abandoned the tabernacle
  of Shiloh,   Jos 18:1

the tent he had set up
    among men.   Eze 8:6
61He sent ⌊the ark of⌋ his might
    into captivity,   Ps 132:8
    his splendor into the hands
    of the enemy.
62He gave his people over to
    the sword;   Dt 28:25
    he was very angry with his
    inheritance.   1Sa 10:1
63Fire consumed their young
    men,   Nu 11:1
    and their maidens had no
    wedding songs;   1Ki 4:32
64their priests were put to the
    sword,   1Sa 4:17
    and their widows could not
    weep.

65Then the Lord awoke as from
    sleep,   Ps 44:23
    as a man wakes from the
    stupor of wine.
66He beat back his enemies;
    he put them to everlasting
    shame.   1Sa 5:6
67Then he rejected the tents of
    Joseph,
    he did not choose the tribe
    of Ephraim;   Jer 7:15
68but he chose the tribe of
    Judah,   Nu 1:7
    Mount Zion, which he
    loved.   Ex 15:17
69He built his sanctuary like
    the heights,   Ps 15:1
    like the earth that he
    established forever.
70He chose David his servant
    and took him from the
    sheep pens;   1Sa 16:1
71from tending the sheep he
    brought him   Ge 37:2

to be the shepherd of his
    people Jacob,   Pr 28:9
    of Israel his inheritance.
72And David shepherded them
    with integrity of heart;
    with skillful hands he led
    them.   Ge 17:1

Psalm 79

A psalm of Asaph.

1O God, the nations have
    invaded your
    inheritance;   Ex 34:9
    they have defiled your holy
    temple,
    they have reduced
    Jerusalem to rubble.
2They have given the dead
    bodies of your servants
    as food to the birds of the
    air,   Rev 19:17-18
    the flesh of your saints to
    the beasts of the earth.
3They have poured out blood
    like water
    all around Jerusalem,
    and there is no one to bury
    the dead.   Jer 16:4
4We are objects of reproach to
    our neighbors,
    of scorn and derision to
    those around us.   Ps 39:8

5How long, O Lord? Will you
    be angry forever?   Ps 74:10
    How long will your
    jealousy burn like fire?
6Pour out your wrath on the
    nations   Ps 2:5
    that do not acknowledge
    you,   Ps 147:20

on the kingdoms
  that do not call on your
    name;   Ps 14:4
7for they have devoured Jacob
  and destroyed his
    homeland.   Isa 9:12
8Do not hold against us the
  sins of the fathers;   Ge 9:25
  may your mercy come
    quickly to meet us,
  for we are in desperate
    need.   Ps 116:6

9Help us, O God our Savior,
  for the glory of your name;
deliver us and forgive our
    sins
  for your name's sake.   Ps 25:11
10Why should the nations say,
  "Where is their God?"   Ps 42:3
Before our eyes, make
    known among the
    nations
  that you avenge the
    outpoured blood of
    your servants.   Ps 94:1
11May the groans of the
    prisoners come before
    you;
  by the strength of your arm
  preserve those condemned
    to die.

12Pay back into the laps of our
    neighbors seven times
  the reproach they have
    hurled at you, O Lord.
13Then we your people, the
    sheep of your pasture,
  will praise you forever;   Ps 44:8
from generation to
    generation
  we will recount your
    praise.

Psalm 80

For the director of music. To the
tune of, "The Lilies of the
Covenant." Of Asaph. A psalm.

1Hear us, O Shepherd of
    Israel,
  you who lead Joseph like a
    flock;   Ps 77:20
you who sit enthroned
    between the cherubim,
    shine forth
2 before Ephraim, Benjamin
    and Manasseh.   Ex 25:22
  Awaken your might;   Ps 35:23
  come and save us.   Ps 54:1

3Restore us, O God;   Ps 71:20
  make your face shine upon
    us,
  that we may be saved.

4O LORD God Almighty,
  how long will your anger
    smolder   Ps 74:10
  against the prayers of your
    people?
5You have fed them with the
    bread of tears;   Job 3:24
  you have made them drink
    tears by the bowlful.
6You have made us a source
    of contention to our
    neighbors,
  and our enemies mock us.

7Restore us, O God Almighty;
  make your face shine upon
    us,
  that we may be saved.

8You brought a vine out of
    Egypt;   Isa 5:1-2
  you drove out the nations
    and planted it.   Ex 15:17

9You cleared the ground for it,
  and it took root and filled
    the land.
10The mountains were covered
   with its shade,
  the mighty cedars with its
    branches.
11It sent out its boughs to the
   Sea,a
  its shoots as far as the
    River.b   Ps 72:8

12Why have you broken down
   its walls   Ps 89:40
  so that all who pass by pick
    its grapes?
13Boars from the forest ravage
   it   Jer 5:6
  and the creatures of the
    field feed on it.
14Return to us, O God
   Almighty!
  Look down from heaven
    and see!   Dt 26:15
  Watch over this vine,
15 the root your right hand
    has planted,
  the sonc you have raised up
    for yourself.

16Your vine is cut down, it is
   burned with fire;   Ps 79:1
  at your rebuke your people
    perish.   Dt 28:20
17Let your hand rest on the
   man at your right hand,
  the son of man you have
    raised up for yourself.
18Then we will not turn away
   from you;
  revive us, and we will call
    on your name.   Ps 85:6

19Restore us, O LORD God
   Almighty;
  make your face shine upon
    us,
  that we may be saved.

Psalm 81

For the director of music.
According to *gittith*.d Of Asaph.

1Sing for joy to God our
   strength;
  shout aloud to the God of
    Jacob!   Ps 66:1
2Begin the music, strike the
   tambourine,   Ex 15:20
  play the melodious harp
    and lyre.   Ps 92:3

3Sound the ram's horn at the
   New Moon,   Ex 19:13
  and when the moon is full,
    on the day of our Feast;
4this is a decree for Israel,
  an ordinance of the God of
    Jacob.
5He established it as a statute
   for Joseph
  when he went out against
    Egypt,   Ex 11:4
  where we heard a language
    we did not understand.e

6He says, "I removed the
   burden from their
    shoulders;
  their hands were set free
    from the basket.   Isa 9:4
7In your distress you called
   and I rescued you,   Ex 2:23
  I answered you out of a
    thundercloud;   Ex 19:19

a11 Probably the Mediterranean   b11 That is, the Euphrates   c15 Or *branch*
dTitle: Probably a musical term   e5 Or / *and we heard a voice we had not known*

I tested you at the waters of
Meribah.   *Selah*

8"Hear, O my people, and I
will warn you—   Ps 50:7
if you would but listen to
me, O Israel!
9You shall have no foreign
god among you;   Ex 20:3
you shall not bow down to
an alien god.
10I am the LORD your God,
who brought you up out of
Egypt.   Ex 6:6
Open wide your mouth and
I will fill it.   Eze 2:8

11"But my people would not
listen to me;
Israel would not submit to
me.   Ex 32:1-6
12So I gave them over to their
stubborn hearts   Eze 20:25
to follow their own devices.

13"If my people would but
listen to me,   Dt 5:29
if Israel would follow my
ways,
14how quickly would I subdue
their enemies   Ps 47:3
and turn my hand against
their foes!   Am 1:8
15Those who hate the LORD
would cringe before
him,   2Sa 22:45
and their punishment
would last forever.
16But you would be fed with
the finest of wheat;   Dt 32:14
with honey from the rock I
would satisfy you."

Psalm 82

A psalm of Asaph.

1God presides in the great
assembly;
he gives judgment among
the "gods":   Ps 7:8

2"How long will you[a] defend
the unjust
and show partiality to the
wicked?   *Selah*
3Defend the cause of the weak
and fatherless;   Dt 24:17
maintain the rights of the
poor and oppressed.
4Rescue the weak and needy;
deliver them from the hand
of the wicked.

5"They know nothing, they
understand nothing.
They walk about in
darkness;   Job 30:26
all the foundations of the
earth are shaken.   Jdg 5:4

6"I said, 'You are "gods";
you are all sons of the Most
High.'   Jn 10:34
7But you will die like mere
men;   Ps 49:12
you will fall like every other
ruler."

8Rise up, O God, judge the
earth,   Ps 12:5
for all the nations are your
inheritance.   Ps 2:8

---

[a]2 The Hebrew is plural.

Psalm 83

A song. A psalm of Asaph.

¹O God, do not keep silent;
   be not quiet, O God, be not
   still.   Ps 28:1
²See how your enemies are
   astir,   Ps 2:1
   how your foes rear their
   heads.   Jdg 8:28
³With cunning they conspire
   against your people;
   they plot against those you
   cherish.   Ps 17:14
⁴"Come," they say, "let us
   destroy them as a
   nation,   Est 3:6
   that the name of Israel be
   remembered no more."

⁵With one mind they plot
   together;   Ps 2:2
   they form an alliance
   against you—
⁶the tents of Edom and the
   Ishmaelites,   Ps 137:7
   of Moab and the Hagrites,
⁷Gebal,ᵃ Ammon and
   Amalek,   Ge 14:7
   Philistia, with the people of
   Tyre.   Isa 23:3
⁸Even Assyria has joined
   them   Ge 10:11
   to lend strength to the
   descendants of Lot.
                                        Selah

⁹Do to them as you did to
   Midian,   Ge 25:2
   as you did to Sisera and
   Jabin at the river Kishon,
¹⁰who perished at Endor   1Sa 28:7

and became like refuse on
   the ground.   2Ki 9:37
¹¹Make their nobles like Oreb
   and Zeeb,   Jdg 7:25
   all their princes like Zebah
   and Zalmunna,   Jdg 8:5
¹²who said, "Let us take
   possession   2Ch 20:11
   of the pasturelands of
   God."

¹³Make them like tumbleweed,
   O my God,
   like chaff before the wind.
¹⁴As fire consumes the forest
   or a flame sets the
   mountains ablaze,   Dt 32:22
¹⁵so pursue them with your
   tempest   Ps 50:3
   and terrify them with your
   storm.   Job 9:17
¹⁶Cover their faces with shame
   so that men will seek your
   name, O LORD.   Ps 34:5

¹⁷May they ever be ashamed
   and dismayed;   2Ki 19:26
   may they perish in
   disgrace.   Ps 35:4
¹⁸Let them know that you,
   whose name is the
   LORD—   Ps 68:4
   that you alone are the Most
   High over all the earth.

Psalm 84

*For the director of music.
According to gittith.ᵇ Of the Sons
of Korah. A psalm.*

¹How lovely is your dwelling
   place,
   O LORD Almighty!   Dt 33:27

ᵃ7 That is, Byblos   ᵇTitle: Probably a musical term

[2]My soul yearns, even faints,
  for the courts of the LORD;
my heart and my flesh cry
  out
  for the living God.   Jos 3:10

[3]Even the sparrow has found
  a home,
and the swallow a nest for
  herself,
where she may have her
  young—
a place near your altar,   Ps 43:4
O LORD Almighty, my King
  and my God.   Jer 44:11
[4]Blessed are those who dwell
  in your house;
they are ever praising you.
                    Selah

[5]Blessed are those whose
  strength is in you,   Ps 81:1
who have set their hearts
  on pilgrimage.   Jer 31:6
[6]As they pass through the
  Valley of Baca,
they make it a place of
  springs;   Job 38:26
the autumn rains also cover
  it with pools. [a]   Joel 2:23
[7]They go from strength to
  strength,   Job 17:9
till each appears before God
  in Zion.   1Ki 8:1

[8]Hear my prayer, O LORD
  God Almighty;   Ps 4:1
listen to me, O God of
  Jacob.   *Selah*
[9]Look upon our shield, [b]
  O God;   Ps 59:11
look with favor on your
  anointed one.   1Sa 16:6

[10]Better is one day in your
  courts
  than a thousand elsewhere;
I would rather be a
  doorkeeper in the house
  of my God   1Ch 23:5
than dwell in the tents of
  the wicked.
[11]For the LORD God is a sun
  and shield;   Ge 15:1
the LORD bestows favor and
  honor;
no good thing does he
  withhold
from those whose walk is
  blameless.   Ps 34:10
[12]O LORD Almighty,
  blessed is the man who
  trusts in you.   Ps 2:12

Psalm 85

For the director of music. Of the
Sons of Korah. A psalm.

[1]You showed favor to your
  land, O LORD;
you restored the fortunes of
  Jacob.   Dt 30:3
[2]You forgave the iniquity of
  your people   Nu 14:19
and covered all their sins.
                    Selah
[3]You set aside all your wrath
and turned from your fierce
  anger.   Ex 32:12

[4]Restore us again, O God our
  Savior,   Ps 65:5
and put away your
  displeasure toward us.
[5]Will you be angry with us
  forever?   Ps 50:21

[a]6 Or *blessings*   [b]9 Or *sovereign*

Will you prolong your
  anger through all
  generations?
⁶Will you not revive us again,
  that your people may
  rejoice in you?   Php 3:1
⁷Show us your unfailing love,
  O Lᴏʀᴅ,   Ps 6:4
and grant us your salvation.

⁸I will listen to what God the
  Lᴏʀᴅ will say;
he promises peace to his
  people, his saints—Lev 26:6
but let them not return to
  folly.   Pr 26:11
⁹Surely his salvation is near
  those who fear him,
  that his glory may dwell in
  our land.   Ex 29:43

¹⁰Love and faithfulness meet
  together;   Ps 89:14
  righteousness and peace
  kiss each other.   Ps 72:2-3
¹¹Faithfulness springs forth
  from the earth,
and righteousness looks
  down from heaven. Isa 45:8
¹²The Lᴏʀᴅ will indeed give
  what is good,   Ps 84:11
and our land will yield its
  harvest.   Lev 26:4
¹³Righteousness goes before
  him
and prepares the way for
  his steps.

Psalm 86

A prayer of David.

¹Hear, O Lᴏʀᴅ, and answer
  me,   Ps 17:6
for I am poor and needy.

²Guard my life, for I am
  devoted to you.
You are my God; save your
  servant
who trusts in you. Ps 25:2
³Have mercy on me, O Lord,
  for I call to you all day long.
⁴Bring joy to your servant,
  for to you, O Lord,
I lift up my soul.   Ps 46:5

⁵You are forgiving and good,
  O Lord,
abounding in love to all
  who call to you.   Ex 34:6
⁶Hear my prayer, O Lᴏʀᴅ;
  listen to my cry for mercy.
⁷In the day of my trouble I
  will call to you,   Job 22:27
for you will answer me.

⁸Among the gods there is
  none like you, O Lord;
no deeds can compare with
  yours.
⁹All the nations you have
  made
will come and worship
  before you, O Lord; Ps 66:4
they will bring glory to your
  name.   Isa 43:7
¹⁰For you are great and do
  marvelous deeds;   Ex 3:20
you alone are God.   Dt 6:4

¹¹Teach me your way, O Lᴏʀᴅ,
  and I will walk in your
  truth;   Ps 26:3
give me an undivided heart,
  that I may fear your name.
¹²I will praise you, O Lord my
  God, with all my heart;
I will glorify your name
  forever.   Ps 9:1

¹³For great is your love toward
    me;
  you have delivered me from
    the depths of the grave. ^a

¹⁴The arrogant are attacking
    me, O God;
  a band of ruthless men
    seeks my life—
  men without regard for
    you.   Ps 54:3
¹⁵But you, O Lord, are a
    compassionate and
    gracious God,   Ps 51:1
  slow to anger, abounding in
    love and faithfulness.
¹⁶Turn to me and have mercy
    on me;   Ps 9:13
  grant your strength to your
    servant   Ps 18:1
  and save the son of your
    maidservant. ^b   Ps 116:16
¹⁷Give me a sign of your
    goodness,   Ex 3:12
  that my enemies may see it
    and be put to shame,
  for you, O LORD, have
    helped me and
    comforted me.

Psalm 87

Of the Sons of Korah. A psalm.
A song.

¹He has set his foundation on
    the holy mountain;   Ps 48:1
² the LORD loves the gates of
    Zion   Ps 2:6
  more than all the dwellings
    of Jacob.

³Glorious things are said of
    you,
  O city of God: Selah
⁴"I will record Rahab^c and
    Babylon   Job 9:13
  among those who
    acknowledge me—
  Philistia too, and Tyre, along
    with Cush^d—   2Sa 8:1
  and will say, 'This^e one was
    born in Zion.'"   Isa 19:25

⁵Indeed, of Zion it will be
    said,
  "This one and that one
    were born in her,
  and the Most High himself
    will establish her."
⁶The LORD will write in the
    register of the peoples:
  "This one was born in
    Zion."   Selah
⁷As they make music they will
    sing,   Ps 149:3
  "All my fountains are in
    you."   Ps 36:9

Psalm 88

A song. A psalm of the Sons of
Korah. For the director of music.
According to *mahalath leannoth.*^f
A *maskil*^g of Heman the Ezrahite.

¹O LORD, the God who saves
    me,   Ps 51:14
  day and night I cry out
    before you.   Ps 3:4
²May my prayer come before
    you;
  turn your ear to my cry.

^a13 Hebrew *Sheol*   ^b16 Or *save your faithful son*   ^c4 A poetic name for Egypt
^d4 That is, the upper Nile region   ^e4 Or "*O Rahab and Babylon, / Philistia, Tyre and
Cush, / I will record concerning those who acknowledge me: / 'This*   ^fTitle: Possibly a tune,
"The Suffering of Affliction"   ^gTitle: Probably a literary or musical term

³For my soul is full of trouble
and my life draws near the
grave. *a*   Job 33:22
⁴I am counted among those
who go down to the pit;
I am like a man without
strength.   Ps 18:1
⁵I am set apart with the dead,
like the slain who lie in the
grave,
whom you remember no
more,
who are cut off from your
care.   Ps 31:22

⁶You have put me in the
lowest pit,
in the darkest depths.   Ps 30:1
⁷Your wrath lies heavily upon
me;   Ps 7:11
you have overwhelmed me
with all your waves.
                    Selah
⁸You have taken from me my
closest friends   Job 19:13
and have made me
repulsive to them.
I am confined and cannot
escape;   Job 3:23
⁹ my eyes are dim with grief.

I call to you, O Lᴏʀᴅ, every
day;   Ps 5:2
I spread out my hands to
you.   Job 11:13
¹⁰Do you show your wonders
to the dead?
Do those who are dead rise
up and praise you? *Selah*
¹¹Is your love declared in the
grave,
your faithfulness in
Destruction*b*?   Ps 30:9

¹²Are your wonders known in
the place of darkness,
or your righteous deeds in
the land of oblivion?
¹³But I cry to you for help,
O Lᴏʀᴅ;   Ps 30:2
in the morning my prayer
comes before you.
¹⁴Why, O Lᴏʀᴅ, do you reject
me   Ps 43:2
and hide your face from
me?   Ps 13:1
¹⁵From my youth I have been
afflicted and close to
death;   Ps 9:12
I have suffered your terrors
and am in despair.   2Co 4:8
¹⁶Your wrath has swept over
me;   Ps 7:11
your terrors have destroyed
me.   Job 6:4
¹⁷All day long they surround
me like a flood;   Ps 124:4
they have completely
engulfed me.
¹⁸You have taken my
companions and loved
ones from me;   Ps 38:11
the darkness is my closest
friend.

Psalm 89

A *maskilc* of Ethan the Ezrahite.

¹I will sing of the Lᴏʀᴅ's great
love forever;   Ps 59:16
with my mouth I will make
your faithfulness known
through all generations.
²I will declare that your love
stands firm forever,

---

*a*3 Hebrew *Sheol*   *b*11 Hebrew *Abaddon*   *c*Title: Probably a literary or musical term

that you established your
    faithfulness in heaven
    itself.   Ps 36:5

³You said, "I have made a
    covenant with my
    chosen one,
I have sworn to David my
    servant,
⁴'I will establish your line
    forever
and make your throne firm
    through all
    generations.' "   *Selah*

⁵The heavens praise your
    wonders, O LORD,   Ps 19:1
    your faithfulness too, in the
    assembly of the holy
    ones.   Ps 1:5
⁶For who in the skies above
    can compare with the
    LORD?
Who is like the LORD
    among the heavenly
    beings?   Ge 1:26
⁷In the council of the holy
    ones God is greatly
    feared;   Ps 111:1
he is more awesome than
    all who surround him.
⁸O LORD God Almighty, who
    is like you?   Isa 6:3
You are mighty, O LORD,
    and your faithfulness
    surrounds you.

⁹You rule over the surging
    sea;
    when its waves mount up,
    you still them.   Ps 65:7
¹⁰You crushed Rahab like one
    of the slain;   Job 9:13

with your strong arm you
    scattered your enemies.
¹¹The heavens are yours, and
    yours also the earth;
you founded the world and
    all that is in it.   Ge 1:1
¹²You created the north and
    the south;
Tabor and Hermon sing for
    joy at your name.   Jos 19:22
¹³Your arm is endued with
    power;
    your hand is strong, your
    right hand exalted.   Jos 4:24

¹⁴Righteousness and justice are
    the foundation of your
    throne;   Ps 97:2
love and faithfulness go
    before you.   Ps 85:10-11
¹⁵Blessed are those who have
    learned to acclaim you,
who walk in the light of
    your presence, O LORD.
¹⁶They rejoice in your name all
    day long;   Ps 30:4
    they exult in your
    righteousness.
¹⁷For you are their glory and
    strength,   Ps 18:1
and by your favor you exalt
    our horn. *ᵃ*   Ps 75:10
¹⁸Indeed, our shield*ᵇ* belongs
    to the LORD,   Ps 18:2
our king to the Holy One of
    Israel.   Ps 47:9

¹⁹Once you spoke in a vision,
to your faithful people you
    said:
"I have bestowed strength on
    a warrior;

ᵃ17 *Horn* here symbolizes strong one.   ᵇ18 Or *sovereign*

I have exalted a young man
  from among the people.
20I have found David my
  servant;   Ac 13:22
with my sacred oil I have
  anointed him.   Ex 29:7
21My hand will sustain him;
  surely my arm will
  strengthen him.   Ps 18:35
22No enemy will subject him to
  tribute;   Jdg 3:15
no wicked man will oppress
  him.   2Sa 7:10
23I will crush his foes before
  him   Ps 18:40
and strike down his
  adversaries.   2Sa 7:9
24My faithful love will be with
  him,   2Sa 7:15
and through my name his
  horn*a* will be exalted.
25I will set his hand over the
  sea,
his right hand over the
  rivers.   Ps 72:8
26He will call out to me, 'You
  are my Father,   2Sa 7:14
my God, the Rock my
  Savior.'   Ps 62:2
27I will also appoint him my
  firstborn,   Col 1:18
the most exalted of the
  kings of the earth.   Nu 24:7
28I will maintain my love to
  him forever,
and my covenant with him
  will never fail.   Isa 55:3
29I will establish his line
  forever,
his throne as long as the
  heavens endure.

30"If his sons forsake my law

and do not follow my
  statutes,
31if they violate my decrees
  and fail to keep my
  commands,
32I will punish their sin with
  the rod,
  their iniquity with flogging;
33but I will not take my love
  from him,   2Sa 7:15
nor will I ever betray my
  faithfulness.
34I will not violate my covenant
  or alter what my lips have
  uttered.   Nu 23:19
35Once for all, I have sworn by
  my holiness—
  and I will not lie to David—
36that his line will continue
  forever
  and his throne endure
  before me like the sun;
37it will be established forever
  like the moon,
  the faithful witness in the
  sky."   *Selah*

38But you have rejected, you
  have spurned,   1Ch 28:9
you have been very angry
  with your anointed
  one.
39You have renounced the
  covenant with your
  servant
and have defiled his crown
  in the dust.   La 5:16
40You have broken through all
  his walls   Ps 80:12
and reduced his
  strongholds to ruins.
41All who pass by have
  plundered him;   Jdg 2:14

---

a24 Horn here symbolizes strength.

he has become the scorn of
  his neighbors.   Ps 44:13
⁴²You have exalted the right
  hand of his foes;
you have made all his
  enemies rejoice.   Ps 13:2
⁴³You have turned back the
  edge of his sword
and have not supported
  him in battle.   Ps 44:10
⁴⁴You have put an end to his
  splendor
and cast his throne to the
  ground.
⁴⁵You have cut short the days
  of his youth;   Ps 39:5
you have covered him with
  a mantle of shame. *Selah*

⁴⁶How long, O LORD? Will you
  hide yourself forever?
How long will your wrath
  burn like fire?   Ps 79:5
⁴⁷Remember how fleeting is
  my life.   Ge 47:9
For what futility you have
  created all men!
⁴⁸What man can live and not
  see death,
or save himself from the
  power of the grave*a*?
                          Selah
⁴⁹O Lord, where is your former
  great love,
which in your faithfulness
  you swore to David?
⁵⁰Remember, Lord, how your
  servant has*b* been
  mocked,   Ps 69:19
how I bear in my heart the
  taunts of all the
  nations,

⁵¹the taunts with which your
  enemies have mocked,
  O LORD,
with which they have
  mocked every step of
  your anointed one.   Ps 74:10

⁵²Praise be to the LORD forever!
  Amen and Amen.   Ps 41:13

BOOK IV

Psalms 90–106

Psalm 90

A prayer of Moses the man of
God.

¹Lord, you have been our
  dwelling place   Dt 33:27
  throughout all generations.
²Before the mountains were
  born   Job 15:7
or you brought forth the
  earth and the world,
from everlasting to
  everlasting you are God.

³You turn men back to dust,
  saying, "Return to dust,
  O sons of men."   Ge 2:7
⁴For a thousand years in your
  sight
are like a day that has just
  gone by,
or like a watch in the night.
⁵You sweep men away in the
  sleep of death;   Ge 19:15
they are like the new grass
  of the morning—
⁶though in the morning it
  springs up new,

---

a48 Hebrew *Sheol*   *b50* Or *your servants have*

by evening it is dry and
   withered.   Isa 40:6-8

⁷We are consumed by your
   anger
and terrified by your
   indignation.
⁸You have set our iniquities
   before you,
our secret sins in the light
   of your presence.   Ps 19:12
⁹All our days pass away
   under your wrath;
we finish our years with a
   moan.   Ps 78:33
¹⁰The length of our days is
   seventy years—   Isa 23:15
or eighty, if we have the
   strength;   2Sa 19:35
yet their span*ᵃ* is but trouble
   and sorrow,   Job 5:7
for they quickly pass, and
   we fly away.   Job 20:8

¹¹Who knows the power of
   your anger?
For your wrath is as great
   as the fear that is due
   you.   Ps 76:7
¹²Teach us to number our days
   aright,   Ps 39:4
that we may gain a heart of
   wisdom.   Dt 32:29

¹³Relent, O Lᴏʀᴅ! How long
   will it be?   Ps 6:3
Have compassion on your
   servants.   Dt 32:36
¹⁴Satisfy us in the morning
   with your unfailing love,
that we may sing for joy
   and be glad all our days.

¹⁵Make us glad for as many
   days as you have
   afflicted us,
for as many years as we
   have seen trouble.
¹⁶May your deeds be shown to
   your servants,
your splendor to their
   children.   Ps 44:1

¹⁷May the favor*ᵇ* of the Lord
   our God rest upon us;
establish the work of our
   hands for us—
yes, establish the work of
   our hands.   Isa 26:12

Psalm 91

¹He who dwells in the shelter
   of the Most High   Ex 33:22
will rest in the shadow of
   the Almighty.*ᶜ*   Ps 63:7
²I will say*ᵈ* of the Lᴏʀᴅ, "He
   is my refuge and my
   fortress,   2Sa 22:2
my God, in whom I trust."

³Surely he will save you from
   the fowler's snare Ps 124:7
and from the deadly
   pestilence.   1Ki 8:37
⁴He will cover you with his
   feathers,
and under his wings you
   will find refuge;   Ru 2:12
his faithfulness will be your
   shield and rampart. Dt 32:10
⁵You will not fear the terror of
   night,   Job 5:21
nor the arrow that flies by
   day,

ᵃ10 Or *yet the best of them*   *ᵇ17* Or *beauty*   *ᶜ1* Hebrew *Shaddai*   *ᵈ2* Or *He says*

⁶nor the pestilence that stalks
in the darkness,
    nor the plague that destroys
    at midday.
⁷A thousand may fall at your
side,
    ten thousand at your right
    hand,
    but it will not come near
    you.
⁸You will only observe with
your eyes
    and see the punishment of
    the wicked.   Ps 37:34

⁹If you make the Most High
your dwelling—
    even the LORD, who is my
    refuge—
¹⁰then no harm will befall you,
    no disaster will come near
    your tent.
¹¹For he will command his
angels concerning you
    to guard you in all your
    ways;   Ps 34:7
¹²they will lift you up in their
hands,
    so that you will not strike
    your foot against a
    stone.   Mt 4:6
¹³You will tread upon the lion
and the cobra;
    you will trample the great
    lion and the serpent.

¹⁴"Because he loves me," says
the LORD, "I will rescue
him;
    I will protect him, for he
    acknowledges my name.
¹⁵He will call upon me, and I
will answer him;
    I will be with him in
    trouble,

I will deliver him and honor
him.   1Sa 2:30
¹⁶With long life will I satisfy
him   Dt 6:2
    and show him my
    salvation."   Ps 50:23

Psalm 92

A psalm. A song. For the Sabbath
day.

¹It is good to praise the LORD
    and make music to your
        name, O Most High, Ps 9:2
²to proclaim your love in the
        morning   Ps 55:17
    and your faithfulness at
        night,
³to the music of the
        ten-stringed lyre   Ps 71:22
    and the melody of the harp.

⁴For you make me glad by
        your deeds, O LORD;
    I sing for joy at the works of
        your hands.   Ps 8:6
⁵How great are your works,
        O LORD,   Job 36:24
    how profound your
        thoughts!   Ps 40:5
⁶The senseless man does not
        know,   Ps 73:22
    fools do not understand,
⁷that though the wicked
        spring up like grass
    and all evildoers flourish,
they will be forever
        destroyed.   Ps 37:2

⁸But you, O LORD, are exalted
forever.

⁹For surely your enemies,
        O LORD,   Ps 45:5

surely your enemies will
perish;
all evildoers will be
scattered.   Ps 68:1
10You have exalted my horn[a]
like that of a wild ox;
fine oils have been poured
upon me.   Ps 23:5
11My eyes have seen the defeat
of my adversaries;
my ears have heard the rout
of my wicked foes.   Ps 54:7

12The righteous will flourish
like a palm tree,   Ps 72:7
they will grow like a cedar
of Lebanon;   Ps 1:3
13planted in the house of the
LORD,
they will flourish in the
courts of our God.   Ps 135:2
14They will still bear fruit in old
age,   Jn 15:2
they will stay fresh and
green,
15proclaiming, "The LORD is
upright;
he is my Rock, and there is
no wickedness in him."

Psalm 93

1The LORD reigns, he is robed
in majesty;   Job 40:10
the LORD is robed in
majesty
and is armed with strength.
The world is firmly
established;   Ps 24:2
it cannot be moved.   1Ch 16:30
2Your throne was established
long ago;
you are from all eternity.   2Sa 7:16

3The seas have lifted up,
O LORD,   Ps 96:11
the seas have lifted up their
voice;   Ps 46:3
the seas have lifted up their
pounding waves.   Job 9:8
4Mightier than the thunder of
the great waters,   Ps 65:7
mightier than the breakers
of the sea—   Ps 18:4
the LORD on high is mighty.

5Your statutes stand firm;
holiness adorns your house
for endless days, O LORD.

Psalm 94

1O LORD, the God who
avenges,   Ge 4:24
O God who avenges, shine
forth.   Dt 33:2
2Rise up, O Judge of the
earth;   Ge 18:25
pay back to the proud what
they deserve.   Ps 31:23
3How long will the wicked,
O LORD;
how long will the wicked be
jubilant?   Ps 13:2

4They pour out arrogant
words;   Jer 43:2
all the evildoers are full of
boasting.   Ps 52:1
5They crush your people,
O LORD,   Ps 44:2
they oppress your
inheritance.   Ps 28:9
6They slay the widow and the
alien;   Dt 10:18
they murder the fatherless.

---

[a]10 *Horn* here symbolizes strength.

⁷They say, "The LORD does
    not see;   Job 22:14
the God of Jacob pays no
    heed."   Ge 24:12

⁸Take heed, you senseless
    ones among the
    people;
you fools, when will you
    become wise?
⁹Does he who implanted the
    ear not hear?
Does he who formed the
    eye not see?   Ex 4:11
¹⁰Does he who disciplines
    nations not punish?
Does he who teaches man
    lack knowledge?   Ex 35:34
¹¹The LORD knows the
    thoughts of man;   Ps 139:2
he knows that they are
    futile.   1Co 3:20

¹²Blessed is the man you
    discipline, O LORD,   Job 5:17
the man you teach from
    your law;   Dt 8:3
¹³you grant him relief from
    days of trouble,   Ps 86:7
till a pit is dug for the
    wicked.   Ps 7:15
¹⁴For the LORD will not reject
    his people;   Dt 31:6
he will never forsake his
    inheritance.
¹⁵Judgment will again be
    founded on
    righteousness,   Ps 97:2
and all the upright in heart
    will follow it.   Ps 7:10

¹⁶Who will rise up for me
    against the wicked?

Who will take a stand for
    me against evildoers?
¹⁷Unless the LORD had given
    me help,   Ps 124:2
I would soon have dwelt in
    the silence of death.
¹⁸When I said, "My foot is
    slipping,"   Dt 32:35
your love, O LORD,
    supported me.
¹⁹When anxiety was great
    within me,   Ecc 11:10
your consolation brought
    joy to my soul.   Job 6:10

²⁰Can a corrupt throne be
    allied with you—   Jer 22:30
one that brings on misery
    by its decrees?   Ps 58:2
²¹They band together against
    the righteous   Ps 56:6
and condemn the innocent
    to death.   Ge 18:23
²²But the LORD has become my
    fortress,
and my God the rock in
    whom I take refuge.
²³He will repay them for their
    sins   Ex 32:34
and destroy them for their
    wickedness;   Ps 9:5
the LORD our God will
    destroy them.

Psalm 95

¹Come, let us sing for joy to
    the LORD;   Ps 5:11
let us shout aloud to the
    Rock of our salvation.
²Let us come before him with
    thanksgiving   Ps 100:2
and extol him with music
    and song.   Ps 81:2

³For the LORD is the great
God,   Ps 48:1
the great King above all
gods.   Ps 96:4
⁴In his hand are the depths of
the earth,   Ps 63:9
and the mountain peaks
belong to him.
⁵The sea is his, for he made
it,
and his hands formed the
dry land.   Ge 1:9

⁶Come, let us bow down in
worship,   2Sa 12:16
let us kneel before the LORD
our Maker;   Ps 100:3
⁷for he is our God
and we are the people of
his pasture,   Ps 74:1
the flock under his care.

Today, if you hear his voice,
⁸ do not harden your hearts
as you did at Meribah,ᵃ
as you did that day at
Massahᵇ in the
desert,
⁹where your fathers tested
and tried me,   Nu 14:22
though they had seen what
I did.
¹⁰For forty years I was angry
with that generation;
I said, "They are a people
whose hearts go astray,
and they have not known
my ways."   Dt 8:6
¹¹So I declared on oath in my
anger,   Nu 14:23
"They shall never enter my
rest."   Dt 1:35

Psalm 96

¹Sing to the LORD a new song;
sing to the LORD, all the
earth.   Ps 33:3
²Sing to the LORD, praise his
name;   Ps 68:4
proclaim his salvation day
after day.   Ps 27:1
³Declare his glory among the
nations,   Ps 8:1
his marvelous deeds among
all peoples.   Ps 71:17

⁴For great is the LORD and
most worthy of praise;
he is to be feared above all
gods.   Ps 95:3
⁵For all the gods of the
nations are idols,   Lev 19:4
but the LORD made the
heavens.   Ge 1:1
⁶Splendor and majesty are
before him;   Ps 21:5
strength and glory are in
his sanctuary.   Ps 29:1

⁷Ascribe to the LORD,
O families of nations,
ascribe to the LORD glory
and strength.   Ps 22:27
⁸Ascribe to the LORD the glory
due his name;
bring an offering and come
into his courts.   Ps 65:4
⁹Worship the LORD in the
splendor of hisᶜ
holiness;   Ps 93:5
tremble before him, all the
earth.   Ps 33:8

¹⁰Say among the nations, "The
LORD reigns."   Ps 97:1

ᵃ8 *Meribah* means *quarreling.*   ᵇ8 *Massah* means *testing.*   ᶜ9 Or LORD *with the splendor of*

The world is firmly
established, it cannot be
moved; Ps 24:2
he will judge the peoples
with equity. Ps 67:4
11Let the heavens rejoice, let
the earth be glad; Ps 97:1
let the sea resound, and all
that is in it;
12 let the fields be jubilant,
and everything in them.
Then all the trees of the
forest will sing for joy;
13 they will sing before the
LORD, for he comes,
he comes to judge the
earth. Rev 19:11
He will judge the world in
righteousness Ps 7:11
and the peoples in his
truth. Ps 86:11

Psalm 97

1The LORD reigns, let the
earth be glad; Ps 96:11
let the distant shores
rejoice. Est 10:1

2Clouds and thick darkness
surround him; Ex 19:9
righteousness and justice
are the foundation of his
throne. Ps 89:14
3Fire goes before him Isa 9:19
and consumes his foes on
every side. 2Sa 22:9
4His lightning lights up the
world; Job 36:30
the earth sees and trembles.
5The mountains melt like wax
before the LORD, Ps 46:2
before the Lord of all the
earth. Jos 3:11

6The heavens proclaim his
righteousness, Ps 50:6
and all the peoples see his
glory. Ps 19:1

7All who worship images are
put to shame, Lev 26:1
those who boast in idols—
worship him, all you gods!

8Zion hears and rejoices
and the villages of Judah
are glad Ps 9:2
because of your judgments,
O LORD. Ps 48:11
9For you, O LORD, are the
Most High over all the
earth; Job 34:29
you are exalted far above all
gods. Ps 47:9

10Let those who love the LORD
hate evil, Job 28:28
for he guards the lives of
his faithful ones Ps 31:23
and delivers them from the
hand of the wicked.
11Light is shed upon the
righteous Ps 11:5
and joy on the upright in
heart. Ps 7:10
12Rejoice in the LORD, you who
are righteous, Job 22:19
and praise his holy name.

Psalm 98

A psalm.

1Sing to the LORD a new song,
for he has done marvelous
things; Ps 96:3
his right hand and his holy
arm Jos 4:24
have worked salvation for
him. Ps 44:3

²The LORD has made his
    salvation known   Isa 52:10
and revealed his
    righteousness to the
    nations.   Ps 67:2
³He has remembered his love
and his faithfulness to the
    house of Israel;   1Ch 16:15
all the ends of the earth have
    seen
    the salvation of our God.

⁴Shout for joy to the LORD, all
    the earth,   Ps 20:5
    burst into jubilant song
    with music;
⁵make music to the LORD with
    the harp,   Ps 33:2
    with the harp and the
    sound of singing,   Isa 51:3
⁶with trumpets and the blast
    of the ram's horn— Ex 19:13
    shout for joy before the
    LORD, the King.   Ps 2:6

⁷Let the sea resound, and
    everything in it,   Ps 93:3
    the world, and all who live
    in it.   Ps 24:1
⁸Let the rivers clap their
    hands,   2Ki 11:12
    let the mountains sing
    together for joy;   Ps 148:9
⁹let them sing before the
    LORD,
    for he comes to judge the
    earth.
He will judge the world in
    righteousness
    and the peoples with
    equity.   Ps 96:10

Psalm 99

¹The LORD reigns,   1Ch 16:31
    let the nations tremble;
he sits enthroned between
    the cherubim,   Ex 25:22
    let the earth shake.
²Great is the LORD in Zion;
    he is exalted over all the
    nations.   Ex 15:1
³Let them praise your great
    and awesome name—
    he is holy.   Ex 15:11

⁴The King is mighty, he loves
    justice—   1Ki 10:9
    you have established
    equity;   Ps 98:9
in Jacob you have done
    what is just and right.
⁵Exalt the LORD our God
    and worship at his
    footstool;
    he is holy.   Ex 15:2

⁶Moses and Aaron were
    among his priests,   Ex 28:1
    Samuel was among those
    who called on his name;
they called on the LORD
    and he answered them.
⁷He spoke to them from the
    pillar of cloud;   Ex 13:21
    they kept his statutes and
    the decrees he gave
    them.

⁸O LORD our God,
    you answered them;
    you were to Israel*ᵃ* a
    forgiving God,   Ex 22:27

*ᵃ*8 Hebrew *them*

though you punished their
   misdeeds[a]   Lev 26:18
9Exalt the LORD our God
   and worship at his holy
      mountain,
for the LORD our God is
   holy.

Psalm 100

A psalm. For giving thanks.

1Shout for joy to the LORD, all
   the earth.   Ps 98:6
2 Worship the LORD with
      gladness;   Dt 10:12
come before him with joyful
   songs.   Ps 95:2
3Know that the LORD is God.
It is he who made us, and
   we are his[b];   Job 10:3
we are his people, the
   sheep of his pasture.

4Enter his gates with
      thanksgiving   Ps 42:4
and his courts with praise;
give thanks to him and
   praise his name.   Ps 116:17
5For the LORD is good and his
   love endures forever;
his faithfulness continues
   through all generations.

Psalm 101

Of David. A psalm.

1I will sing of your love and
   justice;   Ps 33:1
to you, O LORD, I will sing
   praise.

2I will be careful to lead a
   blameless life—   Ge 17:1
when will you come to me?

I will walk in my house
   with blameless heart.   1Ki 3:14
3I will set before my eyes
   no vile thing.   Jer 16:18

The deeds of faithless men I
   hate;   Ps 5:5
they will not cling to me.
4Men of perverse heart shall
   be far from me;   Pr 3:32
I will have nothing to do
   with evil.

5Whoever slanders his
   neighbor in secret,   Ex 20:16
him will I put to silence;
whoever has haughty eyes
   and a proud heart,   Ps 10:5
him will I not endure.

6My eyes will be on the
   faithful in the land,
that they may dwell with
   me;
he whose walk is blameless
   will minister to me.   Ps 119:1

7No one who practices deceit
   will dwell in my house;
no one who speaks falsely
   will stand in my presence.

8Every morning I will put to
   silence   Ps 5:3
all the wicked in the land;
I will cut off every evildoer
   from the city of the LORD.

a8 Or / an avenger of the wrongs done to them   b3 Or and not we ourselves

Psalm 102

A prayer of an afflicted man.
When he is faint and pours out
his lament before the LORD.

[1] Hear my prayer, O LORD;
  let my cry for help come to
    you.   Ex 2:23
[2] Do not hide your face from
    me
  when I am in distress. Ps 22:24
Turn your ear to me;   2Ki 19:16
  when I call, answer me
    quickly.

[3] For my days vanish like
    smoke;   Ps 37:20
  my bones burn like glowing
    embers.   La 1:13
[4] My heart is blighted and
    withered like grass; Ps 37:2
  I forget to eat my food. 1Sa 1:7
[5] Because of my loud groaning
  I am reduced to skin and
    bones.   Ps 6:6
[6] I am like a desert owl, Job 30:29
  like an owl among the
    ruins.
[7] I lie awake; I have become
  like a bird alone on a roof.
[8] All day long my enemies
    taunt me;   Ps 42:10
  those who rail against me
    use my name as a curse.
[9] For I eat ashes as my food
  and mingle my drink with
    tears   Ps 6:6
[10] because of your great wrath,
  for you have taken me up
    and thrown me aside.
[11] My days are like the evening
    shadow;   1Ch 29:15
  I wither away like grass.

[12] But you, O LORD, sit
    enthroned forever;
  your renown endures
    through all
    generations.
[13] You will arise and have
    compassion on Zion,
  for it is time to show favor
    to her;   Ps 77:7
  the appointed time has
    come.   Ex 13:10
[14] For her stones are dear to
    your servants;
  her very dust moves them
    to pity.
[15] The nations will fear the
    name of the LORD,
  all the kings of the earth
    will revere your glory.
[16] For the LORD will rebuild
    Zion   Ps 51:18
  and appear in his glory.
[17] He will respond to the prayer
    of the destitute;   1Ki 8:29
  he will not despise their
    plea.

[18] Let this be written for a
    future generation,   Ro 4:24
  that a people not yet
    created may praise the
    LORD: Ps 22:31
[19] "The LORD looked down
    from his sanctuary on
    high,   Ps 53:2
  from heaven he viewed the
    earth,
[20] to hear the groans of the
    prisoners   Ps 68:6
  and release those
    condemned to death."
[21] So the name of the LORD will
    be declared in Zion
  and his praise in Jerusalem

²²when the peoples and the
    kingdoms
  assemble to worship the
    LORD.   Ps 22:27

²³In the course of my life^a he
    broke my strength;
  he cut short my days.   Ps 39:5
²⁴So I said:
  "Do not take me away,
    O my God, in the midst
    of my days;
  your years go on through
    all generations.   Ge 21:33
²⁵In the beginning you laid the
    foundations of the earth,
  and the heavens are the
    work of your hands.
²⁶They will perish, but you
    remain;   Isa 13:10
  they will all wear out like a
    garment.
  Like clothing you will change
    them
  and they will be discarded.
²⁷But you remain the same,
  and your years will never
    end.   Ps 9:7
²⁸The children of your servants
    will live in your
    presence;   Ps 69:36
  their descendants will be
    established before you."

Psalm 103

Of David.

¹Praise the LORD, O my soul;
  all my inmost being, praise
    his holy name.   Ps 30:4
²Praise the LORD, O my soul,

and forget not all his
    benefits—   Dt 6:12
³who forgives all your sins
  and heals all your diseases,
⁴who redeems your life from
    the pit   Ps 34:22
  and crowns you with love
    and compassion,   Ps 8:5
⁵who satisfies your desires
    with good things   Ps 90:14
  so that your youth is
    renewed like the eagle's.

⁶The LORD works
    righteousness
  and justice for all the
    oppressed.   Ps 74:21

⁷He made known his ways to
    Moses,   Ex 33:13
  his deeds to the people of
    Israel: Ps 106:22
⁸The LORD is compassionate
    and gracious,   Ex 22:27
  slow to anger, abounding in
    love.
⁹He will not always accuse,
  nor will he harbor his anger
    forever;   Ps 30:5
¹⁰he does not treat us as our
    sins deserve   Ezr 9:13
  or repay us according to our
    iniquities.
¹¹For as high as the heavens
    are above the earth,
  so great is his love for those
    who fear him;   2Ch 6:31
¹²as far as the east is from the
    west,
  so far has he removed our
    transgressions from us.
¹³As a father has compassion
  on his children,   Mal 3:17

a23 Or By his power

so the LORD has
  compassion on those
  who fear him;
14for he knows how we are
  formed,   Ps 119:73
  he remembers that we are
  dust.   Ge 2:7
15As for man, his days are like
  grass,   Ps 37:2
  he flourishes like a flower
  of the field;   Job 14:2
16the wind blows over it and it
  is gone,   Isa 40:7
  and its place remembers it
  no more.   Job 7:8
17But from everlasting to
  everlasting
  the LORD's love is with
  those who fear him,
  and his righteousness with
  their children's
  children—   Ge 48:11
18with those who keep his
  covenant   Dt 29:9
  and remember to obey his
  precepts.   Nu 15:40

19The LORD has established his
  throne in heaven,   Ps 47:8
  and his kingdom rules over
  all.   Ps 22:28

20Praise the LORD, you his
  angels,   Ne 9:6
  you mighty ones who do
  his bidding,   Ps 107:25
  who obey his word.
21Praise the LORD, all his
  heavenly hosts,   1Ki 22:19
  you his servants who do his
  will.   Ne 7:73
22Praise the LORD, all his works

everywhere in his
  dominion.   Ps 19:1
Praise the LORD, O my soul.

Psalm 104

1Praise the LORD, O my soul.

O LORD my God, you are
  very great;
  you are clothed with
  splendor and majesty.
2He wraps himself in light as
  with a garment;   Ps 18:12
  he stretches out the
  heavens like a tent   Ps 19:4
3 and lays the beams of his
  upper chambers on their
  waters.   Ps 24:2
He makes the clouds his
  chariot   2Ki 2:11
  and rides on the wings of
  the wind.   Ps 18:10
4He makes winds his
  messengers,a   Ps 148:8
  flames of fire his servants.

5He set the earth on its
  foundations;   1Sa 2:8
  it can never be moved.
6You covered it with the deep
  as with a garment;   Ge 7:19
  the waters stood above the
  mountains.   2Pe 3:6
7But at your rebuke the waters
  fled,   Ps 18:15
  at the sound of your
  thunder they took to
  flight;   Ex 9:23
8they flowed over the
  mountains,
  they went down into the
  valleys,

a4 Or *angels*

to the place you assigned
   for them.   Ps 33:7
⁹You set a boundary they
   cannot cross;   Ge 1:9
never again will they cover
   the earth.

¹⁰He makes springs pour water
   into the ravines;   Ps 107:33
it flows between the
   mountains.
¹¹They give water to all the
   beasts of the field;
the wild donkeys quench
   their thirst.   Ge 16:12
¹²The birds of the air nest by
   the waters;   Mt 8:20
they sing among the
   branches.   Mt 13:32
¹³He waters the mountains
   from his upper
   chambers;   Lev 26:4
the earth is satisfied by the
   fruit of his work.   Am 9:6
¹⁴He makes grass grow for the
   cattle,   Job 38:27
and plants for man to
   cultivate—
bringing forth food from
   the earth: Ge 1:30
¹⁵wine that gladdens the heart
   of man,   Ge 14:18
oil to make his face shine,
and bread that sustains his
   heart.   Dt 8:3
¹⁶The trees of the LORD are
   well watered,   Ge 1:11
the cedars of Lebanon that
   he planted.   Ps 72:16
¹⁷There the birds make their
   nests;
the stork has its home in
   the pine trees.

¹⁸The high mountains belong
   to the wild goats; Dt 14:5
the crags are a refuge for
   the coneys. ᵃ   Pr 30:26
¹⁹The moon marks off the
   seasons,   Ge 1:14
and the sun knows when to
   go down.   Ps 19:6
²⁰You bring darkness, it
   becomes night, Ps 74:16
and all the beasts of the
   forest prowl.   Ps 50:10
²¹The lions roar for their prey
and seek their food from
   God.   Ps 145:15
²²The sun rises, and they steal
   away;
they return and lie down in
   their dens.   Job 37:8
²³Then man goes out to his
   work,   Ge 3:19
to his labor until evening.

²⁴How many are your works,
   O LORD!
In wisdom you made them
   all;   Ge 1:31
the earth is full of your
   creatures.   Ps 24:1
²⁵There is the sea, vast and
   spacious,   Ps 69:34
teeming with creatures
   beyond number—
living things both large and
   small.   Eze 47:10
²⁶There the ships go to and fro,
and the leviathan, which
   you formed to frolic
   there.   Job 40:20
²⁷These all look to you
to give them their food at
   the proper time. Job 36:31

ᵃ18 That is, the hyrax or rock badger

²⁸When you give it to them,
    they gather it up;
when you open your hand,
    they are satisfied with good
        things.   Ps 103:5
²⁹When you hide your face,
    they are terrified;   Dt 31:17
when you take away their
    breath,
they die and return to the
    dust.   Job 7:21
³⁰When you send your Spirit,
    they are created,
and you renew the face of
    the earth.   Ge 1:2

³¹May the glory of the LORD
    endure forever;   Ex 40:35
may the LORD rejoice in his
    works—   Ge 1:4
³²he who looks at the earth,
    and it trembles,   Ps 97:4
who touches the
    mountains, and they
    smoke.   Ps 144:5

³³I will sing to the LORD all my
    life;   Ex 15:1
I will sing praise to my God
    as long as I live.
³⁴May my meditation be
    pleasing to him,
as I rejoice in the LORD.
³⁵But may sinners vanish from
    the earth   Ps 37:38
and the wicked be no
    more.

Praise the LORD, O my soul.

Praise the LORD.^a   Ps 28:6

Psalm 105

¹Give thanks to the LORD, call
    on his name;   Ps 80:18
make known among the
    nations what he has
    done.
²Sing to him, sing praise to
    him;   Ps 30:4
tell of all his wonderful
    acts.   Ps 75:1
³Glory in his holy name;
    let the hearts of those who
    seek the LORD rejoice.
⁴Look to the LORD and his
    strength;
seek his face always.   Ps 24:6

⁵Remember the wonders he
    has done,   Ps 40:5
his miracles, and the
    judgments he
    pronounced,   Dt 7:18
⁶O descendants of Abraham
    his servant,
O sons of Jacob, his chosen
    ones.   Dt 10:15
⁷He is the LORD our God;
    his judgments are in all the
    earth.

⁸He remembers his covenant
    forever,   Ge 9:15
the word he commanded,
    for a thousand
    generations,
⁹the covenant he made with
    Abraham,   Ge 12:7
the oath he swore to Isaac.
¹⁰He confirmed it to Jacob as a
    decree,   Ge 28:13-15
to Israel as an everlasting
    covenant: Isa 55:3

^a35 Hebrew *Hallelu Yah*; in the Septuagint this line stands at the beginning of Psalm 105.

11"To you I will give the land
    of Canaan   Ge 12:7
  as the portion you will
    inherit."   Nu 34:2

12When they were but few in
    number,   Dt 7:7
  few indeed, and strangers
    in it,   Ge 23:4
13they wandered from nation
    to nation,   Ge 15:13-16
  from one kingdom to
    another.
14He allowed no one to
    oppress them;   Ge 35:5
  for their sake he rebuked
    kings: Ge 12:17-20
15"Do not touch my anointed
    ones;   Ge 26:11
  do my prophets no harm."

16He called down famine on
    the land   Ge 12:10
  and destroyed all their
    supplies of food;
17and he sent a man before
    them—
  Joseph, sold as a slave.
18They bruised his feet with
    shackles,   Ge 40:15
  his neck was put in irons,
19till what he foretold came to
    pass,   Ge 12:10
  till the word of the LORD
    proved him true.   Ge 41:40
20The king sent and released
    him,
  the ruler of peoples set him
    free.   Ge 41:14
21He made him master of his
    household,
  ruler over all he possessed,
22to instruct his princes as he
    pleased   Ge 41:43-44

and teach his elders
    wisdom.   Ge 41:40

23Then Israel entered Egypt;
  Jacob lived as an alien in
    the land of Ham.   Ps 78:51
24The LORD made his people
    very fruitful;
  he made them too
    numerous for their foes,
25whose hearts he turned to
    hate his people,   Ex 4:21
  to conspire against his
    servants.   Ex 1:6-10
26He sent Moses his servant,
  and Aaron, whom he had
    chosen.   Nu 16:5
27They performed his
    miraculous signs among
    them,   Ex 4:17
  his wonders in the land of
    Ham.   Ex 3:20
28He sent darkness and made
    the land dark—
  for had they not rebelled
    against his words?   Ex 7:22
29He turned their waters into
    blood,   Ps 78:44
  causing their fish to die.
30Their land teemed with
    frogs,   Ex 8:2,6
  which went up into the
    bedrooms of their rulers.
31He spoke, and there came
    swarms of flies,   Ex 8:21-24
  and gnats throughout their
    country.   Ex 8:16-18
32He turned their rain into hail,
  with lightning throughout
    their land;   Ex 9:22-25
33he struck down their vines
    and fig trees   Ps 78:47
  and shattered the trees of
    their country.

³⁴He spoke, and the locusts
came,   Ex 10:4,12-15
grasshoppers without
number;   Joel 1:16
³⁵they ate up every green thing
in their land,
ate up the produce of their
soil.
³⁶Then he struck down all the
firstborn in their land,
the firstfruits of all their
manhood.   Ex 4:23

³⁷He brought out Israel, laden
with silver and gold,
and from among their tribes
no one faltered.   Ex 3:21
³⁸Egypt was glad when they
left,
because dread of Israel had
fallen on them.   Ex 15:16
³⁹He spread out a cloud as a
covering,   Ex 13:21
and a fire to give light at
night.   Ps 78:14
⁴⁰They asked, and he brought
them quail   Ps 78:18
and satisfied them with the
bread of heaven.   Ex 16:4
⁴¹He opened the rock, and
water gushed out;   Nu 20:11
like a river it flowed in the
desert.

⁴²For he remembered his holy
promise   Ge 12:1-3
given to his servant
Abraham.
⁴³He brought out his people
with rejoicing,   Ex 15:1-18
his chosen ones with shouts
of joy;

⁴⁴he gave them the lands of the
nations,   Ex 32:13
and they fell heir to what
others had toiled for—
⁴⁵that they might keep his
precepts
and observe his laws.

Praise the LORD.^a   Ps 104:35

Psalm 106

¹Praise the LORD.^b   Ps 22:23

Give thanks to the LORD, for
he is good;   Ps 119:68
his love endures forever.
²Who can proclaim the mighty
acts of the LORD   Ps 71:16
or fully declare his praise?
³Blessed are they who
maintain justice,   Ps 112:5
who constantly do what is
right.   Ps 15:2
⁴Remember me, O LORD,
when you show favor to
your people,   Ps 77:7
come to my aid when you
save them,   Ge 50:24
⁵that I may enjoy the
prosperity of your
chosen ones,   Ps 105:6
that I may share in the joy
of your nation   Ps 20:5
and join your inheritance in
giving praise.   Ex 34:9

⁶We have sinned, even as our
fathers did;   1Ki 8:47
we have done wrong and
acted wickedly.   Ne 1:7
⁷When our fathers were in
Egypt,

^a45 Hebrew *Hallelu Yah*   ^b1 Hebrew *Hallelu Yah*; also in verse 48

they gave no thought to
  your miracles;   Jdg 3:7
they did not remember your
  many kindnesses,
and they rebelled by the
  sea, the Red Sea.ᵃ   Ex 14:11
⁸Yet he saved them for his
  name's sake,   Ex 9:16
to make his mighty power
  known.   Ex 14:31
⁹He rebuked the Red Sea, and
  it dried up;   Na 1:4
he led them through the
  depths as through a
  desert.   Ps 78:13
¹⁰He saved them from the
  hand of the foe;   Ps 78:53
from the hand of the enemy
  he redeemed them.
¹¹The waters covered their
  adversaries;   Ex 14:28
not one of them survived.
¹²Then they believed his
  promises
and sang his praise.   Ex 15:1-21

¹³But they soon forgot what he
  had done   Ex 15:24
and did not wait for his
  counsel.   Ex 16:28
¹⁴In the desert they gave in to
  their craving;   Ps 78:40
in the wasteland they put
  God to the test.   Ex 17:2
¹⁵So he gave them what they
  asked for,   Ex 16:13
but sent a wasting disease
  upon them.   Nu 11:33

¹⁶In the camp they grew
  envious of Moses
and of Aaron, who was
  consecrated to the LORD.

¹⁷The earth opened up and
  swallowed Dathan;
it buried the company of
  Abiram.   Nu 16:1
¹⁸Fire blazed among their
  followers;   Lev 10:2
a flame consumed the
  wicked.

¹⁹At Horeb they made a calf
  and worshiped an idol cast
  from metal.
²⁰They exchanged their Glory
  for an image of a bull,
  which eats grass.   Jer 2:11
²¹They forgot the God who
  saved them,   Ps 78:1
who had done great things
  in Egypt,   Dt 10:21
²²miracles in the land of Ham
  and awesome deeds by the
  Red Sea.   Ex 3:20
²³So he said he would destroy
  them—   Ex 32:10
had not Moses, his chosen
  one,
stood in the breach before
  him   Ex 32:11-14
to keep his wrath from
  destroying them.

²⁴Then they despised the
  pleasant land;   Dt 8:7
they did not believe his
  promise.   Nu 14:11
²⁵They grumbled in their tents
  and did not obey the LORD.
²⁶So he swore to them with
  uplifted hand   Nu 14:23
that he would make them
  fall in the desert,   Dt 2:14
²⁷make their descendants fall
  among the nations

ᵃ7 Hebrew *Yam Suph*; that is, Sea of Reeds; also in verses 9 and 22

and scatter them
   throughout the lands.

²⁸They yoked themselves to
   the Baal of Peor
and ate sacrifices offered to
   lifeless gods;   Nu 23:28
²⁹they provoked the LORD to
   anger by their wicked
   deeds,   Ps 64:2
and a plague broke out
   among them.   Nu 16:46
³⁰But Phinehas stood up and
   intervened,   Ex 6:25
and the plague was
   checked.   Nu 25:8
³¹This was credited to him as
   righteousness   Ge 15:6
for endless generations to
   come.   Ps 49:11

³²By the waters of Meribah
   they angered the LORD,
and trouble came to Moses
   because of them;
³³for they rebelled against the
   Spirit of God,   Ex 23:21
and rash words came from
   Moses' lips. ^a   Ex 17:4-7

³⁴They did not destroy the
   peoples   Jos 9:15
as the LORD had
   commanded them, Ex 23:24
³⁵but they mingled with the
   nations   Jdg 3:5-6
and adopted their customs.
³⁶They worshiped their idols,
   which became a snare to
   them.   Ex 10:7
³⁷They sacrificed their sons
   and their daughters to
   demons.   Ex 22:20
³⁸They shed innocent blood,

the blood of their sons and
   daughters,   Lev 18:21
whom they sacrificed to the
   idols of Canaan,
and the land was
   desecrated by their
   blood.
³⁹They defiled themselves by
   what they did;   Ge 3:17
by their deeds they
   prostituted themselves.

⁴⁰Therefore the LORD was
   angry with his people
and abhorred his
   inheritance.   Ex 34:9
⁴¹He handed them over to the
   nations,   Jdg 2:14
and their foes ruled over
   them.
⁴²Their enemies oppressed
   them   Jdg 4:3
and subjected them to their
   power.
⁴³Many times he delivered
   them,   Jos 10:14
but they were bent on
   rebellion   Jdg 2:16-19
and they wasted away in
   their sin.

⁴⁴But he took note of their
   distress
when he heard their cry;
⁴⁵for their sake he remembered
   his covenant   Ge 9:15
and out of his great love he
   relented.   Ex 32:14
⁴⁶He caused them to be pitied
   by all who held them
   captive.   Ex 3:21

⁴⁷Save us, O LORD our God,

---

^a33 Or *against his spirit, / and rash words came from his lips*

and gather us from the
   nations,   Ps 107:3
that we may give thanks to
   your holy name   Ps 30:4
and glory in your praise.

⁴⁸Praise be to the LORD, the
   God of Israel,
from everlasting to
   everlasting.
Let all the people say,
   "Amen!"   Ps 41:13

Praise the LORD.

BOOK V

Psalms 107–150

Psalm 107

¹Give thanks to the LORD, for
   he is good;   1Ch 16:8
his love endures forever.
²Let the redeemed of the
   LORD say this—   Ps 106:10
those he redeemed from the
   hand of the foe,
³those he gathered from the
   lands,   Ne 1:9
from east and west, from
   north and south. ᵃ

⁴Some wandered in desert
   wastelands,   Jos 5:6
finding no way to a city
   where they could settle.
⁵They were hungry and
   thirsty,   Ex 15:22
and their lives ebbed away.
⁶Then they cried out to the
   LORD in their trouble,
and he delivered them from
   their distress.   Ex 14:10

⁷He led them by a straight
   way   Eze 8:21
to a city where they could
   settle.
⁸Let them give thanks to the
   LORD for his unfailing
   love   Ps 6:4
and his wonderful deeds
   for men,   Ps 75:1
⁹for he satisfies the thirsty
and fills the hungry with
   good things.   Ps 22:26

¹⁰Some sat in darkness and the
   deepest gloom,   Ps 88:6
prisoners suffering in iron
   chains,   Job 36:8
¹¹for they had rebelled against
   the words of God   Ps 5:10
and despised the counsel of
   the Most High.   1Ki 22:5
¹²So he subjected them to
   bitter labor;
they stumbled, and there
   was no one to help.
¹³Then they cried to the LORD
   in their trouble,
and he saved them from
   their distress.   Ps 106:8
¹⁴He brought them out of
   darkness and the
   deepest gloom   Ps 86:13
and broke away their
   chains.   Job 36:8
¹⁵Let them give thanks to the
   LORD for his unfailing
   love   Ps 105:1
and his wonderful deeds
   for men,   Ps 75:1
¹⁶for he breaks down gates of
   bronze
and cuts through bars of
   iron.

ᵃ3 Hebrew *north and the sea*

¹⁷Some became fools through
their rebellious ways
and suffered affliction
because of their
iniquities.   Lev 26:16

¹⁸They loathed all food
and drew near the gates of
death.   Job 17:16

¹⁹Then they cried to the LORD
in their trouble,
and he saved them from
their distress.   Ps 34:4

²⁰He sent forth his word and
healed them;   Dt 32:2
he rescued them from the
grave.   Ps 16:10

²¹Let them give thanks to the
LORD for his unfailing
love   Ps 6:4
and his wonderful deeds
for men.   Ps 75:1

²²Let them sacrifice thank
offerings   Lev 7:12
and tell of his works with
songs of joy.   Job 8:21

²³Others went out on the sea
in ships;   Ps 104:26
they were merchants on the
mighty waters.

²⁴They saw the works of the
LORD,   Ps 64:9
his wonderful deeds in the
deep.

²⁵For he spoke and stirred up a
tempest   Ps 50:3
that lifted high the waves.

²⁶They mounted up to the
heavens and went down
to the depths;
in their peril their courage
melted away.   Jos 2:11

²⁷They reeled and staggered
like drunken men;

they were at their wits' end.

²⁸Then they cried out to the
LORD in their trouble,
and he brought them out of
their distress.   Jnh 1:6

²⁹He stilled the storm to a
whisper;   Lk 8:24
the waves of the sea were
hushed.   Ps 65:7

³⁰They were glad when it grew
calm,
and he guided them to their
desired haven.

³¹Let them give thanks to the
LORD for his unfailing
love   Ps 6:4
and his wonderful deeds
for men.

³²Let them exalt him in the
assembly of the people
and praise him in the
council of the elders.

³³He turned rivers into a
desert,   1Ki 17:1
flowing springs into thirsty
ground,   Ps 104:10

³⁴and fruitful land into a salt
waste,   Ge 13:10
because of the wickedness
of those who lived
there.

³⁵He turned the desert into
pools of water   2Ki 3:17
and the parched ground
into flowing springs;

³⁶there he brought the hungry
to live,
and they founded a city
where they could settle.

³⁷They sowed fields and
planted vineyards
that yielded a fruitful
harvest;   2Ki 19:29

[38]he blessed them, and their
    numbers greatly
    increased,   Ge 12:2
and he did not let their
    herds diminish.   Ge 49:25

[39]Then their numbers
    decreased, and they
    were humbled   Ps 44:9
by oppression, calamity and
    sorrow;
[40]he who pours contempt on
    nobles   Job 12:18
made them wander in a
    trackless waste.   Dt 32:10
[41]But he lifted the needy out of
    their affliction   1Sa 2:8
and increased their families
    like flocks.   Job 21:11
[42]The upright see and rejoice,
    but all the wicked shut their
    mouths.   Job 5:16

[43]Whoever is wise, let him
    heed these things
and consider the great love
    of the LORD.   Ps 103:11

Psalm 108

A song. A psalm of David.

[1]My heart is steadfast, O God;
    I will sing and make music
    with all my soul.   Ps 18:49
[2]Awake, harp and lyre!   Job 21:12
    I will awaken the dawn.
[3]I will praise you, O LORD,
    among the nations;
    I will sing of you among the
    peoples.
[4]For great is your love, higher
    than the heavens;

your faithfulness reaches to
    the skies.   Ps 36:5
[5]Be exalted, O God, above the
    heavens,   Ps 8:1
and let your glory be over
    all the earth.   Ps 57:5

[6]Save us and help us with
    your right hand,   Job 40:14
that those you love may be
    delivered.
[7]God has spoken from his
    sanctuary: Ps 68:35
"In triumph I will parcel
    out Shechem   Ge 12:6
and measure off the Valley
    of Succoth.   Ge 33:17
[8]Gilead is mine, Manasseh is
    mine;
    Ephraim is my helmet,
    Judah my scepter.   Ps 78:68
[9]Moab is my washbasin,
    upon Edom I toss my
    sandal;   2Sa 8:13-14
    over Philistia I shout in
    triumph."   2Sa 8:1

[10]Who will bring me to the
    fortified city?
    Who will lead me to
    Edom?
[11]Is it not you, O God, you
    who have rejected us
and no longer go out with
    our armies?   Ps 44:9
[12]Give us aid against the
    enemy,
    for the help of man is
    worthless.   Ps 118:8
[13]With God we will gain the
    victory,
    and he will trample down
    our enemies.   Ps 44:5

Psalm 109

For the director of music. Of
David. A psalm.

[1]O God, whom I praise,
  do not remain silent, Job 34:29
[2]for wicked and deceitful men
  have opened their mouths
  against me;
  they have spoken against
  me with lying tongues.
[3]With words of hatred they
  surround me; Ps 69:4
  they attack me without
  cause. Ps 35:7
[4]In return for my friendship
  they accuse me,
  but I am a man of prayer.
[5]They repay me evil for good,
  and hatred for my
  friendship. Ge 44:4

[6]Appoint[a] an evil man[b] to
  oppose him;
  let an accuser[c] stand at his
  right hand. 1Ch 21:1
[7]When he is tried, let him be
  found guilty, Ps 1:5
  and may his prayers
  condemn him. Pr 28:9
[8]May his days be few; Job 15:32
  may another take his place
  of leadership. Ac 1:20
[9]May his children be
  fatherless
  and his wife a widow. Ex 22:24
[10]May his children be
  wandering beggars;
  may they be driven[d] from
  their ruined homes.

[11]May a creditor seize all he
  has; Ne 5:3
  may strangers plunder the
  fruits of his labor. Job 20:18
[12]May no one extend kindness
  to him
  or take pity on his
  fatherless children.
[13]May his descendants be cut
  off, Job 20:19
  their names blotted out
  from the next
  generation. Nu 14:12
[14]May the iniquity of his
  fathers be remembered
  before the LORD; Ex 20:5
  may the sin of his mother
  never be blotted out.
[15]May their sins always remain
  before the LORD, Ps 90:8
  that he may cut off the
  memory of them from
  the earth. Ex 17:14

[16]For he never thought of
  doing a kindness,
  but hounded to death the
  poor
  and the needy and the
  brokenhearted. Job 20:19
[17]He loved to pronounce a
  curse—
  may it[e] come on him; Pr 28:27
  he found no pleasure in
  blessing—
  may it be[f] far from him.
[18]He wore cursing as his
  garment; Ps 10:7
  it entered into his body like
  water, Nu 5:22
  into his bones like oil.

---

[a]6 Or *They say:* "Appoint (with quotation marks at the end of verse 19)   [b]6 Or *the Evil One*   [c]6 Or *let Satan*   [d]10 Septuagint; Hebrew *sought*   [e]17 Or *curse, / and it has*   [f]17 Or *blessing, / and it is*

¹⁹May it be like a cloak
        wrapped about him,
    like a belt tied forever
        around him.   Ps 73:6
²⁰May this be the LORD's
        payment to my
        accusers,
    to those who speak evil of
        me.   Ps 71:10

²¹But you, O Sovereign LORD,
    deal well with me for your
        name's sake;   Ex 9:16
    out of the goodness of your
        love, deliver me.   Ps 3:7
²²For I am poor and needy,
    and my heart is wounded
        within me.
²³I fade away like an evening
        shadow;   Job 14:2
    I am shaken off like a
        locust.
²⁴My knees give way from
        fasting;   Ps 35:13
    my body is thin and gaunt.
²⁵I am an object of scorn to my
        accusers;   Ps 22:6
    when they see me, they
        shake their heads.   Job 16:4

²⁶Help me, O LORD my God;
    save me in accordance with
        your love.   Ps 12:1
²⁷Let them know that it is your
        hand,   Job 37:7
    that you, O LORD, have
        done it.
²⁸They may curse, but you will
        bless;
    when they attack they will
        be put to shame,   2Sa 16:12
    but your servant will
        rejoice.   Ps 66:4

²⁹My accusers will be clothed
        with disgrace
    and wrapped in shame as
        in a cloak.   Ps 35:26

³⁰With my mouth I will greatly
        extol the LORD;
    in the great throng I will
        praise him.   Ps 35:18
³¹For he stands at the right
        hand of the needy one,
    to save his life from those
        who condemn him.

Psalm 110

Of David. A psalm.

¹The LORD says to my Lord:
    "Sit at my right hand
until I make your enemies
    a footstool for your feet."

²The LORD will extend your
        mighty scepter from
        Zion;   Ps 2:6
    you will rule in the midst of
        your enemies.   Ps 72:8
³Your troops will be willing
    on your day of battle.
Arrayed in holy majesty,
    from the womb of the dawn
you will receive the dew of
    your youth. ᵃ   Mic 5:7

⁴The LORD has sworn
    and will not change his
        mind: Nu 23:19
    "You are a priest forever,
    in the order of
        Melchizedek."   Ge 14:18

⁵The Lord is at your right
        hand;   Ps 16:8

ᵃ3 Or / your young men will come to you like the dew

he will crush kings on the
day of his wrath.   Ps 2:5
⁶He will judge the nations,
heaping up the dead
and crushing the rulers of
the whole earth.   Ps 18:38
⁷He will drink from a brook
beside the wayᵃ;
therefore he will lift up his
head.   Ps 3:3; 27:6

Psalm 111ᵇ

¹Praise the LORD.ᶜ

I will extol the LORD with all
my heart   Ps 34:1
in the council of the upright
and in the assembly.

²Great are the works of the
LORD;   Job 36:24
they are pondered by all
who delight in them.
³Glorious and majestic are his
deeds,
and his righteousness
endures forever.   Ps 112:3
⁴He has caused his wonders
to be remembered;
the LORD is gracious and
compassionate.   Dt 4:31
⁵He provides food for those
who fear him;   Ge 1:30
he remembers his covenant
forever.   1Ch 16:15
⁶He has shown his people the
power of his works,
giving them the lands of
other nations.   Ps 105:44
⁷The works of his hands are
faithful and just;   Ps 92:4

all his precepts are
trustworthy.   Ps 19:7
⁸They are steadfast for ever
and ever,   Ps 119:89
done in faithfulness and
uprightness.
⁹He provided redemption for
his people;   Ps 34:22
he ordained his covenant
forever—
holy and awesome is his
name.   Ps 30:4

¹⁰The fear of the LORD is the
beginning of wisdom;
all who follow his precepts
have good
understanding.   Dt 4:6
To him belongs eternal
praise.   Ps 28:6

Psalm 112ᵇ

¹Praise the LORD.ᶜ   Ps 33:2

Blessed is the man who fears
the LORD,   Job 1:8
who finds great delight in
his commands.   Ps 1:2

²His children will be mighty
in the land;   Ps 25:13
the generation of the
upright will be blessed.
³Wealth and riches are in his
house,   Dt 8:18
and his righteousness
endures forever.   Ps 37:6
⁴Even in darkness light dawns
for the upright,   Ps 18:28
for the gracious and

ᵃ7 Or / *The One who grants succession will set him in authority*   ᵇThis psalm is an
acrostic poem, the lines of which begin with the successive letters of the Hebrew
alphabet.   ᶜ1 Hebrew *Hallelu Yah*

compassionate and
righteous man. *a*   Ps 5:12
5Good will come to him who
is generous and lends
freely,   Ps 37:21
who conducts his affairs
with justice.
6Surely he will never be
shaken;   Ps 15:5
a righteous man will be
remembered forever.
7He will have no fear of bad
news;
his heart is steadfast,
trusting in the LORD.
8His heart is secure, he will
have no fear;   Ps 3:6
in the end he will look in
triumph on his foes.
9He has scattered abroad his
gifts to the poor,   Lk 19:8
his righteousness endures
forever;   Ps 111:3
his horn *b* will be lifted high
in honor.   Ps 75:10
10The wicked man will see and
be vexed,   Ps 86:17
he will gnash his teeth and
waste away;   Ps 37:12
the longings of the wicked
will come to nothing.

Psalm 113

1Praise the LORD. *c*   Ps 22:23

Praise, O servants of the
LORD,   Ps 34:22
praise the name of the
LORD.
2Let the name of the LORD be
praised,   Ps 30:4

both now and forevermore.
3From the rising of the sun to
the place where it sets,
the name of the LORD is to
be praised.   Isa 24:15
4The LORD is exalted over all
the nations,   Ps 99:2
his glory above the
heavens.   Ps 8:1
5Who is like the LORD our
God,   Ex 8:10
the One who sits enthroned
on high,   Job 16:19
6who stoops down to look
on the heavens and the
earth?   Ps 11:4
7He raises the poor from the
dust   1Sa 2:8
and lifts the needy from the
ash heap;   Ps 107:41
8he seats them with princes,
with the princes of their
people.   2Sa 9:11
9He settles the barren woman
in her home   1Sa 2:5
as a happy mother of
children.

Praise the LORD.

Psalm 114

1When Israel came out of
Egypt,   Ex 13:3
the house of Jacob from a
people of foreign
tongue,
2Judah became God's
sanctuary,   Ex 15:17
Israel his dominion.
3The sea looked and fled,

a4 Or / *for the* LORD *is gracious and compassionate and righteous*   *b9* Horn *here*
symbolizes dignity.   *c1* Hebrew *Hallelu Yah;* also in verse 9

the Jordan turned back;
⁴the mountains skipped like
   rams,   Jdg 5:5
the hills like lambs.

⁵Why was it, O sea, that you
   fled,   Ex 14:21
O Jordan, that you turned
   back,
⁶you mountains, that you
   skipped like rams,
   you hills, like lambs?

⁷Tremble, O earth, at the
   presence of the Lord,
at the presence of the God
   of Jacob,   Ex 15:14
⁸who turned the rock into a
   pool,
the hard rock into springs
   of water.   Ex 17:6

Psalm 115

¹Not to us, O LORD, not to us
   but to your name be the
   glory,   Ps 29:2
because of your love and
   faithfulness.   Ex 34:6

²Why do the nations say,
   "Where is their God?"   Ps 42:3
³Our God is in heaven;   Ezr 5:11
   he does whatever pleases
   him.   Ps 135:6
⁴But their idols are silver and
   gold,   Rev 9:20
   made by the hands of men.
⁵They have mouths, but
   cannot speak,   Jer 10:5
   eyes, but they cannot see;
⁶they have ears, but cannot
   hear,
   noses, but they cannot
   smell;

⁷they have hands, but cannot
   feel,
   feet, but they cannot walk;
   nor can they utter a sound
   with their throats.
⁸Those who make them will
   be like them,
   and so will all who trust in
   them.

⁹O house of Israel, trust in the
   LORD—   Ps 37:3
   he is their help and shield.
¹⁰O house of Aaron, trust in
   the LORD—   Ex 30:30
   he is their help and shield.
¹¹You who fear him, trust in
   the LORD—   Ps 22:23
   he is their help and shield.

¹²The LORD remembers us and
   will bless us: Ge 12:2
He will bless the house of
   Israel,
   he will bless the house of
   Aaron,
¹³he will bless those who fear
   the LORD—   Ps 112:1
   small and great alike.

¹⁴May the LORD make you
   increase,   Dt 1:11
   both you and your children.
¹⁵May you be blessed by the
   LORD,
   the Maker of heaven and
   earth.   Ge 1:1

¹⁶The highest heavens belong
   to the LORD,   Ps 89:11
   but the earth he has given
   to man.   Ge 1:28
¹⁷It is not the dead who praise
   the LORD,   Ps 88:10-12
   those who go down to
   silence;

18it is we who extol the LORD,
both now and forevermore.

Praise the LORD. *a*   Ps 28:6

Psalm 116

1I love the LORD, for he heard
my voice;   Ps 18:1
he heard my cry for mercy.
2Because he turned his ear to
me,   Ps 5:1
I will call on him as long as
I live.

3The cords of death entangled
me,   2Sa 22:6
the anguish of the grave*b*
came upon me;
I was overcome by trouble
and sorrow.
4Then I called on the name of
the LORD: Ps 80:18
"O LORD, save me!"   Ps 80:2

5The LORD is gracious and
righteous;   Ex 9:27
our God is full of
compassion.   Ex 22:27
6The LORD protects the
simplehearted;
when I was in great need,
he saved me.   Ps 18:3

7Be at rest once more, O my
soul,   Ps 46:10
for the LORD has been good
to you.   Ps 13:6

8For you, O LORD, have
delivered my soul from
death,   Ps 86:13
my eyes from tears,
my feet from stumbling,

9that I may walk before the
LORD   Ge 5:22
in the land of the living.
10I believed; therefore*c* I said,
"I am greatly afflicted."
11And in my dismay I said,
"All men are liars."   Hos 7:13

12How can I repay the LORD
for all his goodness to me?
13I will lift up the cup of
salvation
and call on the name of the
LORD.   Ps 105:1
14I will fulfill my vows to the
LORD   Nu 30:2
in the presence of all his
people.

15Precious in the sight of the
LORD   Ps 72:14
is the death of his saints.
16O LORD, truly I am your
servant;   Ps 119:125
I am your servant, the son
of your maidservant*d*;
you have freed me from my
chains.   Ps 86:16

17I will sacrifice a thank
offering to you   Lev 7:12
and call on the name of the
LORD.
18I will fulfill my vows to the
LORD   Lev 22:18
in the presence of all his
people,
19in the courts of the house of
the LORD—   Ps 92:13
in your midst, O Jerusalem.

Praise the LORD. *a*

---

*a*18,19 Hebrew *Hallelu Yah*   *b*3 Hebrew *Sheol*   *c*10 Or *believed even when*
*d*16 Or *servant, your faithful son*

Psalm 117

1Praise the LORD, all you
    nations;
                     Ro 15:11
extol him, all you peoples.
2For great is his love toward
    us,
                     Ps 17:7
and the faithfulness of the
    LORD endures forever.

Praise the LORD.*a*

Psalm 118

1Give thanks to the LORD, for
    he is good;
                    1Ch 16:8
his love endures forever.

2Let Israel say:
                    Ps 115:9
    "His love endures forever."
3Let the house of Aaron say:
    "His love endures forever."
4Let those who fear the LORD
    say:
                  Ps 115:11
    "His love endures forever."

5In my anguish I cried to the
    LORD,
                 Ps 18:6
and he answered by setting
    me free.
6The LORD is with me; I will
    not be afraid.
                 Dt 31:6
What can man do to me?
7The LORD is with me; he is
    my helper.
                 Dt 33:29
I will look in triumph on
    my enemies.
                Ps 54:7

8It is better to take refuge in
    the LORD
                 Ps 2:12
than to trust in man.
                 Isa 2:22
9It is better to take refuge in
    the LORD
than to trust in princes.

10All the nations surrounded
    me,
but in the name of the LORD
    I cut them off.
                Ps 37:9
11They surrounded me on
    every side,
                Ps 88:17
but in the name of the LORD
    I cut them off.
12They swarmed around me
    like bees,
                Dt 1:44
but they died out as quickly
    as burning thorns;
               Ps 58:9
in the name of the LORD I
    cut them off.
                Ps 37:9

13I was pushed back and about
    to fall,
but the LORD helped me.
14The LORD is my strength and
    my song;
                Ex 15:2
he has become my
    salvation.
                Ps 62:2

15Shouts of joy and victory
    resound in the tents of the
    righteous:
                Job 8:21
    "The LORD's right hand has
    done mighty things!
16   The LORD's right hand is
    lifted high;
    the LORD's right hand has
    done mighty things!"

17I will not die but live,
    and will proclaim what the
    LORD has done.
                Dt 32:3
18The LORD has chastened me
    severely,
                Jer 31:18
but he has not given me
    over to death.
                Ps 86:13

19Open for me the gates of
    righteousness;
                Ps 24:7

*a*2 Hebrew *Hallelu Yah*

I will enter and give thanks
   to the LORD.   Ps 100:4
20This is the gate of the LORD
   through which the
   righteous may enter.
21I will give you thanks, for
   you answered me;
   you have become my
   salvation.   Ps 27:1

22The stone the builders
   rejected   Isa 8:14
   has become the capstone;
23the LORD has done this,
   and it is marvelous in our
   eyes.   Mt 21:42
24This is the day the LORD has
   made;
   let us rejoice and be glad
   in it.   Ps 70:4

25O LORD, save us;   Ps 28:9
   O LORD, grant us success.
26Blessed is he who comes in
   the name of the LORD.
   From the house of the LORD
   we bless you. *a*   Ps 129:8
27The LORD is God,   1Ki 18:21
   and he has made his light
   shine upon us.   Ps 27:1
   With boughs in hand, join in
   the festal procession
   up*b* to the horns of the
   altar.   Ex 27:2

28You are my God, and I will
   give you thanks;
   you are my God, and I will
   exalt you.   Ex 15:2

29Give thanks to the LORD, for
   he is good;
   his love endures forever.

Psalm 119*c*

א   Aleph

1Blessed are they whose
   ways are blameless,
   who walk according to the
   law of the LORD.   Ps 128:1
2Blessed are they who keep
   his statutes   Ps 99:7
   and seek him with all their
   heart.   Dt 10:12
3They do nothing wrong;
   they walk in his ways.
4You have laid down precepts
   that are to be fully obeyed.
5Oh, that my ways were
   steadfast
   in obeying your decrees!
6Then I would not be put to
   shame
   when I consider all your
   commands.
7I will praise you with an
   upright heart
   as I learn your righteous
   laws.   Dt 4:8
8I will obey your decrees;
   do not utterly forsake me.

ב   Beth

9How can a young man keep
   his way pure?   Ps 39:1
   By living according to your
   word.
10I seek you with all my heart;
   do not let me stray from
   your commands.
11I have hidden your word in
   my heart   Dt 6:6

a26 The Hebrew is plural.   *b27* Or *Bind the festal sacrifice with ropes / and take it*
*c*This psalm is an acrostic poem; the verses of each stanza begin with the same letter of
the Hebrew alphabet.

that I might not sin against
   you.   Ps 18:22-23
12Praise be to you, O LORD;
   teach me your decrees.
13With my lips I recount
   all the laws that come from
      your mouth.
14I rejoice in following your
      statutes
   as one rejoices in great
      riches.
15I meditate on your precepts
   and consider your ways.
16I delight in your decrees;
   I will not neglect your
      word.

ג   Gimel

17Do good to your servant, and
   I will live;   Ps 13:6
   I will obey your word.
18Open my eyes that I may see
   wonderful things in your
      law.
19I am a stranger on earth;
   do not hide your
      commands from me.
20My soul is consumed with
      longing   Ps 42:2
   for your laws at all times.
21You rebuke the arrogant,
   who are cursed   Job 30:1
   and who stray from your
      commands.
22Remove from me scorn and
      contempt,   Ps 39:8
   for I keep your statutes.
23Though rulers sit together
   and slander me,
   your servant will meditate
      on your decrees.
24Your statutes are my delight;
   they are my counselors.

ד   Daleth

25I am laid low in the dust;
   preserve my life according
      to your word.   Ps 143:4
26I recounted my ways and
      you answered me;
   teach me your decrees.
27Let me understand the
      teaching of your
      precepts;
   then I will meditate on your
      wonders.   Ps 105:2
28My soul is weary with
      sorrow;   Ps 6:7
   strengthen me according to
      your word.   Ps 18:1
29Keep me from deceitful
      ways;   Ps 26:4
   be gracious to me through
      your law.   Nu 6:25
30I have chosen the way of
      truth;   Ps 26:3
   I have set my heart on your
      laws.   Ps 108:1
31I hold fast to your statutes,
   O LORD;   Dt 10:20
   do not let me be put to
      shame.
32I run in the path of your
      commands,
   for you have set my heart
      free.

ה   He

33Teach me, O LORD, to follow
      your decrees;
   then I will keep them to the
      end.
34Give me understanding, and
   I will keep your law
   and obey it with all my
      heart.   Dt 6:25

³⁵Direct me in the path of your
   commands,   Ps 25:4-5
 for there I find delight.
³⁶Turn my heart toward your
   statutes   Jos 24:23
 and not toward selfish
   gain.
³⁷Turn my eyes away from
   worthless things;
 preserve my life according
   to your word. ᵃ   Ps 71:20
³⁸Fulfill your promise to your
   servant,   Nu 23:19
 so that you may be feared.
³⁹Take away the disgrace I
   dread,   Ps 69:9
 for your laws are good.
⁴⁰How I long for your precepts!
 Preserve my life in your
   righteousness.

ו Waw

⁴¹May your unfailing love
   come to me, O LORD,
 your salvation according to
   your promise;
⁴²then I will answer the one
   who taunts me,   Ps 42:10
 for I trust in your word.
⁴³Do not snatch the word of
   truth from my mouth,
 for I have put my hope in
   your laws.
⁴⁴I will always obey your
   law,
 for ever and ever.   Dt 6:25
⁴⁵I will walk about in freedom,
 for I have sought out your
   precepts.
⁴⁶I will speak of your statutes
   before kings   Mt 10:18

and will not be put to
   shame,
⁴⁷for I delight in your
   commands   Ps 112:1
 because I love them.
⁴⁸I lift up my hands to ᵇ your
   commands, which I
   love,
 and I meditate on your
   decrees.   Ge 24:63

ז Zayin

⁴⁹Remember your word to
   your servant,
 for you have given me
   hope.
⁵⁰My comfort in my suffering
   is this:
 Your promise preserves my
   life.
⁵¹The arrogant mock me
   without restraint,   Job 16:10
 but I do not turn from your
   law.   Job 23:11
⁵²I remember your ancient
   laws, O LORD,   Ps 103:18
 and I find comfort in
   them.
⁵³Indignation grips me because
   of the wicked,   Ex 32:19
 who have forsaken your
   law.   Ps 89:30
⁵⁴Your decrees are the theme
   of my song
 wherever I lodge.   Ps 101:1
⁵⁵In the night I remember your
   name, O LORD,   Ps 1:2
 and I will keep your
   law.
⁵⁶This has been my practice:
 I obey your precepts.

ᵃ37 Two manuscripts of the Masoretic Text and Dead Sea Scrolls; most manuscripts of
the Masoretic Text *life in your way*   ᵇ48 Or *for*

ח   Heth

⁵⁷You are my portion, O Lᴏʀᴅ;
   I have promised to obey
   your words.
⁵⁸I have sought your face with
   all my heart;   Dt 4:29
   be gracious to me according
   to your promise.
⁵⁹I have considered my ways
   and have turned my steps
   to your statutes.   Ps 39:1
⁶⁰I will hasten and not delay
   to obey your commands.
⁶¹Though the wicked bind me
   with ropes,
   I will not forget your law.
⁶²At midnight I rise to give you
   thanks   Ac 16:25
   for your righteous laws.
⁶³I am a friend to all who fear
   you,   Ps 15:4
   to all who follow your
   precepts.   Ps 111:10
⁶⁴The earth is filled with your
   love, O Lᴏʀᴅ;   Ps 33:5
   teach me your decrees.

ט   Teth

⁶⁵Do good to your servant
   according to your word,
   O Lᴏʀᴅ.
⁶⁶Teach me knowledge and
   good judgment,   Ps 51:6
   for I believe in your
   commands.
⁶⁷Before I was afflicted I went
   astray,   Ps 116:10
   but now I obey your word.
⁶⁸You are good, and what you
   do is good;   Ps 100:5
   teach me your decrees.
⁶⁹Though the arrogant have
   smeared me with lies,

I keep your precepts with
   all my heart.   Job 13:4
⁷⁰Their hearts are callous and
   unfeeling,   Ps 17:10
   but I delight in your law.
⁷¹It was good for me to be
   afflicted
   so that I might learn your
   decrees.
⁷²The law from your mouth is
   more precious to me
   than thousands of pieces of
   silver and gold.   Job 28:17

י   Yodh

⁷³Your hands made me and
   formed me;   Ge 1:27
   give me understanding to
   learn your commands.
⁷⁴May those who fear you
   rejoice when they see
   me,   Ps 34:2
   for I have put my hope in
   your word.
⁷⁵I know, O Lᴏʀᴅ, that your
   laws are righteous,
   and in faithfulness you
   have afflicted me.
⁷⁶May your unfailing love be
   my comfort,   Ps 6:4
   according to your promise
   to your servant.
⁷⁷Let your compassion come to
   me that I may live,
   for your law is my delight.
⁷⁸May the arrogant be put to
   shame for wronging me
   without cause;   Ps 35:19
   but I will meditate on your
   precepts.
⁷⁹May those who fear you turn
   to me,

those who understand your
　statutes.
80May my heart be blameless
　　toward your decrees,
　that I may not be put to
　　shame.

** כ Kaph**

81My soul faints with longing
　　for your salvation,
　but I have put my hope in
　　your word.
82My eyes fail, looking for your
　　promise; Ps 6:7
　I say, "When will you
　　comfort me?"
83Though I am like a wineskin
　　in the smoke,
　I do not forget your
　　decrees.
84How long must your servant
　　wait? Ps 6:3
　When will you punish my
　　persecutors? Jer 12:3
85The arrogant dig pitfalls for
　　me, Ps 35:7
　contrary to your law.
86All your commands are
　　trustworthy;
　help me, for men persecute
　　me without cause.
87They almost wiped me from
　　the earth,
　but I have not forsaken
　　your precepts. Isa 1:4
88Preserve my life according to
　　your love, Ps 51:1
　and I will obey the statutes
　　of your mouth.

ל Lamedh

89Your word, O LORD, is
　　eternal; Ps 111:8

it stands firm in the
　heavens.
90Your faithfulness continues
　　through all generations;
　you established the earth,
　　and it endures. Job 8:19
91Your laws endure to this day,
　for all things serve you.
92If your law had not been my
　　delight, Ps 37:4
　I would have perished in
　　my affliction.
93I will never forget your
　　precepts,
　for by them you have
　　preserved my life.
94Save me, for I am yours;
　I have sought out your
　　precepts.
95The wicked are waiting to
　　destroy me, Ps 69:4
　but I will ponder your
　　statutes.
96To all perfection I see a limit;
　but your commands are
　　boundless. Ps 19:7

מ Mem

97Oh, how I love your law!
　I meditate on it all day
　　long.
98Your commands make me
　　wiser than my enemies,
　for they are ever with me.
99I have more insight than all
　　my teachers,
　for I meditate on your
　　statutes.
100I have more understanding
　　than the elders,
　for I obey your precepts.
101I have kept my feet from
　　every evil path

so that I might obey your
word.
102I have not departed from
your laws,   Dt 17:20
for you yourself have
taught me.   Dt 4:5
103How sweet are your words
to my taste,
sweeter than honey to my
mouth!   Ps 19:10
104I gain understanding from
your precepts;
therefore I hate every
wrong path.   Ps 111:10

נ Nun

105Your word is a lamp to my
feet   Pr 20:27
and a light for my path.
106I have taken an oath and
confirmed it,   Ne 10:29
that I will follow your
righteous laws.
107I have suffered much;
preserve my life, O LORD,
according to your word.
108Accept, O LORD, the willing
praise of my mouth,
and teach me your laws.
109Though I constantly take my
life in my hands,
I will not forget your law.
110The wicked have set a snare
for me,   Ps 25:15
but I have not strayed from
your precepts.
111Your statutes are my
heritage forever;
they are the joy of my
heart.
112My heart is set on keeping
your decrees
to the very end.   Ps 108:1

ס Samekh

113I hate double-minded men,
but I love your law.   Jas 1:8
114You are my refuge and my
shield;   Ge 15:1
I have put my hope in your
word.
115Away from me, you
evildoers,   Ps 6:8
that I may keep the
commands of my God!
116Sustain me according to your
promise, and I will live;
do not let my hopes be
dashed.   Ro 5:5
117Uphold me, and I will be
delivered;   Isa 41:10
I will always have regard
for your decrees.
118You reject all who stray from
your decrees,
for their deceitfulness is in
vain.
119All the wicked of the earth
you discard like dross;
therefore I love your
statutes.
120My flesh trembles in fear of
you;   Job 4:14
I stand in awe of your laws.

ע Ayin

121I have done what is
righteous and just;
do not leave me to my
oppressors.   2Sa 8:15
122Ensure your servant's
well-being;   Job 17:3
let not the arrogant oppress
me.   Ps 106:42
123My eyes fail, looking for
your salvation,

looking for your righteous
   promise.
[124]Deal with your servant
   according to your love
and teach me your decrees.
[125]I am your servant; give me
   discernment   Ps 116:16
that I may understand your
   statutes.
[126]It is time for you to act,
   O Lord;
your law is being broken.
[127]Because I love your
   commands
more than gold, more than
   pure gold,   Ps 19:10
[128]and because I consider all
   your precepts right,
I hate every wrong path.

פ Pe

[129]Your statutes are wonderful;
   therefore I obey them.
[130]The unfolding of your words
   gives light;
it gives understanding to
   the simple.   Ps 19:7
[131]I open my mouth and pant,
   longing for your
   commands.   Ps 42:1
[132]Turn to me and have mercy
   on me,   Ps 6:4
as you always do to those
   who love your name.
[133]Direct my footsteps
   according to your word;
let no sin rule over me.
[134]Redeem me from the
   oppression of men,
that I may obey your
   precepts.
[135]Make your face shine upon
   your servant   Nu 6:25

and teach me your decrees.
[136]Streams of tears flow from
   my eyes,   Ps 6:6
for your law is not obeyed.

צ Tsadhe

[137]Righteous are you, O Lord,
   and your laws are right.
[138]The statutes you have laid
   down are righteous;
they are fully trustworthy.
[139]My zeal wears me out,
   for my enemies ignore your
   words.   Ps 69:9
[140]Your promises have been
   thoroughly tested,
and your servant loves
   them.
[141]Though I am lowly and
   despised,
I do not forget your
   precepts.   Ps 22:6
[142]Your righteousness is
   everlasting
and your law is true.
[143]Trouble and distress have
   come upon me,
but your commands are my
   delight.
[144]Your statutes are forever
   right;
give me understanding that
   I may live.

ק Qoph

[145]I call with all my heart;
   answer me, O Lord,
and I will obey your
   decrees.
[146]I call out to you; save me
   and I will keep your
   statutes.

¹⁴⁷I rise before dawn and cry
for help; *Ps 5:3*
I have put my hope in your
word.
¹⁴⁸My eyes stay open through
the watches of the
night,
that I may meditate on your
promises.
¹⁴⁹Hear my voice in accordance
with your love; *Ps 27:7*
preserve my life, O LORD,
according to your
laws.
¹⁵⁰Those who devise wicked
schemes are near,
but they are far from your
law.
¹⁵¹Yet you are near, O LORD,
and all your commands are
true.
¹⁵²Long ago I learned from
your statutes
that you established them
to last forever. *Ps 111:8*

ר Resh

¹⁵³Look upon my suffering and
deliver me, *Ps 13:3*
for I have not forgotten
your law. *Ps 44:17*
¹⁵⁴Defend my cause and
redeem me; *Ps 35:1*
preserve my life according
to your promise.
¹⁵⁵Salvation is far from the
wicked,
for they do not seek out
your decrees.
¹⁵⁶Your compassion is great,
O LORD; *Ne 9:27*
preserve my life according
to your laws.

¹⁵⁷Many are the foes who
persecute me, *Ps 7:1*
but I have not turned from
your statutes. *Ps 44:18*
¹⁵⁸I look on the faithless with
loathing, *Ex 32:19*
for they do not obey your
word.
¹⁵⁹See how I love your
precepts;
preserve my life, O LORD,
according to your love.
¹⁶⁰All your words are true;
all your righteous laws are
eternal.

ש Sin and Shin

¹⁶¹Rulers persecute me without
cause, *1Sa 24:14-15*
but my heart trembles at
your word.
¹⁶²I rejoice in your promise
like one who finds great
spoil. *1Sa 30:16*
¹⁶³I hate and abhor falsehood
but I love your law.
¹⁶⁴Seven times a day I praise
you
for your righteous laws.
¹⁶⁵Great peace have they who
love your law, *Ps 37:11*
and nothing can make them
stumble. *Ps 37:24*
¹⁶⁶I wait for your salvation,
O LORD,
and I follow your
commands.
¹⁶⁷I obey your statutes,
for I love them greatly.
¹⁶⁸I obey your precepts and
your statutes,
for all my ways are known
to you. *Job 10:4*

ת Taw

169May my cry come before
    you, O LORD;   Job 16:18
 give me understanding
    according to your word.
170May my supplication come
    before you;   1Ki 8:30
 deliver me according to
    your promise.   Ps 3:7
171May my lips overflow with
    praise,   Ps 51:15
 for you teach me your
    decrees.   Ps 94:12
172May my tongue sing of your
    word,   Ps 51:14
 for all your commands are
    righteous.
173May your hand be ready to
    help me,   Ps 37:24
 for I have chosen your
    precepts.   Jos 24:22
174I long for your salvation,
    O LORD,
 and your law is my delight.
175Let me live that I may praise
    you,
 and may your laws sustain
    me.
176I have strayed like a lost
    sheep.   Ps 95:10
 Seek your servant,
 for I have not forgotten
    your commands.   Ps 44:17

Psalm 120

A song of ascents.

1I call on the LORD in my
    distress,   Ps 18:6
 and he answers me.
2Save me, O LORD, from lying
    lips   Ps 31:18
 and from deceitful tongues.

3What will he do to you,
 and what more besides,
    O deceitful tongue?
4He will punish you with a
    warrior's sharp arrows,
 with burning coals of the
    broom tree.   Dt 32:23
5Woe to me that I dwell in
    Meshech,
 that I live among the tents
    of Kedar!   Ge 25:13
6Too long have I lived
 among those who hate
    peace.
7I am a man of peace;
 but when I speak, they are
    for war.

Psalm 121

A song of ascents.

1I lift up my eyes to the hills—
 where does my help come
    from?
2My help comes from the
    LORD,
 the Maker of heaven and
    earth.   Ps 104:5

3He will not let your foot
    slip—
 he who watches over you
    will not slumber;
4indeed, he who watches over
    Israel
 will neither slumber nor
    sleep.   Ps 127:1
5The LORD watches over
    you—   Ps 1:6
 the LORD is your shade at
    your right hand;
6the sun will not harm you by
    day,   Isa 49:10

nor the moon by night.
7The LORD will keep you from
   all harm—   Ps 9:9
he will watch over your life;
8the LORD will watch over
   your coming and going
both now and forevermore.

Psalm 122

A song of ascents. Of David.

1I rejoiced with those who
   said to me,
   "Let us go to the house of
   the LORD."
2Our feet are standing
   in your gates, O Jerusalem.

3Jerusalem is built like a city
   that is closely compacted
   together.
4That is where the tribes go
   up,
   the tribes of the LORD,
to praise the name of the
   LORD
   according to the statute
   given to Israel.
5There the thrones for
   judgment stand,
   the thrones of the house of
   David.

6Pray for the peace of
   Jerusalem:
   "May those who love you
   be secure.   Ps 26:8
7May there be peace within
   your walls   1Sa 25:6
   and security within your
   citadels."   Ps 48:3
8For the sake of my brothers
   and friends,

I will say, "Peace be within
   you."
9For the sake of the house of
   the LORD our God,
I will seek your prosperity.

Psalm 123

A song of ascents.

1I lift up my eyes to you,
   to you whose throne is in
   heaven.   Ps 68:5
2As the eyes of slaves look to
   the hand of their master,
   as the eyes of a maid look
   to the hand of her
   mistress,
so our eyes look to the LORD
   our God,   Ps 25:15
   till he shows us his mercy.

3Have mercy on us, O LORD,
   have mercy on us,
   for we have endured much
   contempt.
4We have endured much
   ridicule from the
   proud,
   much contempt from the
   arrogant.

Psalm 124

A song of ascents. Of David.

1If the LORD had not been on
   our side—
   let Israel say—   Ps 129:1
2if the LORD had not been on
   our side
   when men attacked us,
3when their anger flared
   against us,

they would have swallowed
us alive;
[4]the flood would have
engulfed us,   Ps 88:17
the torrent would have
swept over us,   Ps 18:4
[5]the raging waters
would have swept us away.

[6]Praise be to the LORD,
who has not let us be torn
by their teeth.
[7]We have escaped like a bird
out of the fowler's snare;
the snare has been broken,
and we have escaped.
[8]Our help is in the name of
the LORD,   1Sa 17:45
the Maker of heaven and
earth.   Ge 1:1

Psalm 125

A song of ascents.

[1]Those who trust in the LORD
are like Mount Zion,
which cannot be shaken but
endures forever.   Ps 46:5
[2]As the mountains surround
Jerusalem,   1Ch 21:15
so the LORD surrounds his
people   Ps 32:10
both now and forevermore.

[3]The scepter of the wicked
will not remain   Ps 89:22
over the land allotted to the
righteous,
for then the righteous might
use
their hands to do evil.

[4]Do good, O LORD, to those
who are good,   Ps 119:65
to those who are upright in
heart.   Ps 36:10
[5]But those who turn to
crooked ways   Job 23:11
the LORD will banish with
the evildoers.   Ps 92:7

Peace be upon Israel.   Ps 128:6

Psalm 126

A song of ascents.

[1]When the LORD brought back
the captives to[a] Zion,
we were like men who
dreamed.[b]
[2]Our mouths were filled with
laughter,   Ge 21:6
our tongues with songs of
joy.   Job 8:21
Then it was said among the
nations,
"The LORD has done great
things for them."   Dt 10:21
[3]The LORD has done great
things for us,
and we are filled with
joy.

[4]Restore our fortunes,[c]
O LORD,   Dt 30:3
like streams in the Negev.
[5]Those who sow in tears
will reap with songs of joy.
[6]He who goes out weeping,
carrying seed to sow,
will return with songs of joy,
carrying sheaves with him.

[a]1 Or LORD restored the fortunes of   [b]1 Or men restored to health   [c]4 Or Bring back our
captives

Psalm 127

A song of ascents. Of Solomon.

¹Unless the LORD builds the
house,   Ps 78:69
its builders labor in vain.
Unless the LORD watches
over the city,   Ps 121:4
the watchmen stand guard
in vain.
²In vain you rise early
and stay up late,
toiling for food to eat—   Ge 3:17
for he grants sleep to*a* those
he loves.   Nu 6:26

³Sons are a heritage from the
LORD,
children a reward from
him.   Ge 1:28
⁴Like arrows in the hands of a
warrior   Ps 112:2
are sons born in one's
youth.
⁵Blessed is the man
whose quiver is full of
them.   Ps 128:2-3
They will not be put to
shame
when they contend with
their enemies in the
gate.   Ge 24:60

Psalm 128

A song of ascents.

¹Blessed are all who fear the
LORD,   Ps 103:11
who walk in his ways.
²You will eat the fruit of your
labor;   Ps 58:11

blessings and prosperity
will be yours.   Ge 39:3
³Your wife will be like a
fruitful vine   Ge 49:22
within your house;
your sons will be like olive
shoots   Job 29:5
around your table.
⁴Thus is the man blessed
who fears the LORD.

⁵May the LORD bless you from
Zion   Ps 20:2
all the days of your life;
may you see the prosperity
of Jerusalem,   Ps 122:9
⁶ and may you live to see
your children's children.

Peace be upon Israel.   Ps 125:5

Psalm 129

A song of ascents.

¹They have greatly oppressed
me from my youth—
let Israel say—   Ps 124:1
²they have greatly oppressed
me from my youth,
but they have not gained
the victory over me.
³Plowmen have plowed my
back
and made their furrows
long.
⁴But the LORD is righteous;
he has cut me free from the
cords of the wicked.

⁵May all who hate Zion
be turned back in shame.
⁶May they be like grass on the
roof,   Isa 37:27

*a*2 Or eat— / for while they sleep he provides for

which withers before it can
  grow;   2Ki 19:26
⁷with it the reaper cannot fill
  his hands,   Dt 28:38
nor the one who gathers fill
  his arms.
⁸May those who pass by not
  say,
"The blessing of the LORD
  be upon you;
we bless you in the name of
  the LORD."   Ps 118:26

Psalm 130

A song of ascents.

¹Out of the depths I cry to
  you, O LORD;   Ps 22:2
² O Lord, hear my voice.
Let your ears be attentive
  to my cry for mercy.   Ps 28:6

³If you, O LORD, kept a record
  of sins,
O Lord, who could stand?
⁴But with you there is
  forgiveness;   Ex 34:7
therefore you are feared.

⁵I wait for the LORD, my soul
  waits,   Ps 27:14
and in his word I put my
  hope.   Ps 119:74
⁶My soul waits for the Lord
more than watchmen wait
  for the morning,
more than watchmen wait
  for the morning.   2Sa 23:4

⁷O Israel, put your hope in
  the LORD,   Ps 25:5
for with the LORD is
  unfailing love   1Ch 21:13
and with him is full
  redemption.   Ps 111:9

⁸He himself will redeem Israel
from all their sins.   Lk 1:68

Psalm 131

A song of ascents. Of David.

¹My heart is not proud,
  O LORD,   Ps 101:5
my eyes are not haughty;
I do not concern myself with
  great matters   Jer 45:5
or things too wonderful for
  me.   Job 5:9
²But I have stilled and quieted
  my soul;   Ps 116:7
like a weaned child with its
  mother,
like a weaned child is my
  soul within me.   Mt 18:3

³O Israel, put your hope in
  the LORD   Ps 25:5
both now and forevermore.

Psalm 132

A song of ascents.

¹O LORD, remember David
and all the hardships he
  endured.   1Sa 18:11
²He swore an oath to the
  LORD
and made a vow to the
  Mighty One of Jacob:
³"I will not enter my house
or go to my bed—   2Sa 7:2
⁴I will allow no sleep to my
  eyes,
no slumber to my eyelids,
⁵till I find a place for the
  LORD,   1Ki 8:17
a dwelling for the Mighty
  One of Jacob."

⁶We heard it in Ephrathah,
we came upon it in the
fields of Jaar*ᵃ:ᵇ*   Jos 9:17
⁷"Let us go to his dwelling
place;   2Sa 15:25
let us worship at his
footstool—   1Ch 28:2
⁸arise, O LORD, and come to
your resting place,
you and the ark of your
might.
⁹May your priests be clothed
with righteousness;
may your saints sing for
joy."   Ps 16:3

¹⁰For the sake of David your
servant,
do not reject your anointed
one.

¹¹The LORD swore an oath to
David,   Ps 89:3-4
a sure oath that he will not
revoke:
"One of your own
descendants   1Ch 17:11-14
I will place on your
throne—
¹²if your sons keep my
covenant   2Ch 6:16
and the statutes I teach
them,
then their sons will sit
on your throne for ever and
ever."   Lk 1:32

¹³For the LORD has chosen
Zion,   Ex 15:17
he has desired it for his
dwelling: 1Ki 8:13

¹⁴"This is my resting place for
ever and ever;   Ps 68:16
here I will sit enthroned, for
I have desired it—   2Sa 6:2
¹⁵I will bless her with
abundant provisions;
her poor will I satisfy with
food.   Ps 107:9
¹⁶I will clothe her priests with
salvation,   2Ch 6:41
and her saints will ever sing
for joy.   Job 8:21

¹⁷"Here I will make a horn*ᶜ*
grow for David   1Sa 2:10
and set up a lamp for my
anointed one.   1Ki 11:36
¹⁸I will clothe his enemies with
shame,   Job 8:22
but the crown on his head
will be resplendent."

Psalm 133

A song of ascents. Of David.

¹How good and pleasant it is
when brothers live together
in unity!   Jn 17:11
²It is like precious oil poured
on the head,   Ex 29:7
running down on the
beard,
running down on Aaron's
beard,
down upon the collar of his
robes.
³It is as if the dew of Hermon
were falling on Mount
Zion.   Ex 15:17
For there the LORD bestows
his blessing,   Lev 25:21

ᵃ6 That is, Kiriath Jearim   *ᵇ6* Or *heard of it in Ephrathah, / we found it in the fields of
Jaar.* (And no quotes around verses 7-9)   *ᶜ17 Horn* here symbolizes strong one, that
is, king.

even life forevermore.

Psalm 134

A song of ascents.

¹Praise the LORD, all you
    servants of the LORD
who minister by night in
    the house of the LORD.
²Lift up your hands in the
    sanctuary   Ps 28:2
    and praise the LORD.   Ps 33:2

³May the LORD, the Maker of
    heaven and earth,
    bless you from Zion.   Lev 25:21

Psalm 135

¹Praise the LORD.*ᵃ*

Praise the name of the LORD;
    praise him, you servants of
    the LORD,   Ne 7:73
²you who minister in the
    house of the LORD,
    in the courts of the house of
    our God.   Ps 116:19

³Praise the LORD, for the LORD
    is good;   1Ch 16:34
    sing praise to his name, for
    that is pleasant.   Ps 92:1
⁴For the LORD has chosen
    Jacob to be his own,
    Israel to be his treasured
    possession.   Ex 19:5

⁵I know that the LORD is
    great,   Ps 48:1
    that our Lord is greater
    than all gods.   Ex 12:12
⁶The LORD does whatever
    pleases him,   Ps 115:3

in the heavens and on the
    earth,
    in the seas and all their   Mt 6:10
    depths.
⁷He makes clouds rise from
    the ends of the earth;
he sends lightning with the
    rain   Job 5:10
and brings out the wind
    from his storehouses.

⁸He struck down the firstborn
    of Egypt,   Ex 4:23
    the firstborn of men and
    animals.
⁹He sent his signs and
    wonders into your
    midst, O Egypt,   Ex 7:9
    against Pharaoh and all his
    servants.   Ps 136:10-15
¹⁰He struck down many
    nations
    and killed mighty kings—
¹¹Sihon king of the Amorites,
    Og king of Bashan   Nu 21:33
    and all the kings of
    Canaan—   Jos 24:12
¹²and he gave their land as an
    inheritance,   Dt 29:8
    an inheritance to his people
    Israel.

¹³Your name, O LORD, endures
    forever,   Ex 3:15
    your renown, O LORD,
    through all generations.
¹⁴For the LORD will vindicate
    his people   1Sa 24:15
    and have compassion on
    his servants.   Dt 32:36
¹⁵The idols of the nations are
    silver and gold,   Ps 96:5
    made by the hands of men.

ᵃ1 Hebrew *Hallelu Yah*; also in verses 3 and 21

16They have mouths, but
cannot speak,   1Ki 18:26
eyes, but they cannot see;
17they have ears, but cannot
hear,
nor is there breath in their
mouths.   Jer 10:14
18Those who make them will
be like them,
and so will all who trust in
them.

19O house of Israel, praise the
LORD;   Ps 22:23
O house of Aaron, praise
the LORD;
20O house of Levi, praise the
LORD;
you who fear him, praise
the LORD.
21Praise be to the LORD from
Zion,   Ps 128:5
to him who dwells in
Jerusalem.   1Ki 8:13

Praise the LORD.

Psalm 136

1Give thanks to the LORD, for
he is good.   Ps 105:1
His love endures forever.
2Give thanks to the God of
gods.   Dt 10:17
His love endures forever.
3Give thanks to the Lord of
lords:
His love endures forever.

4to him who alone does great
wonders,   Ex 3:20
His love endures forever.

5who by his understanding
made the heavens,
His love endures forever.
6who spread out the earth
upon the waters,   Isa 42:5
His love endures forever.
7who made the great lights—
His love endures forever.
8the sun to govern the day,
His love endures forever.
9the moon and stars to govern
the night;
His love endures forever.

10to him who struck down the
firstborn of Egypt   Ex 4:23
His love endures forever.
11and brought Israel out from
among them   Ex 6:6
His love endures forever.
12with a mighty hand and
outstretched arm;   Dt 9:29
His love endures forever.

13to him who divided the Red
Sea[a] asunder   Ps 78:13
His love endures forever.
14and brought Israel through
the midst of it,   Ex 14:22
His love endures forever.
15but swept Pharaoh and his
army into the Red Sea;
His love endures forever.

16to him who led his people
through the desert,   Ex 13:18
His love endures forever.
17who struck down great
kings,   Nu 21:23-25
His love endures forever.
18and killed mighty kings—
His love endures forever.
19Sihon king of the Amorites
His love endures forever.

a13 Hebrew *Yam Suph*; that is, Sea of Reeds; also in verse 15

²⁰and Og king of Bashan—
His love endures forever.
²¹and gave their land as an
inheritance,   Jos 12:1
His love endures forever.
²²an inheritance to his servant
Israel;   Dt 29:8
His love endures forever.

²³to the One who remembered
us in our low estate
His love endures forever.
²⁴and freed us from our
enemies,   Jos 10:14
His love endures forever.
²⁵and who gives food to every
creature.   Ge 1:30
His love endures forever.

²⁶Give thanks to the God of
heaven.   Ps 115:3
His love endures forever.

Psalm 137

¹By the rivers of Babylon we
sat and wept   Ne 1:4
when we remembered
Zion.   Isa 3:26
²There on the poplars
we hung our harps,   Job 30:31
³for there our captors asked
us for songs,   Ps 79:1-4
our tormentors demanded
songs of joy;   Job 30:9
they said, "Sing us one of
the songs of Zion!"

⁴How can we sing the songs
of the LORD   Ne 12:46
while in a foreign land?
⁵If I forget you, O Jerusalem,
may my right hand forget
its skill.   Isa 2:3

⁶May my tongue cling to the
roof of my mouth   Ps 22:15
if I do not remember you,
if I do not consider Jerusalem
my highest joy.   Dt 4:29

⁷Remember, O LORD, what
the Edomites did
on the day Jerusalem fell.
"Tear it down," they cried,
"tear it down to its
foundations!"   Ps 74:7

⁸O Daughter of Babylon,
doomed to destruction,
happy is he who repays
you
for what you have done to
us—   Isa 13:1
⁹he who seizes your infants
and dashes them against
the rocks.   2Ki 8:12

Psalm 138

Of David.

¹I will praise you, O LORD,
with all my heart;
before the "gods" I will
sing your praise.   Ps 95:3
²I will bow down toward your
holy temple   1Ki 8:29
and will praise your name
for your love and your
faithfulness,   Ps 108:4
for you have exalted above
all things
your name and your word.
³When I called, you answered
me;   Ps 118:5
you made me bold and
stouthearted.   Pr 28:1
⁴May all the kings of the earth
praise you, O LORD,

when they hear the words
of your mouth.
⁵May they sing of the ways of
the LORD,   Ps 51:14
for the glory of the LORD is
great.   Ps 21:5

⁶Though the LORD is on high,
he looks upon the lowly,
but the proud he knows
from afar.   Ps 40:4
⁷Though I walk in the midst
of trouble,   Ps 23:4
you preserve my life;   Ps 41:2
you stretch out your hand
against the anger of my
foes,   Ps 7:6
with your right hand you
save me.   Ps 17:7
⁸The LORD will fulfill his
purpose for me;   Php 1:6
your love, O LORD, endures
forever—   Ezr 3:11
do not abandon the works
of your hands.   Ps 51:11

Psalm 139

For the director of music. Of
David. A psalm.

¹O LORD, you have searched
me   Ps 17:3
and you know me.   Ps 44:21
²You know when I sit and
when I rise;   2Ki 19:27
you perceive my thoughts
from afar.   Ps 94:11
³You discern my going out
and my lying down;
you are familiar with all my
ways.   Job 31:4

⁴Before a word is on my
tongue
you know it completely,
O LORD.   Heb 4:13

⁵You hem me in—behind and
before;   1Sa 25:16
you have laid your hand
upon me.
⁶Such knowledge is too
wonderful for me,
too lofty for me to attain.

⁷Where can I go from your
Spirit?
Where can I flee from your
presence?   Jer 23:24
⁸If I go up to the heavens, you
are there;   Dt 30:12-15
if I make my bed in the
depths,ᵃ you are there.
⁹If I rise on the wings of the
dawn,
if I settle on the far side of
the sea,
¹⁰even there your hand will
guide me,   Ps 23:3
your right hand will hold
me fast.   Ps 108:6

¹¹If I say, "Surely the darkness
will hide me
and the light become night
around me,"
¹²even the darkness will not be
dark to you;   Job 34:22
the night will shine like the
day,
for darkness is as light to
you.

¹³For you created my inmost
being;   Ps 119:73

ᵃ8 Hebrew *Sheol*

you knit me together in my
    mother's womb.   Isa 44:2
14I praise you because I am
    fearfully and
    wonderfully made;
your works are wonderful,
    I know that full well.   Job 40:19
15My frame was not hidden
    from you
when I was made in the
    secret place.   Ecc 11:5
When I was woven together
    in the depths of the
    earth,   Ps 63:9
16 your eyes saw my
    unformed body.
All the days ordained for me
    were written in your book
    before one of them came
    to be.   Job 33:29

17How precious toᵃ me are
    your thoughts, O God!
How vast is the sum of
    them!   Job 5:9
18Were I to count them,
    they would outnumber the
    grains of sand.   Job 29:18
When I awake,
    I am still with you.   Ps 3:5

19If only you would slay the
    wicked, O God!   Ps 5:6
Away from me, you
    bloodthirsty men!   Ps 59:2
20They speak of you with evil
    intent;
    your adversaries misuse
    your name.   Ps 65:7
21Do I not hate those who hate
    you, O LORD,   2Ch 19:2
    and abhor those who rise
    up against you?   Ps 26:5

22I have nothing but hatred for
    them;
    I count them my enemies.

23Search me, O God, and
    know my heart;   Job 31:6
test me and know my
    anxious thoughts.
24See if there is any offensive
    way in me,   Jer 25:5
and lead me in the way
    everlasting.   Ps 5:8

Psalm 140

For the director of music.
A psalm of David.

1Rescue me, O LORD, from
    evil men;   Ps 17:13
protect me from men of
    violence,   Ps 86:14
2who devise evil plans in their
    hearts   Ps 36:4
    and stir up war every day.
3They make their tongues as
    sharp as a serpent's;
the poison of vipers is on
    their lips.   *Selah*

4Keep me, O LORD, from the
    hands of the wicked;
protect me from men of
    violence
who plan to trip my feet.
5Proud men have hidden a
    snare for me;   Job 34:30
they have spread out the
    cords of their net   Job 18:8
and have set traps for me
    along my path.   *Selah*

6O LORD, I say to you, "You
    are my God."   Ps 16:2

ᵃ17 Or *concerning*

Hear, O LORD, my cry for
  mercy.   Ps 28:2
7O Sovereign LORD, my
  strong deliverer,   Ps 68:20
who shields my head in the
  day of battle—
8do not grant the wicked their
  desires, O LORD;
do not let their plans
  succeed,
or they will become proud.
                                              Selah

9Let the heads of those who
  surround me
be covered with the trouble
  their lips have caused.
10Let burning coals fall upon
  them;
may they be thrown into
  the fire,   Ps 11:6
into miry pits, never to rise.
11Let slanderers not be
  established in the land;
may disaster hunt down
  men of violence.   Ps 34:21

12I know that the LORD secures
  justice for the poor
and upholds the cause of
  the needy.   Ps 35:10
13Surely the righteous will
  praise your name
and the upright will live
  before you.   Ps 16:11

Psalm 141

A psalm of David.

1O LORD, I call to you; come
  quickly to me.   Ps 22:19
Hear my voice when I call
  to you.   Ps 4:1

2May my prayer be set before
  you like incense;   Lk 1:9
may the lifting up of my
  hands be like the
  evening sacrifice.   Ex 29:39

3Set a guard over my mouth,
  O LORD;   Ps 34:13
keep watch over the door of
  my lips.   Ps 12:2
4Let not my heart be drawn to
  what is evil,   Jos 24:23
to take part in wicked deeds
with men who are evildoers;
let me not eat of their
  delicacies.   Pr 23:1-3

5Let a righteous man*a* strike
  me—it is a kindness;
let him rebuke me—it is oil
  on my head.   Pr 9:8
My head will not refuse it.

Yet my prayer is ever against
  the deeds of evildoers;
6 their rulers will be thrown
  down from the cliffs,
and the wicked will learn
  that my words were well
  spoken.   2Ch 25:12
7They will say, "As one
  plows and breaks up the
  earth,   Ps 129:3
so our bones have been
  scattered at the mouth of
  the grave.*b*"   Nu 16:30

8But my eyes are fixed on
  you, O Sovereign LORD;
in you I take refuge—do not
  give me over to death.
9Keep me from the snares
  they have laid for me,

---

*a*5 Or *Let the Righteous One*   *b*7 Hebrew *Sheol*

from the traps set by
evildoers.   Ps 38:12
¹⁰Let the wicked fall into their
own nets,   Ps 7:15
while I pass by in safety.

Psalm 142

*A maskil[a] of David. When he was
in the cave. A prayer.*

¹I cry aloud to the LORD;
I lift up my voice to the
LORD for mercy.   Ps 30:8
²I pour out my complaint
before him;   Ps 64:1
before him I tell my trouble.

³When my spirit grows faint
within me,   Ps 6:2
it is you who know my
way.
In the path where I walk
men have hidden a snare
for me.
⁴Look to my right and see;
no one is concerned for me.
I have no refuge;   Jer 25:35
no one cares for my life.

⁵I cry to you, O LORD;
I say, "You are my refuge,
my portion in the land of
the living."   Job 28:13
⁶Listen to my cry,   Ps 17:1
for I am in desperate need;
rescue me from those who
pursue me,   Ps 25:20
for they are too strong for
me.   Jer 31:11
⁷Set me free from my prison,
that I may praise your
name.   Ps 7:17

Then the righteous will
gather about me
because of your goodness
to me.   2Ch 6:41

Psalm 143

A psalm of David.

¹O LORD, hear my prayer,
listen to my cry for mercy;
in your faithfulness and
righteousness
come to my relief.   Ps 71:2
²Do not bring your servant
into judgment,
for no one living is
righteous before you.

³The enemy pursues me,
he crushes me to the
ground;
he makes me dwell in
darkness   Ps 107:10
like those long dead.
⁴So my spirit grows faint
within me;
my heart within me is
dismayed.   Ps 30:7

⁵I remember the days of long
ago;   Ps 77:6
I meditate on all your works
and consider what your
hands have done.
⁶I spread out my hands to
you;   Ex 9:29
my soul thirsts for you like
a parched land.   *Selah*

⁷Answer me quickly, O LORD;
my spirit fails.   Ps 142:3

[a]Title: Probably a literary or musical term

Do not hide your face from
    me   <small>Ps 22:24</small>
or I will be like those who
    go down to the pit.
⁸Let the morning bring me
    word of your unfailing
    love,   <small>Ps 6:4</small>
for I have put my trust in
    you.
Show me the way I should
    go,   <small>Ex 33:13</small>
for to you I lift up my soul.
⁹Rescue me from my enemies,
    O LORD,   <small>Ps 18:17</small>
for I hide myself in you.
¹⁰Teach me to do your will,
    for you are my God;   <small>Ps 31:14</small>
may your good Spirit
    lead me on level ground.

¹¹For your name's sake,
    O LORD, preserve my
    life;
in your righteousness,
    bring me out of trouble.
¹²In your unfailing love,
    silence my enemies;
destroy all my foes,
    for I am your servant.<small>Ps 116:16</small>

Psalm 144

Of David.

¹Praise be to the LORD my
    Rock,   <small>Ge 49:24</small>
who trains my hands for
    war,
    my fingers for battle.
²He is my loving God and my
    fortress,   <small>Ps 59:9</small>
my stronghold and my
    deliverer,   <small>Ps 27:1</small>

my shield, in whom I take
    refuge,   <small>Ge 15:1</small>
who subdues peoples^a
    under me.   <small>Jdg 4:23</small>

³O LORD, what is man that
    you care for him,
the son of man that you
    think of him?   <small>Heb 2:6</small>
⁴Man is like a breath;
    his days are like a fleeting
    shadow.   <small>1Ch 29:15</small>

⁵Part your heavens, O LORD,
    and come down;   <small>Ge 11:5</small>
touch the mountains, so
    that they smoke.   <small>Ps 104:32</small>
⁶Send forth lightning and
    scatter the enemies;
shoot your arrows and rout
    them.   <small>Ps 7:12-13</small>
⁷Reach down your hand from
    on high;   <small>2Sa 22:17</small>
deliver me and rescue me
from the mighty waters,
    from the hands of
    foreigners   <small>Ps 18:44</small>
⁸whose mouths are full of lies,
    whose right hands are
    deceitful.   <small>Ps 36:3</small>

⁹I will sing a new song to you,
    O God;   <small>Ps 28:7</small>
on the ten-stringed lyre I
    will make music to you,
¹⁰to the One who gives victory
    to kings,   <small>2Sa 8:14</small>
who delivers his servant
    David from the deadly
    sword.   <small>Job 5:20</small>

¹¹Deliver me and rescue me

---

^a2 Many manuscripts of the Masoretic Text, Dead Sea Scrolls, Aquila, Jerome and
Syriac; most manuscripts of the Masoretic Text *subdues my people*

from the hands of
  foreigners   Ps 18:44
whose mouths are full of lies,
  whose right hands are
  deceitful.   Ps 12:2

¹²Then our sons in their youth
  will be like well-nurtured
  plants,   Ps 92:12-14
and our daughters will be
  like pillars   SS 4:4
carved to adorn a palace.
¹³Our barns will be filled
  with every kind of
  provision.   Pr 3:10
Our sheep will increase by
  thousands,
  by tens of thousands in our
  fields;
¹⁴ our oxen will draw heavy
  loads.*a*   Pr 14:4
There will be no breaching of
  walls,   2Ki 25:11
no going into captivity,
no cry of distress in our
  streets.   Isa 24:11

¹⁵Blessed are the people of
  whom this is true;   Dt 28:3
blessed are the people
  whose God is the LORD.

Psalm 145*b*

A psalm of praise. Of David.

¹I will exalt you, my God the
  King;   Ps 2:6
I will praise your name for
  ever and ever.   Ps 54:6
²Every day I will praise you

and extol your name for
  ever and ever.   Ps 34:1

³Great is the LORD and most
  worthy of praise;   2Sa 24:4
his greatness no one can
  fathom.   Job 5:9
⁴One generation will
  commend your works to
  another;   Ps 22:30
they will tell of your mighty
  acts.   Ps 71:16
⁵They will speak of the
  glorious splendor of
  your majesty,   Ps 96:6
and I will meditate on your
  wonderful works.*c*
⁶They will tell of the power of
  your awesome works,
and I will proclaim your
  great deeds.   Dt 32:3
⁷They will celebrate your
  abundant goodness
and joyfully sing of your
  righteousness.   Ps 138:5

⁸The LORD is gracious and
  compassionate,   Ps 86:15
slow to anger and rich in
  love.   Ps 86:5
⁹The LORD is good to all;
he has compassion on all he
  has made.   Ps 103:13-14
¹⁰All you have made will
  praise you, O LORD;
your saints will extol you.
¹¹They will tell of the glory of
  your kingdom
and speak of your might,
¹²so that all men may know of
  your mighty acts

---

*a*14 Or *our chieftains will be firmly established*
verses of which (including verse 13b) begin with the successive letters of the Hebrew
alphabet.   *c*5 Dead Sea Scrolls and Syriac (see also Septuagint); Masoretic Text *On
the glorious splendor of your majesty / and on your wonderful works I will meditate*

*b*This psalm is an acrostic poem, the

and the glorious splendor
of your kingdom.   Ps 103:19

[13]Your kingdom is an
everlasting kingdom,
and your dominion endures
through all generations.

The LORD is faithful to all his
promises   Dt 7:9
and loving toward all he
has made. [a]

[14]The LORD upholds all those
who fall   Ps 37:17
and lifts up all who are
bowed down.   1Sa 2:8

[15]The eyes of all look to you,
and you give them their
food at the proper time.

[16]You open your hand
and satisfy the desires of
every living thing.

[17]The LORD is righteous in all
his ways   Ex 9:27
and loving toward all he
has made.

[18]The LORD is near to all who
call on him,   Nu 23:21
to all who call on him in
truth.

[19]He fulfills the desires of
those who fear him;
he hears their cry and saves
them.   Ps 31:22

[20]The LORD watches over all
who love him,   Ps 1:6
but all the wicked he will
destroy.   Ps 94:23

[21]My mouth will speak in
praise of the LORD.   Ps 71:8

Let every creature praise his
holy name   Ps 65:2
for ever and ever.

Psalm 146

[1]Praise the LORD. [b]

Praise the LORD, O my soul.
[2] I will praise the LORD all
my life;   Ps 104:23
I will sing praise to my God
as long as I live.   Ps 105:2

[3]Do not put your trust in
princes,   Ps 118:9
in mortal men, who cannot
save.   Ps 60:11
[4]When their spirit departs,
they return to the
ground;   Ge 3:19
on that very day their plans
come to nothing.   Ps 33:10

[5]Blessed is he whose help is
the God of Jacob,
whose hope is in the LORD
his God,   Ps 33:18
[6]the Maker of heaven and
earth,   2Ch 2:12
the sea, and everything in
them—
the LORD, who remains
faithful forever.   Dt 7:9
[7]He upholds the cause of the
oppressed   Ps 103:6
and gives food to the
hungry.   Ps 107:9
The LORD sets prisoners free,
[8] the LORD gives sight to the
blind,   Pr 20:12

---

[a]13 One manuscript of the Masoretic Text, Dead Sea Scrolls and Syriac (see also
Septuagint); most manuscripts of the Masoretic Text do not have the last two lines of
verse 13.   [b]1 Hebrew *Hallelu Yah*; also in verse 10

the LORD lifts up those who
    are bowed down,   Ps 38:6
the LORD loves the
    righteous.   Dt 7:13
⁹The LORD watches over the
    alien   Lev 19:34
and sustains the fatherless
    and the widow,   Ex 22:22
but he frustrates the ways
    of the wicked.

¹⁰The LORD reigns forever,
    your God, O Zion, for all
    generations.   Ge 21:33

Praise the LORD.

Psalm 147

¹Praise the LORD. *ᵃ*

How good it is to sing praises
    to our God,
how pleasant and fitting to
    praise him!   Ps 135:3
²The LORD builds up
    Jerusalem;   Ps 51:18
he gathers the exiles of
    Israel.   Ps 106:47
³He heals the brokenhearted
    and binds up their wounds.

⁴He determines the number of
    the stars   Ge 15:5
and calls them each by
    name.
⁵Great is our Lord and mighty
    in power;   Ex 14:31
his understanding has no
    limit.   Ps 145:3
⁶The LORD sustains the
    humble   2Ch 33:23
but casts the wicked to the
    ground.   Ps 37:9-10

⁷Sing to the LORD with
    thanksgiving;   Ps 42:4
make music to our God on
    the harp.   Ps 98:5
⁸He covers the sky with
    clouds;   Job 26:8
he supplies the earth with
    rain   Dt 11:14
and makes grass grow on
    the hills.   Job 28:26
⁹He provides food for the
    cattle   Ge 1:30
and for the young ravens
    when they call.   Ge 8:7

¹⁰His pleasure is not in the
    strength of the horse,
nor his delight in the legs of
    a man;
¹¹the LORD delights in those
    who fear him,   Ps 33:18
who put their hope in his
    unfailing love.   Ps 119:43

¹²Extol the LORD, O Jerusalem;
    praise your God, O Zion,
¹³for he strengthens the bars of
    your gates   Dt 33:25
and blesses your people
    within you.   Lev 25:21
¹⁴He grants peace to your
    borders   Lev 26:6
and satisfies you with the
    finest of wheat.   Dt 32:14
¹⁵He sends his command to
    the earth;   Job 37:12
his word runs swiftly.
¹⁶He spreads the snow like
    wool   Ps 148:8
and scatters the frost like
    ashes.   Job 37:12
¹⁷He hurls down his hail like
    pebbles.   Ex 9:22-23

ᵃ1 Hebrew *Hallelu Yah*; also in verse 20

Who can withstand his icy
blast?

¹⁸He sends his word and melts
them; Ps 33:9
he stirs up his breezes, and
the waters flow. Ps 50:3

¹⁹He has revealed his word to
Jacob, Ps 78:5
his laws and decrees to
Israel. Dt 33:4
²⁰He has done this for no
other nation; Dt 4:7-8
they do not know his
laws.

Praise the LORD. Ps 33:2

Psalm 148

¹Praise the LORD. *a*

Praise the LORD from the
heavens, Ps 19:1
praise him in the heights
above.
²Praise him, all his angels,
praise him, all his heavenly
hosts. 1Ki 22:19
³Praise him, sun and moon,
praise him, all you shining
stars.
⁴Praise him, you highest
heavens Dt 10:14
and you waters above the
skies. Ge 1:7
⁵Let them praise the name of
the LORD, Ps 145:21
for he commanded and
they were created.
⁶He set them in place for ever
and ever;

he gave a decree that will
never pass away. Jer 33:25

⁷Praise the LORD from the
earth, Ps 33:2
you great sea creatures and
all ocean depths, Dt 33:13
⁸lightning and hail, snow and
clouds, Ex 9:18
stormy winds that do his
bidding, Job 37:11-12
⁹you mountains and all hills,
fruit trees and all cedars,
¹⁰wild animals and all cattle,
small creatures and flying
birds,
¹¹kings of the earth and all
nations, Ps 102:15
you princes and all rulers
on earth,
¹²young men and maidens,
old men and children.

¹³Let them praise the name of
the LORD, Ps 113:2
for his name alone is
exalted;
his splendor is above the
earth and the heavens.
¹⁴He has raised up for his
people a horn, *b*
the praise of all his saints,
of Israel, the people close to
his heart. Dt 26:19

Praise the LORD.

Psalm 149

¹Praise the LORD. *c* Ps 33:2

Sing to the LORD a new song,
his praise in the assembly
of the saints. Ps 1:5

a1 Hebrew *Hallelu Yah*; also in verse 14
is, king. *c1* Hebrew *Hallelu Yah*; also in verse 9 *b14* *Horn* here symbolizes strong one, that

²Let Israel rejoice in their
   Maker;   Job 10:3
let the people of Zion be
   glad in their King. Ps 10:16
³Let them praise his name
   with dancing   Ex 15:20
and make music to him
   with tambourine and
   harp.   Ps 57:8
⁴For the LORD takes delight in
   his people;   Ps 35:27
he crowns the humble with
   salvation.   Ps 132:16
⁵Let the saints rejoice in this
   honor
and sing for joy on their
   beds.   Job 35:10

⁶May the praise of God be in
   their mouths   Ps 66:17
and a double-edged sword
   in their hands,   Ne 4:17
⁷to inflict vengeance on the
   nations   Nu 31:3
and punishment on the
   peoples,   Ps 81:15
⁸to bind their kings with
   fetters,   2Sa 3:34
their nobles with shackles
   of iron,   2Ch 33:11
⁹to carry out the sentence
   written against them.

This is the glory of all his
   saints.   Ps 145:10

Praise the LORD.

Psalm 150

¹Praise the LORD.ᵃ   Ps 112:1
Praise God in his sanctuary;
   praise him in his mighty
     heavens.   Ps 148:1
²Praise him for his acts of
   power;   Dt 3:24
praise him for his
   surpassing greatness.
³Praise him with the sounding
   of the trumpet,   Nu 10:2
praise him with the harp
   and lyre,   Ps 57:8
⁴praise him with tambourine
   and dancing,   Ex 15:20
praise him with the strings
   and flute,   Ps 45:8
⁵praise him with the clash of
   cymbals,   2Sa 6:5
praise him with resounding
   cymbals.

⁶Let everything that has
   breath praise the LORD.

Praise the LORD.

ᵃ1 Hebrew *Hallelu Yah*; also in verse 6

Proverbs

Introduction:

Proverbs is a collection of wise sayings and good advice for daily living. The book begins by reminding us that "The fear of the LORD is the beginning of knowledge" (1:7). The first four chapters go on to discuss the importance of wisdom.

Following this, the author includes a collection of short and powerful two-line sayings that cover many different subjects including: marriage, social behavior, friendship, justice, folly, poverty, wealth, family, love, laziness, and warnings against drinking and adultery.

Many of these proverbs came from King Solomon. Others were copied by the men of Hezekiah. Agur and Lemuel wrote the last two chapters.

Outline of contents:

Instructions on wisdom and foolishness (1:1–9:18)
The proverbs of Solomon (10:1–22:16)
Sayings of the wise (22:17–24:34)
More proverbs of Solomon (25:1–29:27)
Sayings of Agur and Lemuel (30:1–31:31)

Prologue: Purpose and Theme

1 The proverbs of Solomon son of David, king of Israel:

²for attaining wisdom and discipline;
for understanding words of insight;
³for acquiring a disciplined and prudent life,
doing what is right and just and fair;   Pr 8:5

⁴for giving prudence to the simple,   Pr 8:12
knowledge and discretion to the young—   Pr 9:9
⁵let the wise listen and add to their learning,
and let the discerning get guidance—
⁶for understanding proverbs and parables,   Ps 49:4
the sayings and riddles of the wise.   Pr 22:17

⁷The fear of the LORD is the beginning of knowledge,

but fools[a] despise wisdom
and discipline.   Pr 9:7-9

Exhortations to Embrace Wisdom

Warning Against Enticement

8Listen, my son, to your
father's instruction
and do not forsake your
mother's teaching.   Dt 21:18
9They will be a garland to
grace your head
and a chain to adorn your
neck.   Pr 3:21-22

10My son, if sinners entice you,
do not give in to them.
11If they say, "Come along
with us;
let's lie in wait for
someone's blood,   Ps 10:8
let's waylay some harmless
soul;
12let's swallow them alive, like
the grave,[b]   Ps 35:25
and whole, like those who
go down to the pit;
13we will get all sorts of
valuable things
and fill our houses with
plunder;
14throw in your lot with us,
and we will share a
common purse"—
15my son, do not go along with
them,
do not set foot on their
paths;   Ge 49:6

16for their feet rush into sin,
they are swift to shed
blood.   Pr 6:18
17How useless to spread a net
in full view of all the birds!
18These men lie in wait for
their own blood;   Ps 71:10
they waylay only
themselves!
19Such is the end of all who go
after ill-gotten gain;
it takes away the lives of
those who get it.   Pr 11:19

Warning Against Rejecting Wisdom

20Wisdom calls aloud in the
street,   Job 28:12
she raises her voice in the
public squares;
21at the head of the noisy
streets[c] she cries out,
in the gateways of the city
she makes her speech:

22"How long will you simple
ones[d] love your simple
ways?   Pr 6:32
How long will mockers
delight in mockery
and fools hate knowledge?
23If you had responded to my
rebuke,
I would have poured out
my heart to you
and made my thoughts
known to you.
24But since you rejected me
when I called   Isa 65:12

---

[a]7 The Hebrew words rendered *fool* in Proverbs, and often elsewhere in the Old
Testament, denote one who is morally deficient.   [b]12 Hebrew *Sheol*   [c]21 Hebrew;
Septuagint / *on the tops of the walls*   [d]22 The Hebrew word rendered *simple* in
Proverbs generally denotes one without moral direction and inclined to evil.

and no one gave heed
    when I stretched out my
    hand,   1Sa 8:19
²⁵since you ignored all my
    advice
and would not accept my
    rebuke,
²⁶I in turn will laugh at your
    disaster;   Ps 2:4
I will mock when calamity
    overtakes you—   Dt 28:63
²⁷when calamity overtakes you
    like a storm,
when disaster sweeps over
    you like a whirlwind,
when distress and trouble
    overwhelm you.   Ps 18:18

²⁸"Then they will call to me
    but I will not answer;
they will look for me but
    will not find me.   Job 27:9
²⁹Since they hated knowledge
    and did not choose to fear
    the LORD,   Job 21:14
³⁰since they would not accept
    my advice
and spurned my rebuke,
³¹they will eat the fruit of their
    ways
and be filled with the fruit
    of their schemes.   2Ch 36:16
³²For the waywardness of the
    simple will kill them,
and the complacency of
    fools will destroy them;
³³but whoever listens to me
    will live in safety
and be at ease, without fear
    of harm."   Ps 112:8

Moral Benefits of Wisdom

2 My son, if you accept my
    words   Pr 1:8

and store up my commands
    within you,
²turning your ear to wisdom
    and applying your heart to
    understanding,   Pr 22:17
³and if you call out for insight
    and cry aloud for
    understanding,   Jas 1:5
⁴and if you look for it as for
    silver
and search for it as for
    hidden treasure,   Job 3:21
⁵then you will understand the
    fear of the LORD
and find the knowledge of
    God.   Dt 4:6
⁶For the LORD gives wisdom,
    and from his mouth come
    knowledge and
    understanding.   Job 9:4
⁷He holds victory in store for
    the upright,
he is a shield to those
    whose walk is
    blameless,   Ge 6:9
⁸for he guards the course of
    the just
and protects the way of his
    faithful ones.   1Sa 2:9

⁹Then you will understand
    what is right and just
and fair—every good path.
¹⁰For wisdom will enter your
    heart,   Pr 14:33
and knowledge will be
    pleasant to your soul.
¹¹Discretion will protect you,
    and understanding will
    guard you.   Pr 4:6

¹²Wisdom will save you from
    the ways of wicked men,
from men whose words are
    perverse,   Pr 4:5

13who leave the straight paths
  to walk in dark ways,   Pr 4:19
14who delight in doing wrong
  and rejoice in the
    perverseness of evil,
15whose paths are crooked
  and who are devious in
    their ways.   Pr 21:8

16It will save you also from the
  adulteress,   Pr 5:1-6
  from the wayward wife
    with her seductive
    words,
17who has left the partner of
  her youth
  and ignored the covenant
    she made before God. a
18For her house leads down to
  death
  and her paths to the spirits
    of the dead.   Pr 5:5
19None who go to her return
  or attain the paths of life.

20Thus you will walk in the
  ways of good men
  and keep to the paths of the
    righteous.
21For the upright will live in
  the land,   Ps 37:29
  and the blameless will
    remain in it;
22but the wicked will be cut off
  from the land,   Ps 5:4
  and the unfaithful will be
    torn from it.   Dt 28:63

Further Benefits of Wisdom

3 My son, do not forget my
  teaching,   Ps 44:17
  but keep my commands in
    your heart,

2for they will prolong your life
  many years   Dt 11:21
  and bring you prosperity.

3Let love and faithfulness
  never leave you;
  bind them around your
    neck,
  write them on the tablet of
    your heart.   Ex 13:9
4Then you will win favor and
  a good name
  in the sight of God and
    man.   1Sa 2:26

5Trust in the LORD with all
  your heart   Ps 4:5
  and lean not on your own
    understanding;
6in all your ways acknowledge
  him,
  and he will make your
    paths straight. b   Ps 5:8

7Do not be wise in your own
  eyes;   Pr 26:5
  fear the LORD and shun
    evil.   Ex 20:20
8This will bring health to your
  body   Ps 38:3
  and nourishment to your
    bones.   Job 21:24

9Honor the LORD with your
  wealth,
  with the firstfruits of all
    your crops;   Ex 22:29
10then your barns will be filled
  to overflowing,   Ps 144:13
  and your vats will brim
    over with new wine.

11My son, do not despise the
  LORD's discipline   Job 5:17

---

a17 Or covenant of her God   b6 Or will direct your paths

and do not resent his
  rebuke,
¹²because the LORD disciplines
    those he loves,   Pr 13:24
  as a father*a* the son he
    delights in.   Dt 8:5

¹³Blessed is the man who finds
    wisdom,
  the man who gains
    understanding,
¹⁴for she is more profitable
    than silver
  and yields better returns
    than gold.   Job 28:15
¹⁵She is more precious than
    rubies;   Job 28:18
  nothing you desire can
    compare with her.
¹⁶Long life is in her right hand;
  in her left hand are riches
    and honor.
¹⁷Her ways are pleasant ways,
  and all her paths are peace.
¹⁸She is a tree of life to those
    who embrace her;
  those who lay hold of her
    will be blessed.   Pr 2:12

¹⁹By wisdom the LORD laid the
    earth's foundations,
  by understanding he set the
    heavens in place;   Pr 8:27
²⁰by his knowledge the deeps
    were divided,
  and the clouds let drop the
    dew.

²¹My son, preserve sound
    judgment and
    discernment,   Pr 1:8-9
  do not let them out of your
    sight;   Pr 4:20-22

²²they will be life for you,
  an ornament to grace your
    neck.   Pr 1:8-9
²³Then you will go on your
    way in safety,   Pr 1:33
  and your foot will not
    stumble;   Ps 37:24
²⁴when you lie down, you will
    not be afraid;   Ps 91:5
  when you lie down, your
    sleep will be sweet.
²⁵Have no fear of sudden
    disaster
  or of the ruin that overtakes
    the wicked,
²⁶for the LORD will be your
    confidence   2Ki 18:5
  and will keep your foot
    from being snared. Job 5:19

²⁷Do not withhold good from
    those who deserve it,
  when it is in your power to
    act.
²⁸Do not say to your neighbor,
  "Come back later; I'll give it
    tomorrow"—
  when you now have it with
    you.   Lev 19:13
²⁹Do not plot harm against
    your neighbor,
  who lives trustfully near
    you.   Zec 8:17
³⁰Do not accuse a man for no
    reason—
  when he has done you no
    harm.
³¹Do not envy a violent man
  or choose any of his ways,
³²for the LORD detests a
    perverse man   Ps 101:4

a12 Hebrew; Septuagint / *and he punishes*

but takes the upright into
   his confidence.   Job 29:4

33The LORD's curse is on the
   house of the wicked,
but he blesses the home of
   the righteous.   Ps 37:22
34He mocks proud mockers
   but gives grace to the
   humble.   Ps 18:25-27
35The wise inherit honor,
   but fools he holds up to
   shame.

Wisdom Is Supreme

4 Listen, my sons, to a
      father's instruction;
pay attention and gain
   understanding.   Job 8:10
2I give you sound learning,
   so do not forsake my
   teaching.
3When I was a boy in my
   father's house,
still tender, and an only
   child of my mother,
4he taught me and said,
   "Lay hold of my words
      with all your heart;   1Ki 9:4
keep my commands and
   you will live.   Pr 7:2
5Get wisdom, get
   understanding;   Pr 2:12
do not forget my words or
   swerve from them.
6Do not forsake wisdom, and
   she will protect you;
love her, and she will watch
   over you.   Pr 2:11
7Wisdom is supreme;
   therefore get wisdom.

Though it cost all you
   have, a get
   understanding.   Pr 23:23
8Esteem her, and she will
   exalt you;
embrace her, and she will
   honor you.   Pr 3:18
9She will set a garland of
   grace on your head
and present you with a
   crown of splendor."

10Listen, my son, accept what I
   say,   Ps 34:11
and the years of your life
   will be many.   Dt 11:21
11I guide you in the way of
   wisdom
and lead you along straight
   paths.   2Sa 22:37
12When you walk, your steps
   will not be hampered;
when you run, you will not
   stumble.   Job 18:7
13Hold on to instruction, do
   not let it go;
guard it well, for it is your
   life.   Pr 3:22
14Do not set foot on the path of
   the wicked
or walk in the way of evil
   men.   Ps 1:1
15Avoid it, do not travel on it;
   turn from it and go on your
   way.
16For they cannot sleep till they
   do evil;   Ps 36:4
they are robbed of slumber
   till they make someone
   fall.
17They eat the bread of
   wickedness

a7 Or *Whatever else you get*

and drink the wine of
violence.   Ge 49:5

¹⁸The path of the righteous is
like the first gleam of
dawn,   Job 22:28
shining ever brighter till the
full light of day.   2Sa 23:4
¹⁹But the way of the wicked is
like deep darkness;
they do not know what
makes them stumble.

²⁰My son, pay attention to
what I say;   Ps 34:11
listen closely to my words.
²¹Do not let them out of your
sight,
keep them within your
heart;
²²for they are life to those who
find them
and health to a man's
whole body.   Pr 3:8
²³Above all else, guard your
heart,   2Ki 10:31
for it is the wellspring of
life.   Pr 10:11
²⁴Put away perversity from
your mouth;
keep corrupt talk far from
your lips.
²⁵Let your eyes look straight
ahead,   Job 31:1
fix your gaze directly before
you.
²⁶Make level^a paths for your
feet   Heb 12:13
and take only ways that are
firm.
²⁷Do not swerve to the right or
the left;   Lev 10:11
keep your foot from evil.

Warning Against Adultery

5 My son, pay attention to
my wisdom,   Pr 1:8
listen well to my words of
insight,   Pr 4:30
²that you may maintain
discretion
and your lips may preserve
knowledge.
³For the lips of an adulteress
drip honey,
and her speech is smoother
than oil;   Ps 55:21
⁴but in the end she is bitter as
gall,   Ecc 7:26
sharp as a double-edged
sword.
⁵Her feet go down to death;
her steps lead straight to
the grave. ^b   Ps 9:17
⁶She gives no thought to the
way of life;
her paths are crooked, but
she knows it not.   Pr 9:13

⁷Now then, my sons, listen to
me;   Pr 1:8-9
do not turn aside from what
I say.
⁸Keep to a path far from her,
do not go near the door of
her house,
⁹lest you give your best
strength to others
and your years to one who
is cruel,
¹⁰lest strangers feast on your
wealth
and your toil enrich another
man's house.   Pr 29:3
¹¹At the end of your life you
will groan,

---

^a26 Or *Consider the*   ^b5 Hebrew *Sheol*

when your flesh and body
are spent.
12You will say, "How I hated
discipline!
How my heart spurned
correction!   Pr 12:1
13I would not obey my teachers
or listen to my instructors.
14I have come to the brink of
utter ruin   Pr 1:24-27
in the midst of the whole
assembly."   Pr 31:3

15Drink water from your own
cistern,
running water from your
own well.
16Should your springs
overflow in the streets,
your streams of water in the
public squares?
17Let them be yours alone,
never to be shared with
strangers.
18May your fountain be
blessed,   SS 4:12-15
and may you rejoice in the
wife of your youth.
19A loving doe, a graceful
deer—
may her breasts satisfy you
always,
may you ever be captivated
by her love.
20Why be captivated, my son,
by an adulteress?
Why embrace the bosom of
another man's wife?

21For a man's ways are in full
view of the LORD,
and he examines all his
paths.   Job 10:4
22The evil deeds of a wicked
man ensnare him;   Ps 9:16

the cords of his sin hold
him fast.   Nu 32:23
23He will die for lack of
discipline,
led astray by his own great
folly.   Job 34:21-25

Warnings Against Folly

6 My son, if you have put up
security for your
neighbor,   Pr 17:18
if you have struck hands in
pledge for another,
2if you have been trapped by
what you said,
ensnared by the words of
your mouth,
3then do this, my son, to free
yourself,
since you have fallen into
your neighbor's hands:
Go and humble yourself;
press your plea with your
neighbor!
4Allow no sleep to your eyes,
no slumber to your eyelids.
5Free yourself, like a gazelle
from the hand of the
hunter,   2Sa 2:18
like a bird from the snare of
the fowler.   Ps 91:3

6Go to the ant, you sluggard;
consider its ways and be
wise!   Pr 20:4
7It has no commander,
no overseer or ruler,
8yet it stores its provisions in
summer
and gathers its food at
harvest.   Pr 10:4

9How long will you lie there,
you sluggard?   Pr 24:30-34

When will you get up from
   your sleep?
¹⁰A little sleep, a little slumber,
   a little folding of the hands
      to rest—   Pr 24:33
¹¹and poverty will come on
      you like a bandit
   and scarcity like an armed
      man.ᵃ   Pr 20:13

¹²A scoundrel and villain,
   who goes about with a
      corrupt mouth,
¹³ who winks with his eye,
   signals with his feet
   and motions with his
      fingers,   Isa 58:9
¹⁴ who plots evil with deceit
      in his heart—
   he always stirs up
      dissension.   Ps 140:2
¹⁵Therefore disaster will
      overtake him in an
      instant;   Ps 55:15
   he will suddenly be
      destroyed—without
      remedy.   Pr 14:32

¹⁶There are six things the LORD
      hates,   Pr 3:32
   seven that are detestable to
      him:
¹⁷ haughty eyes,   Job 41:34
   a lying tongue,   Pr 12:22
   hands that shed innocent
      blood,   Dt 19:10
¹⁸ a heart that devises
      wicked schemes,
   feet that are quick to rush
      into evil,   Job 15:31
¹⁹ a false witness who pours
      out lies   Dt 19:16

and a man who stirs up
      dissension among
      brothers.   Pr 15:18

Warning Against Adultery

²⁰My son, keep your father's
      commands   Pr 3:21
   and do not forsake your
      mother's teaching.
²¹Bind them upon your heart
      forever;
   fasten them around your
      neck.   Dt 6:8
²²When you walk, they will
      guide you;
   when you sleep, they will
      watch over you;
   when you awake, they will
      speak to you.
²³For these commands are a
      lamp,
   this teaching is a light,
   and the corrections of
      discipline
   are the way to life,   Pr 10:17
²⁴keeping you from the
      immoral woman,
   from the smooth tongue of
      the wayward wife.   Ge 39:8
²⁵Do not lust in your heart
      after her beauty
   or let her captivate you with
      her eyes,
²⁶for the prostitute reduces you
      to a loaf of bread,
   and the adulteress preys
      upon your very life.   Pr 7:22
²⁷Can a man scoop fire into his
      lap
   without his clothes being
      burned?
²⁸Can a man walk on hot coals

ᵃ11 Or *like a vagrant / and scarcity like a beggar*

without his feet being scorched?
[29]So is he who sleeps with another man's wife;
no one who touches her will go unpunished.

[30]Men do not despise a thief if he steals
to satisfy his hunger when he is starving.
[31]Yet if he is caught, he must pay sevenfold,   Ex 32:1-14
though it costs him all the wealth of his house.
[32]But a man who commits adultery lacks judgment;
whoever does so destroys himself.
[33]Blows and disgrace are his lot,
and his shame will never be wiped away;   Pr 5:9-14
[34]for jealousy arouses a husband's fury,   Ge 34:7
and he will show no mercy when he takes revenge.
[35]He will not accept any compensation;
he will refuse the bribe, however great it is.

Warning Against the Adulteress

7 My son, keep my words and store up my commands within you.
[2]Keep my commands and you will live;   Pr 4:4
guard my teachings as the apple of your eye.
[3]Bind them on your fingers;

write them on the tablet of your heart.   Pr 3:3
[4]Say to wisdom, "You are my sister,"
and call understanding your kinsman;
[5]they will keep you from the adulteress,
from the wayward wife with her seductive words.   Job 31:9

[6]At the window of my house I looked out through the lattice.
[7]I saw among the simple, I noticed among the young men,
a youth who lacked judgment.   Pr 1:22
[8]He was going down the street near her corner,
walking along in the direction of her house
[9]at twilight, as the day was fading,   Job 24:15
as the dark of night set in.

[10]Then out came a woman to meet him,
dressed like a prostitute and with crafty intent.
[11](She is loud and defiant, her feet never stay at home;
[12]now in the street, now in the squares,
at every corner she lurks.)
[13]She took hold of him and kissed him   Ge 39:12
and with a brazen face she said: Pr 1:20
[14]"I have fellowship offerings[a] at home;   Lev 7:11-18

a14 Traditionally *peace offerings*

today I fulfilled my vows.
15So I came out to meet you;
    I looked for you and have
        found you!
16I have covered my bed
    with colored linens from
        Egypt.
17I have perfumed my bed
    with myrrh, aloes and
        cinnamon.   Ge 37:25
18Come, let's drink deep of
    love till morning;
    let's enjoy ourselves with
        love!   Ge 39:7
19My husband is not at home;
    he has gone on a long
        journey.
20He took his purse filled with
    money
    and will not be home till
        full moon."

21With persuasive words she
    led him astray;
    she seduced him with her
        smooth talk.
22All at once he followed her
    like an ox going to the
        slaughter,
    like a deera stepping into a
        nooseb   Job 18:10
23   till an arrow pierces his
        liver,   Job 15:22
    like a bird darting into a
        snare,
    little knowing it will cost
        him his life.   Pr 6:26

24Now then, my sons, listen
    to me;   Pr 1:8-9
    pay attention to what I
        say.

25Do not let your heart turn to
    her ways
    or stray into her paths.
26Many are the victims she has
    brought down;
    her slain are a mighty
        throng.
27Her house is a highway to
    the grave,c
    leading down to the
        chambers of death.

Wisdom's Call

8 Does not wisdom call out?
    Does not understanding
        raise her voice?
2On the heights along the
    way,
    where the paths meet, she
        takes her stand;
3beside the gates leading into
    the city,
    at the entrances, she cries
        aloud: Pr 7:6-13
4"To you, O men, I call out;
    I raise my voice to all
        mankind.
5You who are simple, gain
    prudence;   Pr 1:22
    you who are foolish, gain
        understanding.
6Listen, for I have worthy
    things to say;
    I open my lips to speak
        what is right.
7My mouth speaks what is
    true,   Jn 8:14
    for my lips detest
        wickedness.
8All the words of my mouth
    are just;

a22 Syriac (see also Septuagint); Hebrew *fool*
this line is uncertain.   c27 Hebrew *Sheol*   b22 The meaning of the Hebrew for

none of them is crooked or
    perverse.
[9]To the discerning all of them
    are right;
they are faultless to those
    who have knowledge.
[10]Choose my instruction
    instead of silver,
knowledge rather than
    choice gold,   Job 28:17
[11]for wisdom is more precious
    than rubies,   Job 28:7-19
and nothing you desire can
    compare with her.

[12]"I, wisdom, dwell together
    with prudence;
I possess knowledge and
    discretion.   Pr 1:4
[13]To fear the LORD is to hate
    evil;   Ex 20:20
I hate pride and arrogance,
evil behavior and perverse
    speech.
[14]Counsel and sound
    judgment are mine;
I have understanding and
    power.   Job 9:4
[15]By me kings reign
and rulers make laws that
    are just;   Ps 2:10
[16]by me princes govern,
and all nobles who rule on
    earth.[a]
[17]I love those who love me,
and those who seek me find
    me.   1Ch 16:11
[18]With me are riches and
    honor,   1Ki 3:13
enduring wealth and
    prosperity.   Dt 8:18

[19]My fruit is better than fine
    gold;   Job 28:17-19
what I yield surpasses
    choice silver.   Pr 3:13-14
[20]I walk in the way of
    righteousness,   Ps 5:8
along the paths of justice,
[21]bestowing wealth on those
    who love me
and making their treasuries
    full.   Pr 15:6

[22]"The LORD brought me forth
    as the first of his works,[b,c]
before his deeds of old;
[23]I was appointed[d] from
    eternity,
from the beginning, before
    the world began.
[24]When there were no oceans,
    I was given birth,
when there were no springs
    abounding with water;
[25]before the mountains were
    settled in place,   Job 38:6
before the hills, I was given
    birth,   Job 15:7
[26]before he made the earth or
    its fields
or any of the dust of the
    world.   Ps 90:2
[27]I was there when he set the
    heavens in place,   Job 26:7
when he marked out the
    horizon on the face of
    the deep,   Job 22:14
[28]when he established the
    clouds above   Job 36:29
and fixed securely the
    fountains of the deep,
[29]when he gave the sea its
    boundary   Ge 1:9

---

[a]16 Many Hebrew manuscripts and Septuagint; most Hebrew manuscripts *and
nobles—all righteous rulers*   [b]22 Or *way;* or *dominion*   [c]22 Or *The LORD
possessed me*   [d]23 Or *fashioned*

so the waters would not
overstep his command,
and when he marked out the
foundations of the earth.
30 Then I was the craftsman at
his side. Pr 3:19-20
I was filled with delight day
after day,
rejoicing always in his
presence,
31rejoicing in his whole world
and delighting in mankind.

32"Now then, my sons, listen
to me; Pr 7:24
blessed are those who keep
my ways. 2Sa 22:22
33Listen to my instruction and
be wise;
do not ignore it.
34Blessed is the man who
listens to me, 1Ki 10:8
watching daily at my doors,
waiting at my doorway.
35For whoever finds me finds
life Ps 9:6
and receives favor from the
LORD. Job 33:26
36But whoever fails to find me
harms himself; Pr 15:32
all who hate me love
death." Job 28:22

Invitations of Wisdom and of Folly

9 Wisdom has built her
house; Eph 2:20-22
she has hewn out its seven
pillars.
2She has prepared her meat
and mixed her wine;
she has also set her table.
3She has sent out her maids,
and she calls Pr 1:20

from the highest point of
the city.
4"Let all who are simple come
in here!" Pr 1:22
she says to those who lack
judgment.
5"Come, eat my food
and drink the wine I have
mixed. Ps 42:2
6Leave your simple ways and
you will live; Pr 8:35
walk in the way of
understanding. Pr 3:1-2

7"Whoever corrects a mocker
invites insult;
whoever rebukes a wicked
man incurs abuse. Pr 23:9
8Do not rebuke a mocker or
he will hate you; Pr 15:12
rebuke a wise man and he
will love you. Ps 141:5
9Instruct a wise man and he
will be wiser still;
teach a righteous man and
he will add to his
learning. Pr 1:5,7

10"The fear of the LORD is the
beginning of wisdom,
and knowledge of the Holy
One is understanding.
11For through me your days
will be many,
and years will be added to
your life. Ge 15:15
12If you are wise, your wisdom
will reward you;
if you are a mocker, you
alone will suffer."

13The woman Folly is loud;
she is undisciplined and
without knowledge.

14She sits at the door of her
house,
on a seat at the highest
point of the city, Eze 16:25
15calling out to those who pass
by, Pr 1:20
who go straight on their
way.
16"Let all who are simple come
in here!"
she says to those who lack
judgment. Pr 1:22
17"Stolen water is sweet;
food eaten in secret is
delicious!" Pr 20:17
18But little do they know that
the dead are there,
that her guests are in the
depths of the grave. a

Proverbs of Solomon

10 The proverbs of Solomon:
A wise son brings joy to
his father, Pr 15:20
but a foolish son grief to his
mother.

2Ill-gotten treasures are of no
value, Pr 13:11
but righteousness delivers
from death. Pr 11:4

3The LORD does not let the
righteous go hungry
but he thwarts the craving
of the wicked. Pr 13:25

4Lazy hands make a man
poor, Pr 6:6-8
but diligent hands bring
wealth. Pr 12:24

5He who gathers crops in
summer is a wise son,
but he who sleeps during
harvest is a disgraceful
son. Pr 24:30-34

6Blessings crown the head of
the righteous,
but violence overwhelms
the mouth of the
wicked. b Pr 12:13

7The memory of the righteous
will be a blessing,
but the name of the wicked
will rot. Job 18:17

8The wise in heart accept
commands,
but a chattering fool comes
to ruin. Job 33:33

9The man of integrity walks
securely, Ps 37:24
but he who takes crooked
paths will be found out.

10He who winks maliciously
causes grief, Ps 35:19
and a chattering fool comes
to ruin.

11The mouth of the righteous is
a fountain of life,
but violence overwhelms
the mouth of the
wicked. Pr 17:9

12Hatred stirs up dissension,
but love covers over all
wrongs. Pr 17:9

13Wisdom is found on the lips
of the discerning,

a18 Hebrew *Sheol*   b6 Or *but the mouth of the wicked conceals violence*; also in verse 11

but a rod is for the back of
him who lacks
judgment. Dt 25:2

14Wise men store up
knowledge,
but the mouth of a fool
invites ruin. Ps 59:12

15The wealth of the rich is their
fortified city, Pr 18:11
but poverty is the ruin of
the poor. Pr 19:7

16The wages of the righteous
bring them life, Dt 30:15
but the income of the
wicked brings them
punishment. Pr 11:18-19

17He who heeds discipline
shows the way to life,
but whoever ignores
correction leads others
astray. Pr 6:23

18He who conceals his hatred
has lying lips, Ps 31:18
and whoever spreads
slander is a fool.

19When words are many, sin is
not absent,
but he who holds his
tongue is wise. Job 1:22

20The tongue of the righteous
is choice silver,
but the heart of the wicked
is of little value.

21The lips of the righteous
nourish many,
but fools die for lack of
judgment. Pr 5:22-23

22The blessing of the LORD
brings wealth,

and he adds no trouble
to it. 2Ch 25:9

23A fool finds pleasure in evil
conduct, Pr 2:14
but a man of understanding
delights in wisdom.

24What the wicked dreads will
overtake him;
what the righteous desire
will be granted. Ps 37:4

25When the storm has swept
by, the wicked are gone,
but the righteous stand firm
forever. Ps 20:8

26As vinegar to the teeth and
smoke to the eyes,
so is a sluggard to those
who send him. Pr 13:17

27The fear of the LORD adds
length to life, Dt 11:9
but the years of the wicked
are cut short. Job 15:32

28The prospect of the righteous
is joy,
but the hopes of the wicked
come to nothing. Est 7:10

29The way of the LORD is a
refuge for the righteous,
but it is the ruin of those
who do evil. Pr 21:15

30The righteous will never be
uprooted,
but the wicked will not
remain in the land.

31The mouth of the righteous
brings forth wisdom,
but a perverse tongue will
be cut out. Ps 52:4

³²The lips of the righteous
know what is fitting,
but the mouth of the
wicked only what is
perverse. <small>Ps 59:7</small>

11 The LORD abhors
dishonest scales,
but accurate weights are his
delight. <small>Pr 16:11</small>

²When pride comes, then
comes disgrace,
but with humility comes
wisdom. <small>Pr 18:12</small>

³The integrity of the upright
guides them,
but the unfaithful are
destroyed by their
duplicity. <small>Pr 13:6</small>

⁴Wealth is worthless in the
day of wrath, <small>Job 20:20</small>
but righteousness delivers
from death. <small>Pr 10:2</small>

⁵The righteousness of the
blameless makes a
straight way for them,
but the wicked are brought
down by their own
wickedness. <small>Pr 5:21-23</small>

⁶The righteousness of the
upright delivers them,
but the unfaithful are
trapped by evil desires.

⁷When a wicked man dies, his
hope perishes; <small>Job 8:13</small>
all he expected from his
power comes to nothing.

⁸The righteous man is rescued
from trouble,
and it comes on the wicked
instead. <small>Pr 21:18</small>

⁹With his mouth the godless
destroys his neighbor,
but through knowledge the
righteous escape.

¹⁰When the righteous prosper,
the city rejoices;
when the wicked perish,
there are shouts of joy.

¹¹Through the blessing of the
upright a city is exalted,
but by the mouth of the
wicked it is destroyed.

¹²A man who lacks judgment
derides his neighbor,
but a man of understanding
holds his tongue. <small>Job 6:24</small>

¹³A gossip betrays a
confidence, <small>Pr 20:19</small>
but a trustworthy man
keeps a secret. <small>Pr 10:14</small>

¹⁴For lack of guidance a nation
falls, <small>Pr 20:18</small>
but many advisers make
victory sure. <small>2Sa 15:34</small>

¹⁵He who puts up security for
another will surely
suffer,
but whoever refuses to
strike hands in pledge is
safe. <small>Pr 17:18</small>

¹⁶A kindhearted woman gains
respect, <small>Pr 31:31</small>
but ruthless men gain only
wealth.

¹⁷A kind man benefits himself,
but a cruel man brings
trouble on himself.

¹⁸The wicked man earns
deceptive wages,

but he who sows
   righteousness reaps a
   sure reward.   Ex 1:20

19The truly righteous man
   attains life,   Dt 30:15
but he who pursues evil
   goes to his death.   1Sa 2:6

20The LORD detests men of
   perverse heart   Pr 3:32
but he delights in those
   whose ways are
   blameless.   1Ch 29:17

21Be sure of this: The wicked
   will not go unpunished,
but those who are righteous
   will go free.   Pr 16:5

22Like a gold ring in a pig's
   snout
   is a beautiful woman who
   shows no discretion.

23The desire of the righteous
   ends only in good,
but the hope of the wicked
   only in wrath.

24One man gives freely, yet
   gains even more;
another withholds unduly,
   but comes to poverty.

25A generous man will
   prosper;   1Ch 29:17
he who refreshes others
   will himself be
   refreshed.   Pr 22:9

26People curse the man who
   hoards grain,
but blessing crowns him
   who is willing to sell.

27He who seeks good finds
   goodwill,

but evil comes to him who
   searches for it.   Ps 7:15-16

28Whoever trusts in his riches
   will fall,   Job 31:24-28
but the righteous will thrive
   like a green leaf.   Ps 52:8

29He who brings trouble on his
   family will inherit only
   wind,
and the fool will be servant
   to the wise.   Pr 14:19

30The fruit of the righteous is a
   tree of life,   Ge 2:9
and he who wins souls is
   wise.

31If the righteous receive their
   due on earth,   Jer 25:29
how much more the
   ungodly and the sinner!

12 Whoever loves discipline
   loves knowledge,
but he who hates correction
   is stupid.   Pr 5:11-14

2A good man obtains favor
   from the LORD,   Job 33:26
but the LORD condemns a
   crafty man.   2Sa 15:3

3A man cannot be established
   through wickedness,
but the righteous cannot be
   uprooted.   Pr 10:25

4A wife of noble character is
   her husband's crown,
but a disgraceful wife is like
   decay in his bones.

5The plans of the righteous
   are just,
but the advice of the wicked
   is deceitful.

⁶The words of the wicked lie
in wait for blood,
but the speech of the
upright rescues them.

⁷Wicked men are overthrown
and are no more,
but the house of the
righteous stands firm.

⁸A man is praised according
to his wisdom,
but men with warped
minds are despised.

⁹Better to be a nobody and yet
have a servant
than pretend to be
somebody and have no
food.

¹⁰A righteous man cares for the
needs of his animal,
but the kindest acts of the
wicked are cruel.

¹¹He who works his land will
have abundant food,
but he who chases fantasies
lacks judgment.   Pr 28:19

¹²The wicked desire the
plunder of evil men,
but the root of the righteous
flourishes.

¹³An evil man is trapped by his
sinful talk,   Ps 59:12
but a righteous man
escapes trouble.   Pr 21:23

¹⁴From the fruit of his lips a
man is filled with good
things   Pr 13:2
as surely as the work of his
hands rewards him.

¹⁵The way of a fool seems right
to him,   Pr 14:12
but a wise man listens to
advice.   Pr 9:7-9

¹⁶A fool shows his annoyance
at once,   Job 5:2
but a prudent man
overlooks an insult.

¹⁷A truthful witness gives
honest testimony,
but a false witness tells lies.

¹⁸Reckless words pierce like a
sword,   Ps 55:21
but the tongue of the wise
brings healing.   Pr 15:4

¹⁹Truthful lips endure forever,
but a lying tongue lasts
only a moment.

²⁰There is deceit in the hearts
of those who plot evil,
but joy for those who
promote peace.   Ro 14:19

²¹No harm befalls the
righteous,   Job 4:7
but the wicked have their
fill of trouble.

²²The LORD detests lying lips,
but he delights in men who
are truthful.   Pr 11:20

²³A prudent man keeps his
knowledge to himself,
but the heart of fools blurts
out folly.   Ps 38:5

²⁴Diligent hands will rule,
but laziness ends in slave
labor.   Pr 10:4

²⁵An anxious heart weighs a
man down,   Pr 15:13

but a kind word cheers him
up.

26A righteous man is cautious
in friendship,[a]
but the way of the wicked
leads them astray.   Ps 95:10

27The lazy man does not roast[b]
his game,
but the diligent man prizes
his possessions.

28In the way of righteousness
there is life;   Dt 30:15
along that path is
immortality.

13 A wise son heeds his
father's instruction,
but a mocker does not listen
to rebuke.   Pr 12:1

2From the fruit of his lips a
man enjoys good things,
but the unfaithful have a
craving for violence.

3He who guards his lips
guards his life,   Pr 10:6
but he who speaks rashly
will come to ruin.   Job 1:22

4The sluggard craves and gets
nothing,   Pr 21:25-26
but the desires of the
diligent are fully
satisfied.

5The righteous hate what is
false,   Ps 119:128
but the wicked bring shame
and disgrace.

6Righteousness guards the
man of integrity,

but wickedness overthrows
the sinner.   Pr 11:3

7One man pretends to be rich,
yet has nothing;   Rev 3:17
another pretends to be
poor, yet has great
wealth.   2Co 6:10

8A man's riches may ransom
his life,
but a poor man hears no
threat.   Pr 15:16

9The light of the righteous
shines brightly,
but the lamp of the wicked
is snuffed out.   Job 18:5

10Pride only breeds quarrels,
but wisdom is found in
those who take advice.

11Dishonest money dwindles
away,   Pr 10:2
but he who gathers money
little by little makes it
grow.

12Hope deferred makes the
heart sick,
but a longing fulfilled is a
tree of life.   Pr 10:11

13He who scorns instruction
will pay for it,   Nu 15:31
but he who respects a
command is rewarded.

14The teaching of the wise is a
fountain of life,   Pr 10:11
turning a man from the
snares of death.   Pr 14:27

15Good understanding wins
favor,

---

a26 Or *man is a guide to his neighbor*   b27 The meaning of the Hebrew for this word is
uncertain.

but the way of the
unfaithful is hard. *a*

¹⁶Every prudent man acts out
of knowledge,
but a fool exposes his folly.

¹⁷A wicked messenger falls
into trouble,   Pr 10:26
but a trustworthy envoy
brings healing.   Pr 25:13

¹⁸He who ignores discipline
comes to poverty and
shame,   Pr 1:7
but whoever heeds
correction is honored.

¹⁹A longing fulfilled is sweet to
the soul,   Pr 10:11
but fools detest turning
from evil.

²⁰He who walks with the wise
grows wise,
but a companion of fools
suffers harm.   2Ch 10:8

²¹Misfortune pursues the
sinner,   2Sa 3:39
but prosperity is the reward
of the righteous.   Ps 32:10

²²A good man leaves an
inheritance for his
children's children,
but a sinner's wealth is
stored up for the
righteous.   Est 8:2

²³A poor man's field may
produce abundant food,
but injustice sweeps it
away.

²⁴He who spares the rod hates
his son,   2Sa 7:14

but he who loves him is
careful to discipline him.

²⁵The righteous eat to their
hearts' content,
but the stomach of the
wicked goes hungry.

14 The wise woman builds
her house,   Ru 3:11
but with her own hands the
foolish one tears hers
down.

²He whose walk is upright
fears the LORD,
but he whose ways are
devious despises him.

³A fool's talk brings a rod to
his back,   Pr 10:14
but the lips of the wise
protect them.   Pr 10:13

⁴Where there are no oxen, the
manger is empty,
but from the strength of an
ox comes an abundant
harvest.   Ps 144:14

⁵A truthful witness does not
deceive,
but a false witness pours
out lies.   Ps 12:2

⁶The mocker seeks wisdom
and finds none,
but knowledge comes easily
to the discerning.   Pr 9:9

⁷Stay away from a foolish
man,
for you will not find
knowledge on his lips.

⁸The wisdom of the prudent is

---

*a*15 Or *unfaithful does not endure*

to give thought to their
ways,   Pr 15:28
but the folly of fools is
deception.

⁹Fools mock at making
amends for sin,
but goodwill is found
among the upright.

¹⁰Each heart knows its own
bitterness,
and no one else can share
its joy.

¹¹The house of the wicked will
be destroyed,   Job 8:22
but the tent of the upright
will flourish.   Ps 72:7

¹²There is a way that seems
right to a man,   Pr 12:15
but in the end it leads to
death.   Pr 16:25

¹³Even in laughter the heart
may ache,   Ecc 2:2
and joy may end in grief.

¹⁴The faithless will be fully
repaid for their ways,
and the good man
rewarded for his.   2Ch 15:7

¹⁵A simple man believes
anything,
but a prudent man gives
thought to his steps.

¹⁶A wise man fears the LORD
and shuns evil,   Ex 20:20
but a fool is hotheaded and
reckless.   1Sa 25:25

¹⁷A quick-tempered man does
foolish things,   2Ki 5:12
and a crafty man is hated.

¹⁸The simple inherit folly,
but the prudent are
crowned with
knowledge.

¹⁹Evil men will bow down in
the presence of the
good,
and the wicked at the gates
of the righteous.   Pr 11:29

²⁰The poor are shunned even
by their neighbors,
but the rich have many
friends.   Pr 19:4,7

²¹He who despises his
neighbor sins,   Pr 11:12
but blessed is he who is
kind to the needy.

²²Do not those who plot evil go
astray?   Pr 4:16-17
But those who plan what is
good find*a* love and
faithfulness.

²³All hard work brings a profit,
but mere talk leads only to
poverty.

²⁴The wealth of the wise is
their crown,
but the folly of fools yields
folly.

²⁵A truthful witness saves
lives,
but a false witness is
deceitful.   Pr 12:17

²⁶He who fears the LORD has a
secure fortress,   Pr 18:10
and for his children it will
be a refuge.   Ps 9:9

a22 Or *show*

²⁷The fear of the LORD is a
　　fountain of life, _Pr 10:11_
turning a man from the
　　snares of death. _Ps 18:5_

²⁸A large population is a king's
　　glory,
but without subjects a
　　prince is ruined. _2Sa 19:7_

²⁹A patient man has great
　　understanding, _2Ki 5:12_
but a quick-tempered man
　　displays folly. _Ecc 7:8-9_

³⁰A heart at peace gives life to
　　the body,
but envy rots the bones.

³¹He who oppresses the poor
　　shows contempt for
　　their Maker, _Pr 17:5_
but whoever is kind to the
　　needy honors God. _Dt 24:14_

³²When calamity comes, the
　　wicked are brought
　　down, _Ps 34:21_
but even in death the
　　righteous have a refuge.

³³Wisdom reposes in the heart
　　of the discerning _Pr 2:6-10_
and even among fools she
　　lets herself be known. ᵃ

³⁴Righteousness exalts a
　　nation, _Pr 11:11_
but sin is a disgrace to any
　　people.

³⁵A king delights in a wise
　　servant,
but a shameful servant
　　incurs his wrath. _Est 8:2_

15 A gentle answer turns
　　away wrath, _1Ki 12:7_
but a harsh word stirs up
　　anger.

²The tongue of the wise
　　commends knowledge,
but the mouth of the fool
　　gushes folly. _Pr 25:15_

³The eyes of the LORD are
　　everywhere, _2Ch 16:9_
keeping watch on the
　　wicked and the good.

⁴The tongue that brings
　　healing is a tree of life,
but a deceitful tongue
　　crushes the spirit. _Pr 12:18_

⁵A fool spurns his father's
　　discipline,
but whoever heeds
　　correction shows
　　prudence. _Pr 10:17_

⁶The house of the righteous
　　contains great treasure,
but the income of the
　　wicked brings them
　　trouble. _Pr 10:16_

⁷The lips of the wise spread
　　knowledge; _Pr 10:13_
not so the hearts of fools.

⁸The LORD detests the sacrifice
　　of the wicked, _Ps 51:17_
but the prayer of the
　　upright pleases him.

⁹The LORD detests the way of
　　the wicked _Pr 6:16_
but he loves those who
　　pursue righteousness.

ᵃ33 Hebrew; Septuagint and Syriac / _but in the heart of fools she is not known_

¹⁰Stern discipline awaits him
who leaves the path;
he who hates correction will
die. Pr 1:31-32

¹¹Death and Destruction*ᵃ* lie
open before the LORD—
how much more the hearts
of men! 1Sa 2:3

¹²A mocker resents correction;
he will not consult the wise.

¹³A happy heart makes the
face cheerful,
but heartache crushes the
spirit. Pr 12:25

¹⁴The discerning heart seeks
knowledge, Pr 18:15
but the mouth of a fool
feeds on folly.

¹⁵All the days of the oppressed
are wretched,
but the cheerful heart has a
continual feast.

¹⁶Better a little with the fear of
the LORD
than great wealth with
turmoil. Ps 37:16-17

¹⁷Better a meal of vegetables
where there is love
than a fattened calf with
hatred. Pr 17:1

¹⁸A hot-tempered man stirs up
dissension, Pr 6:16-19
but a patient man calms a
quarrel. Ge 13:8

¹⁹The way of the sluggard is
blocked with thorns,
but the path of the upright
is a highway. Pr 22:5

²⁰A wise son brings joy to his
father, Pr 10:1
but a foolish man despises
his mother.

²¹Folly delights a man who
lacks judgment, Pr 2:14
but a man of understanding
keeps a straight course.

²²Plans fail for lack of counsel,
but with many advisers
they succeed. Pr 11:14

²³A man finds joy in giving an
apt reply— Pr 12:14
and how good is a timely
word! Pr 25:11

²⁴The path of life leads upward
for the wise
to keep him from going
down to the grave. *ᵇ*

²⁵The LORD tears down the
proud man's house
but he keeps the widow's
boundaries intact. Dt 19:14

²⁶The LORD detests the
thoughts of the wicked,
but those of the pure are
pleasing to him. Ps 18:26

²⁷A greedy man brings trouble
to his family,
but he who hates bribes will
live. Ex 23:8

²⁸The heart of the righteous
weighs its answers,
but the mouth of the
wicked gushes evil.

²⁹The LORD is far from the
wicked

ᵃ11 Hebrew *Sheol and Abaddon*   *ᵇ24* Hebrew *Sheol*

but he hears the prayer of
the righteous.   Job 15:31

30A cheerful look brings joy to
the heart,
and good news gives health
to the bones.   Pr 25:25

31He who listens to a
life-giving rebuke
will be at home among the
wise.   Pr 9:7-9

32He who ignores discipline
despises himself,   Pr 1:7
but whoever heeds
correction gains
understanding.   Pr 12:1

33The fear of the LORD teaches
a man wisdom,a
and humility comes before
honor.   Pr 16:18

16 To man belong the plans
of the heart,
but from the LORD comes
the reply of the tongue.

2All a man's ways seem
innocent to him,   Pr 12:15
but motives are weighed by
the LORD.   2Ch 6:30

3Commit to the LORD
whatever you do,
and your plans will
succeed.   2Ch 20:20

4The LORD works out
everything for his own
ends—   Ex 9:16
even the wicked for a day
of disaster.   2Ch 34:24

5The LORD detests all the
proud of heart.   Ps 40:4

Be sure of this: They will
not go unpunished.

6Through love and
faithfulness sin is atoned
for;
through the fear of the
LORD a man avoids evil.

7When a man's ways are
pleasing to the LORD,
he makes even his enemies
live at peace with him.

8Better a little with
righteousness
than much gain with
injustice.   Pr 15:16

9In his heart a man plans his
course,
but the LORD determines
his steps.

10The lips of a king speak as an
oracle,
and his mouth should not
betray justice.   Pr 17:7

11Honest scales and balances
are from the LORD;
all the weights in the bag
are of his making.   Pr 11:1

12Kings detest wrongdoing,
for a throne is established
through righteousness.

13Kings take pleasure in honest
lips;
they value a man who
speaks the truth.   Pr 22:11

14A king's wrath is a
messenger of death, Ge 40:2
but a wise man will
appease it.   Pr 25:15

a33 Or Wisdom teaches the fear of the LORD

¹⁵When a king's face brightens,
    it means life;   Ge 40:2
  his favor is like a rain cloud
    in spring.   Pr 19:12

¹⁶How much better to get
    wisdom than gold,
  to choose understanding
    rather than silver!   Job 28:15

¹⁷The highway of the upright
    avoids evil;
  he who guards his way
    guards his life.   Pr 19:16

¹⁸Pride goes before
    destruction,   1Sa 17:42
  a haughty spirit before a
    fall.   Est 5:12

¹⁹Better to be lowly in spirit
    and among the
    oppressed
  than to share plunder with
    the proud.

²⁰Whoever gives heed to
    instruction prospers,
  and blessed is he who
    trusts in the LORD. Ps 32:10

²¹The wise in heart are called
    discerning,
  and pleasant words
    promote instruction.ᵃ

²²Understanding is a fountain
    of life to those who
    have it,   Pr 10:11
  but folly brings punishment
    to fools.

²³A wise man's heart guides
    his mouth,   Job 15:5
  and his lips promote
    instruction.ᵇ

²⁴Pleasant words are a
    honeycomb,   1Sa 14:27
  sweet to the soul and
    healing to the bones.

²⁵There is a way that seems
    right to a man,   Pr 12:15
  but in the end it leads to
    death.   Est 3:6

²⁶The laborer's appetite works
    for him;
  his hunger drives him on.

²⁷A scoundrel plots evil,
  and his speech is like a
    scorching fire.   Jas 3:6

²⁸A perverse man stirs up
    dissension,   Pr 14:17
  and a gossip separates close
    friends.   Pr 17:9

²⁹A violent man entices his
    neighbor
  and leads him down a path
    that is not good.   Pr 1:10

³⁰He who winks with his eye is
    plotting perversity; Pr 6:13
  he who purses his lips is
    bent on evil.

³¹Gray hair is a crown of
    splendor;   Pr 20:29
  it is attained by a righteous
    life.

³²Better a patient man than a
    warrior,
  a man who controls his
    temper than one who
    takes a city.

³³The lot is cast into the lap,
  but its every decision is
    from the LORD.   Jos 7:14

ᵃ21 Or *words make a man persuasive*   ᵇ23 Or *mouth / and makes his lips persuasive*

17

Better a dry crust with peace and quiet
than a house full of feasting,*a* with strife.

2A wise servant will rule over a disgraceful son,
and will share the inheritance as one of the brothers.

3The crucible for silver and the furnace for gold,
but the LORD tests the heart.   1Ch 29:17

4A wicked man listens to evil lips;
a liar pays attention to a malicious tongue.

5He who mocks the poor shows contempt for their Maker;   Pr 14:31
whoever gloats over disaster will not go unpunished.   Eze 25:3

6Children's children are a crown to the aged,
and parents are the pride of their children.

7Arrogant*b* lips are unsuited to a fool—
how much worse lying lips to a ruler!   Pr 16:10

8A bribe is a charm to the one who gives it;
wherever he turns, he succeeds.   Ex 23:8

9He who covers over an offense promotes love,
but whoever repeats the matter separates close friends.   Pr 16:28

10A rebuke impresses a man of discernment
more than a hundred lashes a fool.

11An evil man is bent only on rebellion;
a merciless official will be sent against him.

12Better to meet a bear robbed of her cubs
than a fool in his folly.

13If a man pays back evil for good,   Ge 44:4
evil will never leave his house.

14Starting a quarrel is like breaching a dam;
so drop the matter before a dispute breaks out.

15Acquitting the guilty and condemning the innocent—   Ps 94:21
the LORD detests them both.   Ex 23:6-7

16Of what use is money in the hand of a fool,
since he has no desire to get wisdom?   Pr 23:23

17A friend loves at all times,
and a brother is born for adversity.   2Sa 15:21

18A man lacking in judgment strikes hands in pledge
and puts up security for his neighbor.   Pr 6:1-5

---

a1 Hebrew *sacrifices*   *b7* Or *Eloquent*

¹⁹He who loves a quarrel loves
  sin;
  he who builds a high gate
    invites destruction.

²⁰A man of perverse heart does
    not prosper;
  he whose tongue is
    deceitful falls into
    trouble.

²¹To have a fool for a son
    brings grief;
  there is no joy for the father
    of a fool.   Pr 10:1

²²A cheerful heart is good
    medicine,
  but a crushed spirit dries up
    the bones.   Ex 12:46

²³A wicked man accepts a bribe
    in secret   Ex 18:21
  to pervert the course of
    justice.   Job 34:33

²⁴A discerning man keeps
    wisdom in view,
  but a fool's eyes wander to
    the ends of the earth.

²⁵A foolish son brings grief to
    his father
  and bitterness to the one
    who bore him.   Pr 10:1

²⁶It is not good to punish an
    innocent man,   Ps 94:21
  or to flog officials for their
    integrity.

²⁷A man of knowledge uses
    words with restraint,
  and a man of
    understanding is
    even-tempered.   Pr 14:29

²⁸Even a fool is thought wise if
    he keeps silent,
  and discerning if he holds
    his tongue.   Job 2:13

18 An unfriendly man
     pursues selfish ends;
  he defies all sound
    judgment.

²A fool finds no pleasure in
    understanding
  but delights in airing his
    own opinions.   Pr 12:23

³When wickedness comes, so
    does contempt,
  and with shame comes
    disgrace.

⁴The words of a man's mouth
    are deep waters,   Ps 18:16
  but the fountain of wisdom
    is a bubbling brook.

⁵It is not good to be partial to
    the wicked   Pr 24:23-25
  or to deprive the innocent
    of justice.   Ps 82:2

⁶A fool's lips bring him strife,
  and his mouth invites a
    beating.   Pr 10:14

⁷A fool's mouth is his
    undoing,
  and his lips are a snare to
    his soul.   Ps 64:8

⁸The words of a gossip are
    like choice morsels;
  they go down to a man's
    inmost parts.   Pr 26:22

⁹One who is slack in his work
  is brother to one who
    destroys.   Pr 28:24

¹⁰The name of the Lord is a
strong tower;   Ps 61:3
the righteous run to it and
are safe.   Ps 20:1

¹¹The wealth of the rich is their
fortified city;   Pr 10:15
they imagine it an
unscalable wall.

¹²Before his downfall a man's
heart is proud,
but humility comes before
honor.   Pr 11:2

¹³He who answers before
listening—
that is his folly and his
shame.   Pr 20:25

¹⁴A man's spirit sustains him
in sickness,
but a crushed spirit who
can bear?   Pr 15:13

¹⁵The heart of the discerning
acquires knowledge;
the ears of the wise seek it
out.   Pr 15:14

¹⁶A gift opens the way for the
giver   Ge 32:13
and ushers him into the
presence of the great.

¹⁷The first to present his case
seems right,
till another comes forward
and questions him.

¹⁸Casting the lot settles
disputes
and keeps strong
opponents apart.

¹⁹An offended brother is more
unyielding than a
fortified city,   1Sa 17:28
and disputes are like the
barred gates of a citadel.

²⁰From the fruit of his mouth a
man's stomach is filled;
with the harvest from his
lips he is satisfied.   Pr 12:14

²¹The tongue has the power of
life and death,   Ps 12:4
and those who love it will
eat its fruit.   Pr 13:2-3

²²He who finds a wife finds
what is good   Pr 12:4
and receives favor from the
Lord.   Job 33:26

²³A poor man pleads for
mercy,
but a rich man answers
harshly.

²⁴A man of many companions
may come to ruin,
but there is a friend who
sticks closer than a
brother.   1Sa 20:42

19 Better a poor man whose
walk is blameless
than a fool whose lips are
perverse.   Pr 28:6

²It is not good to have zeal
without knowledge,
nor to be hasty and miss
the way.   Pr 29:20

³A man's own folly ruins his
life,   Ps 14:1
yet his heart rages against
the Lord.   Jas 1:13-15

⁴Wealth brings many friends,
but a poor man's friend
deserts him.   Pr 14:20

⁵A false witness will not go
    unpunished,   Ps 56:7
and he who pours out lies
    will not go free.   Dt 19:19

⁶Many curry favor with a
    ruler,   Pr 29:26
and everyone is the friend
    of a man who gives
    gifts.   Pr 17:8

⁷A poor man is shunned by all
    his relatives—
how much more do his
    friends avoid him!
Though he pursues them
    with pleading,
they are nowhere to be
    found.ᵃ

⁸He who gets wisdom loves
    his own soul;
he who cherishes
    understanding prospers.

⁹A false witness will not go
    unpunished,
and he who pours out lies
    will perish.   Dt 19:19

¹⁰It is not fitting for a fool to
    live in luxury—   Pr 26:1
how much worse for a slave
    to rule over princes!

¹¹A man's wisdom gives him
    patience;   2Ki 5:12
it is to his glory to overlook
    an offense.

¹²A king's rage is like the roar
    of a lion,   Pr 20:2
but his favor is like dew on
    the grass.   Est 1:12

¹³A foolish son is his father's
    ruin,   Pr 10:1
and a quarrelsome wife is
    like a constant dripping.

¹⁴Houses and wealth are
    inherited from parents,
but a prudent wife is from
    the LORD.   Pr 18:22

¹⁵Laziness brings on deep
    sleep,
and the shiftless man goes
    hungry.   Pr 10:4

¹⁶He who obeys instructions
    guards his life,
but he who is
    contemptuous of his
    ways will die.   Pr 16:17

¹⁷He who is kind to the poor
    lends to the LORD,   Dt 24:14
and he will reward him for
    what he has done.

¹⁸Discipline your son, for in
    that there is hope;
do not be a willing party to
    his death.   Pr 13:24

¹⁹A hot-tempered man must
    pay the penalty;
if you rescue him, you will
    have to do it again.

²⁰Listen to advice and accept
    instruction,   Pr 4:1
and in the end you will be
    wise.   Pr 12:15

²¹Many are the plans in a
    man's heart,
but it is the LORD's purpose
    that prevails.   Ps 33:11

ᵃ7 The meaning of the Hebrew for this sentence is uncertain.

²²What a man desires is
  unfailing love*ª*;
  better to be poor than a liar.

²³The fear of the LORD leads to
  life:
  Then one rests content,
  untouched by trouble.

²⁴The sluggard buries his hand
  in the dish;
  he will not even bring it
  back to his mouth!   Pr 26:15

²⁵Flog a mocker, and the
  simple will learn
  prudence;
  rebuke a discerning man,
  and he will gain
  knowledge.   Pr 9:9

²⁶He who robs his father and
  drives out his mother
  is a son who brings shame
  and disgrace.   Pr 28:24

²⁷Stop listening to instruction,
  my son,   Pr 1:8
  and you will stray from the
  words of knowledge.

²⁸A corrupt witness mocks at
  justice,
  and the mouth of the
  wicked gulps down evil.

²⁹Penalties are prepared for
  mockers,
  and beatings for the backs
  of fools.   Dt 25:2

20 Wine is a mocker and
  beer a brawler;   1Sa 25:36
  whoever is led astray by
  them is not wise.   Pr 31:4

²A king's wrath is like the roar
  of a lion;   Pr 19:12
  he who angers him forfeits
  his life.   Est 7:7

³It is to a man's honor to
  avoid strife,
  but every fool is quick to
  quarrel.   Ge 13:8

⁴A sluggard does not plow in
  season;   Pr 6:6
  so at harvest time he looks
  but finds nothing.

⁵The purposes of a man's
  heart are deep waters,
  but a man of understanding
  draws them out.   Ps 18:16

⁶Many a man claims to have
  unfailing love,
  but a faithful man who can
  find?   Ps 12:1

⁷The righteous man leads a
  blameless life;   Ps 26:1
  blessed are his children
  after him.   Ps 37:25-26

⁸When a king sits on his
  throne to judge,   1Ki 7:7
  he winnows out all evil
  with his eyes.   Pr 25:4-5

⁹Who can say, "I have kept
  my heart pure;   Job 15:14
  I am clean and without
  sin"?   1Ki 8:46

¹⁰Differing weights and
  differing measures—
  the LORD detests them
  both.   Pr 11:1

¹¹Even a child is known by his
  actions,

ª22 Or A man's greed is his shame

by whether his conduct is
pure and right.   Ps 39:1

¹²Ears that hear and eyes that
see—
the Lord has made them
both.   Ps 94:9

¹³Do not love sleep or you will
grow poor;   Pr 6:11
stay awake and you will
have food to spare.

¹⁴"It's no good, it's no good!"
says the buyer;
then off he goes and boasts
about his purchase.

¹⁵Gold there is, and rubies in
abundance,
but lips that speak
knowledge are a rare
jewel.

¹⁶Take the garment of one who
puts up security for a
stranger;
hold it in pledge if he does
it for a wayward
woman.   Pr 27:13

¹⁷Food gained by fraud tastes
sweet to a man,   Pr 9:17
but he ends up with a
mouth full of gravel.

¹⁸Make plans by seeking
advice;
if you wage war, obtain
guidance.   Pr 11:14

¹⁹A gossip betrays a
confidence;   Pr 11:13
so avoid a man who talks
too much.

²⁰If a man curses his father or
mother,   Pr 30:11
his lamp will be snuffed out
in pitch darkness.   Ex 21:17

²¹An inheritance quickly
gained at the beginning
will not be blessed at the
end.

²²Do not say, "I'll pay you
back for this wrong!"
Wait for the Lord, and he
will deliver you.   Isa 37:20

²³The Lord detests differing
weights,
and dishonest scales do not
please him.   Dt 25:13

²⁴A man's steps are directed by
the Lord.   Ps 90:12
How then can anyone
understand his own
way?   Pr 19:21

²⁵It is a trap for a man to
dedicate something
rashly
and only later to consider
his vows.   Pr 10:19

²⁶A wise king winnows out the
wicked;
he drives the threshing
wheel over them.

²⁷The lamp of the Lord
searches the spirit of a
man^a;   Ps 119:105
it searches out his inmost
being.   Pr 16:2

²⁸Love and faithfulness keep a
king safe;

---

^a27 Or *The spirit of man is the Lord's lamp*

through love his throne is
made secure. Pr 16:12

²⁹The glory of young men is
their strength,
gray hair the splendor of
the old. Pr 16:31

³⁰Blows and wounds cleanse
away evil, Ps 51:2
and beatings purge the
inmost being. Isa 1:5

21 The king's heart is in the
hand of the LORD;
he directs it like a
watercourse wherever
he pleases. Est 5:1

²All a man's ways seem right
to him,
but the LORD weighs the
heart. Pr 16:2

³To do what is right and just
is more acceptable to the
LORD than sacrifice.

⁴Haughty eyes and a proud
heart, Job 41:34
the lamp of the wicked, are
sin!

⁵The plans of the diligent lead
to profit Pr 10:4
as surely as haste leads to
poverty.

⁶A fortune made by a lying
tongue
is a fleeting vapor and a
deadly snare. ᵃ Pr 10:2

⁷The violence of the wicked
will drag them away,

for they refuse to do what is
right. Pr 11:5

⁸The way of the guilty is
devious, Pr 2:15
but the conduct of the
innocent is upright.

⁹Better to live on a corner of
the roof
than share a house with a
quarrelsome wife. Pr 19:13

¹⁰The wicked man craves evil;
his neighbor gets no mercy
from him.

¹¹When a mocker is punished,
the simple gain wisdom;
when a wise man is
instructed, he gets
knowledge. Pr 19:25

¹²The Righteous Oneᵇ takes
note of the house of the
wicked
and brings the wicked to
ruin. Pr 14:11

¹³If a man shuts his ears to the
cry of the poor,
he too will cry out and not
be answered. Job 29:12

¹⁴A gift given in secret soothes
anger,
and a bribe concealed in the
cloak pacifies great
wrath. Ge 32:20

¹⁵When justice is done, it
brings joy to the
righteous
but terror to evildoers.

ᵃ6 Some Hebrew manuscripts, Septuagint and Vulgate; most Hebrew manuscripts *vapor
for those who seek death*   ᵇ12 Or *The righteous man*

¹⁶A man who strays from the
  path of understanding
comes to rest in the
  company of the dead.

¹⁷He who loves pleasure will
  become poor;
whoever loves wine and oil
  will never be rich.

¹⁸The wicked become a ransom
  for the righteous,   Pr 11:8
and the unfaithful for the
  upright.

¹⁹Better to live in a desert
  than with a quarrelsome
  and ill-tempered wife.

²⁰In the house of the wise are
  stores of choice food and
  oil,
but a foolish man devours
  all he has.

²¹He who pursues
  righteousness and love
finds life, prosperity*a* and
  honor.   Mt 5:6

²²A wise man attacks the city
  of the mighty   Pr 8:14
and pulls down the
  stronghold in which
  they trust.

²³He who guards his mouth
  and his tongue   Ps 34:13
  keeps himself from
  calamity.   Pr 10:19

²⁴The proud and arrogant
  man—"Mocker" is his
  name;   Jer 43:2
he behaves with
  overweening pride.

²⁵The sluggard's craving will
  be the death of him,
  because his hands refuse to
  work.   Pr 13:4

²⁶All day long he craves for
  more,
but the righteous give
  without sparing.   Lev 25:35

²⁷The sacrifice of the wicked is
  detestable—   1Ki 14:24
how much more so when
  brought with evil intent!

²⁸A false witness will perish,
  and whoever listens to him
  will be destroyed
  forever.*b*   Isa 29:21

²⁹A wicked man puts up a bold
  front,
but an upright man gives
  thought to his ways.

³⁰There is no wisdom, no
  insight, no plan
that can succeed against the
  LORD.   2Ch 13:12

³¹The horse is made ready for
  the day of battle,
but victory rests with the
  LORD.   Ps 33:12-19

22 A good name is more
  desirable than great
  riches;
to be esteemed is better
  than silver or gold.

²Rich and poor have this in
  common:
  The LORD is the Maker of
  them all.   Job 31:15

---

a21 Or *righteousness*   *b28* Or / *but the words of an obedient man will live on*

³A prudent man sees danger
　　and takes refuge,　Pr 14:16
but the simple keep going
　　and suffer for it.　Pr 27:12

⁴Humility and the fear of the
　　LORD
　　bring wealth and honor and
　　life.　Pr 10:27

⁵In the paths of the wicked lie
　　thorns and snares,
but he who guards his soul
　　stays far from them.

⁶Train^a a child in the way he
　　should go,　Eph 6:4
and when he is old he will
　　not turn from it.　Dt 6:7

⁷The rich rule over the poor,
　　and the borrower is servant
　　to the lender.

⁸He who sows wickedness
　　reaps trouble,
and the rod of his fury will
　　be destroyed.　Hos 8:7

⁹A generous man will himself
　　be blessed,　Dt 14:29
for he shares his food with
　　the poor.　Pr 11:25

¹⁰Drive out the mocker, and
　　out goes strife;
quarrels and insults are
　　ended.　Pr 26:20

¹¹He who loves a pure heart
　　and whose speech is
　　gracious
will have the king for his
　　friend.　Pr 16:13

¹²The eyes of the LORD keep
　　watch over knowledge,

but he frustrates the words
　　of the unfaithful.

¹³The sluggard says, "There is
　　a lion outside!"　Pr 26:13
or, "I will be murdered in
　　the streets!"

¹⁴The mouth of an adulteress is
　　a deep pit;　Pr 5:3-5
he who is under the LORD's
　　wrath will fall into it.

¹⁵Folly is bound up in the heart
　　of a child,
but the rod of discipline will
　　drive it far from him.

¹⁶He who oppresses the poor
　　to increase his wealth
and he who gives gifts to
　　the rich—both come to
　　poverty.

Sayings of the Wise

¹⁷Pay attention and listen to
　　the sayings of the wise;
apply your heart to what I
　　teach,　Pr 2:2
¹⁸for it is pleasing when you
　　keep them in your heart
and have all of them ready
　　on your lips.
¹⁹So that your trust may be in
　　the LORD,
I teach you today, even
　　you.
²⁰Have I not written thirty^b
　　sayings for you,
sayings of counsel and
　　knowledge,
²¹teaching you true and
　　reliable words,　Ecc 12:10

^a6 Or *Start*　　^b20 Or *not formerly written; or not written excellent*

so that you can give sound
answers
to him who sent you?

22Do not exploit the poor
because they are poor
and do not crush the needy
in court,   Ex 23:6
23for the LORD will take up
their case   Job 29:16
and will plunder those who
plunder them.   Est 8:1

24Do not make friends with a
hot-tempered man,
do not associate with one
easily angered,
25or you may learn his ways
and get yourself ensnared.

26Do not be a man who strikes
hands in pledge
or puts up security for
debts;   Pr 6:1-5
27if you lack the means to pay,
your very bed will be
snatched from under
you.   Pr 11:15

28Do not move an ancient
boundary stone   Dt 19:14
set up by your forefathers.

29Do you see a man skilled in
his work?   1Ki 11:28
He will serve before kings;
he will not serve before
obscure men.

23 When you sit to dine
with a ruler,
note well what*a* is before
you,
2and put a knife to your throat

if you are given to gluttony.
3Do not crave his delicacies,
for that food is deceptive.

4Do not wear yourself out to
get rich;
have the wisdom to show
restraint.
5Cast but a glance at riches,
and they are gone,
for they will surely sprout
wings
and fly off to the sky like an
eagle.   Pr 27:24

6Do not eat the food of a
stingy man,
do not crave his delicacies;
7for he is the kind of man
who is always thinking
about the cost.*b*
"Eat and drink," he says to
you,
but his heart is not with
you.
8You will vomit up the little
you have eaten
and will have wasted your
compliments.

9Do not speak to a fool,
for he will scorn the
wisdom of your words.

10Do not move an ancient
boundary stone   Dt 19:14
or encroach on the fields of
the fatherless,
11for their Defender is strong;
he will take up their case
against you.   Ex 22:22-24

12Apply your heart to
instruction   Pr 2:2

*a*1 Or *who*   *b*7 Or *for as he thinks within himself, / so he is; or for as he puts on a feast, / so he is*

and your ears to words of knowledge.

¹³Do not withhold discipline from a child;
if you punish him with the rod, he will not die.
¹⁴Punish him with the rod and save his soul from death. *a*
Pr 13:24

¹⁵My son, if your heart is wise, then my heart will be glad;
¹⁶my inmost being will rejoice when your lips speak what is right.
Pr 27:11

¹⁷Do not let your heart envy sinners, Ps 37:1
but always be zealous for the fear of the LORD.
¹⁸There is surely a future hope for you,
and your hope will not be cut off.
Ps 9:18

¹⁹Listen, my son, and be wise, and keep your heart on the right path.
²⁰Do not join those who drink too much wine Isa 5:11
or gorge themselves on meat,
²¹for drunkards and gluttons become poor, Pr 21:17
and drowsiness clothes them in rags.

²²Listen to your father, who gave you life,
and do not despise your mother when she is old.
²³Buy the truth and do not sell it;

get wisdom, discipline and understanding. Pr 4:7
²⁴The father of a righteous man has great joy;
he who has a wise son delights in him.
²⁵May your father and mother be glad;
may she who gave you birth rejoice!
Pr 10:1

²⁶My son, give me your heart and let your eyes keep to my ways, Ps 18:21
²⁷for a prostitute is a deep pit and a wayward wife is a narrow well.
²⁸Like a bandit she lies in wait, and multiplies the unfaithful among men.

²⁹Who has woe? Who has sorrow?
Who has strife? Who has complaints?
Who has needless bruises? Who has bloodshot eyes?
³⁰Those who linger over wine, who go to sample bowls of mixed wine. Isa 5:11
³¹Do not gaze at wine when it is red,
when it sparkles in the cup, when it goes down smoothly!
³²In the end it bites like a snake and poisons like a viper.
³³Your eyes will see strange sights
and your mind imagine confusing things.

---

*a*14 Hebrew *Sheol*

³⁴You will be like one sleeping
    on the high seas,
lying on top of the rigging.
³⁵"They hit me," you will say,
    "but I'm not hurt!
They beat me, but I don't
    feel it!
When will I wake up
    so I can find another
    drink?"   Pr 20:1

24 Do not envy wicked
    men,   Pr 3:31-32
 do not desire their
    company;
²for their hearts plot violence,
    and their lips talk about
    making trouble.   Ps 10:7

³By wisdom a house is built,
    and through understanding
    it is established;   Pr 14:1
⁴through knowledge its rooms
    are filled
with rare and beautiful
    treasures.   Pr 8:21

⁵A wise man has great power,
    and a man of knowledge
    increases strength;
⁶for waging war you need
    guidance,
    and for victory many
    advisers.   Pr 11:14

⁷Wisdom is too high for a fool;
    in the assembly at the gate
    he has nothing to say.

⁸He who plots evil
    will be known as a
    schemer.
⁹The schemes of folly are sin,
    and men detest a mocker.

¹⁰If you falter in times of
    trouble,

how small is your strength!
¹¹Rescue those being led away
    to death;
hold back those staggering
    toward slaughter.
¹²If you say, "But we knew
    nothing about this,"
does not he who weighs the
    heart perceive it?   1Sa 2:3
Does not he who guards
    your life know it?
Will he not repay each
    person according to
    what he has done?

¹³Eat honey, my son, for it is
    good;
honey from the comb is
    sweet to your taste.
¹⁴Know also that wisdom is
    sweet to your soul;
if you find it, there is a
    future hope for you,
    and your hope will not be
    cut off.   Ps 119:103

¹⁵Do not lie in wait like an
    outlaw against a
    righteous man's house,
    do not raid his dwelling
    place;
¹⁶for though a righteous man
    falls seven times, he
    rises again,
but the wicked are brought
    down by calamity.   Job 5:19

¹⁷Do not gloat when your
    enemy falls;   Ob 12
when he stumbles, do not
    let your heart rejoice,
¹⁸or the LORD will see and
    disapprove
and turn his wrath away
    from him.   Job 31:29

¹⁹Do not fret because of evil
    men   Ps 37:1
  or be envious of the
    wicked,
²⁰for the evil man has no
    future hope,
  and the lamp of the wicked
    will be snuffed out. Job 18:5

²¹Fear the LORD and the king,
    my son,   Rom 13:1-5
  and do not join with the
    rebellious,
²²for those two will send
    sudden destruction
    upon them,   Ps 73:19
  and who knows what
    calamities they can
    bring?

Further Sayings of the Wise

²³These also are sayings of the
wise: Pr 1:6

  To show partiality in judging
    is not good: Ex 18:16
²⁴Whoever says to the guilty,
    "You are innocent"—
  peoples will curse him and
    nations denounce him.
²⁵But it will go well with those
    who convict the guilty,
  and rich blessing will come
    upon them.

²⁶An honest answer
  is like a kiss on the lips.

²⁷Finish your outdoor work
  and get your fields ready;
  after that, build your house.

²⁸Do not testify against your
    neighbor without cause,
  or use your lips to deceive.
²⁹Do not say, "I'll do to him as
    he has done to me;
  I'll pay that man back for
    what he did."   Pr 20:22

³⁰I went past the field of the
    sluggard,   Pr 6:6-11
  past the vineyard of the
    man who lacks
    judgment;
³¹thorns had come up
    everywhere,
  the ground was covered
    with weeds,
  and the stone wall was in
    ruins.
³²I applied my heart to what I
    observed
  and learned a lesson from
    what I saw:
³³A little sleep, a little slumber,
  a little folding of the hands
    to rest—   Pr 6:10
³⁴and poverty will come on
    you like a bandit
  and scarcity like an armed
    man. ᵃ   Pr 10:4

More Proverbs of Solomon

25 These are more proverbs
of Solomon, copied by
the men of Hezekiah king of
Judah: Pr 1:1

²It is the glory of God to
    conceal a matter;
  to search out a matter is the
    glory of kings.   Pr 16:10-15

ᵃ34 Or *like a vagrant / and scarcity like a beggar*

³As the heavens are high and
　　the earth is deep,
　so the hearts of kings are
　　unsearchable.

⁴Remove the dross from the
　　silver,
　and out comes material for*ᵃ*
　　the silversmith;
⁵remove the wicked from the
　　king's presence,　　Pr 20:8
　and his throne will be
　　established through
　　righteousness.　　Pr 16:12

⁶Do not exalt yourself in the
　　king's presence,
　and do not claim a place
　　among great men;
⁷it is better for him to say to
　　you, "Come up here,"
　than for him to humiliate
　　you before a nobleman.

What you have seen with
　　your eyes
⁸　do not bring*ᵇ* hastily to
　　court,
　for what will you do in the
　　end
　　if your neighbor puts you to
　　shame?　　Mt 5:25-26

⁹If you argue your case with a
　　neighbor,
　do not betray another
　　man's confidence,
¹⁰or he who hears it may
　　shame you
　and you will never lose
　　your bad reputation.

¹¹A word aptly spoken
　is like apples of gold in
　　settings of silver.　　Pr 15:23

¹²Like an earring of gold or an
　　ornament of fine gold
　is a wise man's rebuke to a
　　listening ear.　　Ps 141:5

¹³Like the coolness of snow at
　　harvest time
　is a trustworthy messenger
　　to those who send him;
　he refreshes the spirit of his
　　masters.　　Pr 10:26

¹⁴Like clouds and wind
　　without rain
　is a man who boasts of gifts
　　he does not give.

¹⁵Through patience a ruler can
　　be persuaded,　　Ecc 10:4
　and a gentle tongue can
　　break a bone.　　Pr 15:1

¹⁶If you find honey, eat just
　　enough—
　too much of it, and you will
　　vomit.
¹⁷Seldom set foot in your
　　neighbor's house—
　too much of you, and he
　　will hate you.

¹⁸Like a club or a sword or a
　　sharp arrow
　is the man who gives false
　　testimony against his
　　neighbor.　　Pr 12:18

¹⁹Like a bad tooth or a lame
　　foot
　is reliance on the unfaithful
　　in times of trouble.

²⁰Like one who takes away a
　　garment on a cold day,
　or like vinegar poured on
　　soda,

ᵃ4 Or *comes a vessel from*　　*ᵇ7,8* Or *nobleman / on whom you had set your eyes. / 8Do not go*

is one who sings songs to a heavy heart.

²¹If your enemy is hungry,
    give him food to eat;
if he is thirsty, give him
    water to drink.
²²In doing this, you will heap
    burning coals on his
    head,   Ps 18:8
and the LORD will reward
    you.   Mt 5:44

²³As a north wind brings rain,
    so a sly tongue brings angry
    looks.

²⁴Better to live on a corner of
    the roof
    than share a house with a
    quarrelsome wife.   Pr 21:9

²⁵Like cold water to a weary
    soul
    is good news from a distant
    land.   Pr 15:30

²⁶Like a muddied spring or a
    polluted well
    is a righteous man who
    gives way to the wicked.

²⁷It is not good to eat too much
    honey,
    nor is it honorable to seek
    one's own honor.   Pr 27:2

²⁸Like a city whose walls are
    broken down
    is a man who lacks
    self-control.

26 Like snow in summer or
    rain in harvest,   1Sa 12:17
honor is not fitting for a
    fool.   Pr 19:10

²Like a fluttering sparrow or a
    darting swallow,
an undeserved curse does
    not come to rest.   Dt 23:5

³A whip for the horse, a halter
    for the donkey,   Ps 32:9
and a rod for the backs of
    fools!   Pr 10:13

⁴Do not answer a fool
    according to his folly,
    or you will be like him
    yourself.   Isa 36:21

⁵Answer a fool according to
    his folly,
    or he will be wise in his
    own eyes.   Pr 3:7

⁶Like cutting off one's feet or
    drinking violence
    is the sending of a message
    by the hand of a fool.

⁷Like a lame man's legs that
    hang limp
    is a proverb in the mouth of
    a fool.

⁸Like tying a stone in a sling
    is the giving of honor to a
    fool.

⁹Like a thornbush in a
    drunkard's hand
    is a proverb in the mouth of
    a fool.

¹⁰Like an archer who wounds
    at random
    is he who hires a fool or
    any passer-by.

¹¹As a dog returns to its vomit,
    so a fool repeats his folly.

¹²Do you see a man wise in his
    own eyes?   Pr 3:7

There is more hope for a
  fool than for him.   Pr 29:20

¹³The sluggard says, "There is
  a lion in the road,
a fierce lion roaming the
  streets!"   Pr 22:13

¹⁴As a door turns on its hinges,
  so a sluggard turns on his
  bed.   Pr 6:9

¹⁵The sluggard buries his hand
  in the dish;
he is too lazy to bring it
  back to his mouth.   Pr 19:24

¹⁶The sluggard is wiser in his
  own eyes
than seven men who
  answer discreetly.

¹⁷Like one who seizes a dog by
  the ears
is a passer-by who meddles
  in a quarrel not his own.

¹⁸Like a madman shooting
  firebrands or deadly arrows
¹⁹is a man who deceives his
  neighbor
and says, "I was only
  joking!"

²⁰Without wood a fire goes
  out;
without gossip a quarrel
  dies down.   Pr 22:10

²¹As charcoal to embers and as
  wood to fire,
so is a quarrelsome man for
  kindling strife.   Pr 14:17

²²The words of a gossip are
  like choice morsels;

they go down to a man's
  inmost parts.   Pr 18:8

²³Like a coating of glaze[a] over
  earthenware
are fervent lips with an evil
  heart.

²⁴A malicious man disguises
  himself with his lips,
but in his heart he harbors
  deceit.   Ps 41:6

²⁵Though his speech is
  charming, do not believe
  him,   Ps 28:3
for seven abominations fill
  his heart.   Jer 9:4

²⁶His malice may be concealed
  by deception,
but his wickedness will be
  exposed in the
  assembly.

²⁷If a man digs a pit, he will
  fall into it;   Est 6:13
if a man rolls a stone, it will
  roll back on him.   Est 2:23

²⁸A lying tongue hates those it
  hurts,
and a flattering mouth
  works ruin.   Ps 12:3

27 Do not boast about
  tomorrow,   1Ki 20:11
for you do not know what a
  day may bring forth. Mt 6:34

²Let another praise you, and
  not your own mouth;
someone else, and not your
  own lips.   Pr 25:27

³Stone is heavy and sand a
  burden,   Job 6:3

---

a23   With a different word division of the Hebrew; Masoretic Text *of silver dross*

but provocation by a fool is
   heavier than both.

⁴Anger is cruel and fury
   overwhelming,
but who can stand before
   jealousy? Nu 5:14

⁵Better is open rebuke
   than hidden love.

⁶Wounds from a friend can be
   trusted,
but an enemy multiplies
   kisses. Ps 141:5

⁷He who is full loathes honey,
but to the hungry even
   what is bitter tastes
   sweet.

⁸Like a bird that strays from
   its nest Isa 16:2
is a man who strays from
   his home.

⁹Perfume and incense bring
   joy to the heart, Est 2:12
and the pleasantness of
   one's friend springs
   from his earnest
   counsel.

¹⁰Do not forsake your friend
   and the friend of your
   father,
and do not go to your
   brother's house when
   disaster strikes you—
better a neighbor nearby
   than a brother far
   away.

¹¹Be wise, my son, and bring
   joy to my heart; Pr 10:1

then I can answer anyone
   who treats me with
   contempt. Ge 24:60

¹²The prudent see danger and
   take refuge,
but the simple keep going
   and suffer for it. Pr 22:3

¹³Take the garment of one who
   puts up security for a
   stranger;
hold it in pledge if he does
   it for a wayward
   woman. Pr 20:16

¹⁴If a man loudly blesses his
   neighbor early in the
   morning,
it will be taken as a curse.

¹⁵A quarrelsome wife is like
a constant dripping on a
   rainy day; Est 1:18
¹⁶restraining her is like
   restraining the wind
or grasping oil with the
   hand.

¹⁷As iron sharpens iron,
so one man sharpens
   another.

¹⁸He who tends a fig tree will
   eat its fruit, 1Co 9:7
and he who looks after his
   master will be honored.

¹⁹As water reflects a face,
so a man's heart reflects the
   man.

²⁰Death and Destruction^a are
   never satisfied, Pr 30:15-16
and neither are the eyes of
   man. Ecc 1:8

^a20 Hebrew *Sheol and Abaddon*

²¹The crucible for silver and
　　the furnace for gold,
　but man is tested by the
　　praise he receives.　　Pr 17:3

²²Though you grind a fool in a
　　mortar,
　grinding him like grain with
　　a pestle,
　you will not remove his
　　folly from him.

²³Be sure you know the
　　condition of your flocks,
　give careful attention to
　　your herds;
²⁴for riches do not endure
　　forever,　　Pr 23:5
　and a crown is not secure
　　for all generations.
²⁵When the hay is removed
　　and new growth appears
　and the grass from the hills
　　is gathered in,
²⁶the lambs will provide you
　　with clothing,
　and the goats with the price
　　of a field.
²⁷You will have plenty of
　　goats' milk
　to feed you and your family
　and to nourish your servant
　　girls.

28 The wicked man flees
　　though no one pursues,
　but the righteous are as
　　bold as a lion.　　Ps 138:3

²When a country is rebellious,
　　it has many rulers,
　but a man of understanding
　　and knowledge
　　maintains order.

³A ruler*ᵃ* who oppresses the
　　poor
　is like a driving rain that
　　leaves no crops.

⁴Those who forsake the law
　　praise the wicked,
　but those who keep the law
　　resist them.

⁵Evil men do not understand
　　justice,
　but those who seek the
　　LORD understand it
　　fully.

⁶Better a poor man whose
　　walk is blameless
　than a rich man whose
　　ways are perverse.　　Pr 19:1

⁷He who keeps the law is a
　　discerning son,
　but a companion of gluttons
　　disgraces his father.

⁸He who increases his wealth
　　by exorbitant interest
　amasses it for another, who
　　will be kind to the poor.

⁹If anyone turns a deaf ear to
　　the law,
　even his prayers are
　　detestable.　　Ps 109:7

¹⁰He who leads the upright
　　along an evil path
　will fall into his own trap,
　but the blameless will
　　receive a good
　　inheritance.　　Ps 57:6

¹¹A rich man may be wise in
　　his own eyes,

ᵃ3 Or A poor man

but a poor man who has
discernment sees
through him.

¹²When the righteous triumph,
there is great elation;
but when the wicked rise to
power, men go into
hiding.   Job 24:4

¹³He who conceals his sins
does not prosper, 2Sa 12:13
but whoever confesses and
renounces them finds
mercy.   Ps 32:1-5

¹⁴Blessed is the man who
always fears the LORD,
but he who hardens his
heart falls into trouble.

¹⁵Like a roaring lion or a
charging bear
is a wicked man ruling over
a helpless people.

¹⁶A tyrannical ruler lacks
judgment,
but he who hates ill-gotten
gain will enjoy a long
life.

¹⁷A man tormented by the
guilt of murder
will be a fugitive till death;
let no one support him.

¹⁸He whose walk is blameless
is kept safe,   Jer 39:18
but he whose ways are
perverse will suddenly
fall.   Est 6:13

¹⁹He who works his land will
have abundant food,
but the one who chases
fantasies will have his
fill of poverty.   Pr 12:11

²⁰A faithful man will be richly
blessed,
but one eager to get rich
will not go unpunished.

²¹To show partiality is not
good—   Ps 94:21
yet a man will do wrong for
a piece of bread.   Eze 13:19

²²A stingy man is eager to get
rich
and is unaware that poverty
awaits him.

²³He who rebukes a man will
in the end gain more
favor
than he who has a flattering
tongue.   Pr 27:5-6

²⁴He who robs his father or
mother   Pr 19:26
and says, "It's not
wrong"—
he is partner to him who
destroys.   Pr 18:9

²⁵A greedy man stirs up
dissension,   Pr 14:17
but he who trusts in the
LORD will prosper.

²⁶He who trusts in himself is a
fool,   Ps 4:5
but he who walks in
wisdom is kept safe.

²⁷He who gives to the poor will
lack nothing,   Dt 24:19
but he who closes his eyes
to them receives many
curses.   Ps 109:17

²⁸When the wicked rise to
power, people go into
hiding;   Job 20:19
but when the wicked

perish, the righteous thrive.

29 A man who remains stiff-necked after many rebukes Ex 32:9
will suddenly be destroyed—without remedy. 2Ch 36:16

2When the righteous thrive, the people rejoice; 2Ki 11:20
when the wicked rule, the people groan. Pr 30:22

3A man who loves wisdom brings joy to his father, but a companion of prostitutes squanders his wealth. Pr 5:8-10

4By justice a king gives a country stability, Pr 8:15-16
but one who is greedy for bribes tears it down.

5Whoever flatters his neighbor is spreading a net for his feet. Job 32:21

6An evil man is snared by his own sin, Job 5:13
but a righteous one can sing and be glad.

7The righteous care about justice for the poor, but the wicked have no such concern. Pr 31:8-9

8Mockers stir up a city, but wise men turn away anger. Pr 11:11

9If a wise man goes to court with a fool, the fool rages and scoffs, and there is no peace.

10Bloodthirsty men hate a man of integrity and seek to kill the upright.

11A fool gives full vent to his anger, Job 15:13
but a wise man keeps himself under control.

12If a ruler listens to lies, all his officials become wicked. Job 34:30

13The poor man and the oppressor have this in common:
The LORD gives sight to the eyes of both. Pr 22:2

14If a king judges the poor with fairness, his throne will always be secure. Ps 72:1-5

15The rod of correction imparts wisdom, but a child left to himself disgraces his mother.

16When the wicked thrive, so does sin, but the righteous will see their downfall. Ps 91:8

17Discipline your son, and he will give you peace; he will bring delight to your soul.

18Where there is no revelation, the people cast off restraint; but blessed is he who keeps the law. Ps 1:1-2

19A servant cannot be corrected by mere words;

though he understands, he
will not respond.

20Do you see a man who
speaks in haste?
There is more hope for a
fool than for him.   Pr 19:2

21If a man pampers his servant
from youth,
he will bring grief^a in the
end.

22An angry man stirs up
dissension,
and a hot-tempered one
commits many sins.

23A man's pride brings him
low,   Est 5:12
but a man of lowly spirit
gains honor.   Pr 11:2

24The accomplice of a thief is
his own enemy;
he is put under oath and
dare not testify.   Lev 5:1

25Fear of man will prove to be
a snare,
but whoever trusts in the
LORD is kept safe.   Pr 16:20

26Many seek an audience with
a ruler,   Pr 19:6
but it is from the LORD that
man gets justice.   Pr 16:33

27The righteous detest the
dishonest;
the wicked detest the
upright.

Sayings of Agur

30 The sayings of Agur son
of Jakeh—an oracle^b:

This man declared to Ithiel,
to Ithiel and to Ucal:^c

2"I am the most ignorant of
men;
I do not have a man's
understanding.
3I have not learned wisdom,
nor have I knowledge of the
Holy One.   Pr 9:10
4Who has gone up to heaven
and come down?   Dt 30:12
Who has gathered up the
wind in the hollow of
his hands?   Isa 40:12
Who has wrapped up the
waters in his cloak?
Who has established all the
ends of the earth?
What is his name, and the
name of his son?   Rev 19:12
Tell me if you know!

5"Every word of God is
flawless;   Ps 12:6
he is a shield to those who
take refuge in him.
6Do not add to his words,
or he will rebuke you and
prove you a liar.   Dt 4:2

7"Two things I ask of you,
O LORD;
do not refuse me before I
die:
8Keep falsehood and lies far
from me;

---

^a21 The meaning of the Hebrew for this word is uncertain.   ^b1 Or Jakeh of Massa
^c1 Masoretic Text; with a different word division of the Hebrew declared, "I am weary,
O God; / I am weary, O God, and faint.

give me neither poverty nor
riches,
but give me only my daily
bread.   Mt 6:11
9Otherwise, I may have too
much and disown you
and say, 'Who is the LORD?'
Or I may become poor and
steal,
and so dishonor the name
of my God.   Dt 8:12

10"Do not slander a servant to
his master,
or he will curse you, and
you will pay for it.

11"There are those who curse
their fathers
and do not bless their
mothers;   Pr 20:20
12those who are pure in their
own eyes   Pr 16:2
and yet are not cleansed of
their filth;   Jer 2:23,25
13those whose eyes are ever so
haughty,   2Sa 22:28
whose glances are so
disdainful;
14those whose teeth are swords
and whose jaws are set
with knives   Ps 57:4
to devour the poor from the
earth,   Am 8:4
the needy from among
mankind.   Job 19:22

15"The leech has two
daughters.
'Give! Give!' they cry.

"There are three things that
are never satisfied,

four that never say,
'Enough!':   Pr 27:20
16the grave,ᵃ the barren womb,
land, which is never
satisfied with water,
and fire, which never says,
'Enough!'

17"The eye that mocks a father,
that scorns obedience to a
mother,
will be pecked out by the
ravens of the valley,
will be eaten by the
vultures.   Job 15:23

18"There are three things that
are too amazing for me,
four that I do not
understand:
19the way of an eagle in the
sky,
the way of a snake on a
rock,
the way of a ship on the high
seas,
and the way of a man with
a maiden.

20"This is the way of an
adulteress:
She eats and wipes her
mouth
and says, 'I've done
nothing wrong.'   Pr 5:6

21"Under three things the
earth trembles,
under four it cannot bear
up:
22a servant who becomes king,
a fool who is full of food,
23an unloved woman who is
married,

ᵃ16 Hebrew *Sheol*

and a maidservant who
   displaces her mistress.

24"Four things on earth are
   small,
  yet they are extremely wise:
25Ants are creatures of little
   strength,
  yet they store up their food
   in the summer;   Pr 6:6-8
26coneys*a* are creatures of little
   power,   Ps 104:18
  yet they make their home in
   the crags;
27locusts have no king,   Ex 10:4
  yet they advance together
   in ranks;
28a lizard can be caught with
   the hand,
  yet it is found in kings'
   palaces.

29"There are three things that
   are stately in their stride,
  four that move with stately
   bearing:
30a lion, mighty among beasts,
  who retreats before
   nothing;
31a strutting rooster, a he-goat,
  and a king with his army
   around him.*b*

32"If you have played the fool
   and exalted yourself,
  or if you have planned evil,
  clap your hand over your
   mouth!   Job 29:9
33For as churning the milk
   produces butter,
  and as twisting the nose
   produces blood,

so stirring up anger
   produces strife."

Sayings of King Lemuel

31 The sayings of King
   Lemuel—an oracle*c* his
mother taught him: Pr 22:17
2"O my son, O son of my
   womb,
  O son of my vows,*d*   Jdg 11:30
3do not spend your strength
   on women,
  your vigor on those who
   ruin kings.   Dt 17:17

4"It is not for kings,
   O Lemuel—
  not for kings to drink wine,
  not for rulers to crave beer,
5lest they drink and forget
   what the law decrees,
  and deprive all the
   oppressed of their
   rights.   Pr 16:12
6Give beer to those who are
   perishing,
  wine to those who are in
   anguish;   Ge 14:18
7let them drink and forget
   their poverty   Est 1:10
  and remember their misery
   no more.

8"Speak up for those who
   cannot speak for
   themselves,   1Sa 19:4
  for the rights of all who are
   destitute.
9Speak up and judge fairly;
   defend the rights of the
   poor and needy."   Pr 24:23

---

a26 That is, the hyrax or rock badger   *b31* Or *king secure against revolt*   *c1* Or *of*
Lemuel king of Massa, which   *d2* Or / *the answer to my prayers*

Epilogue: The Wife of Noble Character

10 ^aA wife of noble character
who can find?   Ru 3:11
She is worth far more than
rubies.

11Her husband has full
confidence in her   Ge 2:18
and lacks nothing of
value.

12She brings him good, not
harm,
all the days of her life.

13She selects wool and flax
and works with eager
hands.   1Ti 2:9-10

14She is like the merchant
ships,
bringing her food from
afar.

15She gets up while it is still
dark;
she provides food for her
family
and portions for her servant
girls.

16She considers a field and
buys it;
out of her earnings she
plants a vineyard.

17She sets about her work
vigorously;
her arms are strong for her
tasks.

18She sees that her trading is
profitable,
and her lamp does not go
out at night.

19In her hand she holds the
distaff

and grasps the spindle with
her fingers.

20She opens her arms to the
poor
and extends her hands to
the needy.   Dt 15:11

21When it snows, she has no
fear for her household;
for all of them are clothed
in scarlet.

22She makes coverings for her
bed;
she is clothed in fine linen
and purple.

23Her husband is respected at
the city gate,
where he takes his seat
among the elders of the
land.   Ex 3:16

24She makes linen garments
and sells them,
and supplies the merchants
with sashes.

25She is clothed with strength
and dignity;
she can laugh at the days to
come.

26She speaks with wisdom,
and faithful instruction is
on her tongue.   Pr 10:31

27She watches over the affairs
of her household
and does not eat the bread
of idleness.

28Her children arise and call
her blessed;
her husband also, and he
praises her:

---

^a10 Verses 10-31 are an acrostic, each verse beginning with a successive letter of the
Hebrew alphabet.

29"Many women do noble
things,
but you surpass them
all."
30Charm is deceptive, and
beauty is fleeting;

but a woman who fears the
Lord is to be praised.
31Give her the reward she has
earned,
and let her works bring her
praise at the city gate.

Ecclesiastes

Introduction:

Ecclesiastes studies the meaning of life. The "Teacher" looks at wisdom, pleasure, work, power, riches, religion, and other things. All of these have some value and are useful in the proper time and place, but they have lasting value only if God is at the center of man's life. Reverence and respect for God and a real devotion in serving God are the most important in making life have meaning. Without God, the "Teacher" says, "everything is meaningless."

Outline of contents:

Everything Is Meaningless

1 The words of the Teacher,[a] son of David, king in Jerusalem: Pr 1:1

2"Meaningless! Meaningless!"
  says the Teacher.
 "Utterly meaningless!
  Everything is meaningless."

3What does man gain from all
    his labor
  at which he toils under the
    sun?   Ecc 2:11,22
4Generations come and
    generations go,
  but the earth remains
    forever.   Job 8:19
5The sun rises and the sun
    sets,
  and hurries back to where it
    rises.   Ps 19:5-6
6The wind blows to the south
    and turns to the north;
  round and round it goes,
    ever returning on its
    course.
7All streams flow into the sea,
  yet the sea is never full.
 To the place the streams
    come from,
  there they return again.

a1 Or leader of the assembly; also in verses 2 and 12

⁸All things are wearisome,
more than one can say.
The eye never has enough of
seeing,   Pr 27:20
nor the ear its fill of
hearing.
⁹What has been will be again,
what has been done will be
done again;   Ecc 2:12
there is nothing new under
the sun.
¹⁰Is there anything of which
one can say,
"Look! This is something
new"?
It was here already, long ago;
it was here before our time.
¹¹There is no remembrance of
men of old,   Ge 40:23
and even those who are yet
to come
will not be remembered
by those who follow.

Wisdom Is Meaningless

¹²I, the Teacher, was king
over Israel in Jerusalem. ¹³I devoted myself to study and to explore by wisdom all that is done
under heaven. What a heavy
burden God has laid on men! ¹⁴I
have seen all the things that are
done under the sun; all of them
are meaningless, a chasing after
the wind.   Job 28:3; Ecc 2:16

¹⁵What is twisted cannot be
straightened;   Ecc 7:13
what is lacking cannot be
counted.

¹⁶I thought to myself, "Look,
I have grown and increased in
wisdom more than anyone who
has ruled over Jerusalem before

me; I have experienced much of
wisdom and knowledge."
¹⁷Then I applied myself to the
understanding of wisdom, and
also of madness and folly, but I
learned that this, too, is a chasing after the wind.   1Ki 3:12; Ecc 2:3

¹⁸For with much wisdom
comes much sorrow;
the more knowledge, the
more grief.   Ecc 12:12

Pleasures Are Meaningless

2 I thought in my heart,
"Come now, I will test you
with pleasure to find out what is
good." But that also proved to
be meaningless. ²"Laughter," I
said, "is foolish. And what does
pleasure accomplish?" ³I tried
cheering myself with wine, and
embracing folly—my mind still
guiding me with wisdom. I
wanted to see what was worthwhile for men to do under
heaven during the few days of
their lives.   Jdg 9:13; Ecc 7:4

⁴I undertook great projects: I
built houses for myself and
planted vineyards. ⁵I made gardens and parks and planted all
kinds of fruit trees in them. ⁶I
made reservoirs to water groves
of flourishing trees. ⁷I bought
male and female slaves and had
other slaves who were born in
my house. I also owned more
herds and flocks than anyone in
Jerusalem before me. ⁸I
amassed silver and gold for myself, and the treasure of kings
and provinces. I acquired men
and women singers, and a

harem*a* as well—the delights of the heart of man. 9I became greater by far than anyone in Jerusalem before me. In all this my wisdom stayed with me.

10I denied myself nothing my eyes desired;
  I refused my heart no pleasure.
My heart took delight in all my work,
  and this was the reward for all my labor.
11Yet when I surveyed all that my hands had done
  and what I had toiled to achieve,
everything was meaningless,
  a chasing after the wind;
nothing was gained under the sun.   Ecc 1:3

Wisdom and Folly Are Meaningless

12Then I turned my thoughts to consider wisdom,
  and also madness and folly.
What more can the king's successor do
  than what has already been done?   Ecc 1:9
13I saw that wisdom is better than folly,   Ecc 7:11-12
  just as light is better than darkness.
14The wise man has eyes in his head,
  while the fool walks in the darkness;

but I came to realize
  that the same fate overtakes them both.   Ps 49:10

15Then I thought in my heart,

"The fate of the fool will overtake me also.
What then do I gain by being wise?"   Ecc 6:8
I said in my heart,
  "This too is meaningless."
16For the wise man, like the fool, will not be long remembered;   Ps 112:6
in days to come both will be forgotten.   Ecc 1:11
Like the fool, the wise man too must die!   Ps 49:10

Toil Is Meaningless

17So I hated life, because the work that is done under the sun was grievous to me. All of it is meaningless, a chasing after the wind. 18I hated all the things I had toiled for under the sun, because I must leave them to the one who comes after me. 19And who knows whether he will be a wise man or a fool? Yet he will have control over all the work into which I have poured my effort and skill under the sun. This too is meaningless. 20So my heart began to despair over all my toilsome labor under the sun. 21For a man may do his work with wisdom, knowledge and skill, and then he must leave all he owns to someone who has not worked for it. This

---

a8 The meaning of the Hebrew for this phrase is uncertain.

too is meaningless and a great misfortune. ²²What does a man get for all the toil and anxious striving with which he labors under the sun? ²³All his days his work is pain and grief; even at night his mind does not rest. This too is meaningless.

²⁴A man can do nothing better than to eat and drink and find satisfaction in his work. This too, I see, is from the hand of God, ²⁵for without him, who can eat or find enjoyment? ²⁶To the man who pleases him, God gives wisdom, knowledge and happiness, but to the sinner he gives the task of gathering and storing up wealth to hand it over to the one who pleases God. This too is meaningless, a chasing after the wind.　　Ps 39:6

A Time for Everything

3 There is a time for everything,　　Ecc 8:6
and a season for every activity under heaven:

² 　a time to be born and a time to die,
a time to plant and a time to uproot,　　Isa 28:24
³ 　a time to kill and a time to heal,　　Dt 5:17
a time to tear down and a time to build,
⁴ 　a time to weep and a time to laugh,
a time to mourn and a time to dance,

⁵ 　a time to scatter stones and a time to gather them,
a time to embrace and a time to refrain,
⁶ 　a time to search and a time to give up,
a time to keep and a time to throw away,
⁷ 　a time to tear and a time to mend,
a time to be silent and a time to speak,　　Est 4:14
⁸ 　a time to love and a time to hate,
a time for war and a time for peace.

⁹What does the worker gain from his toil? ¹⁰I have seen the burden God has laid on men. ¹¹He has made everything beautiful in its time. He has also set eternity in the hearts of men; yet they cannot fathom what God has done from beginning to end. ¹²I know that there is nothing better for men than to be happy and do good while they live. ¹³That everyone may eat and drink, and find satisfaction in all his toil—this is the gift of God. ¹⁴I know that everything God does will endure forever; nothing can be added to it and nothing taken from it. God does it so that men will revere him.　　Ecc 2:3; 5:7; Ps 34:12

¹⁵Whatever is has already been,　　Ecc 6:10
and what will be has been before;　　Ecc 1:9

and God will call the past to account. *a*

16And I saw something else under the sun:

In the place of judgment—
    wickedness was there,
in the place of justice—
    wickedness was there.

17I thought in my heart,

"God will bring to judgment
    both the righteous and the
        wicked,   Job 19:29
for there will be a time for
    every activity,
a time for every deed."

18I also thought, "As for men, God tests them so that they may see that they are like the animals. 19Man's fate is like that of the animals; the same fate awaits them both: As one dies, so dies the other. All have the same breath;*b* man has no advantage over the animal. Everything is meaningless. 20All go to the same place; all come from dust, and to dust all return. 21Who knows if the spirit of man rises upward and if the spirit of the animal*c* goes down into the earth?"   Ps 73:22; Ecc 12:7

22So I saw that there is nothing better for a man than to enjoy his work, because that is his lot. For who can bring him to see what will happen after him?

Oppression, Toil, Friendlessness

4 Again I looked and saw all the oppression that was taking place under the sun: Ps 12:5

I saw the tears of the
    oppressed—
and they have no
    comforter;
power was on the side of
    their oppressors—
and they have no
    comforter.   La 1:16
2And I declared that the dead,
    who had already died,
are happier than the living,
    who are still alive.   Job 3:17
3But better than both
    is he who has not yet been,
who has not seen the evil
    that is done under the sun.

4And I saw that all labor and all achievement spring from man's envy of his neighbor. This too is meaningless, a chasing after the wind.   Ecc 1:14

5The fool folds his hands
    and ruins himself.   Pr 6:10
6Better one handful with
    tranquillity
than two handfuls with toil
    and chasing after the wind.

7Again I saw something meaningless under the sun:

8There was a man all alone;
    he had neither son nor
        brother.
There was no end to his toil,

---

*a*15 Or *God calls back the past*   *b*19 Or *spirit*   *c*21 Or *Who knows the spirit of man,*
which rises upward, or the spirit of the animal, which

yet his eyes were not
    content with his wealth.
"For whom am I toiling," he
    asked,
"and why am I depriving
    myself of enjoyment?"
This too is meaningless—
    a miserable business!

⁹Two are better than one,
    because they have a good
    return for their work:
¹⁰If one falls down,
    his friend can help him up.
But pity the man who falls
    and has no one to help him
    up!
¹¹Also, if two lie down
    together, they will keep
    warm.
But how can one keep
    warm alone?
¹²Though one may be
    overpowered,
    two can defend themselves.
A cord of three strands is not
    quickly broken.

Advancement Is Meaningless

¹³Better a poor but wise youth
than an old but foolish king
who no longer knows how to
take warning. ¹⁴The youth may
have come from prison to the
kingship, or he may have been
born in poverty within his kingdom. ¹⁵I saw that all who lived
and walked under the sun followed the youth, the king's
successor. ¹⁶There was no end
to all the people who were before them. But those who came
later were not pleased with the
successor. This too is meaning-

less, a chasing after the wind.

Stand in Awe of God

5 Guard your steps when you
    go to the house of God. Go
near to listen rather than to offer
the sacrifice of fools, who do not
know that they do wrong.

²Do not be quick with your
    mouth,
    do not be hasty in your
    heart
    to utter anything before
    God.   Jdg 11:35
God is in heaven
    and you are on earth,
    so let your words be few.
³As a dream comes when
    there are many cares,
    so the speech of a fool
    when there are many
    words.   Ecc 10:14

⁴When you make a vow to
God, do not delay in fulfilling it.
He has no pleasure in fools; fulfill your vow. ⁵It is better not to
vow than to make a vow and
not fulfill it. ⁶Do not let your
mouth lead you into sin. And
do not protest to the ₗtempleⱼ
messenger, "My vow was a
mistake." Why should God be
angry at what you say and destroy the work of your hands?
⁷Much dreaming and many
words are meaningless. Therefore stand in awe of God. Dt 23:21

Riches Are Meaningless

⁸If you see the poor op-
pressed in a district, and justice
and rights denied, do not be
surprised at such things; for one

official is eyed by a higher one, and over them both are others higher still. ⁹The increase from the land is taken by all; the king himself profits from the fields.

¹⁰Whoever loves money never
    has money enough;
whoever loves wealth is
    never satisfied with his
    income.
This too is meaningless.

¹¹As goods increase,
    so do those who consume
    them.
And what benefit are they to
    the owner
except to feast his eyes on
    them?

¹²The sleep of a laborer is
    sweet,
whether he eats little or
    much,
but the abundance of a rich
    man
permits him no sleep. Job 20:20

¹³I have seen a grievous evil
under the sun: Ecc 6:1-2

wealth hoarded to the harm
    of its owner,
¹⁴ or wealth lost through
    some misfortune,
so that when he has a son
    there is nothing left for
    him.
¹⁵Naked a man comes from his
    mother's womb,
and as he comes, so he
    departs.   Job 1:21
He takes nothing from his
    labor   Ps 49:17

that he can carry in his
    hand.   Ecc 1:3

¹⁶This too is a grievous evil:

As a man comes, so he
    departs,
and what does he gain,
    since he toils for the wind?
¹⁷All his days he eats in
    darkness,
with great frustration,
    affliction and anger.

¹⁸Then I realized that it is good and proper for a man to eat and drink, and to find satisfaction in his toilsome labor under the sun during the few days of life God has given him—for this is his lot. ¹⁹Moreover, when God gives any man wealth and possessions, and enables him to enjoy them, to accept his lot and be happy in his work—this is a gift of God. ²⁰He seldom reflects on the days of his life, because God keeps him occupied with gladness of heart.   Job 31:2; Ecc 2:24

6 I have seen another evil under the sun, and it weighs heavily on men: ²God gives a man wealth, possessions and honor, so that he lacks nothing his heart desires, but God does not enable him to enjoy them, and a stranger enjoys them instead. This is meaningless, a grievous evil.   Ecc 5:13,19

³A man may have a hundred children and live many years; yet no matter how long he lives, if he cannot enjoy his prosperity and does not receive proper burial, I say that a stillborn child

is better off than he. ⁴It comes without meaning, it departs in darkness, and in darkness its name is shrouded. ⁵Though it never saw the sun or knew anything, it has more rest than does that man— ⁶even if he lives a thousand years twice over but fails to enjoy his prosperity. Do not all go to the same place?

⁷All man's efforts are for his
    mouth,
  yet his appetite is never
    satisfied.   Pr 27:20
⁸What advantage has a wise
    man
  over a fool?   Ecc 2:15
  What does a poor man gain
  by knowing how to conduct
    himself before others?
⁹Better what the eye sees
  than the roving of the
    appetite.
  This too is meaningless,
  a chasing after the wind.

¹⁰Whatever exists has already
    been named,   Ecc 3:15
  and what man is has been
    known;
  no man can contend
  with one who is stronger
    than he.
¹¹The more the words,
  the less the meaning,
  and how does that profit
    anyone?

¹²For who knows what is good for a man in life, during the few and meaningless days he passes through like a shadow? Who can tell him what will happen under the sun after he is gone?   1Ch 29:15; Job 14:2

Wisdom

7 A good name is better than
    fine perfume,   Pr 22:1
  and the day of death better
    than the day of birth.
²It is better to go to a house of
    mourning
  than to go to a house of
    feasting,
  for death is the destiny of
    every man;   Ecc 2:14
  the living should take this
    to heart.
³Sorrow is better than
    laughter,   Pr 14:13
  because a sad face is good
    for the heart.
⁴The heart of the wise is in the
    house of mourning,
  but the heart of fools is in
    the house of pleasure.
⁵It is better to heed a wise
    man's rebuke   Pr 13:18
  than to listen to the song of
    fools.
⁶Like the crackling of thorns
    under the pot,   Ps 58:9
  so is the laughter of fools.
  This too is meaningless.

⁷Extortion turns a wise man
    into a fool,
  and a bribe corrupts the
    heart.   Ex 18:21

⁸The end of a matter is better
    than its beginning,
  and patience is better than
    pride.   Pr 14:29
⁹Do not be quickly provoked
    in your spirit,   Mt 5:22

for anger resides in the lap
of fools.   Pr 14:29

¹⁰Do not say, "Why were the
old days better than
these?"   Ps 77:5
For it is not wise to ask
such questions.

¹¹Wisdom, like an inheritance,
is a good thing   Ecc 2:13
and benefits those who see
the sun.   Ecc 11:7
¹²Wisdom is a shelter
as money is a shelter,
but the advantage of
knowledge is this:
that wisdom preserves the
life of its possessor.

¹³Consider what God has
done: Ecc 2:24

Who can straighten
what he has made crooked?
¹⁴When times are good, be
happy;
but when times are bad,
consider:
God has made the one
as well as the other.   Job 1:21
Therefore, a man cannot
discover
anything about his future.

¹⁵In this meaningless life of
mine I have seen both of these:

a righteous man perishing in
his righteousness,
and a wicked man living
long in his wickedness.
¹⁶Do not be overrighteous,
neither be overwise—
why destroy yourself?

¹⁷Do not be overwicked,
and do not be a fool—
why die before your time?
¹⁸It is good to grasp the one
and not let go of the other.
The man who fears God
will avoid all ⌊extremes⌋.ᵃ

¹⁹Wisdom makes one wise
man more powerful
than ten rulers in a city.

²⁰There is not a righteous man
on earth   Ps 14:3
who does what is right and
never sins.   2Ch 6:36

²¹Do not pay attention to every
word people say,
or you may hear your
servant cursing you—
²²for you know in your heart
that many times you
yourself have cursed
others.

²³All this I tested by wisdom
and I said,

"I am determined to be
wise"—   Ecc 1:17
but this was beyond me.
²⁴Whatever wisdom may be,
it is far off and most
profound—
who can discover it?
²⁵So I turned my mind to
understand,
to investigate and to search
out wisdom and the
scheme of things   Job 28:3
and to understand the
stupidity of wickedness
and the madness of folly.

ᵃ18 Or will follow them both

26I find more bitter than death
　the woman who is a snare,
　whose heart is a trap
　　and whose hands are
　　　chains.　　　　　　Ex 10:7
The man who pleases God
　will escape her,
　but the sinner she will
　　ensnare.　　　　　　Pr 2:16-19

27"Look," says the Teacher,[a]
"this is what I have discovered:

"Adding one thing to
　　another to discover the
　　scheme of things—
28　while I was still searching
　but not finding—
I found one ˌuprightˌ man
　　among a thousand,
　but not one ˌuprightˌ
　　woman among them all.
29This only have I found:
　God made mankind
　　upright,
　but men have gone in
　　search of many
　　schemes."

8 Who is like the wise man?
　Who knows the explanation
　of things?
Wisdom brightens a man's
　face
and changes its hard
　appearance.

Obey the King

2Obey the king's command, I
say, because you took an oath
before God. 3Do not be in a hurry to leave the king's presence.
Do not stand up for a bad cause,
for he will do whatever he
pleases. 4Since a king's word is
supreme, who can say to him,
"What are you doing?"　　Ecc 10:4

5Whoever obeys his command
　will come to no harm,
　and the wise heart will
　　know the proper time
　　and procedure.
6For there is a proper time
　and procedure for every
　matter,　　　　　　Ecc 3:1
though a man's misery
　weighs heavily upon
　him.

7Since no man knows the
　future,
　who can tell him what is to
　　come?
8No man has power over the
　wind to contain it[b];
　so no one has power over
　　the day of his death.
As no one is discharged in
　time of war,
　so wickedness will not
　　release those who
　　practice it.

9All this I saw, as I applied my
mind to everything done under
the sun. There is a time when a
man lords it over others to his
own[c] hurt. 10Then too, I saw the
wicked buried—those who
used to come and go from the
holy place and receive praise[d] in
the city where they did this.

a27 Or *leader of the assembly*　　b8 Or *over his spirit to retain it*　　c9 Or *to their*
d10 Some Hebrew manuscripts and Septuagint (Aquila); most Hebrew manuscripts *and
are forgotten*

This too is meaningless.   Ecc 1:11

[11]When the sentence for a crime is not quickly carried out, the hearts of the people are filled with schemes to do wrong. [12]Although a wicked man commits a hundred crimes and still lives a long time, I know that it will go better with God-fearing men, who are reverent before God. [13]Yet because the wicked do not fear God, it will not go well with them, and their days will not lengthen like a shadow.   Dt 12:28; Ecc 3:14

[14]There is something else meaningless that occurs on earth: righteous men who get what the wicked deserve, and wicked men who get what the righteous deserve. This too, I say, is meaningless. [15]So I commend the enjoyment of life, because nothing is better for a man under the sun than to eat and drink and be glad. Then joy will accompany him in his work all the days of the life God has given him under the sun.   Job 21:7

[16]When I applied my mind to know wisdom and to observe man's labor on earth—his eyes not seeing sleep day or night— [17]then I saw all that God has done. No one can comprehend what goes on under the sun. Despite all his efforts to search it out, man cannot discover its meaning. Even if a wise man claims he knows, he cannot really comprehend it.   Job 28:3

A Common Destiny for All

9 So I reflected on all this and concluded that the righteous and the wise and what they do are in God's hands, but no man knows whether love or hate awaits him. [2]All share a common destiny—the righteous and the wicked, the good and the bad,[a] the clean and the unclean, those who offer sacrifices and those who do not.   Ecc 10:14

As it is with the good man,
  so with the sinner;
as it is with those who take
    oaths,
  so with those who are
    afraid to take them. Job 9:22

[3]This is the evil in everything that happens under the sun: The same destiny overtakes all. The hearts of men, moreover, are full of evil and there is madness in their hearts while they live, and afterward they join the dead. [4]Anyone who is among the living has hope[b]—even a live dog is better off than a dead lion!   Job 9:22; Jer 11:8

[5]For the living know that they
    will die,
  but the dead know nothing;
they have no further reward,
  and even the memory of
    them is forgotten.   Ecc 1:11
[6]Their love, their hate
  and their jealousy have
  long since vanished;

---

[a]2 Septuagint (Aquila), Vulgate and Syriac; Hebrew does not have *and the bad*.
[b]4 Or *What then is to be chosen? With all who live, there is hope*

never again will they have a
　part
in anything that happens
　under the sun.　Job 21:21

[7]Go, eat your food with gladness, and drink your wine with
a joyful heart, for it is now that
God favors what you do. [8]Al-
ways be clothed in white, and
always anoint your head with
oil. [9]Enjoy life with your wife,
whom you love, all the days of
this meaningless life that God
has given you under the sun—
all your meaningless days. For
this is your lot in life and in your
toilsome labor under the sun.
[10]Whatever your hand finds to
do, do it with all your might, for
in the grave,[a] where you are going, there is neither working
nor planning nor knowledge
nor wisdom.　Nu 6:20; 1Sa 10:7

[11]I have seen something else
under the sun:

The race is not to the swift
　or the battle to the strong,
nor does food come to the
　wise　Job 32:13
　or wealth to the brilliant
　or favor to the learned;
but time and chance happen
　to them all.　Ecc 2:14

[12]Moreover, no man knows
when his hour will come:

As fish are caught in a cruel
　net,
　or birds are taken in a
　snare,

so men are trapped by evil
　times　Pr 29:6
that fall unexpectedly upon
　them.　Ps 73:22

Wisdom Better Than Folly

[13]I also saw under the sun this
example of wisdom that greatly
impressed me: [14]There was once
a small city with only a few
people in it. And a powerful
king came against it, surrounded it and built huge siegeworks
against it. [15]Now there lived in
that city a man poor but wise,
and he saved the city by his wisdom. But nobody remembered
that poor man. [16]So I said, "Wisdom is better than strength."
But the poor man's wisdom is
despised, and his words are no
longer heeded.　2Sa 20:22; Est 6:3

[17]The quiet words of the wise
　are more to be heeded
than the shouts of a ruler of
　fools.
[18]Wisdom is better than
　weapons of war,　Ecc 2:13
but one sinner destroys
　much good.

10 As dead flies give
　　perfume a bad smell,
so a little folly outweighs
　wisdom and honor.
[2]The heart of the wise inclines
　to the right,
but the heart of the fool to
　the left.
[3]Even as he walks along the
　road,
　the fool lacks sense

and shows everyone how
  stupid he is.   Pr 13:16
⁴If a ruler's anger rises against
  you,
  do not leave your post; Ecc 8:3
  calmness can lay great
  errors to rest.   Pr 16:14

⁵There is an evil I have seen
  under the sun,
  the sort of error that arises
  from a ruler:
⁶Fools are put in many high
  positions,   Pr 29:2
  while the rich occupy the
  low ones.
⁷I have seen slaves on
  horseback,
  while princes go on foot
  like slaves.   Pr 19:10

⁸Whoever digs a pit may fall
  into it;   Ps 57:6
  whoever breaks through a
  wall may be bitten by a
  snake.   Est 2:23
⁹Whoever quarries stones may
  be injured by them;
  whoever splits logs may be
  endangered by them.

¹⁰If the ax is dull
  and its edge unsharpened,
  more strength is needed
  but skill will bring success.

¹¹If a snake bites before it is
  charmed,
  there is no profit for the
  charmer.   Ps 58:5

¹²Words from a wise man's
  mouth are gracious, Pr 10:32
  but a fool is consumed by
  his own lips.

¹³At the beginning his words
  are folly;
  at the end they are wicked
  madness—
¹⁴ and the fool multiplies
    words.   Ecc 5:3

No one knows what is
  coming—
  who can tell him what will
  happen after him?   Ecc 9:1

¹⁵A fool's work wearies him;
  he does not know the way
  to town.

¹⁶Woe to you, O land whose
  king was a servant[a]
  and whose princes feast in
  the morning.   Isa 3:4-5
¹⁷Blessed are you, O land
  whose king is of noble
  birth
  and whose princes eat at a
  proper time—
  for strength and not for
  drunkenness.   Dt 14:26

¹⁸If a man is lazy, the rafters
  sag;
  if his hands are idle, the
  house leaks.   Pr 20:4

¹⁹A feast is made for laughter,
  and wine makes life merry,
  but money is the answer for
  everything.   Ge 14:18

²⁰Do not revile the king even
  in your thoughts,   Ex 22:28
  or curse the rich in your
  bedroom,
  because a bird of the air may
  carry your words,

[a]16 Or king is a child

and a bird on the wing may
report what you say.

Bread Upon the Waters

11 Cast your bread upon
the waters,   Isa 32:20
for after many days you will
find it again.   Dt 24:19
²Give portions to seven, yes
to eight,
for you do not know what
disaster may come upon
the land.

³If clouds are full of water,
they pour rain upon the
earth.
Whether a tree falls to the
south or to the north,
in the place where it falls,
there will it lie.
⁴Whoever watches the wind
will not plant;
whoever looks at the clouds
will not reap.

⁵As you do not know the path
of the wind,   Jn 3:8
or how the body is formed*ᵃ*
in a mother's womb,
so you cannot understand
the work of God,
the Maker of all things.

⁶Sow your seed in the
morning,
and at evening let not your
hands be idle,   Ecc 9:10
for you do not know which
will succeed,
whether this or that,
or whether both will do
equally well.

Remember Your Creator While Young

⁷Light is sweet,
and it pleases the eyes to
see the sun.   Ecc 7:11
⁸However many years a man
may live,
let him enjoy them all.
But let him remember the
days of darkness,   Ecc 12:1
for they will be many.
Everything to come is
meaningless.

⁹Be happy, young man, while
you are young,
and let your heart give you
joy in the days of your
youth.
Follow the ways of your
heart
and whatever your eyes
see,
but know that for all these
things
God will bring you to
judgment.   Job 19:29
¹⁰So then, banish anxiety from
your heart   Ps 94:19
and cast off the troubles of
your body,
for youth and vigor are
meaningless.   Ecc 2:24

12 Remember your Creator
in the days of your
youth,   Ecc 11:8
before the days of trouble
come   2Sa 19:35
and the years approach
when you will say,

ᵃ5 Or *know how life* (or *the spirit*) / *enters the body being formed*

"I find no pleasure in
    them"—
²before the sun and the light
    and the moon and the stars
    grow dark,
    and the clouds return after
    the rain;
³when the keepers of the
    house tremble,
    and the strong men stoop,
    when the grinders cease
        because they are few,
    and those looking through
        the windows grow dim;
⁴when the doors to the street
    are closed
    and the sound of grinding
    fades;
    when men rise up at the
        sound of birds,
    but all their songs grow
        faint;   Jer 25:10
⁵when men are afraid of
    heights
    and of dangers in the
    streets;
    when the almond tree
    blossoms
    and the grasshopper drags
        himself along
    and desire no longer is
    stirred.
    Then man goes to his eternal
        home   Job 10:21
    and mourners go about the
        streets.   Jer 9:17

⁶Remember him—before the
    silver cord is severed,
    or the golden bowl is
    broken;
    before the pitcher is
        shattered at the spring,

or the wheel broken at the
    well,
⁷and the dust returns to the
    ground it came from,
    and the spirit returns to
    God who gave it.   Job 20:8

⁸"Meaningless! Meaningless!"
    says the Teacher. ª   Ecc 1:1
"Everything is
    meaningless!"   Ecc 1:2

The Conclusion of the Matter

⁹Not only was the Teacher
wise, but also he imparted
knowledge to the people. He
pondered and searched out and
set in order many proverbs.
¹⁰The Teacher searched to find
just the right words, and what
he wrote was upright and true.

¹¹The words of the wise are
like goads, their collected sayings like firmly embedded
nails—given by one Shepherd.
¹²Be warned, my son, of anything in addition to them.   Ezr 9:8

Of making many books there
is no end, and much study wearies the body.   Ecc 1:18

¹³Now all has been heard;
    here is the conclusion of the
        matter:
    Fear God and keep his
        commandments,   Dt 4:2
    for this is the whole ⌊duty⌋
        of man.   Dt 4:6
¹⁴For God will bring every
        deed into judgment,
    including every hidden
        thing,   Job 34:21
    whether it is good or evil.

ª 8 Or *the leader of the assembly*; also in verses 9 and 10

Song of Songs

Introduction:

Although some scholars view Song of Songs as being a picture of Christ's love for his people, the more accepted view of Song of Songs is that it is a collection of love poems between a lover and his beloved. It is a beautiful picture of ideal human love and marriage.

Outline of contents:

---

1 Solomon's Song of Songs.

Beloveda

²Let him kiss me with the
  kisses of his mouth—
for your love is more
  delightful than wine.
³Pleasing is the fragrance of
  your perfumes;   Est 2:12
your name is like perfume
  poured out.
No wonder the maidens
  love you!   Ps 45:14
⁴Take me away with you—let
  us hurry!
Let the king bring me into
  his chambers.   Ps 45:15

Friends

We rejoice and delight in
  you*b*;   SS 2:3
we will praise your love
  more than wine.

Beloved

How right they are to adore
  you!

⁵Dark am I, yet lovely,   SS 2:14
  O daughters of Jerusalem,
  dark like the tents of Kedar,
  like the tent curtains of
    Solomon.*c*   Ge 25:13
⁶Do not stare at me because I
  am dark,

---

*a*Primarily on the basis of the gender of the Hebrew pronouns used, male and female speakers are indicated in the margins by the captions *Lover* and *Beloved* respectively. The words of others are marked *Friends*. In some instances the divisions and their captions are debatable.   *b*4 The Hebrew is masculine singular.   *c*5 Or *Salma*

because I am darkened by
        the sun.
My mother's sons were
        angry with me
and made me take care of
        the vineyards;   SS 2:15
my own vineyard I have
        neglected.
⁷Tell me, you whom I love,
        where you graze your
        flock
and where you rest your
        sheep at midday.   Isa 13:20
Why should I be like a veiled
        woman
        Ge 24:65
beside the flocks of your
        friends?

Friends

⁸If you do not know, most
        beautiful of women,
follow the tracks of the
        sheep
and graze your young goats
        by the tents of the
        shepherds.

Lover

⁹I liken you, my darling, to a
        mare
        harnessed to one of the
        chariots of Pharaoh.
¹⁰Your cheeks are beautiful
        with earrings,   SS 5:13
your neck with strings of
        jewels.
        Isa 61:10
¹¹We will make you earrings of
        gold,
        studded with silver.

Beloved

¹²While the king was at his
        table,
        my perfume spread its
        fragrance.   SS 4:11-14
¹³My lover is to me a sachet of
        myrrh
        Ge 37:25
        resting between my breasts.
¹⁴My lover is to me a cluster of
        henna blossoms   SS 4:13
        from the vineyards of En
        Gedi.
        1Sa 23:29

Lover

¹⁵How beautiful you are, my
        darling!   SS 4:7
        Oh, how beautiful!
        Your eyes are doves.   Ps 74:19

Beloved

¹⁶How handsome you are, my
        lover!
        Oh, how charming!
        And our bed is verdant.

Lover

¹⁷The beams of our house are
        cedars;   1Ki 6:9
        our rafters are firs.

*Beloved*ᵃ

2 I am a roseᵇ of Sharon,
        a lily of the valleys.   SS 5:13

Lover

²Like a lily among thorns
        is my darling among the
        maidens.

ᵃ1 Or *Lover*   ᵇ1 Possibly a member of the crocus family

Beloved

³Like an apple tree among the
    trees of the forest
is my lover among the
    young men.   SS 1:14
I delight to sit in his shade,
    and his fruit is sweet to my
    taste.   SS 4:16
⁴He has taken me to the
    banquet hall,   Est 1:11
and his banner over me is
    love.   Nu 1:52
⁵Strengthen me with raisins,
    refresh me with apples,
    for I am faint with love. SS 5:8
⁶His left arm is under my
    head,
and his right arm embraces
    me.   SS 8:3
⁷Daughters of Jerusalem, I
    charge you   SS 5:8
by the gazelles and by the
    does of the field:
Do not arouse or awaken
    love
until it so desires.   SS 3:5

⁸Listen! My lover!
    Look! Here he comes,
leaping across the
    mountains,
bounding over the hills.
⁹My lover is like a gazelle or a
    young stag.   SS 8:14
Look! There he stands
    behind our wall,
gazing through the windows,
    peering through the lattice.
¹⁰My lover spoke and said to
    me,
"Arise, my darling,
    my beautiful one, and come
    with me.

¹¹See! The winter is past;
    the rains are over and
    gone.
¹²Flowers appear on the earth;
    the season of singing has
    come,
the cooing of doves
    is heard in our land.
¹³The fig tree forms its early
    fruit;   Isa 28:4
the blossoming vines
    spread their
    fragrance.
Arise, come, my darling;
    my beautiful one, come
    with me.''

Lover

¹⁴My dove in the clefts of the
    rock,   Ge 8:8
in the hiding places on the
    mountainside,
show me your face,
    let me hear your voice;
for your voice is sweet,
    and your face is lovely.
¹⁵Catch for us the foxes,
    the little foxes   Jdg 15:4
that ruin the vineyards,
    our vineyards that are in
    bloom.   SS 7:12

Beloved

¹⁶My lover is mine and I am
    his;   SS 7:10
he browses among the
    lilies.   SS 4:5
¹⁷Until the day breaks
    and the shadows flee,
turn, my lover,
    and be like a gazelle

or like a young stag
on the rugged hills. *a*

3 All night long on my bed
I looked for the one my
heart loves;   SS 5:6
I looked for him but did not
find him.
²I will get up now and go
about the city,
through its streets and
squares;
I will search for the one my
heart loves.
So I looked for him but did
not find him.
³The watchmen found me
as they made their rounds
in the city.   SS 5:7
"Have you seen the one my
heart loves?"
⁴Scarcely had I passed them
when I found the one my
heart loves.
I held him and would not let
him go
till I had brought him to my
mother's house,   SS 8:2
to the room of the one who
conceived me.   SS 6:9
⁵Daughters of Jerusalem, I
charge you   SS 2:7
by the gazelles and by the
does of the field:
Do not arouse or awaken
love
until it so desires.   SS 8:4

⁶Who is this coming up from
the desert   SS 8:5
like a column of smoke,
perfumed with myrrh and
incense   SS 4:6

made from all the spices of
the merchant?   Ex 30:34
⁷Look! It is Solomon's
carriage,
escorted by sixty warriors,
the noblest of Israel,
⁸all of them wearing the
sword,
all experienced in battle,
each with his sword at his
side,
prepared for the terrors of
the night.   Job 15:22
⁹King Solomon made for
himself the carriage;
he made it of wood from
Lebanon.
¹⁰Its posts he made of silver,
its base of gold.
Its seat was upholstered with
purple,
its interior lovingly inlaid
by*b* the daughters of
Jerusalem.
¹¹Come out, you daughters of
Zion,   Isa 3:16
and look at King Solomon
wearing the crown,
the crown with which his
mother crowned him
on the day of his wedding,
the day his heart rejoiced.

Lover

4 How beautiful you are, my
darling!
Oh, how beautiful!
Your eyes behind your veil
are doves.   SS 1:15
Your hair is like a flock of
goats

---

a17 Or *the hills of Bether*   *b10* Or *its inlaid interior a gift of love / from*

descending from Mount
  Gilead.   Ge 37:25
[2]Your teeth are like a flock of
  sheep just shorn,
  coming up from the
  washing.
Each has its twin;
  not one of them is alone.
[3]Your lips are like a scarlet
  ribbon;
  your mouth is lovely.   SS 1:5
Your temples behind your
  veil
are like the halves of a
  pomegranate.
[4]Your neck is like the tower of
  David,   Ps 144:12
  built with elegance[a];
on it hang a thousand
  shields,   Eze 27:10
all of them shields of
  warriors.
[5]Your two breasts are like two
  fawns,   SS 7:3
like twin fawns of a gazelle
  that browse among the
  lilies.   SS 2:16
[6]Until the day breaks
  and the shadows flee, SS 2:17
I will go to the mountain of
  myrrh   SS 3:6
and to the hill of incense.
[7]All beautiful you are, my
  darling;   SS 1:15
  there is no flaw in you. SS 5:2

[8]Come with me from
  Lebanon, my bride,   SS 5:1
come with me from
  Lebanon.
Descend from the crest of
  Amana,

from the top of Senir, the
  summit of Hermon,
from the lions' dens
  and the mountain haunts of
  the leopards.
[9]You have stolen my heart,
  my sister, my bride;
you have stolen my heart
with one glance of your eyes,
with one jewel of your
  necklace.   Ge 41:42
[10]How delightful is your love,
  my sister, my bride!
How much more pleasing is
  your love than wine,
and the fragrance of your
  perfume than any spice!
[11]Your lips drop sweetness as
  the honeycomb, my
  bride;
milk and honey are under
  your tongue.   Ps 19:10
The fragrance of your
  garments is like that of
  Lebanon.   Hos 14:6
[12]You are a garden locked up,
  my sister, my bride;
you are a spring enclosed, a
  sealed fountain.   Pr 5:15-18
[13]Your plants are an orchard of
  pomegranates   SS 7:12
  with choice fruits,
with henna and nard,   SS 1:14
[14] nard and saffron,
  calamus and cinnamon,
with every kind of incense
  tree,
with myrrh and aloes   Nu 24:6
and all the finest spices.
[15]You are[b] a garden fountain,
  a well of flowing water Pr 5:18

---

[a]4 The meaning of the Hebrew for this word is uncertain.   [b]15 Or *I am* (spoken by
the *Beloved*)

streaming down from
Lebanon.

Beloved

16Awake, north wind,
and come, south wind!
Blow on my garden,
that its fragrance may
spread abroad.
Let my lover come into his
garden   SS 7:13
and taste its choice fruits.

Lover

5 I have come into my
garden, my sister, my
bride;   SS 4:8
I have gathered my myrrh
with my spice.
I have eaten my honeycomb
and my honey;
I have drunk my wine and
my milk.   SS 4:11

Friends

Eat, O friends, and drink;
drink your fill, O lovers.

Beloved

2I slept but my heart was
awake.
Listen! My lover is
knocking:
"Open to me, my sister, my
darling,
my dove, my flawless one.
My head is drenched with
dew,
my hair with the dampness
of the night."
3I have taken off my robe—

must I put it on again?
I have washed my feet—
must I soil them again?
4My lover thrust his hand
through the
latch-opening;
my heart began to pound
for him.
5I arose to open for my lover,
and my hands dripped with
myrrh,
my fingers with flowing
myrrh,
on the handles of the lock.
6I opened for my lover,   SS 6:1
but my lover had left; he
was gone.   SS 6:2
My heart sank at his
departure.*a*
I looked for him but did not
find him.   SS 3:1
I called him but he did not
answer.
7The watchmen found me
as they made their rounds
in the city.   SS 3:3
They beat me, they bruised
me;
they took away my cloak,
those watchmen of the
walls!
8O daughters of Jerusalem, I
charge you—   SS 2:7
if you find my lover,   SS 1:14
what will you tell him?
Tell him I am faint with
love.   SS 2:5

Friends

9How is your beloved better
than others,
most beautiful of women?

---

a6 Or heart had gone out to him when he spoke

How is your beloved better
than others,
that you charge us so?

Beloved

[10]My lover is radiant and
ruddy,
outstanding among ten
thousand.   Ps 45:2
[11]His head is purest gold;
his hair is wavy
and black as a raven.
[12]His eyes are like doves SS 1:15
by the water streams,
washed in milk,   Ge 49:12
mounted like jewels.
[13]His cheeks are like beds of
spice   SS 6:2
yielding perfume.
His lips are like lilies SS 2:1
dripping with myrrh.
[14]His arms are rods of gold
set with chrysolite.
His body is like polished
ivory
decorated with sapphires.[a]
[15]His legs are pillars of marble
set on bases of pure gold.
His appearance is like
Lebanon,   1Ki 4:33
choice as its cedars.
[16]His mouth is sweetness itself;
he is altogether lovely.
This is my lover, this my
friend,   SS 7:9
O daughters of Jerusalem.

Friends

6 Where has your lover gone,
most beautiful of women?
Which way did your lover
turn,

that we may look for him
with you?

Beloved

[2]My lover has gone down to
his garden,   SS 4:12
to the beds of spices, SS 5:13
to browse in the gardens
and to gather lilies.
[3]I am my lover's and my lover
is mine;   SS 7:10
he browses among the
lilies.   SS 2:16

Lover

[4]You are beautiful, my
darling, as Tirzah, Jos 12:24
lovely as Jerusalem,
majestic as troops with
banners.   Nu 1:52
[5]Turn your eyes from me;
they overwhelm me.
Your hair is like a flock of
goats
descending from Gilead.
[6]Your teeth are like a flock of
sheep
coming up from the
washing.
Each has its twin,
not one of them is alone.
[7]Your temples behind your
veil   Ge 24:65
are like the halves of a
pomegranate. SS 4:3
[8]Sixty queens there may be,
and eighty concubines,
and virgins beyond
number;
[9]but my dove, my perfect one,
is unique,   SS 5:2

---

[a]14 Or *lapis lazuli*

the only daughter of her
mother,
the favorite of the one who
bore her.　　　　SS 3:4
The maidens saw her and
called her blessed;
the queens and concubines
praised her.

Friends

¹⁰Who is this that appears like
the dawn,
fair as the moon, bright as
the sun,
majestic as the stars in
procession?

Lover

¹¹I went down to the grove of
nut trees
to look at the new growth
in the valley,
to see if the vines had
budded
or the pomegranates were
in bloom.　　　　SS 7:12
¹²Before I realized it,
my desire set me among the
royal chariots of my
people.ᵃ

Friends

¹³Come back, come back,
O Shulammite;
come back, come back, that
we may gaze on you!

Lover

Why would you gaze on the
Shulammite

as on the dance of
Mahanaim?　　　　Ex 15:20

7 How beautiful your
sandaled feet,
O prince's daughter!　　Ps 45:13
Your graceful legs are like
jewels,
the work of a craftsman's
hands.
²Your navel is a rounded
goblet
that never lacks blended
wine.
Your waist is a mound of
wheat
encircled by lilies.
³Your breasts are like two
fawns,　　　　SS 4:5
twins of a gazelle.
⁴Your neck is like an ivory
tower.　　　　Ps 144:12
Your eyes are the pools of
Heshbon　　　　Nu 21:26
by the gate of Bath Rabbim.
Your nose is like the tower of
Lebanon　　　　SS 5:15
looking toward Damascus.
⁵Your head crowns you like
Mount Carmel.　　Isa 35:2
Your hair is like royal
tapestry;
the king is held captive by
its tresses.
⁶How beautiful you are and
how pleasing,　　SS 1:15
O love, with your delights!
⁷Your stature is like that of the
palm,
and your breasts like
clusters of fruit.　　SS 4:5
⁸I said, "I will climb the palm
tree;

ᵃ12 Or *among the chariots of Amminadab; or among the chariots of the people of the prince*

I will take hold of its fruit.''
May your breasts be like the
　　clusters of the vine,
　　the fragrance of your breath
　　　like apples,　　　　ss 2:5
9 and your mouth like the
　　best wine.

Beloved

May the wine go straight to
　　my lover,　　　　ss 1:16
　　flowing gently over lips and
　　teeth.ᵃ
10I belong to my lover,
　　and his desire is for me.
11Come, my lover, let us go to
　　the countryside,
　　let us spend the night in the
　　villages.ᵇ
12Let us go early to the
　　vineyards　　　　ss 1:6
　　to see if the vines have
　　　budded,　　　　ss 2:15
　　if their blossoms have
　　　opened,　　　　ss 2:13
　　and if the pomegranates are
　　　in bloom—　　　ss 4:13
　　there I will give you my
　　love.
13The mandrakes send out
　　their fragrance,　　Ge 30:14
　　and at our door is every
　　delicacy,
　　both new and old,
　　that I have stored up for
　　you, my lover.　　ss 4:16

8 If only you were to me like
　　a brother,
　　who was nursed at my
　　mother's breasts!
Then, if I found you outside,

I would kiss you,
　　and no one would despise
　　me.
2I would lead you
　　and bring you to my
　　　mother's house—　ss 3:4
　　she who has taught me.
I would give you spiced wine
　　to drink,
　　the nectar of my
　　　pomegranates.
3His left arm is under my
　　head
　　and his right arm embraces
　　me.　　　　　ss 2:6
4Daughters of Jerusalem, I
　　charge you:
Do not arouse or awaken
　　love
　　until it so desires.　ss 2:7

Friends

5Who is this coming up from
　　the desert　　　ss 3:6
　　leaning on her lover?

Beloved

Under the apple tree I roused
　　you;
　　there your mother
　　　conceived you,　　ss 3:4
　　there she who was in labor
　　gave you birth.
6Place me like a seal over your
　　heart,
　　like a seal on your arm;
for love is as strong as death,
　　its jealousyᶜ unyielding as
　　the grave.ᵈ
　　　　　　　　Nu 5:14
It burns like blazing fire,
　　like a mighty flame.ᵉ

ᵃ9 Septuagint, Aquila, Vulgate and Syriac; Hebrew *lips of sleepers*　　ᵇ11 Or *henna bushes*　　ᶜ6 Or *ardor*　　ᵈ6 Hebrew *Sheol*　　ᵉ6 Or *I like the very flame of the* LORD

⁷Many waters cannot quench
   love;
  rivers cannot wash it away.
If one were to give
  all the wealth of his house
    for love,
  it*ᵃ* would be utterly
    scorned.   Pr 6:35

Friends

⁸We have a young sister,
  and her breasts are not yet
    grown.
What shall we do for our
    sister
  for the day she is spoken
    for?
⁹If she is a wall,
  we will build towers of
    silver on her.
If she is a door,
  we will enclose her with
    panels of cedar.

Beloved

¹⁰I am a wall,
  and my breasts are like
    towers.
Thus I have become in his
    eyes

like one bringing
    contentment.
¹¹Solomon had a vineyard in
    Baal Hamon;   Ecc 2:4
  he let out his vineyard to
    tenants.
Each was to bring for its fruit
  a thousand shekels*ᵇ* of
    silver.   Isa 7:23
¹²But my own vineyard is mine
    to give;   SS 1:6
  the thousand shekels are
    for you, O Solomon,
  and two hundred*ᶜ* are for
    those who tend its fruit.

Lover

¹³You who dwell in the
    gardens
  with friends in attendance,
  let me hear your voice!

Beloved

¹⁴Come away, my lover,
  and be like a gazelle   Pr 5:19
  or like a young stag   SS 2:9
  on the spice-laden
    mountains.   SS 2:8

---

*ᵃ*7 Or *he*   *ᵇ*11 That is, about 25 pounds (about 11.5 kilograms); also in verse 12
*ᶜ*12 That is, about 5 pounds (about 2.3 kilograms)

Isaiah

Introduction:

Isaiah prophesied in Judah during the reigns of Kings Uzziah, Jotham, Ahaz, and Hezekiah. According to tradition Isaiah was martyred under Manasseh, the wicked son of Hezekiah, about 680 B.C.

Isaiah repeatedly warned the people that Jerusalem and Judah would be judged because of their wickedness. In chapter 39 he predicted the Babylonian exile. But he also held to the hope that the kingdom would be restored again.

Beginning in chapter 40 Isaiah offered comfort with these promises from God: 1) the Babylonian exiles would be allowed to return to Jerusalem; 2) a righteous, suffering servant would bring salvation; 3) God would set up a new, righteous kingdom.

Outline of contents:

Judgment and hope of restoration (1:1–6:13)
Hopes in Assyria or God (7:1–12:6)
Prophecies about nations (13:1–23:18)
Israel's judgment and deliverance (24:1–27:13)
Warnings and Zion restored (28:1–35:10)
King Hezekiah withstands Assyria (36:1–39:8)
Promises of divine deliverance (40:1–56:8)
The final kingdom established (56:9–66:24)

---

1 The vision concerning Judah and Jerusalem that Isaiah son of Amoz saw during the reigns of Uzziah, Jotham, Ahaz and Hezekiah, kings of Judah.

A Rebellious Nation

²Hear, O heavens! Listen,
  O earth!   Dt 4:26
  For the LORD has spoken:
"I reared children and
  brought them up,
but they have rebelled
  against me.   Isa 24:5
³The ox knows his master,
  the donkey his owner's
    manger,   Ge 42:27
but Israel does not know,
  my people do not
    understand."   Dt 32:28
⁴Ah, sinful nation,
  a people loaded with
    guilt,
a brood of evildoers,   Isa 9:17

children given to
corruption! Ps 14:3
They have forsaken the
LORD; Dt 32:15
they have spurned the Holy
One of Israel
and turned their backs on
him. Pr 30:9
⁵Why should you be beaten
anymore? Pr 20:30
Why do you persist in
rebellion? Isa 31:6
Your whole head is injured,
your whole heart afflicted.
⁶From the sole of your foot to
the top of your head
there is no soundness—
only wounds and welts
and open sores, Isa 53:5
not cleansed or bandaged
or soothed with oil. 2Sa 14:2

⁷Your country is desolate,
your cities burned with fire;
your fields are being stripped
by foreigners Lev 26:16
right before you,
laid waste as when
overthrown by
strangers. 2Ki 18:13
⁸The Daughter of Zion is left
like a shelter in a vineyard,
like a hut in a field of
melons, Job 27:18
like a city under siege.
⁹Unless the LORD Almighty
had left us some survivors,
we would have become like
Sodom,
we would have been like
Gomorrah. Ge 19:24

¹⁰Hear the word of the LORD,
you rulers of Sodom; Ge 13:13

listen to the law of our God,
you people of Gomorrah!
¹¹"The multitude of your
sacrifices—
what are they to me?" says
the LORD.
"I have more than enough of
burnt offerings,
of rams and the fat of
fattened animals; Ps 50:8
I have no pleasure
in the blood of bulls and
lambs and goats. 1Sa 15:22
¹²When you come to appear
before me,
who has asked this of you,
this trampling of my courts?
¹³Stop bringing meaningless
offerings! Pr 15:8
Your incense is detestable
to me. 1Ki 14:24
New Moons, Sabbaths and
convocations— 1Ch 23:31
I cannot bear your evil
assemblies.
¹⁴Your New Moon festivals
and your appointed
feasts
my soul hates. Ps 11:5
They have become a burden
to me; Job 7:12
I am weary of bearing
them.
¹⁵When you spread out your
hands in prayer,
I will hide my eyes from
you; Dt 31:17
even if you offer many
prayers,
I will not listen. Dt 1:45
Your hands are full of blood;
¹⁶ wash and make yourselves
clean. Mt 27:24
Take your evil deeds

out of my sight!
Stop doing wrong,
17 learn to do right!   Ps 34:14
Seek justice,
encourage the oppressed. *a*
Defend the cause of the
    fatherless,
plead the case of the
    widow.   Ex 22:22

18"Come now, let us reason
    together,"
says the LORD.   1Sa 2:25
"Though your sins are like
    scarlet,
they shall be as white as
    snow;   Ps 51:7
though they are red as
    crimson,
they shall be like wool. Isa 55:7
19If you are willing and
    obedient,
you will eat the best from
    the land;   Dt 30:15-16
20but if you resist and rebel,
you will be devoured by the
    sword."   Job 15:22
        For the mouth of the
        LORD has spoken.

21See how the faithful city
    has become a harlot!   Jer 2:20
She once was full of justice;
    righteousness used to dwell
    in her—
but now murderers!   Pr 6:17
22Your silver has become
    dross,
your choice wine is diluted
    with water.   Ps 119:119
23Your rulers are rebels,
    companions of thieves;
they all love bribes

and chase after gifts.   Ex 23:8
They do not defend the cause
    of the fatherless;
the widow's case does not
    come before them.   Isa 10:2
24Therefore the Lord, the LORD
    Almighty,
the Mighty One of Israel,
    declares: Ge 49:24
"Ah, I will get relief from my
    foes
and avenge myself on my
    enemies.   Dt 32:43
25I will turn my hand against
    you;   Dt 28:63
I will thoroughly purge
    away your dross
and remove all your
    impurities.   2Ch 29:15
26I will restore your judges as
    in days of old,   Jer 33:7
your counselors as at the
    beginning.
Afterward you will be called
    the City of Righteousness,
    the Faithful City."   Isa 4:3

27Zion will be redeemed with
    justice,
her penitent ones with
    righteousness.   Isa 30:15
28But rebels and sinners will
    both be broken,
and those who forsake the
    LORD will perish.   Ps 9:5

29"You will be ashamed
    because of the sacred
    oaks   Isa 57:5
in which you have
    delighted;
you will be disgraced because
    of the gardens   Isa 65:3

that you have chosen.
30You will be like an oak with
    fading leaves,   Ps 1:3
 like a garden without
    water.
31The mighty man will become
    tinder
 and his work a spark;
 both will burn together,
  with no one to quench the
    fire."   Isa 4:4

The Mountain of the Lord

2 This is what Isaiah son of
Amoz saw concerning Judah
and Jerusalem: Isa 1:1

2In the last days

the mountain of the Lord's
  temple will be
  established
as chief among the
  mountains;   Isa 65:9
it will be raised above the
  hills,
and all nations will stream
  to it.   Ps 102:15

3Many peoples will come and
say,   Isa 45:23

"Come, let us go up to the
  mountain of the Lord,
 to the house of the God of
  Jacob.   Dt 33:19
He will teach us his ways,
 so that we may walk in his
  paths."
The law will go out from
  Zion,   Isa 1:10
 the word of the Lord from
  Jerusalem.   Lk 24:47

4He will judge between the
  nations
 and will settle disputes for
  many peoples.   Ge 49:10
They will beat their swords
  into plowshares
 and their spears into
  pruning hooks.   Joel 3:10
Nation will not take up
  sword against nation,
 nor will they train for war
  anymore.   Ps 46:9

5Come, O house of Jacob,
 let us walk in the light of
  the Lord.   Isa 60:1

The Day of the Lord

6You have abandoned your
  people,
 the house of Jacob.   Jer 12:7
They are full of superstitions
  from the East;
 they practice divination like
  the Philistines
 and clasp hands with
  pagans.   2Ki 16:7
7Their land is full of silver and
  gold;   Dt 17:17
 there is no end to their
  treasures.   Ps 17:14
Their land is full of horses;
 there is no end to their
  chariots.   Ge 41:43
8Their land is full of idols;
 they bow down to the work
  of their hands,
 to what their fingers have
  made.   Isa 17:8
9So man will be brought low
 and mankind humbled—
 do not forgive them. a   Ne 4:5

a9 Or not raise them up

¹⁰Go into the rocks,
    hide in the ground   Na 3:11
  from dread of the LORD
  and the splendor of his
    majesty!   Ps 145:12
¹¹The eyes of the arrogant man
    will be humbled
  and the pride of men
    brought low;   Job 40:11
  the LORD alone will be
    exalted in that day. Ps 46:10

¹²The LORD Almighty has a
    day in store   Isa 13:6
  for all the proud and lofty,
  for all that is exalted   Ps 76:12
  (and they will be humbled),
¹³for all the cedars of Lebanon,
    tall and lofty,   Jdg 9:15
  and all the oaks of Bashan,
¹⁴for all the towering
    mountains
  and all the high hills,
¹⁵for every lofty tower   Isa 30:25
  and every fortified wall,
¹⁶for every trading ship*a*
  and every stately vessel.
¹⁷The arrogance of man will be
    brought low   2Sa 22:28
  and the pride of men
    humbled;
  the LORD alone will be
    exalted in that day,
¹⁸ and the idols will totally
    disappear.   Dt 9:21

¹⁹Men will flee to caves in the
    rocks   Jdg 6:2
  and to holes in the ground
  from dread of the LORD
  and the splendor of his
    majesty,   Ps 145:12

when he rises to shake the
    earth.   Job 9:6
²⁰In that day men will throw
    away
  to the rodents and bats
  their idols of silver and idols
    of gold,
  which they made to
    worship.   Eze 7:19-20
²¹They will flee to caverns in
    the rocks   Ex 33:22
  and to the overhanging
    crags
  from dread of the LORD
  and the splendor of his
    majesty,
  when he rises to shake the
    earth.   Isa 33:10

²²Stop trusting in man,
  who has but a breath in his
    nostrils.   Ps 118:6
  Of what account is he? Job 12:19

Judgment on Jerusalem and Judah

3 See now, the Lord,
  the LORD Almighty,
  is about to take from
    Jerusalem and Judah
  both supply and support:
  all supplies of food and all
    supplies of water,   Isa 5:13
² the hero and warrior,
  the judge and prophet,
  the soothsayer and elder,
³the captain of fifty and man
    of rank,   Job 22:8
  the counselor, skilled
    craftsman and clever
    enchanter.   Ecc 10:11

---

a16 Hebrew *every ship of Tarshish*

⁴I will make boys their
    officials;
  mere children will govern
    them.   Ecc 10:16
⁵People will oppress each
    other—
  man against man, neighbor
    against neighbor.   Ps 28:3
  The young will rise up
    against the old,
  the base against the
    honorable.

⁶A man will seize one of his
    brothers
  at his father's home, and
    say,
  "You have a cloak, you be
    our leader;
  take charge of this heap of
    ruins!"
⁷But in that day he will cry
    out,   Isa 2:11
  "I have no remedy.   Jer 30:12
  I have no food or clothing in
    my house;   Joel 1:16
  do not make me the leader
    of the people."   Isa 24:2

⁸Jerusalem staggers,
  Judah is falling;   Isa 1:7
  their words and deeds are
    against the LORD,   2Ch 33:6
  defying his glorious
    presence.   Job 1:11
⁹The look on their faces
    testifies against
    them;
  they parade their sin like
    Sodom;   Ge 13:13
  they do not hide it.
  Woe to them!
  They have brought disaster
    upon themselves.   Ro 6:23

¹⁰Tell the righteous it will be
    well with them,   Dt 5:33
  for they will enjoy the fruit
    of their deeds.   Ge 15:1
¹¹Woe to the wicked! Disaster
    is upon them!   Job 9:13
  They will be paid back for
    what their hands have
    done.   Jer 21:14

¹²Youths oppress my people,
  women rule over them.
  O my people, your guides
    lead you astray;   Isa 9:16
  they turn you from the
    path.

¹³The LORD takes his place in
    court;   Job 10:2
  he rises to judge the
    people.   Ps 82:1
¹⁴The LORD enters into
    judgment   1Sa 12:7
  against the elders and
    leaders of his people:
  "It is you who have ruined
    my vineyard;
  the plunder from the poor
    is in your houses.   Job 24:9
¹⁵What do you mean by
    crushing my people
  and grinding the faces of
    the poor?"   Isa 10:6
    declares the Lord,
    the LORD Almighty.

¹⁶The LORD says,
  "The women of Zion are
    haughty,   SS 3:11
  walking along with
    outstretched necks,
  flirting with their eyes,
  tripping along with mincing
    steps,

with ornaments jingling on
their ankles.
17Therefore the Lord will bring
sores on the heads of the
women of Zion;
the LORD will make their
scalps bald.''　　　　Eze 27:31

18In that day the Lord will
snatch away their finery: the
bangles and headbands and
crescent necklaces, 19the earrings and bracelets and veils,
20the headdresses and ankle
chains and sashes, the perfume
bottles and charms, 21the signet
rings and nose rings, 22the fine
robes and the capes and cloaks,
the purses 23and mirrors, and
the linen garments and tiaras
and shawls.　　　Isa 2:11; Eze 16:10

24Instead of fragrance there
　　will be a stench;　　Isa 4:4
　instead of a sash, a rope;
　instead of well-dressed hair,
　　baldness;　　　　Lev 13:40
　instead of fine clothing,
　　sackcloth;　　　　Ge 37:34
　instead of beauty,
　　branding.　　　　2Sa 10:4
25Your men will fall by the
　　sword,　　　　　Isa 1:20
　your warriors in battle.
26The gates of Zion will lament
　　and mourn;　　　Ps 137:1
　destitute, she will sit on the
　　ground.　　　　Job 2:13

4 In that day seven women
will take hold of one man
and say, ''We will eat our
own food

and provide our own
　clothes;　　　　Isa 13:12
only let us be called by your
　name.
Take away our disgrace!''

The Branch of the LORD

2In that day the Branch of the
LORD will be beautiful and glorious, and the fruit of the land
will be the pride and glory of the
survivors in Israel. 3Those who
are left in Zion, who remain in
Jerusalem, will be called holy,
all who are recorded among the
living in Jerusalem. 4The Lord
will wash away the filth of the
women of Zion; he will cleanse
the bloodstains from Jerusalem
by a spirit*a* of judgment and a
spirit*a* of fire. 5Then the LORD
will create over all of Mount
Zion and over those who assemble there a cloud of smoke
by day and a glow of flaming
fire by night; over all the glory
will be a canopy. 6It will be a
shelter and shade from the heat
of the day, and a refuge and
hiding place from the storm and
rain.　　　　　　Ps 27:5; Isa 52:13

The Song of the Vineyard

5 I will sing for the one I love
a song about his vineyard:
My loved one had a vineyard
　on a fertile hillside.
2He dug it up and cleared it of
　stones
　and planted it with the
　　choicest vines.　　Ex 15:17
He built a watchtower in it

and cut out a winepress as
well.   Job 24:11
Then he looked for a crop of
good grapes,
but it yielded only bad fruit.

³"Now you dwellers in
Jerusalem and men of
Judah,
judge between me and my
vineyard.   Mt 21:40
⁴What more could have been
done for my vineyard
than I have done for it?
When I looked for good
grapes,
why did it yield only bad?
⁵Now I will tell you
what I am going to do to
my vineyard:
I will take away its hedge,
and it will be destroyed;
I will break down its wall,
and it will be trampled.
⁶I will make it a wasteland,
neither pruned nor
cultivated,
and briers and thorns will
grow there.   Isa 7:23-24
I will command the clouds
not to rain on it."   Dt 28:24

⁷The vineyard of the LORD
Almighty
is the house of Israel,   Ps 80:8
and the men of Judah
are the garden of his
delight.
And he looked for justice,
but saw bloodshed;
for righteousness, but
heard cries of distress.

Woes and Judgments

⁸Woe to you who add house
to house
and join field to field   Job 20:19
till no space is left
and you live alone in the
land.

⁹The LORD Almighty has declared in my hearing: Jer 44:11

"Surely the great houses will
become desolate,   Isa 6:11-12
the fine mansions left
without occupants.
¹⁰A ten-acreᵃ vineyard will
produce only a bathᵇ of
wine,
a homerᶜ of seed only an
ephahᵈ of grain."   Lev 26:26

¹¹Woe to those who rise early
in the morning
to run after their drinks,
who stay up late at night
till they are inflamed with
wine.   1Sa 25:36
¹²They have harps and lyres at
their banquets,
tambourines and flutes and
wine,   Job 21:12
but they have no regard for
the deeds of the LORD,
no respect for the work of
his hands.   Ps 28:5
¹³Therefore my people will go
into exile   Isa 49:21
for lack of understanding;
their men of rank will die of
hunger   Job 22:8
and their masses will be
parched with thirst.

ᵃ10 Hebrew *ten-yoke*, that is, the land plowed by 10 yoke of oxen in one day
ᵇ10 That is, probably about 6 gallons (about 22 liters)   ᶜ10 That is, probably about 6
bushels (about 220 liters)   ᵈ10 That is, probably about 3/5 bushel (about 22 liters)

¹⁴Therefore the grave*a* enlarges
      its appetite   Pr 30:16
   and opens its mouth
      without limit;   Nu 16:30
   into it will descend their
      nobles and masses
   with all their brawlers and
      revelers.   Isa 22:2
¹⁵So man will be brought low
      and mankind humbled,
   the eyes of the arrogant
      humbled.   Isa 2:11
¹⁶But the LORD Almighty will
      be exalted by his justice,
   and the holy God will show
      himself holy by his
      righteousness.   Lev 10:3
¹⁷Then sheep will graze as in
      their own pasture;   Isa 7:25
   lambs will feed*b* among the
      ruins of the rich.

¹⁸Woe to those who draw sin
      along with cords of
      deceit,   Hos 11:4
   and wickedness as with cart
      ropes,   Jer 23:14
¹⁹to those who say, "Let God
      hurry,
   let him hasten his work
      so we may see it.   Isa 60:22
   Let it approach,
   let the plan of the Holy One
      of Israel come,   Isa 1:4
   so we may know it."   Jer 17:15

²⁰Woe to those who call evil
      good
   and good evil,   Ge 18:25
   who put darkness for light
      and light for darkness,
   who put bitter for sweet
      and sweet for bitter.   Am 5:7

²¹Woe to those who are wise in
      their own eyes
   and clever in their own
      sight.   Pr 3:7

²²Woe to those who are heroes
      at drinking wine   1Sa 25:36
   and champions at mixing
      drinks,   Pr 31:4
²³who acquit the guilty for a
      bribe,   Ex 23:8
   but deny justice to the
      innocent.   Ps 94:21
²⁴Therefore, as tongues of fire
      lick up straw   Isa 47:14
   and as dry grass sinks
      down in the flames,
   so their roots will decay
   and their flowers blow
      away like dust;   Job 24:24
   for they have rejected the law
      of the LORD Almighty
   and spurned the word of
      the Holy One of Israel.
²⁵Therefore the LORD's anger
      burns against his people;
   his hand is raised and he
      strikes them down.
   The mountains shake,   Ex 19:18
   and the dead bodies are like
      refuse in the streets.

   Yet for all this, his anger is
      not turned away,   Jer 4:8
   his hand is still upraised.

²⁶He lifts up a banner for the
      distant nations,   Ps 20:5
   he whistles for those at the
      ends of the earth.   Isa 7:18
   Here they come,
      swiftly and speedily!
²⁷Not one of them grows tired
      or stumbles,   Isa 14:31

---

*a*14 Hebrew *Sheol*   *b*17 Septuagint; Hebrew / *strangers will eat*

not one slumbers or sleeps;
not a belt is loosened at the
    waist,   Job 12:18
not a sandal thong is
    broken.   Joel 2:7-8
28Their arrows are sharp,
    all their bows are strung;
    their horses' hoofs seem like
        flint,   Eze 26:11
    their chariot wheels like a
        whirlwind.   2Ki 2:1
29Their roar is like that of the
        lion,   2Ki 17:25
    they roar like young lions;
    they growl as they seize their
        prey
    and carry it off with no one
        to rescue.   Isa 42:22
30In that day they will roar
        over it
    like the roaring of the sea.
    And if one looks at the land,
    he will see darkness and
        distress;   1Sa 2:9
    even the light will be
        darkened by the
        clouds.

Isaiah's Commission

6 In the year that King Uzziah
died, I saw the Lord seated
on a throne, high and exalted,
and the train of his robe filled
the temple. 2Above him were
seraphs, each with six wings:
With two wings they covered
their faces, with two they
covered their feet, and with two
they were flying. 3And they
were calling to one another:

"Holy, holy, holy is the LORD
    Almighty;   Ex 15:11; Ps 89:8
the whole earth is full of his
    glory."   Ex 16:7; Isa 11:9

4At the sound of their voices
the doorposts and thresholds
shook and the temple was filled
with smoke.   Ex 19:18

5"Woe to me!" I cried. "I am
ruined! For I am a man of unclean lips, and I live among a
people of unclean lips, and my
eyes have seen the King, the
LORD Almighty."   Job 42:5; Isa 5:8

6Then one of the seraphs flew
to me with a live coal in his
hand, which he had taken with
tongs from the altar. 7With it he
touched my mouth and said,
"See, this has touched your lips;
your guilt is taken away and
your sin atoned for."   Lev 10:1

8Then I heard the voice of the
Lord saying, "Whom shall I
send? And who will go for us?"

And I said, "Here am I. Send
me!"   Ge 22:1

9He said, "Go and tell this
people: Eze 3:11

" 'Be ever hearing, but never
    understanding;
be ever seeing, but never
    perceiving.'   Jer 5:21
10Make the heart of this people
    calloused;   Ex 4:21
    make their ears dull
    and close their eyes.[a] Isa 29:9
Otherwise they might see
    with their eyes,
    hear with their ears,   Dt 29:4

---

[a]9,10 Hebrew; Septuagint 'You will be ever hearing, but never understanding; / you will be
ever seeing, but never perceiving.' / 10This people's heart has become calloused; / they hardly hear
with their ears, / and they have closed their eyes

understand with their
    hearts,
and turn and be healed."

[11]Then I said, "For how long,
O Lord?"   Ps 79:5
And he answered:

"Until the cities lie ruined
    and without inhabitant,
until the houses are left
    deserted
and the fields ruined and
    ravaged,   Ps 79:1
[12]until the Lord has sent
    everyone far away
and the land is utterly
    forsaken.   Isa 5:5
[13]And though a tenth remains
    in the land,   Isa 1:9
it will again be laid waste.
But as the terebinth and oak
    leave stumps when they are
    cut down,   Job 14:8
so the holy seed will be the
    stump in the land."Job 14:7

The Sign of Immanuel

7 When Ahaz son of Jotham,
    the son of Uzziah, was king
of Judah, King Rezin of Aram
and Pekah son of Remaliah king
of Israel marched up to fight
against Jerusalem, but they
could not overpower it.   Isa 8:6

[2]Now the house of David was
told, "Aram has allied itself
with[a] Ephraim"; so the hearts of
Ahaz and his people were shak-
en, as the trees of the forest are
shaken by the wind.

[3]Then the Lord said to Isaiah,
"Go out, you and your son

Shear-Jashub,[b] to meet Ahaz at
the end of the aqueduct of the
Upper Pool, on the road to the
Washerman's Field. [4]Say to
him, 'Be careful, keep calm and
don't be afraid. Do not lose
heart because of these two
smoldering stubs of firewood—
because of the fierce anger of
Rezin and Aram and of
the son of Remaliah. [5]Aram,
Ephraim and Remaliah's son
have plotted your ruin, saying,
[6]"Let us invade Judah; let us
tear it apart and divide it among
ourselves, and make the son of
Tabeel king over it." [7]Yet this is
what the Sovereign Lord says:

" 'It will not take place,
    it will not happen, Ps 2:1
[8]for the head of Aram is
    Damascus,   Ge 14:15
and the head of Damascus
    is only Rezin.   Isa 9:11
Within sixty-five years
    Ephraim will be too
    shattered to be a
    people.
[9]The head of Ephraim is
    Samaria,   2Ki 15:29
and the head of Samaria is
    only Remaliah's son.
If you do not stand firm in
    your faith,   2Ch 20:20
you will not stand at all.' "

[10]Again the Lord spoke to
Ahaz, [11]"Ask the Lord your
God for a sign, whether in the
deepest depths or in the highest
heights."   Ex 7:9; Ps 139:8

[12]But Ahaz said, "I will not

---

[a]2 Or *has set up camp in*   [b]3 *Shear-Jashub* means *a remnant will return.*

ask; I will not put the LORD to the test."   Dt 4:34

¹³Then Isaiah said, "Hear now, you house of David! Is it not enough to try the patience of men? Will you try the patience of my God also? ¹⁴Therefore the Lord himself will give you[a] a sign: The virgin will be with child and will give birth to a son, and[b] will call him Immanuel.[c] ¹⁵He will eat curds and honey when he knows enough to reject the wrong and choose the right. ¹⁶But before the boy knows enough to reject the wrong and choose the right, the land of the two kings you dread will be laid waste. ¹⁷The LORD will bring on you and on your people and on the house of your father a time unlike any since Ephraim broke away from Judah—he will bring the king of Assyria."   Ge 30:15; 1Ki 12:16

¹⁸In that day the LORD will whistle for flies from the distant streams of Egypt and for bees from the land of Assyria. ¹⁹They will all come and settle in the steep ravines and in the crevices in the rocks, on all the thornbushes and at all the water holes. ²⁰In that day the Lord will use a razor hired from beyond the River[d]—the king of Assyria—to shave your head and the hair of your legs, and to take off your beards also. ²¹In that day, a man will keep alive a young cow and two goats. ²²And because of the abundance of the milk they give, he will have curds to eat. All who remain in the land will eat curds and honey. ²³In that day, in every place where there were a thousand vines worth a thousand silver shekels,[e] there will be only briers and thorns. ²⁴Men will go there with bow and arrow, for the land will be covered with briers and thorns. ²⁵As for all the hills once cultivated by the hoe, you will no longer go there for fear of the briers and thorns; they will become places where cattle are turned loose and where sheep run.   Isa 2:11

Assyria, the LORD's Instrument

8 The LORD said to me, "Take a large scroll and write on it with an ordinary pen: Maher-Shalal-Hash-Baz.[f] ²And I will call in Uriah the priest and Zechariah son of Jeberekiah as reliable witnesses for me."   Dt 27:8

³Then I went to the prophetess, and she conceived and gave birth to a son. And the LORD said to me, "Name him Maher-Shalal-Hash-Baz. ⁴Before the boy knows how to say 'My father' or 'My mother,' the wealth of Damascus and the plunder of Samaria will be carried off by the king of Assyria."   Isa 7:16

⁵The LORD spoke to me again:

---

a14 The Hebrew is plural.   b14 Masoretic Text; Dead Sea Scrolls and he or and they   c14 Immanuel means God with us.   d20 That is, the Euphrates   e23 That is, about 25 pounds (about 11.5 kilograms)   f1 Maher-Shalal-Hash-Baz means quick to the plunder, swift to the spoil; also in verse 3.

6"Because this people has
rejected
the gently flowing waters of
Shiloah　　　　　Ne 3:15
and rejoices over Rezin
and the son of Remaliah,
7therefore the Lord is about to
bring against them
the mighty floodwaters of
the River*a*—　　　Isa 17:12-13
the king of Assyria with all
his pomp.　　　　Isa 10:16
It will overflow all its
channels,
run over all its banks　Jos 3:15
8and sweep on into Judah,
swirling over it,　　Isa 28:15
passing through it and
reaching up to the neck.
Its outspread wings will
cover the breadth of
your land,
O Immanuel*b*!"　　　Isa 7:14

9Raise the war cry,*c* you
nations, and be
shattered!　　　　Job 34:24
Listen, all you distant
lands.
Prepare for battle, and be
shattered!　　　　Jer 6:4
Prepare for battle, and be
shattered!
10Devise your strategy, but it
will be thwarted;　　Job 5:12
propose your plan, but it
will not stand,　　Pr 19:21
for God is with us.*d*　　Isa 7:14

Fear God

11The LORD spoke to me with
his strong hand upon me, warning me not to follow the way of
this people. He said:　　Eze 2:8

12"Do not call conspiracy
everything that these
people call conspiracy*e*;
do not fear what they fear,
and do not dread it.　Isa 7:4
13The LORD Almighty is the
one you are to regard as
holy,　　　　　Nu 20:12
he is the one you are to
fear,　　　　　Ex 20:20
he is the one you are to
dread,　　　　Isa 29:23
14and he will be a sanctuary;
but for both houses of Israel
he will be
a stone that causes men to
stumble　　　　Jer 6:21
and a rock that makes them
fall.　　　　　Lk 2:34
And for the people of
Jerusalem he will be
a trap and a snare.　Ps 119:110
15Many of them will stumble;
they will fall and be broken,
they will be snared and
captured."　　　Pr 4:19

16Bind up the testimony
and seal up the law among
my disciples.　　Isa 29:11-12
17I will wait for the LORD,
who is hiding his face from
the house of Jacob.　Dt 31:17
I will put my trust in him.

18Here am I, and the children
the LORD has given me. We are
signs and symbols in Israel from

---

a7 That is, the Euphrates　　*b8* *Immanuel* means *God with us.*　　*c9* Or *Do your worst*
d10 Hebrew *Immanuel*　　*e12* Or *Do not call for a treaty / every time these people call for a*
treaty

the Lord Almighty, who dwells on Mount Zion.   Ps 9:11

¹⁹When men tell you to consult mediums and spiritists, who whisper and mutter, should not a people inquire of their God? Why consult the dead on behalf of the living? ²⁰To the law and to the testimony! If they do not speak according to this word, they have no light of dawn. ²¹Distressed and hungry, they will roam through the land; when they are famished, they will become enraged and, looking upward, will curse their king and their God. ²²Then they will look toward the earth and see only distress and darkness and fearful gloom, and they will be thrust into utter darkness.   Ru 4:7

To Us a Child Is Born

9 Nevertheless, there will be no more gloom for those who were in distress. In the past he humbled the land of Zebulun and the land of Naphtali, but in the future he will honor Galilee of the Gentiles, by the way of the sea, along the Jordan—   2Ki 15:29; Job 15:24

²The people walking in
    darkness   Ps 82:5
  have seen a great light; Ps 36:9
on those living in the land of
    the shadow of death[a]
  a light has dawned.   Isa 58:8
³You have enlarged the nation
  and increased their joy;

they rejoice before you
  as people rejoice at the
    harvest,
as men rejoice
  when dividing the
    plunder.
⁴For as in the day of Midian's
    defeat,   Jdg 7:25
  you have shattered
the yoke that burdens them,
  the bar across their
    shoulders,   Ps 81:6
  the rod of their oppressor.
⁵Every warrior's boot used in
    battle
  and every garment rolled in
    blood
will be destined for burning,
  will be fuel for the fire.   Isa 2:4
⁶For to us a child is born, Ge 3:15
  to us a son is given,   Jn 3:16
and the government will be
  on his shoulders.   Isa 22:22
And he will be called
  Wonderful Counselor,[b]Job 15:8
    Mighty God,   Dt 7:21
  Everlasting Father, Prince
    of Peace.   Isa 26:3,12
⁷Of the increase of his
    government and peace
  there will be no end.   Da 2:44
He will reign on David's
    throne
  and over his kingdom,
establishing and upholding it
  with justice and
    righteousness   Ps 72:2
from that time on and
    forever.   2Sa 7:13
The zeal of the Lord
    Almighty
  will accomplish this.   2Ki 19:31

The LORD's Anger Against Israel

⁸The Lord has sent a message
  against Jacob;   Dt 32:2
it will fall on Israel.
⁹All the people will know it—
  Ephraim and the
      inhabitants of Samaria—
who say with pride
and arrogance of heart,
¹⁰"The bricks have fallen
      down,
  but we will rebuild with
      dressed stone;   Ge 11:3
the fig trees have been felled,
but we will replace them
  with cedars."   1Ki 7:2-3
¹¹But the LORD has
      strengthened Rezin's
      foes against them
and has spurred their
      enemies on.   Isa 7:8
¹²Arameans from the east and
      Philistines from the west
have devoured Israel with
      open mouth.   Ps 79:7

Yet for all this, his anger is
      not turned away, Job 40:11
his hand is still upraised.

¹³But the people have not
      returned to him who
      struck them,   Jer 5:3
nor have they sought the
      LORD Almighty.   Isa 2:3
¹⁴So the LORD will cut off from
      Israel both head and tail,
both palm branch and reed
      in a single day;   Rev 18:8
¹⁵the elders and prominent
      men are the head, Isa 5:13

the prophets who teach lies
      are the tail.   Job 13:4
¹⁶Those who guide this people
      mislead them,   Mt 15:14
and those who are guided
      are led astray.   Isa 3:12
¹⁷Therefore the Lord will take
      no pleasure in the young
      men,   Jer 9:21
nor will he pity the
      fatherless and widows,
for everyone is ungodly and
      wicked,   Isa 1:4
every mouth speaks
      vileness.   Isa 3:8

Yet for all this, his anger is
      not turned away,
his hand is still upraised.

¹⁸Surely wickedness burns like
      a fire;   Dt 29:23
  it consumes briers and
      thorns,   Isa 5:6
  it sets the forest thickets
      ablaze,   Ps 83:14
  so that it rolls upward in a
      column of smoke.
¹⁹By the wrath of the LORD
      Almighty
  the land will be scorched
and the people will be fuel
      for the fire;   Ps 97:3
  no one will spare his
      brother.   Isa 3:5
²⁰On the right they will
      devour,
  but still be hungry;
on the left they will eat,
  but not be satisfied. Isa 49:26
Each will feed on the flesh of
      his own offspring[a]:

^a20 Or arm

21 Manasseh will feed on
    Ephraim, and Ephraim
    on Manasseh;   Jdg 7:22
  together they will turn
    against Judah.   2Ch 28:6

Yet for all this, his anger is
  not turned away,
  his hand is still upraised.

10 Woe to those who make
   unjust laws,   Isa 5:8
  to those who issue
    oppressive decrees,
2 to deprive the poor of their
    rights
  and withhold justice from
    the oppressed of my
    people,   Isa 5:23
  making widows their prey
  and robbing the fatherless.
3 What will you do on the day
    of reckoning,   Job 31:14
  when disaster comes from
    afar?   Ps 59:5
  To whom will you run for
    help?   Ps 108:12
  Where will you leave your
    riches?
4 Nothing will remain but to
    cringe among the
    captives
  or fall among the slain. Isa 22:2

Yet for all this, his anger is
  not turned away,
  his hand is still upraised.

God's Judgment on Assyria

5 "Woe to the Assyrian, the
    rod of my anger,   Isa 14:5
  in whose hand is the club of
    my wrath!   Isa 9:4
6 I send him against a godless
    nation,   Isa 9:17

I dispatch him against a
  people who anger me,
  to seize loot and snatch
    plunder,   Jdg 6:4
  and to trample them down
    like mud in the streets.
7 But this is not what he
    intends,   Ge 50:20
  this is not what he has in
    mind;
  his purpose is to destroy,
  to put an end to many
    nations.
8 'Are not my commanders all
    kings?' he says.   2Ki 18:24
9 'Has not Calno fared like
    Carchemish?   2Ch 35:20
  Is not Hamath like Arpad,
    and Samaria like
    Damascus?   Ge 14:15
10 As my hand seized the
    kingdoms of the idols,
  kingdoms whose images
    excelled those of
    Jerusalem and Samaria—
11 shall I not deal with
    Jerusalem and her
    images
  as I dealt with Samaria and
    her idols?' "   2Ki 19:13

12 When the Lord has finished
all his work against Mount Zion
and Jerusalem, he will say, "I
will punish the king of Assyria
for the willful pride of his heart
and the haughty look in his
eyes. 13 For he says: Isa 30:31-33

" 'By the strength of my
    hand I have done this,
  and by my wisdom,
    because I have
    understanding.   Dt 32:26-27

I removed the boundaries of
   nations,
  I plundered their treasures;
  like a mighty one I
   subdued*a* their kings.
¹⁴As one reaches into a nest,
  so my hand reached for the
   wealth of the nations;
  as men gather abandoned
   eggs,
  so I gathered all the
   countries;   Isa 14:6
  not one flapped a wing,
  or opened its mouth to
   chirp.' "   2Ki 19:22-24

¹⁵Does the ax raise itself above
   him who swings it,
  or the saw boast against
   him who uses it?   Isa 7:20
  As if a rod were to wield him
   who lifts it up,
  or a club brandish him who
   is not wood!
¹⁶Therefore, the Lord, the
   Lᴏʀᴅ Almighty,
  will send a wasting disease
   upon his sturdy
   warriors;   Nu 11:33; Ps 78:31
  under his pomp a fire will be
   kindled
  like a blazing flame.   Jer 21:14
¹⁷The Light of Israel will
   become a fire,   Job 41:21
  their Holy One a flame;
  in a single day it will burn
   and consume
  his thorns and his briers.
¹⁸The splendor of his forests
   and fertile fields
  it will completely destroy,
  as when a sick man wastes
   away.   2Ki 19:23

¹⁹And the remaining trees of
   his forests will be so few
  that a child could write
   them down.   Isa 17:6

The Remnant of Israel

²⁰In that day the remnant of
   Israel,
  the survivors of the house
   of Jacob,   Isa 1:9
  will no longer rely on him
  who struck them down
  but will truly rely on the
   Lᴏʀᴅ,   2Ch 14:11
  the Holy One of Israel.
²¹A remnant will return,*b* a
   remnant of Jacob
  will return to the Mighty
   God.   Isa 9:6
²²Though your people,
   O Israel, be like the sand
   by the sea,   Ge 12:2
  only a remnant will return.
  Destruction has been
   decreed,   Isa 28:22
  overwhelming and
   righteous.
²³The Lord, the Lᴏʀᴅ
   Almighty, will carry out
  the destruction decreed
  upon the whole land.

²⁴Therefore, this is what the
Lord, the Lᴏʀᴅ Almighty, says:

"O my people who live in
   Zion,   Ps 87:5-6
  do not be afraid of the
   Assyrians,   Isa 7:4
  who beat you with a rod
  and lift up a club against
   you, as Egypt did.

---

*a*13 Or *I subdued the mighty,*   *b*21 Hebrew *shear-jashub*; also in verse 22

²⁵"Very soon my anger against
you will end   Isa 17:14
and my wrath will be
directed to their
destruction."   Mic 5:6

²⁶The LORD Almighty will lash
them with a whip,
as when he struck down
Midian at the rock of
Oreb;   Isa 9:4
and he will raise his staff
over the waters,
as he did in Egypt.   Ex 14:16
²⁷In that day their burden will
be lifted from your
shoulders,   Ps 66:11
their yoke from your neck;
the yoke will be broken
because you have grown so
fat.^a   Jer 30:8

²⁸They enter Aiath;
they pass through Migron;
they store supplies at
Micmash.   1Sa 13:2
²⁹They go over the pass, and
say,
"We will camp overnight at
Geba."   Jos 18:24
Ramah trembles;
Gibeah of Saul flees.   Isa 15:5
³⁰Cry out, O Daughter of
Gallim!   1Sa 25:44
Listen, O Laishah!
Poor Anathoth!   Ne 1:32
³¹Madmenah is in flight;
the people of Gebim take
cover.
³²This day they will halt at
Nob;   1Sa 21:1
they will shake their fist

at the mount of the Daughter
of Zion,   Ps 9:14
at the hill of Jerusalem.

³³See, the Lord, the LORD
Almighty,
will lop off the boughs with
great power.   Isa 18:5
The lofty trees will be felled,
the tall ones will be brought
low.   Isa 5:15
³⁴He will cut down the forest
thickets with an ax;   Na 1:12
Lebanon will fall before the
Mighty One.   Ge 49:24

The Branch From Jesse

11 A shoot will come up
from the stump of Jesse;
from his roots a Branch will
bear fruit.   2Ki 19:30
²The Spirit of the LORD will
rest on him—   Jdg 3:10
the Spirit of wisdom and of
understanding,   Ex 28:3
the Spirit of counsel and of
power,   Isa 9:6
the Spirit of knowledge and
of the fear of the LORD—
³and he will delight in the fear
of the LORD.   Isa 33:6

He will not judge by what he
sees with his eyes,   Jn 7:24
or decide by what he hears
with his ears;   Jn 2:25
⁴but with righteousness he
will judge the needy,
with justice he will give
decisions for the poor of
the earth.   Job 5:16
He will strike the earth with
the rod of his mouth;

---

^a27 Hebrew; Septuagint *broken / from your shoulders*

with the breath of his lips
he will slay the wicked.
⁵Righteousness will be his
belt
and faithfulness the sash
around his waist.   Eph 6:14

⁶The wolf will live with the
lamb,   Isa 65:25
the leopard will lie down
with the goat,
the calf and the lion and the
yearling*ᵃ* together;
and a little child will lead
them.
⁷The cow will feed with the
bear,
their young will lie down
together,
and the lion will eat straw
like the ox.   Job 40:15
⁸The infant will play near the
hole of the cobra,   Isa 65:20
and the young child put his
hand into the viper's
nest.   Isa 14:29
⁹They will neither harm nor
destroy
on all my holy mountain,
for the earth will be full of
the knowledge of the
LORD   Ex 7:5
as the waters cover the sea.

¹⁰In that day the Root of Jesse
will stand as a banner for the
peoples; the nations will rally to
him, and his place of rest will be
glorious. ¹¹In that day the Lord
will reach out his hand a second
time to reclaim the remnant that
is left of his people from As-

syria, from Lower Egypt, from
Upper Egypt,*ᵇ* from Cush,*ᶜ*
from Elam, from Babylonia,*ᵈ*
from Hamath and from the islands of the sea.   Isa 10:20; 49:12

¹²He will raise a banner for the
nations   Ps 20:5
and gather the exiles of
Israel;   Ne 1:9
he will assemble the
scattered people of
Judah
from the four quarters of
the earth.   Ps 48:10
¹³Ephraim's jealousy will
vanish,
and Judah's enemies*ᵉ* will
be cut off;
Ephraim will not be jealous
of Judah,
nor Judah hostile toward
Ephraim.   2Ch 28:6
¹⁴They will swoop down on
the slopes of Philistia to
the west;   2Ch 26:6
together they will plunder
the people to the east.
They will lay hands on Edom
and Moab,   Nu 24:18
and the Ammonites will be
subject to them.   Isa 25:3
¹⁵The LORD will dry up
the gulf of the Egyptian sea;
with a scorching wind he will
sweep his hand
over the Euphrates River.*ᶠ*
He will break it up into seven
streams
so that men can cross over
in sandals.   Ex 14:29
¹⁶There will be a highway for

ᵃ6 Hebrew; Septuagint *lion will feed*   *ᵇ11* Hebrew *from Pathros*   *ᶜ11* That is, the
upper Nile region   *ᵈ11* Hebrew *Shinar*   *ᵉ13* Or *hostility*   *ᶠ15* Hebrew *the River*

the remnant of his
people   Ge 45:7
that is left from Assyria,
as there was for Israel
when they came up from
Egypt.   Ex 14:26-31

Songs of Praise

12 In that day you will say:
"I will praise you,
   O Lord.   Ps 9:1
Although you were angry
   with me,
your anger has turned away
   and you have comforted
   me.   Ps 71:21
²Surely God is my salvation;
   I will trust and not be
   afraid.   Job 13:15
The Lord, the Lord, is my
   strength and my song;
he has become my
   salvation."   Ex 15:2
³With joy you will draw water
from the wells of salvation.

⁴In that day you will say:

"Give thanks to the Lord,
   call on his name;   Ex 3:15
make known among the
   nations what he has
   done,   Isa 54:5
and proclaim that his name
   is exalted.   Ps 113:2
⁵Sing to the Lord, for he has
   done glorious things;
let this be known to all the
   world.   Ps 98:1
⁶Shout aloud and sing for joy,
   people of Zion,   Ge 21:6
for great is the Holy One of
   Israel among you."   Ps 46:5

a6 Hebrew Shaddai

A Prophecy Against Babylon

13 An oracle concerning
Babylon that Isaiah son of
Amoz saw: Isa 1:1

²Raise a banner on a bare
   hilltop,
   shout to them;   Ps 20:5
beckon to them
   to enter the gates of the
   nobles.   Isa 24:12
³I have commanded my holy
   ones;
   I have summoned my
   warriors to carry out my
   wrath—   Isa 21:2
those who rejoice in my
   triumph.   Ps 149:2

⁴Listen, a noise on the
   mountains,
   like that of a great
   multitude!   Joel 3:14
Listen, an uproar among the
   kingdoms,   Ps 46:6
like nations massing
   together!
The Lord Almighty is
   mustering
   an army for war.   Isa 42:13
⁵They come from faraway
   lands,
   from the ends of the
   heavens—   Isa 5:26
the Lord and the weapons of
   his wrath—   Isa 45:1
to destroy the whole
   country.   Jos 6:17
⁶Wail, for the day of the Lord
   is near;   Isa 2:12
it will come like destruction
   from the Almighty.ᵃ

⁷Because of this, all hands will
   go limp,   2Ki 19:26
  every man's heart will melt.
⁸Terror will seize them,
  pain and anguish will grip
    them;   Ex 15:14
  they will writhe like a
    woman in labor.   Ge 3:16
They will look aghast at each
   other,
  their faces aflame.   Joel 2:6

⁹See, the day of the LORD is
   coming
  —a cruel day, with wrath
    and fierce anger—   Isa 9:19
to make the land desolate
  and destroy the sinners
    within it.
¹⁰The stars of heaven and their
   constellations
  will not show their light.
The rising sun will be
    darkened   Isa 24:23
  and the moon will not give
    its light.   Eze 32:7
¹¹I will punish the world for its
   evil,
  the wicked for their sins.
I will put an end to the
   arrogance of the
    haughty   Ps 10:5
  and will humble the pride
    of the ruthless.   Isa 25:3
¹²I will make man scarcer than
   pure gold,
  more rare than the gold of
    Ophir.   Ge 10:29
¹³Therefore I will make the
   heavens tremble;   Ps 102:26
  and the earth will shake
    from its place   Job 9:6

at the wrath of the LORD
   Almighty,
  in the day of his burning
    anger.   Job 9:5

¹⁴Like a hunted gazelle,
  like sheep without a
    shepherd,   1Ki 22:17
each will return to his own
   people,
  each will flee to his native
    land.   Jer 46:16
¹⁵Whoever is captured will be
   thrust through;
  all who are caught will fall
    by the sword.   Isa 14:19
¹⁶Their infants will be dashed
   to pieces before their
    eyes;   Nu 16:27
  their houses will be looted
   and their wives
    ravished.   Ge 34:29

¹⁷See, I will stir up against
   them the Medes,
  who do not care for silver
  and have no delight in
    gold.   2Ki 18:14-16
¹⁸Their bows will strike down
   the young men;   Dt 32:25
  they will have no mercy on
    infants   Isa 47:6
nor will they look with
   compassion on children.
¹⁹Babylon, the jewel of
   kingdoms,   Isa 47:5
  the glory of the
    Babylonians'ᵃ pride,
will be overthrown by God
  like Sodom and Gomorrah.
²⁰She will never be inhabited
  or lived in through all
    generations;   Isa 14:23

ᵃ19 Or Chaldeans'

no Arab will pitch his tent
  there,
  no shepherd will rest his
  flocks there.   2Ch 17:11
21But desert creatures will lie
  there,   Ps 74:14
  jackals will fill her houses;
there the owls will dwell,
  and there the wild goats
  will leap about.   Lev 17:7
22Hyenas will howl in her
  strongholds,
  jackals in her luxurious
  palaces.   Isa 34:13
Her time is at hand,
  and her days will not be
  prolonged.   Jer 50:39

14 The LORD will have
     compassion on Jacob;
  once again he will choose
    Israel
  and will settle them in their
    own land.   Jer 3:18
Aliens will join them
  and unite with the house of
    Jacob.   Ex 14:23
2Nations will take them
  and bring them to their
    own place.   Isa 11:12
And the house of Israel will
    possess the nations
  as menservants and
    maidservants in the
    LORD's land.   Ps 49:14
They will make captives of
    their captors   Ps 149:8
  and rule over their
    oppressors.   Isa 60:14

3On the day the LORD gives
you relief from suffering and
turmoil and cruel bondage,
4you will take up this taunt
against the king of Babylon:

How the oppressor has come
  to an end!   Isa 9:4
How his fury[a] has ended!
5The LORD has broken the rod
  of the wicked,   Isa 10:15
  the scepter of the rulers,
6which in anger struck down
    peoples
  with unceasing blows, Isa 10:14
and in fury subdued nations
  with relentless aggression.
7All the lands are at rest and
    at peace;   Nu 6:26
  they break into singing.
8Even the pine trees and the
    cedars of Lebanon
  exult over you and say,
"Now that you have been
    laid low,
  no woodsman comes to cut
    us down."   2Ki 19:23

9The grave[b] below is all astir
  to meet you at your coming;
it rouses the spirits of the
    departed to greet
    you—
  all those who were leaders
    in the world;   Zec 10:3
it makes them rise from their
    thrones—
  all those who were kings
    over the nations.   Job 3:14
10They will all respond,
  they will say to you,
"You also have become
    weak, as we are;
  you have become like us."

---

a4 Dead Sea Scrolls, Septuagint and Syriac; the meaning of the word in the Masoretic
Text is uncertain.   b9 Hebrew Sheol; also in verses 11 and 15

¹¹All your pomp has been
  brought down to the
  grave,   Nu 16:30
along with the noise of your
  harps;   Isa 5:12
maggots are spread out
  beneath you
and worms cover you. Job 21:26

¹²How you have fallen from
  heaven,
  O morning star, son of the
  dawn!   2Pe 1:19
You have been cast down to
  the earth,
you who once laid low the
  nations!   Eze 26:17
¹³You said in your heart,
  "I will ascend to heaven;
I will raise my throne
  above the stars of God;
I will sit enthroned on the
  mount of assembly,
on the utmost heights of
  the sacred mountain. ᵃ
¹⁴I will ascend above the tops
  of the clouds;   Job 20:6
I will make myself like the
  Most High."   Ge 3:5
¹⁵But you are brought down to
  the grave,   Job 21:13
to the depths of the pit.

¹⁶Those who see you stare at
  you,
they ponder your fate: Jer 50:23
"Is this the man who shook
  the earth
and made kingdoms
  tremble,   Isa 2:19
¹⁷the man who made the world
  a desert,   Isa 15:6
who overthrew its cities

and would not let his
  captives go home?" Ex 7:14

¹⁸All the kings of the nations
  lie in state,
each in his own tomb.
¹⁹But you are cast out of your
  tomb
like a rejected branch;
you are covered with the
  slain,   Isa 34:3
with those pierced by the
  sword,   Isa 13:15
those who descend to the
  stones of the pit.   Jer 41:7-9
Like a corpse trampled
  underfoot,
²⁰ you will not join them in
  burial,   1Ki 21:19
for you have destroyed your
  land
and killed your people.

The offspring of the wicked
will never be mentioned
  again.   Isa 1:4
²¹Prepare a place to slaughter
  his sons
  for the sins of their
  forefathers;   Ge 9:25
they are not to rise to inherit
  the land
and cover the earth with
  their cities.

²²"I will rise up against them,"
  declares the LORD
  Almighty.   Ps 94:16
"I will cut off from Babylon
  her name and survivors,
her offspring and
  descendants,"   2Sa 18:18
  declares the LORD.

ᵃ13 Or *the north*; Hebrew *Zaphon*

23"I will turn her into a place
    for owls   Lev 11:16-18
and into swampland;
I will sweep her with the
    broom of destruction,"
declares the LORD
    Almighty.   Isa 10:3

A Prophecy Against Assyria

24The LORD Almighty has
sworn,   Isa 45:23

"Surely, as I have planned,
    so it will be,
and as I have purposed, so
    it will stand.   Isa 19:12,17
25I will crush the Assyrian in
    my land;   Isa 10:5,12
on my mountains I will
    trample him down.
His yoke will be taken from
    my people,   Isa 9:4
and his burden removed
    from their shoulders."

26This is the plan determined
    for the whole world;
this is the hand stretched
    out over all nations.
27For the LORD Almighty has
    purposed, and who can
    thwart him?   Jer 49:20
His hand is stretched out,
    and who can turn it
    back?   2Ch 20:6

A Prophecy Against the Philistines

28This oracle came in the year
King Ahaz died: 2Ki 16:1

29Do not rejoice, all you
    Philistines,   Jos 13:3
that the rod that struck you
    is broken;

from the root of that snake
    will spring up a viper,
its fruit will be a darting,
    venomous serpent.   Dt 8:15
30The poorest of the poor will
    find pasture,
and the needy will lie down
    in safety.   Isa 3:15
But your root I will destroy
    by famine;   Isa 8:21
it will slay your survivors.

31Wail, O gate! Howl, O city!
    Melt away, all you
        Philistines!   Ge 10:14
A cloud of smoke comes
    from the north,   Isa 41:25
and there is not a straggler
    in its ranks.   Isa 5:27
32What answer shall be given
    to the envoys of that
        nation?   Isa 37:9
"The LORD has established
    Zion,   Ps 51:18
and in her his afflicted
    people will find refuge."

A Prophecy Against Moab

15 An oracle concerning
    Moab: Nu 22:3-6

Ar in Moab is ruined,
    destroyed in a night!   Nu 21:15
Kir in Moab is ruined,
    destroyed in a night!   2Ki 3:25
2Dibon goes up to its temple,
    to its high places to weep;
Moab wails over Nebo and
        Medeba.   Nu 32:38
Every head is shaved
    and every beard cut off.
3In the streets they wear
    sackcloth;   Isa 3:24
on the roofs and in the
    public squares

they all wail,   Isa 14:31
  prostrate with weeping.
4Heshbon and Elealeh cry
    out,
  their voices are heard all
    the way to Jahaz.   Nu 21:23
Therefore the armed men of
    Moab cry out,
  and their hearts are faint.

5My heart cries out over
    Moab;   Isa 16:11
  her fugitives flee as far as
    Zoar,   Nu 21:29
  as far as Eglath Shelishiyah.
They go up the way to
    Luhith,
  weeping as they go;
  on the road to Horonaim
  they lament their
    destruction.   Jer 4:20
6The waters of Nimrim are
    dried up   Isa 19:5-7
  and the grass is withered;
  the vegetation is gone
  and nothing green is left.
7So the wealth they have
    acquired and stored up
  they carry away over the
    Ravine of the Poplars.
8Their outcry echoes along the
    border of Moab;
  their wailing reaches as far
    as Eglaim,
  their lamentation as far as
    Beer Elim.   Nu 21:16
9Dimon'sa waters are full of
    blood,
  but I will bring still more
    upon Dimona—
  a lion upon the fugitives of
    Moab   Eze 25:8-11

and upon those who
  remain in the land.

16 Send lambs as tribute
    to the ruler of the land,
  from Sela, across the desert,
  to the mount of the
    Daughter of Zion.   Isa 10:32
2Like fluttering birds
    pushed from the nest,
  so are the women of Moab
  at the fords of the Arnon.

3"Give us counsel,
  render a decision.
Make your shadow like
    night—
  at high noon.
Hide the fugitives,   1Ki 18:4
  do not betray the refugees.
4Let the Moabite fugitives stay
    with you;
  be their shelter from the
    destroyer."   Isa 58:7

The oppressor will come to
    an end,   Isa 9:4
  and destruction will cease;
  the aggressor will vanish
    from the land.
5In love a throne will be
    established;   Pr 20:28
  in faithfulness a man will sit
    on it—
  one from the houseb of
    David—   Isa 7:2
  one who in judging seeks
    justice
  and speeds the cause of
    righteousness.   Isa 9:7

6We have heard of Moab's
    pride—   Lev 26:19

a9 Masoretic Text; Dead Sea Scrolls, some Septuagint manuscripts and Vulgate *Dibon*
b5 Hebrew *tent*

her overweening pride and
  conceit,
her pride and her insolence—
but her boasts are empty.
7Therefore the Moabites wail,
  they wail together for
  Moab.   Isa 13:6
Lament and grieve
  for the men*a* of Kir
  Hareseth.   1Ch 16:3
8The fields of Heshbon
  wither,   Isa 15:6
  the vines of Sibmah also.
The rulers of the nations
  have trampled down the
  choicest vines,   Isa 5:2
which once reached Jazer
  and spread toward the
  desert.   Nu 21:32
Their shoots spread out
  and went as far as the sea.
9So I weep, as Jazer weeps,
  for the vines of Sibmah.
O Heshbon, O Elealeh,
  I drench you with tears!
The shouts of joy over your
  ripened fruit
  and over your harvests
  have been stilled.   Jer 40:12
10Joy and gladness are taken
  away from the
  orchards;
  no one sings or shouts in
  the vineyards;   Jer 25:30
no one treads out wine at the
  presses,   Job 24:11
for I have put an end to the
  shouting.
11My heart laments for Moab
  like a harp,   Job 30:31
  my inmost being for Kir
  Hareseth.   Isa 63:15

12When Moab appears at her
  high place,   1Ki 11:7
she only wears herself out;
when she goes to her shrine
  to pray,
  it is to no avail.   1Ki 18:29

13This is the word the LORD
has already spoken concerning
Moab. 14But now the LORD says:
"Within three years, as a servant bound by contract would
count them, Moab's splendor
and all her many people will be
despised, and her survivors will
be very few and feeble."   Isa 20:3

An Oracle Against Damascus

17 An oracle concerning
  Damascus: Isa 13:1

"See, Damascus will no
  longer be a city
but will become a heap of
  ruins.   Dt 13:16
2The cities of Aroer will be
  deserted
and left to flocks, which
  will lie down,   Isa 27:10
with no one to make them
  afraid.   Lev 26:6
3The fortified city will
  disappear from
  Ephraim,   Isa 25:2
and royal power from
  Damascus;
the remnant of Aram will be
  like the glory of the
  Israelites,"   Isa 7:8
  declares the LORD
  Almighty.

a7 Or "*raisin cakes,*" a wordplay

⁴"In that day the glory of
    Jacob will fade;   Isa 2:11
the fat of his body will
    waste away.   Isa 10:16
⁵It will be as when a reaper
    gathers the standing
    grain
and harvests the grain with
    his arm—   Isa 33:4
as when a man gleans heads
    of grain
in the Valley of Rephaim.
⁶Yet some gleanings will
    remain,   Dt 4:27
as when an olive tree is
    beaten,   Isa 27:12
leaving two or three olives
    on the topmost
    branches,
four or five on the fruitful
    boughs,"
            declares the LORD,
            the God of Israel.

⁷In that day men will look to
    their Maker   Ps 95:6
and turn their eyes to the
    Holy One of Israel. Isa 12:6
⁸They will not look to the
    altars,
the work of their hands,
and they will have no regard
    for the Asherah
    poles[a]
and the incense altars their
    fingers have made.   Isa 2:8

⁹In that day their strong cities, which they left because of
the Israelites, will be like places
abandoned to thickets and undergrowth. And all will be desolation.   Isa 7:19

¹⁰You have forgotten God your
    Savior;   Dt 6:12
you have not remembered
    the Rock, your fortress.
Therefore, though you set
    out the finest plants
and plant imported vines,
¹¹though on the day you set
    them out, you make
    them grow,
and on the morning when
    you plant them, you
    bring them to bud,
yet the harvest will be as
    nothing
in the day of disease and
    incurable pain.   Dt 28:39

¹²Oh, the raging of many
    nations—   Isa 41:11
they rage like the raging
    sea!   Ps 18:4
Oh, the uproar of the
    peoples—
they roar like the roaring of
    great waters!   Isa 8:7
¹³Although the peoples roar
    like the roar of surging
    waters,
when he rebukes them they
    flee far away,   Dt 28:20
driven before the wind like
    chaff on the hills,   Job 13:25
like tumbleweed before a
    gale.   Job 21:18
¹⁴In the evening, sudden
    terror!   Isa 33:18
Before the morning, they
    are gone!   2Ki 19:35
This is the portion of those
    who loot us,
the lot of those who
    plunder us.

---

[a]8 That is, symbols of the goddess Asherah

A Prophecy Against Cush

18 Woe to the land of
whirring wings[a]   Isa 5:8
along the rivers of Cush,[b]
² which sends envoys by sea
in papyrus boats over the
water.   Ex 2:3

Go, swift messengers,
to a people tall and
smooth-skinned,   Ge 41:14
to a people feared far and
wide,
an aggressive nation of
strange speech,   Ge 10:8-9
whose land is divided by
rivers.

³ All you people of the world,
you who live on the earth,
when a banner is raised on
the mountains,   Ps 60:4
you will see it,
and when a trumpet sounds,
you will hear it.   Jos 6:20
⁴ This is what the LORD says to
me:
"I will remain quiet and will
look on from my
dwelling place,   Isa 26:21
like shimmering heat in the
sunshine,   Jdg 5:31
like a cloud of dew in the
heat of harvest."   2Sa 1:21
⁵ For, before the harvest, when
the blossom is gone
and the flower becomes a
ripening grape,
he will cut off the shoots
with pruning knives,
and cut down and take
away the spreading
branches.   Isa 17:10-11

⁶ They will all be left to the
mountain birds of prey
and to the wild animals;
the birds will feed on them
all summer,
the wild animals all winter.

⁷ At that time gifts will be
brought to the LORD Almighty

from a people tall and
smooth-skinned,   Ge 41:14
from a people feared far
and wide,   Hab 1:7
an aggressive nation of
strange speech,
whose land is divided by
rivers—   Ps 68:31

the gifts will be brought to
Mount Zion, the place of the
Name of the LORD Almighty.

A Prophecy About Egypt

19 An oracle concerning
Egypt: Ex 12:12

See, the LORD rides on a
swift cloud   Dt 10:14
and is coming to Egypt.
The idols of Egypt tremble
before him,
and the hearts of the
Egyptians melt within
them.   Jos 2:11

² "I will stir up Egyptian
against Egyptian—
brother will fight against
brother,   Jdg 7:22
neighbor against neighbor,
city against city,
kingdom against kingdom.
³ The Egyptians will lose heart,

---

a1 Or of locusts   *b1 That is, the upper Nile region*

and I will bring their plans
　　to nothing;　　　2Ch 10:13
they will consult the idols
　　and the spirits of the
　　dead,
　　the mediums and the
　　spiritists.　　　Lev 19:31
⁴I will hand the Egyptians
　　over
　　to the power of a cruel
　　master,
and a fierce king will rule
　　over them,"　　　Isa 20:4
declares the Lord, the LORD
　　Almighty.

⁵The waters of the river will
　　dry up,　　　Isa 44:27
and the riverbed will be
　　parched and dry.　2Sa 14:14
⁶The canals will stink;　Ex 7:18
　　the streams of Egypt will
　　dwindle and dry up.
The reeds and rushes will
　　wither,
⁷　also the plants along the
　　Nile,　　　Nu 11:5
　　at the mouth of the river.
Every sown field along the
　　Nile
　　will become parched, will
　　blow away and be no
　　more.　　　Zec 10:11
⁸The fishermen will groan and
　　lament,　　　Nu 11:5
all who cast hooks into the
　　Nile;　　　Am 4:2
those who throw nets on the
　　water
　　will pine away.
⁹Those who work with
　　combed flax will
　　despair,

the weavers of fine linen
　　will lose hope.　　Pr 7:16
¹⁰The workers in cloth will be
　　dejected,
　　and all the wage earners
　　will be sick at heart.

¹¹The officials of Zoan are
　　nothing but fools;
　　the wise counselors of
　　Pharaoh give senseless
　　advice.
How can you say to Pharaoh,
　　"I am one of the wise men,
　　a disciple of the ancient
　　kings"?　　　1Ki 4:30

¹²Where are your wise men
　　now?　　　1Co 1:20
　　Let them show you and
　　make known
　　what the LORD Almighty
　　has planned against Egypt.
¹³The officials of Zoan have
　　become fools,　　Nu 13:22
　　the leaders of Memphisᵃ are
　　deceived;　　　Jer 2:16
the cornerstones of her
　　peoples
　　have led Egypt astray. Ps 118:22
¹⁴The LORD has poured into
　　them
　　a spirit of dizziness;　Pr 12:8
they make Egypt stagger in
　　all that she does,
　　as a drunkard staggers
　　around in his vomit.
¹⁵There is nothing Egypt can
　　do—
　　head or tail, palm branch or
　　reed.　　　Isa 19:14

¹⁶In that day the Egyptians
will be like women. They will

ᵃ13 Hebrew *Noph*

shudder with fear at the uplift-ed hand that the LORD Almighty raises against them. ¹⁷And the land of Judah will bring terror to the Egyptians; everyone to whom Judah is mentioned will be terrified, because of what the LORD Almighty is planning against them.   Ge 35:5; Isa 2:17

¹⁸In that day five cities in Egypt will speak the language of Canaan and swear allegiance to the LORD Almighty. One of them will be called the City of Destruction.ᵃ   Isa 10:20; Zep 3:9

¹⁹In that day there will be an altar to the LORD in the heart of Egypt, and a monument to the LORD at its border. ²⁰It will be a sign and witness to the LORD Almighty in the land of Egypt. When they cry out to the LORD because of their oppressors, he will send them a savior and de-fender, and he will rescue them. ²¹So the LORD will make himself known to the Egyptians, and in that day they will acknowledge the LORD. They will worship with sacrifices and grain offer-ings; they will make vows to the LORD and keep them. ²²The LORD will strike Egypt with a plague; he will strike them and heal them. They will turn to the LORD, and he will respond to their pleas and heal them.

²³In that day there will be a highway from Egypt to Assyria. The Assyrians will go to Egypt and the Egyptians to Assyria.

The Egyptians and Assyrians will worship together. ²⁴In that day Israel will be the third, along with Egypt and Assyria, a blessing on the earth. ²⁵The LORD Almighty will bless them, saying, "Blessed be Egypt my people, Assyria my handiwork, and Israel my inheritance."

A Prophecy Against Egypt and Cush

20 In the year that the su-preme commander, sent by Sargon king of Assyria, came to Ashdod and attacked and captured it— ²at that time the LORD spoke through Isaiah son of Amoz. He said to him, "Take off the sackcloth from your body and the sandals from your feet." And he did so, going around stripped and barefoot.

³Then the LORD said, "Just as my servant Isaiah has gone stripped and barefoot for three years, as a sign and portent against Egypt and Cush,ᵇ ⁴so the king of Assyria will lead away stripped and barefoot the Egyptian captives and Cushite exiles, young and old, with but-tocks bared—to Egypt's shame. ⁵Those who trusted in Cush and boasted in Egypt will be afraid and put to shame. ⁶In that day the people who live on this coast will say, 'See what has happened to those we relied on, those we fled to for help and

---

ᵃ18 Most manuscripts of the Masoretic Text; some manuscripts of the Masoretic Text, Dead Sea Scrolls and Vulgate *City of the Sun* (that is, Heliopolis)   ᵇ3 That is, the upper Nile region; also in verse 5

deliverance from the king of Assyria! How then can we escape?' "   Isa 22:20; Jer 46:25

A Prophecy Against Babylon

21 An oracle concerning the
Desert by the Sea: Isa 13:21

Like whirlwinds sweeping
     through the southland,
an invader comes from the
     desert,
  from a land of terror. Job 1:19

2A dire vision has been shown
     to me: Eze 4:1-12
The traitor betrays, the
     looter takes loot. Isa 24:16
Elam, attack! Media, lay
     siege!   Ge 10:22
I will bring to an end all the
     groaning she caused.

3At this my body is racked
     with pain,   Job 14:22
pangs seize me, like those
     of a woman in labor;
I am staggered by what I
     hear,
I am bewildered by what I
     see.   Da 7:28
4My heart falters,   Isa 7:4
  fear makes me tremble;
the twilight I longed for
  has become a horror to me.

5They set the tables,
  they spread the rugs,
  they eat, they drink! Isa 5:12
Get up, you officers,
  oil the shields!   2Sa 1:21
6This is what the Lord says to
me:

"Go, post a lookout
  and have him report what
     he sees.   2Ki 9:17
7When he sees chariots
  with teams of horses,
riders on donkeys
  or riders on camels,
let him be alert,
  fully alert.' "   Jdg 6:5

8And the lookout*a* shouted,

"Day after day, my lord, I
     stand on the
     watchtower;
every night I stay at my
     post.
9Look, here comes a man in a
     chariot
with a team of horses.
And he gives back the
     answer:
  'Babylon has fallen, has
     fallen!   Isa 47:11
All the images of its gods
  lie shattered on the
     ground!' "   Isa 2:18

10O my people, crushed on the
     threshing floor,   Isa 27:12
I tell you what I have heard
from the LORD Almighty,
  from the God of Israel.

A Prophecy Against Edom

11An   oracle   concerning
Dumah*b*:   Ge 25:14

Someone calls to me from
     Seir,   Ge 32:3
  "Watchman, what is left of
     the night?

---

a8 Dead Sea Scrolls and Syriac; Masoretic Text *A lion*   *b11 Dumah* means *silence* or
stillness, a wordplay on *Edom*.

Watchman, what is left of
    the night?"
¹²The watchman replies,
    "Morning is coming, but
    also the night.
If you would ask, then ask;
    and come back yet again."

A Prophecy Against Arabia

¹³An   oracle   concerning
Arabia: 2Ch 9:14

You caravans of Dedanites,
    who camp in the thickets of
    Arabia,
¹⁴ bring water for the thirsty;
    you who live in Tema,   Ge 25:15
    bring food for the fugitives.
¹⁵They flee from the sword,
    from the drawn sword,
    from the bent bow
    and from the heat of battle.

¹⁶This is what the Lord says to
me: "Within one year, as a servant bound by contract would
count it, all the pomp of Kedar
will come to an end. ¹⁷The survivors of the bowmen, the warriors of Kedar, will be few." The
LORD, the God of Israel, has
spoken.   Lev 25:50; Dt 4:27

A Prophecy About Jerusalem

22 An oracle concerning the
    Valley of Vision: Ps 125:2

What troubles you now,
    that you have all gone up
    on the roofs,   Jos 2:8
²O town full of commotion,
    O city of tumult and
    revelry?   Isa 5:14
Your slain were not killed by
    the sword,   2Ki 25:3

nor did they die in battle.
³All your leaders have fled
    together;   Isa 13:14
they have been captured
    without using the bow.
All you who were caught
    were taken prisoner
    together,
having fled while the
    enemy was still far
    away.
⁴Therefore I said, "Turn away
    from me;
let me weep bitterly.   Isa 15:3
Do not try to console me
    over the destruction of my
    people."   Jer 9:1

⁵The Lord, the LORD
    Almighty, has a day
    of tumult and trampling
    and terror   2Sa 22:43
in the Valley of Vision,
a day of battering down walls
    and of crying out to the
    mountains.
⁶Elam takes up the quiver,
    with her charioteers and
    horses;   Ps 46:9
Kir uncovers the shield.
⁷Your choicest valleys are full
    of chariots,   Jos 15:8
and horsemen are posted at
    the city gates;   2Ch 32:1-2
⁸ the defenses of Judah are
    stripped away.

And you looked in that day
    to the weapons in the
    Palace of the Forest;
⁹you saw that the City of
    David
    had many breaches in its
    defenses;   Ne 1:3
you stored up water

in the Lower Pool.   2Ki 18:17

¹⁰You counted the buildings in
Jerusalem
and tore down houses to
strengthen the wall..Jer 33:4
¹¹You built a reservoir between
the two walls
for the water of the Old
Pool,   2Ch 32:4
but you did not look to the
One who made it,
or have regard for the One
who planned it long
ago.   2Ki 19:25

¹²The Lord, the LORD
Almighty,
called you on that day
to weep and to wail,   Joel 1:9
to tear out your hair and
put on sackcloth.   Isa 3:21
¹³But see, there is joy and
revelry,   Isa 21:5
slaughtering of cattle and
killing of sheep,
eating of meat and drinking
of wine!   1Sa 25:36
"Let us eat and drink," you
say,
"for tomorrow we die!"

¹⁴The LORD Almighty has revealed this in my hearing: "Till
your dying day this sin will not
be atoned for," says the Lord,
the LORD Almighty.   Isa 30:13-14

¹⁵This is what the Lord, the
LORD Almighty, says:

"Go, say to this steward,
to Shebna, who is in charge
of the palace: 2Ki 6:30
¹⁶What are you doing here and

who gave you
permission
to cut out a grave for
yourself here,   Ge 50:5
hewing your grave on the
height
and chiseling your resting
place in the rock?

¹⁷"Beware, the LORD is about
to take firm hold of you
and hurl you away, O you
mighty man.   Jer 10:18
¹⁸He will roll you up tightly
like a ball
and throw you into a large
country.   Job 18:11
There you will die
and there your splendid
chariots will remain—
you disgrace to your
master's house!
¹⁹I will depose you from your
office,
and you will be ousted from
your position.   Lk 16:3

²⁰"In that day I will summon
my servant, Eliakim son of Hilkiah. ²¹I will clothe him with
your robe and fasten your sash
around him and hand your authority over to him. He will be a
father to those who live in
Jerusalem and to the house of
Judah. ²²I will place on his
shoulder the key to the house of
David; what he opens no one
can shut, and what he shuts no
one can open. ²³I will drive him
like a peg into a firm place; he
will be a seatᵃ of honor for the
house of his father. ²⁴All the

ᵃ23 Or *throne*

glory of his family will hang on him: its offspring and off-shoots—all its lesser vessels, from the bowls to all the jars.

²⁵"In that day," declares the LORD Almighty, "the peg driven into the firm place will give way; it will be sheared off and will fall, and the load hang-ing on it will be cut down." The LORD has spoken.   Isa 46:11

A Prophecy About Tyre

23 An oracle concerning Tyre: Jos 19:23

Wail, O ships of Tarshish!
    For Tyre is destroyed
    and left without house or
        harbor.   Eze 26:4
From the land of Cyprusᵃ
    word has come to them.

²Be silent, you people of the
        island
    and you merchants of
        Sidon,   Jdg 1:31
    whom the seafarers have
        enriched.
³On the great waters
    came the grain of the
        Shihor;   Ge 41:5
    the harvest of the Nileᵇ was
        the revenue of Tyre, Ps 83:7
    and she became the
        marketplace of the
        nations.

⁴Be ashamed, O Sidon, and
        you, O fortress of the
        sea,   Ge 10:15,19

for the sea has spoken:
"I have neither been in labor
        nor given birth;   Isa 54:1
I have neither reared sons
        nor brought up
        daughters."
⁵When word comes to Egypt,
    they will be in anguish at
        the report from Tyre.

⁶Cross over to Tarshish;
    wail, you people of the
        island.
⁷Is this your city of revelry,
    the old, old city,
    whose feet have taken her
    to settle in far-off lands?
⁸Who planned this against
        Tyre,
    the bestower of crowns,
    whose merchants are
        princes,   Na 3:16
    whose traders are
        renowned in the
        earth?
⁹The LORD Almighty planned
        it,   Isa 14:24
    to bring low the pride of all
        glory
    and to humble all who are
        renowned on the earth.

¹⁰Tillᶜ your land as along the
        Nile,
    O Daughter of Tarshish,
    for you no longer have a
        harbor.
¹¹The LORD has stretched out
        his hand over the sea
    and made its kingdoms
        tremble.   Ps 46:6

ᵃ1 Hebrew *Kittim*   ᵇ2,3 Masoretic Text; one Dead Sea Scroll *Sidon, / who cross over the sea; / your envoys* ³*are on the great waters. / The grain of the Shihor, / the harvest of the Nile,*   ᶜ10 Dead Sea Scrolls and some Septuagint manuscripts; Masoretic Text *Go through*

He has given an order
    concerning Phoenicia*ᵃ*
that her fortresses be
    destroyed.   Isa 25:2
¹²He said, "No more of your
    reveling,   Rev 18:22
O Virgin Daughter of
    Sidon, now crushed!

"Up, cross over to Cyprus*ᵇ*;
    even there you will find no
    rest."   Ge 10:4
¹³Look at the land of the
    Babylonians,*ᶜ*   Isa 43:14
this people that is now of
    no account!
The Assyrians have made it
    a place for desert creatures;
they raised up their siege
    towers,   2Ki 25:1
they stripped its fortresses
    bare
and turned it into a ruin.

¹⁴Wail, you ships of Tarshish;
    your fortress is destroyed!

¹⁵At that time Tyre will be forgotten for seventy years, the
span of a king's life. But at the
end of these seventy years, it
will happen to Tyre as in the
song of the prostitute: Jer 25:22

¹⁶"Take up a harp, walk
    through the city,
O prostitute forgotten;   Pr 7:10
play the harp well, sing
    many a song,
so that you will be
    remembered."

¹⁷At the end of seventy years,
the LORD will deal with Tyre.
She will return to her hire as a
prostitute and will ply her trade
with all the kingdoms on the
face of the earth. ¹⁸Yet her profit
and her earnings will be set
apart for the LORD; they will not
be stored up or hoarded. Her
profits will go to those who live
before the LORD, for abundant
food and fine clothes.   Dt 23:17-18

The LORD's Devastation of the Earth

24 See, the LORD is going to
    lay waste the earth
and devastate it;   Jos 6:17
he will ruin its face
    and scatter its inhabitants—
²it will be the same
    for priest as for people,
    for master as for servant,
    for mistress as for maid,
    for seller as for buyer,
    for borrower as for lender,
    for debtor as for creditor.
³The earth will be completely
    laid waste   Ge 6:13
and totally plundered.
        The LORD has spoken
            this word.

⁴The earth dries up and
    withers,
the world languishes and
    withers,   Jer 12:11
the exalted of the earth
    languish.   Isa 3:26
⁵The earth is defiled by its
    people;   Ge 3:17
they have disobeyed the
    laws,
violated the statutes

---

*ᵃ*11 Hebrew *Canaan*   *ᵇ*12 Hebrew *Kittim*   *ᶜ*13 Or *Chaldeans*

and broken the everlasting
  covenant.   Ge 9:11
⁶Therefore a curse consumes
  the earth;   Jos 23:15
its people must bear their
  guilt.
Therefore earth's inhabitants
  are burned up,
and very few are left.   Isa 1:31
⁷The new wine dries up and
  the vine withers;   Isa 7:23
all the merrymakers groan.
⁸The gaiety of the
  tambourines is stilled,
the noise of the revelers has
  stopped,   Isa 5:14
the joyful harp is silent.
⁹No longer do they drink
  wine with a song;   Isa 5:11
the beer is bitter to its
  drinkers.   Isa 5:20
¹⁰The ruined city lies desolate;
the entrance to every house
  is barred.
¹¹In the streets they cry out for
  wine;   La 2:12
all joy turns to gloom,
all gaiety is banished from
  the earth.
¹²The city is left in ruins,
its gate is battered to pieces.
¹³So will it be on the earth
  and among the nations,
as when an olive tree is
  beaten,   Dt 30:4
or as when gleanings are
  left after the grape
  harvest.   Ob 5

¹⁴They raise their voices, they
  shout for joy;   Isa 12:6
from the west they acclaim
  the LORD's majesty.

¹⁵Therefore in the east give
  glory to the LORD;
exalt the name of the LORD,
  the God of Israel,
in the islands of the sea.
¹⁶From the ends of the earth
  we hear singing: Ps 65:8
"Glory to the Righteous
  One."   Ezr 9:15

But I said, "I waste away, I
  waste away!   Lev 26:39
Woe to me!   1Sa 4:8
The treacherous betray!
With treachery the
  treacherous betray!"
¹⁷Terror and pit and snare
  await you,   Isa 8:14
O people of the earth.
¹⁸Whoever flees at the sound
  of terror   Job 20:24
will fall into a pit;
whoever climbs out of the pit
  will be caught in a snare.

The floodgates of the
  heavens are opened,
the foundations of the earth
  shake.   Jdg 5:4
¹⁹The earth is broken up,
the earth is split asunder,
the earth is thoroughly
  shaken.   Dt 11:6
²⁰The earth reels like a
  drunkard,   Job 12:25
it sways like a hut in the
  wind;   Job 27:18
so heavy upon it is the guilt
  of its rebellion   Isa 1:2
that it falls—never to rise
  again.   Job 12:14

²¹In that day the LORD will
  punish

the powers in the heavens
above
and the kings on the earth
below.   Isa 2:12
22They will be herded together
like prisoners bound in a
dungeon;   Isa 42:7
they will be shut up in prison
and be punished*a* after
many days.   Eze 38:8
23The moon will be abashed,
the sun ashamed;   Isa 13:10
for the Lord Almighty will
reign
on Mount Zion and in
Jerusalem,
and before its elders,
gloriously.   Isa 28:5

Praise to the Lord

25 O Lord, you are my
God;   Isa 7:13
I will exalt you and praise
your name,
for in perfect faithfulness
you have done marvelous
things,   Ps 40:5
things planned long ago.
2You have made the city a
heap of rubble,   Isa 17:1
the fortified town a ruin,
the foreigners' stronghold a
city no more;   Isa 13:22
it will never be rebuilt.
3Therefore strong peoples will
honor you;   Ex 6:2
cities of ruthless nations
will revere you.   Isa 13:11
4You have been a refuge for
the poor,   Isa 3:14
a refuge for the needy in his
distress,   Isa 14:30

a shelter from the storm
and a shade from the heat.
For the breath of the ruthless
is like a storm driving
against a wall
5 and like the heat of the
desert.   Isa 29:5
You silence the uproar of
foreigners;   Ps 18:44
as heat is reduced by the
shadow of a cloud,
so the song of the ruthless
is stilled.   Isa 13:11

6On this mountain the Lord
Almighty will prepare
a feast of rich food for all
peoples,   Ge 29:22
a banquet of aged wine—
the best of meats and the
finest of wines.   Ps 36:8
7On this mountain he will
destroy
the shroud that enfolds all
peoples,   Job 4:9
the sheet that covers all
nations;
8 he will swallow up death
forever.
The Sovereign Lord will
wipe away the tears
from all faces;   Isa 15:3
he will remove the disgrace
of his people
from all the earth.   Ge 30:23
       The Lord has spoken.

9In that day they will say,

"Surely this is our God; Isa 40:9
we trusted in him, and he
saved us.   Ps 145:19
This is the Lord, we trusted
in him;

*a*22 Or *released*

let us rejoice and be glad in
  his salvation." Ps 13:5

¹⁰The hand of the LORD will
    rest on this mountain;
  but Moab will be trampled
    under him
  as straw is trampled down
    in the manure. Ge 19:37
¹¹They will spread out their
    hands in it,
  as a swimmer spreads out
    his hands to swim.
  God will bring down their
    pride
  despite the cleverness*ᵃ* of
    their hands. Lev 26:19
¹²He will bring down your
    high fortified walls
  and lay them low; Job 40:11
  he will bring them down to
    the ground,
  to the very dust.

A Song of Praise

26 In that day this song will
    be sung in the land of
Judah: Isa 30:29

  We have a strong city; Isa 14:32
  God makes salvation
    its walls and ramparts. Ps 48:13
²Open the gates
  that the righteous nation
    may enter, Ps 24:3-4
  the nation that keeps
    faith.
³You will keep in perfect
    peace
  him whose mind is
    steadfast, Job 22:21
  because he trusts in you.

⁴Trust in the LORD forever,
  for the LORD, the LORD, is
    the Rock eternal. Ge 49:24
⁵He humbles those who dwell
    on high,
  he lays the lofty city low;
  he levels it to the ground
  and casts it down to the
    dust. Isa 25:2
⁶Feet trample it down—
  the feet of the oppressed,
  the footsteps of the poor.

⁷The path of the righteous is
    level; Ps 26:12
  O upright One, you make
    the way of the righteous
    smooth. Ex 14:19
⁸Yes, LORD, walking in the
    way of your laws,*ᵇ*
  we wait for you; Dt 18:18
  your name and renown
  are the desire of our hearts.
⁹My soul yearns for you in the
    night; Ps 119:55
  in the morning my spirit
    longs for you. Ps 63:1
  When your judgments come
    upon the earth,
  the people of the world
    learn righteousness.
¹⁰Though grace is shown to the
    wicked, Mt 5:45
  they do not learn
    righteousness;
  even in a land of uprightness
    they go on doing evil
  and regard not the majesty
    of the LORD. 1Sa 12:24
¹¹O LORD, your hand is lifted
    high, Ps 10:12
  but they do not see it. Isa 18:3
  Let them see your zeal for

ᵃ11 The meaning of the Hebrew for this word is uncertain.   ᵇ8 Or *judgments*

your people and be put
  to shame;   Mic 7:16
let the fire reserved for your
  enemies consume them.

¹²Lord, you establish peace for
  us;   Ps 119:165
all that we have
  accomplished you have
  done for us.   Ps 68:28
¹³O Lord, our God, other lords
  besides you have ruled
  over us,   Isa 2:8
but your name alone do we
  honor.   Isa 12:4
¹⁴They are now dead, they live
  no more;   Dt 4:28
those departed spirits do
  not rise.   Job 26:5
You punished them and
  brought them to ruin;
you wiped out all memory
  of them.   Ps 9:6
¹⁵You have enlarged the
  nation, O Lord;
you have enlarged the
  nation.   Job 12:23
You have gained glory for
  yourself;
you have extended all the
  borders of the land.

¹⁶Lord, they came to you in
  their distress;   Jdg 6:2
when you disciplined them,
  they could barely whisper a
  prayer.ᵃ   Isa 29:4
¹⁷As a woman with child and
  about to give birth
writhes and cries out in her
  pain,   Isa 21:3
so were we in your
  presence, O Lord.

¹⁸We were with child, we
  writhed in pain,
but we gave birth to wind.
We have not brought
  salvation to the earth;
we have not given birth to
  people of the world.

¹⁹But your dead will live;
  their bodies will rise.
You who dwell in the dust,
  wake up and shout for joy.
Your dew is like the dew of
  the morning;   Ge 27:28
the earth will give birth to
  her dead.   Isa 66:24

²⁰Go, my people, enter your
  rooms
and shut the doors behind
  you;   Ex 12:23
hide yourselves for a little
  while
until his wrath has passed
  by.   Isa 10:25
²¹See, the Lord is coming out
  of his dwelling   Isa 18:4
to punish the people of the
  earth for their sins.   Isa 13:9
The earth will disclose the
  blood shed upon her;
she will conceal her slain no
  longer.   Job 16:18

Deliverance of Israel

27In that day,
  the Lord will punish
  with his sword,   Ge 3:24
his fierce, great and
  powerful sword,
Leviathan the gliding
  serpent,   Job 3:8

ᵃ16 The meaning of the Hebrew for this clause is uncertain.

Leviathan the coiling
  serpent;
he will slay the monster of
  the sea.   Ps 68:30

2In that day—

"Sing about a fruitful
  vineyard: Jer 2:21
3 I, the LORD, watch over it;
  I water it continually. Isa 58:11
I guard it day and night
  so that no one may harm it.
4 I am not angry.
If only there were briers and
  thorns confronting me!
I would march against them
  in battle;
I would set them all on fire.
5Or else let them come to me
  for refuge;   Isa 25:4
let them make peace with
  me,   Job 22:21
yes, let them make peace
  with me."

6In days to come Jacob will
  take root,   2Ki 19:30
Israel will bud and blossom
and fill all the world with
  fruit.   Ps 72:16

7Has ˻the LORD˼ struck her
  as he struck down those
  who struck her?   Isa 10:26
Has she been killed
  as those were killed who
  killed her?
8By warfareª and exile you
  contend with her—
with his fierce blast he
  drives her out,   Isa 49:14

as on a day the east wind
  blows.   Ge 41:6
9By this, then, will Jacob's
  guilt be atoned for,
and this will be the full
  fruitage of the removal
  of his sin: Ro 11:27
When he makes all the altar
  stones
to be like chalk stones
  crushed to pieces,   Ex 23:24
no Asherah poles[b] or incense
  altars
will be left standing.   Lev 26:30
10The fortified city stands
  desolate,   Ge 1:2
an abandoned settlement,
  forsaken like the
  desert;
there the calves graze,
  there they lie down;   Isa 5:17
they strip its branches bare.
11When its twigs are dry, they
  are broken off   Isa 10:33
and women come and make
  fires with them.   Isa 33:12
For this is a people without
  understanding;   Dt 32:28
so their Maker has no
  compassion on them,
and their Creator shows
  them no favor.   Isa 9:17

12In that day the LORD will
thresh from the flowing Euphrates[c] to the Wadi of Egypt,
and you, O Israelites, will be
gathered up one by one. 13And
in that day a great trumpet will
sound. Those who were perishing in Assyria and those who
were exiled in Egypt will come

ª8 See Septuagint; the meaning of the Hebrew for this word is uncertain.   b9 That
is, symbols of the goddess Asherah   c12 Hebrew *River*

and worship the LORD on the holy mountain in Jerusalem.

Woe to Ephraim

28 Woe to that wreath, the pride of Ephraim's drunkards,   Isa 7:2
to the fading flower, his glorious beauty,
set on the head of a fertile valley—
to that city, the pride of those laid low by wine!
²See, the Lord has one who is powerful and strong.
Like a hailstorm and a destructive wind,   Isa 29:6
like a driving rain and a flooding downpour,
he will throw it forcefully to the ground.
³That wreath, the pride of Ephraim's drunkards,
will be trampled underfoot.
⁴That fading flower, his glorious beauty,
set on the head of a fertile valley,
will be like a fig ripe before harvest—   SS 2:13
as soon as someone sees it and takes it in his hand,
he swallows it.

⁵In that day the LORD Almighty   1Sa 10:20
will be a glorious crown,
a beautiful wreath
for the remnant of his people.   Isa 1:9
⁶He will be a spirit of justice

to him who sits in judgment,   Isa 4:4
a source of strength
to those who turn back the battle at the gate.   Jdg 9:44

⁷And these also stagger from wine
and reel from beer: Lev 10:9
Priests and prophets stagger from beer
and are befuddled with wine;   Isa 9:15
they reel from beer,
they stagger when seeing visions,   Isa 1:1
they stumble when rendering decisions.
⁸All the tables are covered with vomit
and there is not a spot without filth.   Jer 48:26

⁹"Who is it he is trying to teach?   Ps 32:8
To whom is he explaining his message?   Isa 52:7
To children weaned from their milk,   Heb 5:12-13
to those just taken from the breast?
¹⁰For it is:
Do and do, do and do,
rule on rule, rule on rule[a];
a little here, a little there."

¹¹Very well then, with foreign lips and strange tongues
God will speak to this people,   Eze 3:5
¹²to whom he said,
"This is the resting place,
let the weary rest";   Ex 14:14

---

[a]10 Hebrew / *sav lasav sav lasav* / *kav lakav kav lakav* (possibly meaningless sounds; perhaps a mimicking of the prophet's words); also in verse 13

and, "This is the place of
repose"—
but they would not listen.
¹³So then, the word of the
Lord to them will
become:
Do and do, do and do,
rule on rule, rule on rule;
a little here, a little there—
so that they will go and fall
backward,
be injured and snared and
captured.   Isa 8:15

¹⁴Therefore hear the word of
the Lord, you scoffers
who rule this people in
Jerusalem.   2Ch 36:16
¹⁵You boast, "We have entered
into a covenant with
death,   Job 5:23
with the grave[a] we have
made an agreement.
When an overwhelming
scourge sweeps by,
it cannot touch us,   Isa 8:7
for we have made a lie our
refuge
and falsehood[b] our hiding
place."   Jdg 9:35

¹⁶So this is what the Sover-
eign Lord says:

"See, I lay a stone in Zion,
a tested stone,   Isa 14:32
a precious cornerstone for a
sure foundation;   Jer 51:26
the one who trusts will
never be dismayed.
¹⁷I will make justice the
measuring line

and righteousness the
plumb line;   2Ki 21:13
hail will sweep away your
refuge, the lie,
and water will overflow
your hiding place.
¹⁸Your covenant with death
will be annulled;
your agreement with the
grave will not stand.
When the overwhelming
scourge sweeps by,
you will be beaten down
by it.   Isa 5:5
¹⁹As often as it comes it will
carry you away;   2Ki 24:2
morning after morning, by
day and by night,
it will sweep through."

The understanding of this
message
will bring sheer terror.
²⁰The bed is too short to
stretch out on,
the blanket too narrow to
wrap around you.
²¹The Lord will rise up as he
did at Mount Perazim,
he will rouse himself as in
the Valley of Gibeon—
to do his work, his strange
work,   Isa 10:12
and perform his task, his
alien task.
²²Now stop your mocking,
or your chains will become
heavier;   2Ch 36:16
the Lord, the Lord
Almighty, has told me
of the destruction decreed
against the whole land.

---

^a15 Hebrew *Sheol*; also in verse 18   ^b15 Or *false gods*

23Listen and hear my voice;
　　pay attention and hear
　　　what I say.　　Isa 32:9
24When a farmer plows for
　　planting, does he plow
　　continually?　　Ecc 3:2
　Does he keep on breaking
　　up and harrowing the
　　soil?
25When he has leveled the
　　surface,
　does he not sow caraway
　　and scatter cummin?
　Does he not plant wheat in
　　its place,*a*
　barley in its plot,*a*　　Ex 9:31
　and spelt in its field?　　Eze 4:9
26His God instructs him
　and teaches him the right
　　way.　　Ps 94:10

27Caraway is not threshed with
　　a sledge,　　Isa 21:10
　nor is a cartwheel rolled
　　over cummin;
　caraway is beaten out with a
　　rod,　　Isa 10:5
　and cummin with a stick.
28Grain must be ground to
　　make bread;
　so one does not go on
　　threshing it forever.
　Though he drives the wheels
　　of his threshing cart
　　over it,　　Isa 21:10
　his horses do not grind it.
29All this also comes from the
　　LORD Almighty,
　wonderful in counsel and
　　magnificent in
　　wisdom.

Woe to David's City

29 Woe to you, Ariel, Ariel,
　　the city where David
　　settled!　　2Sa 5:7
　Add year to year
　and let your cycle of
　　festivals go on.　　Isa 1:14
2Yet I will besiege Ariel;　　Isa 3:26
　she will mourn and lament,
　she will be to me like an
　　altar hearth.*b*　　Eze 43:15
3I will encamp against you all
　　around;
　I will encircle you with
　　towers
　and set up my siege works
　　against you.　　2Ki 25:1
4Brought low, you will speak
　　from the ground;
　your speech will mumble
　　out of the dust.　　Isa 8:19
　Your voice will come
　　ghostlike from the earth;
　out of the dust your speech
　　will whisper.　　Isa 26:16

5But your many enemies will
　　become like fine dust,
　the ruthless hordes like
　　blown chaff.　　Isa 17:13
　Suddenly, in an instant,
6　the LORD Almighty will
　　come
　with thunder and earthquake
　　and great noise,　　Mt 24:7
　with windstorm and
　　tempest and flames of a
　　devouring fire.　　Lev 10:2
7Then the hordes of all the
　　nations that fight against
　　Ariel,　　Mic 4:11-12

---

a25 The meaning of the Hebrew for this word is uncertain.　　*b2* The Hebrew for *altar hearth* sounds like the Hebrew for *Ariel*.

that attack her and her
  fortress and besiege her,
will be as it is with a dream,
  with a vision in the night—
8as when a hungry man
  dreams that he is eating,
but he awakens, and his
  hunger remains; Ps 73:20
as when a thirsty man
  dreams that he is
  drinking,
but he awakens faint, with
  his thirst unquenched.
So will it be with the hordes
  of all the nations
that fight against Mount
  Zion. Isa 17:12-14

9Be stunned and amazed,
  blind yourselves and be
  sightless; Isa 6:10
be drunk, but not from wine,
  stagger, but not from beer.
10The LORD has brought over
  you a deep sleep: Jdg 4:21
He has sealed your eyes
  (the prophets); Mic 3:6
he has covered your heads
  (the seers). 1Sa 9:9

11For you this whole vision is
nothing but words sealed in a
scroll. And if you give the scroll
to someone who can read, and
say to him, "Read this, please,"
he will answer, "I can't; it is
sealed." 12Or if you give the
scroll to someone who cannot
read, and say, "Read this,
please," he will answer, "I
don't know how to read." Isa 28:7

13The Lord says:

"These people come near to
  me with their mouth
and honor me with their
  lips, Ps 50:16
but their hearts are far from
  me. Ps 119:70
Their worship of me
  is made up only of rules
  taught by men. a Col 2:22
14Therefore once more I will
  astound these people
with wonder upon wonder;
the wisdom of the wise will
  perish,
  the intelligence of the
  intelligent will vanish."
15Woe to those who go to great
  depths
  to hide their plans from the
  LORD, Ge 3:8
who do their work in
  darkness and think,
  "Who sees us? Who will
  know?" 2Ki 21:16
16You turn things upside
  down,
  as if the potter were
  thought to be like the
  clay! Job 10:9
Shall what is formed say to
  him who formed it,
  "He did not make me"?
Can the pot say of the potter,
  "He knows nothing"?

17In a very short time, will not
  Lebanon be turned into
  a fertile field
and the fertile field seem
  like a forest? Isa 32:15
18In that day the deaf will hear
  the words of the scroll,

a13 Hebrew; Septuagint *They worship me in vain; / their teachings are but rules taught by men*

and out of gloom and
darkness
the eyes of the blind will
see.   Ps 146:8
¹⁹Once more the humble will
rejoice in the LORD;   Ps 25:9
the needy will rejoice in the
Holy One of Israel.   Ps 72:4
²⁰The ruthless will vanish,
the mockers will disappear,
and all who have an eye for
evil will be cut down—
²¹those who with a word make
a man out to be guilty,
who ensnare the defender
in court
and with false testimony
deprive the innocent of
justice.   Isa 5:23; 32:7

²²Therefore this is what the
LORD, who redeemed Abra-
ham, says to the house of Jacob:

"No longer will Jacob be
ashamed;   Ps 22:5
no longer will their faces
grow pale.   Jer 30:6
²³When they see among them
their children,   Isa 53:10
the work of my hands,
they will keep my name holy;
they will acknowledge the
holiness of the Holy One
of Jacob,   Isa 5:19
and will stand in awe of the
God of Israel.
²⁴Those who are wayward in
spirit will gain
understanding;   Isa 1:3
those who complain will
accept instruction."

Woe to the Obstinate Nation

30 "Woe to the obstinate
children,"   Dt 21:18
declares the LORD,
"to those who carry out
plans that are not mine,
forming an alliance, but not
by my Spirit,   2Ki 17:4
heaping sin upon sin;
²who go down to Egypt
without consulting me;
who look for help to
Pharaoh's protection,
to Egypt's shade for refuge.
³But Pharaoh's protection will
be to your shame,
Egypt's shade will bring
you disgrace.   Jdg 9:8-15
⁴Though they have officials in
Zoan   Nu 13:22
and their envoys have
arrived in Hanes,
⁵everyone will be put to
shame
because of a people useless
to them,   2Ki 18:21
who bring neither help nor
advantage,
but only shame and
disgrace."   Eze 17:15

⁶An oracle concerning the
animals of the Negev: Jdg 1:9

Through a land of hardship
and distress,   Ex 1:13
of lions and lionesses,
of adders and darting
snakes,   Dt 8:15
the envoys carry their riches
on donkeys' backs,   Ge 42:26
their treasures on the
humps of camels,

to that unprofitable nation,
7   to Egypt, whose help is
        utterly useless.   2Ki 18:21
Therefore I call her
Rahab the Do-Nothing.

⁸Go now, write it on a tablet
        for them,   Dt 27:8
    inscribe it on a scroll,   Ex 17:14
that for the days to come
it may be an everlasting
        witness.   Jos 24:26-27
⁹These are rebellious people,
    deceitful children,
children unwilling to listen
    to the LORD's
    instruction.   Isa 1:10
¹⁰They say to the seers,
    "See no more visions!" Jer 11:21
and to the prophets,
    "Give us no more visions of
    what is right!
Tell us pleasant things,   1Ki 22:8
    prophesy illusions.   Jer 23:26
¹¹Leave this way,
    get off this path,
and stop confronting us
    with the Holy One of
        Israel!"   Isa 29:19

¹²Therefore, this is what the
Holy One of Israel says: Isa 5:19

"Because you have rejected
    this message,   Isa 5:24
    relied on oppression
and depended on deceit,
¹³this sin will become for you
    like a high wall, cracked
        and bulging,   Ne 2:17
    that collapses suddenly, in
        an instant.   Isa 17:14
¹⁴It will break in pieces like
        pottery,   Ps 2:9
    shattered so mercilessly

that among its pieces not a
    fragment will be found
for taking coals from a
    hearth
or scooping water out of a
    cistern."

¹⁵This is what the Sovereign
LORD, the Holy One of Israel,
says: Jer 7:20

"In repentance and rest is
    your salvation,   Ex 14:14
in quietness and trust is
    your strength,   2Ch 20:12
but you would have none
    of it.   Isa 8:6
¹⁶You said, 'No, we will flee on
    horses.'   Dt 17:16
Therefore you will flee!
You said, 'We will ride off on
    swift horses.'
Therefore your pursuers
    will be swift!
¹⁷A thousand will flee
    at the threat of one;
at the threat of five   Lev 26:8
    you will all flee away,
till you are left
    like a flagstaff on a
        mountaintop,
    like a banner on a hill."

¹⁸Yet the LORD longs to be
    gracious to you;   Ge 43:31
he rises to show you
    compassion.   Ps 78:38
For the LORD is a God of
    justice.   Ps 11:7
Blessed are all who wait for
    him!   Ps 27:14

¹⁹O people of Zion, who live
in Jerusalem, you will weep no
more. How gracious he will be
when you cry for help! As soon

as he hears, he will answer you.
²⁰Although the Lord gives you the bread of adversity and the water of affliction, your teachers will be hidden no more; with your own eyes you will see them. ²¹Whether you turn to the right or to the left, your ears will hear a voice behind you, saying, "This is the way; walk in it." ²²Then you will defile your idols overlaid with silver and your images covered with gold; you will throw them away like a menstrual cloth and say to them, "Away with you!" Ps 50:15

²³He will also send you rain for the seed you sow in the ground, and the food that comes from the land will be rich and plentiful. In that day your cattle will graze in broad meadows. ²⁴The oxen and donkeys that work the soil will eat fodder and mash, spread out with fork and shovel. ²⁵In the day of great slaughter, when the towers fall, streams of water will flow on every high mountain and every lofty hill. ²⁶The moon will shine like the sun, and the sunlight will be seven times brighter, like the light of seven full days, when the Lord binds up the bruises of his people and heals the wounds he inflicted. Isa 62:8

²⁷See, the Name of the Lord
        comes from afar, 1Ki 18:24
    with burning anger and
        dense clouds of smoke;
his lips are full of wrath,
    and his tongue is a
        consuming fire. Job 41:21

²⁸His breath is like a rushing
        torrent, Ps 50:3
    rising up to the neck. Isa 8:8
He shakes the nations in the
        sieve of destruction; Am 9:9
he places in the jaws of the
        peoples
    a bit that leads them astray.
²⁹And you will sing
    as on the night you
        celebrate a holy festival;
your hearts will rejoice
    as when people go up with
        flutes 1Sa 10:5
to the mountain of the Lord,
    to the Rock of Israel. Ge 49:24
³⁰The Lord will cause men to
        hear his majestic voice
    and will make them see his
        arm coming down
with raging anger and
        consuming fire, Isa 4:4
    with cloudburst,
        thunderstorm and hail.
³¹The voice of the Lord will
        shatter Assyria; Isa 10:5
    with his scepter he will
        strike them down. Isa 11:4
³²Every stroke the Lord lays
        on them
    with his punishing rod
will be to the music of
        tambourines and harps,
    as he fights them in battle
        with the blows of his
        arm. Isa 11:15
³³Topheth has long been
        prepared; 2Ki 23:10
    it has been made ready for
        the king.
Its fire pit has been made
        deep and wide,
    with an abundance of fire
        and wood;

the breath of the LORD,
   like a stream of burning
      sulfur,
   sets it ablaze.   Isa 1:31

Woe to Those Who Rely on Egypt

31 Woe to those who go
         down to Egypt for help,
   who rely on horses,   Isa 30:16
   who trust in the multitude of
      their chariots   Isa 2:7
   and in the great strength of
      their horsemen,
   but do not look to the Holy
      One of Israel,   Job 6:10
   or seek help from the
      LORD.
² Yet he too is wise and can
      bring disaster;   Ps 92:5
   he does not take back his
      words.   Nu 23:19
   He will rise up against the
      house of the wicked,
   against those who help
      evildoers.   Isa 1:4
³ But the Egyptians are men
      and not God;   Ps 9:20
   their horses are flesh and
      not spirit.   Isa 30:16
   When the LORD stretches out
      his hand,   Ne 1:10
   he who helps will stumble,
   he who is helped will fall;
   both will perish together.

⁴ This is what the LORD says to
me:

   "As a lion growls,   Nu 24:9
   a great lion over his prey—
   and though a whole band of
      shepherds

is called together against
      him,   Jer 3:15
   he is not frightened by their
      shouts
   or disturbed by their
      clamor—   Ps 74:23
   so the LORD Almighty will
      come down   Isa 42:13
   to do battle on Mount Zion
      and on its heights.
⁵ Like birds hovering
      overhead,   Ge 1:2
   the LORD Almighty will
      shield Jerusalem;   Ps 91:4
   he will shield it and deliver
      it,   Ps 34:7
   he will 'pass over' it and
      will rescue it."   Ex 12:23

⁶ Return to him you have so
greatly revolted against, O Israelites. ⁷ For in that day every one
of you will reject the idols of silver and gold your sinful hands
have made.   Job 22:23; Isa 29:18

⁸ "Assyria will fall by a sword
      that is not of man;   Isa 10:12
   a sword, not of mortals,
      will devour them.   Ex 12:12
   They will flee before the
      sword
   and their young men will
      be put to forced labor.
⁹ Their stronghold will fall
      because of terror;   Dt 32:31
   at sight of the battle
      standard their
      commanders will
      panic,"   Jer 51:9
   declares the LORD,
   whose fire is in Zion,
   whose furnace is in
      Jerusalem.   Ps 21:9

The Kingdom of Righteousness

32 See, a king will reign in righteousness
and rulers will rule with justice. ^{Ps 72:1-4}
²Each man will be like a shelter from the wind
and a refuge from the storm, ^{Ps 55:8}
like streams of water in the desert
and the shadow of a great rock in a thirsty land.

³Then the eyes of those who see will no longer be closed, ^{Isa 29:18}
and the ears of those who hear will listen. ^{Dt 29:4}
⁴The mind of the rash will know and understand,
and the stammering tongue will be fluent and clear.
⁵No longer will the fool be called noble
nor the scoundrel be highly respected. ^{1Sa 25:25}
⁶For the fool speaks folly,
his mind is busy with evil:
He practices ungodliness
and spreads error ^{Isa 3:12}
concerning the LORD;
the hungry he leaves empty
and from the thirsty he withholds water.
⁷The scoundrel's methods are wicked, ^{Jer 5:26-28}
he makes up evil schemes
to destroy the poor with lies,
even when the plea of the needy is just. ^{Isa 29:21}

⁸But the noble man makes noble plans,
and by noble deeds he stands. ^{Isa 14:24}

The Women of Jerusalem

⁹You women who are so complacent, ^{Isa 4:1}
rise up and listen to me;
you daughters who feel secure,
hear what I have to say!
¹⁰In little more than a year
you who feel secure will tremble;
the grape harvest will fail,
and the harvest of fruit will not come. ^{Isa 5:5-6}
¹¹Tremble, you complacent women; ^{Isa 33:14}
shudder, you daughters who feel secure!
Strip off your clothes,
put sackcloth around your waists. ^{Isa 3:24}
¹²Beat your breasts for the pleasant fields, ^{Na 2:7}
for the fruitful vines
¹³and for the land of my people,
a land overgrown with thorns and briers— ^{Isa 5:6}
yes, mourn for all houses of merriment ^{Isa 24:11}
and for this city of revelry.
¹⁴The fortress will be abandoned, ^{Isa 13:22}
the noisy city deserted;
citadel and watchtower will become a wasteland forever,
the delight of donkeys, a pasture for flocks,

¹⁵till the Spirit is poured upon
us from on high,
and the desert becomes a
fertile field, _{Ps 107:35}
and the fertile field seems
like a forest. _{Isa 29:17}
¹⁶Justice will dwell in the
desert _{Isa 9:7}
and righteousness live in
the fertile field. _{Ps 48:1}
¹⁷The fruit of righteousness
will be peace; _{Ps 85:10}
the effect of righteousness
will be quietness and
confidence forever._{Isa 30:15}
¹⁸My people will live in
peaceful dwelling
places, _{Isa 2:4}
in secure homes, _{Isa 26:1}
in undisturbed places of
rest. _{Jos 1:13}
¹⁹Though hail flattens the
forest _{Isa 28:17}
and the city is leveled
completely, _{Job 40:11}
²⁰how blessed you will be,
sowing your seed by every
stream, _{Dt 28:12}
and letting your cattle and
donkeys range free.

Distress and Help

33 Woe to you,
O destroyer, _{2Ki 19:21}
you who have not been
destroyed!
Woe to you, O traitor,
you who have not been
betrayed!
When you stop destroying,
you will be destroyed; _{Isa 31:8}

when you stop betraying,
you will be betrayed. _{Isa 21:2}

²O LORD, be gracious to us;
we long for you. _{Ge 43:29}
Be our strength every
morning,
our salvation in time of
distress. _{Ps 13:5}
³At the thunder of your voice,
the peoples flee; _{Ps 68:1}
when you rise up, the
nations scatter. _{Nu 10:35}
⁴Your plunder, O nations, is
harvested as by young
locusts; _{Joel 1:4}
like a swarm of locusts men
pounce on it.

⁵The LORD is exalted, for he
dwells on high; _{Isa 5:16}
he will fill Zion with justice
and righteousness. _{Isa 1:26}
⁶He will be the sure
foundation for your
times,
a rich store of salvation and
wisdom and knowledge;
the fear of the LORD is the
key to this treasure. ^a

⁷Look, their brave men cry
aloud in the streets;
the envoys of peace weep
bitterly. _{2Ki 18:37}
⁸The highways are deserted,
no travelers are on the
roads. _{Jdg 5:6}
The treaty is broken,
its witnesses^b are despised,
no one is respected. _{2Ki 18:14}
⁹The land mourns^c and
wastes away, _{Isa 3:26}

^a6 Or *is a treasure from him*   ^b8 Dead Sea Scrolls; Masoretic Text / *the cities*   ^c9 Or
dries up

Lebanon is ashamed and
    withers;   Isa 15:6
Sharon is like the Arabah,
    and Bashan and Carmel
        drop their leaves.   Mic 7:14

¹⁰"Now will I arise," says the
    LORD.   Isa 2:21
"Now will I be exalted; Isa 5:16
now will I be lifted up.
¹¹You conceive chaff,
    you give birth to straw;
    your breath is a fire that
        consumes you.   Isa 1:31
¹²The peoples will be burned
    as if to lime;   Am 2:1
    like cut thornbushes they
        will be set ablaze." Isa 10:17

¹³You who are far away, hear
    what I have done;   Ps 48:10
    you who are near,
        acknowledge my power!
¹⁴The sinners in Zion are
    terrified;   Isa 1:28
    trembling grips the godless:
"Who of us can dwell with
    the consuming fire?
Who of us can dwell with
    everlasting burning?"
¹⁵He who walks righteously
    and speaks what is right,
    who rejects gain from
        extortion   Eze 22:13
    and keeps his hand from
        accepting bribes,   Pr 15:27
    who stops his ears against
        plots of murder
    and shuts his eyes against
        contemplating evil—
¹⁶this is the man who will
    dwell on the heights,
    whose refuge will be the
        mountain fortress. Isa 26:1

His bread will be supplied,
    and water will not fail him.

¹⁷Your eyes will see the king in
    his beauty   Isa 4:2
    and view a land that
        stretches afar.   Isa 26:15
¹⁸In your thoughts you will
    ponder the former
        terror: Isa 17:14
"Where is that chief officer?
Where is the one who took
    the revenue?
Where is the officer in
    charge of the towers?"
¹⁹You will see those arrogant
    people no more,   Ps 5:5
    those people of an obscure
        speech,
    with their strange,
        incomprehensible
        tongue.   Ge 11:7

²⁰Look upon Zion, the city of
    our festivals;   Ps 125:1
    your eyes will see
        Jerusalem,
    a peaceful abode, a tent that
        will not be moved; Ps 46:5
    its stakes will never be pulled
        up,
    nor any of its ropes broken.
²¹There the LORD will be our
    Mighty One.   Isa 10:34
    It will be like a place of
        broad rivers and
        streams.   Ex 17:6
No galley with oars will ride
    them,
    no mighty ship will sail
        them.   Isa 23:1
²²For the LORD is our judge,
    the LORD is our lawgiver,
    the LORD is our king; Ps 89:18
    it is he who will save us.

23Your rigging hangs loose:
   The mast is not held secure,
   the sail is not spread.
Then an abundance of spoils
   will be divided
and even the lame will
   carry off plunder.   2Ki 7:8
24No one living in Zion will
   say, "I am ill";   Isa 30:26
and the sins of those who
   dwell there will be
   forgiven.   Nu 23:21

Judgment Against the Nations

34 Come near, you nations,
      and listen;   Isa 33:13
pay attention, you peoples!
Let the earth hear, and all
   that is in it,
   the world, and all that
   comes out of it!   Ps 24:1
2The LORD is angry with all
   nations;
his wrath is upon all their
   armies.   Isa 10:25
He will totally destroy[a] them,
   he will give them over to
   slaughter.   Isa 30:25
3Their slain will be thrown
   out,
   their dead bodies will send
   up a stench;   Joel 2:20
the mountains will be
   soaked with their blood.
4All the stars of the heavens
   will be dissolved   Job 9:7
and the sky rolled up like a
   scroll;   Isa 38:12
all the starry host will fall

like withered leaves from
   the vine,   Job 8:12
like shriveled figs from the
   fig tree.
5My sword has drunk its fill in
   the heavens;   Dt 32:41-42
see, it descends in
   judgment on Edom,
   the people I have totally
   destroyed.   Dt 13:15
6The sword of the LORD is
   bathed in blood,   Isa 27:1
it is covered with fat—
the blood of lambs and goats,
   fat from the kidneys of
   rams.
For the LORD has a sacrifice
   in Bozrah
and a great slaughter in
   Edom.   Isa 30:25
7And the wild oxen will fall
   with them,   Nu 23:22
   the bull calves and the great
   bulls.   Ps 68:30
Their land will be drenched
   with blood,   2Sa 1:22
and the dust will be soaked
   with fat.

8For the LORD has a day of
   vengeance,   Isa 1:24
a year of retribution, to
   uphold Zion's cause.
9Edom's streams will be
   turned into pitch,
her dust into burning
   sulfur;   Ge 19:24
her land will become
   blazing pitch!
10It will not be quenched night
   and day;   Isa 1:31

---

a2 The Hebrew term refers to the irrevocable giving over of things or persons to the LORD, often by totally destroying them; also in verse 5.

its smoke will rise forever.
From generation to
    generation it will lie
    desolate;   Isa 13:20
no one will ever pass
    through it again.
[11]The desert owl[a] and screech
    owl[a] will possess it;
the great owl[a] and the
    raven will nest there.
God will stretch out over
    Edom
the measuring line of
    chaos
and the plumb line of
    desolation.   2Ki 21:13
[12]Her nobles will have nothing
    there to be called a
    kingdom,
all her princes will vanish
    away.   Isa 29:20
[13]Thorns will overrun her
    citadels,
nettles and brambles her
    strongholds.   Isa 13:22
She will become a haunt for
    jackals,
a home for owls.   Lev 11:16-18
[14]Desert creatures will meet
    with hyenas,   Isa 13:22
and wild goats will bleat to
    each other;
there the night creatures will
    also repose   Rev 18:2
and find for themselves
    places of rest.
[15]The owl will nest there and
    lay eggs,
she will hatch them, and
    care for her young under
    the shadow of her
    wings;   Ps 17:8

there also the falcons will
    gather,
each with its mate.   Dt 14:13
[16]Look in the scroll of the
LORD and read: Isa 30:8

None of these will be
    missing,   Isa 40:26
not one will lack her mate.
For it is his mouth that has
    given the order,
and his Spirit will gather
    them together.   Isa 1:20
[17]He allots their portions;
his hand distributes them
    by measure.   Isa 17:14
They will possess it forever
and dwell there from
    generation to
    generation.

Joy of the Redeemed

35 The desert and the
    parched land will be
    glad;   Isa 27:10
the wilderness will rejoice
    and blossom.   Isa 27:6
Like the crocus, [2]it will burst
    into bloom;   SS:21
it will rejoice greatly and
    shout for joy.   Ge 21:6
The glory of Lebanon will be
    given to it,   Ezr 3:7
the splendor of Carmel and
    Sharon;   1Ch 27:29
they will see the glory of the
    LORD,   Ex 16:7
the splendor of our God.

[3]Strengthen the feeble hands,
    steady the knees that give
    way;   Job 4:4

---

[a]11 The precise identification of these birds is uncertain.

⁴say to those with fearful
hearts,
"Be strong, do not fear;
your God will come,
he will come with
vengeance;   Isa 1:24
with divine retribution
he will come to save you."

⁵Then will the eyes of the
blind be opened   Ps 146:8
and the ears of the deaf
unstopped.
⁶Then will the lame leap like a
deer,   2Sa 22:34
and the mute tongue shout
for joy.   Ps 20:5
Water will gush forth in the
wilderness
and streams in the desert.
⁷The burning sand will
become a pool,
the thirsty ground bubbling
springs.   Ps 107:35
In the haunts where jackals
once lay,
grass and reeds and
papyrus will grow.   Job 8:11

⁸And a highway will be there;
it will be called the Way of
Holiness.   Isa 4:3
The unclean will not journey
on it;   Isa 52:1
it will be for those who
walk in that Way;
wicked fools will not go
about on it. ᵃ
⁹No lion will be there,   Isa 30:6
nor will any ferocious beast
get up on it;   Isa 11:6
they will not be found
there.

But only the redeemed will
walk there,   Ex 6:6
10 and the ransomed of the
LORD will return.   Job 19:25
They will enter Zion with
singing;   Isa 30:29
everlasting joy will crown
their heads.   Ps 4:7
Gladness and joy will
overtake them,   Ps 51:8
and sorrow and sighing will
flee away.   Isa 30:19

Sennacherib Threatens Jerusalem

36 In the fourteenth year of
King Hezekiah's reign,
Sennacherib king of Assyria attacked all the fortified cities of
Judah and captured them.
²Then the king of Assyria sent
his field commander with a
large army from Lachish to King
Hezekiah at Jerusalem. When
the commander stopped at the
aqueduct of the Upper Pool, on
the road to the Washerman's
Field, ³Eliakim son of Hilkiah
the palace administrator, Shebna the secretary, and Joah son
of Asaph the recorder went out
to him.   2Ki 18:9; Isa 22:20-21

⁴The field commander said to
them, "Tell Hezekiah,

" 'This is what the great
king, the king of Assyria,
says: On what are you
basing this confidence
of yours? ⁵You say you
have strategy and military
strength—but you speak

ᵃ8 Or / the simple will not stray from it

only empty words. On whom are you depending, that you rebel against me? [6]Look now, you are depending on Egypt, that splintered reed of a staff, which pierces a man's hand and wounds him if he leans on it! Such is Pharaoh king of Egypt to all who depend on him. [7]And if you say to me, "We are depending on the Lord our God"—isn't he the one whose high places and altars Hezekiah removed, saying to Judah and Jerusalem, "You must worship before this altar"?

[8]" 'Come now, make a bargain with my master, the king of Assyria: I will give you two thousand horses—if you can put riders on them! [9]How then can you repulse one officer of the least of my master's officials, even though you are depending on Egypt for chariots and horsemen? [10]Furthermore, have I come to attack and destroy this land without the Lord? The Lord himself told me to march against this country and destroy it.' "   Ps 20:7

[11]Then Eliakim, Shebna and Joah said to the field commander, "Please speak to your servants in Aramaic, since we understand it. Don't speak to us in Hebrew in the hearing of the people on the wall."   Ezr 4:7

[12]But the commander replied, "Was it only to your master and you that my master sent me to say these things, and not to the men sitting on the wall—who, like you, will have to eat their own filth and drink their own urine?"   2Ki 6:25; Eze 4:12

[13]Then the commander stood and called out in Hebrew, "Hear the words of the great king, the king of Assyria! [14]This is what the king says: Do not let Hezekiah deceive you. He cannot deliver you! [15]Do not let Hezekiah persuade you to trust in the Lord when he says, 'The Lord will surely deliver us; this city will not be given into the hand of the king of Assyria.'

[16]"Do not listen to Hezekiah. This is what the king of Assyria says: Make peace with me and come out to me. Then every one of you will eat from his own vine and fig tree and drink water from his own cistern, [17]until I come and take you to a land like your own—a land of grain and new wine, a land of bread and vineyards.   1Ki 4:25

[18]"Do not let Hezekiah mislead you when he says, 'The Lord will deliver us.' Has the god of any nation ever delivered his land from the hand of the king of Assyria? [19]Where are the gods of Hamath and Arpad? Where are the gods of Sepharvaim? Have they rescued Samaria from my hand? [20]Who of all the gods of these countries has been able to save his land from me? How then can the

LORD deliver Jerusalem from my hand?"   2Ki 17:24; 18:34

²¹But the people remained silent and said nothing in reply, because the king had commanded, "Do not answer him."

²²Then Eliakim son of Hilkiah the palace administrator, Shebna the secretary, and Joah son of Asaph the recorder went to Hezekiah, with their clothes torn, and told him what the field commander had said.

Jerusalem's Deliverance Foretold

37 When King Hezekiah heard this, he tore his clothes and put on sackcloth and went into the temple of the LORD. ²He sent Eliakim the palace administrator, Shebna the secretary, and the leading priests, all wearing sackcloth, to the prophet Isaiah son of Amoz. ³They told him, "This is what Hezekiah says: This day is a day of distress and rebuke and disgrace, as when children come to the point of birth and there is no strength to deliver them. ⁴It may be that the LORD your God will hear the words of the field commander, whom his master, the king of Assyria, has sent to ridicule the living God, and that he will rebuke him for the words the LORD your God has heard. Therefore pray for the remnant that still survives."

⁵When King Hezekiah's officials came to Isaiah, ⁶Isaiah said to them, "Tell your master, 'This is what the LORD says: Do not be afraid of what you have heard—those words with which the underlings of the king of Assyria have blasphemed me. ⁷Listen! I am going to put a spirit in him so that when he hears a certain report, he will return to his own country, and there I will have him cut down with the sword.' "

⁸When the field commander heard that the king of Assyria had left Lachish, he withdrew and found the king fighting against Libnah.   Nu 33:20; Jos 10:3

⁹Now Sennacherib received a report that Tirhakah, the Cushite*ᵃ* king of Egypt, was marching out to fight against him. When he heard it, he sent messengers to Hezekiah with this word: ¹⁰"Say to Hezekiah king of Judah: Do not let the god you depend on deceive you when he says, 'Jerusalem will not be handed over to the king of Assyria.' ¹¹Surely you have heard what the kings of Assyria have done to all the countries, destroying them completely. And will you be delivered? ¹²Did the gods of the nations that were destroyed by my forefathers deliver them—the gods of Gozan, Haran, Rezeph and the people of Eden who were in Tel Assar? ¹³Where is the king of Hamath, the king of Arpad, the king of the city of Sepharvaim, or of Hena or Ivvah?"   2Ch 32:1,11,15

ᵃ 9 That is, from the upper Nile region

Hezekiah's Prayer

¹⁴Hezekiah received the letter from the messengers and read it. Then he went up to the temple of the LORD and spread it out before the LORD. ¹⁵And Hezekiah prayed to the LORD: ¹⁶"O LORD Almighty, God of Israel, enthroned between the cherubim, you alone are God over all the kingdoms of the earth. You have made heaven and earth. ¹⁷Give ear, O LORD, and hear; open your eyes, O LORD, and see; listen to all the words Sennacherib has sent to insult the living God. 2Ch 32:17

¹⁸"It is true, O LORD, that the Assyrian kings have laid waste all these peoples and their lands. ¹⁹They have thrown their gods into the fire and destroyed them, for they were not gods but only wood and stone, fashioned by human hands. ²⁰Now, O LORD our God, deliver us from his hand, so that all kingdoms on earth may know that you alone, O LORD, are God.ᵃ"

Sennacherib's Fall

²¹Then Isaiah son of Amoz sent a message to Hezekiah: "This is what the LORD, the God of Israel, says: Because you have prayed to me concerning Sennacherib king of Assyria, ²²this is the word the LORD has spoken against him:

"The Virgin Daughter of
  Zion   Isa 10:32
despises and mocks you.
The Daughter of Jerusalem
  tosses her head as you flee.
²³Who is it you have insulted
  and blasphemed?   Nu 15:30
Against whom have you
  raised your voice
and lifted your eyes in pride?
Against the Holy One of
  Israel!   Isa 1:4
²⁴By your messengers
  you have heaped insults on
  the Lord.
And you have said,
  'With my many chariots
I have ascended the heights
  of the mountains,
  the utmost heights of
  Lebanon.   1Ki 7:2
I have cut down its tallest
  cedars,
  the choicest of its pines.
I have reached its remotest
  heights,
  the finest of its forests.
²⁵I have dug wells in foreign
  landsᵇ
and drunk the water there.
With the soles of my feet
I have dried up all the
  streams of Egypt.'   Dt 11:10

²⁶"Have you not heard?
  Long ago I ordained it. Ac 2:23
In days of old I planned it;
  now I have brought it to
  pass,
that you have turned fortified
  cities

ᵃ20 Dead Sea Scrolls (see also 2 Kings 19:19); Masoretic Text *alone are the LORD*
ᵇ25 Dead Sea Scrolls (see also 2 Kings 19:24); Masoretic Text does not have *in foreign lands.*

into piles of stone.   Dt 13:16
27Their people, drained of
    power,
are dismayed and put to
    shame.
They are like plants in the
    field,
like tender green shoots,
like grass sprouting on the
    roof,   Ps 129:6
scorched[a] before it grows
    up.

28"But I know where you stay
and when you come and go
and how you rage against
    me.   Ps 2:1
29Because you rage against me
and because your insolence
    has reached my ears,
I will put my hook in your
    nose   2Ch 33:11
and my bit in your mouth,
and I will make you return
by the way you came.

30"This will be the sign for
you, O Hezekiah: Isa 20:3

"This year you will eat what
    grows by itself,   Isa 32:10
and the second year what
    springs from that.
But in the third year sow and
    reap,
plant vineyards and eat
    their fruit.   Ps 107:37
31Once more a remnant of the
    house of Judah
will take root below and
    bear fruit above.   Isa 27:6

32For out of Jerusalem will
    come a remnant,   Isa 11:11
and out of Mount Zion a
    band of survivors.   Isa 1:9
The zeal of the LORD
    Almighty
will accomplish this.   Isa 9:7

33"Therefore this is what the
LORD says concerning the king
of Assyria:

"He will not enter this city
    or shoot an arrow here.
He will not come before it
    with shield
or build a siege ramp
    against it.   2Sa 20:15
34By the way that he came he
    will return;
    he will not enter this city,"
        declares the LORD.
35"I will defend this city and
    save it,   Isa 31:5
    for my sake and for the
    sake of David my
    servant!"   1Ch 17:19

36Then the angel of the LORD
went out and put to death a
hundred and eighty-five thousand men in the Assyrian camp.
When the people got up the
next morning—there were all
the dead bodies! 37So Sennacherib king of Assyria broke camp
and withdrew. He returned to
Nineveh and stayed there.
    38One day, while he was wor-
shiping in the temple of his god
Nisroch, his sons Adrammelech

---

a27 Some manuscripts of the Masoretic Text, Dead Sea Scrolls and some Septuagint
manuscripts (see also 2 Kings 19:26); most manuscripts of the Masoretic Text *roofs and
terraced fields*

and Sharezer cut him down with the sword, and they escaped to the land of Ararat. And Esarhaddon his son succeeded him as king. Ge 8:4; Jer 51:27

Hezekiah's Illness

38 In those days Hezekiah became ill and was at the point of death. The prophet Isaiah son of Amoz went to him and said, "This is what the LORD says: Put your house in order, because you are going to die; you will not recover."

²Hezekiah turned his face to the wall and prayed to the LORD, ³"Remember, O LORD, how I have walked before you faithfully and with wholehearted devotion and have done what is good in your eyes." And Hezekiah wept bitterly.

⁴Then the word of the LORD came to Isaiah: ⁵"Go and tell Hezekiah, 'This is what the LORD, the God of your father David, says: I have heard your prayer and seen your tears; I will add fifteen years to your life. ⁶And I will deliver you and this city from the hand of the king of Assyria. I will defend this city. 1Sa 13:13; Isa 31:5

⁷" 'This is the LORD's sign to you that the LORD will do what he has promised: ⁸I will make the shadow cast by the sun go back the ten steps it has gone down on the stairway of Ahaz.' " So the sunlight went back the ten steps it had gone down. Ge 24:14; Jos 10:13

⁹A writing of Hezekiah king of Judah after his illness and recovery:

¹⁰I said, "In the prime of my life
    must I go through the gates
        of death*ᵃ* Job 17:16
and be robbed of the rest of
        my years?" Job 17:11
¹¹I said, "I will not again see
        the LORD,
    the LORD, in the land of the
        living; Job 28:13
no longer will I look on
        mankind,
    or be with those who now
        dwell in this world.ᵇ
¹²Like a shepherd's tent my
        house
    has been pulled down and
        taken from me. Isa 33:20
Like a weaver I have rolled
        up my life, Isa 34:4
    and he has cut me off from
        the loom; Nu 11:15
    day and night you made an
        end of me. Ps 32:4
¹³I waited patiently till dawn,
    but like a lion he broke all
        my bones; Job 10:16
    day and night you made an
        end of me.
¹⁴I cried like a swift or thrush,
    I moaned like a mourning
        dove. Ge 8:8
    My eyes grew weak as I
        looked to the heavens.

ᵃ10 Hebrew *Sheol*   ᵇ11 A few Hebrew manuscripts; most Hebrew manuscripts *in the place of cessation*

I am troubled; O Lord,
　　come to my aid!''　　Ge 50:24

15But what can I say?　　2Sa 7:20
　He has spoken to me, and
　　he himself has done
　　this.　　Ps 39:9
　I will walk humbly all my
　　years
　because of this anguish of
　　my soul.　　Job 7:11
16Lord, by such things men
　　live;
　and my spirit finds life in
　　them too.
　You restored me to health
　　and let me live.　　Ps 119:25
17Surely it was for my benefit
　　that I suffered such
　　anguish.　　Ps 119:71
　In your love you kept me
　　from the pit of destruction;
　you have put all my sins
　　behind your back.　　Ps 103:12
18For the grave*a* cannot praise
　　you,
　death cannot sing your
　　praise;　　Ps 6:5
　those who go down to the pit
　　cannot hope for your
　　faithfulness.
19The living, the living—they
　　praise you,　　Ps 118:17
　as I am doing today;
　fathers tell their children
　　about your faithfulness.

20The Lord will save me,
　　and we will sing with
　　　stringed instruments
　all the days of our lives
　　in the temple of the Lord.
21Isaiah had said, ''Prepare a

poultice of figs and apply it to
the boil, and he will recover.''
22Hezekiah had asked, ''What
will be the sign that I will go up
to the temple of the Lord?''

Envoys From Babylon

39 At that time Merodach-
Baladan son of Baladan
king of Babylon sent Hezekiah
letters and a gift, because he
had heard of his illness and
recovery. 2Hezekiah received
the envoys gladly and showed
them what was in his storehouses—the silver, the gold,
the spices, the fine oil, his entire
armory and everything found
among his treasures. There was
nothing in his palace or in all his
kingdom that Hezekiah did not
show them.　　2Ch 32:31
3Then Isaiah the prophet
went to King Hezekiah and
asked, ''What did those men
say, and where did they come
from?''
　''From a distant land,'' Hezekiah replied. ''They came to me
from Babylon.''　　Dt 28:49
4The prophet asked, ''What
did they see in your palace?''
　''They saw everything in my
palace,'' Hezekiah said. ''There
is nothing among my treasures
that I did not show them.''
5Then Isaiah said to Hezekiah, ''Hear the word of the
Lord Almighty: 6The time will
surely come when everything in
your palace, and all that your
fathers have stored up until this

day, will be carried off to Babylon. Nothing will be left, says the LORD. 7And some of your descendants, your own flesh and blood who will be born to you, will be taken away, and they will become eunuchs in the palace of the king of Babylon."

8"The word of the LORD you have spoken is good," Hezekiah replied. For he thought, "There will be peace and security in my lifetime." Jdg 10:15

Comfort for God's People

40 Comfort, comfort my people, Isa 12:1
says your God.
2Speak tenderly to Jerusalem,
and proclaim to her
that her hard service has
been completed, Isa 49:25
that her sin has been paid
for, Lev 26:41
that she has received from
the LORD's hand
double for all her sins. Isa 51:19

3A voice of one calling:
"In the desert prepare
the way for the LORDª;
make straight in the
wilderness
a highway for our God. b
4Every valley shall be raised
up, Isa 49:11
every mountain and hill
made low; Isa 2:14
the rough ground shall
become level, Ps 26:12
the rugged places a plain.

5And the glory of the LORD
will be revealed, Ex 16:7
and all mankind together
will see it. Isa 52:10
For the mouth of the
LORD has spoken."

6A voice says, "Cry out."
And I said, "What shall I
cry?"

"All men are like grass,
and all their glory is like the
flowers of the field.
7The grass withers and the
flowers fall, Job 8:12
because the breath of the
LORD blows on them.
Surely the people are grass.
8The grass withers and the
flowers fall, Isa 5:24
but the word of our God
stands forever." Ps 119:89

9You who bring good tidings
to Zion, Isa 41:27
go up on a high mountain.
You who bring good tidings
to Jerusalem, c Isa 1:1
lift up your voice with a
shout,
lift it up, do not be afraid;
say to the towns of Judah,
"Here is your God!" Isa 25:9
10See, the Sovereign LORD
comes with power, Isa 28:2
and his arm rules for him.
See, his reward is with him,
and his recompense
accompanies him. Isa 35:4
11He tends his flock like a
shepherd: Ge 48:15

ª3 Or *A voice of one calling in the desert:* / *"Prepare the way for the LORD*   b3 Hebrew;
Septuagint *make straight the paths of our God*   c9 Or *O Zion, bringer of good tidings,* / *go
up on a high mountain.* / *O Jerusalem, bringer of good tidings*

He gathers the lambs in his
    arms   Nu 11:12
and carries them close to his
    heart;   Dt 26:19
    he gently leads those that
    have young.   Ge 33:13

¹²Who has measured the
    waters in the hollow of
    his hand,   Pr 30:4
    or with the breadth of his
    hand marked off the
    heavens?   Job 38:5
Who has held the dust of the
    earth in a basket,
    or weighed the mountains
    on the scales
and the hills in a balance?
¹³Who has understood the
    mind*a* of the LORD,
    or instructed him as his
    counselor?   Job 15:8
¹⁴Whom did the LORD consult
    to enlighten him,
    and who taught him the
    right way?
Who was it that taught him
    knowledge   Job 21:22
    or showed him the path of
    understanding?   Job 12:13

¹⁵Surely the nations are like a
    drop in a bucket;
    they are regarded as dust
    on the scales;   Ps 62:9
    he weighs the islands as
    though they were fine
    dust.   Dt 9:21
¹⁶Lebanon is not sufficient for
    altar fires,   Isa 33:9
    nor its animals enough for
    burnt offerings.   Ps 50:9-11

¹⁷Before him all the nations are
    as nothing;   Job 12:19
    they are regarded by him as
    worthless
    and less than nothing. Isa 37:19
¹⁸To whom, then, will you
    compare God?   Ex 8:10
    What image will you
    compare him to?   Dt 4:15
¹⁹As for an idol, a craftsman
    casts it,   Ex 20:4
    and a goldsmith overlays it
    with gold   Isa 2:20
    and fashions silver chains
    for it.
²⁰A man too poor to present
    such an offering
    selects wood that will not
    rot.   Isa 44:19
    He looks for a skilled
    craftsman
    to set up an idol that will
    not topple.   1Sa 5:3

²¹Do you not know?
    Have you not heard?   2Ki 19:25
    Has it not been told you from
    the beginning?   Ge 1:1
    Have you not understood
    since the earth was
    founded?   Isa 48:13
²²He sits enthroned above the
    circle of the earth,   2Ch 6:18
    and its people are like
    grasshoppers.   Nu 13:33
    He stretches out the heavens
    like a canopy,   Ge 1:8
    and spreads them out like a
    tent to live in.   Job 36:29
²³He brings princes to naught
    and reduces the rulers of
    this world to nothing.

^a13 Or *Spirit;* or *spirit*

²⁴No sooner are they planted,
  no sooner are they sown,
  no sooner do they take root
    in the ground,   Job 5:3
than he blows on them and
    they wither,   Job 8:12
and a whirlwind sweeps
    them away like chaff.

²⁵"To whom will you compare
    me?   1Sa 2:2
  Or who is my equal?" says
    the Holy One.   Isa 1:4
²⁶Lift your eyes and look to the
    heavens: Isa 51:6
Who created all these?
He who brings out the starry
    host one by one,   2Ki 17:16
and calls them each by
    name.
Because of his great power
    and mighty strength,
not one of them is missing.

²⁷Why do you say, O Jacob,
  and complain, O Israel,
  "My way is hidden from the
    LORD;
  my cause is disregarded by
    my God"?   Job 6:29
²⁸Do you not know?
  Have you not heard?
The LORD is the everlasting
    God,   Dt 33:27
the Creator of the ends of
    the earth.   Isa 37:16
He will not grow tired or
    weary,   Isa 44:12
and his understanding no
    one can fathom.   Ps 147:5
²⁹He gives strength to the
    weary   Isa 50:4

and increases the power of
    the weak.
³⁰Even youths grow tired and
    weary,
  and young men stumble
    and fall;   Ps 20:8
³¹but those who hope in the
    LORD
  will renew their strength.
They will soar on wings like
    eagles;   Ex 19:4
they will run and not grow
    weary,
they will walk and not be
    faint.   2Co 4:1

The Helper of Israel

41 "Be silent before me,
  you islands!   Isa 11:11
Let the nations renew their
    strength!   1Sa 2:4
Let them come forward and
    speak;   Isa 48:16
let us meet together at the
    place of judgment.

²"Who has stirred up one
    from the east,   Isa 13:4
  calling him in righteousness
    to his service^a?   Isa 44:28
He hands nations over to
    him
  and subdues kings before
    him.
He turns them to dust with
    his sword,   2Sa 22:43
to windblown chaff with his
    bow.   Isa 13:18
³He pursues them and moves
    on unscathed,   Da 8:4
by a path his feet have not
    traveled before.

^a2 Or / whom victory meets at every step

⁴Who has done this and
    carried it through,
  calling forth the generations
    from the beginning?
  I, the LORD—with the first of
    them
  and with the last—I am
    he."   Dt 32:39; Isa 44:6

⁵The islands have seen it and
    fear;   Isa 11:11
  the ends of the earth
    tremble.
  They approach and come
    forward;
6   each helps the other
  and says to his brother, "Be
    strong!"   Jos 1:6
⁷The craftsman encourages
    the goldsmith,   Isa 40:19
  and he who smooths with
    the hammer
  spurs on him who strikes
    the anvil.
  He says of the welding, "It is
    good."
  He nails down the idol so it
    will not topple.   1Sa 5:3

⁸"But you, O Israel, my
    servant,   Ps 136:22
  Jacob, whom I have chosen,
  you descendants of
    Abraham my friend,
⁹I took you from the ends of
    the earth,   Isa 11:12
  from its farthest corners I
    called you.
  I said, 'You are my servant';
  I have chosen you and have
    not rejected you.   Dt 7:6
¹⁰So do not fear, for I am with
    you;   Dt 3:22
  do not be dismayed, for I
    am your God.

I will strengthen you and
    help you;   Ps 68:35
  I will uphold you with my
    righteous right hand.

¹¹"All who rage against you
  will surely be ashamed and
    disgraced;   Isa 29:22
  those who oppose you
  will be as nothing and
    perish.   Ex 23:22
¹²Though you search for your
    enemies,
  you will not find them.
  Those who wage war against
    you
  will be as nothing at all.
¹³For I am the LORD, your God,
  who takes hold of your
    right hand   Ps 73:23
  and says to you, Do not fear;
  I will help you.
¹⁴Do not be afraid, O worm
    Jacob,   Ge 15:1
  O little Israel,
  for I myself will help you,"
    declares the LORD,
  your Redeemer, the Holy
    One of Israel.   Ex 15:13
¹⁵"See, I will make you into a
    threshing sledge,   Job 41:30
  new and sharp, with many
    teeth.
  You will thresh the
    mountains and crush
    them,   Ex 19:18
  and reduce the hills to
    chaff.
¹⁶You will winnow them, the
    wind will pick them up,
  and a gale will blow them
    away.   Da 2:35
  But you will rejoice in the
    LORD

and glory in the Holy One
of Israel. Mk 1:24

17"The poor and needy search
for water, Isa 43:20
but there is none;
their tongues are parched
with thirst. Isa 35:7
But I the LORD will answer
them;
I, the God of Israel, will not
forsake them. Dt 31:6
18I will make rivers flow on
barren heights, Isa 30:25
and springs within the
valleys.
I will turn the desert into
pools of water, Isa 43:19
and the parched ground
into springs. Job 38:26
19I will put in the desert
the cedar and the acacia,
the myrtle and the
olive.
I will set pines in the
wasteland, Isa 37:24
the fir and the cypress
together, Isa 60:13
20so that people may see and
know, Ex 6:7
may consider and
understand, Isa 29:24
that the hand of the LORD
has done this,
that the Holy One of Israel
has created it. Isa 4:5

21"Present your case," says the
LORD.
"Set forth your
arguments," says Jacob's
King. Isa 43:15
22"Bring in your idols, to tell
us

what is going to happen.
Tell us what the former
things were, Isa 43:18
so that we may consider
them
and know their final
outcome.
Or declare to us the things to
come, Isa 42:9
23 tell us what the future
holds,
so we may know that you
are gods. Isa 45:3
Do something, whether good
or bad, Jer 10:5
so that we will be dismayed
and filled with fear.
24But you are less than nothing
and your works are utterly
worthless; 1Sa 12:21
he who chooses you is
detestable. Ps 109:7

25"I have stirred up one from
the north, and he
comes— Jer 50:9
one from the rising sun
who calls on my name.
He treads on rulers as if they
were mortar,
as if he were a potter
treading the clay. 2Sa 22:43
26Who told of this from the
beginning, so we could
know,
or beforehand, so we could
say, 'He was right'?
No one told of this,
no one foretold it, Isa 52:6
no one heard any words
from you. 1Ki 18:26
27I was the first to tell Zion,
'Look, here they are!'
I gave to Jerusalem a

messenger of good
tidings.   Isa 40:9
²⁸I look but there is no one—
no one among them to give
counsel,   Isa 40:13-14
no one to give answer
when I ask them. 1Ki 18:26
²⁹See, they are all false!
Their deeds amount to
nothing;   1Sa 12:21
their images are but wind
and confusion.   Jer 5:13

The Servant of the LORD

42 "Here is my servant,
whom I uphold,   Isa 20:3
my chosen one in whom I
delight;   Mt 3:17
I will put my Spirit on him
and he will bring justice to
the nations.   Ge 49:10
²He will not shout or cry out,
or raise his voice in the
streets.   Pr 8:1-4
³A bruised reed he will not
break,   Job 30:24
and a smoldering wick he
will not snuff out. Job 13:25
In faithfulness he will bring
forth justice;   Ps 72:2
⁴ he will not falter or be
discouraged
till he establishes justice on
earth.   Isa 2:4
In his law the islands will
put their hope."

⁵This is what God the LORD
says—
he who created the heavens
and stretched them out,
who spread out the earth
and all that comes out
of it,   Ge 1:1

who gives breath to its
people,   Ge 2:7
and life to those who walk
on it:
⁶"I, the LORD, have called you
in righteousness; Ex 31:2
I will take hold of your
hand.   Isa 41:13
I will keep you and will make
you
to be a covenant for the
people   Isa 49:8
and a light for the Gentiles,
⁷to open eyes that are blind,
to free captives from prison
and to release from the
dungeon those who sit
in darkness.   Ps 107:10

⁸"I am the LORD; that is my
name!   Ex 3:15
I will not give my glory to
another
or my praise to idols.   Ex 8:10
⁹See, the former things have
taken place,
and new things I declare;
before they spring into being
I announce them to you."

Song of Praise to the LORD

¹⁰Sing to the LORD a new song,
his praise from the ends of
the earth,   Dt 30:4
you who go down to the sea,
and all that is in it,
you islands, and all who
live in them.   Isa 11:11
¹¹Let the desert and its towns
raise their voices; Isa 32:16
let the settlements where
Kedar lives rejoice. Ge 25:13
Let the people of Sela sing
for joy;   Jdg 1:36

let them shout from the
  mountaintops.   Isa 52:7
¹²Let them give glory to the
  Lord
                                   1Ch 16:24
and proclaim his praise in
  the islands.   Isa 11:11
¹³The Lord will march out like
  a mighty man,   Isa 9:6
like a warrior he will stir up
  his zeal;   Isa 26:11
with a shout he will raise the
  battle cry
and will triumph over his
  enemies.   Isa 66:14

¹⁴"For a long time I have kept
  silent,   Est 4:14
I have been quiet and held
  myself back.   Ge 43:31
But now, like a woman in
  childbirth,
I cry out, I gasp and pant.
¹⁵I will lay waste the
  mountains and hills
and dry up all their
  vegetation;   Eze 38:20
I will turn rivers into islands
and dry up the pools. Isa 11:15
¹⁶I will lead the blind by ways
  they have not known,
along unfamiliar paths I will
  guide them;
I will turn the darkness into
  light before them
and make the rough places
  smooth.   Isa 26:7
These are the things I will
  do;
I will not forsake them. Dt 4:31
¹⁷But those who trust in idols,
  who say to images, 'You are
  our gods,'   Ex 32:4
will be turned back in utter
  shame.   Ps 97:7

Israel Blind and Deaf

¹⁸"Hear, you deaf;
  look, you blind, and see!
¹⁹Who is blind but my servant,
  and deaf like the messenger
  I send?   Isa 44:26
Who is blind like the one
  committed to me,
blind like the servant of the
  Lord?   Isa 26:3
²⁰You have seen many things,
  but have paid no
  attention;
your ears are open, but you
  hear nothing."   Isa 6:9-10
²¹It pleased the Lord
for the sake of his
  righteousness
to make his law great and
  glorious.   2Co 3:7
²²But this is a people
  plundered and looted,
all of them trapped in pits
  or hidden away in prisons.
They have become plunder,
  with no one to rescue them;
they have been made loot,
  with no one to say, "Send
  them back."   Isa 5:29

²³Which of you will listen to
  this
or pay close attention in
  time to come?   Dt 32:29
²⁴Who handed Jacob over to
  become loot,
and Israel to the
  plunderers?   2Ki 17:6
Was it not the Lord,
  against whom we have
  sinned?   Isa 10:5-6
For they would not follow his
  ways;   Isa 30:15

they did not obey his law.
25So he poured out on them
his burning anger,
the violence of war.   2Ki 22:13
It enveloped them in flames,
yet they did not
understand;   2Ki 25:9
it consumed them, but they
did not take it to heart.

Israel's Only Savior

43 But now, this is what the
Lord says—
he who created you,
O Jacob,   Isa 27:11
he who formed you,
O Israel: Ge 32:28
"Fear not, for I have
redeemed you;   Ex 6:6
I have summoned you by
name; you are mine.
2When you pass through the
waters,
I will be with you;   Isa 8:7
and when you pass through
the rivers,
they will not sweep over
you.
When you walk through the
fire,   Isa 29:6
you will not be burned;
the flames will not set you
ablaze.   Ps 66:12
3For I am the Lord, your God,
the Holy One of Israel, your
Savior;   Ex 14:30
I give Egypt for your ransom,
Cush*a* and Seba in your
stead.   Ge 10:7
4Since you are precious and
honored in my sight,
and because I love you,

I will give men in exchange
for you,
and people in exchange for
your life.
5Do not be afraid, for I am
with you;   Ge 21:22
I will bring your children
from the east   Isa 41:8
and gather you from the
west.   Isa 24:14
6I will say to the north, 'Give
them up!'
and to the south, 'Do not
hold them back.'   Ps 107:3
Bring my sons from afar
and my daughters from the
ends of the earth—   Dt 30:4
7everyone who is called by my
name,   Isa 48:1
whom I created for my
glory,   Ps 86:9
whom I formed and made."

8Lead out those who have
eyes but are blind,   Isa 6:9-10
who have ears but are deaf.
9All the nations gather
together   Isa 41:1
and the peoples assemble.
Which of them foretold this
and proclaimed to us the
former things?   Isa 41:26
Let them bring in their
witnesses to prove they
were right,
so that others may hear and
say, "It is true."
10"You are my witnesses,"
declares the Lord,   Jos 24:22
"and my servant whom I
have chosen,   Isa 20:3
so that you may know and
believe me   Ex 6:7

---

*a*3 That is, the upper Nile region

and understand that I am
  he.
Before me no god was
  formed,   Ps 86:10
nor will there be one after
  me.
[11]I, even I, am the LORD,
  and apart from me there is
  no savior.   Ps 3:8
[12]I have revealed and saved
  and proclaimed—
  I, and not some foreign god
  among you.   Dt 32:12
You are my witnesses,"
  declares the LORD, "that
  I am God.
[13] Yes, and from ancient days
  I am he.   Ps 90:2
No one can deliver out of my
  hand.
  When I act, who can
  reverse it?"   Nu 23:8

God's Mercy and Israel's Unfaithfulness

[14]This is what the LORD says—
  your Redeemer, the Holy
  One of Israel: Isa 1:4
"For your sake I will send to
  Babylon
  and bring down as fugitives
  all the Babylonians,[a]
  in the ships in which they
  took pride.   Isa 23:13
[15]I am the LORD, your Holy
  One,
  Israel's Creator, your
  King."   Isa 41:21

[16]This is what the LORD says—
  he who made a way
  through the sea,

a path through the mighty
  waters,   Ex 14:29
[17]who drew out the chariots
  and horses,   Ex 14:22
  the army and
  reinforcements together,
  and they lay there, never to
  rise again,   Ps 76:5-6
  extinguished, snuffed out
  like a wick: Job 13:25
[18]"Forget the former things;
  do not dwell on the past.
[19]See, I am doing a new thing!
  Now it springs up; do you
  not perceive it?
  I am making a way in the
  desert
  and streams in the
  wasteland.   Ps 126:4
[20]The wild animals honor me,
  the jackals and the owls,
  because I provide water in
  the desert
  and streams in the
  wasteland,   Nu 20:8
  to give drink to my people,
  my chosen,
[21] the people I formed for
  myself   Mal 3:17
  that they may proclaim my
  praise.   Ps 66:2

[22]"Yet you have not called
  upon me, O Jacob,
  you have not wearied
  yourselves for me,
  O Israel.   Jos 22:5
[23]You have not brought me
  sheep for burnt
  offerings,   Ex 29:41
  nor honored me with your
  sacrifices.   Am 5:25

---

[a]14 Or *Chaldeans*

I have not burdened you
with grain offerings
nor wearied you with
demands for incense.
24You have not bought any
fragrant calamus for me,
or lavished on me the fat of
your sacrifices.   Lev 3:9
But you have burdened me
with your sins
and wearied me with your
offenses.   Jer 44:22

25"I, even I, am he who blots
out
your transgressions, for my
own sake,   2Sa 12:13
and remembers your sins
no more.   Isa 64:9
26Review the past for me,
let us argue the matter
together;   Isa 1:18
state the case for your
innocence.   Isa 41:1
27Your first father sinned;
your spokesmen rebelled
against me.   Isa 24:20
28So I will disgrace the
dignitaries of your
temple,
and I will consign Jacob to
destruction[a]   Nu 5:27
and Israel to scorn.   Ps 39:8

Israel the Chosen

44 "But now listen,
O Jacob, my servant,
Israel, whom I have chosen.
2This is what the LORD says—
he who made you, who
formed you in the
womb,   Ge 2:7

and who will help you:
Do not be afraid, O Jacob,
my servant,   Jer 30:10
Jeshurun, whom I have
chosen.   Nu 23:21
3For I will pour water on the
thirsty land,
and streams on the dry
ground;   Pr 9:5
I will pour out my Spirit on
your offspring,   Isa 11:2
and my blessing on your
descendants.   Isa 61:9
4They will spring up like grass
in a meadow,   Job 5:25
like poplar trees by flowing
streams.   Job 40:22
5One will say, 'I belong to the
LORD';
another will call himself by
the name of Jacob;
still another will write on his
hand, 'The LORD's,'
and will take the name
Israel.   Isa 60:3

The LORD, Not Idols

6"This is what the LORD
says—
Israel's King and Redeemer,
the LORD Almighty: Isa 41:21
I am the first and I am the
last;   Rev 1:8,17
apart from me there is no
God.   Dt 6:4
7Who then is like me? Let him
proclaim it.   Dt 32:39
Let him declare and lay out
before me
what has happened since I

---

a28 The Hebrew term refers to the irrevocable giving over of things or persons to the
LORD, often by totally destroying them.

established my ancient
people,
and what is yet to come—
yes, let him foretell what
will come.   Isa 41:22
⁸Do not tremble, do not be
afraid.
Did I not proclaim this and
foretell it long ago? Isa 40:21
You are my witnesses. Is
there any God besides
me?   Isa 43:10
No, there is no other Rock;
I know not one."   Ge 49:24

⁹All who make idols are
nothing,   Ex 20:4
and the things they treasure
are worthless.   Isa 41:24
Those who would speak up
for them are blind;
they are ignorant, to their
own shame.   Isa 26:11
¹⁰Who shapes a god and casts
an idol,   Isa 40:19
which can profit him
nothing?
¹¹He and his kind will be put
to shame;   Isa 1:29
craftsmen are nothing but
men.
Let them all come together
and take their stand;
they will be brought down
to terror and infamy.

¹²The blacksmith takes a tool
and works with it in the
coals;   Isa 40:19
he shapes an idol with
hammers,
he forges it with the might
of his arm.   Ac 17:29
He gets hungry and loses his
strength;

he drinks no water and
grows faint.   Isa 40:28
¹³The carpenter measures with
a line
and makes an outline with
a marker;   Isa 41:7
he roughs it out with chisels
and marks it with
compasses.
He shapes it in the form of
man,   Ps 115:4-7
of man in all his glory,
that it may dwell in a
shrine.   Jdg 17:4-5
¹⁴He cut down cedars,
or perhaps took a cypress
or oak.
He let it grow among the
trees of the forest,
or planted a pine, and the
rain made it grow. Isa 41:19
¹⁵It is man's fuel for burning;
some of it he takes and
warms himself,
he kindles a fire and bakes
bread.
But he also fashions a god
and worships it;   Ex 20:5
he makes an idol and bows
down to it.   2Ch 25:14
¹⁶Half of the wood he burns in
the fire;
over it he prepares his
meal,
he roasts his meat and eats
his fill.
He also warms himself and
says,
"Ah! I am warm; I see the
fire."   Isa 47:14
¹⁷From the rest he makes a
god, his idol;
he bows down to it and
worships.   Ex 20:5

He prays to it and says,
  "Save me; you are my
    god."   Jdg 10:14
[18]They know nothing, they
    understand nothing;
  their eyes are plastered over
    so they cannot see,
  and their minds closed so
    they cannot understand.
[19]No one stops to think,
  no one has the knowledge
    or understanding to say,
  "Half of it I used for fuel;
  I even baked bread over its
    coals,   Dt 27:15
  I roasted meat and I ate.
  Shall I make a detestable
    thing from what is left?
  Shall I bow down to a block
    of wood?"   Isa 40:20
[20]He feeds on ashes, a deluded
    heart misleads him;
  he cannot save himself, or
    say,
  "Is not this thing in my
    right hand a lie?"   Isa 59:3

[21]"Remember these things,
    O Jacob,   Isa 46:8
  for you are my servant,
    O Israel.   Isa 43:1
  I have made you, you are my
    servant;   Ps 136:22
  O Israel, I will not forget
    you.   Ps 27:10
[22]I have swept away your
    offenses like a cloud,
  your sins like the morning
    mist.
  Return to me,
  for I have redeemed you."

[23]Sing for joy, O heavens, for
    the LORD has done this;
  shout aloud, O earth
    beneath.   1Ch 16:31
  Burst into song, you
    mountains,   Ps 98:8
  you forests and all your
    trees,   Ps 65:13
  for the LORD has redeemed
    Jacob,   Ex 6:6
  he displays his glory in
    Israel.   Ex 16:7

Jerusalem to Be Inhabited

[24]"This is what the LORD
    says—
  your Redeemer, who
    formed you in the
    womb: Ps 139:13

  I am the LORD,
  who has made all things,
  who alone stretched out the
    heavens,   Ge 2:1
  who spread out the earth by
    myself,   Ge 1:1

[25]who foils the signs of false
    prophets   Ps 33:10
  and makes fools of diviners,
  who overthrows the learning
    of the wise   Job 5:13
  and turns it into nonsense,
[26]who carries out the words of
    his servants   Isa 59:21
  and fulfills the predictions
    of his messengers,   Isa 46:10

  who says of Jerusalem, 'It
    shall be inhabited,'
  of the towns of Judah,
    'They shall be built,'
  and of their ruins, 'I will
    restore them,'   Ezr 9:9
[27]who says to the watery deep,
    'Be dry,

and I will dry up your
　　streams,'　　　　　Isa 11:15
²⁸who says of Cyrus, 'He is my
　　shepherd
and will accomplish all that
　　I please;
he will say of Jerusalem,
　　"Let it be rebuilt,"
and of the temple, "Let its
　　foundations be laid." '

45 "This is what the LORD
　　says to his anointed,
to Cyrus, whose right hand
　　I take hold of　　　2Ch 36:22
to subdue nations before him
　　and to strip kings of their
　　　armor,　　　　　Isa 48:14
to open doors before him
　　so that gates will not be
　　　shut:
²I will go before you
　　and will level the
　　　mountains*a*;　　　Isa 40:4
I will break down gates of
　　bronze　　　　　　Isa 13:2
and cut through bars of
　　iron.　　　　　　Ps 107:16
³I will give you the treasures
　　of darkness,
riches stored in secret
　　places,　　　　　Jer 41:8
so that you may know that I
　　am the LORD,　　　Isa 41:23
the God of Israel, who
　　summons you by
　　name.
⁴For the sake of Jacob my
　　servant,　　　　　Isa 14:1
of Israel my chosen,
I summon you by name

and bestow on you a title of
　　honor,
though you do not
　　acknowledge me.　Ac 17:23
⁵I am the LORD, and there is
　　no other;　　　　Isa 44:8
apart from me there is no
　　God.　　　　　　Dt 32:12
I will strengthen you,
　　though you have not
　　acknowledged me,
⁶so that from the rising of the
　　sun
to the place of its setting
men may know there is none
　　besides me.　　　Isa 14:13-14
I am the LORD, and there is
　　no other.
⁷I form the light and create
　　darkness,　　　　Ge 1:4
I bring prosperity and
　　create disaster;　　Isa 14:15
I, the LORD, do all these
　　things.

⁸"You heavens above, rain
　　down righteousness;
let the clouds shower it
　　down.　　　　　Ps 72:6
Let the earth open wide,
　　let salvation spring up,
let righteousness grow with
　　it;　　　　　　　Ps 85:9
I, the LORD, have created it.

⁹"Woe to him who quarrels
　　with his Maker,　Job 33:13
to him who is but a
　　potsherd among the
　　potsherds on the
　　ground.　　　　　Ps 22:15

---

*a*2 Dead Sea Scrolls and Septuagint; the meaning of the word in the Masoretic Text is
uncertain.

Does the clay say to the
    potter,
    'What are you making?'
Does your work say,
    'He has no hands'?   Isa 10:15
10Woe to him who says to his
    father,
    'What have you begotten?'
    or to his mother,
    'What have you brought to
    birth?'

11"This is what the LORD
    says—
    the Holy One of Israel, and
    its Maker: Ps 149:2
Concerning things to come,
    do you question me about
    my children,
    or give me orders about the
    work of my hands?   Ps 8:6
12It is I who made the earth
    and created mankind
    upon it.   Ge 1:1
My own hands stretched out
    the heavens;   Ge 2:1
I marshaled their starry
    hosts.   Ne 9:6
13I will raise up Cyrus[a] in my
    righteousness: 2Ch 36:22
    I will make all his ways
    straight.   1Ki 8:36
He will rebuild my city
    and set my exiles free,   Ezr 1:2
    but not for a price or reward,
    says the LORD Almighty."

14This is what the LORD says:

"The products of Egypt and
    the merchandise of
    Cush,[b]   2Sa 8:2
    and those tall Sabeans—

they will come over to you
    and will be yours;
they will trudge behind you,
    coming over to you in
    chains.   2Sa 3:34
They will bow down before
    you
    and plead with you, saying,
    'Surely God is with you, and
    there is no other;   1Co 14:25
    there is no other god.' "

15Truly you are a God who
    hides himself,   Dt 31:17
    O God and Savior of Israel.
16All the makers of idols will
    be put to shame and
    disgraced;   Ps 35:4
    they will go off into
    disgrace together.
17But Israel will be saved by
    the LORD
    with an everlasting
    salvation;   Isa 12:2
you will never be put to
    shame or disgraced,
    to ages everlasting.   Ge 30:23

18For this is what the LORD
    says—
he who created the heavens,
    he is God;
he who fashioned and made
    the earth,   Ge 1:1
    he founded it;
he did not create it to be
    empty,   Ge 1:2
    but formed it to be
    inhabited—   Ge 1:26
he says:
"I am the LORD,
    and there is no other.   Dt 4:35
19I have not spoken in secret,

---

[a]13 Hebrew *him*   [b]14 That is, the upper Nile region

from somewhere in a land
of darkness;   Jer 2:31
I have not said to Jacob's
descendants,
'Seek me in vain.'   Dt 4:29
I, the LORD, speak the truth;
I declare what is right.

20"Gather together and come;
assemble, you fugitives
from the nations.   Isa 43:9
Ignorant are those who carry
about idols of wood,
who pray to gods that
cannot save.   Dt 32:37
21Declare what is to be,
present it—
let them take counsel
together.
Who foretold this long ago,
who declared it from the
distant past?   Isa 46:10
Was it not I, the LORD?
And there is no God apart
from me,   Ps 46:10
a righteous God and a Savior;
there is none but me.   Ps 3:8

22"Turn to me and be saved,
all you ends of the earth;
for I am God, and there is
no other.   Hos 13:4
23By myself I have sworn,
my mouth has uttered in all
integrity
a word that will not be
revoked: Isa 55:11
Before me every knee will
bow;
by me every tongue will
swear.   Ps 63:11
24They will say of me, 'In the
LORD alone

are righteousness and
strength.' "   Dt 33:29
All who have raged against
him
will come to him and be put
to shame.   Isa 41:11
25But in the LORD all the
descendants of Israel
will be found righteous and
will exult.   Isa 24:23

Gods of Babylon

46 Bel bows down, Nebo
stoops low;   Isa 21:9
their idols are borne by
beasts of burden. a   1Sa 5:2
The images that are carried
about are burdensome,
a burden for the weary.
2They stoop and bow down
together;
unable to rescue the
burden,
they themselves go off into
captivity.   Jdg 18:17-18

3"Listen to me, O house of
Jacob,   Isa 48:12
all you who remain of the
house of Israel,
you whom I have upheld
since you were
conceived,   Ps 139:13
and have carried since your
birth.   Ps 22:10
4Even to your old age and
gray hairs   Ps 71:18
I am he, I am he who will
sustain you.   Dt 32:39
I have made you and I will
carry you;

a1 Or are but beasts and cattle

I will sustain you and I will
    rescue you.   Ps 18:35

5"To whom will you compare
    me or count me equal?
To whom will you liken me
    that we may be
    compared?   Ex 15:11
6Some pour out gold from
    their bags
and weigh out silver on the
    scales;
they hire a goldsmith to
    make it into a god,
and they bow down and
    worship it.   Ex 20:5
7They lift it to their shoulders
    and carry it;
they set it up in its place,
    and there it stands.
From that spot it cannot
    move.   1Sa 5:3
Though one cries out to it, it
    does not answer;   1Ki 18:26
it cannot save him from his
    troubles.   Isa 44:17

8"Remember this, fix it in
    mind,
take it to heart, you rebels.
9Remember the former things,
    those of long ago;   Isa 41:22
I am God, and there is no
    other;
I am God, and there is none
    like me.   Ex 8:10
10I make known the end from
    the beginning,   Isa 41:4
from ancient times, what is
    still to come.   Isa 45:21
I say: My purpose will stand,
    and I will do all that I
    please.   Pr 19:21

11From the east I summon a
    bird of prey;   Isa 8:8
from a far-off land, a man
    to fulfill my purpose.
What I have said, that will I
    bring about;
what I have planned, that
    will I do.   Ge 41:25
12Listen to me, you
    stubborn-hearted,
you who are far from
    righteousness.   Ps 119:150
13I am bringing my
    righteousness near,
it is not far away;   Isa 1:26
and my salvation will not
    be delayed.   Ps 85:9
I will grant salvation to Zion,
    my splendor to Israel.   Isa 44:23

The Fall of Babylon

47 "Go down, sit in the
    dust,   Job 2:13
Virgin Daughter of Babylon;
sit on the ground without a
    throne,
Daughter of the
    Babylonians. *a*   Ps 137:8
No more will you be called
    tender or delicate.   Dt 28:56
2Take millstones and grind
    flour;   Ex 11:5
take off your veil.   Ge 24:65
Lift up your skirts, bare your
    legs,   Isa 32:11
and wade through the
    streams.
3Your nakedness will be
    exposed   Ge 2:25
and your shame uncovered.
I will take vengeance;   Isa 1:24
I will spare no one."   Isa 13:18-19

---

a1 Or *Chaldeans*; also in verse 5

⁴Our Redeemer—the LORD
   Almighty is his name—
   is the Holy One of Israel.

⁵"Sit in silence, go into
   darkness,   Isa 9:2
   Daughter of the
   Babylonians;   Isa 21:9
no more will you be called
   queen of kingdoms.   La 1:1
⁶I was angry with my people
   and desecrated my
      inheritance;   Dt 13:15
I gave them into your hand,
   and you showed them no
      mercy.   Isa 14:6
Even on the aged
   you laid a very heavy yoke.
⁷You said, 'I will continue
   forever—   Isa 10:13
   the eternal queen!'   Rev 18:7
But you did not consider
   these things
   or reflect on what might
      happen.   Dt 32:29

⁸"Now then, listen, you
   wanton creature,
   lounging in your security
and saying to yourself,
   'I am, and there is none
      besides me.   Isa 45:6
I will never be a widow
   or suffer the loss of
      children.'   Isa 49:21
⁹Both of these will overtake
   you
   in a moment, on a single
      day: Ps 55:15
   loss of children and
      widowhood.   Isa 4:1
They will come upon you in
   full measure,
   in spite of your many
      sorceries   Na 3:4

and all your potent spells.
¹⁰You have trusted in your
   wickedness   Job 15:31
and have said, 'No one sees
   me.'   2Ki 21:16
Your wisdom and knowledge
   mislead you   Isa 44:20
when you say to yourself,
   'I am, and there is none
      besides me.'
¹¹Disaster will come upon you,
   and you will not know how
      to conjure it away.   Isa 10:3
A calamity will fall upon you
   that you cannot ward off
      with a ransom;
a catastrophe you cannot
      foresee
   will suddenly come upon
      you.   Ps 55:15

¹²"Keep on, then, with your
   magic spells
   and with your many
      sorceries,   Ex 7:11
which you have labored at
   since childhood.
Perhaps you will succeed,
   perhaps you will cause
      terror.
¹³All the counsel you have
   received has only worn
      you out!   Isa 57:10
Let your astrologers come
   forward,   Isa 19:3
those stargazers who make
   predictions month by
      month,
   let them save you from
      what is coming upon
      you.   Isa 5:29
¹⁴Surely they are like stubble;
   the fire will burn them
      up.

They cannot even save
   themselves
from the power of the
   flame.   Isa 10:17
Here are no coals to warm
   anyone;
   here is no fire to sit by.
15That is all they can do for
   you—
   these you have labored
     with
   and trafficked with since
     childhood.   Rev 18:11
Each of them goes on in his
   error;
   there is not one that can
     save you.   Isa 44:17

Stubborn Israel

48 "Listen to this, O house
   of Jacob,
   you who are called by the
     name of Israel   Ge 17:5
   and come from the line of
     Judah,
   you who take oaths in the
     name of the LORD
   and invoke the God of
     Israel—   1Sa 20:42
   but not in truth or
     righteousness—   Isa 59:14
2you who call yourselves
     citizens of the holy city
   and rely on the God of
     Israel—   Isa 10:20
   the LORD Almighty is his
     name: Isa 47:4
3I foretold the former things
     long ago,   Isa 41:22
   my mouth announced them
   and I made them
     known;   Isa 40:21

then suddenly I acted, and
   they came to pass. Isa 17:14
4For I knew how stubborn
     you were;   Isa 9:9
   the sinews of your neck
     were iron,   Ex 32:9
   your forehead was bronze.
5Therefore I told you these
     things long ago;
   before they happened I
     announced them to you
so that you could not say,
   'My idols did them;
   my wooden image and
     metal god ordained
     them.'
6You have heard these things;
   look at them all.
   Will you not admit them?

"From now on I will tell you
   of new things,
   of hidden things unknown
     to you.   Isa 41:22
7They are created now, and
     not long ago;   Isa 45:21
   you have not heard of them
     before today.
So you cannot say,
   'Yes, I knew of them.' Ex 6:7
8You have neither heard nor
     understood;   Isa 1:3
   from of old your ear has not
     been open.   Dt 29:4
Well do I know how
     treacherous you are;
   you were called a rebel
     from birth.   Dt 9:7
9For my own name's sake I
     delay my wrath; Job 9:13
   for the sake of my praise I
     hold it back from you,
   so as not to cut you off.

¹⁰See, I have refined you,
   though not as silver;
I have tested you in the
   furnace of affliction.
¹¹For my own sake, for my
   own sake, I do this.
How can I let myself be
   defamed?   Lev 18:21
I will not yield my glory to
   another.   Isa 42:8

Israel Freed

¹²"Listen to me, O Jacob,
   Israel, whom I have called:
I am he;   Isa 43:13
I am the first and I am the
   last.   Rev 1:17
¹³My own hand laid the
   foundations of the
   earth,
and my right hand spread
   out the heavens;   Ge 2:1
when I summon them,
   they all stand up together.

¹⁴"Come together, all of you,
   and listen: Isa 43:9
Which of the idols has
   foretold these things?
The LORD's chosen ally
will carry out his purpose
   against Babylon;   Isa 21:9
his arm will be against the
   Babylonians.ᵃ
¹⁵I, even I, have spoken;
   yes, I have called him. Jdg 4:10
I will bring him,
   and he will succeed in his
   mission.   Isa 44:28

¹⁶"Come near me and listen
to this: Isa 33:13

"From the first
   announcement I have
   not spoken in secret;
at the time it happens, I am
   there."

And now the Sovereign LORD
   has sent me,   Isa 50:5
with his Spirit.

¹⁷This is what the LORD says—
   your Redeemer, the Holy
   One of Israel: Isa 47:4
"I am the LORD your God,
who teaches you what is
   best for you,   Isa 28:9
who directs you in the way
   you should go.   Isa 30:11
¹⁸If only you had paid
   attention to my
   commands,   Isa 42:23
your peace would have
   been like a river,   Isa 33:21
your righteousness like the
   waves of the sea.   Isa 1:26
¹⁹Your descendants would
   have been like the sand,
your children like its
   numberless grains; Job 5:25
their name would never be
   cut off   Isa 56:5
nor destroyed from before
   me."

²⁰Leave Babylon,
   flee from the Babylonians!
Announce this with shouts of
   joy
and proclaim it.
Send it out to the ends of the
   earth;   Ge 49:10
say, "The LORD has
   redeemed his servant
   Jacob."   Ex 6:6

ᵃ14 Or *Chaldeans*; also in verse 20

21They did not thirst when he
    led them through the
    deserts;   Isa 33:16
he made water flow for
    them from the rock;
he split the rock
    and water gushed out.

22"There is no peace," says the
    LORD, "for the wicked."

The Servant of the LORD

49 Listen to me, you
    islands;   Isa 11:11
hear this, you distant
    nations:
Before I was born the LORD
    called me;   Isa 7:14
from my birth he has made
    mention of my name.
2He made my mouth like a
    sharpened sword,
in the shadow of his hand
    he hid me;   Ex 33:22
he made me into a polished
    arrow
and concealed me in his
    quiver.   Dt 32:23
3He said to me, "You are my
    servant,   Isa 20:3
Israel, in whom I will
    display my splendor."
4But I said, "I have labored to
    no purpose;
I have spent my strength in
    vain and for nothing.
Yet what is due me is in the
    LORD's hand,
and my reward is with my
    God."   Job 27:2

5And now the LORD says—
    he who formed me in the
    womb to be his servant
to bring Jacob back to him
    and gather Israel to himself,
for I am honored in the eyes
    of the LORD   Isa 43:4
and my God has been my
    strength—   Ps 18:1
6he says:
"It is too small a thing for
    you to be my servant
to restore the tribes of Jacob
    and bring back those of
    Israel I have kept.
I will also make you a light
    for the Gentiles,   Isa 9:2
that you may bring my
    salvation to the ends of
    the earth."   Dt 30:4

7This is what the LORD says—
    the Redeemer and Holy
    One of Israel—   Isa 48:17
to him who was despised
    and abhorred by the
    nation,   Ps 22:6
to the servant of rulers:
"Kings will see you and rise
    up,   Ezr 1:2
princes will see and bow
    down,   Ge 27:29
because of the LORD, who is
    faithful,   Dt 7:9
the Holy One of Israel, who
    has chosen you."   Isa 14:1

Restoration of Israel

8This is what the LORD says:

"In the time of my favor I
    will answer you,   Ps 69:13
and in the day of salvation I
    will help you;   Isa 41:10
I will keep you and will make
    you
to be a covenant for the
    people,   Isa 42:6

to restore the land
and to reassign its desolate
inheritances,　　Nu 34:13
⁹to say to the captives, 'Come
out,'　　Isa 42:7
and to those in darkness,
'Be free!'　　Ps 107:10

"They will feed beside the
roads
and find pasture on every
barren hill.　　Isa 41:18
¹⁰They will neither hunger nor
thirst,　　Isa 33:16
nor will the desert heat or
the sun beat upon them.
He who has compassion on
them will guide them
and lead them beside
springs of water.　　Isa 33:21
¹¹I will turn all my mountains
into roads,
and my highways will be
raised up.　　Isa 40:4
¹²See, they will come from
afar—　　Isa 2:3
some from the north, some
from the west,
some from the region of
Aswan.ᵃ"　　Isa 59:19

¹³Shout for joy, O heavens;
rejoice, O earth;　　Ps 96:11
burst into song,
O mountains!　　Ps 98:4
For the LORD comforts his
people　　Ps 71:21
and will have compassion
on his afflicted ones.

¹⁴But Zion said, "The LORD has
forsaken me,　　Ps 9:10
the Lord has forgotten me."

¹⁵"Can a mother forget the
baby at her breast
and have no compassion on
the child she has borne?
Though she may forget,
I will not forget you!　　Isa 44:21
¹⁶See, I have engraved you on
the palms of my hands;
your walls are ever before
me.　　Ps 48:12-13
¹⁷Your sons hasten back,
and those who laid you
waste depart from
you.
¹⁸Lift up your eyes and look
around;
all your sons gather and
come to you.　　Isa 11:12
As surely as I live," declares
the LORD,　　Nu 14:21
"you will wear them all as
ornaments;　　Isa 52:1
you will put them on, like a
bride.

¹⁹"Though you were ruined
and made desolate
and your land laid waste,
now you will be too small for
your people,　　Eze 36:10-11
and those who devoured
you will be far away.
²⁰The children born during
your bereavement
will yet say in your hearing,
'This place is too small for us;
give us more space to live
in.'　　Zec 2:4
²¹Then you will say in your
heart,
'Who bore me these?　　Isa 29:23
I was bereaved and barren;
I was exiled and rejected.

ᵃ12 Dead Sea Scrolls; Masoretic Text *Sinim*

Who brought these up?
I was left all alone,　Isa 1:8
but these—where have they
　come from?' "

22This is what the Sovereign
Lord says:　Ge 15:2

"See, I will beckon to the
　Gentiles,
I will lift up my banner to
　the peoples;　Isa 11:10
they will bring your sons in
　their arms　Isa 11:12
and carry your daughters
　on their shoulders.
23Kings will be your foster
　fathers,　Isa 60:3
and their queens your
　nursing mothers.
They will bow down before
　you with their faces to
　the ground;　Ge 27:29
they will lick the dust at
　your feet.
Then you will know that I am
　the Lord;　Ge 3:14
those who hope in me will
　not be disappointed."

24Can plunder be taken from
　warriors,
or captives rescued from
　the fierce[a]?

25But this is what the Lord
says:

"Yes, captives will be taken
　from warriors,　Isa 14:2
and plunder retrieved from
　the fierce;　Isa 13:11
I will contend with those
　who contend with you,

and your children I will
　save.　Isa 25:9
26I will make your oppressors
　eat their own flesh;　Isa 9:20
they will be drunk on their
　own blood, as with
　wine.　Nu 23:24
Then all mankind will know
　that I, the Lord, am your
　Savior,　Isa 25:9
your Redeemer, the Mighty
　One of Jacob."　Ge 49:24

Israel's Sin and the Servant's Obedience

50 This is what the Lord
　says:

"Where is your mother's
　certificate of divorce　Dt 24:1
with which I sent her away?
Or to which of my creditors
　did I sell you?　Ne 5:5
Because of your sins you
　were sold;　Dt 32:30
because of your
　transgressions your
　mother was sent away.
2When I came, why was there
　no one?
When I called, why was
　there no one to answer?
Was my arm too short to
　ransom you?　Nu 11:23
Do I lack the strength to
　rescue you?　Ge 18:14
By a mere rebuke I dry up
　the sea,　Ex 14:22
I turn rivers into a desert;
　their fish rot for lack of water
　and die of thirst.

a24 Dead Sea Scrolls, Vulgate and Syriac (see also Septuagint and verse 25); Masoretic
Text righteous

³I clothe the sky with
  darkness
  and make sackcloth its
  covering."   Ex 10:22 Rev 6:12

⁴The Sovereign LORD has
  given me an instructed
  tongue,   Isa 61:1
to know the word that
  sustains the weary.   Mt 11:28
He wakens me morning by
  morning,   Ps 5:3
wakens my ear to listen like
  one being taught.   Isa 28:9
⁵The Sovereign LORD has
  opened my ears,   Isa 35:5
and I have not been
  rebellious;   Eze 2:8
I have not drawn back.
⁶I offered my back to those
  who beat me,   Isa 53:5
my cheeks to those who
  pulled out my beard;
I did not hide my face
from mocking and spitting.
⁷Because the Sovereign LORD
  helps me,   Isa 41:10
I will not be disgraced.
Therefore have I set my face
  like flint,   Jer 1:18
and I know I will not be put
  to shame.   Isa 28:16
⁸He who vindicates me is
  near.   Ps 34:18
Who then will bring
  charges against me?
Let us face each other!   Isa 41:1
Who is my accuser?
Let him confront me!
⁹It is the Sovereign LORD who
  helps me.   Isa 48:16
Who is he that will
  condemn me?   Ro 8:1

They will all wear out like a
  garment;
  the moths will eat them up.
¹⁰Who among you fears the
  LORD   Pr 1:7
and obeys the word of his
  servant?   Isa 49:3
Let him who walks in the
  dark,
who has no light,   Ps 107:14
trust in the name of the LORD
and rely on his God.   Isa 10:20
¹¹But now, all you who light
  fires
and provide yourselves
  with flaming torches,
go, walk in the light of your
  fires   Isa 1:31
and of the torches you have
  set ablaze.
This is what you shall receive
  from my hand: Pr 26:27
You will lie down in
  torment.   Job 15:20

Everlasting Salvation for Zion

51 "Listen to me, you who
  pursue righteousness
and who seek the LORD:
Look to the rock from which
  you were cut   Isa 17:10
and to the quarry from
  which you were hewn;
²look to Abraham, your
  father,   Ge 17:6
and to Sarah, who gave you
  birth.
When I called him he was
  but one,
and I blessed him and made
  him many.   Ge 12:2

³The Lord will surely comfort
Zion   Isa 40:1
and will look with
compassion on all her
ruins;   Isa 44:26
he will make her deserts like
Eden,   Ge 2:8
her wastelands like the
garden of the Lord.
Joy and gladness will be
found in her,   Isa 25:9
thanksgiving and the sound
of singing.   Jer 17:26

⁴"Listen to me, my people;
hear me, my nation: Ps 78:1
The law will go out from me;
my justice will become a
light to the nations.
⁵My righteousness draws near
speedily,
my salvation is on the way,
and my arm will bring
justice to the nations.
The islands will look to me
and wait in hope for my
arm.   Ge 49:10
⁶Lift up your eyes to the
heavens,
look at the earth beneath;
the heavens will vanish like
smoke,   Ps 37:20
the earth will wear out like
a garment   Ps 102:25-26
and its inhabitants die like
flies.
But my salvation will last
forever,   Ps 119:89
my righteousness will never
fail.   Ps 89:33

⁷"Hear me, you who know
what is right,
you people who have my
law in your hearts: Dt 6:6

Do not fear the reproach of
men
or be terrified by their
insults.   Ps 119:39
⁸For the moth will eat them
up like a garment;   Jas 5:2
the worm will devour them
like wool.   Isa 14:11
But my righteousness will
last forever,
my salvation through all
generations."

⁹Awake, awake! Clothe
yourself with strength,
O arm of the Lord;   Ps 98:1
awake, as in days gone by,
as in generations of old.
Was it not you who cut
Rahab to pieces,   Job 9:13
who pierced that monster
through?
¹⁰Was it not you who dried up
the sea,   Ex 14:22
the waters of the great
deep,   Ex 15:5
who made a road in the
depths of the sea
so that the redeemed might
cross over?   Ex 15:13
¹¹The ransomed of the Lord
will return.   Isa 35:9
They will enter Zion with
singing;   Ps 109:28
everlasting joy will crown
their heads.
Gladness and joy will
overtake them,   Isa 48:20
and sorrow and sighing will
flee away.   Isa 30:19

¹²"I, even I, am he who
comforts you.   Isa 40:1
Who are you that you fear
mortal men,   2Ki 1:15

the sons of men, who are
but grass,   Isa 15:6
[13]that you forget the LORD
your Maker,   Job 4:17
who stretched out the
heavens   Isa 48:13
and laid the foundations of
the earth,
that you live in constant
terror every day   Isa 7:4
because of the wrath of the
oppressor,
who is bent on destruction?
For where is the wrath of the
oppressor?   Isa 9:4
[14]   The cowering prisoners will
soon be set free;   Isa 42:7
they will not die in their
dungeon,
nor will they lack bread.
[15]For I am the LORD your God,
who churns up the sea so
that its waves roar—
the LORD Almighty is his
name.   Isa 13:4
[16]I have put my words in your
mouth
and covered you with the
shadow of my hand—
I who set the heavens in
place,
who laid the foundations of
the earth,   Isa 48:13
and who say to Zion, 'You
are my people.' "   Jer 7:23

The Cup of the LORD's Wrath

[17]Awake, awake!   Jdg 5:12
Rise up, O Jerusalem,
you who have drunk from
the hand of the LORD
the cup of his wrath,   Job 21:20

you who have drained to its
dregs   Ps 75:8
the goblet that makes men
stagger.   Ps 60:3
[18]Of all the sons she bore
there was none to guide
her;   Job 31:18
of all the sons she reared
there was none to take her
by the hand.   Isa 41:13
[19]These double calamities have
come upon you—   Isa 40:2
who can comfort you?—
ruin and destruction, famine
and sword—   Isa 60:18
who can[a] console you?
[20]Your sons have fainted;
they lie at the head of every
street,   Isa 5:25
like antelope caught in a
net.   Job 18:10
They are filled with the
wrath of the LORD
and the rebuke of your
God.   Dt 28:20

[21]Therefore hear this, you
afflicted one,   Isa 14:32
made drunk, but not with
wine.   Isa 29:9
[22]This is what your Sovereign
LORD says,
your God, who defends his
people: Isa 49:25
"See, I have taken out of
your hand
the cup that made you
stagger;   Jer 25:15
from that cup, the goblet of
my wrath,
you will never drink again.
[23]I will put it into the hands of
your tormentors,   Isa 14:4

---

[a]19 Dead Sea Scrolls, Septuagint, Vulgate and Syriac; Masoretic Text / how can I

who said to you,
'Fall prostrate that we may
    walk over you.'   Jos 10:24
And you made your back like
    the ground,
like a street to be walked
    over."   Ps 66:12

52 Awake, awake, O Zion,
clothe yourself with
    strength.   1Sa 2:4
Put on your garments of
    splendor,
O Jerusalem, the holy city.
The uncircumcised and
    defiled   Ge 34:14
will not enter you again.
²Shake off your dust;   Isa 29:4
    rise up, sit enthroned,
    O Jerusalem.
Free yourself from the chains
    on your neck,   Ps 81:6
O captive Daughter of Zion.

³For this is what the LORD
says:

"You were sold for nothing,
    and without money you
    will be redeemed."   Isa 1:27

⁴For this is what the Sovereign LORD says:

"At first my people went
    down to Egypt to live;
lately, Assyria has
    oppressed them.   Isa 10:24

⁵"And now what do I have
here?" declares the LORD.

"For my people have been
    taken away for nothing,

and those who rule them
    mock,ᵃ"
        declares the LORD.
"And all day long
    my name is constantly
    blasphemed.   Isa 37:23
⁶Therefore my people will
    know my name;   Ex 6:3
therefore in that day they
    will know
that it is I who foretold it.
    Yes, it is I."

⁷How beautiful on the
    mountains   Isa 42:11
are the feet of those who
    bring good news,
who proclaim peace,   Na 1:15
    who bring good tidings,
    who proclaim salvation,
who say to Zion,
    "Your God reigns!"   1Ch 16:31
⁸Listen! Your watchmen lift
    up their voices;   1Sa 14:16
together they shout for joy.
When the LORD returns to
    Zion,   Isa 59:20
    they will see it with their
    own eyes.
⁹Burst into songs of joy
    together,   Ps 98:4
you ruins of Jerusalem,
for the LORD has comforted
    his people,   Isa 40:1
    he has redeemed Jerusalem.
¹⁰The LORD will lay bare his
    holy arm   2Ch 32:8
in the sight of all the
    nations,   Isa 66:18
and all the ends of the earth
    will see
    the salvation of our God.

¹¹Depart, depart, go out from
 there!   Isa 48:20
 Touch no unclean thing!
 Come out from it and be
   pure,   Nu 8:6
 you who carry the vessels
   of the LORD.   2Ch 36:10
¹²But you will not leave in
 haste
 or go in flight;   Ex 12:11
 for the LORD will go before
   you,   Mic 2:13
 the God of Israel will be
   your rear guard.   Ex 14:19

The Suffering and Glory of the Servant

¹³See, my servant will act
 wisely[a];   Jos 1:8
 he will be raised and lifted
   up and highly exalted.
¹⁴Just as there were many who
   were appalled at him[b]—
 his appearance was so
   disfigured beyond that
   of any man   2Sa 10:4
 and his form marred
   beyond human
   likeness—   Job 2:12
¹⁵so will he sprinkle many
   nations,[c]   Lev 14:7
 and kings will shut their
   mouths because of him.
 For what they were not told,
   they will see,
 and what they have not
   heard, they will
   understand.   Ro 15:21

53 Who has believed our
 message   Isa 28:9

and to whom has the arm
 of the LORD been
 revealed?   Jn 12:38
²He grew up before him like a
 tender shoot,   2Ki 19:26
 and like a root out of dry
 ground.   Isa 11:10
 He had no beauty or majesty
 to attract us to him,
 nothing in his appearance
 that we should desire
 him.   Isa 52:14
³He was despised and
 rejected by men,
 a man of sorrows, and
 familiar with suffering.
 Like one from whom men
 hide their faces   Dt 31:17
 he was despised, and we
 esteemed him not.   1Sa 2:30

⁴Surely he took up our
 infirmities
 and carried our sorrows,
 yet we considered him
 stricken by God,
 smitten by him, and
 afflicted.   Ge 12:17
⁵But he was pierced for our
 transgressions,   Ps 22:16
 he was crushed for our
 iniquities;   Ps 34:18
 the punishment that brought
 us peace was upon him,
 and by his wounds we are
 healed.   Dt 32:39
⁶We all, like sheep, have gone
 astray,   Ps 95:10
 each of us has turned to his
 own way;   1Sa 8:3
 and the LORD has laid on him
 the iniquity of us all.   Ex 28:38

---

[a]13 Or will prosper   [b]14 Hebrew you   [c]15 Hebrew; Septuagint so will many nations
marvel at him

7He was oppressed and
     afflicted,   Isa 49:26
  yet he did not open his
     mouth;   Mk 14:61
  he was led like a lamb to the
     slaughter,   Ps 44:22
  and as a sheep before her
     shearers is silent,
  so he did not open his
     mouth.
8By oppression*a* and
     judgment he was taken
     away.   Mk 14:49
  And who can speak of his
     descendants?
  For he was cut off from the
     land of the living;   Ps 88:5
  for the transgression of my
     people he was stricken.*b*
9He was assigned a grave
     with the wicked,   Mt 27:38
  and with the rich in his
     death,   Mt 27:57-60
  though he had done no
     violence,   Isa 42:1-3
  nor was any deceit in his
     mouth.   Job 16:17

10Yet it was the LORD's will to
     crush him and cause
     him to suffer,   Ge 12:17
  and though the LORD
     makes*c* his life a guilt
     offering,   Lev 5:15
  he will see his offspring and
     prolong his days,   Ps 22:30
  and the will of the LORD
     will prosper in his
     hand.

11After the suffering of his
     soul,   Jn 10:14-18
  he will see the light ⌐of life⌐*d*
     and be satisfied*e*;   Job 33:30
  by his knowledge*f* my
     righteous servant will
     justify many,   Isa 6:7
  and he will bear their
     iniquities.   Ex 28:38
12Therefore I will give him a
     portion among the
     great,*g*   Isa 6:1
  and he will divide the spoils
     with the strong,*h*   Ex 15:9
  because he poured out his
     life unto death,   Mt 26:28
  and was numbered with the
     transgressors.   Mt 27:38
  For he bore the sin of many,
  and made intercession for
     the transgressors.   Isa 59:16

The Future Glory of Zion

54 "Sing, O barren woman,
  you who never bore a
     child;   Ge 30:1
  burst into song, shout for
     joy,   Ge 21:6
  you who were never in
     labor;   Isa 66:7
  because more are the
     children of the desolate
     woman   Isa 49:19
  than of her who has a
     husband,"   1Sa 2:5
     says the LORD.
2"Enlarge the place of your
     tent,   Ge 26:22

---

*a*8 Or *From arrest*   *b*8 Or *away.* / *Yet who of his generation considered* / *that he was cut off from the land of the living* / *for the transgression of my people,* / *to whom the blow was due?*
*c*10 Hebrew *though you make*   *d*11 Dead Sea Scrolls (see also Septuagint); Masoretic Text does not have *the light ⌐of life⌐.*   *e*11 Or (with Masoretic Text) 11*He will see the result of the suffering of his soul* / *and be satisfied*   *f*11 Or *by knowledge of him*   *g*12 Or *many*   *h*12 Or *numerous*

stretch your tent curtains
  wide,
do not hold back;
lengthen your cords,
  strengthen your stakes.
³For you will spread out to the
  right and to the left;
your descendants will
  dispossess nations Ge 13:14
and settle in their desolate
  cities.   Isa 49:19

⁴"Do not be afraid; you will
  not suffer shame. Jer 30:10
Do not fear disgrace; you
  will not be humiliated.
You will forget the shame of
  your youth   Ps 25:7
and remember no more the
  reproach of your
  widowhood.   Isa 47:8
⁵For your Maker is your
  husband—   Ps 95:6
the LORD Almighty is his
  name—
the Holy One of Israel is your
  Redeemer;   Isa 48:17
he is called the God of all
  the earth.   Isa 6:3
⁶The LORD will call you back
  as if you were a wife
  deserted and distressed
  in spirit—
a wife who married young,
  only to be rejected," says
  your God.   Ex 20:14
⁷"For a brief moment I
  abandoned you,   Ps 71:11
but with deep compassion I
  will bring you back.
⁸In a surge of anger
I hid my face from you for a
  moment,   Isa 1:15

but with everlasting kindness
I will have compassion on
  you,"   Ps 102:13
says the LORD your
  Redeemer.   Isa 48:17

⁹"To me this is like the days
  of Noah,
when I swore that the
  waters of Noah would
  never again cover the
  earth.   Ge 8:21
So now I have sworn not to
  be angry with you, Ps 13:1
never to rebuke you again.
¹⁰Though the mountains be
  shaken   Rev 6:14
and the hills be removed,
yet my unfailing love for you
  will not be shaken
nor my covenant of peace
  be removed,"   Ge 9:16
says the LORD, who has
  compassion on you.

¹¹"O afflicted city, lashed by
  storms and not
  comforted,   Isa 51:19
I will build you with stones
  of turquoise,ᵃ   1Ch 29:2
your foundations with
  sapphires.ᵇ   Ex 24:10
¹²I will make your battlements
  of rubies,
your gates of sparkling
  jewels,   Rev 21:21
and all your walls of
  precious stones.
¹³All your sons will be taught
  by the LORD,   Isa 28:9
and great will be your
  children's peace. Lev 26:6

ᵃ11 The meaning of the Hebrew for this word is uncertain.   ᵇ11 Or *lapis lazuli*

14In righteousness you will be
   established: Isa 26:2
Tyranny will be far from
   you;
  you will have nothing to
   fear.   Zep 3:15
Terror will be far removed;
  it will not come near you.
15If anyone does attack you, it
   will not be my doing;
  whoever attacks you will
   surrender to you.   Isa 41:11

16"See, it is I who created the
   blacksmith   Isa 44:12
  who fans the coals into
   flame
  and forges a weapon fit for
   its work.   Isa 10:5
And it is I who have created
   the destroyer to work
   havoc;   Isa 13:5
17   no weapon forged against
   you will prevail,   Isa 29:8
  and you will refute every
   tongue that accuses
   you.
This is the heritage of the
   servants of the LORD,
  and this is their vindication
   from me,"   Ps 17:2
     declares the LORD.

Invitation to the Thirsty

55 "Come, all you who are
   thirsty,   Pr 9:5
  come to the waters;   Jer 2:13
and you who have no
   money,
  come, buy and eat!   La 5:4
Come, buy wine and milk
  without money and without
   cost.   Hos 14:4

2Why spend money on what
  is not bread,
  and your labor on what
   does not satisfy?   Ps 22:26
Listen, listen to me, and eat
  what is good,   Isa 1:19
  and your soul will delight
   in the richest of fare.
3Give ear and come to me;
  hear me, that your soul
   may live.   Ps 78:1
I will make an everlasting
   covenant with you,
  my faithful love promised
   to David.   Isa 54:8
4See, I have made him a
   witness to the peoples,
  a leader and commander of
   the peoples.   1Sa 13:14
5Surely you will summon
   nations you know not,
  and nations that do not
   know you will hasten to
   you,   Isa 2:3
because of the LORD your
   God,
  the Holy One of Israel,
  for he has endowed you
   with splendor."   Isa 44:23

6Seek the LORD while he may
   be found;   Ps 32:6
  call on him while he is
   near.
7Let the wicked forsake his
   way   2Ch 7:14
  and the evil man his
   thoughts.   Isa 32:7
Let him turn to the LORD,
  and he will have mercy
   on him,   Isa 54:10
  and to our God, for he will
   freely pardon.   2Ch 6:21

8"For my thoughts are not
your thoughts,   Php 2:5
neither are your ways my
ways,"   Isa 53:6
          declares the LORD.
9"As the heavens are higher
than the earth,   Job 11:8
so are my ways higher than
your ways
and my thoughts than your
thoughts.   Nu 23:19
10As the rain and the snow
come down from heaven,
and do not return to it
without watering the earth
and making it bud and
flourish,   Lev 25:19
so that it yields seed for the
sower and bread for the
eater,   2Co 9:10
11so is my word that goes out
from my mouth: Dt 32:2
It will not return to me
empty,   Isa 40:8
but will accomplish what I
desire
and achieve the purpose for
which I sent it.   Pr 19:21
12You will go out in joy
and be led forth in peace;
the mountains and hills
will burst into song before
you,   Ps 65:12-13
and all the trees of the field
will clap their hands.   Ps 98:8
13Instead of the thornbush will
grow the pine tree,
and instead of briers the
myrtle will grow.   Isa 41:9
This will be for the LORD's
renown,   Ps 102:12
for an everlasting sign,
which will not be
destroyed."

Salvation for Others

56 This is what the LORD
says:

"Maintain justice
and do what is right,   Isa 26:8
for my salvation is close at
hand   Ps 85:9
and my righteousness will
soon be revealed.   Jer 23:6
2Blessed is the man who does
this,   Ps 149:2
the man who holds it fast,
who keeps the Sabbath
without desecrating it,
and keeps his hand from
doing any evil."

3Let no foreigner who has
bound himself to the
LORD say,   Ex 12:43
"The LORD will surely
exclude me from his
people."   Dt 23:3
And let not any eunuch
complain,   Lev 21:20
"I am only a dry tree."

4For this is what the LORD
says:

"To the eunuchs who keep
my Sabbaths,
who choose what pleases
me
and hold fast to my
covenant—   Ex 31:13
5to them I will give within my
temple and its walls
a memorial and a name
better than sons and
daughters;   Nu 32:42
I will give them an
everlasting name
that will not be cut off.   Isa 48:19

6And foreigners who bind
    themselves to the LORD
  to serve him,   1Ch 22:2
  to love the name of the LORD,
  and to worship him,
  all who keep the Sabbath
    without desecrating it
  and who hold fast to my
    covenant—
7these I will bring to my holy
    mountain   Isa 2:2
  and give them joy in my
    house of prayer.
  Their burnt offerings and
    sacrifices   Isa 19:21
  will be accepted on my
    altar;
  for my house will be called
    a house of prayer for all
    nations."   Mt 21:13
8The Sovereign LORD
    declares—
  he who gathers the exiles of
    Israel:
  "I will gather still others to
    them   Dt 30:4
  besides those already
    gathered."

God's Accusation Against the Wicked

9Come, all you beasts of the
    field,   Isa 18:6
  come and devour, all you
    beasts of the forest!
10Israel's watchmen are blind,
  they all lack knowledge;
  they are all mute dogs,
  they cannot bark;
  they lie around and dream,
  they love to sleep.   Na 3:18
11They are dogs with mighty
    appetites;

they never have enough.
  They are shepherds who lack
    understanding;   Isa 1:3
  they all turn to their own
    way,   Isa 53:6
  each seeks his own gain.
12"Come," each one cries, "let
    me get wine!   Lev 10:9
  Let us drink our fill of beer!
  And tomorrow will be like
    today,
  or even far better."   Ps 10:6

57 The righteous perish,
     and no one ponders it in
     his heart;   Isa 42:25
  devout men are taken away,
  and no one understands
  that the righteous are taken
    away
  to be spared from evil.
2Those who walk uprightly
  enter into peace;   Isa 26:7
  they find rest as they lie in
    death.   Da 12:13

3"But you—come here, you
    sons of a sorceress,
  you offspring of adulterers
    and prostitutes!   Isa 1:21
4Whom are you mocking?
  At whom do you sneer
  and stick out your tongue?
  Are you not a brood of
    rebels,   Isa 1:2
  the offspring of liars?
5You burn with lust among
    the oaks   Isa 1:29
  and under every spreading
    tree;   Dt 12:2
  you sacrifice your children in
    the ravines   Lev 18:21
  and under the overhanging
    crags.

⁶₍The idols₎ among the smooth
　　stones of the ravines are
　　your portion;　　2Ki 17:10
they, they are your lot.
Yes, to them you have
　　poured out drink
　　offerings　　Jer 7:18
and offered grain offerings.
In the light of these things,
　　should I relent?　　Jer 5:9
⁷You have made your bed on
　　a high and lofty hill;
there you went up to offer
　　your sacrifices.　　Isa 65:7
⁸Behind your doors and your
　　doorposts
you have put your pagan
　　symbols.
Forsaking me, you
　　uncovered your
　　bed,
you climbed into it and
　　opened it wide;
you made a pact with those
　　whose beds you love,
and you looked on their
　　nakedness.　　Eze 16:15
⁹You went to Molechᵃ with
　　olive oil　　Lev 18:21
and increased your
　　perfumes.　　SS 4:10
You sent your ambassadorsᵇ
　　far away;　　Eze 23:16
you descended to the
　　graveᶜ itself!　　Isa 8:19
¹⁰You were wearied by all your
　　ways,
but you would not say, 'It is
　　hopeless.'　　Jer 2:25
You found renewal of your
　　strength,　　1Sa 2:4
and so you did not faint.

¹¹"Whom have you so dreaded
　　and feared　　2Ki 1:15
that you have been false to
　　me,
and have neither
　　remembered me
nor pondered this in your
　　hearts?　　Isa 42:23
Is it not because I have long
　　been silent　　Est 4:14
that you do not fear me?
¹²I will expose your
　　righteousness and your
　　works,　　Isa 29:15
and they will not benefit
　　you.
¹³When you cry out for help,
　　let your collection ₍of idols₎
　　save you!　　Jdg 10:14
The wind will carry all of
　　them off,
a mere breath will blow
　　them away.　　Isa 40:7
But the man who makes me
　　his refuge
will inherit the land
and possess my holy
　　mountain."　　Isa 2:2-3

Comfort for the Contrite

¹⁴And it will be said:

"Build up, build up, prepare
　　the road!　　Isa 11:16
Remove the obstacles out of
　　the way of my people."
¹⁵For this is what the high and
　　lofty One says—　　Isa 52:13
he who lives forever, whose
　　name is holy:　　Dt 33:27
"I live in a high and holy
　　place,　　Job 16:19
but also with him who is

ᵃ9 Or *to the king*　　ᵇ9 Or *idols*　　ᶜ9 Hebrew *Sheol*

contrite and lowly in
spirit,   Ps 147:3
to revive the spirit of the
lowly
and to revive the heart of
the contrite.   2Ki 22:19
16I will not accuse forever,
nor will I always be angry,
for then the spirit of man
would grow faint before
me—   Ps 103:9
the breath of man that I
have created.   Ge 2:7
17I was enraged by his sinful
greed;   Isa 56:11
I punished him, and hid my
face in anger,   Isa 1:15
yet he kept on in his willful
ways.   Isa 1:4
18I have seen his ways, but I
will heal him;   Dt 32:39
I will guide him and restore
comfort to him,   Isa 49:13
19 creating praise on the lips
of the mourners in
Israel.   Isa 6:7
Peace, peace, to those far and
near,"   Ac 2:39
says the LORD. "And I will
heal them."
20But the wicked are like the
tossing sea,   Ge 49:4
which cannot rest,
whose waves cast up mire
and mud.   Ps 69:14
21"There is no peace," says my
God, "for the wicked."

True Fasting

58 "Shout it aloud, do not
hold back.   Isa 40:6
Raise your voice like a
trumpet.   Ex 20:18

Declare to my people their
rebellion   Isa 24:20
and to the house of Jacob
their sins.   Isa 57:12
2For day after day they seek
me out;   Isa 48:1
they seem eager to know
my ways,
as if they were a nation that
does what is right
and has not forsaken the
commands of its God.
They ask me for just
decisions
and seem eager for God to
come near them.   Isa 29:13
3'Why have we fasted,' they
say,   Lev 16:29
and you have not seen it?
Why have we humbled
ourselves,   Ex 10:3
and you have not noticed?'

"Yet on the day of your
fasting, you do as you
please   Isa 22:13
and exploit all your
workers.
4Your fasting ends in
quarreling and strife,
and in striking each other
with wicked fists.
You cannot fast as you do
today
and expect your voice to be
heard on high.   1Sa 8:18
5Is this the kind of fast I have
chosen,   Zec 7:5
only a day for a man to
humble himself?   1Ki 21:27
Is it only for bowing one's
head like a reed   Isa 36:6
and for lying on sackcloth
and ashes?   Job 2:8

Is that what you call a fast,
a day acceptable to the
Lord?

6"Is not this the kind of
fasting I have chosen:
to loose the chains of
injustice   Ne 5:10-11
and untie the cords of the
yoke,
to set the oppressed free
and break every yoke?   Isa 9:4
7Is it not to share your food
with the hungry   Job 22:7
and to provide the poor
wanderer with
shelter—
when you see the naked, to
clothe him,   Mt 25:36
and not to turn away from
your own flesh and
blood?   Ge 29:14
8Then your light will break
forth like the dawn,
and your healing will
quickly appear;   Isa 1:5
then your righteousness[a] will
go before you,   Isa 26:2
and the glory of the Lord
will be your rear guard.
9Then you will call, and the
Lord will answer;   Job 8:6
you will cry for help, and
he will say: Here am I.

"If you do away with the
yoke of oppression,
with the pointing finger
and malicious talk,   Ps 12:2
10and if you spend yourselves
in behalf of the hungry
and satisfy the needs of the
oppressed,   Dt 15:7-8

then your light will rise in
the darkness,   Isa 42:16
and your night will become
like the noonday.   Job 11:17
11The Lord will guide you
always;   Ps 48:14
he will satisfy your needs in
a sun-scorched land
and will strengthen your
frame.   Pr 72:16
You will be like a
well-watered garden,
like a spring whose waters
never fail.   Isa 35:7
12Your people will rebuild the
ancient ruins   Isa 49:8
and will raise up the
age-old foundations;
you will be called Repairer of
Broken Walls,   Ne 2:17
Restorer of Streets with
Dwellings.

13"If you keep your feet from
breaking the Sabbath
and from doing as you
please on my holy day,
if you call the Sabbath a
delight   Ps 37:4
and the Lord's holy day
honorable,
and if you honor it by not
going your own way
and not doing as you please
or speaking idle words,
14then you will find your joy in
the Lord,   Job 22:36
and I will cause you to ride
on the heights of the
land   Dt 32:13
and to feast on the
inheritance of your
father Jacob."   Ps 105:10-11

The mouth of the LORD
has spoken.

Sin, Confession and Redemption

59 Surely the arm of the
LORD is not too short to
save,   Isa 50:2
nor his ear too dull to hear.
²But your iniquities have
separated
you from your God;   Jer 5:25
your sins have hidden his
face from you,
so that he will not hear.
³For your hands are stained
with blood,   2Ki 21:16
your fingers with guilt.
Your lips have spoken lies,
and your tongue mutters
wicked things.   Isa 3:8
⁴No one calls for justice; Isa 5:23
no one pleads his case with
integrity.
They rely on empty
arguments and speak
lies;   Isa 44:20
they conceive trouble and
give birth to evil.   Job 4:8
⁵They hatch the eggs of vipers
and spin a spider's web.
Whoever eats their eggs will
die,
and when one is broken, an
adder is hatched.
⁶Their cobwebs are useless for
clothing;
they cannot cover
themselves with what
they make.   Isa 28:20
Their deeds are evil deeds,
and acts of violence are in
their hands.   Ps 55:9

⁷Their feet rush into sin;
they are swift to shed
innocent blood.
Their thoughts are evil
thoughts;   Pr 24:2
ruin and destruction mark
their ways.   Ro 3:15-17
⁸The way of peace they do not
know;
there is no justice in their
paths.
They have turned them into
crooked roads;   Jdg 5:6
no one who walks in them
will know peace.   Isa 57:21

⁹So justice is far from us,
and righteousness does not
reach us.
We look for light, but all is
darkness;   Job 19:8
for brightness, but we walk
in deep shadows.
¹⁰Like the blind we grope
along the wall,   Dt 28:29
feeling our way like men
without eyes.
At midday we stumble as if it
were twilight;   Job 3:23
among the strong, we are
like the dead.   La 3:6
¹¹We all growl like bears;
we moan mournfully like
doves.   Ge 8:8
We look for justice, but find
none;
for deliverance, but it is far
away.

¹²For our offenses are many in
your sight,   Ezr 9:6
and our sins testify against
us.
Our offenses are ever with
us,

and we acknowledge our
   iniquities: Ps 51:3
[13]rebellion and treachery
   against the LORD,   Isa 46:8
turning our backs on our
   God,   Nu 11:20
fomenting oppression and
   revolt,   Ps 12:5
uttering lies our hearts have
   conceived.   Isa 3:8
[14]So justice is driven back,
   and righteousness stands at
   a distance;   Isa 1:21
truth has stumbled in the
   streets,   Isa 48:1
   honesty cannot enter.
[15]Truth is nowhere to be
   found,   Jer 7:28
   and whoever shuns evil
   becomes a prey.

The LORD looked and was
   displeased
that there was no justice.
[16]He saw that there was no
   one,   Isa 41:28
   he was appalled that there
   was no one to intervene;
so his own arm worked
   salvation for him,   Isa 51:5
and his own righteousness
   sustained him.   Isa 45:8
[17]He put on righteousness as
   his breastplate,   Eph 6:14
and the helmet of salvation
   on his head;   Eph 6:7
he put on the garments of
   vengeance   Job 27:6
and wrapped himself in
   zeal as in a cloak.   Isa 9:7
[18]According to what they have
   done,
   so will he repay   Lev 26:28

wrath to his enemies
   and retribution to his foes;
he will repay the islands
   their due.   Isa 11:11
[19]From the west, men will fear
   the name of the LORD,
and from the rising of the
   sun, they will revere his
   glory.   Ps 97:6
For he will come like a
   pent-up flood
that the breath of the LORD
   drives along. [a]   Isa 11:4

[20]"The Redeemer will come to
   Zion,   Isa 52:8
to those in Jacob who
   repent of their sins,"
      declares the LORD.

[21]"As for me, this is my covenant with them," says the
LORD. "My Spirit, who is on
you, and my words that I have
put in your mouth will not depart from your mouth, or from
the mouths of your children, or
from the mouths of their descendants from this time on and
forever," says the LORD. Ge 9:16

The Glory of Zion

60 "Arise, shine, for your
   light has come,   Ps 36:9
and the glory of the LORD
   rises upon you.   Ex 16:7
[2]See, darkness covers the
   earth   1Sa 2:9
and thick darkness is over
   the peoples,   Jer 13:16
but the LORD rises upon you
   and his glory appears over
   you.

[a]19 Or *When the enemy comes in like a flood, / the Spirit of the* LORD *will put him to flight*

³Nations will come to your
   light,   Isa 9:2
  and kings to the brightness
   of your dawn.   Isa 49:23

⁴"Lift up your eyes and look
   about you:
  All assemble and come to
   you;   Isa 11:12
  your sons come from afar,
   and your daughters are
   carried on the arm.   Isa 43:6
⁵Then you will look and be
   radiant,   Ex 34:29
  your heart will throb and
   swell with joy;   Isa 35:2
  the wealth on the seas will be
   brought to you,   Dt 33:19
  to you the riches of the
   nations will come.
⁶Herds of camels will cover
   your land,   Jdg 6:5
  young camels of Midian
   and Ephah.   Ge 25:4
  And all from Sheba will
   come,   Ge 10:4
  bearing gold and incense
  and proclaiming the praise
   of the LORD.   1Ki 5:7
⁷All Kedar's flocks will be
   gathered to you,   Ge 25:13
  the rams of Nebaioth will
   serve you;
  they will be accepted as
   offerings on my altar,
  and I will adorn my
   glorious temple.   Hag 2:3

⁸"Who are these that fly along
   like clouds,   Isa 19:1
  like doves to their nests?
⁹Surely the islands look to me;

in the lead are the ships of
   Tarshish,ᵃ   Ge 10:4
  bringing your sons from afar,
  with their silver and gold,
  to the honor of the LORD
   your God,   Ps 22:23
  the Holy One of Israel,
  for he has endowed you
   with splendor.   Isa 44:23

¹⁰"Foreigners will rebuild your
   walls,   Ex 1:11
  and their kings will serve
   you.   Ezr 1:2
  Though in anger I struck
   you,
  in favor I will show you
   compassion.   Ps 102:13
¹¹Your gates will always stand
   open,   Ps 24:7
  they will never be shut, day
   or night,
  so that men may bring you
   the wealth of the
   nations—   Isa 61:6
  their kings led in triumphal
   procession.   Ps 149:8
¹²For the nation or kingdom
   that will not serve you
   will perish;   Isa 11:14
  it will be utterly ruined.

¹³"The glory of Lebanon will
   come to you,   Ezr 3:7
  the pine, the fir and the
   cypress together,   Isa 41:19
  to adorn the place of my
   sanctuary;
  and I will glorify the place
   of my feet.   1Ch 28:2
¹⁴The sons of your oppressors
   will come bowing before
   you;   Isa 14:2

ᵃ9 Or *the trading ships*

all who despise you will
bow down at your
feet
and will call you the City of
the LORD,   Ge 32:28
Zion of the Holy One of
Israel.   Heb 12:22

15"Although you have been
forsaken and hated,
with no one traveling
through,   Isa 33:8
I will make you the
everlasting pride
and the joy of all
generations.   Ps 126:5
16You will drink the milk of
nations
and be nursed at royal
breasts.   Ex 6:2
Then you will know that I,
the LORD, am your
Savior,   Ex 14:30
your Redeemer, the Mighty
One of Jacob.   Ge 49:24
17Instead of bronze I will bring
you gold,   1Ki 10:21
and silver in place of iron.
Instead of wood I will bring
you bronze,
and iron in place of stones.
I will make peace your
governor   Ps 85:8
and righteousness your
ruler.   Isa 9:7
18No longer will violence be
heard in your land,
nor ruin or destruction
within your borders,
but you will call your walls
Salvation   Isa 33:6
and your gates Praise.
19The sun will no more be your
light by day,

nor will the brightness of
the moon shine on you,
for the LORD will be your
everlasting light,   Ps 36:9
and your God will be your
glory.   Ps 85:9
20Your sun will never set
again,   Isa 30:26
and your moon will wane
no more;
the LORD will be your
everlasting light,
and your days of sorrow
will end.   Isa 30:19
21Then will all your people be
righteous   Isa 4:3
and they will possess the
land forever.   Ps 37:11
They are the shoot I have
planted,   Ex 15:17
the work of my hands,
for the display of my
splendor.   Lev 10:3
22The least of you will become
a thousand,
the smallest a mighty
nation.   Ge 12:2
I am the LORD;
in its time I will do this
swiftly."   Isa 5:19

The Year of the LORD's Favor

61 The Spirit of the
Sovereign LORD is on
me,   Isa 11:2
because the LORD has
anointed me
to preach good news to the
poor.   2Sa 18:26
He has sent me to bind up
the brokenhearted,2Ki 22:19
to proclaim freedom for the
captives   Ps 68:6

and release from darkness
for the prisoners, ^a
²to proclaim the year of the
LORD's favor   Isa 49:8
and the day of vengeance of
our God,   Isa 1:24
to comfort all who mourn,
³ and provide for those who
grieve in Zion—
to bestow on them a crown
of beauty   Isa 3:23
instead of ashes,   Job 2:8
the oil of gladness
instead of mourning,   Jer 31:13
and a garment of praise
instead of a spirit of
despair.
They will be called oaks of
righteousness,
a planting of the LORD
for the display of his
splendor.   Isa 44:23

⁴They will rebuild the ancient
ruins   Isa 44:26
and restore the places long
devastated;
they will renew the ruined
cities
that have been devastated
for generations.
⁵Aliens will shepherd your
flocks;   Isa 14:1-2
foreigners will work your
fields and vineyards.
⁶And you will be called priests
of the LORD,   Ex 19:6
you will be named
ministers of our God.
You will feed on the wealth
of nations,   Dt 33:19
and in their riches you will
boast.

⁷Instead of their shame
my people will receive a
double portion,
and instead of disgrace
they will rejoice in their
inheritance;
and so they will inherit a
double portion in their
land,   Isa 60:21
and everlasting joy will be
theirs.   Ps 126:5

⁸"For I, the LORD, love justice;
I hate robbery and iniquity.
In my faithfulness I will
reward them
and make an everlasting
covenant with them.
⁹Their descendants will be
known among the
nations   Isa 43:5
and their offspring among
the peoples.
All who see them will
acknowledge
that they are a people the
LORD has blessed."   Ge 12:2

¹⁰I delight greatly in the LORD;
my soul rejoices in my God.
For he has clothed me with
garments of salvation
and arrayed me in a robe of
righteousness,   Job 27:6
as a bridegroom adorns his
head like a priest,
and as a bride adorns
herself with her jewels.
¹¹For as the soil makes the
sprout come up
and a garden causes seeds
to grow,   Ge 47:23
so the Sovereign LORD will

^a1 Hebrew; Septuagint *the blind*

make righteousness and
praise   Isa 45:8
spring up before all nations.

Zion's New Name

62 For Zion's sake I will not
keep silent,   Est 4:14
for Jerusalem's sake I will
not remain quiet,
till her righteousness shines
out like the dawn,
her salvation like a blazing
torch.   Ps 67:2
²The nations will see your
righteousness,   Isa 40:5
and all kings your glory;
you will be called by a new
name   Ge 32:28
that the mouth of the LORD
will bestow.
³You will be a crown of
splendor in the LORD's
hand,   Isa 28:5
a royal diadem in the hand
of your God.
⁴No longer will they call you
Deserted,   Lev 26:43
or name your land
Desolate.   Isa 49:19
But you will be called
Hephzibah,ᵃ   2Ki 21:1
and your land Beulahᵇ;
for the LORD will take delight
in you,   Isa 65:19
and your land will be
married.   Isa 54:5
⁵As a young man marries a
maiden,
so will your sonsᶜ marry
you;
as a bridegroom rejoices over
his bride,

so will your God rejoice
over you.   Dt 28:63

⁶I have posted watchmen on
your walls, O Jerusalem;
they will never be silent day
or night.
You who call on the LORD,
give yourselves no rest,
⁷and give him no rest till he
establishes Jerusalem
and makes her the praise of
the earth.   Dt 26:19

⁸The LORD has sworn by his
right hand   Ge 22:16
and by his mighty arm:
"Never again will I give your
grain   Dt 28:30-33
as food for your enemies,
and never again will
foreigners drink the new
wine
for which you have toiled;
⁹but those who harvest it will
eat it   Isa 1:19
and praise the LORD,
and those who gather the
grapes will drink it
in the courts of my
sanctuary."   Lev 33:39

¹⁰Pass through, pass through
the gates!   Ps 24:7
Prepare the way for the
people.
Build up, build up the
highway!   Isa 57:14
Remove the stones.
Raise a banner for the
nations.   Isa 11:10

¹¹The LORD has made
proclamation

ᵃ4 *Hephzibah* means *my delight is in her.*   ᵇ4 *Beulah* means *married.*   ᶜ5 Or *Builder*

to the ends of the earth:
"Say to the Daughter of
Zion,   Ps 9:14
'See, your Savior comes!
See, his reward is with him,
and his recompense
accompanies him.'"
¹²They will be called the Holy
People,   Ge 32:28; Ex 19:6
the Redeemed of the LORD;
and you will be called Sought
After,
the City No Longer
Deserted.   Ps 27:9

God's Day of Vengeance and Redemption

63 Who is this coming from
Edom,   2Ch 28:17
from Bozrah, with his
garments stained
crimson?   Rev 19:13
Who is this, robed in
splendor,
striding forward in the
greatness of his
strength?   Job 9:4

"It is I, speaking in
righteousness,
mighty to save."   Isa 46:13

²Why are your garments red,
like those of one treading
the winepress?   Ge 49:11

³"I have trodden the
winepress alone;   Jdg 6:11
from the nations no one
was with me.
I trampled them in my anger
and trod them down in my
wrath;   Isa 22:5
their blood spattered my
garments,   Rev 19:13

and I stained all my
clothing.
⁴For the day of vengeance was
in my heart,   Isa 1:24
and the year of my
redemption has come.
⁵I looked, but there was no
one to help,   2Ki 14:26
I was appalled that no one
gave support;
so my own arm worked
salvation for me,
and my own wrath
sustained me.   Isa 59:16
⁶I trampled the nations in my
anger;   Job 40:12
in my wrath I made them
drunk   Isa 29:9
and poured their blood on
the ground."   Isa 34:3

Praise and Prayer

⁷I will tell of the kindnesses of
the LORD,   Isa 54:8
the deeds for which he is to
be praised,
according to all the LORD
has done for us—
yes, the many good things he
has done
for the house of Israel,   Ex 18:9
according to his compassion
and many kindnesses.
⁸He said, "Surely they are my
people,   Ps 100:3
sons who will not be false
to me";
and so he became their
Savior.   Ex 14:30
⁹In all their distress he too
was distressed,
and the angel of his
presence saved them.

In his love and mercy he
   redeemed them;   Dt 7:7-8
he lifted them up and
   carried them
all the days of old.   Dt 1:31
[10]Yet they rebelled
   and grieved his Holy Spirit.
So he turned and became
   their enemy   Ps 106:40
and he himself fought
   against them.   Jos 10:14

[11]Then his people recalled[a] the
   days of old,
   the days of Moses and his
      people—
where is he who brought
   them through the sea,
   with the shepherd of his
      flock?   Ps 77:20
Where is he who set
   his Holy Spirit among
      them,   Nu 11:17
[12]who sent his glorious arm of
   power
   to be at Moses' right hand,
who divided the waters
   before them,   Ex 14:21-22
to gain for himself
   everlasting renown,
[13]who led them through the
   depths?   Ex 14:22
Like a horse in open country,
   they did not stumble;   Ps 119:11
[14]like cattle that go down to
   the plain,
   they were given rest by the
      Spirit of the LORD.   Ex 33:14
This is how you guided your
   people
to make for yourself a
   glorious name.

[15]Look down from heaven and
   see   Dt 26:15
from your lofty throne, holy
   and glorious.   1Ki 22:19
Where are your zeal and
   your might?   Isa 9:7
Your tenderness and
   compassion are withheld
   from us.   Ge 43:31
[16]But you are our Father,
   though Abraham does not
      know us   Ex 4:22
or Israel acknowledge us;
you, O LORD, are our Father,
   our Redeemer from of old is
      your name.   Isa 41:14
[17]Why, O LORD, do you make
   us wander from your
      ways   Ge 20:13
and harden our hearts so
   we do not revere you?
Return for the sake of your
   servants,   Nu 10:36
   the tribes that are your
      inheritance.   Ex 34:9
[18]For a little while your people
   possessed your holy
      place,   Dt 4:26
but now our enemies have
   trampled down your
      sanctuary.   Lev 26:31
[19]We are yours from of old;
   but you have not ruled over
      them,
they have not been called
   by your name.[b]   Isa 43:7

64 Oh, that you would rend
   the heavens and come
      down,   Ps 18:9
that the mountains would
   tremble before you!

---

[a]11 Or But may he recall   [b]19 Or We are like those you have never ruled, / like those never
called by your name

²As when fire sets twigs
  ablaze
and causes water to boil,
come down to make your
    name known to your
    enemies   Isa 30:27
and cause the nations to
    quake before you!   Ps 99:1
³For when you did awesome
    things that we did not
    expect,   Ps 65:5
you came down, and the
    mountains trembled
    before you.   Ps 18:7
⁴Since ancient times no one
    has heard,
  no ear has perceived,
no eye has seen any God
    besides you,   Isa 43:10-11
who acts on behalf of those
    who wait for him. Isa 30:18
⁵You come to the help of
    those who gladly do
    right,   Isa 26:8
  who remember your ways.
But when we continued to
    sin against them,
  you were angry.   Isa 10:4
  How then can we be
    saved?
⁶All of us have become like
    one who is unclean,
and all our righteous acts
    are like filthy rags;
we all shrivel up like a leaf,
and like the wind our sins
    sweep us away.   Ps 1:4
⁷No one calls on your name
  or strives to lay hold of
    you;
  for you have hidden your
    face from us   Dt 31:18
and made us waste away
    because of our sins.

⁸Yet, O LORD, you are our
    Father.   Ex 4:22
We are the clay, you are the
    potter;   Isa 29:16
we are all the work of your
    hand.   Job 10:3
⁹Do not be angry beyond
    measure, O LORD;
  do not remember our sins
    forever.   Isa 43:25
Oh, look upon us, we pray,
  for we are all your people.
¹⁰Your sacred cities have
    become a desert;   Ps 78:54
even Zion is a desert,
    Jerusalem a desolation.
¹¹Our holy and glorious
    temple, where our
    fathers praised you,
has been burned with fire,
and all that we treasured
    lies in ruins.   La 1:7
¹²After all this, O LORD, will
    you hold yourself
    back?
Will you keep silent and
    punish us beyond
    measure?   Est 4:14

Judgment and Salvation

65 "I revealed myself to
    those who did not ask
    for me;
  I was found by those who
    did not seek me. Hos 1:10
To a nation that did not call
    on my name,   Ps 14:4
  I said, 'Here am I, here
    am I.'
²All day long I have held out
    my hands
  to an obstinate people, Ps 78:8
who walk in ways not good,

pursuing their own
 imaginations— Ps 81:11-12
³a people who continually
 provoke me
to my very face, Job 1:11
offering sacrifices in gardens
and burning incense on
 altars of brick; Lev 2:2
⁴who sit among the graves
and spend their nights
 keeping secret vigil;
who eat the flesh of pigs,
and whose pots hold broth
 of unclean meat; Lev 11:7
⁵who say, 'Keep away; don't
 come near me,
for I am too sacred for you!'
Such people are smoke in my
 nostrils, Pr 10:26
a fire that keeps burning all
 day.

⁶"See, it stands written before
 me:
I will not keep silent but
 will pay back in full;
I will pay it back into their
 laps— Ps 79:12
⁷both your sins and the sins of
 your fathers," Isa 22:14
says the LORD.
"Because they burned
 sacrifices on the
 mountains
and defied me on the hills,
I will measure into their laps
 the full payment for their
 former deeds." Pr 10:24

⁸This is what the LORD says:

"As when juice is still found
 in a cluster of grapes
and men say, 'Don't
 destroy it, Isa 5:2

there is yet some good in
 it,'
so will I do in behalf of my
 servants; Isa 54:17
I will not destroy them all.
⁹I will bring forth descendants
 from Jacob, Isa 45:19
and from Judah those who
 will possess my
 mountains; Nu 34:13
my chosen people will inherit
 them, Isa 14:1
and there will my servants
 live. Isa 32:18
¹⁰Sharon will become a pasture
 for flocks, Jer 31:12
and the Valley of Achor a
 resting place for herds,
for my people who seek
 me. Isa 51:1
¹¹"But as for you who forsake
 the LORD Dt 28:20
and forget my holy
 mountain, Dt 33:19
who spread a table for
 Fortune
and fill bowls of mixed
 wine for Destiny, Isa 5:22
¹²I will destine you for the
 sword, Isa 1:20
and you will all bend down
 for the slaughter; Isa 30:25
for I called but you did not
 answer, Pr 1:24-25
I spoke but you did not
 listen. 2Ch 36:15-16
You did evil in my sight
 and chose what displeases
 me." Ps 149:7

¹³Therefore this is what the
Sovereign LORD says:

"My servants will eat, Isa 1:19

but you will go hungry;
my servants will drink, Isa 33:16
but you will go thirsty;
my servants will rejoice,
but you will be put to
shame. Isa 44:9
¹⁴My servants will sing
out of the joy of their
hearts, Ps 109:28
but you will cry out
from anguish of heart
and wail in brokenness of
spirit. Isa 15:2
¹⁵You will leave your name
to my chosen ones as a
curse; Nu 5:27
the Sovereign LORD will put
you to death,
but to his servants he will
give another name.
¹⁶Whoever invokes a blessing
in the land Dt 29:19
will do so by the God of
truth; Ps 31:5
he who takes an oath in the
land
will swear by the God of
truth. Ps 63:11
For the past troubles will be
forgotten Job 11:16
and hidden from my eyes.

New Heavens and a New Earth

¹⁷"Behold, I will create
new heavens and a new
earth. Isa 41:22
The former things will not be
remembered, Isa 43:18
nor will they come to mind.
¹⁸But be glad and rejoice
forever Dt 32:43

in what I will create,
for I will create Jerusalem to
be a delight
and its people a joy. Rev 21:2
¹⁹I will rejoice over Jerusalem
and take delight in my
people; Dt 30:9
the sound of weeping and of
crying Isa 25:8
will be heard in it no more.

²⁰"Never again will there be
in it
an infant who lives but a
few days, Isa 11:8
or an old man who does not
live out his years; Ge 5:1-32
he who dies at a hundred
will be thought a mere
youth;
he who fails to reachᵃ a
hundred
will be considered
accursed.
²¹They will build houses and
dwell in them; Isa 32:18
they will plant vineyards
and eat their fruit. 2Ki 19:29
²²No longer will they build
houses and others live in
them, Dt 28:30
or plant and others eat.
For as the days of a tree,
so will be the days of my
people; Ps 21:4
my chosen ones will long
enjoy
the works of their hands.
²³They will not toil in vain
or bear children doomed to
misfortune; Dt 28:32
for they will be a people
blessed by the LORD,

ᵃ20 Or / the sinner who reaches

they and their descendants
with them.   Isa 44:3
²⁴Before they call I will answer;
while they are still speaking
I will hear.   Da 9:20-23
²⁵The wolf and the lamb will
feed together,   Isa 11:6
and the lion will eat straw
like the ox,   Job 40:15
but dust will be the
serpent's food.   Ge 3:14
They will neither harm nor
destroy
on all my holy mountain,"
says the LORD.

Judgment and Hope

66 This is what the LORD
says:

"Heaven is my throne,
and the earth is my
footstool.   1Ki 8:27
Where is the house you will
build for me?   2Sa 7:7
Where will my resting place
be?
²Has not my hand made all
these things,   Isa 40:26
and so they came into
being?"
declares the LORD.

"This is the one I esteem:
he who is humble and
contrite in spirit,   Isa 57:15
and trembles at my word.
³But whoever sacrifices a bull
is like one who kills a man,
and whoever offers a lamb,
like one who breaks a dog's
neck;
whoever makes a grain
offering

is like one who presents
pig's blood,   Lev 11:7
and whoever burns memorial
incense,   Lev 2:2
like one who worships an
idol.
They have chosen their own
ways,   Isa 57:17
and their souls delight in
their abominations;
⁴so I also will choose harsh
treatment for them
and will bring upon them
what they dread.   Pr 10:24
For when I called, no one
answered,   1Sa 8:19
when I spoke, no one
listened.
They did evil in my sight
and chose what displeases
me."   Isa 65:12

⁵Hear the word of the LORD,
you who tremble at his
word: Ezr 9:4
"Your brothers who hate
you,   Ps 38:20
and exclude you because of
my name, have said,
'Let the LORD be glorified,
that we may see your joy!'
Yet they will be put to
shame.   Isa 44:9
⁶Hear that uproar from the
city,
hear that noise from the
temple!
It is the sound of the LORD
repaying his enemies all
they deserve.   Lev 26:28

⁷"Before she goes into labor,
she gives birth;   Isa 54:1
before the pains come upon
her,

she delivers a son.   Lev 12:5
⁸Who has ever heard of such a
    thing?
Who has ever seen such
    things?   Isa 64:4
Can a country be born in a
    day   Isa 49:20
or a nation be brought forth
    in a moment?
Yet no sooner is Zion in labor
than she gives birth to her
    children.   Isa 49:31
⁹Do I bring to the moment of
    birth
and not give delivery?"
    says the LORD.   Isa 37:3
"Do I close up the womb
    when I bring to delivery?"
    says your God.
¹⁰"Rejoice with Jerusalem and
    be glad for her,   Dt 32:43
all you who love her;
rejoice greatly with her,
all you who mourn over
    her.   Isa 57:19
¹¹For you will nurse and be
    satisfied   Nu 11:12
    at her comforting breasts;
you will drink deeply
    and delight in her
    overflowing
    abundance."   Nu 25:1

¹²For this is what the LORD
says:

"I will extend peace to her
    like a river,   Ps 119:165
and the wealth of nations
    like a flooding stream;
you will nurse and be carried
    on her arm   Nu 11:12

and dandled on her knees.
¹³As a mother comforts her
    child,   Isa 49:15
so will I comfort you;   Isa 40:1
and you will be comforted
    over Jerusalem."

¹⁴When you see this, your
    heart will rejoice   Isa 25:9
and you will flourish like
    grass;   Ps 72:16
the hand of the LORD will be
    made known to his
    servants,   Isa 54:17
but his fury will be shown
    to his foes.   Isa 10:5
¹⁵See, the LORD is coming with
    fire,   Isa 1:31
and his chariots are like a
    whirlwind;   2Ki 2:1
he will bring down his anger
    with fury,
and his rebuke with flames
    of fire.   Dt 28:20
¹⁶For with fire and with his
    sword   Isa 1:20
the LORD will execute
    judgment upon all men,
and many will be those
    slain by the LORD.   Isa 10:4

¹⁷"Those who consecrate and
purify themselves to go into the
gardens, following the one in
the midst of[a] those who eat the
flesh of pigs and rats and other
abominable things—they will
meet their end together," declares the LORD.   Ps 37:20

¹⁸"And I, because of their actions and their imaginations,
am about to come[b] and gather

---

[a]17 Or gardens behind one of your temples, and
this clause is uncertain.

[b]18 The meaning of the Hebrew for

all nations and tongues, and they will come and see my glory. Pr 24:2; Zec 12:3

¹⁹"I will set a sign among them, and I will send some of those who survive to the nations—to Tarshish, to the Libyans[a] and Lydians (famous as archers), to Tubal and Greece, and to the distant islands that have not heard of my fame or seen my glory. They will proclaim my glory among the nations. ²⁰And they will bring all your brothers, from all the nations, to my holy mountain in Jerusalem as an offering to the LORD—on horses, in chariots and wagons, and on mules and camels," says the LORD. "They will bring them, as the Israelites bring their grain offerings, to the temple of the LORD in ceremonially clean vessels. ²¹And I will select some of them also to be priests and Levites," says the LORD. Ex 19:6; Isa 11:10

²²"As the new heavens and the new earth that I make will endure before me," declares the LORD, "so will your name and descendants endure. ²³From one New Moon to another and from one Sabbath to another, all mankind will come and bow down before me," says the LORD. ²⁴"And they will go out and look upon the dead bodies of those who rebelled against me; their worm will not die, nor will their fire be quenched, and they will be loathsome to all mankind." Isa 65:17; Mt 25:41

Jeremiah

Introduction:

Jeremiah, like Isaiah, was a young man called by God to warn Judah about its wickedness. He spent the first twenty years of his ministry under Josiah, a good king who tried to bring the people of Judah back to God. After this Jeremiah was often in danger from political and religious leaders who were angry because of his messages. Through all this God protected Jeremiah so he could continue to warn the wicked and comfort those who trusted in God.

After Jerusalem was destroyed in 586 B.C., Jeremiah chose to remain with the people, and eventually went with them to Egypt.

Since the messages of Jeremiah are not arranged in chronological order, it is helpful to read the history of Judah as found in Kings and Chronicles to better understand Jeremiah's messages.

Outline of contents:

1 The words of Jeremiah son of Hilkiah, one of the priests at Anathoth in the territory of Benjamin. ²The word of the LORD came to him in the thirteenth year of the reign of Josiah son of Amon king of Judah, ³and through the reign of Jehoiakim son of Josiah king of Judah, down to the fifth month of the eleventh year of Zedekiah son of Josiah king of Judah, when the people of Jerusalem went into exile.   Jos 21:18; Hos 1:1

The Call of Jeremiah

⁴The word of the Lᴏʀᴅ came to me, saying,

⁵"Before I formed you in the
    womb I knew*ᵃ* you,
before you were born I set
    you apart;   Jn 10:36
I appointed you as a
    prophet to the nations."

⁶"Ah, Sovereign Lᴏʀᴅ," I said, "I do not know how to speak; I am only a child." Ex 3:11

⁷But the Lᴏʀᴅ said to me, "Do not say, 'I am only a child.' You must go to everyone I send you to and say whatever I command you. ⁸Do not be afraid of them, for I am with you and will rescue you," declares the Lᴏʀᴅ.

⁹Then the Lᴏʀᴅ reached out his hand and touched my mouth and said to me, "Now, I have put my words in your mouth. ¹⁰See, today I appoint you over nations and kingdoms to uproot and tear down, to destroy and overthrow, to build and to plant." Isa 6:7; Jer 25:17

¹¹The word of the Lᴏʀᴅ came to me: "What do you see, Jeremiah?" Jer 24:3

"I see the branch of an almond tree," I replied.

¹²The Lᴏʀᴅ said to me, "You have seen correctly, for I am watching*ᵇ* to see that my word is fulfilled." Job 29:2; Jer 44:27

¹³The word of the Lᴏʀᴅ came to me again: "What do you see?" Jer 24:3

"I see a boiling pot, tilting away from the north," I answered.

¹⁴The Lᴏʀᴅ said to me, "From the north disaster will be poured out on all who live in the land. ¹⁵I am about to summon all the peoples of the northern kingdoms," declares the Lᴏʀᴅ.

"Their kings will come and
    set up their thrones
in the entrance of the gates
    of Jerusalem;
they will come against all her
    surrounding walls
and against all the towns of
    Judah.   Jer 4:16
¹⁶I will pronounce my
    judgments on my people
because of their wickedness
    in forsaking me, Jer 2:13
in burning incense to other
    gods   Ex 20:3
and in worshiping what
    their hands have made.

¹⁷"Get yourself ready! Stand up and say to them whatever I command you. Do not be terrified by them, or I will terrify you before them. ¹⁸Today I have made you a fortified city, an iron pillar and a bronze wall to stand against the whole land—against the kings of Judah, its officials, its priests and the people of the land. ¹⁹They will fight against you but will not overcome you, for I am with you and will rescue you," declares the Lᴏʀᴅ. Isa 50:7

---

*ᵃ*5 Or *chose*   *ᵇ*12 The Hebrew for *watching* sounds like the Hebrew for *almond tree*.

Israel Forsakes God

2 The word of the LORD came to me: [2]"Go and proclaim in the hearing of Jerusalem:

" 'I remember the devotion
    of your youth,   Ps 71:17
how as a bride you loved
    me
and followed me through the
    desert,   Ex 13:21
through a land not sown.
[3]Israel was holy to the LORD,
    the firstfruits of his harvest;
all who devoured her were
    held guilty,   Isa 41:11
and disaster overtook
    them,' "
        declares the LORD.

[4]Hear the word of the LORD,
    O house of Jacob,
all you clans of the house of
    Israel.

[5]This is what the LORD says:

"What fault did your fathers
    find in me,
that they strayed so far
    from me?
They followed worthless
    idols   Dt 32:21
and became worthless
    themselves.
[6]They did not ask, 'Where is
    the LORD,
who brought us up out of
    Egypt   Ex 6:6
and led us through the
    barren wilderness,

through a land of deserts
    and rifts,   Dt 1:19
a land of drought and
    darkness,[a]
a land where no one travels
    and no one lives?'   Jer 51:43
[7]I brought you into a fertile
    land
to eat its fruit and rich
    produce.   Nu 13:27
But you came and defiled my
    land
and made my inheritance
    detestable.   Ps 106:34-39
[8]The priests did not ask,
    'Where is the LORD?'
Those who deal with the law
    did not know me;   1Sa 2:12
the leaders rebelled against
    me.   Jer 3:15
The prophets prophesied by
    Baal,   1Ki 18:22
following worthless idols.

[9]"Therefore I bring charges
    against you again,"
        declares the LORD.
"And I will bring charges
    against your children's
    children.
[10]Cross over to the coasts of
    Kittim[b] and look,   Ge 10:4
send to Kedar[c] and observe
    closely;   Ge 25:13
see if there has ever been
    anything like this:
[11]Has a nation ever changed its
    gods?
(Yet they are not gods at
    all.)   Isa 37:19

---

[a]6 Or and the shadow of death   [b]10 That is, Cyprus and western coastlands
[c]10 The home of Bedouin tribes in the Syro-Arabian desert

But my people have
    exchanged their[a] Glory
    for worthless idols.   1Sa 4:21
[12]Be appalled at this,
    O heavens,
and shudder with great
    horror,"
            declares the Lord.
[13]"My people have committed
    two sins:
They have forsaken me,   Dt 31:16
    the spring of living water,
and have dug their own
    cisterns,
broken cisterns that cannot
    hold water.
[14]Is Israel a servant, a slave by
    birth?   Ex 4:22
Why then has he become
    plunder?
[15]Lions have roared;   Jer 4:7
    they have growled at
    him.
They have laid waste his
    land;   Isa 1:7
his towns are burned and
    deserted.   Lev 26:43
[16]Also, the men of Memphis[b]
    and Tahpanhes   Isa 19:13
have shaved the crown of
    your head.[c]
[17]Have you not brought this on
    yourselves   Jer 4:18
by forsaking the Lord your
    God   Isa 1:28
when he led you in the
    way?
[18]Now why go to Egypt
    to drink water from the
    Shihor[d]?   Jos 13:3
And why go to Assyria

to drink water from the
    River[e]?   Isa 7:20
[19]Your wickedness will punish
    you;
your backsliding will
    rebuke you.   Isa 3:9
Consider then and realize
    how evil and bitter it is for
    you   Job 20:14
when you forsake the Lord
    your God
and have no awe of me,"
            declares the Lord,
            the Lord Almighty.

[20]"Long ago you broke off
    your yoke   Lev 26:13
and tore off your bonds;
you said, 'I will not serve
    you!'   Job 21:14
Indeed, on every high hill
and under every spreading
    tree   Dt 12:2
you lay down as a
    prostitute.   Isa 1:21
[21]I had planted you like a
    choice vine   Ps 80:8
of sound and reliable stock.
How then did you turn
    against me
into a corrupt, wild vine?
[22]Although you wash yourself
    with soda   Job 9:30
and use an abundance of
    soap,
the stain of your guilt is still
    before me,"
            declares the Sovereign
            Lord.
[23]"How can you say, 'I am not
    defiled;   Pr 30:12

---

[a]11 Masoretic Text; an ancient Hebrew scribal tradition *my*   [b]16 Hebrew *Noph*
[c]16 Or *have cracked your skull*   [d]18 That is, a branch of the Nile   [e]18 That is, the
Euphrates

I have not run after the
Baals'?   Jer 9:14
See how you behaved in the
valley;   2Ki 23:10
consider what you have
done.
You are a swift she-camel
running here and there,
²⁴a wild donkey accustomed to
the desert,   Job 39:6
sniffing the wind in her
craving—
in her heat who can restrain
her?
Any males that pursue her
need not tire
themselves;
at mating time they will
find her.
²⁵Do not run until your feet are
bare
and your throat is dry.
But you said, 'It's no use!
I love foreign gods,   Dt 32:16
and I must go after them.'

²⁶"As a thief is disgraced when
he is caught,   Jer 48:27
so the house of Israel is
disgraced—
they, their kings and their
officials,
their priests and their
prophets.   Jer 32:32
²⁷They say to wood, 'You are
my father,'   Jer 10:8
and to stone, 'You gave me
birth.'   Jer 3:9
They have turned their backs
to me
and not their faces;   Jer 18:17
yet when they are in trouble,
they say,
'Come and save us!'   Isa 37:20

²⁸Where then are the gods you
made for yourselves?
Let them come if they can
save you
when you are in trouble!
For you have as many gods
as you have towns,
O Judah.   2Ki 17:29

²⁹"Why do you bring charges
against me?
You have all rebelled
against me,"   Jer 5:1
declares the LORD.
³⁰"In vain I punished your
people;
they did not respond to
correction.   Lev 26:23
Your sword has devoured
your prophets
like a ravening lion.   Ne 9:26

³¹"You of this generation,
consider the word of the LORD:

"Have I been a desert to
Israel
or a land of great darkness?
Why do my people say, 'We
are free to roam;
we will come to you no
more'?   Job 21:14
³²Does a maiden forget her
jewelry,
a bride her wedding
ornaments?
Yet my people have forgotten
me,
days without number.   Dt 32:18
³³How skilled you are at
pursuing love!
Even the worst of women
can learn from your
ways.

³⁴On your clothes men find
the lifeblood of the innocent
poor,   2Ki 21:16
though you did not catch
them breaking in.   Ex 22:2
Yet in spite of all this
³⁵ you say, 'I am innocent;
he is not angry with me.'
But I will pass judgment on
you   Isa 66:16
because you say, 'I have not
sinned.'   2Sa 12:13
³⁶Why do you go about so
much,
changing your ways? Jer 31:22
You will be disappointed by
Egypt
as you were by Assyria.
³⁷You will also leave that place
with your hands on your
head,   2Sa 23:19
for the LORD has rejected
those you trust;
you will not be helped by
them.   Jer 37:7

3 "If a man divorces his wife
and she leaves him and
marries another man,
should he return to her
again?   Dt 24:1-4
Would not the land be
completely defiled?
But you have lived as a
prostitute with many
lovers—   2Ki 16:7
would you now return to
me?"   Hos 2:7
declares the LORD.
²"Look up to the barren
heights and see.
Is there any place where

you have not been
ravished?
By the roadside you sat
waiting for lovers,
sat like a nomad*a* in the
desert.   Ge 38:14
You have defiled the land
with your prostitution and
wickedness.   Nu 15:39
³Therefore the showers have
been withheld,   Lev 26:19
and no spring rains have
fallen.   Dt 11:14
Yet you have the brazen look
of a prostitute;   Eze 3:7
you refuse to blush with
shame.   Jer 6:15
⁴Have you not just called to
me:
'My Father, my friend from
my youth,   Jer 2:2
⁵will you always be angry?
Will your wrath continue
forever?'
This is how you talk,
but you do all the evil you
can."

Unfaithful Israel

⁶During the reign of King Josiah, the LORD said to me,
"Have you seen what faithless
Israel has done? She has gone
up on every high hill and under
every spreading tree and has
committed adultery there. ⁷I
thought that after she had done
all this she would return to me
but she did not, and her unfaithful sister Judah saw it. ⁸I
gave faithless Israel her certificate of divorce and sent her

---

*a*2 Or *an Arab*

away because of all her adulteries. Yet I saw that her unfaithful sister Judah had no fear; she also went out and committed adultery. ⁹Because Israel's immorality mattered so little to her, she defiled the land and committed adultery with stone and wood. ¹⁰In spite of all this, her unfaithful sister Judah did not return to me with all her heart, but only in pretense," declares the LORD. 1Ch 3:14

¹¹The LORD said to me, "Faithless Israel is more righteous than unfaithful Judah. ¹²Go, proclaim this message toward the north: Eze 16:52

" 'Return, faithless Israel,'
    declares the LORD, Dt 4:30
'I will frown on you no
    longer,
for I am merciful,' declares
    the LORD, 1Ki 3:26
'I will not be angry forever.
¹³Only acknowledge your
    guilt— Dt 30:1-3
you have rebelled against
    the LORD your God,
you have scattered your
    favors to foreign gods
under every spreading tree,
and have not obeyed me,' "
    declares the LORD.

¹⁴"Return, faithless people," declares the LORD, "for I am your husband. I will choose you—one from a town and two from a clan—and bring you to Zion. ¹⁵Then I will give you shepherds after my own heart, who will lead you with knowledge and understanding. ¹⁶In those days, when your numbers have increased greatly in the land," declares the LORD, "men will no longer say, 'The ark of the covenant of the LORD.' It will never enter their minds or be remembered; it will not be missed, nor will another one be made. ¹⁷At that time they will call Jerusalem The Throne of the LORD, and all nations will gather in Jerusalem to honor the name of the LORD. No longer will they follow the stubbornness of their evil hearts. ¹⁸In those days the house of Judah will join the house of Israel, and together they will come from a northern land to the land I gave your forefathers as an inheritance. Job 22:23; Eze 37:19

¹⁹"I myself said,

" 'How gladly would I treat
    you like sons
and give you a desirable
    land, Dt 8:7
the most beautiful
    inheritance of any
    nation.' Ps 106:24
I thought you would call me
    'Father' Ex 4:22
and not turn away from
    following me.
²⁰But like a woman unfaithful
    to her husband,
so you have been unfaithful
    to me, O house of
    Israel," Isa 24:16
    declares the LORD.

²¹A cry is heard on the barren
    heights,
    the weeping and pleading
    of the people of Israel,

because they have perverted
their ways
and have forgotten the
LORD their God.   Jer 57:11

²²"Return, faithless people;
I will cure you of
backsliding."   Jer 2:19

"Yes, we will come to you,
for you are the LORD our
God.
²³Surely the ⌊idolatrous⌋
commotion on the hills
and mountains is a
deception;   Jer 2:20
surely in the LORD our God
is the salvation of Israel.
²⁴From our youth shameful
gods have consumed
the fruits of our fathers'
labor—   Jer 11:13
their flocks and herds,
their sons and daughters.
²⁵Let us lie down in our
shame,   Ezr 9:6
and let our disgrace cover
us.
We have sinned against the
LORD our God,   Jdg 10:10
both we and our fathers;
from our youth till this day
we have not obeyed the
LORD our God."   Eze 2:3

4 "If you will return,
O Israel,   Dt 4:30
return to me,"
declares the LORD.
"If you put your detestable
idols out of my sight
and no longer go astray,
²and if in a truthful, just and
righteous way

you swear, 'As surely as the
LORD lives,'   Nu 14:21
then the nations will be
blessed by him   Ge 12:2
and in him they will glory."

³This is what the LORD says to
the men of Judah and to Jerusalem:

"Break up your unplowed
ground   Hos 10:12
and do not sow among
thorns.   Mk 4:18
⁴Circumcise yourselves to the
LORD,
circumcise your hearts,
you men of Judah and
people of Jerusalem,
or my wrath will break out
and burn like fire
because of the evil you have
done—   Ex 32:22
burn with no one to quench
it.   Isa 1:31

Disaster From the North

⁵"Announce in Judah and
proclaim in Jerusalem
and say: Jer 5:20
'Sound the trumpet
throughout the land!'
Cry aloud and say:
'Gather together!
Let us flee to the fortified
cities!'   Jos 10:20
⁶Raise the signal to go to Zion!
Flee for safety without
delay!
For I am bringing disaster
from the north,   Jer 11:11
even terrible destruction."

⁷A lion has come out of his
lair;   Jer 25:38

a destroyer of nations has
    set out.   Jer 6:26
He has left his place
to lay waste your land.
Your towns will lie in ruins
    without inhabitant.   Lev 26:31
8So put on sackcloth,
    lament and wail,   1Ki 21:27
for the fierce anger of the
    LORD
has not turned away from
    us.   Isa 10:4

9"In that day," declares the
    LORD,
    "the king and the officials
        will lose heart,   1Sa 17:32
    the priests will be horrified,
    and the prophets will be
        appalled."   Isa 24:9

10Then I said, "Ah, Sovereign
LORD, how completely you
have deceived this people and
Jerusalem by saying, 'You will
have peace,' when the sword is
at our throats."   Ex 5:23
11At that time this people and
Jerusalem will be told, "A
scorching wind from the barren
heights in the desert blows
toward my people, but not to
winnow or cleanse; 12a wind too
strong for that comes from me. a
Now I pronounce my judg-
ments against them."   Isa 64:6

13Look! He advances like the
    clouds,   2Sa 22:10
    his chariots come like a
        whirlwind,   Isa 66:15
    his horses are swifter than
        eagles.   Dt 28:49
    Woe to us! We are ruined!

14O Jerusalem, wash the evil
    from your heart and be
    saved.   Isa 45:22
    How long will you harbor
        wicked thoughts?   Ps 6:3
15A voice is announcing from
    Dan,   Ge 30:6
    proclaiming disaster from
        the hills of Ephraim.
16"Tell this to the nations,
    proclaim it to Jerusalem:
    'A besieging army is coming
        from a distant land,
    raising a war cry against the
        cities of Judah.   Eze 21:22
17They surround her like men
    guarding a field,   2Ki 25:1
    because she has rebelled
        against me,' "   1Sa 12:15
            declares the LORD.
18"Your own conduct and
    actions   Ps 107:17
    have brought this upon
        you.   Jer 2:17
    This is your punishment.
        How bitter it is!   Jer 2:19
        How it pierces to the
            heart!"

19Oh, my anguish, my
    anguish!   Isa 22:4
    I writhe in pain.   Job 6:10
    Oh, the agony of my heart!
    My heart pounds within
        me,   Job 37:1
    I cannot keep silent.   Job 4:2
    For I have heard the sound of
        the trumpet;   Nu 10:2
    I have heard the battle cry.
20Disaster follows disaster;
    the whole land lies in ruins.
    In an instant my tents are
        destroyed,   Nu 24:5

a12 Or comes at my command

my shelter in a moment.
²¹How long must I see the
  battle standard   Nu 2:2
and hear the sound of the
  trumpet?   Jos 6:20

²²"My people are fools;   Jer 5:21
  they do not know me.
They are senseless children;
  they have no
    understanding.   Ps 14:4
They are skilled in doing evil;
  they know not how to do
    good."   Ps 36:3

²³I looked at the earth,
  and it was formless and
    empty;   Ge 1:2
and at the heavens,
  and their light was gone.
²⁴I looked at the mountains,
  and they were quaking;
all the hills were swaying.
²⁵I looked, and there were no
    people;
every bird in the sky had
    flown away.   Jer 7:20
²⁶I looked, and the fruitful land
    was a desert;   Ge 13:10
all its towns lay in ruins
before the LORD, before his
    fierce anger.   Jer 12:13

²⁷This is what the LORD says:

"The whole land will be
    ruined,
though I will not destroy it
    completely.   Lev 26:44
²⁸Therefore the earth will
    mourn   Jer 12:4
and the heavens above
    grow dark,
because I have spoken and
    will not relent,   Nu 23:19

I have decided and will not
  turn back."   Jer 23:20

²⁹At the sound of horsemen
  and archers   Jer 6:23
every town takes to flight.
Some go into the thickets;
  some climb up among the
    rocks.   Ex 33:22
All the towns are deserted;
  no one lives in them.   Isa 6:12

³⁰What are you doing,
  O devastated one?
Why dress yourself in
    scarlet
and put on jewels of gold?
Why shade your eyes with
    paint?   2Ki 9:30
You adorn yourself in vain.
Your lovers despise you;
  they seek your life.   Ps 35:4

³¹I hear a cry as of a woman in
    labor,   Ge 3:16
  a groan as of one bearing
    her first child—
the cry of the Daughter of
  Zion gasping for breath,
stretching out her hands
  and saying,   Isa 1:15
"Alas! I am fainting;
  my life is given over to
    murderers."   Dt 32:25

Not One Is Upright

5 "Go up and down the
    streets of Jerusalem,
look around and consider,
  search through her squares.
If you can find but one
    person   Ge 18:32
who deals honestly and
  seeks the truth,   Jer 14:14
I will forgive this city.

²Although they say, 'As
surely as the LORD lives,'
still they are swearing
falsely."   Lev 19:12

³O LORD, do not your eyes
look for truth?   2Ch 16:9
You struck them, but they
felt no pain;   Isa 9:13
you crushed them, but they
refused correction.
They made their faces harder
than stone   Jer 7:26
and refused to repent.   Isa 1:5
⁴I thought, "These are only
the poor;
they are foolish,   Jer 4:22
for they do not know the
way of the LORD,   Pr 10:21
the requirements of their
God.
⁵So I will go to the leaders
and speak to them;   Mic 3:1
surely they know the way of
the LORD,
the requirements of their
God."
But with one accord they too
had broken off the yoke
and torn off the bonds.
⁶Therefore a lion from the
forest will attack them,
a wolf from the desert will
ravage them,   Lev 26:22
a leopard will lie in wait near
their towns   Hos 13:7
to tear to pieces any who
venture out,
for their rebellion is great
and their backslidings
many.   Jer 14:7

⁷"Why should I forgive you?
Your children have
forsaken me

and sworn by gods that are
not gods.   Dt 32:21
I supplied all their needs,
yet they committed
adultery   Nu 25:1
and thronged to the houses
of prostitutes.   Jer 13:27
⁸They are well-fed, lusty
stallions,
each neighing for another
man's wife.   Jer 29:23
⁹Should I not punish them for
this?"   Jer 9:9
declares the LORD.
"Should I not avenge myself
on such a nation as this?

¹⁰"Go through her vineyards
and ravage them,
but do not destroy them
completely.   Jer 4:27
Strip off her branches,
for these people do not
belong to the LORD.
¹¹The house of Israel and the
house of Judah
have been utterly unfaithful
to me,"   1Ki 19:10
declares the LORD.

¹²They have lied about the
LORD;   Isa 28:15
they said, "He will do
nothing!
No harm will come to us;
we will never see sword or
famine.   Jer 14:13
¹³The prophets are but wind
and the word is not in
them;   2Ch 36:16
so let what they say be
done to them."

¹⁴Therefore this is what the
LORD God Almighty says:

"Because the people have
    spoken these words,
I will make my words in
    your mouth a fire   Ps 39:3
and these people the wood
    it consumes.   Isa 1:31
¹⁵O house of Israel," declares
    the LORD,
"I am bringing a distant
    nation against you—
an ancient and enduring
    nation,
a people whose language
    you do not know,   Ge 11:7
whose speech you do not
    understand.
¹⁶Their quivers are like an
    open grave;   Job 39:23
all of them are mighty
    warriors.
¹⁷They will devour your
    harvests and food,   Isa 1:7
devour your sons and
    daughters;   Jer 50:7
they will devour your flocks
    and herds,   Dt 28:31
devour your vines and fig
    trees.   Nu 16:14
With the sword they will
    destroy
the fortified cities in which
    you trust.   Dt 28:33

¹⁸"Yet even in those days,"
declares the LORD, "I will not
destroy you completely. ¹⁹And
when the people ask, 'Why has
the LORD our God done all this
to us?' you will tell them, 'As
you have forsaken me and
served foreign gods in your
own land, so now you will serve
foreigners in a land not your
own.'   Dt 4:28; Jer 4:27

²⁰"Announce this to the house
    of Jacob
and proclaim it in Judah:
²¹Hear this, you foolish and
    senseless people,
who have eyes but do not
    see,   Isa 6:10
who have ears but do not
    hear: Dt 29:4
²²Should you not fear me?"
    declares the LORD.
"Should you not tremble in
    my presence?   Job 4:14
I made the sand a boundary
    for the sea,   Ge 1:9
an everlasting barrier it
    cannot cross.
The waves may roll, but they
    cannot prevail;
they may roar, but they
    cannot cross it.   Ps 46:3
²³But these people have
    stubborn and rebellious
    hearts;   Dt 21:18
they have turned aside and
    gone away.   Ps 14:3
²⁴They do not say to
    themselves,
'Let us fear the LORD our
    God,   Dt 6:24
who gives autumn and
    spring rains in season,
who assures us of the
    regular weeks of
    harvest.'   Ge 8:22
²⁵Your wrongdoings have kept
    these away;
your sins have deprived
    you of good.   Ps 84:11

²⁶"Among my people are
    wicked men   Mt 7:15
who lie in wait like men
    who snare birds   Ps 10:8

and like those who set traps
    to catch men.   Ecc 9:12
27Like cages full of birds,
    their houses are full of
        deceit;   Jer 8:5
they have become rich and
    powerful   Jer 12:1
28   and have grown fat and
        sleek.   Dt 32:15
    Their evil deeds have no
        limit;
    they do not plead the case
        of the fatherless to win
        it,   Zec 7:10
    they do not defend the
        rights of the poor.   Ps 82:3
29Should I not punish them for
    this?"
    declares the LORD.
    "Should I not avenge myself
        on such a nation as this?

30"A horrible and shocking
        thing
    has happened in the land:
31The prophets prophesy lies,
    the priests rule by their
        own authority,   La 4:13
    and my people love it this
        way.
    But what will you do in the
        end?   Hos 9:5

Jerusalem Under Siege

6 "Flee for safety, people of
        Benjamin!
    Flee from Jerusalem!
    Sound the trumpet in Tekoa!
    Raise the signal over Beth
        Hakkerem!   Ne 3:14
    For disaster looms out of the
        north,   Jer 4:6
    even terrible destruction.

2I will destroy the Daughter of
        Zion,   Ps 9:14
    so beautiful and delicate.
3Shepherds with their flocks
    will come against her;
    they will pitch their tents
        around her,   2Ki 25:4
    each tending his own
        portion."

4"Prepare for battle against
        her!
    Arise, let us attack at noon!
    But, alas, the daylight is
        fading,
    and the shadows of evening
        grow long.
5So arise, let us attack at night
    and destroy her fortresses!"

6This is what the LORD Almighty says:

    "Cut down the trees   Dt 20:19-20
    and build siege ramps
        against Jerusalem.   2Sa 20:15
    This city must be punished;
        it is filled with oppression.
7As a well pours out its water,
    so she pours out her
        wickedness.
    Violence and destruction
        resound in her;   Ps 55:9
    her sickness and wounds
        are ever before me.
8Take warning, O Jerusalem,
    or I will turn away from
        you   Eze 23:18
    and make your land desolate
    so no one can live in it."

9This is what the LORD Almighty says:

    "Let them glean the remnant
        of Israel   Ge 45:7

as thoroughly as a vine;
pass your hand over the
   branches again,
like one gathering grapes."

¹⁰To whom can I speak and
   give warning?
Who will listen to me?
Their ears are closed^a
   so they cannot hear.   Isa 42:20
The word of the LORD is
   offensive to them; Jer 15:10
they find no pleasure in it.
¹¹But I am full of the wrath of
   the LORD,   Jer 7:20
and I cannot hold it in.

"Pour it out on the children
   in the street
and on the young men
   gathered together; 2Ch 36:17
both husband and wife will
   be caught in it,
and the old, those weighed
   down with years.   La 2:21
¹²Their houses will be turned
   over to others,   Dt 28:30
together with their fields
   and their wives,   1Ki 11:4
when I stretch out my hand
   against those who live in
   the land,"
          declares the LORD.
¹³"From the least to the
   greatest,
all are greedy for gain; Isa 56:11
prophets and priests alike,
   all practice deceit.   La 4:13
¹⁴They dress the wound of my
   people
as though it were not
   serious.

'Peace, peace,' they say,
   when there is no peace.
¹⁵Are they ashamed of their
   loathsome conduct?
No, they have no shame at
   all;
they do not even know how
   to blush.   Jer 3:3
So they will fall among the
   fallen;
they will be brought down
   when I punish them,"
             says the LORD.

¹⁶This is what the LORD says:

"Stand at the crossroads and
   look;
ask for the ancient paths,
ask where the good way is,
   and walk in it,   1Ki 8:36
and you will find rest for
   your souls.   Jos 1:13
But you said, 'We will not
   walk in it.'
¹⁷I appointed watchmen over
   you and said,   Isa 52:8
'Listen to the sound of the
   trumpet!'   Ex 20:18
But you said, 'We will not
   listen.'   Jer 11:7-8
¹⁸Therefore hear, O nations;
   observe, O witnesses,
what will happen to them.
¹⁹Hear, O earth: Dt 4:26
I am bringing disaster on this
   people,   Jos 23:15
the fruit of their schemes,
because they have not
   listened to my words
and have rejected my law.
²⁰What do I care about incense
   from Sheba   Ge 10:7

^a10 Hebrew *uncircumcised*

or sweet calamus from a
distant land?   Ex 30:23
Your burnt offerings are not
acceptable;   Am 5:22
your sacrifices do not please
me."   Isa 1:11

²¹Therefore this is what the
Lord says:

"I will put obstacles before
this people.
Fathers and sons alike will
stumble over them;
neighbors and friends will
perish."   Lev 26:37

²²This is what the Lord says:

"Look, an army is coming
from the land of the north;
a great nation is being stirred
up
from the ends of the earth.
²³They are armed with bow
and spear;
they are cruel and show no
mercy.   Isa 13:18
They sound like the roaring
sea   Ps 18:4
as they ride on their horses;
they come like men in battle
formation
to attack you, O Daughter
of Zion."

²⁴We have heard reports about
them,
and our hands hang limp.
Anguish has gripped us,
pain like that of a woman in
labor.   Jer 4:31
²⁵Do not go out to the fields
or walk on the roads,
for the enemy has a sword,

and there is terror on every
side.   Job 15:21
²⁶O my people, put on
sackcloth   Jer 4:8
and roll in ashes;   Job 2:8
mourn with bitter wailing
as for an only son,   Ge 21:16
for suddenly the destroyer
will come upon us.   Ex 12:23

²⁷"I have made you a tester of
metals   Jer 9:7
and my people the ore,
that you may observe
and test their ways.
²⁸They are all hardened rebels,
going about to slander.
They are bronze and iron;
they all act corruptly.
²⁹The bellows blow fiercely
to burn away the lead with
fire,
but the refining goes on in
vain;   Mal 3:3
the wicked are not purged
out.
³⁰They are called rejected
silver,   Pr 17:3
because the Lord has
rejected them."   Ps 53:5

False Religion Worthless

7 This is the word that came to
Jeremiah from the Lord:
²"Stand at the gate of the Lord's
house and there proclaim this
message: Jer 17:19
" 'Hear the word of the Lord,
all you people of Judah who
come through these gates to
worship the Lord. ³This is what
the Lord Almighty, the God of
Israel, says: Reform your ways
and your actions, and I will let

you live in this place. 4Do not trust in deceptive words and say, "This is the temple of the LORD, the temple of the LORD, the temple of the LORD!" 5If you really change your ways and your actions and deal with each other justly, 6if you do not oppress the alien, the fatherless or the widow and do not shed innocent blood in this place, and if you do not follow other gods to your own harm, 7then I will let you live in this place, in the land I gave your forefathers for ever and ever. 8But look, you are trusting in deceptive words that are worthless.   Jer 18:11

9" 'Will you steal and murder, commit adultery and perjury,*a* burn incense to Baal and follow other gods you have not known, 10and then come and stand before me in this house, which bears my Name, and say, "We are safe"—safe to do all these detestable things? 11Has this house, which bears my Name, become a den of robbers to you? But I have been watching! declares the LORD.   Ex 20:15

12" 'Go now to the place in Shiloh where I first made a dwelling for my Name, and see what I did to it because of the wickedness of my people Israel. 13While you were doing all these things, declares the LORD, I spoke to you again and again, but you did not listen; I called you, but you did not answer. 14Therefore, what I did to Shiloh

I will now do to the house that bears my Name, the temple you trust in, the place I gave to you and your fathers. 15I will thrust you from my presence, just as I did all your brothers, the people of Ephraim.'   Ge 4:14; Jos 18:1

16"So do not pray for this people nor offer any plea or petition for them; do not plead with me, for I will not listen to you. 17Do you not see what they are doing in the towns of Judah and in the streets of Jerusalem? 18The children gather wood, the fathers light the fire, and the women knead the dough and make cakes of bread for the Queen of Heaven. They pour out drink offerings to other gods to provoke me to anger. 19But am I the one they are provoking? declares the LORD. Are they not rather harming themselves, to their own shame?

20" 'Therefore this is what the Sovereign LORD says: My anger and my wrath will be poured out on this place, on man and beast, on the trees of the field and on the fruit of the ground, and it will burn and not be quenched.   Isa 30:15; La 4:11

21" 'This is what the LORD Almighty, the God of Israel, says: Go ahead, add your burnt offerings to your other sacrifices and eat the meat yourselves! 22For when I brought your forefathers out of Egypt and spoke to them, I did not just give them commands about burnt offerings

a9 Or and swear by false gods

and sacrifices, 23but I gave them this command: Obey me, and I will be your God and you will be my people. Walk in all the ways I command you, that it may go well with you. 24But they did not listen or pay attention; instead, they followed the stubborn inclinations of their evil hearts. They went backward and not forward. 25From the time your forefathers left Egypt until now, day after day, again and again I sent you my servants the prophets. 26But they did not listen to me or pay attention. They were stiff-necked and did more evil than their forefathers.'   2Ch 36:16; Jer 6:20

27"When you tell them all this, they will not listen to you; when you call to them, they will not answer. 28Therefore say to them, 'This is the nation that has not obeyed the LORD its God or responded to correction. Truth has perished; it has vanished from their lips. 29Cut off your hair and throw it away; take up a lament on the barren heights, for the LORD has rejected and abandoned this generation that is under his wrath.

The Valley of Slaughter

30" 'The people of Judah have done evil in my eyes, declares the LORD. They have set up their detestable idols in the house that bears my Name and have defiled it. 31They have built the high places of Topheth in the Valley of Ben Hinnom to burn their sons and daughters in the fire—something I did not command, nor did it enter my mind. 32So beware, the days are coming, declares the LORD, when people will no longer call it Topheth or the Valley of Ben Hinnom, but the Valley of Slaughter, for they will bury the dead in Topheth until there is no more room. 33Then the carcasses of this people will become food for the birds of the air and the beasts of the earth, and there will be no one to frighten them away. 34I will bring an end to the sounds of joy and gladness and to the voices of bride and bridegroom in the towns of Judah and the streets of Jerusalem, for the land will become desolate.   Jer 32:34

8 " 'At that time, declares the LORD, the bones of the kings and officials of Judah, the bones of the priests and prophets, and the bones of the people of Jerusalem will be removed from their graves. 2They will be exposed to the sun and the moon and all the stars of the heavens, which they have loved and served and which they have followed and consulted and worshiped. They will not be gathered up or buried, but will be like refuse lying on the ground. 3Wherever I banish them, all the survivors of this evil nation will prefer death to life, declares the LORD Almighty.'   Job 3:22; Ps 53:5

Sin and Punishment

4"Say to them, 'This is what the LORD says:

'' 'When men fall down, do
　　they not get up?　　Pr 24:16
When a man turns away,
　　does he not return?
5Why then have these people
　　turned away?
Why does Jerusalem always
　　turn away?
They cling to deceit;　　Jer 5:27
　　they refuse to return.　　Zec 7:11
6I have listened attentively,
　　but they do not say what is
　　right.　　Mal 3:16
No one repents of his
　　wickedness,　　Rev 9:20
　　saying, "What have I
　　done?"
Each pursues his own course
　　like a horse charging into
　　battle.
7Even the stork in the sky
　　knows her appointed
　　seasons,
and the dove, the swift and
　　the thrush
　　observe the time of their
　　migration.
But my people do not know
　　the requirements of the
　　LORD.　　Dt 32:28

8'' 'How can you say, "We are
　　wise,
for we have the law of the
　　LORD,"　　Ro 2:17
when actually the lying pen
　　of the scribes
　　has handled it falsely?
9The wise will be put to
　　shame;　　Isa 29:14
they will be dismayed and
　　trapped.　　Job 5:13

Since they have rejected the
　　word of the LORD,
　　what kind of wisdom do
　　they have?　　Pr 1:7
10Therefore I will give their
　　wives to other men
　　and their fields to new
　　owners.　　Jer 6:12
From the least to the
　　greatest,
　　all are greedy for gain;
prophets and priests alike,
　　all practice deceit.　　Jer 23:11
11They dress the wound of my
　　people
　　as though it were not
　　serious.
"Peace, peace," they say,
　　when there is no peace.
12Are they ashamed of their
　　loathsome conduct?
No, they have no shame at
　　all;　　Jer 3:3
they do not even know how
　　to blush.
So they will fall among the
　　fallen;
　　they will be brought down
　　when they are
　　punished,　　Ps 52:5-7
　　　　says the LORD.

13'' 'I will take away their
　　harvest,
　　　　declares the LORD.
There will be no grapes on
　　the vine.　　Hos 2:12
There will be no figs on the
　　tree,　　Lk 13:6
　　and their leaves will wither.
What I have given them
　　will be taken from them. a' ''

---

a13 The meaning of the Hebrew for this sentence is uncertain.

¹⁴"Why are we sitting here?
　Gather together!
Let us flee to the fortified
　cities
and perish there! Jos 10:20
For the LORD our God has
　doomed us to perish
and given us poisoned
　water to drink, Dt 29:18
because we have sinned
　against him. Jer 14:7
¹⁵We hoped for peace
　but no good has come,
for a time of healing
　but there was only terror.
¹⁶The snorting of the enemy's
　horses Jer 4:29
　is heard from Dan; Ge 30:6
at the neighing of their
　stallions
the whole land trembles.
They have come to devour
　the land and everything
　in it, Jer 5:17
the city and all who live
　there."

¹⁷"See, I will send venomous
　snakes among you,
vipers that cannot be
　charmed, Ps 58:5
and they will bite you,"
　　　declares the LORD.

¹⁸O my Comforter[a] in sorrow,
　my heart is faint within me.
¹⁹Listen to the cry of my
　people
from a land far away: Dt 28:64
"Is the LORD not in Zion?
　Is her King no longer
　there?" Mic 4:9

"Why have they provoked
　me to anger with their
　images, Jer 44:3
with their worthless foreign
　idols?" Isa 41:24

²⁰"The harvest is past,
　the summer has ended,
　and we are not saved."

²¹Since my people are crushed,
　I am crushed; Ps 94:5
I mourn, and horror grips
　me. Ps 78:40
²²Is there no balm in Gilead?
　Is there no physician there?
Why then is there no healing
　for the wound of my
　people? Isa 1:6

9 ¹Oh, that my head were a
　　spring of water
and my eyes a fountain of
　tears! Ps 119:136
I would weep day and night
　for the slain of my people.
²Oh, that I had in the desert
　a lodging place for
　travelers, Ps 55:7
so that I might leave my
　people
and go away from them;
for they are all adulterers,
　a crowd of unfaithful
　people. 1Ki 19:10

³"They make ready their
　tongue
like a bow, to shoot lies;
it is not by truth
　that they triumph[b] in the
　land.
They go from one sin to
　another;

---

[a]18 The meaning of the Hebrew for this word is uncertain.　　[b]3 Or lies; / they are not valiant for truth

they do not acknowledge
   me,"   Isa 1:3
      declares the LORD.
[4]"Beware of your friends;
   do not trust your brothers.
For every brother is a
   deceiver,[a]   Ge 27:35
and every friend a
   slanderer.   Ex 20:16
[5]Friend deceives friend,
   and no one speaks the
   truth.   Ps 15:2
They have taught their
   tongues to lie;   Ps 52:3
they weary themselves with
   sinning.
[6]You[b] live in the midst of
   deception;   Jer 5:27
in their deceit they refuse to
   acknowledge me,"
      declares the LORD.

[7]Therefore this is what the
LORD Almighty says:

"See, I will refine and test
   them,   Jer 6:27
for what else can I do
because of the sin of my
   people?
[8]Their tongue is a deadly
   arrow;   Ps 35:20
it speaks with deceit.
With his mouth each speaks
   cordially to his
   neighbor,
but in his heart he sets a
   trap for him.   Jer 5:26
[9]Should I not punish them for
   this?"
   declares the LORD.
"Should I not avenge myself
   on such a nation as this?"

[10]I will weep and wail for the
   mountains
and take up a lament
   concerning the desert
   pastures.   Jer 23:10
They are desolate and
   untraveled,
and the lowing of cattle is
   not heard.
The birds of the air have fled
   and the animals are gone.

[11]"I will make Jerusalem a
   heap of ruins,   Jer 26:18
   a haunt of jackals;   Job 30:29
and I will lay waste the
   towns of Judah
so no one can live there."

[12]What man is wise enough to
understand this? Who has been
instructed by the LORD and can
explain it? Why has the land
been ruined and laid waste like
a desert that no one can cross?

[13]The LORD said, "It is because they have forsaken my
law, which I set before them;
they have not obeyed me or followed my law. [14]Instead, they
have followed the stubbornness
of their hearts; they have followed the Baals, as their fathers
taught them." [15]Therefore, this
is what the LORD Almighty, the
God of Israel, says: "See, I will
make this people eat bitter food
and drink poisoned water. [16]I
will scatter them among nations
that neither they nor their fathers have known, and I will
pursue them with the sword
until I have destroyed them."

---

[a]4 Or *a deceiving Jacob*   [b]6 That is, Jeremiah (the Hebrew is singular)

¹⁷This is what the LORD Almighty says:

"Consider now! Call for the
   wailing women to come;
   send for the most skillful of
   them.
¹⁸Let them come quickly
   and wail over us
till our eyes overflow with
      tears
   and water streams from our
      eyelids.   Ps 119:136
¹⁹The sound of wailing is
   heard from Zion:
   'How ruined we are!   Jer 4:13
   How great is our shame!
We must leave our land
   because our houses are in
   ruins.' "

²⁰Now, O women, hear the
   word of the LORD;
   open your ears to the words
   of his mouth.   Jer 23:16
Teach your daughters how to
   wail;
   teach one another a lament.
²¹Death has climbed in
   through our windows
   and has entered our
   fortresses;
   it has cut off the children
   from the streets
   and the young men from
   the public squares.

²²Say, "This is what the LORD
declares:

" 'The dead bodies of men
   will lie
like refuse on the open
   field,   2Ki 9:37

like cut grain behind the
   reaper,
   with no one to gather
   them.' "

²³This is what the LORD says:

"Let not the wise man boast
   of his wisdom   Job 4:12
   or the strong man boast of
   his strength   1Ki 20:11
   or the rich man boast of his
   riches,   Ps 62:10
²⁴but let him who boasts boast
   about this: Ps 34:2
   that he understands and
   knows me,   Ps 36:10
that I am the LORD, who
   exercises kindness,
   justice and righteousness
   on earth,   Ps 36:6
   for in these I delight,"
           declares the LORD.

²⁵"The days are coming," declares the LORD, "when I will
punish all who are circumcised
only in the flesh— ²⁶Egypt,
Judah, Edom, Ammon, Moab
and all who live in the desert in
distant places. ᵃ For all these nations are really uncircumcised,
and even the whole house of Israel is uncircumcised in heart."

God and Idols

10 Hear what the LORD says
      to you, O house of Israel.
²This is what the LORD says:

"Do not learn the ways of the
   nations   Ex 23:24
   or be terrified by signs in
   the sky,   Ge 1:14

ᵃ26 Or *desert and who clip the hair by their foreheads*

though the nations are
　　terrified by them.
[3]For the customs of the
　　peoples are worthless;
they cut a tree out of the
　　forest,
and a craftsman shapes it
　　with his chisel.　　Dt 9:21
[4]They adorn it with silver and
　　gold;　　　　　　Ps 135:15
they fasten it with hammer
　　and nails
so it will not totter.　　1Sa 5:3
[5]Like a scarecrow in a melon
　　patch,
their idols cannot speak;
they must be carried
because they cannot walk.
Do not fear them;
　　they can do no harm
nor can they do any good."

[6]No one is like you, O LORD;
　　you are great,
and your name is mighty in
　　power.　　　　　2Sa 7:22
[7]Who should not revere you,
　　O King of the nations?
This is your due.
Among all the wise men of
　　the nations
and in all their kingdoms,
　　there is no one like you.
[8]They are all senseless and
　　foolish;　　　　　Isa 44:18
they are taught by
　　worthless wooden
　　idols.
[9]Hammered silver is brought
　　from Tarshish　　Ge 10:4
and gold from Uphaz.
What the craftsman and
　　goldsmith have made

is then dressed in blue and
　　purple—　　　　Ps 115:4
all made by skilled workers.
[10]But the LORD is the true God;
　　he is the living God, the
　　eternal King.　　Ge 21:33
When he is angry, the earth
　　trembles;　　　　Jdg 5:4
the nations cannot endure
　　his wrath.　　　Ps 76:7

[11]"Tell them this: 'These
gods, who did not make the
heavens and the earth, will perish from the earth and from under the heavens.' "[a]　　Isa 2:18

[12]But God made the earth by
　　his power;　　　　1Sa 2:8
he founded the world by
　　his wisdom　　　Ge 1:31
and stretched out the
　　heavens by his
　　understanding.　Ge 1:1,8
[13]When he thunders, the
　　waters in the heavens
　　roar;　　　　　Job 36:29
he makes clouds rise from
　　the ends of the earth.
He sends lightning with the
　　rain　　　　　Ps 104:13
and brings out the wind
　　from his storehouses.

[14]Everyone is senseless and
　　without knowledge;
every goldsmith is shamed
　　by his idols.　　Ps 97:7
His images are a fraud;
　　they have no breath in
　　them.　　　　　Isa 44:20
[15]They are worthless, the
　　objects of mockery;

---

[a]11 The text of this verse is in Aramaic.

when their judgment
comes, they will perish.
¹⁶He who is the Portion of
Jacob is not like these,
for he is the Maker of all
things,   Jer 32:17
including Israel, the tribe of
his inheritance—   Ex 34:9
the LORD Almighty is his
name.   Jer 31:35

Coming Destruction

¹⁷Gather up your belongings to
leave the land,   Eze 12:3
you who live under siege.
¹⁸For this is what the LORD
says:
"At this time I will hurl out
those who live in this land;
I will bring distress on them
so that they may be
captured."   Dt 28:52

¹⁹Woe to me because of my
injury!
My wound is incurable!
Yet I said to myself,
"This is my sickness, and I
must endure it."   Mic 7:9
²⁰My tent is destroyed;   Jer 4:20
all its ropes are snapped.
My sons are gone from me
and are no more;
no one is left now to pitch
my tent
or to set up my shelter.
²¹The shepherds are senseless
and do not inquire of the
LORD;
so they do not prosper   Isa 56:10
and all their flock is
scattered.   Jer 23:2
²²Listen! The report is
coming—

a great commotion from the
land of the north!   Jer 6:22
It will make the towns of
Judah desolate,
a haunt of jackals.   Isa 34:13

Jeremiah's Prayer

²³I know, O LORD, that a man's
life is not his own;
it is not for man to direct
his steps.   Job 33:29
²⁴Correct me, LORD, but only
with justice—
not in your anger,   Ps 6:1
lest you reduce me to
nothing.   Jer 30:11
²⁵Pour out your wrath on the
nations   Ps 69:24
that do not acknowledge
you,
on the peoples who do not
call on your name.   Ps 14:4
For they have devoured
Jacob;   Ps 79:7
they have devoured him
completely
and destroyed his
homeland.   Ps 79:6-7

The Covenant Is Broken

11 This is the word that
came to Jeremiah from
the LORD: ²"Listen to the terms
of this covenant and tell them to
the people of Judah and to those
who live in Jerusalem. ³Tell
them that this is what the LORD,
the God of Israel, says: 'Cursed
is the man who does not obey
the terms of this covenant—
⁴the terms I commanded your
forefathers when I brought
them out of Egypt, out of the

iron-smelting furnace.' I said, 'Obey me and do everything I command you, and you will be my people, and I will be your God. ⁵Then I will fulfill the oath I swore to your forefathers, to give them a land flowing with milk and honey'—the land you possess today." Dt 5:2; 11:26-28

I answered, "Amen, LORD."

⁶The LORD said to me, "Proclaim all these words in the towns of Judah and in the streets of Jerusalem: 'Listen to the terms of this covenant and follow them. ⁷From the time I brought your forefathers up from Egypt until today, I warned them again and again, saying, "Obey me." ⁸But they did not listen or pay attention; instead, they followed the stubbornness of their evil hearts. So I brought on them all the curses of the covenant I had commanded them to follow but that they did not keep.' " Jer 4:5

⁹Then the LORD said to me, "There is a conspiracy among the people of Judah and those who live in Jerusalem. ¹⁰They have returned to the sins of their forefathers, who refused to listen to my words. They have followed other gods to serve them. Both the house of Israel and the house of Judah have broken the covenant I made with their forefathers. ¹¹Therefore this is what the LORD says: 'I will bring on them a disaster they cannot escape. Although they cry out to me, I will not listen to them. ¹²The towns of Judah and the people of Jerusalem will go and cry out to the gods to whom they burn incense, but they will not help them at all when disaster strikes. ¹³You have as many gods as you have towns, O Judah; and the altars you have set up to burn incense to that shameful god Baal are as many as the streets of Jerusalem.'

¹⁴"Do not pray for this people nor offer any plea or petition for them, because I will not listen when they call to me in the time of their distress. Ex 32:10

¹⁵"What is my beloved doing
    in my temple
  as she works out her evil
      schemes with many?
  Can consecrated meat avert
    ⌐your punishment⌐?
When you engage in your
      wickedness,
    then you rejoice. *a*"

¹⁶The LORD called you a
    thriving olive tree
  with fruit beautiful in form.
But with the roar of a mighty
    storm
  he will set it on fire,
  and its branches will be
    broken. Isa 27:11

¹⁷The LORD Almighty, who planted you, has decreed disaster for you, because the house of Israel and the house of Judah have done evil and provoked

---

a15 Or *Could consecrated meat avert your punishment? / Then you would rejoice*

me to anger by burning incense to Baal.   _{Ex 15:17; Jer 12:2}

Plot Against Jeremiah

¹⁸Because the Lᴏʀᴅ revealed their plot to me, I knew it, for at that time he showed me what they were doing. ¹⁹I had been like a gentle lamb led to the slaughter; I did not realize that they had plotted against me, saying,   _{Ps 44:22; Jer 18:18}

"Let us destroy the tree and
    its fruit;
  let us cut him off from the
    land of the living, _{Job 28:13}
  that his name be
    remembered no more."
²⁰But, O Lᴏʀᴅ Almighty, you
    who judge righteously
  and test the heart and
    mind,   _{1Sa 2:3}
  let me see your vengeance
    upon them,   _{Ps 58:10}
  for to you I have committed
    my cause.

²¹"Therefore this is what the Lᴏʀᴅ says about the men of Anathoth who are seeking your life and saying, 'Do not prophesy in the name of the Lᴏʀᴅ or you will die by our hands'— ²²therefore this is what the Lᴏʀᴅ Almighty says: 'I will punish them. Their young men will die by the sword, their sons and daughters by famine. ²³Not even a remnant will be left to them, because I will bring disaster on the men of Anathoth in the year of their punishment.'"

Jeremiah's Complaint

12 You are always
    righteous, O Lᴏʀᴅ,
  when I bring a case before
    you.   _{Job 5:8}
Yet I would speak with you
    about your justice:
  Why does the way of the
    wicked prosper?   _{Job 21:7}
  Why do all the faithless live
    at ease?
²You have planted them, and
    they have taken root;
  they grow and bear fruit.
  You are always on their lips
    but far from their hearts.
³Yet you know me, O Lᴏʀᴅ;
  you see me and test my
    thoughts about you.
  Drag them off like sheep to
    be butchered!   _{Ps 44:11}
  Set them apart for the day
    of slaughter!   _{Jer 16:18}
⁴How long will the land lie
    parched[a]
  and the grass in every field
    be withered?   _{Jer 4:26}
  Because those who live in it
    are wicked,
  the animals and birds have
    perished.   _{Dt 28:15-18}
  Moreover, the people are
    saying,
  "He will not see what
    happens to us."

God's Answer

⁵"If you have raced with men
    on foot
  and they have worn you
    out,

_{a4 Or land mourn}

how can you compete with
    horses?
If you stumble in safe
    country,[a]
how will you manage in the
    thickets by[b] the Jordan?
⁶Your brothers, your own
    family—
even they have betrayed
    you;
they have raised a loud cry
    against you.   Pr 26:24-25
Do not trust them,
though they speak well of
    you.   Ps 12:2

⁷"I will forsake my house,
    abandon my inheritance;
I will give the one I love
into the hands of her
    enemies.   Jer 17:4
⁸My inheritance has become
    to me
like a lion in the forest.
She roars at me;
    therefore I hate her.   Ps 5:5
⁹Has not my inheritance
    become to me
like a speckled bird of prey
that other birds of prey
    surround and attack?
Go and gather all the wild
    beasts;
bring them to devour.   Dt 28:26
¹⁰Many shepherds will ruin my
    vineyard   Jer 23:1
and trample down my field;
they will turn my pleasant
    field
into a desolate wasteland.
¹¹It will be made a wasteland,
    parched and desolate before
    me;   Jer 9:12

the whole land will be laid
    waste
because there is no one
    who cares.
¹²Over all the barren heights in
    the desert
destroyers will swarm,
for the sword of the LORD
    will devour   Eze 21:3-4
from one end of the land to
    the other;   Jer 3:2
no one will be safe.   Jer 7:10
¹³They will sow wheat but reap
    thorns;
they will wear themselves
    out but gain nothing.
So bear the shame of your
    harvest
because of the LORD's fierce
    anger."   Ex 15:7

¹⁴This is what the LORD says:
"As for all my wicked neighbors
who seize the inheritance I gave
my people Israel, I will uproot
them from their lands and I will
uproot the house of Judah from
among them. ¹⁵But after I
uproot them, I will again have
compassion and will bring each
of them back to his own inheritance and his own country.
¹⁶And if they learn well the
ways of my people and swear
by my name, saying, 'As surely
as the LORD lives'—even as they
once taught my people to swear
by Baal—then they will be
established among my people.
¹⁷But if any nation does not listen, I will completely uproot
and destroy it," declares the
LORD.   Ge 27:29; Lev 26:20

---

[a]5 Or *If you put your trust in a land of safety*   [b]5 Or *the flooding of*

A Linen Belt

13 This is what the LORD said to me: "Go and buy a linen belt and put it around your waist, but do not let it touch water." ²So I bought a belt, as the LORD directed, and put it around my waist. Isa 20:2

³Then the word of the LORD came to me a second time: ⁴"Take the belt you bought and are wearing around your waist, and go now to Perath*a* and hide it there in a crevice in the rocks." ⁵So I went and hid it at Perath, as the LORD told me.

⁶Many days later the LORD said to me, "Go now to Perath and get the belt I told you to hide there." ⁷So I went to Perath and dug up the belt and took it from the place where I had hidden it, but now it was ruined and completely useless.

⁸Then the word of the LORD came to me: ⁹"This is what the LORD says: 'In the same way I will ruin the pride of Judah and the great pride of Jerusalem. ¹⁰These wicked people, who refuse to listen to my words, who follow the stubbornness of their hearts and go after other gods to serve and worship them, will be like this belt—completely useless! ¹¹For as a belt is bound around a man's waist, so I bound the whole house of Israel and the whole house of Judah to me,' declares the LORD, 'to be my people for my renown and praise and honor. But they have not listened.' Lev 26:19; Isa 63:12

Wineskins

¹²"Say to them: 'This is what the LORD, the God of Israel, says: Every wineskin should be filled with wine.' And if they say to you, 'Don't we know that every wineskin should be filled with wine?' ¹³then tell them, 'This is what the LORD says: I am going to fill with drunkenness all who live in this land, including the kings who sit on David's throne, the priests, the prophets and all those living in Jerusalem. ¹⁴I will smash them one against the other, fathers and sons alike, declares the LORD. I will allow no pity or mercy or compassion to keep me from destroying them.' "

Threat of Captivity

¹⁵Hear and pay attention,
  do not be arrogant,
  for the LORD has spoken.
¹⁶Give glory to the LORD your
    God Jos 7:19
  before he brings the
    darkness,
before your feet stumble
  on the darkening hills.
You hope for light,
  but he will turn it to thick
    darkness
  and change it to deep
    gloom. 1Sa 2:9
¹⁷But if you do not listen,
  I will weep in secret
  because of your pride;

---

*a*4 Or possibly *the Euphrates*; also in verses 5-7

my eyes will weep bitterly,
overflowing with tears,
because the LORD's flock
will be taken captive.

18Say to the king and to the
queen mother,   1Ki 2:19
"Come down from your
thrones,
for your glorious crowns
will fall from your heads."
19The cities in the Negev will
be shut up,
and there will be no one to
open them.
All Judah will be carried into
exile,   Jer 20:4
carried completely away.

20Lift up your eyes and see
those who are coming from
the north.   Jer 6:22
Where is the flock that was
entrusted to you,
the sheep of which you
boasted?   Jer 23:2
21What will you say when ⌞the
LORD⌟ sets over you
those you cultivated as your
special allies?
Will not pain grip you
like that of a woman in
labor?   Jer 4:31
22And if you ask yourself,
"Why has this happened to
me?"—   1Ki 9:9
it is because of your many
sins   Jer 9:2-6
that your skirts have been
torn off   Isa 20:4
and your body mistreated.
23Can the Ethiopian*a* change
his skin

or the leopard its spots?
Neither can you do good
who are accustomed to
doing evil.   2Ch 6:36

24"I will scatter you like chaff
driven by the desert wind.
25This is your lot,
the portion I have decreed
for you,"   Job 20:29
declares the LORD,
"because you have forgotten
me   Isa 17:10
and trusted in false gods.
26I will pull up your skirts over
your face
that your shame may be
seen—   La 1:8
27your adulteries and lustful
neighings,
your shameless
prostitution!   Eze 23:29
I have seen your detestable
acts
on the hills and in the
fields.   Isa 57:7
Woe to you, O Jerusalem!
How long will you be
unclean?"   Hos 8:5

Drought, Famine, Sword

14 This is the word of the
LORD to Jeremiah con-
cerning the drought: Dt 28:22

2"Judah mourns,   Isa 3:26
her cities languish;
they wail for the land,
and a cry goes up from
Jerusalem.
3The nobles send their
servants for water;
they go to the cisterns

---

*a23 Hebrew *Cushite* (probably a person from the upper Nile region)

but find no water. Dt 28:48
They return with their jars
  unfilled;
dismayed and despairing,
  they cover their heads.
⁴The ground is cracked
  because there is no rain in
    the land; Jer 3:3
the farmers are dismayed
  and cover their heads.
⁵Even the doe in the field
  deserts her newborn fawn
  because there is no grass.
⁶Wild donkeys stand on the
    barren heights Job 39:5-6
  and pant like jackals;
their eyesight fails
  for lack of pasture." Ge 47:4

⁷Although our sins testify
    against us,
  O Lᴏʀᴅ, do something for
    the sake of your name.
For our backsliding is great;
  we have sinned against
    you. Jer 8:14
⁸O Hope of Israel, Ps 9:18
  its Savior in times of
    distress, Ps 46:1
why are you like a stranger
    in the land,
like a traveler who stays
    only a night?
⁹Why are you like a man
    taken by surprise,
  like a warrior powerless to
    save? Isa 50:2
You are among us, O Lᴏʀᴅ,
  and we bear your name;
do not forsake us! Ps 27:9

¹⁰This is what the Lᴏʀᴅ says
about this people:

"They greatly love to
    wander;
they do not restrain their
    feet. Ps 119:101
So the Lᴏʀᴅ does not accept
    them; Jer 6:20
he will now remember their
    wickedness
and punish them for their
    sins." Jer 44:21-23

¹¹Then the Lᴏʀᴅ said to me,
"Do not pray for the well-being
of this people. ¹²Although they
fast, I will not listen to their cry;
though they offer burnt offerings
and grain offerings, I will
not accept them. Instead, I will
destroy them with the sword,
famine and plague." Ex 32:10
¹³But I said, "Ah, Sovereign
Lᴏʀᴅ, the prophets keep telling
them, 'You will not see the
sword or suffer famine. Indeed,
I will give you lasting peace in
this place.'" Dt 18:22; Jer 27:14
¹⁴Then the Lᴏʀᴅ said to me,
"The prophets are prophesying
lies in my name. I have not sent
them or appointed them or
spoken to them. They are
prophesying to you false visions,
divinations, idolatries[a]
and the delusions of their own
minds. ¹⁵Therefore, this is what
the Lᴏʀᴅ says about the prophets
who are prophesying in my
name: I did not send them, yet
they are saying, 'No sword or
famine will touch this land.'
Those same prophets will perish
by sword and famine. ¹⁶And
the people they are prophesy-

---

a14 Or *visions, worthless divinations*

ing to will be thrown out into the streets of Jerusalem because of the famine and sword. There will be no one to bury them or their wives, their sons or their daughters. I will pour out on them the calamity they deserve.

¹⁷"Speak this word to them:

" 'Let my eyes overflow with
  tears   Ps 119:136
  night and day without
    ceasing;
for my virgin daughter—my
    people—   2Ki 19:21
  has suffered a grievous
    wound,
  a crushing blow.   Jer 8:21
¹⁸If I go into the country,
  I see those slain by the
    sword;
if I go into the city,
  I see the ravages of famine.
Both prophet and priest
  have gone to a land they
    know not.' "   2Ch 36:10

¹⁹Have you rejected Judah
    completely?   Jer 7:29
  Do you despise Zion?
Why have you afflicted us
  so that we cannot be
    healed?   Isa 1:6
We hoped for peace
  but no good has come,
for a time of healing
  but there is only terror.
²⁰O LORD, we acknowledge
    our wickedness
  and the guilt of our fathers;
  we have indeed sinned
    against you.   Jdg 10:10
²¹For the sake of your name do
  not despise us;   Jos 7:9

do not dishonor your
    glorious throne.
Remember your covenant
    with us
  and do not break it.   Ex 2:24
²²Do any of the worthless idols
    of the nations bring
    rain?   1Ki 8:36
Do the skies themselves
    send down showers?
No, it is you, O LORD our
    God.
Therefore our hope is in
    you,
  for you are the one who
    does all this.   Isa 43:10

15 Then the LORD said to me: "Even if Moses and Samuel were to stand before me, my heart would not go out to this people. Send them away from my presence! Let them go! ²And if they ask you, 'Where shall we go?' tell them, 'This is what the LORD says: Ex 32:11

" 'Those destined for death,
    to death;
those for the sword, to the
    sword;   Jer 42:22
those for starvation, to
    starvation;   Dt 28:26
those for captivity, to
    captivity.'   Eze 12:11

³"I will send four kinds of destroyers against them," declares the LORD, "the sword to kill and the dogs to drag away and the birds of the air and the beasts of the earth to devour and destroy. ⁴I will make them abhorrent to all the kingdoms of the earth because of what Ma-

nasseh son of Hezekiah king of
Judah did in Jerusalem.   Nu 33:4

5"Who will have pity on you,
    O Jerusalem?   Isa 27:11
  Who will mourn for you?
  Who will stop to ask how
    you are?
6You have rejected me,"
    declares the LORD.   Dt 32:15
  "You keep on backsliding.
  So I will lay hands on you
    and destroy you;   Isa 31:3
  I can no longer show
    compassion.   Jer 7:20
7I will winnow them with a
    winnowing fork   Isa 41:16
  at the city gates of the land.
  I will bring bereavement and
    destruction on my
    people,   Isa 3:26
  for they have not changed
    their ways.   2Ch 28:22
8I will make their widows
    more numerous
  than the sand of the sea.
  At midday I will bring a
    destroyer   Jer 4:7
  against the mothers of their
    young men;
  suddenly I will bring down
    on them
  anguish and terror.   Job 18:11
9The mother of seven will
    grow faint
  and breathe her last.   Job 8:13
  Her sun will set while it is
    still day;
  she will be disgraced and
    humiliated.   Jer 7:19
  I will put the survivors to the
    sword   Jer 21:7

before their enemies,"
        declares the LORD.
10Alas, my mother, that you
    gave me birth,   Job 3:1
  a man with whom the
    whole land strives and
    contends!   Jer 1:19
  I have neither lent nor
    borrowed,   Lev 25:36
  yet everyone curses me.

11The LORD said,

"Surely I will deliver you for
    a good purpose;   Jer 40:4
  surely I will make your
    enemies plead with you
  in times of disaster and
    times of distress.

12"Can a man break iron—
    iron from the north—or
    bronze?   Dt 28:48
13Your wealth and your
    treasures   2Ki 25:15
  I will give as plunder,
    without charge,
  because of all your sins
    throughout your country.
14I will enslave you to your
    enemies
  ina a land you do not know,
  for my anger will kindle a fire
    that will burn against you."

15You understand, O LORD;
  remember me and care for
    me.
  Avenge me on my
    persecutors.   Jdg 16:28
  You are long-suffering—do
    not take me away;   Ex 34:6

<hr>

a14 Some Hebrew manuscripts, Septuagint and Syriac (see also Jer. 17:4); most Hebrew
manuscripts *I will cause your enemies to bring you / into*

think of how I suffer
  reproach for your sake.
¹⁶When your words came, I ate
  them;   Eze 2:8
they were my joy and my
  heart's delight,   Job 15:11
for I bear your name,
O LORD God Almighty.
¹⁷I never sat in the company of
  revelers,   Ru 3:3
never made merry with
  them;
I sat alone because your hand
  was on me   2Ki 3:15
and you had filled me with
  indignation.
¹⁸Why is my pain unending
and my wound grievous
  and incurable?   Job 6:4
Will you be to me like a
  deceptive brook,
like a spring that fails? Job 6:15

¹⁹Therefore this is what the
LORD says:

"If you repent, I will restore
  you
that you may serve me;
if you utter worthy, not
  worthless, words,
you will be my spokesman.
Let this people turn to you,
  but you must not turn to
  them.
²⁰I will make you a wall to this
  people,   Isa 50:7
a fortified wall of bronze;
they will fight against you
  but will not overcome you,
for I am with you
  to rescue and save you,"
           declares the LORD.
²¹"I will save you from the
  hands of the wicked

and redeem you from the
  grasp of the cruel." Ge 48:16

Day of Disaster

16 Then the word of the
LORD came to me: ²"You
must not marry and have sons
or daughters in this place." ³For
this is what the LORD says about
the sons and daughters born in
this land and about the women
who are their mothers and the
men who are their fathers:
⁴"They will die of deadly dis-
eases. They will not be
mourned or buried but will be
like refuse lying on the ground.
They will perish by sword and
famine, and their dead bodies
will become food for the birds of
the air and the beasts of the
earth."   Jer 25:33; Mt 19:12
  ⁵For this is what the LORD
says: "Do not enter a house
where there is a funeral meal;
do not go to mourn or show
sympathy, because I have withdrawn my blessing, my love
and my pity from this people,"
declares the LORD. ⁶"Both high
and low will die in this land.
They will not be buried or
mourned, and no one will cut
himself or shave his head for
them. ⁷No one will offer food to
comfort those who mourn for
the dead—not even for a father
or a mother—nor will anyone
give them a drink to console
them.   2Sa 3:35; Jer 15:5
  ⁸"And do not enter a house
where there is feasting and sit
down to eat and drink. ⁹For this
is what the LORD Almighty, the

God of Israel, says: Before your eyes and in your days I will bring an end to the sounds of joy and gladness and to the voices of bride and bridegroom in this place.   Ex 32:6; Isa 24:8

¹⁰"When you tell these people all this and they ask you, 'Why has the LORD decreed such a great disaster against us? What wrong have we done? What sin have we committed against the LORD our God?' ¹¹then say to them, 'It is because your fathers forsook me,' declares the LORD, 'and followed other gods and served and worshiped them. They forsook me and did not keep my law. ¹²But you have behaved more wickedly than your fathers. See how each of you is following the stubbornness of his evil heart instead of obeying me. ¹³So I will throw you out of this land into a land neither you nor your fathers have known, and there you will serve other gods day and night, for I will show you no favor.'   Dt 29:24; 2Ch 7:20

¹⁴"However, the days are coming," declares the LORD, "when men will no longer say, 'As surely as the LORD lives, who brought the Israelites up out of Egypt,' ¹⁵but they will say, 'As surely as the LORD lives, who brought the Israelites up out of the land of the north and out of all the countries where he had banished them.' For I will restore them to the land I gave their forefathers.

¹⁶"But now I will send for many fishermen," declares the LORD, "and they will catch them. After that I will send for many hunters, and they will hunt them down on every mountain and hill and from the crevices of the rocks. ¹⁷My eyes are on all their ways; they are not hidden from me, nor is their sin concealed from my eyes. ¹⁸I will repay them double for their wickedness and their sin, because they have defiled my land with the lifeless forms of their vile images and have filled my inheritance with their detestable idols."   Nu 35:34; Am 4:2

¹⁹O LORD, my strength and my
     fortress,
my refuge in time of
     distress,   2Sa 22:3
to you the nations will come
     from the ends of the earth
     and say,   Isa 2:2
"Our fathers possessed
     nothing but false gods,
     worthless idols that did
     them no good.   Isa 40:19
²⁰Do men make their own
     gods?
     Yes, but they are not gods!"

²¹"Therefore I will teach
     them—
     this time I will teach them
     my power and might.
Then they will know
     that my name is the LORD.

17 "Judah's sin is engraved
     with an iron tool,   Job 19:24
inscribed with a flint point,
on the tablets of their hearts

and on the horns of their
　　altars.　　　　　　　Ex 27:2
²Even their children
　　remember
　　their altars and Asherah
　　poles[a]　　　　　　2Ch 24:18
beside the spreading trees
and on the high hills.
³My mountain in the land
and your[b] wealth and all
　　your treasures
I will give away as plunder,
together with your high
　　places,　　　　　Jer 26:18
because of sin throughout
　　your country.　　Jer 15:13
⁴Through your own fault you
　　will lose
the inheritance I gave you.
I will enslave you to your
　　enemies　　　　　Dt 28:48
in a land you do not know,
for you have kindled my
　　anger,
and it will burn forever.''

⁵This is what the LORD says:

''Cursed is the one who
　　trusts in man,　　Ps 108:12
who depends on flesh for
　　his strength
and whose heart turns
　　away from the LORD.
⁶He will be like a bush in the
　　wastelands;
he will not see prosperity
　　when it comes.
He will dwell in the parched
　　places of the desert,
in a salt land where no one
　　lives.　　　　　　Dt 29:23

⁷''But blessed is the man who
　　trusts in the LORD,　Ps 26:1
whose confidence is in him.
⁸He will be like a tree planted
　　by the water
that sends out its roots by
　　the stream.　　　　Job 14:9
It does not fear when heat
　　comes;
its leaves are always green.
It has no worries in a year of
　　drought　　　　　Jer 14:1-6
and never fails to bear
　　fruit.''　　　　　　Ps 1:3

⁹The heart is deceitful above
　　all things　　　　　Ecc 9:3
and beyond cure.
Who can understand it?

¹⁰''I the LORD search the heart
　　and examine the mind, Ps 17:3
to reward a man according to
　　his conduct,　　　Lev 26:28
according to what his deeds
　　deserve.''　　　　Jer 12:13

¹¹Like a partridge that hatches
　　eggs it did not lay
is the man who gains riches
　　by unjust means.
When his life is half gone,
　　they will desert him,
and in the end he will
　　prove to be a fool.

¹²A glorious throne, exalted
　　from the beginning,
is the place of our
　　sanctuary.　　　　Jer 3:17
¹³O LORD, the hope of Israel,
all who forsake you will be
　　put to shame.　　Jer 2:17

---

[a]2 That is, symbols of the goddess Asherah
land. / Your

[b]2,3 Or hills / ³and the mountains of the

Those who turn away from
  you will be written in
  the dust   Ps 69:28
because they have forsaken
  the LORD,
the spring of living water.

¹⁴Heal me, O LORD, and I will
  be healed;   Isa 30:26
save me and I will be saved,
  for you are the one I praise.
¹⁵They keep saying to me,
  "Where is the word of the
  LORD?
Let it now be fulfilled!"
¹⁶I have not run away from
  being your shepherd;
you know I have not
  desired the day of
  despair.
What passes my lips is
  open before you.   Ps 139:4
¹⁷Do not be a terror to me;
  you are my refuge in the
  day of disaster.   Ps 18:18
¹⁸Let my persecutors be put to
  shame,
but keep me from shame;
let them be terrified,
but keep me from terror.
Bring on them the day of
  disaster;
destroy them with double
  destruction.   Ps 35:1-8

Keeping the Sabbath Holy

¹⁹This is what the LORD said
to me: "Go and stand at the gate
of the people, through which
the kings of Judah go in and out;
stand also at all the other gates
of Jerusalem. ²⁰Say to them,
'Hear the word of the LORD, O
kings of Judah and all people of
Judah and everyone living in
Jerusalem who come through
these gates. ²¹This is what the
LORD says: Be careful not to carry a load on the Sabbath day or
bring it through the gates of
Jerusalem. ²²Do not bring a load
out of your houses or do any
work on the Sabbath, but keep
the Sabbath day holy, as I commanded your forefathers. ²³Yet
they did not listen or pay attention; they were stiff-necked and
would not listen or respond to
discipline. ²⁴But if you are careful to obey me, declares the
LORD, and bring no load
through the gates of this city on
the Sabbath, but keep the Sabbath day holy by not doing any
work on it, ²⁵then kings who sit
on David's throne will come
through the gates of this city
with their officials. They and
their officials will come riding in
chariots and on horses, accompanied by the men of Judah and
those living in Jerusalem, and
this city will be inhabited forever. ²⁶People will come from
the towns of Judah and the villages around Jerusalem, from
the territory of Benjamin and
the western foothills, from the
hill country and the Negev,
bringing burnt offerings and
sacrifices, grain offerings, incense and thank offerings to the
house of the LORD. ²⁷But if you
do not obey me to keep the Sabbath day holy by not carrying
any load as you come through
the gates of Jerusalem on the
Sabbath day, then I will kindle

an unquenchable fire in the gates of Jerusalem that will consume her fortresses.' " _{Jer 19:3}

At the Potter's House

18 This is the word that came to Jeremiah from the LORD: ²"Go down to the potter's house, and there I will give you my message." ³So I went down to the potter's house, and I saw him working at the wheel. ⁴But the pot he was shaping from the clay was marred in his hands; so the potter formed it into another pot, shaping it as seemed best to him. _{Jer 19:1,2}

⁵Then the word of the LORD came to me: ⁶"O house of Israel, can I not do with you as this potter does?" declares the LORD. "Like clay in the hand of the potter, so are you in my hand, O house of Israel. ⁷If at any time I announce that a nation or kingdom is to be uprooted, torn down and destroyed, ⁸and if that nation I warned repents of its evil, then I will relent and not inflict on it the disaster I had planned. ⁹And if at another time I announce that a nation or kingdom is to be built up and planted, ¹⁰and if it does evil in my sight and does not obey me, then I will reconsider the good I had intended to do for it. _{Isa 29:16; Eze 33:18}

¹¹"Now therefore say to the people of Judah and those living in Jerusalem, 'This is what the LORD says: Look! I am preparing a disaster for you and devising a plan against you. So turn from your evil ways, each one of you, and reform your ways and your actions.' ¹²But they will reply, 'It's no use. We will continue with our own plans; each of us will follow the stubbornness of his evil heart.' " _{2Ki 22:16; Isa 57:10}

¹³Therefore this is what the LORD says:

"Inquire among the nations:
   Who has ever heard
      anything like this? _{Isa 66:8}
A most horrible thing has
      been done _{Jer 5:30}
   by Virgin Israel. _{2Ki 19:21}
¹⁴Does the snow of Lebanon
   ever vanish from its rocky
      slopes?
Do its cool waters from
      distant sources
   ever cease to flow?ᵃ
¹⁵Yet my people have forgotten
      me; _{Isa 17:10}
   they burn incense to
      worthless idols, _{Jer 10:15}
which made them stumble in
      their ways _{Eze 44:12}
   and in the ancient paths.
They made them walk in
      bypaths
   and on roads not built up.
¹⁶Their land will be laid waste,
   an object of lasting scorn;
all who pass by will be
      appalled _{Lev 26:32}
   and will shake their heads.
¹⁷Like a wind from the east,
   I will scatter them before
      their enemies; _{Job 7:10}

ᵃ14 The meaning of the Hebrew for this sentence is uncertain.

I will show them my back
  and not my face   2Ch 29:6
in the day of their disaster.''

¹⁸They said, "Come, let's
make plans against Jeremiah;
for the teaching of the law by
the priest will not be lost, nor
will counsel from the wise, nor
the word from the prophets. So
come, let's attack him with our
tongues and pay no attention to
anything he says.''   Jer 11:19

¹⁹Listen to me, O Lord;
  hear what my accusers are
    saying!   Ps 71:13
²⁰Should good be repaid with
    evil?   Ge 44:4
  Yet they have dug a pit for
    me.   Ps 35:7
  Remember that I stood before
    you   Jer 15:1
  and spoke in their behalf
  to turn your wrath away
    from them.
²¹So give their children over to
    famine;   Jer 11:22
  hand them over to the
    power of the sword.
  Let their wives be made
    childless and widows;
  let their men be put to
    death,
  their young men slain by
    the sword in battle.
²²Let a cry be heard from their
    houses   Jer 6:26
  when you suddenly bring
    invaders against them,
  for they have dug a pit to
    capture me   Ps 119:85
  and have hidden snares for
    my feet.   Ps 35:15
²³But you know, O Lord,

all their plots to kill me.
Do not forgive their crimes
  or blot out their sins from
    your sight.   Ne 4:5
Let them be overthrown
  before you;
  deal with them in the time
    of your anger.   Ps 59:5

19 This is what the Lord
says: "Go and buy a clay
jar from a potter. Take along
some of the elders of the people
and of the priests ²and go out to
the Valley of Ben Hinnom, near
the entrance of the Potsherd
Gate. There proclaim the words
I tell you, ³and say, 'Hear the
word of the Lord, O kings of
Judah and people of Jerusalem.
This is what the Lord Al-
mighty, the God of Israel, says:
Listen! I am going to bring a
disaster on this place that will
make the ears of everyone who
hears of it tingle. ⁴For they have
forsaken me and made this a
place of foreign gods; they have
burned sacrifices in it to gods
that neither they nor their fathers nor the kings of Judah
ever knew, and they have filled
this place with the blood of the
innocent. ⁵They have built the
high places of Baal to burn their
sons in the fire as offerings to
Baal—something I did not command or mention, nor did it enter my mind. ⁶So beware, the
days are coming, declares the
Lord, when people will no
longer call this place Topheth or
the Valley of Ben Hinnom, but
the Valley of Slaughter.   Jer 17:20

7"'In this place I will ruin*a* the plans of Judah and Jerusalem. I will make them fall by the sword before their enemies, at the hands of those who seek their lives, and I will give their carcasses as food to the birds of the air and the beasts of the earth. 8I will devastate this city and make it an object of scorn; all who pass by will be appalled and will scoff because of all its wounds. 9I will make them eat the flesh of their sons and daughters, and they will eat one another's flesh during the stress of the siege imposed on them by the enemies who seek their lives.' Lev 26:29; Ps 33:10-11

10"Then break the jar while those who go with you are watching, 11and say to them, 'This is what the LORD Almighty says: I will smash this nation and this city just as this potter's jar is smashed and cannot be repaired. They will bury the dead in Topheth until there is no more room. 12This is what I will do to this place and to those who live here, declares the LORD. I will make this city like Topheth. 13The houses in Jerusalem and those of the kings of Judah will be defiled like this place, Topheth—all the houses where they burned incense on the roofs to all the starry hosts and poured out drink offerings to other gods.'" Ps 2:9

14Jeremiah then returned from Topheth, where the LORD had sent him to prophesy, and stood in the court of the LORD's temple and said to all the people, 15"This is what the LORD Almighty, the God of Israel, says: 'Listen! I am going to bring on this city and the villages around it every disaster I pronounced against them, because they were stiff-necked and would not listen to my words.'" 2Ch 20:5; Jer 11:11

Jeremiah and Pashhur

20 When the priest Pashhur son of Immer, the chief officer in the temple of the LORD, heard Jeremiah prophesying these things, 2he had Jeremiah the prophet beaten and put in the stocks at the Upper Gate of Benjamin at the LORD's temple. 3The next day, when Pashhur released him from the stocks, Jeremiah said to him, "The LORD's name for you is not Pashhur, but Magor-Missabib.*b* 4For this is what the LORD says: 'I will make you a terror to yourself and to all your friends; with your own eyes you will see them fall by the sword of their enemies. I will hand all Judah over to the king of Babylon, who will carry them away to Babylon or put them to the sword. 5I will hand over to their enemies all the wealth of this city—all its products, all its valuables and all the treasures

a7 The Hebrew for *ruin* sounds like the Hebrew for *jar* (see verses 1 and 10).
b3 Magor-Missabib means *terror on every side.*

of the kings of Judah. They will take it away as plunder and carry it off to Babylon. ⁶And you, Pashhur, and all who live in your house will go into exile to Babylon. There you will die and be buried, you and all your friends to whom you have prophesied lies.'" 1Ch 24:14

Jeremiah's Complaint

⁷O Lord, you deceived*ᵃ* me,
and I was deceived*ᵃ*;
you overpowered me and
prevailed. Isa 8:11
I am ridiculed all day long;
everyone mocks me. Job 17:2
⁸Whenever I speak, I cry out
proclaiming violence and
destruction. Jer 6:7
So the word of the Lord has
brought me
insult and reproach all day
long. 2Ch 36:16
⁹But if I say, "I will not
mention him
or speak any more in his
name," Jer 44:16
his word is in my heart like
a fire, Ps 39:3
a fire shut up in my
bones.
I am weary of holding it in;
indeed, I cannot. Job 4:2
¹⁰I hear many whispering,
"Terror on every side! Jer 6:25
Report him! Let's report
him!" Ne 6:6-13
All my friends
are waiting for me to slip,
saying, Ps 57:4
"Perhaps he will be deceived;

then we will prevail over
him 1Ki 19:2
and take our revenge on
him." 1Sa 18:25

¹¹But the Lord is with me like
a mighty warrior; Jer 1:8
so my persecutors will
stumble and not prevail.
They will fail and be
thoroughly disgraced;
their dishonor will never be
forgotten.
¹²O Lord Almighty, you who
examine the righteous
and probe the heart and
mind, Ps 7:9
let me see your vengeance
upon them, Dt 32:35
for to you I have committed
my cause. Ps 62:8

¹³Sing to the Lord!
Give praise to the Lord!
He rescues the life of the
needy Ps 34:6
from the hands of the
wicked. Ps 97:10

¹⁴Cursed be the day I was
born! Job 3:8
May the day my mother
bore me not be blessed!
¹⁵Cursed be the man who
brought my father the
news,
who made him very glad,
saying,
"A child is born to you—a
son!"
¹⁶May that man be like the
towns Ge 19:25
the Lord overthrew
without pity.

May he hear wailing in the
 morning,   Jer 6:26
 a battle cry at noon.
¹⁷For he did not kill me in the
 womb,   Job 3:16
 with my mother as my
  grave,
 her womb enlarged
  forever.
¹⁸Why did I ever come out of
 the womb   Job 3:10-11
 to see trouble and sorrow
 and to end my days in
  shame?   1Ki 19:4

God Rejects Zedekiah's Request

21 The word came to Jeremiah from the Lord when King Zedekiah sent to him Pashhur son of Malkijah and the priest Zephaniah son of Maaseiah. They said: ²"Inquire now of the Lord for us because Nebuchadnezzar*ᵃ* king of Babylon is attacking us. Perhaps the Lord will perform wonders for us as in times past so that he will withdraw from us."   2Ki 24:18

³But Jeremiah answered them, "Tell Zedekiah, ⁴'This is what the Lord, the God of Israel, says: I am about to turn against you the weapons of war that are in your hands, which you are using to fight the king of Babylon and the Babylonians*ᵇ* who are outside the wall besieging you. And I will gather them inside this city. ⁵I myself will fight against you with an out-

stretched hand and a mighty arm in anger and fury and great wrath. ⁶I will strike down those who live in this city—both men and animals—and they will die of a terrible plague. ⁷After that, declares the Lord, I will hand over Zedekiah king of Judah, his officials and the people in this city who survive the plague, sword and famine, to Nebuchadnezzar king of Babylon and to their enemies who seek their lives. He will put them to the sword; he will show them no mercy or pity or compassion.'   2Ki 25:7; Jer 32:5

⁸"Furthermore, tell the people, 'This is what the Lord says: See, I am setting before you the way of life and the way of death. ⁹Whoever stays in this city will die by the sword, famine or plague. But whoever goes out and surrenders to the Babylonians who are besieging you will live; he will escape with his life. ¹⁰I have determined to do this city harm and not good, declares the Lord. It will be given into the hands of the king of Babylon, and he will destroy it with fire.'   Dt 30:15; Jer 44:27

¹¹"Moreover, say to the royal house of Judah, 'Hear the word of the Lord; ¹²O house of David, this is what the Lord says:

" 'Administer justice every
 morning;   Ex 22:22
 rescue from the hand of his
  oppressor   Ps 27:11

ᵃ2 Hebrew *Nebuchadrezzar*, of which *Nebuchadnezzar* is a variant; here and often in Jeremiah and Ezekiel   *ᵇ4* Or *Chaldeans*; also in verse 9

the one who has been
robbed,
or my wrath will break out
and burn like fire   Isa 42:25
because of the evil you have
done—   Jer 23:2
burn with no one to quench
it.   Isa 1:31

13I am against you, Jerusalem,
you who live above this
valley   Ps 125:2
on the rocky plateau,
declares the Lord—
you who say, "Who can
come against us?
Who can enter our refuge?"
14I will punish you as your
deeds deserve,   Pr 1:31
declares the Lord.
I will kindle a fire in your
forests   2Ki 19:23
that will consume
everything around
you.'"

Judgment Against Evil Kings

22 This is what the Lord
says: "Go down to the
palace of the king of Judah and
proclaim this message there:
2'Hear the word of the Lord, O
king of Judah, you who sit on
David's throne—you, your officials and your people who come
through these gates. 3This is
what the Lord says: Do what is
just and right. Rescue from the
hand of his oppressor the one
who has been robbed. Do no
wrong or violence to the alien,
the fatherless or the widow, and
do not shed innocent blood in
this place. 4For if you are careful
to carry out these commands,

then kings who sit on David's
throne will come through the
gates of this palace, riding in
chariots and on horses, accompanied by their officials and
their people. 5But if you do not
obey these commands, declares
the Lord, I swear by myself that
this palace will become a
ruin.'"   Jer 13:18; Heb 6:13

6For this is what the Lord
says about the palace of the king
of Judah:

"Though you are like Gilead
to me,   Ge 31:21
like the summit of Lebanon,
I will surely make you like a
desert,   Mic 3:12
like towns not inhabited.
7I will send destroyers against
you,   Jer 4:7
each man with his
weapons,
and they will cut up your
fine cedar beams   Ps 74:5
and throw them into the
fire.   2Ch 36:19

8"People from many nations
will pass by this city and will ask
one another, 'Why has the Lord
done such a thing to this great
city?' 9And the answer will be:
'Because they have forsaken the
covenant of the Lord their God
and have worshiped and served
other gods.'"   Dt 29:25-26; Jer 16:11

10Do not weep for the dead
king or mourn his loss;
rather, weep bitterly for
him who is exiled,
because he will never return

nor see his native land
again. Jer 24:9

¹¹For this is what the LORD says about Shallum[a] son of Josiah, who succeeded his father as king of Judah but has gone from this place: "He will never return. ¹²He will die in the place where they have led him captive; he will not see this land again." 2Ki 23:31,34

¹³"Woe to him who builds his
palace by
unrighteousness, Mic 3:10
his upper rooms by
injustice,
making his countrymen work
for nothing,
not paying them for their
labor. Lev 19:13
¹⁴He says, 'I will build myself a
great palace Isa 5:8-9
with spacious upper
rooms.'
So he makes large windows
in it,
panels it with cedar 2Sa 7:2
and decorates it in red.

¹⁵"Does it make you a king
to have more and more
cedar?
Did not your father have
food and drink?
He did what was right and
just, 2Ki 23:25
so all went well with him.
¹⁶He defended the cause of the
poor and needy, Ps 72:1-4
and so all went well.
Is that not what it means to
know me?" Ps 36:10

declares the LORD.
¹⁷"But your eyes and your
heart
are set only on dishonest
gain, Isa 56:11
on shedding innocent blood
and on oppression and
extortion." Dt 28:33

¹⁸Therefore this is what the LORD says about Jehoiakim son of Josiah king of Judah:

"They will not mourn for
him: 2Sa 1:26
'Alas, my brother! Alas, my
sister!'
They will not mourn for him:
'Alas, my master! Alas, his
splendor!'
¹⁹He will have the burial of a
donkey— 2Ki 24:6
dragged away and thrown
outside the gates of
Jerusalem." Jer 8:2
²⁰"Go up to Lebanon and cry
out, Isa 57:13
let your voice be heard in
Bashan, Ps 68:15
cry out from Abarim,
for all your allies are
crushed. Jer 30:14
²¹I warned you when you felt
secure, Zec 7:7
but you said, 'I will not
listen!'
This has been your way from
your youth; Dt 9:7
you have not obeyed me.
²²The wind will drive all your
shepherds away, Jer 10:21
and your allies will go into
exile.

Then you will be ashamed
and disgraced   Jer 7:19
because of all your
wickedness.
23You who live in 'Lebanon,^a'
who are nestled in cedar
buildings,
how you will groan when
pangs come upon you,
pain like that of a woman in
labor!   Jer 4:31

24"As surely as I live," declares the LORD, "even if you, Jehoiachin^b son of Jehoiakim king of Judah, were a signet ring on my right hand, I would still pull you off. 25I will hand you over to those who seek your life, those you fear—to Nebuchadnezzar king of Babylon and to the Babylonians.^c 26I will hurl you and the mother who gave you birth into another country, where neither of you was born, and there you both will die. 27You will never come back to the land you long to return to."   1Ki 2:19; 2Ki 24:6,8

28Is this man Jehoiachin a
despised, broken pot,
an object no one wants?
Why will he and his children
be hurled out,   Jer 15:1
cast into a land they do not
know?   Jer 17:4
29O land, land, land,   Jer 6:19
hear the word of the LORD!
30This is what the LORD says:
"Record this man as if
childless,   1Ch 3:18

a man who will not prosper
in his lifetime,   Jer 10:21
for none of his offspring will
prosper,   Job 18:19
none will sit on the throne
of David   Ps 94:20
or rule anymore in Judah."

The Righteous Branch

23 "Woe to the shepherds who are destroying and scattering the sheep of my pasture!" declares the LORD. 2Therefore this is what the LORD, the God of Israel, says to the shepherds who tend my people: "Because you have scattered my flock and driven them away and have not bestowed care on them, I will bestow punishment on you for the evil you have done," declares the LORD. 3"I myself will gather the remnant of my flock out of all the countries where I have driven them and will bring them back to their pasture, where they will be fruitful and increase in number. 4I will place shepherds over them who will tend them, and they will no longer be afraid or terrified, nor will any be missing," declares the LORD.   Jer 10:21

5"The days are coming,"
declares the LORD,
"when I will raise up to
David^d a righteous
Branch,   2Ki 19:26
a King who will reign wisely
and do what is just and
right in the land.   Mt 2:2

---

^a23 That is, the palace in Jerusalem (see 1 Kings 7:2) of *Jehoiachin*; also in verse 28   ^c25 Or *Chaldeans*   ^b24 Hebrew *Coniah*, a variant   ^d5 Or *up from David's line*

⁶In his days Judah will be
saved
and Israel will live in safety.
This is the name by which he
will be called: Ex 23:21
The LORD Our
Righteousness.   Ezr 9:15

⁷"So then, the days are coming," declares the LORD, "when
people will no longer say, 'As
surely as the LORD lives, who
brought the Israelites up out of
Egypt,' ⁸but they will say, 'As
surely as the LORD lives, who
brought the descendants of Israel up out of the land of the
north and out of all the countries where he had banished
them.' Then they will live in
their own land."   Isa 14:1; Jer 30:3

Lying Prophets

⁹Concerning the prophets:

My heart is broken within
me;   Jer 4:19
all my bones tremble.
I am like a drunken man,
like a man overcome by
wine,
because of the LORD
and his holy words.   Jer 20:8-9
¹⁰The land is full of adulterers;
because of the curse*a* the
land lies parched*b*
and the pastures in the
desert are withered.
The ˌprophetsˌ follow an evil
course
and use their power
unjustly.

¹¹"Both prophet and priest are
godless;   Jer 6:13
even in my temple I find
their wickedness,"
declares the LORD.
¹²"Therefore their path will
become slippery;   Dt 32:35
they will be banished to
darkness
and there they will fall.
I will bring disaster on them
in the year they are
punished,"   Jer 11:23
declares the LORD.

¹³"Among the prophets of
Samaria
I saw this repulsive thing:
They prophesied by Baal
and led my people Israel
astray.   Isa 3:12
¹⁴And among the prophets of
Jerusalem
I have seen something
horrible: Jer 5:30
They commit adultery and
live a lie.   Jer 29:23
They strengthen the hands of
evildoers,   Isa 5:18
so that no one turns from
his wickedness.
They are all like Sodom to
me;   Ge 18:20
the people of Jerusalem are
like Gomorrah."   Jer 20:16

¹⁵Therefore, this is what the
LORD Almighty says concerning
the prophets:

"I will make them eat bitter
food
and drink poisoned water,

---

*a*10 Or *because of these things*   *b*10 Or *land mourns*

because from the prophets of
  Jerusalem
ungodliness has spread
  throughout the land."

¹⁶This is what the LORD Almighty says:

"Do not listen to what the
  prophets are
  prophesying to you;
they fill you with false
  hopes.   Jer 27:9-10
They speak visions from their
  own minds,   Jer 14:14
not from the mouth of the
  LORD.   Jer 9:20
¹⁷They keep saying to those
  who despise me,
'The LORD says: You will
  have peace.'   1Ki 22:8
And to all who follow the
  stubbornness of their
  hearts   Jer 13:10
they say, 'No harm will
  come to you.'   Jer 5:12
¹⁸But which of them has stood
  in the council of the
  LORD   1Ki 22:19
to see or to hear his word?
Who has listened and heard
  his word?
¹⁹See, the storm of the LORD
  will burst out in wrath,
a whirlwind swirling down
  on the heads of the wicked.
²⁰The anger of the LORD will
    not turn back   2Ki 23:26
until he fully accomplishes
  the purposes of his heart.
In days to come
  you will understand it
  clearly.
²¹I did not send these
  prophets,   Jer 27:15

yet they have run with their
  message;
I did not speak to them,
  yet they have prophesied.
²²But if they had stood in my
  council,   1Ki 22:19
they would have
  proclaimed my words to
  my people   Dt 33:10
and would have turned them
  from their evil ways
  and from their evil deeds.

²³"Am I only a God nearby,"
    declares the LORD,
"and not a God far away?
²⁴Can anyone hide in secret
  places   Ge 3:8
so that I cannot see him?"
    declares the LORD.
"Do not I fill heaven and
  earth?"   1Ki 8:27
    declares the LORD.

²⁵"I have heard what the
prophets say who prophesy lies
in my name. They say, 'I had a
dream! I had a dream!' ²⁶How
long will this continue in the
hearts of these lying prophets,
who prophesy the delusions of
their own minds? ²⁷They think
the dreams they tell one another
will make my people forget my
name, just as their fathers forgot my name through Baal worship. ²⁸Let the prophet who has
a dream tell his dream, but let
the one who has my word speak
it faithfully. For what has straw
to do with grain?" declares the
LORD. ²⁹"Is not my word like
fire," declares the LORD, "and
like a hammer that breaks a rock
in pieces?   Ps 39:3; Jer 27:10

30"Therefore," declares the LORD, "I am against the prophets who steal from one another words supposedly from me. 31Yes," declares the LORD, "I am against the prophets who wag their own tongues and yet declare, 'The LORD declares.' 32Indeed, I am against those who prophesy false dreams," declares the LORD. "They tell them and lead my people astray with their reckless lies, yet I did not send or appoint them. They do not benefit these people in the least," declares the LORD. Ps 34:16

False Oracles and False Prophets

33"When these people, or a prophet or a priest, ask you, 'What is the oracle[a] of the LORD?' say to them, 'What oracle?[b] I will forsake you, declares the LORD.' 34If a prophet or a priest or anyone else claims, 'This is the oracle of the LORD,' I will punish that man and his household. 35This is what each of you keeps on saying to his friend or relative: 'What is the LORD's answer?' or 'What has the LORD spoken?' 36But you must not mention 'the oracle of the LORD' again, because every man's own word becomes his oracle and so you distort the words of the living God, the LORD Almighty, our God. 37This is what you keep saying to a prophet: 'What is the LORD's answer to you?' or 'What has the LORD spoken?' 38Although you claim, 'This is the oracle of the LORD,' this is what the LORD says: You used the words, 'This is the oracle of the LORD,' even though I told you that you must not claim, 'This is the oracle of the LORD.' 39Therefore, I will surely forget you and cast you out of my presence along with the city I gave to you and your fathers. 40I will bring upon you everlasting disgrace—everlasting shame that will not be forgotten." Jer 33:3

Two Baskets of Figs

24 After Jehoiachin[c] son of Jehoiakim king of Judah and the officials, the craftsmen and the artisans of Judah were carried into exile from Jerusalem to Babylon by Nebuchadnezzar king of Babylon, the LORD showed me two baskets of figs placed in front of the temple of the LORD. 2One basket had very good figs, like those that ripen early; the other basket had very poor figs, so bad they could not be eaten. 2Ki 24:16

3Then the LORD asked me, "What do you see, Jeremiah?"

"Figs," I answered. "The good ones are very good, but the poor ones are so bad they cannot be eaten." Jer 1:11; Am 8:2

4Then the word of the LORD came to me: 5"This is what the

---

a33 Or *burden* (see Septuagint and Vulgate)   *b33* Hebrew; Septuagint and Vulgate *'You are the burden.* (The Hebrew for *oracle* and *burden* is the same.)   *c1* Hebrew *Jeconiah,* a variant of *Jehoiachin*

LORD, the God of Israel, says: 'Like these good figs, I regard as good the exiles from Judah, whom I sent away from this place to the land of the Babylonians.*a* ⁶My eyes will watch over them for their good, and I will bring them back to this land. I will build them up and not tear them down; I will plant them and not uproot them. ⁷I will give them a heart to know me, that I am the LORD. They will be my people, and I will be their God, for they will return to me with all their heart.   Jer 29:4

⁸"'But like the poor figs, which are so bad they cannot be eaten,' says the LORD, 'so will I deal with Zedekiah king of Judah, his officials and the survivors from Jerusalem, whether they remain in this land or live in Egypt. ⁹I will make them abhorrent and an offense to all the kingdoms of the earth, a reproach and a byword, an object of ridicule and cursing, wherever I banish them. ¹⁰I will send the sword, famine and plague against them until they are destroyed from the land I gave to them and their fathers.'"   Isa 51:19; Jer 29:17

Seventy Years of Captivity

25 The word came to Jeremiah concerning all the people of Judah in the fourth year of Jehoiakim son of Josiah king of Judah, which was the first year of Nebuchadnezzar king of Babylon. ²So Jeremiah the prophet said to all the people of Judah and to all those living in Jerusalem: ³For twenty-three years—from the thirteenth year of Josiah son of Amon king of Judah until this very day—the word of the LORD has come to me and I have spoken to you again and again, but you have not listened.

⁴And though the LORD has sent all his servants the prophets to you again and again, you have not listened or paid any attention. ⁵They said, "Turn now, each of you, from your evil ways and your evil practices, and you can stay in the land the LORD gave to you and your fathers for ever and ever. ⁶Do not follow other gods to serve and worship them; do not provoke me to anger with what your hands have made. Then I will not harm you."   Jer 6:17

⁷"But you did not listen to me," declares the LORD, "and you have provoked me with what your hands have made, and you have brought harm to yourselves."   Dt 32:21; Jer 30:14

⁸Therefore the LORD Almighty says this: "Because you have not listened to my words, ⁹I will summon all the peoples of the north and my servant Nebuchadnezzar king of Babylon," declares the LORD, "and I will bring them against this land and its inhabitants and against all the surrounding nations. I

a5 Or Chaldeans

will completely destroy[a] them and make them an object of horror and scorn, and an everlasting ruin. [10]I will banish from them the sounds of joy and gladness, the voices of bride and bridegroom, the sound of millstones and the light of the lamp. [11]This whole country will become a desolate wasteland, and these nations will serve the king of Babylon seventy years.

[12]"But when the seventy years are fulfilled, I will punish the king of Babylon and his nation, the land of the Babylonians,[b] for their guilt," declares the LORD, "and will make it desolate forever. [13]I will bring upon that land all the things I have spoken against it, all that are written in this book and prophesied by Jeremiah against all the nations. [14]They themselves will be enslaved by many nations and great kings; I will repay them according to their deeds and the work of their hands."

                                    Isa 14:6; Jer 27:7

The Cup of God's Wrath

[15]This is what the LORD, the God of Israel, said to me: "Take from my hand this cup filled with the wine of my wrath and make all the nations to whom I send you drink it. [16]When they drink it, they will stagger and go mad because of the sword I will send among them."   Isa 51:17

[17]So I took the cup from the LORD's hand and made all the nations to whom he sent me drink it: [18]Jerusalem and the towns of Judah, its kings and officials, to make them a ruin and an object of horror and scorn and cursing, as they are today; [19]Pharaoh king of Egypt, his attendants, his officials and all his people, [20]and all the foreign people there; all the kings of Uz; all the kings of the Philistines (those of Ashkelon, Gaza, Ekron, and the people left at Ashdod); [21]Edom, Moab and Ammon; [22]all the kings of Tyre and Sidon; the kings of the coastlands across the sea; [23]Dedan, Tema, Buz and all who are in distant places[c]; [24]all the kings of Arabia and all the kings of the foreign people who live in the desert; [25]all the kings of Zimri, Elam and Media; [26]and all the kings of the north, near and far, one after the other—all the kingdoms on the face of the earth. And after all of them, the king of Sheshach[d] will drink it too.   2Ch 9:14; Jer 1:10

[27]"Then tell them, 'This is what the LORD Almighty, the God of Israel, says: Drink, get drunk and vomit, and fall to rise no more because of the sword I will send among you.' [28]But if they refuse to take the cup from your hand and drink, tell them, 'This is what the LORD Almighty says: You must drink it! [29]See, I am beginning to bring disaster

---

[a]9 The Hebrew term refers to the irrevocable giving over of things or persons to the LORD, often by totally destroying them.   [b]12 Or *Chaldeans*   [c]23 Or *who clip the hair by their foreheads*   [d]26 *Sheshach* is a cryptogram for Babylon.

on the city that bears my Name, and will you indeed go unpunished? You will not go unpunished, for I am calling down a sword upon all who live on the earth, declares the LORD Almighty.' 2Sa 5:7; Isa 29:9

30"Now prophesy all these words against them and say to them:

"'The LORD will roar from on high; Isa 16:10
he will thunder from his holy dwelling Ps 46:6
and roar mightily against his land.
He will shout like those who tread the grapes, Isa 63:3
shout against all who live on the earth.
31The tumult will resound to the ends of the earth,
for the LORD will bring charges against the nations; Jer 2:9
he will bring judgment on all mankind 1Sa 12:7
and put the wicked to the sword,'" Jer 15:9
declares the LORD.

32This is what the LORD Almighty says:

"Look! Disaster is spreading from nation to nation; Isa 34:2
a mighty storm is rising from the ends of the earth."

33At that time those slain by the LORD will be everywhere—from one end of the earth to the other. They will not be mourned or gathered up or buried, but will be like refuse lying on the ground. Isa 66:16

34Weep and wail, you shepherds; Jer 2:8
roll in the dust, you leaders of the flock. Jer 6:26
For your time to be slaughtered has come;
you will fall and be shattered like fine pottery. Jer 22:28
35The shepherds will have nowhere to flee,
the leaders of the flock no place to escape. Job 11:20
36Hear the cry of the shepherds,
the wailing of the leaders of the flock, Jer 23:1
for the LORD is destroying their pasture.
37The peaceful meadows will be laid waste
because of the fierce anger of the LORD.
38Like a lion he will leave his lair,
and their land will become desolate Jer 44:22
because of the sword[a] of the oppressor Jer 46:16
and because of the LORD'S fierce anger. Ex 15:7

Jeremiah Threatened With Death

26 Early in the reign of Jehoiakim son of Josiah king of Judah, this word came

---

a38 Some Hebrew manuscripts and Septuagint (see also Jer. 46:16 and 50:16); most Hebrew manuscripts *anger*

from the LORD: ²"This is what the LORD says: Stand in the courtyard of the LORD's house and speak to all the people of the towns of Judah who come to worship in the house of the LORD. Tell them everything I command you; do not omit a word. ³Perhaps they will listen and each will turn from his evil way. Then I will relent and not bring on them the disaster I was planning because of the evil they have done. ⁴Say to them, 'This is what the LORD says: If you do not listen to me and follow my law, which I have set before you, ⁵and if you do not listen to the words of my servants the prophets, whom I have sent to you again and again (though you have not listened), ⁶then I will make this house like Shiloh and this city an object of cursing among all the nations of the earth.'"

⁷The priests, the prophets and all the people heard Jeremiah speak these words in the house of the LORD. ⁸But as soon as Jeremiah finished telling all the people everything the LORD had commanded him to say, the priests, the prophets and all the people seized him and said, "You must die! ⁹Why do you prophesy in the LORD's name that this house will be like Shiloh and this city will be desolate and deserted?" And all the people crowded around Jeremiah in the house of the LORD.

¹⁰When the officials of Judah heard about these things, they went up from the royal palace to the house of the LORD and took their places at the entrance of the New Gate of the LORD's house. ¹¹Then the priests and the prophets said to the officials and all the people, "This man should be sentenced to death because he has prophesied against this city. You have heard it with your own ears!"

¹²Then Jeremiah said to all the officials and all the people: "The LORD sent me to prophesy against this house and this city all the things you have heard. ¹³Now reform your ways and your actions and obey the LORD your God. Then the LORD will relent and not bring the disaster he has pronounced against you. ¹⁴As for me, I am in your hands; do with me whatever you think is good and right. ¹⁵Be assured, however, that if you put me to death, you will bring the guilt of innocent blood on yourselves and on this city and on those who live in it, for in truth the LORD has sent me to you to speak all these words in your hearing." Dt 19:10; Jer 34:19

¹⁶Then the officials and all the people said to the priests and the prophets, "This man should not be sentenced to death! He has spoken to us in the name of the LORD our God." Ac 23:9

¹⁷Some of the elders of the land stepped forward and said to the entire assembly of people, ¹⁸"Micah of Moresheth prophesied in the days of Hezekiah king of Judah. He told all

the people of Judah, 'This is what the LORD Almighty says:

" 'Zion will be plowed like a
    field,   Isa 2:3
Jerusalem will become a
    heap of rubble,   2Ki 25:9
the temple hill a mound
    overgrown with
    thickets.'ᵃ   Jer 17:3

¹⁹"Did Hezekiah king of Judah or anyone else in Judah put him to death? Did not Hezekiah fear the LORD and seek his favor? And did not the LORD relent, so that he did not bring the disaster he pronounced against them? We are about to bring a terrible disaster on ourselves!"

²⁰(Now Uriah son of Shemaiah from Kiriath Jearim was another man who prophesied in the name of the LORD; he prophesied the same things against this city and this land as Jeremiah did. ²¹When King Jehoiakim and all his officers and officials heard his words, the king sought to put him to death. But Uriah heard of it and fled in fear to Egypt. ²²King Jehoiakim, however, sent Elnathan son of Acbor to Egypt, along with some other men. ²³They brought Uriah out of Egypt and took him to King Jehoiakim, who had him struck down with a sword and his body thrown into the burial place of the common people.)

²⁴Furthermore, Ahikam son

of Shaphan supported Jeremiah, and so he was not handed over to the people to be put to death.   2Ki 22:12

Judah to Serve Nebuchadnezzar

27 Early in the reign of Zedekiahᵇ son of Josiah king of Judah, this word came to Jeremiah from the LORD: ²This is what the LORD said to me: "Make a yoke out of straps and crossbars and put it on your neck. ³Then send word to the kings of Edom, Moab, Ammon, Tyre and Sidon through the envoys who have come to Jerusalem to Zedekiah king of Judah. ⁴Give them a message for their masters and say, 'This is what the LORD Almighty, the God of Israel, says: "Tell this to your masters: ⁵With my great power and outstretched arm I made the earth and its people and the animals that are on it, and I give it to anyone I please. ⁶Now I will hand all your countries over to my servant Nebuchadnezzar king of Babylon; I will make even the wild animals subject to him. ⁷All nations will serve him and his son and his grandson until the time for his land comes; then many nations and great kings will subjugate him.

⁸" ' "If, however, any nation or kingdom will not serve

ᵃ18 Micah 3:12   ᵇ1 A few Hebrew manuscripts and Syriac (see also Jer. 27:3, 12 and 28:1); most Hebrew manuscripts *Jehoiakim* (Most Septuagint manuscripts do not have this verse.)

Nebuchadnezzar king of Babylon or bow its neck under his yoke, I will punish that nation with the sword, famine and plague, declares the LORD, until I destroy it by his hand. 9So do not listen to your prophets, your diviners, your interpreters of dreams, your mediums or your sorcerers who tell you, 'You will not serve the king of Babylon.' 10They prophesy lies to you that will only serve to remove you far from your lands; I will banish you and you will perish. 11But if any nation will bow its neck under the yoke of the king of Babylon and serve him, I will let that nation remain in its own land to till it and to live there, declares the LORD." ' "   Dt 6:2; Jer 9:16

12I gave the same message to Zedekiah king of Judah. I said, "Bow your neck under the yoke of the king of Babylon; serve him and his people, and you will live. 13Why will you and your people die by the sword, famine and plague with which the LORD has threatened any nation that will not serve the king of Babylon? 14Do not listen to the words of the prophets who say to you, 'You will not serve the king of Babylon,' for they are prophesying lies to you. 15'I have not sent them,' declares the LORD. 'They are prophesying lies in my name. Therefore, I will banish you and you will perish, both you and

the prophets who prophesy to you.' "   Jer 17:4; Mt 15:12-14

16Then I said to the priests and all these people, "This is what the LORD says: Do not listen to the prophets who say, 'Very soon now the articles from the LORD's house will be brought back from Babylon.' They are prophesying lies to you. 17Do not listen to them. Serve the king of Babylon, and you will live. Why should this city become a ruin? 18If they are prophets and have the word of the LORD, let them plead with the LORD Almighty that the furnishings remaining in the house of the LORD and in the palace of the king of Judah and in Jerusalem not be taken to Babylon. 19For this is what the LORD Almighty says about the pillars, the Sea, the movable stands and the other furnishings that are left in this city, 20which Nebuchadnezzar king of Babylon did not take away when he carried Jehoiachin[a] son of Jehoiakim king of Judah into exile from Jerusalem to Babylon, along with all the nobles of Judah and Jerusalem— 21yes, this is what the LORD Almighty, the God of Israel, says about the things that are left in the house of the LORD and in the palace of the king of Judah and in Jerusalem: 22'They will be taken to Babylon and there they will remain until the day I come for them,' declares the LORD. 'Then I will bring

a20 Hebrew Jeconiah, a variant of Jehoiachin

them back and restore them to this place.' " Dt 13:5; 1Ki 7:48-50

The False Prophet Hananiah

28 In the fifth month of that same year, the fourth year, early in the reign of Zedekiah king of Judah, the prophet Hananiah son of Azzur, who was from Gibeon, said to me in the house of the LORD in the presence of the priests and all the people: ²"This is what the LORD Almighty, the God of Israel, says: 'I will break the yoke of the king of Babylon. ³Within two years I will bring back to this place all the articles of the LORD's house that Nebuchadnezzar king of Babylon removed from here and took to Babylon. ⁴I will also bring back to this place Jehoiachin[a] son of Jehoiakim king of Judah and all the other exiles from Judah who went to Babylon,' declares the LORD, 'for I will break the yoke of the king of Babylon.' " Jer 13:17

⁵Then the prophet Jeremiah replied to the prophet Hananiah before the priests and all the people who were standing in the house of the LORD. ⁶He said, "Amen! May the LORD do so! May the LORD fulfill the words you have prophesied by bringing the articles of the LORD's house and all the exiles back to this place from Babylon. ⁷Nevertheless, listen to what I have to say in your hearing and in the hearing of all the people:

⁸From early times the prophets who preceded you and me have prophesied war, disaster and plague against many countries and great kingdoms. ⁹But the prophet who prophesies peace will be recognized as one truly sent by the LORD only if his prediction comes true." Jer 30:19

¹⁰Then the prophet Hananiah took the yoke off the neck of the prophet Jeremiah and broke it, ¹¹and he said before all the people, "This is what the LORD says: 'In the same way will I break the yoke of Nebuchadnezzar king of Babylon off the neck of all the nations within two years.' " At this, the prophet Jeremiah went on his way. 2Ch 36:21; Ps 40:5

¹²Shortly after the prophet Hananiah had broken the yoke off the neck of the prophet Jeremiah, the word of the LORD came to Jeremiah: ¹³"Go and tell Hananiah, 'This is what the LORD says: You have broken a wooden yoke, but in its place you will get a yoke of iron. ¹⁴This is what the LORD Almighty, the God of Israel, says: I will put an iron yoke on the necks of all these nations to make them serve Nebuchadnezzar king of Babylon, and they will serve him. I will even give him control over the wild animals.' " Hos 2:23; Zep 3:12

¹⁵Then the prophet Jeremiah said to Hananiah the prophet, "Listen, Hananiah! The LORD

---

*a*4 Hebrew *Jeconiah*, a variant of *Jehoiachin*

has not sent you, yet you have persuaded this nation to trust in lies. [16]Therefore, this is what the LORD says: 'I am about to remove you from the face of the earth. This very year you are going to die, because you have preached rebellion against the LORD.'" Ge 7:4; Jer 29:31

[17]In the seventh month of that same year, Hananiah the prophet died. 2Ki 1:17

A Letter to the Exiles

29 This is the text of the letter that the prophet Jeremiah sent from Jerusalem to the surviving elders among the exiles and to the priests, the prophets and all the other people Nebuchadnezzar had carried into exile from Jerusalem to Babylon. [2](This was after King Jehoiachin[a] and the queen mother, the court officials and the leaders of Judah and Jerusalem, the craftsmen and the artisans had gone into exile from Jerusalem.) [3]He entrusted the letter to Elasah son of Shaphan and to Gemariah son of Hilkiah, whom Zedekiah king of Judah sent to King Nebuchadnezzar in Babylon. It said: 2Ch 36:10

[4]This is what the LORD Almighty, the God of Israel, says to all those I carried into exile from Jerusalem to Babylon: [5]"Build houses and settle down; plant gardens and eat what they produce. [6]Marry and have sons

and daughters; find wives for your sons and give your daughters in marriage, so that they too may have sons and daughters. Increase in number there; do not decrease. [7]Also, seek the peace and prosperity of the city to which I have carried you into exile. Pray to the LORD for it, because if it prospers, you too will prosper." [8]Yes, this is what the LORD Almighty, the God of Israel, says: "Do not let the prophets and diviners among you deceive you. Do not listen to the dreams you encourage them to have. [9]They are prophesying lies to you in my name. I have not sent them," declares the LORD. Jer 24:5; La 2:14

[10]This is what the LORD says: "When seventy years are completed for Babylon, I will come to you and fulfill my gracious promise to bring you back to this place. [11]For I know the plans I have for you," declares the LORD, "plans to prosper you and not to harm you, plans to give you hope and a future. [12]Then you will call upon me and come and pray to me, and I will listen to you. [13]You will seek me and find me when you seek me with all your heart. [14]I will be found by you," declares the LORD, "and will

---

[a]2 Hebrew *Jeconiah*, a variant of *Jehoiachin*

bring you back from captivity.[a] I will gather you from all the nations and places where I have banished you," declares the LORD, "and will bring you back to the place from which I carried you into exile."

15You may say, "The LORD has raised up prophets for us in Babylon," 16but this is what the LORD says about the king who sits on David's throne and all the people who remain in this city, your countrymen who did not go with you into exile— 17yes, this is what the LORD Almighty says: "I will send the sword, famine and plague against them and I will make them like poor figs that are so bad they cannot be eaten. 18I will pursue them with the sword, famine and plague and will make them abhorrent to all the kingdoms of the earth and an object of cursing and horror, of scorn and reproach, among all the nations where I drive them. 19For they have not listened to my words," declares the LORD, "words that I sent to them again and again by my servants the prophets. And you exiles have not listened either," declares the LORD.

20Therefore, hear the word of the LORD, all you exiles whom I have sent away from Jerusalem to Babylon. 21This is what the LORD Almighty, the God of Israel, says about Ahab son of Kolaiah and Zedekiah son of Maaseiah, who are prophesying lies to you in my name: "I will hand them over to Nebuchadnezzar king of Babylon, and he will put them to death before your very eyes. 22Because of them, all the exiles from Judah who are in Babylon will use this curse: 'The LORD treat you like Zedekiah and Ahab, whom the king of Babylon burned in the fire.' 23For they have done outrageous things in Israel; they have committed adultery with their neighbors' wives and in my name have spoken lies, which I did not tell them to do. I know it and am a witness to it," declares the LORD.

Message to Shemaiah

24Tell Shemaiah the Nehelamite, 25"This is what the LORD Almighty, the God of Israel, says: You sent letters in your own name to all the people in Jerusalem, to Zephaniah son of Maaseiah the priest, and to all the other priests. You said to Zephaniah, 26'The LORD has appointed you priest in place of Jehoiada to be in charge of the house of the LORD; you should put any madman who acts like a

---

a14 Or *will restore your fortunes*

prophet into the stocks and neck-irons. [27]So why have you not reprimanded Jeremiah from Anathoth, who poses as a prophet among you? [28]He has sent this message to us in Babylon: It will be a long time. Therefore build houses and settle down; plant gardens and eat what they produce.' " 2Ki 25:18

[29]Zephaniah the priest, however, read the letter to Jeremiah the prophet. [30]Then the word of the LORD came to Jeremiah: [31]"Send this message to all the exiles: 'This is what the LORD says about Shemaiah the Nehelamite: Because Shemaiah has prophesied to you, even though I did not send him, and has led you to believe a lie, [32]this is what the LORD says: I will surely punish Shemaiah the Nehelamite and his descendants. He will have no one left among this people, nor will he see the good things I will do for my people, declares the LORD, because he has preached rebellion against me.' " Jer 21:1; 28:16

Restoration of Israel

30 This is the word that came to Jeremiah from the LORD: [2]"This is what the LORD, the God of Israel, says: 'Write in a book all the words I have spoken to you. [3]The days are coming,' declares the LORD, 'when I will bring my people Israel and Judah back from captivity[a] and restore them to the

land I gave their forefathers to possess,' says the LORD." Jer 36:2

[4]These are the words the LORD spoke concerning Israel and Judah: [5]"This is what the LORD says:

" 'Cries of fear are heard—
  terror, not peace. Jer 6:25
[6]Ask and see:
  Can a man bear children?
Then why do I see every
    strong man
  with his hands on his
    stomach like a woman in
    labor, Jer 4:31
  every face turned deathly
    pale? Isa 29:22
[7]How awful that day will be!
  None will be like it.
It will be a time of trouble for
    Jacob, Isa 22:5
  but he will be saved out
    of it. Jer 23:3

[8]" ' In that day,' declares the
    LORD Almighty,
  'I will break the yoke off
    their necks Isa 9:4
and will tear off their bonds;
  no longer will foreigners
    enslave them. Jer 25:14
[9]Instead, they will serve the
    LORD their God
  and David their king,
  whom I will raise up for
    them. 1Sa 13:14

[10]" 'So do not fear, O Jacob my
    servant;
    Isa 44:2
  do not be dismayed,
    O Israel,'
      declares the LORD.

---

[a]3 Or *will restore the fortunes of my people Israel and Judah*

'I will surely save you out of
a distant place, Jer 29:14
your descendants from the
land of their exile.
Jacob will again have peace
and security, Isa 35:9
and no one will make him
afraid. Isa 29:22
¹¹I am with you and will save
you,' Jos 1:5
declares the LORD.
'Though I completely destroy
all the nations
among which I scatter you,
I will not completely
destroy you. Lev 26:44
I will discipline you but only
with justice; Jer 10:24
I will not let you go entirely
unpunished.' Hos 11:9

¹²"This is what the LORD says:

" 'Your wound is incurable,
your injury beyond healing.
¹³There is no one to plead your
cause, Jdg 6:31
no remedy for your sore,
no healing for you. Jer 8:22
¹⁴All your allies have forgotten
you; Jer 22:20
they care nothing for you.
I have struck you as an
enemy would Job 13:24
and punished you as would
the cruel, Job 30:21
because your guilt is so great
and your sins so many.
¹⁵Why do you cry out over
your wound,
your pain that has no cure?
Because of your great guilt
and many sins
I have done these things to
you. Pr 1:31; La 1:5

¹⁶" 'But all who devour you
will be devoured;
all your enemies will go
into exile. Isa 14:2
Those who plunder you will
be plundered;
all who make spoil of you I
will despoil.
¹⁷But I will restore you to
health
and heal your wounds,'
declares the LORD,
'because you are called an
outcast, Isa 6:12
Zion for whom no one
cares.' Ps 142:4

¹⁸"This is what the LORD says:

" 'I will restore the fortunes
of Jacob's tents Nu 24:5
and have compassion on
his dwellings; Ps 102:13
the city will be rebuilt on her
ruins, Jer 31:4
and the palace will stand in
its proper place.
¹⁹From them will come songs
of thanksgiving Isa 51:3
and the sound of rejoicing.
I will add to their numbers,
and they will not be
decreased; Ge 15:5
I will bring them honor,
and they will not be
disdained. Isa 44:23
²⁰Their children will be as in
days of old, Isa 54:13
and their community will
be established before
me; Isa 54:14
I will punish all who
oppress them. Ex 23:22
²¹Their leader will be one of
their own;

their ruler will arise from
   among them.   Dt 17:15
I will bring him near and he
   will come close to me,
for who is he who will
   devote himself
to be close to me?'
         declares the LORD.
22" 'So you will be my people,
   and I will be your God.' "

23See, the storm of the LORD
   will burst out in wrath,
a driving wind swirling
   down
on the heads of the wicked.
24The fierce anger of the LORD
   will not turn back
until he fully accomplishes
   the purposes of his heart.
In days to come
   you will understand this.

31 "At that time," declares
the LORD, "I will be the
God of all the clans of Israel,
and they will be my people."

2This is what the LORD says:

"The people who survive the
   sword
will find favor in the desert;
I will come to give rest to
   Israel."   Ex 33:14

3The LORD appeared to us in
the past,ª saying:

"I have loved you with an
   everlasting love;   Dt 4:37
I have drawn you with
   loving-kindness.   Hos 11:4
4I will build you up again

and you will be rebuilt,
   O Virgin Israel.   2Ki 19:21
Again you will take up your
   tambourines   Ge 31:27
and go out to dance with
   the joyful.   Jer 30:19
5Again you will plant
   vineyards
on the hills of Samaria;
the farmers will plant them
   and enjoy their fruit. Isa 37:30
6There will be a day when
   watchmen cry out
on the hills of Ephraim,
'Come, let us go up to Zion,
   to the LORD our God.' "

7This is what the LORD says:

"Sing with joy for Jacob;
   shout for the foremost of
   the nations.   Dt 28:13
Make your praises heard,
   and say,
'O LORD, save your people,
   the remnant of Israel.'
8See, I will bring them from
   the land of the north
and gather them from the
   ends of the earth. Ge 33:13
Among them will be the
   blind and the lame,
expectant mothers and
   women in labor;
a great throng will return.
9They will come with
   weeping;   Ezr 3:12
they will pray as I bring
   them back.
I will lead them beside
   streams of water   Nu 20:8
on a level path where they
   will not stumble,   Isa 40:4

ª3 Or LORD *has appeared to us from afar*

because I am Israel's father,
and Ephraim is my firstborn
son. Ex 4:22

10"Hear the word of the LORD,
O nations;
proclaim it in distant
coastlands: Isa 49:1
'He who scattered Israel will
gather them Dt 30:4
and will watch over his
flock like a shepherd.'
11For the LORD will ransom
Jacob
and redeem them from the
hand of those stronger
than they. Ps 142:6
12They will come and shout for
joy on the heights of
Zion; Eze 17:23
they will rejoice in the
bounty of the LORD—
the grain, the new wine and
the oil, Nu 18:12
the young of the flocks and
herds. Isa 65:10
They will be like a
well-watered garden,
and they will sorrow no
more. Isa 30:19
13Then maidens will dance and
be glad,
young men and old as
well.
I will turn their mourning
into gladness; Isa 61:3
I will give them comfort
and joy instead of
sorrow. Ps 30:11
14I will satisfy the priests with
abundance, Lev 7:35-36
and my people will be filled
with my bounty,"
declares the LORD.

15This is what the LORD says:

"A voice is heard in Ramah,
mourning and great
weeping,
Rachel weeping for her
children
and refusing to be
comforted, Ge 37:35
because her children are no
more." Jer 10:20

16This is what the LORD says:

"Restrain your voice from
weeping
and your eyes from tears,
for your work will be
rewarded," Ru 2:12
declares the LORD.
"They will return from the
land of the enemy.
17So there is hope for your
future," Job 8:7
declares the LORD.
"Your children will return
to their own land. Jer 30:20
18"I have surely heard
Ephraim's moaning:
'You disciplined me like an
unruly calf, Jer 50:11
and I have been disciplined.
Restore me, and I will return,
because you are the LORD
my God.
19After I strayed,
I repented; Ps 95:10
after I came to understand,
I beat my breast. Eze 21:12
I was ashamed and
humiliated Ezr 9:6
because I bore the disgrace
of my youth.' Ps 25:7
20Is not Ephraim my dear son,
the child in whom I delight?

Though I often speak against
him,
I still remember him. Isa 44:21
Therefore my heart yearns
for him;
I have great compassion for
him," 1Ki 3:26
declares the LORD.

21"Set up road signs;
put up guideposts. Eze 21:19
Take note of the highway,
the road that you take. Isa 35:8
Return, O Virgin Israel,
return to your towns.
22How long will you wander,
O unfaithful daughter?
The LORD will create a new
thing on earth—
a woman will surround[a] a
man." Dt 32:10

23This is what the LORD Almighty, the God of Israel, says:
"When I bring them back from
captivity,[b] the people in the
land of Judah and in its towns
will once again use these words:
'The LORD bless you, O righteous dwelling, O sacred mountain.' 24People will live together
in Judah and all its towns—
farmers and those who move
about with their flocks. 25I will
refresh the weary and satisfy
the faint." Jer 30:18; Jn 4:14
26At this I awoke and looked
around. My sleep had been
pleasant to me. Zec 4:1
27"The days are coming," declares the LORD, "when I will
plant the house of Israel and the

house of Judah with the offspring of men and of animals.
28Just as I watched over them to
uproot and tear down, and to
overthrow, destroy and bring
disaster, so I will watch over
them to build and to plant," declares the LORD. 29"In those
days people will no longer say,

'The fathers have eaten sour
grapes, Ge 9:25
and the children's teeth are
set on edge.' Eze 18:2

30Instead, everyone will die for
his own sin; whoever eats sour
grapes—his own teeth will be
set on edge. 2Ki 14:6

31"The time is coming,"
declares the LORD,
"when I will make a new
covenant Dt 29:14
with the house of Israel
and with the house of
Judah.
32It will not be like the
covenant
I made with their
forefathers Dt 5:3
when I took them by the
hand
to lead them out of Egypt,
because they broke my
covenant,
though I was a husband to[c]
them,[d]" Isa 54:5
declares the LORD.
33"This is the covenant I will
make with the house of
Israel

after that time," declares
the LORD.
"I will put my law in their
minds   Ex 4:15
and write it on their hearts.
I will be their God,
and they will be my people.
34No longer will a man teach
his neighbor,   1Jn 2:7
or a man his brother,
saying, 'Know the
LORD,'
because they will all know
me,   Isa 11:9
from the least of them to
the greatest,"
            declares the LORD.
"For I will forgive their
wickedness   Ps 85:2
and will remember their
sins no more."   Job 7:21

35This is what the LORD says,

he who appoints the sun
to shine by day,   Ps 136:7-9
who decrees the moon and
stars
to shine by night,   Ge 1:16
who stirs up the sea
so that its waves roar—Ps 93:3
the LORD Almighty is his
name: Jer 10:16
36"Only if these decrees vanish
from my sight,"   Job 38:33
declares the LORD,
"will the descendants of
Israel ever cease Ps 89:36-37
to be a nation before me."

37This is what the LORD says:

"Only if the heavens above
can be measured   Job 38:5
and the foundations of the

earth below be searched
out
will I reject all the
descendants of Israel
because of all they have
done,"   Jer 33:24-26
declares the LORD.

38"The days are coming," declares the LORD, "when this city
will be rebuilt for me from the
Tower of Hananel to the Corner
Gate. 39The measuring line will
stretch from there straight to the
hill of Gareb and then turn to
Goah. 40The whole valley where
dead bodies and ashes are
thrown, and all the terraces out
to the Kidron Valley on the east
as far as the corner of the Horse
Gate, will be holy to the LORD.
The city will never again be
uprooted or demolished." Jer 2:23

Jeremiah Buys a Field

32 This is the word that
came to Jeremiah from
the LORD in the tenth year of
Zedekiah king of Judah, which
was the eighteenth year of
Nebuchadnezzar. 2The army of
the king of Babylon was then
besieging Jerusalem, and Jeremiah the prophet was confined
in the courtyard of the guard in
the royal palace of Judah. 2Ki 25:1

3Now Zedekiah king of Judah
had imprisoned him there, saying, "Why do you prophesy as
you do? You say, 'This is what
the LORD says: I am about to
hand this city over to the king of
Babylon, and he will capture it.
4Zedekiah king of Judah will not

escape out of the hands of the Babylonians*a* but will certainly be handed over to the king of Babylon, and will speak with him face to face and see him with his own eyes. 5He will take Zedekiah to Babylon, where he will remain until I deal with him, declares the LORD. If you fight against the Babylonians, you will not succeed.'"   Jer 26:8-9

6Jeremiah said, "The word of the LORD came to me: 7Hanamel son of Shallum your uncle is going to come to you and say, 'Buy my field at Anathoth, because as nearest relative it is your right and duty to buy it.'   Jer 39:7

8"Then, just as the LORD had said, my cousin Hanamel came to me in the courtyard of the guard and said, 'Buy my field at Anathoth in the territory of Benjamin. Since it is your right to redeem it and possess it, buy it for yourself.'

"I knew that this was the word of the LORD; 9so I bought the field at Anathoth from my cousin Hanamel and weighed out for him seventeen shekels*b* of silver. 10I signed and sealed the deed, had it witnessed, and weighed out the silver on the scales. 11I took the deed of purchase—the sealed copy containing the terms and conditions, as well as the unsealed copy— 12and I gave this deed to Baruch son of Neriah, the son of Mahseiah, in the presence of my

cousin Hanamel and of the witnesses who had signed the deed and of all the Jews sitting in the courtyard of the guard.   Jer 37:12

13"In their presence I gave Baruch these instructions: 14'This is what the LORD Almighty, the God of Israel, says: Take these documents, both the sealed and unsealed copies of the deed of purchase, and put them in a clay jar so they will last a long time. 15For this is what the LORD Almighty, the God of Israel, says: Houses, fields and vineyards will again be bought in this land.'   Isa 8:16

16"After I had given the deed of purchase to Baruch son of Neriah, I prayed to the LORD:

17"Ah, Sovereign LORD, you have made the heavens and the earth by your great power and outstretched arm. Nothing is too hard for you. 18You show love to thousands but bring the punishment for the fathers' sins into the laps of their children after them. O great and powerful God, whose name is the LORD Almighty, 19great are your purposes and mighty are your deeds. Your eyes are open to all the ways of men; you reward everyone according to his conduct and as his deeds deserve. 20You performed miraculous signs and wonders in Egypt and have con-

---

*a*4 Or *Chaldeans*; also in verses 5, 24, 25, 28, 29 and 43 (about 200 grams)   *b*9 That is, about 7 ounces

tinued them to this day, both in Israel and among all mankind, and have gained the renown that is still yours. ²¹You brought your people Israel out of Egypt with signs and wonders, by a mighty hand and an out-stretched arm and with great terror. ²²You gave them this land you had sworn to give their fore-fathers, a land flowing with milk and honey. ²³They came in and took posses-sion of it, but they did not obey you or follow your law; they did not do what you commanded them to do. So you brought all this disaster upon them.   Dt 9:29

²⁴"See how the siege ramps are built up to take the city. Because of the sword, famine and plague, the city will be handed over to the Babylonians who are attacking it. What you said has happened, as you now see. ²⁵And though the city will be handed over to the Babylonians, you, O Sover-eign LORD, say to me, 'Buy the field with silver and have the transaction wit-nessed.'"   2Sa 20:15; Isa 8:2

²⁶Then the word of the LORD came to Jeremiah: ²⁷"I am the LORD, the God of all mankind. Is anything too hard for me? ²⁸Therefore, this is what the LORD says: I am about to hand

this city over to the Babylonians and to Nebuchadnezzar king of Babylon, who will capture it. ²⁹The Babylonians who are at-tacking this city will come in and set it on fire; they will burn it down, along with the houses where the people provoked me to anger by burning incense on the roofs to Baal and by pouring out drink offerings to other gods.   Nu 16:22; 2Ch 36:19

³⁰"The people of Israel and Judah have done nothing but evil in my sight from their youth; indeed, the people of Is-rael have done nothing but pro-voke me with what their hands have made, declares the LORD. ³¹From the day it was built until now, this city has so aroused my anger and wrath that I must remove it from my sight. ³²The people of Israel and Judah have provoked me by all the evil they have done—they, their kings and officials, their priests and prophets, the men of Judah and the people of Jerusalem. ³³They turned their backs to me and not their faces; though I taught them again and again, they would not listen or respond to discipline. ³⁴They set up their abominable idols in the house that bears my Name and defiled it. ³⁵They built high places for Baal in the Valley of Ben Hin-nom to sacrifice their sons and daughters*a* to Molech, though I never commanded, nor did it enter my mind, that they

---

a35 Or to make their sons and daughters pass through the fire

should do such a detestable thing and so make Judah sin.

36"You are saying about this city, 'By the sword, famine and plague it will be handed over to the king of Babylon'; but this is what the LORD, the God of Israel, says: 37I will surely gather them from all the lands where I banish them in my furious anger and great wrath; I will bring them back to this place and let them live in safety. 38They will be my people, and I will be their God. 39I will give them singleness of heart and action, so that they will always fear me for their own good and the good of their children after them. 40I will make an everlasting covenant with them: I will never stop doing good to them, and I will inspire them to fear me, so that they will never turn away from me. 41I will rejoice in doing them good and will assuredly plant them in this land with all my heart and soul.   Dt 28:63; Isa 11:12

42"This is what the LORD says: As I have brought all this great calamity on this people, so I will give them all the prosperity I have promised them. 43Once more fields will be bought in this land of which you say, 'It is a desolate waste, without men or animals, for it has been handed over to the Babylonians.' 44Fields will be bought for silver, and deeds will be signed, sealed and witnessed in the territory of Benjamin, in the villages around Jerusalem, in the towns of Judah and in the towns of the hill country, of the western foothills and of the Negev, because I will restore their fortunes,[a] declares the LORD."   Ru 4:9; La 3:38

Promise of Restoration

33 While Jeremiah was still confined in the courtyard of the guard, the word of the LORD came to him a second time: 2"This is what the LORD says, he who made the earth, the LORD who formed it and established it—the LORD is his name: 3'Call to me and I will answer you and tell you great and unsearchable things you do not know.' 4For this is what the LORD, the God of Israel, says about the houses in this city and the royal palaces of Judah that have been torn down to be used against the siege ramps and the sword 5in the fight with the Babylonians[b]: 'They will be filled with the dead bodies of the men I will slay in my anger and wrath. I will hide my face from this city because of all its wickedness.   Dt 31:17; Ps 88:8

6" 'Nevertheless, I will bring health and healing to it; I will heal my people and will let them enjoy abundant peace and security. 7I will bring Judah and Israel back from captivity[c] and will rebuild them as they were before. 8I will cleanse them from

a44 Or will bring them back from captivity fortunes of Judah and Israel   b5 Or Chaldeans   c7 Or will restore the

all the sin they have committed against me and will forgive all their sins of rebellion against me. ⁹Then this city will bring me renown, joy, praise and honor before all nations on earth that hear of all the good things I do for it; and they will be in awe and will tremble at the abundant prosperity and peace I provide for it.'   Dt 32:39; Isa 55:13

¹⁰"This is what the LORD says: 'You say about this place, "It is a desolate waste, without men or animals." Yet in the towns of Judah and the streets of Jerusalem that are deserted, inhabited by neither men nor animals, there will be heard once more ¹¹the sounds of joy and gladness, the voices of bride and bridegroom, and the voices of those who bring thank offerings to the house of the LORD, saying,   Lev 7:12; Jer 32:43

"Give thanks to the LORD
    Almighty,
for the LORD is good;
    his love endures forever."

For I will restore the fortunes of the land as they were before,' says the LORD.   Ps 14:7

¹²"This is what the LORD Almighty says: 'In this place, desolate and without men or animals—in all its towns there will again be pastures for shepherds to rest their flocks. ¹³In the towns of the hill country, of the western foothills and of the Negev, in the territory of Benja-

min, in the villages around Jerusalem and in the towns of Judah, flocks will again pass under the hand of the one who counts them,' says the LORD.

¹⁴" 'The days are coming,' declares the LORD, 'when I will fulfill the gracious promise I made to the house of Israel and to the house of Judah.   Dt 28:1-14

¹⁵" 'In those days and at that
    time
I will make a righteous
    Branch sprout from
    David's line;   2Sa 7:12
he will do what is just and
    right in the land.
¹⁶In those days Judah will be
    saved   Isa 45:17
and Jerusalem will live in
    safety.   Jer 17:25
This is the name by which it[a]
    will be called: Isa 59:14
The LORD Our
    Righteousness.'   1Co 1:30

¹⁷For this is what the LORD says: 'David will never fail to have a man to sit on the throne of the house of Israel, ¹⁸nor will the priests, who are Levites, ever fail to have a man to stand before me continually to offer burnt offerings, to burn grain offerings and to present sacrifices.'"   Nu 25:11-13; 2Sa 7:13

¹⁹The word of the LORD came to Jeremiah: ²⁰"This is what the LORD says: 'If you can break my covenant with the day and my covenant with the night, so that day and night no longer come at

their appointed time, ²¹then my covenant with David my servant—and my covenant with the Levites who are priests ministering before me—can be broken and David will no longer have a descendant to reign on his throne. ²²I will make the descendants of David my servant and the Levites who minister before me as countless as the stars of the sky and as measureless as the sand on the seashore.'" _{Ge 12:2; Ps 89:36}

²³The word of the LORD came to Jeremiah: ²⁴"Have you not noticed that these people are saying, 'The LORD has rejected the two kingdomsᵃ he chose'? So they despise my people and no longer regard them as a nation. ²⁵This is what the LORD says: 'If I have not established my covenant with day and night and the fixed laws of heaven and earth, ²⁶then I will reject the descendants of Jacob and David my servant and will not choose one of his sons to rule over the descendants of Abraham, Isaac and Jacob. For I will restore their fortunesᵇ and have compassion on them.'"

Warning to Zedekiah

34 While Nebuchadnezzar king of Babylon and all his army and all the kingdoms and peoples in the empire he ruled were fighting against Jerusalem and all its surrounding towns, this word came to Jeremiah from the LORD: ²"This is what the LORD, the God of Israel, says: Go to Zedekiah king of Judah and tell him, 'This is what the LORD says: I am about to hand this city over to the king of Babylon, and he will burn it down. ³You will not escape from his grasp but will surely be captured and handed over to him. You will see the king of Babylon with your own eyes, and he will speak with you face to face. And you will go to Babylon. _{Jer 21:7; 27:7}

⁴"'Yet hear the promise of the LORD, O Zedekiah king of Judah. This is what the LORD says concerning you: You will not die by the sword; ⁵you will die peacefully. As people made a funeral fire in honor of your fathers, the former kings who preceded you, so they will make a fire in your honor and lament, "Alas, O master!" I myself make this promise, declares the LORD.'" _{2Ch 16:14; Jer 52:11}

⁶Then Jeremiah the prophet told all this to Zedekiah king of Judah, in Jerusalem, ⁷while the army of the king of Babylon was fighting against Jerusalem and the other cities of Judah that were still holding out—Lachish and Azekah. These were the only fortified cities left in Judah.

Freedom for Slaves

⁸The word came to Jeremiah from the LORD after King Zede-

ᵃ24 Or *families*   ᵇ26 Or *will bring them back from captivity*

kiah had made a covenant with all the people in Jerusalem to proclaim freedom for the slaves. [9]Everyone was to free his Hebrew slaves, both male and female; no one was to hold a fellow Jew in bondage. [10]So all the officials and people who entered into this covenant agreed that they would free their male and female slaves and no longer hold them in bondage. They agreed, and set them free. [11]But afterward they changed their minds and took back the slaves they had freed and enslaved them again.   2Ki 11:17; Ps 78:37

[12]Then the word of the LORD came to Jeremiah: [13]"This is what the LORD, the God of Israel, says: I made a covenant with your forefathers when I brought them out of Egypt, out of the land of slavery. I said, [14]'Every seventh year each of you must free any fellow Hebrew who has sold himself to you. After he has served you six years, you must let him go free.'[a] Your fathers, however, did not listen to me or pay attention to me. [15]Recently you repented and did what is right in my sight: Each of you proclaimed freedom to his countrymen. You even made a covenant before me in the house that bears my Name. [16]But now you have turned around and profaned my name; each of you has taken back the male and female slaves you had set free to go where they wished. You have forced them to become your slaves again.   Ex 24:8

[17]"Therefore, this is what the LORD says: You have not obeyed me; you have not proclaimed freedom for your fellow countrymen. So I now proclaim 'freedom' for you, declares the LORD—'freedom' to fall by the sword, plague and famine. I will make you abhorrent to all the kingdoms of the earth. [18]The men who have violated my covenant and have not fulfilled the terms of the covenant they made before me, I will treat like the calf they cut in two and then walked between its pieces. [19]The leaders of Judah and Jerusalem, the court officials, the priests and all the people of the land who walked between the pieces of the calf, [20]I will hand over to their enemies who seek their lives. Their dead bodies will become food for the birds of the air and the beasts of the earth.   Eze 16:27; Mt 7:2

[21]"I will hand Zedekiah king of Judah and his officials over to their enemies who seek their lives, to the army of the king of Babylon, which has withdrawn from you. [22]I am going to give the order, declares the LORD, and I will bring them back to this city. They will fight against it, take it and burn it down. And I will lay waste the towns of Judah so no one can live there."

[a]14 Deut. 15:12

The Recabites

35 This is the word that came to Jeremiah from the LORD during the reign of Jehoiakim son of Josiah king of Judah: ²"Go to the Recabite family and invite them to come to one of the side rooms of the house of the LORD and give them wine to drink."   2Ch 36:5

³So I went to get Jaazaniah son of Jeremiah, the son of Habazziniah, and his brothers and all his sons—the whole family of the Recabites. ⁴I brought them into the house of the LORD, into the room of the sons of Hanan son of Igdaliah the man of God. It was next to the room of the officials, which was over that of Maaseiah son of Shallum the doorkeeper. ⁵Then I set bowls full of wine and some cups before the men of the Recabite family and said to them, "Drink some wine."

⁶But they replied, "We do not drink wine, because our forefather Jonadab son of Recab gave us this command: 'Neither you nor your descendants must ever drink wine. ⁷Also you must never build houses, sow seed or plant vineyards; you must never have any of these things, but must always live in tents. Then you will live a long time in the land where you are nomads.' ⁸We have obeyed everything our forefather Jonadab son of Recab commanded us. Neither

we nor our wives nor our sons and daughters have ever drunk wine ⁹or built houses to live in or had vineyards, fields or crops. ¹⁰We have lived in tents and have fully obeyed everything our forefather Jonadab commanded us. ¹¹But when Nebuchadnezzar king of Babylon invaded this land, we said, 'Come, we must go to Jerusalem to escape the Babylonian*a* and Aramean armies.' So we have remained in Jerusalem."   2Ki 10:15

¹²Then the word of the LORD came to Jeremiah, saying: ¹³"This is what the LORD Almighty, the God of Israel, says: Go and tell the men of Judah and the people of Jerusalem, 'Will you not learn a lesson and obey my words?' declares the LORD. ¹⁴'Jonadab son of Recab ordered his sons not to drink wine and this command has been kept. To this day they do not drink wine, because they obey their forefather's command. But I have spoken to you again and again, yet you have not obeyed me. ¹⁵Again and again I sent all my servants the prophets to you. They said, "Each of you must turn from your wicked ways and reform your actions; do not follow other gods to serve them. Then you will live in the land I have given to you and your fathers." But you have not paid attention or listened to me. ¹⁶The descendants of Jonadab son of

---

a 11 Or *Chaldean*

Recab have carried out the command their forefather gave them, but these people have not obeyed me.'   Lev 20:9; Jer 11:6

17"Therefore, this is what the LORD God Almighty, the God of Israel, says: 'Listen! I am going to bring on Judah and on everyone living in Jerusalem every disaster I pronounced against them. I spoke to them, but they did not listen; I called to them, but they did not answer.' " Pr 1:24

18Then Jeremiah said to the family of the Recabites, "This is what the LORD Almighty, the God of Israel, says: 'You have obeyed the command of your forefather Jonadab and have followed all his instructions and have done everything he ordered.' 19Therefore, this is what the LORD Almighty, the God of Israel, says: 'Jonadab son of Recab will never fail to have a man to serve me.' "   Ge 31:35

Jehoiakim Burns Jeremiah's Scroll

36 In the fourth year of Jehoiakim son of Josiah king of Judah, this word came to Jeremiah from the LORD: 2"Take a scroll and write on it all the words I have spoken to you concerning Israel, Judah and all the other nations from the time I began speaking to you in the reign of Josiah till now. 3Perhaps when the people of Judah hear about every disaster I plan to inflict on them, each of them will turn from his wicked way;

then I will forgive their wickedness and their sin."   2Ch 36:5

4So Jeremiah called Baruch son of Neriah, and while Jeremiah dictated all the words the LORD had spoken to him, Baruch wrote them on the scroll. 5Then Jeremiah told Baruch, "I am restricted; I cannot go to the LORD's temple. 6So you go to the house of the LORD on a day of fasting and read to the people from the scroll the words of the LORD that you wrote as I dictated. Read them to all the people of Judah who come in from their towns. 7Perhaps they will bring their petition before the LORD, and each will turn from his wicked ways, for the anger and wrath pronounced against this people by the LORD are great."   Jer 32:12; 37:20

8Baruch son of Neriah did everything Jeremiah the prophet told him to do; at the LORD's temple he read the words of the LORD from the scroll. 9In the ninth month of the fifth year of Jehoiakim son of Josiah king of Judah, a time of fasting before the LORD was proclaimed for all the people in Jerusalem and those who had come from the towns of Judah. 10From the room of Gemariah son of Shaphan the secretary, which was in the upper courtyard at the entrance of the New Gate of the temple, Baruch read to all the people at the LORD's temple the words of Jeremiah from the scroll.   2Ch 20:3

11When Micaiah son of Gema-

riah, the son of Shaphan, heard all the words of the LORD from the scroll, [12]he went down to the secretary's room in the royal palace, where all the officials were sitting: Elishama the secretary, Delaiah son of Shemaiah, Elnathan son of Acbor, Gemariah son of Shaphan, Zedekiah son of Hananiah, and all the other officials. [13]After Micaiah told them everything he had heard Baruch read to the people from the scroll, [14]all the officials sent Jehudi son of Nethaniah, the son of Shelemiah, the son of Cushi, to say to Baruch, "Bring the scroll from which you have read to the people and come." So Baruch son of Neriah went to them with the scroll in his hand. [15]They said to him, "Sit down, please, and read it to us."

So Baruch read it to them. [16]When they heard all these words, they looked at each other in fear and said to Baruch, "We must report all these words to the king." [17]Then they asked Baruch, "Tell us, how did you come to write all this? Did Jeremiah dictate it?"　　　Ps 36:1

[18]"Yes," Baruch replied, "he dictated all these words to me, and I wrote them in ink on the scroll."　　　2Co 3:3

[19]Then the officials said to Baruch, "You and Jeremiah, go and hide. Don't let anyone know where you are."　　　Jer 26:16

[20]After they put the scroll in the room of Elishama the secretary, they went to the king in the courtyard and reported everything to him. [21]The king sent Jehudi to get the scroll, and Jehudi brought it from the room of Elishama the secretary and read it to the king and all the officials standing beside him. [22]It was the ninth month and the king was sitting in the winter apartment, with a fire burning in the firepot in front of him. [23]Whenever Jehudi had read three or four columns of the scroll, the king cut them off with a scribe's knife and threw them into the firepot, until the entire scroll was burned in the fire. [24]The king and all his attendants who heard all these words showed no fear, nor did they tear their clothes. [25]Even though Elnathan, Delaiah and Gemariah urged the king not to burn the scroll, he would not listen to them. [26]Instead, the king commanded Jerahmeel, a son of the king, Seraiah son of Azriel and Shelemiah son of Abdeel to arrest Baruch the scribe and Jeremiah the prophet. But the LORD had hidden them.

[27]After the king burned the scroll containing the words that Baruch had written at Jeremiah's dictation, the word of the LORD came to Jeremiah: [28]"Take another scroll and write on it all the words that were on the first scroll, which Jehoiakim king of Judah burned up. [29]Also tell Jehoiakim king of Judah, 'This is what the LORD says: You burned that scroll and said, "Why did you write on it that the king of Babylon would cer-

tainly come and destroy this land and cut off both men and animals from it?" ³⁰Therefore, this is what the LORD says about Jehoiakim king of Judah: He will have no one to sit on the throne of David; his body will be thrown out and exposed to the heat by day and the frost by night. ³¹I will punish him and his children and his attendants for their wickedness; I will bring on them and those living in Jerusalem and the people of Judah every disaster I pronounced against them, because they have not listened.' " Jer 33:12

³²So Jeremiah took another scroll and gave it to the scribe Baruch son of Neriah, and as Jeremiah dictated, Baruch wrote on it all the words of the scroll that Jehoiakim king of Judah had burned in the fire. And many similar words were added to them. Ex 34:1; Jer 30:2

Jeremiah in Prison

37 Zedekiah son of Josiah was made king of Judah by Nebuchadnezzar king of Babylon; he reigned in place of Jehoiachin*a* son of Jehoiakim. ²Neither he nor his attendants nor the people of the land paid any attention to the words the LORD had spoken through Jeremiah the prophet. 2Ki 24:17

³King Zedekiah, however, sent Jehucal son of Shelemiah with the priest Zephaniah son of Maaseiah to Jeremiah the prophet with this message: "Please pray to the LORD our God for us." Jer 38:14

⁴Now Jeremiah was free to come and go among the people, for he had not yet been put in prison. ⁵Pharaoh's army had marched out of Egypt, and when the Babylonians*b* who were besieging Jerusalem heard the report about them, they withdrew from Jerusalem. Jer 32:2

⁶Then the word of the LORD came to Jeremiah the prophet: ⁷"This is what the LORD, the God of Israel, says: Tell the king of Judah, who sent you to inquire of me, 'Pharaoh's army, which has marched out to support you, will go back to its own land, to Egypt. ⁸Then the Babylonians will return and attack this city; they will capture it and burn it down.' Ge 25:22; Jer 38:3

⁹"This is what the LORD says: Do not deceive yourselves, thinking, 'The Babylonians will surely leave us.' They will not! ¹⁰Even if you were to defeat the entire Babylonian*c* army that is attacking you and only wounded men were left in their tents, they would come out and burn this city down." Jer 21:10; 29:8

¹¹After the Babylonian army had withdrawn from Jerusalem because of Pharaoh's army, ¹²Jeremiah started to leave the city to go to the territory of Benjamin to get his share of the

---

*a*1 Hebrew *Coniah*, a variant of *Jehoiachin* and 14   *c*10 Or *Chaldean*; also in verse 11

*b*5 Or *Chaldeans*; also in verses 8, 9, 13

property among the people there. ¹³But when he reached the Benjamin Gate, the captain of the guard, whose name was Irijah son of Shelemiah, the son of Hananiah, arrested him and said, "You are deserting to the Babylonians!"   Jer 32:9

¹⁴"That's not true!" Jeremiah said. "I am not deserting to the Babylonians." But Irijah would not listen to him; instead, he arrested Jeremiah and brought him to the officials. ¹⁵They were angry with Jeremiah and had him beaten and imprisoned in the house of Jonathan the secretary, which they had made into a prison.   Isa 58:6; Jer 20:2

¹⁶Jeremiah was put into a vaulted cell in a dungeon, where he remained a long time. ¹⁷Then King Zedekiah sent for him and had him brought to the palace, where he asked him privately, "Is there any word from the LORD?"   Ge 25:22

"Yes," Jeremiah replied, "you will be handed over to the king of Babylon."   Jer 21:7

¹⁸Then Jeremiah said to King Zedekiah, "What crime have I committed against you or your officials or this people, that you have put me in prison? ¹⁹Where are your prophets who prophesied to you, 'The king of Babylon will not attack you or this land'? ²⁰But now, my lord the king, please listen. Let me bring my petition before you: Do not send me back to the house of

Jonathan the secretary, or I will die there."   1Sa 26:18; Ac 25:8

²¹King Zedekiah then gave orders for Jeremiah to be placed in the courtyard of the guard and given bread from the street of the bakers each day until all the bread in the city was gone. So Jeremiah remained in the courtyard of the guard.   Lev 26:26

Jeremiah Thrown Into a Cistern

38 Shephatiah son of Mattan, Gedaliah son of Pashhur, Jehucal*ᵃ* son of Shelemiah, and Pashhur son of Malkijah heard what Jeremiah was telling all the people when he said, ²"This is what the LORD says: 'Whoever stays in this city will die by the sword, famine or plague, but whoever goes over to the Babylonians*ᵇ* will live. He will escape with his life; he will live.' ³And this is what the LORD says: 'This city will certainly be handed over to the army of the king of Babylon, who will capture it.'"   1Ch 9:12; Jer 21:4

⁴Then the officials said to the king, "This man should be put to death. He is discouraging the soldiers who are left in this city, as well as all the people, by the things he is saying to them. This man is not seeking the good of these people but their ruin."

⁵"He is in your hands," King Zedekiah answered. "The king can do nothing to oppose you."

⁶So they took Jeremiah and

ᵃ1 Hebrew *Jucal*, a variant of *Jehucal*   *ᵇ2* Or *Chaldeans*; also in verses 18, 19 and 23

put him into the cistern of Malkijah, the king's son, which was in the courtyard of the guard. They lowered Jeremiah by ropes into the cistern; it had no water in it, only mud, and Jeremiah sank down into the mud.

⁷But Ebed-Melech, a Cushite,ᵃ an officialᵇ in the royal palace, heard that they had put Jeremiah into the cistern. While the king was sitting in the Benjamin Gate, ⁸Ebed-Melech went out of the palace and said to him, ⁹"My lord the king, these men have acted wickedly in all they have done to Jeremiah the prophet. They have thrown him into a cistern, where he will starve to death when there is no longer any bread in the city."

¹⁰Then the king commanded Ebed-Melech the Cushite, "Take thirty men from here with you and lift Jeremiah the prophet out of the cistern before he dies." Pr 16:15

¹¹So Ebed-Melech took the men with him and went to a room under the treasury in the palace. He took some old rags and worn-out clothes from there and let them down with ropes to Jeremiah in the cistern. ¹²Ebed-Melech the Cushite said to Jeremiah, "Put these old rags and worn-out clothes under your arms to pad the ropes." Jeremiah did so, ¹³and they pulled him up with the ropes and lifted him out of the cistern.

And Jeremiah remained in the courtyard of the guard. Jos 2:15

Zedekiah Questions Jeremiah Again

¹⁴Then King Zedekiah sent for Jeremiah the prophet and had him brought to the third entrance to the temple of the LORD. "I am going to ask you something," the king said to Jeremiah. "Do not hide anything from me." Jer 37:3

¹⁵Jeremiah said to Zedekiah, "If I give you an answer, will you not kill me? Even if I did give you counsel, you would not listen to me." Lk 22:67

¹⁶But King Zedekiah swore this oath secretly to Jeremiah: "As surely as the LORD lives, who has given us breath, I will neither kill you nor hand you over to those who are seeking your life." Isa 42:5; Jer 37:17

¹⁷Then Jeremiah said to Zedekiah, "This is what the LORD God Almighty, the God of Israel, says: 'If you surrender to the officers of the king of Babylon, your life will be spared and this city will not be burned down; you and your family will live. ¹⁸But if you will not surrender to the officers of the king of Babylon, this city will be handed over to the Babylonians and they will burn it down; you yourself will not escape from their hands.' " Jer 27:8; 37:8

¹⁹King Zedekiah said to Jeremiah, "I am afraid of the Jews

ᵃ7 Probably from the upper Nile region   ᵇ7 Or *a eunuch*

who have gone over to the Babylonians, for the Babylonians may hand me over to them and they will mistreat me." Isa 51:12

²⁰"They will not hand you over," Jeremiah replied. "Obey the LORD by doing what I tell you. Then it will go well with you, and your life will be spared. ²¹But if you refuse to surrender, this is what the LORD has revealed to me: ²²All the women left in the palace of the king of Judah will be brought out to the officials of the king of Babylon. Those women will say to you: Jer 11:4

" 'They misled you and
overcame you—
those trusted friends of
yours. Job 19:14
Your feet are sunk in the
mud; Job 30:19
your friends have deserted
you.'

²³"All your wives and children will be brought out to the Babylonians. You yourself will not escape from their hands but will be captured by the king of Babylon; and this city will* be burned down." 2Ki 25:6

²⁴Then Zedekiah said to Jeremiah, "Do not let anyone know about this conversation, or you may die. ²⁵If the officials hear that I talked with you, and they come to you and say, 'Tell us what you said to the king and what the king said to you; do not hide it from us or we will kill you,' ²⁶then tell them, 'I was pleading with the king not to send me back to Jonathan's house to die there.' " Jer 37:17

²⁷All the officials did come to Jeremiah and question him, and he told them everything the king had ordered him to say. So they said no more to him, for no one had heard his conversation with the king. 1Sa 10:15-16

²⁸And Jeremiah remained in the courtyard of the guard until the day Jerusalem was captured. Jer 37:21; 39:14

The Fall of Jerusalem

39 This is how Jerusalem was taken: ¹In the ninth year of Zedekiah king of Judah, in the tenth month, Nebuchadnezzar king of Babylon marched against Jerusalem with his whole army and laid siege to it. ²And on the ninth day of the fourth month of Zedekiah's eleventh year, the city wall was broken through. ³Then all the officials of the king of Babylon came and took seats in the Middle Gate: Nergal-Sharezer of Samgar, Nebo-Sarsekim* a chief officer, Nergal-Sharezer a high official and all the other officials of the king of Babylon. ⁴When Zedekiah king of Judah and all the soldiers saw them, they fled; they left the city at night by way of the king's garden, through the gate between

---

*a23 Or and you will cause this city to   *b3 Or Nergal-Sharezer, Samgar-Nebo, Sarsekim

the two walls, and headed toward the Arabah. *a* _{Jer 25:29}

⁵But the Babylonian*b* army pursued them and overtook Zedekiah in the plains of Jericho. They captured him and took him to Nebuchadnezzar king of Babylon at Riblah in the land of Hamath, where he pronounced sentence on him. ⁶There at Riblah the king of Babylon slaughtered the sons of Zedekiah before his eyes and also killed all the nobles of Judah. ⁷Then he put out Zedekiah's eyes and bound him with bronze shackles to take him to Babylon. _{Isa 34:12; Jer 24:8}

⁸The Babylonians*c* set fire to the royal palace and the houses of the people and broke down the walls of Jerusalem. ⁹Nebuzaradan commander of the imperial guard carried into exile to Babylon the people who remained in the city, along with those who had gone over to him, and the rest of the people. ¹⁰But Nebuzaradan the commander of the guard left behind in the land of Judah some of the poor people, who owned nothing; and at that time he gave them vineyards and fields.

¹¹Now Nebuchadnezzar king of Babylon had given these orders about Jeremiah through Nebuzaradan commander of the imperial guard: ¹²"Take him and look after him; don't harm him but do for him whatever he asks." ¹³So Nebuzaradan the commander of the guard, Nebushazban a chief officer, Nergal-Sharezer a high official and all the other officers of the king of Babylon ¹⁴sent and had Jeremiah taken out of the courtyard of the guard. They turned him over to Gedaliah son of Ahikam, the son of Shaphan, to take him back to his home. So he remained among his own people. _{Ne 3:25; Pr 16:7}

¹⁵While Jeremiah had been confined in the courtyard of the guard, the word of the LORD came to him: ¹⁶"Go and tell Ebed-Melech the Cushite, 'This is what the LORD Almighty, the God of Israel, says: I am about to fulfill my words against this city through disaster, not prosperity. At that time they will be fulfilled before your eyes. ¹⁷But I will rescue you on that day, declares the LORD; you will not be handed over to those you fear. ¹⁸I will save you; you will not fall by the sword but will escape with your life, because you trust in me, declares the LORD.' "

Jeremiah Freed

40 The word came to Jeremiah from the LORD after Nebuzaradan commander of the imperial guard had released him at Ramah. He had found Jeremiah bound in chains among all the captives from Jerusalem and Judah who were being carried into exile to Babylon. ²When the commander of

---

_{a4 Or the Jordan Valley   b5 Or Chaldean   c8 Or Chaldeans}

the guard found Jeremiah, he said to him, "The LORD your God decreed this disaster for this place. ³And now the LORD has brought it about; he has done just as he said he would. All this happened because you people sinned against the LORD and did not obey him. ⁴But today I am freeing you from the chains on your wrists. Come with me to Babylon, if you like, and I will look after you; but if you do not want to, then don't come. Look, the whole country lies before you; go wherever you please." ⁵However, before Jeremiah turned to go,ᵃ Nebuzaradan added, "Go back to Gedaliah son of Ahikam, the son of Shaphan, whom the king of Babylon has appointed over the towns of Judah, and live with him among the people, or go anywhere else you please."

Then the commander gave him provisions and a present and let him go. ⁶So Jeremiah went to Gedaliah son of Ahikam at Mizpah and stayed with him among the people who were left behind in the land.   Jdg 20:1

Gedaliah Assassinated

⁷When all the army officers and their men who were still in the open country heard that the king of Babylon had appointed Gedaliah son of Ahikam as governor over the land and had put him in charge of the men,

women and children who were the poorest in the land and who had not been carried into exile to Babylon, ⁸they came to Gedaliah at Mizpah—Ishmael son of Nethaniah, Johanan and Jonathan the sons of Kareah, Seraiah son of Tanhumeth, the sons of Ephai the Netophathite, and Jaazaniahᵇ the son of the Maacathite, and their men. ⁹Gedaliah son of Ahikam, the son of Shaphan, took an oath to reassure them and their men. "Do not be afraid to serve the Babylonians,ᶜ" he said. "Settle down in the land and serve the king of Babylon, and it will go well with you. ¹⁰I myself will stay at Mizpah to represent you before the Babylonians who come to us, but you are to harvest the wine, summer fruit and oil, and put them in your storage jars, and live in the towns you have taken over."   Ge 41:41; Ex 23:16

¹¹When all the Jews in Moab, Ammon, Edom and all the other countries heard that the king of Babylon had left a remnant in Judah and had appointed Gedaliah son of Ahikam, the son of Shaphan, as governor over them, ¹²they all came back to the land of Judah, to Gedaliah at Mizpah, from all the countries where they had been scattered. And they harvested an abundance of wine and summer fruit.   Nu 21:11; Jer 43:5

¹³Johanan son of Kareah and

all the army officers still in the open country came to Gedaliah at Mizpah ¹⁴and said to him, "Don't you know that Baalis king of the Ammonites has sent Ishmael son of Nethaniah to take your life?" But Gedaliah son of Ahikam did not believe them. Ge 19:38; Jer 42:1

¹⁵Then Johanan son of Kareah said privately to Gedaliah in Mizpah, "Let me go and kill Ishmael son of Nethaniah, and no one will know it. Why should he take your life and cause all the Jews who are gathered around you to be scattered and the remnant of Judah to perish?" Dt 5:17

¹⁶But Gedaliah son of Ahikam said to Johanan son of Kareah, "Don't do such a thing! What you are saying about Ishmael is not true." Jer 43:2

41 In the seventh month Ishmael son of Nethaniah, the son of Elishama, who was of royal blood and had been one of the king's officers, came with ten men to Gedaliah son of Ahikam at Mizpah. While they were eating together there, ²Ishmael son of Nethaniah and the ten men who were with him got up and struck down Gedaliah son of Ahikam, the son of Shaphan, with the sword, killing the one whom the king of Babylon had appointed as governor over the land. ³Ishmael also killed all the Jews who were with Gedaliah at Mizpah, as

well as the Babylonian*ᵃ* soldiers who were there. Ps 41:9; Jer 40:8

⁴The day after Gedaliah's assassination, before anyone knew about it, ⁵eighty men who had shaved off their beards, torn their clothes and cut themselves came from Shechem, Shiloh and Samaria, bringing grain offerings and incense with them to the house of the LORD. ⁶Ishmael son of Nethaniah went out from Mizpah to meet them, weeping as he went. When he met them, he said, "Come to Gedaliah son of Ahikam." ⁷When they went into the city, Ishmael son of Nethaniah and the men who were with him slaughtered them and threw them into a cistern. ⁸But ten of them said to Ishmael, "Don't kill us! We have wheat and barley, oil and honey, hidden in a field." So he let them alone and did not kill them with the others. ⁹Now the cistern where he threw all the bodies of the men he had killed along with Gedaliah was the one King Asa had made as part of his defense against Baasha king of Israel. Ishmael son of Nethaniah filled it with the dead. Lev 19:27; Jdg 6:2

¹⁰Ishmael made captives of all the rest of the people who were in Mizpah—the king's daughters along with all the others who were left there, over whom Nebuzaradan commander of the imperial guard had appointed Gedaliah son of Ahi-

*ᵃ*3 Or *Chaldean*

kam. Ishmael son of Nethaniah took them captive and set out to cross over to the Ammonites.

¹¹When Johanan son of Kareah and all the army officers who were with him heard about all the crimes Ishmael son of Nethaniah had committed, ¹²they took all their men and went to fight Ishmael son of Nethaniah. They caught up with him near the great pool in Gibeon. ¹³When all the people Ishmael had with him saw Johanan son of Kareah and the army officers who were with him, they were glad. ¹⁴All the people Ishmael had taken captive at Mizpah turned and went over to Johanan son of Kareah. ¹⁵But Ishmael son of Nethaniah and eight of his men escaped from Johanan and fled to the Ammonites. Ex 14:14; Job 21:30

Flight to Egypt

¹⁶Then Johanan son of Kareah and all the army officers who were with him led away all the survivors from Mizpah whom he had recovered from Ishmael son of Nethaniah after he had assassinated Gedaliah son of Ahikam: the soldiers, women, children and court officials he had brought from Gibeon. ¹⁷And they went on, stopping at Geruth Kimham near Bethlehem on their way to Egypt ¹⁸to escape the Babylonians.ᵃ They were afraid of them because Ishmael son of Nethaniah had killed Gedaliah son of Ahikam, whom the king of Babylon had appointed as governor over the land. Nu 14:9; Jer 42:1

42 Then all the army officers, including Johanan son of Kareah and Jezaniahᵇ son of Hoshaiah, and all the people from the least to the greatest approached ²Jeremiah the prophet and said to him, "Please hear our petition and pray to the LORD your God for this entire remnant. For as you now see, though we were once many, now only a few are left. ³Pray that the LORD your God will tell us where we should go and what we should do." Jer 40:13

⁴"I have heard you," replied Jeremiah the prophet. "I will certainly pray to the LORD your God as you have requested; I will tell you everything the LORD says and will keep nothing back from you." Ex 8:29

⁵Then they said to Jeremiah, "May the LORD be a true and faithful witness against us if we do not act in accordance with everything the LORD your God sends you to tell us. ⁶Whether it is favorable or unfavorable, we will obey the LORD our God, to whom we are sending you, so that it will go well with us, for we will obey the LORD our God." Dt 5:29; 1Ki 22:16

⁷Ten days later the word of the LORD came to Jeremiah. ⁸So he called together Johanan son of Kareah and all the army offi-

ᵃ18 Or *Chaldeans*   ᵇ1 Hebrew; Septuagint (see also 43:2) *Azariah*

cers who were with him and all the people from the least to the greatest. ⁹He said to them, "This is what the Lord, the God of Israel, to whom you sent me to present your petition, says: ¹⁰'If you stay in this land, I will build you up and not tear you down; I will plant you and not uproot you, for I am grieved over the disaster I have inflicted on you. ¹¹Do not be afraid of the king of Babylon, whom you now fear. Do not be afraid of him, declares the Lord, for I am with you and will save you and deliver you from his hands. ¹²I will show you compassion so that he will have compassion on you and restore you to your land.'   Ex 3:21; Jer 41:16

¹³"However, if you say, 'We will not stay in this land,' and so disobey the Lord your God, ¹⁴and if you say, 'No, we will go and live in Egypt, where we will not see war or hear the trumpet or be hungry for bread,' ¹⁵then hear the word of the Lord, O remnant of Judah. This is what the Lord Almighty, the God of Israel, says: 'If you are determined to go to Egypt and you do go to settle there, ¹⁶then the sword you fear will overtake you there, and the famine you dread will follow you into Egypt, and there you will die. ¹⁷Indeed, all who are determined to go to Egypt to settle there will die by the sword, famine and plague; not one of

them will survive or escape the disaster I will bring on them.' ¹⁸This is what the Lord Almighty, the God of Israel, says: 'As my anger and wrath have been poured out on those who lived in Jerusalem, so will my wrath be poured out on you when you go to Egypt. You will be an object of cursing and horror, of condemnation and reproach; you will never see this place again.'   Dt 11:28; 2Ch 12:7

¹⁹"O remnant of Judah, the Lord has told you, 'Do not go to Egypt.' Be sure of this: I warn you today ²⁰that you made a fatal mistake*a* when you sent me to the Lord your God and said, 'Pray to the Lord our God for us; tell us everything he says and we will do it.' ²¹I have told you today, but you still have not obeyed the Lord your God in all he sent me to tell you. ²²So now, be sure of this: You will die by the sword, famine and plague in the place where you want to go to settle."   Isa 1:28; Jer 40:15

43 When Jeremiah finished telling the people all the words of the Lord their God—everything the Lord had sent him to tell them— ²Azariah son of Hoshaiah and Johanan son of Kareah and all the arrogant men said to Jeremiah, "You are lying! The Lord our God has not sent you to say, 'You must not go to Egypt to settle there.' ³But Baruch son of Neriah is inciting you against us

to hand us over to the Babylonians,[a] so they may kill us or carry us into exile to Babylon."

[4]So Johanan son of Kareah and all the army officers and all the people disobeyed the LORD's command to stay in the land of Judah. [5]Instead, Johanan son of Kareah and all the army officers led away all the remnant of Judah who had come back to live in the land of Judah from all the nations where they had been scattered. [6]They also led away all the men, women and children and the king's daughters whom Nebuzaradan commander of the imperial guard had left with Gedaliah son of Ahikam, the son of Shaphan, and Jeremiah the prophet and Baruch son of Neriah. [7]So they entered Egypt in disobedience to the LORD and went as far as Tahpanhes.

[8]In Tahpanhes the word of the LORD came to Jeremiah: [9]"While the Jews are watching, take some large stones with you and bury them in clay in the brick pavement at the entrance to Pharaoh's palace in Tahpanhes. [10]Then say to them, 'This is what the LORD Almighty, the God of Israel, says: I will send for my servant Nebuchadnezzar king of Babylon, and I will set his throne over these stones I have buried here; he will spread his royal canopy above them. [11]He will come and attack Egypt, bringing death to those destined for death, captivity to those destined for captivity, and the sword to those destined for the sword. [12]He[b] will set fire to the temples of the gods of Egypt; he will burn their temples and take their gods captive. As a shepherd wraps his garment around him, so will he wrap Egypt around himself and depart from there unscathed. [13]There in the temple of the sun[c] in Egypt he will demolish the sacred pillars and will burn down the temples of the gods of Egypt.' "

Dt 4:19; Ps 139:7

Disaster Because of Idolatry

44 This word came to Jeremiah concerning all the Jews living in Lower Egypt—in Migdol, Tahpanhes and Memphis[d]—and in Upper Egypt[e]: [2]"This is what the LORD Almighty, the God of Israel, says: You saw the great disaster I brought on Jerusalem and on all the towns of Judah. Today they lie deserted and in ruins [3]because of the evil they have done. They provoked me to anger by burning incense and by worshiping other gods that neither they nor you nor your fathers ever knew. [4]Again and again I sent my servants the prophets, who said, 'Do not do this detestable thing that I hate!' [5]But they did not listen or pay attention; they did not turn

---

[a]3 Or *Chaldeans*   [b]12 Or *I*   [c]13 Or *in Heliopolis*   [d]1 Hebrew *Noph*
[e]1 Hebrew *in Pathros*

from their wickedness or stop burning incense to other gods. ⁶Therefore, my fierce anger was poured out; it raged against the towns of Judah and the streets of Jerusalem and made them the desolate ruins they are today.

⁷"Now this is what the LORD God Almighty, the God of Israel, says: Why bring such great disaster on yourselves by cutting off from Judah the men and women, the children and infants, and so leave yourselves without a remnant? ⁸Why provoke me to anger with what your hands have made, burning incense to other gods in Egypt, where you have come to live? You will destroy yourselves and make yourselves an object of cursing and reproach among all the nations on earth. ⁹Have you forgotten the wickedness committed by your fathers and by the kings and queens of Judah and the wickedness committed by you and your wives in the land of Judah and the streets of Jerusalem? ¹⁰To this day they have not humbled themselves or shown reverence, nor have they followed my law and the decrees I set before you and your fathers. 2Ki 25:26; Isa 45:1

¹¹"Therefore, this is what the LORD Almighty, the God of Israel, says: I am determined to bring disaster on you and to destroy all Judah. ¹²I will take away the remnant of Judah who were determined to go to Egypt to settle there. They will all perish in Egypt; they will fall by the sword or die from famine. From the least to the greatest, they will die by sword or famine. They will become an object of cursing and horror, of condemnation and reproach. ¹³I will punish those who live in Egypt with the sword, famine and plague, as I punished Jerusalem. ¹⁴None of the remnant of Judah who have gone to live in Egypt will escape or survive to return to the land of Judah, to which they long to return and live; none will return except a few fugitives." Jer 46:13-26

¹⁵Then all the men who knew that their wives were burning incense to other gods, along with all the women who were present—a large assembly—and all the people living in Lower and Upper Egypt,^a said to Jeremiah, ¹⁶"We will not listen to the message you have spoken to us in the name of the LORD! ¹⁷We will certainly do everything we said we would: We will burn incense to the Queen of Heaven and will pour out drink offerings to her just as we and our fathers, our kings and our officials did in the towns of Judah and in the streets of Jerusalem. At that time we had plenty of food and were well off and suffered no harm. ¹⁸But ever since we stopped burning incense to the Queen of Heaven and pouring

^a15 Hebrew *in Egypt and Pathros*

out drink offerings to her, we have had nothing and have been perishing by sword and famine." _{Lev 23:18; Pr 31:10}

¹⁹The women added, "When we burned incense to the Queen of Heaven and poured out drink offerings to her, did not our husbands know that we were making cakes like her image and pouring out drink offerings to her?" _{Jer 18:15; Ac 17:29}

²⁰Then Jeremiah said to all the people, both men and women, who were answering him, ²¹"Did not the LORD remember and think about the incense burned in the towns of Judah and the streets of Jerusalem by you and your fathers, your kings and your officials and the people of the land? ²²When the LORD could no longer endure your wicked actions and the detestable things you did, your land became an object of cursing and a desolate waste without inhabitants, as it is today. ²³Because you have burned incense and have sinned against the LORD and have not obeyed him or followed his law or his decrees or his stipulations, this disaster has come upon you, as you now see." _{1Ki 9:6; Isa 64:9}

²⁴Then Jeremiah said to all the people, including the women, "Hear the word of the LORD, all you people of Judah in Egypt. ²⁵This is what the LORD Almighty, the God of Israel, says: You and your wives have shown by your actions what you promised when you said, 'We will certainly carry out the vows we made to burn incense and pour out drink offerings to the Queen of Heaven.' _{Jer 43:7}

"Go ahead then, do what you promised! Keep your vows! ²⁶But hear the word of the LORD, all Jews living in Egypt: 'I swear by my great name,' says the LORD, 'that no one from Judah living anywhere in Egypt will ever again invoke my name or swear, "As surely as the Sovereign LORD lives." ²⁷For I am watching over them for harm, not for good; the Jews in Egypt will perish by sword and famine until they are all destroyed. ²⁸Those who escape the sword and return to the land of Judah from Egypt will be very few. Then the whole remnant of Judah who came to live in Egypt will know whose word will stand—mine or theirs. _{Ac 19:13}

²⁹" 'This will be the sign to you that I will punish you in this place,' declares the LORD, 'so that you will know that my threats of harm against you will surely stand.' ³⁰This is what the LORD says: 'I am going to hand Pharaoh Hophra king of Egypt over to his enemies who seek his life, just as I handed Zedekiah king of Judah over to Nebuchadnezzar king of Babylon, the enemy who was seeking his life.' " _{Ge 24:14; Jer 25:19}

A Message to Baruch

45 This is what Jeremiah the prophet told Baruch son of Neriah in the fourth year of

Jehoiakim son of Josiah king of Judah, after Baruch had written on a scroll the words Jeremiah was then dictating: ²"This is what the LORD, the God of Israel, says to you, Baruch: ³You said, 'Woe to me! The LORD has added sorrow to my pain; I am worn out with groaning and find no rest.' " Jer 32:12

⁴The LORD said, "Say this to him: 'This is what the LORD says: I will overthrow what I have built and uproot what I have planted, throughout the land. ⁵Should you then seek great things for yourself? Seek them not. For I will bring disaster on all people, declares the LORD, but wherever you go I will let you escape with your life.' " Ps 131:1; Jer 42:10

A Message About Egypt

46 This is the word of the LORD that came to Jeremiah the prophet concerning the nations: Jer 1:10

²Concerning Egypt:

This is the message against the army of Pharaoh Neco king of Egypt, which was defeated at Carchemish on the Euphrates River by Nebuchadnezzar king of Babylon in the fourth year of Jehoiakim son of Josiah king of Judah: 2Ki 23:29; Jer 1:3

³"Prepare your shields, both
        large and small, Isa 21:5
    and march out for battle!

⁴Harness the horses,
    mount the steeds!
Take your positions
    with helmets on!
Polish your spears,
    put on your armor! 1Sa 17:5
⁵What do I see?
    They are terrified,
they are retreating,
    their warriors are defeated.
They flee in haste
    without looking back, Jer 48:44
and there is terror on every
        side," Ps 31:13
            declares the LORD.
⁶"The swift cannot flee Isa 30:16
    nor the strong escape.
In the north by the River
    Euphrates Ge 2:14
    they stumble and fall.

⁷"Who is this that rises like
        the Nile,
    like rivers of surging
        waters? Jer 47:2
⁸Egypt rises like the Nile, Eze 29:3
    like rivers of surging
        waters.
She says, 'I will rise and
        cover the earth;
    I will destroy cities and
        their people.' Da 11:10
⁹Charge, O horses!
    Drive furiously,
        O charioteers! Jer 47:3
March on, O warriors—
    men of Cush ͣ and Put who
        carry shields, Ge 10:6
    men of Lydia who draw the
        bow. Isa 66:19
¹⁰But that day belongs to the
    Lord, the LORD
    Almighty— Eze 32:10

ͣ9 That is, the upper Nile region

a day of vengeance, for
vengeance on his foes.
The sword will devour till it
is satisfied,   Dt 32:42
till it has quenched its thirst
with blood.
For the Lord, the LORD
Almighty, will offer
sacrifice   Lev 3:9
in the land of the north by
the River Euphrates.

11"Go up to Gilead and get
balm,   Ge 37:25
O Virgin Daughter of
Egypt.   2Ki 19:21
But you multiply remedies in
vain;
there is no healing for you.
12The nations will hear of your
shame;
your cries will fill the earth.
One warrior will stumble
over another;
both will fall down
together."   Isa 19:4

13This is the message the
LORD spoke to Jeremiah the
prophet about the coming of
Nebuchadnezzar king of Babylon to attack Egypt: Eze 32:11

14"Announce this in Egypt,
and proclaim it in
Migdol;
proclaim it also in
Memphis*a* and
Tahpanhes: Isa 19:13
'Take your positions and get
ready,
for the sword devours those
around you.'   Dt 32:42

15Why will your warriors be
laid low?
They cannot stand, for the
LORD will push them
down.   Jos 23:5
16They will stumble repeatedly;
they will fall over each
other.
They will say, 'Get up, let us
go back
to our own people and our
native lands,   Isa 13:14
away from the sword of the
oppressor.'   Jer 25:38
17There they will exclaim,
'Pharaoh king of Egypt is
only a loud noise;
he has missed his
opportunity.'   Isa 19:11-16

18"As surely as I live," declares
the King,   Jer 48:15
whose name is the LORD
Almighty,
"one will come who is like
Tabor among the
mountains,   Jos 19:22
like Carmel by the sea.
19Pack your belongings for
exile,   Isa 20:4
you who live in Egypt,
for Memphis will be laid
waste   Eze 29:10,12
and lie in ruins without
inhabitant.

20"Egypt is a beautiful heifer,
but a gadfly is coming
against her from the north.
21The mercenaries in her ranks
are like fattened calves.
They too will turn and flee
together,   Job 20:24

a14 Hebrew *Noph;* also in verse 19

they will not stand their
    ground,
for the day of disaster is
    coming upon them, Ps 18:18
the time for them to be
    punished.   Job 18:20
²²Egypt will hiss like a fleeing
    serpent
  as the enemy advances in
    force;
they will come against her
    with axes,
  like men who cut down
    trees.   Ps 74:5
²³They will chop down her
    forest,"
          declares the LORD,
  "dense though it be.
They are more numerous
    than locusts,   Dt 28:42
  they cannot be counted.
²⁴The Daughter of Egypt will
    be put to shame,
  handed over to the people
    of the north."   2Ki 24:7

²⁵The LORD Almighty, the
God of Israel, says: "I am about
to bring punishment on Amon
god of Thebes,^a on Pharaoh, on
Egypt and her gods and her
kings, and on those who rely on
Pharaoh. ²⁶I will hand them
over to those who seek their
lives, to Nebuchadnezzar king
of Babylon and his officers.
Later, however, Egypt will be
inhabited as in times past," declares the LORD.   Eze 30:14

²⁷"Do not fear, O Jacob my
    servant;   Isa 44:2

do not be dismayed,
    O Israel.
I will surely save you out of a
    distant place,
  your descendants from the
    land of their exile. Isa 11:11
Jacob will again have peace
    and security,
  and no one will make him
    afraid.
²⁸Do not fear, O Jacob my
    servant,
  for I am with you," declares
    the LORD.   Ex 14:22
"Though I completely
    destroy all the nations
  among which I scatter you,
  I will not completely
    destroy you.
I will discipline you but only
    with justice;
  I will not let you go entirely
    unpunished."

A Message About the Philistines

47 This is the word of the
LORD that came to Jere-
miah the prophet concerning
the Philistines before Pharaoh
attacked Gaza: Ge 10:14

²This is what the LORD says:

"See how the waters are
    rising in the north; Isa 14:31
  they will become an
    overflowing torrent.
They will overflow the land
    and everything in it,
  the towns and those who
    live in them.

^a25 Hebrew *No*

The people will cry out;
all who dwell in the land
will wail   Isa 15:3
³at the sound of the hoofs of
galloping steeds,
at the noise of enemy
chariots   Jer 46:9
and the rumble of their
wheels.
Fathers will not turn to help
their children;
their hands will hang
limp.
⁴For the day has come
to destroy all the Philistines
and to cut off all survivors
who could help Tyre and
Sidon.   Isa 23:1
The LORD is about to destroy
the Philistines,   Ge 10:14
the remnant from the coasts
of Caphtor. ᵃ   Dt 2:23
⁵Gaza will shave her head in
mourning;   Jer 41:5
Ashkelon will be silenced.
O remnant on the plain,
how long will you cut
yourselves?   Lev 19:28

⁶" 'Ah, sword of the LORD,'
⌊you cry,⌋
'how long till you rest?
Return to your scabbard;
cease and be still.'   Eze 21:30
⁷But how can it rest
when the LORD has
commanded it,
when he has ordered it
to attack Ashkelon and the
coast?"   Eze 25:15-17

A Message About Moab

48 Concerning Moab: Ge 19:37

This is what the LORD Almighty, the God of Israel, says:

"Woe to Nebo, for it will be
ruined.   Nu 32:38
Kiriathaim will be disgraced
and captured;   Nu 32:37
the stronghold ᵇ will be
disgraced and shattered.
²Moab will be praised no
more;   Isa 16:14
in Heshbon ᶜ men will plot
her downfall: Nu 21:25
'Come, let us put an end to
that nation.'
You too, O Madmen, ᵈ will be
silenced;
the sword will pursue you.
³Listen to the cries from
Horonaim,   Isa 15:5
cries of great havoc and
destruction.
⁴Moab will be broken;
her little ones will cry out. ᵉ
⁵They go up the way to
Luhith,   Isa 15:5
weeping bitterly as they go;
on the road down to
Horonaim
anguished cries over the
destruction are heard.
⁶Flee! Run for your lives; Ge 19:17
become like a bush ᶠ in the
desert.   Jer 17:6
⁷Since you trust in your deeds
and riches,   Ps 49:6

ᵃ4 That is, Crete   ᵇ1 Or / Misgab   ᶜ2 The Hebrew for Heshbon sounds like the Hebrew for plot.   ᵈ2 The name of the Moabite town Madmen sounds like the Hebrew for be silenced.   ᵉ4 Hebrew; Septuagint / proclaim it to Zoar   ᶠ6 Or like Aroer

you too will be taken
　　captive,
and Chemosh will go into
　　exile,　　　　　　　Nu 21:29
together with his priests
　　and officials.　　　Am 2:3

⁸The destroyer will come
　　against every town,
and not a town will escape.
The valley will be ruined
and the plateau destroyed,
because the LORD has
　　spoken.　　　　　　Jos 13:9

⁹Put salt on Moab,
for she will be laid waste*ᵃ*;
her towns will become
　　desolate,
with no one to live in
　　them.

¹⁰"A curse on him who is lax
　　in doing the LORD's
　　work!
A curse on him who keeps
　　his sword from
　　bloodshed!　　　　1Sa 15:11

¹¹"Moab has been at rest from
　　youth,　　　　　　Zec 1:15
like wine left on its dregs,
not poured from one jar to
　　another—
she has not gone into exile.
So she tastes as she did,
and her aroma is
　　unchanged.

¹²But days are coming,"
　　declares the LORD,
"when I will send men who
　　pour from jars,
and they will pour her out;
they will empty her jars
and smash her jugs.

¹³Then Moab will be ashamed
　　of Chemosh,
as the house of Israel was
　　ashamed
when they trusted in
　　Bethel.　　　　　　Jos 7:2

¹⁴"How can you say, 'We are
　　warriors,　　　　　Ps 33:16
men valiant in battle'?

¹⁵Moab will be destroyed and
　　her towns invaded;
her finest young men will
　　go down in the
　　slaughter,"　　　　Isa 9:17
declares the King, whose
　　name is the LORD
　　Almighty.　　　　　Jer 51:57

¹⁶"The fall of Moab is at hand;
　　her calamity will come
　　quickly.

¹⁷Mourn for her, all who live
　　around her,
all who know her fame;
say, 'How broken is the
　　mighty scepter,　　Ps 110:2
how broken the glorious
　　staff!'

¹⁸"Come down from your
　　glory
and sit on the parched
　　ground,　　　　　　Isa 47:1
O inhabitants of the
　　Daughter of Dibon,
for he who destroys Moab
will come up against you
and ruin your fortified
　　cities.

¹⁹Stand by the road and watch,
you who live in Aroer.　Nu 32:34
Ask the man fleeing and the
　　woman escaping,

ᵃ9 Or *Give wings to Moab, / for she will fly away*

ask them, 'What has
   happened?'
²⁰Moab is disgraced, for she is
   shattered.
Wail and cry out!   Isa 16:7
Announce by the Arnon
   that Moab is destroyed.
²¹Judgment has come to the
   plateau—   Jos 13:9
to Holon, Jahzah and
   Mephaath,   Jos 13:18
²² to Dibon, Nebo and Beth
   Diblathaim,   Nu 21:30
²³ to Kiriathaim, Beth Gamul
   and Beth Meon,
²⁴ to Kerioth and Bozrah—
to all the towns of Moab,
   far and near.   Isa 15:1
²⁵Moab's horn*ᵃ* is cut off;
her arm is broken,"
   declares the LORD.

²⁶"Make her drunk,   Jer 25:16
for she has defied the
   LORD.
Let Moab wallow in her
   vomit;   Isa 28:8
let her be an object of
   ridicule.
²⁷Was not Israel the object of
   your ridicule?   Jer 2:26
Was she caught among
   thieves,   2Ki 17:3-6
that you shake your head in
   scorn
whenever you speak of
   her?
²⁸Abandon your towns and
   dwell among the rocks,
you who live in Moab.
Be like a dove that makes its
   nest   Ge 8:8
at the mouth of a cave.

²⁹"We have heard of Moab's
   pride—   Lev 26:19
her overweening pride and
   conceit,
her pride and arrogance
and the haughtiness of her
   heart.   Ps 10:5
³⁰I know her insolence but it is
   futile,"
   declares the LORD,
"and her boasts accomplish
   nothing.   Ps 10:3
³¹Therefore I wail over Moab,
for all Moab I cry out,
I moan for the men of Kir
   Hareseth.   2Ki 3:25
³²I weep for you, as Jazer
   weeps,   Jos 13:25
O vines of Sibmah.   Nu 32:3
Your branches spread as far
   as the sea;
they reached as far as the
   sea of Jazer.
The destroyer has fallen
on your ripened fruit and
   grapes.
³³Joy and gladness are gone
from the orchards and
   fields of Moab.
I have stopped the flow of
   wine from the presses;
no one treads them with
   shouts of joy.   Joel 1:12
Although there are shouts,
they are not shouts of joy.

³⁴"The sound of their cry rises
from Heshbon to Elealeh
   and Jahaz,   Nu 21:23
from Zoar as far as Horonaim
   and Eglath Shelishiyah,
for even the waters of
   Nimrim are dried up.

ᵃ25 Horn here symbolizes strength.

³⁵In Moab I will put an end
    to those who make
        offerings on the high
            places   Isa 15:2
    and burn incense to their
        gods,"   Jer 11:13
            declares the LORD.
³⁶"So my heart laments for
    Moab like a flute;   2Ki 3:25
    it laments like a flute for the
        men of Kir Hareseth.
    The wealth they acquired is
        gone.   Isa 15:7
³⁷Every head is shaved
    and every beard cut off;
    every hand is slashed
    and every waist is covered
        with sackcloth.   Ge 37:34
³⁸On all the roofs in Moab
    and in the public squares
    there is nothing but
        mourning,   Isa 15:3
    for I have broken Moab
    like a jar that no one
        wants,"   Jer 22:28
            declares the LORD.
³⁹"How shattered she is! How
    they wail!   Jer 50:23
    How Moab turns her back
        in shame!
    Moab has become an object
        of ridicule,
    an object of horror to all
        those around her."

⁴⁰This is what the LORD says:

"Look! An eagle is swooping
    down,   Dt 28:49
    spreading its wings over
        Moab.   Isa 8:8
⁴¹Keriothᵃ will be captured
    and the strongholds taken.

In that day the hearts of
    Moab's warriors
    will be like the heart of a
        woman in labor.   Isa 21:3
⁴²Moab will be destroyed as a
    nation   Isa 16:14
    because she defied the
        LORD.
⁴³Terror and pit and snare
    await you,   Jer 49:5
    O people of Moab,"
            declares the LORD.
⁴⁴"Whoever flees from the
    terror
    will fall into a pit,   1Ki 19:17
    whoever climbs out of the pit
    will be caught in a snare;
    for I will bring upon Moab
    the year of her
        punishment,"   Jer 11:23
            declares the LORD.

⁴⁵"In the shadow of Heshbon
    the fugitives stand helpless,
    for a fire has gone out from
        Heshbon,
    a blaze from the midst of
        Sihon;   Nu 21:21
    it burns the foreheads of
        Moab,
    the skulls of the noisy
        boasters.   Nu 24:17
⁴⁶Woe to you, O Moab!
    The people of Chemosh are
        destroyed;
    your sons are taken into exile
    and your daughters into
        captivity.
⁴⁷"Yet I will restore the
    fortunes of Moab
    in days to come,"   Ps 14:7
            declares the LORD.

ᵃ41 Or The cities

Here ends the judgment on Moab.

A Message About Ammon

49 Concerning the Ammonites: Ge 19:38

This is what the LORD says:

"Has Israel no sons?
Has she no heirs?
Why then has Molech*a* taken
    possession of Gad? Ge 30:11
Why do his people live in
    its towns?
²But the days are coming,"
    declares the LORD,
"when I will sound the battle
    cry Jer 4:19
against Rabbah of the
    Ammonites; Dt 3:11
it will become a mound of
    ruins, Dt 13:16
and its surrounding villages
    will be set on fire.
Then Israel will drive out
    those who drove her out,"
    says the LORD.
³"Wail, O Heshbon, for Ai is
    destroyed! Jos 13:26
Cry out, O inhabitants of
    Rabbah!
Put on sackcloth and mourn;
    rush here and there inside
    the walls,
for Molech will go into exile,
    together with his priests
    and officials.
⁴Why do you boast of your
    valleys,
boast of your valleys so
    fruitful?
O unfaithful daughter, Jer 3:6

you trust in your riches and
    say, Jer 9:23
'Who will attack me?' Jer 21:13
⁵I will bring terror on you
    from all those around you,"
        declares the Lord,
        the LORD Almighty.
"Every one of you will be
    driven away,
and no one will gather the
    fugitives. Jer 44:14
⁶"Yet afterward, I will restore
    the fortunes of the
    Ammonites," Jer 12:14-17
        declares the LORD.

A Message About Edom

⁷Concerning Edom: Ge 25:30

This is what the LORD Almighty says:

"Is there no longer wisdom
    in Teman? Ge 36:11
Has counsel perished from
    the prudent?
Has their wisdom decayed?
⁸Turn and flee, hide in deep
    caves, Jdg 6:2
you who live in Dedan,
for I will bring disaster on
    Esau
at the time I punish him.
⁹If grape pickers came to you,
    would they not leave a few
    grapes?
If thieves came during the
    night,
would they not steal only as
    much as they wanted?
¹⁰But I will strip Esau bare;
    I will uncover his hiding
    places, Ge 3:8

---

*a*1 Or *their king*; Hebrew *malcam*; also in verse 3

so that he cannot conceal
himself.
His children, relatives and
neighbors will perish,
and he will be no more.
¹¹Leave your orphans; I will
protect their lives.
Your widows too can trust
in me." Dt 10:18

¹²This is what the LORD says:
"If those who do not deserve to
drink the cup must drink it,
why should you go unpunished? You will not go unpunished, but must drink it. ¹³I
swear by myself," declares the
LORD, "that Bozrah will become
a ruin and an object of horror, of
reproach and of cursing; and all
its towns will be in ruins forever." Ge 22:16; Isa 51:23

¹⁴I have heard a message from
the LORD:
An envoy was sent to the
nations to say,
"Assemble yourselves to
attack it!
Rise up for battle!"

¹⁵"Now I will make you small
among the nations,
despised among men.
¹⁶The terror you inspire
and the pride of your heart
have deceived you,
you who live in the clefts of
the rocks, Job 39:28
who occupy the heights of
the hill.
Though you build your nest
as high as the eagle's,
from there I will bring you

down," declares the LORD.
¹⁷"Edom will become an object
of horror;
all who pass by will be
appalled and will
scoff
because of all its wounds.
¹⁸As Sodom and Gomorrah
were overthrown,
along with their Jer 23:14
neighboring towns,"
says the LORD,
"so no one will live there;
no man will dwell in it.

¹⁹"Like a lion coming up from
Jordan's thickets 1Sa 17:34
to a rich pastureland,
I will chase Edom from its
land in an instant.
Who is the chosen one I
will appoint for this?
Who is like me and who can
challenge me? Ex 8:10
And what shepherd can
stand against me?"1Sa 17:35
²⁰Therefore, hear what the
LORD has planned
against Edom, Isa 34:5
what he has purposed
against those who live in
Teman: Isa 14:27
The young of the flock will
be dragged away; Jer 50:45
he will completely destroy
their pasture because of
them. Ob 10
²¹At the sound of their fall the
earth will tremble; Ps 114:7
their cry will resound to the
Red Sea.ᵃ
²²Look! An eagle will soar and
swoop down, Dt 28:49

ᵃ21 Hebrew *Yam Suph*; that is, Sea of Reeds

spreading its wings over
Bozrah. <small>Ge 36:33</small>
In that day the hearts of
Edom's warriors <small>Jer 50:36</small>
will be like the heart of a
woman in labor. <small>Isa 13:8</small>

A Message About Damascus

²³Concerning Damascus:

"Hamath and Arpad are
dismayed, <small>1Ki 8:65</small>
for they have heard bad
news.
They are disheartened,
troubled like^a the restless
sea. <small>Ge 49:4</small>
²⁴Damascus has become feeble,
she has turned to flee
and panic has gripped her;
anguish and pain have seized
her,
pain like that of a woman in
labor. <small>Jer 13:21</small>
²⁵Why has the city of renown
not been abandoned,
the town in which I delight?
²⁶Surely, her young men will
fall in the streets; <small>Isa 9:17</small>
all her soldiers will be
silenced in that day,"
declares the LORD
Almighty.
²⁷"I will set fire to the walls of
Damascus; <small>Jer 21:14</small>
it will consume the
fortresses of
Ben-Hadad." <small>1Ki 15:18</small>

A Message About Kedar and Hazor

²⁸Concerning Kedar and the

kingdoms of Hazor, which
Nebuchadnezzar king of Bab-
ylon attacked: <small>Ge 25:13</small>

This is what the LORD says:

"Arise, and attack Kedar
and destroy the people of
the East. <small>Jdg 6:3</small>
²⁹Their tents and their flocks
will be taken;
their shelters will be carried
off
with all their goods and
camels.
Men will shout to them,
'Terror on every side!' <small>Jer 6:25</small>

³⁰"Flee quickly away!
Stay in deep caves, you
who live in Hazor,"
declares the LORD.
"Nebuchadnezzar king of
Babylon has plotted
against you;
he has devised a plan
against you.

³¹"Arise and attack a nation at
ease,
which lives in confidence,"
declares the LORD,
"a nation that has neither
gates nor bars; <small>Eze 38:11</small>
its people live alone.
³²Their camels will become
plunder, <small>Jdg 6:5</small>
and their large herds will be
booty.
I will scatter to the winds
those who are in distant
places^b <small>Jer 9:26</small>
and will bring disaster on

^a23 Hebrew *on* or *by*   ^b32 Or *who clip the hair by their foreheads*

them from every side,"
declares the LORD.
³³"Hazor will become a haunt
of jackals, Jos 11:1
a desolate place forever.
No one will live there;
no man will dwell in it."

A Message About Elam

³⁴This is the word of the LORD
that came to Jeremiah the
prophet concerning Elam, early
in the reign of Zedekiah king of
Judah: Ge 10:22

³⁵This is what the LORD Al-
mighty says:

"See, I will break the bow of
Elam, Ps 37:15
the mainstay of their might.
³⁶I will bring against Elam the
four winds
from the four quarters of
the heavens; Da 11:4
I will scatter them to the four
winds,
and there will not be a
nation
where Elam's exiles do not
go.
³⁷I will shatter Elam before
their foes,
before those who seek their
lives;
I will bring disaster upon
them,
even my fierce anger,"
declares the LORD.
"I will pursue them with the
sword Jer 9:16
until I have made an end of
them.

³⁸I will set my throne in Elam
and destroy her king and
officials,"
declares the LORD.

³⁹"Yet I will restore the
fortunes of Elam Jer 48:47
in days to come,"
declares the LORD.

A Message About Babylon

50 This is the word the LORD
spoke through Jeremiah
the prophet concerning Babylon and the land of the Babylo-
nians^a: Ge 10:10

²"Announce and proclaim
among the nations,
lift up a banner and
proclaim it; Ps 20:5
keep nothing back, but say,
'Babylon will be captured;
Bel will be put to shame,
Marduk filled with terror.
Her images will be put to
shame
and her idols filled with
terror.' Lev 26:30
³A nation from the north will
attack her
and lay waste her land.
No one will live in it; Isa 14:22-23
both men and animals will
flee away. Zep 1:3

⁴"In those days, at that time,"
declares the LORD,
"the people of Israel and the
people of Judah together
will go in tears to seek the
LORD their God. Ezr 3:12
⁵They will ask the way to Zion

---

^a1 Or *Chaldeans*; also in verses 8, 25, 35 and 45

and turn their faces toward
it.
They will come and bind
themselves to the LORD
in an everlasting covenant
that will not be forgotten.

6"My people have been lost
sheep;   Ps 119:176
their shepherds have led
them astray   Ps 95:10
and caused them to roam
on the mountains.
They wandered over
mountain and hill   Jer 3:6
and forgot their own resting
place.
7Whoever found them
devoured them;   Jer 5:17
their enemies said, 'We are
not guilty,   Jer 2:3
for they sinned against the
LORD, their true
pasture,
the LORD, the hope of their
fathers.'   Jer 14:8

8"Flee out of Babylon;   Isa 48:20
leave the land of the
Babylonians,
and be like the goats that
lead the flock.
9For I will stir up and bring
against Babylon   Isa 13:17
an alliance of great nations
from the land of the
north.   Isa 41:25
They will take up their
positions against her,
and from the north she will
be captured.
Their arrows will be like
skilled warriors   Isa 13:18

who do not return
empty-handed.
10So Babyloniaᵃ will be
plundered;   Isa 47:11
all who plunder her will
have their fill,"
declares the LORD.

11"Because you rejoice and are
glad,
you who pillage my
inheritance,   Isa 47:6
because you frolic like a
heifer threshing grain
and neigh like stallions,
12your mother will be greatly
ashamed;
she who gave you birth will
be disgraced.   Jer 51:47
She will be the least of the
nations—
a wilderness, a dry land, a
desert.   Isa 21:1
13Because of the LORD's anger
she will not be inhabited
but will be completely
desolate.   Jer 9:11
All who pass Babylon will be
horrified and scoff   Jer 51:41
because of all her wounds.

14"Take up your positions
around Babylon,
all you who draw the bow.
Shoot at her! Spare no
arrows,   Dt 29:22
for she has sinned against
the LORD.
15Shout against her on every
side!   Jer 51:14
She surrenders, her towers
fall,
her walls are torn down.

Since this is the vengeance of
the LORD,   Isa 10:3
take vengeance on her;
do to her as she has done to
others.   Ps 137:8
16Cut off from Babylon the
sower,
and the reaper with his
sickle at harvest.
Because of the sword of the
oppressor   Jer 25:38
let everyone return to his
own people,   Isa 13:14
let everyone flee to his own
land.   Jer 51:9

17"Israel is a scattered flock
that lions have chased
away.   2Ki 24:1
The first to devour him
was the king of Assyria;
the last to crush his bones
was Nebuchadnezzar king
of Babylon."   Jer 51:34

18Therefore this is what the
LORD Almighty, the God of Israel, says:

"I will punish the king of
Babylon and his land
as I punished the king of
Assyria.   Eze 31:3
19But I will bring Israel back to
his own pasture   Jer 31:10
and he will graze on Carmel
and Bashan;
his appetite will be satisfied
on the hills of Ephraim and
Gilead.   Mic 7:14
20In those days, at that time,"
declares the LORD,

"search will be made for
Israel's guilt,
but there will be none,
and for the sins of Judah,
but none will be found,
for I will forgive the
remnant I spare.   Ge 45:7

21"Attack the land of
Merathaim
and those who live in
Pekod.   Eze 23:23
Pursue, kill and completely
destroya them,"
declares the LORD.
"Do everything I have
commanded you.
22The noise of battle is in the
land,   Jer 4:19-21
the noise of great
destruction!
23How broken and shattered
is the hammer of the whole
earth!   Isa 10:5
How desolate is Babylon
among the nations!   Isa 14:16
24I set a trap for you,
O Babylon,   Jer 51:12
and you were caught before
you knew it;
you were found and
captured   Jer 57:31
because you opposed the
LORD.   Job 9:4
25The LORD has opened his
arsenal
and brought out the
weapons of his wrath,
for the Sovereign LORD
Almighty has work to do
in the land of the
Babylonians.   Jer 51:25

a21 The Hebrew term refers to the irrevocable giving over of things or persons to the
LORD, often by totally destroying them; also in verse 26.

²⁶Come against her from afar.
Break open her granaries;
pile her up like heaps of
grain.   Ru 3:7
Completely destroy her
and leave her no remnant.
²⁷Kill all her young bulls; Ps 68:30
let them go down to the
slaughter!   Isa 30:25
Woe to them! For their day
has come,   Job 18:20
the time for them to be
punished.   Jer 51:6
²⁸Listen to the fugitives and
refugees from Babylon
declaring in Zion
how the LORD our God has
taken vengeance,
vengeance for his temple.

²⁹"Summon archers against
Babylon,
all those who draw the
bow.
Encamp all around her;
let no one escape.   Isa 13:18
Repay her for her deeds;
do to her as she has done.
For she has defied the LORD,
the Holy One of Israel.
³⁰Therefore, her young men
will fall in the streets;
all her soldiers will be
silenced in that day,"
declares the LORD.
³¹"See, I am against you,
O arrogant one,"   Jer 21:13
declares the Lord, the LORD
Almighty,
"for your day has come,
the time for you to be
punished.
³²The arrogant one will
stumble and fall   Ps 20:8

and no one will help her
up;   Am 5:2
I will kindle a fire in her
towns   Jer 49:27
that will consume all who
are around her."

³³This is what the LORD Almighty says:

"The people of Israel are
oppressed,   Isa 58:6
and the people of Judah as
well.
All their captors hold them
fast,
refusing to let them go.
³⁴Yet their Redeemer is strong;
the LORD Almighty is his
name.   Jer 31:35
He will vigorously defend
their cause   Ps 119:154
so that he may bring rest to
their land,   Isa 14:7
but unrest to those who live
in Babylon.

³⁵"A sword against the
Babylonians!"   Jer 47:6
declares the LORD—
"against those who live in
Babylon
and against her officials and
wise men!   Da 5:7
³⁶A sword against her false
prophets!
They will become fools.
A sword against her
warriors!   Jer 49:22
They will be filled with
terror.   Jer 51:30
³⁷A sword against her horses
and chariots   2Ki 19:23
and all the foreigners in her
ranks!

They will become women.
A sword against her
  treasures! Isa 45:3
They will be plundered.
[38] A drought on[a] her waters!
They will dry up. Isa 11:15
For it is a land of idols,
  idols that will go mad with
  terror.

[39] "So desert creatures and
    hyenas will live there,
and there the owl will
  dwell.
It will never again be
  inhabited
or lived in from generation
  to generation. Isa 13:19-22
[40] As God overthrew Sodom
    and Gomorrah Ge 19:24
along with their
  neighboring towns,"
        declares the Lord,
"so no one will live there;
no man will dwell in it.

[41] "Look! An army is coming
    from the north; Isa 41:25
a great nation and many
  kings
are being stirred up from
  the ends of the earth.
[42] They are armed with bows
  and spears;
they are cruel and without
  mercy. Job 30:21
They sound like the roaring
  sea Isa 5:30
as they ride on their horses;
they come like men in battle
  formation
to attack you, O Daughter
  of Babylon. Isa 47:1

[43] The king of Babylon has
    heard reports about
    them,
and his hands hang limp.
Anguish has gripped him,
  pain like that of a woman in
  labor. Jer 6:22-24
[44] Like a lion coming up from
    Jordan's thickets Jer 12:5
to a rich pastureland,
I will chase Babylon from its
  land in an instant.
Who is the chosen one I
  will appoint for this?
Who is like me and who can
  challenge me? Job 41:10
And what shepherd can
  stand against me?"
[45] Therefore, hear what the
    Lord has planned
    against Babylon,
what he has purposed
  against the land of the
  Babylonians: Isa 48:14
The young of the flock will
  be dragged away;
he will completely destroy
  their pasture because of
  them.
[46] At the sound of Babylon's
    capture the earth will
    tremble; Jdg 5:4
its cry will resound among
  the nations. Job 24:12

51 This is what the Lord
    says:

"See, I will stir up the spirit
  of a destroyer Isa 13:17
against Babylon and the
  people of Leb Kamai.[b]

---

[a] 38 Or *A sword against*   [b] 1 *Leb Kamai* is a cryptogram for Chaldea, that is, Babylonia.

²I will send foreigners to
   Babylon   Isa 13:5
to winnow her and to
   devastate her land;
they will oppose her on
   every side
in the day of her disaster.
³Let not the archer string his
   bow,   Jer 50:29
nor let him put on his
   armor.   Jer 46:4
Do not spare her young
   men;
completely destroy[a] her
   army.
⁴They will fall down slain in
   Babylon,[b]   Isa 13:15
fatally wounded in her
   streets.   Isa 13:18
⁵For Israel and Judah have not
   been forsaken   Lev 26:44
by their God, the LORD
   Almighty,
though their land[c] is full of
   guilt   Hos 4:1
before the Holy One of
   Israel.

⁶"Flee from Babylon!   Isa 48:20
Run for your lives!
Do not be destroyed
   because of her sins.
It is time for the LORD's
   vengeance;   Isa 1:24
he will pay her what she
   deserves.   Dt 32:35
⁷Babylon was a gold cup in
   the LORD's hand; Isa 51:22
she made the whole earth
   drunk.
The nations drank her wine;

therefore they have now
   gone mad.
⁸Babylon will suddenly fall
   and be broken.   Isa 14:15
Wail over her!
Get balm for her pain; Jer 8:22
   perhaps she can be healed.

⁹" 'We would have healed
   Babylon,
but she cannot be healed;
let us leave her and each go
   to his own land, Isa 13:14
for her judgment reaches to
   the skies,   Rev 18:4-5
it rises as high as the
   clouds.'

¹⁰" 'The LORD has vindicated
   us;   Mic 7:9
come, let us tell in Zion
what the LORD our God has
   done.'   Ps 64:9

¹¹"Sharpen the arrows, Jer 50:9
take up the shields! Isa 21:5
The LORD has stirred up the
   kings of the Medes, Isa 13:3
because his purpose is to
   destroy Babylon.
The LORD will take
   vengeance,   Lev 26:25
vengeance for his temple.
¹²Lift up a banner against the
   walls of Babylon! Ps 20:5
Reinforce the guard,
station the watchmen, 2Sa 18:24
prepare an ambush! Jer 50:24
The LORD will carry out his
   purpose,   Ps 33:11
his decree against the
   people of Babylon.

[a]3 The Hebrew term refers to the irrevocable giving over of things or persons to the
LORD, often by totally destroying them.   [b]4 Or *Chaldea*   [c]5 Or *I and the land of the
Babylonians*

¹³You who live by many
        waters   Jer 50:38
    and are rich in treasures,
your end has come,
    the time for you to be cut
        off.   Jer 50:3
¹⁴The LORD Almighty has
        sworn by himself: Ge 22:16
    I will surely fill you with
        men, as with a swarm of
        locusts,   Am 7:1
    and they will shout in
        triumph over you.

¹⁵"He made the earth by his
        power;
    he founded the world by
        his wisdom   Ps 104:24
    and stretched out the
        heavens by his
        understanding.   Ps 136:5
¹⁶When he thunders, the
        waters in the heavens
        roar;   Ps 18:13
    he makes clouds rise from
        the ends of the earth.
    He sends lightning with the
        rain   Job 28:26
    and brings out the wind
        from his storehouses.

¹⁷"Every man is senseless and
        without knowledge;
    every goldsmith is shamed
        by his idols.
    His images are a fraud; Isa 44:20
    they have no breath in
        them.
¹⁸They are worthless, the
        objects of mockery;Jer 18:15
    when their judgment
        comes, they will
        perish.

¹⁹He who is the Portion of
        Jacob is not like these,
    for he is the Maker of all
        things,
    including the tribe of his
        inheritance—   Ex 34:9
    the LORD Almighty is his
        name.

²⁰"You are my war club,   Isa 10:5
    my weapon for battle—
    with you I shatter nations,
    with you I destroy
        kingdoms,   Isa 45:1
²¹with you I shatter horse and
        rider,   Ex 15:1
    with you I shatter chariot
        and driver,   Isa 43:17
²²with you I shatter man and
        woman,
    with you I shatter old man
        and youth,
    with you I shatter young
        man and maiden,   2Ch 36:17
²³with you I shatter shepherd
        and flock,
    with you I shatter farmer
        and oxen,
    with you I shatter
        governors and officials.

²⁴"Before your eyes I will
repay Babylon and all who live
in Babylonia*a* for all the wrong
they have done in Zion," declares the LORD.   Dt 32:41

²⁵"I am against you,
        O destroying mountain,
    you who destroy the whole
        earth,"   Jer 50:23
        declares the LORD.
    "I will stretch out my hand
        against you,   Ex 3:20

a24 Or Chaldea; also in verse 35

roll you off the cliffs,
and make you a burned-out
mountain.   Zec 4:7
²⁶No rock will be taken from
you for a cornerstone,
nor any stone for a
foundation,
for you will be desolate
forever,"   Isa 13:19-22
    declares the Lord.

²⁷"Lift up a banner in the land!
Blow the trumpet among
the nations!
Prepare the nations for battle
against her;
summon against her these
kingdoms: Jer 25:14
Ararat, Minni and
Ashkenaz.   Ge 8:4
Appoint a commander
against her;
send up horses like a
swarm of locusts.
²⁸Prepare the nations for battle
against her—
the kings of the Medes,
their governors and all their
officials,
and all the countries they
rule.
²⁹The land trembles and
writhes,   Jdg 5:4
for the Lord's purposes
against Babylon stand—
to lay waste the land of
Babylon   Jer 48:9
so that no one will live
there.   Isa 13:20
³⁰Babylon's warriors have
stopped fighting;   Jer 50:36
they remain in their
strongholds.

Their strength is exhausted;
they have become like
women.   Isa 19:16
Her dwellings are set on fire;
the bars of her gates are
broken.   Isa 45:2
³¹One courier follows another
and messenger follows
messenger   2Sa 18:19-31
to announce to the king of
Babylon
that his entire city is
captured,   Jer 50:2
³²the river crossings seized,
the marshes set on fire,
and the soldiers terrified."

³³This is what the Lord Almighty, the God of Israel, says:

"The Daughter of Babylon is
like a threshing floor
at the time it is trampled;
the time to harvest her will
soon come."   Isa 13:22

³⁴"Nebuchadnezzar king of
Babylon has devoured
us,   Jer 50:17
he has thrown us into
confusion,
he has made us an empty
jar.
Like a serpent he has
swallowed us
and filled his stomach with
our delicacies,
and then has spewed us
out.   Lev 18:25
³⁵May the violence done to our
flesh*ᵃ* be upon
Babylon,"   Joel 3:19
say the inhabitants of Zion.

ᵃ35 Or *done to us and to our children*

"May our blood be on those
 who live in Babylonia,"
says Jerusalem.   Ps 137:8

36Therefore, this is what the
LORD says:

"See, I will defend your
 cause
 and avenge you;   Jer 20:12
 I will dry up her sea   Isa 11:15
 and make her springs dry.
37Babylon will be a heap of
 ruins,
 a haunt of jackals,   Isa 13:22
 an object of horror and scorn,
 a place where no one lives.
38Her people all roar like
 young lions,   Isa 5:29
 they growl like lion cubs.
39But while they are aroused,
 I will set out a feast for
 them
 and make them drunk,
so that they shout with
 laughter—
 then sleep forever and not
 awake,"   Ps 13:3
 declares the LORD.
40"I will bring them down
 like lambs to the slaughter,
 like rams and goats.   Eze 39:18

41"How Sheshach[a] will be
 captured,   Jer 25:26
 the boast of the whole earth
 seized!
 What a horror Babylon will
 be
 among the nations!   Jer 50:13
42The sea will rise over
 Babylon;
 its roaring waves will cover
 her.   Ps 18:4

43Her towns will be desolate,
 a dry and desert land,
 a land where no one lives,
 through which no man
 travels.   Isa 13:20
44I will punish Bel in Babylon
 and make him spew out
 what he has swallowed.
 The nations will no longer
 stream to him.
 And the wall of Babylon
 will fall.   2Ki 25:4

45"Come out of her, my
 people!
 Run for your lives!   Isa 48:20
 Run from the fierce anger of
 the LORD.   Ps 76:10
46Do not lose heart or be afraid
 when rumors are heard in
 the land;   2Ki 19:7
 one rumor comes this year,
 another the next,
 rumors of violence in the
 land
 and of ruler against ruler.
47For the time will surely come
 when I will punish the idols
 of Babylon;   Isa 46:1-2
 her whole land will be
 disgraced   Jer 50:12
 and her slain will all lie
 fallen within her.   Jer 27:7
48Then heaven and earth and
 all that is in them
 will shout for joy over
 Babylon,   Job 3:7
 for out of the north
 destroyers will attack her,"
 declares the LORD.

49"Babylon must fall because of
 Israel's slain,

a41 *Sheshach* is a cryptogram for Babylon.

just as the slain in all the
    earth
have fallen because of
    Babylon.   Ps 137:8
⁵⁰You who have escaped the
    sword,
leave and do not linger!
Remember the LORD in a
    distant land,   Jer 23:23
and think on Jerusalem.''

⁵¹''We are disgraced,   Ps 44:13-16
for we have been insulted
and shame covers our faces,
because foreigners have
    entered
the holy places of the
    LORD's house.''   La 1:10

⁵²''But days are coming,''
    declares the LORD,
''when I will punish her
    idols,
and throughout her land
the wounded will groan.
⁵³Even if Babylon reaches the
    sky   Ge 11:4
and fortifies her lofty
    stronghold,
I will send destroyers
    against her,''   Job 15:21
    declares the LORD.

⁵⁴''The sound of a cry comes
    from Babylon,   Job 24:12
the sound of great
    destruction   Jer 50:22
from the land of the
    Babylonians.ᵃ
⁵⁵The LORD will destroy
    Babylon;
he will silence her noisy
    din.   Isa 25:5

Waves ʟof enemies˩ will rage
    like great waters;   Ps 18:4
the roar of their voices will
    resound.
⁵⁶A destroyer will come against
    Babylon;   Job 15:21
her warriors will be
    captured,
and their bows will be
    broken.   Ps 46:9
For the LORD is a God of
    retribution;
he will repay in full.   Ge 4:24
⁵⁷I will make her officials and
    wise men drunk,   Isa 21:5
her governors, officers and
    warriors as well;
they will sleep forever and
    not awake,''   Ps 76:5
declares the King, whose
    name is the LORD
    Almighty.   Isa 6:5

⁵⁸This is what the LORD Almighty says:

''Babylon's thick wall will be
    leveled   2Ki 25:4
and her high gates set on
    fire;   Isa 13:2
the peoples exhaust
    themselves for nothing,
the nations' labor is only
    fuel for the flames.''Isa 47:14

⁵⁹This is the message Jeremiah gave to the staff officer Seraiah son of Neriah, the son of Mahseiah, when he went to Babylon with Zedekiah king of Judah in the fourth year of his reign. ⁶⁰Jeremiah had written on a scroll about all the disasters that would come upon Bab-

ᵃ54 Or *Chaldeans*

ylon—all that had been recorded concerning Babylon.
61He said to Seraiah, "When
you get to Babylon, see that you
read all these words aloud.
62Then say, 'O LORD, you have
said you will destroy this place,
so that neither man nor animal
will live in it; it will be desolate
forever.' 63When you finish
reading this scroll, tie a stone to
it and throw it into the Euphrates. 64Then say, 'So will Babylon
sink to rise no more because of
the disaster I will bring upon
her. And her people will fall.' "

The words of Jeremiah end
here.   Job 31:40

The Fall of Jerusalem

52 Zedekiah was twenty-
one years old when he
became king, and he reigned in
Jerusalem eleven years. His
mother's name was Hamutal
daughter of Jeremiah; she was
from Libnah. 2He did evil in the
eyes of the LORD, just as Jehoiakim had done. 3It was because
of the LORD's anger that all this
happened to Jerusalem and
Judah, and in the end he thrust
them from his presence. 2Ki 24:17

Now Zedekiah rebelled
against the king of Babylon.

4So in the ninth year of Zedekiah's reign, on the tenth day of
the tenth month, Nebu-
chadnezzar king of Babylon
marched against Jerusalem with
his whole army. They camped
outside the city and built siege
works all around it. 5The city
was kept under siege until the
eleventh year of King Zedekiah.

6By the ninth day of the
fourth month the famine in the
city had become so severe that
there was no food for the people
to eat. 7Then the city wall was
broken through, and the whole
army fled. They left the city at
night through the gate between
the two walls near the king's
garden, though the Babylo-
niansa were surrounding the
city. They fled toward the Arabah,b 8but the Babylonianc
army pursued King Zedekiah
and overtook him in the plains
of Jericho. All his soldiers were
separated from him and scattered, 9and he was captured.

He was taken to the king of
Babylon at Riblah in the land of
Hamath, where he pronounced
sentence on him. 10There at Riblah the king of Babylon slaughtered the sons of Zedekiah before his eyes; he also killed all
the officials of Judah. 11Then he
put out Zedekiah's eyes, bound
him with bronze shackles and
took him to Babylon, where he
put him in prison till the day of
his death.   Jer 22:30; Eze 12:13

12On the tenth day of the fifth
month, in the nineteenth year
of Nebuchadnezzar king of Babylon, Nebuzaradan commander
of the imperial guard, who
served the king of Babylon,

a7 Or Chaldeans; also in verse 17   b7 Or the Jordan Valley   c8 Or Chaldean; also in
verse 14

came to Jerusalem. [13]He set fire to the temple of the LORD, the royal palace and all the houses of Jerusalem. Every important building he burned down. [14]The whole Babylonian army under the commander of the imperial guard broke down all the walls around Jerusalem. [15]Nebuzaradan the commander of the guard carried into exile some of the poorest people and those who remained in the city, along with the rest of the craftsmen[a] and those who had gone over to the king of Babylon. [16]But Nebuzaradan left behind the rest of the poorest people of the land to work the vineyards and fields.

[17]The Babylonians broke up the bronze pillars, the movable stands and the bronze Sea that were at the temple of the LORD and they carried all the bronze to Babylon. [18]They also took away the pots, shovels, wick trimmers, sprinkling bowls, dishes and all the bronze articles used in the temple service. [19]The commander of the imperial guard took away the basins, censers, sprinkling bowls, pots, lampstands, dishes and bowls used for drink offerings—all that were made of pure gold or silver.   Ex 25:29; 1Ki 7:15

[20]The bronze from the two pillars, the Sea and the twelve bronze bulls under it, and the movable stands, which King Solomon had made for the temple of the LORD, was more than could be weighed. [21]Each of the pillars was eighteen cubits high and twelve cubits in circumference[b]; each was four fingers thick, and hollow. [22]The bronze capital on top of the one pillar was five cubits[c] high and was decorated with a network and pomegranates of bronze all around. The other pillar, with its pomegranates, was similar. [23]There were ninety-six pomegranates on the sides; the total number of pomegranates above the surrounding network was a hundred.   Ex 28:33; 1Ki 7:25

[24]The commander of the guard took as prisoners Seraiah the chief priest, Zephaniah the priest next in rank and the three doorkeepers. [25]Of those still in the city, he took the officer in charge of the fighting men, and seven royal advisers. He also took the secretary who was chief officer in charge of conscripting the people of the land and sixty of his men who were found in the city. [26]Nebuzaradan the commander took them all and brought them to the king of Babylon at Riblah. [27]There at Riblah, in the land of Hamath, the king had them executed.

So Judah went into captivity, away from her land. [28]This is the number of the people Nebuchadnezzar carried into exile:

in the seventh year, 3,023 Jews;

---

[a]15 Or *populace*   [b]21 That is, about 27 feet (about 8.1 meters) high and 18 feet (about 5.4 meters) in circumference   [c]22 That is, about 7 1/2 feet (about 2.3 meters)

²⁹in Nebuchadnezzar's eighteenth year,
832 people from Jerusa-
lem;
³⁰in his twenty-third year,
745 Jews taken into exile
by Nebuzaradan the
commander of the im-
perial guard.   Jer 43:3
There were 4,600 people
in all.   Jer 13:19

Jehoiachin Released

³¹In the thirty-seventh year of
the exile of Jehoiachin king of
Judah, in the year Evil-
Merodach^a became king of Babylon, he released Jehoiachin
king of Judah and freed him
from prison on the twenty-fifth
day of the twelfth month. ³²He
spoke kindly to him and gave
him a seat of honor higher than
those of the other kings who
were with him in Babylon. ³³So
Jehoiachin put aside his prison
clothes and for the rest of his life
ate regularly at the king's table.
³⁴Day by day the king of Babylon gave Jehoiachin a regular
allowance as long as he lived,
till the day of his death.   2Sa 9:10

ᵃ31 Also called *Amel-Marduk*.

Lamentations

Introduction:

The title of this book means "funeral songs." The author was probably Jeremiah, and he was grieving about the destruction of Jerusalem.

In the original language, Hebrew, the twenty-two verses in each of chapters 1, 2, and 4 use the twenty-two letters of the Hebrew alphabet to start the verse. The third chapter has sixty-six verses and every third verse starts a new letter of the Hebrew alphabet. This is called an acrostic.

Jeremiah reflects here on the total destruction that has happened to Jerusalem and the temple. But he recognizes that all of this is the judgment of a righteous God. Knowing that God is merciful he appeals for mercy in prayer to God.

Outline of contents:

Jerusalem's total destruction (1:1–22)
God's anger—search for comfort (2:1–22)
Thoughts on suffering—hope in God (3:1–66)
The old glory of Jerusalem—present misery (4:1–22)
A prayer for God's mercy (5:1–22)

---

1 [a] How deserted lies the city,
  once so full of people! Jer 42:2
How like a widow is she,
  who once was great among the nations! 1Ki 4:21
She who was queen among the provinces
  has now become a slave.

2 Bitterly she weeps at night,
  tears are upon her cheeks.
Among all her lovers
  there is none to comfort her. Jer 3:1
All her friends have betrayed her; Jer 4:30
  they have become her enemies. Jer 30:14

3 After affliction and harsh labor,
  Judah has gone into exile.
She dwells among the nations;
  she finds no resting place.

[a] This chapter is an acrostic poem, the verses of which begin with the successive letters of the Hebrew alphabet.

All who pursue her have
overtaken her   Ex 15:9
in the midst of her distress.

⁴The roads to Zion mourn,
for no one comes to her
appointed feasts.   Ps 137:1
All her gateways are
desolate,   Isa 27:10
her priests groan,
her maidens grieve,
and she is in bitter anguish.

⁵Her foes have become her
masters;
her enemies are at ease.
The LORD has brought her
grief   Isa 22:5
because of her many sins.
Her children have gone into
exile,   Jer 10:20
captive before the foe.

⁶All the splendor has
departed
from the Daughter of Zion.
Her princes are like deer
that find no pasture;
in weakness they have fled
before the pursuer.   Lev 26:36

⁷In the days of her affliction
and wandering
Jerusalem remembers all
the treasures
that were hers in days of
old.
When her people fell into
enemy hands,
there was no one to help
her.   2Ki 14:26
Her enemies looked at her
and laughed at her
destruction.   Jer 2:26

⁸Jerusalem has sinned greatly

and so has become unclean.
All who honored her despise
her,
for they have seen her
nakedness;   Jer 13:22,26
she herself groans
and turns away.   Ps 6:6

⁹Her filthiness clung to her
skirts;
she did not consider her
future.   Dt 32:28-29
Her fall was astounding;
there was none to comfort
her.   Ecc 4:1
"Look, O LORD, on my
affliction,   Ps 25:18
for the enemy has
triumphed."

¹⁰The enemy laid hands
on all her treasures; Isa 64:11
she saw pagan nations
enter her sanctuary—   Ps 74:7-8
those you had forbidden
to enter your assembly. Dt 23:3

¹¹All her people groan
as they search for bread;
they barter their treasures for
food
to keep themselves alive.
"Look, O LORD, and
consider,
for I am despised."

¹²"Is it nothing to you, all you
who pass by?   Jer 18:16
Look around and see.
Is any suffering like my
suffering
that was inflicted on me,
that the LORD brought on me
in the day of his fierce
anger?   Isa 10:4

¹³"From on high he sent fire,
  sent it down into my bones.
He spread a net for my feet
  and turned me back.   Job 18:8
He made me desolate,
  faint all the day long.   Jer 44:6

¹⁴"My sins have been bound
  into a yoke[a];   Dt 28:48
  by his hands they were
  woven together.
They have come upon my
  neck
and the Lord has sapped
  my strength.
He has handed me over
  to those I cannot withstand.

¹⁵"The Lord has rejected
  all the warriors in my
  midst;   Jer 37:10
he has summoned an army
  against me
to[b] crush my young men.
In his winepress the Lord has
  trampled   Jdg 6:11
  the Virgin Daughter of
  Judah.   Jer 14:17

¹⁶"This is why I weep
  and my eyes overflow with
  tears.   Job 7:3
No one is near to comfort
  me,   Ps 69:20
  no one to restore my spirit.
My children are destitute
  because the enemy has
  prevailed."   Jer 13:17

¹⁷Zion stretches out her hands,
  but there is no one to
  comfort her.   Jer 4:31

The Lᴏʀᴅ has decreed for
  Jacob
that his neighbors become
  his foes;   Ex 23:21
Jerusalem has become
  an unclean thing among
  them.   Jer 2:22

¹⁸"The Lᴏʀᴅ is righteous,
  yet I rebelled against his
  command.   1Sa 12:14
Listen, all you peoples;
  look upon my suffering.
My young men and maidens
  have gone into exile.   Dt 28:32

¹⁹"I called to my allies
  but they betrayed me.
My priests and my elders
  perished in the city
while they searched for food
  to keep themselves alive.

²⁰"See, O Lᴏʀᴅ, how
  distressed I am!   Jer 4:19
I am in torment within,
and in my heart I am
  disturbed,   Job 20:2
  for I have been most
  rebellious.
Outside, the sword bereaves;
  inside, there is only death.

²¹"People have heard my
  groaning,   Ps 6:6
  but there is no one to
  comfort me.
All my enemies have heard
  of my distress;
they rejoice at what you
  have done.   La 2:15
May you bring the day you
  have announced   Isa 47:11

---

[a]14 Most Hebrew manuscripts; Septuagint *He kept watch over my sins*   [b]15 Or *has set a time for me / when he will*

so they may become like
me.

22"Let all their wickedness
come before you;
deal with them
as you have dealt with me
because of all my sins.
My groans are many
and my heart is faint."

2 ^aHow the Lord has covered
the Daughter of Zion
with the cloud of his
anger^b!
He has hurled down the
splendor of Israel
from heaven to earth;
he has not remembered his
footstool   Jer 14:17
in the day of his anger.

2Without pity the Lord has
swallowed up
all the dwellings of Jacob;
in his wrath he has torn
down
the strongholds of the
Daughter of Judah.
He has brought her kingdom
and its princes
down to the ground in
dishonor.   Isa 25:12

3In fierce anger he has cut off
every horn^c of Israel.   Ps 75:5
He has withdrawn his right
hand
at the approach of the
enemy.   Ps 74:11

He has burned in Jacob like a
flaming fire
that consumes everything
around it.   Isa 42:25

4Like an enemy he has strung
his bow;   Job 3:23
his right hand is ready.
Like a foe he has slain
all who were pleasing to the
eye;
he has poured out his wrath
like fire   Isa 42:25
on the tent of the Daughter
of Zion.   Jer 4:20

5The Lord is like an enemy;
he has swallowed up Israel.
He has swallowed up all her
palaces
and destroyed her
strongholds.
He has multiplied mourning
and lamentation
for the Daughter of Judah.

6He has laid waste his
dwelling like a garden;
he has destroyed his place
of meeting.   Jer 52:13
The LORD has made Zion
forget
her appointed feasts and
her Sabbaths;   Zep 3:18
in his fierce anger he has
spurned
both king and priest.

7The Lord has rejected his
altar
and abandoned his
sanctuary.   Lev 26:31

---

^aThis chapter is an acrostic poem, the verses of which begin with the successive letters
of the Hebrew alphabet.   ^b1 Or *How the Lord in his anger / has treated the Daughter of
Zion with contempt*   ^c3 Or / *all the strength;* or *every king; horn* here symbolizes
strength.

He has handed over to the
> enemy
the walls of her palaces;
they have raised a shout in
> the house of the Lord
as on the day of an
> appointed feast.

⁸The Lord determined to tear
> down
the wall around the
> Daughter of Zion.
He stretched out a measuring
> line   2Ki 21:13
and did not withhold his
> hand from destroying.
He made ramparts and walls
> lament;   Ps 48:13
together they wasted away.

⁹Her gates have sunk into the
> ground;   Ne 1:3
their bars he has broken
> and destroyed.   Isa 45:2
Her king and her princes are
> exiled among the
> nations,   Dt 28:36
the law is no more,
and her prophets no longer
> find   1Sa 3:1
visions from the Lord.

¹⁰The elders of the Daughter of
> Zion
sit on the ground in silence;
they have sprinkled dust on
> their heads   Jos 7:6
and put on sackcloth. Isa 3:24
The young women of
> Jerusalem
have bowed their heads to
> the ground.   Job 2:13

¹¹My eyes fail from weeping,
I am in torment within,

my heart is poured out on
> the ground
because my people are
> destroyed,   Jer 9:1
because children and infants
> faint   La 4:4
in the streets of the city.

¹²They say to their mothers,
> "Where is bread and
> wine?"   Isa 24:11
as they faint like wounded
> men
in the streets of the city,
as their lives ebb away
in their mothers' arms. La 4:4

¹³What can I say for you?
With what can I compare
> you,
O Daughter of Jerusalem?
To what can I liken you,
that I may comfort you,
O Virgin Daughter of Zion?
Your wound is as deep as the
> sea.   Jer 14:17
Who can heal you?

¹⁴The visions of your prophets
> were false and worthless;
they did not expose your sin
> to ward off your captivity.
The oracles they gave you
> were false and misleading.

¹⁵All who pass your way
clap their hands at you;
they scoff and shake their
> heads
at the Daughter of
> Jerusalem: La 1:21
"Is this the city that was
> called
the perfection of beauty,
the joy of the whole earth?"

16All your enemies open their
　　mouths
　　wide against you;　　　Ps 22:13
　they scoff and gnash their
　　teeth　　　　　　　　Job 16:9
　and say, "We have
　　swallowed her up.
　This is the day we have
　　waited for;
　we have lived to see it."

17The Lord has done what he
　　planned;
　he has fulfilled his word,
　　which he decreed long ago.
　He has overthrown you
　　without pity,　　　　Eze 5:11
　he has let the enemy gloat
　　over you,　　　　　Ps 22:17
　he has exalted the horn*a* of
　　your foes.　　　　　Ps 89:42

18The hearts of the people
　　cry out to the Lord.　Ps 119:145
　O wall of the Daughter of
　　Zion,
　let your tears flow like a
　　river
　　day and night;　　　Jer 9:1
　give yourself no relief,
　　your eyes no rest.　　La 3:49

19Arise, cry out in the night,
　　as the watches of the night
　　begin;
　pour out your heart like
　　water　　　　　　　1Sa 1:15
　in the presence of the Lord.
　Lift up your hands to him
　for the lives of your
　　children,

who faint from hunger　Isa 51:20
　at the head of every street.

20"Look, O Lord, and
　　consider:
　Whom have you ever
　　treated like this?
　Should women eat their
　　offspring,　　　　　Dt 28:53
　the children they have
　　cared for?　　　　　La 4:10
　Should priest and prophet be
　　killed
　in the sanctuary of the
　　Lord?　　　　　　　La 1:19

21"Young and old lie together
　　in the dust of the streets;
　my young men and maidens
　　have fallen by the sword.
　You have slain them in the
　　day of your anger;
　you have slaughtered them
　　without pity.　　　　Jer 13:14

22"As you summon to a feast
　　day,
　so you summoned against
　　me terrors on every side.
　In the day of the Lord's
　　anger
　no one escaped or survived;
　those I cared for and reared,
　　my enemy has destroyed."

3 *b*I am the man who has
　　seen affliction　　Jer 15:17-18
　by the rod of his wrath.
2He has driven me away and
　　made me walk
　in darkness rather than
　　light;　　　　　　　Job 19:8

---

a17 Horn here symbolizes strength.　　*b*This chapter is an acrostic poem; the verses of
each stanza begin with the successive letters of the Hebrew alphabet, and the verses
within each stanza begin with the same letter.

³indeed, he has turned his
hand against me
again and again, all day
long.   Ps 38:2

⁴He has made my skin and
my flesh grow old Job 30:30
and has broken my bones.
⁵He has besieged me and
surrounded me
with bitterness and
hardship.   Jer 23:15
⁶He has made me dwell in
darkness
like those long dead. Ps 88:5-6

⁷He has walled me in so I
cannot escape;   Job 3:23
he has weighed me down
with chains.
⁸Even when I call out or cry
for help,   Ps 5:2
he shuts out my prayer.
⁹He has barred my way with
blocks of stone;   Job 19:8
he has made my paths
crooked.   Job 9:24

¹⁰Like a bear lying in wait,
like a lion in hiding, Hos 13:8
¹¹he dragged me from the path
and mangled me
and left me without help.
¹²He drew his bow   La 2:4
and made me the target for
his arrows.   Job 16:12

¹³He pierced my heart
with arrows from his
quiver.   Job 6:4
¹⁴I became the laughingstock
of all my people;   Job 17:2
they mock me in song all
day long.
¹⁵He has filled me with bitter
herbs

and sated me with gall. Jer 9:15

¹⁶He has broken my teeth with
gravel;   Pr 20:17
he has trampled me in the
dust.   Ps 7:5
¹⁷I have been deprived of
peace;
I have forgotten what
prosperity is.
¹⁸So I say, "My splendor is
gone
and all that I had hoped
from the LORD."   Job 17:15

¹⁹I remember my affliction and
my wandering,
the bitterness and the gall.
²⁰I well remember them,
and my soul is downcast
within me.   Ps 42:11
²¹Yet this I call to mind
and therefore I have hope:

²²Because of the LORD's great
love we are not
consumed,   Ps 103:11
for his compassions never
fail.
²³They are new every morning;
great is your faithfulness.
²⁴I say to myself, "The LORD is
my portion;   Ps 119:57
therefore I will wait for
him."

²⁵The LORD is good to those
whose hope is in him,
to the one who seeks him;
²⁶it is good to wait quietly
for the salvation of the
LORD.   Ps 37:7
²⁷It is good for a man to bear
the yoke
while he is young.

²⁸Let him sit alone in silence,
  for the LORD has laid it on
    him.   Jer 15:17
²⁹Let him bury his face in the
  dust—   Job 2:8
  there may yet be hope.
³⁰Let him offer his cheek to
  one who would strike
    him,   Ps 94:14
  and let him be filled with
    disgrace.   Mic 5:1

³¹For men are not cast off
  by the Lord forever.   Ps 94:14
³²Though he brings grief, he
    will show compassion,
  so great is his unfailing
    love.   Ps 78:38
³³For he does not willingly
    bring affliction
  or grief to the children of
    men.   Job 37:23

³⁴To crush underfoot
  all prisoners in the land,
³⁵to deny a man his rights
  before the Most High,
³⁶to deprive a man of justice—
  would not the Lord see
    such things?   Ps 140:12

³⁷Who can speak and have it
    happen
  if the Lord has not decreed
    it?   Ps 33:9-11
³⁸Is it not from the mouth of
    the Most High
  that both calamities and
    good things come?   Job 2:10
³⁹Why should any living man
    complain
  when punished for his sins?

⁴⁰Let us examine our ways and
    test them,   2Co 13:5

and let us return to the
  LORD.   Ps 119:59
⁴¹Let us lift up our hearts and
  our hands
  to God in heaven, and say:
⁴²"We have sinned and
    rebelled   Jer 14:20
  and you have not forgiven.

⁴³"You have covered yourself
    with anger and pursued
    us;
  you have slain without pity.
⁴⁴You have covered yourself
    with a cloud   Ps 97:2
  so that no prayer can get
    through.   Isa 58:4
⁴⁵You have made us scum and
    refuse   1Co 4:13
  among the nations.

⁴⁶"All our enemies have
    opened their mouths
  wide against us.   Ps 22:13
⁴⁷We have suffered terror and
    pitfalls,   Jer 48:43
  ruin and destruction."
⁴⁸Streams of tears flow from
  my eyes   Ps 119:136
  because my people are
    destroyed.   La 2:11

⁴⁹My eyes will flow
    unceasingly,
  without relief,   Jer 14:17
⁵⁰until the LORD looks down
  from heaven and sees.   Ps 14:2
⁵¹What I see brings grief to my
    soul
  because of all the women of
    my city.

⁵²Those who were my enemies
    without cause
  hunted me like a bird.   Ps 35:7

⁵³They tried to end my life in a
　pit
　　　　　　　　　　　Jer 37:16
　and threw stones at me;
⁵⁴the waters closed over my
　head,
　　　　　　　　　　　Ps 69:2
　and I thought I was about
　　to be cut off.　　Ps 88:5

⁵⁵I called on your name,
　O Lᴏʀᴅ,
　from the depths of the pit.
⁵⁶You heard my plea: "Do not
　close your ears
　to my cry for relief."　Ps 55:1
⁵⁷You came near when I called
　you,
　and you said, "Do not
　　fear."　　　　　　Isa 41:10

⁵⁸O Lord, you took up my
　case;
　　　　　　　　　　　Jer 51:36
　you redeemed my life.
⁵⁹You have seen, O Lᴏʀᴅ, the
　wrong done to me.
　Uphold my cause!　Ps 35:23
⁶⁰You have seen the depth of
　their vengeance,
　all their plots against me.

⁶¹O Lᴏʀᴅ, you have heard
　their insults,
　all their plots against me—
⁶²what my enemies whisper
　and mutter
　against me all day long.
⁶³Look at them! Sitting or
　standing,
　they mock me in their
　　songs.　　　　　　Job 30:9

⁶⁴Pay them back what they
　deserve, O Lᴏʀᴅ,

for what their hands have
　done.　　　　　　　Ps 28:4
⁶⁵Put a veil over their hearts,
　and may your curse be on
　them!
⁶⁶Pursue them in anger and
　destroy them
　from under the heavens of
　the Lᴏʀᴅ.

4 ᵃHow the gold has lost its
　luster,
　the fine gold become dull!
The sacred gems are
　scattered
　at the head of every street.

²How the precious sons of
　Zion,　　　　　　　Isa 51:18
　once worth their weight in
　gold,
　are now considered as pots
　of clay,
　the work of a potter's
　hands!

³Even jackals offer their
　breasts
　to nurse their young,
but my people have become
　heartless
　like ostriches in the desert.

⁴Because of thirst the infant's
　tongue
　sticks to the roof of its
　　mouth;　　　　　　Ps 22:15
the children beg for bread,
　but no one gives it to them.

⁵Those who once ate
　delicacies
　are destitute in the streets.

ᵃThis chapter is an acrostic poem, the verses of which begin with the successive letters
of the Hebrew alphabet.

Those nurtured in purple
　now lie on ash heaps.　Isa 3:26

⁶The punishment of my
　　people
　is greater than that of
　　Sodom,　　　　　Ge 19:25
　which was overthrown in a
　　moment
　without a hand turned to
　　help her.

⁷Their princes were brighter
　　than snow
　and whiter than milk,
　their bodies more ruddy than
　　rubies,
　their appearance like
　　sapphires. ᵃ

⁸But now they are blacker
　　than soot;　　　Job 30:28
　they are not recognized in
　　the streets.
　Their skin has shriveled on
　　their bones;　　Ps 102:3-5
　it has become as dry as a
　　stick.

⁹Those killed by the sword are
　　better off
　than those who die of
　　famine;　　　　2Ki 25:3
　racked with hunger, they
　　waste away
　for lack of food from the
　　field.　　　　　Jer 15:2

¹⁰With their own hands
　　compassionate women
　have cooked their own
　　children,　　　Lev 26:29
　who became their food
　　when my people were
　　destroyed.

¹¹The LORD has given full vent
　　to his wrath;　　Job 20:23
　he has poured out his fierce
　　anger.　　　　　Na 1:6
　He kindled a fire in Zion
　　that consumed her
　　foundations.　　Jer 17:27

¹²The kings of the earth did
　　not believe,
　nor did any of the world's
　　people,
　that enemies and foes could
　　enter
　the gates of Jerusalem.　1Ki 9:9

¹³But it happened because of
　　the sins of her prophets
　and the iniquities of her
　　priests,　　　　Jer 5:31
　who shed within her
　　the blood of the righteous.

¹⁴Now they grope through the
　　streets
　like men who are blind.
　They are so defiled with
　　blood　　　　　Jer 19:4
　that no one dares to touch
　　their garments.

¹⁵"Go away! You are unclean!"
　　men cry to them.
　"Away! Away! Don't touch
　　us!"
　When they flee and wander
　　about,　　　　Jer 44:14
　people among the nations
　　say,
　"They can stay here no
　　longer."　　　　Lev 13:46

¹⁶The LORD himself has
　　scattered them;

ᵃ7 Or *lapis lazuli*

he no longer watches over
them.   Isa 9:14-16
The priests are shown no
honor,
the elders no favor.   La 2:6

¹⁷Moreover, our eyes failed,
looking in vain for help;
from our towers we watched
for a nation that could not
save us.   Jer 37:7

¹⁸Men stalked us at every step,
so we could not walk in our
streets.
Our end was near, our days
were numbered,
for our end had come.

¹⁹Our pursuers were swifter
than eagles in the sky; Dt 28:49
they chased us over the
mountains   Lev 26:36
and lay in wait for us in the
desert.   Jer 52:7

²⁰The Lᴏʀᴅ's anointed, our
very life breath,   1Sa 26:9
was caught in their traps.
We thought that under his
shadow
we would live among the
nations.   Ps 91:1

²¹Rejoice and be glad,
O Daughter of Edom,
you who live in the land of
Uz.   Ge 10:23
But to you also the cup will
be passed;   Ps 16:5
you will be drunk and
stripped naked.   Isa 34:6-10

²²O Daughter of Zion, your
punishment will end;
he will not prolong your
exile.

But, O Daughter of Edom, he
will punish your sin
and expose your
wickedness.   Ps 137:7

5 Remember, O Lᴏʀᴅ, what
has happened to us;
look, and see our disgrace.
²Our inheritance has been
turned over to aliens,
our homes to foreigners.
³We have become orphans
and fatherless,
our mothers like widows.
⁴We must buy the water we
drink;   Isa 55:1
our wood can be had only
at a price.   Isa 3:1
⁵Those who pursue us are at
our heels;
we are weary and find no
rest.   Jos 1:13
⁶We submitted to Egypt and
Assyria   Jer 2:36
to get enough bread.
⁷Our fathers sinned and are
no more,
and we bear their
punishment.   Jer 14:20
⁸Slaves rule over us,
and there is none to free us
from their hands.   Zec 11:6
⁹We get our bread at the risk
of our lives
because of the sword in the
desert.
¹⁰Our skin is hot as an oven,
feverish from hunger.
¹¹Women have been ravished
in Zion,   Ge 34:29
and virgins in the towns of
Judah.
¹²Princes have been hung up
by their hands;

elders are shown no
respect. Lev 19:32
¹³Young men toil at the
millstones;
boys stagger under loads of
wood.
¹⁴The elders are gone from the
city gate;
the young men have
stopped their music.
¹⁵Joy is gone from our hearts;
our dancing has turned to
mourning. Jer 25:10
¹⁶The crown has fallen from
our head. Job 19:9
Woe to us, for we have
sinned! Isa 3:11
¹⁷Because of this our hearts are
faint, Jer 8:18
because of these things our
eyes grow dim Ps 6:7

¹⁸for Mount Zion, which lies
desolate, Ps 74:2-3
with jackals prowling
over it.

¹⁹You, O LORD, reign forever;
your throne endures from
generation to
generation. Ps 45:6
²⁰Why do you always forget
us? Ps 13:1
Why do you forsake us so
long? Ps 71:11
²¹Restore us to yourself,
O LORD, that we
may return;
renew our days as of old
²²unless you have utterly
rejected us Ps 53:5
and are angry with us
beyond measure. Isa 64:9

Ezekiel

Introduction:

This book is named after the prophet Ezekiel, which means "God is strong." His messages are dated between the years 593–571 B.C. and were given to his fellow exiles in Babylonian captivity.

Born in 623 B.C. to a priestly family, Ezekiel grew up in the surroundings of the temple in Jerusalem. In 597 B.C. he was included in the exile to Babylon. It was in 593 B.C. that he was called by God in a divine revelation to be a prophet.

During the first part of his ministry Ezekiel proclaimed basically the same message given by Jeremiah—Jerusalem and the temple were doomed to destruction because of the sinfulness and idolatry of the people.

After the news reached Babylon that Jerusalem actually had been destroyed in 586 B.C. Ezekiel proclaimed a new message of hope and restoration—God would regather the Israelites from the ends of the earth and re-establish them in their own land. The nations who challenged Israel's return would be defeated and judged.

Outline of contents:

The Living Creatures and the Glory of the LORD

1 In the*ᵃ* thirtieth year, in the fourth month on the fifth day, while I was among the exiles by the Kebar River, the heavens were opened and I saw visions of God.   Dt 21:10; Mt 3:16

²On the fifth of the month—it was the fifth year of the exile of King Jehoiachin— ³the word of the LORD came to Ezekiel the priest, the son of Buzi,ᵇ by the Kebar River in the land of the

ᵃ1 Or ⸤my⸥   ᵇ3 Or *Ezekiel son of Buzi the priest*

Babylonians.^a There the hand
of the LORD was upon him.

4I looked, and I saw a windstorm coming out of the
north—an immense cloud with
flashing lightning and surrounded by brilliant light. The
center of the fire looked like
glowing metal, 5and in the fire
was what looked like four living
creatures. In appearance their
form was that of a man, 6but
each of them had four faces and
four wings. 7Their legs were
straight; their feet were like
those of a calf and gleamed like
burnished bronze. 8Under their
wings on their four sides they
had the hands of a man. All four
of them had faces and wings,
9and their wings touched one
another. Each one went straight
ahead; they did not turn as they
moved.   Job 38:1; Eze 10:22; 40:3

10Their faces looked like this:
Each of the four had the face of a
man, and on the right side each
had the face of a lion, and on the
left the face of an ox; each also
had the face of an eagle. 11Such
were their faces. Their wings
were spread out upward; each
had two wings, one touching
the wing of another creature on
either side, and two wings
covering its body. 12Each one
went straight ahead. Wherever
the spirit would go, they would
go, without turning as they
went. 13The appearance of the
living creatures was like burning coals of fire or like torches.

Fire moved back and forth
among the creatures; it was
bright, and lightning flashed
out of it. 14The creatures sped
back and forth like flashes of
lightning.   Ps 29:7; Eze 10:14

15As I looked at the living
creatures, I saw a wheel on the
ground beside each creature
with its four faces. 16This was
the appearance and structure of
the wheels: They sparkled like
chrysolite, and all four looked
alike. Each appeared to be made
like a wheel intersecting a
wheel. 17As they moved, they
would go in any one of the four
directions the creatures faced;
the wheels did not turn about^b
as the creatures went. 18Their
rims were high and awesome,
and all four rims were full of
eyes all around.   Eze 3:13; Rev 4:6

19When the living creatures
moved, the wheels beside them
moved; and when the living
creatures rose from the ground,
the wheels also rose. 20Wher-
ever the spirit would go, they
would go, and the wheels
would rise along with them, because the spirit of the living
creatures was in the wheels.
21When the creatures moved,
they also moved; when the creatures stood still, they also stood
still; and when the creatures
rose from the ground, the
wheels rose along with them,
because the spirit of the living
creatures was in the wheels.

22Spread out above the heads

of the living creatures was what looked like an expanse, sparkling like ice, and awesome. ²³Under the expanse their wings were stretched out one toward the other, and each had two wings covering its body. ²⁴When the creatures moved, I heard the sound of their wings, like the roar of rushing waters, like the voice of the Almighty,ᵃ like the tumult of an army. When they stood still, they lowered their wings.   Ps 46:3; Eze 10:1

²⁵Then there came a voice from above the expanse over their heads as they stood with lowered wings. ²⁶Above the expanse over their heads was what looked like a throne of sapphire,ᵇ and high above on the throne was a figure like that of a man. ²⁷I saw that from what appeared to be his waist up he looked like glowing metal, as if full of fire, and that from there down he looked like fire; and brilliant light surrounded him. ²⁸Like the appearance of a rainbow in the clouds on a rainy day, so was the radiance around him.   1Ki 22:19; Eze 8:2

This was the appearance of the likeness of the glory of the LORD. When I saw it, I fell facedown, and I heard the voice of one speaking.   Ge 17:3; Ex 16:7

Ezekiel's Call

2 He said to me, "Son of man, stand up on your feet and I will speak to you." ²As he

spoke, the Spirit came into me and raised me to my feet, and I heard him speaking to me.

³He said: "Son of man, I am sending you to the Israelites, to a rebellious nation that has rebelled against me; they and their fathers have been in revolt against me to this very day. ⁴The people to whom I am sending you are obstinate and stubborn. Say to them, 'This is what the Sovereign LORD says.' ⁵And whether they listen or fail to listen—for they are a rebellious house—they will know that a prophet has been among them. ⁶And you, son of man, do not be afraid of them or their words. Do not be afraid, though briers and thorns are all around you and you live among scorpions. Do not be afraid of what they say or terrified by them, though they are a rebellious house. ⁷You must speak my words to them, whether they listen or fail to listen, for they are rebellious. ⁸But you, son of man, listen to what I say to you. Do not rebel like that rebellious house; open your mouth and eat what I give you."   Jer 3:25

⁹Then I looked, and I saw a hand stretched out to me. In it was a scroll, ¹⁰which he unrolled before me. On both sides of it were written words of lament and mourning and woe.

3 And he said to me, "Son of man, eat what is before you, eat this scroll; then go and

---

ᵃ24 Hebrew *Shaddai*   ᵇ26 Or *lapis lazuli*

speak to the house of Israel."
²So I opened my mouth, and he
gave me the scroll to eat.

³Then he said to me, "Son of
man, eat this scroll I am giving
you and fill your stomach with
it." So I ate it, and it tasted as
sweet as honey in my mouth.

⁴He then said to me: "Son of
man, go now to the house of
Israel and speak my words to
them. ⁵You are not being sent to
a people of obscure speech and
difficult language, but to the
house of Israel— ⁶not to many
peoples of obscure speech and
difficult language, whose
words you cannot understand.
Surely if I had sent you to them,
they would have listened to
you. ⁷But the house of Israel is
not willing to listen to you because they are not willing to listen to me, for the whole house
of Israel is hardened and obstinate. ⁸But I will make you as
unyielding and hardened as
they are. ⁹I will make your forehead like the hardest stone,
harder than flint. Do not be
afraid of them or terrified by
them, though they are a rebellious house." Jer 3:25

¹⁰And he said to me, "Son of
man, listen carefully and take to
heart all the words I speak to
you. ¹¹Go now to your countrymen in exile and speak to them.
Say to them, 'This is what the
Sovereign LORD says,' whether
they listen or fail to listen."

¹²Then the Spirit lifted me up,
and I heard behind me a loud
rumbling sound—May the
glory of the LORD be praised in
his dwelling place!— ¹³the
sound of the wings of the living
creatures brushing against each
other and the sound of the
wheels beside them, a loud
rumbling sound. ¹⁴The Spirit
then lifted me up and took me
away, and I went in bitterness
and in the anger of my spirit,
with the strong hand of the
LORD upon me. ¹⁵I came to the
exiles who lived at Tel Abib near
the Kebar River. And there,
where they were living, I sat
among them for seven days—
overwhelmed. Eze 8:3

Warning to Israel

¹⁶At the end of seven days the
word of the LORD came to me:
¹⁷"Son of man, I have made you
a watchman for the house of Israel; so hear the word I speak
and give them warning from
me. ¹⁸When I say to a wicked
man, 'You will surely die,' and
you do not warn him or speak
out to dissuade him from his
evil ways in order to save his
life, that wicked man will die
for[a] his sin, and I will hold you
accountable for his blood. ¹⁹But
if you do warn the wicked man
and he does not turn from his
wickedness or from his evil
ways, he will die for his sin; but
you will have saved yourself.

²⁰"Again, when a righteous
man turns from his righteous-

---

a18 Or in; also in verses 19 and 20

ness and does evil, and I put a stumbling block before him, he will die. Since you did not warn him, he will die for his sin. The righteous things he did will not be remembered, and I will hold you accountable for his blood. 21But if you do warn the righteous man not to sin and he does not sin, he will surely live because he took warning, and you will have saved yourself." Ac 20:31

22The hand of the LORD was upon me there, and he said to me, "Get up and go out to the plain, and there I will speak to you." 23So I got up and went out to the plain. And the glory of the LORD was standing there, like the glory I had seen by the Kebar River, and I fell face-down. Ge 17:3; Eze 1:3

24Then the Spirit came into me and raised me to my feet. He spoke to me and said: "Go, shut yourself inside your house. 25And you, son of man, they will tie with ropes; you will be bound so that you cannot go out among the people. 26I will make your tongue stick to the roof of your mouth so that you will be silent and unable to rebuke them, though they are a rebellious house. 27But when I speak to you, I will open your mouth and you shall say to them, 'This is what the Sovereign LORD says.' Whoever will listen let him listen, and whoever will refuse let him refuse; for they are a rebellious house. Eze 2:2

Siege of Jerusalem Symbolized

4 "Now, son of man, take a clay tablet, put it in front of you and draw the city of Jerusalem on it. 2Then lay siege to it: Erect siege works against it, build a ramp up to it, set up camps against it and put battering rams around it. 3Then take an iron pan, place it as an iron wall between you and the city and turn your face toward it. It will be under siege, and you shall besiege it. This will be a sign to the house of Israel.

4"Then lie on your left side and put the sin of the house of Israel upon yourself.a You are to bear their sin for the number of days you lie on your side. 5I have assigned you the same number of days as the years of their sin. So for 390 days you will bear the sin of the house of Israel. Nu 14:34; 18:1

6"After you have finished this, lie down again, this time on your right side, and bear the sin of the house of Judah. I have assigned you 40 days, a day for each year. 7Turn your face toward the siege of Jerusalem and with bared arm prophesy against her. 8I will tie you up with ropes so that you cannot turn from one side to the other until you have finished the days of your siege. Ex 28:38; Eze 3:25

9"Take wheat and barley, beans and lentils, millet and spelt; put them in a storage jar

a4 Or your side

and use them to make bread for yourself. You are to eat it during the 390 days you lie on your side. ¹⁰Weigh out twenty shekels*a* of food to eat each day and eat it at set times. ¹¹Also measure out a sixth of a hin*b* of water and drink it at set times. ¹²Eat the food as you would a barley cake; bake it in the sight of the people, using human excrement for fuel." ¹³The LORD said, "In this way the people of Israel will eat defiled food among the nations where I will drive them." Isa 28:25; Hos 9:3

¹⁴Then I said, "Not so, Sovereign LORD! I have never defiled myself. From my youth until now I have never eaten anything found dead or torn by wild animals. No unclean meat has ever entered my mouth."

¹⁵"Very well," he said, "I will let you bake your bread over cow manure instead of human excrement."

¹⁶He then said to me: "Son of man, I will cut off the supply of food in Jerusalem. The people will eat rationed food in anxiety and drink rationed water in despair, ¹⁷for food and water will be scarce. They will be appalled at the sight of each other and will waste away because of*c* their sin. Ps 105:16; La 5:4

5 "Now, son of man, take a sharp sword and use it as a barber's razor to shave your head and your beard. Then take a set of scales and divide up the hair. ²When the days of your siege come to an end, burn a third of the hair with fire inside the city. Take a third and strike it with the sword all around the city. And scatter a third to the wind. For I will pursue them with drawn sword. ³But take a few strands of hair and tuck them away in the folds of your garment. ⁴Again, take a few of these and throw them into the fire and burn them up. A fire will spread from there to the whole house of Israel. Nu 6:5

⁵"This is what the Sovereign LORD says: This is Jerusalem, which I have set in the center of the nations, with countries all around her. ⁶Yet in her wickedness she has rebelled against my laws and decrees more than the nations and countries around her. She has rejected my laws and has not followed my decrees. Dt 4:6; 2Ki 17:15

⁷"Therefore this is what the Sovereign LORD says: You have been more unruly than the nations around you and have not followed my decrees or kept my laws. You have not even*d* conformed to the standards of the nations around you. 2Ki 21:9

⁸"Therefore this is what the Sovereign LORD says: I myself am against you, Jerusalem, and I will inflict punishment on you in the sight of the nations. ⁹Because of all your detestable

a10 That is, about 8 ounces (about 0.2 kilogram)   *b11* That is, about 2/3 quart (about 0.6 liter)   *c17* Or *away in*   *d7* Most Hebrew manuscripts; some Hebrew manuscripts and Syriac *You have*

idols, I will do to you what I have never done before and will never do again. [10]Therefore in your midst fathers will eat their children, and children will eat their fathers. I will inflict punishment on you and will scatter all your survivors to the winds. [11]Therefore as surely as I live, declares the Sovereign LORD, because you have defiled my sanctuary with all your vile images and detestable practices, I myself will withdraw my favor; I will not look on you with pity or spare you. [12]A third of your people will die of the plague or perish by famine inside you; a third will fall by the sword outside your walls; and a third I will scatter to the winds and pursue with drawn sword.Da 9:12

[13]"Then my anger will cease and my wrath against them will subside, and I will be avenged. And when I have spent my wrath upon them, they will know that I the LORD have spoken in my zeal.　　2Ch 12:7

[14]"I will make you a ruin and a reproach among the nations around you, in the sight of all who pass by. [15]You will be a reproach and a taunt, a warning and an object of horror to the nations around you when I inflict punishment on you in anger and in wrath and with stinging rebuke. I the LORD have spoken. [16]When I shoot at you with my deadly and destructive arrows of famine, I will shoot to destroy you. I will bring more and more famine upon you and cut off your supply of food. [17]I will send famine and wild beasts against you, and they will leave you childless. Plague and bloodshed will sweep through you, and I will bring the sword against you. I the LORD have spoken."　　Lev 26:32

A Prophecy Against the Mountains of Israel

6 The word of the LORD came to me: [2]"Son of man, set your face against the mountains of Israel; prophesy against them [3]and say: 'O mountains of Israel, hear the word of the Sovereign LORD. This is what the Sovereign LORD says to the mountains and hills, to the ravines and valleys: I am about to bring a sword against you, and I will destroy your high places. [4]Your altars will be demolished and your incense altars will be smashed; and I will slay your people in front of your idols. [5]I will lay the dead bodies of the Israelites in front of their idols, and I will scatter your bones around your altars. [6]Wherever you live, the towns will be laid waste and the high places demolished, so that your altars will be laid waste and devastated, your idols smashed and ruined, your incense altars broken down, and what you have made wiped out. [7]Your people will fall slain among you, and you will know that I am the LORD.　　Eze 4:7; Zec 13:2

[8]" 'But I will spare some, for

some of you will escape the sword when you are scattered among the lands and nations. ⁹Then in the nations where they have been carried captive, those who escape will remember me—how I have been grieved by their adulterous hearts, which have turned away from me, and by their eyes, which have lusted after their idols. They will loathe themselves for the evil they have done and for all their detestable practices. ¹⁰And they will know that I am the LORD; I did not threaten in vain to bring this calamity on them.   Dt 28:52; Ps 68:20

¹¹" 'This is what the Sovereign LORD says: Strike your hands together and stamp your feet and cry out "Alas!" because of all the wicked and detestable practices of the house of Israel, for they will fall by the sword, famine and plague. ¹²He that is far away will die of the plague, and he that is near will fall by the sword, and he that survives and is spared will die of famine. So will I spend my wrath upon them. ¹³And they will know that I am the LORD, when their people lie slain among their idols around their altars, on every high hill and on all the mountaintops, under every spreading tree and every leafy oak—places where they offered fragrant incense to all their idols. ¹⁴And I will stretch out my

hand against them and make the land a desolate waste from the desert to Diblah[a]— wherever they live. Then they will know that I am the LORD.' "   Ex 7:5; Jer 42:22

The End Has Come

7 The word of the LORD came to me: ²"Son of man, this is what the Sovereign LORD says to the land of Israel: The end! The end has come upon the four corners of the land. ³The end is now upon you and I will unleash my anger against you. I will judge you according to your conduct and repay you for all your detestable practices. ⁴I will not look on you with pity or spare you; I will surely repay you for your conduct and the detestable practices among you. Then you will know that I am the LORD.   Jer 13:14; Am 8:2

⁵"This is what the Sovereign LORD says: Disaster! An unheard-of[b] disaster is coming. ⁶The end has come! The end has come! It has roused itself against you. It has come! ⁷Doom has come upon you—you who dwell in the land. The time has come, the day is near; there is panic, not joy, upon the mountains. ⁸I am about to pour out my wrath on you and spend my anger against you; I will judge you according to your conduct and repay you for all your detestable practices. ⁹I will not

---

[a]14 Most Hebrew manuscripts; a few Hebrew manuscripts *Riblah*   [b]5 Most Hebrew manuscripts; some Hebrew manuscripts and Syriac *Disaster after*

look on you with pity or spare you; I will repay you in accordance with your conduct and the detestable practices among you. Then you will know that it is I the LORD who strikes the blow.

10"The day is here! It has come! Doom has burst forth, the rod has budded, arrogance has blossomed! 11Violence has grown into*a* a rod to punish wickedness; none of the people will be left, none of that crowd—no wealth, nothing of value. 12The time has come, the day has arrived. Let not the buyer rejoice nor the seller grieve, for wrath is upon the whole crowd. 13The seller will not recover the land he has sold as long as both of them live, for the vision concerning the whole crowd will not be reversed. Because of their sins, not one of them will preserve his life. 14Though they blow the trumpet and get everything ready, no one will go into battle, for my wrath is upon the whole crowd.

15"Outside is the sword, inside are plague and famine; those in the country will die by the sword, and those in the city will be devoured by famine and plague. 16All who survive and escape will be in the mountains, moaning like doves of the valleys, each because of his sins. 17Every hand will go limp, and every knee will become as weak as water. 18They will put on sackcloth and be clothed with terror. Their faces will be covered with shame and their heads will be shaved. 19They will throw their silver into the streets, and their gold will be an unclean thing. Their silver and gold will not be able to save them in the day of the LORD's wrath. They will not satisfy their hunger or fill their stomachs with it, for it has made them stumble into sin. 20They were proud of their beautiful jewelry and used it to make their detestable idols and vile images. Therefore I will turn these into an unclean thing for them. 21I will hand it all over as plunder to foreigners and as loot to the wicked of the earth, and they will defile it. 22I will turn my face away from them, and they will desecrate my treasured place; robbers will enter it and desecrate it.   Nu 14:3; Dt 32:25

23"Prepare chains, because the land is full of bloodshed and the city is full of violence. 24I will bring the most wicked of the nations to take possession of their houses; I will put an end to the pride of the mighty, and their sanctuaries will be desecrated. 25When terror comes, they will seek peace, but there will be none. 26Calamity upon calamity will come, and rumor upon rumor. They will try to get a vision from the prophet; the teaching of the law by the priest will be lost, as will the counsel of the elders. 27The king will mourn,

a11 Or *The violent one has become*

the prince will be clothed with despair, and the hands of the people of the land will tremble. I will deal with them according to their conduct, and by their own standards I will judge them. Then they will know that I am the LORD.'" Eze 11:6

Idolatry in the Temple

8 In the sixth year, in the sixth month on the fifth day, while I was sitting in my house and the elders of Judah were sitting before me, the hand of the Sovereign LORD came upon me there. ²I looked, and I saw a figure like that of a man.ᵃ From what appeared to be his waist down he was like fire, and from there up his appearance was as bright as glowing metal. ³He stretched out what looked like a hand and took me by the hair of my head. The Spirit lifted me up between earth and heaven and in visions of God he took me to Jerusalem, to the entrance to the north gate of the inner court, where the idol that provokes to jealousy stood. ⁴And there before me was the glory of the God of Israel, as in the vision I had seen in the plain. Dt 32:16

⁵Then he said to me, "Son of man, look toward the north." So I looked, and in the entrance north of the gate of the altar I saw this idol of jealousy. Ps 78:58

⁶And he said to me, "Son of man, do you see what they are doing—the utterly detestable things the house of Israel is doing here, things that will drive me far from my sanctuary? But you will see things that are even more detestable." Ps 78:60

⁷Then he brought me to the entrance to the court. I looked, and I saw a hole in the wall. ⁸He said to me, "Son of man, now dig into the wall." So I dug into the wall and saw a doorway there.

⁹And he said to me, "Go in and see the wicked and detestable things they are doing here." ¹⁰So I went in and looked, and I saw portrayed all over the walls all kinds of crawling things and detestable animals and all the idols of the house of Israel. ¹¹In front of them stood seventy elders of the house of Israel, and Jaazaniah son of Shaphan was standing among them. Each had a censer in his hand, and a fragrant cloud of incense was rising. Eze 11:1-2

¹²He said to me, "Son of man, have you seen what the elders of the house of Israel are doing in the darkness, each at the shrine of his own idol? They say, 'The LORD does not see us; the LORD has forsaken the land.'" ¹³Again, he said, "You will see them doing things that are even more detestable."

¹⁴Then he brought me to the entrance to the north gate of the house of the LORD, and I saw women sitting there, mourning

---

ᵃ2 Or *saw a fiery figure*

for Tammuz. ¹⁵He said to me, "Do you see this, son of man? You will see things that are even more detestable than this."

¹⁶He then brought me into the inner court of the house of the Lord, and there at the entrance to the temple, between the portico and the altar, were about twenty-five men. With their backs toward the temple of the Lord and their faces toward the east, they were bowing down to the sun in the east. ^{Joel 2:17}

¹⁷He said to me, "Have you seen this, son of man? Is it a trivial matter for the house of Judah to do the detestable things they are doing here? Must they also fill the land with violence and continually provoke me to anger? Look at them putting the branch to their nose! ¹⁸Therefore I will deal with them in anger; I will not look on them with pity or spare them. Although they shout in my ears, I will not listen to them." ^{Eze 16:2}

Idolaters Killed

9 Then I heard him call out in a loud voice, "Bring the guards of the city here, each with a weapon in his hand." ²And I saw six men coming from the direction of the upper gate, which faces north, each with a deadly weapon in his hand. With them was a man clothed in linen who had a writing kit at his side. They came in and stood beside the bronze altar.

³Now the glory of the God of Israel went up from above the cherubim, where it had been, and moved to the threshold of the temple. Then the Lord called to the man clothed in linen who had the writing kit at his side ⁴and said to him, "Go throughout the city of Jerusalem and put a mark on the foreheads of those who grieve and lament over all the detestable things that are done in it." ^{Lev 16:4}

⁵As I listened, he said to the others, "Follow him through the city and kill, without showing pity or compassion. ⁶Slaughter old men, young men and maidens, women and children, but do not touch anyone who has the mark. Begin at my sanctuary." So they began with the elders who were in front of the temple. ^{Ge 4:15; Jer 13:14}

⁷Then he said to them, "Defile the temple and fill the courts with the slain. Go!" So they went out and began killing throughout the city. ⁸While they were killing and I was left alone, I fell facedown, crying out, "Ah, Sovereign Lord! Are you going to destroy the entire remnant of Israel in this outpouring of your wrath on Jerusalem?" ^{Jos 7:6; Eze 6:7}

⁹He answered me, "The sin of the house of Israel and Judah is exceedingly great; the land is full of bloodshed and the city is full of injustice. They say, 'The Lord has forsaken the land; the Lord does not see.' ¹⁰So I will not look on them with pity or spare them, but I will bring

down on their own heads what they have done." Ps 58:2; Jer 13:14

[11]Then the man in linen with the writing kit at his side brought back word, saying, "I have done as you commanded." Ge 6:22

The Glory Departs From the Temple

10 I looked, and I saw the likeness of a throne of sapphire[a] above the expanse that was over the heads of the cherubim. [2]The LORD said to the man clothed in linen, "Go in among the wheels beneath the cherubim. Fill your hands with burning coals from among the cherubim and scatter them over the city." And as I watched, he went in. Eze 9:2; Rev 4:2

[3]Now the cherubim were standing on the south side of the temple when the man went in, and a cloud filled the inner court. [4]Then the glory of the LORD rose from above the cherubim and moved to the threshold of the temple. The cloud filled the temple, and the court was full of the radiance of the glory of the LORD. [5]The sound of the wings of the cherubim could be heard as far away as the outer court, like the voice of God Almighty[b] when he speaks.

[6]When the LORD commanded the man in linen, "Take fire from among the wheels, from among the cherubim," the man went in and stood beside a wheel. [7]Then one of the cherubim reached out his hand to the fire that was among them. He took up some of it and put it into the hands of the man in linen, who took it and went out. [8](Under the wings of the cherubim could be seen what looked like the hands of a man.) Da 7:9

[9]I looked, and I saw beside the cherubim four wheels, one beside each of the cherubim; the wheels sparkled like chrysolite. [10]As for their appearance, the four of them looked alike; each was like a wheel intersecting a wheel. [11]As they moved, they would go in any one of the four directions the cherubim faced; the wheels did not turn about[c] as the cherubim went. The cherubim went in whatever direction the head faced, without turning as they went. [12]Their entire bodies, including their backs, their hands and their wings, were completely full of eyes, as were their four wheels. [13]I heard the wheels being called "the whirling wheels." [14]Each of the cherubim had four faces: One face was that of a cherub, the second the face of a man, the third the face of a lion, and the fourth the face of an eagle.

[15]Then the cherubim rose upward. These were the living creatures I had seen by the Kebar River. [16]When the cherubim moved, the wheels beside them moved; and when the cherubim spread their wings to rise from

---

[a]1 Or *lapis lazuli*   [b]5 Hebrew *El-Shaddai*   [c]11 Or *aside*

the ground, the wheels did not leave their side. [17]When the cherubim stood still, they also stood still; and when the cherubim rose, they rose with them, because the spirit of the living creatures was in them.   Isa 6:2

[18]Then the glory of the LORD departed from over the threshold of the temple and stopped above the cherubim. [19]While I watched, the cherubim spread their wings and rose from the ground, and as they went, the wheels went with them. They stopped at the entrance to the east gate of the LORD's house, and the glory of the God of Israel was above them.   1Sa 4:21

[20]These were the living creatures I had seen beneath the God of Israel by the Kebar River, and I realized that they were cherubim. [21]Each had four faces and four wings, and under their wings was what looked like the hands of a man. [22]Their faces had the same appearance as those I had seen by the Kebar River. Each one went straight ahead.   Eze 1:1; 41:18

Judgment on Israel's Leaders

11 Then the Spirit lifted me up and brought me to the gate of the house of the LORD that faces east. There at the entrance to the gate were twenty-five men, and I saw among them Jaazaniah son of Azzur and Pelatiah son of Benaiah, leaders of the people. [2]The

LORD said to me, "Son of man, these are the men who are plotting evil and giving wicked advice in this city. [3]They say, 'Will it not soon be time to build houses?[a] This city is a cooking pot, and we are the meat.' [4]Therefore prophesy against them; prophesy, son of man."

[5]Then the Spirit of the LORD came upon me, and he told me to say: "This is what the LORD says: That is what you are saying, O house of Israel, but I know what is going through your mind. [6]You have killed many people in this city and filled its streets with the dead.

[7]"Therefore this is what the Sovereign LORD says: The bodies you have thrown there are the meat and this city is the pot, but I will drive you out of it. [8]You fear the sword, and the sword is what I will bring against you, declares the Sovereign LORD. [9]I will drive you out of the city and hand you over to foreigners and inflict punishment on you. [10]You will fall by the sword, and I will execute judgment on you at the borders of Israel. Then you will know that I am the LORD. [11]This city will not be a pot for you, nor will you be the meat in it; I will execute judgment on you at the borders of Israel. [12]And you will know that I am the LORD, for you have not followed my decrees or kept my laws but have

---

[a]3 Or This is not the time to build houses.

conformed to the standards of the nations around you."   Jer 1:13

¹³Now as I was prophesying, Pelatiah son of Benaiah died. Then I fell facedown and cried out in a loud voice, "Ah, Sovereign Lord! Will you completely destroy the remnant of Israel?"

¹⁴The word of the Lord came to me: ¹⁵"Son of man, your brothers—your brothers who are your blood relatives*a* and the whole house of Israel—are those of whom the people of Jerusalem have said, 'They are*b* far away from the Lord; this land was given to us as our possession.'   Eze 33:24

Promised Return of Israel

¹⁶"Therefore say: 'This is what the Sovereign Lord says: Although I sent them far away among the nations and scattered them among the countries, yet for a little while I have been a sanctuary for them in the countries where they have gone.'   Ps 31:20; Isa 4:6

¹⁷"Therefore say: 'This is what the Sovereign Lord says: I will gather you from the nations and bring you back from the countries where you have been scattered, and I will give you back the land of Israel again.'

¹⁸"They will return to it and remove all its vile images and detestable idols. ¹⁹I will give them an undivided heart and put a new spirit in them; I will remove from them their heart of stone and give them a heart of flesh. ²⁰Then they will follow my decrees and be careful to keep my laws. They will be my people, and I will be their God. ²¹But as for those whose hearts are devoted to their vile images and detestable idols, I will bring down on their own heads what they have done, declares the Sovereign Lord."   2Ch 30:12

²²Then the cherubim, with the wheels beside them, spread their wings, and the glory of the God of Israel was above them. ²³The glory of the Lord went up from within the city and stopped above the mountain east of it. ²⁴The Spirit lifted me up and brought me to the exiles in Babylonia*c* in the vision given by the Spirit of God.   Ex 24:16

Then the vision I had seen went up from me, ²⁵and I told the exiles everything the Lord had shown me.   Eze 3:4,11

The Exile Symbolized

12 The word of the Lord came to me: ²"Son of man, you are living among a rebellious people. They have eyes to see but do not see and ears to hear but do not hear, for they are a rebellious people.   Ps 78:40

³"Therefore, son of man, pack your belongings for exile and in the daytime, as they watch, set out and go from where you are to another place.

---

*a*15 Or *are in exile with you* (see Septuagint and Syriac)   *b*15 Or *those to whom the people of Jerusalem have said, 'Stay*   *c*24 Or *Chaldea*

Perhaps they will understand, though they are a rebellious house. ⁴During the daytime, while they watch, bring out your belongings packed for exile. Then in the evening, while they are watching, go out like those who go into exile. ⁵While they watch, dig through the wall and take your belongings out through it. ⁶Put them on your shoulder as they are watching and carry them out at dusk. Cover your face so that you cannot see the land, for I have made you a sign to the house of Israel." Jer 36:3

⁷So I did as I was commanded. During the day I brought out my things packed for exile. Then in the evening I dug through the wall with my hands. I took my belongings out at dusk, carrying them on my shoulders while they watched.

⁸In the morning the word of the LORD came to me: ⁹"Son of man, did not that rebellious house of Israel ask you, 'What are you doing?' Eze 17:12

¹⁰"Say to them, 'This is what the Sovereign LORD says: This oracle concerns the prince in Jerusalem and the whole house of Israel who are there.' ¹¹Say to them, 'I am a sign to you.'

"As I have done, so it will be done to them. They will go into exile as captives. Isa 8:18

¹²"The prince among them will put his things on his shoulder at dusk and leave, and a hole will be dug in the wall for him to go through. He will

cover his face so that he cannot see the land. ¹³I will spread my net for him, and he will be caught in my snare; I will bring him to Babylonia, the land of the Chaldeans, but he will not see it, and there he will die. ¹⁴I will scatter to the winds all those around him—his staff and all his troops—and I will pursue them with drawn sword. Jer 39:4

¹⁵"They will know that I am the LORD, when I disperse them among the nations and scatter them through the countries. ¹⁶But I will spare a few of them from the sword, famine and plague, so that in the nations where they go they may acknowledge all their detestable practices. Then they will know that I am the LORD." Lev 26:33

¹⁷The word of the LORD came to me: ¹⁸"Son of man, tremble as you eat your food, and shudder in fear as you drink your water. ¹⁹Say to the people of the land: 'This is what the Sovereign LORD says about those living in Jerusalem and in the land of Israel: They will eat their food in anxiety and drink their water in despair, for their land will be stripped of everything in it because of the violence of all who live there. ²⁰The inhabited towns will be laid waste and the land will be desolate. Then you will know that I am the LORD.'"

²¹The word of the LORD came to me: ²²"Son of man, what is this proverb you have in the land of Israel: 'The days go by and every vision comes to noth-

ing'? ²³Say to them, 'This is what the Sovereign Lord says: I am going to put an end to this proverb, and they will no longer quote it in Israel.' Say to them, 'The days are near when every vision will be fulfilled. ²⁴For there will be no more false visions or flattering divinations among the people of Israel. ²⁵But I the Lord will speak what I will, and it shall be fulfilled without delay. For in your days, you rebellious house, I will fulfill whatever I say, declares the Sovereign Lord.'"   Eze 7:7

²⁶The word of the Lord came to me: ²⁷"Son of man, the house of Israel is saying, 'The vision he sees is for many years from now, and he prophesies about the distant future.'   Eze 11:3

²⁸"Therefore say to them, 'This is what the Sovereign Lord says: None of my words will be delayed any longer; whatever I say will be fulfilled, declares the Sovereign Lord.'"

False Prophets Condemned

13 The word of the Lord came to me: ²"Son of man, prophesy against the prophets of Israel who are now prophesying. Say to those who prophesy out of their own imagination: 'Hear the word of the Lord! ³This is what the Sovereign Lord says: Woe to the foolish*ᵃ* prophets who follow their own spirit and have seen nothing! ⁴Your prophets, O Is-

rael, are like jackals among ruins. ⁵You have not gone up to the breaks in the wall to repair it for the house of Israel so that it will stand firm in the battle on the day of the Lord. ⁶Their visions are false and their divinations a lie. They say, "The Lord declares," when the Lord has not sent them; yet they expect their words to be fulfilled. ⁷Have you not seen false visions and uttered lying divinations when you say, "The Lord declares," though I have not spoken?   Isa 9:15; 30:10

⁸" 'Therefore this is what the Sovereign Lord says: Because of your false words and lying visions, I am against you, declares the Sovereign Lord. ⁹My hand will be against the prophets who see false visions and utter lying divinations. They will not belong to the council of my people or be listed in the records of the house of Israel, nor will they enter the land of Israel. Then you will know that I am the Sovereign Lord.   Jer 21:13

¹⁰" 'Because they lead my people astray, saying, "Peace," when there is no peace, and because, when a flimsy wall is built, they cover it with whitewash, ¹¹therefore tell those who cover it with whitewash that it is going to fall. Rain will come in torrents, and I will send hailstones hurtling down, and violent winds will burst forth. ¹²When the wall collapses, will

people not ask you, "Where is the whitewash you covered it with?" Jer 23:13; Eze 38:22

13" 'Therefore this is what the Sovereign LORD says: In my wrath I will unleash a violent wind, and in my anger hailstones and torrents of rain will fall with destructive fury. 14I will tear down the wall you have covered with whitewash and will level it to the ground so that its foundation will be laid bare. When it*a* falls, you will be destroyed in it; and you will know that I am the LORD. 15So I will spend my wrath against the wall and against those who covered it with whitewash. I will say to you, "The wall is gone and so are those who whitewashed it, 16those prophets of Israel who prophesied to Jerusalem and saw visions of peace for her when there was no peace, declares the Sovereign LORD." ' Jos 10:11; Isa 57:21

17"Now, son of man, set your face against the daughters of your people who prophesy out of their own imagination. Prophesy against them 18and say, 'This is what the Sovereign LORD says: Woe to the women who sew magic charms on all their wrists and make veils of various lengths for their heads in order to ensnare people. Will you ensnare the lives of my people but preserve your own? 19You have profaned me among my people for a few handfuls of barley and scraps of bread. By lying to my people, who listen to lies, you have killed those who should not have died and have spared those who should not live. Jer 44:26; Eze 4:7

20" 'Therefore this is what the Sovereign LORD says: I am against your magic charms with which you ensnare people like birds and I will tear them from your arms; I will set free the people that you ensnare like birds. 21I will tear off your veils and save my people from your hands, and they will no longer fall prey to your power. Then you will know that I am the LORD. 22Because you disheartened the righteous with your lies, when I had brought them no grief, and because you encouraged the wicked not to turn from their evil ways and so save their lives, 23therefore you will no longer see false visions or practice divination. I will save my people from your hands. And then you will know that I am the LORD.' " Ne 6:12; Ps 124:7

Idolaters Condemned

14 Some of the elders of Israel came to me and sat down in front of me. 2Then the word of the LORD came to me: 3"Son of man, these men have set up idols in their hearts and put wicked stumbling blocks before their faces. Should I let them inquire of me at all? 4Therefore speak to them and

tell them, 'This is what the Sovereign LORD says: When any Israelite sets up idols in his heart and puts a wicked stumbling block before his face and then goes to a prophet, I the LORD will answer him myself in keeping with his great idolatry. ⁵I will do this to recapture the hearts of the people of Israel, who have all deserted me for their idols.'   Dt 32:15; Eze 8:1

⁶"Therefore say to the house of Israel, 'This is what the Sovereign LORD says: Repent! Turn from your idols and renounce all your detestable practices!

⁷" 'When any Israelite or any alien living in Israel separates himself from me and sets up idols in his heart and puts a wicked stumbling block before his face and then goes to a prophet to inquire of me, I the LORD will answer him myself. ⁸I will set my face against that man and make him an example and a byword. I will cut him off from my people. Then you will know that I am the LORD.

⁹" 'And if the prophet is enticed to utter a prophecy, I the LORD have enticed that prophet, and I will stretch out my hand against him and destroy him from among my people Israel. ¹⁰They will bear their guilt—the prophet will be as guilty as the one who consults him. ¹¹Then the people of Israel will no longer stray from me, nor will they defile themselves anymore with all their sins. They will be my people, and I will be their God, declares the Sovereign LORD.' "   Jer 14:15

Judgment Inescapable

¹²The word of the LORD came to me: ¹³"Son of man, if a country sins against me by being unfaithful and I stretch out my hand against it to cut off its food supply and send famine upon it and kill its men and their animals, ¹⁴even if these three men—Noah, Daniel[a] and Job—were in it, they could save only themselves by their righteousness, declares the Sovereign LORD.   Ge 6:8; Pr 13:21

¹⁵"Or if I send wild beasts through that country and they leave it childless and it becomes desolate so that no one can pass through it because of the beasts, ¹⁶as surely as I live, declares the Sovereign LORD, even if these three men were in it, they could not save their own sons or daughters. They alone would be saved, but the land would be desolate.   Ge 19:29; Eze 5:17

¹⁷"Or if I bring a sword against that country and say, 'Let the sword pass throughout the land,' and I kill its men and their animals, ¹⁸as surely as I live, declares the Sovereign LORD, even if these three men were in it, they could not save

---

[a]14 Or *Danel*; the Hebrew spelling may suggest a person other than the prophet Daniel; also in verse 20.

their own sons or daughters. They alone would be saved.

¹⁹"Or if I send a plague into that land and pour out my wrath upon it through bloodshed, killing its men and their animals, ²⁰as surely as I live, declares the Sovereign LORD, even if Noah, Daniel and Job were in it, they could save neither son nor daughter. They would save only themselves by their righteousness. Eze 7:8; 38:22

²¹"For this is what the Sovereign LORD says: How much worse will it be when I send against Jerusalem my four dreadful judgments—sword and famine and wild beasts and plague—to kill its men and their animals! ²²Yet there will be some survivors—sons and daughters who will be brought out of it. They will come to you, and when you see their conduct and their actions, you will be consoled regarding the disaster I have brought upon Jerusalem—every disaster I have brought upon it. ²³You will be consoled when you see their conduct and their actions, for you will know that I have done nothing in it without cause, declares the Sovereign LORD."

Jerusalem, A Useless Vine

15 The word of the LORD came to me: ²"Son of man, how is the wood of a vine better than that of a branch on any of the trees in the forest? ³Is wood ever taken from it to make anything useful? Do they make pegs from it to hang things on? ⁴And after it is thrown on the fire as fuel and the fire burns both ends and chars the middle, is it then useful for anything? ⁵If it was not useful for anything when it was whole, how much less can it be made into something useful when the fire has burned it and it is charred? Jn 15:6

⁶"Therefore this is what the Sovereign LORD says: As I have given the wood of the vine among the trees of the forest as fuel for the fire, so will I treat the people living in Jerusalem. ⁷I will set my face against them. Although they have come out of the fire, the fire will yet consume them. And when I set my face against them, you will know that I am the LORD. ⁸I will make the land desolate because they have been unfaithful, declares the Sovereign LORD."

An Allegory of Unfaithful Jerusalem

16 The word of the LORD came to me: ²"Son of man, confront Jerusalem with her detestable practices ³and say, 'This is what the Sovereign LORD says to Jerusalem: Your ancestry and birth were in the land of the Canaanites; your father was an Amorite and your mother a Hittite. ⁴On the day you were born your cord was not cut, nor were you washed with water to make you clean, nor were you rubbed with salt or wrapped in cloths. ⁵No one

looked on you with pity or had compassion enough to do any of these things for you. Rather, you were thrown out into the open field, for on the day you were born you were despised.

6" 'Then I passed by and saw you kicking about in your blood, and as you lay there in your blood I said to you, "Live!"ᵃ ⁷I made you grow like a plant of the field. You grew up and developed and became the most beautiful of jewels.ᵇ Your breasts were formed and your hair grew, you who were naked and bare.   Ex 19:4; Dt 1:10

8" 'Later I passed by, and when I looked at you and saw that you were old enough for love, I spread the corner of my garment over you and covered your nakedness. I gave you my solemn oath and entered into a covenant with you, declares the Sovereign LORD, and you became mine.   Ru 3:9; Jer 11:10

9" 'I bathedᶜ you with water and washed the blood from you and put ointments on you. ¹⁰I clothed you with an embroidered dress and put leather sandals on you. I dressed you in fine linen and covered you with costly garments. ¹¹I adorned you with jewelry: I put bracelets on your arms and a necklace around your neck, ¹²and I put a ring on your nose, earrings on your ears and a beautiful crown on your head. ¹³So you were adorned with gold and silver; your clothes were of fine linen and costly fabric and embroidered cloth. Your food was fine flour, honey and olive oil. You became very beautiful and rose to be a queen. ¹⁴And your fame spread among the nations on account of your beauty, because the splendor I had given you made your beauty perfect, declares the Sovereign LORD.

15" 'But you trusted in your beauty and used your fame to become a prostitute. You lavished your favors on anyone who passed by and your beauty became his.ᵈ ¹⁶You took some of your garments to make gaudy high places, where you carried on your prostitution. Such things should not happen, nor should they ever occur. ¹⁷You also took the fine jewelry I gave you, the jewelry made of my gold and silver, and you made for yourself male idols and engaged in prostitution with them. ¹⁸And you took your embroidered clothes to put on them, and you offered my oil and incense before them. ¹⁹Also the food I provided for you—the fine flour, olive oil and honey I gave you to eat—you offered as fragrant incense before them. That is what happened, declares the Sovereign LORD.   Isa 57:8

ᵃ6 A few Hebrew manuscripts, Septuagint and Syriac; most Hebrew manuscripts *"Live!" And as you lay there in your blood I said to you, "Live!"*   ᵇ7 Or *became mature*   ᶜ9 Or *I had bathed*   ᵈ15 Most Hebrew manuscripts; one Hebrew manuscript (see some Septuagint manuscripts) *by. Such a thing should not happen*

²⁰" 'And you took your sons and daughters whom you bore to me and sacrificed them as food to the idols. Was your prostitution not enough? ²¹You slaughtered my children and sacrificed them*a* to the idols. ²²In all your detestable practices and your prostitution you did not remember the days of your youth, when you were naked and bare, kicking about in your blood. Ps 106:37-38; Hos 2:15

²³" 'Woe! Woe to you, declares the Sovereign LORD. In addition to all your other wickedness, ²⁴you built a mound for yourself and made a lofty shrine in every public square. ²⁵At the head of every street you built your lofty shrines and degraded your beauty, offering your body with increasing promiscuity to anyone who passed by. ²⁶You engaged in prostitution with the Egyptians, your lustful neighbors, and provoked me to anger with your increasing promiscuity. ²⁷So I stretched out my hand against you and reduced your territory; I gave you over to the greed of your enemies, the daughters of the Philistines, who were shocked by your lewd conduct. ²⁸You engaged in prostitution with the Assyrians too, because you were insatiable; and even after that, you still were not satisfied. ²⁹Then you increased your promiscuity to include Babylonia,*b* a land of merchants, but even with this you were not satisfied. Eze 24:6

³⁰" 'How weak-willed you are, declares the Sovereign LORD, when you do all these things, acting like a brazen prostitute! ³¹When you built your mounds at the head of every street and made your lofty shrines in every public square, you were unlike a prostitute, because you scorned payment. Isa 52:3; Jer 3:3

³²" 'You adulterous wife! You prefer strangers to your own husband! ³³Every prostitute receives a fee, but you give gifts to all your lovers, bribing them to come to you from everywhere for your illicit favors. ³⁴So in your prostitution you are the opposite of others; no one runs after you for your favors. You are the very opposite, for you give payment and none is given to you. Ge 30:15; Hos 8:9-10

³⁵" 'Therefore, you prostitute, hear the word of the LORD! ³⁶This is what the Sovereign LORD says: Because you poured out your wealth*c* and exposed your nakedness in your promiscuity with your lovers, and because of all your detestable idols, and because you gave them your children's blood, ³⁷therefore I am going to gather all your lovers, with whom you found pleasure, those you loved as well as those you hated. I will gather them against you from all around and will

*a*21 Or and made them pass through ⌊the fire⌋   *b*29 Or Chaldea   *c*36 Or lust

strip you in front of them, and they will see all your nakedness. ³⁸I will sentence you to the punishment of women who commit adultery and who shed blood; I will bring upon you the blood vengeance of my wrath and jealous anger. ³⁹Then I will hand you over to your lovers, and they will tear down your mounds and destroy your lofty shrines. They will strip you of your clothes and take your fine jewelry and leave you naked and bare. ⁴⁰They will bring a mob against you, who will stone you and hack you to pieces with their swords. ⁴¹They will burn down your houses and inflict punishment on you in the sight of many women. I will put a stop to your prostitution, and you will no longer pay your lovers. ⁴²Then my wrath against you will subside and my jealous anger will turn away from you; I will be calm and no longer angry.   Jer 19:5

⁴³" 'Because you did not remember the days of your youth but enraged me with all these things, I will surely bring down on your head what you have done, declares the Sovereign LORD. Did you not add lewdness to all your other detestable practices?   Ex 15:24

⁴⁴" 'Everyone who quotes proverbs will quote this proverb about you: "Like mother, like daughter." ⁴⁵You are a true daughter of your mother, who despised her husband and her children; and you are a true sister of your sisters, who despised their husbands and their children. Your mother was a Hittite and your father an Amorite. ⁴⁶Your older sister was Samaria, who lived to the north of you with her daughters; and your younger sister, who lived to the south of you with her daughters, was Sodom. ⁴⁷You not only walked in their ways and copied their detestable practices, but in all your ways you soon became more depraved than they. ⁴⁸As surely as I live, declares the Sovereign LORD, your sister Sodom and her daughters never did what you and your daughters have done.   Ps 49:4; Mt 10:15

⁴⁹" 'Now this was the sin of your sister Sodom: She and her daughters were arrogant, overfed and unconcerned; they did not help the poor and needy. ⁵⁰They were haughty and did detestable things before me. Therefore I did away with them as you have seen. ⁵¹Samaria did not commit half the sins you did. You have done more detestable things than they, and have made your sisters seem righteous by all these things you have done. ⁵²Bear your disgrace, for you have furnished some justification for your sisters. Because your sins were more vile than theirs, they appear more righteous than you. So then, be ashamed and bear your disgrace, for you have made your sisters appear righteous.   Isa 1:10; Jer 3:11

⁵³" 'However, I will restore the fortunes of Sodom and her daughters and of Samaria and her daughters, and your fortunes along with them, ⁵⁴so that you may bear your disgrace and be ashamed of all you have done in giving them comfort. ⁵⁵And your sisters, Sodom with her daughters and Samaria with her daughters, will return to what they were before; and you and your daughters will return to what you were before. ⁵⁶You would not even mention your sister Sodom in the day of your pride, ⁵⁷before your wickedness was uncovered. Even so, you are now scorned by the daughters of Edom*a* and all her neighbors and the daughters of the Philistines—all those around you who despise you. ⁵⁸You will bear the consequences of your lewdness and your detestable practices, declares the LORD.

⁵⁹" 'This is what the Sovereign LORD says: I will deal with you as you deserve, because you have despised my oath by breaking the covenant. ⁶⁰Yet I will remember the covenant I made with you in the days of your youth, and I will establish an everlasting covenant with you. ⁶¹Then you will remember your ways and be ashamed when you receive your sisters, both those who are older than you and those who are younger. I will give them to you as daughters, but not on the basis of my covenant with you. ⁶²So I will establish my covenant with you, and you will know that I am the LORD. ⁶³Then, when I make atonement for you for all you have done, you will remember and be ashamed and never again open your mouth because of your humiliation, declares the Sovereign LORD.' "

Two Eagles and a Vine

17 The word of the LORD came to me: ²"Son of man, set forth an allegory and tell the house of Israel a parable. ³Say to them, 'This is what the Sovereign LORD says: A great eagle with powerful wings, long feathers and full plumage of varied colors came to Lebanon. Taking hold of the top of a cedar, ⁴he broke off its topmost shoot and carried it away to a land of merchants, where he planted it in a city of traders.

⁵" 'He took some of the seed of your land and put it in fertile soil. He planted it like a willow by abundant water, ⁶and it sprouted and became a low, spreading vine. Its branches turned toward him, but its roots remained under it. So it became a vine and produced branches and put out leafy boughs. Dt 8:7-9

⁷" 'But there was another great eagle with powerful wings and full plumage. The vine now

---

a57 Many Hebrew manuscripts and Syriac; most Hebrew manuscripts, Septuagint and Vulgate *Aram*

sent out its roots toward him from the plot where it was planted and stretched out its branches to him for water. ⁸It had been planted in good soil by abundant water so that it would produce branches, bear fruit and become a splendid vine.'   Job 18:19; Eze 31:4

⁹"Say to them, 'This is what the Sovereign LORD says: Will it thrive? Will it not be uprooted and stripped of its fruit so that it withers? All its new growth will wither. It will not take a strong arm or many people to pull it up by the roots. ¹⁰Even if it is transplanted, will it thrive? Will it not wither completely when the east wind strikes it—wither away in the plot where it grew?' "   Jer 42:10; Hos 12:1

¹¹Then the word of the LORD came to me: ¹²"Say to this rebellious house, 'Do you not know what these things mean?' Say to them: 'The king of Babylon went to Jerusalem and carried off her king and her nobles, bringing them back with him to Babylon. ¹³Then he took a member of the royal family and made a treaty with him, putting him under oath. He also carried away the leading men of the land, ¹⁴so that the kingdom would be brought low, unable to rise again, surviving only by keeping his treaty. ¹⁵But the king rebelled against him by sending his envoys to Egypt to get horses and a large army. Will he succeed? Will he who does such things escape? Will he break the treaty and yet escape?   Jer 52:3; Eze 12:8

¹⁶" 'As surely as I live, declares the Sovereign LORD, he shall die in Babylon, in the land of the king who put him on the throne, whose oath he despised and whose treaty he broke. ¹⁷Pharaoh with his mighty army and great horde will be of no help to him in war, when ramps are built and siege works erected to destroy many lives. ¹⁸He despised the oath by breaking the covenant. Because he had given his hand in pledge and yet did all these things, he shall not escape.   1Ch 29:24; Eze 12:13

¹⁹" 'Therefore this is what the Sovereign LORD says: As surely as I live, I will bring down on his head my oath that he despised and my covenant that he broke. ²⁰I will spread my net for him, and he will be caught in my snare. I will bring him to Babylon and execute judgment upon him there because he was unfaithful to me. ²¹All his fleeing troops will fall by the sword, and the survivors will be scattered to the winds. Then you will know that I the LORD have spoken.   Jer 7:9; Eze 12:14

²²" 'This is what the Sovereign LORD says: I myself will take a shoot from the very top of a cedar and plant it; I will break off a tender sprig from its topmost shoots and plant it on a high and lofty mountain. ²³On the mountain heights of Israel I will plant it; it will produce branches and bear fruit and

become a splendid cedar. Birds of every kind will nest in it; they will find shelter in the shade of its branches. ²⁴All the trees of the field will know that I the LORD bring down the tall tree and make the low tree grow tall. I dry up the green tree and make the dry tree flourish.

" 'I the LORD have spoken, and I will do it.' "   Ps 96:12

The Soul Who Sins Will Die

18 The word of the LORD came to me: ²"What do you people mean by quoting this proverb about the land of Israel:

" 'The fathers eat sour
      grapes,
and the children's teeth are
      set on edge'?   Job 21:19

³"As surely as I live, declares the Sovereign LORD, you will no longer quote this proverb in Israel. ⁴For every living soul belongs to me, the father as well as the son—both alike belong to me. The soul who sins is the one who will die.   Ps 49:4; Isa 42:5

⁵"Suppose there is a righteous
      man
   who does what is just and
      right.
⁶He does not eat at the
      mountain shrines   Eze 6:2
   or look to the idols of the
      house of Israel.   Dt 4:19
He does not defile his
      neighbor's wife

or lie with a woman during
      her period.   Eze 6:2
⁷He does not oppress anyone,
   but returns what he took in
      pledge for a loan.   Ex 22:26
He does not commit robbery
   but gives his food to the
      hungry   Job 22:7
   and provides clothing for
      the naked.   Dt 15:11
⁸He does not lend at usury
   or take excessive interest. ^a
He withholds his hand from
      doing wrong
   and judges fairly between
      man and man.   Jer 22:3
⁹He follows my decrees
   and faithfully keeps my
      laws.   Lev 19:37
That man is righteous;
   he will surely live,   Hab 2:4
      declares the Sovereign
      LORD.

¹⁰"Suppose he has a violent son, who sheds blood or does any of these other things^b ¹¹(though the father has done none of them):   Ex 21:12; Eze 22:6

"He eats at the mountain
      shrines.   Eze 22:9
He defiles his neighbor's
      wife.
¹²He oppresses the poor and
      needy.   Ex 22:22
He commits robbery.
He does not return what he
      took in pledge.   Ex 22:27
He looks to the idols.
He does detestable things.
¹³He lends at usury and takes
      excessive interest.   Ex 22:25

^a8 Or *take interest*; similarly in verses 13 and 17   ^b10 Or *things to a brother*

Will such a man live? He will not! Because he has done all these detestable things, he will surely be put to death and his blood will be on his own head.

14"But suppose this son has a son who sees all the sins his father commits, and though he sees them, he does not do such things: 2Ch 34:21

15"He does not eat at the
     mountain shrines
  or look to the idols of the
     house of Israel.   Ps 24:4
  He does not defile his
     neighbor's wife.
16He does not oppress anyone
  or require a pledge for a
     loan.
  He does not commit robbery
  but gives his food to the
     hungry   Isa 58:7
  and provides clothing for
     the naked.   Ps 41:1
17He withholds his hand from
     sin[a]
  and takes no usury or
     excessive interest.
  He keeps my laws and
     follows my decrees.   Ps 1:2

He will not die for his father's sin; he will surely live. 18But his father will die for his own sin, because he practiced extortion, robbed his brother and did what was wrong among his people.

19"Yet you ask, 'Why does the son not share the guilt of his father?' Since the son has done what is just and right and has been careful to keep all my de-crees, he will surely live. 20The soul who sins is the one who will die. The son will not share the guilt of the father, nor will the father share the guilt of the son. The righteousness of the righteous man will be credited to him, and the wickedness of the wicked will be charged against him.   Ex 20:5; Nu 15:31

21"But if a wicked man turns away from all the sins he has committed and keeps all my decrees and does what is just and right, he will surely live; he will not die. 22None of the offenses he has committed will be remembered against him. Because of the righteous things he has done, he will live. 23Do I take any pleasure in the death of the wicked? declares the Sovereign LORD. Rather, am I not pleased when they turn from their ways and live?   Jer 18:8

24"But if a righteous man turns from his righteousness and commits sin and does the same detestable things the wicked man does, will he live? None of the righteous things he has done will be remembered. Because of the unfaithfulness he is guilty of and because of the sins he has committed, he will die.   Pr 21:16; Jer 34:16

25"Yet you say, 'The way of the Lord is not just.' Hear, O house of Israel: Is my way un-just? Is it not your ways that are unjust? 26If a righteous man turns from his righteousness

---

[a]17 Septuagint (see also verse 8); Hebrew *from the poor*

and commits sin, he will die for it; because of the sin he has committed he will die. ²⁷But if a wicked man turns away from the wickedness he has committed and does what is just and right, he will save his life. ²⁸Because he considers all the offenses he has committed and turns away from them, he will surely live; he will not die. ²⁹Yet the house of Israel says, 'The way of the Lord is not just.' Are my ways unjust, O house of Israel? Is it not your ways that are unjust?   Isa 55:7; Jer 2:29

³⁰"Therefore, O house of Israel, I will judge you, each one according to his ways, declares the Sovereign LORD. Repent! Turn away from all your offenses; then sin will not be your downfall. ³¹Rid yourselves of all the offenses you have committed, and get a new heart and a new spirit. Why will you die, O house of Israel? ³²For I take no pleasure in the death of anyone, declares the Sovereign LORD. Repent and live!   Isa 1:27; 55:7

A Lament for Israel's Princes

19 "Take up a lament concerning the princes of Israel ²and say: 2Ki 24:6

" 'What a lioness was your mother
    among the lions!   Nu 23:24
She lay down among the young lions
    and reared her cubs.   Ge 49:9

³She brought up one of her cubs,
    and he became a strong lion.
He learned to tear the prey
    and he devoured men.
⁴The nations heard about him,
    and he was trapped in their pit.
They led him with hooks
    to the land of Egypt.   Job 41:2

⁵" 'When she saw her hope unfulfilled,
    her expectation gone,
she took another of her cubs
    and made him a strong lion.   2Ki 23:34
⁶He prowled among the lions,
    for he was now a strong lion.
He learned to tear the prey
    and he devoured men.   2Ki 24:9
⁷He broke down[a] their strongholds
    and devastated their towns.
The land and all who were in it
    were terrified by his roaring.
⁸Then the nations came against him,   2Ki 24:2
    those from regions round about.
They spread their net for him,   Eze 13:13
    and he was trapped in their pit.   2Ki 24:11
⁹With hooks they pulled him into a cage   2Ki 19:28
    and brought him to the king of Babylon.   2Ki 25:7
They put him in prison,

---

[a]7 Targum (see Septuagint); Hebrew *He knew*

so his roar was heard no
    longer   Zec 11:3
on the mountains of Israel.

10" 'Your mother was like a
    vine in your vineyard*a*
planted by the water;   Jer 17:8
it was fruitful and full of
    branches
because of abundant
    water.
11Its branches were strong,
    fit for a ruler's scepter.
It towered high
    above the thick foliage,
conspicuous for its height
and for its many branches.
12But it was uprooted in fury
    and thrown to the ground.
The east wind made it
    shrivel,   Ge 41:6
    it was stripped of its fruit;
its strong branches withered
and fire consumed them.
13Now it is planted in the
    desert,   Eze 20:35
    in a dry and thirsty land.
14Fire spread from one of its
    main*b* branches
and consumed its fruit.
No strong branch is left on it
    fit for a ruler's scepter.'Eze 15:4

This is a lament and is to be
used as a lament."

Rebellious Israel

20 In the seventh year, in
the fifth month on the
tenth day, some of the elders of
Israel came to inquire of the
LORD, and they sat down in
front of me.   Ge 25:22
    2Then the word of the LORD
came to me: 3"Son of man,
speak to the elders of Israel and
say to them, 'This is what the
Sovereign LORD says: Have you
come to inquire of me? As surely as I live, I will not let you
inquire of me, declares the Sov-
ereign LORD.'   Eze 7:26; Am 8:12
    4"Will you judge them? Will
you judge them, son of man?
Then confront them with the
detestable practices of their fathers 5and say to them: 'This is
what the Sovereign LORD says:
On the day I chose Israel, I
swore with uplifted hand to the
descendants of the house of
Jacob and revealed myself to
them in Egypt. With uplifted
hand I said to them, "I am the
LORD your God." 6On that day I
swore to them that I would
bring them out of Egypt into a
land I had searched out for
them, a land flowing with milk
and honey, the most beautiful
of all lands. 7And I said to them,
"Each of you, get rid of the vile
images you have set your eyes
on, and do not defile yourselves
with the idols of Egypt. I am the
LORD your God."   Eze 6:9; 16:2
    8" 'But they rebelled against
me and would not listen to me;
they did not get rid of the vile
images they had set their eyes
on, nor did they forsake the
idols of Egypt. So I said I would

*a*10 Two Hebrew manuscripts; most Hebrew manuscripts *your blood*   *b*14 Or *from
under its*

pour out my wrath on them and spend my anger against them in Egypt. ⁹But for the sake of my name I did what would keep it from being profaned in the eyes of the nations they lived among and in whose sight I had revealed myself to the Israelites by bringing them out of Egypt. ¹⁰Therefore I led them out of Egypt and brought them into the desert. ¹¹I gave them my decrees and made known to them my laws, for the man who obeys them will live by them. ¹²Also I gave them my Sabbaths as a sign between us, so they would know that I the LORD made them holy.   Ex 20:10; Dt 9:7

¹³" 'Yet the people of Israel rebelled against me in the desert. They did not follow my decrees but rejected my laws—although the man who obeys them will live by them—and they utterly desecrated my Sabbaths. So I said I would pour out my wrath on them and destroy them in the desert. ¹⁴But for the sake of my name I did what would keep it from being profaned in the eyes of the nations in whose sight I had brought them out. ¹⁵Also with uplifted hand I swore to them in the desert that I would not bring them into the land I had given them—a land flowing with milk and honey, most beautiful of all lands— ¹⁶because they rejected my laws and did not follow my decrees and desecrated my Sabbaths. For their hearts were devoted to their idols. ¹⁷Yet I looked on them with pity and did not destroy them or put an end to them in the desert. ¹⁸I said to their children in the desert, "Do not follow the statutes of your fathers or keep their laws or defile yourselves with their idols. ¹⁹I am the LORD your God; follow my decrees and be careful to keep my laws. ²⁰Keep my Sabbaths holy, that they may be a sign between us. Then you will know that I am the LORD your God."   Ps 78:40; Jer 17:22

²¹" 'But the children rebelled against me: They did not follow my decrees, they were not careful to keep my laws—although the man who obeys them will live by them—and they desecrated my Sabbaths. So I said I would pour out my wrath on them and spend my anger against them in the desert. ²²But I withheld my hand, and for the sake of my name I did what would keep it from being profaned in the eyes of the nations in whose sight I had brought them out. ²³Also with uplifted hand I swore to them in the desert that I would disperse them among the nations and scatter them through the countries, ²⁴because they had not obeyed my laws but had rejected my decrees and desecrated my Sabbaths, and their eyes lusted after their fathers' idols. ²⁵I also gave them over to statutes that were not good and laws they could not live by; ²⁶I let them become defiled

through their gifts—the sacrifice of every firstborn[a]—that I might fill them with horror so they would know that I am the LORD.'   2Ki 17:17; Jer 7:26

27"Therefore, son of man, speak to the people of Israel and say to them, 'This is what the Sovereign LORD says: In this also your fathers blasphemed me by forsaking me: 28When I brought them into the land I had sworn to give them and they saw any high hill or any leafy tree, there they offered their sacrifices, made offerings that provoked me to anger, presented their fragrant incense and poured out their drink offerings. 29Then I said to them: What is this high place you go to?' " (It is called Bamah[b] to this day.)   Ps 78:57; Eze 16:16

Judgment and Restoration

30"Therefore say to the house of Israel: 'This is what the Sovereign LORD says: Will you defile yourselves the way your fathers did and lust after their vile images? 31When you offer your gifts—the sacrifice of your sons in[c] the fire—you continue to defile yourselves with all your idols to this day. Am I to let you inquire of me, O house of Israel? As surely as I live, declares the Sovereign LORD, I will not let you inquire of me. Jer 16:12

32" 'You say, "We want to be like the nations, like the peoples of the world, who serve wood and stone." But what you have in mind will never happen. 33As surely as I live, declares the Sovereign LORD, I will rule over you with a mighty hand and an outstretched arm and with outpoured wrath. 34I will bring you from the nations and gather you from the countries where you have been scattered—with a mighty hand and an outstretched arm and with outpoured wrath. 35I will bring you into the desert of the nations and there, face to face, I will execute judgment upon you. 36As I judged your fathers in the desert of the land of Egypt, so I will judge you, declares the Sovereign LORD. 37I will take note of you as you pass under my rod, and I will bring you into the bond of the covenant. 38I will purge you of those who revolt and rebel against me. Although I will bring them out of the land where they are living, yet they will not enter the land of Israel. Then you will know that I am the LORD.   2Co 6:17

39" 'As for you, O house of Israel, this is what the Sovereign LORD says: Go and serve your idols, every one of you! But afterward you will surely listen to me and no longer profane my holy name with your gifts and idols. 40For on my holy mountain, the high mountain of Israel, declares the Sovereign LORD, there in the land the en-

---

[a]26 Or —making every firstborn pass through the fire   [b]29 Bamah means high place.
[c]31 Or —making your sons pass through

tire house of Israel will serve me, and there I will accept them. There I will require your offerings and your choice gifts,ᵃ along with all your holy sacrifices. ⁴¹I will accept you as fragrant incense when I bring you out from the nations and gather you from the countries where you have been scattered, and I will show myself holy among you in the sight of the nations. ⁴²Then you will know that I am the LORD, when I bring you into the land of Israel, the land I had sworn with uplifted hand to give to your fathers. ⁴³There you will remember your conduct and all the actions by which you have defiled yourselves, and you will loathe yourselves for all the evil you have done. ⁴⁴You will know that I am the LORD, when I deal with you for my name's sake and not according to your evil ways and your corrupt practices, O house of Israel, declares the Sovereign LORD.' "   Ps 109:21; Jer 44:25

Prophecy Against the South

⁴⁵The word of the LORD came to me: ⁴⁶"Son of man, set your face toward the south; preach against the south and prophesy against the forest of the southland. ⁴⁷Say to the southern forest: 'Hear the word of the LORD. This is what the Sovereign LORD says: I am about to set fire to you, and it will consume all your trees, both green and dry.

The blazing flame will not be quenched, and every face from south to north will be scorched by it. ⁴⁸Everyone will see that I the LORD have kindled it; it will not be quenched.' "   Jer 7:20; Eze 4:3

⁴⁹Then I said, "Ah, Sovereign LORD! They are saying of me, 'Isn't he just telling parables?' "

Babylon, God's Sword of Judgment

21 The word of the LORD came to me: ²"Son of man, set your face against Jerusalem and preach against the sanctuary. Prophesy against the land of Israel ³and say to her: 'This is what the LORD says: I am against you. I will draw my sword from its scabbard and cut off from you both the righteous and the wicked. ⁴Because I am going to cut off the righteous and the wicked, my sword will be unsheathed against everyone from south to north. ⁵Then all people will know that I the LORD have drawn my sword from its scabbard; it will not return again.'   Isa 34:5; Eze 20:1

⁶"Therefore groan, son of man! Groan before them with broken heart and bitter grief. ⁷And when they ask you, 'Why are you groaning?' you shall say, 'Because of the news that is coming. Every heart will melt and every hand go limp; every spirit will become faint and every knee become as weak as water.' It is coming! It will sure-

---

ᵃ40 Or and the gifts of your firstfruits

ly take place, declares the Sovereign LORD." <small>Job 23:2; Isa 22:4</small>

⁸The word of the LORD came to me: ⁹"Son of man, prophesy and say, 'This is what the Lord says: <small>Dt 32:41</small>

" 'A sword, a sword,
  sharpened and polished—
¹⁰sharpened for the slaughter,
  polished to flash like
    lightning! <small>Ps 110:5-6</small>

" 'Shall we rejoice in the scepter of my son ⌊Judah⌋? The sword despises every such stick.

¹¹" 'The sword is appointed to
    be polished, <small>Jer 46:4</small>
  to be grasped with the
    hand;
  it is sharpened and polished,
    made ready for the hand of
    the slayer.
¹²Cry out and wail, son of
    man,
  for it is against my people;
  it is against all the princes
    of Israel.
They are thrown to the
    sword
  along with my people.
Therefore beat your breast.

¹³" 'Testing will surely come. And what if the scepter ⌊of Judah⌋, which the sword despises, does not continue? declares the Sovereign LORD.'

¹⁴"So then, son of man,
    prophesy
  and strike your hands
    together. <small>Nu 24:10</small>
Let the sword strike twice,

even three times.
It is a sword for slaughter—
  a sword for great slaughter,
  closing in on them from
    every side. <small>Eze 6:11</small>
¹⁵So that hearts may melt
  and the fallen be many,
I have stationed the sword
  for slaughter[a]
  at all their gates.
Oh! It is made to flash like
    lightning,
  it is grasped for slaughter.
¹⁶O sword, slash to the right,
    then to the left,
  wherever your blade is
    turned.
¹⁷I too will strike my hands
    together, <small>Eze 22:13</small>
  and my wrath will subside.
I the LORD have spoken."

¹⁸The word of the LORD came to me: ¹⁹"Son of man, mark out two roads for the sword of the king of Babylon to take, both starting from the same country. Make a signpost where the road branches off to the city. ²⁰Mark out one road for the sword to come against Rabbah of the Ammonites and another against Judah and fortified Jerusalem. ²¹For the king of Babylon will stop at the fork in the road, at the junction of the two roads, to seek an omen: He will cast lots with arrows, he will consult his idols, he will examine the liver. ²²Into his right hand will come the lot for Jerusalem, where he is to set up battering rams, to give the command to slaughter,

---

<small>ª15 Septuagint; the meaning of the Hebrew for this word is uncertain.</small>

to sound the battle cry, to set battering rams against the gates, to build a ramp and to erect siege works. ²³It will seem like a false omen to those who have sworn allegiance to him, but he will remind them of their guilt and take them captive.

²⁴"Therefore this is what the Sovereign LORD says: 'Because you people have brought to mind your guilt by your open rebellion, revealing your sins in all that you do—because you have done this, you will be taken captive.   Nu 32:23

²⁵" 'O profane and wicked prince of Israel, whose day has come, whose time of punishment has reached its climax, ²⁶this is what the Sovereign LORD says: Take off the turban, remove the crown. It will not be as it was: The lowly will be exalted and the exalted will be brought low. ²⁷A ruin! A ruin! I will make it a ruin! It will not be restored until he comes to whom it rightfully belongs; to him I will give it.'   Eze 22:4

²⁸"And you, son of man, prophesy and say, 'This is what the Sovereign LORD says about the Ammonites and their insults: Ge 19:38; Zep 2:8

" 'A sword, a sword,
   drawn for the slaughter,
   polished to consume
   and to flash like lightning!
²⁹Despite false visions
   concerning you
   and lying divinations about
   you,   Jer 27:9

it will be laid on the necks
   of the wicked who are to be
   slain,
whose day has come,
   whose time of punishment
   has reached its climax.
³⁰Return the sword to its
   scabbard.   Jer 47:6
In the place where you
   were created,
in the land of your ancestry,
   I will judge you.
³¹I will pour out my wrath
   upon you
   and breathe out my fiery
   anger against you;   Ps 79:6
I will hand you over to brutal
   men,
   men skilled in destruction.
³²You will be fuel for the fire,
   your blood will be shed in
   your land,
you will be remembered no
   more;   Eze 25:10
for I the LORD have
   spoken.' "

Jerusalem's Sins

22 The word of the LORD came to me: ²"Son of man, will you judge her? Will you judge this city of bloodshed? Then confront her with all her detestable practices ³and say: 'This is what the Sovereign LORD says: O city that brings on herself doom by shedding blood in her midst and defiles herself by making idols, ⁴you have become guilty because of the blood you have shed and have become defiled by the idols you have made. You have brought your days to a close,

and the end of your years has come. Therefore I will make you an object of scorn to the nations and a laughingstock to all the countries. ⁵Those who are near and those who are far away will mock you, O infamous city, full of turmoil. Isa 22:2; Eze 24:6

⁶" 'See how each of the princes of Israel who are in you uses his power to shed blood. ⁷In you they have treated father and mother with contempt; in you they have oppressed the alien and mistreated the fatherless and the widow. ⁸You have despised my holy things and desecrated my Sabbaths. ⁹In you are slanderous men bent on shedding blood; in you are those who eat at the mountain shrines and commit lewd acts. ¹⁰In you are those who dishonor their fathers' bed; in you are those who violate women during their period, when they are ceremonially unclean. ¹¹In you one man commits a detestable offense with his neighbor's wife, another shamefully defiles his daughter-in-law, and another violates his sister, his own father's daughter. ¹²In you men accept bribes to shed blood; you take usury and excessive interestᵃ and make unjust gain from your neighbors by extortion. And you have forgotten me, declares the Sovereign LORD. Dt 27:25; Eze 11:6

¹³" 'I will surely strike my hands together at the unjust gain you have made and at the blood you have shed in your midst. ¹⁴Will your courage endure or your hands be strong in the day I deal with you? I the LORD have spoken, and I will do it. ¹⁵I will disperse you among the nations and scatter you through the countries; and I will put an end to your uncleanness. ¹⁶When you have been defiledᵇ in the eyes of the nations, you will know that I am the LORD.' "

¹⁷Then the word of the LORD came to me: ¹⁸"Son of man, the house of Israel has become dross to me; all of them are the copper, tin, iron and lead left inside a furnace. They are but the dross of silver. ¹⁹Therefore this is what the Sovereign LORD says: 'Because you have all become dross, I will gather you into Jerusalem. ²⁰As men gather silver, copper, iron, lead and tin into a furnace to melt it with a fiery blast, so will I gather you in my anger and my wrath and put you inside the city and melt you. ²¹I will gather you and I will blow on you with my fiery wrath, and you will be melted inside her. ²²As silver is melted in a furnace, so you will be melted inside her, and you will know that I the LORD have poured out my wrath upon you.' " Ps 119:119; Isa 1:25

²³Again the word of the LORD came to me: ²⁴"Son of man, say to the land, 'You are a land that

---

ᵃ12 Or usury and interest   ᵇ16 Or When I have allotted you your inheritance

has had no rain or showers*ª* in the day of wrath.' ²⁵There is a conspiracy of her princes*ᵇ* within her like a roaring lion tearing its prey; they devour people, take treasures and precious things and make many widows within her. ²⁶Her priests do violence to my law and profane my holy things; they do not distinguish between the holy and the common; they teach that there is no difference between the unclean and the clean; and they shut their eyes to the keeping of my Sabbaths, so that I am profaned among them. ²⁷Her officials within her are like wolves tearing their prey; they shed blood and kill people to make unjust gain. ²⁸Her prophets whitewash these deeds for them by false visions and lying divinations. They say, 'This is what the Sovereign LORD says'—when the LORD has not spoken. ²⁹The people of the land practice extortion and commit robbery; they oppress the poor and needy and mistreat the alien, denying them justice.

³⁰"I looked for a man among them who would build up the wall and stand before me in the gap on behalf of the land so I would not have to destroy it, but I found none. ³¹So I will pour out my wrath on them and consume them with my fiery anger, bringing down on their own heads all they have done,

declares the Sovereign LORD."

Two Adulterous Sisters

23 The word of the LORD came to me: ²"Son of man, there were two women, daughters of the same mother. ³They became prostitutes in Egypt, engaging in prostitution from their youth. In that land their breasts were fondled and their virgin bosoms caressed. ⁴The older was named Oholah, and her sister was Oholibah. They were mine and gave birth to sons and daughters. Oholah is Samaria, and Oholibah is Jerusalem.   Jer 3:7; Eze 16:46

⁵"Oholah engaged in prostitution while she was still mine; and she lusted after her lovers, the Assyrians—warriors ⁶clothed in blue, governors and commanders, all of them handsome young men, and mounted horsemen. ⁷She gave herself as a prostitute to all the elite of the Assyrians and defiled herself with all the idols of everyone she lusted after. ⁸She did not give up the prostitution she began in Egypt, when during her youth men slept with her, caressed her virgin bosom and poured out their lust upon her.

⁹"Therefore I handed her over to her lovers, the Assyrians, for whom she lusted. ¹⁰They stripped her naked, took away her sons and daughters and killed her with the sword.

ª24 Septuagint; Hebrew *has not been cleansed or rained on*   *ᵇ25* Septuagint; Hebrew *prophets*

She became a byword among women, and punishment was inflicted on her. 2Ki 18:11; Hos 2:10

11"Her sister Oholibah saw this, yet in her lust and prostitution she was more depraved than her sister. 12She too lusted after the Assyrians—governors and commanders, warriors in full dress, mounted horsemen, all handsome young men. 13I saw that she too defiled herself; both of them went the same way. Jer 3:7; Hos 12:2

14"But she carried her prostitution still further. She saw men portrayed on a wall, figures of Chaldeans*a* portrayed in red, 15with belts around their waists and flowing turbans on their heads; all of them looked like Babylonian chariot officers, natives of Chaldea.*b* 16As soon as she saw them, she lusted after them and sent messengers to them in Chaldea. 17Then the Babylonians came to her, to the bed of love, and in their lust they defiled her. After she had been defiled by them, she turned away from them in disgust. 18When she carried on her prostitution openly and exposed her nakedness, I turned away from her in disgust, just as I had turned away from her sister. 19Yet she became more and more promiscuous as she recalled the days of her youth, when she was a prostitute in Egypt. 20There she lusted after her lovers, whose genitals were like those of donkeys and whose emission was like that of horses. 21So you longed for the lewdness of your youth, when in Egypt your bosom was caressed and your young breasts fondled.*c* Eze 8:10; 16:26

22"Therefore, Oholibah, this is what the Sovereign LORD says: I will stir up your lovers against you, those you turned away from in disgust, and I will bring them against you from every side— 23the Babylonians and all the Chaldeans, the men of Pekod and Shoa and Koa, and all the Assyrians with them, handsome young men, all of them governors and commanders, chariot officers and men of high rank, all mounted on horses. 24They will come against you with weapons,*d* chariots and wagons and with a throng of people; they will take up positions against you on every side with large and small shields and with helmets. I will turn you over to them for punishment, and they will punish you according to their standards. 25I will direct my jealous anger against you, and they will deal with you in fury. They will cut off your noses and your ears, and those of you who are left will fall by the sword. They will take away your sons and daughters, and those of you who are left will be consumed

---

*a*14 Or *Babylonians*   *b*15 Or *Babylonia;* also in verse 16   *c*21 Syriac (see also verse 3); Hebrew *caressed because of your young breasts*   *d*24 The meaning of the Hebrew for this word is uncertain.

by fire. 26They will also strip you of your clothes and take your fine jewelry. 27So I will put a stop to the lewdness and prostitution you began in Egypt. You will not look on these things with longing or remember Egypt anymore.   Jer 4:30; Eze 16:41

28"For this is what the Sovereign LORD says: I am about to hand you over to those you hate, to those you turned away from in disgust. 29They will deal with you in hatred and take away everything you have worked for. They will leave you naked and bare, and the shame of your prostitution will be exposed. Your lewdness and promiscuity 30have brought this upon you, because you lusted after the nations and defiled yourself with their idols. 31You have gone the way of your sister; so I will put her cup into your hand.   2Ki 21:13; Jer 34:20

32"This is what the Sovereign LORD says:

"You will drink your sister's
    cup,
  a cup large and deep;
it will bring scorn and
    derision,   Ps 44:13
  for it holds so much.   Ps 60:3
33You will be filled with
    drunkenness and
    sorrow,
  the cup of ruin and
    desolation,
  the cup of your sister
    Samaria.   Jer 25:15-16

34You will drink it and drain it
    dry;   Ps 16:5
  you will dash it to pieces
  and tear your breasts.

I have spoken, declares the Sovereign LORD.   Jer 25:27

35"Therefore this is what the Sovereign LORD says: Since you have forgotten me and thrust me behind your back, you must bear the consequences of your lewdness and prostitution."

36The LORD said to me: "Son of man, will you judge Oholah and Oholibah? Then confront them with their detestable practices, 37for they have committed adultery and blood is on their hands. They committed adultery with their idols; they even sacrificed their children, whom they bore to me,a as food for them. 38They have also done this to me: At that same time they defiled my sanctuary and desecrated my Sabbaths. 39On the very day they sacrificed their children to their idols, they entered my sanctuary and desecrated it. That is what they did in my house.   2Ki 21:4; Eze 16:2

40"They even sent messengers for men who came from far away, and when they arrived you bathed yourself for them, painted your eyes and put on your jewelry. 41You sat on an elegant couch, with a table spread before it on which you had placed the incense and oil that belonged to me.   Isa 57:9

---

a37 Or even made the children they bore to me pass through ⌈the fire⌉

⁴²"The noise of a carefree crowd was around her; Sabeans*a* were brought from the desert along with men from the rabble, and they put bracelets on the arms of the woman and her sister and beautiful crowns on their heads. ⁴³Then I said about the one worn out by adultery, 'Now let them use her as a prostitute, for that is all she is.' ⁴⁴And they slept with her. As men sleep with a prostitute, so they slept with those lewd women, Oholah and Oholibah. ⁴⁵But righteous men will sentence them to the punishment of women who commit adultery and shed blood, because they are adulterous and blood is on their hands.   Ps 73:5; Eze 22:3

⁴⁶"This is what the Sovereign Lord says: Bring a mob against them and give them over to terror and plunder. ⁴⁷The mob will stone them and cut them down with their swords; they will kill their sons and daughters and burn down their houses. Eze 16:40

⁴⁸"So I will put an end to lewdness in the land, that all women may take warning and not imitate you. ⁴⁹You will suffer the penalty for your lewdness and bear the consequences of your sins of idolatry. Then you will know that I am the Sovereign Lord."   Eze 24:13; 2Pe 2:6

The Cooking Pot

24 In the ninth year, in the tenth month on the tenth day, the word of the Lord came to me: ²"Son of man, record this date, this very date, because the king of Babylon has laid siege to Jerusalem this very day. ³Tell this rebellious house a parable and say to them: 'This is what the Sovereign Lord says: Eze 8:1

" 'Put on the cooking pot;
    put it on
  and pour water into it. Eze 11:3
⁴Put into it the pieces of meat,
  all the choice pieces—the
    leg and the shoulder.
Fill it with the best of these
    bones;   Eze 11:7
⁵ take the pick of the flock.
Pile wood beneath it for the
    bones;
  bring it to a boil
  and cook the bones in it.

⁶" 'For this is what the Sovereign Lord says:

" 'Woe to the city of
    bloodshed,   Eze 22:2
  to the pot now encrusted,
  whose deposit will not go
    away!
Empty it piece by piece
  without casting lots for
    them.   Job 6:27; Eze 11:11

⁷" 'For the blood she shed is
    in her midst:
  She poured it on the bare
    rock;
  she did not pour it on the
    ground,
  where the dust would
    cover it.   Lev 17:13

⁸To stir up wrath and take
    revenge
  I put her blood on the bare
    rock,
  so that it would not be
    covered.

⁹" 'Therefore this is what the
Sovereign Lord says:

" 'Woe to the city of
    bloodshed!
  I, too, will pile the wood
    high.
¹⁰So heap on the wood
  and kindle the fire.
  Cook the meat well,
    mixing in the spices;
  and let the bones be
    charred.
¹¹Then set the empty pot on
    the coals
  till it becomes hot and its
    copper glows
  so its impurities may be
    melted
  and its deposit burned
    away.   Jer 21:10
¹²It has frustrated all efforts;
  its heavy deposit has not
    been removed,
  not even by fire.

¹³" 'Now your impurity is
lewdness. Because I tried to
cleanse you but you would not
be cleansed from your impurity,
you will not be clean again until
my wrath against you has subsided.   Isa 22:14; Hos 7:1

¹⁴" 'I the Lord have spoken.
The time has come for me to act.
I will not hold back; I will not
have pity, nor will I relent. You

will be judged according to your
conduct and your actions, declares the Sovereign Lord.' "

Ezekiel's Wife Dies

¹⁵The word of the Lord came
to me: ¹⁶"Son of man, with one
blow I am about to take away
from you the delight of your
eyes. Yet do not lament or weep
or shed any tears. ¹⁷Groan quietly; do not mourn for the dead.
Keep your turban fastened and
your sandals on your feet; do
not cover the lower part of your
face or eat the customary food
of mourners."   Ex 28:39; Ps 39:10

¹⁸So I spoke to the people in
the morning, and in the evening
my wife died. The next morning
I did as I had been commanded.

¹⁹Then the people asked me,
"Won't you tell us what these
things have to do with us?"

²⁰So I said to them, "The
word of the Lord came to me:
²¹Say to the house of Israel,
'This is what the Sovereign
Lord says: I am about to desecrate my sanctuary—the stronghold in which you take pride,
the delight of your eyes, the object of your affection. The sons
and daughters you left behind
will fall by the sword. ²²And you
will do as I have done. You will
not cover the lower part of your
face or eat the customary food
of mourners. ²³You will keep
your turbans on your heads and
your sandals on your feet. You
will not mourn or weep but will

waste away because of[a] your sins and groan among yourselves. 24Ezekiel will be a sign to you; you will do just as he has done. When this happens, you will know that I am the Sovereign LORD.' Lev 26:31; Eze 1:3

25"And you, son of man, on the day I take away their stronghold, their joy and glory, the delight of their eyes, their heart's desire, and their sons and daughters as well— 26on that day a fugitive will come to tell you the news. 27At that time your mouth will be opened; you will speak with him and will no longer be silent. So you will be a sign to them, and they will know that I am the LORD.'' La 2:4

A Prophecy Against Ammon

25 The word of the LORD came to me: 2"Son of man, set your face against the Ammonites and prophesy against them. 3Say to them, 'Hear the word of the Sovereign LORD. This is what the Sovereign LORD says: Because you said "Aha!" over my sanctuary when it was desecrated and over the land of Israel when it was laid waste and over the people of Judah when they went into exile, 4therefore I am going to give you to the people of the East as a possession. They will set up their camps and pitch their tents among you; they will eat your fruit and drink your milk. 5I will turn Rabbah into a pasture for camels and Ammon into a resting place for sheep. Then you will know that I am the LORD. 6For this is what the Sovereign LORD says: Because you have clapped your hands and stamped your feet, rejoicing with all the malice of your heart against the land of Israel, 7therefore I will stretch out my hand against you and give you as plunder to the nations. I will cut you off from the nations and exterminate you from the countries. I will destroy you, and you will know that I am the LORD.' '' Eze 13:17

A Prophecy Against Moab

8"This is what the Sovereign LORD says: 'Because Moab and Seir said, "Look, the house of Judah has become like all the other nations," 9therefore I will expose the flank of Moab, beginning at its frontier towns—Beth Jeshimoth, Baal Meon and Kiriathaim—the glory of that land. 10I will give Moab along with the Ammonites to the people of the East as a possession, so that the Ammonites will not be remembered among the nations; 11and I will inflict punishment on Moab. Then they will know that I am the LORD.' '' Ge 19:37; Isa 15:9

A Prophecy Against Edom

12"This is what the Sovereign LORD says: 'Because Edom took revenge on the house of Judah

and became very guilty by doing so, [13]therefore this is what the Sovereign LORD says: I will stretch out my hand against Edom and kill its men and their animals. I will lay it waste, and from Teman to Dedan they will fall by the sword. [14]I will take vengeance on Edom by the hand of my people Israel, and they will deal with Edom in accordance with my anger and my wrath; they will know my vengeance, declares the Sovereign LORD.' "   2Sa 8:13-14; Am 1:11

A Prophecy Against Philistia

[15]"This is what the Sovereign LORD says: 'Because the Philistines acted in vengeance and took revenge with malice in their hearts, and with ancient hostility sought to destroy Judah, [16]therefore this is what the Sovereign LORD says: I am about to stretch out my hand against the Philistines, and I will cut off the Kerethites and destroy those remaining along the coast. [17]I will carry out great vengeance on them and punish them in my wrath. Then they will know that I am the LORD, when I take vengeance on them.' "   Nu 31:3; Jos 13:3

A Prophecy Against Tyre

26 In the eleventh year, on the first day of the month, the word of the LORD came to me: [2]"Son of man, because Tyre has said of Jerusalem, 'Aha! The gate to the nations is broken, and its doors have swung open to me; now that she lies in ruins I will prosper,' [3]therefore this is what the Sovereign LORD says: I am against you, O Tyre, and I will bring many nations against you, like the sea casting up its waves. [4]They will destroy the walls of Tyre and pull down her towers; I will scrape away her rubble and make her a bare rock. [5]Out in the sea she will become a place to spread fishnets, for I have spoken, declares the Sovereign LORD. She will become plunder for the nations, [6]and her settlements on the mainland will be ravaged by the sword. Then they will know that I am the LORD.   Eze 24:1; 29:1

[7]"For this is what the Sovereign LORD says: From the north I am going to bring against Tyre Nebuchadnezzar[a] king of Babylon, king of kings, with horses and chariots, with horsemen and a great army. [8]He will ravage your settlements on the mainland with the sword; he will set up siege works against you, build a ramp up to your walls and raise his shields against you. [9]He will direct the blows of his battering rams against your walls and demolish your towers with his weapons. [10]His horses will be so

---

[a]7 Hebrew *Nebuchadrezzar*, of which *Nebuchadnezzar* is a variant; here and often in Ezekiel and Jeremiah

many that they will cover you with dust. Your walls will tremble at the noise of the war horses, wagons and chariots when he enters your gates as men enter a city whose walls have been broken through. [11]The hoofs of his horses will trample all your streets; he will kill your people with the sword, and your strong pillars will fall to the ground. [12]They will plunder your wealth and loot your merchandise; they will break down your walls and demolish your fine houses and throw your stones, timber and rubble into the sea. [13]I will put an end to your noisy songs, and the music of your harps will be heard no more. [14]I will make you a bare rock, and you will become a place to spread fishnets. You will never be rebuilt, for I the LORD have spoken, declares the Sovereign LORD.

[15]"This is what the Sovereign LORD says to Tyre: Will not the coastlands tremble at the sound of your fall, when the wounded groan and the slaughter takes place in you? [16]Then all the princes of the coast will step down from their thrones and lay aside their robes and take off their embroidered garments. Clothed with terror, they will sit on the ground, trembling every moment, appalled at you. [17]Then they will take up a lament concerning you and say to you: Ex 26:36; Isa 41:5

" 'How you are destroyed,
    O city of renown,
  peopled by men of the sea!
You were a power on the
    seas,
  you and your citizens;
  you put your terror
    on all who lived there.
[18]Now the coastlands tremble
    on the day of your fall;
  the islands in the sea
  are terrified at your
    collapse.'   Isa 23:5; Eze 27:35

[19]"This is what the Sovereign LORD says: When I make you a desolate city, like cities no longer inhabited, and when I bring the ocean depths over you and its vast waters cover you, [20]then I will bring you down with those who go down to the pit, to the people of long ago. I will make you dwell in the earth below, as in ancient ruins, with those who go down to the pit, and you will not return or take your place[a] in the land of the living. [21]I will bring you to a horrible end and you will be no more. You will be sought, but you will never again be found, declares the Sovereign LORD."

A Lament for Tyre

27 The word of the LORD came to me: [2]"Son of man, take up a lament concerning Tyre. [3]Say to Tyre, situated at the gateway to the sea, merchant of peoples on many coasts, 'This is what the Sovereign LORD says: Ps 83:7; Eze 19:1

---

[a]20 Septuagint; Hebrew *return, and I will give glory*

" 'You say, O Tyre,
  "I am perfect in beauty."
⁴Your domain was on the
    high seas;
  your builders brought your
    beauty to perfection.
⁵They made all your timbers
    of pine trees from Senir*ᵃ*;
  they took a cedar from
    Lebanon   Isa 2:13
  to make a mast for you.
⁶Of oaks from Bashan   Nu 21:33
    they made your oars;
  of cypress wood*ᵇ* from the
    coasts of Cyprus*ᶜ*   Ge 10:4
  they made your deck, inlaid
    with ivory.
⁷Fine embroidered linen from
    Egypt was your sail
  and served as your banner;
  your awnings were of blue
    and purple   Ex 25:4
  from the coasts of Elishah.
⁸Men of Sidon and Arvad
    were your oarsmen;
  your skilled men, O Tyre,
    were aboard as your
    seamen.   1Ki 9:27
⁹Veteran craftsmen of Gebal*ᵈ*
    were on board   Jos 13:5
  as shipwrights to caulk
    your seams.
All the ships of the sea and
    their sailors   Ps 104:26
  came alongside to trade for
    your wares.

¹⁰" 'Men of Persia, Lydia and
    Put
  served as soldiers in your
    army.   2Ch 36:20

They hung their shields and
    helmets on your walls,
  bringing you splendor.
¹¹Men of Arvad and Helech
    manned your walls on
    every side;
  men of Gammad
    were in your towers.
  They hung their shields
    around your walls;
  they brought your beauty to
    perfection.

¹²" 'Tarshish did business
with you because of your great
wealth of goods; they ex-
changed silver, iron, tin and
lead for your merchandise.Ge 10:4
¹³" 'Greece, Tubal and Meshech traded with you; they exchanged slaves and articles of
bronze for your wares.   Joel 3:6
¹⁴" 'Men of Beth Togarmah
exchanged work horses, war
horses and mules for your merchandise.   Ge 10:3
¹⁵" 'The men of Rhodes*ᵉ* traded with you, and many coastlands were your customers;
they paid you with ivory tusks
and ebony.   Ge 10:7; 1Ki 10:22
¹⁶" 'Aram*ᶠ* did business with
you because of your many products; they exchanged turquoise,
purple fabric, embroidered
work, fine linen, coral and rubies for your merchandise.Jdg 10:6
¹⁷" 'Judah and Israel traded
with you; they exchanged
wheat from Minnith and con-

ᵃ5 That is, Hermon   *ᵇ6* Targum; the Masoretic Text has a different division of the
consonants.   *ᶜ6* Hebrew *Kittim*   *ᵈ9* That is, Byblos   *ᵉ15* Septuagint; Hebrew
Dedan   *ᶠ16* Most Hebrew manuscripts; some Hebrew manuscripts and Syriac *Edom*

fections,ᵃ honey, oil and balm for your wares. 1Ki 5:9; Ac 12:20

¹⁸" 'Damascus, because of your many products and great wealth of goods, did business with you in wine from Helbon and wool from Zahar. Ge 14:15

¹⁹" 'Danites and Greeks from Uzal bought your merchandise; they exchanged wrought iron, cassia and calamus for your wares. Ge 10:2; Ex 30:24

²⁰" 'Dedan traded in saddle blankets with you. Ge 10:7

²¹" 'Arabia and all the princes of Kedar were your customers; they did business with you in lambs, rams and goats. 2Ch 9:14

²²" 'The merchants of Sheba and Raamah traded with you; for your merchandise they exchanged the finest of all kinds of spices and precious stones, and gold. Ge 10:7,28; Rev 18:12

²³" 'Haran, Canneh and Eden and merchants of Sheba, Asshur and Kilmad traded with you. ²⁴In your marketplace they traded with you beautiful garments, blue fabric, embroidered work and multicolored rugs with cords twisted and tightly knotted. Ge 11:26; Nu 24:24

²⁵" 'The ships of Tarshish serve Ge 10:4
as carriers for your wares.
You are filled with heavy cargo
in the heart of the sea. Rev 18:3
²⁶Your oarsmen take you out to the high seas.

But the east wind will break
you to pieces Ge 41:6
in the heart of the sea.
²⁷Your wealth, merchandise and wares, Pr 11:4
your mariners, seamen and shipwrights,
your merchants and all your soldiers,
and everyone else on board
will sink into the heart of the sea Eze 28:8
on the day of your shipwreck.
²⁸The shorelands will quake
when your seamen cry out.
²⁹All who handle the oars
will abandon their ships;
the mariners and all the seamen
will stand on the shore.
³⁰They will raise their voice
and cry bitterly over you;
they will sprinkle dust on their heads Jos 7:6
and roll in ashes. Jer 6:26
³¹They will shave their heads because of you Lev 13:40
and will put on sackcloth.
They will weep over you
with anguish of soul
and with bitter mourning.
³²As they wail and mourn over you,
they will take up a lament concerning you: Eze 19:1
"Who was ever silenced like Tyre,
surrounded by the sea?"
³³When your merchandise went out on the seas,
you satisfied many nations;

ᵃ17 The meaning of the Hebrew for this word is uncertain.

with your great wealth and
　　your wares　　　　Eze 28:4-5
you enriched the kings of
　　the earth.
³⁴Now you are shattered by
　　the sea
　　in the depths of the waters;
your wares and all your
　　company
have gone down with you.
³⁵All who live in the coastlands
　　are appalled at you;　Lev 26:32
their kings shudder with
　　horror
and their faces are distorted
　　with fear.　　　　Eze 26:17-18
³⁶The merchants among the
　　nations hiss at you;　Jer 19:8
you have come to a horrible
　　end
and will be no more.' " Ps 37:10

A Prophecy Against the King of Tyre

28 The word of the LORD
　　came to me: ²"Son of
man, say to the ruler of Tyre,
'This is what the Sovereign
LORD says:　　　　　　Isa 13:11

" 'In the pride of your heart
　　you say, "I am a god;
I sit on the throne of a god
　　in the heart of the seas."
But you are a man and not a
　　god,
　　though you think you are
　　　as wise as a god.　　Ge 3:5
³Are you wiser than Daniel*ᵃ*?
　　Is no secret hidden from
　　　you?

⁴By your wisdom and
　　understanding
　　you have gained wealth for
　　　yourself
and amassed gold and silver
　　in your treasuries.　Isa 10:13
⁵By your great skill in trading
　　you have increased your
　　　wealth,　　　　　Jer 9:23
and because of your wealth
　　your heart has grown
　　　proud.　　　　　Job 31:25

⁶" 'Therefore this is what the
Sovereign LORD says:

" 'Because you think you are
　　wise,
　　as wise as a god,
⁷I am going to bring
　　foreigners against you,
　　the most ruthless of
　　　nations;　　　　Eze 30:11
they will draw their swords
　　against your beauty and
　　　wisdom　　　　　Jer 9:23
and pierce your shining
　　splendor.　　　　Eze 7:24
⁸They will bring you down to
　　the pit,　　　　　Ps 55:23
and you will die a violent
　　death　　　　　　Rev 18:7
　　in the heart of the seas.
⁹Will you then say, "I am a
　　god,"
　　in the presence of those
　　who kill you?
You will be but a man, not a
　　god,　　　　　　Isa 31:3
　　in the hands of those who
　　slay you.　　　　Eze 16:49
¹⁰You will die the death of the
　　uncircumcised　　1Sa 14:6

ᵃ3 Or *Danel*; the Hebrew spelling may suggest a person other than the prophet Daniel.

at the hands of foreigners.

I have spoken, declares the Sovereign LORD.' "

¹¹The word of the LORD came to me: ¹²"Son of man, take up a lament concerning the king of Tyre and say to him: 'This is what the Sovereign LORD says:

" 'You were the model of
        perfection,
    full of wisdom and perfect
        in beauty.   Eze 27:2-4
¹³You were in Eden,   Ge 2:8
    the garden of God;   Eze 31:8-9
    every precious stone adorned
        you: Rev 17:4
    ruby, topaz and emerald,
    chrysolite, onyx and jasper,
    sapphire,ᵃ turquoise and
        beryl.ᵇ   Eze 27:16
    Your settings and
        mountingsᶜ were made
        of gold;
    on the day you were
        created they were
        prepared.   Isa 14:11
¹⁴You were anointed as a
        guardian cherub,   Ex 30:26
    for so I ordained you.
    You were on the holy mount
        of God;
    you walked among the fiery
        stones.
¹⁵You were blameless in your
        ways
    from the day you were
        created
    till wickedness was found
        in you.

¹⁶Through your widespread
        trade
    you were filled with
        violence,   Ge 6:11
    and you sinned.
    So I drove you in disgrace
        from the mount of
        God,
    and I expelled you,
        O guardian cherub, Ge 3:24
    from among the fiery
        stones.
¹⁷Your heart became proud
    on account of your beauty,
    and you corrupted your
        wisdom
    because of your splendor.
    So I threw you to the earth;
    I made a spectacle of you
        before kings.   Eze 19:12
¹⁸By your many sins and
        dishonest trade
    you have desecrated your
        sanctuaries.
    So I made a fire come out
        from you,   Ob 18
    and it consumed you,
    and I reduced you to ashes
        on the ground   Mal 4:3
    in the sight of all who were
        watching.   Zec 9:2-4
¹⁹All the nations who knew
        you
    are appalled at you;   Lev 26:32
    you have come to a horrible
        end
    and will be no more.' "Jer 51:64

A Prophecy Against Sidon

²⁰The word of the LORD came to me: ²¹"Son of man, set your

ᵃ13 Or *lapis lazuli*   ᵇ13 The precise identification of some of these precious stones is
uncertain.   ᶜ13 The meaning of the Hebrew for this phrase is uncertain.

face against Sidon; prophesy against her [22]and say: 'This is what the Sovereign LORD says:

" 'I am against you, O Sidon,
    and I will gain glory within
    you.   Eze 39:13
They will know that I am the
    LORD,
    when I inflict punishment
        on her   Eze 30:19
    and show myself holy
        within her.   Lev 10:3
[23]I will send a plague upon her
    and make blood flow in her
    streets.
The slain will fall within her,
    with the sword against her
    on every side.
Then they will know that I
    am the LORD.   Eze 5:17

[24]" 'No longer will the people of Israel have malicious neighbors who are painful briers and sharp thorns. Then they will know that I am the Sovereign LORD.   Isa 5:6; Eze 2:6

[25]" 'This is what the Sovereign LORD says: When I gather the people of Israel from the nations where they have been scattered, I will show myself holy among them in the sight of the nations. Then they will live in their own land, which I gave to my servant Jacob. [26]They will live there in safety and will build houses and plant vineyards; they will live in safety when I inflict punishment on all their neighbors who maligned them. Then they will know that I am the LORD their God.' "Dt 20:6

A Prophecy Against Egypt

29 In the tenth year, in the tenth month on the twelfth day, the word of the LORD came to me: [2]"Son of man, set your face against Pharaoh king of Egypt and prophesy against him and against all Egypt. [3]Speak to him and say: 'This is what the Sovereign LORD says: Isa 19:1-17; Eze 26:1

" 'I am against you, Pharaoh
    king of Egypt,   Jer 44:30
you great monster lying
    among your streams.
You say, "The Nile is mine;
    I made it for myself." Jer 46:8
[4]But I will put hooks in your
    jaws   2Ki 19:28
and make the fish of your
    streams stick to your
    scales.
I will pull you out from
    among your streams,
    with all the fish sticking to
    your scales.   Eze 38:4
[5]I will leave you in the desert,
    you and all the fish of your
    streams.
You will fall on the open field
    and not be gathered or
    picked up.   Jer 8:2
I will give you as food
    to the beasts of the earth
    and the birds of the air.

[6]Then all who live in Egypt will know that I am the LORD.

" 'You have been a staff of reed for the house of Israel. [7]When they grasped you with their hands, you splintered and you tore open their shoulders;

when they leaned on you, you broke and their backs were wrenched. *a*   2Ki 18:21; Isa 36:6

8" 'Therefore this is what the Sovereign LORD says: I will bring a sword against you and kill your men and their animals. 9Egypt will become a desolate wasteland. Then they will know that I am the LORD.   Eze 25:13

" 'Because you said, "The Nile is mine; I made it," 10therefore I am against you and against your streams, and I will make the land of Egypt a ruin and a desolate waste from Migdol to Aswan, as far as the border of Cush. *b* 11No foot of man or animal will pass through it; no one will live there for forty years. 12I will make the land of Egypt desolate among devastated lands, and her cities will lie desolate forty years among ruined cities. And I will disperse the Egyptians among the nations and scatter them through the countries.   Jer 21:13

13" 'Yet this is what the Sovereign LORD says: At the end of forty years I will gather the Egyptians from the nations where they were scattered. 14I will bring them back from captivity and return them to Upper Egypt, *c* the land of their ancestry. There they will be a lowly kingdom. 15It will be the lowliest of kingdoms and will never again exalt itself above the other nations. I will make it so weak that it will never again rule over the nations. 16Egypt will no longer be a source of confidence for the people of Israel but will be a reminder of their sin in turning to her for help. Then they will know that I am the Sovereign LORD.' "   Isa 11:11

17In the twenty-seventh year, in the first month on the first day, the word of the LORD came to me: 18"Son of man, Nebuchadnezzar king of Babylon drove his army in a hard campaign against Tyre; every head was rubbed bare and every shoulder made raw. Yet he and his army got no reward from the campaign he led against Tyre. 19Therefore this is what the Sovereign LORD says: I am going to give Egypt to Nebuchadnezzar king of Babylon, and he will carry off its wealth. He will loot and plunder the land as pay for his army. 20I have given him Egypt as a reward for his efforts because he and his army did it for me, declares the Sovereign LORD.   Isa 43:3; Eze 24:1

21"On that day I will make a horn*d* grow for the house of Israel, and I will open your mouth among them. Then they will know that I am the LORD." Lk 1:69

A Lament for Egypt

30 The word of the LORD came to me: 2"Son of man, prophesy and say: 'This is

---

*a*7 Syriac (see also Septuagint and Vulgate); Hebrew *and you caused their backs to stand* *b*10 That is, the upper Nile region *c*14 Hebrew *to Pathros* *d*21 *Horn* here symbolizes strength.

what the Sovereign Lord says:

" 'Wail and say,   Isa 13:6
"Alas for that day!"'
[3]For the day is near,   Eze 7:7
the day of the Lord is
near—   Eze 7:12
a day of clouds,
a time of doom for the
nations.
[4]A sword will come against
Egypt,   Jer 25:19
and anguish will come
upon Cush.[a]   Ge 10:6
When the slain fall in Egypt,
her wealth will be carried
away
and her foundations torn
down.   Eze 29:19

[5]Cush and Put, Lydia and all
Arabia, Libya[b] and the people
of the covenant land will fall by
the sword along with Egypt.

[6]" 'This is what the Lord
says:

" 'The allies of Egypt will fall
and her proud strength will
fail.
From Migdol to Aswan Eze 29:10
they will fall by the sword
within her,
declares the Sovereign
Lord.
[7]" 'They will be desolate
among desolate lands,
and their cities will lie
among ruined cities.   Eze 29:12
[8]Then they will know that I
am the Lord,
when I set fire to Egypt

and all her helpers are
crushed.   Eze 29:9

[9]" 'On that day messengers
will go out from me in ships to
frighten Cush out of her complacency. Anguish will take
hold of them on the day of
Egypt's doom, for it is sure to
come.   Ge 10:6; Isa 23:5

[10]" 'This is what the Sovereign Lord says:

" 'I will put an end to the
hordes of Egypt
by the hand of
Nebuchadnezzar king of
Babylon.   Jer 39:1
[11]He and his army—the most
ruthless of nations—
will be brought in to
destroy the land.   Eze 28:7
They will draw their swords
against Egypt
and fill the land with the
slain.
[12]I will dry up the streams of
the Nile   Isa 19:6
and sell the land to evil
men;
by the hand of foreigners
I will lay waste the land and
everything in it.   Eze 19:7
I the Lord have spoken.

[13]" 'This is what the Sovereign Lord says:

" 'I will destroy the idols
and put an end to the
images in Memphis.[c]

---

[a]4 That is, the upper Nile region; also in verses 5 and 9   [b]5 Hebrew *Cub*
[c]13 Hebrew *Noph*; also in verse 16

No longer will there be a
   prince in Egypt,   Zec 10:11
and I will spread fear
   throughout the land.
14I will lay waste Upper
   Egypt,ᵃ   Eze 29:14
set fire to Zoan   Nu 13:22
and inflict punishment on
   Thebes.ᵇ   Jer 46:25
15I will pour out my wrath on
   Pelusium,ᶜ
the stronghold of Egypt,
and cut off the hordes of
   Thebes.
16I will set fire to Egypt;   Jos 7:15
Pelusium will writhe in
   agony.
Thebes will be taken by
   storm;
Memphis will be in
   constant distress.   Isa 19:13
17The young men of
   Heliopolisᵈ and
   Bubastisᵉ   Ge 41:45
will fall by the sword,
and the cities themselves
   will go into captivity.
18Dark will be the day at
   Tahpanhes   Jer 43:7
when I break the yoke of
   Egypt;   Lev 26:13
there her proud strength
   will come to an end.
She will be covered with
   clouds,
and her villages will go into
   captivity.
19So I will inflict punishment
   on Egypt,   Eze 28:22
and they will know that I
   am the LORD.'"

20In the eleventh year, in the first month on the seventh day, the word of the LORD came to me: 21"Son of man, I have broken the arm of Pharaoh king of Egypt. It has not been bound up for healing or put in a splint so as to become strong enough to hold a sword. 22Therefore this is what the Sovereign LORD says: I am against Pharaoh king of Egypt. I will break both his arms, the good arm as well as the broken one, and make the sword fall from his hand. 23I will disperse the Egyptians among the nations and scatter them through the countries. 24I will strengthen the arms of the king of Babylon and put my sword in his hand, but I will break the arms of Pharaoh, and he will groan before him like a mortally wounded man. 25I will strengthen the arms of the king of Babylon, but the arms of Pharaoh will fall limp. Then they will know that I am the LORD, when I put my sword into the hand of the king of Babylon and he brandishes it against Egypt. 26I will disperse the Egyptians among the nations and scatter them through the countries. Then they will know that I am the LORD."   1Ch 21:12; Eze 26:1

A Cedar in Lebanon

31 In the eleventh year, in the third month on the

ᵃ14 Hebrew *waste Pathros*   ᵇ14 Hebrew *No*; also in verses 15 and 16   ᶜ15 Hebrew
Sin; also in verse 16   ᵈ17 Hebrew *Awen* (or *On*)   ᵉ17 Hebrew *Pi Beseth*

first day, the word of the LORD came to me: ²"Son of man, say to Pharaoh king of Egypt and to his hordes: _{Jer 52:5; Eze 30:20}

" 'Who can be compared
  with you in majesty?
³Consider Assyria, once a
    cedar in Lebanon, _{2Ki 19:23}
  with beautiful branches
    overshadowing the
    forest;
  it towered on high,
    its top above the thick
    foliage. _{Isa 10:34}
⁴The waters nourished it,
  deep springs made it grow
    tall; _{Eze 17:7}
  their streams flowed
  all around its base
and sent their channels
  to all the trees of the field.
⁵So it towered higher
  than all the trees of the
    field;
  its boughs increased
  and its branches grew
    long,
  spreading because of
    abundant waters. _{Nu 24:6}
⁶All the birds of the air
  nested in its boughs,
all the beasts of the field
  gave birth under its
    branches; _{Ge 31:7-9}
all the great nations
  lived in its shade. _{Eze 17:23}
⁷It was majestic in beauty,
  with its spreading boughs,
for its roots went down
  to abundant waters. _{Job 14:9}
⁸The cedars in the garden of
    God
  could not rival it, _{Ps 80:10}

nor could the pine trees
  equal its boughs,
nor could the plane trees
  compare with its
    branches— _{Ge 30:37}
no tree in the garden of God
  could match its beauty._{Ge 2:8-9}
⁹I made it beautiful
  with abundant branches,
the envy of all the trees of
    Eden
  in the garden of God. _{Ge 13:10}

¹⁰" 'Therefore this is what the Sovereign LORD says: Because it towered on high, lifting its top above the thick foliage, and because it was proud of its height, ¹¹I handed it over to the ruler of the nations, for him to deal with according to its wickedness. I cast it aside, ¹²and the most ruthless of foreign nations cut it down and left it. Its boughs fell on the mountains and in all the valleys; its branches lay broken in all the ravines of the land. All the nations of the earth came out from under its shade and left it. ¹³All the birds of the air settled on the fallen tree, and all the beasts of the field were among its branches. ¹⁴Therefore no other trees by the waters are ever to tower proudly on high, lifting their tops above the thick foliage. No other trees so well-watered are ever to reach such a height; they are all destined for death, for the earth below, among mortal men, with those who go down to the pit. _{Isa 2:11}

¹⁵" 'This is what the Sovereign LORD says: On the day it

was brought down to the grave[a] I covered the deep springs with mourning for it; I held back its streams, and its abundant waters were restrained. Because of it I clothed Lebanon with gloom, and all the trees of the field withered away. [16]I made the nations tremble at the sound of its fall when I brought it down to the grave with those who go down to the pit. Then all the trees of Eden, the choicest and best of Lebanon, all the trees that were well-watered, were consoled in the earth below. [17]Those who lived in its shade, its allies among the nations, had also gone down to the grave with it, joining those killed by the sword. 2Sa 1:21

[18]" 'Which of the trees of Eden can be compared with you in splendor and majesty? Yet you, too, will be brought down with the trees of Eden to the earth below; you will lie among the uncircumcised, with those killed by the sword. Jer 9:26

" 'This is Pharaoh and all his hordes, declares the Sovereign LORD.' "

A Lament for Pharaoh

32 In the twelfth year, in the twelfth month on the first day, the word of the LORD came to me: [2]"Son of man, take up a lament concerning Pharaoh king of Egypt and say to him:

" 'You are like a lion among the nations; 2Ki 24:1

you are like a monster in the seas Job 3:8

thrashing about in your streams, churning the water with your feet and muddying the streams.

[3]" 'This is what the Sovereign LORD says:

" 'With a great throng of people I will cast my net over you, and they will haul you up in my net. Eze 12:13

[4]I will throw you on the land and hurl you on the open field.

I will let all the birds of the air settle on you and all the beasts of the earth gorge themselves on you. Isa 18:6

[5]I will spread your flesh on the mountains and fill the valleys with your remains. Eze 31:12

[6]I will drench the land with your flowing blood all the way to the mountains, Isa 34:3 and the ravines will be filled with your flesh.

[7]When I snuff you out, I will cover the heavens and darken their stars; I will cover the sun with a cloud, and the moon will not give its light. Isa 13:10

[8]All the shining lights in the heavens

---

[a]15 Hebrew *Sheol*; also in verses 16 and 17

I will darken over you;
I will bring darkness over
  your land,   Job 9:7
    declares the Sovereign
      LORD.
⁹I will trouble the hearts of
  many peoples
when I bring about your
    destruction among the
    nations,
  among*a* lands you have not
    known.
¹⁰I will cause many peoples to
  be appalled at you,
and their kings will
    shudder with horror
    because of you
when I brandish my sword
    before them.   Isa 30:32
On the day of your downfall
  each of them will tremble
  every moment for his life.

¹¹" 'For this is what the Sovereign LORD says:

" 'The sword of the king of
    Babylon   Isa 19:4; Eze 21:19
  will come against you.
¹²I will cause your hordes to
    fall
  by the swords of mighty
    men—
  the most ruthless of all
    nations.   Eze 28:7
They will shatter the pride of
    Egypt,
  and all her hordes will be
    overthrown.   Eze 31:11-12
¹³I will destroy all her cattle
  from beside abundant
    waters

no longer to be stirred by the
    foot of man
  or muddied by the hoofs of
    cattle.   Eze 29:8
¹⁴Then I will let her waters
    settle
  and make her streams flow
    like oil,
    declares the Sovereign
      LORD.
¹⁵When I make Egypt desolate
  and strip the land of
    everything in it,
when I strike down all who
    live there,
  then they will know that I
    am the LORD.'   Ex 7:5

¹⁶"This is the lament they will
chant for her. The daughters of
the nations will chant it; for
Egypt and all her hordes they
will chant it, declares the Sovereign LORD."   Ge 50:10; Eze 19:1

¹⁷In the twelfth year, on the
fifteenth day of the month, the
word of the LORD came to me:
¹⁸"Son of man, wail for the
hordes of Egypt and consign to
the earth below both her and
the daughters of mighty nations, with those who go down
to the pit. ¹⁹Say to them, 'Are
you more favored than others?
Go down and be laid among the
uncircumcised.' ²⁰They will fall
among those killed by the
sword. The sword is drawn; let
her be dragged off with all her
hordes. ²¹From within the
grave*b* the mighty leaders will

---

*a*9 Hebrew; Septuagint *bring you into captivity among the nations, / to*   *b*21 Hebrew
Sheol; also in verse 27

say of Egypt and her allies, 'They have come down and they lie with the uncircumcised, with those killed by the sword.'

²²"Assyria is there with her whole army; she is surrounded by the graves of all her slain, all who have fallen by the sword. ²³Their graves are in the depths of the pit and her army lies around her grave. All who had spread terror in the land of the living are slain, fallen by the sword.   Isa 14:15

²⁴"Elam is there, with all her hordes around her grave. All of them are slain, fallen by the sword. All who had spread terror in the land of the living went down uncircumcised to the earth below. They bear their shame with those who go down to the pit. ²⁵A bed is made for her among the slain, with all her hordes around her grave. All of them are uncircumcised, killed by the sword. Because their terror had spread in the land of the living, they bear their shame with those who go down to the pit; they are laid among the slain.   Ge 10:22; Eze 28:10

²⁶"Meshech and Tubal are there, with all their hordes around their graves. All of them are uncircumcised, killed by the sword because they spread their terror in the land of the living. ²⁷Do they not lie with the other uncircumcised warriors who have fallen, who went down to the grave with their weapons of war, whose swords were placed under their heads?

The punishment for their sins rested on their bones, though the terror of these warriors had stalked through the land of the living.   Eze 27:13; 28:10

²⁸"You too, O Pharaoh, will be broken and will lie among the uncircumcised, with those killed by the sword.

²⁹"Edom is there, her kings and all her princes; despite their power, they are laid with those killed by the sword. They lie with the uncircumcised, with those who go down to the pit.

³⁰"All the princes of the north and all the Sidonians are there; they went down with the slain in disgrace despite the terror caused by their power. They lie uncircumcised with those killed by the sword and bear their shame with those who go down to the pit.   Isa 14:31; Jer 25:26

³¹"Pharaoh—he and all his army—will see them and he will be consoled for all his hordes that were killed by the sword, declares the Sovereign LORD. ³²Although I had him spread terror in the land of the living, Pharaoh and all his hordes will be laid among the uncircumcised, with those killed by the sword, declares the Sovereign LORD."   Lev 26:25; Eze 14:22

Ezekiel a Watchman

33 The word of the LORD came to me: ²"Son of man, speak to your countrymen and say to them: 'When I bring the sword against a land, and the people of the land choose

they will know that a prophet has been among them." 1Sa 3:20

Shepherds and Sheep

34 The word of the LORD came to me: 2"Son of man, prophesy against the shepherds of Israel; prophesy and say to them: 'This is what the Sovereign LORD says: Woe to the shepherds of Israel who only take care of themselves! Should not shepherds take care of the flock? 3You eat the curds, clothe yourselves with the wool and slaughter the choice animals, but you do not take care of the flock. 4You have not strengthened the weak or healed the sick or bound up the injured. You have not brought back the strays or searched for the lost. You have ruled them harshly and brutally. 5So they were scattered because there was no shepherd, and when they were scattered they became food for all the wild animals. 6My sheep wandered over all the mountains and on every high hill. They were scattered over the whole earth, and no one searched or looked for them. Ps 78:70-72; Jer 50:6

7" 'Therefore, you shepherds, hear the word of the LORD: 8As surely as I live, declares the Sovereign LORD, because my flock lacks a shepherd and so has been plundered and has become food for all the wild animals, and because my shepherds did not search for my flock but cared for themselves rather than for my flock, 9therefore, O shepherds, hear the word of the LORD: 10This is what the Sovereign LORD says: I am against the shepherds and will hold them accountable for my flock. I will remove them from tending the flock so that the shepherds can no longer feed themselves. I will rescue my flock from their mouths, and it will no longer be food for them.

11" 'For this is what the Sovereign LORD says: I myself will search for my sheep and look after them. 12As a shepherd looks after his scattered flock when he is with them, so will I look after my sheep. I will rescue them from all the places where they were scattered on a day of clouds and darkness. 13I will bring them out from the nations and gather them from the countries, and I will bring them into their own land. I will pasture them on the mountains of Israel, in the ravines and in all the settlements in the land. 14I will tend them in a good pasture, and the mountain heights of Israel will be their grazing land. There they will lie down in good grazing land, and there they will feed in a rich pasture on the mountains of Israel. 15I myself will tend my sheep and have them lie down, declares the Sovereign LORD. 16I will search for the lost and bring back the strays. I will bind up the injured and strengthen the weak, but the sleek and the

strong I will destroy. I will shepherd the flock with justice.Lk 19:10

17" 'As for you, my flock, this is what the Sovereign LORD says: I will judge between one sheep and another, and between rams and goats. 18Is it not enough for you to feed on the good pasture? Must you also trample the rest of your pasture with your feet? Is it not enough for you to drink clear water? Must you also muddy the rest with your feet? 19Must my flock feed on what you have trampled and drink what you have muddied with your feet? Ge 30:15

20" 'Therefore this is what the Sovereign LORD says to them: See, I myself will judge between the fat sheep and the lean sheep. 21Because you shove with flank and shoulder, butting all the weak sheep with your horns until you have driven them away, 22I will save my flock, and they will no longer be plundered. I will judge between one sheep and another. 23I will place over them one shepherd, my servant David, and he will tend them; he will tend them and be their shepherd. 24I the LORD will be their God, and my servant David will be prince among them. I the LORD have spoken. Mt 25:32

25" 'I will make a covenant of peace with them and rid the land of wild beasts so that they may live in the desert and sleep in the forests in safety. 26I will bless them and the places surrounding my hill.a I will send down showers in season; there will be showers of blessing. 27The trees of the field will yield their fruit and the ground will yield its crops; the people will be secure in their land. They will know that I am the LORD, when I break the bars of their yoke and rescue them from the hands of those who enslaved them. 28They will no longer be plundered by the nations, nor will wild animals devour them. They will live in safety, and no one will make them afraid. 29I will provide for them a land renowned for its crops, and they will no longer be victims of famine in the land or bear the scorn of the nations. 30Then they will know that I, the LORD their God, am with them and that they, the house of Israel, are my people, declares the Sovereign LORD. 31You my sheep, the sheep of my pasture, are people, and I am your God, declares the Sovereign LORD.' "

A Prophecy Against Edom

35 The word of the LORD came to me: 2"Son of man, set your face against Mount Seir; prophesy against it 3and say: 'This is what the Sovereign LORD says: I am against you, Mount Seir, and I will stretch out my hand against you and make you a desolate waste. 4I will turn your towns into

---

a26 Or I will make them and the places surrounding my hill a blessing

ruins and you will be desolate. Then you will know that I am the LORD.   Ge 14:6; Jer 44:2

5" 'Because you harbored an ancient hostility and delivered the Israelites over to the sword at the time of their calamity, the time their punishment reached its climax, 6therefore as surely as I live, declares the Sovereign LORD, I will give you over to bloodshed and it will pursue you. Since you did not hate bloodshed, bloodshed will pursue you. 7I will make Mount Seir a desolate waste and cut off from it all who come and go. 8I will fill your mountains with the slain; those killed by the sword will fall on your hills and in your valleys and in all your ravines. 9I will make you desolate forever; your towns will not be inhabited. Then you will know that I am the LORD.   Ps 63:10; Ob 10

10" 'Because you have said, "These two nations and countries will be ours and we will take possession of them," even though I the LORD was there, 11therefore as surely as I live, declares the Sovereign LORD, I will treat you in accordance with the anger and jealousy you showed in your hatred of them and I will make myself known among them when I judge you. 12Then you will know that I the LORD have heard all the contemptible things you have said against the mountains of Israel. You said, "They have been laid waste and have been given over to us to devour." 13You boasted against

me and spoke against me without restraint, and I heard it. 14This is what the Sovereign LORD says: While the whole earth rejoices, I will make you desolate. 15Because you rejoiced when the inheritance of the house of Israel became desolate, that is how I will treat you. You will be desolate, O Mount Seir, you and all of Edom. Then they will know that I am the LORD.' "

A Prophecy to the Mountains of Israel

36 "Son of man, prophesy to the mountains of Israel and say, 'O mountains of Israel, hear the word of the LORD. 2This is what the Sovereign LORD says: The enemy said of you, "Aha! The ancient heights have become our possession." ' 3Therefore prophesy and say, 'This is what the Sovereign LORD says: Because they ravaged and hounded you from every side so that you became the possession of the rest of the nations and the object of people's malicious talk and slander, 4therefore, O mountains of Israel, hear the word of the Sovereign LORD: This is what the Sovereign LORD says to the mountains and hills, to the ravines and valleys, to the desolate ruins and the deserted towns that have been plundered and ridiculed by the rest of the nations around you— 5this is what the Sovereign LORD says: In my burning zeal I have

spoken against the rest of the nations, and against all Edom, for with glee and with malice in their hearts they made my land their own possession so that they might plunder its pastureland.' 6Therefore prophesy concerning the land of Israel and say to the mountains and hills, to the ravines and valleys: 'This is what the Sovereign LORD says: I speak in my jealous wrath because you have suffered the scorn of the nations. 7Therefore this is what the Sovereign LORD says: I swear with uplifted hand that the nations around you will also suffer scorn. Nu 14:30; Eze 17:22

8" 'But you, O mountains of Israel, will produce branches and fruit for my people Israel, for they will soon come home. 9I am concerned for you and will look on you with favor; you will be plowed and sown, 10and I will multiply the number of people upon you, even the whole house of Israel. The towns will be inhabited and the ruins rebuilt. 11I will increase the number of men and animals upon you, and they will be fruitful and become numerous. I will settle people on you as in the past and will make you prosper more than before. Then you will know that I am the LORD. 12I will cause people, my people Israel, to walk upon you. They will possess you, and you will be their inheritance; you will never again deprive them of their children. Isa 4:2; Zec 10:8

13" 'This is what the Sovereign LORD says: Because people say to you, "You devour men and deprive your nation of its children," 14therefore you will no longer devour men or make your nation childless, declares the Sovereign LORD. 15No longer will I make you hear the taunts of the nations, and no longer will you suffer the scorn of the peoples or cause your nation to fall, declares the Sovereign LORD.' " Nu 13:32; Isa 54:4

16Again the word of the LORD came to me: 17"Son of man, when the people of Israel were living in their own land, they defiled it by their conduct and their actions. Their conduct was like a woman's monthly uncleanness in my sight. 18So I poured out my wrath on them because they had shed blood in the land and because they had defiled it with their idols. 19I dispersed them among the nations, and they were scattered through the countries; I judged them according to their conduct and their actions. 20And wherever they went among the nations they profaned my holy name, for it was said of them, 'These are the LORD's people, and yet they had to leave his land.' 21I had concern for my holy name, which the house of Israel profaned among the nations where they had gone.

22"Therefore say to the house of Israel, 'This is what the Sovereign LORD says: It is not for your sake, O house of Israel,

that I am going to do these things, but for the sake of my holy name, which you have profaned among the nations where you have gone. ²³I will show the holiness of my great name, which has been profaned among the nations, the name you have profaned among them. Then the nations will know that I am the LORD, declares the Sovereign LORD, when I show myself holy through you before their eyes.

²⁴" 'For I will take you out of the nations; I will gather you from all the countries and bring you back into your own land. ²⁵I will sprinkle clean water on you, and you will be clean; I will cleanse you from all your impurities and from all your idols. ²⁶I will give you a new heart and put a new spirit in you; I will remove from you your heart of stone and give you a heart of flesh. ²⁷And I will put my Spirit in you and move you to follow my decrees and be careful to keep my laws. ²⁸You will live in the land I gave your forefathers; you will be my people, and I will be your God. ²⁹I will save you from all your uncleanness. I will call for the grain and make it plentiful and will not bring famine upon you. ³⁰I will increase the fruit of the trees and the crops of the field, so that you will no longer suffer disgrace among the nations because of famine. ³¹Then you will remember your evil ways and wicked deeds, and you will

loathe yourselves for your sins and detestable practices. ³²I want you to know that I am not doing this for your sake, declares the Sovereign LORD. Be ashamed and disgraced for your conduct, O house of Israel!

³³" 'This is what the Sovereign LORD says: On the day I cleanse you from all your sins, I will resettle your towns, and the ruins will be rebuilt. ³⁴The desolate land will be cultivated instead of lying desolate in the sight of all who pass through it. ³⁵They will say, "This land that was laid waste has become like the garden of Eden; the cities that were lying in ruins, desolate and destroyed, are now fortified and inhabited." ³⁶Then the nations around you that remain will know that I the LORD have rebuilt what was destroyed and have replanted what was desolate. I the LORD have spoken, and I will do it.'

³⁷"This is what the Sovereign LORD says: Once again I will yield to the plea of the house of Israel and do this for them: I will make their people as numerous as sheep, ³⁸as numerous as the flocks for offerings at Jerusalem during her appointed feasts. So will the ruined cities be filled with flocks of people. Then they will know that I am the LORD."

The Valley of Dry Bones

37 The hand of the LORD was upon me, and he brought me out by the Spirit of the LORD and set me in the mid-

dle of a valley; it was full of bones. ²He led me back and forth among them, and I saw a great many bones on the floor of the valley, bones that were very dry. ³He asked me, "Son of man, can these bones live?"

I said, "O Sovereign LORD, you alone know."   Dt 32:39

⁴Then he said to me, "Prophesy to these bones and say to them, 'Dry bones, hear the word of the LORD! ⁵This is what the Sovereign LORD says to these bones: I will make breath*a* enter you, and you will come to life. ⁶I will attach tendons to you and make flesh come upon you and cover you with skin; I will put breath in you, and you will come to life. Then you will know that I am the LORD.' "   Ex 6:2; Jer 22:29

⁷So I prophesied as I was commanded. And as I was prophesying, there was a noise, a rattling sound, and the bones came together, bone to bone. ⁸I looked, and tendons and flesh appeared on them and skin covered them, but there was no breath in them.   Eze 38:19

⁹Then he said to me, "Prophesy to the breath; prophesy, son of man, and say to it, 'This is what the Sovereign LORD says: Come from the four winds, O breath, and breathe into these slain, that they may live.' " ¹⁰So I prophesied as he commanded me, and breath entered them; they came to life

and stood up on their feet—a vast army.   Ps 104:30; Eze 12:7

¹¹Then he said to me: "Son of man, these bones are the whole house of Israel. They say, 'Our bones are dried up and our hope is gone; we are cut off.' ¹²Therefore prophesy and say to them: 'This is what the Sovereign LORD says: O my people, I am going to open your graves and bring you up from them; I will bring you back to the land of Israel. ¹³Then you, my people, will know that I am the LORD, when I open your graves and bring you up from them. ¹⁴I will put my Spirit in you and you will live, and I will settle you in your own land. Then you will know that I the LORD have spoken, and I have done it, declares the LORD.' "   Ex 6:2; Job 17:15

One Nation Under One King

¹⁵The word of the LORD came to me: ¹⁶"Son of man, take a stick of wood and write on it, 'Belonging to Judah and the Israelites associated with him.' Then take another stick of wood, and write on it, 'Ephraim's stick, belonging to Joseph and all the house of Israel associated with him.' ¹⁷Join them together into one stick so that they will become one in your hand.   1Ki 12:20; Isa 11:13

¹⁸"When your countrymen ask you, 'Won't you tell us what you mean by this?' ¹⁹say to them, 'This is what the Sover-

---

*a*5 The Hebrew for this word can also mean *wind* or *spirit* (see verses 6-14).

eign LORD says: I am going to take the stick of Joseph—which is in Ephraim's hand—and of the Israelite tribes associated with him, and join it to Judah's stick, making them a single stick of wood, and they will become one in my hand.' ²⁰Hold before their eyes the sticks you have written on ²¹and say to them, 'This is what the Sovereign LORD says: I will take the Israelites out of the nations where they have gone. I will gather them from all around and bring them back into their own land. ²²I will make them one nation in the land, on the mountains of Israel. There will be one king over all of them and they will never again be two nations or be divided into two kingdoms. ²³They will no longer defile themselves with their idols and vile images or with any of their offenses, for I will save them from all their sinful backsliding,ᵃ and I will cleanse them. They will be my people, and I will be their God.   Eze 24:19

²⁴'' 'My servant David will be king over them, and they will all have one shepherd. They will follow my laws and be careful to keep my decrees. ²⁵They will live in the land I gave to my servant Jacob, the land where your fathers lived. They and their children and their children's children will live there forever, and David my servant will be their prince forever. ²⁶I will make a covenant of peace with them; it will be an everlasting covenant. I will establish them and increase their numbers, and I will put my sanctuary among them forever. ²⁷My dwelling place will be with them; I will be their God, and they will be my people. ²⁸Then the nations will know that I the LORD make Israel holy, when my sanctuary is among them forever.' ''   Ex 31:13; Isa 55:4

A Prophecy Against Gog

38 The word of the LORD came to me: ²"Son of man, set your face against Gog, of the land of Magog, the chief prince ofᵇ Meshech and Tubal; prophesy against him ³and say: 'This is what the Sovereign LORD says: I am against you, O Gog, chief prince ofᶜ Meshech and Tubal. ⁴I will turn you around, put hooks in your jaws and bring you out with your whole army—your horses, your horsemen fully armed, and a great horde with large and small shields, all of them brandishing their swords. ⁵Persia, Cushᵈ and Put will be with them, all with shields and helmets, ⁶also Gomer with all its troops, and Beth Togarmah from the far north with all its troops—the many nations with you.   Eze 39:11

⁷'' 'Get ready; be prepared, you and all the hordes gathered

ᵃ23 Many Hebrew manuscripts (see also Septuagint); most Hebrew manuscripts *all their dwelling places where they sinned*   ᵇ2 Or *the prince of Rosh,*   ᶜ3 Or *Gog, prince of Rosh,*   ᵈ5 That is, the upper Nile region

about you, and take command of them. ⁸After many days you will be called to arms. In future years you will invade a land that has recovered from war, whose people were gathered from many nations to the mountains of Israel, which had long been desolate. They had been brought out from the nations, and now all of them live in safety. ⁹You and all your troops and the many nations with you will go up, advancing like a storm; you will be like a cloud covering the land.   Isa 8:9

¹⁰" 'This is what the Sovereign LORD says: On that day thoughts will come into your mind and you will devise an evil scheme. ¹¹You will say, "I will invade a land of unwalled villages; I will attack a peaceful and unsuspecting people—all of them living without walls and without gates and bars. ¹²I will plunder and loot and turn my hand against the resettled ruins and the people gathered from the nations, rich in livestock and goods, living at the center of the land." ¹³Sheba and Dedan and the merchants of Tarshish and all her villages*a* will say to you, "Have you come to plunder? Have you gathered your hordes to loot, to carry off silver and gold, to take away livestock and goods and to seize much plunder?" '   Jer 17:10

¹⁴"Therefore, son of man, prophesy and say to Gog: 'This is what the Sovereign LORD says: In that day, when my people Israel are living in safety, will you not take notice of it? ¹⁵You will come from your place in the far north, you and many nations with you, all of them riding on horses, a great horde, a mighty army. ¹⁶You will advance against my people Israel like a cloud that covers the land. In days to come, O Gog, I will bring you against my land, so that the nations may know me when I show myself holy through you before their eyes.

¹⁷" 'This is what the Sovereign LORD says: Are you not the one I spoke of in former days by my servants the prophets of Israel? At that time they prophesied for years that I would bring you against them. ¹⁸This is what will happen in that day: When Gog attacks the land of Israel, my hot anger will be aroused, declares the Sovereign LORD. ¹⁹In my zeal and fiery wrath I declare that at that time there shall be a great earthquake in the land of Israel. ²⁰The fish of the sea, the birds of the air, the beasts of the field, every creature that moves along the ground, and all the people on the face of the earth will tremble at my presence. The mountains will be overturned, the cliffs will crumble and every wall will fall to the ground. ²¹I will summon a sword against Gog on all my mountains, declares the Sover-

---

a13 Or *her strong lions*

eign LORD. Every man's sword will be against his brother. ²²I will execute judgment upon him with plague and bloodshed; I will pour down torrents of rain, hailstones and burning sulfur on him and on his troops and on the many nations with him. ²³And so I will show my greatness and my holiness, and I will make myself known in the sight of many nations. Then they will know that I am the LORD.'

Isa 24:18; Eze 20:42

39 "Son of man, prophesy against Gog and say: 'This is what the Sovereign LORD says: I am against you, O Gog, chief prince of*ᵃ* Meshech and Tubal. ²I will turn you around and drag you along. I will bring you from the far north and send you against the mountains of Israel. ³Then I will strike your bow from your left hand and make your arrows drop from your right hand. ⁴On the mountains of Israel you will fall, you and all your troops and the nations with you. I will give you as food to all kinds of carrion birds and to the wild animals. ⁵You will fall in the open field, for I have spoken, declares the Sovereign LORD. ⁶I will send fire on Magog and on those who live in safety in the coastlands, and they will know that I am the LORD.

Eze 30:8; Rev 20:8

⁷" 'I will make known my holy name among my people Is-rael. I will no longer let my holy name be profaned, and the nations will know that I the LORD am the Holy One in Israel. ⁸It is coming! It will surely take place, declares the Sovereign LORD. This is the day I have spoken of.

⁹" 'Then those who live in the towns of Israel will go out and use the weapons for fuel and burn them up—the small and large shields, the bows and arrows, the war clubs and spears. For seven years they will use them for fuel. ¹⁰They will not need to gather wood from the fields or cut it from the forests, because they will use the weapons for fuel. And they will plunder those who plundered them and loot those who looted them, declares the Sovereign LORD.

Ps 76:3; Hab 2:8

¹¹" 'On that day I will give Gog a burial place in Israel, in the valley of those who travel east toward*ᵇ* the Sea.*ᶜ* It will block the way of travelers, because Gog and all his hordes will be buried there. So it will be called the Valley of Hamon Gog.*ᵈ*

Isa 34:3; Eze 38:2

¹²" 'For seven months the house of Israel will be burying them in order to cleanse the land. ¹³All the people of the land will bury them, and the day I am glorified will be a memorable day for them, declares the Sovereign LORD.

Dt 21:23; Eze 28:22

ᵃ1 Or *Gog, prince of Rosh,*   *ᵇ11* Or *of*   *ᶜ11* That is, the Dead Sea   *ᵈ11* *Hamon Gog* means *hordes of Gog.*

¹⁴" 'Men will be regularly employed to cleanse the land. Some will go throughout the land and, in addition to them, others will bury those that remain on the ground. At the end of the seven months they will begin their search. ¹⁵As they go through the land and one of them sees a human bone, he will set up a marker beside it until the gravediggers have buried it in the Valley of Hamon Gog. ¹⁶(Also a town called Hamonah^a will be there.) And so they will cleanse the land.'

¹⁷"Son of man, this is what the Sovereign LORD says: Call out to every kind of bird and all the wild animals: 'Assemble and come together from all around to the sacrifice I am preparing for you, the great sacrifice on the mountains of Israel. There you will eat flesh and drink blood. ¹⁸You will eat the flesh of mighty men and drink the blood of the princes of the earth as if they were rams and lambs, goats and bulls—all of them fattened animals from Bashan. ¹⁹At the sacrifice I am preparing for you, you will eat fat till you are glutted and drink blood till you are drunk. ²⁰At my table you will eat your fill of horses and riders, mighty men and soldiers of every kind,' declares the Sovereign LORD.

²¹"I will display my glory among the nations, and all the nations will see the punishment I inflict and the hand I lay upon them. ²²From that day forward the house of Israel will know that I am the LORD their God. ²³And the nations will know that the people of Israel went into exile for their sin, because they were unfaithful to me. So I hid my face from them and handed them over to their enemies, and they all fell by the sword. ²⁴I dealt with them according to their uncleanness and their offenses, and I hid my face from them.   Ex 9:16; 2Ki 17:23

²⁵"Therefore this is what the Sovereign LORD says: I will now bring Jacob back from captivity^b and will have compassion on all the people of Israel, and I will be zealous for my holy name. ²⁶They will forget their shame and all the unfaithfulness they showed toward me when they lived in safety in their land with no one to make them afraid. ²⁷When I have brought them back from the nations and have gathered them from the countries of their enemies, I will show myself holy through them in the sight of many nations. ²⁸Then they will know that I am the LORD their God, for though I sent them into exile among the nations, I will gather them to their own land, not leaving any behind. ²⁹I will no longer hide my face from them, for I will pour out my Spirit on the house of Israel, declares the Sovereign LORD."   Dt 31:17; Jer 33:7

---

^a16 *Hamonah* means *horde.*   ^b25 Or *now restore the fortunes of Jacob*

The New Temple Area

40 In the twenty-fifth year of our exile, at the beginning of the year, on the tenth of the month, in the fourteenth year after the fall of the city—on that very day the hand of the LORD was upon me and he took me there. ²In visions of God he took me to the land of Israel and set me on a very high mountain, on whose south side were some buildings that looked like a city. ³He took me there, and I saw a man whose appearance was like bronze; he was standing in the gateway with a linen cord and a measuring rod in his hand. ⁴The man said to me, "Son of man, look with your eyes and hear with your ears and pay attention to everything I am going to show you, for that is why you have been brought here. Tell the house of Israel everything you see." Dt 6:6; 2Ki 25:7

The East Gate to the Outer Court

⁵I saw a wall completely surrounding the temple area. The length of the measuring rod in the man's hand was six long cubits, each of which was a cubit*a* and a handbreadth.*b* He measured the wall; it was one measuring rod thick and one rod high. Eze 42:20

⁶Then he went to the gate facing east. He climbed its steps and measured the threshold of the gate; it was one rod deep.*c* ⁷The alcoves for the guards were one rod long and one rod wide, and the projecting walls between the alcoves were five cubits thick. And the threshold of the gate next to the portico facing the temple was one rod deep. Eze 8:16

⁸Then he measured the portico of the gateway; ⁹it*d* was eight cubits deep and its jambs were two cubits thick. The portico of the gateway faced the temple.

¹⁰Inside the east gate were three alcoves on each side; the three had the same measurements, and the faces of the projecting walls on each side had the same measurements. ¹¹Then he measured the width of the entrance to the gateway; it was ten cubits and its length was thirteen cubits. ¹²In front of each alcove was a wall one cubit high, and the alcoves were six cubits square. ¹³Then he measured the gateway from the top of the rear wall of one alcove to the top of the opposite one; the distance was twenty-five cubits from one parapet opening to the opposite one. ¹⁴He measured along the faces of the projecting walls all around the inside of the gateway—sixty cubits. The

---

a5 The common cubit was about 1 1/2 feet (about 0.5 meter).   *b5* That is, about 3 inches (about 8 centimeters)   *c6* Septuagint; Hebrew *deep, the first threshold, one rod deep*   *d8,9* Many Hebrew manuscripts, Septuagint, Vulgate and Syriac; most Hebrew manuscripts *gateway facing the temple; it was one rod deep.* *9Then he measured the portico of the gateway; it*

measurement was up to the portico[a] facing the courtyard.[b] 15The distance from the entrance of the gateway to the far end of its portico was fifty cubits. 16The alcoves and the projecting walls inside the gateway were surmounted by narrow parapet openings all around, as was the portico; the openings all around faced inward. The faces of the projecting walls were decorated with palm trees. Ex 27:9

The Outer Court

17Then he brought me into the outer court. There I saw some rooms and a pavement that had been constructed all around the court; there were thirty rooms along the pavement. 18It abutted the sides of the gateways and was as wide as they were long; this was the lower pavement. 19Then he measured the distance from the inside of the lower gateway to the outside of the inner court; it was a hundred cubits on the east side as well as on the north.

The North Gate

20Then he measured the length and width of the gate facing north, leading into the outer court. 21Its alcoves—three on each side—its projecting walls and its portico had the same measurements as those of the first gateway. It was fifty cubits long and twenty-five cubits wide. 22Its openings, its portico and its palm tree decorations had the same measurements as those of the gate facing east. Seven steps led up to it, with its portico opposite them. 23There was a gate to the inner court facing the north gate, just as there was on the east. He measured from one gate to the opposite one; it was a hundred cubits.

The South Gate

24Then he led me to the south side and I saw a gate facing south. He measured its jambs and its portico, and they had the same measurements as the others. 25The gateway and its portico had narrow openings all around, like the openings of the others. It was fifty cubits long and twenty-five cubits wide. 26Seven steps led up to it, with its portico opposite them; it had palm tree decorations on the faces of the projecting walls on each side. 27The inner court also had a gate facing south, and he measured from this gate to the outer gate on the south side; it was a hundred cubits.

Gates to the Inner Court

28Then he brought me into the inner court through the south gate, and he measured the south gate; it had the same measurements as the others.

a14 Septuagint; Hebrew projecting wall   b14 The meaning of the Hebrew for this verse is uncertain.

²⁹Its alcoves, its projecting walls and its portico had the same measurements as the others. The gateway and its portico had openings all around. It was fifty cubits long and twenty-five cubits wide. ³⁰(The porticoes of the gateways around the inner court were twenty-five cubits wide and five cubits deep.) ³¹Its portico faced the outer court; palm trees decorated its jambs, and eight steps led up to it.

³²Then he brought me to the inner court on the east side, and he measured the gateway; it had the same measurements as the others. ³³Its alcoves, its projecting walls and its portico had the same measurements as the others. The gateway and its portico had openings all around. It was fifty cubits long and twenty-five cubits wide. ³⁴Its portico faced the outer court; palm trees decorated the jambs on either side, and eight steps led up to it.

³⁵Then he brought me to the north gate and measured it. It had the same measurements as the others, ³⁶as did its alcoves, its projecting walls and its portico, and it had openings all around. It was fifty cubits long and twenty-five cubits wide. ³⁷Its portico*ᵃ* faced the outer court; palm trees decorated the jambs on either side, and eight steps led up to it.   Eze 44:4

The Rooms for Preparing Sacrifices

³⁸A room with a doorway was by the portico in each of the inner gateways, where the burnt offerings were washed. ³⁹In the portico of the gateway were two tables on each side, on which the burnt offerings, sin offerings and guilt offerings were slaughtered. ⁴⁰By the outside wall of the portico of the gateway, near the steps at the entrance to the north gateway were two tables, and on the other side of the steps were two tables. ⁴¹So there were four tables on one side of the gateway and four on the other—eight tables in all—on which the sacrifices were slaughtered. ⁴²There were also four tables of dressed stone for the burnt offerings, each a cubit and a half long, a cubit and a half wide and a cubit high. On them were placed the utensils for slaughtering the burnt offerings and the other sacrifices. ⁴³And double-pronged hooks, each a handbreadth long, were attached to the wall all around. The tables were for the flesh of the offerings.   Ex 20:25; 2Ch 4:6

Rooms for the Priests

⁴⁴Outside the inner gate, within the inner court, were two rooms, oneᵇ at the side of the north gate and facing south,

---

ᵃ37 Septuagint (see also verses 31 and 34); Hebrew *jambs*   ᵇ44 Septuagint; Hebrew *were rooms for singers, which were*

and another at the side of the south*a* gate and facing north. 45He said to me, "The room facing south is for the priests who have charge of the temple, 46and the room facing north is for the priests who have charge of the altar. These are the sons of Zadok, who are the only Levites who may draw near to the LORD to minister before him." Eze 42:13

47Then he measured the court: It was square—a hundred cubits long and a hundred cubits wide. And the altar was in front of the temple. Eze 41:13-14

The Temple

48He brought me to the portico of the temple and measured the jambs of the portico; they were five cubits wide on either side. The width of the entrance was fourteen cubits and its projecting walls were*b* three cubits wide on either side. 49The portico was twenty cubits wide, and twelve*c* cubits from front to back. It was reached by a flight of stairs,*d* and there were pillars on each side of the jambs. 1Ki 6:2

41 Then the man brought me to the outer sanctuary and measured the jambs; the width of the jambs was six cubits*e* on each side.*f* 2The entrance was ten cubits wide, and the projecting walls on each side of it were five cubits wide. He also measured the outer sanctuary; it was forty cubits long and twenty cubits wide.

3Then he went into the inner sanctuary and measured the jambs of the entrance; each was two cubits wide. The entrance was six cubits wide, and the projecting walls on each side of it were seven cubits wide. 4And he measured the length of the inner sanctuary; it was twenty cubits, and its width was twenty cubits across the end of the outer sanctuary. He said to me, "This is the Most Holy Place." 1Ki 6:20; Heb 9:3-8

5Then he measured the wall of the temple; it was six cubits thick, and each side room around the temple was four cubits wide. 6The side rooms were on three levels, one above another, thirty on each level. There were ledges all around the wall of the temple to serve as supports for the side rooms, so that the supports were not inserted into the wall of the temple. 7The side rooms all around the temple were wider at each successive level. The structure surrounding the temple was built in ascending stages, so that the rooms widened as one went upward. A stairway went up from the lowest floor to the top floor through the middle floor. Eze 40:17

8I saw that the temple had a raised base all around it, form-

*a*44 Septuagint; Hebrew *east*   *b*48 Septuagint; Hebrew *entrance was*
*c*49 Septuagint; Hebrew *eleven*   *d*49 Hebrew; Septuagint *Ten steps led up to it*
*e*1 The common cubit was about 1 1/2 feet (about 0.5 meter).   *f*1 One Hebrew manuscript and Septuagint; most Hebrew manuscripts *side, the width of the tent*

ing the foundation of the side rooms. It was the length of the rod, six long cubits. ⁹The outer wall of the side rooms was five cubits thick. The open area between the side rooms of the temple ¹⁰and the ⌊priests'⌋ rooms was twenty cubits wide all around the temple. ¹¹There were entrances to the side rooms from the open area, one on the north and another on the south; and the base adjoining the open area was five cubits wide all around. Eze 40:5

¹²The building facing the temple courtyard on the west side was seventy cubits wide. The wall of the building was five cubits thick all around, and its length was ninety cubits. Eze 42:1

¹³Then he measured the temple; it was a hundred cubits long, and the temple courtyard and the building with its walls were also a hundred cubits long. ¹⁴The width of the temple courtyard on the east, including the front of the temple, was a hundred cubits. Eze 40:47

¹⁵Then he measured the length of the building facing the courtyard at the rear of the temple, including its galleries on each side; it was a hundred cubits. Eze 42:3

The outer sanctuary, the inner sanctuary and the portico facing the court, ¹⁶as well as the thresholds and the narrow windows and galleries around the three of them—everything

beyond and including the threshold was covered with wood. The floor, the wall up to the windows, and the windows were covered. ¹⁷In the space above the outside of the entrance to the inner sanctuary and on the walls at regular intervals all around the inner and outer sanctuary ¹⁸were carved cherubim and palm trees. Palm trees alternated with cherubim. Each cherub had two faces: ¹⁹the face of a man toward the palm tree on one side and the face of a lion toward the palm tree on the other. They were carved all around the whole temple. ²⁰From the floor to the area above the entrance, cherubim and palm trees were carved on the wall of the outer sanctuary.

²¹The outer sanctuary had a rectangular doorframe, and the one at the front of the Most Holy Place was similar. ²²There was a wooden altar three cubits high and two cubits square*a*; its corners, its base*b* and its sides were of wood. The man said to me, "This is the table that is before the Lᴏʀᴅ." ²³Both the outer sanctuary and the Most Holy Place had double doors. ²⁴Each door had two leaves—two hinged leaves for each door. ²⁵And on the doors of the outer sanctuary were carved cherubim and palm trees like those carved on the walls, and there was a wooden overhang on the front of the portico. ²⁶On the

---

*a*22 Septuagint; Hebrew *long*   *b*22 Septuagint; Hebrew *length*

sidewalls of the portico were narrow windows with palm trees carved on each side. The side rooms of the temple also had overhangs.   Ex 30:1

Rooms for the Priests

42 Then the man led me northward into the outer court and brought me to the rooms opposite the temple courtyard and opposite the outer wall on the north side. [2]The building whose door faced north was a hundred cubits[a] long and fifty cubits wide. [3]Both in the section twenty cubits from the inner court and in the section opposite the pavement of the outer court, gallery faced gallery at the three levels. [4]In front of the rooms was an inner passageway ten cubits wide and a hundred cubits[b] long. Their doors were on the north. [5]Now the upper rooms were narrower, for the galleries took more space from them than from the rooms on the lower and middle floors of the building. [6]The rooms on the third floor had no pillars, as the courts had; so they were smaller in floor space than those on the lower and middle floors. [7]There was an outer wall parallel to the rooms and the outer court; it extended in front of the rooms for fifty cubits. [8]While the row of rooms on the side next to the outer court was fifty cubits long, the row on the side nearest the sanctuary was a hundred cubits long. [9]The lower rooms had an entrance on the east side as one enters them from the outer court.   Ex 27:9; Eze 44:5

[10]On the south side[c] along the length of the wall of the outer court, adjoining the temple courtyard and opposite the outer wall, were rooms [11]with a passageway in front of them. These were like the rooms on the north; they had the same length and width, with similar exits and dimensions. Similar to the doorways on the north [12]were the doorways of the rooms on the south. There was a doorway at the beginning of the passageway that was parallel to the corresponding wall extending eastward, by which one enters the rooms.   Eze 41:12-14

[13]Then he said to me, "The north and south rooms facing the temple courtyard are the priests' rooms, where the priests who approach the LORD will eat the most holy offerings. There they will put the most holy offerings—the grain offerings, the sin offerings and the guilt offerings—for the place is holy. [14]Once the priests enter the holy precincts, they are not to go into the outer court until they leave behind the garments in which they minister, for these are holy. They are to put on other clothes before they go

[a]2 The common cubit was about 1 1/2 feet (about 0.5 meter).   [b]4 Septuagint and Syriac; Hebrew *and one cubit*   [c]10 Septuagint; Hebrew *Eastward*

near the places that are for the people." Lev 16:23; Eze 40:46

¹⁵When he had finished measuring what was inside the temple area, he led me out by the east gate and measured the area all around: ¹⁶He measured the east side with the measuring rod; it was five hundred cubits.ᵃ ¹⁷He measured the north side; it was five hundred cubitsᵇ by the measuring rod. ¹⁸He measured the south side; it was five hundred cubits by the measuring rod. ¹⁹Then he turned to the west side and measured; it was five hundred cubits by the measuring rod. ²⁰So he measured the area on all four sides. It had a wall around it, five hundred cubits long and five hundred cubits wide, to separate the holy from the common. Eze 43:1

The Glory Returns to the Temple

43 Then the man brought me to the gate facing east, ²and I saw the glory of the God of Israel coming from the east. His voice was like the roar of rushing waters, and the land was radiant with his glory. ³The vision I saw was like the vision I had seen when heᶜ came to destroy the city and like the visions I had seen by the Kebar River, and I fell facedown. ⁴The glory of the LORD entered the temple through the gate facing east. ⁵Then the Spirit lifted me up and brought me into the inner court, and the glory of the LORD filled the temple. 1Ch 9:18

⁶While the man was standing beside me, I heard someone speaking to me from inside the temple. ⁷He said: "Son of man, this is the place of my throne and the place for the soles of my feet. This is where I will live among the Israelites forever. The house of Israel will never again defile my holy name—neither they nor their kings—by their prostitutionᵈ and the lifeless idolsᵉ of their kings at their high places. ⁸When they placed their threshold next to my threshold and their doorposts beside my doorposts, with only a wall between me and them, they defiled my holy name by their detestable practices. So I destroyed them in my anger. ⁹Now let them put away from me their prostitution and the lifeless idols of their kings, and I will live among them forever. Lev 26:30; Jer 3:17

¹⁰"Son of man, describe the temple to the people of Israel, that they may be ashamed of their sins. Let them consider the plan, ¹¹and if they are ashamed of all they have done, make known to them the design of the temple—its arrangement, its exits and entrances—its whole design and all its regula-

---

ᵃ16 See Septuagint of verse 17; Hebrew *rods*; also in verses 18 and 19.
ᵇ17 Septuagint; Hebrew *rods*   ᶜ3 Some Hebrew manuscripts and Vulgate; most Hebrew manuscripts *I*   ᵈ7 Or *their spiritual adultery*; also in verse 9   ᵉ7 Or *the corpses*; also in verse 9

tions[a] and laws. Write these down before them so that they may be faithful to its design and follow all its regulations. Eze 16:61

12"This is the law of the temple: All the surrounding area on top of the mountain will be most holy. Such is the law of the temple. Eze 17:22; 42:20

The Altar

13"These are the measurements of the altar in long cubits, that cubit being a cubit[b] and a handbreadth[c]: Its gutter is a cubit deep and a cubit wide, with a rim of one span[d] around the edge. And this is the height of the altar: 14From the gutter on the ground up to the lower ledge it is two cubits high and a cubit wide, and from the smaller ledge up to the larger ledge it is four cubits high and a cubit wide. 15The altar hearth is four cubits high, and four horns project upward from the hearth. 16The altar hearth is square, twelve cubits long and twelve cubits wide. 17The upper ledge also is square, fourteen cubits long and fourteen cubits wide, with a rim of half a cubit and a gutter of a cubit all around. The steps of the altar face east." Ex 20:24; Eze 45:19

18Then he said to me, "Son of man, this is what the Sovereign Lord says: These will be the regulations for sacrificing burnt offerings and sprinkling blood upon the altar when it is built: 19You are to give a young bull as a sin offering to the priests, who are Levites, of the family of Zadok, who come near to minister before me, declares the Sovereign Lord. 20You are to take some of its blood and put it on the four horns of the altar and on the four corners of the upper ledge and all around the rim, and so purify the altar and make atonement for it. 21You are to take the bull for the sin offering and burn it in the designated part of the temple area outside the sanctuary. Ex 40:29

22"On the second day you are to offer a male goat without defect for a sin offering, and the altar is to be purified as it was purified with the bull. 23When you have finished purifying it, you are to offer a young bull and a ram from the flock, both without defect. 24You are to offer them before the Lord, and the priests are to sprinkle salt on them and sacrifice them as a burnt offering to the Lord.

25"For seven days you are to provide a male goat daily for a sin offering; you are also to provide a young bull and a ram from the flock, both without defect. 26For seven days they are to make atonement for the altar and cleanse it; thus they will dedicate it. 27At the end of these

---

[a]11 Some Hebrew manuscripts and Septuagint; most Hebrew manuscripts *regulations and its whole design*   [b]13 The common cubit was about 1 1/2 feet (about 0.5 meter).   [c]13 That is, about 3 inches (about 8 centimeters)   [d]13 That is, about 9 inches (about 22 centimeters)

days, from the eighth day on, the priests are to present your burnt offerings and fellowship offerings*a* on the altar. Then I will accept you, declares the Sovereign Lord." Lev 8:33

The Prince, the Levites, the Priests

44 Then the man brought me back to the outer gate of the sanctuary, the one facing east, and it was shut. ²The Lord said to me, "This gate is to remain shut. It must not be opened; no one may enter through it. It is to remain shut because the Lord, the God of Israel, has entered through it. ³The prince himself is the only one who may sit inside the gateway to eat in the presence of the Lord. He is to enter by way of the portico of the gateway and go out the same way." Eze 43:1

⁴Then the man brought me by way of the north gate to the front of the temple. I looked and saw the glory of the Lord filling the temple of the Lord, and I fell facedown. Eze 40:35; Da 8:17

⁵The Lord said to me, "Son of man, look carefully, listen closely and give attention to everything I tell you concerning all the regulations regarding the temple of the Lord. Give attention to the entrance of the temple and all the exits of the sanctuary. ⁶Say to the rebellious house of Israel, 'This is what the Sovereign Lord says: Enough of your detestable practices, O house of Israel! ⁷In addition to all your other detestable practices, you brought foreigners uncircumcised in heart and flesh into my sanctuary, desecrating my temple while you offered me food, fat and blood, and you broke my covenant. ⁸Instead of carrying out your duty in regard to my holy things, you put others in charge of my sanctuary. ⁹This is what the Sovereign Lord says: No foreigner uncircumcised in heart and flesh is to enter my sanctuary, not even the foreigners who live among the Israelites. Eze 42:9; Joel 3:17

¹⁰" 'The Levites who went far from me when Israel went astray and who wandered from me after their idols must bear the consequences of their sin. ¹¹They may serve in my sanctuary, having charge of the gates of the temple and serving in it; they may slaughter the burnt offerings and sacrifices for the people and stand before the people and serve them. ¹²But because they served them in the presence of their idols and made the house of Israel fall into sin, therefore I have sworn with uplifted hand that they must bear the consequences of their sin, declares the Sovereign Lord. ¹³They are not to come near to serve me as priests or come near any of my holy things or my most holy offer-

a27 Traditionally *peace offerings*

ings; they must bear the shame of their detestable practices. ¹⁴Yet I will put them in charge of the duties of the temple and all the work that is to be done in it.

¹⁵" 'But the priests, who are Levites and descendants of Zadok and who faithfully carried out the duties of my sanctuary when the Israelites went astray from me, are to come near to minister before me; they are to stand before me to offer sacrifices of fat and blood, declares the Sovereign LORD. ¹⁶They alone are to enter my sanctuary; they alone are to come near my table to minister before me and perform my service.   2Sa 8:17; Eze 41:22

¹⁷" 'When they enter the gates of the inner court, they are to wear linen clothes; they must not wear any woolen garment while ministering at the gates of the inner court or inside the temple. ¹⁸They are to wear linen turbans on their heads and linen undergarments around their waists. They must not wear anything that makes them perspire. ¹⁹When they go out into the outer court where the people are, they are to take off the clothes they have been ministering in and are to leave them in the sacred rooms, and put on other clothes, so that they do not consecrate the people by means of their garments.   Rev 19:8

²⁰" 'They must not shave their heads or let their hair grow

long, but they are to keep the hair of their heads trimmed. ²¹No priest is to drink wine when he enters the inner court. ²²They must not marry widows or divorced women; they may marry only virgins of Israelite descent or widows of priests. ²³They are to teach my people the difference between the holy and the common and show them how to distinguish between the unclean and the clean.   Lev 13:50; Eze 5:1

²⁴" 'In any dispute, the priests are to serve as judges and decide it according to my ordinances. They are to keep my laws and my decrees for all my appointed feasts, and they are to keep my Sabbaths holy.

²⁵" 'A priest must not defile himself by going near a dead person; however, if the dead person was his father or mother, son or daughter, brother or unmarried sister, then he may defile himself. ²⁶After he is cleansed, he must wait seven days. ²⁷On the day he goes into the inner court of the sanctuary to minister in the sanctuary, he is to offer a sin offering for himself, declares the Sovereign LORD.   Lev 21:1-4; Nu 3:28

²⁸" 'I am to be the only inheritance the priests have. You are to give them no possession in Israel; I will be their possession. ²⁹They will eat the grain offerings, the sin offerings and the guilt offerings; and everything

in Israel devoted[a] to the LORD will belong to them. 30The best of all the firstfruits and of all your special gifts will belong to the priests. You are to give them the first portion of your ground meal so that a blessing may rest on your household. 31The priests must not eat anything, bird or animal, found dead or torn by wild animals.   Nu 18:20

Division of the Land

45 " 'When you allot the land as an inheritance, you are to present to the LORD a portion of the land as a sacred district, 25,000 cubits long and 20,000[b] cubits wide; the entire area will be holy. 2Of this, a section 500 cubits square is to be for the sanctuary, with 50 cubits around it for open land. 3In the sacred district, measure off a section 25,000 cubits[c] long and 10,000 cubits[d] wide. In it will be the sanctuary, the Most Holy Place. 4It will be the sacred portion of the land for the priests, who minister in the sanctuary and who draw near to minister before the LORD. It will be a place for their houses as well as a holy place for the sanctuary. 5An area 25,000 cubits long and 10,000 cubits wide will belong to the Levites, who serve in the temple, as their possession for towns to live in.[e]   Eze 48:8-9,29

6" 'You are to give the city as its property an area 5,000 cubits wide and 25,000 cubits long, adjoining the sacred portion; it will belong to the whole house of Israel.   Eze 48:15-18

7" 'The prince will have the land bordering each side of the area formed by the sacred district and the property of the city. It will extend westward from the west side and eastward from the east side, running lengthwise from the western to the eastern border parallel to one of the tribal portions. 8This land will be his possession in Israel. And my princes will no longer oppress my people but will allow the house of Israel to possess the land according to their tribes.   Nu 26:53; Eze 48:21

9" 'This is what the Sovereign LORD says: You have gone far enough, O princes of Israel! Give up your violence and oppression and do what is just and right. Stop dispossessing my people, declares the Sovereign LORD. 10You are to use accurate scales, an accurate ephah[f] and an accurate bath.[g] 11The ephah and the bath are to be the same size, the bath containing a tenth of a homer[h] and the ephah a tenth of a homer; the homer is

---

[a]29 The Hebrew term refers to the irrevocable giving over of things or persons to the LORD.   [b]1 Septuagint (see also verses 3 and 5 and 48:9); Hebrew 10,000   [c]3 That is, about 7 miles (about 12 kilometers)   [d]3 That is, about 3 miles (about 5 kilometers)   [e]5 Septuagint; Hebrew temple; they will have as their possession 20 rooms   [f]10 An ephah was a dry measure.   [g]10 A bath was a liquid measure.   [h]11 A homer was a dry measure.

to be the standard measure for both. ¹²The shekel*a* is to consist of twenty gerahs. Twenty shekels plus twenty-five shekels plus fifteen shekels equal one mina.*b*   Nu 3:47; Ps 12:5

Offerings and Holy Days

¹³" 'This is the special gift you are to offer: a sixth of an ephah from each homer of wheat and a sixth of an ephah from each homer of barley. ¹⁴The prescribed portion of oil, measured by the bath, is a tenth of a bath from each cor (which consists of ten baths or one homer, for ten baths are equivalent to a homer). ¹⁵Also one sheep is to be taken from every flock of two hundred from the well-watered pastures of Israel. These will be used for the grain offerings, burnt offerings and fellowship offerings*c* to make atonement for the people, declares the Sovereign LORD. ¹⁶All the people of the land will participate in this special gift for the use of the prince in Israel. ¹⁷It will be the duty of the prince to provide the burnt offerings, grain offerings and drink offerings at the festivals, the New Moons and the Sabbaths—at all the appointed feasts of the house of Israel. He will provide the sin offerings, grain offerings, burnt offerings and fellowship offerings to make atonement for the house of Israel.   Lev 1:4; Nu 10:10

¹⁸" 'This is what the Sovereign LORD says: In the first month on the first day you are to take a young bull without defect and purify the sanctuary. ¹⁹The priest is to take some of the blood of the sin offering and put it on the doorposts of the temple, on the four corners of the upper ledge of the altar and on the gateposts of the inner court. ²⁰You are to do the same on the seventh day of the month for anyone who sins unintentionally or through ignorance; so you are to make atonement for the temple. Ex 12:2

²¹" 'In the first month on the fourteenth day you are to observe the Passover, a feast lasting seven days, during which you shall eat bread made without yeast. ²²On that day the prince is to provide a bull as a sin offering for himself and for all the people of the land. ²³Every day during the seven days of the Feast he is to provide seven bulls and seven rams without defect as a burnt offering to the LORD, and a male goat for a sin offering. ²⁴He is to provide as a grain offering an ephah for each bull and an ephah for each ram, along with a hin*d* of oil for each ephah.

²⁵" 'During the seven days of the Feast, which begins in the seventh month on the fifteenth day, he is to make the same provision for sin offerings,

---

a12 A shekel weighed about 2/5 ounce (about 11.5 grams).   *b12* That is, 60 shekels; the common mina was 50 shekels.   *c15* Traditionally *peace offerings*; also in verse 17
d24 That is, probably about 4 quarts (about 4 liters)

burnt offerings, grain offerings and oil.   Lev 23:34-43; Dt 16:13

46 " 'This is what the Sovereign LORD says: The gate of the inner court facing east is to be shut on the six working days, but on the Sabbath day and on the day of the New Moon it is to be opened. ²The prince is to enter from the outside through the portico of the gateway and stand by the gatepost. The priests are to sacrifice his burnt offering and his fellowship offerings.*a* He is to worship at the threshold of the gateway and then go out, but the gate will not be shut until evening. ³On the Sabbaths and New Moons the people of the land are to worship in the presence of the LORD at the entrance to that gateway. ⁴The burnt offering the prince brings to the LORD on the Sabbath day is to be six male lambs and a ram, all without defect. ⁵The grain offering given with the ram is to be an ephah,*b* and the grain offering with the lambs is to be as much as he pleases, along with a hin*c* of oil for each ephah. ⁶On the day of the New Moon he is to offer a young bull, six lambs and a ram, all without defect. ⁷He is to provide as a grain offering one ephah with the bull, one ephah with the ram, and with the lambs as much as he wants to give, along with a hin of oil with each ephah. ⁸When

the prince enters, he is to go in through the portico of the gateway, and he is to come out the same way.   Eze 40:19; Lk 1:10

⁹" 'When the people of the land come before the LORD at the appointed feasts, whoever enters by the north gate to worship is to go out the south gate; and whoever enters by the south gate is to go out the north gate. No one is to return through the gate by which he entered, but each is to go out the opposite gate. ¹⁰The prince is to be among them, going in when they go in and going out when they go out.   Ex 23:14

¹¹" 'At the festivals and the appointed feasts, the grain offering is to be an ephah with a bull, an ephah with a ram, and with the lambs as much as one pleases, along with a hin of oil for each ephah. ¹²When the prince provides a freewill offering to the LORD—whether a burnt offering or fellowship offerings—the gate facing east is to be opened for him. He shall offer his burnt offering or his fellowship offerings as he does on the Sabbath day. Then he shall go out, and after he has gone out, the gate will be shut.

¹³" 'Every day you are to provide a year-old lamb without defect for a burnt offering to the LORD; morning by morning you shall provide it. ¹⁴You are also to

---

a2 Traditionally *peace offerings*; also in verse 12   *b5* That is, probably about 3/5 bushel (about 22 liters)   *c5* That is, probably about 4 quarts (about 4 liters)

provide with it morning by morning a grain offering, consisting of a sixth of an ephah with a third of a hin of oil to moisten the flour. The presenting of this grain offering to the LORD is a lasting ordinance. ¹⁵So the lamb and the grain offering and the oil shall be provided morning by morning for a regular burnt offering. Ps 5:3; Da 8:11

¹⁶" 'This is what the Sovereign LORD says: If the prince makes a gift from his inheritance to one of his sons, it will also belong to his descendants; it is to be their property by inheritance. ¹⁷If, however, he makes a gift from his inheritance to one of his servants, the servant may keep it until the year of freedom; then it will revert to the prince. His inheritance belongs to his sons only; it is theirs. ¹⁸The prince must not take any of the inheritance of the people, driving them off their property. He is to give his sons their inheritance out of his own property, so that none of my people will be separated from his property.' " 2Ch 21:3

¹⁹Then the man brought me through the entrance at the side of the gate to the sacred rooms facing north, which belonged to the priests, and showed me a place at the western end. ²⁰He said to me, "This is the place where the priests will cook the guilt offering and the sin offering and bake the grain offering,

to avoid bringing them into the outer court and consecrating the people." Lev 6:27; Eze 42:9

²¹He then brought me to the outer court and led me around to its four corners, and I saw in each corner another court. ²²In the four corners of the outer court were enclosed*a* courts, forty cubits long and thirty cubits wide; each of the courts in the four corners was the same size. ²³Around the inside of each of the four courts was a ledge of stone, with places for fire built all around under the ledge. ²⁴He said to me, "These are the kitchens where those who minister at the temple will cook the sacrifices of the people." Eze 44:1

The River From the Temple

47 The man brought me back to the entrance of the temple, and I saw water coming out from under the threshold of the temple toward the east (for the temple faced east). The water was coming down from under the south side of the temple, south of the altar. ²He then brought me out through the north gate and led me around the outside to the outer gate facing east, and the water was flowing from the south side. Isa 55:1; Eze 40:35

³As the man went eastward with a measuring line in his hand, he measured off a thou-

---

*a*22 The meaning of the Hebrew for this word is uncertain.

sand cubits[a] and then led me through water that was ankle-deep. [4]He measured off another thousand cubits and led me through water that was knee-deep. He measured off another thousand and led me through water that was up to the waist. [5]He measured off another thousand, but now it was a river that I could not cross, because the water had risen and was deep enough to swim in—a river that no one could cross. [6]He asked me, "Son of man, do you see this?" Eze 40:3; Hab 2:14

Then he led me back to the bank of the river. [7]When I arrived there, I saw a great number of trees on each side of the river. [8]He said to me, "This water flows toward the eastern region and goes down into the Arabah,[b] where it enters the Sea.[c] When it empties into the Sea,[c] the water there becomes fresh. [9]Swarms of living creatures will live wherever the river flows. There will be large numbers of fish, because this water flows there and makes the salt water fresh; so where the river flows everything will live. [10]Fishermen will stand along the shore; from En Gedi to En Eglaim there will be places for spreading nets. The fish will be of many kinds—like the fish of the Great Sea.[d] [11]But the swamps and marshes will not

become fresh; they will be left for salt. [12]Fruit trees of all kinds will grow on both banks of the river. Their leaves will not wither, nor will their fruit fail. Every month they will bear, because the water from the sanctuary flows to them. Their fruit will serve for food and their leaves for healing." Eze 36:8; Rev 22:2

The Boundaries of the Land

[13]This is what the Sovereign LORD says: "These are the boundaries by which you are to divide the land for an inheritance among the twelve tribes of Israel, with two portions for Joseph. [14]You are to divide it equally among them. Because I swore with uplifted hand to give it to your forefathers, this land will become your inheritance. Ge 12:7; Nu 34:2-12

[15]"This is to be the boundary of the land: Nu 34:2

"On the north side it will run from the Great Sea by the Hethlon road past Lebo[e] Hamath to Zedad, [16]Berothah[f] and Sibraim (which lies on the border between Damascus and Hamath), as far as Hazer Hatticon, which is on the border of Hauran. [17]The boundary will extend from the sea to Hazar Enan,[g] along the

---

[a]3 That is, about 1,500 feet (about 450 meters)   [b]8 Or *the Jordan Valley*   [c]8 That is, the Dead Sea   [d]10 That is, the Mediterranean; also in verses 15, 19 and 20   [e]15 Or *past the entrance to*   [f]15,16 See Septuagint and Ezekiel 48:1; Hebrew *road to go into Zedad,* [16]*Hamath, Berothah*   [g]17 Hebrew *Enon,* a variant of *Enan*

northern border of Damascus, with the border of Hamath to the north. This will be the north boundary.

18"On the east side the boundary will run between Hauran and Damascus, along the Jordan between Gilead and the land of Israel, to the eastern sea and as far as Tamar.*a* This will be the east boundary.   Eze 27:18

19"On the south side it will run from Tamar as far as the waters of Meribah Kadesh, then along the Wadi of Egypt to the Great Sea. This will be the south boundary.

20"On the west side, the Great Sea will be the boundary to a point opposite Lebo*b* Hamath. This will be the west boundary.   Nu 13:21

21"You are to distribute this land among yourselves according to the tribes of Israel. 22You are to allot it as an inheritance for yourselves and for the aliens who have settled among you and who have children. You are to consider them as native-born Israelites; along with you they are to be allotted an inheritance among the tribes of Israel. 23In whatever tribe the alien settles, there you are to give him his inheritance," declares the Sovereign LORD.   Dt 10:19; Eze 36:12

The Division of the Land

48 "These are the tribes, listed by name: At the northern frontier, Dan will have one portion; it will follow the Hethlon road to Lebo*c* Hamath; Hazar Enan and the northern border of Damascus next to Hamath will be part of its border from the east side to the west side.   Ge 30:6; Eze 47:20

2"Asher will have one portion; it will border the territory of Dan from east to west.

3"Naphtali will have one portion; it will border the territory of Asher from east to west.

4"Manasseh will have one portion; it will border the territory of Naphtali from east to west.   Jos 17:1-11

5"Ephraim will have one portion; it will border the territory of Manasseh from east to west.

6"Reuben will have one portion; it will border the territory of Ephraim from east to west.

7"Judah will have one portion; it will border the territory of Reuben from east to west.

8"Bordering the territory of Judah from east to west will be the portion you are to present as a special gift. It will be 25,000 cubits*d* wide, and its length from east to west will equal one of the tribal portions; the sanctuary will be in the center of it.

9"The special portion you are to offer to the LORD will be

a18 Septuagint and Syriac; Hebrew *Israel. You will measure to the eastern sea*   *b20* Or *opposite the entrance to*   *c1* Or *to the entrance to*   *d8* That is, about 7 miles (about 12 kilometers)

25,000 cubits long and 10,000 cubits*a* wide. ¹⁰This will be the sacred portion for the priests. It will be 25,000 cubits long on the north side, 10,000 cubits wide on the west side, 10,000 cubits wide on the east side and 25,000 cubits long on the south side. In the center of it will be the sanctuary of the LORD. ¹¹This will be for the consecrated priests, the Zadokites, who were faithful in serving me and did not go astray as the Levites did when the Israelites went astray. ¹²It will be a special gift to them from the sacred portion of the land, a most holy portion, bordering the territory of the Levites.   2Sa 8:17; Eze 45:1

¹³"Alongside the territory of the priests, the Levites will have an allotment 25,000 cubits long and 10,000 cubits wide. Its total length will be 25,000 cubits and its width 10,000 cubits. ¹⁴They must not sell or exchange any of it. This is the best of the land and must not pass into other hands, because it is holy to the LORD.   Lev 25:34; Eze 45:5

¹⁵"The remaining area, 5,000 cubits wide and 25,000 cubits long, will be for the common use of the city, for houses and for pastureland. The city will be in the center of it ¹⁶and will have these measurements: the north side 4,500 cubits, the south side 4,500 cubits, the east side 4,500 cubits, and the west side 4,500 cubits. ¹⁷The pastureland for the

city will be 250 cubits on the north, 250 cubits on the south, 250 cubits on the east, and 250 cubits on the west. ¹⁸What remains of the area, bordering on the sacred portion and running the length of it, will be 10,000 cubits on the east side and 10,000 cubits on the west side. Its produce will supply food for the workers of the city. ¹⁹The workers from the city who farm it will come from all the tribes of Israel. ²⁰The entire portion will be a square, 25,000 cubits on each side. As a special gift you will set aside the sacred portion, along with the property of the city.   Eze 45:6; Rev 21:16

²¹"What remains on both sides of the area formed by the sacred portion and the city property will belong to the prince. It will extend eastward from the 25,000 cubits of the sacred portion to the eastern border, and westward from the 25,000 cubits to the western border. Both these areas running the length of the tribal portions will belong to the prince, and the sacred portion with the temple sanctuary will be in the center of them. ²²So the property of the Levites and the property of the city will lie in the center of the area that belongs to the prince. The area belonging to the prince will lie between the border of Judah and the border of Benjamin.   Eze 45:7

²³"As for the rest of the tribes:

---

a9 That is, about 3 miles (about 5 kilometers)

Benjamin will have one portion; it will extend from the east side to the west side. Jos 18:11-28

24"Simeon will have one portion; it will border the territory of Benjamin from east to west.

25"Issachar will have one portion; it will border the territory of Simeon from east to west.

26"Zebulun will have one portion; it will border the territory of Issachar from east to west.

27"Gad will have one portion; it will border the territory of Zebulun from east to west.

28"The southern boundary of Gad will run south from Tamar to the waters of Meribah Kadesh, then along the Wadi of Egypt to the Great Sea. *a* Ge 14:7

29"This is the land you are to allot as an inheritance to the tribes of Israel, and these will be their portions," declares the Sovereign LORD. Eze 45:1

The Gates of the City

30"These will be the exits of the city: Beginning on the north side, which is 4,500 cubits long, 31the gates of the city will be named after the tribes of Israel. The three gates on the north side will be the gate of Reuben, the gate of Judah and the gate of Levi. Rev 21:12

32"On the east side, which is 4,500 cubits long, will be three gates: the gate of Joseph, the gate of Benjamin and the gate of Dan.

33"On the south side, which measures 4,500 cubits, will be three gates: the gate of Simeon, the gate of Issachar and the gate of Zebulun.

34"On the west side, which is 4,500 cubits long, will be three gates: the gate of Gad, the gate of Asher and the gate of Naphtali. 2Ch 4:4; Rev 21:12-13

35"The distance all around will be 18,000 cubits.

"And the name of the city from that time on will be:

THE LORD IS THERE." Isa 12:6

a28 That is, the Mediterranean

Daniel

Introduction:

Daniel has traditionally been named the author of this book. The entire book tells of the experiences of Daniel and his friends and the divine revelation that came to Daniel in dreams and visions during his lifetime (about 605–530 B.C.).

Daniel was taken hostage from Jerusalem in 605 B.C. to the Babylonian court. After telling and interpreting Nebuchadnezzar's dream he was given a position of power. He wrote this book during Israel's captivity to encourage the people to trust in God who controls all of history.

In the last six chapters of this book, Daniel describes his visions of the rise and fall of earthly kingdoms and finally the rise of an everlasting kingdom.

Outline of contents:

Daniel's Training in Babylon

1 In the third year of the reign of Jehoiakim king of Judah, Nebuchadnezzar king of Babylon came to Jerusalem and besieged it. ²And the Lord delivered Jehoiakim king of Judah into his hand, along with some of the articles from the temple of God. These he carried off to the temple of his god in Babylonia*a* and put in the treasure house of his god. 2Ki 24:13; Jer 46:2

³Then the king ordered Ashpenaz, chief of his court officials, to bring in some of the Israelites from the royal family and the nobility— ⁴young men without any physical defect, handsome, showing aptitude for every kind of learning, well informed, quick to understand, and qualified to serve in the king's palace. He was to teach

*a*2 Hebrew *Shinar*

them the language and literature of the Babylonians.*a* 5The
king assigned them a daily
amount of food and wine from
the king's table. They were to be
trained for three years, and after
that they were to enter the
king's service.   2Ki 20:18; Est 2:9

6Among these were some
from Judah: Daniel, Hananiah,
Mishael and Azariah. 7The chief
official gave them new names:
to Daniel, the name Belteshazzar; to Hananiah, Shadrach; to
Mishael, Meshach; and to Aza-
riah, Abednego.   Eze 14:14; Da 2:26

8But Daniel resolved not to
defile himself with the royal
food and wine, and he asked
the chief official for permission
not to defile himself this way.
9Now God had caused the official to show favor and sympathy to Daniel, 10but the official
told Daniel, "I am afraid of my
lord the king, who has assigned
your*b* food and drink. Why
should he see you looking
worse than the other young
men your age? The king would
then have my head because of
you."   Ge 39:21; Eze 4:13-14

11Daniel then said to the
guard whom the chief official
had appointed over Daniel,
Hananiah, Mishael and Azariah, 12"Please test your servants for ten days: Give us
nothing but vegetables to eat
and water to drink. 13Then compare our appearance with that
of the young men who eat the
royal food, and treat your servants in accordance with what
you see." 14So he agreed to this
and tested them for ten days.

15At the end of the ten days
they looked healthier and better
nourished than any of the
young men who ate the royal
food. 16So the guard took away
their choice food and the wine
they were to drink and gave
them vegetables instead. Ex 23:25

17To these four young men
God gave knowledge and
understanding of all kinds of literature and learning. And Daniel could understand visions
and dreams of all kinds. Job 12:13

18At the end of the time set by
the king to bring them in, the
chief official presented them to
Nebuchadnezzar. 19The king
talked with them, and he found
none equal to Daniel, Hananiah, Mishael and Azariah; so
they entered the king's service.
20In every matter of wisdom and
understanding about which the
king questioned them, he found
them ten times better than all
the magicians and enchanters in
his whole kingdom.   Ge 41:46

21And Daniel remained there
until the first year of King
Cyrus.   2Ch 36:22; Da 6:28

Nebuchadnezzar's Dream

2 In the second year of his
reign, Nebuchadnezzar had
dreams; his mind was troubled
and he could not sleep. 2So the
king summoned the magicians,

---

*a*4 Or *Chaldeans*   *b*10 The Hebrew for *your* and *you* in this verse is plural.

enchanters, sorcerers and astrologers[a] to tell him what he had dreamed. When they came in and stood before the king, [3]he said to them, "I have had a dream that troubles me and I want to know what it means.[b]"

[4]Then the astrologers answered the king in Aramaic,[c] "O king, live forever! Tell your servants the dream, and we will interpret it."   Ezr 4:7; Ne 2:3

[5]The king replied to the astrologers, "This is what I have firmly decided: If you do not tell me what my dream was and interpret it, I will have you cut into pieces and your houses turned into piles of rubble. [6]But if you tell me the dream and explain it, you will receive from me gifts and rewards and great honor. So tell me the dream and interpret it for me."   Ge 41:32

[7]Once more they replied, "Let the king tell his servants the dream, and we will interpret it."

[8]Then the king answered, "I am certain that you are trying to gain time, because you realize that this is what I have firmly decided: [9]If you do not tell me the dream, there is just one penalty for you. You have conspired to tell me misleading and wicked things, hoping the situation will change. So then, tell me the dream, and I will know that you can interpret it for me."   Est 4:11; Isa 41:22-24

[10]The astrologers answered the king, "There is not a man on earth who can do what the king asks! No king, however great and mighty, has ever asked such a thing of any magician or enchanter or astrologer. [11]What the king asks is too difficult. No one can reveal it to the king except the gods, and they do not live among men."   Da 3:8; 4:7

[12]This made the king so angry and furious that he ordered the execution of all the wise men of Babylon. [13]So the decree was issued to put the wise men to death, and men were sent to look for Daniel and his friends to put them to death.   Da 3:13

[14]When Arioch, the commander of the king's guard, had gone out to put to death the wise men of Babylon, Daniel spoke to him with wisdom and tact. [15]He asked the king's officer, "Why did the king issue such a harsh decree?" Arioch then explained the matter to Daniel. [16]At this, Daniel went in to the king and asked for time, so that he might interpret the dream for him.   Jer 52:12,14

[17]Then Daniel returned to his house and explained the matter to his friends Hananiah, Mishael and Azariah. [18]He urged them to plead for mercy from the God of heaven concerning this mystery, so that he and his friends might not be executed with the rest of the wise men of

---

[a]2 Or *Chaldeans*; also in verses 4, 5 and 10 through chapter 7 is in Aramaic.   [b]3 Or *was*   [c]4 The text from here

Babylon. ¹⁹During the night the mystery was revealed to Daniel in a vision. Then Daniel praised the God of heaven ²⁰and said:

"Praise be to the name of
    God for ever and ever;
    wisdom and power are his.
²¹He changes times and
    seasons;   Da 7:25
    he sets up kings and
    deposes them.   Da 4:17
    He gives wisdom to the wise
    and knowledge to the
    discerning.   2Sa 14:17
²²He reveals deep and hidden
    things;   Ge 40:8
    he knows what lies in
    darkness,   Job 12:22
    and light dwells with him.
²³I thank and praise you,
    O God of my fathers:
    You have given me wisdom
    and power,   Da 1:17
    you have made known to me
    what we asked of you,
    you have made known to
    us the dream of the
    king."   Eze 28:3

Daniel Interprets the Dream

²⁴Then Daniel went to Arioch, whom the king had appointed to execute the wise men of Babylon, and said to him, "Do not execute the wise men of Babylon. Take me to the king, and I will interpret his dream for him."

²⁵Arioch took Daniel to the king at once and said, "I have found a man among the exiles from Judah who can tell the king what his dream means."

²⁶The king asked Daniel (also called Belteshazzar), "Are you able to tell me what I saw in my dream and interpret it?"   Da 1:7

²⁷Daniel replied, "No wise man, enchanter, magician or diviner can explain to the king the mystery he has asked about, ²⁸but there is a God in heaven who reveals mysteries. He has shown King Nebuchadnezzar what will happen in days to come. Your dream and the visions that passed through your mind as you lay on your bed are these: Ge 41:8; Am 4:13

²⁹"As you were lying there, O king, your mind turned to things to come, and the revealer of mysteries showed you what is going to happen. ³⁰As for me, this mystery has been revealed to me, not because I have greater wisdom than other living men, but so that you, O king, may know the interpretation and that you may understand what went through your mind.   Ge 41:25; Isa 45:3

³¹"You looked, O king, and there before you stood a large statue—an enormous, dazzling statue, awesome in appearance. ³²The head of the statue was made of pure gold, its chest and arms of silver, its belly and thighs of bronze, ³³its legs of iron, its feet partly of iron and partly of baked clay. ³⁴While you were watching, a rock was cut out, but not by human hands. It struck the statue on its feet of iron and clay and smashed them. ³⁵Then the iron,

the clay, the bronze, the silver and the gold were broken to pieces at the same time and became like chaff on a threshing floor in the summer. The wind swept them away without leaving a trace. But the rock that struck the statue became a huge mountain and filled the whole earth.   Ps 1:4

[36]"This was the dream, and now we will interpret it to the king. [37]You, O king, are the king of kings. The God of heaven has given you dominion and power and might and glory; [38]in your hands he has placed mankind and the beasts of the field and the birds of the air. Wherever they live, he has made you ruler over them all. You are that head of gold.   Ge 40:12; Jer 27:6

[39]"After you, another kingdom will rise, inferior to yours. Next, a third kingdom, one of bronze, will rule over the whole earth. [40]Finally, there will be a fourth kingdom, strong as iron—for iron breaks and smashes everything—and as iron breaks things to pieces, so it will crush and break all the others. [41]Just as you saw that the feet and toes were partly of baked clay and partly of iron, so this will be a divided kingdom; yet it will have some of the strength of iron in it, even as you saw iron mixed with clay. [42]As the toes were partly iron and partly clay, so this kingdom will be partly strong and partly brittle. [43]And just as you saw the iron mixed with baked clay,

so the people will be a mixture and will not remain united, any more than iron mixes with clay.

[44]"In the time of those kings, the God of heaven will set up a kingdom that will never be destroyed, nor will it be left to another people. It will crush all those kingdoms and bring them to an end, but it will itself endure forever. [45]This is the meaning of the vision of the rock cut out of a mountain, but not by human hands—a rock that broke the iron, the bronze, the clay, the silver and the gold to pieces.   Ge 27:29; Isa 28:16

"The great God has shown the king what will take place in the future. The dream is true and the interpretation is trustworthy."   Ge 41:25; Rev 22:6

[46]Then King Nebuchadnezzar fell prostrate before Daniel and paid him honor and ordered that an offering and incense be presented to him. [47]The king said to Daniel, "Surely your God is the God of gods and the Lord of kings and a revealer of mysteries, for you were able to reveal this mystery."   Da 8:17

[48]Then the king placed Daniel in a high position and lavished many gifts on him. He made him ruler over the entire province of Babylon and placed him in charge of all its wise men. [49]Moreover, at Daniel's request the king appointed Shadrach, Meshach and Abednego administrators over the province of Babylon, while Daniel himself remained at the royal court.

The Image of Gold and the Fiery Furnace

3 King Nebuchadnezzar made an image of gold, ninety feet high and nine feet[a] wide, and set it up on the plain of Dura in the province of Babylon. ²He then summoned the satraps, prefects, governors, advisers, treasurers, judges, magistrates and all the other provincial officials to come to the dedication of the image he had set up. ³So the satraps, prefects, governors, advisers, treasurers, judges, magistrates and all the other provincial officials assembled for the dedication of the image that King Nebuchadnezzar had set up, and they stood before it.   Est 1:1; Da 6:7

⁴Then the herald loudly proclaimed, "This is what you are commanded to do, O peoples, nations and men of every language: ⁵As soon as you hear the sound of the horn, flute, zither, lyre, harp, pipes and all kinds of music, you must fall down and worship the image of gold that King Nebuchadnezzar has set up. ⁶Whoever does not fall down and worship will immediately be thrown into a blazing furnace."   Jer 29:22; Da 4:1

⁷Therefore, as soon as they heard the sound of the horn, flute, zither, lyre, harp and all kinds of music, all the peoples, nations and men of every language fell down and worshiped the image of gold that King Nebuchadnezzar had set up.

⁸At this time some astrologers[b] came forward and denounced the Jews. ⁹They said to King Nebuchadnezzar, "O king, live forever! ¹⁰You have issued a decree, O king, that everyone who hears the sound of the horn, flute, zither, lyre, harp, pipes and all kinds of music must fall down and worship the image of gold, ¹¹and that whoever does not fall down and worship will be thrown into a blazing furnace. ¹²But there are some Jews whom you have set over the affairs of the province of Babylon—Shadrach, Meshach and Abednego—who pay no attention to you, O king. They neither serve your gods nor worship the image of gold you have set up."   Isa 19:3; Da 2:49

¹³Furious with rage, Nebuchadnezzar summoned Shadrach, Meshach and Abednego. So these men were brought before the king, ¹⁴and Nebuchadnezzar said to them, "Is it true, Shadrach, Meshach and Abednego, that you do not serve my gods or worship the image of gold I have set up? ¹⁵Now when you hear the sound of the horn, flute, zither, lyre, harp, pipes and all kinds of music, if you are ready to fall down and worship the image I made, very good. But if you do not worship it, you will be

---

a1 Aramaic *sixty cubits high and six cubits wide* (about 27 meters high and 2.7 meters wide)   *b8* Or *Chaldeans*

thrown immediately into a blazing furnace. Then what god will be able to rescue you from my hand?" 2Ch 32:15; Da 2:12

¹⁶Shadrach, Meshach and Abednego replied to the king, "O Nebuchadnezzar, we do not need to defend ourselves before you in this matter. ¹⁷If we are thrown into the blazing furnace, the God we serve is able to save us from it, and he will rescue us from your hand, O king. ¹⁸But even if he does not, we want you to know, O king, that we will not serve your gods or worship the image of gold you have set up." Jos 24:15; Da 1:7

¹⁹Then Nebuchadnezzar was furious with Shadrach, Meshach and Abednego, and his attitude toward them changed. He ordered the furnace heated seven times hotter than usual ²⁰and commanded some of the strongest soldiers in his army to tie up Shadrach, Meshach and Abednego and throw them into the blazing furnace. ²¹So these men, wearing their robes, trousers, turbans and other clothes, were bound and thrown into the blazing furnace. ²²The king's command was so urgent and the furnace so hot that the flames of the fire killed the soldiers who took up Shadrach, Meshach and Abednego, ²³and these three men, firmly tied, fell into the blazing furnace. Da 1:7

²⁴Then King Nebuchadnezzar leaped to his feet in amazement and asked his advisers, "Weren't there three men that we tied up and threw into the fire?" Mt 13:54

They replied, "Certainly, O king."

²⁵He said, "Look! I see four men walking around in the fire, unbound and unharmed, and the fourth looks like a son of the gods." Isa 43:2

²⁶Nebuchadnezzar then approached the opening of the blazing furnace and shouted, "Shadrach, Meshach and Abednego, servants of the Most High God, come out! Come here!"

So Shadrach, Meshach and Abednego came out of the fire, ²⁷and the satraps, prefects, governors and royal advisers crowded around them. They saw that the fire had not harmed their bodies, nor was a hair of their heads singed; their robes were not scorched, and there was no smell of fire on them. Ps 91:3-11; Da 6:7

²⁸Then Nebuchadnezzar said, "Praise be to the God of Shadrach, Meshach and Abednego, who has sent his angel and rescued his servants! They trusted in him and defied the king's command and were willing to give up their lives rather than serve or worship any god except their own God. ²⁹Therefore I decree that the people of any nation or language who say anything against the God of Shadrach, Meshach and Abednego be cut into pieces and their houses be turned into piles of rubble, for no other god can save in this way." Ps 34:7

³⁰Then the king promoted Shadrach, Meshach and Abednego in the province of Babylon.   Da 2:49

Nebuchadnezzar's Dream of a Tree

4 King Nebuchadnezzar,

To the peoples, nations and men of every language, who live in all the world:

May you prosper greatly!

²It is my pleasure to tell you about the miraculous signs and wonders that the Most High God has performed for me.   Ps 74:9

³How great are his signs,
  how mighty his wonders!
His kingdom is an eternal
    kingdom;
  his dominion endures from
    generation to
    generation.   Da 2:44

⁴I, Nebuchadnezzar, was at home in my palace, contented and prosperous. ⁵I had a dream that made me afraid. As I was lying in my bed, the images and visions that passed through my mind terrified me. ⁶So I commanded that all the wise men of Babylon be brought before me to interpret the dream for me. ⁷When the magicians, enchanters, astrologersᵃ and diviners came, I told them

the dream, but they could not interpret it for me. ⁸Finally, Daniel came into my presence and I told him the dream. (He is called Belteshazzar, after the name of my god, and the spirit of the holy gods is in him.)   Ps 30:6

⁹I said, "Belteshazzar, chief of the magicians, I know that the spirit of the holy gods is in you, and no mystery is too difficult for you. Here is my dream; interpret it for me. ¹⁰These are the visions I saw while lying in my bed: I looked, and there before me stood a tree in the middle of the land. Its height was enormous. ¹¹The tree grew large and strong and its top touched the sky; it was visible to the ends of the earth. ¹²Its leaves were beautiful, its fruit abundant, and on it was food for all. Under it the beasts of the field found shelter, and the birds of the air lived in its branches; from it every creature was fed.   Eze 17:23; Da 2:48

¹³"In the visions I saw while lying in my bed, I looked, and there before me was a messenger,ᵇ a holy one, coming down from heaven. ¹⁴He called in a loud voice: 'Cut down the tree and trim off its branches; strip off its leaves and scatter its fruit. Let the

---

ᵃ7 Or *Chaldeans*   ᵇ13 Or *watchman*; also in verses 17 and 23

animals flee from under it and the birds from its branches. ¹⁵But let the stump and its roots, bound with iron and bronze, remain in the ground, in the grass of the field.   Da 7:1

¹⁶" 'Let him be drenched with the dew of heaven, and let him live with the animals among the plants of the earth. ¹⁶Let his mind be changed from that of a man and let him be given the mind of an animal, till seven times*ᵃ* pass by for him.   Job 14:7-9; Da 7:25

¹⁷" 'The decision is announced by messengers, the holy ones declare the verdict, so that the living may know that the Most High is sovereign over the kingdoms of men and gives them to anyone he wishes and sets over them the lowliest of men.'   Ps 83:18; 103:19

¹⁸"This is the dream that I, King Nebuchadnezzar, had. Now, Belteshazzar, tell me what it means, for none of the wise men in my kingdom can interpret it for me. But you can, because the spirit of the holy gods is in you."   Ge 41:8; Da 5:8

Daniel Interprets the Dream

¹⁹Then Daniel (also called Belteshazzar) was greatly perplexed for a time, and his thoughts terrified him. So the king said, "Belteshazzar, do not let the dream or its meaning alarm you."   Da 7:15,28; 8:27

Belteshazzar answered, "My lord, if only the dream applied to your enemies and its meaning to your adversaries! ²⁰The tree you saw, which grew large and strong, with its top touching the sky, visible to the whole earth, ²¹with beautiful leaves and abundant fruit, providing food for all, giving shelter to the beasts of the field, and having nesting places in its branches for the birds of the air— ²²you, O king, are that tree! You have become great and strong; your greatness has grown until it reaches the sky, and your dominion extends to distant parts of the earth.   Eze 31:6

²³"You, O king, saw a messenger, a holy one, coming down from heaven and saying, 'Cut down the tree and destroy it, but leave the stump, bound with iron and bronze, in the grass of the field, while its roots remain in the ground. Let him be drenched with the dew of heaven; let him live like the wild animals, until seven times pass by for him.'   Da 5:21; 8:13

²⁴"This is the interpreta-

ᵃ16 Or years; also in verses 23, 25 and 32

tion, O king, and this is the decree the Most High has issued against my lord the king: ²⁵You will be driven away from people and will live with the wild animals; you will eat grass like cattle and be drenched with the dew of heaven. Seven times will pass by for you until you acknowledge that the Most High is sovereign over the kingdoms of men and gives them to anyone he wishes. ²⁶The command to leave the stump of the tree with its roots means that your kingdom will be restored to you when you acknowledge that Heaven rules. ²⁷Therefore, O king, be pleased to accept my advice: Renounce your sins by doing what is right, and your wickedness by being kind to the oppressed. It may be that then your prosperity will continue." Job 40:12

The Dream Is Fulfilled

²⁸All this happened to King Nebuchadnezzar. ²⁹Twelve months later, as the king was walking on the roof of the royal palace of Babylon, ³⁰he said, "Is not this the great Babylon I have built as the royal residence, by my mighty power and for the glory of my majesty?" Nu 23:19; Isa 13:19 ³¹The words were still on his lips when a voice came from heaven, "This is what

is decreed for you, King Nebuchadnezzar: Your royal authority has been taken from you. ³²You will be driven away from people and will live with the wild animals; you will eat grass like cattle. Seven times will pass by for you until you acknowledge that the Most High is sovereign over the kingdoms of men and gives them to anyone he wishes."

³³Immediately what had been said about Nebuchadnezzar was fulfilled. He was driven away from people and ate grass like cattle. His body was drenched with the dew of heaven until his hair grew like the feathers of an eagle and his nails like the claws of a bird. 2Sa 22:28; Job 24:8

³⁴At the end of that time, I, Nebuchadnezzar, raised my eyes toward heaven, and my sanity was restored. Then I praised the Most High; I honored and glorified him who lives forever. Job 12:20; Da 12:7

His dominion is an eternal dominion;
his kingdom endures from generation to generation. Ps 145:13
³⁵All the peoples of the earth are regarded as nothing.
He does as he pleases with the powers of heaven and the peoples of the earth.

No one can hold back his
   hand   Isa 14:27
or say to him: "What have
   you done?"   Job 9:4

36At the same time that
my sanity was restored, my
honor and splendor were
returned to me for the glory
of my kingdom. My advis-
ers and nobles sought me
out, and I was restored to
my throne and became
even greater than before.
37Now I, Nebuchadnezzar,
praise and exalt and glorify
the King of heaven, because
everything he does is right
and all his ways are just.
And those who walk in
pride he is able to humble.

The Writing on the Wall

5 King Belshazzar gave a great
banquet for a thousand of
his nobles and drank wine with
them. 2While Belshazzar was
drinking his wine, he gave orders to bring in the gold and
silver goblets that Nebu-
chadnezzar his father*a* had tak-
en from the temple in Jerusalem, so that the king and his
nobles, his wives and his concubines might drink from them.
3So they brought in the gold
goblets that had been taken
from the temple of God in
Jerusalem, and the king and his
nobles, his wives and his concubines drank from them. 4As
they drank the wine, they
praised the gods of gold and silver, of bronze, iron, wood and
stone.   Jdg 16:24; Est 2:14; Da 8:1

5Suddenly the fingers of a human hand appeared and wrote
on the plaster of the wall, near
the lampstand in the royal palace. The king watched the hand
as it wrote. 6His face turned pale
and he was so frightened that
his knees knocked together and
his legs gave way.

7The king called out for the
enchanters, astrologers*b* and diviners to be brought and said to
these wise men of Babylon,
"Whoever reads this writing
and tells me what it means will
be clothed in purple and have a
gold chain placed around his
neck, and he will be made the
third highest ruler in the kingdom."   Ge 41:8; Isa 44:25

8Then all the king's wise men
came in, but they could not read
the writing or tell the king what
it meant. 9So King Belshazzar
became even more terrified and
his face grew more pale. His nobles were baffled.   Ex 8:18

10The queen,*c* hearing the
voices of the king and his nobles, came into the banquet hall.
"O king, live forever!" she said.
"Don't be alarmed! Don't look
so pale! 11There is a man in your
kingdom who has the spirit of
the holy gods in him. In the
time of your father he was
found to have insight and intelligence and wisdom like that of

---

*a*2 Or *ancestor; or predecessor;* also in verses 11, 13 and 18   *b*7 Or *Chaldeans;* also in
verse 11   *c*10 Or *queen mother*

the gods. King Nebuchadnezzar your father—your father the king, I say—appointed him chief of the magicians, enchanters, astrologers and diviners. [12]This man Daniel, whom the king called Belteshazzar, was found to have a keen mind and knowledge and understanding, and also the ability to interpret dreams, explain riddles and solve difficult problems. Call for Daniel, and he will tell you what the writing means."

[13]So Daniel was brought before the king, and the king said to him, "Are you Daniel, one of the exiles my father the king brought from Judah? [14]I have heard that the spirit of the gods is in you and that you have insight, intelligence and outstanding wisdom. [15]The wise men and enchanters were brought before me to read this writing and tell me what it means, but they could not explain it. [16]Now I have heard that you are able to give interpretations and to solve difficult problems. If you can read this writing and tell me what it means, you will be clothed in purple and have a gold chain placed around your neck, and you will be made the third highest ruler in the kingdom."   Est 2:5-6

[17]Then Daniel answered the king, "You may keep your gifts for yourself and give your rewards to someone else. Nevertheless, I will read the writing for the king and tell him what it means.   2Ki 5:16

[18]"O king, the Most High God gave your father Nebuchadnezzar sovereignty and greatness and glory and splendor. [19]Because of the high position he gave him, all the peoples and nations and men of every language dreaded and feared him. Those the king wanted to put to death, he put to death; those he wanted to spare, he spared; those he wanted to promote, he promoted; and those he wanted to humble, he humbled. [20]But when his heart became arrogant and hardened with pride, he was deposed from his royal throne and stripped of his glory. [21]He was driven away from people and given the mind of an animal; he lived with the wild donkeys and ate grass like cattle; and his body was drenched with the dew of heaven, until he acknowledged that the Most High God is sovereign over the kingdoms of men and sets over them anyone he wishes.   Da 8:8

[22]"But you his son,[a] O Belshazzar, have not humbled yourself, though you knew all this. [23]Instead, you have set yourself up against the Lord of heaven. You had the goblets from his temple brought to you, and you and your nobles, your wives and your concubines drank wine from them. You praised the gods of silver and

[a]22 Or descendant; or successor

gold, of bronze, iron, wood and stone, which cannot see or hear or understand. But you did not honor the God who holds in his hand your life and all your ways. ²⁴Therefore he sent the hand that wrote the inscription.

²⁵"This is the inscription that was written:

MENE, MENE, TEKEL, PARSIN^a

²⁶"This is what these words mean:

Mene^b: God has numbered the days of your reign and brought it to an end.
²⁷*Tekel*^c: You have been weighed on the scales and found wanting.   Ps 62:9
²⁸*Peres*^d: Your kingdom is divided and given to the Medes and Persians."   Jer 27:7

²⁹Then at Belshazzar's command, Daniel was clothed in purple, a gold chain was placed around his neck, and he was proclaimed the third highest ruler in the kingdom. Ge 41:42

³⁰That very night Belshazzar, king of the Babylonians,^e was slain, ³¹and Darius the Mede took over the kingdom, at the age of sixty-two. Jer 50:35

Daniel in the Den of Lions

6 It pleased Darius to appoint 120 satraps to rule through-out the kingdom, ²with three administrators over them, one of whom was Daniel. The satraps were made accountable to them so that the king might not suffer loss. ³Now Daniel so distinguished himself among the administrators and the satraps by his exceptional qualities that the king planned to set him over the whole kingdom. ⁴At this, the administrators and the satraps tried to find grounds for charges against Daniel in his conduct of government affairs, but they were unable to do so. They could find no corruption in him, because he was trustworthy and neither corrupt nor negligent. ⁵Finally these men said, "We will never find any basis for charges against this man Daniel unless it has something to do with the law of his God."   Da 5:31; Ac 24:13-16

⁶So the administrators and the satraps went as a group to the king and said: "O King Darius, live forever! ⁷The royal administrators, prefects, satraps, advisers and governors have all agreed that the king should issue an edict and enforce the decree that anyone who prays to any god or man during the next thirty days, except to you, O king, shall be thrown into the lions' den. ⁸Now, O king, issue the decree and put it in writing so that it cannot be altered—in accordance with the laws of the

---

^a25 Aramaic *UPARSIN* (that is, *AND PARSIN*)   ^b26 *Mene* can mean *numbered* or *mina* (a unit of money).   ^c27 *Tekel* can mean *weighed* or *shekel*.   ^d28 *Peres* (the singular of *Parsin*) can mean *divided* or *Persia* or *a half mina* or *a half shekel*.   ^e30 Or *Chaldeans*

Medes and Persians, which cannot be repealed." ⁹So King Darius put the decree in writing.

¹⁰Now when Daniel learned that the decree had been published, he went home to his upstairs room where the windows opened toward Jerusalem. Three times a day he got down on his knees and prayed, giving thanks to his God, just as he had done before. ¹¹Then these men went as a group and found Daniel praying and asking God for help. ¹²So they went to the king and spoke to him about his royal decree: "Did you not publish a decree that during the next thirty days anyone who prays to any god or man except to you, O king, would be thrown into the lions' den?"

The king answered, "The decree stands—in accordance with the laws of the Medes and Persians, which cannot be repealed."   Est 1:19; Da 3:8-12

¹³Then they said to the king, "Daniel, who is one of the exiles from Judah, pays no attention to you, O king, or to the decree you put in writing. He still prays three times a day." ¹⁴When the king heard this, he was greatly distressed; he was determined to rescue Daniel and made every effort until sundown to save him.   Eze 14:14

¹⁵Then the men went as a group to the king and said to him, "Remember, O king, that according to the law of the Medes and Persians no decree or edict that the king issues can be changed."   Est 8:8

¹⁶So the king gave the order, and they brought Daniel and threw him into the lions' den. The king said to Daniel, "May your God, whom you serve continually, rescue you!"   Job 5:19

¹⁷A stone was brought and placed over the mouth of the den, and the king sealed it with his own signet ring and with the rings of his nobles, so that Daniel's situation might not be changed. ¹⁸Then the king returned to his palace and spent the night without eating and without any entertainment being brought to him. And he could not sleep.   Mt 27:66

¹⁹At the first light of dawn, the king got up and hurried to the lions' den. ²⁰When he came near the den, he called to Daniel in an anguished voice, "Daniel, servant of the living God, has your God, whom you serve continually, been able to rescue you from the lions?"   Da 3:17

²¹Daniel answered, "O king, live forever! ²²My God sent his angel, and he shut the mouths of the lions. They have not hurt me, because I was found innocent in his sight. Nor have I ever done any wrong before you, O king."   Ge 32:1; Ne 2:3

²³The king was overjoyed and gave orders to lift Daniel out of the den. And when Daniel was lifted from the den, no wound was found on him, because he had trusted in his God.   Da 3:27

²⁴At the king's command, the

men who had falsely accused Daniel were brought in and thrown into the lions' den, along with their wives and children. And before they reached the floor of the den, the lions overpowered them and crushed all their bones. Dt 19:18-19

25Then King Darius wrote to all the peoples, nations and men of every language throughout the land: Da 3:4

"May you prosper greatly! Da 4:1

26"I issue a decree that in every part of my kingdom people must fear and reverence the God of Daniel. Ps 5:7

"For he is the living God
and he endures forever;
his kingdom will not be
destroyed,
his dominion will never
end. Jos 2:11; Rev 1:18
27He rescues and he saves;
he performs signs and
wonders
in the heavens and on the
earth. Da 4:3
He has rescued Daniel
from the power of the
lions."

28So Daniel prospered during the reign of Darius and the reign of Cyrus*a* the Persian.

Daniel's Dream of Four Beasts

7 In the first year of Belshazzar king of Babylon, Daniel had a dream, and visions passed through his mind as he was lying on his bed. He wrote down the substance of his dream.

2Daniel said: "In my vision at night I looked, and there before me were the four winds of heaven churning up the great sea. 3Four great beasts, each different from the others, came up out of the sea. Eze 37:9; Rev 13:1

4"The first was like a lion, and it had the wings of an eagle. I watched until its wings were torn off and it was lifted from the ground so that it stood on two feet like a man, and the heart of a man was given to it.

5"And there before me was a second beast, which looked like a bear. It was raised up on one of its sides, and it had three ribs in its mouth between its teeth. It was told, 'Get up and eat your fill of flesh!' Da 2:39

6"After that, I looked, and there before me was another beast, one that looked like a leopard. And on its back it had four wings like those of a bird. This beast had four heads, and it was given authority to rule.

7"After that, in my vision at night I looked, and there before me was a fourth beast—terrifying and frightening and very powerful. It had large iron teeth; it crushed and devoured its victims and trampled underfoot whatever was left. It was different from all the

a28 Or Darius, that is, the reign of Cyrus

former beasts, and it had ten horns.   Eze 40:2; Da 2:40

8"While I was thinking about the horns, there before me was another horn, a little one, which came up among them; and three of the first horns were uprooted before it. This horn had eyes like the eyes of a man and a mouth that spoke boastfully.

9"As I looked,

"thrones were set in place,
  and the Ancient of Days
    took his seat.   1Ki 22:19
His clothing was as white as
    snow;   Mt 28:3
  the hair of his head was
    white like wool.   Rev 1:14
His throne was flaming with
    fire,
  and its wheels were all
    ablaze.   Eze 1:15
10A river of fire was flowing,
  coming out from before
    him.   Dt 33:2
Thousands upon thousands
    attended him;
  ten thousand times ten
    thousand stood before
    him.
The court was seated,
  and the books were
    opened.   Ex 32:32

11"Then I continued to watch because of the boastful words the horn was speaking. I kept looking until the beast was slain and its body destroyed and thrown into the blazing fire. 12(The other beasts had been stripped of their authority, but were allowed to live for a period of time.)   Rev 13:5-6; 19:20

13"In my vision at night I looked, and there before me was one like a son of man, coming with the clouds of heaven. He approached the Ancient of Days and was led into his presence. 14He was given authority, glory and sovereign power; all peoples, nations and men of every language worshiped him. His dominion is an everlasting dominion that will not pass away, and his kingdom is one that will never be destroyed.

The Interpretation of the Dream

15"I, Daniel, was troubled in spirit, and the visions that passed through my mind disturbed me. 16I approached one of those standing there and asked him the true meaning of all this.   Job 4:15; Da 4:19

"So he told me and gave me the interpretation of these things: 17'The four great beasts are four kingdoms that will rise from the earth. 18But the saints of the Most High will receive the kingdom and will possess it forever—yes, for ever and ever.'   Da 8:16; Zec 1:9

19"Then I wanted to know the true meaning of the fourth beast, which was different from all the others and most terrifying, with its iron teeth and bronze claws—the beast that crushed and devoured its victims and trampled underfoot whatever was left. 20I also wanted to know about the ten horns

on its head and about the other horn that came up, before which three of them fell—the horn that looked more imposing than the others and that had eyes and a mouth that spoke boastfully. ²¹As I watched, this horn was waging war against the saints and defeating them, ²²until the Ancient of Days came and pronounced judgment in favor of the saints of the Most High, and the time came when they possessed the kingdom.

²³"He gave me this explanation: 'The fourth beast is a fourth kingdom that will appear on earth. It will be different from all the other kingdoms and will devour the whole earth, trampling it down and crushing it. ²⁴The ten horns are ten kings who will come from this kingdom. After them another king will arise, different from the earlier ones; he will subdue three kings. ²⁵He will speak against the Most High and oppress his saints and try to change the set times and the laws. The saints will be handed over to him for a time, times and half a time.ᵃ

²⁶" 'But the court will sit, and his power will be taken away and completely destroyed forever. ²⁷Then the sovereignty, power and greatness of the kingdoms under the whole heaven will be handed over to the saints, the people of the Most High. His kingdom will be an everlasting kingdom, and all

rulers will worship and obey him.'   Isa 14:2

²⁸"This is the end of the matter. I, Daniel, was deeply troubled by my thoughts, and my face turned pale, but I kept the matter to myself."   Isa 21:3

Daniel's Vision of a Ram and a Goat

8 In the third year of King Belshazzar's reign, I, Daniel, had a vision, after the one that had already appeared to me. ²In my vision I saw myself in the citadel of Susa in the province of Elam; in the vision I was beside the Ulai Canal. ³I looked up, and there before me was a ram with two horns, standing beside the canal, and the horns were long. One of the horns was longer than the other but grew up later. ⁴I watched the ram as he charged toward the west and the north and the south. No animal could stand against him, and none could rescue from his power. He did as he pleased and became great.

⁵As I was thinking about this, suddenly a goat with a prominent horn between his eyes came from the west, crossing the whole earth without touching the ground. ⁶He came toward the two-horned ram I had seen standing beside the canal and charged at him in great rage. ⁷I saw him attack the ram furiously, striking the ram and shattering his two horns. The

---

ᵃ25 Or for a year, two years and half a year

ram was powerless to stand against him; the goat knocked him to the ground and trampled on him, and none could rescue the ram from his power. ⁸The goat became very great, but at the height of his power his large horn was broken off, and in its place four prominent horns grew up toward the four winds of heaven. 2Ch 26:16-21

⁹Out of one of them came another horn, which started small but grew in power to the south and to the east and toward the Beautiful Land. ¹⁰It grew until it reached the host of the heavens, and it threw some of the starry host down to the earth and trampled on them. ¹¹It set itself up to be as great as the Prince of the host; it took away the daily sacrifice from him, and the place of his sanctuary was brought low. ¹²Because of rebellion, the host ˎof the saintsˏ*ᵃ* and the daily sacrifice were given over to it. It prospered in everything it did, and truth was thrown to the ground. Da 7:8

¹³Then I heard a holy one speaking, and another holy one said to him, "How long will it take for the vision to be fulfilled—the vision concerning the daily sacrifice, the rebellion that causes desolation, and the surrender of the sanctuary and of the host that will be trampled underfoot?" Dt 33:2; Da 12:6

¹⁴He said to me, "It will take 2,300 evenings and mornings;

then the sanctuary will be reconsecrated." Da 12:11-12

The Interpretation of the Vision

¹⁵While I, Daniel, was watching the vision and trying to understand it, there before me stood one who looked like a man. ¹⁶And I heard a man's voice from the Ulai calling, "Gabriel, tell this man the meaning of the vision." Eze 2:1; Da 9:21

¹⁷As he came near the place where I was standing, I was terrified and fell prostrate. "Son of man," he said to me, "understand that the vision concerns the time of the end." Eze 1:28

¹⁸While he was speaking to me, I was in a deep sleep, with my face to the ground. Then he touched me and raised me to my feet. Eze 2:2; Da 10:9

¹⁹He said: "I am going to tell you what will happen later in the time of wrath, because the vision concerns the appointed time of the end.*ᵇ* ²⁰The two-horned ram that you saw represents the kings of Media and Persia. ²¹The shaggy goat is the king of Greece, and the large horn between his eyes is the first king. ²²The four horns that replaced the one that was broken off represent four kingdoms that will emerge from his nation but will not have the same power. Isa 10:25; Da 10:20

²³"In the latter part of their reign, when rebels have become

ᵃ12 Or *rebellion, the armies*   *ᵇ19* Or *because the end will be at the appointed time*

completely wicked, a stern-faced king, a master of intrigue, will arise. ²⁴He will become very strong, but not by his own power. He will cause astounding devastation and will succeed in whatever he does. He will destroy the mighty men and the holy people. ²⁵He will cause deceit to prosper, and he will consider himself superior. When they feel secure, he will destroy many and take his stand against the Prince of princes. Yet he will be destroyed, but not by human power.   Da 7:25; 11:23

²⁶"The vision of the evenings and mornings that has been given you is true, but seal up the vision, for it concerns the distant future."   Isa 8:16; Da 10:1

²⁷I, Daniel, was exhausted and lay ill for several days. Then I got up and went about the king's business. I was appalled by the vision; it was beyond understanding.   Isa 21:3; Da 10:8

Daniel's Prayer

9 In the first year of Darius son of Xerxes*ᵃ* (a Mede by descent), who was made ruler over the Babylonian*ᵇ* kingdom— ²in the first year of his reign, I, Daniel, understood from the Scriptures, according to the word of the LORD given to Jeremiah the prophet, that the desolation of Jerusalem would last seventy years. ³So I turned to the Lord God and pleaded with him in prayer and petition, in fasting, and in sackcloth and ashes.   2Ch 20:3; Da 5:31

⁴I prayed to the LORD my God and confessed: 1Ki 8:30

"O Lord, the great and awesome God, who keeps his covenant of love with all who love him and obey his commands, ⁵we have sinned and done wrong. We have been wicked and have rebelled; we have turned away from your commands and laws. ⁶We have not listened to your servants the prophets, who spoke in your name to our kings, our princes and our fathers, and to all the people of the land.   Jer 8:14

⁷"Lord, you are righteous, but this day we are covered with shame—the men of Judah and people of Jerusalem and all Israel, both near and far, in all the countries where you have scattered us because of our unfaithfulness to you. ⁸O LORD, we and our kings, our princes and our fathers are covered with shame because we have sinned against you. ⁹The Lord our God is merciful and forgiving, even though we have rebelled against him; ¹⁰we have not obeyed the LORD our God or kept the laws he gave us through his servants the prophets. ¹¹All Is-

ᵃ1 Hebrew *Ahasuerus*   *ᵇ1* Or *Chaldean*

rael has transgressed your law and turned away, refusing to obey you. Ezr 9:15

"Therefore the curses and sworn judgments written in the Law of Moses, the servant of God, have been poured out on us, because we have sinned against you. ¹²You have fulfilled the words spoken against us and against our rulers by bringing upon us great disaster. Under the whole heaven nothing has ever been done like what has been done to Jerusalem. ¹³Just as it is written in the Law of Moses, all this disaster has come upon us, yet we have not sought the favor of the LORD our God by turning from our sins and giving attention to your truth. ¹⁴The LORD did not hesitate to bring the disaster upon us, for the LORD our God is righteous in everything he does; yet we have not obeyed him. Dt 4:29

¹⁵"Now, O Lord our God, who brought your people out of Egypt with a mighty hand and who made for yourself a name that endures to this day, we have sinned, we have done wrong. ¹⁶O Lord, in keeping with all your righteous acts, turn away your anger and your wrath from Jerusalem, your city, your holy hill. Our sins and the iniquities of our fathers have made Jerusalem and your people an object of scorn to all those around us. ¹⁷"Now, our God, hear the prayers and petitions of your servant. For your sake, O Lord, look with favor on your desolate sanctuary. ¹⁸Give ear, O God, and hear; open your eyes and see the desolation of the city that bears your Name. We do not make requests of you because we are righteous, but because of your great mercy. ¹⁹O Lord, listen! O Lord, forgive! O Lord, hear and act! For your sake, O my God, do not delay, because your city and your people bear your Name." Nu 6:24-26

The Seventy "Sevens"

²⁰While I was speaking and praying, confessing my sin and the sin of my people Israel and making my request to the LORD my God for his holy hill— ²¹while I was still in prayer, Gabriel, the man I had seen in the earlier vision, came to me in swift flight about the time of the evening sacrifice. ²²He instructed me and said to me, "Daniel, I have now come to give you insight and understanding. ²³As soon as you began to pray, an answer was given, which I have come to tell you, for you are highly esteemed. Therefore, consider the message and understand the vision: Ezr 10:1

24"Seventy 'sevens'ᵃ are decreed for your people and your holy city to finishᵇ transgression, to put an end to sin, to atone for wickedness, to bring in everlasting righteousness, to seal up vision and prophecy and to anoint the most holy.ᶜ

25"Know and understand this: From the issuing of the decreeᵈ to restore and rebuild Jerusalem until the Anointed One,ᵉ the ruler, comes, there will be seven 'sevens,' and sixty-two 'sevens.' It will be rebuilt with streets and a trench, but in times of trouble. 26After the sixty-two 'sevens,' the Anointed One will be cut off and will have nothing.ᶠ The people of the ruler who will come will destroy the city and the sanctuary. The end will come like a flood: War will continue until the end, and desolations have been decreed. 27He will confirm a covenant with many for one 'seven.'ᵍ In the middle of the 'seven'ᵍ he will put an end to sacrifice and offering. And on a wing ⌊of the temple⌋ he will set up an abomination that causes desolation, until the end that is decreed is poured out on him.ʰ"ⁱ   Isa 28:2

Daniel's Vision of a Man

10 In the third year of Cyrus king of Persia, a revelation was given to Daniel (who

was called Belteshazzar). Its message was true and it concerned a great war.ʲ The understanding of the message came to him in a vision.   Da 1:21; 8:26

2At that time I, Daniel, mourned for three weeks. 3I ate no choice food; no meat or wine touched my lips; and I used no lotions at all until the three weeks were over.   Ezr 9:4

4On the twenty-fourth day of the first month, as I was standing on the bank of the great river, the Tigris, 5I looked up and there before me was a man dressed in linen, with a belt of the finest gold around his waist. 6His body was like chrysolite, his face like lightning, his eyes like flaming torches, his arms and legs like the gleam of burnished bronze, and his voice like the sound of a multitude.

7I, Daniel, was the only one who saw the vision; the men with me did not see it, but such terror overwhelmed them that they fled and hid themselves. 8So I was left alone, gazing at this great vision; I had no strength left, my face turned deathly pale and I was helpless. 9Then I heard him speaking, and as I listened to him, I fell into a deep sleep, my face to the ground.   2Ki 6:17-20

10A hand touched me and set me trembling on my hands and

ᵃ24 Or 'weeks'; also in verses 25 and 26   ᵇ24 Or restrain   ᶜ24 Or Most Holy Place; or most holy One   ᵈ25 Or word   ᵉ25 Or an anointed one; also in verse 26   ᶠ26 Or off and will have no one; or off, but not for himself   ᵍ27 Or 'week'   ʰ27 Or it   ⁱ27 Or And one who causes desolation will come upon the pinnacle of the abominable ⌊temple⌋, until the end that is decreed is poured out on the desolated ⌊city⌋   ʲ1 Or true and burdensome

knees. [11]He said, "Daniel, you who are highly esteemed, consider carefully the words I am about to speak to you, and stand up, for I have now been sent to you." And when he said this to me, I stood up trembling.

[12]Then he continued, "Do not be afraid, Daniel. Since the first day that you set your mind to gain understanding and to humble yourself before your God, your words were heard, and I have come in response to them. [13]But the prince of the Persian kingdom resisted me twenty-one days. Then Michael, one of the chief princes, came to help me, because I was detained there with the king of Persia. [14]Now I have come to explain to you what will happen to your people in the future, for the vision concerns a time yet to come."   Da 9:22; Mt 14:27

[15]While he was saying this to me, I bowed with my face toward the ground and was speechless. [16]Then one who looked like a man[a] touched my lips, and I opened my mouth and began to speak. I said to the one standing before me, "I am overcome with anguish because of the vision, my lord, and I am helpless. [17]How can I, your servant, talk with you, my lord? My strength is gone and I can hardly breathe."   Eze 24:27

[18]Again the one who looked like a man touched me and gave me strength. [19]"Do not be afraid, O man highly esteemed," he said. "Peace! Be strong now; be strong."   Da 8:18

When he spoke to me, I was strengthened and said, "Speak, my lord, since you have given me strength."   Jos 1:9; Da 9:23

[20]So he said, "Do you know why I have come to you? Soon I will return to fight against the prince of Persia, and when I go, the prince of Greece will come; [21]but first I will tell you what is written in the Book of Truth. (No one supports me against them except Michael, your prince. [1]And in the first year of Darius the Mede, I took my stand to support and protect him.)   Da 5:31

The Kings of the South and the North

[2]"Now then, I tell you the truth: Three more kings will appear in Persia, and then a fourth, who will be far richer than all the others. When he has gained power by his wealth, he will stir up everyone against the kingdom of Greece. [3]Then a mighty king will appear, who will rule with great power and do as he pleases. [4]After he has appeared, his empire will be broken up and parceled out toward the four winds of heaven. It will not go to his descendants, nor will it have the power he exercised, because his

---

[a]16 Most manuscripts of the Masoretic Text; one manuscript of the Masoretic Text, Dead Sea Scrolls and Septuagint *Then something that looked like a man's hand*

empire will be uprooted and given to others. Da 7:2; 10:21

5"The king of the South will become strong, but one of his commanders will become even stronger than he and will rule his own kingdom with great power. 6After some years, they will become allies. The daughter of the king of the South will go to the king of the North to make an alliance, but she will not retain her power, and he and his power*a* will not last. In those days she will be handed over, together with her royal escort and her father*b* and the one who supported her.

7"One from her family line will arise to take her place. He will attack the forces of the king of the North and enter his fortress; he will fight against them and be victorious. 8He will also seize their gods, their metal images and their valuable articles of silver and gold and carry them off to Egypt. For some years he will leave the king of the North alone. 9Then the king of the North will invade the realm of the king of the South but will retreat to his own country. 10His sons will prepare for war and assemble a great army, which will sweep on like an irresistible flood and carry the battle as far as his fortress. Isa 8:8

11"Then the king of the South will march out in a rage and fight against the king of the North, who will raise a large army, but it will be defeated. 12When the army is carried off, the king of the South will be filled with pride and will slaughter many thousands, yet he will not remain triumphant. 13For the king of the North will muster another army, larger than the first; and after several years, he will advance with a huge army fully equipped.

14"In those times many will rise against the king of the South. The violent men among your own people will rebel in fulfillment of the vision, but without success. 15Then the king of the North will come and build up siege ramps and will capture a fortified city. The forces of the South will be powerless to resist; even their best troops will not have the strength to stand. 16The invader will do as he pleases; no one will be able to stand against him. He will establish himself in the Beautiful Land and will have the power to destroy it. 17He will determine to come with the might of his entire kingdom and will make an alliance with the king of the South. And he will give him a daughter in marriage in order to overthrow the kingdom, but his plans*c* will not succeed or help him. 18Then he will turn his attention to the coastlands and will take many of them, but a commander will put an end to his insolence and will turn his insolence back upon

---

*a*6 Or *offspring*   *b*6 Or *child* (see Vulgate and Syriac)   *c*17 Or *but she*

him. ¹⁹After this, he will turn back toward the fortresses of his own country but will stumble and fall, to be seen no more.

²⁰"His successor will send out a tax collector to maintain the royal splendor. In a few years, however, he will be destroyed, yet not in anger or in battle.

²¹"He will be succeeded by a contemptible person who has not been given the honor of royalty. He will invade the kingdom when its people feel secure, and he will seize it through intrigue. ²²Then an overwhelming army will be swept away before him; both it and a prince of the covenant will be destroyed. ²³After coming to an agreement with him, he will act deceitfully, and with only a few people he will rise to power. ²⁴When the richest provinces feel secure, he will invade them and will achieve what neither his fathers nor his forefathers did. He will distribute plunder, loot and wealth among his followers. He will plot the overthrow of fortresses—but only for a time.

²⁵"With a large army he will stir up his strength and courage against the king of the South. The king of the South will wage war with a large and very powerful army, but he will not be able to stand because of the plots devised against him. ²⁶Those who eat from the king's provisions will try to destroy him; his army will be swept away, and many will fall in battle. ²⁷The two kings, with their hearts bent on evil, will sit at the same table and lie to each other, but to no avail, because an end will still come at the appointed time. ²⁸The king of the North will return to his own country with great wealth, but his heart will be set against the holy covenant. He will take action against it and then return to his own country.   Ps 64:6; Jer 9:5

²⁹"At the appointed time he will invade the South again, but this time the outcome will be different from what it was before. ³⁰Ships of the western coastlands*a* will oppose him, and he will lose heart. Then he will turn back and vent his fury against the holy covenant. He will return and show favor to those who forsake the holy covenant.   Ge 10:4; 1Sa 17:32

³¹"His armed forces will rise up to desecrate the temple fortress and will abolish the daily sacrifice. Then they will set up the abomination that causes desolation. ³²With flattery he will corrupt those who have violated the covenant, but the people who know their God will firmly resist him.   Hos 3:4

³³"Those who are wise will instruct many, though for a time they will fall by the sword or be burned or captured or plundered. ³⁴When they fall, they will receive a little help, and

---

*a*30 Hebrew of *Kittim*

many who are not sincere will join them. 35Some of the wise will stumble, so that they may be refined, purified and made spotless until the time of the end, for it will still come at the appointed time. Da 12:3; Zec 13:9

The King Who Exalts Himself

36"The king will do as he pleases. He will exalt and magnify himself above every god and will say unheard-of things against the God of gods. He will be successful until the time of wrath is completed, for what has been determined must take place. 37He will show no regard for the gods of his fathers or for the one desired by women, nor will he regard any god, but will exalt himself above them all. 38Instead of them, he will honor a god of fortresses; a god unknown to his fathers he will honor with gold and silver, with precious stones and costly gifts. 39He will attack the mightiest fortresses with the help of a foreign god and will greatly honor those who acknowledge him. He will make them rulers over many people and will distribute the land at a price.ᵃ Rev 13:5-6

40"At the time of the end the king of the South will engage him in battle, and the king of the North will storm out against him with chariots and cavalry and a great fleet of ships. He will invade many countries and sweep through them like a flood. 41He will also invade the Beautiful Land. Many countries will fall, but Edom, Moab and the leaders of Ammon will be delivered from his hand. 42He will extend his power over many countries; Egypt will not escape. 43He will gain control of the treasures of gold and silver and all the riches of Egypt, with the Libyans and Nubians in submission. 44But reports from the east and the north will alarm him, and he will set out in a great rage to destroy and annihilate many. 45He will pitch his royal tents between the seas atᵇ the beautiful holy mountain. Yet he will come to his end, and no one will help him. Isa 21:1

The End Times

12 "At that time Michael, the great prince who protects your people, will arise. There will be a time of distress such as has not happened from the beginning of nations until then. But at that time your people—everyone whose name is found written in the book—will be delivered. 2Multitudes who sleep in the dust of the earth will awake: some to everlasting life, others to shame and everlasting contempt. 3Those who are wiseᶜ will shine like the brightness of the heavens, and those who lead many to righteousness, like the stars for ever and ever. 4But you,

ᵃ39 Or land for a reward   ᵇ45 Or the sea and   ᶜ3 Or who impart wisdom

Daniel, close up and seal the words of the scroll until the time of the end. Many will go here and there to increase knowledge." _{Da 10:13; Jn 11:24; Rev 22:10}

⁵Then I, Daniel, looked, and there before me stood two others, one on this bank of the river and one on the opposite bank. ⁶One of them said to the man clothed in linen, who was above the waters of the river, "How long will it be before these astonishing things are fulfilled?"

⁷The man clothed in linen, who was above the waters of the river, lifted his right hand and his left hand toward heaven, and I heard him swear by him who lives forever, saying, "It will be for a time, times and half a time.ᵃ When the power of the holy people has been finally broken, all these things will be completed."

⁸I heard, but I did not understand. So I asked, "My lord, what will the outcome of all this be?"

⁹He replied, "Go your way, Daniel, because the words are closed up and sealed until the time of the end. ¹⁰Many will be purified, made spotless and refined, but the wicked will continue to be wicked. None of the wicked will understand, but those who are wise will understand. _{Isa 29:11; Hos 14:9}

¹¹"From the time that the daily sacrifice is abolished and the abomination that causes desolation is set up, there will be 1,290 days. ¹²Blessed is the one who waits for and reaches the end of the 1,335 days. _{Ex 29:38}

¹³"As for you, go your way till the end. You will rest, and then at the end of the days you will rise to receive your allotted inheritance." _{Ps 16:5; Isa 57:2}

ᵃ7 Or *a year, two years and half a year*

Hosea

Introduction:

The prophet Hosea was a citizen of the northern kingdom, which he commonly called Ephraim. He probably began his ministry before King Jeroboam II died in 753 B.C. and may have given his messages shortly before the fall of Samaria in 722 B.C.

Chapters 1–3 tell about Hosea's love for his unfaithful wife, Gomer. Her unfaithfulness is a picture of Israel's unfaithfulness in her covenant relationship with God. Instead of responding in thankfulness and love to God for all their blessings, the Israelites used their crops as offerings to idols. The injustice and mistreatment of others reflected their lack of love for God as well as for their fellow citizens.

Outline of contents:

Hosea's experience in family life (1:1–3:5)
Israel's sin (4:1–6:3)
Punishment for Israel (6:4–10:15)
God's judgment and mercy (11:1–14:9)

---

1 The word of the LORD that came to Hosea son of Beeri during the reigns of Uzziah, Jotham, Ahaz and Hezekiah, kings of Judah, and during the reign of Jeroboam son of Jehoash[a] king of Israel: Jer 1:2

Hosea's Wife and Children

2When the LORD began to speak through Hosea, the LORD said to him, "Go, take to yourself an adulterous wife and children of unfaithfulness, because the land is guilty of the vilest adultery in departing from the LORD." 3So he married Gomer daughter of Diblaim, and she conceived and bore him a son.

4Then the LORD said to Hosea, "Call him Jezreel, because I will soon punish the house of Jehu for the massacre at Jezreel, and I will put an end to the kingdom of Israel. 5In that day I will break Israel's bow in the Valley of Jezreel."   Jos 15:56

6Gomer conceived again and gave birth to a daughter. Then the LORD said to Hosea, "Call her Lo-Ruhamah,[b] for I will no longer show love to the house

of Israel, that I should at all forgive them. ⁷Yet I will show love to the house of Judah; and I will save them—not by bow, sword or battle, or by horses and horsemen, but by the LORD their God." Ps 44:6; Hos 2:23

⁸After she had weaned Lo-Ruhamah, Gomer had another son. ⁹Then the LORD said, "Call him Lo-Ammi,ᵃ for you are not my people, and I am not your God. Eze 11:19-20; 1Pe 2:10

¹⁰"Yet the Israelites will be like the sand on the seashore, which cannot be measured or counted. In the place where it was said to them, 'You are not my people,' they will be called 'sons of the living God.' ¹¹The people of Judah and the people of Israel will be reunited, and they will appoint one leader and will come up out of the land, for great will be the day of Jezreel.

2 "Say of your brothers, 'My people,' and of your sisters, 'My loved one.' 1Pe 2:10

Israel Punished and Restored

²"Rebuke your mother, rebuke her, Isa 50:1
for she is not my wife, and I am not her husband.
Let her remove the adulterous look from her face Isa 1:21
and the unfaithfulness from between her breasts.
³Otherwise I will strip her naked Eze 16:37

and make her as bare as on the day she was born;
I will make her like a desert, turn her into a parched land, Isa 32:13-14
and slay her with thirst.
⁴I will not show my love to her children,
because they are the children of adultery.
⁵Their mother has been unfaithful
and has conceived them in disgrace.
She said, 'I will go after my lovers, Jer 3:6
who give me my food and my water,
my wool and my linen, my oil and my drink.'
⁶Therefore I will block her path with thornbushes;
I will wall her in so that she cannot find her way.
⁷She will chase after her lovers but not catch them;
she will look for them but not find them. Hos 5:13
Then she will say,
'I will go back to my husband as at first, Isa 54:5
for then I was better off than now.' Eze 16:8
⁸She has not acknowledged that I was the one
who gave her the grain, the new wine and oil, Nu 18:12
who lavished on her the silver and gold— Dt 8:18
which they used for Baal.

ᵃ9 *Lo-Ammi* means *not my people.*

9"Therefore I will take away
my grain when it
ripens,
and my new wine when it
is ready.   Hos 9:2
I will take back my wool and
my linen,
intended to cover her
nakedness.
10So now I will expose her
lewdness   Eze 23:10
before the eyes of her
lovers;   Jer 13:26
no one will take her out of
my hands.   Eze 16:37
11I will stop all her
celebrations: Jer 7:34
her yearly festivals, her
New Moons,
her Sabbath days—all her
appointed feasts.   Isa 1:14
12I will ruin her vines and her
fig trees,   Jer 5:17
which she said were her
pay from her lovers;
I will make them a thicket,
and wild animals will
devour them.   Hos 5:7
13I will punish her for the days
she burned incense to the
Baals;   Isa 65:7
she decked herself with rings
and jewelry,   Eze 16:17
and went after her lovers,
but me she forgot,"   Hos 4:6
declares the LORD.

14"Therefore I am now going
to allure her;
I will lead her into the
desert
and speak tenderly to her.

15There I will give her back her
vineyards,
and will make the Valley of
Achor*a* a door of hope.
There she will sing*b* as in the
days of her youth,   Jer 2:2
as in the day she came up
out of Egypt.   Eze 28:26
16"In that day," declares the
LORD,
"you will call me 'my
husband';   Isa 54:5
you will no longer call me
'my master.*c*'
17I will remove the names of
the Baals from her lips;
no longer will their names
be invoked.   Jos 23:7
18In that day I will make a
covenant for them
with the beasts of the field
and the birds of the air
and the creatures that move
along the ground.   Job 5:22
Bow and sword and battle
I will abolish from the land,
so that all may lie down in
safety.   Job 5:23
19I will betroth you to me
forever;   Isa 62:4
I will betroth you in*d*
righteousness and
justice,   Isa 1:27
in*e* love and compassion.
20I will betroth you in
faithfulness,
and you will acknowledge
the LORD.   Eze 16:8

21"In that day I will respond,"
declares the LORD—

---

*a*15 *Achor* means *trouble.*   *b*15 Or *respond*
in verse 20   *e*19 Or *with*   *c*16 Hebrew *baal*   *d*19 Or *with;* also

"I will respond to the skies,
    and they will respond to
        the earth;   Isa 55:10
22and the earth will respond to
    the grain,
    the new wine and oil,
    and they will respond to
        Jezreel. *a*   Eze 36:29-30
23I will plant her for myself in
    the land;   Jer 31:27
    I will show my love to the
        one I called 'Not my
        loved one.' *b*   Hos 1:6
    I will say to those called 'Not
        my people,' *c* 'You are
        my people';   Isa 19:25
    and they will say, 'You are
        my God.' "

Hosea's Reconciliation With His Wife

3 The LORD said to me, "Go,
    show your love to your wife
again, though she is loved by
another and is an adulteress.
Love her as the LORD loves the
Israelites, though they turn to
other gods and love the sacred
raisin cakes."   2Sa 6:19; Hos 1:2

2So I bought her for fifteen
shekels *d* of silver and about a
homer and a lethek *e* of barley.
3Then I told her, "You are to live
with *f* me many days; you must
not be a prostitute or be intimate with any man, and I will
live with *f* you."   Ru 4:10

4For the Israelites will live
many days without king or
prince, without sacrifice or sacred stones, without ephod or
idol. 5Afterward the Israelites
will return and seek the LORD
their God and David their king.
They will come trembling to the
LORD and to his blessings in the
last days.   Dt 4:29; Hos 13:11

The Charge Against Israel

4 Hear the word of the LORD,
    you Israelites,
because the LORD has a
    charge to bring   Job 10:2
against you who live in the
    land: Joel 1:2,14
"There is no faithfulness, no
    love,   Pr 24:2
no acknowledgment of God
    in the land.   Jer 51:5
2There is only cursing, *g* lying
    and murder,   Hos 5:2
stealing and adultery;
    they break all bounds,
    and bloodshed follows
        bloodshed.   2Ki 21:16
3Because of this the land
    mourns, *h*   Jer 4:28
and all who live in it waste
    away;   Isa 15:6
the beasts of the field and the
    birds of the air
    and the fish of the sea are
        dying.   Jer 4:25

4"But let no man bring a
    charge,
let no man accuse another,
for your people are like those
    who bring charges against a
        priest.   Dt 17:12

---

a22 Jezreel means *God plants.*   *b23* Hebrew *Lo-Ruhamah*   *c23* Hebrew *Lo-Ammi*
d2 That is, about 6 ounces (about 170 grams)   *e2* That is, probably about 10 bushels
(about 330 liters)   *f3* Or *wait for*   *g2* That is, to pronounce a curse upon   *h3* Or
dries up

⁵You stumble day and night,
and the prophets stumble
with you.
So I will destroy your
mother— Hos 2:2
⁶ my people are destroyed
from lack of knowledge.

"Because you have rejected
knowledge,
I also reject you as my
priests;
because you have ignored
the law of your God,
I also will ignore your
children.
⁷The more the priests
increased,
the more they sinned
against me;
they exchanged*ᵃ* their*ᵇ*
Glory for something
disgraceful. Hab 2:16
⁸They feed on the sins of my
people
and relish their wickedness.
⁹And it will be: Like people,
like priests. Isa 24:2
I will punish both of them
for their ways
and repay them for their
deeds. Jer 5:31

¹⁰"They will eat but not have
enough; Lev 26:26
they will engage in
prostitution but not
increase, Eze 22:9
because they have deserted
the LORD Hos 7:14
to give themselves ¹¹to
prostitution, Hos 5:4

to old wine and new, Lev 10:9
which take away the
understanding ¹²of my
people. Pr 20:1
They consult a wooden idol
and are answered by a stick
of wood. Jer 2:27
A spirit of prostitution leads
them astray;
they are unfaithful to their
God. Ps 73:27
¹³They sacrifice on the
mountaintops
and burn offerings on the
hills,
under oak, poplar and
terebinth, Isa 1:29
where the shade is
pleasant. Jer 3:6
Therefore your daughters
turn to prostitution
and your daughters-in-law
to adultery. Hos 2:13

¹⁴"I will not punish your
daughters
when they turn to
prostitution,
nor your daughters-in-law
when they commit
adultery,
because the men themselves
consort with harlots
and sacrifice with shrine
prostitutes— Ge 38:21
a people without
understanding will come
to ruin! Pr 10:21

¹⁵"Though you commit
adultery, O Israel,
let not Judah become guilty.

ᵃ7 Syriac and an ancient Hebrew scribal tradition; Masoretic Text *I will exchange*
ᵇ7 Masoretic Text; an ancient Hebrew scribal tradition *my*

"Do not go to Gilgal;   Hos 9:15
  do not go up to Beth
    Aven.ᵃ   Jos 7:2
And do not swear, 'As
  surely as the LORD lives!'
¹⁶The Israelites are stubborn,
  like a stubborn heifer.   Jer 31:18
How then can the LORD
  pasture them
  like lambs in a meadow?
¹⁷Ephraim is joined to idols;
  leave him alone!
¹⁸Even when their drinks are
    gone,
  they continue their
    prostitution;
  their rulers dearly love
    shameful ways.
¹⁹A whirlwind will sweep
    them away,   Hos 12:1
  and their sacrifices will
    bring them shame.   Isa 1:29

Judgment Against Israel

5 "Hear this, you priests!
  Pay attention, you
    Israelites!
  Listen, O royal house!
  This judgment is against
    you: Job 10:2
  You have been a snare at
    Mizpah,   Hos 6:9
  a net spread out on Tabor.
²The rebels are deep in
    slaughter.   Hos 4:2
  I will discipline all of them.
³I know all about Ephraim;
  Israel is not hidden from
    me.   Am 5:12
Ephraim, you have now
    turned to prostitution;
  Israel is corrupt.   Eze 23:7

⁴"Their deeds do not permit
    them
  to return to their God.   Hos 7:10
A spirit of prostitution is in
    their heart;   Hos 4:11
  they do not acknowledge
    the LORD.   Jer 4:22
⁵Israel's arrogance testifies
  against them;   Isa 3:9
  the Israelites, even
    Ephraim, stumble in
    their sin;   Eze 14:7
Judah also stumbles with
    them.   Hos 14:1
⁶When they go with their
    flocks and herds
  to seek the LORD,   Mic 6:6-7
  they will not find him;
  he has withdrawn himself
    from them.   Pr 1:28
⁷They are unfaithful to the
    LORD;   Isa 24:16
  they give birth to
    illegitimate children.
Now their New Moon
    festivals   Isa 1:14
  will devour them and their
    fields.   Hos 2:11-12

⁸"Sound the trumpet in
    Gibeah,   Jdg 19:12
  the horn in Ramah.   Isa 10:29
Raise the battle cry in Beth
    Avenᵃ;
  lead on, O Benjamin.
⁹Ephraim will be laid waste
  on the day of reckoning.
Among the tribes of Israel
  I proclaim what is certain.
¹⁰Judah's leaders are like those
  who move boundary
    stones.   Dt 19:14

ᵃ15,8 *Beth Aven* means *house of wickedness* (a name for Bethel, which means *house of God*).

I will pour out my wrath on
   them   Eze 7:8
like a flood of water.
[11]Ephraim is oppressed,
   trampled in judgment,
   intent on pursuing idols. [a]
[12]I am like a moth to Ephraim,
   like rot to the people of
   Judah.   Job 18:16

[13]"When Ephraim saw his
   sickness,
   and Judah his sores,
then Ephraim turned to
   Assyria,   Eze 23:5
   and sent to the great king
   for help.   La 5:6
But he is not able to cure
   you,   Isa 3:7
   not able to heal your sores.
[14]For I will be like a lion to
   Ephraim,   Job 10:16
   like a great lion to Judah.
I will tear them to pieces and
   go away;   Hos 6:1
   I will carry them off, with
   no one to rescue them.
[15]Then I will go back to my
   place   Isa 18:4
   until they admit their guilt.
And they will seek my face;
   in their misery they will
   earnestly seek me."

Israel Unrepentant

6 "Come, let us return to the
      LORD.   Isa 10:20
He has torn us to pieces
   but he will heal us;   Nu 12:13
he has injured us
   but he will bind up our
   wounds.   Dt 32:39

[2]After two days he will revive
   us;   Ps 30:5
on the third day he will
   restore us,   Ps 71:20
that we may live in his
   presence.
[3]Let us acknowledge the
   LORD;
   let us press on to
   acknowledge him.
As surely as the sun rises,
   he will appear;
he will come to us like the
   winter rains,   Job 4:3
   like the spring rains that
   water the earth."   Ps 72:6

[4]"What can I do with you,
   Ephraim?   Hos 11:8
What can I do with you,
   Judah?
Your love is like the morning
   mist,
   like the early dew that
   disappears.   Hos 7:1
[5]Therefore I cut you in pieces
   with my prophets,
   I killed you with the words
   of my mouth;   Jer 1:9-10
   my judgments flashed like
   lightning upon you.
[6]For I desire mercy, not
   sacrifice,   1Sa 15:22
   and acknowledgment of
   God rather than burnt
   offerings.   Ps 40:6
[7]Like Adam, [b] they have
   broken the covenant—
   they were unfaithful to me
   there.   Hos 5:7
[8]Gilead is a city of wicked
   men,   Hos 12:11

---

[a]11 The meaning of the Hebrew for this word is uncertain.   [b]7 Or As at Adam; or Like
men

stained with footprints of
blood.
⁹As marauders lie in ambush
for a man, Ps 10:8
so do bands of priests;
they murder on the road to
Shechem, Hos 4:2
committing shameful
crimes. Jer 5:30-31
¹⁰I have seen a horrible thing
in the house of Israel.
There Ephraim is given to
prostitution
and Israel is defiled. Jer 23:14

¹¹"Also for you, Judah,
a harvest is appointed. Joel 3:13

"Whenever I would restore
the fortunes of my
people, Ps 126:1
7 ¹whenever I would heal
Israel,
the sins of Ephraim are
exposed
and the crimes of Samaria
revealed. Eze 24:13
They practice deceit,
thieves break into houses,
bandits rob in the streets;
²but they do not realize
that I remember all their
evil deeds. Job 35:15
Their sins engulf them; Jer 2:19
they are always before me.

³"They delight the king with
their wickedness,
the princes with their lies.
⁴They are all adulterers, Jer 9:2
burning like an oven
whose fire the baker need
not stir
from the kneading of the
dough till it rises.

⁵On the day of the festival of
our king
the princes become
inflamed with wine, Isa 28:1
and he joins hands with the
mockers. Ps 1:1
⁶Their hearts are like an oven;
they approach him with
intrigue.
Their passion smolders all
night;
in the morning it blazes like
a flaming fire.
⁷All of them are hot as an
oven;
they devour their rulers.
All their kings fall, Hos 13:10
and none of them calls on
me. Ps 14:4
⁸"Ephraim mixes with the
nations; Ps 106:35
Ephraim is a flat cake not
turned over.
⁹Foreigners sap his strength,
but he does not realize it.
His hair is sprinkled with
gray,
but he does not notice.
¹⁰Israel's arrogance testifies
against him, Hos 5:5
but despite all this
he does not return to the
Lord his God
or search for him. Isa 9:13

¹¹"Ephraim is like a dove,
easily deceived and
senseless— Ge 8:8
now calling to Egypt, Hos 9:6
now turning to Assyria.
¹²When they go, I will throw
my net over them; Eze 12:13
I will pull them down like
birds of the air.

When I hear them flocking
     together,
I will catch them.
[13]Woe to them,   Hos 9:12
     because they have strayed
          from me!   Jer 14:10
Destruction to them,
     because they have rebelled
          against me!
I long to redeem them
     but they speak lies against
          me.   Ps 116:11
[14]They do not cry out to me
     from their hearts
but wail upon their beds.
They gather together[a] for
     grain and new wine
but turn away from me.
[15]I trained them and
     strengthened them,
but they plot evil against
     me.   Ps 2:1; 140:2
[16]They do not turn to the Most
     High;
they are like a faulty bow.
Their leaders will fall by the
     sword
because of their insolent
     words.   Mal 3:14
For this they will be
     ridiculed
in the land of Egypt.   Hos 9:3

Israel to Reap the Whirlwind

8 "Put the trumpet to your
     lips!   Nu 10:2
An eagle is over the house
     of the LORD   Dt 28:49
because the people have
     broken my covenant

and rebelled against my
     law.   Hos 4:6
[2]Israel cries out to me,
     'O our God, we
          acknowledge you!'
[3]But Israel has rejected what
     is good;
an enemy will pursue
     him.
[4]They set up kings without
     my consent;
they choose princes without
     my approval.   Hos 13:10
With their silver and gold
     they make idols for
          themselves   Hos 2:8
to their own destruction.
[5]Throw out your calf-idol,
     O Samaria!   Hos 10:5
My anger burns against
     them.
How long will they be
     incapable of purity?
[6] They are from Israel!
This calf—a craftsman has
     made it;
it is not God.   Jer 16:20
It will be broken in pieces,
     that calf of Samaria.   Ex 32:4

[7]"They sow the wind
     and reap the whirlwind.
The stalk has no head;
     it will produce no flour.
Were it to yield grain,
     foreigners would swallow it
          up.   Hos 2:9
[8]Israel is swallowed up;   Jer 51:34
     now she is among the
          nations
like a worthless thing.   Jer 22:28

---

[a]14 Most Hebrew manuscripts; some Hebrew manuscripts and Septuagint *They slash themselves*

⁹For they have gone up to
Assyria   Jer 2:18
like a wild donkey
wandering alone. Ge 16:12
Ephraim has sold herself to
lovers.   Jer 22:20
¹⁰Although they have sold
themselves among the
nations,
I will now gather them
together.   Eze 16:37
They will begin to waste
away   Jer 42:2
under the oppression of the
mighty king.

¹¹"Though Ephraim built
many altars for sin
offerings,
these have become altars
for sinning.   Hos 10:1
¹²I wrote for them the many
things of my law,
but they regarded them as
something alien.
¹³They offer sacrifices given to
me
and they eat the meat, Jer 7:21
but the LORD is not pleased
with them.   Jer 6:20
Now he will remember their
wickedness   Hos 7:2
and punish their sins:
They will return to Egypt.
¹⁴Israel has forgotten his
Maker   Ps 95:6
and built palaces;
Judah has fortified many
towns.
But I will send fire upon their
cities
that will consume their
fortresses."   Jer 5:17

Punishment for Israel

9 Do not rejoice, O Israel;
do not be jubilant like the
other nations.   Isa 22:12-13
For you have been unfaithful
to your God;   Ps 73:27
you love the wages of a
prostitute   Ge 30:15
at every threshing floor.
²Threshing floors and
winepresses will not
feed the people;
the new wine will fail them.
³They will not remain in the
LORD's land;   Lev 25:23
Ephraim will return to
Egypt   Jos 7:16
and eat uncleanᵃ food in
Assyria.   Eze 4:13
⁴They will not pour out wine
offerings to the LORD,
nor will their sacrifices
please him.   Hos 8:13
Such sacrifices will be to
them like the bread of
mourners;   Jer 16:7
all who eat them will be
unclean.   Dt 26:14
This food will be for
themselves;
it will not come into the
temple of the LORD.

⁵What will you do on the day
of your appointed feasts,
on the festival days of the
LORD?   Hos 2:11
⁶Even if they escape from
destruction,
Egypt will gather them,
and Memphis will bury
them.   Isa 19:13

ᵃ3 That is, ceremonially unclean

Their treasures of silver will
    be taken over by briers,
and thorns will overrun
    their tents.   Isa 5:6
⁷The days of punishment are
    coming,   Isa 34:8
the days of reckoning are at
    hand.   Job 31:14
Let Israel know this.
Because your sins are so
    many   Jer 16:18
and your hostility so great,
the prophet is considered a
    fool,   1Sa 10:11
the inspired man a maniac.
⁸The prophet, along with my
    God,
    is the watchman over
        Ephraim,ᵃ
yet snares await him on all
    his paths,   Hos 5:1
and hostility in the house of
    his God.   Eze 22:26
⁹They have sunk deep into
    corruption,   Zep 3:7
as in the days of Gibeah.
God will remember their
    wickedness   Hos 8:13
and punish them for their
    sins.   Hos 4:9

¹⁰"When I found Israel,
    it was like finding grapes in
        the desert;
when I saw your fathers,
    it was like seeing the early
        fruit on the fig tree.
But when they came to Baal
    Peor,   Nu 25:1-5
they consecrated
    themselves to that
        shameful idol   Jer 11:13

and became as vile as the
    thing they loved.
¹¹Ephraim's glory will fly away
    like a bird—   Hos 4:7
no birth, no pregnancy, no
    conception.
¹²Even if they rear children,
    I will bereave them of every
        one.   Eze 24:21
Woe to them
    when I turn away from
        them!   Dt 31:17
¹³I have seen Ephraim, like
    Tyre,
    planted in a pleasant place.
But Ephraim will bring out
    their children to the
        slayer."   Job 15:22

¹⁴Give them, O LORD—
    what will you give them?
Give them wombs that
    miscarry
and breasts that are dry.

¹⁵"Because of all their
    wickedness in Gilgal,
I hated them there.
Because of their sinful deeds,
    I will drive them out of my
        house.   Hos 7:2
I will no longer love them;
    all their leaders are
        rebellious.   Isa 1:23
¹⁶Ephraim is blighted,   Hos 5:11
    their root is withered,
    they yield no fruit.   Job 15:32
Even if they bear children,
    I will slay their cherished
        offspring."

¹⁷My God will reject them

ᵃ8 Or *The prophet is the watchman over Ephraim, / the people of my God*

because they have not
obeyed him; Hos 4:10
they will be wanderers
among the nations. Dt 28:65

10 Israel was a spreading
vine; Eze 5:2
he brought forth fruit for
himself.
As his fruit increased,
he built more altars; 1Ki 14:23
as his land prospered,
he adorned his sacred
stones. Hos 3:4
²Their heart is deceitful,
and now they must bear
their guilt. Hos 13:16
The LORD will demolish their
altars
and destroy their sacred
stones. Mic 5:13

³Then they will say, "We have
no king
because we did not revere
the LORD.
But even if we had a king,
what could he do for us?"
⁴They make many promises,
take false oaths Hos 4:2
and make agreements; Am 5:7
therefore lawsuits spring up
like poisonous weeds in a
plowed field. Am 6:12
⁵The people who live in
Samaria fear
for the calf-idol of Beth
Aven.ᵃ Ex 32:4
Its people will mourn over it,
and so will its idolatrous
priests, 2Ki 23:5

those who had rejoiced over
its splendor,
because it is taken from
them into exile. Hos 8:5
⁶It will be carried to Assyria
as tribute for the great
king.
Ephraim will be disgraced;
Israel will be ashamed of its
wooden idols.ᵇ Jer 48:13
⁷Samaria and its king will float
away Hos 13:11
like a twig on the surface of
the waters.
⁸The high places of
wicknessᶜ will be
destroyed— 1Ki 12:28-30
it is the sin of Israel.
Thorns and thistles will grow
up Hos 9:6
and cover their altars. Isa 32:13
Then they will say to the
mountains, "Cover us!"
and to the hills, "Fall on
us!" Am 7:9

⁹"Since the days of Gibeah,
you have sinned,
O Israel, Jos 7:11
and there you have
remained.ᵈ
Did not war overtake
the evildoers in Gibeah?
¹⁰When I please, I will punish
them; Eze 5:13
nations will be gathered
against them
to put them in bonds for
their double sin.
¹¹Ephraim is a trained heifer
that loves to thresh;

ᵃ5 Beth Aven means house of wickedness (a name for Bethel, which means house of God).
ᵇ6 Or its counsel   ᶜ8 Hebrew aven, a reference to Beth Aven (a derogatory name for
Bethel)   ᵈ9 Or there a stand was taken

so I will put a yoke
on her fair neck.   Jer 15:12
I will drive Ephraim,
Judah must plow,
and Jacob must break up
the ground.
¹²Sow for yourselves
righteousness,   Ecc 11:1
reap the fruit of unfailing
love,
and break up your unplowed
ground;   Jer 4:3
for it is time to seek the
Lord,   Isa 19:22
until he comes
and showers righteousness
on you.   Isa 45:8
¹³But you have planted
wickedness,
you have reaped evil,   Job 4:8
you have eaten the fruit of
deception.   Pr 11:18
Because you have depended
on your own strength
and on your many warriors,
¹⁴the roar of battle will rise
against your people,
so that all your fortresses
will be devastated—
as Shalman devastated Beth
Arbel on the day of
battle,   2Ki 17:3
when mothers were dashed
to the ground with their
children.   Isa 13:16
¹⁵Thus will it happen to you,
O Bethel,
because your wickedness is
great.
When that day dawns,
the king of Israel will be
completely destroyed.

God's Love for Israel

11 "When Israel was a
child, I loved him,   Dt 4:37
and out of Egypt I called
my son.   Ex 4:22
²But the more I ᵃ called Israel,
the further they went from
me. ᵇ
They sacrificed to the Baals
and they burned incense to
images.   2Ki 17:15
³It was I who taught Ephraim
to walk,
taking them by the arms;
but they did not realize
it was I who healed them.
⁴I led them with cords of
human kindness,
with ties of love;   Jer 31:2-3
I lifted the yoke from their
neck   Lev 26:13
and bent down to feed
them.   Jer 31:20

⁵"Will they not return to
Egypt   Hos 7:16
and will not Assyria rule
over them   Hos 10:6
because they refuse to
repent?   Ex 13:17
⁶Swords will flash in their
cities,   Hos 13:16
will destroy the bars of their
gates   La 2:9
and put an end to their
plans.
⁷My people are determined to
turn from me.   Jer 3:6-7
Even if they call to the Most
High,
he will by no means exalt
them.

ᵃ2 Some Septuagint manuscripts; Hebrew *they*   ᵇ2 Septuagint; Hebrew *them*

⁸"How can I give you up,
Ephraim? Hos 6:4
How can I hand you over,
Israel?
How can I treat you like
Admah?
How can I make you like
Zeboiim? Ge 14:8
My heart is changed within
me;
all my compassion is
aroused. 1Ki 3:26
⁹I will not carry out my fierce
anger, Dt 13:17
nor will I turn and
devastate Ephraim.
For I am God, and not man—
the Holy One among you.
I will not come in wrath. ᵃ
¹⁰They will follow the LORD;
he will roar like a lion. Isa 31:4
When he roars,
his children will come
trembling from the west.
¹¹They will come trembling
like birds from Egypt,
like doves from Assyria.
I will settle them in their
homes," Eze 28:26
declares the LORD.

Israel's Sin

¹²Ephraim has surrounded me
with lies, Hos 4:2
the house of Israel with
deceit.
And Judah is unruly against
God,
even against the faithful
Holy One. Dt 7:9

12 ¹Ephraim feeds on the
wind; Ps 78:67

he pursues the east wind all
day
and multiplies lies and
violence. Hos 4:19
He makes a treaty with
Assyria Hos 5:13
and sends olive oil to
Egypt. 2Ki 17:4
²The LORD has a charge to
bring against Judah;
he will punish Jacobᵇ
according to his ways
and repay him according to
his deeds. Hos 4:9
³In the womb he grasped his
brother's heel; Ge 25:26
as a man he struggled with
God. Ge 32:24-29
⁴He struggled with the angel
and overcame him;
he wept and begged for his
favor.
He found him at Bethel
and talked with him
there—
⁵the LORD God Almighty,
the LORD is his name of
renown! Ex 3:15
⁶But you must return to your
God; Isa 19:22
maintain love and justice,
and wait for your God
always. Eze 18:30

⁷The merchant uses dishonest
scales; Lev 19:36
he loves to defraud.
⁸Ephraim boasts, Eze 28:5
"I am very rich; I have
become wealthy. Ps 62:10
With all my wealth they will
not find in me
any iniquity or sin."

ᵃ9 Or *come against any city*   ᵇ2 *Jacob* means *he grasps the heel* (figuratively, *he deceives*).

⁹"I am the LORD your God,
⌊who brought you⌋ out of ᵃ
    Egypt;   Lev 23:43
I will make you live in tents
    again,   Ne 8:17
    as in the days of your
    appointed feasts.
¹⁰I spoke to the prophets,
    gave them many visions
    and told parables through
    them."   Jdg 14:12

¹¹Is Gilead wicked?   Hos 6:8
    Its people are worthless!
Do they sacrifice bulls in
    Gilgal?   Hos 4:15
    Their altars will be like piles
    of stones
    on a plowed field.   Hos 8:11
¹²Jacob fled to the country of
    Aramᵇ;   Ge 28:5
    Israel served to get a wife,
    and to pay for her he
    tended sheep.   Ge 29:18
¹³The LORD used a prophet to
    bring Israel up from
    Egypt,   Hos 11:1
    by a prophet he cared for
    him.   Ex 13:3
¹⁴But Ephraim has bitterly
    provoked him to anger;
    his Lord will leave upon
    him the guilt of his
    bloodshed   Eze 18:13
    and will repay him for his
    contempt.   Da 11:18

The LORD's Anger Against Israel

13 When Ephraim spoke,
        men trembled;   Jdg 12:1
    he was exalted in Israel.

But he became guilty of
    Baal worship and died.
²Now they sin more and
    more;
    they make idols for
    themselves from their
    silver,   Isa 46:6
cleverly fashioned images,
    all of them the work of
    craftsmen.   Hos 14:3
It is said of these people,
    "They offer human sacrifice
    and kissᶜ the calf-idols."
³Therefore they will be like
    the morning mist,
    like the early dew that
    disappears,   Hos 6:4
    like chaff swirling from a
    threshing floor,   Job 13:25
    like smoke escaping
    through a window.   Ps 68:2

⁴"But I am the LORD your
    God,
    ⌊who brought you⌋ out of ᵃ
    Egypt.   Jer 2:6
You shall acknowledge no
    God but me,   Ex 20:3
    no Savior except me.   Dt 28:29
⁵I cared for you in the desert,
    in the land of burning heat.
⁶When I fed them, they were
    satisfied;
    when they were satisfied,
    they became proud;
    then they forgot me.   Dt 32:18
⁷So I will come upon them
    like a lion,   Job 10:16
    like a leopard I will lurk by
    the path.
⁸Like a bear robbed of her
    cubs,   2Sa 17:8

ᵃ9,4 Or God / ever since you were in   ᵇ12 That is, Northwest Mesopotamia   ᶜ2 Or
"Men who sacrifice / kiss

I will attack them and rip
　　them open.
Like a lion I will devour
　　them;　　　　　1Sa 17:34
　　a wild animal will tear them
　　　apart.　　　　　Ps 50:22

9 "You are destroyed, O Israel,
　　because you are against me,
　　against your helper.
10 Where is your king, that he
　　may save you?　　2Ki 17:4
　　Where are your rulers in all
　　your towns,
　　of whom you said,
　　'Give me a king and
　　　princes'?　　　　1Sa 8:6
11 So in my anger I gave you a
　　king,　　　　　Nu 11:20
　　and in my wrath I took him
　　away.　　　　　Jos 24:20
12 The guilt of Ephraim is
　　stored up,
　　his sins are kept on record.
13 Pains as of a woman in
　　childbirth come to him,
　　but he is a child without
　　wisdom;
　　when the time arrives,
　　he does not come to the
　　opening of the womb.

14 "I will ransom them from the
　　power of the grave*a*;
　　I will redeem them from
　　death.　　　　　Isa 25:8
　　Where, O death, are your
　　plagues?
　　Where, O grave, *a* is your
　　destruction?　　1Co 15:55

　　"I will have no compassion,
15 　even though he thrives
　　among his brothers.

An east wind from the LORD
　　will come,　　Job 1:19
　　blowing in from the desert;
　　his spring will fail
　　and his well dry up.　Jer 51:36
　　His storehouse will be
　　plundered
　　of all its treasures.　Jer 20:5
16 The people of Samaria must
　　bear their guilt,　　2Ki 17:5
　　because they have rebelled
　　against their God.　Hos 7:14
　　They will fall by the sword;
　　their little ones will be
　　dashed to the ground,
　　their pregnant women
　　ripped open."　　2Ki 15:16

Repentance to Bring Blessing

14 Return, O Israel, to the
LORD your God.　Isa 19:22
　　Your sins have been your
　　downfall!　　　Hos 4:8
2 Take words with you
　　and return to the LORD.
　　Say to him:
　　"Forgive all our sins　Ex 34:9
　　and receive us graciously,
　　that we may offer the fruit
　　of our lips. *b*　　Heb 13:15
3 Assyria cannot save us;
　　we will not mount
　　war-horses.　　Ps 33:17
　　We will never again say 'Our
　　gods'　　　　Hos 8:6
　　to what our own hands
　　have made,　　Hos 13:2
　　for in you the fatherless
　　find compassion."　Ps 10:14

4 "I will heal their
　　waywardness　　Isa 30:26

---

*a*14 Hebrew *Sheol*　　*b*2 Or *offer our lips as sacrifices of bulls*

and love them freely,
for my anger has turned
away from them. Job 13:16
[5]I will be like the dew to
Israel; Ge 27:28
he will blossom like a lily.
Like a cedar of Lebanon
he will send down his
roots; Job 29:19
[6] his young shoots will grow.
His splendor will be like an
olive tree, Ps 52:8
his fragrance like a cedar of
Lebanon. Ps 92:12
[7]Men will dwell again in his
shade. Ps 91:1-4
He will flourish like the
grain.
He will blossom like a vine,

and his fame will be like the
wine from Lebanon.
[8]O Ephraim, what more have
I[a] to do with idols?
I will answer him and care
for him.
I am like a green pine tree;
your fruitfulness comes
from me." Isa 37:24

[9]Who is wise? He will realize
these things. Ps 107:43
Who is discerning? He will
understand them. Pr 10:29
The ways of the LORD are
right; Ps 111:7-8
the righteous walk in them,
but the rebellious stumble
in them.

Joel

Introduction:

Although the name Joel was common in the Old Testament, nothing is known about this prophet beyond what the book says—he was the son of Pethuel.

In this book Joel gives a detailed description of a severe locust plague that hit Palestine. In this event he saw a sign for the final judgment and warned the people to turn to God in repentance. Joel announced that the "day of the LORD" was coming and would bring even greater judgment.

Outline of contents:

1 The word of the LORD that came to Joel son of Pethuel.

An Invasion of Locusts

²Hear this, you elders;   Joel 2:16
listen, all who live in the
   land.   Hos 4:1
Has anything like this ever
   happened in your days
or in the days of your
   forefathers?   Joel 2:2
³Tell it to your children,   Ex 10:2
and let your children tell it
   to their children,
and their children to the
   next generation.   Ps 71:18
⁴What the locust swarm has
   left   Ex 10:14

the great locusts have
   eaten;
what the great locusts have
   left
the young locusts have
   eaten;
what the young locusts have
   left   Ex 10:5
other locusts[a] have eaten.

⁵Wake up, you drunkards,
   and weep!
Wail, all you drinkers of
   wine;   Joel 3:3
wail because of the new
   wine,
for it has been snatched
   from your lips.   Isa 24:7

---

[a]4 The precise meaning of the four Hebrew words used here for locusts is uncertain.

⁶A nation has invaded my
    land,
powerful and without
    number;   Ps 105:34
it has the teeth of a lion,
    the fangs of a lioness.
⁷It has laid waste my vines
    and ruined my fig trees.
It has stripped off their bark
    and thrown it away,
    leaving their branches
    white.

⁸Mourn like a virgin*ᵃ* in
    sackcloth   Isa 22:12
    grieving for the husband*ᵇ*
    of her youth.
⁹Grain offerings and drink
    offerings   Hos 9:4
are cut off from the house
    of the LORD.
The priests are in mourning,
    those who minister before
    the LORD.
¹⁰The fields are ruined,
    the ground is dried up*ᶜ*;
the grain is destroyed,
    the new wine is dried
    up,
    the oil fails.   Nu 18:12
¹¹Despair, you farmers,
    wail, you vine growers;
grieve for the wheat and the
    barley,   Ex 9:31
because the harvest of the
    field is destroyed.   Isa 17:11
¹²The vine is dried up
    and the fig tree is withered;
the pomegranate, the palm
    and the apple tree—
all the trees of the field—
    are dried up.   Isa 16:8

Surely the joy of mankind
    is withered away.

A Call to Repentance

¹³Put on sackcloth, O priests,
    and mourn;   Ge 37:34
wail, you who minister
    before the altar.   Joel 2:17
Come, spend the night in
    sackcloth,
    you who minister before
    my God;
for the grain offerings and
    drink offerings
are withheld from the
    house of your God.
¹⁴Declare a holy fast;   2Ch 20:3
    call a sacred assembly.
Summon the elders
    and all who live in the land
to the house of the LORD
    your God,
    and cry out to the LORD.

¹⁵Alas for that day!   Isa 2:12
For the day of the LORD is
    near;   Joel 2:1
it will come like destruction
    from the Almighty. *ᵈ*

¹⁶Has not the food been cut off
    before our very eyes—   Isa 3:7
joy and gladness
    from the house of our God?
¹⁷The seeds are shriveled
    beneath the clods. *ᵉ*   Isa 17:10-11
The storehouses are in ruins,
    the granaries have been
    broken down,
for the grain has dried up.
¹⁸How the cattle moan!
    The herds mill about

ᵃ8 Or *young woman*   *ᵇ8* Or *betrothed*   *ᶜ10* Or *ground mourns*   *ᵈ15* Hebrew
Shaddai   *ᵉ17* The meaning of the Hebrew for this word is uncertain.

because they have no
　　pasture;　　　　　　　Ge 47:4
even the flocks of sheep are
　　suffering.　　　　　　　Jer 9:10

¹⁹To you, O LORD, I call,
　　for fire has devoured the
　　　　open pastures　　　　Ps 97:3
and flames have burned up
　　all the trees of the field.
²⁰Even the wild animals pant
　　for you;　　　　　　　Ps 42:1
the streams of water have
　　dried up　　　　　　　1Ki 17:7
and fire has devoured the
　　open pastures.　　　　Joel 2:22

An Army of Locusts

2 Blow the trumpet in Zion;
　　sound the alarm on my
　　　　holy hill.　　　　　Ex 15:17
Let all who live in the land
　　tremble,
　　for the day of the LORD is
　　　　coming.　　　　　　Joel 1:15
It is close at hand—　　Eze 12:23
²　a day of darkness and
　　　　gloom,　　　　　　Eze 34:12
　a day of clouds and
　　　　blackness.　　　　　Zep 1:15
Like dawn spreading across
　　the mountains
　a large and mighty army
　　comes,　　　　　　　Joel 1:6
such as never was of old
　　nor ever will be in ages to
　　　　come.　　　　　　　Joel 1:2

³Before them fire devours,
　　behind them a flame blazes.
Before them the land is like
　　the garden of Eden,
　behind them, a desert
　　waste—　　　　　Ex 10:12-15

nothing escapes them.
⁴They have the appearance of
　　horses;　　　　　　　Rev 9:7
they gallop along like
　　cavalry.
⁵With a noise like that of
　　chariots　　　　　　　Rev 9:9
they leap over the
　　mountaintops,
like a crackling fire
　　consuming stubble,
like a mighty army drawn
　　up for battle.

⁶At the sight of them, nations
　　are in anguish;　　　　Isa 13:8
every face turns pale.　Isa 29:22
⁷They charge like warriors;
　　they scale walls like
　　　　soldiers.
They all march in line,
　　not swerving from their
　　　　course.　　　　　　Isa 5:27
⁸They do not jostle each other;
　　each marches straight
　　　　ahead.
They plunge through
　　defenses
without breaking ranks.
⁹They rush upon the city;
　　they run along the wall.
They climb into the houses;
　　like thieves they enter
　　　　through the windows.

¹⁰Before them the earth
　　shakes,　　　　　　　Ps 18:7
the sky trembles,　　　Eze 38:19
the sun and moon are
　　darkened,
and the stars no longer
　　shine.　　　　　　　Job 9:7
¹¹The LORD thunders
　　at the head of his army;

his forces are beyond
number,
and mighty are those who
obey his command.
The day of the LORD is great;
it is dreadful.
Who can endure it?   Zep 2:11

Rend Your Heart

¹²"Even now," declares the
LORD,
"return to me with all your
heart,   Dt 4:30
with fasting and weeping
and mourning."

¹³Rend your heart
and not your garments.
Return to the LORD your
God,   Isa 19:22
for he is gracious and
compassionate,   Dt 4:31
slow to anger and abounding
in love,   Ex 34:6
and he relents from sending
calamity.   Jer 18:8
¹⁴Who knows? He may turn
and have pity   Am 5:15
and leave behind a
blessing—   Jer 31:14
grain offerings and drink
offerings   Joel 1:13
for the LORD your God.

¹⁵Blow the trumpet in Zion,
declare a holy fast,   2Ch 20:3
call a sacred assembly.
¹⁶Gather the people,
consecrate the assembly;
bring together the elders,
gather the children,
those nursing at the breast.

Let the bridegroom leave his
room   Ps 19:5
and the bride her chamber.
¹⁷Let the priests, who minister
before the LORD,
weep between the temple
porch and the altar. Eze 8:16
Let them say, "Spare your
people, O LORD.
Do not make your
inheritance an object of
scorn,   Dt 9:26-29
a byword among the
nations.   1Ki 9:7
Why should they say among
the peoples,
'Where is their God?'"   Ps 42:3

The LORD's Answer

¹⁸Then the LORD will be jealous
for his land   Isa 26:11
and take pity on his people.

¹⁹The LORD will reply[a] to
them:

"I am sending you grain,
new wine and oil,   Ps 4:7
enough to satisfy you fully;
never again will I make you
an object of scorn to the
nations.   Eze 34:29

²⁰"I will drive the northern
army far from you,
pushing it into a parched
and barren land,
with its front columns going
into the eastern sea[b]
and those in the rear into
the western sea.[c]
And its stench will go up;
its smell will rise."   Isa 34:3

---

[a]18,19 Or LORD was jealous . . . / and took pity . . . / ¹⁹The LORD replied   [b]20 That is, the
Dead Sea   [c]20 That is, the Mediterranean

Surely he has done great
  things. *a*
21 Be not afraid, O land;
  be glad and rejoice.   Ps 9:2
Surely the LORD has done
  great things.   Ps 126:3
22 Be not afraid, O wild
  animals,
for the open pastures are
  becoming green.   Ps 65:12
The trees are bearing their
  fruit;
  the fig tree and the vine
  yield their riches.Joel 1:18-20
23Be glad, O people of Zion,
  rejoice in the LORD your
  God,   Ps 33:21
for he has given you
  the autumn rains in
  righteousness. *b*   Isa 45:8
He sends you abundant
  showers,   Job 36:28
  both autumn and spring
  rains, as before.   Lev 26:4
24The threshing floors will be
  filled with grain;
  the vats will overflow with
  new wine and oil.

25"I will repay you for the
  years the locusts have
  eaten—   Dt 28:39
  the great locust and the
  young locust,
  the other locusts and the
  locust swarm*c*—
my great army that I sent
  among you.   Joel 1:6
26You will have plenty to eat,
  until you are full,   Lev 26:5
and you will praise the

name of the LORD your
  God,
who has worked wonders
  for you;   Ps 126:3
never again will my people
  be shamed.   Isa 29:22
27Then you will know that I am
  in Israel,   Ex 6:7
  that I am the LORD your
  God,   Isa 44:8
and that there is no other;
never again will my people
  be shamed.   Isa 45:17

The Day of the LORD

28"And afterward,
  I will pour out my Spirit on
  all people.   Isa 11:2
Your sons and daughters will
  prophesy,
  your old men will dream
  dreams,   Jer 23:25
  your young men will see
  visions.
29Even on my servants, both
  men and women,
  I will pour out my Spirit in
  those days.   Eze 36:27
30I will show wonders in the
  heavens
  and on the earth,   Lk 21:11
  blood and fire and billows
  of smoke.
31The sun will be turned to
  darkness   Isa 22:5
  and the moon to blood
before the coming of the
  great and dreadful day
  of the LORD.   Joel 1:15
32And everyone who calls

---

a20 Or *rise. / Surely it has done great things."*   *b23* Or / *the teacher for righteousness:*
c25 The precise meaning of the four Hebrew words used here for locusts is uncertain.

on the name of the LORD
  will be saved;   Ps 106:8
for on Mount Zion and in
    Jerusalem   Isa 46:13
  there will be deliverance,
  as the LORD has said,
  among the survivors
    whom the LORD calls.   Ac 2:39

The Nations Judged

3 "In those days and at that
    time,
  when I restore the fortunes
    of Judah and Jerusalem,
²I will gather all nations
  and bring them down to the
    Valley of Jehoshaphat.ᵃ
There I will enter into
    judgment against them
  concerning my inheritance,
    my people Israel,
for they scattered my people
    among the nations
  and divided up my land.
³They cast lots for my people
  and traded boys for
    prostitutes;   Job 6:27
  they sold girls for wine   Joel 1:5
    that they might drink.

⁴"Now what have you
against me, O Tyre and Sidon
and all you regions of Philistia?
Are you repaying me for something I have done? If you are
paying me back, I will swiftly
and speedily return on your
own heads what you have
done. ⁵For you took my silver
and my gold and carried off my
finest treasures to your temples.
⁶You sold the people of Judah

and Jerusalem to the Greeks,
that you might send them far
from their homeland.   Ge 10:15
⁷"See, I am going to rouse
them out of the places to which
you sold them, and I will return
on your own heads what you
have done. ⁸I will sell your sons
and daughters to the people of
Judah, and they will sell them to
the Sabeans, a nation far away."
The LORD has spoken.   Isa 43:5-6

⁹Proclaim this among the
    nations:
  Prepare for war!   Isa 8:9
  Rouse the warriors!   Jer 46:4
  Let all the fighting men
    draw near and attack.
¹⁰Beat your plowshares into
    swords
  and your pruning hooks
    into spears.   Nu 25:7
  Let the weakling say,
  "I am strong!"   Jos 1:6
¹¹Come quickly, all you
    nations from every side,
  and assemble there. Eze 38:15-16

Bring down your warriors,
    O LORD!   Isa 13:3

¹²"Let the nations be roused;
  let them advance into the
    Valley of Jehoshaphat,
for there I will sit
  to judge all the nations on
    every side.   Ps 82:1
¹³Swing the sickle,   Mk 4:29
  for the harvest is ripe.   Isa 17:5
Come, trample the grapes,
  for the winepress is full
  and the vats overflow—

ᵃ2 *Jehoshaphat* means *the LORD judges*; also in verse 12.

so great is their wickedness!"

¹⁴Multitudes, multitudes
  in the valley of decision!
For the day of the LORD is
      near
  in the valley of decision.
¹⁵The sun and moon will be
      darkened,
  and the stars no longer
      shine.   Job 9:7
¹⁶The LORD will roar from Zion
  and thunder from
      Jerusalem;   Am 1:2
  the earth and the sky will
      tremble.   Jdg 5:4
But the LORD will be a refuge
      for his people,
  a stronghold for the people
      of Israel.   2Sa 22:3

Blessings for God's People

¹⁷"Then you will know that I,
      the LORD your God,
  dwell in Zion, my holy
      hill.
Jerusalem will be holy;   Jer 31:40

never again will foreigners
      invade her.   Isa 52:1
¹⁸"In that day the mountains
  will drip new wine,
  and the hills will flow with
      milk;   Ex 3:8
all the ravines of Judah will
      run with water.   Isa 30:25
A fountain will flow out of
      the LORD's house
  and will water the valley of
      acacias. ᵃ   Nu 25:1
¹⁹But Egypt will be desolate,
  Edom a desert waste,
because of violence done to
      the people of Judah,
  in whose land they shed
      innocent blood.   Jer 51:35
²⁰Judah will be inhabited
      forever   Ezr 9:12
  and Jerusalem through all
      generations.
²¹Their bloodguilt, which I
      have not pardoned,
  I will pardon."   Eze 36:25

The LORD dwells in Zion!

ᵃ18 Or Valley of Shittim

Amos

Introduction:

The author's name, Amos, means "burden" or "burdenbearer." Amos was a shepherd called by God to be a prophet in the northern cities of Israel, during a time of riches and wealth for the northern kingdom.

He announced God's judgment on the people for turning away from God, for being cruel to the poor, and for living selfishly.

In a series of five visions, Amos saw the day of doom as being close. He warned the people that they were to prepare to meet God. For those who loved God, however, Amos had a word of hope. The day was coming when the kingdom of David would be re-established and God's people would dwell in safety.

Outline of contents:

1 The words of Amos, one of the shepherds of Tekoa— what he saw concerning Israel two years before the earthquake, when Uzziah was king of Judah and Jeroboam son of Jehoash*a* was king of Israel.

²He said:

"The LORD roars from Zion
  and thunders from
    Jerusalem;   Joel 3:16
the pastures of the shepherds
  dry up,*b*

and the top of Carmel
  withers."   Am 9:3

Judgment on Israel's Neighbors

³This is what the LORD says:

"For three sins of Damascus,
  even for four, I will not turn
    back ₁my wrath₎.   Am 2:6
Because she threshed Gilead
  with sledges having iron
    teeth,
⁴I will send fire upon the
  house of Hazael   1Ki 19:17

a1 Hebrew *Joash*, a variant of *Jehoash*   *b2* Or *shepherds mourn*

that will consume the
    fortresses of Ben-Hadad.
⁵I will break down the gate of
    Damascus;   Jer 51:30
I will destroy the king who
    is in*ᵃ* the Valley of
    Aven*ᵇ*
and the one who holds the
    scepter in Beth Eden.
The people of Aram will go
    into exile to Kir,"   2Ki 16:9
        says the LORD.

⁶This is what the LORD says:

"For three sins of Gaza,
    even for four, I will not turn
    back ˌmy wrathˌ.
Because she took captive
    whole communities
and sold them to Edom,
⁷I will send fire upon the
    walls of Gaza
that will consume her
    fortresses.
⁸I will destroy the king*ᶜ* of
    Ashdod   2Ch 26:6
and the one who holds the
    scepter in Ashkelon.
I will turn my hand against
    Ekron,   Ps 81:14
till the last of the Philistines
    is dead,"   Eze 25:16
      says the Sovereign
        LORD.

⁹This is what the LORD says:

"For three sins of Tyre,
    even for four, I will not turn
    back ˌmy wrathˌ.
Because she sold whole

communities of captives
    to Edom,   1Ki 15:12
disregarding a treaty of
    brotherhood,
¹⁰I will send fire upon the
    walls of Tyre
that will consume her
    fortresses."   Isa 23:1-18

¹¹This is what the LORD says:

"For three sins of Edom,
    even for four, I will not turn
    back ˌmy wrathˌ.
Because he pursued his
    brother with a sword,
    stifling all compassion,*ᵈ*
because his anger raged
    continually
and his fury flamed
    unchecked,   Eze 25:12-14
¹²I will send fire upon Teman
that will consume the
    fortresses of Bozrah."

¹³This is what the LORD says:

"For three sins of Ammon,
    even for four, I will not turn
    back ˌmy wrathˌ.
Because he ripped open the
    pregnant women of
    Gilead   Ge 34:29
in order to extend his
    borders,
¹⁴I will set fire to the walls of
    Rabbah   Dt 3:11
that will consume her
    fortresses   Isa 30:30
amid war cries on the day of
    battle,   Job 39:25
amid violent winds on a
    stormy day.   Jer 23:19

---

*ᵃ*5 Or *the inhabitants of*   *ᵇ*5 *Aven* means *wickedness.*   *ᶜ*8 Or *inhabitants*   *ᵈ*11 Or
sword / and destroyed his allies

¹⁵Her king*ᵃ* will go into exile,
he and his officials
together,"   Jer 25:21
            says the Lord.

2 This is what the Lord says:
"For three sins of Moab,
even for four, I will not turn
back ⸢my wrath⸣.
Because he burned, as if to
lime,   Isa 33:12
the bones of Edom's king,
²I will send fire upon Moab
that will consume the
fortresses of Kerioth. *ᵇ*
Moab will go down in great
tumult
amid war cries and the blast
of the trumpet.   Job 39:25
³I will destroy her ruler
and kill all her officials with
him,"   Isa 40:23
            says the Lord.

⁴This is what the Lord says:

"For three sins of Judah,
even for four, I will not turn
back ⸢my wrath⸣.
Because they have rejected
the law of the Lord
and have not kept his
decrees,   Eze 20:24
because they have been led
astray by false gods,*ᶜ*
the gods*ᵈ* their ancestors
followed,   2Ki 22:13
⁵I will send fire upon Judah
that will consume the
fortresses of Jerusalem."

Judgment on Israel
⁶This is what the Lord says:

"For three sins of Israel,
even for four, I will not turn
back ⸢my wrath⸣.
They sell the righteous for
silver,
and the needy for a pair of
sandals.   Joel 3:3
⁷They trample on the heads of
the poor
as upon the dust of the
ground
and deny justice to the
oppressed.
Father and son use the same
girl
and so profane my holy
name.   Lev 18:21
⁸They lie down beside every
altar
on garments taken in
pledge.   Ex 22:26
In the house of their god
they drink wine taken as
fines.   Hab 2:6

⁹"I destroyed the Amorite
before them,   Nu 21:23-26
though he was tall as the
cedars   Isa 10:33
and strong as the oaks.
I destroyed his fruit above
and his roots below.   2Ki 19:30

¹⁰"I brought you up out of
Egypt,   Ex 6:6
and I led you forty years in
the desert   Dt 2:7
to give you the land of the
Amorites.   Ex 3:8
¹¹I also raised up prophets
from among your sons
and Nazirites from among
your young men.   Jdg 13:5

---

*ᵃ*15 Or / *Molech*; Hebrew *malcam*   *ᵇ*2 Or *of her cities*   *ᶜ*4 Or *by lies*   *ᵈ*4 Or *lies*

Is this not true, people of
Israel?"
            declares the LORD.
12"But you made the Nazirites
    drink wine
  and commanded the
    prophets not to
    prophesy.   Isa 30:10

13"Now then, I will crush you
    as a cart crushes when
    loaded with grain.   Am 7:16
14The swift will not escape,
    the strong will not muster
    their strength,   1Ki 20:11
  and the warrior will not
    save his life.   Ps 33:16
15The archer will not stand his
    ground,   Eze 39:3
  the fleet-footed soldier will
    not get away,
  and the horseman will not
    save his life.   Ex 15:21
16Even the bravest warriors
    will flee naked on that
    day,"   Jer 48:41
            declares the LORD.

Witnesses Summoned Against Israel

3 Hear this word the LORD has
    spoken against you, O
people of Israel—against the
whole family I brought up out
of Egypt: Am 2:10
  2"You only have I chosen
    of all the families of the
        earth;   Ex 19:6
  therefore I will punish you
    for all your sins."   Jer 14:10

3Do two walk together
  unless they have agreed to
    do so?

4Does a lion roar in the thicket
    when he has no prey?
Does he growl in his den
    when he has caught
    nothing?
5Does a bird fall into a trap on
    the ground
  where no snare has been
    set?   Ps 119:110
Does a trap spring up from
    the earth
  when there is nothing to
    catch?
6When a trumpet sounds in a
    city,   Nu 10:2
  do not the people tremble?
When disaster comes to a
    city,   Isa 31:2
  has not the LORD caused it?

7Surely the Sovereign LORD
    does nothing
  without revealing his plan
  to his servants the
    prophets.   Jer 23:22

8The lion has roared—
  who will not fear?   Isa 31:4
The Sovereign LORD has
    spoken—
  who can but prophesy?

9Proclaim to the fortresses of
    Ashdod   Jos 13:3
  and to the fortresses of
    Egypt:
"Assemble yourselves on the
    mountains of Samaria;
  see the great unrest within
    her
  and the oppression among
    her people."

10"They do not know how to
    do right," declares the
    LORD,   Am 5:7

"who hoard plunder and
loot in their fortresses."

[11]Therefore this is what the
Sovereign LORD says:

"An enemy will overrun the
land;
he will pull down your
strongholds
and plunder your
fortresses."   Am 2:5

[12]This is what the LORD says:

"As a shepherd saves from
the lion's mouth   1Sa 17:34
only two leg bones or a
piece of an ear,
so will the Israelites be
saved,
those who sit in Samaria
on the edge of their beds
and in Damascus on their
couches. [a]"   Est 1:6

[13]"Hear this and testify
against the house of Jacob," declares the Lord, the LORD God
Almighty.   Eze 2:7

[14]"On the day I punish Israel
for her sins,   Lev 26:18
I will destroy the altars of
Bethel;   Ge 12:8
the horns of the altar will be
cut off   Ex 27:2
and fall to the ground.
[15]I will tear down the winter
house   Jer 36:22
along with the summer
house;   Jdg 3:20
the houses adorned with
ivory will be destroyed

and the mansions will be
demolished,"   Isa 34:5
declares the LORD.

Israel Has Not Returned to God

4 Hear this word, you cows
of Bashan on Mount
Samaria,   Ps 22:12
you women who oppress
the poor and crush the
needy   Isa 58:6
and say to your husbands,
"Bring us some drinks!"
[2]The Sovereign LORD has
sworn by his holiness:
"The time will surely come
when you will be taken away
with hooks,   2Ki 19:28
the last of you with
fishhooks.
[3]You will each go straight out
through breaks in the wall,
and you will be cast out
toward Harmon, [b]"
declares the LORD.
[4]"Go to Bethel and sin;   Jos 7:2
go to Gilgal and sin yet
more.   Hos 4:15
Bring your sacrifices every
morning,   Nu 28:3
your tithes every three
years. [c]   Dt 14:28
[5]Burn leavened bread as a
thank offering   Lev 7:13
and brag about your
freewill offerings—
boast about them, you
Israelites,
for this is what you love to

---

[a]12 The meaning of the Hebrew for this line is uncertain.   [b]3 Masoretic Text; with a
different word division of the Hebrew (see Septuagint) out, O mountain of oppression
[c]4 Or tithes on the third day

do," declares the Sovereign
Lord.

6"I gave you empty stomachs[a]
in every city
and lack of bread in every
town,
yet you have not returned
to me,"
declares the Lord.

7"I also withheld rain from
you   Jer 3:3
when the harvest was still
three months away.
I sent rain on one town,
but withheld it from
another.   Ex 9:4,26
One field had rain;
another had none and dried
up.
8People staggered from town
to town for water
but did not get enough to
drink,   Hag 1:6
yet you have not returned
to me,"   Jer 3:7
declares the Lord.

9"Many times I struck your
gardens and vineyards,
I struck them with blight
and mildew.   Dt 28:22
Locusts devoured your fig
and olive trees,   Ex 10:13
yet you have not returned
to me,"   Isa 9:13
declares the Lord.

10"I sent plagues among you
as I did to Egypt.   Ex 9:3
I killed your young men with
the sword,   Isa 9:17

along with your captured
horses.
I filled your nostrils with the
stench of your camps,
yet you have not returned
to me,"   Dt 28:21
declares the Lord.

11"I overthrew some of you
as I[b] overthrew Sodom and
Gomorrah.   Ge 19:14
You were like a burning stick
snatched from the fire,
yet you have not returned
to me,"
declares the Lord.

12"Therefore this is what I will
do to you, Israel,
and because I will do this to
you,
prepare to meet your God,
O Israel."

13He who forms the
mountains,
creates the wind,   Ps 135:7
and reveals his thoughts to
man,   Da 2:28
he who turns dawn to
darkness,
and treads the high places
of the earth—   Mic 1:3
the Lord God Almighty is
his name.   Isa 47:4

A Lament and Call to Repentance

5 Hear this word, O house of
Israel, this lament I take up
concerning you: Jer 4:8

2"Fallen is Virgin Israel,
never to rise again,   2Ki 19:21

---

a6 Hebrew *you cleanness of teeth*   b11 Hebrew *God*

deserted in her own land,
  with no one to lift her up.''

³This is what the Sovereign
Lord says:

''The city that marches out a
  thousand strong for
  Israel
will have only a hundred
  left;
the town that marches out a
  hundred strong
will have only ten left.''

⁴This is what the Lord says to
the house of Israel:

''Seek me and live;   Dt 4:29
⁵ do not seek Bethel,
do not go to Gilgal,   1Sa 11:14
  do not journey to
    Beersheba.   Ge 21:31
For Gilgal will surely go into
  exile,
and Bethel will be reduced
  to nothing.ᵃ''   1Sa 7:16
⁶Seek the Lord and live,
  or he will sweep through
    the house of Joseph like
    a fire;   Dt 4:24
it will devour,
  and Bethel will have no one
    to quench it.   Am 3:14

⁷You who turn justice into
    bitterness   Isa 5:20
  and cast righteousness to
    the ground   Am 3:10
⁸(he who made the Pleiades
    and Orion,   Ge 1:16
  who turns blackness into
    dawn   Job 38:12
  and darkens day into night,

who calls for the waters of
  the sea
and pours them out over
  the face of the land—
the Lord is his name—
⁹he flashes destruction on the
  stronghold
  and brings the fortified city
    to ruin),   Mic 5:11
¹⁰you hate the one who
    reproves in court   Isa 29:21
  and despise him who tells
    the truth.   1Ki 22:8

¹¹You trample on the poor
  and force him to give you
    grain.   Am 8:6
Therefore, though you have
  built stone mansions,
you will not live in them;
though you have planted
  lush vineyards,
you will not drink their
  wine.   Jdg 9:27
¹²For I know how many are
    your offenses
  and how great your sins.

You oppress the righteous
  and take bribes   Job 36:18
  and you deprive the poor of
    justice in the courts. Job 5:4
¹³Therefore the prudent man
  keeps quiet in such
    times,   Est 4:14
for the times are evil.

¹⁴Seek good, not evil,
  that you may live.
Then the Lord God
  Almighty will be with
    you,
  just as you say he is.

ᵃ5 Or *grief*; or *wickedness*; Hebrew *aven*, a reference to Beth Aven (a derogatory name for Bethel)

¹⁵Hate evil, love good;   Ge 18:25
  maintain justice in the
    courts.   Isa 1:17
Perhaps the LORD God
    Almighty will have
    mercy   Joel 2:14
  on the remnant of Joseph.

¹⁶Therefore this is what the
Lord, the LORD God Almighty,
says:

"There will be wailing in all
    the streets   Jer 9:17
  and cries of anguish in
    every public square.
The farmers will be
    summoned to weep
  and the mourners to wail.
¹⁷There will be wailing in all
    the vineyards,   Ex 11:6
  for I will pass through your
    midst,"   Eze 12:12
      says the LORD.

The Day of the LORD

¹⁸Woe to you who long
  for the day of the LORD!
Why do you long for the day
    of the LORD?   Jer 30:5
  That day will be darkness,
    not light.   1Sa 2:9
¹⁹It will be as though a man
    fled from a lion
  only to meet a bear,   La 3:10
as though he entered his
    house
  and rested his hand on the
    wall
  only to have a snake bite
    him.   Dt 32:34

²⁰Will not the day of the LORD
    be darkness, not light—
  pitch-dark, without a ray of
    brightness?   Isa 13:10

²¹"I hate, I despise your
    religious feasts;   Lev 26:31
  I cannot stand your
    assemblies.   Eze 23:18
²²Even though you bring me
    burnt offerings and
    grain offerings,   Lev 26:31
  I will not accept them.
Though you bring choice
    fellowship offerings, ᵃ
  I will have no regard for
    them.   Jer 14:12
²³Away with the noise of your
    songs!
  I will not listen to the music
    of your harps.   Am 6:5
²⁴But let justice roll on like a
    river,   Jer 22:3
  righteousness like a
    never-failing stream!

²⁵"Did you bring me sacrifices
    and offerings   Isa 43:23
  forty years in the desert,
    O house of Israel?   Ex 16:35
²⁶You have lifted up the shrine
    of your king,
  the pedestal of your idols,
  the star of your god ᵇ—
which you made for
    yourselves.
²⁷Therefore I will send you into
    exile beyond
    Damascus,"   Am 6:7
  says the LORD, whose name
    is God Almighty.   Dt 32:17

ᵃ22 Traditionally *peace offerings*   ᵇ26 Or *lifted up Sakkuth your king / and Kaiwan your
idols, / your star-gods;* Septuagint *lifted up the shrine of Molech / and the star of your god
Rephan, / their idols*

Woe to the Complacent

6 Woe to you who are
     complacent in Zion,
  and to you who feel secure
     on Mount Samaria,   Am 3:9
  you notable men of the
     foremost nation,
  to whom the people of
     Israel come!   Isa 32:9-11
²Go to Calneh and look at it;
  go from there to great
     Hamath,   2Ki 17:24
  and then go down to Gath
     in Philistia.   Jos 11:22
  Are they better off than your
     two kingdoms?   Na 3:8
  Is their land larger than
     yours?
³You put off the evil day
  and bring near a reign of
     terror.   Isa 56:12
⁴You lie on beds inlaid with
     ivory
  and lounge on your
     couches.   Est 1:6
  You dine on choice lambs
     and fattened calves.   Isa 1:11
⁵You strum away on your
     harps like David   Ps 137:2
  and improvise on musical
     instruments.   1Ch 15:16
⁶You drink wine by the
     bowlful   Isa 28:1
  and use the finest lotions,
  but you do not grieve over
     the ruin of Joseph.
⁷Therefore you will be
     among the first to go
     into exile;
  your feasting and lounging
     will end.   Jer 16:9

The LORD Abhors the Pride of Israel

⁸The Sovereign LORD has
sworn by himself—the LORD
God Almighty declares: Ge 22:16

  "I abhor the pride of Jacob
     and detest his fortresses;
  I will deliver up the city
     and everything in it." Lev 26:19

⁹If ten men are left in one
house, they too will die. ¹⁰And if
a relative who is to burn the
bodies comes to carry them out
of the house and asks anyone
still hiding there, "Is anyone
with you?" and he says, "No,"
then he will say, "Hush! We
must not mention the name of
the LORD."   1Sa 31:12; Am 5:3

¹¹For the LORD has given the
     command,
  and he will smash the great
     house into pieces
  and the small house into
     bits.   Isa 55:11

¹²Do horses run on the rocky
     crags?
  Does one plow there with
     oxen?
  But you have turned justice
     into poison   Hos 10:4
  and the fruit of
     righteousness into
     bitterness—   Isa 1:21
¹³you who rejoice in the
     conquest of Lo Debarᵃ
  and say, "Did we not take
     Karnaimᵇ by our own
     strength?"   Job 8:15

ᵃ13 Lo Debar means nothing.   ᵇ13 Karnaim means horns; horn here symbolizes
strength.

¹⁴For the LORD God Almighty
     declares,
  "I will stir up a nation
     against you, O house of
     Israel,   Jer 5:15
  that will oppress you all the
     way
  from Lebo*a* Hamath to the
     valley of the Arabah."

Locusts, Fire and a Plumb Line

7 This is what the Sovereign
  LORD showed me: He was
preparing swarms of locusts after the king's share had been
harvested and just as the second crop was coming up.
²When they had stripped the
land clean, I cried out, "Sovereign LORD, forgive! How can
Jacob survive? He is so small!"

³So the LORD relented.   Ex 32:14
"This will not happen," the
LORD said.   Hos 11:8

⁴This is what the Sovereign
LORD showed me: The Sovereign LORD was calling for judgment by fire; it dried up the
great deep and devoured the
land. ⁵Then I cried out, "Sovereign LORD, I beg you, stop! How
can Jacob survive? He is so
small!"   Isa 66:16; Jnh 3:10

⁶So the LORD relented.   Ex 32:14
"This will not happen
either," the Sovereign LORD
said.   Jer 42:10

⁷This is what he showed me:
The Lord was standing by a wall
that had been built true to

plumb, with a plumb line in his
hand. ⁸And the LORD asked me,
"What do you see, Amos?"
  "A plumb line," I replied.
  Then the Lord said, "Look, I
am setting a plumb line among
my people Israel; I will spare
them no longer.   Jer 15:6

⁹"The high places of Isaac will
     be destroyed   Lev 26:30
  and the sanctuaries of Israel
     will be ruined;   Lev 26:31
  with my sword I will rise
     against the house of
     Jeroboam."   1Ki 13:34

Amos and Amaziah

¹⁰Then Amaziah the priest of
Bethel sent a message to Jeroboam king of Israel: "Amos is
raising a conspiracy against you
in the very heart of Israel. The
land cannot bear all his words.
¹¹For this is what Amos is saying:

  " 'Jeroboam will die by the
     sword,
  and Israel will surely go
     into exile,   Am 5:27
  away from their native
     land.' "   Jer 36:16

¹²Then Amaziah said to
Amos, "Get out, you seer! Go
back to the land of Judah. Earn
your bread there and do your
prophesying there. ¹³Don't
prophesy anymore at Bethel,
because this is the king's sanctuary and the temple of the
kingdom."   Jos 7:2; 1Sa 9:9

¹⁴Amos answered Amaziah,

a14 Or *from the entrance to*

"I was neither a prophet nor a prophet's son, but I was a shepherd, and I also took care of sycamore-fig trees. ¹⁵But the LORD took me from tending the flock and said to me, 'Go, prophesy to my people Israel.' ¹⁶Now then, hear the word of the LORD. You say,   Zec 13:5

" 'Do not prophesy against
    Israel,   Eze 20:46
and stop preaching against
    the house of Isaac.'

¹⁷"Therefore this is what the LORD says:

" 'Your wife will become a
    prostitute in the city,
and your sons and
    daughters will fall by the
    sword.
Your land will be measured
    and divided up,
and you yourself will die in
    a pagan^a country.
And Israel will certainly go
    into exile,   Am 5:27
away from their native
    land.' "   2Ki 17:6

A Basket of Ripe Fruit

8 This is what the Sovereign LORD showed me: a basket of ripe fruit. ²"What do you see, Amos?" he asked.   Jer 1:13
    "A basket of ripe fruit," I answered.   Ge 40:16
    Then the LORD said to me, "The time is ripe for my people Israel; I will spare them no longer.   La 4:18
    ³"In that day," declares the Sovereign LORD, "the songs in the temple will turn to wailing.^b Many, many bodies—flung everywhere! Silence!"   Am 5:16

⁴Hear this, you who trample
    the needy
and do away with the poor
    of the land,   Pr 30:14

⁵saying,

"When will the New Moon
    be over   Nu 10:10
that we may sell grain,
and the Sabbath be ended
    that we may market
    wheat?"—   Isa 58:13
skimping the measure,
    boosting the price
and cheating with
    dishonest scales,   Dt 25:15
⁶buying the poor with silver
and the needy for a pair of
    sandals,   Am 5:11
selling even the sweepings
    with the wheat.   Am 2:6

⁷The LORD has sworn by the Pride of Jacob: "I will never forget anything they have done.

⁸"Will not the land tremble for
    this,   Job 9:6
and all who live in it
    mourn?
The whole land will rise like
    the Nile;
it will be stirred up and
    then sink
like the river of Egypt.   Ps 18:7

⁹"In that day," declares the Sovereign LORD,

---

^a17 Hebrew *an unclean*   ^b3 Or *"the temple singers will wail*

"I will make the sun go
    down at noon
and darken the earth in
    broad daylight.   Job 5:14
¹⁰I will turn your religious
    feasts into mourning
and all your singing into
    weeping.   La 5:15
I will make all of you wear
    sackcloth   Joel 1:8
and shave your heads.
I will make that time like
    mourning for an only
    son   Ge 21:16
and the end of it like a
    bitter day.   Jer 2:19

¹¹"The days are coming,"
    declares the Sovereign
    LORD,   Jer 30:3
    "when I will send a famine
    through the land—
not a famine of food or a
    thirst for water,
but a famine of hearing the
    words of the LORD.
¹²Men will stagger from sea to
    sea
and wander from north to
    east,
searching for the word of the
    LORD,
but they will not find it.

¹³"In that day

"the lovely young women
    and strong young men
will faint because of thirst.
¹⁴They who swear by the
    shame*ᵃ* of Samaria,
or say, 'As surely as your
    god lives, O Dan,'

or, 'As surely as the godᵇ of
    Beersheba lives'—   Am 5:5
they will fall,
    never to rise again."   Am 5:2

Israel to Be Destroyed

9 I saw the Lord standing by
    the altar, and he said:

"Strike the tops of the pillars
    so that the thresholds
    shake.
Bring them down on the
    heads of all the people;
those who are left I will kill
    with the sword.
Not one will get away,
    none will escape.   Jer 11:11
²Though they dig down to the
    depths of the grave,ᶜ
from there my hand will
    take them.
Though they climb up to the
    heavens,   Jer 51:53
from there I will bring them
    down.   Ob 4
³Though they hide themselves
    on the top of Carmel,
there I will hunt them
    down and seize them.
Though they hide from me at
    the bottom of the sea,
there I will command the
    serpent to bite them.
⁴Though they are driven into
    exile by their enemies,
there I will command the
    sword to slay them.
I will fix my eyes upon them
    for evil and not for good."

⁵The Lord, the LORD
    Almighty,

ᵃ14 Or by Ashima; or by the idol   ᵇ14 Or power   ᶜ2 Hebrew to Sheol

he who touches the earth
and it melts,   Ps 46:2
and all who live in it
mourn—
the whole land rises like the
Nile,
then sinks like the river of
Egypt—   Am 8:8
[6] he who builds his lofty
palace[a] in the heavens
and sets its foundation[b] on
the earth,   Jer 43:9
who calls for the waters of
the sea
and pours them out over
the face of the land—
the LORD is his name.   Ps 104:1

[7] "Are not you Israelites
the same to me as the
Cushites[c]?"   2Ch 12:3
declares the LORD.
"Did I not bring Israel up
from Egypt,
the Philistines from
Caphtor[d]   Ge 10:14
and the Arameans from
Kir?   2Ki 16:9

[8] "Surely the eyes of the
Sovereign LORD
are on the sinful kingdom.
I will destroy it   Jer 4:27
from the face of the earth—
yet I will not totally destroy
the house of Jacob,"
declares the LORD.
[9] "For I will give the
command,

and I will shake the house
of Israel
among all the nations
as grain is shaken in a sieve,
and not a pebble will reach
the ground.   Jer 31:36
[10] All the sinners among my
people
will die by the sword,   Jer 49:37
all those who say,
'Disaster will not overtake
or meet us.'   Jer 5:12

Israel's Restoration

[11] "In that day I will restore
David's fallen tent.   Ge 26:22
I will repair its broken places,
restore its ruins,   Ps 53:6
and build it as it used to be,
[12] so that they may possess the
remnant of Edom   Nu 24:18
and all the nations that bear
my name,[e]"   Isa 43:7
declares the LORD,
who will do these things.

[13] "The days are coming," declares the LORD,   Jer 31:38

"when the reaper will be
overtaken by the
plowman   Lev 26:5
and the planter by the one
treading grapes.   Jdg 9:27
New wine will drip from the
mountains   Joel 2:24
and flow from all the hills.
[14] I will bring back my exiled[f]
people Israel;   Jer 33:7

---

a6 The meaning of the Hebrew for this phrase is uncertain.   *b6* The meaning of the Hebrew for this word is uncertain.   *c7* That is, people from the upper Nile region   *d7* That is, Crete   *e12* Hebrew; Septuagint *so that the remnant of men / and all the nations that bear my name may seek the Lord*   *f14* Or *will restore the fortunes of my*

they will rebuild the ruined
cities and live in them.
They will plant vineyards
and drink their wine;
they will make gardens and
eat their fruit.　　Isa 62:9

¹⁵I will plant Israel in their own
land,　　Ex 15:17
never again to be uprooted
from the land I have given
them,"　　Isa 65:9

says the LORD your God.

Obadiah

Introduction:

The name Obadiah means "servant of Jehovah." Nothing more is known about this prophet than this short book containing his prophecy.

Obadiah is a book of prophecy against the nation of Edom. This country had invaded and plundered Jerusalem at least four times, so Obadiah announced God's judgment against them and prophesied that their kingdom would be destroyed.

The Edomites are heard of no more after the destruction of Jerusalem in A.D. 70.

Outline of contents:

The doom of Edom (1–14)
Edom in the day of the Lord (15–21)

---

¹The vision of Obadiah. Isa 1:1

This is what the Sovereign LORD says about Edom— Ge 25:14

We have heard a message
  from the LORD:
An envoy was sent to the
  nations to say, Isa 18:2
"Rise, and let us go against
  her for battle"— Jer 6:4-5
²"See, I will make you small
  among the nations;
you will be utterly
  despised. Nu 24:18
³The pride of your heart has
  deceived you, Isa 16:6
you who live in the clefts of
  the rocks*ᵃ* Isa 16:1

and make your home on
  the heights,
you who say to yourself,
  'Who can bring me down to
  the ground?' 2Ch 25:11-12
⁴Though you soar like the
  eagle
and make your nest among
  the stars, Isa 10:14
from there I will bring you
  down," Isa 14:13
            declares the LORD.
⁵"If thieves came to you,
  if robbers in the night—
Oh, what a disaster awaits
  you—
would they not steal only as
  much as they wanted?
If grape pickers came to you,

ᵃ3 Or of Sela

would they not leave a few
  grapes?   Dt 4:27
⁶But how Esau will be
  ransacked,
  his hidden treasures
    pillaged!
⁷All your allies will force you
    to the border;   Jer 30:14
  your friends will deceive
    and overpower you;
  those who eat your bread
    will set a trap for
    you,ᵃ
  but you will not detect it.

⁸"In that day," declares the
    LORD,
  "will I not destroy the wise
    men of Edom,   Job 5:12
  men of understanding in
    the mountains of
    Esau?
⁹Your warriors, O Teman,
    will be terrified,   Ge 36:11
  and everyone in Esau's
    mountains
  will be cut down in the
    slaughter.
¹⁰Because of the violence
    against your brother
    Jacob,   Joel 3:19
  you will be covered with
    shame;
  you will be destroyed
    forever.   Ps 137:7
¹¹On the day you stood aloof
  while strangers carried off
    his wealth
  and foreigners entered his
    gates
  and cast lots for Jerusalem,
  you were like one of them.

¹²You should not look down
    on your brother
  in the day of his
    misfortune,   Job 31:29
  nor rejoice over the people of
    Judah   Ex 35:15
  in the day of their
    destruction,   Pr 17:5
  nor boast so much
  in the day of their trouble.
¹³You should not march
    through the gates of my
    people
  in the day of their disaster,
  nor look down on them in
    their calamity
  in the day of their disaster,
  nor seize their wealth
  in the day of their disaster.
¹⁴You should not wait at the
    crossroads
  to cut down their fugitives,
  nor hand over their survivors
  in the day of their trouble.

¹⁵"The day of the LORD is near
    for all nations.   Jer 46:10
  As you have done, it will be
    done to you;
  your deeds will return upon
    your own head.   Jer 50:29
¹⁶Just as you drank on my holy
    hill,   Isa 51:17
  so all the nations will drink
    continually;   Jer 25:15
  they will drink and drink
  and be as if they had never
    been.   La 4:21
¹⁷But on Mount Zion will be
    deliverance;   Ps 69:35
  it will be holy,   Ps 74:2
  and the house of Jacob
    will possess its inheritance.

ᵃ7 The meaning of the Hebrew for this clause is uncertain.

[18]The house of Jacob will be a
    fire
  and the house of Joseph a
    flame;
  the house of Esau will be
    stubble,
  and they will set it on fire
    and consume it.   Isa 1:31
  There will be no survivors
  from the house of Esau."
        The LORD has spoken.

[19]People from the Negev will
    occupy
  the mountains of Esau,
  and people from the foothills
    will possess
  the land of the Philistines.

They will occupy the fields of
    Ephraim and Samaria,
  and Benjamin will possess
    Gilead.   Nu 1:36
[20]This company of Israelite
    exiles who are in Canaan
  will possess ⌊the land⌋ as far
    as Zarephath;   1Ki 17:9-10
  the exiles from Jerusalem
    who are in Sepharad
  will possess the towns of
    the Negev.   Jer 33:13
[21]Deliverers will go up on[a]
    Mount Zion   Dt 28:29
  to govern the mountains of
    Esau.
  And the kingdom will be
    the LORD's.   Ps 22:28

Jonah

Introduction:

Jonah was a prophet whom God called to preach in the foreign city of Nineveh. Jonah tried to run away from God and was swallowed by a great fish.

When the fish returned him to land, Jonah went to Nineveh and warned the people about God's judgment. Jonah learned, to his dismay, that God would forgive even a heathen city if the people were sorry for their sins.

Outline of contents:

Jonah Flees From the LORD

1 The word of the LORD came to Jonah son of Amittai: ²"Go to the great city of Nineveh and preach against it, because its wickedness has come up before me."   Mt 12:39-41

³But Jonah ran away from the LORD and headed for Tarshish. He went down to Joppa, where he found a ship bound for that port. After paying the fare, he went aboard and sailed for Tarshish to flee from the LORD.

⁴Then the LORD sent a great wind on the sea, and such a violent storm arose that the ship threatened to break up. ⁵All the sailors were afraid and each cried out to his own god. And they threw the cargo into the sea to lighten the ship. Ps 107:23-26

But Jonah had gone below deck, where he lay down and fell into a deep sleep. ⁶The captain went to him and said, "How can you sleep? Get up and call on your god! Maybe he will take notice of us, and we will not perish."   Ps 107:28; Jnh 3:8

⁷Then the sailors said to each other, "Come, let us cast lots to find out who is responsible for this calamity." They cast lots and the lot fell on Jonah. Nu 32:23

⁸So they asked him, "Tell us, who is responsible for making all this trouble for us? What do you do? Where do you come from? What is your country?

From what people are you?"

⁹He answered, "I am a Hebrew and I worship the LORD, the God of heaven, who made the sea and the land."   Ps 96:9

¹⁰This terrified them and they asked, "What have you done?" (They knew he was running away from the LORD, because he had already told them so.)

¹¹The sea was getting rougher and rougher. So they asked him, "What should we do to you to make the sea calm down for us?"   2Sa 24:17

¹²"Pick me up and throw me into the sea," he replied, "and it will become calm. I know that it is my fault that this great storm has come upon you."

¹³Instead, the men did their best to row back to land. But they could not, for the sea grew even wilder than before. ¹⁴Then they cried to the LORD, "O LORD, please do not let us die for taking this man's life. Do not hold us accountable for killing an innocent man, for you, O LORD, have done as you pleased." ¹⁵Then they took Jonah and threw him overboard, and the raging sea grew calm. ¹⁶At this the men greatly feared the LORD, and they offered a sacrifice to the LORD and made vows to him.   Pr 21:30

¹⁷But the LORD provided a great fish to swallow Jonah, and Jonah was inside the fish three days and three nights.   Jnh 4:6-7

Jonah's Prayer

2 From inside the fish Jonah prayed to the LORD his God. ²He said:

"In my distress I called to the
    LORD,   La 3:55
and he answered me.
From the depths of the
      grave*a* I called for help,
  and you listened to my cry.
³You hurled me into the deep,
  into the very heart of the
      seas,   Ps 88:6
and the currents swirled
      about me;
all your waves and breakers
      swept over me.   2Sa 22:5
⁴I said, 'I have been banished
      from your sight;
yet I will look again
  toward your holy temple.'
⁵The engulfing waters
      threatened me,*b*
  the deep surrounded me;
seaweed was wrapped
      around my head.   Ps 69:1-2
⁶To the roots of the mountains
      I sank down;   Job 28:9
  the earth beneath barred
      me in forever.
But you brought my life up
      from the pit,   Job 17:16
  O LORD my God.

⁷"When my life was ebbing
      away,
  I remembered you, LORD,
and my prayer rose to you,
  to your holy temple.   Ps 11:4

⁸"Those who cling to
      worthless idols   Dt 32:21

---

*a*2 Hebrew *Sheol*   *b*5 Or *waters were at my throat*

forfeit the grace that could
be theirs.
⁹But I, with a song of
thanksgiving, Ps 42:4
will sacrifice to you. Ps 50:14
What I have vowed I will
make good. Nu 30:2
Salvation comes from the
LORD." Ex 15:2

¹⁰And the LORD commanded
the fish, and it vomited Jonah
onto dry land.

Jonah Goes to Nineveh

3 Then the word of the LORD
came to Jonah a second time:
²"Go to the great city of Nineveh and proclaim to it the message I give you." Jnh 1:1

³Jonah obeyed the word of
the LORD and went to Nineveh.
Now Nineveh was a very important city—a visit required
three days. ⁴On the first day,
Jonah started into the city. He
proclaimed: "Forty more days
and Nineveh will be over-
turned." ⁵The Ninevites believed God. They declared a
fast, and all of them, from the
greatest to the least, put on
sackcloth. Jer 18:7-10; Da 9:3

⁶When the news reached the
king of Nineveh, he rose from
his throne, took off his royal
robes, covered himself with
sackcloth and sat down in the
dust. ⁷Then he issued a proclamation in Nineveh: Est 4:1-3

"By the decree of the king
and his nobles:

Do not let any man or
beast, herd or flock, taste
anything; do not let them
eat or drink. ⁸But let man
and beast be covered with
sackcloth. Let everyone call
urgently on God. Let them
give up their evil ways
and their violence. ⁹Who
knows? God may yet relent
and with compassion turn
from his fierce anger so that
we will not perish." 2Sa 12:22

¹⁰When God saw what they
did and how they turned from
their evil ways, he had compassion and did not bring upon
them the destruction he had
threatened. Jer 18:8; Am 7:6

Jonah's Anger at the LORD's Compassion

4 But Jonah was greatly displeased and became angry.
²He prayed to the LORD, "O
LORD, is this not what I said
when I was still at home? That is
why I was so quick to flee to
Tarshish. I knew that you are a
gracious and compassionate
God, slow to anger and abounding in love, a God who relents
from sending calamity. ³Now,
O LORD, take away my life, for it
is better for me to die than to
live." Jer 8:3; Mt 20:11

⁴But the LORD replied, "Have
you any right to be angry?"

⁵Jonah went out and sat
down at a place east of the city.
There he made himself a shelter, sat in its shade and waited
to see what would happen to
the city. ⁶Then the LORD God

provided a vine and made it grow up over Jonah to give shade for his head to ease his discomfort, and Jonah was very happy about the vine. ⁷But at dawn the next day God provided a worm, which chewed the vine so that it withered. ⁸When the sun rose, God provided a scorching east wind, and the sun blazed on Jonah's head so that he grew faint. He wanted to die, and said, "It would be better for me to die than to live." Joel 1:12; Jnh 1:17

⁹But God said to Jonah, "Do you have a right to be angry about the vine?"

"I do," he said. "I am angry enough to die."

¹⁰But the LORD said, "You have been concerned about this vine, though you did not tend it or make it grow. It sprang up overnight and died overnight. ¹¹But Nineveh has more than a hundred and twenty thousand people who cannot tell their right hand from their left, and many cattle as well. Should I not be concerned about that great city?" Jnh 1:2; 3:10

Micah

Introduction:

This book contains the writings of the prophet Micah who lived in the countryside of Judah during the reigns of Jotham, Ahaz and Hezekiah. Micah warned about God's judgment against the capital cities of both kingdoms, Jerusalem and Samaria, because of the sinfulness of their rulers, prophets and priests. The poor were oppressed and people's lives did not show that they belonged to a holy God.

But Micah promised the restoration of Zion and a kingdom of peace for those who trusted in God. He prophesied that a ruler born in Bethlehem would set up a kingdom that would last forever.

Outline of contents:

Judgment against Samaria and Jerusalem (1:1–16)
Leaders guilty of oppression (2:1–3:12)
Divine restoration (4:1–5:15)
Judgment and mercy (6:1–7:20)

---

1 The word of the LORD that came to Micah of Moresheth during the reigns of Jotham, Ahaz and Hezekiah, kings of Judah—the vision he saw concerning Samaria and Jerusalem.

²Hear, O peoples, all of you,
listen, O earth and all who
are in it,   Jer 6:19
that the Sovereign LORD
may witness against
you,
the Lord from his holy
temple.   Ps 11:4

Judgment Against Samaria and Jerusalem

³Look! The LORD is coming
from his dwelling place;
he comes down and treads
the high places of the
earth.   Isa 64:1
⁴The mountains melt beneath
him   Ps 46:2,6
and the valleys split apart,
like wax before the fire, Nu 16:31
like water rushing down a
slope.
⁵All this is because of Jacob's
transgression,

because of the sins of the
house of Israel.
What is Jacob's
transgression?
Is it not Samaria?   Am 8:14
What is Judah's high place?
Is it not Jerusalem?

6"Therefore I will make
Samaria a heap of
rubble,
a place for planting
vineyards.   Dt 20:6
I will pour her stones into the
valley   Am 5:11
and lay bare her
foundations.   Eze 13:14
7All her idols will be broken to
pieces;   Ex 32:20
all her temple gifts will be
burned with fire;
I will destroy all her
images.   Dt 9:21
Since she gathered her gifts
from the wages of
prostitutes,   Dt 23:17-18
as the wages of prostitutes
they will again be used."

Weeping and Mourning

8Because of this I will weep
and wail;   Isa 15:3
I will go about barefoot and
naked.   Isa 20:2
I will howl like a jackal
and moan like an owl.
9For her wound is incurable;
it has come to Judah.   2Ki 18:13

It*a* has reached the very gate
of my people,   Isa 3:26
even to Jerusalem itself.
10Tell it not in Gath*b*;
weep not at all. *c*
In Beth Ophrah*d*
roll in the dust.
11Pass on in nakedness and
shame,   Eze 23:29
you who live in Shaphir. *e*
Those who live in Zaanan*f*
will not come out.
Beth Ezel is in mourning;
its protection is taken from
you.
12Those who live in Maroth*g*
writhe in pain,
waiting for relief,   Jer 14:19
because disaster has come
from the Lord,   Jer 40:2
even to the gate of
Jerusalem.
13You who live in Lachish, *h*
harness the team to the
chariot.
You were the beginning of
sin
to the Daughter of Zion,
for the transgressions of
Israel
were found in you.
14Therefore you will give
parting gifts
to Moresheth Gath.   2Ki 16:8
The town of Aczib*i* will
prove deceptive   Jos 15:44
to the kings of Israel.
15I will bring a conqueror
against you

---

*a*9 Or *He*   *b*10 *Gath* sounds like the Hebrew for *tell.*   *c*10 Hebrew; Septuagint may
suggest *not in Acco.* The Hebrew for *in Acco* sounds like the Hebrew for *weep.*
*d*10 *Beth Ophrah* means *house of dust.*   *e*11 *Shaphir* means *pleasant.*   *f*11 *Zaanan*
sounds like the Hebrew for *come out.*   *g*12 *Maroth* sounds like the Hebrew for *bitter.*
*h*13 *Lachish* sounds like the Hebrew for *team.*   *i*14 *Aczib* means *deception.*

who live in Mareshah. *a*
He who is the glory of Israel
   will come to Adullam. Jos 12:15
16Shave your heads in
      mourning   Lev 13:40
   for the children in whom
      you delight;
   make yourselves as bald as
      the vulture,
   for they will go from you
      into exile.   Dt 4:27

Man's Plans and God's

2 Woe to those who plan
      iniquity,
   to those who plot evil on
      their beds!   Isa 29:20
   At morning's light they carry
      it out
   because it is in their power
      to do it.
2They covet fields and seize
      them,   Isa 5:8
   and houses, and take them.
   They defraud a man of his
      home,   Jer 22:17
   a fellowman of his
      inheritance.   1Sa 8:14

3Therefore, the LORD says:

"I am planning disaster
   against this people,
from which you cannot
   save yourselves.
You will no longer walk
   proudly,   Isa 2:12
for it will be a time of
   calamity.
4In that day men will ridicule
   you;
they will taunt you with
   this mournful song:

'We are utterly ruined; Lev 26:41
   my people's possession is
      divided up.   Jer 6:12
He takes it from me!
   He assigns our fields to
      traitors.' "

5Therefore you will have no
      one in the assembly of
      the LORD
   to divide the land by lot.

False Prophets

6"Do not prophesy," their
      prophets say.
   "Do not prophesy about
      these things;
   disgrace will not overtake
      us."   Ps 44:13
7Should it be said, O house of
      Jacob:
   "Is the Spirit of the LORD
      angry?
   Does he do such things?"

"Do not my words do good
   to him whose ways are
      upright?   Ps 15:2
8Lately my people have risen
      up
   like an enemy.
You strip off the rich robe
   from those who pass by
      without a care,
   like men returning from
      battle.
9You drive the women of my
      people
   from their pleasant homes.
You take away my blessing
   from their children forever.
10Get up, go away!

For this is not your resting
　　place,　　　　　　　　Dt 12:9
because it is defiled,　Lev 18:25-29
　it is ruined, beyond all
　　remedy.
[11]If a liar and deceiver comes
　　and says,　　　　　　2Ch 36:16
'I will prophesy for you
　　plenty of wine and
　　beer,'　　　　　　　Lev 10:9
he would be just the
　　prophet for this people!

Deliverance Promised

[12]"I will surely gather all of
　　you, O Jacob;
I will surely bring together
　　the remnant of Israel.
I will bring them together
　　like sheep in a pen,
like a flock in its pasture;
　the place will throng with
　　people.　　　　　　　Ne 1:9
[13]One who breaks open the
　　way will go up before
　　them;　　　　　　　Isa 52:12
they will break through the
　　gate and go out.　Isa 60:11
Their king will pass through
　　before them,
the LORD at their head."

Leaders and Prophets Rebuked

3 Then I said,
　　"Listen, you leaders of
　　Jacob,　　　　　　　Jer 5:5
　you rulers of the house of
　　Israel.
Should you not know justice,
[2]　you who hate good and
　　love evil;

who tear the skin from my
　　people
and the flesh from their
　　bones;　　　　　　　Ps 53:4
[3]who eat my people's flesh,
　strip off their skin
and break their bones in
　　pieces;　　　　　　　Eze 34:4
who chop them up like meat
　　for the pan,　　　　Job 24:14
　like flesh for the pot?"　Eze 11:7

[4]Then they will cry out to the
　　LORD,
but he will not answer
　　them.　　　　　　　Dt 1:45
At that time he will hide his
　　face from them　　　Dt 31:17
because of the evil they
　　have done.　　　　　Job 15:31

[5]This is what the LORD says:

"As for the prophets
　who lead my people astray,
if one feeds them,
　they proclaim 'peace';　Jer 4:10
if he does not,
　they prepare to wage war
　　against him.
[6]Therefore night will come
　　over you, without
　　visions,
and darkness, without
　　divination.　　　　Isa 8:19-22
The sun will set for the
　　prophets,　　　　　Isa 29:10
and the day will go dark for
　　them.　　　　　　　Eze 7:26
[7]The seers will be ashamed
　and the diviners disgraced.
They will all cover their faces
　because there is no answer
　　from God."　　　　Eze 20:3

⁸But as for me, I am filled
        with power,
    with the Spirit of the Lord,
    and with justice and might,
    to declare to Jacob his
        transgression,
    to Israel his sin.   Isa 57:12
⁹Hear this, you leaders of the
        house of Jacob,
    you rulers of the house of
        Israel,
    who despise justice
    and distort all that is right;
¹⁰who build Zion with
        bloodshed,   Isa 59:7
    and Jerusalem with
        wickedness.   Jer 22:17
¹¹Her leaders judge for a bribe,
    her priests teach for a price,
    and her prophets tell
        fortunes for money. Isa 1:23
    Yet they lean upon the Lord
        and say,   Isa 10:20
    "Is not the Lord among us?
    No disaster will come upon
        us."   Jer 7:4
¹²Therefore because of you,
    Zion will be plowed like a
        field,
    Jerusalem will become a heap
        of rubble,   2Ki 25:9
    the temple hill a mound
        overgrown with
        thickets.   Lev 26:31

The Mountain of the Lord

4 In the last days
    the mountain of the Lord's
        temple will be
        established   Ps 48:1
    as chief among the
        mountains;

    it will be raised above the
        hills,   Eze 17:22
    and peoples will stream
        to it.   Ps 22:27

²Many nations will come and
say,

    "Come, let us go up to the
        mountain of the Lord,
    to the house of the God of
        Jacob.   Zec 2:11
    He will teach us his ways,
    so that we may walk in his
        paths."   Ps 119:171
    The law will go out from
        Zion,   Dt 18:18
    the word of the Lord from
        Jerusalem.
³He will judge between many
        peoples
    and will settle disputes for
        strong nations far and
        wide.
    They will beat their swords
        into plowshares
    and their spears into
        pruning hooks.   Joel 3:10
    Nation will not take up
        sword against nation,
    nor will they train for war
        anymore.   Ps 46:9
⁴Every man will sit under his
        own vine
    and under his own fig tree,
    and no one will make them
        afraid,   Lev 26:6
    for the Lord Almighty has
        spoken.   Isa 1:20
⁵All the nations may walk
    in the name of their gods;
    we will walk in the name of
        the Lord
    our God for ever and ever.

The LORD's Plan

6"In that day," declares the LORD,

"I will gather the lame;   Jer 31:8
I will assemble the exiles
and those I have brought to
grief.   Eze 34:13
7I will make the lame a
remnant,   Joel 2:32
those driven away a strong
nation.   Ge 12:2
The LORD will rule over them
in Mount Zion   Isa 2:2
from that day and forever.
8As for you, O watchtower of
the flock,
O stronghold[a] of the
Daughter of Zion,
the former dominion will be
restored to you;   Isa 1:26
kingship will come to the
Daughter of Jerusalem."

9Why do you now cry aloud—
have you no king?   Jer 8:19
Has your counselor perished,
that pain seizes you like
that of a woman in
labor?   Ge 3:16
10Writhe in agony, O Daughter
of Zion,
like a woman in labor,
for now you must leave the
city
to camp in the open field.
You will go to Babylon;   Dt 21:10
there you will be rescued.
There the LORD will redeem
you   Isa 48:20
out of the hand of your
enemies.

11But now many nations
are gathered against you.
They say, "Let her be
defiled,
let our eyes gloat over
Zion!"   La 2:16
12But they do not know
the thoughts of the LORD;
they do not understand his
plan,   Ge 50:20
he who gathers them like
sheaves to the threshing
floor.
13"Rise and thresh,
O Daughter of Zion,
for I will give you horns of
iron;
I will give you hoofs of
bronze
and you will break to pieces
many nations."   Isa 45:1

You will devote their
ill-gotten gains to the
LORD,   Isa 23:18
their wealth to the Lord of
all the earth.

A Promised Ruler
From Bethlehem

5 Marshal your troops, O city
  of troops,[b]
for a siege is laid against us.
They will strike Israel's ruler
on the cheek with a rod.

2"But you, Bethlehem
Ephrathah,   Ge 35:16
though you are small
among the clans[c] of
Judah,
out of you will come for me

---

[a]8 Or *hill*   [b]1 Or *Strengthen your walls, O walled city*   [c]2 Or *rulers*

one who will be ruler over
Israel,   Nu 24:19
whose origins[a] are from of
old,   Ps 102:25
from ancient times.[b]"   Mt 2:6

³Therefore Israel will be
abandoned   Jer 7:29
until the time when she
who is in labor gives
birth
and the rest of his brothers
return
to join the Israelites.

⁴He will stand and shepherd
his flock   Isa 40:11
in the strength of the LORD,
in the majesty of the name
of the LORD his God.
And they will live securely,
for then his greatness
will reach to the ends of the
earth.   Isa 52:13
5   And he will be their peace.

Deliverance and Destruction

When the Assyrian invades
our land   Isa 8:7
and marches through our
fortresses,
we will raise against him
seven shepherds,
even eight leaders of men.
⁶They will rule[c] the land of
Assyria with the sword,
the land of Nimrod with
drawn sword.[d]   Zep 2:13
He will deliver us from the
Assyrian
when he invades our land

and marches into our
borders.   Na 2:11-13

⁷The remnant of Jacob will be
in the midst of many
peoples   Am 5:15
like dew from the LORD,
like showers on the grass,
which do not wait for man
or linger for mankind.
⁸The remnant of Jacob will be
among the nations,
in the midst of many
peoples,
like a lion among the beasts
of the forest,   Ge 49:9
like a young lion among
flocks of sheep,
which mauls and mangles as
it goes,   Mic 4:13
and no one can rescue.
⁹Your hand will be lifted up in
triumph over your
enemies,   Ps 10:12
and all your foes will be
destroyed.

¹⁰"In that day," declares the
LORD,

"I will destroy your horses
from among you
and demolish your chariots.
¹¹I will destroy the cities of
your land   Dt 29:23
and tear down all your
strongholds.   La 2:2
¹²I will destroy your witchcraft
and you will no longer cast
spells.   Dt 18:10-12
¹³I will destroy your carved
images   Na 1:14

---

*a*2 Hebrew *goings out*   *b*2 Or *from days of eternity*   *c*6 Or *crush*   *d*6 Or *Nimrod in its gates*

and your sacred stones
　　from among you;　Hos 10:2
you will no longer bow down
　　to the work of your hands.
[14]I will uproot from among you
　　your Asherah poles[a]
and demolish your cities.
[15]I will take vengeance in
　　anger and wrath　Isa 65:12
upon the nations that have
　　not obeyed me."

The LORD's Case Against Israel

6 Listen to what the LORD
　says:

"Stand up, plead your case
　　before the mountains;
let the hills hear what you
　　have to say.
[2]Hear, O mountains, the
　　LORD's accusation;　Hos 12:2
listen, you everlasting
　　foundations of the earth.
For the LORD has a case
　　against his people;
he is lodging a charge
　　against Israel.　Ps 50:7

[3]"My people, what have I
　　done to you?
How have I burdened you?
　　Answer me.　Jer 2:5
[4]I brought you up out of
　　Egypt　Ex 3:10
and redeemed you from the
　　land of slavery.　Dt 7:8
I sent Moses to lead you,
　　also Aaron and Miriam.　Ex 4:16
[5]My people, remember

what Balak king of Moab
　　counseled　Nu 22:2
and what Balaam son of
　　Beor answered.
Remember ˎyour journeyˌ
　　from Shittim to Gilgal,
that you may know the
　　righteous acts of the
　　LORD."　Jdg 5:11

[6]With what shall I come
　　before the LORD　Ps 95:2
and bow down before the
　　exalted God?
Shall I come before him with
　　burnt offerings,
with calves a year old?
[7]Will the LORD be pleased
　　with thousands of rams,
with ten thousand rivers of
　　oil?　Ps 50:8-10
Shall I offer my firstborn for
　　my transgression,　Lev 18:21
the fruit of my body for the
　　sin of my soul?　Hos 5:6
[8]He has showed you, O man,
　　what is good.
And what does the LORD
　　require of you?
To act justly and to love
　　mercy　Isa 1:17
and to walk humbly with
　　your God.　2Ki 22:19

Israel's Guilt and Punishment

[9]Listen! The LORD is calling to
　　the city—
and to fear your name is
　　wisdom—
"Heed the rod and the One
　　who appointed it.[b]　Ge 17:1

---

[a]14 That is, symbols of the goddess Asherah line is uncertain.　　[b]9 The meaning of the Hebrew for this

¹⁰Am I still to forget, O wicked
   house,
   your ill-gotten treasures
   and the short ephah,ᵃ
   which is accursed? Eze 45:9
¹¹Shall I acquit a man with
   dishonest scales, Lev 19:36
   with a bag of false weights?
¹²Her rich men are violent;
   her people are liars
   and their tongues speak
   deceitfully. Ps 35:20
¹³Therefore, I have begun to
   destroy you, Isa 1:7
   to ruin you because of your
   sins.
¹⁴You will eat but not be
   satisfied; Isa 9:20
   your stomach will still be
   empty.ᵇ
   You will store up but save
   nothing, Isa 30:6
   because what you save I
   will give to the sword.
¹⁵You will plant but not
   harvest; Dt 28:38
   you will press olives but not
   use the oil on
   yourselves,
   you will crush grapes but
   not drink the wine. Job 24:11
¹⁶You have observed the
   statutes of Omri 1Ki 16:25
   and all the practices of
   Ahab's house, 1Ki 16:19-33
   and you have followed their
   traditions. Jer 7:24
   Therefore I will give you over
   to ruin Jer 25:9
   and your people to
   derision;

you will bear the scorn of
   the nations.ᶜ'' Dt 28:37

Israel's Misery

7 What misery is mine!
   I am like one who gathers
   summer fruit
   at the gleaning of the
   vineyard;
   there is no cluster of grapes
   to eat,
   none of the early figs that I
   crave. SS 2:13
²The godly have been swept
   from the land; Ps 12:1
   not one upright man
   remains. Jer 2:29
   All men lie in wait to shed
   blood; Pr 6:17
   each hunts his brother with
   a net. Isa 3:5
³Both hands are skilled in
   doing evil; Pr 4:16
   the ruler demands gifts,
   the judge accepts bribes,
   the powerful dictate what
   they desire—
   they all conspire together.
⁴The best of them is like a
   brier, Nu 33:55
   the most upright worse
   than a thorn hedge.
   The day of your watchmen
   has come,
   the day God visits you.
   Now is the time of their
   confusion. Job 31:14
⁵Do not trust a neighbor;
   put no confidence in a
   friend. Jer 9:4

ᵃ10 An ephah was a dry measure.   ᵇ14 The meaning of the Hebrew for this word is
uncertain.   ᶜ16 Septuagint; Hebrew *scorn due my people*

Even with her who lies in
   your embrace
be careful of your words.
⁶For a son dishonors his
   father,
a daughter rises up against
   her mother,   Eze 22:7
a daughter-in-law against her
   mother-in-law—
a man's enemies are the
   members of his own
   household.   Mt 10:35-36

⁷But as for me, I watch in
   hope for the LORD,   Isa 21:8
I wait for God my Savior;
my God will hear me.   Ps 4:3

Israel Will Rise

⁸Do not gloat over me, my
   enemy!   Ps 22:17
Though I have fallen, I will
   rise.   Ps 20:8
Though I sit in darkness,
   the LORD will be my light.
⁹Because I have sinned
   against him,
I will bear the LORD's
   wrath,   La 3:39-40
until he pleads my case
and establishes my right.
He will bring me out into the
   light;   Ps 107:10
I will see his righteousness.
¹⁰Then my enemy will see it
and will be covered with
   shame,   Ps 35:26
she who said to me,
   "Where is the LORD your
   God?"   Ps 42:3
My eyes will see her
   downfall;   Isa 51:23

even now she will be
   trampled underfoot
like mire in the streets.

¹¹The day for building your
   walls will come,   Isa 54:11
the day for extending your
   boundaries.
¹²In that day people will come
   to you
from Assyria and the cities
   of Egypt,   Isa 11:11
even from Egypt to the
   Euphrates
and from sea to sea
and from mountain to
   mountain.   Isa 19:23-25
¹³The earth will become
   desolate because of its
   inhabitants,
as the result of their
   deeds.

Prayer and Praise

¹⁴Shepherd your people with
   your staff,   Ps 28:9
the flock of your
   inheritance,
which lives by itself in a
   forest,
in fertile pasturelands. ᵃ
Let them feed in Bashan and
   Gilead   Isa 33:9
as in days long ago.   Eze 36:11

¹⁵"As in the days when you
   came out of Egypt,
I will show them my
   wonders."   Ex 3:20

¹⁶Nations will see and be
   ashamed,   Isa 26:11

ᵃ14 Or *in the middle of Carmel*

deprived of all their power.
They will lay their hands on
 their mouths   Jdg 18:19
and their ears will become
 deaf.
¹⁷They will lick dust like a
 snake,   Ge 3:14
like creatures that crawl on
 the ground.
They will come trembling out
 of their dens;   2Sa 22:46
they will turn in fear to the
 LORD our God   Isa 25:3
and will be afraid of you.
¹⁸Who is a God like you,
 who pardons sin and
 forgives the
 transgression   Isa 43:25

of the remnant of his
 inheritance?   Joel 2:32
You do not stay angry
 forever   Ps 103:9
but delight to show mercy.
¹⁹You will again have
 compassion on us;
you will tread our sins
 underfoot
and hurl all our iniquities
 into the depths of the
 sea.   Isa 43:25
²⁰You will be true to Jacob,
 and show mercy to
 Abraham,   Gal 3:16
as you pledged on oath to
 our fathers   Dt 7:8
in days long ago.   Ps 108:4

Nahum

Introduction:

Nahum was a prophet in the last half of the seventh century B.C. He prophesied at the same time as Zephaniah, Jeremiah, and Habakkuk.

Nahum is a book of prophecy against Nineveh, the capital of Assyria. The prophet describes the cruelty of the Assyrians as they conquered nation after nation. He predicts the seige and destruction of Nineveh and the end of the kingdom of Assyria.

Nahum's only advice to Judah was that they observe their religious feasts, since the Assyrians would never again threaten Jerusalem.

Outline of contents:

1 An oracle concerning Nineveh. The book of the vision of Nahum the Elkoshite. Ge 10:11

The LORD's Anger Against Nineveh

2The LORD is a jealous and
    avenging God; Ex 20:5
the LORD takes vengeance
    and is filled with wrath.
The LORD takes vengeance
    on his foes
and maintains his wrath
    against his enemies.
3The LORD is slow to anger
    and great in power; Ne 9:17
the LORD will not leave the
    guilty unpunished. Ex 34:7
His way is in the whirlwind
    and the storm, Ex 14:21
and clouds are the dust of
    his feet. 2Sa 22:10
4He rebukes the sea and dries
    it up; Ex 14:22
he makes all the rivers run
    dry.
Bashan and Carmel wither
    and the blossoms of
    Lebanon fade. Isa 33:9
5The mountains quake before
    him Ex 19:18
and the hills melt away.
The earth trembles at his
    presence, Joel 2:10
the world and all who live
    in it. Eze 38:20

6Who can withstand his
    indignation?   Ps 130:3
Who can endure his fierce
    anger?   Ps 76:7
His wrath is poured out like
    fire;   Isa 5:24-25
the rocks are shattered
    before him.   1Ki 19:11

7The LORD is good,   Jer 33:11
    a refuge in times of trouble.
He cares for those who trust
    in him,   Ps 1:6
8 but with an overwhelming
    flood   Isa 8:7
he will make an end of
    ⌊Nineveh⌋;
he will pursue his foes into
    darkness.

9Whatever they plot against
    the LORD   Hos 7:15
he*a* will bring to an end;
trouble will not come a
    second time.
10They will be entangled
    among thorns   2Sa 23:6
and drunk from their wine;
they will be consumed like
    dry stubble. *b*
11From you, ⌊O Nineveh,⌋ has
    one come forth
who plots evil against the
    LORD
and counsels wickedness.

12This is what the LORD says:

"Although they have allies
    and are numerous,
they will be cut off and pass
    away.   Isa 10:34

Although I have afflicted
    "you, ⌊O Judah,⌋
I will afflict you no more.
13Now I will break their yoke
    from your neck   Isa 9:4
and tear your shackles
    away."   Job 12:18

14The LORD has given a
    command concerning
    you, ⌊Nineveh⌋:
"You will have no
    descendants to bear
    your name.   Isa 14:22
I will destroy the carved
    images and cast idols
that are in the temple of
    your gods.
I will prepare your grave,
    for you are vile."   Jer 28:8

15Look, there on the
    mountains,
the feet of one who brings
    good news,   Isa 40:9
who proclaims peace!   Isa 52:7
Celebrate your festivals,
    O Judah,   Lev 23:2-4
and fulfill your vows.
No more will the wicked
    invade you;   Isa 52:1
they will be completely
    destroyed.

Nineveh to Fall

2 An attacker advances
    against you, ⌊Nineveh⌋.
Guard the fortress,
watch the road,
brace yourselves,
marshal all your strength!

---

a9 Or *What do you foes plot against the LORD?* / *He*
this verse is uncertain.   *b10* The meaning of the Hebrew for

²The Lord will restore the
	splendor of Jacob Isa 60:15
  like the splendor of Israel,
though destroyers have laid
		them waste
  and have ruined their
		vines.

³The shields of his soldiers are
		red;
	the warriors are clad in
		scarlet. Eze 23:14-15
The metal on the chariots
		flashes
	on the day they are made
		ready;
	the spears of pine are
		brandished. ᵃ
⁴The chariots storm through
		the streets, Jer 4:13
	rushing back and forth
		through the squares.
They look like flaming
		torches;
	they dart about like
		lightning.

⁵He summons his picked
		troops,
	yet they stumble on their
		way. Jer 46:12
They dash to the city wall;
	the protective shield is put
		in place.
⁶The river gates are thrown
		open Isa 45:1
  and the palace collapses.
⁷It is decreed ᵇ that ⌊the city⌋
	be exiled and carried away.
Its slave girls moan like
		doves Ge 8:8
  and beat upon their breasts.

⁸Nineveh is like a pool,
	and its water is draining
		away.
"Stop! Stop!" they cry,
	but no one turns back.
⁹Plunder the silver!
	Plunder the gold!
The supply is endless,
	the wealth from all its
		treasures!
¹⁰She is pillaged, plundered,
		stripped!
	Hearts melt, knees give
		way, Jos 2:11
	bodies tremble, every face
		grows pale. Isa 29:22

¹¹Where now is the lions' den,
	the place where they fed
		their young,
where the lion and lioness
		went,
	and the cubs, with nothing
		to fear?
¹²The lion killed enough for his
		cubs Jer 51:34
	and strangled the prey for
		his mate,
filling his lairs with the kill
	and his dens with the prey.

¹³"I am against you,"   Isa 10:5-13
	declares the Lord
		Almighty.
"I will burn up your chariots
		in smoke, Ps 46:9
	and the sword will devour
		your young lions. 2Sa 2:26
I will leave you no prey on
		the earth.
The voices of your
		messengers

ᵃ3 Hebrew; Septuagint and Syriac / *the horsemen rush to and fro*   ᵇ7 The meaning of
the Hebrew for this word is uncertain.

will no longer be heard."

Woe to Nineveh

3 Woe to the city of blood,
full of lies,   Ps 12:2
  full of plunder,
    never without victims!
²The crack of whips,
    the clatter of wheels,
  galloping horses
    and jolting chariots!
³Charging cavalry,
    flashing swords
    and glittering spears!
  Many casualties,
    piles of dead,
  bodies without number,
    people stumbling over the
      corpses—   2Ki 19:35
⁴all because of the wanton lust
    of a harlot,
  alluring, the mistress of
    sorceries,   Isa 47:9
  who enslaved nations by her
    prostitution   Isa 23:17
  and peoples by her
    witchcraft.

⁵"I am against you," declares
    the LORD Almighty.
  "I will lift your skirts over
    your face.   Isa 20:4
  I will show the nations your
    nakedness   Isa 47:3
  and the kingdoms your
    shame.
⁶I will pelt you with filth,
  I will treat you with
    contempt   1Sa 2:30
  and make you a spectacle.
⁷All who see you will flee
    from you and say,   Isa 13:14

'Nineveh is in ruins—who
    will mourn for her?'
  Where can I find anyone to
    comfort you?"   Isa 51:19

⁸Are you better than Thebes,[a]
    situated on the Nile,   Isa 19:6-9
  with water around her?
  The river was her defense,
    the waters her wall.
⁹Cush[b] and Egypt were her
    boundless strength;
  Put and Libya were among
    her allies.   Eze 27:10
¹⁰Yet she was taken captive
    and went into exile.   Isa 20:4
  Her infants were dashed to
    pieces   2Ki 8:12
  at the head of every street.
  Lots were cast for her nobles,
  and all her great men were
    put in chains.   Jer 40:1
¹¹You too will become drunk;
  you will go into hiding
  and seek refuge from the
    enemy.   Isa 2:10

¹²All your fortresses are like fig
    trees
  with their first ripe fruit;
  when they are shaken,
    the figs fall into the mouth
    of the eater.   Isa 28:4
¹³Look at your troops—
    they are all women!   Isa 19:16
  The gates of your land
  are wide open to your
    enemies;   Na 2:6
  fire has consumed their
    bars.   Isa 45:2
¹⁴Draw water for the siege,
    strengthen your defenses!
  Work the clay,

---

[a]8 Hebrew *No Amon*   [b]9 That is, the upper Nile region

tread the mortar,
repair the brickwork!
¹⁵There the fire will devour
you;   Isa 27:1
the sword will cut you
down   2Sa 2:26
and, like grasshoppers,
consume you.
Multiply like grasshoppers,
multiply like locusts!   Jer 51:14
¹⁶You have increased the
number of your
merchants
till they are more than the
stars of the sky,
but like locusts they strip the
land   Ex 10:13
and then fly away.
¹⁷Your guards are like locusts,
your officials like swarms of
locusts

that settle in the walls on a
cold day—
but when the sun appears
they fly away,
and no one knows where.

¹⁸O king of Assyria, your
shepherds*ᵃ* slumber;
your nobles lie down to
rest.   Isa 56:10
Your people are scattered on
the mountains   1Ki 22:17
with no one to gather them.
¹⁹Nothing can heal your
wound;   Jer 30:13
your injury is fatal.
Everyone who hears the
news about you
claps his hands at your fall,
for who has not felt
your endless cruelty?   Isa 37:18

ᵃ18 Or *rulers*

Habakkuk

Introduction:

Habakkuk was written as a dialogue or conversation between God and the prophet. Habakkuk saw that the leaders in Judah were oppressing the poor, so he asked the question as to why God allowed those wicked people to prosper. When God told him that the Babylonians would come to punish Judah, Habakkuk became more concerned. He did not understand how God could use the Babylonians, who were actually more wicked than the wicked Jews, to bring judgment on God's chosen people. God's answer was that the just would live by faith in God and that they had the assurance that God was doing what was right. God told Habakkuk that in due time the Babylonians too would be judged and that justice would come about for the people of God. Habakkuk ends his book with a prayer of praise.

Outline of contents:

---

1 The oracle that Habakkuk the prophet received.   Na 1:1

Habakkuk's Complaint

2How long, O LORD, must I
  call for help,   Ps 6:3
  but you do not listen? Ps 13:1-2
Or cry out to you,
  "Violence!"
  but you do not save?   Jer 14:9
3Why do you make me look at
  injustice?
Why do you tolerate
  wrong?   Job 9:23
Destruction and violence are
  before me;   Jer 20:8
there is strife, and conflict
  abounds.   Ps 55:9
4Therefore the law is
  paralyzed,   Ps 119:126
and justice never prevails.
The wicked hem in the
  righteous,
so that justice is perverted.

The LORD's Answer

5"Look at the nations and
  watch—

and be utterly amazed.
For I am going to do
    something in your days
that you would not believe,
    even if you were told. Ac 13:41
⁶I am raising up the
    Babylonians,ᵃ   Dt 28:49
that ruthless and impetuous
    people,
who sweep across the whole
    earth   Rev 20:9
to seize dwelling places not
    their own.   Jer 13:20
⁷They are a feared and
    dreaded people;   Isa 18:7
they are a law to
    themselves
and promote their own
    honor.
⁸Their horses are swifter than
    leopards,   Jer 4:13
fiercer than wolves at dusk.
Their cavalry gallops
    headlong;
their horsemen come from
    afar.
They fly like a vulture
    swooping to devour;
⁹ they all come bent on
    violence.
Their hordesᵇ advance like a
    desert wind
and gather prisoners like
    sand.   Hab 2:5
¹⁰They deride kings
    and scoff at rulers. 2Ch 36:6
They laugh at all fortified
    cities;
they build earthen ramps
    and capture them.   Jer 33:4
¹¹Then they sweep past like
    the wind and go on—

guilty men, whose own
    strength is their god."

Habakkuk's Second Complaint

¹²O LORD, are you not from
    everlasting?   Ge 21:33
My God, my Holy One, we
    will not die.   Isa 31:1
O LORD, you have appointed
    them to execute
    judgment;   Isa 10:6
O Rock, you have ordained
    them to punish.   Ge 49:24
¹³Your eyes are too pure to
    look on evil;   Ps 18:26
you cannot tolerate wrong.
Why then do you tolerate the
    treacherous?   Ps 25:3
Why are you silent while
    the wicked
swallow up those more
    righteous than
    themselves?   Job 21:7
¹⁴You have made men like fish
    in the sea,
like sea creatures that have
    no ruler.
¹⁵The wicked foe pulls all of
    them up with hooks,
he catches them in his net,
he gathers them up in his
    dragnet;
and so he rejoices and is
    glad.
¹⁶Therefore he sacrifices to his
    net
and burns incense to his
    dragnet,   Jer 44:8
for by his net he lives in
    luxury

ᵃ6 Or *Chaldeans*   ᵇ9 The meaning of the Hebrew for this word is uncertain.

and enjoys the choicest
    food.
¹⁷Is he to keep on emptying his
    net,
    destroying nations without
        mercy?   Isa 14:6

2 I will stand at my watch
    and station myself on the
        ramparts;   Ps 48:13
I will look to see what he will
    say to me,
and what answer I am to
    give to this complaint.^a

The LORD's Answer

²Then the LORD replied:

"Write down the revelation
    and make it plain on tablets
    so that a herald^b may run
        with it.   Isa 30:8
³For the revelation awaits an
        appointed time;   Da 11:27
    it speaks of the end   Da 8:17
    and will not prove false.
    Though it linger, wait for it;
    it^c will certainly come and
        will not delay.   Eze 12:25

⁴"See, he is puffed up;
    his desires are not
        upright—
    but the righteous will live
        by his faith^d—   Ro 1:17
⁵indeed, wine betrays him;
    he is arrogant and never at
        rest.   Isa 2:11
Because he is as greedy as
    the grave^e
and like death is never
    satisfied,   Pr 27:20

he gathers to himself all the
    nations
and takes captive all the
    peoples.   Hab 1:9

⁶"Will not all of them taunt
him with ridicule and scorn,
saying,   Isa 14:4

" 'Woe to him who piles up
    stolen goods
and makes himself wealthy
    by extortion!   Am 2:8
How long must this go on?'
⁷Will not your debtors^f
    suddenly arise?
Will they not wake up and
    make you tremble?
Then you will become their
    victim.   Pr 29:1
⁸Because you have plundered
    many nations,
    the peoples who are left
        will plunder you.   Isa 33:1
For you have shed man's
    blood;
    you have destroyed lands
    and cities and everyone
    in them.   Eze 39:10

⁹"Woe to him who builds his
    realm by unjust gain
to set his nest on high,
to escape the clutches of
    ruin!   Job 39:27
¹⁰You have plotted the ruin of
    many peoples,   Jer 26:19
    shaming your own house
    and forfeiting your life.
¹¹The stones of the wall will
    cry out,   Jos 24:27

---

^a1 Or *and what to answer when I am rebuked*   ^b2 Or *so that whoever reads it*   ^c3 Or
Though he linger, wait for him; | he   ^d4 Or *faithfulness*   ^e5 Hebrew *Sheol*   ^f7 Or
creditors

and the beams of the
　　woodwork will echo it.

¹²"Woe to him who builds a
　　city with bloodshed
and establishes a town by
　　crime!　　　　　Eze 22:2
¹³Has not the Lᴏʀᴅ Almighty
　　determined
that the people's labor is
　　only fuel for the fire,
that the nations exhaust
　　themselves for nothing?
¹⁴For the earth will be filled
　　with the knowledge of
　　the glory of the Lᴏʀᴅ,
　as the waters cover the sea.

¹⁵"Woe to him who gives drink
　　to his neighbors,　Pr 23:20
pouring it from the
　　wineskin till they are
　　drunk,
so that he can gaze on their
　　naked bodies.
¹⁶You will be filled with shame
　　instead of glory.　Eze 23:32
Now it is your turn! Drink
　　and be exposedᵃ!　Lev 10:9
The cup from the Lᴏʀᴅ's
　　right hand is coming
　　around to you,　Ps 16:5
and disgrace will cover your
　　glory.
¹⁷The violence you have done
　　to Lebanon will
　　overwhelm you,　Jer 51:35
and your destruction of
　　animals will terrify you.
For you have shed man's
　　blood;

you have destroyed lands
　　and cities and everyone
　　in them.

¹⁸"Of what value is an idol,
　　since a man has
　　carved it?　　　Jdg 10:14
Or an image that teaches
　　lies?　　　　　Lev 26:1
For he who makes it trusts in
　　his own creation;
he makes idols that cannot
　　speak.　　　　Ps 115:4-5
¹⁹Woe to him who says to
　　wood, 'Come to life!'
Or to lifeless stone, 'Wake
　　up!'　　　　　1Ki 18:27
Can it give guidance?
It is covered with gold and
　　silver;　　　　Jer 10:4
　there is no breath in it.
²⁰But the Lᴏʀᴅ is in his holy
　　temple;　　　　Ps 11:4
let all the earth be silent
　　before him."　　Isa 41:1

Habakkuk's Prayer

3 A prayer of Habakkuk the
prophet. On *shigionoth.*ᵇ

²Lᴏʀᴅ, I have heard of your
　　fame;　　　　Job 26:14
I stand in awe of your
　　deeds, O Lᴏʀᴅ.　Ps 119:120
Renew them in our day,
　in our time make them
　　known;
in wrath remember mercy.

³God came from Teman,
　the Holy One from Mount
　　Paran.　　　　*Selah*ᶜ

ᵃ16 Masoretic Text; Dead Sea Scrolls, Aquila, Vulgate and Syriac (see also Septuagint) *and stagger*　　ᵇ1 Probably a literary or musical term　　ᶜ3 A word of uncertain meaning; possibly a musical term; also in verses 9 and 13

His glory covered the
   heavens   Ps 8:1
and his praise filled the
   earth.   Ps 48:10
4His splendor was like the
   sunrise;   Isa 18:4
rays flashed from his hand,
where his power was
   hidden.   Job 9:6
5Plague went before him;
pestilence followed his
   steps.   Lev 26:25
6He stood, and shook the
   earth;
he looked, and made the
   nations tremble.
The ancient mountains
   crumbled   Ps 46:2
and the age-old hills
   collapsed.   Ge 49:26
   His ways are eternal.   Ge 21:33
7I saw the tents of Cushan in
   distress,
the dwellings of Midian in
   anguish.   Ge 25:2

8Were you angry with the
   rivers, O LORD?   Ex 7:20
Was your wrath against the
   streams?
Did you rage against the sea
when you rode with your
   horses
and your victorious
   chariots?   2Ki 2:11
9You uncovered your bow,
you called for many arrows.
                                   Selah
You split the earth with
   rivers;
10   the mountains saw you and
   writhed.   Ps 77:16

Torrents of water swept by;
the deep roared   Ps 98:7
and lifted its waves on
   high.   Ps 93:3

11Sun and moon stood still in
   the heavens   Jos 10:13
at the glint of your flying
   arrows,   Ps 18:14
at the lightning of your
   flashing spear.   Ps 144:6
12In wrath you strode through
   the earth
and in anger you threshed
   the nations.   Isa 41:15
13You came out to deliver your
   people,   Ex 13:21
to save your anointed one.
You crushed the leader of the
   land of wickedness,
you stripped him from head
   to foot.   Selah
14With his own spear you
   pierced his head
when his warriors stormed
   out to scatter us,   Jdg 7:22
gloating as though about to
   devour
the wretched who were in
   hiding.   Ps 64:2-5
15You trampled the sea with
   your horses,   Job 9:8
churning the great waters.

16I heard and my heart
   pounded,
my lips quivered at the
   sound;
decay crept into my bones,
and my legs trembled.
Yet I will wait patiently for
   the day of calamity

to come on the nation
  invading us.   Ps 37:7
¹⁷Though the fig tree does not
  bud
  and there are no grapes on
    the vines,
though the olive crop fails
  and the fields produce no
    food,   Joel 1:10-12
though there are no sheep in
  the pen
  and no cattle in the stalls,
¹⁸yet I will rejoice in the LORD,

I will be joyful in God my
  Savior.   Ex 15:2

¹⁹The Sovereign LORD is my
  strength;   Dt 33:29
he makes my feet like the
  feet of a deer,
he enables me to go on the
  heights.   Dt 32:13

For the director of music. On
  my stringed
  instruments.

Zephaniah

Introduction:

Zephaniah's ministry is dated in the reign of Josiah (640–609 B.C.). He warned that the day of the Lord would bring judgment on Judah and Jerusalem and he called the Jews to return to God.

Zephaniah then predicted that Judah's neighboring nations would be destroyed as well. With a note of hope, he promised that God would bring his people home.

Outline of contents:

---

1 The word of the LORD that came to Zephaniah son of Cushi, the son of Gedaliah, the son of Amariah, the son of Hezekiah, during the reign of Josiah son of Amon king of Judah: 2Ki 22:1; 1Ch 3:14

Warning of Coming Destruction

2"I will sweep away
    everything
from the face of the earth,"
    declares the LORD.
3"I will sweep away both men
    and animals; Jer 50:3
I will sweep away the birds
    of the air Jer 4:25
and the fish of the sea.
The wicked will have only
    heaps of rubble*a*

when I cut off man from the
    face of the earth," Hos 4:3
    declares the LORD.

Against Judah

4"I will stretch out my hand
    against Judah Jer 6:12
and against all who live in
    Jerusalem.
I will cut off from this place
    every remnant of Baal,
the names of the pagan and
    the idolatrous priests—
5those who bow down on the
    roofs
to worship the starry host,
those who bow down and
    swear by the LORD
and who also swear by
    Molech,*b* Lev 18:21

---

*a*3 The meaning of the Hebrew for this line is uncertain.   *b*5 Hebrew *Malcam*, that is, Milcom

⁶those who turn back from
following the LORD
and neither seek the LORD
nor inquire of him. Hos 7:7
⁷Be silent before the Sovereign
LORD, Isa 41:1
for the day of the LORD is
near. Isa 13:6
The LORD has prepared a
sacrifice; Lev 3:9
he has consecrated those he
has invited.
⁸On the day of the LORD's
sacrifice
I will punish the princes
and the king's sons Jer 39:6
and all those clad
in foreign clothes.
⁹On that day I will punish
all who avoid stepping on
the threshold,ᵃ 1Sa 5:5
who fill the temple of their
gods
with violence and deceit.

¹⁰"On that day," declares the
LORD,
"a cry will go up from the
Fish Gate, 2Ch 33:14
wailing from the New
Quarter, Am 5:16
and a loud crash from the
hills.
¹¹Wail, you who live in the
market districtᵇ; Jas 5:1
all your merchants will be
wiped out,
all who trade withᶜ silver
will be ruined. Hos 9:6
¹²At that time I will search
Jerusalem with lamps
and punish those who are
complacent, Am 6:1

who are like wine left on its
dregs, Jer 48:11
who think, 'The LORD will do
nothing, 2Ki 21:16
either good or bad.' Job 22:13
¹³Their wealth will be
plundered, 2Ki 24:13
their houses demolished.
They will build houses
but not live in them;
they will plant vineyards
but not drink the wine.

The Great Day of the LORD

¹⁴"The great day of the LORD is
near— Eze 7:7
near and coming quickly.
Listen! The cry on the day
of the LORD will be
bitter,
the shouting of the warrior
there.
¹⁵That day will be a day of
wrath,
a day of distress and
anguish,
a day of trouble and ruin,
a day of darkness and
gloom, 1Sa 2:9
a day of clouds and
blackness, Isa 22:5
¹⁶a day of trumpet and battle
cry Jer 4:19
against the fortified cities
and against the corner
towers. Dt 28:52
¹⁷I will bring distress on the
people
and they will walk like
blind men, Isa 59:10
because they have sinned
against the LORD.

ᵃ9 See 1 Samuel 5:5. ᵇ11 Or the Mortar ᶜ11 Or in

Their blood will be poured
   out like dust   Ps 79:3
and their entrails like filth.
18Neither their silver nor their
   gold
will be able to save them
on the day of the LORD's
   wrath.   Job 20:20
In the fire of his jealousy
   the whole world will be
   consumed,   Zep 3:8
for he will make a sudden
   end
of all who live in the earth."

2 Gather together, gather
   together,   2Ch 20:4
   O shameful nation,   Jer 3:3
2before the appointed time
   arrives
and that day sweeps on like
   chaff,   Isa 17:13
before the fierce anger of the
   LORD comes upon you,
before the day of the LORD's
   wrath comes upon you.
3Seek the LORD, all you
   humble of the land,
you who do what he
   commands.
Seek righteousness, seek
   humility;   Ps 45:4
perhaps you will be
   sheltered   Ps 57:1
on the day of the LORD's
   anger.

Against Philistia

4Gaza will be abandoned
   and Ashkelon left in ruins.
At midday Ashdod will be
   emptied

and Ekron uprooted.
5Woe to you who live by the
   sea,
   O Kerethite people;   1Sa 30:14
the word of the LORD is
   against you,   Lev 26:31
   O Canaan, land of the
   Philistines.

"I will destroy you,
   and none will be left."

6The land by the sea, where
   the Kerethites*a* dwell,
will be a place for
   shepherds and sheep
   pens.   Isa 5:17
7It will belong to the remnant
   of the house of Judah;
there they will find pasture.
In the evening they will lie
   down
in the houses of Ashkelon.
The LORD their God will care
   for them;
he will restore their
   fortunes.*b*   Dt 30:3

Against Moab and Ammon

8"I have heard the insults of
   Moab   Jer 48:27
   and the taunts of the
   Ammonites,   Eze 21:28
who insulted my people
and made threats against
   their land.   La 3:61
9Therefore, as surely as I
   live,"
   declares the LORD
   Almighty, the God of
   Israel,

---

a6 The meaning of the Hebrew for this word is uncertain.   *b7* Or *will bring back their captives*

"surely Moab will become
  like Sodom,   Dt 23:6
the Ammonites like
  Gomorrah—
      Jer 49:1-6
a place of weeds and salt
  pits,
a wasteland forever.
The remnant of my people
  will plunder them; Isa 11:14
the survivors of my nation
  will inherit their land."

¹⁰This is what they will get in
  return for their pride,
for insulting and mocking
  the people of the LORD
  Almighty.   Ps 9:6
¹¹The LORD will be awesome to
  them   Joel 2:11
when he destroys all the
  gods of the land.   1Ch 19:1
The nations on every shore
  will worship him,   Ps 86:9
every one in its own land.

Against Cush

¹²"You too, O Cushites,[a]
  will be slain by my sword."

Against Assyria

¹³He will stretch out his hand
  against the north
and destroy Assyria,   Isa 10:5
leaving Nineveh utterly
  desolate   Ge 10:11
and dry as the desert.
¹⁴Flocks and herds will lie
  down there,   Isa 5:17
creatures of every kind.
The desert owl and the
  screech owl   Isa 14:23
will roost on her columns.

Their calls will echo through
  the windows,
rubble will be in the
  doorways,
the beams of cedar will be
  exposed.
¹⁵This is the carefree city
  that lived in safety.   Isa 32:9
She said to herself,
  "I am, and there is none
  besides me."   Eze 28:2
What a ruin she has become,
  a lair for wild beasts! Jer 49:33
All who pass by her scoff
  and shake their fists. Eze 27:36

The Future of Jerusalem

3 Woe to the city of
  oppressors,   Jer 6:6
rebellious and defiled!
²She obeys no one,   Jer 22:21
  she accepts no correction.
She does not trust in the
  LORD,   Dt 1:32
  she does not draw near to
  her God.   Ps 73:28
³Her officials are roaring lions,
  her rulers are evening
  wolves,   Ge 49:27
who leave nothing for the
  morning.   Mic 3:3
⁴Her prophets are arrogant;
  they are treacherous men.
Her priests profane the
  sanctuary
  and do violence to the law.
⁵The LORD within her is
  righteous;   Ezr 9:15
  he does no wrong.   Dt 32:4
Morning by morning he
  dispenses his justice,

ᵃ12 That is, people from the upper Nile region

and every new day he does
    not fail,   La 3:23
yet the unrighteous know
    no shame.   Jer 3:3

6"I have cut off nations;
    their strongholds are
    demolished.
I have left their streets
    deserted,
with no one passing
    through.
Their cities are destroyed;
    no one will be left—no one
    at all.
7I said to the city,
    'Surely you will fear me
    and accept correction!' Jer 7:28
Then her dwelling would not
    be cut off,
    nor all my punishments
    come upon her.
But they were still eager
    to act corruptly in all they
    did.   Hos 9:9
8Therefore wait for me,"
    declares the LORD,   Ps 27:14
    "for the day I will stand up
    to testify.ᵃ
I have decided to assemble
    the nations,   Isa 2:3
    to gather the kingdoms
and to pour out my wrath on
    them—   Ps 79:6
    all my fierce anger.   Jer 10:25
The whole world will be
    consumed   Zep 1:18
by the fire of my jealous
    anger.

9"Then will I purify the lips of
    the peoples,

that all of them may call on
    the name of the LORD
and serve him shoulder to
    shoulder.   Isa 19:18
10From beyond the rivers of
    Cushᵇ   Ge 10:6
    my worshipers, my
    scattered people,
    will bring me offerings.
11On that day you will not be
    put to shame
for all the wrongs you have
    done to me,   Ge 50:15
because I will remove from
    this city
    those who rejoice in their
    pride.   Ps 59:12
Never again will you be
    haughty
    on my holy hill.   Ex 15:17
12But I will leave within you
    the meek and humble,
    who trust in the name of
    the LORD.   Jer 29:12
13The remnant of Israel will do
    no wrong;   Isa 10:21
    they will speak no lies,
    nor will deceit be found in
    their mouths.   Job 16:17
They will eat and lie down
    and no one will make them
    afraid."   Eze 34:15

14Sing, O Daughter of Zion;
    shout aloud, O Israel!
Be glad and rejoice with all
    your heart,   Ps 9:2
    O Daughter of Jerusalem!
15The LORD has taken away
    your punishment,
    he has turned back your
    enemy.

ᵃ8 Septuagint and Syriac; Hebrew *will rise up to plunder*   ᵇ10 That is, the upper Nile region

The LORD, the King of Israel,
  is with you; Eze 37:26-28
never again will you fear
  any harm. Zec 9:9
¹⁶On that day they will say to
  Jerusalem,
"Do not fear, O Zion;
  do not let your hands hang
  limp. 2Ki 19:26
¹⁷The LORD your God is with
  you,
  he is mighty to save. Isa 63:1
He will take great delight in
  you, Dt 28:63
he will quiet you with his
  love, Hos 14:4
he will rejoice over you
  with singing." Isa 40:1

¹⁸"The sorrows for the
  appointed feasts
I will remove from you;

they are a burden and a
  reproach to you. ^a
¹⁹At that time I will deal
  with all who oppressed
  you; Isa 14:2
I will rescue the lame
  and gather those who have
  been scattered. Eze 34:16
I will give them praise and
  honor Isa 60:18
in every land where they
  were put to shame.
²⁰At that time I will gather you;
  at that time I will bring you
  home. Jer 29:14
I will give you honor and
  praise Isa 56:5
among all the peoples of
  the earth
when I restore your fortunes^b
  before your very eyes," Joel 3:1
  says the LORD.

---

^a18 Or "I will gather you who mourn for the appointed feasts; / your reproach is a burden to you
^b20 Or I bring back your captives

Haggai

Introduction:

Eighteen years had passed since Cyrus's decree in 538 B.C. had allowed the Jews to return from exile to Jerusalem. Because they were busy building their own homes, the people still had not finished building God's temple.

Haggai's message was that the time had come to build the house of the Lord. Under the leadership of Zerubbabel and Joshua and with Haggai's prodding the temple was rebuilt during the years 520–515 B.C.

Haggai told the people that the glory of the temple they were building would be greater than that of the former temple, even though the building itself would be less to look at. This temple would be greater because God would fill this house with his glory.

Outline of contents:
> The call to rebuild the temple (1:1–15)
> Hopes for the new temple (2:1–9)
> Promised blessings (2:10–19)
> God's final triumph (2:20–23)

A Call to Build the House of the LORD

1 In the second year of King Darius, on the first day of the sixth month, the word of the LORD came through the prophet Haggai to Zerubbabel son of Shealtiel, governor of Judah, and to Joshua[a] son of Jehozadak, the high priest: Ezr 4:24

²This is what the LORD Almighty says: "These people say, 'The time has not yet come for the LORD's house to be built.'"   Isa 13:4; 29:13

³Then the word of the LORD came through the prophet Haggai: ⁴"Is it a time for you yourselves to be living in your paneled houses, while this house remains a ruin?"   Ezr 5:1

⁵Now this is what the LORD Almighty says: "Give careful thought to your ways. ⁶You have planted much, but have harvested little. You eat, but never have enough. You drink,

---

a1 A variant of *Jeshua*; here and elsewhere in Haggai

but never have your fill. You put on clothes, but are not warm. You earn wages, only to put them in a purse with holes in it." Lev 26:20; La 3:40

7This is what the LORD Almighty says: "Give careful thought to your ways. 8Go up into the mountains and bring down timber and build the house, so that I may take pleasure in it and be honored," says the LORD. 9"You expected much, but see, it turned out to be little. What you brought home, I blew away. Why?" declares the LORD Almighty. "Because of my house, which remains a ruin, while each of you is busy with his own house. 10Therefore, because of you the heavens have withheld their dew and the earth its crops. 11I called for a drought on the fields and the mountains, on the grain, the new wine, the oil and whatever the ground produces, on men and cattle, and on the labor of your hands." 1Ch 14:1

12Then Zerubbabel son of Shealtiel, Joshua son of Jehozadak, the high priest, and the whole remnant of the people obeyed the voice of the LORD their God and the message of the prophet Haggai, because the LORD their God had sent him. And the people feared the LORD. Isa 1:9; Hag 2:2

13Then Haggai, the LORD's messenger, gave this message of the LORD to the people: "I am with you," declares the LORD. 14So the LORD stirred up the spirit of Zerubbabel son of Shealtiel, governor of Judah, and the spirit of Joshua son of Jehozadak, the high priest, and the spirit of the whole remnant of the people. They came and began to work on the house of the LORD Almighty, their God, 15on the twenty-fourth day of the sixth month in the second year of King Darius. Nu 27:21

The Promised Glory of the New House

2 On the twenty-first day of the seventh month, the word of the LORD came through the prophet Haggai: 2"Speak to Zerubbabel son of Shealtiel, governor of Judah, to Joshua son of Jehozadak, the high priest, and to the remnant of the people. Ask them, 3'Who of you is left who saw this house in its former glory? How does it look to you now? Does it not seem to you like nothing? 4But now be strong, O Zerubbabel,' declares the LORD. 'Be strong, O Joshua son of Jehozadak, the high priest. Be strong, all you people of the land,' declares the LORD, 'and work. For I am with you,' declares the LORD Almighty. 5'This is what I covenanted with you when you came out of Egypt. And my Spirit remains among you. Do not fear.' Lev 23:34

6"This is what the LORD Almighty says: 'In a little while I

will once more shake the heavens and the earth, the sea and the dry land. 7I will shake all nations, and the desired of all nations will come, and I will fill this house with glory,' says the LORD Almighty. 8'The silver is mine and the gold is mine,' declares the LORD Almighty. 9'The glory of this present house will be greater than the glory of the former house,' says the LORD Almighty. 'And in this place I will grant peace,' declares the LORD Almighty."   Isa 10:25

Blessings for a Defiled People

10On the twenty-fourth day of the ninth month, in the second year of Darius, the word of the LORD came to the prophet Haggai: 11"This is what the LORD Almighty says: 'Ask the priests what the law says: 12If a person carries consecrated meat in the fold of his garment, and that fold touches some bread or stew, some wine, oil or other food, does it become consecrated?' "   Lev 10:10-11; Hag 1:15

The priests answered, "No."

13Then Haggai said, "If a person defiled by contact with a dead body touches one of these things, does it become defiled?"

"Yes," the priests replied, "it becomes defiled."   Lev 22:4-6

14Then Haggai said, " 'So it is with this people and this nation in my sight,' declares the LORD. 'Whatever they do and what-

ever they offer there is defiled.

15" 'Now give careful thought to this from this day on[a]— consider how things were before one stone was laid on another in the LORD's temple. 16When anyone came to a heap of twenty measures, there were only ten. When anyone went to a wine vat to draw fifty measures, there were only twenty. 17I struck all the work of your hands with blight, mildew and hail, yet you did not turn to me,' declares the LORD. 18'From this day on, from this twenty-fourth day of the ninth month, give careful thought to the day when the foundation of the LORD's temple was laid. Give careful thought: 19Is there yet any seed left in the barn? Until now, the vine and the fig tree, the pomegranate and the olive tree have not borne fruit.   Dt 28:22; Hag 1:5

" 'From this day on I will bless you.' "   Ge 12:2; Lev 25:21

Zerubbabel the LORD's Signet Ring

20The word of the LORD came to Haggai a second time on the twenty-fourth day of the month: 21"Tell Zerubbabel governor of Judah that I will shake the heavens and the earth. 22I will overturn royal thrones and shatter the power of the foreign kingdoms. I will overthrow chariots and their drivers;

horses and their riders will fall, each by the sword of his brother. _{Ezr 5:1; Job 2:13}

²³" 'On that day,' declares the LORD Almighty, 'I will take you, my servant Zerubbabel son of Shealtiel,' declares the LORD, 'and I will make you like my signet ring, for I have chosen you,' declares the LORD Almighty."

Zechariah

Introduction:

Zechariah's prophecies began two months after Haggai's first message (520 B.C.).

In his opening message Zechariah warned the people who had just begun rebuilding the temple that they were to listen to God's message through the prophets. They were also to keep a close relationship with God so that there would be no further judgment.

This opening message is followed by visions that offered encouragement to the builders at a time when they were ready to give up. Zechariah comforted them by telling them God had a long-range plan for Israel.

In chapters 7 and 8 Zechariah called the people to obey God by acting fairly and mercifully to one another. God wanted obedience in his relationship with them.

Chapters 9 through 14 tell of the coming Messiah, the last judgment and the long-range growth of the final kingdom.

Outline of contents:

A Call to Return to the LORD

1 In the eighth month of the second year of Darius, the word of the LORD came to the prophet Zechariah son of Berekiah, the son of Iddo: Ezr 4:24

²"The LORD was very angry with your forefathers. ³Therefore tell the people: This is what the LORD Almighty says: 'Return to me,' declares the LORD Almighty, 'and I will return to you,' says the LORD Almighty. ⁴Do not be like your forefathers, to whom the earlier prophets proclaimed: This is what the LORD Almighty says: 'Turn from your evil ways and your evil practices.' But they would not listen or pay attention to me, declares the LORD. ⁵Where are your forefathers now? And

the prophets, do they live forever? 6But did not my words and my decrees, which I commanded my servants the prophets, overtake your forefathers?

"Then they repented and said, 'The LORD Almighty has done to us what our ways and practices deserve, just as he determined to do.'" Jer 12:14-17

The Man Among the Myrtle Trees

7On the twenty-fourth day of the eleventh month, the month of Shebat, in the second year of Darius, the word of the LORD came to the prophet Zechariah son of Berekiah, the son of Iddo.

8During the night I had a vision—and there before me was a man riding a red horse! He was standing among the myrtle trees in a ravine. Behind him were red, brown and white horses. Zec 6:2-7; Rev 6:4

9I asked, "What are these, my lord?"

The angel who was talking with me answered, "I will show you what they are." Zec 4:1

10Then the man standing among the myrtle trees explained, "They are the ones the LORD has sent to go throughout the earth." Zec 6:5-8

11And they reported to the angel of the LORD, who was standing among the myrtle trees, "We have gone throughout the earth and found the whole world at rest and in peace." Ge 16:7; Isa 14:7

12Then the angel of the LORD said, "LORD Almighty, how long will you withhold mercy from Jerusalem and from the towns of Judah, which you have been angry with these seventy years?" 13So the LORD spoke kind and comforting words to the angel who talked with me.

14Then the angel who was speaking to me said, "Proclaim this word: This is what the LORD Almighty says: 'I am very jealous for Jerusalem and Zion, 15but I am very angry with the nations that feel secure. I was only a little angry, but they added to the calamity.' Isa 26:11

16"Therefore, this is what the LORD says: 'I will return to Jerusalem with mercy, and there my house will be rebuilt. And the measuring line will be stretched out over Jerusalem,' declares the LORD Almighty.

17"Proclaim further: This is what the LORD Almighty says: 'My towns will again overflow with prosperity, and the LORD will again comfort Zion and choose Jerusalem.'" Isa 40:1

Four Horns and Four Craftsmen

18Then I looked up—and there before me were four horns! 19I asked the angel who was speaking to me, "What are these?"

He answered me, "These are

the horns that scattered Judah, Israel and Jerusalem."   Am 6:13

²⁰Then the LORD showed me four craftsmen. ²¹I asked, "What are these coming to do?"

He answered, "These are the horns that scattered Judah so that no one could raise his head, but the craftsmen have come to terrify them and throw down these horns of the nations who lifted up their horns against the land of Judah to scatter its people."   1Ki 22:11; Ps 75:4

A Man With a Measuring Line

2 Then I looked up—and there before me was a man with a measuring line in his hand! ²I asked, "Where are you going?"

He answered me, "To measure Jerusalem, to find out how wide and how long it is."Rev 21:15

³Then the angel who was speaking to me left, and another angel came to meet him ⁴and said to him: "Run, tell that young man, 'Jerusalem will be a city without walls because of the great number of men and livestock in it. ⁵And I myself will be a wall of fire around it,' declares the LORD, 'and I will be its glory within.'   Isa 49:20; Eze 38:11

⁶"Come! Come! Flee from the land of the north," declares the LORD, "for I have scattered you to the four winds of heaven," declares the LORD.   Ps 44:11

⁷"Come, O Zion! Escape, you who live in the Daughter of Babylon!" ⁸For this is what the LORD Almighty says: "After he has honored me and has sent me against the nations that have plundered you—for whoever touches you touches the apple of his eye— ⁹I will surely raise my hand against them so that their slaves will plunder them. ª Then you will know that the LORD Almighty has sent me.

¹⁰"Shout and be glad, O Daughter of Zion. For I am coming, and I will live among you," declares the LORD. ¹¹"Many nations will be joined with the LORD in that day and will become my people. I will live among you and you will know that the LORD Almighty has sent me to you. ¹²The LORD will inherit Judah as his portion in the holy land and will again choose Jerusalem. ¹³Be still before the LORD, all mankind, because he has roused himself from his holy dwelling."   Zep 3:14

Clean Garments for the High Priest

3 Then he showed me Joshuaᵇ the high priest standing before the angel of the LORD, and Satanᶜ standing at his right side to accuse him. ²The LORD said to Satan, "The LORD rebuke you, Satan! The LORD, who has chosen Jerusalem, rebuke you! Is

---

ª8,9 Or says after . . . eye: 9"I . . . plunder them."   ᵇ1 A variant of Jeshua; here and elsewhere in Zechariah   ᶜ1 Satan means accuser.

not this man a burning stick snatched from the fire?" Ezr 2:2

3Now Joshua was dressed in filthy clothes as he stood before the angel. 4The angel said to those who were standing before him, "Take off his filthy clothes."

Then he said to Joshua, "See, I have taken away your sin, and I will put rich garments on you." 2Sa 12:13; Mic 7:18

5Then I said, "Put a clean turban on his head." So they put a clean turban on his head and clothed him, while the angel of the LORD stood by. Ex 29:6

6The angel of the LORD gave this charge to Joshua: 7"This is what the LORD Almighty says: 'If you will walk in my ways and keep my requirements, then you will govern my house and have charge of my courts, and I will give you a place among these standing here. Lev 8:35

8" 'Listen, O high priest Joshua and your associates seated before you, who are men symbolic of things to come: I am going to bring my servant, the Branch. 9See, the stone I have set in front of Joshua! There are seven eyes*a* on that one stone, and I will engrave an inscription on it,' says the LORD Almighty, 'and I will remove the sin of this land in a single day. Hag 1:1

10" 'In that day each of you will invite his neighbor to sit under his vine and fig tree,' declares the LORD Almighty."

The Gold Lampstand and the Two Olive Trees

4 Then the angel who talked with me returned and wakened me, as a man is wakened from his sleep. 2He asked me, "What do you see?" Da 8:18

I answered, "I see a solid gold lampstand with a bowl at the top and seven lights on it, with seven channels to the lights. 3Also there are two olive trees by it, one on the right of the bowl and the other on its left."

4I asked the angel who talked with me, "What are these, my lord?"

5He answered, "Do you not know what these are?" Zec 1:9

"No, my lord," I replied.

6So he said to me, "This is the word of the LORD to Zerubbabel: 'Not by might nor by power, but by my Spirit,' says the LORD Almighty. 1Ch 3:19

7"What*b* are you, O mighty mountain? Before Zerubbabel you will become level ground. Then he will bring out the capstone to shouts of 'God bless it! God bless it!' " Ps 26:12; 118:22

8Then the word of the LORD came to me: 9"The hands of Zerubbabel have laid the foundation of this temple; his hands will also complete it. Then you will know that the LORD Almighty has sent me to you.

10"Who despises the day of small things? Men will rejoice when they see the plumb line in the hand of Zerubbabel. Hag 2:23

*a*9 Or *facets*   *b*7 Or *Who*

"(These seven are the eyes of the Lord, which range throughout the earth.)"   2Ch 16:9

[11] Then I asked the angel, "What are these two olive trees on the right and the left of the lampstand?"   Rev 11:4

[12] Again I asked him, "What are these two olive branches beside the two gold pipes that pour out golden oil?"

[13] He replied, "Do you not know what these are?"

"No, my lord," I said.

[14] So he said, "These are the two who are anointed to[a] serve the Lord of all the earth."   Ex 29:7

The Flying Scroll

5 I looked again—and there before me was a flying scroll!
[2] He asked me, "What do you see?"   Ps 40:7; Jer 1:13

I answered, "I see a flying scroll, thirty feet long and fifteen feet wide.[b]"

[3] And he said to me, "This is the curse that is going out over the whole land; for according to what it says on one side, every thief will be banished, and according to what it says on the other, everyone who swears falsely will be banished. [4] The Lord Almighty declares, 'I will send it out, and it will enter the house of the thief and the house of him who swears falsely by my name. It will remain in his house and destroy it, both its timbers and its stones.'"   Isa 24:6

The Woman in a Basket

[5] Then the angel who was speaking to me came forward and said to me, "Look up and see what this is that is appearing."   Zec 1:9,18

[6] I asked, "What is it?"

He replied, "It is a measuring basket.[c]" And he added, "This is the iniquity[d] of the people throughout the land."   Mic 6:10

[7] Then the cover of lead was raised, and there in the basket sat a woman! [8] He said, "This is wickedness," and he pushed her back into the basket and pushed the lead cover down over its mouth.   Mic 6:11

[9] Then I looked up—and there before me were two women, with the wind in their wings! They had wings like those of a stork, and they lifted up the basket between heaven and earth.   Lev 11:19; Jer 8:7

[10] "Where are they taking the basket?" I asked the angel who was speaking to me.

[11] He replied, "To the country of Babylonia[e] to build a house for it. When it is ready, the basket will be set there in its place."

Four Chariots

6 I looked up again—and there before me were four chariots coming out from between two mountains—mountains of bronze! [2] The first chariot had red hors-

---

[a]14 Or *two who bring oil and appearance*   [b]2 Hebrew *twenty cubits long and ten cubits wide* (about 9 meters long and 4.5 meters wide)   [c]6 Hebrew *an ephah*; also in verses 7-11   [d]6 Or   [e]11 Hebrew *Shinar*

es, the second black, ³the third white, and the fourth dappled—all of them powerful. ⁴I asked the angel who was speaking to me, "What are these, my lord?"   2Ki 2:11; Rev 6:2

⁵The angel answered me, "These are the four spirits*a* of heaven, going out from standing in the presence of the Lord of the whole world. ⁶The one with the black horses is going toward the north country, the one with the white horses toward the west,*b* and the one with the dappled horses toward the south."   Eze 37:9; Mt 24:31

⁷When the powerful horses went out, they were straining to go throughout the earth. And he said, "Go throughout the earth!" So they went throughout the earth.   Zec 1:8

⁸Then he called to me, "Look, those going toward the north country have given my Spirit*c* rest in the land of the north."

A Crown for Joshua

⁹The word of the Lord came to me: ¹⁰"Take silver and gold from the exiles Heldai, Tobijah and Jedaiah, who have arrived from Babylon. Go the same day to the house of Josiah son of Zephaniah. ¹¹Take the silver and gold and make a crown, and set it on the head of the high priest, Joshua son of Jehozadak. ¹²Tell him this is what the Lord Almighty says:

'Here is the man whose name is the Branch, and he will branch out from his place and build the temple of the Lord. ¹³It is he who will build the temple of the Lord, and he will be clothed with majesty and will sit and rule on his throne. And he will be a priest on his throne. And there will be harmony between the two.' ¹⁴The crown will be given to Heldai,*d* Tobijah, Jedaiah and Hen*e* son of Zephaniah as a memorial in the temple of the Lord. ¹⁵Those who are far away will come and help to build the temple of the Lord, and you will know that the Lord Almighty has sent me to you. This will happen if you diligently obey the Lord your God."   Ezr 7:14-16; Isa 60:10

Justice and Mercy, Not Fasting

7 In the fourth year of King Darius, the word of the Lord came to Zechariah on the fourth day of the ninth month, the month of Kislev. ²The people of Bethel had sent Sharezer and Regem-Melech, together with their men, to entreat the Lord ³by asking the priests of the house of the Lord Almighty and the prophets, "Should I mourn and fast in the fifth month, as I have done for so many years?"   2Ki 25:9; Ezr 5:1

⁴Then the word of the Lord Almighty came to me: ⁵"Ask all

---

*a*5 Or *winds*   *b*6 Or *horses after them*   *c*8 Or *spirit*   *d*14 Syriac; Hebrew *Helem*
*e*14 Or *and the gracious one, the*

the people of the land and the priests, 'When you fasted and mourned in the fifth and seventh months for the past seventy years, was it really for me that you fasted? ⁶And when you were eating and drinking, were you not just feasting for yourselves? ⁷Are these not the words the LORD proclaimed through the earlier prophets when Jerusalem and its surrounding towns were at rest and prosperous, and the Negev and the western foothills were settled?' " Isa 1:11-20; 58:5

⁸And the word of the LORD came again to Zechariah: ⁹"This is what the LORD Almighty says: 'Administer true justice; show mercy and compassion to one another. ¹⁰Do not oppress the widow or the fatherless, the alien or the poor. In your hearts do not think evil of each other.'

¹¹"But they refused to pay attention; stubbornly they turned their backs and stopped up their ears. ¹²They made their hearts as hard as flint and would not listen to the law or to the words that the LORD Almighty had sent by his Spirit through the earlier prophets. So the LORD Almighty was very angry.

¹³" 'When I called, they did not listen; so when they called, I would not listen,' says the LORD Almighty. ¹⁴'I scattered them with a whirlwind among all the nations, where they were strangers. The land was left so desolate behind them that no one could come or go. This is

how they made the pleasant land desolate.' " Dt 4:27; Jer 7:27

The LORD Promises to Bless Jerusalem

8 Again the word of the LORD Almighty came to me. ²This is what the LORD Almighty says: "I am very jealous for Zion; I am burning with jealousy for her."

³This is what the LORD says: "I will return to Zion and dwell in Jerusalem. Then Jerusalem will be called the City of Truth, and the mountain of the LORD Almighty will be called the Holy Mountain." Joel 3:21; Zec 1:16

⁴This is what the LORD Almighty says: "Once again men and women of ripe old age will sit in the streets of Jerusalem, each with cane in hand because of his age. ⁵The city streets will be filled with boys and girls playing there." Isa 65:20

⁶This is what the LORD Almighty says: "It may seem marvelous to the remnant of this people at that time, but will it seem marvelous to me?" declares the LORD Almighty.

⁷This is what the LORD Almighty says: "I will save my people from the countries of the east and the west. ⁸I will bring them back to live in Jerusalem; they will be my people, and I will be faithful and righteous to them as their God." Ps 107:3

⁹This is what the LORD Almighty says: "You who now hear these words spoken by the prophets who were there when

the foundation was laid for the house of the LORD Almighty, let your hands be strong so that the temple may be built. [10]Before that time there were no wages for man or beast. No one could go about his business safely because of his enemy, for I had turned every man against his neighbor. [11]But now I will not deal with the remnant of this people as I did in the past," declares the LORD Almighty. Hag 2:4

[12]"The seed will grow well, the vine will yield its fruit, the ground will produce its crops, and the heavens will drop their dew. I will give all these things as an inheritance to the remnant of this people. [13]As you have been an object of cursing among the nations, O Judah and Israel, so will I save you, and you will be a blessing. Do not be afraid, but let your hands be strong."

[14]This is what the LORD Almighty says: "Just as I had determined to bring disaster upon you and showed no pity when your fathers angered me," says the LORD Almighty, [15]"so now I have determined to do good again to Jerusalem and Judah. Do not be afraid. [16]These are the things you are to do: Speak the truth to each other, and render true and sound judgment in your courts; [17]do not plot evil against your neighbor, and do not love to swear falsely. I hate all this," declares the LORD.

[18]Again the word of the LORD Almighty came to me. [19]This is what the LORD Almighty says: "The fasts of the fourth, fifth, seventh and tenth months will become joyful and glad occasions and happy festivals for Judah. Therefore love truth and peace." 2Ki 25:7; Ps 30:11

[20]This is what the LORD Almighty says: "Many peoples and the inhabitants of many cities will yet come, [21]and the inhabitants of one city will go to another and say, 'Let us go at once to entreat the LORD and seek the LORD Almighty. I myself am going.' [22]And many peoples and powerful nations will come to Jerusalem to seek the LORD Almighty and to entreat him." Ps 86:9; Zec 7:2

[23]This is what the LORD Almighty says: "In those days ten men from all languages and nations will take firm hold of one Jew by the hem of his robe and say, 'Let us go with you, because we have heard that God is with you.'" Ps 102:22; 1Co 14:25

Judgment on Israel's Enemies
An Oracle

9 The word of the LORD is
　　against the land of
　　Hadrach
and will rest upon
　　Damascus—　　Isa 17:1
for the eyes of men and all
　　the tribes of Israel
are on the LORD—[a]
[2]and upon Hamath too, which
　　borders on it,　　Jer 49:23

---

[a]1 Or *Damascus. / For the eye of the LORD is on all mankind, / as well as on the tribes of Israel,*

and upon Tyre and Sidon,
though they are very
skillful. Eze 28:1-19
³Tyre has built herself a
stronghold;
she has heaped up silver
like dust,
and gold like the dirt of the
streets. Job 27:16
⁴But the Lord will take away
her possessions
and destroy her power on
the sea, Isa 23:11
and she will be consumed
by fire. Isa 23:1
⁵Ashkelon will see it and fear;
Gaza will writhe in agony,
and Ekron too, for her hope
will wither.
Gaza will lose her king
and Ashkelon will be
deserted.
⁶Foreigners will occupy
Ashdod,
and I will cut off the pride
of the Philistines. Isa 14:30
⁷I will take the blood from
their mouths,
the forbidden food from
between their teeth.
Those who are left will
belong to our God Job 25:2
and become leaders in
Judah,
and Ekron will be like the
Jebusites. Jer 47:1
⁸But I will defend my house
against marauding forces.
Never again will an
oppressor overrun my
people,

for now I am keeping
watch. Isa 52:1

The Coming of Zion's King

⁹Rejoice greatly, O Daughter
of Zion! Isa 62:11
Shout, Daughter of
Jerusalem! 1Ki 1:39
See, your king^a comes to
you, Ps 24:7
righteous and having
salvation, Isa 9:6-7
gentle and riding on a
donkey, Ge 49:11
on a colt, the foal of a
donkey. Mt 21:5
¹⁰I will take away the chariots
from Ephraim
and the war-horses from
Jerusalem,
and the battle bow will be
broken. Hos 1:7
He will proclaim peace to the
nations. Isa 2:4
His rule will extend from
sea to sea
and from the River^b to the
ends of the earth.^c
¹¹As for you, because of the
blood of my covenant
with you, Ex 24:8
I will free your prisoners
from the waterless pit.
¹²Return to your fortress,
O prisoners of hope;
even now I announce that I
will restore twice as
much to you. Dt 21:17
¹³I will bend Judah as I bend
my bow 2Sa 22:35
and fill it with Ephraim.

ᵃ9 Or King ᵇ10 That is, the Euphrates ᶜ10 Or the end of the land

I will rouse your sons,
O Zion,
against your sons,
O Greece,　　　　　　Joel 3:6
and make you like a
warrior's sword.　　Jer 51:20

The Lord Will Appear

14Then the Lord will appear
over them;　　　　Isa 31:5
his arrow will flash like
lightning.　　　　Ps 18:14
The Sovereign Lord will
sound the trumpet; Lev 25:9
he will march in the storms
of the south,
15 and the Lord Almighty will
shield them.　　　Isa 31:5
They will destroy
and overcome with
slingstones.　　　Zec 14:3
They will drink and roar as
with wine;　　　Zec 10:7
they will be full like a bowl
used for sprinkling[a] the
corners of the altar.
16The Lord their God will save
them on that day　Isa 10:20
as the flock of his people.
They will sparkle in his land
like jewels in a crown. Jer 31:11
17How attractive and beautiful
they will be!
Grain will make the young
men thrive,
and new wine the young
women.

The Lord Will Care
for Judah

10 Ask the Lord for rain in
the springtime;

it is the Lord who makes
the storm clouds.
He gives showers of rain to
men,　　　　　Lev 26:4
and plants of the field to
everyone.　　　Job 14:9
2The idols speak deceit,
diviners see visions that lie;
they tell dreams that are
false,　　　　Jer 23:16
they give comfort in vain.
Therefore the people wander
like sheep
oppressed for lack of a
shepherd.　　　Nu 27:17
3"My anger burns against the
shepherds,
and I will punish the
leaders;　　　Isa 14:9
for the Lord Almighty will
care
for his flock, the house of
Judah,
and make them like a proud
horse in battle.　Eze 34:8-10
4From Judah will come the
cornerstone,　　Ps 118:22
from him the tent peg,
from him the battle bow,
from him every ruler.
5Together they[b] will be like
mighty men
trampling the muddy
streets in battle.　2Sa 22:43
Because the Lord is with
them,
they will fight and
overthrow the
horsemen.　　　Am 2:15

6"I will strengthen the house
of Judah　　　Eze 30:24

---

a15 Or bowl, / like　　b4,5 Or ruler, all of them together. / 5They

and save the house of
    Joseph.
I will restore them
because I have compassion
    on them.   Ps 102:13
They will be as though
    I had not rejected them,
for I am the LORD their
    God
and I will answer them.
7The Ephraimites will become
    like mighty men,
and their hearts will be glad
    as with wine.   Zec 9:15
Their children will see it and
    be joyful;
    their hearts will rejoice in
        the LORD.   1Sa 2:1
8I will signal for them   Isa 5:26
    and gather them in.
Surely I will redeem them;
    they will be as numerous as
        before.   Jer 33:22
9Though I scatter them among
    the peoples,
    yet in distant lands they
        will remember me.
They and their children will
    survive,
    and they will return.
10I will bring them back from
    Egypt
    and gather them from
        Assyria.   Isa 11:11
I will bring them to Gilead
    and Lebanon,   Jer 50:19
    and there will not be room
        enough for them.   Isa 49:19
11They will pass through the
    sea of trouble;
    the surging sea will be
        subdued
    and all the depths of the
        Nile will dry up.   Isa 19:5-7

Assyria's pride will be
    brought down   Zep 2:13
and Egypt's scepter will
    pass away.   Eze 30:13
12I will strengthen them in the
    LORD   Eze 30:24
and in his name they will
    walk,"   Mic 4:5
    declares the LORD.

11 Open your doors,
    O Lebanon,   Eze 31:3
so that fire may devour
    your cedars!   2Ch 36:19
2Wail, O pine tree, for the
    cedar has fallen;
    the stately trees are ruined!
Wail, oaks of Bashan;   Isa 2:13
    the dense forest has been
        cut down!   Isa 10:34
3Listen to the wail of the
    shepherds;
    their rich pastures are
        destroyed!
Listen to the roar of the lions;
    the lush thicket of the
        Jordan is ruined!   Jer 2:15

Two Shepherds

4This is what the LORD my
God says: "Pasture the flock
marked for slaughter. 5Their
buyers slaughter them and go
unpunished. Those who sell
them say, 'Praise the LORD, I am
rich!' Their own shepherds do
not spare them. 6For I will no
longer have pity on the people
of the land," declares the LORD.
"I will hand everyone over to
his neighbor and his king. They
will oppress the land, and I will
not rescue them from their
hands."   Jer 50:7; Zec 14:13

⁷So I pastured the flock marked for slaughter, particularly the oppressed of the flock. Then I took two staffs and called one Favor and the other Union, and I pastured the flock. ⁸In one month I got rid of the three shepherds.　　　　　Jer 25:34

The flock detested me, and I grew weary of them ⁹and said, "I will not be your shepherd. Let the dying die, and the perishing perish. Let those who are left eat one another's flesh."

¹⁰Then I took my staff called Favor and broke it, revoking the covenant I had made with all the nations. ¹¹It was revoked on that day, and so the afflicted of the flock who were watching me knew it was the word of the LORD.　　　Ps 89:39; Jer 14:21

¹²I told them, "If you think it best, give me my pay; but if not, keep it." So they paid me thirty pieces of silver.　　Ge 23:16; Mt 26:15

¹³And the LORD said to me, "Throw it to the potter"—the handsome price at which they priced me! So I took the thirty pieces of silver and threw them into the house of the LORD to the potter.　　Ex 21:32; Ac 1:18-19

¹⁴Then I broke my second staff called Union, breaking the brotherhood between Judah and Israel.

¹⁵Then the LORD said to me, "Take again the equipment of a foolish shepherd. ¹⁶For I am going to raise up a shepherd over the land who will not care for the lost, or seek the young, or heal the injured, or feed the healthy, but will eat the meat of the choice sheep, tearing off their hoofs.　　Jer 23:2; Eze 34:2-4

¹⁷"Woe to the worthless
　　shepherd,　　　　Jer 23:1
who deserts the flock!
May the sword strike his arm
　　and his right eye!
May his arm be completely
　　withered,
his right eye totally
　　blinded!"　　　　Jer 23:1

Jerusalem's Enemies to Be Destroyed

An Oracle

12 This is the word of the LORD concerning Israel. The LORD, who stretches out the heavens, who lays the foundation of the earth, and who forms the spirit of man within him, declares: ²"I am going to make Jerusalem a cup that sends all the surrounding peoples reeling. Judah will be besieged as well as Jerusalem. ³On that day, when all the nations of the earth are gathered against her, I will make Jerusalem an immovable rock for all the nations. All who try to move it will injure themselves. ⁴On that day I will strike every horse with panic and its rider with madness," declares the LORD. "I will keep a watchful eye over the house of Judah, but I will blind all the horses of the nations. ⁵Then the leaders of Judah will say in their hearts, 'The people of Jerusalem are strong, because

the Lord Almighty is their God.'　　Ge 1:8; Eze 30:24; Zec 14:2

⁶"On that day I will make the leaders of Judah like a firepot in a woodpile, like a flaming torch among sheaves. They will consume right and left all the surrounding peoples, but Jerusalem will remain intact in her place.　　Isa 10:17-18; Ob 18

⁷"The Lord will save the dwellings of Judah first, so that the honor of the house of David and of Jerusalem's inhabitants may not be greater than that of Judah. ⁸On that day the Lord will shield those who live in Jerusalem, so that the feeblest among them will be like David, and the house of David will be like God, like the Angel of the Lord going before them. ⁹On that day I will set out to destroy all the nations that attack Jerusalem.　　Isa 29:7; Jer 30:18

Mourning for the One They Pierced

¹⁰"And I will pour out on the house of David and the inhabitants of Jerusalem a spirit*a* of grace and supplication. They will look on*b* me, the one they have pierced, and they will mourn for him as one mourns for an only child, and grieve bitterly for him as one grieves for a firstborn son. ¹¹On that day the weeping in Jerusalem will be great, like the weeping of Hadad Rimmon in the plain of

Megiddo. ¹²The land will mourn, each clan by itself, with their wives by themselves: the clan of the house of David and their wives, the clan of the house of Nathan and their wives, ¹³the clan of the house of Levi and their wives, the clan of Shimei and their wives, ¹⁴and all the rest of the clans and their wives.　　Eze 37:9; Mt 24:30

Cleansing From Sin

13 "On that day a fountain will be opened to the house of David and the inhabitants of Jerusalem, to cleanse them from sin and impurity.

²"On that day, I will banish the names of the idols from the land, and they will be remembered no more," declares the Lord Almighty. "I will remove both the prophets and the spirit of impurity from the land. ³And if anyone still prophesies, his father and mother, to whom he was born, will say to him, 'You must die, because you have told lies in the Lord's name.' When he prophesies, his own parents will stab him.　　Dt 13:6-11; Jer 43:12

⁴"On that day every prophet will be ashamed of his prophetic vision. He will not put on a prophet's garment of hair in order to deceive. ⁵He will say, 'I am not a prophet. I am a farmer; the land has been my livelihood since my youth.'*c* ⁶If someone asks him, 'What are these

---

*a*10 Or *the Spirit*　　*b*10 Or *to*　　*c*5 Or *farmer; a man sold me in my youth*

wounds on your body*ᵃ*?' he will answer, 'The wounds I was given at the house of my friends.'

The Shepherd Struck, the Sheep Scattered

⁷"Awake, O sword, against my shepherd,   Isa 40:11
against the man who is close to me!"
declares the Lord Almighty.
"Strike the shepherd,
and the sheep will be scattered,   2Sa 17:2
and I will turn my hand against the little ones.
⁸In the whole land," declares the Lord,
"two-thirds will be struck down and perish;
yet one-third will be left in it.   Eze 5:2-4,12
⁹This third I will bring into the fire;   Isa 4:4
I will refine them like silver and test them like gold.
They will call on my name and I will answer them;
I will say, 'They are my people,'   Lev 26:12
and they will say, 'The Lord is our God.'"   Isa 44:5

The Lord Comes and Reigns

14 A day of the Lord is coming when your plunder will be divided among you.

²I will gather all the nations to Jerusalem to fight against it; the city will be captured, the houses ransacked, and the women raped. Half of the city will go into exile, but the rest of the people will not be taken from the city.   Isa 2:3; Zec 12:3

³Then the Lord will go out and fight against those nations, as he fights in the day of battle. ⁴On that day his feet will stand on the Mount of Olives, east of Jerusalem, and the Mount of Olives will be split in two from east to west, forming a great valley, with half of the mountain moving north and half moving south. ⁵You will flee by my mountain valley, for it will extend to Azel. You will flee as you fled from the earthquake*ᵇ* in the days of Uzziah king of Judah. Then the Lord my God will come, and all the holy ones with him.   Am 1:1; Zec 9:14-15

⁶On that day there will be no light, no cold or frost. ⁷It will be a unique day, without daytime or nighttime—a day known to the Lord. When evening comes, there will be light. Isa 13:10

⁸On that day living water will flow out from Jerusalem, half to the eastern sea*ᶜ* and half to the western sea,*ᵈ* in summer and in winter.   Eze 47:1-12; Jn 7:38

⁹The Lord will be king over the whole earth. On that day there will be one Lord, and his name the only name.   Ps 22:28

¹⁰The whole land, from Geba to Rimmon, south of Jerusalem,

ᵃ6 Or *wounds between your hands*   *ᵇ5* Or *⁵My mountain valley will be blocked and will extend to Azel. It will be blocked as it was blocked because of the earthquake*   *ᶜ8* That is, the Dead Sea   *ᵈ8* That is, the Mediterranean

will become like the Arabah. But Jerusalem will be raised up and remain in its place, from the Benjamin Gate to the site of the First Gate, to the Corner Gate, and from the Tower of Hananel to the royal winepresses. ¹¹It will be inhabited; never again will it be destroyed. Jerusalem will be secure. 1Ki 15:22

¹²This is the plague with which the LORD will strike all the nations that fought against Jerusalem: Their flesh will rot while they are still standing on their feet, their eyes will rot in their sockets, and their tongues will rot in their mouths. ¹³On that day men will be stricken by the LORD with great panic. Each man will seize the hand of another, and they will attack each other. ¹⁴Judah too will fight at Jerusalem. The wealth of all the surrounding nations will be collected—great quantities of gold and silver and clothing. ¹⁵A similar plague will strike the horses and mules, the camels and donkeys, and all the animals in those camps. Isa 11:4

¹⁶Then the survivors from all the nations that have attacked Jerusalem will go up year after year to worship the King, the LORD Almighty, and to celebrate the Feast of Tabernacles. ¹⁷If any of the peoples of the earth do not go up to Jerusalem to worship the King, the LORD Almighty, they will have no rain. ¹⁸If the Egyptian people do not go up and take part, they will have no rain. The LORD^a will bring on them the plague he inflicts on the nations that do not go up to celebrate the Feast of Tabernacles. ¹⁹This will be the punishment of Egypt and the punishment of all the nations that do not go up to celebrate the Feast of Tabernacles. 2Ki 19:31

²⁰On that day HOLY TO THE LORD will be inscribed on the bells of the horses, and the cooking pots in the LORD's house will be like the sacred bowls in front of the altar. ²¹Every pot in Jerusalem and Judah will be holy to the LORD Almighty, and all who come to sacrifice will take some of the pots and cook in them. And on that day there will no longer be a Canaanite^b in the house of the LORD Almighty. Ex 39:30; Ne 8:10

^a18 Or part, then the LORD   ^b21 Or merchant

Malachi

Introduction:

This book records the messages of the prophet, Malachi, who lived during the second half of the fifth century B.C., after the temple had been rebuilt. The Jews' religious life was not in good condition—they had married foreign women, failed to give God what they should have, and even left God.

Malachi's chief concern was that the Israelites' relationship to God was not as it should be. They had forgotten God and treated him with dishonor. They failed to do what God required of them. Because of this, there would be judgment, but the God-fearing people did not need to worry because they were in God's book and would enjoy God's salvation forever.

Outline of contents:

1 An oracle: The word of the LORD to Israel through Malachi.ᵃ   Na 1:1; Ac 7:38

Jacob Loved, Esau Hated

2"I have loved you," says the LORD.   Dt 4:37

"But you ask, 'How have you loved us?'   Mal 2:14

"Was not Esau Jacob's brother?" the LORD says. "Yet I have loved Jacob, 3but Esau I have hated, and I have turned his mountains into a wasteland and left his inheritance to the desert jackals."   Isa 34:10; Lk 14:26

4Edom may say, "Though we have been crushed, we will rebuild the ruins."   Isa 9:10; 11:14

But this is what the LORD Almighty says: "They may build, but I will demolish. They will be called the Wicked Land, a people always under the wrath of the LORD. 5You will see it with your own eyes and say, 'Great is the LORD—even beyond the borders of Israel!'

Blemished Sacrifices

6"A son honors his father, and a servant his master. If I am a father, where is the honor due me? If I am a master, where is

---

ᵃ1 *Malachi* means *my messenger.*

the respect due me?" says the LORD Almighty. "It is you, O priests, who show contempt for my name.   _{Lev 20:9; Lk 6:46}

"But you ask, 'How have we shown contempt for your name?'

7"You place defiled food on my altar.   _{Lev 21:6}

"But you ask, 'How have we defiled you?'

"By saying that the LORD's table is contemptible. 8When you bring blind animals for sacrifice, is that not wrong? When you sacrifice crippled or diseased animals, is that not wrong? Try offering them to your governor! Would he be pleased with you? Would he accept you?" says the LORD Almighty.   _{Lev 1:3}

9"Now implore God to be gracious to us. With such offerings from your hands, will he accept you?"—says the LORD Almighty.   _{Lev 23:33-44; Ps 51:17}

10"Oh, that one of you would shut the temple doors, so that you would not light useless fires on my altar! I am not pleased with you," says the LORD Almighty, "and I will accept no offering from your hands. 11My name will be great among the nations, from the rising to the setting of the sun. In every place incense and pure offerings will be brought to my name, because my name will be great among the nations," says the LORD Almighty.   _{2Ch 28:24}

12"But you profane it by say-

ing of the Lord's table, 'It is defiled,' and of its food, 'It is contemptible.' 13And you say, 'What a burden!' and you sniff at it contemptuously," says the LORD Almighty.   _{Eze 41:22}

"When you bring injured, crippled or diseased animals and offer them as sacrifices, should I accept them from your hands?" says the LORD. 14"Cursed is the cheat who has an acceptable male in his flock and vows to give it, but then sacrifices a blemished animal to the Lord. For I am a great king," says the LORD Almighty, "and my name is to be feared among the nations.   _{Ex 12:5; Ps 95:3}

Admonition for the Priests

2 "And now this admonition is for you, O priests. 2If you do not listen, and if you do not set your heart to honor my name," says the LORD Almighty, "I will send a curse upon you, and I will curse your blessings. Yes, I have already cursed them, because you have not set your heart to honor me.

3"Because of you I will rebuke^a your descendants^b; I will spread on your faces the offal from your festival sacrifices, and you will be carried off with it. 4And you will know that I have sent you this admonition so that my covenant with Levi may continue," says the LORD Almighty. 5"My covenant was with him, a covenant of life and

---

_{a3 Or cut off (see Septuagint)   b3 Or will blight your grain}

peace, and I gave them to him; this called for reverence and he revered me and stood in awe of my name. ⁶True instruction was in his mouth and nothing false was found on his lips. He walked with me in peace and uprightness, and turned many from sin.   Ex 29:14; Dt 33:10

⁷"For the lips of a priest ought to preserve knowledge, and from his mouth men should seek instruction—because he is the messenger of the LORD Almighty. ⁸But you have turned from the way and by your teaching have caused many to stumble; you have violated the covenant with Levi," says the LORD Almighty. ⁹"So I have caused you to be despised and humiliated before all the people, because you have not followed my ways but have shown partiality in matters of the law."   1Sa 2:30; Jer 18:18

Judah Unfaithful

¹⁰Have we not all one Father*a*? Did not one God create us? Why do we profane the covenant of our fathers by breaking faith with one another?   Ex 4:22

¹¹Judah has broken faith. A detestable thing has been committed in Israel and in Jerusalem: Judah has desecrated the sanctuary the LORD loves, by marrying the daughter of a foreign god. ¹²As for the man who does this, whoever he may be, may the LORD cut him off from the tents of Jacob*b*—even though he brings offerings to the LORD Almighty.   Isa 1:13

¹³Another thing you do: You flood the LORD's altar with tears. You weep and wail because he no longer pays attention to your offerings or accepts them with pleasure from your hands. ¹⁴You ask, "Why?" It is because the LORD is acting as the witness between you and the wife of your youth, because you have broken faith with her, though she is your partner, the wife of your marriage covenant.

¹⁵Has not ˻the LORD˼ made them one? In flesh and spirit they are his. And why one? Because he was seeking godly offspring.*c* So guard yourself in your spirit, and do not break faith with the wife of your youth.   Ge 2:24; Mt 19:4-6

¹⁶"I hate divorce," says the LORD God of Israel, "and I hate a man's covering himself*d* with violence as well as with his garment," says the LORD Almighty.   Dt 24:1; Mt 5:31-32

So guard yourself in your spirit, and do not break faith.

The Day of Judgment

¹⁷You have wearied the LORD with your words.   Isa 1:14

"How have we wearied him?" you ask.   Mal 1:2

---

*a*10 Or *father*   *b*12 Or *¹²May the LORD cut off from the tents of Jacob anyone who gives testimony in behalf of the man who does this*   *c*15 Or *¹⁵But the one ˻who is our father˼ did not do this, not as long as life remained in him. And what was he seeking? An offspring from God*   *d*16 Or *his wife*

By saying, "All who do evil are good in the eyes of the LORD, and he is pleased with them" or "Where is the God of justice?"   Ge 18:25

3 "See, I will send my messenger, who will prepare the way before me. Then suddenly the Lord you are seeking will come to his temple; the messenger of the covenant, whom you desire, will come," says the LORD Almighty.   Nu 27:21

2But who can endure the day of his coming? Who can stand when he appears? For he will be like a refiner's fire or a launderer's soap. 3He will sit as a refiner and purifier of silver; he will purify the Levites and refine them like gold and silver. Then the LORD will have men who will bring offerings in righteousness, 4and the offerings of Judah and Jerusalem will be acceptable to the LORD, as in days gone by, as in former years.

5"So I will come near to you for judgment. I will be quick to testify against sorcerers, adulterers and perjurers, against those who defraud laborers of their wages, who oppress the widows and the fatherless, and deprive aliens of justice, but do not fear me," says the LORD Almighty.   Ex 7:11; Isa 47:9

Robbing God

6"I the LORD do not change. So you, O descendants of Jacob, are not destroyed. 7Ever since the time of your forefathers you have turned away from my decrees and have not kept them. Return to me, and I will return to you," says the LORD Almighty.   Nu 23:19; Isa 44:22

"But you ask, 'How are we to return?'   Mal 1:2

8"Will a man rob God? Yet you rob me.   Zec 5:3

"But you ask, 'How do we rob you?'

"In tithes and offerings. 9You are under a curse—the whole nation of you—because you are robbing me. 10Bring the whole tithe into the storehouse, that there may be food in my house. Test me in this," says the LORD Almighty, "and see if I will not throw open the floodgates of heaven and pour out so much blessing that you will not have room enough for it. 11I will prevent pests from devouring your crops, and the vines in your fields will not cast their fruit," says the LORD Almighty. 12"Then all the nations will call you blessed, for yours will be a delightful land," says the LORD Almighty.   Ex 22:29; Isa 61:9

13"You have said harsh things against me," says the LORD.

"Yet you ask, 'What have we said against you?'   Mal 1:2

14"You have said, 'It is futile to serve God. What did we gain by carrying out his requirements and going about like mourners before the LORD Almighty? 15But now we call the arrogant blessed. Certainly the evildoers prosper, and even those who challenge God escape.'"   Ps 119:21

¹⁶Then those who feared the LORD talked with each other, and the LORD listened and heard. A scroll of remembrance was written in his presence concerning those who feared the LORD and honored his name.

¹⁷"They will be mine," says the LORD Almighty, "in the day when I make up my treasured possession.ᵃ I will spare them, just as in compassion a man spares his son who serves him. ¹⁸And you will again see the distinction between the righteous and the wicked, between those who serve God and those who do not.   Ge 18:25; Isa 43:21

The Day of the LORD

4 "Surely the day is coming; it will burn like a furnace. All the arrogant and every evildoer will be stubble, and that day that is coming will set them on fire," says the LORD Almighty. "Not a root or a branch will be left to them. ²But for you who revere my name, the sun of righteousness will rise with healing in its wings. And you will go out and leap like calves released from the stall. ³Then you will trample down the wicked; they will be ashes under the soles of your feet on the day when I do these things," says the LORD Almighty.   Da 7:13

⁴"Remember the law of my servant Moses, the decrees and laws I gave him at Horeb for all Israel.   Dt 28:61; Ps 147:19

⁵"See, I will send you the prophet Elijah before that great and dreadful day of the LORD comes. ⁶He will turn the hearts of the fathers to their children, and the hearts of the children to their fathers; or else I will come and strike the land with a curse."   1Ki 17:1; Lk 1:17

ᵃ17 Or *Almighty, "my treasured possession, in the day when I act*

The
New Testament

Matthew

Introduction:

The book of Matthew tells of the good news that the long-awaited Messiah had come to save people—both Jews and Gentiles. Matthew, one of the twelve disciples, is believed to be the author of this book. It was probably written sometime before the Romans destroyed the temple in Jerusalem in A.D. 70.

Although Mark and Luke also wrote about Jesus' life, Matthew's Gospel has some special things that are different from the others. Matthew uses much of the Gospel to show that Jesus is the promised Messiah of the Old Testament. Matthew quotes the Old Testament often and uses the phrase "kingdom of heaven" from the Old Testament frequently. Because of this many people think he was writing his Gospel to Jewish people.

Matthew also presents Christ as the great teacher who helps us understand God's law and tells the people about the kingdom of God and what it is. Most of Christ's teachings are found in the following five places:

1. The Sermon on the Mount (5:1–7:27)
2. Instruction to the disciples (10:5–42)
3. Teaching through parables (13:3–52)
4. The meaning of discipleship (18:1–35)
5. Teachings about the end of time and the coming of the kingdom of heaven (24:4–25:46)

Outline of contents:

The Genealogy of Jesus

1 A record of the genealogy of Jesus Christ the son of David, the son of Abraham: Ge 22:18

²Abraham was the father of Isaac,   Ge 21:3,12
Isaac the father of Jacob,
Jacob the father of Judah and his brothers,   Ge 29:35
³Judah the father of Perez and Zerah, whose mother was Tamar,
Perez the father of Hezron,
Hezron the father of Ram,
⁴Ram the father of Amminadab,
Amminadab the father of Nahshon,
Nahshon the father of Salmon,
⁵Salmon the father of Boaz, whose mother was Rahab,   Heb 11:31
Boaz the father of Obed, whose mother was Ruth,
Obed the father of Jesse,
⁶and Jesse the father of King David.   1Sa 16:1

David was the father of Solomon, whose mother had been Uriah's wife,
⁷Solomon the father of Rehoboam,
Rehoboam the father of Abijah,
Abijah the father of Asa,
⁸Asa the father of Jehoshaphat,
Jehoshaphat the father of Jehoram,
Jehoram the father of Uzziah,
⁹Uzziah the father of Jotham,
Jotham the father of Ahaz,
Ahaz the father of Hezekiah,
¹⁰Hezekiah the father of Manasseh,   2Ki 20:21
Manasseh the father of Amon,
Amon the father of Josiah,
¹¹and Josiah the father of Jeconiah*a* and his brothers at the time of the exile to Babylon.   2Ki 24:14-16

¹²After the exile to Babylon:
Jeconiah was the father of Shealtiel,   1Ch 3:17
Shealtiel the father of Zerubbabel,
¹³Zerubbabel the father of Abiud,
Abiud the father of Eliakim,
Eliakim the father of Azor,
¹⁴Azor the father of Zadok,
Zadok the father of Akim,
Akim the father of Eliud,
¹⁵Eliud the father of Eleazar,
Eleazar the father of Matthan,
Matthan the father of Jacob,
¹⁶and Jacob the father of Joseph, the husband of Mary, of whom was born Jesus, who is called Christ.   Mt 27:17; Lk 1:27

a11 That is, Jehoiachin; also in verse 12

¹⁷Thus there were fourteen generations in all from Abraham to David, fourteen from David to the exile to Babylon, and fourteen from the exile to the Christ. *a*

The Birth of Jesus Christ

¹⁸This is how the birth of Jesus Christ came about: His mother Mary was pledged to be married to Joseph, but before they came together, she was found to be with child through the Holy Spirit. ¹⁹Because Joseph her husband was a righteous man and did not want to expose her to public disgrace, he had in mind to divorce her quietly.   Dt 24:1; Lk 1:35

²⁰But after he had considered this, an angel of the Lord appeared to him in a dream and said, "Joseph son of David, do not be afraid to take Mary home as your wife, because what is conceived in her is from the Holy Spirit. ²¹She will give birth to a son, and you are to give him the name Jesus,*b* because he will save his people from their sins."   Ps 130:8; Lk 1:31

²²All this took place to fulfill what the Lord had said through the prophet: ²³"The virgin will be with child and will give birth to a son, and they will call him Immanuel"*c*—which means, "God with us."   Is 8:8,10

²⁴When Joseph woke up, he did what the angel of the Lord had commanded him and took Mary home as his wife. ²⁵But he had no union with her until she gave birth to a son. And he gave him the name Jesus.   Lk 1:26-35

The Visit of the Magi

2 After Jesus was born in Bethlehem in Judea, during the time of King Herod, Magi*d* from the east came to Jerusalem ²and asked, "Where is the one who has been born king of the Jews? We saw his star in the east*e* and have come to worship him."

³When King Herod heard this he was disturbed, and all Jerusalem with him. ⁴When he had called together all the people's chief priests and teachers of the law, he asked them where the Christ*f* was to be born. ⁵"In Bethlehem in Judea," they replied, "for this is what the prophet has written:

⁶" 'But you, Bethlehem, in the
    land of Judah,
  are by no means least
    among the rulers of
      Judah;
 for out of you will come a
    ruler
  who will be the shepherd of
    my people Israel.'*g*"   Jn 7:42

⁷Then Herod called the Magi secretly and found out from them the exact time the star had appeared. ⁸He sent them to

---

*a17 Or *Messiah*. "The Christ" (Greek) and "the Messiah" (Hebrew) both mean "the Anointed One."   *b21 *Jesus* is the Greek form of *Joshua*, which means *the LORD saves*.
*c23 Isaiah 7:14   *d1 Traditionally *Wise Men*   *e2 Or *star when it rose*   *f4 Or *Messiah   *g6 Micah 5:2

Bethlehem and said, "Go and make a careful search for the child. As soon as you find him, report to me, so that I too may go and worship him."

⁹After they had heard the king, they went on their way, and the star they had seen in the east*ᵃ* went ahead of them until it stopped over the place where the child was. ¹⁰When they saw the star, they were overjoyed. ¹¹On coming to the house, they saw the child with his mother Mary, and they bowed down and worshiped him. Then they opened their treasures and presented him with gifts of gold and of incense and of myrrh. ¹²And having been warned in a dream not to go back to Herod, they returned to their country by another route.   Ps 72:10

The Escape to Egypt

¹³When they had gone, an angel of the Lord appeared to Joseph in a dream. "Get up," he said, "take the child and his mother and escape to Egypt. Stay there until I tell you, for Herod is going to search for the child to kill him."   Rev 12:4

¹⁴So he got up, took the child and his mother during the night and left for Egypt, ¹⁵where he stayed until the death of Herod. And so was fulfilled what the Lord had said through the prophet: "Out of Egypt I called my son."*ᵇ*

¹⁶When Herod realized that he had been outwitted by the Magi, he was furious, and he gave orders to kill all the boys in Bethlehem and its vicinity who were two years old and under, in accordance with the time he had learned from the Magi. ¹⁷Then what was said through the prophet Jeremiah was fulfilled:

¹⁸"A voice is heard in Ramah,
　　weeping and great
　　　mourning,
　Rachel weeping for her
　　children
　and refusing to be
　　comforted,
because they are no more."*ᶜ*

The Return to Nazareth

¹⁹After Herod died, an angel of the Lord appeared in a dream to Joseph in Egypt ²⁰and said, "Get up, take the child and his mother and go to the land of Israel, for those who were trying to take the child's life are dead."

²¹So he got up, took the child and his mother and went to the land of Israel. ²²But when he heard that Archelaus was reigning in Judea in place of his father Herod, he was afraid to go there. Having been warned in a dream, he withdrew to the district of Galilee, ²³and he went and lived in a town called Nazareth. So was fulfilled what was said through the prophets: "He will be called a Nazarene." Lk 2:39

ᵃ9 Or *seen when it rose*   *ᵇ15* Hosea 11:1   *ᶜ18* Jer. 31:15

John the Baptist Prepares the Way

3 In those days John the Baptist came, preaching in the Desert of Judea ²and saying, "Repent, for the kingdom of heaven is near." ³This is he who was spoken of through the prophet Isaiah: Lk 1:13

> "A voice of one calling in the desert,
> 'Prepare the way for the Lord,
> make straight paths for him.' "ᵃ   Jn 1:23

⁴John's clothes were made of camel's hair, and he had a leather belt around his waist. His food was locusts and wild honey. ⁵People went out to him from Jerusalem and all Judea and the whole region of the Jordan. ⁶Confessing their sins, they were baptized by him in the Jordan River.   2Ki 1:8

⁷But when he saw many of the Pharisees and Sadducees coming to where he was baptizing, he said to them: "You brood of vipers! Who warned you to flee from the coming wrath? ⁸Produce fruit in keeping with repentance. ⁹And do not think you can say to yourselves, 'We have Abraham as our father.' I tell you that out of these stones God can raise up children for Abraham. ¹⁰The ax is already at the root of the trees, and every tree that does not produce good fruit will be cut down and thrown into the fire.   Mt 12:33-34; Jn 15:2,6

¹¹"I baptize you withᵇ water for repentance. But after me will come one who is more powerful than I, whose sandals I am not fit to carry. He will baptize you with the Holy Spirit and with fire. ¹²His winnowing fork is in his hand, and he will clear his threshing floor, gathering his wheat into the barn and burning up the chaff with unquenchable fire."   Mt 13:30; Mk 1:4ff

The Baptism of Jesus

¹³Then Jesus came from Galilee to the Jordan to be baptized by John. ¹⁴But John tried to deter him, saying, "I need to be baptized by you, and do you come to me?"   Mt 3:1

¹⁵Jesus replied, "Let it be so now; it is proper for us to do this to fulfill all righteousness." Then John consented

¹⁶As soon as Jesus was baptized, he went up out of the water. At that moment heaven was opened, and he saw the Spirit of God descending like a dove and lighting on him. ¹⁷And a voice from heaven said, "This is my Son, whom I love; with him I am well pleased."

The Temptation of Jesus

4 Then Jesus was led by the Spirit into the desert to be tempted by the devil. ²After fasting forty days and forty nights, he was hungry. ³The

ᵃ3 Isaiah 40:3   ᵇ11 Or in

tempter came to him and said, "If you are the Son of God, tell these stones to become bread."

[4]Jesus answered, "It is written: 'Man does not live on bread alone, but on every word that comes from the mouth of God.'[a]"   Jn 4:34

[5]Then the devil took him to the holy city and had him stand on the highest point of the temple. [6]"If you are the Son of God," he said, "throw yourself down. For it is written:

" 'He will command his
      angels concerning you,
   and they will lift you up in
      their hands,
   so that you will not strike
      your foot against a
      stone.'[b]"

[7]Jesus answered him, "It is also written: 'Do not put the Lord your God to the test.'[c]"

[8]Again, the devil took him to a very high mountain and showed him all the kingdoms of the world and their splendor. [9]"All this I will give you," he said, "if you will bow down and worship me."

[10]Jesus said to him, "Away from me, Satan! For it is written: 'Worship the Lord your God, and serve him only.'[d]"

[11]Then the devil left him, and angels came and attended him.

Jesus Begins to Preach

[12]When Jesus heard that John had been put in prison, he returned to Galilee. [13]Leaving Nazareth, he went and lived in Capernaum, which was by the lake in the area of Zebulun and Naphtali— [14]to fulfill what was said through the prophet Isaiah:

[15]"Land of Zebulun and land
      of Naphtali,
   the way to the sea, along
      the Jordan,
   Galilee of the Gentiles—
[16]the people living in darkness
      have seen a great light;
   on those living in the land of
      the shadow of death
   a light has dawned."[e] Lk 2:32

[17]From that time on Jesus began to preach, "Repent, for the kingdom of heaven is near."

The Calling of the First Disciples

[18]As Jesus was walking beside the Sea of Galilee, he saw two brothers, Simon called Peter and his brother Andrew. They were casting a net into the lake, for they were fishermen. [19]"Come, follow me," Jesus said, "and I will make you fishers of men." [20]At once they left their nets and followed him.

[21]Going on from there, he saw two other brothers, James son of Zebedee and his brother John. They were in a boat with their father Zebedee, preparing their nets. Jesus called them, [22]and immediately they left the

---

[a]4 Deut. 8:3   [b]6 Psalm 91:11,12   [c]7 Deut. 6:16   [d]10 Deut. 6:13
[e]16 Isaiah 9:1,2

boat and their father and followed him.   Mk 10:28; Jn 1:35ff

Jesus Heals the Sick

23Jesus went throughout Galilee, teaching in their synagogues, preaching the good news of the kingdom, and healing every disease and sickness among the people. 24News about him spread all over Syria, and people brought to him all who were ill with various diseases, those suffering severe pain, the demon-possessed, those having seizures, and the paralyzed, and he healed them. 25Large crowds from Galilee, the Decapolis,*a* Jerusalem, Judea and the region across the Jordan followed him.   Mk 1:39; Lk 6:17-19

The Beatitudes

5 Now when he saw the crowds, he went up on a mountainside and sat down. His disciples came to him, 2and he began to teach them, saying:

3"Blessed are the poor in
    spirit,
  for theirs is the kingdom of
    heaven.   Mt 25:34
4Blessed are those who
    mourn,
  for they will be comforted.
5Blessed are the meek,
  for they will inherit the
    earth.   Ps 37:11
6Blessed are those who
    hunger and thirst for
    righteousness,
  for they will be filled.   Isa 55:1

7Blessed are the merciful,
  for they will be shown
    mercy.   Jos 2:13
8Blessed are the pure in heart,
  for they will see God.   Ps 17:15
9Blessed are the peacemakers,
  for they will be called sons
    of God.   Ro 8:14
10Blessed are those who are
    persecuted because of
    righteousness,
  for theirs is the kingdom of
    heaven.   1Pe 3:14

11"Blessed are you when people insult you, persecute you and falsely say all kinds of evil against you because of me. 12Rejoice and be glad, because great is your reward in heaven, for in the same way they persecuted the prophets who were before you.   Ps 9:2

Salt and Light

13"You are the salt of the earth. But if the salt loses its saltiness, how can it be made salty again? It is no longer good for anything, except to be thrown out and trampled by men.   Mk 9:50

14"You are the light of the world. A city on a hill cannot be hidden. 15Neither do people light a lamp and put it under a bowl. Instead they put it on its stand, and it gives light to everyone in the house. 16In the same way, let your light shine before men, that they may see your good deeds and praise your Father in heaven.   1Co 10:31

a25 That is, the Ten Cities

The Fulfillment of the Law

17"Do not think that I have come to abolish the Law or the Prophets; I have not come to abolish them but to fulfill them. 18I tell you the truth, until heaven and earth disappear, not the smallest letter, not the least stroke of a pen, will by any means disappear from the Law until everything is accomplished. 19Anyone who breaks one of the least of these commandments and teaches others to do the same will be called least in the kingdom of heaven, but whoever practices and teaches these commands will be called great in the kingdom of heaven. 20For I tell you that unless your righteousness surpasses that of the Pharisees and the teachers of the law, you will certainly not enter the kingdom of heaven.   Isa 26:2; 40:8; Lk 16:17

Murder

21"You have heard that it was said to the people long ago, 'Do not murder,*a* and anyone who murders will be subject to judgment.' 22But I tell you that anyone who is angry with his brother*b* will be subject to judgment. Again, anyone who says to his brother, 'Raca,*c*' is answerable to the Sanhedrin. But anyone who says, 'You fool!' will be in danger of the fire of hell.   Ecc 7:9; Jas 1:19,20

23"Therefore, if you are offer-ing your gift at the altar and there remember that your brother has something against you, 24leave your gift there in front of the altar. First go and be reconciled to your brother; then come and offer your gift. 1Jn 3:15

25"Settle matters quickly with your adversary who is taking you to court. Do it while you are still with him on the way, or he may hand you over to the judge, and the judge may hand you over to the officer, and you may be thrown into prison. 26I tell you the truth, you will not get out until you have paid the last penny.*d*   Lk 12:57-59

Adultery

27"You have heard that it was said, 'Do not commit adultery.'*e* 28But I tell you that anyone who looks at a woman lustfully has already committed adultery with her in his heart. 29If your right eye causes you to sin, gouge it out and throw it away. It is better for you to lose one part of your body than for your whole body to be thrown into hell. 30And if your right hand causes you to sin, cut it off and throw it away. It is better for you to lose one part of your body than for your whole body to go into hell.   Pr 6:25; Mk 9:42-47

Divorce

31"It has been said, 'Anyone who divorces his wife must give

*a*21 Exodus 20:13   *b*22 Some manuscripts *brother without cause*   *c*22 An Aramaic term of contempt   *d*26 Greek *kodrantes*   *e*27 Exodus 20:14

her a certificate of divorce.'ᵃ
³²But I tell you that anyone who
divorces his wife, except for
marital unfaithfulness, causes
her to become an adulteress,
and anyone who marries the divorced woman commits adul-
tery.   Lk 16:18

Oaths

³³"Again, you have heard
that it was said to the people
long ago, 'Do not break your
oath, but keep the oaths you
have made to the Lord.' ³⁴But I
tell you, Do not swear at all:
either by heaven, for it is God's
throne; ³⁵or by the earth, for it is
his footstool; or by Jerusalem,
for it is the city of the Great
King. ³⁶And do not swear by
your head, for you cannot make
even one hair white or black.
³⁷Simply let your 'Yes' be 'Yes,'
and your 'No,' 'No'; anything
beyond this comes from the evil
one.   Lev 19:12; Jas 5:12

An Eye for an Eye

³⁸"You have heard that it was
said, 'Eye for eye, and tooth for
tooth.'ᵇ ³⁹But I tell you, Do not
resist an evil person. If someone
strikes you on the right cheek,
turn to him the other also.
⁴⁰And if someone wants to sue
you and take your tunic, let him
have your cloak as well. ⁴¹If
someone forces you to go one
mile, go with him two miles.
⁴²Give to the one who asks you,

and do not turn away from the
one who wants to borrow from
you.   Ex 21:24; Lk 6:29,30

Love for Enemies

⁴³"You have heard that it was
said, 'Love your neighborᶜ and
hate your enemy.' ⁴⁴But I tell
you: Love your enemiesᵈ and
pray for those who persecute
you, ⁴⁵that you may be sons of
your Father in heaven. He
causes his sun to rise on the evil
and the good, and sends rain on
the righteous and the unrighteous. ⁴⁶If you love those who
love you, what reward will you
get? Are not even the tax collectors doing that? ⁴⁷And if you
greet only your brothers, what
are you doing more than others? Do not even pagans do
that? ⁴⁸Be perfect, therefore, as
your heavenly Father is perfect.

Giving to the Needy

6 "Be careful not to do your
'acts of righteousness' before men, to be seen by them. If
you do, you will have no reward from your Father in
heaven.   Mt 5:16; 23:5

²"So when you give to the
needy, do not announce it with
trumpets, as the hypocrites do
in the synagogues and on the
streets, to be honored by men. I
tell you the truth, they have received their reward in full. ³But
when you give to the needy, do
not let your left hand know

ᵃ31 Deut. 24:1   ᵇ38 Exodus 21:24; Lev. 24:20; Deut. 19:21   ᶜ43 Lev. 19:18
ᵈ44 Some late manuscripts enemies, bless those who curse you, do good to those who hate you

what your right hand is doing, [4]so that your giving may be in secret. Then your Father, who sees what is done in secret, will reward you. Ro 12:8

Prayer

[5]"And when you pray, do not be like the hypocrites, for they love to pray standing in the synagogues and on the street corners to be seen by men. I tell you the truth, they have received their reward in full. [6]But when you pray, go into your room, close the door and pray to your Father, who is unseen. Then your Father, who sees what is done in secret, will reward you. [7]And when you pray, do not keep on babbling like pagans, for they think they will be heard because of their many words. [8]Do not be like them, for your Father knows what you need before you ask him. Ecc 5:2; Mk 11:25

[9]"This, then, is how you should pray:

" 'Our Father in heaven,
    hallowed be your name,
[10]your kingdom come,
    your will be done Mt 26:39
    on earth as it is in heaven.
[11]Give us today our daily
    bread. Pr 30:8
[12]Forgive us our debts,
    as we also have forgiven
        our debtors. Mt 18:21-35
[13]And lead us not into
    temptation, Lk 11:2-4

but deliver us from the evil one.[a]' Jas 1:13

[14]For if you forgive men when they sin against you, your heavenly Father will also forgive you. [15]But if you do not forgive men their sins, your Father will not forgive your sins. Mt 18:35

Fasting

[16]"When you fast, do not look somber as the hypocrites do, for they disfigure their faces to show men they are fasting. I tell you the truth, they have received their reward in full. [17]But when you fast, put oil on your head and wash your face, [18]so that it will not be obvious to men that you are fasting, but only to your Father, who is unseen; and your Father, who sees what is done in secret, will reward you. Isa 58:5-7; Zec 7:5

Treasures in Heaven

[19]"Do not store up for yourselves treasures on earth, where moth and rust destroy, and where thieves break in and steal. [20]But store up for yourselves treasures in heaven, where moth and rust do not destroy, and where thieves do not break in and steal. [21]For where your treasure is, there your heart will be also. Lk 12:16-21

[22]"The eye is the lamp of the body. If your eyes are good, your whole body will be full of light. [23]But if your eyes are bad,

---

[a]13 Or *from evil*; some late manuscripts *one, / for yours is the kingdom and the power and the glory forever. Amen.*

your whole body will be full of darkness. If then the light within you is darkness, how great is that darkness! Lk 11:34-36

24"No one can serve two masters. Either he will hate the one and love the other, or he will be devoted to the one and despise the other. You cannot serve both God and Money. Mt 19:21

Do Not Worry

25"Therefore I tell you, do not worry about your life, what you will eat or drink; or about your body, what you will wear. Is not life more important than food, and the body more important than clothes? 26Look at the birds of the air; they do not sow or reap or store away in barns, and yet your heavenly Father feeds them. Are you not much more valuable than they? 27Who of you by worrying can add a single hour to his life*a*? Lk 10:41

28"And why do you worry about clothes? See how the lilies of the field grow. They do not labor or spin. 29Yet I tell you that not even Solomon in all his splendor was dressed like one of these. 30If that is how God clothes the grass of the field, which is here today and tomorrow is thrown into the fire, will he not much more clothe you, O you of little faith? 31So do not worry, saying, 'What shall we eat?' or 'What shall we drink?' or 'What shall we wear?' 32For the pagans run after all these

things, and your heavenly Father knows that you need them. 33But seek first his kingdom and his righteousness, and all these things will be given to you as well. 34Therefore do not worry about tomorrow, for tomorrow will worry about itself. Each day has enough trouble of its own.

Judging Others

7 "Do not judge, or you too will be judged. 2For in the same way you judge others, you will be judged, and with the measure you use, it will be measured to you. Jas 4:11,12

3"Why do you look at the speck of sawdust in your brother's eye and pay no attention to the plank in your own eye? 4How can you say to your brother, 'Let me take the speck out of your eye,' when all the time there is a plank in your own eye? 5You hypocrite, first take the plank out of your own eye, and then you will see clearly to remove the speck from your brother's eye. Lk 6:41,42

6"Do not give dogs what is sacred; do not throw your pearls to pigs. If you do, they may trample them under their feet, and then turn and tear you to pieces. Pr 9:7-8

Ask, Seek, Knock

7"Ask and it will be given to you; seek and you will find; knock and the door will be opened to you. 8For everyone

---

a27 Or single cubit to his height

who asks receives; he who seeks finds; and to him who knocks, the door will be opened. _{1Ki 3:5; Jas 1:5-8}

9"Which of you, if his son asks for bread, will give him a stone? 10Or if he asks for a fish, will give him a snake? 11If you, then, though you are evil, know how to give good gifts to your children, how much more will your Father in heaven give good gifts to those who ask him! 12So in everything, do to others what you would have them do to you, for this sums up the Law and the Prophets. _{Jas 1:17}

The Narrow and Wide Gates

13"Enter through the narrow gate. For wide is the gate and broad is the road that leads to destruction, and many enter through it. 14But small is the gate and narrow the road that leads to life, and only a few find it. _{Lk 13:24; Jn 10:7,9}

A Tree and Its Fruit

15"Watch out for false prophets. They come to you in sheep's clothing, but inwardly they are ferocious wolves. 16By their fruit you will recognize them. Do people pick grapes from thornbushes, or figs from thistles? 17Likewise every good tree bears good fruit, but a bad tree bears bad fruit. 18A good tree cannot bear bad fruit, and a bad tree cannot bear good fruit. 19Every tree that does not bear good fruit is cut down and thrown into the fire. 20Thus, by their fruit you will recognize them. _{Jer 23:16; Mt 3:10}

21"Not everyone who says to me, 'Lord, Lord,' will enter the kingdom of heaven, but only he who does the will of my Father who is in heaven. 22Many will say to me on that day, 'Lord, Lord, did we not prophesy in your name, and in your name drive out demons and perform many miracles?' 23Then I will tell them plainly, 'I never knew you. Away from me, you evildoers!' _{Ps 6:8; Mt 12:50}

The Wise and Foolish Builders

24"Therefore everyone who hears these words of mine and puts them into practice is like a wise man who built his house on the rock. 25The rain came down, the streams rose, and the winds blew and beat against that house; yet it did not fall, because it had its foundation on the rock. 26But everyone who hears these words of mine and does not put them into practice is like a foolish man who built his house on sand. 27The rain came down, the streams rose, and the winds blew and beat against that house, and it fell with a great crash." _{Lk 6:47-49}

28When Jesus had finished saying these things, the crowds were amazed at his teaching, 29because he taught as one who had authority, and not as their teachers of the law. _{Mk 6:2}

The Man With Leprosy

8 When he came down from the mountainside, large crowds followed him. ²A man with leprosy*ᵃ* came and knelt before him and said, "Lord, if you are willing, you can make me clean." Lev 13:45

³Jesus reached out his hand and touched the man. "I am willing," he said. "Be clean!" Immediately he was cured*ᵇ* of his leprosy. ⁴Then Jesus said to him, "See that you don't tell anyone. But go, show yourself to the priest and offer the gift Moses commanded, as a testimony to them." Lev 14:2-32

The Faith of the Centurion

⁵When Jesus had entered Capernaum, a centurion came to him, asking for help. ⁶"Lord," he said, "my servant lies at home paralyzed and in terrible suffering." Mt 4:24

⁷Jesus said to him, "I will go and heal him."

⁸The centurion replied, "Lord, I do not deserve to have you come under my roof. But just say the word, and my servant will be healed. ⁹For I myself am a man under authority, with soldiers under me. I tell this one, 'Go,' and he goes; and that one, 'Come,' and he comes. I say to my servant, 'Do this,' and he does it." Ps 107:20

¹⁰When Jesus heard this, he was astonished and said to those following him, "I tell you the truth, I have not found anyone in Israel with such great faith. ¹¹I say to you that many will come from the east and the west, and will take their places at the feast with Abraham, Isaac and Jacob in the kingdom of heaven. ¹²But the subjects of the kingdom will be thrown outside, into the darkness, where there will be weeping and gnashing of teeth." Lk 13:28,29

¹³Then Jesus said to the centurion, "Go! It will be done just as you believed it would." And his servant was healed at that very hour. Lk 7:1ff

Jesus Heals Many

¹⁴When Jesus came into Peter's house, he saw Peter's mother-in-law lying in bed with a fever. ¹⁵He touched her hand and the fever left her, and she got up and began to wait on him. Mk 1:29ff; Lk 4:38ff

¹⁶When evening came, many who were demon-possessed were brought to him, and he drove out the spirits with a word and healed all the sick. ¹⁷This was to fulfill what was spoken through the prophet Isaiah: Mt 4:23-24

"He took up our infirmities
    and carried our diseases."*ᶜ*

The Cost of Following Jesus

¹⁸When Jesus saw the crowd around him, he gave orders to

ᵃ2 The Greek word was used for various diseases affecting the skin—not necessarily leprosy.   *ᵇ3* Greek *made clean*   *ᶜ17* Isaiah 53:4

cross to the other side of the lake. ¹⁹Then a teacher of the law came to him and said, "Teacher, I will follow you wherever you go."

²⁰Jesus replied, "Foxes have holes and birds of the air have nests, but the Son of Man has no place to lay his head." Mk 2:10

²¹Another disciple said to him, "Lord, first let me go and bury my father."

²²But Jesus told him, "Follow me, and let the dead bury their own dead." Lk 9:57ff

Jesus Calms the Storm

²³Then he got into the boat and his disciples followed him. ²⁴Without warning, a furious storm came up on the lake, so that the waves swept over the boat. But Jesus was sleeping. ²⁵The disciples went and woke him, saying, "Lord, save us! We're going to drown!"

²⁶He replied, "You of little faith, why are you so afraid?" Then he got up and rebuked the winds and the waves, and it was completely calm. Mt 6:30

²⁷The men were amazed and asked, "What kind of man is this? Even the winds and the waves obey him!" Mk 4:36ff

The Healing of Two Demon-possessed Men

²⁸When he arrived at the other side in the region of the Gadarenes, *a* two demon-possessed men coming from the tombs met him. They were so violent that no one could pass that way. ²⁹"What do you want with us, Son of God?" they shouted. "Have you come here to torture us before the appointed time?"

³⁰Some distance from them a large herd of pigs was feeding. ³¹The demons begged Jesus, "If you drive us out, send us into the herd of pigs."

³²He said to them, "Go!" So they came out and went into the pigs, and the whole herd rushed down the steep bank into the lake and died in the water. ³³Those tending the pigs ran off, went into the town and reported all this, including what had happened to the demon-possessed men. ³⁴Then the whole town went out to meet Jesus. And when they saw him, they pleaded with him to leave their region. Mk 5:1ff; Lk 8:26ff

Jesus Heals a Paralytic

9 Jesus stepped into a boat, crossed over and came to his own town. ²Some men brought to him a paralytic, lying on a mat. When Jesus saw their faith, he said to the paralytic, "Take heart, son; your sins are forgiven." Mt 4:13; Jn 16:33

³At this, some of the teachers of the law said to themselves, "This fellow is blaspheming!"

⁴Knowing their thoughts, Jesus said, "Why do you entertain evil thoughts in your

---

a28 Some manuscripts *Gergesenes*; others *Gerasenes*

hearts? [5]Which is easier: to say, 'Your sins are forgiven,' or to say, 'Get up and walk'? [6]But so that you may know that the Son of Man has authority on earth to forgive sins. . . ." Then he said to the paralytic, "Get up, take your mat and go home." [7]And the man got up and went home. [8]When the crowd saw this, they were filled with awe; and they praised God, who had given such authority to men.   Jn 2:25

The Calling of Matthew

[9]As Jesus went on from there, he saw a man named Matthew sitting at the tax collector's booth. "Follow me," he told him, and Matthew got up and followed him.   Mt 4:19

[10]While Jesus was having dinner at Matthew's house, many tax collectors and "sinners" came and ate with him and his disciples. [11]When the Pharisees saw this, they asked his disciples, "Why does your teacher eat with tax collectors and 'sinners'?"   Lk 15:2; 19:7

[12]On hearing this, Jesus said, "It is not the healthy who need a doctor, but the sick. [13]But go and learn what this means: 'I desire mercy, not sacrifice.'[a] For I have not come to call the righteous, but sinners."   Lk 19:10

Jesus Questioned About Fasting

[14]Then John's disciples came and asked him, "How is it that we and the Pharisees fast, but your disciples do not fast?"

[15]Jesus answered, "How can the guests of the bridegroom mourn while he is with them? The time will come when the bridegroom will be taken from them; then they will fast.

[16]"No one sews a patch of unshrunk cloth on an old garment, for the patch will pull away from the garment, making the tear worse. [17]Neither do men pour new wine into old wineskins. If they do, the skins will burst, the wine will run out and the wineskins will be ruined. No, they pour new wine into new wineskins, and both are preserved."   Lk 5:33ff

A Dead Girl and a Sick Woman

[18]While he was saying this, a ruler came and knelt before him and said, "My daughter has just died. But come and put your hand on her, and she will live." [19]Jesus got up and went with him, and so did his disciples.

[20]Just then a woman who had been subject to bleeding for twelve years came up behind him and touched the edge of his cloak. [21]She said to herself, "If I only touch his cloak, I will be healed."   Mt 14:36; Mk 6:56

[22]Jesus turned and saw her. "Take heart, daughter," he said, "your faith has healed you." And the woman was healed from that moment.

[a]13 Hosea 6:6

²³When Jesus entered the ruler's house and saw the flute players and the noisy crowd, ²⁴he said, "Go away. The girl is not dead but asleep." But they laughed at him. ²⁵After the crowd had been put outside, he went in and took the girl by the hand, and she got up. ²⁶News of this spread through all that region. Mk 5:22ff; Lk 8:41ff

Jesus Heals the Blind and Mute

²⁷As Jesus went on from there, two blind men followed him, calling out, "Have mercy on us, Son of David!" Mt 1:1; Mk 10:47

²⁸When he had gone indoors, the blind men came to him, and he asked them, "Do you believe that I am able to do this?"

"Yes, Lord," they replied.

²⁹Then he touched their eyes and said, "According to your faith will it be done to you"; ³⁰and their sight was restored. Jesus warned them sternly, "See that no one knows about this." ³¹But they went out and spread the news about him all over that region. Mt 8:4; Mk 7:36

³²While they were going out, a man who was demon-possessed and could not talk was brought to Jesus. ³³And when the demon was driven out, the man who had been mute spoke. The crowd was amazed and said, "Nothing like this has ever been seen in Israel." Mk 2:12

³⁴But the Pharisees said, "It is by the prince of demons that he drives out demons." Mt 12:22-24

The Workers Are Few

³⁵Jesus went through all the towns and villages, teaching in their synagogues, preaching the good news of the kingdom and healing every disease and sickness. ³⁶When he saw the crowds, he had compassion on them, because they were harassed and helpless, like sheep without a shepherd. ³⁷Then he said to his disciples, "The harvest is plentiful but the workers are few. ³⁸Ask the Lord of the harvest, therefore, to send out workers into his harvest field." Nu 27:17; Jn 4:35

Jesus Sends Out the Twelve

10 He called his twelve disciples to him and gave them authority to drive out evil*a* spirits and to heal every disease and sickness. Mk 3:13-19

²These are the names of the twelve apostles: first, Simon (who is called Peter) and his brother Andrew; James son of Zebedee, and his brother John; ³Philip and Bartholomew; Thomas and Matthew the tax collector; James son of Alphaeus, and Thaddaeus; ⁴Simon the Zealot and Judas Iscariot, who betrayed him. Mt 26:14-16

⁵These twelve Jesus sent out with the following instructions: "Do not go among the Gentiles or enter any town of the Samari-

*a*1 Greek *unclean*

tans. ⁶Go rather to the lost sheep of Israel. ⁷As you go, preach this message: 'The kingdom of heaven is near.' ⁸Heal the sick, raise the dead, cleanse those who have leprosy,ᵃ drive out demons. Freely you have received, freely give. ⁹Do not take along any gold or silver or copper in your belts; ¹⁰take no bag for the journey, or extra tunic, or sandals or a staff; for the worker is worth his keep. Mt 3:2

¹¹"Whatever town or village you enter, search for some worthy person there and stay at his house until you leave. ¹²As you enter the home, give it your greeting. ¹³If the home is deserving, let your peace rest on it; if it is not, let your peace return to you. ¹⁴If anyone will not welcome you or listen to your words, shake the dust off your feet when you leave that home or town. ¹⁵I tell you the truth, it will be more bearable for Sodom and Gomorrah on the day of judgment than for that town. ¹⁶I am sending you out like sheep among wolves. Therefore be as shrewd as snakes and as innocent as doves. Ge 18:20; Mk 6:8ff

¹⁷"Be on your guard against men; they will hand you over to the local councils and flog you in their synagogues. ¹⁸On my account you will be brought before governors and kings as witnesses to them and to the Gentiles. ¹⁹But when they arrest you, do not worry about what to say or how to say it. At that time you will be given what to say, ²⁰for it will not be you speaking, but the Spirit of your Father speaking through you.

²¹"Brother will betray brother to death, and a father his child; children will rebel against their parents and have them put to death. ²²All men will hate you because of me, but he who stands firm to the end will be saved. ²³When you are persecuted in one place, flee to another. I tell you the truth, you will not finish going through the cities of Israel before the Son of Man comes. Mic 7:6

²⁴"A student is not above his teacher, nor a servant above his master. ²⁵It is enough for the student to be like his teacher, and the servant like his master. If the head of the house has been called Beelzebub,ᵇ how much more the members of his household! Mk 3:22; Jn 13:16

²⁶"So do not be afraid of them. There is nothing concealed that will not be disclosed, or hidden that will not be made known. ²⁷What I tell you in the dark, speak in the daylight; what is whispered in your ear, proclaim from the roofs. ²⁸Do not be afraid of those who kill the body but cannot kill the soul. Rather, be afraid of the One who can destroy both soul and body in hell. ²⁹Are not two

---

ᵃ8 The Greek word was used for various diseases affecting the skin—not necessarily leprosy. ᵇ25 Greek *Beezeboul* or *Beelzeboul*

sparrows sold for a penny[a]? Yet not one of them will fall to the ground apart from the will of your Father. [30]And even the very hairs of your head are all numbered. [31]So don't be afraid; you are worth more than many sparrows.   Mt 6:26; Mk 4:22

[32]"Whoever acknowledges me before men, I will also acknowledge him before my Father in heaven. [33]But whoever disowns me before men, I will disown him before my Father in heaven.   Mk 8:38; Ro 10:9

[34]"Do not suppose that I have come to bring peace to the earth. I did not come to bring peace, but a sword. [35]For I have come to turn

" 'a man against his father,
  a daughter against her
    mother,
a daughter-in-law against her
    mother-in-law—
[36] a man's enemies will be the
    members of his own
    household.'[b]

[37]"Anyone who loves his father or mother more than me is not worthy of me; anyone who loves his son or daughter more than me is not worthy of me; [38]and anyone who does not take his cross and follow me is not worthy of me. [39]Whoever finds his life will lose it, and whoever loses his life for my sake will find it.   Lk 14:26,27; Jn 12:25

[40]"He who receives you re-ceives me, and he who receives me receives the one who sent me. [41]Anyone who receives a prophet because he is a prophet will receive a prophet's reward, and anyone who receives a righteous man because he is a righteous man will receive a righteous man's reward. [42]And if anyone gives even a cup of cold water to one of these little ones because he is my disciple, I tell you the truth, he will certainly not lose his reward."

Jesus and John the Baptist

11 After Jesus had finished instructing his twelve disciples, he went on from there to teach and preach in the towns of Galilee.[c]

[2]When John heard in prison what Christ was doing, he sent his disciples [3]to ask him, "Are you the one who was to come, or should we expect someone else?"   Mt 3:1; Ps 118:26

[4]Jesus replied, "Go back and report to John what you hear and see: [5]The blind receive sight, the lame walk, those who have leprosy[d] are cured, the deaf hear, the dead are raised, and the good news is preached to the poor. [6]Blessed is the man who does not fall away on account of me."   Isa 35:4-6

[7]As John's disciples were leaving, Jesus began to speak to the crowd about John: "What did you go out into the desert to

---

[a]29 Greek *an assarion*   [b]36 Micah 7:6   [c]1 Greek *in their towns*   [d]5 The Greek word was used for various diseases affecting the skin—not necessarily leprosy.

see? A reed swayed by the wind? [8]If not, what did you go out to see? A man dressed in fine clothes? No, those who wear fine clothes are in kings' palaces. [9]Then what did you go out to see? A prophet? Yes, I tell you, and more than a prophet. [10]This is the one about whom it is written: Mt 3:1; 14:5

" 'I will send my messenger
      ahead of you,   Jn 3:28
   who will prepare your way
      before you.'[a]

[11]I tell you the truth: Among those born of women there has not risen anyone greater than John the Baptist; yet he who is least in the kingdom of heaven is greater than he. [12]From the days of John the Baptist until now, the kingdom of heaven has been forcefully advancing, and forceful men lay hold of it. [13]For all the Prophets and the Law prophesied until John. [14]And if you are willing to accept it, he is the Elijah who was to come. [15]He who has ears, let him hear.   Mal 4:5; Lk 16:16

[16]"To what can I compare this generation? They are like children sitting in the marketplaces and calling out to others:

[17]" 'We played the flute for
      you,
   and you did not dance;
   we sang a dirge,
      and you did not mourn.'

[18]For John came neither eating nor drinking, and they say, 'He has a demon.' [19]The Son of Man came eating and drinking, and they say, 'Here is a glutton and a drunkard, a friend of tax collectors and "sinners." ' But wisdom is proved right by her actions."   Mt 3:4; 9:11

Woe on Unrepentant Cities

[20]Then Jesus began to denounce the cities in which most of his miracles had been performed, because they did not repent. [21]"Woe to you, Korazin! Woe to you, Bethsaida! If the miracles that were performed in you had been performed in Tyre and Sidon, they would have repented long ago in sackcloth and ashes. [22]But I tell you, it will be more bearable for Tyre and Sidon on the day of judgment than for you. [23]And you, Capernaum, will you be lifted up to the skies? No, you will go down to the depths.[b] If the miracles that were performed in you had been performed in Sodom, it would have remained to this day. [24]But I tell you that it will be more bearable for Sodom on the day of judgment than for you."

Rest for the Weary

[25]At that time Jesus said, "I praise you, Father, Lord of heaven and earth, because you have hidden these things from the wise and learned, and revealed them to little children.

[a]10 Mal. 3:1   [b]23 Greek *Hades*

26Yes, Father, for this was your good pleasure. Lk 22:42

27"All things have been committed to me by my Father. No one knows the Son except the Father, and no one knows the Father except the Son and those to whom the Son chooses to reveal him. Jn 10:15

28"Come to me, all you who are weary and burdened, and I will give you rest. 29Take my yoke upon you and learn from me, for I am gentle and humble in heart, and you will find rest for your souls. 30For my yoke is easy and my burden is light."

Lord of the Sabbath

12 At that time Jesus went through the grainfields on the Sabbath. His disciples were hungry and began to pick some heads of grain and eat them. 2When the Pharisees saw this, they said to him, "Look! Your disciples are doing what is unlawful on the Sabbath."

3He answered, "Haven't you read what David did when he and his companions were hungry? 4He entered the house of God, and he and his companions ate the consecrated bread—which was not lawful for them to do, but only for the priests. 5Or haven't you read in the Law that on the Sabbath the priests in the temple desecrate the day and yet are innocent? 6I tell you that onea greater than the temple is here. 7If you had

known what these words mean, 'I desire mercy, not sacrifice,'b you would not have condemned the innocent. 8For the Son of Man is Lord of the Sabbath." 1Sa 21:6; Mt 9:13

9Going on from that place, he went into their synagogue, 10and a man with a shriveled hand was there. Looking for a reason to accuse Jesus, they asked him, "Is it lawful to heal on the Sabbath?" Mk 3:2

11He said to them, "If any of you has a sheep and it falls into a pit on the Sabbath, will you not take hold of it and lift it out? 12How much more valuable is a man than a sheep! Therefore it is lawful to do good on the Sabbath." Mt 10:31; Lk 14:5

13Then he said to the man, "Stretch out your hand." So he stretched it out and it was completely restored, just as sound as the other. 14But the Pharisees went out and plotted how they might kill Jesus. Ps 71:10

God's Chosen Servant

15Aware of this, Jesus withdrew from that place. Many followed him, and he healed all their sick, 16warning them not to tell who he was. 17This was to fulfill what was spoken through the prophet Isaiah:

18"Here is my servant whom I
    have chosen,
  the one I love, in whom I
    delight; Mt 3:17

---

a6 Or *something*; also in verses 41 and 42   b7 Hosea 6:6

I will put my Spirit on him,
and he will proclaim justice
to the nations. _Jn 3:34_

19He will not quarrel or cry
out;
no one will hear his voice in
the streets.

20A bruised reed he will not
break,
and a smoldering wick he
will not snuff out,
till he leads justice to victory.

21　In his name the nations will
put their hope."_a_

Jesus and Beelzebub

22Then they brought him a
demon-possessed man who
was blind and mute, and Jesus
healed him, so that he could
both talk and see. 23All the
people were astonished and
said, "Could this be the Son of
David?" _Mt 9:27_

24But when the Pharisees
heard this, they said, "It is only
by Beelzebub,_b_ the prince of demons, that this fellow drives out
demons." _Mt 9:34; Mk 3:22_

25Jesus knew their thoughts
and said to them, "Every kingdom divided against itself will
be ruined, and every city or
household divided against itself
will not stand. 26If Satan drives
out Satan, he is divided against
himself. How then can his kingdom stand? 27And if I drive out
demons by Beelzebub, by
whom do your people drive
them out? So then, they will be
your judges. 28But if I drive out

demons by the Spirit of God,
then the kingdom of God has
come upon you. _Mt 3:2_

29"Or again, how can anyone
enter a strong man's house and
carry off his possessions unless
he first ties up the strong man?
Then he can rob his house.

30"He who is not with me is
against me, and he who does
not gather with me scatters.
31And so I tell you, every sin and
blasphemy will be forgiven
men, but the blasphemy against
the Spirit will not be forgiven.
32Anyone who speaks a word
against the Son of Man will be
forgiven, but anyone who
speaks against the Holy Spirit
will not be forgiven, either
in this age or in the age to
come.

33"Make a tree good and its
fruit will be good, or make a tree
bad and its fruit will be bad, for
a tree is recognized by its fruit.
34You brood of vipers, how can
you who are evil say anything
good? For out of the overflow of
the heart the mouth speaks.
35The good man brings good
things out of the good stored up
in him, and the evil man brings
evil things out of the evil stored
up in him. 36But I tell you that
men will have to give account
on the day of judgment for
every careless word they have
spoken. 37For by your words
you will be acquitted, and by
your words you will be condemned." _Job 15:6; Mt 15:18_

_a21_ Isaiah 42:1-4　　_b24_ Greek _Beezeboul_ or _Beelzeboul_; also in verse 27

The Sign of Jonah

³⁸Then some of the Pharisees and teachers of the law said to him, "Teacher, we want to see a miraculous sign from you."

³⁹He answered, "A wicked and adulterous generation asks for a miraculous sign! But none will be given it except the sign of the prophet Jonah. ⁴⁰For as Jonah was three days and three nights in the belly of a huge fish, so the Son of Man will be three days and three nights in the heart of the earth. ⁴¹The men of Nineveh will stand up at the judgment with this generation and condemn it; for they repented at the preaching of Jonah, and now one^a greater than Jonah is here. ⁴²The Queen of the South will rise at the judgment with this generation and condemn it; for she came from the ends of the earth to listen to Solomon's wisdom, and now one greater than Solomon is here. 1Ki 10:1; Lk 11:29ff

⁴³"When an evil^b spirit comes out of a man, it goes through arid places seeking rest and does not find it. ⁴⁴Then it says, 'I will return to the house I left.' When it arrives, it finds the house unoccupied, swept clean and put in order. ⁴⁵Then it goes and takes with it seven other spirits more wicked than itself, and they go in and live there. And the final condition of that man is worse than the first. That is how it will be with this wicked generation." 2Pe 2:20

Jesus' Mother and Brothers

⁴⁶While Jesus was still talking to the crowd, his mother and brothers stood outside, wanting to speak to him. ⁴⁷Someone told him, "Your mother and brothers are standing outside, wanting to speak to you."^c Mt 13:55

⁴⁸He replied to him, "Who is my mother, and who are my brothers?" ⁴⁹Pointing to his disciples, he said, "Here are my mother and my brothers. ⁵⁰For whoever does the will of my Father in heaven is my brother and sister and mother."

The Parable of the Sower

13 That same day Jesus went out of the house and sat by the lake. ²Such large crowds gathered around him that he got into a boat and sat in it, while all the people stood on the shore. ³Then he told them many things in parables, saying: "A farmer went out to sow his seed. ⁴As he was scattering the seed, some fell along the path, and the birds came and ate it up. ⁵Some fell on rocky places, where it did not have much soil. It sprang up quickly, because the soil was shallow. ⁶But when the sun came up, the plants were scorched, and they withered because they had no root. ⁷Other seed fell among

---

^a41 Or *something*; also in verse 42   ^b43 Greek *unclean*   ^c47 Some manuscripts do not have verse 47.

thorns, which grew up and choked the plants. [8]Still other seed fell on good soil, where it produced a crop—a hundred, sixty or thirty times what was sown. [9]He who has ears, let him hear."

[10]The disciples came to him and asked, "Why do you speak to the people in parables?"

[11]He replied, "The knowledge of the secrets of the kingdom of heaven has been given to you, but not to them. [12]Whoever has will be given more, and he will have an abundance. Whoever does not have, even what he has will be taken from him. [13]This is why I speak to them in parables:　Eze 12:2

"Though seeing, they do not see;
　though hearing, they do not hear or understand.

[14]In them is fulfilled the prophecy of Isaiah:

" 'You will be ever hearing but never understanding;
　you will be ever seeing but never perceiving.
[15]For this people's heart has become calloused;
　they hardly hear with their ears,
　and they have closed their eyes.
Otherwise they might see with their eyes,

hear with their ears,
　understand with their hearts
and turn, and I would heal them.'[a]　Ro 11:8

[16]But blessed are your eyes because they see, and your ears because they hear. [17]For I tell you the truth, many prophets and righteous men longed to see what you see but did not see it, and to hear what you hear but did not hear it.　Heb 11:13

[18]"Listen then to what the parable of the sower means: [19]When anyone hears the message about the kingdom and does not understand it, the evil one comes and snatches away what was sown in his heart. This is the seed sown along the path. [20]The one who received the seed that fell on rocky places is the man who hears the word and at once receives it with joy. [21]But since he has no root, he lasts only a short time. When trouble or persecution comes because of the word, he quickly falls away. [22]The one who received the seed that fell among the thorns is the man who hears the word, but the worries of this life and the deceitfulness of wealth choke it, making it unfruitful. [23]But the one who received the seed that fell on good soil is the man who hears the word and understands it. He produces a crop, yielding a hundred, sixty or thirty times what was sown."　Mk 4:1ff; Lk 8:4ff

[a]15　Isaiah 6:9,10

The Parable of the Weeds

24Jesus told them another parable: "The kingdom of heaven is like a man who sowed good seed in his field. 25But while everyone was sleeping, his enemy came and sowed weeds among the wheat, and went away. 26When the wheat sprouted and formed heads, then the weeds also appeared.

27"The owner's servants came to him and said, 'Sir, didn't you sow good seed in your field? Where then did the weeds come from?'

28" 'An enemy did this,' he replied.

"The servants asked him, 'Do you want us to go and pull them up?'

29" 'No,' he answered, 'because while you are pulling the weeds, you may root up the wheat with them. 30Let both grow together until the harvest. At that time I will tell the harvesters: First collect the weeds and tie them in bundles to be burned; then gather the wheat and bring it into my barn.' "

The Parables of the Mustard Seed and the Yeast

31He told them another parable: "The kingdom of heaven is like a mustard seed, which a man took and planted in his field. 32Though it is the smallest of all your seeds, yet when it grows, it is the largest of garden plants and becomes a tree, so that the birds of the air come and perch in its branches."

33He told them still another parable: "The kingdom of heaven is like yeast that a woman took and mixed into a large amount*a* of flour until it worked all through the dough."

34Jesus spoke all these things to the crowd in parables; he did not say anything to them without using a parable. 35So was fulfilled what was spoken through the prophet: Jn 16:25

"I will open my mouth in
    parables,
I will utter things hidden
    since the creation of the
    world."*b*

The Parable of the Weeds Explained

36Then he left the crowd and went into the house. His disciples came to him and said, "Explain to us the parable of the weeds in the field."   Mt 15:15

37He answered, "The one who sowed the good seed is the Son of Man. 38The field is the world, and the good seed stands for the sons of the kingdom. The weeds are the sons of the evil one, 39and the enemy who sows them is the devil. The harvest is the end of the age, and the harvesters are angels.

40"As the weeds are pulled up and burned in the fire, so it will be at the end of the age. 41The Son of Man will send out his

---

*a*33 Greek *three satas* (probably about 1/2 bushel or 22 liters)   *b*35 Psalm 78:2

angels, and they will weed out of his kingdom everything that causes sin and all who do evil. ⁴²They will throw them into the fiery furnace, where there will be weeping and gnashing of teeth. ⁴³Then the righteous will shine like the sun in the kingdom of their Father. He who has ears, let him hear.   Rev 14:15

The Parables of the Hidden Treasure and the Pearl

⁴⁴"The kingdom of heaven is like treasure hidden in a field. When a man found it, he hid it again, and then in his joy went and sold all he had and bought that field.   Mt 19:21

⁴⁵"Again, the kingdom of heaven is like a merchant looking for fine pearls. ⁴⁶When he found one of great value, he went away and sold everything he had and bought it.   Pr 2:4,5

The Parable of the Net

⁴⁷"Once again, the kingdom of heaven is like a net that was let down into the lake and caught all kinds of fish. ⁴⁸When it was full, the fishermen pulled it up on the shore. Then they sat down and collected the good fish in baskets, but threw the bad away. ⁴⁹This is how it will be at the end of the age. The angels will come and separate the wicked from the righteous ⁵⁰and throw them into the fiery furnace, where there will be weeping and gnashing of teeth.

⁵¹"Have you understood all these things?" Jesus asked.

"Yes," they replied.

⁵²He said to them, "Therefore every teacher of the law who has been instructed about the kingdom of heaven is like the owner of a house who brings out of his storeroom new treasures as well as old."

A Prophet Without Honor

⁵³When Jesus had finished these parables, he moved on from there. ⁵⁴Coming to his hometown, he began teaching the people in their synagogue, and they were amazed. "Where did this man get this wisdom and these miraculous powers?" they asked. ⁵⁵"Isn't this the carpenter's son? Isn't his mother's name Mary, and aren't his brothers James, Joseph, Simon and Judas? ⁵⁶Aren't all his sisters with us? Where then did this man get all these things?" ⁵⁷And they took offense at him.

But Jesus said to them, "Only in his hometown and in his own house is a prophet without honor."   Lk 4:24; Jn 4:44

⁵⁸And he did not do many miracles there because of their lack of faith.   Mk 6:5-6

John the Baptist Beheaded

14 At that time Herod the tetrarch heard the reports about Jesus, ²and he said to his attendants, "This is John the Baptist; he has risen from the dead! That is why miraculous powers are at work in him."

³Now Herod had arrested John and bound him and put him in prison because of Herodias, his brother Philip's wife, ⁴for John had been saying to him: "It is not lawful for you to have her." ⁵Herod wanted to kill John, but he was afraid of the people, because they considered him a prophet.   Mt 11:9

⁶On Herod's birthday the daughter of Herodias danced for them and pleased Herod so much ⁷that he promised with an oath to give her whatever she asked. ⁸Prompted by her mother, she said, "Give me here on a platter the head of John the Baptist." ⁹The king was distressed, but because of his oaths and his dinner guests, he ordered that her request be granted ¹⁰and had John beheaded in the prison. ¹¹His head was brought in on a platter and given to the girl, who carried it to her mother. ¹²John's disciples came and took his body and buried it. Then they went and told Jesus.   Ecc 5:2; Mt 17:12

Jesus Feeds the Five Thousand

¹³When Jesus heard what had happened, he withdrew by boat privately to a solitary place. Hearing of this, the crowds followed him on foot from the towns. ¹⁴When Jesus landed and saw a large crowd, he had compassion on them and healed their sick.   Mt 9:36

¹⁵As evening approached, the disciples came to him and said, "This is a remote place, and it's already getting late. Send the crowds away, so they can go to the villages and buy themselves some food."

¹⁶Jesus replied, "They do not need to go away. You give them something to eat."

¹⁷"We have here only five loaves of bread and two fish," they answered.   Mt 16:9

¹⁸"Bring them here to me," he said. ¹⁹And he directed the people to sit down on the grass. Taking the five loaves and the two fish and looking up to heaven, he gave thanks and broke the loaves. Then he gave them to the disciples, and the disciples gave them to the people. ²⁰They all ate and were satisfied, and the disciples picked up twelve basketfuls of broken pieces that were left over. ²¹The number of those who ate was about five thousand men, besides women and children.   Lk 9:10ff; Jn 6:1ff

Jesus Walks on the Water

²²Immediately Jesus made the disciples get into the boat and go on ahead of him to the other side, while he dismissed the crowd. ²³After he had dismissed them, he went up on a mountainside by himself to pray. When evening came, he was there alone, ²⁴but the boat was already a considerable distance[a]

---

[a]24 Greek *many stadia*

from land, buffeted by the waves because the wind was against it.

25During the fourth watch of the night Jesus went out to them, walking on the lake. 26When the disciples saw him walking on the lake, they were terrified. "It's a ghost," they said, and cried out in fear.

27But Jesus immediately said to them: "Take courage! It is I. Don't be afraid."   Da 10:12

28"Lord, if it's you," Peter replied, "tell me to come to you on the water."

29"Come," he said.

Then Peter got down out of the boat, walked on the water and came toward Jesus. 30But when he saw the wind, he was afraid and, beginning to sink, cried out, "Lord, save me!"

31Immediately Jesus reached out his hand and caught him. "You of little faith," he said, "why did you doubt?"   Mt 6:30

32And when they climbed into the boat, the wind died down. 33Then those who were in the boat worshiped him, saying, "Truly you are the Son of God."   Ps 2:7; Mt 4:3

34When they had crossed over, they landed at Gennesaret. 35And when the men of that place recognized Jesus, they sent word to all the surrounding country. People brought all their sick to him 36and begged him to let the sick just touch the edge of his cloak, and all who touched him were healed.

Clean and Unclean

15 Then some Pharisees and teachers of the law came to Jesus from Jerusalem and asked, 2"Why do your disciples break the tradition of the elders? They don't wash their hands before they eat!"   Lk 11:38

3Jesus replied, "And why do you break the command of God for the sake of your tradition? 4For God said, 'Honor your father and mother'a and 'Anyone who curses his father or mother must be put to death.'b 5But you say that if a man says to his father or mother, 'Whatever help you might otherwise have received from me is a gift devoted to God,' 6he is not to 'honor his fatherc' with it. Thus you nullify the word of God for the sake of your tradition. 7You hypocrites! Isaiah was right when he prophesied about you:

8" 'These people honor me
    with their lips,
  but their hearts are far from
    me.
9They worship me in vain;
  their teachings are but rules
    taught by men.'d"

10Jesus called the crowd to him and said, "Listen and understand. 11What goes into a man's mouth does not make him 'unclean,' but what comes

---

a4 Exodus 20:12; Deut. 5:16   b4 Exodus 21:17; Lev. 20:9   c6 Some manuscripts
father or his mother   d9 Isaiah 29:13

out of his mouth, that is what makes him 'unclean.' " Ac 10:14

¹²Then the disciples came to him and asked, "Do you know that the Pharisees were offended when they heard this?"

¹³He replied, "Every plant that my heavenly Father has not planted will be pulled up by the roots. ¹⁴Leave them; they are blind guides.ᵃ If a blind man leads a blind man, both will fall into a pit." Mt 23:16,24

¹⁵Peter said, "Explain the parable to us."

¹⁶"Are you still so dull?" Jesus asked them. ¹⁷"Don't you see that whatever enters the mouth goes into the stomach and then out of the body? ¹⁸But the things that come out of the mouth come from the heart, and these make a man 'unclean.' ¹⁹For out of the heart come evil thoughts, murder, adultery, sexual immorality, theft, false testimony, slander. ²⁰These are what make a man 'unclean'; but eating with unwashed hands does not make him 'unclean.' " Mk 7:1ff

The Faith of the Canaanite Woman

²¹Leaving that place, Jesus withdrew to the region of Tyre and Sidon. ²²A Canaanite woman from that vicinity came to him, crying out, "Lord, Son of David, have mercy on me! My daughter is suffering terribly from demon-possession."

²³Jesus did not answer a word. So his disciples came to him and urged him, "Send her away, for she keeps crying out after us."

²⁴He answered, "I was sent only to the lost sheep of Israel."

²⁵The woman came and knelt before him. "Lord, help me!" she said.

²⁶He replied, "It is not right to take the children's bread and toss it to their dogs." Mt 10:6,7

²⁷"Yes, Lord," she said, "but even the dogs eat the crumbs that fall from their masters' table."

²⁸Then Jesus answered, "Woman, you have great faith! Your request is granted." And her daughter was healed from that very hour. Mk 7:24ff

Jesus Feeds the Four Thousand

²⁹Jesus left there and went along the Sea of Galilee. Then he went up on a mountainside and sat down. ³⁰Great crowds came to him, bringing the lame, the blind, the crippled, the mute and many others, and laid them at his feet; and he healed them. ³¹The people were amazed when they saw the mute speaking, the crippled made well, the lame walking and the blind seeing. And they praised the God of Israel.

³²Jesus called his disciples to him and said, "I have compassion for these people; they have

---

ᵃ14 Some manuscripts guides of the blind

already been with me three days and have nothing to eat. I do not want to send them away hungry, or they may collapse on the way." _{Mt 9:36}

³³His disciples answered, "Where could we get enough bread in this remote place to feed such a crowd?" _{2Ki 4:43}

³⁴"How many loaves do you have?" Jesus asked.

"Seven," they replied, "and a few small fish."

³⁵He told the crowd to sit down on the ground. ³⁶Then he took the seven loaves and the fish, and when he had given thanks, he broke them and gave them to the disciples, and they in turn to the people. ³⁷They all ate and were satisfied. Afterward the disciples picked up seven basketfuls of broken pieces that were left over. ³⁸The number of those who ate was four thousand, besides women and children. ³⁹After Jesus had sent the crowd away, he got into the boat and went to the vicinity of Magadan. _{Mk 7:31ff}

The Demand for a Sign

16 The Pharisees and Sadducees came to Jesus and tested him by asking him to show them a sign from heaven.

²He replied,^a "When evening comes, you say, 'It will be fair weather, for the sky is red,' ³and in the morning, 'Today it will be stormy, for the sky is red and overcast.' You know how to interpret the appearance of the sky, but you cannot interpret the signs of the times. ⁴A wicked and adulterous generation looks for a miraculous sign, but none will be given it except the sign of Jonah." Jesus then left them and went away.

The Yeast of the Pharisees and Sadducees

⁵When they went across the lake, the disciples forgot to take bread. ⁶"Be careful," Jesus said to them. "Be on your guard against the yeast of the Pharisees and Sadducees." _{Lk 12:1}

⁷They discussed this among themselves and said, "It is because we didn't bring any bread." _{Mk 8:11ff}

⁸Aware of their discussion, Jesus asked, "You of little faith, why are you talking among yourselves about having no bread? ⁹Do you still not understand? Don't you remember the five loaves for the five thousand, and how many basketfuls you gathered? ¹⁰Or the seven loaves for the four thousand, and how many basketfuls you gathered? ¹¹How is it you don't understand that I was not talking to you about bread? But be on your guard against the yeast of the Pharisees and Sadducees." ¹²Then they understood that he was not telling them to guard against the yeast used in bread, but against the

_{a2 Some early manuscripts do not have the rest of verse 2 and all of verse 3.}

teaching of the Pharisees and Sadducees. _{Mt 14:17ff; 15:34ff}

Peter's Confession of Christ

¹³When Jesus came to the region of Caesarea Philippi, he asked his disciples, "Who do people say the Son of Man is?"

¹⁴They replied, "Some say John the Baptist; others say Elijah; and still others, Jeremiah or one of the prophets." _{Mt 3:1}

¹⁵"But what about you?" he asked. "Who do you say I am?"

¹⁶Simon Peter answered, "You are the Christ,ᵃ the Son of the living God." _{Ac 14:15}

¹⁷Jesus replied, "Blessed are you, Simon son of Jonah, for this was not revealed to you by man, but by my Father in heaven. ¹⁸And I tell you that you are Peter,ᵇ and on this rock I will build my church, and the gates of Hadesᶜ will not overcome it.ᵈ ¹⁹I will give you the keys of the kingdom of heaven; whatever you bind on earth will beᵉ bound in heaven, and whatever you loose on earth will beᵉ loosed in heaven." ²⁰Then he warned his disciples not to tell anyone that he was the Christ.

Jesus Predicts His Death

²¹From that time on Jesus began to explain to his disciples that he must go to Jerusalem and suffer many things at the hands of the elders, chief priests and teachers of the law, and

that he must be killed and on the third day be raised to life.

²²Peter took him aside and began to rebuke him. "Never, Lord!" he said. "This shall never happen to you!" _{Lk 9:22ff}

²³Jesus turned and said to Peter, "Get behind me, Satan! You are a stumbling block to me; you do not have in mind the things of God, but the things of men."

²⁴Then Jesus said to his disciples, "If anyone would come after me, he must deny himself and take up his cross and follow me. ²⁵For whoever wants to save his lifeᶠ will lose it, but whoever loses his life for me will find it. ²⁶What good will it be for a man if he gains the whole world, yet forfeits his soul? Or what can a man give in exchange for his soul? ²⁷For the Son of Man is going to come in his Father's glory with his angels, and then he will reward each person according to what he has done. ²⁸I tell you the truth, some who are standing here will not taste death before they see the Son of Man coming in his kingdom." _{Jer 17:10}

The Transfiguration

17 After six days Jesus took with him Peter, James and John the brother of James, and led them up a high mountain by themselves. ²There he was transfigured before them. His face shone like the sun, and

---

ᵃ16 Or *Messiah*; also in verse 20   ᵇ18 *Peter* means *rock.*   ᶜ18 Or *hell*   ᵈ18 Or *not prove stronger than it*   ᵉ19 Or *have been*   ᶠ25 The Greek word means either *life* or *soul*; also in verse 26.

his clothes became as white as the light. ³Just then there appeared before them Moses and Elijah, talking with Jesus.

⁴Peter said to Jesus, "Lord, it is good for us to be here. If you wish, I will put up three shelters—one for you, one for Moses and one for Elijah."

⁵While he was still speaking, a bright cloud enveloped them, and a voice from the cloud said, "This is my Son, whom I love; with him I am well pleased. Listen to him!"   Mt 3:17

⁶When the disciples heard this, they fell facedown to the ground, terrified. ⁷But Jesus came and touched them. "Get up," he said. "Don't be afraid." ⁸When they looked up, they saw no one except Jesus.

⁹As they were coming down the mountain, Jesus instructed them, "Don't tell anyone what you have seen, until the Son of Man has been raised from the dead."   Mt 16:21; Mk 8:30

¹⁰The disciples asked him, "Why then do the teachers of the law say that Elijah must come first?"   Mal 4:5,6

¹¹Jesus replied, "To be sure, Elijah comes and will restore all things. ¹²But I tell you, Elijah has already come, and they did not recognize him, but have done to him everything they wished. In the same way the Son of Man is going to suffer at their hands." ¹³Then the disciples understood that he was talking to them about John the Baptist.   Lk 1:16,17

The Healing of a Boy With a Demon

¹⁴When they came to the crowd, a man approached Jesus and knelt before him. ¹⁵"Lord, have mercy on my son," he said. "He has seizures and is suffering greatly. He often falls into the fire or into the water. ¹⁶I brought him to your disciples, but they could not heal him."

¹⁷"O unbelieving and perverse generation," Jesus replied, "how long shall I stay with you? How long shall I put up with you? Bring the boy here to me." ¹⁸Jesus rebuked the demon, and it came out of the boy, and he was healed from that moment.   Mk 9:14ff; Lk 9:37ff

¹⁹Then the disciples came to Jesus in private and asked, "Why couldn't we drive it out?"

²⁰He replied, "Because you have so little faith. I tell you the truth, if you have faith as small as a mustard seed, you can say to this mountain, 'Move from here to there' and it will move. Nothing will be impossible for you. ᵃ"   Mt 21:21; Lk 17:6

²²When they came together in Galilee, he said to them, "The Son of Man is going to be betrayed into the hands of men. ²³They will kill him, and on the third day he will be raised to life." And the disciples were filled with grief.   Mt 16:21

ᵃ20 Some manuscripts *you.* ²¹*But this kind does not go out except by prayer and fasting.*

The Temple Tax

24After Jesus and his disciples arrived in Capernaum, the collectors of the two-drachma tax came to Peter and asked, "Doesn't your teacher pay the temple tax*a*?"   Ex 30:13

25"Yes, he does," he replied.

When Peter came into the house, Jesus was the first to speak. "What do you think, Simon?" he asked. "From whom do the kings of the earth collect duty and taxes—from their own sons or from others?"

26"From others," Peter answered.

"Then the sons are exempt," Jesus said to him. 27"But so that we may not offend them, go to the lake and throw out your line. Take the first fish you catch; open its mouth and you will find a four-drachma coin. Take it and give it to them for my tax and yours."   Ro 13:7

The Greatest in the Kingdom of Heaven

18 At that time the disciples came to Jesus and asked, "Who is the greatest in the kingdom of heaven?"   Mk 9:33ff

2He called a little child and had him stand among them. 3And he said: "I tell you the truth, unless you change and become like little children, you will never enter the kingdom of heaven. 4Therefore, whoever

humbles himself like this child is the greatest in the kingdom of heaven.   Mt 3:2; 19:14

5"And whoever welcomes a little child like this in my name welcomes me. 6But if anyone causes one of these little ones who believe in me to sin, it would be better for him to have a large millstone hung around his neck and to be drowned in the depths of the sea.   Mt 10:40

7"Woe to the world because of the things that cause people to sin! Such things must come, but woe to the man through whom they come! 8If your hand or your foot causes you to sin, cut it off and throw it away. It is better for you to enter life maimed or crippled than to have two hands or two feet and be thrown into eternal fire. 9And if your eye causes you to sin, gouge it out and throw it away. It is better for you to enter life with one eye than to have two eyes and be thrown into the fire of hell.   Lk 17:1; Mt 5:29

The Parable of the Lost Sheep

10"See that you do not look down on one of these little ones. For I tell you that their angels in heaven always see the face of my Father in heaven.*b*

12"What do you think? If a man owns a hundred sheep, and one of them wanders away, will he not leave the ninety-nine

*a*24 Greek *the two drachmas*   *b*10 Some manuscripts *heaven. 11The Son of Man came to save what was lost.*

on the hills and go to look for the one that wandered off? [13]And if he finds it, I tell you the truth, he is happier about that one sheep than about the ninety-nine that did not wander off. [14]In the same way your Father in heaven is not willing that any of these little ones should be lost.

A Brother Who Sins Against You

[15]"If your brother sins against you,[a] go and show him his fault, just between the two of you. If he listens to you, you have won your brother over. [16]But if he will not listen, take one or two others along, so that 'every matter may be established by the testimony of two or three witnesses.'[b] [17]If he refuses to listen to them, tell it to the church; and if he refuses to listen even to the church, treat him as you would a pagan or a tax collector. Jas 5:19,20

[18]"I tell you the truth, whatever you bind on earth will be[c] bound in heaven, and whatever you loose on earth will be[c] loosed in heaven. Mt 16:19

[19]"Again, I tell you that if two of you on earth agree about anything you ask for, it will be done for you by my Father in heaven. [20]For where two or three come together in my name, there am I with them." Mt 7:7

The Parable of the Unmerciful Servant

[21]Then Peter came to Jesus and asked, "Lord, how many times shall I forgive my brother when he sins against me? Up to seven times?" Lk 17:4

[22]Jesus answered, "I tell you, not seven times, but seventy-seven times.[d]

[23]"Therefore, the kingdom of heaven is like a king who wanted to settle accounts with his servants. [24]As he began the settlement, a man who owed him ten thousand talents[e] was brought to him. [25]Since he was not able to pay, the master ordered that he and his wife and his children and all that he had be sold to repay the debt.

[26]"The servant fell on his knees before him. 'Be patient with me,' he begged, 'and I will pay back everything.' [27]The servant's master took pity on him, canceled the debt and let him go.

[28]"But when that servant went out, he found one of his fellow servants who owed him a hundred denarii.[f] He grabbed him and began to choke him. 'Pay back what you owe me!' he demanded.

[29]"His fellow servant fell to his knees and begged him, 'Be patient with me, and I will pay you back.'

[30]"But he refused. Instead, he

---

[a]15 Some manuscripts do not have *against you.*   [b]16 Deut. 19:15   [c]18 Or *have been*   [d]22 Or *seventy times seven*   [e]24 That is, millions of dollars   [f]28 That is, a few dollars

went off and had the man thrown into prison until he could pay the debt. ³¹When the other servants saw what had happened, they were greatly distressed and went and told their master everything that had happened.   Eph 4:31-32

³²"Then the master called the servant in. 'You wicked servant,' he said, 'I canceled all that debt of yours because you begged me to. ³³Shouldn't you have had mercy on your fellow servant just as I had on you?' ³⁴In anger his master turned him over to the jailers to be tortured, until he should pay back all he owed.

³⁵"This is how my heavenly Father will treat each of you unless you forgive your brother from your heart."   Mt 6:14

Divorce

19 When Jesus had finished saying these things, he left Galilee and went into the region of Judea to the other side of the Jordan. ²Large crowds followed him, and he healed them there.

³Some Pharisees came to him to test him. They asked, "Is it lawful for a man to divorce his wife for any and every reason?"

⁴"Haven't you read," he replied, "that at the beginning the Creator 'made them male and female,'ᵃ ⁵and said, 'For this reason a man will leave his father and mother and be united

to his wife, and the two will become one flesh'ᵇ? ⁶So they are no longer two, but one. Therefore what God has joined together, let man not separate."

⁷"Why then," they asked, "did Moses command that a man give his wife a certificate of divorce and send her away?"

⁸Jesus replied, "Moses permitted you to divorce your wives because your hearts were hard. But it was not this way from the beginning. ⁹I tell you that anyone who divorces his wife, except for marital unfaithfulness, and marries another woman commits adultery."

¹⁰The disciples said to him, "If this is the situation between a husband and wife, it is better not to marry."

¹¹Jesus replied, "Not everyone can accept this word, but only those to whom it has been given. ¹²For some are eunuchs because they were born that way; others were made that way by men; and others have renounced marriageᶜ because of the kingdom of heaven. The one who can accept this should accept it."   Mk 10:1ff

The Little Children and Jesus

¹³Then little children were brought to Jesus for him to place his hands on them and pray for them. But the disciples rebuked those who brought them.

¹⁴Jesus said, "Let the little children come to me, and do not

---

ᵃ4 Gen. 1:27   ᵇ5 Gen. 2:24   ᶜ12 Or *have made themselves eunuchs*

hinder them, for the kingdom of heaven belongs to such as these." ¹⁵When he had placed his hands on them, he went on from there. Mk 10:13ff

The Rich Young Man

¹⁶Now a man came up to Jesus and asked, "Teacher, what good thing must I do to get eternal life?" Lk 10:25

¹⁷"Why do you ask me about what is good?" Jesus replied. "There is only One who is good. If you want to enter life, obey the commandments."

¹⁸"Which ones?" the man inquired.

Jesus replied, " 'Do not murder, do not commit adultery, do not steal, do not give false testimony, ¹⁹honor your father and mother,'ᵃ and 'love your neighbor as yourself.'ᵇ" Mt 5:43

²⁰"All these I have kept," the young man said. "What do I still lack?"

²¹Jesus answered, "If you want to be perfect, go, sell your possessions and give to the poor, and you will have treasure in heaven. Then come, follow me." Mt 5:48; Ac 2:45

²²When the young man heard this, he went away sad, because he had great wealth.

²³Then Jesus said to his disciples, "I tell you the truth, it is hard for a rich man to enter the kingdom of heaven. ²⁴Again I tell you, it is easier for a camel to go through the eye of a needle than for a rich man to enter the kingdom of God." 1Tim 6:9,10

²⁵When the disciples heard this, they were greatly astonished and asked, "Who then can be saved?" Ro 1:16

²⁶Jesus looked at them and said, "With man this is impossible, but with God all things are possible." Lk 18:27

²⁷Peter answered him, "We have left everything to follow you! What then will there be for us?" Mt 4:19

²⁸Jesus said to them, "I tell you the truth, at the renewal of all things, when the Son of Man sits on his glorious throne, you who have followed me will also sit on twelve thrones, judging the twelve tribes of Israel. ²⁹And everyone who has left houses or brothers or sisters or father or motherᶜ or children or fields for my sake will receive a hundred times as much and will inherit eternal life. ³⁰But many who are first will be last, and many who are last will be first. Lk 22:28-30

The Parable of the Workers in the Vineyard

20 "For the kingdom of heaven is like a landowner who went out early in the morning to hire men to work in his vineyard. ²He agreed to pay them a denarius for the day and sent them into his vineyard.

³"About the third hour he

ᵃ19 Exodus 20:12-16; Deut. 5:16-20   ᵇ19 Lev. 19:18   ᶜ29 Some manuscripts *mother or wife*

went out and saw others standing in the marketplace doing nothing. ⁴He told them, 'You also go and work in my vineyard, and I will pay you whatever is right.' ⁵So they went.

"He went out again about the sixth hour and the ninth hour and did the same thing. ⁶About the eleventh hour he went out and found still others standing around. He asked them, 'Why have you been standing here all day long doing nothing?'

⁷" 'Because no one has hired us,' they answered.

"He said to them, 'You also go and work in my vineyard.'

⁸"When evening came, the owner of the vineyard said to his foreman, 'Call the workers and pay them their wages, beginning with the last ones hired and going on to the first.'

⁹"The workers who were hired about the eleventh hour came and each received a denarius. ¹⁰So when those came who were hired first, they expected to receive more. But each one of them also received a denarius. ¹¹When they received it, they began to grumble against the landowner. ¹²'These men who were hired last worked only one hour,' they said, 'and you have made them equal to us who have borne the burden of the work and the heat of the day.' Jnh 4:1; Lk 12:55

¹³"But he answered one of them, 'Friend, I am not being unfair to you. Didn't you agree to work for a denarius? ¹⁴Take your pay and go. I want to give the man who was hired last the same as I gave you. ¹⁵Don't I have the right to do what I want with my own money? Or are you envious because I am generous?' Dt 15:9; Mk 7:22

¹⁶"So the last will be first, and the first will be last." Mt 19:30

Jesus Again Predicts His Death

¹⁷Now as Jesus was going up to Jerusalem, he took the twelve disciples aside and said to them, ¹⁸"We are going up to Jerusalem, and the Son of Man will be betrayed to the chief priests and the teachers of the law. They will condemn him to death ¹⁹and will turn him over to the Gentiles to be mocked and flogged and crucified. On the third day he will be raised to life!" Lk 9:51; Ac 2:23

A Mother's Request

²⁰Then the mother of Zebedee's sons came to Jesus with her sons and, kneeling down, asked a favor of him. Mt 4:21

²¹"What is it you want?" he asked.

She said, "Grant that one of these two sons of mine may sit at your right and the other at your left in your kingdom."

²²"You don't know what you are asking," Jesus said to them. "Can you drink the cup I am going to drink?" Mt 26:39-42

"We can," they answered.

²³Jesus said to them, "You

will indeed drink from my cup, but to sit at my right or left is not for me to grant. These places belong to those for whom they have been prepared by my Father."   Ac 12:2; Rev 1:9

24When the ten heard about this, they were indignant with the two brothers. 25Jesus called them together and said, "You know that the rulers of the Gentiles lord it over them, and their high officials exercise authority over them. 26Not so with you. Instead, whoever wants to become great among you must be your servant, 27and whoever wants to be first must be your slave— 28just as the Son of Man did not come to be served, but to serve, and to give his life as a ransom for many."   Php 2:7

Two Blind Men Receive Sight

29As Jesus and his disciples were leaving Jericho, a large crowd followed him. 30Two blind men were sitting by the roadside, and when they heard that Jesus was going by, they shouted, "Lord, Son of David, have mercy on us!"

31The crowd rebuked them and told them to be quiet, but they shouted all the louder, "Lord, Son of David, have mercy on us!"

32Jesus stopped and called them. "What do you want me to do for you?" he asked.

33"Lord," they answered, "we want our sight."

34Jesus had compassion on them and touched their eyes. Immediately they received their sight and followed him.

The Triumphal Entry

21 As they approached Jerusalem and came to Bethphage on the Mount of Olives, Jesus sent two disciples, 2saying to them, "Go to the village ahead of you, and at once you will find a donkey tied there, with her colt by her. Untie them and bring them to me. 3If anyone says anything to you, tell him that the Lord needs them, and he will send them right away."

4This took place to fulfill what was spoken through the prophet:

5"Say to the Daughter of
    Zion,
  'See, your king comes to
    you,
gentle and riding on a
    donkey,
  on a colt, the foal of a
    donkey.' "ᵃ   Isa 62:11

6The disciples went and did as Jesus had instructed them. 7They brought the donkey and the colt, placed their cloaks on them, and Jesus sat on them. 8A very large crowd spread their cloaks on the road, while others cut branches from the trees and spread them on the road. 9The

ᵃ5 Zech. 9:9

crowds that went ahead of him and those that followed shouted,

2Ki 9:13

"Hosanna[a] to the Son of David!"

"Blessed is he who comes in the name of the Lord!"[b]

"Hosanna[a] in the highest!"

10When Jesus entered Jerusalem, the whole city was stirred and asked, "Who is this?" 11The crowds answered, "This is Jesus, the prophet from Nazareth in Galilee."

Lk 7:16

Jesus at the Temple

12Jesus entered the temple area and drove out all who were buying and selling there. He overturned the tables of the money changers and the benches of those selling doves. 13"It is written," he said to them, " 'My house will be called a house of prayer,'[c] but you are making it a 'den of robbers.'[d]"

14The blind and the lame came to him at the temple, and he healed them. 15But when the chief priests and the teachers of the law saw the wonderful things he did and the children shouting in the temple area, "Hosanna to the Son of David," they were indignant.

16"Do you hear what these children are saying?" they asked him.

"Yes," replied Jesus, "have you never read,

" 'From the lips of children and infants you have ordained praise'[e]?"

17And he left them and went out of the city to Bethany, where he spent the night.Mk 11:1ff

The Fig Tree Withers

18Early in the morning, as he was on his way back to the city, he was hungry. 19Seeing a fig tree by the road, he went up to it but found nothing on it except leaves. Then he said to it, "May you never bear fruit again!" Immediately the tree withered.

20When the disciples saw this, they were amazed. "How did the fig tree wither so quickly?" they asked.

Jer 8:13

21Jesus replied, "I tell you the truth, if you have faith and do not doubt, not only can you do what was done to the fig tree, but also you can say to this mountain, 'Go, throw yourself into the sea,' and it will be done. 22If you believe, you will receive whatever you ask for in prayer."

Mt 7:7; Lk 17:6

The Authority of Jesus Questioned

23Jesus entered the temple courts, and, while he was teaching, the chief priests and the elders of the people came to him.

a9 A Hebrew expression meaning "Save!" which became an exclamation of praise; also in verse 15   b9 Psalm 118:26   c13 Isaiah 56:7   d13 Jer. 7:11   e16 Psalm 8:2

"By what authority are you doing these things?" they asked. "And who gave you this authority?" Ac 4:7

24Jesus replied, "I will also ask you one question. If you answer me, I will tell you by what authority I am doing these things. 25John's baptism—where did it come from? Was it from heaven, or from men?" Job 5:13

They discussed it among themselves and said, "If we say, 'From heaven,' he will ask, 'Then why didn't you believe him?' 26But if we say, 'From men'—we are afraid of the people, for they all hold that John was a prophet."

27So they answered Jesus, "We don't know."

Then he said, "Neither will I tell you by what authority I am doing these things. Lk 20:1ff

The Parable of the Two Sons

28"What do you think? There was a man who had two sons. He went to the first and said, 'Son, go and work today in the vineyard.'

29" 'I will not,' he answered, but later he changed his mind and went.

30"Then the father went to the other son and said the same thing. He answered, 'I will, sir,' but he did not go.

31"Which of the two did what his father wanted?"

"The first," they answered.

Jesus said to them, "I tell you the truth, the tax collectors and the prostitutes are entering the kingdom of God ahead of you. 32For John came to you to show you the way of righteousness, and you did not believe him, but the tax collectors and the prostitutes did. And even after you saw this, you did not repent and believe him. Lk 7:29

The Parable of the Tenants

33"Listen to another parable: There was a landowner who planted a vineyard. He put a wall around it, dug a winepress in it and built a watchtower. Then he rented the vineyard to some farmers and went away on a journey. 34When the harvest time approached, he sent his servants to the tenants to collect his fruit. Isa 5:1-7

35"The tenants seized his servants; they beat one, killed another, and stoned a third. 36Then he sent other servants to them, more than the first time, and the tenants treated them the same way. 37Last of all, he sent his son to them. 'They will respect my son,' he said.

38"But when the tenants saw the son, they said to each other, 'This is the heir. Come, let's kill him and take his inheritance.' 39So they took him and threw him out of the vineyard and killed him. Heb 1:2

40"Therefore, when the owner of the vineyard comes, what will he do to those tenants?"

41"He will bring those wretches to a wretched end,"

they replied, "and he will rent the vineyard to other tenants, who will give him his share of the crop at harvest time." Mt 8:11

42Jesus said to them, "Have you never read in the Scriptures:

" 'The stone the builders rejected
has become the capstone[a];
the Lord has done this,
and it is marvelous in our eyes'[b]?

43"Therefore I tell you that the kingdom of God will be taken away from you and given to a people who will produce its fruit. 44He who falls on this stone will be broken to pieces, but he on whom it falls will be crushed."[c] Mt 8:12

45When the chief priests and the Pharisees heard Jesus' parables, they knew he was talking about them. 46They looked for a way to arrest him, but they were afraid of the crowd because the people held that he was a prophet. Jn 7:40

The Parable of the Wedding Banquet

22 Jesus spoke to them again in parables, saying: 2"The kingdom of heaven is like a king who prepared a wedding banquet for his son. 3He sent his servants to those who had been invited to the banquet to tell them to come, but they refused to come. Mt 21:34

4"Then he sent some more servants and said, 'Tell those who have been invited that I have prepared my dinner: My oxen and fattened cattle have been butchered, and everything is ready. Come to the wedding banquet.' Mt 21:36

5"But they paid no attention and went off—one to his field, another to his business. 6The rest seized his servants, mistreated them and killed them. 7The king was enraged. He sent his army and destroyed those murderers and burned their city. Lk 19:27

8"Then he said to his servants, 'The wedding banquet is ready, but those I invited did not deserve to come. 9Go to the street corners and invite to the banquet anyone you find.' 10So the servants went out into the streets and gathered all the people they could find, both good and bad, and the wedding hall was filled with guests.

11"But when the king came in to see the guests, he noticed a man there who was not wearing wedding clothes. 12'Friend,' he asked, 'how did you get in here without wedding clothes?' The man was speechless.

13"Then the king told the attendants, 'Tie him hand and foot, and throw him outside, into the darkness, where there

---

[a]42 Or cornerstone   [b]42 Psalm 118:22,23   [c]44 Some manuscripts do not have
verse 44.

will be weeping and gnashing of teeth.' Mt 8:12

¹⁴"For many are invited, but few are chosen." Lk 14:16ff

Paying Taxes to Caesar

¹⁵Then the Pharisees went out and laid plans to trap him in his words. ¹⁶They sent their disciples to him along with the Herodians. "Teacher," they said, "we know you are a man of integrity and that you teach the way of God in accordance with the truth. You aren't swayed by men, because you pay no attention to who they are. ¹⁷Tell us then, what is your opinion? Is it right to pay taxes to Caesar or not?" Mk 3:6

¹⁸But Jesus, knowing their evil intent, said, "You hypocrites, why are you trying to trap me? ¹⁹Show me the coin used for paying the tax." They brought him a denarius, ²⁰and he asked them, "Whose portrait is this? And whose inscription?"

²¹"Caesar's," they replied.

Then he said to them, "Give to Caesar what is Caesar's, and to God what is God's." Ro 13:7

²²When they heard this, they were amazed. So they left him and went away. Mk 12:13ff

Marriage at the Resurrection

²³That same day the Sadducees, who say there is no resurrection, came to him with a question. ²⁴"Teacher," they said, "Moses told us that if a man dies without having children, his brother must marry the widow and have children for him. ²⁵Now there were seven brothers among us. The first one married and died, and since he had no children, he left his wife to his brother. ²⁶The same thing happened to the second and third brother, right on down to the seventh. ²⁷Finally, the woman died. ²⁸Now then, at the resurrection, whose wife will she be of the seven, since all of them were married to her?"

²⁹Jesus replied, "You are in error because you do not know the Scriptures or the power of God. ³⁰At the resurrection people will neither marry nor be given in marriage; they will be like the angels in heaven. ³¹But about the resurrection of the dead—have you not read what God said to you, ³²'I am the God of Abraham, the God of Isaac, and the God of Jacob'ᵃ? He is not the God of the dead but of the living." Jn 20:9

³³When the crowds heard this, they were astonished at his teaching. Lk 20:27ff

The Greatest Commandment

³⁴Hearing that Jesus had silenced the Sadducees, the Pharisees got together. ³⁵One of them, an expert in the law, tested him with this question: ³⁶"Teacher, which is the great-

ᵃ32 Exodus 3:6

est commandment in the Law?"

³⁷Jesus replied: " 'Love the Lord your God with all your heart and with all your soul and with all your mind.'ᵃ ³⁸This is the first and greatest commandment. ³⁹And the second is like it: 'Love your neighbor as yourself.'ᵇ ⁴⁰All the Law and the Prophets hang on these two commandments."   Mt 7:12

Whose Son Is the Christ?

⁴¹While the Pharisees were gathered together, Jesus asked them, ⁴²"What do you think about the Christᶜ? Whose son is he?"

"The son of David," they replied.

⁴³He said to them, "How is it then that David, speaking by the Spirit, calls him 'Lord'? For he says,

⁴⁴" 'The Lord said to my Lord:
"Sit at my right hand
until I put your enemies
under your feet." 'ᵈ

⁴⁵If then David calls him 'Lord,' how can he be his son?" ⁴⁶No one could say a word in reply, and from that day on no one dared to ask him any more questions.   Lk 20:41ff

Seven Woes

23 Then Jesus said to the crowds and to his disci-

ples: ²"The teachers of the law and the Pharisees sit in Moses' seat. ³So you must obey them and do everything they tell you. But do not do what they do, for they do not practice what they preach. ⁴They tie up heavy loads and put them on men's shoulders, but they themselves are not willing to lift a finger to move them.   Lk 11:46

⁵"Everything they do is done for men to see: They make their phylacteriesᵉ wide and the tassels on their garments long; ⁶they love the place of honor at banquets and the most important seats in the synagogues; ⁷they love to be greeted in the marketplaces and to have men call them 'Rabbi.'   Ex 13:9

⁸"But you are not to be called 'Rabbi,' for you have only one Master and you are all brothers. ⁹And do not call anyone on earth 'father,' for you have one Father, and he is in heaven. ¹⁰Nor are you to be called 'teacher,' for you have one Teacher, the Christ.ᶜ ¹¹The greatest among you will be your servant. ¹²For whoever exalts himself will be humbled, and whoever humbles himself will be exalted.   1Sa 2:8; Mk 9:35

¹³"Woe to you, teachers of the law and Pharisees, you hypocrites! You shut the kingdom of heaven in men's faces. You yourselves do not enter, nor

ᵃ37 Deut. 6:5   ᵇ39 Lev. 19:18   ᶜ42,10 Or Messiah   ᵈ44 Psalm 110:1   ᵉ5 That is, boxes containing Scripture verses, worn on forehead and arm

will you let those enter who are trying to.[a]   Lk 11:52

[15]"Woe to you, teachers of the law and Pharisees, you hypocrites! You travel over land and sea to win a single convert, and when he becomes one, you make him twice as much a son of hell as you are.

[16]"Woe to you, blind guides! You say, 'If anyone swears by the temple, it means nothing; but if anyone swears by the gold of the temple, he is bound by his oath.' [17]You blind fools! Which is greater: the gold, or the temple that makes the gold sacred? [18]You also say, 'If anyone swears by the altar, it means nothing; but if anyone swears by the gift on it, he is bound by his oath.' [19]You blind men! Which is greater: the gift, or the altar that makes the gift sacred? [20]Therefore, he who swears by the altar swears by it and by everything on it. [21]And he who swears by the temple swears by it and by the one who dwells in it. [22]And he who swears by heaven swears by God's throne and by the one who sits on it.   Mt 5:33-35

[23]"Woe to you, teachers of the law and Pharisees, you hypocrites! You give a tenth of your spices—mint, dill and cummin. But you have neglected the more important matters of the law—justice, mercy and faithfulness. You should have prac-

ticed the latter, without neglecting the former. [24]You blind guides! You strain out a gnat but swallow a camel.   Mic 6:8

[25]"Woe to you, teachers of the law and Pharisees, you hypocrites! You clean the outside of the cup and dish, but inside they are full of greed and self-indulgence. [26]Blind Pharisee! First clean the inside of the cup and dish, and then the outside also will be clean.   Lk 11:39

[27]"Woe to you, teachers of the law and Pharisees, you hypocrites! You are like whitewashed tombs, which look beautiful on the outside but on the inside are full of dead men's bones and everything unclean. [28]In the same way, on the outside you appear to people as righteous but on the inside you are full of hypocrisy and wickedness.   Lk 11:44; Ac 23:3

[29]"Woe to you, teachers of the law and Pharisees, you hypocrites! You build tombs for the prophets and decorate the graves of the righteous. [30]And you say, 'If we had lived in the days of our forefathers, we would not have taken part with them in shedding the blood of the prophets.' [31]So you testify against yourselves that you are the descendants of those who murdered the prophets. [32]Fill up, then, the measure of the sin of your forefathers!   Eze 20:4

[33]"You snakes! You brood of

---

[a]13 Some manuscripts to. [14]Woe to you, teachers of the law and Pharisees, you hypocrites! You devour widows' houses and for a show make lengthy prayers. Therefore you will be punished more severely.

vipers! How will you escape being condemned to hell? 34Therefore I am sending you prophets and wise men and teachers. Some of them you will kill and crucify; others you will flog in your synagogues and pursue from town to town. 35And so upon you will come all the righteous blood that has been shed on earth, from the blood of righteous Abel to the blood of Zechariah son of Berekiah, whom you murdered between the temple and the altar. 36I tell you the truth, all this will come upon this generation. Mt 24:34

37"O Jerusalem, Jerusalem, you who kill the prophets and stone those sent to you, how often I have longed to gather your children together, as a hen gathers her chicks under her wings, but you were not willing. 38Look, your house is left to you desolate. 39For I tell you, you will not see me again until you say, 'Blessed is he who comes in the name of the Lord.'ᵃ" 1Ki 9:7; Ps 57:1

Signs of the End of the Age

24 Jesus left the temple and was walking away when his disciples came up to him to call his attention to its buildings. 2"Do you see all these things?" he asked. "I tell you the truth, not one stone here will be left on another; every one will be thrown down."

3As Jesus was sitting on the Mount of Olives, the disciples came to him privately. "Tell us," they said, "when will this happen, and what will be the sign of your coming and of the end of the age?" Lk 17:30

4Jesus answered: "Watch out that no one deceives you. 5For many will come in my name, claiming, 'I am the Christ,'ᵇ and will deceive many. 6You will hear of wars and rumors of wars, but see to it that you are not alarmed. Such things must happen, but the end is still to come. 7Nation will rise against nation, and kingdom against kingdom. There will be famines and earthquakes in various places. 8All these are the beginning of birth pains. Isa 19:2

9"Then you will be handed over to be persecuted and put to death, and you will be hated by all nations because of me. 10At that time many will turn away from the faith and will betray and hate each other, 11and many false prophets will appear and deceive many people. 12Because of the increase of wickedness, the love of most will grow cold, 13but he who stands firm to the end will be saved. 14And this gospel of the kingdom will be preached in the whole world as a testimony to all nations, and then the end will come.

15"So when you see standing in the holy place 'the abomination that causes desolation,'ᶜ spoken of through the prophet

ᵃ39 Psalm 118:26   ᵇ5 Or *Messiah*; also in verse 23   ᶜ15 Daniel 9:27; 11:31; 12:11

Daniel—let the reader understand— [16]then let those who are in Judea flee to the mountains. [17]Let no one on the roof of his house go down to take anything out of the house. [18]Let no one in the field go back to get his cloak. [19]How dreadful it will be in those days for pregnant women and nursing mothers! [20]Pray that your flight will not take place in winter or on the Sabbath. [21]For then there will be great distress, unequaled from the beginning of the world until now—and never to be equaled again. [22]If those days had not been cut short, no one would survive, but for the sake of the elect those days will be shortened. [23]At that time if anyone says to you, 'Look, here is the Christ!' or, 'There he is!' do not believe it. [24]For false Christs and false prophets will appear and perform great signs and miracles to deceive even the elect—if that were possible. [25]See, I have told you ahead of time.　　2Th 2:9

[26]"So if anyone tells you, 'There he is, out in the desert,' do not go out; or, 'Here he is, in the inner rooms,' do not believe it. [27]For as lightning that comes from the east is visible even in the west, so will be the coming of the Son of Man. [28]Wherever there is a carcass, there the vultures will gather.　　Lk 17:23

[29]"Immediately after the distress of those days

" 'the sun will be darkened,
　and the moon will not give
　　its light;
the stars will fall from the
　　sky,
and the heavenly bodies
　　will be shaken.'[a]

[30]"At that time the sign of the Son of Man will appear in the sky, and all the nations of the earth will mourn. They will see the Son of Man coming on the clouds of the sky, with power and great glory. [31]And he will send his angels with a loud trumpet call, and they will gather his elect from the four winds, from one end of the heavens to the other.　　1Th 4:16

[32]"Now learn this lesson from the fig tree: As soon as its twigs get tender and its leaves come out, you know that summer is near. [33]Even so, when you see all these things, you know that it[b] is near, right at the door. [34]I tell you the truth, this generation[c] will certainly not pass away until all these things have happened. [35]Heaven and earth will pass away, but my words will never pass away.　　Jas 5:9

The Day and Hour Unknown

[36]"No one knows about that day or hour, not even the angels in heaven, nor the Son,[d] but only the Father. [37]As it was in the days of Noah, so it will be at the coming of the Son of Man.

[a]29 Isaiah 13:10; 34:4　　[b]33 Or he　　[c]34 Or race　　[d]36 Some manuscripts do not have nor the Son.

³⁸For in the days before the flood, people were eating and drinking, marrying and giving in marriage, up to the day Noah entered the ark; ³⁹and they knew nothing about what would happen until the flood came and took them all away. That is how it will be at the coming of the Son of Man. ⁴⁰Two men will be in the field; one will be taken and the other left. ⁴¹Two women will be grinding with a hand mill; one will be taken and the other left.

⁴²"Therefore keep watch, because you do not know on what day your Lord will come. ⁴³But understand this: If the owner of the house had known at what time of night the thief was coming, he would have kept watch and would not have let his house be broken into. ⁴⁴So you also must be ready, because the Son of Man will come at an hour when you do not expect him.

⁴⁵"Who then is the faithful and wise servant, whom the master has put in charge of the servants in his household to give them their food at the proper time? ⁴⁶It will be good for that servant whose master finds him doing so when he returns. ⁴⁷I tell you the truth, he will put him in charge of all his possessions. ⁴⁸But suppose that servant is wicked and says to himself, 'My master is staying away a long time,' ⁴⁹and he then begins to beat his fellow servants and to eat and drink with drunkards. ⁵⁰The master of that servant will come on a day when he does not expect him and at an hour he is not aware of. ⁵¹He will cut him to pieces and assign him a place with the hypocrites, where there will be weeping and gnashing of teeth.

The Parable of the Ten Virgins

25 "At that time the kingdom of heaven will be like ten virgins who took their lamps and went out to meet the bridegroom. ²Five of them were foolish and five were wise. ³The foolish ones took their lamps but did not take any oil with them. ⁴The wise, however, took oil in jars along with their lamps. ⁵The bridegroom was a long time in coming, and they all became drowsy and fell asleep.   Lk 12:35-38

⁶"At midnight the cry rang out: 'Here's the bridegroom! Come out to meet him!'

⁷"Then all the virgins woke up and trimmed their lamps. ⁸The foolish ones said to the wise, 'Give us some of your oil; our lamps are going out.'

⁹" 'No,' they replied, 'there may not be enough for both us and you. Instead, go to those who sell oil and buy some for yourselves.'

¹⁰"But while they were on their way to buy the oil, the bridegroom arrived. The virgins who were ready went in with him to the wedding banquet. And the door was shut.

11"Later the others also came. 'Sir! Sir!' they said. 'Open the door for us!'   Mt 7:21-23

12"But he replied, 'I tell you the truth, I don't know you.'

13"Therefore keep watch, because you do not know the day or the hour.   Mk 13:35; Lk 12:40

The Parable of the Talents

14"Again, it will be like a man going on a journey, who called his servants and entrusted his property to them. 15To one he gave five talents*a* of money, to another two talents, and to another one talent, each according to his ability. Then he went on his journey. 16The man who had received the five talents went at once and put his money to work and gained five more. 17So also, the one with the two talents gained two more. 18But the man who had received the one talent went off, dug a hole in the ground and hid his master's money.

19"After a long time the master of those servants returned and settled accounts with them. 20The man who had received the five talents brought the other five. 'Master,' he said, 'you entrusted me with five talents. See, I have gained five more.'

21"His master replied, 'Well done, good and faithful servant! You have been faithful with a few things; I will put you in charge of many things. Come and share your master's happiness!'   Mt 24:45,47

22"The man with the two talents also came. 'Master,' he said, 'you entrusted me with two talents; see, I have gained two more.'

23"His master replied, 'Well done, good and faithful servant! You have been faithful with a few things; I will put you in charge of many things. Come and share your master's happiness!'

24"Then the man who had received the one talent came. 'Master,' he said, 'I knew that you are a hard man, harvesting where you have not sown and gathering where you have not scattered seed. 25So I was afraid and went out and hid your talent in the ground. See, here is what belongs to you.'

26"His master replied, 'You wicked, lazy servant! So you knew that I harvest where I have not sown and gather where I have not scattered seed? 27Well then, you should have put my money on deposit with the bankers, so that when I returned I would have received it back with interest.

28" 'Take the talent from him and give it to the one who has the ten talents. 29For everyone who has will be given more, and he will have an abundance. Whoever does not have, even what he has will be taken from him. 30And throw that worth-

a15 A talent was worth more than a thousand dollars.

less servant outside, into the darkness, where there will be weeping and gnashing of teeth.' Lk 8:18; 19:12ff

The Sheep and the Goats

31"When the Son of Man comes in his glory, and all the angels with him, he will sit on his throne in heavenly glory. 32All the nations will be gathered before him, and he will separate the people one from another as a shepherd separates the sheep from the goats. 33He will put the sheep on his right and the goats on his left.

34"Then the King will say to those on his right, 'Come, you who are blessed by my Father; take your inheritance, the kingdom prepared for you since the creation of the world. 35For I was hungry and you gave me something to eat, I was thirsty and you gave me something to drink, I was a stranger and you invited me in, 36I needed clothes and you clothed me, I was sick and you looked after me, I was in prison and you came to visit me.' Jas 1:27; 2:5

37"Then the righteous will answer him, 'Lord, when did we see you hungry and feed you, or thirsty and give you something to drink? 38When did we see you a stranger and invite you in, or needing clothes and clothe you? 39When did we see you sick or in prison and go to visit you?'

40"The King will reply, 'I tell you the truth, whatever you did for one of the least of these brothers of mine, you did for me.' Mt 10:40,42

41"Then he will say to those on his left, 'Depart from me, you who are cursed, into the eternal fire prepared for the devil and his angels. 42For I was hungry and you gave me nothing to eat, I was thirsty and you gave me nothing to drink, 43I was a stranger and you did not invite me in, I needed clothes and you did not clothe me, I was sick and in prison and you did not look after me.' Mt 7:23

44"They also will answer, 'Lord, when did we see you hungry or thirsty or a stranger or needing clothes or sick or in prison, and did not help you?'

45"He will reply, 'I tell you the truth, whatever you did not do for one of the least of these, you did not do for me.' Pr 14:31; 17:5

46"Then they will go away to eternal punishment, but the righteous to eternal life."

The Plot Against Jesus

26 When Jesus had finished saying all these things, he said to his disciples, 2"As you know, the Passover is two days away—and the Son of Man will be handed over to be crucified."

3Then the chief priests and the elders of the people assembled in the palace of the high priest, whose name was Caiaphas, 4and they plotted to arrest Jesus in some sly way and kill him. 5"But not during the

Feast," they said, "or there may be a riot among the people."

Jesus Anointed at Bethany

⁶While Jesus was in Bethany in the home of a man known as Simon the Leper, ⁷a woman came to him with an alabaster jar of very expensive perfume, which she poured on his head as he was reclining at the table. ⁸When the disciples saw this, they were indignant. "Why this waste?" they asked. ⁹"This perfume could have been sold at a high price and the money given to the poor."   Jn 12:1ff

¹⁰Aware of this, Jesus said to them, "Why are you bothering this woman? She has done a beautiful thing to me. ¹¹The poor you will always have with you, but you will not always have me. ¹²When she poured this perfume on my body, she did it to prepare me for burial. ¹³I tell you the truth, wherever this gospel is preached throughout the world, what she has done will also be told, in memory of her."   Dt 15:11; Jn 19:40

Judas Agrees to Betray Jesus

¹⁴Then one of the Twelve—the one called Judas Iscariot—went to the chief priests ¹⁵and asked, "What are you willing to give me if I hand him over to you?" So they counted out for him thirty silver coins. ¹⁶From then on Judas watched for an opportunity to hand him over.   Lk 22:3ff

The Lord's Supper

¹⁷On the first day of the Feast of Unleavened Bread, the disciples came to Jesus and asked, "Where do you want us to make preparations for you to eat the Passover?"   Dt 16:5-8

¹⁸He replied, "Go into the city to a certain man and tell him, 'The Teacher says: My appointed time is near. I am going to celebrate the Passover with my disciples at your house.'" ¹⁹So the disciples did as Jesus had directed them and prepared the Passover.   Jn 7:6

²⁰When evening came, Jesus was reclining at the table with the Twelve. ²¹And while they were eating, he said, "I tell you the truth, one of you will betray me."   Lk 22:21-23

²²They were very sad and began to say to him one after the other, "Surely not I, Lord?"

²³Jesus replied, "The one who has dipped his hand into the bowl with me will betray me. ²⁴The Son of Man will go just as it is written about him. But woe to that man who betrays the Son of Man! It would be better for him if he had not been born."

²⁵Then Judas, the one who would betray him, said, "Surely not I, Rabbi?"   Ps 41:9

Jesus answered, "Yes, it is you."[a]

²⁶While they were eating,

---

[a]25 Or "You yourself have said it"

Jesus took bread, gave thanks and broke it, and gave it to his disciples, saying, "Take and eat; this is my body." Mt 14:19

27Then he took the cup, gave thanks and offered it to them, saying, "Drink from it, all of you. 28This is my blood of the*a* covenant, which is poured out for many for the forgiveness of sins. 29I tell you, I will not drink of this fruit of the vine from now on until that day when I drink it anew with you in my Father's kingdom." Ex 24:6-8; 1Co 10:16

30When they had sung a hymn, they went out to the Mount of Olives.

Jesus Predicts Peter's Denial

31Then Jesus told them, "This very night you will all fall away on account of me, for it is written:

" 'I will strike the shepherd,
   and the sheep of the flock
   will be scattered.'*b* Jn 16:32

32But after I have risen, I will go ahead of you into Galilee." Mt 28:7

33Peter replied, "Even if all fall away on account of you, I never will."

34"I tell you the truth," Jesus answered, "this very night, before the rooster crows, you will disown me three times." Jn 13:38

35But Peter declared, "Even if I have to die with you, I will never disown you." And all the other disciples said the same.

Gethsemane

36Then Jesus went with his disciples to a place called Gethsemane, and he said to them, "Sit here while I go over there and pray." 37He took Peter and the two sons of Zebedee along with him, and he began to be sorrowful and troubled. 38Then he said to them, "My soul is overwhelmed with sorrow to the point of death. Stay here and keep watch with me." Jn 12:27

39Going a little farther, he fell with his face to the ground and prayed, "My Father, if it is possible, may this cup be taken from me. Yet not as I will, but as you will." Ps 40:6-8; Mt 6:10

40Then he returned to his disciples and found them sleeping. "Could you men not keep watch with me for one hour?" he asked Peter. 41"Watch and pray so that you will not fall into temptation. The spirit is willing, but the body is weak." Mt 6:13

42He went away a second time and prayed, "My Father, if it is not possible for this cup to be taken away unless I drink it, may your will be done."

43When he came back, he again found them sleeping, because their eyes were heavy. 44So he left them and went away once more and prayed the third time, saying the same thing.

45Then he returned to the disciples and said to them, "Are you still sleeping and resting? Look, the hour is near, and the

---

*a*28 Some manuscripts *the new*   *b*31 Zech. 13:7

Son of Man is betrayed into the hands of sinners. ⁴⁶Rise, let us go! Here comes my betrayer!"

Jesus Arrested

⁴⁷While he was still speaking, Judas, one of the Twelve, arrived. With him was a large crowd armed with swords and clubs, sent from the chief priests and the elders of the people. ⁴⁸Now the betrayer had arranged a signal with them: "The one I kiss is the man; arrest him." ⁴⁹Going at once to Jesus, Judas said, "Greetings, Rabbi!" and kissed him.

⁵⁰Jesus replied, "Friend, do what you came for."ᵃ

Then the men stepped forward, seized Jesus and arrested him. ⁵¹With that, one of Jesus' companions reached for his sword, drew it out and struck the servant of the high priest, cutting off his ear.   Jn 18:10

⁵²"Put your sword back in its place," Jesus said to him, "for all who draw the sword will die by the sword. ⁵³Do you think I cannot call on my Father, and he will at once put at my disposal more than twelve legions of angels? ⁵⁴But how then would the Scriptures be fulfilled that say it must happen in this way?"   Ge 9:6; Mt 4:11

⁵⁵At that time Jesus said to the crowd, "Am I leading a rebellion, that you have come out with swords and clubs to capture me? Every day I sat in the temple courts teaching, and you did not arrest me. ⁵⁶But this has all taken place that the writings of the prophets might be fulfilled." Then all the disciples deserted him and fled.   Mk 14:43ff

Before the Sanhedrin

⁵⁷Those who had arrested Jesus took him to Caiaphas, the high priest, where the teachers of the law and the elders had assembled. ⁵⁸But Peter followed him at a distance, right up to the courtyard of the high priest. He entered and sat down with the guards to see the outcome.

⁵⁹The chief priests and the whole Sanhedrin were looking for false evidence against Jesus so that they could put him to death. ⁶⁰But they did not find any, though many false witnesses came forward.   Ac 6:13

Finally two came forward ⁶¹and declared, "This fellow said, 'I am able to destroy the temple of God and rebuild it in three days.'"   Jn 2:19

⁶²Then the high priest stood up and said to Jesus, "Are you not going to answer? What is this testimony that these men are bringing against you?" ⁶³But Jesus remained silent.   Mk 14:61

The high priest said to him, "I charge you under oath by the living God: Tell us if you are the Christ,ᵇ the Son of God."   Mt 16:16

⁶⁴"Yes, it is as you say," Jesus replied. "But I say to all of you: In the future you will see the

---

ᵃ50 Or *"Friend, why have you come?"*   ᵇ63 Or *Messiah*; also in verse 68

Son of Man sitting at the right hand of the Mighty One and coming on the clouds of heaven." Mk 16:19; Rev 1:7

⁶⁵Then the high priest tore his clothes and said, "He has spoken blasphemy! Why do we need any more witnesses? Look, now you have heard the blasphemy. ⁶⁶What do you think?" Mk 14:63

"He is worthy of death," they answered. Lev 24:16; Jn 19:7

⁶⁷Then they spit in his face and struck him with their fists. Others slapped him ⁶⁸and said, "Prophesy to us, Christ. Who hit you?" Lk 22:63-65

Peter Disowns Jesus

⁶⁹Now Peter was sitting out in the courtyard, and a servant girl came to him. "You also were with Jesus of Galilee," she said.

⁷⁰But he denied it before them all. "I don't know what you're talking about," he said.

⁷¹Then he went out to the gateway, where another girl saw him and said to the people there, "This fellow was with Jesus of Nazareth."

⁷²He denied it again, with an oath: "I don't know the man!"

⁷³After a little while, those standing there went up to Peter and said, "Surely you are one of them, for your accent gives you away." Lk 22:59

⁷⁴Then he began to call down curses on himself and he swore to them, "I don't know the man!"

Immediately a rooster crowed. ⁷⁵Then Peter remembered the word Jesus had spoken: "Before the rooster crows, you will disown me three times." And he went outside and wept bitterly. Jn 13:38

Judas Hangs Himself

27 Early in the morning, all the chief priests and the elders of the people came to the decision to put Jesus to death. ²They bound him, led him away and handed him over to Pilate, the governor. Mt 20:19

³When Judas, who had betrayed him, saw that Jesus was condemned, he was seized with remorse and returned the thirty silver coins to the chief priests and the elders. ⁴"I have sinned," he said, "for I have betrayed innocent blood."

"What is that to us?" they replied. "That's your responsibility."

⁵So Judas threw the money into the temple and left. Then he went away and hanged himself. Ac 1:18

⁶The chief priests picked up the coins and said, "It is against the law to put this into the treasury, since it is blood money." ⁷So they decided to use the money to buy the potter's field as a burial place for foreigners. ⁸That is why it has been called the Field of Blood to this day. ⁹Then what was spoken by Jeremiah the prophet was fulfilled: "They took the thirty silver coins, the price set on him by the people of Israel, ¹⁰and they

used them to buy the potter's field, as the Lord commanded me."*a*   Ac 1:19

Jesus Before Pilate

11Meanwhile Jesus stood before the governor, and the governor asked him, "Are you the king of the Jews?"   Mt 2:2

"Yes, it is as you say," Jesus replied.

12When he was accused by the chief priests and the elders, he gave no answer. 13Then Pilate asked him, "Don't you hear the testimony they are bringing against you?" 14But Jesus made no reply, not even to a single charge—to the great amazement of the governor.   Mk 14:61

15Now it was the governor's custom at the Feast to release a prisoner chosen by the crowd. 16At that time they had a notorious prisoner, called Barabbas. 17So when the crowd had gathered, Pilate asked them, "Which one do you want me to release to you: Barabbas, or Jesus who is called Christ?" 18For he knew it was out of envy that they had handed Jesus over to him.   Jn 18:39

19While Pilate was sitting on the judge's seat, his wife sent him this message: "Don't have anything to do with that innocent man, for I have suffered a great deal today in a dream because of him."   Jn 19:13

20But the chief priests and the elders persuaded the crowd to ask for Barabbas and to have Jesus executed.   Ac 3:14

21"Which of the two do you want me to release to you?" asked the governor.

"Barabbas," they answered.

22"What shall I do, then, with Jesus who is called Christ?" Pilate asked.

They all answered, "Crucify him!"

23"Why? What crime has he committed?" asked Pilate.

But they shouted all the louder, "Crucify him!"

24When Pilate saw that he was getting nowhere, but that instead an uproar was starting, he took water and washed his hands in front of the crowd. "I am innocent of this man's blood," he said. "It is your responsibility!"   Mt 26:5

25All the people answered, "Let his blood be on us and on our children!"   Jos 2:19

26Then he released Barabbas to them. But he had Jesus flogged, and handed him over to be crucified.   Isa 53:5

The Soldiers Mock Jesus

27Then the governor's soldiers took Jesus into the Praetorium and gathered the whole company of soldiers around him. 28They stripped him and put a scarlet robe on him, 29and then twisted together a crown of thorns and set it on his head. They put a staff in his right hand and knelt in front of him

---

*a10 See Zech. 11:12,13; Jer. 19:1-13; 32:6-9.

and mocked him. "Hail, king of the Jews!" they said. ³⁰They spit on him, and took the staff and struck him on the head again and again. ³¹After they had mocked him, they took off the robe and put his own clothes on him. Then they led him away to crucify him.   Jn 18:28; 19:2,3

The Crucifixion

³²As they were going out, they met a man from Cyrene, named Simon, and they forced him to carry the cross. ³³They came to a place called Golgotha (which means The Place of the Skull). ³⁴There they offered Jesus wine to drink, mixed with gall; but after tasting it, he refused to drink it. ³⁵When they had crucified him, they divided up his clothes by casting lots.ᵃ ³⁶And sitting down, they kept watch over him there. ³⁷Above his head they placed the written charge against him: THIS IS JESUS, THE KING OF THE JEWS. ³⁸Two robbers were crucified with him, one on his right and one on his left. ³⁹Those who passed by hurled insults at him, shaking their heads ⁴⁰and saying, "You who are going to destroy the temple and build it in three days, save yourself! Come down from the cross, if you are the Son of God!"   Heb 13:12

⁴¹In the same way the chief priests, the teachers of the law and the elders mocked him.

⁴²"He saved others," they said, "but he can't save himself! He's the King of Israel! Let him come down now from the cross, and we will believe in him. ⁴³He trusts in God. Let God rescue him now if he wants him, for he said, 'I am the Son of God.'" ⁴⁴In the same way the robbers who were crucified with him also heaped insults on him.

The Death of Jesus

⁴⁵From the sixth hour until the ninth hour darkness came over all the land. ⁴⁶About the ninth hour Jesus cried out in a loud voice, *"Eloi, Eloi,ᵇ lama sabachthani?"*—which means, "My God, my God, why have you forsaken me?"ᶜ   Am 8:9

⁴⁷When some of those standing there heard this, they said, "He's calling Elijah."

⁴⁸Immediately one of them ran and got a sponge. He filled it with wine vinegar, put it on a stick, and offered it to Jesus to drink. ⁴⁹The rest said, "Now leave him alone. Let's see if Elijah comes to save him."   Ps 69:21

⁵⁰And when Jesus had cried out again in a loud voice, he gave up his spirit.   Jn 19:30

⁵¹At that moment the curtain of the temple was torn in two from top to bottom. The earth shook and the rocks split. ⁵²The tombs broke open and the bodies of many holy people who had died were raised to life.

ᵃ35 A few late manuscripts *lots that the word spoken by the prophet might be fulfilled: "They divided my garments among themselves and cast lots for my clothing"* (Psalm 22:18)
ᵇ46 Some manuscripts *Eli, Eli*   ᶜ46 Psalm 22:1

53They came out of the tombs, and after Jesus' resurrection they went into the holy city and appeared to many people.

54When the centurion and those with him who were guarding Jesus saw the earthquake and all that had happened, they were terrified, and exclaimed, "Surely he was the Son*a* of God!"   Mt 17:5

55Many women were there, watching from a distance. They had followed Jesus from Galilee to care for his needs. 56Among them were Mary Magdalene, Mary the mother of James and Joses, and the mother of Zebedee's sons.   Lk 8:2-3; Jn 19:25

The Burial of Jesus

57As evening approached, there came a rich man from Arimathea, named Joseph, who had himself become a disciple of Jesus. 58Going to Pilate, he asked for Jesus' body, and Pilate ordered that it be given to him. 59Joseph took the body, wrapped it in a clean linen cloth, 60and placed it in his own new tomb that he had cut out of the rock. He rolled a big stone in front of the entrance to the tomb and went away. 61Mary Magdalene and the other Mary were sitting there opposite the tomb.

The Guard at the Tomb

62The next day, the one after Preparation Day, the chief priests and the Pharisees went to Pilate. 63"Sir," they said, "we remember that while he was still alive that deceiver said, 'After three days I will rise again.' 64So give the order for the tomb to be made secure until the third day. Otherwise, his disciples may come and steal the body and tell the people that he has been raised from the dead. This last deception will be worse than the first."   Mt 28:13

65"Take a guard," Pilate answered. "Go, make the tomb as secure as you know how." 66So they went and made the tomb secure by putting a seal on the stone and posting the guard.

The Resurrection

28 After the Sabbath, at dawn on the first day of the week, Mary Magdalene and the other Mary went to look at the tomb.   Lk 8:2; Mt 27:56

2There was a violent earthquake, for an angel of the Lord came down from heaven and, going to the tomb, rolled back the stone and sat on it. 3His appearance was like lightning, and his clothes were white as snow. 4The guards were so afraid of him that they shook and became like dead men.

5The angel said to the women, "Do not be afraid, for I know that you are looking for Jesus, who was crucified. 6He is not here; he has risen, just as he said. Come and see the place

*a*54 Or *a son*

where he lay. 7Then go quickly and tell his disciples: 'He has risen from the dead and is going ahead of you into Galilee. There you will see him.' Now I have told you." _{Mt 16:21; 26:32}

8So the women hurried away from the tomb, afraid yet filled with joy, and ran to tell his disciples. 9Suddenly Jesus met them. "Greetings," he said. They came to him, clasped his feet and worshiped him. 10Then Jesus said to them, "Do not be afraid. Go and tell my brothers to go to Galilee; there they will see me." _{Mk 3:34-35; Jn 20:14-18}

The Guards' Report

11While the women were on their way, some of the guards went into the city and reported to the chief priests everything that had happened. 12When the chief priests had met with the elders and devised a plan, they gave the soldiers a large sum of money, 13telling them, "You are to say, 'His disciples came dur-

ing the night and stole him away while we were asleep.' 14If this report gets to the governor, we will satisfy him and keep you out of trouble." 15So the soldiers took the money and did as they were instructed. And this story has been widely circulated among the Jews to this very day. _{Mt 27:64-66}

The Great Commission

16Then the eleven disciples went to Galilee, to the mountain where Jesus had told them to go. 17When they saw him, they worshiped him; but some doubted. 18Then Jesus came to them and said, "All authority in heaven and on earth has been given to me. 19Therefore go and make disciples of all nations, baptizing them in*a* the name of the Father and of the Son and of the Holy Spirit, 20and teaching them to obey everything I have commanded you. And surely I am with you always, to the very end of the age." _{Ac 1:8}

---

a19 Or *into*; see Acts 8:16; 19:5; Romans 6:3; 1 Cor. 1:13; 10:2 and Gal. 3:27.

Mark

Introduction:

Mark, the author of this Gospel, probably was the first to write down the events of Jesus' life. It is believed that he is the same person who worked for many years as a missionary with Paul and Barnabas.

The book of Mark, which stresses facts and actions rather than themes or topics, is the most exciting account of the life of Christ among the Gospels. Although it is the shortest of the four Gospels, it is often the most detailed. From the beginning Mark tells the stories of Christ's ministry, especially his miracles.

Mark shows Jesus as a man of action and authority. He spends one third of the book telling the events of Christ's last week on earth, ending with the Savior's death and resurrection.

Outline of contents:

John the Baptist Prepares the Way

1 The beginning of the gospel about Jesus Christ, the Son of God.[a]

²It is written in Isaiah the prophet:

"I will send my messenger
    ahead of you,
    who will prepare your
        way"[b]—

³"a voice of one calling in the
    desert,
    'Prepare the way for the
        Lord,
    make straight paths for
        him.' "[c]   Jn 1:23

⁴And so John came, baptizing in the desert region and preaching a baptism of repentance for the forgiveness of sins. ⁵The whole Judean countryside and all the people of Jerusalem went out to

---

a1 Some manuscripts do not have *the Son of God.*   *b2* Mal. 3:1   *c3* Isaiah 40:3

him. Confessing their sins, they were baptized by him in the Jordan River. [6]John wore clothing made of camel's hair, with a leather belt around his waist, and he ate locusts and wild honey. [7]And this was his message: "After me will come one more powerful than I, the thongs of whose sandals I am not worthy to stoop down and untie. [8]I baptize you with[a] water, but he will baptize you with the Holy Spirit."   Jn 1:26

The Baptism and Temptation of Jesus

[9]At that time Jesus came from Nazareth in Galilee and was baptized by John in the Jordan. [10]As Jesus was coming up out of the water, he saw heaven being torn open and the Spirit descending on him like a dove. [11]And a voice came from heaven: "You are my Son, whom I love; with you I am well pleased."   Mt 3:17; Jn 1:32

[12]At once the Spirit sent him out into the desert, [13]and he was in the desert forty days, being tempted by Satan. He was with the wild animals, and angels attended him.   Mt 4:1ff; Lk 4:1ff

The Calling of the First Disciples

[14]After John was put in prison, Jesus went into Galilee, proclaiming the good news of God. [15]"The time has come," he said. "The kingdom of God is near. Repent and believe the good news!"   Ro 5:6; Gal 4:4

[16]As Jesus walked beside the Sea of Galilee, he saw Simon and his brother Andrew casting a net into the lake, for they were fishermen. [17]"Come, follow me," Jesus said, "and I will make you fishers of men." [18]At once they left their nets and followed him.   Mt 4:19; 19:27

[19]When he had gone a little farther, he saw James son of Zebedee and his brother John in a boat, preparing their nets. [20]Without delay he called them, and they left their father Zebedee in the boat with the hired men and followed him.

Jesus Drives Out an Evil Spirit

[21]They went to Capernaum, and when the Sabbath came, Jesus went into the synagogue and began to teach. [22]The people were amazed at his teaching, because he taught them as one who had authority, not as the teachers of the law. [23]Just then a man in their synagogue who was possessed by an evil[b] spirit cried out, [24]"What do you want with us, Jesus of Nazareth? Have you come to destroy us? I know who you are—the Holy One of God!"

[25]"Be quiet!" said Jesus sternly. "Come out of him!" [26]The evil spirit shook the man violently and came out of him with a shriek.   Mk 9:20

---

[a]8 Or in   [b]23 Greek *unclean*; also in verses 26 and 27

27The people were all so amazed that they asked each other, "What is this? A new teaching—and with authority! He even gives orders to evil spirits and they obey him." 28News about him spread quickly over the whole region of Galilee.   Mt 9:26

Jesus Heals Many

29As soon as they left the synagogue, they went with James and John to the home of Simon and Andrew. 30Simon's mother-in-law was in bed with a fever, and they told Jesus about her. 31So he went to her, took her hand and helped her up. The fever left her and she began to wait on them.   Lk 4:38ff

32That evening after sunset the people brought to Jesus all the sick and demon-possessed. 33The whole town gathered at the door, 34and Jesus healed many who had various diseases. He also drove out many demons, but he would not let the demons speak because they knew who he was.   Mk 3:12

Jesus Prays in a Solitary Place

35Very early in the morning, while it was still dark, Jesus got up, left the house and went off to a solitary place, where he prayed. 36Simon and his companions went to look for him, 37and when they found him,

they exclaimed: "Everyone is looking for you!"

38Jesus replied, "Let us go somewhere else—to the nearby villages—so I can preach there also. That is why I have come." 39So he traveled throughout Galilee, preaching in their synagogues and driving out demons.   Isa 61:1; Lk 4:42,43

A Man With Leprosy

40A man with leprosy[a] came to him and begged him on his knees, "If you are willing, you can make me clean."

41Filled with compassion, Jesus reached out his hand and touched the man. "I am willing," he said. "Be clean!" 42Immediately the leprosy left him and he was cured.

43Jesus sent him away at once with a strong warning: 44"See that you don't tell this to anyone. But go, show yourself to the priest and offer the sacrifices that Moses commanded for your cleansing, as a testimony to them." 45Instead he went out and began to talk freely, spreading the news. As a result, Jesus could no longer enter a town openly but stayed outside in lonely places. Yet the people still came to him from everywhere.   Lev 14:1-32; Mt 8:4

Jesus Heals a Paralytic

2 A few days later, when Jesus again entered Capernaum,

---

a40 The Greek word was used for various diseases affecting the skin—not necessarily leprosy.

the people heard that he had come home. ²So many gathered that there was no room left, not even outside the door, and he preached the word to them. ³Some men came, bringing to him a paralytic, carried by four of them. ⁴Since they could not get him to Jesus because of the crowd, they made an opening in the roof above Jesus and, after digging through it, lowered the mat the paralyzed man was lying on. ⁵When Jesus saw their faith, he said to the paralytic, "Son, your sins are forgiven."

⁶Now some teachers of the law were sitting there, thinking to themselves, ⁷"Why does this fellow talk like that? He's blaspheming! Who can forgive sins but God alone?"   Isa 43:25

⁸Immediately Jesus knew in his spirit that this was what they were thinking in their hearts, and he said to them, "Why are you thinking these things? ⁹Which is easier: to say to the paralytic, 'Your sins are forgiven,' or to say, 'Get up, take your mat and walk'? ¹⁰But that you may know that the Son of Man has authority on earth to forgive sins . . . ." He said to the paralytic, ¹¹"I tell you, get up, take your mat and go home." ¹²He got up, took his mat and walked out in full view of them all. This amazed everyone and they praised God, saying, "We have never seen anything like this!"   Mt 9:2-8; Lk 5:18-26

The Calling of Levi

¹³Once again Jesus went out beside the lake. A large crowd came to him, and he began to teach them. ¹⁴As he walked along, he saw Levi son of Alphaeus sitting at the tax collector's booth. "Follow me," Jesus told him, and Levi got up and followed him.   Mt 4:19; Jn 6:2

¹⁵While Jesus was having dinner at Levi's house, many tax collectors and "sinners" were eating with him and his disciples, for there were many who followed him. ¹⁶When the teachers of the law who were Pharisees saw him eating with the "sinners" and tax collectors, they asked his disciples: "Why does he eat with tax collectors and 'sinners'?"   Mt 9:9ff

¹⁷On hearing this, Jesus said to them, "It is not the healthy who need a doctor, but the sick. I have not come to call the righteous, but sinners."   Lk 19:10

Jesus Questioned About Fasting

¹⁸Now John's disciples and the Pharisees were fasting. Some people came and asked Jesus, "How is it that John's disciples and the disciples of the Pharisees are fasting, but yours are not?"   Mt 6:16-18

¹⁹Jesus answered, "How can the guests of the bridegroom fast while he is with them? They cannot, so long as they have him with them. ²⁰But the time

will come when the bridegroom will be taken from them, and on that day they will fast. Lk 17:22

21"No one sews a patch of unshrunk cloth on an old garment. If he does, the new piece will pull away from the old, making the tear worse. 22And no one pours new wine into old wineskins. If he does, the wine will burst the skins, and both the wine and the wineskins will be ruined. No, he pours new wine into new wineskins."

Lord of the Sabbath

23One Sabbath Jesus was going through the grainfields, and as his disciples walked along, they began to pick some heads of grain. 24The Pharisees said to him, "Look, why are they doing what is unlawful on the Sabbath?" Mt 12:2

25He answered, "Have you never read what David did when he and his companions were hungry and in need? 26In the days of Abiathar the high priest, he entered the house of God and ate the consecrated bread, which is lawful only for priests to eat. And he also gave some to his companions."

27Then he said to them, "The Sabbath was made for man, not man for the Sabbath. 28So the Son of Man is Lord even of the Sabbath." Ex 23:12; Col 2:16

3 Another time he went into the synagogue, and a man with a shriveled hand was there. 2Some of them were looking for a reason to accuse Jesus, so they watched him closely to see if he would heal him on the Sabbath. 3Jesus said to the man with the shriveled hand, "Stand up in front of everyone." Mk 1:21

4Then Jesus asked them, "Which is lawful on the Sabbath: to do good or to do evil, to save life or to kill?" But they remained silent.

5He looked around at them in anger and, deeply distressed at their stubborn hearts, said to the man, "Stretch out your hand." He stretched it out, and his hand was completely restored. 6Then the Pharisees went out and began to plot with the Herodians how they might kill Jesus. Mt 12:9ff; Mk 12:13

Crowds Follow Jesus

7Jesus withdrew with his disciples to the lake, and a large crowd from Galilee followed. 8When they heard all he was doing, many people came to him from Judea, Jerusalem, Idumea, and the regions across the Jordan and around Tyre and Sidon. 9Because of the crowd he told his disciples to have a small boat ready for him, to keep the people from crowding him. 10For he had healed many, so that those with diseases were pushing forward to touch him. 11Whenever the evila spirits saw him, they fell down before him and cried out, "You are the Son

a11 Greek unclean; also in verse 30

of God." ¹²But he gave them strict orders not to tell who he was.   Mk 1:23-25

The Appointing of the Twelve Apostles

¹³Jesus went up on a mountainside and called to him those he wanted, and they came to him. ¹⁴He appointed twelve—designating them apostles[a]—that they might be with him and that he might send them out to preach ¹⁵and to have authority to drive out demons. ¹⁶These are the twelve he appointed: Simon (to whom he gave the name Peter); ¹⁷James son of Zebedee and his brother John (to them he gave the name Boanerges, which means Sons of Thunder); ¹⁸Andrew, Philip, Bartholomew, Matthew, Thomas, James son of Alphaeus, Thaddaeus, Simon the Zealot ¹⁹and Judas Iscariot, who betrayed him.   Mt 10:1

Jesus and Beelzebub

²⁰Then Jesus entered a house, and again a crowd gathered, so that he and his disciples were not even able to eat. ²¹When his family heard about this, they went to take charge of him, for they said, "He is out of his mind."   Mk 6:31; Jn 10:20

²²And the teachers of the law who came down from Jerusalem said, "He is possessed by Beelzebub[b]! By the prince of de-

mons he is driving out demons."   Jn 10:20,21

²³So Jesus called them and spoke to them in parables: "How can Satan drive out Satan? ²⁴If a kingdom is divided against itself, that kingdom cannot stand. ²⁵If a house is divided against itself, that house cannot stand. ²⁶And if Satan opposes himself and is divided, he cannot stand; his end has come. ²⁷In fact, no one can enter a strong man's house and carry off his possessions unless he first ties up the strong man. Then he can rob his house. ²⁸I tell you the truth, all the sins and blasphemies of men will be forgiven them. ²⁹But whoever blasphemes against the Holy Spirit will never be forgiven; he is guilty of an eternal sin."

³⁰He said this because they were saying, "He has an evil spirit."

Jesus' Mother and Brothers

³¹Then Jesus' mother and brothers arrived. Standing outside, they sent someone in to call him. ³²A crowd was sitting around him, and they told him, "Your mother and brothers are outside looking for you."   Lk 8:19

³³"Who are my mother and my brothers?" he asked.

³⁴Then he looked at those seated in a circle around him and said, "Here are my mother and my brothers! ³⁵Whoever

---

[a]14 Some manuscripts do not have *designating them apostles*.   [b]22 Greek *Beezeboul* or *Beelzeboul*

does God's will is my brother and sister and mother." Mt 12:46ff

The Parable of the Sower

4 Again Jesus began to teach by the lake. The crowd that gathered around him was so large that he got into a boat and sat in it out on the lake, while all the people were along the shore at the water's edge. ²He taught them many things by parables, and in his teaching said: ³"Listen! A farmer went out to sow his seed. ⁴As he was scattering the seed, some fell along the path, and the birds came and ate it up. ⁵Some fell on rocky places, where it did not have much soil. It sprang up quickly, because the soil was shallow. ⁶But when the sun came up, the plants were scorched, and they withered because they had no root. ⁷Other seed fell among thorns, which grew up and choked the plants, so that they did not bear grain. ⁸Still other seed fell on good soil. It came up, grew and produced a crop, multiplying thirty, sixty, or even a hundred times." Col 1:6

⁹Then Jesus said, "He who has ears to hear, let him hear."

¹⁰When he was alone, the Twelve and the others around him asked him about the parables. ¹¹He told them, "The secret of the kingdom of God has been given to you. But to those on the outside everything is said in parables ¹²so that,

"'they may be ever seeing
but never perceiving,
and ever hearing but never
understanding;
otherwise they might turn
and be forgiven!' ᵃ" 1 Th 4:12

¹³Then Jesus said to them, "Don't you understand this parable? How then will you understand any parable? ¹⁴The farmer sows the word. ¹⁵Some people are like seed along the path, where the word is sown. As soon as they hear it, Satan comes and takes away the word that was sown in them. ¹⁶Others, like seed sown on rocky places, hear the word and at once receive it with joy. ¹⁷But since they have no root, they last only a short time. When trouble or persecution comes because of the word, they quickly fall away. ¹⁸Still others, like seed sown among thorns, hear the word; ¹⁹but the worries of this life, the deceitfulness of wealth and the desires for other things come in and choke the word, making it unfruitful. ²⁰Others, like seed sown on good soil, hear the word, accept it, and produce a crop—thirty, sixty or even a hundred times what was sown." Ac 8:4

A Lamp on a Stand

²¹He said to them, "Do you bring in a lamp to put it under a bowl or a bed? Instead, don't you put it on its stand? ²²For whatever is hidden is meant to

be disclosed, and whatever is concealed is meant to be brought out into the open. ²³If anyone has ears to hear, let him hear." Jer 16:17; Mt 5:15

²⁴"Consider carefully what you hear," he continued. "With the measure you use, it will be measured to you—and even more. ²⁵Whoever has will be given more; whoever does not have, even what he has will be taken from him." Mt 25:29

The Parable of the Growing Seed

²⁶He also said, "This is what the kingdom of God is like. A man scatters seed on the ground. ²⁷Night and day, whether he sleeps or gets up, the seed sprouts and grows, though he does not know how. ²⁸All by itself the soil produces grain—first the stalk, then the head, then the full kernel in the head. ²⁹As soon as the grain is ripe, he puts the sickle to it, because the harvest has come."

The Parable of the Mustard Seed

³⁰Again he said, "What shall we say the kingdom of God is like, or what parable shall we use to describe it? ³¹It is like a mustard seed, which is the smallest seed you plant in the ground. ³²Yet when planted, it grows and becomes the largest of all garden plants, with such big branches that the birds of the air can perch in its shade."

³³With many similar parables Jesus spoke the word to them, as much as they could understand. ³⁴He did not say anything to them without using a parable. But when he was alone with his own disciples, he explained everything. Jn 16:12

Jesus Calms the Storm

³⁵That day when evening came, he said to his disciples, "Let us go over to the other side." ³⁶Leaving the crowd behind, they took him along, just as he was, in the boat. There were also other boats with him. ³⁷A furious squall came up, and the waves broke over the boat, so that it was nearly swamped. ³⁸Jesus was in the stern, sleeping on a cushion. The disciples woke him and said to him, "Teacher, don't you care if we drown?" Mk 3:9

³⁹He got up, rebuked the wind and said to the waves, "Quiet! Be still!" Then the wind died down and it was completely calm.

⁴⁰He said to his disciples, "Why are you so afraid? Do you still have no faith?" Mt 14:31

⁴¹They were terrified and asked each other, "Who is this? Even the wind and the waves obey him!" Lk 8:22ff

The Healing of a Demon-possessed Man

5 They went across the lake to the region of the Gera-

senes.ᵃ ²When Jesus got out of the boat, a man with an evilᵇ spirit came from the tombs to meet him. ³This man lived in the tombs, and no one could bind him any more, not even with a chain. ⁴For he had often been chained hand and foot, but he tore the chains apart and broke the irons on his feet. No one was strong enough to subdue him. ⁵Night and day among the tombs and in the hills he would cry out and cut himself with stones.

⁶When he saw Jesus from a distance, he ran and fell on his knees in front of him. ⁷He shouted at the top of his voice, "What do you want with me, Jesus, Son of the Most High God? Swear to God that you won't torture me!" ⁸For Jesus had said to him, "Come out of this man, you evil spirit!"

⁹Then Jesus asked him, "What is your name?"

"My name is Legion," he replied, "for we are many." ¹⁰And he begged Jesus again and again not to send them out of the area.

¹¹A large herd of pigs was feeding on the nearby hillside. ¹²The demons begged Jesus, "Send us among the pigs; allow us to go into them." ¹³He gave them permission, and the evil spirits came out and went into the pigs. The herd, about two thousand in number, rushed down the steep bank into the lake and were drowned.

¹⁴Those tending the pigs ran off and reported this in the town and countryside, and the people went out to see what had happened. ¹⁵When they came to Jesus, they saw the man who had been possessed by the legion of demons, sitting there, dressed and in his right mind; and they were afraid. ¹⁶Those who had seen it told the people what had happened to the demon-possessed man—and told about the pigs as well. ¹⁷Then the people began to plead with Jesus to leave their region.

¹⁸As Jesus was getting into the boat, the man who had been demon-possessed begged to go with him. ¹⁹Jesus did not let him, but said, "Go home to your family and tell them how much the Lord has done for you, and how he has had mercy on you." ²⁰So the man went away and began to tell in the Decapolisᶜ how much Jesus had done for him. And all the people were amazed. Mt 8:28ff

A Dead Girl and a Sick Woman

²¹When Jesus had again crossed over by boat to the other side of the lake, a large crowd gathered around him while he was by the lake. ²²Then one of the synagogue rulers, named Jairus, came there. See-

---

ᵃ1 Some manuscripts *Gadarenes*; other manuscripts *Gergesenes*　　ᵇ2 Greek *unclean*; also in verses 8 and 13　　ᶜ20 That is, the Ten Cities

ing Jesus, he fell at his feet ²³and pleaded earnestly with him, "My little daughter is dying. Please come and put your hands on her so that she will be healed and live." ²⁴So Jesus went with him.   Lk 4:40

A large crowd followed and pressed around him. ²⁵And a woman was there who had been subject to bleeding for twelve years. ²⁶She had suffered a great deal under the care of many doctors and had spent all she had, yet instead of getting better she grew worse. ²⁷When she heard about Jesus, she came up behind him in the crowd and touched his cloak, ²⁸because she thought, "If I just touch his clothes, I will be healed." ²⁹Immediately her bleeding stopped and she felt in her body that she was freed from her suffering.   Lev 15:25-30; Mt 9:18ff

³⁰At once Jesus realized that power had gone out from him. He turned around in the crowd and asked, "Who touched my clothes?"   Lk 6:19

³¹"You see the people crowding against you," his disciples answered, "and yet you can ask, 'Who touched me?'"

³²But Jesus kept looking around to see who had done it. ³³Then the woman, knowing what had happened to her, came and fell at his feet and, trembling with fear, told him the whole truth. ³⁴He said to her, "Daughter, your faith has healed you. Go in peace and be freed from your suffering."

³⁵While Jesus was still speaking, some men came from the house of Jairus, the synagogue ruler. "Your daughter is dead," they said. "Why bother the teacher any more?"

³⁶Ignoring what they said, Jesus told the synagogue ruler, "Don't be afraid; just believe."

³⁷He did not let anyone follow him except Peter, James and John the brother of James. ³⁸When they came to the home of the synagogue ruler, Jesus saw a commotion, with people crying and wailing loudly. ³⁹He went in and said to them, "Why all this commotion and wailing? The child is not dead but asleep." ⁴⁰But they laughed at him.

After he put them all out, he took the child's father and mother and the disciples who were with him, and went in where the child was. ⁴¹He took her by the hand and said to her, *"Talitha koum!"* (which means, "Little girl, I say to you, get up!"). ⁴²Immediately the girl stood up and walked around (she was twelve years old). At this they were completely astonished. ⁴³He gave strict orders not to let anyone know about this, and told them to give her something to eat.   Mt 8:14; Lk 7:14

A Prophet Without Honor

6 Jesus left there and went to his hometown, accompanied by his disciples. ²When the Sabbath came, he began to teach in the synagogue, and

many who heard him were amazed. Mt 2:23

"Where did this man get these things?" they asked. "What's this wisdom that has been given him, that he even does miracles! [3]Isn't this the carpenter? Isn't this Mary's son and the brother of James, Joseph,[a] Judas and Simon? Aren't his sisters here with us?" And they took offense at him. Mt 11:6

[4]Jesus said to them, "Only in his hometown, among his relatives and in his own house is a prophet without honor." [5]He could not do any miracles there, except lay his hands on a few sick people and heal them. [6]And he was amazed at their lack of faith. Mt 13:54ff

Jesus Sends Out the Twelve

Then Jesus went around teaching from village to village. [7]Calling the Twelve to him, he sent them out two by two and gave them authority over evil[b] spirits. Mk 3:13; Lk 10:1

[8]These were his instructions: "Take nothing for the journey except a staff—no bread, no bag, no money in your belts. [9]Wear sandals but not an extra tunic. [10]Whenever you enter a house, stay there until you leave that town. [11]And if any place will not welcome you or listen to you, shake the dust off your feet when you leave, as a testimony against them." Mt 10:14

[12]They went out and preached that people should repent. [13]They drove out many demons and anointed many sick people with oil and healed them. Mt 10:9ff; Lk 9:3ff; Jas 5:14

John the Baptist Beheaded

[14]King Herod heard about this, for Jesus' name had become well known. Some were saying,[c] "John the Baptist has been raised from the dead, and that is why miraculous powers are at work in him."

[15]Others said, "He is Elijah."

And still others claimed, "He is a prophet, like one of the prophets of long ago." Mal 4:5

[16]But when Herod heard this, he said, "John, the man I beheaded, has been raised from the dead!" Lk 3:19,20

[17]For Herod himself had given orders to have John arrested, and he had him bound and put in prison. He did this because of Herodias, his brother Philip's wife, whom he had married. [18]For John had been saying to Herod, "It is not lawful for you to have your brother's wife." [19]So Herodias nursed a grudge against John and wanted to kill him. But she was not able to, [20]because Herod feared John and protected him, knowing him to be a righteous and holy man. When Herod heard John, he was greatly puzzled[d]; yet he liked to listen to him. Mt 4:12

---

[a]3 Greek *Joses*, a variant of *Joseph*   [b]7 Greek *unclean*   [c]14 Some early manuscripts *He was saying*   [d]20 Some early manuscripts *he did many things*

²¹Finally the opportune time came. On his birthday Herod gave a banquet for his high officials and military commanders and the leading men of Galilee. ²²When the daughter of Herodias came in and danced, she pleased Herod and his dinner guests.   Lk 3:1

The king said to the girl, "Ask me for anything you want, and I'll give it to you." ²³And he promised her with an oath, "Whatever you ask I will give you, up to half my kingdom."

²⁴She went out and said to her mother, "What shall I ask for?"

"The head of John the Baptist," she answered.

²⁵At once the girl hurried in to the king with the request: "I want you to give me right now the head of John the Baptist on a platter."

²⁶The king was greatly distressed, but because of his oaths and his dinner guests, he did not want to refuse her. ²⁷So he immediately sent an executioner with orders to bring John's head. The man went, beheaded John in the prison, ²⁸and brought back his head on a platter. He presented it to the girl, and she gave it to her mother. ²⁹On hearing of this, John's disciples came and took his body and laid it in a tomb.   Mt 14:1ff

Jesus Feeds the Five Thousand

³⁰The apostles gathered around Jesus and reported to him all they had done and taught. ³¹Then, because so many people were coming and going that they did not even have a chance to eat, he said to them, "Come with me by yourselves to a quiet place and get some rest."   Mt 10:2; Mk 6:7ff

³²So they went away by themselves in a boat to a solitary place. ³³But many who saw them leaving recognized them and ran on foot from all the towns and got there ahead of them. ³⁴When Jesus landed and saw a large crowd, he had compassion on them, because they were like sheep without a shepherd. So he began teaching them many things.   Mt 9:36

³⁵By this time it was late in the day, so his disciples came to him. "This is a remote place," they said, "and it's already very late. ³⁶Send the people away so they can go to the surrounding countryside and villages and buy themselves something to eat."   Mt 14:13ff; Lk 9:10ff

³⁷But he answered, "You give them something to eat."

They said to him, "That would take eight months of a man's wages[a]! Are we to go and spend that much on bread and give it to them to eat?"   2Ki 4:42ff

³⁸"How many loaves do you have?" he asked. "Go and see."

When they found out, they said, "Five—and two fish."

³⁹Then Jesus directed them to

---

*a*37 Greek *take two hundred denarii*

have all the people sit down in groups on the green grass. ⁴⁰So they sat down in groups of hundreds and fifties. ⁴¹Taking the five loaves and the two fish and looking up to heaven, he gave thanks and broke the loaves. Then he gave them to his disciples to set before the people. He also divided the two fish among them all. ⁴²They all ate and were satisfied, ⁴³and the disciples picked up twelve basketfuls of broken pieces of bread and fish. ⁴⁴The number of the men who had eaten was five thousand.

Jesus Walks on the Water

⁴⁵Immediately Jesus made his disciples get into the boat and go on ahead of him to Bethsaida, while he dismissed the crowd. ⁴⁶After leaving them, he went up on a mountainside to pray.   Lk 3:21

⁴⁷When evening came, the boat was in the middle of the lake, and he was alone on land. ⁴⁸He saw the disciples straining at the oars, because the wind was against them. About the fourth watch of the night he went out to them, walking on the lake. He was about to pass by them, ⁴⁹but when they saw him walking on the lake, they thought he was a ghost. They cried out, ⁵⁰because they all saw him and were terrified.   Lk 24:37

Immediately he spoke to them and said, "Take courage! It is I. Don't be afraid." ⁵¹Then he climbed into the boat with them, and the wind died down. They were completely amazed, ⁵²for they had not understood about the loaves; their hearts were hardened.   Mk 4:39; 8:17-21

⁵³When they had crossed over, they landed at Gennesaret and anchored there. ⁵⁴As soon as they got out of the boat, people recognized Jesus. ⁵⁵They ran throughout that whole region and carried the sick on mats to wherever they heard he was. ⁵⁶And wherever he went—into villages, towns or countryside—they placed the sick in the marketplaces. They begged him to let them touch even the edge of his cloak, and all who touched him were healed.   Mt 14:22ff; Jn 6:15ff

Clean and Unclean

7 The Pharisees and some of the teachers of the law who had come from Jerusalem gathered around Jesus and ²saw some of his disciples eating food with hands that were "unclean," that is, unwashed. ³(The Pharisees and all the Jews do not eat unless they give their hands a ceremonial washing, holding to the tradition of the elders. ⁴When they come from the marketplace they do not eat unless they wash. And they observe many other traditions, such as the washing of cups, pitchers and kettles.ᵃ)   Ac 10:14

⁵So the Pharisees and teach-

ᵃ4 Some early manuscripts *pitchers, kettles and dining couches*

ers of the law asked Jesus, "Why don't your disciples live according to the tradition of the elders instead of eating their food with 'unclean' hands?"

⁶He replied, "Isaiah was right when he prophesied about you hypocrites; as it is written:

" 'These people honor me
    with their lips,
  but their hearts are far from
    me.
⁷They worship me in vain;
  their teachings are but rules
    taught by men.'ᵃ

⁸You have let go of the commands of God and are holding on to the traditions of men."

⁹And he said to them: "You have a fine way of setting aside the commands of God in order to observeᵇ your own traditions! ¹⁰For Moses said, 'Honor your father and your mother,'ᶜ and, 'Anyone who curses his father or mother must be put to death.'ᵈ ¹¹But you say that if a man says to his father or mother: 'Whatever help you might otherwise have received from me is Corban' (that is, a gift devoted to God), ¹²then you no longer let him do anything for his father or mother. ¹³Thus you nullify the word of God by your tradition that you have handed down. And you do many things like that." Heb 4:12

¹⁴Again Jesus called the crowd to him and said, "Listen to me, everyone, and understand this. ¹⁵Nothing outside a man can make him 'unclean' by going into him. Rather, it is what comes out of a man that makes him 'unclean.'ᵉ"

¹⁷After he had left the crowd and entered the house, his disciples asked him about this parable. ¹⁸"Are you so dull?" he asked. "Don't you see that nothing that enters a man from the outside can make him 'unclean'? ¹⁹For it doesn't go into his heart but into his stomach, and then out of his body." (In saying this, Jesus declared all foods "clean.") Ro 14:1-12; 1Ti 4:3-5

²⁰He went on: "What comes out of a man is what makes him 'unclean.' ²¹For from within, out of men's hearts, come evil thoughts, sexual immorality, theft, murder, adultery, ²²greed, malice, deceit, lewdness, envy, slander, arrogance and folly. ²³All these evils come from inside and make a man 'unclean.' " Mt 6:23; 15:1ff

The Faith of a Syrophoenician Woman

²⁴Jesus left that place and went to the vicinity of Tyre.ᶠ He entered a house and did not want anyone to know it; yet he could not keep his presence secret. ²⁵In fact, as soon as she heard about him, a woman whose little daughter was pos-

ᵃ6,7 Isaiah 29:13   ᵇ9 Some manuscripts set up   ᶜ10 Exodus 20:12; Deut. 5:16
ᵈ10 Exodus 21:17; Lev. 20:9   ᵉ15 Some early manuscripts 'unclean.' ¹⁶If anyone has ears
to hear, let him hear.   ᶠ24 Many early manuscripts Tyre and Sidon

sessed by an evil[a] spirit came and fell at his feet. 26The woman was a Greek, born in Syrian Phoenicia. She begged Jesus to drive the demon out of her daughter.

27"First let the children eat all they want," he told her, "for it is not right to take the children's bread and toss it to their dogs."

28"Yes, Lord," she replied, "but even the dogs under the table eat the children's crumbs."

29Then he told her, "For such a reply, you may go; the demon has left your daughter."

30She went home and found her child lying on the bed, and the demon gone.   Mt 15:21ff

The Healing of a Deaf and Mute Man

31Then Jesus left the vicinity of Tyre and went through Sidon, down to the Sea of Galilee and into the region of the Decapolis.[b] 32There some people brought to him a man who was deaf and could hardly talk, and they begged him to place his hand on the man.

33After he took him aside, away from the crowd, Jesus put his fingers into the man's ears. Then he spit and touched the man's tongue. 34He looked up to heaven and with a deep sigh said to him, *"Ephphatha!"* (which means, "Be opened!"). 35At this, the man's ears were opened, his tongue was loos-

ened and he began to speak plainly.   Isa 35:5-6; Mk 8:23

36Jesus commanded them not to tell anyone. But the more he did so, the more they kept talking about it. 37People were overwhelmed with amazement. "He has done everything well," they said. "He even makes the deaf hear and the mute speak."

Jesus Feeds the Four Thousand

8 During those days another large crowd gathered. Since they had nothing to eat, Jesus called his disciples to him and said, 2"I have compassion for these people; they have already been with me three days and have nothing to eat. 3If I send them home hungry, they will collapse on the way, because some of them have come a long distance."   Mt 9:36; 15:32ff

4His disciples answered, "But where in this remote place can anyone get enough bread to feed them?"

5"How many loaves do you have?" Jesus asked.

"Seven," they replied.

6He told the crowd to sit down on the ground. When he had taken the seven loaves and given thanks, he broke them and gave them to his disciples to set before the people, and they did so. 7They had a few small fish as well; he gave thanks for them also and told the disciples to distribute them.

---

[a]25 Greek *unclean*   [b]31 That is, the Ten Cities

[8] The people ate and were satisfied. Afterward the disciples picked up seven basketfuls of broken pieces that were left over. [9] About four thousand men were present. And having sent them away, [10] he got into the boat with his disciples and went to the region of Dalmanutha. Mt 14:19

[11] The Pharisees came and began to question Jesus. To test him, they asked him for a sign from heaven. [12] He sighed deeply and said, "Why does this generation ask for a miraculous sign? I tell you the truth, no sign will be given to it." [13] Then he left them, got back into the boat and crossed to the other side.

The Yeast of the Pharisees and Herod

[14] The disciples had forgotten to bring bread, except for one loaf they had with them in the boat. [15] "Be careful," Jesus warned them. "Watch out for the yeast of the Pharisees and that of Herod." Lk 12:1; 1Co 5:6-8

[16] They discussed this with one another and said, "It is because we have no bread."

[17] Aware of their discussion, Jesus asked them: "Why are you talking about having no bread? Do you still not see or understand? Are your hearts hardened? [18] Do you have eyes but fail to see, and ears but fail to hear? And don't you remember? [19] When I broke the five loaves for the five thousand, how many basketfuls of pieces did you pick up?" Isa 6:9-10; Mk 6:30ff

"Twelve," they replied.

[20] "And when I broke the seven loaves for the four thousand, how many basketfuls of pieces did you pick up?"

They answered, "Seven."

[21] He said to them, "Do you still not understand?" Mk 6:52

The Healing of a Blind Man at Bethsaida

[22] They came to Bethsaida, and some people brought a blind man and begged Jesus to touch him. [23] He took the blind man by the hand and led him outside the village. When he had spit on the man's eyes and put his hands on him, Jesus asked, "Do you see anything?"

[24] He looked up and said, "I see people; they look like trees walking around."

[25] Once more Jesus put his hands on the man's eyes. Then his eyes were opened, his sight was restored, and he saw everything clearly. [26] Jesus sent him home, saying, "Don't go into the village.[a]" Mt 8:4

Peter's Confession of Christ

[27] Jesus and his disciples went on to the villages around Caesarea Philippi. On the way he asked them, "Who do people say I am?" Lk 9:18ff

[28] They replied, "Some say John the Baptist; others say Eli-

---

[a]26 Some manuscripts *Don't go and tell anyone in the village*

jah; and still others, one of the prophets." _{Mal 4:5; Mt 3:1}

²⁹"But what about you?" he asked. "Who do you say I am?"

Peter answered, "You are the Christ.*" _{Jn 6:69; 11:27}

³⁰Jesus warned them not to tell anyone about him. _{Mt 16:13ff}

Jesus Predicts His Death

³¹He then began to teach them that the Son of Man must suffer many things and be rejected by the elders, chief priests and teachers of the law, and that he must be killed and after three days rise again. ³²He spoke plainly about this, and Peter took him aside and began to rebuke him. _{Mt 16:21; Ac 2:23}

³³But when Jesus turned and looked at his disciples, he rebuked Peter. "Get behind me, Satan!" he said. "You do not have in mind the things of God, but the things of men."

³⁴Then he called the crowd to him along with his disciples and said: "If anyone would come after me, he must deny himself and take up his cross and follow me. ³⁵For whoever wants to save his life* will lose it, but whoever loses his life for me and for the gospel will save it. ³⁶What good is it for a man to gain the whole world, yet forfeit his soul? ³⁷Or what can a man give in exchange for his soul? ³⁸If anyone is ashamed of me and my words in this adulter-

ous and sinful generation, the Son of Man will be ashamed of him when he comes in his Father's glory with the holy angels." _{Mt 10:38; Lk 12:9}

9 And he said to them, "I tell you the truth, some who are standing here will not taste death before they see the kingdom of God come with power."

The Transfiguration

²After six days Jesus took Peter, James and John with him and led them up a high mountain, where they were all alone. There he was transfigured before them. ³His clothes became dazzling white, whiter than anyone in the world could bleach them. ⁴And there appeared before them Elijah and Moses, who were talking with Jesus. _{Mt 28:3}

⁵Peter said to Jesus, "Rabbi, it is good for us to be here. Let us put up three shelters—one for you, one for Moses and one for Elijah." ⁶(He did not know what to say, they were so frightened.)

⁷Then a cloud appeared and enveloped them, and a voice came from the cloud: "This is my Son, whom I love. Listen to him!" _{Ex 24:16; Mt 3:17}

⁸Suddenly, when they looked around, they no longer saw anyone with them except Jesus.

⁹As they were coming down the mountain, Jesus gave them orders not to tell anyone what

---

*29 Or *Messiah*. "The Christ" (Greek) and "the Messiah" (Hebrew) both mean "the Anointed One."　　*35 The Greek word means either *life* or *soul*; also in verse 36.

they had seen until the Son of Man had risen from the dead. ¹⁰They kept the matter to themselves, discussing what "rising from the dead" meant. Mk 8:30

¹¹And they asked him, "Why do the teachers of the law say that Elijah must come first?"

¹²Jesus replied, "To be sure, Elijah does come first, and restores all things. Why then is it written that the Son of Man must suffer much and be rejected? ¹³But I tell you, Elijah has come, and they have done to him everything they wished, just as it is written about him."

The Healing of a Boy With an Evil Spirit

¹⁴When they came to the other disciples, they saw a large crowd around them and the teachers of the law arguing with them. ¹⁵As soon as all the people saw Jesus, they were overwhelmed with wonder and ran to greet him.

¹⁶"What are you arguing with them about?" he asked.

¹⁷A man in the crowd answered, "Teacher, I brought you my son, who is possessed by a spirit that has robbed him of speech. ¹⁸Whenever it seizes him, it throws him to the ground. He foams at the mouth, gnashes his teeth and becomes rigid. I asked your disciples to drive out the spirit, but they could not."

¹⁹"O unbelieving generation," Jesus replied, "how long shall I stay with you? How long shall I put up with you? Bring the boy to me."

²⁰So they brought him. When the spirit saw Jesus, it immediately threw the boy into a convulsion. He fell to the ground and rolled around, foaming at the mouth.

²¹Jesus asked the boy's father, "How long has he been like this?"

"From childhood," he answered. ²²"It has often thrown him into fire or water to kill him. But if you can do anything, take pity on us and help us."

²³"'If you can'?" said Jesus. "Everything is possible for him who believes." Mt 21:21; Jn 11:40

²⁴Immediately the boy's father exclaimed, "I do believe; help me overcome my unbelief!"

²⁵When Jesus saw that a crowd was running to the scene, he rebuked the evil*a* spirit. "You deaf and mute spirit," he said, "I command you, come out of him and never enter him again."

²⁶The spirit shrieked, convulsed him violently and came out. The boy looked so much like a corpse that many said, "He's dead." ²⁷But Jesus took him by the hand and lifted him to his feet, and he stood up.

²⁸After Jesus had gone indoors, his disciples asked him

---

a25 Greek unclean

privately, "Why couldn't we drive it out?" Mt 17:14ff; Lk 9:37ff

29He replied, "This kind can come out only by prayer. a"

30They left that place and passed through Galilee. Jesus did not want anyone to know where they were, 31because he was teaching his disciples. He said to them, "The Son of Man is going to be betrayed into the hands of men. They will kill him, and after three days he will rise." 32But they did not understand what he meant and were afraid to ask him about it. Jn 12:16

Who Is the Greatest?

33They came to Capernaum. When he was in the house, he asked them, "What were you arguing about on the road?" 34But they kept quiet because on the way they had argued about who was the greatest. Lk 22:24ff

35Sitting down, Jesus called the Twelve and said, "If anyone wants to be first, he must be the very last, and the servant of all." Mt 18:4; Mk 10:43,44

36He took a little child and had him stand among them. Taking him in his arms, he said to them, 37"Whoever welcomes one of these little children in my name welcomes me; and whoever welcomes me does not welcome me but the one who sent me." Mt 10:40; Lk 9:48

Whoever Is Not Against Us Is for Us

38"Teacher," said John, "we saw a man driving out demons in your name and we told him to stop, because he was not one of us." Nu 11:27-29

39"Do not stop him," Jesus said. "No one who does a miracle in my name can in the next moment say anything bad about me, 40for whoever is not against us is for us. 41I tell you the truth, anyone who gives you a cup of water in my name because you belong to Christ will certainly not lose his reward. Mt 10:42; 12:30; Lk 11:23

Causing to Sin

42"And if anyone causes one of these little ones who believe in me to sin, it would be better for him to be thrown into the sea with a large millstone tied around his neck. 43If your hand causes you to sin, cut it off. It is better for you to enter life maimed than with two hands to go into hell, where the fire never goes out. b 45And if your foot causes you to sin, cut it off. It is better for you to enter life crippled than to have two feet and be thrown into hell. c 47And if your eye causes you to sin, pluck it out. It is better for you to enter the kingdom of God with one eye than to have two

---

a29 Some manuscripts prayer and fasting worm does not die, / and the fire is not quenched.'   b43 Some manuscripts out, 44where / " 'their worm does not die, / and the fire is not quenched.'   c45 Some manuscripts hell, 46where / " 'their worm does not die, / and the fire is not quenched.'

eyes and be thrown into hell, [48]where

> " 'their worm does not die,
>   and the fire is not
>   quenched.' [a]

[49]Everyone will be salted with fire.   Lev 2:13; Mt 5:29; Lk 17:2

[50]"Salt is good, but if it loses its saltiness, how can you make it salty again? Have salt in yourselves, and be at peace with each other."   Mt 5:13; 2Co 13:11; Col 4:6

Divorce

10 Jesus then left that place and went into the region of Judea and across the Jordan. Again crowds of people came to him, and as was his custom, he taught them.   Mk 2:13

[2]Some Pharisees came and tested him by asking, "Is it lawful for a man to divorce his wife?"

[3]"What did Moses command you?" he replied.

[4]They said, "Moses permitted a man to write a certificate of divorce and send her away."

[5]"It was because your hearts were hard that Moses wrote you this law," Jesus replied. [6]"But at the beginning of creation God 'made them male and female.' [b] [7]For this reason a man will leave his father and mother and be united to his wife, [c] [8]and the two will become one flesh.' [d] So they are no longer two, but one. [9]Therefore what God has joined

together, let man not separate."

[10]When they were in the house again, the disciples asked Jesus about this. [11]He answered, "Anyone who divorces his wife and marries another woman commits adultery against her. [12]And if she divorces her husband and marries another man, she commits adultery."   Ro 7:3; 1Co 7:10,11

The Little Children and Jesus

[13]People were bringing little children to Jesus to have him touch them, but the disciples rebuked them. [14]When Jesus saw this, he was indignant. He said to them, "Let the little children come to me, and do not hinder them, for the kingdom of God belongs to such as these. [15]I tell you the truth, anyone who will not receive the kingdom of God like a little child will never enter it." [16]And he took the children in his arms, put his hands on them and blessed them.

The Rich Young Man

[17]As Jesus started on his way, a man ran up to him and fell on his knees before him. "Good teacher," he asked, "what must I do to inherit eternal life?" [Lk 10:25] [18]"Why do you call me good?" Jesus answered. "No one is good—except God alone. [19]You know the commandments: 'Do not murder, do not commit adultery, do not steal,

---

[a]48 Isaiah 66:24   [b]6 Gen. 1:27   [c]7 Some early manuscripts do not have *and be united to his wife*.   [d]8 Gen. 2:24

do not give false testimony, do not defraud, honor your father and mother.'ᵃ" Ex 20:12-16; 1Sa 2:2

²⁰"Teacher," he declared, "all these I have kept since I was a boy." Mt 19:20

²¹Jesus looked at him and loved him. "One thing you lack," he said. "Go, sell everything you have and give to the poor, and you will have treasure in heaven. Then come, follow me." Mt 6:20; Ac 2:45

²²At this the man's face fell. He went away sad, because he had great wealth.

²³Jesus looked around and said to his disciples, "How hard it is for the rich to enter the kingdom of God!" Ps 52:7; Mk 4:19

²⁴The disciples were amazed at his words. But Jesus said again, "Children, how hard it isᵇ to enter the kingdom of God! ²⁵It is easier for a camel to go through the eye of a needle than for a rich man to enter the kingdom of God." Mt 7:13,14; Lk 12:16-20

²⁶The disciples were even more amazed, and said to each other, "Who then can be saved?"

²⁷Jesus looked at them and said, "With man this is impossible, but not with God; all things are possible with God."

²⁸Peter said to him, "We have left everything to follow you!"

²⁹"I tell you the truth," Jesus replied, "no one who has left home or brothers or sisters or mother or father or children or fields for me and the gospel ³⁰will fail to receive a hundred times as much in this present age (homes, brothers, sisters, mothers, children and fields—and with them, persecutions) and in the age to come, eternal life. ³¹But many who are first will be last, and the last first."

Jesus Again Predicts His Death

³²They were on their way up to Jerusalem, with Jesus leading the way, and the disciples were astonished, while those who followed were afraid. Again he took the Twelve aside and told them what was going to happen to him. ³³"We are going up to Jerusalem," he said, "and the Son of Man will be betrayed to the chief priests and teachers of the law. They will condemn him to death and will hand him over to the Gentiles, ³⁴who will mock him and spit on him, flog him and kill him. Three days later he will rise." Mt 16:21; 20:17ff; Lk 18:31ff; Ac 2:23

The Request of James and John

³⁵Then James and John, the sons of Zebedee, came to him. "Teacher," they said, "we want you to do for us whatever we ask." Mt 20:20

³⁶"What do you want me to do for you?" he asked.

ᵃ19 Exodus 20:12-16; Deut. 5:16-20   ᵇ24 Some manuscripts *is for those who trust in riches*

³⁷They replied, "Let one of us sit at your right and the other at your left in your glory." Mt 19:28

³⁸"You don't know what you are asking," Jesus said. "Can you drink the cup I drink or be baptized with the baptism I am baptized with?" Lk 12:50

³⁹"We can," they answered.

Jesus said to them, "You will drink the cup I drink and be baptized with the baptism I am baptized with, ⁴⁰but to sit at my right or left is not for me to grant. These places belong to those for whom they have been prepared." Ac 12:2; Rev 1:9

⁴¹When the ten heard about this, they became indignant with James and John. ⁴²Jesus called them together and said, "You know that those who are regarded as rulers of the Gentiles lord it over them, and their high officials exercise authority over them. ⁴³Not so with you. Instead, whoever wants to become great among you must be your servant, ⁴⁴and whoever wants to be first must be slave of all. ⁴⁵For even the Son of Man did not come to be served, but to serve, and to give his life as a ransom for many." Mt 20:20ff; Mk 9:35

Blind Bartimaeus Receives His Sight

⁴⁶Then they came to Jericho. As Jesus and his disciples, together with a large crowd, were leaving the city, a blind man, Bartimaeus (that is, the Son of Timaeus), was sitting by the roadside begging. ⁴⁷When he heard that it was Jesus of Nazareth, he began to shout, "Jesus, Son of David, have mercy on me!" Mt 20:29ff; Lk 18:35ff

⁴⁸Many rebuked him and told him to be quiet, but he shouted all the more, "Son of David, have mercy on me!"

⁴⁹Jesus stopped and said, "Call him."

So they called to the blind man, "Cheer up! On your feet! He's calling you." ⁵⁰Throwing his cloak aside, he jumped to his feet and came to Jesus.

⁵¹"What do you want me to do for you?" Jesus asked him.

The blind man said, "Rabbi, I want to see."

⁵²"Go," said Jesus, "your faith has healed you." Immediately he received his sight and followed Jesus along the road.

The Triumphal Entry

11 As they approached Jerusalem and came to Bethphage and Bethany at the Mount of Olives, Jesus sent two of his disciples, ²saying to them, "Go to the village ahead of you, and just as you enter it, you will find a colt tied there, which no one has ever ridden. Untie it and bring it here. ³If anyone asks you, 'Why are you doing this?' tell him, 'The Lord needs it and will send it back here shortly.'" Mt 21:1ff; Lk 19:29ff; Jn 12:12ff

⁴They went and found a colt outside in the street, tied at a doorway. As they untied it, ⁵some people standing there

asked, "What are you doing, untying that colt?" ⁶They answered as Jesus had told them to, and the people let them go. ⁷When they brought the colt to Jesus and threw their cloaks over it, he sat on it. ⁸Many people spread their cloaks on the road, while others spread branches they had cut in the fields. ⁹Those who went ahead and those who followed shouted,

"Hosanna!ᵃ"

"Blessed is he who comes in the name of the Lord!"ᵇ

¹⁰"Blessed is the coming kingdom of our father David!"

"Hosanna in the highest!"

¹¹Jesus entered Jerusalem and went to the temple. He looked around at everything, but since it was already late, he went out to Bethany with the Twelve.

Jesus Clears the Temple

¹²The next day as they were leaving Bethany, Jesus was hungry. ¹³Seeing in the distance a fig tree in leaf, he went to find out if it had any fruit. When he reached it, he found nothing but leaves, because it was not the season for figs. ¹⁴Then he said to the tree, "May no one ever eat fruit from you again."

And his disciples heard him say it.   Mt 21:18ff; Lk 13:6-9

¹⁵On reaching Jerusalem, Jesus entered the temple area and began driving out those who were buying and selling there. He overturned the tables of the money changers and the benches of those selling doves, ¹⁶and would not allow anyone to carry merchandise through the temple courts. ¹⁷And as he taught them, he said, "Is it not written:

" 'My house will be called a house of prayer for all nations'ᶜ?

But you have made it 'a den of robbers.' ᵈ"

¹⁸The chief priests and the teachers of the law heard this and began looking for a way to kill him, for they feared him, because the whole crowd was amazed at his teaching.   Mt 21:46

¹⁹When evening came, theyᵉ went out of the city.   Lk 21:37

The Withered Fig Tree

²⁰In the morning, as they went along, they saw the fig tree withered from the roots. ²¹Peter remembered and said to Jesus, "Rabbi, look! The fig tree you cursed has withered!"

²²"Haveᶠ faith in God," Jesus answered. ²³"I tell you the truth, if anyone says to this mountain, 'Go, throw yourself into the sea,' and does not

ᵃ9 A Hebrew expression meaning "Save!" which became an exclamation of praise; also in verse 10   ᵇ9 Psalm 118:25,26   ᶜ17 Isaiah 56:7   ᵈ17 Jer. 7:11   ᵉ19 Some early manuscripts he   ᶠ22 Some early manuscripts If you have

doubt in his heart but believes that what he says will happen, it will be done for him. ²⁴Therefore I tell you, whatever you ask for in prayer, believe that you have received it, and it will be yours. ²⁵And when you stand praying, if you hold anything against anyone, forgive him, so that your Father in heaven may forgive you your sins.^a" Mt 21:21

The Authority of Jesus Questioned

²⁷They arrived again in Jerusalem, and while Jesus was walking in the temple courts, the chief priests, the teachers of the law and the elders came to him. ²⁸"By what authority are you doing these things?" they asked. "And who gave you authority to do this?" Mt 21:23

²⁹Jesus replied, "I will ask you one question. Answer me, and I will tell you by what authority I am doing these things. ³⁰John's baptism—was it from heaven, or from men? Tell me!"

³¹They discussed it among themselves and said, "If we say, 'From heaven,' he will ask, 'Then why didn't you believe him?' ³²But if we say, 'From men' . . . ." (They feared the people, for everyone held that John really was a prophet.)

³³So they answered Jesus, "We don't know."

Jesus said, "Neither will I tell you by what authority I am doing these things."

The Parable of the Tenants

12 He then began to speak to them in parables: "A man planted a vineyard. He put a wall around it, dug a pit for the winepress and built a watchtower. Then he rented the vineyard to some farmers and went away on a journey. ²At harvest time he sent a servant to the tenants to collect from them some of the fruit of the vineyard. ³But they seized him, beat him and sent him away empty-handed. ⁴Then he sent another servant to them; they struck this man on the head and treated him shamefully. ⁵He sent still another, and that one they killed. He sent many others; some of them they beat, others they killed. Isa 5:1-7

⁶"He had one left to send, a son, whom he loved. He sent him last of all, saying, 'They will respect my son.' Heb 1:1-3

⁷"But the tenants said to one another, 'This is the heir. Come, let's kill him, and the inheritance will be ours.' ⁸So they took him and killed him, and threw him out of the vineyard.

⁹"What then will the owner of the vineyard do? He will come and kill those tenants and give the vineyard to others. ¹⁰Haven't you read this scripture:

^a25 Some manuscripts sins. ²⁶But if you do not forgive, neither will your Father who is in heaven forgive your sins.

'' 'The stone the builders
    rejected
has become the capstone*a*;
¹¹the Lord has done this,
    and it is marvelous in our
    eyes'*b*?''

¹²Then they looked for a way
to arrest him because they knew
he had spoken the parable
against them. But they were
afraid of the crowd; so they left
him and went away.   Mk 11:18

Paying Taxes to Caesar

¹³Later they sent some of the
Pharisees and Herodians to
Jesus to catch him in his words.
¹⁴They came to him and said,
"Teacher, we know you are a
man of integrity. You aren't
swayed by men, because you
pay no attention to who they
are; but you teach the way of
God in accordance with the
truth. Is it right to pay taxes to
Caesar or not? ¹⁵Should we pay
or shouldn't we?''   Mt 22:16

But Jesus knew their hypocrisy. "Why are you trying to
trap me?" he asked. "Bring me
a denarius and let me look at it."
¹⁶They brought the coin, and he
asked them, "Whose portrait is
this? And whose inscription?"

"Caesar's," they replied.

¹⁷Then Jesus said to them,
"Give to Caesar what is Cae-
sar's and to God what is
God's.''   Ro 13:7

And they were amazed at
him.

Marriage at the Resurrection

¹⁸Then the Sadducees, who
say there is no resurrection,
came to him with a question.
¹⁹"Teacher," they said, "Moses
wrote for us that if a man's
brother dies and leaves a wife
but no children, the man must
marry the widow and have children for his brother. ²⁰Now
there were seven brothers. The
first one married and died without leaving any children. ²¹The
second one married the widow,
but he also died, leaving no
child. It was the same with the
third. ²²In fact, none of the
seven left any children. Last of
all, the woman died too. ²³At
the resurrection*c* whose wife
will she be, since the seven
were married to her?''   Dt 25:5,6

²⁴Jesus replied, "Are you not
in error because you do not
know the Scriptures or the
power of God? ²⁵When the dead
rise, they will neither marry nor
be given in marriage; they will
be like the angels in heaven.
²⁶Now about the dead ris-
ing—have you not read in the
book of Moses, in the account of
the bush, how God said to him,
'I am the God of Abraham, the
God of Isaac, and the God of
Jacob'*d*? ²⁷He is not the God of
the dead, but of the living. You
are badly mistaken!''   2Ti 3:15-17

The Greatest Commandment

²⁸One of the teachers of the

---

*a*10 Or *cornerstone*   *b*11 Psalm 118:22,23
men rise from the dead,   *d*26 Exodus 3:6

*c*23 Some manuscripts *resurrection, when*

law came and heard them debating. Noticing that Jesus had given them a good answer, he asked him, "Of all the commandments, which is the most important?"   Lk 10:25-28

29"The most important one," answered Jesus, "is this: 'Hear, O Israel, the Lord our God, the Lord is one.ᵃ 30Love the Lord your God with all your heart and with all your soul and with all your mind and with all your strength.'ᵇ 31The second is this: 'Love your neighbor as yourself.'ᶜ There is no commandment greater than these."

32"Well said, teacher," the man replied. "You are right in saying that God is one and there is no other but him. 33To love him with all your heart, with all your understanding and with all your strength, and to love your neighbor as yourself is more important than all burnt offerings and sacrifices."   Dt 4:35

34When Jesus saw that he had answered wisely, he said to him, "You are not far from the kingdom of God." And from then on no one dared ask him any more questions.

Whose Son Is the Christ?

35While Jesus was teaching in the temple courts, he asked, "How is it that the teachers of the law say that the Christᵈ is the son of David? 36David him-

self, speaking by the Holy Spirit, declared:

" 'The Lord said to my Lord:
"Sit at my right hand
until I put your enemies
under your feet." 'ᵉ

37David himself calls him 'Lord.' How then can he be his son?"

The large crowd listened to him with delight.   Jn 12:9

38As he taught, Jesus said, "Watch out for the teachers of the law. They like to walk around in flowing robes and be greeted in the marketplaces, 39and have the most important seats in the synagogues and the places of honor at banquets. 40They devour widows' houses and for a show make lengthy prayers. Such men will be punished most severely."   Lk 11:43

The Widow's Offering

41Jesus sat down opposite the place where the offerings were put and watched the crowd putting their money into the temple treasury. Many rich people threw in large amounts. 42But a poor widow came and put in two very small copper coins,ᶠ worth only a fraction of a penny.ᵍ   2Ki 12:9; Jn 8:20

43Calling his disciples to him, Jesus said, "I tell you the truth, this poor widow has put more into the treasury than all the others. 44They all gave out of their wealth; but she, out of her

---

ᵃ29 Or the Lord our God is one Lord   ᵇ30 Deut. 6:4,5   ᶜ31 Lev. 19:18   ᵈ35 Or Messiah   ᵉ36 Psalm 110:1   ᶠ42 Greek two lepta   ᵍ42 Greek kodrantes

poverty, put in everything—all she had to live on.''   2Co 8:12

Signs of the End of the Age

13 As he was leaving the temple, one of his disciples said to him, ''Look, Teacher! What massive stones! What magnificent buildings!''

2''Do you see all these great buildings?'' replied Jesus. ''Not one stone here will be left on another; every one will be thrown down.''   Lk 19:44

3As Jesus was sitting on the Mount of Olives opposite the temple, Peter, James, John and Andrew asked him privately, 4''Tell us, when will these things happen? And what will be the sign that they are all about to be fulfilled?''

5Jesus said to them: ''Watch out that no one deceives you. 6Many will come in my name, claiming, 'I am he,' and will deceive many. 7When you hear of wars and rumors of wars, do not be alarmed. Such things must happen, but the end is still to come. 8Nation will rise against nation, and kingdom against kingdom. There will be earthquakes in various places, and famines. These are the beginning of birth pains.   1Ti 4:1

9''You must be on your guard. You will be handed over to the local councils and flogged in the synagogues. On account of me you will stand before governors and kings as witnesses to them. 10And the gospel must first be preached to all nations. 11Whenever you are arrested and brought to trial, do not worry beforehand about what to say. Just say whatever is given you at the time, for it is not you speaking, but the Holy Spirit.

12''Brother will betray brother to death, and a father his child. Children will rebel against their parents and have them put to death. 13All men will hate you because of me, but he who stands firm to the end will be saved.   Mic 7:6; Jn 15:21

14''When you see 'the abomination that causes desolation'[a] standing where it[b] does not belong—let the reader understand—then let those who are in Judea flee to the mountains. 15Let no one on the roof of his house go down or enter the house to take anything out. 16Let no one in the field go back to get his cloak. 17How dreadful it will be in those days for pregnant women and nursing mothers! 18Pray that this will not take place in winter, 19because those will be days of distress unequaled from the beginning, when God created the world, until now—and never to be equaled again. 20If the Lord had not cut short those days, no one would survive. But for the sake of the elect, whom he has chosen, he has shortened them. 21At that time if anyone says to you, 'Look, here is the Christ[c]!'

a14 Daniel 9:27; 11:31; 12:11   b14 Or he; also in verse 29   c21 Or Messiah

or, 'Look, there he is!' do not believe it. 22For false Christs and false prophets will appear and perform signs and miracles to deceive the elect—if that were possible. 23So be on your guard; I have told you everything ahead of time. Da 11:31; Joel 2:2

24"But in those days, following that distress,

" 'the sun will be darkened,
    and the moon will not give
        its light;
25the stars will fall from the
    sky,
and the heavenly bodies
    will be shaken.'ᵃ

26"At that time men will see the Son of Man coming in clouds with great power and glory. 27And he will send his angels and gather his elect from the four winds, from the ends of the earth to the ends of the heavens. Zec 2:6; Rev 1:7

28"Now learn this lesson from the fig tree: As soon as its twigs get tender and its leaves come out, you know that summer is near. 29Even so, when you see these things happening, you know that it is near, right at the door. 30I tell you the truth, this generationᵇ will certainly not pass away until all these things have happened. 31Heaven and earth will pass away, but my words will never pass away.

The Day and Hour Unknown

32"No one knows about that day or hour, not even the angels in heaven, nor the Son, but only the Father. 33Be on guard! Be alertᶜ! You do not know when that time will come. 34It's like a man going away: He leaves his house and puts his servants in charge, each with his assigned task, and tells the one at the door to keep watch. Ac 1:7

35"Therefore keep watch because you do not know when the owner of the house will come back—whether in the evening, or at midnight, or when the rooster crows, or at dawn. 36If he comes suddenly, do not let him find you sleeping. 37What I say to you, I say to everyone: 'Watch!' " Lk 12:35-40

Jesus Anointed at Bethany

14 Now the Passover and the Feast of Unleavened Bread were only two days away, and the chief priests and the teachers of the law were looking for some sly way to arrest Jesus and kill him. 2"But not during the Feast," they said, "or the people may riot." Jn 11:55ff

3While he was in Bethany, reclining at the table in the home of a man known as Simon the Leper, a woman came with an alabaster jar of very expensive perfume, made of pure nard. She broke the jar and poured

---

ᵃ25 Isaiah 13:10; 34:4   ᵇ30 Or *race*   ᶜ33 Some manuscripts *alert and pray*

the perfume on his head. [4]Some of those present were saying indignantly to one another, "Why this waste of perfume? [5]It could have been sold for more than a year's wages[a] and the money given to the poor." And they rebuked her harshly.   Mt 26:2ff

[6]"Leave her alone," said Jesus. "Why are you bothering her? She has done a beautiful thing to me. [7]The poor you will always have with you, and you can help them any time you want. But you will not always have me. [8]She did what she could. She poured perfume on my body beforehand to prepare for my burial. [9]I tell you the truth, wherever the gospel is preached throughout the world, what she has done will also be told, in memory of her."

[10]Then Judas Iscariot, one of the Twelve, went to the chief priests to betray Jesus to them. [11]They were delighted to hear this and promised to give him money. So he watched for an opportunity to hand him over.

The Lord's Supper

[12]On the first day of the Feast of Unleavened Bread, when it was customary to sacrifice the Passover lamb, Jesus' disciples asked him, "Where do you want us to go and make preparations for you to eat the Passover?"   Ex 12:1-11; Dt 16:1-4

[13]So he sent two of his disciples, telling them, "Go into the city, and a man carrying a jar of water will meet you. Follow him. [14]Say to the owner of the house he enters, 'The Teacher asks: Where is my guest room, where I may eat the Passover with my disciples?' [15]He will show you a large upper room, furnished and ready. Make preparations for us there."

[16]The disciples left, went into the city and found things just as Jesus had told them. So they prepared the Passover.

[17]When evening came, Jesus arrived with the Twelve. [18]While they were reclining at the table eating, he said, "I tell you the truth, one of you will betray me—one who is eating with me."

[19]They were saddened, and one by one they said to him, "Surely not I?"

[20]"It is one of the Twelve," he replied, "one who dips bread into the bowl with me. [21]The Son of Man will go just as it is written about him. But woe to that man who betrays the Son of Man! It would be better for him if he had not been born."

[22]While they were eating, Jesus took bread, gave thanks and broke it, and gave it to his disciples, saying, "Take it; this is my body."   Mt 14:19

[23]Then he took the cup, gave thanks and offered it to them, and they all drank from it.

[24]"This is my blood of the[b]

---

[a]5 Greek *than three hundred denarii*   [b]24 Some manuscripts *the new*

covenant, which is poured out for many," he said to them. 25"I tell you the truth, I will not drink again of the fruit of the vine until that day when I drink it anew in the kingdom of God."

26When they had sung a hymn, they went out to the Mount of Olives.

Jesus Predicts Peter's Denial

27"You will all fall away," Jesus told them, "for it is written:

" 'I will strike the shepherd,
    and the sheep will be
        scattered.'*a*

28But after I have risen, I will go ahead of you into Galilee." Mk 16:7

29Peter declared, "Even if all fall away, I will not." Jn 13:37-38

30"I tell you the truth," Jesus answered, "today—yes, tonight—before the rooster crows twice*b* you yourself will disown me three times."

31But Peter insisted emphatically, "Even if I have to die with you, I will never disown you." And all the others said the same. Mt 26:47ff; Lk 22:47ff; Jn 18:3ff

Gethsemane

32They went to a place called Gethsemane, and Jesus said to his disciples, "Sit here while I pray." 33He took Peter, James and John along with him, and he began to be deeply distressed and troubled. 34"My soul is overwhelmed with sorrow to the point of death," he said to them. "Stay here and keep watch." Jn 12:27

35Going a little farther, he fell to the ground and prayed that if possible the hour might pass from him. 36"*Abba,c* Father," he said, "everything is possible for you. Take this cup from me. Yet not what I will, but what you will." Mt 26:18

37Then he returned to his disciples and found them sleeping. "Simon," he said to Peter, "are you asleep? Could you not keep watch for one hour? 38Watch and pray so that you will not fall into temptation. The spirit is willing, but the body is weak."

39Once more he went away and prayed the same thing. 40When he came back, he again found them sleeping, because their eyes were heavy. They did not know what to say to him.

41Returning the third time, he said to them, "Are you still sleeping and resting? Enough! The hour has come. Look, the Son of Man is betrayed into the hands of sinners. 42Rise! Let us go! Here comes my betrayer!"

Jesus Arrested

43Just as he was speaking, Judas, one of the Twelve, appeared. With him was a crowd armed with swords and clubs,

---

*a*27 Zech. 13:7   *b*30 Some early manuscripts do not have *twice*.   *c*36 Aramaic for *Father*

sent from the chief priests, the teachers of the law, and the elders.   Jn 18:3-11

⁴⁴Now the betrayer had arranged a signal with them: "The one I kiss is the man; arrest him and lead him away under guard." ⁴⁵Going at once to Jesus, Judas said, "Rabbi!" and kissed him. ⁴⁶The men seized Jesus and arrested him. ⁴⁷Then one of those standing near drew his sword and struck the servant of the high priest, cutting off his ear.

⁴⁸"Am I leading a rebellion," said Jesus, "that you have come out with swords and clubs to capture me? ⁴⁹Every day I was with you, teaching in the temple courts, and you did not arrest me. But the Scriptures must be fulfilled." ⁵⁰Then everyone deserted him and fled.   Isa 53:7-12

⁵¹A young man, wearing nothing but a linen garment, was following Jesus. When they seized him, ⁵²he fled naked, leaving his garment behind.

Before the Sanhedrin

⁵³They took Jesus to the high priest, and all the chief priests, elders and teachers of the law came together. ⁵⁴Peter followed him at a distance, right into the courtyard of the high priest. There he sat with the guards and warmed himself at the fire.

⁵⁵The chief priests and the whole Sanhedrin were looking for evidence against Jesus so that they could put him to death, but they did not find any. ⁵⁶Many testified falsely against him, but their statements did not agree.

⁵⁷Then some stood up and gave this false testimony against him: ⁵⁸"We heard him say, 'I will destroy this man-made temple and in three days will build another, not made by man.'" ⁵⁹Yet even then their testimony did not agree.   Jn 2:19

⁶⁰Then the high priest stood up before them and asked Jesus, "Are you not going to answer? What is this testimony that these men are bringing against you?" ⁶¹But Jesus remained silent and gave no answer.   Isa 53:7; Mt 27:12,14

Again the high priest asked him, "Are you the Christ,ᵃ the Son of the Blessed One?"   Mt 16:16

⁶²"I am," said Jesus. "And you will see the Son of Man sitting at the right hand of the Mighty One and coming on the clouds of heaven."   Rev 1:7

⁶³The high priest tore his clothes. "Why do we need any more witnesses?" he asked. ⁶⁴"You have heard the blasphemy. What do you think?"

They all condemned him as worthy of death. ⁶⁵Then some began to spit at him; they blindfolded him, struck him with their fists, and said, "Prophesy!" And the guards took him and beat him.   Lev 24:16

ᵃ61 Or *Messiah*

Peter Disowns Jesus

⁶⁶While Peter was below in the courtyard, one of the servant girls of the high priest came by. ⁶⁷When she saw Peter warming himself, she looked closely at him.

"You also were with that Nazarene, Jesus," she said.

⁶⁸But he denied it. "I don't know or understand what you're talking about," he said, and went out into the entryway.ᵃ

⁶⁹When the servant girl saw him there, she said again to those standing around, "This fellow is one of them." ⁷⁰Again he denied it.

After a little while, those standing near said to Peter, "Surely you are one of them, for you are a Galilean."

⁷¹He began to call down curses on himself, and he swore to them, "I don't know this man you're talking about."

⁷²Immediately the rooster crowed the second time.ᵇ Then Peter remembered the word Jesus had spoken to him: "Before the rooster crows twiceᶜ you will disown me three times." And he broke down and wept.   Mt 26:69ff; Lk 22:56ff

Jesus Before Pilate

15 Very early in the morning, the chief priests, with the elders, the teachers of the law and the whole Sanhedrin, reached a decision. They bound Jesus, led him away and handed him over to Pilate.

²"Are you the king of the Jews?" asked Pilate.

"Yes, it is as you say," Jesus replied.

³The chief priests accused him of many things. ⁴So again Pilate asked him, "Aren't you going to answer? See how many things they are accusing you of."

⁵But Jesus still made no reply, and Pilate was amazed.   Mk 14:61

⁶Now it was the custom at the Feast to release a prisoner whom the people requested. ⁷A man called Barabbas was in prison with the insurrectionists who had committed murder in the uprising. ⁸The crowd came up and asked Pilate to do for them what he usually did.

⁹"Do you want me to release to you the king of the Jews?" asked Pilate, ¹⁰knowing it was out of envy that the chief priests had handed Jesus over to him. ¹¹But the chief priests stirred up the crowd to have Pilate release Barabbas instead.   Ac 3:14

¹²"What shall I do, then, with the one you call the king of the Jews?" Pilate asked them.

¹³"Crucify him!" they shouted.

¹⁴"Why? What crime has he committed?" asked Pilate.

ᵃ68 Some early manuscripts entryway and the rooster crowed   ᵇ72 Some early manuscripts do not have the second time.   ᶜ72 Some early manuscripts do not have twice.

But they shouted all the louder, "Crucify him!"

¹⁵Wanting to satisfy the crowd, Pilate released Barabbas to them. He had Jesus flogged, and handed him over to be crucified.   Isa 53:6

The Soldiers Mock Jesus

¹⁶The soldiers led Jesus away into the palace (that is, the Praetorium) and called together the whole company of soldiers. ¹⁷They put a purple robe on him, then twisted together a crown of thorns and set it on him. ¹⁸And they began to call out to him, "Hail, king of the Jews!" ¹⁹Again and again they struck him on the head with a staff and spit on him. Falling on their knees, they paid homage to him. ²⁰And when they had mocked him, they took off the purple robe and put his own clothes on him. Then they led him out to crucify him.   Heb 13:12

The Crucifixion

²¹A certain man from Cyrene, Simon, the father of Alexander and Rufus, was passing by on his way in from the country, and they forced him to carry the cross. ²²They brought Jesus to the place called Golgotha (which means The Place of the Skull). ²³Then they offered him wine mixed with myrrh, but he did not take it. ²⁴And they crucified him. Dividing up his clothes, they cast lots to see what each would get.   Ps 22:18

²⁵It was the third hour when they crucified him. ²⁶The written notice of the charge against him read: THE KING OF THE JEWS. ²⁷They crucified two robbers with him, one on his right and one on his left.ᵃ ²⁹Those who passed by hurled insults at him, shaking their heads and saying, "So! You who are going to destroy the temple and build it in three days, ³⁰come down from the cross and save yourself!"

³¹In the same way the chief priests and the teachers of the law mocked him among themselves. "He saved others," they said, "but he can't save himself! ³²Let this Christ,ᵇ this King of Israel, come down now from the cross, that we may see and believe." Those crucified with him also heaped insults on him.

The Death of Jesus

³³At the sixth hour darkness came over the whole land until the ninth hour. ³⁴And at the ninth hour Jesus cried out in a loud voice, *"Eloi, Eloi, lama sabachthani?"*—which means, "My God, my God, why have you forsaken me?"ᶜ   Am 8:9

³⁵When some of those standing near heard this, they said, "Listen, he's calling Elijah."

³⁶One man ran, filled a sponge with wine vinegar, put it on a stick, and offered it to

ᵃ27 Some manuscripts *left, ²⁸and the scripture was fulfilled which says, "He was counted with the lawless ones"* (Isaiah 53:12)   ᵇ32 Or *Messiah*   ᶜ34 Psalm 22:1

Jesus to drink. "Now leave him alone. Let's see if Elijah comes to take him down," he said.

37With a loud cry, Jesus breathed his last.   Jn 19:30

38The curtain of the temple was torn in two from top to bottom. 39And when the centurion, who stood there in front of Jesus, heard his cry and*a* saw how he died, he said, "Surely this man was the Son*b* of God!"

40Some women were watching from a distance. Among them were Mary Magdalene, Mary the mother of James the younger and of Joses, and Salome. 41In Galilee these women had followed him and cared for his needs. Many other women who had come up with him to Jerusalem were also there.   Ps 38:11; Lk 2:2,3

The Burial of Jesus

42It was Preparation Day (that is, the day before the Sabbath). So as evening approached, 43Joseph of Arimathea, a prominent member of the Council, who was himself waiting for the kingdom of God, went boldly to Pilate and asked for Jesus' body. 44Pilate was surprised to hear that he was already dead. Summoning the centurion, he asked him if Jesus had already died. 45When he learned from the centurion that it was so, he gave the body to Joseph. 46So Joseph bought some linen cloth, took down the body, wrapped it in the linen, and placed it in a tomb cut out of rock. Then he rolled a stone against the entrance of the tomb. 47Mary Magdalene and Mary the mother of Joses saw where he was laid.

The Resurrection

16 When the Sabbath was over, Mary Magdalene, Mary the mother of James, and Salome bought spices so that they might go to anoint Jesus' body. 2Very early on the first day of the week, just after sunrise, they were on their way to the tomb 3and they asked each other, "Who will roll the stone away from the entrance of the tomb?"   Lk 23:56; Jn 19:39,40

4But when they looked up, they saw that the stone, which was very large, had been rolled away. 5As they entered the tomb, they saw a young man dressed in a white robe sitting on the right side, and they were alarmed.   Jn 20:12

6"Don't be alarmed," he said. "You are looking for Jesus the Nazarene, who was crucified. He has risen! He is not here. See the place where they laid him. 7But go, tell his disciples and Peter, 'He is going ahead of you into Galilee. There you will see him, just as he told you.' "Jn 21:1ff

8Trembling and bewildered, the women went out and fled from the tomb. They said noth-

---

*a*39 Some manuscripts do not have *heard his cry and*.   *b*39 Or *a son*

ing to anyone, because they were afraid.   Mt 28:8

[The earliest manuscripts and some other ancient witnesses do not have Mark 16:9–20.]

⁹When Jesus rose early on the first day of the week, he appeared first to Mary Magdalene, out of whom he had driven seven demons. ¹⁰She went and told those who had been with him and who were mourning and weeping. ¹¹When they heard that Jesus was alive and that she had seen him, they did not believe it.   Lk 24:11

¹²Afterward Jesus appeared in a different form to two of them while they were walking in the country. ¹³These returned and reported it to the rest; but they did not believe them either.   Lk 24:13-32

¹⁴Later Jesus appeared to the Eleven as they were eating; he rebuked them for their lack of faith and their stubborn refusal to believe those who had seen him after he had risen.   Lk 24:36-43

¹⁵He said to them, "Go into all the world and preach the good news to all creation. ¹⁶Whoever believes and is baptized will be saved, but whoever does not believe will be condemned. ¹⁷And these signs will accompany those who believe: In my name they will drive out demons; they will speak in new tongues; ¹⁸they will pick up snakes with their hands; and when they drink deadly poison, it will not hurt them at all; they will place their hands on sick people, and they will get well."

¹⁹After the Lord Jesus had spoken to them, he was taken up into heaven and he sat at the right hand of God. ²⁰Then the disciples went out and preached everywhere, and the Lord worked with them and confirmed his word by the signs that accompanied it.   Lk 24:50-51

Luke

Introduction:

Luke, the longest of the Gospels, was written by the same author as the book of Acts. Luke's writing shows him to be a highly educated man, who wrote from a Greek background and viewpoint.

Luke tells us in the first four verses of his book that he wrote this Gospel so we would have the true and complete story of Jesus' life. He wrote the fullest, most orderly story of his life.

One of Luke's interests in writing this book was to show that Jesus loved all kinds of people. He often wrote about and identified by name the women Christ met and spoke to. He also gave more attention to children than any other gospel writer. In the parables especially, he wrote about the poor and oppressed. Jesus is shown by Luke as an actual person in history who "came to seek and to save what was lost" (19:10).

The theme of joy is felt throughout this book—from the song of Mary and later the angels at Jesus' birth to the disciples who "returned to Jerusalem with great joy" after Christ's ascension. It is obvious that Luke wanted to tell the good news of Christ and show that his coming brought joy as well as hope and salvation to a sinful world.

Outline of contents:

Introduction

1 Many have undertaken to draw up an account of the things that have been fulfilled[a] among us, ²just as they were handed down to us by those who from the first were eyewitnesses and servants of the word. ³Therefore, since I myself have carefully investigated everything from the beginning, it seemed good also to me to write an orderly account for you, most excellent Theophilus, ⁴so that you may know the certainty of the things you have been taught.   Mk 1:1; Jn 20:31

The Birth of John the Baptist Foretold

⁵In the time of Herod king of Judea there was a priest named Zechariah, who belonged to the priestly division of Abijah; his wife Elizabeth was also a descendant of Aaron. ⁶Both of them were upright in the sight of God, observing all the Lord's commandments and regulations blamelessly. ⁷But they had no children, because Elizabeth was barren; and they were both well along in years.   Ge 6:9

⁸Once when Zechariah's division was on duty and he was serving as priest before God, ⁹he was chosen by lot, according to the custom of the priesthood, to go into the temple of the Lord and burn incense. ¹⁰And when the time for the burning of incense came, all the assembled worshipers were praying outside.   1Ch 24:19

¹¹Then an angel of the Lord appeared to him, standing at the right side of the altar of incense. ¹²When Zechariah saw him, he was startled and was gripped with fear. ¹³But the angel said to him: "Do not be afraid, Zechariah; your prayer has been heard. Your wife Elizabeth will bear you a son, and you are to give him the name John. ¹⁴He will be a joy and delight to you, and many will rejoice because of his birth, ¹⁵for he will be great in the sight of the Lord. He is never to take wine or other fermented drink, and he will be filled with the Holy Spirit even from birth.[b] ¹⁶Many of the people of Israel will he bring back to the Lord their God. ¹⁷And he will go on before the Lord, in the spirit and power of Elijah, to turn the hearts of the fathers to their children and the disobedient to the wisdom of the righteous—to make ready a people prepared for the Lord."   Mal 4:5,6

¹⁸Zechariah asked the angel, "How can I be sure of this? I am an old man and my wife is well along in years."   Ge 17:17

¹⁹The angel answered, "I am Gabriel. I stand in the presence of God, and I have been sent to speak to you and to tell you this good news. ²⁰And now you will be silent and not able to speak until the day this happens, be-

---

[a]1 Or been surely believed   [b]15 Or from his mother's womb

cause you did not believe my words, which will come true at their proper time." Eze 3:6

21Meanwhile, the people were waiting for Zechariah and wondering why he stayed so long in the temple. 22When he came out, he could not speak to them. They realized he had seen a vision in the temple, for he kept making signs to them but remained unable to speak.

23When his time of service was completed, he returned home. 24After this his wife Elizabeth became pregnant and for five months remained in seclusion. 25"The Lord has done this for me," she said. "In these days he has shown his favor and taken away my disgrace among the people." Ge 30:23

The Birth of Jesus Foretold

26In the sixth month, God sent the angel Gabriel to Nazareth, a town in Galilee, 27to a virgin pledged to be married to a man named Joseph, a descendant of David. The virgin's name was Mary. 28The angel went to her and said, "Greetings, you who are highly favored! The Lord is with you."

29Mary was greatly troubled at his words and wondered what kind of greeting this might be. 30But the angel said to her, "Do not be afraid, Mary, you have found favor with God. 31You will be with child and give birth to a son, and you are to

give him the name Jesus. 32He will be great and will be called the Son of the Most High. The Lord God will give him the throne of his father David, 33and he will reign over the house of Jacob forever; his kingdom will never end." Ps 89:3,4; Mt 28:18

34"How will this be," Mary asked the angel, "since I am a virgin?" Isa 7:14

35The angel answered, "The Holy Spirit will come upon you, and the power of the Most High will overshadow you. So the holy one to be born will be calleda the Son of God. 36Even Elizabeth your relative is going to have a child in her old age, and she who was said to be barren is in her sixth month. 37For nothing is impossible with God." Mt 1:18; 19:26

38"I am the Lord's servant," Mary answered. "May it be to me as you have said." Then the angel left her.

Mary Visits Elizabeth

39At that time Mary got ready and hurried to a town in the hill country of Judea, 40where she entered Zechariah's home and greeted Elizabeth. 41When Elizabeth heard Mary's greeting, the baby leaped in her womb, and Elizabeth was filled with the Holy Spirit. 42In a loud voice she exclaimed: "Blessed are you among women, and blessed is the child you will bear! 43But why am I so favored, that the

---

a35 Or So the child to be born will be called holy,

mother of my Lord should come to me? ⁴⁴As soon as the sound of your greeting reached my ears, the baby in my womb leaped for joy. ⁴⁵Blessed is she who has believed that what the Lord has said to her will be accomplished!"

Mary's Song

⁴⁶And Mary said:

"My soul glorifies the Lord
⁴⁷   and my spirit rejoices in
     God my Savior,   Ps 18:46
⁴⁸for he has been mindful
     of the humble state of his
     servant.   Ps 138:6
From now on all generations
     will call me blessed,
⁴⁹   for the Mighty One has
     done great things for
     me—   Ps 71:19
   holy is his name.   Ps 111:9
⁵⁰His mercy extends to those
     who fear him,
   from generation to
     generation.   Ex 20:6
⁵¹He has performed mighty
     deeds with his arm;
   he has scattered those who
     are proud in their
     inmost thoughts.   Ge 11:8
⁵²He has brought down rulers
     from their thrones
   but has lifted up the
     humble.   Mt 23:12
⁵³He has filled the hungry with
     good things   Ps 107:9
   but has sent the rich away
     empty.
⁵⁴He has helped his servant
     Israel,
   remembering to be merciful
⁵⁵to Abraham and his
     descendants forever,
   even as he said to our
     fathers."

⁵⁶Mary stayed with Elizabeth for about three months and then returned home.

The Birth of John the Baptist

⁵⁷When it was time for Elizabeth to have her baby, she gave birth to a son. ⁵⁸Her neighbors and relatives heard that the Lord had shown her great mercy, and they shared her joy.

⁵⁹On the eighth day they came to circumcise the child, and they were going to name him after his father Zechariah, ⁶⁰but his mother spoke up and said, "No! He is to be called John."   Ge 17:12

⁶¹They said to her, "There is no one among your relatives who has that name."

⁶²Then they made signs to his father, to find out what he would like to name the child. ⁶³He asked for a writing tablet, and to everyone's astonishment he wrote, "His name is John." ⁶⁴Immediately his mouth was opened and his tongue was loosed, and he began to speak, praising God. ⁶⁵The neighbors were all filled with awe, and throughout the hill country of Judea people were talking about all these things. ⁶⁶Everyone who heard this wondered about it, asking, "What then is this child going to be?" For the Lord's hand was with him.   Ac 11:21

Zechariah's Song

⁶⁷His father Zechariah was filled with the Holy Spirit and prophesied: Joel 2:28,29

⁶⁸"Praise be to the Lord, the
   God of Israel,   Ge 24:27
   because he has come and
     has redeemed his
     people.   Ps 111:9
⁶⁹He has raised up a horn^a of
     salvation for us   1Sa 2:1
   in the house of his servant
     David   Mt 1:1
⁷⁰(as he said through his holy
     prophets of long ago),
⁷¹salvation from our enemies
   and from the hand of all
     who hate us—
⁷²to show mercy to our fathers
   and to remember his holy
     covenant,   Ps 105:8-9
⁷³ the oath he swore to our
     father Abraham: Ge 22:16-18
⁷⁴to rescue us from the hand of
     our enemies,
   and to enable us to serve
     him without fear   1Jn 4:18
⁷⁵ in holiness and
     righteousness before
     him all our days.   Eph 4:24

⁷⁶And you, my child, will be
   called a prophet of the
   Most High;
   for you will go on before
     the Lord to prepare the
     way for him,   Mt 3:3
⁷⁷to give his people the
   knowledge of salvation
   through the forgiveness of
     their sins,   Jer 31:34

⁷⁸because of the tender mercy
     of our God,
   by which the rising sun will
     come to us from heaven
⁷⁹to shine on those living in
     darkness
   and in the shadow of death,
   to guide our feet into the
     path of peace."   Lk 2:14

⁸⁰And the child grew and became strong in spirit; and he lived in the desert until he appeared publicly to Israel. Lk 2:40,52

The Birth of Jesus

2 In those days Caesar Augustus issued a decree that a census should be taken of the entire Roman world. ²(This was the first census that took place while Quirinius was governor of Syria.) ³And everyone went to his own town to register.

⁴So Joseph also went up from the town of Nazareth in Galilee to Judea, to Bethlehem the town of David, because he belonged to the house and line of David. ⁵He went there to register with Mary, who was pledged to be married to him and was expecting a child. ⁶While they were there, the time came for the baby to be born, ⁷and she gave birth to her firstborn, a son. She wrapped him in cloths and placed him in a manger, because there was no room for them in the inn. Jn 7:42; Lk 1:27

$^a69$ *Horn* here symbolizes strength.

The Shepherds and the Angels

8And there were shepherds living out in the fields nearby, keeping watch over their flocks at night. 9An angel of the Lord appeared to them, and the glory of the Lord shone around them, and they were terrified. 10But the angel said to them, "Do not be afraid. I bring you good news of great joy that will be for all the people. 11Today in the town of David a Savior has been born to you; he is Christ*a* the Lord. 12This will be a sign to you: You will find a baby wrapped in cloths and lying in a manger."

13Suddenly a great company of the heavenly host appeared with the angel, praising God and saying,

14"Glory to God in the highest,
    and on earth peace to men
        on whom his favor
            rests."   Isa 9:6; Mic 5:5

15When the angels had left them and gone into heaven, the shepherds said to one another, "Let's go to Bethlehem and see this thing that has happened, which the Lord has told us about."

16So they hurried off and found Mary and Joseph, and the baby, who was lying in the manger. 17When they had seen him, they spread the word concerning what had been told them about this child, 18and all who heard it were amazed at what the shepherds said to them. 19But Mary treasured up all these things and pondered them in her heart. 20The shepherds returned, glorifying and praising God for all the things they had heard and seen, which were just as they had been told.

Jesus Presented in the Temple

21On the eighth day, when it was time to circumcise him, he was named Jesus, the name the angel had given him before he had been conceived.   Lk 1:31

22When the time of their purification according to the Law of Moses had been completed, Joseph and Mary took him to Jerusalem to present him to the Lord 23(as it is written in the Law of the Lord, "Every firstborn male is to be consecrated to the Lord"*b*), 24and to offer a sacrifice in keeping with what is said in the Law of the Lord: "a pair of doves or two young pigeons."*c*

25Now there was a man in Jerusalem called Simeon, who was righteous and devout. He was waiting for the consolation of Israel, and the Holy Spirit was upon him. 26It had been revealed to him by the Holy Spirit that he would not die before he had seen the Lord's Christ. 27Moved by the Spirit, he went into the temple courts. When

a11 Or *Messiah*. "The Christ" (Greek) and "the Messiah" (Hebrew) both mean "the Anointed One"; also in verse 26.   *b23* Exodus 13:2,12   *c24* Lev. 12:8

the parents brought in the child Jesus to do for him what the custom of the Law required, [28]Simeon took him in his arms and praised God, saying: Lk 1:6

[29]"Sovereign Lord, as you
    have promised,
  you now dismiss[a] your
    servant in peace.
[30]For my eyes have seen your
    salvation,   Isa 40:5
[31] which you have prepared
    in the sight of all people,
[32]a light for revelation to the
    Gentiles
  and for glory to your people
    Israel."   Isa 42:6

[33]The child's father and mother marveled at what was said about him. [34]Then Simeon blessed them and said to Mary, his mother: "This child is destined to cause the falling and rising of many in Israel, and to be a sign that will be spoken against, [35]so that the thoughts of many hearts will be revealed. And a sword will pierce your own soul too."   Isa 8:14; Mt 12:46ff

[36]There was also a prophetess, Anna, the daughter of Phanuel, of the tribe of Asher. She was very old; she had lived with her husband seven years after her marriage, [37]and then was a widow until she was eighty-four.[b] She never left the temple but worshiped night and day, fasting and praying. [38]Coming up to them at that very moment, she gave thanks

to God and spoke about the child to all who were looking forward to the redemption of Jerusalem.   Isa 40:2; Ac 21:9

[39]When Joseph and Mary had done everything required by the Law of the Lord, they returned to Galilee to their own town of Nazareth. [40]And the child grew and became strong; he was filled with wisdom, and the grace of God was upon him.

The Boy Jesus at the Temple

[41]Every year his parents went to Jerusalem for the Feast of the Passover. [42]When he was twelve years old, they went up to the Feast, according to the custom. [43]After the Feast was over, while his parents were returning home, the boy Jesus stayed behind in Jerusalem, but they were unaware of it. [44]Thinking he was in their company, they traveled on for a day. Then they began looking for him among their relatives and friends. [45]When they did not find him, they went back to Jerusalem to look for him. [46]After three days they found him in the temple courts, sitting among the teachers, listening to them and asking them questions. [47]Everyone who heard him was amazed at his understanding and his answers. [48]When his parents saw him, they were astonished. His mother said to him, "Son, why have you treated us like this?

---

[a]29 Or promised, / now dismiss   [b]37 Or widow for eighty-four years

Your father and I have been anxiously searching for you."

49"Why were you searching for me?" he asked. "Didn't you know I had to be in my Father's house?" 50But they did not understand what he was saying to them.　　　　　　　Mk 9:32; Jn 2:16

51Then he went down to Nazareth with them and was obedient to them. But his mother treasured all these things in her heart. 52And Jesus grew in wisdom and stature, and in favor with God and men.　　　　Mt 2:23

John the Baptist Prepares the Way

3 In the fifteenth year of the reign of Tiberius Caesar—when Pontius Pilate was governor of Judea, Herod tetrarch of Galilee, his brother Philip tetrarch of Iturea and Traconitis, and Lysanias tetrarch of Abilene— 2during the high priesthood of Annas and Caiaphas, the word of God came to John son of Zechariah in the desert. 3He went into all the country around the Jordan, preaching a baptism of repentance for the forgiveness of sins. 4As is written in the book of the words of Isaiah the prophet:

"A voice of one calling in the desert,
'Prepare the way for the Lord,
make straight paths for him.

5Every valley shall be filled in,
every mountain and hill
made low.
The crooked roads shall
become straight,
the rough ways smooth.
6And all mankind will see
God's salvation.' "a

7John said to the crowds coming out to be baptized by him, "You brood of vipers! Who warned you to flee from the coming wrath? 8Produce fruit in keeping with repentance. And do not begin to say to yourselves, 'We have Abraham as our father.' For I tell you that out of these stones God can raise up children for Abraham. 9The ax is already at the root of the trees, and every tree that does not produce good fruit will be cut down and thrown into the fire."　　　　　　　Mt 12:34

10"What should we do then?" the crowd asked.　　　Ac 2:37

11John answered, "The man with two tunics should share with him who has none, and the one who has food should do the same."　　　Isa 58:7; Eze 18:7

12Tax collectors also came to be baptized. "Teacher," they asked, "what should we do?"

13"Don't collect any more than you are required to," he told them.　　　　　　　Lk 19:8

14Then some soldiers asked him, "And what should we do?"

He replied, "Don't extort money and don't accuse people

a6 Isaiah 40:3-5

falsely—be content with your pay." Ex 23:1; Lev 19:11

15The people were waiting expectantly and were all wondering in their hearts if John might possibly be the Christ.*a* 16John answered them all, "I baptize you with*b* water. But one more powerful than I will come, the thongs of whose sandals I am not worthy to untie. He will baptize you with the Holy Spirit and with fire. 17His winnowing fork is in his hand to clear his threshing floor and to gather the wheat into his barn, but he will burn up the chaff with unquenchable fire." 18And with many other words John exhorted the people and preached the good news to them.

19But when John rebuked Herod the tetrarch because of Herodias, his brother's wife, and all the other evil things he had done, 20Herod added this to them all: He locked John up in prison. Mt 14:3-4

The Baptism and Genealogy of Jesus

21When all the people were being baptized, Jesus was baptized too. And as he was praying, heaven was opened 22and the Holy Spirit descended on him in bodily form like a dove. And a voice came from heaven: "You are my Son, whom I love; with you I am well pleased."

23Now Jesus himself was about thirty years old when he began his ministry. He was the son, so it was thought, of Joseph, Lk 1:27

the son of Heli, 24the son of Matthat,
the son of Levi, the son of Melki,
the son of Jannai, the son of Joseph,
25the son of Mattathias, the son of Amos,
the son of Nahum, the son of Esli,
the son of Naggai, 26the son of Maath,
the son of Mattathias, the son of Semein,
the son of Josech, the son of Joda,
27the son of Joanan, the son of Rhesa,
the son of Zerubbabel, the son of Shealtiel,
the son of Neri, 28the son of Melki,
the son of Addi, the son of Cosam,
the son of Elmadam, the son of Er,
29the son of Joshua, the son of Eliezer,
the son of Jorim, the son of Matthat,
the son of Levi, 30the son of Simeon,
the son of Judah, the son of Joseph,
the son of Jonam, the son of Eliakim,
31the son of Melea, the son of Menna,

a15 Or *Messiah*　　*b16* Or *in*

the son of Mattatha, the son of Nathan, 2Sa 5:14

the son of David, 32the son of Jesse,

the son of Obed, the son of Boaz,

the son of Salmon,*a* the son of Nahshon,

33the son of Amminadab, the son of Ram,*b*

the son of Hezron, the son of Perez, Ru 4:16-22

the son of Judah, 34the son of Jacob,

the son of Isaac, the son of Abraham,

the son of Terah, the son of Nahor, Ge 11:24

35the son of Serug, the son of Reu,

the son of Peleg, the son of Eber,

the son of Shelah, 36the son of Cainan,

the son of Arphaxad, the son of Shem, Ge 11:12

the son of Noah, the son of Lamech, Ge 5:28-32

37the son of Methuselah, the son of Enoch,

the son of Jared, the son of Mahalalel, Ge 5:12-25

the son of Kenan, 38the son of Enosh,

the son of Seth, the son of Adam,

the son of God. Ge 5:1-2

The Temptation of Jesus

4 Jesus, full of the Holy Spirit, returned from the Jordan and was led by the Spirit in the desert, 2where for forty days he was tempted by the devil. He ate nothing during those days, and at the end of them he was hungry. Lk 1:15,35; 3:3,21

3The devil said to him, "If you are the Son of God, tell this stone to become bread." Mt 4:3

4Jesus answered, "It is written: 'Man does not live on bread alone.'*c*"

5The devil led him up to a high place and showed him in an instant all the kingdoms of the world. 6And he said to him, "I will give you all their authority and splendor, for it has been given to me, and I can give it to anyone I want to. 7So if you worship me, it will all be yours." 1Jn 5:19

8Jesus answered, "It is written: 'Worship the Lord your God and serve him only.'*d*"

9The devil led him to Jerusalem and had him stand on the highest point of the temple. "If you are the Son of God," he said, "throw yourself down from here. 10For it is written:

" 'He will command his
    angels concerning you
  to guard you carefully;
11they will lift you up in their
    hands,
  so that you will not strike
    your foot against a
    stone.'*e*"

12Jesus answered, "It says:

---

a32 Some early manuscripts *Sala*   *b33* Some manuscripts *Amminadab, the son of Admin, the son of Arni;* other manuscripts vary widely.   *c4* Deut. 8:3
d8 Deut. 6:13   *e11* Psalm 91:11,12

'Do not put the Lord your God to the test.'[a]"

¹³When the devil had finished all this tempting, he left him until an opportune time.   Heb 4:15

Jesus Rejected at Nazareth

¹⁴Jesus returned to Galilee in the power of the Spirit, and news about him spread through the whole countryside. ¹⁵He taught in their synagogues, and everyone praised him.

¹⁶He went to Nazareth, where he had been brought up, and on the Sabbath day he went into the synagogue, as was his custom. And he stood up to read. ¹⁷The scroll of the prophet Isaiah was handed to him. Unrolling it, he found the place where it is written: Mt 13:54

¹⁸"The Spirit of the Lord is on me,
    because he has anointed me
        to preach good news to the poor.
    He has sent me to proclaim
        freedom for the prisoners
    and recovery of sight for
        the blind,
    to release the oppressed,   Jn 3:34
¹⁹   to proclaim the year of the
        Lord's favor."[b]

²⁰Then he rolled up the scroll, gave it back to the attendant and sat down. The eyes of everyone in the synagogue were fastened on him, ²¹and he began by saying to them, "Today this scripture is fulfilled in your hearing."   Mt 26:55

²²All spoke well of him and were amazed at the gracious words that came from his lips. "Isn't this Joseph's son?" they asked.   Mt 13:54ff

²³Jesus said to them, "Surely you will quote this proverb to me: 'Physician, heal yourself! Do here in your hometown what we have heard that you did in Capernaum.'"   Mk 1:21-28

²⁴"I tell you the truth," he continued, "no prophet is accepted in his hometown. ²⁵I assure you that there were many widows in Israel in Elijah's time, when the sky was shut for three and a half years and there was a severe famine throughout the land. ²⁶Yet Elijah was not sent to any of them, but to a widow in Zarephath in the region of Sidon. ²⁷And there were many in Israel with leprosy[c] in the time of Elisha the prophet, yet not one of them was cleansed—only Naaman the Syrian."   1Ki 17:8ff; 2Ki 5:1ff; Mt 11:21

²⁸All the people in the synagogue were furious when they heard this. ²⁹They got up, drove him out of the town, and took him to the brow of the hill on which the town was built, in order to throw him down the cliff. ³⁰But he walked right through the crowd and went on his way.

[a]12 Deut. 6:16   [b]19 Isaiah 61:1,2   [c]27 The Greek word was used for various diseases affecting the skin—not necessarily leprosy.

Jesus Drives Out an Evil Spirit

³¹Then he went down to Capernaum, a town in Galilee, and on the Sabbath began to teach the people. ³²They were amazed at his teaching, because his message had authority.

³³In the synagogue there was a man possessed by a demon, an evil*ᵃ* spirit. He cried out at the top of his voice, ³⁴"Ha! What do you want with us, Jesus of Nazareth? Have you come to destroy us? I know who you are—the Holy One of God!"

³⁵"Be quiet!" Jesus said sternly. "Come out of him!" Then the demon threw the man down before them all and came out without injuring him.   Mt 8:26

³⁶All the people were amazed and said to each other, "What is this teaching? With authority and power he gives orders to evil spirits and they come out!" ³⁷And the news about him spread throughout the surrounding area.   Mk 1:21ff

Jesus Heals Many

³⁸Jesus left the synagogue and went to the home of Simon. Now Simon's mother-in-law was suffering from a high fever, and they asked Jesus to help her. ³⁹So he bent over her and rebuked the fever, and it left her. She got up at once and began to wait on them.

⁴⁰When the sun was setting, the people brought to Jesus all who had various kinds of sickness, and laying his hands on each one, he healed them. ⁴¹Moreover, demons came out of many people, shouting, "You are the Son of God!" But he rebuked them and would not allow them to speak, because they knew he was the Christ.*ᵇ*

⁴²At daybreak Jesus went out to a solitary place. The people were looking for him and when they came to where he was, they tried to keep him from leaving them. ⁴³But he said, "I must preach the good news of the kingdom of God to the other towns also, because that is why I was sent." ⁴⁴And he kept on preaching in the synagogues of Judea.*ᶜ*   Mt 4:23

The Calling of the First Disciples

5 One day as Jesus was standing by the Lake of Gennesaret,*ᵈ* with the people crowding around him and listening to the word of God, ²he saw at the water's edge two boats, left there by the fishermen, who were washing their nets. ³He got into one of the boats, the one belonging to Simon, and asked him to put out a little from shore. Then he sat down and taught the people from the boat.   Mt 13:2; Heb 4:12

⁴When he had finished speaking, he said to Simon,

---

*ᵃ*33 Greek *unclean*; also in verse 36   *ᵇ*41 Or *Messiah*   *ᶜ*44 Or *the land of the Jews*; some manuscripts *Galilee*   *ᵈ*1 That is, Sea of Galilee

"Put out into deep water, and let down[a] the nets for a catch."

⁵Simon answered, "Master, we've worked hard all night and haven't caught anything. But because you say so, I will let down the nets."   Jn 21:3

⁶When they had done so, they caught such a large number of fish that their nets began to break. ⁷So they signaled their partners in the other boat to come and help them, and they came and filled both boats so full that they began to sink.

⁸When Simon Peter saw this, he fell at Jesus' knees and said, "Go away from me, Lord; I am a sinful man!" ⁹For he and all his companions were astonished at the catch of fish they had taken, ¹⁰and so were James and John, the sons of Zebedee, Simon's partners.   Job 42:6; Isa 6:5

Then Jesus said to Simon, "Don't be afraid; from now on you will catch men." ¹¹So they pulled their boats up on shore, left everything and followed him.   Mt 4:19; Mk 1:16ff; Jn 1:40ff

The Man With Leprosy

¹²While Jesus was in one of the towns, a man came along who was covered with leprosy.[b] When he saw Jesus, he fell with his face to the ground and begged him, "Lord, if you are willing, you can make me clean."   Mt 8:2ff; Lk 17:11-19

¹³Jesus reached out his hand and touched the man. "I am willing," he said. "Be clean!" And immediately the leprosy left him.

¹⁴Then Jesus ordered him, "Don't tell anyone, but go, show yourself to the priest and offer the sacrifices that Moses commanded for your cleansing, as a testimony to them."Lev 14:2-32

¹⁵Yet the news about him spread all the more, so that crowds of people came to hear him and to be healed of their sicknesses. ¹⁶But Jesus often withdrew to lonely places and prayed.

Jesus Heals a Paralytic

¹⁷One day as he was teaching, Pharisees and teachers of the law, who had come from every village of Galilee and from Judea and Jerusalem, were sitting there. And the power of the Lord was present for him to heal the sick. ¹⁸Some men came carrying a paralytic on a mat and tried to take him into the house to lay him before Jesus. ¹⁹When they could not find a way to do this because of the crowd, they went up on the roof and lowered him on his mat through the tiles into the middle of the crowd, right in front of Jesus.   Mt 9:2ff; Lk 6:19

²⁰When Jesus saw their faith, he said, "Friend, your sins are forgiven."   Lk 7:48-49

²¹The Pharisees and the

---

[a]4 The Greek verb is plural.   [b]12 The Greek word was used for various diseases affecting the skin—not necessarily leprosy.

teachers of the law began thinking to themselves, "Who is this fellow who speaks blasphemy? Who can forgive sins but God alone?" Isa 43:25

²²Jesus knew what they were thinking and asked, "Why are you thinking these things in your hearts? ²³Which is easier: to say, 'Your sins are forgiven,' or to say, 'Get up and walk'? ²⁴But that you may know that the Son of Man has authority on earth to forgive sins. . . ." He said to the paralyzed man, "I tell you, get up, take your mat and go home." ²⁵Immediately he stood up in front of them, took what he had been lying on and went home praising God. ²⁶Everyone was amazed and gave praise to God. They were filled with awe and said, "We have seen remarkable things today." Mt 9:8

The Calling of Levi

²⁷After this, Jesus went out and saw a tax collector by the name of Levi sitting at his tax booth. "Follow me," Jesus said to him, ²⁸and Levi got up, left everything and followed him.

²⁹Then Levi held a great banquet for Jesus at his house, and a large crowd of tax collectors and others were eating with them. ³⁰But the Pharisees and the teachers of the law who belonged to their sect complained to his disciples, "Why do you eat and drink with tax collectors and 'sinners'?" Lk 15:1; Ac 23:9

³¹Jesus answered them, "It is not the healthy who need a doctor, but the sick. ³²I have not come to call the righteous, but sinners to repentance." Jn 3:17

Jesus Questioned About Fasting

³³They said to him, "John's disciples often fast and pray, and so do the disciples of the Pharisees, but yours go on eating and drinking." Lk 7:18ff

³⁴Jesus answered, "Can you make the guests of the bridegroom fast while he is with them? ³⁵But the time will come when the bridegroom will be taken from them; in those days they will fast." Lk 9:22; Jn 3:29

³⁶He told them this parable: "No one tears a patch from a new garment and sews it on an old one. If he does, he will have torn the new garment, and the patch from the new will not match the old. ³⁷And no one pours new wine into old wineskins. If he does, the new wine will burst the skins, the wine will run out and the wineskins will be ruined. ³⁸No, new wine must be poured into new wineskins. ³⁹And no one after drinking old wine wants the new, for he says, 'The old is better.'"

Lord of the Sabbath

6 One Sabbath Jesus was going through the grainfields, and his disciples began to pick some heads of grain, rub them in their hands and eat the ker-

nels. 2Some of the Pharisees asked, "Why are you doing what is unlawful on the Sabbath?"   Mt 12:2

3Jesus answered them, "Have you never read what David did when he and his companions were hungry? 4He entered the house of God, and taking the consecrated bread, he ate what is lawful only for priests to eat. And he also gave some to his companions." 5Then Jesus said to them, "The Son of Man is Lord of the Sabbath."   Lev 24:5,9; 1Sa 21:6

6On another Sabbath he went into the synagogue and was teaching, and a man was there whose right hand was shriveled. 7The Pharisees and the teachers of the law were looking for a reason to accuse Jesus, so they watched him closely to see if he would heal on the Sabbath. 8But Jesus knew what they were thinking and said to the man with the shriveled hand, "Get up and stand in front of everyone." So he got up and stood there.   Mt 9:4; 12:10

9Then Jesus said to them, "I ask you, which is lawful on the Sabbath: to do good or to do evil, to save life or to destroy it?"

10He looked around at them all, and then said to the man, "Stretch out your hand." He did so, and his hand was completely restored. 11But they were furious and began to discuss with one another what they might do to Jesus.   Jn 5:18

The Twelve Apostles

12One of those days Jesus went out to a mountainside to pray, and spent the night praying to God. 13When morning came, he called his disciples to him and chose twelve of them, whom he also designated apostles: 14Simon (whom he named Peter), his brother Andrew, James, John, Philip, Bartholomew, 15Matthew, Thomas, James son of Alphaeus, Simon who was called the Zealot, 16Judas son of James, and Judas Iscariot, who became a traitor.

Blessings and Woes

17He went down with them and stood on a level place. A large crowd of his disciples was there and a great number of people from all over Judea, from Jerusalem, and from the coast of Tyre and Sidon, 18who had come to hear him and to be healed of their diseases. Those troubled by evil*a* spirits were cured, 19and the people all tried to touch him, because power was coming from him and healing them all.   Mt 4:25; 9:20

20Looking at his disciples, he said:

"Blessed are you who are
    poor,
  for yours is the kingdom of
    God.

a18 Greek *unclean*

21Blessed are you who hunger
     now,
   for you will be satisfied.
   Blessed are you who weep
     now,
   for you will laugh.   Isa 61:2,3
22Blessed are you when men
     hate you,
   when they exclude you and
     insult you   Isa 51:7
   and reject your name as
     evil,
     because of the Son of Man.

23"Rejoice in that day and
leap for joy, because great is
your reward in heaven. For that
is how their fathers treated the
prophets.   Mt 5:12
24"But woe to you who are
     rich,   Jas 5:1
   for you have already
     received your comfort.
25Woe to you who are well fed
     now,
   for you will go hungry.
   Woe to you who laugh now,
   for you will mourn and
     weep.   Pr 14:13
26Woe to you when all men
     speak well of you,
   for that is how their fathers
     treated the false
     prophets.

Love for Enemies

27"But I tell you who hear me:
Love your enemies, do good to
those who hate you, 28bless
those who curse you, pray for
those who mistreat you. 29If
someone strikes you on one
cheek, turn to him the other
also. If someone takes your
cloak, do not stop him from taking your tunic. 30Give to everyone who asks you, and if anyone takes what belongs to you,
do not demand it back. 31Do to
others as you would have them
do to you.   Mt 5:44; Ro 12:20
32"If you love those who love
you, what credit is that to you?
Even 'sinners' love those who
love them. 33And if you do good
to those who are good to you,
what credit is that to you? Even
'sinners' do that. 34And if you
lend to those from whom you
expect repayment, what credit
is that to you? Even 'sinners'
lend to 'sinners,' expecting to be
repaid in full. 35But love your
enemies, do good to them, and
lend to them without expecting
to get anything back. Then your
reward will be great, and you
will be sons of the Most High,
because he is kind to the ungrateful and wicked. 36Be merciful, just as your Father is merciful.   Mt 5:46; Jas 2:13

Judging Others

37"Do not judge, and you will
not be judged. Do not condemn, and you will not be condemned. Forgive, and you will
be forgiven. 38Give, and it will
be given to you. A good measure, pressed down, shaken together and running over, will be
poured into your lap. For with
the measure you use, it will be
measured to you."   Mt 7:1,2

39He also told them this parable: "Can a blind man lead a
blind man? Will they not both

fall into a pit? ⁴⁰A student is not above his teacher, but everyone who is fully trained will be like his teacher.   Mt 15:14

⁴¹"Why do you look at the speck of sawdust in your brother's eye and pay no attention to the plank in your own eye? ⁴²How can you say to your brother, 'Brother, let me take the speck out of your eye,' when you yourself fail to see the plank in your own eye? You hypocrite, first take the plank out of your eye, and then you will see clearly to remove the speck from your brother's eye.

A Tree and Its Fruit

⁴³"No good tree bears bad fruit, nor does a bad tree bear good fruit. ⁴⁴Each tree is recognized by its own fruit. People do not pick figs from thornbushes, or grapes from briers. ⁴⁵The good man brings good things out of the good stored up in his heart, and the evil man brings evil things out of the evil stored up in his heart. For out of the overflow of his heart his mouth speaks.   Mt 12:33

The Wise and Foolish Builders

⁴⁶"Why do you call me, 'Lord, Lord,' and do not do what I say? ⁴⁷I will show you what he is like who comes to me and hears my words and puts them into practice. ⁴⁸He is like a man building a house, who dug down deep and laid the foundation on rock.

When a flood came, the torrent struck that house but could not shake it, because it was well built. ⁴⁹But the one who hears my words and does not put them into practice is like a man who built a house on the ground without a foundation. The moment the torrent struck that house, it collapsed and its destruction was complete."

The Faith of the Centurion

7 When Jesus had finished saying all this in the hearing of the people, he entered Capernaum. ²There a centurion's servant, whom his master valued highly, was sick and about to die. ³The centurion heard of Jesus and sent some elders of the Jews to him, asking him to come and heal his servant. ⁴When they came to Jesus, they pleaded earnestly with him, "This man deserves to have you do this, ⁵because he loves our nation and has built our synagogue." ⁶So Jesus went with them.   Mt 8:5ff

He was not far from the house when the centurion sent friends to say to him: "Lord, don't trouble yourself, for I do not deserve to have you come under my roof. ⁷That is why I did not even consider myself worthy to come to you. But say the word, and my servant will be healed. ⁸For I myself am a man under authority, with soldiers under me. I tell this one, 'Go,' and he goes; and that one, 'Come,' and he comes. I say to

my servant, 'Do this,' and he does it." Ps 107:20

⁹When Jesus heard this, he was amazed at him, and turning to the crowd following him, he said, "I tell you, I have not found such great faith even in Israel." ¹⁰Then the men who had been sent returned to the house and found the servant well.

Jesus Raises a Widow's Son

¹¹Soon afterward, Jesus went to a town called Nain, and his disciples and a large crowd went along with him. ¹²As he approached the town gate, a dead person was being carried out—the only son of his mother, and she was a widow. And a large crowd from the town was with her. ¹³When the Lord saw her, his heart went out to her and he said, "Don't cry."

¹⁴Then he went up and touched the coffin, and those carrying it stood still. He said, "Young man, I say to you, get up!" ¹⁵The dead man sat up and began to talk, and Jesus gave him back to his mother. Mt 9:25

¹⁶They were all filled with awe and praised God. "A great prophet has appeared among us," they said. "God has come to help his people." ¹⁷This news about Jesus spread throughout Judea[a] and the surrounding country. Lk 1:65; Mt 9:26

Jesus and John the Baptist

¹⁸John's disciples told him about all these things. Calling two of them, ¹⁹he sent them to the Lord to ask, "Are you the one who was to come, or should we expect someone else?"

²⁰When the men came to Jesus, they said, "John the Baptist sent us to you to ask, 'Are you the one who was to come, or should we expect someone else?'"

²¹At that very time Jesus cured many who had diseases, sicknesses and evil spirits, and gave sight to many who were blind. ²²So he replied to the messengers, "Go back and report to John what you have seen and heard: The blind receive sight, the lame walk, those who have leprosy[b] are cured, the deaf hear, the dead are raised, and the good news is preached to the poor. ²³Blessed is the man who does not fall away on account of me." Isa 29:18,19; 35:5,6

²⁴After John's messengers left, Jesus began to speak to the crowd about John: "What did you go out into the desert to see? A reed swayed by the wind? ²⁵If not, what did you go out to see? A man dressed in fine clothes? No, those who wear expensive clothes and indulge in luxury are in palaces. ²⁶But what did you go out to see? A prophet? Yes, I tell you, and more than a prophet. ²⁷This

---

[a]17 Or *the land of the Jews*　　[b]22 The Greek word was used for various diseases affecting the skin—not necessarily leprosy.

is the one about whom it is written:

Mt 11:9

"'I will send my messenger
    ahead of you,
who will prepare your way
    before you.'[a]

28I tell you, among those born of women there is no one greater than John; yet the one who is least in the kingdom of God is greater than he."

29(All the people, even the tax collectors, when they heard Jesus' words, acknowledged that God's way was right, because they had been baptized by John. 30But the Pharisees and experts in the law rejected God's purpose for themselves, because they had not been baptized by John.)

Mt 21:32

31"To what, then, can I compare the people of this generation? What are they like? 32They are like children sitting in the marketplace and calling out to each other:

Mt 11:16

"'We played the flute for
    you,
and you did not dance;
we sang a dirge,
and you did not cry.'

33For John the Baptist came neither eating bread nor drinking wine, and you say, 'He has a demon.' 34The Son of Man came eating and drinking, and you say, 'Here is a glutton and a drunkard, a friend of tax collectors and "sinners."' 35But wisdom is proved right by all her children."

Lk 1:15; 5:29,30

Jesus Anointed by a Sinful Woman

36Now one of the Pharisees invited Jesus to have dinner with him, so he went to the Pharisee's house and reclined at the table. 37When a woman who had lived a sinful life in that town learned that Jesus was eating at the Pharisee's house, she brought an alabaster jar of perfume, 38and as she stood behind him at his feet weeping, she began to wet his feet with her tears. Then she wiped them with her hair, kissed them and poured perfume on them.

39When the Pharisee who had invited him saw this, he said to himself, "If this man were a prophet, he would know who is touching him and what kind of woman she is—that she is a sinner."

Mt 21:11; Lk 24:19

40Jesus answered him, "Simon, I have something to tell you."

"Tell me, teacher," he said.

41"Two men owed money to a certain moneylender. One owed him five hundred denarii,[b] and the other fifty. 42Neither of them had the money to pay him back, so he canceled the debts of both. Now which of them will love him more?"

43Simon replied, "I suppose

---

[a]27 Mal. 3:1   [b]41 A denarius was a coin worth about a day's wages.

the one who had the bigger debt canceled."

"You have judged correctly," Jesus said.

44Then he turned toward the woman and said to Simon, "Do you see this woman? I came into your house. You did not give me any water for my feet, but she wet my feet with her tears and wiped them with her hair. 45You did not give me a kiss, but this woman, from the time I entered, has not stopped kissing my feet. 46You did not put oil on my head, but she has poured perfume on my feet. 47Therefore, I tell you, her many sins have been forgiven—for she loved much. But he who has been forgiven little loves little."

48Then Jesus said to her, "Your sins are forgiven."   Mt 9:2

49The other guests began to say among themselves, "Who is this who even forgives sins?"

50Jesus said to the woman, "Your faith has saved you; go in peace."   Mt 9:22

The Parable of the Sower

8 After this, Jesus traveled about from one town and village to another, proclaiming the good news of the kingdom of God. The Twelve were with him, 2and also some women who had been cured of evil spirits and diseases: Mary (called Magdalene) from whom seven demons had come out; 3Joanna the wife of Cuza, the

manager of Herod's household; Susanna; and many others. These women were helping to support them out of their own means.   Mt 27:55,56

4While a large crowd was gathering and people were coming to Jesus from town after town, he told this parable: 5"A farmer went out to sow his seed. As he was scattering the seed, some fell along the path; it was trampled on, and the birds of the air ate it up. 6Some fell on rock, and when it came up, the plants withered because they had no moisture. 7Other seed fell among thorns, which grew up with it and choked the plants. 8Still other seed fell on good soil. It came up and yielded a crop, a hundred times more than was sown."

When he said this, he called out, "He who has ears to hear, let him hear."   Mt 11:15

9His disciples asked him what this parable meant. 10He said, "The knowledge of the secrets of the kingdom of God has been given to you, but to others I speak in parables, so that,

"'though seeing, they may not see;
though hearing, they may not understand.'a

11"This is the meaning of the parable: The seed is the word of God. 12Those along the path are the ones who hear, and then the devil comes and takes away the

---

a10 Isaiah 6:9

word from their hearts, so that they may not believe and be saved. ¹³Those on the rock are the ones who receive the word with joy when they hear it, but they have no root. They believe for a while, but in the time of testing they fall away. ¹⁴The seed that fell among thorns stands for those who hear, but as they go on their way they are choked by life's worries, riches and pleasures, and they do not mature. ¹⁵But the seed on good soil stands for those with a noble and good heart, who hear the word, retain it, and by persevering produce a crop. Heb 4:12

A Lamp on a Stand

¹⁶"No one lights a lamp and hides it in a jar or puts it under a bed. Instead, he puts it on a stand, so that those who come in can see the light. ¹⁷For there is nothing hidden that will not be disclosed, and nothing concealed that will not be known or brought out into the open. ¹⁸Therefore consider carefully how you listen. Whoever has will be given more; whoever does not have, even what he thinks he has will be taken from him." Mt 5:15; 25:29

Jesus' Mother and Brothers

¹⁹Now Jesus' mother and brothers came to see him, but they were not able to get near him because of the crowd. ²⁰Someone told him, "Your mother and brothers are standing outside, wanting to see you." Jn 7:5

²¹He replied, "My mother and brothers are those who hear God's word and put it into practice." Lk 6:47; 11:28

Jesus Calms the Storm

²²One day Jesus said to his disciples, "Let's go over to the other side of the lake." So they got into a boat and set out. ²³As they sailed, he fell asleep. A squall came down on the lake, so that the boat was being swamped, and they were in great danger.

²⁴The disciples went and woke him, saying, "Master, Master, we're going to drown!"

He got up and rebuked the wind and the raging waters; the storm subsided, and all was calm. ²⁵"Where is your faith?" he asked his disciples. Ps 107:29

In fear and amazement they asked one another, "Who is this? He commands even the winds and the water, and they obey him." Mt 8:23ff; Mk 4:36ff

The Healing of a Demon-possessed Man

²⁶They sailed to the region of the Gerasenes,ᵃ which is across the lake from Galilee. ²⁷When Jesus stepped ashore, he was met by a demon-possessed man from the town. For a long time this man had not worn clothes or lived in a house, but had

ᵃ26 Some manuscripts Gadarenes; other manuscripts Gergesenes; also in verse 37

lived in the tombs. 28When he saw Jesus, he cried out and fell at his feet, shouting at the top of his voice, "What do you want with me, Jesus, Son of the Most High God? I beg you, don't torture me!" 29For Jesus had commanded the evil*a* spirit to come out of the man. Many times it had seized him, and though he was chained hand and foot and kept under guard, he had broken his chains and had been driven by the demon into solitary places.   Mk 1:24

30Jesus asked him, "What is your name?"

"Legion," he replied, because many demons had gone into him. 31And they begged him repeatedly not to order them to go into the Abyss.

32A large herd of pigs was feeding there on the hillside. The demons begged Jesus to let them go into them, and he gave them permission. 33When the demons came out of the man, they went into the pigs, and the herd rushed down the steep bank into the lake and was drowned.

34When those tending the pigs saw what had happened, they ran off and reported this in the town and countryside, 35and the people went out to see what had happened. When they came to Jesus, they found the man from whom the demons had gone out, sitting at Jesus' feet, dressed and in his right mind; and they were afraid. 36Those who had seen it told the people how the demon-possessed man had been cured. 37Then all the people of the region of the Gerasenes asked Jesus to leave them, because they were overcome with fear. So he got into the boat and left.

38The man from whom the demons had gone out begged to go with him, but Jesus sent him away, saying, 39"Return home and tell how much God has done for you." So the man went away and told all over town how much Jesus had done for him.   Mt 8:28ff; Mk 5:1ff

A Dead Girl and a Sick Woman

40Now when Jesus returned, a crowd welcomed him, for they were all expecting him. 41Then a man named Jairus, a ruler of the synagogue, came and fell at Jesus' feet, pleading with him to come to his house 42because his only daughter, a girl of about twelve, was dying.   Mk 5:22ff

As Jesus was on his way, the crowds almost crushed him. 43And a woman was there who had been subject to bleeding for twelve years,*b* but no one could heal her. 44She came up behind him and touched the edge of his cloak, and immediately her bleeding stopped.   Lev 15:25-30

45"Who touched me?" Jesus asked.

When they all denied it, Peter

---

a29 Greek *unclean*   *b43* Many manuscripts *years, and she had spent all she had on doctors*

said, "Master, the people are crowding and pressing against you."

⁴⁶But Jesus said, "Someone touched me; I know that power has gone out from me." Mt 14:36

⁴⁷Then the woman, seeing that she could not go unnoticed, came trembling and fell at his feet. In the presence of all the people, she told why she had touched him and how she had been instantly healed. ⁴⁸Then he said to her, "Daughter, your faith has healed you. Go in peace." Mt 9:22

⁴⁹While Jesus was still speaking, someone came from the house of Jairus, the synagogue ruler. "Your daughter is dead," he said. "Don't bother the teacher any more."

⁵⁰Hearing this, Jesus said to Jairus, "Don't be afraid; just believe, and she will be healed."

⁵¹When he arrived at the house of Jairus, he did not let anyone go in with him except Peter, John and James, and the child's father and mother. ⁵²Meanwhile, all the people were wailing and mourning for her. "Stop wailing," Jesus said. "She is not dead but asleep."

⁵³They laughed at him, knowing that she was dead. ⁵⁴But he took her by the hand and said, "My child, get up!" ⁵⁵Her spirit returned, and at once she stood up. Then Jesus told them to give her something to eat. ⁵⁶Her parents were astonished, but he ordered them not to tell anyone what had happened. Lk 7:14

Jesus Sends Out the Twelve

9 When Jesus had called the Twelve together, he gave them power and authority to drive out all demons and to cure diseases, ²and he sent them out to preach the kingdom of God and to heal the sick. ³He told them: "Take nothing for the journey—no staff, no bag, no bread, no money, no extra tunic. ⁴Whatever house you enter, stay there until you leave that town. ⁵If people do not welcome you, shake the dust off your feet when you leave their town, as a testimony against them." ⁶So they set out and went from village to village, preaching the gospel and healing people everywhere. Mt 10:1

⁷Now Herod the tetrarch heard about all that was going on. And he was perplexed, because some were saying that John had been raised from the dead, ⁸others that Elijah had appeared, and still others that one of the prophets of long ago had come back to life. ⁹But Herod said, "I beheaded John. Who, then, is this I hear such things about?" And he tried to see him. Mt 14:1; Lk 23:8

Jesus Feeds the Five Thousand

¹⁰When the apostles returned, they reported to Jesus what they had done. Then he took them with him and they withdrew by themselves to a town called Bethsaida, ¹¹but the

crowds learned about it and followed him. He welcomed them and spoke to them about the kingdom of God, and healed those who needed healing.

¹²Late in the afternoon the Twelve came to him and said, "Send the crowd away so they can go to the surrounding villages and countryside and find food and lodging, because we are in a remote place here."

¹³He replied, "You give them something to eat."

They answered, "We have only five loaves of bread and two fish—unless we go and buy food for all this crowd." ¹⁴(About five thousand men were there.)

But he said to his disciples, "Have them sit down in groups of about fifty each." ¹⁵The disciples did so, and everybody sat down. ¹⁶Taking the five loaves and the two fish and looking up to heaven, he gave thanks and broke them. Then he gave them to the disciples to set before the people. ¹⁷They all ate and were satisfied, and the disciples picked up twelve basketfuls of broken pieces that were left over. Mt 14:13ff; Jn 6:5ff

Peter's Confession of Christ

¹⁸Once when Jesus was praying in private and his disciples were with him, he asked them, "Who do the crowds say I am?"

¹⁹They replied, "Some say John the Baptist; others say Elijah; and still others, that one of the prophets of long ago has come back to life." 1Ki 18:1ff; Mt 3:11

²⁰"But what about you?" he asked. "Who do you say I am?"

Peter answered, "The Christ[a] of God." Jn 1:49; 11:27

²¹Jesus strictly warned them not to tell this to anyone. ²²And he said, "The Son of Man must suffer many things and be rejected by the elders, chief priests and teachers of the law, and he must be killed and on the third day be raised to life."

²³Then he said to them all: "If anyone would come after me, he must deny himself and take up his cross daily and follow me. ²⁴For whoever wants to save his life will lose it, but whoever loses his life for me will save it. ²⁵What good is it for a man to gain the whole world, and yet lose or forfeit his very self? ²⁶If anyone is ashamed of me and my words, the Son of Man will be ashamed of him when he comes in his glory and in the glory of the Father and of the holy angels. ²⁷I tell you the truth, some who are standing here will not taste death before they see the kingdom of God."

The Transfiguration

²⁸About eight days after Jesus said this, he took Peter, John and James with him and went up onto a mountain to pray. ²⁹As he was praying, the appearance of his face changed,

[a]20 Or Messiah

and his clothes became as bright as a flash of lightning. [30]Two men, Moses and Elijah, [31]appeared in glorious splendor, talking with Jesus. They spoke about his departure, which he was about to bring to fulfillment at Jerusalem. [32]Peter and his companions were very sleepy, but when they became fully awake, they saw his glory and the two men standing with him. [33]As the men were leaving Jesus, Peter said to him, "Master, it is good for us to be here. Let us put up three shelters—one for you, one for Moses and one for Elijah." (He did not know what he was saying.)   Dt 34:10-12; 1Ki 18:1ff

[34]While he was speaking, a cloud appeared and enveloped them, and they were afraid as they entered the cloud. [35]A voice came from the cloud, saying, "This is my Son, whom I have chosen; listen to him." [36]When the voice had spoken, they found that Jesus was alone. The disciples kept this to themselves, and told no one at that time what they had seen.

The Healing of a Boy With an Evil Spirit

[37]The next day, when they came down from the mountain, a large crowd met him. [38]A man in the crowd called out, "Teacher, I beg you to look at my son, for he is my only child. [39]A spirit seizes him and he sud-denly screams; it throws him into convulsions so that he foams at the mouth. It scarcely ever leaves him and is destroy-ing him. [40]I begged your disci-ples to drive it out, but they could not."   Mt 17:14ff

[41]"O unbelieving and per-verse generation," Jesus re-plied, "how long shall I stay with you and put up with you? Bring your son here."   Dt 32:5

[42]Even while the boy was coming, the demon threw him to the ground in a convulsion. But Jesus rebuked the evil[a] spirit, healed the boy and gave him back to his father. [43]And they were all amazed at the greatness of God.   2Pe 1:16

While everyone was marvel-ing at all that Jesus did, he said to his disciples, [44]"Listen care-fully to what I am about to tell you: The Son of Man is going to be betrayed into the hands of men." [45]But they did not under-stand what this meant. It was hidden from them, so that they did not grasp it, and they were afraid to ask him about it.   Mk 9:32

Who Will Be the Greatest?

[46]An argument started among the disciples as to which of them would be the great-est. [47]Jesus, knowing their thoughts, took a little child and had him stand beside him. [48]Then he said to them, "Who-ever welcomes this little child in my name welcomes me; and

[a]42 Greek unclean

whoever welcomes me welcomes the one who sent me. For he who is least among you all—he is the greatest." Lk 22:24

⁴⁹"Master," said John, "we saw a man driving out demons in your name and we tried to stop him, because he is not one of us." Mk 9:33ff

⁵⁰"Do not stop him," Jesus said, "for whoever is not against you is for you." Mt 12:30

Samaritan Opposition

⁵¹As the time approached for him to be taken up to heaven, Jesus resolutely set out for Jerusalem. ⁵²And he sent messengers on ahead, who went into a Samaritan village to get things ready for him; ⁵³but the people there did not welcome him, because he was heading for Jerusalem. ⁵⁴When the disciples James and John saw this, they asked, "Lord, do you want us to call fire down from heaven to destroy them*a*?" ⁵⁵But Jesus turned and rebuked them, ⁵⁶and*b* they went to another village. Mk 16:19

The Cost of Following Jesus

⁵⁷As they were walking along the road, a man said to him, "I will follow you wherever you go." Mt 8:19ff

⁵⁸Jesus replied, "Foxes have holes and birds of the air have nests, but the Son of Man has no place to lay his head."

⁵⁹He said to another man, "Follow me."

But the man replied, "Lord, first let me go and bury my father."

⁶⁰Jesus said to him, "Let the dead bury their own dead, but you go and proclaim the kingdom of God."

⁶¹Still another said, "I will follow you, Lord; but first let me go back and say good-by to my family." 1Ki 19:20

⁶²Jesus replied, "No one who puts his hand to the plow and looks back is fit for service in the kingdom of God."

Jesus Sends Out the Seventy-two

10 After this the Lord appointed seventy-two*c* others and sent them two by two ahead of him to every town and place where he was about to go. ²He told them, "The harvest is plentiful, but the workers are few. Ask the Lord of the harvest, therefore, to send out workers into his harvest field. ³Go! I am sending you out like lambs among wolves. ⁴Do not take a purse or bag or sandals; and do not greet anyone on the road. Mt 10:16; Mk 6:7

⁵"When you enter a house, first say, 'Peace to this house.' ⁶If a man of peace is there, your peace will rest on him; if not, it will return to you. ⁷Stay in that

---

*a*54 Some manuscripts *them, even as Elijah did said, "You do not know what kind of spirit you are of, for the Son of Man did not come to destroy men's lives, but to save them." 56And*　　*b*55,56 Some manuscripts *them. And he*　　*c*1 Some manuscripts *seventy;* also in verse 17

house, eating and drinking whatever they give you, for the worker deserves his wages. Do not move around from house to house.   1Ti 5:18

8"When you enter a town and are welcomed, eat what is set before you. 9Heal the sick who are there and tell them, 'The kingdom of God is near you.' 10But when you enter a town and are not welcomed, go into its streets and say, 11'Even the dust of your town that sticks to our feet we wipe off against you. Yet be sure of this: The kingdom of God is near.' 12I tell you, it will be more bearable on that day for Sodom than for that town.   Mt 10:14,15; 1Co 10:27

13"Woe to you, Korazin! Woe to you, Bethsaida! For if the miracles that were performed in you had been performed in Tyre and Sidon, they would have repented long ago, sitting in sackcloth and ashes. 14But it will be more bearable for Tyre and Sidon at the judgment than for you. 15And you, Capernaum, will you be lifted up to the skies? No, you will go down to the depths.ᵃ

16"He who listens to you listens to me; he who rejects you rejects me; but he who rejects me rejects him who sent me."

17The seventy-two returned with joy and said, "Lord, even the demons submit to us in your name."   Mk 16:17

18He replied, "I saw Satan fall like lightning from heaven. 19I have given you authority to trample on snakes and scorpions and to overcome all the power of the enemy; nothing will harm you. 20However, do not rejoice that the spirits submit to you, but rejoice that your names are written in heaven."

21At that time Jesus, full of joy through the Holy Spirit, said, "I praise you, Father, Lord of heaven and earth, because you have hidden these things from the wise and learned, and revealed them to little children. Yes, Father, for this was your good pleasure.   1Co 1:26-29

22"All things have been committed to me by my Father. No one knows who the Son is except the Father, and no one knows who the Father is except the Son and those to whom the Son chooses to reveal him."

23Then he turned to his disciples and said privately, "Blessed are the eyes that see what you see. 24For I tell you that many prophets and kings wanted to see what you see but did not see it, and to hear what you hear but did not hear it."

The Parable of the Good Samaritan

25On one occasion an expert in the law stood up to test Jesus. "Teacher," he asked, "what must I do to inherit eternal life?"   Mt 19:16; Lk 18:18

ᵃ15 Greek Hades

²⁶"What is written in the Law?" he replied. "How do you read it?"

²⁷He answered: "'Love the Lord your God with all your heart and with all your soul and with all your strength and with all your mind'ᵃ; and, 'Love your neighbor as yourself.'ᵇ"

²⁸"You have answered correctly," Jesus replied. "Do this and you will live."

²⁹But he wanted to justify himself, so he asked Jesus, "And who is my neighbor?"

³⁰In reply Jesus said: "A man was going down from Jerusalem to Jericho, when he fell into the hands of robbers. They stripped him of his clothes, beat him and went away, leaving him half dead. ³¹A priest happened to be going down the same road, and when he saw the man, he passed by on the other side. ³²So too, a Levite, when he came to the place and saw him, passed by on the other side. ³³But a Samaritan, as he traveled, came where the man was; and when he saw him, he took pity on him. ³⁴He went to him and bandaged his wounds, pouring on oil and wine. Then he put the man on his own donkey, took him to an inn and took care of him. ³⁵The next day he took out two silver coinsᶜ and gave them to the innkeeper. 'Look after him,' he said, 'and when I return, I will reimburse you for any extra expense you may have.'

Lk 16:15

³⁶"Which of these three do you think was a neighbor to the man who fell into the hands of robbers?"

³⁷The expert in the law replied, "The one who had mercy on him."

Jesus told him, "Go and do likewise."

At the Home of Martha and Mary

³⁸As Jesus and his disciples were on their way, he came to a village where a woman named Martha opened her home to him. ³⁹She had a sister called Mary, who sat at the Lord's feet listening to what he said. ⁴⁰But Martha was distracted by all the preparations that had to be made. She came to him and asked, "Lord, don't you care that my sister has left me to do the work by myself? Tell her to help me!"

Jn 11:1

⁴¹"Martha, Martha," the Lord answered, "you are worried and upset about many things, ⁴²but only one thing is needed.ᵈ Mary has chosen what is better, and it will not be taken away from her."

Mt 6:25-34

Jesus' Teaching on Prayer

11 One day Jesus was praying in a certain place. When he finished, one of his disciples said to him, "Lord,

---

ᵃ27 Deut. 6:5   ᵇ27 Lev. 19:18   ᶜ35 Greek *two denarii*   ᵈ42 Some manuscripts *but few things are needed—or only one*

teach us to pray, just as John taught his disciples.''

²He said to them, ''When you pray, say:

'' 'Father,ᵃ
hallowed be your name,
your kingdom come.ᵇ
³Give us each day our daily
    bread.
⁴Forgive us our sins,
  for we also forgive
      everyone who sins
      against us.ᶜ   Mt 18:35
And lead us not into
      temptation.ᵈ '' Mt 26:41

⁵Then he said to them, ''Suppose one of you has a friend, and he goes to him at midnight and says, 'Friend, lend me three loaves of bread, ⁶because a friend of mine on a journey has come to me, and I have nothing to set before him.'

⁷''Then the one inside answers, 'Don't bother me. The door is already locked, and my children are with me in bed. I can't get up and give you anything.' ⁸I tell you, though he will not get up and give him the bread because he is his friend, yet because of the man's boldnessᵉ he will get up and give him as much as he needs. Lk 18:1

⁹''So I say to you: Ask and it will be given to you; seek and you will find; knock and the door will be opened to you.

¹⁰For everyone who asks receives; he who seeks finds; and to him who knocks, the door will be opened.   Mt 7:7

¹¹''Which of you fathers, if your son asks forᶠ a fish, will give him a snake instead? ¹²Or if he asks for an egg, will give him a scorpion? ¹³If you then, though you are evil, know how to give good gifts to your children, how much more will your Father in heaven give the Holy Spirit to those who ask him!''

Jesus and Beelzebub

¹⁴Jesus was driving out a demon that was mute. When the demon left, the man who had been mute spoke, and the crowd was amazed. ¹⁵But some of them said, ''By Beelzebub,ᵍ the prince of demons, he is driving out demons.'' ¹⁶Others tested him by asking for a sign from heaven.   Mt 9:32-33; 12:38

¹⁷Jesus knew their thoughts and said to them: ''Any kingdom divided against itself will be ruined, and a house divided against itself will fall. ¹⁸If Satan is divided against himself, how can his kingdom stand? I say this because you claim that I drive out demons by Beelzebub. ¹⁹Now if I drive out demons by Beelzebub, by whom do your followers drive them out? So then, they will be your judges.

ᵃ2 Some manuscripts *Our Father in heaven be done on earth as it is in heaven.*   ᶜ4 Greek *everyone who is indebted to us*   ᵈ4 Some manuscripts *temptation but deliver us from the evil one*   ᵉ8 Or *persistence*   ᶠ11 Some manuscripts *for bread, will give him a stone; or if he asks for*   ᵍ15 Greek *Beezeboul* or *Beelzeboul*; also in verses 18 and 19

²⁰But if I drive out demons by the finger of God, then the kingdom of God has come to you.

²¹"When a strong man, fully armed, guards his own house, his possessions are safe. ²²But when someone stronger attacks and overpowers him, he takes away the armor in which the man trusted and divides up the spoils.   Mt 12:29

²³"He who is not with me is against me, and he who does not gather with me, scatters.

²⁴"When an evilᵃ spirit comes out of a man, it goes through arid places seeking rest and does not find it. Then it says, 'I will return to the house I left.' ²⁵When it arrives, it finds the house swept clean and put in order. ²⁶Then it goes and takes seven other spirits more wicked than itself, and they go in and live there. And the final condition of that man is worse than the first."   2Pe 2:20

²⁷As Jesus was saying these things, a woman in the crowd called out, "Blessed is the mother who gave you birth and nursed you."   Lk 23:29

²⁸He replied, "Blessed rather are those who hear the word of God and obey it."   Heb 4:12,13

The Sign of Jonah

²⁹As the crowds increased, Jesus said, "This is a wicked generation. It asks for a miraculous sign, but none will be given it except the sign of Jonah. ³⁰For

as Jonah was a sign to the Ninevites, so also will the Son of Man be to this generation. ³¹The Queen of the South will rise at the judgment with the men of this generation and condemn them; for she came from the ends of the earth to listen to Solomon's wisdom, and now oneᵇ greater than Solomon is here. ³²The men of Nineveh will stand up at the judgment with this generation and condemn it; for they repented at the preaching of Jonah, and now one greater than Jonah is here. Jnh 1:17

The Lamp of the Body

³³"No one lights a lamp and puts it in a place where it will be hidden, or under a bowl. Instead he puts it on its stand, so that those who come in may see the light. ³⁴Your eye is the lamp of your body. When your eyes are good, your whole body also is full of light. But when they are bad, your body also is full of darkness. ³⁵See to it, then, that the light within you is not darkness. ³⁶Therefore, if your whole body is full of light, and no part of it dark, it will be completely lighted, as when the light of a lamp shines on you."   Mt 5:15,16

Six Woes

³⁷When Jesus had finished speaking, a Pharisee invited him to eat with him; so he went in and reclined at the table. ³⁸But the Pharisee, noticing that

ᵃ24 Greek *unclean*   ᵇ31 Or *something;* also in verse 32

Jesus did not first wash before the meal, was surprised. Mk 7:3-4

39Then the Lord said to him, "Now then, you Pharisees clean the outside of the cup and dish, but inside you are full of greed and wickedness. 40You foolish people! Did not the one who made the outside make the inside also? 41But give what is inside ⌊the dish⌋a to the poor, and everything will be clean for you.

42"Woe to you Pharisees, because you give God a tenth of your mint, rue and all other kinds of garden herbs, but you neglect justice and the love of God. You should have practiced the latter without leaving the former undone. Lk 18:12

43"Woe to you Pharisees, because you love the most important seats in the synagogues and greetings in the marketplaces. Mt 23:6; Lk 14:7

44"Woe to you, because you are like unmarked graves, which men walk over without knowing it." Mt 23:27

45One of the experts in the law answered him, "Teacher, when you say these things, you insult us also."

46Jesus replied, "And you experts in the law, woe to you, because you load people down with burdens they can hardly carry, and you yourselves will not lift one finger to help them.

47"Woe to you, because you build tombs for the prophets, and it was your forefathers who killed them. 48So you testify that you approve of what your forefathers did; they killed the prophets, and you build their tombs. 49Because of this, God in his wisdom said, 'I will send them prophets and apostles, some of whom they will kill and others they will persecute.' 50Therefore this generation will be held responsible for the blood of all the prophets that has been shed since the beginning of the world, 51from the blood of Abel to the blood of Zechariah, who was killed between the altar and the sanctuary. Yes, I tell you, this generation will be held responsible for it all. Mt 23:29-32

52"Woe to you experts in the law, because you have taken away the key to knowledge. You yourselves have not entered, and you have hindered those who were entering."

53When Jesus left there, the Pharisees and the teachers of the law began to oppose him fiercely and to besiege him with questions, 54waiting to catch him in something he might say.

Warnings and Encouragements

12 Meanwhile, when a crowd of many thousands had gathered, so that they were trampling on one another, Jesus began to speak first to his disciples, saying: "Be on your guard against the yeast of

a41 Or what you have

the Pharisees, which is hypocrisy. ²There is nothing concealed that will not be disclosed, or hidden that will not be made known. ³What you have said in the dark will be heard in the daylight, and what you have whispered in the ear in the inner rooms will be proclaimed from the roofs. Mt 16:6ff

⁴"I tell you, my friends, do not be afraid of those who kill the body and after that can do no more. ⁵But I will show you whom you should fear: Fear him who, after the killing of the body, has power to throw you into hell. Yes, I tell you, fear him. ⁶Are not five sparrows sold for two pennies*a*? Yet not one of them is forgotten by God. ⁷Indeed, the very hairs of your head are all numbered. Don't be afraid; you are worth more than many sparrows. Jn 15:14-15

⁸"I tell you, whoever acknowledges me before men, the Son of Man will also acknowledge him before the angels of God. ⁹But he who disowns me before men will be disowned before the angels of God. ¹⁰And everyone who speaks a word against the Son of Man will be forgiven, but anyone who blasphemes against the Holy Spirit will not be forgiven. Lk 15:10

¹¹"When you are brought before synagogues, rulers and authorities, do not worry about how you will defend yourselves or what you will say, ¹²for the Holy Spirit will teach you at that time what you should say."

The Parable of the Rich Fool

¹³Someone in the crowd said to him, "Teacher, tell my brother to divide the inheritance with me."

¹⁴Jesus replied, "Man, who appointed me a judge or an arbiter between you?" ¹⁵Then he said to them, "Watch out! Be on your guard against all kinds of greed; a man's life does not consist in the abundance of his possessions." Job 20:20; Ps 62:10

¹⁶And he told them this parable: "The ground of a certain rich man produced a good crop. ¹⁷He thought to himself, 'What shall I do? I have no place to store my crops.'

¹⁸"Then he said, 'This is what I'll do. I will tear down my barns and build bigger ones, and there I will store all my grain and my goods. ¹⁹And I'll say to myself, "You have plenty of good things laid up for many years. Take life easy; eat, drink and be merry."'

²⁰"But God said to him, 'You fool! This very night your life will be demanded from you. Then who will get what you have prepared for yourself?'

²¹"This is how it will be with anyone who stores up things for himself but is not rich toward God." Ecc 11:9

*a*6 Greek *two assaria*

Do Not Worry

22Then Jesus said to his disciples: "Therefore I tell you, do not worry about your life, what you will eat; or about your body, what you will wear. 23Life is more than food, and the body more than clothes. 24Consider the ravens: They do not sow or reap, they have no storeroom or barn; yet God feeds them. And how much more valuable you are than birds! 25Who of you by worrying can add a single hour to his life*a*? 26Since you cannot do this very little thing, why do you worry about the rest? Ps 147:9

27"Consider how the lilies grow. They do not labor or spin. Yet I tell you, not even Solomon in all his splendor was dressed like one of these. 28If that is how God clothes the grass of the field, which is here today, and tomorrow is thrown into the fire, how much more will he clothe you, O you of little faith! 29And do not set your heart on what you will eat or drink; do not worry about it. 30For the pagan world runs after all such things, and your Father knows that you need them. 31But seek his kingdom, and these things will be given to you as well.

32"Do not be afraid, little flock, for your Father has been pleased to give you the kingdom. 33Sell your possessions and give to the poor. Provide purses for yourselves that will not wear out, a treasure in heaven that will not be exhausted, where no thief comes near and no moth destroys. 34For where your treasure is, there your heart will be also. Jas 5:2

Watchfulness

35"Be dressed ready for service and keep your lamps burning, 36like men waiting for their master to return from a wedding banquet, so that when he comes and knocks they can immediately open the door for him. 37It will be good for those servants whose master finds them watching when he comes. I tell you the truth, he will dress himself to serve, will have them recline at the table and will come and wait on them. 38It will be good for those servants whose master finds them ready, even if he comes in the second or third watch of the night. 39But understand this: If the owner of the house had known at what hour the thief was coming, he would not have let his house be broken into. 40You also must be ready, because the Son of Man will come at an hour when you do not expect him." Mt 24:42,46

41Peter asked, "Lord, are you telling this parable to us, or to everyone?"

42The Lord answered, "Who then is the faithful and wise manager, whom the master puts in charge of his servants to give them their food allowance at the proper time? 43It will be

---

a25 Or *single cubit to his height*

good for that servant whom the master finds doing so when he returns. ⁴⁴I tell you the truth, he will put him in charge of all his possessions. ⁴⁵But suppose the servant says to himself, 'My master is taking a long time in coming,' and he then begins to beat the menservants and maidservants and to eat and drink and get drunk. ⁴⁶The master of that servant will come on a day when he does not expect him and at an hour he is not aware of. He will cut him to pieces and assign him a place with the unbelievers.

⁴⁷"That servant who knows his master's will and does not get ready or does not do what his master wants will be beaten with many blows. ⁴⁸But the one who does not know and does things deserving punishment will be beaten with few blows. From everyone who has been given much, much will be demanded; and from the one who has been entrusted with much, much more will be asked. Lev 5:17

Not Peace but Division

⁴⁹"I have come to bring fire on the earth, and how I wish it were already kindled! ⁵⁰But I have a baptism to undergo, and how distressed I am until it is completed! ⁵¹Do you think I came to bring peace on earth? No, I tell you, but division. ⁵²From now on there will be five in one family divided against

ᵃ59 Greek *lepton*

each other, three against two and two against three. ⁵³They will be divided, father against son and son against father, mother against daughter and daughter against mother, mother-in-law against daughter-in-law and daughter-in-law against mother-in-law." Mt 10:21,22

Interpreting the Times

⁵⁴He said to the crowd: "When you see a cloud rising in the west, immediately you say, 'It's going to rain,' and it does. ⁵⁵And when the south wind blows, you say, 'It's going to be hot,' and it is. ⁵⁶Hypocrites! You know how to interpret the appearance of the earth and the sky. How is it that you don't know how to interpret this present time? Mt 16:2

⁵⁷"Why don't you judge for yourselves what is right? ⁵⁸As you are going with your adversary to the magistrate, try hard to be reconciled to him on the way, or he may drag you off to the judge, and the judge turn you over to the officer, and the officer throw you into prison. ⁵⁹I tell you, you will not get out until you have paid the last penny.ᵃ" Mt 5:25,26

Repent or Perish

13 Now there were some present at that time who told Jesus about the Galileans whose blood Pilate had mixed with their sacrifices. ²Jesus an-

swered, "Do you think that these Galileans were worse sinners than all the other Galileans because they suffered this way? [3]I tell you, no! But unless you repent, you too will all perish. [4]Or those eighteen who died when the tower in Siloam fell on them—do you think they were more guilty than all the others living in Jerusalem? [5]I tell you, no! But unless you repent, you too will all perish."

Jn 9:2-3

[6]Then he told this parable: "A man had a fig tree, planted in his vineyard, and he went to look for fruit on it, but did not find any. [7]So he said to the man who took care of the vineyard, 'For three years now I've been coming to look for fruit on this fig tree and haven't found any. Cut it down! Why should it use up the soil?'

Isa 5:2; Mt 3:10

[8]"'Sir,' the man replied, 'leave it alone for one more year, and I'll dig around it and fertilize it. [9]If it bears fruit next year, fine! If not, then cut it down.'"

A Crippled Woman Healed on the Sabbath

[10]On a Sabbath Jesus was teaching in one of the synagogues, [11]and a woman was there who had been crippled by a spirit for eighteen years. She was bent over and could not straighten up at all. [12]When Jesus saw her, he called her forward and said to her, "Woman, you are set free from your infir-

mity." [13]Then he put his hands on her, and immediately she straightened up and praised God.

Mk 5:23

[14]Indignant because Jesus had healed on the Sabbath, the synagogue ruler said to the people, "There are six days for work. So come and be healed on those days, not on the Sabbath."

Ex 20:9; Mt 12:2

[15]The Lord answered him, "You hypocrites! Doesn't each of you on the Sabbath untie his ox or donkey from the stall and lead it out to give it water? [16]Then should not this woman, a daughter of Abraham, whom Satan has kept bound for eighteen long years, be set free on the Sabbath day from what bound her?"

Lk 14:5

[17]When he said this, all his opponents were humiliated, but the people were delighted with all the wonderful things he was doing.

The Parables of the Mustard Seed and the Yeast

[18]Then Jesus asked, "What is the kingdom of God like? What shall I compare it to? [19]It is like a mustard seed, which a man took and planted in his garden. It grew and became a tree, and the birds of the air perched in its branches."

Lk 17:6

[20]Again he asked, "What shall I compare the kingdom of God to? [21]It is like yeast that a woman took and mixed into a

large amount[a] of flour until it worked all through the dough."

The Narrow Door

22Then Jesus went through the towns and villages, teaching as he made his way to Jerusalem. 23Someone asked him, "Lord, are only a few people going to be saved?"　　　　Lk 9:51

He said to them, 24"Make every effort to enter through the narrow door, because many, I tell you, will try to enter and will not be able to. 25Once the owner of the house gets up and closes the door, you will stand outside knocking and pleading, 'Sir, open the door for us.'

"But he will answer, 'I don't know you or where you come from.'　　　　Mt 7:23; 25:10-12

26"Then you will say, 'We ate and drank with you, and you taught in our streets.'

27"But he will reply, 'I don't know you or where you come from. Away from me, all you evildoers!'

28"There will be weeping there, and gnashing of teeth, when you see Abraham, Isaac and Jacob and all the prophets in the kingdom of God, but you yourselves thrown out. 29People will come from east and west and north and south, and will take their places at the feast in the kingdom of God. 30Indeed there are those who are last who will be first, and first who will be last."　　　　Mt 8:12; 19:30

Jesus' Sorrow for Jerusalem

31At that time some Pharisees came to Jesus and said to him, "Leave this place and go somewhere else. Herod wants to kill you."

32He replied, "Go tell that fox, 'I will drive out demons and heal people today and tomorrow, and on the third day I will reach my goal.' 33In any case, I must keep going today and tomorrow and the next day—for surely no prophet can die outside Jerusalem!　　　　Heb 2:10

34"O Jerusalem, Jerusalem, you who kill the prophets and stone those sent to you, how often I have longed to gather your children together, as a hen gathers her chicks under her wings, but you were not willing! 35Look, your house is left to you desolate. I tell you, you will not see me again until you say, 'Blessed is he who comes in the name of the Lord.'[b]"　　　　Jer 22:5

Jesus at a Pharisee's House

14 One Sabbath, when Jesus went to eat in the house of a prominent Pharisee, he was being carefully watched. 2There in front of him was a man suffering from dropsy. 3Jesus asked the Pharisees and experts in the law, "Is it lawful to heal on the Sabbath or not?" 4But they remained silent. So taking hold of the man, he healed him and sent him away.　　　　Mt 12:10

5Then he asked them, "If one

---

a21 Greek *three satas* (probably about 1/2 bushel or 22 liters)　　　b35 Psalm 118:26

of you has a son[a] or an ox that falls into a well on the Sabbath day, will you not immediately pull him out?" [6]And they had nothing to say.   Lk 13:15

[7]When he noticed how the guests picked the places of honor at the table, he told them this parable: [8]"When someone invites you to a wedding feast, do not take the place of honor, for a person more distinguished than you may have been invited. [9]If so, the host who invited both of you will come and say to you, 'Give this man your seat.' Then, humiliated, you will have to take the least important place. [10]But when you are invited, take the lowest place, so that when your host comes, he will say to you, 'Friend, move up to a better place.' Then you will be honored in the presence of all your fellow guests. [11]For everyone who exalts himself will be humbled, and he who humbles himself will be exalted."   Lk 11:43

[12]Then Jesus said to his host, "When you give a luncheon or dinner, do not invite your friends, your brothers or relatives, or your rich neighbors; if you do, they may invite you back and so you will be repaid. [13]But when you give a banquet, invite the poor, the crippled, the lame, the blind, [14]and you will be blessed. Although they cannot repay you, you will be repaid at the resurrection of the righteous."   Ac 24:15

The Parable of the Great Banquet

[15]When one of those at the table with him heard this, he said to Jesus, "Blessed is the man who will eat at the feast in the kingdom of God."   Isa 25:6

[16]Jesus replied: "A certain man was preparing a great banquet and invited many guests. [17]At the time of the banquet he sent his servant to tell those who had been invited, 'Come, for everything is now ready.'

[18]"But they all alike began to make excuses. The first said, 'I have just bought a field, and I must go and see it. Please excuse me.'

[19]"Another said, 'I have just bought five yoke of oxen, and I'm on my way to try them out. Please excuse me.'

[20]"Still another said, 'I just got married, so I can't come.'

[21]"The servant came back and reported this to his master. Then the owner of the house became angry and ordered his servant, 'Go out quickly into the streets and alleys of the town and bring in the poor, the crippled, the blind and the lame.'

[22]"'Sir,' the servant said, 'what you ordered has been done, but there is still room.'

[23]"Then the master told his servant, 'Go out to the roads and country lanes and make them come in, so that my house will be full. [24]I tell you, not one

---

[a]5 Some manuscripts donkey

of those men who were invited will get a taste of my banquet.' "

The Cost of Being a Disciple

25Large crowds were traveling with Jesus, and turning to them he said: 26"If anyone comes to me and does not hate his father and mother, his wife and children, his brothers and sisters—yes, even his own life—he cannot be my disciple. 27And anyone who does not carry his cross and follow me cannot be my disciple. Mt 10:37-38

28"Suppose one of you wants to build a tower. Will he not first sit down and estimate the cost to see if he has enough money to complete it? 29For if he lays the foundation and is not able to finish it, everyone who sees it will ridicule him, 30saying, 'This fellow began to build and was not able to finish.'

31"Or suppose a king is about to go to war against another king. Will he not first sit down and consider whether he is able with ten thousand men to oppose the one coming against him with twenty thousand? 32If he is not able, he will send a delegation while the other is still a long way off and will ask for terms of peace. 33In the same way, any of you who does not give up everything he has cannot be my disciple. Php 3:7-8

34"Salt is good, but if it loses its saltiness, how can it be made salty again? 35It is fit neither for the soil nor for the manure pile; it is thrown out. Mt 5:13

"He who has ears to hear, let him hear."

The Parable of the Lost Sheep

15 Now the tax collectors and "sinners" were all gathering around to hear him. 2But the Pharisees and the teachers of the law muttered, "This man welcomes sinners and eats with them." Lk 5:29

3Then Jesus told them this parable: 4"Suppose one of you has a hundred sheep and loses one of them. Does he not leave the ninety-nine in the open country and go after the lost sheep until he finds it? 5And when he finds it, he joyfully puts it on his shoulders 6and goes home. Then he calls his friends and neighbors together and says, 'Rejoice with me; I have found my lost sheep.' 7I tell you that in the same way there will be more rejoicing in heaven over one sinner who repents than over ninety-nine righteous persons who do not need to repent. Eze 34:11-16

The Parable of the Lost Coin

8"Or suppose a woman has ten silver coins*a* and loses one. Does she not light a lamp, sweep the house and search carefully until she finds it? 9And when she finds it, she calls her friends and neighbors together

*a*8 Greek *ten drachmas*, each worth about a day's wages

and says, 'Rejoice with me; I have found my lost coin.' [10]In the same way, I tell you, there is rejoicing in the presence of the angels of God over one sinner who repents.''

The Parable of the Lost Son

[11]Jesus continued: ''There was a man who had two sons. [12]The younger one said to his father, 'Father, give me my share of the estate.' So he divided his property between them. Dt 21:17

[13]''Not long after that, the younger son got together all he had, set off for a distant country and there squandered his wealth in wild living. [14]After he had spent everything, there was a severe famine in that whole country, and he began to be in need. [15]So he went and hired himself out to a citizen of that country, who sent him to his fields to feed pigs. [16]He longed to fill his stomach with the pods that the pigs were eating, but no one gave him anything. Lev 11:7,8; Lk 16:1

[17]''When he came to his senses, he said, 'How many of my father's hired men have food to spare, and here I am starving to death! [18]I will set out and go back to my father and say to him: Father, I have sinned against heaven and against you. [19]I am no longer worthy to be called your son; make me like one of your hired

men.' [20]So he got up and went to his father. Lev 26:40-42

''But while he was still a long way off, his father saw him and was filled with compassion for him; he ran to his son, threw his arms around him and kissed him. Gen 46:29

[21]''The son said to him, 'Father, I have sinned against heaven and against you. I am no longer worthy to be called your son. *a* Ps 51:4

[22]''But the father said to his servants, 'Quick! Bring the best robe and put it on him. Put a ring on his finger and sandals on his feet. [23]Bring the fattened calf and kill it. Let's have a feast and celebrate. [24]For this son of mine was dead and is alive again; he was lost and is found.' So they began to celebrate.

[25]''Meanwhile, the older son was in the field. When he came near the house, he heard music and dancing. [26]So he called one of the servants and asked him what was going on. [27]'Your brother has come,' he replied, 'and your father has killed the fattened calf because he has him back safe and sound.'

[28]''The older brother became angry and refused to go in. So his father went out and pleaded with him. [29]But he answered his father, 'Look! All these years I've been slaving for you and never disobeyed your orders. Yet you never gave me even a young goat so I could celebrate

---

*a*21 Some early manuscripts *son. Make me like one of your hired men.*

with my friends. ³⁰But when this son of yours who has squandered your property with prostitutes comes home, you kill the fattened calf for him!'

³¹" 'My son,' the father said, 'you are always with me, and everything I have is yours. ³²But we had to celebrate and be glad, because this brother of yours was dead and is alive again; he was lost and is found.' " Mal 3:17

The Parable of the Shrewd Manager

16 Jesus told his disciples: "There was a rich man whose manager was accused of wasting his possessions. ²So he called him in and asked him, 'What is this I hear about you? Give an account of your management, because you cannot be manager any longer.'

³"The manager said to himself, 'What shall I do now? My master is taking away my job. I'm not strong enough to dig, and I'm ashamed to beg— ⁴I know what I'll do so that, when I lose my job here, people will welcome me into their houses.'

⁵"So he called in each one of his master's debtors. He asked the first, 'How much do you owe my master?'

⁶" 'Eight hundred gallons*a* of olive oil,' he replied.

"The manager told him, 'Take your bill, sit down quickly, and make it four hundred.'

⁷"Then he asked the second, 'And how much do you owe?'

" 'A thousand bushels*b* of wheat,' he replied.

"He told him, 'Take your bill and make it eight hundred.'

⁸"The master commended the dishonest manager because he had acted shrewdly. For the people of this world are more shrewd in dealing with their own kind than are the people of the light. ⁹I tell you, use worldly wealth to gain friends for yourselves, so that when it is gone, you will be welcomed into eternal dwellings. Ps 17:14

¹⁰"Whoever can be trusted with very little can also be trusted with much, and whoever is dishonest with very little will also be dishonest with much. ¹¹So if you have not been trustworthy in handling worldly wealth, who will trust you with true riches? ¹²And if you have not been trustworthy with someone else's property, who will give you property of your own? Mt 25:21,23; Lk 19:17

¹³"No servant can serve two masters. Either he will hate the one and love the other, or he will be devoted to the one and despise the other. You cannot serve both God and Money."

¹⁴The Pharisees, who loved money, heard all this and were sneering at Jesus. ¹⁵He said to

---

*a*6 Greek *one hundred batous* (probably about 3 kiloliters)   *b*7 Greek *one hundred korous* (probably about 35 kiloliters)

them, "You are the ones who justify yourselves in the eyes of men, but God knows your hearts. What is highly valued among men is detestable in God's sight. Rev 2:23

Additional Teachings

16"The Law and the Prophets were proclaimed until John. Since that time, the good news of the kingdom of God is being preached, and everyone is forcing his way into it. 17It is easier for heaven and earth to disappear than for the least stroke of a pen to drop out of the Law.

18"Anyone who divorces his wife and marries another woman commits adultery, and the man who marries a divorced woman commits adultery.

The Rich Man and Lazarus

19"There was a rich man who was dressed in purple and fine linen and lived in luxury every day. 20At his gate was laid a beggar named Lazarus, covered with sores 21and longing to eat what fell from the rich man's table. Even the dogs came and licked his sores. Eze 16:49

22"The time came when the beggar died and the angels carried him to Abraham's side. The rich man also died and was buried. 23In hell,*a* where he was in torment, he looked up and saw Abraham far away, with Lazarus by his side. 24So he called to him, 'Father Abraham, have

pity on me and send Lazarus to dip the tip of his finger in water and cool my tongue, because I am in agony in this fire.' Lk 3:8

25"But Abraham replied, 'Son, remember that in your lifetime you received your good things, while Lazarus received bad things, but now he is comforted here and you are in agony. 26And besides all this, between us and you a great chasm has been fixed, so that those who want to go from here to you cannot, nor can anyone cross over from there to us.'

27"He answered, 'Then I beg you, father, send Lazarus to my father's house, 28for I have five brothers. Let him warn them, so that they will not also come to this place of torment.' Ac 2:40

29"Abraham replied, 'They have Moses and the Prophets; let them listen to them.' Ac 15:21

30" 'No, father Abraham,' he said, 'but if someone from the dead goes to them, they will repent.'

31"He said to him, 'If they do not listen to Moses and the Prophets, they will not be convinced even if someone rises from the dead.' " Jn 12:9-11

Sin, Faith, Duty

17 Jesus said to his disciples: "Things that cause people to sin are bound to come, but woe to that person through whom they come. 2It would be better for him to be

*a*23 Greek *Hades*

thrown into the sea with a millstone tied around his neck than for him to cause one of these little ones to sin. ³So watch yourselves.   Mt 18:7; Lk 10:21

"If your brother sins, rebuke him, and if he repents, forgive him. ⁴If he sins against you seven times in a day, and seven times comes back to you and says, 'I repent,' forgive him."

⁵The apostles said to the Lord, "Increase our faith!"Col 3:13

⁶He replied, "If you have faith as small as a mustard seed, you can say to this mulberry tree, 'Be uprooted and planted in the sea,' and it will obey you.

⁷"Suppose one of you had a servant plowing or looking after the sheep. Would he say to the servant when he comes in from the field, 'Come along now and sit down to eat'? ⁸Would he not rather say, 'Prepare my supper, get yourself ready and wait on me while I eat and drink; after that you may eat and drink'? ⁹Would he thank the servant because he did what he was told to do? ¹⁰So you also, when you have done everything you were told to do, should say, 'We are unworthy servants; we have only done our duty.' "   Lk 12:37

Ten Healed of Leprosy

¹¹Now on his way to Jerusalem, Jesus traveled along the border between Samaria and Galilee. ¹²As he was going into a village, ten men who had leprosyª met him. They stood at a distance ¹³and called out in a loud voice, "Jesus, Master, have pity on us!"   Lk 9:51

¹⁴When he saw them, he said, "Go, show yourselves to the priests." And as they went, they were cleansed.   Lev 14:2

¹⁵One of them, when he saw he was healed, came back, praising God in a loud voice. ¹⁶He threw himself at Jesus' feet and thanked him—and he was a Samaritan.   Mt 10:5

¹⁷Jesus asked, "Were not all ten cleansed? Where are the other nine? ¹⁸Was no one found to return and give praise to God except this foreigner?" ¹⁹Then he said to him, "Rise and go; your faith has made you well."

The Coming of the Kingdom of God

²⁰Once, having been asked by the Pharisees when the kingdom of God would come, Jesus replied, "The kingdom of God does not come with your careful observation, ²¹nor will people say, 'Here it is,' or 'There it is,' because the kingdom of God is withinᵇ you."

²²Then he said to his disciples, "The time is coming when you will long to see one of the days of the Son of Man, but you will not see it. ²³Men will tell

---

ª12 The Greek word was used for various diseases affecting the skin—not necessarily leprosy.   ᵇ21 Or among

you, 'There he is!' or 'Here he is!' Do not go running off after them. ²⁴For the Son of Man in his day[a] will be like the lightning, which flashes and lights up the sky from one end to the other. ²⁵But first he must suffer many things and be rejected by this generation.   Mt 8:20

²⁶"Just as it was in the days of Noah, so also will it be in the days of the Son of Man. ²⁷People were eating, drinking, marrying and being given in marriage up to the day Noah entered the ark. Then the flood came and destroyed them all.   Ge 6:5-8

²⁸"It was the same in the days of Lot. People were eating and drinking, buying and selling, planting and building. ²⁹But the day Lot left Sodom, fire and sulfur rained down from heaven and destroyed them all.   Ge 19:1-28

³⁰"It will be just like this on the day the Son of Man is revealed. ³¹On that day no one who is on the roof of his house, with his goods inside, should go down to get them. Likewise, no one in the field should go back for anything. ³²Remember Lot's wife! ³³Whoever tries to keep his life will lose it, and whoever loses his life will preserve it. ³⁴I tell you, on that night two people will be in one bed; one will be taken and the other left. ³⁵Two women will be grinding grain together; one will be taken and the other left.[b]   Mt 24:41

³⁷"Where, Lord?" they asked.

He replied, "Where there is a dead body, there the vultures will gather."   Mt 24:28

The Parable of the Persistent Widow

18 Then Jesus told his disciples a parable to show them that they should always pray and not give up. ²He said: "In a certain town there was a judge who neither feared God nor cared about men. ³And there was a widow in that town who kept coming to him with the plea, 'Grant me justice against my adversary.'   Isa 40:31

⁴"For some time he refused. But finally he said to himself, 'Even though I don't fear God or care about men, ⁵yet because this widow keeps bothering me, I will see that she gets justice, so that she won't eventually wear me out with her coming!' "

⁶And the Lord said, "Listen to what the unjust judge says. ⁷And will not God bring about justice for his chosen ones, who cry out to him day and night? Will he keep putting them off? ⁸I tell you, he will see that they get justice, and quickly. However, when the Son of Man comes, will he find faith on the earth?"

The Parable of the Pharisee and the Tax Collector

⁹To some who were confident

---

[a]24 Some manuscripts do not have *in his day.*   [b]35 Some manuscripts *left. ³⁶Two men will be in the field; one will be taken and the other left.*

of their own righteousness and looked down on everybody else, Jesus told this parable: 10"Two men went up to the temple to pray, one a Pharisee and the other a tax collector. 11The Pharisee stood up and prayed about[a] himself: 'God, I thank you that I am not like other men—robbers, evildoers, adulterers—or even like this tax collector. 12I fast twice a week and give a tenth of all I get.' Lk 16:15

13"But the tax collector stood at a distance. He would not even look up to heaven, but beat his breast and said, 'God, have mercy on me, a sinner.'

14"I tell you that this man, rather than the other, went home justified before God. For everyone who exalts himself will be humbled, and he who humbles himself will be exalted." Mt 23:12

The Little Children and Jesus

15People were also bringing babies to Jesus to have him touch them. When the disciples saw this, they rebuked them. 16But Jesus called the children to him and said, "Let the little children come to me, and do not hinder them, for the kingdom of God belongs to such as these. 17I tell you the truth, anyone who will not receive the kingdom of God like a little child will never enter it." Mt 11:25; 18:3

The Rich Ruler

18A certain ruler asked him, "Good teacher, what must I do to inherit eternal life?" Lk 10:25

19"Why do you call me good?" Jesus answered. "No one is good—except God alone. 20You know the commandments: 'Do not commit adultery, do not murder, do not steal, do not give false testimony, honor your father and mother.'[b]" Ex 20:12-16

21"All these I have kept since I was a boy," he said.

22When Jesus heard this, he said to him, "You still lack one thing. Sell everything you have and give to the poor, and you will have treasure in heaven. Then come, follow me." Ac 2:45

23When he heard this, he became very sad, because he was a man of great wealth. 24Jesus looked at him and said, "How hard it is for the rich to enter the kingdom of God! 25Indeed, it is easier for a camel to go through the eye of a needle than for a rich man to enter the kingdom of God." Pr 11:28

26Those who heard this asked, "Who then can be saved?"

27Jesus replied, "What is impossible with men is possible with God." Mt 19:26

28Peter said to him, "We have left all we had to follow you!"

29"I tell you the truth," Jesus said to them, "no one who has left home or wife or brothers or

a11 Or to   b20 Exodus 20:12-16; Deut. 5:16-20

parents or children for the sake of the kingdom of God [30]will fail to receive many times as much in this age and, in the age to come, eternal life." Mt 25:46

Jesus Again Predicts His Death

[31]Jesus took the Twelve aside and told them, "We are going up to Jerusalem, and everything that is written by the prophets about the Son of Man will be fulfilled. [32]He will be handed over to the Gentiles. They will mock him, insult him, spit on him, flog him and kill him. [33]On the third day he will rise again."

[34]The disciples did not understand any of this. Its meaning was hidden from them, and they did not know what he was talking about. Mk 9:32

A Blind Beggar Receives His Sight

[35]As Jesus approached Jericho, a blind man was sitting by the roadside begging. [36]When he heard the crowd going by, he asked what was happening. [37]They told him, "Jesus of Nazareth is passing by." Lk 19:1

[38]He called out, "Jesus, Son of David, have mercy on me!"

[39]Those who led the way rebuked him and told him to be quiet, but he shouted all the more, "Son of David, have mercy on me!"

[40]Jesus stopped and ordered the man to be brought to him. When he came near, Jesus asked him, [41]"What do you want me to do for you?"

"Lord, I want to see," he replied.

[42]Jesus said to him, "Receive your sight; your faith has healed you." [43]Immediately he received his sight and followed Jesus, praising God. When all the people saw it, they also praised God. Mt 9:22

Zacchaeus the Tax Collector

19 Jesus entered Jericho and was passing through. [2]A man was there by the name of Zacchaeus; he was a chief tax collector and was wealthy. [3]He wanted to see who Jesus was, but being a short man he could not, because of the crowd. [4]So he ran ahead and climbed a sycamore-fig tree to see him, since Jesus was coming that way. 1Ki 10:27; Lk 18:37

[5]When Jesus reached the spot, he looked up and said to him, "Zacchaeus, come down immediately. I must stay at your house today." [6]So he came down at once and welcomed him gladly.

[7]All the people saw this and began to mutter, "He has gone to be the guest of a 'sinner.'"

[8]But Zacchaeus stood up and said to the Lord, "Look, Lord! Here and now I give half of my possessions to the poor, and if I have cheated anybody out of anything, I will pay back four times the amount." Lev 6:4,5

[9]Jesus said to him, "Today salvation has come to this

house, because this man, too, is a son of Abraham. ¹⁰For the Son of Man came to seek and to save what was lost."   Eze 34:12,16

The Parable of the Ten Minas

¹¹While they were listening to this, he went on to tell them a parable, because he was near Jerusalem and the people thought that the kingdom of God was going to appear at once. ¹²He said: "A man of noble birth went to a distant country to have himself appointed king and then to return. ¹³So he called ten of his servants and gave them ten minas. *a* 'Put this money to work,' he said, 'until I come back.'   Mk 13:34; Lk 17:20

¹⁴"But his subjects hated him and sent a delegation after him to say, 'We don't want this man to be our king.'   Jn 1:11

¹⁵"He was made king, however, and returned home. Then he sent for the servants to whom he had given the money, in order to find out what they had gained with it.

¹⁶"The first one came and said, 'Sir, your mina has earned ten more.'

¹⁷"'Well done, my good servant!' his master replied. 'Because you have been trustworthy in a very small matter, take charge of ten cities.'   Pr 27:18

¹⁸"The second came and said, 'Sir, your mina has earned five more.'

¹⁹"His master answered, 'You take charge of five cities.'

²⁰"Then another servant came and said, 'Sir, here is your mina; I have kept it laid away in a piece of cloth. ²¹I was afraid of you, because you are a hard man. You take out what you did not put in and reap what you did not sow.'

²²"His master replied, 'I will judge you by your own words, you wicked servant! You knew, did you, that I am a hard man, taking out what I did not put in, and reaping what I did not sow? ²³Why then didn't you put my money on deposit, so that when I came back, I could have collected it with interest?'   2Sa 1:16

²⁴"Then he said to those standing by, 'Take his mina away from him and give it to the one who has ten minas.'

²⁵"'Sir,' they said, 'he already has ten!'

²⁶"He replied, 'I tell you that to everyone who has, more will be given, but as for the one who has nothing, even what he has will be taken away. ²⁷But those enemies of mine who did not want me to be king over them—bring them here and kill them in front of me.'"   Mt 25:14-30

The Triumphal Entry

²⁸After Jesus had said this, he went on ahead, going up to Jerusalem. ²⁹As he approached Bethphage and Bethany at the hill called the Mount of Olives,

---

a13 A mina was about three months' wages.

he sent two of his disciples, saying to them, ³⁰"Go to the village ahead of you, and as you enter it, you will find a colt tied there, which no one has ever ridden. Untie it and bring it here. ³¹If anyone asks you, 'Why are you untying it?' tell him, 'The Lord needs it.'"   Mk 10:32; Lk 9:51

³²Those who were sent ahead went and found it just as he had told them. ³³As they were untying the colt, its owners asked them, "Why are you untying the colt?"   Lk 22:13

³⁴They replied, "The Lord needs it."

³⁵They brought it to Jesus, threw their cloaks on the colt and put Jesus on it. ³⁶As he went along, people spread their cloaks on the road.   2Ki 9:13

³⁷When he came near the place where the road goes down the Mount of Olives, the whole crowd of disciples began joyfully to praise God in loud voices for all the miracles they had seen:

³⁸"Blessed is the king who
     comes in the name of
     the Lord!"ᵃ

"Peace in heaven and glory
     in the highest!"   Lk 2:14

³⁹Some of the Pharisees in the crowd said to Jesus, "Teacher, rebuke your disciples!"   Mt 21:15,16

⁴⁰"I tell you," he replied, "if they keep quiet, the stones will cry out."   Hab 2:11

⁴¹As he approached Jerusalem and saw the city, he wept over it ⁴²and said, "If you, even you, had only known on this day what would bring you peace—but now it is hidden from your eyes. ⁴³The days will come upon you when your enemies will build an embankment against you and encircle you and hem you in on every side. ⁴⁴They will dash you to the ground, you and the children within your walls. They will not leave one stone on another, because you did not recognize the time of God's coming to you."

Jesus at the Temple

⁴⁵Then he entered the temple area and began driving out those who were selling. ⁴⁶"It is written," he said to them, " 'My house will be a house of prayer'ᵇ; but you have made it 'a den of robbers.'ᶜ"

⁴⁷Every day he was teaching at the temple. But the chief priests, the teachers of the law and the leaders among the people were trying to kill him. ⁴⁸Yet they could not find any way to do it, because all the people hung on his words.

The Authority of Jesus Questioned

20 One day as he was teaching the people in the temple courts and preaching the gospel, the chief priests and the teachers of the law, together with the elders, came up to him.

ᵃ38 Psalm 118:26   ᵇ46 Isaiah 56:7   ᶜ46 Jer. 7:11

²"Tell us by what authority you are doing these things," they said. "Who gave you this authority?"   Lk 8:1; Ac 4:7

³He replied, "I will also ask you a question. Tell me, ⁴John's baptism—was it from heaven, or from men?"   Mk 1:4

⁵They discussed it among themselves and said, "If we say, 'From heaven,' he will ask, 'Why didn't you believe him?' ⁶But if we say, 'From men,' all the people will stone us, because they are persuaded that John was a prophet."   Lk 7:29,30

⁷So they answered, "We don't know where it was from."

⁸Jesus said, "Neither will I tell you by what authority I am doing these things."

The Parable of the Tenants

⁹He went on to tell the people this parable: "A man planted a vineyard, rented it to some farmers and went away for a long time. ¹⁰At harvest time he sent a servant to the tenants so they would give him some of the fruit of the vineyard. But the tenants beat him and sent him away empty-handed. ¹¹He sent another servant, but that one also they beat and treated shamefully and sent away empty-handed. ¹²He sent still a third, and they wounded him and threw him out.   Isa 5:1-7

¹³"Then the owner of the vineyard said, 'What shall I do? I will send my son, whom I love; perhaps they will respect him.'

¹⁴"But when the tenants saw him, they talked the matter over. 'This is the heir,' they said. 'Let's kill him, and the inheritance will be ours.' ¹⁵So they threw him out of the vineyard and killed him.

"What then will the owner of the vineyard do to them? ¹⁶He will come and kill those tenants and give the vineyard to others."   Lk 19:27

When the people heard this, they said, "May this never be!"

¹⁷Jesus looked directly at them and asked, "Then what is the meaning of that which is written:

" 'The stone the builders rejected
    has become the capstone*ᵃ'*ᵇ?

¹⁸Everyone who falls on that stone will be broken to pieces, but he on whom it falls will be crushed."   Isa 8:14

¹⁹The teachers of the law and the chief priests looked for a way to arrest him immediately, because they knew he had spoken this parable against them. But they were afraid of the people.   Lk 19:47

Paying Taxes to Caesar

²⁰Keeping a close watch on him, they sent spies, who pretended to be honest. They hoped to catch Jesus in something he said so that they might

---

ᵃ17 Or *cornerstone*   *ᵇ17* Psalm 118:22

hand him over to the power and authority of the governor. 21So the spies questioned him: "Teacher, we know that you speak and teach what is right, and that you do not show partiality but teach the way of God in accordance with the truth. 22Is it right for us to pay taxes to Caesar or not?"   Jn 3:2

23He saw through their duplicity and said to them, 24"Show me a denarius. Whose portrait and inscription are on it?"

25"Caesar's," they replied.

He said to them, "Then give to Caesar what is Caesar's, and to God what is God's."   Lk 23:2

26They were unable to trap him in what he had said there in public. And astonished by his answer, they became silent.

The Resurrection and Marriage

27Some of the Sadducees, who say there is no resurrection, came to Jesus with a question. 28"Teacher," they said, "Moses wrote for us that if a man's brother dies and leaves a wife but no children, the man must marry the widow and have children for his brother. 29Now there were seven brothers. The first one married a woman and died childless. 30The second 31and then the third married her, and in the same way the seven died, leaving no children. 32Finally, the woman died too. 33Now then, at the resurrection whose wife will she be, since the seven were married to her?"   Dt 25:5,6

34Jesus replied, "The people of this age marry and are given in marriage. 35But those who are considered worthy of taking part in that age and in the resurrection from the dead will neither marry nor be given in marriage, 36and they can no longer die; for they are like the angels. They are God's children, since they are children of the resurrection. 37But in the account of the bush, even Moses showed that the dead rise, for he calls the Lord 'the God of Abraham, and the God of Isaac, and the God of Jacob.'[a] 38He is not the God of the dead, but of the living, for to him all are alive."   Ex 3:6; Jn 1:12

39Some of the teachers of the law responded, "Well said, teacher!" 40And no one dared to ask him any more questions.

Whose Son Is the Christ?

41Then Jesus said to them, "How is it that they say the Christ[b] is the Son of David? 42David himself declares in the Book of Psalms: Mt 1:1

" 'The Lord said to my Lord:
  "Sit at my right hand
43until I make your enemies
  a footstool for your feet." '[c]

44David calls him 'Lord.' How then can he be his son?"

---

[a]37 Exodus 3:6   [b]41 Or *Messiah*   [c]43 Psalm 110:1

⁴⁵While all the people were listening, Jesus said to his disciples, ⁴⁶"Beware of the teachers of the law. They like to walk around in flowing robes and love to be greeted in the marketplaces and have the most important seats in the synagogues and the places of honor at banquets. ⁴⁷They devour widows' houses and for a show make lengthy prayers. Such men will be punished most severely."

The Widow's Offering

21 As he looked up, Jesus saw the rich putting their gifts into the temple treasury. ²He also saw a poor widow put in two very small copper coins. *ᵃ* ³"I tell you the truth," he said, "this poor widow has put in more than all the others. ⁴All these people gave their gifts out of their wealth; but she out of her poverty put in all she had to live on." Mk 12:41ff; 2Co 8:12

Signs of the End of the Age

⁵Some of his disciples were remarking about how the temple was adorned with beautiful stones and with gifts dedicated to God. But Jesus said, ⁶"As for what you see here, the time will come when not one stone will be left on another; every one of them will be thrown down."

⁷"Teacher," they asked, "when will these things happen? And what will be the sign that they are about to take place?"

⁸He replied: "Watch out that you are not deceived. For many will come in my name, claiming, 'I am he,' and, 'The time is near.' Do not follow them. ⁹When you hear of wars and revolutions, do not be frightened. These things must happen first, but the end will not come right away." Lk 17:23

¹⁰Then he said to them: "Nation will rise against nation, and kingdom against kingdom. ¹¹There will be great earthquakes, famines and pestilences in various places, and fearful events and great signs from heaven. Isa 19:2

¹²"But before all this, they will lay hands on you and persecute you. They will deliver you to synagogues and prisons, and you will be brought before kings and governors, and all on account of my name. ¹³This will result in your being witnesses to them. ¹⁴But make up your mind not to worry beforehand how you will defend yourselves. ¹⁵For I will give you words and wisdom that none of your adversaries will be able to resist or contradict. ¹⁶You will be betrayed even by parents, brothers, relatives and friends, and they will put some of you to death. ¹⁷All men will hate you because of me. ¹⁸But not a hair of your head will perish. ¹⁹By standing firm you will gain life.

*ᵃ*2 Greek *two lepta*

20"When you see Jerusalem being surrounded by armies, you will know that its desolation is near. 21Then let those who are in Judea flee to the mountains, let those in the city get out, and let those in the country not enter the city. 22For this is the time of punishment in fulfillment of all that has been written. 23How dreadful it will be in those days for pregnant women and nursing mothers! There will be great distress in the land and wrath against this people. 24They will fall by the sword and will be taken as prisoners to all the nations. Jerusalem will be trampled on by the Gentiles until the times of the Gentiles are fulfilled.   Lk 19:43

25"There will be signs in the sun, moon and stars. On the earth, nations will be in anguish and perplexity at the roaring and tossing of the sea. 26Men will faint from terror, apprehensive of what is coming on the world, for the heavenly bodies will be shaken. 27At that time they will see the Son of Man coming in a cloud with power and great glory. 28When these things begin to take place, stand up and lift up your heads, because your redemption is drawing near."   2Pe 3:10,12

29He told them this parable: "Look at the fig tree and all the trees. 30When they sprout leaves, you can see for yourselves and know that summer is near. 31Even so, when you see these things happening, you know that the kingdom of God is near.

32"I tell you the truth, this generationª will certainly not pass away until all these things have happened. 33Heaven and earth will pass away, but my words will never pass away.

34"Be careful, or your hearts will be weighed down with dissipation, drunkenness and the anxieties of life, and that day will close on you unexpectedly like a trap. 35For it will come upon all those who live on the face of the whole earth. 36Be always on the watch, and pray that you may be able to escape all that is about to happen, and that you may be able to stand before the Son of Man."   1Th 5:2-7

37Each day Jesus was teaching at the temple, and each evening he went out to spend the night on the hill called the Mount of Olives, 38and all the people came early in the morning to hear him at the temple.   Mt 26:55

Judas Agrees to Betray Jesus

22 Now the Feast of Unleavened Bread, called the Passover, was approaching, 2and the chief priests and the teachers of the law were looking for some way to get rid of Jesus, for they were afraid of the people. 3Then Satan entered Judas, called Iscariot, one of the Twelve. 4And Judas went to the

ª32 Or race

chief priests and the officers of the temple guard and discussed with them how he might betray Jesus. [5]They were delighted and agreed to give him money. [6]He consented, and watched for an opportunity to hand Jesus over to them when no crowd was present.   Zec 11:12; Jn 11:55

The Last Supper

[7]Then came the day of Unleavened Bread on which the Passover lamb had to be sacrificed. [8]Jesus sent Peter and John, saying, "Go and make preparations for us to eat the Passover."   Ex 12:18-20

[9]"Where do you want us to prepare for it?" they asked.

[10]He replied, "As you enter the city, a man carrying a jar of water will meet you. Follow him to the house that he enters, [11]and say to the owner of the house, 'The Teacher asks: Where is the guest room, where I may eat the Passover with my disciples?' [12]He will show you a large upper room, all furnished. Make preparations there."

[13]They left and found things just as Jesus had told them. So they prepared the Passover.

[14]When the hour came, Jesus and his apostles reclined at the table. [15]And he said to them, "I have eagerly desired to eat this Passover with you before I suffer. [16]For I tell you, I will not eat it again until it finds fulfillment in the kingdom of God."   Mt 16:21

[17]After taking the cup, he gave thanks and said, "Take

this and divide it among you. [18]For I tell you I will not drink again of the fruit of the vine until the kingdom of God comes."

[19]And he took bread, gave thanks and broke it, and gave it to them, saying, "This is my body given for you; do this in remembrance of me."   Mt 14:19

[20]In the same way, after the supper he took the cup, saying, "This cup is the new covenant in my blood, which is poured out for you. [21]But the hand of him who is going to betray me is with mine on the table. [22]The Son of Man will go as it has been decreed, but woe to that man who betrays him." [23]They began to question among themselves which of them it might be who would do this.   Ex 24:8

[24]Also a dispute arose among them as to which of them was considered to be greatest. [25]Jesus said to them, "The kings of the Gentiles lord it over them; and those who exercise authority over them call themselves Benefactors. [26]But you are not to be like that. Instead, the greatest among you should be like the youngest, and the one who rules like the one who serves. [27]For who is greater, the one who is at the table or the one who serves? Is it not the one who is at the table? But I am among you as one who serves. [28]You are those who have stood by me in my trials. [29]And I confer on you a kingdom, just as my Father conferred one on me, [30]so that you may eat and drink

at my table in my kingdom and sit on thrones, judging the twelve tribes of Israel.   Mk 9:34,35

31"Simon, Simon, Satan has asked to sift you*a* as wheat. 32But I have prayed for you, Simon, that your faith may not fail. And when you have turned back, strengthen your brothers."   Job 1:6-12; Jn 17:9

33But he replied, "Lord, I am ready to go with you to prison and to death."   Jn 11:16

34Jesus answered, "I tell you, Peter, before the rooster crows today, you will deny three times that you know me."

35Then Jesus asked them, "When I sent you without purse, bag or sandals, did you lack anything?"   Mt 10:9,10

"Nothing," they answered.

36He said to them, "But now if you have a purse, take it, and also a bag; and if you don't have a sword, sell your cloak and buy one. 37It is written: 'And he was numbered with the transgressors'*b*; and I tell you that this must be fulfilled in me. Yes, what is written about me is reaching its fulfillment."

38The disciples said, "See, Lord, here are two swords."

"That is enough," he replied.

Jesus Prays on the Mount of Olives

39Jesus went out as usual to the Mount of Olives, and his disciples followed him. 40On reaching the place, he said to them, "Pray that you will not fall into temptation." 41He withdrew about a stone's throw beyond them, knelt down and prayed, 42"Father, if you are willing, take this cup from me; yet not my will, but yours be done." 43An angel from heaven appeared to him and strengthened him. 44And being in anguish, he prayed more earnestly, and his sweat was like drops of blood falling to the ground.*c*

45When he rose from prayer and went back to the disciples, he found them asleep, exhausted from sorrow. 46"Why are you sleeping?" he asked them. "Get up and pray so that you will not fall into temptation."

Jesus Arrested

47While he was still speaking a crowd came up, and the man who was called Judas, one of the Twelve, was leading them. He approached Jesus to kiss him, 48but Jesus asked him, "Judas, are you betraying the Son of Man with a kiss?"   Mt 26:47

49When Jesus' followers saw what was going to happen, they said, "Lord, should we strike with our swords?" 50And one of them struck the servant of the high priest, cutting off his right ear.

51But Jesus answered, "No more of this!" And he touched the man's ear and healed him.

---

*a*31 The Greek is plural.   *b*37 Isaiah 53:12   *c*44 Some early manuscripts do not have verses 43 and 44.

⁵²Then Jesus said to the chief priests, the officers of the temple guard, and the elders, who had come for him, "Am I leading a rebellion, that you have come with swords and clubs? ⁵³Every day I was with you in the temple courts, and you did not lay a hand on me. But this is your hour—when darkness reigns." Jn 3:20

Peter Disowns Jesus

⁵⁴Then seizing him, they led him away and took him into the house of the high priest. Peter followed at a distance. ⁵⁵But when they had kindled a fire in the middle of the courtyard and had sat down together, Peter sat down with them. ⁵⁶A servant girl saw him seated there in the firelight. She looked closely at him and said, "This man was with him." Mt 26:69-75

⁵⁷But he denied it. "Woman, I don't know him," he said.

⁵⁸A little later someone else saw him and said, "You also are one of them."

"Man, I am not!" Peter replied. Mk 14:66-72

⁵⁹About an hour later another asserted, "Certainly this fellow was with him, for he is a Galilean." Jn 18:16ff

⁶⁰Peter replied, "Man, I don't know what you're talking about!" Just as he was speaking, the rooster crowed. ⁶¹The Lord turned and looked straight at Peter. Then Peter remembered the word the Lord had spoken to him: "Before the rooster crows today, you will disown me three times." ⁶²And he went outside and wept bitterly. Lk 7:13

The Guards Mock Jesus

⁶³The men who were guarding Jesus began mocking and beating him. ⁶⁴They blindfolded him and demanded, "Prophesy! Who hit you?" ⁶⁵And they said many other insulting things to him. Mt 16:21

Jesus Before Pilate and Herod

⁶⁶At daybreak the council of the elders of the people, both the chief priests and teachers of the law, met together, and Jesus was led before them. ⁶⁷"If you are the Christ,ᵃ" they said, "tell us." Mk 15:1

Jesus answered, "If I tell you, you will not believe me, ⁶⁸and if I asked you, you would not answer. ⁶⁹But from now on, the Son of Man will be seated at the right hand of the mighty God."

⁷⁰They all asked, "Are you then the Son of God?" Mt 4:3

He replied, "You are right in saying I am." Mt 27:11

⁷¹Then they said, "Why do we need any more testimony? We have heard it from his own lips." Mt 26:65

23 Then the whole assembly rose and led him off to Pilate. ²And they began to accuse him, saying, "We have found this man subverting our nation.

ᵃ67 Or Messiah

He opposes payment of taxes to Caesar and claims to be Christ,[a] a king."   Lk 20:22ff; Jn 19:12

[3]So Pilate asked Jesus, "Are you the king of the Jews?"

"Yes, it is as you say," Jesus replied.   1Ti 6:13

[4]Then Pilate announced to the chief priests and the crowd, "I find no basis for a charge against this man."   Mt 27:23

[5]But they insisted, "He stirs up the people all over Judea[b] by his teaching. He started in Galilee and has come all the way here."   Mk 1:14

[6]On hearing this, Pilate asked if the man was a Galilean. [7]When he learned that Jesus was under Herod's jurisdiction, he sent him to Herod, who was also in Jerusalem at that time.

[8]When Herod saw Jesus, he was greatly pleased, because for a long time he had been wanting to see him. From what he had heard about him, he hoped to see him perform some miracle. [9]He plied him with many questions, but Jesus gave him no answer. [10]The chief priests and the teachers of the law were standing there, vehemently accusing him. [11]Then Herod and his soldiers ridiculed and mocked him. Dressing him in an elegant robe, they sent him back to Pilate. [12]That day Herod and Pilate became friends— before this they had been enemies.   Lk 9:9; Ac 4:27

[13]Pilate called together the chief priests, the rulers and the people, [14]and said to them, "You brought me this man as one who was inciting the people to rebellion. I have examined him in your presence and have found no basis for your charges against him. [15]Neither has Herod, for he sent him back to us; as you can see, he has done nothing to deserve death. [16]Therefore, I will punish him and then release him.[c]"

[18]With one voice they cried out, "Away with this man! Release Barabbas to us!" [19](Barabbas had been thrown into prison for an insurrection in the city, and for murder.)   Ac 3:13

[20]Wanting to release Jesus, Pilate appealed to them again. [21]But they kept shouting, "Crucify him! Crucify him!"

[22]For the third time he spoke to them: "Why? What crime has this man committed? I have found in him no grounds for the death penalty. Therefore I will have him punished and then release him."

[23]But with loud shouts they insistently demanded that he be crucified, and their shouts prevailed. [24]So Pilate decided to grant their demand. [25]He released the man who had been thrown into prison for insurrection and murder, the one they asked for, and surrendered Jesus to their will.   Ex 23:2

[a]2 Or *Messiah*; also in verses 35 and 39   [b]5 Or *over the land of the Jews*   [c]16 Some manuscripts *him." [17]Now he was obliged to release one man to them at the Feast.*

The Crucifixion

26As they led him away, they seized Simon from Cyrene, who was on his way in from the country, and put the cross on him and made him carry it behind Jesus. 27A large number of people followed him, including women who mourned and wailed for him. 28Jesus turned and said to them, "Daughters of Jerusalem, do not weep for me; weep for yourselves and for your children. 29For the time will come when you will say, 'Blessed are the barren women, the wombs that never bore and the breasts that never nursed!' 30Then

> " 'they will say to the
>   mountains, "Fall on us!"
> and to the hills, "Cover
>   us!" 'a

31For if men do these things when the tree is green, what will happen when it is dry?"

32Two other men, both criminals, were also led out with him to be executed. 33When they came to the place called the Skull, there they crucified him, along with the criminals—one on his right, the other on his left. 34Jesus said, "Father, forgive them, for they do not know what they are doing."b And they divided up his clothes by casting lots.   Isa 53:12; Mt 5:44

35The people stood watching, and the rulers even sneered at him. They said, "He saved others; let him save himself if he is the Christ of God, the Chosen One."   Ps 22:17; Isa 42:1

36The soldiers also came up and mocked him. They offered him wine vinegar 37and said, "If you are the king of the Jews, save yourself."   Ps 22:7

38There was a written notice above him, which read: THIS IS THE KING OF THE JEWS.   Mt 2:2

39One of the criminals who hung there hurled insults at him: "Aren't you the Christ? Save yourself and us!"

40But the other criminal rebuked him. "Don't you fear God," he said, "since you are under the same sentence? 41We are punished justly, for we are getting what our deeds deserve. But this man has done nothing wrong."

42Then he said, "Jesus, remember me when you come into your kingdom.c"   Mt 16:27

43Jesus answered him, "I tell you the truth, today you will be with me in paradise."   Rev 2:7

Jesus' Death

44It was now about the sixth hour, and darkness came over the whole land until the ninth hour, 45for the sun stopped shining. And the curtain of the temple was torn in two. 46Jesus called out with a loud voice, "Father, into your hands I commit my spirit." When he had

---

a30 Hosea 10:8   b34 Some early manuscripts do not have this sentence.
c42 Some manuscripts come with your kingly power

said this, he breathed his last.

47The centurion, seeing what had happened, praised God and said, "Surely this was a righteous man." 48When all the people who had gathered to witness this sight saw what took place, they beat their breasts and went away. 49But all those who knew him, including the women who had followed him from Galilee, stood at a distance, watching these things.

Jesus' Burial

50Now there was a man named Joseph, a member of the Council, a good and upright man, 51who had not consented to their decision and action. He came from the Judean town of Arimathea and he was waiting for the kingdom of God. 52Going to Pilate, he asked for Jesus' body. 53Then he took it down, wrapped it in linen cloth and placed it in a tomb cut in the rock, one in which no one had yet been laid. 54It was Preparation Day, and the Sabbath was about to begin.   Lk 2:25,38

55The women who had come with Jesus from Galilee followed Joseph and saw the tomb and how his body was laid in it. 56Then they went home and prepared spices and perfumes. But they rested on the Sabbath in obedience to the commandment.   Mk 16:1

The Resurrection

24 On the first day of the week, very early in the morning, the women took the spices they had prepared and went to the tomb. 2They found the stone rolled away from the tomb, 3but when they entered, they did not find the body of the Lord Jesus. 4While they were wondering about this, suddenly two men in clothes that gleamed like lightning stood beside them. 5In their fright the women bowed down with their faces to the ground, but the men said to them, "Why do you look for the living among the dead? 6He is not here; he has risen! Remember how he told you, while he was still with you in Galilee: 7'The Son of Man must be delivered into the hands of sinful men, be crucified and on the third day be raised again.' " 8Then they remembered his words.   Jn 2:22

9When they came back from the tomb, they told all these things to the Eleven and to all the others. 10It was Mary Magdalene, Joanna, Mary the mother of James, and the others with them who told this to the apostles. 11But they did not believe the women, because their words seemed to them like nonsense. 12Peter, however, got up and ran to the tomb. Bending over, he saw the strips of linen lying by themselves, and he went away, wondering to himself what had happened.   Jn 20:3-7

On the Road to Emmaus

13Now that same day two of them were going to a village

called Emmaus, about seven miles*a* from Jerusalem. ¹⁴They were talking with each other about everything that had happened. ¹⁵As they talked and discussed these things with each other, Jesus himself came up and walked along with them; ¹⁶but they were kept from recognizing him.   Mk 16:12

¹⁷He asked them, "What are you discussing together as you walk along?"

They stood still, their faces downcast. ¹⁸One of them, named Cleopas, asked him, "Are you only a visitor to Jerusalem and do not know the things that have happened there in these days?"

¹⁹"What things?" he asked.

"About Jesus of Nazareth," they replied. "He was a prophet, powerful in word and deed before God and all the people. ²⁰The chief priests and our rulers handed him over to be sentenced to death, and they crucified him; ²¹but we had hoped that he was the one who was going to redeem Israel. And what is more, it is the third day since all this took place. ²²In addition, some of our women amazed us. They went to the tomb early this morning ²³but didn't find his body. They came and told us that they had seen a vision of angels, who said he was alive. ²⁴Then some of our companions went to the tomb and found it just as the women

had said, but him they did not see."   Mt 16:21; Lk 1:68

²⁵He said to them, "How foolish you are, and how slow of heart to believe all that the prophets have spoken! ²⁶Did not the Christ*b* have to suffer these things and then enter his glory?" ²⁷And beginning with Moses and all the Prophets, he explained to them what was said in all the Scriptures concerning himself.   Isa 53; Heb 2:10

²⁸As they approached the village to which they were going, Jesus acted as if he were going farther. ²⁹But they urged him strongly, "Stay with us, for it is nearly evening; the day is almost over." So he went in to stay with them.

³⁰When he was at the table with them, he took bread, gave thanks, broke it and began to give it to them. ³¹Then their eyes were opened and they recognized him, and he disappeared from their sight. ³²They asked each other, "Were not our hearts burning within us while he talked with us on the road and opened the Scriptures to us?"   Ps 39:3; Mt 14:19

³³They got up and returned at once to Jerusalem. There they found the Eleven and those with them, assembled together ³⁴and saying, "It is true! The Lord has risen and has appeared to Simon." ³⁵Then the two told what had happened on the way, and how Jesus was

---

*a*13 Greek *sixty stadia* (about 11 kilometers)   *b*26 Or *Messiah*; also in verse 46

recognized by them when he
broke the bread.   1Co 15:5

Jesus Appears to the Disciples

36While they were still talking
about this, Jesus himself stood
among them and said to them,
"Peace be with you."   Jn 20:19

37They were startled and
frightened, thinking they saw a
ghost. 38He said to them, "Why
are you troubled, and why do
doubts rise in your minds?
39Look at my hands and my feet.
It is I myself! Touch me and see;
a ghost does not have flesh and
bones, as you see I have."

40When he had said this, he
showed them his hands and
feet. 41And while they still did
not believe it because of joy and
amazement, he asked them,
"Do you have anything here to
eat?" 42They gave him a piece of
broiled fish, 43and he took it and
ate it in their presence.   Ac 10:41

44He said to them, "This is
what I told you while I was still
with you: Everything must be
fulfilled that is written about me
in the Law of Moses, the Prophets and the Psalms."   Lk 18:31-34

45Then he opened their minds
so they could understand the
Scriptures. 46He told them,
"This is what is written: The
Christ will suffer and rise from
the dead on the third day, 47and
repentance and forgiveness of
sins will be preached in his
name to all nations, beginning
at Jerusalem. 48You are witnesses of these things. 49I am
going to send you what my Father has promised; but stay in
the city until you have been
clothed with power from on
high."   Mt 16:21; Jn 14:16

The Ascension

50When he had led them out
to the vicinity of Bethany, he
lifted up his hands and blessed
them. 51While he was blessing
them, he left them and was tak-
en up into heaven. 52Then they
worshiped him and returned to
Jerusalem with great joy. 53And
they stayed continually at the
temple, praising God.   Ac 2:46

John

Introduction:

The fourth Gospel was also written by one of Jesus' twelve disciples—John, "The disciple whom Jesus loved." John wrote this Gospel sometime between A.D. 90–100 so that "you may believe that Jesus is the Christ, the Son of God, and that by believing you may have life in his name" (John 20:31).

Although the book of John gives a general outline of the life and work of Jesus Christ, it is very different from the other three Gospels. John reports five miracles that are not reported by the other Gospels. Only two of the miracles reported in the other Gospels are reported in John. This book contains no parables and seems to stress Jesus' relationships with individuals.

The purpose of this Gospel is to report the signs, usually called miracles in other Gospels. The signs that John reports give proof that Christ is God and has supernatural powers. Although John gives much attention to proving that Jesus is the Son of God he also shows often that Jesus was very much a human by showing that he was tired, sad, hungry and loving.

Outline of contents:

Prologue and theme (1:1–18)
Introduction of Jesus (1:19–4:54)
Jesus' ministry as God's Son (5:1–10:42)
Crises in Jerusalem (11:1–12:50)
Jesus with his disciples (13:1–17:26)
Trial, death and burial (18:1–19:42)
Resurrection and conclusion (20:1–21:25)

The Word Became Flesh

1 In the beginning was the Word, and the Word was with God, and the Word was God. ²He was with God in the beginning. _{Php 2:6; Rev 19:13} ³Through him all things were made; without him nothing was made that has been made. ⁴In him was life, and that life was the light of men. ⁵The light shines in the darkness, but

the darkness has not understood[a] it. Ps 18:28; Jn 5:26; 1Co 8:6

[6]There came a man who was sent from God; his name was John. [7]He came as a witness to testify concerning that light, so that through him all men might believe. [8]He himself was not the light; he came only as a witness to the light. [9]The true light that gives light to every man was coming into the world.[b] Mt 3:1ff

[10]He was in the world, and though the world was made through him, the world did not recognize him. [11]He came to that which was his own, but his own did not receive him. [12]Yet to all who received him, to those who believed in his name, he gave the right to become children of God— [13]children born not of natural descent,[c] nor of human decision or a husband's will, but born of God. Isa 53:3

[14]The Word became flesh and made his dwelling among us. We have seen his glory, the glory of the One and Only,[d] who came from the Father, full of grace and truth. Gal 4:4

[15]John testifies concerning him. He cries out, saying, "This was he of whom I said, 'He who comes after me has surpassed me because he was before me.' " [16]From the fullness of his grace we have all received one blessing after another. [17]For the law was given through Moses; grace and truth came through Jesus Christ. [18]No one has ever seen God, but God the One and Only,[d,e] who is at the Father's side, has made him known.

John the Baptist Denies Being the Christ

[19]Now this was John's testimony when the Jews of Jerusalem sent priests and Levites to ask him who he was. [20]He did not fail to confess, but confessed freely, "I am not the Christ.[f]" Lk 3:15,16; Jn 3:28

[21]They asked him, "Then who are you? Are you Elijah?"

He said, "I am not."

"Are you the Prophet?"[Dt 18:15]

He answered, "No."

[22]Finally they said, "Who are you? Give us an answer to take back to those who sent us. What do you say about yourself?"

[23]John replied in the words of Isaiah the prophet, "I am the voice of one calling in the desert, 'Make straight the way for the Lord.' "[g] Mt 3:1

[24]Now some Pharisees who had been sent [25]questioned him, "Why then do you baptize if you are not the Christ, nor Elijah, nor the Prophet?"

[26]"I baptize with[h] water," John replied, "but among you stands one you do not know. [27]He is the one who comes after

---

[a]5 Or darkness, and the darkness has not overcome   [b]9 Or This was the true light that gives light to every man who comes into the world   [c]13 Greek of bloods   [d]14,18 Or the Only Begotten   [e]18 Some manuscripts but the only (or only begotten) Son   [f]20 Or Messiah. "The Christ" (Greek) and "the Messiah" (Hebrew) both mean "the Anointed One"; also in verse 25.   [g]23 Isaiah 40:3   [h]26 Or in; also in verses 31 and 33

me, the thongs of whose sandals I am not worthy to untie."

28This all happened at Bethany on the other side of the Jordan, where John was baptizing.

Jesus the Lamb of God

29The next day John saw Jesus coming toward him and said, "Look, the Lamb of God, who takes away the sin of the world! 30This is the one I meant when I said, 'A man who comes after me has surpassed me because he was before me.' 31I myself did not know him, but the reason I came baptizing with water was that he might be revealed to Israel." Ge 22:8; Isa 53:7

32Then John gave this testimony: "I saw the Spirit come down from heaven as a dove and remain on him. 33I would not have known him, except that the one who sent me to baptize with water told me, 'The man on whom you see the Spirit come down and remain is he who will baptize with the Holy Spirit.' 34I have seen and I testify that this is the Son of God." Mt 3:16; Mk 1:8

Jesus' First Disciples

35The next day John was there again with two of his disciples. 36When he saw Jesus passing by, he said, "Look, the Lamb of God!"

37When the two disciples heard him say this, they followed Jesus. 38Turning around, Jesus saw them following and asked, "What do you want?"

They said, "Rabbi" (which means Teacher), "where are you staying?"

39"Come," he replied, "and you will see."

So they went and saw where he was staying, and spent that day with him. It was about the tenth hour.

40Andrew, Simon Peter's brother, was one of the two who heard what John had said and who had followed Jesus. 41The first thing Andrew did was to find his brother Simon and tell him, "We have found the Messiah" (that is, the Christ). 42And he brought him to Jesus. Jn 4:25

Jesus looked at him and said, "You are Simon son of John. You will be called Cephas" (which, when translated, is Peter*a*). Mt 16:18

Jesus Calls Philip and Nathanael

43The next day Jesus decided to leave for Galilee. Finding Philip, he said to him, "Follow me." Mt 4:19; Jn 6:5-7

44Philip, like Andrew and Peter, was from the town of Bethsaida. 45Philip found Nathanael and told him, "We have found the one Moses wrote about in the Law, and about whom the prophets also wrote—Jesus of Nazareth, the son of Joseph."

46"Nazareth! Can anything

---

*a*42 Both *Cephas* (Aramaic) and *Peter* (Greek) mean *rock*.

good come from there?" Nathanael asked. Jn 7:41-42

"Come and see," said Philip.

47When Jesus saw Nathanael approaching, he said of him, "Here is a true Israelite, in whom there is nothing false."

48"How do you know me?" Nathanael asked.

Jesus answered, "I saw you while you were still under the fig tree before Philip called you."

49Then Nathanael declared, "Rabbi, you are the Son of God; you are the King of Israel."Jn 12:13

50Jesus said, "You believea because I told you I saw you under the fig tree. You shall see greater things than that." 51He then added, "I tell youb the truth, youb shall see heaven open, and the angels of God ascending and descending on the Son of Man." Ge 28:12; Mt 3:16

Jesus Changes Water to Wine

2 On the third day a wedding took place at Cana in Galilee. Jesus' mother was there, 2and Jesus and his disciples had also been invited to the wedding. 3When the wine was gone, Jesus' mother said to him, "They have no more wine."Jn 4:46

4"Dear woman, why do you involve me?" Jesus replied. "My time has not yet come."

5His mother said to the servants, "Do whatever he tells you."

6Nearby stood six stone water jars, the kind used by the Jews for ceremonial washing, each holding from twenty to thirty gallons.c Mk 7:3-4

7Jesus said to the servants, "Fill the jars with water"; so they filled them to the brim.

8Then he told them, "Now draw some out and take it to the master of the banquet."

They did so, 9and the master of the banquet tasted the water that had been turned into wine. He did not realize where it had come from, though the servants who had drawn the water knew. Then he called the bridegroom aside 10and said, "Everyone brings out the choice wine first and then the cheaper wine after the guests have had too much to drink; but you have saved the best till now."

11This, the first of his miraculous signs, Jesus performed at Cana in Galilee. He thus revealed his glory, and his disciples put their faith in him. Jn 3:2

Jesus Clears the Temple

12After this he went down to Capernaum with his mother and brothers and his disciples. There they stayed for a few days. Mt 4:13; 12:46

13When it was almost time for the Jewish Passover, Jesus went up to Jerusalem. 14In the temple

---

a50 Or Do you believe . . . ?   b51 The Greek is plural.   c6 Greek two to three metretes (probably about 75 to 115 liters)

courts he found men selling cattle, sheep and doves, and others sitting at tables exchanging money. ¹⁵So he made a whip out of cords, and drove all from the temple area, both sheep and cattle; he scattered the coins of the money changers and overturned their tables. ¹⁶To those who sold doves he said, "Get these out of here! How dare you turn my Father's house into a market!"   Lk 2:49

¹⁷His disciples remembered that it is written: "Zeal for your house will consume me."ª

¹⁸Then the Jews demanded of him, "What miraculous sign can you show us to prove your authority to do all this?"   Mt 12:38

¹⁹Jesus answered them, "Destroy this temple, and I will raise it again in three days."

²⁰The Jews replied, "It has taken forty-six years to build this temple, and you are going to raise it in three days?" ²¹But the temple he had spoken of was his body. ²²After he was raised from the dead, his disciples recalled what he had said. Then they believed the Scripture and the words that Jesus had spoken.   Jn 12:16; 1Co 6:19

²³Now while he was in Jerusalem at the Passover Feast, many people saw the miraculous signs he was doing and believed in his name.ᵇ ²⁴But Jesus would not entrust himself to them, for he knew all men. ²⁵He did not

need man's testimony about man, for he knew what was in a man.   Dt 31:21

Jesus Teaches Nicodemus

3 Now there was a man of the Pharisees named Nicodemus, a member of the Jewish ruling council. ²He came to Jesus at night and said, "Rabbi, we know you are a teacher who has come from God. For no one could perform the miraculous signs you are doing if God were not with him."   Jn 7:50; Ac 2:22

³In reply Jesus declared, "I tell you the truth, no one can see the kingdom of God unless he is born again.ᶜ"   Jn 1:13

⁴"How can a man be born when he is old?" Nicodemus asked. "Surely he cannot enter a second time into his mother's womb to be born!"

⁵Jesus answered, "I tell you the truth, no one can enter the kingdom of God unless he is born of water and the Spirit. ⁶Flesh gives birth to flesh, but the Spiritᵈ gives birth to spirit. ⁷You should not be surprised at my saying, 'Youᵉ must be born again.' ⁸The wind blows wherever it pleases. You hear its sound, but you cannot tell where it comes from or where it is going. So it is with everyone born of the Spirit."   Ac 22:16

⁹"How can this be?" Nicodemus asked.

¹⁰"You are Israel's teacher,"

ª17 Psalm 69:9   ᵇ23 Or *and believed in him*   ᶜ3 Or *born from above*; also in verse 7
ᵈ6 Or *but spirit*   ᵉ7 The Greek is plural.

said Jesus, "and do you not understand these things? [11]I tell you the truth, we speak of what we know, and we testify to what we have seen, but still you people do not accept our testimony. [12]I have spoken to you of earthly things and you do not believe; how then will you believe if I speak of heavenly things? [13]No one has ever gone into heaven except the one who came from heaven—the Son of Man.[a] [14]Just as Moses lifted up the snake in the desert, so the Son of Man must be lifted up, [15]that everyone who believes in him may have eternal life.[b]

[16]"For God so loved the world that he gave his one and only Son,[c] that whoever believes in him shall not perish but have eternal life. [17]For God did not send his Son into the world to condemn the world, but to save the world through him. [18]Whoever believes in him is not condemned, but whoever does not believe stands condemned already because he has not believed in the name of God's one and only Son.[d] [19]This is the verdict: Light has come into the world, but men loved darkness instead of light because their deeds were evil. [20]Everyone who does evil hates the light, and will not come into the light for fear that his deeds will be exposed. [21]But whoever lives by the truth comes into the light, so that it may be seen plainly that what he has done has been done through God."[e]   Ro 5:8

John the Baptist's Testimony About Jesus

[22]After this, Jesus and his disciples went out into the Judean countryside, where he spent some time with them, and baptized. [23]Now John also was baptizing at Aenon near Salim, because there was plenty of water, and people were constantly coming to be baptized. [24](This was before John was put in prison.) [25]An argument developed between some of John's disciples and a certain Jew[f] over the matter of ceremonial washing. [26]They came to John and said to him, "Rabbi, that man who was with you on the other side of the Jordan—the one you testified about—well, he is baptizing, and everyone is going to him."

[27]To this John replied, "A man can receive only what is given him from heaven. [28]You yourselves can testify that I said, 'I am not the Christ[g] but am sent ahead of him.' [29]The bride belongs to the bridegroom. The friend who attends the bridegroom waits and listens for him, and is full of joy when he hears the bridegroom's voice. That joy is mine, and it is now complete. [30]He

---

[a]13 Some manuscripts *Man, who is in heaven*   [b]15 Or *believes may have eternal life in* him   [c]16 Or *his only begotten Son*   [d]18 Or *God's only begotten Son*   [e]21 Some interpreters end the quotation after verse 15.   [f]25 Some manuscripts *and certain Jews*   [g]28 Or *Messiah*

must become greater; I must become less. *Jn 1:20,23*

31"The one who comes from above is above all; the one who is from the earth belongs to the earth, and speaks as one from the earth. The one who comes from heaven is above all. 32He testifies to what he has seen and heard, but no one accepts his testimony. 33The man who has accepted it has certified that God is truthful. 34For the one whom God has sent speaks the words of God, for God*ᵃ* gives the Spirit without limit. 35The Father loves the Son and has placed everything in his hands. 36Whoever believes in the Son has eternal life, but whoever rejects the Son will not see life, for God's wrath remains on him."*ᵇ*

Jesus Talks With a Samaritan Woman

4 The Pharisees heard that Jesus was gaining and baptizing more disciples than John, 2although in fact it was not Jesus who baptized, but his disciples. 3When the Lord learned of this, he left Judea and went back once more to Galilee. *Jn 3:22,26*

4Now he had to go through Samaria. 5So he came to a town in Samaria called Sychar, near the plot of ground Jacob had given to his son Joseph. 6Jacob's well was there, and Jesus, tired as he was from the journey, sat down by the well. It was about the sixth hour. *Jos 24:32*

7When a Samaritan woman came to draw water, Jesus said to her, "Will you give me a drink?" 8(His disciples had gone into the town to buy food.)

9The Samaritan woman said to him, "You are a Jew and I am a Samaritan woman. How can you ask me for a drink?" (For Jews do not associate with Samaritans.*ᶜ*) *Isa 44:3; 55:1*

10Jesus answered her, "If you knew the gift of God and who it is that asks you for a drink, you would have asked him and he would have given you living water." *Jer 2:13; Rev 7:17*

11"Sir," the woman said, "you have nothing to draw with and the well is deep. Where can you get this living water? 12Are you greater than our father Jacob, who gave us the well and drank from it himself, as did also his sons and his flocks and herds?" *Rev 21:6*

13Jesus answered, "Everyone who drinks this water will be thirsty again, 14but whoever drinks the water I give him will never thirst. Indeed, the water I give him will become in him a spring of water welling up to eternal life." *Jn 7:38*

15The woman said to him, "Sir, give me this water so that I won't get thirsty and have to keep coming here to draw water." *Jn 6:34,35*

ᵃ34 Greek *he*   *ᵇ36* Some interpreters end the quotation after verse 30.   *ᶜ9* Or *do not use dishes Samaritans have used*

¹⁶He told her, "Go, call your husband and come back."

¹⁷"I have no husband," she replied.

Jesus said to her, "You are right when you say you have no husband. ¹⁸The fact is, you have had five husbands, and the man you now have is not your husband. What you have just said is quite true."

¹⁹"Sir," the woman said, "I can see that you are a prophet. ²⁰Our fathers worshiped on this mountain, but you Jews claim that the place where we must worship is in Jerusalem."

²¹Jesus declared, "Believe me, woman, a time is coming when you will worship the Father neither on this mountain nor in Jerusalem. ²²You Samaritans worship what you do not know; we worship what we do know, for salvation is from the Jews. ²³Yet a time is coming and has now come when the true worshipers will worship the Father in spirit and truth, for they are the kind of worshipers the Father seeks. ²⁴God is spirit, and his worshipers must worship in spirit and in truth."

²⁵The woman said, "I know that Messiah" (called Christ) "is coming. When he comes, he will explain everything to us."

²⁶Then Jesus declared, "I who speak to you am he."   Jn 9:35-37

The Disciples Rejoin Jesus

²⁷Just then his disciples re-

turned and were surprised to find him talking with a woman. But no one asked, "What do you want?" or "Why are you talking with her?"

²⁸Then, leaving her water jar, the woman went back to the town and said to the people, ²⁹"Come, see a man who told me everything I ever did. Could this be the Christ*a*?" ³⁰They came out of the town and made their way toward him.   Mt 12:23

³¹Meanwhile his disciples urged him, "Rabbi, eat something."

³²But he said to them, "I have food to eat that you know nothing about."   Job 23:12

³³Then his disciples said to each other, "Could someone have brought him food?"

³⁴"My food," said Jesus, "is to do the will of him who sent me and to finish his work. ³⁵Do you not say, 'Four months more and then the harvest'? I tell you, open your eyes and look at the fields! They are ripe for harvest. ³⁶Even now the reaper draws his wages, even now he harvests the crop for eternal life, so that the sower and the reaper may be glad together. ³⁷Thus the saying 'One sows and another reaps' is true. ³⁸I sent you to reap what you have not worked for. Others have done the hard work, and you have reaped the benefits of their labor."   Job 31:8; Mt 26:39

*a*29 Or *Messiah*

Many Samaritans Believe

³⁹Many of the Samaritans from that town believed in him because of the woman's testimony, "He told me everything I ever did." ⁴⁰So when the Samaritans came to him, they urged him to stay with them, and he stayed two days. ⁴¹And because of his words many more became believers. Isa 42:1

⁴²They said to the woman, "We no longer believe just because of what you said; now we have heard for ourselves, and we know that this man really is the Savior of the world." Lk 2:11

Jesus Heals the Official's Son

⁴³After the two days he left for Galilee. ⁴⁴(Now Jesus himself had pointed out that a prophet has no honor in his own country.) ⁴⁵When he arrived in Galilee, the Galileans welcomed him. They had seen all that he had done in Jerusalem at the Passover Feast, for they also had been there. Mt 13:57

⁴⁶Once more he visited Cana in Galilee, where he had turned the water into wine. And there was a certain royal official whose son lay sick at Capernaum. ⁴⁷When this man heard that Jesus had arrived in Galilee from Judea, he went to him and begged him to come and heal his son, who was close to death.

⁴⁸"Unless you people see miraculous signs and wonders," Jesus told him, "you will never believe." Da 4:2-3; Ac 2:43

⁴⁹The royal official said, "Sir, come down before my child dies."

⁵⁰Jesus replied, "You may go. Your son will live."

The man took Jesus at his word and departed. ⁵¹While he was still on the way, his servants met him with the news that his boy was living. ⁵²When he inquired as to the time when his son got better, they said to him, "The fever left him yesterday at the seventh hour." Ps 111:7

⁵³Then the father realized that this was the exact time at which Jesus had said to him, "Your son will live." So he and all his household believed. Ac 11:14

⁵⁴This was the second miraculous sign that Jesus performed, having come from Judea to Galilee. Jn 2:11

The Healing at the Pool

5 Some time later, Jesus went up to Jerusalem for a feast of the Jews. ²Now there is in Jerusalem near the Sheep Gate a pool, which in Aramaic is called Bethesda^a and which is surrounded by five covered colonnades. ³Here a great number of disabled people used to lie—the blind, the lame, the paralyzed.^b ⁵One who was there had been

^a2 Some manuscripts *Bethzatha*; other manuscripts *Bethsaida*   ^b3 Some less important manuscripts *paralyzed—and they waited for the moving of the waters. ⁴From time to time an angel of the Lord would come down and stir up the waters. The first one into the pool after each such disturbance would be cured of whatever disease he had.*

an invalid for thirty-eight years. [6]When Jesus saw him lying there and learned that he had been in this condition for a long time, he asked him, "Do you want to get well?" Ne 3:1

[7]"Sir," the invalid replied, "I have no one to help me into the pool when the water is stirred. While I am trying to get in, someone else goes down ahead of me."

[8]Then Jesus said to him, "Get up! Pick up your mat and walk." [9]At once the man was cured; he picked up his mat and walked. Mt 9:5-6

The day on which this took place was a Sabbath, [10]and so the Jews said to the man who had been healed, "It is the Sabbath; the law forbids you to carry your mat." Ne 13:15-22; Mt 12:1-4

[11]But he replied, "The man who made me well said to me, 'Pick up your mat and walk.'"

[12]So they asked him, "Who is this fellow who told you to pick it up and walk?"

[13]The man who was healed had no idea who it was, for Jesus had slipped away into the crowd that was there.

[14]Later Jesus found him at the temple and said to him, "See, you are well again. Stop sinning or something worse may happen to you." [15]The man went away and told the Jews that it was Jesus who had made him well. Mk 2:5; Jn 8:11

Life Through the Son

[16]So, because Jesus was doing these things on the Sabbath, the Jews persecuted him. [17]Jesus said to them, "My Father is always at his work to this very day, and I, too, am working."

[18]For this reason the Jews tried all the harder to kill him; not only was he breaking the Sabbath, but he was even calling God his own Father, making himself equal with God. Lk 2:49

[19]Jesus gave them this answer: "I tell you the truth, the Son can do nothing by himself; he can do only what he sees his Father doing, because whatever the Father does the Son also does. [20]For the Father loves the Son and shows him all he does. Yes, to your amazement he will show him even greater things than these. [21]For just as the Father raises the dead and gives them life, even so the Son gives life to whom he is pleased to give it. [22]Moreover, the Father judges no one, but has entrusted all judgment to the Son, [23]that all may honor the Son just as they honor the Father. He who does not honor the Son does not honor the Father, who sent him. Jn 14:24; Lk 10:16

[24]"I tell you the truth, whoever hears my word and believes him who sent me has eternal life and will not be condemned; he has crossed over from death to life. [25]I tell you the truth, a time is coming and has now come when the dead will hear the voice of the Son of God and those who hear will live. [26]For as the Father has life in

himself, so he has granted the Son to have life in himself. 27And he has given him authority to judge because he is the Son of Man. Ps 36:9; Mt 10:40

28"Do not be amazed at this, for a time is coming when all who are in their graves will hear his voice 29and come out—those who have done good will rise to live, and those who have done evil will rise to be condemned. 30By myself I can do nothing; I judge only as I hear, and my judgment is just, for I seek not to please myself but him who sent me. Da 12:2; Jn 8:16

Testimonies About Jesus

31"If I testify about myself, my testimony is not valid. 32There is another who testifies in my favor, and I know that his testimony about me is valid.

33"You have sent to John and he has testified to the truth. 34Not that I accept human testimony; but I mention it that you may be saved. 35John was a lamp that burned and gave light, and you chose for a time to enjoy his light. Da 12:3; Jn 1:7

36"I have testimony weightier than that of John. For the very work that the Father has given me to finish, and which I am doing, testifies that the Father has sent me. 37And the Father who sent me has himself testified concerning me. You have never heard his voice nor seen his form, 38nor does his word

dwell in you, for you do not believe the one he sent. 39You diligently study*a* the Scriptures because you think that by them you possess eternal life. These are the Scriptures that testify about me, 40yet you refuse to come to me to have life. 1Jn 5:9

41"I do not accept praise from men, 42but I know you. I know that you do not have the love of God in your hearts. 43I have come in my Father's name, and you do not accept me; but if someone else comes in his own name, you will accept him. 44How can you believe if you accept praise from one another, yet make no effort to obtain the praise that comes from the only God*b*? Ro 2:29

45"But do not think I will accuse you before the Father. Your accuser is Moses, on whom your hopes are set. 46If you believed Moses, you would believe me, for he wrote about me. 47But since you do not believe what he wrote, how are you going to believe what I say?" Lk 16:29,31; Jn 9:28,29

Jesus Feeds the Five Thousand

6 Some time after this, Jesus crossed to the far shore of the Sea of Galilee (that is, the Sea of Tiberias), 2and a great crowd of people followed him because they saw the miraculous signs he had performed on the sick. 3Then Jesus went up on

---

*a*39 Or *Study diligently* (the imperative)   *b*44 Some early manuscripts *the Only One*

a mountainside and sat down with his disciples. ⁴The Jewish Passover Feast was near. Jn 11:55

⁵When Jesus looked up and saw a great crowd coming toward him, he said to Philip, "Where shall we buy bread for these people to eat?" ⁶He asked this only to test him, for he already had in mind what he was going to do. Mt 14:14; Jn 1:43

⁷Philip answered him, "Eight months' wages*a* would not buy enough bread for each one to have a bite!"

⁸Another of his disciples, Andrew, Simon Peter's brother, spoke up, ⁹"Here is a boy with five small barley loaves and two small fish, but how far will they go among so many?" Jn 1:40

¹⁰Jesus said, "Have the people sit down." There was plenty of grass in that place, and the men sat down, about five thousand of them. ¹¹Jesus then took the loaves, gave thanks, and distributed to those who were seated as much as they wanted. He did the same with the fish. Mt 14:13-21

¹²When they had all had enough to eat, he said to his disciples, "Gather the pieces that are left over. Let nothing be wasted." ¹³So they gathered them and filled twelve baskets with the pieces of the five barley loaves left over by those who had eaten. Mk 6:32-44

¹⁴After the people saw the miraculous sign that Jesus did, they began to say, "Surely this is the Prophet who is to come into the world." ¹⁵Jesus, knowing that they intended to come and make him king by force, withdrew again to a mountain by himself. Dt 18:15,18; Mt 11:3

Jesus Walks on the Water

¹⁶When evening came, his disciples went down to the lake, ¹⁷where they got into a boat and set off across the lake for Capernaum. By now it was dark, and Jesus had not yet joined them. ¹⁸A strong wind was blowing and the waters grew rough. ¹⁹When they had rowed three or three and a half miles,*b* they saw Jesus approaching the boat, walking on the water; and they were terrified. ²⁰But he said to them, "It is I; don't be afraid." ²¹Then they were willing to take him into the boat, and immediately the boat reached the shore where they were heading. Job 9:8

²²The next day the crowd that had stayed on the opposite shore of the lake realized that only one boat had been there, and that Jesus had not entered it with his disciples, but that they had gone away alone. ²³Then some boats from Tiberias landed near the place where the people had eaten the bread after the Lord had given thanks. ²⁴Once the crowd realized that neither Jesus nor his disciples

a7 Greek *two hundred denarii*   *b19* Greek *rowed twenty-five or thirty stadia* (about 5 or 6 kilometers)

were there, they got into the boats and went to Capernaum in search of Jesus.

Jesus the Bread of Life

25When they found him on the other side of the lake, they asked him, "Rabbi, when did you get here?"

26Jesus answered, "I tell you the truth, you are looking for me, not because you saw miraculous signs but because you ate the loaves and had your fill. 27Do not work for food that spoils, but for food that endures to eternal life, which the Son of Man will give you. On him God the Father has placed his seal of approval."   Isa 55:2; Eph 1:13

28Then they asked him, "What must we do to do the works God requires?"

29Jesus answered, "The work of God is this: to believe in the one he has sent."   1Jn 3:23

30So they asked him, "What miraculous sign then will you give that we may see it and believe you? What will you do? 31Our forefathers ate the manna in the desert; as it is written: 'He gave them bread from heaven to eat.'a"   Nu 11:7-9

32Jesus said to them, "I tell you the truth, it is not Moses who has given you the bread from heaven, but it is my Father who gives you the true bread from heaven. 33For the bread of God is he who comes down from heaven and gives life to the world."   Jn 3:13,31

34"Sir," they said, "from now on give us this bread."   Jn 4:15

35Then Jesus declared, "I am the bread of life. He who comes to me will never go hungry, and he who believes in me will never be thirsty. 36But as I told you, you have seen me and still you do not believe. 37All that the Father gives me will come to me, and whoever comes to me I will never drive away. 38For I have come down from heaven not to do my will but to do the will of him who sent me. 39And this is the will of him who sent me, that I shall lose none of all that he has given me, but raise them up at the last day. 40For my Father's will is that everyone who looks to the Son and believes in him shall have eternal life, and I will raise him up at the last day."   Ex 3:14; Jn 12:44-46

41At this the Jews began to grumble about him because he said, "I am the bread that came down from heaven." 42They said, "Is this not Jesus, the son of Joseph, whose father and mother we know? How can he now say, 'I came down from heaven'?"   Lk 4:22; Jn 7:27-29

43"Stop grumbling among yourselves," Jesus answered. 44"No one can come to me unless the Father who sent me draws him, and I will raise him up at the last day. 45It is written in the Prophets: 'They will all be

a31 Exodus 16:4; Neh. 9:15; Psalm 78:24,25

taught by God.'ᵃ Everyone who listens to the Father and learns from him comes to me. ⁴⁶No one has seen the Father except the one who is from God; only he has seen the Father. ⁴⁷I tell you the truth, he who believes has everlasting life. ⁴⁸I am the bread of life. ⁴⁹Your forefathers ate the manna in the desert, yet they died. ⁵⁰But here is the bread that comes down from heaven, which a man may eat and not die. ⁵¹I am the living bread that came down from heaven. If anyone eats of this bread, he will live forever. This bread is my flesh, which I will give for the life of the world." Jer 31:3

⁵²Then the Jews began to argue sharply among themselves, "How can this man give us his flesh to eat?" Jn 9:16

⁵³Jesus said to them, "I tell you the truth, unless you eat the flesh of the Son of Man and drink his blood, you have no life in you. ⁵⁴Whoever eats my flesh and drinks my blood has eternal life, and I will raise him up at the last day. ⁵⁵For my flesh is real food and my blood is real drink. ⁵⁶Whoever eats my flesh and drinks my blood remains in me, and I in him. ⁵⁷Just as the living Father sent me and I live because of the Father, so the one who feeds on me will live because of me. ⁵⁸This is the bread that came down from heaven. Your forefathers ate manna and died, but he who feeds on this bread will live forever." ⁵⁹He said this while teaching in the synagogue in Capernaum. Mt 26:26; Jn 3:36

Many Disciples Desert Jesus

⁶⁰On hearing it, many of his disciples said, "This is a hard teaching. Who can accept it?"

⁶¹Aware that his disciples were grumbling about this, Jesus said to them, "Does this offend you? ⁶²What if you see the Son of Man ascend to where he was before! ⁶³The Spirit gives life; the flesh counts for nothing. The words I have spoken to you are spiritᵇ and they are life. ⁶⁴Yet there are some of you who do not believe." For Jesus had known from the beginning which of them did not believe and who would betray him. ⁶⁵He went on to say, "This is why I told you that no one can come to me unless the Father has enabled him." 2Co 3:6

⁶⁶From this time many of his disciples turned back and no longer followed him.

⁶⁷"You do not want to leave too, do you?" Jesus asked the Twelve. Mt 10:2

⁶⁸Simon Peter answered him, "Lord, to whom shall we go? You have the words of eternal life. ⁶⁹We believe and know that you are the Holy One of God."

⁷⁰Then Jesus replied, "Have I not chosen you, the Twelve? Yet one of you is a devil!" ⁷¹(He meant Judas, the son of Simon

---

ᵃ45 Isaiah 54:13   ᵇ63 Or Spirit

Iscariot, who, though one of the Twelve, was later to betray him.) Mt 26:14-16; Jn 15:16

Jesus Goes to the Feast of Tabernacles

7 After this, Jesus went around in Galilee, purposely staying away from Judea because the Jews there were waiting to take his life. ²But when the Jewish Feast of Tabernacles was near, ³Jesus' brothers said to him, "You ought to leave here and go to Judea, so that your disciples may see the miracles you do. ⁴No one who wants to become a public figure acts in secret. Since you are doing these things, show yourself to the world." ⁵For even his own brothers did not believe in him.

⁶Therefore Jesus told them, "The right time for me has not yet come; for you any time is right. ⁷The world cannot hate you, but it hates me because I testify that what it does is evil. ⁸You go to the Feast. I am not yet*a* going up to this Feast, because for me the right time has not yet come." ⁹Having said this, he stayed in Galilee.

¹⁰However, after his brothers had left for the Feast, he went also, not publicly, but in secret. ¹¹Now at the Feast the Jews were watching for him and asking, "Where is that man?" Jn 11:56

¹²Among the crowds there was widespread whispering about him. Some said, "He is a good man."

Others replied, "No, he deceives the people." ¹³But no one would say anything publicly about him for fear of the Jews.

Jesus Teaches at the Feast

¹⁴Not until halfway through the Feast did Jesus go up to the temple courts and begin to teach. ¹⁵The Jews were amazed and asked, "How did this man get such learning without having studied?" Mt 13:54

¹⁶Jesus answered, "My teaching is not my own. It comes from him who sent me. ¹⁷If anyone chooses to do God's will, he will find out whether my teaching comes from God or whether I speak on my own. ¹⁸He who speaks on his own does so to gain honor for himself, but he who works for the honor of the one who sent him is a man of truth; there is nothing false about him. ¹⁹Has not Moses given you the law? Yet not one of you keeps the law. Why are you trying to kill me?" Jn 14:24

²⁰"You are demon-possessed," the crowd answered. "Who is trying to kill you?"

²¹Jesus said to them, "I did one miracle, and you are all astonished. ²²Yet, because Moses gave you circumcision (though actually it did not come from Moses, but from the patriarchs), you circumcise a child on the

---

a8 Some early manuscripts do not have *yet.*

Sabbath. 23Now if a child can be circumcised on the Sabbath so that the law of Moses may not be broken, why are you angry with me for healing the whole man on the Sabbath? 24Stop judging by mere appearances, and make a right judgment."

Is Jesus the Christ?

25At that point some of the people of Jerusalem began to ask, "Isn't this the man they are trying to kill? 26Here he is, speaking publicly, and they are not saying a word to him. Have the authorities really concluded that he is the Christ*a*? 27But we know where this man is from; when the Christ comes, no one will know where he is from."

28Then Jesus, still teaching in the temple courts, cried out, "Yes, you know me, and you know where I am from. I am not here on my own, but he who sent me is true. You do not know him, 29but I know him because I am from him and he sent me." Mt 11:27; Jn 8:14

30At this they tried to seize him, but no one laid a hand on him, because his time had not yet come. 31Still, many in the crowd put their faith in him. They said, "When the Christ comes, will he do more miraculous signs than this man?"Jn 10:39

32The Pharisees heard the crowd whispering such things about him. Then the chief priests and the Pharisees sent temple guards to arrest him.

33Jesus said, "I am with you for only a short time, and then I go to the one who sent me. 34You will look for me, but you will not find me; and where I am, you cannot come." Jn 12:35

35The Jews said to one another, "Where does this man intend to go that we cannot find him? Will he go where our people live scattered among the Greeks, and teach the Greeks? 36What did he mean when he said, 'You will look for me, but you will not find me,' and 'Where I am, you cannot come'?"

37On the last and greatest day of the Feast, Jesus stood and said in a loud voice, "If anyone is thirsty, let him come to me and drink. 38Whoever believes in me, as*b* the Scripture has said, streams of living water will flow from within him." 39By this he meant the Spirit, whom those who believed in him were later to receive. Up to that time the Spirit had not been given, since Jesus had not yet been glorified. Isa 55:1; Joel 2:28; Jn 13:31,32

40On hearing his words, some of the people said, "Surely this man is the Prophet." Mt 21:11

41Others said, "He is the Christ."

Still others asked, "How can the Christ come from Galilee? 42Does not the Scripture say that

---

*a*26 Or *Messiah*; also in verses 27, 31, 41 and 42   *b*37,38 Or / *If anyone is thirsty, let him come to me. / And let him drink,* 38*who believes in me. / As*

the Christ will come from David's family[a] and from Bethlehem, the town where David lived?" [43]Thus the people were divided because of Jesus. [44]Some wanted to seize him, but no one laid a hand on him.

Unbelief of the Jewish Leaders

[45]Finally the temple guards went back to the chief priests and Pharisees, who asked them, "Why didn't you bring him in?"

[46]"No one ever spoke the way this man does," the guards declared.   Mt 7:28,29

[47]"You mean he has deceived you also?" the Pharisees retorted. [48]"Has any of the rulers or of the Pharisees believed in him? [49]No! But this mob that knows nothing of the law—there is a curse on them."   Jn 12:42,43

[50]Nicodemus, who had gone to Jesus earlier and who was one of their own number, asked, [51]"Does our law condemn anyone without first hearing him to find out what he is doing?"   Jn 3:1; 19:39

[52]They replied, "Are you from Galilee, too? Look into it, and you will find that a prophet[b] does not come out of Galilee."   Isa 9:1-2

[The earliest manuscripts and many other ancient witnesses do not have John 7:53–8:11.]

[53]Then each went to his own home.

8 But Jesus went to the Mount of Olives. [2]At dawn he appeared again in the temple courts, where all the people gathered around him, and he sat down to teach them. [3]The teachers of the law and the Pharisees brought in a woman caught in adultery. They made her stand before the group [4]and said to Jesus, "Teacher, this woman was caught in the act of adultery. [5]In the Law Moses commanded us to stone such women. Now what do you say?" [6]They were using this question as a trap, in order to have a basis for accusing him.

But Jesus bent down and started to write on the ground with his finger. [7]When they kept on questioning him, he straightened up and said to them, "If any one of you is without sin, let him be the first to throw a stone at her." [8]Again he stooped down and wrote on the ground.   Dt 17:7; Ro 2:1,22

[9]At this, those who heard began to go away one at a time, the older ones first, until only Jesus was left, with the woman still standing there. [10]Jesus straightened up and asked her,

---

[a]42 Greek *seed*   [b]52 Two early manuscripts *the Prophet*

"Woman, where are they? Has no one condemned you?"

[11]"No one, sir," she said.

"Then neither do I condemn you," Jesus declared. "Go now and leave your life of sin." Jn 3:17

The Validity of Jesus' Testimony

[12]When Jesus spoke again to the people, he said, "I am the light of the world. Whoever follows me will never walk in darkness, but will have the light of life." Pr 4:18; Jn 6:35

[13]The Pharisees challenged him, "Here you are, appearing as your own witness; your testimony is not valid." Jn 5:31,32

[14]Jesus answered, "Even if I testify on my own behalf, my testimony is valid, for I know where I came from and where I am going. But you have no idea where I come from or where I am going. [15]You judge by human standards; I pass judgment on no one. [16]But if I do judge, my decisions are right, because I am not alone. I stand with the Father, who sent me. [17]In your own Law it is written that the testimony of two men is valid. [18]I am one who testifies for myself; my other witness is the Father, who sent me." Jn 13:3

[19]Then they asked him, "Where is your father?" Jn 16:3

"You do not know me or my Father," Jesus replied. "If you knew me, you would know my Father also." [20]He spoke these words while teaching in the temple area near the place where the offerings were put. Yet no one seized him, because his time had not yet come. 1 Jn 2:23

[21]Once more Jesus said to them, "I am going away, and you will look for me, and you will die in your sin. Where I go, you cannot come." Eze 3:18

[22]This made the Jews ask, "Will he kill himself? Is that why he says, 'Where I go, you cannot come'?"

[23]But he continued, "You are from below; I am from above. You are of this world; I am not of this world. [24]I told you that you would die in your sins; if you do not believe that I am the one I claim to be,[a] you will indeed die in your sins." Jn 3:31-33

[25]"Who are you?" they asked.

"Just what I have been claiming all along," Jesus replied. [26]"I have much to say in judgment of you. But he who sent me is reliable, and what I have heard from him I tell the world." Jn 7:28

[27]They did not understand that he was telling them about his Father. [28]So Jesus said, "When you have lifted up the Son of Man, then you will know that I am the one I claim to be and that I do nothing on my own but speak just what the Father has taught me. [29]The one who sent me is with me; he has not left me alone, for I always

---

[a]24 Or I am he; also in verse 28

do what pleases him.'' ³⁰Even as he spoke, many put their faith in him.   Jn 7:31; 12:32

The Children of Abraham

³¹To the Jews who had believed him, Jesus said, "If you hold to my teaching, you are really my disciples. ³²Then you will know the truth, and the truth will set you free."   2Jn 9

³³They answered him, "We are Abraham's descendants[a] and have never been slaves of anyone. How can you say that we shall be set free?"   Lk 3:8

³⁴Jesus replied, "I tell you the truth, everyone who sins is a slave to sin. ³⁵Now a slave has no permanent place in the family, but a son belongs to it forever. ³⁶So if the Son sets you free, you will be free indeed. ³⁷I know you are Abraham's descendants. Yet you are ready to kill me, because you have no room for my word. ³⁸I am telling you what I have seen in the Father's presence, and you do what you have heard from your father.[b]"   Jn 5:19,30; Ro 6:16

³⁹"Abraham is our father," they answered.

"If you were Abraham's children," said Jesus, "then you would[c] do the things Abraham did. ⁴⁰As it is, you are determined to kill me, a man who has told you the truth that I heard from God. Abraham did not do

such things. ⁴¹You are doing the things your own father does."

"We are not illegitimate children," they protested. "The only Father we have is God himself."   Isa 63:16

The Children of the Devil

⁴²Jesus said to them, "If God were your Father, you would love me, for I came from God and now am here. I have not come on my own; but he sent me. ⁴³Why is my language not clear to you? Because you are unable to hear what I say. ⁴⁴You belong to your father, the devil, and you want to carry out your father's desire. He was a murderer from the beginning, not holding to the truth, for there is no truth in him. When he lies, he speaks his native language, for he is a liar and the father of lies. ⁴⁵Yet because I tell the truth, you do not believe me! ⁴⁶Can any of you prove me guilty of sin? If I am telling the truth, why don't you believe me? ⁴⁷He who belongs to God hears what God says. The reason you do not hear is that you do not belong to God."   1Jn 5:1

The Claims of Jesus About Himself

⁴⁸The Jews answered him, "Aren't we right in saying that

ᵃ33 Greek *seed*; also in verse 37   *ᵇ38* Or *presence. Therefore do what you have heard from the Father.*   *ᶜ39* Some early manuscripts *"If you are Abraham's children," said Jesus, "then*

you are a Samaritan and de-mon-possessed?"

⁴⁹"I am not possessed by a de-mon," said Jesus, "but I honor my Father and you dishonor me. ⁵⁰I am not seeking glory for myself; but there is one who seeks it, and he is the judge. ⁵¹I tell you the truth, if anyone keeps my word, he will never see death." Jn 5:41ff; 11:26

⁵²At this the Jews exclaimed, "Now we know that you are de-mon-possessed! Abraham died and so did the prophets, yet you say that if anyone keeps your word, he will never taste death. ⁵³Are you greater than our father Abraham? He died, and so did the prophets. Who do you think you are?" Mk 3:22

⁵⁴Jesus replied, "If I glorify myself, my glory means noth-ing. My Father, whom you claim as your God, is the one who glorifies me. ⁵⁵Though you do not know him, I know him. If I said I did not, I would be a liar like you, but I do know him and keep his word. ⁵⁶Your fa-ther Abraham rejoiced at the thought of seeing my day; he saw it and was glad." Jn 16:14

⁵⁷"You are not yet fifty years old," the Jews said to him, "and you have seen Abraham!"

⁵⁸"I tell you the truth," Jesus answered, "before Abraham was born, I am!" ⁵⁹At this, they picked up stones to stone him, but Jesus hid himself, slipping away from the temple grounds.

Jesus Heals a Man Born Blind

9 As he went along, he saw a man blind from birth. ²His disciples asked him, "Rabbi, who sinned, this man or his parents, that he was born blind?" Eze 18:20; Ac 28:4

³"Neither this man nor his parents sinned," said Jesus, "but this happened so that the work of God might be displayed in his life. ⁴As long as it is day, we must do the work of him who sent me. Night is coming, when no one can work. ⁵While I am in the world, I am the light of the world." Jn 1:4; 11:4

⁶Having said this, he spit on the ground, made some mud with the saliva, and put it on the man's eyes. ⁷"Go," he told him, "wash in the Pool of Siloam" (this word means Sent). So the man went and washed, and came home seeing. Mk 7:33ff

⁸His neighbors and those who had formerly seen him begging asked, "Isn't this the same man who used to sit and beg?" ⁹Some claimed that he was. Ac 3:2,10

Others said, "No, he only looks like him."

But he himself insisted, "I am the man."

¹⁰"How then were your eyes opened?" they demanded.

¹¹He replied, "The man they call Jesus made some mud and put it on my eyes. He told me to go to Siloam and wash. So I

went and washed, and then I could see."

¹²"Where is this man?" they asked him.

"I don't know," he said.

The Pharisees Investigate the Healing

¹³They brought to the Pharisees the man who had been blind. ¹⁴Now the day on which Jesus had made the mud and opened the man's eyes was a Sabbath. ¹⁵Therefore the Pharisees also asked him how he had received his sight. "He put mud on my eyes," the man replied, "and I washed, and now I see."

¹⁶Some of the Pharisees said, "This man is not from God, for he does not keep the Sabbath." But others asked, "How can a sinner do such miraculous signs?" So they were divided.

¹⁷Finally they turned again to the blind man, "What have you to say about him? It was your eyes he opened."

The man replied, "He is a prophet."   Mt 21:11

¹⁸The Jews still did not believe that he had been blind and had received his sight until they sent for the man's parents. ¹⁹"Is this your son?" they asked. "Is this the one you say was born blind? How is it that now he can see?"

²⁰"We know he is our son," the parents answered, "and we know he was born blind. ²¹But how he can see now, or who opened his eyes, we don't

know. Ask him. He is of age; he will speak for himself." ²²His parents said this because they were afraid of the Jews, for already the Jews had decided that anyone who acknowledged that Jesus was the Christ*ᵃ* would be put out of the synagogue. ²³That was why his parents said, "He is of age; ask him."   Jn 7:13

²⁴A second time they summoned the man who had been blind. "Give glory to God,*ᵇ*" they said. "We know this man is a sinner."

²⁵He replied, "Whether he is a sinner or not, I don't know. One thing I do know. I was blind but now I see!"

²⁶Then they asked him, "What did he do to you? How did he open your eyes?"

²⁷He answered, "I have told you already and you did not listen. Why do you want to hear it again? Do you want to become his disciples, too?"   Jn 5:25

²⁸Then they hurled insults at him and said, "You are this fellow's disciple! We are disciples of Moses! ²⁹We know that God spoke to Moses, but as for this fellow, we don't even know where he comes from."   Jn 5:45-47

³⁰The man answered, "Now that is remarkable! You don't know where he comes from, yet he opened my eyes. ³¹We know that God does not listen to sinners. He listens to the godly man who does his will. ³²Nobody has ever heard of opening

---

*ᵃ*22 Or *Messiah*   *ᵇ*24 A solemn charge to tell the truth (see Joshua 7:19)

the eyes of a man born blind. ³³If this man were not from God, he could do nothing." Ps 34:15,16

³⁴To this they replied, "You were steeped in sin at birth; how dare you lecture us!" And they threw him out. Isa 66:5

Spiritual Blindness

³⁵Jesus heard that they had thrown him out, and when he found him, he said, "Do you believe in the Son of Man?" Jn 3:15

³⁶"Who is he, sir?" the man asked. "Tell me so that I may believe in him." Ro 10:14

³⁷Jesus said, "You have now seen him; in fact, he is the one speaking with you." Jn 4:26

³⁸Then the man said, "Lord, I believe," and he worshiped him. Mt 28:9

³⁹Jesus said, "For judgment I have come into this world, so that the blind will see and those who see will become blind."

⁴⁰Some Pharisees who were with him heard him say this and asked, "What? Are we blind too?" Ro 2:19

⁴¹Jesus said, "If you were blind, you would not be guilty of sin; but now that you claim you can see, your guilt remains.

The Shepherd and His Flock

10 "I tell you the truth, the man who does not enter the sheep pen by the gate, but climbs in by some other way, is a thief and a robber. ²The man who enters by the gate is the shepherd of his sheep. ³The watchman opens the gate for him, and the sheep listen to his voice. He calls his own sheep by name and leads them out. ⁴When he has brought out all his own, he goes on ahead of them, and his sheep follow him because they know his voice. ⁵But they will never follow a stranger; in fact, they will run away from him because they do not recognize a stranger's voice." ⁶Jesus used this figure of speech, but they did not understand what he was telling them.

⁷Therefore Jesus said again, "I tell you the truth, I am the gate for the sheep. ⁸All who ever came before me were thieves and robbers, but the sheep did not listen to them. ⁹I am the gate; whoever enters through me will be saved.ᵃ He will come in and go out, and find pasture. ¹⁰The thief comes only to steal and kill and destroy; I have come that they may have life, and have it to the full. Jer 23:1,2; Jn 20:31

¹¹"I am the good shepherd. The good shepherd lays down his life for the sheep. ¹²The hired hand is not the shepherd who owns the sheep. So when he sees the wolf coming, he abandons the sheep and runs away. Then the wolf attacks the flock and scatters it. ¹³The man runs away because he is a hired hand and cares nothing for the sheep. Isa 40:11; Zec 11:16-17; Heb 13:20

ᵃ9 Or kept safe

[14]"I am the good shepherd; I know my sheep and my sheep know me— [15]just as the Father knows me and I know the Father—and I lay down my life for the sheep. [16]I have other sheep that are not of this sheep pen. I must bring them also. They too will listen to my voice, and there shall be one flock and one shepherd. [17]The reason my Father loves me is that I lay down my life—only to take it up again. [18]No one takes it from me, but I lay it down of my own accord. I have authority to lay it down and authority to take it up again. This command I received from my Father."　　Eph 2:11-19

[19]At these words the Jews were again divided. [20]Many of them said, "He is demon-possessed and raving mad. Why listen to him?"

[21]But others said, "These are not the sayings of a man possessed by a demon. Can a demon open the eyes of the blind?"　　Ex 4:11; Jn 9:32,33

The Unbelief of the Jews

[22]Then came the Feast of Dedication[a] at Jerusalem. It was winter, [23]and Jesus was in the temple area walking in Solomon's Colonnade. [24]The Jews gathered around him, saying, "How long will you keep us in suspense? If you are the Christ,[b] tell us plainly."　　Lk 22:67

[25]Jesus answered, "I did tell you, but you do not believe. The miracles I do in my Father's name speak for me, [26]but you do not believe because you are not my sheep. [27]My sheep listen to my voice; I know them, and they follow me. [28]I give them eternal life, and they shall never perish; no one can snatch them out of my hand. [29]My Father, who has given them to me, is greater than all[c]; no one can snatch them out of my Father's hand. [30]I and the Father are one."　　Jn 4:26; 17:21-23

[31]Again the Jews picked up stones to stone him, [32]but Jesus said to them, "I have shown you many great miracles from the Father. For which of these do you stone me?"　　Jn 8:59

[33]"We are not stoning you for any of these," replied the Jews, "but for blasphemy, because you, a mere man, claim to be God."　　Lev 24:16; Jn 5:18

[34]Jesus answered them, "Is it not written in your Law, 'I have said you are gods'[d]? [35]If he called them 'gods,' to whom the word of God came—and the Scripture cannot be broken— [36]what about the one whom the Father set apart as his very own and sent into the world? Why then do you accuse me of blasphemy because I said, 'I am God's Son'? [37]Do not believe me unless I do what my Father does. [38]But if I do it, even though you do not believe me,

---

[a]22 That is, Hanukkah　　[b]24 Or *Messiah*　　[c]29 Many early manuscripts *What my Father has given me is greater than all*　　[d]34 Psalm 82:6

believe the miracles, that you may know and understand that the Father is in me, and I in the Father." ³⁹Again they tried to seize him, but he escaped their grasp.   Jn 6:69; 14:10

⁴⁰Then Jesus went back across the Jordan to the place where John had been baptizing in the early days. Here he stayed ⁴¹and many people came to him. They said, "Though John never performed a miraculous sign, all that John said about this man was true." ⁴²And in that place many believed in Jesus.   Jn 1:26-28

The Death of Lazarus

11 Now a man named Lazarus was sick. He was from Bethany, the village of Mary and her sister Martha. ²This Mary, whose brother Lazarus now lay sick, was the same one who poured perfume on the Lord and wiped his feet with her hair. ³So the sisters sent word to Jesus, "Lord, the one you love is sick."   Lk 10:38

⁴When he heard this, Jesus said, "This sickness will not end in death. No, it is for God's glory so that God's Son may be glorified through it." ⁵Jesus loved Martha and her sister and Lazarus. ⁶Yet when he heard that Lazarus was sick, he stayed where he was two more days.

⁷Then he said to his disciples, "Let us go back to Judea."

⁸"But Rabbi," they said, "a short while ago the Jews tried to stone you, and yet you are going back there?"   Jn 10:31

⁹Jesus answered, "Are there not twelve hours of daylight? A man who walks by day will not stumble, for he sees by this world's light. ¹⁰It is when he walks by night that he stumbles, for he has no light."   Jn 9:4

¹¹After he had said this, he went on to tell them, "Our friend Lazarus has fallen asleep; but I am going there to wake him up."   Mt 9:24; Ac 7:60

¹²His disciples replied, "Lord, if he sleeps, he will get better." ¹³Jesus had been speaking of his death, but his disciples thought he meant natural sleep.

¹⁴So then he told them plainly, "Lazarus is dead, ¹⁵and for your sake I am glad I was not there, so that you may believe. But let us go to him."

¹⁶Then Thomas (called Didymus) said to the rest of the disciples, "Let us also go, that we may die with him."

Jesus Comforts the Sisters

¹⁷On his arrival, Jesus found that Lazarus had already been in the tomb for four days. ¹⁸Bethany was less than two miles*ᵃ* from Jerusalem, ¹⁹and many Jews had come to Martha and Mary to comfort them in the loss of their brother. ²⁰When Martha heard that Jesus was coming, she went out to meet him, but Mary stayed at home.

ᵃ18 Greek *fifteen stadia* (about 3 kilometers)

²¹"Lord," Martha said to Jesus, "if you had been here, my brother would not have died. ²²But I know that even now God will give you whatever you ask." _{Jn 9:31}

²³Jesus said to her, "Your brother will rise again."

²⁴Martha answered, "I know he will rise again in the resurrection at the last day." _{Da 12:2}

²⁵Jesus said to her, "I am the resurrection and the life. He who believes in me will live, even though he dies; ²⁶and whoever lives and believes in me will never die. Do you believe this?" _{Jn 1:4; 3:15}

²⁷"Yes, Lord," she told him, "I believe that you are the Christ,ᵃ the Son of God, who was to come into the world."

²⁸And after she had said this, she went back and called her sister Mary aside. "The Teacher is here," she said, "and is asking for you." ²⁹When Mary heard this, she got up quickly and went to him. ³⁰Now Jesus had not yet entered the village, but was still at the place where Martha had met him. ³¹When the Jews who had been with Mary in the house, comforting her, noticed how quickly she got up and went out, they followed her, supposing she was going to the tomb to mourn there. _{Jn 13:13}

³²When Mary reached the place where Jesus was and saw him, she fell at his feet and said,

"Lord, if you had been here, my brother would not have died."

³³When Jesus saw her weeping, and the Jews who had come along with her also weeping, he was deeply moved in spirit and troubled. ³⁴"Where have you laid him?" he asked.

"Come and see, Lord," they replied.

³⁵Jesus wept. _{Lk 19:41}

³⁶Then the Jews said, "See how he loved him!"

³⁷But some of them said, "Could not he who opened the eyes of the blind man have kept this man from dying?" _{Jn 9:6-7}

Jesus Raises Lazarus From the Dead

³⁸Jesus, once more deeply moved, came to the tomb. It was a cave with a stone laid across the entrance. ³⁹"Take away the stone," he said. _{Mt 27:60}

"But, Lord," said Martha, the sister of the dead man, "by this time there is a bad odor, for he has been there four days."

⁴⁰Then Jesus said, "Did I not tell you that if you believed, you would see the glory of God?"

⁴¹So they took away the stone. Then Jesus looked up and said, "Father, I thank you that you have heard me. ⁴²I knew that you always hear me, but I said this for the benefit of the people standing here, that they may believe that you sent me." _{Jn 12:30; 17:1}

⁴³When he had said this,

ᵃ27 Or Messiah

Jesus called in a loud voice, "Lazarus, come out!" 44The dead man came out, his hands and feet wrapped with strips of linen, and a cloth around his face.   Jn 19:40

Jesus said to them, "Take off the grave clothes and let him go."

The Plot to Kill Jesus

45Therefore many of the Jews who had come to visit Mary, and had seen what Jesus did, put their faith in him. 46But some of them went to the Pharisees and told them what Jesus had done. 47Then the chief priests and the Pharisees called a meeting of the Sanhedrin.

"What are we accomplishing?" they asked. "Here is this man performing many miraculous signs. 48If we let him go on like this, everyone will believe in him, and then the Romans will come and take away both our place*a* and our nation."

49Then one of them, named Caiaphas, who was high priest that year, spoke up, "You know nothing at all! 50You do not realize that it is better for you that one man die for the people than that the whole nation perish."

51He did not say this on his own, but as high priest that year he prophesied that Jesus would die for the Jewish nation, 52and not only for that nation but also for the scattered children of God, to bring them together

and make them one. 53So from that day on they plotted to take his life.   Isa 49:6; Jn 10:16

54Therefore Jesus no longer moved about publicly among the Jews. Instead he withdrew to a region near the desert, to a village called Ephraim, where he stayed with his disciples.

55When it was almost time for the Jewish Passover, many went up from the country to Jerusalem for their ceremonial cleansing before the Passover. 56They kept looking for Jesus, and as they stood in the temple area they asked one another, "What do you think? Isn't he coming to the Feast at all?" 57But the chief priests and Pharisees had given orders that if anyone found out where Jesus was, he should report it so that they might arrest him.   Ex 12:13,23,27

Jesus Anointed at Bethany

12 Six days before the Passover, Jesus arrived at Bethany, where Lazarus lived, whom Jesus had raised from the dead. 2Here a dinner was given in Jesus' honor. Martha served, while Lazarus was among those reclining at the table with him. 3Then Mary took about a pint*b* of pure nard, an expensive perfume; she poured it on Jesus' feet and wiped his feet with her hair. And the house was filled with the fragrance of the perfume.   Jn 11:2

4But one of his disciples,

---

*a*48 Or *temple*   *b*3 Greek *a litra* (probably about 0.5 liter)

Judas Iscariot, who was later to betray him, objected, [5]"Why wasn't this perfume sold and the money given to the poor? It was worth a year's wages.[a]" [6]He did not say this because he cared about the poor but because he was a thief; as keeper of the money bag, he used to help himself to what was put into it.   Jn 13:29

[7]"Leave her alone," Jesus replied. "It was intended that she should save this perfume for the day of my burial. [8]You will always have the poor among you, but you will not always have me."   Dt 15:11; Jn 19:40

[9]Meanwhile a large crowd of Jews found out that Jesus was there and came, not only because of him but also to see Lazarus, whom he had raised from the dead. [10]So the chief priests made plans to kill Lazarus as well, [11]for on account of him many of the Jews were going over to Jesus and putting their faith in him.   Jn 11:43-45

The Triumphal Entry

[12]The next day the great crowd that had come for the Feast heard that Jesus was on his way to Jerusalem. [13]They took palm branches and went out to meet him, shouting,

"Hosanna![b]"

"Blessed is he who comes in the name of the Lord!"[c]

"Blessed is the King of Israel!"   Jn 1:49

[14]Jesus found a young donkey and sat upon it, as it is written,

[15]"Do not be afraid,
  O Daughter of Zion;
see, your king is coming,
  seated on a donkey's colt."[d]

[16]At first his disciples did not understand all this. Only after Jesus was glorified did they realize that these things had been written about him and that they had done these things to him.   Mk 9:32; Jn 2:22

[17]Now the crowd that was with him when he called Lazarus from the tomb and raised him from the dead continued to spread the word. [18]Many people, because they had heard that he had given this miraculous sign, went out to meet him. [19]So the Pharisees said to one another, "See, this is getting us nowhere. Look how the whole world has gone after him!"

Jesus Predicts His Death

[20]Now there were some Greeks among those who went up to worship at the Feast. [21]They came to Philip, who was from Bethsaida in Galilee, with a request. "Sir," they said, "we would like to see Jesus." [22]Philip went to tell Andrew; Andrew and Philip in turn told Jesus.   Jn 7:35; Ac 11:20

[23]Jesus replied, "The hour

has come for the Son of Man to be glorified. 24I tell you the truth, unless a kernel of wheat falls to the ground and dies, it remains only a single seed. But if it dies, it produces many seeds. 25The man who loves his life will lose it, while the man who hates his life in this world will keep it for eternal life. 26Whoever serves me must follow me; and where I am, my servant also will be. My Father will honor the one who serves me. Mt 26:18; Jn 14:3

27"Now my heart is troubled, and what shall I say? 'Father, save me from this hour'? No, it was for this very reason I came to this hour. 28Father, glorify your name!" Mt 26:38-39

Then a voice came from heaven, "I have glorified it, and will glorify it again." 29The crowd that was there and heard it said it had thundered; others said an angel had spoken to him. Mt 3:17; Lk 3:22

30Jesus said, "This voice was for your benefit, not mine. 31Now is the time for judgment on this world; now the prince of this world will be driven out. 32But I, when I am lifted up from the earth, will draw all men to myself." 33He said this to show the kind of death he was going to die. Jn 16:11; 18:32

34The crowd spoke up, "We have heard from the Law that the Christ[a] will remain forever, so how can you say, 'The Son of Man must be lifted up'? Who is this 'Son of Man'?" Isa 9:7

35Then Jesus told them, "You are going to have the light just a little while longer. Walk while you have the light, before darkness overtakes you. The man who walks in the dark does not know where he is going. 36Put your trust in the light while you have it, so that you may become sons of light." When he had finished speaking, Jesus left and hid himself from them. Eph 5:8

The Jews Continue in Their Unbelief

37Even after Jesus had done all these miraculous signs in their presence, they still would not believe in him. 38This was to fulfill the word of Isaiah the prophet:

"Lord, who has believed our
    message
and to whom has the arm
    of the Lord been
    revealed?"[b]

39For this reason they could not believe, because, as Isaiah says elsewhere:

40"He has blinded their eyes
    and deadened their hearts,
so they can neither see with
    their eyes,
    nor understand with their
    hearts,
    nor turn—and I would heal
    them."[c]

41Isaiah said this because he saw

___
[a]34 Or *Messiah*   [b]38 Isaiah 53:1   [c]40 Isaiah 6:10

Jesus' glory and spoke about him. Isa 6:1-4

⁴²Yet at the same time many even among the leaders believed in him. But because of the Pharisees they would not confess their faith for fear they would be put out of the synagogue; ⁴³for they loved praise from men more than praise from God. Jn 7:48; 9:22

⁴⁴Then Jesus cried out, "When a man believes in me, he does not believe in me only, but in the one who sent me. ⁴⁵When he looks at me, he sees the one who sent me. ⁴⁶I have come into the world as a light, so that no one who believes in me should stay in darkness. Mt 10:40

⁴⁷"As for the person who hears my words but does not keep them, I do not judge him. For I did not come to judge the world, but to save it. ⁴⁸There is a judge for the one who rejects me and does not accept my words; that very word which I spoke will condemn him at the last day. ⁴⁹For I did not speak of my own accord, but the Father who sent me commanded me what to say and how to say it. ⁵⁰I know that his command leads to eternal life. So whatever I say is just what the Father has told me to say." Mt 25:46; Jn 3:17

Jesus Washes His Disciples' Feet

13 It was just before the Passover Feast. Jesus knew that the time had come for him to leave this world and go to the Father. Having loved his own who were in the world, he now showed them the full extent of his love. ᵃ Jn 16:28

²The evening meal was being served, and the devil had already prompted Judas Iscariot, son of Simon, to betray Jesus. ³Jesus knew that the Father had put all things under his power, and that he had come from God and was returning to God; ⁴so he got up from the meal, took off his outer clothing, and wrapped a towel around his waist. ⁵After that, he poured water into a basin and began to wash his disciples' feet, drying them with the towel that was wrapped around him. Mt 28:18

⁶He came to Simon Peter, who said to him, "Lord, are you going to wash my feet?" Mt 3:14

⁷Jesus replied, "You do not realize now what I am doing, but later you will understand."

⁸"No," said Peter, "you shall never wash my feet."

Jesus answered, "Unless I wash you, you have no part with me." Jn 3:5

⁹"Then, Lord," Simon Peter replied, "not just my feet but my hands and my head as well!"

¹⁰Jesus answered, "A person who has had a bath needs only to wash his feet; his whole body is clean. And you are clean, though not every one of you."

ᵃ1 Or *he loved them to the last*

¹¹For he knew who was going to betray him, and that was why he said not every one was clean.

¹²When he had finished washing their feet, he put on his clothes and returned to his place. "Do you understand what I have done for you?" he asked them. ¹³"You call me 'Teacher' and 'Lord,' and rightly so, for that is what I am. ¹⁴Now that I, your Lord and Teacher, have washed your feet, you also should wash one another's feet. ¹⁵I have set you an example that you should do as I have done for you. ¹⁶I tell you the truth, no servant is greater than his master, nor is a messenger greater than the one who sent him. ¹⁷Now that you know these things, you will be blessed if you do them.   Mt 7:24

Jesus Predicts His Betrayal

¹⁸"I am not referring to all of you; I know those I have chosen. But this is to fulfill the scripture: 'He who shares my bread has lifted up his heel against me.'ᵃ   Jn 6:70

¹⁹"I am telling you now before it happens, so that when it does happen you will believe that I am He. ²⁰I tell you the truth, whoever accepts anyone I send accepts me; and whoever accepts me accepts the one who sent me."   Mt 10:40; Jn 14:29

²¹After he had said this, Jesus was troubled in spirit and testi-fied, "I tell you the truth, one of you is going to betray me."

²²His disciples stared at one another, at a loss to know which of them he meant. ²³One of them, the disciple whom Jesus loved, was reclining next to him. ²⁴Simon Peter motioned to this disciple and said, "Ask him which one he means."   Jn 19:26

²⁵Leaning back against Jesus, he asked him, "Lord, who is it?"   Mt 26:21ff; Jn 21:20

²⁶Jesus answered, "It is the one to whom I will give this piece of bread when I have dipped it in the dish." Then, dipping the piece of bread, he gave it to Judas Iscariot, son of Simon. ²⁷As soon as Judas took the bread, Satan entered into him.   Lk 22:3

"What you are about to do, do quickly," Jesus told him, ²⁸but no one at the meal understood why Jesus said this to him. ²⁹Since Judas had charge of the money, some thought Jesus was telling him to buy what was needed for the Feast, or to give something to the poor. ³⁰As soon as Judas had taken the bread, he went out. And it was night.   Lk 22:53; Jn 12:6

Jesus Predicts Peter's Denial

³¹When he was gone, Jesus said, "Now is the Son of Man glorified and God is glorified in him. ³²If God is glorified in him,ᵇ God will glorify the Son

---

ᵃ18 Psalm 41:9   ᵇ32 Many early manuscripts do not have *If God is glorified in him.*

in himself, and will glorify him at once.   Jn 14:13; 17:1

[33]"My children, I will be with you only a little longer. You will look for me, and just as I told the Jews, so I tell you now: Where I am going, you cannot come.   Jn 7:33-34

[34]"A new command I give you: Love one another. As I have loved you, so you must love one another. [35]By this all men will know that you are my disciples, if you love one another."   Jn 15:12; 1Jn 3:14

[36]Simon Peter asked him, "Lord, where are you going?"

Jesus replied, "Where I am going, you cannot follow now, but you will follow later."   Jn 16:5

[37]Peter asked, "Lord, why can't I follow you now? I will lay down my life for you."   Mt 26:33

[38]Then Jesus answered, "Will you really lay down your life for me? I tell you the truth, before the rooster crows, you will disown me three times!"   Jn 18:27

Jesus Comforts His Disciples

14 "Do not let your hearts be troubled. Trust in God[a]; trust also in me. [2]In my Father's house are many rooms; if it were not so, I would have told you. I am going there to prepare a place for you. [3]And if I go and prepare a place for you, I will come back and take you to be with me that you also may be where I am. [4]You know the way

to the place where I am going."

Jesus the Way to the Father

[5]Thomas said to him, "Lord, we don't know where you are going, so how can we know the way?"   Jn 11:16

[6]Jesus answered, "I am the way and the truth and the life. No one comes to the Father except through me. [7]If you really knew me, you would know[b] my Father as well. From now on, you do know him and have seen him."   Jn 1:18; Eph 2:18

[8]Philip said, "Lord, show us the Father and that will be enough for us."

[9]Jesus answered: "Don't you know me, Philip, even after I have been among you such a long time? Anyone who has seen me has seen the Father. How can you say, 'Show us the Father'? [10]Don't you believe that I am in the Father, and that the Father is in me? The words I say to you are not just my own. Rather, it is the Father, living in me, who is doing his work. [11]Believe me when I say that I am in the Father and the Father is in me; or at least believe on the evidence of the miracles themselves. [12]I tell you the truth, anyone who has faith in me will do what I have been doing. He will do even greater things than these, because I am going to the Father. [13]And I will do whatever you ask in my name, so that the

---

[a]1 Or *You trust in God*   [b]7 Some early manuscripts *If you really have known me, you will know*

Son may bring glory to the Father. [14]You may ask me for anything in my name, and I will do it. Mt 7:7; Jn 10:38; Php 2:6

Jesus Promises the Holy Spirit

[15]"If you love me, you will obey what I command. [16]And I will ask the Father, and he will give you another Counselor to be with you forever— [17]the Spirit of truth. The world cannot accept him, because it neither sees him nor knows him. But you know him, for he lives with you and will be[a] in you. [18]I will not leave you as orphans; I will come to you. [19]Before long, the world will not see me anymore, but you will see me. Because I live, you also will live. [20]On that day you will realize that I am in my Father, and you are in me, and I am in you. [21]Whoever has my commands and obeys them, he is the one who loves me. He who loves me will be loved by my Father, and I too will love him and show myself to him." Jn 15:26,27; 1Jn 2:5

[22]Then Judas (not Judas Iscariot) said, "But, Lord, why do you intend to show yourself to us and not to the world?" Ac 10:41

[23]Jesus replied, "If anyone loves me, he will obey my teaching. My Father will love him, and we will come to him and make our home with him. [24]He who does not love me will not obey my teaching. These words you hear are not my own; they belong to the Father who sent me. Jn 5:19; Ro 8:10

[25]"All this I have spoken while still with you. [26]But the Counselor, the Holy Spirit, whom the Father will send in my name, will teach you all things and will remind you of everything I have said to you. [27]Peace I leave with you; my peace I give you. I do not give to you as the world gives. Do not let your hearts be troubled and do not be afraid. Nu 6:26; Jn 16:13

[28]"You heard me say, 'I am going away and I am coming back to you.' If you loved me, you would be glad that I am going to the Father, for the Father is greater than I. [29]I have told you now before it happens, so that when it does happen you will believe. [30]I will not speak with you much longer, for the prince of this world is coming. He has no hold on me, [31]but the world must learn that I love the Father and that I do exactly what my Father has commanded me. Jn 10:18,29

"Come now; let us leave."

The Vine and the Branches

15 "I am the true vine, and my Father is the gardener. [2]He cuts off every branch in me that bears no fruit, while every branch that does bear fruit he prunes[b] so that it will be even more fruitful. [3]You are already clean because of the word

---

[a]17 Some early manuscripts *and is*   [b]2 The Greek for *prunes* also means *cleans*.

I have spoken to you. ⁴Remain in me, and I will remain in you. No branch can bear fruit by itself; it must remain in the vine. Neither can you bear fruit unless you remain in me. Gal 5:22

⁵"I am the vine; you are the branches. If a man remains in me and I in him, he will bear much fruit; apart from me you can do nothing. ⁶If anyone does not remain in me, he is like a branch that is thrown away and withers; such branches are picked up, thrown into the fire and burned. ⁷If you remain in me and my words remain in you, ask whatever you wish, and it will be given you. ⁸This is to my Father's glory, that you bear much fruit, showing yourselves to be my disciples. Eze 15:4

⁹"As the Father has loved me, so have I loved you. Now remain in my love. ¹⁰If you obey my commands, you will remain in my love, just as I have obeyed my Father's commands and remain in his love. ¹¹I have told you this so that my joy may be in you and that your joy may be complete. ¹²My command is this: Love each other as I have loved you. ¹³Greater love has no one than this, that he lay down his life for his friends. ¹⁴You are my friends if you do what I command. ¹⁵I no longer call you servants, because a servant does not know his master's business. Instead, I have called you friends, for everything that I

learned from my Father I have made known to you. ¹⁶You did not choose me, but I chose you and appointed you to go and bear fruit—fruit that will last. Then the Father will give you whatever you ask in my name. ¹⁷This is my command: Love each other. Jn 17:23-26; Ro 5:7,8

The World Hates the Disciples

¹⁸"If the world hates you, keep in mind that it hated me first. ¹⁹If you belonged to the world, it would love you as its own. As it is, you do not belong to the world, but I have chosen you out of the world. That is why the world hates you. ²⁰Remember the words I spoke to you: 'No servant is greater than his master.'ᵃ If they persecuted me, they will persecute you also. If they obeyed my teaching, they will obey yours also. ²¹They will treat you this way because of my name, for they do not know the One who sent me. ²²If I had not come and spoken to them, they would not be guilty of sin. Now, however, they have no excuse for their sin. ²³He who hates me hates my Father as well. ²⁴If I had not done among them what no one else did, they would not be guilty of sin. But now they have seen these miracles, and yet they have hated both me and my Father. ²⁵But this is to fulfill what is written in their Law:

ᵃ20 John 13:16

'They hated me without reason.'[a]

Isa 66:5; 1Pe 4:14

26"When the Counselor comes, whom I will send to you from the Father, the Spirit of truth who goes out from the Father, he will testify about me. 27And you also must testify, for you have been with me from the beginning.

Lk 24:48; Jn 14:16

16 "All this I have told you so that you will not go astray. 2They will put you out of the synagogue; in fact, a time is coming when anyone who kills you will think he is offering a service to God. 3They will do such things because they have not known the Father or me. 4I have told you this, so that when the time comes you will remember that I warned you. I did not tell you this at first because I was with you.

Jn 15:18-27

The Work of the Holy Spirit

5"Now I am going to him who sent me, yet none of you asks me, 'Where are you going?' 6Because I have said these things, you are filled with grief. 7But I tell you the truth: It is for your good that I am going away. Unless I go away, the Counselor will not come to you; but if I go, I will send him to you. 8When he comes, he will convict the world of guilt[b] in regard to sin and righteousness and judgment: 9in regard to sin, because men do not believe in me; 10in regard to righteousness, because I am going to the Father, where you can see me no longer; 11and in regard to judgment, because the prince of this world now stands condemned.

12"I have much more to say to you, more than you can now bear. 13But when he, the Spirit of truth, comes, he will guide you into all truth. He will not speak on his own; he will speak only what he hears, and he will tell you what is yet to come. 14He will bring glory to me by taking from what is mine and making it known to you. 15All that belongs to the Father is mine. That is why I said the Spirit will take from what is mine and make it known to you.

Mk 4:33; Jn 17:10

16"In a little while you will see me no more, and then after a little while you will see me."

The Disciples' Grief Will Turn to Joy

17Some of his disciples said to one another, "What does he mean by saying, 'In a little while you will see me no more, and then after a little while you will see me,' and 'Because I am going to the Father'?" 18They kept asking, "What does he mean by 'a little while'? We don't understand what he is saying."

19Jesus saw that they wanted to ask him about this, so he said to them, "Are you asking one another what I meant when I said, 'In a little while you will

see me no more, and then after a little while you will see me'? 20I tell you the truth, you will weep and mourn while the world rejoices. You will grieve, but your grief will turn to joy. 21A woman giving birth to a child has pain because her time has come; but when her baby is born she forgets the anguish because of her joy that a child is born into the world. 22So with you: Now is your time of grief, but I will see you again and you will rejoice, and no one will take away your joy. 23In that day you will no longer ask me anything. I tell you the truth, my Father will give you whatever you ask in my name. 24Until now you have not asked for anything in my name. Ask and you will receive, and your joy will be complete.

25"Though I have been speaking figuratively, a time is coming when I will no longer use this kind of language but will tell you plainly about my Father. 26In that day you will ask in my name. I am not saying that I will ask the Father on your behalf. 27No, the Father himself loves you because you have loved me and have believed that I came from God. 28I came from the Father and entered the world; now I am leaving the world and going back to the Father."   Ps 78:2; Jn 13:3

29Then Jesus' disciples said, "Now you are speaking clearly and without figures of speech.

30Now we can see that you know all things and that you do not even need to have anyone ask you questions. This makes us believe that you came from God."   1Ki 17:24

31"You believe at last!"*a* Jesus answered. 32"But a time is coming, and has come, when you will be scattered, each to his own home. You will leave me all alone. Yet I am not alone, for my Father is with me.   Mt 26:31

33"I have told you these things, so that in me you may have peace. In this world you will have trouble. But take heart! I have overcome the world."   Jn 14:27; Ro 8:37

Jesus Prays for Himself

17 After Jesus said this, he looked toward heaven and prayed: Jn 11:41

"Father, the time has come. Glorify your Son, that your Son may glorify you. 2For you granted him authority over all people that he might give eternal life to all those you have given him. 3Now this is eternal life: that they may know you, the only true God, and Jesus Christ, whom you have sent. 4I have brought you glory on earth by completing the work you gave me to do. 5And now, Father, glorify me in your presence with

the glory I had with you before the world began. Php 2:6

Jesus Prays for His Disciples

6"I have revealed you[a] to
those whom you gave me
out of the world. They were
yours; you gave them to me
and they have obeyed your
word. 7Now they know that
everything you have given
me comes from you. 8For I
gave them the words you
gave me and they accepted
them. They knew with cer-
tainty that I came from you,
and they believed that you
sent me. 9I pray for them. I
am not praying for the
world, but for those you
have given me, for they are
yours. 10All I have is yours,
and all you have is mine.
And glory has come to me
through them. 11I will remain in the world no
longer, but they are still in
the world, and I am coming
to you. Holy Father, protect
them by the power of your
name—the name you gave
me—so that they may be
one as we are one. 12While I
was with them, I protected
them and kept them safe by
that name you gave me.
None has been lost except
the one doomed to destruction so that Scripture would
be fulfilled. Jn 1:18; 6:39

13"I am coming to you

now, but I say these things
while I am still in the world,
so that they may have the
full measure of my joy within them. 14I have given them
your word and the world
has hated them, for they are
not of the world any more
than I am of the world. 15My
prayer is not that you take
them out of the world but
that you protect them from
the evil one. 16They are not
of the world, even as I am
not of it. 17Sanctify[b] them by
the truth; your word is
truth. 18As you sent me into
the world, I have sent them
into the world. 19For them I
sanctify myself, that they
too may be truly sancti-
fied.

Jesus Prays for All Believers

20"My prayer is not for
them alone. I pray also for
those who will believe in
me through their message,
21that all of them may be
one, Father, just as you are
in me and I am in you. May
they also be in us so that the
world may believe that you
have sent me. 22I have given
them the glory that you
gave me, that they may be
one as we are one: 23I in
them and you in me. May
they be brought to complete
unity to let the world know
that you sent me and have

[a]6 Greek your name; also in verse 26   [b]17 Greek hagiazo (set apart for sacred use or make holy); also in verse 19

loved them even as you have loved me. Jer 32:39

24"Father, I want those you have given me to be with me where I am, and to see my glory, the glory you have given me because you loved me before the creation of the world. Jn 12:26

25"Righteous Father, though the world does not know you, I know you, and they know that you have sent me. 26I have made you known to them, and will continue to make you known in order that the love you have for me may be in them and that I myself may be in them." Jn 15:9,21

Jesus Arrested

18 When he had finished praying, Jesus left with his disciples and crossed the Kidron Valley. On the other side there was an olive grove, and he and his disciples went into it.

2Now Judas, who betrayed him, knew the place, because Jesus had often met there with his disciples. 3So Judas came to the grove, guiding a detachment of soldiers and some officials from the chief priests and Pharisees. They were carrying torches, lanterns and weapons.

4Jesus, knowing all that was going to happen to him, went out and asked them, "Who is it you want?" Jn 6:64; 13:1,11

5"Jesus of Nazareth," they replied. Mk 1:24

"I am he," Jesus said. (And Judas the traitor was standing there with them.) 6When Jesus said, "I am he," they drew back and fell to the ground.

7Again he asked them, "Who is it you want?"

And they said, "Jesus of Nazareth."

8"I told you that I am he," Jesus answered. "If you are looking for me, then let these men go." 9This happened so that the words he had spoken would be fulfilled: "I have not lost one of those you gave me." [a] Jn 6:39; 17:12

10Then Simon Peter, who had a sword, drew it and struck the high priest's servant, cutting off his right ear. (The servant's name was Malchus.) Mt 26:51

11Jesus commanded Peter, "Put your sword away! Shall I not drink the cup the Father has given me?" Mt 20:22

Jesus Taken to Annas

12Then the detachment of soldiers with its commander and the Jewish officials arrested Jesus. They bound him 13and brought him first to Annas, who was the father-in-law of Caiaphas, the high priest that year. 14Caiaphas was the one who had advised the Jews that it would be good if one man died for the people. Mt 26:3

Peter's First Denial

¹⁵Simon Peter and another disciple were following Jesus. Because this disciple was known to the high priest, he went with Jesus into the high priest's courtyard, ¹⁶but Peter had to wait outside at the door. The other disciple, who was known to the high priest, came back, spoke to the girl on duty there and brought Peter in.

¹⁷"You are not one of his disciples, are you?" the girl at the door asked Peter.

He replied, "I am not."

¹⁸It was cold, and the servants and officials stood around a fire they had made to keep warm. Peter also was standing with them, warming himself. Mk 14:54,67

The High Priest Questions Jesus

¹⁹Meanwhile, the high priest questioned Jesus about his disciples and his teaching.   Mt 26:59

²⁰"I have spoken openly to the world," Jesus replied. "I always taught in synagogues or at the temple, where all the Jews come together. I said nothing in secret. ²¹Why question me? Ask those who heard me. Surely they know what I said."   Mt 4:23

²²When Jesus said this, one of the officials nearby struck him in the face. "Is this the way you answer the high priest?" he demanded.   Mt 16:21

²³"If I said something wrong," Jesus replied, "testify as to what is wrong. But if I spoke the truth, why did you strike me?" ²⁴Then Annas sent him, still bound, to Caiaphas the high priest.ᵃ   Mt 5:39

Peter's Second and Third Denials

²⁵As Simon Peter stood warming himself, he was asked, "You are not one of his disciples, are you?"   Mt 26:69,71

He denied it, saying, "I am not."

²⁶One of the high priest's servants, a relative of the man whose ear Peter had cut off, challenged him, "Didn't I see you with him in the olive grove?" ²⁷Again Peter denied it, and at that moment a rooster began to crow.   Jn 13:38

Jesus Before Pilate

²⁸Then the Jews led Jesus from Caiaphas to the palace of the Roman governor. By now it was early morning, and to avoid ceremonial uncleanness the Jews did not enter the palace; they wanted to be able to eat the Passover. ²⁹So Pilate came out to them and asked, "What charges are you bringing against this man?"   Mt 27:2

³⁰"If he were not a criminal," they replied, "we would not have handed him over to you."

³¹Pilate said, "Take him yourselves and judge him by your own law."

"But we have no right to exe-

ᵃ24 Or (Now Annas had sent him, still bound, to Caiaphas the high priest.)

cute anyone," the Jews objected. ³²This happened so that the words Jesus had spoken indicating the kind of death he was going to die would be fulfilled. Mt 20:19; Jn 3:14

³³Pilate then went back inside the palace, summoned Jesus and asked him, "Are you the king of the Jews?"

³⁴"Is that your own idea," Jesus asked, "or did others talk to you about me?"

³⁵"Am I a Jew?" Pilate replied. "It was your people and your chief priests who handed you over to me. What is it you have done?"

³⁶Jesus said, "My kingdom is not of this world. If it were, my servants would fight to prevent my arrest by the Jews. But now my kingdom is from another place." Mt 26:53; Jn 6:15

³⁷"You are a king, then!" said Pilate.

Jesus answered, "You are right in saying I am a king. In fact, for this reason I was born, and for this I came into the world, to testify to the truth. Everyone on the side of truth listens to me." Jn 3:32

³⁸"What is truth?" Pilate asked. With this he went out again to the Jews and said, "I find no basis for a charge against him. ³⁹But it is your custom for me to release to you one prisoner at the time of the Passover. Do you want me to release 'the king of the Jews'?" Lk 23:4

⁴⁰They shouted back, "No, not him! Give us Barabbas!"

Now Barabbas had taken part in a rebellion. Lk 23:19; Ac 3:14

Jesus Sentenced to be Crucified

19 Then Pilate took Jesus and had him flogged. ²The soldiers twisted together a crown of thorns and put it on his head. They clothed him in a purple robe ³and went up to him again and again, saying, "Hail, king of the Jews!" And they struck him in the face.

⁴Once more Pilate came out and said to the Jews, "Look, I am bringing him out to you to let you know that I find no basis for a charge against him." ⁵When Jesus came out wearing the crown of thorns and the purple robe, Pilate said to them, "Here is the man!"

⁶As soon as the chief priests and their officials saw him, they shouted, "Crucify! Crucify!"

But Pilate answered, "You take him and crucify him. As for me, I find no basis for a charge against him." Ac 3:13

⁷The Jews insisted, "We have a law, and according to that law he must die, because he claimed to be the Son of God." Lev 24:16

⁸When Pilate heard this, he was even more afraid, ⁹and he went back inside the palace. "Where do you come from?" he asked Jesus, but Jesus gave him no answer. ¹⁰"Do you refuse to speak to me?" Pilate said. "Don't you realize I have power

either to free you or to crucify you?"

¹¹Jesus answered, "You would have no power over me if it were not given to you from above. Therefore the one who handed me over to you is guilty of a greater sin." Ro 13:1

¹²From then on, Pilate tried to set Jesus free, but the Jews kept shouting, "If you let this man go, you are no friend of Caesar. Anyone who claims to be a king opposes Caesar." Lk 23:2

¹³When Pilate heard this, he brought Jesus out and sat down on the judge's seat at a place known as the Stone Pavement (which in Aramaic is Gabbatha). ¹⁴It was the day of Preparation of Passover Week, about the sixth hour. Mt 27:19

"Here is your king," Pilate said to the Jews.

¹⁵But they shouted, "Take him away! Take him away! Crucify him!"

"Shall I crucify your king?" Pilate asked.

"We have no king but Caesar," the chief priests answered.

¹⁶Finally Pilate handed him over to them to be crucified.

The Crucifixion

So the soldiers took charge of Jesus. ¹⁷Carrying his own cross, he went out to the place of the Skull (which in Aramaic is called Golgotha). ¹⁸Here they crucified him, and with him two others—one on each side and Jesus in the middle. Lk 23:32

¹⁹Pilate had a notice prepared and fastened to the cross. It read: JESUS OF NAZARETH, THE KING OF THE JEWS. ²⁰Many of the Jews read this sign, for the place where Jesus was crucified was near the city, and the sign was written in Aramaic, Latin and Greek. ²¹The chief priests of the Jews protested to Pilate, "Do not write 'The King of the Jews,' but that this man claimed to be king of the Jews." Heb 13:12

²²Pilate answered, "What I have written, I have written."

²³When the soldiers crucified Jesus, they took his clothes, dividing them into four shares, one for each of them, with the undergarment remaining. This garment was seamless, woven in one piece from top to bottom. ²⁴"Let's not tear it," they said to one another. "Let's decide by lot who will get it."

This happened that the scripture might be fulfilled which said,

"They divided my garments
    among them
and cast lots for my
    clothing."ᵃ

So this is what the soldiers did.

²⁵Near the cross of Jesus stood his mother, his mother's sister, Mary the wife of Clopas, and Mary Magdalene. ²⁶When Jesus saw his mother there, and the disciple whom he loved

ᵃ24 Psalm 22:18

standing nearby, he said to his mother, "Dear woman, here is your son," 27and to the disciple, "Here is your mother." From that time on, this disciple took her into his home.   Mt 27:55-56

The Death of Jesus

28Later, knowing that all was now completed, and so that the Scripture would be fulfilled, Jesus said, "I am thirsty." 29A jar of wine vinegar was there, so they soaked a sponge in it, put the sponge on a stalk of the hyssop plant, and lifted it to Jesus' lips. 30When he had received the drink, Jesus said, "It is finished." With that, he bowed his head and gave up his spirit.

31Now it was the day of Preparation, and the next day was to be a special Sabbath. Because the Jews did not want the bodies left on the crosses during the Sabbath, they asked Pilate to have the legs broken and the bodies taken down. 32The soldiers therefore came and broke the legs of the first man who had been crucified with Jesus, and then those of the other. 33But when they came to Jesus and found that he was already dead, they did not break his legs. 34Instead, one of the soldiers pierced Jesus' side with a spear, bringing a sudden flow of blood and water. 35The man who saw it has given testimony, and his testimony is true. He knows that he tells the truth, and he testifies so that you also may believe. 36These things happened so that the scripture would be fulfilled: "Not one of his bones will be broken,"a 37and, as another scripture says, "They will look on the one they have pierced."b   Dt 21:23

The Burial of Jesus

38Later, Joseph of Arimathea asked Pilate for the body of Jesus. Now Joseph was a disciple of Jesus, but secretly because he feared the Jews. With Pilate's permission, he came and took the body away. 39He was accompanied by Nicodemus, the man who earlier had visited Jesus at night. Nicodemus brought a mixture of myrrh and aloes, about seventy-five pounds.c 40Taking Jesus' body, the two of them wrapped it, with the spices, in strips of linen. This was in accordance with Jewish burial customs. 41At the place where Jesus was crucified, there was a garden, and in the garden a new tomb, in which no one had ever been laid. 42Because it was the Jewish day of Preparation and since the tomb was nearby, they laid Jesus there.   Mt 26:12; Jn 7:13

The Empty Tomb

20 Early on the first day of the week, while it was

---

a36 Exodus 12:46; Num. 9:12; Psalm 34:20   b37 Zech. 12:10   c39 Greek a hundred litrai (about 34 kilograms)

still dark, Mary Magdalene went to the tomb and saw that the stone had been removed from the entrance. ²So she came running to Simon Peter and the other disciple, the one Jesus loved, and said, "They have taken the Lord out of the tomb, and we don't know where they have put him!" Mt 27:60,66; Lk 8:2

³So Peter and the other disciple started for the tomb. ⁴Both were running, but the other disciple outran Peter and reached the tomb first. ⁵He bent over and looked in at the strips of linen lying there but did not go in. ⁶Then Simon Peter, who was behind him, arrived and went into the tomb. He saw the strips of linen lying there, ⁷as well as the burial cloth that had been around Jesus' head. The cloth was folded up by itself, separate from the linen. ⁸Finally the other disciple, who had reached the tomb first, also went inside. He saw and believed. ⁹(They still did not understand from Scripture that Jesus had to rise from the dead.) Lk 24:12

Jesus Appears to Mary Magdalene

¹⁰Then the disciples went back to their homes, ¹¹but Mary stood outside the tomb crying. As she wept, she bent over to look into the tomb ¹²and saw two angels in white, seated where Jesus' body had been, one at the head and the other at the foot. Mt 28:2; Mk 16:5

¹³They asked her, "Woman, why are you crying?"

"They have taken my Lord away," she said, "and I don't know where they have put him." ¹⁴At this, she turned around and saw Jesus standing there, but she did not realize that it was Jesus. Mk 16:9

¹⁵"Woman," he said, "why are you crying? Who is it you are looking for?"

Thinking he was the gardener, she said, "Sir, if you have carried him away, tell me where you have put him, and I will get him."

¹⁶Jesus said to her, "Mary."

She turned toward him and cried out in Aramaic, "Rabboni!" (which means Teacher).

¹⁷Jesus said, "Do not hold on to me, for I have not yet returned to the Father. Go instead to my brothers and tell them, 'I am returning to my Father and your Father, to my God and your God.'" Mt 28:10; Jn 7:33

¹⁸Mary Magdalene went to the disciples with the news: "I have seen the Lord!" And she told them that he had said these things to her. Lk 24:10,22-23

Jesus Appears to His Disciples

¹⁹On the evening of that first day of the week, when the disciples were together, with the doors locked for fear of the Jews, Jesus came and stood among them and said, "Peace be with you!" ²⁰After he said

this, he showed them his hands and side. The disciples were overjoyed when they saw the Lord. _{Lk 24:39-40}

²¹Again Jesus said, "Peace be with you! As the Father has sent me, I am sending you." ²²And with that he breathed on them and said, "Receive the Holy Spirit. ²³If you forgive anyone his sins, they are forgiven; if you do not forgive them, they are not forgiven." _{Jn 3:17}

Jesus Appears to Thomas

²⁴Now Thomas (called Didymus), one of the Twelve, was not with the disciples when Jesus came. ²⁵So the other disciples told him, "We have seen the Lord!" _{Jn 11:16}

But he said to them, "Unless I see the nail marks in his hands and put my finger where the nails were, and put my hand into his side, I will not believe it." _{Mk 16:11}

²⁶A week later his disciples were in the house again, and Thomas was with them. Though the doors were locked, Jesus came and stood among them and said, "Peace be with you!" ²⁷Then he said to Thomas, "Put your finger here; see my hands. Reach out your hand and put it into my side. Stop doubting and believe." _{Jn 14:27}

²⁸Thomas said to him, "My Lord and my God!"

²⁹Then Jesus told him, "Because you have seen me, you have believed; blessed are those who have not seen and yet have believed." _{Jn 3:15; 1Pe 1:8}

³⁰Jesus did many other miraculous signs in the presence of his disciples, which are not recorded in this book. ³¹But these are written that you may*ᵃ* believe that Jesus is the Christ, the Son of God, and that by believing you may have life in his name. _{Jn 2:11; 3:15; 19:35}

Jesus and the Miraculous Catch of Fish

21 Afterward Jesus appeared again to his disciples, by the Sea of Tiberias.ᵇ It happened this way: ²Simon Peter, Thomas (called Didymus), Nathanael from Cana in Galilee, the sons of Zebedee, and two other disciples were together. ³"I'm going out to fish," Simon Peter told them, and they said, "We'll go with you." So they went out and got into the boat, but that night they caught nothing. _{Lk 5:5}

⁴Early in the morning, Jesus stood on the shore, but the disciples did not realize that it was Jesus. _{Lk 24:16; Jn 20:14}

⁵He called out to them, "Friends, haven't you any fish?" _{Lk 24:41}

"No," they answered.

⁶He said, "Throw your net on the right side of the boat and you will find some." When they did, they were unable to haul

---

_{*ᵃ*31 Some manuscripts *may continue to*   ᵇ1 That is, Sea of Galilee}

the net in because of the large number of fish. Lk 5:4-7

7Then the disciple whom Jesus loved said to Peter, "It is the Lord!" As soon as Simon Peter heard him say, "It is the Lord," he wrapped his outer garment around him (for he had taken it off) and jumped into the water. 8The other disciples followed in the boat, towing the net full of fish, for they were not far from shore, about a hundred yards. a 9When they landed, they saw a fire of burning coals there with fish on it, and some bread.

10Jesus said to them, "Bring some of the fish you have just caught."

11Simon Peter climbed aboard and dragged the net ashore. It was full of large fish, 153, but even with so many the net was not torn. 12Jesus said to them, "Come and have breakfast." None of the disciples dared ask him, "Who are you?" They knew it was the Lord. 13Jesus came, took the bread and gave it to them, and did the same with the fish. 14This was now the third time Jesus appeared to his disciples after he was raised from the dead. Jn 20:19,26

Jesus Reinstates Peter

15When they had finished eating, Jesus said to Simon Peter, "Simon son of John, do you truly love me more than these?"

"Yes, Lord," he said, "you know that I love you." Mt 26:33,35

Jesus said, "Feed my lambs."

16Again Jesus said, "Simon son of John, do you truly love me?"

He answered, "Yes, Lord, you know that I love you."

Jesus said, "Take care of my sheep." Ac 20:28; 1Pe 5:2,3

17The third time he said to him, "Simon son of John, do you love me?" Jn 16:30

Peter was hurt because Jesus asked him the third time, "Do you love me?" He said, "Lord, you know all things; you know that I love you."

Jesus said, "Feed my sheep. 18I tell you the truth, when you were younger you dressed yourself and went where you wanted; but when you are old you will stretch out your hands, and someone else will dress you and lead you where you do not want to go." 19Jesus said this to indicate the kind of death by which Peter would glorify God. Then he said to him, "Follow me!" Jn 13:36

20Peter turned and saw that the disciple whom Jesus loved was following them. (This was the one who had leaned back against Jesus at the supper and had said, "Lord, who is going to betray you?") 21When Peter saw him, he asked, "Lord, what about him?"

22Jesus answered, "If I want

a8 Greek about two hundred cubits (about 90 meters)

him to remain alive until I return, what is that to you? You must follow me." ²³Because of this, the rumor spread among the brothers that this disciple would not die. But Jesus did not say that he would not die; he only said, "If I want him to remain alive until I return, what is that to you?"

²⁴This is the disciple who testifies to these things and who wrote them down. We know that his testimony is true.

²⁵Jesus did many other things as well. If every one of them were written down, I suppose that even the whole world would not have room for the books that would be written.

Acts

Introduction:

The Acts of the Apostles is the second part of Luke's history. It was written so we would have the true story of how the Christian church began and grew.

This book especially tells about the work of two of the apostles—Peter and Paul. Peter is the central person involved in beginning the church in Jerusalem and Paul is the important missionary who went out to nearby countries to tell others about Christ. Acts can also be called "The Acts of the Holy Spirit" because it teaches about the coming and work of the Spirit.

The book of Acts teaches three things about the early church: 1) what the message of the early church was; 2) how the Jews rejected this message and how God sent the apostles to the Gentiles, who accepted the Gospel; and 3) how the early church was treated by the local and Roman governments.

Outline of contents:

Jesus Taken Up Into Heaven

1 In my former book, Theophilus, I wrote about all that Jesus began to do and to teach ²until the day he was taken up to heaven, after giving instructions through the Holy Spirit to the apostles he had chosen. ³After his suffering, he showed himself to these men and gave many convincing proofs that he was alive. He appeared to them over a period of forty days and spoke about the kingdom of God. ⁴On one occasion, while he was eating with them, he gave them this command: "Do not leave Jerusalem, but wait for

the gift my Father promised, which you have heard me speak about. ⁵For John baptized with*ᵃ* water, but in a few days you will be baptized with the Holy Spirit." Mk 1:4; Lk 1:1-4

⁶So when they met together, they asked him, "Lord, are you at this time going to restore the kingdom to Israel?" Ac 3:21

⁷He said to them: "It is not for you to know the times or dates the Father has set by his own authority. ⁸But you will receive power when the Holy Spirit comes on you; and you will be my witnesses in Jerusalem, and in all Judea and Samaria, and to the ends of the earth." Dt 29:29

⁹After he said this, he was taken up before their very eyes, and a cloud hid him from their sight. Mk 16:19

¹⁰They were looking intently up into the sky as he was going, when suddenly two men dressed in white stood beside them. ¹¹"Men of Galilee," they said, "why do you stand here looking into the sky? This same Jesus, who has been taken from you into heaven, will come back in the same way you have seen him go into heaven." Mt 16:27

Matthias Chosen to Replace Judas

¹²Then they returned to Jerusalem from the hill called the Mount of Olives, a Sabbath day's walk*ᵇ* from the city.

¹³When they arrived, they went upstairs to the room where they were staying. Those present were Peter, John, James and Andrew; Philip and Thomas, Bartholomew and Matthew; James son of Alphaeus and Simon the Zealot, and Judas son of James. ¹⁴They all joined together constantly in prayer, along with the women and Mary the mother of Jesus, and with his brothers. Lk 24:52

¹⁵In those days Peter stood up among the believers*ᶜ* (a group numbering about a hundred and twenty) ¹⁶and said, "Brothers, the Scripture had to be fulfilled which the Holy Spirit spoke long ago through the mouth of David concerning Judas, who served as guide for those who arrested Jesus— ¹⁷he was one of our number and shared in this ministry." Jn 6:70,71

¹⁸(With the reward he got for his wickedness, Judas bought a field; there he fell headlong, his body burst open and all his intestines spilled out. ¹⁹Everyone in Jerusalem heard about this, so they called that field in their language Akeldama, that is, Field of Blood.) Mt 26:14-16

²⁰"For," said Peter, "it is written in the book of Psalms,

" 'May his place be deserted; let there be no one to dwell in it,'*ᵈ*

and,

ᵃ5 Or *in*   *ᵇ12* That is, about 3/4 mile (about 1,100 meters)   *ᶜ15* Greek *brothers*
ᵈ20 Psalm 69:25

" 'May another take his place of leadership.' [a]

21Therefore it is necessary to choose one of the men who have been with us the whole time the Lord Jesus went in and out among us, 22beginning from John's baptism to the time when Jesus was taken up from us. For one of these must become a witness with us of his resurrection." Lk 24:48

23So they proposed two men: Joseph called Barsabbas (also known as Justus) and Matthias. 24Then they prayed, "Lord, you know everyone's heart. Show us which of these two you have chosen 25to take over this apostolic ministry, which Judas left to go where he belongs." 26Then they cast lots, and the lot fell to Matthias; so he was added to the eleven apostles. Ac 6:6

The Holy Spirit Comes at Pentecost

2 When the day of Pentecost came, they were all together in one place. 2Suddenly a sound like the blowing of a violent wind came from heaven and filled the whole house where they were sitting. 3They saw what seemed to be tongues of fire that separated and came to rest on each of them. 4All of them were filled with the Holy Spirit and began to speak in other tongues[b] as the Spirit enabled them. Lev 23:15; Lk 1:15

5Now there were staying in Jerusalem God-fearing Jews from every nation under heaven. 6When they heard this sound, a crowd came together in bewilderment, because each one heard them speaking in his own language. 7Utterly amazed, they asked: "Are not all these men who are speaking Galileans? 8Then how is it that each of us hears them in his own native language? 9Parthians, Medes and Elamites; residents of Mesopotamia, Judea and Cappadocia, Pontus and Asia, 10Phrygia and Pamphylia, Egypt and the parts of Libya near Cyrene; visitors from Rome 11(both Jews and converts to Judaism); Cretans and Arabs—we hear them declaring the wonders of God in our own tongues!" 12Amazed and perplexed, they asked one another, "What does this mean?" Lk 2:25

13Some, however, made fun of them and said, "They have had too much wine.[c]" 1Co 14:23

Peter Addresses the Crowd

14Then Peter stood up with the Eleven, raised his voice and addressed the crowd: "Fellow Jews and all of you who live in Jerusalem, let me explain this to you; listen carefully to what I say. 15These men are not drunk, as you suppose. It's only nine in the morning! 16No, this is what was spoken by the prophet Joel:

17" 'In the last days, God says,

---

[a]20 Psalm 109:8   [b]4 Or *languages*; also in verse 11   [c]13 Or *sweet wine*

I will pour out my Spirit on
    all people.   Nu 11:25
Your sons and daughters will
    prophesy,   Ac 21:9
your young men will see
    visions,
your old men will dream
    dreams.
[18]Even on my servants, both
    men and women,
I will pour out my Spirit in
    those days,
and they will prophesy.
[19]I will show wonders in the
    heaven above
and signs on the earth
    below,   Lk 21:11
blood and fire and billows
    of smoke.
[20]The sun will be turned to
    darkness
and the moon to blood Mt 24:29
before the coming of the
    great and glorious day of
    the Lord.
[21]And everyone who calls
    on the name of the Lord
    will be saved.'[a]

[22]"Men of Israel, listen to this:
Jesus of Nazareth was a man accredited by God to you by miracles, wonders and signs, which
God did among you through
him, as you yourselves know.
[23]This man was handed over to
you by God's set purpose and
foreknowledge; and you, with
the help of wicked men,[b] put
him to death by nailing him to
the cross. [24]But God raised him

from the dead, freeing him from
the agony of death, because it
was impossible for death to
keep its hold on him. [25]David
said about him: Eph 1:20

" 'I saw the Lord always
    before me.
Because he is at my right
    hand,
I will not be shaken.
[26]Therefore my heart is glad
    and my tongue rejoices;
my body also will live in
    hope,
[27]because you will not
    abandon me to the
    grave,
nor will you let your Holy
    One see decay.
[28]You have made known to me
    the paths of life;
you will fill me with joy in
    your presence.'[c]

[29]"Brothers, I can tell you
confidently that the patriarch
David died and was buried, and
his tomb is here to this day.
[30]But he was a prophet and
knew that God had promised
him on oath that he would place
one of his descendants on his
throne. [31]Seeing what was
ahead, he spoke of the resurrection of the Christ,[d] that he was
not abandoned to the grave, nor
did his body see decay. [32]God
has raised this Jesus to life, and
we are all witnesses of the fact.
[33]Exalted to the right hand of
God, he has received from the

a21 Joel 2:28-32   b23 Or *of those not having the law* (that is, Gentiles)
c28 Psalm 16:8-11   d31 Or *Messiah*. "The Christ" (Greek) and "the Messiah"
(Hebrew) both mean "the Anointed One"; also in verse 36.

Father the promised Holy Spirit and has poured out what you now see and hear. ³⁴For David did not ascend to heaven, and yet he said, _{Jn 15:26}

" 'The Lord said to my Lord:
    "Sit at my right hand
³⁵until I make your enemies
    a footstool for your feet." ' ᵃ

³⁶"Therefore let all Israel be assured of this: God has made this Jesus, whom you crucified, both Lord and Christ." _{Mt 28:18}
³⁷When the people heard this, they were cut to the heart and said to Peter and the other apostles, "Brothers, what shall we do?" _{Ac 16:30}
³⁸Peter replied, "Repent and be baptized, every one of you, in the name of Jesus Christ for the forgiveness of your sins. And you will receive the gift of the Holy Spirit. ³⁹The promise is for you and your children and for all who are far off—for all whom the Lord our God will call." _{Isa 44:3; Ac 8:12,16,36}
⁴⁰With many other words he warned them; and he pleaded with them, "Save yourselves from this corrupt generation." ⁴¹Those who accepted his message were baptized, and about three thousand were added to their number that day. _{Dt 32:5}

The Fellowship of the Believers

⁴²They devoted themselves to the apostles' teaching and to the fellowship, to the breaking of bread and to prayer. ⁴³Everyone was filled with awe, and many wonders and miraculous signs were done by the apostles. ⁴⁴All the believers were together and had everything in common. ⁴⁵Selling their possessions and goods, they gave to anyone as he had need. ⁴⁶Every day they continued to meet together in the temple courts. They broke bread in their homes and ate together with glad and sincere hearts, ⁴⁷praising God and enjoying the favor of all the people. And the Lord added to their number daily those who were being saved. _{Mt 28:20}

Peter Heals the Crippled Beggar

3 One day Peter and John were going up to the temple at the time of prayer—at three in the afternoon. ²Now a man crippled from birth was being carried to the temple gate called Beautiful, where he was put every day to beg from those going into the temple courts. ³When he saw Peter and John about to enter, he asked them for money. ⁴Peter looked straight at him, as did John. Then Peter said, "Look at us!" ⁵So the man gave them his attention, expecting to get something from them. _{Ac 14:8}
⁶Then Peter said, "Silver or gold I do not have, but what I have I give you. In the name of

Jesus Christ of Nazareth, walk." [7]Taking him by the right hand, he helped him up, and instantly the man's feet and ankles became strong. [8]He jumped to his feet and began to walk. Then he went with them into the temple courts, walking and jumping, and praising God. [9]When all the people saw him walking and praising God, [10]they recognized him as the same man who used to sit begging at the temple gate called Beautiful, and they were filled with wonder and amazement at what had happened to him.

Peter Speaks to the Onlookers

[11]While the beggar held on to Peter and John, all the people were astonished and came running to them in the place called Solomon's Colonnade. [12]When Peter saw this, he said to them: "Men of Israel, why does this surprise you? Why do you stare at us as if by our own power or godliness we had made this man walk? [13]The God of Abraham, Isaac and Jacob, the God of our fathers, has glorified his servant Jesus. You handed him over to be killed, and you disowned him before Pilate, though he had decided to let him go. [14]You disowned the Holy and Righteous One and asked that a murderer be released to you. [15]You killed the author of life, but God raised

him from the dead. We are witnesses of this. [16]By faith in the name of Jesus, this man whom you see and know was made strong. It is Jesus' name and the faith that comes through him that has given this complete healing to him, as you can all see.   Ac 2:24

[17]"Now, brothers, I know that you acted in ignorance, as did your leaders. [18]But this is how God fulfilled what he had foretold through all the prophets, saying that his Christ[a] would suffer. [19]Repent, then, and turn to God, so that your sins may be wiped out, that times of refreshing may come from the Lord, [20]and that he may send the Christ, who has been appointed for you—even Jesus. [21]He must remain in heaven until the time comes for God to restore everything, as he promised long ago through his holy prophets. [22]For Moses said, 'The Lord your God will raise up for you a prophet like me from among your own people; you must listen to everything he tells you. [23]Anyone who does not listen to him will be completely cut off from among his people.'[b]   Lk 23:34

[24]"Indeed, all the prophets from Samuel on, as many as have spoken, have foretold these days. [25]And you are heirs of the prophets and of the covenant God made with your fathers. He said to Abraham,

---

[a]18 Or *Messiah*; also in verse 20   [b]23 Deut. 18:15,18,19

'Through your offspring all peoples on earth will be blessed.'*a* ²⁶When God raised up his servant, he sent him first to you to bless you by turning each of you from your wicked ways." Lk 24:27

Peter and John Before the Sanhedrin

4 The priests and the captain of the temple guard and the Sadducees came up to Peter and John while they were speaking to the people. ²They were greatly disturbed because the apostles were teaching the people and proclaiming in Jesus the resurrection of the dead. ³They seized Peter and John, and because it was evening, they put them in jail until the next day. ⁴But many who heard the message believed, and the number of men grew to about five thousand. Lk 22:4; Ac 2:41

⁵The next day the rulers, elders and teachers of the law met in Jerusalem. ⁶Annas the high priest was there, and so were Caiaphas, John, Alexander and the other men of the high priest's family. ⁷They had Peter and John brought before them and began to question them: "By what power or what name did you do this?" Lk 23:13

⁸Then Peter, filled with the Holy Spirit, said to them: "Rulers and elders of the people! ⁹If we are being called to account today for an act of kindness shown to a cripple and are asked how he was healed, ¹⁰then know this, you and all the people of Israel: It is by the name of Jesus Christ of Nazareth, whom you crucified but whom God raised from the dead, that this man stands before you healed. ¹¹He is

" 'the stone you builders
    rejected,
which has become the
    capstone.*b'c*

¹²Salvation is found in no one else, for there is no other name under heaven given to men by which we must be saved." Mt 1:21

¹³When they saw the courage of Peter and John and realized that they were unschooled, ordinary men, they were astonished and they took note that these men had been with Jesus. ¹⁴But since they could see the man who had been healed standing there with them, there was nothing they could say. ¹⁵So they ordered them to withdraw from the Sanhedrin and then conferred together. ¹⁶"What are we going to do with these men?" they asked. "Everybody living in Jerusalem knows they have done an outstanding miracle, and we cannot deny it. ¹⁷But to stop this thing from spreading any further among the people, we must warn these men to speak no longer to anyone in this name." Mk 3:14; Jn 11:47; Ac 3:6-10

¹⁸Then they called them in

---

*a*25 Gen. 22:18; 26:4   *b*11 Or *cornerstone*   *c*11 Psalm 118:22

again and commanded them not to speak or teach at all in the name of Jesus. [19]But Peter and John replied, "Judge for yourselves whether it is right in God's sight to obey you rather than God. [20]For we cannot help speaking about what we have seen and heard."   Job 32:18

[21]After further threats they let them go. They could not decide how to punish them, because all the people were praising God for what had happened. [22]For the man who was miraculously healed was over forty years old.

The Believers' Prayer

[23]On their release, Peter and John went back to their own people and reported all that the chief priests and elders had said to them. [24]When they heard this, they raised their voices together in prayer to God. "Sovereign Lord," they said, "you made the heaven and the earth and the sea, and everything in them. [25]You spoke by the Holy Spirit through the mouth of your servant, our father David:

" 'Why do the nations rage
     and the peoples plot in
         vain?
[26]The kings of the earth take
     their stand
   and the rulers gather
       together
against the Lord
   and against his Anointed
     One.'[a][b]

[27]Indeed Herod and Pontius Pilate met together with the Gentiles and the people[c] of Israel in this city to conspire against your holy servant Jesus, whom you anointed. [28]They did what your power and will had decided beforehand should happen. [29]Now, Lord, consider their threats and enable your servants to speak your word with great boldness. [30]Stretch out your hand to heal and perform miraculous signs and wonders through the name of your holy servant Jesus."   Ps 138:3

[31]After they prayed, the place where they were meeting was shaken. And they were all filled with the Holy Spirit and spoke the word of God boldly.   Ac 2:2

The Believers Share Their Possessions

[32]All the believers were one in heart and mind. No one claimed that any of his possessions was his own, but they shared everything they had. [33]With great power the apostles continued to testify to the resurrection of the Lord Jesus, and much grace was upon them all. [34]There were no needy persons among them. For from time to time those who owned lands or houses sold them, brought the money from the sales [35]and put it at the apostles' feet, and it was distributed to anyone as he had need. Ac 2:44

[36]Joseph, a Levite from Cyprus, whom the apostles called

---

[a]26 That is, Christ or Messiah   [b]26 Psalm 2:1,2   [c]27 The Greek is plural.

Barnabas (which means Son of Encouragement), [37]sold a field he owned and brought the money and put it at the apostles' feet.   Ac 9:27; 1Co 9:6

Ananias and Sapphira

5 Now a man named Ananias, together with his wife Sapphira, also sold a piece of property. [2]With his wife's full knowledge he kept back part of the money for himself, but brought the rest and put it at the apostles' feet.   Jos 7:11; Ac 4:35

[3]Then Peter said, "Ananias, how is it that Satan has so filled your heart that you have lied to the Holy Spirit and have kept for yourself some of the money you received for the land? [4]Didn't it belong to you before it was sold? And after it was sold, wasn't the money at your disposal? What made you think of doing such a thing? You have not lied to men but to God."

[5]When Ananias heard this, he fell down and died. And great fear seized all who heard what had happened. [6]Then the young men came forward, wrapped up his body, and carried him out and buried him.

[7]About three hours later his wife came in, not knowing what had happened. [8]Peter asked her, "Tell me, is this the price you and Ananias got for the land?"

"Yes," she said, "that is the price."

[9]Peter said to her, "How could you agree to test the Spirit of the Lord? Look! The feet of the men who buried your husband are at the door, and they will carry you out also."

[10]At that moment she fell down at his feet and died. Then the young men came in and, finding her dead, carried her out and buried her beside her husband. [11]Great fear seized the whole church and all who heard about these events.   Ac 19:17

The Apostles Heal Many

[12]The apostles performed many miraculous signs and wonders among the people. And all the believers used to meet together in Solomon's Colonnade. [13]No one else dared join them, even though they were highly regarded by the people. [14]Nevertheless, more and more men and women believed in the Lord and were added to their number. [15]As a result, people brought the sick into the streets and laid them on beds and mats so that at least Peter's shadow might fall on some of them as he passed by. [16]Crowds gathered also from the towns around Jerusalem, bringing their sick and those tormented by evil[a] spirits, and all of them were healed.   Jn 4:48

The Apostles Persecuted

[17]Then the high priest and all his associates, who were mem-

[a]16 Greek *unclean*

bers of the party of the Sadducees, were filled with jealousy. [18]They arrested the apostles and put them in the public jail. [19]But during the night an angel of the Lord opened the doors of the jail and brought them out. [20]"Go, stand in the temple courts," he said, "and tell the people the full message of this new life."   Jn 6:63,68

[21]At daybreak they entered the temple courts, as they had been told, and began to teach the people.

When the high priest and his associates arrived, they called together the Sanhedrin—the full assembly of the elders of Israel—and sent to the jail for the apostles. [22]But on arriving at the jail, the officers did not find them there. So they went back and reported, [23]"We found the jail securely locked, with the guards standing at the doors; but when we opened them, we found no one inside." [24]On hearing this report, the captain of the temple guard and the chief priests were puzzled, wondering what would come of this.   Ac 12:18,19

[25]Then someone came and said, "Look! The men you put in jail are standing in the temple courts teaching the people." [26]At that, the captain went with his officers and brought the apostles. They did not use force, because they feared that the people would stone them.

[27]Having brought the apostles, they made them appear before the Sanhedrin to be questioned by the high priest. [28]"We gave you strict orders not to teach in this name," he said. "Yet you have filled Jerusalem with your teaching and are determined to make us guilty of this man's blood."   Ac 2:23

[29]Peter and the other apostles replied: "We must obey God rather than men! [30]The God of our fathers raised Jesus from the dead—whom you had killed by hanging him on a tree. [31]God exalted him to his own right hand as Prince and Savior that he might give repentance and forgiveness of sins to Israel. [32]We are witnesses of these things, and so is the Holy Spirit, whom God has given to those who obey him."   Ex 1:17; Lk 24:48

[33]When they heard this, they were furious and wanted to put them to death. [34]But a Pharisee named Gamaliel, a teacher of the law, who was honored by all the people, stood up in the Sanhedrin and ordered that the men be put outside for a little while. [35]Then he addressed them: "Men of Israel, consider carefully what you intend to do to these men. [36]Some time ago Theudas appeared, claiming to be somebody, and about four hundred men rallied to him. He was killed, all his followers were dispersed, and it all came to nothing. [37]After him, Judas the Galilean appeared in the days of the census and led a band of people in revolt. He too was killed, and all his followers

were scattered. [38]Therefore, in the present case I advise you: Leave these men alone! Let them go! For if their purpose or activity is of human origin, it will fail. [39]But if it is from God, you will not be able to stop these men; you will only find yourselves fighting against God." Pr 21:30

[40]His speech persuaded them. They called the apostles in and had them flogged. Then they ordered them not to speak in the name of Jesus, and let them go. Mt 10:17

[41]The apostles left the Sanhedrin, rejoicing because they had been counted worthy of suffering disgrace for the Name. [42]Day after day, in the temple courts and from house to house, they never stopped teaching and proclaiming the good news that Jesus is the Christ.[a] Mt 5:12

The Choosing of the Seven

6 In those days when the number of disciples was increasing, the Grecian Jews among them complained against the Hebraic Jews because their widows were being overlooked in the daily distribution of food. [2]So the Twelve gathered all the disciples together and said, "It would not be right for us to neglect the ministry of the word of God in order to wait on tables. [3]Brothers, choose seven men from among you who are known to be full of the Spirit and wisdom. We will turn this responsibility over to them [4]and will give our attention to prayer and the ministry of the word." Heb 4:12

[5]This proposal pleased the whole group. They chose Stephen, a man full of faith and of the Holy Spirit; also Philip, Procorus, Nicanor, Timon, Parmenas, and Nicolas from Antioch, a convert to Judaism. [6]They presented these men to the apostles, who prayed and laid their hands on them. Ac 7:55-60

[7]So the word of God spread. The number of disciples in Jerusalem increased rapidly, and a large number of priests became obedient to the faith.

Stephen Seized

[8]Now Stephen, a man full of God's grace and power, did great wonders and miraculous signs among the people. [9]Opposition arose, however, from members of the Synagogue of the Freedmen (as it was called)—Jews of Cyrene and Alexandria as well as the provinces of Cilicia and Asia. These men began to argue with Stephen, [10]but they could not stand up against his wisdom or the Spirit by whom he spoke. Lk 21:15

[11]Then they secretly persuaded some men to say, "We have heard Stephen speak words of blasphemy against Moses and against God." 1Ki 21:10

[12]So they stirred up the

[a]42 Or Messiah

people and the elders and the teachers of the law. They seized Stephen and brought him before the Sanhedrin. ¹³They produced false witnesses, who testified, "This fellow never stops speaking against this holy place and against the law. ¹⁴For we have heard him say that this Jesus of Nazareth will destroy this place and change the customs Moses handed down to us."   Ex 23:1; Ac 21:21

¹⁵All who were sitting in the Sanhedrin looked intently at Stephen, and they saw that his face was like the face of an angel.

Stephen's Speech to the Sanhedrin

7 Then the high priest asked him, "Are these charges true?"   Jn 7:51

²To this he replied: "Brothers and fathers, listen to me! The God of glory appeared to our father Abraham while he was still in Mesopotamia, before he lived in Haran. ³'Leave your country and your people,' God said, 'and go to the land I will show you.'ᵃ   Ge 12:1

⁴"So he left the land of the Chaldeans and settled in Haran. After the death of his father, God sent him to this land where you are now living. ⁵He gave him no inheritance here, not even a foot of ground. But God promised him that he and his descendants after him

would possess the land, even though at that time Abraham had no child. ⁶God spoke to him in this way: 'Your descendants will be strangers in a country not their own, and they will be enslaved and mistreated four hundred years. ⁷But I will punish the nation they serve as slaves,' God said, 'and afterward they will come out of that country and worship me in this place.'ᵇ ⁸Then he gave Abraham the covenant of circumcision. And Abraham became the father of Isaac and circumcised him eight days after his birth. Later Isaac became the father of Jacob, and Jacob became the father of the twelve patriarchs.

⁹"Because the patriarchs were jealous of Joseph, they sold him as a slave into Egypt. But God was with him ¹⁰and rescued him from all his troubles. He gave Joseph wisdom and enabled him to gain the goodwill of Pharaoh king of Egypt; so he made him ruler over Egypt and all his palace.   Ge 37:4,11; Ge 39:2,21,23

¹¹"Then a famine struck all Egypt and Canaan, bringing great suffering, and our fathers could not find food. ¹²When Jacob heard that there was grain in Egypt, he sent our fathers on their first visit. ¹³On their second visit, Joseph told his brothers who he was, and Pharaoh learned about Joseph's family. ¹⁴After this, Joseph sent for his father Jacob and his whole

ᵃ3 Gen. 12:1   ᵇ7 Gen. 15:13,14

family, seventy-five in all. ¹⁵Then Jacob went down to Egypt, where he and our fathers died. ¹⁶Their bodies were brought back to Shechem and placed in the tomb that Abraham had bought from the sons of Hamor at Shechem for a certain sum of money. Ge 23:16-20

¹⁷"As the time drew near for God to fulfill his promise to Abraham, the number of our people in Egypt greatly increased. ¹⁸Then another king, who knew nothing about Joseph, became ruler of Egypt. ¹⁹He dealt treacherously with our people and oppressed our forefathers by forcing them to throw out their newborn babies so that they would die. Ex 1:7,16

²⁰"At that time Moses was born, and he was no ordinary child. ᵃ For three months he was cared for in his father's house. ²¹When he was placed outside, Pharaoh's daughter took him and brought him up as her own son. ²²Moses was educated in all the wisdom of the Egyptians and was powerful in speech and action. Ex 2:2; 1Ki 4:30

²³"When Moses was forty years old, he decided to visit his fellow Israelites. ²⁴He saw one of them being mistreated by an Egyptian, so he went to his defense and avenged him by killing the Egyptian. ²⁵Moses thought that his own people would realize that God was us-ing him to rescue them, but they did not. ²⁶The next day Moses came upon two Israelites who were fighting. He tried to reconcile them by saying, 'Men, you are brothers; why do you want to hurt each other?'

²⁷"But the man who was mistreating the other pushed Moses aside and said, 'Who made you ruler and judge over us? ²⁸Do you want to kill me as you killed the Egyptian yesterday?'ᵇ ²⁹When Moses heard this, he fled to Midian, where he settled as a foreigner and had two sons. Ex 2:11-15

³⁰"After forty years had passed, an angel appeared to Moses in the flames of a burning bush in the desert near Mount Sinai. ³¹When he saw this, he was amazed at the sight. As he went over to look more closely, he heard the Lord's voice: ³²'I am the God of your fathers, the God of Abraham, Isaac and Jacob.'ᶜ Moses trembled with fear and did not dare to look. Ex 3:1-4

³³"Then the Lord said to him, 'Take off your sandals; the place where you are standing is holy ground. ³⁴I have indeed seen the oppression of my people in Egypt. I have heard their groaning and have come down to set them free. Now come, I will send you back to Egypt.'ᵈ

³⁵"This is the same Moses whom they had rejected with

ᵃ20 Or *was fair in the sight of God*   ᵇ28 Exodus 2:14   ᶜ32 Exodus 3:6
ᵈ34 Exodus 3:5,7,8,10

the words, 'Who made you ruler and judge?' He was sent to be their ruler and deliverer by God himself, through the angel who appeared to him in the bush. 36He led them out of Egypt and did wonders and miraculous signs in Egypt, at the Red Sea[a] and for forty years in the desert.

37"This is that Moses who told the Israelites, 'God will send you a prophet like me from your own people.'[b] 38He was in the assembly in the desert, with the angel who spoke to him on Mount Sinai, and with our fathers; and he received living words to pass on to us.   Lev 27:34; Dt 18:15

39"But our fathers refused to obey him. Instead, they rejected him and in their hearts turned back to Egypt. 40They told Aaron, 'Make us gods who will go before us. As for this fellow Moses who led us out of Egypt—we don't know what has happened to him!'[c] 41That was the time they made an idol in the form of a calf. They brought sacrifices to it and held a celebration in honor of what their hands had made. 42But God turned away and gave them over to the worship of the heavenly bodies. This agrees with what is written in the book of the prophets: Ex 32:1,23

" 'Did you bring me sacrifices
    and offerings

forty years in the desert,
    O house of Israel?
43You have lifted up the shrine
    of Molech
and the star of your god
    Rephan,
    the idols you made to
    worship.
Therefore I will send you into
    exile'[d] beyond Babylon.

44"Our forefathers had the tabernacle of the Testimony with them in the desert. It had been made as God directed Moses, according to the pattern he had seen. 45Having received the tabernacle, our fathers under Joshua brought it with them when they took the land from the nations God drove out before them. It remained in the land until the time of David, 46who enjoyed God's favor and asked that he might provide a dwelling place for the God of Jacob.[e] 47But it was Solomon who built the house for him.

48"However, the Most High does not live in houses made by men. As the prophet says:1Ki 8:27

49" 'Heaven is my throne,
    and the earth is my
        footstool.   Mt 5:34-35
What kind of house will you
    build for me?
            says the Lord.
Or where will my resting
    place be?
50Has not my hand made all
    these things?'[f]

---

[a]36 That is, Sea of Reeds   [b]37 Deut. 18:15
[e]46 Some early manuscripts *the house of Jacob*
[c]40 Exodus 32:1   [d]43 Amos 5:25-27
[f]50 Isaiah 66:1,2

51"You stiff-necked people, with uncircumcised hearts and ears! You are just like your fathers: You always resist the Holy Spirit! 52Was there ever a prophet your fathers did not persecute? They even killed those who predicted the coming of the Righteous One. And now you have betrayed and murdered him— 53you who have received the law that was put into effect through angels but have not obeyed it." Ex 32:9; 1Th 2:15

The Stoning of Stephen

54When they heard this, they were furious and gnashed their teeth at him. 55But Stephen, full of the Holy Spirit, looked up to heaven and saw the glory of God, and Jesus standing at the right hand of God. 56"Look," he said, "I see heaven open and the Son of Man standing at the right hand of God." Ac 5:33

57At this they covered their ears and, yelling at the top of their voices, they all rushed at him, 58dragged him out of the city and began to stone him. Meanwhile, the witnesses laid their clothes at the feet of a young man named Saul. Ac 8:1

59While they were stoning him, Stephen prayed, "Lord Jesus, receive my spirit." 60Then he fell on his knees and cried out, "Lord, do not hold this sin against them." When he had said this, he fell asleep. Ps 31:5

8 And Saul was there, giving approval to his death.

The Church Persecuted and Scattered

On that day a great persecution broke out against the church at Jerusalem, and all except the apostles were scattered throughout Judea and Samaria. 2Godly men buried Stephen and mourned deeply for him. 3But Saul began to destroy the church. Going from house to house, he dragged off men and women and put them in prison.

Philip in Samaria

4Those who had been scattered preached the word wherever they went. 5Philip went down to a city in Samaria and proclaimed the Christ[a] there. 6When the crowds heard Philip and saw the miraculous signs he did, they all paid close attention to what he said. 7With shrieks, evil[b] spirits came out of many, and many paralytics and cripples were healed. 8So there was great joy in that city. Ac 6:5

Simon the Sorcerer

9Now for some time a man named Simon had practiced sorcery in the city and amazed all the people of Samaria. He boasted that he was someone great, 10and all the people, both high and low, gave him their attention and exclaimed, "This man is the divine power known

---

a5 Or *Messiah*   *b7* Greek *unclean*

as the Great Power." ¹¹They followed him because he had amazed them for a long time with his magic. ¹²But when they believed Philip as he preached the good news of the kingdom of God and the name of Jesus Christ, they were baptized, both men and women. ¹³Simon himself believed and was baptized. And he followed Philip everywhere, astonished by the great signs and miracles he saw.

¹⁴When the apostles in Jerusalem heard that Samaria had accepted the word of God, they sent Peter and John to them. ¹⁵When they arrived, they prayed for them that they might receive the Holy Spirit, ¹⁶because the Holy Spirit had not yet come upon any of them; they had simply been baptized into*a* the name of the Lord Jesus. ¹⁷Then Peter and John placed their hands on them, and they received the Holy Spirit.   Mt 28:19; Ac 6:6

¹⁸When Simon saw that the Spirit was given at the laying on of the apostles' hands, he offered them money ¹⁹and said, "Give me also this ability so that everyone on whom I lay my hands may receive the Holy Spirit."

²⁰Peter answered: "May your money perish with you, because you thought you could buy the gift of God with money! ²¹You have no part or share in this ministry, because your heart is not right before God. ²²Repent of this wickedness and pray to the Lord. Perhaps he will forgive you for having such a thought in your heart. ²³For I see that you are full of bitterness and captive to sin."   2Ki 5:16

²⁴Then Simon answered, "Pray to the Lord for me so that nothing you have said may happen to me."   Ex 8:8; Nu 21:7

²⁵When they had testified and proclaimed the word of the Lord, Peter and John returned to Jerusalem, preaching the gospel in many Samaritan villages.

Philip and the Ethiopian

²⁶Now an angel of the Lord said to Philip, "Go south to the road—the desert road—that goes down from Jerusalem to Gaza." ²⁷So he started out, and on his way he met an Ethiopian*b* eunuch, an important official in charge of all the treasury of Candace, queen of the Ethiopians. This man had gone to Jerusalem to worship, ²⁸and on his way home was sitting in his chariot reading the book of Isaiah the prophet. ²⁹The Spirit told Philip, "Go to that chariot and stay near it."   1Ki 8:41-43

³⁰Then Philip ran up to the chariot and heard the man reading Isaiah the prophet. "Do you understand what you are reading?" Philip asked.

³¹"How can I," he said, "unless someone explains it to me?"

*a*16 Or *in*   *b*27 That is, from the upper Nile region

So he invited Philip to come up and sit with him. Isa 56:3-7

³²The eunuch was reading this passage of Scripture:

"He was led like a sheep to
the slaughter,
and as a lamb before the
shearer is silent,
so he did not open his
mouth.
³³In his humiliation he was
deprived of justice.
Who can speak of his
descendants?
For his life was taken from
the earth."*a*

³⁴The eunuch asked Philip, "Tell me, please, who is the prophet talking about, himself or someone else?" ³⁵Then Philip began with that very passage of Scripture and told him the good news about Jesus. Lk 24:27

³⁶As they traveled along the road, they came to some water and the eunuch said, "Look, here is water. Why shouldn't I be baptized?"*b* ³⁸And he gave orders to stop the chariot. Then both Philip and the eunuch went down into the water and Philip baptized him. ³⁹When they came up out of the water, the Spirit of the Lord suddenly took Philip away, and the eunuch did not see him again, but went on his way rejoicing. ⁴⁰Philip, however, appeared at

Azotus and traveled about, preaching the gospel in all the towns until he reached Caesarea. Ac 2:38

Saul's Conversion

9 Meanwhile, Saul was still breathing out murderous threats against the Lord's disciples. He went to the high priest ²and asked him for letters to the synagogues in Damascus, so that if he found any there who belonged to the Way, whether men or women, he might take them as prisoners to Jerusalem. ³As he neared Damascus on his journey, suddenly a light from heaven flashed around him. ⁴He fell to the ground and heard a voice say to him, "Saul, Saul, why do you persecute me?"

⁵"Who are you, Lord?" Saul asked.

"I am Jesus, whom you are persecuting," he replied. ⁶"Now get up and go into the city, and you will be told what you must do." Eze 3:22

⁷The men traveling with Saul stood there speechless; they heard the sound but did not see anyone. ⁸Saul got up from the ground, but when he opened his eyes he could see nothing. So they led him by the hand into Damascus. ⁹For three days he was blind, and did not eat or drink anything. Da 10:7; Jn 12:29

¹⁰In Damascus there was a

---

a33 Isaiah 53:7,8   *b36* Some late manuscripts *baptized?" ³⁷Philip said, "If you believe with all your heart, you may." The eunuch answered, "I believe that Jesus Christ is the Son of God."*

disciple named Ananias. The Lord called to him in a vision, "Ananias!"   Ac 10:3; 12:9

"Yes, Lord," he answered.

[11]The Lord told him, "Go to the house of Judas on Straight Street and ask for a man from Tarsus named Saul, for he is praying. [12]In a vision he has seen a man named Ananias come and place his hands on him to restore his sight."   Mk 5:23

[13]"Lord," Ananias answered, "I have heard many reports about this man and all the harm he has done to your saints in Jerusalem. [14]And he has come here with authority from the chief priests to arrest all who call on your name."   Ac 26:10

[15]But the Lord said to Ananias, "Go! This man is my chosen instrument to carry my name before the Gentiles and their kings and before the people of Israel. [16]I will show him how much he must suffer for my name."   Ac 13:2; 2Co 6:4-10

[17]Then Ananias went to the house and entered it. Placing his hands on Saul, he said, "Brother Saul, the Lord—Jesus, who appeared to you on the road as you were coming here—has sent me so that you may see again and be filled with the Holy Spirit." [18]Immediately, something like scales fell from Saul's eyes, and he could see again. He got up and was baptized, [19]and after taking some food, he regained his strength.

Saul in Damascus and Jerusalem

Saul spent several days with the disciples in Damascus. [20]At once he began to preach in the synagogues that Jesus is the Son of God. [21]All those who heard him were astonished and asked, "Isn't he the man who raised havoc in Jerusalem among those who call on this name? And hasn't he come here to take them as prisoners to the chief priests?" [22]Yet Saul grew more and more powerful and baffled the Jews living in Damascus by proving that Jesus is the Christ. [a]   Ac 8:3; 17:3

[23]After many days had gone by, the Jews conspired to kill him, [24]but Saul learned of their plan. Day and night they kept close watch on the city gates in order to kill him. [25]But his followers took him by night and lowered him in a basket through an opening in the wall.

[26]When he came to Jerusalem, he tried to join the disciples, but they were all afraid of him, not believing that he really was a disciple. [27]But Barnabas took him and brought him to the apostles. He told them how Saul on his journey had seen the Lord and that the Lord had spoken to him, and how in Damascus he had preached fearlessly in the name of Jesus. [28]So Saul stayed with them and moved about freely in Jerusalem, speaking boldly in the

[a]22 Or Messiah

name of the Lord. [29]He talked and debated with the Grecian Jews, but they tried to kill him. [30]When the brothers learned of this, they took him down to Caesarea and sent him off to Tarsus.   2Co 11:26

[31]Then the church throughout Judea, Galilee and Samaria enjoyed a time of peace. It was strengthened; and encouraged by the Holy Spirit, it grew in numbers, living in the fear of the Lord.

Aeneas and Dorcas

[32]As Peter traveled about the country, he went to visit the saints in Lydda. [33]There he found a man named Aeneas, a paralytic who had been bedridden for eight years. [34]"Aeneas," Peter said to him, "Jesus Christ heals you. Get up and take care of your mat." Immediately Aeneas got up. [35]All those who lived in Lydda and Sharon saw him and turned to the Lord.

[36]In Joppa there was a disciple named Tabitha (which, when translated, is Dorcas[a]), who was always doing good and helping the poor. [37]About that time she became sick and died, and her body was washed and placed in an upstairs room. [38]Lydda was near Joppa; so when the disciples heard that Peter was in Lydda, they sent two men to him and urged him, "Please come at once!"   Tit 3:8

[39]Peter went with them, and when he arrived he was taken upstairs to the room. All the widows stood around him, crying and showing him the robes and other clothing that Dorcas had made while she was still with them.   1Ti 5:3

[40]Peter sent them all out of the room; then he got down on his knees and prayed. Turning toward the dead woman, he said, "Tabitha, get up." She opened her eyes, and seeing Peter she sat up. [41]He took her by the hand and helped her to her feet. Then he called the believers and the widows and presented her to them alive. [42]This became known all over Joppa, and many people believed in the Lord. [43]Peter stayed in Joppa for some time with a tanner named Simon.

Cornelius Calls for Peter

10 At Caesarea there was a man named Cornelius, a centurion in what was known as the Italian Regiment. [2]He and all his family were devout and God-fearing; he gave generously to those in need and prayed to God regularly. [3]One day at about three in the afternoon he had a vision. He distinctly saw an angel of God, who came to him and said, "Cornelius!"

[4]Cornelius stared at him in fear. "What is it, Lord?" he asked.

The angel answered, "Your prayers and gifts to the poor

---

[a]36 Both *Tabitha* (Aramaic) and *Dorcas* (Greek) mean *gazelle*.

have come up as a memorial offering before God. ⁵Now send men to Joppa to bring back a man named Simon who is called Peter. ⁶He is staying with Simon the tanner, whose house is by the sea." Ps 20:3; Ac 9:43

⁷When the angel who spoke to him had gone, Cornelius called two of his servants and a devout soldier who was one of his attendants. ⁸He told them everything that had happened and sent them to Joppa.

Peter's Vision

⁹About noon the following day as they were on their journey and approaching the city, Peter went up on the roof to pray. ¹⁰He became hungry and wanted something to eat, and while the meal was being prepared, he fell into a trance. ¹¹He saw heaven opened and something like a large sheet being let down to earth by its four corners. ¹²It contained all kinds of four-footed animals, as well as reptiles of the earth and birds of the air. ¹³Then a voice told him, "Get up, Peter. Kill and eat."

¹⁴"Surely not, Lord!" Peter replied. "I have never eaten anything impure or unclean."

¹⁵The voice spoke to him a second time, "Do not call anything impure that God has made clean." Ge 9:3; Mt 15:11

¹⁶This happened three times, and immediately the sheet was taken back to heaven.

¹⁷While Peter was wondering about the meaning of the vision, the men sent by Cornelius found out where Simon's house was and stopped at the gate. ¹⁸They called out, asking if Simon who was known as Peter was staying there. Ac 9:10

¹⁹While Peter was still thinking about the vision, the Spirit said to him, "Simon, three*ᵃ* men are looking for you. ²⁰So get up and go downstairs. Do not hesitate to go with them, for I have sent them." Ac 15:7-9

²¹Peter went down and said to the men, "I'm the one you're looking for. Why have you come?"

²²The men replied, "We have come from Cornelius the centurion. He is a righteous and God-fearing man, who is respected by all the Jewish people. A holy angel told him to have you come to his house so that he could hear what you have to say." ²³Then Peter invited the men into the house to be his guests. Ac 11:14

Peter at Cornelius' House

The next day Peter started out with them, and some of the brothers from Joppa went along. ²⁴The following day he arrived in Caesarea. Cornelius was expecting them and had called together his relatives and close friends. ²⁵As Peter entered the house, Cornelius met him and fell at his feet in reverence.

ᵃ19 One early manuscript *two*; other manuscripts do not have the number.

26But Peter made him get up. "Stand up," he said, "I am only a man myself."   Ac 14:15; Rev 19:10

27Talking with him, Peter went inside and found a large gathering of people. 28He said to them: "You are well aware that it is against our law for a Jew to associate with a Gentile or visit him. But God has shown me that I should not call any man impure or unclean. 29So when I was sent for, I came without raising any objection. May I ask why you sent for me?"   Jn 4:9

30Cornelius answered: "Four days ago I was in my house praying at this hour, at three in the afternoon. Suddenly a man in shining clothes stood before me 31and said, 'Cornelius, God has heard your prayer and remembered your gifts to the poor. 32Send to Joppa for Simon who is called Peter. He is a guest in the home of Simon the tanner, who lives by the sea.' 33So I sent for you immediately, and it was good of you to come. Now we are all here in the presence of God to listen to everything the Lord has commanded you to tell us."

34Then Peter began to speak: "I now realize how true it is that God does not show favoritism 35but accepts men from every nation who fear him and do what is right. 36You know the message God sent to the people of Israel, telling the good news of peace through Jesus Christ, who is Lord of all. 37You know what has happened throughout Judea, beginning in Galilee after the baptism that John preached— 38how God anointed Jesus of Nazareth with the Holy Spirit and power, and how he went around doing good and healing all who were under the power of the devil, because God was with him.   Dt 10:17; Gal 2:6

39"We are witnesses of everything he did in the country of the Jews and in Jerusalem. They killed him by hanging him on a tree, 40but God raised him from the dead on the third day and caused him to be seen. 41He was not seen by all the people, but by witnesses whom God had already chosen—by us who ate and drank with him after he rose from the dead. 42He commanded us to preach to the people and to testify that he is the one whom God appointed as judge of the living and the dead. 43All the prophets testify about him that everyone who believes in him receives forgiveness of sins through his name."

44While Peter was still speaking these words, the Holy Spirit came on all who heard the message. 45The circumcised believers who had come with Peter were astonished that the gift of the Holy Spirit had been poured out even on the Gentiles. 46For they heard them speaking in tongues*a* and praising God.   Mk 16:17; Ac 8:15

a46 Or other languages

Then Peter said, [47]"Can anyone keep these people from being baptized with water? They have received the Holy Spirit just as we have." [48]So he ordered that they be baptized in the name of Jesus Christ. Then they asked Peter to stay with them for a few days. Ac 8:36

Peter Explains His Actions

11 The apostles and the brothers throughout Judea heard that the Gentiles also had received the word of God. [2]So when Peter went up to Jerusalem, the circumcised believers criticized him [3]and said, "You went into the house of uncircumcised men and ate with them." Ac 10:28,45; Gal 2:12

[4]Peter began and explained everything to them precisely as it had happened: [5]"I was in the city of Joppa praying, and in a trance I saw a vision. I saw something like a large sheet being let down from heaven by its four corners, and it came down to where I was. [6]I looked into it and saw four-footed animals of the earth, wild beasts, reptiles, and birds of the air. [7]Then I heard a voice telling me, 'Get up, Peter. Kill and eat.' Ac 10:9-32

[8]"I replied, 'Surely not, Lord! Nothing impure or unclean has ever entered my mouth.'

[9]"The voice spoke from heaven a second time, 'Do not call anything impure that God has made clean.' [10]This hap-

pened three times, and then it was all pulled up to heaven again.

[11]"Right then three men who had been sent to me from Caesarea stopped at the house where I was staying. [12]The Spirit told me to have no hesitation about going with them. These six brothers also went with me, and we entered the man's house. [13]He told us how he had seen an angel appear in his house and say, 'Send to Joppa for Simon who is called Peter. [14]He will bring you a message through which you and all your household will be saved.'

[15]"As I began to speak, the Holy Spirit came on them as he had come on us at the beginning. [16]Then I remembered what the Lord had said: 'John baptized with[a] water, but you will be baptized with the Holy Spirit.' [17]So if God gave them the same gift as he gave us, who believed in the Lord Jesus Christ, who was I to think that I could oppose God?" Ac 10:44

[18]When they heard this, they had no further objections and praised God, saying, "So then, God has granted even the Gentiles repentance unto life." 2Co 7:10

The Church in Antioch

[19]Now those who had been scattered by the persecution in connection with Stephen traveled as far as Phoenicia, Cyprus and Antioch, telling the mes-

[a]16 Or *in*

sage only to Jews. ²⁰Some of them, however, men from Cyprus and Cyrene, went to Antioch and began to speak to Greeks also, telling them the good news about the Lord Jesus. ²¹The Lord's hand was with them, and a great number of people believed and turned to the Lord. Ac 8:1,4

²²News of this reached the ears of the church at Jerusalem, and they sent Barnabas to Antioch. ²³When he arrived and saw the evidence of the grace of God, he was glad and encouraged them all to remain true to the Lord with all their hearts. ²⁴He was a good man, full of the Holy Spirit and faith, and a great number of people were brought to the Lord. Ac 4:36

²⁵Then Barnabas went to Tarsus to look for Saul, ²⁶and when he found him, he brought him to Antioch. So for a whole year Barnabas and Saul met with the church and taught great numbers of people. The disciples were called Christians first at Antioch. Ac 9:11

²⁷During this time some prophets came down from Jerusalem to Antioch. ²⁸One of them, named Agabus, stood up and through the Spirit predicted that a severe famine would spread over the entire Roman world. (This happened during the reign of Claudius.) ²⁹The disciples, each according to his ability, decided to provide help for the brothers living in Judea. ³⁰This they did, sending their gift to the elders by Barnabas and Saul. Ac 13:1; Ro 15:26

Peter's Miraculous Escape From Prison

12 It was about this time that King Herod arrested some who belonged to the church, intending to persecute them. ²He had James, the brother of John, put to death with the sword. ³When he saw that this pleased the Jews, he proceeded to seize Peter also. This happened during the Feast of Unleavened Bread. ⁴After arresting him, he put him in prison, handing him over to be guarded by four squads of four soldiers each. Herod intended to bring him out for public trial after the Passover. Mt 14:1; Jn 11:55

⁵So Peter was kept in prison, but the church was earnestly praying to God for him. Ac 1:14

⁶The night before Herod was to bring him to trial, Peter was sleeping between two soldiers, bound with two chains, and sentries stood guard at the entrance. ⁷Suddenly an angel of the Lord appeared and a light shone in the cell. He struck Peter on the side and woke him up. "Quick, get up!" he said, and the chains fell off Peter's wrists. Ps 107:14; Ac 16:26

⁸Then the angel said to him, "Put on your clothes and sandals." And Peter did so. "Wrap your cloak around you and follow me," the angel told him. ⁹Peter followed him out of the

prison, but he had no idea that what the angel was doing was really happening; he thought he was seeing a vision. [10]They passed the first and second guards and came to the iron gate leading to the city. It opened for them by itself, and they went through it. When they had walked the length of one street, suddenly the angel left him.   Ac 5:19

[11]Then Peter came to himself and said, "Now I know without a doubt that the Lord sent his angel and rescued me from Herod's clutches and from everything the Jewish people were anticipating."   Ps 34:7; 2Co 1:10

[12]When this had dawned on him, he went to the house of Mary the mother of John, also called Mark, where many people had gathered and were praying. [13]Peter knocked at the outer entrance, and a servant girl named Rhoda came to answer the door. [14]When she recognized Peter's voice, she was so overjoyed she ran back without opening it and exclaimed, "Peter is at the door!"

[15]"You're out of your mind," they told her. When she kept insisting that it was so, they said, "It must be his angel."

[16]But Peter kept on knocking, and when they opened the door and saw him, they were astonished. [17]Peter motioned with his hand for them to be quiet and described how the Lord had brought him out of prison. "Tell James and the brothers about this," he said, and then he left for another place.

[18]In the morning, there was no small commotion among the soldiers as to what had become of Peter. [19]After Herod had a thorough search made for him and did not find him, he cross-examined the guards and ordered that they be executed.

Herod's Death

Then Herod went from Judea to Caesarea and stayed there a while. [20]He had been quarreling with the people of Tyre and Sidon; they now joined together and sought an audience with him. Having secured the support of Blastus, a trusted personal servant of the king, they asked for peace, because they depended on the king's country for their food supply.

[21]On the appointed day Herod, wearing his royal robes, sat on his throne and delivered a public address to the people. [22]They shouted, "This is the voice of a god, not of a man." [23]Immediately, because Herod did not give praise to God, an angel of the Lord struck him down, and he was eaten by worms and died.   Ac 5:19

[24]But the word of God continued to increase and spread.

[25]When Barnabas and Saul had finished their mission, they returned from[a] Jerusalem, tak-

[a]25 Some manuscripts to

ing with them John, also called
Mark.   Ac 4:36; 11:30

Barnabas and Saul Sent Off

13 In the church at Antioch
there were prophets and
teachers: Barnabas, Simeon
called Niger, Lucius of Cyrene,
Manaen (who had been brought
up with Herod the tetrarch) and
Saul. 2While they were worshiping the Lord and fasting,
the Holy Spirit said, "Set apart
for me Barnabas and Saul for
the work to which I have called
them." 3So after they had fasted
and prayed, they placed their
hands on them and sent them
off.   Ac 9:15; 14:26; Eph 4:11

On Cyprus

4The two of them, sent on
their way by the Holy Spirit,
went down to Seleucia and
sailed from there to Cyprus.
5When they arrived at Salamis,
they proclaimed the word of
God in the Jewish synagogues.
John was with them as their
helper.   Heb 4:12
6They traveled through the
whole island until they came to
Paphos. There they met a
Jewish sorcerer and false
prophet named Bar-Jesus, 7who
was an attendant of the proconsul, Sergius Paulus. The proconsul, an intelligent man, sent
for Barnabas and Saul because
he wanted to hear the word of
God. 8But Elymas the sorcerer
(for that is what his name
means) opposed them and tried
to turn the proconsul from the

faith. 9Then Saul, who was also
called Paul, filled with the Holy
Spirit, looked straight at Elymas
and said, 10"You are a child of
the devil and an enemy of
everything that is right! You are
full of all kinds of deceit and
trickery. Will you never stop
perverting the right ways of the
Lord? 11Now the hand of the
Lord is against you. You are going to be blind, and for a time
you will be unable to see the
light of the sun."   Ps 32:4; Ac 8:9
Immediately mist and dark-
ness came over him, and he
groped about, seeking someone
to lead him by the hand. 12When
the proconsul saw what had
happened, he believed, for he
was amazed at the teaching
about the Lord.

In Pisidian Antioch

13From Paphos, Paul and his
companions sailed to Perga in
Pamphylia, where John left
them to return to Jerusalem.
14From Perga they went on to
Pisidian Antioch. On the Sabbath they entered the synagogue and sat down. 15After the
reading from the Law and the
Prophets, the synagogue rulers
sent word to them, saying,
"Brothers, if you have a message of encouragement for the
people, please speak."   Ac 15:21
16Standing up, Paul motioned
with his hand and said: "Men of
Israel and you Gentiles who
worship God, listen to me!
17The God of the people of Israel
chose our fathers; he made the

people prosper during their stay in Egypt, with mighty power he led them out of that country, [18]he endured their conduct[a] for about forty years in the desert, [19]he overthrew seven nations in Canaan and gave their land to his people as their inheritance. [20]All this took about 450 years.   Ex 6:6

"After this, God gave them judges until the time of Samuel the prophet. [21]Then the people asked for a king, and he gave them Saul son of Kish, of the tribe of Benjamin, who ruled forty years. [22]After removing Saul, he made David their king. He testified concerning him: 'I have found David son of Jesse a man after my own heart; he will do everything I want him to do.'

[23]"From this man's descendants God has brought to Israel the Savior Jesus, as he promised. [24]Before the coming of Jesus, John preached repentance and baptism to all the people of Israel. [25]As John was completing his work, he said: 'Who do you think I am? I am not that one. No, but he is coming after me, whose sandals I am not worthy to untie.'   Mt 1:1

[26]"Brothers, children of Abraham, and you God-fearing Gentiles, it is to us that this message of salvation has been sent. [27]The people of Jerusalem and their rulers did not recognize Jesus, yet in condemning him they fulfilled the words of the prophets that are read every Sabbath. [28]Though they found no proper ground for a death sentence, they asked Pilate to have him executed. [29]When they had carried out all that was written about him, they took him down from the tree and laid him in a tomb. [30]But God raised him from the dead, [31]and for many days he was seen by those who had traveled with him from Galilee to Jerusalem. They are now his witnesses to our people.

[32]"We tell you the good news: What God promised our fathers [33]he has fulfilled for us, their children, by raising up Jesus. As it is written in the second Psalm:

" 'You are my Son;
    today I have become your
        Father.[b][c]

[34]The fact that God raised him from the dead, never to decay, is stated in these words:

" 'I will give you the holy
    and sure blessings
        promised to David.'[d]

[35]So it is stated elsewhere:

" 'You will not let your Holy
    One see decay.'[e]

[36]"For when David had served God's purpose in his own generation, he fell asleep; he was buried with his fathers and his body decayed. [37]But the

---

[a]18 Some manuscripts and cared for them   [b]33 Or have begotten you   [c]33 Psalm 2:7
[d]34 Isaiah 55:3   [e]35 Psalm 16:10

one whom God raised from the dead did not see decay. Ac 2:24

³⁸"Therefore, my brothers, I want you to know that through Jesus the forgiveness of sins is proclaimed to you. ³⁹Through him everyone who believes is justified from everything you could not be justified from by the law of Moses. ⁴⁰Take care that what the prophets have said does not happen to you:

⁴¹" 'Look, you scoffers,
    wonder and perish,
for I am going to do
        something in your days
    that you would never
        believe,
    even if someone told
        you.'*a*"

⁴²As Paul and Barnabas were leaving the synagogue, the people invited them to speak further about these things on the next Sabbath. ⁴³When the congregation was dismissed, many of the Jews and devout converts to Judaism followed Paul and Barnabas, who talked with them and urged them to continue in the grace of God.

⁴⁴On the next Sabbath almost the whole city gathered to hear the word of the Lord. ⁴⁵When the Jews saw the crowds, they were filled with jealousy and talked abusively against what Paul was saying. Ac 18:6

⁴⁶Then Paul and Barnabas answered them boldly: "We had to speak the word of God to you first. Since you reject it and do not consider yourselves worthy of eternal life, we now turn to the Gentiles. ⁴⁷For this is what the Lord has commanded us:

" 'I have made you*b* a light
        for the Gentiles,   Lk 2:32
    that you*b* may bring
        salvation to the ends of
        the earth.'*c*"

⁴⁸When the Gentiles heard this, they were glad and honored the word of the Lord; and all who were appointed for eternal life believed.

⁴⁹The word of the Lord spread through the whole region. ⁵⁰But the Jews incited the God-fearing women of high standing and the leading men of the city. They stirred up persecution against Paul and Barnabas, and expelled them from their region. ⁵¹So they shook the dust from their feet in protest against them and went to Iconium. ⁵²And the disciples were filled with joy and with the Holy Spirit.   1Th 2:16

In Iconium

14 At Iconium Paul and Barnabas went as usual into the Jewish synagogue. There they spoke so effectively that a great number of Jews and Gentiles believed. ²But the Jews who refused to believe stirred up the Gentiles and poisoned their minds against the brothers. ³So Paul and Barnabas

a41 Hab. 1:5   *b47* The Greek is singular.   *c47* Isaiah 49:6

spent considerable time there, speaking boldly for the Lord, who confirmed the message of his grace by enabling them to do miraculous signs and wonders. [4]The people of the city were divided; some sided with the Jews, others with the apostles. [5]There was a plot afoot among the Gentiles and Jews, together with their leaders, to mistreat them and stone them. [6]But they found out about it and fled to the Lycaonian cities of Lystra and Derbe and to the surrounding country, [7]where they continued to preach the good news.

In Lystra and Derbe

[8]In Lystra there sat a man crippled in his feet, who was lame from birth and had never walked. [9]He listened to Paul as he was speaking. Paul looked directly at him, saw that he had faith to be healed [10]and called out, "Stand up on your feet!" At that, the man jumped up and began to walk.   Eze 2:1; Ac 3:2

[11]When the crowd saw what Paul had done, they shouted in the Lycaonian language, "The gods have come down to us in human form!" [12]Barnabas they called Zeus, and Paul they called Hermes because he was the chief speaker. [13]The priest of Zeus, whose temple was just outside the city, brought bulls and wreaths to the city gates because he and the crowd wanted to offer sacrifices to them.

[14]But when the apostles Barnabas and Paul heard of this, they tore their clothes and rushed out into the crowd, shouting: [15]"Men, why are you doing this? We too are only men, human like you. We are bringing you good news, telling you to turn from these worthless things to the living God, who made heaven and earth and sea and everything in them. [16]In the past, he let all nations go their own way. [17]Yet he has not left himself without testimony: He has shown kindness by giving you rain from heaven and crops in their seasons; he provides you with plenty of food and fills your hearts with joy." [18]Even with these words, they had difficulty keeping the crowd from sacrificing to them.

[19]Then some Jews came from Antioch and Iconium and won the crowd over. They stoned Paul and dragged him outside the city, thinking he was dead. [20]But after the disciples had gathered around him, he got up and went back into the city. The next day he and Barnabas left for Derbe.   2Co 11:25; 2Ti 3:11

The Return to Antioch in Syria

[21]They preached the good news in that city and won a large number of disciples. Then they returned to Lystra, Iconium and Antioch, [22]strengthening the disciples and encouraging them to remain true to the faith. "We must go through many hardships to enter the

kingdom of God," they said. [23]Paul and Barnabas appointed elders[a] for them in each church and, with prayer and fasting, committed them to the Lord, in whom they had put their trust. [24]After going through Pisidia, they came into Pamphylia, [25]and when they had preached the word in Perga, they went down to Attalia.   Jn 16:33

[26]From Attalia they sailed back to Antioch, where they had been committed to the grace of God for the work they had now completed. [27]On arriving there, they gathered the church together and reported all that God had done through them and how he had opened the door of faith to the Gentiles. [28]And they stayed there a long time with the disciples.   1Co 16:9

The Council at Jerusalem

15 Some men came down from Judea to Antioch and were teaching the brothers: "Unless you are circumcised, according to the custom taught by Moses, you cannot be saved." [2]This brought Paul and Barnabas into sharp dispute and debate with them. So Paul and Barnabas were appointed, along with some other believers, to go up to Jerusalem to see the apostles and elders about this question. [3]The church sent them on their way, and as they traveled through Phoenicia and Samaria, they told how the Gentiles had been converted. This news made all the brothers very glad. [4]When they came to Jerusalem, they were welcomed by the church and the apostles and elders, to whom they reported everything God had done through them.

[5]Then some of the believers who belonged to the party of the Pharisees stood up and said, "The Gentiles must be circumcised and required to obey the law of Moses."

[6]The apostles and elders met to consider this question. [7]After much discussion, Peter got up and addressed them: "Brothers, you know that some time ago God made a choice among you that the Gentiles might hear from my lips the message of the gospel and believe. [8]God, who knows the heart, showed that he accepted them by giving the Holy Spirit to them, just as he did to us. [9]He made no distinction between us and them, for he purified their hearts by faith. [10]Now then, why do you try to test God by putting on the necks of the disciples a yoke that neither we nor our fathers have been able to bear? [11]No! We believe it is through the grace of our Lord Jesus that we are saved, just as they are."

[12]The whole assembly became silent as they listened to Barnabas and Paul telling about the miraculous signs and wonders God had done among the

[a]23 Or *Barnabas ordained elders*; or *Barnabas had elders elected*

Gentiles through them. ¹³When they finished, James spoke up: "Brothers, listen to me. ¹⁴Simon*ª* has described to us how God at first showed his concern by taking from the Gentiles a people for himself. ¹⁵The words of the prophets are in agreement with this, as it is written:

¹⁶" 'After this I will return
      and rebuild David's fallen
      tent.
   Its ruins I will rebuild,
      and I will restore it,
¹⁷that the remnant of men may
      seek the Lord,
   and all the Gentiles who
      bear my name,
   says the Lord, who does
      these things'*ᵇ*
¹⁸   that have been known for
      ages.*ᶜ*   Isa 45:21

¹⁹"It is my judgment, therefore, that we should not make it difficult for the Gentiles who are turning to God. ²⁰Instead we should write to them, telling them to abstain from food polluted by idols, from sexual immorality, from the meat of strangled animals and from blood. ²¹For Moses has been preached in every city from the earliest times and is read in the synagogues on every Sabbath."

The Council's Letter to Gentile Believers

²²Then the apostles and elders, with the whole church, decided to choose some of their own men and send them to Antioch with Paul and Barnabas. They chose Judas (called Barsabbas) and Silas, two men who were leaders among the brothers. ²³With them they sent the following letter: Ac 11:30

The apostles and elders, your brothers,

To the Gentile believers in Antioch, Syria and Cilicia:

Greetings.

²⁴We have heard that some went out from us without our authorization and disturbed you, troubling your minds by what they said. ²⁵So we all agreed to choose some men and send them to you with our dear friends Barnabas and Paul— ²⁶men who have risked their lives for the name of our Lord Jesus Christ. ²⁷Therefore we are sending Judas and Silas to confirm by word of mouth what we are writing. ²⁸It seemed good to the Holy Spirit and to us not to burden you with anything beyond the following requirements: ²⁹You are to abstain from food sacrificed to idols, from blood, from the meat of strangled animals and from sexual immoral-

ª14 Greek *Simeon,* a variant of *Simon;* that is, Peter   *ᵇ17* Amos 9:11,12
ᶜ17,18 Some manuscripts *things'— / ¹⁸known to the Lord for ages is his work*

ity. You will do well to avoid these things.

Farewell. Gal 1:7

30The men were sent off and went down to Antioch, where they gathered the church together and delivered the letter. 31The people read it and were glad for its encouraging message. 32Judas and Silas, who themselves were prophets, said much to encourage and strengthen the brothers. 33After spending some time there, they were sent off by the brothers with the blessing of peace to return to those who had sent them.*a* 35But Paul and Barnabas remained in Antioch, where they and many others taught and preached the word of the Lord. Ac 8:4; 1Co 16:11

Disagreement Between Paul and Barnabas

36Some time later Paul said to Barnabas, "Let us go back and visit the brothers in all the towns where we preached the word of the Lord and see how they are doing." 37Barnabas wanted to take John, also called Mark, with them, 38but Paul did not think it wise to take him, because he had deserted them in Pamphylia and had not continued with them in the work. 39They had such a sharp disagreement that they parted company. Barnabas took Mark and sailed for Cyprus, 40but

Paul chose Silas and left, commended by the brothers to the grace of the Lord. 41He went through Syria and Cilicia, strengthening the churches.

Timothy Joins Paul and Silas

16 He came to Derbe and then to Lystra, where a disciple named Timothy lived, whose mother was a Jewess and a believer, but whose father was a Greek. 2The brothers at Lystra and Iconium spoke well of him. 3Paul wanted to take him along on the journey, so he circumcised him because of the Jews who lived in that area, for they all knew that his father was a Greek. 4As they traveled from town to town, they delivered the decisions reached by the apostles and elders in Jerusalem for the people to obey. 5So the churches were strengthened in the faith and grew daily in numbers. Ac 9:31; 15:28,29; 1Co 4:17

Paul's Vision of the Man of Macedonia

6Paul and his companions traveled throughout the region of Phrygia and Galatia, having been kept by the Holy Spirit from preaching the word in the province of Asia. 7When they came to the border of Mysia, they tried to enter Bithynia, but the Spirit of Jesus would not allow them to. 8So they passed by Mysia and went down to Troas. 9During the night Paul had a vi-

---

*a*33 Some manuscripts *them,* 34*but Silas decided to remain there*

sion of a man of Macedonia standing and begging him, "Come over to Macedonia and help us." [10]After Paul had seen the vision, we got ready at once to leave for Macedonia, concluding that God had called us to preach the gospel to them.

Lydia's Conversion in Philippi

[11]From Troas we put out to sea and sailed straight for Samothrace, and the next day on to Neapolis. [12]From there we traveled to Philippi, a Roman colony and the leading city of that district of Macedonia. And we stayed there several days.

[13]On the Sabbath we went outside the city gate to the river, where we expected to find a place of prayer. We sat down and began to speak to the women who had gathered there. [14]One of those listening was a woman named Lydia, a dealer in purple cloth from the city of Thyatira, who was a worshiper of God. The Lord opened her heart to respond to Paul's message. [15]When she and the members of her household were baptized, she invited us to her home. "If you consider me a believer in the Lord," she said, "come and stay at my house." And she persuaded us.   Lk 24:45

Paul and Silas in Prison

[16]Once when we were going to the place of prayer, we were met by a slave girl who had a spirit by which she predicted the future. She earned a great deal of money for her owners by fortune-telling. [17]This girl followed Paul and the rest of us, shouting, "These men are servants of the Most High God, who are telling you the way to be saved." [18]She kept this up for many days. Finally Paul became so troubled that he turned around and said to the spirit, "In the name of Jesus Christ I command you to come out of her!" At that moment the spirit left her.   Mk 5:7; 16:17

[19]When the owners of the slave girl realized that their hope of making money was gone, they seized Paul and Silas and dragged them into the marketplace to face the authorities. [20]They brought them before the magistrates and said, "These men are Jews, and are throwing our city into an uproar [21]by advocating customs unlawful for us Romans to accept or practice."   Est 3:8; Ac 19:25-26

[22]The crowd joined in the attack against Paul and Silas, and the magistrates ordered them to be stripped and beaten. [23]After they had been severely flogged, they were thrown into prison, and the jailer was commanded to guard them carefully. [24]Upon receiving such orders, he put them in the inner cell and fastened their feet in the stocks.

[25]About midnight Paul and Silas were praying and singing hymns to God, and the other prisoners were listening to

them. [26]Suddenly there was such a violent earthquake that the foundations of the prison were shaken. At once all the prison doors flew open, and everybody's chains came loose. [27]The jailer woke up, and when he saw the prison doors open, he drew his sword and was about to kill himself because he thought the prisoners had escaped. [28]But Paul shouted, "Don't harm yourself! We are all here!" Ps 119:55; Ac 12:19

[29]The jailer called for lights, rushed in and fell trembling before Paul and Silas. [30]He then brought them out and asked, "Sirs, what must I do to be saved?" Ac 2:37,38

[31]They replied, "Believe in the Lord Jesus, and you will be saved—you and your household." [32]Then they spoke the word of the Lord to him and to all the others in his house. [33]At that hour of the night the jailer took them and washed their wounds; then immediately he and all his family were baptized. [34]The jailer brought them into his house and set a meal before them; he was filled with joy because he had come to believe in God—he and his whole family. Jn 3:15; Ac 11:14

[35]When it was daylight, the magistrates sent their officers to the jailer with the order: "Release those men." [36]The jailer told Paul, "The magistrates have ordered that you and Silas

be released. Now you can leave. Go in peace." Ac 15:33

[37]But Paul said to the officers: "They beat us publicly without a trial, even though we are Roman citizens, and threw us into prison. And now do they want to get rid of us quietly? No! Let them come themselves and escort us out." Ac 22:25-29

[38]The officers reported this to the magistrates, and when they heard that Paul and Silas were Roman citizens, they were alarmed. [39]They came to appease them and escorted them from the prison, requesting them to leave the city. [40]After Paul and Silas came out of the prison, they went to Lydia's house, where they met with the brothers and encouraged them. Then they left. Mt 8:34; Ac 22:29

In Thessalonica

17 When they had passed through Amphipolis and Apollonia, they came to Thessalonica, where there was a Jewish synagogue. [2]As his custom was, Paul went into the synagogue, and on three Sabbath days he reasoned with them from the Scriptures, [3]explaining and proving that the Christ[a] had to suffer and rise from the dead. "This Jesus I am proclaiming to you is the Christ,[a]" he said. [4]Some of the Jews were persuaded and joined Paul and Silas, as did a large number of God-fearing

[a]3 Or *Messiah*

Greeks and not a few prominent women. Lk 24:26,46; Ac 18:28

5But the Jews were jealous; so they rounded up some bad characters from the market-place, formed a mob and started a riot in the city. They rushed to Jason's house in search of Paul and Silas in order to bring them out to the crowd. *a* 6But when they did not find them, they dragged Jason and some other brothers before the city officials, shouting: "These men who have caused trouble all over the world have now come here, 7and Jason has welcomed them into his house. They are all de-fying Caesar's decrees, saying that there is another king, one called Jesus." 8When they heard this, the crowd and the city offi-cials were thrown into turmoil. 9Then they made Jason and the others post bond and let them go.   Mt 24:14; Lk 23:2; Ac 16:20

In Berea

10As soon as it was night, the brothers sent Paul and Silas away to Berea. On arriving there, they went to the Jewish synagogue. 11Now the Bereans were of more noble character than the Thessalonians, for they received the message with great eagerness and examined the Scriptures every day to see if what Paul said was true. 12Many of the Jews believed, as did also a number of prominent Greek women and many Greek men.

13When the Jews in Thessalo-nica learned that Paul was preaching the word of God at Berea, they went there too, agi-tating the crowds and stirring them up. 14The brothers immediately sent Paul to the coast, but Silas and Timothy stayed at Berea. 15The men who escorted Paul brought him to Athens and then left with in-structions for Silas and Timo-thy to join him as soon as pos-sible.

In Athens

16While Paul was waiting for them in Athens, he was greatly distressed to see that the city was full of idols. 17So he rea-soned in the synagogue with the Jews and the God-fearing Greeks, as well as in the market-place day by day with those who happened to be there. 18A group of Epicurean and Stoic philosophers began to dispute with him. Some of them asked, "What is this babbler trying to say?" Others remarked, "He seems to be advocating foreign gods." They said this because Paul was preaching the good news about Jesus and the resur-rection. 19Then they took him and brought him to a meeting of the Areopagus, where they said to him, "May we know what this new teaching is that you are presenting? 20You are bringing some strange ideas to our ears, and we want to know what they

mean." 21(All the Athenians and the foreigners who lived there spent their time doing nothing but talking about and listening to the latest ideas.)   Ac 13:32,33

22Paul then stood up in the meeting of the Areopagus and said: "Men of Athens! I see that in every way you are very religious. 23For as I walked around and looked carefully at your objects of worship, I even found an altar with this inscription: TO AN UNKNOWN GOD. Now what you worship as something unknown I am going to proclaim to you.

24"The God who made the world and everything in it is the Lord of heaven and earth and does not live in temples built by hands. 25And he is not served by human hands, as if he needed anything, because he himself gives all men life and breath and everything else. 26From one man he made every nation of men, that they should inhabit the whole earth; and he determined the times set for them and the exact places where they should live. 27God did this so that men would seek him and perhaps reach out for him and find him, though he is not far from each one of us. 28'For in him we live and move and have our being.' As some of your own poets have said, 'We are his offspring.'   Isa 42:5-7

29"Therefore since we are God's offspring, we should not think that the divine being is like gold or silver or stone—an image made by man's design and skill. 30In the past God overlooked such ignorance, but now he commands all people everywhere to repent. 31For he has set a day when he will judge the world with justice by the man he has appointed. He has given proof of this to all men by raising him from the dead."Ro 1:23; 3:25

32When they heard about the resurrection of the dead, some of them sneered, but others said, "We want to hear you again on this subject." 33At that, Paul left the Council. 34A few men became followers of Paul and believed. Among them was Dionysius, a member of the Areopagus, also a woman named Damaris, and a number of others.

In Corinth

18 After this, Paul left Athens and went to Corinth. 2There he met a Jew named Aquila, a native of Pontus, who had recently come from Italy with his wife Priscilla, because Claudius had ordered all the Jews to leave Rome. Paul went to see them, 3and because he was a tentmaker as they were, he stayed and worked with them. 4Every Sabbath he reasoned in the synagogue, trying to persuade Jews and Greeks.   Ro 16:3; 1 Th 2:9

5When Silas and Timothy came from Macedonia, Paul devoted himself exclusively to preaching, testifying to the Jews

that Jesus was the Christ. *a* 6But when the Jews opposed Paul and became abusive, he shook out his clothes in protest and said to them, "Your blood be on your own heads! I am clear of my responsibility. From now on I will go to the Gentiles." Eze 3:17-19

7Then Paul left the synagogue and went next door to the house of Titius Justus, a worshiper of God. 8Crispus, the synagogue ruler, and his entire household believed in the Lord; and many of the Corinthians who heard him believed and were baptized. Ac 16:14; 1Co 1:14

9One night the Lord spoke to Paul in a vision: "Do not be afraid; keep on speaking, do not be silent. 10For I am with you, and no one is going to attack and harm you, because I have many people in this city." 11So Paul stayed for a year and a half, teaching them the word of God.

12While Gallio was proconsul of Achaia, the Jews made a united attack on Paul and brought him into court. 13"This man," they charged, "is persuading the people to worship God in ways contrary to the law."

14Just as Paul was about to speak, Gallio said to the Jews, "If you Jews were making a complaint about some misdemeanor or serious crime, it would be reasonable for me to listen to you. 15But since it involves questions about words

and names and your own law—settle the matter yourselves. I will not be a judge of such things." 16So he had them ejected from the court. 17Then they all turned on Sosthenes the synagogue ruler and beat him in front of the court. But Gallio showed no concern whatever.

Priscilla, Aquila and Apollos

18Paul stayed on in Corinth for some time. Then he left the brothers and sailed for Syria, accompanied by Priscilla and Aquila. Before he sailed, he had his hair cut off at Cenchrea because of a vow he had taken. 19They arrived at Ephesus, where Paul left Priscilla and Aquila. He himself went into the synagogue and reasoned with the Jews. 20When they asked him to spend more time with them, he declined. 21But as he left, he promised, "I will come back if it is God's will." Then he set sail from Ephesus. 22When he landed at Caesarea, he went up and greeted the church and then went down to Antioch. Nu 6:2,5,18; Jas 4:15

23After spending some time in Antioch, Paul set out from there and traveled from place to place throughout the region of Galatia and Phrygia, strengthening all the disciples. Ac 14:22

24Meanwhile a Jew named Apollos, a native of Alexandria, came to Ephesus. He was a learned man, with a thorough

*a*5 Or *Messiah;* also in verse 28

knowledge of the Scriptures. ²⁵He had been instructed in the way of the Lord, and he spoke with great fervor*a* and taught about Jesus accurately, though he knew only the baptism of John. ²⁶He began to speak boldly in the synagogue. When Priscilla and Aquila heard him, they invited him to their home and explained to him the way of God more adequately.   Ro 12:11

²⁷When Apollos wanted to go to Achaia, the brothers encouraged him and wrote to the disciples there to welcome him. On arriving, he was a great help to those who by grace had believed. ²⁸For he vigorously refuted the Jews in public debate, proving from the Scriptures that Jesus was the Christ.

Paul in Ephesus

19 While Apollos was at Corinth, Paul took the road through the interior and arrived at Ephesus. There he found some disciples ²and asked them, "Did you receive the Holy Spirit when*b* you believed?"   Jn 20:22

They answered, "No, we have not even heard that there is a Holy Spirit."

³So Paul asked, "Then what baptism did you receive?"

"John's baptism," they replied.

⁴Paul said, "John's baptism was a baptism of repentance.

He told the people to believe in the one coming after him, that is, in Jesus." ⁵On hearing this, they were baptized into*c* the name of the Lord Jesus. ⁶When Paul placed his hands on them, the Holy Spirit came on them, and they spoke in tongues*d* and prophesied. ⁷There were about twelve men in all.   Mk 1:4

⁸Paul entered the synagogue and spoke boldly there for three months, arguing persuasively about the kingdom of God. ⁹But some of them became obstinate; they refused to believe and publicly maligned the Way. So Paul left them. He took the disciples with him and had discussions daily in the lecture hall of Tyrannus. ¹⁰This went on for two years, so that all the Jews and Greeks who lived in the province of Asia heard the word of the Lord.   Ac 20:31; 28:23

¹¹God did extraordinary miracles through Paul, ¹²so that even handkerchiefs and aprons that had touched him were taken to the sick, and their illnesses were cured and the evil spirits left them.   Ac 5:15; 8:13

¹³Some Jews who went around driving out evil spirits tried to invoke the name of the Lord Jesus over those who were demon-possessed. They would say, "In the name of Jesus, whom Paul preaches, I command you to come out." ¹⁴Seven sons of Sceva, a Jewish chief priest, were doing this.

---

*a*25 Or *with fervor in the Spirit*   *b*2 Or *after*   *c*5 Or *in*   *d*6 Or *other languages*

¹⁵ₗOne dayⱼ the evil spirit answered them, "Jesus I know, and I know about Paul, but who are you?" ¹⁶Then the man who had the evil spirit jumped on them and overpowered them all. He gave them such a beating that they ran out of the house naked and bleeding.   Mt 12:27

¹⁷When this became known to the Jews and Greeks living in Ephesus, they were all seized with fear, and the name of the Lord Jesus was held in high honor. ¹⁸Many of those who believed now came and openly confessed their evil deeds. ¹⁹A number who had practiced sorcery brought their scrolls together and burned them publicly. When they calculated the value of the scrolls, the total came to fifty thousand drachmas.ᵃ ²⁰In this way the word of the Lord spread widely and grew in power.   Ac 6:7

²¹After all this had happened, Paul decided to go to Jerusalem, passing through Macedonia and Achaia. "After I have been there," he said, "I must visit Rome also." ²²He sent two of his helpers, Timothy and Erastus, to Macedonia, while he stayed in the province of Asia a little longer.

The Riot in Ephesus

²³About that time there arose a great disturbance about the Way. ²⁴A silversmith named Demetrius, who made silver shrines of Artemis, brought in no little business for the craftsmen. ²⁵He called them together, along with the workmen in related trades, and said: "Men, you know we receive a good income from this business. ²⁶And you see and hear how this fellow Paul has convinced and led astray large numbers of people here in Ephesus and in practically the whole province of Asia. He says that man-made gods are no gods at all. ²⁷There is danger not only that our trade will lose its good name, but also that the temple of the great goddess Artemis will be discredited, and the goddess herself, who is worshiped throughout the province of Asia and the world, will be robbed of her divine majesty."   Ac 9:2; Rev 9:20

²⁸When they heard this, they were furious and began shouting: "Great is Artemis of the Ephesians!" ²⁹Soon the whole city was in an uproar. The people seized Gaius and Aristarchus, Paul's traveling companions from Macedonia, and rushed as one man into the theater. ³⁰Paul wanted to appear before the crowd, but the disciples would not let him. ³¹Even some of the officials of the province, friends of Paul, sent him a message begging him not to venture into the theater.

³²The assembly was in confu-

ᵃ19 A drachma was a silver coin worth about a day's wages.

sion: Some were shouting one thing, some another. Most of the people did not even know why they were there. ³³The Jews pushed Alexander to the front, and some of the crowd shouted instructions to him. He motioned for silence in order to make a defense before the people. ³⁴But when they realized he was a Jew, they all shouted in unison for about two hours: "Great is Artemis of the Ephesians!" Ac 21:34

³⁵The city clerk quieted the crowd and said: "Men of Ephesus, doesn't all the world know that the city of Ephesus is the guardian of the temple of the great Artemis and of her image, which fell from heaven? ³⁶Therefore, since these facts are undeniable, you ought to be quiet and not do anything rash. ³⁷You have brought these men here, though they have neither robbed temples nor blasphemed our goddess. ³⁸If, then, Demetrius and his fellow craftsmen have a grievance against anybody, the courts are open and there are proconsuls. They can press charges. ³⁹If there is anything further you want to bring up, it must be settled in a legal assembly. ⁴⁰As it is, we are in danger of being charged with rioting because of today's events. In that case we would not be able to account for this commotion, since there is no reason for it." ⁴¹After he had said this, he dismissed the assembly.

Through Macedonia and Greece

20 When the uproar had ended, Paul sent for the disciples and, after encouraging them, said good-by and set out for Macedonia. ²He traveled through that area, speaking many words of encouragement to the people, and finally arrived in Greece, ³where he stayed three months. Because the Jews made a plot against him just as he was about to sail for Syria, he decided to go back through Macedonia. ⁴He was accompanied by Sopater son of Pyrrhus from Berea, Aristarchus and Secundus from Thessalonica, Gaius from Derbe, Timothy also, and Tychicus and Trophimus from the province of Asia. ⁵These men went on ahead and waited for us at Troas. ⁶But we sailed from Philippi after the Feast of Unleavened Bread, and five days later joined the others at Troas, where we stayed seven days.

Eutychus Raised From the Dead at Troas

⁷On the first day of the week we came together to break bread. Paul spoke to the people and, because he intended to leave the next day, kept on talking until midnight. ⁸There were many lamps in the upstairs room where we were meeting. ⁹Seated in a window was a young man named Eutychus, who was sinking into a deep

sleep as Paul talked on and on. When he was sound asleep, he fell to the ground from the third story and was picked up dead. [10]Paul went down, threw himself on the young man and put his arms around him. "Don't be alarmed," he said. "He's alive!" [11]Then he went upstairs again and broke bread and ate. After talking until daylight, he left. [12]The people took the young man home alive and were greatly comforted.   Mt 9:23,24

Paul's Farewell to the Ephesian Elders

[13]We went on ahead to the ship and sailed for Assos, where we were going to take Paul aboard. He had made this arrangement because he was going there on foot. [14]When he met us at Assos, we took him aboard and went on to Mitylene. [15]The next day we set sail from there and arrived off Kios. The day after that we crossed over to Samos, and on the following day arrived at Miletus. [16]Paul had decided to sail past Ephesus to avoid spending time in the province of Asia, for he was in a hurry to reach Jerusalem, if possible, by the day of Pentecost.

[17]From Miletus, Paul sent to Ephesus for the elders of the church. [18]When they arrived, he said to them: "You know how I lived the whole time I was with you, from the first day I came

into the province of Asia. [19]I served the Lord with great humility and with tears, although I was severely tested by the plots of the Jews. [20]You know that I have not hesitated to preach anything that would be helpful to you but have taught you publicly and from house to house. [21]I have declared to both Jews and Greeks that they must turn to God in repentance and have faith in our Lord Jesus.   Ps 40:10

[22]"And now, compelled by the Spirit, I am going to Jerusalem, not knowing what will happen to me there. [23]I only know that in every city the Holy Spirit warns me that prison and hardships are facing me. [24]However, I consider my life worth nothing to me, if only I may finish the race and complete the task the Lord Jesus has given me—the task of testifying to the gospel of God's grace.   2Co 4:1

[25]"Now I know that none of you among whom I have gone about preaching the kingdom will ever see me again. [26]Therefore, I declare to you today that I am innocent of the blood of all men. [27]For I have not hesitated to proclaim to you the whole will of God. [28]Keep watch over yourselves and all the flock of which the Holy Spirit has made you overseers. [a] Be shepherds of the church of God, [b] which he bought with his own blood. [29]I know that after I leave, savage

---

[a]28 Traditionally *bishops*   [b]28 Many manuscripts *of the Lord*

wolves will come in among you and will not spare the flock. ³⁰Even from your own number men will arise and distort the truth in order to draw away disciples after them. ³¹So be on your guard! Remember that for three years I never stopped warning each of you night and day with tears. Jn 21:16

³²"Now I commit you to God and to the word of his grace, which can build you up and give you an inheritance among all those who are sanctified. ³³I have not coveted anyone's silver or gold or clothing. ³⁴You yourselves know that these hands of mine have supplied my own needs and the needs of my companions. ³⁵In everything I did, I showed you that by this kind of hard work we must help the weak, remembering the words the Lord Jesus himself said: 'It is more blessed to give than to receive.'" 2Co 7:2

³⁶When he had said this, he knelt down with all of them and prayed. ³⁷They all wept as they embraced him and kissed him. ³⁸What grieved them most was his statement that they would never see his face again. Then they accompanied him to the ship. Ac 21:5

On to Jerusalem

21 After we had torn ourselves away from them, we put out to sea and sailed straight to Cos. The next day we went to Rhodes and from there to Patara. ²We found a ship crossing over to Phoenicia, went on board and set sail. ³After sighting Cyprus and passing to the south of it, we sailed on to Syria. We landed at Tyre, where our ship was to unload its cargo. ⁴Finding the disciples there, we stayed with them seven days. Through the Spirit they urged Paul not to go on to Jerusalem. ⁵But when our time was up, we left and continued on our way. All the disciples and their wives and children accompanied us out of the city, and there on the beach we knelt to pray. ⁶After saying good-by to each other, we went aboard the ship, and they returned home. Ac 20:23

⁷We continued our voyage from Tyre and landed at Ptolemais, where we greeted the brothers and stayed with them for a day. ⁸Leaving the next day, we reached Caesarea and stayed at the house of Philip the evangelist, one of the Seven. ⁹He had four unmarried daughters who prophesied. Ac 2:17

¹⁰After we had been there a number of days, a prophet named Agabus came down from Judea. ¹¹Coming over to us, he took Paul's belt, tied his own hands and feet with it and said, "The Holy Spirit says, 'In this way the Jews of Jerusalem will bind the owner of this belt and will hand him over to the Gentiles.'" Ac 11:28

¹²When we heard this, we and the people there pleaded with Paul not to go up to Jerusa-

lem. ¹³Then Paul answered, "Why are you weeping and breaking my heart? I am ready not only to be bound, but also to die in Jerusalem for the name of the Lord Jesus." ¹⁴When he would not be dissuaded, we gave up and said, "The Lord's will be done."   Mt 26:39; Ac 20:24

¹⁵After this, we got ready and went up to Jerusalem. ¹⁶Some of the disciples from Caesarea accompanied us and brought us to the home of Mnason, where we were to stay. He was a man from Cyprus and one of the early disciples.

Paul's Arrival at Jerusalem

¹⁷When we arrived at Jerusalem, the brothers received us warmly. ¹⁸The next day Paul and the rest of us went to see James, and all the elders were present. ¹⁹Paul greeted them and reported in detail what God had done among the Gentiles through his ministry.   Ac 14:27

²⁰When they heard this, they praised God. Then they said to Paul: "You see, brother, how many thousands of Jews have believed, and all of them are zealous for the law. ²¹They have been informed that you teach all the Jews who live among the Gentiles to turn away from Moses, telling them not to circumcise their children or live according to our customs. ²²What shall we do? They will certainly hear that you have come, ²³so do what we tell you. There are four men with us who have made a vow. ²⁴Take these men, join in their purification rites and pay their expenses, so that they can have their heads shaved. Then everybody will know there is no truth in these reports about you, but that you yourself are living in obedience to the law. ²⁵As for the Gentile believers, we have written to them our decision that they should abstain from food sacrificed to idols, from blood, from the meat of strangled animals and from sexual immorality."

²⁶The next day Paul took the men and purified himself along with them. Then he went to the temple to give notice of the date when the days of purification would end and the offering would be made for each of them.   Nu 6:13-20; Ac 24:18

Paul Arrested

²⁷When the seven days were nearly over, some Jews from the province of Asia saw Paul at the temple. They stirred up the whole crowd and seized him, ²⁸shouting, "Men of Israel, help us! This is the man who teaches all men everywhere against our people and our law and this place. And besides, he has brought Greeks into the temple area and defiled this holy place." ²⁹(They had previously seen Trophimus the Ephesian in the city with Paul and assumed that Paul had brought him into the temple area.)

³⁰The whole city was aroused, and the people came

running from all directions. Seizing Paul, they dragged him from the temple, and immediately the gates were shut. ³¹While they were trying to kill him, news reached the commander of the Roman troops that the whole city of Jerusalem was in an uproar. ³²He at once took some officers and soldiers and ran down to the crowd. When the rioters saw the commander and his soldiers, they stopped beating Paul.   Ac 26:21

³³The commander came up and arrested him and ordered him to be bound with two chains. Then he asked who he was and what he had done. ³⁴Some in the crowd shouted one thing and some another, and since the commander could not get at the truth because of the uproar, he ordered that Paul be taken into the barracks. ³⁵When Paul reached the steps, the violence of the mob was so great he had to be carried by the soldiers. ³⁶The crowd that followed kept shouting, "Away with him!"   Lk 23:18; Ac 19:32

Paul Speaks to the Crowd

³⁷As the soldiers were about to take Paul into the barracks, he asked the commander, "May I say something to you?"

"Do you speak Greek?" he replied. ³⁸"Aren't you the Egyptian who started a revolt and led four thousand terrorists out into the desert some time ago?"   Ac 5:36

³⁹Paul answered, "I am a Jew, from Tarsus in Cilicia, a citizen of no ordinary city. Please let me speak to the people."   Ac 9:11

⁴⁰Having received the commander's permission, Paul stood on the steps and motioned to the crowd. When they were all silent, he said to them in Aramaic*a*: ²²¹"Brothers and fathers, listen now to my defense."   Ac 7:2

²When they heard him speak to them in Aramaic, they became very quiet.

Then Paul said: ³"I am a Jew, born in Tarsus of Cilicia, but brought up in this city. Under Gamaliel I was thoroughly trained in the law of our fathers and was just as zealous for God as any of you are today. ⁴I persecuted the followers of this Way to their death, arresting both men and women and throwing them into prison, ⁵as also the high priest and all the Council can testify. I even obtained letters from them to their brothers in Damascus, and went there to bring these people as prisoners to Jerusalem to be punished.

⁶"About noon as I came near Damascus, suddenly a bright light from heaven flashed around me. ⁷I fell to the ground and heard a voice say to me, 'Saul! Saul! Why do you persecute me?'   Ac 9:3,4

⁸"'Who are you, Lord?' I asked.

---

*a*40 Or possibly *Hebrew*; also in 22:2

" 'I am Jesus of Nazareth, whom you are persecuting,' he replied. ⁹My companions saw the light, but they did not understand the voice of him who was speaking to me. 　Ac 26:13

¹⁰ 'What shall I do, Lord?' I asked.

" 'Get up,' the Lord said, 'and go into Damascus. There you will be told all that you have been assigned to do.' ¹¹My companions led me by the hand into Damascus, because the brilliance of the light had blinded me. 　Ac 9:8

¹²"A man named Ananias came to see me. He was a devout observer of the law and highly respected by all the Jews living there. ¹³He stood beside me and said, 'Brother Saul, receive your sight!' And at that very moment I was able to see him. 　Ac 9:17

¹⁴"Then he said: 'The God of our fathers has chosen you to know his will and to see the Righteous One and to hear words from his mouth. ¹⁵You will be his witness to all men of what you have seen and heard. ¹⁶And now what are you waiting for? Get up, be baptized and wash your sins away, calling on his name.' 　Ac 7:52; Eph 5:26

¹⁷"When I returned to Jerusalem and was praying at the temple, I fell into a trance ¹⁸and saw the Lord speaking. 'Quick!' he said to me. 'Leave Jerusalem immediately, because they will not accept your testimony about me.' 　Ac 9:26

¹⁹" 'Lord,' I replied, 'these men know that I went from one synagogue to another to imprison and beat those who believe in you. ²⁰And when the blood of your martyr[a] Stephen was shed, I stood there giving my approval and guarding the clothes of those who were killing him.' 　Ac 7:57-60; 8:3

²¹"Then the Lord said to me, 'Go; I will send you far away to the Gentiles.' " 　Ac 9:15; 13:46

Paul the Roman Citizen

²²The crowd listened to Paul until he said this. Then they raised their voices and shouted, "Rid the earth of him! He's not fit to live!" 　Ac 21:36; 25:24

²³As they were shouting and throwing off their cloaks and flinging dust into the air, ²⁴the commander ordered Paul to be taken into the barracks. He directed that he be flogged and questioned in order to find out why the people were shouting at him like this. ²⁵As they stretched him out to flog him, Paul said to the centurion standing there, "Is it legal for you to flog a Roman citizen who hasn't even been found guilty?"

²⁶When the centurion heard this, he went to the commander and reported it. "What are you going to do?" he asked. "This man is a Roman citizen."

²⁷The commander went to

---

[a]20 Or witness

Paul and asked, "Tell me, are you a Roman citizen?"

"Yes, I am," he answered.

28Then the commander said, "I had to pay a big price for my citizenship."

"But I was born a citizen," Paul replied.

29Those who were about to question him withdrew immediately. The commander himself was alarmed when he realized that he had put Paul, a Roman citizen, in chains.

Before the Sanhedrin

30The next day, since the commander wanted to find out exactly why Paul was being accused by the Jews, he released him and ordered the chief priests and all the Sanhedrin to assemble. Then he brought Paul and had him stand before them.   Ac 23:28

23 Paul looked straight at the Sanhedrin and said, "My brothers, I have fulfilled my duty to God in all good conscience to this day." 2At this the high priest Ananias ordered those standing near Paul to strike him on the mouth. 3Then Paul said to him, "God will strike you, you whitewashed wall! You sit there to judge me according to the law, yet you yourself violate the law by commanding that I be struck!"

4Those who were standing near Paul said, "You dare to insult God's high priest?"

5Paul replied, "Brothers, I did not realize that he was the high priest; for it is written: 'Do not speak evil about the ruler of your people.'a"

6Then Paul, knowing that some of them were Sadducees and the others Pharisees, called out in the Sanhedrin, "My brothers, I am a Pharisee, the son of a Pharisee. I stand on trial because of my hope in the resurrection of the dead." 7When he said this, a dispute broke out between the Pharisees and the Sadducees, and the assembly was divided. 8(The Sadducees say that there is no resurrection, and that there are neither angels nor spirits, but the Pharisees acknowledge them all.)   Ac 24:15,21; 26:5

9There was a great uproar, and some of the teachers of the law who were Pharisees stood up and argued vigorously. "We find nothing wrong with this man," they said. "What if a spirit or an angel has spoken to him?" 10The dispute became so violent that the commander was afraid Paul would be torn to pieces by them. He ordered the troops to go down and take him away from them by force and bring him into the barracks.

11The following night the Lord stood near Paul and said, "Take courage! As you have testified about me in Jerusalem, so you must also testify in Rome."

a5 Exodus 22:28

The Plot to Kill Paul

[12]The next morning the Jews formed a conspiracy and bound themselves with an oath not to eat or drink until they had killed Paul. [13]More than forty men were involved in this plot. [14]They went to the chief priests and elders and said, "We have taken a solemn oath not to eat anything until we have killed Paul. [15]Now then, you and the Sanhedrin petition the commander to bring him before you on the pretext of wanting more accurate information about his case. We are ready to kill him before he gets here."   Ac 20:3

[16]But when the son of Paul's sister heard of this plot, he went into the barracks and told Paul.

[17]Then Paul called one of the centurions and said, "Take this young man to the commander; he has something to tell him." [18]So he took him to the commander.

The centurion said, "Paul, the prisoner, sent for me and asked me to bring this young man to you because he has something to tell you."

[19]The commander took the young man by the hand, drew him aside and asked, "What is it you want to tell me?"

[20]He said: "The Jews have agreed to ask you to bring Paul before the Sanhedrin tomorrow on the pretext of wanting more accurate information about him. [21]Don't give in to them, be-cause more than forty of them are waiting in ambush for him. They have taken an oath not to eat or drink until they have killed him. They are ready now, waiting for your consent to their request."

[22]The commander dismissed the young man and cautioned him, "Don't tell anyone that you have reported this to me."

Paul Transferred to Caesarea

[23]Then he called two of his centurions and ordered them, "Get ready a detachment of two hundred soldiers, seventy horsemen and two hundred spearmen[a] to go to Caesarea at nine tonight. [24]Provide mounts for Paul so that he may be taken safely to Governor Felix."Ac 24:1-3

[25]He wrote a letter as follows:

[26]Claudius Lysias,

To His Excellency, Governor Felix:

Greetings.

[27]This man was seized by the Jews and they were about to kill him, but I came with my troops and rescued him, for I had learned that he is a Roman citizen. [28]I wanted to know why they were accusing him, so I brought him to their Sanhedrin. [29]I found that the accusation had to do with questions about their law, but

[a]23 The meaning of the Greek for this word is uncertain.

there was no charge against him that deserved death or imprisonment. ³⁰When I was informed of a plot to be carried out against the man, I sent him to you at once. I also ordered his accusers to present to you their case against him.   Ac 20:3; 21:32

³¹So the soldiers, carrying out their orders, took Paul with them during the night and brought him as far as Antipatris. ³²The next day they let the cavalry go on with him, while they returned to the barracks. ³³When the cavalry arrived in Caesarea, they delivered the letter to the governor and handed Paul over to him. ³⁴The governor read the letter and asked what province he was from. Learning that he was from Cilicia, ³⁵he said, "I will hear your case when your accusers get here." Then he ordered that Paul be kept under guard in Herod's palace.

The Trial Before Felix

24 Five days later the high priest Ananias went down to Caesarea with some of the elders and a lawyer named Tertullus, and they brought their charges against Paul before the governor. ²When Paul was called in, Tertullus presented his case before Felix: "We have enjoyed a long period of peace under you, and your foresight has brought about reforms in this nation. ³Everywhere and in every way, most excellent Felix, we acknowledge this with profound gratitude. ⁴But in order not to weary you further, I would request that you be kind enough to hear us briefly.   Ac 23:30,35

⁵"We have found this man to be a troublemaker, stirring up riots among the Jews all over the world. He is a ringleader of the Nazarene sect ⁶and even tried to desecrate the temple; so we seized him. ⁸By*a* examining him yourself you will be able to learn the truth about all these charges we are bringing against him."   Ac 16:20; 21:28

⁹The Jews joined in the accusation, asserting that these things were true.

¹⁰When the governor motioned for him to speak, Paul replied: "I know that for a number of years you have been a judge over this nation; so I gladly make my defense. ¹¹You can easily verify that no more than twelve days ago I went up to Jerusalem to worship. ¹²My accusers did not find me arguing with anyone at the temple, or stirring up a crowd in the synagogues or anywhere else in the city. ¹³And they cannot prove to you the charges they are now making against me. ¹⁴However, I admit that I wor-

---

a6-8 Some manuscripts *him and wanted to judge him according to our law.* ⁷*But the commander, Lysias, came and with the use of much force snatched him from our hands* ⁸*and ordered his accusers to come before you. By*

ship the God of our fathers as a follower of the Way, which they call a sect. I believe everything that agrees with the Law and that is written in the Prophets, [15]and I have the same hope in God as these men, that there will be a resurrection of both the righteous and the wicked. [16]So I strive always to keep my conscience clear before God and man. Ac 26:6,22

[17]"After an absence of several years, I came to Jerusalem to bring my people gifts for the poor and to present offerings. [18]I was ceremonially clean when they found me in the temple courts doing this. There was no crowd with me, nor was I involved in any disturbance. [19]But there are some Jews from the province of Asia, who ought to be here before you and bring charges if they have anything against me. [20]Or these who are here should state what crime they found in me when I stood before the Sanhedrin— [21]unless it was this one thing I shouted as I stood in their presence: 'It is concerning the resurrection of the dead that I am on trial before you today.'" Ac 11:29; 23:6

[22]Then Felix, who was well acquainted with the Way, adjourned the proceedings. "When Lysias the commander comes," he said, "I will decide your case." [23]He ordered the centurion to keep Paul under guard but to give him some freedom and permit his friends to take care of his needs. Ac 28:16

[24]Several days later Felix came with his wife Drusilla, who was a Jewess. He sent for Paul and listened to him as he spoke about faith in Christ Jesus. [25]As Paul discoursed on righteousness, self-control and the judgment to come, Felix was afraid and said, "That's enough for now! You may leave. When I find it convenient, I will send for you." [26]At the same time he was hoping that Paul would offer him a bribe, so he sent for him frequently and talked with him. Ac 10:42; 20:21; Gal 5:23

[27]When two years had passed, Felix was succeeded by Porcius Festus, but because Felix wanted to grant a favor to the Jews, he left Paul in prison.

The Trial Before Festus

25 Three days after arriving in the province, Festus went up from Caesarea to Jerusalem, [2]where the chief priests and Jewish leaders appeared before him and presented the charges against Paul. [3]They urgently requested Festus, as a favor to them, to have Paul transferred to Jerusalem, for they were preparing an ambush to kill him along the way. [4]Festus answered, "Paul is being held at Caesarea, and I myself am going there soon. [5]Let some of your leaders come with me and press charges against the man there, if he has done anything wrong."

[6]After spending eight or ten days with them, he went down

to Caesarea, and the next day he convened the court and ordered that Paul be brought before him. [7]When Paul appeared, the Jews who had come down from Jerusalem stood around him, bringing many serious charges against him, which they could not prove.   Mk 15:3

[8]Then Paul made his defense: "I have done nothing wrong against the law of the Jews or against the temple or against Caesar."   Ac 28:17

[9]Festus, wishing to do the Jews a favor, said to Paul, "Are you willing to go up to Jerusalem and stand trial before me there on these charges?"   Ac 24:27

[10]Paul answered: "I am now standing before Caesar's court, where I ought to be tried. I have not done any wrong to the Jews, as you yourself know very well. [11]If, however, I am guilty of doing anything deserving death, I do not refuse to die. But if the charges brought against me by these Jews are not true, no one has the right to hand me over to them. I appeal to Caesar!"   Ac 26:32; 28:19

[12]After Festus had conferred with his council, he declared: "You have appealed to Caesar. To Caesar you will go!"

Festus Consults King Agrippa

[13]A few days later King Agrippa and Bernice arrived at Caesarea to pay their respects to Festus. [14]Since they were spending many days there, Festus discussed Paul's case with the king. He said: "There is a man here whom Felix left as a prisoner. [15]When I went to Jerusalem, the chief priests and elders of the Jews brought charges against him and asked that he be condemned.   Ac 24:1

[16]"I told them that it is not the Roman custom to hand over any man before he has faced his accusers and has had an opportunity to defend himself against their charges. [17]When they came here with me, I did not delay the case, but convened the court the next day and ordered the man to be brought in. [18]When his accusers got up to speak, they did not charge him with any of the crimes I had expected. [19]Instead, they had some points of dispute with him about their own religion and about a dead man named Jesus who Paul claimed was alive. [20]I was at a loss how to investigate such matters; so I asked if he would be willing to go to Jerusalem and stand trial there on these charges. [21]When Paul made his appeal to be held over for the Emperor's decision, I ordered him held until I could send him to Caesar."

[22]Then Agrippa said to Festus, "I would like to hear this man myself."

He replied, "Tomorrow you will hear him."   Ac 9:15

Paul Before Agrippa

[23]The next day Agrippa and

Bernice came with great pomp and entered the audience room with the high ranking officers and the leading men of the city. At the command of Festus, Paul was brought in. 24Festus said: "King Agrippa, and all who are present with us, you see this man! The whole Jewish community has petitioned me about him in Jerusalem and here in Caesarea, shouting that he ought not to live any longer. 25I found he had done nothing deserving of death, but because he made his appeal to the Emperor I decided to send him to Rome. 26But I have nothing definite to write to His Majesty about him. Therefore I have brought him before all of you, and especially before you, King Agrippa, so that as a result of this investigation I may have something to write. 27For I think it is unreasonable to send on a prisoner without specifying the charges against him." Ac 23:9; 26:30

26 Then Agrippa said to Paul, "You have permission to speak for yourself." Ac 9:15

So Paul motioned with his hand and began his defense: 2"King Agrippa, I consider myself fortunate to stand before you today as I make my defense against all the accusations of the Jews, 3and especially so because you are well acquainted with all the Jewish customs and controversies. Therefore, I beg you to listen to me patiently. Ps 119:46

4"The Jews all know the way I have lived ever since I was a child, from the beginning of my life in my own country, and also in Jerusalem. 5They have known me for a long time and can testify, if they are willing, that according to the strictest sect of our religion, I lived as a Pharisee. 6And now it is because of my hope in what God has promised our fathers that I am on trial today. 7This is the promise our twelve tribes are hoping to see fulfilled as they earnestly serve God day and night. O king, it is because of this hope that the Jews are accusing me. 8Why should any of you consider it incredible that God raises the dead? Gal 1:13,14

9"I too was convinced that I ought to do all that was possible to oppose the name of Jesus of Nazareth. 10And that is just what I did in Jerusalem. On the authority of the chief priests I put many of the saints in prison, and when they were put to death, I cast my vote against them. 11Many a time I went from one synagogue to another to have them punished, and I tried to force them to blaspheme. In my obsession against them, I even went to foreign cities to persecute them. 1Ti 1:13

12"On one of these journeys I was going to Damascus with the authority and commission of the chief priests. 13About noon, O king, as I was on the road, I saw a light from heaven, brighter than the sun, blazing around

me and my companions. ¹⁴We all fell to the ground, and I heard a voice saying to me in Aramaic,ª 'Saul, Saul, why do you persecute me? It is hard for you to kick against the goads.'

¹⁵"Then I asked, 'Who are you, Lord?'

"'I am Jesus, whom you are persecuting,' ¹⁶'Now get up and stand on your feet. I have appeared to you to appoint you as a servant and as a witness of what you have seen of me and what I will show you. ¹⁷I will rescue you from your own people and from the Gentiles. I am sending you to them ¹⁸to open their eyes and turn them from darkness to light, and from the power of Satan to God, so that they may receive forgiveness of sins and a place among those who are sanctified by faith in me.' Isa 42:7,16

¹⁹"So then, King Agrippa, I was not disobedient to the vision from heaven. ²⁰First to those in Damascus, then to those in Jerusalem and in all Judea, and to the Gentiles also, I preached that they should repent and turn to God and prove their repentance by their deeds. ²¹That is why the Jews seized me in the temple courts and tried to kill me. ²²But I have had God's help to this very day, and so I stand here and testify to small and great alike. I am saying nothing beyond what the prophets and Moses said would

happen— ²³that the Christᵇ would suffer and, as the first to rise from the dead, would proclaim light to his own people and to the Gentiles." Isa 50:5

²⁴At this point Festus interrupted Paul's defense. "You are out of your mind, Paul!" he shouted. "Your great learning is driving you insane." Jn 10:20

²⁵"I am not insane, most excellent Festus," Paul replied. "What I am saying is true and reasonable. ²⁶The king is familiar with these things, and I can speak freely to him. I am convinced that none of this has escaped his notice, because it was not done in a corner. ²⁷King Agrippa, do you believe the prophets? I know you do."

²⁸Then Agrippa said to Paul, "Do you think that in such a short time you can persuade me to be a Christian?" Ac 11:26

²⁹Paul replied, "Short time or long—I pray God that not only you but all who are listening to me today may become what I am, except for these chains."

³⁰The king rose, and with him the governor and Bernice and those sitting with them. ³¹They left the room, and while talking with one another, they said, "This man is not doing anything that deserves death or imprisonment."

³²Agrippa said to Festus, "This man could have been set free if he had not appealed to Caesar." Ac 25:11; 28:18

ª14 Or Hebrew   ᵇ23 Or Messiah

Paul Sails for Rome

27 When it was decided that we would sail for Italy, Paul and some other prisoners were handed over to a centurion named Julius, who belonged to the Imperial Regiment. ²We boarded a ship from Adramyttium about to sail for ports along the coast of the province of Asia, and we put out to sea. Aristarchus, a Macedonian from Thessalonica, was with us.

³The next day we landed at Sidon; and Julius, in kindness to Paul, allowed him to go to his friends so they might provide for his needs. ⁴From there we put out to sea again and passed to the lee of Cyprus because the winds were against us. ⁵When we had sailed across the open sea off the coast of Cilicia and Pamphylia, we landed at Myra in Lycia. ⁶There the centurion found an Alexandrian ship sailing for Italy and put us on board. ⁷We made slow headway for many days and had difficulty arriving off Cnidus. When the wind did not allow us to hold our course, we sailed to the lee of Crete, opposite Salmone. ⁸We moved along the coast with difficulty and came to a place called Fair Havens, near the town of Lasea.

⁹Much time had been lost, and sailing had already become dangerous because by now it was after the Fast.ᵃ So Paul warned them, ¹⁰"Men, I can see that our voyage is going to be disastrous and bring great loss to ship and cargo, and to our own lives also." ¹¹But the centurion, instead of listening to what Paul said, followed the advice of the pilot and of the owner of the ship. ¹²Since the harbor was unsuitable to winter in, the majority decided that we should sail on, hoping to reach Phoenix and winter there. This was a harbor in Crete, facing both southwest and northwest.

The Storm

¹³When a gentle south wind began to blow, they thought they had obtained what they wanted; so they weighed anchor and sailed along the shore of Crete. ¹⁴Before very long, a wind of hurricane force, called the "northeaster," swept down from the island. ¹⁵The ship was caught by the storm and could not head into the wind; so we gave way to it and were driven along. ¹⁶As we passed to the lee of a small island called Cauda, we were hardly able to make the lifeboat secure. ¹⁷When the men had hoisted it aboard, they passed ropes under the ship itself to hold it together. Fearing that they would run aground on the sandbars of Syrtis, they lowered the sea anchor and let the ship be driven along. ¹⁸We took such

---

ᵃ9 That is, the Day of Atonement (Yom Kippur)

a violent battering from the storm that the next day they began to throw the cargo overboard. ¹⁹On the third day, they threw the ship's tackle overboard with their own hands. ²⁰When neither sun nor stars appeared for many days and the storm continued raging, we finally gave up all hope of being saved.   Jnh 1:5

²¹After the men had gone a long time without food, Paul stood up before them and said: "Men, you should have taken my advice not to sail from Crete; then you would have spared yourselves this damage and loss. ²²But now I urge you to keep up your courage, because not one of you will be lost; only the ship will be destroyed. ²³Last night an angel of the God whose I am and whom I serve stood beside me ²⁴and said, 'Do not be afraid, Paul. You must stand trial before Caesar; and God has graciously given you the lives of all who sail with you.' ²⁵So keep up your courage, men, for I have faith in God that it will happen just as he told me. ²⁶Nevertheless, we must run aground on some island."   Ac 5:19; Ro 4:20-21

The Shipwreck

²⁷On the fourteenth night we were still being driven across the Adriatic[a] Sea, when about midnight the sailors sensed

they were approaching land. ²⁸They took soundings and found that the water was a hundred and twenty feet[b] deep. A short time later they took soundings again and found it was ninety feet[c] deep. ²⁹Fearing that we would be dashed against the rocks, they dropped four anchors from the stern and prayed for daylight. ³⁰In an attempt to escape from the ship, the sailors let the lifeboat down into the sea, pretending they were going to lower some anchors from the bow. ³¹Then Paul said to the centurion and the soldiers, "Unless these men stay with the ship, you cannot be saved." ³²So the soldiers cut the ropes that held the lifeboat and let it fall away.

³³Just before dawn Paul urged them all to eat. "For the last fourteen days," he said, "you have been in constant suspense and have gone without food—you haven't eaten anything. ³⁴Now I urge you to take some food. You need it to survive. Not one of you will lose a single hair from his head." ³⁵After he said this, he took some bread and gave thanks to God in front of them all. Then he broke it and began to eat. ³⁶They were all encouraged and ate some food themselves. ³⁷Altogether there were 276 of us on board. ³⁸When they had eaten as much as they wanted, they

---

a27 In ancient times the name referred to an area extending well south of Italy.
b28 Greek *twenty orguias* (about 37 meters)   c28 Greek *fifteen orguias* (about 27 meters)

lightened the ship by throwing the grain into the sea. Mt 10:30

39When daylight came, they did not recognize the land, but they saw a bay with a sandy beach, where they decided to run the ship aground if they could. 40Cutting loose the anchors, they left them in the sea and at the same time untied the ropes that held the rudders. Then they hoisted the foresail to the wind and made for the beach. 41But the ship struck a sandbar and ran aground. The bow stuck fast and would not move, and the stern was broken to pieces by the pounding of the surf. Ac 28:1; 2Co 11:25

42The soldiers planned to kill the prisoners to prevent any of them from swimming away and escaping. 43But the centurion wanted to spare Paul's life and kept them from carrying out their plan. He ordered those who could swim to jump overboard first and get to land. 44The rest were to get there on planks or on pieces of the ship. In this way everyone reached land in safety. 2Pe 2:9

Ashore on Malta

28 Once safely on shore, we found out that the island was called Malta. 2The islanders showed us unusual kindness. They built a fire and welcomed us all because it was raining and cold. 3Paul gathered a pile of brushwood and, as he put it on the fire, a viper, driven out by

the heat, fastened itself on his hand. 4When the islanders saw the snake hanging from his hand, they said to each other, "This man must be a murderer; for though he escaped from the sea, Justice has not allowed him to live." 5But Paul shook the snake off into the fire and suffered no ill effects. 6The people expected him to swell up or suddenly fall dead, but after waiting a long time and seeing nothing unusual happen to him, they changed their minds and said he was a god.

7There was an estate nearby that belonged to Publius, the chief official of the island. He welcomed us to his home and for three days entertained us hospitably. 8His father was sick in bed, suffering from fever and dysentery. Paul went in to see him and, after prayer, placed his hands on him and healed him. 9When this had happened, the rest of the sick on the island came and were cured. 10They honored us in many ways and when we were ready to sail, they furnished us with the supplies we needed. Jas 5:14

Arrival at Rome

11After three months we put out to sea in a ship that had wintered in the island. It was an Alexandrian ship with the figurehead of the twin gods Castor and Pollux. 12We put in at Syracuse and stayed there three days. 13From there we set sail and arrived at Rhegium. The

next day the south wind came up, and on the following day we reached Puteoli. ¹⁴There we found some brothers who invited us to spend a week with them. And so we came to Rome. ¹⁵The brothers there had heard that we were coming, and they traveled as far as the Forum of Appius and the Three Taverns to meet us. At the sight of these men Paul thanked God and was encouraged. ¹⁶When we got to Rome, Paul was allowed to live by himself, with a soldier to guard him. Ac 27:3

Paul Preaches at Rome Under Guard

¹⁷Three days later he called together the leaders of the Jews. When they had assembled, Paul said to them: "My brothers, although I have done nothing against our people or against the customs of our ancestors, I was arrested in Jerusalem and handed over to the Romans. ¹⁸They examined me and wanted to release me, because I was not guilty of any crime deserving death. ¹⁹But when the Jews objected, I was compelled to appeal to Caesar—not that I had any charge to bring against my own people. ²⁰For this reason I have asked to see you and talk with you. It is because of the hope of Israel that I am bound with this chain." Ac 26:6

²¹They replied, "We have not received any letters from Judea

concerning you, and none of the brothers who have come from there has reported or said anything bad about you. ²²But we want to hear what your views are, for we know that people everywhere are talking against this sect." Ac 24:5

²³They arranged to meet Paul on a certain day, and came in even larger numbers to the place where he was staying. From morning till evening he explained and declared to them the kingdom of God and tried to convince them about Jesus from the Law of Moses and from the Prophets. ²⁴Some were convinced by what he said, but others would not believe. ²⁵They disagreed among themselves and began to leave after Paul had made this final statement: "The Holy Spirit spoke the truth to your forefathers when he said through Isaiah the prophet:

²⁶" 'Go to this people and say,
"You will be ever hearing but never understanding;
you will be ever seeing but never perceiving."
²⁷For this people's heart has become calloused; Ps 119:70
they hardly hear with their ears,
and they have closed their eyes.
Otherwise they might see with their eyes,
hear with their ears,
understand with their hearts

and turn, and I would heal them.'[a]

28"Therefore I want you to know that God's salvation has been sent to the Gentiles, and they will listen!"[b]   Lk 2:30; Ac 13:46

30For two whole years Paul stayed there in his own rented house and welcomed all who came to see him. 31Boldly and without hindrance he preached the kingdom of God and taught about the Lord Jesus Christ.

---

[a]27 Isaiah 6:9,10   [b]28 Some manuscripts *listen!" 29After he said this, the Jews left, arguing vigorously among themselves.*

Romans

Introduction:

This letter was written by Paul to the church in Rome in A.D. 56 or 57 as he was finishing his third missionary journey. Paul had hoped to first go to Jerusalem and then on to Rome and Spain. He probably wrote this letter in preparation for his visit.

The theme of this letter is righteousness. Paul teaches in this letter that: 1) no human being is righteous; 2) Jesus Christ is perfectly righteous; 3) if we have faith in Jesus, we are freed from the power of sin, given a new life, and returned to a right relationship with God; 4) we should live Christian lives that are "holy and pleasing to God."

Outline of contents:

---

1 Paul, a servant of Christ Jesus, called to be an apostle and set apart for the gospel of God— ²the gospel he promised beforehand through his prophets in the Holy Scriptures ³regarding his Son, who as to his human nature was a descendant of David, ⁴and who through the Spirit*a* of holiness was declared with power to be the Son of God*b* by his resurrection from the dead: Jesus Christ our Lord. ⁵Through him and for his name's sake, we received grace and apostleship to call people from among all the Gentiles to the obedience that comes from faith. ⁶And you also are among those who are called to belong to Jesus Christ.   1Ti 1:14; Jude 1

⁷To all in Rome who are loved by God and called to be saints:

Grace and peace to you from God our Father and from the Lord Jesus Christ.   1Co 1:3

---

a4 Or *who as to his spirit*   *b4* Or *was appointed to be the Son of God with power*

Paul's Longing to Visit Rome

[8]First, I thank my God through Jesus Christ for all of you, because your faith is being reported all over the world. [9]God, whom I serve with my whole heart in preaching the gospel of his Son, is my witness how constantly I remember you [10]in my prayers at all times; and I pray that now at last by God's will the way may be opened for me to come to you.   1Sa 12:23,24

[11]I long to see you so that I may impart to you some spiritual gift to make you strong— [12]that is, that you and I may be mutually encouraged by each other's faith. [13]I do not want you to be unaware, brothers, that I planned many times to come to you (but have been prevented from doing so until now) in order that I might have a harvest among you, just as I have had among the other Gentiles. Ro 15:23

[14]I am obligated both to Greeks and non-Greeks, both to the wise and the foolish. [15]That is why I am so eager to preach the gospel also to you who are at Rome.   Ro 15:20; 1Co 9:16

[16]I am not ashamed of the gospel, because it is the power of God for the salvation of everyone who believes: first for the Jew, then for the Gentile. [17]For in the gospel a righteousness from God is revealed, a righteousness that is by faith from first to last,[a] just as it is written: "The righteous will live by faith."[b]   Ro 3:21,22; 2Ti 1:8

God's Wrath Against Mankind

[18]The wrath of God is being revealed from heaven against all the godlessness and wickedness of men who suppress the truth by their wickedness, [19]since what may be known about God is plain to them, because God has made it plain to them. [20]For since the creation of the world God's invisible qualities—his eternal power and divine nature—have been clearly seen, being understood from what has been made, so that men are without excuse.   Jn 3:36

[21]For although they knew God, they neither glorified him as God nor gave thanks to him, but their thinking became futile and their foolish hearts were darkened. [22]Although they claimed to be wise, they became fools [23]and exchanged the glory of the immortal God for images made to look like mortal man and birds and animals and reptiles.   Ge 8:21; Dt 4:16-17

[24]Therefore God gave them over in the sinful desires of their hearts to sexual impurity for the degrading of their bodies with one another. [25]They exchanged the truth of God for a lie, and worshiped and served created things rather than the Creator—who is forever praised. Amen.   Ps 81:12; Jer 10:14

---

[a]17 Or *is from faith to faith*   [b]17 Hab. 2:4

26Because of this, God gave them over to shameful lusts. Even their women exchanged natural relations for unnatural ones. 27In the same way the men also abandoned natural relations with women and were inflamed with lust for one another. Men committed indecent acts with other men, and received in themselves the due penalty for their perversion.

28Furthermore, since they did not think it worthwhile to retain the knowledge of God, he gave them over to a depraved mind, to do what ought not to be done. 29They have become filled with every kind of wickedness, evil, greed and depravity. They are full of envy, murder, strife, deceit and malice. They are gossips, 30slanderers, God-haters, insolent, arrogant and boastful; they invent ways of doing evil; they disobey their parents; 31they are senseless, faithless, heartless, ruthless. 32Although they know God's righteous decree that those who do such things deserve death, they not only continue to do these very things but also approve of those who practice them.   Ro 6:23

God's Righteous Judgment

2 You, therefore, have no excuse, you who pass judgment on someone else, for at whatever point you judge the other, you are condemning yourself, because you who pass judgment do the same things. 2Now we know that God's judgment against those who do such things is based on truth. 3So when you, a mere man, pass judgment on them and yet do the same things, do you think you will escape God's judgment? 4Or do you show contempt for the riches of his kindness, tolerance and patience, not realizing that God's kindness leads you toward repentance?   Ro 1:20; 11:22; 1Pe 3:20

5But because of your stubbornness and your unrepentant heart, you are storing up wrath against yourself for the day of God's wrath, when his righteous judgment will be revealed. 6God "will give to each person according to what he has done."a 7To those who by persistence in doing good seek glory, honor and immortality, he will give eternal life. 8But for those who are self-seeking and who reject the truth and follow evil, there will be wrath and anger. 9There will be trouble and distress for every human being who does evil: first for the Jew, then for the Gentile; 10but glory, honor and peace for everyone who does good: first for the Jew, then for the Gentile. 11For God does not show favoritism.

12All who sin apart from the law will also perish apart from the law, and all who sin under the law will be judged by the law. 13For it is not those who

a6 Psalm 62:12; Prov. 24:12

hear the law who are righteous in God's sight, but it is those who obey the law who will be declared righteous. [14](Indeed, when Gentiles, who do not have the law, do by nature things required by the law, they are a law for themselves, even though they do not have the law, [15]since they show that the requirements of the law are written on their hearts, their consciences also bearing witness, and their thoughts now accusing, now even defending them.) [16]This will take place on the day when God will judge men's secrets through Jesus Christ, as my gospel declares.

The Jews and the Law

[17]Now you, if you call yourself a Jew; if you rely on the law and brag about your relationship to God; [18]if you know his will and approve of what is superior because you are instructed by the law; [19]if you are convinced that you are a guide for the blind, a light for those who are in the dark, [20]an instructor of the foolish, a teacher of infants, because you have in the law the embodiment of knowledge and truth— [21]you, then, who teach others, do you not teach yourself? You who preach against stealing, do you steal? [22]You who say that people should not commit adultery, do you commit adultery? You who abhor idols, do you rob temples?

[23]You who brag about the law, do you dishonor God by breaking the law? [24]As it is written: "God's name is blasphemed among the Gentiles because of you." [a]   Eze 36:22; Mic 3:11

[25]Circumcision has value if you observe the law, but if you break the law, you have become as though you had not been circumcised. [26]If those who are not circumcised keep the law's requirements, will they not be regarded as though they were circumcised? [27]The one who is not circumcised physically and yet obeys the law will condemn you who, even though you have the [b] written code and circumcision, are a lawbreaker.   Gal 5:3

[28]A man is not a Jew if he is only one outwardly, nor is circumcision merely outward and physical. [29]No, a man is a Jew if he is one inwardly; and circumcision is circumcision of the heart, by the Spirit, not by the written code. Such a man's praise is not from men, but from God.   Dt 30:6; Mt 3:9

God's Faithfulness

3 What advantage, then, is there in being a Jew, or what value is there in circumcision? [2]Much in every way! First of all, they have been entrusted with the very words of God.   Ro 9:4-5

[3]What if some did not have faith? Will their lack of faith nullify God's faithfulness? [4]Not at

---

[a]24 Isaiah 52:5; Ezek. 36:22   [b]27 Or who, by means of a

all! Let God be true, and every man a liar. As it is written:

> "So that you may be proved
> right when you speak
> and prevail when you
> judge."[a]

[5]But if our unrighteousness brings out God's righteousness more clearly, what shall we say? That God is unjust in bringing his wrath on us? (I am using a human argument.) [6]Certainly not! If that were so, how could God judge the world? [7]Someone might argue, "If my falsehood enhances God's truthfulness and so increases his glory, why am I still condemned as a sinner?" [8]Why not say—as we are being slanderously reported as saying and as some claim that we say—"Let us do evil that good may result"? Their condemnation is deserved.   Ro 5:8

No One Is Righteous

[9]What shall we conclude then? Are we any better[b]? Not at all! We have already made the charge that Jews and Gentiles alike are all under sin. [10]As it is written: 1Ki 8:46,47; 2Ch 6:36,37

> "There is no one righteous,
> not even one;
> [11] there is no one who
> understands,
> no one who seeks God.
> [12]All have turned away,

they have together become
> worthless;
> there is no one who does
> good,
> not even one."[c]
> [13]"Their throats are open
> graves;
> their tongues practice
> deceit."[d]
> "The poison of vipers is on
> their lips."[e]
> [14] "Their mouths are full of
> cursing and bitterness."[f]
> [15]"Their feet are swift to shed
> blood;
> [16] ruin and misery mark their
> ways,
> [17]and the way of peace they do
> not know."[g]
> [18] "There is no fear of God
> before their eyes."[h]

[19]Now we know that whatever the law says, it says to those who are under the law, so that every mouth may be silenced and the whole world held accountable to God. [20]Therefore no one will be declared righteous in his sight by observing the law; rather, through the law we become conscious of sin.   Ro 4:15; Gal 2:16

Righteousness Through Faith

[21]But now a righteousness from God, apart from law, has been made known, to which the Law and the Prophets testify. [22]This righteousness from God

---

[a]4 Psalm 51:4   [b]9 Or *worse*   [c]12 Psalms 14:1-3; 53:1-3; Eccles. 7:20
[d]13 Psalm 5:9   [e]13 Psalm 140:3   [f]14 Psalm 10:7   [g]17 Isaiah 59:7,8
[h]18 Psalm 36:1

comes through faith in Jesus Christ to all who believe. There is no difference, 23for all have sinned and fall short of the glory of God, 24and are justified freely by his grace through the redemption that came by Christ Jesus. 25God presented him as a sacrifice of atonement,*a* through faith in his blood. He did this to demonstrate his justice, because in his forbearance he had left the sins committed beforehand unpunished— 26he did it to demonstrate his justice at the present time, so as to be just and the one who justifies those who have faith in Jesus.

27Where, then, is boasting? It is excluded. On what principle? On that of observing the law? No, but on that of faith. 28For we maintain that a man is justified by faith apart from observing the law. 29Is God the God of Jews only? Is he not the God of Gentiles too? Yes, of Gentiles too, 30since there is only one God, who will justify the circumcised by faith and the uncircumcised through that same faith. 31Do we, then, nullify the law by this faith? Not at all! Rather, we uphold the law.

Abraham Justified by Faith

4 What then shall we say that Abraham, our forefather, discovered in this matter? 2If, in fact, Abraham was justified by works, he had something to boast about—but not before God. 3What does the Scripture say? "Abraham believed God, and it was credited to him as righteousness."*b*   Ro 8:31

4Now when a man works, his wages are not credited to him as a gift, but as an obligation. 5However, to the man who does not work but trusts God who justifies the wicked, his faith is credited as righteousness. 6David says the same thing when he speaks of the blessedness of the man to whom God credits righteousness apart from works: Ro 9:30; 11:6

7"Blessed are they
   whose transgressions are
      forgiven,
   whose sins are covered.
8Blessed is the man
   whose sin the Lord will
      never count against
      him."*c*

9Is this blessedness only for the circumcised, or also for the uncircumcised? We have been saying that Abraham's faith was credited to him as righteousness. 10Under what circumstances was it credited? Was it after he was circumcised, or before? It was not after, but before! 11And he received the sign of circumcision, a seal of the righteousness that he had by faith while he was still uncircumcised. So then, he is the fa-

---

*a25 Or *as the one who would turn aside his wrath, taking away sin*   *b3 Gen. 15:6; also in verse 22   *c8 Psalm 32:1,2

ther of all who believe but have not been circumcised, in order that righteousness might be credited to them. [12]And he is also the father of the circumcised who not only are circumcised but who also walk in the footsteps of the faith that our father Abraham had before he was circumcised.   Ge 17:10; Ro 3:30

[13]It was not through law that Abraham and his offspring received the promise that he would be heir of the world, but through the righteousness that comes by faith. [14]For if those who live by law are heirs, faith has no value and the promise is worthless, [15]because law brings wrath. And where there is no law there is no transgression.

[16]Therefore, the promise comes by faith, so that it may be by grace and may be guaranteed to all Abraham's offspring—not only to those who are of the law but also to those who are of the faith of Abraham. He is the father of us all. [17]As it is written: "I have made you a father of many nations."[a] He is our father in the sight of God, in whom he believed—the God who gives life to the dead and calls things that are not as though they were.   Ro 3:24

[18]Against all hope, Abraham in hope believed and so became the father of many nations, just as it had been said to him, "So shall your offspring be."[b] [19]Without weakening in his faith, he faced the fact that his body was as good as dead—since he was about a hundred years old—and that Sarah's womb was also dead. [20]Yet he did not waver through unbelief regarding the promise of God, but was strengthened in his faith and gave glory to God, [21]being fully persuaded that God had power to do what he had promised. [22]This is why "it was credited to him as righteousness." [23]The words "it was credited to him" were written not for him alone, [24]but also for us, to whom God will credit righteousness—for us who believe in him who raised Jesus our Lord from the dead. [25]He was delivered over to death for our sins and was raised to life for our justification.   Isa 53:5,6,11

Peace and Joy

5 Therefore, since we have been justified through faith, we[c] have peace with God through our Lord Jesus Christ, [2]through whom we have gained access by faith into this grace in which we now stand. And we[c] rejoice in the hope of the glory of God. [3]Not only so, but we[c] also rejoice in our sufferings, because we know that suffering produces perseverance; [4]perseverance, character; and character, hope. [5]And hope does not disappoint us, because God has poured out his love into our

---

[a]17 Gen. 17:5   [b]18 Gen. 15:5   [c]1,2,3 Or let us

hearts by the Holy Spirit, whom he has given us. Ro 4:25; Php 1:20

⁶You see, at just the right time, when we were still powerless, Christ died for the ungodly. ⁷Very rarely will anyone die for a righteous man, though for a good man someone might possibly dare to die. ⁸But God demonstrates his own love for us in this: While we were still sinners, Christ died for us. Jn 3:16; Gal 4:4

⁹Since we have now been justified by his blood, how much more shall we be saved from God's wrath through him! ¹⁰For if, when we were God's enemies, we were reconciled to him through the death of his Son, how much more, having been reconciled, shall we be saved through his life! ¹¹Not only is this so, but we also rejoice in God through our Lord Jesus Christ, through whom we have now received reconciliation.

Death Through Adam, Life Through Christ

¹²Therefore, just as sin entered the world through one man, and death through sin, and in this way death came to all men, because all sinned— ¹³for before the law was given, sin was in the world. But sin is not taken into account when there is no law. ¹⁴Nevertheless, death reigned from the time of Adam to the time of Moses, even over those who did not sin by breaking a command, as did Adam, who was a pattern of the one to come. Ge 3:1-7,17; 1Co 15:22,45

¹⁵But the gift is not like the trespass. For if the many died by the trespass of the one man, how much more did God's grace and the gift that came by the grace of the one man, Jesus Christ, overflow to the many! ¹⁶Again, the gift of God is not like the result of the one man's sin: The judgment followed one sin and brought condemnation, but the gift followed many trespasses and brought justification. ¹⁷For if, by the trespass of the one man, death reigned through that one man, how much more will those who receive God's abundant provision of grace and of the gift of righteousness reign in life through the one man, Jesus Christ. Ac 15:11

¹⁸Consequently, just as the result of one trespass was condemnation for all men, so also the result of one act of righteousness was justification that brings life for all men. ¹⁹For just as through the disobedience of the one man the many were made sinners, so also through the obedience of the one man the many will be made righteous. Ro 4:25; Php 2:8

²⁰The law was added so that the trespass might increase. But where sin increased, grace increased all the more, ²¹so that, just as sin reigned in death, so also grace might reign through righteousness to bring eternal life through Jesus Christ our Lord. Mt 25:46; Ro 3:20; 6:16

Dead to Sin, Alive in Christ

6 What shall we say, then? Shall we go on sinning so that grace may increase? ²By no means! We died to sin; how can we live in it any longer? ³Or don't you know that all of us who were baptized into Christ Jesus were baptized into his death? ⁴We were therefore buried with him through baptism into death in order that, just as Christ was raised from the dead through the glory of the Father, we too may live a new life.

⁵If we have been united with him like this in his death, we will certainly also be united with him in his resurrection. ⁶For we know that our old self was crucified with him so that the body of sin might be done away with,^a that we should no longer be slaves to sin— ⁷because anyone who has died has been freed from sin. Gal 2:20

⁸Now if we died with Christ, we believe that we will also live with him. ⁹For we know that since Christ was raised from the dead, he cannot die again; death no longer has mastery over him. ¹⁰The death he died, he died to sin once for all; but the life he lives, he lives to God. ¹¹In the same way, count yourselves dead to sin but alive to God in Christ Jesus. ¹²Therefore do not let sin reign in your mortal body so that you obey its evil desires. ¹³Do not offer the parts of your body to sin, as instruments of wickedness, but rather offer yourselves to God, as those who have been brought from death to life; and offer the parts of your body to him as instruments of righteousness. ¹⁴For sin shall not be your master, because you are not under law, but under grace. Ro 12:1

Slaves to Righteousness

¹⁵What then? Shall we sin because we are not under law but under grace? By no means! ¹⁶Don't you know that when you offer yourselves to someone to obey him as slaves, you are slaves to the one whom you obey—whether you are slaves to sin, which leads to death, or to obedience, which leads to righteousness? ¹⁷But thanks be to God that, though you used to be slaves to sin, you wholeheartedly obeyed the form of teaching to which you were entrusted. ¹⁸You have been set free from sin and have become slaves to righteousness. 2Pe 2:19

¹⁹I put this in human terms because you are weak in your natural selves. Just as you used to offer the parts of your body in slavery to impurity and to ever-increasing wickedness, so now offer them in slavery to righteousness leading to holiness. ²⁰When you were slaves to sin, you were free from the control of righteousness. ²¹What benefit did you reap at that time from the things you are now

^a6 Or be rendered powerless

ashamed of? Those things result in death! 22But now that you have been set free from sin and have become slaves to God, the benefit you reap leads to holiness, and the result is eternal life. 23For the wages of sin is death, but the gift of God is eternal life in*a* Christ Jesus our Lord.   Gal 6:7,8; 1Pe 2:16

An Illustration From Marriage

7 Do you not know, brothers—for I am speaking to men who know the law—that the law has authority over a man only as long as he lives? 2For example, by law a married woman is bound to her husband as long as he is alive, but if her husband dies, she is released from the law of marriage. 3So then, if she marries another man while her husband is still alive, she is called an adulteress. But if her husband dies, she is released from that law and is not an adulteress, even though she marries another man.   1Co 7:39

4So, my brothers, you also died to the law through the body of Christ, that you might belong to another, to him who was raised from the dead, in order that we might bear fruit to God. 5For when we were controlled by the sinful nature,*b* the sinful passions aroused by the law were at work in our bodies, so that we bore fruit for death.

6But now, by dying to what once bound us, we have been released from the law so that we serve in the new way of the Spirit, and not in the old way of the written code.   Ro 6:6,7; Gal 5:24

Struggling With Sin

7What shall we say, then? Is the law sin? Certainly not! Indeed I would not have known what sin was except through the law. For I would not have known what coveting really was if the law had not said, "Do not covet."*c* 8But sin, seizing the opportunity afforded by the commandment, produced in me every kind of covetous desire. For apart from law, sin is dead. 9Once I was alive apart from law; but when the commandment came, sin sprang to life and I died. 10I found that the very commandment that was intended to bring life actually brought death. 11For sin, seizing the opportunity afforded by the commandment, deceived me, and through the commandment put me to death. 12So then, the law is holy, and the commandment is holy, righteous and good.   Ro 4:15; Gal 3:21

13Did that which is good, then, become death to me? By no means! But in order that sin might be recognized as sin, it produced death in me through what was good, so that through the commandment sin might become utterly sinful.   Ro 6:23

*a*23 Or *through*   *b*5 Or *the flesh*; also in verse 25   *c*7 Exodus 20:17; Deut. 5:21

¹⁴We know that the law is spiritual; but I am unspiritual, sold as a slave to sin. ¹⁵I do not understand what I do. For what I want to do I do not do, but what I hate I do. ¹⁶And if I do what I do not want to do, I agree that the law is good. ¹⁷As it is, it is no longer I myself who do it, but it is sin living in me. ¹⁸I know that nothing good lives in me, that is, in my sinful nature.ᵃ For I have the desire to do what is good, but I cannot carry it out. ¹⁹For what I do is not the good I want to do; no, the evil I do not want to do—this I keep on doing. ²⁰Now if I do what I do not want to do, it is no longer I who do it, but it is sin living in me that does it. Gal 5:17,18,24

²¹So I find this law at work: When I want to do good, evil is right there with me. ²²For in my inner being I delight in God's law; ²³but I see another law at work in the members of my body, waging war against the law of my mind and making me a prisoner of the law of sin at work within my members. ²⁴What a wretched man I am! Who will rescue me from this body of death? ²⁵Thanks be to God—through Jesus Christ our Lord! Ro 6:6; 8:2

So then, I myself in my mind am a slave to God's law, but in the sinful nature a slave to the law of sin. Ro 6:22

Life Through the Spirit

8 Therefore, there is now no condemnation for those who are in Christ Jesus,ᵇ ²because through Christ Jesus the law of the Spirit of life set me free from the law of sin and death. ³For what the law was powerless to do in that it was weakened by the sinful nature,ᶜ God did by sending his own Son in the likeness of sinful man to be a sin offering.ᵈ And so he condemned sin in sinful man,ᵉ ⁴in order that the righteous requirements of the law might be fully met in us, who do not live according to the sinful nature but according to the Spirit.

⁵Those who live according to the sinful nature have their minds set on what that nature desires; but those who live in accordance with the Spirit have their minds set on what the Spirit desires. ⁶The mind of sinful manᶠ is death, but the mind controlled by the Spirit is life and peace; ⁷the sinful mindᵍ is hostile to God. It does not submit to God's law, nor can it do so. ⁸Those controlled by the sinful nature cannot please God.

⁹You, however, are controlled not by the sinful nature but by the Spirit, if the Spirit of God lives in you. And if anyone does not have the Spirit of Christ, he does not belong to

---

ᵃ18 Or my flesh   ᵇ1 Some later manuscripts Jesus, who do not live according to the sinful nature but according to the Spirit,   ᶜ3 Or the flesh; also in verses 4, 5, 8, 9, 12 and 13   ᵈ3 Or man, for sin   ᵉ3 Or in the flesh   ᶠ6 Or mind set on the flesh   ᵍ7 Or the mind set on the flesh

Christ. [10]But if Christ is in you, your body is dead because of sin, yet your spirit is alive because of righteousness. [11]And if the Spirit of him who raised Jesus from the dead is living in you, he who raised Christ from the dead will also give life to your mortal bodies through his Spirit, who lives in you. Gal 5:24,25

[12]Therefore, brothers, we have an obligation—but it is not to the sinful nature, to live according to it. [13]For if you live according to the sinful nature, you will die; but if by the Spirit you put to death the misdeeds of the body, you will live, [14]because those who are led by the Spirit of God are sons of God. [15]For you did not receive a spirit that makes you a slave again to fear, but you received the Spirit of sonship.[a] And by him we cry, "Abba,[b] Father." [16]The Spirit himself testifies with our spirit that we are God's children. [17]Now if we are children, then we are heirs—heirs of God and co-heirs with Christ, if indeed we share in his sufferings in order that we may also share in his glory. Ac 20:32; Gal 3:26; 4:5

Future Glory

[18]I consider that our present sufferings are not worth comparing with the glory that will be revealed in us. [19]The creation waits in eager expectation for the sons of God to be revealed. [20]For the creation was subjected to frustration, not by its own choice, but by the will of the one who subjected it, in hope [21]that[c] the creation itself will be liberated from its bondage to decay and brought into the glorious freedom of the children of God.

[22]We know that the whole creation has been groaning as in the pains of childbirth right up to the present time. [23]Not only so, but we ourselves, who have the firstfruits of the Spirit, groan inwardly as we wait eagerly for our adoption as sons, the redemption of our bodies. [24]For in this hope we were saved. But hope that is seen is no hope at all. Who hopes for what he already has? [25]But if we hope for what we do not yet have, we wait for it patiently. 2Co 5:2,4

[26]In the same way, the Spirit helps us in our weakness. We do not know what we ought to pray for, but the Spirit himself intercedes for us with groans that words cannot express. [27]And he who searches our hearts knows the mind of the Spirit, because the Spirit intercedes for the saints in accordance with God's will. Eph 6:18

More Than Conquerors

[28]And we know that in all things God works for the good of those who love him,[d] who[e]

---

[a]15 Or adoption [b]15 Aramaic for Father [c]20,21 Or subjected it in hope. [21]For
[d]28 Some manuscripts And we know that all things work together for good to those who love God [e]28 Or works together with those who love him to bring about what is good—with those who

have been called according to his purpose. ²⁹For those God foreknew he also predestined to be conformed to the likeness of his Son, that he might be the firstborn among many brothers. ³⁰And those he predestined, he also called; those he called, he also justified; those he justified, he also glorified.   Ge 50:20; 1Co 1:9

³¹What, then, shall we say in response to this? If God is for us, who can be against us? ³²He who did not spare his own Son, but gave him up for us all—how will he not also, along with him, graciously give us all things? ³³Who will bring any charge against those whom God has chosen? It is God who justifies. ³⁴Who is he that condemns? Christ Jesus, who died—more than that, who was raised to life—is at the right hand of God and is also interceding for us. ³⁵Who shall separate us from the love of Christ? Shall trouble or hardship or persecution or famine or nakedness or danger or sword? ³⁶As it is written:

"For your sake we face death
    all day long;
we are considered as sheep
    to be slaughtered."ᵃ

³⁷No, in all these things we are more than conquerors through him who loved us. ³⁸For I am convinced that neither death nor life, neither angels nor demons,ᵇ neither the present nor the future, nor any powers, ³⁹neither height nor depth, nor anything else in all creation, will be able to separate us from the love of God that is in Christ Jesus our Lord.   Ro 5:8; 1Co 15:57

God's Sovereign Choice

9 I speak the truth in Christ—I am not lying, my conscience confirms it in the Holy Spirit— ²I have great sorrow and unceasing anguish in my heart. ³For I could wish that I myself were cursed and cut off from Christ for the sake of my brothers, those of my own race, ⁴the people of Israel. Theirs is the adoption as sons; theirs the divine glory, the covenants, the receiving of the law, the temple worship and the promises. ⁵Theirs are the patriarchs, and from them is traced the human ancestry of Christ, who is God over all, forever praised!ᶜ Amen.   Mt 1:1-16; Jn 1:1; Ro 11:4,28

⁶It is not as though God's word had failed. For not all who are descended from Israel are Israel. ⁷Nor because they are his descendants are they all Abraham's children. On the contrary, "It is through Isaac that your offspring will be reckoned."ᵈ ⁸In other words, it is not the natural children who are God's children, but it is the children of the promise who are regarded as Abraham's offspring. ⁹For this was how the promise

---

ᵃ36 Psalm 44:22   ᵇ38 Or nor heavenly rulers   ᶜ5 Or Christ, who is over all. God be forever praised! Or Christ. God who is over all be forever praised!   ᵈ7 Gen. 21:12

was stated: "At the appointed time I will return, and Sarah will have a son."[a]   Ro 8:14; Gal 3:16

[10]Not only that, but Rebekah's children had one and the same father, our father Isaac. [11]Yet, before the twins were born or had done anything good or bad—in order that God's purpose in election might stand: [12]not by works but by him who calls—she was told, "The older will serve the younger."[b] [13]Just as it is written: "Jacob I loved, but Esau I hated."[c]   Ro 8:28

[14]What then shall we say? Is God unjust? Not at all! [15]For he says to Moses,   2Ch 19:7

"I will have mercy on whom
    I have mercy,
and I will have compassion
    on whom I have
    compassion."[d]

[16]It does not, therefore, depend on man's desire or effort, but on God's mercy. [17]For the Scripture says to Pharaoh: "I raised you up for this very purpose, that I might display my power in you and that my name might be proclaimed in all the earth."[e] [18]Therefore God has mercy on whom he wants to have mercy, and he hardens whom he wants to harden.   Dt 2:30; Eph 2:8

[19]One of you will say to me: "Then why does God still blame us? For who resists his will?" [20]But who are you, O man, to talk back to God? "Shall what is formed say to him who formed it, 'Why did you make me like this?'"[f] [21]Does not the potter have the right to make out of the same lump of clay some pottery for noble purposes and some for common use?   Isa 45:9-12; Ro 11:19

[22]What if God, choosing to show his wrath and make his power known, bore with great patience the objects of his wrath—prepared for destruction? [23]What if he did this to make the riches of his glory known to the objects of his mercy, whom he prepared in advance for glory— [24]even us, whom he also called, not only from the Jews but also from the Gentiles? [25]As he says in Hosea:

"I will call them 'my people'
    who are not my people;
and I will call her 'my loved
    one' who is not my
    loved one,"[g]

[26]and,

"It will happen that in the
    very place where it was
    said to them,
'You are not my people,'
they will be called 'sons of
    the living God.'"[h]

[27]Isaiah cries out concerning Israel:

"Though the number of the
    Israelites be like the
    sand by the sea,   Ge 22:17

[a]9 Gen. 18:10,14   [b]12 Gen. 25:23   [c]13 Mal. 1:2,3   [d]15 Exodus 33:19
[e]17 Exodus 9:16   [f]20 Isaiah 29:16; 45:9   [g]25 Hosea 2:23   [h]26 Hosea 1:10

only the remnant will be
saved.   2Ki 19:4
28For the Lord will carry out
his sentence on earth with
speed and finality."ᵃ

29It is just as Isaiah said previously:

"Unless the Lord Almighty
had left us descendants,
we would have become like
Sodom,
we would have been like
Gomorrah."ᵇ

Israel's Unbelief

30What then shall we say?
That the Gentiles, who did not
pursue righteousness, have obtained it, a righteousness that is
by faith; 31but Israel, who pursued a law of righteousness, has
not attained it. 32Why not? Because they pursued it not by
faith but as if it were by works.
They stumbled over the "stumbling stone." 33As it is written:

"See, I lay in Zion a stone
that causes men to
stumble
and a rock that makes them
fall,
and the one who trusts in
him will never be put to
shame."ᶜ

10 Brothers, my heart's desire and prayer to God for
the Israelites is that they may be
saved. 2For I can testify about
them that they are zealous for

God, but their zeal is not based
on knowledge. 3Since they did
not know the righteousness
that comes from God and
sought to establish their own,
they did not submit to God's
righteousness. 4Christ is the
end of the law so that there may
be righteousness for everyone
who believes.   Ro 1:17; Gal 3:24

5Moses describes in this way
the righteousness that is by the
law: "The man who does these
things will live by them."ᵈ 6But
the righteousness that is by
faith says: "Do not say in your
heart, 'Who will ascend into
heaven?'ᵉ" (that is, to bring
Christ down) 7"or 'Who will descend into the deep?'ᵉ" (that is,
to bring Christ up from the
dead). 8But what does it say?
"The word is near you; it is in
your mouth and in your
heart,"ᶠ that is, the word of
faith we are proclaiming: 9That
if you confess with your mouth,
"Jesus is Lord," and believe in
your heart that God raised him
from the dead, you will be
saved. 10For it is with your heart
that you believe and are justified, and it is with your mouth
that you confess and are saved.
11As the Scripture says, "Anyone who trusts in him will never
be put to shame."ᵍ 12For there is
no difference between Jew and
Gentile—the same Lord is Lord
of all and richly blesses all who
call on him, 13for, "Everyone

ᵃ28 Isaiah 10:22,23   ᵇ29 Isaiah 1:9   ᶜ33 Isaiah 8:14; 28:16   ᵈ5 Lev. 18:5
ᵉ6,7 Deut. 30:13   ᶠ8 Deut. 30:14   ᵍ11 Isaiah 28:16

who calls on the name of the Lord will be saved."[a]

14How, then, can they call on the one they have not believed in? And how can they believe in the one of whom they have not heard? And how can they hear without someone preaching to them? 15And how can they preach unless they are sent? As it is written, "How beautiful are the feet of those who bring good news!"[b]   Na 1:15

16But not all the Israelites accepted the good news. For Isaiah says, "Lord, who has believed our message?"[c] 17Consequently, faith comes from hearing the message, and the message is heard through the word of Christ. 18But I ask: Did they not hear? Of course they did:

"Their voice has gone out
    into all the earth,
their words to the ends of
    the world."[d]

19Again I ask: Did Israel not understand? First, Moses says,

"I will make you envious by
    those who are not a
    nation;   Ro 11:11,14
I will make you angry by a
    nation that has no
    understanding."[e]

20And Isaiah boldly says,

"I was found by those who
    did not seek me;

I revealed myself to those
    who did not ask for
    me."[f]

21But concerning Israel he says,

"All day long I have held out
    my hands
to a disobedient and
    obstinate people."[g]

The Remnant of Israel

11 I ask then: Did God reject his people? By no means! I am an Israelite myself, a descendant of Abraham, from the tribe of Benjamin. 2God did not reject his people, whom he foreknew. Don't you know what the Scripture says in the passage about Elijah—how he appealed to God against Israel: 3"Lord, they have killed your prophets and torn down your altars; I am the only one left, and they are trying to kill me"[h]? 4And what was God's answer to him? "I have reserved for myself seven thousand who have not bowed the knee to Baal."[i] 5So too, at the present time there is a remnant chosen by grace. 6And if by grace, then it is no longer by works; if it were, grace would no longer be grace.[j]   Ps 94:14; Ro 4:4

7What then? What Israel sought so earnestly it did not obtain, but the elect did. The others were hardened, 8as it is written: Ro 9:31

a13 Joel 2:32   b15 Isaiah 52:7   c16 Isaiah 53:1   d18 Psalm 19:4
e19 Deut. 32:21   f20 Isaiah 65:1   g21 Isaiah 65:2   h3 1 Kings 19:10,14
i4 1 Kings 19:18   j6 Some manuscripts by grace. But if by works, then it is no longer grace; if it were, work would no longer be work.

"God gave them a spirit of
stupor,
eyes so that they could not
see
and ears so that they could
not hear,   Mt 13:13-15
to this very day."ᵃ

⁹And David says:

"May their table become a
snare and a trap,
a stumbling block and a
retribution for them.
¹⁰May their eyes be darkened
so they cannot see,
and their backs be bent
forever."ᵇ

Ingrafted Branches

¹¹Again I ask: Did they stumble so as to fall beyond recovery? Not at all! Rather, because of their transgression, salvation has come to the Gentiles to make Israel envious. ¹²But if their transgression means riches for the world, and their loss means riches for the Gentiles, how much greater riches will their fullness bring!   Ac 13:46
¹³I am talking to you Gentiles. Inasmuch as I am the apostle to the Gentiles, I make much of my ministry ¹⁴in the hope that I may somehow arouse my own people to envy and save some of them. ¹⁵For if their rejection is the reconciliation of the world, what will their acceptance be but life from the dead? ¹⁶If the part of the dough offered as firstfruits is holy, then the whole batch is holy; if the root is holy, so are the branches.   1Th 2:16
¹⁷If some of the branches have been broken off, and you, though a wild olive shoot, have been grafted in among the others and now share in the nourishing sap from the olive root, ¹⁸do not boast over those branches. If you do, consider this: You do not support the root, but the root supports you. ¹⁹You will say then, "Branches were broken off so that I could be grafted in." ²⁰Granted. But they were broken off because of unbelief, and you stand by faith. Do not be arrogant, but be afraid. ²¹For if God did not spare the natural branches, he will not spare you either.   Jer 11:16; 1Co 10:12
²²Consider therefore the kindness and sternness of God: sternness to those who fell, but kindness to you, provided that you continue in his kindness. Otherwise, you also will be cut off. ²³And if they do not persist in unbelief, they will be grafted in, for God is able to graft them in again. ²⁴After all, if you were cut out of an olive tree that is wild by nature, and contrary to nature were grafted into a cultivated olive tree, how much more readily will these, the natural branches, be grafted into their own olive tree!   Ro 2:4

All Israel Will Be Saved

²⁵I do not want you to be ignorant of this mystery, broth-

ᵃ8 Deut. 29:4; Isaiah 29:10   ᵇ10 Psalm 69:22,23

ers, so that you may not be conceited: Israel has experienced a hardening in part until the full number of the Gentiles has come in. ²⁶And so all Israel will be saved, as it is written: Ro 1:13

"The deliverer will come
    from Zion;
  he will turn godlessness
    away from Jacob.
²⁷And this is*a* my covenant
    with them
  when I take away their
    sins."*b*

²⁸As far as the gospel is concerned, they are enemies on your account; but as far as election is concerned, they are loved on account of the patriarchs, ²⁹for God's gifts and his call are irrevocable. ³⁰Just as you who were at one time disobedient to God have now received mercy as a result of their disobedience, ³¹so they too have now become disobedient in order that they too may now*c* receive mercy as a result of God's mercy to you. ³²For God has bound all men over to disobedience so that he may have mercy on them all. Ro 3:9; 5:10

Doxology

³³Oh, the depth of the riches of
    the wisdom and*d*
    knowledge of God! Ro 2:4
  How unsearchable his
    judgments,

and his paths beyond
    tracing out! Job 5:9
³⁴"Who has known the mind
    of the Lord?
  Or who has been his
    counselor?"*e*
³⁵"Who has ever given to God,
    that God should repay
    him?"*f*
³⁶For from him and through
    him and to him are all
    things. 1Co 8:6
  To him be the glory forever!
    Amen. Ro 16:27

Living Sacrifices

12 Therefore, I urge you, brothers, in view of God's mercy, to offer your bodies as living sacrifices, holy and pleasing to God—this is your spiritual*g* act of worship. ²Do not conform any longer to the pattern of this world, but be transformed by the renewing of your mind. Then you will be able to test and approve what God's will is—his good, pleasing and perfect will. 1Jn 2:15

³For by the grace given me I say to every one of you: Do not think of yourself more highly than you ought, but rather think of yourself with sober judgment, in accordance with the measure of faith God has given you. ⁴Just as each of us has one body with many members, and these members do not all have the same function, ⁵so in Christ we who are many form

---

*a*27 Or *will be not have now.*   *b*27 Isaiah 59:20,21; 27:9; Jer. 31:33,34   *c*31 Some manuscripts do
*d*33 Or *riches and the wisdom and the*   *e*34 Isaiah 40:13
*f*35 Job 41:11   *g*1 Or *reasonable*

one body, and each member belongs to all the others. ⁶We have different gifts, according to the grace given us. If a man's gift is prophesying, let him use it in proportion to his*a* faith. ⁷If it is serving, let him serve; if it is teaching, let him teach; ⁸if it is encouraging, let him encourage; if it is contributing to the needs of others, let him give generously; if it is leadership, let him govern diligently; if it is showing mercy, let him do it cheerfully.

Love

⁹Love must be sincere. Hate what is evil; cling to what is good. ¹⁰Be devoted to one another in brotherly love. Honor one another above yourselves. ¹¹Never be lacking in zeal, but keep your spiritual fervor, serving the Lord. ¹²Be joyful in hope, patient in affliction, faithful in prayer. ¹³Share with God's people who are in need. Practice hospitality.   1Th 4:9; 1Ti 1:5

¹⁴Bless those who persecute you; bless and do not curse. ¹⁵Rejoice with those who rejoice; mourn with those who mourn. ¹⁶Live in harmony with one another. Do not be proud, but be willing to associate with people of low position.*b* Do not be conceited.   Mt 5:44

¹⁷Do not repay anyone evil for evil. Be careful to do what is right in the eyes of everybody.

¹⁸If it is possible, as far as it depends on you, live at peace with everyone. ¹⁹Do not take revenge, my friends, but leave room for God's wrath, for it is written: "It is mine to avenge; I will repay,"*c* says the Lord. ²⁰On the contrary:

"If your enemy is hungry,
    feed him;
if he is thirsty, give him
    something to drink.
In doing this, you will heap
    burning coals on his
    head."*d*

²¹Do not be overcome by evil, but overcome evil with good.

Submission to the Authorities

13 Everyone must submit himself to the governing authorities, for there is no authority except that which God has established. The authorities that exist have been established by God. ²Consequently, he who rebels against the authority is rebelling against what God has instituted, and those who do so will bring judgment on themselves. ³For rulers hold no terror for those who do right, but for those who do wrong. Do you want to be free from fear of the one in authority? Then do what is right and he will commend you. ⁴For he is God's servant to do you good. But if you do wrong, be afraid, for he does

---

*a*6 Or *in agreement with the*   *b*16 Or *willing to do menial work*   *c*19 Deut. 32:35
*d*20 Prov. 25:21,22

not bear the sword for nothing. He is God's servant, an agent of wrath to bring punishment on the wrongdoer. ⁵Therefore, it is necessary to submit to the authorities, not only because of possible punishment but also because of conscience. Tit 3:1

⁶This is also why you pay taxes, for the authorities are God's servants, who give their full time to governing. ⁷Give everyone what you owe him: If you owe taxes, pay taxes; if revenue, then revenue; if respect, then respect; if honor, then honor. Mt 22:17ff; Lk 23:2

Love, for the Day Is Near

⁸Let no debt remain outstanding, except the continuing debt to love one another, for he who loves his fellowman has fulfilled the law. ⁹The commandments, "Do not commit adultery," "Do not murder," "Do not steal," "Do not covet,"ᵃ and whatever other commandment there may be, are summed up in this one rule: "Love your neighbor as yourself."ᵇ ¹⁰Love does no harm to its neighbor. Therefore love is the fulfillment of the law.

¹¹And do this, understanding the present time. The hour has come for you to wake up from your slumber, because our salvation is nearer now than when we first believed. ¹²The night is nearly over; the day is almost here. So let us put aside the deeds of darkness and put on the armor of light. ¹³Let us behave decently, as in the daytime, not in orgies and drunkenness, not in sexual immorality and debauchery, not in dissension and jealousy. ¹⁴Rather, clothe yourselves with the Lord Jesus Christ, and do not think about how to gratify the desires of the sinful nature.ᶜ Col 3:10,12

The Weak and the Strong

14 Accept him whose faith is weak, without passing judgment on disputable matters. ²One man's faith allows him to eat everything, but another man, whose faith is weak, eats only vegetables. ³The man who eats everything must not look down on him who does not, and the man who does not eat everything must not condemn the man who does, for God has accepted him. ⁴Who are you to judge someone else's servant? To his own master he stands or falls. And he will stand, for the Lord is able to make him stand. Ro 15:1

⁵One man considers one day more sacred than another; another man considers every day alike. Each one should be fully convinced in his own mind. ⁶He who regards one day as special, does so to the Lord. He who eats meat, eats to the Lord, for he gives thanks to God; and he who abstains, does so to the Lord and gives thanks to God. ⁷For none of us lives to himself

ᵃ9 Exodus 20:13-15,17; Deut. 5:17-19,21   ᵇ9 Lev. 19:18   ᶜ14 Or *the flesh*

alone and none of us dies to himself alone. ⁸If we live, we live to the Lord; and if we die, we die to the Lord. So, whether we live or die, we belong to the Lord. _{Gal 2:20; Php 1:20}

⁹For this very reason, Christ died and returned to life so that he might be the Lord of both the dead and the living. ¹⁰You, then, why do you judge your brother? Or why do you look down on your brother? For we will all stand before God's judgment seat. ¹¹It is written:

" 'As surely as I live,' says
   the Lord,
'every knee will bow before
   me;
  every tongue will confess to
   God.' "ᵃ   _{Php 2:10-11}

¹²So then, each of us will give an account of himself to God._{Mt 12:36}

¹³Therefore let us stop passing judgment on one another. Instead, make up your mind not to put any stumbling block or obstacle in your brother's way. ¹⁴As one who is in the Lord Jesus, I am fully convinced that no foodᵇ is unclean in itself. But if anyone regards something as unclean, then for him it is unclean. ¹⁵If your brother is distressed because of what you eat, you are no longer acting in love. Do not by your eating destroy your brother for whom Christ died. ¹⁶Do not allow what you consider good to be spoken of as evil. ¹⁷For the kingdom of

God is not a matter of eating and drinking, but of righteousness, peace and joy in the Holy Spirit, ¹⁸because anyone who serves Christ in this way is pleasing to God and approved by men.   _{2Co 8:21; Eph 5:2}

¹⁹Let us therefore make every effort to do what leads to peace and to mutual edification. ²⁰Do not destroy the work of God for the sake of food. All food is clean, but it is wrong for a man to eat anything that causes someone else to stumble. ²¹It is better not to eat meat or drink wine or to do anything else that will cause your brother to fall.

²²So whatever you believe about these things keep between yourself and God. Blessed is the man who does not condemn himself by what he approves. ²³But the man who has doubts is condemned if he eats, because his eating is not from faith; and everything that does not come from faith is sin.

15 We who are strong ought to bear with the failings of the weak and not to please ourselves. ²Each of us should please his neighbor for his good, to build him up. ³For even Christ did not please himself but, as it is written: "The insults of those who insult you have fallen on me."ᶜ ⁴For everything that was written in the past was written to teach us, so that through endurance and the en-

---

ᵃ11 Isaiah 45:23   ᵇ14 Or *that nothing*   ᶜ3 Psalm 69:9

couragement of the Scriptures we might have hope.   Ro 14:1

⁵May the God who gives endurance and encouragement give you a spirit of unity among yourselves as you follow Christ Jesus, ⁶so that with one heart and mouth you may glorify the God and Father of our Lord Jesus Christ.   Ps 34:3; Ro 12:16

⁷Accept one another, then, just as Christ accepted you, in order to bring praise to God. ⁸For I tell you that Christ has become a servant of the Jews[a] on behalf of God's truth, to confirm the promises made to the patriarchs ⁹so that the Gentiles may glorify God for his mercy, as it is written:

"Therefore I will praise you
    among the Gentiles;
I will sing hymns to your
    name."[b]

¹⁰Again, it says,

"Rejoice, O Gentiles, with
    his people."[c]

¹¹And again,

"Praise the Lord, all you
    Gentiles,
and sing praises to him, all
    you peoples."[d]

¹²And again, Isaiah says,

"The Root of Jesse will spring
    up,
one who will arise to rule
    over the nations;

the Gentiles will hope in
    him."[e]

¹³May the God of hope fill you with all joy and peace as you trust in him, so that you may overflow with hope by the power of the Holy Spirit.   1Th 1:5

Paul the Minister to the Gentiles

¹⁴I myself am convinced, my brothers, that you yourselves are full of goodness, complete in knowledge and competent to instruct one another. ¹⁵I have written you quite boldly on some points, as if to remind you of them again, because of the grace God gave me ¹⁶to be a minister of Christ Jesus to the Gentiles with the priestly duty of proclaiming the gospel of God, so that the Gentiles might become an offering acceptable to God, sanctified by the Holy Spirit.   Ac 9:15; 2Co 8:7

¹⁷Therefore I glory in Christ Jesus in my service to God. ¹⁸I will not venture to speak of anything except what Christ has accomplished through me in leading the Gentiles to obey God by what I have said and done— ¹⁹by the power of signs and miracles, through the power of the Spirit. So from Jerusalem all the way around to Illyricum, I have fully proclaimed the gospel of Christ. ²⁰It has always been my ambition to preach the gospel where Christ was not

---

[a]8 Greek *circumcision*   [b]9 2 Samuel 22:50; Psalm 18:49   [c]10 Deut. 32:43
[d]11 Psalm 117:1   [e]12 Isaiah 11:10

known, so that I would not be building on someone else's foundation. ²¹Rather, as it is written:

"Those who were not told
about him will see,
and those who have not
heard will
understand."ᵃ

²²This is why I have often been hindered from coming to you.

Paul's Plan to Visit Rome

²³But now that there is no more place for me to work in these regions, and since I have been longing for many years to see you, ²⁴I plan to do so when I go to Spain. I hope to visit you while passing through and to have you assist me on my journey there, after I have enjoyed your company for a while. ²⁵Now, however, I am on my way to Jerusalem in the service of the saints there. ²⁶For Macedonia and Achaia were pleased to make a contribution for the poor among the saints in Jerusalem. ²⁷They were pleased to do it, and indeed they owe it to them. For if the Gentiles have shared in the Jews' spiritual blessings, they owe it to the Jews to share with them their material blessings. ²⁸So after I have completed this task and have made sure that they have received this fruit, I will go to Spain and visit you on the way.

²⁹I know that when I come to you, I will come in the full measure of the blessing of Christ. ³⁰I urge you, brothers, by our Lord Jesus Christ and by the love of the Spirit, to join me in my struggle by praying to God for me. ³¹Pray that I may be rescued from the unbelievers in Judea and that my service in Jerusalem may be acceptable to the saints there, ³²so that by God's will I may come to you with joy and together with you be refreshed. ³³The God of peace be with you all. Amen.

Personal Greetings

16 I commend to you our sister Phoebe, a servantᵇ of the church in Cenchrea. ²I ask you to receive her in the Lord in a way worthy of the saints and to give her any help she may need from you, for she has been a great help to many people, including me.

³Greet Priscillaᶜ and Aquila,
my fellow workers in Christ
Jesus. ⁴They risked their
lives for me. Not only I but
all the churches of the Gentiles are grateful to them.
⁵Greet also the church that
meets at their house. 1Co 16:19
Greet my dear friend Epene-
tus, who was the first convert to Christ in the province of Asia.
⁶Greet Mary, who worked very
hard for you.

ᵃ21 Isaiah 52:15   ᵇ1 Or *deaconess*   ᶜ3 Greek *Prisca*, a variant of *Priscilla*

7Greet Andronicus and Junias, my relatives who have been in prison with me. They are outstanding among the apostles, and they were in Christ before I was.

8Greet Ampliatus, whom I love in the Lord.

9Greet Urbanus, our fellow worker in Christ, and my dear friend Stachys.

10Greet Apelles, tested and approved in Christ.

Greet those who belong to the household of Aristobulus.

11Greet Herodion, my relative. Greet those in the household of Narcissus who are in the Lord.

12Greet Tryphena and Tryphosa, those women who work hard in the Lord.

Greet my dear friend Persis, another woman who has worked very hard in the Lord.

13Greet Rufus, chosen in the Lord, and his mother, who has been a mother to me, too.   Mk 15:21

14Greet Asyncritus, Phlegon, Hermes, Patrobas, Hermas and the brothers with them.

15Greet Philologus, Julia, Nereus and his sister, and Olympas and all the saints with them.

16Greet one another with a holy kiss.

All the churches of Christ send greetings.

17I urge you, brothers, to watch out for those who cause divisions and put obstacles in your way that are contrary to the teaching you have learned. Keep away from them. 18For such people are not serving our Lord Christ, but their own appetites. By smooth talk and flattery they deceive the minds of naive people. 19Everyone has heard about your obedience, so I am full of joy over you; but I want you to be wise about what is good, and innocent about what is evil.   Ro 1:8; Gal 1:8,9

20The God of peace will soon crush Satan under your feet.

The grace of our Lord Jesus be with you.

21Timothy, my fellow worker, sends his greetings to you, as do Lucius, Jason and Sosipater, my relatives.   Ac 13:1; 16:1

22I, Tertius, who wrote down this letter, greet you in the Lord.

23Gaius, whose hospitality I and the whole church here enjoy, sends you his greetings.

Erastus, who is the city's director of public works, and our brother Quartus send you their greetings. *a*   Ac 19:22

25Now to him who is able to establish you by my gospel and the proclamation of Jesus

---

*a*23 Some manuscripts *their greetings.* 24*May the grace of our Lord Jesus Christ be with all of you. Amen.*

Christ, according to the revelation of the mystery hidden for long ages past, 26but now revealed and made known through the prophetic writings by the command of the eternal God, so that all nations might believe and obey him— 27to the only wise God be glory forever through Jesus Christ! Amen.

1 Corinthians

Introduction:

This letter was written by Paul to the church in Corinth, probably in the winter of A.D. 55. It was while he was in Ephesus that he sent this letter in response to a letter from the Corinthian church.

Located on the Mediterranean, the city of Corinth was a wealthy trading center. It was also a wicked city and was known for that throughout the Roman world. Because the church in Corinth was new it was hard for the Christians there not to act like their neighbors, so the church had some problems.

The Christians in Corinth were not getting along with one another—they were taking sides. Some of them were living very sinful lives. Paul wrote this letter to scold them and teach them how Christians should act. He tried to teach practical lessons about the Christian life so that people in Corinth would know right from wrong.

Outline of contents:

1 Paul, called to be an apostle of Christ Jesus by the will of God, and our brother Sosthenes, Ro 1:1; Eph 1:1

²To the church of God in Corinth, to those sanctified in Christ Jesus and called to be holy, together with all those everywhere who call on the name of our Lord Jesus Christ—their Lord and ours:

³Grace and peace to you from God our Father and the Lord Jesus Christ. Ro 1:7

Thanksgiving

[4]I always thank God for you because of his grace given you in Christ Jesus. [5]For in him you have been enriched in every way—in all your speaking and in all your knowledge— [6]because our testimony about Christ was confirmed in you. [7]Therefore you do not lack any spiritual gift as you eagerly wait for our Lord Jesus Christ to be revealed. [8]He will keep you strong to the end, so that you will be blameless on the day of our Lord Jesus Christ. [9]God, who has called you into fellowship with his Son Jesus Christ our Lord, is faithful. 1Co 12:1-31

Divisions in the Church

[10]I appeal to you, brothers, in the name of our Lord Jesus Christ, that all of you agree with one another so that there may be no divisions among you and that you may be perfectly united in mind and thought. [11]My brothers, some from Chloe's household have informed me that there are quarrels among you. [12]What I mean is this: One of you says, "I follow Paul"; another, "I follow Apollos"; another, "I follow Cephas[a]"; still another, "I follow Christ." Ro 15:5; 1Co 11:18

[13]Is Christ divided? Was Paul crucified for you? Were you baptized into[b] the name of Paul? [14]I am thankful that I did not baptize any of you except Crispus and Gaius, [15]so no one can say that you were baptized into my name. [16](Yes, I also baptized the household of Stephanas; beyond that, I don't remember if I baptized anyone else.) [17]For Christ did not send me to baptize, but to preach the gospel—not with words of human wisdom, lest the cross of Christ be emptied of its power.

Christ the Wisdom and Power of God

[18]For the message of the cross is foolishness to those who are perishing, but to us who are being saved it is the power of God. [19]For it is written:

"I will destroy the wisdom of
    the wise;
  the intelligence of the
    intelligent I will
    frustrate."[c]

[20]Where is the wise man? Where is the scholar? Where is the philosopher of this age? Has not God made foolish the wisdom of the world? [21]For since in the wisdom of God the world through its wisdom did not know him, God was pleased through the foolishness of what was preached to save those who believe. [22]Jews demand miraculous signs and Greeks look for wisdom, [23]but we preach Christ crucified: a stumbling block to Jews and foolishness to Gentiles, [24]but to those whom God has called, both Jews and

---

*a*12 That is, Peter   *b*13 Or *in*; also in verse 15   *c*19 Isaiah 29:14

Greeks, Christ the power of God and the wisdom of God. [25]For the foolishness of God is wiser than man's wisdom, and the weakness of God is stronger than man's strength. *Jer 8:9*

[26]Brothers, think of what you were when you were called. Not many of you were wise by human standards; not many were influential; not many were of noble birth. [27]But God chose the foolish things of the world to shame the wise; God chose the weak things of the world to shame the strong. [28]He chose the lowly things of this world and the despised things—and the things that are not—to nullify the things that are, [29]so that no one may boast before him. [30]It is because of him that you are in Christ Jesus, who has become for us wisdom from God—that is, our righteousness, holiness and redemption. [31]Therefore, as it is written: "Let him who boasts boast in the Lord." *a* *Jer 9:23,24; Ro 8:28*

2 When I came to you, brothers, I did not come with eloquence or superior wisdom as I proclaimed to you the testimony about God.*b* [2]For I resolved to know nothing while I was with you except Jesus Christ and him crucified. [3]I came to you in weakness and fear, and with much trembling. [4]My message and my preaching were not with wise and persua-sive words, but with a demonstration of the Spirit's power, [5]so that your faith might not rest on men's wisdom, but on God's power. *1Co 1:17; 2Co 4:7; 6:7*

Wisdom From the Spirit

[6]We do, however, speak a message of wisdom among the mature, but not the wisdom of this age or of the rulers of this age, who are coming to nothing. [7]No, we speak of God's secret wisdom, a wisdom that has been hidden and that God destined for our glory before time began. [8]None of the rulers of this age understood it, for if they had, they would not have crucified the Lord of glory. [9]However, as it is written:

"No eye has seen,
  no ear has heard,
 no mind has conceived
  what God has prepared for
    those who love him"*c*—

[10]but God has revealed it to us by his Spirit. *Mt 13:11; Jn 14:26*

The Spirit searches all things, even the deep things of God. [11]For who among men knows the thoughts of a man except the man's spirit within him? In the same way no one knows the thoughts of God except the Spirit of God. [12]We have not received the spirit of the world but the Spirit who is from God, that we may understand what God has freely given us. [13]This

---

a31 Jer. 9:24   *b1* Some manuscripts *as I proclaimed to you God's mystery*
c9 Isaiah 64:4

is what we speak, not in words taught us by human wisdom but in words taught by the Spirit, expressing spiritual truths in spiritual words.[a] [14]The man without the Spirit does not accept the things that come from the Spirit of God, for they are foolishness to him, and he cannot understand them, because they are spiritually discerned. [15]The spiritual man makes judgments about all things, but he himself is not subject to any man's judgment:

[16]"For who has known the
    mind of the Lord
that he may instruct him?"[b]

But we have the mind of Christ.

On Divisions in the Church

3 Brothers, I could not address you as spiritual but as worldly—mere infants in Christ. [2]I gave you milk, not solid food, for you were not yet ready for it. Indeed, you are still not ready. [3]You are still worldly. For since there is jealousy and quarreling among you, are you not worldly? Are you not acting like mere men? [4]For when one says, "I follow Paul," and another, "I follow Apollos," are you not mere men?
    1Co 2:15; Heb 5:12-14

[5]What, after all, is Apollos? And what is Paul? Only servants, through whom you came to believe—as the Lord has assigned to each his task. [6]I planted the seed, Apollos wa-

tered it, but God made it grow. [7]So neither he who plants nor he who waters is anything, but only God, who makes things grow. [8]The man who plants and the man who waters have one purpose, and each will be rewarded according to his own labor. [9]For we are God's fellow workers; you are God's field, God's building.
    Ps 62:12; Mk 16:20

[10]By the grace God has given me, I laid a foundation as an expert builder, and someone else is building on it. But each one should be careful how he builds. [11]For no one can lay any foundation other than the one already laid, which is Jesus Christ. [12]If any man builds on this foundation using gold, silver, costly stones, wood, hay or straw, [13]his work will be shown for what it is, because the Day will bring it to light. It will be revealed with fire, and the fire will test the quality of each man's work. [14]If what he has built survives, he will receive his reward. [15]If it is burned up, he will suffer loss; he himself will be saved, but only as one escaping through the flames.

[16]Don't you know that you yourselves are God's temple and that God's Spirit lives in you? [17]If anyone destroys God's temple, God will destroy him; for God's temple is sacred, and you are that temple.
    1Co 6:19

[18]Do not deceive yourselves. If any one of you thinks he is

---

[a]13 Or Spirit, interpreting spiritual truths to spiritual men   [b]16 Isaiah 40:13

wise by the standards of this age, he should become a "fool" so that he may become wise. [19]For the wisdom of this world is foolishness in God's sight. As it is written: "He catches the wise in their craftiness"[a]; [20]and again, "The Lord knows that the thoughts of the wise are futile."[b] [21]So then, no more boasting about men! All things are yours, [22]whether Paul or Apollos or Cephas[c] or the world or life or death or the present or the future—all are yours, [23]and you are of Christ, and Christ is of God.   Isa 5:21; Ro 8:32

Apostles of Christ

4 So then, men ought to regard us as servants of Christ and as those entrusted with the secret things of God. [2]Now it is required that those who have been given a trust must prove faithful. [3]I care very little if I am judged by you or by any human court; indeed, I do not even judge myself. [4]My conscience is clear, but that does not make me innocent. It is the Lord who judges me. [5]Therefore judge nothing before the appointed time; wait till the Lord comes. He will bring to light what is hidden in darkness and will expose the motives of men's hearts. At that time each will receive his praise from God. 1Co 3:13

[6]Now, brothers, I have applied these things to myself and Apollos for your benefit, so that you may learn from us the meaning of the saying, "Do not go beyond what is written." Then you will not take pride in one man over against another. [7]For who makes you different from anyone else? What do you have that you did not receive? And if you did receive it, why do you boast as though you did not?   Jn 3:27; Ro 12:3,6

[8]Already you have all you want! Already you have become rich! You have become kings—and that without us! How I wish that you really had become kings so that we might be kings with you! [9]For it seems to me that God has put us apostles on display at the end of the procession, like men condemned to die in the arena. We have been made a spectacle to the whole universe, to angels as well as to men. [10]We are fools for Christ, but you are so wise in Christ! We are weak, but you are strong! You are honored, we are dishonored! [11]To this very hour we go hungry and thirsty, we are in rags, we are brutally treated, we are homeless. [12]We work hard with our own hands. When we are cursed, we bless; when we are persecuted, we endure it; [13]when we are slandered, we answer kindly. Up to this moment we have become the scum of the earth, the refuse of the world.   Jer 20:18; Rev 3:17-18

[14]I am not writing this to shame you, but to warn you, as

---

[a]19 Job 5:13   [b]20 Psalm 94:11   [c]22 That is, Peter

my dear children. ¹⁵Even though you have ten thousand guardians in Christ, you do not have many fathers, for in Christ Jesus I became your father through the gospel. ¹⁶Therefore I urge you to imitate me. ¹⁷For this reason I am sending to you Timothy, my son whom I love, who is faithful in the Lord. He will remind you of my way of life in Christ Jesus, which agrees with what I teach everywhere in every church.   Php 3:17

¹⁸Some of you have become arrogant, as if I were not coming to you. ¹⁹But I will come to you very soon, if the Lord is willing, and then I will find out not only how these arrogant people are talking, but what power they have. ²⁰For the kingdom of God is not a matter of talk but of power. ²¹What do you prefer? Shall I come to you with a whip, or in love and with a gentle spirit?   Ro 14:17,18

Expel the Immoral Brother!

5 It is actually reported that there is sexual immorality among you, and of a kind that does not occur even among pagans: A man has his father's wife. ²And you are proud! Shouldn't you rather have been filled with grief and have put out of your fellowship the man who did this? ³Even though I am not physically present, I am with you in spirit. And I have already passed judgment on the one who did this, just as if I were present. ⁴When you are assembled in the name of our Lord Jesus and I am with you in spirit, and the power of our Lord Jesus is present, ⁵hand this man over to Satan, so that the sinful nature*ᵃ* may be destroyed and his spirit saved on the day of the Lord.   Lev 18:8; 1Co 1:8

⁶Your boasting is not good. Don't you know that a little yeast works through the whole batch of dough? ⁷Get rid of the old yeast that you may be a new batch without yeast—as you really are. For Christ, our Passover lamb, has been sacrificed. ⁸Therefore let us keep the Festival, not with the old yeast, the yeast of malice and wickedness, but with bread without yeast, the bread of sincerity and truth.

⁹I have written you in my letter not to associate with sexually immoral people— ¹⁰not at all meaning the people of this world who are immoral, or the greedy and swindlers, or idolaters. In that case you would have to leave this world. ¹¹But now I am writing you that you must not associate with anyone who calls himself a brother but is sexually immoral or greedy, an idolater or a slanderer, a drunkard or a swindler. With such a man do not even eat.

¹²What business is it of mine to judge those outside the church? Are you not to judge those inside? ¹³God will judge

---

ᵃ5 Or that his body; or that the flesh

those outside. "Expel the wicked man from among you."[a]

Lawsuits Among Believers

6 If any of you has a dispute with another, dare he take it before the ungodly for judgment instead of before the saints? [2]Do you not know that the saints will judge the world? And if you are to judge the world, are you not competent to judge trivial cases? [3]Do you not know that we will judge angels? How much more the things of this life! [4]Therefore, if you have disputes about such matters, appoint as judges even men of little account in the church![b] [5]I say this to shame you. Is it possible that there is nobody among you wise enough to judge a dispute between believers? [6]But instead, one brother goes to law against another—and this in front of unbelievers!

Mt 18:17

[7]The very fact that you have lawsuits among you means you have been completely defeated already. Why not rather be wronged? Why not rather be cheated? [8]Instead, you yourselves cheat and do wrong, and you do this to your brothers.

[9]Do you not know that the wicked will not inherit the kingdom of God? Do not be deceived: Neither the sexually immoral nor idolaters nor adulterers nor male prostitutes nor homosexual offenders [10]nor thieves nor the greedy nor drunkards nor slanderers nor swindlers will inherit the kingdom of God. [11]And that is what some of you were. But you were washed, you were sanctified, you were justified in the name of the Lord Jesus Christ and by the Spirit of our God.

Mt 25:34ff

Sexual Immorality

[12]"Everything is permissible for me"—but not everything is beneficial. "Everything is permissible for me"—but I will not be mastered by anything. [13]"Food for the stomach and the stomach for food"—but God will destroy them both. The body is not meant for sexual immorality, but for the Lord, and the Lord for the body. [14]By his power God raised the Lord from the dead, and he will raise us also. [15]Do you not know that your bodies are members of Christ himself? Shall I then take the members of Christ and unite them with a prostitute? Never! [16]Do you not know that he who unites himself with a prostitute is one with her in body? For it is said, "The two will become one flesh."[c] [17]But he who unites himself with the Lord is one with him in spirit.

Ro 8:9-11; 12:1

[18]Flee from sexual immorality. All other sins a man commits are outside his body, but

he who sins sexually sins against his own body. [19]Do you not know that your body is a temple of the Holy Spirit, who is in you, whom you have received from God? You are not your own; [20]you were bought at a price. Therefore honor God with your body. Ro 6:12,13

Marriage

7 Now for the matters you wrote about: It is good for a man not to marry.[a] [2]But since there is so much immorality, each man should have his own wife, and each woman her own husband. [3]The husband should fulfill his marital duty to his wife, and likewise the wife to her husband. [4]The wife's body does not belong to her alone but also to her husband. In the same way, the husband's body does not belong to him alone but also to his wife. [5]Do not deprive each other except by mutual consent and for a time, so that you may devote yourselves to prayer. Then come together again so that Satan will not tempt you because of your lack of self-control. [6]I say this as a concession, not as a command. [7]I wish that all men were as I am. But each man has his own gift from God; one has this gift, another has that. 1Pe 3:7

[8]Now to the unmarried and the widows I say: It is good for them to stay unmarried, as I am. [9]But if they cannot control themselves, they should marry, for it is better to marry than to burn with passion.

[10]To the married I give this command (not I, but the Lord): A wife must not separate from her husband. [11]But if she does, she must remain unmarried or else be reconciled to her husband. And a husband must not divorce his wife. Mal 2:14-16

[12]To the rest I say this (I, not the Lord): If any brother has a wife who is not a believer and she is willing to live with him, he must not divorce her. [13]And if a woman has a husband who is not a believer and he is willing to live with her, she must not divorce him. [14]For the unbelieving husband has been sanctified through his wife, and the unbelieving wife has been sanctified through her believing husband. Otherwise your children would be unclean, but as it is, they are holy.

[15]But if the unbeliever leaves, let him do so. A believing man or woman is not bound in such circumstances; God has called us to live in peace. [16]How do you know, wife, whether you will save your husband? Or, how do you know, husband, whether you will save your wife? Ro 14:19; 1Pe 3:1

[17]Nevertheless, each one should retain the place in life that the Lord assigned to him and to which God has called him. This is the rule I lay down

---

[a]1 Or "It is good for a man not to have sexual relations with a woman."

in all the churches. ¹⁸Was a man already circumcised when he was called? He should not become uncircumcised. Was a man uncircumcised when he was called? He should not be circumcised. ¹⁹Circumcision is nothing and uncircumcision is nothing. Keeping God's commands is what counts. ²⁰Each one should remain in the situation which he was in when God called him. ²¹Were you a slave when you were called? Don't let it trouble you—although if you can gain your freedom, do so. ²²For he who was a slave when he was called by the Lord is the Lord's freedman; similarly, he who was a free man when he was called is Christ's slave. ²³You were bought at a price; do not become slaves of men. ²⁴Brothers, each man, as responsible to God, should remain in the situation God called him to. Ro 12:3

²⁵Now about virgins: I have no command from the Lord, but I give a judgment as one who by the Lord's mercy is trustworthy. ²⁶Because of the present crisis, I think that it is good for you to remain as you are. ²⁷Are you married? Do not seek a divorce. Are you unmarried? Do not look for a wife. ²⁸But if you do marry, you have not sinned; and if a virgin marries, she has not sinned. But those who marry will face many troubles in this life, and I want to spare you this.

²⁹What I mean, brothers, is that the time is short. From now on those who have wives should live as if they had none; ³⁰those who mourn, as if they did not; those who are happy, as if they were not; those who buy something, as if it were not theirs to keep; ³¹those who use the things of the world, as if not engrossed in them. For this world in its present form is passing away. Ro 13:11-12

³²I would like you to be free from concern. An unmarried man is concerned about the Lord's affairs—how he can please the Lord. ³³But a married man is concerned about the affairs of this world—how he can please his wife— ³⁴and his interests are divided. An unmarried woman or virgin is concerned about the Lord's affairs: Her aim is to be devoted to the Lord in both body and spirit. But a married woman is concerned about the affairs of this world—how she can please her husband. ³⁵I am saying this for your own good, not to restrict you, but that you may live in a right way in undivided devotion to the Lord. Ps 86:11; 1 Ti 5:5

³⁶If anyone thinks he is acting improperly toward the virgin he is engaged to, and if she is getting along in years and he feels he ought to marry, he should do as he wants. He is not sinning. They should get married. ³⁷But the man who has settled the matter in his own mind, who is under no compulsion but has control over his own will, and

who has made up his mind not to marry the virgin—this man also does the right thing. ³⁸So then, he who marries the virgin does right, but he who does not marry her does even better. *a*

³⁹A woman is bound to her husband as long as he lives. But if her husband dies, she is free to marry anyone she wishes, but he must belong to the Lord. ⁴⁰In my judgment, she is happier if she stays as she is—and I think that I too have the Spirit of God.   Ro 7:2-3; 2Co 6:14

Food Sacrificed to Idols

8 Now about food sacrificed to idols: We know that we all possess knowledge. *b* Knowledge puffs up, but love builds up. ²The man who thinks he knows something does not yet know as he ought to know. ³But the man who loves God is known by God.   Ac 15:20

⁴So then, about eating food sacrificed to idols: We know that an idol is nothing at all in the world and that there is no God but one. ⁵For even if there are so-called gods, whether in heaven or on earth (as indeed there are many "gods" and many "lords"), ⁶yet for us there is but one God, the Father, from whom all things came and for whom we live; and there is but one Lord, Jesus Christ, through whom all things came and through whom we live.   Ex 34:15

⁷But not everyone knows this. Some people are still so accustomed to idols that when they eat such food they think of it as having been sacrificed to an idol, and since their conscience is weak, it is defiled. ⁸But food does not bring us near to God; we are no worse if we do not eat, and no better if we do.

⁹Be careful, however, that the exercise of your freedom does not become a stumbling block to the weak. ¹⁰For if anyone with a weak conscience sees you who have this knowledge eating in an idol's temple, won't he be emboldened to eat what has been sacrificed to idols? ¹¹So this weak brother, for whom Christ died, is destroyed by your knowledge. ¹²When you sin against your brothers in this way and wound their weak conscience, you sin against Christ. ¹³Therefore, if what I eat causes my brother to fall into sin, I will never eat meat again, so that I will not cause him to fall.   2Co 6:3

The Rights of an Apostle

9 Am I not free? Am I not an apostle? Have I not seen Jesus our Lord? Are you not the result of my work in the Lord?

---

a36-38 Or ³⁶*If anyone thinks he is not treating his daughter properly, and if she is getting along in years, and he feels she ought to marry, he should do as he wants. He is not sinning. He should let her get married.* ³⁷*But the man who has settled the matter in his own mind, who is under no compulsion but has control over his own will, and who has made up his mind to keep the virgin unmarried—this man also does the right thing.* ³⁸*So then, he who gives his virgin in marriage does right, but he who does not give her in marriage does even better.*   *b1* Or *"We all possess knowledge,"* as you say

²Even though I may not be an apostle to others, surely I am to you! For you are the seal of my apostleship in the Lord. 2Co 3:2,3

³This is my defense to those who sit in judgment on me. ⁴Don't we have the right to food and drink? ⁵Don't we have the right to take a believing wife along with us, as do the other apostles and the Lord's brothers and Cephas*ᵃ*? ⁶Or is it only I and Barnabas who must work for a living? Ac 18:3

⁷Who serves as a soldier at his own expense? Who plants a vineyard and does not eat of its grapes? Who tends a flock and does not drink of the milk? ⁸Do I say this merely from a human point of view? Doesn't the Law say the same thing? ⁹For it is written in the Law of Moses: "Do not muzzle an ox while it is treading out the grain."*ᵇ* Is it about oxen that God is concerned? ¹⁰Surely he says this for us, doesn't he? Yes, this was written for us, because when the plowman plows and the thresher threshes, they ought to do so in the hope of sharing in the harvest. ¹¹If we have sown spiritual seed among you, is it too much if we reap a material harvest from you? ¹²If others have this right of support from you, shouldn't we have it all the more? Pr 11:25; Ro 15:27

But we did not use this right. On the contrary, we put up with anything rather than hin-der the gospel of Christ. ¹³Don't you know that those who work in the temple get their food from the temple, and those who serve at the altar share in what is offered on the altar? ¹⁴In the same way, the Lord has commanded that those who preach the gospel should receive their living from the gospel. 2Co 6:3

¹⁵But I have not used any of these rights. And I am not writing this in the hope that you will do such things for me. I would rather die than have anyone deprive me of this boast. ¹⁶Yet when I preach the gospel, I cannot boast, for I am compelled to preach. Woe to me if I do not preach the gospel! ¹⁷If I preach voluntarily, I have a reward; if not voluntarily, I am simply discharging the trust committed to me. ¹⁸What then is my reward? Just this: that in preaching the gospel I may offer it free of charge, and so not make use of my rights in preaching it. Ro 1:14

¹⁹Though I am free and belong to no man, I make myself a slave to everyone, to win as many as possible. ²⁰To the Jews I became like a Jew, to win the Jews. To those under the law I became like one under the law (though I myself am not under the law), so as to win those under the law. ²¹To those not having the law I became like one not having the law (though I am not free from God's law but am under Christ's law), so as to win

those not having the law. ²²To the weak I became weak, to win the weak. I have become all things to all men so that by all possible means I might save some. ²³I do all this for the sake of the gospel, that I may share in its blessings.   1Co 10:33; 2Co 4:5

²⁴Do you not know that in a race all the runners run, but only one gets the prize? Run in such a way as to get the prize. ²⁵Everyone who competes in the games goes into strict training. They do it to get a crown that will not last; but we do it to get a crown that will last forever. ²⁶Therefore I do not run like a man running aimlessly; I do not fight like a man beating the air. ²⁷No, I beat my body and make it my slave so that after I have preached to others, I myself will not be disqualified for the prize.

Warnings From Israel's History

10 For I do not want you to be ignorant of the fact, brothers, that our forefathers were all under the cloud and that they all passed through the sea. ²They were all baptized into Moses in the cloud and in the sea. ³They all ate the same spiritual food ⁴and drank the same spiritual drink; for they drank from the spiritual rock that accompanied them, and that rock was Christ. ⁵Nevertheless, God was not pleased with most of

them; their bodies were scattered over the desert.   Heb 3:17-19

⁶Now these things occurred as examples[a] to keep us from setting our hearts on evil things as they did. ⁷Do not be idolaters, as some of them were; as it is written: "The people sat down to eat and drink and got up to indulge in pagan revelry."[b] ⁸We should not commit sexual immorality, as some of them did—and in one day twenty-three thousand of them died. ⁹We should not test the Lord, as some of them did—and were killed by snakes. ¹⁰And do not grumble, as some of them did—and were killed by the destroying angel.   Nu 16:41; 21:5,6; 25:1-9

¹¹These things happened to them as examples and were written down as warnings for us, on whom the fulfillment of the ages has come. ¹²So, if you think you are standing firm, be careful that you don't fall! ¹³No temptation has seized you except what is common to man. And God is faithful; he will not let you be tempted beyond what you can bear. But when you are tempted, he will also provide a way out so that you can stand up under it.   1Co 1:9; 2Pe 2:9

Idol Feasts and the Lord's Supper

¹⁴Therefore, my dear friends, flee from idolatry. ¹⁵I speak to sensible people; judge for yourselves what I say. ¹⁶Is not the

---

^a6 Or *types*; also in verse 11   ^b7 Exodus 32:6

cup of thanksgiving for which we give thanks a participation in the blood of Christ? And is not the bread that we break a participation in the body of Christ? [17]Because there is one loaf, we, who are many, are one body, for we all partake of the one loaf.   Ro 12:5; 1Jn 5:21

[18]Consider the people of Israel: Do not those who eat the sacrifices participate in the altar? [19]Do I mean then that a sacrifice offered to an idol is anything, or that an idol is anything? [20]No, but the sacrifices of pagans are offered to demons, not to God, and I do not want you to be participants with demons. [21]You cannot drink the cup of the Lord and the cup of demons too; you cannot have a part in both the Lord's table and the table of demons. [22]Are we trying to arouse the Lord's jealousy? Are we stronger than he?

The Believer's Freedom

[23]"Everything is permissible"—but not everything is beneficial. "Everything is permissible"—but not everything is constructive. [24]Nobody should seek his own good, but the good of others.   Php 2:4,21

[25]Eat anything sold in the meat market without raising questions of conscience, [26]for, "The earth is the Lord's, and everything in it."[a]   Ac 10:15

[27]If some unbeliever invites you to a meal and you want to go, eat whatever is put before you without raising questions of conscience. [28]But if anyone says to you, "This has been offered in sacrifice," then do not eat it, both for the sake of the man who told you and for conscience' sake[b]— [29]the other man's conscience, I mean, not yours. For why should my freedom be judged by another's conscience? [30]If I take part in the meal with thankfulness, why am I denounced because of something I thank God for?

[31]So whether you eat or drink or whatever you do, do it all for the glory of God. [32]Do not cause anyone to stumble, whether Jews, Greeks or the church of God— [33]even as I try to please everybody in every way. For I am not seeking my own good but the good of many, so that

11 they may be saved. [1]Follow my example, as I follow the example of Christ.Col 3:17

Propriety in Worship

[2]I praise you for remembering me in everything and for holding to the teachings,[c] just as I passed them on to you.   1Co 15:2-3

[3]Now I want you to realize that the head of every man is Christ, and the head of the woman is man, and the head of Christ is God. [4]Every man who prays or prophesies with his head covered dishonors his

---

[a]26 Psalm 24:1   [b]28 Some manuscripts *conscience' sake, for "the earth is the Lord's and everything in it"*   [c]2 Or *traditions*

head. 5And every woman who prays or prophesies with her head uncovered dishonors her head—it is just as though her head were shaved. 6If a woman does not cover her head, she should have her hair cut off; and if it is a disgrace for a woman to have her hair cut or shaved off, she should cover her head. 7A man ought not to cover his head,*a* since he is the image and glory of God; but the woman is the glory of man. 8For man did not come from woman, but woman from man; 9neither was man created for woman, but woman for man. 10For this reason, and because of the angels, the woman ought to have a sign of authority on her head.

11In the Lord, however, woman is not independent of man, nor is man independent of woman. 12For as woman came from man, so also man is born of woman. But everything comes from God. 13Judge for yourselves: Is it proper for a woman to pray to God with her head uncovered? 14Does not the very nature of things teach you that if a man has long hair, it is a disgrace to him, 15but that if a woman has long hair, it is her glory? For long hair is given to her as a covering. 16If anyone wants to be contentious about this, we have no other prac-

tice—nor do the churches of God. Ge 2:18; Ro 11:36; 1Co 10:32

The Lord's Supper

17In the following directives I have no praise for you, for your meetings do more harm than good. 18In the first place, I hear that when you come together as a church, there are divisions among you, and to some extent I believe it. 19No doubt there have to be differences among you to show which of you have God's approval. 20When you come together, it is not the Lord's Supper you eat, 21for as you eat, each of you goes ahead without waiting for anybody else. One remains hungry, another gets drunk. 22Don't you have homes to eat and drink in? Or do you despise the church of God and humiliate those who have nothing? What shall I say to you? Shall I praise you for this? Certainly not!

23For I received from the Lord what I also passed on to you: The Lord Jesus, on the night he was betrayed, took bread, 24and when he had given thanks, he broke it and said, "This is my body, which is for you; do this in remembrance of me." 25In the same way, after supper he took the cup, saying, "This cup is the new covenant in my blood; do this, whenever you drink it, in

---

a4-7 Or 4Every man who prays or prophesies with long hair dishonors his head. 5And every woman who prays or prophesies with no covering of hair on her head dishonors her head—she is just like one of the "shorn women." 6If a woman has no covering, let her be for now with short hair, but since it is a disgrace for a woman to have her hair shorn or shaved, she should grow it again. 7A man ought not to have long hair

remembrance of me." ²⁶For whenever you eat this bread and drink this cup, you proclaim the Lord's death until he comes.   1Co 10:16; Gal 1:12

²⁷Therefore, whoever eats the bread or drinks the cup of the Lord in an unworthy manner will be guilty of sinning against the body and blood of the Lord. ²⁸A man ought to examine himself before he eats of the bread and drinks of the cup. ²⁹For anyone who eats and drinks without recognizing the body of the Lord eats and drinks judgment on himself. ³⁰That is why many among you are weak and sick, and a number of you have fallen asleep. ³¹But if we judged ourselves, we would not come under judgment. ³²When we are judged by the Lord, we are being disciplined so that we will not be condemned with the world.   Ps 94:12; Heb 10:29

³³So then, my brothers, when you come together to eat, wait for each other. ³⁴If anyone is hungry, he should eat at home, so that when you meet together it may not result in judgment. And when I come I will give further directions.   1Co 4:19

Spiritual Gifts

12 Now about spiritual gifts, brothers, I do not want you to be ignorant. ²You know that when you were pagans, somehow or other you were influenced and led astray to mute idols. ³Therefore I tell you that no one who is speaking by the Spirit of God says, "Jesus be cursed," and no one can say, "Jesus is Lord," except by the Holy Spirit.   1Jn 4:2,3

⁴There are different kinds of gifts, but the same Spirit. ⁵There are different kinds of service, but the same Lord. ⁶There are different kinds of working, but the same God works all of them in all men.   Ro 12:4-8; Eph 4:6

⁷Now to each one the manifestation of the Spirit is given for the common good. ⁸To one there is given through the Spirit the message of wisdom, to another the message of knowledge by means of the same Spirit, ⁹to another faith by the same Spirit, to another gifts of healing by that one Spirit, ¹⁰to another miraculous powers, to another prophecy, to another distinguishing between spirits, to another speaking in different kinds of tongues,ᵃ and to still another the interpretation of tongues.ᵃ ¹¹All these are the work of one and the same Spirit, and he gives them to each one, just as he determines.

One Body, Many Parts

¹²The body is a unit, though it is made up of many parts; and though all its parts are many, they form one body. So it is with Christ. ¹³For we were all baptized byᵇ one Spirit into one body—whether Jews or Greeks,

---

ᵃ10 Or *languages*; also in verse 28   ᵇ13 Or *with*; or *in*

slave or free—and we were all given the one Spirit to drink.

¹⁴Now the body is not made up of one part but of many. ¹⁵If the foot should say, "Because I am not a hand, I do not belong to the body," it would not for that reason cease to be part of the body. ¹⁶And if the ear should say, "Because I am not an eye, I do not belong to the body," it would not for that reason cease to be part of the body. ¹⁷If the whole body were an eye, where would the sense of hearing be? If the whole body were an ear, where would the sense of smell be? ¹⁸But in fact God has arranged the parts in the body, every one of them, just as he wanted them to be. ¹⁹If they were all one part, where would the body be? ²⁰As it is, there are many parts, but one body. Ro 12:5

²¹The eye cannot say to the hand, "I don't need you!" And the head cannot say to the feet, "I don't need you!" ²²On the contrary, those parts of the body that seem to be weaker are indispensable, ²³and the parts that we think are less honorable we treat with special honor. And the parts that are unpresentable are treated with special modesty, ²⁴while our presentable parts need no special treatment. But God has combined the members of the body and has given greater honor to the parts that lacked it, ²⁵so that

there should be no division in the body, but that its parts should have equal concern for each other. ²⁶If one part suffers, every part suffers with it; if one part is honored, every part rejoices with it.

²⁷Now you are the body of Christ, and each one of you is a part of it. ²⁸And in the church God has appointed first of all apostles, second prophets, third teachers, then workers of miracles, also those having gifts of healing, those able to help others, those with gifts of administration, and those speaking in different kinds of tongues. ²⁹Are all apostles? Are all prophets? Are all teachers? Do all work miracles? ³⁰Do all have gifts of healing? Do all speak in tongues*a*? Do all interpret? ³¹But eagerly desire*b* the greater gifts. Eph 1:22,23; 1Co 14:1

Love

And now I will show you the most excellent way.

13 If I speak in the tongues*c* of men and of angels, but have not love, I am only a resounding gong or a clanging cymbal. ²If I have the gift of prophecy and can fathom all mysteries and all knowledge, and if I have a faith that can move mountains, but have not love, I am nothing. ³If I give all I possess to the poor and surrender my body to the flames,*d* but

---

*a*30 Or *other languages*   *b*31 Or *But you are eagerly desiring*   *c*1 Or *languages*
*d*3 Some early manuscripts *body that I may boast*

have not love, I gain nothing.

⁴Love is patient, love is kind. It does not envy, it does not boast, it is not proud. ⁵It is not rude, it is not self-seeking, it is not easily angered, it keeps no record of wrongs. ⁶Love does not delight in evil but rejoices with the truth. ⁷It always protects, always trusts, always hopes, always perseveres.

⁸Love never fails. But where there are prophecies, they will cease; where there are tongues, they will be stilled; where there is knowledge, it will pass away. ⁹For we know in part and we prophesy in part, ¹⁰but when perfection comes, the imperfect disappears. ¹¹When I was a child, I talked like a child, I thought like a child, I reasoned like a child. When I became a man, I put childish ways behind me. ¹²Now we see but a poor reflection as in a mirror; then we shall see face to face. Now I know in part; then I shall know fully, even as I am fully known.

¹³And now these three remain: faith, hope and love. But the greatest of these is love.

Gifts of Prophecy and Tongues

14 Follow the way of love and eagerly desire spiritual gifts, especially the gift of prophecy. ²For anyone who speaks in a tongue*ᵃ* does not speak to men but to God. Indeed, no one understands him; he utters mysteries with his spirit.*ᵇ* ³But everyone who prophesies speaks to men for their strengthening, encouragement and comfort. ⁴He who speaks in a tongue edifies himself, but he who prophesies edifies the church. ⁵I would like every one of you to speak in tongues,*ᶜ* but I would rather have you prophesy. He who prophesies is greater than one who speaks in tongues,*ᶜ* unless he interprets, so that the church may be edified.   1Co 16:14

⁶Now, brothers, if I come to you and speak in tongues, what good will I be to you, unless I bring you some revelation or knowledge or prophecy or word of instruction? ⁷Even in the case of lifeless things that make sounds, such as the flute or harp, how will anyone know what tune is being played unless there is a distinction in the notes? ⁸Again, if the trumpet does not sound a clear call, who will get ready for battle? ⁹So it is with you. Unless you speak intelligible words with your tongue, how will anyone know what you are saying? You will just be speaking into the air. ¹⁰Undoubtedly there are all sorts of languages in the world, yet none of them is without meaning. ¹¹If then I do not grasp the meaning of what someone is saying, I am a foreigner to the

ᵃ2 Or *another language*; also in verses 4, 13, 14, 19, 26 and 27   ᵇ2 Or *by the Spirit*
ᶜ5 Or *other languages*; also in verses 6, 18, 22, 23 and 39

speaker, and he is a foreigner to me. ¹²So it is with you. Since you are eager to have spiritual gifts, try to excel in gifts that build up the church.   Eph 1:17

¹³For this reason anyone who speaks in a tongue should pray that he may interpret what he says. ¹⁴For if I pray in a tongue, my spirit prays, but my mind is unfruitful. ¹⁵So what shall I do? I will pray with my spirit, but I will also pray with my mind; I will sing with my spirit, but I will also sing with my mind. ¹⁶If you are praising God with your spirit, how can one who finds himself among those who do not understand*a* say "Amen" to your thanksgiving, since he does not know what you are saying? ¹⁷You may be giving thanks well enough, but the other man is not edified.   Eph 5:19

¹⁸I thank God that I speak in tongues more than all of you. ¹⁹But in the church I would rather speak five intelligible words to instruct others than ten thousand words in a tongue.

²⁰Brothers, stop thinking like children. In regard to evil be infants, but in your thinking be adults. ²¹In the Law it is written:

"Through men of strange
       tongues
   and through the lips of
       foreigners
   I will speak to this people,

but even then they will not
       listen to me,"*b*
says the Lord.

²²Tongues, then, are a sign, not for believers but for unbelievers; prophecy, however, is for believers, not for unbelievers. ²³So if the whole church comes together and everyone speaks in tongues, and some who do not understand*c* or some unbelievers come in, will they not say that you are out of your mind? ²⁴But if an unbeliever or someone who does not understand*d* comes in while everybody is prophesying, he will be convinced by all that he is a sinner and will be judged by all, ²⁵and the secrets of his heart will be laid bare. So he will fall down and worship God, exclaiming, "God is really among you!"

Orderly Worship

²⁶What then shall we say, brothers? When you come together, everyone has a hymn, or a word of instruction, a revelation, a tongue or an interpretation. All of these must be done for the strengthening of the church. ²⁷If anyone speaks in a tongue, two—or at the most three—should speak, one at a time, and someone must interpret. ²⁸If there is no interpreter, the speaker should keep quiet in the church and speak to himself and God.   Eph 5:19,20

²⁹Two   or   three   prophets

---

a16 Or *among the inquirers or some inquirer*   *b21* Isaiah 28:11,12   *c23* Or *some inquirers*   *d24* Or

should speak, and the others should weigh carefully what is said. ³⁰And if a revelation comes to someone who is sitting down, the first speaker should stop. ³¹For you can all prophesy in turn so that everyone may be instructed and encouraged. ³²The spirits of prophets are subject to the control of prophets. ³³For God is not a God of disorder but of peace.   1Co 13:2

As in all the congregations of the saints, ³⁴women should remain silent in the churches. They are not allowed to speak, but must be in submission, as the Law says. ³⁵If they want to inquire about something, they should ask their own husbands at home; for it is disgraceful for a woman to speak in the church.   1Co 11:5,13

³⁶Did the word of God originate with you? Or are you the only people it has reached? ³⁷If anybody thinks he is a prophet or spiritually gifted, let him acknowledge that what I am writing to you is the Lord's command. ³⁸If he ignores this, he himself will be ignored. ᵃ 2Co 10:7

³⁹Therefore, my brothers, be eager to prophesy, and do not forbid speaking in tongues. ⁴⁰But everything should be done in a fitting and orderly way.

The Resurrection of Christ

15 Now, brothers, I want to remind you of the gospel I preached to you, which you received and on which you have taken your stand. ²By this gospel you are saved, if you hold firmly to the word I preached to you. Otherwise, you have believed in vain.   Isa 40:9; Ro 1:16

³For what I received I passed on to you as of first importanceᵇ: that Christ died for our sins according to the Scriptures, ⁴that he was buried, that he was raised on the third day according to the Scriptures, ⁵and that he appeared to Peter,ᶜ and then to the Twelve. ⁶After that, he appeared to more than five hundred of the brothers at the same time, most of whom are still living, though some have fallen asleep. ⁷Then he appeared to James, then to all the apostles, ⁸and last of all he appeared to me also, as to one abnormally born.   Ac 9:3-6; Gal 1:12

⁹For I am the least of the apostles and do not even deserve to be called an apostle, because I persecuted the church of God. ¹⁰But by the grace of God I am what I am, and his grace to me was not without effect. No, I worked harder than all of them—yet not I, but the grace of God that was with me. ¹¹Whether, then, it was I or they, this is what we preach, and this is what you believed.

The Resurrection of the Dead

¹²But if it is preached that

ᵃ38 Some manuscripts *If he is ignorant of this, let him be ignorant*   ᵇ3 Or *you at the first*
ᶜ5 Greek *Cephas*

Christ has been raised from the dead, how can some of you say that there is no resurrection of the dead? ¹³If there is no resurrection of the dead, then not even Christ has been raised. ¹⁴And if Christ has not been raised, our preaching is useless and so is your faith. ¹⁵More than that, we are then found to be false witnesses about God, for we have testified about God that he raised Christ from the dead. But he did not raise him if in fact the dead are not raised. ¹⁶For if the dead are not raised, then Christ has not been raised either. ¹⁷And if Christ has not been raised, your faith is futile; you are still in your sins. ¹⁸Then those also who have fallen asleep in Christ are lost. ¹⁹If only for this life we have hope in Christ, we are to be pitied more than all men. Ro 4:25; 1Th 4:14

²⁰But Christ has indeed been raised from the dead, the firstfruits of those who have fallen asleep. ²¹For since death came through a man, the resurrection of the dead comes also through a man. ²²For as in Adam all die, so in Christ all will be made alive. ²³But each in his own turn: Christ, the firstfruits; then, when he comes, those who belong to him. ²⁴Then the end will come, when he hands over the kingdom to God the Father after he has destroyed all dominion, authority and power. ²⁵For he must reign until he has put all his enemies under his feet. ²⁶The last enemy to be destroyed is death. ²⁷For he "has put everything under his feet." ^a Now when it says that "everything" has been put under him, it is clear that this does not include God himself, who put everything under Christ. ²⁸When he has done this, then the Son himself will be made subject to him who put everything under him, so that God may be all in all. Php 3:21; 1Pe 1:3

²⁹Now if there is no resurrection, what will those do who are baptized for the dead? If the dead are not raised at all, why are people baptized for them? ³⁰And as for us, why do we endanger ourselves every hour? ³¹I die every day—I mean that, brothers—just as surely as I glory over you in Christ Jesus our Lord. ³²If I fought wild beasts in Ephesus for merely human reasons, what have I gained? If the dead are not raised,

"Let us eat and drink,
 for tomorrow we die." ^b

³³Do not be misled: "Bad company corrupts good character." ³⁴Come back to your senses as you ought, and stop sinning; for there are some who are ignorant of God—I say this to your shame. 1Co 6:9; Gal 4:8,9

The Resurrection Body

³⁵But someone may ask,

^a27 Psalm 8:6   ^b32 Isaiah 22:13

"How are the dead raised? With what kind of body will they come?" ³⁶How foolish! What you sow does not come to life unless it dies. ³⁷When you sow, you do not plant the body that will be, but just a seed, perhaps of wheat or of something else. ³⁸But God gives it a body as he has determined, and to each kind of seed he gives its own body. ³⁹All flesh is not the same: Men have one kind of flesh, animals have another, birds another and fish another. ⁴⁰There are also heavenly bodies and there are earthly bodies; but the splendor of the heavenly bodies is one kind, and the splendor of the earthly bodies is another. ⁴¹The sun has one kind of splendor, the moon another and the stars another; and star differs from star in splendor.

⁴²So will it be with the resurrection of the dead. The body that is sown is perishable, it is raised imperishable; ⁴³it is sown in dishonor, it is raised in glory; it is sown in weakness, it is raised in power; ⁴⁴it is sown a natural body, it is raised a spiritual body.   Da 12:3; Col 3:4

If there is a natural body, there is also a spiritual body. ⁴⁵So it is written: "The first man Adam became a living being"ᵃ; the last Adam, a life-giving spirit. ⁴⁶The spiritual did not come first, but the natural, and after that the spiritual. ⁴⁷The first man was of the dust of the earth, the second man from heaven. ⁴⁸As was the earthly man, so are those who are of the earth; and as is the man from heaven, so also are those who are of heaven. ⁴⁹And just as we have borne the likeness of the earthly man, so shall weᵇ bear the likeness of the man from heaven.   Ge 2:7; Ro 8:29

⁵⁰I declare to you, brothers, that flesh and blood cannot inherit the kingdom of God, nor does the perishable inherit the imperishable. ⁵¹Listen, I tell you a mystery: We will not all sleep, but we will all be changed— ⁵²in a flash, in the twinkling of an eye, at the last trumpet. For the trumpet will sound, the dead will be raised imperishable, and we will be changed. ⁵³For the perishable must clothe itself with the imperishable, and the mortal with immortality. ⁵⁴When the perishable has been clothed with the imperishable, and the mortal with immortality, then the saying that is written will come true: "Death has been swallowed up in victory."ᶜ   Php 3:21; Heb 2:14

⁵⁵"Where, O death, is your
    victory?
  Where, O death, is your
    sting?"ᵈ

⁵⁶The sting of death is sin, and the power of sin is the law. ⁵⁷But

ᵃ45 Gen. 2:7   ᵇ49 Some early manuscripts *so let us*   ᶜ54 Isaiah 25:8
ᵈ55 Hosea 13:14

thanks be to God! He gives us the victory through our Lord Jesus Christ.   Ro 5:12; Heb 2:14

⁵⁸Therefore, my dear brothers, stand firm. Let nothing move you. Always give yourselves fully to the work of the Lord, because you know that your labor in the Lord is not in vain.   Isa 65:23

The Collection for God's People

16 Now about the collection for God's people: Do what I told the Galatian churches to do. ²On the first day of every week, each one of you should set aside a sum of money in keeping with his income, saving it up, so that when I come no collections will have to be made. ³Then, when I arrive, I will give letters of introduction to the men you approve and send them with your gift to Jerusalem. ⁴If it seems advisable for me to go also, they will accompany me.   Ac 24:17; 2Co 9:4,5

Personal Requests

⁵After I go through Macedonia, I will come to you—for I will be going through Macedonia. ⁶Perhaps I will stay with you awhile, or even spend the winter, so that you can help me on my journey, wherever I go. ⁷I do not want to see you now and make only a passing visit; I

hope to spend some time with you, if the Lord permits. ⁸But I will stay on at Ephesus until Pentecost, ⁹because a great door for effective work has opened to me, and there are many who oppose me.   1Co 4:19

¹⁰If Timothy comes, see to it that he has nothing to fear while he is with you, for he is carrying on the work of the Lord, just as I am. ¹¹No one, then, should refuse to accept him. Send him on his way in peace so that he may return to me. I am expecting him along with the brothers.

¹²Now about our brother Apollos: I strongly urged him to go to you with the brothers. He was quite unwilling to go now, but he will go when he has the opportunity.   Ac 18:24

¹³Be on your guard; stand firm in the faith; be men of courage; be strong. ¹⁴Do everything in love.   1Co 1:8; 14:1

¹⁵You know that the household of Stephanas were the first converts in Achaia, and they have devoted themselves to the service of the saints. I urge you, brothers, ¹⁶to submit to such as these and to everyone who joins in the work, and labors at it. ¹⁷I was glad when Stephanas, Fortunatus and Achaicus arrived, because they have supplied what was lacking from you. ¹⁸For they refreshed my spirit and yours also. Such men deserve recognition.

Final Greetings

¹⁹The churches in the province of Asia send you greetings. Aquila and Priscilla*ᵃ* greet you warmly in the Lord, and so does the church that meets at their house. ²⁰All the brothers here send you greetings. Greet one another with a holy kiss.

²¹I, Paul, write this greeting in my own hand.

²²If anyone does not love the Lord—a curse be on him. Come, O Lord*ᵇ*!　　　Eph 6:24

²³The grace of the Lord Jesus be with you.

²⁴My love to all of you in Christ Jesus. Amen.*ᶜ*

ᵃ19 Greek *Prisca,* a variant of *Priscilla*　　*ᵇ22* In Aramaic the expression *Come, O Lord* is *Marana tha.*　　*ᶜ24* Some manuscripts do not have *Amen.*

2 Corinthians

Introduction:

The letter known as 2 Corinthians seems to have been written a few months after the first letter. The divisions and problems that were present in 1 Corinthians were still in the church at Corinth. Paul himself may have made a quick trip to Corinth, but left rather quickly because some of the members in the church there refused to change or believe that Paul was an apostle of God.

After returning to Macedonia, Paul felt much better when Titus brought him the good news that the people in the Corinthian church had seen their problems and sins and were willing to change. It was at this time that Paul wrote his second letter to the Corinthians.

The first part of this letter tells how happy and thankful Paul was when he heard that the Corinthians were sorry for the way they had acted and were now trying to live the way God wanted them to.

In the second part of the letter, Paul defends himself against the people who were angry with him and who were saying untrue things about him.

Outline of contents:

---

1 Paul, an apostle of Christ Jesus by the will of God, and Timothy our brother, Ac 16:1

To the church of God in Corinth, together with all the saints throughout Achaia: 1Co 10:32

²Grace and peace to you from God our Father and the Lord Jesus Christ.

The God of All Comfort

³Praise be to the God and Father of our Lord Jesus Christ, the Father of compassion and the God of all comfort, ⁴who comforts us in all our troubles,

so that we can comfort those in any trouble with the comfort we ourselves have received from God. ⁵For just as the sufferings of Christ flow over into our lives, so also through Christ our comfort overflows. ⁶If we are distressed, it is for your comfort and salvation; if we are comforted, it is for your comfort, which produces in you patient endurance of the same sufferings we suffer. ⁷And our hope for you is firm, because we know that just as you share in our sufferings, so also you share in our comfort.　　　　Isa 51:12; 2Co 4:15

⁸We do not want you to be uninformed, brothers, about the hardships we suffered in the province of Asia. We were under great pressure, far beyond our ability to endure, so that we despaired even of life. ⁹Indeed, in our hearts we felt the sentence of death. But this happened that we might not rely on ourselves but on God, who raises the dead. ¹⁰He has delivered us from such a deadly peril, and he will deliver us. On him we have set our hope that he will continue to deliver us, ¹¹as you help us by your prayers. Then many will give thanks on our*ᵃ* behalf for the gracious favor granted us in answer to the prayers of many.

Paul's Change of Plans

¹²Now this is our boast: Our conscience testifies that we

have conducted ourselves in the world, and especially in our relations with you, in the holiness and sincerity that are from God. We have done so not according to worldly wisdom but according to God's grace. ¹³For we do not write you anything you cannot read or understand. And I hope that, ¹⁴as you have understood us in part, you will come to understand fully that you can boast of us just as we will boast of you in the day of the Lord Jesus.　　　　Ac 23:1; 1Co 1:8

¹⁵Because I was confident of this, I planned to visit you first so that you might benefit twice. ¹⁶I planned to visit you on my way to Macedonia and to come back to you from Macedonia, and then to have you send me on my way to Judea. ¹⁷When I planned this, did I do it lightly? Or do I make my plans in a worldly manner so that in the same breath I say, "Yes, yes" and "No, no"?　　　　1Co 4:19

¹⁸But as surely as God is faithful, our message to you is not "Yes" and "No." ¹⁹For the Son of God, Jesus Christ, who was preached among you by me and Silas*ᵇ* and Timothy, was not "Yes" and "No," but in him it has always been "Yes." ²⁰For no matter how many promises God has made, they are "Yes" in Christ. And so through him the "Amen" is spoken by us to the glory of God. ²¹Now it is God who makes both us and

---

ᵃ11 Many manuscripts *your*　　　*ᵇ19* Greek *Silvanus*, a variant of *Silas*

you stand firm in Christ. He anointed us, [22]set his seal of ownership on us, and put his Spirit in our hearts as a deposit, guaranteeing what is to come.

[23]I call God as my witness that it was in order to spare you that I did not return to Corinth. [24]Not that we lord it over your faith, but we work with you for your joy, because it is by faith **2** you stand firm. [1]So I made up my mind that I would not make another painful visit to you. [2]For if I grieve you, who is left to make me glad but you whom I have grieved? [3]I wrote as I did so that when I came I should not be distressed by those who ought to make me rejoice. I had confidence in all of you, that you would all share my joy. [4]For I wrote you out of great distress and anguish of heart and with many tears, not to grieve you but to let you know the depth of my love for you.   2Co 1:23; 7:8,12

Forgiveness for the Sinner

[5]If anyone has caused grief, he has not so much grieved me as he has grieved all of you, to some extent—not to put it too severely. [6]The punishment inflicted on him by the majority is sufficient for him. [7]Now instead, you ought to forgive and comfort him, so that he will not be overwhelmed by excessive sorrow. [8]I urge you, therefore, to reaffirm your love for him. [9]The reason I wrote you was to see if you would stand the test and be obedient in everything. [10]If you forgive anyone, I also forgive him. And what I have forgiven—if there was anything to forgive—I have forgiven in the sight of Christ for your sake, [11]in order that Satan might not outwit us. For we are not unaware of his schemes.   Gal 6:1

Ministers of the New Covenant

[12]Now when I went to Troas to preach the gospel of Christ and found that the Lord had opened a door for me, [13]I still had no peace of mind, because I did not find my brother Titus there. So I said good-by to them and went on to Macedonia.

[14]But thanks be to God, who always leads us in triumphal procession in Christ and through us spreads everywhere the fragrance of the knowledge of him. [15]For we are to God the aroma of Christ among those who are being saved and those who are perishing. [16]To the one we are the smell of death; to the other, the fragrance of life. And who is equal to such a task? [17]Unlike so many, we do not peddle the word of God for profit. On the contrary, in Christ we speak before God with sincerity, like men sent from God.   Ex 29:18; Jn 3:36; Eph 5:2

3 Are we beginning to commend ourselves again? Or do we need, like some people, letters of recommendation to you or from you? [2]You your-

selves are our letter, written on our hearts, known and read by everybody. ³You show that you are a letter from Christ, the result of our ministry, written not with ink but with the Spirit of the living God, not on tablets of stone but on tablets of human hearts.   Jer 31:33; 1Co 9:2

⁴Such confidence as this is ours through Christ before God. ⁵Not that we are competent in ourselves to claim anything for ourselves, but our competence comes from God. ⁶He has made us competent as ministers of a new covenant—not of the letter but of the Spirit; for the letter kills, but the Spirit gives life.   Eph 3:12

The Glory of the New Covenant

⁷Now if the ministry that brought death, which was engraved in letters on stone, came with glory, so that the Israelites could not look steadily at the face of Moses because of its glory, fading though it was, ⁸will not the ministry of the Spirit be even more glorious? ⁹If the ministry that condemns men is glorious, how much more glorious is the ministry that brings righteousness! ¹⁰For what was glorious has no glory now in comparison with the surpassing glory. ¹¹And if what was fading away came with glory, how much greater is the glory of that which lasts!

¹²Therefore, since we have such a hope, we are very bold. ¹³We are not like Moses, who would put a veil over his face to keep the Israelites from gazing at it while the radiance was fading away. ¹⁴But their minds were made dull, for to this day the same veil remains when the old covenant is read. It has not been removed, because only in Christ is it taken away. ¹⁵Even to this day when Moses is read, a veil covers their hearts. ¹⁶But whenever anyone turns to the Lord, the veil is taken away. ¹⁷Now the Lord is the Spirit, and where the Spirit of the Lord is, there is freedom. ¹⁸And we, who with unveiled faces all reflect*a* the Lord's glory, are being transformed into his likeness with ever-increasing glory, which comes from the Lord, who is the Spirit.   Ro 5:4-5

Treasures in Jars of Clay

4 Therefore, since through God's mercy we have this ministry, we do not lose heart. ²Rather, we have renounced secret and shameful ways; we do not use deception, nor do we distort the word of God. On the contrary, by setting forth the truth plainly we commend ourselves to every man's conscience in the sight of God. ³And even if our gospel is veiled, it is veiled to those who are perishing. ⁴The god of this age has blinded the minds of

---

*a*18 Or *contemplate*

unbelievers, so that they cannot see the light of the gospel of the glory of Christ, who is the image of God. [5]For we do not preach ourselves, but Jesus Christ as Lord, and ourselves as your servants for Jesus' sake. [6]For God, who said, "Let light shine out of darkness,"[a] made his light shine in our hearts to give us the light of the knowledge of the glory of God in the face of Christ.   1Co 1:23; 2Co 5:11

[7]But we have this treasure in jars of clay to show that this all-surpassing power is from God and not from us. [8]We are hard pressed on every side, but not crushed; perplexed, but not in despair; [9]persecuted, but not abandoned; struck down, but not destroyed. [10]We always carry around in our body the death of Jesus, so that the life of Jesus may also be revealed in our body. [11]For we who are alive are always being given over to death for Jesus' sake, so that his life may be revealed in our mortal body. [12]So then, death is at work in us, but life is at work in you.   Ps 37:24; Ro 6:5,6; 2Co 13:9

[13]It is written: "I believed; therefore I have spoken."[b] With that same spirit of faith we also believe and therefore speak, [14]because we know that the one who raised the Lord Jesus from the dead will also raise us with Jesus and present us with you in his presence. [15]All this is for your benefit, so that the grace

that is reaching more and more people may cause thanksgiving to overflow to the glory of God. [16]Therefore we do not lose heart. Though outwardly we are wasting away, yet inwardly we are being renewed day by day. [17]For our light and momentary troubles are achieving for us an eternal glory that far outweighs them all. [18]So we fix our eyes not on what is seen, but on what is unseen. For what is seen is temporary, but what is unseen is eternal.   1Pe 1:6,7

Our Heavenly Dwelling

5 Now we know that if the earthly tent we live in is destroyed, we have a building from God, an eternal house in heaven, not built by human hands. [2]Meanwhile we groan, longing to be clothed with our heavenly dwelling, [3]because when we are clothed, we will not be found naked. [4]For while we are in this tent, we groan and are burdened, because we do not wish to be unclothed but to be clothed with our heavenly dwelling, so that what is mortal may be swallowed up by life. [5]Now it is God who has made us for this very purpose and has given us the Spirit as a deposit, guaranteeing what is to come. [6]Therefore we are always confident and know that as long as we are at home in the body we are away from the Lord. [7]We live by faith, not by sight. [8]We

are confident, I say, and would prefer to be away from the body and at home with the Lord. [9]So we make it our goal to please him, whether we are at home in the body or away from it. [10]For we must all appear before the judgment seat of Christ, that each one may receive what is due him for the things done while in the body, whether good or bad. Ac 10:42; 1Co 13:12

The Ministry of Reconciliation

[11]Since, then, we know what it is to fear the Lord, we try to persuade men. What we are is plain to God, and I hope it is also plain to your conscience. [12]We are not trying to commend ourselves to you again, but are giving you an opportunity to take pride in us, so that you can answer those who take pride in what is seen rather than in what is in the heart. [13]If we are out of our mind, it is for the sake of God; if we are in our right mind, it is for you. [14]For Christ's love compels us, because we are convinced that one died for all, and therefore all died. [15]And he died for all, that those who live should no longer live for themselves but for him who died for them and was raised again.

[16]So from now on we regard no one from a worldly point of view. Though we once regarded Christ in this way, we do so no longer. [17]Therefore, if anyone is in Christ, he is a new creation; the old has gone, the new has come! [18]All this is from God, who reconciled us to himself through Christ and gave us the ministry of reconciliation: [19]that God was reconciling the world to himself in Christ, not counting men's sins against them. And he has committed to us the message of reconciliation. [20]We are therefore Christ's ambassadors, as though God were making his appeal through us. We implore you on Christ's behalf: Be reconciled to God. [21]God made him who had no sin to be sin[a] for us, so that in him we might become the righteousness of God. Ro 6:4; 2Co 6:1

6 As God's fellow workers we urge you not to receive God's grace in vain. [2]For he says,

"In the time of my favor I
    heard you,
and in the day of salvation I
    helped you."[b]

I tell you, now is the time of God's favor, now is the day of salvation.

Paul's Hardships

[3]We put no stumbling block in anyone's path, so that our ministry will not be discredited. [4]Rather, as servants of God we commend ourselves in every way: in great endurance; in troubles, hardships and distresses; [5]in beatings, imprison-

---

[a]21 Or *be a sin offering*   [b]2 Isaiah 49:8

ments and riots; in hard work, sleepless nights and hunger; 6in purity, understanding, patience and kindness; in the Holy Spirit and in sincere love; 7in truthful speech and in the power of God; with weapons of righteousness in the right hand and in the left; 8through glory and dishonor, bad report and good report; genuine, yet regarded as impostors; 9known, yet regarded as unknown; dying, and yet we live on; beaten, and yet not killed; 10sorrowful, yet always rejoicing; poor, yet making many rich; having nothing, and yet possessing everything.

11We have spoken freely to you, Corinthians, and opened wide our hearts to you. 12We are not withholding our affection from you, but you are withholding yours from us. 13As a fair exchange—I speak as to my children—open wide your hearts also.   2Co 7:3; 1Th 2:11

Do Not Be Yoked With Unbelievers

14Do not be yoked together with unbelievers. For what do righteousness and wickedness have in common? Or what fellowship can light have with darkness? 15What harmony is there between Christ and Belial*a*? What does a believer have in common with an unbeliever? 16What agreement is there between the temple of God and idols? For we are the temple of the living God. As God has said:
"I will live with them and walk among them, and I will be their God, and they will be my people."*b*   Ge 24:3; 1Co 10:21

17"Therefore come out from them
   and be separate,   Rev 18:4
         says the Lord.
Touch no unclean thing,
   and I will receive you."*c*
18"I will be a Father to you,
   and you will be my sons
      and daughters,
         says the Lord
            Almighty."*d*

7 Since we have these promises, dear friends, let us purify ourselves from everything that contaminates body and spirit, perfecting holiness out of reverence for God.

Paul's Joy

2Make room for us in your hearts. We have wronged no one, we have corrupted no one, we have exploited no one. 3I do not say this to condemn you; I have said before that you have such a place in our hearts that we would live or die with you. 4I have great confidence in you; I take great pride in you. I am greatly encouraged; in all our troubles my joy knows no bounds.   2Co 6:12-13; 8:24

5For when we came into Macedonia, this body of ours

*a*15 Greek *Beliar*, a variant of *Belial*   *b*16 Lev. 26:12; Jer. 32:38; Ezek. 37:27
*c*17 Isaiah 52:11; Ezek. 20:34,41   *d*18 2 Samuel 7:14; 7:8

had no rest, but we were harassed at every turn—conflicts on the outside, fears within. ⁶But God, who comforts the downcast, comforted us by the coming of Titus, ⁷and not only by his coming but also by the comfort you had given him. He told us about your longing for me, your deep sorrow, your ardent concern for me, so that my joy was greater than ever.   2Co 2:13

⁸Even if I caused you sorrow by my letter, I do not regret it. Though I did regret it—I see that my letter hurt you, but only for a little while— ⁹yet now I am happy, not because you were made sorry, but because your sorrow led you to repentance. For you became sorrowful as God intended and so were not harmed in any way by us. ¹⁰Godly sorrow brings repentance that leads to salvation and leaves no regret, but worldly sorrow brings death. ¹¹See what this godly sorrow has produced in you: what earnestness, what eagerness to clear yourselves, what indignation, what alarm, what longing, what concern, what readiness to see justice done. At every point you have proved yourselves to be innocent in this matter. ¹²So even though I wrote to you, it was not on account of the one who did the wrong or of the injured party, but rather that before God you could see for yourselves how devoted to us you

are. ¹³By all this we are encouraged.   1Co 5:1-2; 2Co 2:2,4

In addition to our own encouragement, we were especially delighted to see how happy Titus was, because his spirit has been refreshed by all of you. ¹⁴I had boasted to him about you, and you have not embarrassed me. But just as everything we said to you was true, so our boasting about you to Titus has proved to be true as well. ¹⁵And his affection for you is all the greater when he remembers that you were all obedient, receiving him with fear and trembling. ¹⁶I am glad I can have complete confidence in you.

Generosity Encouraged

8 And now, brothers, we want you to know about the grace that God has given the Macedonian churches. ²Out of the most severe trial, their overflowing joy and their extreme poverty welled up in rich generosity. ³For I testify that they gave as much as they were able, and even beyond their ability. Entirely on their own, ⁴they urgently pleaded with us for the privilege of sharing in this service to the saints. ⁵And they did not do as we expected, but they gave themselves first to the Lord and then to us in keeping with God's will. ⁶So we urged Titus, since he had earlier made a beginning, to bring also to completion this act of grace on

your part. [7]But just as you excel in everything—in faith, in speech, in knowledge, in complete earnestness and in your love for us[a]—see that you also excel in this grace of giving.

[8]I am not commanding you, but I want to test the sincerity of your love by comparing it with the earnestness of others. [9]For you know the grace of our Lord Jesus Christ, that though he was rich, yet for your sakes he became poor, so that you through his poverty might become rich. Php 2:6-8

[10]And here is my advice about what is best for you in this matter: Last year you were the first not only to give but also to have the desire to do so. [11]Now finish the work, so that your eager willingness to do it may be matched by your completion of it, according to your means. [12]For if the willingness is there, the gift is acceptable according to what one has, not according to what he does not have.

[13]Our desire is not that others might be relieved while you are hard pressed, but that there might be equality. [14]At the present time your plenty will supply what they need, so that in turn their plenty will supply what you need. Then there will be equality, [15]as it is written: "He who gathered much did not have too much, and he who gathered little did not have too little."[b] Ac 4:34,35

Titus Sent to Corinth

[16]I thank God, who put into the heart of Titus the same concern I have for you. [17]For Titus not only welcomed our appeal, but he is coming to you with much enthusiasm and on his own initiative. [18]And we are sending along with him the brother who is praised by all the churches for his service to the gospel. [19]What is more, he was chosen by the churches to accompany us as we carry the offering, which we administer in order to honor the Lord himself and to show our eagerness to help. [20]We want to avoid any criticism of the way we administer this liberal gift. [21]For we are taking pains to do what is right, not only in the eyes of the Lord but also in the eyes of men.

[22]In addition, we are sending with them our brother who has often proved to us in many ways that he is zealous, and now even more so because of his great confidence in you. [23]As for Titus, he is my partner and fellow worker among you; as for our brothers, they are representatives of the churches and an honor to Christ. [24]Therefore show these men the proof of your love and the reason for our pride in you, so that the churches can see it. 2Co 9:2

9 There is no need for me to write to you about this service to the saints. [2]For I know your eagerness to help, and I

---

[a]7 Some manuscripts *in our love for you*   [b]15 Exodus 16:18

have been boasting about it to the Macedonians, telling them that since last year you in Achaia were ready to give; and your enthusiasm has stirred most of them to action. ³But I am sending the brothers in order that our boasting about you in this matter should not prove hollow, but that you may be ready, as I said you would be. ⁴For if any Macedonians come with me and find you unprepared, we—not to say anything about you—would be ashamed of having been so confident. ⁵So I thought it necessary to urge the brothers to visit you in advance and finish the arrangements for the generous gift you had promised. Then it will be ready as a generous gift, not as one grudgingly given. 1Co 16:2

Sowing Generously

⁶Remember this: Whoever sows sparingly will also reap sparingly, and whoever sows generously will also reap generously. ⁷Each man should give what he has decided in his heart to give, not reluctantly or under compulsion, for God loves a cheerful giver. ⁸And God is able to make all grace abound to you, so that in all things at all times, having all that you need, you will abound in every good work. ⁹As it is written: Pr 11:24

"He has scattered abroad his gifts to the poor;

ª9 Psalm 112:9

his righteousness endures forever."ª

¹⁰Now he who supplies seed to the sower and bread for food will also supply and increase your store of seed and will enlarge the harvest of your righteousness. ¹¹You will be made rich in every way so that you can be generous on every occasion, and through us your generosity will result in thanksgiving to God. Mal 3:10

¹²This service that you perform is not only supplying the needs of God's people but is also overflowing in many expressions of thanks to God. ¹³Because of the service by which you have proved yourselves, men will praise God for the obedience that accompanies your confession of the gospel of Christ, and for your generosity in sharing with them and with everyone else. ¹⁴And in their prayers for you their hearts will go out to you, because of the surpassing grace God has given you. ¹⁵Thanks be to God for his indescribable gift! Ro 5:15,16

Paul's Defense of His Ministry

10 By the meekness and gentleness of Christ, I appeal to you—I, Paul, who am "timid" when face to face with you, but "bold" when away! ²I beg you that when I come I may not have to be as bold as I expect

to be toward some people who think that we live by the standards of this world. ³For though we live in the world, we do not wage war as the world does. ⁴The weapons we fight with are not the weapons of the world. On the contrary, they have divine power to demolish strongholds. ⁵We demolish arguments and every pretension that sets itself up against the knowledge of God, and we take captive every thought to make it obedient to Christ. ⁶And we will be ready to punish every act of disobedience, once your obedience is complete.   Ro 12:2; 2Co 9:13

⁷You are looking only on the surface of things.ᵃ If anyone is confident that he belongs to Christ, he should consider again that we belong to Christ just as much as he. ⁸For even if I boast somewhat freely about the authority the Lord gave us for building you up rather than pulling you down, I will not be ashamed of it. ⁹I do not want to seem to be trying to frighten you with my letters. ¹⁰For some say, "His letters are weighty and forceful, but in person he is unimpressive and his speaking amounts to nothing." ¹¹Such people should realize that what we are in our letters when we are absent, we will be in our actions when we are present. Jn 7:24

¹²We do not dare to classify or compare ourselves with some who commend themselves. When they measure themselves by themselves and compare themselves with themselves, they are not wise. ¹³We, however, will not boast beyond proper limits, but will confine our boasting to the field God has assigned to us, a field that reaches even to you. ¹⁴We are not going too far in our boasting, as would be the case if we had not come to you, for we did get as far as you with the gospel of Christ. ¹⁵Neither do we go beyond our limits by boasting of work done by others.ᵇ Our hope is that, as your faith continues to grow, our area of activity among you will greatly expand, ¹⁶so that we can preach the gospel in the regions beyond you. For we do not want to boast about work already done in another man's territory. ¹⁷But, "Let him who boasts boast in the Lord."ᶜ ¹⁸For it is not the one who commends himself who is approved, but the one whom the Lord commends.   Ps 44:8; Ro 15:20

Paul and the False Apostles

11 I hope you will put up with a little of my foolishness; but you are already doing that. ²I am jealous for you with a godly jealousy. I promised you to one husband, to Christ, so

---

ᵃ7 Or *Look at the obvious facts*   ᵇ13-15 Or ¹³*We, however, will not boast about things that cannot be measured, but we will boast according to the standard of measurement that the God of measure has assigned us—a measurement that relates even to you.* ¹⁴ . . . . ¹⁵*Neither do we boast about things that cannot be measured in regard to the work done by others.*   ᶜ17 Jer. 9:24

that I might present you as a pure virgin to him. ³But I am afraid that just as Eve was deceived by the serpent's cunning, your minds may somehow be led astray from your sincere and pure devotion to Christ. ⁴For if someone comes to you and preaches a Jesus other than the Jesus we preached, or if you receive a different spirit from the one you received, or a different gospel from the one you accepted, you put up with it easily enough. ⁵But I do not think I am in the least inferior to those "super-apostles." ⁶I may not be a trained speaker, but I do have knowledge. We have made this perfectly clear to you in every way.   Ro 8:15; Gal 1:6-9

⁷Was it a sin for me to lower myself in order to elevate you by preaching the gospel of God to you free of charge? ⁸I robbed other churches by receiving support from them so as to serve you. ⁹And when I was with you and needed something, I was not a burden to anyone, for the brothers who came from Macedonia supplied what I needed. I have kept myself from being a burden to you in any way, and will continue to do so. ¹⁰As surely as the truth of Christ is in me, nobody in the regions of Achaia will stop this boasting of mine. ¹¹Why? Because I do not love you? God knows I do! ¹²And I will keep on doing what I am doing in order to cut the ground from under those who want an opportunity to be considered equal with us in the things they boast about.

¹³For such men are false apostles, deceitful workmen, masquerading as apostles of Christ. ¹⁴And no wonder, for Satan himself masquerades as an angel of light. ¹⁵It is not surprising, then, if his servants masquerade as servants of righteousness. Their end will be what their actions deserve. Mt 7:15

Paul Boasts About His Sufferings

¹⁶I repeat: Let no one take me for a fool. But if you do, then receive me just as you would a fool, so that I may do a little boasting. ¹⁷In this self-confident boasting I am not talking as the Lord would, but as a fool. ¹⁸Since many are boasting in the way the world does, I too will boast. ¹⁹You gladly put up with fools since you are so wise! ²⁰In fact, you even put up with anyone who enslaves you or exploits you or takes advantage of you or pushes himself forward or slaps you in the face. ²¹To my shame I admit that we were too weak for that!   Gal 2:4; Php 3:3,4

What anyone else dares to boast about—I am speaking as a fool—I also dare to boast about. ²²Are they Hebrews? So am I. Are they Israelites? So am I. Are they Abraham's descendants? So am I. ²³Are they servants of Christ? (I am out of my mind to

talk like this.) I am more. I have worked much harder, been in prison more frequently, been flogged more severely, and been exposed to death again and again. ²⁴Five times I received from the Jews the forty lashes minus one. ²⁵Three times I was beaten with rods, once I was stoned, three times I was shipwrecked, I spent a night and a day in the open sea, ²⁶I have been constantly on the move. I have been in danger from rivers, in danger from bandits, in danger from my own countrymen, in danger from Gentiles; in danger in the city, in danger in the country, in danger at sea; and in danger from false brothers. ²⁷I have labored and toiled and have often gone without sleep; I have known hunger and thirst and have often gone without food; I have been cold and naked. ²⁸Besides everything else, I face daily the pressure of my concern for all the churches. ²⁹Who is weak, and I do not feel weak? Who is led into sin, and I do not inwardly burn? _{Php 3:5}

³⁰If I must boast, I will boast of the things that show my weakness. ³¹The God and Father of the Lord Jesus, who is to be praised forever, knows that I am not lying. ³²In Damascus the governor under King Aretas had the city of the Damascenes guarded in order to arrest me. ³³But I was lowered in a basket from a window in the wall and slipped through his hands.

Paul's Vision and His Thorn

12 I must go on boasting. Although there is nothing to be gained, I will go on to visions and revelations from the Lord. ²I know a man in Christ who fourteen years ago was caught up to the third heaven. Whether it was in the body or out of the body I do not know—God knows. ³And I know that this man—whether in the body or apart from the body I do not know, but God knows— ⁴was caught up to paradise. He heard inexpressible things, things that man is not permitted to tell. ⁵I will boast about a man like that, but I will not boast about myself, except about my weaknesses. ⁶Even if I should choose to boast, I would not be a fool, because I would be speaking the truth. But I refrain, so no one will think more of me than is warranted by what I do or say.

⁷To keep me from becoming conceited because of these surpassingly great revelations, there was given me a thorn in my flesh, a messenger of Satan, to torment me. ⁸Three times I pleaded with the Lord to take it away from me. ⁹But he said to me, "My grace is sufficient for you, for my power is made perfect in weakness." Therefore I will boast all the more gladly about my weaknesses, so that Christ's power may rest on me. ¹⁰That is why, for Christ's sake, I delight in weaknesses, in in-

sults, in hardships, in persecutions, in difficulties. For when I am weak, then I am strong.

Paul's Concern for the Corinthians

[11]I have made a fool of myself, but you drove me to it. I ought to have been commended by you, for I am not in the least inferior to the "super-apostles," even though I am nothing. [12]The things that mark an apostle—signs, wonders and miracles—were done among you with great perseverance. [13]How were you inferior to the other churches, except that I was never a burden to you? Forgive me this wrong!   1Co 9:12; 2Co 11:1

[14]Now I am ready to visit you for the third time, and I will not be a burden to you, because what I want is not your possessions but you. After all, children should not have to save up for their parents, but parents for their children. [15]So I will very gladly spend for you everything I have and expend myself as well. If I love you more, will you love me less? [16]Be that as it may, I have not been a burden to you. Yet, crafty fellow that I am, I caught you by trickery! [17]Did I exploit you through any of the men I sent you? [18]I urged Titus to go to you and I sent our brother with him. Titus did not exploit you, did he? Did we not act in the same spirit and follow the same course?   2Co 11:11,12

[19]Have you been thinking all along that we have been defending ourselves to you? We have been speaking in the sight of God as those in Christ; and everything we do, dear friends, is for your strengthening. [20]For I am afraid that when I come I may not find you as I want you to be, and you may not find me as you want me to be. I fear that there may be quarreling, jealousy, outbursts of anger, factions, slander, gossip, arrogance and disorder. [21]I am afraid that when I come again my God will humble me before you, and I will be grieved over many who have sinned earlier and have not repented of the impurity, sexual sin and debauchery in which they have indulged.   Ro 14:19; 2Co 2:1-4

Final Warnings

13 This will be my third visit to you. "Every matter must be established by the testimony of two or three witnesses."[a] [2]I already gave you a warning when I was with you the second time. I now repeat it while absent: On my return I will not spare those who sinned earlier or any of the others, [3]since you are demanding proof that Christ is speaking through me. He is not weak in dealing with you, but is powerful among you. [4]For to be sure, he was crucified in weakness, yet he lives by God's power. Like-

[a]1 Deut. 19:15

wise, we are weak in him, yet by God's power we will live with him to serve you.   2Co 12:14

⁵Examine yourselves to see whether you are in the faith; test yourselves. Do you not realize that Christ Jesus is in you—unless, of course, you fail the test? ⁶And I trust that you will discover that we have not failed the test. ⁷Now we pray to God that you will not do anything wrong. Not that people will see that we have stood the test but that you will do what is right even though we may seem to have failed. ⁸For we cannot do anything against the truth, but only for the truth. ⁹We are glad whenever we are weak but you are strong; and our prayer is for your perfection. ¹⁰This is

why I write these things when I am absent, that when I come I may not have to be harsh in my use of authority—the authority the Lord gave me for building you up, not for tearing you down.   Ro 8:10; 2Co 1:23,24

Final Greetings

¹¹Finally, brothers, good-by. Aim for perfection, listen to my appeal, be of one mind, live in peace. And the God of love and peace will be with you.   1Th 4:1

¹²Greet one another with a holy kiss. ¹³All the saints send their greetings.

¹⁴May the grace of the Lord Jesus Christ, and the love of God, and the fellowship of the Holy Spirit be with you all.

Galatians

Introduction:

Paul wrote this letter to the Christian churches in the Roman province of Galatia. These churches were being confused by false teachers called Judaizers, who were teaching the gentile Christians that they were not really saved unless they obeyed all the Jewish laws—such as circumcision, eating special foods, and celebrating Jewish feast days. This group also said that Paul did not have God's authority and, therefore, was not to be listened to.

Paul begins the letter by telling the Galatians what gospel it is that he preaches and that his authority is from God. We cannot be saved from our sins by obeying the law; we are saved only by believing in Jesus Christ, Paul adds. Christians are free to live by the law of love, not the law of Moses. Faith, says Paul, must be shown in love and believers must live by the Spirit.

Outline of contents:

---

1 Paul, an apostle—sent not from men nor by man, but by Jesus Christ and God the Father, who raised him from the dead— ²and all the brothers with me,   Ac 9:15

To the churches in Galatia:

³Grace and peace to you from God our Father and the Lord Jesus Christ, ⁴who gave himself for our sins to rescue us from the present evil age, according to the will of our God and Father, ⁵to whom be glory for ever and ever. Amen.   Ro 4:25

No Other Gospel

⁶I am astonished that you are so quickly deserting the one who called you by the grace of Christ and are turning to a different gospel— ⁷which is really no gospel at all. Evidently some people are throwing you into confusion and are trying to per-

vert the gospel of Christ. [8]But even if we or an angel from heaven should preach a gospel other than the one we preached to you, let him be eternally condemned! [9]As we have already said, so now I say again: If anybody is preaching to you a gospel other than what you accepted, let him be eternally condemned!   Ro 16:17; 1Co 15:1,2

[10]Am I now trying to win the approval of men, or of God? Or am I trying to please men? If I were still trying to please men, I would not be a servant of Christ.   Ro 2:29

Paul Called by God

[11]I want you to know, brothers, that the gospel I preached is not something that man made up. [12]I did not receive it from any man, nor was I taught it; rather, I received it by revelation from Jesus Christ.   1Co 15:1,2

[13]For you have heard of my previous way of life in Judaism, how intensely I persecuted the church of God and tried to destroy it. [14]I was advancing in Judaism beyond many Jews of my own age and was extremely zealous for the traditions of my fathers. [15]But when God, who set me apart from birth[a] and called me by his grace, was pleased [16]to reveal his Son in me so that I might preach him among the Gentiles, I did not consult any man, [17]nor did I go up to Jerusalem to see those who were apostles before I was, but I went immediately into Arabia and later returned to Damascus.   Ac 9:2; 26:4-5

[18]Then after three years, I went up to Jerusalem to get acquainted with Peter[b] and stayed with him fifteen days. [19]I saw none of the other apostles—only James, the Lord's brother. [20]I assure you before God that what I am writing you is no lie. [21]Later I went to Syria and Cilicia. [22]I was personally unknown to the churches of Judea that are in Christ. [23]They only heard the report: "The man who formerly persecuted us is now preaching the faith he once tried to destroy." [24]And they praised God because of me.   Ac 9:22-23

Paul Accepted by the Apostles

2 Fourteen years later I went up again to Jerusalem, this time with Barnabas. I took Titus along also. [2]I went in response to a revelation and set before them the gospel that I preach among the Gentiles. But I did this privately to those who seemed to be leaders, for fear that I was running or had run my race in vain. [3]Yet not even Titus, who was with me, was compelled to be circumcised, even though he was a Greek. [4]This matter arose because some false brothers had infiltrated our ranks to spy on the

[a]15 Or from my mother's womb   [b]18 Greek Cephas

freedom we have in Christ Jesus and to make us slaves. [5]We did not give in to them for a moment, so that the truth of the gospel might remain with you.

[6]As for those who seemed to be important—whatever they were makes no difference to me; God does not judge by external appearance—those men added nothing to my message. [7]On the contrary, they saw that I had been entrusted with the task of preaching the gospel to the Gentiles, [a] just as Peter had been to the Jews. [b] [8]For God, who was at work in the ministry of Peter as an apostle to the Jews, was also at work in my ministry as an apostle to the Gentiles. [9]James, Peter[c] and John, those reputed to be pillars, gave me and Barnabas the right hand of fellowship when they recognized the grace given to me. They agreed that we should go to the Gentiles, and they to the Jews. [10]All they asked was that we should continue to remember the poor, the very thing I was eager to do. Ac 10:34,35

Paul Opposes Peter

[11]When Peter came to Antioch, I opposed him to his face, because he was clearly in the wrong. [12]Before certain men came from James, he used to eat with the Gentiles. But when they arrived, he began to draw back and separate himself from the Gentiles because he was afraid of those who belonged to the circumcision group. [13]The other Jews joined him in his hypocrisy, so that by their hypocrisy even Barnabas was led astray. Ac 10:45; 11:2,3

[14]When I saw that they were not acting in line with the truth of the gospel, I said to Peter in front of them all, "You are a Jew, yet you live like a Gentile and not like a Jew. How is it, then, that you force Gentiles to follow Jewish customs? Ac 10:28

[15]"We who are Jews by birth and not 'Gentile sinners' [16]know that a man is not justified by observing the law, but by faith in Jesus Christ. So we, too, have put our faith in Christ Jesus that we may be justified by faith in Christ and not by observing the law, because by observing the law no one will be justified.

[17]"If, while we seek to be justified in Christ, it becomes evident that we ourselves are sinners, does that mean that Christ promotes sin? Absolutely not! [18]If I rebuild what I destroyed, I prove that I am a lawbreaker. [19]For through the law I died to the law so that I might live for God. [20]I have been crucified with Christ and I no longer live, but Christ lives in me. The life I live in the body, I live by faith in the Son of God, who loved me and gave himself for me. [21]I do not set aside the grace of God,

---

[a]7 Greek *uncircumcised*　　[b]7 Greek *circumcised*; also in verses 8 and 9　　[c]9 Greek *Cephas*; also in verses 11 and 14

for if righteousness could be gained through the law, Christ died for nothing!"[a] Ro 8:10

Faith or Observance of the Law

3 You foolish Galatians! Who has bewitched you? Before your very eyes Jesus Christ was clearly portrayed as crucified. [2]I would like to learn just one thing from you: Did you receive the Spirit by observing the law, or by believing what you heard? [3]Are you so foolish? After beginning with the Spirit, are you now trying to attain your goal by human effort? [4]Have you suffered so much for nothing—if it really was for nothing? [5]Does God give you his Spirit and work miracles among you because you observe the law, or because you believe what you heard? Ro 10:17; Gal 2:16

[6]Consider Abraham: "He believed God, and it was credited to him as righteousness."[b] [7]Understand, then, that those who believe are children of Abraham. [8]The Scripture foresaw that God would justify the Gentiles by faith, and announced the gospel in advance to Abraham: "All nations will be blessed through you."[c] [9]So those who have faith are blessed along with Abraham, the man of faith. Ac 3:25; Ro 4:16

[10]All who rely on observing the law are under a curse, for it is written: "Cursed is everyone who does not continue to do everything written in the Book of the Law."[d] [11]Clearly no one is justified before God by the law, because, "The righteous will live by faith."[e] [12]The law is not based on faith; on the contrary, "The man who does these things will live by them."[f] [13]Christ redeemed us from the curse of the law by becoming a curse for us, for it is written: "Cursed is everyone who is hung on a tree."[g] [14]He redeemed us in order that the blessing given to Abraham might come to the Gentiles through Christ Jesus, so that by faith we might receive the promise of the Spirit. Gal 2:16

The Law and the Promise

[15]Brothers, let me take an example from everyday life. Just as no one can set aside or add to a human covenant that has been duly established, so it is in this case. [16]The promises were spoken to Abraham and to his seed. The Scripture does not say "and to seeds," meaning many people, but "and to your seed,"[h] meaning one person, who is Christ. [17]What I mean is this: The law, introduced 430 years later, does not set aside the covenant previously established by God and thus do away with the promise. [18]For if the in-

---

[a]21 Some interpreters end the quotation after verse 14.   [b]6 Gen. 15:6
[c]8 Gen. 12:3; 18:18; 22:18   [d]10 Deut. 27:26   [e]11 Hab. 2:4   [f]12 Lev. 18:5
[g]13 Deut. 21:23   [h]16 Gen. 12:7; 13:15; 24:7

heritance depends on the law, then it no longer depends on a promise; but God in his grace gave it to Abraham through a promise. Ro 4:14,15; 7:1

19What, then, was the purpose of the law? It was added because of transgressions until the Seed to whom the promise referred had come. The law was put into effect through angels by a mediator. 20A mediator, however, does not represent just one party; but God is one.

21Is the law, therefore, opposed to the promises of God? Absolutely not! For if a law had been given that could impart life, then righteousness would certainly have come by the law. 22But the Scripture declares that the whole world is a prisoner of sin, so that what was promised, being given through faith in Jesus Christ, might be given to those who believe. Gal 2:21

23Before this faith came, we were held prisoners by the law, locked up until faith should be revealed. 24So the law was put in charge to lead us to Christ*a* that we might be justified by faith. 25Now that faith has come, we are no longer under the supervision of the law.

Sons of God

26You are all sons of God through faith in Christ Jesus, 27for all of you who were baptized into Christ have clothed yourselves with Christ. 28There is neither Jew nor Greek, slave nor free, male nor female, for you are all one in Christ Jesus. 29If you belong to Christ, then you are Abraham's seed, and heirs according to the promise.

4 What I am saying is that as long as the heir is a child, he is no different from a slave, although he owns the whole estate. 2He is subject to guardians and trustees until the time set by his father. 3So also, when we were children, we were in slavery under the basic principles of the world. 4But when the time had fully come, God sent his Son, born of a woman, born under law, 5to redeem those under law, that we might receive the full rights of sons. 6Because you are sons, God sent the Spirit of his Son into our hearts, the Spirit who calls out, "Abba,*b* Father." 7So you are no longer a slave, but a son; and since you are a son, God has made you also an heir. Ro 8:17; Col 2:8,20

Paul's Concern for the Galatians

8Formerly, when you did not know God, you were slaves to those who by nature are not gods. 9But now that you know God—or rather are known by God—how is it that you are turning back to those weak and miserable principles? Do you wish to be enslaved by them all over again? 10You are observing special days and months and

*a*24 Or *charge until Christ came*   *b*6 Aramaic for *Father*

seasons and years! [11]I fear for you, that somehow I have wasted my efforts on you.   1 Th 3:5

[12]I plead with you, brothers, become like me, for I became like you. You have done me no wrong. [13]As you know, it was because of an illness that I first preached the gospel to you. [14]Even though my illness was a trial to you, you did not treat me with contempt or scorn. Instead, you welcomed me as if I were an angel of God, as if I were Christ Jesus himself. [15]What has happened to all your joy? I can testify that, if you could have done so, you would have torn out your eyes and given them to me. [16]Have I now become your enemy by telling you the truth?   Am 5:10; Mt 10:40

[17]Those people are zealous to win you over, but for no good. What they want is to alienate you from us, so that you may be zealous for them. [18]It is fine to be zealous, provided the purpose is good, and to be so always and not just when I am with you. [19]My dear children, for whom I am again in the pains of childbirth until Christ is formed in you, [20]how I wish I could be with you now and change my tone, because I am perplexed about you!   Gal 2:4, 12

Hagar and Sarah

[21]Tell me, you who want to be under the law, are you not aware of what the law says?

[22]For it is written that Abraham had two sons, one by the slave woman and the other by the free woman. [23]His son by the slave woman was born in the ordinary way; but his son by the free woman was born as the result of a promise.

[24]These things may be taken figuratively, for the women represent two covenants. One covenant is from Mount Sinai and bears children who are to be slaves: This is Hagar. [25]Now Hagar stands for Mount Sinai in Arabia and corresponds to the present city of Jerusalem, because she is in slavery with her children. [26]But the Jerusalem that is above is free, and she is our mother. [27]For it is written:

"Be glad, O barren woman,
  who bears no children;
break forth and cry aloud,
  you who have no labor
    pains;
because more are the
    children of the desolate
    woman
  than of her who has a
    husband."[a]

[28]Now you, brothers, like Isaac, are children of promise. [29]At that time the son born in the ordinary way persecuted the son born by the power of the Spirit. It is the same now. [30]But what does the Scripture say? "Get rid of the slave woman and her son, for the slave woman's son will never share in

_a27_ Isaiah 54:1

the inheritance with the free woman's son."*a* ³¹Therefore, brothers, we are not children of the slave woman, but of the free woman.   Ge 21:9,10; Ro 7:4

Freedom in Christ

5 It is for freedom that Christ has set us free. Stand firm, then, and do not let yourselves be burdened again by a yoke of slavery.   Mt 23:4; Gal 2:4

²Mark my words! I, Paul, tell you that if you let yourselves be circumcised, Christ will be of no value to you at all. ³Again I declare to every man who lets himself be circumcised that he is obligated to obey the whole law. ⁴You who are trying to be justified by law have been alienated from Christ; you have fallen away from grace. ⁵But by faith we eagerly await through the Spirit the righteousness for which we hope. ⁶For in Christ Jesus neither circumcision nor uncircumcision has any value. The only thing that counts is faith expressing itself through love.   Ac 15:1; 1Th 1:3

⁷You were running a good race. Who cut in on you and kept you from obeying the truth? ⁸That kind of persuasion does not come from the one who calls you. ⁹"A little yeast works through the whole batch of dough." ¹⁰I am confident in the Lord that you will take no other view. The one who is throwing you into confusion

will pay the penalty, whoever he may be. ¹¹Brothers, if I am still preaching circumcision, why am I still being persecuted? In that case the offense of the cross has been abolished. ¹²As for those agitators, I wish they would go the whole way and emasculate themselves! Gal 3:1; 6:12

¹³You, my brothers, were called to be free. But do not use your freedom to indulge the sinful nature*b*; rather, serve one another in love. ¹⁴The entire law is summed up in a single command: "Love your neighbor as yourself."*c* ¹⁵If you keep on biting and devouring each other, watch out or you will be destroyed by each other. 1Co 8:9

Life by the Spirit

¹⁶So I say, live by the Spirit, and you will not gratify the desires of the sinful nature. ¹⁷For the sinful nature desires what is contrary to the Spirit, and the Spirit what is contrary to the sinful nature. They are in conflict with each other, so that you do not do what you want. ¹⁸But if you are led by the Spirit, you are not under law. Ro 8:2,4-6

¹⁹The acts of the sinful nature are obvious: sexual immorality, impurity and debauchery; ²⁰idolatry and witchcraft; hatred, discord, jealousy, fits of rage, selfish ambition, dissensions, factions ²¹and envy; drunkenness, orgies, and the like. I warn you, as I did before,

---

*a*30 Gen. 21:10   *b*13 Or *the flesh*; also in verses 16, 17, 19 and 24   *c*14 Lev. 19:18

that those who live like this will not inherit the kingdom of God.

²²But the fruit of the Spirit is love, joy, peace, patience, kindness, goodness, faithfulness, ²³gentleness and self-control. Against such things there is no law. ²⁴Those who belong to Christ Jesus have crucified the sinful nature with its passions and desires. ²⁵Since we live by the Spirit, let us keep in step with the Spirit. ²⁶Let us not become conceited, provoking and envying each other.   Ro 6:6

Doing Good to All

6 Brothers, if someone is caught in a sin, you who are spiritual should restore him gently. But watch yourself, or you also may be tempted. ²Carry each other's burdens, and in this way you will fulfill the law of Christ. ³If anyone thinks he is something when he is nothing, he deceives himself. ⁴Each one should test his own actions. Then he can take pride in himself, without comparing himself to somebody else, ⁵for each one should carry his own load. Ro 12:3

⁶Anyone who receives instruction in the word must share all good things with his instructor.   1Co 9:11; 1Ti 5:17-18

⁷Do not be deceived: God cannot be mocked. A man reaps what he sows. ⁸The one who sows to please his sinful nature, from that nature*ᵃ* will reap destruction; the one who sows to

please the Spirit, from the Spirit will reap eternal life. ⁹Let us not become weary in doing good, for at the proper time we will reap a harvest if we do not give up. ¹⁰Therefore, as we have opportunity, let us do good to all people, especially to those who belong to the family of believers.   Pr 3:27; Hos 10:12,13

Not Circumcision but a New Creation

¹¹See what large letters I use as I write to you with my own hand!

¹²Those who want to make a good impression outwardly are trying to compel you to be circumcised. The only reason they do this is to avoid being persecuted for the cross of Christ. ¹³Not even those who are circumcised obey the law, yet they want you to be circumcised that they may boast about your flesh. ¹⁴May I never boast except in the cross of our Lord Jesus Christ, through which*ᵇ* the world has been crucified to me, and I to the world. ¹⁵Neither circumcision nor uncircumcision means anything; what counts is a new creation. ¹⁶Peace and mercy to all who follow this rule, even to the Israel of God.

¹⁷Finally, let no one cause me trouble, for I bear on my body the marks of Jesus.   Isa 44:5

¹⁸The grace of our Lord Jesus Christ be with your spirit, brothers. Amen.   Ro 16:20

ᵃ8 Or his flesh, from the flesh   ᵇ14 Or whom

Ephesians

Introduction:

This letter was written by Paul during his two-year imprisonment in Rome (about A.D. 60). This letter probably was sent not just to the church at Ephesus but to all the Christian churches near Ephesus. Ephesus was a large, important city at that time, so it was a natural center for the Christian churches.

One of Paul's themes in Ephesians is that of unity and God's purpose "to bring all things in heaven and on earth together under one head, even Christ." Because of this unity, Paul wrote, all Christians are one family in Jesus, and they should act with love toward each other. He gives believers instructions on how to "live a life of love" by addressing the husband-wife, parent-children, and slave-master relationships.

In this letter Paul also writes about the church—not a church building in a certain place but the church that is made up of all Christians who have ever lived. We call this "the church universal." He compares Christ's relationship to the church to the body, a building, and a wife.

Outline of contents:

1 Paul, an apostle of Christ Jesus by the will of God,

To the saints in Ephesus,[a] the faithful[b] in Christ Jesus: Ac 18:19

[2] Grace and peace to you from God our Father and the Lord Jesus Christ.

Spiritual Blessings in Christ

[3] Praise be to the God and Father of our Lord Jesus Christ, who has blessed us in the heavenly realms with every spiritual blessing in Christ. [4] For he chose us in him before the creation of the world to be holy and blame-

---

[a]1 Some early manuscripts do not have *in Ephesus.*   [b]1 Or *believers who are*

less in his sight. In love ⁵he*a* predestined us to be adopted as his sons through Jesus Christ, in accordance with his pleasure and will— ⁶to the praise of his glorious grace, which he has freely given us in the One he loves. ⁷In him we have redemption through his blood, the forgiveness of sins, in accordance with the riches of God's grace ⁸that he lavished on us with all wisdom and understanding. ⁹And he*b* made known to us the mystery of his will according to his good pleasure, which he purposed in Christ, ¹⁰to be put into effect when the times will have reached their fulfillment—to bring all things in heaven and on earth together under one head, even Christ.

¹¹In him we were also chosen,*c* having been predestined according to the plan of him who works out everything in conformity with the purpose of his will, ¹²in order that we, who were the first to hope in Christ, might be for the praise of his glory. ¹³And you also were included in Christ when you heard the word of truth, the gospel of your salvation. Having believed, you were marked in him with a seal, the promised Holy Spirit, ¹⁴who is a deposit guaranteeing our inheritance until the redemption of those who are God's possession—to the praise of his glory. Ro 8:29-30

Thanksgiving and Prayer

¹⁵For this reason, ever since I heard about your faith in the Lord Jesus and your love for all the saints, ¹⁶I have not stopped giving thanks for you, remembering you in my prayers. ¹⁷I keep asking that the God of our Lord Jesus Christ, the glorious Father, may give you the Spirit*d* of wisdom and revelation, so that you may know him better. ¹⁸I pray also that the eyes of your heart may be enlightened in order that you may know the hope to which he has called you, the riches of his glorious inheritance in the saints, ¹⁹and his incomparably great power for us who believe. That power is like the working of his mighty strength, ²⁰which he exerted in Christ when he raised him from the dead and seated him at his right hand in the heavenly realms, ²¹far above all rule and authority, power and dominion, and every title that can be given, not only in the present age but also in the one to come. ²²And God placed all things under his feet and appointed him to be head over everything for the church, ²³which is his body, the fullness of him who fills everything in every way. Mk 16:19

Made Alive in Christ

2 As for you, you were dead in your transgressions and sins, ²in which you used to live

---

a4,5 Or *sight in love.* ⁵*He*   *b8,9* Or *us. With all wisdom and understanding,* ⁹*he*
c11 Or *were made heirs*   *d17* Or *a spirit*

when you followed the ways of this world and of the ruler of the kingdom of the air, the spirit who is now at work in those who are disobedient. ³All of us also lived among them at one time, gratifying the cravings of our sinful nature*a* and following its desires and thoughts. Like the rest, we were by nature objects of wrath. ⁴But because of his great love for us, God, who is rich in mercy, ⁵made us alive with Christ even when we were dead in transgressions—it is by grace you have been saved. ⁶And God raised us up with Christ and seated us with him in the heavenly realms in Christ Jesus, ⁷in order that in the coming ages he might show the incomparable riches of his grace, expressed in his kindness to us in Christ Jesus. ⁸For it is by grace you have been saved, through faith—and this not from yourselves, it is the gift of God— ⁹not by works, so that no one can boast. ¹⁰For we are God's workmanship, created in Christ Jesus to do good works, which God prepared in advance for us to do. Ro 3:24; Col 2:13-15; Tit 2:14

One in Christ

¹¹Therefore, remember that formerly you who are Gentiles by birth and called "uncircumcised" by those who call themselves "the circumcision" (that done in the body by the hands of men)— ¹²remember that at that time you were separate from Christ, excluded from citizenship in Israel and foreigners to the covenants of the promise, without hope and without God in the world. ¹³But now in Christ Jesus you who once were far away have been brought near through the blood of Christ. Isa 14:1; Col 1:20

¹⁴For he himself is our peace, who has made the two one and has destroyed the barrier, the dividing wall of hostility, ¹⁵by abolishing in his flesh the law with its commandments and regulations. His purpose was to create in himself one new man out of the two, thus making peace, ¹⁶and in this one body to reconcile both of them to God through the cross, by which he put to death their hostility. ¹⁷He came and preached peace to you who were far away and peace to those who were near. ¹⁸For through him we both have access to the Father by one Spirit. Jn 14:27; 1Co 12:13

¹⁹Consequently, you are no longer foreigners and aliens, but fellow citizens with God's people and members of God's household, ²⁰built on the foundation of the apostles and prophets, with Christ Jesus himself as the chief cornerstone. ²¹In him the whole building is joined together and rises to become a holy temple in the Lord. ²²And in him you too are being built together to become a

---

a3 Or our flesh

dwelling in which God lives by his Spirit. _{1Co 3:16; 1Pe 2:4-8}

Paul the Preacher to the Gentiles

3 For this reason I, Paul, the prisoner of Christ Jesus for the sake of you Gentiles—

²Surely you have heard about the administration of God's grace that was given to me for you, ³that is, the mystery made known to me by revelation, as I have already written briefly. ⁴In reading this, then, you will be able to understand my insight into the mystery of Christ, ⁵which was not made known to men in other generations as it has now been revealed by the Spirit to God's holy apostles and prophets. ⁶This mystery is that through the gospel the Gentiles are heirs together with Israel, members together of one body, and sharers together in the promise in Christ Jesus.

⁷I became a servant of this gospel by the gift of God's grace given me through the working of his power. ⁸Although I am less than the least of all God's people, this grace was given me: to preach to the Gentiles the unsearchable riches of Christ, ⁹and to make plain to everyone the administration of this mystery, which for ages past was kept hidden in God, who created all things. ¹⁰His intent was that now, through the church, the manifold wisdom of God should be made known to the rulers and authorities in the heavenly realms, ¹¹according to his eternal purpose which he accomplished in Christ Jesus our Lord. ¹²In him and through faith in him we may approach God with freedom and confidence. ¹³I ask you, therefore, not to be discouraged because of my sufferings for you, which are your glory. _{Ro 16:25,26; Eph 2:18}

A Prayer for the Ephesians

¹⁴For this reason I kneel before the Father, ¹⁵from whom his whole family*a* in heaven and on earth derives its name. ¹⁶I pray that out of his glorious riches he may strengthen you with power through his Spirit in your inner being, ¹⁷so that Christ may dwell in your hearts through faith. And I pray that you, being rooted and established in love, ¹⁸may have power, together with all the saints, to grasp how wide and long and high and deep is the love of Christ, ¹⁹and to know this love that surpasses knowledge—that you may be filled to the measure of all the fullness of God. _{Eph 1:23; Col 2:7,10}

²⁰Now to him who is able to do immeasurably more than all we ask or imagine, according to his power that is at work within us, ²¹to him be glory in the church and in Christ Jesus throughout all generations, for ever and ever! Amen. _{2Co 9:8}

a15 Or whom all fatherhood

Unity in the Body of Christ

4 As a prisoner for the Lord, then, I urge you to live a life worthy of the calling you have received. ²Be completely humble and gentle; be patient, bearing with one another in love. ³Make every effort to keep the unity of the Spirit through the bond of peace. ⁴There is one body and one Spirit— just as you were called to one hope when you were called— ⁵one Lord, one faith, one baptism; ⁶one God and Father of all, who is over all and through all and in all.   Dt 6:4; Ro 15:5; Col 3:12,13

⁷But to each one of us grace has been given as Christ apportioned it. ⁸This is why it*ᵃ* says:

"When he ascended on high,
　he led captives in his train
　and gave gifts to men."*ᵇ*

⁹(What does "he ascended" mean except that he also descended to the lower, earthly regions*ᶜ*? ¹⁰He who descended is the very one who ascended higher than all the heavens, in order to fill the whole universe.) ¹¹It was he who gave some to be apostles, some to be prophets, some to be evangelists, and some to be pastors and teachers, ¹²to prepare God's people for works of service, so that the body of Christ may be built up ¹³until we all reach unity in the faith and in the knowledge of the Son of God and become mature, attaining to the whole measure of the fullness of Christ.   1Co 12:27; Php 3:8

¹⁴Then we will no longer be infants, tossed back and forth by the waves, and blown here and there by every wind of teaching and by the cunning and craftiness of men in their deceitful scheming. ¹⁵Instead, speaking the truth in love, we will in all things grow up into him who is the Head, that is, Christ. ¹⁶From him the whole body, joined and held together by every supporting ligament, grows and builds itself up in love, as each part does its work.

Living as Children of Light

¹⁷So I tell you this, and insist on it in the Lord, that you must no longer live as the Gentiles do, in the futility of their thinking. ¹⁸They are darkened in their understanding and separated from the life of God because of the ignorance that is in them due to the hardening of their hearts. ¹⁹Having lost all sensitivity, they have given themselves over to sensuality so as to indulge in every kind of impurity, with a continual lust for more.   Ro 1:21; 2Co 3:14

²⁰You, however, did not come to know Christ that way. ²¹Surely you heard of him and were taught in him in accordance with the truth that is in Jesus. ²²You were taught, with regard to your former way of

---

ᵃ8 Or God　　*ᵇ8* Psalm 68:18　　*ᶜ9* Or *the depths of the earth*

life, to put off your old self, which is being corrupted by its deceitful desires; 23to be made new in the attitude of your minds; 24and to put on the new self, created to be like God in true righteousness and holiness.   Ro 13:14; Col 3:5,8-9

25Therefore each of you must put off falsehood and speak truthfully to his neighbor, for we are all members of one body. 26"In your anger do not sin"*a*: Do not let the sun go down while you are still angry, 27and do not give the devil a foothold. 28He who has been stealing must steal no longer, but must work, doing something useful with his own hands, that he may have something to share with those in need.   Ps 15:2

29Do not let any unwholesome talk come out of your mouths, but only what is helpful for building others up according to their needs, that it may benefit those who listen. 30And do not grieve the Holy Spirit of God, with whom you were sealed for the day of redemption. 31Get rid of all bitterness, rage and anger, brawling and slander, along with every form of malice. 32Be kind and compassionate to one another, forgiving each other, just as in Christ God forgave you.   Mt 12:36

5 Be imitators of God, therefore, as dearly loved children 2and live a life of love, just as Christ loved us and gave

himself up for us as a fragrant offering and sacrifice to God.

3But among you there must not be even a hint of sexual immorality, or of any kind of impurity, or of greed, because these are improper for God's holy people. 4Nor should there be obscenity, foolish talk or coarse joking, which are out of place, but rather thanksgiving. 5For of this you can be sure: No immoral, impure or greedy person—such a man is an idolater—has any inheritance in the kingdom of Christ and of God. *b* 6Let no one deceive you with empty words, for because of such things God's wrath comes on those who are disobedient. 7Therefore do not be partners with them.   1Co 6:18; Eph 2:2

8For you were once darkness, but now you are light in the Lord. Live as children of light 9(for the fruit of the light consists in all goodness, righteousness and truth) 10and find out what pleases the Lord. 11Have nothing to do with the fruitless deeds of darkness, but rather expose them. 12For it is shameful even to mention what the disobedient do in secret. 13But everything exposed by the light becomes visible, 14for it is light that makes everything visible. This is why it is said:

"Wake up, O sleeper,   Ro 13:11
    rise from the dead,   Isa 26:19
and Christ will shine on
    you."

*a*26 Psalm 4:4   *b*5 Or *kingdom of the Christ and God*

¹⁵Be very careful, then, how you live—not as unwise but as wise, ¹⁶making the most of every opportunity, because the days are evil. ¹⁷Therefore do not be foolish, but understand what the Lord's will is. ¹⁸Do not get drunk on wine, which leads to debauchery. Instead, be filled with the Spirit. ¹⁹Speak to one another with psalms, hymns and spiritual songs. Sing and make music in your heart to the Lord, ²⁰always giving thanks to God the Father for everything, in the name of our Lord Jesus Christ. _{Ps 34:1; Col 3:16}

²¹Submit to one another out of reverence for Christ. _{Gal 5:13}

Wives and Husbands

²²Wives, submit to your husbands as to the Lord. ²³For the husband is the head of the wife as Christ is the head of the church, his body, of which he is the Savior. ²⁴Now as the church submits to Christ, so also wives should submit to their husbands in everything. _{Ge 3:16}

²⁵Husbands, love your wives, just as Christ loved the church and gave himself up for her ²⁶to make her holy, cleansing^a her by the washing with water through the word, ²⁷and to present her to himself as a radiant church, without stain or wrinkle or any other blemish, but holy and blameless. ²⁸In this same way, husbands ought to love their wives as their own bodies. He who loves his wife loves himself. ²⁹After all, no one ever hated his own body, but he feeds and cares for it, just as Christ does the church— ³⁰for we are members of his body. ³¹"For this reason a man will leave his father and mother and be united to his wife, and the two will become one flesh."^b ³²This is a profound mystery—but I am talking about Christ and the church. ³³However, each one of you also must love his wife as he loves himself, and the wife must respect her husband. _{Ro 12:5; Col 3:19}

Children and Parents

6 Children, obey your parents in the Lord, for this is right. ²"Honor your father and mother"—which is the first commandment with a promise— ³"that it may go well with you and that you may enjoy long life on the earth."^c _{Pr 6:20}

⁴Fathers, do not exasperate your children; instead, bring them up in the training and instruction of the Lord. _{Col 3:21}

Slaves and Masters

⁵Slaves, obey your earthly masters with respect and fear, and with sincerity of heart, just as you would obey Christ. ⁶Obey them not only to win their favor when their eye is on you, but like slaves of Christ, doing the will of God from your heart. ⁷Serve wholeheartedly,

---

^a26 Or *having cleansed*   ^b31 Gen. 2:24   ^c3 Deut. 5:16

as if you were serving the Lord, not men, ⁸because you know that the Lord will reward everyone for whatever good he does, whether he is slave or free. 1Ti 6:1

⁹And masters, treat your slaves in the same way. Do not threaten them, since you know that he who is both their Master and yours is in heaven, and there is no favoritism with him.

The Armor of God

¹⁰Finally, be strong in the Lord and in his mighty power. ¹¹Put on the full armor of God so that you can take your stand against the devil's schemes. ¹²For our struggle is not against flesh and blood, but against the rulers, against the authorities, against the powers of this dark world and against the spiritual forces of evil in the heavenly realms. ¹³Therefore put on the full armor of God, so that when the day of evil comes, you may be able to stand your ground, and after you have done everything, to stand. ¹⁴Stand firm then, with the belt of truth buckled around your waist, with the breastplate of righteousness in place, ¹⁵and with your feet fitted with the readiness that comes from the gospel of peace. ¹⁶In addition to all this,

take up the shield of faith, with which you can extinguish all the flaming arrows of the evil one. ¹⁷Take the helmet of salvation and the sword of the Spirit, which is the word of God. ¹⁸And pray in the Spirit on all occasions with all kinds of prayers and requests. With this in mind, be alert and always keep on praying for all the saints. Ro 8:26,27

¹⁹Pray also for me, that whenever I open my mouth, words may be given me so that I will fearlessly make known the mystery of the gospel, ²⁰for which I am an ambassador in chains. Pray that I may declare it fearlessly, as I should. 2Co 5:20

Final Greetings

²¹Tychicus, the dear brother and faithful servant in the Lord, will tell you everything, so that you also may know how I am and what I am doing. ²²I am sending him to you for this very purpose, that you may know how we are, and that he may encourage you.

²³Peace to the brothers, and love with faith from God the Father and the Lord Jesus Christ. ²⁴Grace to all who love our Lord Jesus Christ with an undying love. 2Th 3:16

Philippians

Introduction:

Philippians, as well as Colossians, Philemon, and Ephesians, was written by Paul while he was in prison in Rome about A.D. 60. The Philippians had sent Epaphroditus to Paul with a gift. While Epaphroditus was in Rome, he became sick, and the Philippian Christians were worried about him. After he was better, Paul sent him back to Philippi with this letter.

Paul's strong feelings of love for the Philippians is felt throughout this letter and this is the most personal of Paul's letters written to a church. Paul tells of his thankfulness for the love and helpfulness of the Philippians.

Even though Paul was writing from prison this letter is full of joy. The words "joy" or "rejoice" are used fourteen times. Paul here gives his own testimony to the meaning of his present life when he writes "For to me, to live is Christ and to die is gain" (1:21).

As in his other letters Paul gives words of encouragement and instructions for living in harmony with others and in obedience to God.

Outline of contents:

Introduction (1:1–11)
Paul's circumstances and concern (1:12–30)
Imitating Christ's humility (2:1–18)
Paul's messengers (2:19–30)
Warnings and advice (3:1–4:20)
Conclusion (4:21–23)

---

1 Paul and Timothy, servants of Christ Jesus,   Ac 16:1

To all the saints in Christ Jesus at Philippi, together with the overseers[a] and deacons:

²Grace and peace to you from God our Father and the Lord Jesus Christ.

Thanksgiving and Prayer

³I thank my God every time I remember you. ⁴In all my prayers for all of you, I always

---

pray with joy [5]because of your partnership in the gospel from the first day until now, [6]being confident of this, that he who began a good work in you will carry it on to completion until the day of Christ Jesus.   Ps 138:8

[7]It is right for me to feel this way about all of you, since I have you in my heart; for whether I am in chains or defending and confirming the gospel, all of you share in God's grace with me. [8]God can testify how I long for all of you with the affection of Christ Jesus.   2Co 7:3

[9]And this is my prayer: that your love may abound more and more in knowledge and depth of insight, [10]so that you may be able to discern what is best and may be pure and blameless until the day of Christ, [11]filled with the fruit of righteousness that comes through Jesus Christ—to the glory and praise of God.   1Th 3:12

Paul's Chains Advance the Gospel

[12]Now I want you to know, brothers, that what has happened to me has really served to advance the gospel. [13]As a result, it has become clear throughout the whole palace guard[a] and to everyone else that I am in chains for Christ. [14]Because of my chains, most of the brothers in the Lord have been encouraged to speak the word of God more courageously and fearlessly.

[15]It is true that some preach Christ out of envy and rivalry, but others out of goodwill. [16]The latter do so in love, knowing that I am put here for the defense of the gospel. [17]The former preach Christ out of selfish ambition, not sincerely, supposing that they can stir up trouble for me while I am in chains.[b] [18]But what does it matter? The important thing is that in every way, whether from false motives or true, Christ is preached. And because of this I rejoice.   Php 2:3

Yes, and I will continue to rejoice, [19]for I know that through your prayers and the help given by the Spirit of Jesus Christ, what has happened to me will turn out for my deliverance.[c] [20]I eagerly expect and hope that I will in no way be ashamed, but will have sufficient courage so that now as always Christ will be exalted in my body, whether by life or by death. [21]For to me, to live is Christ and to die is gain. [22]If I am to go on living in the body, this will mean fruitful labor for me. Yet what shall I choose? I do not know! [23]I am torn between the two: I desire to depart and be with Christ, which is better by far; [24]but it is more necessary for you that I remain in the body. [25]Convinced of this, I know that I will

---

[a]13 Or *whole palace*   [b]16,17 Some late manuscripts have verses 16 and 17 in reverse order.   [c]19 Or *salvation*

remain, and I will continue with all of you for your progress and joy in the faith, ²⁶so that through my being with you again your joy in Christ Jesus will overflow on account of me.

²⁷Whatever happens, conduct yourselves in a manner worthy of the gospel of Christ. Then, whether I come and see you or only hear about you in my absence, I will know that you stand firm in one spirit, contending as one man for the faith of the gospel ²⁸without being frightened in any way by those who oppose you. This is a sign to them that they will be destroyed, but that you will be saved—and that by God. ²⁹For it has been granted to you on behalf of Christ not only to believe on him, but also to suffer for him, ³⁰since you are going through the same struggle you saw I had, and now hear that I still have.   Ac 14:22; Eph 4:1

Imitating Christ's Humility

2 If you have any encouragement from being united with Christ, if any comfort from his love, if any fellowship with the Spirit, if any tenderness and compassion, ²then make my joy complete by being like-minded, having the same love, being one in spirit and purpose. ³Do nothing out of selfish ambition or vain conceit, but in humility consider others better than yourselves. ⁴Each of you should look not only to your own interests, but also to the interests of others.   Ro 12:10; 1Co 10:24

⁵Your attitude should be the same as that of Christ Jesus:

⁶Who, being in very nature[a]
        God,   Jn 1:1
    did not consider equality
        with God something to
        be grasped,   Jn 5:18
⁷but made himself nothing,
    taking the very nature[b] of a
        servant,   Mt 20:28
    being made in human
        likeness.   Jn 1:14
⁸And being found in
        appearance as a man,
    he humbled himself
    and became obedient to
        death—   Mt 26:39
    even death on a cross!
⁹Therefore God exalted him to
        the highest place   Isa 52:13
    and gave him the name that
        is above every name,
¹⁰that at the name of Jesus
        every knee should bow,
    in heaven and on earth and
        under the earth,   Mt 28:18
¹¹and every tongue confess
        that Jesus Christ is Lord,
    to the glory of God the
        Father.   Jn 13:13

Shining as Stars

¹²Therefore, my dear friends, as you have always obeyed—not only in my presence, but now much more in my absence—continue to work out your salvation with fear and trembling, ¹³for it is God who

---

[a]6 Or *in the form of*   [b]7 Or *the form*

works in you to will and to act according to his good purpose. [14]Do everything without complaining or arguing, [15]so that you may become blameless and pure, children of God without fault in a crooked and depraved generation, in which you shine like stars in the universe [16]as you hold out[a] the word of life—in order that I may boast on the day of Christ that I did not run or labor for nothing. [17]But even if I am being poured out like a drink offering on the sacrifice and service coming from your faith, I am glad and rejoice with all of you. [18]So you too should be glad and rejoice with me.   1Co 10:10; 2Co 12:15

Timothy and Epaphroditus

[19]I hope in the Lord Jesus to send Timothy to you soon, that I also may be cheered when I receive news about you. [20]I have no one else like him, who takes a genuine interest in your welfare. [21]For everyone looks out for his own interests, not those of Jesus Christ. [22]But you know that Timothy has proved himself, because as a son with his father he has served with me in the work of the gospel. [23]I hope, therefore, to send him as soon as I see how things go with me. [24]And I am confident in the Lord that I myself will come soon.

[25]But I think it is necessary to send back to you Epaphroditus, my brother, fellow worker and fellow soldier, who is also your messenger, whom you sent to take care of my needs. [26]For he longs for all of you and is distressed because you heard he was ill. [27]Indeed he was ill, and almost died. But God had mercy on him, and not on him only but also on me, to spare me sorrow upon sorrow. [28]Therefore I am all the more eager to send him, so that when you see him again you may be glad and I may have less anxiety. [29]Welcome him in the Lord with great joy, and honor men like him, [30]because he almost died for the work of Christ, risking his life to make up for the help you could not give me.   1Co 16:17

No Confidence in the Flesh

3 Finally, my brothers, rejoice in the Lord! It is no trouble for me to write the same things to you again, and it is a safeguard for you.   Php 2:18

[2]Watch out for those dogs, those men who do evil, those mutilators of the flesh. [3]For it is we who are the circumcision, we who worship by the Spirit of God, who glory in Christ Jesus, and who put no confidence in the flesh— [4]though I myself have reasons for such confidence.   Ro 15:17; Gal 6:14,15

If anyone else thinks he has reasons to put confidence in the flesh, I have more: [5]circumcised on the eighth day, of the people of Israel, of the tribe of Benja-

min, a Hebrew of Hebrews; in regard to the law, a Pharisee; [6]as for zeal, persecuting the church; as for legalistic righteousness, faultless.   Ro 10:1-4; 2Co 11:22

[7]But whatever was to my profit I now consider loss for the sake of Christ. [8]What is more, I consider everything a loss compared to the surpassing greatness of knowing Christ Jesus my Lord, for whose sake I have lost all things. I consider them rubbish, that I may gain Christ [9]and be found in him, not having a righteousness of my own that comes from the law, but that which is through faith in Christ—the righteousness that comes from God and is by faith. [10]I want to know Christ and the power of his resurrection and the fellowship of sharing in his sufferings, becoming like him in his death, [11]and so, somehow, to attain to the resurrection from the dead.   Mt 13:44

Pressing on Toward the Goal

[12]Not that I have already obtained all this, or have already been made perfect, but I press on to take hold of that for which Christ Jesus took hold of me. [13]Brothers, I do not consider myself yet to have taken hold of it. But one thing I do: Forgetting what is behind and straining toward what is ahead, [14]I press on toward the goal to win the prize for which God has called me heavenward in Christ Jesus.

[15]All of us who are mature should take such a view of things. And if on some point you think differently, that too God will make clear to you. [16]Only let us live up to what we have already attained.   1Co 2:16

[17]Join with others in following my example, brothers, and take note of those who live according to the pattern we gave you. [18]For, as I have often told you before and now say again even with tears, many live as enemies of the cross of Christ. [19]Their destiny is destruction, their god is their stomach, and their glory is in their shame. Their mind is on earthly things. [20]But our citizenship is in heaven. And we eagerly await a Savior from there, the Lord Jesus Christ, [21]who, by the power that enables him to bring everything under his control, will transform our lowly bodies so that they will be like his glorious body.   1Co 4:16; Eph 1:19-23

4 Therefore, my brothers, you whom I love and long for, my joy and crown, that is how you should stand firm in the Lord, dear friends!   1Co 16:13

Exhortations

[2]I plead with Euodia and I plead with Syntyche to agree with each other in the Lord. [3]Yes, and I ask you, loyal yokefellow, [a] help these women who have contended at my side in the cause of the gospel, along

_a3_ Or loyal Syzygus

with Clement and the rest of my fellow workers, whose names are in the book of life.   Php 2:2

4Rejoice in the Lord always. I will say it again: Rejoice! 5Let your gentleness be evident to all. The Lord is near. 6Do not be anxious about anything, but in everything, by prayer and petition, with thanksgiving, present your requests to God. 7And the peace of God, which transcends all understanding, will guard your hearts and your minds in Christ Jesus.   Ro 12:12

8Finally, brothers, whatever is true, whatever is noble, whatever is right, whatever is pure, whatever is lovely, whatever is admirable—if anything is excellent or praiseworthy—think about such things. 9Whatever you have learned or received or heard from me, or seen in me—put it into practice. And the God of peace will be with you.   Ro 15:33

Thanks for Their Gifts

10I rejoice greatly in the Lord that at last you have renewed your concern for me. Indeed, you have been concerned, but you had no opportunity to show it. 11I am not saying this because I am in need, for I have learned to be content whatever the circumstances. 12I know what it is to be in need, and I know what it is to have plenty. I have learned the secret of being content in any and every situation, whether well fed or hun-

gry, whether living in plenty or in want. 13I can do everything through him who gives me strength.   Eph 3:16; 1 Ti 6:6,8

14Yet it was good of you to share in my troubles. 15Moreover, as you Philippians know, in the early days of your acquaintance with the gospel, when I set out from Macedonia, not one church shared with me in the matter of giving and receiving, except you only; 16for even when I was in Thessalonica, you sent me aid again and again when I was in need. 17Not that I am looking for a gift, but I am looking for what may be credited to your account. 18I have received full payment and even more; I am amply supplied, now that I have received from Epaphroditus the gifts you sent. They are a fragrant offering, an acceptable sacrifice, pleasing to God. 19And my God will meet all your needs according to his glorious riches in Christ Jesus.   Ps 23:1; Php 1:7

20To our God and Father be glory for ever and ever. Amen.

Final Greetings

21Greet all the saints in Christ Jesus. The brothers who are with me send greetings. 22All the saints send you greetings, especially those who belong to Caesar's household.

23The grace of the Lord Jesus Christ be with your spirit. Amen. a   Ro 16:20

a23 Some manuscripts do not have Amen.

Colossians

Introduction:

Colossians is the third letter written from prison in Rome (about A.D. 60). Epaphras had come to Rome and told Paul that there were false teachers in Colosse who were telling the people that the Christian faith was incomplete. They were teaching the Colossians to worship angels and to follow special rules and ceremonies.

Paul wrote to the Colossians to oppose these false teachers. He reminded them that Jesus is supreme over everything, that his death is all we need to save us from our sins, and that through him we are free from man-made rules.

Outline of contents:

1 Paul, an apostle of Christ Jesus by the will of God, and Timothy our brother,

²To the holy and faithful*ᵃ* brothers in Christ at Colosse:

Grace and peace to you from God our Father. *ᵇ*

Thanksgiving and Prayer

³We always thank God, the Father of our Lord Jesus Christ, when we pray for you, ⁴because we have heard of your faith in Christ Jesus and of the love you have for all the saints— ⁵the faith and love that spring from the hope that is stored up for you in heaven and that you have already heard about in the word of truth, the gospel ⁶that has come to you. All over the world this gospel is bearing fruit and growing, just as it has been doing among you since the day you heard it and understood God's grace in all its truth. ⁷You learned it from Epaphras, our dear fellow servant, who is a faithful minister of Christ on

---

*ᵃ*2 Or *believing*   *ᵇ*2 Some manuscripts *Father and the Lord Jesus Christ*

our[a] behalf, [8]and who also told us of your love in the Spirit.

[9]For this reason, since the day we heard about you, we have not stopped praying for you and asking God to fill you with the knowledge of his will through all spiritual wisdom and understanding. [10]And we pray this in order that you may live a life worthy of the Lord and may please him in every way: bearing fruit in every good work, growing in the knowledge of God, [11]being strengthened with all power according to his glorious might so that you may have great endurance and patience, and joyfully [12]giving thanks to the Father, who has qualified you[b] to share in the inheritance of the saints in the kingdom of light. [13]For he has rescued us from the dominion of darkness and brought us into the kingdom of the Son he loves, [14]in whom we have redemption,[c] the forgiveness of sins. Ro 3:24; Eph 1:15-17

The Supremacy of Christ

[15]He is the image of the invisible God, the firstborn over all creation. [16]For by him all things were created: things in heaven and on earth, visible and invisible, whether thrones or powers or rulers or authorities; all things were created by him and for him. [17]He is before all things, and in him all things hold to-

gether. [18]And he is the head of the body, the church; he is the beginning and the firstborn from among the dead, so that in everything he might have the supremacy. [19]For God was pleased to have all his fullness dwell in him, [20]and through him to reconcile to himself all things, whether things on earth or things in heaven, by making peace through his blood, shed on the cross. Jn 1:1-3,18; Ro 5:10

[21]Once you were alienated from God and were enemies in your minds because of[d] your evil behavior. [22]But now he has reconciled you by Christ's physical body through death to present you holy in his sight, without blemish and free from accusation— [23]if you continue in your faith, established and firm, not moved from the hope held out in the gospel. This is the gospel that you heard and that has been proclaimed to every creature under heaven, and of which I, Paul, have become a servant. Eph 2:3

Paul's Labor for the Church

[24]Now I rejoice in what was suffered for you, and I fill up in my flesh what is still lacking in regard to Christ's afflictions, for the sake of his body, which is the church. [25]I have become its servant by the commission God gave me to present to you the word of God in its fullness—

---

[a]7 Some manuscripts *your redemption through his blood*   [b]12 Some manuscripts *us*   [d]21 Or *minds, as shown by*   [c]14 A few late manuscripts

26the mystery that has been kept hidden for ages and generations, but is now disclosed to the saints. 27To them God has chosen to make known among the Gentiles the glorious riches of this mystery, which is Christ in you, the hope of glory. Ro 8:10

28We proclaim him, admonishing and teaching everyone with all wisdom, so that we may present everyone perfect in Christ. 29To this end I labor, struggling with all his energy, which so powerfully works in me. 1Co 15:10; Col 3:16

2 I want you to know how much I am struggling for you and for those at Laodicea, and for all who have not met me personally. 2My purpose is that they may be encouraged in heart and united in love, so that they may have the full riches of complete understanding, in order that they may know the mystery of God, namely, Christ, 3in whom are hidden all the treasures of wisdom and knowledge. 4I tell you this so that no one may deceive you by fine-sounding arguments. 5For though I am absent from you in body, I am present with you in spirit and delight to see how orderly you are and how firm your faith in Christ is. Col 1:29

Freedom From Human Regulations Through Life With Christ

6So then, just as you received Christ Jesus as Lord, continue to live in him, 7rooted and built up in him, strengthened in the faith as you were taught, and overflowing with thankfulness.

8See to it that no one takes you captive through hollow and deceptive philosophy, which depends on human tradition and the basic principles of this world rather than on Christ. 1Ti 6:20,21

9For in Christ all the fullness of the Deity lives in bodily form, 10and you have been given fullness in Christ, who is the head over every power and authority. 11In him you were also circumcised, in the putting off of the sinful nature,a not with a circumcision done by the hands of men but with the circumcision done by Christ, 12having been buried with him in baptism and raised with him through your faith in the power of God, who raised him from the dead. Gal 5:24; Php 3:3

13When you were dead in your sins and in the uncircumcision of your sinful nature,b God made youc alive with Christ. He forgave us all our sins, 14having canceled the written code, with its regulations, that was against us and that stood opposed to us; he took it away, nailing it to the cross. 15And having disarmed the powers and authorities, he made a public spectacle

a11 Or the flesh   b13 Or your flesh   c13 Some manuscripts us

of them, triumphing over them by the cross. *a*

Eph 2:1,5; 6:12

[16]Therefore do not let anyone judge you by what you eat or drink, or with regard to a religious festival, a New Moon celebration or a Sabbath day. [17]These are a shadow of the things that were to come; the reality, however, is found in Christ. [18]Do not let anyone who delights in false humility and the worship of angels disqualify you for the prize. Such a person goes into great detail about what he has seen, and his unspiritual mind puffs him up with idle notions. [19]He has lost connection with the Head, from whom the whole body, supported and held together by its ligaments and sinews, grows as God causes it to grow.

Ro 14:3-4

[20]Since you died with Christ to the basic principles of this world, why, as though you still belonged to it, do you submit to its rules: [21]"Do not handle! Do not taste! Do not touch!"? [22]These are all destined to perish with use, because they are based on human commands and teachings. [23]Such regulations indeed have an appearance of wisdom, with their self-imposed worship, their false humility and their harsh treatment of the body, but they lack any value in restraining sensual indulgence.

Ro 6:6; 1Co 6:13

Rules for Holy Living

3 Since, then, you have been raised with Christ, set your hearts on things above, where Christ is seated at the right hand of God. [2]Set your minds on things above, not on earthly things. [3]For you died, and your life is now hidden with Christ in God. [4]When Christ, who is your[b] life, appears, then you also will appear with him in glory.

Ro 6:5; Gal 2:20

[5]Put to death, therefore, whatever belongs to your earthly nature: sexual immorality, impurity, lust, evil desires and greed, which is idolatry. [6]Because of these, the wrath of God is coming.[c] [7]You used to walk in these ways, in the life you once lived. [8]But now you must rid yourselves of all such things as these: anger, rage, malice, slander, and filthy language from your lips. [9]Do not lie to each other, since you have taken off your old self with its practices [10]and have put on the new self, which is being renewed in knowledge in the image of its Creator. [11]Here there is no Greek or Jew, circumcised or uncircumcised, barbarian, Scythian, slave or free, but Christ is all, and is in all.

Eph 4:22

[12]Therefore, as God's chosen people, holy and dearly loved, clothe yourselves with compassion, kindness, humility, gen-

---

*a*15 Or *them in him*   *b*4 Some manuscripts *our*   *c*6 Some early manuscripts *coming*
on those who are disobedient

tleness and patience. ¹³Bear with each other and forgive whatever grievances you may have against one another. Forgive as the Lord forgave you. ¹⁴And over all these virtues put on love, which binds them all together in perfect unity. Eph 4:32

¹⁵Let the peace of Christ rule in your hearts, since as members of one body you were called to peace. And be thankful. ¹⁶Let the word of Christ dwell in you richly as you teach and admonish one another with all wisdom, and as you sing psalms, hymns and spiritual songs with gratitude in your hearts to God. ¹⁷And whatever you do, whether in word or deed, do it all in the name of the Lord Jesus, giving thanks to God the Father through him.

Rules for Christian Households

¹⁸Wives, submit to your husbands, as is fitting in the Lord.
¹⁹Husbands, love your wives and do not be harsh with them.
²⁰Children, obey your parents in everything, for this pleases the Lord. Eph 6:1
²¹Fathers, do not embitter your children, or they will become discouraged. Eph 6:4
²²Slaves, obey your earthly masters in everything; and do it, not only when their eye is on you and to win their favor, but with sincerity of heart and reverence for the Lord. ²³Whatever you do, work at it with all your heart, as working for the Lord, not for men, ²⁴since you know that you will receive an inheritance from the Lord as a reward. It is the Lord Christ you are serving. ²⁵Anyone who does wrong will be repaid for his wrong, and there is no favoritism. Ac 20:32

4 Masters, provide your slaves with what is right and fair, because you know that you also have a Master in heaven.

Further Instructions

²Devote yourselves to prayer, being watchful and thankful. ³And pray for us, too, that God may open a door for our message, so that we may proclaim the mystery of Christ, for which I am in chains. ⁴Pray that I may proclaim it clearly, as I should. ⁵Be wise in the way you act toward outsiders; make the most of every opportunity. ⁶Let your conversation be always full of grace, seasoned with salt, so that you may know how to answer everyone. Lk 18:1

Final Greetings

⁷Tychicus will tell you all the news about me. He is a dear brother, a faithful minister and fellow servant in the Lord. ⁸I am sending him to you for the express purpose that you may know about our*a* circumstances and that he may encourage your

a8 Some manuscripts *that he may know about your*

hearts. [9]He is coming with Onesimus, our faithful and dear brother, who is one of you. They will tell you everything that is happening here.

[10]My fellow prisoner Aristarchus sends you his greetings, as does Mark, the cousin of Barnabas. (You have received instructions about him; if he comes to you, welcome him.) [11]Jesus, who is called Justus, also sends greetings. These are the only Jews among my fellow workers for the kingdom of God, and they have proved a comfort to me. [12]Epaphras, who is one of you and a servant of Christ Jesus, sends greetings. He is always wrestling in prayer for you, that you may stand

firm in all the will of God, mature and fully assured. [13]I vouch for him that he is working hard for you and for those at Laodicea and Hierapolis. [14]Our dear friend Luke, the doctor, and Demas send greetings. [15]Give my greetings to the brothers at Laodicea, and to Nympha and the church in her house. Ac 19:29

[16]After this letter has been read to you, see that it is also read in the church of the Laodiceans and that you in turn read the letter from Laodicea.

[17]Tell Archippus: "See to it that you complete the work you have received in the Lord."

[18]I, Paul, write this greeting in my own hand. Remember my chains. Grace be with you.

1 Thessalonians

Introduction:

Paul started the church at Thessalonica on his second missionary journey. He taught there for about three weeks, but then had to leave because the Jews were opposing him so strongly. On hearing from Timothy about the conditions in Thessalonica, Paul wrote this letter from Corinth to encourage the Thessalonians and to teach them more about Christianity (A.D. 51).

Paul begins by praising the Thessalonians for being brave and not giving up their faith "in spite of severe suffering." He instructs them "how to live in order to please God." And he teaches them about Jesus' second coming. He explains that the time of Jesus' coming is secret, so they should keep working hard until he comes.

Outline of contents:

Introduction and thanksgiving (1:1–10)
Paul's ministry in the church (2:1–3:13)
Instructions on the Lord's coming (4:1–5:11)
Conclusion (5:12–28)

---

1 Paul, Silas*a* and Timothy,

To the church of the Thessalonians in God the Father and the Lord Jesus Christ:

Grace and peace to you.*b*

Thanksgiving for the Thessalonians' Faith

²We always thank God for all of you, mentioning you in our prayers. ³We continually remember before our God and Father your work produced by faith, your labor prompted by love, and your endurance inspired by hope in our Lord Jesus Christ.   Ro 1:8; Jas 2:14-26

⁴For we know, brothers loved by God, that he has chosen you, ⁵because our gospel came to you not simply with words, but also with power, with the Holy Spirit and with deep conviction. You know how we lived among you for your sake. ⁶You became

---

*a*1 Greek *Silvanus*, a variant of *Silas*
*b*1 Some early manuscripts *you from God our Father and the Lord Jesus Christ*

imitators of us and of the Lord; in spite of severe suffering, you welcomed the message with the joy given by the Holy Spirit. [7]And so you became a model to all the believers in Macedonia and Achaia. [8]The Lord's message rang out from you not only in Macedonia and Achaia—your faith in God has become known everywhere. Therefore we do not need to say anything about it, [9]for they themselves report what kind of reception you gave us. They tell how you turned to God from idols to serve the living and true God, [10]and to wait for his Son from heaven, whom he raised from the dead—Jesus, who rescues us from the coming wrath.

Paul's Ministry in Thessalonica

2 You know, brothers, that our visit to you was not a failure. [2]We had previously suffered and been insulted in Philippi, as you know, but with the help of our God we dared to tell you his gospel in spite of strong opposition. [3]For the appeal we make does not spring from error or impure motives, nor are we trying to trick you. [4]On the contrary, we speak as men approved by God to be entrusted with the gospel. We are not trying to please men but God, who tests our hearts. [5]You know we never used flattery, nor did we put on a mask to cover up greed—God is our witness. [6]We were not looking for praise from men, not from you or anyone else.   Ac 14:15; 1Th 1:5,9

As apostles of Christ we could have been a burden to you, [7]but we were gentle among you, like a mother caring for her little children. [8]We loved you so much that we were delighted to share with you not only the gospel of God but our lives as well, because you had become so dear to us. [9]Surely you remember, brothers, our toil and hardship; we worked night and day in order not to be a burden to anyone while we preached the gospel of God to you.   1Jn 3:16

[10]You are witnesses, and so is God, of how holy, righteous and blameless we were among you who believed. [11]For you know that we dealt with each of you as a father deals with his own children, [12]encouraging, comforting and urging you to live lives worthy of God, who calls you into his kingdom and glory.   Gal 4:19; Eph 4:1; 1Th 1:5

[13]And we also thank God continually because, when you received the word of God, which you heard from us, you accepted it not as the word of men, but as it actually is, the word of God, which is at work in you who believe. [14]For you, brothers, became imitators of God's churches in Judea, which are in Christ Jesus: You suffered from your own countrymen the same things those churches suffered from the Jews, [15]who killed the Lord Jesus and the

prophets and also drove us out. They displease God and are hostile to all men [16]in their effort to keep us from speaking to the Gentiles so that they may be saved. In this way they always heap up their sins to the limit. The wrath of God has come upon them at last.[a] 　1Th1:2,6

Paul's Longing to See the Thessalonians

[17]But, brothers, when we were torn away from you for a short time (in person, not in thought), out of our intense longing we made every effort to see you. [18]For we wanted to come to you—certainly I, Paul, did, again and again—but Satan stopped us. [19]For what is our hope, our joy, or the crown in which we will glory in the presence of our Lord Jesus when he comes? Is it not you? [20]Indeed, you are our glory and joy. 1Pe1:7

3 So when we could stand it no longer, we thought it best to be left by ourselves in Athens. [2]We sent Timothy, who is our brother and God's fellow worker[b] in spreading the gospel of Christ, to strengthen and encourage you in your faith, [3]so that no one would be unsettled by these trials. You know quite well that we were destined for them. [4]In fact, when we were with you, we kept telling you that we would be persecuted. And it turned out that way, as

you well know. [5]For this reason, when I could stand it no longer, I sent to find out about your faith. I was afraid that in some way the tempter might have tempted you and our efforts might have been useless. Jn16:33

Timothy's Encouraging Report

[6]But Timothy has just now come to us from you and has brought good news about your faith and love. He has told us that you always have pleasant memories of us and that you long to see us, just as we also long to see you. [7]Therefore, brothers, in all our distress and persecution we were encouraged about you because of your faith. [8]For now we really live, since you are standing firm in the Lord. [9]How can we thank God enough for you in return for all the joy we have in the presence of our God because of you? [10]Night and day we pray most earnestly that we may see you again and supply what is lacking in your faith. 1Th1:2,3

[11]Now may our God and Father himself and our Lord Jesus clear the way for us to come to you. [12]May the Lord make your love increase and overflow for each other and for everyone else, just as ours does for you. [13]May he strengthen your hearts so that you will be blameless and holy in the presence of our

---

[a]16 Or them fully 　[b]2 Some manuscripts brother and fellow worker; other manuscripts brother and God's servant

God and Father when our Lord Jesus comes with all his holy ones. Ps 15; Php 2:15

Living to Please God

4 Finally, brothers, we instructed you how to live in order to please God, as in fact you are living. Now we ask you and urge you in the Lord Jesus to do this more and more. [2]For you know what instructions we gave you by the authority of the Lord Jesus. 2Co 5:9; Eph 4:1

[3]It is God's will that you should be sanctified: that you should avoid sexual immorality; [4]that each of you should learn to control his own body[a] in a way that is holy and honorable, [5]not in passionate lust like the heathen, who do not know God; [6]and that in this matter no one should wrong his brother or take advantage of him. The Lord will punish men for all such sins, as we have already told you and warned you. [7]For God did not call us to be impure, but to live a holy life. [8]Therefore, he who rejects this instruction does not reject man but God, who gives you his Holy Spirit. Eze 36:27; Eph 5:17

[9]Now about brotherly love we do not need to write to you, for you yourselves have been taught by God to love each other. [10]And in fact, you do love all the brothers throughout Macedonia. Yet we urge you,

brothers, to do so more and more. Ro 12:10; 1Th 3:12

[11]Make it your ambition to lead a quiet life, to mind your own business and to work with your hands, just as we told you, [12]so that your daily life may win the respect of outsiders and so that you will not be dependent on anybody. Eph 4:28; 2Th 3:10-12

The Coming of the Lord

[13]Brothers, we do not want you to be ignorant about those who fall asleep, or to grieve like the rest of men, who have no hope. [14]We believe that Jesus died and rose again and so we believe that God will bring with Jesus those who have fallen asleep in him. [15]According to the Lord's own word, we tell you that we who are still alive, who are left till the coming of the Lord, will certainly not precede those who have fallen asleep. [16]For the Lord himself will come down from heaven, with a loud command, with the voice of the archangel and with the trumpet call of God, and the dead in Christ will rise first. [17]After that, we who are still alive and are left will be caught up together with them in the clouds to meet the Lord in the air. And so we will be with the Lord forever. [18]Therefore encourage each other with these words. Ro 14:9; 1Th 5:11; Rev 14:13

5 Now, brothers, about times and dates we do not need to

---

[a]4 Or *learn to live with his own wife*; or *learn to acquire a wife*

write to you, [2]for you know very well that the day of the Lord will come like a thief in the night. [3]While people are saying, "Peace and safety," destruction will come on them suddenly, as labor pains on a pregnant woman, and they will not escape.

Isa 29:5,6; Ac 1:7; 1Co 1:8

[4]But you, brothers, are not in darkness so that this day should surprise you like a thief. [5]You are all sons of the light and sons of the day. We do not belong to the night or to the darkness. [6]So then, let us not be like others, who are asleep, but let us be alert and self-controlled. [7]For those who sleep, sleep at night, and those who get drunk, get drunk at night. [8]But since we belong to the day, let us be self-controlled, putting on faith and love as a breastplate, and the hope of salvation as a helmet. [9]For God did not appoint us to suffer wrath but to receive salvation through our Lord Jesus Christ. [10]He died for us so that, whether we are awake or asleep, we may live together with him. [11]Therefore encourage one another and build each other up, just as in fact you are doing.

Ac 26:18; Eph 4:29

Final Instructions

[12]Now we ask you, brothers, to respect those who work hard among you, who are over you in the Lord and who admonish you. [13]Hold them in the highest regard in love because of their work. Live in peace with each other. [14]And we urge you, brothers, warn those who are idle, encourage the timid, help the weak, be patient with everyone. [15]Make sure that nobody pays back wrong for wrong, but always try to be kind to each other and to everyone else.

[16]Be joyful always; [17]pray continually; [18]give thanks in all circumstances, for this is God's will for you in Christ Jesus.

[19]Do not put out the Spirit's fire; [20]do not treat prophecies with contempt. [21]Test everything. Hold on to the good. [22]Avoid every kind of evil.

[23]May God himself, the God of peace, sanctify you through and through. May your whole spirit, soul and body be kept blameless at the coming of our Lord Jesus Christ. [24]The one who calls you is faithful and he will do it.

Php 1:6; 1Th 3:13

[25]Brothers, pray for us. [26]Greet all the brothers with a holy kiss. [27]I charge you before the Lord to have this letter read to all the brothers.

Eph 6:19

[28]The grace of our Lord Jesus Christ be with you.

2 Thessalonians

Introduction:
  Second Thessalonians was sent from Corinth a few months after the first letter. Some people had misunderstood Paul and were sure Jesus was coming very soon. In fact, they had stopped working and were just waiting for Jesus.
  Paul writes the Thessalonians again and describes to them what Jesus' second coming will be like. He also reminds them to keep working hard until Jesus comes and to use their time wisely.

Outline of contents:

---

1 Paul, Silas*a* and Timothy,

  To the church of the Thessalonians in God our Father and the Lord Jesus Christ: Ac 17:1

  ²Grace and peace to you from God the Father and the Lord Jesus Christ.

Thanksgiving and Prayer

  ³We ought always to thank God for you, brothers, and rightly so, because your faith is growing more and more, and the love every one of you has for each other is increasing. ⁴Therefore, among God's churches we boast about your perseverance and faith in all the persecutions and trials you are enduring.

  ⁵All this is evidence that God's judgment is right, and as a result you will be counted worthy of the kingdom of God, for which you are suffering. ⁶God is just: He will pay back trouble to those who trouble you ⁷and give relief to you who are troubled, and to us as well. This will happen when the Lord Jesus is revealed from heaven in blazing fire with his powerful angels. ⁸He will punish those who do not know God and do not obey the gospel of our Lord Jesus. ⁹They will be punished with everlasting destruction and shut out from the presence of the Lord and from the majesty of his power ¹⁰on the day he comes to be glorified in his holy people and to be marveled at

*a*1 Greek *Silvanus*, a variant of *Silas*

among all those who have believed. This includes you, because you believed our testimony to you.   1Co 3:13; Php 1:28

¹¹With this in mind, we constantly pray for you, that our God may count you worthy of his calling, and that by his power he may fulfill every good purpose of yours and every act prompted by your faith. ¹²We pray this so that the name of our Lord Jesus may be glorified in you, and you in him, according to the grace of our God and the Lord Jesus Christ. ᵃ Php 2:9-11; 1Th 1:3

The Man of Lawlessness

2 Concerning the coming of our Lord Jesus Christ and our being gathered to him, we ask you, brothers, ²not to become easily unsettled or alarmed by some prophecy, report or letter supposed to have come from us, saying that the day of the Lord has already come. ³Don't let anyone deceive you in any way, for ˌthat day will not comeˌ until the rebellion occurs and the man of lawlessnessᵇ is revealed, the man doomed to destruction. ⁴He will oppose and will exalt himself over everything that is called God or is worshiped, so that he sets himself up in God's temple, proclaiming himself to be God. ⁵Don't you remember that when I was with you I used to tell you these things? ⁶And now

you know what is holding him back, so that he may be revealed at the proper time. ⁷For the secret power of lawlessness is already at work; but the one who now holds it back will continue to do so till he is taken out of the way. ⁸And then the lawless one will be revealed, whom the Lord Jesus will overthrow with the breath of his mouth and destroy by the splendor of his coming. ⁹The coming of the lawless one will be in accordance with the work of Satan displayed in all kinds of counterfeit miracles, signs and wonders, ¹⁰and in every sort of evil that deceives those who are perishing. They perish because they refused to love the truth and so be saved. ¹¹For this reason God sends them a powerful delusion so that they will believe the lie ¹²and so that all will be condemned who have not believed the truth but have delighted in wickedness.   Isa 11:4; Ro 1:32

Stand Firm

¹³But we ought always to thank God for you, brothers loved by the Lord, because from the beginning God chose youᶜ to be saved through the sanctifying work of the Spirit and through belief in the truth. ¹⁴He called you to this through our gospel, that you might share in the glory of our Lord Jesus Christ. ¹⁵So then, brothers,

---

ᵃ12 Or God and Lord, Jesus Christ   ᵇ3 Some manuscripts sin   ᶜ13 Some manuscripts because God chose you as his firstfruits

stand firm and hold to the teachings[a] we passed on to you, whether by word of mouth or by letter.

1Co 16:13; Eph 1:4

[16]May our Lord Jesus Christ himself and God our Father, who loved us and by his grace gave us eternal encouragement and good hope, [17]encourage your hearts and strengthen you in every good deed and word.

Request for Prayer

3 Finally, brothers, pray for us that the message of the Lord may spread rapidly and be honored, just as it was with you. [2]And pray that we may be delivered from wicked and evil men, for not everyone has faith. [3]But the Lord is faithful, and he will strengthen and protect you from the evil one. [4]We have confidence in the Lord that you are doing and will continue to do the things we command. [5]May the Lord direct your hearts into God's love and Christ's perseverance.

1Ch 29:18; 1Th 4:1

Warning Against Idleness

[6]In the name of the Lord Jesus Christ, we command you, brothers, to keep away from every brother who is idle and does not live according to the teaching[b] you received from us. [7]For you yourselves know how you ought to follow our example. We were not idle when we

were with you, [8]nor did we eat anyone's food without paying for it. On the contrary, we worked night and day, laboring and toiling so that we would not be a burden to any of you. [9]We did this, not because we do not have the right to such help, but in order to make ourselves a model for you to follow. [10]For even when we were with you, we gave you this rule: "If a man will not work, he shall not eat."

[11]We hear that some among you are idle. They are not busy; they are busybodies. [12]Such people we command and urge in the Lord Jesus Christ to settle down and earn the bread they eat. [13]And as for you, brothers, never tire of doing what is right.

[14]If anyone does not obey our instruction in this letter, take special note of him. Do not associate with him, in order that he may feel ashamed. [15]Yet do not regard him as an enemy, but warn him as a brother. Gal 6:1

Final Greetings

[16]Now may the Lord of peace himself give you peace at all times and in every way. The Lord be with all of you.

[17]I, Paul, write this greeting in my own hand, which is the distinguishing mark in all my letters. This is how I write.

[18]The grace of our Lord Jesus Christ be with you all.

---

[a]15 Or traditions   [b]6 Or tradition

1 Timothy

Introduction:

First and Second Timothy and Titus are commonly called the pastoral letters and were written by Paul. They are called pastoral letters because they deal with the qualifications and duties of pastors.

Timothy was born at Lystra and had a Greek father and a Jewish mother (who taught him the Scriptures from childhood). He went with Paul on his second missionary journey and from then on helped Paul in his work. At the time Paul wrote this letter, Timothy was working as the teacher and leader of the church at Ephesus.

Timothy was quite young to have the important job of leading a church, so Paul wrote this very personal letter to him. In this letter Paul gives him help and advice for his work. He warns him of false teachers and their teachings that are opposite God's commands. Because of Paul's deep care for Timothy he offers him advice on how to be a "man of God."

Outline of contents:

1 Paul, an apostle of Christ Jesus by the command of God our Savior and of Christ Jesus our hope,   Col 1:27

²To Timothy my true son in the faith: Ac 16:1; 1Co 4:17

Grace, mercy and peace from God the Father and Christ Jesus our Lord.

Warning Against False Teachers of the Law

³As I urged you when I went into Macedonia, stay there in Ephesus so that you may command certain men not to teach false doctrines any longer ⁴nor to devote themselves to myths and endless genealogies. These promote controversies rather than God's work—which is by faith. ⁵The goal of this com-

mand is love, which comes from a pure heart and a good conscience and a sincere faith. [6]Some have wandered away from these and turned to meaningless talk. [7]They want to be teachers of the law, but they do not know what they are talking about or what they so confidently affirm. _{Gal 1:6,7; 2Ti 2:14,22}

[8]We know that the law is good if one uses it properly. [9]We also know that law[a] is made not for the righteous but for lawbreakers and rebels, the ungodly and sinful, the unholy and irreligious; for those who kill their fathers or mothers, for murderers, [10]for adulterers and perverts, for slave traders and liars and perjurers—and for whatever else is contrary to the sound doctrine [11]that conforms to the glorious gospel of the blessed God, which he entrusted to me. _{Gal 2:7; 3:19}

The Lord's Grace to Paul

[12]I thank Christ Jesus our Lord, who has given me strength, that he considered me faithful, appointing me to his service. [13]Even though I was once a blasphemer and a persecutor and a violent man, I was shown mercy because I acted in ignorance and unbelief. [14]The grace of our Lord was poured out on me abundantly, along with the faith and love that are in Christ Jesus. _{Ac 8:3; 9:15; 2Ti 1:13}

[15]Here is a trustworthy saying that deserves full acceptance: Christ Jesus came into the world to save sinners—of whom I am the worst. [16]But for that very reason I was shown mercy so that in me, the worst of sinners, Christ Jesus might display his unlimited patience as an example for those who would believe on him and receive eternal life. [17]Now to the King eternal, immortal, invisible, the only God, be honor and glory for ever and ever. Amen. _{Mk 2:17; Jn 3:15-17}

[18]Timothy, my son, I give you this instruction in keeping with the prophecies once made about you, so that by following them you may fight the good fight, [19]holding on to faith and a good conscience. Some have rejected these and so have shipwrecked their faith. [20]Among them are Hymenaeus and Alexander, whom I have handed over to Satan to be taught not to blaspheme. _{2Ti 2:17-18}

Instructions on Worship

2 I urge, then, first of all, that requests, prayers, intercession and thanksgiving be made for everyone— [2]for kings and all those in authority, that we may live peaceful and quiet lives in all godliness and holiness. [3]This is good, and pleases God our Savior, [4]who wants all men to be saved and to come to a knowledge of the truth. [5]For there is one God and one mediator between God and

_{a9 Or that the law}

men, the man Christ Jesus, ⁶who gave himself as a ransom for all men—the testimony given in its proper time. ⁷And for this purpose I was appointed a herald and an apostle—I am telling the truth, I am not lying—and a teacher of the true faith to the Gentiles.   Eph 6:18

⁸I want men everywhere to lift up holy hands in prayer, without anger or disputing.

⁹I also want women to dress modestly, with decency and propriety, not with braided hair or gold or pearls or expensive clothes, ¹⁰but with good deeds, appropriate for women who profess to worship God. 1Pe 3:3,4

¹¹A woman should learn in quietness and full submission. ¹²I do not permit a woman to teach or to have authority over a man; she must be silent. ¹³For Adam was formed first, then Eve. ¹⁴And Adam was not the one deceived; it was the woman who was deceived and became a sinner. ¹⁵But womenᵃ will be savedᵇ through childbearing— if they continue in faith, love and holiness with propriety.

Overseers and Deacons

3 Here is a trustworthy saying: If anyone sets his heart on being an overseer,ᶜ he desires a noble task. ²Now the overseer must be above reproach, the husband of but one wife, temperate, self-con-

trolled, respectable, hospitable, able to teach, ³not given to drunkenness, not violent but gentle, not quarrelsome, not a lover of money. ⁴He must manage his own family well and see that his children obey him with proper respect. ⁵(If anyone does not know how to manage his own family, how can he take care of God's church?) ⁶He must not be a recent convert, or he may become conceited and fall under the same judgment as the devil. ⁷He must also have a good reputation with outsiders, so that he will not fall into disgrace and into the devil's trap.

⁸Deacons, likewise, are to be men worthy of respect, sincere, not indulging in much wine, and not pursuing dishonest gain. ⁹They must keep hold of the deep truths of the faith with a clear conscience. ¹⁰They must first be tested; and then if there is nothing against them, let them serve as deacons.

¹¹In the same way, their wivesᵈ are to be women worthy of respect, not malicious talkers but temperate and trustworthy in everything.   Tit 2:3

¹²A deacon must be the husband of but one wife and must manage his children and his household well. ¹³Those who have served well gain an excellent standing and great assurance in their faith in Christ Jesus.   Mt 25:21

ᵃ15 Greek *she*   ᵇ15 Or *restored*   ᶜ1 Traditionally *bishop*; also in verse 2   ᵈ11 Or
way, deaconesses

¹⁴Although I hope to come to you soon, I am writing you these instructions so that, ¹⁵if I am delayed, you will know how people ought to conduct themselves in God's household, which is the church of the living God, the pillar and foundation of the truth. ¹⁶Beyond all question, the mystery of godliness is great:

1Ti 2:2

He[a] appeared in a body,[b]
  was vindicated by the
    Spirit,   Jn 1:14
  was seen by angels,
  was preached among the
    nations,   Ps 9:11
  was believed on in the world,
  was taken up in glory. Mk 16:19

Instructions to Timothy

4 The Spirit clearly says that in later times some will abandon the faith and follow deceiving spirits and things taught by demons. ²Such teachings come through hypocritical liars, whose consciences have been seared as with a hot iron. ³They forbid people to marry and order them to abstain from certain foods, which God created to be received with thanksgiving by those who believe and who know the truth. ⁴For everything God created is good, and nothing is to be rejected if it is received with thanksgiving, ⁵because it is consecrated by the word of God and prayer.

⁶If you point these things out

to the brothers, you will be a good minister of Christ Jesus, brought up in the truths of the faith and of the good teaching that you have followed. ⁷Have nothing to do with godless myths and old wives' tales; rather, train yourself to be godly. ⁸For physical training is of some value, but godliness has value for all things, holding promise for both the present life and the life to come.   Mk 10:29,30

⁹This is a trustworthy saying that deserves full acceptance ¹⁰(and for this we labor and strive), that we have put our hope in the living God, who is the Savior of all men, and especially of those who believe.

¹¹Command and teach these things. ¹²Don't let anyone look down on you because you are young, but set an example for the believers in speech, in life, in love, in faith and in purity. ¹³Until I come, devote yourself to the public reading of Scripture, to preaching and to teaching. ¹⁴Do not neglect your gift, which was given you through a prophetic message when the body of elders laid their hands on you.   2Ti 1:6; Tit 2:7

¹⁵Be diligent in these matters; give yourself wholly to them, so that everyone may see your progress. ¹⁶Watch your life and doctrine closely. Persevere in them, because if you do, you will save both yourself and your hearers.

---

*a*16 Some manuscripts *God*   *b*16 Or *in the flesh*

Advice About Widows,
Elders and Slaves

5 Do not rebuke an older man harshly, but exhort him as if he were your father. Treat younger men as brothers, ²older women as mothers, and younger women as sisters, with absolute purity.   Lev 19:32; Tit 2:2

³Give proper recognition to those widows who are really in need. ⁴But if a widow has children or grandchildren, these should learn first of all to put their religion into practice by caring for their own family and so repaying their parents and grandparents, for this is pleasing to God. ⁵The widow who is really in need and left all alone puts her hope in God and continues night and day to pray and to ask God for help. ⁶But the widow who lives for pleasure is dead even while she lives. ⁷Give the people these instructions, too, so that no one may be open to blame. ⁸If anyone does not provide for his relatives, and especially for his immediate family, he has denied the faith and is worse than an unbeliever.   Eph 6:1-2

⁹No widow may be put on the list of widows unless she is over sixty, has been faithful to her husband,ᵃ ¹⁰and is well known for her good deeds, such as bringing up children, showing hospitality, washing the feet of the saints, helping those in trouble and devoting herself to all kinds of good deeds.   Ac 9:36

¹¹As for younger widows, do not put them on such a list. For when their sensual desires overcome their dedication to Christ, they want to marry. ¹²Thus they bring judgment on themselves, because they have broken their first pledge. ¹³Besides, they get into the habit of being idle and going about from house to house. And not only do they become idlers, but also gossips and busybodies, saying things they ought not to. ¹⁴So I counsel younger widows to marry, to have children, to manage their homes and to give the enemy no opportunity for slander. ¹⁵Some have in fact already turned away to follow Satan.   1Co 7:9

¹⁶If any woman who is a believer has widows in her family, she should help them and not let the church be burdened with them, so that the church can help those widows who are really in need.

¹⁷The elders who direct the affairs of the church well are worthy of double honor, especially those whose work is preaching and teaching. ¹⁸For the Scripture says, "Do not muzzle the ox while it is treading out the grain,"ᵇ and "The worker deserves his wages."ᶜ ¹⁹Do not entertain an accusation against an elder unless it is brought by two or three wit-

---

ᵃ9 Or *has had but one husband*   ᵇ18 Deut. 25:4   ᶜ18 Luke 10:7

nesses. ²⁰Those who sin are to be rebuked publicly, so that the others may take warning. 1Th 5:12

²¹I charge you, in the sight of God and Christ Jesus and the elect angels, to keep these instructions without partiality, and to do nothing out of favoritism. 1Ti 6:13

²²Do not be hasty in the laying on of hands, and do not share in the sins of others. Keep yourself pure. Ac 6:6

²³Stop drinking only water, and use a little wine because of your stomach and your frequent illnesses.

²⁴The sins of some men are obvious, reaching the place of judgment ahead of them; the sins of others trail behind them. ²⁵In the same way, good deeds are obvious, and even those that are not cannot be hidden.

6 All who are under the yoke of slavery should consider their masters worthy of full respect, so that God's name and our teaching may not be slandered. ²Those who have believing masters are not to show less respect for them because they are brothers. Instead, they are to serve them even better, because those who benefit from their service are believers, and dear to them. These are the things you are to teach and urge on them. Eph 6:5; Phm 16

Love of Money

³If anyone teaches false doctrines and does not agree to the sound instruction of our Lord Jesus Christ and to godly teaching, ⁴he is conceited and understands nothing. He has an unhealthy interest in controversies and quarrels about words that result in envy, strife, malicious talk, evil suspicions ⁵and constant friction between men of corrupt mind, who have been robbed of the truth and who think that godliness is a means to financial gain.

⁶But godliness with contentment is great gain. ⁷For we brought nothing into the world, and we can take nothing out of it. ⁸But if we have food and clothing, we will be content with that. ⁹People who want to get rich fall into temptation and a trap and into many foolish and harmful desires that plunge men into ruin and destruction. ¹⁰For the love of money is a root of all kinds of evil. Some people, eager for money, have wandered from the faith and pierced themselves with many griefs. Ps 49:17; Php 4:11; Heb 13:5

Paul's Charge to Timothy

¹¹But you, man of God, flee from all this, and pursue righteousness, godliness, faith, love, endurance and gentleness. ¹²Fight the good fight of the faith. Take hold of the eternal life to which you were called when you made your good confession in the presence of many witnesses. ¹³In the sight of God, who gives life to everything, and of Christ Jesus, who while testifying before Pontius

Pilate made the good confession, I charge you [14]to keep this command without spot or blame until the appearing of our Lord Jesus Christ, [15]which God will bring about in his own time—God, the blessed and only Ruler, the King of kings and Lord of lords, [16]who alone is immortal and who lives in unapproachable light, whom no one has seen or can see. To him be honor and might forever. Amen. Ps 104:2; 1Co 9:25,26

[17]Command those who are rich in this present world not to be arrogant nor to put their hope in wealth, which is so uncertain, but to put their hope in God, who richly provides us with everything for our enjoyment. [18]Command them to do good, to be rich in good deeds, and to be generous and willing to share. [19]In this way they will lay up treasure for themselves as a firm foundation for the coming age, so that they may take hold of the life that is truly life. Ps 62:10; Mt 6:20,21

[20]Timothy, guard what has been entrusted to your care. Turn away from godless chatter and the opposing ideas of what is falsely called knowledge, [21]which some have professed and in so doing have wandered from the faith. 2Ti 1:12; 2:16

Grace be with you.

2 Timothy

Introduction:

It seems probable that Paul was arrested again sometime after writing 1 Timothy and Titus, and that he wrote this second letter to Timothy from Rome where he was being held a prisoner.

In this letter Paul seems to know that there is little chance of his getting out of prison and that he will soon die. It is for these reasons that he writes to Timothy.

Paul wants not only to see Timothy again but also to encourage Timothy because he would have to continue Paul's missionary work after his death.

Paul gives Timothy more instructions on how to lead a church and warns him to stay away from false teachers. He urges Timothy to be faithful to true Christian teachings.

Outline of contents:

Greeting (1:1,2)
Encouragement to be faithful (1:3–2:13)
The false and the true way (2:14–3:9)
Paul's charge to Timothy (3:10–4:8)
Conclusion (4:9–22)

---

1 Paul, an apostle of Christ Jesus by the will of God, according to the promise of life that is in Christ Jesus, 1Co 1:1

2To Timothy, my dear son:

Grace, mercy and peace from God the Father and Christ Jesus our Lord.

Encouragement to Be Faithful

3I thank God, whom I serve, as my forefathers did, with a clear conscience, as night and day I constantly remember you in my prayers. 4Recalling your tears, I long to see you, so that I may be filled with joy. 5I have been reminded of your sincere faith, which first lived in your grandmother Lois and in your mother Eunice and, I am persuaded, now lives in you also. 6For this reason I remind you to fan into flame the gift of God, which is in you through the laying on of my hands. 7For God did not give us a spirit of timidi-

ty, but a spirit of power, of love and of self-discipline. _{Isa 11:2}

⁸So do not be ashamed to testify about our Lord, or ashamed of me his prisoner. But join with me in suffering for the gospel, by the power of God, ⁹who has saved us and called us to a holy life—not because of anything we have done but because of his own purpose and grace. This grace was given us in Christ Jesus before the beginning of time, ¹⁰but it has now been revealed through the appearing of our Savior, Christ Jesus, who has destroyed death and has brought life and immortality to light through the gospel. ¹¹And of this gospel I was appointed a herald and an apostle and a teacher. ¹²That is why I am suffering as I am. Yet I am not ashamed, because I know whom I have believed, and am convinced that he is able to guard what I have entrusted to him for that day. _{Mk 8:38}

¹³What you heard from me, keep as the pattern of sound teaching, with faith and love in Christ Jesus. ¹⁴Guard the good deposit that was entrusted to you—guard it with the help of the Holy Spirit who lives in us.

¹⁵You know that everyone in the province of Asia has deserted me, including Phygelus and Hermogenes.

¹⁶May the Lord show mercy to the household of Onesiphorus, because he often refreshed me and was not ashamed of my chains. ¹⁷On the contrary, when he was in Rome, he searched hard for me until he found me. ¹⁸May the Lord grant that he will find mercy from the Lord on that day! You know very well in how many ways he helped me in Ephesus. _{Heb 6:10}

2 You then, my son, be strong in the grace that is in Christ Jesus. ²And the things you have heard me say in the presence of many witnesses entrust to reliable men who will also be qualified to teach others. ³Endure hardship with us like a good soldier of Christ Jesus. ⁴No one serving as a soldier gets involved in civilian affairs—he wants to please his commanding officer. ⁵Similarly, if anyone competes as an athlete, he does not receive the victor's crown unless he competes according to the rules. ⁶The hardworking farmer should be the first to receive a share of the crops. ⁷Reflect on what I am saying, for the Lord will give you insight into all this. _{1Co 9:10; Eph 6:10}

⁸Remember Jesus Christ, raised from the dead, descended from David. This is my gospel, ⁹for which I am suffering even to the point of being chained like a criminal. But God's word is not chained. ¹⁰Therefore I endure everything for the sake of the elect, that they too may obtain the salvation that is in Christ Jesus, with eternal glory. _{Ac 2:24; Col 1:24}

¹¹Here is a trustworthy saying:

If we died with him,
 we will also live with him;
[12]if we endure,
 we will also reign with him.
If we disown him,
 he will also disown us; Mt 10:33
[13]if we are faithless,
 he will remain faithful, Ro 3:3
 for he cannot disown
 himself.

A Workman Approved by God

[14]Keep reminding them of these things. Warn them before God against quarreling about words; it is of no value, and only ruins those who listen. [15]Do your best to present yourself to God as one approved, a workman who does not need to be ashamed and who correctly handles the word of truth. [16]Avoid godless chatter, because those who indulge in it will become more and more ungodly. [17]Their teaching will spread like gangrene. Among them are Hymenaeus and Philetus, [18]who have wandered away from the truth. They say that the resurrection has already taken place, and they destroy the faith of some. [19]Nevertheless, God's solid foundation stands firm, sealed with this inscription: "The Lord knows those who are his," [a] and, "Everyone who confesses the name of the Lord must turn away from wickedness." Isa 28:16; 1 Ti 1:4

[20]In a large house there are articles not only of gold and silver, but also of wood and clay; some are for noble purposes and some for ignoble. [21]If a man cleanses himself from the latter, he will be an instrument for noble purposes, made holy, useful to the Master and prepared to do any good work. Eph 2:10

[22]Flee the evil desires of youth, and pursue righteousness, faith, love and peace, along with those who call on the Lord out of a pure heart. [23]Don't have anything to do with foolish and stupid arguments, because you know they produce quarrels. [24]And the Lord's servant must not quarrel; instead, he must be kind to everyone, able to teach, not resentful. [25]Those who oppose him he must gently instruct, in the hope that God will grant them repentance leading them to a knowledge of the truth, [26]and that they will come to their senses and escape from the trap of the devil, who has taken them captive to do his will. 1 Ti 1:5

Godlessness in the Last Days

3 But mark this: There will be terrible times in the last days. [2]People will be lovers of themselves, lovers of money, boastful, proud, abusive, disobedient to their parents, ungrateful, unholy, [3]without love, unforgiving, slanderous, without self-control, brutal, not lovers of the good, [4]treacher-

---

[a]19 Num. 16:5 (see Septuagint)

ous, rash, conceited, lovers of pleasure rather than lovers of God— [5]having a form of godliness but denying its power. Have nothing to do with them.

[6]They are the kind who worm their way into homes and gain control over weak-willed women, who are loaded down with sins and are swayed by all kinds of evil desires, [7]always learning but never able to acknowledge the truth. [8]Just as Jannes and Jambres opposed Moses, so also these men oppose the truth—men of depraved minds, who, as far as the faith is concerned, are rejected. [9]But they will not get very far because, as in the case of those men, their folly will be clear to everyone.　　　Jude 4

Paul's Charge to Timothy

[10]You, however, know all about my teaching, my way of life, my purpose, faith, patience, love, endurance, [11]persecutions, sufferings—what kinds of things happened to me in Antioch, Iconium and Lystra, the persecutions I endured. Yet the Lord rescued me from all of them. [12]In fact, everyone who wants to live a godly life in Christ Jesus will be persecuted, [13]while evil men and impostors will go from bad to worse, deceiving and being deceived. [14]But as for you, continue in what you have learned and have become convinced of, because you know those from whom you learned it, [15]and how

from infancy you have known the holy Scriptures, which are able to make you wise for salvation through faith in Christ Jesus. [16]All Scripture is God-breathed and is useful for teaching, rebuking, correcting and training in righteousness, [17]so that the man of God may be thoroughly equipped for every good work.　　1Ti 4:6; 2Pe 1:20

4 In the presence of God and of Christ Jesus, who will judge the living and the dead, and in view of his appearing and his kingdom, I give you this charge: [2]Preach the Word; be prepared in season and out of season; correct, rebuke and encourage—with great patience and careful instruction. [3]For the time will come when men will not put up with sound doctrine. Instead, to suit their own desires, they will gather around them a great number of teachers to say what their itching ears want to hear. [4]They will turn their ears away from the truth and turn aside to myths. [5]But you, keep your head in all situations, endure hardship, do the work of an evangelist, discharge all the duties of your ministry.　　Isa 30:10; Ac 10:42

[6]For I am already being poured out like a drink offering, and the time has come for my departure. [7]I have fought the good fight, I have finished the race, I have kept the faith. [8]Now there is in store for me the crown of righteousness, which the Lord, the righteous Judge,

will award to me on that day—and not only to me, but also to all who have longed for his appearing. Col 1:5; 1Pe 1:4

Personal Remarks

⁹Do your best to come to me quickly, ¹⁰for Demas, because he loved this world, has deserted me and has gone to Thessalonica. Crescens has gone to Galatia, and Titus to Dalmatia. ¹¹Only Luke is with me. Get Mark and bring him with you, because he is helpful to me in my ministry. ¹²I sent Tychicus to Ephesus. ¹³When you come, bring the cloak that I left with Carpus at Troas, and my scrolls, especially the parchments.

¹⁴Alexander the metalworker did me a great deal of harm. The Lord will repay him for what he has done. ¹⁵You too should be on your guard against him, because he strongly opposed our message. Ps 28:4

¹⁶At my first defense, no one came to my support, but everyone deserted me. May it not be held against them. ¹⁷But the Lord stood at my side and gave me strength, so that through me the message might be fully proclaimed and all the Gentiles might hear it. And I was delivered from the lion's mouth. ¹⁸The Lord will rescue me from every evil attack and will bring me safely to his heavenly kingdom. To him be glory for ever and ever. Amen. Ps 121:7

Final Greetings

¹⁹Greet Priscilla[a] and Aquila and the household of Onesiphorus. ²⁰Erastus stayed in Corinth, and I left Trophimus sick in Miletus. ²¹Do your best to get here before winter. Eubulus greets you, and so do Pudens, Linus, Claudia and all the brothers.

²²The Lord be with your spirit. Grace be with you.

---

[a] 19 Greek Prisca, a variant of Priscilla

Titus

Introduction:

Titus was another friend and helper of Paul's. He had traveled with Paul on some of his missionary journeys, and was working as the leader of the church on Crete. This letter is similar to the two letters to Timothy.

The church in Crete seems to have been an unorganized church and made up of people who needed much instruction in being Christians. Paul tells Titus and the church how God's people should behave. He tells Titus to teach the people the truth of God and instructs him in how to be a good leader of the church.

Outline of contents:

1 Paul, a servant of God and an apostle of Jesus Christ for the faith of God's elect and the knowledge of the truth that leads to godliness— ²a faith and knowledge resting on the hope of eternal life, which God, who does not lie, promised before the beginning of time, ³and at his appointed season he brought his word to light through the preaching entrusted to me by the command of God our Savior,   1Ti 2:6

⁴To Titus, my true son in our common faith:

Grace and peace from God the Father and Christ Jesus our Savior.

Titus' Task on Crete

⁵The reason I left you in Crete was that you might straighten out what was left unfinished and appoint*a* elders in every town, as I directed you. ⁶An elder must be blameless, the husband of but one wife, a man whose children believe and are not open to the charge of being wild and disobedient. ⁷Since an overseer*b* is entrusted with God's work, he must be blame-

*a*5 Or *ordain*   *b*7 Traditionally *bishop*

less—not overbearing, not quick-tempered, not given to drunkenness, not violent, not pursuing dishonest gain. ⁸Rather he must be hospitable, one who loves what is good, who is self-controlled, upright, holy and disciplined. ⁹He must hold firmly to the trustworthy message as it has been taught, so that he can encourage others by sound doctrine and refute those who oppose it.   1Ti 3:1-7

¹⁰For there are many rebellious people, mere talkers and deceivers, especially those of the circumcision group. ¹¹They must be silenced, because they are ruining whole households by teaching things they ought not to teach—and that for the sake of dishonest gain. ¹²Even one of their own prophets has said, "Cretans are always liars, evil brutes, lazy gluttons." ¹³This testimony is true. Therefore, rebuke them sharply, so that they will be sound in the faith ¹⁴and will pay no attention to Jewish myths or to the commands of those who reject the truth. ¹⁵To the pure, all things are pure, but to those who are corrupted and do not believe, nothing is pure. In fact, both their minds and consciences are corrupted. ¹⁶They claim to know God, but by their actions they deny him. They are detestable, disobedient and unfit for doing anything good.   Jer 5:2; Mk 7:14-23

What Must Be Taught to Various Groups

2 You must teach what is in accord with sound doctrine. ²Teach the older men to be temperate, worthy of respect, self-controlled, and sound in faith, in love and in endurance.

³Likewise, teach the older women to be reverent in the way they live, not to be slanderers or addicted to much wine, but to teach what is good. ⁴Then they can train the younger women to love their husbands and children, ⁵to be self-controlled and pure, to be busy at home, to be kind, and to be subject to their husbands, so that no one will malign the word of God.   1Ti 3:11; Tit 1:8

⁶Similarly, encourage the young men to be self-controlled. ⁷In everything set them an example by doing what is good. In your teaching show integrity, seriousness ⁸and soundness of speech that cannot be condemned, so that those who oppose you may be ashamed because they have nothing bad to say about us.   1Ti 5:1; 1Pe 2:12

⁹Teach slaves to be subject to their masters in everything, to try to please them, not to talk back to them, ¹⁰and not to steal from them, but to show that they can be fully trusted, so that in every way they will make the teaching about God our Savior attractive.   Mt 5:16; Eph 6:5

¹¹For the grace of God that brings salvation has appeared to all men. ¹²It teaches us to say "No" to ungodliness and worldly passions, and to live self-controlled, upright and godly lives in this present age, ¹³while we wait for the blessed hope—the glorious appearing of our great God and Savior, Jesus Christ, ¹⁴who gave himself for us to redeem us from all wickedness and to purify for himself a people that are his very own, eager to do what is good.   2Ti 1:10; 1Pe 2:9

¹⁵These, then, are the things you should teach. Encourage and rebuke with all authority. Do not let anyone despise you.

Doing What Is Good

3 Remind the people to be subject to rulers and authorities, to be obedient, to be ready to do whatever is good, ²to slander no one, to be peaceable and considerate, and to show true humility toward all men.   Ro 13:1

³At one time we too were foolish, disobedient, deceived and enslaved by all kinds of passions and pleasures. We lived in malice and envy, being hated and hating one another. ⁴But when the kindness and love of God our Savior appeared, ⁵he saved us, not because of righteous things we had done, but because of his mercy. He saved us through the washing of rebirth and renewal by the Holy Spirit, ⁶whom he poured out on us generously through Jesus Christ our Savior, ⁷so that, having been justified by his grace, we might become heirs having the hope of eternal life. ⁸This is a trustworthy saying. And I want you to stress these things, so that those who have trusted in God may be careful to devote themselves to doing what is good. These things are excellent and profitable for everyone.   Eph 2:2; Tit 1:2

⁹But avoid foolish controversies and genealogies and arguments and quarrels about the law, because these are unprofitable and useless. ¹⁰Warn a divisive person once, and then warn him a second time. After that, have nothing to do with him. ¹¹You may be sure that such a man is warped and sinful; he is self-condemned.   2Ti 2:16

Final Remarks

¹²As soon as I send Artemas or Tychicus to you, do your best to come to me at Nicopolis, because I have decided to winter there. ¹³Do everything you can to help Zenas the lawyer and Apollos on their way and see that they have everything they need. ¹⁴Our people must learn to devote themselves to doing what is good, in order that they may provide for daily necessities and not live unproductive lives.   Tit 2:14

¹⁵Everyone with me sends you greetings. Greet those who love us in the faith.

Grace be with you all.

Philemon

Introduction:

Philemon was a leader of the church at Colosse and a friend of Paul's. Philemon's slave, Onesimus, had stolen money from him and had run away to Rome. While he was there he met Paul and became a Christian.

Paul sends Onesimus back to Philemon with this letter. He begs Philemon to forgive Onesimus and to treat him as a brother in Christ instead of a runaway slave.

This short letter, along with Ephesians, Colossians, and Philippians are often called the prison letters because they were written while Paul was in prison in Rome for the first time (about A.D. 59–61).

Outline of contents:

¹Paul, a prisoner of Christ Jesus, and Timothy our brother,

To Philemon our dear friend and fellow worker, ²to Apphia our sister, to Archippus our fellow soldier and to the church that meets in your home: Col 4:17

³Grace to you and peace from God our Father and the Lord Jesus Christ.

Thanksgiving and Prayer

⁴I always thank my God as I remember you in my prayers, ⁵because I hear about your faith in the Lord Jesus and your love for all the saints. ⁶I pray that you may be active in sharing your faith, so that you will have a full understanding of every good thing we have in Christ. ⁷Your love has given me great joy and encouragement, because you, brother, have refreshed the hearts of the saints. 2Co 7:4,13

Paul's Plea for Onesimus

⁸Therefore, although in Christ I could be bold and order you to do what you ought to do, ⁹yet I appeal to you on the basis of love. I then, as Paul—an old man and now also a prisoner of

Christ Jesus— [10]I appeal to you for my son Onesimus,[a] who became my son while I was in chains. [11]Formerly he was useless to you, but now he has become useful both to you and to me.   1Co 1:10; 1Th 2:11

[12]I am sending him—who is my very heart—back to you. [13]I would have liked to keep him with me so that he could take your place in helping me while I am in chains for the gospel. [14]But I did not want to do anything without your consent, so that any favor you do will be spontaneous and not forced. [15]Perhaps the reason he was separated from you for a little while was that you might have him back for good— [16]no longer as a slave, but better than a slave, as a dear brother. He is very dear to me but even dearer to you, both as a man and as a brother in the Lord.   1Co 7:22

[17]So if you consider me a partner, welcome him as you would welcome me. [18]If he has done you any wrong or owes you anything, charge it to me. [19]I, Paul, am writing this with my own hand. I will pay it back—not to mention that you owe me your very self. [20]I do wish, brother, that I may have some benefit from you in the Lord; refresh my heart in Christ. [21]Confident of your obedience, I write to you, knowing that you will do even more than I ask.

[22]And one thing more: Prepare a guest room for me, because I hope to be restored to you in answer to your prayers.

[23]Epaphras, my fellow prisoner in Christ Jesus, sends you greetings. [24]And so do Mark, Aristarchus, Demas and Luke, my fellow workers.

[25]The grace of the Lord Jesus Christ be with your spirit.

---

[a]10 *Onesimus* means *useful.*

Hebrews

Introduction:

Although the author of Hebrews is unknown, this book was probably written in the late A.D. 60's. During this time persecution was a real problem for the church in Rome. This letter was most likely written to the Jewish Christians in either Palestine or Rome who were ready to give up their faith and return to the Jewish faith because of persecution.

The book of Hebrews was written to teach these Jewish Christians that the Christian faith is better in every way than the Jewish faith. Christ is from God and is better than the angels, Moses and Joshua, any priest, and he is the only complete sacrifice. The author shows how Jesus completed the Jewish faith by making the final sacrifice for sin. After his death, none of the Old Testament sacrifices were needed. Chapter 11—the famous chapter on men and women of faith in Old Testament times—must have given these persecuted Christians great hope and helped them to have faith and trust in God.

Outline of contents:

The Son Superior to Angels

1 In the past God spoke to our forefathers through the prophets at many times and in various ways, ²but in these last days he has spoken to us by his Son, whom he appointed heir of all things, and through whom he made the universe. ³The Son is the radiance of God's glory and the exact representation of his being, sustaining all things by his powerful word. After he had provided purification for sins, he sat down at the right hand of the Majesty in heaven. ⁴So he became as much superior to the angels as the name he has

inherited is superior to theirs.

⁵For to which of the angels did God ever say,

"You are my Son;
today I have become your
Father*ªʺᵇ*?

Or again,

"I will be his Father,
and he will be my Son"*ᶜ*?

⁶And again, when God brings his firstborn into the world, he says,   Jn 3:16; Heb 10:5

"Let all God's angels worship him."*ᵈ*

⁷In speaking of the angels he says,

"He makes his angels winds,
his servants flames of
fire."*ᵉ*

⁸But about the Son he says,

"Your throne, O God, will
last for ever and ever,
and righteousness will be
the scepter of your
kingdom.
⁹You have loved
righteousness and
hated wickedness;
therefore God, your God,
has set you above your
companions   Php 2:9
by anointing you with the
oil of joy."*ᶠ*   Isa 61:1,3

¹⁰He also says,

"In the beginning, O Lord,

you laid the foundations
of the earth,
and the heavens are the
work of your hands.   Ps 8:6
¹¹They will perish, but you
remain;
they will all wear out like a
garment.
¹²You will roll them up like a
robe;   Isa 34:4
like a garment they will be
changed.
But you remain the same,
and your years will never
end."*ᵍ*

¹³To which of the angels did God ever say,

"Sit at my right hand
until I make your enemies
a footstool for your feet"*ʰ*?

¹⁴Are not all angels ministering spirits sent to serve those who will inherit salvation?   Ps 91:11

Warning to Pay Attention

2 We must pay more careful attention, therefore, to what we have heard, so that we do not drift away. ²For if the message spoken by angels was binding, and every violation and disobedience received its just punishment, ³how shall we escape if we ignore such a great salvation? This salvation, which was first announced by the Lord, was confirmed to us by those who heard him. ⁴God also testified to it by signs, wonders

---

ª5 Or *have begotten you*   *ᵇ5* Psalm 2:7   *ᶜ5* 2 Samuel 7:14; 1 Chron. 17:13
ᵈ6 Deut. 32:43 (see Dead Sea Scrolls and Septuagint)   *ᵉ7* Psalm 104:4
ᶠ9 Psalm 45:6,7   *ᵍ12* Psalm 102:25-27   *ʰ13* Psalm 110:1

and various miracles, and gifts of the Holy Spirit distributed according to his will. Heb 1:2

Jesus Made Like His Brothers

⁵It is not to angels that he has subjected the world to come, about which we are speaking. ⁶But there is a place where someone has testified:

"What is man that you are
    mindful of him,
the son of man that you
    care for him? Job 7:17
⁷You made him a little*a* lower
    than the angels;
you crowned him with
    glory and honor
⁸ and put everything under
    his feet."*b*

In putting everything under him, God left nothing that is not subject to him. Yet at present we do not see everything subject to him. ⁹But we see Jesus, who was made a little lower than the angels, now crowned with glory and honor because he suffered death, so that by the grace of God he might taste death for everyone. Ac 3:13-15

¹⁰In bringing many sons to glory, it was fitting that God, for whom and through whom everything exists, should make the author of their salvation perfect through suffering. ¹¹Both the one who makes men holy and those who are made holy are of the same family. So Jesus

is not ashamed to call them brothers. ¹²He says, Ro 11:36

"I will declare your name to
    my brothers;
in the presence of the
    congregation I will sing
    your praises."*c*

¹³And again,

"I will put my trust in him."*d*

And again he says,

"Here am I, and the children
    God has given me."*e*

¹⁴Since the children have flesh and blood, he too shared in their humanity so that by his death he might destroy him who holds the power of death—that is, the devil— ¹⁵and free those who all their lives were held in slavery by their fear of death. ¹⁶For surely it is not angels he helps, but Abraham's descendants. ¹⁷For this reason he had to be made like his brothers in every way, in order that he might become a merciful and faithful high priest in service to God, and that he might make atonement for*f* the sins of the people. ¹⁸Because he himself suffered when he was tempted, he is able to help those who are being tempted. Heb 4:14,15

Jesus Greater Than Moses

3 Therefore, holy brothers, who share in the heavenly calling, fix your thoughts on

a7 Or *him for a little while;* also in verse 9   *b8* Psalm 8:4-6   *c12* Psalm 22:22
d13 Isaiah 8:17   *e13* Isaiah 8:18   *f17* Or *and that he might turn aside God's wrath, taking away*

Jesus, the apostle and high priest whom we confess. ²He was faithful to the one who appointed him, just as Moses was faithful in all God's house. ³Jesus has been found worthy of greater honor than Moses, just as the builder of a house has greater honor than the house itself. ⁴For every house is built by someone, but God is the builder of everything. ⁵Moses was faithful as a servant in all God's house, testifying to what would be said in the future. ⁶But Christ is faithful as a son over God's house. And we are his house, if we hold on to our courage and the hope of which we boast.

Warning Against Unbelief

⁷So, as the Holy Spirit says:

"Today, if you hear his voice,
⁸   do not harden your hearts
as you did in the rebellion,
   during the time of testing in
     the desert,
⁹where your fathers tested
   and tried me
and for forty years saw
   what I did.   Nu 14:33
¹⁰That is why I was angry with
   that generation,
and I said, 'Their hearts are
   always going astray,
and they have not known
   my ways.'
¹¹So I declared on oath in my
   anger,   Dt 1:34-35
'They shall never enter my
   rest.' "ᵃ

¹²See to it, brothers, that none of you has a sinful, unbelieving heart that turns away from the living God. ¹³But encourage one another daily, as long as it is called Today, so that none of you may be hardened by sin's deceitfulness. ¹⁴We have come to share in Christ if we hold firmly till the end the confidence we had at first. ¹⁵As has just been said: Eph 3:12

"Today, if you hear his voice,
   do not harden your hearts
as you did in the rebellion."ᵇ

¹⁶Who were they who heard and rebelled? Were they not all those Moses led out of Egypt? ¹⁷And with whom was he angry for forty years? Was it not with those who sinned, whose bodies fell in the desert? ¹⁸And to whom did God swear that they would never enter his rest if not to those who disobeyedᶜ? ¹⁹So we see that they were not able to enter, because of their unbelief.   Nu 14:2; Ps 78:22

A Sabbath-Rest for the People of God

4 Therefore, since the promise of entering his rest still stands, let us be careful that none of you be found to have fallen short of it. ²For we also have had the gospel preached to us, just as they did; but the message they heard was of no value to them, because those who heard did not combine it with

---

ᵃ11 Psalm 95:7-11   ᵇ15 Psalm 95:7,8   ᶜ18 Or *disbelieved*

faith.ᵃ ³Now we who have believed enter that rest, just as God has said, Heb 12:15

"So I declared on oath in my anger,
'They shall never enter my rest.'"ᵇ

And yet his work has been finished since the creation of the world. ⁴For somewhere he has spoken about the seventh day in these words: "And on the seventh day God rested from all his work."ᶜ ⁵And again in the passage above he says, "They shall never enter my rest."

⁶It still remains that some will enter that rest, and those who formerly had the gospel preached to them did not go in, because of their disobedience. ⁷Therefore God again set a certain day, calling it Today, when a long time later he spoke through David, as was said before: Heb 3:18

"Today, if you hear his voice, do not harden your hearts."ᵈ

⁸For if Joshua had given them rest, God would not have spoken later about another day. ⁹There remains, then, a Sabbath-rest for the people of God; ¹⁰for anyone who enters God's rest also rests from his own work, just as God did from his. ¹¹Let us, therefore, make every effort to enter that rest, so that no one will fall by following their example of disobedience.

¹²For the word of God is living and active. Sharper than any double-edged sword, it penetrates even to dividing soul and spirit, joints and marrow; it judges the thoughts and attitudes of the heart. ¹³Nothing in all creation is hidden from God's sight. Everything is uncovered and laid bare before the eyes of him to whom we must give account. Pr 5:21

Jesus the Great High Priest

¹⁴Therefore, since we have a great high priest who has gone through the heavens,ᵉ Jesus the Son of God, let us hold firmly to the faith we profess. ¹⁵For we do not have a high priest who is unable to sympathize with our weaknesses, but we have one who has been tempted in every way, just as we are—yet was without sin. ¹⁶Let us then approach the throne of grace with confidence, so that we may receive mercy and find grace to help us in our time of need.

5 Every high priest is selected from among men and is appointed to represent them in matters related to God, to offer gifts and sacrifices for sins. ²He is able to deal gently with those who are ignorant and are going astray, since he himself is subject to weakness. ³This is why he has to offer sacrifices for his

---

ᵃ2 Many manuscripts *because they did not share in the faith of those who obeyed*
ᵇ3 Psalm 95:11; also in verse 5   ᶜ4 Gen. 2:2   ᵈ7 Psalm 95:7,8   ᵉ14 Or *gone into heaven*

own sins, as well as for the sins of the people. Lev 9:7; Heb 2:17 [4]No one takes this honor upon himself; he must be called by God, just as Aaron was. [5]So Christ also did not take upon himself the glory of becoming a high priest. But God said to him, Ex 28:1; Jn 8:54

"You are my Son;
today I have become your
Father."[a]"[b]

[6]And he says in another place,

"You are a priest forever,
in the order of
Melchizedek."[c]

[7]During the days of Jesus' life on earth, he offered up prayers and petitions with loud cries and tears to the one who could save him from death, and he was heard because of his reverent submission. [8]Although he was a son, he learned obedience from what he suffered [9]and, once made perfect, he became the source of eternal salvation for all who obey him [10]and was designated by God to be high priest in the order of Melchizedek. Lk 22:41-44; Heb 2:17,18

Warning Against Falling Away

[11]We have much to say about this, but it is hard to explain because you are slow to learn. [12]In fact, though by this time you ought to be teachers, you need someone to teach you the elementary truths of God's word all over again. You need milk, not solid food! [13]Anyone who lives on milk, being still an infant, is not acquainted with the teaching about righteousness. [14]But solid food is for the mature, who by constant use have trained themselves to distinguish good from evil. 1Co 3:2

6 Therefore let us leave the elementary teachings about Christ and go on to maturity, not laying again the foundation of repentance from acts that lead to death,[d] and of faith in God, [2]instruction about baptisms, the laying on of hands, the resurrection of the dead, and eternal judgment. [3]And God permitting, we will do so. Php 3:12-14

[4]It is impossible for those who have once been enlightened, who have tasted the heavenly gift, who have shared in the Holy Spirit, [5]who have tasted the goodness of the word of God and the powers of the coming age, [6]if they fall away, to be brought back to repentance, because[e] to their loss they are crucifying the Son of God all over again and subjecting him to public disgrace. Eph 2:8

[7]Land that drinks in the rain often falling on it and that produces a crop useful to those for whom it is farmed receives the blessing of God. [8]But land that

---

[a]5 Or have begotten you   [b]5 Psalm 2:7   [c]6 Psalm 110:4   [d]1 Or from useless rituals
[e]6 Or repentance while

produces thorns and thistles is worthless and is in danger of being cursed. In the end it will be burned. Ge 3:17-18; Isa 5:6

[9]Even though we speak like this, dear friends, we are confident of better things in your case—things that accompany salvation. [10]God is not unjust; he will not forget your work and the love you have shown him as you have helped his people and continue to help them. [11]We want each of you to show this same diligence to the very end, in order to make your hope sure. [12]We do not want you to become lazy, but to imitate those who through faith and patience inherit what has been promised. 1Th 1:3; Heb 13:7

The Certainty of God's Promise

[13]When God made his promise to Abraham, since there was no one greater for him to swear by, he swore by himself, [14]saying, "I will surely bless you and give you many descendants."[a] [15]And so after waiting patiently, Abraham received what was promised. Ge 21:5

[16]Men swear by someone greater than themselves, and the oath confirms what is said and puts an end to all argument. [17]Because God wanted to make the unchanging nature of his purpose very clear to the heirs of what was promised, he confirmed it with an oath. [18]God

did this so that, by two unchangeable things in which it is impossible for God to lie, we who have fled to take hold of the hope offered to us may be greatly encouraged. [19]We have this hope as an anchor for the soul, firm and secure. It enters the inner sanctuary behind the curtain, [20]where Jesus, who went before us, has entered on our behalf. He has become a high priest forever, in the order of Melchizedek. Ex 22:11; Heb 4:14

Melchizedek the Priest

7 This Melchizedek was king of Salem and priest of God Most High. He met Abraham returning from the defeat of the kings and blessed him, [2]and Abraham gave him a tenth of everything. First, his name means "king of righteousness"; then also, "king of Salem" means "king of peace." [3]Without father or mother, without genealogy, without beginning of days or end of life, like the Son of God he remains a priest forever. Ge 14:18-20

[4]Just think how great he was: Even the patriarch Abraham gave him a tenth of the plunder! [5]Now the law requires the descendants of Levi who become priests to collect a tenth from the people—that is, their brothers—even though their brothers are descended from Abraham. [6]This man, however, did not trace his descent from Levi, yet

---

[a]14 Gen. 22:17

he collected a tenth from Abraham and blessed him who had the promises. [7]And without doubt the lesser person is blessed by the greater. [8]In the one case, the tenth is collected by men who die; but in the other case, by him who is declared to be living. [9]One might even say that Levi, who collects the tenth, paid the tenth through Abraham, [10]because when Melchizedek met Abraham, Levi was still in the body of his ancestor. Ro 4:13; Heb 5:6

Jesus Like Melchizedek

[11]If perfection could have been attained through the Levitical priesthood (for on the basis of it the law was given to the people), why was there still need for another priest to come—one in the order of Melchizedek, not in the order of Aaron? [12]For when there is a change of the priesthood, there must also be a change of the law. [13]He of whom these things are said belonged to a different tribe, and no one from that tribe has ever served at the altar. [14]For it is clear that our Lord descended from Judah, and in regard to that tribe Moses said nothing about priests. [15]And what we have said is even more clear if another priest like Melchizedek appears, [16]one who has become a priest not on the basis of a regulation as to his ancestry but on the basis of the power of an indestructible life. [17]For it is declared:

"You are a priest forever,
    in the order of
        Melchizedek."[a]

[18]The former regulation is set aside because it was weak and useless [19](for the law made nothing perfect), and a better hope is introduced, by which we draw near to God. Ro 8:3

[20]And it was not without an oath! Others became priests without any oath, [21]but he became a priest with an oath when God said to him:

"The Lord has sworn
    and will not change his
        mind: Nu 23:19
'You are a priest forever.' "[a]

[22]Because of this oath, Jesus has become the guarantee of a better covenant. Lk 22:20

[23]Now there have been many of those priests, since death prevented them from continuing in office; [24]but because Jesus lives forever, he has a permanent priesthood. [25]Therefore he is able to save completely[b] those who come to God through him, because he always lives to intercede for them. Ro 8:34

[26]Such a high priest meets our need—one who is holy, blameless, pure, set apart from sinners, exalted above the heavens. [27]Unlike the other high priests, he does not need to offer sacrifices day after day, first

[a]17,21 Psalm 110:4   [b]25 Or *forever*

for his own sins, and then for the sins of the people. He sacrificed for their sins once for all when he offered himself. ²⁸For the law appoints as high priests men who are weak; but the oath, which came after the law, appointed the Son, who has been made perfect forever. Ro 6:10

The High Priest of a New Covenant

8 The point of what we are saying is this: We do have such a high priest, who sat down at the right hand of the throne of the Majesty in heaven, ²and who serves in the sanctuary, the true tabernacle set up by the Lord, not by man.

³Every high priest is appointed to offer both gifts and sacrifices, and so it was necessary for this one also to have something to offer. ⁴If he were on earth, he would not be a priest, for there are already men who offer the gifts prescribed by the law. ⁵They serve at a sanctuary that is a copy and shadow of what is in heaven. This is why Moses was warned when he was about to build the tabernacle: "See to it that you make everything according to the pattern shown you on the mountain."^a ⁶But the ministry Jesus has received is as superior to theirs as the covenant of which he is mediator is superior to the old one, and it is founded on better promises. Heb 2:17; 9:14

⁷For if there had been nothing wrong with that first covenant, no place would have been sought for another. ⁸But God found fault with the people and said^b: Heb 7:11

"The time is coming, declares
  the Lord,
 when I will make a new
  covenant   Lk 22:20
 with the house of Israel
 and with the house of
  Judah.
⁹It will not be like the
  covenant
 I made with their
  forefathers   Ex 19:5-6
 when I took them by the
  hand
 to lead them out of Egypt,
 because they did not remain
  faithful to my covenant,
 and I turned away from
  them,
         declares the Lord.
¹⁰This is the covenant I will
  make with the house of
  Israel
 after that time, declares the
  Lord.
 I will put my laws in their
  minds
 and write them on their
  hearts.   2Co 3:3
 I will be their God,
 and they will be my people.
¹¹No longer will a man teach
  his neighbor,
 or a man his brother,
  saying, 'Know the Lord,'
 because they will all know
  me,   Isa 54:13

---

^a5 Exodus 25:40   ^b8 Some manuscripts may be translated *fault and said to the people.*

from the least of them to the greatest. ¹²For I will forgive their wickedness and will remember their sins no more."^a

¹³By calling this covenant "new," he has made the first one obsolete; and what is obsolete and aging will soon disappear.   2Co 5:17

Worship in the Earthly Tabernacle

9 Now the first covenant had regulations for worship and also an earthly sanctuary. ²A tabernacle was set up. In its first room were the lampstand, the table and the consecrated bread; this was called the Holy Place. ³Behind the second curtain was a room called the Most Holy Place, ⁴which had the golden altar of incense and the gold-covered ark of the covenant. This ark contained the gold jar of manna, Aaron's staff that had budded, and the stone tablets of the covenant. ⁵Above the ark were the cherubim of the Glory, overshadowing the atonement cover.^b But we cannot discuss these things in detail now. Ex 25:8 ⁶When everything had been arranged like this, the priests entered regularly into the outer room to carry on their ministry. ⁷But only the high priest entered the inner room, and that only once a year, and never

without blood, which he offered for himself and for the sins the people had committed in ignorance. ⁸The Holy Spirit was showing by this that the way into the Most Holy Place had not yet been disclosed as long as the first tabernacle was still standing. ⁹This is an illustration for the present time, indicating that the gifts and sacrifices being offered were not able to clear the conscience of the worshiper. ¹⁰They are only a matter of food and drink and various ceremonial washings—external regulations applying until the time of the new order.   Lev 16:11-19; Jn 14:6

The Blood of Christ

¹¹When Christ came as high priest of the good things that are already here,^c he went through the greater and more perfect tabernacle that is not man-made, that is to say, not a part of this creation. ¹²He did not enter by means of the blood of goats and calves; but he entered the Most Holy Place once for all by his own blood, having obtained eternal redemption. ¹³The blood of goats and bulls and the ashes of a heifer sprinkled on those who are ceremonially unclean sanctify them so that they are outwardly clean. ¹⁴How much more, then, will the blood of Christ, who through the eternal Spirit of-

^a12 Jer. 31:31-34   ^b5 Traditionally *the mercy seat*   ^c11 Some early manuscripts *are to come*

fered himself unblemished to God, cleanse our consciences from acts that lead to death, [a] so that we may serve the living God! Heb 2:17; 1Pe 3:18

¹⁵For this reason Christ is the mediator of a new covenant, that those who are called may receive the promised eternal inheritance—now that he has died as a ransom to set them free from the sins committed under the first covenant. Heb 7:22

¹⁶In the case of a will, [b] it is necessary to prove the death of the one who made it, ¹⁷because a will is in force only when somebody has died; it never takes effect while the one who made it is living. ¹⁸This is why even the first covenant was not put into effect without blood. ¹⁹When Moses had proclaimed every commandment of the law to all the people, he took the blood of calves, together with water, scarlet wool and branches of hyssop, and sprinkled the scroll and all the people. ²⁰He said, "This is the blood of the covenant, which God has commanded you to keep." [c] ²¹In the same way, he sprinkled with the blood both the tabernacle and everything used in its ceremonies. ²²In fact, the law requires that nearly everything be cleansed with blood, and without the shedding of blood there is no forgiveness. Lev 8:15; 17:11

²³It was necessary, then, for the copies of the heavenly things to be purified with these sacrifices, but the heavenly things themselves with better sacrifices than these. ²⁴For Christ did not enter a man-made sanctuary that was only a copy of the true one; he entered heaven itself, now to appear for us in God's presence. ²⁵Nor did he enter heaven to offer himself again and again, the way the high priest enters the Most Holy Place every year with blood that is not his own. ²⁶Then Christ would have had to suffer many times since the creation of the world. But now he has appeared once for all at the end of the ages to do away with sin by the sacrifice of himself. ²⁷Just as man is destined to die once, and after that to face judgment, ²⁸so Christ was sacrificed once to take away the sins of many people; and he will appear a second time, not to bear sin, but to bring salvation to those who are waiting for him. 1Pe 2:24

Christ's Sacrifice Once for All

10 The law is only a shadow of the good things that are coming—not the realities themselves. For this reason it can never, by the same sacrifices repeated endlessly year after year, make perfect those who draw near to worship. ²If it

---

[a]14 Or *from useless rituals*   [b]16 Same Greek word as *covenant*; also in verse 17
[c]20 Exodus 24:8

could, would they not have stopped being offered? For the worshipers would have been cleansed once for all, and would no longer have felt guilty for their sins. ³But those sacrifices are an annual reminder of sins, ⁴because it is impossible for the blood of bulls and goats to take away sins. Col 2:17; Heb 9:12

⁵Therefore, when Christ came into the world, he said:

"Sacrifice and offering you did not desire,
  but a body you prepared for me; Heb 2:14
⁶with burnt offerings and sin offerings
  you were not pleased.
⁷Then I said, 'Here I am—it is written about me in the scroll—
  I have come to do your will, O God.'"ᵃ

⁸First he said, "Sacrifices and offerings, burnt offerings and sin offerings you did not desire, nor were you pleased with them" (although the law required them to be made). ⁹Then he said, "Here I am, I have come to do your will." He sets aside the first to establish the second. ¹⁰And by that will, we have been made holy through the sacrifice of the body of Jesus Christ once for all. Mk 12:33

¹¹Day after day every priest stands and performs his religious duties; again and again he offers the same sacrifices, which can never take away sins. ¹²But when this priest had offered for all time one sacrifice for sins, he sat down at the right hand of God. ¹³Since that time he waits for his enemies to be made his footstool, ¹⁴because by one sacrifice he has made perfect forever those who are being made holy. Heb 1:13; 5:1

¹⁵The Holy Spirit also testifies to us about this. First he says:

¹⁶"This is the covenant I will make with them
  after that time, says the Lord.
I will put my laws in their hearts,
  and I will write them on their minds."ᵇ

¹⁷Then he adds:

"Their sins and lawless acts
  I will remember no more."ᶜ

¹⁸And where these have been forgiven, there is no longer any sacrifice for sin.

A Call to Persevere

¹⁹Therefore, brothers, since we have confidence to enter the Most Holy Place by the blood of Jesus, ²⁰by a new and living way opened for us through the curtain, that is, his body, ²¹and since we have a great priest over the house of God, ²²let us draw near to God with a sincere heart in full assurance of faith, having our hearts sprinkled to cleanse us from a guilty conscience and

ᵃ7 Psalm 40:6-8 (see Septuagint)   ᵇ16 Jer. 31:33   ᶜ17 Jer. 31:34

having our bodies washed with pure water. 23Let us hold unswervingly to the hope we profess, for he who promised is faithful. 24And let us consider how we may spur one another on toward love and good deeds. 25Let us not give up meeting together, as some are in the habit of doing, but let us encourage one another—and all the more as you see the Day approaching.   Ac 2:42; Eph 3:12

26If we deliberately keep on sinning after we have received the knowledge of the truth, no sacrifice for sins is left, 27but only a fearful expectation of judgment and of raging fire that will consume the enemies of God. 28Anyone who rejected the law of Moses died without mercy on the testimony of two or three witnesses. 29How much more severely do you think a man deserves to be punished who has trampled the Son of God under foot, who has treated as an unholy thing the blood of the covenant that sanctified him, and who has insulted the Spirit of grace? 30For we know him who said, "It is mine to avenge; I will repay,"*a* and again, "The Lord will judge his people."*b* 31It is a dreadful thing to fall into the hands of the living God.   Heb 6:4-6; 2Pe 2:20

32Remember those earlier days after you had received the light, when you stood your ground in a great contest in the face of suffering. 33Sometimes you were publicly exposed to insult and persecution; at other times you stood side by side with those who were so treated. 34You sympathized with those in prison and joyfully accepted the confiscation of your property, because you knew that you yourselves had better and lasting possessions.   1Pe 1:4,5

35So do not throw away your confidence; it will be richly rewarded. 36You need to persevere so that when you have done the will of God, you will receive what he has promised. 37For in just a very little while,

"He who is coming will come
    and will not delay.
38 But my righteous one*c* will
    live by faith.
And if he shrinks back,
  I will not be pleased with
    him."*d*

39But we are not of those who shrink back and are destroyed, but of those who believe and are saved.   Ac 16:30; 2Pe 2:20

By Faith

11 Now faith is being sure of what we hope for and certain of what we do not see. 2This is what the ancients were commended for.   2Co 4:18

3By faith we understand that the universe was formed at God's command, so that what is

---

a30 Deut. 32:35   *b30* Deut. 32:36; Psalm 135:14   *c38* One early manuscript *But the righteous*   *d38* Hab. 2:3,4

seen was not made out of what was visible.

⁴By faith Abel offered God a better sacrifice than Cain did. By faith he was commended as a righteous man, when God spoke well of his offerings. And by faith he still speaks, even though he is dead.   Ge 4:4

⁵By faith Enoch was taken from this life, so that he did not experience death; he could not be found, because God had taken him away. For before he was taken, he was commended as one who pleased God. ⁶And without faith it is impossible to please God, because anyone who comes to him must believe that he exists and that he rewards those who earnestly seek him.   Ge 5:21-24; Heb 7:19

⁷By faith Noah, when warned about things not yet seen, in holy fear built an ark to save his family. By his faith he condemned the world and became heir of the righteousness that comes by faith.   Ge 6:13-22

⁸By faith Abraham, when called to go to a place he would later receive as his inheritance, obeyed and went, even though he did not know where he was going. ⁹By faith he made his home in the promised land like a stranger in a foreign country; he lived in tents, as did Isaac and Jacob, who were heirs with him of the same promise. ¹⁰For he was looking forward to the city with foundations, whose architect and builder is God.

¹¹By faith Abraham, even though he was past age—and Sarah herself was barren—was enabled to become a father because heᵃ considered him faithful who had made the promise. ¹²And so from this one man, and he as good as dead, came descendants as numerous as the stars in the sky and as countless as the sand on the seashore.   Ge 17:17-19; Ro 4:19

¹³All these people were still living by faith when they died. They did not receive the things promised; they only saw them and welcomed them from a distance. And they admitted that they were aliens and strangers on earth. ¹⁴People who say such things show that they are looking for a country of their own. ¹⁵If they had been thinking of the country they had left, they would have had opportunity to return. ¹⁶Instead, they were longing for a better country—a heavenly one. Therefore God is not ashamed to be called their God, for he has prepared a city for them.   Mt 13:17; 2Ti 4:18

¹⁷By faith Abraham, when God tested him, offered Isaac as a sacrifice. He who had received the promises was about to sacrifice his one and only son, ¹⁸even though God had said to him, "It is through Isaac that your offspringᵇ will be reckoned."ᶜ

ᵃ11 Or *By faith even Sarah, who was past age, was enabled to bear children because she*
ᵇ18 Greek *seed*   ᶜ18 Gen. 21:12

¹⁹Abraham reasoned that God could raise the dead, and figuratively speaking, he did receive Isaac back from death.   Ge 22:1-10

²⁰By faith Isaac blessed Jacob and Esau in regard to their future.   Ge 27:27-29,39-40

²¹By faith Jacob, when he was dying, blessed each of Joseph's sons, and worshiped as he leaned on the top of his staff.

²²By faith Joseph, when his end was near, spoke about the exodus of the Israelites from Egypt and gave instructions about his bones.   Ge 50:24-25

²³By faith Moses' parents hid him for three months after he was born, because they saw he was no ordinary child, and they were not afraid of the king's edict.   Ex 1:16,22; 12:2

²⁴By faith Moses, when he had grown up, refused to be known as the son of Pharaoh's daughter. ²⁵He chose to be mistreated along with the people of God rather than to enjoy the pleasures of sin for a short time. ²⁶He regarded disgrace for the sake of Christ as of greater value than the treasures of Egypt, because he was looking ahead to his reward. ²⁷By faith he left Egypt, not fearing the king's anger; he persevered because he saw him who is invisible. ²⁸By faith he kept the Passover and the sprinkling of blood, so that the destroyer of the firstborn

would not touch the firstborn of Israel.   Ex 2:10; 12:21-23

²⁹By faith the people passed through the Red Sea[a] as on dry land; but when the Egyptians tried to do so, they were drowned.   Ex 14:21-31

³⁰By faith the walls of Jericho fell, after the people had marched around them for seven days.   Jos 6:12-20

³¹By faith the prostitute Rahab, because she welcomed the spies, was not killed with those who were disobedient.[b]

³²And what more shall I say? I do not have time to tell about Gideon, Barak, Samson, Jephthah, David, Samuel and the prophets, ³³who through faith conquered kingdoms, administered justice, and gained what was promised; who shut the mouths of lions, ³⁴quenched the fury of the flames, and escaped the edge of the sword; whose weakness was turned to strength; and who became powerful in battle and routed foreign armies. ³⁵Women received back their dead, raised to life again. Others were tortured and refused to be released, so that they might gain a better resurrection. ³⁶Some faced jeers and flogging, while still others were chained and put in prison. ³⁷They were stoned[c]; they were sawed in two; they were put to death by the sword. They went about in sheepskins and goat-

---

a29 That is, Sea of Reeds   *b31* Or *unbelieving*   *c37* Some early manuscripts *stoned; they were put to the test;*

skins, destitute, persecuted and mistreated— [38]the world was not worthy of them. They wandered in deserts and mountains, and in caves and holes in the ground.   Jdg 6-8; 1Ki 18:4

[39]These were all commended for their faith, yet none of them received what had been promised. [40]God had planned something better for us so that only together with us would they be made perfect.   Heb 10:36; Rev 9:11

God Disciplines His Sons

12 Therefore, since we are surrounded by such a great cloud of witnesses, let us throw off everything that hinders and the sin that so easily entangles, and let us run with perseverance the race marked out for us. [2]Let us fix our eyes on Jesus, the author and perfecter of our faith, who for the joy set before him endured the cross, scorning its shame, and sat down at the right hand of the throne of God. [3]Consider him who endured such opposition from sinful men, so that you will not grow weary and lose heart.   Heb 10:36; Rev 2:3

[4]In your struggle against sin, you have not yet resisted to the point of shedding your blood. [5]And you have forgotten that word of encouragement that addresses you as sons:

"My son, do not make light
   of the Lord's discipline,

and do not lose heart when
   he rebukes you,
[6]because the Lord disciplines
   those he loves,   Ps 94:12
and he punishes everyone
   he accepts as a son."[a]

[7]Endure hardship as discipline; God is treating you as sons. For what son is not disciplined by his father? [8]If you are not disciplined (and everyone undergoes discipline), then you are illegitimate children and not true sons. [9]Moreover, we have all had human fathers who disciplined us and we respected them for it. How much more should we submit to the Father of our spirits and live! [10]Our fathers disciplined us for a little while as they thought best; but God disciplines us for our good, that we may share in his holiness. [11]No discipline seems pleasant at the time, but painful. Later on, however, it produces a harvest of righteousness and peace for those who have been trained by it.   Dt 8:5

[12]Therefore, strengthen your feeble arms and weak knees. [13]"Make level paths for your feet,"[b] so that the lame may not be disabled, but rather healed.

Warning Against Refusing God

[14]Make every effort to live in peace with all men and to be holy; without holiness no one will see the Lord. [15]See to it that

[a]6 Prov. 3:11,12   [b]13 Prov. 4:26

no one misses the grace of God and that no bitter root grows up to cause trouble and defile many. [16]See that no one is sexually immoral, or is godless like Esau, who for a single meal sold his inheritance rights as the oldest son. [17]Afterward, as you know, when he wanted to inherit this blessing, he was rejected. He could bring about no change of mind, though he sought the blessing with tears.

[18]You have not come to a mountain that can be touched and that is burning with fire; to darkness, gloom and storm; [19]to a trumpet blast or to such a voice speaking words that those who heard it begged that no further word be spoken to them, [20]because they could not bear what was commanded: "If even an animal touches the mountain, it must be stoned."[a] [21]The sight was so terrifying that Moses said, "I am trembling with fear."[b]

[22]But you have come to Mount Zion, to the heavenly Jerusalem, the city of the living God. You have come to thousands upon thousands of angels in joyful assembly, [23]to the church of the firstborn, whose names are written in heaven. You have come to God, the judge of all men, to the spirits of righteous men made perfect, [24]to Jesus the mediator of a new covenant, and to the sprinkled blood that speaks a better word than the blood of Abel. Isa 24:23

[25]See to it that you do not refuse him who speaks. If they did not escape when they refused him who warned them on earth, how much less will we, if we turn away from him who warns us from heaven? [26]At that time his voice shook the earth, but now he has promised, "Once more I will shake not only the earth but also the heavens."[c] [27]The words "once more" indicate the removing of what can be shaken—that is, created things—so that what cannot be shaken may remain.

[28]Therefore, since we are receiving a kingdom that cannot be shaken, let us be thankful, and so worship God acceptably with reverence and awe, [29]for our "God is a consuming fire."[d]

Concluding Exhortations

13 Keep on loving each other as brothers. [2]Do not forget to entertain strangers, for by so doing some people have entertained angels without knowing it. [3]Remember those in prison as if you were their fellow prisoners, and those who are mistreated as if you yourselves were suffering. Ro 12:10

[4]Marriage should be honored by all, and the marriage bed kept pure, for God will judge the adulterer and all the sexually immoral. [5]Keep your lives free from the love of money and

---

[a]20 Exodus 19:12,13   [b]21 Deut. 9:19   [c]26 Haggai 2:6   [d]29 Deut. 4:24

be content with what you have, because God has said,   Mal 2:15

"Never will I leave you;
    never will I forsake you."[a]

[6]So we say with confidence,

"The Lord is my helper; I will
    not be afraid.
What can man do to me?"[b]

[7]Remember your leaders, who spoke the word of God to you. Consider the outcome of their way of life and imitate their faith. [8]Jesus Christ is the same yesterday and today and forever.   Ps 102:27; 1Co 16:16

[9]Do not be carried away by all kinds of strange teachings. It is good for our hearts to be strengthened by grace, not by ceremonial foods, which are of no value to those who eat them. [10]We have an altar from which those who minister at the tabernacle have no right to eat.Eph 4:14

[11]The high priest carries the blood of animals into the Most Holy Place as a sin offering, but the bodies are burned outside the camp. [12]And so Jesus also suffered outside the city gate to make the people holy through his own blood. [13]Let us, then, go to him outside the camp, bearing the disgrace he bore. [14]For here we do not have an enduring city, but we are looking for the city that is to come. [15]Through Jesus, therefore, let us continually offer to God a sacrifice of praise—the fruit of lips that confess his name. [16]And do not forget to do good and to share with others, for with such sacrifices God is pleased.   Ro 12:13; 1Pe 2:5

[17]Obey your leaders and submit to their authority. They keep watch over you as men who must give an account. Obey them so that their work will be a joy, not a burden, for that would be of no advantage to you.   Ac 20:28

[18]Pray for us. We are sure that we have a clear conscience and desire to live honorably in every way. [19]I particularly urge you to pray so that I may be restored to you soon.   1Th 5:25

[20]May the God of peace, who through the blood of the eternal covenant brought back from the dead our Lord Jesus, that great Shepherd of the sheep, [21]equip you with everything good for doing his will, and may he work in us what is pleasing to him, through Jesus Christ, to whom be glory for ever and ever. Amen.   2Co 9:8; Php 2:13

[22]Brothers, I urge you to bear with my word of exhortation, for I have written you only a short letter.

[23]I want you to know that our brother Timothy has been released. If he arrives soon, I will come with him to see you.

[24]Greet all your leaders and all God's people. Those from Italy send you their greetings.

[25]Grace be with you all.

[a]5 Deut. 31:6   [b]6 Psalm 118:6,7

James

Introduction:

The book of James may be the earliest of the New Testament letters, written about A.D. 48. This letter, written by the brother of Jesus and one of the leaders of the church in Jerusalem, was addressed to Christians everywhere. The seven books of the New Testament from James through Jude are called the general letters because they are addressed to Christians in general and not to a special church.

James wrote this letter to teach Christians the practice of Christianity. He insists that if we have real faith, we will show it by acting like Christians. He gives practical advice on things like anger and quarreling, showing favoritism, controlling the tongue, boasting, patience and prayer.

Outline of contents:

The heart of true religion (1:1–27)
True faith in practice (2:1–3:12)
True wisdom in practice (3:13–5:12)
The prayer of faith (5:13–20)

---

1 James, a servant of God and of the Lord Jesus Christ,

To the twelve tribes scattered among the nations: Ac 26:7

Greetings.

Trials and Temptations

²Consider it pure joy, my brothers, whenever you face trials of many kinds, ³because you know that the testing of your faith develops perseverance. ⁴Perseverance must finish its work so that you may be mature and complete, not lacking any-thing. ⁵If any of you lacks wisdom, he should ask God, who gives generously to all without finding fault, and it will be given to him. ⁶But when he asks, he must believe and not doubt, because he who doubts is like a wave of the sea, blown and tossed by the wind. ⁷That man should not think he will receive anything from the Lord; ⁸he is a double-minded man, unstable in all he does. Mt 21:21; 1Pe 1:7

⁹The brother in humble circumstances ought to take pride in his high position. ¹⁰But the

one who is rich should take pride in his low position, because he will pass away like a wild flower. 11For the sun rises with scorching heat and withers the plant; its blossom falls and its beauty is destroyed. In the same way, the rich man will fade away even while he goes about his business.　　Mt 23:12

12Blessed is the man who perseveres under trial, because when he has stood the test, he will receive the crown of life that God has promised to those who love him.　　Ge 22:1; 1Pe 3:14

13When tempted, no one should say, "God is tempting me." For God cannot be tempted by evil, nor does he tempt anyone; 14but each one is tempted when, by his own evil desire, he is dragged away and enticed. 15Then, after desire has conceived, it gives birth to sin; and sin, when it is full-grown, gives birth to death.　　Ge 3:6; Job 15:35

16Don't be deceived, my dear brothers. 17Every good and perfect gift is from above, coming down from the Father of the heavenly lights, who does not change like shifting shadows. 18He chose to give us birth through the word of truth, that we might be a kind of firstfruits of all he created.　　Ps 85:12; Jn 1:13

Listening and Doing

19My dear brothers, take note of this: Everyone should be quick to listen, slow to speak and slow to become angry, 20for man's anger does not bring about the righteous life that God desires. 21Therefore, get rid of all moral filth and the evil that is so prevalent and humbly accept the word planted in you, which can save you.　　Eph 4:22

22Do not merely listen to the word, and so deceive yourselves. Do what it says. 23Anyone who listens to the word but does not do what it says is like a man who looks at his face in a mirror 24and, after looking at himself, goes away and immediately forgets what he looks like. 25But the man who looks intently into the perfect law that gives freedom, and continues to do this, not forgetting what he has heard, but doing it—he will be blessed in what he does.　　Ps 19:7; Mt 7:21

26If anyone considers himself religious and yet does not keep a tight rein on his tongue, he deceives himself and his religion is worthless. 27Religion that God our Father accepts as pure and faultless is this: to look after orphans and widows in their distress and to keep oneself from being polluted by the world.　　Ps 34:13; Mt 25:34-36

Favoritism Forbidden

2 My brothers, as believers in our glorious Lord Jesus Christ, don't show favoritism. 2Suppose a man comes into your meeting wearing a gold ring and fine clothes, and a poor man in shabby clothes also comes in. 3If you show special attention to the man wearing

fine clothes and say, "Here's a good seat for you," but say to the poor man, "You stand there" or "Sit on the floor by my feet," ⁴have you not discriminated among yourselves and become judges with evil thoughts?   Dt 1:17; Jn 7:24

⁵Listen, my dear brothers: Has not God chosen those who are poor in the eyes of the world to be rich in faith and to inherit the kingdom he promised those who love him? ⁶But you have insulted the poor. Is it not the rich who are exploiting you? Are they not the ones who are dragging you into court? ⁷Are they not the ones who are slandering the noble name of him to whom you belong?   1Co 1:26-28

⁸If you really keep the royal law found in Scripture, "Love your neighbor as yourself,"ᵃ you are doing right. ⁹But if you show favoritism, you sin and are convicted by the law as lawbreakers. ¹⁰For whoever keeps the whole law and yet stumbles at just one point is guilty of breaking all of it. ¹¹For he who said, "Do not commit adultery,"ᵇ also said, "Do not murder."ᶜ If you do not commit adultery but do commit murder, you have become a lawbreaker.   Mt 5:19

¹²Speak and act as those who are going to be judged by the law that gives freedom, ¹³because judgment without mercy will be shown to anyone who has not been merciful. Mercy triumphs over judgment!

Faith and Deeds

¹⁴What good is it, my brothers, if a man claims to have faith but has no deeds? Can such faith save him? ¹⁵Suppose a brother or sister is without clothes and daily food. ¹⁶If one of you says to him, "Go, I wish you well; keep warm and well fed," but does nothing about his physical needs, what good is it? ¹⁷In the same way, faith by itself, if it is not accompanied by action, is dead.   Mt 25:35,36; Gal 5:6

¹⁸But someone will say, "You have faith; I have deeds."

Show me your faith without deeds, and I will show you my faith by what I do. ¹⁹You believe that there is one God. Good! Even the demons believe that—and shudder.   Mt 8:29; Ro 3:28

²⁰You foolish man, do you want evidence that faith without deeds is uselessᵈ? ²¹Was not our ancestor Abraham considered righteous for what he did when he offered his son Isaac on the altar? ²²You see that his faith and his actions were working together, and his faith was made complete by what he did. ²³And the scripture was fulfilled that says, "Abraham believed God, and it was credited to him as righteousness,"ᵉ and he was called God's friend.

ᵃ8 Lev. 19:18   ᵇ11 Exodus 20:14; Deut. 5:18   ᶜ11 Exodus 20:13; Deut. 5:17
ᵈ20 Some early manuscripts dead   ᵉ23 Gen. 15:6

²⁴You see that a person is justified by what he does and not by faith alone.   1Th 1:3; Heb 11:17

²⁵In the same way, was not even Rahab the prostitute considered righteous for what she did when she gave lodging to the spies and sent them off in a different direction? ²⁶As the body without the spirit is dead, so faith without deeds is dead.

Taming the Tongue

3 Not many of you should presume to be teachers, my brothers, because you know that we who teach will be judged more strictly. ²We all stumble in many ways. If anyone is never at fault in what he says, he is a perfect man, able to keep his whole body in check.

³When we put bits into the mouths of horses to make them obey us, we can turn the whole animal. ⁴Or take ships as an example. Although they are so large and are driven by strong winds, they are steered by a very small rudder wherever the pilot wants to go. ⁵Likewise the tongue is a small part of the body, but it makes great boasts. Consider what a great forest is set on fire by a small spark. ⁶The tongue also is a fire, a world of evil among the parts of the body. It corrupts the whole person, sets the whole course of his life on fire, and is itself set on fire by hell.   Ps 32:9; Pr 16:27

⁷All kinds of animals, birds, reptiles and creatures of the sea are being tamed and have been tamed by man, ⁸but no man can tame the tongue. It is a restless evil, full of deadly poison.Ps 140:3

⁹With the tongue we praise our Lord and Father, and with it we curse men, who have been made in God's likeness. ¹⁰Out of the same mouth come praise and cursing. My brothers, this should not be. ¹¹Can both fresh water and saltᵃ water flow from the same spring? ¹²My brothers, can a fig tree bear olives, or a grapevine bear figs? Neither can a salt spring produce fresh water.   Ge 1:26-27; Mt 7:16

Two Kinds of Wisdom

¹³Who is wise and understanding among you? Let him show it by his good life, by deeds done in the humility that comes from wisdom. ¹⁴But if you harbor bitter envy and selfish ambition in your hearts, do not boast about it or deny the truth. ¹⁵Such "wisdom" does not come down from heaven but is earthly, unspiritual, of the devil. ¹⁶For where you have envy and selfish ambition, there you find disorder and every evil practice.   Jas 2:18; 1Pe 2:12

¹⁷But the wisdom that comes from heaven is first of all pure; then peace-loving, considerate, submissive, full of mercy and good fruit, impartial and sincere. ¹⁸Peacemakers who sow in

---

ᵃ11 Greek *bitter* (see also verse 14)

peace raise a harvest of righteousness.   Mt 5:9; 1Co 2:6

Submit Yourselves to God

4 What causes fights and
quarrels among you? Don't
they come from your desires
that battle within you? ²You
want something but don't get it.
You kill and covet, but you cannot have what you want. You
quarrel and fight. You do not
have, because you do not ask
God. ³When you ask, you do
not receive, because you ask
with wrong motives, that you
may spend what you get on
your pleasures.   Ps 66:18,19; Ro 7:23

⁴You adulterous people,
don't you know that friendship
with the world is hatred toward
God? Anyone who chooses to
be a friend of the world
becomes an enemy of God. ⁵Or
do you think Scripture says
without reason that the spirit he
caused to live in us envies intensely?ᵃ ⁶But he gives us more
grace. That is why Scripture
says: Jn 15:19; 1Co 6:19

"God opposes the proud
     but gives grace to the
     humble."ᵇ

⁷Submit yourselves, then, to
God. Resist the devil, and he
will flee from you. ⁸Come near
to God and he will come near to
you. Wash your hands, you sinners, and purify your hearts,
you double-minded. ⁹Grieve,

mourn and wail. Change your
laughter to mourning and your
joy to gloom. ¹⁰Humble yourselves before the Lord, and he
will lift you up.   Eph 4:27; 1Pe 5:6

¹¹Brothers, do not slander
one another. Anyone who
speaks against his brother or
judges him speaks against the
law and judges it. When you
judge the law, you are not keeping it, but sitting in judgment
on it. ¹²There is only one Lawgiver and Judge, the one who is
able to save and destroy. But
you—who are you to judge
your neighbor?   Isa 33:22; Jas 2:8

Boasting About Tomorrow

¹³Now listen, you who say,
"Today or tomorrow we will go
to this or that city, spend a year
there, carry on business and
make money." ¹⁴Why, you do
not even know what will happen tomorrow. What is your
life? You are a mist that appears
for a little while and then
vanishes. ¹⁵Instead, you ought
to say, "If it is the Lord's will,
we will live and do this or that."
¹⁶As it is, you boast and brag.
All such boasting is evil. ¹⁷Any-
one, then, who knows the good
he ought to do and doesn't do
it, sins.   Ps 39:5; Lk 12:47

Warning to Rich Oppressors

5 Now listen, you rich people,
weep and wail because of
the misery that is coming upon
you. ²Your wealth has rotted,

ᵃ5 Or that God jealously longs for the spirit that he made to live in us; or that the Spirit he
caused to live in us longs jealously   ᵇ6 Prov. 3:34

and moths have eaten your clothes. ³Your gold and silver are corroded. Their corrosion will testify against you and eat your flesh like fire. You have hoarded wealth in the last days. ⁴Look! The wages you failed to pay the workmen who mowed your fields are crying out against you. The cries of the harvesters have reached the ears of the Lord Almighty. ⁵You have lived on earth in luxury and self-indulgence. You have fattened yourselves in the day of slaughter.*ᵃ* ⁶You have condemned and murdered innocent men, who were not opposing you.   Mal 3:5; Lk 6:24

Patience in Suffering

⁷Be patient, then, brothers, until the Lord's coming. See how the farmer waits for the land to yield its valuable crop and how patient he is for the autumn and spring rains. ⁸You too, be patient and stand firm, because the Lord's coming is near. ⁹Don't grumble against each other, brothers, or you will be judged. The Judge is standing at the door!   Ro 13:11; 1Co 4:5

¹⁰Brothers, as an example of patience in the face of suffering, take the prophets who spoke in the name of the Lord. ¹¹As you know, we consider blessed those who have persevered. You have heard of Job's perseverance and have seen what the Lord finally brought about. The Lord is full of compassion and mercy.   Job 1:21-22; 42:10; Mt 5:12

¹²Above all, my brothers, do not swear—not by heaven or by earth or by anything else. Let your "Yes" be yes, and your "No," no, or you will be condemned.   Mt 5:34-37

The Prayer of Faith

¹³Is any one of you in trouble? He should pray. Is anyone happy? Let him sing songs of praise. ¹⁴Is any one of you sick? He should call the elders of the church to pray over him and anoint him with oil in the name of the Lord. ¹⁵And the prayer offered in faith will make the sick person well; the Lord will raise him up. If he has sinned, he will be forgiven. ¹⁶Therefore confess your sins to each other and pray for each other so that you may be healed. The prayer of a righteous man is powerful and effective.   Ps 50:15; Mt 7:7

¹⁷Elijah was a man just like us. He prayed earnestly that it would not rain, and it did not rain on the land for three and a half years. ¹⁸Again he prayed, and the heavens gave rain, and the earth produced its crops.

¹⁹My brothers, if one of you should wander from the truth and someone should bring him back, ²⁰remember this: Whoever turns a sinner from the error of his way will save him from death and cover over a multitude of sins.   Mt 18:15; 1Pe 4:8

ᵃ5 Or *yourselves as in a day of feasting*

1 Peter

Introduction:

First Peter was written by Peter, one of Jesus' twelve disciples, to the Christians who lived in the northern part of Asia Minor. These Christians were being persecuted for their faith, so Peter wrote to encourage them.

He urges them to remember how much Jesus suffered for them and to follow his example by trusting God to care for them. Because God chose them to be his people and because Jesus suffered and died for them, Peter tells these Christians they should live holy lives. He goes on to tell them how they can live as Christians in this sinful world and have hope for the future.

Outline of contents:

Greetings (1:1,2)
Praise to God for salvation (1:3–12)
Holy living (1:13–2:12)
Conduct of the believer (2:13–4:11)
Ministry through suffering (4:12–5:11)
Conclusion (5:12–14)

---

1 Peter, an apostle of Jesus Christ,   Jn 21:17

To God's elect, strangers in the world, scattered throughout Pontus, Galatia, Cappadocia, Asia and Bithynia, ²who have been chosen according to the foreknowledge of God the Father, through the sanctifying work of the Spirit, for obedience to Jesus Christ and sprinkling by his blood: Ro 8:29; 2Th 2:13

Grace and peace be yours in abundance.

Praise to God for a Living Hope

³Praise be to the God and Father of our Lord Jesus Christ! In his great mercy he has given us new birth into a living hope through the resurrection of Jesus Christ from the dead, ⁴and into an inheritance that can never perish, spoil or fade—kept in heaven for you, ⁵who through faith are shielded by God's power until the coming of the salvation that is ready to be revealed in the last time. ⁶In this

you greatly rejoice, though now for a little while you may have had to suffer grief in all kinds of trials. [7]These have come so that your faith—of greater worth than gold, which perishes even though refined by fire—may be proved genuine and may result in praise, glory and honor when Jesus Christ is revealed. [8]Though you have not seen him, you love him; and even though you do not see him now, you believe in him and are filled with an inexpressible and glorious joy, [9]for you are receiving the goal of your faith, the salvation of your souls.   Jn 10:28

[10]Concerning this salvation, the prophets, who spoke of the grace that was to come to you, searched intently and with the greatest care, [11]trying to find out the time and circumstances to which the Spirit of Christ in them was pointing when he predicted the sufferings of Christ and the glories that would follow. [12]It was revealed to them that they were not serving themselves but you, when they spoke of the things that have now been told you by those who have preached the gospel to you by the Holy Spirit sent from heaven. Even angels long to look into these things.

Be Holy

[13]Therefore, prepare your minds for action; be self-controlled; set your hope fully on the grace to be given you when Jesus Christ is revealed. [14]As obedient children, do not conform to the evil desires you had when you lived in ignorance. [15]But just as he who called you is holy, so be holy in all you do; [16]for it is written: "Be holy, because I am holy."[a]   1Jn 3:3

[17]Since you call on a Father who judges each man's work impartially, live your lives as strangers here in reverent fear. [18]For you know that it was not with perishable things such as silver or gold that you were redeemed from the empty way of life handed down to you from your forefathers, [19]but with the precious blood of Christ, a lamb without blemish or defect. [20]He was chosen before the creation of the world, but was revealed in these last times for your sake. [21]Through him you believe in God, who raised him from the dead and glorified him, and so your faith and hope are in God.

[22]Now that you have purified yourselves by obeying the truth so that you have sincere love for your brothers, love one another deeply, from the heart.[b] [23]For you have been born again, not of perishable seed, but of imperishable, through the living and enduring word of God. [24]For,

"All men are like grass,
   and all their glory is like the
    flowers of the field;
the grass withers and the
    flowers fall,

---

[a]16 Lev. 11:44,45; 19:2; 20:7   [b]22 Some early manuscripts *from a pure heart*

25 but the word of the Lord stands forever."*a*

And this is the word that was preached to you.

2 Therefore, rid yourselves of all malice and all deceit, hypocrisy, envy, and slander of every kind. ²Like newborn babies, crave pure spiritual milk, so that by it you may grow up in your salvation, ³now that you have tasted that the Lord is good. Ps 34:8; Eph 4:15,16

The Living Stone and a Chosen People

⁴As you come to him, the living Stone—rejected by men but chosen by God and precious to him— ⁵you also, like living stones, are being built into a spiritual house to be a holy priesthood, offering spiritual sacrifices acceptable to God through Jesus Christ. ⁶For in Scripture it says: Isa 61:6; Eph 2:20-22

"See, I lay a stone in Zion,
    a chosen and precious
        cornerstone,
and the one who trusts in
        him
    will never be put to
        shame."*b*

⁷Now to you who believe, this stone is precious. But to those who do not believe, 2Co 2:16

"The stone the builders
    rejected

has become the
    capstone,*c" d*

⁸and,

"A stone that causes men to
    stumble
    and a rock that makes them
        fall."*e*

They stumble because they disobey the message—which is also what they were destined for.

⁹But you are a chosen people, a royal priesthood, a holy nation, a people belonging to God, that you may declare the praises of him who called you out of darkness into his wonderful light. ¹⁰Once you were not a people, but now you are the people of God; once you had not received mercy, but now you have received mercy. Dt 10:15

¹¹Dear friends, I urge you, as aliens and strangers in the world, to abstain from sinful desires, which war against your soul. ¹²Live such good lives among the pagans that, though they accuse you of doing wrong, they may see your good deeds and glorify God on the day he visits us. Ro 13:14; Php 2:15

Submission to Rulers and Masters

¹³Submit yourselves for the Lord's sake to every authority instituted among men: whether to the king, as the supreme authority, ¹⁴or to governors, who

---

*a*25 Isaiah 40:6-8   *b*6 Isaiah 28:16   *c*7 Or *cornerstone*   *d*7 Psalm 118:22
*e*8 Isaiah 8:14

are sent by him to punish those who do wrong and to commend those who do right. [15]For it is God's will that by doing good you should silence the ignorant talk of foolish men. [16]Live as free men, but do not use your freedom as a cover-up for evil; live as servants of God. [17]Show proper respect to everyone: Love the brotherhood of believers, fear God, honor the king. Ro 12:10; 13:1

[18]Slaves, submit yourselves to your masters with all respect, not only to those who are good and considerate, but also to those who are harsh. [19]For it is commendable if a man bears up under the pain of unjust suffering because he is conscious of God. [20]But how is it to your credit if you receive a beating for doing wrong and endure it? But if you suffer for doing good and you endure it, this is commendable before God. [21]To this you were called, because Christ suffered for you, leaving you an example, that you should follow in his steps. Eph 6:5; Php 1:29

[22]"He committed no sin, 2Co 5:21
  and no deceit was found in
    his mouth."[a]

[23]When they hurled their insults at him, he did not retaliate; when he suffered, he made no threats. Instead, he entrusted himself to him who judges justly. [24]He himself bore our sins in his body on the tree, so that we might die to sins and live for righteousness; by his wounds you have been healed. [25]For you were like sheep going astray, but now you have returned to the Shepherd and Overseer of your souls. Ps 103:3; Isa 53:6

Wives and Husbands

3 Wives, in the same way be submissive to your husbands so that, if any of them do not believe the word, they may be won over without words by the behavior of their wives, [2]when they see the purity and reverence of your lives. [3]Your beauty should not come from outward adornment, such as braided hair and the wearing of gold jewelry and fine clothes. [4]Instead, it should be that of your inner self, the unfading beauty of a gentle and quiet spirit, which is of great worth in God's sight. [5]For this is the way the holy women of the past who put their hope in God used to make themselves beautiful. They were submissive to their own husbands, [6]like Sarah, who obeyed Abraham and called him her master. You are her daughters if you do what is right and do not give way to fear. Ro 7:22; Eph 3:16

[7]Husbands, in the same way be considerate as you live with your wives, and treat them with respect as the weaker partner and as heirs with you of the gra-

cious gift of life, so that nothing will hinder your prayers.

Suffering for Doing Good

⁸Finally, all of you, live in harmony with one another; be sympathetic, love as brothers, be compassionate and humble. ⁹Do not repay evil with evil or insult with insult, but with blessing, because to this you were called so that you may inherit a blessing. ¹⁰For,   Ro 15:5

> "Whoever would love life
>   and see good days
> must keep his tongue from
>   evil
>   and his lips from deceitful
>   speech.
> ¹¹He must turn from evil and
>   do good;
>   he must seek peace and
>   pursue it.
> ¹²For the eyes of the Lord are
>   on the righteous
>   and his ears are attentive to
>   their prayer,
> but the face of the Lord is
>   against those who do
>   evil."ᵃ

¹³Who is going to harm you if you are eager to do good? ¹⁴But even if you should suffer for what is right, you are blessed. "Do not fear what they fearᵇ; do not be frightened."ᶜ ¹⁵But in your hearts set apart Christ as Lord. Always be prepared to give an answer to everyone who asks you to give the reason for the hope that you have. But do this with gentleness and respect, ¹⁶keeping a clear conscience, so that those who speak maliciously against your good behavior in Christ may be ashamed of their slander. ¹⁷It is better, if it is God's will, to suffer for doing good than for doing evil. ¹⁸For Christ died for sins once for all, the righteous for the unrighteous, to bring you to God. He was put to death in the body but made alive by the Spirit, ¹⁹through whomᵈ also he went and preached to the spirits in prison ²⁰who disobeyed long ago when God waited patiently in the days of Noah while the ark was being built. In it only a few people, eight in all, were saved through water, ²¹and this water symbolizes baptism that now saves you also—not the removal of dirt from the body but the pledgeᵉ of a good conscience toward God. It saves you by the resurrection of Jesus Christ, ²²who has gone into heaven and is at God's right hand—with angels, authorities and powers in submission to him.   Tit 2:14; Heb 4:14

Living for God

4 Therefore, since Christ suffered in his body, arm yourselves also with the same attitude, because he who has suffered in his body is done with

---

ᵃ12 Psalm 34:12-16   ᵇ14 Or *not fear their threats*   ᶜ14 Isaiah 8:12   ᵈ18,19 Or
alive in the spirit, ¹⁹*through which*   ᵉ21 Or *response*

sin. [2]As a result, he does not live the rest of his earthly life for evil human desires, but rather for the will of God. [3]For you have spent enough time in the past doing what pagans choose to do—living in debauchery, lust, drunkenness, orgies, carousing and detestable idolatry. [4]They think it strange that you do not plunge with them into the same flood of dissipation, and they heap abuse on you. [5]But they will have to give account to him who is ready to judge the living and the dead. [6]For this is the reason the gospel was preached even to those who are now dead, so that they might be judged according to men in regard to the body, but live according to God in regard to the spirit. Ro 6:2; 1Pe 2:21

[7]The end of all things is near. Therefore be clear minded and self-controlled so that you can pray. [8]Above all, love each other deeply, because love covers over a multitude of sins. [9]Offer hospitality to one another without grumbling. [10]Each one should use whatever gift he has received to serve others, faithfully administering God's grace in its various forms. [11]If anyone speaks, he should do it as one speaking the very words of God. If anyone serves, he should do it with the strength God provides, so that in all things God may be praised through Jesus Christ. To him be the glory and the power for ever and ever. Amen. Ro 12:6-8

Suffering for Being a Christian

[12]Dear friends, do not be surprised at the painful trial you are suffering, as though something strange were happening to you. [13]But rejoice that you participate in the sufferings of Christ, so that you may be overjoyed when his glory is revealed. [14]If you are insulted because of the name of Christ, you are blessed, for the Spirit of glory and of God rests on you. [15]If you suffer, it should not be as a murderer or thief or any other kind of criminal, or even as a meddler. [16]However, if you suffer as a Christian, do not be ashamed, but praise God that you bear that name. [17]For it is time for judgment to begin with the family of God; and if it begins with us, what will the outcome be for those who do not obey the gospel of God? [18]And,

> "If it is hard for the righteous
>   to be saved,
> what will become of the
>   ungodly and the
>   sinner?"[a]

[19]So then, those who suffer according to God's will should commit themselves to their faithful Creator and continue to do good. 1Pe 2:15; 3:17

---

[a]18 Prov. 11:31

To Elders and Young Men

5 To the elders among you, I appeal as a fellow elder, a witness of Christ's sufferings and one who also will share in the glory to be revealed: [2]Be shepherds of God's flock that is under your care, serving as overseers—not because you must, but because you are willing, as God wants you to be; not greedy for money, but eager to serve; [3]not lording it over those entrusted to you, but being examples to the flock. [4]And when the Chief Shepherd appears, you will receive the crown of glory that will never fade away.

[5]Young men, in the same way be submissive to those who are older. All of you, clothe yourselves with humility toward one another, because,   Eph 5:21

"God opposes the proud
but gives grace to the
humble."[a]

[6]Humble yourselves, therefore, under God's mighty hand, that he may lift you up in due time. [7]Cast all your anxiety on him because he cares for you.   Job 5:11

[8]Be self-controlled and alert. Your enemy the devil prowls around like a roaring lion looking for someone to devour. [9]Resist him, standing firm in the faith, because you know that your brothers throughout the world are undergoing the same kind of sufferings.   Jas 4:7

[10]And the God of all grace, who called you to his eternal glory in Christ, after you have suffered a little while, will himself restore you and make you strong, firm and steadfast. [11]To him be the power for ever and ever. Amen.   Ro 8:28; 11:36

Final Greetings

[12]With the help of Silas,[b] whom I regard as a faithful brother, I have written to you briefly, encouraging you and testifying that this is the true grace of God. Stand fast in it.

[13]She who is in Babylon, chosen together with you, sends you her greetings, and so does my son Mark. [14]Greet one another with a kiss of love.

Peace to all of you who are in Christ.

---

[a]5 Prov. 3:34   [b]12 Greek *Silvanus*, a variant of *Silas*

2 Peter

Introduction:

Second Peter was written about A.D. 66 to the same group of Christians as Peter's first letter. These Christians were now not in danger of persecution but were in danger of being confused by false teachers.

Peter reminds the Christians that the best way to resist false teachers is to grow in the knowledge and practice of the Christian faith. He warns them that God would destroy the false teachers. Because Jesus will certainly keep his promise to come again, Peter reminds these Christians to live "holy and godly lives."

Outline of contents:

1 Simon Peter, a servant and apostle of Jesus Christ, Jn 21:17

To those who through the righteousness of our God and Savior Jesus Christ have received a faith as precious as ours: Ro 3:21-26

²Grace and peace be yours in abundance through the knowledge of God and of Jesus our Lord.

Making One's Calling and Election Sure

³His divine power has given us everything we need for life and godliness through our knowledge of him who called us by his own glory and goodness. ⁴Through these he has given us his very great and precious promises, so that through them you may participate in the divine nature and escape the corruption in the world caused by evil desires. Heb 12:10; Jas 1:27

⁵For this very reason, make every effort to add to your faith goodness; and to goodness, knowledge; ⁶and to knowledge, self-control; and to self-control, perseverance; and to perseverance, godliness; ⁷and to godliness, brotherly kindness; and to brotherly kindness, love. ⁸For if you possess these qualities in increasing measure, they will

keep you from being ineffective and unproductive in your knowledge of our Lord Jesus Christ. [9]But if anyone does not have them, he is nearsighted and blind, and has forgotten that he has been cleansed from his past sins. Col 1:10; 1Jn 2:11

[10]Therefore, my brothers, be all the more eager to make your calling and election sure. For if you do these things, you will never fall, [11]and you will receive a rich welcome into the eternal kingdom of our Lord and Savior Jesus Christ. Ps 145:13; Ro 8:28

Prophecy of Scripture

[12]So I will always remind you of these things, even though you know them and are firmly established in the truth you now have. [13]I think it is right to refresh your memory as long as I live in the tent of this body, [14]because I know that I will soon put it aside, as our Lord Jesus Christ has made clear to me. [15]And I will make every effort to see that after my departure you will always be able to remember these things. Php 3:1; 1Jn 2:21

[16]We did not follow cleverly invented stories when we told you about the power and coming of our Lord Jesus Christ, but we were eyewitnesses of his majesty. [17]For he received honor and glory from God the Father when the voice came to him from the Majestic Glory,

saying, "This is my Son, whom I love; with him I am well pleased."[a] [18]We ourselves heard this voice that came from heaven when we were with him on the sacred mountain.

[19]And we have the word of the prophets made more certain, and you will do well to pay attention to it, as to a light shining in a dark place, until the day dawns and the morning star rises in your hearts. [20]Above all, you must understand that no prophecy of Scripture came about by the prophet's own interpretation. [21]For prophecy never had its origin in the will of man, but men spoke from God as they were carried along by the Holy Spirit. 2Ti 3:16; 1Pe 1:10

False Teachers and Their Destruction

2 But there were also false prophets among the people, just as there will be false teachers among you. They will secretly introduce destructive heresies, even denying the sovereign Lord who bought them—bringing swift destruction on themselves. [2]Many will follow their shameful ways and will bring the way of truth into disrepute. [3]In their greed these teachers will exploit you with stories they have made up. Their condemnation has long been hanging over them, and their destruction has not been sleeping. Dt 13:1-3; 2Co 2:17

[a]17 Matt. 17:5; Mark 9:7; Luke 9:35

⁴For if God did not spare angels when they sinned, but sent them to hell,ᵃ putting them into gloomy dungeonsᵇ to be held for judgment; ⁵if he did not spare the ancient world when he brought the flood on its ungodly people, but protected Noah, a preacher of righteousness, and seven others; ⁶if he condemned the cities of Sodom and Gomorrah by burning them to ashes, and made them an example of what is going to happen to the ungodly; ⁷and if he rescued Lot, a righteous man, who was distressed by the filthy lives of lawless men ⁸(for that righteous man, living among them day after day, was tormented in his righteous soul by the lawless deeds he saw and heard)— ⁹if this is so, then the Lord knows how to rescue godly men from trials and to hold the unrighteous for the day of judgment, while continuing their punishment.ᶜ ¹⁰This is especially true of those who follow the corrupt desire of the sinful natureᵈ and despise authority.   Ge 6:1-4; Ps 37:33

Bold and arrogant, these men are not afraid to slander celestial beings; ¹¹yet even angels, although they are stronger and more powerful, do not bring slanderous accusations against such beings in the presence of the Lord. ¹²But these men blaspheme in matters they do not understand. They are like brute beasts, creatures of instinct, born only to be caught and destroyed, and like beasts they too will perish.   Ps 49:12; Jude 9

¹³They will be paid back with harm for the harm they have done. Their idea of pleasure is to carouse in broad daylight. They are blots and blemishes, reveling in their pleasures while they feast with you.ᵉ ¹⁴With eyes full of adultery, they never stop sinning; they seduce the unstable; they are experts in greed—an accursed brood! ¹⁵They have left the straight way and wandered off to follow the way of Balaam son of Beor, who loved the wages of wickedness. ¹⁶But he was rebuked for his wrongdoing by a donkey—a beast without speech—who spoke with a man's voice and restrained the prophet's madness.   Nu 22:21-30; Ro 13:13

¹⁷These men are springs without water and mists driven by a storm. Blackest darkness is reserved for them. ¹⁸For they mouth empty, boastful words and, by appealing to the lustful desires of sinful human nature, they entice people who are just escaping from those who live in error. ¹⁹They promise them freedom, while they themselves are slaves of depravity—for a man is a slave to whatever has mastered him. ²⁰If they have escaped the corruption of the

---

ᵃ4 Greek *Tartarus*   ᵇ4 Some manuscripts *into chains of darkness*   ᶜ9 Or *unrighteous for punishment until the day of judgment*   ᵈ10 Or *the flesh*   ᵉ13 Some manuscripts *in their love feasts*

world by knowing our Lord and Savior Jesus Christ and are again entangled in it and overcome, they are worse off at the end than they were at the beginning. ²¹It would have been better for them not to have known the way of righteousness, than to have known it and then to turn their backs on the sacred command that was passed on to them. ²²Of them the proverbs are true: "A dog returns to its vomit,"ᵃ and, "A sow that is washed goes back to her wallowing in the mud."   Heb 6:4-6

The Day of the Lord

3 Dear friends, this is now my second letter to you. I have written both of them as reminders to stimulate you to wholesome thinking. ²I want you to recall the words spoken in the past by the holy prophets and the command given by our Lord and Savior through your apostles.   2Pe 1:13

³First of all, you must understand that in the last days scoffers will come, scoffing and following their own evil desires. ⁴They will say, "Where is this 'coming' he promised? Ever since our fathers died, everything goes on as it has since the beginning of creation." ⁵But they deliberately forget that long ago by God's word the heavens existed and the earth was formed out of water and by

water. ⁶By these waters also the world of that time was deluged and destroyed. ⁷By the same word the present heavens and earth are reserved for fire, being kept for the day of judgment and destruction of ungodly men.   2Th 1:7; 1Ti 4:1

⁸But do not forget this one thing, dear friends: With the Lord a day is like a thousand years, and a thousand years are like a day. ⁹The Lord is not slow in keeping his promise, as some understand slowness. He is patient with you, not wanting anyone to perish, but everyone to come to repentance.   Ps 90:4

¹⁰But the day of the Lord will come like a thief. The heavens will disappear with a roar; the elements will be destroyed by fire, and the earth and everything in it will be laid bare.ᵇ

¹¹Since everything will be destroyed in this way, what kind of people ought you to be? You ought to live holy and godly lives ¹²as you look forward to the day of God and speed its coming.ᶜ That day will bring about the destruction of the heavens by fire, and the elements will melt in the heat. ¹³But in keeping with his promise we are looking forward to a new heaven and a new earth, the home of righteousness. 1Co 1:7

¹⁴So then, dear friends, since you are looking forward to this, make every effort to be found

---

ᵃ22 Prov. 26:11   ᵇ10 Some manuscripts *be burned up*   ᶜ12 Or *as you wait eagerly for the day of God to come*

spotless, blameless and at peace with him. ¹⁵Bear in mind that our Lord's patience means salvation, just as our dear brother Paul also wrote you with the wisdom that God gave him. ¹⁶He writes the same way in all his letters, speaking in them of these matters. His letters contain some things that are hard to understand, which ignorant and unstable people distort, as

they do the other Scriptures, to their own destruction. _{1Th 3:13}

¹⁷Therefore, dear friends, since you already know this, be on your guard so that you may not be carried away by the error of lawless men and fall from your secure position. ¹⁸But grow in the grace and knowledge of our Lord and Savior Jesus Christ. To him be glory both now and forever! Amen. _{1Co 10:12}

1 John

Introduction:

First, Second and Third John were written by John, the beloved disciple, who also wrote the fourth Gospel. All four books may have been written about the same time, probably about A.D. 90.

The first letter of John was written to warn Christians about dangerous false teachers who were trying to mislead them. These teachers were teaching that the man Jesus was not the Christ, the Son of God. They said that God did not become a man. John tells the Christians he is writing because it is very important to know and believe that Jesus Christ is both God and man.

John also encourages these Christians to keep their faith in Christ strong and to continue loving one another. He says Christians can know they are God's children if they love one another and if they obey God's commands.

Outline of contents:

The Word of Life

1 That which was from the beginning, which we have heard, which we have seen with our eyes, which we have looked at and our hands have touched—this we proclaim concerning the Word of life. ²The life appeared; we have seen it and testify to it, and we proclaim to you the eternal life, which was with the Father and has appeared to us. ³We proclaim to you what we have seen and heard, so that you also may have fellowship with us. And our fellowship is with the Father and with his Son, Jesus Christ. ⁴We write this to make our^a joy complete.　　Jn 1:2,14

Walking in the Light

⁵This is the message we have heard from him and declare to you: God is light; in him there is

^a4 Some manuscripts *your*

no darkness at all. ⁶If we claim to have fellowship with him yet walk in the darkness, we lie and do not live by the truth. ⁷But if we walk in the light, as he is in the light, we have fellowship with one another, and the blood of Jesus, his Son, purifies us from all*a* sin.   Isa 2:5; Jn 3:19-21

⁸If we claim to be without sin, we deceive ourselves and the truth is not in us. ⁹If we confess our sins, he is faithful and just and will forgive us our sins and purify us from all unrighteousness. ¹⁰If we claim we have not sinned, we make him out to be a liar and his word has no place in our lives.   Pr 20:9; 1Jn 5:10

2 My dear children, I write this to you so that you will not sin. But if anybody does sin, we have one who speaks to the Father in our defense—Jesus Christ, the Righteous One. ²He is the atoning sacrifice for our sins, and not only for ours but also for*b* the sins of the whole world.   Ro 3:25; 1Ti 2:5

³We know that we have come to know him if we obey his commands. ⁴The man who says, "I know him," but does not do what he commands is a liar, and the truth is not in him. ⁵But if anyone obeys his word, God's love*c* is truly made complete in him. This is how we know we are in him: ⁶Whoever claims to live in him must walk as Jesus did.   1Jn 3:24; 4:12

⁷Dear friends, I am not writing you a new command but an old one, which you have had since the beginning. This old command is the message you have heard. ⁸Yet I am writing you a new command; its truth is seen in him and you, because the darkness is passing and the true light is already shining.

⁹Anyone who claims to be in the light but hates his brother is still in the darkness. ¹⁰Whoever loves his brother lives in the light, and there is nothing in him*d* to make him stumble. ¹¹But whoever hates his brother is in the darkness and walks around in the darkness; he does not know where he is going, because the darkness has blinded him.   Lev 19:17; Jn 11:9; 1Jn 3:14

¹²I write to you, dear children,
    because your sins have
        been forgiven on
        account of his name.
¹³I write to you, fathers,
    because you have known
        him who is from the
        beginning.   Jn 1:1
I write to you, young men,
    because you have overcome
        the evil one.
I write to you, dear children,
    because you have known
        the Father.
¹⁴I write to you, fathers,
    because you have known
        him who is from the
        beginning.   Jn 1:1
I write to you, young men,

---

a7 Or *every*   *b2* Or *He is the one who turns aside God's wrath, taking away our sins, and not only ours but also*   *c5* Or *word, love for God*   *d10* Or *it*

because you are strong,
and the word of God lives
in you,
and you have overcome the
evil one.

Do Not Love the World

15Do not love the world or anything in the world. If anyone loves the world, the love of the Father is not in him. 16For everything in the world—the cravings of sinful man, the lust of his eyes and the boasting of what he has and does—comes not from the Father but from the world. 17The world and its desires pass away, but the man who does the will of God lives forever. Ro 12:2; Jas 4:4

Warning Against Antichrists

18Dear children, this is the last hour; and as you have heard that the antichrist is coming, even now many antichrists have come. This is how we know it is the last hour. 19They went out from us, but they did not really belong to us. For if they had belonged to us, they would have remained with us; but their going showed that none of them belonged to us. 20But you have an anointing from the Holy One, and all of you know the truth. a 21I do not write to you because you do not know the truth, but because you do know it and because no lie comes from the truth. 22Who is the liar? It is the man who denies that Jesus is the Christ. Such a man is the antichrist—he denies the Father and the Son. 23No one who denies the Son has the Father; whoever acknowledges the Son has the Father also. Jn 8:19; 2Pe 1:12

24See that what you have heard from the beginning remains in you. If it does, you also will remain in the Son and in the Father. 25And this is what he promised us—even eternal life.
26I am writing these things to you about those who are trying to lead you astray. 27As for you, the anointing you received from him remains in you, and you do not need anyone to teach you. But as his anointing teaches you about all things and as that anointing is real, not counterfeit—just as it has taught you, remain in him. 1Co 2:12; 1Jn 3:7

Children of God

28And now, dear children, continue in him, so that when he appears we may be confident and unashamed before him at his coming. Col 3:4; 1Jn 3:2

29If you know that he is righteous, you know that everyone who does what is right has been born of him. 1Jn 3:7

3 How great is the love the Father has lavished on us, that we should be called children of God! And that is what we are! The reason the world does not know us is that it did not know him. 2Dear friends, now we are

a20 Some manuscripts and you know all things

children of God, and what we will be has not yet been made known. But we know that when he appears,[a] we shall be like him, for we shall see him as he is. [3]Everyone who has this hope in him purifies himself, just as he is pure.   Jn 15:21; 16:3; 2Co 7:1

[4]Everyone who sins breaks the law; in fact, sin is lawlessness. [5]But you know that he appeared so that he might take away our sins. And in him is no sin. [6]No one who lives in him keeps on sinning. No one who continues to sin has either seen him or known him.   1Jn 5:17,18

[7]Dear children, do not let anyone lead you astray. He who does what is right is righteous, just as he is righteous. [8]He who does what is sinful is of the devil, because the devil has been sinning from the beginning. The reason the Son of God appeared was to destroy the devil's work. [9]No one who is born of God will continue to sin, because God's seed remains in him; he cannot go on sinning, because he has been born of God. [10]This is how we know who the children of God are and who the children of the devil are: Anyone who does not do what is right is not a child of God; nor is anyone who does not love his brother.   1Jn 2:1

Love One Another

[11]This is the message you heard from the beginning: We should love one another. [12]Do not be like Cain, who belonged to the evil one and murdered his brother. And why did he murder him? Because his own actions were evil and his brother's were righteous. [13]Do not be surprised, my brothers, if the world hates you. [14]We know that we have passed from death to life, because we love our brothers. Anyone who does not love remains in death. [15]Anyone who hates his brother is a murderer, and you know that no murderer has eternal life in him.

[16]This is how we know what love is: Jesus Christ laid down his life for us. And we ought to lay down our lives for our brothers. [17]If anyone has material possessions and sees his brother in need but has no pity on him, how can the love of God be in him? [18]Dear children, let us not love with words or tongue but with actions and in truth. [19]This then is how we know that we belong to the truth, and how we set our hearts at rest in his presence [20]whenever our hearts condemn us. For God is greater than our hearts, and he knows everything.   Jn 10:11; Ro 12:9,10

[21]Dear friends, if our hearts do not condemn us, we have confidence before God [22]and receive from him anything we ask, because we obey his commands and do what pleases

[a]2 Or when it is made known

him. ²³And this is his command: to believe in the name of his Son, Jesus Christ, and to love one another as he commanded us. ²⁴Those who obey his commands live in him, and he in them. And this is how we know that he lives in us: We know it by the Spirit he gave us. 1Jn 4:13,15

Test the Spirits

4 Dear friends, do not believe every spirit, but test the spirits to see whether they are from God, because many false prophets have gone out into the world. ²This is how you can recognize the Spirit of God: Every spirit that acknowledges that Jesus Christ has come in the flesh is from God, ³but every spirit that does not acknowledge Jesus is not from God. This is the spirit of the antichrist, which you have heard is coming and even now is already in the world. Jer 29:8,9; 1Jn 2:22

⁴You, dear children, are from God and have overcome them, because the one who is in you is greater than the one who is in the world. ⁵They are from the world and therefore speak from the viewpoint of the world, and the world listens to them. ⁶We are from God, and whoever knows God listens to us; but whoever is not from God does not listen to us. This is how we recognize the Spirit^a of truth and the spirit of falsehood. Jn 8:47

God's Love and Ours

⁷Dear friends, let us love one another, for love comes from God. Everyone who loves has been born of God and knows God. ⁸Whoever does not love does not know God, because God is love. ⁹This is how God showed his love among us: He sent his one and only Son^b into the world that we might live through him. ¹⁰This is love: not that we loved God, but that he loved us and sent his Son as an atoning sacrifice for^c our sins. ¹¹Dear friends, since God so loved us, we also ought to love one another. ¹²No one has ever seen God; but if we love one another, God lives in us and his love is made complete in us.

¹³We know that we live in him and he in us, because he has given us of his Spirit. ¹⁴And we have seen and testify that the Father has sent his Son to be the Savior of the world. ¹⁵If anyone acknowledges that Jesus is the Son of God, God lives in him and he in God. ¹⁶And so we know and rely on the love God has for us. 1Jn 3:24

God is love. Whoever lives in love lives in God, and God in him. ¹⁷In this way, love is made complete among us so that we will have confidence on the day of judgment, because in this world we are like him. ¹⁸There is no fear in love. But perfect love drives out fear, because fear has

^a6 Or spirit   ^b9 Or his only begotten Son   ^c10 Or as the one who would turn aside his wrath, taking away

2 John

Introduction:

John wrote this letter to "the chosen lady and her children." He might have meant either a Christian woman and her family or a church and its members.

In this letter John writes how important it is for Christians to love one another. He says that to love means to obey God's commandments, and God's commandments tell us to live lives of love.

John again emphasizes the importance of the doctrine that Jesus is God's Son and both man and God. Christians should separate themselves from those who teach that Jesus is not God's Son.

Outline of contents:

---

¹The elder,

To the chosen lady and her children, whom I love in the truth—and not I only, but also all who know the truth— ²because of the truth, which lives in us and will be with us forever: Jn 8:32; 2Pe 1:12

³Grace, mercy and peace from God the Father and from Jesus Christ, the Father's Son, will be with us in truth and love.

⁴It has given me great joy to find some of your children walking in the truth, just as the Father commanded us. ⁵And now, dear lady, I am not writing you a new command but one we have had from the beginning. I ask that we love one another. ⁶And this is love: that we walk in obedience to his commands. As you have heard from the beginning, his command is that you walk in love. 3Jn 3-4

⁷Many deceivers, who do not acknowledge Jesus Christ as coming in the flesh, have gone out into the world. Any such person is the deceiver and the antichrist. ⁸Watch out that you do not lose what you have

worked for, but that you may be rewarded fully. ⁹Anyone who runs ahead and does not continue in the teaching of Christ does not have God; whoever continues in the teaching has both the Father and the Son. ¹⁰If anyone comes to you and does not bring this teaching, do not take him into your house or welcome him. ¹¹Anyone who welcomes him shares in his wicked work. 1Ti 5:22; 1Jn 2:22

¹²I have much to write to you, but I do not want to use paper and ink. Instead, I hope to visit you and talk with you face to face, so that our joy may be complete.

¹³The children of your chosen sister send their greetings.

3 John

Introduction:

Third John was written to Gaius, a friend of John's and a leader in the church. There was a man named Diotrephes in Gaius' church who was refusing to welcome God's messengers. John writes this letter to praise and thank Gaius for his help and to scold Diotrephes for not cooperating. John promises to come to this church soon to deal with this matter himself.

Outline of contents:

---

¹The elder,

To my dear friend Gaius, whom I love in the truth.

²Dear friend, I pray that you may enjoy good health and that all may go well with you, even as your soul is getting along well. ³It gave me great joy to have some brothers come and tell about your faithfulness to the truth and how you continue to walk in the truth. ⁴I have no greater joy than to hear that my children are walking in the truth. _{2Jn 4}

⁵Dear friend, you are faithful in what you are doing for the brothers, even though they are strangers to you. ⁶They have told the church about your love. You will do well to send them on their way in a manner worthy of God. ⁷It was for the sake of the Name that they went out, receiving no help from the pagans. ⁸We ought therefore to show hospitality to such men so that we may work together for the truth. _{Ro 12:13}

⁹I wrote to the church, but Diotrephes, who loves to be first, will have nothing to do with us. ¹⁰So if I come, I will call attention to what he is doing, gossiping maliciously about us. Not satisfied with that, he refuses to welcome the brothers. He also stops those who want to do so and puts them out of the church.

¹¹Dear friend, do not imitate

what is evil but what is good. Anyone who does what is good is from God. Anyone who does what is evil has not seen God. [12]Demetrius is well spoken of by everyone—and even by the truth itself. We also speak well of him, and you know that our testimony is true. *Ps 34:14*

[13]I have much to write you, but I do not want to do so with pen and ink. [14]I hope to see you soon, and we will talk face to face.

Peace to you. The friends here send their greetings. Greet the friends there by name. *Jn 10:3*

Jude

Introduction:

Jude, like James, was a brother of Jesus. He wrote to warn Christians about the same false teachers Peter wrote about in his second letter. These false teachers were not only teaching that Jesus was not the Son of God; they were also leading the people to live sinful lives. Jude warns that God will punish and destroy these false teachers just as he had punished sinners in the Old Testament.

Outline of contents:

Introduction (1,2)
Warnings against false teachers (3–16)
Warning and conclusion (17–25)

---

¹Jude, a servant of Jesus Christ and a brother of James,

To those who have been called, who are loved by God the Father and kept by*a* Jesus Christ: Ro 1:6-7

²Mercy, peace and love be yours in abundance.

The Sin and Doom of Godless Men

³Dear friends, although I was very eager to write to you about the salvation we share, I felt I had to write and urge you to contend for the faith that was once for all entrusted to the saints. ⁴For certain men whose condemnation was written about*b* long ago have secretly slipped in among you. They are godless men, who change the grace of our God into a license for immorality and deny Jesus Christ our only Sovereign and Lord.   Gal 2:4; Tit 1:16

⁵Though you already know all this, I want to remind you that the Lord*c* delivered his people out of Egypt, but later destroyed those who did not believe. ⁶And the angels who did not keep their positions of authority but abandoned their own home—these he has kept in darkness, bound with everlasting chains for judgment on the great Day. ⁷In a similar way, Sodom and Gomorrah and the

---

a1 Or *for;* or *in*   *b4* Or *men who were marked out for condemnation*   *c5* Some early manuscripts *Jesus*

surrounding towns gave themselves up to sexual immorality and perversion. They serve as an example of those who suffer the punishment of eternal fire.

8In the very same way, these dreamers pollute their own bodies, reject authority and slander celestial beings. 9But even the archangel Michael, when he was disputing with the devil about the body of Moses, did not dare to bring a slanderous accusation against him, but said, "The Lord rebuke you!" 10Yet these men speak abusively against whatever they do not understand; and what things they do understand by instinct, like unreasoning animals—these are the very things that destroy them.   2Pe 2:10

11Woe to them! They have taken the way of Cain; they have rushed for profit into Balaam's error; they have been destroyed in Korah's rebellion.

12These men are blemishes at your love feasts, eating with you without the slightest qualm—shepherds who feed only themselves. They are clouds without rain, blown along by the wind; autumn trees, without fruit and uprooted—twice dead. 13They are wild waves of the sea, foaming up their shame; wandering stars, for whom blackest darkness has been reserved forever.   2Pe 2:13

14Enoch, the seventh from Adam, prophesied about these men: "See, the Lord is coming with thousands upon thousands of his holy ones 15to judge everyone, and to convict all the ungodly of all the ungodly acts they have done in the ungodly way, and of all the harsh words ungodly sinners have spoken against him." 16These men are grumblers and faultfinders; they follow their own evil desires; they boast about themselves and flatter others for their own advantage.   Ge 5:18,21-24

A Call to Persevere

17But, dear friends, remember what the apostles of our Lord Jesus Christ foretold. 18They said to you, "In the last times there will be scoffers who will follow their own ungodly desires." 19These are the men who divide you, who follow mere natural instincts and do not have the Spirit.   2Pe 2:1

20But you, dear friends, build yourselves up in your most holy faith and pray in the Holy Spirit. 21Keep yourselves in God's love as you wait for the mercy of our Lord Jesus Christ to bring you to eternal life. Col 2:7

22Be merciful to those who doubt; 23snatch others from the fire and save them; to others show mercy, mixed with fear—hating even the clothing stained by corrupted flesh.

Doxology

24To him who is able to keep

you from falling and to present you before his glorious presence without fault and with great joy— [25]to the only God our Savior be glory, majesty, power and authority, through Jesus Christ our Lord, before all ages, now and forevermore! Amen.

Revelation

Introduction:

The book of Revelation was written by the apostle John during his exile on the island of Patmos. John's purpose in writing this book was to give hope and encouragement to those Christians who were suffering severe persecution for their faith in Jesus Christ. These Christians needed to know that God controls whatever happens here on earth.

Through the imagery and symbols, even though they are sometimes difficult to understand, one thing is made clear, Jesus Christ is the Lord and ruler over everyone and everything—even powerful human governments. He is clearly in control and will someday judge and punish what is evil, even Satan. He will also establish an everlasting kingdom with a new heaven and a new earth.

Outline of contents:

Prologue

1 The revelation of Jesus Christ, which God gave him to show his servants what must soon take place. He made it known by sending his angel to his servant John, ²who testifies to everything he saw—that is, the word of God and the testimony of Jesus Christ. ³Blessed

is the one who reads the words of this prophecy, and blessed are those who hear it and take to heart what is written in it, because the time is near.   Lk 11:28

Greetings and Doxology

⁴John,

To the seven churches in the province of Asia:

Grace and peace to you from him who is, and who was, and who is to come, and from the seven spirits[a] before his throne, ⁵and from Jesus Christ, who is the faithful witness, the firstborn from the dead, and the ruler of the kings of the earth.

To him who loves us and has freed us from our sins by his blood, ⁶and has made us to be a kingdom and priests to serve his God and Father—to him be glory and power for ever and ever! Amen.   1Pe 2:5; Rev 5:10

⁷Look, he is coming with the
   clouds,   Da 7:13
and every eye will see him,
  even those who pierced him;
and all the peoples of the
  earth will mourn
   because of him.   Zec 12:10
    So shall it be! Amen.

⁸"I am the Alpha and the Omega," says the Lord God, "who is, and who was, and who is to come, the Almighty."

One Like a Son of Man

⁹I, John, your brother and companion in the suffering and kingdom and patient endurance that are ours in Jesus, was on the island of Patmos because of the word of God and the testimony of Jesus. ¹⁰On the Lord's Day I was in the Spirit, and I heard behind me a loud voice like a trumpet, ¹¹which said: "Write on a scroll what you see and send it to the seven churches: to Ephesus, Smyrna, Pergamum, Thyatira, Sardis, Philadelphia and Laodicea."

¹²I turned around to see the voice that was speaking to me. And when I turned I saw seven golden lampstands, ¹³and among the lampstands was someone "like a son of man,"[b] dressed in a robe reaching down to his feet and with a golden sash around his chest. ¹⁴His head and hair were white like wool, as white as snow, and his eyes were like blazing fire. ¹⁵His feet were like bronze glowing in a furnace, and his voice was like the sound of rushing waters. ¹⁶In his right hand he held seven stars, and out of his mouth came a sharp double-edged sword. His face was like the sun shining in all its brilliance.   Ex 25:31-40; Rev 2:1

¹⁷When I saw him, I fell at his feet as though dead. Then he placed his right hand on me and said: "Do not be afraid. I am the First and the Last. ¹⁸I am the Liv-

---

ᵃ4 Or *the sevenfold Spirit*   ᵇ13 Daniel 7:13

ing One; I was dead, and behold I am alive for ever and ever! And I hold the keys of death and Hades.   Eze 1:28; Ro 6:9

¹⁹"Write, therefore, what you have seen, what is now and what will take place later. ²⁰The mystery of the seven stars that you saw in my right hand and of the seven golden lampstands is this: The seven stars are the angels^a of the seven churches, and the seven lampstands are the seven churches.   Hab 2:2; Mt 5:14

To the Church in Ephesus

2 "To the angel^b of the church in Ephesus write:

These are the words of him who holds the seven stars in his right hand and walks among the seven golden lampstands: ²I know your deeds, your hard work and your perseverance. I know that you cannot tolerate wicked men, that you have tested those who claim to be apostles but are not, and have found them false. ³You have persevered and have endured hardships for my name, and have not grown weary.   1Jn 4:1

⁴Yet I hold this against you: You have forsaken your first love. ⁵Remember the height from which you have fallen! Repent and do the things you did at first. If you do not repent, I will come to you and remove your lampstand from its place. ⁶But you have this in your favor: You hate the practices of the Nicolaitans, which I also hate.   Jer 2:2; Rev 3:3

⁷He who has an ear, let him hear what the Spirit says to the churches. To him who overcomes, I will give the right to eat from the tree of life, which is in the paradise of God.   Rev 22:2,14,19

To the Church in Smyrna

⁸"To the angel of the church in Smyrna write:

These are the words of him who is the First and the Last, who died and came to life again. ⁹I know your afflictions and your poverty—yet you are rich! I know the slander of those who say they are Jews and are not, but are a synagogue of Satan. ¹⁰Do not be afraid of what you are about to suffer. I tell you, the devil will put some of you in prison to test you, and you will suffer persecution for ten days. Be faithful, even to the point of death, and I will give you the crown of life.

¹¹He who has an ear, let him hear what the Spirit says to the churches. He who overcomes will not be hurt at all by the second death.   Rev 20:6,14; 21:8

---

^a20 Or messengers   ^b1 Or messenger; also in verses 8, 12 and 18

To the Church in Pergamum

¹²"To the angel of the church in Pergamum write:

These are the words of him who has the sharp, double-edged sword. ¹³I know where you live—where Satan has his throne. Yet you remain true to my name. You did not renounce your faith in me, even in the days of Antipas, my faithful witness, who was put to death in your city—where Satan lives.   Rev 14:12

¹⁴Nevertheless, I have a few things against you: You have people there who hold to the teaching of Balaam, who taught Balak to entice the Israelites to sin by eating food sacrificed to idols and by committing sexual immorality. ¹⁵Likewise you also have those who hold to the teaching of the Nicolaitans. ¹⁶Repent therefore! Otherwise, I will soon come to you and will fight against them with the sword of my mouth.   Ac 15:20; 2Pe 2:15

¹⁷He who has an ear, let him hear what the Spirit says to the churches. To him who overcomes, I will give some of the hidden manna. I will also give him a white stone with a new name written on it, known only to him who receives it.

To the Church in Thyatira

¹⁸"To the angel of the church in Thyatira write:

These are the words of the Son of God, whose eyes are like blazing fire and whose feet are like burnished bronze. ¹⁹I know your deeds, your love and faith, your service and perseverance, and that you are now doing more than you did at first.

²⁰Nevertheless, I have this against you: You tolerate that woman Jezebel, who calls herself a prophetess. By her teaching she misleads my servants into sexual immorality and the eating of food sacrificed to idols. ²¹I have given her time to repent of her immorality, but she is unwilling. ²²So I will cast her on a bed of suffering, and I will make those who commit adultery with her suffer intensely, unless they repent of her ways. ²³I will strike her children dead. Then all the churches will know that I am he who searches hearts and minds, and I will repay each of you according to your deeds. ²⁴Now I say to the rest of you in Thyatira, to you who do not hold to her teaching and have not learned Satan's so-called deep secrets (I will not impose any other burden on you): ²⁵Only hold on to

what you have until I come. ²⁶To him who overcomes and does my will to the end, I will give authority over the nations— Mt 10:22; Jn 16:33

²⁷'He will rule them with
    an iron scepter; Rev 12:5
he will dash them to
    pieces like
    pottery'ᵃ—

just as I have received authority from my Father. ²⁸I will also give him the morning star. ²⁹He who has an ear, let him hear what the Spirit says to the churches.

To the Church in Sardis

3 "To the angelᵇ of the church in Sardis write:

These are the words of him who holds the seven spiritsᶜ of God and the seven stars. I know your deeds; you have a reputation of being alive, but you are dead. ²Wake up! Strengthen what remains and is about to die, for I have not found your deeds complete in the sight of my God. ³Remember, therefore, what you have received and heard; obey it, and repent. But if you do not wake up, I will come like a thief, and you will not know at what time I will come to you. Lk 12:39,40; Rev 2:5

⁴Yet you have a few people in Sardis who have not soiled their clothes. They will walk with me, dressed in white, for they are worthy. ⁵He who overcomes will, like them, be dressed in white. I will never blot out his name from the book of life, but will acknowledge his name before my Father and his angels. ⁶He who has an ear, let him hear what the Spirit says to the churches. Jn 16:33; Jude 23

To the Church in Philadelphia

⁷"To the angel of the church in Philadelphia write:

These are the words of him who is holy and true, who holds the key of David. What he opens no one can shut, and what he shuts no one can open. ⁸I know your deeds. See, I have placed before you an open door that no one can shut. I know that you have little strength, yet you have kept my word and have not denied my name. ⁹I will make those who are of the synagogue of Satan, who claim to be Jews though they are not, but are liars—I will make them come and fall down at your feet and acknowledge that I have loved you. ¹⁰Since you have kept my command to endure patiently, I will also

---

ᵃ27 Psalm 2:9 ᵇ1 Or *messenger*; also in verses 7 and 14 ᶜ1 Or *the sevenfold Spirit*

2 John

Introduction:

John wrote this letter to "the chosen lady and her children." He might have meant either a Christian woman and her family or a church and its members.

In this letter John writes how important it is for Christians to love one another. He says that to love means to obey God's commandments, and God's commandments tell us to live lives of love.

John again emphasizes the importance of the doctrine that Jesus is God's Son and both man and God. Christians should separate themselves from those who teach that Jesus is not God's Son.

Outline of contents:

Greeting (1–3)
Advice and warning (4–11)
Conclusion (12,13)

---

[1]The elder,

To the chosen lady and her children, whom I love in the truth—and not I only, but also all who know the truth— [2]because of the truth, which lives in us and will be with us forever: Jn 8:32; 2Pe 1:12

[3]Grace, mercy and peace from God the Father and from Jesus Christ, the Father's Son, will be with us in truth and love.

[4]It has given me great joy to find some of your children walking in the truth, just as the Father commanded us. [5]And now, dear lady, I am not writing you a new command but one we have had from the beginning. I ask that we love one another. [6]And this is love: that we walk in obedience to his commands. As you have heard from the beginning, his command is that you walk in love.   3Jn 3-4

[7]Many deceivers, who do not acknowledge Jesus Christ as coming in the flesh, have gone out into the world. Any such person is the deceiver and the antichrist. [8]Watch out that you do not lose what you have

worked for, but that you may be rewarded fully. ⁹Anyone who runs ahead and does not continue in the teaching of Christ does not have God; whoever continues in the teaching has both the Father and the Son. ¹⁰If anyone comes to you and does not bring this teaching, do not take him into your house or welcome him. ¹¹Anyone who welcomes him shares in his wicked work.   1Ti 5:22; 1Jn 2:22

¹²I have much to write to you, but I do not want to use paper and ink. Instead, I hope to visit you and talk with you face to face, so that our joy may be complete.

¹³The children of your chosen sister send their greetings.

keep you from the hour of trial that is going to come upon the whole world to test those who live on the earth.   Isa 22:22; 2Pe 2:9

[11] I am coming soon. Hold on to what you have, so that no one will take your crown. [12] Him who overcomes I will make a pillar in the temple of my God. Never again will he leave it. I will write on him the name of my God and the name of the city of my God, the new Jerusalem, which is coming down out of heaven from my God; and I will also write on him my new name. [13] He who has an ear, let him hear what the Spirit says to the churches.   Mt 16:27; Rev 22:4

To the Church in Laodicea

[14] "To the angel of the church in Laodicea write:

These are the words of the Amen, the faithful and true witness, the ruler of God's creation. [15] I know your deeds, that you are neither cold nor hot. I wish you were either one or the other! [16] So, because you are lukewarm—neither hot nor cold—I am about to spit you out of my mouth. [17] You say, 'I am rich; I have acquired wealth and do not need a thing.' But you do not realize that you are wretched, pitiful, poor, blind and naked. [18] I counsel you to

buy from me gold refined in the fire, so you can become rich; and white clothes to wear, so you can cover your shameful nakedness; and salve to put on your eyes, so you can see.   Hos 12:8; Rev 16:15

[19] Those whom I love I rebuke and discipline. So be earnest, and repent. [20] Here I am! I stand at the door and knock. If anyone hears my voice and opens the door, I will come in and eat with him, and he with me.   Dt 8:5

[21] To him who overcomes, I will give the right to sit with me on my throne, just as I overcame and sat down with my Father on his throne. [22] He who has an ear, let him hear what the Spirit says to the churches."

The Throne in Heaven

4 After this I looked, and there before me was a door standing open in heaven. And the voice I had first heard speaking to me like a trumpet said, "Come up here, and I will show you what must take place after this." [2] At once I was in the Spirit, and there before me was a throne in heaven with someone sitting on it. [3] And the one who sat there had the appearance of jasper and carnelian. A rainbow, resembling an emerald, encircled the throne. [4] Surrounding the throne were twenty-four other thrones, and seated on them were twenty-four elders. They were dressed

in white and had crowns of gold on their heads. ⁵From the throne came flashes of lightning, rumblings and peals of thunder. Before the throne, seven lamps were blazing. These are the seven spirits*a* of God. ⁶Also before the throne there was what looked like a sea of glass, clear as crystal.   Rev 15:2

In the center, around the throne, were four living creatures, and they were covered with eyes, in front and in back. ⁷The first living creature was like a lion, the second was like an ox, the third had a face like a man, the fourth was like a flying eagle. ⁸Each of the four living creatures had six wings and was covered with eyes all around, even under his wings. Day and night they never stop saying:

"Holy, holy, holy
is the Lord God Almighty,
who was, and is, and is to
    come."   Isa 6:3

⁹Whenever the living creatures give glory, honor and thanks to him who sits on the throne and who lives for ever and ever, ¹⁰the twenty-four elders fall down before him who sits on the throne, and worship him who lives for ever and ever. They lay their crowns before the throne and say: Dt 33:3; Ps 47:8

¹¹"You are worthy, our Lord
    and God,

to receive glory and honor
    and power,   Rev 1:6
for you created all things,
    and by your will they were
        created
    and have their being." Ac 14:15

The Scroll and the Lamb

5 Then I saw in the right hand of him who sat on the throne a scroll with writing on both sides and sealed with seven seals. ²And I saw a mighty angel proclaiming in a loud voice, "Who is worthy to break the seals and open the scroll?" ³But no one in heaven or on earth or under the earth could open the scroll or even look inside it. ⁴I wept and wept because no one was found who was worthy to open the scroll or look inside. ⁵Then one of the elders said to me, "Do not weep! See, the Lion of the tribe of Judah, the Root of David, has triumphed. He is able to open the scroll and its seven seals."   Isa 11:1,10; Rev 4:2

⁶Then I saw a Lamb, looking as if it had been slain, standing in the center of the throne, encircled by the four living creatures and the elders. He had seven horns and seven eyes, which are the seven spirits*a* of God sent out into all the earth. ⁷He came and took the scroll from the right hand of him who sat on the throne. ⁸And when he had taken it, the four living creatures and the twenty-four elders fell down before the

---

a 5,6 Or the sevenfold Spirit

Lamb. Each one had a harp and they were holding golden bowls full of incense, which are the prayers of the saints. [9]And they sang a new song: Ps 141:2; Jn 1:29

"You are worthy to take the scroll
and to open its seals,
because you were slain,
and with your blood you
purchased men for God
from every tribe and
language and people
and nation.   Rev 13:7
[10]You have made them to be a
kingdom and priests to
serve our God,   1Pe 2:5
and they will reign on the
earth."   Rev 3:21

[11]Then I looked and heard the voice of many angels, numbering thousands upon thousands, and ten thousand times ten thousand. They encircled the throne and the living creatures and the elders. [12]In a loud voice they sang: Da 7:10

"Worthy is the Lamb, who
was slain,
to receive power and wealth
and wisdom and
strength
and honor and glory and
praise!"   Rev 1:6; 4:11

[13]Then I heard every creature in heaven and on earth and under the earth and on the sea, and all that is in them, singing:

"To him who sits on the
throne and to the Lamb

be praise and honor and
glory and power,
for ever and ever!"[1Ch 29:11]

[14]The four living creatures said, "Amen," and the elders fell down and worshiped.   Rev 4:6,9

The Seals

6 I watched as the Lamb opened the first of the seven seals. Then I heard one of the four living creatures say in a voice like thunder, "Come!" [2]I looked, and there before me was a white horse! Its rider held a bow, and he was given a crown, and he rode out as a conqueror bent on conquest.   Rev 5:6

[3]When the Lamb opened the second seal, I heard the second living creature say, "Come!" [4]Then another horse came out, a fiery red one. Its rider was given power to take peace from the earth and to make men slay each other. To him was given a large sword.   Zec 1:8; Rev 4:7

[5]When the Lamb opened the third seal, I heard the third living creature say, "Come!" I looked, and there before me was a black horse! Its rider was holding a pair of scales in his hand. [6]Then I heard what sounded like a voice among the four living creatures, saying, "A quart[a] of wheat for a day's wages,[b] and three quarts of barley for a day's wages,[b] and do not damage the oil and the wine!"   Zec 6:2

[7]When the Lamb opened the

---

[a]6 Greek *a choinix* (probably about a liter)   [b]6 Greek *a denarius*

fourth seal, I heard the voice of the fourth living creature say, "Come!" [8]I looked, and there before me was a pale horse! Its rider was named Death, and Hades was following close behind him. They were given power over a fourth of the earth to kill by sword, famine and plague, and by the wild beasts of the earth. _{Jer 24:10; Zec 6:3; Rev 20:13,14}

[9]When he opened the fifth seal, I saw under the altar the souls of those who had been slain because of the word of God and the testimony they had maintained. [10]They called out in a loud voice, "How long, Sovereign Lord, holy and true, until you judge the inhabitants of the earth and avenge our blood?" [11]Then each of them was given a white robe, and they were told to wait a little longer, until the number of their fellow servants and brothers who were to be killed as they had been was completed. _{Ps 79:10; Rev 20:4}

[12]I watched as he opened the sixth seal. There was a great earthquake. The sun turned black like sackcloth made of goat hair, the whole moon turned blood red, [13]and the stars in the sky fell to earth, as late figs drop from a fig tree when shaken by a strong wind. [14]The sky receded like a scroll, rolling up, and every mountain and island was removed from its place. _{Ps 97:4; 2Pe 3:10}

[15]Then the kings of the earth, the princes, the generals, the rich, the mighty, and every slave and every free man hid in caves and among the rocks of the mountains. [16]They called to the mountains and the rocks, "Fall on us and hide us from the face of him who sits on the throne and from the wrath of the Lamb! [17]For the great day of their wrath has come, and who can stand?" _{Joel 1:15; Mal 3:2}

144,000 Sealed

7 After this I saw four angels standing at the four corners of the earth, holding back the four winds of the earth to prevent any wind from blowing on the land or on the sea or on any tree. [2]Then I saw another angel coming up from the east, having the seal of the living God. He called out in a loud voice to the four angels who had been given power to harm the land and the sea: [3]"Do not harm the land or the sea or the trees until we put a seal on the foreheads of the servants of our God." [4]Then I heard the number of those who were sealed: 144,000 from all the tribes of Israel.

[5]From the tribe of Judah
   12,000 were sealed,
from the tribe of Reuben
   12,000,
from the tribe of Gad
   12,000,
[6]from the tribe of Asher
   12,000,
from the tribe of Naphtali
   12,000,
from the tribe of Manasseh
   12,000,

[7]from the tribe of Simeon
　　12,000,
from the tribe of Levi
　　12,000,
from the tribe of Issachar
　　12,000,
[8]from the tribe of Zebulun
　　12,000,
from the tribe of Joseph
　　12,000,
from the tribe of Benjamin
　　12,000.

The Great Multitude in White Robes

[9]After this I looked and there before me was a great multitude that no one could count, from every nation, tribe, people and language, standing before the throne and in front of the Lamb. They were wearing white robes and were holding palm branches in their hands. [10]And they cried out in a loud voice:

"Salvation belongs to our
　　God,　　　Ps 3:8
who sits on the throne,
and to the Lamb."　　Rev 12:10

[11]All the angels were standing around the throne and around the elders and the four living creatures. They fell down on their faces before the throne and worshiped God, [12]saying:

"Amen!
Praise and glory
and wisdom and thanks and
　　honor
and power and strength
be to our God for ever and
　　ever.

Amen!"　　Ro 11:36; Rev 5:12-14

[13]Then one of the elders asked me, "These in white robes—who are they, and where did they come from?"

[14]I answered, "Sir, you know."

And he said, "These are they who have come out of the great tribulation; they have washed their robes and made them white in the blood of the Lamb. [15]Therefore,

"they are before the throne
　　of God
and serve him day and
　　night in his temple; Rev 22:3
and he who sits on the
　　throne will spread his
　　tent over them.
[16]Never again will they
　　hunger;
never again will they thirst.
The sun will not beat upon
　　them,
nor any scorching heat. [17]For the Lamb at the center of
　　the throne will be their
　　shepherd;　　Jn 10:11
he will lead them to springs
　　of living water.　　Jn 4:10
And God will wipe away
　　every tear from their
　　eyes."　　Isa 25:8; 35:10

The Seventh Seal and the Golden Censer

8 When he opened the seventh seal, there was silence in heaven for about half an hour.

[2]And I saw the seven angels

who stand before God, and to them were given seven trumpets. Rev 9:1,13; 11:15

³Another angel, who had a golden censer, came and stood at the altar. He was given much incense to offer, with the prayers of all the saints, on the golden altar before the throne. ⁴The smoke of the incense, together with the prayers of the saints, went up before God from the angel's hand. ⁵Then the angel took the censer, filled it with fire from the altar, and hurled it on the earth; and there came peals of thunder, rumblings, flashes of lightning and an earthquake. Lev 16:12; Rev 5:8

The Trumpets

⁶Then the seven angels who had the seven trumpets prepared to sound them.

⁷The first angel sounded his trumpet, and there came hail and fire mixed with blood, and it was hurled down upon the earth. A third of the earth was burned up, a third of the trees were burned up, and all the green grass was burned up.

⁸The second angel sounded his trumpet, and something like a huge mountain, all ablaze, was thrown into the sea. A third of the sea turned into blood, ⁹a third of the living creatures in the sea died, and a third of the ships were destroyed. Jer 51:25

¹⁰The third angel sounded his trumpet, and a great star, blazing like a torch, fell from the sky on a third of the rivers and on the springs of water— ¹¹the name of the star is Wormwood.ᵃ A third of the waters turned bitter, and many people died from the waters that had become bitter. Isa 14:12; Jer 9:15

¹²The fourth angel sounded his trumpet, and a third of the sun was struck, a third of the moon, and a third of the stars, so that a third of them turned dark. A third of the day was without light, and also a third of the night. Ex 10:21-23; Rev 6:12-13

¹³As I watched, I heard an eagle that was flying in midair call out in a loud voice: "Woe! Woe! Woe to the inhabitants of the earth, because of the trumpet blasts about to be sounded by the other three angels!" Rev 9:12

9 The fifth angel sounded his trumpet, and I saw a star that had fallen from the sky to the earth. The star was given the key to the shaft of the Abyss. ²When he opened the Abyss, smoke rose from it like the smoke from a gigantic furnace. The sun and sky were darkened by the smoke from the Abyss. ³And out of the smoke locusts came down upon the earth and were given power like that of scorpions of the earth. ⁴They were told not to harm the grass of the earth or any plant or tree, but only those people who did not have the seal of God on their foreheads.

ᵃ11 That is, Bitterness

⁵They were not given power to kill them, but only to torture them for five months. And the agony they suffered was like that of the sting of a scorpion when it strikes a man. ⁶During those days men will seek death, but will not find it; they will long to die, but death will elude them.   Job 3:21; Lev 8:10

⁷The locusts looked like horses prepared for battle. On their heads they wore something like crowns of gold, and their faces resembled human faces. ⁸Their hair was like women's hair, and their teeth were like lions' teeth. ⁹They had breastplates like breastplates of iron, and the sound of their wings was like the thundering of many horses and chariots rushing into battle. ¹⁰They had tails and stings like scorpions, and in their tails they had power to torment people for five months. ¹¹They had as king over them the angel of the Abyss, whose name in Hebrew is Abaddon, and in Greek, Apollyon.ᵃ   Joel 2:4

¹²The first woe is past; two other woes are yet to come.

¹³The sixth angel sounded his trumpet, and I heard a voice coming from the hornsᵇ of the golden altar that is before God. ¹⁴It said to the sixth angel who had the trumpet, "Release the four angels who are bound at the great river Euphrates." ¹⁵And the four angels who had been kept ready for this very hour and day and month and year were released to kill a third of mankind. ¹⁶The number of the mounted troops was two hundred million. I heard their number.   Rev 7:1

¹⁷The horses and riders I saw in my vision looked like this: Their breastplates were fiery red, dark blue, and yellow as sulfur. The heads of the horses resembled the heads of lions, and out of their mouths came fire, smoke and sulfur. ¹⁸A third of mankind was killed by the three plagues of fire, smoke and sulfur that came out of their mouths. ¹⁹The power of the horses was in their mouths and in their tails; for their tails were like snakes, having heads with which they inflict injury.   Rev 11:5

²⁰The rest of mankind that were not killed by these plagues still did not repent of the work of their hands; they did not stop worshiping demons, and idols of gold, silver, bronze, stone and wood—idols that cannot see or hear or walk. ²¹Nor did they repent of their murders, their magic arts, their sexual immorality or their thefts.   Rev 2:21

The Angel and the Little Scroll

10 Then I saw another mighty angel coming down from heaven. He was robed in a cloud, with a rainbow above his head; his face was like

---

ᵃ11 *Abaddon* and *Apollyon* mean *Destroyer*.   ᵇ13 That is, projections

the sun, and his legs were like fiery pillars. [2]He was holding a little scroll, which lay open in his hand. He planted his right foot on the sea and his left foot on the land, [3]and he gave a loud shout like the roar of a lion. When he shouted, the voices of the seven thunders spoke. [4]And when the seven thunders spoke, I was about to write; but I heard a voice from heaven say, "Seal up what the seven thunders have said and do not write it down." Da 8:26

[5]Then the angel I had seen standing on the sea and on the land raised his right hand to heaven. [6]And he swore by him who lives for ever and ever, who created the heavens and all that is in them, the earth and all that is in it, and the sea and all that is in it, and said, "There will be no more delay! [7]But in the days when the seventh angel is about to sound his trumpet, the mystery of God will be accomplished, just as he announced to his servants the prophets." Dt 32:40; Am 3:7

[8]Then the voice that I had heard from heaven spoke to me once more: "Go, take the scroll that lies open in the hand of the angel who is standing on the sea and on the land."

[9]So I went to the angel and asked him to give me the little scroll. He said to me, "Take it and eat it. It will turn your stomach sour, but in your mouth it will be as sweet as honey." [10]I took the little scroll from the an-

gel's hand and ate it. It tasted as sweet as honey in my mouth, but when I had eaten it, my stomach turned sour. [11]Then I was told, "You must prophesy again about many peoples, nations, languages and kings."

The Two Witnesses

11 I was given a reed like a measuring rod and was told, "Go and measure the temple of God and the altar, and count the worshipers there. [2]But exclude the outer court; do not measure it, because it has been given to the Gentiles. They will trample on the holy city for 42 months. [3]And I will give power to my two witnesses, and they will prophesy for 1,260 days, clothed in sackcloth." [4]These are the two olive trees and the two lampstands that stand before the Lord of the earth. [5]If anyone tries to harm them, fire comes from their mouths and devours their enemies. This is how anyone who wants to harm them must die. [6]These men have power to shut up the sky so that it will not rain during the time they are prophesying; and they have power to turn the waters into blood and to strike the earth with every kind of plague as often as they want. Eze 40:3

[7]Now when they have finished their testimony, the beast that comes up from the Abyss will attack them, and overpower and kill them. [8]Their bodies will lie in the street of the great

city, which is figuratively called Sodom and Egypt, where also their Lord was crucified. ⁹For three and a half days men from every people, tribe, language and nation will gaze on their bodies and refuse them burial. ¹⁰The inhabitants of the earth will gloat over them and will celebrate by sending each other gifts, because these two prophets had tormented those who live on the earth.   Rev 13:1-4

¹¹But after the three and a half days a breath of life from God entered them, and they stood on their feet, and terror struck those who saw them. ¹²Then they heard a loud voice from heaven saying to them, "Come up here." And they went up to heaven in a cloud, while their enemies looked on.   Eze 37:5,9

¹³At that very hour there was a severe earthquake and a tenth of the city collapsed. Seven thousand people were killed in the earthquake, and the survivors were terrified and gave glory to the God of heaven.

¹⁴The second woe has passed; the third woe is coming soon.

The Seventh Trumpet

¹⁵The seventh angel sounded his trumpet, and there were loud voices in heaven, which said: Rev 16:17; 19:1

"The kingdom of the world
    has become the kingdom
    of our Lord and of his
    Christ,   Rev 12:10

and he will reign for ever
    and ever."   Ps 145:13

¹⁶And the twenty-four elders, who were seated on their thrones before God, fell on their faces and worshiped God, ¹⁷saying: Rev 4:4,10

"We give thanks to you,
    Lord God Almighty,
  the One who is and who
    was,   Rev 1:4
because you have taken your
    great power
  and have begun to reign.
¹⁸The nations were angry; Ps 2:1
    and your wrath has come.
  The time has come for
    judging the dead, Rev 20:12
  and for rewarding your
    servants the prophets
  and your saints and those
    who reverence your
    name,
  both small and great—Rev 19:5
  and for destroying those who
    destroy the earth."

¹⁹Then God's temple in heaven was opened, and within his temple was seen the ark of his covenant. And there came flashes of lightning, rumblings, peals of thunder, an earthquake and a great hailstorm.   Rev 15:5,8

The Woman and the Dragon

12 A great and wondrous sign appeared in heaven: a woman clothed with the sun, with the moon under her feet and a crown of twelve stars on her head. ²She was pregnant and cried out in pain as she was

about to give birth. ³Then another sign appeared in heaven: an enormous red dragon with seven heads and ten horns and seven crowns on his heads. ⁴His tail swept a third of the stars out of the sky and flung them to the earth. The dragon stood in front of the woman who was about to give birth, so that he might devour her child the moment it was born. ⁵She gave birth to a son, a male child, who will rule all the nations with an iron scepter. And her child was snatched up to God and to his throne. ⁶The woman fled into the desert to a place prepared for her by God, where she might be taken care of for 1,260 days.   Ps 2:9; Da 7:7,20

⁷And there was war in heaven. Michael and his angels fought against the dragon, and the dragon and his angels fought back. ⁸But he was not strong enough, and they lost their place in heaven. ⁹The great dragon was hurled down—that ancient serpent called the devil, or Satan, who leads the whole world astray. He was hurled to the earth, and his angels with him.   Ge 3:1-7; Jude 9

¹⁰Then I heard a loud voice in heaven say:

"Now have come the
    salvation and the power
    and the kingdom of our
    God,   Rev 7:10
and the authority of his
    Christ.

For the accuser of our
    brothers,   Job 1:9-11
who accuses them before
    our God day and night,
    has been hurled down.
¹¹They overcame him
    by the blood of the Lamb
    and by the word of their
    testimony;   Rev 6:9
they did not love their lives
    so much
    as to shrink from death.
¹²Therefore rejoice, you
    heavens   Ps 96:11
and you who dwell in
    them!
But woe to the earth and the
    sea,   Rev 8:13
because the devil has gone
    down to you!
He is filled with fury,
    because he knows that his
    time is short."

¹³When the dragon saw that he had been hurled to the earth, he pursued the woman who had given birth to the male child. ¹⁴The woman was given the two wings of a great eagle, so that she might fly to the place prepared for her in the desert, where she would be taken care of for a time, times and half a time, out of the serpent's reach. ¹⁵Then from his mouth the serpent spewed water like a river, to overtake the woman and sweep her away with the torrent. ¹⁶But the earth helped the woman by opening its mouth and swallowing the river that the dragon had spewed out of his mouth. ¹⁷Then the dragon

was enraged at the woman and went off to make war against the rest of her offspring—those who obey God's commandments and hold to the testi-

13 mony of Jesus. [1]And the dragon[a] stood on the shore of the sea.   Ge 3:15

The Beast out of the Sea

And I saw a beast coming out of the sea. He had ten horns and seven heads, with ten crowns on his horns, and on each head a blasphemous name. [2]The beast I saw resembled a leopard, but had feet like those of a bear and a mouth like that of a lion. The dragon gave the beast his power and his throne and great authority. [3]One of the heads of the beast seemed to have had a fatal wound, but the fatal wound had been healed. The whole world was astonished and followed the beast. [4]Men worshiped the dragon because he had given authority to the beast, and they also worshiped the beast and asked, "Who is like the beast? Who can make war against him?"   Da 7:1-6

[5]The beast was given a mouth to utter proud words and blasphemies and to exercise his authority for forty-two months. [6]He opened his mouth to blaspheme God, and to slander his name and his dwelling place and those who live in heaven. [7]He was given power to make war against the saints and to conquer them. And he was given authority over every tribe, people, language and nation. [8]All inhabitants of the earth will worship the beast—all whose names have not been written in the book of life belonging to the Lamb that was slain from the creation of the world.[b]   Da 7:8,11

[9]He who has an ear, let him hear.

[10]If anyone is to go into
   captivity,
   into captivity he will go.
If anyone is to be killed[c] with
   the sword,
   with the sword he will be
   killed.   Jer 15:2; 43:11

This calls for patient endurance and faithfulness on the part of the saints.   Rev 14:12

The Beast out of the Earth

[11]Then I saw another beast, coming out of the earth. He had two horns like a lamb, but he spoke like a dragon. [12]He exercised all the authority of the first beast on his behalf, and made the earth and its inhabitants worship the first beast, whose fatal wound had been healed. [13]And he performed great and miraculous signs, even causing fire to come down from heaven to earth in full view of men. [14]Because of the signs he was given power to do on behalf of the first beast, he deceived the

inhabitants of the earth. He ordered them to set up an image in honor of the beast who was wounded by the sword and yet lived. 15He was given power to give breath to the image of the first beast, so that it could speak and cause all who refused to worship the image to be killed. 16He also forced everyone, small and great, rich and poor, free and slave, to receive a mark on his right hand or on his forehead, 17so that no one could buy or sell unless he had the mark, which is the name of the beast or the number of his name.

18This calls for wisdom. If anyone has insight, let him calculate the number of the beast, for it is man's number. His number is 666.   Rev 15:2; 17:9

The Lamb and the 144,000

14 Then I looked, and there before me was the Lamb, standing on Mount Zion, and with him 144,000 who had his name and his Father's name written on their foreheads. 2And I heard a sound from heaven like the roar of rushing waters and like a loud peal of thunder. The sound I heard was like that of harpists playing their harps. 3And they sang a new song before the throne and before the four living creatures and the elders. No one could learn the song except the 144,000 who had been redeemed from the earth. 4These are those who did not defile themselves with women, for they kept themselves pure. They follow the Lamb wherever he goes. They were purchased from among men and offered as firstfruits to God and the Lamb. 5No lie was found in their mouths; they are blameless.   Ps 2:6; Zep 3:13

The Three Angels

6Then I saw another angel flying in midair, and he had the eternal gospel to proclaim to those who live on the earth—to every nation, tribe, language and people. 7He said in a loud voice, "Fear God and give him glory, because the hour of his judgment has come. Worship him who made the heavens, the earth, the sea and the springs of water."   Ps 34:9; Rev 15:4

8A second angel followed and said, "Fallen! Fallen is Babylon the Great, which made all the nations drink the maddening wine of her adulteries."   Isa 21:9

9A third angel followed them and said in a loud voice: "If anyone worships the beast and his image and receives his mark on the forehead or on the hand, 10he, too, will drink of the wine of God's fury, which has been poured full strength into the cup of his wrath. He will be tormented with burning sulfur in the presence of the holy angels and of the Lamb. 11And the smoke of their torment rises for ever and ever. There is no rest day or night for those who worship the beast and his image, or for anyone who receives the mark of his name." 12This calls

for patient endurance on the part of the saints who obey God's commandments and remain faithful to Jesus.   Jn 14:15

¹³Then I heard a voice from heaven say, "Write: Blessed are the dead who die in the Lord from now on."   1Th 4:16

"Yes," says the Spirit, "they will rest from their labor, for their deeds will follow them."

The Harvest of the Earth

¹⁴I looked, and there before me was a white cloud, and seated on the cloud was one "like a son of man"[a] with a crown of gold on his head and a sharp sickle in his hand. ¹⁵Then another angel came out of the temple and called in a loud voice to him who was sitting on the cloud, "Take your sickle and reap, because the time to reap has come, for the harvest of the earth is ripe." ¹⁶So he who was seated on the cloud swung his sickle over the earth, and the earth was harvested.   Jer 51:33

¹⁷Another angel came out of the temple in heaven, and he too had a sharp sickle. ¹⁸Still another angel, who had charge of the fire, came from the altar and called in a loud voice to him who had the sharp sickle, "Take your sharp sickle and gather the clusters of grapes from the earth's vine, because its grapes are ripe." ¹⁹The angel swung his sickle on the earth, gathered its grapes and threw them into the great winepress of God's wrath. ²⁰They were trampled in the winepress outside the city, and blood flowed out of the press, rising as high as the horses' bridles for a distance of 1,600 stadia.[b]   Isa 63:3; Joel 3:13

Seven Angels With Seven Plagues

15 I saw in heaven another great and marvelous sign: seven angels with the seven last plagues—last, because with them God's wrath is completed. ²And I saw what looked like a sea of glass mixed with fire and, standing beside the sea, those who had been victorious over the beast and his image and over the number of his name. They held harps given them by God ³and sang the song of Moses the servant of God and the song of the Lamb: Ex 15:1

"Great and marvelous are
    your deeds,   Ps 111:2
Lord God Almighty.   Rev 1:8
Just and true are your ways,
    King of the ages.   Ps 145:17
⁴Who will not fear you,
    O Lord,   Jer 10:7
and bring glory to your
    name?   Ps 86:9
For you alone are holy.
All nations will come
    and worship before you,
for your righteous acts have
    been revealed."

⁵After this I looked and in heaven the temple, that is, the

---

[a]14 Daniel 7:13   [b]20 That is, about 180 miles (about 300 kilometers)

tabernacle of the Testimony, was opened. 6Out of the temple came the seven angels with the seven plagues. They were dressed in clean, shining linen and wore golden sashes around their chests. 7Then one of the four living creatures gave to the seven angels seven golden bowls filled with the wrath of God, who lives for ever and ever. 8And the temple was filled with smoke from the glory of God and from his power, and no one could enter the temple until the seven plagues of the seven angels were completed.

The Seven Bowls of God's Wrath

16 Then I heard a loud voice from the temple saying to the seven angels, "Go, pour out the seven bowls of God's wrath on the earth."   Zep 3:8

2The first angel went and poured out his bowl on the land, and ugly and painful sores broke out on the people who had the mark of the beast and worshiped his image.

3The second angel poured out his bowl on the sea, and it turned into blood like that of a dead man, and every living thing in the sea died.

4The third angel poured out his bowl on the rivers and springs of water, and they became blood. 5Then I heard the angel in charge of the waters say: Ex 7:17-21

"You are just in these judgments,   Rev 15:3
you who are and who were, the Holy One,
because you have so judged;   Rev 6:10
6for they have shed the blood of your saints and prophets,   Lk 11:49-51
and you have given them blood to drink as they deserve."   Isa 49:26

7And I heard the altar respond:

"Yes, Lord God Almighty, true and just are your judgments."   Rev 1:8; 15:3

8The fourth angel poured out his bowl on the sun, and the sun was given power to scorch people with fire. 9They were seared by the intense heat and they cursed the name of God, who had control over these plagues, but they refused to repent and glorify him.   Rev 2:21

10The fifth angel poured out his bowl on the throne of the beast, and his kingdom was plunged into darkness. Men gnawed their tongues in agony 11and cursed the God of heaven because of their pains and their sores, but they refused to repent of what they had done.

12The sixth angel poured out his bowl on the great river Euphrates, and its water was dried up to prepare the way for the kings from the East. 13Then I saw three evil*a* spirits that

a13 Greek *unclean*

looked like frogs; they came out of the mouth of the dragon, out of the mouth of the beast and out of the mouth of the false prophet. ¹⁴They are spirits of demons performing miraculous signs, and they go out to the kings of the whole world, to gather them for the battle on the great day of God Almighty.

¹⁵"Behold, I come like a thief! Blessed is he who stays awake and keeps his clothes with him, so that he may not go naked and be shamefully exposed." Lk 12:39

¹⁶Then they gathered the kings together to the place that in Hebrew is called Armageddon.

¹⁷The seventh angel poured out his bowl into the air, and out of the temple came a loud voice from the throne, saying, "It is done!" ¹⁸Then there came flashes of lightning, rumblings, peals of thunder and a severe earthquake. No earthquake like it has ever occurred since man has been on earth, so tremendous was the quake. ¹⁹The great city split into three parts, and the cities of the nations collapsed. God remembered Babylon the Great and gave her the cup filled with the wine of the fury of his wrath. ²⁰Every island fled away and the mountains could not be found. ²¹From the sky huge hailstones of about a hundred pounds each fell upon men. And they cursed God on account of the plague of hail, because the plague was so terrible. Eze 13:13; Rev 14:8

The Woman on the Beast

17 One of the seven angels who had the seven bowls came and said to me, "Come, I will show you the punishment of the great prostitute, who sits on many waters. ²With her the kings of the earth committed adultery and the inhabitants of the earth were intoxicated with the wine of her adulteries."

³Then the angel carried me away in the Spirit into a desert. There I saw a woman sitting on a scarlet beast that was covered with blasphemous names and had seven heads and ten horns. ⁴The woman was dressed in purple and scarlet, and was glittering with gold, precious stones and pearls. She held a golden cup in her hand, filled with abominable things and the filth of her adulteries. ⁵This title was written on her forehead:

MYSTERY
BABYLON THE GREAT Rev 14:8
THE MOTHER OF PROSTITUTES
AND OF THE ABOMINATIONS OF
THE EARTH.

⁶I saw that the woman was drunk with the blood of the saints, the blood of those who bore testimony to Jesus. Rev 16:6

When I saw her, I was greatly astonished. ⁷Then the angel said to me: "Why are you astonished? I will explain to you the mystery of the woman and of the beast she rides, which has the seven heads and ten horns. ⁸The beast, which you saw,

once was, now is not, and will come up out of the Abyss and go to his destruction. The inhabitants of the earth whose names have not been written in the book of life from the creation of the world will be astonished when they see the beast, because he once was, now is not, and yet will come.   Lk 8:31

⁹"This calls for a mind with wisdom. The seven heads are seven hills on which the woman sits. ¹⁰They are also seven kings. Five have fallen, one is, the other has not yet come; but when he does come, he must remain for a little while. ¹¹The beast who once was, and now is not, is an eighth king. He belongs to the seven and is going to his destruction.

¹²"The ten horns you saw are ten kings who have not yet received a kingdom, but who for one hour will receive authority as kings along with the beast. ¹³They have one purpose and will give their power and authority to the beast. ¹⁴They will make war against the Lamb, but the Lamb will overcome them because he is Lord of lords and King of kings—and with him will be his called, chosen and faithful followers."   Jn 16:33

¹⁵Then the angel said to me, "The waters you saw, where the prostitute sits, are peoples, multitudes, nations and languages. ¹⁶The beast and the ten horns you saw will hate the prostitute. They will bring her to ruin and leave her naked; they will eat her flesh and burn her with fire. ¹⁷For God has put it into their hearts to accomplish his purpose by agreeing to give the beast their power to rule, until God's words are fulfilled. ¹⁸The woman you saw is the great city that rules over the kings of the earth."

The Fall of Babylon

18 After this I saw another angel coming down from heaven. He had great authority, and the earth was illuminated by his splendor. ²With a mighty voice he shouted:

"Fallen! Fallen is Babylon the
    Great!   Rev 14:8
She has become a home for
    demons
and a haunt for every evil[a]
    spirit,   Rev 16:13
a haunt for every unclean
    and detestable bird.
³For all the nations have
    drunk
the maddening wine of her
    adulteries.   Rev 14:8
The kings of the earth
    committed adultery with
    her,   Rev 17:2
and the merchants of the
    earth grew rich from her
    excessive luxuries."

⁴Then I heard another voice from heaven say:

"Come out of her, my
    people,   Isa 48:20

---

a2 Greek *unclean*

so that you will not share in
her sins,
so that you will not receive
any of her plagues; Ge 19:15
⁵for her sins are piled up to
heaven, 2Ch 28:9
and God has remembered
her crimes. Rev 16:19
⁶Give back to her as she has
given;
pay her back double for
what she has done.
Mix her a double portion
from her own cup. Rev 14:10
⁷Give her as much torture and
grief
as the glory and luxury she
gave herself. Eze 28:2-8
In her heart she boasts,
'I sit as queen; I am not a
widow,
and I will never mourn.' Ps 10:6
⁸Therefore in one day her
plagues will overtake
her:
death, mourning and
famine.
She will be consumed by fire,
for mighty is the Lord God
who judges her. Rev 17:16

⁹"When the kings of the earth
who committed adultery with
her and shared her luxury see
the smoke of her burning, they
will weep and mourn over her.
¹⁰Terrified at her torment, they
will stand far off and cry:

" 'Woe! Woe, O great city,
O Babylon, city of power!
In one hour your doom has
come!'

¹¹"The merchants of the earth
will weep and mourn over her
because no one buys their
cargoes any more— ¹²cargoes of
gold, silver, precious stones
and pearls; fine linen, purple,
silk and scarlet cloth; every sort
of citron wood, and articles of
every kind made of ivory, costly
wood, bronze, iron and marble;
¹³cargoes of cinnamon and
spice, of incense, myrrh and
frankincense, of wine and olive
oil, of fine flour and wheat; cattle and sheep; horses and car-
riages; and bodies and souls of
men. Eze 27:12-31
¹⁴"They will say, 'The fruit
you longed for is gone from
you. All your riches and splendor have vanished, never to be
recovered.' ¹⁵The merchants
who sold these things and
gained their wealth from her
will stand far off, terrified at her
torment. They will weep and
mourn ¹⁶and cry out:

" 'Woe! Woe, O great city,
dressed in fine linen,
purple and scarlet,
and glittering with gold,
precious stones and
pearls! Rev 17:4
¹⁷In one hour such great
wealth has been brought
to ruin!' Rev 17:12,16

"Every sea captain, and all
who travel by ship, the sailors,
and all who earn their living
from the sea, will stand far off.
¹⁸When they see the smoke of
her burning, they will exclaim,
'Was there ever a city like this
great city?' ¹⁹They will throw

dust on their heads, and with weeping and mourning cry out:

" 'Woe! Woe, O great city,
　where all who had ships on
　　the sea
　became rich through her
　　wealth!   Rev 17:18
In one hour she has been
　　brought to ruin!   Rev 17:16
20Rejoice over her, O heaven!
　Rejoice, saints and apostles
　　and prophets!   Jer 51:48
God has judged her for the
　　way she treated you.' "

21Then a mighty angel picked up a boulder the size of a large millstone and threw it into the sea, and said:

"With such violence
　the great city of Babylon
　　will be thrown down,
　never to be found again.
22The music of harpists and
　　musicians, flute players
　　and trumpeters,
　will never be heard in you
　　again.   Isa 24:8
No workman of any trade
　will ever be found in you
　　again.
The sound of a millstone
　will never be heard in you
　　again.   Jer 25:10
23The light of a lamp
　will never shine in you
　　again.
The voice of bridegroom and
　　bride
　will never be heard in you
　　again.   Jer 7:34
Your merchants were the
　　world's great men. Isa 23:8

By your magic spell all the
　　nations were led astray.
24In her was found the blood
　of prophets and of the
　　saints,   Rev 16:6; 17:6
and of all who have been
　killed on the earth." Jer 51:49

Hallelujah!

19 After this I heard what sounded like the roar of a great multitude in heaven shouting:

"Hallelujah!
Salvation and glory and
　　power belong to our
　　God,   Rev 4:11; 7:10
2 for true and just are his
　　judgments.   Rev 16:7
He has condemned the great
　　prostitute   Rev 17:1
who corrupted the earth by
　　her adulteries.
He has avenged on her the
　　blood of his servants."

3And again they shouted:

"Hallelujah!
The smoke from her goes up
　　for ever and ever." Isa 34:10

4The twenty-four elders and the four living creatures fell down and worshiped God, who was seated on the throne. And they cried: Rev 4:4,6,10

"Amen, Hallelujah!"

5Then a voice came from the throne, saying:

"Praise our God,
　all you his servants,   Ps 134:1
you who fear him,

both small and great!" Ps 115:13

6Then I heard what sounded like a great multitude, like the roar of rushing waters and like loud peals of thunder, shouting: Rev 1:15

"Hallelujah!
For our Lord God Almighty
reigns. Rev 1:8; 11:15
7Let us rejoice and be glad
and give him glory! Rev 11:13
For the wedding of the Lamb
has come, Mt 22:2
and his bride has made
herself ready. Rev 21:2,9
8Fine linen, bright and clean,
was given her to wear."

(Fine linen stands for the righteous acts of the saints.) Isa 61:10

9Then the angel said to me, "Write: 'Blessed are those who are invited to the wedding supper of the Lamb!' " And he added, "These are the true words of God." Lk 14:15

10At this I fell at his feet to worship him. But he said to me, "Do not do it! I am a fellow servant with you and with your brothers who hold to the testimony of Jesus. Worship God! For the testimony of Jesus is the spirit of prophecy." Rev 22:8,9

The Rider on the White Horse

11I saw heaven standing open and there before me was a white horse, whose rider is called

Faithful and True. With justice he judges and makes war. 12His eyes are like blazing fire, and on his head are many crowns. He has a name written on him that no one knows but he himself. 13He is dressed in a robe dipped in blood, and his name is the Word of God. 14The armies of heaven were following him, riding on white horses and dressed in fine linen, white and clean. 15Out of his mouth comes a sharp sword with which to strike down the nations. "He will rule them with an iron scepter." a He treads the winepress of the fury of the wrath of God Almighty. 16On his robe and on his thigh he has this name written: 1Ti 6:15

KING OF KINGS AND LORD OF
LORDS.

17And I saw an angel standing in the sun, who cried in a loud voice to all the birds flying in midair, "Come, gather together for the great supper of God, 18so that you may eat the flesh of kings, generals, and mighty men, of horses and their riders, and the flesh of all people, free and slave, small and great."

19Then I saw the beast and the kings of the earth and their armies gathered together to make war against the rider on the horse and his army. 20But the beast was captured, and with him the false prophet who had performed the miraculous signs

a15 Psalm 2:9

on his behalf. With these signs he had deluded those who had received the mark of the beast and worshiped his image. The two of them were thrown alive into the fiery lake of burning sulfur. [21]The rest of them were killed with the sword that came out of the mouth of the rider on the horse, and all the birds gorged themselves on their flesh. Da 7:11; Rev 1:16; 13:1

The Thousand Years

20 And I saw an angel coming down out of heaven, having the key to the Abyss and holding in his hand a great chain. [2]He seized the dragon, that ancient serpent, who is the devil, or Satan, and bound him for a thousand years. [3]He threw him into the Abyss, and locked and sealed it over him, to keep him from deceiving the nations anymore until the thousand years were ended. After that, he must be set free for a short time.

[4]I saw thrones on which were seated those who had been given authority to judge. And I saw the souls of those who had been beheaded because of their testimony for Jesus and because of the word of God. They had not worshiped the beast or his image and had not received his mark on their foreheads or their hands. They came to life and reigned with Christ a thousand years. [5](The rest of the dead did not come to life until the thousand years were ended.) This is the first resurrection. [6]Blessed and holy are those who have part in the first resurrection. The second death has no power over them, but they will be priests of God and of Christ and will reign with him for a thousand years. Mt 19:28; Rev 14:13

Satan's Doom

[7]When the thousand years are over, Satan will be released from his prison [8]and will go out to deceive the nations in the four corners of the earth—Gog and Magog—to gather them for battle. In number they are like the sand on the seashore. [9]They marched across the breadth of the earth and surrounded the camp of God's people, the city he loves. But fire came down from heaven and devoured them. [10]And the devil, who deceived them, was thrown into the lake of burning sulfur, where the beast and the false prophet had been thrown. They will be tormented day and night for ever and ever. Rev 12:9

The Dead Are Judged

[11]Then I saw a great white throne and him who was seated on it. Earth and sky fled from his presence, and there was no place for them. [12]And I saw the dead, great and small, standing before the throne, and books were opened. Another book was opened, which is the book of life. The dead were judged according to what they had done as recorded in the books. [13]The sea gave up the dead that

were in it, and death and Hades gave up the dead that were in them, and each person was judged according to what he had done. [14]Then death and Hades were thrown into the lake of fire. The lake of fire is the second death. [15]If anyone's name was not found written in the book of life, he was thrown into the lake of fire. Mt 16:27

The New Jerusalem

21 Then I saw a new heaven and a new earth, for the first heaven and the first earth had passed away, and there was no longer any sea. [2]I saw the Holy City, the new Jerusalem, coming down out of heaven from God, prepared as a bride beautifully dressed for her husband. [3]And I heard a loud voice from the throne saying, "Now the dwelling of God is with men, and he will live with them. They will be his people, and God himself will be with them and be their God. [4]He will wipe every tear from their eyes. There will be no more death or mourning or crying or pain, for the old order of things has passed away." 1Co 15:26; 2Pe 3:13

[5]He who was seated on the throne said, "I am making everything new!" Then he said, "Write this down, for these words are trustworthy and true." Rev 19:9; 22:6

[6]He said to me: "It is done. I am the Alpha and the Omega, the Beginning and the End. To him who is thirsty I will give to drink without cost from the spring of the water of life. [7]He who overcomes will inherit all this, and I will be his God and he will be my son. [8]But the cowardly, the unbelieving, the vile, the murderers, the sexually immoral, those who practice magic arts, the idolaters and all liars—their place will be in the fiery lake of burning sulfur. This is the second death." Isa 55:1

[9]One of the seven angels who had the seven bowls full of the seven last plagues came and said to me, "Come, I will show you the bride, the wife of the Lamb." [10]And he carried me away in the Spirit to a mountain great and high, and showed me the Holy City, Jerusalem, coming down out of heaven from God. [11]It shone with the glory of God, and its brilliance was like that of a very precious jewel, like a jasper, clear as crystal. [12]It had a great, high wall with twelve gates, and with twelve angels at the gates. On the gates were written the names of the twelve tribes of Israel. [13]There were three gates on the east, three on the north, three on the south and three on the west. [14]The wall of the city had twelve foundations, and on them were the names of the twelve apostles of the Lamb. Eze 48:30-35

[15]The angel who talked with me had a measuring rod of gold to measure the city, its gates and its walls. [16]The city was laid out like a square, as long as it was wide. He measured the city

with the rod and found it to be 12,000 stadia[a] in length, and as wide and high as it is long. [17]He measured its wall and it was 144 cubits[b] thick,[c] by man's measurement, which the angel was using. [18]The wall was made of jasper, and the city of pure gold, as pure as glass. [19]The foundations of the city walls were decorated with every kind of precious stone. The first foundation was jasper, the second sapphire, the third chalcedony, the fourth emerald, [20]the fifth sardonyx, the sixth carnelian, the seventh chrysolite, the eighth beryl, the ninth topaz, the tenth chrysoprase, the eleventh jacinth, and the twelfth amethyst.[d] [21]The twelve gates were twelve pearls, each gate made of a single pearl. The great street of the city was of pure gold, like transparent glass.   Isa 54:12; Eze 40:3

[22]I did not see a temple in the city, because the Lord God Almighty and the Lamb are its temple. [23]The city does not need the sun or the moon to shine on it, for the glory of God gives it light, and the Lamb is its lamp. [24]The nations will walk by its light, and the kings of the earth will bring their splendor into it. [25]On no day will its gates ever be shut, for there will be no night there. [26]The glory and honor of the nations will be brought into it. [27]Nothing impure will ever enter it, nor will anyone who does what is shameful or deceitful, but only those whose names are written in the Lamb's book of life.   Isa 52:1; Jn 4:21

The River of Life

22 Then the angel showed me the river of the water of life, as clear as crystal, flowing from the throne of God and of the Lamb [2]down the middle of the great street of the city. On each side of the river stood the tree of life, bearing twelve crops of fruit, yielding its fruit every month. And the leaves of the tree are for the healing of the nations. [3]No longer will there be any curse. The throne of God and of the Lamb will be in the city, and his servants will serve him. [4]They will see his face, and his name will be on their foreheads. [5]There will be no more night. They will not need the light of a lamp or the light of the sun, for the Lord God will give them light. And they will reign for ever and ever.   Ps 36:8

[6]The angel said to me, "These words are trustworthy and true. The Lord, the God of the spirits of the prophets, sent his angel to show his servants the things that must soon take place."Rev 1:1

Jesus Is Coming

[7]"Behold, I am coming soon!

---

[a]16 That is, about 1,400 miles (about 2,200 kilometers)   [b]17 That is, about 200 feet (about 65 meters)   [c]17 Or *high*   [d]20 The precise identification of some of these precious stones is uncertain.

Blessed is he who keeps the words of the prophecy in this book."   Mt 16:27; Rev 1:3

8I, John, am the one who heard and saw these things. And when I had heard and seen them, I fell down to worship at the feet of the angel who had been showing them to me. 9But he said to me, "Do not do it! I am a fellow servant with you and with your brothers the prophets and of all who keep the words of this book. Worship God!"   Rev 1:1; 19:10

10Then he told me, "Do not seal up the words of the prophecy of this book, because the time is near. 11Let him who does wrong continue to do wrong; let him who is vile continue to be vile; let him who does right continue to do right; and let him who is holy continue to be holy."   Eze 3:27; Da 8:26

12"Behold, I am coming soon! My reward is with me, and I will give to everyone according to what he has done. 13I am the Alpha and the Omega, the First and the Last, the Beginning and the End.   Mt 16:27; Rev 1:8,17

14"Blessed are those who wash their robes, that they may have the right to the tree of life and may go through the gates into the city. 15Outside are the dogs, those who practice magic arts, the sexually immoral, the murderers, the idolaters and everyone who loves and practices falsehood.   Gal 5:19-21; Rev 7:14

16"I, Jesus, have sent my angel to give you[a] this testimony for the churches. I am the Root and the Offspring of David, and the bright Morning Star."   Rev 1:1

17The Spirit and the bride say, "Come!" And let him who hears say, "Come!" Whoever is thirsty, let him come; and whoever wishes, let him take the free gift of the water of life. Jn 4:10

18I warn everyone who hears the words of the prophecy of this book: If anyone adds anything to them, God will add to him the plagues described in this book. 19And if anyone takes words away from this book of prophecy, God will take away from him his share in the tree of life and in the holy city, which are described in this book.   Dt 4:2

20He who testifies to these things says, "Yes, I am coming soon."   Mt 16:27; Rev 1:2

Amen. Come, Lord Jesus.

21The grace of the Lord Jesus be with God's people. Amen.

---

a16 The Greek is plural.

Table of Weights and Measures

BIBLICAL UNIT		APPROXIMATE AMERICAN EQUIVALENT	APPROXIMATE METRIC EQUIVALENT
WEIGHTS			
talent	(60 minas)	75 pounds	34 kilograms
mina	(50 shekels)	1 1/4 pounds	0.6 kilogram
shekel	(2 bekas)	2/5 ounce	11.5 grams
pim	(2/3 shekel)	1/3 ounce	7.6 grams
beka	(10 gerahs)	1/5 ounce	5.5 grams
gerah		1/50 ounce	0.6 gram
LENGTH			
cubit		18 inches	0.5 meter
span		9 inches	23 centimeters
handbreadth		3 inches	8 centimeters
CAPACITY			
Dry Measure			
cor [homer]	(10 ephahs)	6 bushels	220 liters
lethek	(5 ephahs)	3 bushels	110 liters
ephah	(10 omers)	3/5 bushel	22 liters
seah	(1/3 ephah)	7 quarts	7.3 liters
omer	(1/10 ephah)	2 quarts	2 liters
cab	(1/18 ephah)	1 quart	1 liter
Liquid Measure			
bath	(1 ephah)	6 gallons	22 liters
hin	(1/6 bath)	4 quarts	4 liters
log	(1/72 bath)	1/3 quart	0.3 liter

The figures of the table are calculated on the basis of a shekel equaling 11.5 grams, a cubit equaling 18 inches and an ephah equaling 22 liters. The quart referred to is either a dry quart (slightly larger than a liter) or a liquid quart (slightly smaller than a liter), whichever is applicable. The ton referred to in the footnotes is the American ton of 2,000 pounds.

This table is based upon the best available information, but it is not intended to be mathematically precise; like the measurement equivalents in the footnotes, it merely gives approximate amounts and distances. Weights and measures differed somewhat at various times and places in the ancient world. There is uncertainty particularly about the ephah and the bath; further discoveries may give more light on these units of capacity.

A
Concordance
to the
NEW INTERNATIONAL
VERSION

ZONDERVAN BIBLE PUBLISHERS

GRAND RAPIDS, MICHIGAN

Introduction

The NIV Concordance, created by Edward W. Goodrick and John R. Kohlenberger III, has been developed specifically for use with the New International Version. Like all concordances, it is a special index which contains an alphabetical listing of words used in the Bible text. By looking up key words, readers can find verses and passages for which they remember a word or two but not their location.

This concordance contains 2,000 word entries, with some 13,000 Scripture references. Each word entry is followed by the Scripture references in which that particular word is found, as well as by a brief excerpt from the surrounding context. The first letter of the entry word is italicized to conserve space and to allow for a longer context excerpt. Variant spellings due to number and tense and compound forms follow the entry in parentheses, and direct the reader to check other forms of that word in locating a passage.

This concordance contains a number of "block entries," which highlight some of the key events and characteristics in the lives of certain Bible figures. The descriptive phrases replace the brief context surrounding each occurrence of the name. In those instances where more than one Bible character has the same name, that name is placed under one block entry, and each person is given a number (1), (2), etc. Insignificant names are not included.

Word or block entries marked with an asterisk (*) list every verse in the Bible in which the word appears.

This concordance is a valuable tool for Bible study. While one of its key purposes is to help the reader find forgotten references to verses, it can also be used to do word studies and to locate and trace biblical themes. Be sure to use this concordance as more than just a verse finder. Whenever you look up a verse, aim to discover the intended meaning of the verse in context. Give special attention to the flow of thought from the beginning of the passage to the end.

ABBREVIATIONS FOR THE BOOKS OF THE BIBLE

Genesis	Ge	Nahum	Na
Exodus	Ex	Habakkuk	Hab
Leviticus	Lev	Zephaniah	Zep
Numbers	Nu	Haggai	Hag
Deuteronomy	Dt	Zechariah	Zec
Joshua	Jos	Malachi	Mal
Judges	Jdg	Matthew	Mt
Ruth	Ru	Mark	Mk
1 Samuel	1Sa	Luke	Lk
2 Samuel	2Sa	John	Jn
1 Kings	1Ki	Acts	Ac
2 Kings	2Ki	Romans	Ro
1 Chronicles	1Ch	1 Corinthians	1Co
2 Chronicles	2Ch	2 Corinthians	2Co
Ezra	Ezr	Galatians	Gal
Nehemiah	Ne	Ephesians	Eph
Esther	Est	Philippians	Php
Job	Job	Colossians	Col
Psalms	Ps	1 Thessalonians	1Th
Proverbs	Pr	2 Thessalonians	2Th
Ecclesiastes	Ecc	1 Timothy	1Ti
Song of Songs	SS	2 Timothy	2Ti
Isaiah	Isa	Titus	Tit
Jeremiah	Jer	Philemon	Phm
Lamentations	La	Hebrews	Heb
Ezekiel	Eze	James	Jas
Daniel	Da	1 Peter	1Pe
Hosea	Hos	2 Peter	2Pe
Joel	Joel	1 John	1Jn
Amos	Am	2 John	2Jn
Obadiah	Ob	3 John	3Jn
Jonah	Jnh	Jude	Jude
Micah	Mic	Revelation	Rev

AARON

Priesthood of (Ex 28:1; Nu 17; Heb 5:1-4; 7), garments (Ex 28; 39), consecration (Ex 29), ordination (Lev 8).

Spokesman for Moses (Ex 4:14-16, 27-31; 7:1-2). Supported Moses' hands in battle (Ex 17:8-13). Built golden calf (Ex 32; Dt 9:20). Talked against Moses (Nu 12). Priesthood opposed (Nu 16); staff budded (Nu 17). Forbidden to enter land (Nu 20:1-12). Death (Nu 20:22-29; 33:38-39).

ABANDON

Dt   4:31 he will not *a* or destroy you
1Ti   4: 1 in later times some will *a* the faith

ABBA

Ro   8:15 And by him we cry, "*A*, Father."
Gal   4: 6 the Spirit who calls out, "*A*, Father

ABEL

Second son of Adam (Ge 4:2). Offered proper sacrifice (Ge 4:4; Heb 11:4). Murdered by Cain (Ge 4:8; Mt 23:35; Lk 11:51; 1Jn 3:12).

ABHORS

Pr   11: 1 The LORD *a* dishonest scales,

ABIGAIL

Wife of Nabal (1Sa 25:30); pled for his life with David (1Sa 25:14-35). Became David's wife (1Sa 25:36-42).

ABIJAH

Son of Rehoboam; king of Judah (1Ki 14:31-15:8; 2Ch 12:16-14:1).

ABILITY (ABLE)

Ezr   2:69 According to their *a* they gave
2Co   1: 8 far beyond our *a* to endure,
       8: 3 were able, and even beyond their *a*.

ABIMELECH

1. King of Gerar who took Abraham's wife Sarah, believing her to be his sister (Ge 20). Later made a covenant with Abraham (Ge 21:22-33).

2. King of Gerar who took Isaac's wife Rebekah, believing her to be his sister (Ge 26:1-11). Later made a covenant with Isaac (Ge 26:12-31).

ABLE (ABILITY ENABLE ENABLED ENABLES)

Eze   7:19 and gold will not be *a* to save them
Da   3:17 the God we serve is *a* to save us
Ro   8:39 will be *a* to separate us
       14: 4 for the Lord is *a* to make him stand
       16:25 to him who is *a* to establish you
2Co   9: 8 God is *a* to make all grace abound
Eph   3:20 him who is *a* to do immeasurably
2Ti   1:12 and am convinced that he is *a*
       3:15 which are *a* to make you wise
Heb   7:25 he is *a* to save completely
Jude   :24 To him who is *a* to keep you
Rev   5: 5 He is *a* to open the scroll

ABOLISH

Mt   5:17 that I have come to *a* the Law

ABOMINATION

Da   11:31 set up the *a* that causes desolation.

ABOUND (ABOUNDING)

2Co   9: 8 able to make all grace *a* to you,
Php   1: 9 that your love may *a* more

ABOUNDING (ABOUND)

Ex   34: 6 slow to anger, *a* in love
Ps   86: 5 *a* in love to all who call to you.

ABRAHAM

Covenant relation with the LORD (Ge 12:1-3; 13:14-17; 15; 17; 22:15-18; Ex 2:24; Ne 9:8; Ps 105; Mic 7:20; Lk 1:68-75; Ro 4; Heb 6:13-15).

Called from Ur, via Haran, to Canaan (Ge 12:1; Ac 7:2-4; Heb 11:8-10). Moved to Egypt, nearly lost Sarah to Pharaoh (Ge 12:10-20). Divided the land with Lot (Ge 13). Saved Lot from four kings (Ge 14:1-16); blessed by Melchizedek (Ge 14:17-20; Heb 7:1-20). Declared righteous by faith (Ge 15:6; Ro 4:3; Gal 3:6-9). Fathered Ishmael by Hagar (Ge 16).

Name changed from Abram (Ge 17:5; Ne 9:7). Circumcised (Ge 17; Ro 4:9-12). Entertained three visitors (Ge 18); promised a son by Sarah (Ge 18:9-15; 17:16). Moved to Gerar; nearly lost Sarah to Abimelech (Ge 20). Fathered Isaac by Sarah (Ge 21:1-7; Ac 7:8; Heb 11:11-12); sent away Hagar and Ishmael (Ge 21:8-21; Gal 4:22-30). Tested by offering Isaac (Ge 22; Heb 11:17-19; Jas 2:21-24). Sarah died; bought field of Ephron for burial (Ge 23). Secured wife for Isaac (Ge 24). Death (Ge 25:7-11).

ABSALOM

Son of David by Maacah (2Sa 3:3; 1Ch 3:2). Killed Amnon for rape of his sister Tamar; banished by David (2Sa 13). Returned to Jerusalem; received by David (2Sa 14). Rebelled against David; seized kingdom (2Sa 15-17). Killed (2Sa 18).

ABSTAIN (ABSTAINS)

1Pe   2:11 to *a* from sinful desires,

ABSTAINS* (ABSTAIN)

Ro   14: 6 thanks to God; and he who *a*,

ABUNDANCE (ABUNDANT)

Lk   12:15 consist in the *a* of his possessions."
Jude   : 2 peace and love be yours in *a*.

ABUNDANT (ABUNDANCE)

Dt   28:11 will grant you *a* prosperity—
Ps145: 7 will celebrate your *a* goodness
Pr   28:19 works his land will have *a* food,
Ro   5:17 who receive God's *a* provision

ACCEPT (ACCEPTED ACCEPTS)

Ex   23: 8 "Do not *a* a bribe,
Pr   10: 8 The wise in heart *a* commands,
       19:20 Listen to advice and *a* instruction,
Ro   15: 7 *A* one another, then, just
Jas   1:21 humbly *a* the word planted in you,

ACCEPTED (ACCEPT)

Lk   4:24 "no prophet is *a* in his hometown.

ACCEPTS (ACCEPT)
Ps   6: 9 the LORD *a* my prayer.
Jn 13:20 whoever *a* anyone I send *a* me;

ACCOMPANY
Mk 16:17 these signs will *a* those who believe
Heb   6: 9 your case—things that *a* salvation.

ACCOMPLISH
Isa 55:11 but will *a* what I desire

ACCORD
Nu 24:13 not do anything of my own *a*,
Jn 10:18 but I lay it down of my own *a*.
     12:49 For I did not speak of my own *a*,

ACCOUNT (ACCOUNTABLE)
Mt 12:36 to give *a* on the day of judgment
Ro 14:12 each of us will give an *a* of himself
Heb   4:13 of him to whom we must give *a*.

ACCOUNTABLE (ACCOUNT)
Eze 33: 6 but I will hold the watchman *a*
Ro   3:19 and the whole world held *a* to God.

ACCUSATION (ACCUSE)
1Ti   5:19 Do not entertain an *a*

ACCUSATIONS (ACCUSE)
2Pe   2:11 do not bring slanderous *a*

ACCUSE (ACCUSATION ACCUSATIONS)
Pr   3:30 Do not *a* a man for no reason—
Lk   3:14 and don't *a* people falsely—

ACHAN*
Sin at Jericho caused defeat at Ai; stoned (Jos 7; 22:20; 1Ch 2:7).

ACHE*
Pr 14:13 Even in laughter the heart may *a*,

ACKNOWLEDGE
Mt 10:32 *a* him before my Father in heaven.
1Jn   4: 3 spirit that does not *a* Jesus is not

ACQUIT
Ex 23: 7 to death, for I will not *a* the guilty.

ACTION (ACTIONS ACTIVE ACTS)
Jas   2:17 if it is not accompanied by *a*,
1Pe   1:13 minds for *a*; be self-controlled;

ACTIONS (ACTION)
Mt 11:19 wisdom is proved right by her *a*.''
Gal   6: 4 Each one should test his own *a*.
Tit   1:16 but by their *a* they deny him.

ACTIVE (ACTION)
Heb   4:12 For the word of God is living and *a*

ACTS (ACTION)
Ps 145: 12 all men may know of your mighty *a*
     150: 2 Praise him for his *a* of power;
Isa 64: 6 all our righteous *a* are like filthy
Mt   6: 1 not to do your '*a* of righteousness'

ADAM
First man (Ge 1:26-2:25; Ro 5:14; 1Ti 2:13).

Sin of (Ge 3; Hos 6:7; Ro 5:12-21). Children of (Ge 4:1-5:5). Death of (Ge 5:5; Ro 5:12-21; 1Co 15:22).

ADD
Dt 12:32 do not *a* to it or take away from it.
Pr 30: 6 Do not *a* to his words,
Lk 12:25 by worrying can *a* a single hour
Rev 22:18 God will *a* to him the plagues

ADMIRABLE*
Php   4: 8 whatever is lovely, whatever is *a*—

ADMONISH
Col   3:16 and *a* one another with all wisdom,

ADOPTED (ADOPTION)
Eph   1: 5 In love he predestined us to be *a*

ADOPTION (ADOPTED)
Ro   8:23 as we wait eagerly for our *a* as sons,

ADORE*
SS   1: 4 How right they are to *a* you!

ADORNMENT* (ADORNS)
1Pe   3: 3 should not come from outward *a*,

ADORNS (ADORNMENT)
Ps 93: 5 holiness *a* your house

ADULTERY
Ex 20:14 ''You shall not commit *a*.
Mt   5:27 that it was said, 'Do not commit *a*.'
      5:28 lustfully has already committed *a*
      5:32 the divorced woman commits *a*.
     15:19 murder, *a*, sexual immorality, theft

ADULTS*
1Co 14:20 but in your thinking be *a*.

ADVANCED
Job 32: 7 *a* years should teach wisdom.'

ADVANTAGE
Ex 22:22 ''Do not take *a* of a widow
Dt 24:14 Do not take *a* of a hired man who is
1Th   4: 6 should wrong his brother or take *a*

ADVERSITY
Pr 17:17 and a brother is born for *a*.

ADVICE
1Ki 12: 8 rejected the *a* the elders
     12:14 he followed the *a* of the young men
Pr 12: 5 but the *a* of the wicked is deceitful.
     12:15 but a wise man listens to *a*.
     19:20 Listen to *a* and accept instruction,
     20:18 Make plans by seeking *a*;

AFFLICTION
Ro 12:12 patient in *a*, faithful in prayer.

AFRAID (FEAR)
Ge 26:24 Do not be *a*, for I am with you;
Ex   3: 6 because he was *a* to look at God.
Ps 27: 1 of whom shall I be *a*?
     56: 3 When I am *a*, / I will trust in you.
Pr   3:24 lie down, you will not be *a*;
Jer   1: 8 Do not be *a* of them, for I am

Mt 8:26 You of little faith, why are you so *a*
   10:28 be *a* of the One who can destroy
   10:31 So don't be *a;* you are worth more
Mk 5:36 "Don't be *a;* just believe."
Jn 14:27 hearts be troubled and do not be *a.*
Heb 13: 6 Lord is my helper; I will not be *a.*

AGED

Job 12:12 Is not wisdom found among the *a?*
Pr 17: 6 children are a crown to the *a,*

AGREE

Mt 18:19 on earth *a* about anything you ask
Ro 7:16 want to do, I *a* that the law is good.
Php 4: 2 with Syntyche to *a* with each other

AHAB

Son of Omri; king of Israel (1Ki 16:28-22:40), husband of Jezebel (1Ki 16:31). Promoted Baal worship (1Ki 16:31-33); opposed by Elijah (1Ki 17:1; 18; 21), a prophet (1Ki 20:35-43), Micaiah (1Ki 22:1-28). Defeated Ben-Hadad (1Ki 20). Killed for failing to kill Ben-Hadad and for murder of Naboth (1Ki 20:35-21:40).

AHAZ

Son of Jotham; king of Judah, (2Ki 16; 2Ch 28; Isa 7).

AHAZIAH

1. Son of Ahab; king of Israel (1Ki 22:51-2Ki 1:18; 2Ch 20:35-37).
2. Son of Jehoram; king of Judah (2Ki 8:25-29; 9:14-29), also called Jehoahaz (2Ch 21:17-22:9; 25:23).

AIM

1Co 7:34 Her *a* is to be devoted to the Lord
2Co 13:11 *A* for perfection, listen

AIR

Mt 8:20 and birds of the *a* have nests,
1Co 9:26 not fight like a man beating the *a.*
Eph 2: 2 of the ruler of the kingdom of the *a,*
1Th 4:17 clouds to meet the Lord in the *a.*

ALABASTER

Mt 26: 7 came to him with an *a* jar

ALERT

Jos 8: 4 All of you be on the *a.*
Mk 13:33 Be *a!* You do not know
Eph 6:18 be *a* and always keep on praying
1Th 5: 6 but let us be *a* and self-controlled.

ALIEN (ALIENATED)

Ex 22:21 "Do not mistreat an *a*

ALIENATED (ALIEN)

Gal 5: 4 by law have been *a* from Christ;

ALIVE (LIVE)

Ac 1: 3 convincing proofs that he was *a.*
Ro 6:11 but *a* to God in Christ Jesus.
1Co 15:22 so in Christ all will be made *a.*

ALMIGHTY (MIGHT)

Ge 17: 1 "I am God *A;* walk before me

Job 11: 7 Can you probe the limits of the *A?*
   33: 4 the breath of the *A* gives me life.
Ps 91: 1 will rest in the shadow of the *A.*
Isa 6: 3 "Holy, holy, holy is the LORD *A;*

ALTAR

Ge 22: 9 his son Isaac and laid him on the *a,*
Ex 27: 1 "Build an *a* of acacia wood,
1Ki 18:30 and he repaired the *a* of the LORD
2Ch 4: 1 made a bronze *a* twenty cubits
   4:19 the golden *a;* the tables

ALWAYS

Ps 16: 8 I have set the LORD *a* before me.
   51: 3 and my sin is *a* before me.
Mt 26:11 The poor you will *a* have with you,
   28:20 And surely I will be with you *a,*
1Co 13: 7 *a* protects, *a* trusts, *a* hopes, *a*
Php 4: 4 Rejoice in the Lord *a.*
1Pe 3:15 *A* be prepared to give an answer

AMAZIAH

Son of Joash; king of Judah (2Ki 14; 2Ch 25).

AMBASSADORS

2Co 5:20 We are therefore Christ's *a,*

AMBITION

Ro 15:20 It has always been my *a*
1Th 4:11 Make it your *a* to lead a quiet life,

AMON

Son of Manasseh; king of Judah (2Ki 21:18-26; 1Ch 3:14; 2Ch 33:21-25).

ANANIAS

1. Husband of Sapphira; died for lying to God (Ac 5:1-11).
2. Disciple who baptized Saul (Ac 9:10-19).
3. High priest at Paul's arrest (Ac 22:30-24:1).

ANCHOR

Heb 6:19 We have this hope as an *a*

ANCIENT

Da 7: 9 and the *A* of Days took his seat.

ANDREW*

Apostle; brother of Simon Peter (Mt 4:18; 10: 2; Mk 1:16-18, 29; 3:18; 13:3; Lk 6:14; Jn 1: 35-44; 6:8-9; 12:22; Ac 1:13).

ANGEL (ANGELS ARCHANGEL)

Ps 34: 7 The *a* of the LORD encamps
Ac 6:15 his face was like the face of an *a.*
2Co 11:14 Satan himself masquerades as an *a*
Gal 1: 8 or an *a* from heaven should preach

ANGELS (ANGEL)

Ps 91:11 command his *a* concerning you
Mt 18:10 For I tell you that their *a*
   25:41 prepared for the devil and his *a.*
Lk 20:36 for they are like the *a.*
1Co 6: 3 you not know that we will judge *a?*
Heb 1: 4 as much superior to the *a*
   1:14 Are not all *a* ministering spirits
   2: 7 made him a little lower than the *a;*
   13: 2 some people have entertained *a*

1Pe 1:12 Even *a* long to look
2Pe 2: 4 For if God did not spare *a*

ANGER (ANGERED ANGRY)

Ex 32:10 alone so that my *a* may burn
34: 6 slow to *a*, abounding in love
Dt 29:28 In furious *a* and in great wrath
2Ki 22:13 Great is the LORD's *a* that burns
Ps 30: 5 For his *a* lasts only a moment,
Pr 15: 1 but a harsh word stirs up *a*.
29:11 A fool gives full vent to his *a*,

ANGERED (ANGER)

Pr 22:24 do not associate with one easily *a*,
1Co 13: 5 it is not easily *a*, it keeps no record

ANGRY (ANGER)

Ps 2:12 Kiss the Son, lest he be *a*
Pr 29:22 An *a* man stirs up dissension,
Jas 1:19 slow to speak and slow to become *a*

ANGUISH

Ps118: 5 In my *a* I cried to the LORD,

ANOINT

Ps 23: 5 You *a* my head with oil;
Jas 5:14 and *a* him with oil in the name

ANT*

Pr 6: 6 Go to the *a*, you sluggard;

ANTICHRIST

1Jn 2:18 have heard that the *a* is coming,
2Jn : 7 person is the deceiver and the *a*.

ANTIOCH

Ac 11:26 were called Christians first at *A*.

ANXIETY (ANXIOUS)

1Pe 5: 7 Cast all your *a* on him

ANXIOUS (ANXIETY)

Pr 12:25 An *a* heart weighs a man down,
Php 4: 6 Do not be *a* about anything,

APOLLOS*

Christian from Alexandria, learned in the Scriptures; instructed by Aquila and Priscilla (Ac 18:24-28). Ministered at Corinth (Ac 19:1; 1Co 1:12; 3; Tit 3:13).

APOSTLES

See also Andrew, Bartholomew, James, John, Judas, Matthew, Nathanael, Paul, Peter, Philip, Simon, Thaddaeus, Thomas.
Mk 3:14 twelve—designating them *a*—
Ac 1:26 so he was added to the eleven *a*.
2:43 signs were done by the *a*.
1Co 12:28 God has appointed first of all *a*,
15: 9 For I am the least of the *a*
2Co 11:13 masquerading as *a* of Christ.
Eph 2:20 built on the foundation of the *a*

APPEAR (APPEARANCE APPEARING)

Mk 13:22 false prophets will *a* and perform
2Co 5:10 we must all *a* before the judgment
Col 3: 4 also will *a* with him in glory.
Heb 9:24 now to *a* for us in God's presence.

Heb 9:28 and he will *a* a second time,

APPEARANCE (APPEAR)

1Sa 16: 7 Man looks at the outward *a*,
Gal 2: 6 God does not judge by external *a*—

APPEARING (APPEAR)

2Ti 4: 8 to all who have longed for his *a*.
Tit 2:13 the glorious *a* of our great God

APPLY

Pr 22:17 *a* your heart to what I teach,
23:12 *A* your heart to instruction

APPROACH

Eph 3:12 in him we may *a* God with freedom
Heb 4:16 Let us then *a* the throne of grace

APPROVED

2Ti 2:15 to present yourself to God as one *a*,

AQUILA*

Husband of Priscilla; co-worker with Paul, instructor of Apollos (Ac 18; Ro 16:3; 1Co 16:19; 2Ti 4:19).

ARARAT

Ge 8: 4 came to rest on the mountains of *A*.

ARCHANGEL* (ANGEL)

1Th 4:16 with the voice of the *a*
Jude : 9 *a* Michael, when he was disputing

ARCHITECT*

Heb 11:10 whose *a* and builder is God.

ARK

Ge 6:14 So make yourself an *a*
Dt 10: 5 put the tablets in the *a* I had made,
2Ch 35: 3 "Put the sacred *a* in the temple that
Heb 9: 4 This *a* contained the gold jar

ARM (ARMY)

Nu 11:23 "Is the LORD's *a* too short?
1Pe 4: 1 *a* yourselves also with the same

ARMAGEDDON*

Rev 16:16 that in Hebrew is called *A*.

ARMOR (ARMY)

1Ki 20:11 on his *a* should not boast like one
Eph 6:11 Put on the full *a* of God
6:13 Therefore put on the full *a* of God,

ARMS (ARMY)

Dt 33:27 underneath are the everlasting *a*.
Ps 18:32 It is God who *a* me with strength
Pr 31:20 She opens her *a* to the poor
Isa 40:11 He gathers the lambs in his *a*
Mk 10:16 And he took the children in his *a*,

ARMY (ARM ARMOR ARMS)

Ps 33:16 No king is saved by the size of his *a*
Rev 19:19 the rider on the horse and his *a*.

AROMA

2Co 2:15 For we are to God the *a* of Christ

ARRAYED*

Ps110: 3 *A* in holy majesty,
Isa 61:10 and *a* me in a robe of righteousness

ARROGANT
Ro 11:20 Do not be *a*, but be afraid.

ARROWS
Eph 6:16 you can extinguish all the flaming *a*

ASA
King of Judah (1Ki 15:8-24; 1Ch 3:10; 2Ch 14-16).

ASCENDED
Eph 4: 8 "When he *a* on high,

ASCRIBE
1Ch 16:28 *a* to the LORD glory and strength,
Job 36: 3 I will *a* justice to my Maker.
Ps 29: 2 *A* to the LORD the glory due his

ASHAMED (SHAME)
Lk 9:26 If anyone is *a* of me and my words,
Ro 1:16 I am not *a* of the gospel,
2Ti 1: 8 So do not be *a* to testify about our
2:15 who does not need to be *a*

ASSIGNED
Mk 13:34 with his *a* task, and tells the one
1Co 3: 5 as the Lord has *a* to each his task.
7:17 place in life that the Lord *a* to him

ASSOCIATE
Pr 22:24 do not *a* with one easily angered,
Ro 12:16 but be willing to *a* with people
1Co 5:11 am writing you that you must not *a*
2Th 3:14 Do not *a* with him,

ASSURANCE
Heb 10:22 with a sincere heart in full *a* of faith

ASTRAY
Pr 10:17 ignores correction leads others *a*.
Isa 53: 6 We all, like sheep, have gone *a*,
Jer 50: 6 their shepherds have led them *a*
Jn 16: 1 you so that you will not go *a*.
1Pe 2:25 For you were like sheep going *a*,
1Jn 3: 7 do not let anyone lead you *a*.

ATHALIAH
Evil queen of Judah (2Ki 11; 2Ch 23).

ATHLETE*
2Ti 2: 5 if anyone competes as an *a*,

ATONEMENT
Ex 25:17 "Make an *a* cover of pure gold—
30:10 Once a year Aaron shall make *a*
Lev 17:11 it is the blood that makes *a*
23:27 this seventh month is the Day of *A*.
Nu 25:13 and made *a* for the Israelites."
Ro 3:25 presented him as a sacrifice of *a*,
Heb 2:17 that he might make *a* for the sins

ATTENTION
Pr 4: 1 pay *a* and gain understanding.
5: 1 My son, pay *a* to my wisdom,
22:17 Pay *a* and listen to the sayings
Tit 1:14 and will pay no *a* to Jewish myths

ATTITUDE (ATTITUDES)
Eph 4:23 new in the *a* of your minds;

ATTITUDES (ATTITUDE)
Php 2: 5 Your *a* should be the same
1Pe 4: 1 yourselves also with the same *a*,

ATTITUDES (ATTITUDE)
Heb 4:12 it judges the thoughts and *a*

ATTRACTIVE
Tit 2:10 teaching about God our Savior *a*.

AUTHORITIES (AUTHORITY)
Ro 13: 5 it is necessary to submit to the *a*,
13: 6 for the *a* are God's servants,
Tit 3: 1 people to be subject to rulers and *a*,
1Pe 3:22 *a* and powers in submission to him.

AUTHORITY (AUTHORITIES)
Mt 7:29 because he taught as one who had *a*
9: 6 the Son of Man has *a* on earth
28:18 "All *a* in heaven and on earth has
Ro 13: 1 for there is no *a* except that which
13: 2 rebels against the *a* is rebelling
1Co 11:10 to have a sign of *a* on her head.
1Ti 2: 2 for kings and all those in *a*,
2:12 to teach or to have *a* over a man;
Heb 13:17 your leaders and submit to their *a*.

AVENGE (VENGEANCE)
Dt 32:35 It is mine to *a*; I will repay.

AVOID
Pr 20: 3 It is to a man's honor to *a* strife,
20:19 so *a* a man who talks too much.
1Th 4: 3 you should *a* sexual immorality;
5:22 *A* every kind of evil.
2Ti 2:16 *A* godless chatter, because those
Tit 3: 9 But *a* foolish controversies

AWAKE
Ps 17:15 when I *a*, I will be satisfied

AWE (AWESOME)
Job 25: 2 "Dominion and *a* belong to God;
Ps 119:120 I stand in *a* of your laws.
Ecc 5: 7 Therefore stand in *a* of God.
Isa 29:23 will stand in *a* of the God of Israel.
Jer 33: 9 they will be in *a* and will tremble
Hab 3: 2 I stand in *a* of your deeds,
Mal 2: 5 and stood in *a* of my name.
Mt 9: 8 They were filled with *a*;
Lk 7:16 They were all filled with *a*
Ac 2:43 Everyone was filled with *a*,
Heb 12:28 acceptably with reverence and *a*,

AWESOME (AWE)
Ge 28:17 and said, "How *a* is this place!
Ex 15:11 *a* in glory,
Dt 7:21 is among you, is a great and *a* God.
10:17 the great God, mighty and *a*,
28:58 revere this glorious and *a* name—
Jdg 13: 6 like an angel of God, very *a*.
Ne 1: 5 of heaven, the great and *a* God,
9:32 the great, mighty and *a* God,
Job 10:16 again display your *a* power
37:22 God comes in *a* majesty.
Ps 45: 4 let your right hand display *a* deeds.
47: 2 How *a* is the LORD Most High,

Ps 66: 5 how *a* his works in man's behalf!
68:35 You are *a*, O God,
89: 7 he is more *a* than all who surround
99: 3 praise your great and *a* name—
111: 9 holy and *a* is his name.
145: 6 of the power of your *a* works,
Da 9: 4 "O Lord, the great and *a* God,

BAAL
1Ki 18:25 Elijah said to the prophets of *B*,

BAASHA
King of Israel (1Ki 15:16-16:7; 2Ch 16:1-6).

BABIES (BABY)
Lk 18:15 also bringing *b* to Jesus
1Pe 2: 2 Like newborn *b*, crave pure

BABY (BABIES)
Isa 49:15 "Can a mother forget the *b*
Lk 1:44 the *b* in my womb leaped for joy.
2:12 You will find a *b* wrapped in strips
Jn 16:21 but when her *b* is born she forgets

BABYLON
Ps 137: 1 By the rivers of *B* we sat and wept

BACKSLIDING
Jer 3:22 I will cure you of *b*."
14: 7 For our *b* is great;
Eze 37:23 them from all their sinful *b*,

BALAAM
Prophet who attempted to curse Israel (Nu 22-24; Dt 23:4-5; 2Pe 2:15; Jude 11). Killed (Nu 31:8; Jos 13:22).

BALM
Jer 8:22 Is there no *b* in Gilead?

BANISH
Jer 25:10 I will *b* from them the sounds of joy

BANQUET
SS 2: 4 He has taken me to the *b* hall,
Lk 14:13 when you give a *b*, invite the poor,

BAPTIZE (BAPTIZED)
Mt 3:11 He will *b* you with the Holy Spirit
Mk 1: 8 he will *b* you with the Holy Spirit."
1Co 1:17 For Christ did not send me to *b*,

BAPTIZED (BAPTIZE)
Mt 3: 6 they were *b* by him in the Jordan
Mk 1: 9 and was *b* by John in the Jordan.
10:38 or be *b* with the baptism I am
16:16 believes and is *b* will be saved,
Jn 4: 2 in fact it was not Jesus who *b*,
Ac 1: 5 but in a few days you will be *b*

BARABBAS
Mt 27:26 Then he released *B* to them.

BARBS*
Nu 33:55 allow to remain will become *b*

BARE
Heb 4:13 and laid *b* before the eyes of him

BARNABAS*
Disciple, originally Joseph (Ac 4:36), prophet (Ac 13:1), apostle (Ac 14:14). Brought Paul to apostles (Ac 9:27), Antioch (Ac 11:22-29; Gal 2:1-13), on the first missionary journey (Ac 13-14). Together at Jerusalem Council, they separated over John Mark (Ac 15). Later co-workers (1Co 9:6; Col 4:10).

BARREN
Ps 113: 9 He settles the *b* woman

BARTHOLOMEW*
Apostle (Mt 10:3; Mk 3:18; Lk 6:14; Ac 1:13). Possibly also known as Nathanael (Jn 1:45-49; 21:2).

BATH
Jn 13:10 person who has had a *b* needs only

BATHSHEBA
Wife of Uriah who committed adultery with and became wife of David (2Sa 11), mother of Solomon (2Sa 12:24; 1Ki 1-2; 1Ch 3:5).

BATTLE
2Ch 20:15 For the *b* is not yours, but God's.
Ps 24: 8 the LORD mighty in *b*.
Ecc 9:11 or the *b* to the strong,

BEAR (BEARING BIRTH BIRTHRIGHT BORN FIRSTBORN NEWBORN)
Ge 4:13 punishment is more than I can *b*.
Ps 38: 4 like a burden too heavy to *b*.
Isa 53:11 and he will *b* their iniquities.
Da 7: 5 beast, which looked like a *b*.
Mt 7:18 A good tree cannot *b* bad fruit,
Jn 15: 2 branch that does *b* fruit he prunes
15:16 and appointed you to go and *b* fruit—
Ro 15: 1 ought to *b* with the failings
1Co 10:13 tempted beyond what you can *b*.
Col 3:13 *B* with each other and forgive

BEARING (BEAR)
Eph 4: 2 *b* with one another in love.
Col 1:10 *b* fruit in every good work,

BEAST
Rev 13:18 him calculate the number of the *b*,

BEAT (BEATING)
Isa 2: 4 They will *b* their swords
Joel 3:10 *B* your plowshares into swords
1Co 9:27 I *b* my body and make it my slave

BEATING (BEAT)
1Co 9:26 I do not fight like a man *b* the air.
1Pe 2:20 if you receive a *b* for doing wrong

BEAUTIFUL (BEAUTY)
Ge 6: 2 that the daughters of men were *b*,
12:11 "I know what a *b* woman you are.
12:14 saw that she was a very *b* woman.
24:16 The girl was very *b*, a virgin;
26: 7 of Rebekah, because she is *b*."
29:17 Rachel was lovely in form, and *b*.
Job 38:31 "Can you bind the *b* Pleiades?

Pr 11:22 is a *b* woman who shows no
Ecc 3:11 He has made everything *b*
Isa 4: 2 of the LORD will be *b*
52: 7 How *b* on the mountains
Eze 20: 6 and honey, the most *b* of all lands.
Zec 9:17 How attractive and *b* they will be!
Mt 23:27 which look *b* on the outside
26:10 She has done a *b* thing to me.
Ro 10:15 "How *b* are the feet
1Pe 3: 5 in God used to make themselves *b*.

BEAUTY (BEAUTIFUL)

Ps 27: 4 to gaze upon the *b* of the LORD
45:11 The king is enthralled by your *b;*
Pr 31:30 is deceptive, and *b* is fleeting;
Isa 33:17 Your eyes will see the king in his *b*
53: 2 He had no *b* or majesty
61: 3 to bestow on them a crown of *b*
Eze 28:12 full of wisdom and perfect in *b*.
1Pe 3: 4 the unfading *b* of a gentle

BED

Heb 13: 4 and the marriage *b* kept pure,

BEELZEBUB

Lk 11:15 "By *B*, the prince of demons,

BEER

Pr 20: 1 Wine is a mocker and *b* a brawler;

BEERSHEBA

Jdg 20: 1 all the Israelites from Dan to *B*

BEGINNING

Ge 1: 1 In the *b* God created the heavens
Ps 102: 25 In the *b* you laid the foundations
111: 10 of the LORD is the *b* of wisdom;
Pr 1: 7 of the LORD is the *b* of knowledge
Jn 1: 1 In the *b* was the Word,
1Jn 1: 1 That which was from the *b*,
Rev 21: 6 and the Omega, the *B* and the End.

BEHAVE

Ro 13:13 Let us *b* decently, as in the daytime

BELIEVE (BELIEVED BELIEVER BELIEVERS BELIEVES BELIEVING)

Mt 18: 6 one of these little ones who *b* in me
21:22 If you *b*, you will receive whatever
Mk 1:15 Repent and *b* the good news!"
9:24 "I do *b*; help me overcome my
16:17 signs will accompany those who *b:*
Lk 8:50 just *b*, and she will be healed."
24:25 to *b* all that the prophets have
Jn 1: 7 that through him all men might *b*.
3:18 does not *b* stands condemned
6:29 to *b* in the one he has sent."
10:38 you do not *b* me, *b* the miracles,
11:27 "I *b* that you are the Christ,
14:11 *B* me when I say that I am
16:30 This makes us *b* that you came
16:31 "You *b* at last!" Jesus answered.
17:21 that the world may *b* that you have
20:27 Stop doubting and *b*."
20:31 written that you may *b* that Jesus is
Ac 16:31 They replied, "*B* in the Lord Jesus,

Ac 24:14 I *b* everything that agrees
Ro 3:22 faith in Jesus Christ to all who *b*.
4:11 he is the father of all who *b*
10: 9 *b* in your heart that God raised him
10:14 And how can they *b* in the one
16:26 so that all nations might *b*
1Th 4:14 We *b* that Jesus died and rose again
2Th 2:11 delusion so that they will *b* the lie
1Ti 4:10 and especially of those who *b*.
Tit 1: 6 a man whose children *b*
Heb 11: 6 comes to him must *b* that he exists
Jas 2:19 Even the demons *b* that—
1Jn 4: 1 Dear friends, do not *b* every spirit,

BELIEVED (BELIEVE)

Ge 15: 6 Abram *b* the LORD, and he
Jnh 3: 5 The Ninevites *b* God.
Jn 1:12 to those who *b* in his name,
2:22 Then they *b* the Scripture
3:18 because he has not *b* in the name
20: 8 He saw and *b*.
20:29 who have not seen and yet have *b*."
Ac 13:48 were appointed for eternal life *b*.
Ro 4: 3 Scripture say? "Abraham *b* God,
10:14 call on the one they have not *b* in?
1Co 15: 2 Otherwise, you have *b* in vain.
Gal 3: 6 Consider Abraham: "He *b* God,
2Ti 1:12 because I know whom I have *b*,
Jas 2:23 that says, "Abraham *b* God,

BELIEVER (BELIEVE)

1Co 7:12 brother has a wife who is not a *b*
2Co 6:15 What does a *b* have in common

BELIEVERS (BELIEVE)

Ac 4:32 All the *b* were one in heart
5:12 And all the *b* used to meet together
1Co 6: 5 to judge a dispute between *b*?
1Ti 4:12 set an example for the *b* in speech,
1Pe 2:17 Love the brotherhood of *b*,

BELIEVES (BELIEVE)

Pr 14:15 A simple man *b* anything,
Mk 9:23 is possible for him who *b*."
11:23 *b* that what he says will happen,
16:16 Whoever *b* and is baptized will be
Jn 3:16 that whoever *b* in him shall not
3:36 Whoever *b* in the Son has eternal
5:24 *b* him who sent me has eternal life
6:35 and he who *b* in me will never be
6:40 and *b* in him shall have eternal life,
6:47 he who *b* has everlasting life.
7:38 Whoever *b* in me, as the Scripture
11:26 and *b* in me will never die.
Ro 1:16 for the salvation of everyone who *b*
10: 4 righteousness for everyone who *b*.
1Jn 5: 1 Everyone who *b* that Jesus is
5: 5 Only he who *b* that Jesus is the Son

BELIEVING (BELIEVE)

Jn 20:31 and that by *b* you may have life

BELONG (BELONGS)

Dt 29:29 The secret things *b*
Job 25: 2 "Dominion and awe *b* to God;

Ps 47: 9 for the kings of the earth *b* to God;
95: 4 and the mountain peaks *b* to him.
Jn 8:44 You *b* to your father, the devil,
15:19 As it is, you do not *b* to the world,
Ro 1: 6 called to *b* to Jesus Christ.
7: 4 that you might *b* to another,
14: 8 we live or die, we *b* to the Lord.
Gal 5:24 Those who *b* to Christ Jesus have
1Th 5: 8 But since we *b* to the day, let us be

BELONGS (BELONG)
Job 41:11 Everything under heaven *b* to me.
Ps111: 10 To him *b* eternal praise.
Eze 18: 4 For every living soul *b* to me,
Jn 8:47 He who *b* to God hears what God
Ro 12: 5 each member *b* to all the others.

BELOVED (LOVE)
Dt 33:12 "Let the *b* of the LORD rest secure

BELT
Isa 11: 5 Righteousness will be his *b*
Eph 6:14 with the *b* of truth buckled

BENEFIT (BENEFITS)
Ro 6:22 the *b* you reap leads to holiness,
2Co 4:15 All this is for your *b*,

BENEFITS (BENEFIT)
Ps103: 2 and forget not all his *b*.
Jn 4:38 you have reaped the *b* of their labor

BENJAMIN
Twelfth son of Jacob by Rachel (Ge 35:16-24; 46:19-21; 1Ch 2:2). Jacob refused to send him to Egypt, but relented (Ge 42-45).

BEREANS*
Ac 17:11 the *B* were of more noble character

BESTOWS
Ps 84:11 the LORD *b* favor and honor;

BETHLEHEM
Mt 2: 1 After Jesus was born in *B* in Judea,

BETRAY
Pr 25: 9 do not *b* another man's confidence,

BIND (BINDS)
Dt 6: 8 and *b* them on your foreheads.
Pr 6:21 *B* them upon your heart forever;
Isa 61: 1 me to *b* up the brokenhearted,
Mt 16:19 whatever you *b* on earth will be

BINDS (BIND)
Ps147: 3 and *b* up their wounds.
Isa 30:26 when the LORD *b* up the bruises

BIRDS
Mt 8:20 and *b* of the air have nests,

BIRTH (BEAR)
Ps 58: 3 Even from *b* the wicked go astray;
Mt 1:18 This is how the *b* of Jesus Christ
1Pe 1: 3 great mercy he has given us new *b*

BIRTHRIGHT (BEAR)
Ge 25:34 So Esau despised his *b*.

BLAMELESS
Ge 17: 1 walk before me and be *b*.
Job 1: 1 This man was *b* and upright;
Ps 84:11 from those whose walk is *b*.
119: 1 Blessed are they whose ways are *b*,
Pr 19: 1 Better a poor man whose walk is *b*
1Co 1: 8 so that you will be *b* on the day
Eph 5:27 any other blemish, but holy and *b*.
Php 2:15 so that you may become *b* and pure
1Th 3:13 hearts so that you will be *b*
5:23 and body be kept *b* at the coming
Tit 1: 6 An elder must be *b*, the husband of
Heb 7:26 *b*, pure, set apart from sinners,
2Pe 3:14 effort to be found spotless, *b*

BLASPHEMES
Mk 3:29 whoever *b* against the Holy Spirit

BLEMISH
1Pe 1:19 a lamb without *b* or defect.

BLESS (BLESSED BLESSING BLESSINGS)
Ge 12: 3 I will *b* those who *b* you,
Ro 12:14 Bless those who persecute you; *b*

BLESSED (BLESS)
Ge 1:22 God *b* them and said, "Be fruitful
2: 3 And God *b* the seventh day
22:18 nations on earth will be *b*,
Ps 1: 1 *B* is the man
2:12 *B* are all who take refuge in him.
33:12 *B* is the nation whose God is
41: 1 *B* is he who has regard for the weak
84: 5 *B* are those whose strength is
106: 3 *B* are they who maintain justice,
112: 1 *B* is the man who fears the LORD,
118: 26 *B* is he who comes in the name
Pr 29:18 but *b* is he who keeps the law.
31:28 Her children arise and call her *b*;
Mt 5: 3 saying: "*B* are the poor in spirit,
5: 4 *B* are those who mourn,
5: 5 *B* are the meek,
5: 6 *B* are those who hunger
5: 7 *B* are the merciful,
5: 8 *B* are the pure in heart,
5: 9 *B* are the peacemakers,
5:10 *B* are those who are persecuted
5:11 "*B* are you when people insult you,
Lk 1:48 on all generations will call me *b*,
Jn 12:13 "*B* is he who comes in the name
Ac 20:35 'It is more *b* to give than to receive
Tit 2:13 while we wait for the *b* hope—
Jas 1:12 *B* is the man who perseveres
Rev 1: 3 *B* is the one who reads the words
22:14 "*B* are those who wash their robes,

BLESSING (BLESS)
Eze 34:26 there will be showers of *b*.

BLESSINGS (BLESS)
Pr 10: 6 *B* crown the head of the righteous,

BLIND
Mt 15:14 a *b* man leads a *b* man, both will fall

Mt	23:16	"Woe to you, *b* guides! You say,
Jn	9:25	I was *b* but now I see!''

BLOOD

Ge	9: 6	"Whoever sheds the *b* of man,
Ex	12:13	and when I see the *b*, I will pass
	24: 8	"This is the *b* of the covenant that
Lev	17:11	For the life of a creature is in the *b*,
Ps	72:14	for precious is their *b* in his sight.
Pr	6:17	hands that shed innocent *b*,
Mt	26:28	This is my *b* of the covenant,
Ro	3:25	of atonement, through faith in his *b*
	5: 9	have now been justified by his *b*,
1Co	11:25	cup is the new covenant in my *b*;
Eph	1: 7	we have redemption through his *b*,
	2:13	near through the *b* of Christ.
Col	1:20	by making peace through his *b*,
Heb	9:12	once for all by his own *b*,
	9:22	of *b* there is no forgiveness.
1Pe	1:19	but with the precious *b* of Christ,
1Jn	1: 7	and the *b* of Jesus, his Son,
Rev	1: 5	has freed us from our sins by his *b*,
	5: 9	with your *b* you purchased men
	7:14	white in the *b* of the Lamb.
	12:11	him by the *b* of the Lamb

BLOT (BLOTS)

Ex	32:32	then *b* me out of the book you have
Ps	51: 1	*b* out my transgressions.
Rev	3: 5	I will never *b* out his name

BLOTS (BLOT)

Isa	43:25	"I, even I, am he who *b* out

BLOWN

Eph	4:14	and *b* here and there by every wind
Jas	1: 6	doubts is like a wave of the sea, *b*

BOAST

1Ki	20:11	armor should not *b* like one who
Ps	34: 2	My soul will *b* in the LORD;
	44: 8	In God we make our *b* all day long,
Pr	27: 1	Do not *b* about tomorrow,
1Co	1:31	Let him who boasts *b* in the Lord.''
Gal	6:14	May I never *b* except in the cross
Eph	2: 9	not by works, so that no one can *b*.

BOAZ

Wealthy Bethlehemite who showed favor to Ruth (Ru 2), married her (Ru 4). Ancestor of David (Ru 4:18-22; 1Ch 2:12-15), Jesus (Mt 1: 5-16; Lk 3:23-32).

BODIES (BODY)

Ro	12: 1	to offer your *b* as living sacrifices,
1Co	6:15	not know that your *b* are members
Eph	5:28	to love their wives as their own *b*.

BODY (BODIES)

Zec	13: 6	What are these wounds on your *b*?'
Mt	10:28	afraid of those who kill the *b*
	26:26	saying, "Take and eat; this is my *b*
	26:41	spirit is willing, but the *b* is weak.''
Jn	13:10	wash his feet; his whole *b* is clean.
Ro	6:13	Do not offer the parts of your *b*
	12: 4	us has one *b* with many members,

1Co	6:19	not know that your *b* is a temple
	11:24	"This is my *b*, which is for you;
	12:12	The *b* is a unit, though it is made up
Eph	5:30	for we are members of his *b*.

BOLD (BOLDNESS)

Ps	138: 3	you made me *b* and stouthearted.
Pr	21:29	A wicked man puts up a *b* front,
	28: 1	but the righteous are as *b* as a lion.

BOLDNESS* (BOLD)

Ac	4:29	to speak your word with great *b*.

BONDAGE

Ezr	9: 9	God has not deserted us in our *b*.

BOOK (BOOKS)

Jos	1: 8	Do not let this *B* of the Law depart
Ne	8: 8	They read from the *B* of the Law
Jn	20:30	which are not recorded in this *b*.
Php	4: 3	whose names are in the *b* of life.
Rev	21:27	written in the Lamb's *b* of life.

BOOKS (BOOK)

Ecc	12:12	Of making many *b* there is no end,

BORN (BEAR)

Isa	9: 6	For to us a child is *b*,
Jn	3: 7	at my saying, 'You must be *b* again
1Pe	1:23	For you have been *b* again,
1Jn	4: 7	Everyone who loves has been *b*
	5: 1	believes that Jesus is the Christ is *b*

BORROWER

Pr	22: 7	and the *b* is servant to the lender.

BOUGHT

Ac	20:28	which he *b* with his own blood.
1Co	6:20	You are not your own; you were *b*
	7:23	You were *b* at a price; do not
2Pe	2: 1	the sovereign Lord who *b* them—

BOW

Ps	95: 6	Come, let us *b* down in worship,
Isa	45:23	Before me every knee will *b*;
Ro	14:11	'every knee will *b* before me;
Php	2:10	name of Jesus every knee should *b*,

BRANCH (BRANCHES)

Isa	4: 2	In that day the *B* of the LORD will
Jer	33:15	I will make a righteous *B* sprout

BRANCHES (BRANCH)

Jn	15: 5	"I am the vine; you are the *b*.

BRAVE

2Sa	2: 7	Now then, be strong and *b*,

BREAD

Dt	8: 3	that man does not live on *b* alone
Pr	30: 8	but give me only my daily *b*.
Ecc	11: 1	Cast your *b* upon the waters,
Isa	55: 2	Why spend money on what is not *b*
Mt	4: 4	'Man does not live on *b* alone,
	6:11	Give us today our daily *b*.
Jn	6:35	Jesus declared, "I am the *b* of life.
	21:13	took the *b* and gave it to them,
1Co	11:23	took *b*, and when he had given

BREAK (BREAKING BROKEN)

Nu 30: 2 he must not *b* his word
Jdg 2: 1 'I will never *b* my covenant
Isa 42: 3 A bruised reed he will not *b*,
Mt 12:20 A bruised reed he will not *b*,

BREAKING (BREAK)

Jas 2:10 at just one point is guilty of *b* all

BREASTPIECE (BREASTPLATE)

Ex 28:15 Fashion a *b* for making decisions—

BREASTPLATE* (BREASTPIECE)

Isa 59:17 He put on righteousness as his *b*,
Eph 6:14 with the *b* of righteousness in place
1Th 5: 8 putting on faith and love as a *b*,

BREATHED (GOD-BREATHED)

Ge 2: 7 *b* into his nostrils the breath of life,
Jn 20:22 And with that he *b* on them

BREEDS*

Pr 13:10 Pride only *b* quarrels,

BRIBE

Ex 23: 8 "Do not accept a *b*,
Pr 6:35 will refuse the *b*, however great it

BRIDE

Rev 19: 7 and his *b* has made herself ready,

BRIGHTER (BRIGHTNESS)

Pr 4:18 shining ever *b* till the full light

BRIGHTNESS (BRIGHTER)

2Sa 22:13 Out of the *b* of his presence
Da 12: 3 who are wise will shine like the *b*

BROAD

Mt 7:13 and *b* is the road that leads

BROKEN (BREAK)

Ps 51:17 The sacrifices of God are a *b* spirit;
Ecc 4:12 of three strands is not quickly *b*.
Jn 10:35 and the Scripture cannot be *b*—

BROKENHEARTED* (HEART)

Ps 34:18 The LORD is close to the *b*
109: 16 and the needy and the *b*.
147: 3 He heals the *b*
Isa 61: 1 He has sent me to bind up the *b*,

BROTHER (BROTHER'S BROTHERS)

Pr 17:17 and a *b* is born for adversity.
18:24 a friend who sticks closer than a *b*.
27:10 neighbor nearby than a *b* far away.
Mt 5:24 and be reconciled to your *b*;
18:15 "If your *b* sins against you,
Mk 3:35 Whoever does God's will is my *b*
Lk 17: 3 "If your *b* sins, rebuke him,
1Co 8:13 if what I eat causes my *b* to fall
1Jn 2:10 Whoever loves his *b* lives
4:21 loves God must also love his *b*.

BROTHER'S (BROTHER)

Ge 4: 9 "Am I my *b* keeper?" The LORD

BROTHERS (BROTHER)

Ps 133: 1 is when *b* live together in unity!

Pr 6:19 who stirs up dissension among *b*.
Mt 25:40 one of the least of these *b* of mine,
Mk 10:29 or *b* or sisters or mother or father
Heb 13: 1 Keep on loving each other as *b*.
1Pe 3: 8 be sympathetic, love as *b*,
1Jn 3:14 death to life, because we love our *b*.

BUILD (BUILDING BUILDS BUILT)

Mt 16:18 and on this rock I will *b* my church,
Ac 20:32 which can *b* you up and give you
1Co 14:12 excel in gifts that *b* up the church.
1Th 5:11 one another and *b* each other up,

BUILDING (BUILD)

1Co 3: 9 you are God's field, God's *b*.
2Co 10: 8 us for *b* you up rather
Eph 4:29 helpful for *b* others up according

BUILDS (BUILD)

Ps 127: 1 Unless the LORD *b* the house,
1Co 3:10 one should be careful how he *b*.
8: 1 Knowledge puffs up, but love *b* up.

BUILT (BUILD)

Mt 7:24 is like a wise man who *b* his house
Eph 2:20 *b* on the foundation of the apostles
4:12 the body of Christ may be *b* up

BURDEN (BURDENED BURDENS)

Ps 38: 4 like a *b* too heavy to bear.
Mt 11:30 my yoke is easy and my *b* is light."

BURDENED (BURDEN)

Gal 5: 1 do not let yourselves be *b* again

BURDENS (BURDEN)

Ps 68:19 who daily bears our *b*.
Gal 6: 2 Carry each other's *b*,

BURIED

Ro 6: 4 *b* with him through baptism
1Co 15: 4 that he was *b*, that he was raised

BURNING

Lev 6: 9 the fire must be kept *b* on the altar.
Ro 12:20 you will heap *b* coals on his head."

BUSINESS

Da 8:27 and went about the king's *b*.
1Th 4:11 to mind your own *b* and to work

BUSY

1Ki 20:40 While your servant was *b* here
2Th 3:11 They are not *b*; they are
Tit 2: 5 to be *b* at home, to be kind,

CAESAR

Mt 22:21 "Give to *C* what is Caesar's,

CAIN

Firstborn of Adam (Ge 4:1), murdered brother Abel (Ge 4:1-16; 1Jn 3:12).

CALEB

Judahite who spied out Canaan (Nu 13:6); allowed to enter land because of faith (Nu 13:30-14: 38; Dt 1:36). Possessed Hebron (Jos 14:6-15:19).

CALF
Ex 32: 4 into an idol cast in the shape of a *c,*
Lk 15:23 Bring the fattened *c* and kill it.

CALL (CALLED CALLING CALLS)
Ps 105: 1 to the LORD, *c* on his name;
  145: 18 near to all who *c* on him,
Pr 31:28 children arise and *c* her blessed;
Isa 5:20 Woe to those who *c* evil good
  55: 6 *c* on him while he is near.
  65:24 Before they *c* I will answer;
Jer 33: 3 *'C* to me and I will answer you
Mt 9:13 come to *c* the righteous,
Ro 10:12 and richly blesses all who *c* on him,
  11:29 gifts and his *c* are irrevocable.
1Th 4: 7 For God did not *c* us to be impure,

CALLED (CALL)
1Sa 3: 5 and said, "Here I am; you *c* me."
2Ch 7:14 if my people, who are *c*
Ps 34: 6 This poor man *c,* and the LORD
Mt 21:13 " 'My house will be *c* a house
Ro 8:30 And those he predestined, he also *c*
1Co 7:15 God has *c* us to live in peace.
Gal 5:13 You, my brothers, were *c* to be free
1Pe 2: 9 of him who *c* you out of darkness

CALLING (CALL)
Jn 1:23 I am the voice of one *c* in the desert
Ac 22:16 wash your sins away, *c* on his name
Eph 4: 1 worthy of the *c* you have received.
2Pe 1:10 all the more eager to make your *c*

CALLS (CALL)
Joel 2:32 And everyone who *c*
Jn 10: 3 He *c* his own sheep by name
Ro 10:13 "Everyone who *c* on the name

CAMEL
Mt 19:24 it is easier for a *c* to go
  23:24 strain out a gnat but swallow a *c.*

CANAAN
1Ch 16:18 "To you I will give the land of *C*

CANCELED
Lk 7:42 so he *c* the debts of both.
Col 2:14 having *c* the written code,

CAPITAL
Dt 21:22 guilty of a *c* offense is put to death

CAPSTONE (STONE)
Ps 118: 22 has become the *c;*
1Pe 2: 7 has become the *c,"*

CARE (CAREFUL CARES CARING)
Ps 8: 4 the son of man that you *c* for him?
Pr 29: 7 The righteous *c* about justice
Lk 10:34 him to an inn and took *c* of him.
Jn 21:16 Jesus said, "Take *c* of my sheep."
Heb 2: 6 the son of man that you *c* for him?
1Pe 5: 2 of God's flock that is under your *c,*

CAREFUL (CARE)
Ex 23:13 "Be *c* to do everything I have said
Dt 6: 3 be *c* to obey so that it may go well

CEASE
Jos 23: 6 be *c* to obey all that is written
  23:11 be very *c* to love the LORD your
Pr 13:24 he who loves him is *c*
Mt 6: 1 "Be *c* not to do your 'acts
Ro 12:17 Be *c* to do what is right in the eyes
1Co 3:10 each one should be *c* how he builds
  8: 9 Be *c,* however, that the exercise
Eph 5:15 Be very *c,* then, how you live—

CARELESS
Mt 12:36 for every *c* word they have spoken.

CARES (CARE)
Ps 55:22 Cast your *c* on the LORD
Na 1: 7 He *c* for those who trust in him,
Eph 5:29 but he feeds and *c* for it, just
1Pe 5: 7 on him because he *c* for you.

CARING* (CARE)
1Th 2: 7 like a mother *c* for her little
1Ti 5: 4 practice by *c* for their own family

CARRIED (CARRY)
Ex 19: 4 and how I *c* you on eagles' wings
Isa 53: 4 and *c* our sorrows,
Heb 13: 9 Do not be *c* away by all kinds
2Pe 1:21 as they were *c* along by the Holy

CARRIES (CARRY)
Dt 32:11 and *c* them on its pinions.
Isa 40:11 and *c* them close to his heart;

CARRY (CARRIED CARRIES)
Lk 14:27 anyone who does not *c* his cross
Gal 6: 2 *C* each other's burdens,
  6: 5 for each one should *c* his own load.

CAST
Ps 22:18 and *c* lots for my clothing.
  55:22 *C* your cares on the LORD
Ecc 11: 1 *C* your bread upon the waters,
Jn 19:24 and *c* lots for my clothing."
1Pe 5: 7 *C* all your anxiety on him

CATCH (CAUGHT)
Lk 5:10 from now on you will *c* men."

CATTLE
Ps 50:10 and the *c* on a thousand hills.

CAUGHT (CATCH)
1Th 4:17 and are left will be *c* up together

CAUSE (CAUSES)
Pr 24:28 against your neighbor without *c,*
Ecc 8: 3 Do not stand up for a bad *c,*
Mt 18: 7 of the things that *c* people to sin!
Ro 14:21 else that will *c* your brother
1Co 10:32 Do not *c* anyone to stumble,

CAUSES (CAUSE)
Isa 8:14 a stone that *c* men to stumble
Mt 18: 6 if anyone *c* one of these little ones

CAUTIOUS*
Pr 12:26 A righteous man is *c* in friendship,

CEASE
Ps 46: 9 He makes wars *c* to the ends

CENSER

Lev 16:12 is to take a *c* full of burning coals

CENTURION

Mt 8: 5 had entered Capernaum, a *c* came

CERTAIN (CERTAINTY)

2Pe 1:19 word of the prophets made more *c*,

CERTAINTY* (CERTAIN)

Lk 1: 4 so that you may know the *c*
Jn 17: 8 They knew with *c* that I came

CHAFF

Ps 1: 4 They are like *c*

CHAINED

2Ti 2: 9 But God's word is not *c*.

CHAMPION

Ps 19: 5 like a *c* rejoicing to run his course.

CHANGE (CHANGED)

1Sa 15:29 of Israel does not lie or *c* his mind;
Ps 110: 4 and will not *c* his mind:
Jer 7: 5 If you really *c* your ways
Mal 3: 6 "I the LORD do not *c*.
Mt 18: 3 unless you *c* and become like little
Heb 7:21 and will not *c* his mind:
Jas 1:17 who does not *c* like shifting

CHANGED (CHANGE)

1Co 15:51 but we will all be *c*—in a flash,

CHARACTER

Ru 3:11 that you are a woman of noble *c*.
Pr 31:10 A wife of noble *c* who can find?
Ro 5: 4 perseverance, *c*; and *c*, hope.
1Co 15:33 "Bad company corrupts good *c*."

CHARGE

Ro 8:33 Who will bring any *c*
2Co 11: 7 the gospel of God to you free of *c?*
2Ti 4: 1 I give you this *c*: Preach the Word;

CHARIOTS

2Ki 6:17 and *c* of fire all around Elisha
Ps 20: 7 Some trust in *c* and some in horses,

CHARM

Pr 31:30 *C* is deceptive, and beauty is

CHASES

Pr 12:11 he who *c* fantasies lacks judgment.

CHATTER* (CHATTERING)

1Ti 6:20 Turn away from godless *c*
2Ti 2:16 Avoid godless *c*, because those

CHATTERING* (CHATTER)

Pr 10: 8 but a *c* fool comes to ruin.
10:10 and a *c* fool comes to ruin.

CHEAT* (CHEATED)

Mal 1:14 "Cursed is the *c* who has
1Co 6: 8 you yourselves *c* and do wrong,

CHEATED (CHEAT)

Lk 19: 8 if I have *c* anybody out of anything,
1Co 6: 7 Why not rather be *c*? Instead,

CHEEK

Mt 5:39 someone strikes you on the right *c*,

CHEERFUL* (CHEERS)

Pr 15:13 A happy heart makes the face *c*,
15:15 but the *c* heart has a continual feast
15:30 A *c* look brings joy to the heart,
17:22 A *c* heart is good medicine,
2Co 9: 7 for God loves a *c* giver.

CHEERS (CHEERFUL)

Pr 12:25 but a kind word *c* him up.

CHILD (CHILDISH CHILDREN)

Pr 20:11 Even a *c* is known by his actions,
22: 6 Train a *c* in the way he should go,
22:15 Folly is bound up in the heart of a *c*
23:13 not withhold discipline from a *c;*
29:15 *c* left to himself disgraces his mother.
Isa 7:14 The virgin will be with *c*
9: 6 For to us a *c* is born,
11: 6 and a little *c* will lead them.
66:13 As a mother comforts her *c*,
Mt 1:23 "The virgin will be with *c*
18: 2 He called a little *c* and had him
Lk 1:42 and blessed is the *c* you will bear!
1:80 And the *c* grew and became strong
1Co 13:11 When I was a *c*, I talked like a *c*,
1Jn 5: 1 who loves the father loves his *c*

CHILDISH* (CHILD)

1Co 13:11 When I became a man, I put *c* ways

CHILDREN (CHILD)

Dt 4: 9 Teach them to your *c*
11:19 them to your *c*, talking about them
Ps 8: 2 From the lips of *c* and infants
Pr 17: 6 Children's *c* are a crown
31:28 Her *c* arise and call her blessed;
Mt 7:11 how to give good gifts to your *c*,
11:25 and revealed them to little *c*.
18: 3 you change and become like little *c*
19:14 "Let the little *c* come to me,
21:16 " 'From the lips of *c* and infants
Mk 9:37 one of these little *c* in my name
10:14 "Let the little *c* come to me,
10:16 And he took the *c* in his arms,
13:12 *C* will rebel against their parents
Lk 10:21 and revealed them to little *c*.
18:16 "Let the little *c* come to me,
Ro 8:16 with our spirit that we are God's *c*.
2Co 12:14 parents, but parents for their *c*.
Eph 6: 1 *C*, obey your parents in the Lord,
6: 4 do not exasperate your *c;* instead,
Col 3:20 *C*, obey your parents in everything,
3:21 Fathers, do not embitter your *c*,
1Ti 3: 4 and see that his *c* obey him
3:12 and must manage his *c* and his
5:10 bringing up *c*, showing hospitality,
1Jn 3: 1 that we should be called *c* of God!

CHOOSE (CHOOSES CHOSE CHOSEN)

Dt 30:19 Now *c* life, so that you
Jos 24:15 then *c* for yourselves this day
Pr 8:10 *C* my instruction instead of silver,

Pr 16:16 to *c* understanding rather
Jn 15:16 You did not *c* me, but I chose you

CHOOSES (CHOOSE)

Jn 7:17 If anyone *c* to do God's will,

CHOSE (CHOOSE)

Ge 13:11 So Lot *c* for himself the whole plain
Ps 33:12 the people he *c* for his inheritance.
Jn 15:16 but I *c* you and appointed you to go
1Co 1:27 But God *c* the foolish things
Eph 1: 4 he *c* us in him before the creation
2Th 2:13 from the beginning God *c* you

CHOSEN (CHOOSE)

Isa 41: 8 Jacob, whom I have *c*,
Mt 22:14 For many are invited, but few are *c*
Lk 10:42 Mary has *c* what is better,
    23:35 the Christ of God, the *C* One."
Jn 15:19 but I have *c* you out of the world.
1Pe 1:20 He was *c* before the creation
    2: 9 But you are a *c* people, a royal

CHRIST (CHRIST'S CHRISTIAN CHRISTS)

Mt 1:16 was born Jesus, who is called *C*.
    16:16 Peter answered, "You are the *C*,
    22:42 "What do you think about the *C*?
Jn 1:41 found the Messiah" (that is, the *C*).
    20:31 you may believe that Jesus is the *C*,
Ac 2:36 you crucified, both Lord and *C*."
    5:42 the good news that Jesus is the *C*.
    9:22 by proving that Jesus is the *C*.
    17: 3 proving that the *C* had to suffer
    18:28 the Scriptures that Jesus was the *C*.
    26:23 that the *C* would suffer and,
Ro 3:22 comes through faith in Jesus *C*
    5: 6 we were still powerless, *C* died
    5: 8 While we were still sinners, *C* died
    5:17 life through the one man, Jesus *C*.
    6: 4 as *C* was raised from the dead
    8: 1 for those who are in *C* Jesus,
    8: 9 Spirit of *C*, he does not belong to *C*.
    8:35 us from the love of *C*?
    10: 4 *C* is the end of the law
    14: 9 *C* died and returned to life
    15: 3 For even *C* did not please himself
1Co 1:23 but we preach *C* crucified.
    2: 2 except Jesus *C* and him crucified.
    3:11 one already laid, which is Jesus *C*.
    5: 7 For *C*, our Passover lamb,
    8: 6 and there is but one Lord, Jesus *C*,
    10: 4 them, and that rock was *C*.
    11: 1 as I follow the example of *C*.
    11: 3 the head of every man is *C*,
    12:27 Now you are the body of *C*,
    15: 3 that *C* died for our sins according
    15:14 And if *C* has not been raised,
    15:22 so in *C* all will be made alive.
    15:57 victory through our Lord Jesus *C*.
2Co 3: 3 show that you are a letter from *C*,
    4: 5 not preach ourselves, but Jesus *C*
    5:10 before the judgment seat of *C*,
    5:17 Therefore, if anyone is in *C*,

2Co 11: 2 you to one husband, to *C*,
Gal 2:20 I have been crucified with *C*
    3:13 *C* redeemed us from the curse
    6:14 in the cross of our Lord Jesus *C*,
Eph 1: 3 with every spiritual blessing in *C*.
    3: 8 the unsearchable riches of *C*,
    4:13 measure of the fullness of *C*.
    5: 2 as *C* loved us and gave himself up
    5:23 as *C* is the head of the church,
    5:25 just as *C* loved the church
Php 1:21 to live is *C* and to die is gain.
    1:27 worthy of the gospel of *C*.
    4:19 to his glorious riches in *C* Jesus.
Col 1:27 which is *C* in you, the hope of glory
    1:28 may present everyone perfect in *C*.
    2: 6 as you received *C* Jesus as Lord,
    2:17 the reality, however, is found in *C*.
    3:15 Let the peace of *C* rule
2Th 2: 1 the coming of our Lord Jesus *C*
1Ti 1:15 *C* Jesus came into the world
    2: 5 the man *C* Jesus, who gave himself
2Ti 2: 3 us like a good soldier of *C* Jesus.
    3:15 salvation through faith in *C* Jesus.
Tit 2:13 our great God and Savior, Jesus *C*,
Heb 3:14 to share in *C* if we hold firmly
    9:14 more, then, will the blood of *C*,
    9:15 For this reason *C* is the mediator
    9:28 so *C* was sacrificed once
    10:10 of the body of Jesus *C* once for all.
    13: 8 Jesus *C* is the same yesterday
1Pe 1:19 but with the precious blood of *C*,
    2:21 because *C* suffered for you,
    3:18 For *C* died for sins once for all,
    4:14 insulted because of the name of *C*,
1Jn 2:22 man who denies that Jesus is the *C*.
    3:16 Jesus *C* laid down his life for us.
    5: 1 believes that Jesus is the *C* is born
Rev 20: 4 reigned with *C* a thousand years.

CHRIST'S (CHRIST)

2Co 5:14 For *C* love compels us,
    5:20 We are therefore *C* ambassadors,
    12: 9 so that *C* power may rest on me.

CHRISTIAN (CHRIST)

1Pe 4:16 as a *C*, do not be ashamed,

CHRISTS (CHRIST)

Mt 24:24 For false *C* and false prophets will

CHURCH

Mt 16:18 and on this rock I will build my *c*,
    18:17 if he refuses to listen even to the *c*,
Ac 20:28 Be shepherds of the *c* of God,
1Co 5:12 of mine to judge those outside the *c*
    14: 4 but he who prophesies edifies the *c*.
    14:12 to excel in gifts that build up the *c*.
    14:26 done for the strengthening of the *c*.
Eph 5:23 as Christ is the head of the *c*,
Col 1:24 the sake of his body, which is the *c*.

CIRCUMCISED

Ge 17:10 Every male among you shall be *c*.

CIRCUMSTANCES
Php 4:11 to be content whatever the *c*.
1Th 5:18 continually; give thanks in all *c*,

CITIZENS (CITIZENSHIP)
Eph 2:19 but fellow *c* with God's people

CITIZENSHIP (CITIZENS)
Php 3:20 But our *c* is in heaven.

CITY
Mt 5:14 A *c* on a hill cannot be hidden.
Heb 13:14 here we do not have an enduring *c*,

CIVILIAN*
2Ti 2: 4 a soldier gets involved in *c* affairs—

CLAIM (CLAIMS)
Pr 25: 6 do not *c* a place among great men;
1Jn 1: 6 If we *c* to have fellowship
1: 8 If we *c* to be without sin, we
1:10 If we *c* we have not sinned,

CLAIMS (CLAIM)
Jas 2:14 if a man *c* to have faith
1Jn 2: 6 Whoever *c* to live in him must walk
2: 9 Anyone who *c* to be in the light

CLAP
Ps 47: 1 *C* your hands, all you nations;
Isa 55:12 will *c* their hands.

CLAY
Isa 45: 9 Does the *c* say to the potter,
64: 8 We are the *c*, you are the potter;
Jer 18: 6 "Like *c* in the hand of the potter,
La 4: 2 are now considered as pots of *c*,
Da 2:33 partly of iron and partly of baked *c*.
Ro 9:21 of the same lump of *c* some pottery
2Co 4: 7 we have this treasure in jars of *c*
2Ti 2:20 and *c*; some are for noble purposes

CLEAN
Lev 16:30 you will be *c* from all your sins.
Ps 24: 4 He who has *c* hands and a pure
Mt 12:44 the house unoccupied, swept *c*
23:25 You *c* the outside of the cup
Mk 7:19 Jesus declared all foods "*c*.")
Jn 13:10 to wash his feet; his whole body is *c*
15: 3 are already *c* because of the word
Ac 10:15 impure that God has made *c*."
Ro 14:20 All food is *c*, but it is wrong

CLING (CLINGS)
Ro 12: 9 Hate what is evil; *c* to what is good.

CLINGS (CLING)
Ps 63: 8 My soul *c* to you;

CLOAK
2Ki 4:29 "Tuck your *c* into your belt,

CLOSE (CLOSER)
Ps 34:18 Lord is *c* to the brokenhearted
Isa 40:11 and carries them *c* to his heart;
Jer 30:21 himself to be *c* to me?'

CLOSER (CLOSE)
Ex 3: 5 "Do not come any *c*," God said.

Pr 18:24 there is a friend who sticks *c*

CLOTHE (CLOTHED CLOTHES CLOTHING)
Ps 45: 3 *c* yourself with splendor
Isa 52: 1 *c* yourself with strength.
Ro 13:14 *c* yourselves with the Lord Jesus
Col 3:12 *c* yourselves with compassion,
1Pe 5: 5 *c* yourselves with humility

CLOTHED (CLOTHE)
Ps 30:11 removed my sackcloth and *c* me
Pr 31:25 She is *c* with strength and dignity;
Lk 24:49 until you have been *c* with power

CLOTHES (CLOTHE)
Mt 6:25 the body more important than *c*?
6:28 "And why do you worry about *c*?
Jn 11:44 Take off the grave *c* and let him go

CLOTHING (CLOTHE)
Dt 22: 5 A woman must not wear men's *c*,
Mt 7:15 They come to you in sheep's *c*,

CLOUD (CLOUDS)
Ex 13:21 them in a pillar of *c* to guide them
Isa 19: 1 See, the Lord rides on a swift *c*
Lk 21:27 of Man coming in a *c* with power
Heb 12: 1 by such a great *c* of witnesses,

CLOUDS (CLOUD)
Ps 104: 3 He makes the *c* his chariot
Da 7:13 coming with the *c* of heaven.
Mk 13:26 coming in *c* with great power
1Th 4:17 with them in the *c* to meet the Lord

CO-HEIRS* (INHERIT)
Ro 8:17 heirs of God and *c* with Christ,

COALS
Pr 25:22 you will heap burning *c* on his head
Ro 12:20 you will heap burning *c* on his head

COLD
Pr 25:25 Like *c* water to a weary soul
Mt 10:42 if anyone gives even a cup of *c* water
24:12 the love of most will grow *c*,

COMFORT (COMFORTED COMFORTS)
Ps 23: 4 rod and your staff, they *c* me.
119: 52 and I find *c* in them.
119: 76 May your unfailing love be my *c*,
Zec 1:17 and the Lord will again *c* Zion
1Co 14: 3 encouragement and *c*.
2Co 1: 4 so that we can *c* those
2: 7 you ought to forgive and *c* him,

COMFORTED (COMFORT)
Mt 5: 4 for they will be *c*.

COMFORTS* (COMFORT)
Job 29:25 I was like one who *c* mourners.
Isa 49:13 For the Lord *c* his people
51:12 "I, even I, am he who *c* you.
66:13 As a mother *c* her child,
2Co 1: 4 who *c* us in all our troubles,
7: 6 But God, who *c* the downcast,

COMMAND (COMMANDED COMMANDING COMMANDENT COMMANDMENTS COMMANDS)

Ex   7: 2 You are to say everything I *c* you,
Nu 24:13 to go beyond the *c* of the LORD—
Dt   4: 2 Do not add to what I *c* you
     30:16 For I *c* you today to love
     32:46 so that you may *c* your children
Ps 91:11 For he will *c* his angels concerning
Pr 13:13 but he who respects a *c* is rewarded
Ecc 8: 2 Obey the king's *c*, I say,
Joel 2:11 mighty are those who obey his *c*.
Jn 14:15 love me, you will obey what I *c*.
     15:12 My *c* is this: Love each other
1Co 14:37 writing to you is the Lord's *c*.
Gal 5:14 law is summed up in a single *c:*
1Ti 1: 5 goal of this *c* is love, which comes
Heb 11: 3 universe was formed at God's *c*,
1Jn 3:23 this is his *c:* to believe in the name
2Jn   : 6 his *c* is that you walk in love.

COMMANDED (COMMAND)

Ps 33: 9 he *c*, and it stood firm.
   148: 5 for he *c* and they were created.
Mt 28:20 to obey everything I have *c* you.
1Co 9:14 Lord has *c* that those who preach
1Jn 3:23 and to love one another as he *c* us.

COMMANDING (COMMAND)

2Ti 2: 4 he wants to please his *c* officer.

COMMANDMENT (COMMAND)

Jos 22: 5 But be very careful to keep the *c*
Mt 22:38 This is the first and greatest *c*.
Jn 13:34 "A new *c* I give you: Love one
Ro 7:12 and the *c* is holy, righteous
Eph 6: 2 which is the first *c* with a promise

COMMANDMENTS (COMMAND)

Ex 20: 6 who love me and keep my *c*.
   34:28 of the covenant—the Ten *C*.
Ecc 12:13 Fear God and keep his *c*,
Mt 5:19 one of the least of these *c*
   22:40 the Prophets hang on these two *c*."

COMMANDS (COMMAND)

Dt 7: 9 those who love him and keep his *c*.
  11:27 the blessing if you obey the *c*
Ps112: 1 who finds great delight in his *c*.
 119: 47 for I delight in your *c*
 119: 86 All your *c* are trustworthy;
 119: 98 Your *c* make me wiser
 119:127 Because I love your *c*
 119:143 but your *c* are my delight.
 119:172 for all your *c* are righteous.
Pr 3: 1 but keep my *c* in your heart,
  6:23 For these *c* are a lamp,
 10: 8 The wise in heart accept *c*,
Da 9: 4 all who love him and obey his *c*,
Mt 5:19 teaches these *c* will be called great
Jn 14:21 Whoever has my *c* and obeys them,
Ac 17:30 but now he *c* all people everywhere
1Co 7:19 Keeping God's *c* is what counts.
1Jn 5: 3 And his *c* are not burdensome,

1Jn 5: 3 This is love for God: to obey his *c*.

COMMEND (COMMENDED COMMENDS)

Ecc 8:15 So I *c* the enjoyment of life,
Ro 13: 3 do what is right and he will *c* you.
1Pe 2:14 and to *c* those who do right.

COMMENDED (COMMEND)

Heb 11:39 These were all *c* for their faith,

COMMENDS (COMMEND)

2Co 10:18 not the one who *c* himself who is

COMMIT (COMMITS COMMITTED)

Ex 20:14 "You shall not *c* adultery.
Ps 37: 5 *C* your way to the LORD;
Mt 5:27 that it was said, 'Do not *c* adultery.'
Lk 23:46 into your hands I *c* my spirit."
Ac 20:32 I *c* you to God and to the word
1Co 10: 8 We should not *c* sexual immorality,
1Pe 4:19 to God's will should *c* themselves

COMMITS (COMMIT)

Pr 6:32 man who *c* adultery lacks
  29:22 a hot-tempered one *c* many sins.
Mt 19: 9 marries another woman *c* adultery

COMMITTED (COMMIT)

Nu 5: 7 and must confess the sin he has *c*.
1Ki 8:61 But your hearts must be fully *c*
2Ch 16: 9 those whose hearts are fully *c*
Mt 5:28 lustfully has already *c* adultery
2Co 5:19 And he has *c* to us the message
1Pe 2:22 "He *c* no sin,

COMMON

Pr 22: 2 Rich and poor have this in *c:*
1Co 10:13 has seized you except what is *c*
2Co 6:14 and wickedness have in *c?*

COMPANION (COMPANIONS)

Pr 13:20 but a *c* of fools suffers harm.
  28: 7 a *c* of gluttons disgraces his father.
  29: 3 *c* of prostitutes squanders his

COMPANIONS (COMPANION)

Pr 18:24 A man of many *c* may come to ruin

COMPANY

Pr 24: 1 do not desire their *c;*
Jer 15:17 I never sat in the *c* of revelers,
1Co 15:33 "Bad *c* corrupts good character."

COMPARED (COMPARING)

Eze 31: 2 Who can be *c* with you in majesty?
Php 3: 8 I consider everything a loss *c*

COMPARING* (COMPARED)

Ro 8:18 present sufferings are not worth *c*
2Co 8: 8 the sincerity of your love by *c* it
Gal 6: 4 without *c* himself to somebody else

COMPASSION (COMPASSIONATE COMPASSIONS)

Ex 33:19 I will have *c* on whom I will have *c*.
Ne 9:19 of your great *c* you did not
  9:28 in your *c* you delivered them time

Ps 51: 1 according to your great c
    103: 4 and crowns you with love and c.
    103: 13 As a father has c on his children,
    145: 9 he has c on all he has made.
Isa 49:13 and will have c on his afflicted ones
    49:15 and have no c on the child she has
Hos 2:19 in love and c.
    11: 8 all my c is aroused.
Jnh 3: 9 with c turn from his fierce anger
Mt   9:36 When he saw the crowds, he had c
Mk   8: 2 "I have c for these people;
Ro   9:15 and I will have c on whom I have c
Col 3:12 clothe yourselves with c, kindness,
Jas 5:11 The Lord is full of c and mercy.

COMPASSIONATE (COMPASSION)
Ne   9:17 gracious and c, slow to anger
Ps 103: 8 The LORD is c and gracious,
    112: 4 the gracious and c and righteous
Eph 4:32 Be kind and c to one another,
1Pe 3: 8 love as brothers, be c and humble.

COMPASSIONS* (COMPASSION)
La   3:22 for his c never fail.

COMPELLED (COMPELS)
Ac 20:22 "And now, c by the Spirit,
1Co 9:16 I cannot boast, for I am c to preach.

COMPELS (COMPELLED)
2Co 5:14 For Christ's love c us, because we

COMPETENCE* (COMPETENT)
2Co 3: 5 but our c comes from God.

COMPETENT* (COMPETENCE)
Ro 15:14 and c to instruct one another.
1Co 6: 2 are you not c to judge trivial cases?
2Co 3: 5 Not that we are c in ourselves
    3: 6 He has made us c as ministers

COMPETES*
1Co 9:25 Everyone who c in the games goes
2Ti 2: 5 Similarly, if anyone c as an athlete,
    2: 5 unless he c according to the rules.

COMPLACENT
Am   6: 1 Woe to you who are c in Zion,

COMPLAINING*
Php 2:14 Do everything without c or arguing

COMPLETE
Jn 15:11 and that your joy may be c.
    16:24 will receive, and your joy will be c.
    17:23 May they be brought to c unity
Ac 20:24 c the task the Lord Jesus has given
Php 2: 2 then make my joy c
Col 4:17 to it that you c the work you have
Jas 1: 4 so that you may be mature and c,
    2:22 his faith was made c by what he did

CONCEAL (CONCEALED CONCEALS)
Ps 40:10 I do not c your love and your truth
Pr 25: 2 It is the glory of God to c a matter;

CONCEALED (CONCEAL)
Jer 16:17 nor is their sin c from my eyes.

Mt 10:26 There is nothing c that will not be
Mk   4:22 and whatever is c is meant

CONCEALS (CONCEAL)
Pr 28:13 He who c his sins does not prosper,

CONCEITED
Ro 12:16 Do not be c.
Gal 5:26 Let us not become c, provoking
1Ti 6: 4 he is c and understands nothing.

CONCEIVED
Mt   1:20 what is c in her is from the Holy
1Co 2: 9 no mind has c

CONCERN (CONCERNED)
Eze 36:21 I had c for my holy name, which
1Co 7:32 I would like you to be free from c.
    12:25 that its parts should have equal c
2Co 11:28 of my c for all the churches.

CONCERNED (CONCERN)
Jnh 4:10 "You have been c about this vine,
1Co 7:32 An unmarried man is c about

CONDEMN (CONDEMNATION
CONDEMNED CONDEMNING
CONDEMNS)
Job 40: 8 Would you c me to justify yourself?
Isa 50: 9 Who is he that will c me?
Lk   6:37 Do not c, and you will not be
Jn   3:17 Son into the world to c the world,
    12:48 very word which I spoke will c him
Ro   2:27 yet obeys the law will c you who,
1Jn 3:20 presence whenever our hearts c us.

CONDEMNATION (CONDEMN)
Ro   5:18 of one trespass was c for all men,
    8: 1 there is now no c for those who are

CONDEMNED (CONDEMN)
Ps 34:22 no one will be c who takes refuge
Mt 12:37 and by your words you will be c."
    23:33 How will you escape being c to hell
Jn   3:18 Whoever believes in him is not c,
    5:24 has eternal life and will not be c;
    16:11 prince of this world now stands c.
Ro   4:23 But the man who has doubts is c
1Co 11:32 disciplined so that we will not be c
Heb 11: 7 By his faith he c the world

CONDEMNING (CONDEMN)
Pr 17:15 the guilty and c the innocent—
Ro   2: 1 judge the other, you are c yourself,

CONDEMNS (CONDEMN)
Ro   8:34 Who is he that c? Christ Jesus,
2Co 3: 9 the ministry that c men is glorious,

CONDUCT
Pr 10:23 A fool finds pleasure in evil c,
    20:11 by whether his c is pure and right.
    21: 8 but the c of the innocent is upright.
Ecc 6: 8 how to c himself before others?
Jer 4:18 "Your own c and actions
    17:10 to reward a man according to his c,
Eze 7: 3 I will judge you according to your c

Php 1:27 *c* yourselves in a manner worthy
1Ti 3:15 to *c* themselves in God's household

CONFESS (CONFESSION)

Lev 16:21 and *c* over it all the wickedness
26:40 " 'But if they will *c* their sins
Nu 5: 7 must *c* the sin he has committed.
Ps 38:18 I *c* my iniquity;
Ro 10: 9 That if you *c* with your mouth,
Php 2:11 every tongue *c* that Jesus Christ is
Jas 5:16 Therefore *c* your sins to each other
1Jn 1: 9 If we *c* our sins, he is faithful

CONFESSION (CONFESS)

Ezr 10:11 Now make *c* to the LORD,
2Co 9:13 obedience that accompanies your *c*

CONFIDENCE

Ps 71: 5 my *c* since my youth.
Pr 3:26 for the LORD will be your *c*
11:13 A gossip betrays a *c*,
25: 9 do not betray another man's *c*,
31:11 Her husband has full *c* in her
Isa 32:17 will be quietness and *c* forever.
Jer 17: 7 whose *c* is in him.
Php 3: 3 and who put no *c* in the flesh—
Heb 3:14 till the end the *c* we had at first.
4:16 the throne of grace with *c*,
10:19 since we have *c* to enter the Most
10:35 So do not throw away your *c;*
1Jn 5:14 This is the *c* we have

CONFORM* (CONFORMED)

Ro 12: 2 Do not *c* any longer to the pattern
1Pe 1:14 do not *c* to the evil desires you had

CONFORMED (CONFORM)

Ro 8:29 predestined to be *c* to the likeness

CONQUERORS

Ro 8:37 than *c* through him who loved us.

CONSCIENCE (CONSCIENCES)

Ro 13: 5 punishment but also because of *c*,
1Co 8: 7 since their *c* is weak, it is defiled.
8:12 in this way and wound their weak *c*
10:25 without raising questions of *c,*
10:29 freedom be judged by another's *c?*
Heb 10:22 to cleanse us from a guilty *c*
1Pe 3:16 and respect, keeping a clear *c,*

CONSCIENCES* (CONSCIENCE)

Ro 2:15 their *c* also bearing witness,
1Ti 4: 2 whose *c* have been seared
Tit 1:15 their minds and *c* are corrupted.
Heb 9:14 cleanse our *c* from acts that lead

CONSCIOUS*

Ro 3:20 through the law we become *c* of sin
1Pe 2:19 of unjust suffering because he is *c*

CONSECRATE (CONSECRATED)

Ex 13: 2 "*C* to me every firstborn male."
Lev 20: 7 " '*C* yourselves and be holy,

CONSECRATED (CONSECRATE)

Ex 29:43 and the place will be *c* by my glory.
1Ti 4: 5 because it is *c* by the word of God

CONSIDER (CONSIDERATE CONSIDERED CONSIDERS)

1Sa 12:24 *c* what great things he has done
Job 37:14 stop and *c* God's wonders.
Ps 8: 3 When I *c* your heavens,
107: 43 and *c* the great love of the LORD.
143: 5 and *c* what your hands have done.
Lk 12:24 *C* the ravens: They do not sow
12:27 about the rest? "*C* how the lilies
Php 2: 3 but in humility *c* others better
3: 8 I *c* everything a loss compared
Heb 10:24 And let us *c* how we may spur one
Jas 1: 2 *C* it pure joy, my brothers,

CONSIDERATE* (CONSIDER)

Tit 3: 2 to be peaceable and *c,*
Jas 3:17 then peace-loving, *c,* submissive,
1Pe 2:18 only to those who are good and *c,*
3: 7 in the same way be *c* as you live

CONSIDERED (CONSIDER)

Job 1: 8 "Have you *c* my servant Job?
2: 3 "Have you *c* my servant Job?
Ps 44:22 we are *c* as sheep to be slaughtered.
Isa 53: 4 yet we *c* him stricken by God,
Ro 8:36 we are *c* as sheep to be slaughtered

CONSIDERS (CONSIDER)

Pr 31:16 She *c* a field and buys it;
Ro 14: 5 One man *c* one day more sacred
Jas 1:26 If anyone *c* himself religious

CONSIST

Lk 12:15 a man's life does not *c*

CONSOLATION

Ps 94:19 your *c* brought joy to my soul.

CONSTRUCTIVE*

1Co 10:23 but not everything is *c*.

CONSUME (CONSUMING)

Jn 2:17 "Zeal for your house will *c* me."

CONSUMING (CONSUME)

Dt 4:24 For the LORD your God is a *c* fire,
Heb 12:29 and awe, for our "God is a *c* fire."

CONTAIN

1Ki 8:27 the highest heaven, cannot *c* you.
2Pe 3:16 His letters *c* some things that are

CONTAMINATES*

2Co 7: 1 from everything that *c* body

CONTEMPT

Pr 14:31 He who oppresses the poor shows *c*
17: 5 He who mocks the poor shows *c*
18: 3 When wickedness comes, so does *c*
Da 12: 2 others to shame and everlasting *c.*
Ro 2: 4 Or do you show *c* for the riches
Gal 4:14 you did not treat me with *c*
1Th 5:20 do not treat prophecies with *c.*

CONTEND 22 COURSE

CONTEND (CONTENDING)
Jude : 3 you to *c* for the faith that was once

CONTENDING* (CONTEND)
Php 1:27 *c* as one man for the faith

CONTENT (CONTENTMENT)
Pr 13:25 The righteous eat to their hearts' *c,*
Php 4:11 to be *c* whatever the circumstances
 4:12 I have learned the secret of being *c*
1Ti 6: 8 and clothing, we will be *c* with that.
Heb 13: 5 and be *c* with what you have,

CONTENTMENT (CONTENT)
1Ti 6: 6 But godliness with *c* is great gain.

CONTINUAL (CONTINUE)
Pr 15:15 but the cheerful heart has a *c* feast.

CONTINUE (CONTINUAL)
Php 2:12 *c* to work out your salvation
2Ti 3:14 *c* in what you have learned
1Jn 5:18 born of God does not *c* to sin;
Rev 22:11 and let him who is holy *c* to be holy
 22:11 let him who does right *c* to do right;

CONTRITE*
Ps 51:17 a broken and *c* heart,
Isa 57:15 also with him who is *c* and lowly
 57:15 and to revive the heart of the *c.*
 66: 2 he who is humble and *c* in spirit,

CONTROL (CONTROLLED
SELF-CONTROL SELF-CONTROLLED)
Pr 29:11 a wise man keeps himself under *c.*
1Co 7: 9 But if they cannot *c* themselves,
 7:37 but has *c* over his own will,
1Th 4: 4 you should learn to *c* his own body

CONTROLLED (CONTROL)
Ps 32: 9 but must be *c* by bit and bridle
Ro 8: 6 but the mind *c* by the Spirit is life
 8: 8 Those *c* by the sinful nature cannot

CONTROVERSIES
Tit 3: 9 But avoid foolish *c* and genealogies

CONVERSATION
Col 4: 6 Let your *c* be always full of grace,

CONVERT
1Ti 3: 6 He must not be a recent *c,*

CONVICT
Jn 16: 8 he will *c* the world of guilt in regard

CONVINCED (CONVINCING)
Ro 8:38 For I am *c* that neither death
2Ti 1:12 and am *c* that he is able
 3:14 have learned and have become *c*

CONVINCING* (CONVINCED)
Ac 1: 3 and gave many *c* proofs that he was

CORNELIUS*
Roman to whom Peter preached; first Gentile Christian (Ac 10).

CORNERSTONE (STONE)
Isa 28:16 a precious *c* for a sure foundation;

Eph 2:20 Christ Jesus himself as the chief *c.*
1Pe 2: 6 a chosen and precious *c,*

CORRECT (CORRECTING
CORRECTION CORRECTS)
2Ti 4: 2 *c,* rebuke and encourage—

CORRECTING* (CORRECT)
2Ti 3:16 *c* and training in righteousness,

CORRECTION (CORRECT)
Pr 10:17 whoever ignores *c* leads others
 12: 1 but he who hates *c* is stupid.
 15: 5 whoever heeds *c* shows prudence.
 15:10 he who hates *c* will die.
 29:15 The rod of *c* imparts wisdom,

CORRECTS* (CORRECT)
Job 5:17 "Blessed is the man whom God *c;*
Pr 9: 7 Whoever *c* a mocker invites insult;

CORRUPT (CORRUPTS)
Ge 6:11 Now the earth was *c* in God's sight

CORRUPTS* (CORRUPT)
Ecc 7: 7 and a bribe *c* the heart.
1Co 15:33 "Bad company *c* good character."
Jas 3: 6 It *c* the whole person, sets

COST
Pr 4: 7 Though it *c* all you have, get
Isa 55: 1 milk without money and without *c.*
Rev 21: 6 to drink without *c* from the spring

COUNSEL (COUNSELOR)
1Ki 22: 5 "First seek the *c* of the LORD."
Pr 15:22 Plans fail for lack of *c,*
Rev 3:18 I *c* you to buy from me gold refined

COUNSELOR (COUNSEL)
Isa 9: 6 Wonderful *C,* Mighty God,
Jn 14:16 he will give you another *C* to be
 14:26 But the *C,* the Holy Spirit,

COUNT (COUNTING COUNTS)
Ro 4: 8 whose sin the Lord will never *c*
 6:11 *c* yourselves dead to sin

COUNTING (COUNT)
2Co 5:19 not *c* men's sins against them.

COUNTRY
Jn 4:44 prophet has no honor in his own *c.)*

COUNTS (COUNT)
Jn 6:63 The Spirit gives life; the flesh *c*
1Co 7:19 God's commands is what *c.*
Gal 5: 6 only thing that *c* is faith expressing

COURAGE (COURAGEOUS)
Ac 23:11 "Take *c!* As you have testified
1Co 16:13 stand firm in the faith; be men of *c;*

COURAGEOUS (COURAGE)
Dt 31: 6 Be strong and *c.*
Jos 1: 6 and *c,* because you will lead these

COURSE
Ps 19: 5 a champion rejoicing to run his *c.*
Pr 15:21 of understanding keeps a straight *c.*

COURTS

Ps 84:10 Better is one day in your *c*
   100: 4 and his *c* with praise;

COVENANT (COVENANTS)

Ge 9: 9 "I now establish my *c* with you
Ex 19: 5 if you obey me fully and keep my *c*,
1Ch 16:15 He remembers his *c* forever,
Job 31: 1 "I made a *c* with my eyes
Jer 31:31 "when I will make a new *c*
1Co 11:25 "This cup is the new *c* in my blood;
Gal 4:24 One *c* is from Mount Sinai
Heb 9:15 Christ is the mediator of a new *c*,

COVENANTS (COVENANT)

Ro 9: 4 theirs the divine glory, the *c*,
Gal 4:24 for the women represent two *c*.

COVER (COVER-UP COVERED COVERS)

Ps 91: 4 He will *c* you with his feathers,
Jas 5:20 and *c* over a multitude of sins.

COVER-UP (COVER)

1Pe 2:16 but do not use your freedom as a *c*

COVERED (COVER)

Ps 32: 1 whose sins are *c*.
Isa 6: 2 With two wings they *c* their faces,
Ro 4: 7 whose sins are *c*.
1Co 11: 4 with his head *c* dishonors his head.

COVERS (COVER)

Pr 10:12 but love *c* over all wrongs.
1Pe 4: 8 love *c* over a multitude of sins.

COVET

Ex 20:17 You shall not *c* your neighbor's
Ro 13: 9 "Do not steal," "Do not *c*,"

COWARDLY*

Rev 21: 8 But the *c*, the unbelieving, the vile,

CRAFTINESS (CRAFTY)

1Co 3:19 "He catches the wise in their *c*";

CRAFTY (CRAFTINESS)

Ge 3: 1 the serpent was more *c* than any
2Co 12:16 *c* fellow that I am, I caught you

CRAVE

Pr 23: 3 Do not *c* his delicacies,
1Pe 2: 2 newborn babies, *c* pure spiritual

CREATE (CREATED CREATION CREATOR)

Ps 51:10 *C* in me a pure heart, O God,
Isa 45:18 he did not *c* it to be empty,

CREATED (CREATE)

Ge 1: 1 In the beginning God *c* the heavens
   1:21 God *c* the great creatures of the sea
   1:27 So God *c* man in his own image,
Ps 148: 5 for he commanded and they were *c*
Isa 42: 5 he who *c* the heavens and stretched
Ro 1:25 and served *c* things rather
1Co 11: 9 neither was man *c* for woman,
Col 1:16 For by him all things were *c*:

1Ti 4: 4 For everything God *c* is good,
Rev 10: 6 who *c* the heavens and all that is

CREATION (CREATE)

Mk 16:15 and preach the good news to all *c*.
Jn 17:24 me before the *c* of the world.
Ro 8:19 The *c* waits in eager expectation
   8:39 depth, nor anything else in all *c*,
2Co 5:17 he is a new *c*; the old has gone,
Col 1:15 God, the firstborn over all *c*.
1Pe 1:20 chosen before the *c* of the world,
Rev 13: 8 slain from the *c* of the world.

CREATOR (CREATE)

Ge 14:22 God Most High, *C* of heaven
Ro 1:25 created things rather than the *C*—

CREATURE (CREATURES)

Lev 17:11 For the life of a *c* is in the blood,

CREATURES (CREATURE)

Ge 6:19 bring into the ark two of all living *c*,
Ps 104: 24 the earth is full of your *c*.

CREDIT (CREDITED)

Ro 4:24 to whom God will *c* righteousness
1Pe 2:20 it to your *c* if you receive a beating

CREDITED (CREDIT)

Ge 15: 6 and he *c* it to him as righteousness.
Ro 4: 5 his faith is *c* as righteousness.
Gal 3: 6 and it was *c* to him as righteousness
Jas 2:23 and it was *c* to him as righteousness

CRIED (CRY)

Ps 18: 6 I *c* to my God for help.

CRIMSON

Isa 1:18 though they are red as *c*,

CRIPPLED

Mk 9:45 better for you to enter life *c*

CRITICISM

2Co 8:20 We want to avoid any *c*

CROOKED

Pr 10: 9 he who takes *c* paths will be found
Php 2:15 children of God without fault in a *c*

CROSS

Mt 10:38 and anyone who does not take his *c*
Lk 9:23 take up his *c* daily and follow me.
Ac 2:23 to death by nailing him to the *c*.
1Co 1:17 lest the *c* of Christ be emptied
Gal 6:14 in the *c* of our Lord Jesus Christ,
Php 2: 8 even death on a *c*!
Col 1:20 through his blood, shed on the *c*.
   2:14 he took it away, nailing it to the *c*.
   2:15 triumphing over them by the *c*.
Heb 12: 2 set before him endured the *c*,

CROWD

Ex 23: 2 Do not follow the *c* in doing wrong.

CROWN (CROWNED CROWNS)

Pr 4: 9 present you with a *c* of splendor."
   10: 6 Blessings *c* the head
   12: 4 noble character is her husband's *c*,

Pr 17: 6 Children's children are a *c*
Isa 61: 3 to bestow on them a *c* of beauty
Zec 9:16 like jewels in a *c*.
Mt 27:29 then twisted together a *c* of thorns
1Co 9:25 it to get a *c* that will last forever.
2Ti 4: 8 store for me the *c* of righteousness,
Rev 2:10 and I will give you the *c* of life.

CROWNED (CROWN)

Ps 8: 5 and *c* him with glory and honor.
Pr 14:18 the prudent are *c* with knowledge.
Heb 2: 7 you *c* him with glory and honor

CROWNS (CROWN)

Rev 4:10 They lay their *c* before the throne
19:12 and on his head are many *c*.

CRUCIFIED (CRUCIFY)

Mt 20:19 to be mocked and flogged and *c*.
27:38 Two robbers were *c* with him,
Lk 24: 7 be *c* and on the third day be raised
Jn 19:18 Here they *c* him, and with him two
Ac 2:36 whom you *c*, both Lord and Christ
Ro 6: 6 For we know that our old self was *c*
1Co 1:23 but we preach Christ *c*: a stumbling
2: 2 except Jesus Christ and him *c*.
Gal 2:20 I have been *c* with Christ
5:24 Christ Jesus have *c* the sinful

CRUCIFY (CRUCIFIED CRUCIFYING)

Mt 27:22 They all answered, ''*C* him!'' ''Why
27:31 Then they led him away to *c* him.

CRUCIFYING* (CRUCIFY)

Heb 6: 6 to their loss they are *c* the Son

CRUSH (CRUSHED)

Ge 3:15 he will *c* your head,
Isa 53:10 it was the LORD's will to *c* him
Ro 16:20 The God of peace will soon *c* Satan

CRUSHED (CRUSH)

Ps 34:18 and saves those who are *c* in spirit.
Isa 53: 5 he was *c* for our iniquities;
2Co 4: 8 not *c*; perplexed, but not in despair;

CRY (CRIED)

Ps 34:15 and his ears are attentive to their *c*;
40: 1 he turned to me and heard my *c*.
130: 1 Out of the depths I *c* to you,

CUP

Ps 23: 5 my *c* overflows.
Mt 10:42 if anyone gives even a *c* of cold water
23:25 You clean the outside of the *c*
26:39 may this *c* be taken from me.
1Co 11:25 after supper he took the *c*, saying,

CURSE (CURSED)

Dt 11:26 before you today a blessing and a *c*
21:23 hung on a tree is under God's *c*.
Lk 6:28 bless those who *c* you, pray
Gal 3:13 of the law by becoming a *c* for us,
Rev 22: 3 No longer will there be any *c*.

CURSED (CURSE)

Ge 3:17 ''*C* is the ground because of you;

Dt 27:15 ''*C* is the man who carves an image
27:16 ''*C* is the man who dishonors his
27:17 ''*C* is the man who moves his
27:18 ''*C* is the man who leads the blind
27:19 *C* is the man who withholds justice
27:20 ''*C* is the man who sleeps
27:21 ''*C* is the man who has sexual
27:22 ''*C* is the man who sleeps
27:23 ''*C* is the man who sleeps
27:24 ''*C* is the man who kills his
27:25 ''*C* is the man who accepts a bribe
27:26 ''*C* is the man who does not uphold
Ro 9: 3 I could wish that I myself were *c*
Gal 3:10 ''*C* is everyone who does not

CURTAIN

Ex 26:33 The *c* will separate the Holy Place
Lk 23:45 the *c* of the temple was torn in two.
Heb 10:20 opened for us through the *c*,

CYMBAL*

1Co 13: 1 a resounding gong or a clanging *c*.

DANCE (DANCING)

Ecc 3: 4 a time to mourn and a time to *d*,
Mt 11:17 and you did not *d*;

DANCING (DANCE)

Ps 30:11 You turned my wailing into *d*;
149: 3 Let them praise his name with *d*

DANGER

Pr 27:12 The prudent see *d* and take refuge,
Ro 8:35 famine or nakedness or *d* or sword?

DANIEL

Hebrew exile to Babylon, name changed to Belteshazzar (Da 1:6-7). Refused to eat unclean food (Da 1:8-21). Interpreted Nebuchadnezzar's dreams (Da 2; 4), writing on the wall (Da 5). Thrown into lion's den (Da 6). Visions of (Da 7-12).

DARK (DARKNESS)

Job 34:22 There is no *d* place, no deep
Pr 31:15 She gets up while it is still *d*;
Ro 2:19 a light for those who are in the *d*,
2Pe 1:19 as to a light shining in a *d* place,

DARKNESS (DARK)

Ge 1: 4 he separated the light from the *d*.
2Sa 22:29 the LORD turns my *d* into light.
Jn 3:19 but men loved *d* instead of light
2Co 6:14 fellowship can light have with *d*?
Eph 5: 8 For you were once *d*, but now you
1Pe 2: 9 out of *d* into his wonderful light.
1Jn 1: 5 in him there is no *d* at all.
2: 9 but hates his brother is still in the *d*.

DAUGHTERS

Joel 2:28 sons and *d* will prophesy,

DAVID

Son of Jesse (Ru 4:17-22; 1Ch 2:13-15), ancestor of Jesus (Mt 1:1-17; Lk 3:31).
Anointed king by Samuel (1Sa 16:1-13). Musician to Saul (1Sa 16:14-23; 18:10). Killed Goliath

(1Sa 17). Relation with Jonathan (1Sa 18:1-4; 19-20; 23:16-18; 2Sa 1). Disfavor of Saul (1Sa 18:6-23:29). Spared Saul's life (1Sa 24; 26). Among Philistines (1Sa 21:10-14; 27-30). Lament for Saul and Jonathan (2Sa 1).

Anointed king of Judah (2Sa 2:1-11); of Israel (2Sa 5:1-4; 1Ch 11:1-3). Promised eternal dynasty (2Sa 7; 1Ch 17; Ps 132). Adultery with Bathsheba (2Sa 11-12). Absalom's revolt (2Sa 14-18). Last words (2Sa 23:1-7). Death (1Ki 2:10-12; 1Ch 29:28).

DAWN
Ps   37: 6 your righteousness shine like the d,
Pr   4:18 is like the first gleam of d,

DAY (DAYS)
Ge   1: 5 God called the light "d,"
Ex   20: 8 "Remember the Sabbath d
Lev 23:28 because it is the D of Atonement,
Nu 14:14 before them in a pillar of cloud by d
Jos   1: 8 meditate on it d and night,
Ps   84:10 Better is one d in your courts
       96: 2 proclaim his salvation d after d.
     118: 24 This is the d the Lord has made;
Pr   27: 1 not know what a d may bring forth.
Joel 2:31 and dreadful d of the Lord.
Ob   :15 The d of the Lord is near
Lk   11: 3 Give us each d our daily bread.
Ac   17:11 examined the Scriptures every d
2Co   4:16 we are being renewed d by d.
1Th   5: 2 for you know very well that the d
2Pe   3: 8 With the Lord a d is like

DAYS (DAY)
Dt   17:19 he is to read it all the d, of his life
Ps   23: 6 all the d of my life,
      90:10 The length of our d is seventy years
Ecc 12: 1 Creator in the d of your youth,
Joel 2:29 I will pour out my Spirit in those d.
Mic   4: 1 In the last d
Heb   1: 2 in these last d he has spoken to us
2Pe   3: 3 that in the last d scoffers will come,

DEACONS
1Ti   3: 8 D, likewise, are to be men worthy

DEAD (DIE)
Dt   18:11 or spiritist or who consults the d.
Mt   28: 7 'He has risen from the d
Ro   6:11 count yourselves d to sin
Eph   2: 1 you were d in your transgressions
1Th   4:16 and the d in Christ will rise first.
Jas   2:17 is not accompanied by action, is d.
       2:26 so faith without deeds is d.

DEATH (DIE)
Nu   35:16 the murderer shall be put to d.
Ps   23: 4 the valley of the shadow of d,
     116: 15 is the d of his saints.
Pr   8:36 all who hate me love d."
      14:12 but in the end it leads to d.
Ecc   7: 2 for d is the destiny of every man;
Isa 25: 8 he will swallow up d forever.
      53:12 he poured out his life unto d,

Jn   5:24 he has crossed over from d to life.
Ro   5:12 and in this way d came to all men,
       6:23 For the wages of sin is d,
       8:13 put to d the misdeeds of the body,
1Co 15:21 For since d came through a man,
      15:55 Where, O d, is your sting?"
Rev   1:18 And I hold the keys of d and Hades
      20: 6 The second d has no power
      20:14 The lake of fire is the second d.
      21: 4 There will be no more d

DEBAUCHERY
Ro   13:13 not in sexual immorality and d,
Eph   5:18 drunk on wine, which leads to d.

DEBORAH
Prophetess who led Israel to victory over Canaanites (Jdg 4-5).

DEBT (DEBTORS DEBTS)
Ro   13: 8 Let no d remain outstanding,
      13: 8 continuing d to love one another,

DEBTORS (DEBT)
Mt   6:12 as we also have forgiven our d.

DEBTS (DEBT)
Dt   15: 1 seven years you must cancel d.
Mt   6:12 Forgive us our d,

DECAY
Ps   16:10 will you let your Holy One see d.
Ac   2:27 will you let your Holy One see d.

DECEIT (DECEIVE)
Mk   7:22 greed, malice, d, lewdness, envy,
1Pe   2: 1 yourselves of all malice and all d,
       2:22 and no d was found in his mouth."

DECEITFUL (DECEIVE)
Jer   17: 9 The heart is d above all things
2Co 11:13 men are false apostles, d workmen,

DECEITFULNESS (DECEIVE)
Mk   4:19 the d of wealth and the desires
Heb   3:13 of you may be hardened by sin's d.

DECEIVE (DECEIT DECEITFUL DECEITFULNESS DECEIVED DECEIVES DECEPTIVE)
Lev 19:11 " 'Do not d one another.
Pr   14: 5 A truthful witness does not d,
Mt   24: 5 'I am the Christ,' and will d many.
Ro   16:18 and flattery they d the minds
1Co   3:18 Do not d yourselves.
Eph   5: 6 Let no one d you with empty words
Jas   1:22 to the word, and so d yourselves.
1Jn   1: 8 we d ourselves and the truth is not

DECEIVED (DECEIVE)
Ge   3:13 "The serpent d me, and I ate."
Gal   6: 7 Do not be d: God cannot be
1Ti   2:14 And Adam was not the one d;
2Ti   3:13 to worse, deceiving and being d.
Jas   1:16 Don't be d, my dear brothers.

DECEIVES (DECEIVE)
Gal   6: 3 when he is nothing, he d himself.

Jas 1:26 he *d* himself and his religion is

DECENCY*
1Ti 2: 9 women to dress modestly, with *d*

DECEPTIVE (DECEIVE)
Pr 31:30 Charm is *d*, and beauty is fleeting;
Col 2: 8 through hollow and *d* philosophy,

DECLARE (DECLARED DECLARING)
1Ch 16:24 *D* his glory among the nations,
Ps 19: 1 The heavens *d* the glory of God;
    96: 3 *D* his glory among the nations,
Isa 42: 9 and new things I *d;*

DECLARED (DECLARE)
Mk 7:19 Jesus *d* all foods "clean.")
Ro 2:13 the law who will be *d* righteous.
    3:20 no one will be *d* righteous

DECLARING (DECLARE)
Ps 71: 8 *d* your splendor all day long.
Ac 2:11 we hear them *d* the wonders

DECREED (DECREES)
La 3:37 happen if the Lord has not *d* it?
Lk 22:22 Son of Man will go as it has been *d*,

DECREES (DECREED)
Lev 10:11 Israelites all the *d* the LORD has
Ps 119:112 My heart is set on keeping your *d*

DEDICATE (DEDICATION)
Nu 6:12 He must *d* himself to the LORD
Pr 20:25 for a man to *d* something rashly

DEDICATION (DEDICATE)
1Ti 5:11 sensual desires overcome their *d*

DEED (DEEDS)
Col 3:17 you do, whether in word or *d*,

DEEDS (DEED)
1Sa 2: 3 and by him *d* are weighed.
Ps 65: 5 with awesome *d* of righteousness,
    66: 3 "How awesome are your *d!*
    78: 4 the praiseworthy *d* of the LORD,
    86:10 you are great and do marvelous *d;*
    92: 4 For you make me glad by your *d*,
    111: 3 Glorious and majestic are his *d*,
Hab 3: 2 I stand in awe of your *d*, O LORD.
Mt 5:16 that they may see your good *d*
Ac 26:20 prove their repentance by their *d*.
Jas 2:14 claims to have faith but has no *d?*
    2:20 faith without *d* is useless?
1Pe 2:12 they may see your good *d*

DEEP (DEPTH)
1Co 2:10 all things, even the *d* things
1Ti 3: 9 hold of the *d* truths of the faith

DEER
Ps 42: 1 As the *d* pants for streams of water,

DEFEND (DEFENSE)
Ps 74:22 Rise up, O God, and *d* your cause;
Pr 31: 9 *d* the rights of the poor and needy
Jer 50:34 He will vigorously *d* their cause

DEFENSE (DEFEND)
Ps 35:23 Awake, and rise to my *d!*
Php 1:16 here for the *d* of the gospel.
1Jn 2: 1 speaks to the Father in our *d—*

DEFERRED*
Pr 13:12 Hope *d* makes the heart sick,

DEFILE (DEFILED)
Da 1: 8 Daniel resolved not to *d* himself

DEFILED (DEFILE)
Isa 24: 5 The earth is *d* by its people;

DEFRAUD
Lev 19:13 Do not *d* your neighbor or rob him.

DEITY*
Col 2: 9 of the *D* lives in bodily form,

DELIGHT (DELIGHTS)
1Sa 15:22 "Does the LORD *d*
Ps 1: 2 But his *d* is in the law of the LORD
    16: 3 in whom is all my *d*.
    35: 9 and *d* in his salvation.
    37: 4 *D* yourself in the LORD
    43: 4 to God, my joy and my *d*.
    51:16 You do not *d* in sacrifice,
    119: 77 for your law is my *d*.
Pr 29:17 he will bring *d* to your soul.
Isa 42: 1 my chosen one in whom I *d;*
    55: 2 and your soul will *d* in the richest
    61:10 I *d* greatly in the LORD;
Jer 9:24 for in these I *d*,"
    15:16 they were my joy and my heart's *d*,
Mic 7:18 but *d* to show mercy.
Zep 3:17 He will take great *d* in you,
Mt 12:18 the one I love, in whom I *d;*
1Co 13: 6 Love does not *d* in evil
2Co 12:10 for Christ's sake, I *d* in weaknesses,

DELIGHTS (DELIGHT)
Ps 22: 8 since he *d* in him."
    35:27 who *d* in the well-being
    36: 8 from your river of *d*.
    37:23 if the LORD *d* in a man's way,
Pr 3:12 as a father the son he *d* in.
    12:22 but he *d* in men who are truthful.
    23:24 he who has a wise son *d* in him.

DELILAH*
Woman who betrayed Samson (Jdg 16:4-22).

DELIVER (DELIVERANCE DELIVERED DELIVERER DELIVERS)
Ps 72:12 For he will *d* the needy who cry out
    79: 9 *d* us and forgive our sins
Mt 6:13 but *d* us from the evil one.'
2Co 1:10 hope that he will continue to *d* us,

DELIVERANCE (DELIVER)
Ps 3: 8 From the LORD comes *d*.
    32: 7 and surround me with songs of *d*.
    33:17 A horse is a vain hope for *d;*

DELIVERED (DELIVER)
Ps 34: 4 he *d* me from all my fears.

Ro 4:25 He was *d* over to death for our sins

DELIVERER (DELIVER)

Ps 18: 2 is my rock, my fortress and my *d;*
40:17 You are my help and my *d;*
140: 7 O Sovereign LORD, my strong *d,*
144: 2 my stronghold and my *d,*

DELIVERS (DELIVER)

Ps 34:17 he *d* them from all their troubles.
34:19 but the LORD *d* him from them all
37:40 The LORD helps them and *d* them
37:40 he *d* them from the wicked

DEMANDED

Lk 12:20 This very night your life will be *d*
12:48 been given much, much will be *d;*

DEMONS

Mt 12:27 And if I drive out *d* by Beelzebub,
Mk 5:15 possessed by the legion of *d,*
Ro 8:38 neither angels nor *d,* neither
Jas 2:19 Good! Even the *d* believe that—

DEMONSTRATE (DEMONSTRATES)

Ro 3:26 he did it to *d* his justice

DEMONSTRATES* (DEMONSTRATE)

Ro 5: 8 God *d* his own love for us in this:

DEN

Da 6:16 and threw him into the lions' *d.*
Mt 21:13 you are making it a '*d* of robbers.' ''

DENARIUS

Mk 12:15 Bring me a *d* and let me look at it.''

DENIED (DENY)

1Ti 5: 8 he has *d* the faith and is worse

DENIES (DENY)

1Jn 2:23 No one who *d* the Son has

DENY (DENIED DENIES DENYING)

Ex 23: 6 ''Do not *d* justice to your poor
Job 27: 5 till I die, I will not *d* my integrity.
La 3:35 to *d* a man his rights
Lk 9:23 he must *d* himself and take up his
Tit 1:16 but by their actions they *d* him.

DENYING* (DENY)

Eze 22:29 mistreat the alien, *d* them justice.
2Ti 3: 5 a form of godliness but *d* its power.
2Pe 2: 1 *d* the sovereign Lord who bought

DEPART (DEPARTED)

Ge 49:10 The scepter will not *d* from Judah,
Job 1:21 and naked I will *d.*
Mt 25:41 '*D* from me, you who are cursed,
Php 1:23 I desire to *d* and be with Christ,

DEPARTED (DEPART)

1Sa 4:21 ''The glory has *d* from Israel''—
Ps 119:102 I have not *d* from your laws,

DEPOSIT

2Co 1:22 put his Spirit in our hearts as a *d,*
5: 5 and has given us the Spirit as a *d,*
Eph 1:14 who is a *d* guaranteeing our

2Ti 1:14 Guard the good *d* that was

DEPRAVED (DEPRAVITY)

Ro 1:28 he gave them over to a *d* mind,
Php 2:15 fault in a crooked and *d* generation,

DEPRAVITY (DEPRAVED)

Ro 1:29 of wickedness, evil, greed and *d.*

DEPRIVE

Dt 24:17 Do not *d* the alien or the fatherless
Pr 18: 5 or to *d* the innocent of justice.
Isa 10: 2 to *d* the poor of their rights
29:21 with false testimony *d* the innocent
1Co 7: 5 Do not *d* each other

DEPTH (DEEP)

Ro 8:39 any powers, neither height nor *d,*
11:33 the *d* of the riches of the wisdom

DESERT

Nu 32:13 wander in the *d* forty years,
Ne 9:19 you did not abandon them in the *d.*
Ps 78:19 ''Can God spread a table in the *d?*
78:52 led them like sheep through the *d.*
Mk 1:13 and he was in the *d* forty days,

DESERTED (DESERTS)

Ezr 9: 9 our God has not *d* us
Mt 26:56 all the disciples *d* him and fled.
2Ti 1:15 in the province of Asia has *d* me,

DESERTING (DESERTS)

Gal 1: 6 are so quickly *d* the one who called

DESERTS (DESERTED DESERTING)

Zec 11:17 who *d* the flock!

DESERVE (DESERVES)

Ps 103: 10 he does not treat us as our sins *d*
Jer 21:14 I will punish you as your deeds *d,*
Mt 22: 8 those I invited did not *d* to come.
Ro 1:32 those who do such things *d* death,

DESERVES (DESERVE)

2Sa 12: 5 the man who did this *d* to die!
Lk 10: 7 for the worker *d* his wages.
1Ti 5:18 and ''The worker *d* his wages.''

DESIRABLE (DESIRE)

Pr 22: 1 A good name is more *d*

DESIRE (DESIRABLE DESIRES)

Ge 3:16 Your *d* will be for your husband,
Dt 5:21 You shall not set your *d*
1Ch 29:18 keep this *d* in the hearts
Ps 40: 6 Sacrifice and offering you did not *d*
40: 8 I *d* to do your will, O my God;
73:25 earth has nothing I *d* besides you
Pr 3:15 nothing you *d* can compare
10:24 what the righteous *d* will be
11:23 The *d* of the righteous ends only
Isa 26: 8 are the *d* of our hearts.
53: 2 appearance that we should *d* him.
55:11 but will accomplish what I *d*
Hos 6: 6 For I *d* mercy, not sacrifice,
Mt 9:13 learn what this means: 'I *d* mercy,
Ro 7:18 For I have the *d* to do what is good,

1Co 12:31 But eagerly *d* the greater gifts.
14: 1 and eagerly *d* spiritual gifts,
Php 1:23 I *d* to depart and be with Christ,
Heb 13:18 *d* to live honorably in every way.
Jas 1:15 Then, after *d* has conceived,

DESIRES (DESIRE)
Ge 4: 7 at your door; it *d* to have you,
Ps 34:12 and *d* to see many good days,
37: 4 he will give you the *d* of your heart.
103: 5 satisfies your *d* with good things,
145: 19 He fulfills the *d* of those who fear
Pr 11: 6 the unfaithful are trapped by evil *d*.
19:22 What a man *d* is unfailing love;
Mk 4:19 and the *d* for other things come in
Ro 8: 5 set on what that nature *d*;
13:14 to gratify the *d* of the sinful nature.
Gal 5:16 and you will not gratify the *d*
5:17 the sinful nature *d* what is contrary
1Ti 3: 1 an overseer, he *d* a noble task.
6: 9 and harmful *d* that plunge men
2Ti 2:22 Flee the evil *d* of youth,
Jas 1:20 about the righteous life that God *d*.
4: 1 from your *d* that battle within you?
1Pe 2:11 to abstain from sinful *d*, which war
1Jn 2:17 The world and its *d* pass away,

DESOLATE
Isa 54: 1 are the children of the *d* woman

DESPAIR
Isa 61: 3 instead of a spirit of *d*.
2Co 4: 8 perplexed, but not in *d*; persecuted,

DESPISE (DESPISED DESPISES)
Job 42: 6 Therefore I *d* myself
Pr 1: 7 but fools *d* wisdom and discipline.
3:11 do not *d* the LORD's discipline
23:22 do not *d* your mother
Lk 16:13 devoted to the one and *d* the other.
Tit 2:15 Do not let anyone *d* you.

DESPISED (DESPISE)
Ge 25:34 So Esau *d* his birthright.
Isa 53: 3 He was *d* and rejected by men,
1Co 1:28 of this world and the *d* things—

DESPISES (DESPISE)
Pr 14:21 He who *d* his neighbor sins,
15:20 but a foolish man *d* his mother.
15:32 who ignores discipline *d* himself,
Zec 4:10 "Who *d* the day of small things?

DESTINED (DESTINY)
Lk 2:34 "This child is *d* to cause the falling

DESTINY (DESTINED PREDESTINED)
Ps 73:17 then I understood their final *d*.
Ecc 7: 2 for death is the *d* of every man;

DESTITUTE
Pr 31: 8 for the rights of all who are *d*.
Heb 11:37 *d*, persecuted and mistreated—

DESTROY (DESTROYED DESTROYS DESTRUCTION)
Pr 1:32 complacency of fools will *d* them;

Mt 10:28 of the One who can *d* both soul

DESTROYED (DESTROY)
Job 19:26 And after my skin has been *d*,
Isa 55:13 which will not be *d*."
1Co 8:11 for whom Christ died, is *d*
15:26 The last enemy to be *d* is death.
2Co 5: 1 if the earthly tent we live in is *d*,
Heb 10:39 of those who shrink back and are *d*,
2Pe 3:10 the elements will be *d* by fire,

DESTROYS (DESTROY)
Pr 6:32 whoever does so *d* himself.
11: 9 mouth the godless *d* his neighbor,
18: 9 is brother to one who *d*.
28:24 he is partner to him who *d*.
Ecc 9:18 but one sinner *d* much good.
1Co 3:17 If anyone *d* God's temple,

DESTRUCTION (DESTROY)
Pr 16:18 Pride goes before *d*,
Hos 13:14 Where, O grave, is your *d*?
Mt 7:13 broad is the road that leads to *d*,
Gal 6: 8 from that nature will reap *d*;
2Th 1: 9 punished with everlasting *d*
1Ti 6: 9 that plunge men into ruin and *d*.
2Pe 2: 1 bringing swift *d* on themselves.
3:16 other Scriptures, to their own *d*.

DETERMINED (DETERMINES)
Job 14: 5 Man's days are *d*;
Isa 14:26 This is the plan *d* for the whole
Da 11:36 for what has been *d* must take place
Ac 17:26 and he *d* the times set for them

DETERMINES* (DETERMINED)
Ps 147: 4 He *d* the number of the stars
Pr 16: 9 but the LORD *d* his steps.
1Co 12:11 them to each one, just as he *d*.

DETESTABLE (DETESTS)
Pr 21:27 The sacrifice of the wicked is *d*—
28: 9 even his prayers are *d*.
Isa 1:13 Your incense is *d* to me.
Lk 16:15 among men is *d* in God's sight.
Tit 1:16 They are *d*, disobedient

DETESTS (DETESTABLE)
Dt 22: 5 LORD your God *d* anyone who
23:18 the LORD your God *d* them both.
25:16 LORD your God *d* anyone who
Pr 12:22 The LORD *d* lying lips,
15: 8 The LORD *d* the sacrifice
15: 9 The LORD *d* the way
15:26 The LORD *d* the thoughts
16: 5 The LORD *d* all the proud of heart
17:15 the LORD *d* them both.
20:23 The LORD *d* differing weights,

DEVIL (DEVIL'S)
Mt 13:39 the enemy who sows them is the *d*.
25:41 the eternal fire prepared for the *d*
Lk 4: 2 forty days he was tempted by the *d*.
8:12 then the *d* comes and takes away
Eph 4:27 and do not give the *d* a foothold.
2Ti 2:26 and escape from the trap of the *d*,

Jas   4: 7   Resist the *d*, and he will flee
1Pe   5: 8   Your enemy the *d* prowls
1Jn   3: 8   who does what is sinful is of the *d*,
Rev 12: 9   that ancient serpent called the *d*

DEVIL'S* (DEVIL)

Eph   6:11   stand against the *d* schemes.
1Ti   3: 7   into disgrace and into the *d* trap.
1Jn   3: 8   was to destroy the *d* work.

DEVOTE (DEVOTED DEVOTING DEVOTION DEVOUT)

Job 11:13   "Yet if you *d* your heart to him
Jer 30:21   for who is he who will *d* himself
Col   4: 2   *D* yourselves to prayer, being
1Ti   4:13   *d* yourself to the public reading
Tit   3: 8   may be careful to *d* themselves

DEVOTED (DEVOTE)

Ezr   7:10   For Ezra had *d* himself to the study
Ac   2:42   They *d* themselves
Ro   12:10   Be *d* to one another
1Co   7:34   Her aim is to be *d* to the Lord

DEVOTING (DEVOTE)

1Ti   5:10   *d* herself to all kinds of good deeds.

DEVOTION (DEVOTE)

1Ch 28: 9   and serve him with wholehearted *d*
Eze 33:31   With their mouths they express *d*,
1Co   7:35   way in undivided *d* to the Lord.
2Co 11: 3   from your sincere and pure *d*

DEVOUR

2Sa   2:26   "Must the sword *d* forever?
Mk 12:40   They *d* widows' houses
1Pe   5: 8   lion looking for someone to *d*.

DEVOUT (DEVOTE)

Lk   2:25   Simeon, who was righteous and *d*.

DIE (DEAD DEATH DIED DIES)

Ge   2:17   when you eat of it you will surely *d*
Ex   11: 5   Every firstborn son in Egypt will *d*,
Ru   1:17   Where you *d* I will *d*, and there I
2Ki 14: 6   each is to *d* for his own sins."
Pr   5:23   He will *d* for lack of discipline,
     10:21   but fools *d* for lack of judgment.
     15:10   he who hates correction will *d*.
     23:13   with the rod, he will not *d*.
Ecc   3: 2   a time to be born and a time to *d*,
Isa 66:24   their worm will not *d*, nor will their
Eze   3:18   that wicked man will *d* for his sin,
     18: 4   soul who sins is the one who will *d*.
     33: 8   'O wicked man, you will surely *d*,'
Mt 26:52   "for all who draw the sword will *d*
Jn 11:26   and believes in me will never *d*.
Ro   5: 7   Very rarely will anyone *d*
     14: 8   and if we *d*, we *d* to the Lord.
1Co 15:22   in Adam all *d*, so in Christ all will
     15:31   I *d* every day—I mean that,
Php   1:21   to live is Christ and to *d* is gain.
Heb   9:27   Just as man is destined to *d* once,
Rev 14:13   Blessed are the dead who *d*

DIED (DIE)

Ro   5: 6   we were still powerless, Christ *d*
     6: 2   By no means! We *d* to sin;
     6: 8   if we *d* with Christ, we believe that
     14:15   brother for whom Christ *d*.
1Co   8:11   for whom Christ *d*, is destroyed
     15: 3   that Christ *d* for our sins according
2Co   5:14   *d* for all, and therefore all *d*.
Col   3: 3   For you *d*, and your life is now
1Th   5:10   He *d* for us so that, whether we are
2Ti   2:11   If we *d* with him,
Heb   9:15   now that he has *d* as a ransom
1Pe   3:18   For Christ *d* for sins once for all,
Rev   2: 8   who *d* and came to life again.

DIES (DIE)

Job 14:14   If a man *d*, will he live again?
Pr   11: 7   a wicked man *d*, his hope perishes;
Jn 11:25   in me will live, even though he *d*;
1Co 15:36   does not come to life unless it *d*.

DIFFERENCE (DIFFERENT)

Ro 10:12   For there is no *d* between Jew

DIFFERENT (DIFFERENCE)

1Co 12: 4   There are *d* kinds of gifts,
2Co 11: 4   or a *d* gospel from the one you

DIGNITY

Pr 31:25   She is clothed with strength and *d*;

DIGS

Pr 26:27   If a man *d* a pit, he will fall into it;

DILIGENCE (DILIGENT)

Heb   6:11   to show this same *d* to the very end

DILIGENT (DILIGENCE)

Pr   21: 5   The plans of the *d* lead to profit
1Ti   4:15   Be *d* in these matters; give yourself

DIRECT (DIRECTS)

Ps 119: 35   *D* me in the path of your
     119:133   *D* my footsteps according
Jer 10:23   it is not for man to *d* his steps.
2Th   3: 5   May the Lord *d* your hearts

DIRECTS (DIRECT)

Ps   42: 8   By day the LORD *d* his love,
Isa 48:17   who *d* you in the way you should

DIRGE

Mt 11:17   we sang a *d*,

DISAPPEAR

Mt   5:18   will by any means *d* from the Law
Lk 16:17   earth to *d* than for the least stroke

DISAPPOINT* (DISAPPOINTED)

Ro   5: 5   And hope does not *d* us,

DISAPPOINTED (DISAPPOINT)

Ps   22: 5   in you they trusted and were not *d*.

DISASTER

Ps   57: 1   wings until the *d* has passed.
Pr   3:25   Have no fear of sudden *d*
     17: 5   over *d* will not go unpunished.
Isa 45: 7   I bring prosperity and create *d*;

Eze   7: 5 An unheard-of *d* is coming.

DISCERN (DISCERNING DISCERNMENT)

Ps   19:12 Who can *d* his errors?
   139: 3 You *d* my going out and my lying
Php   1:10 you may be able to *d* what is best

DISCERNING (DISCERN)

Pr   14: 6 knowledge comes easily to the *d*.
   15:14 The *d* heart seeks knowledge,
   17:24 A *d* man keeps wisdom in view,
   17:28 and *d* if he holds his tongue.
   19:25 rebuke a *d* man, and he will gain

DISCERNMENT (DISCERN)

Pr   17:10 A rebuke impresses a man of *d*
   28:11 a poor man who has *d* sees

DISCIPLE (DISCIPLES)

Mt   10:42 these little ones because he is my *d*,
Lk   14:27 and follow me cannot be my *d*.

DISCIPLES (DISCIPLE)

Mt   28:19 Therefore go and make *d*
Jn   8:31 to my teaching, you are really my *d*
   13:35 men will know that you are my *d*
Ac   11:26 The *d* were called Christians first

DISCIPLINE (DISCIPLINED DISCIPLINES)

Ps   38: 1 or *d* me in your wrath.
   39:11 You rebuke and *d* men for their sin;
   94:12 Blessed is the man you *d*, O Lord
Pr   1: 7 but fools despise wisdom and *d*.
    3:11 do not despise the Lord's *d*
    5:12 You will say, "How I hated *d!*
    5:23 He will die for lack of *d*,
    6:23 and the corrections of *d*
   10:17 He who heeds *d* shows the way
   12: 1 Whoever loves *d* loves knowledge,
   13:18 He who ignores *d* comes to poverty
   13:24 who loves him is careful to *d* him.
   15: 5 A fool spurns his father's *d*,
   15:32 He who ignores *d* despises himself,
   19:18 *D* your son, for in that there is hope
   22:15 the rod of *d* will drive it far
   23:13 Do not withhold *d* from a child;
   29:17 *D* your son, and he will give you
Heb 12: 5 do not make light of the Lord's *d*,
   12: 7 as *d*; God is treating you
   12:11 No *d* seems pleasant at the time,
Rev   3:19 Those whom I love I rebuke and *d*.

DISCIPLINED (DISCIPLINE)

Pr   1: 3 for acquiring a *d* and prudent life,
Jer   31:18 'You *d* me like an unruly calf,
1Co 11:32 we are being *d* so that we will not
Tit   1: 8 upright, holy and *d*.
Heb 12: 7 For what son is not *d* by his father?

DISCIPLINES (DISCIPLINE)

Dt   8: 5 your heart that as a man *d* his son,
Pr   3:12 the Lord *d* those he loves,
Heb 12: 6 because the Lord *d* those he loves,
   12:10 but God *d* us for our good,

DISCLOSED

Lk   8:17 is nothing hidden that will not be *d*,

DISCOURAGED

Jos   1: 9 Do not be terrified; do not be *d*,
   10:25 "Do not be afraid; do not be *d*.
1Ch 28:20 or *d*, for the Lord God,
Isa   42: 4 he will not falter or be *d*
Col   3:21 children, or they will become *d*.

DISCREDITED

2Co   6: 3 so that our ministry will not be *d*.

DISCRETION*

1Ch 22:12 May the Lord give you *d*
Pr   1: 4 knowledge and *d* to the young—
    2:11 *D* will protect you,
    5: 2 that you may maintain *d*
    8:12 I possess knowledge and *d*.
   11:22 a beautiful woman who shows no *d*.

DISCRIMINATED*

Jas   2: 4 have you not *d* among yourselves

DISFIGURED

Isa   52:14 his appearance was so *d*

DISGRACE (DISGRACEFUL DISGRACES)

Pr   11: 2 When pride comes, then comes *d*,
   14:34 but sin is a *d* to any people.
   19:26 is a son who brings shame and *d*.
Ac   5:41 of suffering *d* for the Name.
Heb 13:13 the camp, bearing the *d* he bore.

DISGRACEFUL (DISGRACE)

Pr   10: 5 during harvest is a *d* son.
   17: 2 wise servant will rule over a *d* son,

DISGRACES (DISGRACE)

Pr   28: 7 of gluttons *d* his father.
   29:15 but a child left to itself *d* his mother

DISHONEST

Pr   11: 1 The Lord abhors *d* scales,
   29:27 The righteous detest the *d;*
Lk   16:10 whoever is *d* with very little will
1Ti   3: 8 wine, and not pursuing *d* gain.

DISHONOR (DISHONORS)

Lev 18: 7 " 'Do not *d* your father
Pr   30: 9 and so *d* the name of my God.
1Co 15:43 it is sown in *d*, it is raised in glory;

DISHONORS (DISHONOR)

Dt   27:16 Cursed is the man who *d* his father

DISMAYED

Isa   28:16 the one who trusts will never be *d*.
   41:10 do not be *d*, for I am your God.

DISOBEDIENCE (DISOBEY)

Ro   5:19 as through the *d* of the one man
   11:32 to *d* so that he may have mercy
Heb   2: 2 and *d* received its just punishment,
    4: 6 go in, because of their *d*.
    4:11 fall by following their example of *d*.

DISOBEDIENT (DISOBEY)

2Ti   3: 2 proud, abusive, *d* to their parents,
Tit   1: 6 to the charge of being wild and *d*.
    1:16 *d* and unfit for doing anything

DISOBEY (DISOBEDIENCE DISOBEDIENT)

Dt   11:28 the curse if you *d* the commands
2Ch 24:20 'Why do you *d* the LORD's
Ro   1:30 they *d* their parents; they are

DISORDER

1Co 14:33 For God is not a God of *d*
2Co 12:20 slander, gossip, arrogance and *d*.
Jas   3:16 there you find *d* and every evil

DISOWN

Pr   30: 9 I may have too much and *d* you
Mt   10:33 I will *d* him before my Father
    26:35 to die with you, I will never *d* you.''
2Ti   2:12 If we *d* him,

DISPLAY (DISPLAYS)

Eze 39:21 I will *d* my glory among the nations
1Ti   1:16 Christ Jesus might *d* his unlimited

DISPLAYS (DISPLAY)

Isa   44:23 he *d* his glory in Israel.

DISPUTE (DISPUTES)

Pr   17:14 before a *d* breaks out.
1Co   6: 1 If any of you has a *d* with another,

DISPUTES (DISPUTE)

Pr   18:18 Casting the lot settles *d*

DISQUALIFIED

1Co   9:27 I myself will not be *d* for the prize.

DISREPUTE*

2Pe   2: 2 will bring the way of truth into *d*.

DISSENSION*

Pr   6:14 he always stirs up *d*.
    6:19 and a man who stirs up *d*
   10:12 Hatred stirs up *d*,
   15:18 A hot-tempered man stirs up *d*,
   16:28 A perverse man stirs up *d*,
   28:25 A greedy man stirs up *d*,
   29:22 An angry man stirs up *d*,
Ro   13:13 debauchery, not in *d* and jealousy.

DISSIPATION*

Lk   21:34 will be weighed down with *d*,
1Pe   4: 4 with them into the same flood of *d*,

DISTINGUISH

1Ki   3: 9 and to *d* between right and wrong.
Heb   5:14 themselves to *d* good from evil.

DISTORT

2Co   4: 2 nor do we *d* the word of God.
2Pe   3:16 ignorant and unstable people *d*,

DISTRESS (DISTRESSED)

Ps   18: 6 In my *d* I called to the LORD;
Jnh   2: 2 ''In my *d* I called to the LORD,
Jas   1:27 after orphans and widows in their *d*

DISTRESSED (DISTRESS)

Ro   14:15 If your brother is *d*

DIVIDED (DIVISION)

Mt   12:25 household *d* against itself will not
Lk   23:34 they *d* up his clothes by casting lots
1Co   1:13 Is Christ *d*? Was Paul crucified

DIVINATION

Lev 19:26 '' 'Do not practice *d* or sorcery.

DIVINE

Ro   1:20 his eternal power and *d* nature—
2Co 10: 4 they have *d* power
2Pe   1: 4 you may participate in the *d* nature

DIVISION (DIVIDED DIVISIONS DIVISIVE)

Lk   12:51 on earth? No, I tell you, but *d*.
1Co 12:25 so that there should be no *d*

DIVISIONS (DIVISION)

Ro   16:17 to watch out for those who cause *d*
1Co   1:10 another so that there may be no *d*
   11:18 there are *d* among you,

DIVISIVE* (DIVISION)

Tit   3:10 Warn a *d* person once,

DIVORCE

Mal   2:16 ''I hate *d*,'' says the LORD God
Mt   19: 3 for a man to *d* his wife for any
1Co   7:11 And a husband must not *d* his wife.
   7:27 Are you married? Do not seek a *d*.

DOCTOR

Mt   9:12 ''It is not the healthy who need a *d*,

DOCTRINE

1Ti   4:16 Watch your life and *d* closely.
Tit   2: 1 is in accord with sound *d*.

DOMINION

Ps   22:28 for *d* belongs to the LORD

DOOR

Ps 141: 3 keep watch over the *d* of my lips.
Mt   6: 6 close the *d* and pray to your Father
   7: 7 and the *d* will be opened to you.
Rev   3:20 I stand at the *d* and knock.

DOORKEEPER

Ps   84:10 I would rather be a *d* in the house

DOUBLE-EDGED

Heb   4:12 Sharper than any *d* sword,
Rev   1:16 of his mouth came a sharp *d* sword.
   2:12 of him who has the sharp, *d* sword.

DOUBLE-MINDED (MIND)

Ps 119:113 I hate *d* men,
Jas   1: 8 he is a *d* man, unstable

DOUBT

Mt   14:31 he said, ''why did you *d*?''
   21:21 if you have faith and do not *d*,
Mk   11:23 and does not *d* in his heart
Jas   1: 6 he must believe and not *d*,
Jude   :22 Be merciful to those who *d*;

DOWNCAST
Ps 42: 5 Why are you *d*, O my soul?
2Co 7: 6 But God, who comforts the *d*,

DRAW (DRAWING DRAWS)
Mt 26:52 "for all who *d* the sword will die
Jn 12:32 up from the earth, will *d* all men
Heb 10:22 let us *d* near to God

DRAWING (DRAW)
Lk 21:28 because your redemption is *d* near

DRAWS (DRAW)
Jn 6:44 the Father who sent me *d* him,

DREADFUL
Heb 10:31 It is a *d* thing to fall into the hands

DRESS
1Ti 2: 9 I also want women to *d* modestly,

DRINK (DRUNK DRUNKARDS DRUNKENNESS)
Pr 5:15 *D* water from your own cistern,
Lk 12:19 Take life easy; eat, *d* and be merry
Jn 7:37 let him come to me and *d*,
1Co 12:13 were all given the one Spirit to *d*.
Rev 21: 6 to *d* without cost from the spring

DRIVES
1Jn 4:18 But perfect love *d* out fear,

DROP
Pr 17:14 so *d* the matter before a dispute
Isa 40:15 Surely the nations are like a *d*

DRUNK (DRINK)
Eph 5:18 Do not get *d* on wine, which leads

DRUNKARDS (DRINK)
Pr 23:21 for *d* and gluttons become poor,
1Co 6:10 nor the greedy nor *d* nor slanderers

DRUNKENNESS (DRINK)
Lk 21:34 weighed down with dissipation, *d*
Ro 13:13 and *d*, not in sexual immorality
Gal 5:21 factions and envy; *d*, orgies,
1Pe 4: 3 living in debauchery, lust, *d*, orgies,

DRY
Isa 53: 2 and like a root out of *d* ground.
Eze 37: 4 '*D* bones, hear the word

DUST
Ge 2: 7 man from the *d* of the ground
Ps 103: 14 he remembers that we are *d*.
Ecc 3:20 all come from *d*, and to *d* all return.

DUTY
Ecc 12:13 for this is the whole *d* of man.
Ac 23: 1 I have fulfilled my *d* to God
1Co 7: 3 husband should fulfill his marital *d*

DWELL (DWELLING)
1Ki 8:27 "But will God really *d* on earth?
Ps 23: 6 I will *d* in the house of the LORD
Isa 43:18 do not *d* on the past.
Eph 3:17 so that Christ may *d* in your hearts
Col 1:19 to have all his fullness *d* in him,

Col 3:16 the word of Christ *d* in you richly

DWELLING (DWELL)
Eph 2:22 to become a *d* in which God lives

EAGER
Pr 31:13 and works with *e* hands.
1Pe 5: 2 greedy for money, but *e* to serve;

EAGLE'S (EAGLES)
Ps 103: 5 your youth is renewed like the *e*.

EAGLES (EAGLE'S)
Isa 40:31 They will soar on wings like *e*;

EAR (EARS)
1Co 2: 9 no *e* has heard,
12:16 if the *e* should say, "Because I am

EARNED
Pr 31:31 Give her the reward she has *e*,

EARS (EAR)
Job 42: 5 My *e* had heard of you
Ps 34:15 and his *e* are attentive to their cry;
Pr 21:13 If a man shuts his *e* to the cry
2Ti 4: 3 to say what their itching *e* want

EARTH (EARTHLY)
Ge 1: 1 God created the heavens and the *e*.
Ps 24: 1 *e* is the LORD's, and everything
108: 5 and let your glory be over all the *e*.
Isa 6: 3 the whole *e* is full of his glory."
51: 6 the *e* will wear out like a garment
55: 9 the heavens are higher than the *e*,
66: 1 and the *e* is my footstool.
Jer 23:24 "Do not I fill heaven and *e*?"
Hab 2:20 let all the *e* be silent before him."
Mt 6:10 done on *e* as it is in heaven.
16:19 bind on *e* will be bound
24:35 Heaven and *e* will pass away,
28:18 and on *e* has been given to me.
Lk 2:14 on *e* peace to men
1Co 10:26 The *e* is the Lord's, and everything
Php 2:10 in heaven and on *e* and under the *e*,
2Pe 3:13 to a new heaven and a new *e*,

EARTHLY (EARTH)
Php 3:19 Their mind is on *e* things.
Col 3: 2 on things above, not on *e* things.

EAST
Ps 103: 12 as far as the *e* is from the west,

EASY
Mt 11:30 For my yoke is *e* and my burden is

EAT (EATING)
Ge 2:17 but you must not *e* from the tree
Isa 55: 1 come, buy and *e*!
65:25 and the lion will *e* straw like the ox,
Mt 26:26 "Take and *e*; this is my body."
Ro 14: 2 faith allows him to *e* everything,
1Co 8:13 if what I *e* causes my brother to fall
10:31 So whether you *e* or drink
2Th 3:10 man will not work, he shall not *e*."

EATING (EAT)
Ro   14:17 kingdom of God is not a matter of *e*

EDICT
Heb 11:23 they were not afraid of the king's *e*.

EDIFIES
1Co 14: 4 but he who prophesies *e* the church

EFFECT
Isa 32:17 *e* of righteousness will be quietness
Heb   9:18 put into *e* without blood.

EFFORT
Lk   13:24 "Make every *e* to enter
Ro   9:16 depend on man's desire or *e*,
     14:19 make every *e* to do what leads
Eph   4: 3 Make every *e* to keep the unity
Heb   4:11 make every *e* to enter that rest,
     12:14 Make every *e* to live in peace
2Pe   1: 5 make every *e* to add
      3:14 make every *e* to be found spotless,

ELAH
     Son of Baasha; king of Israel (1Ki 16:6-14).

ELDERLY* (ELDERS)
Lev 19:32 show respect for the *e*

ELDERS (ELDERLY)
1Ti   5:17 The *e* who direct the affairs

ELECTION
Ro   9:11 God's purpose in *e* might stand:
2Pe   1:10 to make your calling and *e* sure.

ELI
     High priest in youth of Samuel (1Sa 1-4).
Blessed Hannah (1Sa 1:12-18); raised Samuel
(1Sa 2:11-26).

ELIJAH
     Prophet; predicted famine in Israel (1Ki 17:1;
Jas 5:17). Fed by ravens (1Ki 17:2-6). Raised
Sidonian widow's son (1Ki 17:7-24). Defeated
prophets of Baal at Carmel (1Ki 18:16-46). Ran
from Jezebel (1Ki 19:1-9). Prophesied death of
Azariah (2Ki 1). Succeeded by Elishah (1Ki 19:
19-21; 2Ki 2:1-18). Taken to heaven in whirlwind
(2Ki 2:11-12).
     Return prophesied (Mal 4:5-6); equated with
John the Baptist (Mt 17:9-13; Mk 9:9-13; Lk 1:
17). Appeared with Moses in transfiguration of
Jesus (Mt 17:1-8; Mk 9:1-8).

ELISHA
     Prophet; successor of Elijah (1Ki 19:16-21);
inherited his cloak (2Ki 2:1-18). Miracles of (2Ki
2-6).

ELIZABETH*
     Mother of John the Baptist, relative of Mary
(Lk 1:5-58).

EMBITTER*
Col   3:21 Fathers, do not *e* your children,

EMPTY
Eph   5: 6 no one deceive you with *e* words,

1Pe   1:18 from the *e* way of life handed

ENABLE (ABLE)
Lk   1:74 to *e* us to serve him without fear
Ac   4:29 *e* your servants to speak your word

ENABLED (ABLE)
Lev 26:13 *e* you to walk with heads held high.
Jn   6:65 unless the Father has *e* him."

ENABLES (ABLE)
Php   3:21 by the power that *e* him

ENCAMPS*
Ps   34: 7 The angel of the LORD *e*

ENCOURAGE (ENCOURAGEMENT)
Ps   10:17 you *e* them, and you listen
Isa   1:17 *e* the oppressed.
Ac   15:32 to *e* and strengthen the brothers.
Ro   12: 8 if it is encouraging, let him *e;*
1Th   4:18 Therefore *e* each other
2Ti   4: 2 rebuke and *e*— with great patience
Tit   2: 6 *e* the young men to be
Heb   3:13 But *e* one another daily, as long
     10:25 but let us *e* one another—

ENCOURAGEMENT (ENCOURAGE)
Ac   4:36 Barnabas (which means Son of *E),*
Ro   15: 4 *e* of the Scriptures we might have
     15: 5 and *e* give you a spirit of unity
1Co 14: 3 to men for their strengthening, *e*
Heb 12: 5 word of *e* that addresses you

END
Ps 119: 33 then I will keep them to the *e*.
Pr   14:12 but in the *e* it leads to death.
     19:20 and in the *e* you will be wise.
     23:32 In the *e* it bites like a snake
Ecc 12:12 making many books there is no *e*,
Mt   10:22 firm to the *e* will be saved.
Lk   21: 9 but the *e* will not come right away
Ro   10: 4 Christ is the *e* of the law
1Co 15:24 the *e* will come, when he hands

ENDURANCE (ENDURE)
Ro   15: 4 through *e* and the encouragement
     15: 5 May the God who gives *e*
2Co   1: 6 which produces in you patient *e*
Col   1:11 might so that you may have great *e*
1Ti   6:11 faith, love, *e* and gentleness.
Tit   2: 2 and sound in faith, in love and in *e*.

ENDURE (ENDURANCE ENDURES)
Ps   72:17 May his name *e* forever;
Pr   12:19 Truthful lips *e* forever,
     27:24 for riches do not *e* forever,
Ecc   3:14 everything God does will *e* forever;
Mal   3: 2 who can *e* the day of his coming?
2Ti   2: 3 *E* hardship with us like a good
      2:12 if we *e, I* we will also reign
Heb 12: 7 *E* hardship as discipline; God is
Rev   3:10 kept my command to *e* patiently,

ENDURES (ENDURE)
Ps 112: 9 his righteousness *e* forever;
     136: 1 *His love e forever.*

Da 9:15 made for yourself a name that *e*

ENEMIES (ENEMY)

Ps 23: 5 in the presence of my *e*.
Mic 7: 6 a man's *e* are the members
Mt 5:44 Love your *e* and pray
Lk 20:43 hand until I make your *e*

ENEMY (ENEMIES ENMITY)

Pr 24:17 Do not gloat when your *e* falls;
25:21 If your *e* is hungry, give him food
27: 6 but an *e* multiplies kisses.
1Co 15:26 The last *e* to be destroyed is death.
1Ti 5:14 and to give the *e* no opportunity

ENJOY (JOY)

Dt 6: 2 and so that you may *e* long life.
Eph 6: 3 and that you may *e* long life
Heb 11:25 rather than to *e* the pleasures of sin

ENJOYMENT (JOY)

Ecc 4: 8 and why am I depriving myself of *e*
1Ti 6:17 us with everything for our *e*.

ENLIGHTENED* (LIGHT)

Eph 1:18 that the eyes of your heart may be *e*
Heb 6: 4 for those who have once been *e*,

ENMITY* (ENEMY)

Ge 3:15 And I will put *e*

ENOCH

Walked with God and taken by him (Ge 5:
18-24; Heb 11:5). Prophet (Jude 14).

ENTANGLED (ENTANGLES)

2Pe 2:20 and are again *e* in it and overcome,

ENTANGLES* (ENTANGLED)

Heb 12: 1 and the sin that so easily *e*,

ENTER (ENTERED ENTERS ENTRANCE)

Ps 100: 4 *E* his gates with thanksgiving
Mt 5:20 will certainly not *e* the kingdom
7:13 "*E* through the narrow gate.
18: 8 It is better for you to *e* life maimed
Mk 10:15 like a little child will never *e* it."
10:23 is for the rich to *e* the kingdom

ENTERED (ENTER)

Ro 5:12 as sin *e* the world through one man,
Heb 9:12 but he *e* the Most Holy Place once

ENTERS (ENTER)

Mk 7:18 you see that nothing that *e* a man
Jn 10: 2 The man who *e* by the gate is

ENTERTAIN

1Ti 5:19 Do not *e* an accusation
Heb 13: 2 Do not forget to *e* strangers,

ENTHRALLED*

Ps 45:11 The king is *e* by your beauty;

ENTHRONED (THRONE)

1Sa 4: 4 who is *e* between the cherubim.
Ps 2: 4 The One *e* in heaven laughs;
102: 12 But you, O Lord, sit *e* forever;

Isa 40:22 He sits *e* above the circle

ENTICE

Pr 1:10 My son, if sinners *e* you,
2Pe 2:18 they *e* people who are just escaping

ENTIRE

Gal 5:14 The *e* law is summed up

ENTRUSTED (TRUST)

1Ti 6:20 guard what has been *e* to your care.
2Ti 1:12 able to guard what I have *e* to him
1:14 Guard the good deposit that was *e*
Jude : 3 once for all *e* to the saints.

ENVY

Pr 3:31 Do not *e* a violent man
14:30 but *e* rots the bones.
1Co 13: 4 It does not *e*, it does not boast,

EPHRAIM

1. Second son of Joseph (Ge 41:52; 46:20).
Blessed as firstborn by Jacob (Ge 48).
2. Synonymous with Northern Kingdom (Isa 7:
17; Hos 5).

EQUAL

Isa 40:25 who is my *e*?'' says the Holy One.
Jn 5:18 making himself *e* with God.
1Co 12:25 that its parts should have *e* concern

EQUIP* (EQUIPPED)

Heb 13:21 *e* you with everything good

EQUIPPED (EQUIP)

2Ti 3:17 man of God may be thoroughly *e*

ERROR

Jas 5:20 Whoever turns a sinner from the *e*

ESAU

Firstborn of Isaac, twin of Jacob (Ge 25:21-
26). Also called Edom (Ge 25:30). Sold Jacob his
birthright (Ge 25:29-34); lost blessing (Ge 27).
Reconciled to Jacob (Gen 33).

ESCAPE (ESCAPING)

Ro 2: 3 think you will *e* God's judgment?
Heb 2: 3 how shall we *e* if we ignore such

ESCAPING (ESCAPE)

1Co 3:15 only as one *e* through the flames.

ESTABLISH

Ge 6:18 But I will *e* my covenant with you,
1Ch 28: 7 I will *e* his kingdom forever
Ro 10: 3 God and sought to *e* their own,

ESTEEMED

Pr 22: 1 to be *e* is better than silver or gold.
Isa 53: 3 he was despised, and we *e* him not.

ESTHER

Jewess who lived in Persia; cousin of Mordecai
(Est 2:7). Chosen queen of Xerxes (Est 2:8-18).
Foiled Haman's plan to exterminate the Jews (Est
3-4; 7-9).

ETERNAL (ETERNALLY ETERNITY)

Ps   16:11 with *e* pleasures at your right hand.
   111: 10 To him belongs *e* praise.
   119: 89 Your word, O LORD, is *e;*
Isa   26: 4 LORD, the LORD, is the Rock *e.*
Mt 19:16 good thing must I do to get *e* life?''
   25:41 into the *e* fire prepared for the devil
   25:46 they will go away to *e* punishment,
Jn   3:15 believes in him may have *e* life.
    3:16 him shall not perish but have *e* life.
    3:36 believes in the Son has *e* life,
    4:14 spring of water welling up to *e* life.''
    5:24 believes him who sent me has *e* life
    6:68 You have the words of *e* life.
  10:28 I give them *e* life, and they shall
   17: 3 this is *e* life: that they may know
Ro   1:20 his *e* power and divine nature—
   6:23 but the gift of God is *e* life
2Co 4:17 for us an *e* glory that far outweighs
   4:18 temporary, but what is unseen is *e.*
1Ti 1:16 believe on him and receive *e* life.
   1:17 Now to the King *e,* immortal,
Heb 9:12 having obtained *e* redemption.
1Jn 5:11 God has given us *e* life,
   5:13 you may know that you have *e* life.

ETERNALLY (ETERNAL)

Gal   1: 8 let him be *e* condemned! As we

ETERNITY (ETERNAL)

Ps   93: 2 you are from all *e.*
Ecc   3:11 also set *e* in the hearts of men;

ETHIOPIAN

Jer 13:23 Can the *E* change his skin

EUNUCHS

Mt 19:12 For some are *e* because they were

EVANGELIST (EVANGELISTS)

2Ti   4: 5 hardship, do the work of an *e,*

EVANGELISTS* (EVANGELIST)

Eph 4:11 some to be prophets, some to be *e,*

EVE

2Co 11: 3 as *E* was deceived by the serpent's
1Ti   2:13 For Adam was formed first, then *E*

EVEN-TEMPERED*

Pr   17:27 and a man of understanding is *e.*

EVER (EVERLASTING FOREVER)

Ex 15:18 LORD will reign for *e* and *e.*''
Dt   8:19 If you *e* forget the LORD your
Ps   5:11 let them *e* sing for joy.
  10:16 The LORD is King for *e* and *e;*
   25: 3 will *e* be put to shame,
   26: 3 for your love is *e* before me,
   45: 6 O God, will last for *e* and *e;*
   52: 8 God's unfailing love for *e* and *e.*
  89:33 nor will I *e* betray my faithfulness.
  145: 1 I will praise your name for *e* and *e.*
Pr   4:18 shining *e* brighter till the full light
   5:19 may you *e* be captivated
Isa 66: 8 Who has *e* heard of such a thing?

Jer 31:36 the descendants of Israel *e* cease
Da   7:18 it forever—yes, for *e* and *e.'*
  12: 3 like the stars for *e* and *e.*
Mk   4:12 *e* hearing but never understanding;
Jn   1:18 No one has *e* seen God,
Rev 1:18 and behold I am alive for *e* and *e!*
  22: 5 And they will reign for *e* and *e.*

EVER-INCREASING* (INCREASE)

Ro   6:19 to impurity and to *e* wickedness,
2Co 3:18 into his likeness with *e* glory,

EVERLASTING (EVER)

Dt 33:27 and underneath are the *e* arms.
Ne   9: 5 your God, who is from *e* to *e.*''
Ps   90: 2 from *e* to *e* you are God.
  139: 24 and lead me in the way *e.*
Isa   9: 6 *E* Father, Prince of Peace.
  33:14 Who of us can dwell with *e* burning
  35:10 *e* joy will crown their heads.
  45:17 the LORD with an *e* salvation;
  54: 8 but with *e* kindness
  55: 3 I will make an *e* covenant with you,
  63:12 to gain for himself *e* renown,
Jer 31: 3 ''I have loved you with an *e* love;
Da   9:24 to bring in *e* righteousness,
  12: 2 some to *e* life, others to shame
Jn   6:47 the truth, he who believes has *e* life.
2Th 1: 9 punished with *e* destruction
Jude   : 6 bound with *e* chains for judgment

EVER-PRESENT*

Ps 46: 1 an *e* help in trouble

EVIDENCE (EVIDENT)

Jn 14:11 on the *e* of the miracles themselves.

EVIDENT (EVIDENCE)

Php 4: 5 Let your gentleness be *e* to all.

EVIL

Ge   2: 9 of the knowledge of good and *e.*
Job 1: 1 he feared God and shunned *e.*
   1: 8 a man who fears God and shuns *e.*''
  34:10 Far be it from God to do *e,*
Ps 23: 4 I will fear no *e,*
  34:14 Turn from *e* and do good;
  51: 4 and done what is *e* in your sight,
  97:10 those who love the LORD hate *e,*
  101: 4 I will have nothing to do with *e.*
Pr   8:13 To fear the LORD is to hate *e;*
  10:23 A fool finds pleasure in *e* conduct,
  11:27 *e* comes to him who searches for it.
  24:19 Do not fret because of *e* men
  24:20 for the *e* man has no future hope,
Isa   5:20 Woe to those who call *e* good
  13:11 I will punish the world for its *e,*
  55: 7 and the *e* man his thoughts.
Hab 1:13 Your eyes are too pure to look on *e;*
Mt   5:45 He causes his sun to rise on the *e*
   6:13 but deliver us from the *e* one.'
   7:11 If you, then, though you are *e,*
  12:35 and the *e* man brings *e* things out
Jn 17:15 you protect them from the *e* one.
Ro   2: 9 for every human being who does *e:*

Ro 12: 9 Hate what is *e;* cling
  12:17 Do not repay anyone *e* for *e.*
  16:19 and innocent about what is *e.*
1Co 13: 6 Love does not delight in *e*
  14:20 In regard to *e* be infants,
Eph 6:16 all the flaming arrows of the *e* one.
1Th 5:22 Avoid every kind of *e.*
1Ti 6:10 of money is a root of all kinds of *e.*
2Ti 2:22 Flee the *e* desires of youth,
Jas 1:13 For God cannot be tempted by *e,*
1Pe 2:16 your freedom as a cover-up for *e;*
  3: 9 Do not repay *e* with *e* or insult

EXACT

Heb 1: 3 the *e* representation of his being,

EXALT (EXALTED EXALTS)

Ps 30: 1 I will *e* you, O LORD,
  34: 3 let us *e* his name together.
  118: 28 you are my God, and I will *e* you.
Isa 24:15 *e* the name of the LORD, the God

EXALTED (EXALT)

2Sa 22:47 *E* be God, the Rock, my Savior!
1Ch 29:11 you are *e* as head over all.
Ne 9: 5 and may it be *e* above all blessing
Ps 21:13 Be *e,* O LORD, in your strength;
  46:10 I will be *e* among the nations,
  57: 5 Be *e,* O God, above the heavens;
  97: 9 you are *e* far above all gods.
  99: 2 he is *e* over all the nations.
  108: 5 Be *e,* O God, above the heavens,
  148: 13 for his name alone is *e;*
Isa 6: 1 *e,* and the train of his robe filled
  12: 4 and proclaim that his name is *e.*
  33: 5 The LORD is *e,* for he dwells
Eze 21:26 The lowly will be *e* and the *e* will be
Mt 23:12 whoever humbles himself will be *e.*
Php 1:20 always Christ will be *e* in my body,
  2: 9 Therefore God *e* him

EXALTS (EXALT)

Ps 75: 7 He brings one down, he *e* another.
Pr 14:34 Righteousness *e* a nation,
Mt 23:12 For whoever *e* himself will be

EXAMINE (EXAMINED)

Ps 26: 2 *e* my heart and my mind;
Jer 17:10 and *e* the mind,
La 3:40 Let us *e* our ways and test them,
1Co 11:28 A man ought to *e* himself
2Co 13: 5 *E* yourselves to see whether you

EXAMINED (EXAMINE)

Ac 17:11 *e* the Scriptures every day to see

EXAMPLE (EXAMPLES)

Jn 13:15 have set you an *e* that you should
1Co 11: 1 Follow my *e,* as I follow
1Ti 4:12 set an *e* for the believers in speech,
Tit 2: 7 In everything set them an *e*
1Pe 2:21 leaving you an *e,* that you should

EXAMPLES* (EXAMPLE)

1Co 10: 6 Now these things occurred as *e*
  10:11 as *e* and were written down

1Pe 5: 3 to you, but being *e* to the flock.

EXASPERATE*

Eph 6: 4 Fathers, do not *e* your children;

EXCEL (EXCELLENT)

1Co 14:12 to *e* in gifts that build up the church
2Co 8: 7 But just as you *e* in everything—

EXCELLENT (EXCEL)

1Co 12:31 now I will show you the most *e* way
Php 4: 8 if anything is *e* or praiseworthy—
1Ti 3:13 have served well gain an *e* standing
Tit 3: 8 These things are *e* and profitable

EXCHANGED

Ro 1:23 *e* the glory of the immortal God
  1:25 They *e* the truth of God for a lie,

EXCUSE (EXCUSES)

Jn 15:22 they have no *e* for their sin.
Ro 1:20 so that men are without *e.*

EXCUSES* (EXCUSE)

Lk 14:18 "But they all alike began to make *e.*

EXISTS

Heb 2:10 and through whom everything *e,*
  11: 6 to him must believe that he *e*

EXPECT (EXPECTATION)

Mt 24:44 at an hour when you do not *e* him.

EXPECTATION (EXPECT)

Ro 8:19 waits in eager *e* for the sons
Heb 10:27 but only a fearful *e* of judgment

EXPEL*

1Co 5:13 *E* the wicked man from among you

EXPENSIVE

1Ti 2: 9 or gold or pearls or *e* clothes,

EXPLOIT

Pr 22:22 Do not *e* the poor because they are
2Co 12:17 Did I *e* you through any

EXPOSE

1Co 4: 5 will *e* the motives of men's hearts.
Eph 5:11 of darkness, but rather *e* them.

EXTENDS

Pr 31:20 and *e* her hands to the needy.
Lk 1:50 His mercy *e* to those who fear him,

EXTINGUISHED

2Sa 21:17 the lamp of Israel will not be *e.*"

EXTOL*

Job 36:24 Remember to *e* his work,
Ps 34: 1 I will *e* the LORD at all times;
  68: 4 *e* him who rides on the clouds—
  95: 2 and *e* him with music and song.
  109: 30 mouth I will greatly *e* the LORD;
  111: 1 I will *e* the LORD with all my heart
  115: 18 it is we who *e* the LORD,
  117: 1 *e* him, all you peoples.
  145: 2 and *e* your name for ever and ever.
  145: 10 your saints will *e* you.
  147: 12 *E* the LORD, O Jerusalem;

EXTORT*
Lk   3:14 "Don't *e* money and don't accuse

EYE (EYES)
Ex   21:24 you are to take life for life, *e* for *e*,
Ps   94: 9 Does he who formed the *e* not see?
Mt   5:29 If your right *e* causes you to sin,
      5:38 '*E* for *e*, and tooth for tooth.'
      7: 3 of sawdust in your brother's *e*
1Co   2: 9 "No *e* has seen,
Col   3:22 not only when their *e* is on you
Rev   1: 7 and every *e* will see him,

EYES (EYE)
Nu   33:55 remain will become barbs in your *e*
Jos 23:13 on your backs and thorns in your *e*,
2Ch 16: 9 For the *e* of the LORD range
Job 31: 1 "I made a covenant with my *e*
      36: 7 He does not take his *e*
Ps119: 18 Open my *e* that I may see
      121: 1 I lift up my *e* to the hills—
      141: 8 But my *e* are fixed on you,
Pr   3: 7 Do not be wise in your own *e;*
      4:25 Let your *e* look straight ahead,
      15: 3 The *e* of the LORD are everywhere
Isa   6: 5 and my *e* have seen the King,
Hab   1:13 Your *e* are too pure to look on evil;
Jn   4:35 open your *e* and look at the fields!
2Co   4:18 So we fix our *e* not on what is seen,
Heb 12: 2 Let us fix our *e* on Jesus, the author
Jas   2: 5 poor in the *e* of the world to be rich
1Pe   3:12 For the *e* of the Lord are
Rev   7:17 wipe away every tear from their *e.*"
      21: 4 He will wipe every tear from their *e*

EZEKIEL
   Priest called to be prophet to the exiles (Eze 1-3).

EZRA
   Priest and teacher of the Law who led a return of exiles to Israel to reestablish temple and worship (Ezr 7-8). Corrected intermarriage of priests (Ezr 9-10). Read Law at celebration of Feast of Tabernacles (Neh 8).

FACE (FACES)
Ge   32:30 "It is because I saw God *f* to *f*,
Ex   34:29 was not aware that his *f* was radiant
Nu   6:25 the LORD make his *f* shine
1Ch 16:11 seek his *f* always.
2Ch   7:14 and seek my *f* and turn
Ps   4: 6 Let the light of your *f* shine upon us
      27: 8 Your *f*, LORD, I will seek.
      31:16 Let your *f* shine on your servant;
      105: 4 seek his *f* always.
      119:135 Make your *f* shine
Isa 50: 7 Therefore have I set my *f* like flint,
Mt   17: 2 His *f* shone like the sun,
1Co 13:12 mirror; then we shall see *f* to *f*.
2Co   4: 6 the glory of God in the *f* of Christ.
1Pe   3:12 but the *f* of the Lord is
Rev   1:16 His *f* was like the sun shining

FACES (FACE)
2Co   3:18 who with unveiled *f* all reflect

FACTIONS
Gal   5:20 selfish ambition, dissensions, *f*

FADE
1Pe   5: 4 of glory that will never *f* away.

FAIL (FAILING FAILINGS FAILS)
1Ch 28:20 He will not *f* you or forsake you
2Ch 34:33 they did not *f* to follow the LORD,
Ps   89:28 my covenant with him will never *f*.
Pr   15:22 Plans *f* for lack of counsel,
Isa 51: 6 my righteousness will never *f*.
La   3:22 for his compassions never *f*.
2Co 13: 5 unless, of course, you *f* the test?

FAILING (FAIL)
1Sa 12:23 sin against the LORD by *f* to pray

FAILINGS (FAIL)
Ro   15: 1 ought to bear with the *f* of the weak

FAILS (FAIL)
1Co 13: 8 Love never *f*.

FAINT
Isa 40:31 they will walk and not be *f*.

FAIR
Pr   1: 3 doing what is right and just and *f;*
Col   4: 1 slaves with what is right and *f*,

FAITH (FAITHFUL FAITHFULLY FAITHFULNESS FAITHLESS)
2Ch 20:20 Have *f* in the LORD your God
Hab   2: 4 but the righteous will live by his *f*—
Mt   9:29 According to your *f* will it be done
      17:20 if you have *f* as small as a mustard
      24:10 many will turn away from the *f*
Mk   11:22 "Have *f* in God," Jesus answered.
Lk   7: 9 I have not found such great *f*
      12:28 will he clothe you, O you of little *f!*
      17: 5 "Increase our *f!*" He replied,
      18: 8 will he find *f* on the earth?"
Ac   14: 9 saw that he had *f* to be healed
      14:27 the door of *f* to the Gentiles.
Ro   1:12 encouraged by each other's *f*.
      1:17 is by *f* from first to last,
      1:17 "The righteous will live by *f*."
      3: 3 What if some did not have *f*?
      3:22 comes through *f* in Jesus Christ
      3:25 a sacrifice of atonement, through *f*
      4: 5 his *f* is credited as righteousness.
      5: 1 we have been justified through *f*,
      10:17 *f* comes from hearing the message,
      14: 1 Accept him whose *f* is weak,
      14:23 that does not come from *f* is sin.
1Co 13: 2 and if I have a *f* that can move
      13:13 And now these three remain: *f*,
      16:13 stand firm in the *f*; be men
2Co   5: 7 We live by *f*, not by sight.
      13: 5 to see whether you are in the *f;*
Gal   2:16 Jesus that we may be justified by *f*
      2:20 I live by *f* in the Son of God,

Gal 3:11 "The righteous will live by *f*."
3:24 that we might be justified by *f*.
Eph 2: 8 through *f*— and this not
4: 5 one Lord, one *f*, one baptism;
6:16 to all this, take up the shield of *f*,
Col 1:23 continue in your *f*, established
1Th 5: 8 on *f* and love as a breastplate,
1Ti 2:15 if they continue in *f*, love
4: 1 later times some will abandon the *f*
5: 8 he has denied the *f* and is worse
6:12 Fight the good fight of the *f*.
2Ti 3:15 wise for salvation through *f*
4: 7 finished the race, I have kept the *f*.
Phm : 6 may be active in sharing your *f*,
Heb 10:38 But my righteous one will live by *f*.
11: 1 *f* is being sure of what we hope for
11: 3 By *f* we understand that
11: 5 By *f* Enoch was taken from this life
11: 6 And without *f* it is impossible
11: 7 By *f* Noah, when warned about
11: 8 By *f* Abraham, when called to go
11:17 By *f* Abraham, when God tested
11:20 By *f* Isaac blessed Jacob
11:21 By *f* Jacob, when he was dying,
11:22 By *f* Joseph, when his end was near
11:24 By *f* Moses, when he had grown up
11:31 By *f* the prostitute Rahab,
12: 2 the author and perfecter of our *f*,
Jas 2:14 if a man claims to have *f*
2:17 In the same way, *f* by itself,
2:26 so *f* without deeds is dead.
2Pe 1: 5 effort to add to your *f* goodness;
1Jn 5: 4 overcome the world, even our *f*.
Jude : 3 to contend for the *f* that was once

FAITHFUL (FAITH)

Nu 12: 7 he is *f* in all my house.
Dt 7: 9 your God is God; he is the *f* God,
32: 4 A *f* God who does no wrong,
2Sa 22:26 "To the *f* you show yourself *f*,
Ps 25:10 of the LORD are loving and *f*
31:23 The LORD preserves the *f*,
33: 4 he is *f* in all he does.
37:28 and will not forsake his *f* ones.
97:10 for he guards the lives of his *f* ones
145: 13 The LORD is *f* to all his promises
146: 6 the LORD, who remains *f* forever.
Pr 31:26 and *f* instruction is on her tongue.
Mt 25:21 'Well done, good and *f* servant!
Ro 12:12 patient in affliction, *f* in prayer.
1Co 4: 2 been given a trust must prove *f*.
10:13 And God is *f*; he will not let you be
1Th 5:24 The one who calls you is *f*
2Ti 2:13 he will remain *f*,
Heb 3: 6 But Christ is *f* as a son
10:23 for he who promised is *f*.
1Pe 4:19 themselves to their *f* Creator
1Jn 1: 9 he is *f* and just and will forgive us
Rev 1: 5 who is the *f* witness, the firstborn
2:10 Be *f*, even to the point of death,
19:11 whose rider is called *F* and True.

FAITHFULLY (FAITH)

Dt 11:13 if you *f* obey the commands I am
1Sa 12:24 and serve him *f* with all your heart;
1Ki 2: 4 and if they walk *f* before me
1Pe 4:10 *f* administering God's grace

FAITHFULNESS (FAITH)

Ps 57:10 your *f* reaches to the skies.
85:10 Love and *f* meet together;
86:15 to anger, abounding in love and *f*.
89: 1 mouth I will make your *f* known
89:14 love and *f* go before you.
91: 4 his *f* will be your shield
117: 2 the *f* of the LORD endures forever.
119: 75 and in *f* you have afflicted me.
Pr 3: 3 Let love and *f* never leave you;
Isa 11: 5 and *f* the sash around his waist.
La 3:23 great is your *f*.
Ro 3: 3 lack of faith nullify God's *f*?
Gal 5:22 patience, kindness, goodness, *f*,

FAITHLESS (FAITH)

Ps 119:158 I look on the *f* with loathing,
Jer 3:22 "Return, *f* people;
Ro 1:31 they are senseless, *f*, heartless,
2Ti 2:13 if we are *f*,

FALL (FALLEN FALLING FALLS)

Ps 37:24 though he stumble, he will not *f*,
55:22 he will never let the righteous *f*.
69: 9 of those who insult you *f* on me.
Pr 11:28 Whoever trusts in his riches will *f*.
Lk 11:17 a house divided against itself will *f*.
Ro 3:23 and *f* short of the glory of God,
Heb 6: 6 if they *f* away, to be brought back

FALLEN (FALL)

2Sa 1:19 How the mighty have *f*!
Isa 14:12 How you have *f* from heaven,
1Co 15:20 of those who have *f* asleep.
Gal 5: 4 you have *f* away from grace.
1Th 4:15 precede those who have *f* asleep.

FALLING (FALL)

Jude :24 able to keep you from *f*

FALLS (FALL)

Pr 24:17 Do not gloat when your enemy *f*;
Jn 12:24 a kernel of wheat *f* to the ground
Ro 14: 4 To his own master he stands or *f*.

FALSE (FALSEHOOD FALSELY)

Ex 20:16 "You shall not give *f* testimony
23: 1 "Do not spread *f* reports.
Pr 13: 5 The righteous hate what is *f*,
19: 5 A *f* witness will not go unpunished,
Mt 7:15 "Watch out for *f* prophets.
19:18 not steal, do not give *f* testimony,
24:11 and many *f* prophets will appear
Php 1:18 whether from *f* motives or true,
1Ti 1: 3 not to teach *f* doctrines any longer
2Pe 2: 1 there will be *f* teachers among you.

FALSEHOOD (FALSE)

Ps 119:163 I hate and abhor *f*
Pr 30: 8 Keep *f* and lies far from me;

Eph   4:25 each of you must put off *f*

FALSELY (FALSE)
Lev 19:12 " 'Do not swear *f* by my name
Lk   3:14 and don't accuse people *f*—
1Ti   6:20 ideas of what is *f* called knowledge,

FALTER*
Pr   24:10 If you *f* in times of trouble,
Isa 42: 4 he will not *f* or be discouraged

FAMILIES (FAMILY)
Ps   68: 6 God sets the lonely in *f*,

FAMILY (FAMILIES)
Pr   15:27 greedy man brings trouble to his *f*,
      31:15 she provides food for her *f*
Lk   9:61 go back and say good-by to my *f*."
      12:52 in one *f* divided against each other,
1Ti   3: 4 He must manage his own *f* well
       3: 5 how to manage his own *f*,
       5: 4 practice by caring for their own *f*
       5: 8 and especially for his immediate *f*,

FAMINE
Ge 41:30 seven years of *f* will follow them.
Am   8:11 but a *f* of hearing the words
Ro   8:35 or persecution or *f* or nakedness

FAN*
2Ti   1: 6 you to *f* into flame the gift of God,

FAST
Dt   13: 4 serve him and hold *f* to him.
Jos 22: 5 to hold *f* to him and to serve him
      23: 8 to hold *f* to the LORD your God,
Ps 119: 31 I hold *f* to your statutes, O LORD;
     139: 10 your right hand will hold me *f*.
Mt   6:16 "When you *f*, do not look somber
1Pe   5:12 Stand *f* in it.

FATHER (FATHER'S FATHERLESS FATHERS FOREFATHERS)
Ge   2:24 this reason a man will leave his *f*
      17: 4 You will be the *f* of many nations.
Ex   20:12 "Honor your *f* and your mother,
      21:15 "Anyone who attacks his *f*
      21:17 "Anyone who curses his *f*
Lev 18: 7 " 'Do not dishonor your *f*
      19: 3 you must respect his mother and *f*,
Dt   5:16 "Honor your *f* and your mother,
      21:18 son who does not obey his *f*
Ps   27:10 Though my *f* and mother forsake
      68: 5 A *f* to the fatherless, a defender
Pr   10: 1 A wise son brings joy to his *f*,
      17:21 there is no joy for the *f* of a fool.
      23:22 Listen to your *f*, who gave you life,
      23:24 *f* of a righteous man has great joy;
      28: 7 of gluttons disgraces his *f*.
      29: 3 loves wisdom brings joy to his *f*,
Isa   9: 6 Everlasting *F*, Prince of Peace.
Mt   6: 9 " 'Our *F* in heaven,
      10:37 "Anyone who loves his *f*
      15: 4 'Honor your *f* and mother'
      19: 5 this reason a man will leave his *f*
Lk   12:53 *f* against son and son against *f*,

Lk   23:34 Jesus said, "*F*, forgive them,
Jn   6:44 the *F* who sent me draws him,
       6:46 No one has seen the *F*
       8:44 You belong to your *f*, the devil,
      10:30 I and the *F* are one."
      14: 6 No one comes to the *F*
      14: 9 who has seen me has seen the *F*.
Ro   4:11 he is the *f* of all who believe
2Co   6:18 "I will be a *F* to you,
Eph   6: 2 "Honor your *f* and mother"—
Heb 12: 7 what son is not disciplined by his *f*?

FATHER'S (FATHER)
Pr   13: 1 A wise son heeds his *f* instruction,
      15: 5 A fool spurns his *f* discipline,
      19:13 A foolish son is his *f* ruin,
Lk   2:49 had to be in my *F* house?"
Jn   2:16 How dare you turn my *F* house
      10:29 can snatch them out of my *F* hand.
      14: 2 In my *F* house are many rooms;

FATHERLESS (FATHER)
Dt   10:18 He defends the cause of the *f*
      24:17 Do not deprive the alien or the *f*
      24:19 Leave it for the alien, the *f*
Ps   68: 5 A father to the *f*, a defender
Pr   23:10 or encroach on the fields of the *f*,

FATHERS (FATHER)
Ex   20: 5 for the sin of the *f* to the third
Lk   11:11 "Which of you *f*, if your son asks
Eph   6: 4 *F*, do not exasperate your children;
Col   3:21 *F*, do not embitter your children,

FATHOM*
Job 11: 7 "Can you *f* the mysteries of God?
Ps 145: 3 his greatness no one can *f*.
Ecc   3:11 yet they cannot *f* what God has
Isa 40:28 and his understanding no one can *f*
1Co 13: 2 and can *f* all mysteries and all

FAULT (FAULTS)
Mt   18:15 and show him his *f*, just
Php   2:15 of God without *f* in a crooked
Jas   1: 5 generously to all without finding *f*,
Jude   :24 his glorious presence without *f*

FAULTFINDERS*
Jude   :16 These men are grumblers and *f*;

FAULTS (FAULT)
Ps   19:12 Forgive my hidden *f*.

FAVORITISM*
Ex   23: 3 and do not show *f* to a poor man
Lev 19:15 to the poor or *f* to the great,
Ac   10:34 true it is that God does not show *f*
Ro   2:11 For God does not show *f*.
Eph   6: 9 and there is no *f* with him.
Col   3:25 for his wrong, and there is no *f*.
1Ti   5:21 and to do nothing out of *f*.
Jas   2: 1 Lord Jesus Christ, don't show *f*.
       2: 9 But if you show *f*, you sin

FEAR (AFRAID FEARS)
Dt   6:13 *F* the LORD your God, serve him

Dt 10:12 but to *f* the LORD your God,
    31:12 and learn to *f* the LORD your God
Ps 19: 9 The *f* of the LORD is pure,
    23: 4 I will *f* no evil,
    27: 1 whom shall I *f*?
    91: 5 You will not *f* the terror of night,
  111: 10 *f* of the LORD is the beginning
Pr 8:13 To *f* the LORD is to hate evil;
    9:10 *f* of the LORD is the beginning
  10:27 The *f* of the LORD adds length
  14:27 The *f* of the LORD is a fountain
  15:33 *f* of the LORD teaches a man
  16: 6 through the *f* of the LORD a man
  19:23 The *f* of the LORD leads to life:
  29:25 *F* of man will prove to be a snare,
Isa 11: 3 delight in the *f* of the LORD.
  41:10 So do not *f*, for I am with you;
Lk 12: 5 I will show you whom you should *f*:
Php 2:12 to work out your salvation with *f*
1Jn 4:18 But perfect love drives out *f*,

FEARS (FEAR)
Job 1: 8 a man who *f* God and shuns evil."
Ps 34: 4 he delivered me from all my *f*.
Pr 31:30 a woman who *f* the LORD is
1Jn 4:18 The one who *f* is not made perfect

FEED
Jn 21:15 Jesus said, "*F* my lambs."
  21:17 Jesus said, "*F* my sheep.
Ro 12:20 "If your enemy is hungry, *f* him;
Jude :12 shepherds who *f* only themselves.

FEET (FOOT)
Ps 8: 6 you put everything under his *f*:
  22:16 have pierced my hands and my *f*.
  40: 2 he set my *f* on a rock
  110: 1 a footstool for your *f*."
  119:105 Your word is a lamp to my *f*
Ro 10:15 "How beautiful are the *f*
1Co 12:21 And the head cannot say to the *f*,
  15:25 has put all his enemies under his *f*.
Heb 12:13 "Make level paths for your *f*,"

FELLOWSHIP
2Co 6:14 what *f* can light have with darkness
  13:14 and the *f* of the Holy Spirit be
Php 3:10 the *f* of sharing in his sufferings,
1Jn 1: 6 claim to have *f* with him yet walk
  1: 7 we have *f* with one another,

FEMALE
Ge 1:27 male and *f* he created them.
Gal 3:28 *f*, for you are all one in Christ Jesus

FERVOR
Ro 12:11 but keep your spiritual *f*, serving

FIELD (FIELDS)
Mt 6:28 See how the lilies of the *f* grow.
  13:38 *f* is the world, and the good seed
1Co 3: 9 you are God's *f*, God's building.

FIELDS (FIELD)
Lk 2: 8 were shepherds living out in the *f*
Jn 4:35 open your eyes and look at the *f*!

FIG (FIGS)
Ge 3: 7 so they sewed *f* leaves together

FIGHT (FOUGHT)
Ex 14:14 The LORD will *f* for you; you need
Dt 1:30 going before you, will *f* for you,
  3:22 the LORD your God himself will *f*
Ne 4:20 Our God will *f* for us!''
Ps 35: 1 *f* against those who *f* against me.
Jn 18:36 my servants would *f*
1Co 9:26 I do not *f* like a man beating the air.
2Co 10: 4 The weapons we *f*
1Ti 1:18 them you may *f* the good *f*,
  6:12 Fight the good *f* of the faith.
2Ti 4: 7 fought the good *f*, I have finished

FIGS (FIG)
Lk 6:44 People do not pick *f*

FILL (FILLED FILLS FULL FULLNESS FULLY)
Ge 1:28 and increase in number; *f* the earth
Ps 16:11 you will *f* me with joy
  81:10 wide your mouth and I will *f* it.
Pr 28:19 who chases fantasies will have his *f*
Hag 2: 7 and I will *f* this house with glory,'
Jn 6:26 you ate the loaves and had your *f*.
Ac 2:28 you will *f* me with joy
Ro 15:13 the God of hope *f* you with all joy

FILLED (FILL)
Ps 72:19 may the whole earth be *f*
  119: 64 The earth is *f* with your love,
Eze 43: 5 the glory of the LORD *f* the temple
Hab 2:14 For the earth will be *f*
Lk 1:15 and he will be *f* with the Holy Spirit
  1:41 and Elizabeth was *f* with the Holy
Jn 12: 3 the house was *f* with the fragrance
Ac 2: 4 All of them were *f*
  4: 8 Then Peter, *f* with the Holy Spirit,
  9:17 and be *f* with the Holy Spirit.''
  13: 9 called Paul, *f* with the Holy Spirit,
Eph 5:18 Instead, be *f* with the Spirit.
Php 1:11 *f* with the fruit of righteousness

FILLS (FILL)
Nu 14:21 of the LORD *f* the whole earth,
Ps 107: 9 and *f* the hungry with good things.
Eph 1:23 fullness of him who *f* everything

FILTHY
Isa 64: 6 all our righteous acts are like *f* rags;
Col 3: 8 and *f* language from your lips.
2Pe 2: 7 by the *f* lives of lawless men

FIND (FINDS FOUND)
Nu 32:23 be sure that your sin will *f* you out.
Dt 4:29 you will *f* him if you look for him
1Sa 23:16 and helped him *f* strength in God.
Ps 36: 7 *f* refuge in the shadow
  91: 4 under his wings you will *f* refuge;
Pr 14:22 those who plan what is good *f* love
  31:10 A wife of noble character who can *f*
Jer 6:16 and you will *f* rest for your souls.
Mt 7: 7 seek and you will *f*; knock

Mt 11:29 and you will *f* rest for your souls.
     16:25 loses his life for me will *f* it.
Lk 18: 8 will he *f* faith on the earth?''
Jn 10: 9 come in and go out, and *f* pasture.

FINDS (FIND)

Ps 62: 1 My soul *f* rest in God alone;
    112: 1 who *f* great delight
    119:162 like one who *f* great spoil.
Pr 18:22 He who *f* a wife *f* what is good
Mt   7: 8 he who seeks *f*; and to him who
    10:39 Whoever *f* his life will lose it,
Lk 12:37 whose master *f* them watching
    15: 4 go after the lost sheep until he *f* it?

FINISH (FINISHED)

Jn   4:34 him who sent me and to *f* his work.
     5:36 that the Father has given me to *f*,
Ac 20:24 if only I may *f* the race
2Co 8:11 Now *f* the work, so that your eager
Jas 1: 4 Perseverance must *f* its work

FINISHED (FINISH)

Ge   2: 2 seventh day God had *f* the work he
Jn 19:30 the drink, Jesus said, ''It is *f*.''
2Ti 4: 7 I have *f* the race, I have kept

FIRE

Ex 13:21 in a pillar of *f* to give them light,
Lev 6:12 *f* on the altar must be kept burning;
Isa 30:27 and his tongue is a consuming *f*.
Jer 23:29 my word like *f*,'' declares
Mt   3:11 you with the Holy Spirit and with *f*.
     5:22 will be in danger of the *f* of hell.
    25:41 into the eternal *f* prepared
Mk   9:43 where the *f* never goes out.
Ac   2: 3 to be tongues of *f* that separated
1Co 3:13 It will be revealed with *f*,
1Th 5:19 Do not put out the Spirit's *f*;
Heb 12:29 for our ''God is a consuming *f*.''
Jas 3: 5 set on *f* by a small spark.
2Pe 3:10 the elements will be destroyed by *f*,
Jude   :23 snatch others from the *f*
Rev 20:14 The lake of *f* is the second death.

FIRM

Ex 14:13 Stand *f* and you will see
2Ch 20:17 stand *f* and see the deliverance
Ps 33:11 of the LORD stand *f* forever,
    37:23 he makes his steps *f*;
    40: 2 and gave me a *f* place to stand.
    89: 2 that your love stands *f* forever,
    119: 89 it stands *f* in the heavens.
Pr   4:26 and take only ways that are *f*.
Zec 8:23 nations will take *f* hold of one Jew
Mk 13:13 he who stands *f* to the end will be
1Co 16:13 on your guard; stand *f* in the faith;
2Co 1:24 because it is by faith you stand *f*.
Eph 6:14 Stand *f* then, with the belt
Col 4:12 that you may stand *f* in all the will
2Th 2:15 stand *f* and hold to the teachings
2Ti 2:19 God's solid foundation stands *f*,
Heb 6:19 an anchor for the soul, *f* and secure
1Pe 5: 9 Resist him, standing *f* in the faith,

FIRST

Isa 44: 6 I am the *f* and I am the last;
    48:12 I am the *f* and I am the last.
Mt   5:24 *F* go and be reconciled
     6:33 But seek *f* his kingdom
     7: 5 *f* take the plank out
    20:27 wants to be *f* must be your slave—
    22:38 This is the *f* and greatest
    23:26 *F* clean the inside of the cup
Mk 13:10 And the gospel must *f* be preached
Ac 11:26 disciples were called Christians *f*
Ro   1:16 *f* for the Jew, then for the Gentile.
1Co 12:28 in the church God has appointed *f*
2Co 8: 5 they gave themselves *f* to the Lord
1Ti 2:13 For Adam was formed *f*, then Eve.
Jas 3:17 comes from heaven is *f* of all pure;
1Jn 4:19 We love because he *f* loved us.
3Jn   : 9 but Diotrephes, who loves to be *f*,
Rev 1:17 I am the *F* and the Last.
     2: 4 You have forsaken your *f* love.

FIRSTBORN (BEAR)

Ex 11: 5 Every *f* son in Egypt will die,

FIRSTFRUITS

Ex 23:19 ''Bring the best of the *f* of your soil

FISHERS

Mk   1:17 ''and I will make you *f* of men.''

FITTING*

Ps 33: 1 it is *f* for the upright to praise him.
    147: 1 how pleasant and *f* to praise him!
Pr 10:32 of the righteous know what is *f*,
    19:10 It is not *f* for a fool to live in luxury
    26: 1 honor is not *f* for a fool.
1Co 14:40 everything should be done in a *f*
Col 3:18 to your husbands, as is *f* in the Lord
Heb 2:10 sons to glory, it was *f* that God,

FIX

Dt 11:18 *F* these words of mine
Pr   4:25 *f* your gaze directly before you.
2Co 4:18 we *f* our eyes not on what is seen,
Heb 3: 1 heavenly calling, *f* your thoughts
    12: 2 Let us *f* our eyes on Jesus,

FLAME (FLAMES FLAMING)

2Ti 1: 6 you to fan into *f* the gift of God,

FLAMES (FLAME)

1Co 3:15 only as one escaping through the *f*.
    13: 3 and surrender my body to the *f*,

FLAMING (FLAME)

Eph 6:16 you can extinguish all the *f* arrows

FLASH

1Co 15:52 in a *f*, in the twinkling of an eye,

FLATTER (FLATTERING FLATTERY)

Job 32:21 nor will I *f* any man;
Jude   :16 *f* others for their own advantage.

FLATTERING (FLATTER)

Ps 12: 2 their *f* lips speak with deception.
    12: 3 May the LORD cut off all *f* lips

FLATTERY

Pr 26:28 and a *f* mouth works ruin.

FLATTERY (FLATTER)

Ro 16:18 and *f* they deceive the minds
1Th 2: 5 You know we never used *f*,

FLAWLESS*

2Sa 22:31 the word of the LORD is *f*.
Job 11: 4 You say to God, 'My beliefs are *f*
Ps 12: 6 And the words of the LORD are *f*,
18:30 the word of the LORD is *f*.
Pr 30: 5 "Every word of God is *f*;
SS 5: 2 my dove, my *f* one.

FLEE

Ps 139: 7 Where can I *f* from your presence?
1Co 6:18 *F* from sexual immorality.
10:14 my dear friends, *f* from idolatry.
1Ti 6:11 But you, man of God, *f* from all this
2Ti 2:22 *F* the evil desires of youth,
Jas 4: 7 Resist the devil, and he will *f*

FLEETING

Ps 89:47 Remember how *f* is my life.
Pr 31:30 Charm is deceptive, and beauty is *f*

FLESH

Ge 2:23 and *f* of my *f*;
2:24 and they will become one *f*.
Job 19:26 yet in my *f* I will see God;
Eze 11:19 of stone and give them a heart of *f*.
36:26 of stone and give you a heart of *f*.
Mk 10: 8 and the two will become one *f*.'
Jn 1:14 The Word became *f* and made his
6:51 This bread is my *f*, which I will give
1Co 6:16 "The two will become one *f*."
Eph 5:31 and the two will become one *f*."
6:12 For our struggle is not against *f*

FLOCK (FLOCKS)

Isa 40:11 He tends his *f* like a shepherd:
Eze 34: 2 not shepherds take care of the *f*?
Zec 11:17 who deserts the *f*!
Mt 26:31 the sheep of the *f* will be scattered.'
Ac 20:28 all the *f* of which the Holy Spirit
1Pe 5: 2 Be shepherds of God's *f* that is

FLOCKS (FLOCK)

Lk 2: 8 keeping watch over their *f* at night.

FLOG

Ac 22:25 to *f* a Roman citizen who hasn't

FLOODGATES

Mal 3:10 see if I will not throw open the *f*

FLOURISHING

Ps 52: 8 *f* in the house of God;

FLOW (FLOWING)

Nu 13:27 and it does *f* with milk and honey!
Jn 7:38 streams of living water will *f*

FLOWERS

Isa 40: 7 The grass withers and the *f* fall,

FLOWING (FLOW)

Ex 3: 8 a land *f* with milk and honey—

FOLDING

Pr 6:10 a little *f* of the hands to rest—

FOLLOW (FOLLOWING FOLLOWS)

Ex 23: 2 Do not *f* the crowd in doing wrong.
Lev 18: 4 and be careful to *f* my decrees.
Dt 5: 1 Learn them and be sure to *f* them.
Ps 23: 6 Surely goodness and love will *f* me
Mt 16:24 and take up his cross and *f* me.
Jn 10: 4 his sheep *f* him because they know
1Co 14: 1 *F* the way of love and eagerly
Rev 14: 4 They *f* the Lamb wherever he goes.

FOLLOWING (FOLLOW)

1Ti 1:18 by *f* them you may fight the good

FOLLOWS (FOLLOW)

Jn 8:12 Whoever *f* me will never walk

FOOD (FOODS)

Pr 20:13 you will have *f* to spare.
22: 9 for he shares his *f* with the poor.
25:21 If your enemy is hungry, give him *f*
31:15 she provides *f* for her family
Da 1: 8 to defile himself with the royal *f*
Jn 6:27 Do not work for *f* that spoils,
Ro 14:14 fully convinced that no *f* is unclean
1Co 8: 8 But *f* does not bring us near to God
1Ti 6: 8 But if we have *f* and clothing,
Jas 2:15 sister is without clothes and daily *f*.

FOODS (FOOD)

Mk 7:19 Jesus declared all *f* "clean.")

FOOL (FOOLISH FOOLISHNESS FOOLS)

Ps 14: 1 The *f* says in his heart,
Pr 15: 5 A *f* spurns his father's discipline,
17:28 Even a *f* is thought wise
18: 2 A *f* finds no pleasure
26: 5 Answer a *f* according to his folly,
28:26 He who trusts in himself is a *f*,
Mt 5:22 But anyone who says, 'You *f*!'

FOOLISH (FOOL)

Pr 10: 1 but a *f* son grief to his mother.
17:25 A *f* son brings grief to his father
Mt 7:26 practice is like a *f* man who built
25: 2 of them were *f* and five were wise.
1Co 1:27 God chose the *f* things of the world

FOOLISHNESS (FOOL)

1Co 1:18 of the cross is *f* to those who are
1:25 For the *f* of God is wiser
2:14 for they are *f* to him, and he cannot
3:19 of this world is *f* in God's sight.

FOOLS (FOOL)

Pr 14: 9 *F* mock at making amends for sin,
1Co 4:10 We are *f* for Christ, but you are

FOOT (FEET FOOTHOLD)

Jos 1: 3 every place where you set your *f*,
Isa 1: 6 From the sole of your *f* to the top
1Co 12:15 If the *f* should say, "Because I am

FOOTHOLD (FOOT)
Eph 4:27 and do not give the devil a *f*.

FORBEARANCE*
Ro 3:25 because in his *f* he had left the sins

FORBID
1Co 14:39 and do not *f* speaking in tongues.

FOREFATHERS (FATHER)
Heb 1: 1 spoke to our *f* through the prophets

FOREKNEW* (KNOW)
Ro 8:29 For those God *f* he
11: 2 not reject his people, whom he *f*.

FOREVER (EVER)
1Ch 16:15 He remembers his covenant *f*,
16:34 his love endures *f*.
Ps 9: 7 The LORD reigns *f*;
23: 6 dwell in the house of the LORD *f*.
33:11 the plans of the LORD stand firm *f*
86:12 I will glorify your name *f*.
92: 8 But you, O LORD, are exalted *f*.
110: 4 "You are a priest *f*,
119:111 Your statutes are my heritage *f*;
Jn 6:51 eats of this bread, he will live *f*.
14:16 Counselor to be with you *f*—
1Co 9:25 it to get a crown that will last *f*.
1Th 4:17 And so we will be with the Lord *f*.
Heb 13: 8 same yesterday and today and *f*.
1Pe 1:25 but the word of the Lord stands *f*."
1Jn 2:17 who does the will of God lives *f*.

FORFEIT
Lk 9:25 and yet lose or *f* his very self?

FORGAVE (FORGIVE)
Ps 32: 5 and you *f*
Eph 4:32 just as in Christ God *f* you.
Col 2:13 He *f* us all our sins, having
3:13 Forgive as the Lord *f* you.

FORGET (FORGETS FORGETTING)
Dt 6:12 that you do not *f* the LORD,
Ps 103: 2 and *f* not all his benefits.
137: 5 may my right hand *f* its skill₁.
Isa 49:15 "Can a mother *f* the baby
Heb 6:10 he will not *f* your work

FORGETS (FORGET)
Jn 16:21 her baby is born she *f* the anguish
Jas 1:24 immediately *f* what he looks like.

FORGETTING (FORGET)
Php 3:13 *F* what is behind and straining

FORGIVE (FORGAVE FORGIVENESS FORGIVING)
2Ch 7:14 will *f* their sin and will heal their
Ps 19:12 *F* my hidden faults.
Mt 6:12 *F* us our debts,
6:14 For if you *f* men when they sin
18:21 many times shall I *f* my brother
Mk 11:25 in heaven may *f* you your sins."
Lk 11: 4 *F* us our sins,
23:34 Jesus said, "Father, *f* them,

FORGIVENESS (FORGIVE)
Ps 130: 4 But with you there is *f*;
Ac 10:43 believes in him receives *f* of sins
Eph 1: 7 through his blood, the *f* of sins,
Col 1:14 in whom we have redemption, the *f*
Heb 9:22 the shedding of blood there is no *f*.

FORGIVING (FORGIVE)
Ne 9:17 But you are a *f* God, gracious
Eph 4:32 to one another, *f* each other,

FORMED
Ge 2: 7 And the LORD God *f* man
Ps 103: 14 for he knows how we are *f*,
Isa 45:18 but *f* it to be inhabited—
Ro 9:20 "Shall what is *f* say to him who *f* it,
1Ti 2:13 For Adam was *f* first, then Eve.
Heb 11: 3 understand that the universe was *f*

FORSAKE (FORSAKEN)
Jos 1: 5 I will never leave you nor *f* you.
24:16 "Far be it from us to *f* the LORD
2Ch 15: 2 but if you *f* him, he will *f* you.
Ps 27:10 Though my father and mother *f* me
Isa 55: 7 Let the wicked *f* his way
Heb 13: 5 never will I *f* you."

FORSAKEN (FORSAKE)
Ps 22: 1 my God, why have you *f* me?
37:25 I have never seen the righteous *f*
Mt 27:46 my God, why have you *f* me?"
Rev 2: 4 You have *f* your first love.

FORTRESS
Ps 18: 2 The LORD is my rock, my *f*
71: 3 for you are my rock and my *f*.

FOUGHT (FIGHT)
2Ti 4: 7 I have *f* the good fight, I have

FOUND (FIND)
1Ch 28: 9 If you seek him, he will be *f* by you;
Isa 55: 6 Seek the LORD while he may be *f*;
Da 5:27 on the scales and *f* wanting.
Lk 15: 6 with me; I have *f* my lost sheep.'
15: 9 with me; I have *f* my lost coin.'
Ac 4:12 Salvation is *f* in no one else,

FOUNDATION
Isa 28:16 a precious cornerstone for a sure *f*;
1Co 3:11 For no one can lay any *f* other
Eph 2:20 built on the *f* of the apostles
2Ti 2:19 God's solid *f* stands firm,

FOXES
Mt 8:20 "*F* have holes and birds

FRAGRANCE
2Co 2:16 of death; to the other, the *f* of life.

FREE (FREED FREEDOM FREELY)
Ps 146: 7 The LORD sets prisoners *f*,
Jn 8:32 and the truth will set you *f*."
Ro 6:18 You have been set *f* from sin
Gal 3:28 slave nor *f*, male nor female,

1Pe   2:16 *f* men, but do not use your freedom

FREED (FREE)
Rev   1: 5 has *f* us from our sins by his blood,

FREEDOM (FREE)
Ro   8:21 into the glorious *f* of the children
2Co   3:17 the Spirit of the Lord is, there is *f*.
Gal   5:13 But do not use your *f* to indulge
1Pe   2:16 but do not use your *f* as a cover-up

FREELY (FREE)
Isa   55: 7 and to our God, for he will *f* pardon
Mt   10: 8 Freely you have received, *f* give.
Ro   3:24 and are justified *f* by his grace
Eph   1: 6 which he has *f* given us

FRIEND (FRIENDS)
Ex   33:11 as a man speaks with his *f*.
Pr   17:17 A *f* loves at all times,
      18:24 there is a *f* who sticks closer
      27: 6 Wounds from a *f* can be trusted,
      27:10 Do not forsake your *f* and the *f*
Jas   4: 4 Anyone who chooses to be a *f*

FRIENDS (FRIEND)
Pr   16:28 and a gossip separates close *f*.
Zec   13: 6 given at the house of my *f*.'
Jn   15:13 that he lay down his life for his *f*.

FRUIT (FRUITFUL)
Ps   1: 3 which yields its *f* in season
Pr   11:30 The *f* of the righteous is a tree
Mt   7:16 By their *f* you will recognize them.
Jn   15: 2 branch in me that bears no *f*,
Gal   5:22 But the *f* of the Spirit is love, joy,
Rev   22: 2 of *f*, yielding its *f* every month.

FRUITFUL (FRUIT)
Ge   1:22 "Be *f* and increase in number
Ps   128: 3 Your wife will be like a *f* vine
Jn   15: 2 prunes so that it will be even more *f*.

FULFILL (FULFILLED FULFILLMENT)
Ps   116:14 I will *f* my vows to the LORD
Mt   5:17 come to abolish them but to *f* them.
1Co   7: 3 husband should *f* his marital duty

FULFILLED (FULFILL)
Pr   13:19 A longing *f* is sweet to the soul,
Mk   14:49 But the Scriptures must be *f*."
Ro   13: 8 loves his fellowman has *f* the law.

FULFILLMENT (FULFILL)
Ro   13:10 Therefore love is the *f* of the law.

FULL (FILL)
Ps   127: 5 whose quiver is *f* of them.
Pr   31:11 Her husband has *f* confidence
Isa   6: 3 the whole earth is *f* of his glory."
      11: 9 for the earth will be *f*
Jn   10:10 may have life, and have it to the *f*.
Ac   6: 3 known to be *f* of the Spirit

FULLNESS (FILL)
Col   1:19 to have all his *f* dwell in him,
       2: 9 in Christ all the *f* of the Deity lives

FULLY (FILL)
1Ki   8:61 your hearts must be *f* committed
2Ch   16: 9 whose hearts are *f* committed
Ps   119: 4 that are to be *f* obeyed.
     119:138 they are *f* trustworthy.
1Co   15:58 Always give yourselves *f*

FUTURE
Ps   37:37 there is a *f* for the man of peace.
Pr   23:18 There is surely a *f* hope for you,
Ro   8:38 neither the present nor the *f*,

GABRIEL*
   Angel who interpreted Daniel's visions (Da 8:
16-26; 9:20-27); announced births of John (Lk 1:
11-20), Jesus (Lk 1:26-38).

GAIN (GAINED)
Ps   60:12 With God we will *g* the victory,
Mk   8:36 it for a man to *g* the whole world,
1Co   13: 3 but have not love, I *g* nothing.
Php   1:21 to live is Christ and to die is *g*.
       3: 8 that I may *g* Christ and be found
1Ti   6: 6 with contentment is great *g*.

GAINED (GAIN)
Ro   5: 2 through whom we have *g* access

GALILEE
Isa   9: 1 but in the future he will honor *G*

GALL
Mt   27:34 mixed with *g*; but after tasting it,

GAP
Eze   22:30 stand before me in the *g* on behalf

GARDENER
Jn   15: 1 true vine, and my Father is the *g*.

GARMENT (GARMENTS)
Ps   102:26 they will all wear out like a *g*.
Mt   9:16 of unshrunk cloth on an old *g*,
Jn   19:23 This *g* was seamless, woven

GARMENTS (GARMENT)
Ge   3:21 The LORD God made *g* of skin
Isa   61:10 me with *g* of salvation
      63: 1 with his *g* stained crimson?
Jn   19:24 "They divided my *g* among them

GATE (GATES)
Mt   7:13 For wide is the *g* and broad is
Jn   10: 9 I am the *g*; whoever enters

GATES (GATE)
Ps   100: 4 Enter his *g* with thanksgiving
Mt   16:18 the *g* of Hades will not overcome it

GATHER (GATHERS)
Zec   14: 2 I will *g* all the nations to Jerusalem
Mt   12:30 he who does not *g* with me scatters
      23:37 longed to *g* your children together,

GATHERS (GATHER)
Isa   40:11 He *g* the lambs in his arms
Mt   23:37 a hen *g* her chicks under her wings,

GAVE (GIVE)
Ezr 2:69 According to their ability they *g*
Job 1:21 LORD *g* and the LORD has taken
Jn 3:16 so loved the world that he *g* his one
2Co 8: 5 they *g* themselves first to the Lord
Gal 2:20 who loved me and *g* himself for me
1Ti 2: 6 who *g* himself as a ransom

GAZE
Ps 27: 4 to *g* upon the beauty of the LORD
Pr 4:25 fix your *g* directly before you.

GENEALOGIES
1Ti 1: 4 themselves to myths and endless *g*.

GENERATIONS
Ps 22:30 future *g* will be told about the Lord
 102: 12 your renown endures through all *g*.
 145: 13 dominion endures through all *g*.
Lk 1:48 now on all *g* will call me blessed,
Eph 3: 5 not made known to men in other *g*

GENEROUS
Ps112: 5 Good will come to him who is *g*
Pr 22: 9 A *g* man will himself be blessed,
2Co 9: 5 Then it will be ready as a *g* gift,
1Ti 6:18 and to be *g* and willing to share.

GENTILE (GENTILES)
Ro 1:16 first for the Jew, then for the *G*.
 10:12 difference between Jew and *G*—

GENTILES (GENTILE)
Isa 42: 6 and a light for the *G*,
Ro 3: 9 and *G* alike are all under sin.
 11:13 as I am the apostle to the *G*,
1Co 1:23 block to Jews and foolishness to *G*,

GENTLE (GENTLENESS)
Pr 15: 1 A *g* answer turns away wrath,
Zec 9: 9 *g* and riding on a donkey,
Mt 11:29 for I am *g* and humble in heart,
 21: 5 *g* and riding on a donkey,
1Co 4:21 or in love and with a *g* spirit?
1Pe 3: 4 the unfading beauty of a *g*

GENTLENESS* (GENTLE)
2Co 10: 1 By the meekness and *g* of Christ,
Gal 5:23 faithfulness, *g* and self-control.
Php 4: 5 Let your *g* be evident to all.
Col 3:12 kindness, humility, *g* and patience.
1Ti 6:11 faith, love, endurance and *g*.
1Pe 3: 15 But do this with *g* and respect,

GETHSEMANE
Mt 26:36 disciples to a place called *G*,

GIDEON*
 Judge, also called Jerub-Baal; freed Israel from Midianites (Jdg 6-8; Heb 11:32). Given sign of fleece (Jdg 8:36-40).

GIFT (GIFTS)
Pr 21:14 A *g* given in secret soothes anger,
Mt 5:23 if you are offering your *g*
Ac 2:38 And you will receive the *g*
Ro 6:23 but the *g* of God is eternal life

1Co 7: 7 each man has his own *g* from God;
2Co 8:12 the *g* is acceptable according
 9:15 be to God for his indescribable *g*!
Eph 2: 8 it is the *g* of God—not by works,
1Ti 4:14 not neglect your *g*, which was
2Ti 1: 6 you to fan into flame the *g* of God,
Jas 1:17 and perfect *g* is from above,
1Pe 4:10 should use whatever *g* he has

GIFTS (GIFT)
Ro 11:29 for God's *g* and his call are
 12: 6 We have different *g*, according
1Co 12: 4 There are different kinds of *g*,
 12:31 But eagerly desire the greater *g*.
 14: 1 and eagerly desire spiritual *g*,
 14:12 excel in *g* that build up the church.

GILEAD
Jer 8:22 Is there no balm in *G*?

GIVE (GAVE GIVEN GIVER GIVES GIVING)
Nu 6:26 and *g* you peace.' ''
1Sa 1:11 then I will *g* him to the LORD
2Ch 15: 7 be strong and do not *g* up,
Pr 21:26 but the righteous *g* without sparing
 23:26 My son, *g* me your heart
 30: 8 but *g* me only my daily bread.
 31:31 *G* her the reward she has earned,
Isa 42: 8 I will not *g* my glory to another
Eze 36:26 I will *g* you a new heart
Mt 6:11 *G* us today our daily bread.
 10: 8 Freely you have received, freely *g*.
 22:21 ''*G* to Caesar what is Caesar's,
Mk 8:37 Or what can a man *g* in exchange
Lk 6:38 *G*, and it will be given to you;
 11:13 Father in heaven the Holy Spirit
Jn 10:28 I *g* them eternal life, and they shall
 13:34 ''A new commandment I *g* you:
Ac 20:35 blessed to *g* than to receive.' ''
Ro 12: 8 let him *g* generously;
 13: 7 *G* everyone what you owe him:
 14:12 each of us will *g* an account
2Co 9: 7 Each man should *g* what he has
Rev 14: 7 ''Fear God and *g* him glory,

GIVEN (GIVE)
Nu 8:16 are to be *g* wholly to me.
Ps115: 16 but the earth he has *g* to man.
Isa 9: 6 to us a son is *g*,
Mt 6:33 and all these things will be *g* to you
 7: 7 ''Ask and it will be *g* to you;
Lk 22:19 saying, ''This is my body *g* for you;
Jn 3:27 man can receive only what is *g* him
Ro 5: 5 the Holy Spirit, whom he has *g* us.
1Co 4: 2 those who have been *g* a trust must
 12:13 we were all *g* the one Spirit to drink
Eph 4: 7 to each one of us grace has been *g*

GIVER* (GIVE)
Pr 18:16 A gift opens the way for the *g*
2Co 9: 7 for God loves a cheerful *g*.

GIVES (GIVE)
Ps119:130 The unfolding of your words *g* light;

Pr   14:30 A heart at peace *g* life to the body,
     15:30 good news *g* health to the bones.
     28:27 He who *g* to the poor will lack
Isa 40:29 He *g* strength to the weary
Mt   10:42 if anyone *g* even a cup of cold water
Jn   6:63 The Spirit *g* life; the flesh counts
1Co 15:57 He *g* us the victory
2Co   3: 6 the letter kills, but the Spirit *g* life.

GIVING (GIVE)

Ne   8: 8 *g* the meaning so that the people
Ps   19: 8 *g* joy to the heart.
Mt   6: 4 so that your *g* may be in secret.
2Co   8: 7 also excel in this grace of *g*.

GLAD (GLADNESS)

Ps   31: 7 I will be *g* and rejoice in your love,
     46: 4 whose streams make *g* the city
     97: 1 LORD reigns, let the earth be *g;*
    118: 24 let us rejoice and be *g* in it.
Pr   23:25 May your father and mother be *g;*
Zec   2:10 and be *g*, O Daughter of Zion.
Mt   5:12 be *g*, because great is your reward

GLADNESS (GLAD)

Ps   45:15 They are led in with joy and *g;*
     51: 8 Let me hear joy and *g;*
    100: 2 Serve the LORD with *g;*
Jer 31:13 I will turn their mourning into *g;*

GLORIFIED (GLORY)

Jn   13:31 Son of Man *g* and God is *g* in him.
Ro   8:30 those he justified, he also *g*.
2Th   1:10 comes to be *g* in his holy people

GLORIFY (GLORY)

Ps   34: 3 *G* the LORD with me;
     86:12 I will *g* your name forever.
Jn   13:32 God will *g* the Son in himself,
     17: 1 *G* your Son, that your Son may

GLORIOUS (GLORY)

Ps   45:13 All *g* is the princess
    111: 3 *G* and majestic are his deeds,
    145: 5 of the *g* splendor of your majesty,
Isa   4: 2 the LORD will be beautiful and *g*,
     12: 5 for he has done *g* things;
     42:21 to make his law great and *g*.
     63:15 from your lofty throne, holy and *g*.
Mt   19:28 the Son of Man sits on his *g* throne,
Lk   9:31 appeared in *g* splendor, talking
Ac   2:20 of the great and *g* day of the Lord.
2Co   3: 8 of the Spirit be even more *g?*
Php   3:21 so that they will be like his *g* body.
      4:19 to his *g* riches in Christ Jesus.
Tit   2:13 the *g* appearing of our great God
Jude   :24 before his *g* presence without fault

GLORY (GLORIFIED GLORIFY GLORIOUS)

Ex   15:11 awesome in *g*,
     33:18 Moses said, "Now show me your *g*
1Sa   4:21 "The *g* has departed from Israel"—
1Ch 16:24 Declare his *g* among the nations,
     16:28 ascribe to the LORD *g*

1Ch 29:11 and the *g* and the majesty
Ps   8: 5 and crowned him with *g* and honor
     19: 1 The heavens declare the *g* of God;
     24: 7 that the King of *g* may come in.
     29: 1 ascribe to the LORD *g*
     72:19 the whole earth be filled with his *g*.
     96: 3 Declare his *g* among the nations,
Pr   19:11 it is to his *g* to overlook an offense.
     25: 2 It is the *g* of God to conceal
Isa   6: 3 the whole earth is full of his *g*."
     48:11 I will not yield my *g* to another.
Eze 43: 2 and the land was radiant with his *g*.
Mt   24:30 of the sky, with power and great *g*.
     25:31 the Son of Man comes in his *g*,
Mk   8:38 in his Father's *g* with the holy
     13:26 in clouds with great power and *g*.
Lk   2: 9 and the *g* of the Lord shone
      2:14 saying, "*G* to God in the highest,
Jn   1:14 We have seen his *g*, the *g* of the One
     17: 5 presence with the *g* I had with you
     17:24 to see my *g*, the *g* you have given
Ac   7: 2 The God of *g* appeared
Ro   1:23 exchanged the *g* of the immortal
      3:23 and fall short of the *g* of God,
      8:18 with the *g* that will be revealed
      9: 4 theirs the divine *g*, the covenants,
1Co 10:31 whatever you do, do it all for the *g*
     11: 7 but the woman is the *g* of man.
     15:43 it is raised in *g;* it is sown
2Co   3:10 comparison with the surpassing *g*.
      3:18 faces all reflect the Lord's *g*,
      4:17 us an eternal *g* that far outweighs
Col   1:27 Christ in you, the hope of *g*.
      3: 4 also will appear with him in *g*.
1Ti   3:16 was taken up in *g*.
Heb   1: 3 The Son is the radiance of God's *g*
      2: 7 you crowned him with *g* and honor
1Pe   1:24 and all their *g* is like the flowers
Rev   4:11 to receive *g* and honor and power,
     21:23 for the *g* of God gives it light,

GLUTTONS

Tit   1:12 always liars, evil brutes, lazy *g*."

GNASHING

Mt   8:12 where there will be weeping and *g*

GNAT*

Mt   23:24 You strain out a *g* but swallow

GOAL

2Co   5: 9 So we make it our *g* to please him,
Gal   3: 3 to attain your *g* by human effort?
Php   3:14 on toward the *g* to win the prize

GOAT (GOATS SCAPEGOAT)

Isa 11: 6 the leopard will lie down with the *g*

GOATS (GOAT)

Nu   7:17 five male *g* and five male lambs

GOD (GOD'S GODLINESS GODLY GODS)

Ge   1: 1 In the beginning *G* created
      1: 2 and the Spirit of *G* was hovering

Ge	1:26	Then *G* said, "Let us make man
	1:27	So *G* created man in his own image
	1:31	*G* saw all that he had made,
	2: 3	And *G* blessed the seventh day
	2:22	Then the LORD *G* made a woman
	3:21	The LORD *G* made garments
	3:23	So the LORD *G* banished him
	5:22	Enoch walked with *G* 300 years
	6: 2	sons of *G* saw that the daughters
	9:16	everlasting covenant between *G*
	17: 1	"I am *G* Almighty; walk before me
	21:33	name of the LORD, the Eternal *G*.
	22: 8	"*G* himself will provide the lamb
	28:12	and the angels of *G* were ascending
	32:28	because you have struggled with *G*
	32:30	"It is because I saw *G* face to face,
	35:10	*G* said to him, "Your name is Jacob
	41:51	*G* has made me forget all my
	50:20	but *G* intended it for good
Ex	2:24	*G* heard their groaning
	3: 6	because he was afraid to look at *G*.
	6: 7	own people, and I will be your *G*.
	8:10	is no one like the LORD our *G*.
	13:18	So *G* led the people
	15: 2	He is my *G*, and I will praise him,
	17: 9	with the staff of *G* in my hands."
	19: 3	Then Moses went up to *G*,
	20: 2	the LORD your *G*, who brought
	20: 5	the LORD your *G*, am a jealous *G*,
	20:19	But do not have *G* speak to us
	22:28	"Do not blaspheme *G*
	31:18	inscribed by the finger of *G*.
	34: 6	the compassionate and gracious *G*,
	34:14	name is Jealous, is a jealous *G*.
Lev	18:21	not profane the name of your *G*.
	19: 2	the LORD your *G*, am holy.
	26:12	walk among you and be your *G*,
Nu	22:38	I must speak only what *G* puts
	23:19	*G* is not a man, that he should lie,
Dt	1:17	for judgment belongs to *G*.
	3:22	LORD your *G* himself will fight
	3:24	For what *g* is there in heaven
	4:24	is a consuming fire, a jealous *G*.
	4:31	the LORD your *G* is a merciful *G*;
	4:39	heart this day that the LORD is *G*
	5:11	the name of the LORD your *G*,
	5:14	a Sabbath to the LORD your *G*.
	5:26	of the living *G* speaking out of fire,
	6: 4	LORD our *G*, the LORD is one.
	6: 5	Love the LORD your *G*
	6:13	the LORD your *G*, serve him only
	6:16	Do not test the LORD your *G*
	7: 9	your *G* is *G*; he is the faithful *G*,
	7:12	the LORD your *G* will keep his
	7:21	is a great and awesome *G*.
	8: 5	the LORD your *G* disciplines you.
	10:12	but to fear the LORD your *G*,
	10:14	the LORD your *G* belong
	10:17	For the LORD your *G* is *G* of gods
	11:13	to love the LORD your *G*
	13: 3	The LORD your *G* is testing you
	13: 4	the LORD your *G* you must
Dt	15: 6	the LORD your *G* will bless you
	19: 9	to love the LORD your *G*
	25:16	the LORD your *G* detests anyone
	29:29	belong to the LORD our *G*,
	30: 2	return to the LORD your *G*
	30:16	today to love the LORD your *G*,
	30:20	you may love the LORD your *G*,
	31: 6	for the LORD your *G* goes
	32: 3	Oh, praise the greatness of our *G*!
	32: 4	A faithful *G* who does no wrong,
	33:27	The eternal *G* is your refuge,
Jos	1: 9	for the LORD your *G* will be
	14: 8	the LORD my *G* wholeheartedly.
	22: 5	to love the LORD your *G*,
	22:34	Between Us that the LORD is *G*.
	23:11	careful to love the LORD your *G*.
	23:14	the LORD your *G* gave you has
Jdg	16:28	O *G*, please strengthen me just
Ru	1:16	be my people and your *G* my *G*.
1Sa	2: 2	there is no Rock like our *G*.
	2: 3	for the LORD is a *G* who knows,
	2:25	another man, *G* may mediate
	10:26	men whose hearts *G* had touched.
	12:12	the LORD your *G* was your king.
	17:26	defy the armies of the living *G*?"
	17:46	world will know that there is a *G*
	30: 6	strength in the LORD his *G*.
2Sa	14:14	But *G* does not take away life;
	22: 3	my *G* is my rock, in whom I take
	22:31	"As for *G*, his way is perfect;
1Ki	4:29	*G* gave Solomon wisdom
	8:23	there is no *G* like you in heaven
	8:27	"But will *G* really dwell on earth?
	8:61	committed to the LORD our *G*,
	18:21	If the LORD is *G*, follow him;
	18:37	are *G*, and that you are turning
	20:28	a *g* of the hills and not a *g*
2Ki	19:15	*G* of Israel, enthroned
1Ch	16:35	Cry out, "Save us, O *G* our Savior;
	28: 2	for the footstool of our *G*,
	28: 9	acknowledge the *G* of your father,
	29:10	*G* of our father Israel,
	29:17	my *G*, that you test the heart
2Ch	2: 4	for the Name of the LORD my *G*
	5:14	of the LORD filled the temple of *G*
	6:18	"But will *G* really dwell on earth
	18:13	I can tell him only what my *G* says
	20: 6	are you not the *G* who is in heaven?
	25: 8	for *G* has the power to help
	30: 9	for the LORD your *G* is gracious
	33:12	the favor of the LORD his *G*
Ezr	8:22	"The good hand of our *G* is
	9: 6	"O my *G*, I am too ashamed
	9:13	our *G*, you have punished us less
Ne	1: 5	the great and awesome *G*,
	8: 8	from the Book of the Law of *G*,
	9:17	But you are a forgiving *G*,
	9:32	the great, mighty and awesome *G*,
Job	1: 1	he feared *G* and shunned evil.
	2:10	Shall we accept good from *G*,
	4:17	a mortal be more righteous than *G*?
	5:17	is the man whom *G* corrects;

Job	11: 7	Can you fathom the mysteries of *G*
	19:26	yet in my flesh I will see *G;*
	22:13	Yet you say, 'What does *G* know?
	25: 4	can a man be righteous before *G?*
	33:14	For *G* does speak—now one way,
	34:12	is unthinkable that *G* would do
	36:26	is *G*— beyond our understanding!
	37:22	*G* comes in awesome majesty.
Ps	18: 2	my *G* is my rock, in whom I take
	18:28	my *G* turns my darkness into light.
	19: 1	The heavens declare the glory of *G;*
	22: 1	*G*, my *G*, why have you forsaken
	29: 3	the *G* of glory thunders,
	31:14	I say, "You are my *G*."
	40: 3	a hymn of praise to our *G*.
	40: 8	I desire to do your will, O my *G;*
	42: 2	thirsts for *G*, for the living *G*.
	42:11	Put your hope in *G*,
	45: 6	O *G*, will last for ever and ever;
	46: 1	*G* is our refuge and strength,
	46:10	"Be still, and know that I am *G;*
	47: 7	For *G* is the King of all the earth;
	50: 3	Our *G* comes and will not be silent;
	51: 1	Have mercy on me, O *G*,
	51:10	Create in me a pure heart, O *G*,
	51:17	O *G*, you will not despise.
	62: 7	my honor depend on *G;*
	65: 5	O *G* our Savior,
	66: 1	Shout with joy to *G*, all the earth!
	66:16	listen, all you who fear *G;*
	68: 6	*G* sets the lonely in families,
	71:17	my youth, O *G*, you have taught
	71:19	reaches to the skies, O *G*,
	71:22	harp for your faithfulness, O my *G;*
	73:26	but *G* is the strength of my heart
	77:13	What *g* is so great as our God?
	78:19	Can *G* spread a table in the desert?
	81: 1	Sing for joy to *G* our strength;
	84: 2	out for the living *G*.
	84:10	a doorkeeper in the house of my *G*
	86:12	O Lord my *G*, with all my heart;
	89: 7	of the holy ones *G* is greatly feared;
	90: 2	to everlasting you are *G*.
	91: 2	my *G*, in whom I trust."
	95: 7	for he is our *G*
	100: 3	Know that the LORD is *G*.
	108: 1	My heart is steadfast, O *G;*
	113: 5	Who is like the LORD our *G*,
	139: 23	Search me, O *G*, and know my
Pr	3: 4	in the sight of *G* and man.
	25: 2	of *G* to conceal a matter;
	30: 5	"Every word of *G* is flawless;
Ecc	3:11	cannot fathom what *G* has done
	11: 5	cannot understand the work of *G*,
	12:13	Fear *G* and keep his
Isa	9: 6	Wonderful Counselor, Mighty *G*,
	37:16	you alone are *G* over all
	40: 3	a highway for our *G*.
	40: 8	the word of our *G* stands forever."
	40:28	The LORD is the everlasting *G*,
	41:10	not be dismayed, for I am your *G*.
	44: 6	apart from me there is no *G*.

Isa	52: 7	"Your *G* reigns!"
	55: 7	to our *G*, for he will freely pardon.
	57:21	says my *G*, "for the wicked."
	59: 2	you from your *G;*
	61:10	my soul rejoices in my *G*.
	62: 5	so will your *G* rejoice over you.
Jer	23:23	"Am I only a *G* nearby,"
	31:33	I will be their *G*,
	32:27	"I am the LORD, the *G*
Eze	28:13	the garden of *G;*
Da	3:17	the *G* we serve is able to save us
	9: 4	O Lord, the great and awesome *G*,
Hos	12: 6	and wait for your *G* always.
Joel	2:13	Return to the LORD your *G*,
Am	4:12	prepare to meet your *G*, O Israel."
Mic	6: 8	and to walk humbly with your *G*.
Na	1: 2	LORD is a jealous and avenging *G;*
Zec	14: 5	Then the LORD my *G* will come,
Mal	3: 8	Will a man rob *G*? Yet you rob me.
Mt	1:23	which means, "*G* with us."
	5: 8	for they will see *G*.
	6:24	You cannot serve both *G*
	19: 6	Therefore what *G* has joined
	19:26	but with *G* all things are possible."
	22:21	and to *G* what is God's."
	22:37	" 'Love the Lord your *G*
	27:46	which means, "My *G*, my *G*,
Mk	12:29	the Lord our *G*, the Lord is one.
	16:19	and he sat at the right hand of *G*.
Lk	1:37	For nothing is impossible with *G*."
	1:47	my spirit rejoices in *G* my Savior,
	10: 9	'The kingdom of *G* is near you.'
	10:27	" 'Love the Lord your *G*
	18:19	"No one is good—except *G* alone.
Jn	1: 1	was with *G*, and the Word was *G*.
	1:18	seen *G*, but *G* the One and Only,
	3:16	"For *G* so loved the world that he
	4:24	*G* is spirit, and his worshipers must
	14: 1	Trust in *G;* trust also in me.
	20:28	"My Lord and my *G!*"
Ac	2:24	But *G* raised him from the dead,
	5: 4	You have not lied to men but to *G*
	5:29	"We must obey *G* rather than men!
	7:55	to heaven and saw the glory of *G*,
	17:23	TO AN UNKNOWN *G*.
	20:27	to you the whole will of *G*.
	20:32	"Now I commit you to *G*
Ro	1:17	a righteousness from *G* is revealed,
	2:11	For *G* does not show favoritism.
	3: 4	Let *G* be true, and every man a liar.
	3:23	and fall short of the glory of *G*,
	4:24	to whom *G* will credit
	5: 8	*G* demonstrates his own love for us
	6:23	but the gift of *G* is eternal life
	8:28	in all things *G* works for the good
	11:22	the kindness and sternness of *G;*
	14:12	give an account of himself to *G*.
1Co	1:20	Has not *G* made foolish
	2: 9	what *G* has prepared
	3: 6	watered it, but *G* made it grow.
	6:20	Therefore honor *G* with your body.
	7:24	each man, as responsible to *G*,

1Co 8: 8 food does not bring us near to *G;*
    10:13 *G* is faithful; he will not let you be
    10:31 do it all for the glory of *G.*
    14:33 For *G* is not a *G* of disorder
    15:28 so that *G* may be all in all.
2Co 1: 9 rely on ourselves but on *G,*
    2:14 be to *G,* who always leads us
    3: 5 but our competence comes from *G.*
    4: 7 this all-surpassing power is from *G*
    5:19 that *G* was reconciling the world
    5:21 *G* made him who had no sin
    6:16 we are the temple of the living *G.*
    9: 7 for *G* loves a cheerful giver.
    9: 8 *G* is able to make all grace abound
Gal 2: 6 *G* does not judge by external
    6: 7 not be deceived: *G* cannot be
Eph 2:10 which *G* prepared in advance for us
    4: 6 one baptism; one *G* and Father
    5: 1 Be imitators of *G,* therefore,
Php 2: 6 Who, being in very nature *G,*
    4:19 And my *G* will meet all your needs
1Th 2: 4 trying to please men but *G,*
    4: 7 For *G* did not call us to be impure,
    4: 9 taught by *G* to love each other.
    5: 9 For *G* did not appoint us
1Ti 2: 5 one mediator between *G* and men,
    4: 4 For everything *G* created is good,
    5: 4 for this is pleasing to *G.*
Tit 2:13 glorious appearing of our great *G*
Heb 1: 1 In the past *G* spoke
    4:12 For the word of *G* is living
    6:10 *G* is not unjust; he will not forget
    10:31 to fall into the hands of the living *G*
    11: 6 faith it is impossible to please *G,*
    12:10 but *G* disciplines us for our good,
    12:29 for our ''*G* is a consuming fire.''
    13:15 offer to *G* a sacrifice of praise—
Jas 1:13 For *G* cannot be tempted by evil,
    2:19 You believe that there is one *G.*
    2:23 ''Abraham believed *G,*
    4: 4 the world becomes an enemy of *G.*
    4: 8 Come near to *G* and he will come
1Pe 4:11 it with the strength *G* provides,
2Pe 1:21 but men spoke from *G*
1Jn 1: 5 *G* is light; in him there is no
    3:20 For *G* is greater than our hearts,
    4: 7 for love comes from *G.*
    4: 9 This is how *G* showed his love
    4:11 Dear friends, since *G* so loved us,
    4:12 No one has ever seen *G;*
    4:16 *G* is love.
Rev 4: 8 holy is the Lord *G* Almighty,
    7:17 *G* will wipe away every tear
    19: 6 For our Lord *G* Almighty reigns.

GOD-BREATHED* (BREATHED)

2Ti 3:16 All Scripture is *G* and is useful

GOD'S (GOD)

2Ch 20:15 For the battle is not yours, but *G.*
Job 37:14 stop and consider *G* wonders.
Ps 52: 8 I trust in *G* unfailing love
    69:30 I will praise *G* name in song

Mk 3:35 Whoever does *G* will is my brother
Jn 7:17 If anyone chooses to do *G* will,
    10:36 'I am *G* Son'? Do not believe me
Ro 2: 3 think you will escape *G* judgment?
    2: 4 not realizing that *G* kindness leads
    3: 3 lack of faith nullify *G* faithfulness?
    7:22 in my inner being I delight in *G* law
    9:16 or effort, but on *G* mercy.
    11:29 for *G* gifts and his call are
    12: 2 and approve what *G* will is—
    12:13 Share with *G* people who are
    13: 6 for the authorities are *G* servants,
1Co 7:19 Keeping *G* commands is what
2Co 6: 2 now is the time of *G* favor,
Eph 1: 7 riches of *G* grace that he lavished
1Th 4: 3 It is *G* will that you should be
    5:18 for this is *G* will for you
1Ti 6: 1 so that *G* name and our teaching
2Ti 2:19 *G* solid foundation stands firm,
Tit 1: 7 overseer is entrusted with *G* work,
Heb 1: 3 The Son is the radiance of *G* glory
    9:24 now to appear for us in *G* presence.
    11: 3 was formed at *G* command,
1Pe 2:15 For it is *G* will that
    3: 4 which is of great worth in *G* sight.
1Jn 2: 5 *G* love is truly made complete

GODLINESS (GOD)

1Ti 2: 2 and quiet lives in all *g* and holiness.
    4: 8 but *g* has value for all things,
    6: 6 *g* with contentment is great gain.
    6:11 and pursue righteousness, *g,* faith,

GODLY (GOD)

Ps 4: 3 that the Lord has set apart the *g*
2Co 7:10 *G* sorrow brings repentance that
    11: 2 jealous for you with a *g* jealousy.
2Ti 3:12 everyone who wants to live a *g* life
2Pe 3:11 You ought to live holy and *g* lives

GODS (GOD)

Ex 20: 3 ''You shall have no other *g*
Ac 19:26 He says that man-made *g* are no *g*

GOLD

Job 23:10 tested me, I will come forth as *g.*
Ps 19:10 They are more precious than *g,*
    119:127 more than *g,* more than pure *g,*
Pr 22: 1 esteemed is better than silver or *g.*

GOLGOTHA

Jn 19:17 (which in Aramaic is called *G).*

GOLIATH

    Philistine giant killed by David (1Sa 17; 21:9).

GOOD

Ge 1: 4 God saw that the light was *g,*
    1:31 he had made, and it was very *g.*
    2:18 ''It is not *g* for the man to be alone.
    50:20 but God intended it for *g*
Job 2:10 Shall we accept *g* from God,
Ps 14: 1 there is no one who does *g.*
    34: 8 Taste and see that the Lord is *g;*
    37: 3 Trust in the Lord and do *g;*

Ps	84:11	no *g* thing does he withhold
	86: 5	You are forgiving and *g*, O Lord
	103: 5	satisfies your desires with *g* things,
	119: 68	You are *g*, and what you do is *g*;
	133: 1	How *g* and pleasant it is
	147: 1	How *g* it is to sing praises
Pr	3: 4	you will win favor and a *g* name
	11:27	He who seeks *g* finds *g* will,
	17:22	A cheerful heart is *g* medicine,
	18:22	He who finds a wife finds what is *g*
	22: 1	A *g* name is more desirable
	31:12	She brings him *g*, not harm,
Isa	5:20	Woe to those who call evil *g*
	52: 7	the feet of those who bring *g* news,
Jer	6:16	ask where the *g* way is,
	32:39	the *g* of their children after them.
Mic	6: 8	has showed you, O man, what is *g*.
Mt	5:45	sun to rise on the evil and the *g*,
	7:17	Likewise every *g* tree bears *g* fruit,
	12:35	The *g* man brings *g* things out
	19:17	"There is only One who is *g*.
	25:21	'Well done, *g* and faithful servant!
Mk	3: 4	lawful on the Sabbath: to do *g*
	8:36	What *g* is it for a man
Lk	6:27	do *g* to those who hate you,
Jn	10:11	"I am the *g* shepherd.
Ro	8:28	for the *g* of those who love him,
	10:15	feet of those who bring *g* news!"
	12: 9	Hate what is evil; cling to what is *g*.
1Co	10:24	should seek his own *g*, but the *g*
	15:33	Bad company corrupts *g* character
2Co	9: 8	you will abound in every *g* work.
Gal	6: 9	us not become weary in doing *g*,
	6:10	as we have opportunity, let us do *g*
Eph	2:10	in Christ Jesus to do *g* works,
Php	1: 6	that he who began a *g* work
1Th	5:21	Hold on to the *g*.
1Ti	3: 7	have a *g* reputation with outsiders,
	4: 4	For everything God created is *g*,
	6:12	Fight the *g* fight of the faith.
	6:18	them to do *g*, to be rich in *g* deeds,
2Ti	3:17	equipped for every *g* work.
	4: 7	I have fought the *g* fight, I have
Heb	12:10	but God disciplines us for our *g*,
1Pe	2: 3	you have tasted that the Lord is *g*.
	2:12	Live such *g* lives among the pagans

GOSPEL

Ro	1:16	I am not ashamed of the *g*,
	15:16	duty of proclaiming the *g* of God,
1Co	1:17	to preach the *g*— not with words
	9:16	Woe to me if I do not preach the *g*!
	15: 1	you of the *g* I preached to you,
Gal	1: 7	a different *g*— which is really no *g*
Php	1:27	in a manner worthy of the *g*

GOSSIP

Pr	11:13	A *g* betrays a confidence,
	16:28	and a *g* separates close friends.
	18: 8	of a *g* are like choice morsels;
	26:20	without *g* a quarrel dies down.
2Co	12:20	slander, *g*, arrogance and disorder.

GRACE (GRACIOUS)

Ps	45: 2	lips have been anointed with *g*,
Jn	1:17	*g* and truth came through Jesus
Ac	20:32	to God and to the word of his *g*,
Ro	3:24	and are justified freely by his *g*
	5:15	came by the *g* of the one man,
	5:17	God's abundant provision of *g*
	5:20	where sin increased, *g* increased all
	6:14	you are not under law, but under *g*.
	11: 6	if by *g*, then it is no longer by works
2Co	6: 1	not to receive God's *g* in vain.
	8: 9	For you know the *g*
	9: 8	able to make all *g* abound to you,
	12: 9	"My *g* is sufficient for you,
Gal	2:21	I do not set aside the *g* of God,
	5: 4	you have fallen away from *g*.
Eph	1: 7	riches of God's *g* that he lavished
	2: 5	it is by *g* you have been saved,
	2: 7	the incomparable riches of his *g*,
	2: 8	For it is by *g* you have been saved,
Php	1: 7	all of you share in God's *g* with me.
Col	4: 6	conversation be always full of *g*,
2Th	2:16	and by his *g* gave us eternal
2Ti	2: 1	be strong in the *g* that is
Tit	2:11	For the *g* of God that brings
	3: 7	having been justified by his *g*,
Heb	2: 9	that by the *g* of God he might taste
	4:16	find *g* to help us in our time of need
	4:16	the throne of *g* with confidence,
Jas	4: 6	but gives *g* to the humble."
2Pe	3:18	But grow in the *g* and knowledge

GRACIOUS (GRACE)

Nu	6:25	and be *g* to you;
Pr	22:11	a pure heart and whose speech is *g*
Isa	30:18	Yet the LORD longs to be *g* to you

GRAIN

1Co	9: 9	ox while it is treading out the *g*."

GRANTED

Php	1:29	For it has been *g* to you on behalf

GRASS

Ps 103: 15		As for man, his days are like *g*,
1Pe	1:24	"All men are like *g*,

GRAVE (GRAVES)

Pr	7:27	Her house is a highway to the *g*,
Hos	13:14	Where, O *g*, is your destruction?

GRAVES (GRAVE)

Jn	5:28	are in their *g* will hear his voice
Ro	3:13	"Their throats are open *g*;

GREAT (GREATER GREATEST GREATNESS)

Ge	12: 2	"I will make you into a *g* nation
Dt	10:17	the *g* God, mighty and awesome,
2Sa	22:36	you stoop down to make me *g*.
Ps	19:11	in keeping them there is *g* reward.
	89: 1	of the LORD's *g* love forever;
	103: 11	so *g* is his love for those who fear
	107: 43	consider the *g* love of the LORD.
	108: 4	For *g* is your love, higher

Ps 119:165 *G* peace have they who love your
  145: 3 *G* is the LORD and most worthy
Pr 23:24 of a righteous man has *g* joy;
Isa 42:21 to make his law and glorious.
La 3:23 *g* is your faithfulness.
Mk 10:43 whoever wants to become *g*
Lk 21:27 in a cloud with power and *g* glory.
1Ti 6: 6 with contentment is *g* gain.
Tit 2:13 glorious appearing of our *g* God
Heb 2: 3 if we ignore such a *g* salvation?
1Jn 3: 1 How *g* is the love the Father has

GREATER (GREAT)

Mk 12:31 There is no commandment *g*
Jn 1:50 You shall see *g* things than that."
  15:13 *G* love has no one than this,
1Co 12:31 But eagerly desire the *g* gifts.
Heb 11:26 as of *g* value than the treasures
1Jn 3:20 For God is *g* than our hearts,
  4: 4 is in you is *g* than the one who is

GREATEST (GREAT)

Mt 22:38 is the first and *g* commandment.
Lk 9:48 least among you all—he is the *g*."
1Co 13:13 But the *g* of these is love.

GREATNESS (GREAT)

Ps 145: 3 his *g* no one can fathom.
  150: 2 praise him for his surpassing *g*.
Isa 63: 1 forward in the *g* of his strength?
Php 3: 8 compared to the surpassing *g*

GREED (GREEDY)

Lk 12:15 on your guard against all kinds of *g*
Ro 1:29 kind of wickedness, evil, *g*
Eph 5: 3 or of any kind of impurity, or of *g*,
Col 3: 5 evil desires and *g*, which is idolatry
2Pe 2:14 experts in *g*— an accursed brood!

GREEDY (GREED)

Pr 15:27 A *g* man brings trouble
1Co 6:10 nor thieves nor the *g* nor drunkards
Eph 5: 5 No immoral, impure or *g* person—
1Pe 5: 2 not *g* for money, but eager to serve;

GREEN

Ps 23: 2 makes me lie down in *g* pastures,

GREW (GROW)

Lk 2:52 And Jesus *g* in wisdom and stature,
Ac 16: 5 in the faith and *g* daily in numbers.

GRIEF (GRIEVE)

Ps 10:14 O God, do see trouble and *g*;
Pr 14:13 and joy may end in *g*.
La 3:32 Though he brings *g*, he will show
Jn 16:20 but your *g* will turn to joy.
1Pe 1: 6 had to suffer *g* in all kinds of trials.

GRIEVE (GRIEF)

Eph 4:30 do not *g* the Holy Spirit of God,
1Th 4:13 or to *g* like the rest of men,

GROUND

Ge 3:17 "Cursed is the *g* because of you;
Ex 3: 5 where you are standing is holy *g*."
Eph 6:13 you may be able to stand your *g*,

GROW (GREW)

Pr 13:11 by little makes it *g*.
1Co 3: 6 watered it, but God made it *g*.
2Pe 3:18 But *g* in the grace and knowledge

GRUMBLE (GRUMBLING)

1Co 10:10 And do not *g*, as some of them did
Jas 5: 9 Don't *g* against each other,

GRUMBLING (GRUMBLE)

Jn 6:43 "Stop *g* among yourselves,"
1Pe 4: 9 to one another without *g*.

GUARANTEE (GUARANTEEING)

Heb 7:22 Jesus has become the *g*

GUARANTEEING (GUARANTEE)

2Co 1:22 as a deposit, *g* what is to come.
Eph 1:14 who is a deposit *g* our inheritance

GUARD (GUARDS)

Ps 141: 3 Set a *g* over my mouth, O LORD;
Pr 4:23 Above all else, *g* your heart,
Isa 52:12 the God of Israel will be your rear *g*
Mk 13:33 Be on *g*! Be alert! You do not know
1Co 16:13 Be on your *g*; stand firm in the faith
Php 4: 7 will *g* your hearts and your minds
1Ti 6:20 *g* what has been entrusted

GUARDS (GUARD)

Pr 13: 3 He who *g* his lips *g* his life,
  19:16 who obeys instructions *g* his life,
  21:23 He who *g* his mouth and his tongue
  22: 5 he who *g* his soul stays far

GUIDE

Ex 13:21 of cloud to *g* them on their way
  15:13 In your strength you will *g* them
Ne 9:19 cease to *g* them on their path,
Ps 25: 5 *g* me in your truth and teach me,
  43: 3 let them *g* me;
  48:14 he will be our *g* even to the end.
  67: 4 and *g* the nations of the earth.
  73:24 You *g* me with your counsel,
  139: 10 even there your hand will *g* me,
Pr 4:11 I *g* you in the way of wisdom
  6:22 When you walk, they will *g* you;
Isa 58:11 The LORD will *g* you always;
Jn 16:13 comes, he will *g* you into all truth.

GUILTY

Ex 34: 7 does not leave the *g* unpunished;
Jn 8:46 Can any of you prove me *g* of sin?
Heb 10:22 to cleanse us from a *g* conscience
Jas 2:10 at just one point is *g* of breaking all

HADES

Mt 16:18 the gates of *H* will not overcome it.

HAGAR

Servant of Sarah, wife of Abraham, mother of Ishmael (Ge 16:1-6; 25:12). Driven away by Sarah while pregnant (Ge 16:5-16); after birth of Isaac (Ge 21:9-21; Gal 4:21-31).

HAGGAI*

Post-exilic prophet who encouraged rebuilding

of the temple (Ezr 5:1; 6:14; Hag 1-2).

HAIR (HAIRS)
Lk 21:18 But not a *h* of your head will perish
1Co 11: 6 for a woman to have her *h* cut

HAIRS (HAIR)
Mt 10:30 even the very *h* of your head are all

HALLELUJAH*
Rev 19: 1 3, 4, 6.

HALLOWED (HOLY)
Mt 6: 9 *h* be your name,

HAND (HANDS)
Ps 16: 8 Because he is at my right *h*,
37:24 the LORD upholds him with his *h*.
139: 10 even there your *h* will guide me,
Ecc 9:10 Whatever your *h* finds to do,
Mt 6: 3 know what your right *h* is doing,
Jn 10:28 one can snatch them out of my *h*.
1Co 12:15 I am not a *h*, I do not belong

HANDS (HAND)
Ps 22:16 they have pierced my *h*
24: 4 He who has clean *h* and a pure
31: 5 Into your *h* I commit my spirit;
31:15 My times are in your *h*;
Pr 10: 4 Lazy *h* make a man poor,
31:20 and extends her *h* to the needy.
Isa 55:12 will clap their *h*.
65: 2 All day long I have held out my *h*
Lk 23:46 into your *h* I commit my spirit.''
1Th 4:11 and to work with your *h*,
1Ti 2: 8 to lift up holy *h* in prayer,
5:22 hasty in the laying on of *h*,

HANNAH*
Wife of Elkanah, mother of Samuel (1Sa 1).
Prayer at dedication of Samuel (1Sa 2:1-10).
Blessed (1Sa 2:18-21).

HAPPY
Ps 68: 3 may they be *h* and joyful.
Pr 15:13 A *h* heart makes the face cheerful,
Ecc 3:12 better for men than to be *h*
Jas 5:13 Is anyone *h*? Let him sing songs

HARD (HARDEN HARDSHIP)
Ge 18:14 Is anything too *h* for the LORD?
Mt 19:23 it is *h* for a rich man
1Co 4:12 We work *h* with our own hands.
1Th 5:12 to respect those who work *h*

HARDEN (HARD)
Ro 9:18 he hardens whom he wants to *h*.
Heb 3: 8 do not *h* your hearts

HARDHEARTED* (HEART)
Dt 15: 7 do not be *h* or tightfisted

HARDSHIP (HARD)
Ro 8:35 Shall trouble or *h* or persecution
2Ti 2: 3 Endure *h* with us like a good
4: 5 endure *h*, do the work
Heb 12: 7 Endure *h* as discipline; God is

HARM
Ps 121: 6 the sun will not *h* you by day,
Pr 3:29 not plot *h* against your neighbor,
31:12 She brings him good, not *h*,
Ro 13:10 Love does no *h* to its neighbor.
1Jn 5:18 and the evil one cannot *h* him.

HARMONY
Ro 12:16 Live in *h* with one another.
2Co 6:15 What *h* is there between Christ
1Pe 3: 8 live in *h* with one another;

HARVEST
Mt 9:37 *h* is plentiful but the workers are
Jn 4:35 at the fields! They are ripe for *h*.
Gal 6: 9 at the proper time we will reap a *h*
Heb 12:11 it produces a *h* of righteousness

HASTE (HASTY)
Pr 21: 5 as surely as *h* leads to poverty.
29:20 Do you see a man who speaks in *h*?

HASTY* (HASTE)
Pr 19: 2 nor to be *h* and miss the way.
Ecc 5: 2 do not be *h* in your heart
1Ti 5:22 Do not be *h* in the laying

HATE (HATED HATES HATRED)
Lev 19:17 '' 'Do not *h* your brother
Ps 5: 5 you *h* all who do wrong.
45: 7 righteousness and *h* wickedness;
97:10 those who love the LORD *h* evil,
139: 21 Do I not *h* those who *h* you,
Pr 8:13 To fear the LORD is to *h* evil;
Am 5:15 *H* evil, love good;
Mal 2:16 ''I *h* divorce,'' says the LORD God
Mt 5:43 your neighbor and *h* your enemy.'
10:22 All men will *h* you because of me,
Lk 6:27 do good to those who *h* you,
Ro 12: 9 *H* what is evil; cling to what is good

HATED (HATE)
Ro 9:13 ''Jacob I loved, but Esau I *h*.''
Eph 5:29 no one ever *h* his own body,
Heb 1: 9 righteousness and *h* wickedness;

HATES (HATE)
Pr 6:16 There are six things the LORD *h*,
13:24 He who spares the rod *h* his son,
Jn 3:20 Everyone who does evil *h* the light,
1Jn 2: 9 *h* his brother is still in the darkness.

HATRED (HATE)
Pr 10:12 *H* stirs up dissension,
Jas 4: 4 with the world is *h* toward God?

HAUGHTY
Pr 16:18 a *h* spirit before a fall.

HAY
1Co 3:12 costly stones, wood, *h* or straw,

HEAD (HEADS HOTHEADED)
Ge 3:15 he will crush your *h*,
Ps 23: 5 You anoint my *h* with oil;
Pr 25:22 will heap burning coals on his *h*,
Isa 59:17 and the helmet of salvation on his *h*

Mt   8:20   of Man has no place to lay his *h.*"
Ro   12:20   will heap burning coals on his *h.*"
1Co   11: 3   and the *h* of Christ is God.
      12:21   And the *h* cannot say to the feet,
Eph   5:23   For the husband is the *h* of the wife
2Ti   4: 5   keep your *h* in all situations,
Rev   19:12   and on his *h* are many crowns.

HEADS (HEAD)
Lev   26:13   you to walk with *h* held high.
Isa   35:10   everlasting joy will crown their *h.*

HEAL (HEALED HEALING HEALS)
2Ch   7:14   their sin and will *h* their land.
Ps   41: 4   *h* me, for I have sinned against you
Mt   10: 8   *H* the sick, raise the dead,
Lk   4:23   to me: 'Physician, *h* yourself!
      5:17   present for him to *h* the sick.

HEALED (HEAL)
Isa   53: 5   and by his wounds we are *h.*
Mt   9:22   he said, "your faith has *h* you."
      14:36   and all who touched him were *h.*
Ac   4:10   this man stands before you *h.*
      14: 9   saw that he had faith to be *h*
Jas   5:16   for each other so that you may be *h*
1Pe   2:24   by his wounds you have been *h.*

HEALING (HEAL)
Eze   47:12   for food and their leaves for *h.*"
Mal   4: 2   rise with *h* in its wings.
1Co   12: 9   to another gifts of *h*
      12:30   Do all have gifts of *h?* Do all speak
Rev   22: 2   are for the *h* of the nations.

HEALS (HEAL)
Ex   15:26   for I am the LORD, who *h* you."
Ps   103: 3   and *h* all your diseases;
    147: 3   He *h* the brokenhearted

HEALTH (HEALTHY)
Pr   3: 8   This will bring *h* to your body
      15:30   and good news gives *h* to the bones

HEALTHY (HEALTH)
Mk   2:17   "It is not the *h* who need a doctor,

HEAR (HEARD HEARING HEARS)
Dt   6: 4   *H*, O Israel: The LORD our God,
      31:13   must *h* it and learn
2Ch   7:14   then will I *h* from heaven
Ps   94: 9   he who implanted the ear not *h?*
Isa   29:18   that day the deaf will *h* the words
      65:24   while they are still speaking I will *h*
Mt   11:15   He who has ears, let him *h.*
Jn   8:47   reason you do not *h* is that you do
2Ti   4: 3   what their itching ears want to *h.*

HEARD (HEAR)
Job   42: 5   My ears had *h* of you
Isa   66: 8   Who has ever *h* of such a thing?
Mt   5:21   "You have *h* that it was said
      5:27   "You have *h* that it was said,
      5:33   you have *h* that it was said
      5:38   "You have *h* that it was said,
      5:43   "You have *h* that it was said,

1Co   2: 9   no ear has *h,*
1Th   2:13   word of God, which you *h* from us,
2Ti   1:13   What you *h* from me, keep
Jas   1:25   not forgetting what he has *h,*

HEARING (HEAR)
Ro   10:17   faith comes from *h* the message,

HEARS (HEAR)
Jn   5:24   whoever *h* my word and believes
1Jn   5:14   according to his will, he *h* us.
Rev   3:20   If anyone *h* my voice and opens

HEART (BROKENHEARTED HARDHEARTED HEARTS WHOLEHEARTEDLY)
Ex   25: 2   each man whose *h* prompts him
Lev   19:17   Do not hate your brother in your *h.*
Dt   4:29   if you look for him with all your *h*
      6: 5   LORD your God with all your *h*
      10:12   LORD your God with all your *h*
      15:10   and do so without a grudging *h;*
      30: 6   you may love him with all your *h*
      30:10   LORD your God with all your *h*
Jos   22: 5   and to serve him with all your *h*
1Sa   13:14   sought out a man after his own *h*
      16: 7   but the LORD looks at the *h.*"
2Ki   23: 3   with all his *h* and all his soul,
1Ch   28: 9   for the LORD searches every *h*
2Ch   7:16   and my *h* will always be there.
Job   22:22   and lay up his words in your *h.*
      37: 1   "At this my *h* pounds
Ps   14: 1   The fool says in his *h,*
      19:14   and the meditation of my *h*
      37: 4   will give you the desires of your *h.*
      45: 1   My *h* is stirred by a noble theme
      51:10   Create in me a pure *h,* O God,
      51:17   a broken and contrite *h,*
      66:18   If I had cherished sin in my *h,*
      86:11   give me an undivided *h,*
   119: 11   I have hidden your word in my *h*
   119: 32   for you have set my *h* free.
   139: 23   Search me, O God, and know my *h*
Pr   3: 5   Trust in the LORD with all your *h*
      4:21   keep them within your *h;*
      4:23   Above all else, guard your *h,*
      7: 3   write them on the tablet of your *h.*
      13:12   Hope deferred makes the *h* sick,
      14:13   Even in laughter the *h* may ache,
      15:30   A cheerful look brings joy to the *h,*
      17:22   A cheerful *h* is good medicine,
      24:17   stumbles, do not let your *h* rejoice,
      27:19   so a man's *h* reflects the man.
Ecc   8: 5   wise *h* will know the proper time
SS   4: 9   You have stolen my *h,* my sister,
Isa   40:11   and carries them close to his *h;*
      57:15   and to revive the *h* of the contrite.
Jer   17: 9   The *h* is deceitful above all things
      29:13   when you seek me with all your *h.*
Eze   36:26   I will give you a new *h*
Mt   5: 8   Blessed are the pure in *h,*
      6:21   treasure is, there your *h* will be
      12:34   of the *h* the mouth speaks.

Mt   22:37 the Lord your God with all your *h*
Lk   6:45 overflow of his *h* his mouth speaks.
Ro   2:29 is circumcision of the *h*,
      10:10 is with your *h* that you believe
1Co 14:25 the secrets of his *h* will be laid bare.
Eph   5:19 make music in your *h* to the Lord,
       6: 6 doing the will of God from your *h*.
Col   3:23 work at it with all your *h*,
1Pe   1:22 one another deeply, from the *h*.

HEARTS (HEART)

Dt   11:18 Fix these words of mine in your *h*
1Ki   8:39 for you alone know the *h* of all men
      8:61 your *h* must be fully committed
Ps   62: 8 pour out your *h* to him,
Ecc   3:11 also set eternity in the *h* of men;
Jer 31:33 and write it on their *h*.
Lk   16:15 of men, but God knows your *h*.
     24:32 "Were not our *h* burning within us
Jn   14: 1 "Do not let your *h* be troubled.
Ac   15: 9 for he purified their *h* by faith.
Ro   2:15 of the law are written on their *h*,
2Co   3: 2 written on our *h*, known
       3: 3 but on tablets of human *h*.
       4: 6 shine in our *h* to give us the light
Eph   3:17 dwell in your *h* through faith.
Col   3: 1 set your *h* on things above,
Heb   3: 8 do not harden your *h*
      10:16 I will put my laws in their *h*,
1Jn   3:20 For God is greater than our *h*,

HEAT

2Pe   3:12 and the elements will melt in the *h*.

HEAVEN (HEAVENLY HEAVENS)

Ge   14:19 Creator of *h* and earth.
1Ki   8:27 the highest *h*, cannot contain you.
2Ki   2: 1 up to *h* in a whirlwind,
2Ch   7:14 then will I hear from *h*
Isa 14:12 How you have fallen from *h*,
     66: 1 "*H* is my throne,
Da   7:13 coming with the clouds of *h*.
Mt   6: 9 " 'Our Father in *h*,
      6:20 up for yourselves treasures in *h*,
     16:19 bind on earth will be bound in *h*,
     19:23 man to enter the kingdom of *h*.
     24:35 *H* and earth will pass away,
     26:64 and coming on the clouds of *h*."
     28:18 "All authority in *h*
Mk   16:19 he was taken up into *h*
Lk   15: 7 in *h* over one sinner who repents
     18:22 and you will have treasure in *h*.
Ro   10: 6 'Who will ascend into *h*?' " (that is,
2Co   5: 1 an eternal house in *h*, not built
     12: 2 ago was caught up to the third *h*.
Php   2:10 *h* and on earth and under the earth,
      3:20 But our citizenship is in *h*.
1Th   1:10 and to wait for his Son from *h*,
Heb   8: 5 and shadow of what is in *h*.
      9:24 he entered *h* itself, now to appear
2Pe   3:13 we are looking forward to a new *h*
Rev 21: 1 Then I saw a new *h* and a new earth

HEAVENLY (HEAVEN)

Ps   8: 5 him a little lower than the *h* beings
2Co   5: 2 to be clothed with our *h* dwelling,
Eph   1: 3 in the *h* realms with every spiritual
      1:20 at his right hand in the *h* realms,
2Ti   4:18 bring me safely to his *h* kingdom.
Heb 12:22 to the *h* Jerusalem, the city

HEAVENS (HEAVEN)

Ge   1: 1 In the beginning God created the *h*
1Ki   8:27 The *h*, even the highest heaven,
2Ch   2: 6 since the *h*, even the highest
Ps   8: 3 When I consider your *h*,
     19: 1 The *h* declare the glory of God;
    102: 25 the *h* are the work of your hands.
    108: 4 is your love, higher than the *h*;
    119: 89 it stands firm in the *h*.
    139: 8 If I go up to the *h*, you are there;
Isa 51: 6 Lift up your eyes to the *h*,
     55: 9 "As the *h* are higher than the earth,
     65:17 new *h* and a new earth.
Joel 2:30 I will show wonders in the *h*
Eph   4:10 who ascended higher than all the *h*,
2Pe   3:10 The *h* will disappear with a roar;

HEBREW

Ge   14:13 and reported this to Abram the *H*.

HEEDS

Pr   13: 1 wise son *h* his father's instruction,
     13:18 whoever *h* correction is honored.
     15: 5 whoever *h* correction shows
     15:32 whoever *h* correction gains

HEEL

Ge   3:15 and you will strike his *h*."

HEIRS (INHERIT)

Ro   8:17 then we are *h*— *h* of God
Gal   3:29 and *h* according to the promise.
Eph   3: 6 gospel the Gentiles are *h* together
1Pe   3: 7 as *h* with you of the gracious gift

HELL

Mt   5:22 will be in danger of the fire of *h*.
Lk   16:23 In *h*, where he was in torment,
2Pe   2: 4 but sent them to *h*, putting them

HELMET

Isa 59:17 and the *h* of salvation on his head;
Eph   6:17 Take the *h* of salvation
1Th   5: 8 and the hope of salvation as a *h*.

HELP (HELPED HELPER HELPING HELPS)

Ps   18: 6 I cried to my God for *h*.
     30: 2 my God, I called to you for *h*
     46: 1 an ever-present *h* in trouble.
     79: 9 *H* us, O God our Savior,
    121: 1 where does my *h* come from?
Isa 41:10 I will strengthen you and *h* you;
Jnh   2: 2 depths of the grave I called for *h*,
Mk   9:24 *h* me overcome my unbelief!' "
Ac   16: 9 Come over to Macedonia and *h* us
1Co 12:28 those able to *h* others, those

HELPED (HELP)
1Sa   7:12 "Thus far has the LORD *h* us."

HELPER (HELP)
Ge   2:18 I will make a *h* suitable for him."
Ps   10:14 you are the *h* of the fatherless.
Heb 13: 6 Lord is my *h;* I will not be afraid.

HELPING (HELP)
Ac   9:36 always doing good and *h* the poor.
1Ti   5:10 *h* those in trouble and devoting

HELPS (HELP)
Ro   8:26 the Spirit *h* us in our weakness.

HEN
Mt   23:37 as a *h* gathers her chicks

HERITAGE (INHERIT)
Ps127:   3 Sons are a *h* from the LORD,

HEROD
1. King of Judea who tried to kill Jesus (Mt 2;
Lk 1:5).
2. Son of 1. Tetrarch of Galilee who arrested
and beheaded John the Baptist (Mt 14:1-12; Mk
6:14-29; Lk 3:1, 19-20; 9:7-9); tried Jesus (Lk 23:
6-15).
3. Grandson of 1. King of Judea who killed
James (Ac 12:2); arrested Peter (Ac 12:3-19).
Death (Ac 12:19-23).

HERODIAS
Wife of Herod the Tetrarch who persuaded her
daughter to ask for John the Baptist's head (Mt
14:1-12; Mk 6:14-29).

HEZEKIAH
King of Judah. Restored the temple and worship (2Ch 29-31). Sought the LORD for help
against Assyria (2Ki 18-19; 2Ch 32:1-23; Isa 36-
37). Illness healed (2Ki 20:1-11; 2Ch 32:24-26;
Isa 38). Judged for showing Babylonians his treasures (2Ki 20:12-21; 2Ch 32:31; Isa 39).

HID (HIDE)
Ge   3: 8 and they *h* from the LORD God
Ex   2: 2 she *h* him for three months.
Jos   6:17 because she *h* the spies we sent.
Heb 11:23 By faith Moses' parents *h* him

HIDDEN (HIDE)
Ps   19:12 Forgive my *h* faults.
    119: 11 I have *h* your word in my heart
Pr   2: 4 and search for it as for *h* treasure,
Isa 59: 2 your sins have *h* his face from you,
Mt   5:14 A city on a hill cannot be *h.*
     13:44 of heaven is like treasure *h*
Col   1:26 the mystery that has been kept *h*
      2: 3 in whom are *h* all the treasures
      3: 3 and your life is now *h* with Christ

HIDE (HID HIDDEN)
Ps   17: 8 *h* me in the shadow of your wings
    143: 9 for I *h* myself in you.

HILL (HILLS)
Mt   5:14 A city on a *h* cannot be hidden.

HILLS (HILL)
Ps   50:10 and the cattle on a thousand *h.*
    121: 1 I lift up my eyes to the *h*—

HINDER (HINDERS)
1Sa 14: 6 Nothing can *h* the LORD
Mt   19:14 come to me, and do not *h* them,
1Co   9:12 anything rather than *h* the gospel
1Pe   3: 7 so that nothing will *h* your prayers.

HINDERS (HINDER)
Heb 12: 1 let us throw off everything that *h*

HINT*
Eph   5: 3 even a *h* of sexual immorality,

HOLD
Ex   20: 7 LORD will not *h* anyone guiltless
Lev 19:13 " 'Do not *h* back the wages
Jos 22: 5 to *h* fast to him and to serve him
Ps   73:23 you *h* me by my right hand.
Pr   4: 4 "Lay *h* of my words
Isa 54: 2 do not *h* back;
Mk   11:25 if you *h* anything against anyone,
Php   2:16 as you *h* out the word of life—
      3:12 but I press on to take *h* of that
Col   1:17 and in him all things *h* together.
1Th   5:21 *H* on to the good.
1Ti   6:12 Take *h* of the eternal life
Heb 10:23 Let us *h* unswervingly

HOLINESS (HOLY)
Ex   15:11 majestic in *h,*
Ps   29: 2 in the splendor of his *h.*
     96: 9 in the splendor of his *h;*
Ro   6:19 to righteousness leading to *h.*
2Co   7: 1 perfecting *h* out of reverence
Eph   4:24 God in true righteousness and *h.*
Heb 12:10 that we may share in his *h.*
     12:14 without *h* no one will see the Lord.

HOLY (HALLOWED HOLINESS)
Ex   19: 6 kingdom of priests and a *h* nation.'
     20: 8 the Sabbath day by keeping it *h.*
Lev 11:44 and be *h,* because I am *h.*
     20: 7 " 'Consecrate yourselves and be *h,*
     20:26 You are to be *h* to me because I,
     21: 8 Consider them *h,* because I
     22:32 Do not profane my *h* name.
Ps   16:10 will you let your *H* One see decay.
     24: 3 Who may stand in his *h* place?
     77:13 Your ways, O God, are *h.*
     99: 3 he is *h.*
     99: 5 he is *h.*
     99: 9 for the LORD our God is *h.*
    111: 9 *h* and awesome is his name.
Isa   5:16 the *h* God will show himself *h*
      6: 3 *H, h, h* is the LORD Almighty;
     40:25 who is my equal?" says the *H* One.
     57:15 who lives forever, whose name is *h:*
Eze 28:25 I will show myself *h* among them
Da   9:24 prophecy and to anoint the most *h.*
Hab   2:20 But the LORD is in his *h* temple;
Ac   2:27 will you let your *H* One see decay.
Ro   7:12 and the commandment is *h,*

Ro   12: 1 as living sacrifices, *h* and pleasing
Eph   5: 3 improper for God's *h* people.
2Th   1:10 to be glorified in his *h* people
2Ti   1: 9 saved us and called us to a *h* life—
        3:15 you have known the *h* Scriptures,
Tit   1: 8 upright, *h* and disciplined.
1Pe   1:15 But just as he who called you is *h*,
        1:16 is written: "Be *h*, because I am *h*."
        2: 9 a royal priesthood, a *h* nation,
2Pe   3:11 You ought to live *h* and godly lives
Rev   4: 8 "*H, h, h* is the Lord God

HOME (HOMES)

Dt   6: 7 Talk about them when you sit at *h*
Ps   84: 3 Even the sparrow has found a *h*,
Pr   3:33 but he blesses the *h* of the righteous
Mk   10:29 "no one who has left *h* or brothers
Jn   14:23 to him and make our *h* with him.
Tit   2: 5 to be busy at *h*, to be kind,

HOMES (HOME)

Ne   4:14 daughters, your wives and your *h*."
1Ti   5:14 to manage their *h* and to give

HOMOSEXUAL*

1Co   6: 9 male prostitutes nor *h* offenders

HONEST

Lev   19:36 Use *h* scales and *h* weights,
Dt   25:15 and *h* weights and measures,
Job   31: 6 let God weigh me in *h* scales
Pr   12:17 truthful witness gives *h* testimony,

HONEY

Ex   3: 8 a land flowing with milk and *h*—
Ps   19:10 than *h* from the comb.
     119:103 sweeter than *h* to my mouth!

HONOR (HONORABLE HONORABLY HONORED HONORS)

Ex   20:12 "*H* your father and your mother,
Nu   25:13 he was zealous for the *h* of his God
Dt   5:16 "*H* your father and your mother,
1Sa   2:30 Those who *h* me I will *h*,
Ps   8: 5 and crowned him with glory and *h*.
Pr   3: 9 *H* the LORD with your wealth,
     15:33 and humility comes before *h*.
     20: 3 It is to a man's *h* to avoid strife,
Mt   15: 4 '*H* your father and mother'
Ro   12:10 *H* one another above yourselves.
1Co   6:20 Therefore *h* God with your body.
Eph   6: 2 "*H* your father and mother"—
1Ti   5:17 well are worthy of double *h*,
Heb   2: 7 you crowned him with glory and *h*
Rev   4: 9 *h* and thanks to him who sits

HONORABLE (HONOR)

1Th   4: 4 body in a way that is holy and *h*,

HONORABLY (HONOR)

Heb   13:18 and desire to live *h* in every way.

HONORED (HONOR)

Ps   12: 8 when what is vile is *h* among men.
Pr   13:18 but whoever heeds correction is *h*.
1Co   12:26 if one part is *h*, every part rejoices

Heb   13: 4 Marriage should be *h* by all,

HONORS (HONOR)

Ps   15: 4 but *h* those who fear the LORD,
Pr   14:31 to the needy *h* God.

HOOKS

Isa   2: 4 and their spears into pruning *h*.
Joel   3:10 and your pruning *h* into spears.

HOPE (HOPES)

Job   13:15 Though he slay me, yet will I *h*
Ps   42: 5 Put your *h* in God,
     62: 5 my *h* comes from him.
     119: 74 for I have put my *h* in your word.
     130: 7 O Israel, put your *h* in the LORD,
     147: 11 who put their *h* in his unfailing love
Pr   13:12 *H* deferred makes the heart sick,
Isa   40:31 but those who *h* in the LORD
Ro   5: 4 character; and character, *h*.
     8:24 But *h* that is seen is no *h* at all.
     12:12 Be joyful in *h*, patient in affliction,
     15: 4 of the Scriptures we might have *h*.
1Co   13:13 now these three remain: faith, *h*
     15:19 for this life we have *h* in Christ,
Col   1:27 Christ in you, the *h* of glory.
1Th   5: 8 and the *h* of salvation as a helmet.
1Ti   6:17 but to put their *h* in God,
Tit   2:13 while we wait for the blessed *h*—
Heb   6:19 We have this *h* as an anchor
     11: 1 faith is being sure of what we *h* for
1Jn   3: 3 Everyone who has this *h*

HOPES (HOPE)

1Co   13: 7 always *h*, always perseveres.

HORSE

Ps   147: 10 not in the strength of the *h*,
Pr   26: 3 A whip for the *h*, a halter
Zec   1: 8 before me was a man riding a red *h*
Rev   6: 2 and there before me was a white *h!*
     6: 4 Come!'' Then another *h* came out,
     6: 5 and there before me was a black *h!*
     6: 8 and there before me was a pale *h!*
     19:11 and there before me was a white *h*,

HOSANNA

Mt   21: 9 "*H* in the highest!''

HOSHEA

   Last king of Israel (2Ki 15:30; 17:1-6).

HOSPITABLE* (HOSPITALITY)

1Ti   3: 2 self-controlled, respectable, *h*,
Tit   1: 8 Rather he must be *h*, one who loves

HOSPITALITY (HOSPITABLE)

Ro   12:13 Practice *h*.
1Ti   5:10 as bringing up children, showing *h*,
1Pe   4: 9 Offer *h* to one another

HOSTILE

Ro   8: 7 the sinful mind is *h* to God.

HOT

1Ti   4: 2 have been seared as with a *h* iron.
Rev   3:15 that you are neither cold nor *h*.

HOT-TEMPERED

Pr 15:18 A *h* man stirs up dissension,
    19:19 A *h* man must pay the penalty;
    22:24 Do not make friends with a *h* man,
    29:22 and a *h* one commits many sins.

HOTHEADED (HEAD)

Pr 14:16 but a fool is *h* and reckless.

HOUR

Ecc 9:12 knows when his *h* will come:
Mt 6:27 you by worrying can add a single *h*
Lk 12:40 the Son of Man will come at an *h*
Jn 12:23 The *h* has come for the Son of Man
    12:27 for this very reason I came to this *h*

HOUSE (HOUSEHOLD STOREHOUSE)

Ex 20:17 shall not covet your neighbor's *h*.
Ps 23: 6 I will dwell in the *h* of the LORD
    84:10 a doorkeeper in the *h* of my God
    122: 1 "Let us go to the *h* of the LORD."
    127: 1 Unless the LORD builds the *h*,
Pr 7:27 Her *h* is a highway to the grave,
    21: 9 than share a *h* with a quarrelsome
Isa 56: 7 a *h* of prayer for all nations.'
Zec 13: 6 given at the *h* of my friends.'
Mt 7:24 is like a wise man who built his *h*
    12:29 can anyone enter a strong man's *h*
    21:13 My *h* will be called a *h* of prayer,'
Mk 3:25 If a *h* is divided against itself,
Lk 11:17 a *h* divided against itself will fall.
Jn 2:16 How dare you turn my Father's *h*
    12: 3 the *h* was filled with the fragrance
    14: 2 In my Father's *h* are many rooms;
Heb 3: 3 the builder of a *h* has greater honor

HOUSEHOLD (HOUSE)

Jos 24:15 my *h*, we will serve the LORD."
Mic 7: 6 are the members of his own *h*.
Mt 10:36 will be the members of his own *h*.'
    12:25 or *h* divided against itself will not
1Ti 3:12 manage his children and his *h* well.
    3:15 to conduct themselves in God's *h*,

HUMAN (HUMANITY)

Gal 3: 3 to attain your goal by *h* effort?

HUMANITY* (HUMAN)

Heb 2:14 he too shared in their *h* so that

HUMBLE (HUMBLED HUMBLES HUMILIATE HUMILITY)

2Ch 7:14 will *h* themselves and pray
Ps 25: 9 He guides the *h* in what is right
Pr 3:34 but gives grace to the *h*.
Isa 66: 2 he who is *h* and contrite in spirit,
Mt 11:29 for I am gentle and *h* in heart,
Eph 4: 2 Be completely *h* and gentle;
Jas 4:10 *H* yourselves before the Lord,
1Pe 5: 6 *H* yourselves,

HUMBLED (HUMBLE)

Mt 23:12 whoever exalts himself will be *h*,
Php 2: 8 he *h* himself

HUMBLES (HUMBLE)

Mt 18: 4 whoever *h* himself like this child is
    23:12 whoever *h* himself will be exalted.

HUMILIATE* (HUMBLE)

Pr 25: 7 than for him to *h* you
1Co 11:22 and *h* those who have nothing?

HUMILITY (HUMBLE)

Pr 11: 2 but with *h* comes wisdom.
    15:33 and *h* comes before honor.
Php 2: 3 but in *h* consider others better
Tit 3: 2 and to show true *h* toward all men.
1Pe 5: 5 clothe yourselves with *h*

HUNGRY

Ps 107: 9 and fills the *h* with good things.
    146: 7 and gives food to the *h*.
Pr 25:21 If your enemy is *h*, give him food
Eze 18: 7 but gives his food to the *h*
Mt 25:35 For I was *h* and you gave me
Lk 1:53 He has filled the *h* with good things
Jn 6:35 comes to me will never go *h*,
Ro 12:20 "If your enemy is *h*, feed him;

HURT (HURTS)

Ecc 8: 9 it over others to his own *h*.
Mk 16:18 deadly poison, it will not *h* them
Rev 2:11 He who overcomes will not be *h*

HURTS* (HURT)

Ps 15: 4 even when it *h*,
Pr 26:28 A lying tongue hates those it *h*,

HUSBAND (HUSBAND'S HUSBANDS)

1Co 7: 3 The *h* should fulfill his marital duty
    7:10 wife must not separate from her *h*.
    7:11 And a *h* must not divorce his wife.
    7:13 And if a woman has a *h* who is not
    7:39 A woman is bound to her *h* as long
2Co 11: 2 I promised you to one *h*, to Christ,
Eph 5:23 For the *h* is the head of the wife
    5:33 and the wife must respect her *h*.
1Ti 3: 2 the *h* of but one wife, temperate,

HUSBAND'S (HUSBAND)

Pr 12: 4 of noble character is her *h* crown,
1Co 7: 4 the *h* body does not belong

HUSBANDS (HUSBAND)

Eph 5:22 submit to your *h* as to the Lord.
    5:25 *H*, love your wives, just
Tit 2: 4 the younger women to love their *h*
1Pe 3: 1 same way be submissive to your *h*
    3: 7 *H*, in the same way be considerate

HYMN

1Co 14:26 everyone has a *h*, or a word

HYPOCRISY (HYPOCRITE HYPOCRITES)

Mt 23:28 but on the inside you are full of *h*
1Pe 2: 1 *h*, envy, and slander of every kind.

HYPOCRITE (HYPOCRISY)

Mt 7: 5 You *h*, first take the plank out

HYPOCRITES (HYPOCRISY)
Ps 26: 4 nor do I consort with *h;*
Mt 6: 5 when you pray, do not be like the *h*

HYSSOP
Ps 51: 7 with *h,* and I will be clean;

IDLE (IDLENESS)
1Th 5:14 those who are *i,* encourage
2Th 3: 6 away from every brother who is *i*
1Ti 5:13 they get into the habit of being *i*

IDLENESS* (IDLE)
Pr 31:27 and does not eat the bread of *i.*

IDOL (IDOLATRY IDOLS)
Isa 44:17 From the rest he makes a god, his *i;*
1Co 8: 4 We know that an *i* is nothing at all

IDOLATRY (IDOL)
Col 3: 5 evil desires and greed, which is *i.*

IDOLS (IDOL)
1Co 8: 1 Now about food sacrificed to *i:*

IGNORANT (IGNORE)
1Co 15:34 for there are some who are *i* of God
Heb 5: 2 to deal gently with those who are *i*
1Pe 2:15 good you should silence the *i* talk
2Pe 3:16 which *i* and unstable people distort

IGNORE (IGNORANT IGNORES)
Dt 22: 1 do not *i* it but be sure
Ps 9:12 he does not *i* the cry of the afflicted
Heb 2: 3 if we *i* such a great salvation?

IGNORES (IGNORE)
Pr 10:17 whoever *i* correction leads others
15:32 He who *i* discipline despises

ILLUMINATED*
Rev 18: 1 and the earth was *i* by his splendor.

IMAGE
Ge 1:26 "Let us make man in our *i,*
1:27 So God created man in his own *i,*
1Co 11: 7 since he is the *i* and glory of God;
Col 1:15 He is the *i* of the invisible God,
3:10 in knowledge in the *i* of its Creator.

IMAGINE
Eph 3:20 more than all we ask or *i,*

IMITATE (IMITATORS)
1Co 4:16 Therefore I urge you to *i* me.
Heb 6:12 but to *i* those who through faith
13: 7 of their way of life and *i* their faith.
3Jn :11 do not *i* what is evil but what is

IMITATORS* (IMITATE)
Eph 5: 1 Be *i* of God, therefore,
1Th 1: 6 You became *i* of us and of the Lord
2:14 became *i* of God's churches

IMMANUEL
Isa 7:14 birth to a son, and will call him *I.*
Mt 1:23 and they will call him *I*''—

IMMORAL* (IMMORALITY)
Pr 6:24 keeping you from the *i* woman,

IMMORALITY (IMMORAL)
1Co 6:13 The body is not meant for sexual *i,*
6:18 Flee from sexual *i.*
10: 8 We should not commit sexual *i,*
Gal 5:19 sexual *i,* impurity and debauchery;
Eph 5: 3 must not be even a hint of sexual *i,*
1Th 4: 3 that you should avoid sexual *i;*
Jude : 4 grace of our God into a license for *i*

IMMORTAL* (IMMORTALITY)
Ro 1:23 glory of the *i* God for images made
1Ti 1:17 Now to the King eternal,, *i,*
6:16 who alone is *i* and who lives

IMMORTALITY (IMMORTAL)
Ro 2: 7 honor and *i,* he will give eternal life
1Co 15:53 and the mortal with *i.*
2Ti 1:10 and *i* to light through the gospel.

IMPERISHABLE
1Pe 1:23 not of perishable seed, but of *i,*

IMPORTANCE* (IMPORTANT)
1Co 15: 3 passed on to you as of first *i:*

IMPORTANT (IMPORTANCE)
Mt 6:25 Is not life more *i* than food,
23:23 have neglected the more *i* matters
Mk 12:29 "The most *i* one," answered Jesus,
12:33 as yourself is more *i* than all burnt
Php 1:18 The *i* thing is that in every way,

IMPOSSIBLE
Mt 17:20 Nothing will be *i* for you.''
Lk 1:37 For nothing is *i* with God.''
18:27 "What is *i* with men is possible
Heb 6:18 things in which it is *i* for God to lie,
11: 6 without faith it is *i* to please God,

IMPROPER*
Eph 5: 3 these are *i* for God's holy people.

IMPURE (IMPURITY)
Ac 10:15 not call anything *i* that God has
Eph 5: 5 No immoral, *i* or greedy person—
1Th 4: 7 For God did not call us to be *i,*
Rev 21:27 Nothing *i* will ever enter it,

IMPURITY (IMPURE)
Ro 1:24 hearts to sexual *i* for the degrading
Eph 5: 3 or of any kind of *i,* or of greed,

INCENSE
Ex 40: 5 Place the gold altar of *i* in front
Ps 141: 2 my prayer be set before you like *i;*
Mt 2:11 him with gifts of gold and of *i*

Right column earlier entries:

1Co 5: 9 to associate with sexually *i* people
5:10 the people of this world who are *i,*
5:11 but is sexually *i* or greedy,
6: 9 Neither the sexually *i* nor idolaters
Eph 5: 5 No *i,* impure or greedy person—
Heb 12:16 See that no one is sexually *i,*
13: 4 the adulterer and all the sexually *i.*
Rev 21: 8 the murderers, the sexually *i,*
22:15 the sexually *i,* the murderers,

INCOME
Ecc 5:10 wealth is never satisfied with his *i*.
1Co 16: 2 sum of money in keeping with his *i*,

INCOMPARABLE*
Eph 2: 7 ages he might show the *i* riches

INCREASE (EVER-INCREASING INCREASED INCREASES INCREASING)
Ge 1:22 "Be fruitful and *i* in number
Ps 62:10 though your riches *i*,
Isa 9: 7 Of the *i* of his government
Lk 17: 5 said to the Lord, "*I* our faith!"
1Th 3:12 May the Lord make your love *i*

INCREASED (INCREASE)
Ac 6: 7 of disciples in Jerusalem *i* rapidly,
Ro 5:20 But where sin *i*, grace *i* all the more

INCREASES (INCREASE)
Pr 24: 5 and a man of knowledge *i* strength;

INCREASING (INCREASE)
Ac 6: 1 when the number of disciples was *i*,
2Th 1: 3 one of you has for each other is *i*.
2Pe 1: 8 these qualities in *i* measure,

INDEPENDENT*
1Co 11:11 however, woman is not *i* of man,
11:11 of man, nor is man *i* of woman.

INDESCRIBABLE*
2Co 9:15 Thanks be to God for his *i* gift!

INDISPENSABLE*
1Co 12:22 seem to be weaker are *i*,

INEFFECTIVE*
2Pe 1: 8 they will keep you from being *i*

INEXPRESSIBLE*
2Co 12: 4 He heard *i* things, things that man
1Pe 1: 8 are filled with an *i* and glorious joy,

INFANTS
Mt 21:16 " 'From the lips of children and *i*
1Co 14:20 In regard to evil be *i*,

INFIRMITIES
Isa 53: 4 Surely he took up our *i*

INHERIT (CO-HEIRS HEIRS HERITAGE INHERITANCE)
Ps 37:11 But the meek will *i* the land
37:29 the righteous will *i* the land
Mt 5: 5 for they will *i* the earth.
Mk 10:17 "what must I do to *i* eternal life?"
1Co 15:50 blood cannot *i* the kingdom of God

INHERITANCE (INHERIT)
Dt 4:20 to be the people of his *i*,
Pr 13:22 A good man leaves an *i*
Eph 1:14 who is a deposit guaranteeing our *i*
5: 5 has any *i* in the kingdom of Christ
Heb 9:15 receive the promised eternal *i*—
1Pe 1: 4 and into an *i* that can never perish,

INIQUITIES (INIQUITY)
Ps 78:38 he forgave their *i*

Ps 103: 10 or repay us according to our *i*.
Isa 59: 2 But your *i* have separated
Mic 7:19 and hurl all our *i* into the depths

INIQUITY (INIQUITIES)
Ps 51: 2 Wash away all my *i*
Isa 53: 6 the *i* of us all.

INJUSTICE
2Ch 19: 7 the LORD our God there is no *i*

INNOCENT
Pr 17:26 It is not good to punish an *i* man,
Mt 10:16 shrewd as snakes and as *i* as doves.
27: 4 "for I have betrayed *i* blood."
1Co 4: 4 but that does not make me *i*.

INSCRIPTION
Mt 22:20 And whose *i*?" "Caesar's,"

INSOLENT
Ro 1:30 God-haters, *i*, arrogant

INSTITUTED
Ro 13: 2 rebelling against what God has *i*,
1Pe 2:13 to every authority *i* among men:

INSTRUCT (INSTRUCTION)
Ps 32: 8 I will *i* you and teach you
Pr 9: 9 *I* a wise man and he will be wiser
Ro 15:14 and competent to *i* one another.
2Ti 2:25 who oppose him he must gently *i*,

INSTRUCTION (INSTRUCT)
Pr 1: 8 Listen, my son, to your father's *i*
4: 1 Listen, my sons, to a father's *i;*
4:13 Hold on to *i*, do not let it go;
8:10 Choose my *i* instead of silver,
8:33 Listen to my *i* and be wise;
13: 1 A wise son heeds his father's *i*,
13:13 He who scorns *i* will pay for it,
16:20 Whoever gives heed to *i* prospers,
16:21 and pleasant words promote *i*.
19:20 Listen to advice and accept *i*,
23:12 Apply your heart to *i*
1Co 14: 6 or prophecy or word of *i*?
14:26 or a word of *i*, a revelation,
Eph 6: 4 up in the training and *i* of the Lord.
1Th 4: 8 he who rejects this *i* does not reject
2Th 3:14 If anyone does not obey our *i*
1Ti 1:18 I give you this *i* in keeping
6: 3 to the sound *i* of our Lord Jesus
2Ti 4: 2 with great patience and careful *i*.

INSULT
Pr 9: 7 corrects a mocker invites *i*;
12:16 but a prudent man overlooks an *i*.
Mt 5:11 Blessed are you when people *i* you,
Lk 6:22 when they exclude you and *i* you
1Pe 3: 9 evil with evil or *i* with *i*,

INTEGRITY
1Ki 9: 4 if you walk before me in *i* of heart
Job 2: 3 And he still maintains his *i*,
27: 5 till I die, I will not deny my *i*.
Pr 10: 9 The man of *i* walks securely,
11: 3 The *i* of the upright guides them,

Pr 29:10 Bloodthirsty men hate a man of *i*
Tit 2: 7 your teaching show *i*, seriousness

INTELLIGENCE

Isa 29:14 the *i* of the intelligent will vanish."
1Co 1:19 *i* of the intelligent I will frustrate."

INTELLIGIBLE

1Co 14:19 I would rather speak five *i* words

INTERCEDE (INTERCEDES INTERCESSION)

Heb 7:25 he always lives to *i* for them.

INTERCEDES (INTERCEDE)

Ro 8:26 but the Spirit himself *i* for us

INTERCESSION* (INTERCEDE)

Isa 53:12 and made *i* for the transgressors.
1Ti 2: 1 *i* and thanksgiving be made

INTERESTS

1Co 7:34 his wife—and his *i* are divided.
Php 2: 4 only to your own *i*, but also to the *i*
    2:21 everyone looks out for his own *i*,

INTERMARRY (MARRY)

Dt 7: 3 Do not *i* with them.

INVENTED*

2Pe 1:16 We did not follow cleverly *i* stories

INVESTIGATED

Lk 1: 3 I myself have carefully *i* everything

INVISIBLE

Ro 1:20 of the world God's *i* qualities—
Col 1:15 He is the image of the *i* God,
1Ti 1:17 immortal, *i*, the only God,

INVITE (INVITED INVITES)

Lk 14:13 you give a banquet, *i* the poor,

INVITED (INVITE)

Mt 22:14 For many are *i*, but few are chosen
    25:35 I was a stranger and you *i* me in,

INVITES (INVITE)

1Co 10:27 If some unbeliever *i* you to a meal

INVOLVED

2Ti 2: 4 a soldier gets *i* in civilian affairs—

IRON

1Ti 4: 2 have been seared as with a hot *i*.
Rev 2:27 He will rule them with an *i* scepter;

IRREVOCABLE*

Ro 11:29 for God's gifts and his call are *i*.

ISAAC

Son of Abraham by Sarah (Ge 17:19; 21:1-7; 1Ch 1:28). Offered up by Abraham (Ge 22; Heb 11:17-19). Rebekah taken as wife (Ge 24). Fathered Esau and Jacob (Ge 25:19-26; 1Ch 1:34). Tricked into blessing Jacob (Ge 27). Father of Israel (Ex 3:6; Dt 29:13; Ro 9:10).

ISAIAH

Prophet to Judah (Isa 1:1). Called by the LORD (Isa 6).

ISHMAEL

Son of Abraham by Hagar (Ge 16; 1Ch 1:28). Blessed, but not son of covenant (Ge 17:18-21; Gal 4:21-31). Sent away by Sarah (Ge 21:8-21).

ISRAEL (ISRAELITES)

1. Name given to Jacob (see JACOB).
2. Corporate name of Jacob's descendants; often specifically Northern Kingdom.

Dt 6: 4 Hear, O *I*: The LORD our God,
1Sa 4:21 "The glory has departed from *I*"—
Isa 27: 6 *I* will bud and blossom
Jer 31:10 'He who scattered *I* will gather
Eze 39:23 of *I* went into exile for their sin,
Mk 12:29 'Hear, O *I*, the Lord our God,
Lk 22:30 judging the twelve tribes of *I*.
Ro 9: 6 all who are descended from *I* are *I*.
    11:26 And so all *I* will be saved,
Eph 3: 6 Gentiles are heirs together with *I*,

ISRAELITES (ISRAEL)

Ex 14:22 and the *I* went through the sea
    16:35 The *I* ate manna forty years,
Hos 1:10 "Yet the *I* will be like the sand
Ro 9:27 the number of the *I* be like the sand

ITCHING*

2Ti 4: 3 to say what their *i* ears want to hear

JACOB

Second son of Isaac, twin of Esau (Ge 26:21-26; 1Ch 1:34). Bought Esau's birthright (Ge 26:29-34); tricked Isaac into blessing him (Ge 27:1-37). Abrahamic covenant perpetuated through (Ge 28:13-15; Mal 1:2). Vision at Bethel (Ge 28:10-22). Wives and children (Ge 29:1-30:24; 35:16-26; 1Ch 2-9). Wrestled with God; name changed to Israel (Ge 32:22-32). Sent sons to Egypt during famine (Ge 42-43). Settled in Egypt (Ge 46). Blessed Ephraim and Manasseh (Ge 48). Blessed sons (Ge 49:1-28; Heb 11:21). Death (Ge 49:29-33). Burial (Ge 50:1-14).

JAMES

1. Apostle; brother of John (Mt 4:21-22; 10:2; Mk 3:17; Lk 5:1-10). At transfiguration (Mt 17:1-13; Mk 9:1-13; Lk 9:28-36). Killed by Herod (Ac 12:2).
2. Apostle; son of Alphaeus (Mt 10:3; Mk 3:18; Lk 6:15).
3. Brother of Jesus (Mt 13:55; Mk 6:3; Lk 24:10; Gal 1:19) and Judas (Jude 1). With believers before Pentecost (Ac 1:13). Leader of church at Jerusalem (Ac 12:17; 15; 21:18; Gal 2:9, 12). Author of epistle (Jas 1:1).

JAPHETH

Son of Noah (Ge 5:32; 1Ch 1:4-5). Blessed (Ge 9:18-28).

JARS

2Co 4: 7 we have this treasure in *j* of clay

JEALOUS (JEALOUSY)

Ex 20: 5 the LORD your God, am a *j* God,
    34:14 whose name is Jealous, is a *j* God.

Dt 4:24 God is a consuming fire, a *j* God.
Joel 2:18 the LORD will be *j* for his land
Zec 1:14 I am very *j* for Jerusalem and Zion,
2Co 11: 2 I am *j* for you with a godly jealousy

JEALOUSY (JEALOUS)

1Co 3: 3 For since there is *j* and quarreling
2Co 11: 2 I am jealous for you with a godly *j*.
Gal 5:20 hatred, discord, *j*, fits of rage,

JEHOAHAZ

1. Son of Jehu; king of Israel (2Ki 13:1-9).
2. Son of Josiah; king of Judah (2Ki 23:31-34; 2Ch 36:1-4).

JEHOASH

Son of Jehoahaz; king of Israel (2Ki 13-14; 2Ch 25).

JEHOIACHIN

Son of Jehoiakim; king of Judah exiled by Nebuchadnezzar (2Ki 24:8-17; 2Ch 36:8-10; Jer 22:24-30; 24:1). Raised from prisoner status (2Ki 25:27-30; Jer 52:31-34).

JEHOIAKIM

Son of Josiah; king of Judah (2Ki 23:34-24: 6; 2Ch 36:4-8; Jer 22:18-23; 36).

JEHORAM

Son of Jehoshaphat; king of Judah (2Ki 8:16-24).

JEHOSHAPHAT

Son of Asa; king of Judah (1Ki 22:41-50; 2Ki 3; 2Ch 17-20).

JEHU

King of Israel (1Ki 19:16-19; 2Ki 9-10).

JEPHTHAH

Judge from Gilead who delivered Israel from Ammon (Jdg 10:6-12:7). Made rash vow concerning his daughter (Jdg 11:30-40).

JEREMIAH

Prophet to Judah (Jer 1:1-3). Called by the LORD (Jer 1). Put in stocks (Jer 20:1-3). Threatened for prophesying (Jer 11:18-23; 26). Opposed by Hananiah (Jer 28). Scroll burned (Jer 36). Imprisoned (Jer 37). Thrown into cistern (Jer 38). Forced to Egypt with those fleeing Babylonians (Jer 43).

JEROBOAM

1. Official of Solomon; rebelled to become first king of Israel (1Ki 11:26-40; 12:1-20; 2Ch 10). Idolatry (1Ki 12:25-33); judgment for (1Ki 13-14; 2Ch 13).
2. Son of Jehoash; king of Israel (1Ki 14:23-29).

JERUSALEM

2Ki 23:27 and I will reject *J*, the city I chose,
2Ch 6: 6 now I have chosen *J* for my Name
Ne 2:17 Come, let us rebuild the wall of *J*,
Ps122: 6 Pray for the peace of *J:*
125: 2 As the mountains surround *J*,

Ps137: 5 If I forget you, O *J*,
Isa 40: 9 You who bring good tidings to *J*,
65:18 for I will create *J* to be a delight
Joel 3:17 *J* will be holy;
Zep 3:16 On that day they will say to *J*,
Zec 2: 4 '*J* will be a city without walls
8: 8 I will bring them back to live in *J;*
14: 8 living water will flow out from *J*,
Mt 23:37 "O *J*, *J*, you who kill the prophets
Lk 13:34 die outside *J!* "O *J*, *J*,
21:24 *J* will be trampled
Jn 4:20 where we must worship is in *J*."
Ac 1: 8 and you will be my witnesses in *J*,
Gal 4:25 corresponds to the present city of *J*
Rev 21: 2 I saw the Holy City, the new *J*,

JESUS

LIFE: Genealogy (Mt 1:1-17; Lk 3:21-37). Birth announced (Mt 1:18-25; Lk 1:26-45). Birth (Mt 2:1-12; Lk 2:1-40). Escape to Egypt (Mt 2: 13-23). As a boy in the temple (Lk 2:41-52). Baptism (Mt 3:13-17; Mk 1:9-11; Lk 3:21-22; Jn 1:32-34). Temptation (Mt 4:1-11; Mk 1:12-13; Lk 4:1-13). Ministry in Galilee (Mt 4:12-18:35; Mk 1:14-9:50; Lk 4:14-13:9; Jn 1:35-2:11; 4; 6), Transfiguration (Mt 17:1-8; Mk 9:2-8; Lk 9:28-36), on the way to Jerusalem (Mt 19-20; Mk 10; Lk 13:10-19:27), in Jerusalem (Mt 21-25; Mk 11-13; Lk 19:28-21:38; Jn 2:12-3:36; 5; 7-12). Last supper (Mt 26:17-35; Mk 14:12-31; Lk 22: 1-38; Jn 13-17). Arrest and trial (Mt 26:36-27:31; Mk 14:43-15:20; Lk 22:39-23:25; Jn 18:1-19:16). Crucifixion (Mt 27:32-66; Mk 15:21-47; Lk 23: 26-55; Jn 19:28-42). Resurrection and appearances (Mt 28; Mk 16; Lk 24; Jn 20-21; Ac 1:1-11; 7:56; 9:3-6; 1Co 15:1-8; Rev 1:1-20).

MIRACLES. Healings: official's son (Jn 4:43-54), demoniac in Capernaum (Mk 1:23-26; Lk 4: 33-35), Peter's mother-in-law (Mt 8:14-17; Mk 1: 29-31; Lk 4:38-39), leper (Mt 8:2-4; Mk 1:40-45; Lk 5:12-16), paralytic (Mt 9:1-8; Mk 2:1-12; Lk 5:17-26), cripple (Jn 5:1-9), shriveled hand (Mt 12:10-13; Mk 3:1-5; Lk 6:6-11), centurion's servant (Mt 8:5-13; Lk 7:1-10), widow's son raised (Lk 7:11-17), demoniac (Mt 12:22-23; Lk 11:14), Gadarene demoniacs (Mt 8:28-34; Mk 5:1-20; Lk 8:26-39), woman's bleeding and Jairus' daughter (Mt 9:18-26; Mk 5:21-43; Lk 8:40-56), blind man (Mt 9:27-31), mute man (Mt 9:32-33), Canaanite woman's daughter (Mt 15:21-28; Mk 7:24-30), deaf man (Mk 7:31-37), blind man (Mk 8:22-26), demoniac boy (Mt 17:14-18; Mk 9:14-29; Lk 9: 37-43), ten lepers (Lk 17:11-19), man born blind (Jn 9:1-7), Lazarus raised (Jn 11), crippled woman (Lk 13:11-17), man with dropsy (Lk 14: 1-6), two blind men (Mt 20:29-34; Mk 10:46-52; Lk 18:35-43), Malchus' ear (Lk 22:50-51). Other Miracles: water to wine (Jn 2:1-11), catch of fish (Lk 5:1-11), storm stilled (Mt 8:23-27; Mk 4: 37-41; Lk 8:22-25), 5,000 fed (Mt 14:15-21; Mk 6:35-44; Lk 9:10-17; Jn 6:1-14), walking on water (Mt 14:25-33; Mk 6:48-52; Jn 6:15-21),

4,000 fed (Mt 15:32-39; Mk 8:1-9), money from fish (Mt 17:24-27), fig tree cursed (Mt 21:18-22; Mk 11:12-14), catch of fish (Jn 21:1-14).

MAJOR TEACHING: Sermon on the Mount (Mt 5-7; Lk 6:17-49), to Nicodemus (Jn 3), to Samaritan woman (Jn 4), Bread of Life (Jn 6: 22-59), at Feast of Tabernacles (Jn 7-8), woes to Pharisees (Mt 23; Lk 11:37-54), Good Shepherd (Jn 10:1-18), Olivet Discourse (Mt 24-25; Mk 13; Lk 21:5-36), Upper Room Discourse (Jn 13-16).

PARABLES: Sower (Mt 13:3-23; Mk 4:3-25; Lk 8:5-18), seed's growth (Mk 4:26-29), wheat and weeds (Mt 13:24-30, 36-43), mustard seed (Mt 13:31-32; Mk 4:30-32), yeast (Mt 13:33; Lk 13:20-21), hidden treasure (Mt 13:44), valuable pearl (Mt 13:45-46), net (Mt 13:47-51), house owner (Mt 13:52), good Samaritan (Lk 10: 25-37), unmerciful servant (Mt 18:15-35), lost sheep (Mt 18:10-14; Lk 15:4-7), lost coin (Lk 15: 8-10), prodigal son (Lk 15:11-32), dishonest manager (Lk 16:1-13), rich man and Lazarus (Lk 16:19-31), persistent widow (Lk 18:1-8), Pharisee and tax collector (Lk 18:9-14), payment of workers (Mt 20:1-16), tenants and the vineyard (Mt 21:28-46; Mt 12:1-12; Lk 20:9-19), wedding banquet (Mt 22:1-14), faithful servant (Mt 24: 45-51), ten virgins (Mt 25:1-13), talents (Mt 25: 14-30; Lk 19:12-27).

DISCIPLES see APOSTLES. Call of (Jn 1: 35-51; Mt 4:18-22; 9:9; Mk 1:16-20; 2:13-14; Lk 5:1-11, 27-28). Named Apostles (Mk 3:13-19; Lk 6:12-16). Twelve sent out (Mt 10; Mk 6:7-11; Lk 9:1-5). Seventy sent out (Lk 10:1-24). Defection of (Jn 6:60-71; Mt 26:56; Mk 14:50-52). Final commission (Mt 28:16-20; Jn 21:15-23; Ac 1: 3-8).

Ac	2:32	God has raised this *J* to life.
	9: 5	"I am *J*, whom you are persecuting
	15:11	of our Lord *J* that we are saved,
	16:31	"Believe in the Lord *J*,
Ro	3:24	redemption that came by Christ *J*.
	5:17	life through the one man, *J* Christ.
	8: 1	for those who are in Christ *J*,
1Co	2: 2	except *J* Christ and him crucified.
	8: 6	and there is but one Lord, *J* Christ,
	12: 3	and no one can say, "*J* is Lord,"
2Co	4: 5	not preach ourselves, but *J* Christ
Gal	2:16	but by faith in *J* Christ.
	3:28	for you are all one in Christ *J*.
	5: 6	in Christ *J* neither circumcision
Eph	2:10	created in Christ *J*
	2:20	with Christ *J* himself as the chief
Php	1: 6	until the day of Christ *J*.
	2: 5	be the same as that of Christ *J*:
	2:10	name of *J* every knee should bow,
Col	3:17	do it all in the name of the Lord *J*,
2Th	2: 1	the coming of our Lord *J* Christ
1Ti	1:15	Christ *J* came into the world
2Ti	3:12	life in Christ *J* will be persecuted,
Tit	2:13	our great God and Savior, *J* Christ,
Heb	2: 9	But we see *J*, who was made a little
	3: 1	fix your thoughts on *J*, the apostle
Heb	4:14	through the heavens, *J* the Son
	7:22	*J* has become the guarantee
	7:24	but because *J* lives forever,
	12: 2	Let us fix our eyes on *J*, the author
2Pe	1:16	and coming of our Lord *J* Christ,
1Jn	1: 7	and the blood of *J*, his Son,
	2: 1	*J* Christ, the Righteous One.
	2: 6	to live in him must walk as *J* did.
	4:15	anyone acknowledges that *J* is
Rev	22:20	Come, Lord *J*.

JEW (JEWS JUDAISM)

Zec	8:23	of one *J* by the edge of his robe
Ro	1:16	first for the *J*, then for the Gentile.
	10:12	there is no difference between *J*
1Co	9:20	To the Jews I became like a *J*,
Gal	3:28	There is neither *J* nor Greek,

JEWELRY (JEWELS)

1Pe	3: 3	wearing of gold *j* and fine clothes.

JEWELS (JEWELRY)

Isa	61:10	as a bride adorns herself with her *j*.
Zec	9:16	like *j* in a crown.

JEWS (JEW)

Mt	2: 2	who has been born king of the *J*?
	27:11	"Are you the king of the *J*?" "Yes,
Jn	4:22	for salvation is from the *J*.
Ro	3:29	Is God the God of *J* only?
1Co		*J* demand miraculous signs
	9:20	To the *J* I became like a Jew,
	12:13	whether *J* or Greeks, slave or free
Gal	2: 8	of Peter as an apostle to the *J*,
Rev	3: 9	claim to be *J* though they are not,

JEZEBEL

Sidonian wife of Ahab (1Ki 16:31). Promoted Baal worship (1Ki 16:32-33). Killed prophets of the LORD (1Ki 18:4, 13). Opposed Elijah (1Ki 19: 1-2). Had Naboth killed (1Ki 21). Death prophesied (1Ki 21:17-24). Killed by Jehu (2Ki 9:30-37).

JOASH

Son of Ahaziah; king of Judah. Sheltered from Athaliah by Jehoiada (2Ki 11; 2Ch 22:10-23:21). Repaired temple (2Ki 12; 2Ch 24).

JOB

Wealthy man from Uz; feared God (Job 1:1-5). Righteousness tested by disaster (Job 1:6-22), personal affliction (Job 2). Maintained innocence in debate with three friends (Job 3-31), Elihu (Job 32-37). Rebuked by the LORD (Job 38-41). Vindicated and restored to greater stature by the LORD (Job 42). Example of righteousness (Eze 14:14, 20).

JOHN

1. Son of Zechariah and Elizabeth (Lk 1). Called the Baptist (Mt 3:1-12; Mk 1:2-8). Witness to Jesus (Mt 3:11-12; Mk 1:7-8; Lk 3:15-18; Jn 1: 6-35; 3:27-30; 5:33-36). Doubts about Jesus (Mt 11:2-6; Lk 7:18-23). Arrest (Mt 4:12; Mk 1:14). Execution (Mt 14:1-12; Mk 6:14-29; Lk 9:7-9).

Ministry compared to Elijah (Mt 11:7-19; Mk 9:
11-13; Lk 7:24-35).
   2. Apostle; brother of James (Mt 4:21-22; 10:
2; Mk 3:17; Lk 5:1-10). At transfiguration (Mt 17:
1-13; Mk 9:1-13; Lk 9:28-36). Desire to be greatest (Mk 10:35-45). Leader of church at Jerusalem
(Ac 4:1-3; Gal 2:9). Elder who wrote epistles (2Jn
1; 3Jn 1). Prophet who wrote Revelation (Rev 1:
1; 22:8).
   3. Cousin of Barnabas, co-worker with Paul,
(Ac 12:12-13:13; 15:37), see MARK.

JOIN (JOINED)
Pr   23:20 Do not *j* those who drink too much
     24:21 and do not *j* with the rebellious,
Ro   15:30 to *j* me in my struggle by praying
2Ti   1: 8 *j* with me in suffering for the gospel

JOINED (JOIN)
Mt   19: 6 Therefore what God has *j* together,
Mk   10: 9 Therefore what God has *j* together,
Eph   2:21 him the whole building is *j* together
       4:16 *j* and held together

JOINTS
Heb   4:12 even to dividing soul and spirit, *j*

JOKING
Eph   5: 4 or coarse *j*, which are out of place,

JONAH
   Prophet in days of Jeroboam II (2Ki 14:25).
Called to Nineveh; fled to Tarshish (Jnh 1:1-3).
Cause of storm; thrown into sea (Jnh 1:4-16).
Swallowed by fish (Jnh 1:17). Prayer (Jnh 2).
Preached to Nineveh (Jnh 3). Attitude reproved
by the LORD (Jnh 4). Sign of (Mt 12:39-41; Lk 11:
29-32).

JONATHAN
   Son of Saul (1Sa 13:16; 1Ch 8:33). Valiant
warrior (1Sa 13-14). Relation to David (1Sa 18:
1-4; 19-20; 23:16-18). Killed at Gilboa (1Sa 31).
Mourned by David (2Sa 1).

JORAM
   1. Son of Ahab; king of Israel (2Ki 3; 8-9; 2Ch
22).

JORDAN
Nu   34:12 boundary will go down along the *J*
Jos   4:22 Israel crossed the *J* on dry ground.'
Mt   3: 6 baptized by him in the *J* River.

JOSEPH
   1. Son of Jacob by Rachel (Ge 30:24; 1Ch 2:
2). Favored by Jacob, hated by brothers (Ge 37:
3-4). Dreams (Ge 37:5-11). Sold by brothers (Ge
37:12-36). Served Potiphar; imprisoned by false
accusation (Ge 39). Interpreted dreams of Pharaoh's servants (Ge 40), of Pharaoh (Ge 41:4-40).
Made greatest in Egypt (Ge 41:41-57). Sold grain
to brothers (Ge 42-45). Brought Jacob and sons to
Egypt (Ge 46-47). Sons Ephraim and Manasseh blessed (Ge 48). Blessed (Ge 49:22-26;
Dt 33:13-17). Death (Ge 50:22-26; Ex 13:19;

Heb 11:22). 12,000 from (Rev 7:8).
   2. Husband of Mary, mother of Jesus (Mt 1:
16-24; 2:13-19; Lk 1:27; 2; Jn 1:45).
   3. Disciple from Arimathea, who gave his
tomb for Jesus' burial (Mt 27:57-61; Mk 15:43-
47; Lk 24:50-52).
   4. Original name of Barnabas (Ac 4:36).

JOSHUA
   1. Son of Nun; name changed from Hoshea (Nu
13:8, 16; 1Ch 7:27). Fought Amalekites under
Moses (Ex 17:9-14). Servant of Moses on Sinai
(Ex 24:13; 32:17). Spied Canaan (Nu 13). With
Caleb, allowed to enter land (Nu 14:6, 30). Succeeded Moses (Dt 1:38; 31:1-8; 34:9).
   Charged Israel to conquer Canaan (Jos 1).
Crossed Jordan (Jos 3-4). Circumcised sons of
wilderness wanderings (Jos 5). Conquered Jericho (Jos 6), Ai (Jos 7-8), five kings at Gibeon (Jos
10:1-28), southern Canaan (Jos 10:29-43), northern Canaan (Jos 11-12). Defeated at Ai (Jos 7).
Deceived by Gibeonites (Jos 9). Renewed covenant (Jos 8:30-35; 24:1-27). Divided land among
tribes (Jos 13-22). Last words (Jos 23). Death
(Jos 24:28-31).
   2. High priest during rebuilding of temple (Hag
1-2; Zec 3:1-9; 6:11).

JOSIAH
   Son of Amon; king of Judah (2Ki 22-23; 2Ch
34-35).

JOTHAM
   Son of Azariah (Uzziah); king of Judah (2Ki
15:32-38; 2Ch 26:21-27:9).

JOY (ENJOY ENJOYMENT JOYFUL
OVERJOYED REJOICE REJOICES
REJOICING)
Dt   16:15 and your *j* will be complete.
1Ch 16:27 strength and *j* in his dwelling place.
Ne   8:10 for the *j* of the LORD is your
Est   9:22 their sorrow was turned into *j*
Job 38: 7 and all the angels shouted for *j?*
Ps   4: 7 have filled my heart with greater *j*
     21: 6 with the *j* of your presence.
     30:11 sackcloth and clothed me with *j*,
     43: 4 to God, my *j* and my delight.
     51:12 to me the *j* of your salvation
     66: 1 Shout with *j* to God, all the earth!
     96:12 the trees of the forest will sing for *j*;
    107: 22 and tell of his works with songs of *j*
    119:111 they are the *j* of my heart.
Pr   10: 1 A wise son brings *j* to his father,
     10:28 The prospect of the righteous is *j*,
     12:20 but *j* for those who promote peace.
Isa 35:10 everlasting *j* will crown their heads
     51:11 Gladness and *j* will overtake them,
     55:12 You will go out in *j*
Lk   1:44 the baby in my womb leaped for *j*.
      2:10 news of great *j* that will be
Jn   15:11 and that your *j* may be complete.
     16:20 but your grief will turn to *j*.
2Co   8: 2 their overflowing *j* and their

Php 2: 2 then make my *j* complete
4: 1 and long for, my *j* and crown,
1Th 2:19 For what is our hope, our *j*,
Phm : 7 Your love has given me great *j*
Heb 12: 2 for the *j* set before him endured
Jas 1: 2 Consider it pure *j*, my brothers,
1Pe 1: 8 with an inexpressible and glorious *j*
2Jn : 4 It has given me great *j* to find some
3Jn : 4 I have no greater *j*

JOYFUL (JOY)
Ps 100: 2 come before him with *j* songs.
Hab 3:18 I will be *j* in God my Savior.
1Th 5:16 Be *j* always; pray continually;

JUDAH
1. Son of Jacob by Leah (Ge 29:35; 35:23; 1Ch 2:1). Tribe of blessed as ruling tribe (Ge 49:8-12; Dt 33:7).
2. Name used for people and land of Southern Kingdom.
Jer 13:19 All *J* will be carried into exile,
Zec 10: 4 From *J* will come the cornerstone,
Heb 7:14 that our Lord descended from *J*,

JUDAISM (JEW)
Gal 1:13 of my previous way of life in *J*,

JUDAS
1. Apostle (Lk 6:16; Jn 14:22; Ac 1:13). Probably also called Thaddaeus (Mt 10:3; Mk 3:18).
2. Brother of James and Jesus (Mt 13:55; Mk 6:3), also called Jude (Jude 1).
3. Apostle, also called Iscariot, who betrayed Jesus (Mt 10:4; 26:14-56; Mk 3:19; 14:10-50; Lk 6:16; 22:3-53; Jn 6:71; 12:4; 13:2-30; 18:2-11). Suicide of (Mt 27:3-5; Ac 1:16-25).

JUDGE (JUDGED JUDGES JUDGING JUDGMENT)
Ge 18:25 Will not the *J* of all the earth do
1Ch 16:33 for he comes to *j* the earth.
Ps 9: 8 He will *j* the world in righteousness
Joel 3:12 sit to *j* all the nations on every side.
Mt 7: 1 Do not *j*, or you too will be judged.
Jn 12:47 For I did not come to *j* the world,
Ac 17:31 a day when he will *j* the world
Ro 2:16 day when God will *j* men's secrets
1Co 4: 3 indeed, I do not even *j* myself.
6: 2 that the saints will *j* the world?
Gal 2: 6 not *j* by external appearance—
2Ti 4: 1 who will *j* the living and the dead,
4: 8 which the Lord, the righteous *J*,
Jas 4:12 There is only one Lawgiver and *J*,
4:12 who are you to *j* your neighbor?
Rev 20: 4 who had been given authority to *j*.

JUDGED (JUDGE)
Mt 7: 1 "Do not judge, or you too will be *j*.
1Co 11:31 But if we *j* ourselves, we would not
Jas 3: 1 who teach will be *j* more strictly.
Rev 20:12 The dead were *j* according

JUDGES (JUDGE)
Jdg 2:16 Then the LORD raised up *j*,

Ps 58:11 there is a God who *j* the earth."
Heb 4:12 it *j* the thoughts and attitudes
Rev 19:11 With justice he *j* and makes war.

JUDGING (JUDGE)
Mt 19:28 *j* the twelve tribes of Israel.
Jn 7:24 Stop *j* by mere appearances,

JUDGMENT (JUDGE)
Dt 1:17 of any man, for *j* belongs to God.
Ps 1: 5 the wicked will not stand in the *j*,
119: 66 Teach me knowledge and good *j*,
Pr 6:32 man who commits adultery lacks *j*;
12:11 but he who chases fantasies lacks *j*.
Ecc 12:14 God will bring every deed into *j*,
Isa 66:16 the LORD will execute *j*
Mt 5:21 who murders will be subject to *j*.'
10:15 on the day of *j* than for that town.
12:36 have to give account on the day of *j*
Jn 5:22 but has entrusted all *j* to the Son,
7:24 appearances, and make a right *j*."
16: 8 to sin and righteousness and *j*:
Ro 14:10 stand before God's *j* seat.
14:13 Therefore let us stop passing *j*
1Co 11:29 body of the Lord eats and drinks *j*
2Co 5:10 appear before the *j* seat of Christ,
Heb 9:27 to die once, and after that to face *j*,
10:27 but only a fearful expectation of *j*
1Pe 4:17 For it is time for *j* to begin
Jude : 6 bound with everlasting chains for *j*

JUST (JUSTICE JUSTIFICATION JUSTIFIED JUSTIFY JUSTLY)
Dt 32: 4 and all his ways are *j*.
Ps 37:28 For the LORD loves the *j*
111: 7 of his hands are faithful and *j*;
Pr 1: 3 doing what is right and *j* and fair;
2: 8 for he guards the course of the *j*
Da 4:37 does is right and all his ways are *j*.
Ro 3:26 as to be *j* and the one who justifies
Heb 2: 2 received its *j* punishment,
1Jn 1: 9 and *j* and will forgive us our sins
Rev 16: 7 true and *j* are your judgments."

JUSTICE (JUST)
Ex 23: 2 do not pervert *j* by siding
23: 6 "Do not deny *j* to your poor people
Job 37:23 in his *j* and great righteousness,
Ps 9: 8 he will govern the peoples with *j*.
9:16 The LORD is known by his *j*;
11: 7 he loves *j*;
45: 6 a scepter of *j* will be the scepter
101: 1 I will sing of your love and *j*;
106: 3 Blessed are they who maintain *j*,
Pr 21:15 When *j* is done, it brings joy
28: 5 Evil men do not understand *j*,
29: 4 By *j* a king gives a country stability
29:26 from the LORD that man gets *j*.
Isa 9: 7 it with *j* and righteousness
28:17 I will make *j* the measuring line
30:18 For the LORD is a God of *j*.
42: 1 and he will bring *j* to the nations.
42: 4 till he establishes *j* on earth.
56: 1 "Maintain *j*

Isa 61: 8 "For I, the LORD, love *j;*
Jer 30:11 I will discipline you but only with *j;*
Eze 34:16 I will shepherd the flock with *j.*
Am 5:15 maintain *j* in the courts.
    5:24 But let *j* roll on like a river,
Zec 7: 9 'Administer true *j;* show mercy
Lk 11:42 you neglect *j* and the love of God.
Ro 3:25 He did this to demonstrate his *j,*

JUSTIFICATION (JUST)
Ro 4:25 and was raised to life for our *j.*
    5:18 of righteousness was *j* that brings

JUSTIFIED (JUST)
Ac 13:39 him everyone who believes is *j*
Ro 3:24 and are *j* freely by his grace
    3:28 For we maintain that a man is *j*
    5: 1 since we have been *j* through faith,
    5: 9 Since we have now been *j*
    8:30 those he called, he also *j;* those he *j,*
1Co 6:11 you were *j* in the name
Gal 2:16 observing the law no one will be *j.*
    3:11 Clearly no one is *j* before God
    3:24 to Christ that we might be *j* by faith
Jas 2:24 You see that a person is *j*

JUSTIFY (JUST)
Gal 3: 8 that God would *j* the Gentiles

JUSTLY (JUST)
Mic 6: 8 To act *j* and to love mercy

KEEP (KEEPER KEEPING KEEPS KEPT)
Ge 31:49 "May the LORD *k* watch
Ex 20: 6 and *k* my commandments.
Nu 6:24 and *k* you;
Ps 18:28 You, O LORD, *k* my lamp burning
    19:13 *K* your servant also from willful
    119: 9 can a young man *k* his way pure?
    121: 7 The LORD will *k* you
    141: 3 *k* watch over the door of my lips.
Pr 4:24 *k* corrupt talk far from your lips.
Isa 26: 3 You will *k* in perfect peace
Mt 10:10 for the worker is worth his *k.*
Lk 12:35 and *k* your lamps burning,
Gal 5:25 let us *k* in step with the Spirit.
Eph 4: 3 Make every effort to *k* the unity
1Ti 5:22 *K* yourself pure.
2Ti 4: 5 *k* your head in all situations,
Heb 13: 5 *K* your lives free from the love
Jas 1:26 and yet does not *k* a tight rein
    2: 8 If you really *k* the royal law found
Jude :24 able to *k* you from falling

KEEPER (KEEP)
Ge 4: 9 I my brother's *k?*" The LORD

KEEPING (KEEP)
Ex 20: 8 the Sabbath day by *k* it holy.
Ps 19:11 in *k* them there is great reward.
Mt 3: 8 Produce fruit in *k* with repentance.
Lk 2: 8 *k* watch over their flocks at night.
1Co 7:19 *K* God's commands is what counts.
2Pe 3: 9 Lord is not slow in *k* his promise,

KEEPS (KEEP)
Pr 17:28 a fool is thought wise if he *k* silent,
Am 5:13 Therefore the prudent man *k* quiet
1Co 13: 5 is not easily angered, it *k* no record
Jas 2:10 For whoever *k* the whole law

KEPT (KEEP)
Ps 130: 3 If you, O LORD, *k* a record of sins,
2Ti 4: 7 finished the race, I have *k* the faith.
1Pe 1: 4 spoil or fade—*k* in heaven for you,

KEYS
Mt 16:19 I will give you the *k* of the kingdom

KILL (KILLS)
Mt 17:23 They will *k* him, and on the third

KILLS (KILL)
Lev 24:21 but whoever *k* a man must be put
2Co 3: 6 for the letter *k,* but the Spirit gives

KIND (KINDNESS KINDS)
Ge 1:24 animals, each according to its *k.*"
2Ch 10: 7 "If you will be *k* to these people
Pr 11:17 A *k* man benefits himself,
    12:25 but a *k* word cheers him up.
    14:21 blessed is he who is *k* to the needy
    14:31 whoever is *k* to the needy honors
    19:17 He who is *k* to the poor lends
Da 4:27 by being *k* to the oppressed.
Lk 6:35 because he is *k* to the ungrateful
1Co 13: 4 Love is patient, love is *k.*
    15:35 With what *k* of body will they
Eph 4:32 Be *k* and compassionate
1Th 5:15 but always try to be *k* to each other
2Ti 2:24 instead, he must be *k* to everyone,
Tit 2: 5 to be busy at home, to be *k,*

KINDNESS (KIND)
Ac 14:17 He has shown *k* by giving you rain
Ro 11:22 Consider therefore the *k*
Gal 5:22 peace, patience, *k,* goodness,
Eph 2: 7 expressed in his *k* to us
2Pe 1: 7 brotherly *k;* and to brotherly *k,*

KINDS (KIND)
1Co 12: 4 There are different *k* of gifts,
1Ti 6:10 of money is a root of all *k* of evil.

KING (KINGDOM KINGS)
1. Kings of Judah and Israel: see Saul, David, Solomon.
2. Kings of Judah: see Rehoboam, Abijah, Asa, Jehoshaphat, Jehoram, Ahaziah, Athaliah (Queen), Joash, Amaziah, Uzziah, Jotham, Ahaz, Hezekiah, Manasseh, Amon, Josiah, Jehoahaz, Jehoiakim, Jehoiachin, Zedekiah.
3. Kings of Israel: see Jeroboam I, Nadab, Baasha, Elah, Zimri, Tibni, Omri, Ahab, Ahaziah, Joram, Jehu, Jehoahaz, Jehoash, Jeroboam II, Zechariah, Shallum, Menahem, Pekah, Pekahiah, Hoshea.
Jdg 17: 6 In those days Israel had no *k;*
1Sa 12:12 the LORD your God was your *k.*
Ps 24: 7 that the *K* of glory may come in.
Isa 32: 1 See, a *k* will reign in righteousness

Zec 9: 9 See, your *k* comes to you,
1Ti 6:15 the *K* of kings and Lord of lords,
1Pe 2:17 of believers, fear God, honor the *k*.
Rev 19:16 *K* OF KINGS AND LORD

KINGDOM (KING)

Ex 19: 6 you will be for me a *k* of priests
1Ch 29:11 Yours, O LORD, is the *k;*
Ps 45: 6 justice will be the scepter of your *k*.
Da 4: 3 His *k* is an eternal *k;*
Mt 3: 2 Repent, for the *k* of heaven is near
 5: 3 for theirs is the *k* of heaven.
 6:10 your *k* come,
 6:33 But seek first his *k* and his
 7:21 Lord,' will enter the *k* of heaven,
 11:11 least in the *k* of heaven is greater
 13:24 "The *k* of heaven is like a man who
 13:31 *k* of heaven is like a mustard seed,
 13:33 "The *k* of heaven is like yeast that
 13:44 *k* of heaven is like treasure hidden
 13:45 the *k* of heaven is like a merchant
 13:47 *k* of heaven is like a net that was let
 16:19 the keys of the *k* of heaven;
 18:23 the *k* of heaven is like a king who
 19:24 for a rich man to enter the *k* of God
 24: 7 rise against nation, and *k* against *k*.
 24:14 gospel of the *k* will be preached
 25:34 the *k* prepared for you
Mk 9:47 better for you to enter the *k* of God
 10:14 for the *k* of God belongs to such
 10:23 for the rich to enter the *k* of God!''
Lk 10: 9 'The *k* of God is near you.'
 12:31 seek his *k*, and these things will be
 17:21 because the *k* of God is within you
Jn 3: 5 no one can enter the *k* of God
 18:36 ''My *k* is not of this world.
1Co 6: 9 the wicked will not inherit the *k*
 15:24 hands over the *k* to God the Father
Rev 1: 6 has made us to be a *k* and priests
 11:15 of the world has become the *k*

KINGS (KING)

Ps 2: 2 The *k* of the earth take their stand
 72:11 All *k* will bow down to him
Da 7:24 ten horns are ten *k* who will come
1Ti 2: 2 for *k* and all those in authority,
Rev 1: 5 and the ruler of the *k* of the earth.

KINSMAN-REDEEMER (REDEEM)

Ru 3: 9 over me, since you are a *k*.''

KISS

Ps 2:12 *K* the Son, lest he be angry
Pr 24:26 is like a *k* on the lips.
Lk 22:48 the Son of Man with a *k?*''

KNEE (KNEES)

Isa 45:23 Before me every *k* will bow;
Ro 14:11 'every *k* will bow before me;
Php 2:10 name of Jesus every *k* should bow,

KNEES (KNEE)

Isa 35: 3 steady the *k* that give way;
Heb 12:12 your feeble arms and weak *k*.

KNEW (KNOW)

Job 23: 3 If only I *k* where to find him;
Jnh 4: 2 I *k* that you are a gracious
Mt 7:23 tell them plainly, 'I never *k* you.

KNOCK

Mt 7: 7 *k* and the door will be opened
Rev 3:20 I am! I stand at the door and *k*.

KNOW (FOREKNEW KNEW KNOWING KNOWLEDGE KNOWN KNOWS)

Dt 18:21 ''How can we *k* when a message
Job 19:25 I *k* that my Redeemer lives,
 42: 3 things too wonderful for me to *k*.
Ps 46:10 ''Be still, and *k* that I am God;
 139: 1 and you *k* me.
 139: 23 Search me, O God, and *k* my heart;
Pr 27: 1 for you do not *k* what a day may
Jer 24: 7 I will give them a heart to *k* me,
 31:34 his brother, saying, '*K* the LORD,
Mt 6: 3 let your left hand *k* what your right
 24:42 you do not *k* on what day your
Lk 1: 4 so that you may *k* the certainty
Jn 3:11 we speak of what we *k*,
 4:22 we worship what we do *k*,
 9:25 One thing I do *k*.
 10:14 I *k* my sheep and my sheep *k* me—
 17: 3 that they may *k* you, the only true
 21:24 We *k* that his testimony is true.
Ac 1: 7 ''It is not for you to *k* the times
Ro 6: 6 For we *k* that our old self was
 7:18 I *k* that nothing good lives in me,
 8:28 we *k* that in all things God works
1Co 2: 2 For I resolved to *k* nothing
 6:15 Do you not *k* that your bodies are
 6:19 Do you not *k* that your body is
 13:12 Now I *k* in part; then I shall *k* fully,
 15:58 because you *k* that your labor
Php 3:10 I want to *k* Christ and the power
2Ti 1:12 because I *k* whom I have believed,
Jas 4:14 *k* what will happen tomorrow.
1Jn 2: 4 The man who says, ''I *k* him,''
 3:14 We *k* that we have passed
 3:16 This is how we *k* what love is:
 5: 2 This is how we *k* that we love
 5:13 so that you may *k* that you have

KNOWING (KNOW)

Ge 3: 5 and you will be like God, *k* good
Php 3: 8 of *k* Christ Jesus my Lord,

KNOWLEDGE (KNOW)

Ge 2: 9 the tree of the *k* of good and evil.
Job 42: 3 obscures my counsel without *k?*'
Ps 19: 2 night after night they display *k*.
 73:11 Does the Most High have *k?*''
 139: 6 Such *k* is too wonderful for me,
Pr 1: 7 of the LORD is the beginning of *k*,
 10:14 Wise men store up *k*,
 12: 1 Whoever loves discipline loves *k*,
 13:16 Every prudent man acts out of *k*,
 19: 2 to have zeal without *k*,
Isa 11: 9 full of the *k* of the LORD
Hab 2:14 filled with the *k* of the glory

Ro 11:33 riches of the wisdom and *k* of God!
1Co 8: 1 *K* puffs up, but love builds up.
    8:11 Christ died, is destroyed by your *k*.
    13: 2 can fathom all mysteries and all *k*,
2Co 2:14 everywhere the fragrance of the *k*
    4: 6 light of the *k* of the glory of God
Eph 3:19 to know this love that surpasses *k*
Col 2: 3 all the treasures of wisdom and *k*.
1Ti 6:20 ideas of what is falsely called *k*,
2Pe 3:18 grow in the grace and *k* of our Lord

KNOWN (KNOW)
Ps 16:11 You have made *k* to me the path
  105: 1 make *k* among the nations what he
Isa 46:10 *k* the end from the beginning,
Mt 10:26 or hidden that will not be made *k*.
Ro 1:19 since what may be *k* about God is
    11:34 "Who has *k* the mind of the Lord?
    15:20 the gospel where Christ was not *k*,
2Co 3: 2 written on our hearts, *k*
2Pe 2:21 than to have *k* it and then

KNOWS (KNOW)
1Sa 2: 3 for the Lord is a God who *k*,
Job 23:10 But he *k* the way that I take;
Ps 44:21 since he *k* the secrets of the heart?
  94:11 The Lord *k* the thoughts of man;
Ecc 8: 7 Since no man *k* the future,
Mt 6: 8 for your Father *k* what you need
  24:36 "No one *k* about that day or hour,
Ro 8:27 who searches our hearts *k* the mind
1Co 8: 2 who thinks he *k* something does
2Ti 2:19 The Lord *k* those who are his," and

LABAN
Brother of Rebekah (Ge 24:29-51), father of Rachel and Leah (Ge 29-31).

LABOR
Ex 20: 9 Six days you shall *l* and do all your
Isa 55: 2 and your *l* on what does not satisfy
Mt 6:28 They do not *l* or spin.
1Co 3: 8 rewarded according to his own *l*.
  15:58 because you know that your *l*

LACK (LACKING LACKS)
Pr 15:22 Plans fail for *l* of counsel,
Ro 3: 3 Will their *l* of faith nullify God's
Col 2:23 *l* any value in restraining sensual

LACKING (LACK)
Ro 12:11 Never be *l* in zeal, but keep your
Jas 1: 4 and complete, not *l* anything.

LACKS (LACK)
Pr 6:32 who commits adultery *l* judgment;
  12:11 he who chases fantasies *l* judgment
Jas 1: 5 any of you *l* wisdom, he should ask

LAID (LAY)
Isa 53: 6 and the Lord has *l* on him
1Co 3:11 other than the one already *l*,
1Jn 3:16 Jesus Christ *l* down his life for us.

LAKE
Rev 19:20 into the fiery *l* of burning sulfur.

Rev 20:14 The *l* of fire is the second death.

LAMB (LAMB'S LAMBS)
Ge 22: 8 "God himself will provide the *l*
Ex 12:21 and slaughter the Passover *l*.
Isa 11: 6 The wolf will live with the *l*,
  53: 7 he was led like a *l* to the slaughter,
Jn 1:29 *L* of God, who takes away the sin
1Co 5: 7 our Passover *l*, has been sacrificed.
1Pe 1:19 a *l* without blemish or defect.
Rev 5: 6 Then I saw a *L*, looking
  5:12 "Worthy is the *L*, who was slain,
  14: 4 They follow the *L* wherever he

LAMB'S (LAMB)
Rev 21:27 written in the *L* book of life.

LAMBS (LAMB)
Lk 10: 3 I am sending you out like *l*
Jn 21:15 Jesus said, "Feed my *l*."

LAMENT
2Sa 1:17 took up this *l* concerning Saul

LAMP (LAMPS)
2Sa 22:29 You are my *l*, O Lord;
Ps 18:28 You, O Lord, keep my *l* burning;
  119:105 Your word is a *l* to my feet
Pr 31:18 and her *l* does not go out at night.
Lk 8:16 "No one lights a *l* and hides it
Rev 21:23 gives it light, and the Lamb is its *l*.

LAMPS (LAMP)
Mt 25: 1 be like ten virgins who took their *l*
Lk 12:35 for service and keep your *l* burning,

LAND
Ge 1:10 God called the dry ground "*l*,"
  1:11 "Let the *l* produce vegetation:
  12: 7 To your offspring I will give this *l*."
Ex 3: 8 a *l* flowing with milk and honey—
Nu 35:33 Do not pollute the *l* where you are.
Dt 34: 1 Lord showed him the whole *l*—
Jos 13: 2 "This is the *l* that remains:
  14: 4 Levites received no share of the *l*
2Ch 7:14 their sin and will heal their *l*.
  7:20 then I will uproot Israel from my *l*,
Eze 36:24 and bring you back into your own *l*.

LANGUAGE
Ge 11: 1 Now the whole world had one *l*
Ps 19: 3 There is no speech or *l*
Jn 8:44 When he lies, he speaks his native *l*
Ac 2: 6 heard them speaking in his own *l*.
Col 3: 8 slander, and filthy *l* from your lips.
Rev 5: 9 from every tribe and *l* and people

LAST (LASTING LASTS LATTER)
2Sa 23: 1 These are the *l* words of David:
Isa 44: 6 I am the first and I am the *l*;
Mt 19:30 But many who are first will be *l*,
Mk 10:31 are first will be *l*, and the *l* first."
Jn 15:16 and bear fruit—fruit that will *l*.
Ro 1:17 is by faith from first to *l*,
2Ti 3: 1 will be terrible times in the *l* days.
2Pe 3: 3 in the *l* days scoffers will come,

Rev   1:17 I am the First and the L.
       22:13 the First and the L, the Beginning

LASTING (LAST)

Ex   12:14 to the LORD—a l ordinance.
Lev 24: 8 of the Israelites, as a l covenant.
Nu   25:13 have a covenant of a l priesthood,
Heb 10:34 had better and l possessions.

LASTS (LAST)

Ps   30: 5 For his anger l only a moment,
2Co   3:11 greater is the glory of that which l!

LATTER (LAST)

Job 42:12 The LORD blessed the l part

LAUGH (LAUGHS)

Ecc   3: 4 a time to weep and a time to l,

LAUGHS (LAUGH)

Ps   2: 4 The One enthroned in heaven l;
       37:13 but the Lord l at the wicked,

LAVISHED

Eph   1: 8 of God's grace that he l on us
1Jn   3: 1 great is the love the Father has l

LAW (LAWS)

Dt   31:11 you shall read this l before them
       31:26 "Take this Book of the L
Jos   1: 8 of the L depart from your mouth;
Ne   8: 8 from the Book of the L of God,
Ps   1: 2 and on his l he meditates day
       19: 7 The l of the LORD is perfect,
      119: 18 wonderful things in your l.
      119: 72 l from your mouth is more precious
      119: 97 Oh, how I love your l!
      119:165 peace have they who love your l,
Isa   8:20 To the l and to the testimony!
Jer   31:33 "I will put my l in their minds
Mt   5:17 that I have come to abolish the L
       7:12 sums up the L and the Prophets.
       22:40 All the L and the Prophets hang
Lk   16:17 stroke of a pen to drop out of the L.
Jn   1:17 For the l was given through Moses;
Ro   2:12 All who sin apart from the l will
       2:15 of the l are written on their hearts,
       5:13 for before the l was given,
       5:20 l was added so that the trespass
       6:14 because you are not under l,
       7: 6 released from the l so that we serve
       7:12 l is holy, and the commandment is
       8: 3 For what the l was powerless to do
       10: 4 Christ is the end of the l
       13:10 love is the fulfillment of the l.
Gal   3:13 curse of the l by becoming a curse
       3:24 So the l was put in charge to lead us
       5: 3 obligated to obey the whole l.
       5: 4 justified by l have been alienated
       5:14 The entire l is summed up
Heb   7:19 (for the l made nothing perfect),
       10: 1 The l is only a shadow
Jas   1:25 intently into the perfect l that gives
       2:10 For whoever keeps the whole l

LAWLESSNESS*

2Th   2: 3 and the man of l is revealed,
       2: 7 power of l is already at work;
1Jn   3: 4 sins breaks the law; in fact, sin is l.

LAWS (LAW)

Lev 25:18 and be careful to obey my l,
Ps 119: 30 I have set my heart on your l.
      119:120 I stand in awe of your l.
Heb   8:10 I will put my l in their minds
       10:16 I will put my l in their hearts,

LAY (LAID LAYING)

Job 22:22 and l up his words in your heart.
Isa   28:16 "See, I l a stone in Zion,
Mt   8:20 of Man has no place to l his head."
Jn   10:15 and I l down my life for the sheep.
       15:13 that he l down his life
1Co   3:11 no one can l any foundation other
1Jn   3:16 And we ought to l down our lives
Rev   4:10 They l their crowns

LAYING (LAY)

1Ti   5:22 Do not be hasty in the l on of hands
Heb   6: 1 not l again the foundation

LAZARUS

   1. Poor man in Jesus' parable (Lk 16:19-31).
   2. Brother of Mary and Martha whom Jesus
raised from the dead (Jn 11:1-12:19).

LAZY

Pr   10: 4 L hands make a man poor,
Heb   6:12 We do not want you to become l,

LEAD (LEADERS LEADERSHIP LEADS LED)

Ex   15:13 "In your unfailing love you will l
Ps   27:11 l me in a straight path
       61: 2 l me to the rock that is higher
      139: 24 and l me in the way everlasting.
      143: 10 l me on level ground.
Ecc   5: 6 Do not let your mouth l you
Isa   11: 6 and a little child will l them.
Da   12: 3 those who l many to righteousness,
Mt   6:13 And l us not into temptation,
1Jn   3: 7 do not let anyone l you astray.

LEADERS (LEAD)

Heb 13: 7 Remember your l, who spoke
       13:17 Obey your l and submit

LEADERSHIP (LEAD)

Ro   12: 8 if it is l, let him govern diligently;

LEADS (LEAD)

Ps   23: 2 he l me beside quiet waters,
Pr   19:23 The fear of the LORD l to life:
Isa   40:11 he gently l those that have young.
Mt   7:13 and broad is the road that l
       15:14 If a blind man l a blind man,
Jn   10: 3 sheep by name and l them out.
Ro   14:19 effort to do what l to peace
2Co   2:14 always l us in triumphal procession

LEAH

   Wife of Jacob (Ge 29:16-30); bore six sons and

one daughter (Ge 29:31-30:21; 34:1; 35:23).

LEAN
Pr   3: 5 *l* not on your own understanding;

LEARN (LEARNED LEARNING)
Isa   1:17 *l* to do right!
Mt   11:29 yoke upon you and *l* from me,

LEARNED (LEARN)
Php   4:11 for I have *l* to be content whatever
2Ti   3:14 continue in what you have *l*

LEARNING (LEARN)
Pr   1: 5 let the wise listen and add to their *l*,
2Ti   3: 7 always *l* but never able

LED (LEAD)
Ps   68:18 you *l* captives in your train;
Isa   53: 7 he was *l* like a lamb to the slaughter
Am   2:10 and I *l* you forty years in the desert
Ro   8:14 those who are *l* by the Spirit
Eph   4: 8 he *l* captives in his train

LEFT
Jos   1: 7 turn from it to the right or to the *l*,
Pr   4:27 Do not swerve to the right or the *l*;
Mt   6: 3 do not let your *l* hand know what
     25:33 on his right and the goats on his *l*.

LEGION
Mk   5: 9 "My name is *L*," he replied,

LEND (LENDS)
Dt   15: 8 freely *l* him whatever he needs.
Ps   37:26 are always generous and *l* freely;
Lk   6:34 if you *l* to those from whom you

LENDS (LEND)
Pr   19:17 to the poor *l* to the LORD,

LENGTH (LONG)
Ps   90:10 The *l* of our days is seventy years—
Pr   10:27 The fear of the LORD adds *l* to life

LEPROSY
2Ki   7: 3 men with *l* at the entrance

LETTER (LETTERS)
Mt   5:18 not the smallest *l*, not the least
2Co   3: 2 You yourselves are our *l*, written
     3: 6 for the *l* kills, but the Spirit gives
2Th   3:14 not obey our instruction in this *l*,

LETTERS (LETTER)
2Co   3: 7 which was engraved in *l* on stone,
     10:10 "His *l* are weighty and forceful,
2Pe   3:16 His *l* contain some things that are

LEVEL
Ps 143: 10 lead me on *l* ground.
Pr   4:26 Make *l* paths for your feet
Isa 26: 7 The path of the righteous is *l*;
Heb 12:13 "Make *l* paths for your feet,"

LEVI (LEVITES)
   1. Son of Jacob by Leah (Ge 29:34; 46:11; 1Ch 2:1). Tribe of blessed (Ge 49:5-7; Dt 33:8-11), chosen as priests (Nu 3-4), numbered (Nu 3:39;

26:62), allotted cities, but not land (Nu 18; 35; Dt 10:9; Jos 13:14; 21), land (Eze 48:8-22), 12,000 from (Rev 7:7).
   2. See MATTHEW.

LEVITES (LEVI)
Nu   1:53 The *L* are to be responsible
     8: 6 "Take the *L* from among the other
     18:21 I give to the *L* all the tithes in Israel

LEWDNESS
Mk   7:22 malice, deceit, *l*, envy, slander,

LIAR (LIE)
Pr   19:22 better to be poor than a *l*.
Jn   8:44 for he is a *l* and the father of lies.
Ro   3: 4 Let God be true, and every man a *l*.

LIBERATED*
Ro   8:21 that the creation itself will be *l*

LIE (LIAR LIED LIES LYING)
Lev 19:11 " 'Do not *l*.
Nu   23:19 God is not a man, that he should *l*,
Dt   6: 7 when you *l* down and when you get
Ps   23: 2 me *l* down in green pastures,
Isa 11: 6 leopard will *l* down with the goat,
Eze 34:14 they will *l* down in good grazing
Ro   1:25 exchanged the truth of God for a *l*,
Col   3: 9 Do not *l* to each other,
Heb   6:18 which it is impossible for God to *l*,

LIED (LIE)
Ac   5: 4 You have not *l* to men but to God."

LIES (LIE)
Ps   34:13 and your lips from speaking *l*.
Jn   8:44 for he is a liar and the father of *l*.

LIFE (LIVE)
Ge   2: 7 into his nostrils the breath of *l*,
     2: 9 of the garden were the tree of *l*
     9:11 Never again will all *l* be cut
Ex   21:23 you are to take *l* for *l*, eye for eye,
Lev 17:14 the *l* of every creature is its blood.
     24:18 must make restitution—*l* for *l*.
Dt   30:19 Now choose *l*, so that you
Ps   16:11 known to me the path of *l*;
     23: 6 all the days of my *l*,
     34:12 Whoever of you loves *l*
     39: 4 let me know how fleeting is my *l*.
     49: 7 No man can redeem the *l*
     104: 33 I will sing to the LORD all my *l*;
Pr   1: 3 a disciplined and prudent *l*,
     6:23 are the way to *l*,
     7:23 little knowing it will cost him his *l*.
     8:35 For whoever finds me finds *l*
     11:30 of the righteous is a tree of *l*,
     21:21 finds *l*, prosperity and honor.
Jer 10:23 that a man's *l* is not his own;
Eze 37: 5 enter you, and you will come to *l*.
Da   12: 2 some to everlasting *l*, others
Mt   6:25 Is not *l* more important than food,
     7:14 and narrow the road that leads to *l*,
     10:39 Whoever finds his *l* will lose it,
     16:25 wants to save his *l* will lose it,

Mt 20:28 to give his *l* as a ransom for many.''
Mk 10:45 to give his *l* as a ransom for many.''
Lk 12:15 a man's *l* does not consist
 12:22 do not worry about your *l*,
 14:26 even his own *l*— he cannot be my
Jn 1: 4 In him was *l*, and that *l* was
 3:15 believes in him may have eternal *l*.
 3:36 believes in the Son has eternal *l*,
 4:14 of water welling up to eternal *l*.''
 5:24 him who sent me has eternal *l*
 6:35 Jesus declared, ''I am the bread of *l*
 6:47 he who believes has everlasting *l*.
 6:68 You have the words of eternal *l*.
 10:10 I have come that they may have *l*,
 10:15 and I lay down my *l* for the sheep.
 10:28 I give them eternal *l*, and they shall
 11:25 ''I am the resurrection and the *l*.
 14: 6 am the way and the truth and the *l*.
 15:13 lay down his *l* for his friends.
 20:31 that by believing you may have *l*
Ac 13:48 appointed for eternal *l* believed.
Ro 4:25 was raised to *l* for our justification.
 6:13 have been brought from death to *l*;
 6:23 but the gift of God is eternal *l*
 8:38 convinced that neither death nor *l*,
1Co 15:19 If only for this *l* we have hope
2Co 3: 6 letter kills, but the Spirit gives *l*.
Gal 2:20 The *l* I live in the body, I live
Eph 4: 1 I urge you to live a *l* worthy
Php 2:16 as you hold out the word of *l*—
Col 1:10 order that you may live a *l* worthy
1Th 4:12 so that your daily *l* may win
1Ti 4: 8 for both the present *l* and the *l*
 4:16 Watch your *l* and doctrine closely.
 6:19 hold of the *l* that is truly *l*.
2Ti 3:12 to live a godly *l* in Christ Jesus will
Jas 1:12 crown of *l* that God has promised
 3:13 Let him show it by his good *l*,
1Pe 3:10 ''Whoever would love *l*
2Pe 1: 3 given us everything we need for *l*
1Jn 3:14 we have passed from death to *l*,
 5:11 has given us eternal *l*, and this *l* is
Rev 13: 8 written in the book of *l* belonging
 20:12 was opened, which is the book of *l*.
 21:27 written in the Lamb's book of *l*.
 22: 2 side of the river stood the tree of *l*,

LIFT (LIFTED)

Ps 121: 1 I *l* up my eyes to the hills—
 134: 2 *L* up your hands in the sanctuary
La 3:41 Let us *l* up our hearts and our
1Ti 2: 8 everywhere to *l* up holy hands

LIFTED (LIFT)

Ps 40: 2 He *l* me out of the slimy pit,
Jn 3:14 Moses *l* up the snake in the desert,
 12:32 when I am *l* up from the earth,

LIGHT (ENLIGHTENED)

Ge 1: 3 ''Let there be *l*,'' and there was *l*.
2Sa 22:29 LORD turns my darkness into *l*.
Job 38:19 ''What is the way to the abode of *l*?
Ps 4: 6 Let the *l* of your face shine upon us

Ps 19: 8 giving *l* to the eyes.
 27: 1 LORD is my *l* and my salvation—
 56:13 God in the *l* of life.
 76: 4 You are resplendent with *l*,
 104: 2 He wraps himself in *l*
 119:105 and a *l* for my path.
 119:130 The unfolding of your words gives *l*;
Isa 2: 5 let us walk in the *l* of the LORD.
 9: 2 have seen a great *l*;
 49: 6 also make you a *l* for the Gentiles,
Mt 4:16 have seen a great *l*;
 5:16 let your *l* shine before men,
 11:30 yoke is easy and my burden is *l*.''
Jn 3:19 but men loved darkness instead of *l*
 8:12 he said, ''I am the *l* of the world.
2Co 4: 6 made his *l* shine in our hearts
 6:14 Or what fellowship can *l* have
 11:14 masquerades as an angel of *l*.
1Ti 6:16 and who lives in unapproachable *l*,
1Pe 2: 9 of darkness into his wonderful *l*.
1Jn 1: 5 God is *l*; in him there is no
 1: 7 But if we walk in the *l*,
Rev 21:23 for the glory of God gives it *l*,

LIGHTNING

Da 10: 6 his face like *l*, his eyes like flaming
Mt 24:27 For as the *l* that comes from the east
 28: 3 His appearance was like *l*,

LIKENESS

Ge 1:26 man in our image, in our *l*,
Ps 17:15 I will be satisfied with seeing your *l*
Isa 52:14 his form marred beyond human *l*—
Ro 8: 3 Son in the *l* of sinful man
 8:29 to be conformed to the *l* of his Son,
2Co 3:18 his *l* with ever-increasing glory,
Php 2: 7 being made in human *l*.
Jas 3: 9 who have been made in God's *l*.

LILIES

Lk 12:27 ''Consider how the *l* grow.

LION

Isa 11: 7 and the *l* will eat straw like the ox.
1Pe 5: 8 around like a roaring *l* looking
Rev 5: 5 See, the *L* of the tribe of Judah,

LIPS

Ps 8: 2 From the *l* of children and infants
 34: 1 his praise will always be on my *l*.
 119:171 May my *l* overflow with praise,
Pr 13: 3 He who guards his *l* guards his life,
 27: 2 someone else, and not your own *l*.
Isa 6: 5 For I am a man of unclean *l*,
Mt 21:16 '' 'From the *l* of children
Col 3: 8 and filthy language from your *l*.

LISTEN (LISTENING LISTENS)

Dt 30:20 *l* to his voice, and hold fast to him.
Pr 1: 5 let the wise *l* and add
Jn 10:27 My sheep *l* to my voice; I know
Jas 1:19 Everyone should be quick to *l*,
 1:22 Do not merely *l* to the word,

LISTENING (LISTEN)

| 1Sa | 3: 9 | Speak, LORD, for your servant is l |
| Pr | 18:13 | He who answers before l— |

LISTENS (LISTEN)

Pr 12:15 but a wise man l to advice.

LIVE (ALIVE LIFE LIVES LIVING)

Ex 20:12 so that you may l long
33:20 for no one may see me and l.''
Dt 8: 3 to teach you that man does not l
Job 14:14 If a man dies, will he l again?
Ps119:175 Let me l that I may praise you,
Isa 55: 3 hear me, that your soul may l.
Eze 37: 3 can these bones l?'' I said,
Hab 2: 4 but the righteous will l by his faith
Mt 4: 4 'Man does not l on bread alone,
Ac 17:24 does not l in temples built by hands
17:28 'For in him we l and move
Ro 1:17 ''The righteous will l by faith.''
2Co 5: 7 We l by faith, not by sight.
Gal 2:20 The life I l in the body, I l by faith
5:25 Since we l by the Spirit, let us keep
Php 1:21 to l is Christ and to die is gain.
1Th 5:13 L in peace with each other.
2Ti 3:12 who wants to l a godly life
Heb 12:14 Make every effort to l in peace
1Pe 1:17 l your lives as strangers here

LIVES (LIVE)

Job 19:25 I know that my Redeemer l,
Isa 57:15 he who l forever, whose name is
Da 3:28 to give up their l rather than serve
Jn 14:17 for he l with you and will be in you.
Ro 7:18 I know that nothing good l in me,
14: 7 For none of us l to himself alone
1Co 3:16 and that God's Spirit l in you?
Gal 2:20 I no longer live, but Christ l in me.
Heb 13: 5 Keep your l free from the love
2Pe 3:11 You ought to live holy and godly l
1Jn 3:16 to lay down our l for our brothers.
4:16 Whoever l in love l in God,

LIVING (LIVE)

Ge 2: 7 and man became a l being.
Jer 2:13 the spring of l water,
Mt 22:32 the God of the dead but of the l.''
Jn 7:38 streams of l water will flow
Ro 12: 1 to offer your bodies as l sacrifices,
Heb 4:12 For the word of God is l and active.
10:31 to fall into the hands of the l God.
Rev 1:18 I am the L One; I was dead,

LOAD

Gal 6: 5 for each one should carry his own l.

LOCUSTS

Mt 3: 4 His food was l and wild honey.

LOFTY

Ps139: 6 too l for me to attain.
Isa 57:15 is what the high and l One says—

LONELY

Ps 68: 6 God sets the l in families,

LONG (LENGTH LONGED LONGING LONGS)

1Ki 18:21 ''How l will you waver
Jn 9: 4 As l as it is day, we must do
Eph 3:18 to grasp how wide and l and high
1Pe 1:12 Even angels l to look

LONGED (LONG)

Mt 13:17 righteous men l to see what you see
23:37 how often I have l
2Ti 4: 8 to all who have l for his appearing.

LONGING (LONG)

Pr 13:19 A l fulfilled is sweet to the soul,
2Co 5: 2 l to be clothed with our heavenly

LONGS (LONG)

Isa 30:18 Yet the LORD l to be gracious

LOOK (LOOKING LOOKS)

Dt 4:29 you will find him if you l for him
Job 31: 1 not to l lustfully at a girl.
Ps 34: 5 Those who l to him are radiant;
Pr 4:25 Let your eyes l straight ahead,
Isa 60: 5 Then you will l and be radiant,
Hab 1:13 Your eyes are too pure to l on evil;
Zec 12:10 They will l on me, the one they
Mk 13:21 'L, here is the Christ!' or, 'L,
Lk 24:39 L at my hands and my feet.
Jn 1:36 he said, ''L, the Lamb of God!''
4:35 open your eyes and l at the fields!
19:37 ''They will l on the one they have
Jas 1:27 to l after orphans and widows
1Pe 1:12 long to l into these things.

LOOKING (LOOK)

2Co 10: 7 You are l only on the surface
Rev 5: 6 I saw a Lamb, l as if it had been

LOOKS (LOOK)

1Sa 16: 7 Man l at the outward appearance,
Lk 9:62 and l back is fit for service
Php 2:21 For everyone l out

LORD† (LORD'S† LORDING)

Ne 4:14 Remember the L, who is great
Job 28:28 'The fear of the L— that is wisdom,
Ps 54: 4 the L is the one who sustains me.
62:12 and that you, O L, are loving.
86: 5 You are forgiving and good, O L,
110: 1 The LORD says to my L:
147: 5 Great is our L and mighty in power
Isa 6: 1 I saw the L seated on a throne,
Da 9: 4 ''O L, the great and awesome God,
Mt 3: 3 'Prepare the way for the L,
4: 7 'Do not put the L your God
7:21 ''Not everyone who says to me, 'L,
22:37 '' 'Love the L your God
22:44 For he says, '' 'The L said to my L:
Mk 12:11 the L has done this,
12:29 the L our God, the L is one.
Lk 2: 9 glory of the L shone around them,
6:46 ''Why do you call me, 'L, L,'
10:27 '' 'Love the L your God
Ac 2:21 on the name of the L will be saved.'

Ac	16:31	replied, "Believe in the *L* Jesus,
Ro	10: 9	with your mouth, "Jesus is *L*,"
	10:13	on the name of the *L* will be saved
	12:11	your spiritual fervor, serving the *L*.
	14: 8	we live to the *L;* and if we die,
1Co	1:31	Let him who boasts boast in the *L*."
	3: 5	the *L* has assigned to each his task.
	7:34	to be devoted to the *L* in both body
	10: 9	We should not test the *L*,
	11:23	For I received from the *L* what I
	12: 3	"Jesus is *L*," except by the Holy
	15:57	victory through our *L* Jesus Christ.
	16:22	If anyone does not love the *L*—
2Co	3:17	Now the *L* is the Spirit,
	8: 5	they gave themselves first to the *L*
	10:17	Let him who boasts boast in the *L*."
Gal	6:14	in the cross of our *L* Jesus Christ,
Eph	4: 5	one *L*, one faith, one baptism;
	5:10	and find out what pleases the *L*.
	5:19	make music in your heart to the *L*,
Php	2:11	confess that Jesus Christ is *L*,
	3: 1	my brothers, rejoice in the *L!*
	4: 4	Rejoice in the *L* always.
Col	2: 6	as you received Christ Jesus as *L*,
	3:17	do it all in the name of the *L* Jesus,
	3:23	as working for the *L*, not for men,
	4:17	work you have received in the *L*."
1Th	3:12	May the *L* make your love increase
	5: 2	day of the *L* will come like a thief
	5:23	at the coming of our *L* Jesus Christ.
2Th	2: 1	the coming of our *L* Jesus Christ
2Ti	2:19	"The *L* knows those who are his,"
Heb	12:14	holiness no one will see the *L*.
	13: 6	*L* is my helper; I will not be afraid.
Jas	4:10	Humble yourselves before the *L*,
1Pe	1:25	the word of the *L* stands forever."
	2: 3	you have tasted that the *L* is good.
	3:15	in your hearts set apart Christ as *L*.
2Pe	1:16	and coming of our *L* Jesus Christ,
	2: 1	the sovereign *L* who bought
	3: 9	The *L* is not slow in keeping his
Jude	:14	the *L* is coming with thousands
Rev	4: 8	holy, holy is the *L* God Almighty,
	4:11	"You are worthy, our *L* and God,
	17:14	he is *L* of lords and King of kings—
	22:20	Come, *L* Jesus.

LORD'S† (LORD†)

Ac	21:14	and said, "The *L* will be done."
1Co	10:26	"The earth is the *L*, and everything
	11:26	you proclaim the *L* death
2Co	3:18	faces all reflect the *L* glory,
2Ti	2:24	And the *L* servant must not quarrel
Jas	4:15	you ought to say, "If it is the *L* will,

LORDING* (LORD†)

1Pe	5: 3	not *l* it over those entrusted to you,

LORD‡ (LORD'S‡)

Ge	2: 4	When the *L* God made the earth

Ge	2: 7	the *L* God formed the man
	3:21	The *L* God made garments of skin
	7:16	Then the *L* shut him in.
	15: 6	Abram believed the *L*,
	18:14	Is anything too hard for the *L*?
	31:49	"May the *L* keep watch
Ex	3: 2	the angel of the *L* appeared to him
	9:12	the *L* hardened Pharaoh's heart
	14:30	That day the *L* saved Israel
	20: 2	"I am the *L* your God, who
	33:11	The *L* would speak to Moses face
	40:34	glory of the *L* filled the tabernacle.
Lev	19: 2	'Be holy because I, the *L* your God,
Nu	8: 5	*L* said to Moses: "Take the Levites
	14:21	glory of the *L* fills the whole earth,
Dt	2: 7	forty years the *L* your God has
	5: 9	the *L* your God, am a jealous God,
	6: 4	The *L* our God, the *L* is one.
	6: 5	Love the *L* your God
	6:16	Do not test the *L* your God
	10:14	To the *L* your God belong
	10:17	For the *L* your God is God of gods
	11: 1	Love the *L* your God and keep his
	28: 1	If you fully obey the *L* your God
	30:16	today to love the *L* your God,
	30:20	For the *L* is your life, and he will
	31: 6	for the *L* your God goes with you;
Jos	22: 5	to love the *L* your God, to walk
	24:15	my household, we will serve the *L*
1Sa	1:28	So now I give him to the *L*.
	2: 2	"There is no one holy like the *L;*
	7:12	"Thus far has the *L* helped us."
	12:22	his great name the *L* will not reject
	15:22	"Does the *L* delight
2Sa	22: 2	"The *L* is my rock, my fortress
1Ki	2: 3	and observe what the *L* your God
	8:11	the glory of the *L* filled his temple.
	8:61	fully committed to the *L* our God,
	18:21	If the *L* is God, follow him;
2Ki	13:23	But the *L* was gracious to them
1Ch	16: 8	Give thanks to the *L*, call
	16:23	Sing to the *L*, all the earth;
	28: 9	for the *L* searches every heart
	29:11	O *L*, is the greatness and the power
2Ch	5:14	the glory of the *L* filled the temple
	16: 9	of the *L* range throughout the earth
	19: 6	judging for man but for the *L*,
	30: 9	for the *L* your God is gracious
Ne	1: 5	Then I said: "O *L*, God of heaven,
Job	1:21	*L* gave and the *L* has taken away;
	38: 1	the *L* answered Job out
	42: 9	and the *L* accepted Job's prayer.
Ps	1: 2	But his delight is in the law of the *L*
	9: 9	The *L* is a refuge for the oppressed,
	12: 6	And the words of the *L* are flawless
	16: 8	I have set the *L* always before me.
	18:30	the word of the *L* is flawless.
	19: 7	The law of the *L* is perfect,
	19:14	O *L*, my Rock and my Redeemer.

Ps 23: 1 The *L* is my shepherd, I shall not be
23: 6 I will dwell in the house of the *L*
27: 1 The *L* is my light and my salvation
27: 4 to gaze upon the beauty of the *L*
29: 1 Ascribe to the *L*, O mighty ones,
32: 2 whose sin the *L* does not count
33:12 is the nation whose God is the *L*,
33:18 But the eyes of the *L* are
34: 3 Glorify the *L* with me;
34: 7 The angel of the *L* encamps
34: 8 Taste and see that the *L* is good;
34:18 The *L* is close to the brokenhearted
37: 4 Delight yourself in the *L*
40: 1 I waited patiently for the *L*;
47: 2 How awesome is the *L* Most High,
48: 1 Great is the *L*, and most worthy
55:22 Cast your cares on the *L*
75: 8 In the hand of the *L* is a cup
84:11 For the *L* God is a sun and shield;
86:11 Teach me your way, O *L*,
89: 5 heavens praise your wonders, O *L*,
91: 2 I will say of the *L*, "He is my refuge
95: 1 Come, let us sing for joy to the *L*;
96: 1 Sing to the *L* a new song;
98: 4 Shout for joy to the *L*, all the earth,
100: 1 Shout for joy to the *L*, all the earth.
103: 1 Praise the *L*, O my soul;
103: 8 The *L* is compassionate
104: 1 O *L* my God, you are very great;
107: 8 to the *L* for his unfailing love
110: 1 The *L* says to my Lord:
113: 4 *L* is exalted over all the nations,
115: 1 Not to us, O *L*, not to us
116: 15 Precious in the sight of the *L*
118: 1 Give thanks to the *L*, for he is good
118: 24 This is the day the *L* has made;
121: 2 My help comes from the *L*,
121: 5 The *L* watches over you—
125: 2 so the *L* surrounds his people
127: 1 Unless the *L* builds the house,
127: 3 Sons are a heritage from the *L*,
130: 3 If you, O *L*, kept a record of sins,
135: 6 The *L* does whatever pleases him,
136: 1 Give thanks to the *L*, for he is good
139: 1 O *L*, you have searched me
144: 3 O *L*, what is man that you care
145: 3 Great is the *L* and most worthy
145: 18 The *L* is near to all who call on him
Pr 1: 7 The fear of the *L* is the beginning
3: 5 Trust in the *L* with all your heart
3: 9 Honor the *L* with your wealth,
3:12 the *L* disciplines those he loves,
3:19 By wisdom the *L* laid the earth's
5:21 are in full view of the *L*,
6:16 There are six things the *L* hates,
10:27 The fear of the *L* adds length to life
11: 1 The *L* abhors dishonest scales,
12:22 The *L* detests lying lips,
14:26 He who fears the *L* has a secure
15: 3 The eyes of the *L* are everywhere,
16: 2 but motives are weighed by the *L*.
16: 4 The *L* works out everything

Pr 16: 9 but the *L* determines his steps.
16:33 but its every decision is from the *L*.
18:10 The name of the *L* is a strong tower
18:22 and receives favor from the *L*.
19:14 but a prudent wife is from the *L*.
19:17 to the poor lends to the *L*,
21: 3 to the *L* than sacrifice.
21:30 that can succeed against the *L*.
21:31 but victory rests with the *L*.
22: 2 The *L* is the Maker of them all.
24:18 or the *L* will see and disapprove
31:30 a woman who fears the *L* is
Isa 6: 3 holy, holy is the *L* Almighty;
11: 2 The Spirit of the *L* will rest on him
11: 9 full of the knowledge of the *L*
12: 2 The *L*, the *L*, is my strength
24: 1 the *L* is going to lay waste the earth
25: 8 The Sovereign *L* will wipe away
29:15 to hide their plans from the *L*,
33: 6 the fear of the *L* is the key
35:10 the ransomed of the *L* will return.
40: 5 the glory of the *L* will be revealed,
40: 7 the breath of the *L* blows on them.
40:10 the Sovereign *L* comes with power,
40:28 The *L* is the everlasting God,
40:31 but those who hope in the *L*
42: 8 "I am the *L*; that is my name!
43:11 I, even I, am the *L*,
44:24 I am the *L*,
45: 5 I am the *L*, and there is no other;
45:21 Was it not I, the *L*?
51:11 The ransomed of the *L* will return.
53: 6 and the *L* has laid on him
53:10 and the will of the *L* will prosper
55: 6 Seek the *L* while he may be found;
58: 8 of the *L* will be your rear guard.
58:11 The *L* will guide you always;
59: 1 the arm of the *L* is not too short
61: 3 a planting of the *L*
61:10 I delight greatly in the *L*;
Jer 1: 9 Then the *L* reached out his hand
9:24 I am the *L*, who exercises kindness,
16:19 O *L*, my strength and my fortress,
17: 7 is the man who trusts in the *L*,
La 3:40 and let us return to the *L*.
Eze 1:28 of the likeness of the glory of the *L*.
Hos 1: 7 horsemen, but by the *L* their God."
3: 5 They will come trembling to the *L*
6: 1 "Come, let us return to the *L*.
Joel 2: 1 for the day of the *L* is coming.
2:11 The day of the *L* is great;
3:14 For the day of the *L* is near
Am 5:18 long for the day of the *L*?
Jnh 1: 3 But Jonah ran away from the *L*
Mic 4: 2 up to the mountain of the *L*,
6: 8 And what does the *L* require of you
Na 1: 2 The *L* takes vengeance on his foes
1: 3 The *L* is slow to anger
Hab 2:14 knowledge of the glory of the *L*,
2:20 But the *L* is in his holy temple;
Zep 3:17 The *L* your God is with you,
Zec 1:17 and the *L* will again comfort Zion

Zec   9:16   The *L* their God will save them
    14:   5   Then the *L* my God will come,
    14:   9   The *L* will be king
Mal   4:   5   and dreadful day of the *L* comes.

LORD'S‡ (LORD‡)

Ex   34:34   he entered the *L* presence
Nu   14:41   you disobeying the *L* command?
Dt   6:18   is right and good in the *L* sight,
    32:   9   For the *L* portion is his people,
Jos   21:45   Not one of all the *L* good promises
Ps   24:   1   The earth is the *L*, and everything
    32:10   but the *L* unfailing love
    89:   1   of the *L* great love forever;
    103:   17   *L* love is with those who fear him,
Pr   3:11   do not despise the *L* discipline
Isa   24:14   west they acclaim the *L* majesty.
    62:   3   of splendor in the *L* hand,
Jer   48:10   lax in doing the *L* work!
La   3:22   of the *L* great love we are not
Mic   4:   1   of the *L* temple will be established

LOSE (LOSES LOSS LOST)

1Sa   17:32   "Let no one *l* heart on account
Mt   10:39   Whoever finds his life will *l* it,
Lk   9:25   and yet *l* or forfeit his very self?
Jn   6:39   that I shall *l* none of all that he has
Heb 12:   3   will not grow weary and *l* heart.
    12:   5   do not *l* heart when he rebukes you

LOSES (LOSE)

Mt   5:13   But if the salt *l* its saltiness,
Lk   15:   4   you has a hundred sheep and *l* one
    15:   8   has ten silver coins and *l* one.

LOSS (LOSE)

Ro   11:12   and their *l* means riches
1Co   3:15   he will suffer *l;* he himself will be
Php   3:   8   I consider everything a *l* compared

LOST (LOSE)

Ps   73:   2   I had nearly *l* my foothold.
Jer   50:   6   "My people have been *l* sheep;
Eze   34:   4   the strays or searched for the *l*.
    34:16   for the *l* and bring back the strays.
Mt   18:14   any of these little ones should be *l*.
Lk   15:   4   go after the *l* sheep until he finds it?
    15:   6   with me; I have found my *l* sheep.'
    15:   9   with me; I have found my *l* coin.'
    15:24   is alive again; he was *l* and is found
    19:10   to seek and to save what was *l*."
Php   3:   8   for whose sake I have *l* all things.

LOT (LOTS)

Nephew of Abraham (Ge 11:27; 12:5). Chose to live in Sodom (Ge 13). Rescued from four kings (Ge 14). Rescued from Sodom (Ge 19:1-29; 2Pe 2:7). Fathered Moab and Ammon by his daughters (Ge 19:30-38).
Est   3:   7   the *l)* in the presence of Haman
    9:24   the *l)* for their ruin and destruction.
Pr   16:33   The *l* is cast into the lap,
    18:18   Casting the *l* settles disputes
Ecc   3:22   his work, because that is his *l*.
Ac   1:26   Then they drew lots, and the *l* fell

LOTS (LOT)

Ps   22:18   and cast *l* for my clothing.
Mt   27:35   divided up his clothes by casting *l*.

LOVE (BELOVED LOVED LOVELY LOVER LOVERS LOVES LOVING)

Ge   22:   2   your only son, Isaac, whom you *l*,
Ex   15:13   "In your unfailing *l* you will lead
    20:   6   showing *l* to a thousand generations
    20:   6   of those who *l* me
    34:   6   abounding in *l* and faithfulness,
Lev   19:18   but *l* your neighbor as yourself.
    19:34   *L* him as yourself,
Nu   14:18   abounding in *l* and forgiving sin
Dt   5:10   showing *l* to a thousand generations
    5:10   of those who *l* me
    6:   5   *L* the LORD your God
    7:13   He will *l* you and bless you
    10:12   to walk in all his ways, to *l* him,
    11:13   to *l* the LORD your God
    13:   6   wife you *l*, or your closest friend
    30:   6   so that you may *l* him
Jos   22:   5   to *l* the LORD your God, to walk
1Ki   3:   3   Solomon showed his *l*
    8:23   you who keep your covenant of *l*
2Ch   5:13   his *l* endures forever."
Ne   1:   5   covenant of *l* with those who *l* him
Ps   18:   1   I *l* you, O LORD, my strength.
    23:   6   Surely goodness and *l* will follow
    25:   6   O LORD, your great mercy and *l*,
    31:16   save me in your unfailing *l*.
    32:10   but the LORD's unfailing *l*
    33:   5   the earth is full of his unfailing *l*.
    33:18   whose hope is in his unfailing *l*,
    36:   5   Your *l*, O LORD, reaches
    36:   7   How priceless is your unfailing *l!*
    45:   7   You *l* righteousness and hate
    51:   1   according to your unfailing *l;*
    57:10   For great is your *l*, reaching
    63:   3   Because your *l* is better than life,
    66:20   or withheld his *l* from me!
    70:   4   may those who *l* your salvation
    77:   8   Has his unfailing *l* vanished forever
    85:   7   Show us your unfailing *l*, O LORD
    85:10   *L* and faithfulness meet together;
    86:13   For great is your *l* toward me;
    89:   1   of the LORD's great *l* forever;
    89:33   but I will not take my *l* from him,
    92:   2   to proclaim your *l* in the morning
    94:18   your *l*, O LORD, supported me.
    100:   5   is good and his *l* endures forever;
    101:   1   I will sing of your *l* and justice;
    103:   4   crowns you with *l* and compassion.
    103:   8   slow to anger, abounding in *l*.
    103:   11   so great is his *l* for those who fear
    107:   8   to the LORD for his unfailing *l*
    108:   4   For great is your *l*, higher
    116:   1   I *l* the LORD, for he heard my
    118:   1   his *l* endures forever.
    119:   47   because I *l* them.
    119:   64   The earth is filled with your *l*,
    119:   76   May your unfailing *l* be my

Ps 119: 97 Oh, how I *l* your law!
  119:119 therefore I *l* your statutes.
  119:124 your servant according to your *l*
  119:132 to those who *l* your name.
  119:159 O LORD, according to your *l*.
  119:163 but I *l* your law.
  119:165 peace have they who *l* your law,
  122: 6 "May those who *l* you be secure.
  130: 7 for with the LORD is unfailing *l*
  136: 1 -26 *His l endures forever*.
  143: 8 of your unfailing *l*,
  145: 8 slow to anger and rich in *l*.
  145: 20 over all who *l* him,
  147: 11 who put their hope in his unfailing *l*
Pr 3: 3 Let *l* and faithfulness never leave
    4: 6 *l* her, and she will watch over you.
  5:19 you ever be captivated by her *l*.
  8:17 I *l* those who *l* me,
  9: 8 rebuke a wise man and he will *l* you
  10:12 but *l* covers over all wrongs.
  14:22 those who plan what is good find *l*
  15:17 of vegetables where there is *l*
  17: 9 over an offense promotes *l*,
  19:22 What a man desires is unfailing *l*;
  20: 6 claims to have unfailing *l*,
  20:13 Do not *l* sleep or you will grow
  20:28 through *l* his throne is made secure
  21:21 who pursues righteousness and *l*
  27: 5 rebuke than hidden *l*.
Ecc 9: 6 Their *l*, their hate
  9: 9 life with your wife, whom you *l*,
SS 2: 4 and his banner over me is *l*.
  8: 6 for *l* is as strong as death,
  8: 7 Many waters cannot quench *l*;
  8: 7 all the wealth of his house for *l*,
Isa 5: 1 I will sing for the one I *l*
  16: 5 In *l* a throne will be established;
  38:17 In your *l* you kept me
  54:10 yet my unfailing *l* for you will not
  55: 3 my faithful *l* promised to David.
  61: 8 "For I, the LORD, *l* justice;
  63: 9 In his *l* and mercy he redeemed
Jer 5:31 and my people *l* it this way.
  31: 3 you with an everlasting *l*;
  32:18 You show *l* to thousands
  33:11 his *l* endures forever."
La 3:22 of the LORD's great *l* we are not
  3:32 so great is his unfailing *l*.
Eze 33:32 more than one who sings *l* songs
Da 9: 4 covenant of *l* with all who *l* him
Hos 2:19 in *l* and compassion.
  3: 1 Go, show your *l* to your wife again,
  11: 4 with ties of *l*;
  12: 6 maintain *l* and justice,
Joel 2:13 slow to anger and abounding in *l*,
Am 5:15 Hate evil, *l* good;
Mic 3: 2 you who hate good and *l* evil;
  6: 8 To act justly and to *l* mercy
Zep 3:17 he will quiet you with his *l*,
Zec 8:19 Therefore *l* truth and peace."
Mt 3:17 "This is my Son, whom I *l*;
  5:44 *L* your enemies and pray

Mt 6:24 he will hate the one and *l* the other,
  17: 5 "This is my Son, whom I *l*;
  19:19 and '*l* your neighbor as yourself.' "
  22:37 " '*L* the Lord your God
Lk 6:32 Even 'sinners' *l* those who *l* them.
  7:42 which of them will *l* him more?"
  20:13 whom I *l*; perhaps they will respect
Jn 13:34 I give you: *L* one another.
  13:35 disciples, if you *l* one another."
  14:15 "If you *l* me, you will obey what I
  15:13 Greater *l* has no one than this,
  15:17 This is my command: *L* each other.
  21:15 do you truly *l* me more than these
Ro 5: 5 because God has poured out his *l*
  5: 8 God demonstrates his own *l* for us
  8:28 for the good of those who *l* him,
  8:35 us from the *l* of Christ?
  8:39 us from the *l* of God that is
  12: 9 *L* must be sincere.
  12:10 to one another in brotherly *l*.
  13: 8 continuing debt to *l* one another,
  13: 9 "*L* your neighbor as yourself."
  13:10 Therefore *l* is the fulfillment
  13:10 *L* does no harm to its neighbor.
1Co 2: 9 prepared for those who *l* him"—
  8: 1 Knowledge puffs up, but *l* builds up
  13: 1 have not *l*, I am only a resounding
  13: 2 but have not *l*, I am nothing.
  13: 3 but have not *l*, I gain nothing.
  13: 4 Love is patient, *l* is kind.
  13: 4 *L* is patient, love is kind.
  13: 6 *L* does not delight in evil
  13: 8 *L* never fails.
  13:13 But the greatest of these is *l*.
  13:13 three remain: faith, hope and *l*.
  14: 1 way of *l* and eagerly desire spiritual
  16:14 Do everything in *l*.
2Co 5:14 For Christ's *l* compels us,
  8: 8 sincerity of your *l* by comparing it
  8:24 show these men the proof of your *l*
Gal 5: 6 is faith expressing itself through *l*.
  5:13 rather, serve one another in *l*.
  5:22 But the fruit of the Spirit is *l*, joy,
Eph 1: 4 In *l* he predestined us
  2: 4 But because of his great *l* for us,
  3:17 being rooted and established in *l*,
  3:18 and high and deep is the *l* of Christ,
  3:19 and to know this *l* that surpasses
  4: 2 bearing with one another in *l*.
  4:15 Instead, speaking the truth in *l*,
  5: 2 loved children and live a life of *l*,
  5:25 *l* your wives, just as Christ loved
  5:28 husbands ought to *l* their wives
  5:33 each one of you also must *l* his wife
Php 1: 9 that your *l* may abound more
  2: 2 having the same *l*, being one
Col 1: 5 *l* that spring from the hope that is
  2: 2 in heart and united in *l*,
  3:14 And over all these virtues put on *l*,
  3:19 *l* your wives and do not be harsh
1Th 1: 3 your labor prompted by *l*,
  4: 9 taught by God to *l* each other.

1Th	5: 8	on faith and *l* as a breastplate,
2Th	3: 5	direct your hearts into God's *l*
1Ti	1: 5	The goal of this command is *l*,
	2:15	*l* and holiness with propriety.
	4:12	in life, in *l*, in faith and in purity.
	6:10	For the *l* of money is a root
	6:11	faith, *l*, endurance and gentleness.
2Ti	1: 7	of power, of *l* and of self-discipline.
	2:22	and pursue righteousness, faith, *l*
	3:10	faith, patience, *l*, endurance,
Tit	2: 4	women to *l* their husbands
Phm	: 9	yet I appeal to you on the basis of *l*.
Heb	6:10	and the *l* you have shown him
	10:24	may spur one another on toward *l*
	13: 5	free from the *l* of money
Jas	1:12	promised to those who *l* him.
	2: 5	he promised those who *l* him?
	2: 8	"*L* your neighbor as yourself,"
1Pe	1:22	the truth so that you have sincere *l*
	1:22	*l* one another deeply,
	2:17	*L* the brotherhood of believers,
	3: 8	be sympathetic, *l* as brothers,
	3:10	"Whoever would *l* life
	4: 8	Above all, *l* each other deeply,
	4: 8	*l* covers over a multitude of sins.
	5:14	Greet one another with a kiss of *l*.
2Pe	1: 7	and to brotherly kindness, *l*.
	1:17	"This is my Son, whom I *l;*
1Jn	2: 5	God's *l* is truly made complete
	2:15	Do not *l* the world or anything
	3: 1	How great is the *l* the Father has
	3:10	anyone who does not *l* his brother.
	3:11	We should *l* one another.
	3:14	Anyone who does not *l* remains
	3:16	This is how we know what *l* is:
	3:18	let us not *l* with words or tongue
	3:23	to *l* one another as he commanded
	4: 7	Dear friends, let us *l* one another,
	4: 7	for *l* comes from God.
	4: 8	Whoever does not *l* does not know
	4: 9	This is how God showed his *l*
	4:10	This is *l:* not that we loved God,
	4:11	we also ought to *l* one another.
	4:12	and his *l* is made complete in us.
	4:16	God is *l.*
	4:16	Whoever lives in *l* lives in God,
	4:17	*l* is made complete among us
	4:18	But perfect *l* drives out fear,
	4:19	We *l* because he first loved us.
	4:20	If anyone says, "I *l* God,"
	4:21	loves God must also *l* his brother.
	5: 2	we know that we *l* the children
	5: 3	This is *l* for God: to obey his
2Jn	: 5	I ask that we *l* one another.
	: 6	his command is that you walk in *l*.
	: 6	this is *l:* that we walk in obedience
Jude	:12	men are blemishes at your *l* feasts,
	:21	Keep yourselves in God's *l*
Rev	2: 4	You have forsaken your first *l*.
	3:19	Those whom I *l* I rebuke
	12:11	they did not *l* their lives so much

LOVED (LOVE)

Ge	24:67	she became his wife, and he *l* her;
	29:30	and he *l* Rachel more than Leah.
	37: 3	Now Israel *l* Joseph more than any
Dt	7: 8	But it was because the LORD *l* you
1Sa	1: 5	a double portion because he *l* her,
	20:17	because he *l* him as he *l* himself.
Ps	44: 3	light of your face, for you *l* them.
Jer	2: 2	how as a bride you *l* me
	31: 3	"I have *l* you with an everlasting
Hos	2:23	to the one I called 'Not my *l* one.'
	3: 1	though she is *l* by another
	9:10	became as vile as the thing they *l*.
	11: 1	"When Israel was a child, I *l* him,
Mal	1: 2	"But you ask, 'How have you *l* us?'
Mk	12: 6	left to send, a son, whom he *l*.
Jn	3:16	so *l* the world that he gave his one
	3:19	but men *l* darkness instead of light
	11: 5	Jesus *l* Martha and her sister
	12:43	for they *l* praise from men more
	13: 1	Having *l* his own who were
	13:23	the disciple whom Jesus *l,*
	13:34	As I have *l* you, so you must love
	14:21	He who loves me will be *l*
	15: 9	the Father has *l* me, so have I *l* you.
	15:12	Love each other as I have *l* you.
	19:26	the disciple whom he *l* standing
Ro	8:37	conquerors through him who *l* us.
	9:13	"Jacob I *l,* but Esau I hated."
	9:25	her 'my *l* one' who is not my *l* one,"
	11:28	they are *l* on account
Gal	2:20	who *l* me and gave himself for me.
Eph	5: 2	as Christ *l* us and gave himself up
	5:25	just as Christ *l* the church
2Th	2:16	who *l* us and by his grace gave us
2Ti	4:10	for Demas, because he *l* this world,
Heb	1: 9	You have *l* righteousness
1Jn	4:10	This is love: not that we *l* God,
	4:11	Dear friends, since God so *l* us,
	4:19	We love because he first *l* us.

LOVELY (LOVE)

Ps	84: 1	How *l* is your dwelling place,
SS	2:14	and your face is *l.*
	5:16	he is altogether *l.*
Php	4: 8	whatever is *l,* whatever is

LOVER (LOVE)

SS	2:16	*Beloved* My *l* is mine and I am his;
	7:10	I belong to my *l,*
1Ti	3: 3	not quarrelsome, not a *l* of money.

LOVERS (LOVE)

2Ti	3: 2	People will be *l* of themselves,
	3: 3	without self-control, brutal, not *l*
	3: 4	*l* of pleasure rather than *l* of God—

LOVES (LOVE)

Ps	11: 7	he *l* justice;
	33: 5	The LORD *l* righteousness
	34:12	Whoever of you *l* life
	91:14	Because he *l* me," says the LORD,
	127: 2	for he grants sleep to those he *l*.
Pr	3:12	the LORD disciplines those he *l,*

Pr	12: 1	Whoever *l* discipline *l* knowledge,
	13:24	he who *l* him is careful
	17:17	A friend *l* at all times,
	17:19	He who *l* a quarrel *l* sin;
	22:11	He who *l* a pure heart and whose
Ecc	5:10	whoever *l* wealth is never satisfied
Mt	10:37	anyone who *l* his son or daughter
Lk	7:47	has been forgiven little *l* little.''
Jn	3:35	Father *l* the Son and has placed
	10:17	reason my Father *l* me is that I lay
	12:25	The man who *l* his life will lose it,
	14:21	obeys them, who *l* me is the one who *l* me.
	14:23	Jesus replied, ''If anyone *l* me,
Ro	13: 8	for he who *l* his fellowman has
2Co	9: 7	for God *l* a cheerful giver.
Eph	5:28	He who *l* his wife *l* himself,
	5:33	must love his wife as he *l* himself,
Heb	12: 6	the Lord disciplines those he *l*,
1Jn	2:10	Whoever *l* his brother lives
	2:15	If anyone *l* the world, the love
	4: 7	Everyone who *l* has been born
	4:21	Whoever *l* God must also love his
	5: 1	who *l* the father *l* his child
3Jn	: 9	but Diotrephes, who *l* to be first,
Rev	1: 5	To him who *l* us and has freed us

LOVING (LOVE)

Ps	25:10	All the ways of the LORD are *l*
	62:12	and that you, O Lord, are *l*.
	145: 17	and *l* toward all he has made.
Heb	13: 1	Keep on *l* each other as brothers.
1Jn	5: 2	by *l* God and carrying out his

LOWLY

Job	5:11	The *l* he sets on high,
Pr	29:23	but a man of *l* spirit gains honor.
Isa	57:15	also with him who is contrite and *l*
Eze	21:26	*l* will be exalted and the exalted
1Co	1:28	He chose the *l* things of this world

LUKE*

Co-worker with Paul (Col 4:14; 2Ti 4:11; Phm 24).

LUKEWARM*

Rev	3:16	So, because you are *l*— neither hot

LUST

Pr	6:25	Do not *l* in your heart
Col	3: 5	sexual immorality, impurity, *l*,
1Th	4: 5	not in passionate *l* like the heathen,
1Jn	2:16	the *l* of his eyes and the boasting

LYING (LIE)

Pr	6:17	a *l* tongue,
	26:28	A *l* tongue hates those it hurts,

MACEDONIA

Ac	16: 9	''Come over to *M* and help us.''

MADE (MAKE)

Ge	1:16	He also *m* the stars.
	1:25	God *m* the wild animals according
	2:22	Then the LORD God *m* a woman
2Ki	19:15	You have *m* heaven and earth.
Ps	95: 5	The sea is his, for he *m* it,

Ps	100: 3	It is he who *m* us, and we are his;
	118: 24	This is the day the LORD has *m;*
	139: 14	I am fearfully and wonderfully *m;*
Ecc	3:11	He has *m* everything beautiful
Mk	2:27	''The Sabbath was *m* for man,
Jn	1: 3	Through him all things were *m;*
Ac	17:24	''The God who *m* the world
Heb	1: 2	through whom he *m* the universe
Rev	14: 7	Worship him who *m* the heavens,

MAGI

Mt	2: 1	*M* from the east came to Jerusalem

MAGOG

Eze	38: 2	of the land of *M*, the chief prince
	39: 6	I will send fire on *M*
Rev	20: 8	and *M*— to gather them for battle.

MAIDEN

Pr	30:19	and the way of a man with a *m*.
Isa	62: 5	As a young man marries a *m*,
Jer	2:32	Does a *m* forget her jewelry,

MAIMED

Mt	18: 8	It is better for you to enter life *m*

MAJESTIC (MAJESTY)

Ex	15: 6	was *m* in power.
	15:11	*m* in holiness,
Ps	8: 1	how *m* is your name in all the earth
	29: 4	the voice of the LORD is *m*.
	111: 3	Glorious and *m* are his deeds,
SS	6:10	*m* as the stars in procession?
2Pe	1:17	came to him from the *M* Glory,

MAJESTY (MAJESTIC)

Ex	15: 7	In the greatness of your *m*
Dt	33:26	and on the clouds in his *m*.
1Ch	16:27	Splendor and *m* are before him;
Est	1: 4	the splendor and glory of his *m*.
Job	37:22	God comes in awesome *m*.
	40:10	and clothe yourself in honor and *m*
Ps	45: 4	In your *m* ride forth victoriously
	93: 1	The LORD reigns, he is robed in *m*
	110: 3	Arrayed in holy *m*,
	145: 5	of the glorious splendor of your *m*,
Isa	53: 2	or *m* to attract us to him,
Eze	31: 2	can be compared with you in *m?*
2Pe	1:16	but we were eyewitnesses of his *m*.
Jude	:25	only God our Savior be glory, *m*,

MAKE (MADE MAKER MAKES MAKING)

Ge	1:26	''Let us *m* man in our image,
	2:18	I will *m* a helper suitable for him.''
	12: 2	''I will *m* you into a great nation
Ex	22: 3	thief must certainly *m* restitution,
Nu	6:25	the LORD *m* his face shine
Ps	108: 1	*m* music with all my soul.
Isa	14:14	I will *m* myself like the Most High
	29:16	''He did not *m* me''?
Jer	31:31	''when I will *m* a new covenant
Mt	3: 3	*m* straight paths for him.' ''
	28:19	and *m* disciples of all nations,
Mk	1:17	''and I will *m* you fishers of men.''

MAKER

Lk	13:24	"*M* every effort to enter
	14:23	country lanes and *m* them come in,
Ro	14:19	*m* every effort to do what leads
2Co	5: 9	So we *m* it our goal to please him,
Eph	4: 3	*M* every effort to keep the unity
Col	4: 5	*m* the most of every opportunity.
1Th	4:11	*M* it your ambition
Heb	4:11	*m* every effort to enter that rest,
	12:14	*M* every effort to live in peace
2Pe	1: 5	*m* every effort to add
	3:14	*m* every effort to be found spotless,

MAKER (MAKE)

Job	4:17	Can a man be more pure than his *M*
	36: 3	I will ascribe justice to my *M*.
Ps	95: 6	kneel before the Lord our *M;*
Pr	22: 2	The Lord is the *M* of them all.
Isa	45: 9	to him who quarrels with his *M,*
	54: 5	For your *M* is your husband—
Jer	10:16	for he is the *M* of all things,

MAKES (MAKE)

1Co	3: 7	but only God, who *m* things grow.

MAKING (MAKE)

Ps	19: 7	*m* wise the simple.
Ecc	12:12	Of *m* many books there is no end,
Jn	5:18	*m* himself equal with God.
Eph	5:16	*m* the most of every opportunity,

MALE

Ge	1:27	*m* and female he created them.
Gal	3:28	slave nor free, *m* nor female,

MALICE (MALICIOUS)

Ro	1:29	murder, strife, deceit and *m*.
Col	3: 8	*m,* slander, and filthy language
1Pe	2: 1	rid yourselves of all *m*

MALICIOUS (MALICE)

Pr	26:24	A *m* man disguises himself
1Ti	3:11	not *m* talkers but temperate
	6: 4	*m* talk, evil suspicions

MAN (MEN WOMAN WOMEN)

Ge	1:26	"Let us make *m* in our image,
	2: 7	God formed the *m* from the dust
	2:18	for the *m* to be alone
	2:23	she was taken out of *m*.
	9: 6	Whoever sheds the blood of *m,*
Dt	8: 3	*m* does not live on bread
1Sa	13:14	a *m* after his own heart
	15:29	he is not a *m* that he
Job	14: 1	*M* born of woman is of few
	14:14	If a *m* dies, will he live
Ps	1: 1	Blessed is the *m* who does
	8: 4	what is *m* that you are
	119: 9	can a young *m* keep his
	127: 5	Blessed is the *m* whose quiver
Pr	14:12	that seems right to a *m,*
	30:19	way of a *m* with a maiden.
Isa	53: 3	a *m* of sorrows,
Mt	19: 5	a *m* will leave his father
Mk	8:36	What good is it for a *m*
Lk	4: 4	'*M* does not live on bread

Ro	5:12	entered the world through one *m*
1Co	7: 2	each *m* should have his own
	11: 3	head of every *m* is Christ,
	11: 3	head of woman is *m,*
	13:11	When I became a *m,*
Php	2: 8	found in appearance as a *m,*
1Ti	2: 5	the *m* Christ Jesus,
	2:11	have authority over a *m;*
Heb	9:27	as *m* is destined to die

MANAGE

Jer	12: 5	how will you *m* in the thickets
1Ti	3: 4	He must *m* his own family well
	3:12	one wife and must *m* his children
	5:14	to *m* their homes and to give

MANASSEH

1. Firstborn of Joseph (Ge 41:51; 46:20). Blessed (Ge 48).

2. Son of Hezekiah; king of Judah (2Ki 21: 1-18; 2Ch 33:1-20).

MANGER

Lk	2:12	in strips of cloth and lying in a *m.*"

MANNA

Ex	16:31	people of Israel called the bread *m.*
Dt	8:16	He gave you *m* to eat in the desert,
Jn	6:49	Your forefathers ate the *m*
Rev	2:17	I will give some of the hidden *m.*

MANNER

1Co	11:27	in an unworthy *m* will be guilty
Php	1:27	conduct yourselves in a *m* worthy

MARITAL* (MARRY)

Ex	21:10	of her food, clothing and *m* rights.
Mt	5:32	except for *m* unfaithfulness,
	19: 9	except for *m* unfaithfulness,
1Co	7: 3	husband should fulfill his *m* duty

MARK (MARKS)

Cousin of Barnabas (Col 4:10; 2Ti 4:11; Phm 24; 1Pe 5:13), see JOHN.

Ge	4:15	Then the Lord put a *m* on Cain
Rev	13:16	to receive a *m* on his right hand

MARKS (MARK)

Jn	20:25	Unless I see the nail *m* in his hands
Gal	6:17	bear on my body the *m* of Jesus.

MARRED

Isa	52:14	his form *m* beyond human likeness

MARRIAGE (MARRY)

Mt	22:30	neither marry nor be given in *m;*
	24:38	marrying and giving in *m,*
Ro	7: 2	she is released from the law of *m.*
Heb	13: 4	by all, and the *m* bed kept pure,

MARRIED (MARRY)

Ro	7: 2	by law a *m* woman is bound
1Co	7:27	Are you *m?* Do not seek a divorce.
	7:33	But a *m* man is concerned about
	7:36	They should get *m.*

MARRIES (MARRY)

Mt	5:32	and anyone who *m* the divorced

Mt 19: 9 and *m* another woman commits
Lk 16:18 the man who *m* a divorced woman

MARRY (INTERMARRY MARITAL MARRIAGE MARRIED MARRIES)

Mt 22:30 resurrection people will neither *m*
1Co 7: 1 It is good for a man not to *m*,
     7: 9 control themselves, they should *m*,
1Ti 5:14 So I counsel younger widows to *m*,

MARTHA*

Sister of Mary and Lazarus (Lk 10:38-42; Jn 11; 12:2).

MARVELED

Lk 2:33 mother *m* at what was said about

MARY

1. Mother of Jesus (Mt 1:16-25; Lk 1:27-56; 2:1-40). With Jesus at temple (Lk 2:41-52), at the wedding in Cana (Jn 2:1-5), questioning his sanity (Mk 3:21), at the cross (Jn 19:25-27). Among disciples after Ascension (Ac 1:14).
2. Magdalene; former demoniac (Lk 8:2). Helped support Jesus' ministry (Lk 8:1-3). At the cross (Mt 27:56; Mk 15:40; Jn 19:25), burial (Mt 27:61; Mk 15:47). Saw angel after resurrection (Mt 28:1-10; Mk 16:1-9; Lk 24:1-12); also Jesus (Jn 20:1-18).
3. Sister of Martha and Lazarus (Jn 11). Washed Jesus' feet (Jn 12:1-8).

MASQUERADES*

2Co 11:14 for Satan himself *m* as an angel

MASTER (MASTERED MASTERS)

Mt 10:24 nor a servant above his *m*.
    23: 8 for you have only one *M*
    24:46 that servant whose *m* finds him
    25:21 "His *m* replied, 'Well done,
Ro   6:14 For sin shall not be your *m*,
    14: 4 To his own *m* he stands or falls.
2Ti 2:21 useful to the *M* and prepared

MASTERED* (MASTER)

1Co 6:12 but I will not be *m* by anything.
2Pe 2:19 a slave to whatever has *m* him.

MASTERS (MASTER)

Mt   6:24 "No one can serve two *m*.
Eph 6: 5 obey your earthly *m* with respect
     6: 9 And *m*, treat your slaves
Tit 2: 9 subject to their *m* in everything,

MATTHEW*

Apostle; former tax collector (Mt 9:9-13; 10:3; Mk 3:18; Lk 6:15; Ac 1:13). Also called Levi (Mk 2:14-17; Lk 5:27-32).

MATURE (MATURITY)

Eph 4:13 of the Son of God and become *m*,
Php 3:15 of us who are *m* should take such
Heb 5:14 But solid food is for the *m*,
Jas 1: 4 work so that you may be *m*

MATURITY* (MATURE)

Heb 6: 1 about Christ and go on to *m*,

MEAL

Pr 15:17 Better a *m* of vegetables where
1Co 10:27 some unbeliever invites you to a *m*
Heb 12:16 for a single *m* sold his inheritance

MEANING

Ne   8: 8 and giving the *m* so that the people

MEANS

1Co 9:22 by all possible *m* I might save some

MEAT

Ro 14: 6 He who eats *m*, eats to the Lord,
    14:21 It is better not to eat *m*

MEDIATOR

1Ti 2: 5 and one *m* between God and men,
Heb 8: 6 of which he is *m* is superior
     9:15 For this reason Christ is the *m*
    12:24 to Jesus the *m* of a new covenant,

MEDICINE*

Pr 17:22 A cheerful heart is good *m*,

MEDITATE (MEDITATES MEDITATION)

Jos   1: 8 from your mouth; *m* on it day
Ps 119: 15 I *m* on your precepts
    119: 78 but I will *m* on your precepts.
    119: 97 I *m* on it all day long.
    145: 5 I will *m* on your wonderful works.

MEDITATES* (MEDITATE)

Ps   1: 2 and on his law he *m* day and night.

MEDITATION* (MEDITATE)

Ps 19:14 of my mouth and the *m* of my heart
   104: 34 May my *m* be pleasing to him,

MEDIUM

Lev 20:27 " 'A man or woman who is a *m*

MEEK (MEEKNESS)

Ps 37:11 But the *m* will inherit the land
Mt   5: 5 Blessed are the *m*,

MEEKNESS* (MEEK)

2Co 10: 1 By the *m* and gentleness of Christ,

MEET (MEETING)

Ps 85:10 Love and faithfulness *m* together;
Am   4:12 prepare to *m* your God, O Israel."
1Th 4:17 them in the clouds to *m* the Lord

MEETING (MEET)

Heb 10:25 Let us not give up *m* together,

MELCHIZEDEK

Ge 14:18 *M* king of Salem brought out bread
Ps 110: 4 in the order of *M*."
Heb 7:11 in the order of *M*, not in the order

MELT

2Pe 3:12 and the elements will *m* in the heat.

MEMBERS

Mic 7: 6 a man's enemies are the *m*
Ro   7:23 law at work in the *m* of my body,
    12: 4 of us has one body with many *m*,
1Co 6:15 not know that your bodies are *m*

1Co 12:24 But God has combined the *m*
Eph 4:25 for we are all *m* of one body.
Col 3:15 as *m* of one body you were called

MEN (MAN)

Mt 4:19 will make you fishers of *m*
5:16 your light shine before *m*
12:36 *m* will have to give account
Jn 12:32 will draw all *m* to myself
Ac 5:29 obey God rather than *m*!
Ro 1:27 indecent acts with other *m*,
5:12 death came to all *m*,
1Co 9:22 all things to all *m*
2Co 5:11 we try to persuade *m*.
1Ti 2: 4 wants all *m* to be saved
2Ti 2: 2 entrust to reliable *m*
2Pe 1:21 but *m* spoke from God

MENAHEM

King of Israel (2Ki 15:17-22).

MERCIFUL (MERCY)

Dt 4:31 the LORD your God is a *m* God;
Ne 9:31 for you are a gracious and *m* God.
Mt 5: 7 Blessed are the *m*,
Lk 6:36 Be *m*, just as your Father is *m*.
Heb 2:17 in order that he might become a *m*
Jude :22 Be *m* to those who doubt; snatch

MERCY (MERCIFUL)

Ex 33:19 *m* on whom I will have *m*,
Ps 25: 6 O LORD, your great *m* and love,
Isa 63: 9 and *m* he redeemed them;
Hos 6: 6 For I desire *m*, not sacrifice,
Mic 6: 8 To act justly and to love *m*
Hab 3: 2 in wrath remember *m*.
Mt 12: 7 'I desire *m*, not sacrifice,' you
23:23 justice, *m* and faithfulness.
Ro 9:15 "I will have *m* on whom I have *m*,
Eph 2: 4 who is rich in *m*, made us alive
Jas 2:13 *M* triumphs over judgment!
1Pe 1: 3 In his great *m* he has given us new

MESSAGE

Isa 53: 1 Who has believed our *m*
Jn 12:38 "Lord, who has believed our *m*
Ro 10:17 faith comes from hearing the *m*,
1Co 1:18 For the *m* of the cross is
2Co 5:19 to us the *m* of reconciliation.

MESSIAH*

Jn 1:41 "We have found the *M*" (that is,
4:25 "I know that *M*" (called Christ) "is

METHUSELAH

Ge 5:27 Altogether, *M* lived 969 years,

MICHAEL

Archangel (Jude 9); warrior in angelic realm,
protector of Israel (Da 10:13, 21; 12:1; Rev 12:7).

MIDWIVES

Ex 1:17 The *m*, however, feared God

MIGHT (ALMIGHTY MIGHTY)

Jdg 16:30 Then he pushed with all his *m*,
2Sa 6:14 before the LORD with all his *m*,

Ps 21:13 we will sing and praise your *m*.
Zec 4: 6 'Not by *m* nor by power,
1Ti 6:16 To him be honor and *m* forever.

MIGHTY (MIGHT)

Ex 6: 1 of my *m* hand he will drive them
Dt 7: 8 he brought you out with a *m* hand
2Sa 1:19 How the *m* have fallen!
23: 8 the names of David's *m* men:
Ps 24: 8 The LORD strong and *m*,
50: 1 The *M* One, God, the LORD,
89: 8 You are *m*, O LORD,
136: 12 with a *m* hand and outstretched
147: 5 Great is our Lord and *m* in power;
Isa 9: 6 Wonderful Counselor, *M* God,
Zep 3:17 he is *m* to save.
Eph 6:10 in the Lord and in his *m* power.

MILE*

Mt 5:41 If someone forces you to go one *m*,

MILK

Ex 3: 8 a land flowing with *m* and honey—
Isa 55: 1 Come, buy wine and *m*
1Co 3: 2 I gave you *m*, not solid food,
Heb 5:12 You need *m*, not solid food!
1Pe 2: 2 babies, crave pure spiritual *m*,

MILLSTONE (STONE)

Lk 17: 2 sea with a *m* tied around his neck

MIND (DOUBLE-MINDED MINDFUL MINDS)

1Sa 15:29 Israel does not lie or change his *m*;
1Ch 28: 9 devotion and with a willing *m*,
Ps 26: 2 examine my heart and my *m*;
Isa 26: 3 him whose *m* is steadfast,
Mt 22:37 all your soul and with all your *m*.'
Ac 4:32 believers were one in heart and *m*.
Ro 7:25 I myself in my *m* am a slave
8: 7 the sinful *m* is hostile to God.
12: 2 by the renewing of your *m*.
1Co 2: 9 no *m* has conceived
14:14 spirit prays, but my *m* is unfruitful.
2Co 13:11 be of one *m*, live in peace.
Php 3:19 Their *m* is on earthly things.
1Th 4:11 to *m* your own business
Heb 7:21 and will not change his *m*:

MINDFUL* (MIND)

Ps 8: 4 what is man that you are *m* of him,
Lk 1:48 God my Savior, for he has been *m*
Heb 2: 6 What is man that you are *m* of him,

MINDS (MIND)

Ps 7: 9 who searches *m* and hearts,
Jer 31:33 "I will put my law in their *m*
Eph 4:23 new in the attitude of your *m*;
Col 3: 2 Set your *m* on things above,
Heb 8:10 I will put my laws in their *m*
Rev 2:23 I am he who searches hearts and *m*,

MINISTERING (MINISTRY)

Heb 1:14 Are not all angels *m* spirits sent

MINISTRY (MINISTERING)

Ac 6: 4 to prayer and the *m* of the word."
2Co 5:18 gave us the *m* of reconciliation:
2Ti 4: 5 discharge all the duties of your *m*.

MIRACLES (MIRACULOUS)

1Ch 16:12 his *m*, and the judgments he
Ps 77:14 You are the God who performs *m;*
Mt 11:20 most of his *m* had been performed,
11:21 If the *m* that were performed
24:24 and perform great signs and *m*
Mk 6: 2 does *m!* Isn't this the carpenter?
Jn 10:32 "I have shown you many great *m*
14:11 the evidence of the *m* themselves.
Ac 2:22 accredited by God to you by *m*,
19:11 God did extraordinary *m*
1Co 12:28 third teachers, then workers of *m*,
Heb 2: 4 it by signs, wonders and various *m*,

MIRACULOUS (MIRACLES)

Jn 3: 2 could perform the *m* signs you are
9:16 "How can a sinner do such *m* signs
20:30 Jesus did many other *m* signs
1Co 1:22 Jews demand *m* signs and Greeks

MIRE

Ps 40: 2 out of the mud and *m;*
Isa 57:20 whose waves cast up *m* and mud.

MIRIAM

Sister of Moses and Aaron (Nu 26:59). Led dancing at Red Sea (Ex 15:20-21). Struck with leprosy for criticizing Moses (Nu 12). Death (Nu 20:1).

MIRROR

Jas 1:23 a man who looks at his face in a *m*

MISERY

Ex 3: 7 "I have indeed seen the *m*
Jdg 10:16 he could bear Israel's *m* no longer.
Hos 5:15 in their *m* they will earnestly seek
Ro 3:16 ruin and *m* mark their ways,
Jas 5: 1 of the *m* that is coming upon you.

MISLED

1Co 15:33 Do not be *m:* "Bad company

MISS

Pr 19: 2 nor to be hasty and *m* the way.

MIST

Hos 6: 4 Your love is like the morning *m*,
Jas 4:14 You are a *m* that appears for a little

MISUSE*

Ex 20: 7 "You shall not *m* the name
Dt 5:11 "You shall not *m* the name
Ps139: 20 your adversaries *m* your name.

MOCK (MOCKED MOCKER MOCKERS MOCKING)

Ps 22: 7 All who see me *m* me;
Pr 14: 9 Fools *m* at making amends for sin,
Mk 10:34 who will *m* him and spit on him,

MOCKED (MOCK)

Mt 27:29 knelt in front of him and *m* him.

Mt 27:41 of the law and the elders *m* him.
Gal 6: 7 not be deceived: God cannot be *m*.

MOCKER (MOCK)

Pr 9: 7 corrects a *m* invites insult;
9:12 if you are a *m*, you alone will suffer
20: 1 Wine is a *m* and beer a brawler;
22:10 Drive out the *m*, and out goes strife

MOCKERS (MOCK)

Ps 1: 1 or sit in the seat of *m*.

MOCKING (MOCK)

Isa 50: 6 face from *m* and spitting.

MODEL*

Eze 28:12 " 'You were the *m* of perfection,
1Th 1: 7 And so you became a *m*
2Th 3: 9 to make ourselves a *m* for you

MOMENT

Job 20: 5 the joy of the godless lasts but a *m*.
Ps 30: 5 For his anger lasts only a *m*,
Isa 66: 8 or a nation be brought forth in a *m*?
Gal 2: 5 We did not give in to them for a *m*,

MONEY

Ecc 5:10 Whoever loves *m* never has *m*
Isa 55: 1 and you who have no *m*,
Mt 6:24 You cannot serve both God and *M*.
Lk 9: 3 no bread, no *m*, no extra tunic.
1Co 16: 2 set aside a sum of *m* in keeping
1Ti 3: 3 not quarrelsome, not a lover of *m*.
6:10 For the love of *m* is a root
2Ti 3: 2 lovers of *m*, boastful, proud,
Heb 13: 5 free from the love of *m*
1Pe 5: 2 not greedy for *m*, but eager to serve

MOON

Ps121: 6 nor the *m* by night.
Joel 2:31 and the *m* to blood
1Co 15:41 *m* another and the stars another;

MORNING

Ge 1: 5 and there was *m*— the first day.
Dt 28:67 In the *m* you will say, "If only it
Ps 5: 3 In the *m*, O LORD,
2Pe 1:19 and the *m* star rises in your hearts.
Rev 22:16 of David, and the bright *M* Star."

MORTAL

1Co 15:53 and the *m* with immortality.

MOSES

Levite; brother of Aaron (Ex 6:20; 1Ch 6:3). Put in basket into Nile; discovered and raised by Pharaoh's daughter (Ex 2:1-10). Fled to Midian after killing Egyptian (Ex 2:11-15). Married to Zipporah, fathered Gershom (Ex 2:16-22).

Called by the LORD to deliver Israel (Ex 3-4). Pharaoh's resistance (Ex 5). Ten plagues (Ex 7-11). Passover and Exodus (Ex 12-13). Led Israel through Red Sea (Ex 14). Song of deliverance (Ex 15:1-21). Brought water from rock (Ex 17:1-7). Raised hands to defeat Amalekites (Ex 17:8-16). Delegated judges (Ex 18; Dt 1:9-18).

Received Law at Sinai (Ex 19-23; 25-31; Jn 1:

17). Announced Law to Israel (Ex 19:7-8; 24;
35). Broke tablets because of golden calf (Ex 32;
Dt 9). Saw glory of the LORD (Ex 33-34). Supervised building of tabernacle (Ex 36-40). Set apart
Aaron and priests (Lev 8-9). Numbered tribes (Nu
1-4; 26). Opposed by Aaron and Miriam (Nu 12).
Sent spies into Canaan (Nu 13). Announced forty
years of wandering for failure to enter land (Nu
14). Opposed by Korah (Nu 16). Forbidden to
enter land for striking rock (Nu 20:1-13; Dt 1:37).
Lifted bronze snake for healing (Nu 21:4-9; Jn 3:
14). Final address to Israel (Dt 1-33). Succeeded
by Joshua (Nu 27:12-23; Dt 34). Death (Dt 34:
5-12).
"Law of Moses" (1Ki 2:3; Ezr 3:2; Mk 12:26;
Lk 24:44). "Book of Moses" (2Ch 25:12; Ne 13:
1). "Song of Moses" (Ex 15:1-21; Rev 15:3).
"Prayer of Moses" (Ps 90).

MOTH
Mt   6:19 where *m* and rust destroy,

MOTHER (MOTHER'S)
Ge   2:24 and *m* and be united to his wife,
      3:20 because she would become the *m*
Ex 20:12 "Honor your father and your *m*,
Lev 20: 9 " 'If anyone curses his father or *m*,
Dt   5:16 "Honor your father and your *m*,
    21:18 who does not obey his father and *m*
    27:16 who dishonors his father or his *m*."
1Sa 2:19 Each year his *m* made him a little
Ps 113: 9 as a happy *m* of children.
Pr 23:25 May your father and *m* be glad;
    29:15 child left to himself disgraces his *m*.
    31: 1 an oracle his *m* taught him:
Isa 49:15 "Can a *m* forget the baby
    66:13 As a *m* comforts her child,
Mt 10:37 or *m* more than me is not worthy
    15: 4 'Honor your father and *m*'
    19: 5 and *m* and be united to his wife,
Mk   7:10 'Honor your father and your *m*,'
    10:19 honor your father and *m*.' "
Jn 19:27 to the disciple, "Here is your *m*."

MOTHER'S (MOTHER)
Job   1:21 "Naked I came from my *m* womb,
Pr   1: 8 and do not forsake your *m* teaching

MOTIVES*
Pr 16: 2 but *m* are weighed by the LORD.
1Co 4: 5 will expose the *m* of men's hearts.
Php 1:18 whether from false *m* or true,
1Th 2: 3 spring from error or impure *m*,
Jas 4: 3 because you ask with wrong *m*,

MOUNTAIN (MOUNTAINS)
Mic 4: 2 let us go up to the *m* of the LORD,
Mt 17:20 say to this *m*, 'Move from here

MOUNTAINS (MOUNTAIN)
Isa 52: 7 How beautiful on the *m*
    55:12 the *m* and hills
1Co 13: 2 if I have a faith that can move *m*,

MOURN (MOURNING)
Ecc 3: 4 a time to *m* and a time to dance,
Isa 61: 2 to comfort all who *m*,
Mt   5: 4 Blessed are those who *m*,
Ro 12:15 *m* with those who *m*.

MOURNING (MOURN)
Jer 31:13 I will turn their *m* into gladness;
Rev 21: 4 There will be no more death or *m*

MOUTH
Jos   1: 8 of the Law depart from your *m;*
Ps 19:14 May the words of my *m*
    40: 3 He put a new song in my *m*,
 119:103 sweeter than honey to my *m!*
Pr 16:23 A wise man's heart guides his *m*,
    27: 2 praise you, and not your own *m;*
Isa 51:16 I have put my words in your *m*
Mt 12:34 overflow of the heart the *m* speaks.
    15:11 into a man's *m* does not make him
Ro 10: 9 That if you confess with your *m*,

MUD
Ps 40: 2 out of the *m* and mire;
Isa 57:20 whose waves cast up mire and *m*.
2Pe 2:22 back to her wallowing in the *m*."

MULTITUDE (MULTITUDES)
Isa 31: 1 who trust in the *m* of their chariots
1Pe 4: 8 love covers over a *m* of sins.
Rev 7: 9 me was a great *m* that no one could

MULTITUDES (MULTITUDE)
Joel 3:14 *M*, *m* in the valley of decision!

MURDER (MURDERER MURDERERS)
Ex 20:13 "You shall not *m*.
Mt 15:19 *m*, adultery, sexual immorality,
Ro 13: 9 "Do not *m*," "Do not steal,"
Jas 2:11 adultery," also said, "Do not *m*."

MURDERER (MURDER)
Nu 35:16 he is a *m;* the *m* shall be put
Jn   8:44 He was a *m* from the beginning,
1Jn 3:15 who hates his brother is a *m*,

MURDERERS (MURDER)
1Ti 1: 9 for *m*, for adulterers and perverts,
Rev 21: 8 the *m*, the sexually immoral,

MUSIC
Jdg 5: 3 I will make *m* to the LORD,
Ps 27: 6 and make *m* to the LORD.
    95: 2 and extol him with *m* and song.
    98: 4 burst into jubilant song with *m;*
  108: 1 make *m* with all my soul.
Eph 5:19 make *m* in your heart to the Lord,

MUSTARD
Mt 13:31 kingdom of heaven is like a *m* seed,
    17:20 you have faith as small as a *m* seed,

MUZZLE
Dt 25: 4 Do not *m* an ox while it is treading
Ps 39: 1 I will put a *m* on my mouth
1Co 9: 9 "Do not *m* an ox while it is

MYRRH
Mt 2:11 of gold and of incense and of *m*.
Mk 15:23 offered him wine mixed with *m*,

MYSTERY
Ro 16:25 to the revelation of the *m* hidden
1Co 15:51 I tell you a *m*: We will not all sleep,
Eph 5:32 This is a profound *m*—
Col 1:26 the *m* that has been kept hidden
1Ti 3:16 the *m* of godliness is great:

MYTHS
1Ti 4: 7 Have nothing to do with godless *m*

NADAB
Son of Jeroboam I; king of Israel (1Ki 15:
25-32).

NAIL* (NAILING)
Jn 20:25 "Unless I see the *n* marks

NAILING* (NAIL)
Ac 2:23 him to death by *n* him to the cross.
Col 2:14 he took it away, *n* it to the cross.

NAKED
Ge 2:25 The man and his wife were both *n*,
Job 1:21 *N* I came from my mother's womb,
Isa 58: 7 when you see the *n*, to clothe him,
2Co 5: 3 are clothed, we will not be found *n*.

NAME
Ex 3:15 This is my *n* forever, the *n*
20: 7 "You shall not misuse the *n*
Dt 5:11 "You shall not misuse the *n*
28:58 this glorious and awesome *n*—
1Ki 5: 5 will build the temple for my *N*.'
2Ch 7:14 my people, who are called by my *n*,
Ps 34: 3 let us exalt his *n* together.
103: 1 my inmost being, praise his holy *n*.
147: 4 and calls them each by *n*.
Pr 22: 1 A good *n* is more desirable
30: 4 What is his *n*, and the *n* of his son?
Isa 40:26 and calls them each by *n*.
57:15 who lives forever, whose *n* is holy:
Jer 14: 7 do something for the sake of your *n*
Da 12: 1 everyone whose *n* is found written
Joel 2:32 on the *n* of the LORD will be saved
Zec 14: 9 one LORD, and his *n* the only *n*.
Mt 1:21 and you are to give him the *n* Jesus,
6: 9 hallowed be your *n*,
18:20 or three come together in my *n*,
Jn 10: 3 He calls his own sheep by *n*
16:24 asked for anything in my *n*.
Ac 4:12 for there is no other *n*
Ro 10:13 "Everyone who calls on the *n*
Php 2: 9 him the *n* that is above every *n*,
Col 3:17 do it all in the *n* of the Lord Jesus,
Heb 1: 4 as the *n* he has inherited is superior
Rev 20:15 If anyone's *n* was not found written

NAOMI
Mother-in-law of Ruth (Ru 1). Advised Ruth to
seek marriage with Boaz (Ru 2-4).

NARROW
Mt 7:13 "Enter through the *n* gate.

NATHANAEL
Apostle (Jn 1:45-49; 21:2). Probably also
called Bartholomew (Mt 10:3).

NATION (NATIONS)
Ge 12: 2 "I will make you into a great *n*
Ps 33:12 Blessed is the *n* whose God is
Pr 14:34 Righteousness exalts a *n*,
Isa 65: 1 To a *n* that did not call on my name
1Pe 2: 9 a royal priesthood, a holy *n*,
Rev 7: 9 from every *n*, tribe, people

NATIONS (NATION)
Ge 17: 4 You will be the father of many *n*.
18:18 and all *n* on earth will be blessed
Ex 19: 5 of all *n* you will be my treasured
Ne 1: 8 I will scatter you among the *n*,
Ps 96: 3 Declare his glory among the *n*,
Isa 40:15 Surely the *n* are like a drop
Eze 36:23 *n* will know that I am the LORD,
Hag 2: 7 and the desired of all *n* will come,
Zec 8:23 *n* will take firm hold of one Jew
14: 2 I will gather all the *n* to Jerusalem
Mt 28:19 and make disciples of all *n*,
Rev 21:24 The *n* will walk by its light,

NATURAL (NATURE)
Ro 6:19 you are weak in your *n* selves.
1Co 15:44 If there is a *n* body, there is

NATURE (NATURAL)
Ro 8: 4 do not live according to the sinful *n*
8: 8 by the sinful *n* cannot please God.
Gal 5:19 The acts of the sinful *n* are obvious:
5:24 Jesus have crucified the sinful *n*
Php 2: 6 Who, being in very *n* God,

NAZARENE
Mt 2:23 prophets: "He will be called a *N*."

NAZIRITE
Jdg 13: 7 because the boy will be a *N* of God

NECESSARY
Ro 13: 5 it is *n* to submit to the authorities,

NEED (NEEDS NEEDY)
Ps 116: 6 when I was in great *n*, he saved me.
Mt 6: 8 for your Father knows what you *n*
Ro 12:13 with God's people who are in *n*.
1Co 12:21 say to the hand, "I don't *n* you!"
1Jn 3:17 sees his brother in *n* but has no pity

NEEDLE
Mt 19:24 go through the eye of a *n*

NEEDS (NEED)
Isa 58:11 he will satisfy your *n*
Php 4:19 God will meet all your *n* according

NEEDY
Pr 14:21 blessed is he who is kind to the *n*.
14:31 to the *n* honors God.
31:20 and extends her hands to the *n*.
Mt 6: 2 "So when you give to the *n*,

NEGLECT (NEGLECTED)
Ne 10:39 We will not *n* the house of our God
Ps119: 16 I will not *n* your word.
Ac 6: 2 for us to *n* the ministry of the word
1Ti 4:14 Do not *n* your gift, which was

NEGLECTED (NEGLECT)
Mt 23:23 But you have *n* the more important

NEHEMIAH
Cupbearer of Artaxerxes (Ne 2:1); governor of Israel (Ne 8:9). Returned to Jerusalem to rebuild walls (Ne 2-6). With Ezra, reestablished worship (Ne 8). Prayer confessing nation's sin (Ne 9). Dedicated wall (Ne 12).

NEIGHBOR (NEIGHBOR'S)
Ex 20:16 give false testimony against your *n*.
Lev 19:13 Do not defraud your *n* or rob him.
19:18 but love your *n* as yourself.
Pr 27:10 better a *n* nearby than a brother far
Mt 19:19 and 'love your *n* as yourself.' "
Lk 10:29 who is my *n?*" In reply Jesus said:
Ro 13:10 Love does no harm to its *n*.

NEIGHBOR'S (NEIGHBOR)
Ex 20:17 You shall not covet your *n* wife,
Dt 5:21 not set your desire on your *n* house
19:14 not move your *n* boundary stone
Pr 25:17 Seldom set foot in your *n* house—

NEW
Ps 40: 3 He put a *n* song in my mouth,
Ecc 1: 9 there is nothing *n* under the sun.
Isa 65:17 *n* heavens and a *n* earth.
Jer 31:31 "when I will make a *n* covenant
Eze 36:26 give you a *n* heart and put a *n* spirit
Mt 9:17 Neither do men pour *n* wine
Lk 22:20 "This cup is the *n* covenant
2Co 5:17 he is a *n* creation; the old has gone,
Eph 4:24 and to put on the *n* self, created
2Pe 3:13 to a *n* heaven and a *n* earth,
1Jn 2: 8 Yet I am writing you a *n* command;

NEWBORN (BEAR)
1Pe 2: 2 Like *n* babies, crave pure spiritual

NEWS
Isa 52: 7 the feet of those who bring good *n*,
Mk 1:15 Repent and believe the good *n!*"
16:15 preach the good *n* to all creation.
Lk 2:10 I bring you good *n*
Ac 5:42 proclaiming the good *n* that Jesus
17:18 preaching the good *n* about Jesus
Ro 10:15 feet of those who bring good *n!*"

NICODEMUS*
Pharisee who visted Jesus at night (Jn 3). Argued fair treatment of Jesus (Jn 7:50-52). With Joseph, prepared Jesus for burial (Jn 19:38-42).

NIGHT
Job 35:10 who gives songs in the *n*,
Ps 1: 2 on his law he meditates day and *n*.
91: 5 You will not fear the terror of *n*,
Jn 3: 2 He came to Jesus at *n* and said,

1Th 5: 2 Lord will come like a thief in the *n*.
5: 5 We do not belong to the *n*
Rev 21:25 for there will be no *n* there.

NOAH
Righteous man (Eze 14:14, 20) called to build ark (Ge 6-8; Heb 11:7; 1Pe 3:20; 2Pe 2:5). God's covenant with (Ge 9:1-17). Drunkenness of (Ge 9:18-23). Blessed sons, cursed Canaan (Ge 9:24-27).

NOBLE
Ru 3:11 you are a woman of *n* character.
Ps 45: 1 My heart is stirred by a *n* theme
Pr 12: 4 of *n* character is her husband's
31:10 A wife of *n* character who can find?
31:29 "Many women do *n* things,
Isa 32: 8 But the *n* man makes *n* plans,
Lk 8:15 good soil stands for those with a *n*
Ro 9:21 of clay some pottery for *n* purposes
Php 4: 8 whatever is *n*, whatever is right,
2Ti 2:20 some are for *n* purposes

NOTHING
Ne 9:21 in the desert; they lacked *n*,
Jer 32:17 *N* is too hard for you
Jn 15: 5 apart from me you can do *n*.

NULLIFY
Ro 3:31 Do we, then, *n* the law by this faith

OATH
Dt 7: 8 and kept the *o* he swore

OBEDIENCE (OBEY)
2Ch 31:21 in *o* to the law and the commands,
Pr 30:17 that scorns *o* to a mother,
Ro 1: 5 to the *o* that comes from faith.
6:16 to *o*, which leads to righteousness?
2Jn 6 that we walk in *o* to his commands.

OBEDIENT (OBEY)
Lk 2:51 with them and was *o* to them.
Php 2: 8 and became *o* to death—
1Pe 1:14 As *o* children, do not conform

OBEY (OBEDIENCE OBEDIENT OBEYED)
Ex 12:24 "*O* these instructions as a lasting
Dt 6: 3 careful to *o* so that it may go well
13: 4 Keep his commands and *o* him;
21:18 son who does not *o* his father
30: 2 and *o* him with all your heart
32:46 children to *o* carefully all the words
1Sa 15:22 To *o* is better than sacrifice,
Ps119: 34 and *o* it with all my heart.
Mt 28:20 to *o* everything I have commanded
Jn 14:23 loves me, he will *o* my teaching.
Ac 5:29 "We must *o* God rather than men!
Ro 6:16 slaves to the one whom you *o*—
Gal 5: 3 obligated to *o* the whole law.
Eph 6: 1 *o* your parents in the Lord,
6: 5 *o* your earthly masters with respect
Col 3:20 *o* your parents in everything,
1Ti 3: 4 and see that his children *o* him
Heb 13:17 *O* your leaders and submit

1Jn 5: 3 love for God: to *o* his commands.

OBEYED (OBEY)

Ps 119: 4 that are to be fully *o*.
Jnh 3: 3 Jonah *o* the word of the LORD
Jn 17: 6 and they have *o* your word.
Ro 6:17 you wholeheartedly *o* the form
Heb 11: 8 *o* and went, even though he did not
1Pe 3: 6 who *o* Abraham and called him her

OBLIGATED

Ro 1:14 I am *o* both to Greeks
Gal 5: 3 himself be circumcised that he is *o*

OBSCENITY

Eph 5: 4 Nor should there be *o*, foolish talk

OBSOLETE

Heb 8:13 he has made the first one *o*;

OBTAINED

Ro 9:30 not pursue righteousness, have *o* it,
Php 3:12 Not that I have already *o* all this,
Heb 9:12 having *o* eternal redemption.

OFFENDED (OFFENSE)

Pr 18:19 An *o* brother is more unyielding

OFFENSE (OFFENDED OFFENSIVE)

Pr 17: 9 over an *o* promotes love,
    19:11 it is to his glory to overlook an *o*.

OFFENSIVE (OFFENSE)

Ps 139: 24 See if there is any *o* way in me,

OFFER (OFFERED OFFERING OFFERINGS)

Ro 12: 1 to *o* your bodies as living sacrifices,
Heb 13:15 therefore, let us continually *o*

OFFERED (OFFER)

Heb 7:27 once for all when he *o* himself.
    11: 4 By faith Abel *o* God a better

OFFERING (OFFER)

Ge 22: 8 provide the lamb for the burnt *o*,
Ps 40: 6 Sacrifice and *o* you did not desire,
Isa 53:10 the LORD makes his life a guilt *o*,
Mt 5:23 if you are *o* your gift at the altar
Eph 5: 2 as a fragrant *o* and sacrifice to God.
Heb 10: 5 "Sacrifice and *o* you did not desire,

OFFERINGS (OFFER)

Mal 3: 8 do we rob you?' "In tithes and *o*.
Mk 12:33 is more important than all burnt *o*

OFFICER

2Ti 2: 4 wants to please his commanding *o*.

OFFSPRING

Ge 3:15 and between your *o* and hers;
    12: 7 "To your *o* I will give this land."

OIL

Ps 23: 5 You anoint my head with *o*;
Isa 61: 3 the *o* of gladness
Heb 1: 9 by anointing you with the *o* of joy."

OLIVE (OLIVES)

Zec 4: 3 Also there are two *o* trees by it,

Ro 11:17 and you, though a wild *o* shoot,
Rev 11: 4 These are the two *o* trees

OLIVES (OLIVE)

Jas 3:12 a fig tree bear *o*, or a grapevine bear

OMEGA

Rev 1: 8 "I am the Alpha and the *O*,"

OMRI

King of Israel (1Ki 16:21-26).

OPINIONS*

1Ki 18:21 will you waver between two *o*?
Pr 18: 2 but delights in airing his own *o*.

OPPORTUNITY

Ro 7:11 seizing the *o* afforded
Gal 6:10 as we have *o*, let us do good
Eph 5:16 making the most of every *o*,
Col 4: 5 make the most of every *o*.
1Ti 5:14 to give the enemy no *o* for slander.

OPPOSES

Jas 4: 6 "God *o* the proud
1Pe 5: 5 because, "God *o* the proud

OPPRESS (OPPRESSED)

Ex 22:21 "Do not mistreat an alien or *o* him,
Zec 7:10 Do not *o* the widow

OPPRESSED (OPPRESS)

Ps 9: 9 The LORD is a refuge for the *o*,
Isa 53: 7 He was *o* and afflicted,
Zec 10: 2 *o* for lack of a shepherd.

ORDAINED

Ps 8: 2 you have *o* praise

ORDERLY

1Co 14:40 done in a fitting and *o* way.
Col 2: 5 and delight to see how *o* you are

ORGIES*

Ro 13:13 not in *o* and drunkenness,
Gal 5:21 drunkenness, *o*, and the like.
1Pe 4: 3 *o*, carousing and detestable

ORIGIN

2Pe 1:21 For prophecy never had its *o*

ORPHANS

Jn 14:18 will not leave you as *o*; I will come
Jas 1:27 to look after *o* and widows

OUTCOME

Heb 13: 7 Consider the *o* of their way of life
1Pe 4:17 what will the *o* be for those who do

OUTSIDERS*

Col 4: 5 wise in the way you act toward *o*;
1Th 4:12 daily life may win the respect of *o*
1Ti 3: 7 also have a good reputation with *o*,

OUTSTANDING

SS 5:10 *o* among ten thousand.
Ro 13: 8 no debt remain *o*,

OUTSTRETCHED

Ex 6: 6 and will redeem you with an *o* arm
Jer 27: 5 and *o* arm I made the earth

Eze 20:33 an *o* arm and with outpoured wrath

OUTWEIGHS
2Co   4:17 an eternal glory that far *o* them all.

OVERCOME (OVERCOMES)
Mt   16:18 and the gates of Hades will not *o* it.
Mk   9:24 I do believe; help me *o* my unbelief
Jn   16:33 But take heart! I have *o* the world.''
Ro   12:21 Do not be *o* by evil, but *o* evil
1Jn   5: 4 is the victory that has *o* the world,
Rev 17:14 but the Lamb will *o* them

OVERCOMES* (OVERCOME)
1Jn   5: 4 born of God *o* the world.
      5: 5 Who is it that *o* the world?
Rev   2: 7 To him who *o*, I will give the right
      2:11 He who *o* will not be hurt at all
      2:17 To him who *o*, I will give some
      2:26 To him who *o* and does my will
      3: 5 He who *o* will, like them, be
      3:12 Him who *o* I will make a pillar
      3:21 To him who *o*, I will give the right
     21: 7 He who *o* will inherit all this,

OVERFLOW (OVERFLOWS)
Ps 119:171 May my lips *o* with praise,
Lk   6:45 out of the *o* of his heart his mouth
Ro   15:13 so that you may *o* with hope
2Co   4:15 to *o* to the glory of God.
1Th   3:12 *o* for each other and for everyone

OVERFLOWS* (OVERFLOW)
Ps   23: 5 my cup *o*.
2Co   1: 5 also through Christ our comfort *o*.

OVERJOYED* (JOY)
Da   6:23 The king was *o* and gave orders
Mt   2:10 they saw the star, they were *o*.
Jn   20:20 the disciples were *o*
Ac   12:14 she was so *o* she ran back
1Pe   4:13 so that you may be *o*

OVERSEER (OVERSEERS)
1Ti   3: 1 anyone sets his heart on being an *o*,
      3: 2 Now the *o* must be above reproach,
Tit   1: 7 Since an *o* is entrusted

OVERSEERS* (OVERSEER)
Ac   20:28 the Holy Spirit has made you *o*.
Php   1: 1 together with the *o* and deacons:
1Pe   5: 2 as *o*— not because you must,

OVERWHELMED
Ps   38: 4 My guilt has *o* me
     65: 3 When we were *o* by sins,
Mt   26:38 ''My soul is *o* with sorrow
Mk   7:37 People were *o* with amazement.

OWE
Ro   13: 7 If you *o* taxes, pay taxes; if revenue
Phm   :19 to mention that you *o* me your very

OX
Dt   25: 4 Do not muzzle an *o*
Isa 11: 7 and the lion will eat straw like the *o*
1Co   9: 9 ''Do not muzzle an *o*

PAGANS
Mt   5:47 Do not even *p* do that? Be perfect,
1Pe   2:12 such good lives among the *p* that,

PAIN (PAINFUL)
Ge   3:16 with *p* you will give birth
Job 33:19 may be chastened on a bed of *p*
Jn   16:21 woman giving birth to a child has *p*

PAINFUL (PAIN)
Ge   3:17 through *p* toil you will eat of it
Heb 12:11 seems pleasant at the time, but *p*.
1Pe   4:12 at the *p* trial you are suffering,

PALMS
Isa 49:16 you on the *p* of my hands;

PANTS
Ps   42: 1 As the deer *p* for streams of water,

PARADISE*
Lk   23:43 today you will be with me in *p*.''
2Co 12: 4 God knows—was caught up to *p*.
Rev   2: 7 of life, which is in the *p* of God.

PARALYTIC
Mk   2: 3 bringing to him a *p*, carried by four

PARDON (PARDONS)
Isa 55: 7 and to our God, for he will freely *p*.

PARDONS* (PARDON)
Mic   7:18 who *p* sin and forgives

PARENTS
Pr   17: 6 and *p* are the pride of their children
Lk   18:29 left home or wife or brothers or *p*
     21:16 You will be betrayed even by *p*,
Ro   1:30 they disobey their *p*; they are
2Co 12:14 for their *p*, but *p* for their children.
Eph   6: 1 Children, obey your *p* in the Lord,
Col   3:20 obey your *p* in everything,
2Ti   3: 2 disobedient to their *p*, ungrateful,

PARTIALITY
Dt   10:17 who shows no *p* and accepts no
2Ch 19: 7 our God there is no injustice or *p*
Lk   20:21 and that you do not show *p*

PARTICIPATION
1Co 10:16 is not the bread that we break a *p*

PASS
Ex   12:13 and when I see the blood, I will *p*
La   1:12 to you, all you who *p* by?
Lk   21:33 Heaven and earth will *p* away,
1Co 13: 8 there is knowledge, it will *p* away.

PASSION (PASSIONS)
1Co   7: 9 better to marry than to burn with *p*.

PASSIONS (PASSION)
Gal   5:24 crucified the sinful nature with its *p*
Tit   2:12 to ungodliness and worldly *p*,

PASSOVER
Ex   12:11 Eat it in haste; it is the LORD's *P*.
Dt   16: 1 celebrate the *P* of the LORD your
1Co   5: 7 our *P* lamb, has been sacrificed.

PAST
Isa 43:18 do not dwell on the *p*.
Ro 15: 4 in the *p* was written to teach us,
Heb 1: 1 In the *p* God spoke

PASTORS*
Eph 4:11 and some to be *p* and teachers,

PASTURE (PASTURES)
Ps 37: 3 dwell in the land and enjoy safe *p*.
100: 3 we are his people, the sheep of his *p*
Jer 50: 7 against the LORD, their true *p*,
Eze 34:13 I will *p* them on the mountains
Jn 10: 9 come in and go out, and find *p*.

PASTURES (PASTURE)
Ps 23: 2 He makes me lie down in green *p*,

PATCH
Mt 9:16 No one sews a *p* of unshrunk cloth

PATH (PATHS)
Ps 27:11 lead me in a straight *p*
119:105 and a light for my *p*.
Pr 15:19 the *p* of the upright is a highway.
15:24 The *p* of life leads upward
Isa 26: 7 The *p* of the righteous is level;
Lk 1:79 to guide our feet into the *p* of peace
2Co 6: 3 no stumbling block in anyone's *p*,

PATHS (PATH)
Ps 23: 3 He guides me in *p* of righteousness
25: 4 teach me your *p*;
Pr 3: 6 and he will make your *p* straight.
Ro 11:33 and his *p* beyond tracing out!
Heb 12:13 "Make level *p* for your feet,"

PATIENCE (PATIENT)
Pr 19:11 A man's wisdom gives him *p*;
2Co 6: 6 understanding, *p* and kindness;
Gal 5:22 joy, peace, *p*, kindness, goodness,
Col 1:11 may have great endurance and *p*,
3:12 humility, gentleness and *p*.

PATIENT (PATIENCE PATIENTLY)
Pr 15:18 but a *p* man calms a quarrel.
Ro 12:12 Be joyful in hope, *p* in affliction,
1Co 13: 4 Love is *p*, love is kind.
Eph 4: 2 humble and gentle; be *p*,
1Th 5:14 help the weak, be *p* with everyone.

PATIENTLY (PATIENT)
Ps 40: 1 I waited *p* for the LORD;
Ro 8:25 we do not yet have, we wait for it *p*.

PATTERN
Ro 5:14 who was a *p* of the one to come.
12: 2 longer to the *p* of this world,
2Ti 1:13 keep as the *p* of sound teaching,

PAUL
Also called Saul (Ac 13:9). Pharisee from Tarsus (Ac 9:11; Php 3:5). Apostle (Gal 1). At stoning of Stephen (Ac 8:1). Persecuted Church (Ac 9:1-2; Gal 1:13). Vision of Jesus on road to Damascus (Ac 9:4-9; 26:12-18). In Arabia (Gal 1:17). Preached in Damascus; escaped death through the wall in a basket (Ac 9:19-25). In Jerusalem; sent back to Tarsus (Ac 9:26-30).
Brought to Antioch by Barnabas (Ac 11:22-26). First missionary journey to Cyprus and Galatia (Ac 13-14). Stoned at Lystra (Ac 14:19-20). At Jerusalem council (Ac 15). Split with Barnabas over Mark (Ac 15:36-41).
Second missionary journey with Silas (Ac 16-20). Called to Macedonia (Ac 16:6-10). Freed from prison in Philippi (Ac 16:16-40). In Thessalonica (Ac 17:1-9). Speech in Athens (Ac 17:16-33). In Corinth (Ac 18). In Ephesus (Ac 19). Return to Jerusalem (Ac 20). Farewell to Ephesian elders (Ac 20:13-38). Arrival in Jerusalem (Ac 21:1-26). Arrested (Ac 21:27-36). Addressed crowds (Ac 22), Sanhedrin (Ac 23:1-11). Transferred to Caesarea (Ac 23:12-35). Trial before Felix (Ac 24), Festus (Ac 25:1-12). Before Agrippa (Ac 25:13-26:32). Voyage to Rome; shipwreck (Ac 27). Arrival in Rome (Ac 28).

PAY (REPAID REPAY)
Lev 26:43 They will *p* for their sins
Pr 22:17 *P* attention and listen
Mt 22:17 Is it right to *p* taxes to Caesar
Ro 13: 6 This is also why you *p* taxes,
2Pe 1:19 you will do well to *p* attention to it,

PEACE (PEACEMAKERS)
Nu 6:26 and give you *p*.' '
Ps 34:14 seek *p* and pursue it.
85:10 righteousness and *p* kiss each other
119:165 Great *p* have they who love your
122: 6 Pray for the *p* of Jerusalem:
Pr 14:30 A heart at *p* gives life to the body,
17: 1 Better a dry crust with *p* and quiet
Isa 9: 6 Everlasting Father, Prince of *P*.
26: 3 You will keep in perfect *p*
48:22 "There is no *p*," says the LORD,
Zec 9:10 He will proclaim *p* to the nations.
Mt 10:34 I did not come to bring *p*,
Lk 2:14 on earth *p* to men on whom his
Jn 14:27 *P* I leave with you; my *p*
16:33 so that in me you may have *p*.
Ro 5: 1 we have *p* with God
1Co 7:15 God has called us to live in *p*.
14:33 a God of disorder but of *p*.
Gal 5:22 joy, *p*, patience, kindness,
Eph 2:14 he himself is our *p*, who has made
Php 4: 7 the *p* of God, which transcends all
Col 1:20 by making *p* through his blood,
3:15 Let the *p* of Christ rule
1Th 5: 3 While people are saying, "*P*
2Th 3:16 the Lord of *p* himself give you *p*
2Ti 2:22 righteousness, faith, love and *p*,
1Pe 3:11 he must seek *p* and pursue it.
Rev 6: 4 power to take *p* from the earth

PEACEMAKERS* (PEACE)
Mt 5: 9 Blessed are the *p*,
Jas 3:18 *P* who sow in peace raise a harvest

PEARL* (PEARLS)
Rev 21:21 each gate made of a single *p*.

PEARLS (PEARL)
Mt   7: 6 do not throw your *p* to pigs.
    13:45 like a merchant looking for fine *p*.
1Ti   2: 9 or gold or *p* or expensive clothes,
Rev 21:21 The twelve gates were twelve *p*,

PEKAH
  King of Israel (2Ki 16:25-31; Isa 7:1).

PEKAHIAH*
  Son of Menahem; king of Israel (2Ki 16:22-26).

PEN
Mt   5:18 letter, not the least stroke of a *p*,

PENTECOST
Ac   2: 1 of *P* came, they were all together

PEOPLE (PEOPLES)
Dt 32: 9 the LORD's portion is his *p*,
Ru   1:16 Your *p* will be my *p*
2Ch 7:14 if my *p*, who are called
Jer 24: 7 They will be my *p*,
Zec 2:11 and will become my *p*.
Lk   2:10 joy that will be for all the *p*.
Ac 15:14 from the Gentiles a *p*.
2Co 6:16 and they will be my *p*.''
Tit 2:14 a *p* that are his very own,
1Pe 2: 9 you are a chosen *p*,
Rev 21: 3 They will be his *p*,

PEOPLES (PEOPLE)
Da   7:14 all *p*, nations and men
Mic 4: 1 and *p* will stream to it.

PERCEIVING
Isa   6: 9 be ever seeing, but never *p*.'

PERFECT (PERFECTER PERFECTION)
SS   6: 9 but my dove, my *p* one, is unique,
Isa 26: 3 You will keep in *p* peace
Mt   5:48 as your heavenly Father is *p*.
Ro 12: 2 his good, pleasing and *p* will.
2Co 12: 9 for my power is made *p*
Col   1:28 so that we may present everyone *p*
    3:14 binds them all together in *p* unity.
Heb 9:11 and more *p* tabernacle that is not
  10:14 he has made *p* forever those who
Jas   1:17 Every good and *p* gift is from above
    1:25 into the *p* law that gives freedom,
    3: 2 he is a *p* man, able
1Jn 4:18 But *p* love drives out fear,

PERFECTER* (PERFECT)
Heb 12: 2 the author and *p* of our faith,

PERFECTION (PERFECT)
Ps 119: 96 To all *p* I see a limit;
2Co 13:11 Aim for *p*, listen to my appeal,
Heb 7:11 If *p* could have been attained

PERFORMS
Ps 77:14 You are the God who *p* miracles;

PERISH (PERISHABLE)
Ps   1: 6 but the way of the wicked will *p*.
 102: 26 They will *p*, but you remain;
Lk 13: 3 unless you repent, you too will all *p*
Jn 10:28 eternal life, and they shall never *p*;
Col 2:22 These are all destined to *p* with use,
Heb 1:11 They will *p*, but you remain;
2Pe 3: 9 not wanting anyone to *p*,

PERISHABLE (PERISH)
1Co 15:42 The body that is sown is *p*,

PERJURERS
1Ti 1:10 for slave traders and liars and *p*—

PERMISSIBLE (PERMIT)
1Co 10:23 ''Everything is *p*''— but not

PERMIT (PERMISSIBLE)
1Ti 2:12 I do not *p* a woman to teach

PERSECUTE (PERSECUTED PERSECUTION)
Mt   5:11 *p* you and falsely say all kinds
Jn 15:20 they persecuted me, they will *p* you
Ac   9: 4 why do you *p* me?'' ''Who are you,
Ro 12:14 Bless those who *p* you; bless

PERSECUTED (PERSECUTE)
1Co 4:12 when we are *p*, we endure it;
2Ti 3:12 life in Christ Jesus will be *p*,

PERSECUTION (PERSECUTE)
Ro   8:35 or hardship or *p* or famine

PERSEVERANCE (PERSEVERE)
Ro   5: 3 we know that suffering produces *p*;
    5: 4 *p*, character; character, hope.
Heb 12: 1 run with *p* the race marked out
Jas   1: 3 the testing of your faith develops *p*.
2Pe 1: 6 *p*; and to *p*, godliness;

PERSEVERE* (PERSEVERANCE PERSEVERED PERSEVERES)
1Ti 4:16 *P* in them, because if you do,
Heb 10:36 You need to *p* so that

PERSEVERED* (PERSEVERE)
Heb 11:27 he *p* because he saw him who is
Jas   5:11 consider blessed those who have *p*.
Rev 2: 3 You have *p* and have endured

PERSEVERES* (PERSEVERE)
1Co 13: 7 trusts, always hopes, always *p*.
Jas   1:12 Blessed is the man who *p*

PERSUADE
2Co 5:11 is to fear the Lord, we try to *p* men.

PERVERSION (PERVERT)
Lev 18:23 sexual relations with it; that is a *p*.
Jude : 7 up to sexual immorality and *p*.

PERVERT (PERVERSION PERVERTS)
Gal 1: 7 are trying to *p* the gospel of Christ.

PERVERTS* (PERVERT)
1Ti 1:10 for murderers, for adulterers and *p*,

PESTILENCE
Ps 91: 6 nor the *p* that stalks in the darkness

PETER
Apostle, brother of Andrew, also called Simon (Mt 10:2; Mk 3:16; Lk 6:14; Ac 1:13), and Cephas (Jn 1:42). Confession of Christ (Mt 16:13-20; Mk 8:27-30; Lk 9:18-27). At transfiguration (Mt 17:1-8; Mk 9:2-8; Lk 9:28-36; 2Pe 1:16-18). Caught fish with coin (Mt 17:24-27). Denial of Jesus predicted (Mt 26:31-35; Mk 14:27-31; Lk 22:31-34; Jn 13:31-38). Denied Jesus (Mt 26:69-75; Mk 14:66-72; Lk 22:54-62; Jn 18:15-27). Commissioned by Jesus to shepherd his flock (Jn 21:15-23).

Speech at Pentecost (Ac 2). Healed beggar (Ac 3:1-10). Speech at temple (Ac 3:11-26), before Sanhedrin (Ac 4:1-22). In Samaria (Ac 8:14-25). Sent by vision to Cornelius (Ac 10). Announced salvation of Gentiles in Jerusalem (Ac 11; 15). Freed from prison (Ac 12). Inconsistency at Antioch (Gal 2:11-21). At Jerusalem Council (Ac 15).

PHARISEES
Mt 5:20 surpasses that of the *P*

PHILIP
1. Apostle (Mt 10:3; Mk 3:18; Lk 6:14; Jn 1:43-48; 14:8; Ac 1:13).
2. Deacon (Ac 6:1-7); evangelist in Samaria (Ac 8:4-25), to Ethiopian (Ac 8:26-40).

PHILOSOPHY*
Col 2: 8 through hollow and deceptive *p*,

PHYLACTERIES*
Mt 23: 5 They make their *p* wide

PHYSICAL
1Ti 4: 8 For *p* training is of some value,
Jas 2:16 but does nothing about his *p* needs,

PIECES
Ge 15:17 and passed between the *p*.
Jer 34:18 and then walked between its *p*.

PIERCED
Ps 22:16 they have *p* my hands and my feet.
Isa 53: 5 But he was *p* for our transgressions,
Zec 12:10 look on me, the one they have *p*,
Jn 19:37 look on the one they have *p*.''

PIGS
Mt 7: 6 do not throw your pearls to *p*.

PILATE
Governor of Judea. Questioned Jesus (Mt 27:1-26; Mk 15:15; Lk 22:66-23:25; Jn 18:28-19:16); sent him to Herod (Lk 23:6-12); consented to his crucifixion when crowds chose Barabbas (Mt 27:15-26; Mk 15:6-15; Lk 23:13-25; Jn 19:1-10).

PILLAR
Ge 19:26 and she became a *p* of salt.
Ex 13:21 ahead of them in a *p* of cloud
1Ti 3:15 the *p* and foundation of the truth.

PIT
Ps 40: 2 He lifted me out of the slimy *p*,
103: 4 who redeems your life from the *p*
Mt 15:14 a blind man, both will fall into a *p*.''

PITIED
1Co 15:19 we are to be *p* more than all men.

PLAGUE
2Ch 6:28 ''When famine or *p* comes

PLAIN
Ro 1:19 what may be known about God is *p*

PLAN (PLANNED PLANS)
Job 42: 2 no *p* of yours can be thwarted.
Pr 14:22 those who *p* what is good find love
Eph 1:11 predestined according to the *p*

PLANK
Mt 7: 3 attention to the *p* in your own eye?
Lk 6:41 attention to the *p* in your own eye?

PLANNED (PLAN)
Ps 40: 5 The things you *p* for us
Isa 46:11 what I have *p*, that will I do.
Heb 11:40 God had *p* something better for us

PLANS (PLAN)
Ps 20: 4 and make all your *p* succeed.
33:11 *p* of the LORD stand firm forever,
Pr 20:18 Make *p* by seeking advice;
Isa 32: 8 But the noble man makes noble *p*,

PLANTED (PLANTS)
Ps 1: 3 He is like a tree *p* by streams
Mt 15:13 Father has not *p* will be pulled
1Co 3: 6 I *p* the seed, Apollos watered it,

PLANTS (PLANTED)
1Co 3: 7 So neither he who *p* nor he who
9: 7 Who *p* a vineyard and does not eat

PLATTER
Mk 6:25 head of John the Baptist on a *p*.''

PLAYED
Lk 7:32 '' 'We *p* the flute for you,
1Co 14: 7 anyone know what tune is being *p*

PLEADED
2Co 12: 8 Three times I *p* with the Lord

PLEASANT (PLEASE)
Ps 16: 6 for me in *p* places;
133: 1 How good and *p* it is
147: 1 how *p* and fitting to praise him!
Heb 12:11 No discipline seems *p* at the time,

PLEASE (PLEASANT PLEASED PLEASES PLEASING PLEASURE PLEASURES)
Pr 20:23 and dishonest scales do not *p* him.
Jer 6:20 your sacrifices do not *p* me.''
Jn 5:30 for I seek not to *p* myself
Ro 8: 8 by the sinful nature cannot *p* God.
15: 2 Each of us should *p* his neighbor
1Co 7:32 affairs—how he can *p* the Lord.
10:33 I try to *p* everybody in every way.

2Co 5: 9 So we make it our goal to *p* him,
Gal 1:10 or of God? Or am I trying to *p* men
1Th 4: 1 how to live in order to *p* God,
2Ti 2: 4 wants to *p* his commanding officer.
Heb 11: 6 faith it is impossible to *p* God,

PLEASED (PLEASE)

Mt 3:17 whom I love; with him I am well *p*
1Co 1:21 God was *p* through the foolishness
Col 1:19 For God was *p* to have all his
Heb 11: 5 commended as one who *p* God.
2Pe 1:17 whom I love; with him I am well *p*

PLEASES (PLEASE)

Ps 135: 6 The LORD does whatever *p* him,
Pr 15: 8 but the prayer of the upright *p* him.
Jn 3: 8 The wind blows wherever it *p*.
     8:29 for I always do what *p* him.''
Col 3:20 in everything, for this *p* the Lord.
1Ti 2: 3 This is good, and *p* God our Savior,
1Jn 3:22 his commands and do what *p* him.

PLEASING (PLEASE)

Ps 104: 34 May my meditation be *p* to him,
Ro 12: 1 *p* to God—which is your spiritual
Php 4:18 an acceptable sacrifice, *p* to God.
Heb 13:21 may he work in us what is *p* to him,

PLEASURE (PLEASE)

Ps 5: 4 You are not a God who takes *p*
    147: 10 His *p* is not in the strength
Pr 21:17 He who loves *p* will become poor;
Eze 18:32 For I take no *p* in the death
Eph 1: 5 in accordance with his *p* and will—
     1: 9 of his will according to his good *p*,
2Ti 3: 4 lovers of *p* rather than lovers

PLEASURES (PLEASE)

Ps 16:11 with eternal *p* at your right hand.
Heb 11:25 rather than to enjoy the *p* of sin
2Pe 2:13 reveling in their *p* while they feast

PLENTIFUL

Mt 9:37 harvest is *p* but the workers are

PLOW (PLOWSHARES)

Lk 9:62 ''No one who puts his hand to the *p*

PLOWSHARES (PLOW)

Isa 2: 4 They will beat their swords into *p*
Joel 3:10 Beat your *p* into swords

PLUNDER

Ex 3:22 And so you will *p* the Egyptians.''

POINT

Jas 2:10 yet stumbles at just one *p* is guilty

POISON

Mk 16:18 and when they drink deadly *p*,
Jas 3: 8 It is a restless evil, full of deadly *p*.

POLLUTE* (POLLUTED)

Nu 35:33 '' 'Do not *p* the land where you are.
Jude : 8 these dreamers *p* their own bodies,

POLLUTED* (POLLUTE)

Ezr 9:11 entering to possess is a land *p*

Pr 25:26 Like a muddied spring or a *p* well
Ac 15:20 to abstain from food *p* by idols,
Jas 1:27 oneself from being *p* by the world.

PONDER

Ps 64: 9 and *p* what he has done.
    119: 95 but I will *p* your statutes.

POOR (POVERTY)

Dt 15: 4 there should be no *p* among you,
    15:11 There will always be *p* people
Ps 34: 6 This *p* man called, and the LORD
    82: 3 maintain the rights of the *p*
    112: 9 scattered abroad his gifts to the *p*,
Pr 10: 4 Lazy hands make a man *p*,
    13: 7 to be *p*, yet has great wealth.
    14:31 oppresses the *p* shows contempt
    19: 1 Better a *p* man whose walk is
    19:17 to the *p* lends to the LORD,
    22: 2 Rich and *p* have this in common:
    22: 9 for he shares his food with the *p*.
    28: 6 Better a *p* man whose walk is
    31:20 She opens her arms to the *p*
Isa 61: 1 me to preach good news to the *p*.
Mt 5: 3 saying: ''Blessed are the *p* in spirit,
    11: 5 the good news is preached to the *p*.
    19:21 your possessions and give to the *p*,
    26:11 The *p* you will always have
Mk 12:42 But a *p* widow came and put
Ac 10: 4 and gifts to the *p* have come up
1Co 13: 3 If I give all I possess to the *p*,
2Co 8: 9 yet for your sakes he became *p*,
Jas 2: 2 and a *p* man in shabby clothes

PORTION

Dt 32: 9 For the LORD's *p* is his people,
2Ki 2: 9 ''Let me inherit a double *p*
La 3:24 to myself, ''The LORD is my *p*;

POSSESS (POSSESSING POSSESSION POSSESSIONS)

Nu 33:53 for I have given you the land to *p*.
Jn 5:39 that by them you *p* eternal life.

POSSESSING* (POSSESS)

2Co 6:10 nothing, and yet *p* everything.

POSSESSION (POSSESS)

Ge 15: 7 to give you this land to take *p* of it
Nu 13:30 ''We should go up and take *p*
Eph 1:14 of those who are God's *p*—

POSSESSIONS (POSSESS)

Lk 12:15 consist in the abundance of his *p*.
2Co 12:14 what I want is not your *p* but you.
1Jn 3:17 If anyone has material *p*

POSSIBLE

Mt 19:26 but with God all things are *p*.''
Mk 9:23 ''Everything is *p* for him who
    10:27 all things are *p* with God.''
Ro 12:18 If it is *p*, as far as it depends on you,
1Co 9:22 by all *p* means I might save some.

POT (POTSHERD POTTER POTTERY)

2Ki 4:40 there is death in the *p!*''
Jer 18: 4 But the *p* he was shaping

POTSHERD (POT)

Isa 45: 9 a *p* among the potsherds

POTTER (POT)

Isa 29:16 Can the pot say of the *p*,
    45: 9 Does the clay say to the *p*,
    64: 8 We are the clay, you are the *p;*
Jer 18: 6 ''Like clay in the hand of the *p*,
Ro 9:21 Does not the *p* have the right

POTTERY (POT)

Ro 9:21 of clay some *p* for noble purposes

POUR (POURED)

Ps 62: 8 *p* out your hearts to him,
Joel 2:28 I will *p* out my Spirit on all people.
Mal 3:10 *p* out so much blessing that you
Ac 2:17 I will *p* out my Spirit on all people.

POURED (POUR)

Ac 10:45 of the Holy Spirit had been *p* out
Ro 5: 5 because God has *p* out his love

POVERTY (POOR)

Pr 14:23 but mere talk leads only to *p*.
    21: 5 as surely as haste leads to *p*.
    30: 8 give me neither *p* nor riches,
Mk 12:44 out of her *p*, put in everything—
2Co 8: 2 and their extreme *p* welled up
    8: 9 through his *p* might become rich.

POWER (POWERFUL POWERS)

1Ch 29:11 LORD, is the greatness and the *p*
2Ch 32: 7 for there is a greater *p* with us
Job 36:22 ''God is exalted in his *p*.
Ps 63: 2 and beheld your *p* and your glory.
  68:34 Proclaim the *p* of God,
  147: 5 Great is our Lord and mighty in *p;*
Pr 24: 5 A wise man has great *p*,
Isa 40:10 the Sovereign LORD comes with *p*
Zec 4: 6 nor by *p*, but by my Spirit,'
Mt 22:29 do not know the Scriptures or the *p*
  24:30 on the clouds of the sky, with *p*
Ac 1: 8 you will receive *p* when the Holy
    4:33 With great *p* the apostles
  10:38 with the Holy Spirit and *p*,
Ro 1:16 it is the *p* of God for the salvation
1Co 1:18 to us who are being saved it is the *p*
  15:56 of death is sin, and the *p*
2Co 12: 9 for my *p* is made perfect
Eph 1:19 and his incomparably great *p*
Php 3:10 and the *p* of his resurrection
Col 1:11 strengthened with all *p* according
2Ti 1: 7 but a spirit of *p*, of love
Heb 7:16 of the *p* of an indestructible life.
Rev 4:11 to receive glory and honor and *p*,
  19: 1 and glory and *p* belong to our God,
  20: 6 The second death has no *p*

POWERFUL (POWER)

Ps 29: 4 The voice of the LORD is *p;*
Lk 24:19 *p* in word and deed before God

2Th 1: 7 in blazing fire with his *p* angels.
Heb 1: 3 sustaining all things by his *p* word.
Jas 5:16 The prayer of a righteous man is *p*

POWERLESS

Ro 5: 6 when we were still *p*, Christ died
    8: 3 For what the law was *p* to do

POWERS (POWER)

Ro 8:38 nor any *p*, neither height nor depth
1Co 12:10 to another miraculous *p*,
Col 1:16 whether thrones or *p* or rulers
    2:15 And having disarmed the *p*

PRACTICE

Lev 19:26 '' 'Do not *p* divination or sorcery.
Mt 23: 3 for they do not *p* what they preach.
Lk 8:21 hear God's word and put it into *p*.''
Ro 12:13 *P* hospitality.
1Ti 5: 4 to put their religion into *p* by caring

PRAISE (PRAISED PRAISES PRAISING)

Ex 15: 2 He is my God, and I will *p* him,
Dt 32: 3 Oh, *p* the greatness of our God!
Ru 4:14 said to Naomi: ''*P* be to the LORD,
2Sa 22:47 The LORD lives! *P* be to my Rock
1Ch 16:25 is the LORD and most worthy of *p;*
2Ch 20:21 and to *p* him for the splendor
Ps 8: 2 you have ordained *p*
    33: 1 it is fitting for the upright to *p* him.
    34: 1 his *p* will always be on my lips.
    40: 3 a hymn of *p* to our God.
    48: 1 the LORD, and most worthy of *p*,
  68:19 *P* be to the Lord, to God our Savior
  89: 5 The heavens *p* your wonders,
  100: 4 and his courts with *p;*
  105: 2 Sing to him, sing *p* to him;
  106: 1 *P* the LORD.
  119:175 Let me live that I may *p* you,
  139: 14 I *p* you because I am fearfully
  145: 21 Let every creature *p* his holy name
  146: 1 *P* the LORD, O my soul.
  150: 2 *p* him for his surpassing greatness.
  150: 6 that has breath *p* the LORD.
Pr 27: 2 Let another *p* you, and not your
  27:21 man is tested by the *p* he receives.
  31:31 let her works bring her *p*
Mt 5:16 and *p* your Father in heaven.
  21:16 you have ordained *p*'?''
Jn 12:43 for they loved *p* from men more
Eph 1: 6 to the *p* of his glorious grace,
    1:12 might be for the *p* of his glory.
    1:14 to the *p* of his glory.
Heb 13:15 offer to God a sacrifice of *p*—
Jas 5:13 happy? Let him sing songs of *p*.

PRAISED (PRAISE)

1Ch 29:10 David *p* the LORD in the presence
Ne 8: 6 Ezra *p* the LORD, the great God;
Da 2:19 Then Daniel *p* the God of heaven
Ro 9: 5 who is God over all, forever *p!*
1Pe 4:11 that in all things God may be *p*

PRAISES (PRAISE)

2Sa 22:50 I will sing *p* to your name.

Ps 47: 6 Sing *p* to God, sing *p;*
   147:   1 How good it is to sing *p* to our God,
Pr 31:28 her husband also, and he *p* her:

PRAISING (PRAISE)

Ac 10:46 speaking in tongues and *p* God.
1Co 14:16 If you are *p* God with your spirit,

PRAY (PRAYED PRAYER PRAYERS PRAYING)

Dt   4: 7 is near us whenever we *p* to him?
1Sa 12:23 the Lord by failing to *p* for you.
2Ch 7:14 will humble themselves and *p*
Job 42: 8 My servant Job will *p* for you,
Ps 122: 6 *P* for the peace of Jerusalem:
Mt   5:44 and *p* for those who persecute you,
     6: 5 "And when you *p*, do not be like
     6: 9 "This, then, is how you should *p:*
  26:36 Sit here while I go over there and *p*
Lk   6:28 *p* for those who mistreat you.
  18: 1 them that they should always *p*
  22:40 "*P* that you will not fall
Ro   8:26 do not know what we ought to *p*,
1Co 14:13 in a tongue should *p* that he may
1Th 5:17 Be joyful always; *p* continually;
Jas   5:13 one of you in trouble? He should *p*.
   5:16 *p* for each other so that you may be

PRAYED (PRAY)

1Sa 1:27 I *p* for this child, and the Lord
Jnh 2: 1 From inside the fish Jonah *p*
Mk 14:35 *p* that if possible the hour might

PRAYER (PRAY)

2Ch 30:27 for their *p* reached heaven,
Ezr 8:23 about this, and he answered our *p*.
Ps   6: 9 the Lord accepts my *p*.
  86: 6 Hear my *p*, O Lord;
Pr   15: 8 but the *p* of the upright pleases him
Isa 56: 7 a house of *p* for all nations."
Mt 21:13 house will be called a house of *p*,'
Mk 11:24 whatever you ask for in *p*,
Jn 17:15 My *p* is not that you take them out
Ac   6: 4 and will give our attention to *p*
Php 4: 6 but in everything, by *p* and petition
Jas   5:15 *p* offered in faith will make the sick
1Pe 3:12 and his ears are attentive to their *p*,

PRAYERS (PRAY)

1Ch 5:20 He answered their *p*, because they
Mk 12:40 and for a show make lengthy *p*.
1Pe 3: 7 so that nothing will hinder your *p*.
Rev 5: 8 which are the *p* of the saints.

PRAYING (PRAY)

Mk 11:25 And when you stand *p*,
Jn 17: 9 I am not *p* for the world,
Ac 16:25 and Silas were *p* and singing hymns
Eph 6:18 always keep on *p* for all the saints.

PREACH (PREACHED PREACHING)

Mt 23: 3 they do not practice what they *p*.
Mk 16:15 and *p* the good news to all creation.
Ac   9:20 At once he began to *p*
Ro 10:15 how can they *p* unless they are sent

Ro 15:20 to *p* the gospel where Christ was
1Co 1:17 to *p* the gospel—not with words
   1:23 wisdom, but we *p* Christ crucified:
   9:14 that those who *p* the gospel should
   9:16 Woe to me if I do not *p* the gospel!
2Co 10:16 so that we can *p* the gospel
Gal 1: 8 from heaven should *p* a gospel
2Ti 4: 2 I give you this charge: *P* the Word;

PREACHED (PREACH)

Mk 13:10 And the gospel must first be *p*
Ac   8: 4 had been scattered *p* the word
1Co 9:27 so that after I have *p* to others,
  15: 1 you of the gospel I *p* to you,
2Co 11: 4 other than the Jesus we *p*,
Gal 1: 8 other than the one we *p* to you,
Php 1:18 false motives or true, Christ is *p*.
1Ti 3:16 was *p* among the nations,

PREACHING (PREACH)

Ro 10:14 hear without someone *p* to them?
1Co 9:18 in *p* the gospel I may offer it free
1Ti 4:13 the public reading of Scripture, to *p*
   5:17 especially those whose work is *p*

PRECEPTS

Ps 19: 8 The *p* of the Lord are right,
  111: 7 all his *p* are trustworthy.
  111: 10 who follow his *p* have good
  119: 40 How I long for your *p!*
  119: 69 I keep your *p* with all my heart.
  119:104 I gain understanding from your *p;*
  119:159 See how I love your *p;*

PRECIOUS

Ps 19:10 They are more *p* than gold,
  116: 15 *P* in the sight of the Lord
Pr   8:11 for wisdom is more *p* than rubies,
Isa 28:16 a *p* cornerstone for a sure
1Pe 1:19 but with the *p* blood of Christ,
   2: 6 a chosen and *p* cornerstone,
2Pe 1: 4 us his very great and *p* promises,

PREDESTINED* (DESTINY)

Ro 8:29 *p* to be conformed to the likeness
   8:30 And those he *p*, he also called;
Eph 1: 5 In love he *p* us to be adopted
   1:11 having been *p* according

PREDICTION*

Jer 28: 9 only if his *p* comes true."

PREPARE (PREPARED)

Ps 23: 5 You *p* a table before me
Am 4:12 *p* to meet your God, O Israel."
Jn 14: 2 there to *p* a place for you.
Eph 4:12 to *p* God's people for works

PREPARED (PREPARE)

Mt 25:34 the kingdom *p* for you
1Co 2: 9 what God has *p* for those who love
Eph 2:10 which God *p* in advance for us
2Ti 4: 2 be *p* in season and out of season;
1Pe 3:15 Always be *p* to give an answer

PRESENCE (PRESENT)

Ex 25:30 Put the bread of the *P* on this table
Ezr 9:15 one of us can stand in your *p*.''
Ps 31:20 the shelter of your *p* you hide them
89:15 who walk in the light of your *p*,
90: 8 our secret sins in the light of your *p*
139: 7 Where can I flee from your *p*?
Jer 5:22 ''Should you not tremble in my *p*?
Heb 9:24 now to appear for us in God's *p*.
Jude :24 before his glorious *p* without fault

PRESENT (PRESENCE)

2Co 11: 2 so that I might *p* you as a pure
Eph 5:27 and to *p* her to himself
2Ti 2:15 Do your best to *p* yourself to God

PRESERVES

Ps 119:50 Your promise *p* my life.

PRESS (PRESSED PRESSURE)

Php 3:14 I *p* on toward the goal

PRESSED (PRESS)

Lk 6:38 *p* down, shaken together

PRESSURE (PRESS)

2Co 1: 8 We were under great *p*, far
11:28 I face daily the *p* of my concern

PREVAILS

1Sa 2: 9 ''It is not by strength that one *p*;

PRICE

Job 28:18 the *p* of wisdom is beyond rubies.
1Co 6:20 your own; you were bought at a *p*.
7:23 bought at a *p*; do not become slaves

PRIDE (PROUD)

Pr 8:13 I hate *p* and arrogance,
16:18 *P* goes before destruction,
Da 4:37 And those who walk in *p* he is able
Gal 6: 4 Then he can take *p* in himself,
Jas 1: 9 ought to take *p* in his high position.

PRIEST (PRIESTHOOD PRIESTS)

Heb 4:14 have a great high *p* who has gone
4:15 do not have a high *p* who is unable
7:26 Such a high *p* meets our need—
8: 1 We do have such a high *p*,

PRIESTHOOD (PRIEST)

Heb 7:24 lives forever, he has a permanent *p*.
1Pe 2: 5 into a spiritual house to be a holy *p*,
2: 9 you are a chosen people, a royal *p*,

PRIESTS (PRIEST)

Ex 19: 6 you will be for me a kingdom of *p*
Rev 5:10 to be a kingdom and *p*

PRINCE

Isa 9: 6 Everlasting Father, *P* of Peace.
Jn 12:31 now the *p* of this world will be
Ac 5:31 as *P* and Savior that he might give

PRISON (PRISONER)

Isa 42: 7 to free captives from *p*
Mt 25:36 I was in *p* and you came to visit me
1Pe 3:19 spirits in *p* who disobeyed long ago

Rev 20: 7 Satan will be released from his *p*

PRISONER (PRISON)

Ro 7:23 and making me a *p* of the law of sin
Gal 3:22 declares that the whole world is a *p*
Eph 3: 1 the *p* of Christ Jesus for the sake

PRIVILEGE*

2Co 8: 4 pleaded with us for the *p* of sharing

PRIZE

1Co 9:24 Run in such a way as to get the *p*.
Php 3:14 on toward the goal to win the *p*

PROCLAIM (PROCLAIMED PROCLAIMING)

1Ch 16:23 *p* his salvation day after day.
Ps 19: 1 the skies *p* the work of his hands.
50: 6 the heavens *p* his righteousness,
68:34 *P* the power of God,
118: 17 will *p* what the LORD has done.
Zec 9:10 He will *p* peace to the nations.
Ac 20:27 hesitated to *p* to you the whole will
1Co 11:26 you *p* the Lord's death

PROCLAIMED (PROCLAIM)

Ro 15:19 I have fully *p* the gospel of Christ.
Col 1:23 that has been *p* to every creature

PROCLAIMING (PROCLAIM)

Ro 10: 8 the word of faith we are *p*:

PRODUCE (PRODUCES)

Mt 3: 8 *P* fruit in keeping with repentance.
3:10 tree that does not *p* good fruit will

PRODUCES (PRODUCE)

Pr 30:33 so stirring up anger *p* strife.''
Ro 5: 3 that suffering *p* perseverance;
Heb 12:11 it *p* a harvest of righteousness

PROFANE

Lev 22:32 Do not *p* my holy name.

PROFESS*

1Ti 2:10 for women who *p* to worship God.
Heb 4:14 let us hold firmly to the faith we *p*.
10:23 unswervingly to the hope we *p*,

PROMISE (PROMISED PROMISES)

1Ki 8:20 The LORD has kept the *p* he made
Ac 2:39 The *p* is for you and your children
Gal 3:14 that by faith we might receive the *p*
1Ti 4: 8 holding *p* for both the present life
2Pe 3: 9 Lord is not slow in keeping his *p*,

PROMISED (PROMISE)

Ex 3:17 And I have *p* to bring you up out
Dt 26:18 his treasured possession as he *p*,
Ps119: 57 I have *p* to obey your words.
Ro 4:21 power to do what he had *p*.
Heb 10:23 for he who *p* is faithful.
2Pe 3: 4 ''Where is this 'coming' he *p*?

PROMISES (PROMISE)

Jos 21:45 one of all the LORD's good *p*
Ro 9: 4 the temple worship and the *p*.
2Pe 1: 4 us his very great and precious *p*,

PROMPTED

1Th 1: 3 your labor *p* by love, and your
2Th 1:11 and every act *p* by your faith.

PROPHECIES (PROPHESY)

1Co 13: 8 where there are *p*, they will cease;
1Th 5:20 do not treat *p* with contempt.

PROPHECY (PROPHESY)

1Co 14: 1 gifts, especially the gift of *p*.
2Pe 1:20 you must understand that no *p*

PROPHESY (PROPHECIES PROPHECY PROPHESYING PROPHET PROPHETS)

Joel 2:28 Your sons and daughters will *p*,
Mt 7:22 Lord, did we not *p* in your name,
1Co 14:39 my brothers, be eager to *p*,

PROPHESYING (PROPHESY)

Ro 12: 6 If a man's gift is *p*, let him use it

PROPHET (PROPHESY)

Dt 18:18 up for them a *p* like you
Am 7:14 "I was neither a *p* nor a prophet's
Mt 10:41 Anyone who receives a *p*
Lk 4:24 "no *p* is accepted in his hometown.

PROPHETS (PROPHESY)

Ps 105: 15 do my *p* no harm."
Mt 5:17 come to abolish the Law or the *P*;
7:12 for this sums up the Law and the *P*.
24:24 false Christs and false *p* will appear
Lk 24:25 believe all that the *p* have spoken!
Ac 10:43 All the *p* testify about him that
1Co 12:28 second *p*, third teachers, then
14:32 The spirits of *p* are subject
Eph 2:20 foundation of the apostles and *p*,
Heb 1: 1 through the *p* at many times
1Pe 1:10 Concerning this salvation, the *p*,
2Pe 1:19 word of the *p* made more certain,

PROSPER (PROSPERITY PROSPERS)

Pr 28:25 he who trusts in the Lord will *p*.

PROSPERITY (PROSPER)

Ps 73: 3 when I saw the *p* of the wicked.
Pr 13:21 but *p* is the reward of the righteous.

PROSPERS (PROSPER)

Ps 1: 3 Whatever he does *p*.

PROSTITUTE (PROSTITUTES)

1Co 6:15 of Christ and unite them with a *p*?

PROSTITUTES (PROSTITUTE)

Lk 15:30 property with *p* comes home,
1Co 6: 9 male *p* nor homosexual offenders

PROSTRATE

Dt 9:18 again I fell *p* before the Lord

PROTECT (PROTECTS)

Ps 32: 7 you will *p* me from trouble
Pr 2:11 Discretion will *p* you,
Jn 17:11 *p* them by the power of your name

PROTECTS (PROTECT)

1Co 13: 7 It always *p*, always trusts,

PROUD (PRIDE)

Pr 16: 5 The Lord detests all the *p*
Ro 12:16 Do not be *p*, but be willing
1Co 13: 4 it does not boast, it is not *p*.

PROVE

Ac 26:20 *p* their repentance by their deeds.
1Co 4: 2 been given a trust must *p* faithful.

PROVIDE (PROVIDED PROVIDES)

Ge 22: 8 "God himself will *p* the lamb
Isa 43:20 because I *p* water in the desert
1Ti 5: 8 If anyone does not *p*

PROVIDED (PROVIDE)

Jnh 1:17 But the Lord *p* a great fish
4: 6 Then the Lord God *p* a vine
4: 7 dawn the next day God *p* a worm,
4: 8 God *p* a scorching east wind,

PROVIDES (PROVIDE)

1Ti 6:17 who richly *p* us with everything
1Pe 4:11 it with the strength God *p*,

PROVOKED

Ecc 7: 9 Do not be quickly *p* in your spirit,

PRUDENT

Pr 14:15 a *p* man gives thought to his steps.
19:14 but a *p* wife is from the Lord.
Am 5:13 Therefore the *p* man keeps quiet

PRUNING

Isa 2: 4 and their spears into *p* hooks.
Joel 3:10 and your *p* hooks into spears.

PSALMS

Eph 5:19 Speak to one another with *p*,
Col 3:16 and as you sing *p*, hymns

PUBLICLY

Ac 20:20 have taught you *p* and from house
1Ti 5:20 Those who sin are to be rebuked *p*,

PUFFS

1Co 8: 1 Knowledge *p* up, but love builds up

PULLING

2Co 10: 8 building you up rather than *p* you

PUNISH (PUNISHED PUNISHES)

Ex 32:34 I will *p* them for their sin."
Pr 23:13 if you *p* him with the rod, he will
Isa 13:11 I will *p* the world for its evil,
1Pe 2:14 by him to *p* those who do wrong

PUNISHED (PUNISH)

La 3:39 complain when *p* for his sins?
2Th 1: 9 be *p* with everlasting destruction
Heb 10:29 to be *p* who has trampled the Son

PUNISHES (PUNISH)

Heb 12: 6 and he *p* everyone he accepts

PURE (PURIFIES PURIFY PURITY)

2Sa 22:27 to the *p* you show yourself *p*,
Ps 24: 4 who has clean hands and a *p* heart,
51:10 Create in me a *p* heart, O God,
119: 9 can a young man keep his way *p*?

Pr   20: 9 can say, "I have kept my heart *p;*
Isa   52:11 Come out from it and be *p,*
Hab   1:13 Your eyes are too *p* to look on evil;
Mt   5: 8 Blessed are the *p* in heart,
2Co 11: 2 I might present you as a *p* virgin
Php   4: 8 whatever is *p,* whatever is lovely,
1Ti   5:22 Keep yourself *p.*
Tit   1:15 To the *p,* all things are *p,*
      2: 5 to be self-controlled and *p,*
Heb 13: 4 and the marriage bed kept *p,*
1Jn   3: 3 him purifies himself, just as he is *p.*

PURGE

Pr   20:30 and beatings *p* the inmost being.

PURIFIES* (PURE)

1Jn   1: 7 of Jesus, his Son, *p* us from all sin.
      3: 3 who has this hope in him *p* himself,

PURIFY (PURE)

Tit   2:14 to *p* for himself a people that are
1Jn   1: 9 and *p* us from all unrighteousness.

PURITY (PURE)

2Co   6: 6 in *p,* understanding, patience
1Ti   4:12 in life, in love, in faith and in *p.*

PURPOSE

Pr   19:21 but it is the LORD's *p* that prevails
Isa   55:11 and achieve the *p* for which I sent it
Ro   8:28 have been called according to his *p.*
Php   2: 2 love, being one in spirit and *p.*

PURSES

Lk   12:33 Provide *p* for yourselves that will

PURSUE

Ps   34:14 seek peace and *p* it.
2Ti   2:22 and *p* righteousness, faith,
1Pe   3:11 he must seek peace and *p* it.

QUALITIES (QUALITY)

2Pe   1: 8 For if you possess these *q*

QUALITY (QUALITIES)

1Co   3:13 and the fire will test the *q*

QUARREL (QUARRELSOME)

Pr   15:18 but a patient man calms a *q.*
      17:14 Starting a *q* is like breaching a dam;
      17:19 He who loves a *q* loves sin;
2Ti   2:24 And the Lord's servant must not *q;*

QUARRELSOME (QUARREL)

Pr   19:13 a *q* wife is like a constant dripping.
1Ti   3: 3 not violent but gentle, not *q,*

QUICK-TEMPERED

Tit   1: 7 not *q,* not given to drunkenness,

QUIET (QUIETNESS)

Ps   23: 2 he leads me beside *q* waters,
Zep   3:17 he will *q* you with his love,
Lk   19:40 he replied, "if they keep *q,*
1Ti   2: 2 we may live peaceful and *q* lives
1Pe   3: 4 beauty of a gentle and *q* spirit,

QUIETNESS (QUIET)

Isa   30:15 in *q* and trust is your strength,

Isa   32:17 the effect of righteousness will be *q*
1Ti   2:11 A woman should learn in *q*

QUIVER

Ps 127: 5 whose *q* is full of them.

RACE

Ecc   9:11 The *r* is not to the swift
1Co   9:24 that in a *r* all the runners run,
2Ti   4: 7 I have finished the *r,* I have kept
Heb 12: 1 perseverance the *r* marked out

RACHEL

   Daughter of Laban (Ge 29:16); wife of Jacob
(Ge 29:28); bore two sons (Ge 30:22-24; 35:16-
24; 46:19).

RADIANCE (RADIANT)

Heb   1: 3 The Son is the *r* of God's glory

RADIANT (RADIANCE)

Ex   34:29 he was not aware that his face was *r*
Ps   34: 5 Those who look to him are *r;*
SS   5:10 *Beloved* My lover is *r* and ruddy,
Isa   60: 5 Then you will look and be *r,*
Eph   5:27 her to himself as a *r* church,

RAIN (RAINBOW)

Mt   5:45 and sends *r* on the righteous

RAINBOW (RAIN)

Ge   9:13 I have set my *r* in the clouds,

RAISED (RISE)

Ro   4:25 was *r* to life for our justification.
      10: 9 in your heart that God *r* him
1Co 15: 4 that he was *r* on the third day

RAN (RUN)

Jnh   1: 3 But Jonah *r* away from the LORD

RANSOM

Mt   20:28 and to give his life as a *r* for many."
Heb   9:15 as a *r* to set them free

RAVENS

1Ki 17: 6 The *r* brought him bread
Lk   12:24 Consider the *r:* They do not sow

READ (READS)

Jos   8:34 Joshua *r* all the words of the law—
Ne   8: 8 They *r* from the Book of the Law
2Co   3: 2 known and *r* by everybody.

READS (READ)

Rev   1: 3 Blessed is the one who *r* the words

REAL (REALITY)

Jn   6:55 is *r* food and my blood is *r* drink.

REALITY* (REAL)

Col   2:17 the *r,* however, is found in Christ.

REAP (REAPS)

Job   4: 8 and those who sow trouble *r* it.
2Co   9: 6 generously will also *r* generously.

REAPS (REAP)

Gal   6: 7 A man *r* what he sows.

REASON
Isa 1:18 "Come now, let us *r* together,"
1Pe 3:15 to give the *r* for the hope that you

REBEKAH
Sister of Laban, secured as bride for Isaac (Ge 24). Mother of Esau and Jacob (Ge 25:19-26). Taken by Abimelech as sister of Isaac; returned (Ge 26:1-11). Encouraged Jacob to trick Isaac out of blessing (Ge 27:1-17).

REBEL
Mt 10:21 children will *r* against their parents

REBUKE (REBUKED REBUKING)
Pr 9: 8 *r* a wise man and he will love you.
27: 5 Better is open *r*
Lk 17: 3 "If your brother sins, *r* him,
2Ti 4: 2 correct, *r* and encourage—
Rev 3:19 Those whom I love I *r*

REBUKED (REBUKE)
1Ti 5:20 Those who sin are to be *r* publicly,

REBUKING (REBUKE)
2Ti 3:16 *r*, correcting and training

RECEIVE (RECEIVED RECEIVES)
Ac 1: 8 you will *r* power when the Holy
20:35 'It is more blessed to give than to *r*
2Co 6:17 and I will *r* you."
Rev 4:11 to *r* glory and honor and power,

RECEIVED (RECEIVE)
Mt 6: 2 they have *r* their reward in full.
10: 8 Freely you have *r*, freely give.
1Co 11:23 For I *r* from the Lord what I
Col 2: 6 just as you *r* Christ Jesus as Lord,
1Pe 4:10 should use whatever gift he has *r*

RECEIVES (RECEIVE)
Mt 7: 8 everyone who asks *r;* he who seeks
10:40 he who *r* me *r* the one who sent me.
Ac 10:43 believes in him *r* forgiveness of sins

RECKONING
Isa 10: 3 What will you do on the day of *r*,

RECOGNIZE (RECOGNIZED)
Mt 7:16 By their fruit you will *r* them.

RECOGNIZED (RECOGNIZE)
Mt 12:33 for a tree is *r* by its fruit.
Ro 7:13 in order that sin might be *r* as sin,

RECOMPENSE
Isa 40:10 and his *r* accompanies him.

RECONCILE (RECONCILED RECONCILIATION)
Eph 2:16 in this one body to *r* both of them

RECONCILED (RECONCILE)
Mt 5:24 First go and be *r* to your brother;
Ro 5:10 we were *r* to him through the death
2Co 5:18 who *r* us to himself through Christ

RECONCILIATION* (RECONCILE)
Ro 5:11 whom we have now received *r*.
11:15 For if their rejection is the *r*
2Co 5:18 and gave us the ministry of *r:*
5:19 committed to us the message of *r*.

RECORD
Ps 130: 3 If you, O LORD, kept a *r* of sins,

RED
Isa 1:18 though they are *r* as crimson,

REDEEM (KINSMAN-REDEEMER REDEEMED REDEEMER REDEMPTION)
2Sa 7:23 on earth that God went out to *r*
Ps 49: 7 No man can *r* the life of another
Gal 4: 5 under law, to *r* those under law,

REDEEMED (REDEEM)
Gal 3:13 Christ *r* us from the curse
1Pe 1:18 or gold that you were *r*

REDEEMER (REDEEM)
Job 19:25 I know that my *R* lives,

REDEMPTION (REDEEM)
Ps 130: 7 and with him is full *r*.
Lk 21:28 because your *r* is drawing near."
Ro 8:23 as sons, the *r* of our bodies.
Eph 1: 7 In him we have *r* through his blood
Col 1:14 in whom we have *r*, the forgiveness
Heb 9:12 having obtained eternal *r*.

REFLECT
2Co 3:18 unveiled faces all *r* the Lord's

REFUGE
Nu 35:11 towns to be your cities of *r*,
Dt 33:27 The eternal God is your *r*,
Ru 2:12 wings you have come to take *r*."
Ps 46: 1 God is our *r* and strength,
91: 2 "He is my *r* and my fortress,

REHOBOAM
Son of Solomon (1Ki 11:43; 1Ch 3:10). Harsh treatment of subjects caused divided kingdom (1Ki 12:1-24; 14:21-31; 2Ch 10-12).

REIGN
Ex 15:18 The LORD will *r*
Ro 6:12 Therefore do not let sin *r*
1Co 15:25 For he must *r* until he has put all
2Ti 2:12 we will also *r* with him.
Rev 20: 6 will *r* with him for a thousand years

REJECTED (REJECTS)
Ps 118: 22 The stone the builders *r*
Isa 53: 3 He was despised and *r* by men,
1Ti 4: 4 nothing is to be *r* if it is received
1Pe 2: 4 *r* by men but chosen by God
2: 7 "The stone the builders *r*

REJECTS (REJECTED)
Lk 10:16 but he who *r* me *r* him who sent me
Jn 3:36 whoever *r* the Son will not see life,

REJOICE (JOY)
Ps 2:11 and *r* with trembling.

Ps   66: 6 come, let us *r* in him.
    118: 24 let us *r* and be glad in it.
Pr   5:18 may you *r* in the wife of your youth
Lk 10:20 but *r* that your names are written
     15: 6 '*R* with me; I have found my lost
Ro 12:15 Rejoice with those who *r;* mourn
Php   4: 4 *R* in the Lord always.

REJOICES (JOY)

Isa 61:10 my soul *r* in my God.
Lk   1:47 and my spirit *r* in God my Savior,
1Co 12:26 if one part is honored, every part *r*
     13: 6 delight in evil but *r* with the truth.

REJOICING (JOY)

Ps   30: 5 but *r* comes in the morning.
Lk   15: 7 in the same way there will be more *r*
Ac   5:41 *r* because they had been counted

RELIABLE

2Ti   2: 2 witnesses entrust to *r* men who will

RELIGION

1Ti   5: 4 all to put their *r* into practice
Jas   1:27 *R* that God our Father accepts

REMAIN (REMAINS)

Nu 33:55 allow to *r* will become barbs
Jn   15: 7 If you *r* in me and my words
Ro   13: 8 Let no debt *r* outstanding,
1Co 13:13 And now these three *r:* faith,
2Ti   2:13 he will *r* faithful,

REMAINS (REMAIN)

Ps 146: 6 the LORD, who *r* faithful forever.
Heb   7: 3 Son of God he *r* a priest forever.

REMEMBER (REMEMBERS REMEMBRANCE)

Ex   20: 8 "*R* the Sabbath day
1Ch 16:12 *R* the wonders he has done,
Ecc 12: 1 *R* your Creator
Jer 31:34 and will *r* their sins no more."
Gal   2:10 we should continue to *r* the poor,
Php   1: 3 I thank my God every time I *r* you.
Heb   8:12 and will *r* their sins no more."

REMEMBERS (REMEMBER)

Ps 103: 14 he *r* that we are dust.
    111:   5 he *r* his covenant forever.
Isa 43:25 and *r* your sins no more.

REMEMBRANCE (REMEMBER)

1Co 11:24 which is for you; do this in *r* of me

REMIND

Jn 14:26 will *r* you of everything I have said

REMOVED

Ps   30:11 you *r* my sackcloth and clothed me
    103: 12 so far has he *r* our transgressions
Jn   20: 1 and saw that the stone had been *r*

RENEW (RENEWED RENEWING)

Ps   51:10 and *r* a steadfast spirit within me.
Isa 40:31 will *r* their strength.

RENEWED (RENEW)

Ps 103:   5 that your youth is *r* like the eagle's.
2Co   4:16 yet inwardly we are being *r* day

RENEWING (RENEW)

Ro   12: 2 transformed by the *r* of your mind.

RENOUNCE (RENOUNCES)

Da   4:27 *R* your sins by doing what is right,

RENOUNCES (RENOUNCE)

Pr   28:13 confesses and *r* them finds

RENOWN

Isa 63:12 to gain for himself everlasting *r*,
Jer 32:20 have gained the *r* that is still yours.

REPAID (PAY)

Lk   14:14 you will be *r* at the resurrection
Col   3:25 Anyone who does wrong will be *r*

REPAY (PAY)

Dt   32:35 It is mine to avenge; I will *r*.
Ru   2:12 May the LORD *r* you
Ps 116: 12 How can I *r* the LORD
Ro   12:19 "It is mine to avenge; I will *r*,"
1Pe   3: 9 Do not *r* evil with evil

REPENT (REPENTANCE REPENTS)

Job 42: 6 and *r* in dust and ashes."
Jer 15:19 "If you *r*, I will restore you
Mt   4:17 "*R*, for the kingdom of heaven is
Lk   3: 3 unless you *r*, you too will all perish.
Ac   2:38 Peter replied, "*R* and be baptized,
     17:30 all people everywhere to *r*.

REPENTANCE (REPENT)

Lk   3: 8 Produce fruit in keeping with *r*.
      5:32 call the righteous, but sinners to *r*."
Ac   26:20 and prove their *r* by their deeds.
2Co   7:10 Godly sorrow brings *r* that leads

REPENTS (REPENT)

Lk   15:10 of God over one sinner who *r*."
     17: 3 rebuke him, and if he *r*, forgive him

REPROACH

1Ti   3: 2 Now the overseer must be above *r*,

REPUTATION

1Ti   3: 7 also have a good *r* with outsiders,

REQUESTS

Ps   20: 5 May the LORD grant all your *r*.
Php   4: 6 with thanksgiving, present your *r*

REQUIRE

Mic   6: 8 And what does the LORD *r* of you

RESCUE (RESCUES)

Da   6:20 been able to *r* you from the lions?"
2Pe   2: 9 how to *r* godly men from trials

RESCUES (RESCUE)

1Th   1:10 who *r* us from the coming wrath.

RESIST

Jas   4: 7 *R* the devil, and he will flee
1Pe   5: 9 *R* him, standing firm in the faith,

RESOLVED

Ps 17: 3 I have *r* that my mouth will not sin.
Da 1: 8 But Daniel *r* not to defile himself
1Co 2: 2 For I *r* to know nothing while I was

RESPECT (RESPECTABLE)

Lev 19: 3 " 'Each of you must *r* his mother
19:32 show *r* for the elderly and revere
Pr 11:16 A kindhearted woman gains *r*,
Mal 1: 6 where is the *r* due me?'' says
1Th 4:12 so that your daily life may win the *r*
5:12 to *r* those who work hard
1Ti 3: 4 children obey him with proper *r*.
1Pe 2:17 Show proper *r* to everyone:
3: 7 them with *r* as the weaker partner

RESPECTABLE* (RESPECT)

1Ti 3: 2 self-controlled, *r*, hospitable,

REST

Ex 31:15 the seventh day is a Sabbath of *r*,
Ps 91: 1 will *r* in the shadow
Jer 6:16 and you will find *r* for your souls.
Mt 11:28 and burdened, and I will give you *r*.

RESTITUTION

Ex 22: 3 "A thief must certainly make *r*,
Lev 6: 5 He must make *r* in full, add a fifth

RESTORE (RESTORES)

Ps 51:12 *R* to me the joy of your salvation
Gal 6: 1 are spiritual should *r* him gently.

RESTORES (RESTORE)

Ps 23: 3 he *r* my soul.

RESURRECTION

Mt 22:30 At the *r* people will neither marry
Lk 14:14 repaid at the *r* of the righteous.''
Jn 11:25 Jesus said to her, ''I am the *r*
Ro 1: 4 Son of God by his *r* from the dead:
1Co 15:12 some of you say that there is no *r*
Php 3:10 power of his *r* and the fellowship
Rev 20: 5 This is the first *r*.

RETRIBUTION

Jer 51:56 For the LORD is a God of *r*;

RETURN

2Ch 30: 9 If you *r* to the LORD, then your
Ne 1: 9 but if you *r* to me and obey my
Isa 55:11 It will not *r* to me empty,
Hos 6: 1 ''Come, let us *r* to the LORD.
Joel 2:12 ''*r* to me with all your heart,

REVEALED (REVELATION)

Dt 29:29 but the things *r* belong to us
Isa 40: 5 the glory of the LORD will be *r*,
Mt 11:25 and *r* them to little children.
Ro 1:17 a righteousness from God is *r*,
8:18 with the glory that will be *r* in us.

REVELATION (REVEALED)

Gal 1:12 I received it by *r* from Jesus Christ.
Rev 1: 1 *r* of Jesus Christ, which God gave

REVENGE (VENGEANCE)

Lev 19:18 " 'Do not seek *r* or bear a grudge

Ro 12:19 Do not take *r*, my friends,

REVERE (REVERENCE)

Ps 33: 8 let all the people of the world *r* him

REVERENCE (REVERE)

Lev 19:30 and have *r* for my sanctuary.
Ps 5: 7 in *r* will I bow down
Col 3:22 of heart and *r* for the Lord.
1Pe 3: 2 when they see the purity and *r*

REVIVE (REVIVING)

Ps 85: 6 Will you not *r* us again,
Isa 57:15 to *r* the spirit of the lowly

REVIVING (REVIVE)

Ps 19: 7 *r* the soul.

REWARD (REWARDED)

Ps 19:11 in keeping them there is great *r*.
127: 3 children a *r* from him.
Pr 19:17 he will *r* him for what he has done.
25:22 and the LORD will *r* you.
31:31 Give her the *r* she has earned,
Jer 17:10 to *r* a man according to his conduct
Mt 5:12 because great is your *r* in heaven,
6: 5 they have received their *r* in full.
16:27 and then he will *r* each person
1Co 3:14 built survives, he will receive his *r*.
Rev 22:12 I am coming soon! My *r* is with me

REWARDED (REWARD)

Ru 2:12 May you be richly *r* by the LORD,
Ps 18:24 The LORD has *r* me according
Pr 14:14 and the good man *r* for his.
1Co 3: 8 and each will be *r* according

RICH (RICHES)

Pr 23: 4 Do not wear yourself out to get *r*;
Jer 9:23 or the *r* man boast of his riches,
Mt 19:23 it is hard for a *r* man
2Co 6:10 yet making many *r*; having nothing
8: 9 he was *r*, yet for your sakes he
1Ti 6:17 Command those who are *r*

RICHES (RICH)

Ps 119: 14 as one rejoices in great *r*.
Pr 30: 8 give me neither poverty nor *r*,
Isa 10: 3 Where will you leave your *r*?
Ro 9:23 to make the *r* of his glory known
11:33 the depth of the *r* of the wisdom
Eph 2: 7 he might show the incomparable *r*
3: 8 to the Gentiles the unsearchable *r*
Col 1:27 among the Gentiles the glorious *r*

RID

Ge 21:10 ''Get *r* of that slave woman
1Co 5: 7 Get *r* of the old yeast that you may
Gal 4:30 ''Get *r* of the slave woman

RIGHT (RIGHTS)

Ge 18:25 the Judge of all the earth do *r*?''
Ex 15:26 and do what is *r* in his eyes,
Dt 5:32 do not turn aside to the *r*
Ps 16: 1 Because he is at my *r* hand,
19: 8 The precepts of the LORD are *r*,
63: 8 your *r* hand upholds me.

Ps 110: 1 "Sit at my *r* hand
Pr 4:27 Do not swerve to the *r* or the left;
14:12 There is a way that seems *r*
Isa 1:17 learn to do *r!*
Jer 23: 5 and do what is just and *r* in the land
Hos 14: 9 The ways of the LORD are *r;*
Mt 6: 3 know what your *r* hand is doing,
Jn 1:12 he gave the *r* to become children
Ro 9:21 Does not the potter have the *r*
12:17 careful to do what is *r* in the eyes
Eph 1:20 and seated him at his *r* hand
Php 4: 8 whatever is *r,* whatever is pure,
2Th 3:13 never tire of doing what is *r.*

RIGHTEOUS (RIGHTEOUSNESS)

Ps 34:15 The eyes of the LORD are on the *r*
37:25 yet I have never seen the *r* forsaken
119:137 *R* are you, O LORD,
143: 2 for no one living is *r* before you.
Pr 3:33 but he blesses the home of the *r.*
11:30 The fruit of the *r* is a tree of life,
18:10 the *r* run to it and are safe.
Isa 64: 6 and all our *r* acts are like filthy rags
Hab 2: 4 but the *r* will live by his faith—
Mt 5:45 rain on the *r* and the unrighteous.
9:13 For I have not come to call the *r,*
13:49 and separate the wicked from the *r*
25:46 to eternal punishment, but the *r*
Ro 1:17 as it is written: "The *r* will live
3:10 "There is no one *r,* not even one;
1Ti 1: 9 that law is made not for the *r*
1Pe 3:18 the *r* for the unrighteous,
1Jn 3: 7 does what is right is *r,* just as he is *r.*
Rev 19: 8 stands for the *r* acts of the saints.)

RIGHTEOUSNESS (RIGHTEOUS)

Ge 15: 6 and he credited it to him as *r.*
1Sa 26:23 LORD rewards every man for his *r*
Ps 9: 8 He will judge the world in *r;*
23: 3 He guides me in paths of *r*
45: 7 You love *r* and hate wickedness;
85:10 *r* and peace kiss each other.
89:14 *R* and justice are the foundation
111: 3 and his *r* endures forever.
Pr 14:34 *R* exalts a nation,
21:21 He who pursues *r* and love
Isa 5:16 will show himself holy by his *r.*
59:17 He put on *r* as his breastplate,
Eze 18:20 The *r* of the righteous man will be
Da 9:24 to bring in everlasting *r,*
12: 3 and those who lead many to *r,*
Mal 4: 2 the sun of *r* will rise with healing
Mt 5: 6 those who hunger and thirst for *r,*
5:20 unless your *r* surpasses that
6:33 But seek first his kingdom and his *r*
Ro 4: 3 and it was credited to him as *r."*
4: 9 faith was credited to him as *r.*
6:13 body to him as instruments of *r.*
2Co 5:21 that in him we might become the *r*
Gal 2:21 for if *r* could be gained
3: 6 and it was credited to him as *r."*
Eph 6:14 with the breastplate of *r* in place,
Php 3: 9 not having a *r* of my own that

2Ti 3:16 correcting and training in *r,*
4: 8 is in store for me the crown of *r,*
Heb 11: 7 became heir of the *r* that comes
2Pe 2:21 not to have known the way of *r,*

RIGHTS (RIGHT)

La 3:35 to deny a man his *r*
Gal 4: 5 that we might receive the full *r*

RISE (RAISED)

Isa 26:19 their bodies will *r.*
Mt 27:63 'After three days I will *r* again.'
Jn 5:29 those who have done good will *r*
1Th 4:16 and the dead in Christ will *r* first.

ROAD

Mt 7:13 and broad is the *r* that leads

ROBBERS

Jer 7:11 become a den of *r* to you?
Mk 15:27 They crucified two *r* with him,
Lk 19:46 but you have made it 'a den of *r.'* "
Jn 10: 8 came before me were thieves and *r,*

ROCK

Ps 18: 2 The LORD is my *r,* my fortress
40: 2 he set my feet on a *r*
Mt 7:24 man who built his house on the *r.*
16:18 and on this *r* I will build my church
Ro 9:33 and a *r* that makes them fall,
1Co 10: 4 the spiritual *r* that accompanied

ROD

Ps 23: 4 your *r* and your staff,
Pr 13:24 He who spares the *r* hates his son,
23:13 if you punish him with the *r,*

ROOM (ROOMS)

Mt 6: 6 But when you pray, go into your *r,*
Lk 2: 7 there was no *r* for them in the inn.
Jn 21:25 the whole world would not have *r*

ROOMS (ROOM)

Jn 14: 2 In my Father's house are many *r;*

ROOT

Isa 53: 2 and like a *r* out of dry ground.
1Ti 6:10 of money is a *r* of all kinds of evil.

ROYAL

Jas 2: 8 If you really keep the *r* law found
1Pe 2: 9 a *r* priesthood, a holy nation,

RUBBISH*

Php 3: 8 I consider them *r,* that I may gain

RUDE*

1Co 13: 5 It is not *r,* it is not self-seeking,

RUIN (RUINS)

Pr 18:24 many companions may come to *r,*
1Ti 6: 9 desires that plunge men into *r*

RUINS (RUIN)

Pr 19: 3 A man's own folly *r* his life,
2Ti 2:14 and only *r* those who listen.

RULE (RULER RULERS RULES)

1Sa 12:12 'No, we want a king to *r* over us'—
Ps 2: 9 You will *r* them with an iron
119:133 let no sin *r* over me.
Zec 9:10 His *r* will extend from sea to sea
Col 3:15 the peace of Christ *r* in your hearts,
Rev 2:27 He will *r* them with an iron scepter;

RULER (RULE)

Ps 8: 6 You made him *r* over the works
Eph 2: 2 of the *r* of the kingdom of the air,
1Ti 6:15 God, the blessed and only *R*,

RULERS (RULE)

Ps 2: 2 and the *r* gather together
Col 1:16 or powers or *r* or authorities;

RULES (RULE)

Ps103: 19 and his kingdom *r* over all.
Lk 22:26 one who *r* like the one who serves.
2Ti 2: 5 he competes according to the *r*.

RUMORS

Mt 24: 6 You will hear of wars and *r* of wars,

RUN (RAN)

Isa 40:31 they will *r* and not grow weary,
1Co 9:24 *R* in such a way as to get the prize.
Heb 12: 1 let us *r* with perseverance the race

RUST

Mt 6:19 where moth and *r* destroy,

RUTH*

Moabitess; widow who went to Bethlehem with mother-in-law Naomi (Ru 1). Gleaned in field of Boaz; shown favor (Ru 2). Proposed marriage to Boaz (Ru 3). Married (Ru 4:1-12); bore Obed, ancestor of David (Ru 4:13-22), Jesus (Mt 1:5).

SABBATH

Ex 20: 8 "Remember the *S* day
Dt 5:12 "Observe the *S* day
Col 2:16 a New Moon celebration or a *S* day

SACKCLOTH

Mt 11:21 would have repented long ago in *s*

SACRED

Mt 7: 6 "Do not give dogs what is *s*;
1Co 3:17 for God's temple is *s*, and you are

SACRIFICE (SACRIFICED SACRIFICES)

Ge 22: 2 *S* him there as a burnt offering
Ex 12:27 'It is the Passover *s* to the LORD,
1Sa 15:22 To obey is better than *s*,
Hos 6: 6 For I desire mercy, not *s*,
Mt 9:13 this means: 'I desire mercy, not *s*.'
Heb 9:26 away with sin by the *s* of himself.
13:15 offer to God a *s* of praise,
1Jn 2: 2 He is the atoning *s* for our sins,

SACRIFICED (SACRIFICE)

1Co 5: 7 our Passover lamb, has been *s*.
8: 1 Now about food *s* to idols:
Heb 9:28 so Christ was *s* once

SACRIFICES (SACRIFICE)

Ps 51:17 The *s* of God are a broken spirit;
Ro 12: 1 to offer your bodies as living *s*,

SADDUCEES

Mk 12:18 *S*, who say there is no resurrection,

SAFE (SAVE)

Ps 37: 3 in the land and enjoy *s* pasture.
Pr 18:10 the righteous run to it and are *s*.

SAFETY (SAVE)

Ps 4: 8 make me dwell in *s*.
1Th 5: 3 people are saying, "Peace and *s*,"

SAINTS

Ps116: 15 is the death of his *s*.
Ro 8:27 intercedes for the *s* in accordance
Eph 1:18 of his glorious inheritance in the *s*,
6:18 always keep on praying for all the *s*
Rev 5: 8 which are the prayers of the *s*.
19: 8 for the righteous acts of the *s*.)

SAKE

Ps 44:22 Yet for your *s* we face death all day
Php 3: 7 loss for the *s* of Christ.
Heb 11:26 He regarded disgrace for the *s*

SALT

Ge 19:26 and she became a pillar of *s*.
Mt 5:13 "You are the *s* of the earth.

SALVATION (SAVE)

Ex 15: 2 he has become my *s*.
1Ch 16:23 proclaim his *s* day after day.
Ps 27: 1 The LORD is my light and my *s*—
51:12 Restore to me the joy of your *s*
62: 1 He alone is my rock and my *s*;
85: 9 Surely his *s* is near those who fear
96: 2 proclaim his *s* day after day.
Isa 25: 9 let us rejoice and be glad in his *s*."
45:17 the LORD with an everlasting *s*;
51: 6 But my *s* will last forever,
59: 6 and the helmet of *s* on his head;
61:10 me with garments of *s*
Jnh 2: 9 *S* comes from the LORD."
Zec 9: 9 righteous and having *s*,
Lk 2:30 For my eyes have seen your *s*,
Jn 4:22 for *s* is from the Jews.
Ac 4:12 *S* is found in no one else,
13:47 that you may bring *s* to the ends
Ro 11:11 *s* has come to the Gentiles
2Co 7:10 brings repentance that leads to *s*
Eph 6:17 Take the helmet of *s* and the sword
Php 2:12 to work out your *s* with fear
1Th 5: 8 and the hope of *s* as a helmet.
2Ti 3:15 wise for *s* through faith
Heb 2: 3 escape if we ignore such a great *s*?
6: 9 case—things that accompany *s*.
1Pe 1:10 Concerning this *s*, the prophets,
2: 2 by it you may grow up in your *s*,

SAMARITAN

Lk 10:33 But a *S*, as he traveled, came where

SAMSON

Danite judge. Birth promised (Jdg 13). Married to Philistine (Jdg 14). Vengeance on Philistines (Jdg 15). Betrayed by Delilah (Jdg 16:1-22). Death (Jdg 16:23-31). Feats of strength: killed lion (Jdg 14:6), 30 Philistines (Jdg 14:19), 1,000 Philistines with jawbone (Jdg 15:13-17), carried off gates of Gaza (Jdg 16:3), pushed down temple of Dagon (Jdg 16:25-30).

SAMUEL

Ephraimite judge and prophet (Heb 11:32). Birth prayed for (1Sa 1:10-18). Dedicated to temple by Hannah (1Sa 1:21-28). Raised by Eli (1Sa 2:11, 18-26). Called as prophet (1Sa 3). Led Israel to victory over Philistines (1Sa 7). Asked by Israel for a king (1Sa 8). Anointed Saul as king (1Sa 9-10). Farewell speech (1Sa 12). Rebuked Saul for sacrifice (1Sa 13). Announced rejection of Saul (2Sa 15). Anointed David as king (1Sa 16). Protected David from Saul (1Sa 19:18-24). Death (1Sa 25:1). Returned from dead to condemn Saul (1Sa 28).

SANCTIFIED (SANCTIFY)

Ac 20:32 among all those who are *s*.
Ro 15:16 to God, *s* by the Holy Spirit.
1Co 6:11 But you were washed, you were *s*,
7:14 and the unbelieving wife has been *s*
Heb 10:29 blood of the covenant that *s* him,

SANCTIFY (SANCTIFIED SANCTIFYING)

1Th 5:23 *s* you through and through.

SANCTIFYING (SANCTIFY)

2Th 2:13 through the *s* work of the Spirit

SANCTUARY

Ex 25: 8 "Then have them make a *s* for me,

SAND

Ge 22:17 and as the *s* on the seashore.
Mt 7:26 man who built his house on *s*.

SANDALS

Ex 3: 5 off your *s*, for the place where you
Jos 5:15 off your *s*, for the place where you

SANG (SING)

Job 38: 7 while the morning stars *s* together
Rev 5: 9 And they *s* a new song:

SARAH

Wife of Abraham, originally named Sarai; barren (Ge 11:29-31; 1Pe 3:6). Taken by Pharaoh as Abraham's sister; returned (Ge 12:10-20). Gave Hagar to Abraham; sent her away in pregnancy (Ge 16). Name changed; Isaac promised (Ge 17: 15-21; 18:10-15; Heb 11:11). Taken by Abimelech as Abraham's sister; returned (Ge 20). Isaac born; Hagar and Ishmael sent away (Ge 21:1-21; Gal 4:21-31). Death (Ge 23).

SATAN

Job 1: 6 and *S* also came with them.
Zec 3: 2 said to *S*, "The LORD rebuke you,

Mk 4:15 *S* comes and takes away the word
2Co 11:14 for *S* himself masquerades
12: 7 a messenger of *S*, to torment me.
Rev 12: 9 serpent called the devil, or *S*,
20: 2 or *S*, and bound him for a thousand
20: 7 *S* will be released from his prison

SATISFIED (SATISFY)

Isa 53:11 he will see the light ,of life, and be *s*

SATISFIES (SATISFY)

Ps 103: 5 who *s* your desires with good things,

SATISFY (SATISFIED SATISFIES)

Isa 55: 2 and your labor on what does not *s*?

SAUL

1. Benjamite; anointed by Samuel as first king of Israel (1Sa 9-10). Defeated Ammonites (1Sa 11). Rebuked for offering sacrifice (1Sa 13:1-15). Defeated Philistines (1Sa 14). Rejected as king for failing to annihilate Amalekites (1Sa 15). Soothed from evil spirit by David (1Sa 16:14-23). Sent David against Goliath (1Sa 17). Jealousy and attempted murder of David (1Sa 18:1-11). Gave David Michal as wife (1Sa 18:12-30). Second attempt to kill David (1Sa 19). Anger at Jonathan (1Sa 20:26-34). Pursued David: killed priests at Nob (1Sa 22), went to Keilah and Ziph (1Sa 23), life spared by David at En Gedi (1Sa 24) and in his tent (1Sa 26). Rebuked by Samuel's spirit for consulting witch at Endor (1Sa 28). Wounded by Philistines; took his own life (1Sa 31; 1Ch 10).

2. See PAUL

SAVE (SAFE SAFETY SALVATION SAVED SAVIOR)

Isa 63: 1 mighty to *s*."
Da 3:17 the God we serve is able to *s* us
Zep 3:17 he is mighty to *s*.
Mt 1:21 he will *s* his people from their sins
16:25 wants to *s* his life will lose it,
Lk 19:10 to seek and to *s* what was lost."
Jn 3:17 but to *s* the world through him.
1Ti 1:15 came into the world to *s* sinners—
Jas 5:20 of his way will *s* him from death

SAVED (SAVE)

Ps 34: 6 he *s* him out of all his troubles.
Isa 45:22 "Turn to me and be *s*,
Joel 2:32 on the name of the LORD will be *s*;
Mk 13:13 firm to the end will be *s*.
16:16 believes and is baptized will be *s*,
Jn 10: 9 enters through me will be *s*.
Ac 4:12 to men by which we must be *s*."
16:30 do to be *s*?" They replied,
Ro 9:27 only the remnant will be *s*.
10: 9 him from the dead, you will be *s*.
1Co 3:15 will suffer loss; he himself will be *s*,
15: 2 By this gospel you are *s*,
Eph 2: 5 it is by grace you have been *s*.
2: 8 For it is by grace you have been *s*,
1Ti 2: 4 who wants all men to be *s*

SAVIOR (SAVE)

Ps   89:26 my God, the Rock my *S*.'
Isa   43:11 and apart from me there is no *s*.
Hos 13: 4 no *S* except me.
Lk   1:47 and my spirit rejoices in God my *S*,
         2:11 of David a *S* has been born to you;
Jn   4:42 know that this man really is the *S*
Eph   5:23 his body, of which he is the *S*.
1Ti   4:10 who is the *S* of all men,
Tit   2:10 about God our *S* attractive.
         2:13 appearing of our great God and *S*,
         3: 4 and love of God our *S* appeared,
1Jn   4:14 Son to be the *S* of the world.
Jude   :25 to the only God our *S* be glory,

SCALES

Lev   19:36 Use honest *s* and honest weights,
Da   5:27 You have been weighed on the *s*

SCAPEGOAT (GOAT)

Lev   16:10 by sending it into the desert as a *s*.

SCARLET

Isa   1:18 "Though your sins are like *s*,

SCATTERED

Jer   31:10 'He who *s* Israel will gather them
Ac   8: 4 who had been *s* preached the word

SCEPTER

Rev   19:15 "He will rule them with an iron *s*."

SCHEMES

2Co   2:11 For we are not unaware of his *s*.
Eph   6:11 stand against the devil's *s*.

SCOFFERS

2Pe   3: 3 that in the last days *s* will come,

SCORPION

Rev   9: 5 sting of a *s* when it strikes a man.

SCRIPTURE (SCRIPTURES)

Jn   10:35 and the *S* cannot be broken—
1Ti   4:13 yourself to the public reading of *S*,
2Ti   3:16 All *S* is God-breathed
2Pe   1:20 that no prophecy of *S* came about

SCRIPTURES (SCRIPTURE)

Lk   24:27 said in all the *S* concerning himself.
Jn   5:39 These are the *S* that testify about
Ac   17:11 examined the *S* every day to see

SCROLL

Eze   3: 1 eat what is before you, eat this *s*;

SEA

Ex   14:16 go through the *s* on dry ground.
Isa   57:20 the wicked are like the tossing *s*,
Mic   7:19 iniquities into the depths of the *s*.
Jas   1: 6 who doubts is like a wave of the *s*,
Rev   13: 1 I saw a beast coming out of the *s*.

SEAL (SEALS)

Jn   6:27 God the Father has placed his *s*
2Co   1:22 set his *s* of ownership on us,
Eph   1:13 you were marked in him with a *s*,

SEALS (SEAL)

Rev   5: 2 "Who is worthy to break the *s*
         6: 1 opened the first of the seven *s*.

SEARCH (SEARCHED SEARCHES SEARCHING)

Ps   4: 4 *s* your hearts and be silent.
      139: 23 *S* me, O God, and know my heart;
Pr   2: 4 and *s* for it as for hidden treasure,
Jer   17:10 "I the LORD *s* the heart
Eze 34:16 I will *s* for the lost and bring back
Lk   15: 8 and *s* carefully until she finds it?

SEARCHED (SEARCH)

Ps 139: 1 O LORD, you have *s* me

SEARCHES (SEARCH)

Ro   8:27 And he who *s* our hearts knows
1Co   2:10 The Spirit *s* all things,

SEARCHING (SEARCH)

Am   8:12 *s* for the word of the LORD,

SEARED

1Ti   4: 2 whose consciences have been *s*

SEASON

2Ti   4: 2 be prepared in *s* and out of *s*;

SEAT (SEATED SEATS)

Ps   1: 1 or sit in the *s* of mockers.
Da   7: 9 and the Ancient of Days took his *s*.
2Co   5:10 before the judgment *s* of Christ,

SEATED (SEAT)

Ps   47: 8 God is *s* on his holy throne.
Isa   6: 1 I saw the Lord *s* on a throne,
Col   3: 1 where Christ is *s* at the right hand

SEATS (SEAT)

Lk   11:43 you love the most important *s*

SECRET (SECRETS)

Dt   29:29 The *s* things belong
Jdg   16: 6 Tell me the *s* of your great strength
Ps   90: 8 our *s* sins in the light
Pr   11:13 but a trustworthy man keeps a *s*.
Mt   6: 4 so that your giving may be in *s*.
2Co   4: 2 we have renounced *s* and shameful
Php   4:12 I have learned the *s*

SECRETS (SECRET)

Ps   44:21 since he knows the *s* of the heart?
1Co 14:25 the *s* of his heart will be laid bare.

SECURE (SECURITY)

Ps 112: 8 His heart is *s*, he will have no fear;
Heb   6:19 an anchor for the soul, firm and *s*.

SECURITY (SECURE)

Job   31:24 or said to pure gold, 'You are my *s*,'

SEED (SEEDS)

Lk   8:11 of the parable: The *s* is the word
1Co   3: 6 I planted the *s*, Apollos watered it,
2Co   9:10 he who supplies *s* to the sower
Gal   3:29 then you are Abraham's *s*,
1Pe   1:23 not of perishable *s*,

SEEDS (SEED)
Jn 12:24 But if it dies, it produces many *s*.
Gal 3:16 Scripture does not say "and to *s*,"

SEEK (SEEKS SELF-SEEKING)
Dt 4:29 if from there you *s* the LORD your
1Ch 28: 9 If you *s* him, he will be found
2Ch 7:14 themselves and pray and *s* my face
Ps119: 10 I *s* you with all my heart;
Isa 55: 6 *S* the LORD while he may be
65: 1 found by those who did not *s* me.
Mt 6:33 But *s* first his kingdom
Lk 19:10 For the Son of Man came to *s*
Ro 10:20 found by those who did not *s* me;
1Co 7:27 you married? Do not *s* a divorce.

SEEKS (SEEK)
Jn 4:23 the kind of worshipers the Father *s*.

SEER
1Sa 9: 9 of today used to be called a *s*.)

SELF-CONTROL (CONTROL)
1Co 7: 5 you because of your lack of *s*.
Gal 5:23 faithfulness, gentleness and *s*.
2Pe 1: 6 and to knowledge, *s*; and to *s*,

SELF-CONTROLLED* (CONTROL)
1Th 5: 6 are asleep, but let us be alert and *s*.
5: 8 let us be *s*, putting on faith and love
1Ti 3: 2 *s*, respectable, hospitable,
Tit 1: 8 who is *s*, upright, holy
2: 2 worthy of respect, *s*, and sound
2: 5 to be *s* and pure, to be busy at home
2: 6 encourage the young men to be *s*.
2:12 to live *s*, upright and godly lives
1Pe 1:13 prepare your minds for action; be *s*;
4: 7 and *s* so that you can pray.
5: 8 Be *s* and alert.

SELF-INDULGENCE
Mt 23:25 inside they are full of greed and *s*.

SELF-SEEKING (SEEK)
1Co 13: 5 it is not *s*, it is not easily angered,

SELFISH*
Ps119: 36 and not toward *s* gain.
Pr 18: 1 An unfriendly man pursues *s* ends;
Gal 5:20 fits of rage, *s* ambition, dissensions,
Php 1:17 preach Christ out of *s* ambition,
2: 3 Do nothing out of *s* ambition
Jas 3:14 and *s* ambition in your hearts,
3:16 you have envy and *s* ambition,

SEND (SENDING SENT)
Isa 6: 8 *S* me!" He said, "Go and tell this
Mt 9:38 to *s* out workers into his harvest
Jn 16: 7 but if I go, I will *s* him to you.

SENDING (SEND)
Jn 20:21 Father has sent me, I am *s* you."

SENSES*
Lk 15:17 "When he came to his *s*, he said,
1Co 15:34 Come back to your *s* as you ought,
2Ti 2:26 and that they will come to their *s*

SENSUAL
Col 2:23 value in restraining *s* indulgence.

SENT (SEND)
Isa 55:11 achieve the purpose for which I *s* it.
Mt 10:40 me receives the one who *s* me.
Jn 4:34 "is to do the will of him who *s* me
Ro 10:15 can they preach unless they are *s*?
1Jn 4:10 but that he loved us and *s* his Son

SEPARATE (SEPARATED SEPARATES)
Mt 19: 6 has joined together, let man not *s*."
Ro 8:35 Who shall *s* us from the love
1Co 7:10 wife must not *s* from her husband.
2Co 6:17 and be *s*, says the Lord.

SEPARATED (SEPARATE)
Isa 59: 2 But your iniquities have *s*

SEPARATES (SEPARATE)
Pr 16:28 and a gossip *s* close friends.

SERPENT
Ge 3: 1 the *s* was more crafty than any
Rev 12: 9 that ancient *s* called the devil

SERVANT (SERVANTS)
1Sa 3:10 "Speak, for your *s* is listening."
Mt 20:26 great among you must be your *s*,
25:21 'Well done, good and faithful *s*!
Lk 16:13 "No *s* can serve two masters.
Php 2: 7 taking the very nature of a *s*,
2Ti 2:24 And the Lord's *s* must not quarrel;

SERVANTS (SERVANT)
Lk 17:10 should say, 'We are unworthy *s*;
Jn 15:15 longer call you *s*, because a servant

SERVE (SERVICE SERVING)
Dt 10:12 to *s* the LORD your God
Jos 22: 5 and to *s* him with all your heart
24:15 this day whom you will *s*,
Mt 4:10 Lord your God, and *s* him only.'"
6:24 "No one can *s* two masters.
20:28 but to *s*, and to give his life
Eph 6: 7 *S* wholeheartedly,

SERVICE (SERVE)
1Co 12: 5 There are different kinds of *s*,
Eph 4:12 God's people for works of *s*,

SERVING (SERVE)
Ro 12:11 your spiritual fervor, *s* the Lord.
Eph 6: 7 as if you were *s* the Lord, not men,
Col 3:24 It is the Lord Christ you are *s*.
2Ti 2: 4 No one *s* as a soldier gets involved

SEVEN (SEVENTH)
Ge 7: 2 Take with you *s* of every kind
Jos 6: 4 march around the city *s* times,
1Ki 19:18 Yet I reserve *s* thousand in Israel—
Pr 6:16 *s* that are detestable to him:
24:16 a righteous man falls *s* times,
Isa 4: 1 In that day *s* women
Da 9:25 comes, there will be *s* 'sevens,'
Mt 18:21 Up to *s* times?" Jesus answered,
Lk 11:26 takes *s* other spirits more wicked

Ro   11: 4 for myself *s* thousand who have not
Rev   1: 4 To the *s* churches in the province
       6: 1 opened the first of the *s* seals.
       8: 2 and to them were given *s* trumpets.
      10: 4 And when the *s* thunders spoke,
      15: 7 to the *s* angels *s* golden bowls filled

SEVENTH (SEVEN)
Ge   2: 2 By the *s* day God had finished
Ex   23:12 but on the *s* day do not work,

SEXUAL (SEXUALLY)
1Co   6:13 body is not meant for *s* immorality,
       6:18 Flee from *s* immorality.
      10: 8 should not commit *s* immorality,
Eph   5: 3 even a hint of *s* immorality,
1Th   4: 3 that you should avoid *s* immorality

SEXUALLY (SEXUAL)
1Co   5: 9 to associate with *s* immoral people
       6:18 he who sins *s* sins against his own

SHADOW
Ps   23: 4 through the valley of the *s* of death,
      36: 7 find refuge in the *s* of your wings.
Heb 10: 1 The law is only a *s*

SHALLUM
King of Israel (2Ki 15:10-16).

SHAME (ASHAMED)
Ps   34: 5 their faces are never covered with *s*
Pr   13:18 discipline comes to poverty and *s*,
Heb 12: 2 endured the cross, scorning its *s*,

SHARE (SHARED)
Ge   21:10 that slave woman's son will never *s*
Lk   3:11 "The man with two tunics should *s*
Gal   4:30 the slave woman's son will never *s*
       6: 6 in the word must *s* all good things
Eph   4:28 something to *s* with those in need.
1Ti   6:18 and to be generous and willing to *s*.
Heb 12:10 that we may *s* in his holiness.
      13:16 to do good and to *s* with others,

SHARED (SHARE)
Heb   2:14 he too *s* in their humanity so that

SHARON
SS   2: 1 I am a rose of *S*,

SHARPER*
Heb   4:12 *S* than any double-edged sword,

SHED (SHEDDING)
Ge   9: 6 by man shall his blood be *s*;
Col   1:20 through his blood, *s* on the cross.

SHEDDING (SHED)
Heb   9:22 without the *s* of blood there is no

SHEEP
Ps 100: 3 we are his people, the *s*
     119:176 I have strayed like a lost *s*.
Isa 53: 6 We all, like *s*, have gone astray,
Jer 50: 6 "My people have been lost *s*;
Eze 34:11 I myself will search for my *s*
Mt   9:36 helpless, like *s* without a shepherd.

Jn   10: 3 He calls his own *s* by name
      10:15 and I lay down my life for the *s*.
      10:27 My *s* listen to my voice; I know
      21:17 Jesus said, "Feed my *s*.
1Pe   2:25 For you were like *s* going astray,

SHELTER
Ps   61: 4 take refuge in the *s* of your wings.
      91: 1 in the *s* of the Most High

SHEM
Son of Noah (Ge 5:32; 6:10). Blessed (Ge 9:
26). Descendants (Ge 10:21-31; 11:10-32).

SHEPHERD (SHEPHERDS)
Ps   23: 1 LORD is my *s*, I shall not be in want.
Isa 40:11 He tends his flock like a *s*:
Jer 31:10 will watch over his flock like a *s*."
Eze 34:12 As a *s* looks after his scattered
Zec 11:17 "Woe to the worthless *s*,
Mt   9:36 and helpless, like sheep without a *s*.
Jn   10:11 The good *s* lays down his life
      10:16 there shall be one flock and one *s*.
1Pe   5: 4 And when the Chief *S* appears,

SHEPHERDS (SHEPHERD)
Jer 23: 1 "Woe to the *s* who are destroying
Lk   2: 8 there were *s* living out in the fields
Ac   20:28 Be *s* of the church of God,
1Pe   5: 2 Be *s* of God's flock that is

SHIELD
Ps   28: 7 LORD is my strength and my *s*;
Eph   6:16 to all this, take up the *s* of faith,

SHINE (SHONE)
Ps   4: 6 Let the light of your face *s* upon us,
      80: 1 between the cherubim, *s* forth
Isa 60: 1 "Arise, *s*, for your light has come,
Da   12: 3 are wise will *s* like the brightness
Mt   5:16 let your light *s* before men,
      13:43 the righteous will *s* like the sun
2Co   4: 6 made his light *s* in our hearts
Eph   5:14 and Christ will *s* on you."

SHIPWRECKED*
2Co 11:25 I was stoned, three times I was *s*,
1Ti   1:19 and so have *s* their faith.

SHONE (SHINE)
Mt   17: 2 His face *s* like the sun,
Lk   2: 9 glory of the Lord *s* around them,
Rev 21:11 It *s* with the glory of God,

SHORT
Isa 59: 1 of the LORD is not too *s* to save,
Ro   3:23 and fall *s* of the glory of God,

SHOULDERS
Isa   9: 6 and the government will be on his *s*
Lk   15: 5 he joyfully puts it on his *s*

SHOWED
1Jn   4: 9 This is how God *s* his love

SHREWD
Mt   10:16 Therefore be as *s* as snakes and

SHUN*

Job 28:28 and to *s* evil is understanding.' ''
Pr   3: 7 fear the LORD and *s* evil.

SICK

Pr 13:12 Hope deferred makes the heart *s*,
Mt   9:12 who need a doctor, but the *s*.
    25:36 I was *s* and you looked after me,
Jas   5:14 of you *s?* He should call the elders

SICKLE

Joel 3:13 Swing the *s*,

SIDE

Ps 91: 7 A thousand may fall at your *s*,
  124: 1 If the LORD had not been on our *s*
2Ti 4:17 But the Lord stood at my *s*

SIGHT

Ps 90: 4 For a thousand years in your *s*
  116: 15 Precious in the *s* of the LORD
2Co 5: 7 We live by faith, not by *s*.
1Pe 3: 4 which is of great worth in God's *s*.

SIGN (SIGNS)

Isa   7:14 the Lord himself will give you a *s;*

SIGNS (SIGN)

Mk 16:17 these *s* will accompany those who
Jn 20:30 Jesus did many other miraculous *s*

SILENT

Pr 17:28 a fool is thought wise if he keeps *s*,
Isa 53: 7 as a sheep before her shearers is *s*,
Hab 2:20 let all the earth be *s* before him.''
1Co 14:34 women should remain *s*
1Ti 2:12 over a man; she must be *s*.

SILVER

Pr 25:11 is like apples of gold in settings of *s*.
Hag 2: 8 'The *s* is mine and the gold is mine,'
1Co 3:12 *s*, costly stones, wood, hay or straw

SIMON

  1. See PETER.
  2. Apostle, called the Zealot (Mt 10:4; Mk 3:
18; Lk 6:15; Ac 1:13).
  3. Samaritan sorcerer (Ac 8:9-24).

**SIN (SINFUL SINNED SINNER
SINNERS SINNING SINS)**

Nu   5: 7 and must confess the *s* he has
  32:23 be sure that your *s* will find you
Dt 24:16 each is to die for his own *s*.
1Ki 8:46 for there is no one who does not *s*
2Ch 7:14 and will forgive their *s* and will heal
Ps   4: 4 In your anger do not *s;*
  32: 2 whose *s* the LORD does not count
  32: 5 Then I acknowledged my *s* to you
  51: 2 and cleanse me from my *s*.
  66:18 If I had cherished *s* in my heart,
  119: 11 that I might not *s* against you.
  119:133 let no *s* rule over me.
Isa   6: 7 is taken away and your *s* atoned
Mic 7:18 who pardons *s* and forgives
Mt 18: 6 little ones who believe in me to *s*,
Jn   1:29 who takes away the *s* of the world!

Jn   8:34 everyone who sins is a slave to *s*.
Ro   5:12 as *s* entered the world
  5:20 where *s* increased, grace increased
  6:11 count yourselves dead to *s*
  6:23 For the wages of *s* is death,
  14:23 that does not come from faith is *s*.
2Co 5:21 God made him who had no *s* to be *s*
Gal   6: 1 if someone is caught in a *s*,
Heb 9:26 to do away with *s* by the sacrifice
  11:25 the pleasures of *s* for a short time.
  12: 1 and the *s* that so easily entangles,
1Pe 2:22 ''He committed no *s*,
1Jn 1: 8 If we claim to be without *s*,
  3: 4 in fact, *s* is lawlessness.
  3: 5 And in him is no *s*.
  3: 9 born of God will continue to *s*,
  5:18 born of God does not continue to *s;*

SINCERE

Ro 12: 9 Love must be *s*.
Heb 10:22 near to God with a *s* heart

SINFUL (SIN)

Ps 51: 5 Surely I was *s* at birth
  51: 5 *s* from the time my mother
Ro   7: 5 we were controlled by the *s* nature,
  8: 4 not live according to the *s* nature
  8: 9 are controlled not by the *s* nature
Gal 5:19 The acts of the *s* nature are obvious
  5:24 Jesus have crucified the *s* nature
1Pe 2:11 abstain from *s* desires, which war

SING (SANG SINGING SONG SONGS)

Ps 30: 4 *S* to the LORD, you saints of his;
  47: 6 *S* praises to God, *s* praises;
  59:16 But I will *s* of your strength,
  89: 1 I will *s* of the LORD's great love
  101: 1 I will *s* of your love and justice;
Eph 5:19 *S* and make music in your heart

SINGING (SING)

Ps 63: 5 with *s* lips my mouth will praise
Ac 16:25 Silas were praying and *s* hymns

SINNED (SIN)

2Sa 12:13 ''I have *s* against the LORD.''
Job 1: 5 ''Perhaps my children have *s*
Ps 51: 4 Against you, you only, have I *s*
Da 9: 5 we have *s* and done wrong.
Mic 7: 9 Because I have *s* against him,
Lk 15:18 I have *s* against heaven
Ro   3:23 for all have *s* and fall short
1Jn 1:10 claim we have not *s*, we make him

SINNER (SIN)

Ecc 9:18 but one *s* destroys much good.
Lk 15: 7 in heaven over one *s* who repents
  18:13 'God, have mercy on me, a *s*.'
1Co 14:24 convinced by all that he is a *s*
Jas 5:20 Whoever turns a *s* from the error
1Pe 4:18 become of the ungodly and the *s?*''

SINNERS (SIN)

Ps   1: 1 or stand in the way of *s*
Pr 23:17 Do not let your heart envy *s*,

Mt	9:13	come to call the righteous, but s.''
Ro	5: 8	While we were still s, Christ died
1Ti	1:15	came into the world to save s—

SINNING (SIN)

Ex	20:20	be with you to keep you from s.''
1Co	15:34	stop s; for there are some who are
Heb	10:26	If we deliberately keep on s
1Jn	3: 6	No one who lives in him keeps on s
	3: 9	go on s, because he has been born

SINS (SIN)

2Ki	14: 6	each is to die for his own s.''
Ezr	9: 6	our s are higher than our heads
Ps	19:13	your servant also from willful s;
	32: 1	whose s are covered.
	103: 3	who forgives all your s
	130: 3	O Lord, kept a record of s,
Pr	28:13	who conceals his s does not
Isa	1:18	"Though your s are like scarlet,
	43:25	and remembers your s no more.
	59: 2	your s have hidden his face
Eze	18: 4	soul who s is the one who will die.
Mt	1:21	he will save his people from their s
	18:15	"If your brother s against you,
Lk	11: 4	Forgive us our s,
	17: 3	"If your brother s, rebuke him,
Ac	22:16	be baptized and wash your s away,
1Co	15: 3	died for our s according
Eph	2: 1	dead in your transgressions and s,
Col	2:13	us all our s, having canceled
Heb	1: 3	he had provided purification for s,
	7:27	He sacrificed for their s once for all
	8:12	and will remember their s no more
	10:12	for all time one sacrifice for s,
Jas	4:17	ought to do and doesn't do it, s.
	5:16	Therefore confess your s
	5:20	and cover over a multitude of s.
1Pe	2:24	He himself bore our s in his body
	3:18	For Christ died for s once for all,
1Jn	1: 9	If we confess our s, he is faithful
Rev	1: 5	has freed us from our s by his blood

SITS

Ps	99: 1	s enthroned between the cherubim,
Isa	40:22	He s enthroned above the circle
Mt	19:28	of Man s on his glorious throne,
Rev	4: 9	thanks to him who s on the throne

SKIN

Job	19:20	with only the s of my teeth.
	19:26	And after my s has been destroyed,
Jer	13:23	Can the Ethiopian change his s

SLAIN (SLAY)

Rev	5:12	"Worthy is the Lamb, who was s,

SLANDER (SLANDERED SLANDERERS)

Lev	19:16	" 'Do not go about spreading s
1Ti	5:14	the enemy no opportunity for s.
Tit	3: 2	to s no one, to be peaceable

SLANDERED (SLANDER)

1Co	4:13	when we are s, we answer kindly.

SLANDERERS (SLANDER)

Ro	1:30	They are gossips, s, God-haters,
1Co	6:10	nor the greedy nor drunkards nor s
Tit	2: 3	not to be s or addicted

SLAUGHTER

Isa	53: 7	he was led like a lamb to the s,

SLAVE (SLAVERY SLAVES)

Ge	21:10	"Get rid of that s woman
Mt	20:27	wants to be first must be your s—
Jn	8:34	everyone who sins is a s to sin.
1Co	12:13	whether Jews or Greeks, s or free
Gal	3:28	s nor free, male nor female,
	4:30	Get rid of the s woman and her son
2Pe	2:19	a man is a s to whatever has

SLAVERY (SLAVE)

Ro	6:19	parts of your body in s to impurity
Gal	4: 3	were in s under the basic principles

SLAVES (SLAVE)

Ro	6: 6	that we should no longer be s to sin
	6:22	and have become s to God,

SLAY (SLAIN)

Job	13:15	Though he s me, yet will I hope

SLEEP (SLEEPING)

Ps	121: 4	will neither slumber nor s.
1Co	15:51	We will not all s, but we will all be

SLEEPING (SLEEP)

Mk	13:36	suddenly, do not let him find you s.

SLOW

Ex	34: 6	and gracious God, s to anger,
Jas	1:19	s to speak and s to become angry,
2Pe	3: 9	The Lord is not s in keeping his

SLUGGARD

Pr	6: 6	Go to the ant, you s;
	20: 4	A s does not plow in season;

SLUMBER

Ps	121: 3	he who watches over you will not s;
Pr	6:10	A little sleep, a little s,
Ro	13:11	for you to wake up from your s,

SNAKE (SNAKES)

Nu	21: 8	"Make a s and put it up on a pole;
Pr	23:32	In the end it bites like a s
Jn	3:14	Moses lifted up the s in the desert,

SNAKES (SNAKE)

Mt	10:16	as shrewd as s and as innocent
Mk	16:18	they will pick up s with their hands;

SNATCH

Jn	10:28	no one can s them out of my hand.
Jude	:23	s others from the fire and save

SNOW

Ps	51: 7	and I will be whiter than s.

SOAR

Isa	40:31	They will s on wings like eagles;

SODOM

Ge	19:24	rained down burning sulfur on S

Ro 9:29 we would have become like *S*,

SOIL

Ge 4: 2 kept flocks, and Cain worked the *s*.
Mt 13:23 on good *s* is the man who hears

SOLDIER

1Co 9: 7 as a *s* at his own expense?
2Ti 2: 3 with us like a good *s* of Christ Jesus

SOLE

Dt 28:65 place for the *s* of your foot.
Isa 1: 6 From the *s* of your foot to the top

SOLID

2Ti 2:19 God's *s* foundation stands firm,
Heb 5:12 You need milk, not *s* food!

SOLOMON

Son of David by Bathsheba; king of Judah (2Sa 12:24; 1Ch 3:5, 10). Appointed king by David (1Ki 1); adversaries Adonijah, Joab, Shimei killed by Benaiah (1Ki 2). Asked for wisdom (1Ki 3; 2Ch 1). Judged between two prostitutes (1Ki 3:16-28). Built temple (1Ki 5-7; 2Ch 2-5); prayer of dedication (1Ki 8; 2Ch 6). Visited by Queen of Sheba (1Ki 10; 2Ch 9). Wives turned his heart from God (1Ki 11:1-13). Jeroboam rebelled against (1Ki 11:26-40). Death (1Ki 11:41-43; 2Ch 9:29-31).

Proverbs of (1Ki 4:32; Pr 1:1; 10:1; 25:1); psalms of (Ps 72; 127); song of (SS 1:1).

SON (SONS)

Ge 22: 2 "Take your *s*, your only *s*, Isaac,
Ex 11: 5 Every firstborn *s* in Egypt will die,
Dt 21:18 rebellious *s* who does not obey his
Ps 2: 7 He said to me, "You are my *S;*
    2:12 Kiss the *S*, lest he be angry
Pr 10: 1 A wise *s* brings joy to his father,
    13:24 He who spares the rod hates his *s*,
    29:17 Discipline your *s*, and he will give
Isa 7:14 with child and will give birth to a *s*,
Hos 11: 1 and out of Egypt I called my *s*.
Mt 2:15 "Out of Egypt I called my *s*."
    3:17 "This is my *S*, whom I love;
    11:27 one knows the *S* except the Father,
    16:16 "You are the Christ, the *S*
    17: 5 "This is my *S*, whom I love;
    20:18 and the *S* of Man will be betrayed
    24:30 They will see the *S* of Man coming
    24:44 the *S* of Man will come at an hour
    27:54 "Surely he was the *S* of God!"
    28:19 and of the *S* and of the Holy Spirit,
Mk 10:45 even the *S* of Man did not come
    14:62 you will see the *S* of Man sitting
Lk 9:58 but the *S* of Man has no place
    18: 8 when the *S* of Man comes,
    19:10 For the *S* of Man came to seek
Jn 3:14 so the *S* of Man must be lifted up,
    3:16 that he gave his one and only *S*,
    17: 1 Glorify your *S*, that your *S* may
Ro 8:29 conformed to the likeness of his *S*,
    8:32 He who did not spare his own *S*,
1Co 15:28 then the *S* himself will be made

Gal 4:30 rid of the slave woman and her *s*,
1Th 1:10 and to wait for his *S* from heaven,
Heb 1: 2 days he has spoken to us by his *S*,
    10:29 punished who has trampled the *S*
1Jn 1: 7 his *S*, purifies us from all sin.
    4: 9 only *S* into the world that we might
    5: 5 he who believes that Jesus is the *S*
    5:11 eternal life, and this life is in his *S*.

SONG (SING)

Ps 40: 3 He put a new *s* in my mouth,
    96: 1 Sing to the LORD a new *s;*
  149: 1 Sing to the LORD a new *s*,
Isa 49:13 burst into *s*, O mountains!
    55:12 will burst into *s* before you,
Rev 5: 9 And they sang a new *s:*
    15: 3 and sang the *s* of Moses the servant

SONGS (SING)

Job 35:10 who gives *s* in the night,
Ps 100: 2 come before him with joyful *s*.
Eph 5:19 with psalms, hymns and spiritual *s*.
Jas 5:13 Is anyone happy? Let him sing *s*

SONS (SON)

Joel 2:28 Your *s* and daughters will prophesy
Jn 12:36 so that you may become *s* of light."
Ro 8:14 by the Spirit of God are *s* of God.
2Co 6:18 and you will be my *s* and daughters
Gal 4: 5 we might receive the full rights of *s*.
Heb 12: 7 discipline; God is treating you as *s*.

SORROW (SORROWS)

Jer 31:12 and they will *s* no more.
Ro 9: 2 I have great *s* and unceasing
2Co 7:10 Godly *s* brings repentance that

SORROWS (SORROW)

Isa 53: 3 a man of *s*, and familiar

SOUL (SOULS)

Dt 6: 5 with all your *s* and with all your
    10:12 all your heart and with all your *s*,
Jos 22: 5 with all your heart and all your *s*."
Ps 23: 3 he restores my *s*.
    42: 1 so my *s* pants for you, O God.
    42:11 Why are you downcast, O my *s?*
  103: 1 Praise the LORD, O my *s;*
Pr 13:19 A longing fulfilled is sweet to the *s*,
Isa 55: 2 your *s* will delight in the richest
Mt 10:28 kill the body but cannot kill the *s*.
    16:26 yet forfeits his *s?* Or what can
    22:37 with all your *s* and with all your
Heb 4:12 even to dividing *s* and spirit,

SOULS (SOUL)

Pr 11:30 and he who wins *s* is wise.
Jer 6:16 and you will find rest for your *s*.
Mt 11:29 and you will find rest for your *s*.

SOUND

1Co 14: 8 if the trumpet does not *s* a clear call
    15:52 the trumpet will *s*, the dead will
2Ti 4: 3 men will not put up with *s* doctrine.

SOVEREIGN
Da   4:25 that the Most High is *s*

SOW (SOWS)
Job   4: 8 and those who *s* trouble reap it.
Mt   6:26 they do not *s* or reap or store away
2Pe   2:22 and, ''A *s* that is washed goes back

SOWS (SOW)
Pr   11:18 he who *s* righteousness reaps a sure
    22: 8 He who *s* wickedness reaps trouble
2Co   9: 6 Whoever *s* sparingly will
Gal   6: 7 A man reaps what he *s*.

SPARE (SPARES)
Ro   8:32 He who did not *s* his own Son,
    11:21 natural branches, he will not *s* you

SPARES (SPARE)
Pr   13:24 He who *s* the rod hates his son,

SPEARS
Isa   2: 4 and their *s* into pruning hooks.
Joel   3:10 and your pruning hooks into *s*.
Mic   4: 3 and their *s* into pruning hooks.

SPECTACLE
1Co   4: 9 We have been made a *s*
Col   2:15 he made a public *s* of them,

SPIN
Mt   6:28 They do not labor or *s*.

SPIRIT (SPIRIT'S SPIRITS SPIRITUAL SPIRITUALLY)
Ge   1: 2 and the *S* of God was hovering
    6: 3 ''My *S* will not contend
2Ki   2: 9 inherit a double portion of your *s*,''
Job   33: 4 The *S* of God has made me;
Ps   31: 5 Into your hands I commit my *s*;
    51:10 and renew a steadfast *s* within me.
    51:11 or take your Holy *S* from me.
    51:17 sacrifices of God are a broken *s*;
    139: 7 Where can I go from your *S*?
Isa   57:15 him who is contrite and lowly in *s*,
    63:10 and grieved his Holy *S*.
Eze   11:19 an undivided heart and put a new *s*
    36:26 you a new heart and put a new *s*
Joel   2:28 I will pour out my *S* on all people.
Zec   4: 6 but by my *S*,' says the LORD
Mt   1:18 to be with child through the Holy *S*
    3:11 will baptize you with the Holy *S*
    3:16 he saw the *S* of God descending
    4: 1 led by the *S* into the desert
    5: 3 saying: ''Blessed are the poor in *s*,
    26:41 *s* is willing, but the body is weak.''
    28:19 and of the Son and of the Holy *S*,
Lk   1:80 child grew and became strong in *s*;
    11:13 Father in heaven give the Holy *S*
Jn   4:24 God is *s*, and his worshipers must
    7:39 Up to that time the *S* had not been
    14:26 But the Counselor, the Holy *S*,
    16:13 But when he, the *S* of truth, comes,
    20:22 and said, ''Receive the Holy *S*.
Ac   1: 5 will be baptized with the Holy *S*.''
    2: 4 of them were filled with the Holy *S*

    2:38 will receive the gift of the Holy *S*.
    6: 3 who are known to be full of the *S*
    19: 2 ''Did you receive the Holy *S*
Ro   8: 9 And if anyone does not have the *S*
    8:26 the *S* helps us in our weakness.
1Co   2:10 God has revealed it to us by his *S*.
    2:14 man without the *S* does not accept
    6:19 body is a temple of the Holy *S*,
    12:13 baptized by one *S* into one body—
2Co   3: 6 the letter kills, but the *S* gives life.
    5: 5 and has given us the *S* as a deposit,
Gal   5:16 by the *S*, and you will not gratify
    5:22 But the fruit of the *S* is love, joy,
    5:25 let us keep in step with the *S*.
Eph   1:13 with a seal, the promised Holy *S*,
    4:30 do not grieve the Holy *S* of God,
    5:18 Instead, be filled with the *S*.
    6:17 of salvation and the sword of the *S*,
2Th   2:13 the sanctifying work of the *S*
Heb   4:12 even to dividing soul and *s*,
1Pe   3: 4 beauty of a gentle and quiet *s*,
2Pe   1:21 carried along by the Holy *S*.
1Jn   4: 1 Dear friends, do not believe every *s*

SPIRIT'S (SPIRIT)
1Th   5:19 not put out the *S* fire; do not treat

SPIRITS (SPIRIT)
1Co   12:10 to another distinguishing between *s*,
    14:32 The *s* of prophets are subject
1Jn   4: 1 test the *s* to see whether they are

SPIRITUAL (SPIRIT)
Ro   12: 1 this is your *s* act of worship.
    12:11 but keep your *s* fervor, serving
1Co   2:13 expressing *s* truths in *s* words.
    3: 1 I could not address you as *s* but
    12: 1 Now about *s* gifts, brothers,
    14: 1 of love and eagerly desire *s* gifts,
    15:44 a natural body, it is raised a *s* body.
Gal   6: 1 you who are *s* should restore him
Eph   1: 3 with every *s* blessing in Christ.
    5:19 with psalms, hymns and *s* songs.
    6:12 and against the *s* forces of evil
1Pe   2: 2 newborn babies, crave pure *s* milk,
    2: 5 are being built into a *s* house

SPIRITUALLY (SPIRIT)
1Co   2:14 because they are *s* discerned.

SPLENDOR
1Ch   16:29 the LORD in the *s* of his holiness.
    29:11 the glory and the majesty and the *s*,
Job   37:22 of the north he comes in golden *s*;
Ps   29: 2 in the *s* of his holiness.
    45: 3 clothe yourself with *s* and majesty.
    96: 6 *S* and majesty are before him;
    96: 9 in the *s* of his holiness;
    104: 1 you are clothed with *s* and majesty.
    145: 5 of the glorious *s* of your majesty,
Isa   61: 3 the LORD for the display of his *s*.
    63: 1 Who is this, robed in *s*,
Lk   9:31 appeared in glorious *s*, talking
2Th   2: 8 and destroy by the *s* of his coming.

SPOIL
Ps119:162 like one who finds great *s*.

SPOTLESS
2Pe 3:14 make every effort to be found *s*,

SPREAD (SPREADING)
Ac 12:24 of God continued to increase and *s*.
19:20 the word of the Lord *s* widely

SPREADING (SPREAD)
1Th 3: 2 God's fellow worker in *s* the gospel

SPRING
Jer 2:13 the *s* of living water,
Jn 4:14 in him a *s* of water welling up
Jas 3:12 can a salt *s* produce fresh water.

SPUR*
Heb 10:24 how we may *s* one another

SPURNS*
Pr 15: 5 A fool *s* his father's discipline,

STAFF
Ps 23: 4 your rod and your *s*,

STAKES
Isa 54: 2 strengthen your *s*.

STAND (STANDING STANDS)
Ex 14:13 *S* firm and you will see
2Ch 20:17 *s* firm and see the deliverance
Ps 1: 5 Therefore the wicked will not *s*
40: 2 and gave me a firm place to *s*.
119:120 I *s* in awe of your laws.
Eze 22:30 *s* before me in the gap on behalf
Zec 14: 4 On that day his feet will *s*
Mt 12:25 divided against itself will not *s*.
Ro 14:10 we will all *s* before God's judgment
1Co 10:13 out so that you can *s* up under it.
15:58 Therefore, my dear brothers, *s* firm
Eph 6:14 *S* firm then, with the belt
2Th 2:15 *s* firm and hold to the teachings we
Jas 5: 8 You too, be patient and *s* firm,
Rev 3:20 Here I am! I *s* at the door

STANDING (STAND)
Ex 3: 5 where you are *s* is holy ground."
Jos 5:15 the place where you are *s* is holy."
1Pe 5: 9 Resist him, *s* firm in the faith,

STANDS (STAND)
Ps 89: 2 that your love *s* firm forever,
119: 89 it *s* firm in the heavens.
Mt 10:22 but he who *s* firm to the end will be
2Ti 2:19 God's solid foundation *s* firm,
1Pe 1:25 but the word of the Lord *s* forever

STAR (STARS)
Nu 24:17 A *s* will come out of Jacob;
Rev 22:16 and the bright Morning *S*."

STARS (STAR)
Da 12: 3 like the *s* for ever and ever.
Php 2:15 in which you shine like *s*

STATURE
Lk 2:52 And Jesus grew in wisdom and *s*,

STEADFAST
Ps 51:10 and renew a *s* spirit within me.
Isa 26: 3 him whose mind is *s*,
1Pe 5:10 and make you strong, firm and *s*.

STEAL
Ex 20:15 "You shall not *s*.
Mt 19:18 do not *s*, do not give false
Eph 4:28 has been stealing must *s* no longer,

STEP (STEPS)
Gal 5:25 let us keep in *s* with the Spirit.

STEPS (STEP)
Pr 16: 9 but the LORD determines his *s*.
Jer 10:23 it is not for man to direct his *s*.
1Pe 2:21 that you should follow in his *s*.

STICKS
Pr 18:24 there is a friend who *s* closer

STIFF-NECKED
Ex 34: 9 Although this is a *s* people,

STILL
Ps 46:10 "Be *s*, and know that I am God;
Zec 2:13 Be *s* before the LORD, all mankind

STIRS
Pr 6:19 and a man who *s* up dissension
10:12 Hatred *s* up dissension,
15: 1 but a harsh word *s* up anger.
15:18 hot-tempered man *s* up dissension,
16:28 A perverse man *s* up dissension,
28:25 A greedy man *s* up dissension,
29:22 An angry man *s* up dissension,

STONE (CAPSTONE CORNERSTONE MILLSTONE)
1Sa 17:50 the Philistine with a sling and a *s;*
Isa 8:14 a *s* that causes men to stumble
Eze 11:19 remove from them their heart of *s*
Mk 16: 3 "Who will roll the *s* away
Lk 4: 3 tell this *s* to become bread."
Jn 8: 7 the first to throw a *s* at her."
2Co 3: 3 not on tablets of *s* but on tablets

STOOP
2Sa 22:36 you *s* down to make me great.

STORE
Pr 10:14 Wise men *s* up knowledge,
Mt 6:19 not *s* up for yourselves treasures

STOREHOUSE (HOUSE)
Mal 3:10 Bring the whole tithe into the *s*,

STRAIGHT
Pr 3: 6 and he will make your paths *s*.
4:25 Let your eyes look *s* ahead,
15:21 of understanding keeps a *s* course.
Jn 1:23 'Make *s* the way for the Lord.' "

STRAIN
Mt 23:24 You *s* out a gnat but swallow

STRANGER (STRANGERS)
Mt 25:35 I was a *s* and you invited me in,
Jn 10: 5 But they will never follow a *s;*

STRANGERS (STRANGER)
1Pe 2:11 as aliens and *s* in the world,

STREAMS
Ps 1: 3 He is like a tree planted by *s*
46: 4 is a river whose *s* make glad
Ecc 1: 7 All *s* flow into the sea,
Jn 7:38 *s* of living water will flow

STRENGTH (STRONG)
Ex 15: 2 The LORD is my *s* and my song;
Dt 6: 5 all your soul and with all your *s.*
2Sa 22:33 It is God who arms me with *s*
Ne 8:10 for the joy of the LORD is your *s.''*
Ps 28: 7 The LORD is my *s* and my shield;
46: 1 God is our refuge and *s,*
96: 7 ascribe to the LORD glory and *s.*
118: 14 The LORD is my *s* and my song;
147: 10 not in the *s* of the horse,
Isa 40:31 will renew their *s.*
Mk 12:30 all your mind and with all your *s.'*
1Co 1:25 of God is stronger than man's *s.*
Php 4:13 through him who gives me *s.*
1Pe 4:11 it with the *s* God provides,

STRENGTHEN (STRONG)
2Ch 16: 9 to *s* those whose hearts are fully
Ps119: 28 *s* me according to your word.
Isa 35: 3 *S* the feeble hands,
41:10 I will *s* you and help you;
Eph 3:16 of his glorious riches he may *s* you
2Th 2:17 and *s* you in every good deed
Heb 12:12 *s* your feeble arms and weak knees.

STRENGTHENING (STRONG)
1Co 14:26 done for the *s* of the church.

STRIFE
Pr 20: 3 It is to a man's honor to avoid *s,*
22:10 out the mocker, and out goes *s;*

STRIKE (STRIKES)
Ge 3:15 and you will *s* his heel.''
Zec 13: 7 *''S* the shepherd,
Mt 26:31 '' 'I will *s* the shepherd,

STRIKES (STRIKE)
Mt 5:39 If someone *s* you on the right

STRONG (STRENGTH STRENGTHEN STRENGTHENING)
Dt 31: 6 Be *s* and courageous.
1Ki 2: 2 ''So be *s,* show yourself a man,
Pr 18:10 The name of the LORD is a *s* tower
31:17 her arms are *s* for her tasks.
SS 8: 6 for love is as *s* as death,
Lk 2:40 And the child grew and became *s;*
Ro 15: 1 We who are *s* ought to bear
1Co 1:27 things of the world to shame the *s.*
16:13 in the faith; be men of courage; be *s*
2Co 12:10 For when I am weak, then I am *s.*
Eph 6:10 be *s* in the Lord and in his mighty

STRUGGLE
Ro 15:30 me in my *s* by praying to God
Eph 6:12 For our *s* is not against flesh

Heb 12: 4 In your *s* against sin, you have not

STUDY
Ezr 7:10 Ezra had devoted himself to the *s*
Ecc 12:12 and much *s* wearies the body.
Jn 5:39 You diligently *s* the Scriptures

STUMBLE (STUMBLING)
Ps 37:24 though he *s,* he will not fall,
119:165 and nothing can make them *s.*
Isa 8:14 a stone that causes men to *s*
Jer 31: 9 a level path where they will not *s,*
Eze 7:19 for it has made them *s* into sin.
1Co 10:32 Do not cause anyone to *s,*
1Pe 2: 8 and, ''A stone that causes men to *s*

STUMBLING (STUMBLE)
Ro 14:13 up your mind not to put any *s* block
1Co 8: 9 freedom does not become a *s* block
2Co 6: 3 We put no *s* block in anyone's path,

SUBDUE
Ge 1:28 in number; fill the earth and *s* it.

SUBJECT (SUBJECTED)
1Co 14:32 of prophets are *s* to the control
15:28 then the Son himself will be made *s*
Tit 2: 5 and to be *s* to their husbands,
2: 9 slaves to be *s* to their masters
3: 1 Remind the people to be *s* to rulers

SUBJECTED (SUBJECT)
Ro 8:20 For the creation was *s*

SUBMISSION (SUBMIT)
1Co 14:34 but must be in *s,* as the Law says.
1Ti 2:11 learn in quietness and full *s.*

SUBMISSIVE (SUBMIT)
Jas 3:17 then peace-loving, considerate, *s,*
1Pe 3: 1 in the same way be *s*
5: 5 in the same way be *s*

SUBMIT (SUBMISSION SUBMISSIVE SUBMITS)
Ro 13: 1 Everyone must *s* himself
13: 5 necessary to *s* to the authorities,
1Co 16:16 to *s* to such as these
Eph 5:21 *S* to one another out of reverence
Col 3:18 Wives, *s* to your husbands,
Heb 12: 9 How much more should we *s*
13:17 Obey your leaders and *s*
Jas 4: 7 *S* yourselves, then, to God.
1Pe 2:18 *s* yourselves to your masters

SUBMITS* (SUBMIT)
Eph 5:24 Now as the church *s* to Christ,

SUCCESSFUL
Jos 1: 7 that you may be *s* wherever you go.
2Ki 18: 7 he was *s* in whatever he undertook.
2Ch 20:20 in his prophets and you will be *s.''*

SUFFER (SUFFERED SUFFERING SUFFERINGS SUFFERS)
Isa 53:10 to crush him and cause him to *s,*
Mk 8:31 the Son of Man must *s* many things
Lk 24:26 the Christ have to *s* these things

Lk   24:46 The Christ will *s* and rise
Php   1:29 to *s* for him, since you are going
1Pe   4:16 However, if you *s* as a Christian,

SUFFERED (SUFFER)
Heb   2: 9 and honor because he *s* death,
         2:18 Because he himself *s*
1Pe   2:21 Christ *s* for you, leaving you

SUFFERING (SUFFER)
Isa   53: 3 of sorrows, and familiar with *s*.
Ac   5:41 worthy of *s* disgrace for the Name.
2Ti   1: 8 But join with me in *s* for the gospel,
Heb   2:10 of their salvation perfect through *s*.

SUFFERINGS (SUFFER)
Ro   8:17 share in his *s* in order that we may
         8:18 that our present *s* are not worth
2Co   1: 5 as the *s* of Christ flow
Php   3:10 the fellowship of sharing in his *s*,

SUFFERS (SUFFER)
Pr   13:20 but a companion of fools *s* harm.
1Co 12:26 If one part *s*, every part *s* with it;

SUFFICIENT
2Co 12: 9 said to me, "My grace is *s* for you,

SUITABLE
Ge   2:18 I will make a helper *s* for him."

SUN
Ecc   1: 9 there is nothing new under the *s*.
Mal   4: 2 the *s* of righteousness will rise
Mt   5:45 He causes his *s* to rise on the evil
        17: 2 His face shone like the *s*,
Rev   1:16 His face was like the *s* shining
        21:23 The city does not need the *s*

SUPERIOR
Heb   1: 4 he became as much *s* to the angels
         8: 6 ministry Jesus has received is as *s*

SUPERVISION
Gal   3:25 longer under the *s* of the law.

SUPREMACY* (SUPREME)
Col   1:18 in everything he might have the *s*.

SUPREME (SUPREMACY)
Pr   4: 7 Wisdom is *s;* therefore get wisdom.

SURE
Nu   32:23 you may be *s* that your sin will find
Dt   6:17 Be *s* to keep the commands
        14:22 Be *s* to set aside a tenth
Isa   28:16 cornerstone for a *s* foundation;
Heb 11: 1 faith is being *s* of what we hope for
2Pe   1:10 to make your calling and election *s*.

SURPASS* (SURPASSES SURPASSING)
Pr   31:29 but you *s* them all."

SURPASSES (SURPASS)
Mt   5:20 unless your righteousness *s* that
Eph   3:19 to know this love that *s* knowledge

SURPASSING* (SURPASS)
Ps 150:   2 praise him for his *s* greatness.

2Co   3:10 in comparison with the *s* glory.
         9:14 of the *s* grace God has given you.
Php   3: 8 the *s* greatness of knowing Christ

SURROUNDED
Heb 12: 1 since we are *s* by such a great cloud

SUSPENDS*
Job 26: 7 he *s* the earth over nothing.

SUSTAINING* (SUSTAINS)
Heb   1: 3 *s* all things by his powerful word.

SUSTAINS (SUSTAINING)
Ps   18:35 and your right hand *s* me;
        146:   9 and *s* the fatherless and the widow,
        147:   6 The LORD *s* the humble
Isa   50: 4 to know the word that *s* the weary.

SWALLOWED
1Co 15:54 "Death has been *s* up in victory."
2Co   5: 4 so that what is mortal may be *s* up

SWEAR
Mt   5:34 Do not *s* at all: either by heaven,

SWORD (SWORDS)
Ps   45: 3 Gird your *s* upon your side,
Pr   12:18 Reckless words pierce like a *s*,
Mt   10:34 come to bring peace, but a *s*.
        26:52 all who draw the *s* will die by the *s*.
Lk   2:35 a *s* will pierce your own soul too."
Ro   13: 4 for he does not bear the *s*
Eph   6:17 of salvation and the *s* of the Spirit,
Heb   4:12 Sharper than any double-edged *s*,
Rev   1:16 came a sharp double-edged *s*.

SWORDS (SWORD)
Isa   2: 4 They will beat their *s*
Joel 3:10 Beat your plowshares into *s*

SYMPATHETIC*
1Pe   3: 8 in harmony with one another; be *s*,

SYNAGOGUE
Lk   4:16 the Sabbath day he went into the *s*,
Ac   17: 2 custom was, Paul went into the *s*,

TABERNACLE
Ex   40:34 the glory of the LORD filled the *t*.

TABLE (TABLES)
Ps   23: 5 You prepare a *t* before me

TABLES (TABLE)
Ac   6: 2 word of God in order to wait on *t*.

TABLET (TABLETS)
Pr   3: 3 write them on the *t* of your heart.
         7: 3 write them on the *t* of your heart.

TABLETS (TABLET)
Ex   31:18 he gave him the two *t*
Dt   10: 5 and put the *t* in the ark I had made,
2Co   3: 3 not on *t* of stone but on *t*

TAKE (TAKEN TAKES TAKING TOOK)
Dt   12:32 do not add to it or *t* away from it.
        31:26 "*T* this Book of the Law
Job 23:10 But he knows the way that I *t;*

TAKEN

Ps 49:17 for he will *t* nothing with him
51:11 or *t* your Holy Spirit from me.
Mt 10:38 anyone who does not *t* his cross
11:29 *T* my yoke upon you and learn
16:24 deny himself and *t* up his cross

TAKEN (TAKE)

Lev 6: 4 must return what he has stolen or *t*
Isa 6: 7 your guilt is *t* away and your sin
Mt 24:40 one will be *t* and the other left.
Mk 16:19 he was *t* up into heaven
1Ti 3:16 was *t* up in glory.

TAKES (TAKE)

1Ki 20:11 should not boast like one who *t* it
Ps 5: 4 You are not a God who *t* pleasure
Jn 1:29 who *t* away the sin of the world!
Rev 22:19 And if anyone *t* words away

TAKING (TAKE)

Ac 15:14 by *t* from the Gentiles a people
Php 2: 7 *t* the very nature of a servant,

TALENT

Mt 25:15 to another one *t*, each according

TAME*

Jas 3: 8 but no man can *t* the tongue.

TASK

Mk 13:34 each with his assigned *t*,
Ac 20:24 complete the *t* the Lord Jesus has
1Co 3: 5 the Lord has assigned to each his *t*.
2Co 2:16 And who is equal to such a *t?*

TASTE (TASTED)

Ps 34: 8 *T* and see that the LORD is good;
Col 2:21 Do not *t!* Do not touch!''?
Heb 2: 9 the grace of God he might *t* death

TASTED (TASTE)

1Pe 2: 3 now that you have *t* that the Lord

TAUGHT (TEACH)

Mt 7:29 he *t* as one who had authority,
1Co 2:13 but in words *t* by the Spirit,
Gal 1:12 nor was I *t* it; rather, I received it

TAXES

Mt 22:17 Is it right to pay *t* to Caesar or not
Ro 13: 7 If you owe *t*, pay *t;* if revenue,

TEACH (TAUGHT TEACHER
TEACHERS TEACHES TEACHING)

Ex 33:13 *t* me your ways so I may know you
Dt 4: 9 *T* them to your children
8: 3 to *t* you that man does not live
11:19 *T* them to your children, talking
1Sa 12:23 I will *t* you the way that is good
Ps 32: 8 *t* you in the way you should go;
51:13 I will *t* transgressors your ways,
90:12 *T* us to number our days aright,
143: 10 *T* me to do your will,
Jer 31:34 No longer will a man *t* his neighbor
Lk 11: 1 said to him, ''Lord, *t* us to pray,
Jn 14:26 will *t* you all things and will remind
1Ti 2:12 I do not permit a woman to *t*

1Ti 3: 2 respectable, hospitable, able to *t*,
Tit 2: 1 You must *t* what is in accord
Heb 8:11 No longer will a man *t* his neighbor
Jas 3: 1 know that we who *t* will be judged
1Jn 2:27 you do not need anyone to *t* you.

TEACHER (TEACH)

Mt 10:24 ''A student is not above his *t*,
Jn 13:14 and *T*, have washed your feet,

TEACHERS (TEACH)

1Co 12:28 third *t*, then workers of miracles,
Eph 4:11 and some to be pastors and *t*,
Heb 5:12 by this time you ought to be *t*,

TEACHES (TEACH)

1Ti 6: 3 If anyone *t* false doctrines

TEACHING (TEACH)

Pr 1: 8 and do not forsake your mother's *t*.
Mt 28:20 *t* them to obey everything I have
Jn 7:17 whether my *t* comes from God or
14:23 loves me, he will obey my *t*.
1Ti 4:13 of Scripture, to preaching and to *t*.
2Ti 3:16 is God-breathed and is useful for *t*,
Tit 2: 7 In your *t* show integrity,

TEAR (TEARS)

Rev 7:17 God will wipe away every *t*

TEARS (TEAR)

Ps 126: 5 Those who sow in *t*
Php 3:18 and now say again even with *t*,

TEETH (TOOTH)

Mt 8:12 will be weeping and gnashing of *t*.''

TEMPERATE*

1Ti 3: 2 *t*, self-controlled, respectable,
3:11 not malicious talkers but *t*
Tit 2: 2 Teach the older men to be *t*,

TEMPEST

Ps 55: 8 far from the *t* and storm.''

TEMPLE (TEMPLES)

1Ki 8:27 How much less this *t* I have built!
Hab 2:20 But the LORD is in his holy *t*;
1Co 3:16 that you yourselves are God's *t*
6:19 you not know that your body is a *t*
2Co 6:16 For we are the *t* of the living God.

TEMPLES (TEMPLE)

Ac 17:24 does not live in *t* built by hands.

TEMPT (TEMPTATION TEMPTED)

1Co 7: 5 again so that Satan will not *t* you

TEMPTATION (TEMPT)

Mt 6:13 And lead us not into *t*,
26:41 pray so that you will not fall into *t*.
1Co 10:13 No *t* has seized you except what is

TEMPTED (TEMPT)

Mt 4: 1 into the desert to be *t* by the devil.
1Co 10:13 he will not let you be *t*
Heb 2:18 he himself suffered when he was *t*,
4:15 but we have one who has been *t*
Jas 1:13 For God cannot be *t* by evil,

TEN (TENTH TITHE TITHES)
Ex   34:28   covenant—the *T* Commandments.
Ps   91: 7   *t* thousand at your right hand,
Mt   25:28   it to the one who has the *t* talents.
Lk   15: 8   suppose a woman has *t* silver coins

TENTH (TEN)
Dt   14:22   Be sure to set aside a *t*

TERRIBLE (TERROR)
2Ti   3: 1   There will be *t* times

TERROR (TERRIBLE)
Ps   91: 5   You will not fear the *t* of night,
Lk   21:26   Men will faint from *t*, apprehensive
Ro   13: 3   For rulers hold no *t*

TEST (TESTED TESTS)
Dt   6:16   Do not *t* the LORD your God
Ps 139: 23   *t* me and know my anxious
Ro   12: 2   Then you will be able to *t*
1Co   3:13   and the fire will *t* the quality
1Jn   4: 1   *t* the spirits to see whether they are

TESTED (TEST)
Ge   22: 1   Some time later God *t* Abraham.
Job   23:10   when he has *t* me, I will come forth
Pr   27:21   man is *t* by the praise he receives.
1Ti   3:10   They must first be *t*; and then

TESTIFY (TESTIMONY)
Jn   5:39   are the Scriptures that *t* about me,
2Ti   1: 8   ashamed to *t* about our Lord,

TESTIMONY (TESTIFY)
Isa   8:20   and to the *t!* If they do not speak
Lk   18:20   not give false *t*, honor your father

TESTS (TEST)
Pr   17: 3   but the LORD *t* the heart.
1Th   2: 4   but God, who *t* our hearts.

THADDAEUS
    Apostle (Mt 10:3; Mk 3:18); probably also known as Judas son of James (Lk 6:16; Ac 1:13).

THANKFUL (THANKS)
Heb 12:28   let us be *t*, and so worship God

THANKS (THANKFUL THANKSGIVING)
1Ch 16: 8   Give *t* to the LORD, call
Ne   12:31   assigned two large choirs to give *t*.
Ps 100: 4   give *t* to him and praise his name.
1Co 15:57   *t* be to God! He gives us the victory
2Co   2:14   *t* be to God, who always leads us
     9:15   *T* be to God for his indescribable
1Th   5:18   give *t* in all circumstances,

THANKSGIVING (THANKS)
Ps   95: 2   Let us come before him with *t*
    100: 4   Enter his gates with *t*
Php   4: 6   by prayer and petition, with *t*,
1Ti   4: 3   created to be received with *t*

THIEF (THIEVES)
Ex   22: 3   A *t* must certainly make restitution
1Th   5: 2   day of the Lord will come like a *t*

Rev 16:15   I come like a *t!* Blessed is he who

THIEVES (THIEF)
1Co   6:10   nor homosexual offenders nor *t*

THINK (THOUGHT THOUGHTS)
Ro   12: 3   Do not *t* of yourself more highly
Php   4: 8   praiseworthy—*t* about such things

THIRST (THIRSTY)
Ps   69:21   and gave me vinegar for my *t*.
Mt   5: 6   Blessed are those who hunger and *t*
Jn   4:14   the water I give him will never *t*.

THIRSTY (THIRST)
Isa   55: 1   "Come, all you who are *t*,
Jn   7:37   "If anyone is *t*, let him come to me
Rev 22:17   Whoever is *t*, let him come;

THOMAS
    Apostle (Mt 10:3; Mk 3:18; Lk 6:15; Jn 11:16; 14:5; 21:2; Ac 1:13). Doubted resurrection (Jn 20:24-28).

THONGS
Mk   1: 7   *t* of whose sandals I am not worthy

THORN (THORNS)
2Co 12: 7   there was given me a *t* in my flesh,

THORNS (THORN)
Nu   33:55   in your eyes and *t* in your sides.
Mt   27:29   then twisted together a crown of *t*
Heb   6: 8   But land that produces *t*

THOUGHT (THINK)
Pr   14:15   a prudent man gives *t* to his steps.
1Co 13:11   I talked like a child, I *t* like a child,

THOUGHTS (THINK)
Ps   94:11   The LORD knows the *t* of man;
    139: 23   test me and know my anxious *t*.
Isa   55: 8   "For my *t* are not your *t*,
Heb   4:12   it judges the *t* and attitudes

THREE
Ecc   4:12   of *t* strands is not quickly broken.
Mt   12:40   *t* nights in the belly of a huge fish,
    18:20   or *t* come together in my name,
    27:63   'After *t* days I will rise again.'
1Co 13:13   And now these *t* remain: faith,
    14:27   or at the most *t*— should speak,
2Co 13: 1   testimony of two or *t* witnesses."

THRESHING
2Sa 24:18   an altar to the LORD on the *t* floor

THRONE (ENTHRONED)
2Sa   7:16   your *t* will be established forever
Ps   45: 6   Your *t*, O God, will last for ever
    47: 8   God is seated on his holy *t*.
Isa   6: 1   I saw the Lord seated on a *t*,
    66: 1   "Heaven is my *t*
Heb   4:16   Let us then approach the *t* of grace
    12: 2   at the right hand of the *t* of God.
Rev   4:10   They lay their crowns before the *t*
    20:11   Then I saw a great white *t*
    22: 3   *t* of God and of the Lamb will be

THROW

Jn   8: 7   the first to *t* a stone at her.''
Heb 10:35   So do not *t* away your confidence;
     12: 1   let us *t* off everything that hinders

THWART*

Isa 14:27   has purposed, and who can *t* him?

TIBNI

King of Israel (1Ki 16:21-22).

TIME (TIMES)

Est   4:14   come to royal position for such a *t*
Da   7:25   to him for a *t*, times and half a *t*.
Hos 10:12   for it is *t* to seek the LORD,
Ro   9: 9   ''At the appointed *t* I will return,
Heb   9:28   and he will appear a second *t*,
     10:12   for all *t* one sacrifice for sins,
1Pe   4:17   For it is *t* for judgment to begin

TIMES (TIME)

Ps   9: 9   a stronghold in *t* of trouble.
     31:15   My *t* are in your hands;
     62: 8   Trust in him at all *t*, O people;
Pr   17:17   A friend loves at all *t*,
Am   5:13   for the *t* are evil.
Mt   18:21   how many *t* shall I forgive my
Ac   1: 7   ''It is not for you to know the *t*
Rev 12:14   *t* and half a time, out

TIMIDITY*

2Ti   1: 7   For God did not give us a spirit of *t*

TIMOTHY

Believer from Lystra (Ac 16:1). Joined Paul on second missionary journey (Ac 16-20). Sent to settle problems at Corinth (1Co 4:17; 16:10). Led church at Ephesus (1Ti 1:3). Co-writer with Paul (1Th 1:1; 2Th 1:1; Phm 1).

TIRE (TIRED)

2Th   3:13   never *t* of doing what is right.

TIRED (TIRE)

Ex   17:12   When Moses' hands grew *t*,
Isa   40:28   He will not grow *t* or weary,

TITHE (TEN)

Lev 27:30   '' 'A *t* of everything from the land,
Dt   12:17   eat in your own towns the *t*
Mal   3:10   the whole *t* into the storehouse,

TITHES (TEN)

Mal   3: 8   'How do we rob you?' ''In *t*

TITUS

Gentile co-worker of Paul (Gal 2:1-3; 2Ti 4:10); sent to Corinth (2Co 2:13; 7-8; 12:18), Crete (Tit 1:4-5).

TODAY

Mt   6:11   Give us *t* our daily bread.
Lk   23:43   *t* you will be with me in paradise.''
Heb   3:13   daily, as long as it is called *T*,
     13: 8   Christ is the same yesterday and *t*

TOIL

Ge   3:17   through painful *t* you will eat of it

TOLERATE

Hab   1:13   you cannot *t* wrong.
Rev   2: 2   that you cannot *t* wicked men,

TOMB

Mt   27:65   make the *t* as secure as you know
Lk   24: 2   the stone rolled away from the *t*,

TOMORROW

Pr   27: 1   Do not boast about *t*,
Isa   22:13   ''for *t* we die!''
Mt   6:34   Therefore do not worry about *t*,
Jas   4:13   ''Today or *t* we will go to this

TONGUE (TONGUES)

Ps   39: 1   and keep my *t* from sin;
Pr   12:18   but the *t* of the wise brings healing.
1Co 14: 2   speaks in a *t* does not speak to men
     14: 4   He who speaks in a *t* edifies himself
     14:13   in a *t* should pray that he may
     14:19   than ten thousand words in a *t*.
Php   2:11   every *t* confess that Jesus Christ is
Jas   1:26   does not keep a tight rein on his *t*,
     3: 8   but no man can tame the *t*.

TONGUES (TONGUE)

Isa   28:11   with foreign lips and strange *t*
     66:18   and gather all nations and *t*,
Mk   16:17   in new *t*; they will pick up snakes
Ac   2: 4   and began to speak in other *t*
     10:46   For they heard them speaking in *t*
     19: 6   and they spoke in *t* and prophesied
1Co 12:30   Do all speak in *t*? Do all interpret?
     14:18   speak in *t* more than all of you.
     14:39   and do not forbid speaking in *t*.

TOOK (TAKE)

1Co 11:23   the night he was betrayed, *t* bread,
Php   3:12   for which Christ Jesus *t* hold of me.

TOOTH (TEETH)

Ex   21:24   eye for eye, *t* for *t*, hand for hand,
Mt   5:38   'Eye for eye, and *t* for *t*.'

TORMENTED

Rev 20:10   They will be *t* day and night

TORN

Gal   4:15   you would have *t* out your eyes
Php   1:23   I do not know! I am *t*

TOUCH (TOUCHED)

Ps 105: 15   ''Do not *t* my anointed ones;
Lk   24:39   It is I myself! *T* me and see;
2Co   6:17   *T* no unclean thing,
Col   2:21   Do not taste! Do not *t*!'' ?

TOUCHED (TOUCH)

1Sa 10:26   men whose hearts God had *t*.
Mt   14:36   and all who *t* him were healed.

TOWER

Ge   11: 4   with a *t* that reaches to the heavens
Pr   18:10   of the LORD is a strong *t*;

TOWNS

Nu   35: 2   to give the Levites *t* to live
     35:15   These six *t* will be a place of refuge

TRACING*
Ro 11:33 and his paths beyond *t* out!

TRADITION
Mt 15: 6 word of God for the sake of your *t*.
Col 2: 8 which depends on human *t*

TRAIN (TRAINING)
Pr 22: 6 *T* a child in the way he should go,
Eph 4: 8 he led captives in his *t*

TRAINING (TRAIN)
1Co 9:25 in the games goes into strict *t*.
2Ti 3:16 correcting and *t* in righteousness,

TRAMPLED
Lk 21:24 Jerusalem will be *t*
Heb 10:29 to be punished who has *t* the Son

TRANCE
Ac 10:10 was being prepared, he fell into a *t*.

TRANSCENDS*
Php 4: 7 which *t* all understanding,

TRANSFIGURED
Mt 17: 2 There he was *t* before them.

TRANSFORM* (TRANSFORMED)
Php 3:21 will *t* our lowly bodies

TRANSFORMED (TRANSFORM)
Ro 12: 2 be *t* by the renewing of your mind.
2Co 3:18 are being *t* into his likeness

TRANSGRESSION (TRANSGRESSIONS TRANSGRESSORS)
Isa 53: 8 for the *t* of my people he was
Ro 4:15 where there is no law there is no *t*.

TRANSGRESSIONS (TRANSGRESSION)
Ps 32: 1 whose *t* are forgiven,
51: 1 blot out my *t*.
103: 12 so far has he removed our *t* from us
Isa 53: 5 But he was pierced for our *t*,
Eph 2: 1 you were dead in your *t* and sins,

TRANSGRESSORS (TRANSGRESSION)
Ps 51:13 Then I will teach *t* your ways,
Isa 53:12 and made intercession for the *t*.
53:12 and was numbered with the *t*.

TREADING
Dt 25: 4 an ox while it is *t* out the grain.
1Co 9: 9 an ox while it is *t* out the grain."

TREASURE (TREASURED TREASURES)
Isa 33: 6 of the LORD is the key to this *t*.
Mt 6:21 For where your *t* is, there your
2Co 4: 7 But we have this *t* in jars of clay

TREASURED (TREASURE)
Dt 7: 6 to be his people, his *t* possession.
Lk 2:19 But Mary *t* up all these things

TREASURES (TREASURE)
Mt 6:19 up for yourselves *t* on earth,
Col 2: 3 in whom are hidden all the *t*
Heb 11:26 of greater value than the *t* of Egypt,

TREAT
Lev 22: 2 sons to *t* with respect the sacred
1Ti 5: 1 *T* younger men as brothers,
1Pe 3: 7 and *t* them with respect

TREATY
Dt 7: 2 Make no *t* with them, and show

TREE
Ge 2: 9 and the *t* of the knowledge of good
2: 9 of the garden were the *t* of life
Dt 21:23 hung on a *t* is under God's curse.
Ps 1: 3 He is like a *t* planted by streams
Mt 3:10 every *t* that does not produce good
12:33 for a *t* is recognized by its fruit.
Gal 3:13 is everyone who is hung on a *t*."
Rev 22:14 they may have the right to the *t*

TREMBLE (TREMBLING)
1Ch 16:30 *T* before him, all the earth!
Ps 114: 7 *T*, O earth, at the presence

TREMBLING (TREMBLE)
Ps 2:11 and rejoice with *t*.
Php 2:12 out your salvation with fear and *t*,

TRESPASS
Ro 5:17 For if, by the *t* of the one man,

TRIALS
1Th 3: 3 one would be unsettled by these *t*.
Jas 1: 2 whenever you face *t* of many kinds,
2Pe 2: 9 how to rescue godly men from *t*

TRIBES
Ge 49:28 All these are the twelve *t* of Israel,
Mt 19:28 judging the twelve *t* of Israel.

TRIBULATION*
Rev 7:14 who have come out of the great *t*;

TRIUMPHAL* (TRIUMPHING)
Isa 60:11 their kings led in *t* procession.
2Co 2:14 us in *t* procession in Christ

TRIUMPHING* (TRIUMPHAL)
Col 2:15 of them, *t* over them by the cross.

TROUBLE (TROUBLED TROUBLES)
Job 14: 1 is of few days and full of *t*.
Ps 46: 1 an ever-present help in *t*.
107: 13 they cried to the LORD in their *t*,
Pr 11:29 He who brings *t* on his family will
24:10 If you falter in times of *t*,
Mt 6:34 Each day has enough *t* of its own.
Jn 16:33 In this world you will have *t*.
Ro 8:35 Shall *t* or hardship or persecution

TROUBLED (TROUBLE)
Jn 14: 1 "Do not let your hearts be *t*.
14:27 Do not let your hearts be *t*

TROUBLES (TROUBLE)
1Co 7:28 those who marry will face many *t*
2Co 1: 4 who comforts us in all our *t*,
4:17 and momentary *t* are achieving

TRUE (TRUTH)
Dt 18:22 does not take place or come *t*,

1Sa 9: 6 and everything he says comes *t*.
Ps119:160 All your words are *t;*
Jn 17: 3 the only *t* God, and Jesus Christ,
Ro 3: 4 Let God be *t*, and every man a liar.
Php 4: 8 whatever is *t*, whatever is noble,
Rev 22: 6 These words are trustworthy and *t*.

TRUMPET

1Co 14: 8 if the *t* does not sound a clear call,
15:52 For the *t* will sound, the dead will

TRUST (ENTRUSTED TRUSTED TRUSTS TRUSTWORTHY)

Ps 20: 7 we *t* in the name of the LORD our
37: 3 *T* in the LORD and do good;
56: 4 in God I *t;* I will not be afraid.
119: 42 for I *t* in your word.
Pr 3: 5 *T* in the LORD with all your heart
Isa 30:15 in quietness and *t* is your strength,
Jn 14: 1 *T* in God; *t* also in me.
1Co 4: 2 been given a *t* must prove faithful.

TRUSTED (TRUST)

Ps 26: 1 I have *t* in the LORD
Isa 25: 9 we *t* in him, and he saved us.
Da 3:28 They *t* in him and defied the king's
Lk 16:10 *t* with very little can also be *t*

TRUSTS (TRUST)

Ps 32:10 surrounds the man who *t* in him.
Pr 11:28 Whoever *t* in his riches will fall,
28:26 He who *t* in himself is a fool,
Ro 9:33 one who *t* in him will never be put

TRUSTWORTHY (TRUST)

Ps119:138 they are fully *t*.
Pr 11:13 but a *t* man keeps a secret.
Rev 22: 6 "These words are *t* and true.

TRUTH (TRUE TRUTHFUL TRUTHS)

Ps 51: 6 Surely you desire *t*
Isa 45:19 I, the LORD, speak the *t;*
Zec 8:16 are to do: Speak the *t* to each other,
Jn 4:23 worship the Father in spirit and *t*,
8:32 Then you will know the *t*,
8:32 and the *t* will set you free."
14: 6 I am the way and the *t* and the life.
16:13 comes, he will guide you into all *t*.
18:38 "What is *t?*" Pilate asked.
Ro 1:25 They exchanged the *t* of God
1Co 13: 6 in evil but rejoices with the *t*.
2Co 13: 8 against the *t*, but only for the *t*.
Eph 4:15 Instead, speaking the *t* in love,
6:14 with the belt of *t* buckled
2Th 2:10 because they refused to love the *t*
1Ti 2: 4 to come to a knowledge of the *t*.
3:15 the pillar and foundation of the *t*.
2Ti 2:15 correctly handles the word of *t*.
3: 7 never able to acknowledge the *t*.
Heb 10:26 received the knowledge of the *t*,
1Pe 1:22 by obeying the *t* so that you have
2Pe 2: 2 the way of *t* into disrepute.
1Jn 1: 6 we lie and do not live by the *t*.
1: 8 deceive ourselves and the *t* is not

TRUTHFUL (TRUTH)

Pr 12:22 but he delights in men who are *t*.
Jn 3:33 it has certified that God is *t*.

TRUTHS (TRUTH)

1Co 2:13 expressing spiritual *t*
1Ti 3: 9 hold of the deep *t* of the faith
Heb 5:12 to teach you the elementary *t*

TRY (TRYING)

Ps 26: 2 Test me, O LORD, and *t* me,
Isa 7:13 enough to *t* the patience of men?
1Co 14:12 *t* to excel in gifts that build up
2Co 5:11 is to fear the Lord, we *t*
1Th 5:15 always *t* to be kind to each other

TRYING (TRY)

2Co 5:12 We are not *t* to commend ourselves
1Th 2: 4 We are not *t* to please men but God

TUNIC

Lk 6:29 do not stop him from taking your *t*.

TURN (TURNED TURNS)

Ex 32:12 *T* from your fierce anger; relent
Dt 5:32 do not *t* aside to the right
28:14 Do not *t* aside from any
Jos 1: 7 do not *t* from it to the right
2Ch 7:14 and *t* from their wicked ways,
30: 9 He will not *t* his face from you
Ps 78: 6 they in *t* would tell their children.
Pr 22: 6 when he is old he will not *t* from it.
Isa 29:16 You *t* things upside down,
30:21 Whether you *t* to the right
45:22 "*T* to me and be saved,
55: 7 Let him *t* to the LORD,
Eze 33:11 *T! T* from your evil ways!
Mal 4: 6 He will *t* the hearts of the fathers
Mt 5:39 you on the right cheek, *t*
10:35 For I have come to *t*
Jn 12:40 nor *t*— and I would heal them."
Ac 3:19 Repent, then, and *t* to God,
26:18 and *t* them from darkness to light,
1Ti 6:20 *T* away from godless chatter
1Pe 3:11 He must *t* from evil and do good;

TURNED (TURN)

Ps 30:11 You *t* my wailing into dancing;
40: 1 he *t* to me and heard my cry.
Isa 53: 6 each of us has *t* to his own way;
Hos 7: 8 Ephraim is a flat cake not *t* over.
Joel 2:31 The sun will be *t* to darkness
Ro 3:12 All have *t* away,

TURNS (TURN)

2Sa 22:29 the LORD *t* my darkness into light
Pr 15: 1 A gentle answer *t* away wrath,
Isa 44:25 and *t* it into nonsense,
Jas 5:20 Whoever *t* a sinner from the error

TWELVE

Ge 49:28 All these are the *t* tribes of Israel,
Mt 10: 1 He called his *t* disciples to him

TWINKLING*

1Co 15:52 in a flash, in the *t* of an eye,

UNAPPROACHABLE*
1Ti 6:16 immortal and who lives in *u* light,

UNBELIEF (UNBELIEVER UNBELIEVERS UNBELIEVING)
Mk   9:24 help me overcome my *u!*''
Ro 11:20 they were broken off because of *u,*
Heb 3:19 able to enter, because of their *u.*

UNBELIEVER* (UNBELIEF)
1Co 7:15 But if the *u* leaves, let him do so.
      10:27 If some *u* invites you to a meal
      14:24 if an *u* or someone who does not
2Co 6:15 have in common with an *u?*
1Ti 5: 8 the faith and is worse than an *u.*

UNBELIEVERS (UNBELIEF)
1Co 6: 6 another—and this in front of *u!*
2Co 6:14 Do not be yoked together with *u.*

UNBELIEVING (UNBELIEF)
1Co 7:14 For the *u* husband has been
Rev 21: 8 But the cowardly, the *u,* the vile,

UNCERTAIN*
1Ti 6:17 which is so *u,* but to put their hope

UNCHANGEABLE*
Heb 6:18 by two *u* things in which it is

UNCIRCUMCISED
1Sa 17:26 Who is this *u* Philistine that he
Col 3:11 circumcised or *u,* barbarian,

UNCIRCUMCISION
1Co 7:19 is nothing and *u* is nothing.
Gal 5: 6 neither circumcision nor *u* has any

UNCLEAN
Isa 6: 5 ruined! For I am a man of *u* lips,
Ro 14:14 fully convinced that no food is *u*
2Co 6:17 Touch no *u* thing,

UNCONCERNED*
Eze 16:49 were arrogant, overfed and *u;*

UNCOVERED
Heb 4:13 Everything is *u* and laid bare

UNDERSTAND (UNDERSTANDING UNDERSTANDS)
Job 42: 3 Surely I spoke of things I did not *u,*
Ps 73:16 When I tried to *u* all this,
    119:125 that I may *u* your statutes.
Lk 24:45 so they could *u* the Scriptures.
Ac   8:30 "Do you *u* what you are reading?"
Ro   7:15 I do not *u* what I do.
1Co 2:14 and he cannot *u* them,
Eph 5:17 but *u* what the Lord's will is.
2Pe 3:16 some things that are hard to *u,*

UNDERSTANDING (UNDERSTAND)
Ps 119:104 I gain *u* from your precepts;
    147: 5 his *u* has no limit.
Pr   3: 5 and lean not on your own *u;*
     4: 7 Though it cost all you have, get *u.*
    10:23 but a man of *u* delights in wisdom.
    11:12 but a man of *u* holds his tongue.

UNDERSTANDS (UNDERSTAND)
1Ch 28: 9 and *u* every motive
1Ti 6: 4 he is conceited and *u* nothing.

UNDIVIDED*
1Ch 12:33 to help David with *u* loyalty—
Ps 86:11 give me an *u* heart,
Eze 11:19 I will give them an *u* heart
1Co 7:35 way in *u* devotion to the Lord.

UNDOING
Pr 18: 7 A fool's mouth is his *u,*

UNDYING*
Eph 6:24 Lord Jesus Christ with an *u* love.

UNFADING*
1Pe 3: 4 the *u* beauty of a gentle

UNFAILING
Ps 33: 5 the earth is full of his *u* love.
    119: 76 May your *u* love be my comfort,
    143: 8 bring me word of your *u* love,
Pr 19:22 What a man desires is *u* love;
La   3:32 so great is his *u* love.

UNFAITHFUL (UNFAITHFULNESS)
Lev 6: 2 is *u* to the LORD by deceiving his
1Ch 10:13 because he was *u* to the LORD;
Pr 13:15 but the way of the *u* is hard.

UNFAITHFULNESS (UNFAITHFUL)
Mt   5:32 except for marital *u,* causes her
     19: 9 for marital *u,* and marries another

UNFOLDING
Ps 119:130 the *u* of your words gives light;

UNGODLINESS
Tit 2:12 It teaches us to say "No" to *u*

UNIT
1Co 12:12 body is a *u,* though it is made up

UNITED (UNITY)
Ro   6: 5 If we have been *u* with him
Php 2: 1 from being *u* with Christ,
Col 2: 2 encouraged in heart and *u* in love,

UNITY (UNITED)
Ps 133: 1 is when brothers live together in *u!*
Ro 15: 5 a spirit of *u* among yourselves
Eph 4: 3 effort to keep the *u* of the Spirit
     4:13 up until we all reach *u* in the faith
Col 3:14 them all together in perfect *u.*

UNIVERSE
Php 2:15 which you shine like stars in the *u*
Heb 1: 2 and through whom he made the *u.*

UNDERSTANDS (UNDERSTAND) column (right, top):
Pr 15:21 a man of *u* keeps a straight course.
    15:32 whoever heeds correction gains *u.*
    23:23 get wisdom, discipline and *u.*
Isa 40:28 and his *u* no one can fathom.
Da   5:12 a keen mind and knowledge and *u,*
Mk   4:12 and ever hearing but never *u;*
    12:33 with all your *u* and with all your
Php 4: 7 of God, which transcends all *u,*

UNKNOWN
Ac 17:23 TO AN *U* GOD.

UNLEAVENED
Ex 12:17 "Celebrate the Feast of *U* Bread,

UNPROFITABLE
Tit 3: 9 because these are *u* and useless.

UNPUNISHED
Ex 34: 7 Yet he does not leave the guilty *u;*
Pr 19: 5 A false witness will not go *u,*

UNREPENTANT*
Ro 2: 5 stubbornness and your *u* heart,

UNRIGHTEOUS*
Zep 3: 5 yet the *u* know no shame.
Mt 5:45 rain on the righteous and the *u.*
1Pe 3:18 the righteous for the *u,* to bring you
2Pe 2: 9 and to hold the *u* for the day

UNSEARCHABLE
Ro 11:33 How *u* his judgments,
Eph 3: 8 preach to the Gentiles the *u* riches

UNSEEN
2Co 4:18 on what is seen, but on what is *u.*
4:18 temporary, but what is *u* is eternal.

UNSTABLE*
Jas 1: 8 he is a double-minded man, *u*
2Pe 2:14 they seduce the *u;* they are experts
3:16 ignorant and *u* people distort,

UNTHINKABLE*
Job 34:12 It is *u* that God would do wrong,

UNVEILED*
2Co 3:18 with *u* faces all reflect the Lord's

UNWORTHY
Job 40: 4 "I am *u*— how can I reply to you?
Lk 17:10 should say, 'We are *u* servants;

UPRIGHT
Job 1: 1 This man was blameless and *u;*
Pr 2: 7 He holds victory in store for the *u,*
15: 8 but the prayer of the *u* pleases him.
Tit 1: 8 who is self-controlled, *u,* holy
2:12 *u* and godly lives in this present

UPROOTED
Jude 12 without fruit and *u*— twice dead.

USEFUL
2Ti 2:21 *u* to the Master and prepared
3:16 Scripture is God-breathed and is *u*

USELESS
1Co 15:14 our preaching is *u*
Jas 2:20 faith without deeds is *u?*

USURY
Ne 5:10 But let the exacting of *u* stop!

UTTER
Ps 78: 2 I will *u* hidden things, things from of

UZZIAH
Son of Amaziah; king of Judah also known as Azariah (2Ki 15:1-7; 1Ch 6:24; 2Ch 26).

VAIN
Ps 33:17 A horse is a *v* hope for deliverance;
Isa 65:23 They will not toil in *v*
1Co 15: 2 Otherwise, you have believed in *v.*
15:58 labor in the Lord is not in *v.*
2Co 6: 1 not to receive God's grace in *v.*

VALLEY
Ps 23: 4 walk through the *v* of the shadow
Isa 40: 4 Every *v* shall be raised up,
Joel 3:14 multitudes in the *v* of decision!

VALUABLE (VALUE)
Lk 12:24 And how much more *v* you are

VALUE (VALUABLE)
Mt 13:46 When he found one of great *v,*
1Ti 4: 8 For physical training is of some *v,*
Heb 11:26 as of greater *v* than the treasures

VEIL
Ex 34:33 to them, he put a *v* over his face.
2Co 3:14 for to this day the same *v* remains

VENGEANCE (AVENGE REVENGE)
Isa 34: 8 For the LORD has a day of *v,*

VICTORIES (VICTORY)
Ps 18:50 He gives his king great *v;*
21: 1 great is his joy in the *v* you give!

VICTORIOUSLY* (VICTORY)
Ps 45: 4 In your majesty ride forth *v*

VICTORY (VICTORIES VICTORIOUSLY)
Ps 60:12 With God we will gain the *v,*
1Co 15:54 "Death has been swallowed up in *v*
15:57 He gives us the *v* through our Lord
1Jn 5: 4 This is the *v* that has overcome

VINDICATED
1Ti 3:16 was *v* by the Spirit,

VINE
Jn 15: 1 "I am the true *v,* and my Father is

VINEGAR
Mk 15:36 filled a sponge with wine *v,*

VIOLATION
Heb 2: 2 every *v* and disobedience received

VIOLENCE
Isa 60:18 No longer will *v* be heard
Eze 45: 9 Give up your *v* and oppression

VIPERS
Ro 3:13 "The poison of *v* is on their lips."

VIRGIN
Isa 7:14 The *v* will be with child
Mt 1:23 "The *v* will be with child
2Co 11: 2 that I might present you as a pure *v*

VIRTUES*
Col 3:14 And over all these *v* put on love,

VISION
Ac 26:19 disobedient to the *v* from heaven.

VOICE
Ps 95: 7 Today, if you hear his *v*,
Isa 30:21 your ears will hear a *v* behind you,
Jn 5:28 are in their graves will hear his *v*
10: 3 and the sheep listen to his *v*.
Heb 3: 7 "Today, if you hear his *v*,
Rev 3:20 If anyone hears my *v* and opens

VOMIT
Pr 26:11 As a dog returns to its *v*,
2Pe 2:22 "A dog returns to its *v*," and,

VOW
Nu 30: 2 When a man makes a *v*

WAGES
Lk 10: 7 for the worker deserves his *w*.
Ro 4: 4 his *w* are not credited to him
6:23 For the *w* of sin is death,

WAILING
Ps 30:11 You turned my *w* into dancing;

WAIST
2Ki 1: 8 with a leather belt around his *w*."
Mt 3: 4 he had a leather belt around his *w*.

WAIT (WAITED WAITS)
Ps 27:14 *W* for the LORD;
130: 5 I *w* for the LORD, my soul waits,
Isa 30:18 Blessed are all who *w* for him!
Ac 1: 4 *w* for the gift my Father promised,
Ro 8:23 as we *w* eagerly for our adoption
1Th 1:10 and to *w* for his Son from heaven,
Tit 2:13 while we *w* for the blessed hope—

WAITED (WAIT)
Ps 40: 1 I *w* patiently for the LORD;

WAITS (WAIT)
Ro 8:19 creation *w* in eager expectation

WALK (WALKED WALKS)
Dt 11:19 and when you *w* along the road,
Ps 1: 1 who does not *w* in the counsel
23: 4 Even though I *w*
89:15 who *w* in the light of your presence
Isa 2: 5 let us *w* in the light of the LORD.
30:21 saying, "This is the way; *w* in it."
40:31 they will *w* and not be faint.
Jer 6:16 ask where the good way is, and *w*
Da 4:37 And those who *w* in pride he is able
Am 3: 3 Do two *w* together
Mic 6: 8 and to *w* humbly with your God.
Mk 2: 9 'Get up, take your mat and *w*'?
Jn 8:12 Whoever follows me will never *w*
1Jn 1: 7 But if we *w* in the light,
2Jn : 6 his command is that you *w* in love.

WALKED (WALK)
Ge 5:24 Enoch *w* with God; then he was no
Jos 14: 9 which your feet have *w* will be your
Mt 14:29 *w* on the water and came toward

WALKS (WALK)
Pr 13:20 He who *w* with the wise grows wise

WALL
Jos 6:20 *w* collapsed; so every man charged
Ne 2:17 let us rebuild the *w* of Jerusalem,
Rev 21:12 It had a great, high *w*

WALLOWING
2Pe 2:22 back to her *w* in the mud."

WANT (WANTED WANTING WANTS)
1Sa 8:19 "We *w* a king over us.
Ps 23: 1 is my shepherd, I shall not be in *w*.
Lk 19:14 'We don't *w* this man to be our king
Ro 7:15 For what I *w* to do I do not do,
Php 3:10 I *w* to know Christ and the power

WANTED (WANT)
1Co 12:18 of them, just as he *w* them to be.

WANTING (WANT)
Da 5:27 weighed on the scales and found *w*.
2Pe 3: 9 with you, not *w* anyone to perish,

WANTS (WANT)
Mt 20:26 whoever *w* to become great
Mk 8:35 For whoever *w* to save his life will
Ro 9:18 he hardens whom he *w* to harden.
1Ti 2: 4 who *w* all men to be saved

WAR (WARS)
Isa 2: 4 nor will they train for *w* anymore.
Da 9:26 *W* will continue until the end,
2Co 10: 3 we do not wage *w* as the world does
Rev 19:11 With justice he judges and makes *w*

WARN (WARNED WARNINGS)
Eze 3:19 But if you do *w* the wicked man
33: 9 if you do *w* the wicked man to turn

WARNED (WARN)
Ps 19:11 By them is your servant *w*;

WARNINGS (WARN)
1Co 10:11 and were written down as *w* for us,

WARS (WAR)
Ps 46: 9 He makes *w* cease to the ends
Mt 24: 6 You will hear of *w* and rumors of *w*,

WASH (WASHED WASHING)
Ps 51: 7 *w* me, and I will be whiter
Jn 13: 5 and began to *w* his disciples' feet,
Ac 22:16 be baptized and *w* your sins away,
Rev 22:14 Blessed are those who *w* their robes

WASHED (WASH)
1Co 6:11 you were *w*, you were sanctified,
Rev 7:14 they have *w* their robes

WASHING (WASH)
Eph 5:26 cleansing her by the *w* with water
Tit 3: 5 us through the *w* of rebirth

WATCH (WATCHES WATCHING WATCHMAN)
Ge 31:49 "May the LORD keep *w*
Jer 31:10 will *w* over his flock like a shepherd

Mt   24:42 "Therefore keep w, because you do
     26:41 W and pray so that you will not fall
Lk   2: 8 keeping w over their flocks at night
1Ti   4:16 W your life and doctrine closely.

WATCHES (WATCH)

Ps   1: 6 For the LORD w over the way
    121: 3 he who w over you will not slumber

WATCHING (WATCH)

Lk   12:37 whose master finds them w

WATCHMAN (WATCH)

Eze   3:17 I have made you a w for the house

WATER (WATERED WATERS)

Ps   1: 3 like a tree planted by streams of w,
     22:14 I am poured out like w,
Pr   25:21 if he is thirsty, give him w to drink.
Isa 49:10 and lead them beside springs of w.
Jer   2:13 broken cisterns that cannot hold w.
Zec 14: 8 On that day living w will flow out
Mk   9:41 anyone who gives you a cup of w
Jn   4:10 he would have given you living w."
      7:38 streams of living w will flow
Eph   5:26 washing with w through the word,
1Pe   3:21 this w symbolizes baptism that now
Rev 21: 6 cost from the spring of the w of life.

WATERED (WATER)

1Co   3: 6 I planted the seed, Apollos w it,

WATERS (WATER)

Ps   23: 2 he leads me beside quiet w,
Ecc 11: 1 Cast your bread upon the w,
Isa 58:11 like a spring whose w never fail.
1Co   3: 7 plants nor he who w is anything,

WAVE (WAVES)

Jas   1: 6 he who doubts is like a w of the sea,

WAVES (WAVE)

Isa 57:20 whose w cast up mire and mud.
Mt   8:27 Even the winds and the w obey him
Eph   4:14 tossed back and forth by the w,

WAY (WAYS)

Dt   1:33 to show you the w you should go.
2Sa 22:31 "As for God, his w is perfect;
Job 23:10 But he knows the w that I take;
Ps   1: 1 or stand in the w of sinners
     37: 5 Commit your w to the LORD;
    119: 9 can a young man keep his w pure?
    139: 24 See if there is any offensive w in me
Pr   14:12 There is a w that seems right
     16:17 he who guards his w guards his life.
     22: 6 Train a child in the w he should go,
Isa 30:21 saying, "This is the w; walk in it."
     53: 6 each of us has turned to his own w;
     55: 7 Let the wicked forsake his w
Mt   3: 3 'Prepare the w for the Lord,
Jn   14: 6 "I am the w and the truth
1Co 10:13 also provide a w out so that you can
     12:31 will show you the most excellent w.
Heb   4:15 who has been tempted in every w,
      9: 8 was showing by this that the w

Heb 10:20 and living w opened for us

WAYS (WAY)

Ex   33:13 teach me your w so I may know
Ps   25:10 All the w of the LORD are loving
     51:13 I will teach transgressors your w,
Pr   3: 6 in all your w acknowledge him,
Isa 55: 8 neither are your w my w,"
Jas   3: 2 We all stumble in many w.

WEAK (WEAKER WEAKNESS)

Mt   26:41 spirit is willing, but the body is w."
Ro   14: 1 Accept him whose faith is w,
1Co   1:27 God chose the w things
      8: 9 become a stumbling block to the w.
      9:22 To the w I became w, to win the w.
2Co 12:10 For when I am w, then I am strong.
Heb 12:12 your feeble arms and w knees.

WEAKER (WEAK)

1Co 12:22 seem to be w are indispensable,
1Pe   3: 7 them with respect as the w partner

WEAKNESS (WEAK)

Ro   8:26 the Spirit helps us in our w.
1Co   1:25 and the w of God is stronger
2Co 12: 9 for my power is made perfect in w
Heb   5: 2 since he himself is subject to w.

WEALTH

Pr   3: 9 Honor the LORD with your w,
Mk   10:22 away sad, because he had great w.
Lk   15:13 and there squandered his w

WEAPONS

2Co 10: 4 The w we fight with are not

WEARIES (WEARY)

Ecc 12:12 and much study w the body.

WEARY (WEARIES)

Isa 40:31 they will run and not grow w,
Mt   11:28 all you who are w and burdened,
Gal   6: 9 Let us not become w in doing good,

WEDDING

Mt   22:11 who was not wearing w clothes.
Rev 19: 7 For the w of the Lamb has come,

WEEP (WEEPING WEPT)

Ecc   3: 4 a time to w and a time to laugh,
Lk   6:21 Blessed are you who w now,

WEEPING (WEEP)

Ps   30: 5 w may remain for a night,
    126: 6 He who goes out w,
Mt   8:12 where there will be w and gnashing

WELCOMES

Mt   18: 5 whoever w a little child like this
2Jn   :11 Anyone who w him shares

WELL

Lk   17:19 your faith has made you w."
Jas   5:15 in faith will make the sick person w

WEPT (WEEP)

Ps 137: 1 of Babylon we sat and w
Jn   11:35 Jesus w.

WEST
Ps 103: 12 as far as the east is from the *w*,

WHIRLWIND (WIND)
2Ki 2: 1 to take Elijah up to heaven in a *w*,
Hos 8: 7 and reap the *w*.
Na 1: 3 His way is in the *w* and the storm,

WHITE (WHITER)
Isa 1:18 they shall be as *w* as snow;
Da 7: 9 His clothing was as *w* as snow;
Rev 1:14 hair were *w* like wool, as *w* as snow,
3: 4 dressed in *w*, for they are worthy.
20:11 Then I saw a great *w* throne

WHITER (WHITE)
Ps 51: 7 and I will be *w* than snow.

WHOLE
Mt 16:26 for a man if he gains the *w* world,
24:14 will be preached in the *w* world
Jn 13:10 to wash his feet; his *w* body is clean
21:25 the *w* world would not have room
Ac 20:27 proclaim to you the *w* will of God.
Ro 3:19 and the *w* world held accountable
8:22 know that the *w* creation has been
Gal 3:22 declares that the *w* world is
5: 3 obligated to obey the *w* law.
Eph 4:13 attaining to the *w* measure
Jas 2:10 For whoever keeps the *w* law
1Jn 2: 2 but also for the sins of the *w* world.

WHOLEHEARTEDLY (HEART)
Dt 1:36 because he followed the LORD *w*
Eph 6: 7 Serve *w*, as if you were serving

WICKED (WICKEDNESS)
Ps 1: 1 walk in the counsel of the *w*
1: 5 Therefore the *w* will not stand
73: 3 when I saw the prosperity of the *w*.
Pr 10:20 the heart of the *w* is of little value.
11:21 The *w* will not go unpunished,
Isa 53: 9 He was assigned a grave with the *w*
55: 7 Let the *w* forsake his way
57:20 But the *w* are like the tossing sea,
Eze 3:18 that *w* man will die for his sin,
18:23 pleasure in the death of the *w*?
33:14 to the *w* man, 'You will surely die,'

WICKEDNESS (WICKED)
Eze 28:15 created till *w* was found in you.

WIDE
Isa 54: 2 stretch your tent curtains *w*,
Mt 7:13 For *w* is the gate and broad is
Eph 3:18 to grasp how *w* and long and high

WIDOW (WIDOWS)
Dt 10:18 cause of the fatherless and the *w*,
Lk 21: 2 saw a poor *w* put in two very small

WIDOWS (WIDOW)
Jas 1:27 look after orphans and *w*

WIFE (WIVES)
Ge 2:24 and mother and be united to his *w*,
24:67 she became his *w*, and he loved her;
Ex 20:17 shall not covet your neighbor's *w*,
Dt 5:21 shall not covet your neighbor's *w*.
Pr 5:18 in the *w* of your youth.
12: 4 *w* of noble character is her
18:22 He who finds a *w* finds what is
19:13 quarrelsome *w* is like a constant
31:10 *w* of noble character who can find?
Mt 19: 3 for a man to divorce his *w* for any
1Co 7: 2 each man should have his own *w*,
7:33 how he can please his *w*—
Eph 5:23 the husband is the head of the *w*
5:33 must love his *w* as he loves himself,
1Ti 3: 2 husband of but one *w*, temperate,
Rev 21: 9 I will show you the bride, the *w*

WILD
Lk 15:13 squandered his wealth in *w* living.
Ro 11:17 and you, though a *w* olive shoot,

WILL (WILLING WILLINGNESS)
Ps 40: 8 I desire to do your *w*, O my God;
143: 10 Teach me to do your *w*,
Isa 53:10 Yet it was the LORD's *w*
Mt 6:10 your *w* be done
26:39 Yet not as I *w*, but as you *w*."
Jn 7:17 If anyone chooses to do God's *w*,
Ac 20:27 to you the whole *w* of God.
Ro 12: 2 and approve what God's *w* is—
1Co 7:37 but has control over his own *w*,
Eph 5:17 understand what the Lord's *w* is.
Php 2:13 for it is God who works in you to *w*
1Th 4: 3 God's *w* that you should be
5:18 for this is God's *w* for you
Heb 9:16 In the case of a *w*, it is necessary
10: 7 I have come to do your *w*, O God
Jas 4:15 "If it is the Lord's *w*,
1Jn 5:14 we ask anything according to his *w*,
Rev 4:11 and by your *w* they were created

WILLING (WILL)
Ps 51:12 grant me a *w* spirit, to sustain me.
Da 3:28 were *w* to give up their lives rather
Mt 18:14 Father in heaven is not *w* that any
23:37 her wings, but you were not *w*.
26:41 The spirit is *w*, but the body is weak

WILLINGNESS (WILL)
2Co 8:12 For if the *w* is there, the gift is

WIN (WINS)
Php 3:14 on toward the goal to *w* the prize
1Th 4:12 your daily life may *w* the respect

WIND (WHIRLWIND)
Jas 1: 6 blown and tossed by the *w*.

WINE
Pr 20: 1 *W* is a mocker and beer a brawler;
Isa 55: 1 Come, buy *w* and milk
Mt 9:17 Neither do men pour new *w*
Lk 23:36 They offered him *w* vinegar
Ro 14:21 not to eat meat or drink *w*
Eph 5:18 on *w*, which leads to debauchery.

WINESKINS
Mt 9:17 do men pour new wine into old *w*.

WINGS

Ru   2:12 under whose *w* you have come
Ps 17: 8 hide me in the shadow of your *w*
Isa 40:31 They will soar on *w* like eagles;
Mal 4: 2 rise with healing in its *w*.
Lk 13:34 hen gathers her chicks under her *w*,

WINS (WIN)

Pr 11:30 and he who *w* souls is wise.

WIPE

Rev 7:17 God will *w* away every tear

WISDOM (WISE)

1Ki 4:29 God gave Solomon *w* and very
Ps111: 10 of the LORD is the beginning of *w*;
Pr 31:26 She speaks with *w*,
Jer 10:12 he founded the world by his *w*
Mt 11:19 But *w* is proved right by her actions
Lk   2:52 And Jesus grew in *w* and stature,
Ro 11:33 the depth of the riches of the *w*
Col 2: 3 are hidden all the treasures of *w*
Jas 1: 5 of you lacks *w*, he should ask God,

WISE (WISDOM WISER)

1Ki 3:12 give you a *w* and discerning heart,
Job 5:13 He catches the *w* in their craftiness
Ps 19: 7 making *w* the simple.
Pr   3: 7 Do not be *w* in your own eyes;
       9: 8 rebuke a *w* man and he will love
    10: 1 A *w* son brings joy to his father,
    11:30 and he who wins souls is *w*.
    13:20 He who walks with the *w* grows *w*,
    17:28 Even a fool is thought *w*
Da 12: 3 Those who are *w* will shine like
Mt 11:25 hidden these things from the *w*
1Co 1:27 things of the world to shame the *w*;
2Ti 3:15 able to make you *w* for salvation

WISER (WISE)

1Co 1:25 of God is *w* than man's wisdom,

WITHER (WITHERS)

Ps 1: 3 and whose leaf does not *w*.

WITHERS (WITHER)

Isa 40: 7 The grass *w* and the flowers fall,
1Pe 1:24 the grass *w* and the flowers fall,

WITHHOLD

Ps 84:11 no good thing does he *w*
Pr 23:13 Do not *w* discipline from a child;

WITNESS (WITNESSES)

Jn 1: 8 he came only as a *w* to the light.

WITNESSES (WITNESS)

Dt 19:15 by the testimony of two or three *w*.
Ac 1: 8 and you will be my *w* in Jerusalem,

WIVES (WIFE)

Eph 5:22 *W*, submit to your husbands
     5:25 love your *w*, just as Christ loved
1Pe 3: 1 words by the behavior of their *w*,

WOE

Isa 6: 5 "*W* to me!" I cried.

WOLF

Isa 65:25 *w* and the lamb will feed together,

WOMAN (MAN)

Ge 2:22 God made a *w* from
    3:15 between you and the *w*,
Lev 20:13 as one lies with a *w*,
Dt 22: 5 *w* must not wear men's
Ru 3:11 a *w* of noble character
Pr 31:30 a *w* who fears the LORD
Mt 5:28 looks at a *w* lustfully
Jn 8: 3 a *w* caught in adultery.
Ro 7: 2 a married *w* is bound to
1Co 11: 3 the head of the *w* is man,
    11:13 a *w* to pray to God with
1Ti 2:11 A *w* should learn in

WOMEN (MAN)

Lk 1:42 Blessed are you among *w*,
1Co 14:34 *w* should remain silent in
1Ti 2: 9 want *w* to dress modestly
Tit 2: 3 teach the older *w* to be
1Pe 3: 5 the holy *w* of the past

WOMB

Job 1:21 Naked I came from my mother's *w*,
Jer 1: 5 you in the *w* I knew you,
Lk 1:44 the baby in my *w* leaped for joy.

WONDER (WONDERFUL WONDERS)

Ps 17: 7 Show the *w* of your great love,

WONDERFUL (WONDER)

Job 42: 3 things too *w* for me to know.
Ps 31:21 for he showed his *w* love to me
   119: 18 *w* things in your law.
   119:129 Your statutes are *w*;
    139: 6 Such knowledge is too *w* for me,
Isa 9: 6 *W* Counselor, Mighty God,
1Pe 2: 9 out of darkness into his *w* light.

WONDERS (WONDER)

Job 37:14 stop and consider God's *w*.
Ps119: 27 then I will meditate on your *w*.
Joel 2:30 I will show *w* in the heavens
Ac 2:19 I will show *w* in the heaven above

WOOD

Isa 44:19 Shall I bow down to a block of *w*?"
1Co 3:12 costly stones, *w*, hay or straw,

WORD (WORDS)

Dt 8: 3 but on every *w* that comes
2Sa 22:31 the *w* of the LORD is flawless.
Ps119: 9 By living according to your *w*.
   119: 11 I have hidden your *w* in my heart
   119:105 Your *w* is a lamp to my feet
Pr 12:25 but a kind *w* cheers him up.
    25:11 A *w* aptly spoken
    30: 5 "Every *w* of God is flawless;
Isa 55:11 so is my *w* that goes out
Jn 1: 1 was the *W*, and the *W* was
    1:14 The *W* became flesh and made his
2Co 2:17 we do not peddle the *w* of God
    4: 2 nor do we distort the *w* of God.
Eph 6:17 of the Spirit, which is the *w* of God.

Php 2:16 as you hold out the *w* of life—
Col 3:16 Let the *w* of Christ dwell
2Ti 2:15 and who correctly handles the *w*
Heb 4:12 For the *w* of God is living
Jas 1:22 Do not merely listen to the *w*,
2Pe 1:19 And we have the *w* of the prophets

WORDS (WORD)

Dt 11:18 Fix these *w* of mine in your hearts
Ps 119:103 How sweet are your *w* to my taste
119:130 The unfolding of your *w* gives light;
119:160 All your *w* are true;
Pr 30: 6 Do not add to his *w*,
Jer 15:16 When your *w* came, I ate them;
Mt 24:35 but my *w* will never pass away.
Jn 6:68 You have the *w* of eternal life.
15: 7 in me and my *w* remain in you,
1Co 14:19 rather speak five intelligible *w*
Rev 22:19 And if anyone takes *w* away

WORK (WORKER WORKERS WORKING WORKMAN WORKMANSHIP WORKS)

Ex 23:12 "Six days do your *w*,
Nu 8:11 ready to do the *w* of the LORD.
Dt 5:14 On it you shall not do any *w*,
Ecc 5:19 his lot and be happy in his *w*—
Jer 48:10 lax in doing the LORD's *w!*
Jn 6:27 Do not *w* for food that spoils,
9: 4 we must do the *w* of him who sent
1Co 3:13 test the quality of each man's *w*.
Php 1: 6 that he who began a good *w*
2:12 continue to *w* out your salvation
Col 3:23 Whatever you do, *w* at it
1Th 5:12 to respect those who *w* hard
2Th 3:10 If a man will not *w*, he shall not eat
2Ti 3:17 equipped for every good *w*.
Heb 6:10 he will not forget your *w*

WORKER (WORK)

Lk 10: 7 for the *w* deserves his wages.
1Ti 5:18 and "The *w* deserves his wages."

WORKERS (WORK)

Mt 9:37 is plentiful but the *w* are few.
1Co 3: 9 For we are God's fellow *w;*

WORKING (WORK)

Col 3:23 as *w* for the Lord, not for men,

WORKMAN (WORK)

2Ti 2:15 a *w* who does not need

WORKMANSHIP* (WORK)

Eph 2:10 For we are God's *w*, created

WORKS (WORK)

Pr 31:31 let her *w* bring her praise
Ro 8:28 in all things God *w* for the good
Eph 2: 9 not by *w*, so that no one can boast.
4:12 to prepare God's people for *w*

WORLD (WORLDLY)

Ps 50:12 for the *w* is mine, and all that is in it
Isa 13:11 I will punish the *w* for its evil,
Mt 5:14 "You are the light of the *w*.

Mt 16:26 for a man if he gains the whole *w*,
Mk 16:15 into all the *w* and preach the good
Jn 1:29 who takes away the sin of the *w!*
3:16 so loved the *w* that he gave his one
8:12 he said, "I am the light of the *w*.
15:19 As it is, you do not belong to the *w*,
16:33 In this *w* you will have trouble.
18:36 "My kingdom is not of this *w*.
Ro 3:19 and the whole *w* held accountable
1Co 3:19 the wisdom of this *w* is foolishness
2Co 5:19 that God was reconciling the *w*
10: 3 For though we live in the *w*,
1Ti 6: 7 For we brought nothing into the *w*,
1Jn 2: 2 but also for the sins of the whole *w*.
2:15 not love the *w* or anything in the *w*.
Rev 13: 8 slain from the creation of the *w*.

WORLDLY (WORLD)

Tit 2:12 to ungodliness and *w* passions,

WORM

Mk 9:48 " 'their *w* does not die,

WORRY (WORRYING)

Mt 6:25 I tell you, do not *w* about your life,
10:19 do not *w* about what to say

WORRYING (WORRY)

Mt 6:27 of you by *w* can add a single hour

WORSHIP

1Ch 16:29 *w* the LORD in the splendor
Ps 95: 6 Come, let us bow down in *w*,
Mt 2: 2 and have come to *w* him."
Jn 4:24 and his worshipers must *w* in spirit
Ro 12: 1 this is your spiritual act of *w*.

WORTH (WORTHY)

Job 28:13 Man does not comprehend its *w;*
Pr 31:10 She is *w* far more than rubies.
Mt 10:31 are *w* more than many sparrows.
Ro 8:18 sufferings are not *w* comparing
1Pe 1: 7 of greater *w* than gold,
3: 4 which is of great *w* in God's sight.

WORTHLESS

Pr 11: 4 Wealth is *w* in the day of wrath,
Jas 1:26 himself and his religion is *w*.

WORTHY (WORTH)

1Ch 16:25 For great is the LORD and most *w*
Eph 4: 1 to live a life *w* of the calling you
Php 1:27 in a manner *w* of the gospel
3Jn : 6 on their way in a manner *w* of God.
Rev 5: 2 "Who is *w* to break the seals

WOUNDS

Pr 27: 6 *W* from a friend can be trusted,
Isa 53: 5 and by his *w* we are healed.
Zec 13: 6 'What are these *w* on your body?'
1Pe 2:24 by his *w* you have been healed.

WRATH

2Ch 36:16 scoffed at his prophets until the *w*
Ps 2: 5 and terrifies them in his *w*, saying,
76:10 Surely your *w* against men brings
Pr 15: 1 A gentle answer turns away *w*,

Jer 25:15 filled with the wine of my *w*
Ro 1:18 The *w* of God is being revealed
5: 9 saved from God's *w* through him!
1Th 5: 9 God did not appoint us to suffer *w*
Rev 6:16 and from the *w* of the Lamb!

WRESTLED

Ge 32:24 and a man *w* with him till daybreak

WRITE (WRITING WRITTEN)

Dt 6: 9 *W* them on the doorframes
Pr 7: 3 *w* them on the tablet of your heart.
Heb 8:10 and *w* them on their hearts.

WRITING (WRITE)

1Co 14:37 him acknowledge that what I am *w*

WRITTEN (WRITE)

Jos 1: 8 careful to do everything *w* in it.
Da 12: 1 everyone whose name is found *w*
Lk 10:20 but rejoice that your names are *w*
Jn 20:31 these are *w* that you may believe
1Co 4: 6 "Do not go beyond what is *w*."
2Co 3: 3 *w* not with ink but with the Spirit
Col 2:14 having canceled the *w* code,
Heb 12:23 whose names are *w* in heaven.

WRONG (WRONGDOING WRONGED WRONGS)

Ex 23: 2 Do not follow the crowd in doing *w*
Nu 5: 7 must make full restitution for his *w*,
Job 34:12 unthinkable that God would do *w*,
1Th 5:15 that nobody pays back *w* for *w*,

WRONGDOING (WRONG)

Job 1:22 sin by charging God with *w*.

WRONGED (WRONG)

1Co 6: 7 not rather be *w*? Why not rather

WRONGS (WRONG)

Pr 10:12 but love covers over all *w*.
1Co 13: 5 angered, it keeps no record of *w*.

YEARS

Ps 90: 4 For a thousand *y* in your sight
90:10 The length of our days is seventy *y*
2Pe 3: 8 the Lord a day is like a thousand *y*,
Rev 20: 2 and bound him for a thousand *y*.

YESTERDAY

Heb 13: 8 Jesus Christ is the same *y*

YOKE (YOKED)

Mt 11:29 Take my *y* upon you and learn

YOKED (YOKE)

2Co 6:14 Do not be *y* together

YOUNG (YOUTH)

Ps 119: 9 How can a *y* man keep his way
1Ti 4:12 down on you because you are *y*,

YOUTH (YOUNG)

Ps 103: 5 so that your *y* is renewed like
Ecc 12: 1 Creator in the days of your *y*,
2Ti 2:22 Flee the evil desires of *y*,

ZEAL

Pr 19: 2 to have *z* without knowledge,
Ro 12:11 Never be lacking in *z*,

ZECHARIAH

1. Son of Jeroboam II; king of Israel (2Ki 15:8-12).

2. Post-exilic prophet who encouraged rebuilding of temple (Ezr 5:1; 6:14; Zec 1:1).

3. Father of John the Baptist (Lk 1:13; 3:2).

ZEDEKIAH

Mattaniah, son of Josiah (1Ch 3:15), made king of Judah by Nebuchadnezzar (2Ki 24:17-25:7; 2Ch 36:10-14; Jer 37-39; 52:1-11).

ZERUBBABEL

Descendant of David (1Ch 3:19; Mt 1:3). Led return from exile (Ezr 2-3; Ne 7:7; Hag 1-2; Zec 4).

ZIMRI

King of Israel (1Ki 16:9-20).

ZION

Ps 137: 3 "Sing us one of the songs of *Z!*"
Jer 50: 5 They will ask the way to *Z*
Ro 9:33 I lay in *Z* a stone that causes men
11:26 "The deliverer will come from *Z;*

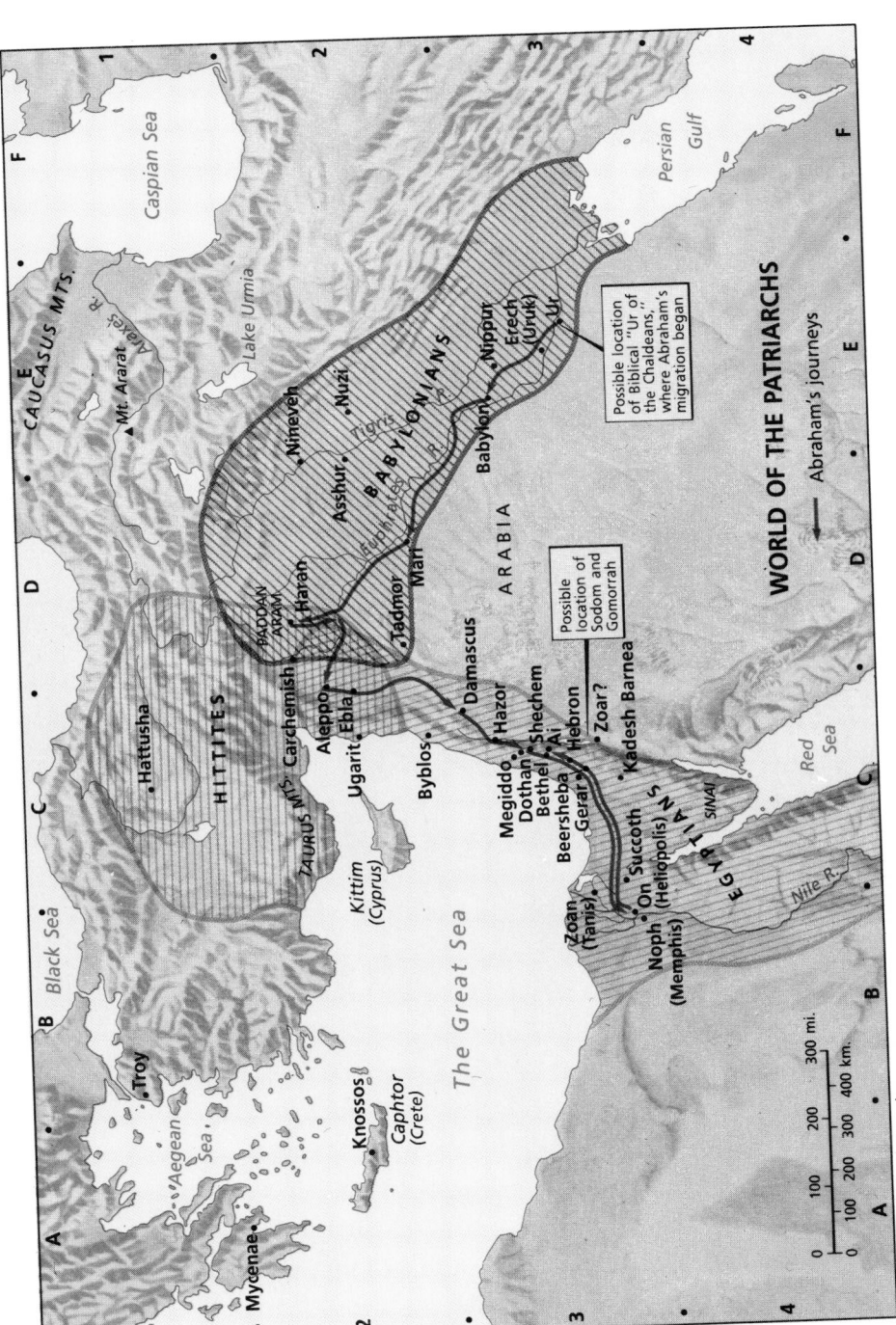

WORLD OF THE PATRIARCHS

→ Abraham's journeys

Possible location of Biblical "Ur of the Chaldeans," where Abraham's migration began

Possible location of Sodom and Gomorrah

Seas and Waters: Caspian Sea, Black Sea, Aegean Sea, The Great Sea, Red Sea, Persian Gulf, Lake Urmia, Nile R., Tigris R., Euphrates R., Araxes R.

Regions and Peoples: CAUCASUS MTS., HITTITES, TAURUS MTS., BABYLONIANS, ARABIA, EGYPTIANS, SINAI, Kittim (Cyprus), Caphtor (Crete)

Places: Troy, Mycenae, Knossos, Hattusha, Mt. Ararat, Nineveh, Asshur, Nuzi, Carchemish, Haran, PADDAN ARAM, Ugarit, Ebla, Aleppo, Tadmor, Mari, Babylon, Nippur, Erech (Uruk), Ur, Byblos, Damascus, Hazor, Megiddo, Dothan, Shechem, Bethel, Ai, Hebron, Zoar?, Beersheba, Gerar, Kadesh Barnea, Zoan (Tanis), Succoth, On (Heliopolis), Noph (Memphis)

0   100   200   300 mi.
0 100 200 300 400 km.

© 1986 The Zondervan Corporation

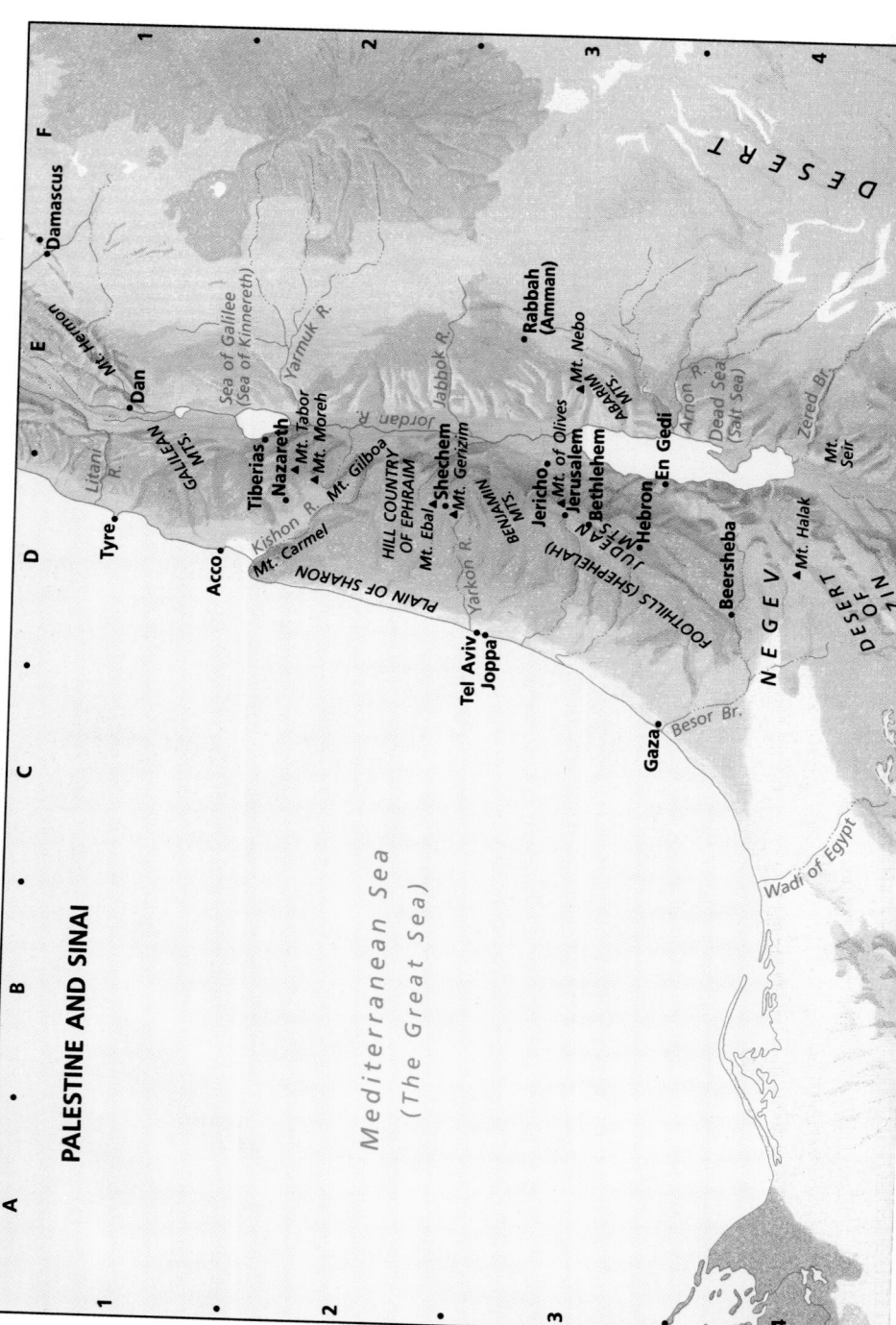

PALESTINE AND SINAI

Mediterranean Sea
(The Great Sea)

Damascus

Mt. Hermon

Litani R.

Dan

GALILEAN MTS.

Tyre

Sea of Galilee
(Sea of Kinnereth)

Yarmuk R.

Tiberias

Nazareth
Mt. Tabor
Mt. Moreh

Kishon R.
Mt. Gilboa

Acco

Mt. Carmel

PLAIN OF SHARON

HILL COUNTRY
OF EPHRAIM

Jordan R.

Jabbok R.

Shechem
Mt. Ebal
Mt. Gerizim

Rabbah
(Amman)

Mt. Nebo

ABARIM MTS.

Yarkon R.

BENJAMIN MTS.

Tel Aviv
Joppa

Jericho
Mt. of Olives
Jerusalem
Bethlehem

FOOTHILLS (SHEPHELAH)

JUDEAN MTS.

Hebron

En Gedi

Dead Sea
(Salt Sea)

Arnon R.

Gaza

Besor Br.

Beersheba

N E G E V

Mt. Halak

DESERT
OF
ZIN

Mt. Seir

Zered Br.

Wadi of Egypt

D E S E R T

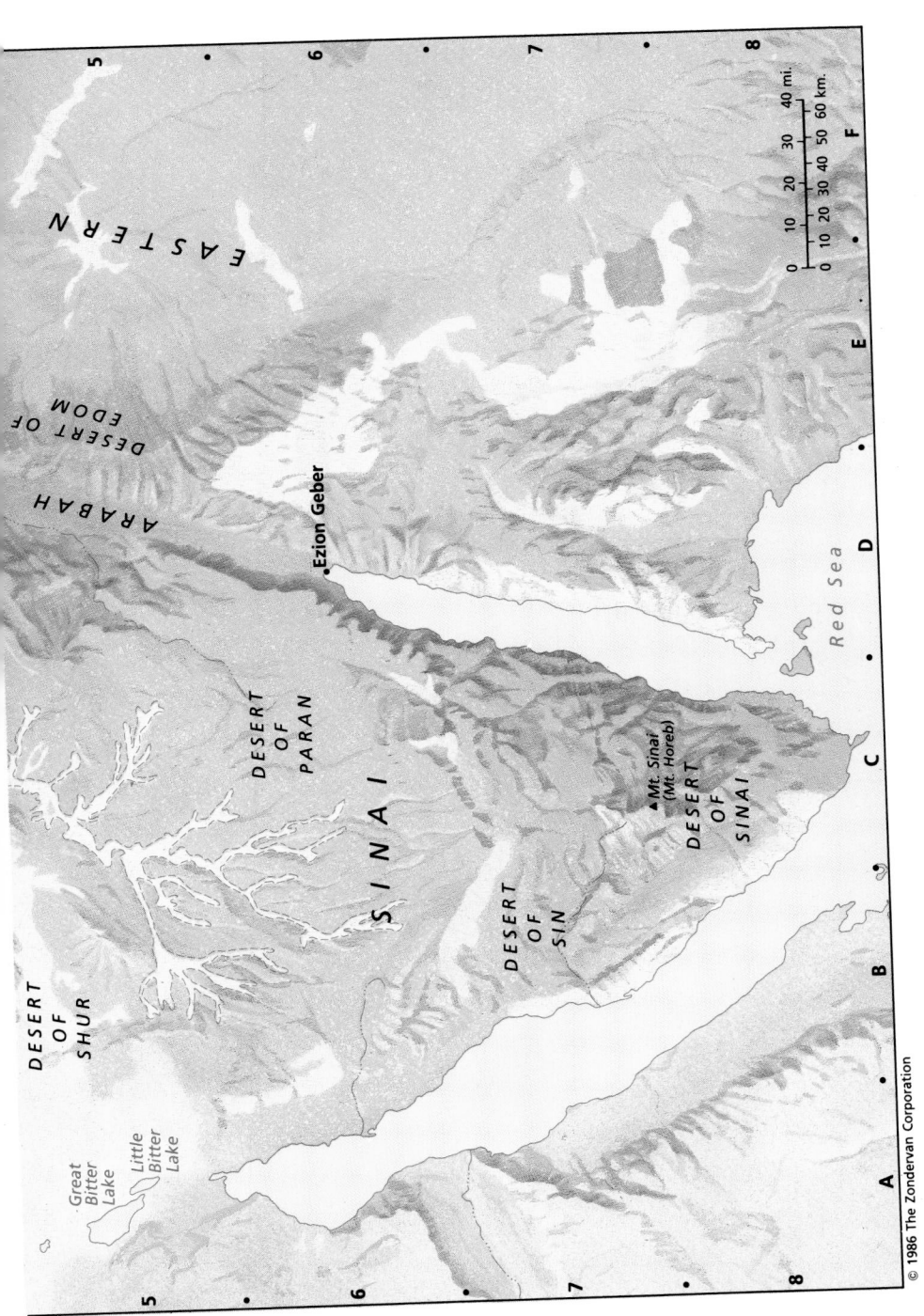

DESERT
OF
SHUR

Great
Bitter
Lake

Little
Bitter
Lake

DESERT
OF
PARAN

S I N A I

DESERT
OF
SIN

DESERT
OF
SINAI

▲Mt. Sinai
(Mt. Horeb)

ARABAH

DESERT OF
EDOM

EASTERN

Ezion Geber

Red Sea

0   10   20   30   40 mi.
0 10 20 30 40 50 60 km.

A   B   C   D   E   F

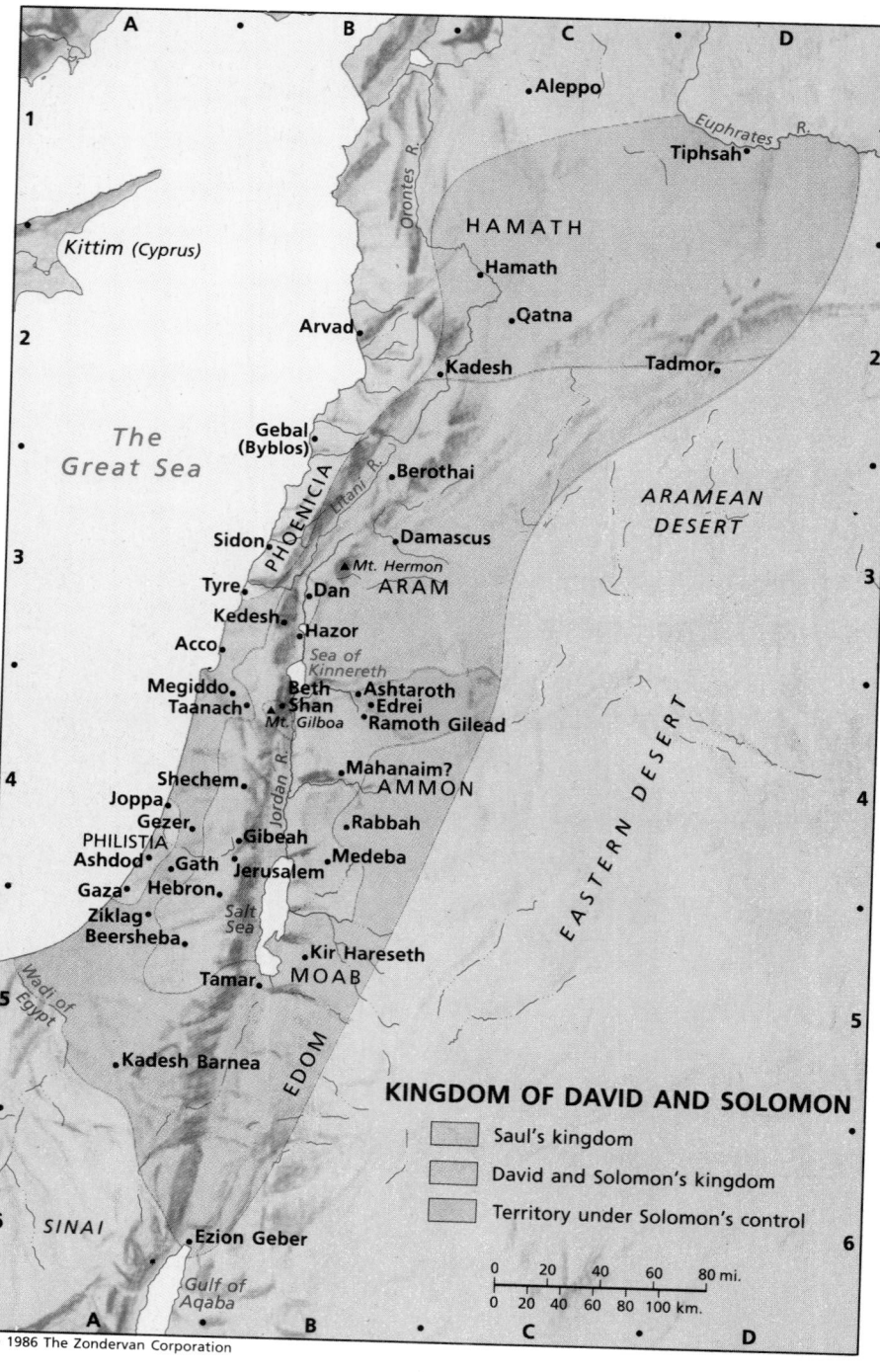

KINGDOM OF DAVID AND SOLOMON

	Saul's kingdom
	David and Solomon's kingdom
	Territory under Solomon's control

0   20   40   60   80 mi.

0 20 40 60 80 100 km.

A · B · C · D
1 ·Aleppo 1
Euphrates R.
Tiphsah·
Orontes R.
HAMATH
Kittim (Cyprus) ·Hamath
·Qatna
Arvad· 2
2 Kadesh· Tadmor·
Gebal ARAMEAN
(Byblos)· DESERT
The ·Berothai
Great Sea PHOENICIA Litani R.
Sidon· ·Damascus
3 Tyre· ▲Mt. Hermon 3
·Dan ARAM
Kedesh·
Acco· ·Hazor
Sea of
Kinnereth
Megiddo· Beth ·Ashtaroth EASTERN DESERT
Taanach· Shan ·Edrei
Mt. Gilboa ·Ramoth Gilead
Jordan R.
Shechem· Mahanaim?
4 Joppa· AMMON 4
Gezer· ·Rabbah
PHILISTIA ·Gibeah
Ashdod· ·Gath ·Medeba
Gaza· Hebron· Jerusalem
Ziklag· Salt
Beersheba· Sea
·Kir Hareseth
Tamar· MOAB
5 5
Wadi of EDOM
Egypt
·Kadesh Barnea

6 SINAI 6
·Ezion Geber
Gulf of
Aqaba
A B C D

© 1986 The Zondervan Corporation

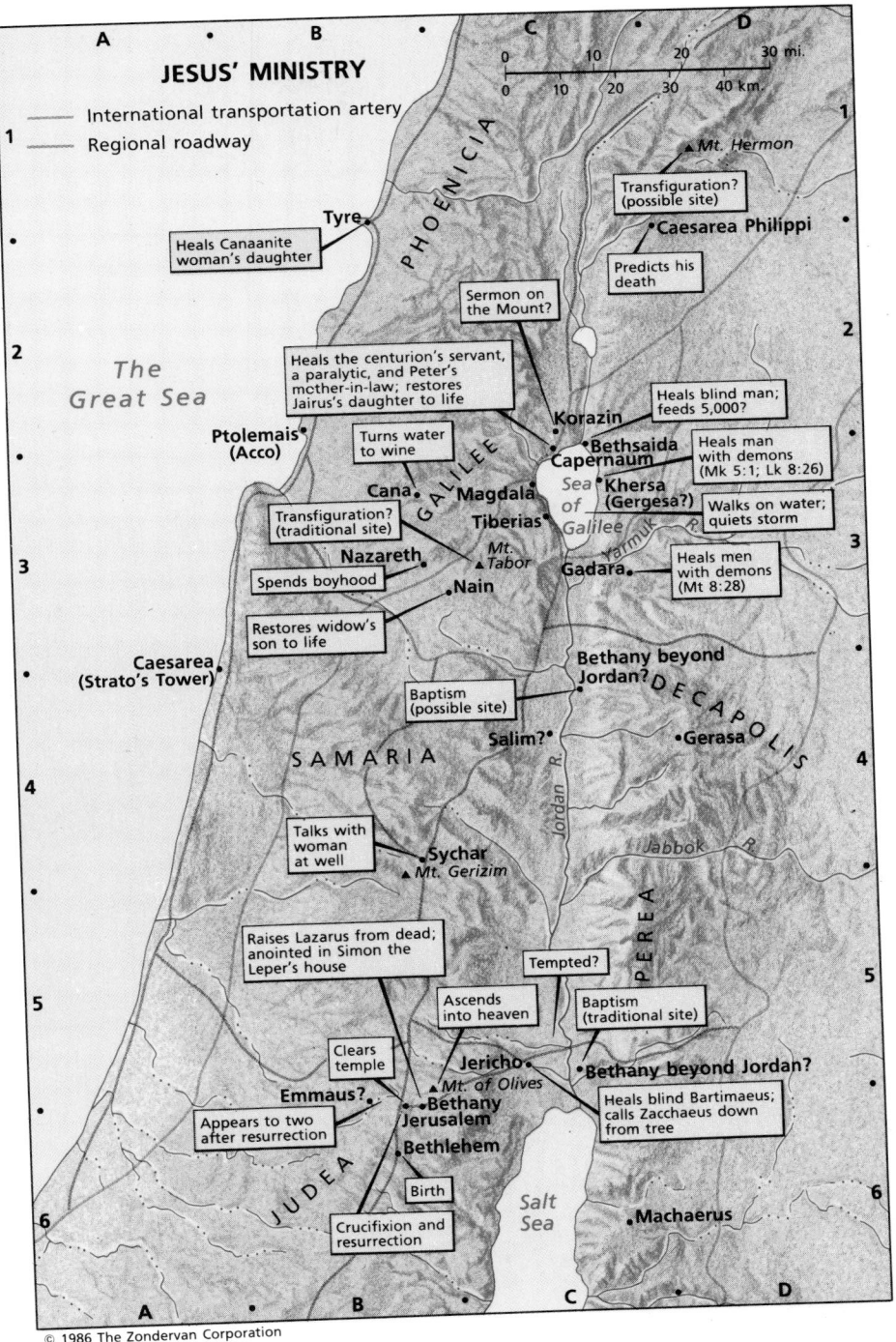

JESUS' MINISTRY

International transportation artery
Regional roadway

The Great Sea

PHOENICIA

Tyre

Heals Canaanite woman's daughter

Transfiguration? (possible site)

▲Mt. Hermon

Caesarea Philippi

Predicts his death

Sermon on the Mount?

Heals the centurion's servant, a paralytic, and Peter's mother-in-law; restores Jairus's daughter to life

Heals blind man; feeds 5,000?

Korazin

Ptolemais (Acco)

Turns water to wine

GALILEE

Bethsaida
Capernaum

Heals man with demons (Mk 5:1; Lk 8:26)

Cana
Magdala

Sea of Galilee

Khersa (Gergesa?)

Walks on water; quiets storm

Transfiguration? (traditional site)

Tiberias

Mt. Tabor

Nazareth

Spends boyhood

Nain

Restores widow's son to life

Gadara

Yarmuk R.

Heals men with demons (Mt 8:28)

Caesarea (Strato's Tower)

Bethany beyond Jordan?

DECAPOLIS

Baptism (possible site)

Salim?

Gerasa

SAMARIA

Talks with woman at well

Sychar
▲ Mt. Gerizim

Jordan R.

Jabbok R.

PEREA

Raises Lazarus from dead; anointed in Simon the Leper's house

Tempted?

Ascends into heaven

Baptism (traditional site)

Clears temple

Jericho

Bethany beyond Jordan?

Emmaus?

Mt. of Olives
Bethany
Jerusalem

Heals blind Bartimaeus; calls Zacchaeus down from tree

Appears to two after resurrection

Bethlehem

JUDEA

Birth

Salt Sea

Crucifixion and resurrection

Machaerus

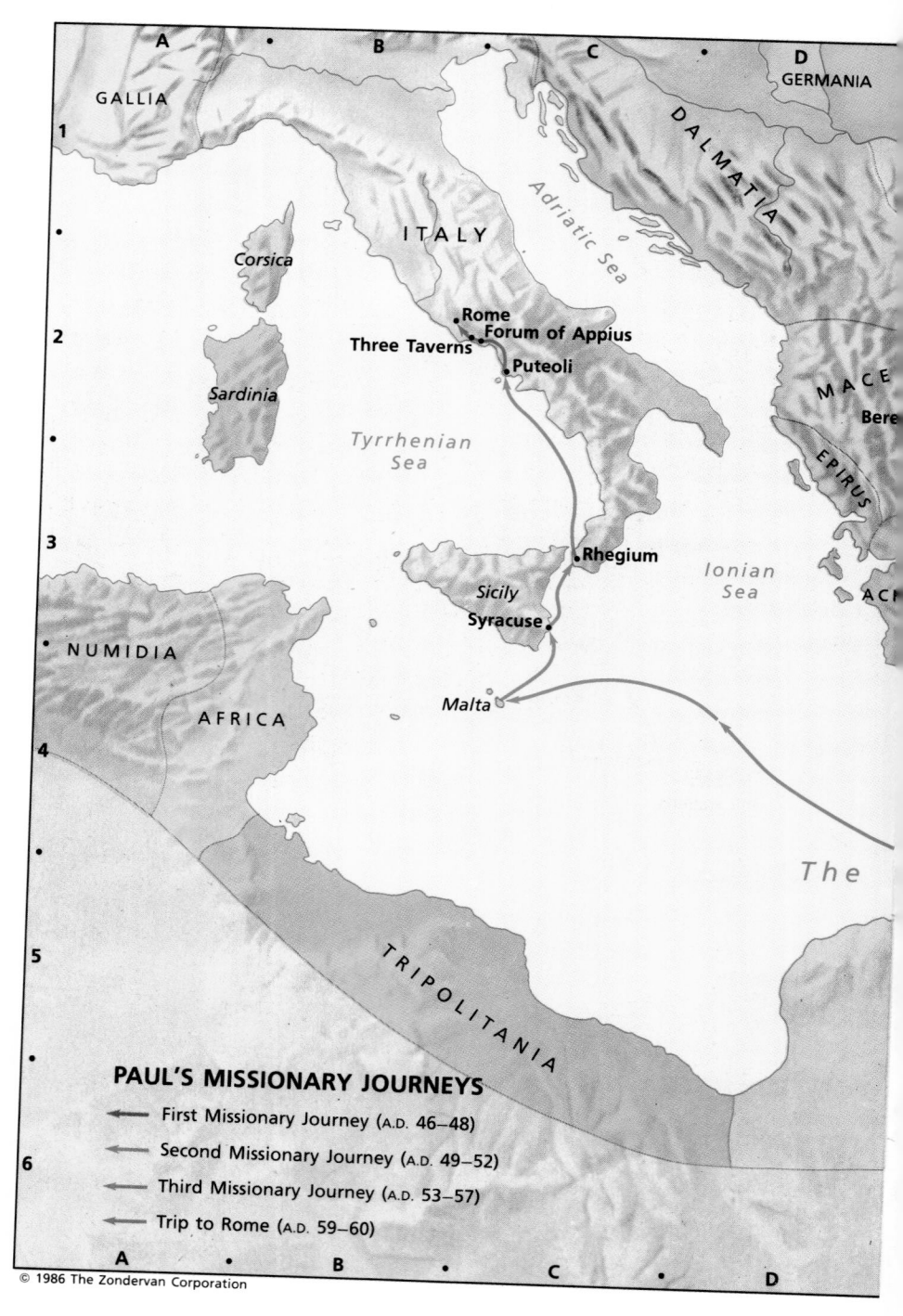

PAUL'S MISSIONARY JOURNEYS

First Missionary Journey (A.D. 46–48)

Second Missionary Journey (A.D. 49–52)

Third Missionary Journey (A.D. 53–57)

Trip to Rome (A.D. 59–60)

© 1986 The Zondervan Corporation

E   **F**   **G**   **H**

D A C I A

1

Black Sea

M O E S I A

T H R A C E

2

Philippi
Neapolis
mphipolis
Apollonia
Samothrace
Thessalonica
lt. Olympus
NIA
BITHYNIA AND PONTUS
G A L A T I A

CAPPADOCIA

COMMAGENE

Troas
Assos
Mitylene
MYSIA
Pergamum
A S I A
Thyatira
Sardis.
Philadelphia
Pisidian
Antioch
LYCAONIA
Aegean
Sea
Kios
Smyrna
LYDIA
Ephesus
PHRYGIA
Iconium
Lystra
Derbe
CILICIA
Euphrates R.
3
Delphi
orinth
Athens
Samos
Laodicea
Colosse
PISIDIA
Tarsus
Issus
Aleppo
AIA
Miletus
PAMPHYLIA
Antioch
enchrea
Sparta
Patmos
Attalia
LYCIA
Perga
Seleucia
Cos
Cnidus
Patara
S Y R I A

Rhodes
Myra
Cyprus
Salamis
Paphos

Phoenix
Crete
Lasea
Salmone
Sidon
PHOENICIA
ABILENE
Damascus
4
Fair Havens
Tyre
Ptolemais
Caesarea
J U D E A
Jordan R.
Jerusalem
Salt Sea
5

G r e a t   S e a

A R A B I A

C Y R E N A I C A

E G Y P T

Nile R.

6

Red
Sea

0   100   200 mi.
0   100   200   300 km.

E   **F**   **G**   **H**

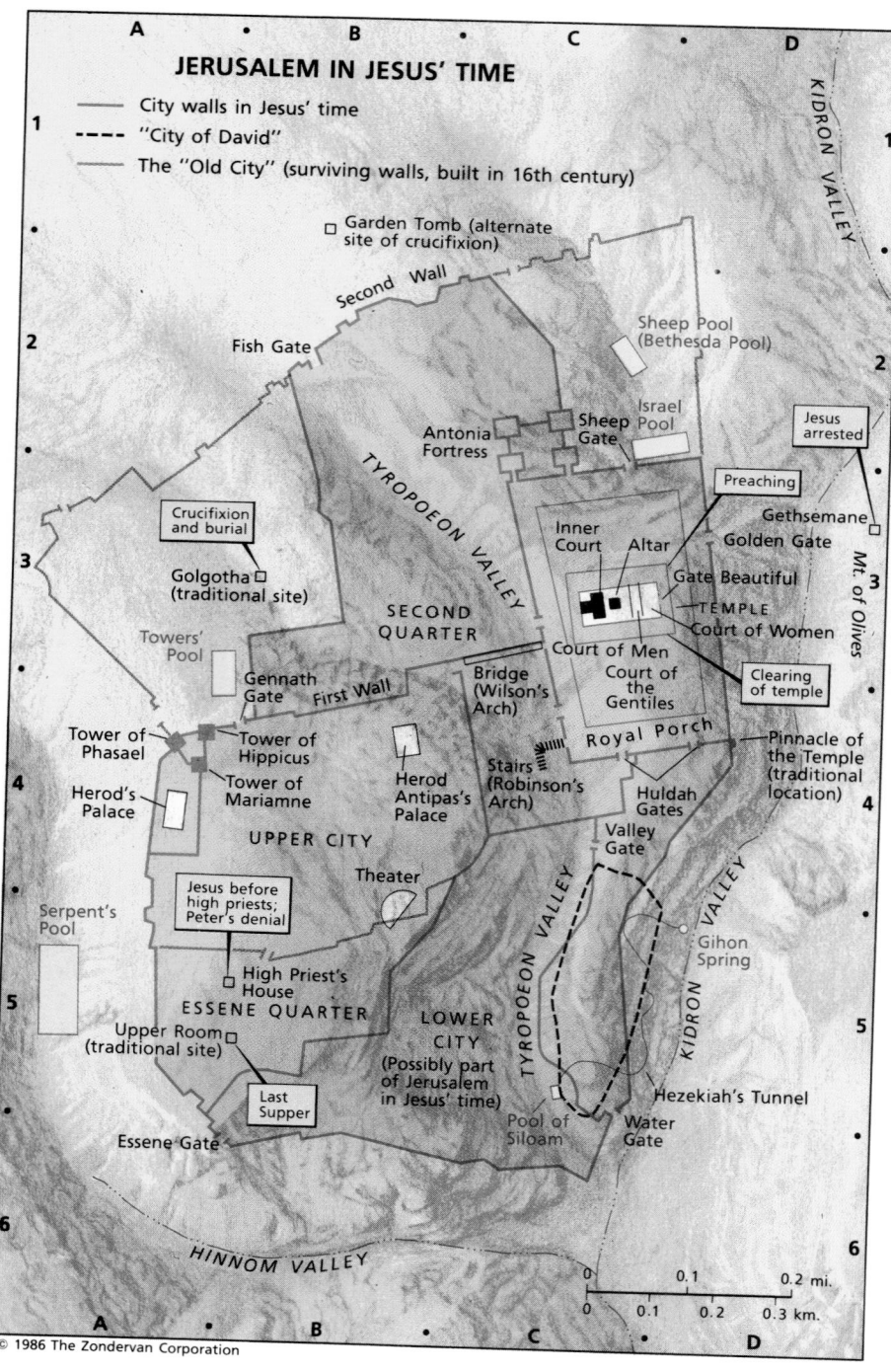

JERUSALEM IN JESUS' TIME

City walls in Jesus' time
"City of David"
The "Old City" (surviving walls, built in 16th century)

KIDRON VALLEY

Garden Tomb (alternate site of crucifixion)

Second Wall

Fish Gate

Sheep Pool (Bethesda Pool)

Israel Pool

Antonia Fortress

Sheep Gate

TYROPOEON VALLEY

Jesus arrested

Preaching

Inner Court

Altar

Golden Gate

Gate Beautiful

Gethsemane

Mt. of Olives

Crucifixion and burial

Golgotha (traditional site)

SECOND QUARTER

TEMPLE

Court of Women

Towers' Pool

Gennath Gate

First Wall

Bridge (Wilson's Arch)

Court of Men

Court of the Gentiles

Clearing of temple

Tower of Phasael

Tower of Hippicus

Tower of Mariamne

Herod's Palace

Herod Antipas's Palace

Stairs (Robinson's Arch)

Royal Porch

Pinnacle of the Temple (traditional location)

Huldah Gates

UPPER CITY

Theater

Valley Gate

Serpent's Pool

Jesus before high priests; Peter's denial

High Priest's House

ESSENE QUARTER

LOWER CITY (Possibly part of Jerusalem in Jesus' time)

TYROPOEON VALLEY

KIDRON VALLEY

Gihon Spring

Upper Room (traditional site)

Last Supper

Hezekiah's Tunnel

Essene Gate

Pool of Siloam

Water Gate

HINNOM VALLEY

0   0.1   0.2 mi.

0   0.1   0.2   0.3 km.